I0877087

COMPARATIVE ESKIMO DICTIONARY
With Aleut Cognates

Michael Fortescue
Steven Jacobson
Lawrence Kaplan

Alaska Native Language Center
Research Paper Number 9
University of Alaska Fairbanks

Second Edition
2010

© 2010, 1994 Alaska Native Language Center

Printed in the United States of America
All rights reserved

Library of Congress Cataloging-in-Publication Data:
Fortescue, Michael D.
Comparative Eskimo dictionary : with Aleut cognates / Michael Fortescue, Steven Jacobson, Lawrence Kaplan. -- 2nd ed.
p. cm.
Includes bibliographical references and index.
Summary: "Compares cognates found in the modern Eskimo languages ranging from northeastern Siberia, across Alaska and Canada, to East Greenland. Includes five Inuit dialect groups, the four Yupik languages, and Sirenikski. Aleut cognates are added when available"--Provided by publisher.
ISBN 978-1-55500-109-4 (alk. paper)
1. Eskimo languages--Grammar, Comparative--Dictionaries. 2. Eskimo languages--Cognates--Dictionaries. 3. Eskimo languages--Dictionaries--English. 4. English language--Dictionaries--Eskimo. I. Jacobson, Steven. II. Kaplan, Lawrence. III. Title.
PM50.Z5F65 2010
497'.1--dc22
2010039028

First edition	1994	300 copies
Second printing	1996	400 copies
Second edition	2010	500 copies

Address correspondence to:
Alaska Native Language Center
University of Alaska Fairbanks
P.O. Box 757680
Fairbanks, AK 99775-7680

It is the policy of the University of Alaska to provide equal education and employment opportunities and to provide services and benefits to all students and employees without regard to race, color, religion, national origin, sex, age, disability, status as a Vietnam-era or disabled veteran, marital status, changes in marital status, pregnancy, or parenthood, pursuant to laws enforced by the Department of Education and the Department of Labor, including Presidential Executive Order 11246, as amended, Title VI and Title VII of the 1964 Civil Rights Act, Title IX of the Education Amendments of 1972, the Public Health Service Act of 1971, the Veteran's Readjustment Assistance Act of 1974, the Vocational Rehabilitation Act of 1973, the Age Discrimination Act of 1967, the Equal Pay Act of 1963, the 14th Amendment, EEOC's Sex Discrimination Guidelines, and Alaska Statutes 18.80.010 et seq. and 14.80.010 et seq. Inquiries regarding application of these and other regulations should be directed either to the University of Alaska Fairbanks, Director of Employee Relations; to the Office of Civil Rights, Department of Education, Washington, D.C.; or to the Office of Federal Contract Compliance Programs, Department of Labor, Washington, D.C.

CONTENTS

PREFACE TO THE SECOND EDITION

Early explorers and ethnographers collected and compiled vocabularies of the Eskimo languages they encountered, and much of their work already in the eighteenth century was comparative in nature (e.g. Cook and King). Important figures in comparative Eskimo, whose work included phonological correspondences and morphology as well as lexicon, were Rask, Rink, Miller, Thalbitzer, Uhlenbeck, Birket-Smith, Hammerich, Jenness, Rasmussen, Menovshchikov, Swadesh, Bergsland, and Emel'yanova. Notable among those who compiled comparative lists in this century are Birket-Smith, Jenness, and Rasmussen. Erik Holtved compiled by far the most extensive comparative lexical files, with a view to eventually producing a major dictionary.

Work on the present *Comparative Eskimo Dictionary* began in 1985, when Steven Jacobson and Lawrence Kaplan started to compose comparative sets from their field notes and files, from material in the archives of the Alaska Native Language Center, and from published Eskimo dictionaries. They received a Faculty Grant from the University of Alaska Fairbanks to pursue the work. Michael Fortescue joined the project and spent the spring of 1988 working on the comparative files in Fairbanks. He has since been responsible for the sections on postbases and proto-Eskimo inflectional endings and for the integration of the Aleut cognates from Knut Bergsland. Kaplan spent a sabbatical year at the Institute of Eskimology in Copenhagen in 1988–1989, where he and Fortescue used Holtved's files to flesh out existing sets and develop new ones. A draft manuscript was produced from computer files in 1989 and was subsequently enlarged and refined to include the results of lexical research done by Darlene Orr in 1993 with the remaining speakers of Sirenikski. For a history of early comparative Eskimo work, see Krauss 1973.

The most significant new materials integrated into this second edition (by Fortescue) are the bulk of D. Pryde's manuscript dictionary of the western Canadian dialects (only the a's were available for the first edition), made available to the Institute of Eskimology following the author's death thanks to John MacDonald, plus the dictionaries of Naukanski and Nunivak Yupik assembled at the Alaska Native Language Center. Also, indices for Central Siberian Yupik and North Alaskan Inuit have been added, and numerous additions and corrections have been made by the authors on the basis of new information that has since come to light, notably from newer versions of the ANLC's Central Alaskan Yupik and Central Siberian Yupik dictionaries. Also, the original page on forms from single Eskimo languages with proposed cognates in Aleut has been replaced by a new list of Proto-Aleut bases with no obvious (or only a doubtful) Eskimo cognate. This broadens the dictionary's coverage of the Eskimo-Aleut family so that all bases found in at least two of the three Aleut dialects in Bergsland (1994) without a known cognate (or with a doubtful cognate) in Eskimo are listed separately.

Thanks (now, alas, posthumous) are due to Knut Bergsland for his careful reading of the original manuscript and for his detailed comments and suggestions. Thanks go also to David Lipscomb for the Tarramiut index, to Bent Nielsen for the Central Siberian Yupik index, to Nikolai Vakhtin for access to Sirenikski data, to Evgeni Golovko for access to Naukanski data, to Darlene Orr for field research in Sirenikski, to Michael Krauss for his support and encouragement, and to Jeff Leer for access to his Alutiiq lexical files, which contain Eskimo comparisons (not necessarily followed here) and for helpful critical advice. Darlene Orr and Joe Kwaraceius deserve recognition for their help in preparing the typed manuscript at various stages, as do Tom Alton and Leon Unruh, who prepared the final manuscripts for publication. We also thank Vye, N. Enmenkau, V. S. Qagaq, A. Verbitskaya, A. Ivanova, I. Leonova-Teplilek, and Yakov Taghyuq for providing Sirenikski and Naukanski forms, and Jean Briggs for access to her manuscript Utkusiksalingmiut dictionary. Thanks also to Christian Berthelsen and the late Gaba Thorning for information on West Greenlandic, and to Louis-Jacques Dorais for commenting on Eastern Canadian Inuit forms.

A collaborative project of this nature always entails compromises on certain issues when there is a difference of opinion on the part of the authors; these differences have not been noted but are sometimes responsible for qualifying words and phrases, such as "perhaps" and "possible relationship to" concerning derivational relationships. We recognize that this dictionary will never be truly complete but we hope that the layout of dictionary entries will make it useful to both scholars and laymen as a tool for elicitation of further Eskimo lexical material.

DIALECT MAPS WITH LISTS OF SETTLEMENTS

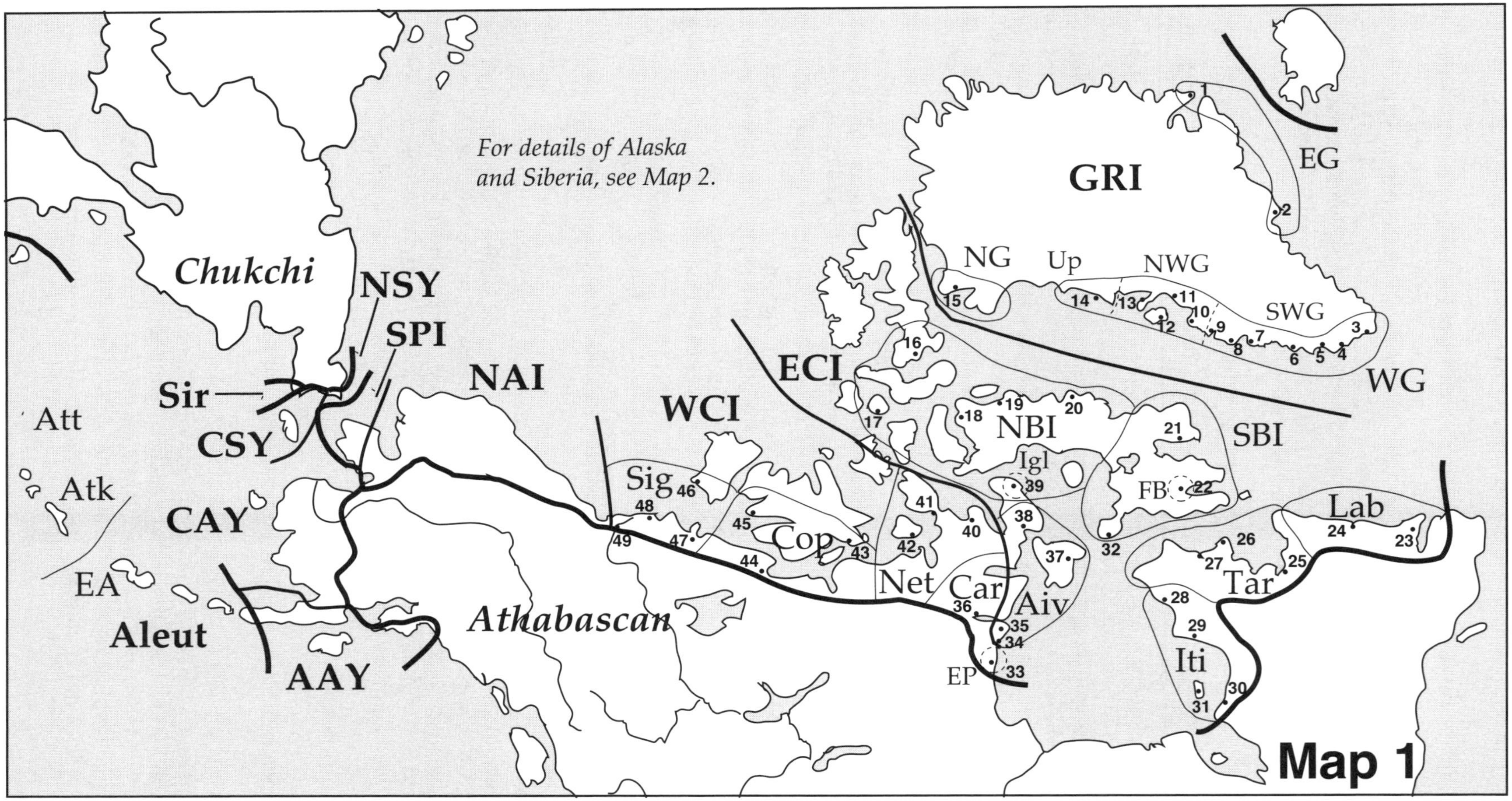

Notes to Map 1:

1) This map (and Map 2) are not meant to be thorough presentations of Eskimo-Aleut dialectology, but represent simply the dialects and languages of the source materials for this work. Also, smaller settlements are generally not shown.

2) Utkusiksalingmiut now live, along with others, in Gjoa Haven. No Utkusiksalingmiut region is shown on this map; it formerly occupied the area south of Gjoa Haven.

3) Within West Greenland SWG can be split into Central West Greenlandic, our default dialect and basis of the literary language (towns 7-9) and the southern 'i-dialects' (towns 3-6), which in turn can be broken up into the sub-dialects of Paamiut, Nanortalik-Qaqortoq and phonologically divergent Kap Farvel. NWG is also referred to as the Kangaatsiaq-Uummannaq sub-dialect.

4) The modern variety of Car spoken at Baker Lake is intermediate between WCI and ECI, according to Dorais.

Key to villages and towns on Map 1 (note that names are given first in their Euro-American version or form and then in the local standard Eskimo orthography)

1. Scoresbysund / Ittoqqortoormiit
2. Ammassalik / Tasiilaq
3. Kap Farvel: Frederiksdal / Narsaq Kujalleq
4. Nanortalik
5. Julianehåb / Qaqortoq
6. Frederikshåb / Paamiut
7. Godthåb / Nuuk
8. Sukkertoppen / Maniitsoq
9. Holsteinsborg / Sisimiut
10. Egedesminde / Aasiaat
11. Jacobshavn / Ilulissat
12. Godhavn / Qeqertarsuaq
13. Umanak / Uummannaq
14. Upernavik
15. Thule / Qaanaaq
16. Grise Fiord / Ausuittuq
17. Resolute Bay / Qausuittuq
18. Arctic Bay / Ikpiarjuk
19. Pond Inlet / Mittimatalik
20. Clyde River / Kangiqługaapik
21. Pangnirtung / Pangniqtuuq
22. Frobisher Bay / Iqaluit
23. Rigolet / Tikiraqsuarusik
24. Nain / Naini
25. Fort Chimo / Kuujjuaq
26. Wakeham Bay / Kangiqsujuaq
27. Saglouc / Salluit
28. Povungnituk / Puvirnituq
29. Port Harrison / Inujjuaq
30. Great Whale River / Kuujjuaraapik
31. Belcher Islands / Sanikiluaq
32. Cape Dorset / Kinngait
33. Eskimo Point / Arviat
34. Rankin Inlet / Kangiqłiniq
35. Chesterfield Inlet / Igluligaarjuk
36. Baker Lake / Qamanittuaq
37. Coral Harbour / Sagliq
38. Repulse Bay / Naujat
39. Igloolik / Iglulik
40. Pelly Bay / Arviligjuaq
41. Spence Bay / Talurjuaq
42. Gjoa Haven / Uqsuqtuuq
43. Cambridge Bay / Iqaluktuuttiaq
44. Coppermine / Qurluqtuq
45. Holman Island / Ulukhaqtuuq
46. Sachs Harbour / Ikaasuk
47. Paulatuk / Paulatuuq
48. Tuktuyaktuk / Tuktuujaqtuuq
49. Inuvik / Inuuvik

Key to abbreviations on map 1

AAY	Alutiiq Alaskan Yupik
Aiv	Aivilik
Atk	Atkan
Att	Attuan
Car	Caribou
CAY	Central Alaskan Yupik
Cop	Copper
CSY	Central Siberian Yupik
EA	Eastern Aleut
ECI	Eastern Canadian Inuit
EG	East Greenlandic
EP	Eskimo Point
FB	Frobisher Bay
GRI	Greenlandic Inuit
Igl	Iglulik
Iti	Itivimmiut
Lab	Labrador
NAI	North Alaskan Inuit
NBI	North Baffin-Iglulik
Net	Netsilik
NG	North Greenlandic/Polar Eskimo
NSY	Naukanski Siberian Yupik
NWG	Northwest Greenlandic
SB	South Baffin
Sig	Siglit
Sir	Sirenik(ski)
SPI	Seward Peninsula Inuit
SWG	Southwest Greenlandic
Tar	Tarramiut
Up	Upernavik
WCI	Western Canadian Inuit
WG	West Greenlandic

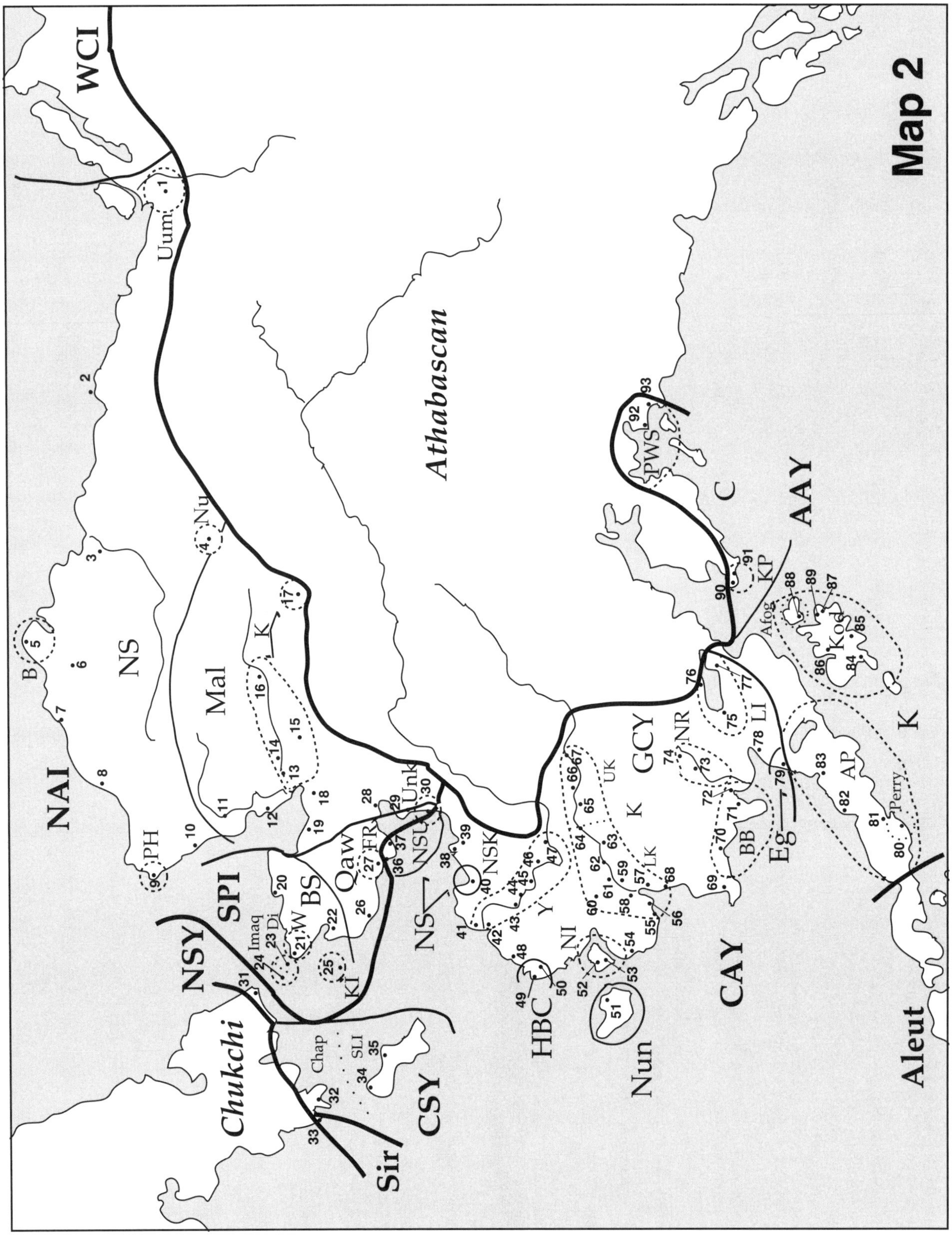
Map 2
Athabascan
Chukchi
Aleut
NAI
WCI
NSY
SPI
CSY
Sir
CAY
AAY
GCY
Nun
NS
Mal
BS
Qaw
Unk
NSK
HBC
PWS
Uum
Chap
SLI
Imaq
Perry
Afog
Kod

Notes to Map 2:
1) Atkasuk, Nuiqsut, Wainwright, Point Lay, and Kaktovik in NS_{NAI} resemble Barrow dialectally.
2) Brevig Mission and Shishmaref in BS_{SPI} resemble Wales dialectally. Teller includes speakers of Qaw_{SPI} and of BS_{SPI}.
3) Nome includes speakers of various SPI dialects, and CSY.
4) Elim and Golovin both include speakers of NS_{CAY} and Qaw_{SPI}
5) Unalakleet includes speakers of NS_{CAY}, Mal_{NAI} and Qaw_{SPI} (Unk subdialect).
6) Stebbins in GCY_{CAY} resembles NI_{GCY}.
7) Other CAY villages not included in (sub)dialect boundaries are dialectally transitional between nearby (sub)dialects.

Key to villages and towns on Map 2 (note that names are given first in their Euro-American version or form and then in the local standard Eskimo orthography):
1. Aklavik / Akłarvik
2. Kaktovik / Qaaktuġvik
3. Nuiqsut / Nuiqsat
4. Anaktuvuk Pass / Anaqtuuvak/Naqsraq
5. Barrow / Utqiaġvik
6. Atkasuk / Atqasuk
7. Wainwright / Ulġuniq
8. Pt. Lay / Kali
9. Point Hope / Tikiġaq
10. Kivalina / Kivaliñiq
11. Noatak / Nuataaq
12. Kotzebue / Qikiqtaġruk
13. Noorvik / Nuurvik
14. Kiana / Katyaak
15. Selawik / Siiḷivik / Akuliġaq
16. Shungnak / Isiŋnaq, Ambler / Ivisaappaat
17. Alatna / Alaasuq
18. Buckland / Kaŋiq
19. Deering / Ipnaitchiaq
20. Shishmaref / Qigiqtaq
21. Wales / Kiŋigin
22. Teller / Tala
23. Little Diomede / Iŋaliq
24. Big Diomede/ Imaqłiq
25. King Island / Ugiuvak (population moved to Nome)
26. Nome / Sitŋasuaq
27. White Mountain / Nasirvik
28. Koyuk / Kuuyuk
29. Shaktoolik / Saktuliq
30. Unalakleet / Uŋalaqłiit-Ungalaqliq
31. Naukan / Nuvuqaq (population moved elsewhere)
32. New Chaplino / Ungaziq
33. Sireniki / Sigheneg
34. Gambell / Sivuqaq
35. Savoonga / Sivungaq
36. Golovin / Siŋik-Cingik
37. Elim / Neviarcaurluq
38. Stebbins / Tapraq
39. St. Michael / Taciq
40. Kotlik / Qerrulliik
41. Emmonak / Imangaq
42. Alakanuk / Alarneq
43. Mountain Village / Asaacarsaq
44. St. Mary's / Negeqliq
45. Pilot Station / Tuutalgaq
46. Marshall / Masserculleq
47. Russian Mission / Iqugmiut
48. Scammon Bay / Marayaarmiut
49. Hooper Bay / Naparyaarmiut
50. Chevak / Cev'aq
51. Mekoryuk / Mikuryaq
52. Tununak / Tununeq
53. Toksook Bay /Nunakauyaq
54. Chefornak / Cevv'arneq, Kipnuk / Qipneq
55. Kwigillingok / Kuigilnguq
56. Kongiganak / Kangirnaq
57. Eek / Iik
58. Tuntutuliak / Tuntutuliaq
59. Napakiak / Naparyarraq
60. Kasigluk / Kassigluq Nunapitchuk / Nunapicuar,
    Atmautluak /Atmaulluaq
61. Bethel / Mamterilleq,
    Napaskiaq / Napaskiaq
62. Kwethluk / Kuiggluk,
    Akiachuk / Akiacuar,
    Akiak / Akiaq
63. Tuluksak / Tuulkessaaq
64. Kalskag / Qalqaq
65. Aniak / Anyaraq
66. Chuathbaluk / Curarpalek
67. Sleetmiut / Cellitemiut
68. Quinhagak / Kuinerraq
69. Goodnews Bay / Mamterat
70. Togiak / Tuyuryaq
71. Manokotak / Manuquutaq
72. Dillingham / Curyung
73. New Stuyahok / Cetuyaraq
74. Koliganek / Qalirneq
75. Igiugig / Igyaraq, Levelock / Liivlek
76. Newhalen/ Nuuriileng
77. Kokhonok / Qarr'unaq
78. Naknek / Nakneq
79. Egegik / Igyagiiq
80. Perryville
81. Chignik / Cirniq, Chignik Lake / Igyaraq
82. Port Heiden / Masrriq
83. Pilot Point / Agisaq
84. Akhiok / Kasukuak
85. Old Harbor / Nuniaq
86. Larsen Bay / Uyaqsaq, Karluk / Kal'ut
87. Kodiak / Sun'aq
88. Afognak (population moved elsewhere)
89. Ouzinkie / Uusenkaaq, Port Lions / Masiqsirraq
90. English Bay / Nanwalek
91. Port Graham / Paluwik
92. Tatitlek / Tatiillaaq
93. Cordova–Eyak / Igya'aq

Key to Abbreviations on Map 2:
AAY Alutiiq Alaskan Yupik
Afog Afognak
AP Alaska Peninsula
B Barrow
BB Bristol Bay
BS Bering Strait
C Chugach
CAY Central Alaskan Yupik
Chap Chaplinski
CSY Central Siberian Yupik
Di Little Diomede
Eg Egegik
FR Fish River
GCY General Central Yupik
HBC Hooper Bay-Chevak
Imaq Imaqliq or Big Diomede
K Kobuk (NAI)
K Koniag (AAY)
K Kuskokwim (CAY)
KI King Island
Kod Kodiak
KP Kenai Peninsula
LI Lake Iliamna
LK Lower Kuskokwim
Mal Malimiut
NAI North Alaskan Inuit
NI Nelson Island
NR Nushagak River
NS North Slope (NAI)
NS Norton Sound (CAY)
NSK Norton Sound Kotlik
NSU Norton Sound Unaliq
NSY Naukan(ski) Yupik
Nu Nunamiut
Nun Nunivak
Perry Perryville
PH Point Hope
PWS Prince William Sound
Qaw Qawiaraq
Sir Sirenik(ski)
SLI St. Lawrence Island
SPI Seward Peninsula Inuit
UK Upper Kuskokwim
Unk Unalakleet
Uum Uummarmiut
W Cape Prince of Wales
WCI Western Canadian Inuit
Y Yukon

INTRODUCTION

Eskimo-Aleut languages are spoken across the top of North America, from the Aleutian Islands to East Greenland, and on the coast of the Chukchi Peninsula, the eastern extremity of the Asian continent. Although relationships to other language families are open to question, the connection between the Eskimo and Aleut branches is certain, first suggested in Cook and King (1784) and formulated by Rask in 1819 (Thalbitzer 1916 and 1921). The Eskimo sub-family in turn comprises at least two branches: Yupik and Inuit. For this reason it is impossible to use any other word than 'Eskimo' to cover both branches, although 'Inuit' is preferred by many (especially in Canada) for the people who speak any of these languages—here it is to be understood as a purely technical linguistic term. Sirenikski has been proposed as a third branch, as discussed below.

The Yupik languages, spoken in an area that probably included the Eskimo 'homeland' (see Map 1), are more sharply differentiated than the different varieties of Inuit, which form a rough dialect continuum (see Map 2). For the purpose of this introduction, these varieties will be referred to as languages, since the dictionary represents them in a parallel fashion to the Yupik languages. Some transitions within Inuit are more abrupt than others. Intelligibility today between the two ends of the continuum is minimal. At one end of the continuum, the Seward Peninsula dialects are distanced from neighboring Inuit by the phonological influence of a Yupik substrate. In earlier times, probably less than five hundred years ago, there must have been a Yupik continuum from St. Lawrence Island and the opposing shore of Chukotka northward and across the Bering Strait, through the Seward Peninsula and south to the Pacific coast of Alaska, later broken by the Inuit intrusion onto the Seward Peninsula. At the other end, East Greenlandic has undergone massive word replacement (owing to ritual name avoidance) on top of certain accelerated phonological developments (but not so much so nor so deeply so as to be considered an Inuit grouping separate from other Greenlandic in this work). North Greenlandic, note, is a late intrusion from Canada, but it has been drawn lexically more and more into the Greenlandic group of dialects in recent times.

More problematical is the relationship to the rest of the family of Sirenikski, formerly spoken in Chukotka but now extinct. This highly divergent form of Eskimo has unique traits both archaic and innovative, and it has undergone strong influence from neighboring Chukchi (as have the two other Eskimo languages in Chukotka). Sirenikski has apparently borrowed extensively from neighboring and dominant Central Siberian Yupik, often with total or partial adjustment to fit Sirenikski phonology. Today, Sirenikski is closer to Yupik than to Inuit. However, Sirenikski may actually be a third branch of Eskimo along with Yupik and Inuit. Thus PY-S (Proto-Yupik-Sirenikski) may be a fictitious entity but is used here for convenience, since in many cases where a Proto-Yupik form is also represented in Sirenikski (but not Inuit), it is impossible to determine whether it was borrowed from Central Siberian Yupik.

The basic criterion for setting up a PE (Proto-Eskimo) comparative set in this dictionary is that attested cognates should exist in at least two of the ten languages (or dialect groupings, in the case of Inuit) including at least one from each side of the family. A similar principle holds for PY (Proto-Yupik) and PI (Proto-Inuit) sets *mutatis mutandis.* The homogeneity of these hypothetical proto-phases in space and time is subject to doubt, however, as innovative traits, both phonological and lexical, have diffused across boundaries at different stages. The break between PY and PI is nevertheless abrupt enough in terms of phonological and lexical isoglosses to sanction the traditional division between the two major branches of the family.

In some cases a form in a modern language may include morphemes that extend the posited protoform. Occasionally, certain modern forms may not include suffix morphemes found in posited protoforms. No distinction has been made in this edition between cases where a derived word in a daughter language is derivable from the posited protoform purely by recognized processes (described below) and those cases where the derived word—while clearly belonging to the comparative set—is derived by other than recognized processes, i.e. through unexplained correspondence sub-rules, contaminations, anomalous changes, etc.

A dash indicates that there is no attested cognate in a given language. That is, either no cognate exists or else none is recorded in available sources. In general, no distinction has been made between the following cases: (1) a cognate has been sought by elicitation from a range of speakers of the language in question but has not been found and therefore presumably does not presently exist in that language, and (2) no cognate is attested in available sources but one may yet exist in the language and might be found by elicitation.

The symbol ➞ found in a main set indicates that although no direct reflex is given in the main set, a reflex will be found in a derivative set beneath the main entry. Notice that derived forms cited for individual languages under main entries are usually not analysed—this would of course be desirable in a future expanded version of the dictionary.

When cognates on successive lines bear exactly the same meaning, the gloss has not been repeated but can be assumed to carry down from above. Glosses from original sources in other languages are given in English translation, and all forms are phonemicized unless there is some reason for uncertainty. In such cases, forms are cited as given in the source named. Uncertain protoform glosses are followed by a question mark. The criterion for entering a cognate set indented as a derivative beneath a main entry is that it should not be completely predictable from the constituent base plus postbase(s) but should contain morphological or semantic idiosyncracies of linguistic interest. Cross-references to ingredient postbases are given when these postbases have been set up as protoform sets in the postbase section. The criteria for postbase sets are the same as for base sets. When a decision between two competing protoform reconstructions is problematical, both of them are given, separated by 'or'. Two protoforms separated by 'and' are given when there are two different formative patterns for a derivative set embodying the same idea. It should be borne in mind that parallel derivatives may develop independently in the different languages. (Thus it is possible to reconstruct a 'proto-Eskimo' form *qinəʀun for 'telescope'!) Moreover, some derivatives must have spread locally, so, strictly speaking, their assignment to a particular proto-stage is not always justified.

Probable cognates in Aleut, a much more distantly — but clearly — related language, are cited in brackets following PE, PY, PY-S or PI forms. A PY (or PY-S or PI) form that has an Aleut cognate must have been present in PE as well; however, since it is attested today only in Yupik (or Yupik-Sirenik or Inuit) the protoform reconstruction is in PY (or PY-S or PI) and not PE. Proto-Eskimo-Aleut reconstructions have not been attempted, but the sound correspondences necessary for reconstruction can be found in Bergsland 1986. (Only the most important ones are mentioned below.) Such reconstructions would not look very different from the PE ones except in distinguishing a PE-A t_1 and t_2 (the latter perhaps from an affricate *c) and apparently also a PE-A c_1 and c_2.

The dictionary also contains 'old' loan words, that is, from Aleut, Chukchi, Old Norse and Athabaskan languages, that meet our distributional criteria for inclusion. The forms given are reconstructions of the original borrowings and are not preceded by 'PE', 'PI' or 'PY'. In fact many if not most of these loan words were borrowed independently into several of the present-day languages or borrowed into one and diffused to other(s), rather than being borrowed at a proto-stage. Chukchi loans found only in the Siberian Eskimo languages are only exceptionally included since they are probably of more recent date, and for the same reason Russian and English loans are categorically excluded. Note that Bergsland (1994) in his Appendix 10 gives a list of loans and diffusions between Eskimo languages and Aleut.

As a reasonable estimate, one could suggest that our reconstructed PE belongs to a period some time around two thousand years ago, whereas hypothetical PE-A would belong to a period of around two thousand years earlier than that (cf. Dumond 1987 and Fortescue 1985). PI can be dated to around a thousand years ago in North Alaska, about the same time as the linguistic ancestor of Alaskan Yupik moved down onto the Alaska Peninsula and the Gulf of Alaska. The extension of Canadian and Greenlandic Inuit south from the High Arctic to Labrador and southern Greenland (along both coasts) took place gradually over the following centuries. Aleut is believed to have been spoken on the Aleutian archipelago for at least three thousand years, but with a later partial overlay of a single eastern dialect of the language obscuring earlier variation so that the dialect variation today is not so great as might be expected. Eskimo has been spoken on the Chukchi Peninsula for at least two thousand years, with Sirenikski possibly representing a first wave of arrivals from what is believed to be the point of origin of Eskimo culture on the Alaskan side of Bering Strait.

Forms unmarked as to dialect represent either the default dialect, as explained below, or are present throughout the language. Other dialect forms follow these default or general forms and are marked as to their dialect. Exceptions to this pattern are made clear by punctuation and dialect markings.

PE (AND LATER) PHONEMES

(Notes to the two charts in this section appear on page xx.)

Non-PE phonemes are given in parentheses

Consonants

	p	t		c[1]			k	q	(ʼ)[2]
v	(w)	ð	l	(z)	(ž)[3]	y	ɣ	ʀ	
(f)	(w̥)		ł	(s)	(š)[3]	(y̥)	(x)	(X)	(h)
	m	n					ŋ	(ʀ̃)	
	(m̥)	(n̥)					(ŋ̊)		

Palatalization and labialization (both non-PE) are shown with superscripts: l^y, ɬ^y, n^y, k^w, q^w, ɣ^w, ʀ^w, x^w, X^w, ŋ^w, and ŋ̊^{w}. Possible PE n^y is not indicated (see under A 13 below). Gemination is shown by doubling consonants.

Vowels

i/ɨ[4]   u

ə

a

Length is shown by doubling vowels.

For purposes of alphabetization ð counts as d, ə as e, ɣ as g, and ʀ as r. ŋ follows n, X follows x, a symbol with a diacritic follows the corresponding symbol without the diacritic, and a labialized or palatalized consonant follows the corresponding plain consonant. Thus the alphabetic order is: a, c, ð, ə, f, ɣ, ɣ^w, h, i, ɨ, k, k^w, l, l^y, ɬ, ɬ^y, m, m̥, n, n^y, n̥, ŋ, ŋ^w, ŋ̊, ŋ̊^{w}, p, q, q^w, ʀ, ʀ^w, ʀ̃ ,s, š, t, u, v, w, w̥, x, x^w, X, X^w, y, y̥, z, ž, ‘. (In practice, alphabetization in the bases and postbases sections applies only to PE, PI, and PY forms and loans, and therefore does not involve all of the above symbols.) Material in parentheses indicates uncertain elements within a form and does not count in alphabetization.

The reader is directed to the works listed in the bibliography for information on standard practical writing systems—in Cyrillic, Roman, and Syllabics—used with the various Aleut and Eskimo languages. Brief discussions of the equivalences between standard writing and that used in this work will be found in the Aleut, Central Alaskan Yupik, Eastern Canadian Inuit, and Western Greenlandic protoform index sections.

LANGUAGES, DIALECTS, AND ABBREVIATIONS

Division into dialects is problematical and uneven and often reflects available sources of information more than actual dialect differences. Note that in the following list of subdialects of a given dialect is not necessarily exhaustive for the dialect, but represents only the varieties considered especially relevant for this work and where documentation is available (and likewise for sub-subdialects). Dialects and subdialects are listed in rough geographical order.

<u>Alutiiq</u> (**AAY—**Alutiiq Alaskan Yupik), also called Pacific Yupik or Sugpiaq, is spoken in Alaska on the shores of Prince William Sound, at the tip of Kenai Peninsula, on Kodiak Island, and on the Alaska Peninsula.

Dialects and subdialects:

- Chugach (**C**)
  - Prince William Sound (**PWS**)
  - Kenai Peninsula (**KP**)
- Koniag (**K**)
  - Kodiak (**Kod**)
    - Afognak (**Afog**)
  - Alaska Peninsula (**AP**)
    - Perryville (**Perry**)

<u>Central Alaskan Yupik</u> (**CAY**) is spoken in south-western Alaska around Bristol Bay and the lower drainages of the Yukon and Kuskokwim Rivers.

Dialects and subdialects:

- Egegik (**Eg**)
- General Central Yupik (**GCY**)
  - Lake Iliamna (**LI**)
  - Nushagak River (**NR**)
  - Bristol Bay (**BB**)
  - Kuskokwim (**K**)
    - Lower Kuskokwim (**LK**)
    - Upper Kuskokwim (**UK**)
  - Nelson Island (**NI**)
  - Yukon (**Y**)
- Hooper Bay-Chevak (**HBC**)
- Nunivak (**Nun**)
- Norton Sound (**NS**)
  - Norton Sound Kotlik (**NSK**)
  - Norton Sound Unaliq (**NSU**)

For some purposes it is desirable to group Y, LI, and UK as ‘peripheral’ GCY, and LK and BB as ‘core’ GCY, with NR and NI falling somewhat in between peripheral and core.

<u>Naukan(ski)</u> (**NSY—**Naukan Siberian Yupik) is actually intermediate between Central Alaskan and Central Siberian Yupik, with the term “Siberian” reflecting geographical rather than linguistic position. It was spoken at East Cape on the Chukchi Peninsula of the (former) Soviet Far East, until the population was relocated to Lavrentiya and other settlements in 1958.

<u>Central Siberian Yupik</u> (**CSY**) is spoken on St. Lawrence Island, Alaska, and on the opposite coast of Chukotka.

Varieties:

- Chaplinski (**Chap**)
- St. Lawrence Island (**SLI**)

Note that separate designations for SLI and Chap represent a difference in sources more than an actual dialect difference, although traces of subdialectal variation are present in both varieties.

<u>Sirenik(ski)</u> (**Sir**) was spoken in Sireniki, Chukotka, and recently became extinct. At the time of the first edition it was remembered by two elderly persons, of whom Vye was Orr’s, Krupnik’s, and Vakhtin’s primary informant.

<u>Seward Peninsula Inuit</u> (**SPI**) is spoken on the Seward Peninsula in northwestern Alaska and on adjacent islands in Bering Strait.

Dialects:

- Bering Strait (**BS**)
  - Imaqliq or Big Diomede (**Imaq**)
  - Little Diomede (**Di**)

King Island (**KI**)
Cape Prince of Wales (**W**)
Qawiaraq (**Qaw**)
Fish River (**FR**)
Unalakleet (**Unk**)

Note that separate designations for Di and Imaq represent a difference in sources more than an actual sub-dialect difference.

North Alaskan Inuit (**NAI**) is spoken in northern and northwestern Alaska with extensions to Norton Sound and into Canada.

Dialects:

Malimiut (**Mal**)
Kobuk (**K**)
North Slope (**NS**)
Point Hope (**PH**)
Barrow (**B**)
Nunamiut (**Nu**)
Uummarmiut (**Uum**)

Western Canadian Inuit (**WCI**) is spoken in northwestern Canada from the Mackenzie Delta to the (south)western shore of Hudson Bay.

Dialects:

Siglit (**Sig**)
Copper (**Cop**)
Caribou (**Car**)
Eskimo Point (**EP**)
Netsilik (**Net**)
Utkusiksalingmiut (**Utk**)

Note that Dorais 1990b treats Car as an eastern dialect—this probably reflects recent influence from the east there and we have kept our original boundary between WCI and ECI in this version of the dictionary.

Eastern Canadian Inuit (**ECI**) is spoken in the eastern Canadian Arctic, including part of the western shore of Hudson Bay, and extending to the Davis Strait, including Labrador.

Dialects:

Aivilik (**Aiv**)
South Baffin (**SB**)—including Frobisher Bay (**FB**)
Tarramiut (**Tar**)
North Baffin-Iglulik (**NBI**)
Iglulik (**Igl**)
Itivimmiut (**Iti**)
Labrador (**Lab**)

Greenlandic Inuit (**GRI**)

Dialects:

North Greenlandic/Polar Eskimo (**NG**)
West Greenlandic (**WG**)
Upernavik (**Up**)
Southwest Greenlandic (**SWG**)
Central West Greenlandic (**CWG**)
Northwest Greenlandic (**NWG**)
East Greenlandic (**EG**)

NWG corresponds to Schultz-Lorentzen's 'N.G.', and SWG to his 'S.G.' minus CWG around Nuuk (which he included under it, so some forms marked 'SWG' are indeed used in Nuuk, where sub-dialects have become somewhat mixed today). SWG proper can be divided into Paamiut, Qaqortoq-Nanortalik, and Kap Farvel sub-dialects, although the differences are mainly phonological rather than lexical.

DEFAULT DIALECTS, DEFAULT AND OTHER SOURCES, AND ORTHOGRAPHIC ISSUES FOR INDIVIDUAL LANGUAGES

Alutiiq Alaskan Yupik (AAY)
Default dialect: Kenai Peninsula
Default sources: (J. Leer's dictionaries and files)
Additional sources: Birket-Smith 1953

An apostrophe is used when prosody indicates that a consonant has dropped intervocalically but that consonant is not determinable within AAY. Consonants that appear only in some forms in some dialects are in angled brackets.

Entries are given in their preprosodic forms, that is, without indication of rhythmic length or prosodically caused gemination or fortition. Compressed like vowels are written long (double) if and only if it is ascertainable within AAY that they are indeed compressed and not underlyingly short. (See Leer in Krauss 1985 for information on compression, fortition, and AAY prosody.)

Central Alaskan Yupik (CAY)
Default dialect: General Central Yupik
Default source: Jacobson 1984
Additional sources: Holtved's notes for Mountain Village and Hooper Bay, Hammerich's ms. lexicon and Lantis's notes for Nunivak, and the Cup'ig Eskimo Dictionary (2003) for Nunivak (newer forms from there are marked 'ANLC').

Entries are given in their preprosodic forms, that is, without indication of rhythmic length or prosodically caused gemination. ə deleted for prosodic reasons (in dialects other than NSU) is not written. ə that appears only in some forms is in angled brackets. In those dialects (Eg, Nun, and HBC) in which compression occurs, compressed like vowels are written long (double) if and only if it is ascertainable within that dialect that they are indeed compressed and not underlyingly short.

Nun forms are written as pronounced with final fricatives rather than stops, and with geminated fricatives devoiced. However, if a Nun form differs from the form used elsewhere only in one or both of these two ways, then the Nun form is not listed separately.

w is distinguished from v and y from z even though in some dialects w becomes v under certain conditions and similarly y becomes z. w is distinguished from γ^w even though they are in complementary distribution except when geminated. w̥ as written here is equivalent to xʷ. Initial ua, ui, and ia are indistinguishable from waa, wii, and yaa, respectively, and are written here in the latter form. Initial ə is written even when silent or almost silent and its presence ascertainable mostly—and sometimes only—from its effect on prosody.

Naukanski Siberian Yupik (NSY)
Default source: Menovshchikov 1975
Additional sources: Manuscript dictionary by Teplilek-Leonova (we regret the spurious attribution in the first edition), dictionary files by Emel'yanova (annotated by E. Golovko), wordlist by Tasyan Tein from *I Bylo Tak*, and forms received via S. Taghyuq from Akukin by D. Orr and from N. Enmenkau and other Naukan speakers present at the 7th Inuit Studies Conference in Fairbanks; all of this and more recently elicited forms have been integrated into the Naukan Eskimo dictionary published by Alaska Native Language Center in 2004 (newer forms from there are abbreviated 'ANLC').

Underlying ia and ai are phonetically identical, realized as [e:] and written ē in Soviet sources. There is a slight diphthongization of this sound, giving something close to [ea] (see Krauss 1985). We write ia for all such vowels, whether the source is ai or ia. On the other hand, underlying au and ua are phonetically distinct. Underlying au is realized as [a:]; written ā in Soviet sources, and we write aa here. Slightly diphthongized ua sounds like [ɔa] and is written ō in Soviet sources and ua in this work. (Underlying iu is realized as [i:] and written here as ii; ui undergoes no change.)

The present/habitual postbase aqə- is deleted from verbal forms as cited in Soviet sources.

Central Siberian Yupik (CSY)
Default source: Badten et al. 1987, rev. 2008
Additional sources: Rubtsova 1971, Vakhtin and Emel'yanova 1988

Entries are given in their preprosodic forms, that is, without indication of rhythmic vowel length or "overlength" (see Krauss 1975).

w as written here is equivalent to ɣʷ, and w̥ as written here is equivalent to xʷ.

The present/habitual postbase aqə- is deleted from verbal forms as cited in Soviet sources.

Sirenikski (Sir)
Default source: Menovshchikov 1964
Additional sources: N. Vakhtin's Sir dictionary files compiled from texts gathered by Men., Rubtsova and himself (now published, 2000), dictionary files by Emel'yanova, word list from Miller, forms received from Vye by I. Krupnik and D. Orr

The present/habitual postbase cəqəʀ- is deleted from verbal forms as cited in Soviet sources. With transitive forms as customarily cited (because of the addition of certain postbases), it is not usually possible to distinguish ɣ/ʀ bases from xtə/Xtə. Vowel length is problematical. Theoretically, long vowels should not exist; however, vowel length is sometimes indicated in the default source marked here with an acute accent perhaps actually indicating prototonic stress. Also forms that may be borrowings from CSY (rather than cognates) sometimes apparently have shortened the original long vowels. It is not always possible to distinguish between cognates and recent CSY borrowings which have undergone partial or complete adaptation to Sirenikski phonology. Nevertheless, all forms reported by our informants as Sirenikski rather than CSY are included with the understanding that some may in fact be borrowed.

Seward Peninsula Inuit (SPI)
Default dialect: King Island
Default source: L. Kaplan's ms. dictionary—King Island unless otherwise specified
Additional sources: Menovshchikov 1980 for Imaqliq, essentially the same dialect as Diomede; Kaplan's Diomede files; Kaplan's Qawiaraq ms. dictionary; Jenness 1928 for Wales

Forms are given with consonants deleted or lenited by consonant weakening (see Kaplan in Krauss 1985). Geminate consonants are contrastive only after the first short vowel of the stem. Otherwise, length of intervocalic consonants is not contrastive and depends on position in the word, so all such consonants are written single. The present/habitual postbase žaq/taq/ɣaq- is deleted from verbal forms as cited in Soviet sources. Although phonemically triple vowels may result from consonant deletions in the King Island dialect, these are almost always across morpheme boundaries and do not figure here. Half-long a (written a·) results from deletion of a syllable-final uvular following the vowel a.

North Alaskan Inuit (NAI)
Default dialect: Barrow
Default source: ANLC ms. dictionary (MacLean et al.)
Additional sources: Kobuk Junior Dictionary (Sun et al. 1979) and/or W. Seiler's manuscript dictionary for Malimiut (now published, 2005)

Intervocalic recessive continuants that appear only in certain forms/derivatives are in angled brackets. Palatalized t is written c. For Kobuk (northern Malimiut), diphthongs that are leveled and assimilated are written as if they were full contrasting diphthongs. Reflexes of *ə are written ɨ to distinguish them from reflexes of *i which cause palatalization of alveolars and—in Malimiut—some velars. i and ɨ are almost always indistinguishable phonetically. In other varieties of Inuit, this distinction is not nearly so important as in NAI and is therefore not noted. (See Kaplan 1976 and Rischel 1974.)

Western Canadian Inuit (WCI)
Default dialect: Copper
Default source: M. Métayer 1953
Additional sources: Lowe 1983, 1984b, Rasmussen's texts for Net and Car, etc.; D. Pryde's ms. dictionary (all dialects), Dorais 1990 for Net and Baker Lake, Owingayak 1986 for EP, and Briggs' ms dictionary for Utk.

Where dialect forms have either s or h, only the s form is given. Net, Car and Cop always have geminate xx, XX and ff for C+*s, and have h initially and intervocalically rather than single s, but these dialects do have ts (tt in Cop).

Glottal stop (written apostrophe) is indicated only when phonologically distinctive.

y before another continuant (including a second y) is written as in other WCI but pronounced as an alveopalatal affricate in Sig; ts is written as in other WCI but pronounced tc in Sig.

Eastern Canadian Inuit (ECI)
Default dialect: Tarramiut and other Eastern Canadian dialects as given in Schneider
Default source: L. Schneider 1966, 1985
Additional sources: L.-J. Dorais 1978, 1975b, etc., for NBI and SB; Spalding 1979 for NBI and R. Jeddore—or Peck where noted—for Lab; also Mark Saul's comments for Tar, which refers substantially to Qumaq 1990; note that Schn.'s 'adg' usually means Car but sometimes refers to Aiv

For ECI ʀs is written rather than qs as further west, though the actual phonetic difference may not be as great as the difference in writing suggests. Also ʀ plus a stop is written even for Tar though q plus the stop might be more accurate phonetically. For consistency yy and qq and ʀʀ are written rather than ty, ʀq or qʀ as in Schn. and y is written for Iti ž. Syllable-final consonants deleted by 'Schneider's law' (discussed below) are indicated in brackets. (When there is doubt C is written.) Labials or velars plus C are given in their assimilated Tar forms (i.e. CC, or ts for *Cs/Cł). For modern Lab (which has largely neutralized the uvular/velar distinction, especially finally and before a consonant) ɣ and xx (Jed.'s qq) are written for *ɣ/ʀ and *ɣɣ/ʀʀ (except when the citation is of an earlier pre-neutralized form, e.g. Bourquin, who also has the q/k distinction finally), and qq is written for Jed.'s kq. For consistency, yy is written for Jed.'s tj and ff for Jed.'s pv.

Greenlandic Inuit (GRI)
Default dialect: West Greenlandic (central)
Default source: Schultz-Lorentzen and Berthelsen et al. (Ordbogi/Oqaatsit) Additional sources: M. Fortescue's ms. word list for Up; Fortescue 1991 supplemented by Holtved's files for NG; M. Vebæk's 2001 texts for southernmost WG; Robbe and Dorais 1986 for EG; and a newer EG ms. word-list made available by Robbe and Mennecier for the first edition—now supplemented by Tersis 2008.

Forms are cited with all assimilations as in the new orthography, but s and š are distinguished as in the old (Kleinschmidt) orthography. Verbal ɣ-final and t-final bases are distinguished as in the old orthography, although this is sometimes spurious. Verb-forms ending in -ɣpoq in the old orthography are given as t-final bases.

The old orthographic forms are cited when they show relevant unassimilated clusters of consonants or vowels. Assimilation processes were being generalized at the time when old spellings were fixed, ca. 1850–1870. Sometimes, old orthographic clusters are spurious (i.e. attempts at historical reconstruction), and we note these cases.

For phonetic accuracy, c rather than s is written word-initially for EG, and C is written at the end of historical ɣ-final or t-final verbal bases.

For phonetic accuracy, h is written for NG corresponding to a single s (or š) in WG, but as in WG ss is written when double. Earlier labial plus C clusters are given in assimilated (CC) form. NG (unlike WG, which is the basis for the practical orthography) has syllable-final q and k on verb bases and they are written as such. Very recent vowel sequence changes are not indicated, e.g. *ua to aa and *ui to ii.

Aleut (Al)
Default dialect: Atkan
Source: Bergsland 1980, 1986, and 1994 supplemented with additional items and comments from Bergsland

Forms cited have been converted to the phonemic orthography employed in the present work, with nominal vowel-final bases indicated by a hyphen before final X. Eastern Aleut (EA) and Attuan (Att) dialect forms are indicated where appropriate.

Additional points:
'Positional (nominal) bases' and 'emotional (verbal) roots' (see Jacobson 1984) are marked accordingly: the former are followed by a hyphen to indicate obligatory possessed marking, and the latter are given with yuɣ- (a typical postbase for such roots) in parentheses following them. 'Deep roots' (usually monosyllabic and occuring as part of a longer base) are not treated as independent entries, but a relationship between bases containing a particular deep root is indicated by 'cf.' and information in square brackets. Yupik 'postural roots' (see Jacobson 1983) are given without any of the obligatory suffixes.

Yupik verbal tə-final bases usually correspond to PE bases ending in t; in Sir there is a fluctuation between tə bases of this sort and bases in final t (compare under t-[1]). In Inuit east of NAI, verbal bases in ut(i)- ('with, for') are cited with the i in parentheses, since this regularly drops except before truncating postbases. Nominal bases are cited in absolutive citation form, not as underlying bases (except the positional bases mentioned above and certain others requiring obligatory possessor marking).

Final 'strong' q (or ʀ) behaves under suffixation in a manner parallel to k (or ɣ) as regards truncation. Strong q (written as q*) is differentiated only for CAY, CSY, NAI, and GRI. Parentheses for the latter indicate fluctuation—usually strong in singular only. Where q* does not follow ə (or VV in CSY), it may reflect a contraction. Not all available information concerning q* is incorporated into this edition; for some languages information on this point is not readily available, and moreover, in many cases the distinction between q* and 'weak' q is highly variable depending on speaker or is totally absent.

It is assumed that PE had no double vowel sequences and had syllable-final obstruents that could have been stops or fricatives (written here as the latter except for t). Original geminate consonants are assumed, though reduced in Yup and Sir, though the status of some PI geminates is in doubt (the second consonant is then written in parentheses). Original continuant + stop and continuant + continuant clusters are assumed, also stop + continuant with deleted ə. PE ł is assumed to derive from pre-Eskimo (perhaps pre-Eskimo-Aleut) clusters like *tl (if not from contact devoicing). ł is written in PE forms intervocalically and next to a fricative but not next to a stop, where neutralization is assumed.

PI forms have word-final stops (as do PY and PY-S nominal forms). Unlike PE forms, PI forms may have vowel sequences. They also have ž rather than ð, as do PY and PY-S forms, but ə and c like PE and PY; s and š are assumed for both PI and PY in certain positions. Voicing neutralization in protoform consonant clusters is only partially reflected: s and š are written next to a voiceless consonant rather than y or ž in PY (š also in PI, except following p or t, where most non-Greenlandic reflexes have a voiced cluster today), whereas l, ɣ, and ʀ are retained in similar contexts (a purely orthographical convention).

PRINCIPAL SOUND CHANGES FROM PROTO-ESKIMO TO THE MODERN LANGUAGES

Subscripts on abbreviations in the following indicate to which of the ten Eskimo languages (as considered in this work) the dialect in question belongs. Thus, K$_{AAY}$ is the K dialect of AAY, that is, the Koniag dialect of Alutiiq Alaskan Yupik, while K$_{CAY}$ is the K dialect of CAY, that is, the Kuskokwim dialect of Central Alaskan Yupik. In discussing Inu, "original i" means i from PE i rather from PE ə, that is, not ɨ.

A. Consonants

1. PE k: Intervocalic *k goes to ɣ in Inu, except after initial vowels of words. Remaining k, and other stops, may reflect earlier geminates or clusters. More generally *k goes to ɣ non-initially in EG$_{GRI}$ and in 'weak' position in non-Qaw SPI. *qVk- goes to qVq- in WG$_{GRI}$ and EG$_{GRI}$. *k goes to c following original i(C) in northern Mal$_{NAI}$ in some morphemes. Final *k goes to x in Sir and Nun$_{CAY}$. Initial *k is dropped in some words (including when from PE t) before ə in GCY$_{CAY}$ and NS$_{CAY}$ (e.g. əntə- from *tənət- by way of kəntə-), and when followed by əx in AAY and CSY. Final k goes to ŋ in NG$_{GRI}$ (if not just unexploded), and similarly with all stops (replaced by nasals finally).

2. PE q: Intervocalically *q goes to ʀ in Inu, except after initial vowels of words. Remaining q, and other stops, may reflect earlier geminates or clusters. More generally *q goes to ʀ non-initially in EG$_{GRI}$ and in 'weak' position in SPI, and to X in Tar$_{ECI}$ and Lab$_{ECI}$, but in the latter neutralized to k word-finally and to kx when geminate. Final *q goes to X in Sir and Nun$_{CAY}$. Initial *q is dropped when followed by əX in AAY and CSY.

3. PE p and t: *p and *t are generally preserved, but *p is weakened to v in 'weak' position in non-Qaw SPI. *t is assibilated to [t^s] before i in WG$_{GRI}$. Intervocalically, *t goes to l in EG$_{GRI}$. Final *t goes to y in Sir when from plural inflection t (via *ð?) and in PH$_{NAI}$ generally (where it is a strident fricative). *t goes to s after original i in NAI and GRI (less regularly also in NBI$_{ECI}$ and Net$_{WCI}$) and in NAI to c finally. *tət usually goes to cət (AAY cəst; CSY əst) in Yup, but in HBC$_{CAY}$ to cit, and in NSY to sit.

Note that Eskimo *p corresponds to Aleut h initially and m̥ medially. Eskimo *t may correspond to either t (*t$_1$) or to c (*t$_2$) in Aleut (or medially to s before ə). Note also that there is no t before i (and no c before ə) in PE, a fact that may be related to the complex t ~ c ~ s relationships between Eskimo and Aleut.

4. PE c: *c is preserved in AAY, CAY, and FR$_{SPI}$ and is also found in older Sig$_{WCI}$, NSY, CSY and Alaskan Inuit lexical data. Cases of s rather than c in AAY and CAY may reflect (apart from loan words) various sources, including *əcV-, *cəC-, *tð, and *ty. Otherwise *c goes to s, but with traces of c remaining in NAI geminate/cluster tc (which is ts in WCI, ECI, and GRI and tt in NBI$_{ECI}$, Cop$_{WCI}$, southernmost SWG$_{GRI}$ (before a and u), and NWG$_{GRI}$ but not Up$_{GRI}$). *c is preserved initially in EG$_{GRI}$. *c goes to h (or h-like allophones) in Nu$_{NAI}$, Uum$_{NAI}$, Cop$_{WCI}$, Net$_{WCI}$, Car$_{WCI}$, and NG$_{GRI}$, with PI *ks and *qs usually becoming xx and XX respectively and *ps often becoming ff (but ss in NG$_{GRI}$). Intervocalically *c goes to š (except after original i) in Mal$_{NAI}$ and into z in 'weak' position in non-Qaw SPI. PI *ss and *šš go to ts in Up$_{GRI}$ and *ss goes to ts in EG$_{GRI}$. Initial *c is dropped before ə in some words in core GCY$_{CAY}$ (e.g. əła from cəła in other CAY, ultimately from *cila).

Note that Eskimo c may correspond to Aleut c (*c_1) or to Aleut s (*c_2).

5. PE ð: *ð is usually dropped between full vowels (except when geminated or after i from *ə—i.e. ɨ—in Inu) in Yup and Inu, in the former also following a consonant (and otherwise merged with y intervocalically). Preconsonantally and intervocalically before ə, ð falls together in Yup with PE y (q.v.). In Sir *ð goes to ž (before a full vowel) and to c (before ə, apparently under Chukchi influence). In CSY and NSY, *ð sometimes goes to ž intervocalically or in clusters with other continuants. There are various reflexes of *ð in Inu: (retroflex) ž in SPI, NAI, and Net$_{WCI}$; y in other WCI and ECI; retroflex š in older WG$_{GRI}$; h in NG$_{GRI}$; and l in EG$_{GRI}$ (becoming tt when geminated) and also in Cop$_{WCI}$ and PH$_{NAI}$ before other continuants. In many instances a recessive ž in nominal bases in Inu (written in this work in angle brackets for NAI) does not represent the reflex of *ð, and the same is true of recessive ɣ in verbal bases. *ð may go to s before i (e.g. Inu isiq, Yup (ə)səq from *əðiʀ) or to l (see *aðiʀ), but in CSY *ð may also go to z (along with *y). *ð is dropped before *ə in Inu bases like qaa- from *qaðə-, kuuk from *kuðəɣ and qiiq from *qiðəʀ. In AAY and CAY *Vðə goes to Vi in such cases (in CSY and NSY only in the case of *iðə and *uðə). *ð becomes š after a stop in SPI and NAI (except Nu$_{NAI}$, where after k and q it becomes ž). Furthermore š from *ð merges with s in WCI (ecept Net$_{WCI}$) and ECI, (and in recent WG$_{GRI}$ š merges with s also intervocalically—though not in conservative central WG$_{GRI}$). *ð goes to ɣ before v or ɣ in ECI.

Note that *ð alternates with t after a consonant in postbases and inflections such as PE indicative *ðuʀ, tuʀ.

(Proto)-Eskimo *ð corresponds to ð in Aleut (where the proto-Eskimo-Aleut value is preserved or has gone to z, especially in certain Atkan postbases). In some cases the protophoneme has been preserved in Aleut but has gone to *y in PE between full vowels other than i.

6. PE y: Intervocalically *y goes to s before ə in AP$_{AAY}$, to z before ə in CAY (except in HBC$_{CAY}$ and Eg$_{CAY}$). In Nun$_{CAY}$ *y goes to z before a consonant, and to s before a consonant in K$_{AAY}$. When geminated *y goes to s in Nun$_{CAY}$ and Perry$_{AAY}$—in the latter, *y also goes to s after a consonant before VV. *y goes to z only before i in CSY, but in most CAY *y goes to z when geminated within morphemes (in NS$_{CAY}$ before any double vowel) or before a voiced consonant. Next to a stop, *y goes to s (as in uksuq from *ukyuʀ) except in Sir and NSY, where *y is devoiced, (i.e. y̥). Geminated *y (non-productively) goes to tc in Inu (GRI ts), and to c in Sir. Initial *iy- goes to is- in Inu, but it falls together with *iŋ- before vowels in certain bases in Yup as y-, except as c- in HBC$_{CAY}$ and Nun$_{CAY}$, and as s- in AAY but only when not underlyingly from iu- or ia- (and in some Y$_{CAY}$ as s- even if from such a source). *y goes to s also in some forms in Inu when initiating closed syllables as in pisuk- from *piyuɣ-. *y is usually vocalized to i before or after a consonant in Inu (e.g. ukiuq from *ukyuʀ) but to n before ŋ. *y is also vocalized to i when in combination with ə (e.g. tui from *tuyə). *y is neutralized with *ð as ž in Iti$_{ECI}$ (and as an alveopalatal affricate before a consonant or when geminate in Sig$_{WCI}$), and is dropped between two morpheme-internal u's in EG$_{GRI}$.

7. PE l: *l is generally preserved except in some bases in Sir that have c (e.g. ucəma- from *ulima). *l is devoiced when geminated in Nun$_{CAY}$ and Perry$_{AAY}$ (where it is also devoiced when before another consonant or between a consonant and VV). *l goes to ž before another continuant in Point Barrow NAI and (optionally?) in Net$_{WCI}$. *l goes to tt when geminated in EG$_{GRI}$, corresponding to (recent) NG$_{GRI}$ glottalized l and general WG$_{GRI}$ łł but Kap Farvel retroflex affricate dj (from C plus l). *l goes to l^y in NAI following original i (but not in PH$_{NAI}$ or southern Mal$_{NAI}$).

8. PE ł: *ł is generally preserved in Yup and Sir, though sometimes it goes to s intervocalically in the latter (as in si- from *əłi-). In Inu, *ł is usually merged with l intervocalically (except in e.g. iłuaq- outside of GRI), but otherwise *ł has various reflexes in more easterly dialects: t in southeastern SB$_{ECI}$, s in southwestern SB$_{ECI}$ and Tar$_{ECI}$. In Cop$_{WCI}$, *ł is merged with *s as h, and also in 'past' contemporative inflections like -xuni, -Xuni (Nu$_{NAI}$ -xxuni, -XXuni) in NS$_{NAI}$ (alongside -xłuni, -Xłuni). Although geminate WG$_{GRI}$ łł (EG$_{GRI}$ tt) is secondary, EG$_{GRI}$ distinguishes Cs (coming from *Cł) from tt. *ł goes to $ł^y$ after original i in NAI (but not in southern Mal$_{NAI}$ or PH$_{NAI}$), and *ł goes to l in 'weak' position in non-Qaw SPI.

Note that ł is largely merged with l in Aleut (completely so in eastern EA).

9. PE v: *v is generally preserved intervocalically in Inu, though weakened to w in various dialects (in SPI regularly in 'weak' position). Initial *iv- goes to uy- in WG$_{GRI}$ and EG$_{GRI}$ and to yu- in GCY$_{CAY}$, NS$_{CAY}$ and C$_{AAY}$. *v is dropped between certain vowels in GCY$_{CAY}$ and NS$_{CAY}$, also WG$_{GRI}$ and EG$_{GRI}$, leaving optional glide (note WG$_{GRI}$ siu-, EG$_{GRI}$ suu-, CAY ciu-, AAY cuu- corresponding to CSY sivu-). In Yup initial *uva- goes to w̥a- except to wa- in HBC$_{CAY}$, NS$_{CAY}$ and NSY, and to k^wa- in Nun$_{CAY}$, and to mə- in Sir. Otherwise *v is preserved in all NSY, CSY, HBC$_{CAY}$ and Eg$_{CAY}$. In core GCY$_{CAY}$, *v goes to w when non-geminated between vowels except before ə or morpheme boundary. In AAY, *v goes to w or (u)$ɣ^{(w)}$, though sometimes it is dropped in PWS$_{AAY}$ before a single vowel intervocalically, and in AP$_{AAY}$ *v goes to (u)ɣ or (u)x before a consonant (thus kuɣluku and qauxcin corresponding to CAY kuvluku, qafcin). Geminated v is devoiced in WG$_{GRI}$ (but goes to pp in EG$_{GRI}$ and Up$_{GRI}$ and to kk in Kap Farvel), Lab$_{ECI}$, Nun$_{CAY}$, and Perry$_{AAY}$, but is glottalized in Iti$_{ECI}$ and (recent) NG$_{GRI}$. In Perry$_{AAY}$,* v goes to x^w also between a consonant and VV.

Note that v alternates with p after a consonant in postbases and inflections such as Inu indicative -vuq/puq. Eskimo v corresponds to Aleut m medially, and Eskimo uv- corresponds to Aleut w- (Atkan m-).

10. PE ɣ: Intervocalically *ɣ is usually dropped within morphemes in AAY, CAY, and NSY except next to ə (and in HBC_{CAY} and Eg_{CAY} sometimes it is retained elsewhere too). In AAY, CAY, and NSY *ɣ is also dropped under productive 'velar dropping' (dropping of ɣ, ʀ, and ŋ between single vowels), and *aɣa goes to ii in these areas. A retained ɣ in these areas may reflect an original geminate or *ɣð. *ɣ is dropped intervocalically within morphemes in Inu except when geminated or after *ə (though in more easterly dialects also after the latter). Intervocalic *ɣ is more widely dropped in EG and also between two i's in NG_{GRI} and in 'weak' position in SPI. Postbase-initial *ɣ is usually lost in both Yup and Inu. In EG_{GRI} and WG_{GRI} 'fringe' dialects (including all NWG_{GRI}), intervocalic *ɣ goes to ŋ when preserved, and in northern Mal_{NAI} it goes to y following original i in some morphemes. Geminated ɣ is devoiced in WG_{GRI}, EG_{GRI} (to kk as also in Up_{GRI} and Kap Farvel GRI), Lab_{ECI}, Nun_{CAY}, and K_{AAY}, but glottalized in Iti_{ECI} and (recent) NG_{GRI}. Often dropped before a single vowel in AAY (especially in C_{AAY}), with resulting gemination of preceding consonant (as in kammuk, but kamɣua). There is no phonemic distinction in the voicing of ɣ in most K_{AAY}, where it is usually voiceless.

11. PE ʀ: In Yup *ʀ is sometimes dropped intervocalically, but rarely when following after the first syllable vowel; it is also dropped by productive 'velar dropping' (dropping of ɣ, ʀ, and ŋ between single vowels). In Inu *ʀ is dropped intervocalically within morphemes except when geminated or after *ə (though in more easterly dialects also after the latter). Intervocalic *ʀ is more widely dropped in EG and also in 'weak' position in non-Qaw SPI. In EG_{GRI} and Up_{GRI} *ʀ is nasalized to ʀ̃ when preserved. In modern (Nain) Lab_{ECI} ʀ is neutralized with ɣ (more uvular variant between a's). Geminated ʀ is devoiced in WG_{GRI}, EG_{GRI} (to qq, as also in Up_{GRI} and Kap Farvel GRI), Lab_{ECI}, Nun_{CAY} and K_{AAY} (but glottalized in Iti_{ECI} and recent NG_{GRI}, with stop-like onset in Tar_{ECI}). *ʀ is often dropped before a single vowel in AAY (especially in C_{AAY}), with resulting gemination of preceding consonant. There is no phonemic distinction in the voicing of ʀ in most K_{AAY}, where it is usually voiceless.

12. PE ŋ: Intervocalically *ŋ is often dropped within morphemes in AAY, CSY, and NSY except next to ə (in HBC_{CAY} and Eg_{CAY} sometimes retained elsewhere too). In AAY, CAY, and NSY, *ŋ is also dropped under productive 'velar dropping' (dropping of ɣ, ʀ, and ŋ between single vowels), and *aŋa goes to ii in these areas. In AAY and CAY, initial *iŋ- before a vowel goes to y- (or c- or s-, as for *iy- under m̥) before a, and in some bases in all Yup and Sir also before other vowels (cf. PE iŋuɣ). *ŋ is sometimes also dropped intervocalically in Inu, most widely so in EG. Word-finally *ŋ goes to k in more easterly Inu (except NG_{GRI}). *ŋ goes to nʸ after original i in northern Mal_{NAI} in some morphemes.

13. PE m and n: Word-final *m goes to p in more easterly Inu, but is otherwise preserved. Initial *n is dropped in Yup and Sir before i (which becomes y, but s for some Y_{CAY}, before an immediately following vowel). In Sir it corresponds to y before other vowels in many bases, possibly reflecting a PE *nʸ, though this could be a general development for initial *n that is blocked before a nasal or alveolar/palatal consonant beginning the next syllable (there are many exceptions, however, only some of which are loans from CSY). In some bases initial *n has dropped also before əl/ən in GCY_{CAY} at least (e.g. ənəq from *nənəʀ and ələʀ(-) from *nələʀ(-)). Single *n between two i's is dropped in EG_{GRI} morpheme-internally. Word-finally *m and *n go to p and t in more easterly Inu (except NG_{GRI}). *n goes to nʸ after original i(C) in NAI (except for PH_{NAI} or southern Mal_{NAI}).

Eskimo m corresponds to Aleut h initially, and n to Aleut t initially (though Aleut like Yupik drops initial n before i, and also usually before *ə-).

B. Consonant Clusters

A cluster of a fricative plus a stop goes to stop plus stop in Inu, but in WG_{GRI} and EG_{GRI} and much of ECI a cluster of a uvular consonant plus stop produces a pharyngealized geminate of the second consonant. A cluster of a nasal plus another consonant goes to the corresponding non-nasal (fricative if the second consonant of the cluster is a fricative, and stop if it is a stop) plus consonant in Inu following an earlier change of n+C to ŋ+C in WCI and ECI (as in aɣlu, tuktu, B_{NAI} allu, tuttu, from *anlu, *tuntu). *nq goes to qq and *lq goes to tq in SPI (both go to tq in NAI). *l plus stop generally goes to t plus stop in Inu, but goes to k plus stop in the eastern part of Inu (before assimilation)—compare also under alpaɣ- and (for possible parallel *ðv to ɣv change also in NAI) qaɣvaʀ-. These changes are apparently the result of the diffusion of innovations within Inu such that PI itself must be posited as still having nasal+non-nasal clusters. *kl and *ql go to kł and qł except in Nu_{NAI}, where they go to xl and Xl. *pl goes to pł (but in CSY to fł) in Yup, and to pl in Mal_{NAI} and Nu_{NAI}, to, pł in SPI, and to vl in the rest of Inu. There is some variation in Inu as regards other original labial plus non-labial fric. clusters (p + fric. favored as the outcome in SPI, Mal_{NAI} and WCI, v + fric. in B_{NAI}, though p + corresponding stop is also found). *n plus consonant and *ŋ plus consonant are largely neutralized to ŋ plus consonant in CSY (in most bases), but to n plus consonant in the case of a following coronal consonant in NSY. Increasing regressive assimilation in clusters to the east within Inu: stop plus continuant goes to geminate continuant outside of Mal_{NAI} (where the stop is represented by a glottalized element as also in Nu_{NAI}, Net_{WCI}, and Car_{WCI}) and SPI. In the latter, however, *tž, *tl, and *tc go to šš, łł, and ss respectively (also Yup and Sir have ł from *tl), and in Qaw_{SPI} and PI *ty goes to ss, as in WG_{GRI} (EG_{GRI} ts)—see pumyuɣ- —though PE ty seems to have produced Inu s(i) in early derivations such as tasiuq- under PE tatyuʀ- (and compare katyuɣ-). Alveolar plus other consonant (labial or alveolar) goes to velar plus consonant in ECI and GRI (though *tl, *tž remain as ll and žž/yy- as in B$_{NAI}$ and WCI—and PI ts, NAI tc, remains as such). In WCI, however, voiced continuant clusters of this type go as ECI (e.g. naŋmak-, NAI nanmak-) whereas *l + stop goes to t + consonant as in NAI (thus atpa—compare ECI akpa). Labial plus another consonant into geminate consonant east of—and including—Melville Peninsula ECI (not Aiv$_{ECI}$), but PI *pc goes to ts (and in NBI$_{ECI}$ to ss). Velar plus other consonant to geminate consonant in Tar$_{ECI}$ and Lab$_{ECI}$ (where *ks goes to ts, however) and in GRI apart from NG$_{GRI}$. Uvular plus other consonant goes to geminate consonant in Lab$_{ECI}$. In Yup and Sir, *ty goes to s or ts (and NSY y̥, which seems to vary with š intervocalically and before other consonants, although it is apparently distinct from š < *ð after a voiceless consonant at least). Productively at the morpheme-boundary t+y goes to c in CAY. Also *tð has produced s (in NSY y̥). There is some fluctuation with stop plus nasal clusters in Yup. In NSY *t plus nasal usually to k plus nasal. In Inu *km goes to pm in Mal$_{NAI}$ (B$_{NAI}$ mm), and farther east to ŋm or ʼm. Metathesis of *nʀ and *lʀ (and *mʀ) is regular in Di$_{SPI}$, ECI (ʀŋ, but *lʀ, is assimilated to ʀʀ), and GRI (ʀn, ʀŋ—and in SWG$_{GRI}$ also ʀm—and ʀł), and in Net$_{WCI}$ *nʀ regularly goes to nŋ (also in Cop$_{WCI}$ at Holman Island according to Lowe—also elsewhere acc. Pryde). Elsewhere (including within Yup) sporadic metathesis of other continuant clusters occurs. In NAI *łʀ goes to łX (and also WCI), and *qv goes to Xf (in Nu$_{NAI}$ to Xv). In Net., l (or ł) + C and ž + C are neutralized (with variation). Clusters of stop plus voiceless fricative go to two corresponding voiced fricatives in PH$_{NAI}$ (and sporadically also farther east). Stop plus continuant or stop plus stop clusters in Yup are usually by loss of intervening ə (these often involve v, in early alternation with p after a stop—thus most Yup has qv or kv whereas Inu and NSY have qp and kp). Voiceless nasals in Yup arise from (previous) adjacency of a stop.

C. Vowels

1. PE ə (schwa): *ə is merged with i in Inu except for Di$_{SPI}$/Imaq$_{SPI}$, where there is a tendency to regressive assimilation (or neutralization) from ə to an *i (or vice versa) in the preceding syllable and also *i to ə before ž. Traces of the distinction are left in most NAI in the form of a palatalized series of consonants after original i only. There is some fluctuation, however, and in B$_{NAI}$ at least *əli and *əni have generally become ilʸi and inʸi and everywhere a final *ə on disyllabic verb bases has become 'strong' (i.e. palatalizing) i after a fricative or n (so the distinction of original i vs. non-palatalizing i, written as ɨ, does not always correspond to the distinction pattern of *i vs. *ə). Sometimes ə has become a (especially before another vowel) or has been dropped in Inu. In Sir and in Yup (except in NSY, where it has apparently been restored word-finally) word-final ə becomes a (and this includes ə from reduced vowels in the latter). ə-adjustments (deletion and insertion to break up clusters) occur in most Yup, with rhythmically stressed ə deleted in AAY (but only in the second syllable) and in CAY outside of NSU$_{CAY}$. Devoicing of fricatives before voiceless consonants resulting from this deletion of rhythmically stressed ə in core GCY$_{CAY}$ and non-Perry K$_{AAY}$. Initial ə is usually dropped in CSY (but not NSY) before a single consonant, as is also common to varying degrees in AAY and CAY (most markedly in AAY, least in Nun$_{CAY}$). This results in first syllable lengthening when it occurs in CSY and in AAY. *əʀ- usually into aʀ- in CSY. NSY initial ə sometimes goes to i, especially before a following syllable with i, or to u before a syllable with u.

Eskimo ə corresponds to Aleut a or i or has been dropped in Aleut: the correspondences are complicated further by vowel harmony between adjacent syllables, for which see Bergsland 1986.

2. PE i, a and u: *i, *a, and *u are often reduced to ə in Sir, except in the first syllable (and there is no distinction of vowel length after the first syllable; length marking in Menovshchikov's writing probably just indicates prototonic stress). Under suffixation such a Sir ə will sometimes resume its underlying identity except when followed by a velar or uvular. For example, PE yaquʀ is Sir yaqəX 'arm', but yaqun 'your arm' shows the u. Even when followed by a uvular or velar, this ə behaves differently from an original unreduced ə, viz. by not undergoing deletion before suffixes which cause other ə to delete. Many postbases retain a full vowel, and there is a tendency to retain them also after original geminates. (Note that in neighboring Chukchi ə is the only vowel not involved in vowel harmony alternations.) *i goes to ə between alveolar consonants in Yup except in NSY, HBC$_{CAY}$ and Eg$_{CAY}$ (thus CAY (c)əła, CSY əsła but Eg$_{CAY}$ HBC$_{CAY}$ ciła, NSY siła). Initial vowels are lengthened in CSY when ə is dropped in the following syllable. *u goes to i in certain positions other than the first syllable in EG$_{GRI}$, Up$_{GRI}$, and southern SWG$_{GRI}$ (at least when not before a labial consonant or following a syllable with *u). *ua goes to iva (but in Paamiut$_{GRI}$ and some Up$_{GRI}$ to ava). EG$_{GRI}$ also has aʀ̃a from *iʀa and more sporadic vowel harmony-like changes. *kVɣ- goes to x- before a vowel in CSY and AAY, in NSY usually to voiced ɣ- and in CAY to k(ə)x-. Similarly, *qVʀ- goes to X- in CSY and AAY, in NSY usually to voiced ʀ-, and in CAY to q(ə)X-. This Yup denaturization of vowels sometimes also occurs later within morphemes. In CSY *qVq- often goes to aXq-. In AAY and CAY medial *qaʀ goes to qəʀ, and in CAY aʀ is sometimes dropped (or goes to ə).

D. Diphthongs

Diphthongs are leveled out in CSY and NSY (perhaps under Chukchi influence) with labialization of a flanking velar and uvular consonant in certain positions if the diphthong contained a *u (thus CSY sikʷaa from *sikua). In CSY *au and *ua go to aa, *iu and *ui to ii, as also *ai and *ia. In NSY *ai and *ia go to [e:], *ua goes to [o:] (though these still may be shallow diphthongs), and *iu (but not *ui) goes to ii. Non-initial *ai and *au go to ii and uu in PWS_{AAY} and *ia goes to aa in all AAY after s, c, or y. Nun_{CAY} *ai goes to aa except in endings. In WG_{GRI} and EG_{GRI} *au and *ai go to aa, though final ai is preserved in WG_{GRI} and goes to ii before a uvular in NG_{GRI}. Diphthongs are flattened and merged in northern Mal_{NAI} (ai and ia into [e:], au and ua into [o:] and iu into ii); in SPI this involves only *ai and *au.

E. Suprasegmental Phenomena
Following the reduction of original geminates in Yup and Sir, a major prosodic shift spread through Yup, rhythmically stressing (and lengthening) alternate open short syllables after the first (or after primary stress, which lies on double vowels or—in AAY, NSY, and CAY—on closed initial syllables). The most complex rules of adjustment (with 'stress retraction' from short open syllables to preceding short closed syllables, and with "compression" of long Vs) are to be found in AAY, and the simplest in CSY. In Sir the pattern has been recently superimposed on an apparently initial-syllable-stressed prosody. In AAY and CAY there is secondary gemination of consonants before double vowels, and in AAY (where this occurs only after the first syllable vowel) there is a stress-related distinction between fortis and lenis C articulation. The details are not relevant to the present comparative work since Yup forms are cited in their pre-prosodic shape (before predictable lengthening, contraction, and gemination). However, non-predictable gemination in Alaskan Yup is indicated: in most cases (esp. in disyllabic verbal bases ending in ə) the gemination is a means of maintaining primary stress on the base. CSY lengthens an initial full vowel in similar contexts (and in NSY an initial full vowel is lengthened before ŋ + C).

A Yup substratum has produced a related system of alternating 'weak' and 'strong' consonant positions in SPI (less marked in Qaw_{SPI}, where only *q, *v, and some *ɣ are regularly weakened). These correspond to positions following unstressed and stressed syllables respectively in neighboring Yup. Clusters may also be affected, the details varying from sub-dialect to sub-dialect; in KI_{SPI}, at least, a *q before another stop in weak position is deleted and a preceding aa vowel is partially lengthened. The distinction between geminate and non-geminate Cs is lost after the first syllable boundary. For details on Yup prosody, including its effects on SPI, see the papers in Krauss 1985.

In Tar_{ECI} and Lab_{ECI} 'Schneider's law' reduces C_1C_2 (geminate or cluster) to C_2 following syllables that also begin with a geminate or a cluster. This applies also to recent Sig_{WCI} as regards geminate but not cluster reduction (see Lowe 1985a).

Notes to charts on pages xi and xii.

1. A palatal affricate, [č], with the following exceptions: an alveo-palatal affricate, [ts], in Central Alaskan Yupik when followed by ə, a dental affricate, [t̪s], in Sirenikski, and a palatalized dental stop, [tʸ], when followed by another consonant in North Alaskan Inuit. (The sounds in daughter languages are of course not all derived from *c.)
2. Glottal stop in some Inuit; however, an apostrophe is also used for Alutiiq Alaskan Yupik to indicate a dropped intervocalic consonant which continues to affect the prosody.
3. Degree of retroflexion varies with language and dialect.
4. Reflexes of *ə, phonetically identical to ɨ (see Kaplan 1981a).

ABBREVIATIONS

Sources

Avt.	Avtonova
B.-S.	Birket-Smith
Berg.	Bergsland
Bogo.	Bogoraz
Bourq.	Bourquin
Dor.	Dorais
Eg.	Egede
Em.	Emel'yanova
Enm.	Enmenkau
Fab.	Fabricius
Hamm.	Hammerich
Holt.	Holtved
Jen.	Jenness
Kl.	Kleinschmidt
Krup.	Krupnik
Math.	Mathiesen
Men.	Menovshchikov
Met.	Metayer
Ow.	Owingayak
Pet.	Petitot
Ras.	Rasmussen
Rez.	Rezanov
Rub.	Rubtsova
Schn.	Schneider
Spald.	Spalding
S.-L.	Schultz-Lorentzen
Thal.	Thalbitzer
Vakh.	Vakhtin

Miscellaneous

acc.	according to
aeq.	aequalis
all.	allative
contam.	contamination
dem.	demonstrative
du.	dual
emot.	emotional
encl.	enclitic
esp.	especially
gem.	geminate
indep.	independent
infl.	inflection
intr.	intransitive
lit.	literally
loc.	locative
nom.	nominal
ortho.	orthography
p.b.	postbase
pl.	plural
posit.	positional
poss.	possible
post.	postural
prob.	probably
rel.	relative
relat.	relation
s.o.	someone
s.th.	something
trans.	transitive
vial.	vialis

BASES

A

PE a(a) 'oh no (exclamation of dismay or surprise)'
AAY C aalaa 'darn, gee!'
CAY alaa, alai 'eek!'
NSY aaa 'wow!' [ANLC]
CSY aa [with breathy voice] 'expression of exasperation'
Sir — [for a-a 'yes' see a(a)ŋ]
SPI —
NAI aa 'listen, oops!' [expression of dismay or exasperation; also aallalii 'shame on you, not like that!']
WCI alii 'expression of fright or surprise' [Pryde; Schn. has aa 'exclamation of pain' for 'adg']
ECI [aala(ɣit) 'listen!', aalakkualuk 'what rubbish!']
GRI aali 'fancy, just think!' [with enclitic li; note also aa (enclitic or proclitic) 'hey!', alaa 'that was close!', aaʀit 'just see!']

PI aa(k) 'lateral point of dart or hook' [cf. aɣ(ɣ)a(ʀ)-, aaɣiaq and aaɣžuuk; for Aleut aɣalu-X 'tooth, fang, barb' see aɣluʀ]
Yup [for AAY, CAY aɣaq 'hook' see aɣ(ɣ)a(ʀ)-]
Sir [for aɣaX 'hook' see aɣ(ɣ)a(ʀ)-]
SPI —
NAI —
WCI —
ECI SB a(a), pl. aŋit 'lateral point of bird dart' [Boas], Lab a(a), du. aik, pl ait 'horn with a hook used as bird arrow' [Peck]
GRI aaq [Fab. ak, Kl. pl. ait], EG aayak 'lateral point of bird dart', NG aaq 'hook', aatit- '(lift with a) hook'

PI aaci(in) 'stop (exclamation)?' [cf. a(a) and acu]
Yup [note AAY acianaa 'no, don't!']
SPI aasin 'stop, let's go!'
NAI aasi(i), aasiinʸ 'and then' [also enclitic], aasi 'stop!' [and with expressive gemination aatcikaaŋ 'what a narrow escape!']
WCI Sig aasin 'and then' [Pryde has asi 'furthermore' for Paulatuuq, which Met. has as an exclam. of wonder]
ECI a(a)siit 'again' [also enclitic]
GRI aasiit, aasit 'again as usual' [usually with disapproving connotation; can also be enclitic; note also aasik 'no, I won't!' (child's expression)]

PI aacivak 'spider' [cf. p.b. vaɣ]
Yup [note NSY apayapak, CSY apayapayiiq 'spider']
SPI —
NAI aasivak 'large spider'
WCI aasivak
ECI a(a)sivaq, Igl aasivak 'large spider' [B.-S. for the latter; Saul has aasivalaaq for Iti]
GRI aasiak, NG aahivak 'spider' [WG also aasiaq; old ortho. ausiak, ausiaq (Fab. ausiek), probably by contam. with aðuʀ-; NG also auhi(v)ak]

PI aaɣiaq 'prong of antler' [cf. aa(k), and yaʀ?]
SPI —
NAI aaɣiaq, Nu aaɣiužaq 'prong of antler'
WCI Cop, Net aaɣiaq [Pryde; B.-S. has Car aaɣiaqtaat 'branches on antlers, the Pleiades'; Jen. has aɣiattat 'unidentified constellation' for Net and Cop]
ECI Baf a(a)ɣia(q), pl. a(a)ɣiyyat 'prong, tine of antler' [Boas; Math. has aɣiatta(i)t 'the Pleiades']
GRI aaɣiaq 'prong of antler', NG 'tip of sledge upright'

PI aaɣžuuk 'constellation of two stars appearing around winter solstice' [cf. aa(k), aaɣiaq and/or aɣ(ɣ)a(ʀ)-, and p.b. yuɣ, ðuɣ, in the dual; i.e. '(constellation) like two lateral blades of a dart pointing toward where the sun will start to rise again after the solstice'?]
Yup [note CSY aayɣuk 'pair of stars seen at dawn (Altair and Tarazed in the Eagle?)', as if the dual of aayɣu 'arrow' — compare Chukchi ə'uygən 'pointer, spit, spur' — but it could rather be a loan from Inu with contam. from the Chukchi base (which is apparently used in an expression for the North Star in that language acc. de Reuse) and/or metathesis]
SPI —
NAI aaɣžuuk [du.] 'constellation consisting of two stars which appear above the horizon in late December, an indication that the solstice is past and that days will soon grow longer again'
WCI Cop aaɣyuuk 'Altair and Beta Aquilae in the constellation Aquila' [Pryde — also in Ras. for Cop, Net and Car]
ECI a(a)yyuuk 'two stars appearing early in the morning and disappearing last during part of winter (December)' [aayyuuk refers to Altair and Tarazed of the Eagle acc. Saul]
GRI aaššu(u)tit [old ortho. âgssûtit] 'constellation appearing on the shortest day of the year' [Ordbogêraq; also aašši(ɣ)it, which may be an i-dialect form but seems to be by contamination with aaššik 'butterfly larva' — q.v. under aužvik; Fab. has aiksuk with the original u; in NG aaxxuuk = 'a large and a small star appearing in a northerly direction' — Holt.]

PI aak- 'skin a small animal or bird'
SPI W aak- 'skin a bird' [Ras.]
NAI aak- 'skin an animal without cutting the fur, peeling back the skin, turning it inside out'
WCI aak- 'skin an animal' [Pryde has aaktuq- rather for Cop, Net, Car; Ras. distinguishes aak- 'skin a bird' from aaktuq- 'skin an animal' for Cop, Net]
ECI aattu(q)- 'skin an animal' [Peck has aak- 'skin a bird' and aaktuq- 'skin an animal' for Lab, the same distinction B.-S. has for Igl, with the first form also used for foxes]
GRI aaɣ-, NG aak- 'skin a small animal', NG 'skin a bird', aattuʀ- 'skin a reindeer' [and note axxaatsuq — old ortho. aggaitsoq — 'one who sleeps with his clothes on'?]

PI aanakliq 'whitefish or brook trout'
Yup [note CAY BB anəXłuaq 'saltwater trout'?]
SPI —
NAI aanaakłiq 'Arctic cisco (large whitefish)', Nu aanaaqłiiŋiq 'whitefish'
WCI Sig aanakłiiq, Cop aanaaxxiiq 'whitefish' [Schn.

has analliq 'whitefish (salmon trout)' for 'adg.']
ECI Lab aanaałłik 'brook trout' [and Tar aana = 'salmon trout'; Saul has aanaakkiq for Iti]
GRI aanaʀłiq 'small red brook trout' [Fab. — who spells it aunardlek, by contam. with aunaaʀ- 'bleed' from aðuɣ?]

a(a)-a(a)ŋliʀ 'oldsquaw duck' [now preferably called 'long-tailed duck'; the first two syllables onomatopoeic with some sort of glottal constriction between them; note also ałɣiʀ (and its Aleut cognates), which is either related to this set or at least has contaminated some forms]
AAY C aXaŋkiluk, AP aaXaaŋiiq, Kod aaXalaq, aaXalak, aaXaliiq, aaXaliik 'oldsquaw duck' [B.S. has aXaŋkiluk 'long-tailed duck']
CAY aaXaaŋiiq, aaXaaliq 'oldsquaw duck'
NSY aa'aaliq
CSY aahaaŋᵂliq
Sir —
SPI aa'aaŋiq
NAI aaXaaliq, aaXaalliq, Nu aahaaliq [Lowe has ahaaliq for Uum]
WCI Cop aahaŋiq, Sig ahaanliq [Lowe], Utku aahaalliq [Ras., who spells it aahaikLeq], Car EP aa'aaŋiq [Ow.] 'long-tailed duck' [Pryde has asaalliq, B.-S. has a'aaniq, Ras. a·aŋ·eq]
ECI [Schn. reports that the form a('a)aŋiq is used by children in W. Bay]
GRI — [but this bird (ałłiq — cf. ałɣiʀ) is said to produce the call a'aliq in WG]

PI aaʀiak '(area between) shoulder blades' [cf. aɣaʀluʀ-?]
SPI aariaq 'area across shoulders and upper back'
NAI aaʀiak, du. aaʀižžak
WCI Cop, Net aaʀiak 'area between shoulder blades, place where river issues from lake' [Pryde; Pet. has aridjerk 'shoulder blade' and arealik 'end of lake' for Sig; Ras. cites ariarLeq as a 'frequently used name for a river bed' in Car]
ECI aaʀiak 'upper back and shoulders'
GRI aaʀiak, aʀiak 'area between shoulder blades, place where river issues from lake'

PE a(C)aʀłuɣ 'killer whale' [from *aɣaʀłuɣ with p.b. łuɣ?; cf. Aleut aɣlu-X 'killer whale'; there may be a ʀelat. to aa(k) and/or aɣaʀluʀ-]
AAY aXłuk 'killer whale'
CAY aXłuk
NSY aXłuk
CSY — [but note aaʀlu 'meteor — traditionally thought to be connected with creature dwelling in rocks behind Gambell']
Sir —
SPI aaʀlu 'killer whale'
NAI aaʀlu
WCI Net, Cop aaʀluk, Sig aaʀlu 'killer whale' [Ras. for the first two forms; Met. and Pryde have Cop aaʀlu 'dark-colored wolf'; Lowe has aʀluk for Holman Island Cop, as Dor. for Net]
ECI aaʀluk 'killer whale' [aʀluasiaq 'whitebeak dolphin']
GRI aaʀłuk 'killer whale' [and note aaʀłiʀi- 'be afraid of']

PI aat- 'take' [cf. Aleut aɣa- 'go away', aɣat- 'take away' with t-[1], also aɣə- though the relat. is obscure (compare naɣət- for the vowel)]
Sir — [for aɣətət- 'send s.o. to fetch' see aɣə-]
SPI aat- 'take away'
NAI aat- 'take away from, take someone somewhere' [for aɣɣaq- 'come loose' see aɣ(ɣ)a(ʀ)-]
WCI aat- 'bring'
ECI aat- 'take away, offer, bring'
GRI aat- 'bring'

PY aatunaq 'sourdock'
AAY K aatunaq 'sourdock'
CAY Y, HBC aatunaq 'sourdock'
NSY —
CSY —

PY aavcaaq 'dart' [cf. avət- under avəɣ-?]
AAY K auxca<ʀ>aq, PWS auxcaq 'dart'
CAY aafcaaq
NSY —
CSY —

PE acaluʀ 'kayak tray for line' [cf. at(ə)- and p.b. lu(ʀ)?]
AAY —
CAY acaluq 'kayak tray for harpoon line' [and acaluʀuaq 'snowshoe with upturned front']
NSY —
CSY [note asaluʀaq 'anvil']
Sir —
SPI azaluuk
NAI —
WCI —
ECI Baf asallut 'kayak tray for harpoon line' [Boas; Peck has it as 'sort of leather strap on the boat or a basin to receive seal in' for Lab; Math. has asaluk for Igl in the same sense as Boas]
GRI asaluq [usually pl. asałłut] 'frame for harpoon line coiled up on front of kayak'

PE accaɣ 'paternal aunt' [cf. acuʀaʀ]
AAY aca(k), acaaq 'paternal aunt'
CAY acak
NSY asik [L.-T.]
CSY asak
Sir asəx [Orr]
SPI assak
NAI atcak
WCI Net atsak, Cop attak
ECI atsa, atsak
GRI atsa(k), EG also atsaaq

PY-S aci[1] 'area below' [cf. at(ə)- and atliʀ under it, with which the first Sir forms may belong; the origin of the final vowel is obscure, but compare aki(-) and note especially the Alaskan *tət to cət (NSY sit) change

mentioned under at(ə)-; it could otherwise be the same as aci[2], which can also function as a positional root as in Yupik]
AAY aci- 'area below'
CAY aci- 'area below' [and aci(q) 'mattress, bed', LI 'wild potato', also NS aciłquq 'root']
NSY asi 'area below, skirt of garment'
CSY asi- 'area below' [also in Chap 'area in winter tent where head of bed located, tip of harpoon tied to a rope, back part of a quadruped'; asiŋani 'under it, lower part of it', asiiq 'fancy border on hem of parka', asiŋiʀ- 'put beneath']
Sir asəX, asiX '(area) below, border of parka', asa 'ground, tundra' [Vakh. has asəŋani 'below, around (it)' — Em. has asa 'area below, coastal part of mainland, bottom of cliff', asəX 'wide fur border at hem of fur coat', asiX 'lower one', asiməžuʀ- 'go down' and asəŋəʀ- 'put beneath']
Inu [note SPI azini 'on the ground or floor', Qaw asi 'ground, floor', Imaq asa '(area) below, skirt (of garment)' — from Yup?]

PY-S acivaʀ- 'go down' [cf. vaʀ-]
AAY aciwaʀ- K 'go or come down', C 'go down (to beach) after seafood' [note also Kod aciwaXtə, AP aciwaxtə 'be sound asleep']
CAY acivaʀ- 'go down' [also acivaqaniʀ-, for homonym of which in sense 'lower, curse' see acciʀ- (under atəʀ); note also acivaxtə 'be fast asleep']
NSY asivaʀ- 'go down' [and asivakanaXtu 'west' (ANLC) — compare Imaq azivaq- under PI acivaq- (aci[2])]
CSY asivaʀ- 'lower, go down' [and asivaq 'east (wind)']
Sir asəvaniʀ- 'lower (thing or self)', asəvaʀ- 'go down' [Vakh. for the latter]

PI aci[2] 'somewhere or something vague or remote' [the relat. — if any to aci[1] and ali is obscure; this base may go rather with Aleut aði-m haða-a 'the landward side, the shore', aðaŋa- 'landward side, back or other side' (unless this goes with ali), in which case it should be PI asi]
Sir — [for asa 'tundra' see aci[1]]
SPI Qaw asi 'surrounding area' [note azitquq- 'miss (aiming at target)'; azivak- 'be worn out', KI, Di azitnaq- 'be or act bad, cause trouble' may go rather with Yup asiitə- 'be bad' under asiʀ-]
NAI asi 'not a specific or usual place, s.th. insignificant' [and note asinʸi 'out in the open, not in usual place', asitqut- 'miss target', asiŋŋuŋa- 'be pale']
WCI Cop ahi 'somewhere else, away from settlement', Net 'another person' [Ras.]
ECI asi [plus possessed ending] 'another (person)', asiani 'elsewhere'
GRI asi 'place away from settlement, distant' [and note asiŋa- 'be pale']

PI aciɣə- 'scorn or ignore' [cf. kə-[1]]
SPI —
NAI asikšuq- 'insult'
WCI —
ECI asiɣiyaaq- 'treat (s.o.) as if he were s.o. else'
GRI asiɣi-, asiššuʀ- 'scorn, reject'

PI aciʀuq- 'become spoiled' [cf. ʀuq- under ŋ(ŋ)uʀ-]
Yup — [but note NSY asaxtiuʀ- 'destroy']
SPI [note aziŋuq- 'ruin, become spoiled']
NAI asiʀuq- 'become useless' [and asiŋŋuq- 'begin not to go right']
WCI Sig asiʀuq- 'be spoiled (fruit, etc.)', Cop, Net ahiʀuq- 'damage, be broken'
ECI asiʀuq- 'destroy, be destroyed'
GRI asiʀuʀ- 'break, be broken', NG ahiʀuq- 'have got wet (clothing)' [Holt.]

PI aciu- 'be useless or wasted' [cf. ŋu-]
SPI aziu- 'be bad'
NAI asiu- 'be useless', PH 'be bad'
WCI Sig asiuyi- 'become spoilt'
ECI asiu- 'be lost' [asiuyi- 'have lost s.th.']
GRI asiu- 'be spoiled, have disappeared, be rotten', NG ahiu- 'be wasted'

PI acivaq- 'go away from settlement' [cf. vaʀ-]
SPI Imaq azivaq- 'blow a northwest wind' [also nom. — compare NSY asivakanaXtu under PY-S acivaʀ- (aci[1])]]
NAI asivaq- 'stray from course', PH, Nu 'move away'
WCI Baker Lake ahivaq- 'get out of the way, move off, shift, remove' [trans. sense also Net — Pryde, who also has Perry River asiqpaq- 'shift, put elsewhere']
ECI asivaq- 'go hunting on pack ice'
GRI asiaʀ- 'go elsewhere, aside, into the wilds' [for EG sense 'pluck berries' see atyaʀ]

PI acini(la)- 'be loose' [cf. aci[2]?]
SPI aziniŋa- 'be loose (clothing or skin)'
NAI asinʸilʸa- 'be baggy'
WCI —
ECI —
GRI asiila- 'be baggy'

PE acu 'indeed (exclamation)?'
AAY —
CAY —
NSY asuŋa 'well, let's see'
CSY asunaq, asunan 'soon'
Sir —
SPI azukiaq 'too bad', Imaq azuŋa 'however, rather, let - ', azuqtauŋ 'of course'
NAI asulu you're right!', Nu asu 'apparently, indeed' [and asuɣupta 'luckily', also atcu(u), atcukii, 'I don't know' — with expressive gemination?]
WCI Cop ahu, Sig asulu 'sure, perhaps', Net ahu 'maybe, isn't it', Car ahu 'stop!' [Pryde; B.-S. has ahuila 'at last']
ECI asuila 'at last!', asuɣuuq 'it's true', Iti asu 'is that so?', asuinna 'it's him right enough' [and Tar, Lab

aatsu(u)k 'I don't know'; Peck has asu 'thus it is (?), what a pity!' for Lab; Saul has Iti asuu 'OK, now I get it, I understand' rather]
GRI asu 'at last, enough', asuki(aq) 'I don't know', NG ahu 'it's true (countering incredulity), ahukiaʀli, ahulluaq 'sure ', EG asiq '(not) again!', asiina 'how —!' [Tersis; and note asuli 'thoughtlessly, as a joke, in vain']

PE acu- 'have sex with a woman not one's wife'
AAY C acuniaʀ- 'try to coerce into sex'
CAY acuniaʀ- 'rape, come stealthily and have sex with a woman other than one's wife'
NSY —
CSY asutǝ- 'exchange wives temporarily'
Sir —
SPI azu- 'leave the men's house'
NAI Nu asu- 'sleep with someone other than one's spouse'
WCI —
ECI asu- 'go to bed with a woman' [uncommon word acc. Schn.; Ras. has asuaq- 'give self to a woman' for Igl.]
GRI asu- 'chase women' [Fab.]

PE acuʀaʀ 'aunt by marriage' [cf. accaɣ if not acu-]
AAY C, Kod acu<ʀ>aq 'aunt by marriage'
CAY acuʀaq
NSY —
CSY —
Sir —
SPI azuʀaq
NAI asuʀaq 'paternal aunt-in-law'
WCI —
ECI —
GRI —

PE að(ð)a(a) 'oh no (exclamation of surprise or pain)?'
AAY —
CAY aaʀ- 'emit sound, say ah' [also aaʀa- 'scream, moan', aaʀnaXqǝ- 'be dangerous']
NSY —
CSY ažaʀ- 'scream'
Sir —
SPI Qaw ažaa 'ouch, gosh, darn!'
NAI ažaa 'oh no, too much!' [and ažaaq- 'be excessive, too loud or talkative', ažaq 'how big!', ažii 'ouch!']
WCI [Schn. has ayyia 'exclamation of admiration' for 'adg']
ECI —
GRI aššaa, aššaaššakkaak 'exclamation of surprise or admiration' [and note NG assak 'a good provider, a diligent person', assauŋŋiihuk- 'be sorry', assauŋŋitsuq 'that was annoying!']

PE aðɣa(ʀ) and **aðɣaɣ** 'hand' [cf. perhaps Aleut atXu-X (from *aðqu-X?), EA also aðqu-X 'finger, toe' — with p.b. qu(ʀ)?]
AAY aixaq 'hand'
CAY aixaq, NSU aixa [base aixǝ-], Nun aaxaX 'hand, seal flipper' [and NSU aixaʀ- 'dig']
NSY aɣ̣xaq 'hand, glove'
CSY iixa 'hand' [base iixǝ; also iixǝ- 'dig']
Sir acxǝX 'hand'
SPI aɣžak, aɣžaq 'hand' [verbal = 'scratch ice when seal-hunting'; Qaw ažɣauži- 'shake hands']
NAI ažɣak 'hand' [verbal = 'dig with hands or paws, scratch ice when hunting seal'; also ažɣautɨ- 'bury']
WCI Cop alɣak, Sig ayɣak, Net ažɣak 'hand' [and verbally = 'dig with hands' or acc. Pryde 'scratch, paw ground, burrow']
ECI ayɣak 'hand' [verbal = dig with hands'; and note ayɣaa(q)- 'make seal come by scraping on ice']
GRI aššak 'hand' [and aššaɣ- 'dig', aššaat(i)- 'bury']

PE aðɣa(C)aʀ 'glove' [cf. p.b. aʀ]
AAY —
CAY Y aazɣaaq, aizɣaaq, K aiɣzaaq, HBC aiyɣaaq, aɣyaaq 'glove'
NSY aɣ̣xaq [Orr and L.-T.]
CSY [iixaq 'glove' may be directly from aðɣa(ʀ)]
Sir —
SPI aɣžaaq 'glove'
NAI ažɣaaq
WCI Sig ayɣaaq
ECI ayɣayaak (dual)
GRI —

PE aðɣaʀuðaʀ 'starfish' [cf. ŋ(ŋ)uðaʀ; the AAY, CAY and CSY forms via *aixšaq?]
AAY [note C, Kod axsiq 'starfish']
CAY [note aaxsak, aaxsaq 'starfish']
NSY aɣ̣xaʀuaq 'starfish'
CSY [note iyǝksak 'starfish']
Sir —
SPI —
NAI —
WCI Cop alɣauyaq, Net alɣaɣiaq 'starfish' [Pryde for the latter form]
ECI ayɣauyaq 'starfish'
GRI aššaašat

PI ažɣaun 'forearm' [cf. un]
SPI aɣžaun 'wrist'
NAI ažɣaun 'wrist', ažɣautit 'metacarpal bones'
WCI —
ECI ayɣauti 'radius, forearm'
GRI aššaat 'lower arm'

PI ažɣaɣmik- 'do finger pull' [cf. miɣ-]
SPI aɣžaŋmik- 'do finger pull (contest)'
NAI ažɣaɣmik-
WCI —
ECI [ayɣamik- 'touch with hand']
GRI aššamiɣ- 'do finger pull' [for NG aXXaʀaaq- 'compete at (arm) pulling' see aʀcaʀ-]

PE aðɣiʀ- 'roast' [cf. Aleut aðaɣ- 'roast over open fire']
AAY K asxiʀ- 'roast, bake'
CAY NS, Nun azɣiʀ- 'roast, fry'
NSY aɣ̣xiʀ- 'roast, bake, cook flippers or hoofs, fry pancakes' [aɣ̣xiʀvik '(frying) pan']

CSY —
Sir —
SPI ayžiq- 'fry, roast over open fire, esp. bread' [nom. = 'bread roasted over a fire']
NAI ažɣiq-, PH alɣiq- 'roast meat on spit' [also nominally of the meat]
WCI Sig ayɣiqsi-, Cop alɣiXXi- 'roast meat' [and Pryde has alɣiq- 'scorch' for Cop, Net and Car]
ECI —
GRI —

PE aðɣuʀ- 'go against current or wind' [cf. Aleut aðɣuʀ- 'rebuke, forbid']
AAY KP ayɣuaʀ-, PWS ay<ɣ>uʀ-, K asxuʀ- 'go against the current or the wind'
CAY azɣuʀ-, ayɣuʀ- 'go against wind or current' [and azɣuʀaq 'obstacle']
NSY ayɣuq 'north', ayɣumun 'going against the wind' [L.-T.; also ajɣəsqə 'north', directly from Chukchi, as below]
CSY ayɣuʀ- 'go against wind or current, go north', ayɣuq, aywa- 'north'
Sir — [Vakh. has ayɣəsqəX 'north', but this is from probably unrelated Chukchi eygəsqən]
SPI ayžuq- 'travel eastward', ayžuq 'northeast side', Qaw ažɣuq- 'go against the wind' [and Jen. has ažɣuaq 'windward side']
NAI ažɣuq- 'go against the wind', ažɣu(q) 'line of wind direction' [usually a positional root]
WCI Sig ayɣuq- 'go against wind', Cop alɣu 'headwind', Net ažɣu 'windward' [the latter Dor., who also has ałɣuani 'upstream' — for ažɣuani?]
ECI ayɣuq- 'go against wind', ayɣu 'windward'
GRI aššuʀ- 'go against wind', aššuq, EG attu(a) 'windward' [and aššuʀtuʀ- 'contradict, quarrel with']

PE aðɣuʀa- 'be stubborn or unwilling' [cf. p.b. a-]
AAY K assu'a-, C ayɣu'a- 'doubt, disbelieve' (emotional root)
CAY azɣuʀakə- 'not believe'
NSY ayɣuʀi- 'not believe, doubt'
CSY ayɣuʀikə- 'doubt'
Sir —
SPI Qaw ažɣuayi- 'doubt', ažɣuaŋa- 'be stubborn'
NAI ažɣuaŋa- 'be bold, undaunted', PH ažɣuaɣi- 'be undaunted by'
WCI Sig ayɣuaŋa-, Cop alɣuaŋa- 'be proud'
ECI —
GRI aššuaʀi- 'reprove, have s.th. against (s.o.)'

PE aðiʀ 'sleeve' [cf. Aleut aði-X 'lip, edge']
AAY AP, C aliq 'sleeve'
CAY aliq* 'sleeve' [and note aliʀuaq 'razor clam', aliiman, aliuman 'mitten']
NSY aliq 'sleeve' [and aliʀ- 'put arms in sleeves' (ANLC)]
CSY aliq 'sleeve' [also apparently 'lean-to at side of house']
Sir siX 'sleeve'
SPI assiq, Qaw assi, FR atciq 'sleeve' [and aiq- 'put arm in sleeve']
NAI asiq*, Mal aiq 'sleeve' [and aiq- 'put arm in sleeve']
WCI Sig asiq, Cop ahiq, aiq 'sleeve' [the last form also Net and Car acc. Pryde]
ECI aiq 'sleeve' [and verbal = 'put arm in sleeve']
GRI aaq [rel. atsip] 'sleeve' [old ortho. âq, but Fab. has aek; for homonym meaning 'lateral point' see aa(k); aaʀ- 'put arm in sleeve']

PI aitqan 'mitten' [cf. p.b. qan?]
SPI aiqan 'mitten'
NAI aitqan, aatqan, aaqqan
WCI aiqqatik 'mittens'
ECI [aiqqavaq 'long-sleeved mitten']
GRI aaqqat 'mitten'

PE aðuɣ 'blood' [for Inu homonym auk- 'melt' see aʀu-]
AAY auk 'blood
CAY auk
NSY aak^{w} 'blood' [and aaɣuqə - 'bleed']
CSY aak^{w} 'blood' [verbal = 'bleed']
Sir acəx 'blood' [Vakh. also has ažux]
SPI auk 'blood' [and verbal = 'bleed, menstruate']
NAI a<ž>uk [also verbal 'bleed', PH 'bleed from nose', ažžiq- 'give or get blood transfusion']
WCI auk 'blood' [verbal = 'bleed', Cop 'bleed from nose']
ECI auk 'blood' [verbal = 'bleed from nose']
GRI aak 'blood' [and aaɣ- 'bleed from nose', aššiʀ- 'spill blood on, mix blood with'; EG also aakkat 'veins' — Robbe and Menn.]

PE aðuɣɣaʀ 'clotted blood' [cf. ɣaʀ]
AAY C auɣɣaq 'bloodshot part, blood clot, or blister'
CAY auɣɣaq 'dark mole on skin'
NSY aawɣaq [Orr]
CSY aawɣaq 'blood clot'
Sir aawɣaX [Orr; long vowel may indicate a borrowing from CSY]
SPI auɣiaq 'clotted blood' [verbal = 'have blood clots']
NAI auɣiaq
WCI auɣiaq
ECI auɣiaq
GRI aaviak, aaɣiak 'clotted blood' [aaviaɣ-, aaɣiaɣ- 'have blood clots']

PE aðun(ə)ʀaʀ- 'bleed' [cf. p.b. n(ə)ʀaʀ(aʀ)(-)]
AAY —
CAY aunʀaʀ- 'bleed'
NSY —
CSY —
Sir —
SPI aunaaq- 'bleed, menstruate'
NAI aunaaq(šuq)-
WCI Cop aunaaq- [Pryde]
ECI aunaaq- 'bleed, menstruate'
GRI aanaaʀ-

PI **aukpaluk-** 'be red' [cf. valuk-]
SPI — [note KI aukpalitiŋiq 'red phalarope']
NAI —
WCI Car aupaluk- 'be red' [and aupayaaq- 'be blood red' acc. Dor., which Lowe also has for Cop; Net aukpalaaq- 'be red' acc. Dor., but Pryde has aupalaaq-; Met. has Cop aupiaq-, Sig ausuk- 'be red']
ECI aupaluutaq 'red, egg yoke', aupaqtuq 'red', Lab aupaluk- 'be red' [the latter Bourq., who also has aupayaaq- 'be reddish'; Saul has aupaluttaq 'yolk' for Fort Chimo]
GRI aappaluɣ- [old ortho. augpalug-] 'be red', aappalaaʀ- 'be (bright) red' [NG aukpilat- 'be red' —Holt. has aukpayaaq-, aukpilak-; aappaluttuʀtaq 'yolk']

PI **ažžiuq-** '.th. bloody; work with s.th. bloody' [cf. li(C)uʀ-]
SPI ažžiuq- 'work with s.th. bloody, menstruate'
NAI ažžiuq- 'mix blood with water to make broth'
WCI —
ECI —
GRI aššiuʀ-

PE **aðuʀ-** 'crawl' [cf. Aleut aðuʀ- 'swim with flapping wings, skim (puffin or duck)']
AAY PWS auxə-, Kod auXtə- 'crawl'
CAY auXə-
NSY —
CSY aaX^{w}ə- 'crawl'
Sir acXupəcəXaʀ- 'crawl' [Vakh. has acXəpəsXaʀ-; Orr has acXupəsXaʀ-; acəXpaʀənəqcəX 'one who is hunting a whale']
SPI auq- 'stalk a seal'
NAI auq- 'stalk animal on ice by crawling'
WCI auq-
ECI Lab aunniava- 'crawl toward (animal one is stalking)' [Andersen et al.; and note NBI aaʀnasuk- 'hunt' in Dor.]
GRI aaʀ-, NG auʀiaq- 'stalk animal on ice by crawling'

PE **aɣa-** 'have convulsions or faint'
AAY ii- 'run out of breath and turn blue from crying hard'
CAY ii- 'turn blue from crying too hard (baby)'
NSY —
CSY [aɣalʀu- 'stagger', perhaps influenced by aɣalu(ʀ)-]
Sir —
SPI aat-, W aa- 'cry hard, holding breath (baby)' [and aanŋuq- 'knock unconscious']
NAI aa- 'cry convulsively, followed by fainting' [and aanŋu- 'feel faint']
WCI Sig aaya-, aamaŋa- 'not pay attention (from distraction)', aamaŋasi- 'no longer be in possession of one's reason (from suffering so much)' [Ras. has Cop, Net au- for aa- 'faint, have falling sickness']
ECI aa- 'faint (from illness, laughter, etc.)' [and aamai- 'be dizzy (from weakness)']
GRI aa- [old ortho. â-] 'have convulsions, falling sickness'

PI **aaŋa-** 'be lightheaded' [cf. ŋa-[1]]
Yup — [for CAY NS aŋazaaʀ- 'sway' see aŋa(yəɣ)-]
SPI —
NAI aaŋayaaq- 'be partly conscious, lightheaded'
WCI Car aaŋayaaq- 'act silly or drunk' [Pryde; Schn. has aaŋa- 'be irritated, stupid' for 'adg']
ECI aaŋayaak-, SB, NBI aaŋayaaq- 'be drunk'
GRI aaŋa- 'be unclear, have a faint voice' [old ortho. aunga- (also Fab.) perhaps due to contam. from auk- under aʀu-; also aaŋŋaa- 'fall asleep, lose from sight'; for aŋa- 'hang head, be depressed' see aɣ(ɣ)a(ʀ)-]

PE **aɣ(ɣ)a(ʀ)-** 'hang' [or perhaps aɣða(ʀ)-, given the first NAI form — but the retention of the sequence aɣa in CAY could be due to the original geminate, as in demonstrative forms like paɣaa-i < *paɣɣa-i, etc.; cf. aa(k), aaɣiaq, and perhaps aɣaʀluʀ-]
AAY aɣaq 'handle, hook (for hanging), collarbone', K also 'doorknob', C aɣa'aXtə- 'get hung up'
CAY aɣa- 'hang (intr.)', aɣaʀ- 'hang (post.)', Nun aɣaX 'earring (with hook)'
NSY —
CSY aɣaʀ- 'hang' [and aɣaqšaq 'peg, hook (for hanging)']
Sir aɣaʀ- 'hang', aɣaX 'hook'
SPI —
NAI [note aɣžaq 'mitten or knife string' but also aɣɣaq- 'come loose, slip off' and aɣɣaʀiitkuq 'barb on spear to prevent speared object from falling off']
WCI — [for aɣɣaq- 'raise head' see aɣaʀluʀ-]
ECI —
GRI [aŋa- 'hang head, be depressed (because others have gone away)' — note such *ɣ to *ŋ changes in WG as under taɣi(C)uʀ- and əɣumə(t)-; compare also NG aaq 'hook' under aa(k)]

PE **aɣ(ɣ)aɣ-** 'tease or be a troublemaker'
AAY Kod aɣaxsaaʀ- 'tease'
CAY [note NSU aɣɣaŋa- 'be arrogant']
NSY —
CSY —
Sir —
SPI aɣɣaŋa- 'be haughty, belligerent', aɣaaq- 'have hurt feelings', Imaq aɣak- 'get angry'
NAI aɣak- 'tease' [as nom. = 'a tease'; aɣɣaŋa- 'be a tease, troublemaker']
WCI —
ECI —
GRI —

PE **aɣanʀu(Caʀ)** 'amulet' [cf. aɣ(ɣ)a(ʀ)- and nəʀ[1] plus ŋ(ŋ)uðaʀ?]
AAY C iinnu 'amulet' [B.-S.]
CAY iinʀu(q) 'amulet, medicine' [Ras. has änʀəq 'amulet' for Nun]
NSY —
CSY — [Men. has aʀinʀ^{w}aq 'amulet' and Rub. aʀnəʀ^{w}aalək 'one with amulets', but these go with aʀʀi(t)naʀ, with which there is probably contam. here]
Sir —

SPI aanRuaq 'amulet'
NAI aanRu<ž>aq 'amulet'
WCI aanRuaq 'amulet' [Schn. has aRŋuaq 'medicine' for Baker Lake but 'object belonging to the dead' for EP; Ow. has aaŋŋuaq 'medicine' for the latter]
ECI aRŋuaq 'amulet'
GRI aaRnuaq [pl. aaRnuššat] 'amulet'

PE aɣaRluR- 'raise head' [there may be a relationship to aɣ(ɣ)a(R)-]
AAY —
CAY —
NSY aɣaRluR- 'have head raised', aɣaRluXtə- 'raise one's head' [ANLC]
CSY —
Sir —
SPI aaRluq- 'raise head, look up' [and note aaqsuq- 'raise using block and tackle']
NAI aaRluq- 'look up, raise chin' [and aaq- 'raise head, sit up']
WCI aaRluq- 'raise head' [and note aɣɣaq- 'raise head (like seal on ice)']
ECI aaRlu(q)- 'raise head'
GRI aaRłuR- 'look up'

PY aɣayu- 'celebrate mask ceremony' [cf. aɣ(ɣ)a(R)-; a nominal form as in Nun below may lie behind this set; for a parallel to the dancing/praying connection in Inu see yuRžaR-; the forms with ŋ could be from contam. with aŋayu- 'dance' under aŋa(yəɣ)-]
AAY aɣayu- 'pray, cross self' [and aɣayuik 'church'; the stem appears in early word lists in a pre-Christian ceremonial sense]
CAY aɣayu- 'pray', Nun aɣayu 'traditional mask' [and aɣayuvik 'church' — aŋayuvik in NSU (by contamin. with aŋayuɣ or the Inu forms below?; Hinz, citing Nelson, has agaiyo 'divine service, great mask ceremony' and agaiyun 'God, s.th. possessing supernatural power, e.g. talisman']
NSY aŋayu- 'pray' [and aŋayułtə 'priest']
CSY —
Inu [SPI aɣaayu-, aŋaayu- 'pray', NAI aŋaayyu-, Mal aɣaayyu-, aŋaayyu- 'pray', Nu aɣaayyut- hold a funeral for s.o.', WCI aŋa(a)yyu(k)- 'pray' (Met.), aŋaayyuvik 'church' (Lowe) are borrowed from Yup as the long vowels indicate]

aɣayuuq 'cormorant' [loan from Aleut a(a)ɣayuuX 'cormorant']
AAY C aɣayuuq, K aɣasuuq 'cormorant'
CAY Y aɣayuuq, NS aɣazuuq
NSY —
CSY —
SPI Qaw aɣaayuuq is a loan from CAY.

PY aɣciun 'paddle' [cf. aɣə- and un]
AAY Perry axcuun 'paddle'
CAY axciun 'paddle' [and note axsuun, aɣsuun 'fishing spear']
NSY —
CSY —

PE aɣə- 'go (over or past)' [cf. Aleut aɣ- 'pass, go through or by', also PI aat-]
AAY aɣə- 'go (along or through)' [and aɣutə- 'carry, take along' as opposed to axtə- 'move, set in motion, PWS also 'pass (s.th.) on to (s.o.)']
CAY aɣə- 'go over (land, water, etc.), drift over (snow)' [aɣutə- 'take over']
NSY aɣə- 'go over or off or past' [aɣəlRia 'one that is passing', aɣusiɣqə- 'tell to take away']
CSY aaɣ- 'stop on the way, make a side trip' [aaɣutə- 'make a side trip for'; for aɣlaR- 'go home' see aŋilRaR- under aŋit-]
Sir aɣə- 'go after s.th., stop in somewhere on the way', aɣətət- 'send s.o. for' [Vakh.; Men. has aɣəšaxkiR- 'go quickly' and aɣtat(ə)- 'chase away']
SPI ai- 'go home, fetch, land far away (of s.th. thrown)' [half trans. aikłiq-]
NAI ai- 'go home, fetch' [half trans. aikł^{y}iq-; aɣɣisi- 'bring home']
WCI ai- 'go, come home, fetch' [half trans. aikłiq-]
ECI ai- 'go, fetch' [half trans. aitsi-]
GRI aa- [old ortho. ai-, NG ai-] 'fetch' [half trans. aałłiR-, EG aarsiR-]

PE aɣɣiR- 'come' [or *aɣəɣiR- — compare anəɣiR- (under anə-) and taɣɣiq-]
AAY —
CAY aɣiiXtə- 'approach from a distance', NSU aɣɣiR- 'invite to feast' [the second form could be borrowed from Inu]
NSY aɣiiXtə- 'return, pass' [ANLC — Orr has aɣiXtə-'come']
CSY —
Sir —
SPI aɣɣiq- 'be visible, coming in distance'
NAI aɣɣiq- 'come, arrive'
WCI aɣɣiq- 'come from afar'
ECI aɣɣi(q)-
GRI axxiR- 'come'

PY aɣnəq 'a certain distance' [cf. nər[1]]
AAY aɣnəq KP 'layer', PWS 'course, wake'
CAY aɣnəq* 'a mile's distance'
NSY aɣnəq 'measure of length, crotch of pants' [ANLC]
CSY aaɣnəq* 'one step or pace'

PE aɣnəR 'snowstorm' [compare aɣnəq above, a parallel formation]
AAY —
CAY aɣnəq* 'snow bank'
NSY aɣnəq 'hurricane'
CSY —
Sir —
SPI Qaw aŋniq- 'be a snowstorm'
NAI aɣniq, aŋniq 'blizzard' [also verbal]
WCI —
ECI —
GRI —

PY aɣtaʀ- 'shoot at something far away'
AAY —
CAY axtaʀ- 'shoot or cause to flow up and out in an arc'
NSY axtaʀ- 'shoot at s.th. far away, fling' [ANLC]
CSY aaxtaʀ- 'shoot at even though it is far'

PI aɣžaq- 'transport' [cf. ðaʀ-]
SPI aɣžaq- 'haul with repeated trips'
NAI aɣžaq-
WCI Net aɣžaq- 'transport' [Pryde; Ras. has akyaʀ-, i.e. aɣyaq-, for Car]
ECI aɣya(q)- 'carry' [and Ras. has agyaq 'means of conveyance' as a shaman's word for Igl]
GRI aššaq [old ortho. agssaq] 'load, cargo', aššaʀtuʀ- 'transport' [Egede has it as a shaman's word for 'kayak']

PI aittuq- 'give' [cf. t-[1] and tuʀ-[2]]
SPI ait(t)uq- 'give a present'
NAI aitcuq- 'give'
WCI aittuq-
ECI aittu(q)-
GRI aatsuʀ- 'infect' [SWG and NWG (aattuʀ-) but not CWG; note also aatsuiniq* 'sacrifice to spirits in clefts, etc.']

PE aɣi 'brother- or sister-in-law of opposite sex' [cf. Aleut aɣi- as in aɣiit- 'another', aɣiituða-a 'his brother or her sister' and Atkan aɣiiða-X 'guest', as verb 'visit'; compare also a(C)ippaʀ]
AAY ai, aisaaq 'sister-in-law (either brother's wife or wife's sister), brother-in-law (either sister's husband or husband's brother)'
CAY —
NSY —
CSY aɣi 'opposite sex spouse of sibling or sibling of spouse, i.e. man's sister-in-law (either brother's wife or wife's sister), woman's brother-in-law (either sister's husband or husband's brother)'
Sir aɣə- 'brother-in-law' [Vakh. from Rub.'s texts]
SPI —
NAI aiʀaaluk 'husband's brother' [and Ras. has Nu ainaaq 'younger brother's wife, husband's sister'; for an[y]n[y]aq 'female cousin' see an(ə)ɣaʀ(aʀ)]
WCI Sig aiʀaaluk 'man's sister-in-law' [Lowe], 'woman's brother-in-law' [Met.], Cop ainnuaq 'man's sister-in-law', Net ainnuaq 'wife's sister, brother's wife', B. Lake ai 'brother or sister-in-law of opposite sex' [Dor.; Pryde has ai 'sister-in-law (of man)' for Cop]
ECI ai Lab 'sister-in-law', NBI 'brother or sister-in-law of opposite sex, first cousin-in-law' [the latter is aikuluk in Tar — Saul also has aiʀaaqquq]
GRI [note EG aaviaaq 'second cousin']

PE aɣiɣ- 'file or rub' [cf. Atkan Aleut aɣiɣ-, aɣiʀ- 'rub, be rubbed (e.g. boat against dock)', EA aɣiX 'round stone']
AAY —
CAY —
NSY —
CSY aaxaʀ- 'sharpen' [from *aɣiɣaʀ-?]
Sir aɣiɣžaqutaX 'grindstone'
SPI Qaw aɣiaq- 'file' [nom. = 'grindstone']
NAI aɣik-, aɣiaq- 'rub, file' [and aɣiaq 'grindstone', aɣɣiq* 's.th. filed down']
WCI aɣik- 'file (a single stroke)', aɣiaq- 'file' [nom. = 'file, grindstone' — Pryde]
ECI aɣiaq- 'file' [also nom. 'file'; aɣɣiut(i)- 'polish with stone or file', NBI aɣiaɣaq 'violin']
GRI aɣiaʀ- 'rub, file, play violin' [also taɣiaʀ-, taŋiaʀ- 'rub', influenced by tanəɣ-?; aɣiaq '(shaman's) grindstone, violin']

PE aɣiɣ(aʀ)un 'grindstone' [cf. un]
AAY —
CAY —
NSY —
CSY aaxaata 'whetstone'
Sir —
SPI —
NAI aɣiun 'file'
WCI Car? aɣiut 'grindstone' [Schn. 'adg'; Met. has aɣ(ɣ)iaun 'file']
ECI [Iti aɣɣiuti 'brush']
GRI aɣiut 'file, grindstone, violin bow' [and note SWG taɣiut 'bow']

PI aɣiuppak 'wall of sheered ice?' [cf. vaɣ]
SPI —
NAI aɣiuppak 'wall of ice sheered off along edge of open lead formed by vertical grinding action of free ice'
WCI Car EP aɣiuppiniq 'snow bank' [Ow.]
ECI aɣiuppiniq 'steep edge at low tide of ice stuck to a cliff' [with p.b. li-[1]]
GRI NG aɣiuppiniq 'wave-like snow drift on frozen sea or inland ice caused by wind'

PY-S aɣiɣtə- 'watch from vantage point' [cf. aɣɣuʀ- and Aleut aɣisa-X 'lookout, observation hill']
AAY —
CAY —
NSY aɣixtaaʀvik 'observation hill (from which people watch shore)' [ANLC]
CSY aɣixtə- 'peek over, look around from a vantage place', Chap aɣixsəlʀaq 'elevated vantage point'
Sir aɣixtə- 'hide', aɣixcəʀə- 'observe' [and aɣixtəqəkcəX 'secret', Em. has aɣəɣit(ə)- 'come together on hilltop from different directions']

PE aɣittaʀ- 'open mouth' [cf. ainnəq and Aleut aɣi- 'open (mouth, eyes, clam, etc.), aɣit- 'open (eyes, clam, book, etc.), spread (clothes)']
AAY aitaʀ- 'open mouth'
CAY aitaʀ- 'gape, spread open' [and LI aitaqci- 'yawn']
NSY iataʀ- 'yawn, open mouth' [ANLC]
CSY aɣitaʀ- 'open mouth', aɣitaʀa- 'yawn'
Sir aɣətaʀ- 'yawn'
SPI aitaq- 'open mouth'
NAI aatcaq-
WCI aittaq-

ECI aitta(q)- 'open (e.g. trap)'
GRI aatsaʀ- 'open mouth, gape'

PE aɣittaʀuʀ- 'yawn' [cf. (C)uʀ-]
AAY aitauʀ-, PWS aituaʀ- 'yawn'
CAY aitauʀ-
NSY —
CSY —
Sir —
SPI aitauq-
NAI aatcauq-
WCI aittauq-
ECI aittau(q)-
GRI aatsaaʀ-, NG aitsauq-

PI aɣlaan 'even (though)' [cf. 3s rel. mood alternant -ŋan in Inu; there may be a link to aŋilʀaʀ- under aŋit- — note the possible parallel to iŋilʀaan under iŋilʀa-]
SPI aɣlaan 'but', W 'unfortunately, I can't', Imaq aɣlaa 'when, then, there you are, but'
NAI aɣlaan 'but, however, up to, even'
WCI Net aɣlaat 'up to' [Pryde, who says it is obsolete in daily speech; Ras. has it in sense 'even (then)' for Sig]
ECI allaat 'even'
GRI ałłaat

PE aɣləʀ(-) '(observe) taboo'
AAY —
CAY aɣləʀ- 'menstruate'
NSY aɣləʀ- 'follow taboo, abstain, fast' [Tein]
CSY aɣləq 'sacred thing', aɣləʀu- 'follow traditional abstinence patterns'
Sir aɣləX 'sacred thing' [Orr; Em. has aɣləʀnəłiʀəX, aɣləɣnəX 'taboo', and aɣləʀə- 'observe period of mourning after a death']
SPI aɣliq- 'menstruate' [Jen. also has 'miscarry' for W and Ras. has W aɣliʀi- 'refrain from on account of taboo']
NAI aɣliʀi- 'shun in accordance with taboo', PH aɣliq- 'menstruate' [also aalʀu- 'menstruate']
WCI aɣliq- 'refrain from s.th. on account of taboo' [and Ras. has aɣliqtuq 'menstruating woman' for Net]
ECI alli(q)- 'refrain from doing s.th.' [allituni 'Sunday']
GRI ałłiʀ- 'miscarry, refrain from on account of taboo'

PY aɣluɣ- 'rummage'
AAY aɣluɣ- 'rummage'
CAY aɣluɣ-
NSY aɣluɣ- 'work'
CSY aɣluɣ- 'rummage'

PE aɣluʀ 'jaw (of whale)' [cf. perhaps Aleut aɣalu-X 'tooth, tusk, barb', unless this goes with aa(k)]
AAY ➠
CAY aɣluq 'ridgepole, center beam'
NSY aɣluk 'rainbow, arc, crosspiece on skin stretcher, walrus-bone strut for whale boat' [ANLC; Men. has aɣlu 'whale's jaw']
CSY aɣluk 'jaw, rainbow'
Sir aɣləX 'jaw'
SPI aɣlu 'boat keel, sled runner' [and aɣluk 'two jawbones of whale used for doorframe of house' — Jen.]
NAI aɣlu 'whale jawbone, sled runner shoe' [and aɣluq- 'remove jawbone']
WCI aɣluit 'sledge runners of bone — esp. whalebone'
ECI allu(q)- 'remove or disjoint jaw' [also 'open up a bird, revealing its interior']
GRI ałłuʀ- 'pull jawbone out of joint'

PE aɣluquʀ 'jawbone' [cf. quʀ; the Inu (esp. WG) forms may be influenced by atliʀ under at(ə)-]
AAY AP aɣluquq, Kod auɣlułquq, KP aɣlułquq 'jawbone'
CAY aɣluquq
NSY aɣləquq 'jaw' [ANLC — Men. has aɣləkuk, L.-T. has aɣləqxuq or aɣləqxuq]
CSY —
Sir —
SPI aɣliuq 'jawbone'
NAI aɣliʀuq
WCI —
ECI alliʀuq
GRI ałłiʀuq '(lower) jaw'

PY aɣluʀyaq 'rainbow' [cf. yaʀ?]
AAY K aɣluʀyaq, C aɣlu<y>aq 'rainbow'
CAY aɣluʀyaq
NSY — [note aɣlutə 'rainbow' (L.-T.)]
CSY — [see aɣluk above]

PE aɣtuʀ- 'touch'
AAY axtuʀ- 'touch'
CAY axtuʀ-
NSY axsiqə- 'touch', axtuqaʀ- 'touch lightly' [ANLC]
CSY axtuʀ-
Sir axtəʀ- [Orr]
SPI aktuʀit-
NAI [note aksik- 'touch', aksiŋa- 'be sore to touch']
WCI aktuq- 'touch'
ECI attu(q)-
GRI attuʀ-

PY-S aɣuʀ- 'bend' [cf. aɣu(C)ummaʀ]
AAY —
CAY —
NSY —
CSY aɣuʀ- 'bend, turn'
Sir aɣuʀ- 'bend', aɣuʀməlŋuX 'bent, crooked'

PE aɣu(C)ummaʀ 'woven object' [cf. aummin, but also aɣuʀ-]
AAY —
CAY aɣuumaq 'woven object, basket' [and note aɣuumaʀ(aq*) 'beach swallow']
NSY —
CSY —
Sir —
SPI Qaw aɣɣuumaq 'basket' [borrowed from CAY]
NAI aɣuummak, aɣuummaq* 'woven basket'
WCI —
ECI —
GRI —

PY aɣyaq 'star' [cf. aɣ(ɣ)a(ʀ)- and yaʀ? — compare also aaɣžuuk]
AAY aɣyaq 'star'
CAY aɣyaq
NSY —
CSY —
Inu — [for Pryde's Net aɣiattaat 'unidentified constellation' see aaɣiaq]

PY aɣyumiʀ- 'whisper'
AAY AP aɣyumia<ʀ>aʀ-, PWS aɣyumiʀuaʀ- 'whisper'
CAY aɣyumiʀ-, aɣyumciaʀ(aʀ)-, aɣyimciaʀ(aʀ)-
NSY —
CSY —

PE aɣyuʀ- 'hover over' [cf. aɣiɣtə-?]
AAY PWS aɣyuuʀ- 'hover over (with romantic interest)'
CAY aɣyauʀ- 'desire, hover over'
NSY aɣyaaʀ- 'soar (bird)' [Enm. et al.]
CSY aŋyii- 'hover over'
Sir —
SPI —
NAI —
WCI Cop aɣiuqtuq 'evil spirit causing sickness and death in human beings and dogs' [perhaps with contam. from aliuqtuq; note also aɣiuqtuyaq- 'confess']
ECI —
GRI aɣiuʀ-, aɣiuaaʀ-, aŋiuaaʀ- 'hover over'

PY aɣži(ʀ)- or **ažʀiʀ-** 'act mischievously' [there seems to be some contam. from ayuʀiʀ-]
AAY [Kod asʀiq 'fool' — Pinart]
CAY azʀiq, HBC ayʀiq 'mischievous child, brat'
NSY aɣžiXtə 'gambol, romp' [ANLC; also aɣžiʀnəq 'mischievous child, brat']
CSY aɣziXtə- 'stubbornly and sullenly delay in doing what one has been told to do' [and SLI ayʀiyuɣniqə- 'be spoiled, obstinate (child)' — Chap ayʀiʀyuɣumalʀii 'pestering']
Inu [note NAI aɣžutaq 'bothersome person']

PY aɣʷitə- 'move aside' [cf. av(v)ar(iʀ)- and avðaʀ[2] — there appears to be contamination here; the first consonant may be due to dem. root av- (and its derivs. like avan) — note that av- can mean 'one going away' in CAY]
AAY K awitə- 'get out of the way'
CAY awitə-
NSY awitə- 'move aside, put aside, separate', awiyutə- 'take away, part' [and awiaXtə- 'jump aside' (ANLC); Men. writes awgitə-, etc.]
CSY awitə- 'get out of way', awiqə- 'take aside' [for aviitə- 'be absent' see av(v)aʀ-]
Sir — [for avətəŋəɣət(ə)- 'disappear' see avataŋiʀ- under avan]

PY aɣʷtaʀ- 'feel uncertain or uncomfortable' [cf. aɣʷitə- and/or avəɣ-?]
AAY K auxtaʀ(yuɣ)-, C auxta(yuɣ)- 'feel uncertain', PWS 'feel one has not received one's share'
CAY aw̥taʀ(yuɣ)- 'feel inhibited, uncomfortable, hesitant'
NSY —
CSY —

PI ailitaq 'wall skin' [cf. aʀu- and ŋilitaʀ?]
SPI —
NAI —
WCI Car ailitaq 'wall skin' [B.-S.; Ow. has 'canvas windbreak' for EP and Ras. has Net aalisaq — for ailisaq]
ECI ailitaq 'rampart, shield of snow at door of house', Lab ailitak 'tapestry, hangings' [Peck]
GRI aalisaq, EG aalitsaq 'tapestry', NG ailihaq also 'picture' [and compare uŋalisaq under uŋan]

PI ainnəq 'open lead' [cf. aɣittaʀ- and nəʀ[1]]
SPI [note Imaq ainaituq 'unpassable' and ainiq 'storm']
NAI [note ainʸɨq* 'pocket']
WCI ainniq 'open lead in water' [and Sig ainiq 'pocket', also aimatqutak 'bay, inlet' — 'harbor' acc. Lowe]
ECI —
GRI NG ainniq 'open lead' [Holt.]

PE a(C)ippaʀ 'companion' [there may be a link to aɣi; compare also alupaq- and alʀapak (aləʀ) for the final element]
AAY aipaq 'companion, spouse, other'
CAY aipaq
NSY aɣ̥paq 'fellow traveler, companion, other' [ANLC — Men. has aɣ̥pii '(the) second', aɣ̥paqutaq 'companion']
CSY —
Sir —
SPI aippaq 'companion, spouse, other of two'
NAI aippaq* 'mate, other of two, co-wife'
WCI aippaq 'companion, spouse, other of two'
ECI aippaq
GRI aappa(q*) 'companion, spouse, other of two' [and NG (older) also aippaq 'father of woman', aippaxxaq 'father of man' acc. Søby, presumably by contam. with ap(p)a; note also aappaʀ-'get married']

PI aiʀaq 'black oxytrope *(Oxytropis nigrescens)*'
SPI —
NAI aiʀaq 'black oxytrope (plant with edible root)'
WCI Cop, Net aiʀaq [Pryde]
ECI aiʀaq
GRI —

PI aiviqižak 'bird (wading) [cf. ayvəʀ?]
SPI —
NAI aiviqi<ž>ak 'pectoral sandpiper'
WCI Net aiviqiak
ECI aiviqiak 'black-bellied plover or hyperboreal phalarope'
GRI —

PE aka(a) and **akəka** 'ouch (exclamation of pain)' [cf. akka?]
AAY —

CAY akəka(taki), akkatak, NI, HBC akaa 'ouch! (reaction to anything in excess)' [and akakaaŋ 'expression of sympathy to child'
NSY [note kəka 'exclamatory warning' — also kəkka 'hot!' (ANLC)]
CSY [note kəka 'ouch!' — which de Reuse, however, regards as a loan from Chukchi keke 'women's interjection of surprise']
Sir aka-kaa 'expression of surprise' [and Vakh. has kəka as an exclamation 'oh!' from Rub.'s texts]
SPI [note Qaw a'aa, KI aa'aa 'almost, that was close!']
NAI —
WCI —
ECI [note a'aa (Saul has aataa) 'cry of pain', also NBI aak(k)a, SB aɣɣaq, Aiv aaka, Tar auka, Lab aukak 'no' — entangled with na-[1]?; note Lab aɣalak 'moan, sound made when in pain' — Andersen et al.]
GRI EG aɣaa 'ouch!' [= NG (h)a'aa; for WG na'aa see na-[1]]

PE a(a)kaʀ 'older female relative' [with expressive gemination of first vowel as in a(a)na?]
AAY aakaaq 'older sister'
CAY NSU aakaq 'mother'
NSY aakaq 'older sister'
CSY aakaq* 'older sister of female'
Sir aakaX [Orr; the long vowel may indicate borrowing from CSY]
SPI aaka 'mother'
NAI aaka 'mother' [and aakiyaq, aakatciaq, aaxxaa 'eldest sister']
WCI Sig aakaq [Met.], aakaaʀaaluk 'older sister'
ECI —
GRI —

PI akcut 'hard or with effort'
SPI —
NAI —
WCI Cop, Net, Car axxut 'hard, strongly' [Pryde; Met. has gloss 'go ahead!' for Cop and Pet. has 'again, strongly' for Sig; Met. has Cop axxuqtuq- 'make an effort' but Pryde has axxuuq- 'do one's best, labor, try to prevail upon, urge']
ECI atsut, Lab atsuut 'go ahead!' [Dor. has aksut for the former; Lab atsuɣuk-, NBI aksuʀuq- 'exert oneself' — Saul has aʀsuʀaq- for Tar]
GRI assut [old ortho. agsut] 'very, quickly' [assuʀu(u)ʀ- 'exert oneself']

PE akðaɣ- 'roll or turn over'
AAY akaɣ- 'roll', akaɣŋa- 'be round'
CAY akaɣ- 'roll', akalʀia 'wheel' [and Y, NS akaxtaq 'dough']
NSY akaʀ- 'roll downhill, collapse' [ANLC; Men. has akakə-, akaXtə- 'roll, rush down', akaɣałqiitaʀ- 'roll', akaɣžak 'wheel', and akamłuruaq 'circle']
CSY akamka 'circle', Chap akamkəxtaq 'cylindrical object'
Sir —
SPI akšak- 'roll, knead dough', Qaw akšalak- 'roll over, begin to roll', akšaktuaq 'wheeled vehicle' [and Imaq akšaq 'ball' — contam. with aqšaq under aqə-]
NAI akšak- 'roll, slide like caribou killed on slope', akšaliɣaq 'wheel, tire' [and PH aɣžalɣun 'wheeled vehicle']
WCI aksak- 'roll' [nominal = 's.th. round'; aksaʀniq 'snow slide', aksaluɣaq 'wheel' — Cop axxaluaq (Pryde)]
ECI atsa(k)- 'roll, turn round or over', atsakaa(q)- 'roll along' [nominal = 'ball of snow made by rolling'; atsaluaq 'wheel', atsalua- 'turn (wheel)']
GRI aššakaʀ- 'turn over, roll over', aššakaa- 'roll' [and aššakaašuq 'wheel', aššałłaɣ- 'turn over, around, on side']

PI akšaɣiitkutaq 'device for preventing implements from rolling off kayak deck' [note ɣiit- and un]
SPI —
NAI akšaɣiitkutaq 'barrier to keep s.th. from rolling off (e.g. rails along kayak deck)'
WCI Perry River aksaɣiipkutik 'rest on kayak for (caribou) spear' [Pryde]
ECI atsaɣiikkuti 'chock, s.th. to prevent wheel from rolling'
GRI aššaɣiikkut 'holder for harpoon on kayak deck'

PI akšalək- 'roll between hands' [cf. ləɣ-]
SPI Imaq akšaləq- 'roll dough'
NAI [note akšalik- 'roll (away)']
WCI aksaliɣaq- 'roll in hands, pulverize', Cop axxalik- 'rub hands together' [Pryde for the latter]
ECI atsalik- 'roll between hands'
GRI aššaliɣ- 'roll between hands, pulverize'

PE akðanquʀ 'upper arm' [cf. akðaɣ- and quʀ?]
AAY —
CAY isaquq 'humerus', Nun akłanquX 'part of seal's front flipper bones' [the former influenced by yaquq 'wing'?]
NSY —
CSY — [aymałqa 'humerus, femur' is from the Chukchi]
Sir —
SPI —
NAI Nu akšatquq 'upper arm' [Ras.; B (Web. and Zib.) aXfaluaq, Mal aqšavaluqtaq 'upper arm muscle' are probably influenced by aXfaluq-, aqšavaluq- 'be round' — see aŋvaluʀ- under aŋva(ʀ)-]
WCI aksatquq 'upper arm' [Lowe has axxatquq for Cop and aksaʀuq for Sig]
ECI aʀsaquq, Lab atsaquk 'upper arm, humerus'
GRI aššaqquq 'upper arm, humerus' [in SWG also 'second cousin' acc. S.-L.]

PY-S akəqə- 'promise'
AAY akəqə- 'promise (tr.)', akqi- 'promise (intr.)'
CAY ak(ə)qə- 'promise'
NSY akəqə-
CSY akəqə-

Sir akəqə- [Vakh.]
Inu [note Qaw akiqšuq- 'promise', from the Yup?]

PE akəquʀ 'knot in wood' [cf. akəʀ and qur?]
AAY —
CAY Y, HBC akquq 'knot in wood'
NSY —
CSY [akaŋquq 'knot in wood']
Sir [akaŋqəX 'knot in wood' — Vakh. from Rub.'s texts]
SPI aɣiʀuq 'knot in wood'
NAI akiʀuq 'knot in wood, branch', Nu 'tine of antler'
WCI akiʀuq 'knot in wood, branch' [Pryde]
ECI akiʀuq 'knot in wood, branch' [Saul; Schn. has Iti akiʀuaʀuq 'leaf, wheat']
GRI akiʀuq 'knot in wood'

PE akəʀ 'barb'
AAY akəq 'harpoon barb'
CAY akəq*
NSY [note akn̥əq 'end, sharp edge' — ANLC]
CSY →
Sir →
SPI —
NAI aki 'gaff, barb' [and akit- 'hook']
WCI —
ECI aki Iti 'barbed point of fish hook or arrow', Lab 'harpoon point' [Bourq. for the latter]
GRI akik, EG aɣiq, Up akiq 'harpoon barb' [and akiliʀ-, ałłiʀ- 'put a barb on', akitat, akiʀsat 'jigging hook(s)', akkit- 'catch on s.th. (hook)']

PE akləɣaʀ 'bird dart (with bladder float)' [cf. aklək below and aʀ, also Aleut akliɣa-X 'harpoon with bladder float', possibly borrowed from the Esk.]
AAY [note akłəɣaq 'small auklet']
CAY akłəɣaq 'bird arrow, spear with line and float attached'
NSY —
CSY akłəɣaq 'arrow used on birds'
Sir —
SPI —
NAI —
WCI —
ECI —
GRI ałłiɣaq [Egede akliak], EG atsiŋaq 'bladder dart'

PY-S aklək 'barb or notch in arrow?' [cf. ləɣ]
AAY [note akłək 'auklet']
CAY —
NSY —
CSY akłək 'barb, notch in arrow' [also du. for one]
Sir akłəx 'barb, notch in arrow'

PE aki(-) '(thing) opposite or answer' [cf. Aleut aki-X 'price, payment', aki- 'pay, buy' and akiit- 'limit, border'; there may be a link to dem. roots aɣ-, akəm-, etc.]
AAY aki 'other side (of)' [posit. root; as verb = 'reciprocate, fight back'; also aki(q) 'coin, money']
CAY aki 'equivalent, value, price, response' [as posit. root = 'other side (of)', as verb 'reciprocate, answer, take revenge'; also aki(q) 'coin']
NSY aki 'value, price, s.th. to exchange' [as verb = 'take revenge, reciprocate, reward', and as posit. root = 'other side (of), area across (from)']
CSY aki 'equivalent, price, money' [as verb = 'reciprocate', as posit. root = 'other side (of)', akitə- 'answer, take revenge']
Sir aka 'price, value', akit(ə)- 'answer' [and akitəʀ- 'revenge, pay back', akitəX 'revenge', akəsaʀvəx 'shop'; Vakh. has akisaX 'trade' from Men.'s texts and aki- 'revenge' from Rub.'s texts]
SPI aɣi, Qaw aki 'money' [as posit. root = 'across from', as verb = 'take revenge'; and aɣisaq- 'go to trade', Qaw akiaq- 'take over from, relieve']
NAI aki 'cost, price, value' [as verb = 'respond (esp. with gestures to someone far off)', as posit. root = 'opposite side (of)'; akiaq- 'relieve someone']
WCI aki 'payment, price' [as posit. root = 'other side (of)'; akiaq- 'take someone's place']
ECI aki 'cost, side platform in snow house where lamps kept' [as verb = 'answer, revenge oneself', as posit. root = 'other side (of)']
GRI aki 'price, cost, front platform in trad. house' [as verb aki- 'answer', as posit. root = 'other side (of)'; and NG akia 'North America', akiqaq- 'trade']

PE akiɣaʀ- and **akiʀaʀ-** 'carry between two' [cf. aʀ-?]
AAY C aki<ʀ>aʀ- 'carry between two or more people'
CAY akiɣaʀ- 'carry on a stretcher'
NSY —
CSY —
Sir —
SPI aɣiɣaq- 'carry with arms extended as by handle'
NAI akiɣaq- 'carry across shoulders or between two people'
WCI akiraq- 'carry between two people'
ECI akiʀaq- 'carry between two' [Saul; Bourquin has Lab akiɣaq- 'carry between two people']
GRI akiaʀ- 'carry between two'

PE akiliʀ- 'pay for' [cf. liʀ-]
AAY akiliʀ- 'pay (for)'
CAY akiliʀ-
NSY akiliʀ- 'pay' [ANLC]
CSY akiləXtuʀ-
Sir akəcəʀ-
SPI aɣiliq- 'buy'
NAI akilʸiq- 'pay (for)'
WCI akiliq-
ECI akiliq-
GRI akiliʀ-

PE akil(l)iʀ and **akiqliʀ** '(one) opposite' [cf. l(l)iʀ and for the second form qliʀ, containing qaʀ as in PI akiʀaq below?]
AAY akiqłiq, AP akiliq 'one opposite, opponent'
CAY akiqłiq* 'one opposite'

CSY —
NSY —
Sir —
SPI Qaw akiliq
NAI akilʸlʸiq* 'opponent' [and akilʸinʸaaq 'north side of Point Barrow']
WCI Perry River akilliq 'the one opposite' [Pryde]
ECI akiliq 'one on opposite side', akilliq 's.o living at opposite end of village', Iti 'adversary'
GRI akiliq* 'place on opposite side of fjord, s.o. living opposite' [and akiliniq* 'land on other side, North American coast opposite Greenland']

PI akima- 'win or surpass' [cf. (u)ma-?]
SPI aɣima- 'win game, beat'
NAI akima- 'win'
WCI akima-
ECI akima- 'answer back', akimayuk- 'be undefeated, defend self' [and note akit- 'surpass']
GRI akima- 'be distinguished, prominent' [and akit-, akimuʀ- 'surpass']

PE akimiɣaʀ 'fifteen' [cf. ECI, GRI akit- under akima- above and also akitmi(C)- below]
AAY K akimiaq 'fifteen'
CAY akimiaq
NSY akimiaq
CSY akimiɣaq
Sir —
SPI aɣimiaq
NAI akimiaq
WCI Sig akimiaq [Lowe]
ECI —
GRI — [but note akimmik 'still more']

PE akin 'headrest' [cf. un]
AAY akin 'pillow'
CAY akin, akitaq, akitəq 'pillow'
NSY akin
CSY akin
Sir akəta
SPI aɣin
NAI akinʸ, akisi
WCI akin
ECI akiti
GRI akit, EG aɣisiq 'pillow, head of bed'

PE akini(C)aʀ- 'retaliate' [cf. ni(C)aʀ-]
AAY —
CSY —
NSY akiniaʀ- 'reciprocate' [ANLC]
CSY akiniiʀ- 'retaliate, raise objections'
Sir —
SPI —
NAI —
WCI —
ECI akiniaq- 'take revenge'
GRI akiniaʀ-

PE akiŋit- 'be free or cheap' [cf. ŋit-]
AAY akiitə- 'have no money', C 'be inexpensive' [akiilŋuq 'debt']
CAY akiitə- 'be free or valueless' [akiilŋuq 'debt']
CSY akiŋitə- 'be free or cheap'
NSY akiitə- 'be cheap' [ANLC; Men. has akiilŋuq 'cheap, free']
Sir —
SPI aɣiit- 'be inexpensive'
NAI akiit- 'be cheap, lose game' [and akiilʸaq 'debt', as verb 'buy on credit'; akiitcuq 'prostitute']
WCI akiit- 'have no money, lose game' [and Car? akiittuq 'free, worthless, debt' — Schn. 'adg']
ECI —
GRI akiit- 'be free' [akiitsuʀ- 'get s.th. free or on credit, owe a debt', akiitsuɣaq 'debt']

PY akiʀ- 'shine' [cf. liʀ-?; compare with akiʀᴜʀ- below]
AAY akiʀ- 'shine, shed light'
CAY [note akəXta 'sun' and akinqaʀ- 'reflect']
NSY [for akiiXʷtə- 'reflect' see akiʀᴜʀ- below]
CSY akisqaXtə- 'shine, flash, reflect light (on)'

PI akiʀaq 'enemy' [cf. qaʀ?]
SPI —
NAI —
WCI akiʀaq 'adversary'
ECI akiʀaq 'enemy'
GRI akiʀaq

PE akiʀᴜʀ- 'answer back'
AAY akiuʀ- 'echo, fight back'
CAY akiuʀ- 'fight back' [and akiuxtə- 'echo']
NSY akiiXʷtə- 'reflect (light)'
CSY [note akiiŋqʷaXtə- 'echo', akilʀuu(ʀ)- 'yell']
Sir [note akəʀᴜʀ- 'shout' — but Vakh. has akəlʀᴜʀ- — from the CSY?; Em. also has akəłəX 'shout']
SPI aɣiuq- 'echo, fight back'
NAI akiuq- 'be opposed, keep responding'
WCI akiuq- 'respond, echo, revenge oneself'
ECI akiuq- 'revenge oneself'
GRI akiuʀ- 'answer back, be unwilling to give in'

PI akisuk- 'reflect' [cf. yuɣ-]
Yup — [but note CAY akiuxtə- under akiʀᴜʀ- above]
NAI [note akilʸuk 'beam of light' and akiłʸuk(-) 'echo']
WCI akisuk- 'reflect, shine on (sun)'
ECI akisuk-
GRI akisuɣ- 'reflect, shine, echo', EG aɣisiC- 'be white' [and note EG aɣittiliʀ- 'dawn', aɣiittuq 'copper']

PE akitnaʀ 'wall' [note akin above and naʀ]
AAY — [but note place name Akitŋ̥aq in AP]
CAY Nun akitnax 'wall, modern house' [Lantis — for akitŋ̥aX?]
NSY —
CSY —
Sir —
SPI —
NAI —

WCI Perry River akinnaq 'mountainside' [Pryde]
ECI akinnaq 'side of mountain, wall'
GRI NG akinnaq 'mountainside'

PE akitmi(C)- 'knock against' [cf. akin under aki(-) and p.b. miɣ-?]
AAY PWS akitm̥iʀ- 'sideswipe'
CAY akitm̥itə- bump into s.th. sideways, be halted', akitm̥iaʀ- 'bump into' [and akitm̥iɣ- 'carry (a burden)']
NSY —
CSY —
Sir —
SPI —
NAI —
WCI Cop akimiɣaq- 'jostle, push around' [Pryde]
ECI akimmi(C)- 'be pushed, knock against', akimmia(q)- 'be heated by contact, give off heat', Iti 'reflect (image)' [and akimmiaq 'reflected, absorbed heat']
GRI akimmit- [also akingmig- in old ortho.] 'bump into, strike against' [and note NG akimmiXXaq- 'be in breathing hole (seal)']

PE akiviɣ- 'prop up (boat)' [cf. akkiʀ-]
AAY akiwik 'baidar, open boat with flat bottom and protruding bow'
CAY akivixtə- 'prop up'
NSY akivixtə- [ANLC]
CSY akivixtə- 'prop a boat on its side' [and note Chap akəvəxtə- 'turn over']
Sir —
SPI —
NAI akivik- 'prop a boat on its side'
WCI —
ECI [akivik- 'go from one side to another (on swing or rollers)']
GRI —

PE akka 'so much (exclamation)?' [cf. aka(a), but also ak(k)uvaʀ — the relat. is obscure]
AAY —
CAY akka 'past, a long time, already', akkakika 'so far away, so many!' [and NSU akkami'i 'that's all!', probably borrowed from SPI]
NSY —
CSY —
Sir — [for akəvʀaʀmiʀaX 'recently' see ak(k)uvaʀ]
SPI akkaa, akkakaa 'how big, so much, be quiet!', akkamii 'the end (of story)'
NAI akkakaa 'what a lot, enough!' [and note aaqqaa, Uum aqqaa 'it stinks!']
WCI Car? akka 'get out of the way and let me work!' [Schn. for 'adg', = B. Lake aqqami; Sig aqqali 'my goodness (surprise or disgust)']
ECI Lab akka 'here, catch it!' [perhaps by contam. with ak under a(a)ŋ; Schn. has Aiv aqa 'get out of my way' and Tar aqali 'goodbye' (influenced by aqaɣu?); note also akau- 'be good, fine' and akauɣi- 'find agreeable' — perhaps influenced by naku(a)q(-)]
GRI [note kakkaak 'wow!', kakaɣ- 'be very clever, be too much', kak(k)aɣi- 'be impressed by (s.o.)', perhaps also akaaʀi- 'like']

PI akkak 'uncle (paternal)'
SPI W akkak 'paternal uncle' [Jen.], akkaluuʀaq 'uncle as term of affection'
NAI akkaaka, Mal akkak 'paternal uncle' [the first form in Nu apparently for both maternal and paternal uncle]
WCI Net akka(k) 'paternal uncle'
ECI akka(k)
GRI akka(k), EG akkaq

PE akkiʀ- 'lift up' [cf. aku(ʀ) and liʀ-?]
AAY — [for akiʀ- 'shine' see akiʀ- under aki(-)]
CAY Nun akiʀ- 'hold up, lift'
NSY —
CSY akiʀ- 'support, prop up'
Sir akəʀətaX 'lever'
SPI akkiq- 'help someone up, providing a foothold'
NAI akkiq- 'catch someone or s.th. from falling'
WCI —
ECI akki(q)- 'help s.o. up, pushing from behind'
GRI akkiʀ- 'lift (from below)', Up 'catch with hook' [there is probably contam. with akəʀ in the latter form]

PI aklaq 'bear (brown)'
Yup [NSY akłaq 'brown bear' is presumably borrowed from Inu, but note also NS akłanquXun 'weasel, ermine'; for AAY laqłaq 'brown bear' see aləməqaʀ-]
SPI akłaq 'brown bear'
NAI akłaq, Nu aklaq
WCI akłaq, Cop axxaq 'brown bear' [Lowe has 'grizzly bear' for Sig; Pet. distinguishes akłaq 'black bear' from akvik 'yellow land bear']
ECI atsaq 'brown bear'
GRI ałłaq

PE aklu- 'be needy'
AAY akłu(u)q Kod, AP 's.th. picked up and saved', C 'bead', akłu(u)ʀ- 'pick up and save' [and Kod, PWS akłuun 'store']
CAY akłu(q) 'merchandise, clothing, bedding'
NSY akłu- 'be in need'
CSY akłu- 'be in need, lack' [and akłuŋi 'wealth, riches', akłunaq 's.th. needed, time of scarcity']
Sir akłə- 'be in need' [Orr]
SPI —
NAI —
WCI —
ECI atsu- 'be poor' [NBI akłuyuq 'poor person', akłuittuq 'rich person']
GRI —

PI akluna(a)q 'rope' [cf. aklu-?]
Yup — [but note CSY akłunaq 's.th. needed' under aklu-]
SPI akłunaaq 'rope'
NAI akłuna<ž>aq
WCI akłunaaq, axxunaaq 'thong of seal skin'
ECI atsunaaq 'rope made of bearded seal skin', atsunayaq 'cord, rope'
GRI ałłunaaq, EG atsinaaq 'rope'

PI akmaaq 'flint'
SPI Qaw akmaaq 'flint'
NAI aɣmaaq, Mal, Nu akmaaq
WCI anmaaq
ECI ammaaq, Aiv aŋmaaq
GRI ammaaq

PY akmaliaʀaq 'least auklet'
AAY —
CAY [note akm̥aliaʀaɬɬəX(aq) 'raven']
NSY akm̥aliaXaq 'least auklet' [ANLC]
CSY akm̥aliiʀaq

PI akpət- 'start to sing or talk' [there may be a link to aku(ʀ)]
Yup [note perhaps CSY akuzi- 'speak' if from *akvət-; for CAY akuzʀaXtə- 'fool around, make a commotion' see akut- under aku(ʀ)]
SPI akpit- 'begin to sing'
NAI akpɨt- 'begin to talk, sing'
WCI akpit- 'get s.th. off one's chest, make a request or remark' [and akpiuti- 'tell, address'; Schn. has for B. Lake akpik- 'speak out of turn for no reason']
ECI Lab akpitsi- 'lead the choir' [Peck], SB akpiliq- 'begin a song' [Boas]
GRI appit- 'start singing, talking' [and appiut(i)- 'reply to, sing in s.o.'s place', NG akpiut(i)- 'scold']

PE aku(ʀ) 'space between or lower part (widening out)' [there may be two different bases here but note the flap of the traditional parka (between the legs) for the second sense; cf. ak(k)uvaʀ and akkiʀ-]
AAY akuq 'skirt'
CAY aku(q) 'skirt, lower part of garment'
NSY akuq 'root, skirt'
CSY akuq 'root of plant'
Sir akəX 'root'
SPI aɣuq 'skirt', Qaw aku(q) 'hem of skirt, root', Imaq aɣuq 'root'
NAI akuq 'lower part of garment' [for akku 'a while ago' see ak(k)uvaʀ]
WCI aku 'lower part of garment', Cop akuq 'thigh bone of seal' [Pryde], Car 'river flowing into lake' [Dor. for Baker Lake; Ow. has akuq 'mouth of river' for EP]
ECI akuq 'tail of women's parka, seal bone between femur and pelvis' [and akukittut 'Greenlanders' (due to short flaps of the Polar Eskimo parka, apparently), akuilitaq 'waterproof garment covering whole body for kayaking']
GRI aku(q) 'mouth of river, thigh bone of seal, rib of umiak, lower flap of parka', NG akuq 'parka tail' [Holt.; and akuilisaq 'waterproof half-jacket for kayaking']

PE akulə- 'space between'
AAY akulə- 'amidst' [posit. root]
CAY akula [as posit. root akulə-] 'midsection, area between, tundra'
NSY akulə- '(space) between'
CSY akulə- 'middle, midst, space between ' [posit. root]
Sir akələ-
SPI aɣulaq 'interval, space between'
NAI akullaq 'distance between'
WCI —
ECI Lab akulait- 'be close together', akulaittumik 'not very often' [Andersen et al.]
GRI akulaaq 'crotch'

PY akulipaq or **akulipəq** 'middle finger' [cf. akul(l)iʀ below; compare qətəqliq under qətəʀ, also alqiliq; the present set may be a more local innovation]
AAY K akuləpaq, Kod also akulimaq, AP akilipaq, Perry akuləpaaq 'middle finger' [compare PWS akulək, akuləkaq 'ring finger']
CAY akulipəq*, akulipXaq 'middle finger' [and note HBC əkiliq, ikilipik 'ring finger' — contam. with source of mikəliʀaq under mikə-?]
NSY —
CSY —

PE akul(l)iʀ 'middle thing' [cf. l(l)iʀ; compare qulə- and its deriv. qulliʀ]
AAY akuləqɬiq, PWS akuliq 'middle part'
CAY akuliq 'middle'
NSY akuliq 'interval'
CSY akuliq 'middle'
Sir —
SPI —
NAI Nu akulliq* 'middle one'
WCI [Dor. has akuliq 'skin for clothes' for B. Lake]
ECI akulliq 'middle one'
GRI akuɬɬiq*

PE akul(l)iʀaʀ 'bridge of nose' [cf. akul(l)iʀ above and aʀ]
AAY —
CAY akuliʀaq 'bridge of nose'
NSY —
CSY —
Sir —
SPI aɣuliaq
NAI akuliaq
WCI akuliaq 'bridge of nose' [Cop 'face' acc. Lowe]
ECI akuliaq 'space between eyes'
GRI akuliaq 'bridge of nose'

PY akulqucuk 'gap or crack' [cf. akulə- above]
AAY akuɬcuqaq K 'groin', C 'fly of pants'
CAY akuɬqucuk, akuɬtuqucuk 'gap, crack between boards'
NSY akuɬqusuk 'gap' [ANLC]
CSY akuɬqusuk 'crack between boards or rocks'

PE akultu- 'be far apart' [cf. akulə above and tu-[1]]
AAY Kod akuɬtu- 'be far apart'
CAY akuɬtu-
NSY —
CSY akuɬtu-
Sir —
SPI —
NAI akuttu-

WCI akuttu- 'be far apart' [and Pryde has Cop, Net akuttuyuuk 'constellation appearing at twilight associated with lengthening of day after midwinter']
ECI akuttuyumik 'at infrequent, distant intervals' [and akuttuyut 'spread out from one another' acc. Saul (Schn. has akuttutut); MacDonald has akuttuyuuk 'constellation formed by Betelgeuse and Bellatrix' for Igl]
GRI akuttu- 'be far apart'

PI akunnak- 'pass between' [cf. akunnəq below and p.b. nəɣ-?]
SPI —
NAI akunna(a)q- 'pass between or through'
WCI [Net akunnaaq 'opening or passage between two interlocking snowhouses' — Pryde]
ECI akunna(C)- Iti 'pass between two hills', Lab 'enter' [Bourq.; akunnaaq 'space between two parts of a thing', akunnaɣi- 'put off til later, make a pause']
GRI akunnaɣ- 'take the middle way, be medium large, not quite fit' [akunnaɣi- 'think it too late to begin s.th.']

PI akunnəq 'interval between' [cf. akulə- above and nəʀ[1]]
Yup — [note NSY akunəq clan name acc. L.-T.]
SPI aɣuniq 'interval between', Qaw akuniq 'groin'
NAI akunniq* 'interval between'
WCI akunniq 'between' [posit. root; 3s poss. akunʀa-]
ECI akunniq, akuʀŋa-
GRI akunniq*, akuʀna- 'between' [and note akuʀnut 'hindrance']

PE akuʀaʀ '(lower) abdomen' [cf. aʀ]
AAY aku<ʀ>aq 'groin'
CAY akuʀaq 'lower abdomen'
NSY— [but note akuʀaat 'knots in wood' — Orr]
CSY akuʀaq 'groin'
Sir [akəʀcəɣəX 'groin' — Vakh.]
SPI Qaw akuaq 'lower belly'
NAI Nu, PH akuaq 'lower belly'
WCI Perry River akuaq [Pryde]
ECI akuaq 'lower belly'
GRI akuaq 'lower belly, stomach' [and EG pl. aɣittat 'abdomen, entrails' (the latter meaning in Robbe and Menn.)]

PE akut- 'mix' [cf. t-[1]]
AAY akuutə- 'mix'
CAY akutə- 'mix' [note also akuzʀaXtə- 'fool around, make a commotion, commit adultery']
NSY akutə- 'mix, knead' [ANLC]
CSY akuutə- 'mix'
Sir —
SPI aɣut- 'mix, stir'
NAI akut- 'mix' -
WCI Sig akutsi- 'mix' [also 'adg' aku- acc. Schn.]
ECI akut- 'mix'
GRI aku-, akut-

PE akutaʀ 'edible mixture' [cf. akut- above and ðaʀ]
AAY —
CAY akutaq 'Eskimo ice cream'
NSY akutaq 'mixture (or reindeer fat, meat and blood and plant roots), dough' [L.-T.]
CSY akuutaq 'Eskimo ice cream'
Sir —
SPI aɣutaq 'Eskimo ice cream'
NAI akutaq 'dough' [and akutuq 'Eskimo ice cream']
WCI Car akutaq 'mixture of contents of caribou stomach and seal blubber' [Ras]
ECI —
GRI [note parallel deriv. akutaq 's.o. with light hair']

PE akuʀ-[1] 'catch' [cf. aku(ʀ)]
AAY akuʀ- 'wrestle', C akuqaʀ-, K akiqaʀ- 'catch with hands'
CAY akuXtuʀ- 'receive', akuqaʀ- 'catch with hands'
NSY akuqaʀ- 'catch' [ANLC; Men. has akuqə- 'catch', akuXtuʀ- 'take, receive']
CSY akuXtuʀ- 'reach, stretch out to reach', akuqaʀ- 'catch, grab'
Sir akuXtuʀ- 'stretch out to reach' [Vakh. from Men. and Rub.]
SPI aɣuqtuq- 'receive', akkuaq- 'catch s.th. thrown' [and Imaq aɣuta(q)- 'wrestle']
NAI akuqtuq- 'accept, acknowledge', akkuaq- 'catch'
WCI akuq- 'catch in the air'
ECI akuq-
GRI akuʀ- 'catch in the air, play ball with s.o.' [and note akuiʀi- 'agree']

PY-S akuʀ-[2] 'dip (in liquid)' [cf. aku(ʀ)]
AAY —
CAY akuXtə- 'dip into liquid'
NSY —
CSY akuXtə- 'apply water, soak, dilute, mix seal oil and water'
Sir akuqšəskay '(things) dipped or soaked' [Vakh. from Men.'s texts]

PE ak(k)uvaʀ 'yesterday or the other day' [cf. perhaps aku(ʀ) and vaʀ-, also dem. root akəm-]
AAY akxʷaq 'the other day, akxua<ʀ>aq 'evening, night'
CAY akxʷauɣaq 'yesterday', akxʷaXpak 'forever'
NSY —
CSY akuɣaaq 'the other day, yesterday'
Sir [akfasitaX 's.th. from today', akəvʀaʀmiraX 'recently', akəvʀaX 'the day after tomorrow'; note also akfasitaʀnun 'still more strongly', akfaʀninun 'as he approached' and exclamatory akfa 'and so (as I told you)' — Vakh. from Men.'s texts; Em. has akəvɣažuxlax (for akəvɣažuxłax?) 'long ago']
SPI akkuni 'a while ago' [Jen. has aqquni, Imaq akuni 'today, now']
NAI akku ' a while ago', akkupak 'right now', akkusaaq 'a long while ago, earlier in the day' [and akkumman 'after some time']
WCI Sig akkuɣu 'in a moment, later' [Lowe]

ECI akuni 'for a long time'
GRI akuni, SWG akunit 'for a long time, hurryɣ' [and note EG akki 'morning' (Ras. 'early in the morning') and akkiilu 'since early morning' acc. Robbe and Menn. (from *akkuni-lu?)]

PY ala- 'desire' [cf. Aleut ala- 'want, need (e.g. food)', and perhaps ala-X 'whale'; there may be a relat. to alaŋkaʀ-]
AAY K ala(yuk)- 'be stingy' [emot. root; for alaŋ<ʀ>u- 'be critical' see alaŋru-]
CAY alakə-, alaŋə- 'be attracted to a member of the opposite sex' [the former also 'encounter, notice', for which see alaŋkaʀ-]
NSY —
CSY — [for alaŋʀu- 'miss, be at a loss' see alaŋʀu-]
Sir — [but note alaqa 'vagina'?] an unattested
Inu — [but note Qaw alaun 'lover (not spouse)', a borrowing from an unattested CAY form?]

alaɣnaq 'type of red berry' [cf. naʀ; probably from Aleut halaɣna-X 'salmonberry', though the loan could have been the other way; perhaps the NSY form, with another p.b., is the cognate of the Aleut base]
AAY K, KP alaɣnaq 'high bush salmonberry'
CAY BB alaɣnaq 'type of red berry'
NSY [alaɣlukaq 'bearberry']
CSY —

PE alaŋkaʀ- 'observe or catch sight of' [cf. p.b.s nəɣ- and k(k)aʀ- and perhaps bases alaŋʀu- and alapənʀaʀ-]
AAY alaŋkaXtə- AP 'observe (as animal trying not to be seen)', Kod, KP 'check up on, go visit'
CAY [note alakə- 'notice, encounter']
NSY —
CSY —
Sir —
SPI alakaq- 'go check on,' Qaw 'peek' [also Qaw alakauq- 'peek']
NAI alatkaq- 'peer over barrier, reach point where one can see, rise over horizon (sun)'
WCI alatkaq- 'go and look' [and Ras. has Cop alakkaq- 'get a view over'; Pet. has alayuaq- 'spy on' and alan͡taq 'coward' for Sig]
ECI alakka(q)- 'appear, make appear, see what one sought to see'
GRI alakkaʀ- 'catch sight of, rise (sun), look in for a moment', EG 'become visible' (Robbe and Menn. have 'appear behind'), NG alikkaq- 'appear (before), go and see'

PY alaŋʀu- 'be taken by surprise' [cf. alaʀ- (esp. for the Qaw and Cop forms below) and alapənʀaʀ-]
AAY [note alaŋ<ʀ>u- 'be critical' — with contam. from naŋʀu(ʀ)-?]
CAY alaŋʀu(q) 'unexpected discovery or visitor, ghost' [and note alaŋaaʀ- 'be surprised']
NSY —
CSY [alaŋʀu(yuɣ)- 'miss, be at a loss' — there appears to be contam. with ala-]
Inu [note Qaw a(a)laaŋaaq- 'find amazing', alaaŋaa 'great!' — from the Yup?; for Qaw alatquq-, Cop alatqu- 'be taken by surprise' see alaʀ- — though they could belong directly here]

PE alapənʀaʀ- 'surprise' [cf. alaʀ- and alaŋʀu- and p.b. n(ə)ʀaʀ(aʀ)]
AAY —
CAY alapənnəXtə-, alapəŋŋəXtə- 'surprise'
NSY alapaŋilŋuq 'talkative (person)' [L.-T.]
CSY —
Sir —
SPI —
NAI [alapiɣɨ- 'pay no attention to, not notice', alapɨt- 'become confused, shuffle (cards)', alavži- 'confuse, become confused', Mal alapyaŋaaq- 'be absent-minded']
WCI —
ECI Lab alapiʀnaq- 'spy on, do unnoticed' [Peck]
GRI alapiʀnaat- 'catch the eye, be visible everywhere, be inquisitive, intrusive', alapiʀnaaʀsuʀ-, EG alipiʀnaaʀsuuʀ- [Robbe and Menn.] 'observe, keep an eye on', NG alupiʀŋaq- 'surprise, creep up on', alupiʀŋaqtaili- 'keep an eye on'

PI alappaa 'how cold (exclamation)'
Yup [CAY Y, NS alappaa 'oh, it's cold' is from the Inu]
SPI alapaa 'oh, it's cold'
NAI alappaa, alappuu
WCI alappaa
ECI —
GRI —

PI ala(a)q 'sole' [cf. at(ə)- and alu(ʀ)]
Yup — [note NSY has alalɣək 'mittens made from caribou leg skins (with palm of sealskin)'; Holt. has aLaksat 'moccasins' for Mountain Village CAY — though this is probably for ałiqsak under ałiʀtə]
SPI —
NAI alaaq 'sole of animal's paw, part of mittens covering palm' [and PH alannaaq 'palm of hand']
WCI alaq 'piece of skin sewn to bottom of boot or to interior of mitten' [for Cop Pryde has ala, and Ras has alaaxxaq 'skin of caribou head and neck for boot soles']
ECI ala 'sole of shoe', alaq 'sole of boot lining' [the latter in Lab the whole sole, not just inner part; Saul has alaaq rather for Tar]
GRI alaaq [pl. alaššat] 'sole, sledge shoeing' [and note EG alinnaa 'forward cushion on sole of foot' acc. Robbe and Menn. — contam. with alu(ʀ)?]

PE alaʀ- 'look away' [cf. alaŋʀu-, alapənʀaʀ- and EA alaqaaða- 'wonder']
AAY alaXtə- 'make a mistake'
CAY alaXtə- 'make a mistake, be in error'
NSY —
CSY — [for alaŋʀu- 'miss, be at a loss' see under alaŋʀu-]
Sir ałaXqə- 'make a mistake'
SPI Imaq alaq- 'turn away' [and note Qaw alatquq- 'take by surprise', alatquqtaili- 'be on the alert, watching for s.o.']

NAI alaq- 'look away, give up trying to catch'
WCI alaq- 'look away' [and Cop alatqu- 'pass without being seen']
ECI alaq- 'look away'
GRI alaʀ- 'look away from, not touch', NG alaq- 'cease doing, put aside, let be ', NG alaXXinnaq- 'not care about' [and note alaŋŋa(a)ʀ- 'read or know by heart', alaŋŋuq 'shady side e.g. of fjord)', NWG alaatsinaat(i)- 'watch']

PY aləɣ- 'feel confident'
AAY aləɣ(yuɣ)-, C also aməɣ(yuɣ)- 'be confident, self-assured'
CAY Nun alaɣ(yuɣ)- 'feel confident, ałke- 'consider feasible'
NSY —
CSY —

PE aləmqaʀ- 'eat greedily' [cf. alqimaʀ- and alqutaq; the relat. with aluɣ- is obscure]
AAY [note łaqłaq 'brown bear' — a deformation of aklaq?; for aXməɣ- 'be a hog, take more than one should' see ᴀʀcᴀʀ-]
CAY aləmqaʀ- 'sneak a taste', Y, HBC almə- 'taste, lick' [and note laqaʀ-, NSU ałqaʀ- 'gobble up food', Nun, NS amqaʀ- 'eat berries while picking them']
NSY —
CSY [amqəXtə- 'bite']
Sir [note aləqaʀ- 'lick', but Vakh. has amqaʀ- 'bite' from Rub. and Men.]
SPI Qaw ałXaq- 'eat hurriedly'
NAI apqałak- 'eat quickly'
WCI —
ECI aqqala- 'eat quickly' alumiʀaq-, 'water (mouth)'
GRI aqqaʀ- [old ortho. avqar-] 'be greedy, wasteful of food', aqqala- 'eat greedily'

PI aləq 'harpoon line'
Yup — [for aliq 'sleeve' see aðiʀ]
SPI aliq 'rawhide sealskin thong', etc.', Imaq alaqpak '(harpoon) line' [probably for aləqpak, and KI, W aliq 'heavy harpoon line for hunting — Jen.]
NAI PH aliq* 'harpoon line'
WCI aliq
ECI aliq
GRI aliq*, pl. aʀłit

PE aləqa(ʀ) 'older sister (of man)' [cf. aləʀ?]
AAY alqaq, Perry ałqaq 'older sister'
CAY ałqaq, HBC alqaq, NSU ałəqaq
NSY —
CSY —
Sir —
SPI — [but note KI, W aliqaʀa(a) 'he takes care of him' acc. Jen.]
NAI aliqa(q) 'older sister' [Jen.]
WCI aliqak, aliqaq 'older sister of male'
ECI NBI aliqannaq [B.-S. has aliqaa for Igl]
GRI aliqaq, NG aliqa, EG alaʀa 'older sister of male'

PE aləʀ 'other (of pair)' [Aleut a(a)lax, Att ulax 'two' (dual) is probably not related acc. Berg. — cf. rather p.b. ŋu- and the dual ending]
AAY ałəq '(its) other, companion, placenta' [Lisianski has az'l'xa 'two', and Veniaminov al'akha 'second']
CAY ➡
NSY —
CSY aləq* 'other of pair, companion, afterbirth', aalʀaq 'other of cooperating pair of boats, hunting partner, another family in same clan'
Sir aləX 'companion', alʀəX 'partner, other of pair' [Orr for former, Em. for latter form; also alʀəʀa 'second', and Vakh. has alʀan '(its) other']
SPI ➡
NAI alʀa(i) 'other one of pair'
WCI [Met. has alʀaiɣit 'their equivalent, other of a pair'; Ras. has alʀaa 'two' for Utku and Dor. has alʀaak 'two' for B. Lake — also 'seven, twelve, seventeen']
ECI ➡
GRI aʀła(ʀ)- 'one of them' [and aʀłaanisaq 'land animal in its second year', aʀłałłit, EG aʀtaʀaʀtit 'several']

PE alʀani and **alʀaku** 'next or last year' [i.e. with 3s poss. locative and p.b. ku respectively]
AAY Kod, KP ałXani, PWS ałłani 'once in a while'
CAY ałXaɣni 'last year', ałXaɣniku, ałXaku 'next year' [and ałXakuq 'year'; HBC alXaɣni, etc.]
NSY —
CSY —
Sir —
SPI —
NAI alʀaani 'a long time ago'
WCI Cop alʀaani 'a year or more ago or hence' [Jen.], Car 'last year', alʀaaɣu 'next year' [Pryde; also Utk acc. Briggs]
ECI aʀʀaani 'last year', aʀʀaaɣu 'next year'
GRI NG aʀlaani 'last year', aʀlaaɣu 'next year' [and note WG aʀłaaɣut 'at an earlier time']

PY alʀapak 'partner' [or alʀapaq; cf. vaɣ(-)?]
AAY —
CAY alʀapak, alʀapaq 'back-to-back sitting partner (in kayak)'
NSY —
CSY alʀapak 'companion, partner, second wife'

PE al(ə)ʀaʀ(aʀ) 'placenta' [cf. ʀaʀ]
AAY—
CAY alləXpak 'placenta'
NSY alʀaXpak [L.-T.]
CSY —
Sir —
SPI aʀlaaq 'placenta, afterbirth'
NAI alʀaaq 'afterbirth'
WCI alʀaq 'reticulum of caribou used as bag for carrying blood', Cop alʀaaq 'afterbirth' [Pryde for the latter]
ECI Lab axxaak 'placenta' [Bourq.]
GRI aʀłaaq 'afterbirth'

PI alʀa(a)ʀuciq '(second) stomach of ruminant' [cf. p.b. ɣuciq]
SPI —
NAI alʀaaʀusiq* 'large flat part of caribou's digestive system'
WCI alʀausiq 'second stomach of ruminant'
ECI —
GRI —

PE alǝraqðuʀ- advise (to do s.th.)'
AAY C ałǝXquʀ- 'advise'
CAY alǝXquʀ-, HBC alaXquʀ- 'advise, tell to do s.th.'
NSY —
CSY alǝXquʀ- 'speak to another person, advise'
Sir —
SPI Qaw alʀaqšuq- 'teach lesson, give instructions to'
NAI alʀaqšuq- 'preach, counsel, teach'
WCI —
ECI —
GRI —

PY-S alɣu- 'covet' [cf. EA alɣu- 'be jealous']
AAY —
CAY aɣluma- 'desire, covet' [contam. with aɣluɣ-?]
NSY aɣluma- 'desire, covet' [ANLC — but Men. has alɣuma-]
CSY alɣuma- 'be envious, covet', alɣumakǝ- 'be envious of'
Sir [Vakh. has alǝɣɣuqǝ- 'envy' from Rub.'s texts; Em. has alǝɣ- 'be envious']

PE ali 'far away' [cf. aliɣa-, alikǝ- and aliŋit-, but compare also aci[2]]
AAY —
CAY —
NSY —
CSY ali- 'out of sight'
Sir alimǝŋ 'from afar' [ab. case — Vakh.]
SPI —
NAI —
WCI ali(sik)- 'have gone or be far', alivani 'in the distance' [and note Cop aliaqtuq- 'go by sledge' — Met. p. 103]
ECI alivaq- 'retreat a little'
GRI ali- 'move away, distance oneself' [and alikkaʀ- 'have moved away a bit', alimasiɣ- 'be some distance away']

PE aliɣa- 'be lonely' [cf. ali; the same (emotional) root is found in ali(C)uʀtuʀ-, alikǝ- and aliŋǝ-, q.v.; observe the flip-flop 'good/bad' senses within Inu]
AAY alia(yuɣ)-, Perry ałia(yuɣ)- 'be lonely, depressed'
CAY alia(yuɣ)-, alai(yuɣ)- 'be lonesome'
NSY aliałǝq 'homesickness' [L.-T. has aliatǝ- 'be bored'; alianiiʀʷ- 'be bored' (ANLC)]
CSY aliɣa- 'long to go somewhere'
Sir —
SPI alianaq 'be sad, gloomy, dark', aliasuk- 'be sorry to leave an enjoyable situation' [and aliat- 'be eager to go somewhere']
NAI alianaq- 'be boring', [Dor.] 'unpleasant', aliasuk- 'feel lonely, sad'
WCI Cop aliahuk- 'be happy', Sig aliasuk- 'be sad, scared of being alone', alianaq- Sig 'be boring', Cop, Net 'be nice, splendid' [Ras. for the latter; and Cop aliaɣi- 'long for', Sig aliɣanaiq- 'have many, be great']
ECI alianaq- NBI 'be frightening', Tar 'be wonderful, fun', aliasuk- NBI 'be timid', Tar, Lab 'be happy' [and aliaɣi- NBI 'be afraid of', Tar, Lab 'enjoy', aliaC- 'be happy'; Ras. has alianaq- 'be joyful' also for Igl]
GRI alianaʀ-, aliasuɣ- 'be sad', NG aliahuk- 'be afraid (esp. of ghost)'

PE aliɣanaʀit- 'be amusing or entertaining' [cf. naʀ- and ŋit-]
AAY alianaitǝ-, Perry ałianaitǝ- 'be entertaining'
CAY —
NSY —
CSY —
Sir —
SPI alianait- 'be cheery, bright'
NAI alianait- 'be amusing'
WCI alianait- Cop 'be boring', Sig 'be amusing' [Schn. has the latter sense also for 'adg']
ECI alianait- NBI 'be pleasant, amusing' [Saul also for Tar; Schn. has 'be unpleasant', alongside exclamation alianai 'what funɣ' and alianaigi- 'take pleasure in, find amusing'; Saul has alianaŋŋit- rather in the 'be unpleasant' sense — in NB alianaiŋŋit- acc. Dor.]
GRI alianaat- 'be wonderful'

PI aliɣuq 'rock crystal' [cf. ali(C)uʀtuʀ-?]
SPI —
NAI —
WCI aliɣuq 'hailstone', Car 'glass, bottle' [Pryde — who also has it as 'mouth' in Perry River shaman language; Sch. has alikut 'small hail (stone?)' for 'adg']
ECI aliɣuq 'translucent quartz' [Bourq. has alikut for Lab]
GRI aliɣuq 'rock crystal' [aliɣuqqik 'diamond']

PE alikǝ- 'be afraid of' [cf. ali, aliŋǝ-, p.b. kǝ-[1] and perhaps Aleut alitxu-X 'war, warrior, army, crew' — as a verb 'wage war, assault']
AAY alikǝ- 'be afraid of'
CAY alikǝ-
NSY ➡
CSY alikǝ-
Sir —
SPI —
NAI —
WCI —
ECI —
GRI aliɣi- 'consider big', alinnaʀ- 'be big' [and NG aliŋnak 's.th. bad or ugly']

PY aliɣnaʀ- 'be frightening' [cf. naʀ-; compare the Yup forms under p.b. yuknaʀ- for the ɣ]
AAY —
CAY —

NSY aliɣnaʀ- 'be scary' [ANLC; Men. has aliɣnaq 'danger', aliɣnalʀia 's.th. dangerous, shaman']
CSY aliɣnaʀ- 'practice shamanism' [and aliɣnaq 'shaman's power', aliɣnalʀii 'shaman']

PY aliŋə- 'be afraid' [cf. ali, alikə-, aliŋit-, aliɣa- and p.b. nəɣ-]
AAY aliŋə- 'be afraid'
CAY aliŋə-
NSY aliŋə- 'be afraid' [also aliɣ- (ANLC)]
CSY aliŋə- 'be afraid' [and aliŋnaq 'frightening thing or person']
Sir [Vakh. has aliŋuʀ- 'defend oneself']
Inu [for NG aliŋnak 's.th. bad or ugly' see alikə- above)

PY aliŋtaʀ- 'be cowardly' [cf. (t)taʀ-]
AAY aliŋtaʀ- 'be fearful by nature'
CAY aliŋtaʀ- 'be cowardly'
NSY aliŋtaʀ- 'be cowardly' [ANLC; also aliŋtaq 'coward' (L.-T.)]
CSY aliŋtaʀ- 'be cowardly'

PE aliŋit- 'be fearless' [cf. aliɣa-, aliŋə-, and p.b. ŋit-]
AAY —
CAY aliŋitə- 'be fearless'
NSY aliŋitə- 'be brave' [ANLC; Men. has aliŋilŋuq 'brave']
CSY aliŋitə- 'be fearless' [as opposed to aliitə- 'be visible' under allaʀitə- (allaʀ(iʀ)-)]
Sir aliŋtiłəX 'bravery'
SPI [note aliitkun 'pastime, hobby, companion']
NAI aliit- 'not feel lonely though living alone' [aliitkun 'entertainment, passtime']
WCI aliŋit- 'become wild'
ECI aliŋit- 'feel aversion, reject, leave unpleasant place', aliŋiɣi- 'dislike'
GRI [aliikkutaq, Up aliakkitaq 'entertainment', NG aliŋiattaq 'wild animal']

PE ali(C)uʀtuʀ- 'see a ghost' [cf. aliŋə- and aliɣa-]
AAY —
CAY aliuXtuʀ- 'be surprised by an unexpected sight, see a ghost' [aliuXtuq 'unexpected sight, ghost']
NSY aliiXʷtuʀ- 'see a ghost' [ANLC; and L.-T. has aliuXtuq 'ghost']
CSY —
Sir —
SPI aliuqtuq- 'see an apparition'
NAI aliuq- 'be amazed, astonished, marvel'
WCI aliuqtuq 'see a ghost, have a vision'
ECI —
GRI aliuʀtuʀ-, NG aliuqtuaq- 'be surprised by an unexpected sight, see a ghost'

PE alivtuʀ- 'miscarry'
AAY —
CAY aliftuʀ- 'miscarry'
NSY aliftuʀ- 'miscarry' [ANLC; and aliftuq 'miscarriage' (L.-T.)]
CSY aliftuʀ- 'miscarry'
Sir —
SPI Qaw aliptuq-
NAI alifsuk- 'miscarry' [and nom. = 'premature baby']
WCI Car? aliptuq- 'have an abortion' [and aliptuɣaq 'abortion' — Schn. 'adg']
ECI Lab aliptuq- 'miscarry' [Peck; Ras. has alubsuaŋu- 'emerge as an abortion' for Igl]
GRI alussuʀ-, alussuɣ- [old ortho. with -gs-] 'abort' [and alussuɣaq 'abortion, child born in concealment']

PI allaq '(s.th.) 'ripped (off)' [cf. ałəɣ-[1] and q under nəʀ[1] — there could be parallel formations here]
SPI allaq 'tear, rip, hole in clothing' [for W Jen. has 'breast (meat of bird)']
NAI allaq* 'perforation, hole, breast meat of bird' [and allaiq- 'no longer have any holes']
WCI allaq 'piece ripped off, shred, breast meat of bird' [Pryde]
ECI allaaq 'breast meat of bird'
GRI ałłaq*

PE allaʀ(iʀ)- '(make or get) clear?' [cf. ŋiʀ- and note ECI nominal base allaq below; compare the parallel here with av(v)aʀiʀ- and əppaʀiʀ-]
AAY alaiʀ-, Perry ałaiʀ-, PWS aliiʀ- 'appear'
CAY alaiʀ- 'appear' [also perhaps alaʀutə- 'approach']
NSY aliaʀ- 'appear, clear up (weather)' [and aliaXtə- 'show, show up' (ANLC)]
CSY aliiʀ- 'appear, clear up' [note also ałxəʀ- 'appear, be born' — influenced by ałəɣ-[2]?]
Sir alaʀiʀ- 'appear' [Vakh. also 'see'; Em. has alaʀəŋəlŋuX 'invisible'; note also aləqiʀ- 'wipe dry', alaʀiqcəX 'newborn' and alałqižaX 'thawed patch'; Vakh. has also ałxəqə- 'appear' from Men.'s texts (from CSY?) and aləʀ-, ałəʀ- 'appear, become thus, remain', ałəqə(s)-, aləqə(s)- 'become thus', and Em. has aləŋuX 'similar, thus, equal' and aləkə(s)- 'be similar to', perhaps reflecting contam. with aləʀ and/or əliʀ- under əli-]
SPI KI, W allaq- 'be clear (weather)' [Jen.]
NAI PH allaq- 'be clear (weather)' [Jen. has also for B; note Mal allaʀun 'napkin, towel']
WCI allaq- 'be clear (weather), wipe', Cop allaq 'patch of clear sky' [Pryde]
ECI allaqi-, Aiv allaq- 'clear up (sky)', allai(q)-, Lab also allaq- 'wipe' [as nom. allaq = 'dirt on an object, humid patch to be wiped' and allaqi = 'clearing in sky']
GRI ałłaʀ- 'be clear (sky)' [and ałłikaʀ- 'come out (e.g. sun)' — old ortho. aglikar- but Fab. has allikaʀ- 'clear up'; EG attaŋŋit- 'be dirty', attinaʀ- 'be clean']

PY-S alaʀitə- 'be clearly visible' [with ŋit- rather than ŋiʀ-]
AAY —
CAY alaitə- 'be visible or audible'
NSY alianəxtaq '(s.th.) clearly visible'
CSY aliitə- 'be visible'
Sir alaritə(qət)- 'be visible' [Vakh.]

PI allaqtəq- 'wipe off' [cf. təʀ-]
SPI —
NAI —
WCI allaqtiq- allaqsi- 'wipe (dry)' [and Pryde has

Net allaqtiʀun 's.th. to wipe with, cloth']
ECI allatiq- 'wipe'
GRI ałłartiʀ- 'wipe off'

PY-S almiɣžaq 'bearded seal'
AAY —
CAY NS almiɣaq 'bearded seal'
NSY —
CSY —
Sir almiɣcəX 'bearded seal' [Orr; Men. almiʀžaX, Amos Pinaya acc. Krauss almiɣžaX]

PE alŋaʀ(-) 'mark or pattern' [with metathesis in Inu; cf. perhaps Aleut aluX 'line, letter']
AAY C alŋaq 'natural coloration, pattern', PWS alŋaʀ- 'color'
CAY alŋaq 'mark, symbol, hanging decoration on parka or boot', Y, HBC, Nun, NS alŋaʀ- 'write'
NSY alŋaq 'sheet of paper, tattoo on face', alŋaʀ- 'write' [and alŋaʀuaq 'picture, pattern']
CSY [atŋaʀun 'woman's facial tattoo, front seam with piping on skin boot']
Sir —
SPI aɣlak- 'write' [as noun = 'letter, character']
NAI aɣlak- 'write' [as noun = 'letter, printed pattern', aɣlaɣaaq 'design, stripe']
WCI Sig aɣlak- 'write', aɣlait 'letters', Car (?) 'decorative drawing' [Schn. 'adg'; Cop aɣlalik 'with a pattern' — Ras.]
ECI allaq 'letter, sign, decorative drawing', alla(k)-, alla(q)- 'write' [Bourquin has both forms for Lab; Cape Dorset aɣlait 'religious book']
GRI ałłak 'stripe, pattern' [old ortho. agdlak], ałłaɣ- 'write' [and ałłakkat 'book', ałłattuuq 'young Greenland seal']

PE alŋaʀun 'instrument for drawing or writing' [cf. un]
AAY PWS alŋaun 'marking pen, crayon'
CAY [Y, NS, HBC alŋaʀin, alŋaXcuun 'writing implement']
NSY —
CSY —
Sir —
SPI aɣlaun 'pencil, pen'
NAI aɣlaun
WCI Sig aɣlaun
ECI allauti
GRI ałłaat 'piece of chalk, pen'

PE alpa(ɣ) 'murre' [cf. alpaɣ-, but also perhaps ałəɣ-²]
AAY ałpaq 'murre'
CAY ałpa
NSY —
CSY ałpa
Sir ałpa
SPI atpa
NAI atpa, PH aqpa, Mal akpak
WCI atpa, atpak 'murre, guillemot'
ECI appaq, NBI akpa
GRI appa, NG akpa

PE alpaɣ- 'come through' [cf. ałəɣ-¹ and alpa(ɣ), though the relationship is not completely clear — perhaps originally referring to skinning a bird]
AAY ałpaɣ- 'get over, pull through'
CAY ałpaɣ- 'rip' [by contamination with ałəɣ-¹?]
NSY ałpaɣ- 'protrude, poke out' [ANLC; Men. has ałpaʀ- 'stick through']
CSY ałpaɣ- 'pass by'
Sir ałpəɣaʀ- 'go past' [Vakh. has ałpəʀ- 'go through' from Rub., who also has ałpəɣ- in this sense, but in Men.'s texts this is 'approach']
SPI —
NAI akpak- 'come up through entrance hole, come through door, reach top, overcome a crisis', Mal 'step up' [compare the shift from PE alpa(ɣ) to akpak in Mal]
WCI akpak- 'overcome s.th.' [Ras. has 'get through' for Sig]
ECI [for appai- 'sleep deeply' see atpaq- under at-]
GRI appakaʀ- [old ortho. agpakar-] 'come through' [for appaa- 'be dying' see atpaq- under at(ə)-]

PY alqəɣkaq 'arctic dock *(Rumex arcticus)*'
AAY —
CAY —
NSY ałqəxkaq 'arctic dock'
CSY ałqəxkaq

PY alqiliq 'middle finger' [cf. atʀilŋuq, with which there is considerable contam., and alqimaʀ- and l(l)iʀ; compare also akulipaq under aku(ʀ)]
AAY [for K qilimaq 'ring finger' see atʀilŋuq]
CAY ałqiliq 'middle finger' [note also aliqiliqiaq 'ring finger' in naming jingle]
NSY [atqilŋə 'middle finger' — contam. with atʀilŋuq?]
CSY [note atXilək 'middle finger', also alaŋquq 'ring finger' — Men. has the two reversed on his comp. list; Miller has alankoka '(my) ring finger']

PY alqimaʀ- 'lick food from fingers' [cf. aləmqaʀ-, from which this could be metathesized]
AAY —
CAY ałqimaʀ- 'taste food with one's fingers'
NSY ałqimaʀ- 'lick' [ANLC]
CSY ałqimaʀ- 'lick, taste'
Sir [for aləqaʀ- 'lick' see aləmqaʀ-]

PE alqunaʀ- 'hurt oneself' [cf. ałəɣ-?]
AAY —
CAY ałqunaq 'suddenly', ałqunaqaʀ- 'die suddenly'
NSY —
CSY [note alŋunaXqə- 'act carelessly']
Sir [note ałəquʀaʀ- 'dislocate' and aqənaqə(s)- 'hurt, maim', perhaps influenced by aq(ə)nəʀ- under atŋiʀ-]
SPI atqunaq- 'hurt self severely' [Jen.]
NAI atqunaq- 'be numerous, do in excess', PH 'hurt a lot, do too much to someone'
WCI atqunaq- 'be severely wounded, have caught many foxes or caribou, be severe (storm)'
ECI aqqunaq- 'wound, hurt seriously, have fractured bone, blow hard (storm)' [Saul has aqqunaaq- 'hurt

oneself seriously' and aqqunaq 'storm']
GRI aqqunaʀ- 'be hurt, injure', NG aqqunaluqi- 'hurt oneself' [and EG aqqinaq 'storm']

PY-S alqutaq 'spoon' [cf. alǝmqaʀ- and un]
AAY —
CAY —
NSY ałqu(u)taq 'spoon'
CSY ałqutaq 'spoon'
Sir [ałqǝsǝɣaX 'spoon' — Vakh.]
Inu [SPI aałXuutaq 'spoon' is from the Yup]

PE alu(ʀ) 'sole' [cf. at(ǝ)- and lu(ʀ), also alaq]
AAY —
CAY alu(q) 'sole of boot or foot'
NSY alu 'sole of foot' [ANLC]
CSY [aluq 'blade of paddle or oar']
Sir —
SPI alu(q)
NAI alu 'sole'
WCI aluq
ECI aluq 'sole, central runner or keel span of kayak, bottom of sea or lake'
GRI aluq 'sole' [and NG alut 'underside of sled runners' — Holt.]

PE aluɣ- 'lick' [cf. alqimaʀ- and alǝmqaʀ-]
AAY aluŋǝ- 'lick'
CAY aluŋǝ- 'lap with tongue', aluŋa 'home-made dogfood'
NSY —
CSY aluŋǝ- 'lick'
Sir alǝɣ- 'lick' [and aluminaʀ- 'lick s.th.']
SPI aluk- 'lick, lap' [and aluk 'crowberry', aluqfik 'dog dish']
NAI aluk- 'lick' [and aluk 'dog mush']
WCI aluk- 'lick'
ECI aluk-
GRI aluɣ-

PI alumǝʀaq- and **alupǝq-** 'lick one's lips'
Sir [note alǝɣǝpiɣ- 'eat greedily' — Orr]
SPI —
NAI [note alumiʀait- 'lack hospitality and regard for others', influenced by alupaq-?]
WCI Cop alupiq- 'lick one's lips' [Pryde]
ECI alupiq- 'lick avidly (dog)'
GRI alumiʀaʀ- 'lick one's lips'

PE alu(C)un 'spoon' [cf. un]
AAY Kod aluŋun 'spoon' [and alutaq 'plate']
CAY aluŋun 'dog-feeding trough', K, BB 'tongue' [and Y alusiq 'spoon']
NSY —
CSY —
Sir —
SPI Di, Imaq aluun 'tongue'
NAI aluuttaq, aluuttaun, Mal aluutaq 'spoon' [Jen. has aluun for Mal]
WCI aluuttaq 'spoon' [Ras. has aluut for Cop, Net, and Met. has allun 'shovel for removing ice from hole']
ECI Aiv aluut 'spoon'
GRI [note alušše̞aat 'spoon', and EG alittuut 'tongue']

PI aluktǝtnǝq 'snow cliff' [cf. aluɣ-]
Yup [note CSY aluŋutǝłǝq* 'area in lee of building without much snow (because it looks licked out)' and alukanǝq* 'wavy surface caused by drifting snow', though the latter could go rather with Aleut aalu-X 'swell, wave']
SPI —
NAI aluktɨnnɨq* 'snow cliff'
WCI —
ECI aluttiniq 'hollow under overhanging ice or snow'
GRI alutsinniq* 'steep side of snow drift, moist ice'

PI alupaq- or **alupak-** 'look after s.o.' [cf. alutuʀ-]
SPI —
NAI alupaaʀiik 'pair of whales swimming together' [and Spencer has alupaak- 'leave wife with partner or neighbor while one is off traveling']
WCI —
ECI [alupaq-, alupak- 'clean by licking' — contam. with aluɣ-?]
GRI alupaaʀ- 'have wife along on sledge, stick together all the time (man and wife, female seal and pups)' [alupaat, alupaaʀiit 'husband and wife always together']

PY aluqaq 'castor' [cf. aluɣ- and qaʀ?]
AAY PWS aluqaq 'castor (beaver's scent gland)'
CAY aluqaq, aluqun, aluqan
NSY —
CSY —
Sir — [but note alǝqiqa 'delicacy', probably going with alǝqaʀ- 'lick' under alǝmqaʀ- — Vakh. from Men.'s texts]

PE alutuʀ- 'be a good provider?' [cf. alupaq- and tuʀ-[2]]
AAY —
CAY Y, NS alutuʀ-, alutukǝ- 'take care of' [alutuXta 'provider']
NSY —
CSY —
Sir —
SPI —
NAI —
WCI —
ECI —
GRI alutuʀɴaʀ- 'be wonderful', alutuʀi- 'think wonderful, admire'

PY aluvik 'tear(drop)' [the relat. — if any — to qulvi (qv.) is obscure]
AAY K, KP alu<w>iq, PWS alu<w>ik, KP also alu<ɣ>aq 'stream of tears'
CAY aluvik, aluwik 'teardrop'
NSY alivik 'tear' [L.-T.]
CSY —

ałayaq 'cutting board' [loan from Aleut ałaya-X 'board']
AAY ałłaq 'cutting board'
CAY ayałaq, Nun alasaX 'cutting board (for skin sewing)'
NSY ayałaq
CSY ayałaʀaaq
Sir —
Inu [Imaq has ayałaq 'board for scraping skin on' from Yup]

PE ałəɣ-[1] 'tear' [cf. allaq]
AAY —
CAY ałəɣ- 'tear' [for Eg ałəxtuʀ- 'wipe dishes' see ałəɣ-[2]]
NSY aləɣ- 'tear' [ANLC; L.-T. has aləɣnəq, alələq 'tear on clothes']
CSY —
Sir [note ałəquʀaʀ- 'sprain']
SPI alik- 'tear'
NAI ałik-
WCI alik-
ECI alik-
GRI aliɣ-

PI aləktuq- 'tear up' [cf. tuʀ-[2]]
Yup [NSY aləxtułəq 'tearing' L.-T.]
SPI aliktuq- 'tear up'
NAI —
WCI aliktuq- 'tear up'
ECI alittu(q)-
GRI alittuʀ-

PY-S ałəɣ-[2] 'wipe or sweep' [a possible but unlikely link to ałəɣ-[1] is suggested by alpa(ɣ), a bird whose skin might be torn off and used for such purposes as cleaning, etc.]
AAY ałəɣ- 'wipe, erase, dry (dishes)' [and K ałxutaq, PWS ałxuutaq 'cloth for wiping']
CAY Eg ałəxtuʀ- 'wipe dishes'
NSY ałəɣ- 'sweep' and ałxutaq 'broom'
CSY ałəɣ- 'sweep, brush off' [and compare pałəɣ- 'brush off snow or dust' — contam. with pəłuɣ-?]
Sir ałxutaX 'broom' [and Vakh. has ałxiniqə- 'shake off dirt, cleanse (shaman)' from Rub.'s texts]

PE ałɣiʀ 'oldsquaw duck' [i.e. 'long-tailed duck'; cf. EA aalŋaaX, aalŋaaX, Atkan aŋlaaX, aŋalaaX 'oldsquaw duck', also a(a)-a(a)ŋliʀ and perhaps alpa(ɣ)]
AAY —
CAY ałxiaʀ(aq*) 'oldsquaw duck'
NSY —
CSY [aɣləkəsəɣaq 'Steller's eider']
Sir [aɣləkəsəɣaX 'Steller's eider' — Vye acc. Orr]
SPI —
NAI Point Barrow ažɣiq 'oldsquaw duck'
WCI Net alɣiq 'oldsquaw duck' [B.- S.; Pryde has aalɣiq for Perry River, Dor. has ayɣi'naaq, alɣi'naaq 'mallard' for B. Lake]
ECI aɣɣiq 'small migratory duck with long tail'
GRI ałłiq*, NG aɣliq 'long-tailed duck' [Tersis has EG cognate attiq as *Clangula hyemalis*]

PE ałiʀtə 'stocking' [cf. atliʀ under at(ə)-]
AAY —
CAY NSU ałiXtət 'pants with attached fur socks' [and note ałiqsak, ałiqsaq 'woven boot liner']
NSY aliXtə 'fur sock, woven grass sock' [ANLC]
CSY ałiXta 'sock of deerskin (woman's) or sealskin (man's)'
Sir asiXta 'stocking'
SPI Qaw aliqtik 'old style woman's underpants', Imaq aliqti 'skin stocking' [KI aliqšuzuk 'sock']
NAI aliqsik 'pair of high fur socks', PH 'pair of woman's breeches with fur inside'
WCI Cop, Net, Car aliqti 'stocking' [Ras.]
ECI aliqtiik 'pair of stockings'
GRI aliʀsi 'stocking' [3s possessed = aliʀsaa; Tersis has EG aliʀsiq 'stocking, inside boot']

PE ałŋiɣ 'patch on sole' [there may be a link to ałəɣ-[1] if not at(ə)-]
AAY —
CAY ałŋik 'patch on sole of boot' [and ałŋiɣ- 'patch sole'; note also ałŋiɣuaq 'coltsfoot plant']
NSY ałŋik 'patch on sole of boot' [L.-T.]
CSY ałŋik 'patch on bottom of sole' [and ałŋiɣ- 'sew patch on sole']
Sir ałŋəx 'sole patch' [Orr; note also ałŋiʀnəX 'butterfly' — Orr has ałŋiɣnəX; note also ałka 'patch', verbal ałkə- — but the last two items may be influenced by Chukchi ałpənŋəlɣən 'patch']
SPI annŋik 'patch for sole' [also verbal 'patch sole']
NAI annŋik
WCI —
ECI aŋŋi(C)- 'sew a patch on sole of boot'
GRI aŋŋik 'patch on sole of boot' [also verbal aŋŋiɣ-]

PY-S ałunžak ' bottom part (of container)' [cf. at(ə)- and alu(ʀ)]
AAY —
CAY ałuŋak 'bottom part or piece of container'
NSY aluŋak 'sole of shoe' [ANLC — for ałuŋak?]
CSY ałuŋak 'bottom or base part of container'
Sir ałəŋcəx [Orr]

PY-S ałuʀ- 'take from'
AAY ałuXtə- 'take s.th. from'
CAY ałuXtə-
NSY ałuquʀi- 'receive guests' [Tein]
CSY ałuXqi- 'adopt'
Sir ałuXqi- [Orr]

PE ama(C)- 'suckle' [cf. also mamaʀ- — there may be only a single proto-form here]
AAY amaaʀ-, AP aamaʀ- 'nurse a baby' [and amaaq, AP aamaq 'female breast']
CAY aamaʀ- 'suckle' [and aamaq 'breast']
NSY —
CSY —
Sir —
SPI maamak- 'suckle'

NAI amaamak- 'suckle'
WCI amaamak 'mother's milk' [also verbal 'suckle']
ECI amaamak 'breast' [also verbal]
GRI amaama(k) 'breast (child's word)' [also amaamaɣ- 'suckle' — Ordbogêraq]

PI amaaq 'shoot (of plant)'
SPI [note Qaw amaalik 'heel of bread'?]
NAI amaaq 'small secondary roots of plant (e.g. spruce root for basket weaving)'
WCI amaaq
ECI ama(a)q 'hard inedible roots' [Peck has Lab amaak 'small root' and Schn. also has amaalik 'turnip']
GRI amaaq 'tree shoot' [pl. = 'wicker basket']

PE amaquʀ 'wolf' [cf. p.b. quʀ]
AAY —
CAY —
NSY —
CSY amaa 'wolf' [apparently with loss of the p.b., the former presence of which is suggested by the (originally rhythmical) lengthening of the final vowel]
Sir —
SPI amaʀuq 'wolf'
NAI amaʀuq [pl. amaqqut]
WCI amaʀuq
ECI amaʀuq
GRI amaʀuq

PE amaʀ- 'carry on back'
AAY amaʀ- 'carry on back', Kod, KP 'carry in arms' [and amaq 's.th. carried that way' but in AP, PWS also 'amber', perhaps for the 'load' of a ring]
CAY amaʀ- 'carry on back' [and amaq 'load carried on back', also 'stone of ring' — see under AAY; for atm̥aɣ- 'carry on back' see natmaɣ-]
NSY amaʀ- 'carry on back' [ANLC, also for nom. amaq 'load on back']
CSY amaʀ- 'carry on back'
Sir amaʀ- [Orr]
SPI amaq- 'put baby on back to carry it', amaaq- 'carry baby on back'
NAI amaq- 'put on back', amaaq- 'carry on back' [and amaaq 'load carried on back']
WCI amaq- 'put baby on back' [Pryde], amaaq- 'carry baby on back'
ECI amaaq- 'carry baby on back' [amaq 'baby or object carried on back', but Igl amaaq 'baby carried in amaut' in Ras.]
GRI amaʀ- 'take baby on back', amaaʀ- 'carry baby on back', NWG 'be drunk' [amaaq 'baby carried on back']

PI amaun 'hood for carrying baby in' [cf. un]
SPI amaun 'parka hood, sth. to carry baby on back'
NAI —
WCI amaut 'carrying pouch (hood) for baby'
ECI amaut
GRI amaat, EG amaaʀ̃ut

PE amaʀtuʀ 'humpback salmon' [cf. amaʀ-]
AAY amaXtuq 'humpback salmon'
CAY amaqsuq, Nun amaqsux
NSY amaqtuq [ANLC also amaXtuq]
CSY amaXtu
Sir —
SPI amaqtuq
NAI amaqtuq
WCI —
ECI —
GRI —

PE amaʀutləɣ '(male) eider' [cf. amaun under amaʀ- and p.b. ləɣ]
AAY —
CAY — [but Jen. has Nun ama·ruLix 'snow bunting']
NSY amaʀułək 'eider'
CSY —
Sir —
SPI Imaq amaʀuliq 'eider with black breast and white back' [may be loan from NSY]
NAI amaullɨk 'male common eider' [Ras. has as 'snow bunting' for Nu; Jen. has amarullik for 'Ingl.']
WCI amaulik 'male common eider' [Pryde]
ECI Iti amaulik 'drake' [Lab 'male of eider duck' — Peck]
GRI amaalik 'male eider'

PI amautləɣaq 'snow bunting' [cf. aʀ]
SPI —
NAI amaułłiɣaaluk, Nu amautliɣaq, Mal amautliɣaužaq 'snow bunting' [Jen. has amauliɣaq for B]
WCI amauliɣaq, Sig amauliɣaaluk 'snow sparrow (sic)'
ECI amaulliɣaaq
GRI SWG amaaliɣa(a)q 'snow bunting' [Oqaatsit — reported by R. Petersen for Qassimiut and Fiskenaeset]

PE ama(C)uʀ 'great grandparent' [cf. əma and compare ap(p)a[1]]
AAY PWS amuuq 'great-grandparent'
CAY amauq*, Nun amauXłuɣaX 'great-grandparent'
NSY —
CSY —
Sir —
SPI amau 'great-grandparent, great-grandchild'
NAI amau, amaułuk
WCI Sig amaukłuk 'great-grandparent', Net amauq 'great-grandmother' [Ras.]
ECI amauʀaq 'great-grandmother'
GRI NG amauq 'great-grandparent'

PE aməcu- 'many' [cf. aməl(ə)ʀa(ʀ)- and aməɣaq-]
AAY —
CAY —
NSY —
CSY —
Sir amsəpɨɣ- 'be many' [Vakh.; Men. has amtuʀəŋ 'much', amtuʀ- 'increase' with tu-[1]; Vakh. and Orr also have amtəvałaX 'many' and, from Men.'s texts, amtəyaɣəcəX 'big' and amtupixtəɣaʀ- 'become much or many']

SPI —
NAI [Jen. has amisut 'many']
WCI Cop, Net, Car amihut 'many', Perry River amilli- 'increase in numbers' [Pryde; Schn. has amit- 'be very numerous' for 'adg']
ECI amisut 'many'
GRI amisut 'pod of seals or white whales' [NG amihuussihut 'group of seals at hole in ice']

PI aməɣaq- 'be insufficient' [cf. aməcu-]
Sir — [but Vakh. has amkətaʀ- 'be little (of)', amkəqižaʀaX 'a few' from Men.'s texts]
SPI Imaq amiɣanəq 'small part of s.th.' [amiɣaluɣu 'a little'; and note Qaw amayaqtuužau- 'be few']
NAI amiɣaq- 'be insufficient' [and amikkit- 'run short of s.th.']
WCI Cop amiɣaq- 'be insufficient' [and amiɣaiq- 'become numerous, multiply' — Pryde]
ECI amiɣaʀi- 'have a shortage of'
GRI amiɣaʀ- 'be insufficient' [and amikkit- 'not be enough, run short of, get nothing']

PY-S amələ 'width or space between legs' [cf. amłuʀ- and amit-]
AAY aməłkitə- 'be narrow', aməłtu- 'be wide'
CAY amlək 'crotch' [and aməłkitə- 'be narrow', aməłtu- 'be wide']
NSY amələ 'crotch' [ANLC]
CSY amla 'crotch and upper leg area' [and aməłkəstaaXaq 'narrow thing', aməłtu- 'be wide']
Sir amlə- 'crotch, fork of legs' [and amkəłkaʀəncəX 'small' Vakh. from Men.'s texts]

PE aməl(ə)ʀa(ʀ)- 'be many' [cf. aməcu-, also Atkan Aleut amna- 'number, set', EA amnaʀu- 'be many, much']
AAY amləXtə-, K, KP amləʀ-, PWS amłəʀ- 'be many' [and participial C amləXqat, K amləsqat 'many']
CAY amłəq 'much', amłəʀ- 'be much, many'
NSY —
CSY —
Sir [for amtuʀəŋ 'much', amtuʀ- 'increase' see aməcu-]
SPI amiʀlat, amiʀla(q)tut 'many', Imaq amaʀla-, W amalʀa(q)- 'be many' [and note amiʀlauti- 'gang up on, all work on']
NAI amižʀaq- 'be many' [a Point Barrow form? — Jen. has amilʀat 'many'; note also amilluti- 'gang up on']
WCI Cop amilʀat 'herd of musk oxen', Net, Car 'herd of caribou' [Schn. has Car amilʀait 'very numerous' and Pryde has amilʀiq- 'arrive — of caribou migration' for Net, but Ras. has amilʀaq- 'be many' for the latter]
ECI —
GRI amiʀła- 'be many' [and amiʀłi- 'become more']

PY-S amik 'door' [probably a reanalysis of the dual of amiq 'skin']
AAY amiik 'door'
CAY amiik, Y amik, HBC avik 'door' [the latter form by contam. with avəɣ-?]
NSY amik 'passageway in men's house, hallway' [L.-T.]
CSY amik 'door'
Sir aməx

PE amik(k)uʀ 'octopus or related creature' [cf. amir and k(k)uʀ?; also EA amʀu-X 'octopus']
AAY amikuq 'octopus' [and PWS amikuʀniilŋuq 'squid']
CAY amikuk 'legendary octopus-like creature'
NSY —
CSY —
Sir —
SPI —
NAI —
WCI —
ECI —
GRI amikuq 'cuttlefish' [for amiku 'old skin covering' see amiʀ]

PE aminaʀ 'leftover' [for similar dropping of intervocalic n in Inuit by dissimilation see nanit- and nunanniʀ-; the relat. — if any — with minaʀ- is obscure]
AAY C aminaq, aminałXət 'leftover food' [aminaqə- 'have it left over']
CAY aminaq, Nun aminkux 'leftover food'
NSY —
CSY aminaqə- 'leave for someone else'
Sir —
SPI amiaku(q) 'remainder, s.th. left'
NAI amižžiaq 'remainder, food left over from preparing meal'
WCI amiakkuq 's.th. left over, remainder' [Pryde]
ECI amiakku
GRI amiakku

PE amiʀ 'skin' [cf. Aleut amu-X 'piece of clothing', amu- 'dress']
AAY amiq 'skin, hide'
CAY amiq
NSY amiq
CSY amiq 'skin, hide' [and amiʀ- 'cover (skin boat)'
Sir aməX 'reindeer hide' [Vakh.; Men. has amiX, amižaX 'hide, skin']
SPI amiq 'hide, skin'
NAI amiq 'hide, skin' [as verb = 'cover (skin boat)'; amiku 'remainder from cutting skin']
WCI amiq [also verbal]
ECI amiq 'hide, skin, cover' [and Lab 'bark'; amiq- 'cover (skin boat)']
GRI amiq 'hide, skin' [and amiʀ- 'cover (skin boat)', NWG 'paint'; amiku 'stripped off skin covering']

PY aminʀaq 'old (seal) skin' [cf. p.b. n(ə)ʀaʀ(aʀ)(-)]
AAY —
CAY aminʀaq 'darkened aged skin used for making boot soles'
NSY aminʀaq 'walrus hide' [ANLC]
CSY aminʀaq 'trimming from skin covering of boat'

PE amiʀaʀ 'bark or fish skin' [cf. aʀ]
AAY ami<ʀ>ak 'fish skin', PWS ami<ʀ>aq 'dried fish skin'
CAY amiʀaq, amiʀak 'fish skin for clothing'
NSY —
CSY amiʀaq 'skin prepared for use on hull of skin

boat, newly covered boat'
Sir [note aminʀaX 'skin prepared for use on hull of skin boat, newly covered boat' — Orr]
SPI Qaw amiʀaq 'tree bark, dried fish skin'
NAI amiʀaq 'tree bark, velvet on caribou antlers, waterproof stitching' [esp. for skin boat, also verbal for such stitching]
WCI amiʀaq 'bark, velvet on caribou antlers'
ECI amiʀaq 'skin of fruit, bark, fish scales'
GRI amiʀaq 'bark, paint'

PY amiʀluq 'cloud' [cf. amiʀ?]
AAY amiʀluq 'cloud' [amiʀlu- 'be cloudy']
CAY amiʀluq 'cloud' [and amiʀliʀ-, amiXtu- 'be cloudy']
NSY —
CSY —

PE amit- 'be narrow' [cf. amələ and Aleut am- as in amni- 'be tight, firmly fastened', EA amiðɣi-n 'calf of leg, shank' and Atkan amiðɣi-s 'metacarpal bones'; this base could have a parallel source to aməłkitə- under amələ, i.e. with neg. p.b. ŋit-]
AAY amitə- 'be small in girth, thin'
CAY amitə- 'be small in girth, thin' [with tə ~ l alternation as for other contrary adj. bases and p.b.s]
NSY amitaʀaq 'narrow (thing)' [and amitaʀaʀ- 'be thin around' (ANLC)]
CSY aməstaaXaq 'narrow thing' [and note amsakaXtaq 'small thing']
Sir amətaʀałəʀəX 'narrow (thing)' [and aməkəžaʀaX 'very thin']
SPI Qaw amit- 'be narrow', KI amituužaq 's.th. narrow'
NAI amit- 'be narrow'
WCI amit-
ECI amit- 'be narrow' [and amittukaaq 'oblong']
GRI amit- 'be narrow'

PE amiləqaʀ and **amitə(l)qaʀ** 'ulna (arm bone)' [cf. qaʀ? — there may be contam. with aməl(ə)ʀa(ʀ)-]
AAY —
CAY aməlʀaq 'ulna, large bone of forearm' [sic]
NSY —
CSY amitəłqaq 'radius (?), thin bone in arm'
Sir amitəłqaX [Orr]
SPI —
NAI amil^{y}ʀaq, amižʀaq 'ulna, fibula', Nu 'radius (?) bone in forearm' [compare amižʀaq- 'be many' under PE aməlʀa(ʀ)-]
WCI amiliʀaq 'fibula, bone of lower leg' [Pryde]
ECI amiliʀaq 'thinner of forearm bones'
GRI amiliʀaq 'radius (?), fibula'

PI amilʀuq 'narrow part' [cf. quʀ]
SPI —
NAI amil^{y}ʀuq 'narrow part'
WCI —
ECI amiʀʀuq 'back (narrow) part of beluga'
GRI amiʀłuq 'narrow watercourse'

PY-S amitatuk 'weasel'
AAY amitatuk 'weasel'
CAY Eg, HBC, amitatuk
NSY amitatuk
CSY [amikłuk 'weasel']
Sir amitatux 'weasel'
Inu — [but Men. has amitatak 'weasel' also for Imaq]

PE amitli- 'get narrower' [cf. li-[2]]
AAY —
CAY amili- 'get narrow'
NSY amili- 'get narrow, thin around' [ANLC]
CSY —
Sir —
SPI amili-, Qaw amiɣli- 'grow narrower'
NAI amikł^{y}i- 'grow narrower', amiɣl^{y}i- 'wane (moon), grow narrower'
WCI amilisi- 'get narrower'
ECI —
GRI amili-

a(a)miyu(u) 'king salmon' [from EA a(a)miyuuŋ, amiyuX 'king salmon'; reconstruction of a proto-form lying behind this and the possible direct cognate in CSY is problematical and is further complicated by the existence of Koryak ewec(u), Itelmen c'u(vaj) 'chavycha (kind of salmon)', perhaps indicative of the ultimate source of the loan]
AAY K aamasuuk, aamasaaq 'large king salmon'
CAY —
NSY —
CSY [awisu 'king salmon' may be a cognate if it is not a Chukotko-Kamchatkan loan]
Sir [note acu 'hump-backed salmon']

PE amłuʀ- 'step (over)' [or amluʀ-?; cf. amələ]
AAY amłiʀ- 'step' [compare under CAY]
CAY amłiʀ- 'step over' [contaminated by amlək 'crotch' under amələ and p.b. liʀ-?; note aməlvaɣ- 'take a big step']
NSY amłuʀ- 'take a step, step across'
CSY amłuʀ- 'take a step'
Sir amləqaʀ- 'take a step', amləqanəX 'step' [and Orr has amlər- 'have legs spread apart'; Vakh. has amłəʀ- 'spread legs, step across' from Men.'s texts; Em. has amłuʀ- 'step (across)', amłənəX 'step']
SPI avlu(q)- 'take a step'
NAI avluq-, Mal, Nu apluq- 'take a step'
WCI avluq- 'take a step' [Lowe has aabluq- for Sig, also aablurniqtu- 'take a big step', corresponding to Cop aptuniqtu-; Ow. has apluʀaaq- 'run by stepping on stones' for EP]
ECI allu(q)- 'step over' [and allu(ʀ)niqtu- 'make big strides']
GRI ałłuʀ- 'step (over), straddle'

PI aməluʀəq 'threshold' [cf. yaʀ?]
SPI —
NAI —
WCI avluʀiq 'threshold, doorstep'
ECI alluʀaq 'doorstep, start of entry porch of snow house'
GRI ałłuʀiq 'board for tent door'

PE amma 'also' [adverbial/exclamatory form of dem. root am-; cf. Aleut ama 'and'; de Reuse regards Yup a(a)mta as a loan from Chukchi amto 'well, what news?', but this may be coincidence — compare rather enclitic ptauq, which is ingredient in some of the Inu forms below]
AAY —
CAY [Barnum has am 'again' — but cf. under p.b. (ŋ) am; note also amtału 'but', amatiiɣni 'the day before (the day before) yesterday', and amatiiku 'the day after (the day after) tomorrow' (the unbracketed meanings NI only)]
NSY amałi 'of course, indeed' [and a(a)mta 'also, if', amatŋani 'the day before yesterday', amatŋaku 'the day after tomorrow']
CSY ama 'also' [saama, as if from dem. root sam- is also used this way, but this is apparently from Chukchi cama of that meaning; note also aamta 'as we know from experience']
Sir ama 'also, and'
SPI —
NAI —
WCI Baker Lake ammalu 'furthermore' [Pryde; note also Net aapta 'again' in Ras. — inflected forms aptuma, etc., from amna]
ECI amma(lu) 'further(more), again, also'
GRI aamma(lu) 'also, further(more)' [and NG aatta — Holt. aa^{w}ta — 'again, also, and then', from *aapta]

amʀaq 'sleeve' [from Aleut hamʀa-X 'sleeve', later EA amʀa-X, western EA amXa-X]
AAY AP amʀaq 'sleeve'
CAY amʀaq
NSY —
CSY —

PE amu- 'pull' [cf. Aleut amilʀi-X 'fishing place' and/or EA amlu- 'draw, bail']
AAY amu- 'pull up, out, off'
CAY amu- 'pull out'
NSY amu-
CSY amu- 'pull (rope, etc.)'
Sir amə- 'pull out' [Vakh.]
SPI amu-
NAI amu-
WCI amu-
ECI amu-
GRI amu-

PE ammun 'net rope' [cf. un]
AAY —
CAY amun 'net rope'
NSY amun [ANLC]
CSY —
Sir —
SPI Qaw ammun
NAI ammun
WCI [Met. has Cop ammaun 'net rope']
ECI ammuti 'pulley'
GRI ammut 'net rope'

PE amuʀaʀ- 'haul up' [cf. ʀaq-?]
AAY —
CAY —
NSY —
CSY Chap amuʀaqə- 'pull fishing line out of water'
Sir —
SPI —
NAI amuaq- 'pull up and out'
WCI amuaq- 'pull s.th. requiring effort'
ECI amuaq- 'draw to self with rope, etc.'
GRI amuaʀ- 'haul up'

PY amyak 'mussel'
AAY amyak 'mussel'
CAY amyak 'small clam, black on ends'
NSY amyak 'mussel'
CSY amyak 'mussel'
Inu [SPI avyak 'mussel' is probably borrowed from Yup]

PE a(a)na 'grandmother, mother' [with expressive gemination of the first vowel? — cf. ana(a)na and NAI aapa under ap(p)a[1]]
AAY aana 'mother'
CAY aana
NSY aana
CSY naa
Sir nana [written by Men. nána; Vakh. has nanə]
SPI aana 'grandmother'
NAI aana 'grandmother', Mal 'mother' [aanaak 'parents', Nu 'grandparents', aanaluk 'old woman']
WCI Sig aana 'grandmother'
ECI aana 'paternal grandmother, paternal great aunt' [for homophone meaning 'salmon trout' see aanakliq]
GRI aanak, aanaq 'grandmother'

PY a(a)nakaq 'stepmother' [cf. kðaʀ]
AAY —
CAY —
NSY aanaxkaq 'stepmother'
CSY naakaXqaq
Sir — [note nanəsəx 'stepmother']
Inu [note ECI anaatsaq 'stepmother', also 'adg' in Schn.]

PE an(n)aɣ- '(try to) surpass or beat at game' [there may be a link to annaɣ-]
AAY anaxtə- 'beat in competition'
CAY anaxtə- 'surpass'
NSY —
CSY [note anaxtə- 'miss the mark, irritate, confuse' and anaɣŋa- 'be incorrect']
Sir —
SPI anak- 'surpass', anaktauti- 'compete at sport', Qaw anaktaq- 'play a competition sport' [and Qaw annaušaq- 'play Eskimo football']
NAI anak- 'surpass' [and anaʀvik- 'beat soundly at a game' (prob. contam. with anaq), anaktaq- 'hold competitive games']
WCI [note annaaqtuq- 'argue back and forth']

ECI [annaatu(q)- 'contradict', annaatuuti- 'argue']
GRI [annaaʀtuʀ- 'contradict, argue' — old ortho. angnârtor- with spurious ng]

PY-S anaɣutə- 'overdo it?' [cf. utə-]
AAY ana<ɣ>utə-, Kod also anaɣua'utə- 'get out of control, overdo, get worse'
CAY anaɣutə- 'misbehave'
NSY —
CSY [anaxute- 'be mixed up, confused']
Sir anaxut(ə)-, anaɣŋa- 'do s.th. wrong' [Em.]
Inu [Qaw anaɣaʀuti- 'overdo it' — from Yup?]

PE anaɣu- 'hit (with club)' [cf. Aleut anax, EA also aŋ̊ax 'club, stick (for clubbing animals or big fish)', anaɣ- 'hit with club or stick']
AAY KP anuuɣ-, Kod anauʀ-, Perry anauɣ- 'club, hit'
CAY anau-, Nun, NS anauʀ- 'hit with stick or club'
NSY anaa(w)-
CSY anaɣu-
Sir anəɣə- [Vakh. from Rub.]
SPI anau-
NAI anau- 'hit with stick or club' [and note anaɣɣusimaaq- 'be leaning securely against']
WCI anau- 'hit with stick or club'
ECI anau-
GRI anaa- 'hit with stick or whip' [and anaxxut(i)- 'support firmly against s.th. (e.g. gun, telescope, or other long rigid thing)', EG anakkut(i)- 'aim at (with gun)']

PE anaɣutaʀ 'club' [cf. un]
AAY KP anuu'utaq, Kod anau'utaq 'club'
CAY anautaq
NSY anaataq
CSY anaɣutaq
Sir —
SPI anautaq
NAI anautaq 'upper hind leg', anauttaq 'axe'
WCI anautaq 'club'
ECI anautaq
GRI EG anaalaq

PE ana(a)na 'older female relative' [cf. a(a)na, of which this could be a doubling, and Aleut ana-X 'mother, mother's sister']
AAY anaana(k), anaanaaq 'maternal aunt'
CAY anaana 'maternal aunt, stepmother'
NSY anaana 'maternal aunt'
CSY anaana
Sir anána [Orr]
SPI —
NAI [Ras. has Nu anaanažuaq 'mother-in-law']
WCI Sig anaanak, Car anaanatsiaq 'grandmother', Cop anaanattiaq 'grandmother', Net anaana 'mother' [also Car acc. B.-S., Cop 'stepmother' acc. Ras.]
ECI anaana 'mother', Lake Harbor anaanatsiaq 'maternal grandmother'
GRI anaana 'mother (hypocoristic)', NG anaanak 'grandmother' [anaanaššaq 'stepmother']

PI anaqa 'later or in the evening' [cf. aqaɣu and ataku under ata² for possible sources of contam. in NAI at least]
SPI anaqaqsi- 'become evening' [and note naanaan 'wait', naanaakun 'wait, in a while']
NAI anaqami 'in the evening', anaqapak 'this evening' [aannaɣu, aannuɣu, Nu aatnaɣu 'wait a bit, in a while' (Lowe has Uum aatnuɣu) and Nu aatnapak 'this evening' appear to have a different source]
WCI Sig anaqai 'in a moment', anaqan(an) 'later'
ECI —
GRI [Fab. has annaket — for anaqat? — 'later, some time in the evening']

PE anaʀ(-) 'excrement' [and as verb 'defecate'; cf. anə-]
AAY anaq 'feces, excrement' [and as verb anaʀ- 'defecate']
CAY anaq 'excrement' [and as verb anaʀ- 'defecate']
NSY anaq 'excrement' [and anaʀ- 'defecate'; note also anaqata(ʀ)- 'rust']
CSY anaq 'excrement, rust' [and as verb anaʀ- 'defecate']
Sir anəX 'excrement ' [and anaXtatə- 'rust' (trans.)']
SPI anaq 'excrement' [and as verb anaq- 'defecate', as in all other Inu.]
NAI anaq
WCI anaq
ECI anaq
GRI anaq

PY anaqyaʀtuʀ- 'go to defecate' [cf. yaʀ(tuʀ)-, also məqyaʀtuʀ- under əməʀ(-)]
AAY anaqsaXtuʀ-, anaqsatuʀ- 'go to defecate'
CAY anaqsaXtuʀ-
NSY anaqy̥aXtuʀ- [ANLC]
CSY —

PY anaqyuɣ- 'feel the urge to defecate' [cf. qyuɣ-, also məqyuɣ- under əməʀ(-)]
AAY anaqsuɣ- 'feel the urge to defecate'
CAY anaqsuɣ-
NSY anaqy̥uɣ-
CSY anaqsuɣ-

PE anaʀiʀ(yaʀ) 'dung fly' [cf. (C)iʀ]
AAY Kod anaayak, C anaayaq 'type of small brown fly'
CAY anaiq* 'dung fly', Nun anaʀaʀiʀyaX 'fly'
NSY —
CSY —
Sir —
SPI —
NAI —
WCI Sig anaʀiatsiaq 'dung fly'
ECI —
GRI anaʀiaq

PI anaʀluk 'impurity in ice' [cf. łuɣ]
Yup — [but note CAY anaXłuk 'feces stain on diaper']
SPI anaʀluk 'black sediment on ice, faces of newborn'

NAI anaʀlu 'black sediment on ice visible when ice melts in spring'
WCI Sig anaʀluit 'black impurities in ice seen from afar in spring'
ECI —
GRI anaʀɬuk 'dirty piece of calved ice'

PE ana(C)uvaɣ 'catcher for birds' [apparently from anaɣu- and vaɣ, but the loss of ɣ in CSY problematical]
AAY —
CAY —
NSY anaavan 'catcher for birds'
CSY anaavak 'net on pole for catching birds'
Sir anaavax [Orr; long vowel may indicate a borrowing from CSY]
SPI [KI anauvaktuun; Imaq anauvan is prob. from NSY]
NAI PH anauvak
WCI —
ECI —
GRI —

PI anaya- 'be careful with' [cf. aninqə-]
SPI aniyasuk- 'be cautious (with s.th.)'
NAI anaya(suk)-
WCI Sig anaya(suk)-, anayaɣi- 'pay attention (to)'
ECI —
GRI NG anayaɣi- 'be careful with' [and anayaŋnaŋŋit- 'be strong or solid']

PI anə 'woman's older brother' [cf. anəŋaʀ, also anə-]
Sir — [note anta 'brother' — Vakh. also has antə(X) 'sibling' from Men.'s texts]
SPI —
NAI Nu anik 'sister's elder brother' [Ras.]
WCI ani(k) 'older brother of female', Net ani 'older or younger brother of female' [Pryde]
ECI ani(k) 'brother of female'
GRI ani(k), Up aniq 'older brother of female'

PE anə- 'go out' [cf. anə, anəlɣun, annaɣ- and Aleut analuX 'ladder (to hatchway), hatchway (down through roof)', anqa- 'stand up, set out' (cf. p.b. k(k) aʀ-), aniiðа-X 'young of sea animal, pup' and aniqðu-X 'child']
AAY anə- 'go, come out'
CAY anə- 'go out, be born' [and anətm̥un 'out, downriver']
NSY anə- 'go out, get free'
CSY aanə- 'go out'
Sir anə-
SPI ani- 'go out, be born' [and aniaqan 'sibling']
NAI ani- 'go out, be born' [and aniqan 'sibling', ania- 'go out as group']
WCI ani- 'go out, be born'
ECI ani- 'go out, leave' [and ania- 'go out as group']
GRI ani- 'go out' [ania- 'go out as group'; and Ges. has EG anittaʀ- 'be born']

PE an(ə)caʀnəʀ 'seaward wind or current' [cf. caʀ-[1] and nəʀ[1]]
AAY [anca<y>uxtə- 'blow out from river or bay']
CAY ancaʀnəq* 'mist of cold air coming into house when door is open', Nun 'outgoing tide'
NSY —
CSY —
Sir —
SPI anisa.niq 'outgoing tide'
NAI atcaʀniq* 'easterly wind', atcaʀnaq 'ocean current flowing away from shore' [and atcaʀmun 'out to ocean via a current']
WCI aksaʀniq 'avalanche, landslide, outgoing current'
ECI Lab aksa(a)ʀniq 'seaward current' [Peck; aksaʀniq is also the local name for Chesterfield Inlet in NBI; note also Baffin anisaʀniq 'east wind' given by Keenainak for Pangnirtung — Boas has aksaʀniq]
GRI assaʀniq* [old ortho. agsarneq] 'east wind, wind from land or fjord' [also anisaʀniq*, e.g. in Up; note assaʀ- '(several) move out']

PE anəɣiʀ- 'go outside' [cf. ayyiʀ- under ayə- and tayyiq-]
AAY AP anɣiʀ- 'go on a hunting trip'
CAY Y, Nun, NS anɣiʀ- 'go outside for fresh air, play outside'
NSY anɣiʀ- 'go for a walk'
CSY anɣiʀ- 'go outside for fresh air, play outside'
Sir —
SPI aniiq- 'stay or play outside'
NAI aniiq- 'be outside' [aniiqsuaq- 'relax or play outside']
WCI aniiq-
ECI aniiqtuq 'one who deliberately stays outside'
GRI aniiʀ- 'be outside' [aniiʀsuaʀ- 'go outside for some fresh air']

PY-S anəlɣun 'sibling' [cf. lɣun]
AAY K anəlɣun, Perry anɬun, C anəɬun 'full sibling'
CAY anəlɣun 'sibling'
NSY anəɬxutə 'brother' [ANLC 'sibling']
CSY aanəlɣun 'littermate, peer'
Sir anəɬxute 'brother' [Vakh.]

PE anət- 'put out' [cf. t-[1]]
AAY antə- 'take or put out' [compare anutə- 'carry or bring out', with utə-]
CAY antə- 'take or put out' [compare anutə- 'carry or bring out']
NSY [compare anutə- 'take out']
CSY aantə- 'take or put out' [compare aanutə- 'take out' with utə-]
Sir antə-
SPI anit- 'throw out, put out'
NAI anit- 'put or throw out, begin (speech or song)'
WCI —
ECI anit- 'take out'
GRI anit- 'put or throw out, present (one's thoughts)'

PI aniciq- 'depart (suddenly)'
SPI anisiq- 'depart suddenly'
NAI anisiq- 'depart because of ill feelings'
WCI —
ECI —
GRI anisiʀ- 'move one's tent in the spring, leave one's house and move in with others (while it is still winter)'

PI aniɣuq- 'pass through' [cf. (C)uʀ-]
SPI —
NAI aniɣuq- 'pass through, come out on other side'
WCI aniɣuq- 'pass'
ECI aniɣuq- 'pass through' [and aniɣɣuq 'escape hole of bullet or harpoon through body']
GRI aniɣuʀ- 'pass through unhurt, escape' [and anixxuq 'mouth of fjord']

PI aniŋa- 'stick out' [cf. ŋa-[1]]
SPI aniŋa- 'have a bump or protuberance' [and nom. aniŋažuaq 'bump']
NAI aniŋa- 'have a bump or lump on it, be convex'
WCI —
ECI aniŋa- 'be convex, rounded'
GRI aniiŋa- 'stick out (s.th. projecting)' [from or influenced by aniiʀ- under anəɣiʀ- above?; EG aniŋaliq 'round epiphysis of bone' — Ges.]

PE annəviɣ and **anəðviɣ** 'place or time of going out' [cf. ðviɣ]
AAY anwik 'exit'
CAY anvik 'exit' [also place name Anvik]
NSY anvik 'exit, co-uterine sibling (?)'
CSY aanvik 'outlet, exit'
Sir anvəx
SPI annuik, Qaw anniwik 'birthday, birthplace'
NAI annivik
WCI annivik 'birthday, birthplace' [and Schn. has anivvik 'exit' for 'adg']
ECI —
GRI annivik, aniffik 'place or time of going out', EG annivik 'mother'

PI annitə- 'take out' [cf. utə- — a later derivation than the Yup forms with utə- under anət- above since it presupposes ani- < *anə-, reflecting a regular process in Inu — see Intro. C1]
SPI anniti- 'take out'
NAI annisi-
WCI anniti- 'take out' [Pryde]
ECI —
GRI annit-, annisi- 'take out (with one)'

PE antat 'midden' [cf. anət- above, of which this is a pl. pass. participial form]
AAY —
CAY —
NSY [note Orr has ansiivik and L.-T. has ansivik for 'dump']
CSY aantat 'dump (for rubbish)'
Sir —
SPI attaq 'dump'
NAI attat 'dumping area for honey buckets'
WCI [Sig aktakkun 'garbage']
ECI [Peck has aktak 'fish or meat brought out of the house to be kept for later' for Lab]
GRI attat 'dump, midden'

PE an(ə)ɣaʀ(aʀ) 'woman's nephew or niece' [cf. anəŋaʀ and aʀ — there could be dissimilation in Yup if from *anəŋaʀaʀ, otherwise assimilation in Inu]
AAY KP anɣaaq 'woman's nephew or niece'
CAY anɣaʀaq 'woman's nephew or niece via her brother'
NSY —
CSY anɣaʀaq
Sir anɣəX [Orr]
SPI anaŋa 'younger sibling, cousin (affectionate term)', Qaw anaŋa 'younger sibling'
NAI PH anaŋŋaq 'cousin, sibling' [and note anaŋŋaa 'how cute!', also PH anaaq 'cousin', B an^{y}n^{y}aq 'female cousin, cousin of opposite sex']
WCI Cop anŋaq 'child of brother (or male cousin) of female'
ECI aŋŋaq 'nephew or niece of a paternal aunt'
GRI aŋŋak 'woman's nephew (through brother)'

PE anəŋaʀ '(woman's) older brother' [cf. anə and an(ə)ɣaʀ(aʀ); the link to the moon in Inu is to be found in the old Eskimo myth of the incestuous brother and sister who became respectively the moon and the sun — see also under ciqinəʀ]
AAY anŋaq, K, PWS aniŋaaq 'older brother' [voc. anŋaa, aniŋaa, Perry also naŋaa]
CAY anŋaq, NSU anəŋaq 'older brother'
NSY anəŋaq
CSY anəŋaq
Sir —
SPI — [for anaŋa 'younger sibling' see an(ə)ŋaʀ(aʀ)]
NAI aniŋa, aniŋak 'older brother'
WCI Net, Car aniŋaaq 'the moon' [Ras.]
ECI Igl aniŋaat 'the moon' [Ras.; Boas has aniŋa 'her brother (the moon)']
GRI aniŋaaq WG 'the moon', NG, EG 'moon, month' [old word from myths in WG — note modern aniŋaašaq 'coin']

PY-S anəq 'spark or ember'
AAY —
CAY —
NSY anəq 'spark, lightning, ember'
CSY anəq 'burning or glowing ember' [aanʀutə- 'spark from friction']
Sir anəX 'spark, embers'

PE anəʀ- 'breathe (out)' [cf. Aleut anʀ(i)- 'breathe, blow', as nom. = 'breath, voice, ghost, life, spirit, soul', anrari- 'live, be alive'; there may be a relat. to anə-]
AAY ➡
CAY ➡

NSY anəXtukaʀ- 'take a breath' [ANLC; Men. has anəʀnəʀiʀ(aʀ)- 'get out of breath', anəXłukita(a)ʀ- 'gasp']
CSY anəXtə- 'breathe, continue to function normally'
Sir anəcəcəXtəX 'breath' [and Vakh. and Orr have anəXt(ə)- 'breathe'
SPI ➟
NAI aniq- 'speak'
WCI ➟
ECI ➟
GRI ➟

PE anəʀnəʀ 'breath or spirit' [cf. nəʀ[1]]
AAY anəʀrnəq 'breath, spirit'
CAY anəʀnəq* 'spirit, soul, breath'
NSY anəʀnəq 'breath' [ANLC]
CSY anərnəq* 'breath, the way things are'
Sir anəʀnəX 'breath' [Orr]
SPI aniʀniq 'breath'
NAI aniʀniq* 'breath'
WCI aniʀniq 'breath', Cop also 'soul' [and Car 'spirit' in Schn.]
ECI aniʀniq 'breath, spirit'
GRI aniʀniq*

PE anəʀtəqə- 'breathe' [cf. p.b. təʀ-]
AAY anəXtəqə- 'breathe'
CAY anəXtəqə- 'live, breathe'
NSY —
CSY —
Sir [Men. has anəXsaqə(s)- 'breathe']
SPI —
NAI aniqtiʀi- 'breathe'
WCI aniqtiʀi-
ECI aniqtiʀi-
GRI aniʀtiʀi- 'breathe deeply, groan'

PE anəʀya(C)aʀ- 'take a breath' [cf. yaʀaʀ-?]
AAY anəʀyaaʀ- 'sigh'
CAY anəʀyaaʀ- 'take a breath, sigh'
NSY [note anʀayuʀiŋ̣ałəq 'catching one's breath' (L.-T.)]
CSY —
Sir —
SPI aniqsaaq- 'breathe' [and Imaq anəqsaaʀ- 'mention']
NAI aniqsaaq- 'take a breath'
WCI aniqsaaq- 'breathe'
ECI aniʀsaatuq- 'breathe'
GRI aniʀsaaʀ- 'breathe', aniʀsaaq 'spirit, ghost'

PI an(ə)ʀilək- 'gasp for breath' [cf. ləɣ-?]
SPI —
NAI —
WCI [note Cop anrayuktuq- 'be out of breath']
ECI arŋilik- 'hurt oneself in pit of stomach' [and as noun = 'pit of stomach'; note Lab aŋŋayuɣak- 'pant because too warm (dog)']
GRI arŋili(ɣ)- 'gasp for breath'

PE aniɣu 'snow (fallen)'
AAY aniu, aniuq 'fallen snow'
CAY NS aniu 'fallen snow' [Jen. has aniu for any kind of snow in Nun]
NSY anii 'fallen snow'
CSY aniɣu 'fallen snow'
Sir anəɣa 'snow'
SPI aniu
NAI aniu 'packed snow'
WCI aniu 'snow for making water'
ECI aniu
GRI [Fab. has anigorvirkssuaq as a shaman's word for 'snow' = NG aniong according to Kroeber]

PE aniɣutyaʀ 'snow shelter' [compare NAI apuyyaq under apun (apə-)]
AAY —
CAY aniɣuyaq 'snow shelter' [used even outside of NS though aniu (above) is NS only]
NSY —
CSY aziɣutaq 'snow or rock shelter', Chap. 'shelter around hole in ice for fishing' [perhaps by contamination with aziɣuXtə- 'begin to warm up']
Sir —
SPI —
NAI aniɣuyyaq, Nu aniɣutyaq, Mal aniuyutyaq 'snow hut, winter den of female bear'
WCI —
ECI —
GRI —

PY aninqə- 'be careful with' [cf. anaya-, also nəʀ[1] and kə-[1]?]
AAY KP, Kod aninqə-, Perry aŋinqə- [also PWS qaɣinqə-] 'be careful or thrifty with'
CAY aninqə-
NSY —
CSY —

PY aniŋuaq 'boil or abcess' [cf. anə- and ŋ(ŋ)uðaʀ?]
AAY aniŋua<ʀ>aq, AP aniŋuaq 'boil, abcess'
CAY aniŋuaq 'boil'
NSY aniŋuaq [L.-T.]
CSY aniŋ^{w}aaq
Inu [compare SPI aniŋažuaq under aniŋa- (anə-)]

PY-S anipa 'snowy owl' [cf. aniɣu?]
AAY anipaq, KP anipak 'snowy owl'
CAY anipa(q)
NSY —
CSY anipa
Sir anipa

PE aniʀta 'how fortunate (exclamation)'
AAY aniXta, K, KP 'it's a good thing', KP also 'no wonder!', PWS 'you remember the time that -'
CAY aniXta 'how fortunate!'
NSY aniXta 'good!' [L.-T.]
CSY aniXta 'it used to be (wistfully)'
Sir aniXta [Orr]
SPI aniqta 'how fortunate'
NAI aniqsa 'luckily'

WCI Cop aniqtak 'but of course'
ECI aniqta 'luckily', Lab 'at last, this is good!' [Peck]
GRI aniʀsa 'that was lucky, I hope so, I wonder', aniʀsalu 'thanks, that was good of you'

PE anlu 'seal's breathing hole in ice' [cf. anə- and lu(ʀ)]
AAY ➡
CAY anlu 'seal's breathing hole'
NSY ➡
CSY aŋlu
Sir —
SPI allu
NAI allu
WCI aɣlu
ECI allu
GRI ałłu [old ortho. agdlo], EG attiq

PE anlu(C)aʀ 'hole in ice for fishing through [cf. aʀ]
AAY AP anluaq, Kod anłuaq 'hole cut in ice for fishing through'
CAY anluaq, NSU aŋłuaq 'fishing hole through ice' [contam. from aŋłuʀ- in the latter form?]
NSY anluaq 'hole in ice for fishing through'
CSY aŋlaaq
Sir [aŋluvəX 'hole in ice' — Vakh. has aŋluyəX from Men.'s texts]
SPI alluaq 'hole in ice for fishing'
NAI alluaq 'hole in ice for fishing (or seal's breathing hole)'
WCI alluaq 'hole in ice for fishing'
ECI alluaq
GRI ałłuaq

PY anłəq 'type of tuber' [cf. anə-?]
AAY AP, Kod anłəq 'type of tuber'
CAY anłəq* 'tuber of tall cottongrass'
NSY anłəq 'sprout' [ANLC]
CSY —

PE annaɣ- 'escape' [cf. anə-, esp. the NSY form, also p.b.s nnak- and nəɣ-?]
AAY anaɣ- 'escape'
CAY anaɣ- 'escape' [and note aniXtuʀ- 'rescue']
NSY anaɣ- 'flee' [ANLC]
CSY anaɣ- 'flee, escape'
Sir anaɣ- 'run away, escape'
SPI annak- 'escape'
NAI annak-
WCI annak-
ECI anna(k)-
GRI annaɣ-

PE annaɣutə- 'save' [cf. utə-]
AAY ana'utə- 'escape, get away with'
CAY anautə- 'help escape, deliver from danger'
NSY anaatə- 'save' [and ana(a)siłtə 'savior']
CSY anaɣutə- 'save'
Sir [Vakh. has anəʀətə- 'run away with' and Men. has anaxtuxta 'savior']
SPI annauti- 'save from danger'
NAI annauti- 'save'
WCI annauti- [Lowe]
ECI —
GRI annaat(i)- 'save'

PI annəq(tu)- '(broad) extent' [cf. nəʀ[1] and tu-[1] and probably at(ə)- — compare esp. atətu- and atnəq under it; there appears to be contam. with aunnəqtu-]
SPI —
NAI —
WCI —
ECI annitu- 'be wide and flat, last long' [Bourquin has annertu- 'last long'; note also anniq 'flat part of object or terrain, top part of teeth worn flat' and annikit- 'have little flat ground, be of short duration' — Bourquin has 'be not much, short-lived']
GRI anniʀtu- [old ortho. angnertu-] 'be wide below, last long, be reliable' [and annikit- 'be tapering, of small extent or duration — Fabricius has 'lack support, have a small foot or root']

PE annuʀaqə- 'feel constrained' [or 'force oneself to do s.th.'; cf. annut-]
AAY —
CAY anuʀaqə- 'feel restrained from doing what one wants, wait patiently'
NSY anuʀaqəsaʀ- 'encourage, approve, inspire' [ANLC]
CSY anuʀaqə 'train oneself physically, exercise'
Sir —
SPI Qaw anuaʀi- 'hold one's feelings or intentions back' [anuaqši- 'force to do s.th.']
NAI anuaqun 'reason for being moved to compassion or vulnerability' [and anuaqšuit- 'be emotionally vulnerable', anuqšu- 'be stoic']
WCI Car annualaq- 'admonish', annuaqsaq- 'persist though tired, obey after refusing' [Schn. 'adg']
ECI [Lab annusaC- 'admonish' — Andersen et al.]
GRI —

PE annut- and **annuci-** 'look serious (having learned one's lesson)' [cf. annuʀaqə-]
AAY anuci- 'learn one's lesson' [and anucicaʀ- 'teach s.o. a lesson']
CAY anuciŋə- 'learn one's lesson'
NSY ➡
CSY anusiɣaa-, anusiyaa- 'be tired of'
Sir ➡
SPI ➡
NAI annut- 'frown, pout'
WCI annut- 'look serious, sad', Car annutsiyaq 'one who has had enough' [Schn. 'adg', who also has annulaqsai- 'be tired after a long effort' for B. Lake; Pryde has anusi- 'regain one's appetite' for Perry River]
ECI Lab annut- 'become sad or bored' [Andersen et al.], Baffin annuq- 'become bored, sad' [biblical acc. Schn.; Dorais has annutaq- for Igl, also annuq- 'frown' for Lake Harbor; note also NBI anullaksiq- 'be jailed']
GRI annuɣ- 'look serious, cross', anusiɣi- 'teach s.o. a lesson' [and anuliŋiak- 'be nervous of s.th. one has had a bad experience with']

PI annucinŋu(q)- 'have learned one's lesson' [cf. lŋu-]
SPI anusiŋuq- 'be deterred, give up' [Jen.]

NAI anusin^{y}ŋu(q)- 'be so affected by an experience that one doesn't want to repeat it'
WCI Car annusiŋuq- 'have had enough' [Schn.; Met. has Sig an(n)usinŋuq- 'be so effected by an experience one doesn't want to repeat it' and an(n)usinŋuqsaq- 'punish']
ECI Lab annusiŋ(ŋ)uq- 'have learned one's lesson, be discouraged' [Peck]
GRI NG anuhiŋŋuXXaq- 'teach a lesson to (child)'

PY-S anucimiʀ- 'learn or teach a lesson' [cf. miqə-]
AAY —
CAY anucimiXqə- 'repent', anucimiXqəfkaʀ- 'make not want to do again'
NSY anusimiʀ- 'teach one a lesson (through punishment)' [ANLC; Men. has anusiminłaʀvik 'jail']
CSY anusimiXtə- 'have learned one's lesson' [and anusimiŋłaʀ- 'punish']
Sir anəsimiXtə- 'have learned one's lesson' [Em. has ansəmiʀ- 'lose patience', also ansəmiŋłaʀ- 'punish' — from CSY?]

PY an(ə)ŋanquq or **an(ə)ŋašquq** 'ankle bone' [cf. aniŋa- under anə- and aniŋuaq, and compare aŋənquq under aŋə- for the ending]
AAY —
CAY —
NSY anŋanquq 'ankle bone'
CSY Chap aanŋəšquq, aŋaŋašquq 'ankle bone'

PI anqaluk 'woman's younger brother' [cf. NAI aniqan under anə- and p.b. ʀuluk?]
SPI —
NAI aqqaluk 'woman's younger brother'
WCI Cop aqqaluaq 'woman's younger brother' [Lowe; B.-S. has atqaluaq for Car and Net, and Dor. has atqaluaqtaaq 'woman's preferred brother' for B. Lake]
ECI —
GRI aqqaluk, aqqaluaq 'woman's younger brother'

PE an(ə)ʀutaʀ 'stomach of mammal' [cf. anəʀ- and un?]
AAY —
CAY anʀutaq 'stomach of mammal'
NSY —
CSY [note anʀuŋitə- 'eat greedily, gobble food']
Sir —
SPI aʀʀutaq 'walrus stomach container'
NAI aʀʀutaq 'dried stomach or bladder used as a container'
WCI —
ECI —
GRI —

PE anu 'harness'
AAY —
CAY anu(k) 'harness'
NSY —
CSY —
Sir —
SPI anu [as verb = 'put harness on', as in all Inu]
NAI anu 'harness'
WCI anu
ECI anu
GRI anu

PE anuqə 'wind'
AAY K anuqa 'wind' [base anuqə]
CAY anuqa [base anuqə]
NSY anuqə
CSY anuqa [base anuqə]
Sir —
SPI anuʀi
NAI anuʀɨ
WCI anuʀi 'wind' [anuʀsaʀiktuq 'good wind', Perry River anuXXaaq- 'be a light breeze' — Pryde]
ECI anuʀi 'wind'
GRI anuʀi 'wind' [and anuʀšarissi-, Up aniʀsaʀ-, aniʀsaʀžitsi- 'have risen (wind)', NG anuXXaaq- 'blow (wind)']

PE anuqliʀ- 'be windy' [cf. liʀ-]
AAY AP anuqiʀ- 'be windy'
CAY anuqłiʀ- 'be windy'
NSY anuqłiʀ- 'be windy' [ANLC]
CSY anuqłiʀ- 'get or be windy'
Sir —
SPI anuqłiq- 'be windy'
NAI anuqłiq-
WCI anuqłiq-, Cop anuXXiq-
ECI anuʀsili- 'be windy', Lab anuʀłiq- 'become windy' [Peck]
GRI anuʀłiʀ-, EG aniʀsiʀ- 'be windy' [and EG aniʀsiq 'wind']

PE a(a)ŋ 'yes (here you are)' [cf. Aleut aaŋ 'yes', aŋa- 'say yes' and compare i(i)[1]; the Inu forms ending in m/p probably influenced by a(a)mi(ila) below]
AAY aa-a 'yes'
CAY aa-aŋ
NSY aŋ 'here you are'
CSY aŋ 'here you are' [and aa, aa-a 'yes']
Sir aŋ 'here you are' [and Vakh. has a-a 'yes, I don't know']
SPI Imaq aŋ 'here you are'
NAI aaŋ, aa 'yes', aŋ 'here you are'
WCI Cop ak 'here, take it' [Pryde; Lowe further has aapkiaq 'maybe' for Sig and Jen. has aam 'yes' for Cop]
ECI aa, Lab aaŋ 'yes'
GRI aap 'yes', NG 'isn't it?' [Uummannaq aa 'yes' rather; also WG ak, aak, NWG akki 'here you are']

PI a(a)mi(ila) 'indeed?' [cf. perhaps enclitic mi, also ila[2]]
SPI —
NAI amii 'that's right, isn't it?', amiami 'well, just the same' [and PH amay 'I don't know', Uum amiunniin 'OK, you're welcome']
WCI Sig ami 'yes indeed', Car B. Lake aamilaa 'indeed' [Pryde Schn. has amilaq for 'adg' and

Ras. aamilaung for Sig; Dor. has amiahuk 'I don't know' for B. Lake]
ECI amila 'in truth' [marked 'rare' for Wakeham Bay; also NBI aamai 'I don't know'; Schn. has ami 'let me see!' for Baf.]
GRI NG aamilaa 'yes, indeed' [for EG iimilaa in this sense see i(i)[2]]

PE aŋəʀ- 'say yes' [cf. p.b. (a)ʀ-?]
CAY aŋəʀ- 'say yes, agree'
NSY aŋəʀ-
CSY aŋəʀ-
Sir aŋəʀ-
SPI aŋiq-
NAI aŋɨq- 'say yes' [and aŋŋaq- 'keep saying or nodding yes']
WCI aŋiq-
ECI aŋiq- 'say yes' [and aŋŋaa- 'agree']
GRI aŋiʀ- 'say yes, agree' [and aŋŋaa- 'say yes several times', aŋŋałłaɣ- 'nod yes']

PY-S aŋa(ʀ)- 'travel or move' [cf. aŋalkuʀ, aŋaqə-, aŋatuʀ-, also PE aŋa(yəɣ)-]
AAY K, KP aŋŋa- 'travel, behave in a certain way' [continuative = aŋauʀ-; aŋŋatə-, aŋŋaquʀ- 'take along with one, manage s.th.']
CAY aŋŋaqə- 'take along' [and aŋaqun 'tow-line']
NSY aŋaXtə- 'take along, carry'
CSY aŋaXqə- 'take along, transport' [for aŋałqataq 'sling or hook for birds or seals' see iŋilqaʀ]
Sir aŋaXqəʀ- 'take along, transport'

PE aŋa(yəɣ)- or **aŋayu(ɣ)-** 'sway?' [cf. aŋa(ʀ)- and aŋala-? — there may be a further link to aŋalkuʀ]
AAY —
CAY aŋayiitə- 'suffer motion sickness', NS aŋazaaʀ- 'sway', HBC aɣayəxtə- 'slant (s.th. meant to be straight)' [and note aŋya(a)q 'swamp']
NSY —
CSY —
Sir —
SPI aŋayu- 'perform a religious rite' [compare aŋaayu- under aɣayu-, with which there appears to be entanglement]
NAI aŋayu- 'dance Inupiaq style' [acc. Pryde used specifically of women's part in traditional dances, i.e. referring to their swaying motion back and forth? — compare under aɣayu-]
WCI —
ECI —
GRI — [for aŋa- 'hang head, be depressed' see aɣ(ɣ)a(ʀ)-]

PE aŋaɣ 'maternal uncle' [cf. aŋə-?]
AAY aŋak 'maternal uncle'
CAY aŋak
NSY aŋak
CSY aŋak
Sir aŋax [Orr]
SPI aŋak
NAI aŋak
WCI aŋak
ECI aŋak
GRI aŋak, Up aŋaq

PE aŋala- 'move about' [cf. aŋa(ʀ)-, aŋa(yəɣ)- and p.b. la(ʀ)-]
AAY —
CAY aŋala- 'flutter, wobble, move back and forth'
NSY —
CSY —
Sir —
SPI aŋala- 'move about'
NAI aŋala-
WCI —
ECI —
GRI aŋala- 'travel, be in motion' [and aŋałłat(i)- 'carry about']

PE aŋalat- 'stir' [cf. t-[1]]
AAY —
CAY aŋalaci- 'wave', K aŋulatə- 'stir, mix' [the former with p.b. ðiə-, the latter influenced by ᴀʀulat- under ᴀʀula-]
NSY —
CSY —
Sir —
SPI aŋalat- 'stir'
NAI aŋalat- 'stir, manipulate'
WCI aŋalat-
ECI —
GRI —

PE aŋalkuʀ 'shaman' [cf. CSY aŋałkə- under aŋaqə- and/or aŋala- and perhaps p.b. kə(-)[2], also aŋa(yəɣ)-; note probably unrelated Chukchi eŋeŋəlʼn 'shaman' from eŋeŋ 'spirit']
AAY aŋałkuq 'shaman'
CAY aŋałkuq, aŋałkuk 'shaman' [and aŋaʀvak 'powerful shaman']
NSY aŋałkuq 'shaman'
CSY —
Sir —
SPI aŋatkuq
NAI aŋatkuq
WCI aŋatkuq
ECI aŋakkuq
GRI aŋakkuq

PI aŋatkuaq- 'shamanize'
SPI aŋatkuaq- 'practice magic'
NAI aŋatkuaq-, Nu aŋatkuk- 'work as shaman, cast spell on'
WCI aŋatku(a)q- 'perform sorcery on'
ECI Lab aŋakkuaq- 'practice sorcery' [Peck]
GRI aŋakkuaʀ-

PY-S aŋaqə- and **aŋalkə-** 'strain to get free' [cf. aŋa(ʀ)-, aŋatu(ʀ)- and aŋalkuʀ]
AAY K, KP aŋaqə- 'try hard to reach destination'
CAY aŋaqə- 'strain at leash, eager to go (dog)'
NSY aŋaqə- 'strain at the leash', aŋałitə- 'strain at leash,

try to reach for, try to break free from' [ANLC]
CSY aŋałkə- 'jerk on rope to get free (animal)' [note also aŋałqataq 'white wagtail']
Sir aŋałkəʀ- 'jerk on rope to get free, strain to get free, long to go to s.o' [Orr and Em.]

PY aŋatu(ʀ)- 'be in a hurry' [cf. aŋa(ʀ)-]
AAY —
CAY —
NSY aŋatuʀnəq '(doing) quick, in a hurry', aŋatuʀi- 'hurry' [nom. aŋatuʀisałəq]
CSY aŋatuxqə- 'hurry over', aŋatuməŋ 'quickly'
Sir [note aŋəsaqnaməŋ 'in a hurry', aŋəsaqə(s)- 'hurry']

PE aŋayuɣ 'elder sibling of same sex' [cf. perhaps aŋə- and/or aŋaɣ plus yuɣ-, also old Atkan Aleut aŋax 'power, steward', aŋaɣ- 'reign']
AAY aŋa<y>uk 'partner, buddy'
CAY BB aŋayuk 'partner'
NSY aŋayuk 'older relative'
CSY ➟
Sir ➟
SPI aŋayuk 'older brother', Qaw 'elder sibling of same sex'
NAI Nu aŋayuk
WCI aŋayuk Cop 'elder sibling of same sex', Sig 'older brother of boy'
ECI aŋayuk 'elder sibling of same sex'
GRI aŋayu(q), EG aŋiiq

PI aŋayukliʀ 'oldest one' [cf. l(l)iʀ]
Yup [note CAY NS aŋayukłiq* 'bearded seal' from Inu]
SPI aŋayuɣliq 'oldest child'
NAI aŋayukłiq* 'elder or eldest one'
WCI Sig aŋayukłiq, Cop aŋayuxxiqun [Lowe]
ECI aŋayutsiq 'elder one'
GRI aŋayułłiq*, NG aŋayuɣliq, EG aŋiitsiq; 'elder or eldest one'

PI aŋayunʀuq 'senior co-in-law' [cf. nukaunʀuq under nukaʀ]
SPI —
NAI aŋayunʀuq 'senior co-in-law, spouse's older same sex sibling's spouse'
WCI —
ECI aŋayuʀŋuq
GRI aŋayuʀnuq

PE aŋayuq(q)ᴀʀ 'parent or leader'
AAY aŋa<y>uqaq 'leader, boss', aŋa<y>uqak 'parents' [and note Biblical qilam aŋayuqasinaa 'king of heaven']
CAY aŋayuqaq 'boss, chief, parent'
NSY aŋayuqaq 'relative'
CSY aŋayuqaq 'parent, boss'
Sir aŋayuqaʀiy 'parents'
SPI aŋayuʀaaq 'parent', aŋayuʀakšaq 'old man'
NAI aŋayuqaak 'parents', aŋayuqak, aŋayuqakšaq 'old man'
WCI Sig aŋayuqaq [Met.], aŋayuqaksaq 'old man' [Lowe]
ECI aŋayuqqaaq 'boss, head of family'
GRI aŋayuqqaat 'parents'

PE aŋə- 'be big' [cf. Aleut aŋuna-X 'big', aŋuna- 'be big, much']
AAY aŋə- 'be big'
CAY aŋə-
NSY [anłuk 'big', aŋənəXpiɣaq 'very big thing', and note aiɣitaʀaq 'small']
CSY aaŋə- 'be big' [and a(a)ŋənəq* 's.th. bigger']
Sir aŋəpalaʀ- 'be big' [and aŋuʀ- 'grow'; Vakh. and Orr have aŋəpalaX 'big one']
SPI ➟
NAI aŋɨ- 'be big'
WCI aŋi-
ECI aŋi-
GRI aŋi- 'be big' [and aŋisuuq, NG aŋihuuq 'big', anniq* 'bigger or biggest thing', EG 'bearded seal']

PI aŋənaaq- 'make too big' [cf. naaq-]
SPI aŋnaaq- 'make too large'
NAI aŋ(ɨ)naaq-, Nu aknaaq-
WCI —
ECI aŋinaaq- 'be too big for'
GRI annaaʀ- 'make or consider too big'

PY aŋənquq 'big toe' [cf. qur; compare with an(ə)ŋanquq]
AAY AP aŋənquq, Kod aŋənquyuk 'big toe'
CAY NS, Eg aŋənquq, Nun aŋənquyux, HBC aŋunquyuk, Canineq aŋunquq
NSY —
CSY —

PE aŋ(ə)li- 'become bigger' [cf. li-[2]]
AAY aŋli- 'become bigger, grow'
CAY aŋli- 'become bigger' [aŋlicaʀ- raise (child)']
NSY anli- 'bnecome bigger' [anlisaʀ- 'raise (child)']
CSY aŋli- 'become bigger' [aŋlisaʀ- 'raise (child)']
Sir —
SPI aɣli- 'grow' [aɣlizaq- 'raise (child)']
NAI aɣli- 'grow' [aɣlilʸaaq- 'enlarge']
WCI aɣli- 'grow'
ECI aŋili-
GRI ałłi- 'grow, have s.th. grow' [ałłisaʀ- 'raise (child)']

PE aŋtuʀ(ᴀʀ) ' big thing' [cf. žuaq, tuaq under ðuʀ?]
AAY AP aŋtu<ʀ>aq 'big thing'
CAY aŋtuaq
NSY —
CSY aŋtaaq* 'mature bearded seal', aŋtuXpak 'walrus bull'
Sir aŋtaX 'mature bearded seal' [Orr]
SPI aktuaq 's.th. big'
NAI Nu akturžuaq 'fully grown animal'
WCI Net, Perry River aktuaqtaq 'large ringed seal' [Ras., Pryde]
ECI attuq 'adult bearded seal', Iti 'big thing'
GRI —

PY aŋəq 'pitch or resin'
AAY K aŋəq 'pitch of tree, resin, chewing gum' [and K, KP aŋəqcuk, K also aŋəʀnak, AP also aŋəʀsuk 'pitch']
CAY aŋəq* 'chewing gum' [and aŋiyaq 'pitch of tree used for chewing, aŋəʀyuk, aŋəʀnak 'pitch of tree']
NSY— [for ayŋun 'blubber chewed as gum' see ayŋun]
CSY— [for ayŋusi- 'make chewing gum from blubber' see ayŋun]

PE aŋi- 'loosen (by soaking)' [cf. Aleut aŋi- 'start out, begin', but also PE aŋit-?]
AAY C aŋiqqaʀ- 'get wet and soft', aŋitə- 'soak, dunk'
CAY aŋi- 'come loose', aŋitə- 'loosen'
NSY aŋitə- 'untwist, unwrap, unscrew' [and aŋiqun 'wrapper, screwdriver']
CSY aŋi- 'come undone' aŋitə-, aŋiqə- 'untie'
Sir aŋitə- 'untie, release, undo, unwind' [Orr and Em.]
SPI aŋivžaq- 'loosen, untie, undo', aŋit- W 'wet, soak' [Jen.], Imaq 'twist, unscrew'
NAI aŋivit-, aŋivžaq- 'become loose, loosen'
WCI Cop aŋivit- 'untie (a knot)' [Ras.]
ECI Lab aŋivit- 'be thoroughly wet' [Peck]
GRI aŋit- 'soak'

PE aŋit- 'come back'
AAY aŋitə- 'return (esp. home)', aŋitm̥un 'homeward'
CAY aŋimuXtə- 'go back into original condition'
NSY —
CSY aŋiitə- 'arrive, finish on time'
Sir [note aŋutə- 'arrive, finish on time' acc. Orr]
SPI aŋi- 'come back to life, revive', aŋiinaq- 'fail to make a kill'
NAI aŋi- come back to life, revive' [and aŋilʸuŋaq-, aŋiinʸnʸaq- 'fail to obtain']
WCI aŋit(i)- 'return without obtaining anything'
ECI aŋiinna(q)- 'return empty-handed from hunt'
GRI aŋiluttuʀ- 'come home empty-handed'

PE aŋilluʀ- 'go in reverse direction (current)' [cf. luʀ-]
AAY aŋiluXtə- 'current reverses direction'
CAY —
NSY —
CSY —
Sir —
SPI —
NAI —
WCI Car? aŋilluqtuq 'whirlpool in current of pool' [Schn. 'adg']
ECI aŋillutaq 'whirlpool in current'
GRI aŋiłłuq, aŋiʀłuq 'whirlpool, wake', aŋiłłuʀtaq 'cross current (going across main one)'

PE aŋilʀaʀ- 'return home' [cf. ʀaq- and compare the relat. between əɣlər- and iŋilʀa- for the variation in the Yup forms]
AAY —
CAY BB ilɣaʀ- 'go home after evening activities' [and Nun anəlʀaʀ-, alʀaʀ- 'go toward exit, downriver', as if from anə-]
NSY —
CSY aɣlaʀ- 'go home'
Sir —
SPI aŋiʀlaq- 'return home from hunting trip'
NAI aŋilʸʀaq-, Mal aŋilʸaa- 'go home' [and compare under iŋilʀa-]
WCI aŋilʀaq- 'return home from hunting trip', Net aŋižʀaq-, aŋižʀau- [Ras. has aŋilʀaq-, aŋilʀau- — for the second form note ɨɣlau- alongside ɨɣlɨq- 'travel' in NAI under əɣlər-]
ECI aŋiʀʀa(q)-, Iti anaʀʀa(q)- 'go home' [and aŋiʀʀaq 'home', aŋiʀʀamut 'homeward']
GRI aŋiʀłaʀ- 'go home, travel back' [and aŋiʀłamut 'homeward']

PY-S aŋla- 'enjoy' [cf. aŋniʀ-]
AAY aŋlanaʀ- 'be greedy', aŋlani- 'watch closely'
CAY aŋlani- 'have fun, enjoy, watch', aŋlanaXqə- 'be enjoyable'
NSY anlanaq 'interesting thing, pageant', anlani- 'watch' [ANLC; Men. has anlanitəkə- 'watch']
CSY aŋlanaʀ- 'be beautiful (esp. of sounds)'
Sir aŋlaniłəʀəX 'beautiful, wonderful' [Em.]

PE aŋłuʀ- 'dive into water' [or aŋluʀ-?]
AAY aŋłuʀ- 'dive into water (esp. bird)' [in PWS of any animal, not necessarily diving]
CAY aŋłuʀ- 'dive, be submerged, be baptized'
NSY [note anłəʀnaʀ- 'be wet' — Orr]
CSY ałŋuʀ- 'dive, submerge' [and ałŋuqayuk — Men. ałŋuqaq — 's.th. that has dived down' (in Rub. 'submarine')]
Sir aŋlər- 'dive' [Vakh. has ałŋəʀ-]
SPI aɣluq- 'dive into water (bird)'
NAI aɣluq- 'dive into water'
WCI aɣluq-
ECI allu(q)- 'dive into water (bird)'
GRI ałłuʀ- [old ortho. agdlor-]

PI aŋmaq 'small fish (like capelin)' [cf. aŋva-?]
SPI —
NAI aŋmaʀuq 'little trout', Nu aŋmaɣaužaq 'smelt'
WCI Car aŋmaxxak 'capelin' [B.-S.]
ECI Fort Chimo ammayaq 'sand eel' ['capelin' acc. Saul, which Schn. only has for Iti; Peck has Lab anmayak, anmatyak 'kind of small sea fish']
GRI ammaššak [old ortho. angmagssak] 'capelin'

PY aŋniʀ- 'arouse interest or be happy?' [cf. aŋla-; from *aŋnəʀ plus liʀ-?]
AAY aŋniʀ- 'be potentially useful', aŋniqə- 'consider potentially useful'
CAY aŋniʀ- 'be happy' [and aŋniq 'happiness']
NSY —
CSY —
Inu — [but note Sig aŋiqqi- 'pass the time agreeably']

PI aŋŋi- 'conceal (a secret)' [cf. perhaps Aleut aŋayuʀ- 'steal, appropriate' (if that is not related to aŋa(ʀ)- as Berg. suggests); the relat., if any, to a(a)tsaqə- is obscure]
SPI aŋŋii- 'deny, not say'

NAI aŋŋiqi- 'deny knowledge of', PH aŋŋikuti- 'keep s.th. a secret' [and aŋŋiiyaq- 'set a situation right with s.o.']
WCI [Met. has aŋiyi- 'keep s.th. a secret' and aŋ(ŋ)i(i)yaq- 'confess'; Dor. has aŋŋiniq 'ghost' for Net]
ECI aŋiaq 's.th. one hides, does not want to say'
GRI aŋŋiaq 'child born under concealment of pregnancy (or its ghost)', aŋŋiɣi- 'keep s.th. a secret' [and aŋŋiuʀ- 'do s.th. secretively', aŋŋiiaʀ- 'confess', EG aŋŋiiʀ- 'steal']

PE aŋŋu 'stop (exclamation)'
AAY C aŋu, PWS also aŋa 'don't!'
CAY aŋu, aɣu, aŋu'u 'don't, no!' [and Nun aŋuqa 'or']
NSY —
CSY —
Sir —
SPI Qaw aŋŋu 'don't do it!'
NAI aŋŋuu(ŋ) 'stop that!'
WCI — [Schn. has aŋu 'it's urgent' for 'adg', perhaps by contam. with aŋuðuʀ-]
ECI Lab aŋŋuu 'stop, don't!'
GRI NWG aŋŋuuna 'and suddenly there was -' [note also aŋusuu 'exclamation of surprise']

PY-S aŋqaq 'ball' [cf. aqšaq under aqə- and aŋvaluʀ- under aŋva- — there appears to be contamination between these two here]
AAY AP aŋqaaq 'ball'
CAY aŋqaq 'ball'
NSY aŋqaq 'ball'
CSY aaŋqaq 'ball' [and aaŋqaʀ- 'play ball']
Sir aŋqaX 'ball' [Vakh. also has this as 'stone' from Rub.'s texts]

PY aŋqutə- 'stumble' [there may be a link to aqə-]
AAY K aŋqutə- 'stumble, trip'
CAY Y, NS aŋqutə- 'stumble, fall down'
NSY —
CSY —

PE aŋu- 'catch (up)' [cf. aŋuðaʀ-]
AAY aŋu- 'catch up with, overtake, reach in time'
CAY aŋu- 'catch (after hunting), overtake, have experienced during one's life' [aŋusaaɣ- 'hunt']
NSY aŋu- 'catch up with, chase, reach'
CSY aŋu- 'catch up with, overtake'
Sir aŋə- 'come across, catch' [Men. also has aŋəcəʀ-]
SPI aŋu- 'catch (after hunting), catch up with'
NAI aŋu- 'catch (up with), have experienced during one's life' [and aŋŋun 'game animal']
WCI aŋu- 'catch, catch up with' [and aŋuniaq- 'go hunting', Cop aŋŋun 'game animal', Net aŋŋutaq 'game caught' — Dor.]
ECI aŋu- 'catch' [and NBI, Aiv aŋŋutaq 'game caught']
GRI aŋu- '(trans.) catch up with, reach, (intr.) catch seal', NG aŋunialuk- 'go hunting'

PE aŋuma- 'keep up (with)' [cf. (u)ma-]
AAY —
CAY aŋuma- 'keep up with'
NSY —
CSY [note aumaasitaaʀ- 'search for s.th. lost', aŋumaasqitaXtə- 'be delayed', and Chap aŋumaasqitaʀ- 'try to get more than others']
Sir —
SPI —
NAI —
WCI —
ECI aŋuma-, aŋummat(i)- 'maintain same speed as'
GRI aŋummat(i)-, aŋumaršaʀi- 'keep up with (at full speed)' [and note aŋumiʀi- 'reach s.o. before he or she leaves'; Robbe and Menn. have EG aŋimii- 'catch up with (a seal?)', aŋimmaliʀ- 'catch (seal) in a net']

PE aŋuyu(ʀ)- 'be a good hunter' [cf. yu-, ðu-]
AAY —
CAY aŋuyu- 'be good at catching game'
NSY aŋuyu- [ANLC]
CSY aŋuyu-
Sir —
SPI aŋusuq- 'be a good hunter'
NAI aŋusuq-
WCI aŋusuq-
ECI aŋusuqtuq, aŋusuyuq, Iti aŋusuttuq 'good hunter'
GRI aŋuʀsuɣ-, NG aŋuxxuq- 'be good at catching seals'

PE aŋuðaʀ- 'paddle' [cf. aŋu- and ðaʀ- and Aleut aŋaaʀu-X 'single-bladed paddle for skin boat' from aŋa- 'longitudinal half, side, match', old Atkan also 'adversary', for which compare aŋuyaɣ]
AAY AP, Kod aŋuaʀ- 'row'
CAY aŋuaʀ- 'paddle'
NSY aŋuaʀ- 'paddle, row'
CSY aŋʷaaʀ- 'paddle'
Sir aŋəcəʀ- 'paddle, row' [Vakh. also has aŋužaʀ- from Rub.]
SPI aŋuaq- 'paddle'
NAI aŋuaq-
WCI Sig aŋuaq-
ECI aŋuaq- 'swim, advance in water' [Peck has 'row' for Lab]
GRI aŋuaʀ- 'paddle'

PE aŋuðaʀun 'paddle' [cf. un]
AAY aŋua<ʀ>un 'oar, paddle, caudal fin'
CAY aŋuaʀun 'single-bladed paddle, propeller'
NSY aŋuaʀun 'oar'
CSY aŋʷaaʀun 'paddle'
Sir aŋəcəʀəta 'oar'
SPI aŋuun 'short oar, paddle, fish fin'
NAI aŋuun
WCI aŋuun 'paddle, lateral fin, propeller'
ECI aŋuuti 'fin, propeller'
GRI aŋuut 'single-bladed paddle, fin'

PE aŋuðuʀ- 'urinate or defecate involuntarily' [cf. aŋu-?]
AAY aŋuuʀ- 'urinate involuntarily'

CAY aŋuuʀ- 'urinate involuntarily (in one's pants), release amniotic fluid'
NSY —
CSY aŋuuʀ- 'be stormbound or otherwise delayed by unforeseen circumstances'
Sir aŋuʀ- 'be stormbound' [Orr; for aŋəcəʀ- 'come upon' see aŋu-]
SPI Qaw aŋuuq- 'urinate or defecate accidentally, give birth before reaching hospital' [and trans. = 'be caught in storm']
NAI aŋuuq- 'urinate or defecate accidentally, give birth before reaching hospital' [not the trans. meaning]
WCI aŋu(u)q- 'need to urinate or defecate urgently'
ECI aŋuuq- 'go in one's pants' [in Iti 'urinate or defecate (of women only)' acc. Saul]
GRI aŋuuʀ- 'need to urinate or defecate urgently, go in one's pants' [and perhaps EG aŋi(i)aaʀ- 'defecate' — Gessain et al. have aŋiiʀ-]

PY aŋukaq 'plant (wild rhubarb?)' [cf. aŋun and kðaʀ?]
AAY —
CAY K aŋukaq 'wild rhubarb'
NSY [note aŋkužʀaq 'bistort' (L.-T.)]
CSY aŋukaq 'dwarf fireweed'

PE aŋula- 'chew (to soften)'
AAY aŋula- 'chew'
CAY aŋula- 'chew on skin to soften for sewing' [for K aŋulatə- 'stir' see aŋalat- under aŋala-]
NSY —
CSY —
Sir —
SPI aŋula- 'chew' [Jen.]
NAI aŋula- 'scrape (for chew?) fat from bird skin'
WCI aŋula- 'chew to soften (skin or sole)'
ECI aŋula- 'chew fat from skin' [nom. = 'fat of bird or fox']
GRI aŋula- 'soften bird skin by chewing or sucking fat off'

PE aŋun 'man (male human)' [cf. aŋə- and un?; probably not from aŋu-, since there is no gemination in Inu forms — compare NAI, WCI aŋŋun under aŋu-]
AAY aŋun 'old man' [informally also 'husband']
CAY aŋun 'man'
NSY aŋukaʀaq 'old man'
CSY —
Sir aŋəta 'father'
SPI aŋun 'man, father'
NAI aŋun 'man' [and aŋutaat 'her husband']
WCI aŋun, aŋut 'man, father'
ECI aŋuti 'man, husband, male animal'
GRI aŋut 'man, father'

PE aŋucalluʀ 'male'
AAY AP aŋusaluq 'male animal'
CAY aŋucaluq 'male animal, woman's lover'
NSY —
CSY —
Sir —
SPI aŋusaluq 'male animal'
NAI aŋusalluq
WCI aŋusalluk 'male animal', B. Lake aŋuhalluk 'almost adult male caribou' [Dor.]
ECI aŋusalluk 'male bird, whale or seal (except bearded seal)'
GRI aŋusałłuk 'male fish'

PY aŋukaʀaq 'old man' [cf. kaʀaq]
AAY K aŋuka<ʀ>aq 'little old man'
CAY aŋukaʀaq 'old man'
NSY aŋukaʀaq
CSY —

PI aŋutəkšaq 'stepfather' [cf. kðaʀ]
SPI aŋutiɣžaq 'stepfather'
NAI —
WCI aŋutiksaq 'adoptive father' [Lowe has Cop aŋutixxaq 'step-father' — Car 'male partner in extra-marital sexual acts' acc. Schn.; Dor. has 'stepfather, foster father' for B. Lake]
ECI [Lab angititsak 'husband to be, fiance' — Andersen et al.]
GRI aŋutiššaq 'stepfather' [compare aŋutisiaq 'foster father']

PI aŋutəviaq 'male bird' [cf. piɣ and aʀ]
SPI —
NAI —
WCI —
ECI aŋutiviaq 'male bird'
GRI aŋutiviaq

PI aŋutnaq 'garment for men' [cf. naʀ]
SPI aŋutnaq 'man's garment'
NAI aŋunnaq 's.th. used by a man'
WCI Car B. Lake aŋunnaq 'man's clothing' [Dor.]
ECI —
GRI aŋunnaq 'short outer half-jacket'

PE aŋutŋunəʀ 'woman's male relative or lover?' [cf. ŋu- and nəʀ[1]?]
AAY PWS aŋutŋunəq 'woman's younger brother'
CAY Nun, HBC aŋutŋunəq* 'brother'
NSY aŋutŋunəq
CSY —
Sir —
SPI aŋutnuniq 'brother of woman'
NAI aŋunnuniq*, Nu aŋutnuniq* 'husband, male maternal parallel cousin'
WCI Car, Net aŋu'nuniq 'temporary husband' [B.-S.]
ECI Igl aŋunnuniq [B.-S.]
GRI aŋunnuniq* 'adulterer', NG 'woman's husband or lover' [Holt.]

PI aŋuviɣaq 'lance' [cf. aŋu-]
SPI aŋuviaq 'toggle harpoon head'
NAI Nu aŋuviɣaq [Ras.] 'lance'
WCI —
ECI aŋuviɣaq
GRI aŋuiɣaq

PE aŋuyaɣ(-) 'enemy, wage war' [cf. aŋu-, but also Aleut aŋaðuuti-X 'enemy', Atkan 'war', related further by Bergsland to aŋa- 'half, match' — compare aŋuðaʀ-]
AAY aŋuyak 'warrior' [aŋuyaɣ- 'wage war']
CAY aŋuyak 'battle, warrior' [aŋuyaɣ- 'fight in battle']
NSY aŋuyak 'outsider, foreigner, Russian'
CSY aŋuyak 'enemy'
Sir aŋəyəx
SPI aŋuyak- 'fight, do battle', Qaw aŋuyak 'warrior'
NAI aŋuyak- 'wage war'
WCI aŋuyak-
ECI —
GRI —

PE aŋva- 'be open'
AAY →
CAY aŋpaŋqa-, Nun aŋvaŋqa- 'be open'
NSY —
CSY →
Sir →
SPI aŋma- 'be open, free of ice (lake)' [aŋmaq 'hole']
NAI aɣma-, Mal aŋma- 'be open' [and Nu, PH aŋmaq 'hole, opening']
WCI aŋma- 'be open' [and aŋmak (for aŋmaq?) 's.th. round or open']
ECI ammaniq 'opening' [and note ammaniriik 'two snow houses joined by a common passage through a hole where they touch']
GRI amma- 'be open' [ammaniq*, EG ammaliq 'opening' — note also EG ammalivatsiaq 'star']

> **PE aŋvaluʀ-** 'be round' [cf. lu(ʀ)?; compare also aŋqaq]
> AAY —
> CAY —
> NSY —
> CSY aŋvałuqəxtaq 'oval-shaped thing'
> Sir —
> SPI aŋmaluaʀik- 'be round'
> NAI aŋmaluaq- 'be round' [Jen.; MacLean has it as a nom. in Nu = 'bone labret with beads in it'; for 'be round' she has aXfaluq-, which in Mal is aqšavaluq-, by contam. with aqšaq 'ball']
> WCI aŋmaluʀik- 'be round' [Met.], Car, Net aŋmaluqtuq 's.th. round' [Ras.]
> ECI ammaluʀik- 'be round'
> GRI ammaluʀ -

> **PY-S aŋvanəq** 'hollow above collarbone or below shoulderblade?' [cf. nəʀ[1]]
> AAY —
> CAY aŋvanuq 'sternum, breastbone'
> NSY —
> CSY aŋvanəq* 'hollow beneath shoulder blade or above collarbone'
> Sir aŋvanəX

> **PE aŋvaʀ-** 'open' [cf. ʀ- under ŋ(ŋ)uʀ-]
> AAY ampaʀ- 'open (s.th. sealed or sky clearing)'
> CAY aŋpaʀ-, Nun aŋvaʀ- 'open' [postural root]
> NSY —
> CSY —
> Sir —
> SPI aŋmaq- 'open'
> NAI aɣmaq-, Mal aŋmaq- '(become or make) open'
> WCI aŋmaq- 'open'
> ECI amma(q)- 'open, be open'
> GRI ammaʀ- '(become or make) open'

PY aŋyaq 'open skin boat' [cf. aŋu- and yaʀ]
AAY aŋyaq 'boat'
CAY aŋyaq 'boat (other than kayak)' [aŋyaʀ- 'ride in a boat', aŋyaXłuk 'raft']
NSY anyaq 'whaling boat' [anyaXłuk 'ship']
CSY aŋyaq 'boat (esp. open skin one)' [aŋyaʀ- 'go hunting with a boat, use a boat', aŋyalək 'captain, boat's owner']
Sir aŋyəX 'boat' [Vakh. also has aŋyiʀ- (for aŋyəʀ-?) 'go hunting', and aŋyəłəX 'hunter' from Men.'s texts]
Inu — [note GRI WG aksak (in old ortho.) 'boat' in shaman's language according to Egede and Fabricius as reported by Rink]

PE ap(p)a[1] 'grandfather' [compare ama(C)uʀ]
AAY apa, apaaq 'grandfather' [and note apaacua<r>aq, AP apaŋcuk 'uncle']
CAY apa(q), appa 'grandfather' [and note Nun apakcux 'sea lion']
NSY apa, apaya 'grandfather' [and apaXpak 'great grandfather' acc. Orr]
CSY apa 'grandfather'
Sir apa 'grandfather' [and apałqusiX, apamłəX 'great grandparent' acc. Orr]
SPI ava 'grandfather' [and avaak 'grandfather and grandmother']
NAI aapa 'father' [and apaaluk 'grandfather', aapi(y)aq 'elder brother'; Ras. has PH apagssuk — for apaɣžuk? — 'sea horse' (sic! — for 'sea lion?')]
WCI aappak 'father' [and Pet. has abba 'seal with pointed nose']
ECI [Peck has abba 'kind of sea dog, seal' for Lab and Boas has SB apaa 'bladder-nose seal with white belly and black back']
GRI — [for NG aippaq in the sense 'father' see a(C)ippaʀ]

> **PY apaʀuʀluq** and **apaʀuʀluɣaq** '(great) grandfather? [cf. ʀuʀluq]
> AAY [note Kod apaXłuk, C apału<ɣ>aq 'uncle']
> CAY apauʀluq*, Nun, HBC apaXłuɣaq* 'grandfather'
> NSY —
> CSY Chap apaʀuʀluq 'great grandfather'

PE ap(p)a[2] 'food (child's word)'
AAY —
CAY pappa 'child's word for food'
NSY —
CSY —
SPI [Jen. has W avaapen — for avaapa? — 'child's word when it desires food']
NAI —

WCI Cop, Car, Net aappa 'food' [Ras.]
ECI apaapa 'child's word for food'
GRI apaapa

PY-S apałuk 'words of song' [cf. apəʀ- and łuɣ]
AAY apałut 'words of a song' [archaic acc. Leer]
CAY apałuk 'stanza, lyric of dance song'
NSY apałuq 'lyrics' [ANLC; L.-T. has apałuk]
CSY apałuq 'chorus of song, reason, cause'
Sir [note apələqəlmi 'for that reason' — Vakh. from Rub.'s texts]

PY apaʀ- 'gesture to come' [cf. apəʀ-?]
AAY —
CAY —
NSY apa(ʀ)- 'gesticulate to come, lure'
CSY apaʀ- 'beckon to come' [apaqu- 'gesture, direct, instruct']

PI apcak- 'make loud noise (by pounding)'
SPI —
NAI Nu apsaktaq- 'pound repeatedly' [and note afsak- 'make a noise by falling', afsaluk- 'make a loud noise with s.th.']
WCI Car? apsaq- 'make a noise nearby (ice, ground, thunder)' [Schn. 'adg'; also nom.]
ECI atsataq- 'call by knocking s.th., drum on s.th. with fingers' [and Iti atsatauti 'drum']
GRI assaɣ- [old ortho. agsag-] 'beat (drum) to produce sound'

PE apə- 'become covered in snow' [there may be a link to apuʀ-]
AAY —
CAY ➟
NSY apə- 'become covered with snow' [and nominal apə 'snow' (ANLC)]
CSY apənʀaan 'fluffy new snow'
Sir apət- 'become covered with snow'
SPI avi-
NAI apɨ-
WCI api-
ECI api- 'become snowed in '
GRI api- 'become covered in snow' [today also just 'snow']

PI apətciq 'female polar bear's den in snowdrift'
SPI —
NAI apitciq* 'snowdrift, female polar bear which bears its young in a hollow snowdrift'
WCI apitsiuvik 'polar bear's den in the snow' [and Pryde has Cop apittiq 'birthing den of polar bear']
ECI —
GRI apissiq* 'polar bear's den in snow'

PE apun 'snow (on ground)' [cf. un]
AAY —
CAY NS apun 'snow on ground'
NSY apun 'snow on ground' [ANLC]
CSY [apumək 'soft snow or dirt']
Sir apəta 'snow'
SPI avun 'snow on ground'
NAI apun 'snow on ground' [and apuyyaq, Nu aputyaq 'snow house or shelter']
WCI apun 'snow on ground'
ECI aput 'snow on ground' [and apuyyaq 's.th. snowed in', apuyyasuq- 'shovel out from snow']
GRI aput 'snow on ground' [and apusiniq* 'snow drift', which in EG is 'glacier' acc. Ras. — Ges. has apusiq 'Inland Ice (of Greenland)'; NG apussaXXuq- 'shovel (out)']

PI apəktət- 'be fastened or fit tight?' [cf. apəŋə- and p.b. tət-]
SPI —
NAI apɨktɨt- 'be fastened or fit snugly, fasten tight'
WCI —
ECI [note apaak- 'come undone (stitches)']
GRI apissit- [old ortho. apigsit-] 'come right in so as to knock against (e.g. bottom)' [and note NG apaussaaq- 'untie, untangle', apaŋniq 'mooring rope' — Holt. also has apak- 'moor' and apak 'bollard']

PY apəŋə- 'bend or fold' [cf. apəktət-]
AAY PWS apəŋə- 'lose rigidity and bend over, drop', apəŋtə- 'fold, hem, cross legs'
CAY ap(ə)ŋə- 'bend' [for Y pəŋə- 'return to original shape after being bent' see pətɣəʀ-]
NSY —
CSY apəŋqə- 'be folded over, stooped with age', apəŋtə- 'fold'

PY-S apəʀ- 'speak' [cf. apət(ə)- and apəʀə-, though the relat. is not clear — perhaps apət(ə)- contains t-[1]]
AAY apəʀ- 'say, pronounce'
CAY apəʀ-
NSY apəʀ- 'speak, designate, mention, betray, confess', apəqəŋaq 's.th. said' [and note apətuqaq 'liar']
CSY apəʀ- 'tell, confess', apəXtuʀ- 'teach' [and apətaq 'tattletale, informer']
Sir apəʀ- 'tell' [Em. and Vakh. from Rub.'s and Men.'s texts], apəXtəʀ- 'explain, designate' [and apəʀžista 'chatterbox, liar']

PI apəʀə- 'ask' [cf. apət(ə)- and ʀqə-]
SPI aviʀi- 'ask'
NAI apiʀi-
WCI apiʀi-
ECI apiʀi-
GRI apiʀi-

PI apəqšuq- 'question' [cf. qðuʀ-]
SPI aviqšuq- 'ask (repeatedly)'
NAI apiqšuq-
WCI apiqsuq- 'question (insistently)'
ECI apiʀsu(q)- 'interrogate'
GRI apiʀšuʀ- 'question'

PY-S apət(ə)- 'ask' [cf. apəʀ-, apəʀə- and Aleut am̥at- 'ask', am̥ayaaʀ- 'ask, try to find out']
AAY K ap<ə>tə- 'ask'

CAY ap<ə>tə- 'enquire, ask question'
NSY apətə- 'ask'
CSY aaptə-
Sir apət- 'ask' [Vakh.]

PY-S apəqaʀ- 'ask (repeatedly)' [cf. qqaʀ-]
AAY C apqaʀ- 'ask' [continuative apqauʀ-]
CAY apqaʀa- 'ask about s.th.', apqauʀ- 'ask questions'
NSY apəqaʀ- 'question, interrogate'
CSY —
Sir apəqaʀ- 'ask'

PE apʀun 'trail' [cf. un; there may be a link to apəʀə-]
AAY apXun 'path, trail'
CAY apXun 'trail'
NSY —
CSY —
Sir —
SPI apqun 'path cleared through snow', Qaw 'road, well-used trail'
NAI apqun 'road, trl'
WCI apqun
ECI aqquti
GRI aqqut, EG also aqqulaq

PI apqucaaq- 'go via' [cf. caʀ-]
SPI apquzaaq- 'stop by and pick up'
NAI apqusaaq- 'travel through, experience, meet by chance'
WCI apqusaaq- 'pass s.o. on the way'
ECI aqqusaa(q)- 'pass on way, land in passing at'
GRI aqqusaaʀ- 'go via, pick up s.o. on the way'

PI apqucinəq 'trail (beaten)' [cf. li-[1] and nəʀ[1]]
SPI —
NAI [note apqusi- 'make a trail or road']
WCI apqusiniq 'trail'
ECI aqqusiniq 'road in the snow'
GRI aqqusiniq* 'beaten trail, road'

PE apummaʀ 'gunwale of kayak' [cf. apuʀ-, but also apəktət-?]
AAY apamaq 'gunwale of kayak'
CAY apamaq
NSY —
CSY —
Sir —
SPI avumaaq
NAI apummak, apummaaq 'side lathe of kayak'
WCI apummaq 'gunwale of kayak'
ECI apummaq
GRI apummak 'side lathe of kayak' [and note apuma- 'knock against', going with apuʀ-]

PE apuʀ- 'knock up against'
AAY —
CAY apuʀ- 'reach, arrive, run up against'
NSY —
CSY —
Sir [Vakh. has apuXt(ə)- 'stab' from Men.'s texts; Orr has 'get a splinter']
SPI avuq- 'meet s.o.', Qaw also 'bump into'
NAI apuq- 'bump into, reach shore'
WCI apuq- 'arrive, come across, knock into'
ECI apuq- 'bump against'
GRI apuʀ- 'knock into, run up against', apuut(i)- 'arrive'

PE apyuʀ 'smoke or haze'
AAY apsuq 'smoke'
CAY apsuq 'smoke, haze, dust in air' [apsuʀi- 'be hazy or smoky]
NSY apy̨uq 'smoke'
CSY aɣəpsuq 'smoke, steam' [and aɣəpsuʀ- 'be smoky']
Sir apy̨əX 'smoke'
SPI apyuq 'smoke, haze, mist'
NAI avyuq 'smoke, haze, mist', Mal apyuq 'dust' [verbal = 'smoke, be dusty']
WCI —
ECI —
GRI —

PE aqaɣ- 'sing to or caress (a child)'
AAY — [note aqamiɣ- 'feel lethargic' — impersonal trans. base]
CAY — [note aaqucuŋuq 'doll']
NSY [aqasaŋalʀia 'very drunk (person)' (L.-T.)]
CSY ➟
Sir aqəmaʀ- 'love, be good, beautiful, happy' [Vakh. also 'strong'; he also has aqəmaʀuʀ- 'recover, settle down, make better, cure, pacify']
SPI [Jen. has KI, W agrator- 'caress a child' — for aʀaktuq-?]
NAI aqak- 'sing to a baby'
WCI Net aqaq- 'communicate tenderly with s.o. by speech or gesture' [Briggs; Ras. has aqattuaq 'one whom one sings love songs to'; B.-S. has aq(q)auc·iaq 'made lullaby' for Car]
ECI aqaq- 'sing lullaby to baby'
GRI aqaʀ- 'caress or sing to a child' [Robbe and Menn. have EG aaʀ- 'lull baby to sleep']

PE aqaɣcuɣ- 'lull baby to sleep'
AAY —
CAY —
NSY —
CSY aXsuɣ- 'put baby down to sleep'
Sir əXsəɣ- [Orr]
SPI —
NAI —
WCI Cop aXXuk- 'put baby to sleep during the day'
ECI aʀsu(k)- 'put a baby to sleep'
GRI aqassuɣ- [old ortho. aqagsug-], aʀsuɣ- 'pet, caress'

PI aqaɣu 'tomorrow or in a while' [cf. p.b. ku, ataku under ata[2], and anaqa, though the relat. is obscure]
Yup — [but note CAY ataku 'this evening' under ata[2]]
SPI aʀaɣun 'tomorrow'
NAI aaqaɣu(n), aaqan 'wait a bit, in a while' [Jen.

has aqagu; for aannaɣu, Nu aatnaɣu in the same meaning and Barrow anaqapak 'this evening' see anaqa]
WCI aqaɣu 'tomorrow', Cop aqaɣuani 'the day after tomorrow'
ECI aqaɣuani 'the day after tomorrow', Aiv aqaɣu 'tomorrow' [and Lab aqaɣuk- 'expect to leave (e.g. tomorrow)' — also Iti acc. Saul in sense 'be leaving tomorrow']
GRI aqaɣu 'tomorrow', aqaɣuani 'the day after tomorrow' [Robbe and Menn. have ᴀʀaŋit 'tomorrow' for EG; aqaɣut- 'put off till next day']

PE aqayaɣ '(s.th.) soft and slimy' [cf. aqit-?]
AAY Kod aqayak 'algae'
CAY HBC aqak, NS aqatak 'mold or fungus on dried fish'
NSY aqayak 'green mold, slime'
CSY aqaža 'frozen layer of ice and snow over the ground'
Sir aqayəX [Orr]
SPI Qaw ᴀʀaya 'slimy mud, e.g. at creek bottom or at hot springs'
NAI aqaya, aqiya 'mud' [Ras. has the latter as 'swamp']
WCI Net aqayak [Ras.], Cop aqayait 'seaweed'
ECI aqayaq 'fine, soft slippery grass growing by rivers or hair-like seaweed'
GRI NG ᴀʀayak 'slimy seaweed' [Holt.; and note WG ayaʀᴀᴀʀ-, ayaʀᴀaɣ- 'be slimy' and shaman's word ayaʀaq 'spit' — Fab.]

PI aqci- 'have plenty' [there may be a relat. to ᴀʀcᴀʀ-]
SPI KI, W aqsi- 'have plenty' [Jen.]
NAI —
WCI Perry River aqsi- 'waste food supply' [Pryde]
ECI ᴀʀsi- 'have plenty'
GRI ᴀʀsi- 'have in excess'

PE aqə- 'kick (ball)' [cf. aqu(C)i-]
AAY — [note perhaps aqqalaʀ- 'fall or dive into water', K also 'jump (fish)']
CAY NSU aqə- 'kick' [Jen. also has for Nun]
NSY —
CSY —
Sir —
SPI ᴀʀi- 'kick (a ball)'
NAI aqɨ- 'kick' [and aqšaq- 'kick repeatedly']
WCI Perry River aqi- 'kick' [Pryde]
ECI aqi-
GRI aqi- 'kick (ball)'

PI aqšaq 'ball' [cf. ðᴀʀ and compare aŋqaq; note that the northern lights are supposed to contain the souls of the dead playing Eskimo football]
SPI aqšaq 'ball' [verbal = 'play football']
NAI aqšaaq, PH ᴀʀžaq 'ball' [for aXfaluq-, Mal aqšavaluq- 'be round' see aŋva(ʀ)-]
WCI aqsaq, aXXaq 'ball' [also 'northern lights' for Net and Car acc. Ras. — for this Jen. has aXkarniq for Cop; Cop aXXaq (shaman's language) 'weather' acc. Pryde — who also has Perry River aXXaliŋianniq 'northern lights', corresponding to Lowe's aXXaliŋiiq- 'for there to be northern lights' in Cop; Jen. has aXXarniq rather for the latter]
ECI Baffin ᴀʀsaq 'ball' [Schn.; and Tar ᴀʀsaniq, Lab atsanik, Baf ᴀʀsᴀʀniq 'northern lights']
GRI ᴀʀšaq 'ball', ᴀʀšᴀʀ- 'play football' [and ᴀʀšᴀʀniq* 'northern lights']

PE aqəðɣiʀ 'ptarmigan' [cf. Aleut ᴀʀðiika-X 'ptarmigan', though the relat. is not regular]
AAY —
CAY aqəzɣiq 'ptarmigan'
NSY aqažɣiq
CSY aqəžɣiiq
Sir aqəžɣiX
SPI ᴀʀaɣžiq
NAI aqažɣiq, Nu qažɣiq
WCI Sig aqiɣɣiq, Cop aqilɣiq 'ptarmigan' [B.-S. has Car, Net aqigzeq, but Dor. has Net aqiɬɣiq, aqižɣiq]
ECI aqiɣɣiq 'ptarmigan'
GRI aqiššiq, NG aqixxiq

PY-S aqəlqaq 'stranger or guest' [cf. aqu(C)i-?]
AAY —
CAY NS aqəɬqaq 'stranger' [and note K aqəɬquʀ- 'go from one point to another', Y aqəɬquXtə- 'fall off']
NSY aqəɬqaq 'guest'
CSY aqəɬqaq 'guest', aqəɬqaXtə- 'be a guest'
Sir aqəɬqəX 'guest, person from another tribe'

PY-S aqəstə- 'sneeze' [cf. Aleut haqiša-, haqisxa- 'sneeze' (with secondary h)]
AAY aqəsŋiiʀ-, aqəsŋaaʀ-, aqəsŋaiʀ- 'sneeze'
CAY aqəstə-, aqəsŋaaʀ-
NSY —
CSY aqəsxiiʀ-
Sir aqəsxiiʀ-

PE aqəvðiɣ 'cloudberry' [cf. EA aqamða-X 'cloudberry', also PY aqəvləʀ-?]
AAY aqaɣwik 'cloudberry'
CAY HBC aqəvyik, NS aqavzik
NSY aqpik
CSY aqavzik
Sir aqavzix
SPI aqpik
NAI aqpik
WCI aqpik
ECI aqpik
GRI —

PY aqəvləʀ- 'dangle'
AAY Kod aquɣləXtə-, AP aqəɣʷləXtə- 'hang, dangle'
CAY aqəvla-, aqəvləXtə- 'dangle, lower on a rope, be ready to penetrate sexually' [and Nun aqəvyax 'dangling ornament of wolverine fur and beads on parka']
NSY aqəvləʀ-, aqəvləXtə- 'hang' [and aqəvləʀaq 'hanging ornament on a parka' (L.-T.)]
CSY [aqəvləʀaq 'small dangling decoration on parka']

PE aqit- 'be soft'
AAY aqili- 'chew'
CAY [note Y aqixtə- 'start melting (snow)']
NSY aqitaʀaʀ- 'be soft, flabby, find oneself in a delicate situation' [ANLC; aqitaʀaq 'flabby, soft, delicate thing']
CSY —
Sir ➟
SPI aʀituužau-, Qaw aʀit- 'be soft, soak'
NAI aqit- 'be soft, tender'
WCI aqit- 'be soft', aqili- 'become soft'
ECI aqit- 'be soft', aqili- 'become soft' [and aqittuq 'lead']
GRI aqit- 'be soft', aqili- 'become soft'

PI aqilluk 'soft snow' [cf. ług(-)]
Yup — [but note AAY PWS aqiluqə- 'soften (skin by chewing, etc.)']
SPI [Jen. has KI ariluq 'slush ice']
NAI aqil^{y}l^{y}uk 'bank of deep soft snow' [Ras. has 'swamp' for Nu], aqil^{y}uqqaq, Nu aqil^{y}l^{y}uq 'soft snow'
WCI aqilluqaq 'soft snow'
ECI aqilluqaaq 'bank of soft snow after a snowfall, mixed snow and water that is thawing'
GRI aqiłłuɣ- 'have become soft (snow in spring)'

PE aqilʀuʀ '(s.th.) soft' [cf. quʀ]
AAY —
CAY K aqəlʀuXtə- 'be gelatinous'
NSY aqilʀuq 'swamp' [Ras.]
CSY —
Sir aqələłəʀaX 's.th. soft' [Vakh. from Men.'s texts]
SPI —
NAI aqil^{y}ʀuq 'soft spot'
WCI aqilʀuq Cop 'lead', Sig 'softest part of s.th. (e.g. snow to cross)' [Ras. has 'swamp' for Net, but also aqer^{t}lroq 'lead']
ECI —
GRI aqiʀłuq 'lead, tin, bullet' [Tersis has aqaʀtiq for EG]

PY aqituʀ- 'be full of food'
AAY K, KP aqituXtə- 'be or become full of food'
CAY aqituXtə- 'lack firmness of flesh (fish), be full of food'
NSY aqituXtə- 'eat one's fill, be full'
CSY —

PI aqiun 'magic song' [cf. un]
SPI aʀiun 'incantation, magic song' [Jen.]
NAI Nu aqiun 'healing song' [Jen. has this as 'magic song' also for B]
WCI Cop aqiun 'magic song' [Jen.]
ECI —
GRI —

PE aqla- 'be drafty'
AAY aqłaq 'wind', aqłaXtə-, aqłatə- 'be windy'
CAY aqłatə- 'be in motion (air), emanate odor', Nun aqłaʀniʀ- 'get windy' [and aqłayun 'fan']
NSY —
CSY aqłaʀ- 'dry up after rain (ground)', aqłaʀa 'cold air' [and aqłaʀatə- 'be cold outside']
Sir aqłaʀ- 'dry up after rain (ground)' [Orr]
SPI aqłaq- 'be a draft of air, be blown by air'
NAI aqła 'draft' [and verbal = 'be a draft'; aqłanaaq 'breeze' — also verbal]
WCI aqłak 'air or atmosphere', aqłaiq- 'make a draft', Net aqła 'wind' [Ras.]
ECI aʀsa(C)- 'be windy' [and arsaiʀaut 'fan']
GRI aʀłaarsaʀ- 'fan s.o.'

PY aqlin 'earring' [cf. aqəvləʀ-, li-^{1} and un]
AAY Kod aqłin 'earring' [and note PWS aqłi- 'dress up']
CAY aqłin, aqłitaq 'earring'
NSY —
CSY —
Inu [SPI aqlin 'dance mitten with dangling pieces of ivory' is probably borrowed from Yup]

PI aqpik- 'be encumbered (by)'
SPI aqpii- 'not want s.o. around and send him away'
NAI aqpiɣi- 'find s.o.'s presence undesirable, send away, not want', Nu aqpik- 'dislike, not want (big load in boat or sled)'
WCI aqpiɣiaɣi- [for aqpiŋiaɣi-?] 'leave to s.o. else, not want to carry s.th. oneself'
ECI —
GRI arpiŋiaɣ- 'feel encumbered by s.th.' [trans. aʀpiŋiaɣi-]

PE aqu 'stern' [cf. aqumə- and Atkan Aleut aqul(a) 'lee, behind (it)', EA aquli-X 'gate, door']
AAY PWS aqu 'stern of boat'
CAY NS aqu 'stern'
NSY aquq 'stern'
CSY ➟
Sir [note aqista 'steersman' (Vakh. from Rub., and Orr)] ➟
SPI aʀu 'stern'
NAI aqu 'back part, stern, (as posit. root) time after' [and aqulliq* 'last']
WCI aqu 'back of sled or boat, lower part of s.th.'
ECI aqu 'back part, stern'
GRI aqu, EG aʀiq 'stern' [as posit. root 'astern (of)']

PE aqut- 'steer' [cf. p.b. t-^{1}]
AAY PWS, Kod aqu(tə)-, KP aʀu(tə)- 'steer a boat'
CAY aqutə- 'be last in a race', NS 'steer a boat'
NSY aquXtə- 'steer'
CSY aquutaq 'rudder', aquutaʀ- 'to steer'
Sir [Orr has aqitaX 'rudder' (pl. aqitaʀiy) and aqit- 'steer']
SPI aʀut- 'steer'
NAI aqut- 'steer, pilot boat'
WCI aqut- 'steer'
ECI aqut-
GRI aqut-

PE aqu(ʀu)n 'rudder' [cf. un]
AAY Kod aqun, KP aʀun 'rudder'
CAY NS aqutaq

NSY aquʀun [Taghyuq]
CSY —
Sir —
SPI ᴀʀuun
NAI aquun
WCI aqu(u)n, aquut
ECI aquuti
GRI aquut

PE aqu(C)i- 'walk around' [cf. aqva-?]
AAY —
CAY aqui- 'play actively (out of doors usually)'
NSY aqui- 'walk, make one's way (e.g. on thin ice or swampy ground)'
CSY aqii- 'take a pleasure trip'
Sir —
SPI ᴀʀui- 'walk'
NAI aqui- 'travel' [Jen.]
WCI aqui- 'travel to see s.o., visit' [and Net 'go to pick up a cache of meat' acc. Pryde, Car 'fetch caribou meat in winter cached in autumn' — Ras.]
ECI aqui- 'go hunting (for several days)'
GRI NG aqui(luk)- 'go hunting at seal's breathing hole'

PE aqumə- and **aquvət-** 'sit down' [cf. aqu and vət- under vaʀ-?]
AAY aqumə- 'sit down'
CAY aqumə-
NSY aqumə- 'sit down, land (bird)'
CSY aqumə- 'sit down'
Sir — [for aqəmaʀ- 'be good, beautiful, happy', aqəmaʀuʀ- 'recover, settle down, pacify' see aqaɣ-]
SPI ᴀʀuvit-
NAI aquvit-
WCI ➟
ECI aquvit- 'squat'
GRI aquit-, aquimi- 'squat'

PY aqumɣa- 'be sitting' [cf. a-?]
AAY aqum<ɣ>a- 'be sitting'
CAY aqumɣa-
NSY aqumɣa-
CSY aqumɣa-

PY aqumkałaɣ- 'fall on buttocks'
AAY K, KP aqumqałaɣ-, PWS aqumqəłaɣ- 'sit down involuntarily or too hard'
CAY aqumkałaɣ- 'fall on buttocks'
NSY aqumkałaʀ-
CSY —

PY aqumłəq 'seat' [cf. łeʀ]
AAY aqumłəq 'chair, seat, couch'
CAY aqumłəq* 'chair, seat' [also aqumłin, aqumvik]
NSY —
CSY —

PI aqup(p)i- 'be sitting'
Yup [note CSY aqupiləʀ(yuɣ)- 'feel uneasy, be tired of asking']
SPI ᴀʀupi- 'be sitting'
NAI aquppi-
WCI aqupi- 'lie down (animal)'
ECI aqupi- 'curl up in ball (animal)'
GRI aqup(p)i- 'sit on its tail (animal)'

PE aqva- 'run' [cf. Atkan Aleut aqi-, EA iqi- 'run away', also aqui-?]
AAY aqx^{w}a- 'fetch' [half-trans. aqx^{w}atə- 'fetch s.th. (for him)']
CAY aqvə- 'run hard, in straight line', aqfa- 'fetch' [half-trans. of the latter
aqfatə-; aqfautə- 'run in a race']
NSY aXpa- 'fetch', aXpatə- 'run' [ANLC for the former]
CSY aqfaʀ- 'fetch', aqfaatə- 'run' [half-trans. of former aqfatə-]
Sir —
SPI aqpa- 'run'
NAI aqpat-
WCI Cop aqpat- [and Schn. has aqpak- 'run at a trot' for 'adg'; Ras. has Net aqpaaq- 'fetch']
ECI aqpasua-, aqpaŋiq- 'run', Lab appaŋik- 'run' [and aqpaa(q)- 'run to fetch']
GRI ᴀʀpaɣ-, EG appaC- 'run', ᴀʀpat- 'run after or for' [and Fab. has akpar- — for arpaaʀ-? — 'inform (e.g. that it is time to set off)']

PY aqvaquʀ- 'run (around)' [cf. qðuʀ-]
AAY —
CAY aqfaquʀ- 'run'
NSY aXpaquʀ- 'run on a sport track' [ANLC]
CSY aqfaquʀ- 'jog, run for excercise'

PE aq(ə)yaʀ 'belly' [cf. Aleut a(a)qaya-x, Attuan aaqiyaaya-x 'hips']
AAY aqsaq 'belly'
CAY aqsaq
NSY aqɣ̥aq [ANLC also aqɣ̥ak]
CSY aqsa
Sir aqi 'belly' [Krup. reports aqəy; note also aqɣ̥aX 'strength'?]
SPI ➟
NAI aqiaq '(upper) belly'
WCI aqiaq 'soft underbelly (just under ribs)'
ECI aqiaq '(lower) belly'
GRI aqayak 'belly'

PE aqyamuɣ '(underside of) fish belly'
AAY —
CAY aqsamuq 'outside part of fish belly'
NSY —
CSY aqsamuk 'salmon belly'
Sir —
SPI ᴀʀiamuk 'underside, belly of fish'
NAI —
WCI Cop aqiamuk 'lower belly'
ECI —
GRI —

PE aq(ə)yaquʀ 'stomach' [cf. quʀ]
AAY AP, C aqsaquq 'stomach, animal stomach used as float'

CAY aqsaquq 'stomach'
NSY aqɣ̥aquq
CSY aqsaquq
Sir aqiXqəX
SPI ariaʀuq
NAI aqiaʀuq
WCI aqiaʀuq
ECI aqiaʀuq
GRI aqayaʀuq, NG aqiaʀuq 'stomach' [NG also 'earlobe' acc. Holt.]

PY-S aʀaʀ- 'move' [there may be a relat. to aʀula-; for the voiceless fric. in CSY compare ayaʀaʀaʀ for example]
AAY —
CAY —
NSY —
CSY aaXtə-, aaXaXtə- 'move a little, budge, convince, change one's mind, be an earthquake', aaXə- 'move freely' [also aʀəłqutə- 'move a little']
Sir aʀaʀ- 'go' [within village or immediate vicinity acc. Em., who also has aʀəʀ- 'come loose', and aʀəmiqə- 'turn' — Vakh. from Rub.'s texts]
Inu [note NAI aʀyuk-, PH aʀiyuk- 'travel around, stroll'?]

PE aʀcaʀ- 'grab or otherwise act excessively' [cf. aʀli(C)-]
AAY AP aXcaʀ- 'act greedy', aXcaʀi- 'get worse' [and K (Tyzh.) aXcaqə-, aXcakə- 'cast away (Biblical — from God's presence)' and PWS aʀsakə- 'depend on'; note also aXcaq AP 'greedy!', KP 'nonsense!', PWS 'I dare you!']
CAY [note aXcaqə-, aXcakə- 'favor, consider important, treat in excessive way' and aXca 'hush, stop!']
NSY aXsaXtə- 'be greedy', aXsaʀnəq 'greedy person' [ANLC, also for aXsi- 'have plenty' and aXsaan 'softly, quietly'; Men. has aXsai- 'be plenty, acquire plenty']
CSY aXsaXtə- 'overdo, act in excessive way, annoy' [and aXsaan 'too much', also aXsaʀmətə- 'be good weather, favor']
Sir [note aXtənəX 'excess, plenty']
SPI aqsaq- 'make noise', Qaw 'be excessive'
NAI aqsak- 'grab from, cheat' [and note aqtaq- 'take away from repeatedly']
WCI [B.-S. has Car aXXaʀaq 'handle for trials of strength', Net aXXaʀaqtut 'tug-of-war' (Ras.), and Ow. has aXXaaʀaʀniq 'hand-pull game' for EP] ➟
ECI [note aqtaq- 'take back s.th. stolen or taken', also Iti aqtaq 'shaft of seal harpoon'?] ➟
GRI [EG aʀsalaaʀ- 'pull, be drafty', also aʀsi- 'possess a lot of things', aʀsi(ŋ)i- 'have too much -' (Robbe and Menn.), NG aXXaʀak 'handle for trials of strength' (as in WG aʀsaaʀutit under aʀcaaq- below), verbal aXXaʀaaq- for competing with this apparatus — Holt.]

PI aqcaaq- remove by force from (s.o.)' [cf. aʀ-?]
SPI aqsaaq- 'fight over'
NAI aqsaaq- 'grab away from, play handle-pulling game'
WCI aqsaaq- 'take away from, rob'
ECI aʀsaa(q)- 'remove by force from'
GRI aʀsaaʀ- 'take away from' [and aʀsaaʀutit, aʀsaaqqat 'two bits of wood connected by strap to test strength with', EG aʀsaaliŋaq 'strap used for test of strength' (Robbe and Menn.) — compare the NG under aʀcaʀ- above]

PY aʀ(caʀ)maɣ- or aʀ(caʀ)məɣ- 'be greedy'
AAY aXm̥əɣ- 'be greedy, a hog'
CAY —
NSY —
CSY aXm̥axtə- 'take or use all'

PE aʀða 'ash'
AAY aʀaq 'ash'
CAY aʀaq 'ash from birch fungus, used with chewing tobacco'
NSY aʀa 'medicine', aʀža 'gunpowder'
CSY aʀa 'medicine, amulet'
Sir —
SPI aʀža 'ash, gunpowder' [Jen. has also 'fireplace, coal' for W]
NAI aʀža 'ash, gunpowder'
WCI aʀya 'ash, gunpowder' [Utk aqžaq acc. Briggs]
ECI Lab ayyak 'ash' [Saul gives aʀya 'shot powder' for older Tar]
GRI aʀšat 'ash'

PE aʀənqiɣ- 'fix or arrange' [cf. nqiɣ-[1]]
AAY aʀənqiɣ-, Kod also anqiɣ- [Tyzh.] 'be opportune, handy'
CAY aʀənqiɣ- 'be or make satisfactory'
NSY —
CSY aʀənqiɣnəq* 'right hand'
Sir [note aʀənəqat- 'force to do, insist s.o. does s.th.' — Vakh. from Rub.'s texts]
SPI aaqik- 'store away'
NAI aatqik- 'straighten or make bed', PH 'stand up straight, turn over on back (whale)'
WCI Car aatqik- 'repair' [B.-S.; Schn. has aaqqisuiviksaq 'notebook for collecting faults to be corrected' for 'adg'; Met. has Cop a(a)q(q)ik- 'sweep' and Pryde has P. River aatqiktit- 'feed (dogs)']
ECI aaqqi(k)- 'cure, manage, repair', aaqqisuʀ- 'arrange, put in order'
GRI aaqqiɣ- 'fix, make or get better', aaqqiššuʀ- 'arrange, set right' [and note aaqqiak 'friend'; Ges. has EG aaqqitsivi- 'work, make' as an old word, and Ras. has aaqqissut(i)- 'invoke spirits for s.o.']

PE aʀi(t)- 'become wet' [cf. aʀu- and aʀipa-]
AAY a<ʀ>i- 'become soggy, wet'
CAY aʀi- 'get mashed'
NSY [note aʀipaXsit 'clothing' acc. Orr]
CSY aʀi- 'be, become wet'
Sir aʀimžukaʀ- 'become very wet' [Vakh. from Men.'s texts]
SPI [for aʀit- 'be soft, soak' see aqit-: there seems to be conflation here] ➟
NAI aʀit- 'become wet or damp'
WCI aʀit- 'become wet'
ECI ➟
GRI ➟

PE aʀiɬaʀ- 'be damp' [cf. la(ʀ)-?]
AAY a<ʀ>iɬaq 'steam'
CAY Nun aʀiɬa 'moisture' [verbal = 'be moist']
NSY [aʀiɬanaq 'slush, mire' (L.-T.)]
CSY —
Sir —
SPI ailaq- 'be damp' [Qaw nom. = 'moisture, dew']
NAI ail^{y}aq- 'be damp' [ail^{y}l^{y}aq 'dampness, s.th. damp']
WCI Sig ailaq- 'be damp, wet' [and nom. = 'dampness, drizzle (esp. penetrating dampness in spring)'; Ras. also has it as 'vapor, dampness' for Cop]
ECI ailaq- 'be damp (ground)' [and nom. = 'dew, drizzle, fog' in Lab acc. Peck; Boas has it as 'sweat' for Igl]
GRI aalaʀ- [old ortho. ailaʀ-], aaɬɬiʀ- 'get covered in moisture (e.g. window), sweat', aalaq 'dampness, vapor, sweat'

PE aʀinaʀ- 'be rotten or damp' [cf. naʀ-]
AAY a<ʀ>inaq 's.th. rotten or smelly (esp. food)'
CAY aʀinaq 'rotten food' [aʀinaʀ- 'be rotten']
NSY aʀinaq 'rotten odor' [ANLC]
CSY aʀinaq 'wet weather'
Sir —
SPI aʀinaq- 'become rotten, strong smelling'
NAI aʀin^{y}aq- 'be soft, damp, remain moist (meat)', PH aʀin^{y}n^{y}aq- 'be damp'
WCI Sig aʀinaq- 'be soft'
ECI Iti aʀanaq 'very soft or rotten meat'
GRI —

PY-S aʀin 'mitten' [cf. aʀʀi(t)naʀ]
AAY aʀin, Perry a'in 'mitten'
CAY aʀin, aʀiɬuk, aʀitfak 'waterproof skin mitten'
NSY aʀitfak, aʀiɬuk 'mitten' [ANLC]
CSY aʀiɬuk 'skin mitten'
Sir aʀəsikaX 'mitten' [Vakh. from Men.'s texts]

PE aʀipa- 'be raw' [cf. aʀi(t)-]
AAY —
CAY aʀipa- 'be raw, eat raw food'
NSY aʀipatə- 'be damp' [ANLC; Men. has aʀipalŋuq 'damp']
CSY aʀipa 'wetness, moisture' [and aʀipatə- 'be wet']
Sir —
SPI aipa- 'be raw' [and Jen. has aipan 'food']
NAI Mal aipa- [and NS aʀipažaq 'fresh, untanned skin']
WCI Net, Car aipa- [Pryde and Ras. respectively — the latter also has Net aip·a·t 'food' as a shaman's word]
ECI aipa- 'be half-cooked' [and Boas has aipat 'food' as a shaman's word on Baf.]
GRI aapa- 'be raw', NG aipaaq- 'not be completely cooked' [and Fab. has aipat 'food', also verbal 'eat', a shaman's word acc. Kroeber; and note EG aammaqqaaq, earlier aappaqqaaq 'blubber']

PE aʀiva- 'scold or quarrel' [cf. aʀʀi- and/or aʀyuʀ-?]
AAY AP aʀiftə- 'abuse verbally'
CAY aʀiftə- 'abuse verbally', NS aʀiva- 'argue'
NSY aʀi-, aʀitə- 'shout', aʀiva- 'quarrel, shout at' [and nom. aʀi 'scream, cry', aʀiva 'verbal abuse, bad language' (ANLC)]
CSY aʀiva- 'bawl out'
Sir — [for aʀyuXt(ə)- 'bawl out' see aʀyuʀ-]
SPI [Jen. has KI aʀavit- 'be busy'; Men. has Imaq aʀivak 'loud voice']
NAI Nu aiva- 'quarrel' [Met. has aiviluk- 'grumble']
WCI Net aiva- 'quarrel' [Pryde; Ow. has 'argue' for EP]
ECI aiva- 'quarrel'
GRI —

PE aʀli(C)- 'be overwhelmed or overburdened' [cf. aʀcaʀ-?]
AAY aXɬiaʀ- 'struggle, be loaded down' [aXɬiaq 'burden, strain']
CAY Y aʀliaʀ- 'be busy'
NSY aʀlukaxtu- 'be overwhelmed' [ANLC]
CSY aʀliiʀ(yuɣ)-, aʀliiʀnapiɣ- 'be overwhelmed'
Sir aʀliʀnəpiɣ- [Orr]
SPI —
NAI aʀlik- 'leave behind some part of a load'
WCI [Schn. has Baker Lake aʀlia(q)- 'work hard to finish job, expect to receive a bonus'; Ras. has Net aʀliŋnaq- 'make one tired of s.th.] ➟
ECI aʀli(k)- 'leave s.th. behind because it is too big for transporting, receive more than expected, be delighted', Iti 'be overwhelmed' [and Peck has for Lab aʀlik- 'for there not to be want', aʀliaq- 'have one's hands full', aʀliŋnaq- 'be great, cause surprise']
GRI aʀɬiɣ- 'make much of, exaggerate (e.g. number of seals)', aʀɬiaʀ- 'have too much to carry' [and aʀɬiaʀi- 'cannot take it along']

PI aʀliɣə- 'consider (s.th.) to be too much?' [cf. kə-^{1}]
SPI —
NAI aʀliɣɨ- 'feel bad about doing so'
WCI Cop aʀliɣi- 'be surprised at, wonder at'
ECI aʀliɣi- 'leave behind because one considers it too much or too heavy' [Peck has 'esteem as the greatest' for Lab]
GRI —

aʀli(ɣ)aq 'albatross' [loan from Aleut aʀliɣa-X 'albatross']
AAY aʀliaq 'albatross'
CAY aʀliaq, Nushagak River taʀliaq 'mew-gull, black-legged kittiwake'
NSY —
CSY —

PY aʀ(aʀ)naq 'sea otter' [cf. aʀaʀ- unless there is a link to aʀcaʀ- rather]
AAY Kod aXn̥aq 'sea otter'
CAY BB aXn̥aq
NSY —
CSY —

PE aʀnaʀ 'woman'
AAY aʀnaq 'woman' [and note AP aʀyaɣaq, Kod (archaic) aʀya<ɣ>aq 'unmarried young woman' with p.b. yaɣaq 'little']
CAY aʀnaq 'woman'
NSY aʀnaq
CSY aʀnaq
Sir ➟
SPI aʀnaq
NAI aʀnaq
WCI aʀnaq 'woman' [and note Net aʀnaktaq- 'change into an animal (shaman)' — Ras., who adds 'literally get a mother']
ECI aʀnaq 'woman'
GRI aʀnaq 'woman, (when possessed) mother' [and note aʀnaɣ- 'be possessed by a dead person', NG aʀnaktaq- 'change at will into a seal or dog' — Holt., also given in that meaning for EG by Thal.]

PE aʀnacalluʀ 'female animal' [compare aŋucalluʀ under aŋun]
AAY aʀnasaluq 'female animal'
CAY aʀnacaluq
NSY [aʀnasaluk 'pelvic bone' acc. L.-T.]
CSY aʀnasalək 'female walrus'
Sir aʀnasaləx 'female animal' [Vakh. from Rub.]
SPI aʀnazaluq
NAI aʀnasalluq
WCI —
ECI [Spalding has aʀnalluq 'female animal' for NBI — compare Tar aʀnaluk 'female bird, bitch, naughty woman']
GRI —

PY aʀnalɣun 'parallel cousin on mother's side [cf. lɣun]
AAY —
CAY —
NSY aʀnalɣun, aʀnalɣutə 'parallel cousin on mother's side'
CSY aʀnalɣun

PE aʀnalqu(C)aʀ 'old woman' [cf. lqu(C)aq]
AAY —
CAY NI, Nun, HBC aʀnałquaʀ(aq*) 'old woman'
NSY aʀəłquaʀaq 'old woman'
CSY aʀnałqʷaaq* 'old woman' [also aʀnasqʷaaq* acc. de Reuse]
Sir —
SPI aʀnaʀukšaq, Qaw aʀnatqukšaq, W aʀniʀukšaq 'old woman' [and note aʀnaʀuaq-, W aʀniʀuaq 'grow old (woman)']
NAI aaquk, aaquakšaq 'old woman' [and aaquaq-, PH aʀnaʀuaq- 'grow old (woman)']
WCI aaquaq, Sig aaquaksaq 'old woman' [and verbal aaquaq- = 'be old (woman)'], Net aʀnaqquaksa(a)q 'old woman' [Ras.]
ECI Baf aʀnaq(q)uaksaq [Boas], Igl aaquaksaaluk 'old woman' [Ras.]
GRI aʀnaqquaššaaq 'old woman' [also the mythical figure at the bottom of the sea, = sanna 'she down there' on Baffin at least]

PY aʀnaʀaq 'girl' [cf. ʀaʀ]
AAY —
CAY NSU aʀnaʀaq 'girl'
NSY aʀnaʀaq
CSY aʀnaʀaq*

PE aʀnaʀunəʀ 'man's female relative or lover' [cf. ŋu- and nəʀ[1] — compare aŋutŋunəʀ under aŋun]
AAY AP aʀnaunəq 'man's sister'
CAY Nun, HBC aʀnaunəq* 'sister'
NSY —
CSY aʀnaanəq* 'female bird, fish or seal'
Sir —
SPI —
NAI aʀnauniq* 'wife, woman along on hunting party', Nu 'female maternal parallel cousin of man'
WCI —
ECI —
GRI aʀnaaniq* 'promiscuous woman, whore', NG aʀnauniq 'female lover, wife'

PY aʀnauciq 'effeminate man' [cf. ɣuciq]
AAY KP, K aʀnauciq, PWS aʀnuuciq 'effeminate man' [old word]
CAY —
NSY aʀnaasiq
CSY aʀnaasiq

PI aʀnaviaq 'female bird' [cf. piɣ]
SPI —
NAI aʀnaviaq 'female eider duck'
WCI aʀnaviaq 'female duck'
ECI aʀnaviaq 'female bird'
GRI aʀnaviaq [pl. aʀnaviššat] 'female animal'

PE aʀniqə- 'play around sexually with women' [cf. liqə-]
AAY —
CAY aʀniqə- 'be obsessed with sex (male)'
NSY —
CSY —
Sir —
SPI aʀniʀi- 'womanize, play around sexually with a woman'
NAI aʀniqɨ-
WCI —
ECI —
GRI aʀniʀi- 'womanize', NG 'make love to (a woman)' [Holt.]

PY aʀnaʀuq 'small edible sea creature' [cf. aʀnaʀ?]
AAY —
CAY Nun aʀnauX 'small, pinkish, edible sea creature'
NSY aʀnaʀq 'edible sea creature, sea turnip' [ANLC]
CSY aʀnaʀuq 'edible sea creature found on beaches'

PE aʀʀi- 'hurry?' [cf. aʀiva- and also Aleut aXa- 'dance' if this does not go rather with aʀula-; there may be a further link to aʀli(C)-]
AAY K aʀiɣnaaʀ-, Perry aʀʀiɣnaaʀ-, C aiɣnaaʀ- 'be busy with s.th.'

CAY [for Y aʀliaʀ- 'be busy' see aʀli(C)- and for aviʀluXtə- 'make a noise' see avi(ʀ)luʀ-]
NSY —
CSY —
Sir —
SPI aʀʀi- 'celebrate, have a good time, do Eskimo dance' [and Jen. has aʀʀɨsuk- 'hurry']
NAI aʀʀi- 'do Inupiaq dance'
WCI Net aʀʀi- 'play (in song)' [Pryde]
ECI aʀʀi- 'flow quickly down (blood from wound, water from roof)' [and aʀʀitit- 'make move rapidly', aʀʀiit- 'make move slowly, irregularly']
GRI aXXi- 'be in a hurry' [and aXXiit- 'be slow', southern SWG aXXi-, EG aqqi- 'be homesick' — perhaps influenced by aʀ(ə)yu-]

PE aʀʀi(t)naʀ 'bag for hunting' [cf. aʀin and naʀ]
AAY —
CAY Y, HBC, NS aʀʀinaq 'sealskin hunting bag'
NSY aʀikŋ̥aažaq 'pocket', aʀikŋ̥aq 'bag for hunting' [ANLC]
CSY aʀin^{w}aaq 'sealskin bag holding articles used to ensure good whale hunting' [influenced by aɣanʀu(Caʀ)]
Sir —
SPI aʀʀinaq, Qaw aʀʀitnaq 'sealskin hunting bag'
NAI aʀʀin^{y}n^{y}aq 'knapsack, bag for hunting gear'
WCI Sig aʀʀinaq 'traveling bag'
ECI —
GRI —

PE aʀtuʀ- 'be unable' [cf. aʀli(C)- and aʀ(ə)yu-?]
AAY aXtunaʀ- 'be heavy' [aXtunaq 'weight']
CAY aXtuʀ- 'be unable to handle or manage' [aXtuʀnaXqə- 'be unmanageable']
NSY aXtuʀ- 'not be able'
CSY aXtuʀ- 'be unable to bear or withstand'
Sir aXtəʀ- 'not be able' [Vakh.]
SPI aqtuq- 'be unable to manage, lack strength to move'
NAI aqtuq-
ECI aqtuq 'fat, heavy (person or animal)', Igl, Lab aqtuq- 'cannot manage or move' [Ras., Bourq.]
GRI artuʀ- 'cannot manage or move' [artuʀnaʀ- 'be difficult, impossible'; Tersis has aʀtiʀ- 'be heavy, difficult' for EG]

PE aʀu- 'rot' [cf. aʀi(t)-?]
AAY aʀu- 'rot'
CAY aʀu- 'rot, ripen'
NSY aʀu- 'rot' [ANLC; Men. has aʀunalʀia 'rotten']
CSY aʀu- 'rot'
Sir aʀə-
SPI au-
NAI au- 'rot, decay (tooth, wood, ice, etc.)'
WCI au- 'be rotten, suppurate (wound)'
ECI au- 'be rotten' [and auma- 'be soft']
GRI aa- 'be rotten', NG au- 'go off, spoil (food)' [and note aʀuma-, aʀama- 'swelter, be immobile from the heat']

PI auk- 'melt' [cf. aðuɣ for probable source of contamination here]
Yup — [but compare PY uʀuɣ- 'melt' under uʀə-]
SPI auk- 'melt, thaw' [homophonous with 'bleed' under aðuɣ; auksiq- 'thaw']
NAI auk- 'melt' [different from a<ž>uk- 'bleed'; auksiq, auksiaq- 'warm oneself up']
WCI auktuq- 'melt, thaw' [Pryde; auksiq- 'warm oneself up']
ECI auk- 'melt, thaw' [autsa(q)- 'thaw, warm self up (with hot drink)']
GRI aaɣ- 'melt, thaw' [and note aXXuʀ- 'dissolve' and NG aunaʀi(tsiq)- 'warm up']

PI aunəq 'rotten ice' [cf. nəʀ[1]; the forms with double n may contain liʀ-]
SPI Qaw auniq 'rotten ice, rotten part of s.th.'
NAI aunɨq* 'rotten area of s.th.', aunniq* 'rotten ice' [also auniq- 'melt, become unsafe (ice)']
WCI auniq 's.th. rotten'
ECI aunniq 'ground uncovered by melting snow in spring' [and Iti auniq- 'rot']
GRI aanniʀšaq 'hole caused by current'

PI aupkaʀnəq 'ice that has been melted through' [cf. vkaʀ- and nəʀ[1]]
SPI aupka(ʀ)niq 'hole where sea ice has melted through'
NAI aupkaʀnɨq*
WCI —
ECI aukkaniq 'stretch of unfrozen water (autumn) or melted sea ice (spring)'
GRI aakkaʀniq* 'ice cut by currents, hole in ice' [aakkaʀ- 'be cut by currents (ice)']

PI aužaq 'summer'[cf. ðaʀ-?]
SPI —
NAI Mal aužaq 'summer'
WCI auyaq
ECI auyaq- 'thaw, become summer', Iti, Lab, NBI, SB auyaq 'summer'
GRI aašaq 'summer' [aašaʀ- 'become summer']

PE aʀula- 'move' [cf. aʀaʀ-; for Aleut aXa- 'dance' see aʀʀi-]
AAY aʀula-, aula- 'move, shake, sway'
CAY aʀula- 'move, be loosely attached' [aʀulaq 'men's Eskimo dance']
NSY aʀula- 'rock, sway'
CSY aʀula- 'rock back and forth, dance Eskimo style' [for aʀəɬqutə- 'move a little' see aʀaʀ-]
Sir aʀulanʀuʀ- 'dance' [and Vakh. has arəɬmiqə- 'wave'; Orr has aʀəlmiqaʀ- 'shake']
SPI aula- 'move about'
NAI aula- 'move about'
WCI aula- 'move'
ECI aula- 'move, have gone on a journey'
GRI aala- 'move about'

PE aʀula(ŋ)iʀ- 'stop' [cf. ŋiʀ-]
AAY K aʀulaiʀ-, KP auliiʀ-, PWS aʀuliiʀ- 'stop'
CAY aʀulaiʀ-
NSY aʀulaiʀ- 'stop' [ANLC]
CSY aʀuliiʀ-
Sir —
SPI aulaiq-
NAI —
WCI —
ECI [aulaikkaq 's.th. immobile']
GRI [aalaakkaa- 'be steady, stand firm']

PE aʀulat- 'stir or move' [cf. t-[1]]
AAY a<ʀ>ulatə- 'cause to move back and forth, shake, sway', PWS also 'take charge of'
CAY aʀulatə- 'stir'
NSY aʀulatə- 'shake, wave, move'
CSY aʀulatə- 'shake'
Sir —
SPI —
NAI aulat- 'move, be in charge of'
WCI [note aulatsi- 'fish with a fising line']
ECI aulat- 'govern'
GRI aalat- 'shake, move, stir'

PE aʀullaʀ- 'leave' [cf. ʀ- under ŋ(ŋ)uʀ-]
AAY aʀulaXtə- 'run away'
CAY —
NSY aʀulaXqə- 'gather greens' [aʀulaXquq 'gathered greens' (L.-T.)]
CSY aʀulaqə- 'leave', aʀulaXquʀ- 'go and gather greens'
Sir aʀəlaʀ- 'leave', aʀəlaʀət(ə)- 'take away' [and aʀəłəktətiłəX 'displacement, shift'; Vakh. also has aʀəlaq(ə)- 'leave' from Men.'s texts]
SPI aulaʀi- 'leave', aulaq- 'go berry gathering'
NAI aullaq- 'leave' [aullai- 'have s.th. go out of one's control, accidently fire (gun)']
WCI aullaq- 'leave'
ECI aulla(q)-
GRI aałłaʀ- 'leave' [aałłaa- 'shoot', with ði-]

PI aulacaq- 'jig for fish' [cf. caʀ-]
SPI aulazaq- 'jig for fish'
NAI aulasaq-
WCI Car aulahaq- [Pryde]
ECI aulasaq- 'fish through ice'
GRI aalisaʀ- 'fish' [and aalisaɣaq, Maniitsoq aalasaɣaq 'fish' (acc. R. Petersen for the latter), EG aalisaʀ̃aq 'cod']

PI aulait- 'be whole' [cf. ŋit-]
SPI aulait- 'be complete, whole'
NAI aulait- 'be whole, uncut' [aulailʸaq 'whole, complete']
WCI Sig aulait- 'be whole'
ECI —
GRI [aalaŋŋaat 'whole, unbroken', aalaŋŋit- 'be firm, untouched']

PI aulay(y)aŋiq- 'stop moving' [cf. aulayyak- below and ŋiʀ-]
SPI —
NAI aulay(y)aiq- '(cause to) become motionless or secure'
WCI —
ECI aulayaiq- 'be unable to move, make immobile'
GRI aalayaŋiʀ- 'be motionless, fix, decide'

PI aulayyak- 'be in motion' [cf. ya- and k- under nəɣ-?]
SPI Qaw aulayak- 'move, cause to move'
NAI aulayyak- 'begin to move, come free, budge'
WCI Cop aulayyaaq- 'be unsteady, shaky' [Pryde]
ECI aulayya(k)- 'begin to stir, move, start'
GRI aalassaɣ- [old ortho. aulagsag- but Fab. has auleisak-] 'become agitated, restless (sea)', make sudden movement and dive (seal)'

PI aullaaq- 'travel (out to camp)' [cf. aʀullaʀ- above and aʀ-]
SPI aullaaq 's.o. out picking berries or greens'
NAI aullaaq- 'go camping'
WCI Cop, Net aullaaq- 'leave with all one's gear, make a long trip' [Pryde]
ECI aullaaq- 'go a long distance, go to summer camp' [aullaat 'travelers, people moving']
GRI aałłaaʀ- 'travel in a group, move out with family, move to summer camp'

PI aullaʀniq- 'begin' [cf. aʀullaʀ- above, nəʀ[1] and liʀ-]
SPI aula(ʀ)nii- 'begin'
NAI aullaʀnii-
WCI —
ECI —
GRI aałłaʀniʀ- 'begin' [aałłaʀniivik 'starting point']

PY aʀuqə- 'distribute shares of catch'
AAY —
CAY aʀuqə- 'distribute shares of a catch or gifts'
NSY aʀuqə- [ANLC]
CSY aʀuqə-

PE aʀuvəʀ(aʀ) 'roof beam or pole?' [for the old p.b. here compare taŋpəq]
AAY —
CAY —
NSY —
CSY aʀvəʀaɣətaq 'pole in center of house'
Sir aʀvəʀaX 'roof'
SPI [Jen. has W avva 'roof beam']
NAI —
WCI auviq 'snow block' [but Sig 'pole' acc. Pet., Net 'roofing timber, pillar, bone' acc. Ras.]
ECI auviq 'snow block for building house' [Lab 'roof rafter' acc. Peck; Ras. has Igl shaman's word auviʀaksaq 'bone']
GRI aaviq* 'piece of timber for roofing' [aaviʀ- 'put roofing timber on (house)']

PE arvaɣ 'edge of hand' [cf. arvir-]
AAY ➡
CAY Nun, HBC arvak 'palm of hand'
NSY ➡
CSY arvak 'edge of hand away from thumb'
Sir arvax [Orr]
SPI [Jen. has KI, W arvaq 'outer edge of hand']
NAI arvak 'edge of hand, fleshy part of palm, balls of fingers and thumb']
WCI arvait 'edge of one's fingers'
ECI ➡
GRI arfak, arfaq 'outer edge of hand'

PE arvin(ə)ləɣ 'six' [cf. li-[1], nər[1] and ləɣ?; counting above five begins by shifting across to the edge of the second hand in traditional counting; 'seven' and 'eight' in the oldest system were probably malruɣnəŋ arvinələɣ and piŋayunəŋ arvinələɣ, with respectively malruɣ and piŋayut, as in NSY today (and Sig malruŋnik arvinilik, piŋasunik arvinilik acc. Dor.); it is possible that the GRI and old Lab forms for 'sixteen' given below reflect the original PE form for this number, with akimiɣar 'fifteen' under aki(-) a neologism from the west — compare Lab arviqtaq- under arvir- though the p.b., may be ta- rather than ðar-]
AAY arwinlən 'six'
CAY arvinləɣən
NSY arvinələk
CSY arvinlək
Sir arvinilit
SPI arvinilik [Men. has arviŋilik for Imaq.]
NAI —
WCI arvinilik 'six' [and note Net qulit arviŋmat 'eleven' acc. Dor.]
ECI Baffin arvinilik, Aiv arviniqtuq 'six' [Dor.; note Peck has arvaŋat 'six' and arviqtaŋat 'sixteen' for Lab.]
GRI arfiniłłit, NG arviniɣlit 'six' [arfirsaniłłit, EG appasirniq 'sixteen' — Gessain et al. arpirsarnattit, also arpiniq 'six' (arpiittit in Robbe and Dorais)]

PE arvər 'whale (bowhead)' [compare the second syllable of ayvər; the CSY form in brackets may represent a clue to the origin of the base]
AAY arwəq, arwaq, arruq 'bowhead whale'
CAY arvəq*
NSY arvəq 'whale'
CSY arvəq* 'whale' [note also arvəqutə- 'plunge, fall forward']
Sir arvəX 'whale'
SPI arviq 'bowhead whale'
NAI arviq* 'bowhead whale'
WCI arviq 'bowhead whale'
ECI arviq, Lab affik
GRI arfiq* 'whale', EG arpiq 'whale, Greenland (bowhead) whale'

PE arəvcaɣ 'bowhead whale' [or arvəmcaɣ — cf. mcaɣ-?]
AAY —
CAY —
NSY arəfsak, arvəsak 'bowhead or Greenland whale' [ANLC - Men. has arəfsaq]
CSY arvəsak 'large (bowhead) whale' [and arvəsiiq 'humpback whale']
Sir —
SPI aapsak 'bowhead whale'
NAI PH aapsavak 'large whale'
WCI —
ECI —
GRI —

PI arvak- 'catch a whale' [cf. k- under nəɣ-]
SPI arvak- 'catch a whale'
NAI arvak-, PH arvaaq-
WCI [note Cop arviq- 'catch a whale']
ECI —
GRI arfaɣ- 'catch a whale'

PE arvəpiɣ 'bowhead whale' [cf. piɣ]
AAY —
CAY —
NSY arvəpik 'bowhead whale'
CSY arvəpik
Sir arvəpix
SPI —
NAI —
WCI —
ECI —
GRI arfivik 'Greenland (bowhead) whale'

PI arvərluaq 'gray whale'
SPI arvaluaq 'gray whale'
NAI arvɨrluaq 'gray whale'
WCI —
ECI —
GRI —

PE arvətu(C)ar 'porpoise (or dolphin)' [compare the ending of iŋutur?]
AAY —
CAY —
NSY arvətuaq 'porpoise'
CSY Chap arvətuq [on Men.'s comp. list; and note arvəŋəXtaq 'porpoise']
Sir [note arvəqəŋəstaX 'porpoise' on Men.'s comp. list]
SPI [Imaq arvətuaq 'gray whale' probably from the NSY]
NAI arvisuaq 'porpoise' [with unexplained s]
WCI —
ECI —
GRI —

PE arvir- 'cross over' [cf. arvaɣ and p.b. lir-?]
AAY arwir- 'cross over'
CAY arvir-
NSY arvir-
CSY arvir-
Sir arvər-
SPI arvi(q)taq- 'go in and out, pace back and forth'
NAI PH arviqtaq- 'pace back and forth'

WCI aʀviq- Cop 'go on a visit' [Ras.], Sig 'go over a portage' [Met.; Jen. has aʀviqtaqtiʀluaq for Cop 'seal that goes from one hole to another']
ECI aʀvitaq- 'prowl about' [and aʀvitaqtuq 'a child who goes here and there all around', Lab affitak- 'go from place to place' — Bourq. aʀviqtaq- 'wander about']
GRI NG aʀviq- 'go visiting'

PE aʀ(ə)yu- 'be tired or homesick' [cf. aʀtuʀ-, aʀyuʀ- and iyaŋa-, though the relat. is obscure]
AAY AP aʀyu- 'become worn down, ready to collapse', PWS aʀyuʀ(yuɣ)- 'be homesick'
CAY ➟
NSY ➟
CSY aʀyuʀ- 'get old, age'
Sir aʀyuʀ- 'get old' [Vakh.]
SPI aʀiu- 'tire of s.th.'
NAI aʀiu- 'stop, die after lengthy illness, have nothing more to do with'
WCI Perry River aʀiu- 'be tired of' [Pryde — Jen. has it as 'stop' in Cop; Car? aʀiuk- 'play at remaining slumped down' — Schn. 'adg'; for Sig yaʀa- 'be tired' see iyaŋa-]
ECI aʀiu- 'be rejected by loved one', aʀiuk- 'reject' [Saul has aʀiut- 'reject'; note also ariuniku 's.th. discarded']
GRI aʀayuɣ- [Eg. has aʀiu(t)-] 'have become tired of s.th., go down and stay down (whale)', NG aʀiu- (trans. aʀiut-) 'not like, be tired of s.th.', EG aa(y)ii- 'have had enough of, be tired of' [the latter Robbe and Menn.; note also aʀayutsi- 'not notice'; for aXXi- 'be homesick' see aʀʀi-]

PY-S aʀyuqə- 'be homesick for' [cf. kə-[2]]
AAY PWS aʀyuqə- 'be homesick for'
CAY aʀyuqə-, iʀyuqə- 'be glad to see s.o. after a long time'
NSY aʀyuqə- 'miss, be homesick, be bored'
CSY aʀyuqə- 'be homesick, tired of s.th.'
Sir aʀyəqə- 'miss, be bored' [listed as aʀyiqə- in Men.; Orr has the form given here, and Em. has aʀyiqə(s)-]
Inu [for EG aqqi- 'be homesick' see aʀʀi-]

PY-S aʀyuʀ- 'scold' [cf. aʀ(ə)yu- but also aʀiva- — contam.?]
AAY —
CAY Nun aʀyua- 'scold'
NSY —
CSY aʀyuuʀ- 'scold'
Sir aʀyuXt(ə)- 'bawl out' [Vakh. from Men.'s texts]

PY asiɣaʀnaq 'white whale' [cf. naʀ]
AAY AP asi<ɣ>aʀnaq 'white whale'
CAY LI, BB, Eg asiɣaʀnaq
NSY —
CSY —

PY asiʀ- 'be good' [cf. perhaps ata- and liʀ- and compare CAY asiʀnəq under aciʀnəʀ (at(ə)-), but note SPI azitnaq- 'be bad' under aci[2], also PI sets aciu- and aciʀuq- there — the relationship is obscure]
AAY asiʀ- 'be good' [and asiitə- 'be bad', asii'aXtə- 'ruin, break, make angry']
CAY asiʀ- 'be good' [and asqiɣ- 'be right, satisfactory' (with p.b. kig-), aspiaʀ- 'be excellent', asiitə- 'be bad']
NSY —
CSY [for asiʀ- 'be tied in bundle' see ata-]

PY asikə- 'like' [cf. kə-[1]]
AAY asikə- 'like'
CAY asikə-
NSY —
CSY —

PY as(q)iɣtə- 'dance' [cf. CAY asqiɣ- under asiʀ-?]
AAY Kod asqixtə- 'make dancing motions, sway to music'
CAY Nun asixtə- 'dance Eskimo style', HBC axixtə- 'dance vigorously' [and note asqiɣ- 'be satisfactory, right' under asiʀ-]
NSY —
CSY —
Inu — [but note NAI asiq- 'nod head while watching others dance']

PE at(ə)- 'down' [cf. aci[1] and Aleut ac-a 'the lower part of it' (with the regular reflex of at- before a), atmuðaʀan 'downward' and ay̥u-x 'buttocks' (from *atyu-x); the Yup forms go more directly with aci[1] but compare atəqaʀ and note that *tət goes to cət in Alaskan Yup, NSY and HBC sit, so the combinations with tmən, tmun given below may be a clue as to the origin of the former]
AAY [note acitm̥ən 'down' from aci with allative case variant tm̥ən on posit. roots] ➟
CAY [note acitm̥un 'down', acitm̥uXtə- 'go downward', also K asiŋaq 'sled runner' and asipaq, asipek 'cutting board']
NSY [note asitm̥un 'down' — from *atətmun?; also aspik 'anvil', ašpiɣaq 'saucer, s.th. put under s.th. else']
CSY [note asitm̥un 'down'] ➟
Sir [note asəmənu 'down' from asəX '(area) down' under aci[1] — Vakh. has asitm̥un, from CSY?] ➟
SPI at(i)- 'area below' [posit. root; atmun 'downward']
NAI at(ɨ)- 'area below' [anmun 'down']
WCI at(i)- 'area below' [anmun 'down']
ECI at(i)- 'area below' [ammut 'down']
GRI at(i)- 'area below' [ammut 'down']

PY aciɣtaq or **asiɣtaq** 'tray or s.th. put underneath' [cf. atcik- below?]
AAY K acixta, acixtaq 's.th. put underneath, foundation'
CAY asixtaq 'vessel, tray, boat'
NSY asixtaq 'bottom item in a stack' [ANLC]
CSY —
Sir [note asəŋiɣətaX 'underlayer']

PE aciʀnəʀ 'underside' [cf. liʀ- and nəʀ[1]]
AAY PWS aciʀnəʀ- '(its) underside'
CAY asiʀnəq*, HBC aciʀnəq* 'sled runner, bottom of boat or other vessel' [for K asiŋaq 'sled runner' see at(ə)- above]

NSY —
CSY —
Sir —
SPI —
NAI asiʀn^{y}ɨq* 'bent bow of sled, snowshoe tip'
WCI —
ECI —
GRI asiʀniq* 'eaves of roof'

PI ataaq- 'go down (toward coast)' [cf. ðaʀ-?]
SPI Qaw ataaq- 'travel downriver'
NAI ataaq- 'travel downriver' [and ataaqtuq- 'be out whaling, camped on ice', PH 'move down to beach to hunting camp (inland people)'; note also Nu atažžatmun 'downriver']
WCI Cop, Net ataaq- 'come to coast from interior' [Pryde]
ECI ataaq-
GRI ataaʀ- NWG 'ski (down)', Maniitsoq 'come down to coast from hunting caribou inland'

PY atatak or **atatək** 'salt-water duck?'
AAY K, KP atatak, PWS atata<ʀ>aq 'grebe, small loon (?)'
CAY Nun atatək 'salt-water duck'
NSY —
CSY —

PI atcik- 'be far down' [cf. ðiɣ-, also perhaps aciɣtaq above]
SPI Qaw assik-, FR atcik- 'be low'
NAI atcik- 'be far down, be deep or low, be humble'
WCI atsik- 'be far down or low'
ECI —
GRI atsiɣ- 'be low (down)'

PE atəʀ- 'go down (to shore)'
AAY atəʀ- 'go out (to sea, etc.)'
CAY Nun, NS atəʀ- 'go down'
NSY atəʀ- 'go down' [ANLC has atəX- 'get down, slip down, make a move, visit another house, come to wrestle']
CSY atəʀ- 'go down'
Sir atəʀ- 'go down' [Vakh. and Orr; Em. has 'go down from ice floe into water (sea mammal)']
SPI atiq- 'go down to shore'
NAI atɨq- 'go down after hunting inland, go out to whaling camp on ice' [and atɨqtaq 'one-year-old polar bear cub (brought down to coast by mother)']
WCI atiq- 'hunt seals' [and B. Lake atiqtuq 'first caribou after winter' — Dor.]
ECI atiq- 'come down to sea (bear)' [also of people going to greet arriving boats, acc. Saul; for Igl Ras. has 'go out on ice']
GRI atiʀ- 'go down' [atiʀtaq 'polar bear cub']

PY atəʀtə- 'drift (out to sea)' [cf. atəʀ- above and t-[1]]
AAY atəXtə- 'drift (out)'
CAY atəXtə- 'drift (with current)'
NSY atəXtaaʀ- 'drift' [ANLC]
CSY [atəXtə- 'take down']

PE atətu- 'be wide below' [cf. tu-[1]]
AAY —
CAY atəxtu- 'be deep (net)'
NSY —
CSY aastu- 'be wide'
Sir astəvalaX 'wide thing' [Orr]
SPI atitu- 'be far down (open water from shore)'
NAI atɨtu- 'be far out or down (lead or open water)'
WCI at(t)itu- 'be wider below' [opp. = at(t)ikit-]
ECI —
GRI atitu- 'have wide lower part (e.g. isthmus), be broad in proportion to height' [opp. = atikit-]

PE atliqaʀ 'underlayer or s.th. put underneath' [cf. atliʀ below and qaʀ]
AAY ałiqaq 'mattress, s.th. to lie on'
CAY ałiqaq 's.th. used as working surface'
NSY ałiqaq 'bowl, vessel'
CSY —
Sir —
SPI Qaw ałłiʀaq 'pad, willow twig tent floor' [KI ałłiaq found below under atliʀaʀ may in fact belong here.]
NAI alliʀaq 'bottom skin of bedding' [and alliʀaužaq 'saucer']
WCI Car? alliʀaq 'big plate' [Schn. 'adg']
ECI alliʀaq 'carpet, anything for putting things on'
GRI — [for ałłiaq 'foundation, underlayer' see atliʀaʀ below]

PE atliʀ 'lower thing' [cf. p.b. l(l)iʀ]
AAY atłiq, aciqłiq 'lower one or part' [note aci[1] for the second, presumably newer form with related p.b. qliʀ]
CAY atłiq*, Y acłiq* 'thing underneath, cellar, saucer'
NSY —
CSY [note asiliq 'one below' and asiliqutaq 's.th. put under to raise, base' from aci[1]]
Sir [for asiX 'lower one' (Em.) see aci[1], though it may belong here]
SPI ałłiq 'bottom one'
NAI alliq*, Mal atliq*
WCI Sig alliq 'bottom one' [Ras.; Pryde has alliqutak 'saucer', also Cop a(a)lliniq 'mattress']
ECI alliq 'the lower of two'
GRI ałłiq* 'lower (esp. lower of two lamps in trad. house)' [and ałłiqutaq 'tray, foundation', NG alliniq 'mattress]

PE atliʀaʀ 'bedding' [cf. atliʀ above and aʀ]
AAY AP ałiʀaq, Perry, Kod, PWS ałi<ʀ>aq, KP ałiʀaaq 'hide with fur on used for sleeping on'
CAY ałiʀaq 'insole, mattress, bedding skin'
NSY ałiʀaq 'bedding'
CSY ałiʀaq 'mattress'
Sir —
SPI ałłiaq 'mat'
NAI alliaq, Nu atliaq 'floor made of willow twigs, etc.'

WCI Net alliaq 'mattress' [Pryde, who also has a(a)lliaq 'sledge (runner)' for Cop — Lowe has alliak 'sled']
ECI alliaq 'mattress (esp. of twigs)'
GRI ałłiaq 'foundation, underlayer (to lie on)', EG attiaʀut 'mattress of twigs'

PY atnəq 'cape' [cf. atəʀ- above and nəʀ[1]]
AAY —
CAY atŋ̥əq* 'Cape Darby (place name)'
NSY atŋ̥əq 'cape' [ANLC — Men. has akneq]
CSY aatŋ̥əq* 'slope near beach, land extending into water', atŋ̥əʀaq 'cape'
Inu [note Qaw place name Atniq 'Cape Darby', from the Yup]

PI atpaq- 'go down or sink' [cf. vaʀ-]
SPI atpazik- 'be located far down'
NAI atpaq-, ažvaq- 'go down'
WCI atpaq- 'go down, sink, lower'
ECI appa(q)- [older akpaq-] 'go down, sink' [and Lab appai- 'sleep profoundly, be dead' — Bourq.]
GRI appaʀ- 'go down, sink' [Fab. akpak- 'go down', akpai- 'lose one's breath by fainting or dying', the latter appaa- 'die of a heart attack' in Oqaatsit]

PE atʀanələɣ 'eleven' [cf. atʀaʀ- below, nəʀ[1] and ləɣ: the reference is to moving down to the toes in the traditional counting system; the truncating form of nəʀ[1] here may be due to analogy from aʀvin(ə)ləɣ under aʀvaɣ — compare also GRI isikkaniłłit under itəɣaʀ (itəɣ)]
AAY [note atXaXtuq 'eleven' in old sources such as Lis.]
CAY —
NSY atXanələk 'eleven' [and malʀuɣnəŋ atXanilək 'twelve', piŋayunəŋ atXanilək 'thirteen']
CSY —
Sir — [but note unɣamu 'eleven', from demonstrative root unəɣ- also refering to 'down']
SPI Imaq atqanələk 'eleven' [prob. borrowed from NSY]
NAI —
WCI Net Utku atqanʀat, Car atqaniq 'eleven' [B.-S.; Dor. has atqaŋaq for B. Lake]
ECI Aiv atqanilit 'eleven' [Schn.; Lab aqqaŋat 'eleven' — Peck, for atqanʀat, an old form acc. Dor.]
GRI aqqaniq*, aqqaniłłit 'eleven'

PE atʀaʀ- 'go down' [cf. p.b. aʀ-, also perhaps Aleut asXa- 'die']
AAY atXaʀ- 'go down'
CAY atXaʀ-
NSY atXaʀ- [Taghyuq]
CSY atXaʀ-
Sir atXaʀ- 'go down' [Vakh. also 'go away']
SPI atqaq- 'go down'
NAI atqaq-
WCI atqaq- 'go down'
ECI aqqa(q)- 'descend, dive down'
GRI aqqaʀ- 'descend'

PE ata[1] 'father' [cf. ata(a)ta and Aleut aða-X 'father', though the Aleut ð ~ Esk. t correspondence here is not regular — compare however ciðu- under citu-]
AAY ata 'father'
CAY ata, aata
NSY ata
CSY ata
Sir ata
SPI ata
NAI —
WCI —
ECI [Andersen et al. have ataa 'saying 'dad' 'for Lab]
GRI aatak, aataq 'grandfather'

PY atakaq 'stepfather' [cf. kðaʀ]
AAY —
CAY —
NSY ataxkaq 'stepfather'
CSY atakaXqaq

PY atalɣun 'parallel cousin on father's side' [cf. lɣun]
AAY —
CAY —
NSY atalɣun 'parallel cousin on father's side'
CSY atalɣun

PE ataʀ[2] 'listen (exclamation)'
AAY ata 'let's see, listen, excuse me' [and K atam 'you see, but then, and yet']
CAY ata, ata'a, atak(i) 'let me see, well then' [and atam 'look!', atata 'later on']
NSY — [ataw 'any way' is from Chukchi ataw 'on purpose', also atawqun 'all the same']
CSY aatak, aataqun 'do it, give it a try!' [also aataw — from Chukchi — and atax^{w}a 'you know, you see']
Sir ataqun 'now' [also ataw 'now' and atam ataw 'sure' — from Chukchi, as is probably the p.b. qun, found also in CSY; Vakh. has ata 'well then']
SPI ata 'don't do that!', W 'move!' [and Imaq has ataw 'not in vain' — from CSY? — and ata(a)ka 'now']
NAI atta, Nu ata(a) 'listen, be quiet', Nu ataŋ 'look!' [and atakkii 'because', ataxii 'oh, look at that!']
WCI ata 'listen, be quiet' [and Net atai 'go ahead, let's go' — Pryde; Ras. has atatau 'take care' for Cop]
ECI atai, atii 'go ahead!'
GRI ata 'listen, be quiet!'

PE ataku 'let's see?' [cf. ku]
AAY —
CAY ataku 'this evening' [compare aqaɣu for the meaning — contam.?]
NSY —
CSY — [note aataqun under ata[2] above]
Sir — [note ataqun above]
SPI Qaw ataɣum, atuɣum, Imaq ataɣun 'hey look!'
NAI ataɣuna 'look at this, give it to me!'
WCI Cop ataɣu 'look out!' [Pryde]
ECI attaɣu 'let's go!'
GRI ataɣu 'listen, let's see now' [Fab. has atuɣu(t); NG atu(ɣ)ulu 'more!' — Holt.]

PE ata- 'be attached or persisting' [cf. Atkan Aleut ataqi-X, EA atiqi-X 'end part of kayak keel'; the Inu forms with a geminate may be secondary]
AAY ata- 'become attached'
CAY ata- 'be attached, dependent' [and atax^{w}a 'benefit', ataXtə- 'copulate'; compare also PY asiʀ-]
NSY ata- 'be kept or contained in s.th.' [ANLC — Men. has 'consist in']
CSY [note asiʀ- 'be tied in bundle' — with p.b. liʀ- attached to a nominalized form *at(t)aq?]
Sir [asiqəlmi 'tied together' — Vakh. from Men.'s texts; for atinaX 'together' see atunəm] ➟
SPI atta- 'be attached', ataniq 'isthmus, attached thing' [and note Qaw attaiq- 'be cute']
NAI ata- 'be attached' [and atažamik 'continually']
WCI ata- 'be attached' [and Car ataniq 'portage' — B.-S.; Met. has ataʀamik 'always' for Sig, corresponding to Cop atayumik in Pryde]
ECI ata- 'adhere, be attached, be faithful' [and perhaps atauq 'that's good!' unless this goes with ata[2]]
GRI ata- 'be attached, persist, manage' [and ataqqi- 'honor', ataniq* 'coherence, watershed (in place-names)', attaʀmik 'together']

PE atanəʀ 'boss' [cf. nəʀ[1]]
AAY atanəq* 'boss, lord'
CAY atanəq
NSY atanəXtaq 'elder' [ANLC, also for atanəq 'crescent moon, root of plant or of family, horizontal beam of ceiling']
CSY atanəq* 'boss, leader, lord' [Chap also 'head of family']
Sir atanəX 'boss, beam (wooden)' [and see under ata- above]
SPI ataniq 'boss, lord, foundation post' [and see under ata- above]
NAI ataniq* 'boss'
WCI ataniq 'boss' [but see Car ataniq above]
ECI ataniq 'king'
GRI — [see above for ataniq]

PI attan 'means for holding s.th. together' [cf. un]
SPI —
NAI —
WCI attavik, Cop attat 'hinge' [Pryde for the latter]
ECI [note atauti 'support']
GRI attat 'button, splint, means to hold s.th. together' [and attataq 's.th. attached']

PI attaq- 'pay back (in return)'
SPI attaun 'salary', attausiq- 'pay, salary'
NAI attaqsi- 'borrow', attausiq- 'pay'
WCI —
ECI attatuq-, Lab attasik- 'borrow'
GRI attaʀtuʀ- 'borrow, rent', NWG attaat 'compensation for loan, interest, duty'

PI a(a)ta(a)q 'seal (harp)' [cf. Aleut aataax 'bull of fur seal or sea lion' — perhaps related to ataata, hence the lengthened vowels — compare also apakcuk, etc. under ap(p)a[1]]
Yup [note AAY, CAY aataak 'fur seal' is probably from the Aleut]
SPI —
NAI —
WCI —
ECI [Boas has ataq 'harp seal' as a shaman's word for Baf.]
GRI aataaq 'saddle-back (harp) seal'

PE ataʀuciʀ 'one' [cf. ata- and p.b. uciʀ? — also Aleut ataqan 'one', atuuŋ 'six']
AAY PWS atauciq, atuuciq 'first'
CAY atauciq 'one'
NSY ataasiq
CSY ataasiq
Sir atəʀəsəX
SPI atausiq
NAI atausiq
WCI atausiq
ECI atausiq
GRI ataasiq

PE ataʀuccikun 'together (at same time)' [vial. case]
AAY —
CAY ataucikun 'all together'
NSY ataasikun
CSY Chap ataasiku 'at once, all together'
Sir atəʀəsiku
SPI atausiɣun 'together, at same time'
NAI atautcikun
WCI atautsikun
ECI atautsikut
GRI ataatsikkut

PI atauciʀaq- 'do once' [cf. ʀaq-?]
Yup — [but note CSY ataasiʀaaXtə- 'be only one in number']
SPI atausiaq- 'do all at once, at one attempt'
NAI atausiaq- 'do once, complete at one attempt' [and atausiʀaaq 'individual']
WCI atausiʀaq- 'get one'
ECI atausiaq- 'do once, get or kill one', Iti atausiʀaaq- 'get one'
GRI ataasiaʀ-, ataasiʀiaʀ- 'do once' [ataasiʀaaʀ- 'get one', ataasiaq 'a single one']

PE ata(a)ta 'older male relative?' [cf. ata[1], of which this is probably a doubling, also Aleut taata-X 'father, dad']
AAY ataata, ataaq 'paternal uncle'
CAY ataata
NSY ataata
CSY ataata
Sir atata
SPI ataata 'father' [and Qaw ataatakšaq 'stepfather']
NAI ataata, Nu taata 'grandfather, great uncle', Mal ataata, taata, PH ataata 'father'
WCI Sig ataatak 'grandfather', Cop ataatattiaq 'grandfather', Car ataatatsiaq 'grandfather'
ECI ataata 'father', SB ataatatsiaq 'grandfather, Lab ataatak 'father', ataatsiak 'grandfather', Tar ataatatsiaq 'great-uncle'

GRI ataata, EG ataataq 'father', NG ataatak 'grandfather' [and ataataššaq 'stepfather']

PE atə- 'put on' [cf. atəkə and atuʀ-]
AAY attə- 'put on (garment)'
CAY attə-
NSY atə-
CSY aatə- 'put on' [and atii 'garment one is wearing'; Chap. asiɣalŋuq 's.th. that is not put on (garment)']
Sir [Vakh. has asitəkə- 'dress (s.o.)' from Men. and Rub. and asəɣułkə 's.th. not put on; for atəXt(ə)- 'dress' see atuʀ-]
SPI ati- 'put on (garment)'
NAI atɨ-
WCI ati-
ECI ati-
GRI ati- 'put on (garment)' [and atiššat 'clothes']

PI atnuʀaaq 'clothing' [perhaps from *atŋuʀaaq — compare aŋutŋunəʀ under aŋun for the cons. cluster]
SPI atnuʀaaq 'article of clothing'
NAI annuʀaaq, Nu atnuraaq
WCI annuʀaaq
ECI annuʀaaq 'piece of clothing', Iti 'dress with sleeves'
GRI annuʀaaq 'anorak' [earlier 'clothing, dress', pl. annuʀaššat], EG ᴀʀnaʀ̃aat 'clothes', arnaʀ̃aaq 'dress'

PY atšaʀ- 'put on (fine clothing)' [from *atðaʀ-? — cf. atžuq- below and p.b. žaʀaq]
AAY [ayyaXtaʀuat 'jacket' is from a different p.b.]
CAY [azzaXcaʀaq 'pullover clothing is from a different p.b.]
NSY ašaʀ- 'put on new clothes' [ANLC; Men. has ašaʀuaŋʀalʀia 'dressed in fine clothes']
CSY aašaʀ- 'dress in fancy clothes' [note p.b. šaʀ- 'in a fancy way' under žaʀaʀ-]

PI atžuq- 'put on clothes' [cf. (C)uʀ- and/or ðuʀaʀ-]
Yup — [but note CAY azzun 'pullover' perhaps with a different p.b.]
SPI Qaw aššuq- 'keep putting on clothes'
NAI —
WCI ayyuq- 'disguise oneself in another's clothes'
ECI ayyu(q)- 'put on a coat, disguise oneself in another's clothes'
GRI aššuʀ- 'put on clothes — esp. fine Sunday ones' [Tersis has EG atsuaq- 'wear one's best clothes']

PE atə(ði)- 'be the same' [cf. Aleut at- 'straight or even position or shape' as in atiim akuX 'it is straight' and atxaʀ- 'be straight, even, smooth, right']
AAY —
CAY [NSU atikŋui-, atəkŋui- 'tell stories, illustrating them with story knife']
NSY —
CSY —
Sir atəqinaʀ- 'imitate'
SPI ati- 'be the same', ašši 'copy, likeness'
NAI atɨ- 'be the same, treat equally', ažži, atiži, Mal atži 'copy, likeness'
WCI ayyi 'copy, likeness' [and Net a'ziɣiit 'similar ones' acc. Briggs — Dor. has atži 'picture']
ECI Aiv ayyi 'likeness, picture, photograph', Lab ayyik 'likeness' [and Tar ayyitaaq- 'reflect image, photograph', ayyiqaŋŋituq 'its has no equal']
GRI ašši(k), EG atsiq 'picture, photograph' [and note aššiɣi- 'be the same as', also perhaps EG atsiŋa 'even']

PI atžili- 'copy' [cf. li-[1]]
SPI aššili- 'copy, imitate'
NAI aždžilʸi- 'draw, photograph, copy'
WCI —
ECI —
GRI aššili-

PE atəkə and **atəkuɣ** 'parka' [cf. atə- and p.b. kə[2], perhaps reformulated as a dual in Yup — compare under kaməɣ]
AAY atkuk 'article of clothing, coat, parka' [and atkuɣ- 'put on clothes or parka']
CAY atkuk, NSU atəkuk, atəɣuk 'parka' [atkuɣ- 'put on parka']
NSY atəkuk 'parka'
CSY atkuk 'parka' [atkuɣ- 'put on parka']
Sir —
SPI atiɣi 'parka'
NAI atiɣɨ
WCI atiɣi 'parka' [in B. Lake 'with short fur' acc. Dor.]
ECI atiɣi 'inner parka'
GRI atiɣiq 'woman's jacket', NG ati(ɣ)it, EG aliɣiq 'birdskin inner garment [Holt. and Ges. for the latter two forms]

PE atəkluɣ 'outer parka or shirt' [cf. łuɣ(-)?]
AAY —
CAY —
NSY atəkłuk 'garment, shirt'
CSY —
Sir —
SPI atikłuk 'shirt'
NAI atɨkłuk 'fur parka cloth cover, snowshirt'
WCI Sig atikłuk 'outer parka of cloth'
ECI —
GRI EG alatsuk 'outer fur garment'

PE atəʀ 'name' [cf. Aleut asa- 'name'; there may be a relat. to atə(ði)-]
AAY atəq 'name, namesake'
CAY atəq*
NSY atəq 'name'
CSY atəq*
Sir atəX 'name' [Vakh.; Men. has atiqusłux (for atəqusłux?) 'nickname']
SPI atiq 'name'
NAI atɨq* 'name, namesake' [atiʀusiq 'given name rarely used']
WCI atiq 'name' [also 'namesake' in Sig acc. Lowe; Met. has atiqqat(i) 's.o. with same name as one']

ECI atiq 'name' [and Lab atitsiak 'namesake']
GRI atiq* 'name' [atiiq, atiik, NG atiqqat, Up atiisaq (Søby) 'namesake'; atiqaat 'person s.o. is named after', atiʀusiq 'nickname']

PE acciʀ- 'name' [cf. liʀ-]
AAY aciʀ- 'name'
CAY aciʀ- 'name' [and note acivaqaniʀ- 'curse']
NSY asiʀ- 'name' [ANLC]
CSY [atiʀ- 'name, say', atiXtuʀ- 'read']
Sir [note atiXtuʀ- 'read']
SPI assiq- 'name'
NAI atciq-
WCI atsiq- 'name' [and note atsiqtui- 'insult, call names']
ECI atsi(q)-
GRI atsiʀ- 'name' [atsiaʀi- 'be named after a dead relative'; Tersis has EG atsiaq 's.o. named after a dead person']

PE acciʀutə- 'name after' [cf. acciʀ- above and utə-]
AAY —
CAY aciutə- 'give as name to s.o.'
NSY asiitə- 'name baby after a dead relative'
CSY — [note atiiqə- 'name after']
Sir —
SPI assiuti- 'name after s.o. else'
NAI atciuti-
WCI —
ECI atsiuti- 'give s.o. another's name acc. Inuit custom' [Saul]
GRI atsiut(i)- 'name (child) after s.o. who has died'

PY atʀilŋuq 'ring finger' [cf. ŋit- and ŋuq and compare Russian bezymyanny palets 'ring finger (lit. nameless finger)', of which the present set appears to be a calque — so not real PY; compare alqiliq, with which there is contam.]
AAY AP atXilŋuq 'ring finger' [Kod has qilimaq]
CAY atXilŋuq 'ring finger' [for aquq, qaquq 'middle finger' see qaqu(ʀ) and for HBC əkiliq 'ring finger' see akulipaq under aku(ʀ)]
NSY [note atqilaʀžuk 'ring finger'; for atqilŋə 'middle finger' see alqiliq]
CSY [for atXilək 'middle finger' and alaŋquq 'ring finger' see under alqiliq]
Sir — [alələmənayaki 'ring finger' (Orr — Men. has alima(na)yaki) is from or contam. with Chukchi enənnəki 'ring finger' (and compare also Chukchi aləm- 'extra'?)]

PE atəʀaʀ 'boot (for indoors)' [cf. at(ə)-]
AAY K, AP acciqaq 'shoe', Kod 'slipper'
CAY Nun acciqaX 'high skin boot'
NSY —
CSY —
Sir —
SPI [note attuaq 'slipper' — influenced by atuʀ- or atuŋaʀ?]
NAI atiʀaq PH 'slipper', Nu 'boot covering calf' [and PH atiqqak 'high fur socks']
WCI atiʀaq Net 'calf', Cop 'indoor shoe' [Ras.; Jen. has 'leg-bone, tibia' for Sig; Met. has atiqqak 'long caribou skin indoor boots' for Sig]
ECI — [but note Iti atiʀaq 'board for scraping skins']
GRI atiʀaašaq 'slipper' [Fab. has atterak 'slipper'; note also EG atiʀaq 'inner clothing' in Ras.]

atɣiyaq 'arctic cod' [loan from Aleut atxiða-X 'arctic cod']
AAY K, KP atxiaq 'arctic cod'
CAY Nun atxiiyaX, BB atxiaq
NSY —
CSY —

PE atla 'other' [cf. atə(ði)- and Aleut asl-a 'time, position or point corresponding to or level with (it)', aslixt- 'meet, find, come together with', EA also 'get hold of, catch', aslita- 'be worthy of' — unless some of these go with PE naɫə- rather]
AAY aɫa '(an)other'
CAY aɫa
NSY aɫa
CSY aɫa
Sir aɫa '(an)other' [and aɫəqət(ə)- 'separate']
SPI aɫɫa '(an)other'
NAI alla, Mal, Uum atla
WCI alla '(an)other' [and Net a'latqiit 'dissimilar ones' acc. Briggs]
ECI alla 'Indian'
GRI aɫɫa 'other' [old ortho. avdla spurious — Fabricius has adla; note also NG allaXXuaq 'North American Eskimo/Inuk']

PE atlakkaʀ 'alone or strange (thing)'
AAY —
CAY aɫakaq 'strange, different thing', aɫakaʀ- 'alone, separately' [in indep. relative construction]
NSY aɫakai- 'separately' [ANLC]
CSY aɫakaʀ- 'alone, separately' [in indep. relative construction]
Sir aɫəkaʀmi 'separately'
SPI —
NAI —
WCI —
ECI —
GRI aɫɫakkayaaq '(s.th.) strange'

PE atlanəʀ 'stranger' [cf. nəʀ[1]]
AAY C aɫanəq, K aɫanəXtaq 'stranger, visitor, guest' [and aɫanaʀ- 'be unsettling']
CAY aɫanəq* 'stranger, visitor'
NSY —
CSY —
Sir —
SPI —
NAI [note allanaq- 'be strange']
WCI Cop? allaniq 'stranger' [Schn. 'adg'; Met. has allanitat for Cop]
ECI allaniq 'stranger'
GRI aɫɫaniʀtaq 'foreigner, stranger' [and aɫɫanniʀ-, aɫɫanaʀ- 'have become different']

PE atlayuɣ- 'feel strange' [cf. yuɣ-]
AAY ałayuɣ- 'feel out of place'
CAY ałayuk 's.th. strange'
NSY ałayuɣniXtə- 'grow dark'
CSY ałayuɣ- 'feel strange'
Sir ałayuɣ- [Orr]
SPI ałłayuaq- 'be fearful of strangers'
NAI allayuaq- 'be shy (small child), have a vision, see s.th. strange'
WCI Sig allayuaq- 'be afraid (young child at seeing s.o. he or she doesn't know)'
ECI —
GRI NG allayuaq- 'be shy or embarrassed'

PE atŋiʀ- 'be in pain' [with forms like akŋiʀ- by assimilation and with forms like aŋqiXtə- and aqniʀ- either influenced by aŋqutə- or aqə- or due to the final uvular, undergoing metathesis in some languages; compare aŋutŋunəʀ under aŋun for the Inu development]
AAY aŋqəXtə- 'be in pain', aŋqiaXtə- 'get hurt (suddenly)'
CAY akn̥iXtə-, akŋ̊iXtə-, Nun aŋqiXtə-, HBC aqŋ̊iXtə-, aqn̥iXtə- 'hurt, get hurt', akŋ̊ia-, etc. 'suffer pain' [and akŋ̊iq 'nerve']
NSY aŋqiʀ- 'be ill' [and aŋqiXtə- 'hurt, get hurt' (ANLC)]
CSY aqn̥iʀ-, aŋqiʀ- 'be in pain', aqn̥iXtə- 'hurt, get hurt'
Sir aqn̥əʀ- 'be ill' [note also aqənaqə(s)- 'hurt' under alqunaʀ-; Orr has aqənaʀ-]
SPI atniq-, Imaq atŋiq- 'be hurt'
NAI anniq-, Mal, Uum atniq- 'hurt, get hurt'
WCI anniq-, Cop aanniq- 'hurt oneself' [the latter acc. Lowe], Net a'niq- 'hurt' [Briggs]
ECI aanni(q)- 'hurt, feel pain'
GRI anniʀ- 'have pain' [and anniq 'pain', EG annikkaʀ- 'suffer' — '- hurt' acc. Robbe and Menn.]

PI atniaq- 'be ill or in pain [cf. aʀ-]
SPI atniaq- 'hurt'
NAI anniaq- 'be in pain'
WCI anniaq-, Cop aanniaq- 'be ill' [the latter acc. Lowe]
ECI aannia(q)- 'feel constant pain, be ill'
GRI anniaʀ- 'suffer'

PE atŋiqə- 'yearn for' [cf. p.b. kə-[1]]
AAY —
CAY —
NSY —
CSY aqn̥iqə- 'grieve, yearn for'
Sir — [aqnəqə(s)- 'grieve, be sorry for' — Em.]
SPI —
NAI anniʀi-, Nu atniʀi- 'be protective about, refuse to share'
WCI anniʀi- 'keep for oneself, not want to part with', anniʀusuk- 'be protective toward one's things, be miserly'
ECI anniʀi- 'want s.th.', anniʀusuk-, anniʀitta- 'refuse to share one's things'
GRI anniʀi- 'have pain in one's -' [and note NG anniʀihuk- 'be in pain'; Robbe and Menn. have EG anniinaʀ- '(be) envious']

PY a(a)tsaqə- or **a(a)tyaqə-** 'keep s.th. secret' [there may be a relat. to aŋŋi-, though the relat. is obscure]
AAY —
CAY aasaqə- 'keep a secret, hide' [and aasaqəq 'shield' — there may be contam. with avðaʀ[2] here]
NSY aay̥aqə- 'keep s.th. secret' [ANLC; Men. has a voiced y, but compare iliy̥utə- under əlit-]
CSY aksaqə- 'keep a secret, hide'

PE atunəm 'equally' [cf. EA atuuɣ- 'both', also PE ata-]
AAY atunəm 'by both sides, in a matching pair'
CAY atunəm 'matching, mutually, conforming'
NSY —
CSY atunəm 'together' [and Chap atunəkitə- 'be equal to or level with']
Sir [note atinaX (for atənaX?) 'together' — Vakh.; Em. has atunəkəsiʀ- 'be equal to or level with']
SPI atunim, W atanim 'equally, the same'
NAI atunim 'equally'
WCI atuni(m) 'each'
ECI atunit
GRI —

PE atuŋaʀ 'sole of boot' [cf. at(ə)-]
AAY —
CAY Nun atuŋaX 'sole of foot or boot'
NSY atuŋaq 'skin of bearded seal'
CSY atuŋaq 'sole of boot', atuŋak 'hide of female walrus (for boat covering)'
Sir —
SPI atuŋak 'boot sole from skin of bearded seal'
NAI atuŋak
WCI atuŋaq Sig 'sole made of bearded seal skin' [Met. has 'bleached seal skin' for Cop]
ECI atuŋaq 'boot sole'
GRI atuŋak 'boot sole', NG atuŋaq 'skin for boot sole'

PE atuʀ- 'use' [also 'wear' and 'sing'; cf. atə- and (C)uʀ-?]
AAY atuʀ- 'use, wear, experience, follow, sing', atuq 'useful thing, s.th. used, song'
CAY atuʀ- 'use, wear, sing, follow (tracks, rules)', atuq 'useful thing'
NSY atuʀ- 'use, sing'
CSY atuʀ- 'use, sing' [and atuq 'useful thing']
Sir atəʀ- 'use, put on (clothing)' [Vakh.; Men. has 'fulfil, carry out', also atəXt(ə)- 'dress', atuʀaʀ- 'sing' and atəʀyuqcəX 's.th. necessary or set aside for s.th.', atəqy̥a- 'borrow']
SPI atuq- 'use, sing, wear' [for attuaq 'slipper' see atəʀaq, atuʀaq- 'play piano or organ']
NAI atuq- 'sing, use, wear' [and attuq 's.th. worn out', Nu atuɣaq, atukkaq 's.th. borrowed']
WCI atuq- 'use, sing, be in use, borrow' [and atuɣaq 's.th. borrowed', atukkiq- 'be in debt', atukkit- 'lend']
ECI atuq- 'use'
GRI atuʀ- 'use, be used, borrow, experience, have intercourse with (woman), sing' [and atukkit- 'lend', Up atiŋaq, EG atiʀniaŋaq 's.th. borrowed']

PI atuaq- 'follow' [cf. aʀ-?]
SPI —
NAI atuaʀniq* 'southeast wind (following coast)'
WCI [note Cop atuaqtaut 'axe', atuaqtaq- 'cut with axe'?]
ECI atuaq- 'repeat, read' [also 'follow (coastline or trail)' acc. Saul; and atuarniq 'wind following coast']
GRI atuaʀ- 'read, follow (track)' [and atuɣaq 'book'; NG atuaʀnaq 's.w. wind' — Holt.]

PE atu(ʀ)un 'song' [cf. un]
AAY atuun 'song, record'
CAY atuun 'song' [also 'useful thing']
NSY atu(u)n 'dance song'
CSY atuun 'Eskimo song'
Sir [atuʀaʀəta 'song']
SPI Qaw atuun 'song'
NAI atuun 'song, record' [and atuułłuk 'shaman's magic song for hunting']
WCI atuun 'song'
ECI Igl atuut 'song' [Ras.]
GRI —

PE atyaʀ 'berry' [cf. at(ə)- and yaʀ and compare tatyuʀ- for the cons. cluster]
AAY atsaq 'blueberry'
CAY atsaq, acsaq, NS accaq 'berry, fruit'
NSY —
CSY —
Sir — [for asa 'land, tundra' see aci[1]]
SPI aziaq 'saxifrage' [and Qaw aciacaaq 'wild lettuce']
NAI asi<ž>aq 'berry or fruit (esp. blueberry)' [as verb = 'pick berries'; and note asiaʀžuaq 'potato']
WCI asiaq 'berry or other fruit' [asiyyiaq- 'go berry-picking']
ECI —
GRI asiaʀpak 'butterfly orchid', EG asiaʀ- 'pluck berries' [Ras.]

PY a(C)ulukə- 'watch over' [cf. kə-[1]]
AAY aulukə- 'watch over, tend to'
CAY aulukə- 'watch over, tend to' [and aułu 'watch out!']
NSY aluake- 'take care of, tend' [L.-T.]
CSY [ažuuʀ- 'watch for sea mammals on the ice, call out for s.o. whose arrival is anticipated']

PE a(C)umaʀ 'ember' [cf. perhaps Aleut amu- 'flash (lightning)' — also nom. 'lightning']
AAY aumaʀaq 'ember, glowing coal' [B.-S. has aumaq]
CAY aumaq, aumak
NSY —
CSY [aamak 'berry species' is perhaps not a cognate]
Sir —
SPI auma, aumaq 'ember, glowing coal'
NAI auma 'ember, coal' [and verbal = 'be live (coal)']
WCI auma 'ember, coal'
ECI auma, aumaq 'ember, glowing coal' [aumayaaq- 'be very hot']
GRI aama(q) 'ember, glowing coal' [aamaaʀ- 'be glowing']

PI aummin 'bedding or blanket' [cf. ayu(C)ummaʀ and un]
Yup —
SPI —
NAI aummisit PH 'bedding', Nu 'caribou skin blanket'
WCI Car? aummiti 'blanket, mattress' [Schn. 'adg']
ECI aummiti 'blanket, matress' [aummisiq- 'go to bed, wrap self in blanket, bandage']
GRI aammit 'winding cloth (for corpse)'

PI aunnəqtu- 'last long' [there may be a link to aunəq under aʀu- relating to melting snow, as Kleinschmidt suggested, at least as a source of contamination — compare annəq(tu)-]
SPI —
NAI —
WCI —
ECI aunnitu- 'last a long time, be durable' [Bourquin has aumnertu- 'lasy long (e.g. food)']
GRI aanniʀtu- 'last a long time, be durable' [Fab. has has aunertu-]

PI auqcaaq- 'swoop down' [cf. aðuʀ- and caʀ-?]
SPI —
NAI —
WCI auqsaaq- 'swoop down on (bird of prey)'
ECI auʀsaa(q)-
GRI aaʀsaaʀ- 'swoop down'

PI auvaq- 'hunt caribou' [cf. aðuʀ-?]
SPI —
NAI —
WCI auvaq- 'hunt caribou' [Ras. for Cop, Sig — he also has auv(v)aq 'caribou hunter' for Cop]
ECI Igl auvaq- 'hunt caribou' [Ras.]
GRI aavaʀ- 'go on caribou hunt' [and aaffaq* 'caribou-hunting area']

PI aužvik or **aužviq** 'caterpillar (larva)' [cf. aðuʀ- and ðviɣ?]
SPI Qaw aužvik 'hairy caterpillar'
NAI aužviq, Nu aužvik 'hairy caterpillar' [Jen. has auʀ(u)viq 'larva']
WCI Sig auyviq, Cop aulvik 'hairy caterpillar' [Lowe; Pryde has Cop, Net aulviq, and Ras. has Net arveq, also auffeq 'larva' — for aužviq?]
ECI auvvik 'caterpillar'
GRI aaššik [old ortho. âgssik], NG aussiq 'butterfly larva' [also aaffaffak 'legendary creature with short legs and a horn on its nose', contaminated with ayvəʀ?]

PE ava- 'feel faint' [cf. avaŋitə-]
AAY K, KP awa- 'become numb, feel faint' [and awatə- K 'numb', KP 'cause to feel faint', perhaps also awaʀnaq 'pain in chest']
CAY awatə-, avatə-, əvatə- 'strangle (putting pressure on carotid artery)'
NSY —
CSY avaaʀ- 'be relieved of pain'
Sir —
SPI Qaw awat- 'strangle' [and awataaq- 'press on carotid

artery to cause to feel faint']
NAI ➟
WCI ➟
ECI Lab avaaŋu- 'stunned, knocked out' [Andersen et al.; Saul has Tar avat- 'hang oneself']
GRI avaaʀ- 'have had enough, learned one's lesson', avaaŋu- 'feel giddy, tired of s.th.' [and avaaʀut(i)- 'be heartily tired of', avaaŋŋunaʀ- 'be boring']

PI avaaq- 'knock out (with blow on head)' [cf. p.b. aʀ-?]
SPI —
NAI avaaq- 'knock or be knocked unconscious'
WCI avaaq- 'kill outright', Net 'hit on head' [Ras.; also avaaqtaun 'club']
ECI avaaq- 'be killed or hit in vital spot' [and Peck has 'beat, shoot in the head' for Lab — but avaak- 'be knocked out' in Andersen et al.]
GRI avaaʀ- 'hit on back of head (and kill that way)', avaaq 'back of head' [and avaaʀtaat 'club']

PI avaaɣə- 'be charitable toward' [cf. kə-[1], also avaliʀ-?]
SPI —
NAI —
WCI Car avaaɣi- 'give food to' [Ras.]
ECI ava(a)ɣi- 'be charitable toward'
GRI avaaɣi- 'be good toward', NG avaaxxui- 'show sympathy'

PI avaala- 'shout'
SPI awaalak- 'cry out in pain, holler'
NAI avaala- 'yell'
WCI [Jen. and Pryde have avaalaq- 'yell' for Cop]
ECI avaala- 'cry loudly', avaalaa- 'shout so as to stun seal on ice'
GRI avaala-, avaalaaʀ- 'howl, hoot' [Robbe and Menn. have the latter as 'mock by pointing at s.o.' for EG]

PI avaalaqiaq 'dwarf birch' [cf. avayaq]
SPI —
NAI —
WCI Cop avaalaqiaq 'dwarf birch' [Pryde; in pl. 'birch twig mat on sleeping platform']
ECI avaalaqiaq 'dwarf birch'
GRI avaalaqiak, avaalaɣiaq

PE avaliʀ- 'take along' [cf. avvaq under avəɣ- and liʀ-? — compare also avaqutaq and/or avaaɣə-]
AAY —
CAY awaliq, HBC avaliq 'thing one has with one, foster child', avaliitə- 'be lacking s.th.', avaliŋqəX- 'have s.th. on hand' [and avaliqə- 'watch over']
NSY —
CSY —
Sir —
SPI [note avvazaaq 's.o. with same name as one' under avvaq (avəɣ-); for Imaq awaliq- 'be removing, separating' compare av(v)aʀ(iʀ)-, here with p.b. liq-]
NAI [for PH avvasaaq 'close relative or friend' see avvaq (avəɣ-)]
WCI Cop avaliq- 'accompany', avaliiq- 'leave alone', avaliit- 'be left alone' [and note Sig avaŋiq- 'accompany' and avayaiq- 'leave alone', also avayak 'spouse']
ECI —
GRI —

PE avan (avatə) 'area around' [from demonst. root av- and p.b. tə; cf. avataq and avayaq]
AAY awatə 'area around' [posit. root; also 'bank (of river)']
CAY awatə 'area around'
NSY awatə 'surroundings, wall'
CSY awata 'area on other side'
Sir [Vakh. has avətə, also avaciʀnəʀ- 'behind'; for avəta 'cause, reason' see avun] ➟
SPI awan 'limb, surrounding area'
NAI avan, avatɨ 'limb, surrounding area' [and avat- 'surround', avala- 'move one's arms and legs about']
WCI avat(i) 'surrounding area' [and avatait 'limbs'; Pryde has Cop avalak- 'veer to one side']
ECI avat(i) 'surrounding area' [Lab also 'limb'; avatit 'twenty']
GRI avat(i) 'limb, surrounding area, off from land', EG avat, avaliq 'hand' [the latter also 'pancreas', 'cape' and 'joint' acc. Robbe and Menn. — Ges. also has avaliʀti 'pericardium'; note also avalaɣ- 'move out, set off', avannaq 'north wind' (= avaŋŋaq 'east wind' in EG acc. Robbe and Menn., but 'north wind' acc. Tersis — from WG)]

PE aval(l)iʀ 'outermost or far off thing' [cf. l(l)iʀ; there appears to be an earlier and a later parallel derivation (the former derived directly from the dem. root) as with civul(l)iʀ under civu-]
AAY —
CAY —
NSY awaliq 'outermost one' [ANLC]
CSY awaliq 'one on other side'
Sir avəcəX 'far (thing)'
SPI awaliq 'farthest one in a direction'
NAI avalliq* 'one farthest to one side'
WCI avalliq 'outermost'
ECI —
GRI avałłiq* 'outermost', EG avattiq 'little finger' [and avaliq(*) 'that which lies outside (e.g. land)'; avaliqut 'branch', possibly also EG avalisaq 'kayak lance']

PI avalu 'fence or border' [cf. lu(ʀ)]
SPI —
NAI avalu 'fence, border' [as verb = 'fence or be fenced in']
WCI avalu 'fence'
ECI avalua 'its surrounding area', NBI, Lab avaluk, SB avaluaq 'fence'
GRI —

PE avatəŋiʀ- 'surround' [cf. ŋiʀ-]
AAY awataiʀ- 'go around'
CAY —
NSY —

CSY awatiiʀ- 'lose s.th. by its escaping'
Sir avətəŋiʀ- 'hide (behind s.th.)' [Vakh. — Men. has avatəŋəɣət(ə)- 'disappear']
SPI awataŋia- 'surround'
NAI PH avataŋia-
WCI Cop avataŋiq- 'go around or past, get to the far side off' [Pryde]
ECI avataŋiq-
GRI avataŋiʀ- 'surround, keep close to but outside of'

PY-S avaŋitə- 'be absent' [cf. ŋit-; the relat. with ava- and/or av(v)aʀ(iʀ)- and aɣ^{w}itə- is obscure]
AAY —
CAY —
NSY aviatə- 'be absent'
CSY aviitə-, Chap [Men.] avaŋitə- 'be absent, gone'
Sir avəŋət- 'not have (any)' [Vakh., who also has avaŋiʀət(ə)- 'not have any (left)' — for Men. 'remove'; note avatəŋiʀ- under avan for avətəŋəɣət(ə)- 'disappear']

PY avaqutaq 'offspring' [cf. avaliʀ- and q(q)un?]
AAY K awaqutaq 'son'
CAY Nun awaqutaX 'son' [and HBC avankuq 'son']
NSY avaqutaq 'infant, child'
CSY avaqutaq 'child, offspring'
Sir [avaqutaX 'child, offspring' (Orr) probably borrowed from CSY]

PE av(v)aʀiʀ- 'remove or be removed (by wiping)' [cf. allaʀ(iʀ)- and əppaʀiʀ- for parallel semantics — the forms with iʀ, etc., from p.b. ŋiʀ-, suggest an original nominal base *av(v)aʀ, like allaʀ under allaʀ(iʀ)-, perhaps 'impurity, obscurity', ultimately from avəɣ- plus geminating nominalizer q under nəʀ[1] (see avvaq under avəɣ-); there seems to be some entanglement with aɣ^{w}itə- in Yup]
AAY K awwaʀ-, C aɣ^{w}ɣ^{w}aʀ- 'move aside', aɣ^{w}aiʀ- 'become clear (sky)', AP 'clean off', C aɣuiʀ- 'clean off', Kod (Rez.) [and note aɣuinəq 'clear sky', K aɣ^{w}aitə- 'be clear (weather)']
CAY aɣ^{w}ɣ^{w}aʀ-, Nun aɣuɣaʀ- 'come off, remove', avaiʀ- 'be clear (weather)' [and aɣ^{w}ɣ^{w}aʀitə- 'forgive']
NSY aviaʀ- 'wipe, dry'
CSY aviiʀ- 'wipe', aviiʀutə- 'not be there any more, die, disappear' [and avaXqaXiiʀutə- 'be nothing left' — Men. has 'take away'; for avaaʀ- 'be relieved of pain' see ava(C)uʀ-]
Sir —
SPI Imaq awaʀ- 'separate, remove' [and await- Qaw 'be clear (weather)', Imaq 'be possible, probable']
NAI [note avaʀniq- 'reappear after absence' and nom. avaʀniq* 'time taken to reappear after an absence']
WCI —
ECI — [but note SB (Boas) ava(a)-, Lab (Peck) avaava- 'be always out hunting'?]
GRI —

PE avataʀ '(sealskin) float' [cf. avan]
AAY AP awataq 'sealskin float' [in old sources]
CAY awataXpak, NS awataq 'sealskin float' [Lantis has awata- for Nun]
NSY awataq 'sealskin poke' [and awataXpak 'sealskin float']
CSY awataXpak 'sealskin float'
Sir [aɣətəXpəx 'sealskin float' — Vakh.]
SPI awataq 'sealskin poke or float'
NAI avataq
WCI avataq 'hunting bladder (float)'
ECI avataq [Saul, also Ras. for Igl]
GRI avataq

PY ava(C)uʀ- 'forget' [cf. ava- and (C)uʀ-?]
AAY C aɣuuʀ- 'forget'
CAY avauʀ- 'forget to take along'
NSY avaaʀ^{w}- 'forget'
CSY— [for avaaʀ- 'be relieved of pain' see ava-]

PY-S avayaq 'branch' [cf. avaalaqiaq]
AAY —
CAY awayaq, HBC avayaq 'branch', Nun awayaX 'knot in wood' [the latter by contam. with avðaʀ[1]? — note also Nun, NSU qiwayuq 'branch']
NSY —
CSY avayaq 'branch'
Sir avayəx 'branch' [Vakh.]
Inu [note Qaw awayak, qiwaya 'branch' — from the Yup? — but also GRI avaliqut 'branch' under aval(l)iʀ (avan)]

PE avðaʀ[1] 'wart' [there may be a link to avðaʀ[2]]
AAY —
CAY awaq 'cyst' [for Nun awayaX 'knot in wood' see avayaq]
NSY —
CSY ava 'cyst'
Sir [Orr has ava, pl. avay 'cyst' — probably borrowed from CSY]
SPI avžaq 'mole, wart-like growth on body'
NAI avžaq
WCI —
ECI —
GRI aššaq 'protuberance (soft and smooth), wart' [old ortho. agssaq by contam. with homonym meaning 'load'? — see aɣžaq-]

PE avðaʀ[2] 'hindrance or protection'
AAY awaʀ(yuɣ)- 'feel annoyed at s.th. or s.o. in the way, want to be alone'
CAY [for aasaqəq 'shield' see a(a)tsaqə-] ➡
NSY avža 'clothes' [and avžataq 'place for hanging clothes']
CSY —
Sir avžaX, pl. avžaŋy 'clothes' [Orr]
SPI avžaiq- 'straighten up, remove obstacles' [and note perhaps avžak 'guts']
NAI PH avžat 'bedding'
WCI —
ECI ➡
GRI aššaq 'defense, shield, curtain' [also aššiq, see below; and aššaaʀ-, aššiu- 'get out of the way (of)']

PE avðiR- 'hinder or protect' [cf. liR-]
AAY awi<R>aR- 'hinder, get in the way'
CAY awiRautə- 'be in the way', awiRa(yuɣ)- 'not want around' [emot. root; note that even HBC has w rather than v here, suggesting contam. with demon. root av- and/or aɣ^{w}itə-]
NSY —
CSY —
Sir —
SPI avžiaq- 'be an obstacle, in the way'
NAI avžiaq-, Mal avžiaqutau- 'be an obstacle, in the way'
WCI —
ECI avvia(q)-, NBI aɣviaq- 'be an obstacle'
GRI aššiR- [old ortho. avsser-] 'protect, shield', aššiaq 'obstacle', aššiq 'defense, shield, curtain', aššiaR-, aššiu- 'be in s.o.'s way'

PE avəɣ- 'divide or separate' [cf. av(v)aR(iR)-, also perhaps Aleut amax, amɣi-X 'night']
AAY awək 'half', AP, PWS awəɣ-, AP also auxtə-, KP awəxtə-, Kod a'uxtə- 'divide, split'
CAY avəɣ- 'divide in two', avək 'half'
NSY [avəxtuRaq 'tobacco'; avəxtuRvik 'kitchen board' (L.-T.)]
CSY avəɣ- 'divide in two', avək, aavnəq* 'half' [and avəxtuRaq 'pipe tobacco']
Sir avəɣ- 'cut up' [Vakh.; also av(ə)nəX 'half', avənəR- 'break, smash' and avəqaqəłəX 'piece']
SPI awik- 'divide in two'
NAI avik- 'divide' [and aviktaq 'piece cut from s.th.']
WCI avik- 'divide'
ECI avik-
GRI aviɣ- 'separate' [and avittaR- 'embroider']

PE avət- 'separate' [probably via *avəɣt-]
AAY [cf. awəxtə- under avəɣ- above]
CAY aftə- 'divide, separate'
NSY aftə- [ANLC]
CSY aaftə- 'separate' [and afta- 'cut up game']
Sir — [for aftalRaR- 'work' see avta-]
SPI awit- 'separate, get a divorce'
NAI avit- 'get a divorce, split one's pants'
WCI avit- 'separate' [Sig also aptiq-; note also Car, Net avunnivik 'month in which seals miscarry' acc. Ras. — at B. Lake 'January' acc. Dor.; the latter also has avunniniq 'female caribou with fetus']
ECI Iti avit- 'separate (from wife), fire (employee)' [and avut(i)- 'be separated (baby seal from mother)', avuyuq 'young seal separated from mother']
GRI avit- 'halve, give change (for coin), divorce'

PE avɣuR- 'cut up' [cf. (C)uR-, also EA amɣu- 'dig (ground), cut up (wood)']
AAY —
CAY avɣuR- 'cut up or divide with repeated acts'
NSY avɣułəq 'piece, part' [ANLC]
CSY aavɣuR- 'cut up thoroughly'
Sir —
SPI Qaw avɣuq- 'pick up, collect, slice up'
NAI avɣuq- 'skin, cut up'
WCI avɣuq- 'cut up'
ECI aɣɣu(q)- 'share, divide, deal'
GRI axxuR- 'separate, divide, cut up'

PI avvaq 'half' [cf. q under nəR[1]]
SPI avvaq 'half'
NAI avvaq*
WCI avvaq
ECI avvaq
GRI affaq* 'half' [old ortho. agfaq with spurious g — Fab. has àuako]

PI avvasaaq 'relative'
SPI avvazaaq 's.o. with same name'
NAI PH avvasaaq 'close relative or friend'
WCI —
ECI —
GRI —

PE avəlŋaR or **avəłŋaR** 'lemming' [cf. perhaps avət- under avəɣ- and compare NAI aviŋaaq- 'be undecided between two things', GRI aviŋŋaRut(i)- 'become separated from others']
AAY AP apłəŋaq, Perry apłiŋaŋuaq 'vole' [note KP qupilŋaq with the same meaning, but with qupə- 'split in two' in place of avəɣ- (as in CAY) which may have been assumed to mean 'split in two', here by folk etymology]
CAY avəlŋaq*, Y, NS afcəłŋaq* 'vole, mouse'
NSY avəsŋaaXaq [ANLC; Men. has avəšaXaq]
CSY afsəŋaq*
Sir afsəŋaX
SPI Qaw awiŋaq 'lemming'
NAI aviŋŋaq*, PH avinŋaq*
WCI aviŋŋaq
ECI aviŋŋaq
GRI aviŋŋaq(*)

PE avi(R)luR- 'make a noise' [from *aviRuluR-? — cf. aviRu- and luR-]
AAY Kod awiRluXtə- 'make a noise, ring, rattle, rumble', awiRluq 'noise'
CAY aviRluXtə-, aRivluXtə- 'be noisy, clanging' [the latter by contam. with aRiva-?]
NSY aviluɣ- [aviluXqə- acc. L.-T.] 'make noise', aviluk 'noise, thunder'
CSY —
Sir —
SPI Qaw awiRluq- 'ring', Imaq awiluk 'thunder'
NAI avil^{y}uq- 'make a banging noise'
WCI aviluRaq- 'sound (bell)'
ECI aviliuq- 'sound, ring'
GRI aviluR- 'ring'

PE aviRu- 'shout' [cf. avi(R)luR- and Aleut amilɣi-X 'voice', amliɣ- 'shout, cry']
AAY —
CAY aviu- 'scream, yell' [and aviuqaXtə- 'make food offering to the dead', aviuRnaXqə- 'be of interest'?]
NSY avii 'cry of seal under water', avii- 'invite to dance

(during whale festival)' [and aviža- 'escape danger by shouting'; avii 'bearded seal staying in one place and making a call from under water' (ANLC)]
CSY avii- 'have ringing in one's ears, signal (by shouts or flags)' [and note aviʀaatə- 'keep thinking about s.th.'?]
Sir avəʀə- 'have ringing in ears' [Orr; Em. has avəɣə- 'call people to gather for a ceremony']
SPI ayuu-, W awiu- 'cheer, cry out in victory'
NAI aviu- 'shoot, cheep, ring (ears)', PH aviuʀi- 'call when a catch is made'
WCI Sig aviu- 'ring (ears)' [also Net in Ras.], aviuq- 'groan (bearded seal under water)'
ECI aviuyi- 'have ringing in ears', aviuq- 'cry (male bearded seal)'
GRI aviu- 'have ringing in ears', aviuʀ- 'cry (bearded seal in rut)' [and EG aviilaaʀ- 'cry for help (from kayak)']

PE avləʀ- 'spread one's legs' [cf. avəɣ-]
AAY auɣləʀ- 'spread one's legs'
CAY avləʀ-
NSY avləʀ-
CSY avləʀ-
Sir avlaʀ-
SPI avlaak- 'spread legs' [Imaq avləvaq-, also avlək 'gusset in trouser crotch']
NAI avlaak-, Nu apla(a)k- 'spread legs' [compare Mal apluq- under PE amłuʀ-; Jen. has 'fork of legs' as a nominal]
WCI avla(a)ŋa- 'have legs apart'
ECI allaa(k)- 'open legs, straddle', allaaŋa- 'have legs apart', Great Whale River 'be bandy-legged'
GRI ałłaat-, ałłaaŋa- 'stand astride'

PY avləqaʀtaq 'bolas'
AAY —
CAY —
NSY avləqaXtaq 'bolas' [ANLC]
CSY avləqaXtaq

PY av(ə)ŋuq 'burl (in wood)' [cf. avðaʀ[1]?]
AAY —
CAY Y avŋuq 'burl' [and NS, Y, LI avŋulək 'balsam poplar']
NSY avəŋuq 'crust, bark of tree' [ANLC]
CSY aavŋuq 'burl'

PE avta- 'be busy' [cf. avət- under avəɣ- and p.b. a-?]
AAY —
CAY —
NSY aftayaʀ- 'be busy' [ANLC]
CSY —
Sir aftalʀaʀ- 'work' [and Vakh. has aftə- 'fall behind' from Rub.'s texts]
SPI apta- 'work on things one after another'
NAI apta-
WCI —
ECI —
GRI —

PE avu- 'supplement one's diet (e.g. during pregnancy)' [there may be a link to avuʀ-]
AAY aɣuq 'slice of bread to go with tea or coffee, thickener for soup'
CAY awu-, au-, HBC avu- 'supplement, eat bread with tea or coffee'
NSY [note avuɣatət 'whale cartilege formed into balls' (ANLC)]
CSY —
Sir —
SPI au- 'add an ingredient, mix in' [and auɣit 'ingredients']
NAI avu- 'add sugar to' [nominal = 'sugar, extra ingredient'], avusuk- 'crave a change of diet (pregnant woman)'
WCI Sig avu- 'mix' [nominal = 'sugar, s.th. mixed in']
ECI [Peck has avusuk- 'long for s.th.' for Lab]
GRI avu- 'grow lean from giving suck', avusuɣ-, aɣusuk- 'crave a change of diet (pregnant woman)' [S.-L. has 'be dainty'; Holt. has avuhuk- 'crave s.th. special to eat' for NG]

PE avun 'reason for blame' [cf. un; there may be a link to avuʀ-]
AAY —
CAY —
NSY —
CSY avun 'reason', avutkə- 'blame'
Sir avəta 'cause, reason', avətəqə(s)- 'suspect, blame'
SPI autqak- 'reprimand'
NAI avutqak- 'scold, criticize'
WCI —
ECI —
GRI avuqqaaʀi-, aŋuqqaaʀi- [half-trans. avuqqaaʀłiʀ-]

PY-S avuʀ- 'gather or sort' [cf. avəɣ-?]
AAY auʀ- 'gather', Kod 'separate and clean (berries)'
CAY awuʀ-, auʀ-, HBC avuʀ- 'gather'
NSY avuʀ- 'gather' [avuɣaq 'picked up (thing)' (L.-T.)]
CSY avuʀ- 'sort' [and Chap avułiq 'selection, choice']
Sir avuʀ- 'sort (e.g. beads)' [Vakh.]

PE ay 'what did you say?'
AAY ai 'what did you say?'
CAY ai
NSY ay 'what did you say?' [ANLC]
CSY ay
Sir —
SPI —
NAI ai 'OK?', aiy 'is that so?' [also enclitic]
WCI ai 'OK?, isn't it?' [Pryde; also enclitic]
ECI ai 'hi!' [also emphatic enclitic]
GRI ai 'what did you say?', aat [old ortho. ait] 'OK, won't you?', NG ai(t) 'isn't that so?' [the latter two forms may be enclitic; EG aa 'what did you say?, aai 'what did you say?, please' — Tersis]

PE ayaɣ- 'thrust or push with a pole' [cf. Aleut ayɣaɣ- 'walk', ayaquðaax 'sea otter spear, small harpoon', ayaqu-X 'fish spear', EA ayaasaqa-X 'harpoon with float and line']

AAY ayaɣ- 'push with pole, go with walking stick'
CAY ayaɣ- 'leave'
NSY ayaɣ- 'push away, lean, push off (from shore)' [ANLC, also for ayaɣaq 'deck stiffener in kayak'; Men. has ayaq 'shaft of whale harpoon', ayaqə- 'lean against']
CSY ayaɣ- 'push off, reject'
Sir ayəɣ- 'push against s.th., raise s.th. above one's head, push away' [Em.; Men. has ayəɣtəʀ- 'lean against, chase away']
SPI ayak 'tent pole, house post'
NAI ayak- 'push, launch boat, prop up, depart', ayak 'harpoon or spear pole'
WCI ayak, ayaq 'support' [and ayaun 'pole for pushing boat']
ECI ayak- 'shove', Lab ayak- 'lean on, shove' [but in Andersen et al. also 'touch, gently touch s.o. on shoulder to see if they are OK' — conflation with PI ažak-?]
GRI ayaɣ- 'push away, prop up, hit (in throwing game)' [and ayaššaat 'fork']

PI ayaɣaq 'ring-and-pin game'
SPI ayaɣaq 'ring and pin game'
NAI ayaɣaq 'first neck vertebra of caribou, toy made of this', ayaɣaaq 'game played with this toy (catching neckbone on string through hole in stick)' [also verbal]
WCI ayaɣaq 'ring and pin game'
ECI [Math. has Igl ayaɣaq 'game']
GRI ayaɣaq 'ring and pin game' [and ayaɣaʀ- 'play this game' — these words are also used of the 'cat's cradle' game, for which see ayaʀaʀaʀ; note also ayaɣaatit 'knucklebones (game)' in S.-L.]

PE ayaɣaʀ 'crosspiece of kayak'
AAY aya<ɣ>aq 'crosspiece of baidarka'
CAY ayaɣaq 'kayak deck stiffener or support'
NSY —
CSY Chap ayaɣaq 'stone or weights on pole for training in lifting'
Sir ayaɣaX 'stone or pole with weights for lifting' [Em.]
SPI ayaɣaq 'bone toss game'
NAI ayaaʀun 'crosspiece on bed of sled', Nu 'kayak cross-bar'
WCI [Met. has ayaq — for ayaaq? — 'support']
ECI ayaaq 'kayak cross-bar' [Saul]
GRI ayaaq

PY ayaɣta 'pole or support' [compare ayaɣun below]
AAY ayaxta 'pole, support, prop'
CAY ayaxta 'prop, support, spreader for drying fish'
NSY [ayatat 'poles in hallway' (L.-T.)]
CSY —
Sir [note ayaxsiʀəta 'support']

PE ayaɣtuʀ- 'push away' [cf. tuʀ-[2]]
AAY [ayaxtuʀ- 'have a miscarriage', AP ayakutaq 'prop']
CAY ayaxtuutaq 'prop'
NSY —
CSY —
Sir [ayəxtəʀ- 'support oneself against s.th.']
SPI ayaktuq- 'reject'
NAI ayaktuq- 'pole (a boat), reject, keep at a distance, bend into shape' [ayaktuun 'pole for poling a boat']
WCI —
ECI —
GRI ayattuʀ- 'push s.o. away, pole boat along with oar, reject'

PE ayaɣun 'push pole' [cf. un and compare ayakutaq below]
AAY KP, Kod aya'un, aya'utaq 'pole for poling boat'
CAY K, BB ayaun 'thumb'
NSY ayaʀun [for ayaɣun?] 'pole'
CSY ayaɣun 'push pole'
Sir ayəɣətəX 'pole supporting trad. dwelling' [Vakh. from Rub.]
SPI Qaw ayautaq 'pole, e.g. to push off boat'
NAI ayaɣutaq 'post, support'
WCI ayaɣutaq Cop 'support', Sig 'rainbow'
ECI [ayaɣutaq 'rainbow' (Saul)]
GRI aya(a)ɣutaq 'support, prop' [also verbal ayaɣutaʀ-]

PY ayakutaq 'side of face (temple)' [compare ayaɣun above]
AAY ayakutaq Kod 'temple', AP 'support, prop'
CAY ayakutaʀ(aq*) 'temple, side of face' [and LI ayakuttə- 'rest one's chin on one's hands (with elbows on table)']
NSY [ayakutaq 'forked prop in yaranga' (ANLC)]
CSY Chap ayakutaq 'side of face'

PE ayapəʀ- 'lean against'
AAY ayapəʀ- 'support oneself holding on to s.th.' [ayapəq 's.th. to lean on']
CAY ayapəʀ- 'lean against (with) hand'
NSY ayapəʀ- [L.-T.], ayəpəʀ- [Dob.]
CSY ayapəʀ-
Sir ay(ə)pəʀ- 'lean against' [Vakh. has 'attack']
SPI ayapiq- 'lean against with hand'
NAI ayapɨq-, ayappak-
WCI —
ECI ayapiq- 'arrive at right time'
GRI ayapiʀ- 'lean against (with) hand' [and note EG ayipiʀtiŋaq 'knee' — Ges. has ayipiʀtiq 'kneecap' (compare ayapʀun below)]

PY-S ayapʀun 'bone in lower arm' [cf. ayapəʀ- above and un]
AAY —
CAY —
NSY ayəpXun 'elbow bone'
CSY ayapXun 'bone in lower arm (radius?)' [on Men.'s comp. list as 'elbow bone']
Sir ayapXuta 'elbow bone' [on Men.'s comp. list]

PE ayaʀuʀ and **aya(ʀu)viʀaʀ** 'walking stick' [cf. Atkan Aleut ayaXu-X, EA ayaaʀu-X, Att ayaʀu-X 'walking stick'; in Inu there seems to be reinterpretation of the second form as containing p.b. piɣ]
AAY aya<ʀ>uq 'walking stick, cane'
CAY ayaʀuq 'walking stick' [NS azaupiaq 'walking stick' is probably borrowed from Inuit]
NSY ayaviaq 'walking stick'
CSY ayaviiq*
Sir ayəvəʀaX 'stick'
SPI ayaupiaq 'walking stick'
NAI ayauppiaq
ECI ayauppiak
GRI ayaappiaq 'walking stick', EG 'ice pick'

PI ayak 'maternal aunt' [compare accaɣ]
SPI ayak 'maternal aunt'
NAI PH ayak, ayauluk 'paternal aunt' [sic — for 'maternal aunt'?; note also ayaayak 'older sister']
WCI Sig aya 'maternal aunt' [Pet.]
ECI NBI aya(k), Tar ayakuluk 'maternal aunt' [Peck has the former also for Lab]
GRI aya(k), NG ayaaXXuk 'maternal aunt' [Robbe and Menn. have ayaq, ayaaq for EG]

PE ayalu(ʀ)- 'walk bent over' [cf. PE ayaɣ- and luʀ-?; also perhaps Aleut aya- Atkan 'fall, tumble down', EA 'menstruate', ayu- 'fall, collapse', Att aya-n 'menstrual discharge' and perhaps even Aleut ayaɣa-X 'woman']
AAY AP, Kod ayalu-, PWS ayaluXtə-, K ayalua- 'walk off balance', PWS 'walk bent over', Kod 'walk having to hold onto things', AP 'stagger' [and note Kod aya- 'have one's first menstrual period' (Rez.), ayanaXaq 'girl who has just had her first period']
CAY ayaluʀ- 'lean', ayalua- 'stagger'
NSY —
CSY — [for aɣalʀu- 'stagger' see aɣa-]
Sir —
SPI —
NAI ayalu- 'collapse'
WCI —
ECI —
GRI ayalu(ʀ)-

PY ayani(ʀ)- 'have endurance'
AAY C ayaniʀ- 'be able to withstand or cope with pain, be tough (physically or emotionally)'
CAY ayani- 'have stamina, endurance'
NSY —
CSY ayaniqə- 'feel nostalgia'

PE ayaʀaʀaʀ 'string figure' [cf. ayaɣ- and ʀaʀaʀ-?]
AAY aixaq, KP also aiXaq 'cat's cradle (string used in telling stories, etc.)' [also verbal aixaʀ-, aiXaʀ-; aixaq may be influenced by ayaɣ-]
CAY aiXaq, Nun, BB aaXaq, NSU ayaXXaq 'cat's cradle' [also verbal aiXaʀ-, etc. 'tell a string story']
NSY ayXaʀ- 'make cat's cradle figures' [Em.; nom. ayXaq 'cat's cradle']
CSY iiXaq* 'string story, cat's cradle' [and iiXaata 'string used for making figures']
Sir icəʀaX 'string story, cat's cradle' [Orr — from *iyyaʀaʀ?; and icəʀaʀəta 'string used for making figures'; Em. has iXaʀəta and iXa — from the CSY']
SPI ayaXaaq 'string game'
NAI ayaXaaq, ayaʀaaq [verbal = 'play string game, tell string story']
WCI ayaʀaaq 'string game'
ECI ayaʀaaq 'string game' [Saul, also as verb]
GRI NG ayaʀaaq, EG ayaŋaaliiʀniq 'string game' [also ayaŋaaliiʀ- as a verb in Ges.; Holt. also has NG ayaʀʀaaʀutit 'string figures'; for the WG equivalent see under ayaɣaq (ayaɣ-)]

PY ayaʀi- 'covet' [there may be a link to ayi-]
AAY aya<ʀ>i- 'covet, envy'
CAY HBC ayaʀi-, ayaʀa- 'covet, desire'
NSY —
CSY —

PE aya(C)u- 'be blind'
AAY —
CAY —
NSY ayaa(w)- 'go blind' [ANLC; L.-T. also has ayama- 'be blind', probably for ayaama-]
CSY ayaa- 'become blind'
SPI ayau-
NAI ayau-
WCI —
ECI —
GRI —

PY-S ayəmə- 'break in two'
AAY ayəmə-, aimə-, Kod also ayumə- 'break in two (long, slender objects)' [and aimaaXtə- 'snap off suddenly', ayəmqaq, aimqaq 'portage']
CAY azmə-, HBC aymə- 'break in two' [and note azvaitə-, ayvaitə- 'be solid']
NSY ayəmə- 'break in two (s.th. long and thin)'
CSY ayəmə- 'break off' [and note ayəmqə-, ayəmquʀ- 'break a long, thin thing', ayəpsuɣitə- 'be sturdy', also ayva- 'be gravely ill']
Sir ayəmquʀ- 'break' [Vakh.]
Inu — [but note NAI aimaʀnaq 'antlerless or barren female caribou']

PY ayəməɣtə- 'cut hair'
AAY —
CAY azməxtə- 'cut hair short'
NSY ayməxtə- 'cut hair' [ANLC, also for ayməɣnəq 'haircut']
CSY —

PY ayi- 'get whatever one wants'
AAY —
CAY ayi- 'be satiated, get whatever one wants'
NSY —
CSY azi- 'get whatever one wants'

PE ayŋun 'rancid oil' [the NSY, CSY and Sir meanings by contam. with aŋəq?; cf. un]
AAY —
CAY —[but note Y, Nun azəXtə- 'rub something against something']
NSY ayŋun 'blubber chewed as gum' [and ayŋuXtə- 'paint' — Men. has ayŋuʀusiʀ-]
CSY [ayŋusi- 'make chewing gum from blubber']
Sir [ayŋusaX- 'make chewing gum from cooked oil' — Orr]
SPI anŋun 'rancid oil for caulking boat'
NAI anŋun, PH anŋuk 'rancid oil for caulking boat'
WCI —
ECI —
GRI —

PE ayu- 'go ahead or further' [cf. Aleut aðu- 'be long', also perhaps PI ayu(ž)aq and ayuktaq-; Aleut ayuɣ- 'leave (by boat)' may also be related but compare PE ayaɣ- — the PE set here could represent a conflation of two distinct sets reflected in Aleut; for Aleut ayu- 'fall' see ayalu(ʀ)-]
AAY AP, KP ayu- 'progress, get bigger, spread' [ayu<ɣ>i-, K, KP also aiwi-, KP also ayyu- 'leave (by boat)' are probably borrowed directly from Aleut ayuɣ- (pres. ayuɣi-kuX, etc.) above; note B.-S. has ayuɣi- 'travel, hunt (sea animals)']
CAY ayu- 'progress, go further, spread (e.g. rash)'
NSY ayu- 'go far' [ANLC; ayuʀ- 'hold out, hold on'; Men. also has ayuŋalʀia 'distant', ayułəq 'distance']
CSY ayu- 'progress, keep going'
Sir ayə- 'go far off' [Em.]
SPI ayu- 'get a head's start, progress, die', Qaw ayuuqi- 'put off doing s.th.' [and W ayu- 'carry away (ice)' — Jen.]
NAI ayu- 'go ahead, have head's start, die', ayuuq- 'go far, progress', ayuuqqi-, Mal ayuuqi- 'put off doing s.th.' [and Jen. has ayuk- 'flee', which could go with Aleut ayuɣ- above]
WCI [Sig ayuulɣu- 'go far (rock, bullet)' is perhaps rather Uum acc. Met.] ⟶
ECI ayu- 'run away, break loose, run off inland (angry person)' [and ayutit- 'free', ayuuʀvik 'goal (football)']
GRI ayuut(i)- 'kick toward goal (football)'

PY-S ayumiq 'long ago'
AAY —
CAY —
NSY —
CSY ayumiq* 'long ago, year' [ayumiqun 'next year', ayumiXtaq 'thing from long ago']
Sir ayəmiX 'long ago, last year' [and Em. has ayəmiku 'next year', ayəmisitaX 'thing from long ago']

PE ayut- 'extend or enlarge' [cf. t-[1] and Aleut aðut- 'make longer']
AAY —
CAY ayutə- 'enlarge'
NSY ayutə- 'enlarge' [ANLC]
CSY —
Sir [Vakh. has ayələɣaʀ- 'move aside (trans.)']
SPI [note Imaq ayut- 'move away (trans.)']
NAI —
WCI —
ECI Lab ayu(t)- 'enlarge' [Peck]
GRI ayut- 'extend, stretch (shoes)'

PI ayuži- 'have s.th. get away from one' [cf. ði-]
SPI —
NAI Nu ayuži- 'have get away from one'
WCI Sig ayuy(y)i- 'lose ground on s.o.' [Cop ayuXXi- of the same meaning may be due to contam. with ayuq-]
ECI ayuyi- 'have run away from one (one's dogs)'
GRI ayuši- 'have s.th. get away from one'

PI ayu(ž)aq 'boil (sore)'
SPI ayuaq, pl. ayužat 'boil'
NAI ayuaq 'boil, sore' [verbal = 'develop a boil']
WCI ayuaq
ECI ayuaq 'boil' [verbal = 'have a boil']
GRI ayuaq 'boil' [pl. ayuššat; ayuaʀ- 'have a boil']

PY-S ayuɣ- 'be loose' [there may be a link to ayuktaq-]
AAY KP ayuɣnəq, PWS ayuʀnəq 'joint (on body)'
CAY — [but note aʀivnəq* 'hinge, knuckle, joint'?]
NSY —
CSY ayuɣiʀ- 'tighten', ayuɣitə- 'be durable'
Sir ayuɣiqət(ə)- 'strengthen, be durable (boat)'

PI ayuktaq- 'play game with ball' [the relat. — if any — with ayu- and ayyutaʀ- is obscure; cf. also ayuɣ-?]
SPI —
NAI ayuktaq- 'play football' [nom. = 'ball'; Jen. has ayuk 'football']
WCI —
ECI ayutta(q)- 'play football' [as nom. = 'football'; Peck has ayuk- 'sling, hit (ball)' and ayuktaut 'sling used by two men, line for beating and playing at ball' for Lab]
GRI NG ayuktaq- 'roll ball up a slope in game' [Holt. — also nom. ayuktaq 'ball made of caribou bone for playing game with']

PI ayuq- 'be unable to reach or do' [cf. Aleut ayqiXta- 'find difficult'; there may be a link to ayuʀiʀ-]
Yup — [but B.-S. has AAY ayuuqenta 'difficult']
SPI ayuq- 'be unable to reach'
NAI ayuq- 'be unable to reach, be in desperate need of s.th.'
WCI Sig ayuq- 'be unable to reach', Cop 'cannot do, be incompetent']
ECI ayuq-, ayuʀi- 'cannot do' [and ayuɣaq 'someone unbeatable, difficulty', NBI, Aiv ayuŋŋit- 'be clever']
GRI ayuʀ- WG 'cannot, does not, be bad', EG 'be bad', NG ayuq- 'cannot' [note also ayuʀši- 'cannot manage', ayuʀi- 'not like', ayuŋŋit- 'be good', NG 'be able to', ayuɣaq 'superior', ayuɣaa- 'win', ayuqut 'hindrance']

PI ayuqšaq- 'suffer want' [compare capəqšaq- under capə-]
SPI —

NAI —
WCI [Sig ayuqsaR- 'try to catch (but cannot)']
ECI ayuRsa(q)- 'be in need, impoverished'
GRI ayuRšaR- 'suffer want, lack, lose'

PI ayuqšit- 'become unable to do anything'
SPI —
NAI —
WCI Sig ayuqsit- 'be stuck, unable to do s.th.'
ECI ayuRsit- 'become impossible to dislodge'
GRI ayuRšit- 'give up'

PI ayuRnaq- 'be impossible to do' [cf. naR-]
SPI —
NAI ayuRnaq- 'be scarce, hard to catch'
WCI Cop ayuRnaq- 'be impossible' [Jen.; Briggs has 'cannot be helped' for Net]
ECI ayuRna(q)- 'be impossible' [Saul]
GRI ayuRnaR- 'be impossible' [and NG ayuRnaŋŋuayu 'how good, how clever!']

PE ayuqə- 'resemble' [cf. ayuRiR-]
AAY ayuqə- 'resemble, be like'
CAY ayuqə-
NSY ayuqə-
CSY ayuqə- 'resemble, be like' [and note ayuqłiq(*) 'mainland Alaskan Eskimo']
Sir —
SPI [for ayuuqi- 'become fixed' see ayuRiR-] ➡
NAI ➡
WCI Car? ayuqasi- 'imitate' [Schn. 'adg']
ECI [for Lab ayuɣik- 'imitate' see ayuRiR-] ➡
GRI ➡

PE ayuquciRtuR- 'instruct' [cf. un, liR- and tuR-[2]; the preserved q in Inu suggests the contraction that is involved]
AAY [note Kod ayuqutaXcista 'teacher']
CAY ayuquciXtuR- 'instruct'
NSY ayuqəsiXtusi- 'explain, show how'
CSY —
Sir —
SPI Qaw ayuqiqtuq- 'instruct', KI ayuqatuq- 'show how to behave'
NAI ayuqiqsuq- 'give moral instruction' [and ayuqiqsuun 'good teachings']
WCI —
ECI ayuqiq-, ayuqiqtu(q)- 'teach, preach'
GRI ayuqiR-, ayuqiRsuR- 'instruct', ayuqi, SWG ayuqiit 'catechist' [the former nominal a back-formation; note also ayuqiRsuut 'teaching']

PE ayuRiR- 'get used to or fixed' [cf. ayuqə-, also ayuq- and ŋiR-?]
AAY —
CAY —
NSY ayuRiR- 'get used to'
CSY ayRiR- 'get accustomed to s.th.'
Sir ayRiR- 'get used to'
SPI [note ayuuqi- 'become fixed' and Imaq ayu(u)siq 'habit']
NAI ayuRak- 'get used to, become fixed', ayuRit- 'form a habit'
WCI ayuRak- 'go dead (limb), get folded wrongly (garment)', ayuRit- 'have the habit of -ing'
ECI ayuRiR- 'get used to', ayuRit- 'get a habit' [and Lab ayuɣik- 'imitate']
GRI [ayuRiŋŋuR-, ayuRuŋŋuR-, EG ajaaŋŋuR- 'be stiff, unable to return to earlier shape']

PY-S ayva- 'be weak?'
AAY K asɣʷaitə-, KP aywaitə-, PWS aywiitə- 'be made to last, sturdy, secure, strong (spiritually)'
CAY azvaitə- 'be solid, stable, immovable', azvaiR- 'stabilize, solidify'
NSY —
CSY ayva- 'be gravely ill'
Sir ayvatalər- 'be sad' [Vakh. from Rub.'s texts]

PE ayvəR 'walrus' [there may be a link to ayaɣ-; compare also the second syllable of arvəR]
AAY C ayyuq, AP aswəq, Kod asɣuq 'walrus'
CAY azvəq*
NSY ayvəq
CSY ayvəq*
Sir ayvəX
SPI aiviq
NAI aiviq*
WCI aiviq
ECI aiviq
GRI aaviq* [old ortho. auveq spurious] 'walrus' [pl. aaffit, aaXXit, NG pl. auRRit, rel. sing. aiRRup]

PI aivvak- 'catch a walrus' [cf. nəɣ-]
SPI aivak- 'catch a walrus'
NAI aivvak-
WCI [Pryde has aiviq-]
ECI aivva(k)- 'catch a walrus'
GRI aaffaɣ-

PE ayyutaR- 'play game like hockey' [compare ayuktaq-, though the relat. is obscure — perhaps there is contam. with ayaɣutaR under ayaɣ-]
AAY —
CAY ayyutaR- 'play hockey', ayyutaq 'hockey stick'
NSY —
CSY —
Sir —
SPI ayyutaq 'game like hockey played on ice', Qaw 'hockey stick', ayyutaq- 'play Eskimo ice hockey'
NAI PH ayyutaq- 'play (Inupiaq version of) ice hockey, play golf', ayyutaaq 'hockey stick, etc.'
WCI —
ECI [ayuttauti 'hockey stick']
GRI —

PI ažak- 'be gentle with' [two bases may have fallen together here]
SPI ažak- 'comfort'
NAI ažak- 'comfort, encourage, soothe, placate' [note the Mal 'half transitive' form ažaknik- with nnək-; ažaaRi- 'keep encouraging tenderly']

WCI —
ECI Iti ayak- 'wash (plates and bowls)' [Schn. for Richmond Gulf; note Tar asaC- 'clean (house, self or clothes)' acc. Qumaq — Schn. has trans. asa-; the s is unexplained, but there may be contam. from uasaq- 'wash' under URAR- if not from the GRI below (via the missionaries?); note also Lab ayak- 'gently touch s.o. on shoulder to see if they are OK' under ayaɣ-, which may belong here rather]
GRI ašattuaʀ- 'go gently', ašattuut(i)- 'spare, bear with s.o.' [and WG, EG asa- 'love, be loving or friendly toward' (already in Top, but perhaps a NWG or southern SWG form from earlier *aša(ɣ)-), WG asaaʀi- 'love tenderly' — cf. NAI ažaaʀi- above, and compare also the half-trans. form of asa-, asanniɣ-, with the Mal above, suggesting reanalysis of the ɣ as going with the p.b. (old ortho. ngnig — see under nnək-); also ašaɣ- (half.-trans. ašaa-), EG asaɣ- (not expected *alaɣ-, so probably from WG) 'wash (e.g. self or floor)' (specifically 'wash face' in NWG), NG ahak- 'wash self', ahai- 'wash floor' — in Fab. this is glossed 'look after, clean, be economical with', i.e. clearly the same base as in his ašektor- 'preserve, look after' (Egede has ašak- 'look after, treat well', not in Top)]

C

PY caaʀin 'alder'
AAY AP caa<ʀ>in 'alder'
CAY caaʀin 'white alder'
NSY —
CSY —

PI caat-[1] 'be thin' [the intervocalic ɣ in NAI may not be historic, so there is probably a link to PY-S całək and/or PY canəɣ(ə)t-, though the relat. is obscure — compare the loss of intervocalic n in Inu under nanit-]
SPI saatuužau-, Qaw saat- 'be thin' [and saałuʀayak 'thin, flat stone'; W saalɣužaq 'thin ice']
NAI sa<ɣ>at- 'be soft, thin, pliable, have thin hair' [and saalʀuq 'thinner area of s.th. (esp. thin ice)', Nu saɣɣutyaq 'snow house made of soft new snow', saatuquyak, Nu saapaqayak 'thin, flat stone']
WCI saat- 'be thin'
ECI saat- 'be thin' [Dor. has NBI saak-; note also saattuʀayaq, saattuyaaq 's.th. thin (cloth, iron sheet, etc.)']
GRI saat- 'be thin' [and saaʀłuq 'bald patch (from bad haircut)', saattuq 'thin, flat rock', saattuʀalaaq, saanniʀalaaq 'shirting'; for saniɣuʀ- 'become emaciated' see canəɣ(ə)t-]

PI caakli- 'become thin' [cf. li-[2]]
SPI Qaw saaɣli- 'become thin (esp. ice)'
NAI saakłi-, saaɣli- 'become thin, make pliable (skin)'
WCI saɣli- 'become thinner'
ECI saalli- 'have thinned s.th. down', sallili(q)- 'thin down' [and sallitaq 'plank']
GRI sałłi-, saali- 'become or make thin' [sałłilisaq 'plank']

PI caavʀaq 'snipe'
SPI —
NAI saavʀaq 'snipe'
WCI haavʀaq Net 'snipe', Cop 'redshank' [Ras.; Dor. has 'sandpiper' for B. Lake]
ECI saaʀvak 'red phalarope'
GRI saaʀfaaʀšuk 'snipe'

PY caayuʀ(y)aq 'silver salmon'
AAY —
PWS caayuaq 'silver salmon'
CAY Nun, NS caayuʀyaq
NSY —
CSY —

PE caðə- 'front (of body)' [see under p.b. tə as regards the second syllable; cf. Aleut sað- 'outside, side toward sea', Atkan saðaʀu-X 'northwest', and perhaps sa- 'blade of knife, face' as in sam kaðan 'front of the face' and 'steep promontory' in place names; there may be a remote relat. to dem. roots cam-, cakəm-, etc.]
AAY K cai- 'front of body'
CAY — [for cayaq 'chest, lungpower' see caya(ɣ)]
NSY sayə- 'front', sayət chest' [ANLC sayə in both senses]
CSY saya 'front of body' [and Chap sayəŋuʀžuk 'chest']
Sir saca 'chest' [also caca 'front of object or clothing', Vakh. saca; and Em. has lum sacəŋa 'walrus skin cover over entrance to winter dwelling']
SPI saa- 'front of body'
NAI saa- 'front of body', sanmun 'toward ocean'
WCI Sig saa- 'in front, toward sea', Cop haa- 'in front, south'
ECI saa- 'in front', saa 'table' [and savvik, NBI, SB saɣvik 'chest']
GRI saaq, saa- 'front' [in EG caaq also 'chest' and 'palm' acc. Robbe and Menn. — Robbe and Dor. have caaya 'chest', a possessed form; sammut 'toward the front or west', saaqqutit 'implements on front of kayak' — EG caaqqit 'harpoon used from kayak'; NG haŋmuak- 'go out to sea']

PI caat-[2] 'face' [cf. t-[1]]
SPI saat- 'face, turn toward'
NAI saat-
WCI saat-
ECI saat-
GRI saat- 'face, turn toward' [and saaššut(i)- 'turn in anger toward, attack']

PI caavət- 'go out to sea' [cf. vət- under VAR-]
SPI saavit- 'go out in front of a group to dance'
NAI saavɨt- 'go out to sea or river, go down to hunt on ice or beach, go out in front of a group, put boat out to sea'
WCI saavit-, saavik- 'go out to sea (of boat or floating thing)' [Ras. also has for Cop haavik- 'drift away

from land, (poetic) jump forward to sing a reply in song contest']
ECI saavik- 'go out to sea'
GRI saaviɣ-, saavit- 'be driven off by wind or current'

PE caðəŋilitaʀ 'apron' [cf. ŋilitaʀ]
AAY —
CAY —
NSY [sayəʀailitaq 'apron']
CSY saayŋiitaq 'apron'
Sir sayŋitaX, pl. sayŋitaʀy [Orr]
SPI [saamiilitaq 'apron']
NAI [note saaʀu<ž>aq 'apron, bib']
WCI Cop haaŋilitaq 'apron' [Pryde; and note Sig saamiʀun, saamiʀuaq 'apron, bib']
ECI saaŋilitaq 'apron'
GRI [note saarułłik 'sea cod', EG caarʀ̌ittik 'murre' with ləɣ, both creatures with 'bibs']

PI ca(a)lliq and **caaʀliq** 'foremost' [cf. l(l)iʀ — the second form with related qliʀ rather]
SPI salliq 'one toward the ocean'
NAI salliq* 'one in front, most toward ocean'
WCI saalliq 'most toward sea'
ECI saaʀsiq 's.th. farther ahead' [and note place name Salliq 'Coral Harbor']
GRI saarłiq* 'foremost', sałłiq* 'foremost, farthest out to sea' [old ortho. sagdleq for the latter, but Fab. has sellek; EG cattiq 'rower nearest steersman'; note also EG caʀti- 'be off the coast' in Robbe and Menn.]

PI canmi- 'turn toward' [cf. p.b. umi-?]
SPI [Jen. has KI saɣmi- 'be very fond of']
NAI sanmi-, PH saŋmi- 'turn to face'
WCI sanmi-, hanmi-
ECI sammituq- 'come toward shore (wave)', sammiut(i)- 'face one another'
GRI sammi- [old ortho. sangmi-] 'turn toward, be occupied with'

PI cažʀutə- 'pass in front' [cf. tʀutə-]
SPI sažʀut(i)- 'pass by in front or along shore'
NAI sažʀut(ɨ)- 'pass by in front (of)'
WCI Sig sayʀut(i)-, Cop halʀuti- [Pryde] 'pass offshore', Car EP halʀuti- 'pass by without stopping' [Ow.]
ECI saʀʀut(i)- 'pass in front of' [intr. also 'come to surface and pass close in front (seal, whale)']
GRI saʀšut(i)- 'pass in front of, pass by'

PI cažvaq- 'move forward' [cf. vaʀ-]
SPI savžaq- 'lay out, put or go forward'
NAI sažvaq- 'move forward or toward ocean'
WCI Sig sa(a)yvakun 'at large, far out to sea'
ECI savva(q)- 'put in front of, wager, present self as partner (for work)', saʀva(q)- 'place oneself in front of (another)' [contam. with caʀvaʀ? — see the homonym there meaning 'lie on a slope'; Spald. has saɣuaq- 'put down in front or nearer to sea' for NBI]
GRI [saʀšaʀ- 'move forward, bring forward, set out (food)' — influenced by cažʀutə- above?]

PI cažvasik- 'be out in front' [cf. cažvaq- above and ðiɣ-]
SPI savžazik- 'be nearby, near the edge'
NAI sažvasik- 'lie far out to sea, out of reach' [and satcik- 'be far out in front or at sea']
WCI Cop halvahik- 'be out at sea'
ECI savvasik- 'be close in front'
GRI [satsiɣ- 'be far out to sea or in the west']

PE caðəɣ(iʀ) 'wormwood (artemesia)'
AAY C, AP caik 'wormwood' [and AP caixłuk 'bushy place', PWS caisiq 'yarrow']
CAY caixłuk, NSU caxłuk 'wormwood, artemesia'
NSY saaɣ̥xə [ANLC]
CSY žiixłuk
Sir əcixłux [Orr]
SPI saɣžiq 'blade of grass, stinkweed'
NAI PH sažɣɨq, sažɣiʀžuaq, PH salɣiʀžuaq 'artemesia, stinkweed'
WCI Cop halɣiq 'groundsel' [Pryde]
ECI —
GRI —

PE caðəɣuʀ 'fence or partition' [cf. caðə-]
AAY K cazɣuq 'fence'
CAY cazɣuq, HBC cayɣuq 'fence, partition'
NSY [sayutaq 'curtain']
CSY saayɣu 'tunnel entrance to semi-subterranean house'
Sir sayɣu [Orr]
SPI [saayu 'cache on roof of house']
NAI [saiʀut 'stockade made of large willows']
WCI —
ECI saiɣuq 'fence, grillwork' [as verb = 'keep captive in cage, behind fence, etc.]
GRI saaɣuq, EG caaʀžiq 'curtain, hanging, veil' [and saaɣu- 'pull a curtain in front of', NG haayuq 'curtain', haarut 'trouser flap' — Holt.]

PE caðku 'weapon or tool' [cf. caðə-, also EA sat- 'pierce, wound (game)' with p.b. t-[1]]
AAY C caskuk 'hunting equipment'
CAY caskuk, caskuq, saskuk, saskuq 'weapon, tool'
NSY saɣku 'bow' [L.-T.; for saanqutə 'ware' see canqun]
CSY— [for sanqun 'ware' see canqun]
Sir —
SPI satkuq 'bow'
NAI satku(q) 'weapon' [satku- 'strike with harpoon, shoot at animal']
WCI satku 'weapon' [B. Lake hakku 'bullet, ammunition' — Dor.; Schn. has sakkuaq- 'have wounded (game, with harpoon)' for 'adg']
ECI sakku 'weapon, bullet', NBI also 'tip of sealing harpoon', Frobisher Bay 'ammunition' [and Iti sakkua(q)- 'have wounded with weapon', an old word

from legends, acc. Schn.]
GRI sakku 'weapon, tool, implement', EG cakkiq 'woman's knife', NG hakkuq 'thin harpoon blade for harpooning narwhal' [note also sakkuaʀ- 'attack, use weapon against']

PY caɣəlmak 'plover'
AAY —
CAY ciilmak 'black turnstone, black-bellied plover, American golden plover'
NSY —
CSY saɣəlmak 'plover, turnstone'

PI caɣɣaq 'thin-haired skin' [there may be a link to ciðaɣ- but see also caat-[1]]
Yup [CAY caɣinʀaq 'caribou skin taken just after long winter hair has been shed in spring' probably goes with ciðaɣ-]
SPI —
NAI saɣɣaq* 'caribou or caribou skin with new hair'
WCI saɣɣaq 'short hair (just beginning to grow)', Car Baker Lake 'skin bitten by insects' [Dor. for the latter, Met. for the former; Met. also has sanraq in this sense for Sig — influenced by kanʀaq-?; Schn. has hayɣamaktiq 'caribou skin that is almost hairless' for B. Lake]
ECI saɣɣaq 'short hair', Iti saɣɣa(q)- 'Iti 'have short fur' [but in Tar 'unearth by digging or scraping, hoe']
GRI saxxaq* 'thin-haired skin, light fog, thin layer of snow', EG cakkaq 'ringed seal' [and note saxxaʀ- 'spread, push aside by force']

caɣiq 'halibut' [loan from Aleut caɣi-X]
AAY saɣiq 'halibut'
CAY caɣiq, saɣiq 'flounder', Nun 'halibut'
NSY —
CSY —

PY-S caɣiqə- 'persist or make an effort' [cf. caɣŋi- and ʀqə-, also cakə(t)-]
AAY —
CAY —
NSY saɣiqaXtaʀ- 'make effort to do s.th., be difficult, harden oneself physically', saɣiqn̥aq 'difficulty' [and saɣiqn̥aXqə- 'make difficulties'; ANLC has saɣiqn̥aʀ- 'be difficult', saɣiqaXtə- 'find difficult, harden, endeavor to do']
CSY saɣiqə- 'persist, insist, urge on' [saɣiqn̥ailŋuq 'easy']
Sir saXqə- 'work hard', saXqat(ə)- 'strain, make effort' [saXqənəɬəʀəX 'difficult', saXqənəʀəlŋuX 'easy']
Inu [for SPI saɣiqi- 'work hard' see cakə(t)-]

PI caɣlu- 'tell a lie'
SPI saɣlu- 'tell a lie'
NAI saɣlu-
WCI saɣlu-
ECI sallu-
GRI saɬɬu-

PI caɣluqə(C)- 'tell a lie to' [cf. ʀqə-?]
SPI —
NAI saɣluqɨ- 'tell a lie to'
WCI Cop haɣluqit-, Car haɣluqitaaq- 'fool, deceive' [Pryde]
ECI salluqi(C)- 'tell a lie'
GRI saɬɬuqittaʀ-

PE caɣnəʀ- 'ache (have sore muscles)' [cf. caɣŋi-]
AAY AP saɣnəʀ- 'have sore muscles'
CAY caɣnəʀ-
NSY —
CSY —
Sir —
SPI saŋniq- 'have sore muscles from hard work'
NAI saŋniq-
WCI —
ECI sanni(q)- 'be aching all over'
GRI NG haŋniq- 'be sore in one's muscles' [Holt.]

PE caɣŋi- 'be taut or strong' [cf. caɣnəʀ-, also caɣiqə-]
AAY AP saɣni(tə)- 'be taut'
CAY caɣni-
NSY —
CSY saɣniin 'cord sewn along boot sole seam to keep threads taut'
Sir saɣnita [Orr]
SPI saŋŋit- 'tighten', saŋŋima- 'be taut'
NAI saŋŋi- 'be strong' [and saŋŋiqšuq- 'exert great force'], saŋŋit- 'be taut', PH 'form cirrus clouds', Mal saŋŋiit- 'be weak'
WCI Sig saŋŋi- 'be strong', saŋŋit- 'tighten'
ECI saŋŋiit- 'be weak' [Dorais], Lab saŋ(ŋ)i-, Iti saŋŋi- 'be strong, mighty' [Peck and Saul respectively]
GRI saŋŋi-, NWG saŋŋit- 'be strong', saŋŋiit- 'be weak'

PY-S caɣuyaq[1] 'drum' [cf. Aleut caaya-x 'drum' (dual) — borrowed from Eskimo]
AAY cauyat (pl.) 'music'
CAY cauyaq 'drum'
NSY saayaq 'drum' [and saayaʀ- 'dance (woman)' (ANLC)']
CSY saɣuyaq
Sir saɣəyaX 'drum' [and saɣəɬəx 'shaman' — Vakh. has saɣiɬəx 'shaman, helping spirit']
Inu [SPI sauyaq 'drum' is probably borrowed from Yup]

caɣuyaq[2] 'conical wooden hat' [from Aleut caxuða-X 'conical wooden hat, visor', ultimately perhaps from Tlingit]
AAY saku<ʀ>aq 'conical wooden hat'
CAY Nun caɣuyaX
NSY —
CSY —

PI caɣvi(q)- 'become visible' [the relat. with caðə- is obscure but compare qaɣvaʀ- — the cluster may reflect a parallel change to the n + C to ŋ + C shift east of Alaska]
SPI [for savžaq- 'lay out, put or go forward' see cažvaq- under caðə-]

NAI saɣviq- 'bring into the open, explain, come into view', Nu saɣvi- 'become visible'
WCI saɣviq- 'appear' [and Schn. has savviq- 'lose bet, lose sight of' for 'adg']
ECI — [for savva(q)- 'put in front of' see under cažvaq- (caðə-)]
GRI —

PI cail(l)i- 'feel at ease' [cf. caima-]
SPI —
NAI sailʸlʸi- 'relax, recover after stress'
WCI Cop haili- 'laze about' [Pryde]
ECI saili- 'feel at ease'
GRI saali- 'be at home (while others are out)'

PI caima- 'become calm' [cf. cail(l)i- and (u)ma-]
SPI saimaq- 'stop crying'
NAI saima- 'be quiet, not cry', saimmaq- 'stop crying' [and note saʀimasuk- 'feel appreciated'; Dor. has haima- 'be happy']
WCI saimaq- 'become calm, stop crying' [and note B. Lake haʀima- 'be happy to have got what one wanted' — Schn.]
ECI saimmaC- 'calm after anger', saimma- 'be calm, at peace' [and saimmati 'flag'?]
GRI saama- 'be kind, mild, tractable, satisfied'

PI caka- or **caɣɣa-** 'rock back and forth' [compare Aiv saɣɣamaktaq under cakamaktaq for the geminate]
SPI —
NAI —
WCI Car B. Lake haka- 'practice sorcery' [Dor.; but Schn. has saɣɣa- 'perform sorcery on sick person' for 'adg']
ECI Igl saka- 'shamanize' [Ras.; Schn. has sakka- for non-Car 'adg']
GRI saka- 'rock back and forth' [and sakaɣ- 'shove, jostle (into s.o. carelessly)']

PI cakamaktaq 'raised cache or cairn' [cf. caka-?]
SPI —
NAI —
WCI Net hakamaktuq 'cairn-like rock structure built for amusement with top and sides of equal dimensions', hence also 'square braiding of dog-whip' [Pryde; for Baker Lake haɣɣamaktiq 'caribou skin that is almost hairless' see caɣɣaq]
ECI Aiv saɣɣamaktaq 'cache of food raised on snow' [by contam. with caɣɣaq?]
GRI NG hakamaktaq 'cairn' [compare WG sakamattaq 'knob on end of s.th.' — Kl. 'a head-shaped knob on the end of s.th., a toy of this kind', sakamaɣ- 'put knob on end of, plait straws layed across each other (as a toy)']

PI cakcakiq 'redpoll (or similar small bird)' [cf. ceqtaaq]
SPI —
NAI saksakiq, Nu saksaŋiq 'redpoll' [also saksaɣiaq, saksaŋiaq]
WCI saksaɣialuk 'kind of robin'
ECI satsaɣiaq 'little bird (Hudsonian chaffinch, sparrow)' [Bourq. has 'birch siskin' for Lab]
GRI —

PE cakə(t)- 'struggle or have a hard time' [cf. cakla-, also caɣiqə-, cakəvət- with which there appears to be some contamination]
AAY cakŋ̥əʀ-, Kod cakŋ̥iuʀ-, AP cakuuɣ-, Kod, KP cakuɣ-, C caktuuɣ- 'have difficulty, a hard time' [and note perhaps PWS cakuxtə- 'rummage through s.th.']
CAY cakfiuʀ- 'have a hard time', NSU cakətə- 'work hard' [Eg caktə- 'be small' is prob. from a different base], also cakŋ̥əʀ- 'struggle to function']
NSY —
CSY sakŋ̥iqə- 'exert oneself, yearn for s.th., be anxious'
Sir —
SPI saɣiqi-, Qaw sakiqi- 'have a hard time, work hard' [there may be conflation of two bases here — compare under caɣiqə-]
NAI sakiʀi- 'feel unable to accomplish', sakiʀnaq- 'be hard to do' [and sakuuk- 'be busy, work hard', sakkiq- 'begin s.th.', Nu 'work hard, depart'; Mal sakiq-. sakiʀi- 'feel incapable', sakiqnaq 'hardship, difficulty', sakkaq-, sakiqi- 'work hard' — compare the latter forms with SPI above]
WCI Sig sakiʀnaq- 'be a little hard to do' [and sakuq- 'be hard at work']
ECI —
GRI saki- 'struggle to get free (e.g. animal in trap)' [and sakimmiʀi- 'be hard to get (s.th. one likes)']

PE cakəvət- and **caku-** 'scrape skin' [cf. caki(tə)- and also cakə(t)-, with which there is contamination; forms like cakuuɣ- may be further influenced by caluɣ-]
AAY —
CAY NSU cakuuɣ-, HBC, Nun, NS cakiftə- 'tan by scraping (skin)'
NSY —
CSY sakətə- 'make thinner'
Sir —
SPI saɣivit- 'scrape skin', saɣuuk- 'stretch, soften skin after tanning'
NAI sakivɨt- 'scrape skin'
WCI sakipsi-, sakivit- 'scrape sealskin', Net hakuut 'sharp skin scraper' [Ras.]
ECI sakuuk- 'soften a skin with an instrument' [and Iti sakiuti 'instrument for softening skin']
GRI —

PE caki 'father- or mother-in-law' [cf. Aleut cikiiða- 'wife's brother, (man's) sister's husband']
AAY caki(k) 'father-in-law'
CAY cakiq 'father-in-law, mother-in-law'
NSY saki
CSY saki
Sir saki
SPI saɣiq
NAI ➟
WCI saki 'in-law'
ECI saki 'father- or mother-in-law'
GRI saki, EG caɣiq, Up sakiq 'father- or mother-in-law'

PE cakiʀaʀ 'brother- or sister-in-law' [cf. aʀ]
AAY C caki<ʀ>aq 'brother-in-law or sister-in-law (only in sense of spouse's sibling)'

CAY cakiʀaq
NSY sakiʀaq 'sibling of spouse' [ANLC]
CSY sakiiq* 'husband's sister', sakiiʀaq* 'wife's brother'
Sir sakiX 'husband's sister', sakəʀaX 'wife's brother' [Orr]
SPI sagiʀaq 'spouse's sibling'
NAI sakiʀaq 'spouse's sibling, sister-in-law or brother-in-law, older sister's husband', PH 'in-law' [and sakialuk 'husband's sister']
WCI Cop hakiaq 'brother-in-law (of man)' [Pryde]
ECI sakiaq 'uncle- or aunt-in- law, brother- or sister-in-law'
GRI [sakiatsiaq 'brother- or sister-in-law']

PY-S caki(tə)- 'chop or cut into' [cf. cakəvət-?]
AAY cakitə- 'hew, carve'
CAY caki- 'cut out a small piece, plane (wood)', cakitə- 'chop, cut into accidentally' [and caki(y)un 'chopping device']
NSY —
CSY [sakəʀ- 'cut in one stroke, slash']
Sir sakit(ə)- 'chop, dig with front paws (animal)' [Em.; sakitəqəX 'kind of small hoe or hatchet' — Vakh. from Men's texts; Em. has sakita for this]

PE caki(C)aɣ 'rib cage' [cf. Aleut sakiix, pl. Atkan sakiiɣis, EA sakiiɣin 'rib (the back bony part)']
AAY cakia<ʀ>aq 'rib (of animal, Kod also of boat)'
CAY cakiak, cakiaq 'breastbone'
NSY saɣiq 'breast' [Jen.]
CSY sakimak 'chest'
Sir sakəməx 'chest'
SPI saɣiat, W saɣiaɣit [pl. in Jen.] 'chest'
NAI sakiak, pl. sakiaɣic 'breastbone', sakkiak 'front middle part of animal'
WCI sakiyyat [pl.] 'chest'
ECI sakiat [pl.] 'chest, rib cage, bones of thorax'
GRI sakiak, EG saɣiaq 'rib cage', pl. sakiššat 'chest', NG hakiq '(upper part of) chest' [the šš in the WG form probably does not reflect a historical *ð]

PI cakla- 'move about busily' [cf. cakə(t)-]
SPI sakła- 'move about constantly'
NAI PH saɣla- 'be constantly busy'
WCI —
ECI —
GRI sałła- 'move around quickly' [sałłaat- 'be slow, be gentle']

PY calaʀaq 'east or fine weather?' [this assumes that weather from the east on Kenai Peninsula is generally of this nature]
AAY KP cal<ʀ>aq 'fine clear weather'
CAY calaʀaq 'east'
NSY —
CSY —

PI caliaq- 'cross hillside' [cf. caðə- and liyaʀ-?]
SPI [note sanniaq- traverse a hillside', influenced by cani-?]
NAI saliaq- 'traverse, walk along a hillside, slope, or beach' [and salik- 'travel swiftly parallel to s.th.' — the Nu homonym meaning 'wave arms when sighting caribou' may not be related; saliuržuk- 'slip sideaways (sled)']
WCI [note Sig saliɣniuq- 'slip sideways (of sled)'; for saliktaq- 'gesture for s.o. to come' compare the Nu above]
ECI saliaq- 'go along edge of sea, around base of mountain' [and saliak- 'slide to the side (of sled)']
GRI NG haliaq- 'move forward along mountain slope a little way up it' [Holt.]

PY caliɣaq 'flat rock' [there could be a link to całiɣ-[1]]
AAY PWS saliyaʀnaq 'flat rock, slab of rock'
CAY Nun caliɣaX 'large flat rock'
NSY —
CSY —
Inu [compare ECI saliɣaq- 'smooth and flatten blocks of snow for snow house' under całiɣ-[1]]

PE caluɣ- 'be dried out or dry out (esp. skin in sun)' [cf. western Aleut saalu-X 'dry weather', also PE całiɣ-[1], with which there appears to be considerable entanglement]
AAY —
CAY caluxtə- 'tan by scraping'
NSY saluɣ- 'be dying of thirst' [Taghyuq]
CSY saluɣ- 'be in dire need of water, dying of thirst'
Sir saluxt(ə)- 'dry, be dried out'
SPI saluk- 'tan, die of starvation'
NAI saluksi- 'clean skin by hitting with stick (tanning process)', Nu saluk- 'scrape skin'
WCI Cop haluk- 'scrape skin' [contam. with całiɣ-[1]?; and Ow. has haluʀaq 'dry ground' for EP]
ECI saluk- 'have slimmed' [and sallu 'thin thing']
GRI saluɣ- 'be thin' [and saluaʀ-, salummaʀ- ' have been dried in sun (skin, etc.), saluaʀsaʀ- 'scrape or wipe dry (skin, etc.)', sałłuu- 'be lean']

PE cała- 'be dozy from heat'
AAY cała- 'be idle, have nothing to do' [K has ciłi-]
CAY [note cała- 'spread open']
NSY —
CSY sałaqi- 'have a comfortable life, be relaxed'
Sir —
SPI Qaw sała- 'sleep fitfully' [Jen. has sala- 'suffer from heat', W salama- 'be dry weather']
NAI —
WCI salai- 'lie on back' [Pryde has Cop hala- 'lie down for a rest']
ECI Lab salausuk- 'sleep quietly (child)' [Peck]
GRI sala- 'suffer from heat, lie dozing, be thinly dressed', NG halaɣama- 'feel lazy, not want to work'

PY-S całək 'thin ice' [cf. caat-[1], and note in particular NAI saalʀuq there in this sense]
AAY —
CAY —
NSY sałək 'slush ice' [ANLC; Men. has sałəq 'thin ice on sea']

CSY sałək 'rotten ice'
Sir salxiX 'thin ice' [Vakh. from Rub.'s texts]

PE całiɣ-^{1} 'scrape hair or fat from skin' [cf. EA saalikðaasiX 'scraper (for skin)'; there is some entanglement with caluɣ- and całiɣ-^{2}]
AAY —
CAY [note tałəxtə- 'scratch, scour' — contam. with təluɣ-?]
NSY —
CSY sałixtə-, sałəxtə- 'scrape (esp. fat from skin)' [also satəxtə- 'scrape hairless side of skin, scrub' perhaps by contamination with catə]
Sir sałixtə- 'scrape (esp. fat from skin)' [Orr; also satəxtə- 'scrape hairless side of skin, scrub' perhaps by contamination with catə if not borrowed from CSY]
SPI sali- 'cut with scissors' [and note also Qaw sałik- 'be messy']
NAI sali- 'cut with scissors', saliɣuq- 'remove blubber from sea mammal'
WCI Car EP haliɣuut 'skin scraper' [Ow.]
ECI sali- 'clean by scraping (ice off snow house window), cut hair short', salik- 'clip hair', saliɣuq- 'scrape s.th., thinning it' [for saliɣaq- 'smooth, flatten blocks of snow for snow house' see całiɣ-^{2}]
GRI sali- 'scrape hair off skin with razor'

PE całiɣ-^{2} 'sweep or clean away' [cf. całiɣ-^{1}?]
AAY [note PWS całixtə- 'sort through s.th.']
CAY całixtə- 'move s.th. out of way, scatter'
NSY —
CSY [note sałaxtə- 'clean in rough, preliminary manner']
Sir sałixtə- 'sweep'
SPI [Qaw sałik- 'be messy, disorderly']
NAI Mal salikuq- 'sweep the floor'
WCI Net halik- 'remove snow from over-clothes' [Ras.]
ECI [saliɣaq- 'smooth, flatten blocks of snow for snow house']
GRI saliɣ- 'clean (e.g. house), brush', saliɣar- 'clean', NG halik- 'sweep', halik 'sweepings, dust'

> **PI caluma-** 'be clean' [cf. (u)ma-]
> SPI —
> NAI saluma- 'be clean'
> WCI Sig saluma-, Cop halima- 'be clean' [but Car halima- be dry' (Ras.) — influenced by caluɣ-?]
> ECI saluma- 'be clean', Igl 'be dry' [Ras. for the latter, infl. by caluɣ-]
> GRI —

PY całmak 'patch'
AAY całm̥ak 'patch [also verbal całm̥aɣ-]
CAY K, BB całm̥ak 'patch on clothing' [całm̥aɣ- 'patch']
NSY —
CSY sałm̥ak 'patch on sole of boot' [sałm̥aɣ- 'patch a boot sole']
Inu [note PH salɣu- 'patch']

PY cama-i 'greeting' [probably from dem. root cam-]
AAY cama-i 'hello, pleased to meet you (said while shaking hands)'
CAY K, BB cama-i
NSY — [samaa 'what happened?' is presumably from the Chukchi below]
CSY — [saama 'also, too' is from Chukchi cama 'also' mentioned under amma]

PY camataq 'metal head ornament'
AAY —
CAY camataq 'metal head ornament'
NSY —
CSY samataq 'iron forehead ornament given by shaman to patient as remedy' [from Bogoraz 1913 song text 11]

PE cana(ʀ)- 'carve or make' [there may be a relat. with can(n)a(q)- and/or canaʀtə-]
AAY K cana- 'make, carve', AP also 'put to use'
CAY cana(ʀ)- 'carve wood, whittle'
NSY — [for sanaXtə- 'process, tan a skin' see canaʀtə-]
Sir — [for sanaXtə- 'process, manufacture' see canaʀtə-]
SPI sana- 'carve' [Imaq also 'make']
NAI sana- 'whittle, carve' [sannan 'carving knife']
WCI sana- 'work, make, carve' [sannalʀutit 'tools']
ECI sana- 'work, make, carve' [sanaɣaq 's.th. home-made', sannati 'tool']
GRI sana- 'make, carve' [sanaaq 's.th. made', sannat 'tool, whittling knife']

> **PI canatu-** 'be skillful at making things' [cf. tu-^{1}]
> SPI sanatu- 'carve a lot'
> NAI sanatu- 'be skillful, productive'
> WCI sanatu- [Pryde]
> ECI NBI, Iti sanatu-
> GRI EG canali- 'be good at building, making'

> **PI cannaq** 'shaving or chip' [cf. q under nəʀ^{1}]
> Yup [note AAY canaŋuat 'shavings']
> SPI —
> NAI sannaq* 'curved chip from whittling'
> WCI sannakut, sannait 'shavings'
> ECI sannaku 'shavings, sawdust'
> GRI sannakut, sannarłukut

PI can(n)a(q)- 'prepare to leave' [there may be a relat. to cana(ʀ)- and/or canaʀtə-]
SPI sanaʀi- 'prepare to travel to mainland from K. Island,' Imaq sanažuaq- 'get ready for s.th.'
NAI sanaɣɨ- 'prepare to leave'
WCI Sig sannaiyaq- 'get ready', Cop hannaiq- 'be ready', hannailimaiq- 'take a long time getting ready' [Lowe]
ECI [note Iti sanaʀvaisima- 'have put in order (many things)', apparently going with Tar saniʀva(q)-, sanaʀva(q)- under canivaq- (cani-), but the second form may be by contam. with the present set]
GRI NWG sanaʀšuʀ- 'put clothes on, get ready to leave' [and sanaʀšuiaʀ- 'undress']

PY-S canaʀtə- 'process (a skin)' [cf. cana(ʀ)- and/or can(n)a(q)- and t-^{1}]
AAY —
CAY —

NSY sanaXtə- 'manufacture, process a skin'
CSY sanaXtə- 'process, tan a skin'
Sir sanaXtə- 'process, manufacture'
Inu [note WG sanarfi-, Kap Farvel sanaqqi- 'work on, prepare (esp. seal for towing)'

PE canəɣ 'dirt?' [cf. caniʀ-]
AAY —
CAY canək 'grass' [canəxtə-, canəxtaʀ- 'gather grass']
NSY —
CSY [for saŋixtə- 'wipe, clean off (spilled liquid)' see caniʀ-]
Sir —
SPI W sanik 'dust' [Jen.; also Qaw sanikłuk 'dirt, dust']
NAI sanik 'speck of dust, caribou hair on clothings or floor' [also sanɣu- 'be dusty, full of animal hairs', sanniqi- 'shed, lose or remove hair']
WCI sanik, pl. sannit or sanŋit 'dust'
ECI sanik, pl. saniit 'dust, dirt, twigs in picked fruit', Lab also 'weeds or dirt in fishing nets'
GRI sanik, pl. saŋŋit, sannit 'dust'

PI canŋiyaq- or **canɣiyaq-** 'clean (removing dirt or hairs)' [cf. ŋiyaʀ-]
SPI —
NAI sanŋiyaq- 'remove lint, dust or animal hairs from'
WCI saŋiyaq- 'dust off' [for sanŋiyaq-? — note also san(n)iiq- 'sweep']
ECI saniiyaq- 'remove dirt (from eider down)' [saniiyauti 'sieve to remove dust from eider down found in duck's nest, vacuum cleaner']
GRI saŋŋiaʀ-, sanniaʀ-, saniiaʀ- 'brush off'

PY canəɣ(ə)t- 'be thin' [cf. can(n)u-; with a variant of p.b. ŋit- apparently — for the possible relat. to PI caat-[1] compare the loss of intervocalic n in Inu under nanit-]
AAY K canəxtə- 'be thin'
CAY Y canxətə-, NSU canəxətə- 'be thin (skin, ice, wall)' [with the tə ~ l alternation]
NSY sanɣi- 'become thin' [ANLC; L.-T. has sanəxtaʀaq 'thin thing']
CSY —
Inu [note GRI saniɣuʀ- 'become emaciated']

PE cani- 'area beside' [cf. Aleut sana- 'be sufficient, equal, amount to'?]
AAY cani- 'area beside' [posit. root]
CAY cani-
NSY sani- 'area besides' [ANLC; Taghyuq has saniani 'beside (him)']
CSY sani- 'area beside' [posit. root; and sani- 'build addition on side of building']
Sir sanə- 'area beside' [posit. root]
SPI sani- 'area beside'
NAI sani-
WCI sani-
ECI sani-
GRI sani-

PE canil(l)iʀ 'one beside' [cf. l(l)iʀ]
AAY PWS caniliq 'one beside or next to' [Rez.; elsewhere = caniqłiq — from caniqaʀ below?]
CAY —
NSY —
CSY —
Sir —
SPI saniliʀiik 'two people side by side'
NAI —
WCI saniliʀiik 'two dogs side by side'
ECI sanilliq 's.th. situated by the side (of s.th.)', sanilliʀiik 'neighbors'
GRI saniliq* 'neighbor' [saniliʀiit- 'be neighbors', saniliqut, saniliaq 'spouse']

PY caniŋuʀtaq 'quiver' [cf. p.b. taʀ and also EA cŋayuXta-X 'quiver' and Att caɣyuXta-X 'skin bag' — from the Esk.?]
AAY —
CAY caniuXtaq 'quiver, gun case'
NSY —
CSY saniŋuXtaq 'quiver'

PE caniqaʀ 'side' [cf. qaʀ]
AAY caniqaq 'side'
CAY caniqaq 'side (of body), appendix, wall'
NSY saniqaq 'side of body, wall' [ANLC]
CSY —
Sir sanəqəX 'side' [Orr]
SPI saniʀaq
NAI saniʀaq
WCI saniʀaq
ECI saniʀaq
GRI saniʀaq, EG canaȓaq

PI caniqqiaq- 'sail with sidewind' [cf. caniqaʀ above and liyaʀ-]
Yup [note AAY K caniqi- 'go crosswise, at a slant across']
SPI —
NAI —
WCI saniqqiaq- 'sail with a sidewind'
ECI saniqqia(q)-
GRI saniqqiar-

PE canivaʀ- 'move to adjacent area' [cf. vaʀ-]
AAY —
CAY canivaʀ- 'move to side'
NSY sanivaʀaq 'voyage, trip' [L.-T.]
CSY sanivaʀ- 'move to side'
Sir —
SPI sanivaq- 'travel to a new place'
NAI sanivaq- 'move to uninhabited place'
WCI Cop hanivaq- 'place alongside' [Pryde]
ECI [note saniʀva(q)-, sanaʀva(q)- 'put to one side' — Saul has sanavvaq- for Iti]
GRI NG hanivaq- 'go hunting' [compare WG sanipiɣ- 'move sideways']

PE canniqun and **canniʀun** 'crosspiece' [cf. un, q(q)un and canniʀ- below]
AAY AP, KP caniqun, caniqutaq 'crosspiece'
CAY caniʀun 'axle, crosspiece'
NSY —
CSY saniquun 'centerboard of boat'
Sir —
SPI sanniutaq 'crossbar, boom, horizontal beam'
NAI sanniʀutaq 'crossbar on door, crosspiece on bed of sled, boom', PH 'cross'
WCI Sig sanniʀutaq 'crossbar of anchor'
ECI sanniʀutaq 'anything that crosses s.th. else (like bars of chair)'
GRI sanniʀut 'crosspiece (e.g. on mast), bolt of door', NG hanniʀut 'crosspiece between sled uprights' [but Holt. has haniʀaut 'gunwale']

PE canniʀ- 'turn on side' [cf. liʀ-]
AAY caniʀ- 'turn or put on side'
CAY caniʀ-
NSY saniʀ- [ANLC]
CSY saniʀ- [saniʀyaq 'barrier, obstacle, bar across door to prevent entry']
Sir [saniʀyəX 'barrier, bar' — Em.]
SPI sanniq- 'turn sideways'
NAI sanniq- 'turn or put sideways', Nu 'cross (e.g. road)'
WCI [Cop hanniŋayulik 'cross']
ECI sanni(q)- 'cross a vertical line or form a horizontal base to', sanniŋa- 'lie across' [and sanniŋayulik 'cross']
GRI sanniʀ- 'turn sideways', sanniŋa- 'lie across, be parallel with coast (e.g. island)' [and sanniŋašulik 'cross']

PE caniʀ- 'sweep' [cf. canəɣ and p.b. ŋiʀ-?]
AAY —
CAY caniʀ- 'sweep'
NSY saniłəq 'sweepings, dust' [Em.]
CSY [note saŋixtə- 'wipe, clean up (spilled liquid)' — contam. with caŋiɣ-?]
Sir [note samixtə- 'wipe, clean up' — Orr]
Sir —
SPI saniq- 'clean (house)', Qaw 'sweep'
NAI —
WCI saniq- 'sweep'
ECI saniq- 'sweep', NBI 'scrub (floor)' [saniku 'garbage']
GRI saniʀ- 'sweep, clean (house)'

PY-S canqun 'ware or object' [cf. q(q)un and also cana(ʀ)- if not catqummiq-]
AAY —
CAY —
NSY sanqutə 'thing, equipment' [Em. has saanqutə 'ware']
CSY sanqun Chap 'ware', SLI 'tool, equipment, weapon' [meaning of the latter perhaps by contam. with caðku]
Sir sanquta(X) 'goods, ware, object'
Inu [Imaq satqun 'ware, object' may be from Yup — the tq rather than qq perhaps under the influence of satkuq under caðku]

PY can(n)u- 'be thick' [cf. canəɣ(ə)t- and compare CAY əttu- under ətə-, with tu-[1]]
AAY K cannu- 'be thick'
CAY Y cannu-
NSY sanu- 'be thick (ice, cloth)' [L.-T.]
CSY —

PY caŋaɣ- 'object to s.th.' [cf. caŋiak-]
AAY AP caŋaɣ(yuɣ)- 'object to s.th.'
CAY caŋa(yuɣ)- 'dislike or reject s.th.' [and note caŋatə- 'have s.th. amiss' with the tə ~ l alternation]
NSY —
CSY —

PI caŋiak- 'be jealous' [cf. caŋaɣ-, caŋyaʀ- and caŋimmiʀ-, though the relat. is not clear]
SPI saŋiak- 'be jealous (man of woman)'
NAI saŋiak- 'be sexually jealous'
WCI saŋiak- 'be jealous (man)'
ECI [for saŋiak- 'delouse' see caŋiɣ-]
GRI saŋiaɣ- 'be jealous (man)' [and saŋiut(i)- 'be jealous of']

PE caŋiɣ- 'delouse'
AAY caŋiɣ- 'fondle, feel with fingers (formerly esp. for lice)'
CAY caŋiɣaʀ- 'massage'
NSY saŋiɣ- 'delouse'
CSY [for saŋixtə- 'wipe, clean off' see caniʀ-]
Sir —
SPI saŋik- 'delouse' [Jen.]
NAI saŋik-
WCI —
ECI saŋiak- 'delouse'
GRI saŋiɣ- 'delouse' [for saŋiut(i)- 'be jealous of' see caŋiak-]

PE caŋimmiʀ- 'want more' [cf. caŋiak-]
AAY AP caŋimiXtə- 'want more'
CAY caŋimiXtə-
NSY —
CSY —
Sir —
SPI Qaw saŋimiq-
NAI saŋimmiq-
WCI —
ECI —
GRI —

PE caŋu- 'turn (to the side)' [cf. caŋuʀ- and ca(C)u-]
AAY caŋu- 'swerve, turn to the side'
CAY Nun, NS caŋu- 'turn back', Nun also 'walk', HBC 'look for eggs'
NSY —
CSY —
Sir [saŋəXpaqaʀ- 'rock or sway from side to side']
SPI Imaq saŋu(žak)- 'make way (across difficult terrain)', KI, W 'twist, wind, be tortuous' [Jen.]
NAI —

WCI Sig saŋu- 'go from side to side', Net 'turn aside' [Ras.]
ECI saŋu- 'change direction' [saŋuyaʀaq- 'change direction all the time']
GRI saŋu-, EG caŋiC- 'turn (to the side), curve, wind' [and saŋuyuʀaaʀ-, saŋuyaaʀ- 'meander, wind']

PY-S caŋuʀ- 'be twisted or bent down' [cf. caŋu- and Aleut saŋuXta- 'have a wry mouth' and saŋus (pl.) as a name of bays]
AAY caŋuʀ- 'bend, twist, distort' [postural root]
CAY caŋuʀ-, caŋuŋqa- 'lack symmetry, pull a face' [postural root]
NSY —
CSY —
Sir saŋuXtə- 'bend down, incline' [and saŋuʀmalŋuX 'tilted'; Em. has saŋuʀən 'crooked, bent']
Inu [note GRI saŋuŋa- 'be crooked' and NAI saŋut- 'gossip maliciously about']

PY caŋyaʀ- 'be hard to move' [cf. perhaps Atkan Aleut saŋaXta- 'honor, respect' with p.b. Xta-]
AAY K caŋyaʀ-, C saŋyaʀ- 'be hard to move' [and caŋyaitə-, saŋyaitə- 'be easy to move']
CAY —
NSY —
CSY saŋyaʀ- 'be hard to move, slow of learning', saŋyitə- 'not slide easily because of friction'

PI capaŋaq 'bead' [there may be a link to capək-]
SPI —
NAI [sapaŋiak, sapaŋiẑẑaq 'piece of wood or bone to hold when throwing seal line']
WCI Car hapaŋaqtalik 'bead' [Ras.; Pet. has Sig siapaŋa 'bracelet']
ECI sapaŋaq 'bead'
GRI sapaŋaq, EG capaȓaq

PE capə- 'block' [cf. Atkan Aleut cam̥it-, EA cim̥it-, cimit- 'block, plug', also capəʀnaʀ-]
AAY sapu- 'fence off, dam up', saputə- 'confine by blocking off' [and sapuʀ- 'be weathered in']
CAY capa (base: capə) 'barrier, curtain', capə- 'block (ice), cover up'
NSY sapə- 'cover'
CSY saapə- 'cover, herd to a new place (reindeer)', safkaaʀ- 'block (view)'
Sir sapuXt(ə)- 'cover', sapuʀəta 'curtain' [and Vakh. has sapuʀ- 'plug' from Men.'s texts; savləX 'winter, year' may also belong here — compare quvə- under qupə-]
SPI savi- 'block', savak 'door' [and verbal = 'close door'; note also Di savək- 'block' — influenced by savak?; Imaq savəq- 'close' (for savək-?)]
NAI sapi- 'block, obstruct, be blocked' [savži- 'block, prevent', sappit- 'give up, quit']
WCI sapi- 'block'
ECI saput(i)- 'protect, defend'
GRI sapi- 'block, drive together' [and saššsi- (old ortho. savssi-) 'find crowd of sea mammals trapped in ice — esp. narwhales', saššaʀ- 'catch sea mammals in open hole in ice']

PI capiqšaq- 'be inhibited or in need' [cf. capiʀ- below and compare ayuqšaq- under ayuq-]
SPI saviqšaq- 'be apprehensive of asking s.th. of s.o.'
NAI sapiqšaq- 'be reserved, shy' [sapiqšalait- 'be bold']
WCI sapiqsait- 'can do anything, be omnipotent'
ECI sapiʀsait-
GRI sapiʀšaʀ- 'cannot do or get s.th., be in need'

PE capiʀ- 'block or be blocked' [cf. liʀ-?]
AAY —
CAY capiʀ- 'impede, block'
NSY sapiʀ- 'block, close' [and sapiXsaʀ- 'lose desire to do s.th., give up']
CSY —
Sir —
SPI saviq- 'feel one cannot do s.th.'
NAI sapiq- 'not try to do from feeling that it's impossible, be weary of'
WCI sapiq- 'be unable to do', Car 'be lazy' [Ras. and Schn. for Baker Lake]
ECI sapiq- 'become discouraged and not want to do', Aiv 'cannot do' [and sapiʀʀia(C)- 'not want any more, give up']
GRI sapiʀ- 'cannot, not dare', NWG, Up 'be extremely fond of' [and sapiit- 'be bold']

PE cap(p)un 'fish weir' [cf. un]
AAY sapun, saputaq, KP, Kod sapuq 'gate, barrier, dam'
CAY capun 'weir' [and capu- 'cover' — also nominal]
NSY sapun 'partition, wall, obstacle' [L.-T.; ANLC also has saputə 'obstacle', saputaq 'partition, barrier']
CSY sa(a)putaq 'cover, lid'
Sir [note sapuʀəta 'curtain' and sapuʀ- 'cover']
SPI sappun 'dam, blockage, barrier'
NAI sapun 'dam, barrier, fence', Nu saputit 'fish weir'
WCI saputit 'fish weir'
ECI saput
GRI saputit

PI capək- and **capkut-** 'drop' [cf. Aleut sam̥i- 'jerk to the side', sam̥iisa- 'fling (to side or ground)']
SPI saviktuq- 'have s.th. slip from one's grasp'
NAI [note sipiksaq- 'come undone, slip off, grow suddenly or quickly', sipiksaa(ʀa)q- 'not engage (arrow on bow), not get a grip on' — contam. with cipkiq- under cipə(ɣ)-?]
WCI Car? sapku- 'release' [Schn. 'adg.'; Pryde has Cop, Net hapkut- 'let go']
ECI sakku(C)- [half tr. sakkui-, Lab sakkutsi- in Peck] 'release', sapiyyi(C)- 'drop'
GRI sapaŋit-, sapašši(t)- 'drop, release'

PE capəʀnaʀ- 'be difficult or formidable' [cf. naʀ- and probably capə-]
AAY —

CAY capəXn̥aXqə- 'be difficult'
NSY [sapn̥aq 'emergency stop in bad weather' (L.-T.)]
CSY sapəXn̥aʀ- 'be very cold', sapəXn̥aq 'very cold weather'
Sir —
SPI saviʀnaq- 'be strong', Qaw sapiʀnaq- 'be talented, be difficult'
NAI sapɨʀnaq- 'be formidable, seem impossible', PH 'be strong'
WCI sapiʀnaq- 'be impossible, be difficult'
ECI —
GRI sapiʀnaʀ- 'be difficult', NWG 'be great'

PE caqə-[1] 'turn or move' [cf. caqu-[1], caqələkitaʀ, and caqviɣ]
AAY caʀi(tə)- 'tilt, swerve, weave'
CAY caqiʀ- 'turn' [and see caqəlŋa- 'hop, flit' under caqələkitaʀ]
NSY saqiɣ- 'push aside' [Enm.]
CSY —
Sir [note saqiɬux 'tundra animal']
SPI saʀit- 'put aside', Qaw saʀik-, Imaq saʀit- 'push aside'
NAI saqɨt- 'push, move out of the way'
WCI Sig saqi- 'change direction', saqiuʀaq- 'zig-zag'
ECI saqi- 'change direction (wind), push away because it is annoying', Lab saqitsik- 'scatter, knock down'
GRI saqi- 'wander about, serve', NG haqi- 'change direction', EG caʀi- 'be out hunting in kayak' [and saqiaɬɬaɣ- 'change direction', saqiɣ- 'move aside', saʀmiɣ- 'push, jostle', also EG caqqit 'kayak']

PY caqə-[2] 'break or chip' [cf. caqšanəkut?]
AAY caqtə- 'rip, tear'
CAY caqətə- 'chip' [and note Nun, HBC caqəXtə-, Eg caqiXtə- 'rip']
NSY [saqšək 'fragment, shell' (L.-T.)]
CSY saqəXqə-, saqiXqə- 'break to pieces, chip off bits', saqəXtə- 'chip off a piece'

PE caqələkitaʀ and **caqəlŋataq** 'butterfly' [cf. caqə-[1] and ləɣ-, referring to the zig-zag path of the insect; with different final p.b.s in Yup and Inu?]
AAY KP caqaɬŋaataaq, PWS caqaɬŋatak, Kod saqalŋatak, AP saqilŋatak 'butterfly, moth'
CAY caqəlŋataq* [note caqəlŋa-, Nun caqiɬŋa- 'hop, flit']
NSY yaqəɬəŋusiq [influenced by yaquq 'wing' (under iyaɣ-); L.-T. has yaqaɬuŋusiaq]
CSY yaqəɬəŋətaq [influenced by yaquq 'wing'; for səŋəɬqaʀ- 'hop' see cəŋələ-]
Sir — [note siɣəsqətataʀ- 'hop' — Em.]
SPI saʀaɬaŋitaq 'butterfly' [Jen. has sirininitaq for W]
NAI Nu taqalukisaq 'butterfly' [and note B taqɨlakisaaq 'northern buttercup']
WCI Sig saqalukitaq [Met.], saqalikitaaq [Lowe], Cop haqalikitaq [Lowe], Net haqalikitaaq, Utku taqalikitaaq [Ras.], Car taqalikitaaq [B.-S., but Dor. has taʀalikitaaq for B. Lake and Pryde has taqalikisaaq for Net]
ECI taqalikitaaq, taʀalikitaaq, saʀalikitaaq, Igl taʀʀalikisaaq [B.-S. — several of these forms seem to indicate contamination with taʀʀaq 'shade']
GRI NG taqulikihaaq, NWG taqaliqisaaq 'butterfly', SWG taXXaliqisaaq 'moth, ray (fish)' [EG isaqqiiq — Thal. isaqqiliq — 'butterfly' is influenced by iyaqqi- under iyaɣ-]

PE caqlaɣ 'roseroot' [may be PY borrowed into SPI, or PI borrowed into NSY and CSY; cf. cuqlaɣ]
AAY —
CAY HBC caqɬak 'roseroot'
NSY saqɬak 'roseroot' [L.-T.]
CSY saqɬak
SPI saqɬak
NAI —
WCI —
ECI —
NAI —

PI caqšanəkut 'waste' [cf. caqə-[2], ðaʀ-, nəʀ[1] and k(k)uʀ?]
SPI [note Qaw saXiq- 'clean (a place)']
NAI saqšanikut 'waste, offal, leftovers'
WCI [note Sig saqaq 'dirt, s.th. dirty'?]
ECI —
GRI saʀɬanikut 'waste, offal, leftovers'

PE caqu-[1] 'veer to the side' [cf. caqə-[1]]
AAY —
CAY —
NSY —
CSY saqustə- 'glide to side (bird)'
Sir —
SPI saʀu- 'swerve, veer, change direction'
NAI saqu- 'change direction', saquŋa- 'be crooked or bent'
WCI saquŋayuq 'oblique, crooked (road)'
ECI —
GRI —

PY-S caqu-[2] 'wrap around' [there may be contam. with iyaquʀ under iyaɣ- in NSY and CSY here]
AAY saqun 'diaper'
CAY caqu- 'wrap' [as noun = 'container, poke, mother']
NSY saqumiɣ-, saqumiaʀ- 'put under one's arm' [ANLC; Men. has saqumiɬəq 'underarm' — Enm. has saqumik and L.-T. saqumiaq 'armload']
CSY saqumiɣ- 'hold in crook of arm' [and perhaps also saquk 'edge of skin cut off and discarded', saquɣnəq* 'triangle']
Sir saqəməɣ- 'embrace, surround'

PE caqviɣ 'tail of whale' [cf. caqə-[1]]
AAY K caqX^{w}ik 'tail of whale, propeller'
CAY →
NSY saqpik 'whale's tail, propeller'
CSY →
Sir —
SPI saqpik 'tail of whale'
NAI saqpik
WCI saqpik
ECI saqpik
GRI saʀpik 'tail of whale, propeller' ['propeller' is haqpinaq in NG]

PE caqviʀ- or **caqviɣ-** 'walk splay-footed'
AAY Kod caqXʷiɣ-, Perry caqiʀ-, PWS caqxʷiʀ- 'walk splay-footed' [post. root]
CAY caqfiʀ- 'walk splay-footed, put shoes on wrong feet' [post. root]
NSY saqpiʀ- 'walk splay-footed' [ANLC]
CSY saqfiʀ- 'walk splay-footed' [post. root]
Sir —
SPI Qaw saqpiŋa- 'be splay-footed', KI saqpilik- 'turn one's feet out, cross one's legs'
NAI saqpik- 'turn feet out' [also nom. of one with feet that way]
WCI Sig saqpiluaq- 'turn feet out' [Jen.]
ECI saqpiŋa- 'have feet turned out' [and saqpiqut(i)- 'shoot past too far to right']
GRI saʀpiŋa- 'walk with feet turned out' [and note NG haqpit- 'be cross-eyed' — Holt.]

PI caʀaq- and **caqaq-** 'make a loud noise' [there appears to be contam. with ciqəʀ- and/or caʀat- here]
SPI Imaq saʀaq, saqaq 'noise'
NAI saʀaaluk- 'make splashing or crashing sound', saʀʀalliqsiq- 'make a splashing sound (water)' [and saʀmak- 'talk loudly', saqłak-, Nu saqmak- 'shout']
WCI saʀaq- 'yell, make noise (child)'
ECI [note saʀʀaa(C)-, saʀaliq- 'wet s.th. by splashing']
GRI —

PI caʀat- 'be moist or slippery on surface'
SPI —
NAI [note saʀayak- 'be spoiled (food)']
WCI —
ECI saʀat- 'be lightly dampened on surface (waterproof object)' [also 'adg' acc. Schn.; sarait- 'be dry on surface']
GRI saʀat- 'glisten (with moisture)', saʀayaɣ- 'be slippery to touch, be silly or peculiar' [and saʀassi- 'slip out of one's hand']

PY caʀayak 'monster' [cf. perhaps cu(na) and AAY p.b. laayak 'horrible' under la(C)aʀ-]
AAY K caʀaayak 'monster, apparition'
CAY caʀayak 'monster, ghost, bear'
NSY —
CSY [note saʀiiʀayuɣ- 'be shocked'?]

PY caʀəvə- 'collapse'
AAY —
CAY —
NSY saʀavə- 'collapse' [ANLC; Men. has saʀəvə-]
CSY saʀəvə- 'collapse, crumble' [and note also saqəmə- 'crumble to pieces' — by contam. with ciqumə(t)-?]

PY cariaʀ- 'gnaw'
AAY —
CAY cariaʀ- 'gnaw'
NSY sariaʀ-
CSY —

PE caʀliyaʀ 'child held in lap' [cf. Aleut caʀalix, caʀaliɣi-X 'young seal that has (just) left its mother']
AAY caʀliaq 'child, baby, young (of animal)' [as verb caʀliaq- = K 'have a child', KP 'hold (child) on lap or belly']
CAY LI, HBC caʀliaq 'last child in family'
NSY saʀliaq 'young child (on lap)' [Enm. has saʀliiq; L.-T. has saɣliaqseq 'bitch with pups']
CSY saʀliɣaq 'female dog or other quadruped'
Sir —
SPI Qaw saʀliaq 's.th. held on the lap'
NAI saʀliaq 's.th. or s.o. sitting in one's lap' [Jen. has also 'child'; as verb 'rock on the lap']
WCI Net saʀliaqtuq 'bitch with pups' [Ras.]
ECI saʀliaq- 'carry in front of one,' Lab saaʀliak 'animal with young' [Peck; Saul has saʀliaq 'child held in lap' for Tar, as a verb = 'hold or cuddle child or animal in one's lap, sit on eggs (bird)']
GRI saʀłiaq 'infant in arms, dog with young' [as verb saʀłiaʀ- = 'have a child (or s.th.) in lap']

caʀsa(q) 'hot beverage' [from Aleut caXsa-X 'fish soup'; compare PE qayuʀ for the conflation of tea and soup here]
AAY saʀsaq 'tea'
CAY saXsa-, caʀca- 'drink tea'
NSY —
CSY —

PE caʀumiɣ 'left (hand)' [cf. miɣ- and perhaps caqu-[1]?]
AAY —
CAY caʀumik 'left hand or side'
NSY [for saqumik 'armpit' see caqu-[2]]
CSY saʀumik 'left side' [saʀuya 'left hand']
Sir —
SPI saumik 'left hand or side'
NAI saumik
WCI saumik
ECI saumik
GRI saamik

PE caʀvaʀ 'current' [cf. Aleut caʀ- in Atkan caʀna-X 'outgoing surf', EA caʀat- 'go out to the open sea, fall down (into pit), sink (into snow)']
AAY caʀwaq 'current' [and KP caʀʀu-, PWS caʀ<ɣ>u- 'slide (snow, earth, mud)']
CAY caʀvaq 'current, rapidly flowing stream' [and note caʀvə-, caʀvaʀ-' flow (of current)']
NSY —
CSY —
Sir saʀvətələX 'drift'
SPI saʀvaq 'current', saʀvaq- 'flow (of current)'
NAI saʀvaq 'current', saʀvaq- 'have a strong current, be carried away by current'
WCI saʀvaq 'current' [and Baker Lake as verb = 'go downstream']
ECI saʀvaq 'river rapids' [also 'bed on a slope' and as verb 'lie on a slope']
GRI saʀfaq 'current, river rapids', saʀfaʀ- 'have a current (river)'

PY-S catə 'inside or skin-side of a pelt'
AAY AP, KP cata 'inside or skin-side of a pelt'
CAY cata

NSY —
CSY sata
Sir sata [borrowed from CSY?]

PI catqaq 'front part' [cf. caðə- and qaʀ?]
SPI —
NAI satqak 'one side of chest', Mal 'chest'
WCI satqak 'front (e.g. of chest)', Net, Cop satqaq 'breast'
ECI saqqaq 'exposed, visible part, part of a place that can be seen in all directions to the horizon' [for saqqit- 'show, appear' see catqummiq-]
GRI saqqaq 'front, sunny side (e.g. northern side of fjord)', EG also 'visible part of s.th., face' [saqqaʀ- 'turn (front) toward s.o.', saqqisaaʀ- 'bask in sun']

PI catqummiq- 'display or appear' [there may be a link to caðə- and/or canqun though the t in SPI is problematical in the latter case; compare p.b. miqə-]
SPI satqumiq- 'display, get ready'
NAI satqummiq-, satqummiaq- 'show, display'
WCI satqum(m)iq- 'appear'
ECI [saqqit- 'show, appear', as if from saqqaq 'exposed place' — see catqaq — and p.b. łit-; note also saqqiyaaq- 'show or appear for a while', corresponding to GRI saqqisaaʀ- under catqaq]
GRI saqqummiʀ- 'appear, be displayed' [and saqqumi- 'be exposed, visible']

PI catuq- 'take back'
SPI satuuti- 'give up on'
NAI tasuq- 'repossess, take back, redeem, ransom', Mal satuq- 'take back'
WCI sattu- 'take back what one has given, regain s.th. lost' [Pryde has satuq- 'rejoin, recover, return to']
ECI satuq- 'recover, regain possession'
GRI —

PI cau- 'strew (with earth or snow)' [the relat. — if any — to ciʀu- is obscure]
SPI sau- 'bury, cover with earth or snow' [Jen. has as noun 'loose earth or snow covering s.th.']
NAI sau- [and as noun 'snow, sand or earth covering']
WCI sauk 'earth, stones, orsnow covering s.th., skirting of house', sau- 'cover with earth'
ECI sau- 'cover with earth or snow'
GRI saa- 'sprinkle, cover or be covered (e.g. with earth or snow)', saaq 'fine earth or snow strewn on s.th., humus, soil on a traditional Greenlandic house roof'

PY ca(C)u- 'turn and face' [cf. caŋu-]
AAY cau- 'turn and face'
CAY cau-
NSY saaw- 'turn' [and saak^{w}aʀ- 'look back, look around']
CSY [note saaq^{w} 'side']

PI caulluq- 'remove marrow' [cf. caunəq]
SPI —
NAI saulluq 'spinal cord (esp. of caribou)' [as verb = 'remove through a narrow opening like marrow from a bone, PH saulluk- 'extract marrow']
WCI saulluq- 'take marrow from a bone'
ECI saullu(C)- 'remove contents with a long instrument through a narrow opening (brain from skull, marrow from bone)'
GRI —

PI caunəq 'bone or pit' [cf. nəʀ[1]]
SPI sauniq 'bone'
NAI sauniq* 'bone, pit, seed in fruit', [in pl. saunʀic is also 'boat frame'], saunaaq 'eggshell, pit, seed of fruit, small fishbone'
WCI sauniq 'bone, pit' [Pryde also has 'eggshell, shaft of feather, kernel']
ECI sauniq 'bone, fishbone, eggshell', saunaq 'seed, pit'
GRI saaniq* 'knuckle, bone, pit (in fruit)' [old ortho. = sauneq; note saaʀni 'its bones, ribs of boat']

> **PI caunnit-** 'have a bone stuck in one's throat' [cf. łit-; compare nənəqitə- under nənəq]
> SPI saunit- 'have a bone stuck in throat'
> NAI saunnit-
> WCI saunik- [for saunnit-?]
> ECI saunnit-
> GRI saannit-

PE cavaɣ- 'work'
AAY — [AP cawaɣ- 'do what so hard?' from ca- 'what' and waɣ 'hard', can hardly be related since ca- corresponds to su- in Inuit (see cu(na))]
CAY NS cavəɣ- 'work' [by contamination with cavət-? — see cavizʀa- 'make s.th.' under cavət- 'touch']
NSY —
CSY —
Sir —
SPI sawaaq 'work, job', W sawak- 'work' [Jen.; for sawit- 'work' see cavət-]
NAI savak- 'work (on)'
WCI savak-
ECI Iti savak- 'succeed'
GRI —

PE cavəɣ 'harpoon or spear head' [the relat. — if any — to caviɣ is obscure]
AAY Kod cawək 'type of arrow or spear for small sea animals'
CAY Y, HBC cavək 'harpoon, big spear'
NSY savək 'harpoon'
CSY savək 'head of whaling harpoon', savəɣ- 'harpoon'
Sir savəɣəX 'spearhead' [for homonym in sense 'knife' see caviɣ]
SPI —
NAI —
WCI — [for Car havɣut 'snow probe' see cavət-]
ECI savik- 'mount harpoon head on harpoon'
GRI saviɣ- [half-trans. savittuʀ-] 'mount harpoon head', saxxuššaaʀ- [old ortho. savguŝssaer-] 'take harpoon head off shaft', EG caviɣattaq, cavuɣattaq, cavaɣattaq 'harpoon head', cavattarpik 'base of harpoon tip', NG haɣɣut 'short strap for attaching line to breathing hole harpoon' [Holt.; note also WG suuɣaq, Up saŋuaq 'iron head of bird dart']

PE cavət- 'touch or feel' [cf. Aleut cam- 'scrape, clean (skin) by scraping']
AAY cauxtə- 'touch' [and note witə- 'switch around, rearrange'?]
CAY caftə-, caaftə-, LI saftə- 'touch' [and note NSU cavizʀa- 'make s.th.'; for NS cavəɣ- 'work' see cavaɣ-]
NSY ➟
CSY saaftə- 'touch, feel'
Sir —
SPI sawit- 'work, palpate, adjust' [contam. with cavaɣ-?]
NAI savɨt- 'touch' [and savɨtu- 'be handy', savɨnnaq- 'be time-consuming']
WCI savit- 'touch, work on s.th. guided by touch (e.g. in poor light)' [and savitu- 'touch everything'; note also Schn. 'adg' havɣut 'snow probe' — Cop havɣut, Car havɣun acc. Pryde — and havɣuhaq- 'test snow with snow rod', infl. by cavəɣ?]
ECI [Aiv saggut 'snow probe' — Pryde]
GRI savit- 'touch' [and savitu- 'be handy']

PI captək- 'grope'
SPI saptik-, saptaaq- 'grope'
NAI saptaq- 'grope, palpate, examine by touch'
WCI saptik- 'grope, feel way'
ECI tatsi(C)- 'touch with eyes closed or in the dark to find, recognize', Lab tapsik- 'feel, finger, touch' [Peck]
GRI satsiɣ- 'grope', sattaɣ-, NG hattaaq- 'grope way forward'

PY-S cavłəɣ- 'handle' [cf. ləɣ-]
AAY —
CAY cafłiuʀ- 'do housework'
NSY sapłəɣ- 'touch, feel' [Enm. and Orr]
CSY safłəɣ- 'handle'
Sir safłəɣ- 'feel' [Vakh.]

PE caviɣ 'knife' [Aleut saami-X EA 'stone knife, dagger', Att 'knife, spear point, iron', Atkan saami-X, saam̥i-X 'iron, steel'; the relat. with cavəɣ is obscure — perhaps the original meaning of this set was 'metal (surface iron?) for tools']
AAY K cawik 'iron, metal'
CAY cavik 'knife, metal, iron', Nun 'curved knife', Y, HBC, NI cavixaq 'cutting knife']
NSY savik 'knife' [and saviɣ- 'plane', saviłquyuk 'iron']
CSY savik 'knife' [and savikənʀaaq 'tin, metal', saviłquq 'small curved knife']
Sir savəɣəX 'knife' [Vakh. also saviɣəx; savipəstaʀ- 'plane']
SPI sawik 'knife' [sawiłhaq, sawisXaq 'metal', sawiłhaq- 'plane', sawiviniq 'piece of metal']
NAI savik, savɨk 'knife' [the latter by contam. with cavəɣ; saviłhaq 'iron, metal']
WCI savik 'knife, iron' [savisuk 'piece of iron']
ECI savik 'knife' [and savik- 'plane', Iti, SB, NBI saviʀayaq 'metal']
GRI savik 'knife' [saviɣ- 'prune, whittle to fit', saviminiq*, NG haviɣluk 'iron']

PE caviʀuʀ- 'whittle'
AAY —
CAY —
NSY —
CSY saviXə- 'whittle, carve'
Sir saviXqə(s)-
SPI —
NAI saviʀuq- 'trim or smooth (piece of metal or bone)'
WCI Car? haviʀuq- 'scrape with a knife' [Schn. 'adg']
ECI —
GRI saviʀuʀ- 'whittle' [and savirurtitsi- 'gnash one's teeth']

PI caviužaq- 'cut blocks of snow' [cf. ŋ(ŋ)uðaʀ(-)]
SPI —
NAI —
WCI saviuyaq- 'cut blocks of snow' [saviuyaqtuʀnikkut 'debris left after cutting snow blocks']
ECI saviuyaqtu(q)- 'cut blocks of snow' [saviuyaʀniku 'debris from cutting snow blocks']
GRI NG haviuhaqtuq- 'cut blocks of snow', haviuhaq 'knife' [haviuhaqtuɣaq 'snow block, sugar cube']

PY cayak 'red salmon'
AAY AP sayak 'red salmon'
CAY cayak, sayak
NSY —
CSY —

PE caya(ɣ) 'strength or fortitude'
AAY cayaxtə- 'be angry'
CAY cayaq 'chest, lungpower', cayaitə-, NS casaitə- 'lack fortitude' [there appears to be contam. with caðə- here]
NSY — [for sayət 'chest' see caðə-]
CSY —
Sir —
SPI sayak 'strength', sayait- 'be weak'
NAI sayak 'health, strength', sayait- 'be weak'
WCI —
ECI —
GRI [note saya- 'be tired of work, bungle, be careless', sayaat- 'be diligent']

PE cayuɣ- 'pull or twitch' [cf. Aleut sayu- 'pull' and sayɣi-x 'bow' (du.)]
AAY cayuɣ- 'pull, tug toward self'
CAY cayuɣ- 'pull toward self, twitch'
NSY tayuɣ- 'pull', tayuxtə- twitch, kick' [and tayuxpag- 'tremble, be alarmed' — contam. with tayu(ɣ)-?; ANLC has tayuɣ- 'pull toward one, twitch', sayuɣ- 'pull toward one']
CSY sayuɣ- 'pull, tug' [and sayuxpaxtaʀ- 'pull by jerking, twitch']
Sir sayəɣ- 'pull' [note also sayəkayux 'bow']
SPI sayuk- 'quake, tremble, shiver, twitch'
NAI sayuk- 'twitch'
WCI Sig sayuk- 'move'

ECI sayuk- 'tremble, shake'
GRI sayuɣ- 'tremble'

PE cayuʀ- 'dance' [there could be a link to cayuɣ-]
AAY —
CAY cayuXtə- 'Eskimo dance (of man)'
NSY sayuʀ- 'dance'
CSY sayuʀ- 'dance a set, non-improvised Eskimo dance'
Sir sayəX 'celebration, festival' [Em.]
SPI sayuq- 'Eskimo dance' [Qaw of women]
NAI sayuq- 'do a motion dance'
WCI sayuq- 'dance'
ECI —
GRI —

cəqtaaq 'kind of (noisy) bird' [onomatopoeic, perhaps from *təqcaaq or *təʀatəʀaaq — cf. cakcakiq and also təðatəða(C)iʀ, which may in fact represent the same set]
AAY C səqtaaq, səqtaq 'mallard'
CAY cəqcaaq 'northern phalarope' [and cətaaq, cətaaʀ(aq*) 'little bird', Y cəqpilunaq 'sparrow' — compare cəqcəXtə- 'be excitedly alive, making lots of noise']
NSY [səqəžʀaaXaq 'gray seagull']
CSY — [but note təžatəžiiq 'red phalarope, sandpiper' under təðatəða(C)iʀ]

PE ci(ð)aɣanəʀ 'lengthwise lathe in kayak' [cf. ciðaɣ- and nəʀ[1]]
AAY —
CAY caaɣanəq, saaɣanəq 'kayak stringer'
NSY —
CSY —
Sir —
SPI siaaniq 'lengthwise strip in side of kayak frame'
NAI Nu sianiq* 'lengthwise piece in bottom of kayak frame'
WCI sianiq [Pryde]
ECI sianiq
GRI siaaniq* 'lengthwise piece in bottom of kayak frame'

PI cialʀi- 'slide' [there may be a link to ciðaɣ-]
SPI Qaw sialʀi- 'glide through air, over water, slide on ice'
NAI sialʀi-, Mal sailʸʀi- 'slide on slippery surface, glide'
WCI Cop halʀi(y)aq- 'skate' [halʀi(y)autit 'ice skates']
ECI siaʀʀi(C)- 'slip unintentionally' [siaʀʀiyauti 'ice skate', Lab siaXXiyaaC- 'ski, skate']
GRI saXXi(t)- 'slide out, slip', saaʀɫi- 'slide on ice' [and NWG saaʀɫisaaʀut 'skate']

PE ciðaɣ- 'spread out' [cf. Aleut ciðaɣ- 'stretch'; note the Yup contraction leaving initial s-; compare also caɣɣaq]
AAY saxtə- 'spread out, stretch out' [and saɣləʀ- 'spread out, sprawl, C cuɣu-, cuɣləʀ- 'be scattered, messed up'; saxtə- conflates with base yaxtə-, caxtə- 'stretch one's arm out' under iyaɣ-]
CAY caxtə-, saxtə- 'scatter, spread' [for ciikaʀ- 'have diarrhea' see ətəɣ(taʀ)-]
NSY saxtə- 'smooth out, straighten, scatter, spread' [and saɣvitəkə- 'scatter']
CSY saaɣ- 'get scattered, spread'
Sir sižaɣ- 'smoothen, spread out' [Vakh. has it as 'stretch or straighten out' from Rub.]
SPI siak- 'spread out, scatter' [and Imaq saktuma- 'be straightened, smoothed out']
NAI siak- 'arrange, be arranged in a row', PH 'scatter, be scattered'
WCI siak- 'scatter' [and note siaqtit- (for siaaqtit-?) 'reattach a rope farther away']
ECI siak- 'be placed side by side', Lab 'be placed in a line or row'
GRI siaɣ- 'arrange, be arranged in a row, let run out (harpoon line)', siaaʀ- 'distend, extend' [and note NG hiaXXaq 'taut rope']

PE ciðaɣma(ʀ)- 'get scattered' [cf. maʀ-, but also ciðamə(t)- below, with which there is some entanglement]
AAY saɣmə- 'get scattered'
CAY caɣmaʀ- 'lose'
NSY saɣma(ʀ)- 'lose, be lost'
CSY —
Sir —
SPI —
NAI —
WCI Cop hiammak- 'spread out, extend' [Pryde]
ECI siamma(ŋa)- 'be scattered'
GRI siammaʀ- 'scatter, get scattered'

PE ciðamə(t)- 'scatter or crumble' [compare ciqumə(t)-]
AAY —
CAY ciamə- 'crumble, crush'
NSY siamə- 'get crushed, break up, crumble, quieten down (child)' [and siamquvžiapiɣ- 'crush']
CSY —
Sir —
SPI siamit- 'scatter, disorganize'
NAI siamɨt- 'spread, scatter', PH 'lose'
WCI siamit- 'scatter'
ECI — [for siamma(ŋa)- 'be spread out' see ciðaɣma(ʀ)- above]
GRI siamat- 'be scattered'

PE ciðamʀu '(small piece of) driftwood' [cf. ciðamə(t)- above and EA caamʀu-X 'small piece of driftwood', caamʀu- 'pick up pieces of driftwood', borrowed from Esk.?]
AAY camʀu(q) 'small piece of driftwood' [short a probably due to compression]
CAY Y, NS ciamʀuq 'small piece of driftwood'
NSY siamʀuq [ANLC]
CSY siimʀu 'small stick used for kindling'
Sir —
SPI siaʀmuq 'small piece of driftwood'
NAI siamʀu
WCI Sig siamʀu

ECI —
GRI —

PE ciðəɣ- 'cut open (fish or animal)' [compare ciðaɣ- for the Yup contractions and cf. also ciɣɣaq-]
AAY səɣə- 'cut fish' [and note PWS sia<ʀ>aʀ- 'make a cut or slit in', siaXtə- 'graze, nick']
CAY cəɣ-, səɣ-, Nun əsəɣ- 'cut fish'
NSY əsəɣ- 'cut fish' [Enm.; also əsəxtuʀ- 'rip open']
CSY səxə- 'cut open, slash'
Sir sicəɣ- 'cut up, slit' [Vakh.]
SPI siik- 'cut lengthwise through belly (seal, fish)'
NAI siik- 'tear lengthwise'
WCI siik- 'disembowel animal'
ECI siik- 'open animal down middle'
GRI siiɣ- 'cut up (animal along belly), burst' [and siššaɣ- 'gape, spread apart']

PI cižžaq 'split' [cf. q under nəʀ[1]]
SPI Qaw sižžaq 'hairlip' [and KI sižžuaq- 'tear a seam']
NAI sižžaq* 'split section of garment or skin'
WCI siyyaq 'long split in garment'
ECI —
GRI siššaq* 'split in garment, fly' [old ortho. sivssaq by contam. with cipə(ɣ)-?]

PE ciɣəðquʀ 'knee' [cf. Aleut ciðiɣi-X, EA ciiðɣiiða-X 'knee', also p.b. quʀ]
AAY cisquq 'knee' [short i probably due to compression]
CAY ciisquq 'knee' [also cisquq reported for areas where it has not been established that compression occurs]
NSY siiXquq 'kneecap' [Jen. and L.-T.; Taghyuq has siixquq 'knee', Enm. et al. both forms]
CSY səɣəsquq 'knee' [seɣəsquʀ- 'kneel'; for əsłəquq 'flipper' see cil(ə)quʀ]
Sir siɣəsqəX 'knee' [Orr; Men. has siɣəkəX]
SPI siitquq 'knee'
NAI siicquq 'knee' [also sicquq — contam. with cil(ə)quʀ?; siicquq-, Mal sitquq- 'kneel']
WCI siitquq 'knee'
ECI siiqquq 'knee' [siiqqu(q)- 'kneel']
GRI siiqquq 'knee'

PE ciɣəðqu(C)aʀ 'kneecap' [cf. aʀ]
AAY —
CAY —
NSY siiXquaq 'kneecap' [ANLC]
CSY səɣəsqʷaaq
Sir —
SPI siitquaq 'kneecap'
NAI siicquaq, Mal sitquaq 'kneecap' [Seiler]
WCI siitquaq
ECI siiqquaq
GRI siiqquaq 'kneecap, small bone in seal's back flipper' [the latter probably by contam. with cil(ə)quʀ]

PE ciɣəðqumiɣ- 'kneel' [cf. miɣ-]
AAY cisqumiɣ- 'kneel, put in kneeling position' [postural root]
CAY ciisqumiɣ-
NSY siiXquXm̥iɣ-
CSY —
Sir —
SPI —
NAI [sicquɣmik- 'press down with one's knees']
WCI siitqumiaq- 'kneel for a moment'
ECI siiqqumiaq- 'be kneeling' [siiqqumiɣaq- 'walk on knees']
GRI siiqqumiaʀ- 'be kneeling', siiqqummiʀ- 'kneel down'

PI ciitqinəq '(baggy) trouser knee' [cf. li-[1] and nəʀ[1]]
SPI siitqaniq 'trouser knee that has become baggy from wear'
NAI siicqinʸ(nʸ)ɨq*
WCI —
ECI siiqqiniq 'deformation of trousers at the knee'
GRI siiqqiʀnit 'women's trousers, knee trousers for men', EG ciiqqiniit 'woman's trousers made of sealskin'

PI ciɣɣaq- 'make tearing or sizzling noise' [note that the ɣɣ here need not be historical, so there is probably a link to ciðəɣ- — compare ciiq-[2]]
SPI —
NAI siɣɣaq- 'make sizzling noise', siɣaala-, Nun 'make noise of running water', PH siɣatit- 'spurt, gush, make sound of s.th. tearing'
WCI siɣ(ɣ)aq- 'tear cleanly, make ripping sound' [Schn. has siɣaqpallaq- 'make cracking sounds' for 'adg']
ECI siɣaq- 'make the noise of s.th. dry tearing', Lab 'crackle, crack' [Peck; also siɣalak- 'make cracking sound in fire']
GRI sixxaʀ- 'whistle'

PE ciɣi- and **ciɣɣi(t)-** 'be brittle or crack' [cf. ciimik- and Aleut sixsa- (intr.), sixsi- (tr.) 'break in two', also siɣna-X 'rest, surplus'?]
AAY cii- 'get smashed, squashed', ciitə- 'squash flat'
CAY cii- 'get smashed, chapped, squashed (s.th. soft with hard outside)'
NSY —
CSY siɣiqə- 'break, shatter (s.th. brittle)'
Sir [note siɣnəX 'remains' and compare Aleut siɣna-X above]
SPI siɣɣit- 'tear, of s.th. dry'
NAI siɣɣit- 'break, crack cleanly'
WCI Net siɣ(ɣ)it- 'crack' [Briggs]
ECI siɣɣi(t)- 'crack through, break'
GRI sixxit- 'be brittle, crack, break' [and siiʀłak 's.th. fragile, that bursts easily (e.g. clothing)']

PY ci(ɣ)iləʀtə- 'crackle'
AAY K, KP ciiləXtə- 'crackle, rustle'
CAY ciiləXtə- 'be crisp, crackly'
NSY —
CSY —

PY ciilʀaq 'dragonfly' [cf. niulʀiq]
AAY cilʀayuk 'dragonfly'
CAY ciilʀaq, LI ciiləʀnaq
NSY —
CSY —

PE ciɣun 'ear' [cf. un?]
AAY cuun 'ear'
CAY ciun
NSY siitə
CSY siɣuta
Sir siɣəta
SPI siun
NAI siun
WCI siun
ECI siuti
GRI siut

PE ciɣutəquʀ 'snail shell' [cf. quʀ]
AAY —
CAY ciutəquluk, ciutəmquq 'snail shell'
NSY —
CSY —
Sir —
SPI —
NAI siutiʀu(q) 'seashell'
WCI siutiʀuq 'welk-like spiral sea-shell' [Pryde]
ECI Lab siutiʀuq 'snail, slug' [Bourq.]
GRI siutiʀuq 'snail'

PY ci(ɣ)utaiq 'kind of beetle' [cf. (C)iʀ]
AAY KP cuutaiq, PWS cuutiq 'type of beetle said to crawl into people's ears as they sleep'
CAY ciutaiq, ciutaiʀ(aq*)
NSY —
CSY —

PY ciɣuq or **ciɣuʀaq** 'kind of murrelet' [cf. ciuʀaq (from earlier PE ciɣuʀaʀ?), perhaps a matter of the mottled, sand-colored coloration of this bird]
AAY C, Kod cuu<ʀ>aq, Perry suu'aŋuaq 'pigeon guillemot, ancient murrelet'
CAY ciɣuq, ciɣuʀ(aq*), Nun ciɣuʀaX 'Kittlitz's murrelet'
NSY —
CSY —

PY ciɣvik 'nose bead'
AAY PWS ciɣwik 'nose bead' [old sources only]
CAY ciɣvik 'nose bead'
NSY —
CSY —

cii(q) 'sheefish, inconnu' [acc. Krauss, an Athabaskan loan, rather than an Eskimo loan to Ath. — cf. Kutchin šʳia: of this meaning]
AAY —
CAY ciiq 'inconnu, sheefish'
NSY —
CSY —
Sir —
SPI Qaw sii
NAI sii
WCI siiʀaq 'sheefish' [Pryde has Net siiq 'kind of whitefish']
ECI —
GRI —

PY ciilavik 'kind of grass?' [cf. ciilqa(a)q and perhaps ciɣi-]
AAY AP ciilawik, KP cuulawik, PWS cuula<w>ik 'eelgrass'
CAY ciilavik 'spreading wood fern'
NSY —
CSY —

PY ciilqa(a)q 'fireweed' [cf. ciilavik]
AAY ciłqaq 'fireweed'
CAY ciiłqaaq
NSY —
CSY —

PI ciimik- 'press down on or squeeze?' [cf. ciɣi- and miɣ-?]
Yup — [for CAY, AAY cii- 'get smashed or squashed' see ciɣi-]
SPI [for Qaw siimak- 'gather strength for s.th., be determined to win' see ciʀi-]
NAI siimik- 'overload, press to ground when wrestling', Nu 'grind protruding middle finger against s.o. to hurt them'
WCI —
ECI siimik- 'squeeze (between two things)'
GRI SWG siimiɣ- 'snap one's fingers at', NG hiimik-, hiimixxaq- 'beat, punch'

PI ciiq-[1] 'ooze out' [cf. ci(i)qiak]
SPI siiq- 'become sour, fermented (of food)'
NAI siiq- 'ooze, seep (like a sore), leak out (of air)', PH 'sweat, perspire' [and siiqsipkaq- 'sweat']
WCI siiqsipkaq- 'make someone sweat' [and siiʀlaŋu- 'have heartburn'?]
ECI siiq- 'taste bitterness', Lab 'let dampness go through'
GRI siiʀ- 'get sour taste in mouth' [for homonym meaning 'make hissing noise' see ciiq-[2]; note also siiʀi- 'get water in the mouth, ooze out, be shy', NG hiiʀahaaq 'swampy place']

PI ciiqtənnəq 'water oozing up through ice' [cf. tət- and nəʀ[1]]
SPI —
NAI siiqsɨnnɨq* 'water flowing through crack in ground, on top of ice, overflow' [siiqsɨt- 'ooze, flow out through crack']
WCI siiqtin(n)iq 'a spring', overflow on ice'
ECI —
GRI siiʀsinniq* 'ice swollen with water oozing up from below' [and siiʀsit- 'swell that way']

PI ciiʀnaq- 'be sour' [cf. naʀ-]
Yup [note CAY NSU ciiʀnaXqə- 'be sour' — from the Inu? — and CSY siiʀnaq 'walrus stomach']

SPI siiʀnaq- 'be sour' [as noun = 's.th. sour']
NAI siiʀnʸaq- 'be sour, sweet, tart'
WCI siiʀnaq- 'be sour' [siiʀnat 'conserved fruit']
ECI siiʀnatuq 's.th. that causes one to salivate, produces an acid taste in mouth', Lab siiʀnaqtuq 'yeast, vinegar' [Peck]
GRI siiʀnaʀ- 'be sour' [and siiʀnaq 'sorrel']

PI ciiq-[2] 'sizzle or hiss' [cf. ciqəʀ- and ciɣɣaq-]
SPI —
NAI siilʸak- 'sizzle, make a tearing noise,'
WCI siiʀaq- 'sizzle (lamp or stove)', Car? 'whistle in ears' [Schn. 'adg'; Pryde has hiiʀaq- 'hiss, sing (kettle), thunder (surf)' for Cop, siʀaaq- 'spurt (frying bacon)' for Sig, also Cop hiqanaxxiq- 'fry', hiqanitaut 'frying pan']
ECI siʀaaq- 'buzz, make noise (static)'
GRI siiʀ- 'make hissing noise' [and NG hiʀaalataq 'meat roasted on flat stone rubbed with tallow or blubber']

PY ciivak 'fly' [cf. vaɣ, and compare PI nəvyuvak — cf. nəvyuʀ for the initial cons., also PI niulʀiq]
AAY ciiwak 'housefly' [perhaps influenced by ciɣi- — compare the words for dragonfly there]
CAY ciivak, ciuvak 'housefly'
NSY [for ŋuyŋuaXaq 'housefly' see nəvyuvak]
CSY [for ŋuuyŋaaʀaq 'housefly' see under nəvyuvak]

PY cika(C)aq 'capelin (eulachon)'
AAY cikəq 'capelin, smelt'
CAY cikaaq, cikaaʀ(aq*)
NSY sikaaq 'small fish'
CSY sikaaq* 'smelt'
Sir [Orr has sikaX, pl. sikaʀiy in this sense, probably borrowed from CSY]

PI cikaq- or **cikak-** 'be stiff' [cf. Aleut sakaʀ-, Atkan also sakaɣ- 'be stiff (e.g. sinew)']
Yup [note AAY cikiaʀ-, sikiaʀ- 'roast split fish' (compare to GRI sikaɣ-)]
SPI —
NAI —
WCI —
ECI sikaŋa- 'be clumsy' [and note Lab sikkaq- 'be soft', sikkaniq 'soft part of walrus tooth — Peck; NBI sikkaŋa- 'be dissipated, provocative']
GRI sikaɣ- 'be or make hard and brittle, roast over a fire', EG ciɣaʀ- 'be hard'

PI cikcuiq- 'be attentive or careful'
SPI —
NAI —
WCI Car B. Lake hitsuiq- [for hixxuiq-?] 'be careful, think about how to do a task', hitsuitsia- 'have forethought' [Schn., who also has sitsiq-, siksiq- 'be intelligent' for 'adg', also 'be water-absorbant, soaked', conflating this with the entry under citciq-]
ECI —
GRI NWG sissuiʀ- [old ortho. sigssuer- or sigsuer- in Ordbogêraq] 'be attentive, pay attention'

PE cikðiɣ 'squirrel'
AAY —
CAY NS cikik 'arctic ground squirrel' [also elsewhere in cikixpak 'marmot' and cikiɣnaq 'lake trout' with naʀ]
NSY —
CSY sikik 'arctic ground squirrel'
Sir —
SPI sikšik
NAI sikšik 'arctic ground squirrel', sikšaaq 'young ground squirrel', sikšikpak 'hoary marmot'
WCI siksik 'squirrel', Cop, Car, Net 'marmot' [Ras.]
ECI Igl siksik 'marmot' [Ras.], Lab 'squirrel' [Peck]
GRI siššiŋŋuaq 'squirrel' [Kl. has siššik 'squirrel', old ortho. sigssik; for siššiŋit 'small bones in head of fish, scales in ear' see təkðə(ʀ)]

PE cikə(t)- 'lower head' [cf. Aleut ciiki- 'be atilt, in disorder', ciikit- 'tilt, put into disorder']
AAY ciktə- 'lower head, dive, bow'
CAY cikətə- 'close in (weather, hole), bend over, bow'
NSY səkətə- 'bow head', səkəXqa- 'nod' [Enm.]
CSY səkətə- 'dunk or bury one's head in s.th., bend forward', sikm̥uutə- 'lunge forward' [and sikłaatə- 'fall over'; Chap sikm̥uxtə- 'bend' in Rub.]
Sir sikətə- 'bow, dunk' [Orr; Em. also has sikmuxtə- 'bend (head below knees)' and sikəłXət(ə)- 'fall down (person)']
SPI siɣit- 'bow, lower head, bend over, bend forward', Qaw siɣžaaʀaq- 'dip face repeatedly into water (as a moose looking for food)'
NAI siki- 'lower or hang head'
WCI siki-
ECI siki- 'drink from surface of water' [and sikiŋa- 'be bent over in that position'; Lab sikit- 'drink without a cup']
GRI siki- 'stand in a bending position', sikiɣ- 'stoop, bend' [and sikiŋa- 'stand or sit with bent head']

PY cikiʀ- ' give (to)' [from PE cu(na), kðaʀ and liʀ-? — compare the Kod form below and CAY pikitə- 'give to' from pi(-), kðaʀ and lit-]
AAY K, KP cikiʀ- 'give (to)' [Kod caqaʀ- rather]
CAY cikiʀ- 'give to'
NSY —
CSY —

PE ciklaʀ 'pickaxe' [cf. Atkan Aleut sikli-X 'notch (e.g. in wood), notched (as of knife)']
AAY cikłaʀ- 'chop'
CAY cikłaq 'pickaxe'
NSY sikłaq [Taghyuq]
CSY sikłaq
Sir sikəłəʀaX
SPI sikłaq
NAI sikłʸaq* 'pickaxe', Nu 'incisor' [as verb = 'use pickaxe on']
WCI sikłaq 'pickaxe'
ECI Lab tiłłak 'pickaxe' [and Igl tikłaʀaut 'that with which one stabs', tikłaʀalik 'walrus' — Ras.]
GRI siłłaq(*) [old ortho. sigdlaq] 'pickaxe, crowbar' [siłłaʀ- 'hack loose (e.g. from frozen earth)']

PY cikmiʀ- 'close eyes' [cf. cikunʀiq-]
AAY cikm̥iʀ- 'close one's eyes'
CAY cikm̥iʀ-, cikm̥ə- 'close one's eyes, become blind'
NSY sikm̥iʀ-'blink'
CSY —
Inu [Qaw sipmiq- 'close eyes' may be a borrowing from Yup]

PE cikna- 'be jealous'
AAY cikn̥a(yuɣ)-, K cikn̥a- 'envy, be jealous', cikn̥akə- 'be jealous of'
CAY cikn̥a- 'be jealous, envious'
NSY sikn̥ažaaʀ- 'be envious' [Enm. has sikn̥ažaɣ-]
CSY sikn̥a(yuɣ)- 'feel possessive'
Sir siknəkə(s)- 'feel possessive about' [Em.].
SPI siknak- 'be jealous' [influenced by caŋiak-?]
NAI siɣnʸa- 'refuse to share, be stingy', Mal siqnʸa- 'be jealous, envious' [contam. with ciqni-?; siɣnʸaɣi-, Nu siknʸaɣɨ- 'be stingy with']
WCI siŋna- 'be jealous' [siŋnaɣi- 'not want to part with (its food, of dog)']
ECI sinna-, NBI, SB siŋna- 'be jealous' [Saul — Schn. has Tar siŋŋa-; sinnaɣi- 'be jealous of']
GRI siŋŋa(ɣi)- 'be jealous (of)'

PE ciku 'ice' [also verbal 'freeze over']
AAY ciku 'ice'
CAY ciku
CSU siku
NSY siku
Sir —
SPI siɣu
NAI siku
WCI siku
ECI siku
GRI siku, EG ciɣiq 'ice' [in pl. 'lumps of ice'; sikuršuit, EG ciɣiviit 'pack ice']

PE ciku(C)aʀ '(thin) ice ' [cf. aʀ]
AAY cikuaq 'thin ice (on water)'
CAY cikuaq
NSY sikuaq [ANLC]
CSY sikʷaavžəʀaq 'very thin ice'
Sir —
SPI siɣuaq 'thin new ice'
NAI sikuaq 'thin ice on water' [as verb = 'become covered with thin ice']
WCI sikuaq 'thin ice' [also verbal acc. Lowe]
ECI sikuaq 'first thin ice on water'
GRI sikuaq, pl. sikuššat 'thin ice' [sikuaʀ- 'be covered with thin ice']

PI cikulaaq '(slushy) ice ' [cf. la(C)aʀ(-)]
Yup [note CAY cikulʀaq, cikulʀaaʀ(aq*) 'glare ice on river or lake']
SPI —
NAI sikulaaq- 'develop slush ice (fishing hole)'
WCI —
ECI sikullaaq 'piece of floating ice'
GRI sikulaaq 'brittle ice'

PI cikuliaq '(new) ice ' [cf. li(C)aʀ]
SPI siɣuliaq 'young ice'
NAI sikuliaq 'young ice formed around edge of old solid ice on open lead'
WCI sikuliaq 'young ice'
ECI sikuliaq 'new ice' [as verb = 'fall (freezing rain)']
GRI sikuliaq 'new ice'

PE cikuŋiʀ- 'break up (ice)' [cf. ŋiʀ-]
AAY cikuiʀ- 'have become free of ice'
CAY cikuiʀ- 'have become free of ice' [and cikuiłquq, cikuiʀnəq* 'open hole in river ice, soft spot on baby's head']
NSY —
CSY —
Sir —
SPI siɣuiq- 'break up (ice)'
NAI sikuiʀvik 'ice break-up time'
WCI —
ECI sikuiq- 'have broken up (ice at break-up time)'
GRI sikuiʀ- 'have become free of ice, open water'

PI cikunʀiq- 'close eyes' [cf. cikmiʀ-]
SPI siɣuʀniq- 'close one's eyes'
NAI siqu- 'fall asleep,' PH 'close eyes', Mal siqunʀiq- 'close eyes'
WCI sikunŋi- 'close eyes' [Lowe; Ow. has hiquŋiqtiq- 'blink at' for EP]
ECI sikuŋŋit- 'close eyes'
GRI siquŋŋiʀ-, NG hikuʀŋiq-, NWG sikuʀniʀ-, Up siqiʀniʀ-, EG ciʀiʀniʀ- 'close eyes'

PE cikuʀ 'needle or sharp tip'
AAY —
CAY Nun cikuX 'needle'
NSY sikuq
CSY sikuq*
Sir —
SPI siɣuq 'point, tip'
NAI sikuq 'drill bit, stone spearhead or arrow'
WCI —
ECI —
GRI —

PE cila or **cił̣a** '(spirit of) weather or outside world' [also 'awareness'; cila or cilam iŋuɣa/inuɣa (see iŋuɣ) is the spirit of the weather in the old Esk legends; cf. Aleut sla-X, Att ła-X 'wind, weather, compass point']
AAY ła 'weather, world, outside, awareness'
CAY Y, NS, UK, LI cəła, K, BB, Nun əła, HBC, Eg ciła 'weather, world, outside, awareness' [and note əłam yua 'God']
NSY siła 'weather, world, outside, awareness'
CSY əsła
Sir siła [Vakh. and Orr; Men. has sila]
SPI sila
NAI silʸa 'weather, outside, atmosphere, air'
WCI sila
ECI sila 'weather, air, atmosphere, atmosphere, the world, intelligence'

GRI sila, Kap Farvel silaq 'weather, outside, the world, intelligence' [and silaannaq* 'air'; note also siani- 'notice, be reasonable', sianiut 'nerve, sense']

PE cilakiɣ- 'be good weather' [cf. kiɣ-]
AAY KP łaakəxtə-, AP łakkəxci- 'be good weather'
CAY cəłakəɣ- 'be good weather' [and cəłakəxcivaa 'how nice the weather is!']
NSY —
CSY —
Sir —
SPI silaɣik-
NAI silʸaɣik-
WCI silaɣik-
ECI [compare silaqqi(C)- 'be good weather']
GRI silaɣiɣ- 'be good weather' [silaɣik 'good weather']

PI cilali- 'become bleached by the sun' [cf. li-²?]
Yup [note HBC ciła- 'become weathered']
SPI Qaw silali- 'get suntanned'
NAI silʸali- 'get a tan, get faded by sun'
WCI Cop, Net hilali- 'be weather-beaten' [Pryde]
ECI — [but note silaaʀniq 's.th. weathered in the air']
GRI silali- 'become weathered, bleached by the sun'

PE cilalliʀ and **cilaqliʀ** 'outside part or neighbor' [cf. l(l)iʀ; the latter form with related qliʀ]
AAY łaqłiq 'outside (part)'
CAY əlaqłiq* 'one immediately outside, neighbor'
NSY —
CSY —
Sir —
SPI silaliq 'outermost one, neighbor'
NAI silʸalliq* 'outside part, neighbor'
WCI silalliq 'exterior (e.g. door)', Sig also 'neighbor'
ECI silalliq 'outermost part'
GRI silaʀłiq* 'porch, front yard' [Robbe and Menn. have EG silaʀtiq 'exterior']

PE cilałuɣ 'rain or bad weather' [cf. p.b. łuɣ(-)]
AAY KP łaałuxtə-, AP łałłuxtə- 'be bad weather', AP łałłuk 'squall'
CAY əłałuk, cəłałuk 'rain' [əłałiʀ-, cəłałiʀ- 'rain']
NSY siłałuk 'rain'
CSY əsłałuk 'rain' [əsłałuɣuuXtə- 'rain']
Sir siłalux 'bad weather'
SPI silaluk-, silaqłuk- 'be bad weather'
NAI silʸaluk, sialuk 'rain' [also verbal]
WCI Sig silaluk 'rain' [also verbal]
ECI silaluk
GRI sialuk 'rain' [siałłiʀ- 'rain', silaʀłuk 'bad weather']

PE cilan (cilatə) 'outside' [cf. tə; usually with possessor endings]
AAY łaatə 'outside part of s.th.'
CAY cəłatə 'area outside' [also əlatə- 'area outside']
NSY siłatə
CSY əsłatə
Sir siłta 'area outside' [Orr; also siłtinaʀətə- 'be outside']
SPI silati 'outside of s.th.'
NAI silan, silatɨ 'outside of s.th., immediate surroundings, right side (fabric)'
WCI silati 'outside of s.th.'
ECI silati
GRI silat(i) 'outside of s.th., area outside'

PE cilaŋiʀutə- 'lose one's senses' [cf. ŋiʀutə-]
AAY —
CAY cəłaiʀutə-, əłaiʀutə- 'lose one's senses'
NSY —
CSY —
Sir —
SPI [silaiq- 'lose one's senses, become suddenly dark']
NAI silʸaiʀutɨ-
WCI —
ECI —
GRI silaaʀut(i)- 'have lost one's senses, act crazily, be drunk'

PE cilaŋit- 'be out of one's mind' [cf. ŋit-]
AAY əłaitə- 'not be aware of what one is doing, be foolish'
CAY cəłaitə-, Nun, K, HBC əłaitə-
NSY —
CSY —
Sir —
SPI Qaw silait- 'be out of one's mind'
NAI silʸait- 'pay no attention to whether it is night or day'
WCI Cop hilait- 'be stupid' [Pryde]
ECI silait- 'be stupid, crazy'
GRI silaat- 'do s.th. hurtful or foolish on purpose'

PI cilatu- 'be wise' [cf. tu-¹]
SPI —
NAI [silʸɣatu- 'be wise, in one's prime']
WCI silatu- 'be sensible, wise' [Pryde]
ECI silatu- 'be wise, cunning, intelligent'
GRI silatu- 'be sensible, clever, miserly'

PY cilatuqaq 'enclosed porch' [cf. tu-¹ and qaʀ?]
AAY Kod łaatuqaq 'enclosed porch'
CAY əlatuXaq
NSY —
CSY —

PE ciləɣ-¹ 'be thick or wide' [or ciłəɣ-?; cf. Aleut slaɣ- 'be wide']
AAY łəɣə- 'be thick in diameter'
CAY K əłəɣ-, Y cəłəɣ-, HBC ciłəɣ-
NSY siłəɣ- [Enm. and L.-T.]
CSY əsłəɣə- 'be stout, thick'
Sir —
SPI silik- 'be stout, thick', Qaw 'be wide'
NAI silʸɨk- 'be wide'
WCI silik-
ECI silik-
GRI siliɣ-

PE ciləɣ-[2] 'be full' [cf. ciləɣ-[1]?]
AAY —
CAY [note Nun əłm̥aʀ- 'be full']
NSY —
CSY əsłəqə- 'be full'
Sir [note simləqaʀ- 'be full', simlaXt(ə)- 'fill' acc. Vakh. from Men.'s texts, and Orr]
SPI —
NAI silʸivɨt- 'become full (stomach, etc.), fill completely'
WCI Car hiliŋu- 'have a full stomach, suffer from indigestion' [Schn.]
ECI siliC- 'leave the rest (having had enough)' [and silinniku 'remainder, leftover']
GRI [note siłłima- 'be ready', siłłimmaʀ- 'make ready', siłłimmat 'spare, s.th. kept in readiness, insurance']

PE cili- or ciłi- 'sharpen'
AAY —
CAY cəłi-, əłi-, HBC ciłi- 'whet, sharpen'
NSY [siluak 'whetstone' acc. L.-T.]
CSY —
Sir —
SPI W sili- 'whet, sharpen'
NAI silʸi-
WCI Sig silimmak- 'sharpen' [and silimmaun 'whetstone']
ECI sili- 'sharpen'
GRI sili-

PE cillin or ciłin 'whetstone' [cf. un]
AAY —
CAY cəłin, əłin 'whetstone'
NSY —
CSY —
Sir —
SPI sillin
NAI silʸlʸinʸ
WCI Car B. Lake hillit [Dor.]
ECI silliti
GRI siłłit

PI ciliʀak- 'glide' [cf. ciluk- and ciluʀ-]
SPI Qaw siliak- 'glide (esp. through air)'
NAI silʸiak- 'swoop down on, be blown along with wind, glide'
WCI siliak- 'glide downward (of bird)'
ECI —
GRI siliʀaɣ- 'go obliquely, tack'

PE cil(ə)quʀ or cił(ə)quʀ '(hind) flipper' [cf. ciləɣ-[1] and quʀ?; there is some entanglement with ciɣəðquʀ]
AAY —
CAY —
NSY —
CSY əsłəquq 'flipper'
Sir siłəqəX [Orr]
SPI sitquq 'hind flipper'
NAI sicquq, sicquaq 'hind flipper of seal' [also 'knee' — see ciɣəðquʀ]
WCI sitquq 'hind flipper'
ECI siqquq
GRI siqquq

PI cilu 'carcass of sea mammal'
SPI silu 'animal carcass drifted ashore, floating carcass' [Men. has 's.th. thrown up by the sea' for Imaq]
NAI silʸu 'sea mammal carcass drifted ashore'
WCI silu
ECI silu
GRI silu

PI ciluli- 'find an animal carcass' [cf. łit- if not li-[1]]
SPI siluli- 'find a drifted carcass on the beach' [and note Imaq siluak- 'find s.th. thrown up by sea']
NAI silʸuli-, silʸut- 'come across an animal carcass drifted ashore or floating'
WCI —
ECI siluli- 'find a dead animal'
GRI siluli- 'come across a carcass at sea or on the beach'

PI ciluk- 'lift arms?' [cf. ciluʀ- and ciliʀak-]
Yup — [for CSY siluk 'wing' see culuɣ]
SPI siluk- 'glide through the air, soar' [influenced by ciliʀak-?]
NAI silʸuk- 'cross over by holding onto s.th. overhead and raising legs, kick'
WCI siluktaq- 'lift oneself by the force of one's wrists'
ECI siluk- 'be about to go off, strike (gun, clock, etc.)'
GRI siluɣ- 'have arm lifted for blow or to throw, be cocked (of gun)'

PY ciluʀ- 'slide or glide' [cf. ciluk-]
AAY łuʀ- 'slide (down)'
CAY ciluʀ- 'glide, skip on water', Y cəłuʀ-, HBC ciłuʀ-, K əłuʀ- 'slide down, dive through air'
NSY —
CSY əsłuʀ- 'go south, travel with wind'

PE ciłuvaɣ 'fish egg' [compare the loss of intervocalic l in Inu sialuk under cilałuɣ (cila); cf. perhaps Aleut cisu-X 'fish eggs', in du. 'vulva', for which compare the s in qisa- under qiłəʀ- — also macu(ɣ), where fish eggs and female genitals are also denoted by the same term in AAY]
AAY łuuwak 'fish egg' [also sisuq 'roe, fish eggs' in K, borrowed directly from the Aleut]
CAY HBC ciłuvak 'fish egg' [and NS cuak 'aged fish roe' — from Inu? — but see also cu(C)aniʀ]
NSY siłəvak 'fish egg' [Taghyuq]
CSY əsłəvak 'fish egg' [note ałavak 'vagina']
Sir siłəvəx 'fish egg' [Orr has siłəvax]
SPI suak
NAI suvak
WCI suvak
ECI suvak
GRI suak 'fish egg' [suaašaq 'gruel', Up suaat 'female genitals']

PI cimək- 'plug'
SPI [simiaq 'wound plug for sea mammal']
NAI simik- 'stop with a plug'
WCI simik- 'plug' [as noun = 'stopper, plug']
ECI simik- 'plug' [as noun = 'stopper, plug']
GRI simiɣ- 'plug' [also noun simik; simmiʀ- 'plug, cork', EG cimi 'cotton grass']

PE cimmiʀ- 'exchange or replace'
AAY cimiʀ- 'change, exchange, trade, replace'
CAY cimiʀ- 'change, substitute, exchange' [and cimiq 'substituted item']
NSY simiʀ- 'change, substitute' [Enm.]
CSY simiʀ- 'change, exchange, replace'
Sir siməɣ- 'change, exchange' [for siməʀ-?; Vakh. has simət- 'change (clothes)']
SPI simmiq- 'change, exchange'
NAI simmiq-
WCI simmiq-
ECI —
GRI simiʀ- 'penetrate, soak into, be influenced (e.g. by European ways)' [for sinniʀ- 'replace' see cip(ə)nəʀ under cipə(t)-; note also siʀŋut(i)-, siʀmut(i)- 'penetrate and form a spot (liquid), be influenced by another's dialect']

PY cin(n)aq 'aged fish' [cf. cu(C)aniʀ, which could be the same set, with the present one influenced bypiɣinaq]
AAY cinnaq 'aged fish'
CAY Y, HBC, Nun, Eg, LI cinnaq 'cheese-like fish aged in pit'
NSY —
CSY —

PE cinə 'shore or edge' [cf. Aleut sn(a)- as in snaŋa- 'side, sea side of bank', snaanu- 'go to the side', Atkan also snamuðaran 'in all directions', snuuʀi-X 'subject', EA 'being on one side, alien']
AAY K cənə-, C sənə- '(its) shore, edge'
CAY cən̥a, HBC cina 'shore, edge'
NSY sinə 'shore, edge'
CSY əsn̥a 'edge' [base əsn̥ə-], əsn̥aq 'shore'
Sir [Orr has sincəX, probably the same as 'shore' under ciŋðaʀ]
SPI Qaw sini 'shore, edge' [and KI sitka 'shore, edge' from poss. 'its edge']
NAI sinʸɨ 'shore, edge'
WCI sinaa '(its) shore, edge' [Pryde, who also has Cop hini 'edge of parka bottom'; and note ethnonym Siglit — 'those most toward the shore'?]
ECI sini 'shore, edge'
GRI sini 'shore, edge' [and siniʀiak 'coast', NG hiɣliaq- 'travel out to ice edge', WG sinaʀɬiq* 's.th. most toward edge', EG ciaʀtiq 'edge, ice edge' (Robbe and Menn.)]

PY cəniq 'beaver' [cf. (C)iʀ]
AAY sn̥i(i)q 'beaver'
CAY NSU cən̥iqqaq
NSY —
CSY —

PE cinəʀaʀ 'edge of ice or channel?' [cf. aʀ]
AAY —
CAY [note cəŋŋaq 'sandy beach']
NSY —
CSY əsn̥əʀaq 'lagoon opening to sea'
Sir —
SPI siʀnaq
NAI sinʸaʀaq PH 'channel from sea into lagoon', Nu 'strait'
WCI —
ECI sinaaq 'ice edge, corner (e.g. of eye)'
GRI sinaaq, EG ciaa(q) 'edge (e.g. of ice)'

PEciniʀ- 'go along edge or shore' [cf. liʀ-?]
AAY K cəniXtə-, PWS sn̥iXtə- 'go along edge or shore'
CAY cən̥iXtə-, Nun cəniXtə-, HBC ciniXtə- 'visit (within village), walk along shore'
NSY —
CSY əsn̥iXtə- 'go along shore'
Sir — [for siŋžiXt(ə)- 'go past' see under ciŋðaʀ]
SPI [siniqšaq- 'travel along shore', Qaw 'come to visit from somewhere else']
NAI [siniqšaq- 'travel along shore, go in and out along a row of houses']
WCI —
ECI Wakeham Bay siniqtuq 'even, flat surface' [and siniʀsu(q)- 'follow coast']
GRI siniʀ- 'follow the edge of s.th. (e.g. bank or shore)' [siniʀšuʀ- 'travel along coast (past fjords)']

PY-S cinək 'bruise' [cf. cinkutaɣ]
AAY cənəɣ-, sənəɣ- 'be bruised' [and cənəɣnəq, sənəɣnəq, sənəxtaq 'bruise, black eye']
CAY cənək, HBC cinək 'bruise'
NSY sinəɣ- 'bruise' [ANLC; Em. has sinəŋɣalʀia 'one that has become blue', and L.-T. has siniɬək 'bruise']
CSY əsnək 'bruise'
Sir sinəx [Orr]

PI cinək- 'sleep' [from *ciŋək-? — cf. Aleut sŋaɣ- 'dream']
SPI sinik- 'sleep' [and sinŋuziq 'night dress']
NAI sinʸik- 'sleep'
WCI sinik-
ECI sinik-
GRI siniɣ- 'sleep' [note also siŋŋusiq 'night dress', sinnartuuʀ- 'oversleep', siŋŋaniiʀ- 'surprise in one's sleep']

PI cinəɣvik 'bed' [cf. ðviɣ]
SPI siniɣvik 'bed'
NAI sinʸɨɣvik
WCI siniɣvik
ECI sinivvik 'sleeping bag'
GRI siniffik 'bed'

PI cinnaktuq- or **ciŋnaktuq-** 'dream' [cf. nəɣ- and tuʀ-²?]
SPI sinnaktuq- 'dream'
NAI sinʸnʸaktuq-

WCI sinnaktuq- [Lowe has siŋnaktuq-]
ECI sinnatuuma-, NBI, SB siŋnaktuuma- 'dream' [also 'adg' acc. Schn.]
GRI sinnattuʀ-, NG hinnaktuq- 'dream' [nominal sinnattuɣaq — old ortho. singnagtugaq, but Fab. has sinektugak; NG hinnaqtuq 'dream']

PI cinnaʀliuq- 'sleep badly' [cf. łuɣ(-) and li(C)uʀ-]
SPI —
NAI sinʸnʸaʀliuq- 'sleep fitfully, have a nightmare'
WCI —
ECI sinnaliuq- 'find it hard to sleep, try to sleep'
GRI sinnaʀłiuʀ- 'sleep badly'

PE cinkutaɣ 'sty in eye' [cf. cinək]
AAY ciŋkutak, ciŋkutaq 'sty in eye', cikutak 'infection or growth in eye'
CAY cənkutak, HBC cinkutak 'sty in the eye' [and note cikutaq 'bladder of small mammal such as squirrel']
NSY —
CSY —
Sir —
SPI sikkutak 'sty in the eye'
NAI sickutaq, sikkutaq
WCI sitkutak- 'have a sty'
ECI sikkutaq 'sty, swelling or pus on edge of eyelid'
GRI sikkutak 'sty' [sikkutaɣ- 'get a sty']

PI ciŋai- 'be pregnant'
SPI siŋai(yau)- 'be pregnant' [siŋaiq 'fetus']
NAI siŋai(yau)- 'be pregnant (of human)'
WCI siŋa(i)- 'be pregnant'
ECI siŋai- 'be pregnant' [as noun = 'fetus']
GRI NG hiŋaiyaq 'pregnant bitch (or other animal)' [Holt.]

PI ciŋaq- 'be grayish?'
SPI —
NAI —
WCI Car B. Lake hiŋaqtit 'wolves (shaman's word)' [Schn.]
ECI siŋaqti 'wolf (shaman's word)', sinarnaq, NBI, Aiv siaʀnaq 'gray (fur)' [Lab sinaanak 'gray' can also be verbal]
GRI siŋaʀnaq, NG hinaʀnaq 'yellowish gray dog (the most wolf-like type)'

PE ciŋaʀ- 'crush?'
AAY ciŋaʀ- 'kiss in the older style by pressing the nose against the face and sniffing softly' [ciŋaq 'kiss']
CAY ciŋaʀ- 'kiss'
NSY siŋaʀ- 'kiss with nose' [Enm.]
CSY Chap siŋaʀ- 'kiss'
Sir siŋəʀ- 'kiss, press noses together, sniff s.th. or s.o.' [Em.]
SPI —
NAI —
WCI siŋaq- 'be smashed, crushed'
ECI siŋaq- 'burst from being crushed'
GRI siŋaʀ- 'strike, crush flat'

PE ciŋða(C)aʀ 'sled cover'
AAY C cimyaq 'dehaired seal hide used as cover'
CAY ciŋyaaq, ciŋsaaq 'tarpaulin cover for sled or boat'
NSY siŋžaq 'dried walrus skin' [Tein]
CSY —
Sir —
SPI siɣžaaq
NAI siɣžaaq
WCI siɣyaaq 'sled cover'
ECI —
GRI —

PE ciŋðaʀ 'beach or shore' [cf. ciŋə(t)-, ciŋða(C)aʀ and ciŋiɣ]
AAY —
CAY [note ciŋsiik, siŋsiiyaq 'elf, dwarf'? — compare NG hixxaʀmiut below]
NSY —
CSY —
Sir siŋcəX 'shore' [Vakh. also has siŋžaX, and siŋžiXtə- 'travel past' from Rub.]
SPI —
NAI [Jen. has siɣžaq 'shore on either side of river mouth']
WCI Sig siɣyaq 'shore'
ECI siyyaq 'shore, beach, wave breaking on shore', Igl and Baffin 'shore covered with ice' [and note Iti sitsalukaa- 'form waves'?]
GRI siššaq [old ortho. sigssaq] 'shore, beach, legendary sea monster' [Fab. also 'saltwater fish'], NG hixxaq 'shore, zone between sea ice and ice edge' [and NG hixxat 'Milky Way' or 'pressure ridges of ice along shore'; hixxaʀmiut refers to small, benign spirits living on beaches, like the WG inniʀšuit or the qunniʀaʀšuit living in cracks in icebergs — Søby]

PI ciŋžaʀiaq '(kind of) shore bird' [cf. yaʀ]
SPI —
NAI —
WCI siɣyaʀiaq 'shore bird' ['dunlin' at Baker Lake acc. Dor.]
ECI siyyaʀiaq 'shore bird'
GRI NWG siššaʀiaʀšuk, EG cittaʀmiilaq 'shore snipe, sandpiper'

PE ciŋə(t)- 'shove' [cf. ciŋuk-, also perhaps Aleut caŋa- 'enter, crawl into (e.g. hole of baydarka)']
AAY ciŋə- 'give a push, shove to'
CAY ciŋə- 'push'
NSY ciŋtə- [Enm]
CSY siiŋə- 'push, shove'
Sir siŋ(ə)t(ə)- 'leave, be left', siŋəlaʀət(ə)- 'push off from shore' [Vakh. from Rub.; Em. has siŋə- 'push aside, chase away', siŋut(ə)- 'make one's way through a crowd']
SPI siŋit- 'throw s.th. in the water, push someone in the water'
NAI siŋit- 'immerse in water while holding or while s.th. is staked, anchored to land,' PH 'throw, heave into water, over a cliff'
WCI Net, Sig siŋit- 'throw, fling' [Ras.]

ECI siŋit- 'place in the water', Lab 'push away' [Peck], Iti 'fall into water, squeeze out' [see ciŋuk- for the probable contamination behind the latter sense']
GRI siŋiɣ- 'push s.th. down or out, squeeze contents out', siŋit- 'lower boat into water', NG also 'push down' [Holt.]

PY ciŋələ- 'hop' [possible related to CAY caqəlŋa- under caqələkitaʀ — contam.?]
AAY —
CAY — [for caqəlŋa- 'hop, flit' see caqələkitaʀ]
NSY siŋiłquXaʀ- 'hop, jump on foot' [ANLC; L.-T. has siŋiłquXaq 'hop, jump on one foot']
CSY səŋəłqaʀ- 'hop' [siŋləpəXtə-, səŋləpəXtə- 'limp']

PE ciŋiɣ 'point (of land)' [cf. Aleut ciŋa-X, EA (Nikolski) ciŋa-X 'impassable place on beach (because of cliff or rocks going down to the sea)', also ciŋə(t)- and ciŋðaʀ?]
AAY ciŋik 'point of land' [Kod 'penis']
CAY ciŋik 'point, tip'
NSY —
CSY siŋik 'point, tip' [and siŋiɣ- 'come to a point']
Sir siŋəx 'point, tip' [Vakh. from Men.'s texts]
SPI [Siŋik 'Golovin (place name)' — from Yupik?]
NAI —
WCI siŋik 'point of land which extends into sea'
ECI —
GRI —

PY ciŋilək 'arrow or spear with point' [cf. ləɣ]
AAY K ciŋilək 'arrow or spear with point'
CAY ciŋilək, ciŋiləɣaq
NSY —
CSY —
Sir — [but note siŋləʀaX 'plane']

PE ciŋiʀ 'bootlace'
AAY ciŋiq 'armband, garter, sleeveholder'
CAY ciŋiq 'bootlace, boot strap' [and ciŋiʀ- 'tie bootlaces']
NSY siŋiq 'bootlace' [Enm.]
CSY siŋiq 'bootlace' [and siŋiʀ- 'tie bootlaces']
Sir —
SPI siŋiq 'bootlace'
NAI siŋiq 'bootlace' [and as verb = 'tie bootlaces', as in all Inu]
WCI siŋiq
ECI siŋiq
GRI siŋiq 'bootlace' [siŋiʀ- 'tie bootlaces']

PY ciŋiłəq 'ankle' [cf. li-[1] and łəʀ?]
AAY KP, Kod ciŋiłəq, K, PWS ciŋiłquq 'ankle, small of leg'
CAY ciŋiłəq* 'ankle'
NSY —
CSY —

PI ciŋiʀnəq 'ankle' [cf. nəʀ[1]]
SPI siŋiʀniq 'ankle'
NAI siŋiʀnʸiq*
WCI siŋiʀniq [Pryde]
ECI siŋiʀniq 'round (part) of the ankle, round (part) of a low boat, (felt) inner lining at ankle'
GRI siŋiʀniq* 'instep, ankle'

PE ciŋquʀ- 'crack or crackle'
AAY K ciŋquq, C cəŋquq 'crackling noise'
CAY ciŋqə- 'crackle'
NSY siŋquXtə- 'pop' [ANLC]
CSY —
Sir —
SPI siqquq- 'be hard', Qaw 'crack (e.g. of knuckles, joints)'
NAI siqquq- 'be hard, tough, opinionated', siqqutɨt- 'snap with loud noise'
WCI siqquq- 'loud crack', siqquʀiaq- 'shoot a gun', Cop hiqquun 'gun' [Lowe; Ras. has Net seqqorsiksut — for siqquʀsižžut? — 'gun']
ECI siqquq- 'clap', siqquqtit- 'shoot with a gun' [and Aiv siqquqtiyyut 'gun']
GRI siqquʀ- 'crack, rattle, go off with a bang', NWG, Up 'shoot', NG hiqquqtaaq- 'shoot' [and NG hiqquut 'gun']

PI ciŋuk- 'strain' [cf. ciŋə(t)-, cuŋaʀ-, and ciŋuʀ-, but also təŋuqə- (the relat. is obscure)]
SPI siŋutniq-, Qaw siŋuk- 'push, strain with abdominal muscles'
NAI siŋuk- 'strain at stool or in labor contractions' [siŋŋuktɨt- 'become red in the face from exertion']
WCI —
ECI siŋu- 'swell, become congested (weather, river or human face)' [and siŋutit- 'become congested with blood', Iti siŋu(q)- 'squeeze out, be squeezed out' and siŋŋutit- 'pop (a boil)']
GRI siŋŋuʀ- 'be red-faced', siŋŋuʀtit- 'become red-faced' [and siŋunniʀ- 'strain so one's veins stand out']

PI ciŋulluq- 'strain at stool' [cf. luʀ-]
SPI —
NAI siŋulluq- 'strain at stool'
WCI Cop hiŋulluq- 'strain (esp. at stool)' [Pryde]
ECI siŋullu(q)- 'become red in face, strain to relieve oneself'
GRI siŋułłuʀ- 'strain at stool'

PY ciŋuʀ- 'overflow' [cf. ciŋuk-?]
AAY əsŋuʀ- 'overflow and ice over (river)' [and note əsŋiʀ- 'squirt, spurt', and perhaps AP ciŋuʀuuq 'sun' — compare the relat. of ciqinəʀ to ciqəʀ-]
CAY əsŋuʀ-, səŋŋuʀ-, NS cəŋŋuʀ- 'overflow' [also əsm̥iaʀ-; NS cəŋŋuq 'spring', HBC əsŋuq 'pus']
NSY —
CSY —

PE cipə(ɣ)- 'split or burst' [cf. cipə(t)- and cipyaʀ, also Atkan Aleut sim̥i- 'whip, spank', sim̥it- 'get startled'?]
AAY cipəxtə- 'squeeze liquid out' [and compare cipsaʀ 'spread legs' under cipyaʀ]
CAY cipəxtə- 'squeeze out liquid or slime (from tube, etc.)'
NSY sipəxtə- [Enm. et al.]

CSY sipəxtə- 'strip leaves from stem, squeeze out liquid' [and note səfkaXtə- 'accidentally burst' (compare səfkaʀ- 'accidentally cut' under civə-)]
Sir sipəxtə- 'strip leaves from stem, squeeze out liquid' [Orr]
SPI sipłiq- 'change from female to male in womb (traditional belief)'
NAI sipi-
WCI —
ECI sipi- 'change to female in womb (male child)' [and sikkaaqi- 'explode', sippi(C)- 'crack around edge (e.g. dish), split on side, add piece of cloth to edge or center of garment']
GRI sipi- 'split, be split, cut up, separate, burst', NG hipit- 'burst', EG cipiC- 'change into a girl (baby boy in womb)' [and sippaq* 'crack', siłłiq* (old ortho. sivdleq) 'middle line where animal is split open', sippiʀ- 'cut open (to widen garment)'; for EG cipuluuʀ- 'break wind' see cupə-]

PI cipkiq- 'burst out'
SPI —
NAI sipkiq- 'burst out laughing, bud, sprout' [for sipiksaq- 'grow suddenly or quickly' see capək-]
WCI si(i)pkiq- 'try to stifle one's laughter', Car hikkiʀaq- 'spit a jet of saliva', hipqiq- [for hipkiq-?] 'shoot, burst out laughing' [Schn., who also has the latter for Aiv]
ECI sikki(q)- 'go off (gun), burst out laughing, squirt' [Schn. also has Iti sikki- 'fire or detonate unintentionally']
GRI sikkiʀ- [old ortho. sivkeʀ-] 'bud, sprout, burst out laughing'

PE cipə(t)- 'exceed or be left over' [there may be a relat. to cipə(ɣ)-; cf. also cimmiʀ-]
AAY ciptə- 'exceed'
CAY cipətə- 'have s.th. left over, in excess', Nun 'overflow' [also used in counting higher numerals]
NSY səpətə- 'be left, leave a remainder' [ANLC; Men. also has it as 'press' — influenced by cipə(ɣ)-?; səpłəq 'remains']
CSY siiptə- 'have s.th. left over, in excess'
Sir ➟
SPI Qaw sipik- 'have some left over' [contam. from cipə(ɣ)-?]
NAI sipit- 'exceed, get more than expected', sippiq- 'exceed' [for sipi- 'change from male to female in womb' see cipə(ɣ)-]
WCI [Cop hipitait- 'have everything, all' (Pryde)]
ECI sipit- 'exclude, pass s.o. by, keep to one side'
GRI sippuʀut(i)-, NWG sipput(i)- 'lack space for', sippuʀ- 'exceed'

PE cip(ə)nəʀ 'excess' [cf. nəʀ[1]]
AAY Kod [Tyzh.], PWS cipŋəq 'excess'
CAY cipnaq 'excess, leftover'
NSY —
CSY siipŋ̥əq* 'excess, leftover' [and note qula maalʀuk siipŋ̥əqłukək 'twelve', etc.]
Sir sipŋ̥əX 'remains' [Vakh. from Men.'s texts]
SPI —
NAI —
WCI —
ECI sinniku, sipinniku 'remainder, excess'
GRI sinniq* [old ortho. sivneq] 'surplus, remainder' [and sinniʀ- 'replace, do on s.o.'s behalf, be more than (in counting)' — the first two senses with contam. from cimmiʀ-?]

PI cippaq 'leftover' [cf. q under nəʀ[1]]
SPI sippaq 'remnant, leftover'
NAI sippaq* 'surplus'
WCI sippalik 'having too much'
ECI —
GRI — [for sippaq* 'crack' see cipə(ɣ)-]

PE cipyaʀ 'hip' [cf. cipə(ɣ)- and yaʀ?]
AAY KP cipsaʀ-, PWS sipsaʀ- 'spread one's legs or knees'
CAY NS cipsaq 'hip'
NSY sipɣ̥aq [ANLC]
CSY sipsaq
Sir sipɣ̥əX 'pelvis'
SPI sipyaq, Qaw also sipsaq 'hip'
NAI sivviaq, Mal sipyaaq
WCI sivviaq
ECI sivviaq
GRI siffiaq

PE ciqəʀ- and **ciq(q)i-** 'splash' [the second form perhaps with li-[1]; cf. Aleut ciXi- 'make wet, dip', ciXt- 'become wet' and ciXta- 'be wet, rain' and ciʀana-X 'river', alongside EA ciqa- 'splash']
AAY ciqi- 'throw or splash water on', C ciqəq 'splash, waves, wake' [and K ciqŋ̥əq 'splashing noise']
CAY ciqi- 'bale a boat', ciqəʀ-, ciqXutə-, ciqəXtaʀ- 'splash'
NSY [note səqsəXtanəq 'sound of grinding ice', perhaps influenced by təðə(ʀ)-] ➟
CSY [note suqsuq 'noise of splashing or running water', but also isiqXutə-, əsiqXutə- 'toss out liquid', and əsiqXuutə-, isiqXuutə- 'fall into water with a splash', perhaps reflecting contamination with the source of əžət-] ➟
Sir [note siqətəʀ- 'gulp down']
SPI siʀi- 'splash'
NAI siqi-, siqiłʸłʸak- 'splash'
WCI Cop hiqiq- 'make a splash' [and Baker Lake hiqqiʀaq- 'spit' — Schn.]
ECI siqiʀaq- 'sprinkle' Lab siqqiɣai- 'sprinkle'
GRI siqiʀ- 'splash', SWG 'shine on'

PE ciq(q)it- 'pour out or dump with a splash' [cf. t-[1]]
AAY ciqitə- 'throw, splash, dump (water, in AP also garbage)'
CAY ciqitə- 'pour out, dump'
NSY —
CSY siqitə- 'splash'
Sir —
SPI —

NAI —
WCI —
ECI —
GRI siqit-, siqqit- 'splash (trans.) on to s.th., throw out (water)'

PE ciqpaɣ- or **ciqpaʀ-** 'splash (a lot)' [cf. vaɣ]
AAY —
CAY ciqpaɣ- 'throw a lot of water' [and ciqfałəXtə- 'splash']
NSY siqpaXtə- [Enm. et al.], siqpaʀ- [L.-T.] 'splash'
CSY —
Sir —
SPI siqpaq-
NAI PH siqpaɣɨ- 'throw around indiscriminately' [and siqpan 'blubber used as stove fuel' — influenced by ciiq-²?]
WCI Cop hiqpaliɣaq- 'splash' [Pryde]
ECI siqpa(k)- 'splash (once)'
GRI siʀpaʀ- 'splash'

PI ciqqaq- 'splash or throw out (several)' [cf. qqaʀ-]
Yup [note CSY isiqaXtə-, əsiqaXtə- 'toss out liquid' — compare under ciqəʀ- above]
SPI siqqažaaq- 'throw s.th. out of boat to lighten it'
NAI siqqaq- 'throw things out of a container'
WCI siqqaq- 'splash'
ECI siqqataq- 'throw many objects or times', Lab siqqatai- 'throw into water'
GRI siqqaʀ- 'splash', siqqat- 'throw out (water), splash to to all sides' [the latter form also 'push opponent with elbow'; siqqattaat(i)- 'splash each other']

PI ci(i)qiak 'contents of intestines' [cf. ciiq-¹]
SPI —
NAI siqiak 'contents of stomach or intestines'
WCI Cop hiqiak 'intestinal fluid (of seal, etc.)' [Pryde]
ECI siqiaq, siiqiaɣaq 'contents of stomach or intestines' [and siqiiq- 'empty or be emptied (stomach or intestines)']
GRI siqiak, siqiaq, NG hiqiq 'contents of small intestines' [and note siqayuk, siqiak 's.o. worn out or slack, good-for-nothing', NG hiqayuu- 'be lazy, a bad hunter']

PE ciqinəʀ 'sun or ray of sunlight' [cf. ciq(q)itə- under ciqəʀ- and nəʀ¹; the word may have a specific connection with the myth of the incestuous brother and sister, in which the latter fled into the sky to became the sun bearing a torch (compare GRI maliina under maliɣ-, probably referring to the same myth)]
AAY —
CAY ciqinəq* 'ray of the sun'
NSY siqinəq 'sun' [ANLC]
CSY siqinəq* 'sun'
Sir —
SPI [Jen. has siʀiniq 'sun' for Kl and W]
NAI siqinʸiq* 'sun' [as verb = 'become spoiled in sun (meat)']
WCI siqiniq 'sun' [and 'adg.' siqinniq- 'be sunny' acc. Schn.]
ECI siqiniq 'sun, sunny side, south' [siqinni(q)- 'be sunshine']
GRI siqiniq* 'sun' [and siqiniʀ- 'suffer sun-stroke', siqinniʀ- 'be sunshine', siqiniɣaq 'meat gone off in sun']

PI ciqinnak- 'become sunny' [cf. nəɣ- and/or nnak-]
SPI —
NAI siqinʸnʸak- 'get more sun (as days lengthen)' [and siqinʸnʸaaʀik-, siqinʸnʸažaaq- 'be sunny', siqinʸnʸaasuɣžuk 'February']
WCI siqinnaq- [for siqinnaaq-?] 'appear brightly (sun)', siqinnaʀniq 'ray of sun' [and Sig siqinnaaʀik- 'shine (sun)' — Lowe]
ECI [siqinnaaniq 'ray of sunlight (penetrating room)']
GRI [NG hiqinnaaq 'February' — old word]

PE ciqluɣaʀ '(underground) storage cache'
AAY ciqłuɣaq, ciqluaq 'smokehouse, semi-subterranean house'
CAY Nun ciqłuɣaX 'partially underground food cache'
NSY —
CSY siqłuɣaq 'underground meat cellar'
Sir [note perhaps siXłəX 'dried meat' — Orr; Vakh. has siXła, pl. siXłiy]
SPI siʀluaq, Qaw siqluaq 'underground cold storage cache'
NAI siʀluaq
WCI siʀluaq 'cellar, storeroom'
ECI siʀluaq 'snowhouse cache', NBI 'secondary igloo, room'
GRI NG hiʀluaq 'outhouse for storing skins, tools, etc.' [Holt.]

PE ciqni- 'be protective'
AAY —
CAY —
NSY —
CSY siqn̥i- 'covet'
Sir siqn̥ə- [Orr]
SPI siqnii- 'defend, take someone's side'
NAI siʀnʸiɣi- 'feel protective of, go to the defense of'
WCI siʀniɣi- 'prefer, favor, think s.o. is always right'
ECI siʀnaa(C)-, siʀniɣusuk- 'come to s.o.'s aid, defend, be on s.o.'s side'
GRI siʀniɣi- 'guard, protect'

PE ciqumə(t)- 'break to pieces' [cf. Aleut siXi- 'break to pieces', siXt- 'break, go to pieces']
AAY —
CAY ciqumə- 'break to pieces, crumble'
NSY siqumə- [Enm.]
CSY —
Sir —
SPI siʀumit- 'break to pieces', W siʀimit- 'tear to pieces, break up (ice)' [Jen.], Imaq siʀəmaaq- 'be smashed to pieces' [and siʀupsi- 'break, shatter s.th.']
NAI siqumɨt- 'destroy, crush to pieces' [and siqufsi- 'destroy s.th.', PH siqupsi- 'grind or chop up, pulverize']

WCI Sig siqumit- 'break on purpose'
ECI siqumi(C)- 'break in pieces' [and note siqutsiʀaq 'egg not yet laid, whose shell is not yet hard']
GRI siqumit- 'scatter, be ragged, pulverized', siquɣ- 'break, grind', EG ciʀiC- 'be broken down' [and note NG hiqussiq 'salmon roe, egg inside bird']

PI ciquptəq- 'pulverize' [cf. təʀ-]
SPI siʀuptiq- 'smash to pieces'
NAI siquptɨq- 'crush or break to pieces'
WCI siquptiq- 'crush, grind, chop up' [Pryde)
ECI siqutti(q)- 'break down, demolish (also of fetus by abortion)'
GRI siqutsiʀ- 'grind', EG siʀittaʀ- 'crumble'

PY ciquq 'cottonwood (driftwood)' [cf. ciqumə(t)-]
AAY ciquq 'cottonwood, dish, bowl'
CAY Eg, Nun, HBC ciquq, NSU ciʀuq 'driftwood, cottonwood'
NSY —
CSY —
Inu [SPI Qaw siʀu 'cottonwood which has drifted ashore' is probably a loan from Yup]

PE ciqviɣ 'matter on eyelids?' [cf. ciqəʀ-?]
AAY —
CAY Nun ciXfiX [for ciqfix?] 'eyelash' [Jen.]
NSY siqpiq 'eye mucus' [ANLC; Enm. and L.-T. have siqpik 'eyelash']
CSY —
Sir —
SPI siqpik 'corner of eye, mucus which collects on eyelid'
NAI siqpik 'eyelash'
WCI siqpiit 'eyelashes'
ECI siqpi 'matter in corner of eye'
GRI siʀpiq, siʀpik 'matter on eyelids' [and note siʀpiɣi- 'be careless with, leave lying around']

PE ciʀi- 'be eager or powerful?'
AAY siʀi-, Kod ciʀi- 'be in a good mood, jolly'
CAY ciʀi- 'have an abundance of things'
NSY —
CSY —
Sir —
SPI sixxayuk- 'be willing', Qaw siimak- 'gather strength for s.th., be determined to win'
NAI si<ʀ>i- 'gatheʀ strength for an effort', siimmak- 'become more competetive', PH 'be confident of one's ability to win', siimasaaq- 'encourage to increase effort' [and note also siʀmaaq- 'put all one's efforts into winning', Nu 'be in disagreement']
WCI —
ECI siʀi- 'make traditional cry of thanks on receiving s.th.' [and siʀiilli- 'be discontented because one didn't get what one expected']
GRI siiʀasaaʀ- 'incite, egg on', SWG siʀi- 'be conceited'

PE ciʀlaɣ 's.o. in a weak or critical state?' [cf. ciʀləʀ-]
AAY AP, PWS ciʀlaq 'lazy person' [Petroff has 'weakness']
CAY ciʀlak 'weakling, invalid' [and ciʀlakə- 'overcome, dominate, defeat']
NSY —
CSY siʀla- 'act with strong emotion' [siʀlatkə- 'act with strong emotion because of -']
Sir [Em. has siʀlatəkə(s)- 'do more than necessary or usual, obtain s.th. without effort, hurry to finish s.th.']
SPI —
NAI —
WCI —
ECI siʀlaa(q)- 'just about manage to do s.th.', NBI, SB, Lab siʀlak 'hardly, scarcely' [Lab also siʀlau- 'be in great danger, in a critical state' — Peck]
GRI —

PE ciʀləʀ- 'have a hard time' [cf. ciʀlaɣ]
AAY —
CAY ciʀliqə, iʀliqə- 'have a hard time' [the latter form influenced by iʀ(ə)ləɣ-?]
NSY siʀləʀ- 'be bad' [ANLC; Enm. et al. have siʀləɬtə- 'have a hard time'; L.-T. has siʀləq 'bad']
CSY [səʀləq* 'bad thing or situation', səʀləXqə- 'err, make a mistake']
Sir —
SPI —
NAI siʀl^{y}iqɨ- 'work hard', siʀl^{y}iʀnaq- 'be difficult, obstinate' [there appears to be contam. with ciʀi-, q.v.]
WCI —
ECI siʀliqi- 'feel great physical pain'
GRI siʀɬiʀ- 'be unlucky' [but also iʀɬuqi- 'have a hard time, be pained' (contam. with iʀ(ə)ləɣ-?) and siʀɬiʀi- 'wish s.o. who brings bad luck far away', siʀɬiʀnaʀ- 'be clever at appropriating things, prestidigitate, cause disruptions around one all the time']

PE ciʀmiʀ 'ice (coating)'
AAY —
CAY ciʀmik 'high mountain', ciʀmiutə- 'be iced in (of a squirrel-hole)'
NSY —
CSY —
Sir —
SPI siʀmiq 'frost, ice on an object'
NAI PH siʀmiq 'patch of ice put on sled runners, ice coating on boat, etc.'
WCI siʀmiq 'earth applied to sled runners' [Ow. has 'layer of ice' for EP]
ECI siʀmiq 'coating of ice put on sled runners or used to cement parts of snow house' [and note siʀŋut(i)- 'freeze and be caught in new ice'?]
GRI siʀmiq 'glacier, ice on solid objects' [in EG 'freshwater ice from inland' acc. Tersis; siʀmiʀ- 'be iced over']

PI ciʀʀa- 'recite a charm' [cf. Aleut caʀa-X 'amulet, good luck charm, lure' with vowel harmony; there may be a link to ciʀləʀ-]
SPI Di siʀʀa- 'recite charm' [Jen., p. 107]
NAI siʀʀaqi- 'struggle to overcome s.th.'
WCI —

ECI —
GRI siXXa- 'sing or recite a charm' [Top has 'harm by witchcraft']

PY ciʀu- 'cover' [there could be a relat. to cau-]
AAY KP, K ciʀu-, Perry cu<ʀ>u- 'cover (with dirt, etc.), put a roof on' [and ciʀu(q), Perry cu<ʀ>u(q) 'roof, cover, temporary shelter'; for PWS ciq 'roof' see əciʀ]
CAY ciʀu- 'cover (with earth or snow)' [ciʀu 's.th. used as a cover', Nun, HBC ciʀuq 'covering of snow or dirt']
NSY siʀu- 'cover with dirt, snow, etc.' [ANLC; siʀu 'loose soil, sand']
CSY —

PY-S ciʀunəq 'horn or antler' [cf. ciʀu- and nəʀ[1]?]
AAY ciʀunəq, PWS also ciʀuq 'horn, antler'
CAY ciʀunəq*
NSY siʀunəq [Enm. et al.]
CSY siʀunəq*
Sir siʀənəX

PE ciʀuʀðuɣ(-) '(make an) indistinct noise (like wind)' [cf. yuɣ?]
AAY cəʀyuk 'white noise (of breakers, etc.)'
CAY HBC cəʀyiXpak, Nun cəʀyuX
NSY —
CSY —
Sir —
SPI siuʀžuk- 'make distant, indistinct noise'
NAI siuʀžuk- 'make distant, indistinct hissing or whistling noise' [as noun = 'camp stove']
WCI siuʀyuk- 'make noise of wind blowing' [as noun = 'pressure stove']
ECI Lab siuʀyuk 'roaring of wind' [Peck — also as verb; note also siuʀyuk 'moss']
GRI siuʀšuɣ- 'roar, whistle (air)' [and as noun siuʀšuk, EG ciiʀtuq]

PE citamat 'four' [cf. Atkan Aleut siciŋ, EA (pl.) sici-n 'four'; there may be a distant relat. to citə(ɣ)- 'be hard' via the Eskimo finger-counting system since the index finger is the fourth finger']
AAY staamat 'four'
CAY cətaman, HBC citaman
NSY sitamat
CSY əstamat
Sir sitəməŋiy [Vakh. has sitəmiy]
SPI sitamat
NAI sisamat
WCI sitamat
ECI sitamat, NBI tisamat
GRI sisamat, EG ciamat

PI citciq- 'soak through' [cf. perhaps Atkan, Att Aleut sit- 'sweat']
SPI —
NAI sitciq- 'soak through'
WCI Car hitsiq- 'be water-absorbant, soaked' [also 'be intelligent' (for which see cikcuiq-) acc. Schn., who also has 'adg' tiksiq- 'penetrate, imbibe' and Car hitsuit- 'be waterproof', all entangled with citcuiq-]
ECI sitsituq- 'penetrate (oil, liquid)', sitsiyuit- 'be impermeable, waterproof', Lab sitsitua- 'be wet through and through' [Peck]
GRI sitsiʀ- 'moisten through'

PI citə 'den or lair' [cf. citkik- and Aleut sit- 'be torn or cut off', sitmi- 'cut, corrode'?; compare žiɣtə]
Yup [Jen. has s(ə)tii 'cave' for Nun]
SPI siti 'den, burrow'
NAI sisɨ, sižžaq*, Nu sinʸ
WCI siti, Net hi'žaq 'den, burrow' [Briggs — Dor. has hiti]
ECI siti, NBI tisi 'lair, burrow', siɣyaq, siyyaq 'fox's lair'
GRI sisi, EG citsi 'fox's lair' [for Lab Tersis has cisi, pl. citsit, and Robbe and Menn. have citsik rather]

PE citə(ɣ)- 'be hard' [cf. cituk and Aleut siisaɣ- Atkan 'be stiff', EA, Att 'become stiff (dead person or animal)', also citamat]
AAY —
CAY cətəŋqitə- 'be frozen stiff', cətəxtaq 'frozen fish or meat'
NSY —
CSY əstəqə- 'tense muscles, persevere' [and əstəqaq 'muscle']
Sir [note sisəqnəX 'endurance, self-control' — Em.]
SPI siti- 'be hard' [Jen.], sitiq- 'be stuck', siššuq- 'temper metal'
NAI sisɨ- 'harden', Nu sitži- 'temper metal' [and silʸlʸiq* 'snow made crusty and hard by wind']
WCI sisak 'steel' [as verb = 'harden (steel)'], Cop hiti- 'become hard' [Jen.]
ECI siti-, Igl tisi- 'be hard', sisak 'something hard', Lab 'lead, steel' [and silliq 'limb that has hardened (through illness), kind of black stone']
GRI sisak 'hard, steel', NG hihak 'file' [sisaɣ- 'harden (metal)']

PI citkik- 'be steep or go straight down' [there may be a relat. to citə]
SPI —
NAI sikkik- 'be steep (of ground at water's edge)'
WCI sitkik- 'cut straight', Car? hikkik- 'be clear, limpid, transparent (of ice, water)' [Schn. 'adg.']
ECI sikkitaq 'squaʀe, diamond', Lab sikkik- 'cut straight' [sikkitakutaaq 'parallelogram']
GRI sikkik 'equilateral, s.th. equal sided' [and sikkiłłuɣ- 'be crooked, stupid, careless or sloppily dressed', sikkiɣiɣ- 'have equal sides and smooth planes']

PI cittuqit- 'regurgitate' [cf. qəcuqitə-]
SPI [situvit- 'burp up liquid (of baby)']
NAI sitcuqit- 'vomit (of overfed baby), regurgitate food', sisuɣiaq- 'have a wet burp (of baby)' [and PH sisuvɨt- 'burp up milk (of baby)']
WCI sittuqit- 'choke on food or liquid (food remaining in throat)'
ECI sittuqiC- 'have food come back up one's throat (because of eating too much)'
GRI sitsuqiɣ- 'vomit (child, dog which has eaten too much), retch'

PE cittuʀ- 'sit with legs extended' [cf. citə(ɣ)-]
AAY stuʀ- 'stretch legs out' [postural root]
CAY cətuʀ- [postural root]
NSY situʀ- [L.-T.]
CSY əstuʀ-
Sir situXt(ə)- 'straighten up, stretch out (of person)' [Vakh. from Men.'s texts]
SPI sittuq- 'sit with legs extended'
NAI sitcuq- 'extend legs while sitting on floor'
WCI sittuq- 'extend the leg after it's been bent'
ECI sittuq- 'extend one or both legs'
GRI sitsuʀ- 'sit with legs obliquely downward'

PE citu- 'slide down' [cf. perhaps Aleut ciðu- 'set, go down (sun), slide down']
AAY —
CAY cətu-, HBC citu- 'go with river current, go along shore', Nun 'slide down'
NSY situ- 'slide, og downhill'
CSY əstu-
Sir sitəʀcaʀ- 'skate, slide down' [Vakh. has sitəʀ- 'slide, skate'; note also sitəqaʀ- 'swallow' — Orr]
SPI situ- 'slide down'
NAI sisu- 'slide down' [and sisuuk 'snowslide']
WCI situ- 'slide, slip down (seal into hole)', situʀ- 'be a land or snow slide'
ECI situ- 'slide down, go downriver, slip'
GRI sisu- 'slide down' [Robbe and Menn. have EG tisi-; and sisuat 'landslide', probably also EG citsiŋaliq 'mountain slope']

PE cituʀaʀ- 'slide down (repeatedly)' [cf. ʀaq-]
AAY —
CAY —
NSY situxaʀ- [for situXaʀ-?] 'skate, slide', situʀaʀ- 'slide' [L.-T.]
CSY əstaaʀaʀ- 'slide down repeatedly'
Sir —
SPI situʀaaq-
NAI sisuʀaaq-, sisuXaaq- 'be out sliding'
WCI situʀaq- 'slide down repeatedly' [and situʀautit 'skis'; Pryde has Cop hituaq- 'slide downhill (on sled)']
ECI situʀaq-, Igl tisuʀaq- 'slide downhill repeatedly' [and situʀauti 'ski']
GRI sisuʀaʀ- 'slide down a slope', SWG 'ski' [and sisuʀaatit 'skis'; Kroeber has NG sissoa 'sled' as a shaman's word]

PE citu(C)aʀ 'beluga' [cf. citu- and ðaʀ-?]
AAY —
CAY cətuaq, HBC cituaq 'beluga'
NSY situaq
CSY —
Sir —
SPI situaq
NAI sisu<ž>aq
WCI —
ECI —
GRI —

PY-S cituk 'nail (of finger or toe)' [cf. citə(ɣ)-]
AAY əstuk, stuk 'finger or toe nail'
CAY cətuk, HBC cituk [and note cətuum ciutii 'hangnail', lit. 'nail's ear']
NSY situk 'finger or toe nail, claw'
CSY əstuk 'finger or toe nail' [əstuɣəm siɣutŋa 'hangnail' — convergence with CAY?]
Sir sitəx 'finger or toenail'

PY cituɣmiɣ- 'scratch with nails' [cf. miɣ-]
AAY stuɣmiɣ- 'scratch with nails or claws'
CAY cətuɣmiɣ-
NSY —
CSY —

PY citumquq 'claw' [cf. quʀ]
AAY stumquq 'hoof, hangnail'
CAY citumquq 'claw, hoof, talon, deformed nail'
NSY sitəmquq 'hoof'
CSY —

PI ciuʀaq 'sand' [cf. Aleut cuɣu-X 'sand' (also in names of beaches) and perhaps cuɣ- 'north' (from typical position of house facing northern coast)]
SPI —
NAI siuʀaq 'expanse of fine sand'
WCI siuʀaq 'sand'
ECI siuʀaq
GRI siuʀaq, EG siaʀ̃aq 'grain of sand' [siuʀaʀ- 'strew with sand']

PE civa- 'boil blubber' [cf. civli and EA cm̥a- 'thick, coagulating (blood)', Atkan cmat- 'clot, coagulate']
AAY cuatə-, C cuataaʀ-, Perry suataʀ- 'fry in oil, render oil by frying blubber' [and cuałuk 'sizzling sound']
CAY NUN civacuɣnilaXqə- to taste of cooked seal blubber; *civanʀ(aq)* fibrous leftover piece when seal oil has been obtained by heating diced seal blubber in a pan; crackling; *civatuxtə-* dice seal blubber for boiling.
NSY sivažaXtaq 'boiled blubber', sivažaŋuaq [ANLC sivažaq] 'biscuit, pastry'
CSY —
Sir —
SPI W siaʀaq 'boiling seal blubber' [Jen.]
NAI siaʀaq- 'cook blubber', PH sivaʀaaq 'liquid from boiled fat or blubber'
WCI sivaaq-, sivvaqtu- 'make noise (of pressure lamp or heater)'
ECI siva 'solid part of blubber or fat remaining after melting', Lab 'cooked cod liver' [and sivaya 'oil produced by this cooking', sivat- 'melt fat over fire, be thus melted']
GRI siat- 'fry, melt (blubber or grease)', sialiaq, NG hivahaaq 'melted blubber'

PI civanəq 'ringing sound' [cf. civa- and nəʀ[1]?]
SPI —
NAI sivanɨq- 'be an unpleasant, high-pitched noise', sivanau- 'ring (of ears)', sivanɨqtaq- 'jingle (of bell), PH sivanuaq- 'echo'

WCI sivayaqtaun, Cop hivayaun 'bell' [Lowe]
ECI sivaniq 'bell', Lab sivanik- 'ring'
GRI sianiq* 'bell, tingle' [sianiʀ- 'ring']

PY-S civ(v)aʀ- 'go downhill' [cf. civəŋa- and perhaps civə-]
AAY K əsx^{w}aʀ- 'go downhill, downland (toward beach or shore)'
CAY Y cəffaXtə- 'emerge from trees into open area' [and note cəvak 'low altitude, area near ground']
NSY —
CSY —
Sir [Vakh. has sivəX 'place where one puts s.th. (e.g. a shelf)', also sivəqłaʀ- 'put or take off, put aside or down']

PY civə- 'cut through' [there may be a relat. to civəŋa- and civ(v)aʀ-]
AAY suɣə- 'be cut through by water (of land)' [also cuuɣutaq, PWS cuu<ɣ>uk 'adze', verbal 'chop, plane with an adze']
CAY cəvə- 'get cut through (land)' [cəvvaq 'place where river has cut a channel through'; for cəvak 'low altitude, area near ground' see civ(v)aʀ- and for civə- 'chase sea mammal' see civtə-]
NSY [note siviʀ- 'interupt s.o., get in s.o.'s way']
CSY səvə- 'cut or tear along a straight line' [and səfkaʀ- 'accidently cut through', as opposed to səfkaXtə- 'accidently burst' under cipə(ɣ)-]

PI civəŋa- 'slope upward' [from *civiŋa-? — cf. ŋa-[1] and civ(v)aʀ-; there may be a relat. to civə-]
SPI suviŋa- 'slope gently, not be level'
NAI siviiŋa- 'be gently sloping (hill)', siviinaaq 'slope', siviŋaaq-, sivaaŋa- 'be sloping'
WCI Net siviŋŋaʀik- 'fall off steeply (slope)' [Pryde]
ECI —
GRI siviŋa- 'slope obliquely up (hill)'

PI civi 'duration'
SPI —
NAI sivikit- 'be of short duration', sivisu- 'be of long duration' [and note siviksiq- 'happen, occur']
WCI sivikit- 'be of short duration', sivitu- 'be of long duration'
ECI sivi 'distance', sivitu- 'be a long distance', sivikit- 'be a short distance'
GRI sivi 'duration', sivikit- 'be of short duration', sivisu- 'be of long duration'

PI civli 'sediment in oil lamp' [cf. cipə(t)-?]
SPI sivliit 'sediment from oil in lamp' [Jen.]
NAI —
WCI —
ECI [Peck has Lab sigviniq 'fibrous remains of blubber in lamp']
GRI siłłi, siłłiniq* 'sediment in lamp' [old ortho. sivdle; Holm has cittiq 'baleen' for EG]

PY-S civtə- 'set net or trap'
AAY cuxtə-, Kod also ciuxtə- [Tyzh.] 'set (net or trap)' [C also 'spread out', and note cuɣə- 'become scattered, messed up']
CAY ciftə- 'set (fishnet or trap)' [and note civə- 'chase a sea mammal']
NSY siftə- 'set a net' [ANLC; L.-T. has sifŋ̥əq or sifłəq 'setting a net']
CSY siiftə- 'set (net or trap)' [and note sifturʀ- 'bury, crush or trap under a weight']
Sir [sivləXt(ə)- 'set nets' — Vakh. from Men.'s texts]

PE civu- 'area or part in front'
AAY cuu-, PWS also ciu- 'area in front of, time before' [posit. root]
CAY ciu-, HBC, Nun civu- [posit. root, also 'bow of boat']
NSY sivu 'area in front' [also 'front of vehicle, time before']
CSY sivu 'front, bow of boat'
Sir siva 'front part or side of s.th.' [also 'time before' — Vakh.]
SPI siu- 'area in front (of)' [also 'front of boat or sled']
NAI sivu- 'area or time before' [posit. root, also 'bow of boat'; sivut- 'navigate from bow of boat']
WCI sivu- 'what is in front or before' [but as possessed posit. root also sivunʀa, etc., from sivuniq]
ECI sivu 'front part of s.th. (e.g. vehicle or forehead)' [but as possessed posit. root sivuʀŋa, etc., from sivuniq; sivuvaq- 'go ahead,' sivuvaaq 'ancestor']
GRI siu [old ortho. suju] 'front of kayak', siumut 'forward' [as posit. root siuʀna, etc., from civunəʀ below — compare EG cuumut 'forward' and cuuʀnani 'in front of it'; siuttuq 'harpooner (at bow of whaling boat)', siuaʀ- 'go before', siuaašaq 'ancestor']

PE civu(C)aʀ 'incisor tooth' [cf. civuqaʀ below — here with p.b. aʀ rather]
AAY —
CAY civuaq 'incisor tooth'
NSY —
CSY sivaaq
Sir sivaX 'front lower tooth' [Orr]
SPI siyuaq 'incisor tooth'
NAI sivuaq 'incisor tooth' [for PH sivuʀaq in this sense see civuqaʀ below and for sivuɣaq 'promontory at end of ridge' see civ(v)uɣ-]
WCI [for sivuʀaq in the sense 'incisor' see civuqaʀ]
ECI sivuaq 'incisor tooth'
GRI siuaq, NG hivuaq

PE civuləɣ- 'go or do before' [cf. ləɣ-?]
AAY —
CAY ciułəxtə- 'get ahead of'
NSY —
CSY —
Sir —
SPI siulik- 'precede, do before'
NAI sivulik- 'do before, cut in line in front of'
WCI sivulik- 'get ahead, arrive before' [Pryde; and note sivulliq- 'go ahead of, arrive before'; Schn. has sivuliŋa- 'go first, flirt (girl)' for 'adg']
ECI [sivuliq- 'be at head of line, go ahead of']

GRI siuliɣ- 'prime (give first coat of paint), dictate to', siulittuR- 'warn of s.th. in advance'

PE civul(l)iR 'first one' [cf. l(l)iR and compare civuqliR and civuliRaR below; there may be two derivations here, an earlier (civuliR) and a later one (civulliR) — compare qaliR and qaðliR under qaðə-]
AAY —
CAY —
NSY sivuliq 'first one'
CSY sivuliq(*)
Sir sivəcəX
SPI siuliq 'first one, front one, Monday'
NAI sivulliq* 'first one, ancestor, foreleg' [also 'Arcturus']
WCI sivulliq 'first one, ancestor' [and B. Lake hivuliqti 'sailor' — Dor.; Jen. has Cop hivulliq 'Arcturus', Ras. has it in the dual for Sig as 'a constellation'; and Ow. has hivulliik 'forelegs of caribou' for EP]
ECI sivulliq 'first or front one, ancestor' [also 'Arcturus' — Math.]
GRI siułłiq* 'first, ancestor', siuliq(*) 'predecessor, ancestor', siułłiiq 'foreleg of animal' [and NG hiuliqatuit 'ancestors'; Holt. has NG hiulliik 'constellation of two stars' — Arcturus and Muphrid?]

PE civuliRaR 'ancestor' [cf. civul(l)iR above and p.b. aR]
AAY cuuli<R>aq 'ancestor'
CAY ciuliaq, HBC civuliaq
NSY —
CSY —
Sir —
SPI —
NAI Nu sivulliaRžuit 'ancestors'
WCI —
ECI —
GRI siułłiaRšuit

PI civulliqtə 'lead dog' [cf. civul(l)iR above and p.b.s liR- and ðə, also WCI civulliq- under civuləɣ- above]
Yup [note AAY AP cuulicəsta, CAY ciulista 'lead dog' with li-[1] rather]
SPI Qaw siuliqti 'lead dog'
NAI [sivulliuqtɨ 'lead dog']
WCI Cop hivuliqti, hivuliqtuq 'lead dog' [Pryde]
ECI [sivuliqtaituq, Iti sivulliquti 'lead dog']
GRI —

PE civumiɣ- 'have loaded on front of kayak or other vehicle' [cf. miɣ-]
AAY cuumiɣ- 'keep on bow of boat'
CAY —
NSY —
CSY —
Sir —
SPI —
NAI —
WCI —
ECI sivumik- 'have loaded on front of vehicle'
GRI siumiɣ- 'have loaded on front of kayak'

PI civunəqci- 'understand' [cf. civunəR below and p.b. ci-]
SPI —
NAI sivuniqsi- 'understand'
WCI sivuniqsi-
ECI —
GRI siuniRsi- 'understand' [siuniqaR- 'understand, have insight into s.th.']

PE civunəR 'what lies ahead or before'[cf. nəR[1]]
AAY cuunəq 'what lies ahead'
CAY ciunəq*
NSY sivunəq 'ancestor' [L.-T.]
CSY sivunəq*
Sir sivənəX 'ancestor', pl. sivənay [Orr; Em. has sivənRəy for pl.]
SPI siuniq 'destination', Qaw 'future'
NAI sivuniq* 'destination, meaning' [sivuniRi- 'advance toward']
WCI sivuniq 'destination'
ECI sivuniq 'front of vehicle or foot'
GRI siuniq* 'what lies ahead', NG 'front of kayak' [Holt.], EG cuuniq 'head' [and siuRna 'last year', siuniRi-, siuniRtaRi- 'have as goal']

PE civunniR- 'aim at' [civunəR plus p.b. liR-]
AAY [compare cuun(ə)qə- 'head for' with p.b. kə-[1]]
CAY ciuniR- 'arrive as a guest' [ciunniuR- 'receive as a guest']
NSY —
CSY —
Sir —
SPI —
NAI sivunniq- 'decide', Nu 'head or send in a direction, outline one's course of action' [sivunniuq- 'plan, negotiate', Nu sivunniRvik 'direction one is heading']
WCI sivunniq- 'decide' [sivunniuRutit 'explanation, examples']
ECI [sivunni(q)- 'make a stitch round leg of Inuit boot']
GRI siunniR- 'make a plan for' [siunniRsuR- 'advise, make in advance a plan of action (for or concerning s.o.)', siunniRfik 'goal, plan']

PE civuqaR 'area or part in front' [cf. qaR; there seems to be some entanglement with civu(C)aR above]
AAY cuuqaq 'area or part directly in front'
CAY [note Nun ciuRaX, NS ciuqaq 'St. Lawrence Island']
NSY sivuqaq 'front area' [also 'St. Lawrence Island' — ANLC]
CSY [sivuqaq 'Gambell (St. Lawrence Island)']
Sir —
SPI siuRaq 'front, point of land'
NAI sivuRaq 'space or area in front', PH 'incisor tooth' [and sivuRaqɬiq* 'frontmost one, ancestor']

WCI sivuʀaq 'front of s.th., incisor tooth' [for sivuɣaq 'forehead' see civ(v)uɣ-]
ECI sivuʀaq 'space in front' [sivuʀaʀsiq 'foremost one']
GRI siuʀaq 'front', EG cuuř̃aq 'ridge of nose' [Robbe and Menn. have cuuŋaq; and siuʀaʀłiq* 'frontmost one, outer island', siuʀaa '(area) beyond outer islands, out to sea']

PE civuqliʀ 'first or front one' [cf. qliʀ and compare civul(l)iʀ above — this base may derive from civuqaʀ above]
AAY cuqłiq 'first one in front, front part, senior, ancestor'
CAY ciuqłiq* 'first'
NSY —
CSY sivuqłiq* 'first one, front one'
Sir —
SPI —
NAI sivuqłiq*, PH siuʀli 'sailor' [MacLean adds 'used to sleep in bow of ship']
WCI Net sivu'liq 'foremost one, ancestor' [Pryde, who also has Net sivu'liik 'constellation (Arcturus and Muphrid?)' corresponding to Sig sivulliik under civul(l)iʀ above]
ECI —
GRI siuʀłiq* 'front part (of boat), front rower, foremost one'

PY civuyak 'bow of boat'
AAY —
CAY —
NSY sivuyak 'bow of boat' [ANLC; and L.-T. has sivuyaxtə 'bowman in boat']
CSY sivuyak 'bow of boat' [and sivuyaxta 'bowman in boat']

PE civ(v)uɣ- raise one's head' [cf. civu(C)uʀa-, but also civu-]
AAY cu(u)xtə- 'raise one's head' [cuɣŋa- 'have one's head tilted back'; for PWS cuɣnəq 'bill, beak' see cuɣðuɣ]
CAY ciuɣ-, HBC civuɣ- 'tilt one's head up' [ciuŋqa- 'have one's head tilted up']
NSY —
CSY sivuɣ- 'tilt one's head up' [sivuɣŋa- 'have one's head tilted up']
Sir sivuxtə- 'raise one's head, stick head out' [Vakh. from Rub.'s texts]
SPI —
NAI sivvuŋa- 'have a protruding jaw or lower face' [and note sivuɣaq 'promontory at end of ridge']
WCI [note sivuɣaq 'forehead']
ECI —
GRI —

PE civuʀaʀ or **ciɣuʀaʀ** 'guillemot' [there could be metathesis in the Inu forms via *civ(u)ʀaq]
AAY —
CAY ciɣuʀ(aq*), ciɣuq, ciɣuʀaq 'pigeon guillemot'
NSY sivuʀaq [ANLC]
CSY [for sipəlaaʀaq 'guillemot' see siim̥lu-X under Aleut Proto-forms]
SPI siʀvaq 'guillemot'
NAI siʀvaq 'sea pigeon' [Murdock]
WCI —
ECI NBI siʀvaq 'black guillemot' [Pryde]
GRI siʀfaq 'guillemot'

PE civu(C)uʀa- 'be apprehensive' [cf. civ(v)uɣ-]
AAY —
CAY civuuʀa- 'be concerned, worried or reluctant'
NSY —
CSY sivuuʀaʀ- 'feel unable to proceed, feel defeated'
Sir sivuuʀaʀ- [Orr — from CSY?]
SPI siuuʀa- 'be apprehensive'
NAI sivuuʀa(ɣɨ)- 'be apprehensive, afraid of being blamed (of)'
WCI sivuuʀa-
ECI sivuuʀa- 'be apprehensive, fear in advance'
GRI siuuʀa(ɣi)- 'fear', siuuʀasaaʀ-, EG cuyuř̃asaaʀ- 'threaten' [the latter from Robbe and Menn.]

PE civvuʀ- 'wring out' [Aleut cim̥iɣlu-, cimiɣlu-, Attu civilu- 'wring out', EA 'rinse']
AAY AP, PWS cuuʀ-, Kod, KP cuXtaʀ- 'wring out'
CAY ciuʀ-, HBC civuʀ-
NSY sivuʀ- [Bogo.]
CSY sivuʀ-
Sir sivuʀ-
SPI sivvuq-
NAI sivvuq-
WCI sivvuq- 'wring out'
ECI sivvu(q)- 'wring out' [and sivvu 'liquid which soaks a garment']
GRI siffuʀ- [old ortho. sivfor-], sixxuʀ- [old ortho. sivgor-] 'wring out' [and sixxuut, Up sippuut 'floor cloth']

PE cu(na) 'what' [also verbal 'do what'; everywhere also 'something' or with neg. or deprivative p.b.'s 'nothing, anything'; Yup ca-, sa- is probably a contraction of cuna — compare the abs. singular form of demonstrative pronouns for the -na]
AAY C cacaq 'what', ca- '(do) what' [and note sa 'I don't know', cunaŋ 'actually', K cacəstun 'how']
CAY ca- 'what, do what' [rel. cam, pl. cat ; Nun castun 'how', caluni, etc. 'why', HBC cuyuumiitə- 'not feel like doing anything']
NSY suna, sa- 'what, do what' [pl. sat]
CSY sa- 'what, do what' [pl. saat; and saŋʷaa 'what (is it)', suna, sunami 'suddenly', saa 'I don't know']
Sir saŋəca 'what', sa- '(do) what' [rel. sam, pl. saŋəciy; suna, sunŋuX (Vakh. also sun, suna) 'suddenly']
SPI suna, Qaw sua 'what', su- 'do what' [rel. sum, pl. sut; and suami 'why']
NAI suna, Mal sua 'what', su- 'do what' [rel. sum, pl. sut; sua 'lo and behold!', sulliniq* 'what part']
WCI suna 'what', su- 'do what' [pl. Cop hunat, Sig sut]
ECI suna, sua 'what', su- 'do what' [pl. sunait; also sua 'what did you say?']
GRI suna 'what', su- 'do what' [rel. suup, pl. suut — NG hunap, hunat; suʀłiq* 'which', suami '(only) a bit']

PY-S caŋan and **caŋami** 'why' [3s and ɨ is consecutive/causative mood — compare the NAI forms under cuuq]
AAY cin 'why'
CAY ciin
NSY si(i)mi 'why' [p. 31ɨ of Men., and L.-T.]
CSY saŋan 'why' [this is 'why' with respect to non-reflexive 3rd person singular; 'why' with respect to reflexive 3rd person singular is saŋami, 'why' with respect to 1st person singular is saŋama, etc.; apparently the same pattern is true of NSY and Sir, but in AAY and CAY the 3rd person singular form is lexicalized for all persons]
Sir saŋami 'why'

PI cuaʀžuk 'small thing or belonging' [cf. aʀžuk]
Yup [note CSY SLI saʀya 'thing, household goods, supplies, possession']
SPI [compare Qaw suałuit 'objects, things, possessions' with another p.b.]
NAI suaʀžuit 'possessions,. supplies'
WCI Sig suaʀyuit 'belongings, gear' [Pryde]
ECI —
GRI suaršuk 'small unimportant thing', suaʀšuit 'small things or belongings'

PE cu(na)li 'still (more)' [cf. 3s opt. mood inflection -li?]
AAY cali 'still, more, again' [and note ciła 'always', PWS 'for a long time', by contam. with cila?]
CAY cali 'still, more, again' [also as exclam. '(do it) more']
NSY sali 'still, more, again'
CSY salin
Sir sali
SPI suli
NAI suli
WCI suli
ECI suli
GRI suli 'still, more, again' [NG huli also 'a long time']

PE cu(na)li- 'work' [cf. li-[1]]
AAY cali- 'do what?' [AP also 'work']
CAY cali- 'work'
NSY —
CSY —
Sir —
SPI suli- 'work' [and Imaq suliuq- 'work, make s.th.']
NAI suli- 'make s.th.' [sullivik, sulivik 'October']
WCI suliuq- 'make s.th.', Sig suli- 'work' [Pet.; Dor. has Net, B. Lake Car huli- 'tell the truth, be right']
ECI suliaq '(piece of) work' [and suli- 'speak the truth, be right']
GRI suli- 'work' [and suliaq 'piece of work', suliffik, Up sułłivik 'place or time of work']

PE cu(na)ŋit- 'not have or do anything' [cf. ŋit-]
AAY caitə- 'not have any'
CAY caitə-
NSY siatə- [ANLC]
CSY saŋitə-
Sir —
SPI Qaw suilaq 'he has nothing'
NAI suilʸlʸi- 'relax after being busy' [and suilʸauži- 'do s.th. in secret']
WCI suit-, suiq- 'not have anything'
ECI —
GRI [note suilaaqqut 'entertainment', which Rink defines as 'means to dampen one's sorrow' from suilaaqi- 'not give in to fear on death of a relative', = 'pass the time' today]

PE cuna-uvva 'imagine (exclamation of wonderment)' [cf. uvva]
AAY —
CAY cunaxʷa 'no wonder, so that's why'
NSY —
CSY —
Sir —
SPI suna'uva 'lo and behold'
NAI sunauvva
WCI suna-uvva 'surprisingly enough' [Pryde; Schn. has 'well I never' for 'adg']
ECI sunauvva 'well I never!'
GRI sunaaffa, Kap Farvel sunaaka, EG cunaaʀpa, NG hunauɣɣa 'imagine — that's how it is or was' [and NG hunau 'I see']

PI cuq(q)utə- 's.th. to care about' [cf. p.b. q(q)un]
SPI suqqutiɣi- 'matter, care about', suqqutauŋit- 'not matter'
NAI suqutiɣɨ- 'take notice of, be fond of', suqutau- 'be helpful'
WCI suqutiɣi- 'care about', suqutait- 'have nothing wrong'
ECI suqutiɣi- 'consider important, take umbrage at', suqutauŋŋit- 'not matter', Iti suquti 'change, cause of change', Lab suqutau- 'excert an influence, be efficient' [Bourq.]
GRI suqutiɣi- 'be interested in, care about', suqutaa- 'be of importance', suqutaaŋŋit- 'not matter'

PI cuuq 'why' [cf. ðuʀ?]
SPI —
NAI — [compare summan, Mal sukman, supman 'why', parallel to PY-S caŋan above but with p.b. ŋu-]
WCI suuq 'why' [and Sig suuʀmi, Cop huukiaq 'I don't know' — Pryde has huuʀmi 'that is why' for Cop]
ECI Lab suuq 'why' [compare Tar sumut 'why'; suuʀlu 'as if', suuʀmi 'go ahead', Lab 'but why on earth?', NBI suuqaimma 'naturally']
GRI suuq 'why', suu 'yes' [suuʀłu 'as if', suuʀmi 'but why, why not, indeed']

PE cu(C)aniʀ 'aged or rotting food' [cf. cin(n)aq]
AAY —
CAY — [for NS cuak 'aged fish roe' see ciłuvaɣ]
NSY suaniq 'aged, sour skin of walrus' [ANLC — 'aged walrus meat' acc. Tein, 'old meat' acc. Men.]

CSY —
Sir —
SPI —
NAI —
WCI —
ECI suaniq 's.th. rotting, overripe or soft fruit'
GRI —

PY cuð(ð)u- 'die down (flame)' [compare the CAY entry under qamə- for a possible parallel metaphoric extension to feelings of depression]
AAY AP cuyutə- 'turn down (flame)'
CAY suyutə-, Eg cuyutə- 'turn down (flame)' [and note cuyu- Y 'be meek', NSU 'envy'; for Nun cuŋu- 'die down (flame)' see cuŋu-]
NSY —
CSY —
Sir —
SPI —
NAI sužžuiq- 'recover' [with p.b. ŋiʀ-]
WCI Net hužuužaʀnaq- 'be depressing, make one feel lonely or out of place' [Pryde]
ECI —
GRI — [for NG huyuŋa- 'be ill' see under cuʀ(ʀ)uk(-)]

PE cuɣaɣ- 'scold or raise voice' [cf. Aleut suɣa- 'complain, leak information, tattle']
AAY suɣɣaXqə-, suɣɣatuuɣ- 'bawl out, tell off' [note also cua- 'harden (arteries or veins)']
CAY cuaxtə- 'pout'
NSY suaɣ- 'scold'
CSY suɣaɣ- 'feel offended because of humiliation', Chap suɣaɣniiʀ- 'be angry, offended'
Sir suɣaɣ- 'feel offended because of humiliation', suɣaɣniʀ- 'be angry, offended' [from the CSY?]
SPI suaktaq- 'speak in a loud voice, shout'
NAI suak- 'scold' [sualuk- 'scold lightly']
WCI suak- 'reprimand'
ECI suak- 'argue with, speak in anger, correct, reprimand', NBI 'give a blow' [and suɣaluk- 'exaggerate']
GRI suaɣ- 'harden oneself, make a fuss, beat, scold (child)' [sualuɣ-, NG huɣaluk- 'be bad, violent or extreme', suaaʀ- 'shout']

PI cuaŋa- 'berate or act sternly' [cf. ŋa-[1]]
SPI —
NAI suaŋa- 'be strong'
WCI suaŋa-
ECI suaŋa- 'quarrel, scold'
GRI suaŋa- 'berate, shout at dogs, be ample, powerful, be swollen, distended (boil)'

PE cuɣðuɣ or **ciɣɣuɣ** 'beak or muzzle' [perhaps from *civuɣðuɣ; possibly reformulated from the dual in most languages; the relat. — if any — to cuŋŋuʀ and civ(v)uɣ- is obscure]
AAY C cuxxəq, PWS cuɣnəq, K cuɣɣəq 'beak, lip' [and cuɣɣuk Kod 'forehead', which goes semantically with cuŋŋuʀ; for cu(u)xtə- 'raise head', possible contaminant of the PWS form, see civ(v)uɣ-]
CAY cuxxəq*, suxxəq* 'beak'
NSY suxu 'lip, beak' [and sumžuɣak 'whale lip' (L.-T.)]
CSY suɣžuk 'lip, beak' [and Rub. has suɣžuɣəq 'beak, muzzle, area around mouth' for Chap prob. reformulated as a singular from the dual suɣžuɣək]
Sir suɣžəx
SPI siɣɣuk 'beak'
NAI siɣɣuk, Mal siyyuk 'beak, muzzle'
WCI siɣɣuk
ECI siɣɣuk
GRI sixxuk, EG cikkiq 'snout, beak' [in NG hiɣɣuk also 'lips (human)']

PI cuɣluɣə- 'scorn' [cf. kə-[1]]
SPI suɣlui- 'decline, scorn, refuse s.th. because it's insufficient' [Jen.]
NAI —
WCI Cop huluɣi- 'reject, spurn' [Pryde]
ECI Lab suɣluɣi- 'be too little, small for one' [Peck]
GRI sułłuɣi- 'not be content with s.th., despise' [Kl. has 'think one has gotten too little']

PE cuk(k)a- 'be fast' [cf. perhaps Atkan Aleut sukalu- 'get tired, out of breath']
AAY cuka- 'be fast'
CAY cuka-
NSY [sukažuaq 'quick', sukałuku, sukaməŋ 'quickly', sukalʀia 'fast (thing)' (L.-T.)]
CSY sukatə- 'go fast'
Sir [Em. has sukəžaX 'game (sport or children's)' and sukəžaʀ- 'play, win']
SPI sukka-, Imaq suɣa-, Qaw sukat- 'be or go fast'
NAI suka-, sukat-
WCI suka- 'be fast'
ECI sukat-, Lab sukka- 'be fast'
GRI sukka- 'go fast' [sukkasuuq, EG cukkakkaayu, tukkakkaayu 'fast' — the latter by contam. with tukkaʀ-]

PE cuk(k)aŋit- 'be slow' [cf. ŋit-]
AAY cukaitə- 'be slow'
CAY cukaitə-
NSY sukaiłuku 'slowly'
CSY sukaŋitə- 'be slow'
Sir —
SPI suɣait-
NAI sukait-
WCI sukait-
ECI sukkait-
GRI sukkaat-

PI cukak- 'be tight or tighten' [cf. Aleut suka-X 'baidarka shirt', also cukaʀ?]
SPI —
NAI —
WCI Cop hukat- 'be tight (e.g. screw)' [contam. with cuk(k)a-?]
ECI sukak- 'tighten, stretch, be tightened, stretched, wound up (clock)'
GRI sukaɣ- 'be tightened, hold fast to opinion or intention', sukat- 'tighten' [both with final velar in Fab.]

PE cukaʀ 'post or other support'
AAY —
CAY cuka, Nun cukaX 'post, pole'
NSY —
CSY —
Sir —
SPI Qaw sukaq 'post supporting fish-drying rack'
NAI [note sukaq 'mountain with river at its base']
WCI sukaq 'post, pole, support, scaffolding'
ECI sukaq 'support for wall or roof' [as verb = 'put a support to']
GRI sukaq 'support, post, pillar' [and sukaʀ- 'put support or prop to (house)']

PE cuki(ʀ) 'splinter or thorn'
AAY cukiq 'sliver, thorn, quill, barb, needle (of conifer)'
CAY cukiq, cukilanaq 'quill, thorn'
NSY sukitə- 'get a splinter' [ANLC; Men. has sukiłək 'splinter']
CSY ➟
Sir —
SPI Qaw suki 'porcupine quill' [and sukilaʀnaq 'thorn']
NAI ➟
WCI ➟
ECI ➟
GRI ➟

PE cukkit- 'get a splinter' [cf. łit-]
AAY cukitə- 'get a sliver, etc. in one'
CAY cukitə- 'get s.th. sharp in one's foot' [and compare cuɣitə- 'have a sudden sharp pain']
NSY —
CSY sukitə- 'get a splinter in one's flesh' [sukitun 'splinter']
Sir —
SPI sukkit- 'step on sharp object, get splinter in flesh'
NAI sukkit- 'get a nail, thorn, tack, splinter in one's foot', [sukkiutaq 'splinter, thorn in foot']
WCI sukkit- 'get a splinter'
ECI sukkit- 'hurt self by stepping on a sharp object'
GRI sukkit- 'get a splinter in one's skin' [sukkiut 'splinter in skin']

PY cukilpaq 'crested auklet'
AAY —
CAY Nun cukiłpax 'crested auklet' [ANLC]
NSY —
CSY sukiłpaq

PY cukluk 'dentalia' [cf. EA suklu-n 'pendants to bone ornaments in the nasal cartilage']
AAY Kod cukłuq 'dentalia' [borrowed into Russian as tsukli]
CAY cukłuuk 'hair ornaments worn attached to bangs at side of forehead'
NSY —
CSY SLI sukłuɣžaq 'parakeet auklet' [so named because of its stripes backward from the eyes]
Inu [SPI KI sukłuq 'hair' is probably from Yup]

PI cukuiq- 'distinguish' [cf. ŋiʀ-]
SPI —
NAI sukuiq- 'understand, recognize, distinguish s.th.' [trans. sukuiʀi-]
WCI [note Sig sukuit- 'resemble']
ECI [note sukuuq- 'reprimand, dispute with'?]
GRI sukuiaʀ- 'explain'

PE culuɣ 'wing feather' [also 'sound of bird flapping wings?' — cf. Aleut sulux, sulɣi-X 'noise of running water, thunder, echo', suluɣ- 'make noise, rumble, peep'; note that a number of the 'sound of wind' forms appear to contain p.b. yuɣ and may represent contam. with ciʀuʀðuɣ]
AAY culuk 'feather', K, KP also 'body hair'
CAY culuk 'quill, dorsal fin', culu'uxtə-, Nun culuɣyi- 'whistle (wind)' [and culuɣuyuɣ- 'sigh']
NSY suluk, sulu 'feather'
CSY suluk 'sound of wind', Chap also 'sound of flying birds', suluxtaʀ- 'howl (wind)', siluk 'feather' [note also suŋyuk 'noise of whistling air' and suluŋaq 'crest of auk']
Sir siləx 'feather' [Vakh. also silux 'wing' (from the CSY?); note also suŋyəx 'wind's howl', suŋləɣ- 'make noise']
SPI suluk 'long wing feather, dorsal fin'
NAI suluk 'wing feather' [as verb = 'brush off dirt or snow']
WCI suluk 'big wing or tail feather, fin', Car? huluxxuq- 'make sound of wind' [Schn., who writes suluksuq- for 'adg']
ECI suluk 'big wing or tail feather, cut off tail of bird used as duster', sulutsuk 'sound of wind or bird flapping'
GRI suluk 'wing, wing feather' [and sułłiniq* 'insect']

PE culuɣðuɣun 'dorsal fin' [cf. ðuɣ and un]
AAY C culuxsuun 'dorsal fin'
CAY culuksuk, culuksuɣun 'spine, backbone, hanging decoration on parka'
NSY —
CSY —
Sir —
SPI [Qaw suluun 'fish fin']
NAI [suluun 'dorsal fin']
WCI —
ECI —
GRI sulušsuɣut 'dorsal fin'

PE culuɣpa(C)uɣ 'grayling (or similar fish)' [cf. vaɣ and ðuɣ?]
AAY AP culuxpauq, KP culuxpauwak, PWS culuxpuayak 'sea bass'
CAY culuxpauk, culuxpauɣaq 'arctic grayling'
NSY —
CSY —
Sir —
SPI Qaw sulukpauɣaq
NAI sulukpauɣaq
WCI sulukpauɣaq 'grayling' [Car? also 'chignon (women's hair)' — Schn. 'adg']

ECI suluppauɣaq 'fish shaped like an eel with a double fin the length of its body making it look like a feather', Iti 'head of corn or tall grass'
GRI suluppaavaq 'Norway haddock'

PI culuʀaq 'crack (on whip)?' [cf. ʀᴀʀ]
Yup [note CSY suluXaXtə- 'whip']
SPI —
NAI —
WCI Cop, Net huluʀaq 'lash of dog-whip' [Pryde]
ECI suluʀaq 'little cord attached to whip to make it crack' [also 'sound of wind']
GRI suluʀaq 'crack (attached to whip)' [pl. suluqqat 'feathers attached to bow or toy arrow', suluʀaʀ- 'play badminton']

PY culuʀtə- 'land (boat or sea mammal)'
AAY culuXtə- 'land (boat or sea mammal)'
CAY culuXtə-
NSY —
CSY —

PY-S cułəvnəq 'bad person?'
AAY —
CAY —
NSY —
CSY sułəvnəq* 'bad person who is unconcerned about harm he does to others or who harms through sorcery' [in Rub. 'wicked, naughty, curious, sorceror'; sułəvniqə- 'be bad, destructive' — in Chap 'be bad, naughty, try s.th. out']
Sir sułpənəq 'naughty, crafty' [and sułpəniqə(s)- 'do s.th. bad' — Em.]

PY-S cuməʀ(tə)- 'think or worry' [cf. cumiɣ-, but also icuma(-) — the relat. is obscure]
AAY cuməXtə- C 'work at putting up a supply of food'
CAY cuməXtə- 'worry about food and other necessities and work at providing them'
NSY suməXtaaʀ- 'think, be sad, bored with, suffer' [and suməXtə- 'ponder, be in a low mood, grieve' — ANLC)]
CSY suməq 'mind, thought', suməXtə- 'worry, be concerned about', suməXtaʀaʀ- 'think' [suumqaq 's.th. thought about']
Sir suməXtaʀaʀ- 'think about' [and suməʀnaXpałuX 'clever']
Inu [Imaq suməqtaq- 'think, suffer, be sad' is presumably from the Yup]

PE cumiɣ- 'be anxious or annoyed about s.th.' [cf. cuməʀ(tə)-]
AAY K cuməXtə- 'lose temper' [B.-S. has 'wake up (shaman from trance)' — contam. with PY-S cuməʀ(tə)-?]
CAY cumixtə- 'be anxious, hurry', Nun 'look around' [and cumikə- 'be attentive, take care of']
NSY —
CSY [suumə- 'be drunk, rabid, be in a trance (shaman), go berserk' — but this may go rather with cuməʀ(tə)- above]
Sir [sumə- 'be drunk, rabid, be in a trance (shaman), go berserk' (Orr; but this may go rather with cuməʀ(tə)- above; Em. also has sumərət- 'sober up']
SPI —
NAI —
WCI —
ECI sumiɣi- 'find too little or unsatisfactory', suminaq- 'be insufficient, unsatisfactory'
GRI sumiɣinnaʀ- 'not pay attention to or care about' [and note EG isimiiŋŋiC- 'not pay attention to' and (Robbe and Menn.) isimii- 'be bored, mistreat' — contam. with icumaɣə- (icuma(-))?]

PY cumilŋu- 'be bad tempered' [cf. lŋu-]
AAY cumilŋu- 'be short-tempered'
CAY cumilŋu- 'be peeved at being bested'
NSY —
CSY —

PY cumiŋə- 'come to a boil' [cf. nəɣ-]
AAY sumiŋə- 'come almost to a boil'
CAY cumiŋə- 'come almost to a boil, get angry'
NSY sumiŋə- 'come to a boil, seethe' [ANLC]
CSY —

PI cun(n)iaq- 'affect or work on' [cf. cu(na) and ni(C)aʀ-?]
SPI —
NAI Mal suniaq- 'be working, try to do s.th.' [and note Nu suniʀluk 'illness']
WCI Cop huniaq- 'cast a spell, practice witchcraft on' [Pryde]
ECI —
GRI [sunniʀ- 'affect, work on (e.g. shaman on sick person, positively or negatively acc. Fab.)']

PE cuŋa(ʀ) 'gall' [cf. cuŋitə-; there may be two separate sets for gall and bead, or beads may have originally been greenish (gall-colored); compare PI capaŋaq]
AAY cuŋak, cuŋaq 'gall bladder'
CAY cuŋak 'gall, bile'
NSY suŋaq 'bile, bead'
CSY suŋaq* 'bile, bead', Chap suŋaʀnitə- 'taste bitter'
Sir suŋanəX 'bile', suŋaʀənilŋuX 'bitter' [and Krup. has suŋay 'beads'; Vakh. has suŋəX 'bead' from Men.'s texts]
SPI suŋaq 'bile'
NAI suŋaq 'gall bladder' [and suŋaužaq 'bead']
WCI suŋaq 'gall' [and Car? suŋauyaq 'bead' — Schn. 'adg']
ECI suŋaq 'bile'
GRI suŋaq, EG cuʀ̃aq [Robbe and Menn.] 'gall, bile'

PE cuŋaɣ- or **cuŋaʀ-** 'be green'
AAY cuŋaɣ- 'be green'
CAY cuŋaɣliq*, Nun cuŋaɣɣax 'green'
NSY suŋaʀnitə- 'be green, be bitter' [ANLC; Taghyuq has suŋaʀnilŋuq 'green']
CSY suŋaɣɣaak 'green', suŋaɣɣuk 'blue, green' [the latter with p.b. yuɣ]
Sir suŋ(ə)ʀuʀ- 'become blue, green' [and suʀməlŋuX

'light blue', suxtiłəx 'green']
SPI suŋaq- 'be blue or green'
NAI suŋaaq- 'be green' [also suŋaužaaqtaaq 'a blue thing']
WCI suŋaaq- 'be blue or green' [Lowe has Cop huŋayaaqtaq 'blue or green']
ECI —
GRI suŋaaʀ-, NG huŋaqpaluk- 'be yellow'

PY cuŋaqcuaʀ(naq) 'warbler'
AAY C cuŋaqcua<ʀ>aq 'yellow or Wilson's warbler'
CAY cuŋakcuaʀnaq, cuŋaqcuaʀnaq, cuŋakcuaʀ(aq*) 'yellow, Wilson's or arctic warbler'
NSY —
CSY —

PY cuŋavžəɣaq 'bead' [cf. žaɣaq and/or vžəʀaʀ-]
AAY Kod cuŋauɣɣaq 'bead' [old word]
CAY cuŋavzəq*, cuŋazvəq* 'bead' [also cuŋauzaq,Y, NS cuŋauyaq — perhaps from Inu suŋaužaq — and LI cuŋavləq*]
NSY suŋavžəɣaq
CSY —

PY-S cuŋaʀ- 'become red (from rage or strain)' [cf. ciŋuk-]
AAY — [for AP ciŋuʀuuq 'sun' see ciŋuʀ-, poss. with contam. from the present set]
CAY cuŋaXtəqə- 'suffer anguish'
NSY —
CSY suŋaXtəqə- 'redden in rage', suŋaʀatə- 'be rosy-cheeked'
Sir suŋəɣžaʀiɣləʀəX 'rosy-cheeked' [and Em. has suŋəʀəcəX 'red color on cheeks']

PI cuŋiq- 'settle (down)' [cf. cuŋu-]
SPI suŋiqtuyu- 'be patient' [and Jen. has suŋiq- 'be cheerful']
NAI —
WCI suŋiqtuq- 'feel confidence'
ECI suŋiq- 'arrange' [suŋiuti- 'become used to']
GRI suŋiʀ- 'settle into right shape', suŋiut(i)- 'become accustomed to', suŋiʀsaʀtuʀ- 'encourage, comfort'

PY-S cuŋitə- 'have bitter taste in mouth' [cf. cuŋa(ʀ)- and lit-]
AAY —
CAY cuŋitə- 'whimper, whine'
NSY —
CSY suŋitə- 'feel bitter (taste or emotion)'
Sir suŋit(ə)- 'have bitter taste in mouth' [Em.]

PE cuŋŋuʀ 'brow' [there may be a relat. to cuɣðuɣ]
AAY [for Kod cuɣɣuk 'forehead' see cuɣðuɣ; for cu(u)xtə- 'raise head' see civ(v)uɣ- — there may be contam. here]
CAY cuŋŋuq 'forehead'
NSY —
CSY —
Sir —
SPI Qaw suŋŋuq 'ridge between eyebrows'
NAI Nu suŋŋuq 'area between caribou snout and forehead'
WCI —
ECI —
GRI —

PY cuŋu- 'be in a calm or dreamy state' [cf. cuŋiq-]
AAY —
CAY Nun cuŋu- 'die down (flame)' [perhaps by contam. with cuð(ð)u-]
NSY suŋu- 'be content, quietly happy' [ANLC]
CSY [tuŋu- 'stare vacantly into space, daydream' — contam. with tuŋu-?]

PE cupə-[1] 'blow' [cf. cupluɣ and cuvəq]
AAY K cupə-, C supə- 'blow off, blow on, blow away'
CAY cupə- 'blow on, break up (ice on river)' [cupa 'ice floe']
NSY supə- 'blow' [supłəkaq 'break up of river ice' (L.-T.); ANLC also has supuk 'breeze']
CSY suupə- 'blow' [and supuk 'draft', supuɣ- 'be drafty']
Sir supuɣ- 'blow' [supuʀcəʀ- 'blow away'; Em. also has supət(ə)- 'blow on']
SPI suvi- 'break up (river), shoot with gun', Qaw supi- 'blow, have ice flowing through it during spring break-up (river)'
NAI supi- 'blow, break up and flow (of river)' [supiniq*, sumniq* 'break-up (of river)']
WCI supi- 'blow, break up (ice in river in spring)'
ECI supi- 'blow' [and supiniq 's.th. borne along by river at break-up']
GRI supi- 'blow at, break up (of river)' [and supiniq* 'break-up (of river), thing deposited at mouth of river at break-up', EG cipu- 'blow (up), spout' (influenced by cipə(ɣ)-?); for supi 'draft' see cuviq]

PI cupluaq- 'blow or spout' [cf. cupluɣ?]
Sir [note supłuxpax 'siren']
SPI supłuaq- 'blow, spout (whale)'
NAI suvluaq-, Nu supluaq- 'blow on (once)', spout (whale)'
WCI suvluaq- 'blow on or in' [Schn. has sulluaq- 'blow several times or for a long time' for 'adg']
ECI —
GRI sułłuaʀ- 'blow on, blow away' [and Ras. has EG cipuluuʀ- 'break wind']

PI cupputə- 'carry along with current' [cf. utə-]
SPI —
NAI supput(i)- 'carry or force along (river or air current)'
WCI —
ECI supput(i)- 'carry with current, spit out (walrus, of remains of shellfish it is eating)'
GRI supput(i)- 'wash away, carry along (river breaking up), inundate'

PE cupuʀ- 'blow repeatedly' [cf. (C)uʀ-]
AAY K cupuʀ-, C supuʀ- 'blow continuously'
CAY —
NSY supuʀ- 'blow (e.g. whale)' [ANLC]
CSY supuʀ- 'blow repeatedly'
Sir —
SPI —
NAI —
WCI —
ECI Rep. Bay supuuq- 'smoke'
GRI supuuʀ-, EG cipuuʀ- 'blow on (several times)'

PY cupə-[2] 'be dirty or rancid'
AAY K cupə- 'be rancid' [trans. verb with impersonal subj.]
CAY Nun cupə- 'have oil or fat stuck to it (a skin not well washed)'
NSY —
CSY —

PE cupiɣ- 'turn sideways'
AAY —
CAY Nun cupixtə- 'put boots on wrong feet'
NSY —
CSY —
Sir —
SPI [for suviŋa- 'slope gently' see civiŋa-]
NAI supik- 'turn sideways' [supiaq- 'go diagonally']
WCI supiktaliq- 'lean sideways', supiŋa- 'be turned sideways'
ECI —
GRI supiɣ- 'turn sideways' [and supissaat 'rein', NG hupia- 'jerk hips in drum dance']

PE cupluɣ or **cupluʀ** 'tube' [cf. cupə-[1] and p.b. lu(ʀ) and compare cupluaq- under cupə-]
AAY cupłu<ɣ>aq K 'dry stalk of wild celery', C 'intestines left to dʀy foʀ making rain gear' [and note cupłu-, PWS supłu- 'shoot through a pea-shooter', KP cupłuq 'lung']
CAY cupłuq 'pipe, hose, gun barrel'
NSY supłuk 'tube, place blown through by wind' [ANLC supłu 'pipe']
CSY sufłu(q) 'tube, cavity, cane', sufłuk 'chimney, stovepipe'
Sir supłux 'tube, chimney' [and Vakh. has sufłəɣəX 'opening']
SPI —
NAI suvlu, Nu suplu 'pore, tiny hole, barrel of gun'
WCI suvluk 'nipple of (portable) gas stove'
ECI sulluk 'tube-like hole, strait between mainland and island, gun barrel', Iti 'link of chain' [and Fort Chimo 'esophagus']
GRI sułłuaq 'tube-shaped hole'

PE cuqlaɣ 'root (edible)' [cf. Aleut cuq(i)- 'root, bottom, area beneath']
AAY C cuqłamciq 'plant (*polygonum alpinum*?)' [also PWS cuXqankaq, cuqkamkaq 'edible tuber']
CAY NSU cuqłamcaq 'edible tubers of pink plumes plant'
NSY suqłaq 'edible root' [ANLC suqłak]
CSY suqłak 'a certain edible root' [and note saqłak another 'edible root']
Sir —
SPI — [for saqłak 'roseroot' see caqłaɣ]
NAI —
WCI —
ECI suʀsaq 'edible herb or plant (?)' [and Igl tuʀłiq 'roots of *Silem acaulis*' — Math.]
GRI suʀłak, EG cuʀtaq 'root (esp. roseroot)'

PY-S cuqluʀ- 'dent or get dented'
AAY —
CAY cuqłuʀ- 'get bent out of shape' [post. root; note also cuqiʀ- 'be bent, crooked, windy' and Y cuqpəq*, HBC cuqfəq* 'humpback salmon']
NSY suqłuʀ- 'dent, shrink' [ANLC; Men. has suqłuʀaq 'dent']
CSY suqłuʀ- 'get bashed in, dented, cʀumpled' [post. root; suqłunəq* 'fjord, canyon']
Sir suqłunqaX 'ravine' [and Vakh. has suqəʀaXtə- 'lean on one's elbow' from Men.'s texts]

PE cuqqa(C)aʀ- 'measure'
AAY K cuqa<ʀ>aʀ- 'measure'
CAY cuqa (base cuqə) 'measurement, cord of wood', cuq<ə>tə- 'measure, judge'
NSY —
CSY —
Sir —
SPI [supqaaq- 'estimate, judge']
NAI —
WCI —
ECI suqqaatiq- 'measure length of'
GRI suqqaaʀ- 'mark off with a chalked line'

PE cuqqaʀ 'baleen' [from *cuqəqaʀ? — cf. cuqlaɣ; for Aleut cuqa-X 'throat, gullet' see tuqlu(ʀ)]
AAY Kod suqattaŋiit 'baleen'
CAY cuqaq* 'whale baleen'
NSY suqaq
CSY suqaq* 'baleen' [and suuXqaq* 'edible part of baleen toward gum' — with kðaʀ?]
Sir suqaX 'baleen' [and note suqaʀnəX, pl. suqaʀnay 'sled runner' — Orr]
SPI suqqaq 'baleen'
NAI suqqaq*
WCI suqqaq
ECI suqqaq
GRI suqqaq*

PI cuqula- 'dance and sing in festival'
SPI —
NAI —
WCI Cop huqula- 'dance and sing in festival house'
ECI suqulayuq 'Inuit dance'
GRI suqula- 'take part in festivals with physical feats and singing' [Robbe and Menn. have EG cuʀulaliq 'seated drum player']

PI cuRaiq- 'stop' [cf. cu(na) and ŋiR-, also cuRRait-?]
SPI —
NAI —
WCI Cop huRaiq- 'finish eating' [Pryde; Met. has Sig suRiiq- 'can not do anything more']
ECI Baffin suRaiq- 'stop' [biblical acc. Schn.]
GRI suRaaR- 'stop, retire'

PY cuRaq 'blueberry'
AAY cuRaq 'blueberry'
CAY cuRaq
NSY suXaq 'blueberry'
CSY suuRaq* 'blueberry'
Sir suRəX
Inu [SPI suRa 'blueberry' is probably a loan from Yup]

PE cuRðuɣ- 'attack'
AAY K cuRukaR- 'charge (of animal)'
CAY cuRuɣ- 'go attack'
NSY suRuɣ- [and suRuk 'attack, war']
CSY suRuɣ- 'attack, chase'
Sir suRcəɣ- 'attack' [as nom. = 'war, enemy' — Vakh. from Rub.]
SPI suRžuk- 'go after s.o. who has wronged you'
NAI suRžuk- 'go beRate, quarrel with, attack'
WCI suRyuk- 'attack an enemy' [Schn. has 'encounter, go to quarrel with' for 'adg']
ECI —
GRI suRšuɣ- 'attack, be at war with'

PI cuRləq 'horned grebe'
Yup [note CAY cuRcuRliq, aaqcuRliq, pitəɣcuRliq 'robin']
SPI suuRliq 'grebe'
NAI suRlɨq* 'horned grebe'
WCI Sig suRliq 'mallard' [Pet.]
ECI —
GRI —

PE cuRlu 'nostril' [cf. lu(R); there may be link to cupluɣ]
AAY cuRluq 'nostril'
CAY cuRlu, cuRluq 'nostril, nasal passage, sinus, head of pike fish'
NSY —
CSY —
Sir suRləx 'beak, bill' [Vakh. also has suRlux 'lips' from Men.'s texts]
SPI suRlut 'nasal cavity'
NAI suRlu, suRluq 'nasal cavity'
WCI suRluk 'nasal cavity'
ECI suRluk 'nostrils, nasal passage'
GRI suRłuk, EG cuRtuq 'nostril'

PY cuR(ə)məRaq 'kind of sandpiper'
AAY —
CAY cəRəmRaq 'dunlin'
NSY —
CSY suRməRaq 'red phalarope'

PI cuRRait- 'be healthy or lively' [cf. cuRaiq- and ŋit- and/or cuR(R)uk(-)]
SPI —
NAI suRRait- 'be healthy, doing well' [and note suR(R)ait- 'be whole', which may be influenced by aulait- under aRula-]
WCI Sig suRait- 'be healthy'
ECI suRRait- 'be healthy, unchanged' [and note Aiv suRaq- 'break, destroy'; Saul has suRRa(q)- 'affect' for Tar — in Schn. '(make) change']
GRI suXXaat- SWG 'be cheeky, bold', NWG 'be healthy', EG cuqqaat- 'speak harsh words to s.o.' ['be agressive' acc. Tersis]

PI cuRuciq 'small weak thing?' [cf. cuRuyuk — esp. the WG forms — and/or cuR(R)uk(-), so perhaps from cu(na), Ruyuk under Ruluk, and ɣuciq]
SPI —
NAI —
WCI Cop huRuhiq 'any kind of minute water bug' [Pryde, who also has it in the sense 'animal which plunders a cache or killed game' for B. Inlet]
ECI suRusiq, Iti tuRusiq 'boy', NBI, Fr. Bay 'child', Lab suɣusik 'child'
GRI — [but note sukuRsiq 'lad, boy', suRaluaq 'nephew, niece', and NG huRRuluk 'weakling, handicapped person or animal']

PI cuR(R)uk(-) '(have an) infected wound' [cf. cuRuyuk]
Yup — [but note CAY Y cuqəq 'large open sore on body']
SPI —
NAI —
WCI suR(R)uk 'pus, swollen infected wound' [and Pryde has Cop huRRuq 'putrid meat, festering matter in wound', huRuq- 'fester']
ECI suRRuq 'infected wound' [verbal = 'turn septic (wound), have such a wound']
GRI suXXuk 'swelling filled with matter (on the head)' [suXXuɣ- 'have such a swelling']

PY cuRuq 'something for working or lying on?'
AAY cu<R>uq 'thimble, sailmaker's palm'
CAY cuRuq 'bedding skin'
NSY —
CSY —

PI cuRuyuk 'mud or dirt?' [cf. cuR(R)uk(-) and cuRuciq, also Ruyuk under Ruluk]
Yup [note AAY KP cuRu- 'spray milt to fertilize eggs (of fish)', but also CAY caaRłuk 'dirt']
SPI —
NAI —
WCI —
ECI suRuyuk 'rain' [also verbal; note also suyuk- 'rot, deteriorate from old age or illness' (from *suRuyuk-?), suyuŋa- 'be filthy', suyuRaq- 'damage, destroy, dirty']
GRI suRuyuk 'dirt which sticks to s.th., useless person' [for the latter sense cf. cuRuciq; Egede has sorujúvok 'is dirty'; note NG huyuŋa- 'be ill' and EG cuuyaaRtiq 'ill person' (Ges.), cuiyaaR- 'be ill' (Robbe and Menn.) — Ras. has sorujaar- 'be ill' for EG, so this may be from

*cuʀuyuaʀ-, unless the link for some of the forms is to cuð(ð)u- rather; note also WG suusupaɣi- 'consider worthless, look down on']

PY cuukvak 'pike'
AAY AP cukx^{w}ak 'pike' [old lists only]
CAY cuukfak 'pike'
NSY —
CSY —

PI cuvəq 'draft' [cf. cupə-[1]]
SPI —
NAI —
WCI suviq 'draft' [also verbal 'be drafty']
ECI suviq 'draft' [also verbal]
GRI suiq 'draft' [also supi from cupə-; suiʀ- 'be a draft (on s.o.)' — part. suiʀtuq]

PE cuviŋnit- 'smell of an animal' [cf. nit-]
AAY —
CAY K, BB cuiɣnilŋuq 'otter' [and note Nun civixtə- 'urinate on (animal marking its territory)']
NSY —
CSY —
Sir —
SPI suiŋnit- 'have an unidentified animal odor'
NAI suviŋn^{y}it- 'smell of flesh' [and suviŋn^{y}ɨq 'smell of flesh']
WCI Cop huviŋni 'smell of rutting fox' [Pryde; and note suinnaq 's.th. bad' acc. Met. and Car huikyaʀnik- 'smell of fox' acc. Ras.]
ECI suinnaq 'bad, good for nothing'
GRI suinnit- 'smell of foxes' [noun = suinni]

cuyaq 'willow leaf or twig' [loan from EA cuya-X 'cane, stick, willow twig, white willow']
AAY Kod cuyaq 'branch', C cuaq 'willow'
CAY cuyaq 'leaf, leaf tobacco'
NSY —
CSY —

ə

PE əcəmðuɣ- or **əcumðuɣ-** 'whisper'
AAY Kod icuxsua<ʀ>aʀ- 'whisper'
CAY —
NSY əsumžuɣ- 'whisper' [also əsulɣutau-, with nominalizing postbase lɣun plus ŋu- 'be'?; ANLC has əsəmžuɣ-]
CSY —
Sir —
SPI izivžuaq-, Qaw isivžuaq-, Imaq izuvžuaq- 'whisper' [Jen. has izuvroaq- for W (i.e. izuvžuaq-) and isuisut- (i.e. izivžuk-?) for KI]
NAI isivžuk-, Nu sivžuk- 'whisper'
WCI isivyuk-
ECI isiyyuatuq-, isiyyuʀik-
GRI isuššuɣ-, isuššuʀ- [old ortho. with -vss-; Fab. also has isirvsor-]

PE əciʀ 'drum skin or cover' [cf. əcivət-]
AAY PWS ciq 'roof, cover, temporary, shelter' [but note ciʀu(q), Perry cu<ʀ>u(q) 'roof, cover, temporary shelter' under ciʀu-, with which there appears to be contam.]
CAY əciq 'skin of a drum, windowpane' [for ciʀu 'covering' see ciʀu-]
NSY isi 'skin of drum' [Em.]
CSY sii 'skin of a drum, thin ice on water'
Sir sii 'skin of a drum, thin ice on water' [Orr; may be borrowed from CSY]
SPI izi 'drum skin' [as verb = 'put skin on drum']
NAI isi 'drum skin', isik- 'put skin on drum' [and Nu itciaq 'membrane inside eggshell or around internal organ', verbal = 'stretch a membrane over']
WCI Net isiq 'drum skin' [Ras., who also has Cop ihi(a); Pet. has Sig isi]
ECI isiq 'drum skin'
GRI isi 'skin of drum, violin string' [EG also 'hood' and 'crown of head' acc. Ges.]

PI əcivət- 'stretch out' [cf. əciʀ and vət- under vaʀ-?]
Yup — [for AAY ciitə- 'flatten' see ciɣi-]
SPI izivit- 'stretch out, flatten' [and izitaaq- 'stretch out limbs']
NAI isivɨt- 'be extended, straighten out, stretch fully'
WCI isivik-, isiptiq- 'stretch out'
ECI isiviC- 'stretch' [also isitti(q)- and isiqqit-]
GRI isivit-, isuit- 'spread, stretch out' [and isiqqimišaaʀ- 'stretch lazily', isutsiʀ-, isitsiʀ- 'stretch out gradually']

PE əcuʀ- 'be murky'
AAY cuuʀ- 'be murky, strong (coffee or tea)'
CAY əcuʀ-
NSY əsuʀ- 'to be turbid, murky' [Em.]
CSY suuʀ- 'be murky, muddy'
Sir suʀmətə- [Orr]
SPI izuq- 'be murky (water), brewed strong (tea)' [Qaw isuq- also 'be hazy (weather)']
NAI isuq- 'be opaque, unclear'
WCI isuq- 'be unclear, murky, brownish (water)'
ECI isuqtuq, Iti isuttuq 'unclear (liquid)' [and isuʀsi- 'darken, ruffle (water), isutsiaŋit- 'be pale (tea)', isuqtaq 'gray (of young white whale)', isuaŋayuq 's.th. grayish, whitish or brownish']
GRI isuʀ- 'be opaque, obscure (water, weather)' [and note isuʀtaq 'young white whale', NG ihuqtaaq 'gray (color of young beluga)']

PE əcuʀit- 'be clear' [cf. ŋit-]
AAY əcuitə- 'be clear (water), weak (tea)'
CAY əcuitə-
NSY əsuitə- [ANLC]
CSY suuʀitə- 'be clear, weak' [also siiʀ- 'clear up (weather)']
Sir suʀətə- 'be clear, weak' [Orr]
SPI izuit- 'be thin, weak (soup, coffee, etc.)'
NAI isuit- 'be clear (water)'
WCI isuit-
ECI —
GRI isuit-

PE əðə 'eye' [cf. Aleut ða-X 'eye']
AAY ii 'eye'
CAY ii, Nun iix
NSY ii
CSY iya
Sir əca 'eye' [pl. əciy 'glasses']
SPI iži 'eye'
NAI iži
WCI iyi, Net iži
ECI iyi
GRI iši 'eye'

PE əðəɣmiɣ- 'wink' [cf. miɣ-]
AAY —
CAY iiɣmiuʀ- 'signal with one's eyes' [also iimiutə- 'aim (at)']
NSY —
CSY —
Sir [note əžməɣ- 'look through, sight']
SPI ižimik- 'wink'
NAI iziŋmiɣaq- 'wink (at)'
WCI iyinmiɣ- 'wink (at)' [Lowe has Sig iyimiɣaq-]
ECI iyimmik- [Saul]
GRI išimmiɣ- 'wink'

PE əðəkə- 'watch' [cf. kə-[1]]
AAY —
CAY —
NSY —
CSY iiskuXtə- 'guard, watch over'
Sir [əskə- 'open eyes, watch', intr. only in Men. but with the trans. sense in Vakh. — borrowed from CSY?; compare also əskiɣləʀəX 'sharp-sighted' with kiɣ-]
SPI —
NAI — [but Jen. has igiga(a) 'he looked at it', a misprint?]
WCI iyiyi- 'watch' [Schn. has this intransitively in sense 'follow s.th. with one's eyes' for B. Lake]
ECI —
GRI išiɣi- 'watch', EG ilii- 'watch' [and išikkut(i)- 'stare at', išikku 'appearance', NG ihii- 'watch']

PE əðəłuɣ- 'be blind or have bad eyesight' [cf. łuɣ(-)]
AAY [note K isłuɣ- 'be hard of hearing' as opposed to iskəxtə- 'have good hearing' with kiɣ-]
CAY [note iiłiqə- 'have bad eyes']
NSY iiłuXa- 'become blind'
CSY iyəłuk 'eye trouble'
Sir —
SPI illuk- 'be snowblind' [and Imaq əžəłuaq- 'go blind']
NAI illuk- 'be snowblind' [but ižiluk- 'have bad eyesight']
WCI illuk- Cop 'be snowblind' [Lowe], Car? 'have one's eyes hurt' [Schn. 'adg'; note also Sig iyaʀluk- 'have one's eyes hurt' — Lowe]
ECI illui-, Iti illu(C)- 'be snowblind'
GRI iłłuɣ- 'be snowblind' [but išiluɣ- 'have bad or sore eyes']

PE əð(ə)ɣa(ʀ) '(snow) goggles' [cf. aʀ]
AAY — [but note iiŋaq below]
CAY — [but note iiŋaq below]
NSY —
CSY iyəɣaatək 'eyeglasses'
Sir iyiɣatiy [from CSY]
SPI iɣžaak 'eyeglasses'
NAI ižɣaak 'pair of glasses or (snow) goggles'
WCI iyɣaak
ECI NBI, SB iɣɣaak 'sunglasses' [note Tar iyautiik 'glasses, snow goggles' — but Saul also has iɣɣaak there]
GRI NWG iššat, EG ittaat, Up itsaat, NG ixxaak 'glasses, snow goggles' [for SWG išaʀuššat see əžaʀuaq below]

PY əsɣaʀ(aʀ)- 'open eyes' [cf. aʀaʀtə-? — but compare also əðəkə- above]
AAY əs(x)aʀ- 'wake up', KP əssama- 'be awake'
CAY səxxaʀ-, cəxxaʀ-, Nun əsxaʀ- 'become wide awake, more active'
NSY əsXaʀ- 'see, watch, open eyes'
CSY əsXaʀ- 'open eyes, see'
Sir — [for əskə- 'open eyes' see under əðəkə- above — contam.?]

PY əs(ɣa)ʀapaɣ- 'watch' [cf. əsɣaʀ(aʀ)- above and vaɣ(-)]
AAY —
CAY —
NSY əsXapaɣ- 'watch, look at' [ANLC]
CSY əsXapaɣ-

PI əžaʀuaq 'lens or pupil of eye'
SPI —
NAI [note ižaqumak 'lens, iris']
WCI Car? iyaʀuq, iyaʀuaq 'lens, pupil of eye' [Schn. 'adg'; Met. has iyaʀuvak 'pupil of eye']
ECI iyaʀuvak 'lens of eye' [Bourq. — but not Peck — has iyaʀuyaq for Lab]
GRI išaʀuaq 'lens of eye, spot over dog's eye' [SWG pl. išaʀuššat 'glasses, snow goggles']

PI əžaʀuq- 'hit or hurt in the eye' [cf. ʀuq-]
SPI —
NAI ižaʀuq-, ižaʀuaq- 'hit or hurt eye'
WCI iyaʀuq- 'hurt eye'
ECI iyaʀuq- 'hit in the eye'
GRI išaʀuʀ-

PI əžžit- 'get s.th. in one's eye' [cf. łit-]
SPI ižžit- 'get s.th. in one's eye'
NAI ižžit-
WCI Car B. Lake iyyia- 'get dust in one's eye' [Schn.; Dor. has itži (for ižži?) 'dust in eye' for Net]
ECI iyyi(t)-, iyyi- 'get dust in eye', Iti 'hurt one's eye' [and iyyi 'dust in eye']
GRI iššit- 'get s.th. in eye', iššia- 'get dust in eye'

PY iiŋaq 'eye(ball)'
AAY iiŋaq, iiŋalaq 'eye (esp. individual eye)'
CAY iiŋaq 'eye' [child's form, for some speakers 'eyeball']
NSY iiŋaq 'eye' [child's word]
CSY —

PE əðəŋqi- 'dice or slice food'
AAY C, AP iŋqi- 'slice food into thin slices' [C iŋqiq 'thin slice of food']
CAY iŋqi- 'dice food'
NSY —
CSY —
Sir —
SPI ižaqi- 'dice meat, cut up tobacco' [Di, Imaq əžaqət- 'cut up pieces of cooked meat'; for KI ižaqtu- 'be wide', ižakituuʀaq 's.th. narrow' see iqə-]
NAI ižatqi-, ižaqši-, PH ižɨtqi-, ižaʀži- 'cut into small pieces (meat)' [and ižaqšaq 'crumb of food, pipe tobacco']
WCI Sig iyatqi- 'cut into small pieces' [and iy(y)aʀiktuq 'cigarette tobacco', iyaksaun — for iyaqsaun? — 'pipe tobacco'; Pet. has iyaqsi- 'cut up tobacco']
ECI —
GRI išiqqi- 'cut up, cut into cubes' [S.-L. spells it with s rather than ss in the first sense]

PE əðəʀa(ʀ) 'hollow between neck and shoulder'
AAY AP ii<ʀ>ak 'hollow between neck and collarbone (where carotid arteries are felt)'
CAY iiʀaq 'scar, carotid gland, side of neck, tonsil'
NSY i(i)ʀaq 'scab under nose, growth'
CSY iiʀaq 'swollen gland in neck or side of face', Chap also 'place at side of neck'
Sir əcXa 'shoulder'
SPI —
NAI —
WCI Sig, Car iʀyi 'shoulder' [Pryde has 'bulging extension of a woman's parka' for Cop]
ECI NBI iʀyi 'side of head'
GRI iʀšik 'shoulder hollow'

PE əðəvkaʀ- 'fall or drop from a height' [cf. əžət- and vkaʀ-]
AAY —
CAY iifkaʀ-, HBC, Nun ifkaʀ- 'fall or lower from a height'
NSY ifkə- 'drop', iifkə- 'put out of boat' [and ifkaʀ- 'drop, let s.o. land from boat' — ANLC]
CSY ifkaʀ- 'fall, drop'
Sir —
SPI ižukaq-, Imaq əžukaq- 'drop, fall from a height'
NAI ižukkaqi-, ižupkaq- 'drop, fall from a height' [and also uukkaq-, Nu uupkaq- 'come crashing or sliding down (overhanging ice or snow)']
WCI Sig iyukkaq- 'fall' [but Ras. has iyupkaq-, also for Net; Met. also has u(u)pkaʀniq 'snow or land slide']
ECI iyukka(q)- 'fall from a height'
GRI uukkaʀ- 'topple down, calve (glacier)'

PE əðiʀ 'steam' [cf. Aleut di-X 'soot', also PE kəði- for the phonology]
AAY səʀə- 'sweat'
CAY (ə)səq, (ə)cəq, Nun əsəX 'sweat' [verbal (ə)səʀ-, etc.]
NSY əsaʀ- 'melt', səʀ- 'perspire' [ANLC; the latter perhaps from CSY]
CSY səXə- 'sweat'
Sir əcəX 'smoke, steam'
SPI iziq 'smoke' [as verb = 'make smoke']
NAI isiq 'smoke' [as verb = 'be smoky'; itciala- 'smoke, smoulder (e.g. stove)']
WCI isiq 'smoke, steam'
ECI isiq 'smoke, steam' [in Lab also as a verb 'smoke']
GRI isiq 'smoke, steam (esp. in house)' [and isiʀ- 'give off steam or smoke'; itsi- 'get smoke in eyes']

PE əðiʀyaɣ(-) 'be hazy' [cf. yaɣ-?]
AAY K iʀyaxtə-, iʀyaXtə-'be hazy' [iʀyak, iʀyaq 'haze, light whispy cloud cover']
CAY iʀyaxtə- 'be smoky from a distant fire'
NSY isiʀyak 'haze, blue color of air in summer' [ANLC]
CSY —
Sir —
SPI iziʀiak- 'be smoky from log fire (air)'
NAI isiʀiak- 'be hazy because of fire in distance'
WCI isiʀiaq 'smoke or haze in air in summer' [and Schn. has isiʀiaq- 'make a lot of smoke (stove)' for 'adg']
ECI isiʀiaq- 'be smoky from distant forest fire (air)', isiʀiaq 'smoke from such a source', Lab isiɣiak 'haze'
GRI isiʀiaɣ- 'be misty', isiʀiak 'mist'

PE əɣa- 'cook' [cf. əɣaləʀ]
AAY əɣaa- C 'cook'
CAY əɣa-
NSY əɣa- 'cook', əɣa 'pit for storing meat'
CSY ɣaaʀ-
Sir əɣa-
SPI iɣa- 'cook', Di əɣa 'pit for storing meat, greens'
NAI iɣa- 'cook', iɣa 'cooking area of traditional house'
WCI iɣa- 'cook'
ECI iɣa- 'cook', NBI 'cook outdoors', iɣa 'fireplace or stones on which a cooking utensil is placed'
GRI iɣa- 'cook', iɣa 'cooking pot'

PE əɣa(C)aʀ 'boiled food' [cf. ðaʀ?]
AAY əɣaaq 's.th. cooked'
CAY əɣaaq 'boiled fish or other food'
NSY —
CSY ɣaaʀaq, ɣaaqaq 's.th. cooked'
Sir [əɣákcəX — Orr]
SPI iaaq 'boiled food'
NAI iɣaaq 'boiled food, food being cooked'
WCI iɣak [for iɣaaq?] 'food which is cooked'
ECI [iɣaaʀniq 'smell of cooking'; Andersen et al. have iɣaat 's.th. cooking' for Lab]
GRI iɣaaq 'food which is boiled'

PE əɣama(C)aʀɫuɣ 'partly dried and cooked meat' [cf. ɫuɣ]
AAY —
CAY əɣamaaXɫuk 'half dried then boiled fish'
NSY —
CSY —
Sir —
SPI —
NAI iɣamaaqɫuk 'partly dried meat, cooked and stored in seal oil' [also verbal in Mal of boiling dried meat — Seiler]
WCI —
ECI —
GRI —

PE əɣɣan 'cooking pot' [cf. un]
AAY —
CAY Y, HBC, Nun, NS əɣan 'cooking pot'
NSY —
CSY [ɣaaʀusiq 'cooking pot']
Sir —
SPI iɣɣan 'cooking pot'
NAI iɣɣan
WCI —
ECI —
GRI ixxasiʀ- 'put pot on fire'

PE əɣɣaviɣ and **əɣaðviɣ** 'cooking place' [cf. ðviɣ]
AAY —
CAY —
NSY əɣavik 'kitchen'
CSY —
Sir —
SPI iɣɣawik
NAI iɣɣavik 'kitchen, place for cooking fire'
WCI iɣavik 'cooking place', Sig also 'pot for cooking in, stove'
ECI iɣavik 'kitchen', NBI, F. Bay iɣɣavik 'hearth' [NBI also iɣavvik]
GRI ixxavik, iɣaffik, EG iŋappik 'kitchen, cooking place, stove', NG iɣɣavik 'oudoor cooking place'

PE əɣaləʀ 'smokehole' [cf. əɣa- and ɫəʀ? — also EA ɣalʀ- (as in 3s possessed ɣalʀa), ɣalʀi-X 'doorway, hatch']
AAY ɣaaləq, xaaləq 'window (formally smokehole of trad. Yupik house)'
CAY əɣaləq*, HB also ləɣaləq*
NSY əɣaləq 'smokehole, skylight or vent of stretched gut in yaranga' [ANLC]
CSY —
Sir —
SPI ialiq, Qaw iɣaliq 'window, skylight'
NAI iɣaliq*, iɣalaaq 'skylight window, seal net placed under seal's breathing hole'
WCI Sig iɣaliq, Cop iɣalaaq 'window', Car EP iɣaliq 'chimney' [Ow.]
ECI iɣalaaq 'window'
GRI iɣaliq* 'kitchen (in passage of trad. Greenlandic house)', iɣalaaq 'window, glass'

PE əɣə- 'render oil from blubber' [cf. əɣunaq and Aleut iɣiɣna-X 'fermented seal blubber' with p.b. ɣna- 'result of -ing']
AAY C əɣə- 'render'
CAY əɣə- 'become rendered (fat), release liquid'
NSY əɣəvə- 'melt off' [ANLC has əɣžuaXta- 'render' and əɣəvaʀ- 'flow down, melt down']
CSY əɣə-, ɣəvə- 'render'
Sir əɣvə- [Orr]
SPI iit-, Qaw ii- 'render' [KI also yuuq-]
NAI iɣɨt- 'render oil from blubber, turn to grease by frying'
WCI [Schn. has iɣiuq- 'thicken (liquid)' for Baker Lake]
ECI ➟
GRI iɣi- 'melt (blubber, snow, ice), suppurate (wound)'

PE əɣ(ə)nəʀ 'rendered oil' [cf. nəʀ[1]]
AAY əɣnəq 'rendered oil'
CAY əɣnəq* 'broth (from cooking)'
NSY [əɣnəʀaq 'dough']
CSY —
Sir —
SPI —
NAI ɨɣnɨq* 'rendered oil'
WCI [Sig iɣinniq 'rancid oil' — Ras.]
ECI Lab iŋniq 'broth' [Peck]
GRI [iɣinniq* 'blubber liquefied by decomposition', from trans. *iɣət- as in NAI under əɣə- above]

PE əɣət- 'throw away' [cf. əɣumə(t)- and t-[1] and Aleut iɣni- 'let go' with causative p.b. ni-, iɣlax 'shaft of harpoon']
AAY əxtə- 'throw away'
CAY əxtə-
NSY əxtə- [ANLC also 'shoot' and 'fall (inanimate object)']
CSY əxtə- 'throw away'
Sir əxtə- 'throw away' [and əxtəvəʀca 'shot']
SPI iit- 'throw away'
NAI iɣɨt-
WCI iɣit-
ECI iɣit-
GRI iɣit- 'throw away, shoot' [iššut(i)- 'shoot at']

PE əɣqaʀ- 'throw (several times)' [cf. qqaʀ-]
AAY əxqaqun 'grappling hook for retrieving dead animal'
CAY Nun əxqakun 'net for capturing birds on cliffs'
NSY —
CSY əXqaataqə- 'scatter, spread out'
Sir əXqataqə(s)- 'scatter' [Em.]
SPI [iqqažaaq- 'throw out what belongs to another']
NAI iqqaq- 'throw away several'
WCI Cop iqqahaq- 'fish by casting from shore' [Jen.]
ECI iqqasaq- 'fish by casting line', iqqatai- 'throw around (several things)'
GRI iqqaʀ- 'thrust away or shoot one after the other'

PE əɣtaʀ 's.th. thrown out' [cf. ðaʀ]
AAY əxtaq 'possession of deceased person placed on his grave, something thrown away'

CAY əxtaq
NSY —
CSY əxtaq
Sir —
SPI iktaq 's.th. thrown away'
NAI iktaq
WCI iktau- 'be cursed (biblical)'
ECI ittaniku 's.th. thrown out'
GRI —

PE əɣimaʀ 'foreshaft of harpoon' [cf. əɣumə(t)-]
AAY —
CAY Nun ɣimaX 'foreshaft of harpoon' [i.e. ggimaq in Jen.]
NSY iɣimaq [ANLC]
CSY ɣiimaq 'foreshaft of harpoon'
Sir əɣiməX [Orr]
SPI iimaq 'bare stem between harpoon handle and head' [and Imaq 'socket for couplings (?) on sled']
NAI [Murdoch has igimù 'loose shaft']
WCI Sig, Cop ilimaq 'foreshaft of harpoon' [Jen.; B.-S. has iɣimaq for Car, Ras. also for Net]
ECI iɣimaq 'walrus harpoon', Igl 'harpoon foreshaft' [B.-S.]
GRI iɣimaq 'foreshaft of harpoon', NG iimaq 'breathing hole harpoon' [iɣimaaq 'tip of bladder dart']

əɣiyaaq 'gull or kittiwake' [loan from EA yiðaaX 'black-legged kittiwake']
AAY C əyyaaq, Perry əyi<ʀ>aq, Kod iyya<ʀ>aq, C, Kod 'herring gull', KP also 'mew gull', AP 'black-legged kittiwake'
CAY BB əɣiaq 'mew gull'
NSY —
CSY —

PY-S əɣkuq 'back of house'
AAY əxkuʀ- (plus possessor ending) 'back of (possessor's) house, cave, bay, etc.'
CAY əxkuq 'back wall of house or room'
NSY —
CSY əxkuq 'back of room or land area'
Sir əxkəʀəX 'back wall of house' [Vakh. from Rub.'s texts]

PE əɣləʀ- or **əɣiləʀ-** 'move or travel' [cf. iŋilʀa-; these two bases may in fact belong together, at least there is contam. between them — and with iɣliq-]
AAY K əɣləʀŋa- 'be slow' [and C il<ʀ>a-, K ilʀa-, KP illa-, Perry iɬ(ʀ)a- 'travel (by boat or car)']
CAY əɣləXtə-, K yiləXtə-, Nun ɣilʀauʀ- [and BB, LI, UK əlʀauʀ- 'move, travel'; for əlɣaʀ- 'lie down' see əlɣaʀ- and for BB ilɣaʀ- 'go home' see aŋilʀaʀ- under aŋit-]
NSY əɣləʀ- 'move, travel' [ANLC has əɣləXtə- 'travel, walk', əɣləʀaʀ- 'travel']
CSY iɣləXtə- 'move, travel'
Sir —
SPI iɣli(q)-, Di əɣli(q)-
NAI iɣliq-, iɣlau- 'move, travel' [also iɣlaaq 'traveler, stranger']
WCI Sig iɣliq- 'travel' [Met. also has Sig iɣla(a)t 'uprights on basket sled that resemble travelers from afar'; Pet. has Sig iɣliq- also as 'flow (water)']
ECI —
GRI — [for iɬɬiʀ- 'push, move aside' see iɣliq-, for iɬɬiniq 'sled track' see ənə, and for homonym 'get into kayak' see əkə-[2]]

PI əɣləʀaq 'krill' [cf. əɣləʀ-?]
SPI —
NAI iɣliʀaq 'krill'
WCI iɣliqqat 'small shrimps' [Schn. has 'whale food, plankton' for 'adg']
ECI —
GRI iɬɬiʀaq [old ortho. igdleraq] 'whale food, krill'

PY əɣlu(q) 'thread' [cf. perhaps Aleut EA iŋɬu-X, iŋlu-X, Atkan pl. iŋlu-s 'leader, snell plaited of several sinew threads']
AAY —
CAY əɣlu(q) 'thread, sinew'
NSY əɣlu 'thread perepared by twisting'
CSY —

PE əɣmiʀ- 'do without stopping (esp. a journey)' [there appears to be entanglement with əʀəni(ʀ)- in Yup and Sir here]
AAY əɣmiʀ- 'go straight there without stopping' [and əɣmian 'immediately' — for C equivalent ənʀian see əʀəni(ʀ)-]
CAY Nun, HBC, NS əɣmiʀ- 'keep going (toward goal)' [and əɣmian 'immediately'; for əɣnaaXtə- 'be in a hurry' see əʀəni(ʀ)-]
NSY əɣmi(i)naq 'immediately'
CSY əɣmiʀ- 'rush by without stopping' [and əɣyuɣ- 'act rashly', əɣmiinaq 'hurry up, quickly'; for əɣnaaŋitə- 'be habitually slow' see əʀəni(ʀ)-]
Sir (ə)ɣmiʀ- 'go past, overtake' [Em.; for əɣnaɣan 'quickly', etc., see əʀəni(ʀ)-].
SPI iŋmiq-, Qaw iŋmia- 'travel to one's destination in a single trip without a stopover'
NAI iŋmiq- 'complete a journey in one day'
WCI iŋmiq- 'do at one go, without stopping'
ECI immi(q)- 'reach one's destination in one day without having to stop'
GRI —

PE əɣtuɣ(-) 'loud sound (sharp or whirring)' [cf. əɣtuɣ-]
AAY əxtuk 'repeated sharp noise, whirring, banging, clicking', also 'small eider-like duck' [and KP əxtuxtiliq 'spruce grouse', C əxtuuɣyaʀ- 'make an unexpected sharp noise']
CAY [əxtu(u)k 'spruce grouse']
NSY —
CSY [note əftuq 'sound of gunshot']
Sir əxtəvaʀət(ə)- 'make a (sharp) noise' [Vakh. from Rub.]
SPI [Qaw iktuk 'spruce hen']
NAI ittuk- 'make a repeated sound, e.g. roar'
WCI iktuk 'noise of wind, vibrations of motor' [also verbal]

ECI iktuluk- 'make continuous sound (sea, wind, thunder, motor)', Lab ittuk 'rustling sound' [Schn. — but Peck has 'roar']
GRI ittuk 'roar, rush' [in Fab. 'bang'], ittuɣ- 'rush, roar (e.g. sea)'

PE əɣtuɣ- 'be anxious or timid' [there may be a link to əɣtuɣ(-)]
AAY —
CAY —
NSY —
CSY əxtuɣ- 'be anxious' [emot. root]
Sir əxtuɣ- 'be anxious' [emot. root; Orr and Em.]
SPI —
NAI —
WCI Sig iktu(u)ʀi- 'fear', iktu(u)ʀusuk- 'be timid'
ECI Lab iktuuq- 'be shy' [Peck]
GRI ittuuʀ- [old ortho. igtôr-] 'be shy, ashamed'

PY əɣuaʀ(tə)- 'try to impose ones will'
AAY —
CAY əɣuaXquʀ- 'persuade, urge, convince, exhort'
NSY əɣuaXtə- 'try to be first, try to become leader'
CSY —

PE əɣumə(t)- or **əɣəmə(t)-** 'unravel or come undone' [cf. əɣət- and compare itəmə- and əɣimaʀ]
AAY əɣumə-, Kod əɣemə-, PWS uumə- 'come undone' [and trans. əɣumtə-, etc. 'undo', unravel']
CAY əɣumə-, Nun əŋumə- 'come undone, unravel'
NSY —
CSY —
Sir —
SPI —
NAI iɣumɨt- 'become unraveled, take apart, loosen', iɣuvɨt- 'become unwound, uncoil'
WCI Net Sp. Bay iŋumit- 'undo, unknot' [Pryde]
ECI iɣumii- 'have unknotted, untied it' [and Peck has iɣuptiq- for Lab]
GRI iŋumiɣ-, iŋimiɣ- 'take apart, come apart' [also trans. iŋutsiʀ-, iŋitsiʀ-]

PI əɣunaq 'meat or whale skin left to rot' [cf. əɣə-?]
SPI [Jen. has W iiniʀit 'raw meat']
NAI iɣunaq 'whale skin with blubber left to cure'
WCI Cop, Car iɣunaq 'rotten meat' [Ras.]
ECI iɣunaq NBI, SB 'gamy meat', Lab 'stinking meat' [Peck; Schn. has Tar iɣunaʀuq- 'become rotten (meat)']
GRI iɣunaq 'whale skin left to rot', NG iunaq 'fermented meat — esp. of eider duck' [Holt.]

PE əɣut- 'pierce' [cf. Aleut ɣu- 'pass, go through', ɣu-X 'tube', ɣut- 'put through, pierce']
AAY —
CAY —
NSY ɣusxənalʀia 'contagious' [and ɣutqia- 'touch, rummage in'?]
CSY ɣuutə- 'shoot' [also 'dance vigorously']
Sir —
SPI Qaw iŋuk-, iɣuk- 'suck'
NAI iɣuk- 'suck in' [iɣɣuun 'straw, tube' but iɣuun 'proboscis']
WCI ➟
ECI iɣuuti 'sting, bowsprit', Lab iɣut- 'sting' [Peck]
GRI iɣut- 'sting (insect)', iɣuut 'proboscis' [and note EG iŋiilit 'bee' acc. Robbe and Menn.]

PI əɣutcaq or **əɣutcak** 'bee' [cf. yaʀ?]
SPI iipsak 'bee'
NAI iɣutcaq* 'bumble bee'
WCI iɣutsaq [but Car iɣuppak in B.-S.]
ECI iɣutsaq 'bumble bee' [B.-S. for Igl and Saul for Tar; Peck has 'wasp' for Lab]
GRI iɣutsak, NG ivittaq 'bumble bee' [B.-S. for the latter]

PI əɣžaq or **iɣžaq** 'hole in harpoon head for attaching to shaft?' [cf. əkə-[2] and ðaʀ?]
SPI —
NAI —
WCI —
ECI iɣɣaq 'hole in back of harpoon head to hold it to shaft'
GRI iššaq [old ortho. igssaq] 'end of harpoon line (fixed into holes in harpoon)'

PI əɣžutət 'heather-like plant' [cf. əkə-[1]?]
SPI —
NAI [note ikkuqutit 'heather used for starting fires']
WCI Car B. Lake ixxutit 'heath(er)' [Dor.; Cop ixuun acc. Lowe]
ECI itsuti 'resinous heather-like tundra plant (used for fuel)'
GRI iššutit [old ortho. igssutit] 'heather-like plant used for dying and for fuel'

PE əkə-[1] 'burn' [cf. Aleut hiɣ- 'burn' with secondary h, also ikla-X 'firewood']
AAY ➟
CAY əkə- 'burn' [nominal əka = 'conflagration, fire']
NSY ➟
CSY ➟
Sir ➟
SPI iɣi- 'burn'
NAI iki- 'burn' [and Mal ikɨ 'conflagration']
WCI Sig iki- 'be burnt' [Lowe]
ECI ➟
GRI iki- 'be lit, smoke (lamp)'

PY əkənuʀaq 'lamp'
AAY —
CAY kənuXaq 'lamp'
NSY əkənuʀaq 'candle'
CSY —

PI əkət- 'ignite' [cf. t-[1] and Aleut hixt- 'put fire to']
SPI iɣit- 'ignite'
NAI ikit- 'ignite, be ignited'
WCI ikit- 'ignite'
ECI ikit- 'ignite' [Saul; Schn. has ikisaq- 'ignite']
GRI ikit- 'ignite'

PE ək(ə)nənəɣ- 'catch or strike fire' [cf. ək(ə)nəʀ below and nəɣ-]
AAY kənəŋə- K 'build a fire', C 'fire (shell)'
CAY kənŋə- 'start to burn'
NSY —
CSY —
Sir —
SPI —
NAI —
WCI iŋnak- 'catch fire' [iŋnait 'flintstones']
ECI inna(k)- 'strike fire' [and innaq 'flintstone']
GRI innaɣ- 'strike fire, catch fire' [and NG iŋnaut 'fire-drill, lighter']

PE ək(ə)nəʀ 'fire' [cf. nəʀ[1]]
AAY kənəq 'fire'
CAY kənəq*, NSU kəŋ̥əq*
NSY əkŋ̥əq 'fire, star, light' [and əkŋ̥in 'match'; also əkŋ̥itaq 'lamp' (L.-T.)]
CSY kənəq*
Sir əkŋ̥əX [Krup.]
SPI ikniq, Qaw also itniq 'fire'
NAI iɣniq*, Mal ikniq* 'fire' [and iɣninʸ, ikninʸ 'flint']
WCI iɣniq 'fire' [Lowe has iŋniq for Cop and Sig, and Pryde has i'niq for Net]
ECI inniq 'fire struck with stone, spark from lighter'
GRI inniq* 'fire', SWG and EG also 'match'

PI əkuala- 'burn brightly' [from *əkuma- and la(ʀ)-? — compare AAY, CAY əkua- under əkuma- below and see under the p.b. for the inchoative correlates with (a)llak- here]
SPI iɣuałak- 'burst into flames'
NAI ikuala-, PH ikkuala-, ikualla- 'blaze, burn brightly' [ikuallak- 'burst into flames']
WCI ikuallak- 'burst into flames'
ECI ikuala- 'be smoking (lamp that has burnt too much)' [acc. Saul 'burn brightly' — he also has ikuallak- 'catch fire']
GRI ikuala- 'burn', ikuałłaɣ- 'flare up', EG iɣivattattiq 'fire' [Robbe and Menn.]

PE əkuma- 'be burning' [cf. (u)ma-]
AAY kumaq 'light (e.g. lamp)' [and kuman, kumataq, Kod kumatəkaq 'lamp wick'; note also K kua- 'burn', kuaXtə- 'light']
CAY kuma- 'be lit', kumaXtə- 'ignite' [and Nun kuman 'lamp'; note also əkua- 'burn' — compare əkuala- above]
NSY əkuma- 'burn', əkumaXtə- 'ignite, burn'
CSY kumaʀ- 'burn, ignite', Chap kumaq 'fire, conflagration'
Sir kuməŋə- 'burn', kuməʀ- 'blaze up', kuməX 'flame, glow' [Em.]
SPI iɣuma- 'be burning'
NAI ikuma-
WCI ikuma-
ECI ikuma- 'be burning' [nominal = 'fire, electricity']
GRI ikuma- 'be burning' [and Kroeber has ikuma 'fire' as a shaman's word]

PY (ə)kəniʀ- 'cook' [cf. ək(ə)nəʀ above and liʀ-]
AAY kəniʀ- K, PWS 'cook', C 'build fire under'
CAY kəniʀ- K, BB, NI 'cook', HBC, Y, NS 'build fire under'
NSY —
CSY —

PE əkə-[2] 'get or put in' [cf. əkəvʀaq and əkpan]
AAY əkə- 'get or put into a container or vehicle'
CAY əkə- 'get or put into container or vehicle' [and NSU əksaʀvik 'tool box']
NSY əkə- 'embark' [ANLC 'put in container or vessel, get in'; Men. also has əkutə- 'adjust, adapt']
CSY —
Sir [and ikəmtəX 'case', ikəmtəʀ- 'pack, put in'; Vakh. and Orr have ikəmtə- 'put into a container']
SPI iɣi- 'get or put into vehicle'
NAI iki-, iku- 'get or put into container or vehicle'
WCI iki- 'embark, put in vehicle'
ECI iki- 'embark, get in'
GRI iki- 'embark, get or put in' [and ikkut(i)- 'plant, fix, place over fire', iłłiʀ- 'get into kayak']

PE ək(ə)ðuʀ(aʀ)- 'get or put in (several)' [cf. ðuʀaʀ-]
AAY əkuʀ- 'put or get in (continuously)'
CAY əkkuʀ(aʀ)-
NSY —
CSY —
Sir —
SPI ikšuaq- 'put or get into vehicle one after another, load'
NAI ikšuq- 'embark or put into vehicle'
WCI iksuʀaq- 'put in a hole or container'
ECI —
GRI iššuʀaʀ- 'put into container or vehicle, load things onto vehicle'

PE əkləʀviɣ 'pouch or sack' [cf. ðviɣ, also probably 'half-transitivizer' kłiq- under liq-, as in GRI iłłiʀ- under əkə- above?]
AAY —
CAY kəłaʀvik 'pouch, grass basket, sewing box' [and note BB kəłaʀ- 'put away in container']
NSY əkłaʀvik 'hunter's sack'
CSY —
Sir —
SPI Qaw ikłiʀvik 'small container or sack for belongings' [KI ikłuʀik 'sewing kit']
NAI ikłʸiʀvik 'tool bag or box'
WCI Cop ixxiʀvik 'tool bag' [Jen.]
ECI itsivik, NBI ikłiʀvik, SB iktiʀvik, Lab iłłivik 'box, chest'
GRI iłłiʀfik 'chest, coffin'

PI əkənʀužaq or **ikənʀužaq** 'sole of skin stocking' [cf. əkə-[2]?]
SPI —
NAI ikinʀu<ž>aq 'sole of fur socks'

WCI Car ikinʀuyak 'short sock' [B.-S.; Pryde has Car ikinŋuaq 'caribou skin stocking worn next to skin']
ECI ikiʀŋuaq 'inner sock' [of fur or duffle in Iti]
GRI ikiʀnuk 'shoe, sandal' [old word], ikiʀnuaq 'sole of skin stocking' [and ikiʀnuššiʀ- 'provide stocking with a sole']

PI əkəŋŋun or **ikəŋŋun** 'friend (from childhood)' [cf. un and compare qatəŋŋun]
Yup [note CAY kənəɣ(yuɣ)- 'love']
SPI —
NAI —
WCI Net Spence Bay ikiŋŋun 'close friend, buddy' [Pryde]
ECI Lab ik(k)iŋ(ŋ)ut 'childhood friend, that one has grown up with' [Bourq. — Peck has it as 'good or early friend', and Kublu as 'person born on same day as oneself' in Igl]
GRI ikiŋŋut 'friend'

PE əkəʀ 'bay or sound' [cf. əkəʀaʀ- and əkəʀaʀ]
AAY əkəq 'narrows, strait, sound'
CAY Nun əkʀaX
NSY əkəq
CSY —
Sir —
SPI iɣiq, Di əɣəq 'sound'
NAI ikɨq* 'bay, sound'
WCI ikiq Sig 'open sea' [Met.], Car? 'strait' [Schn. 'adg'; and Jen. has Cop ikiaʀaq 'strait']
ECI ikiq 'narrow part of sea ice (in bay?)' [Peck also has 'middle of bay or river' for Lab]
GRI ikiq* 'sound, fjord' [Kl. also has as 'open space to be crossed']

PI əkəqtu- 'be wide' [cf. tu- [1]]
SPI —
NAI ikɨqtu- 'be wide', ikikit- 'be narrow'
WCI ikiqtu- 'be wide (river, etc.)' [Pryde]
ECI ikiqtu- 'be gaping wide (crevasse)', ikikit- 'be narrow (crevasse)'
GRI ikiʀtu- 'be wide to cross (river)'

PI əkəʀacak 'strait'
SPI —
NAI —
WCI Sig, Net, Car ikiʀahak 'strait' [B.-S.; Ras. also for Cop]
ECI ikiʀasaq 'narrow bay', Lab 'strait' [Peck]
GRI ikiʀasak, EG iɣaasaq 'sound'

PY-S əkəʀ(tu)- 'height' [dimensional root; cf. tu-[1] and compare Inu əkəqtu- under əkəʀ, which may ultimately be the same — there seems to be influence from əkəʀaʀ and/or qəʀaʀ- here]
AAY qəXtu- 'be high', qəXkitə-, PWS qəskitə- 'be low' [for qəXsatu- 'have a high voice' see qaʀi]
CAY qəXtu-, NSU quXtu- 'be high (cliffs, hills)', qəXkitə-, NSU quXkitə- 'be low'
NSY əkəXtu- 'be high' [and əkəXqitaʀaʀ- 'be short' — ANLC; Men. has əkəxtu-, also əkəxkita(a)ʀaq 'low']
CSY [aXqəstaaq, aXqəstaaXaaq 'low or shallow thing', aXqəłi- 'lower, become shallow', aXqitaʀaq 'shallow water']
Sir [əXtəvalaX 'high, deep'; Orr also has əXqətaʀaʀ- 'be shallow, low']

PE əkəʀaʀ 'drying rack' [cf. əkəʀ and aʀ and compare əkəʀaʀ- below]
AAY —
CAY qəʀʀaq, NSU kəʀʀaq 'fish rack' [also plural for one]
NSY —
CSY qəʀaq 'meat rack' [and qəʀaʀ- 'put up a rack'; Rub. has qəʀat 'rack for keeping household things']
Sir qəʀaX 'drying frame' [Vakh.]
SPI iɣiʀat (pl.) 'platform cache' [for iɣiʀaaq 'tent floor' see ikiʀ-]
NAI ikiʀʀat 'drying rack for fish, cache platform on posts'
WCI Cop ikaat, Sig ikiʀat 'meat rack' [Ras.; Pryde has Cop ikaaq 'one of two forked pegs on which harpoon rests while hunter waits at breathing hole']
ECI NBI ikaat 'meat platform' [Ras.; Peck has ikaak 'crossbeam' for Lab]
GRI ikaat 'scaffold (of poles)' [sing. ikaaq = 'a vertical prop with a cross-piece to one on the opposite side (e.g. of a window)' in Kl.; note also EG iɣaaři 'collar-bone' and iɣaařit 'crossbeam of sled']

PE əkəʀaʀ- 'cross' [cf. əkəʀ and aʀ-?]
AAY ək<ʀ>aʀ- 'cross'
CAY qəʀaʀ-, HBC qəʀʀaʀ-, Nun, Eg əkʀaʀ-, NSU kəʀʀaʀ-, Y kəʀaʀ-
NSY əkəʀaʀ- 'cross strait to Alaska' [ANLC]
CSY —
Sir —
SPI ikaaq-
NAI ikaaq- 'cross over' [and ikak- 'cross over water']
WCI ikaaq- 'cross over'
ECI ikaaq-
GRI ikaaʀ- 'cross, go on land, go aboard'

PY-S əkəʀlu(-) 'harness' [cf. əkəʀaʀ-?]
AAY —
CAY —
NSY əkəʀlu 'harness' [ANLC; Men. has əqəʀlu]
CSY qaʀlu 'harness' [also verbal; compare qəʀaq under əkəʀaʀ (əkəʀaʀ-), but there may also be influence from qəʀləʀ-]
Sir qəʀlə- 'harness'

PI əkəvʀaq 'support or base' [cf. əkə-[2]]
SPI iɣiʀvaq 'house foundation post', Qaw ikivʀaq 'prop, support'
NAI ikuvʀaq, ikivʀaq 'mattress (lower of two caribou skins), mat, pad'
WCI ikuvʀaq 'base, sort of stool' [and Schn. has 'step ladder, s.th. used to raise something' for Baker Lake]
ECI ikuʀʀaq 'step ladder, s.th. put under something to raise it up'
GRI ikuʀfaq 'underlayer, s.th. put under something to raise it up'

PE əki 'cut (wound)'
AAY —
CAY əkiq 'cut, wound'
NSY iki 'wound' [L.-T.}
CSY kii
Sir —
SPI iɣi 'cut, wound'
NAI iki 'open wound'
WCI ikiq 'wound'
ECI iki 'severe wound'
GRI iki 'wound'

PE əkiliʀ- 'wound' [cf. liʀ-; for CAY, CSY kiliʀ- 'wound, get cut' see kiliʀ- — there is conflation here]
AAY —
CAY —
NSY ikiliʀ- 'wound, injure' [ANLC; ikiliɬəq 'wound' — compare kili 'cut' under killiʀ (kiliʀ-)]
CSY —
Sir —
SPI iɣiliq- 'wound (animal)'
NAI PH ikiliq- 'wound'
WCI Sig ikiliqtit- 'be wounded' [Ras.]
ECI ikiliq- 'wound'
GRI ikiliʀ- 'wound'

PE əkiðaʀ- 'split into layers'
AAY ➟
CAY [for kii- 'peel off, come off as layer' see kaɣa-] ➟
NSY əkiaʀ- 'form layers' [ANLC 'separate or split into layers, delaminate']
CSY kiiXtə- 'split, separate into parts'
Sir kižaʀ- 'cut into half'
SPI iɣiaq- 'split into layers (e.g. skin for boat cover)'
NAI ikiaq- 'split into layers or in half' [for Nu ikiaʀuk- 'feel cold' see ikki]
WCI Sig ikiaq- 'split in slices' [Pet.; also ikiaqtaq 'slice cut off']
ECI ikiaq- 'split down middle', Iti 'sew in the thick part of material without stitching through it' [and note iki- 'cut block of snow']
GRI ikiaʀ- 'split'

PE əkiðaʀ 'layer or space between' [the above used as a a nominal?]
AAY —
CAY əkiaq 'lining, layer'
NSY əkiaq 'layer, s.th. put between things'
CSY kiiq* 'space between' [and kiiʀmik 'middle layer']
Sir kicəʀəni 'inside' [Vakh. also has kicəX 'inside (part)']
SPI [iɣiaq- 'separate into layers']
NAI ikiaq 'extra wide base of sod house, woman's slip' [and ikɨk 'spinal disk' — the ɨ may be spurious]
WCI ikiaq 'middle'
ECI ikiaq 'space between two surfaces, middle' [posit. root; Peck has 'undergarment, bosom, side of hill' for Lab]
GRI ikiaq 'interval, space between surface and bottom (e.g. of sea)', NG also 'underskirt', ikiaqutit, EG iɣiaʀisit, Up ikiat 'underclothes' [and note ikiaʀuuʀ- ' shine through (surface), be distraught' and NG iki 'spinal disk'; Ges. has EG iɣiaq 'waterproof gutskin frock' and Robbe and Menn. iɣiaa 'space between, marrow']

PY kiaʀnəq 'strip of meat or fish' [cf. nəʀ[1]]
AAY C kiaʀnəq* 'unsalted strip of fish flesh cut from backbone and left to dry'
CAY kiaʀnəq* 'unsalted strip of fish flesh cut from backbone and left to dry'
NSY —
CSY —
Inu [note WG ikiaʀniq* 'longitudinal section']

PE əkli- 'lust for'
AAY ikɬi(yuɣ)-, Kod also əkɬi(yuɣ)- 'have a desire aroused'
CAY əkɬi(yuɣ)- 'lust for, be sexually aroused by s.o.'
NSY qili- 'desire (a woman), lust for' [Em.]
CSY kəɬi(yuɣ)- 'lust for'
Sir [note kəɬəʀəqə(s)- 'be interested in']
SPI ikɬizuk- 'flirt', ikɬii- 'flirt with'
NAI ikɬʸiɣusuk- 'be enticed to do s.th.', ikɬʸiɣɨ- 'desire, covet' [cf. əɬi- for the palatalization]
WCI Sig ikɬiɣi- 'desire' [and Ras. has iglinnakmimai 'what a desire one gets for it' for Car]
ECI itsiɣi- 'desire' [Peck has ikɬiɣi- for Lab]
GRI iɬɬiɣi- 'desire, have an appetite for' [Tersis has itsii- for EG in this meaning]

PI əkpak or **ikpak** 'trouser flap' [cf. əkə-[2]?, and vaɣ and əkvi(C)aʀ]
SPI —
NAI ikpak 'part of trousers in front above belt'
WCI Cop ikpak 'upper front part of trousers' [Pryde; Ras. has ikpaku 'discarded trouser band' and ikpakkuhak 'trouser band']
ECI —
GRI ippak 'trouser flap'

PI əkpan or **ikpan** 'lamp platform' [cf. əkə-[2], vaɣ and un?]
SPI —
NAI —
WCI Cop ikpan 'table (esp. before wife inside the traditional house)' [Met.], Car, Net ikpat 'lamp platform, side platform' [B.-S.]
ECI —
GRI ippat 'lamp table, lamp or side platform in house'

PI əkuq- or **ikuq-** 'go inland to hunt'
SPI —
NAI —
WCI —
ECI ikuq- 'go inland to hunt and fish (the boats being towed upstream by dog sledge)' [and Peck has ikkordlek 'a pond through which reindeer swim across to the other side', and ikkor- 'set out in the summer to

hunt reindeer at such a pond']
GRI Maniitsoq ikuʀ- 'go inland to camp and hunt reindeer' [and Fab. has ikkok 'reindeer hunting (place) up in mountains']

PE əkvi(C)aʀ 'small bag made of skin' [cf. əkə-[2] and ðviɣ and aʀ, also əkpak?; Inu forms have p.b. yuɣ, ðuɣ]
AAY Kod, PWS əkxʷik 'carrying bag' [Fisher has K əkxʷiutat 'woman's sewing bag, man's hunting bag'; B.-S. has C ipigiakun 'tool bag']
CAY —
NSY əkfiqužaq [L.-T.]
CSY [note aqəftaʀaaq* 'bag']
Sir —
SPI ikpiaʀžuk 'duffle bag made of whole sealskin'
NAI ikpiaʀžuk 'small sack for belongings, sewing kit, handbag, jellyfish'
WCI ikpiaʀyuk Sig 'travel bag' [for Cop Met. has 'bag, esp. for tools for repairing bow and arrows'; Pet has ikpiaʀiaq 'pocket' for Sig; note Car? ikpiaq 'baggy part of knee of britches for women' — Schn. 'adg']
ECI ippiayuk 'pocket, kind of bag' [Ras. has 'sewing bag' for Igl]
GRI ippiaʀšuk 'skin bag, sewing bag, jellyfish'

PE əkviɣ '(river) bank' [cf. əkə-[2], and ðviɣ, also əkvi(C)aʀ?]
AAY KP əkxʷik 'cleared-off place for putting baidarka in water'
CAY əkfik 'river bank'
NSY —
CSY —
Sir —
SPI Qaw ikpik 'high river bank, steep place'
NAI ikpik 'river bank, cliff'
WCI Cop ikpik
ECI ippik 'sand dune', ippiɣaq 'steep slope on mountain or rock'
GRI ippik 'cliff'

PE əlaɣ- 'dig' [cf. Aleut la- 'pick, gather, catch, beat (enemy)', Atkan laɣu- 'pick, gather']
AAY laaɣ- 'dig'
CAY əlaɣ-, laaɣ-
NSY əlaɣ- [L.-T.]
CSY laaɣ-
Sir [note laɣlaɣuta- 'tease, torment, rob']
SPI [Jen. has ilak- 'dig' for 'Nome dialect']
NAI ɨlaaq- 'scoop out ice chunks from hole' [and note ɨlak- 'shove aside', ɨlakɬuɣi- 'shove, throw around and leave in a mess']
WCI ilauq- 'use ice scoop'
ECI ➟
GRI ilaʀ- 'remove ice chunks blocking hole in ice'

PY əlaɣayuli 'small bird like a sparrow' [cf. yu-]
AAY AP laaɣayuli 'bird similar to fox sparrow'
CAY əlaɣayuli 'fox sparrow, robin, spotted sandpiper, hermit thrush'
NSY —
CSY —

PY əlaɣɣaq 'pit' [cf. yaʀ]
AAY AP laɣɣaq 'deep hole'
CAY əlaɣɣaq 'partially underground cache, pit for cleaning fish, smoke house'
NSY —
CSY —

PY əlakaq 'hole' [cf. kaʀ]
AAY laakaq 'pit, hole made by digging'
CAY əlakaq 'water hole'
NSY əlakaq 'hole in ice' [ANLC]
CSY laakaq 'hole'

PI əlaun 'ice scoop' [cf. un]
SPI —
NAI ɨlaun 'ice scoop'
WCI ilaut 'shovel for removing ice from water hole'
ECI Igl ilaut 'ice scoop' [B.-S.]
GRI ilaat, NG ilaiyaut 'ice scoop'

PY-S əlaliʀ- 'visit'
AAY —
CAY əlaliXtə- 'visit (within village)'
NSY —
CSY laaliXtə- 'visit'
Sir laliʀ-, laləʀ- 'land (bird)' [Vakh.]

PY əlaʀa- 'be dissatisfied'
AAY AP laa<ʀ>a-, Perry laa'a- 'be dissatisfied, complain that one hasn't been given enough'
CAY əlaʀa- 'be dissatisfied, complain, want more'
NSY əlaʀniɬəq 'offense, grievance' [Em.; ANLC əlaʀniiʀʷ- 'take offense']
CSY —

PY əlavə- 'crouch' [there may be a link to əlaɣ-]
AAY AP lauɣ- 'crouch'
CAY əlavə-, lavə-
NSY —
CSY —

PE ələɣ- 'get burnt' [cf. Aleut ilɣ- 'smell, stench']
AAY ləxtə- 'get scorched, burn, char'
CAY ləɣ-, Nun ləxtə-, HBC ləɣə-
NSY ələk 'fire, conflagration' [L.-T. has ələxtə; ANLC also ələxtə- 'burn (trans.)']
CSY —
Sir —
SPI ilik- 'get scorched, burnt'
NAI ɨlik-
WCI ilik-
ECI Lab i(i)likaq- 'roast (in pan), burn self (in fire)' [Bourq.]
GRI iliɣ- 'be burnt, singed' [iliŋa- 'be curly']

PY əlɣaʀ- 'settle or be settled' [there may be a link to ət-]
AAY K əlɣaXtə-, KP əllaXtə- 'put in order, get settled'
CAY əlɣaʀ- 'be settled', əlɣaXte- 'settle' [postural root; also əɬkaXtə-, HBC ŋəɬkaXtə- 'set, settle on, settle down'; for BB ilɣaʀ- 'go home' see aŋilʀaʀ- under aŋit-]

NSY —
CSY — [for aɣlaʀ- 'go home' see aŋilʀaʀ- under aŋit-]

PI əliciit- 'practice sorcery' [cf. əlit-, with the same strong i in the NAI reflex, also əlitquciq under it — the meaning here probably refers to soul-robbing or to leaving one's body to attack others (Rink)]
SPI [ilisiiq- 'put a curse on'; ilisiit- 'be slow to learn' is from əlit-]
NAI ilʸisiilʸak 'sorcerer' [and ilʸisiiyaq- 'put a curse on']
WCI Net, Car ilihiinniq 'witchcraft' [Ras.; B.-S. has Car ilisiiʀut 'charm']
ECI Lab ilisiit- 'practice witchcraft' [Peck — Ras. also has for Igl]
GRI ilisiit- 'practice sorcery' [ilisiitsuq 'sorcerer'; NG ilihaiq- 'bewitch', ilihaitsuq 'witch' — Holt.]

PI əliktəq- 'cut to a pattern' [cf. əliʀqə- and p.b. təʀ-; there may be a relat. to əlit-; initial ə realized as i rather than ɨ before li in Inu as shown by palatalization in NAI.]
SPI iliktiq- 'cut to pattern'
NAI ilʸiktɨq-
WCI iliktiq-
ECI ilitti(q)-
GRI ilissiʀ- 'cut to pattern', NG ilixxiʀut(i)- 'show how to do, cut to pattern'

PE əlima- 'suspect' [cf. əlit- and p.b. (u)ma-; compare əliktəq- for the initial ə realized as i rather than ɨ in Inu]
AAY —
CAY əlima- 'be knowledgeable'
NSY —
CSY —
Sir [for simaqəɫəXpiɣaX 'well-known' see əlicima- under əlit-]
SPI ilima(zuk)- 'be suspicious, suspect'
NAI ilʸima(suk)- 'be apprehensive', ilʸimaɣɨ- 'suspect' [emot. root]
WCI —
ECI ilima(suk)- 'be apprehensive, on the look out'
GRI ilimasuɣ- 'expect s.th.', ilimaɣi- 'expect', NG ilumahuk-, ilumaɣi- 'expect, dread (s.th. bad)'

PE əlimmaʀ- or **əlummaʀ-** 'fly through air (shaman)' [cf. əlit- and (u)maʀ(aʀ)-?]
AAY —
CAY əlumaʀ- 'fly through air (shaman)'
NSY ilumaʀ- 'fly (of person)'
CSY —
Sir —
SPI ilimaq- ' fly through air (shaman)'
NAI ilʸimmaq- 'metamorphose, make a voyage through air or ocean (shaman)'
WCI Net ilimmaqtuq- 'make voyage through air (shaman)' [Ras. and Pryde]
ECI —
GRI ilimmaʀ-

PE əliʀa- and **əliŋʀa-** 'want to ask for s.th. but not dare?'
AAY liŋŋa- 'be reverent, show respect'
CAY əliŋʀa(yuɣ)- 'be grateful' [but note also iliiʀa- 'ask to have s.th.']
NSY —
CSY liŋʀa(yuɣ)- 'hesitate to ask (again)'
Sir —
SPI iliʀanamik 'thank you!'
NAI ilʸiʀa(suk)- 'be grateful, happy' [emot. root]
WCI Sig iliʀa(suk)- 'be happy, grateful', iliʀa(huk)- Cop 'want to ask for s.th. but not dare', Net 'be afraid' [also 'respect with overtones of fear (of being unkindly treated)' — Briggs; Cop iliʀanaq- 'cause fear (person)', iliʀaŋŋuq- 'become full of depressing thoughts' — Ras.]
ECI iliʀa(suk)- 'fear (embarrassment, criticism,etc.)', Aiv 'be ill at ease' [emot. root]
GRI iliʀasuɣ- 'have a bad conscience', iliʀanaʀ- 'be difficult to approach, be threatening, be taboo' [and iliʀaɣi- 'take care nothing happens to (s.th. belonging to another)', -niq iliʀaɣi- 'not dare -']

PE əliʀqə- 'cut out a pattern' [cf. əliktəq- and p.b. ʀqə-?]
AAY K liXqə-, Kod ciliXqə-, PWS sɫiXqə- 'cut a piece out of (according to pattern for making garment)' [the second form by contam. with ciləɣ-[1] or cili-?]
CAY əliXqə- 'cut out a pattern'
NSY iləXqə- [ANLC]
CSY liiXqə- 'cut out a pattern' [and liiqŋ̥əq* 'remnant of material']
Sir —
SPI iliqniku 'remnants' [and note Qaw iliqun 'sewing pattern']
NAI ilʸiʀnɨq*, ilʸiʀnɨku 'remnants (of material)'
WCI —
ECI iliʀniku 'remnants (esp. of material)' [and note iliq- 'cover with several covers, etc.']
GRI iliʀniku(q) 'piece of cut-off material'

PE əlit- 'learn' [cf. əlima- and compare also əɫi- for the initial vowel change in Inuit]
AAY liitə- 'learn, get used to'
CAY əlitə-, liitə- 'learn, get used to, recognize'
NSY ilitə- 'learn' [ANLC; Enm. et al. have iliɣutə- 'get to know, learn' — Men. iliyutə-, from *əlitðutə-?]
CSY liitə- 'learn'
Sir [Orr has is(tə)- 'learn'; note also siqəXtəʀ- 'recall, bring to awareness' and compare si- under əɫi-]
SPI ilit- 'learn', Qaw ilisuksaq- 'study, learn'
NAI ilʸit- 'learn'
WCI ➡
ECI ilit- 'learn, have learned' [and ilinnia(q)- 'strive to learn']
GRI ilikkaʀ- 'have learned', ilinniaʀ- 'study'

PE əlicaʀ- 'learn or teach' [cf. caʀ-]
AAY —
CAY Y, NI, HBC əlicaʀ- 'study, teach'
NSY ilisaʀ- 'study' [ANLC 'teach, learn a song']
CSY liisaʀ- 'teach, practice'
Sir —
SPI Imaq ilisaq-, KI ilisauti- 'teach'
NAI ilʸisaq- 'study, practice'

WCI ilisaq- 'learn, study'
ECI ilisaq- 'learn, teach'
GRI —

PE əliccuqə- or **əlityuqə-** 'become aware of' [cf. kə-[1], but also yukə-, with variant yuRə- in Inu]
AAY —
CAY —
NSY ilisuqə- 'recognize, discern'
CSY —
Sir —
SPI —
NAI ɨlʸitcuRɨ- 'become aware of, become acquainted with'
WCI ilitsuRi- 'know (s.th. specific)' [Lowe has 'become aware of, learn' for Sig]
ECI —
GRI ilitsuRi- 'become aware or conscious, remember s.th. from earliest childhood (refl.)'

PE əlicima- 'know' [cf. (u)ma-]
AAY —
CAY əlicima- 'know'
NSY ilisimakə- 'understand, know', ilisima- 'be knowledgeable' [the latter ANLC]
CSY liisimakə- 'know'
Sir əsəmə- 'know how to do s.th.' [əsəmələRəX '(one who is) sober', əsəməkax 'knowledgeable about s.th.', əsəməłəXpiɣaX 'educated', əsəmənəX 'right hand' and siməqałəXpiɣaX 'well known'; Vakh. has əsəməkə- 'know' and Em. has (ə)səməkə(s)- 'be conscious']
SPI ilisima- 'know' [also Imaq]
NAI ilʸisima-, Nu ilisima-
WCI ilisima-
ECI ilitsima- [Saul]
GRI ilisima-, EG iisima- 'know' [NG has ilihama- 'wait for s.o.'s arrival', influenced by əlima-?]

PY əliɣaRtə- 'get used to' [cf. aR-?]
AAY lii<y>aXtə-, liiɣuutə-, lii<y>utə- 'get used to' [compare liitə- under əlit- above for the last form]
CAY əliɣaXtə- 'get used to, learn quickly'
NSY —
CSY [note liiɣikə- 'recognize, sense, understand']
Sir [note liɣikə(s)- 'feel, notice' (from the CSY?), liɣikənəqə(s)- 'repeat']

PE əlitaqə- 'recognize' [cf. ðaR and kə-[1]]
AAY liitaqə- 'recognize'
CAY əlitaqə-
NSY —
CSY —
Sir iłtəqə(s)- 'recognize', iłtəqši- 'get to know'
SPI ilitai-, Qaw ilitaRi-, Imaq ilitaə- 'recognize'
NAI ilʸisaRɨ-
WCI ilitaRi-
ECI ilitaRi-
GRI ilisaRi-

PY əlitna(C)uR- 'study or teach' [cf. na(C)uR-]
AAY litn̥auR- 'study, practice, teach'
CAY əlitn̥auR-
NSY —
CSY —

PI əlitquciq 'way of being or doing' [cf. uciR]
SPI ilitqusiq 'habit, way of doing s.th.'
NAI ilʸitqun 'spirit, essence', ilʸitqusiq 'soul' [Pryde has 'soul of deceased person']
WCI ilitqusiq 'soul' [in Cop and Net 'habit, custom', acc. Pryde]
ECI NBI iliqqusiq 'habit, custom'
GRI iliqquq

PY əlivtə- 'flatten'
AAY AP lixʷte-, Kod liuxtə- 'flatten down, smash out'
CAY əliftə-, liftə- 'flatten a standing object'
NSY —
CSY —

PE əlpəkə- 'feel or sense' [the relat. — if any — to ikviɣ- is obscure — conflation in Inu?; co]mpare the cons. cluster of the Inu forms under alpaɣ-]
AAY əłpəɣ(yuɣ)- 'have a feeling, sensation or premonition'
CAY əłpəkə- 'sense, feel' [and əłpəŋə- 'acquire sensation, come to one's senses', əłpəɣitə- 'be numb, insensitive']
NSY əłpəkə- 'feel, sense' [ANLC]
CSY əłpəkə- 'become aware of'
Sir əłpəkə- [Orr]
SPI Qaw ikpii- 'feel sensation' [for homonym 'have one's sleep disturbed by' see ikviɣ-]
NAI ikpiɣɨ 'feel slight pain or discomfort from'
WCI Net Sp. Bay ikpiɣi- 'feel (e.g. breeze or pain)' [Pryde]
ECI Lab ippiɣi- 'be aware (of)' [Andersen et al.]
GRI NG ikpii- 'feel (a sensation)'

PE əlpət or **əłvət** 'you' [cf. ət- and 2s rel. inflection vət, (after C) pət and Atkan Aleut imis, EA imin 'to or for you' — an indep. relative construction like 4s əłmi; compare also əł(ə)ŋa]
AAY əłpət 'you' [pl. əłpəci]
CAY əłpət 'you' [pl. əłpəci, du. əłpətək]
NSY əłpək 'you' [pl. əłpəsi]
CSY əłpək 'you' [pl. əłpəsi]
Sir əłpi 'you' [Orr — Men. has łpi; pl. əłpəsi]
SPI ivlin, W, Qaw ilvin 'you' [pl. ilipsi]
NAI ɨlvic, ɨlivic, ɨlvinʸ 'you' [pl. ɨlifsi, du. ɨlɨptɨk, ɨlifsɨk]
WCI ilvit, Net ilvit, ižvit, Car iɣvit, ilvit 'you' [B.-S. has idwin for Car and itvin for Net, for which Ras. has isfit; Briggs ipžit for Utk; pl. ilipsi, Cop iliffi]
ECI ivvit, Cape Dorset iɣvit 'you' [pl. ilitsi]
GRI iłłit [old ortho. ivdlit] 'you' [pl. ilissi]

PI əlquaRnəq 'smelt'
Yup [NSU əłquaRniq 'boreal smelt' is probably a loan from Inu, but cf. also CAY əłquaq* 'herring eggs or roe' under qəlquðaR and CSY luXtuRaq under iłuuq; cf. also NSY əłquašak 'smelt' (L.-T.)]

SPI iłXuaʀniq 'smelt'
NAI iłXuaʀniq*
WCI —
ECI —
GRI —

PE əlquʀ- 'hit the mark' [cf. əłuʀaʀ-, also ətlu(ʀ)- and ultimately ət- 'be']
AAY —
CAY —
NSY əłquXtə- 'guess, conclude', [Men. also has əłqunʀaaqʷ 'correct, successful']
CSY əłquʀaXtə- 'hit mark, get right', əłquʀutə- 'do s.th. right'
Sir [Orr has əfqaʀaXtə- 'hit mark' which may not be a cognate — Vakh. has it as 'catch' from Rub.'s texts; Em. has əfkaʀ-]
SPI —
NAI itquq- 'sit on eggs in nest' [perhaps influenced by ətəʀ]
WCI itquq- 'guess, hit mark, sit on eggs' [and Schn. has itquqtumik 'the truth' for Baker Lake in conjunction with uqaq- 'say']
ECI iqquq- 'hit target, alight on nest'
GRI iqquʀ- 'hit, strike home' [and note iqqumiit- 'be strange']

PE əlʀaviɣ 'internal organs'
AAY —
CAY Nun əlʀavix lung'
NSY əlʀavit 'internal organs, guts' [ANLC əlʀavik]
CSY —
Sir —
SPI iʀlawik 'intestine', Qaw ilʀawik also 'umbilical cord'
NAI ilʀaviic 'guts'
WCI Cop ilʀaviit [Ras.]
ECI iʀʀaviit
GRI iʀłaviit 'bowels', EG iʀtivik, iʀtiviq 'lung'

PE əltuʀ 'grandchild or grandfather?' [compare iluliʀaʀ under ilu for the same word being used for grandchild and grandfather]
AAY Kodiak, PWS əłtu<ʀ>aq, AP əłtuʀaq, KP əłtuaq 'grandchild'
CAY Nun əłtuʀaX
NSY əłtuʀaq
CSY əłtuʀaq
Sir əłtəX
SPI — [but note ittuu- 'be big']
NAI —
WCI Net ittuq 'grandfather' [Ras., who also has Car iktulukatnaq 'the elder'; Dor. has B. Lake, Net iktuq 'grandfather']
ECI ittuq [Schn. writes 'iktuq'] 'old man', NBI, SB 'grandfather', Lab 'elder in the house' [Peck]
GRI ittuq 'oldest man in household', SWG ittu, EG ittiɣa(y)ik 'grandfather' [Robbe and Menn. for the latter; and NG ittuluk 'old man']

PE əlu(ʀ)- 'all or whole' [perhaps ultimately from ət- 'be' — cf. also əluʀ-, but there are different postbases involved in the various forms, all of which act as 'quantifier/qualifier' roots with rel. person inflections; *əluʀunnaʀ- seems to underlie most forms here]
AAY — [for luuciʀ- 'whole, all' see əluciʀ under ət-; there may be contam. here]
CAY — [for əluciq 'shape, form' under ət-]
NSY [iiʀʷiʀ- 'become whole' (ANLC); Men. has iiɣʷilŋuq — for iiʀʷilŋuq? — also iʀunaq 'whole' (with stress marked on first vowel)]
CSY [iiʀʷiʀ- 'become whole' and iiʀʷitə- 'be whole', also iiŋunaʀ- 'whole, all']
Sir əcəʀunaʀməlŋuX 'all, whole' [Vakh.; Men. has icəʀunaʀməlŋuX; and Em. has itəʀunaʀmi 'completely']
SPI Qaw iluqna(q)-, Imaq əluqna- 'all of' [Jen. has W iluqa(q)-]
NAI iluqa(q)- 'all of'
WCI Sig iluqa(q)-
ECI iluunna-
GRI iluuŋŋaʀ-

PI əlun or **ilun** 'coeval' [cf. ət- and un?]
SPI —
NAI —
WCI —
ECI iluti 's.o. born the same day (Iti the same year?) as one'
GRI ilut 's.o. the same age as one, s.th. from the same time as'

PE əluʀ- 'width' [there may be a relat. to əlu(ʀ)-]
AAY luXtu- 'be wide', luXkitə- 'be narrow' [and luʀiXtə- 'bow one's legs']
CAY əluXtu- 'be wide (garment)', əluXkitə- 'be narrow'
NSY —
CSY [luuʀək (dual) 'line where there is water by shore ice']
Sir luXtəvalaX 'thick (round object)' [Orr; Vakh. has luXtutə(pəyəX) 'fat' and ləʀ(a) '(its) edge' from Men.'s texts]
SPI —
NAI —
WCI iluqtu- 'be wide (e.g. plank)', ilukit- 'be narrow'
ECI Lab ilutu- 'have large capacity', ilukit- 'have small capacity' [Andersen et al.]
GRI —

PE əłi- 'put or act a certain way' [in respective trans. and intrans./reflex. use; pre-Esk. *ətli- from ət- 'be' and p.b. li-^{2}; cf. Aleut li- 'appear', liiða- 'resemble, seem'; note the same development as regards the first vowel in NAI ilʸi- as in əlit-]
AAY łii- 'put, place'
CAY əłi-
NSY łi-
CSY łi- 'put, place' [also łimtaaq 's.th. stored away for the future']
Sir si- 'place' [but Vakh. has łi-; note also siʀcəʀ- 'bury, hide' and simaɣəta 'receptacle' but also łimtaX 'supply, store' from CSY?]

SPI ili- 'put, place, come to resemble, reach a point partway to destination' [also Imaq]
NAI ilʸi-, Nu ili- 'become, make become, put, place, reach a point, come into sight or mind' [in the 'become' sense with a nominal in the aequalis case; half-trans. ilʸiži-]
WCI ili- 'put, place' [and iliuq- 'put several']
ECI ili- 'put, place, store away, behave (thus)', iliuq- 'behave like' [in the 'behave' sense an aequalis case nominal is required; half-trans. ilisi-]
GRI ili- 'behave, treat, become, act, put, bury', iliuʀ- 'do, deal with' [in all except the 'put' senses these require a nominal in the aequalis case or an equivalent adverbial; half-trans. ilisi-]

PY əłiʀ- 'become a certain way' [cf. the ʀ under ŋ(ŋ)uʀ-]
AAY łiʀ- 'get to be thus'
CAY əłiʀ- 'reach a certain point, become a certain way'
NSY łiʀ-
CSY łiiʀ- 'become a certain way'
Sir [for aləʀ-, ałəʀ-, aliʀ- 'become thus, appear, remain' see allaʀ(iʀ)-]

PE əłivəʀ 'grave'
AAY —
CAY Nun əłivəX*, K əlivəq*, Y əlivnəq* 'grave marker, possession of deceased put in grave'
NSY [łiftaq, łimaaq 'possession of deceased left at grave' — ANLC]
CSY łivəq* 'grave'
Sir łivəX [Orr]
SPI [Jen. has W iluvaaq 'grave']
NAI ilʸuvɨq* 'grave, corpse' [influenced by ilu 'interior'; also verbal = 'bury']
WCI iluviq 'grave' [verbal = 'bury']
ECI iluviq 'grave' [verbal = 'bury']
GRI SWG iliviq*, NWG iluiq 'grave' [pl. iliʀfit and iluXXit respectively; iliviʀ- 'bury']

PE əł(ł)iviɣ 'storage place' [cf. ðviɣ]
AAY łiiwik, łiiwiɣuaq, łiiɣʷiutaq 'shelf, storage place'
CAY əłivik K 'elevated cache', NI 'underground cache'
NSY łivik 'place for keeping things' [łivilʀužaq 'shelf']
CSY łivəlʀak 'shelf'
Sir sivəlʀaX 'shelf' [but Vakh. has łivəlʀaX from Men.'s texts]
SPI ilivik 'storage place', Qaw, W illiwik 'shelf, cabinet'
NAI ilʸlʸivik 'chest of drawers, place for storing things'
WCI illiviaq 'plate'
ECI ilivvik 'usual place for storing s.th.' [for Lab iłłivik 'box' see əkləʀvik under əkə-[2]]
GRI NG illivi(ɣ)aq 'box'

PE əłiɣaʀ(aʀ) 'orphan' [there may be a link to əłi-]
AAY KP, K łiiya<ʀ>aq, PWS łii<ʀ>aq 'orphan'
CAY əłiʀaq* 'orphan'
NSY łiʀaq 'poor person'
CSY —
Sir —
SPI iliaʀžuk 'orphan, poor person' [also Imaq; iliapak 'poor outcast, orphan' and iliɣaaʀžuk 'boy']
NAI ilʸiaʀžuk, ilʸiappak 'orphan, poor person' [also ilʸilʸɣa<ʀ>aq 'child']
WCI Cop iliaʀyuk, Sig iliappak, Net iliaqpaluk 'orphan' [also iliŋa- 'be poor', iliaʀuq-, iliŋak- 'become poor']
ECI iliaʀyuk 'orphan, someone one pays no attention to'
GRI iliaršuk 'orphan'

PE əłm̥aʀ(aʀ) 'a little' [cf. ət- and (u)maʀ(aʀ)-?]
AAY əłm̥aa'aq 'a little'
CAY əłm̥aaʀ
NSY əłm̥a(a)ʀaq 'quietly'
CSY əłm̥aaʀaXaq* 'a little bit more'
Sir [note iłəma 'indeed, perhaps', iłəmaqun 'as if' — Vakh. has łəma 'as if']
SPI —
NAI —
WCI — [but note Net iŋma 'expression emphasizing the foregoing' acc. Ras.]
ECI —
GRI imma(ŋŋuaq) 'a little' [old ortho. ingma; NG iŋmaaXXaaq- 'go gently, whisper', EG immaivattit 'a few, a little' (Robbe and Menn.)]

PE əłmi- 'himself or herself' [reflexive pron. corresponding to 3rd person əł(ə)ŋa; cf. Atkan Aleut i(ɣ)im, EA iɣiim 'to himself']
AAY əłm̥i- 'himself, herself'
CAY əłm̥i-
NSY əłm̥i-
CSY əłm̥i-
Sir (ə)łm̥inəŋ 'oneself' [Vakh. has łm̥ə-]
SPI iŋmi-, W, Qaw inmi- 'himself, herself'
NAI ɨnmi-, ilimi-
WCI iŋmi- [Pryde inmi- for Cop]
ECI immi- 'himself, herself' [and imminiiq- 'act on one's own initiative']
GRI immi- [old ortho. ingmi-] 'himself, herself' [and imminiiʀ- 'act on one's own initiative', immikkuuʀ- 'be separate']

PE əł(ə)ŋa 'he or she' [cf. ət- and p.b. łəʀ[1]?; same root as with əłmi and əlpət, etc. but 3rd p. ; cf. Aleut ŋaan 'to him, her', from *əlŋa-ni]
AAY əłiin 'he, she'
CAY əłii
NSY əłŋa
CSY əłŋa 'he, she' [and note łaŋaqa 'it looks or sounds as if']
Sir laŋa 'he, she'
SPI ilaa, Imaq əlaa
NAI ɨlaa 'he, she' [also 'just like' (= Mal enclitic liilaa) — the relat. to ila[2] is obscure]
WCI —
ECI —
GRI —

PY əłŋaʀ- 'leak (liquid)' [compare PI inʀaq-]
AAY əłŋaʀ- 'leak (liquid)'
CAY əłŋaʀ- 'leak (liquid), drip'
NSY əłŋaʀ- 'leak out, drip, spurt out' [ANLC; Men. has əłŋaan 'dirty oil from lamp']
CSY əłŋaʀ- 'leak out (liquid)' [and əłŋaan 'greasy residue from blubber lamp']
Sir [Orr has əłŋəʀ- 'leak out (liquid)' probably borrowed from CSY]
Inu [note ECI Tar iŋŋaniq 'small amount of liquid that remains in the bottom of a container' — Saul]

PE əłuʀaʀ- 'be correct or right' [cf. əlquʀ- and ultimately ət- and l(l)u(C)aʀ-]
AAY əłuaʀ- 'be in order, settled, at peace' [əłuaXtə- 'put in order']
CAY əłuaʀ- 'be correct, perfect' [əłuaXtə- 'correct, fix, make perfect']
NSY əłuaʀaʀ- 'be true' [ANLC]
CSY —
Sir əłəʀaʀən 'truly'
SPI iluaq- 'be right, correct, generous'
NAI iłuaq- [or iluaq-] 'be right' [and iłuamik, iluamik 'properly, correctly']
WCI Sig iluaq-, Cop ihuaq-, Net iłuaq- 'be correct' [Lowe for the first two, Ras. for the last one]
ECI isuaq- 'be useful, practical', NBI iłuaq- 'be suitable, comfortable', Lab iłuaC- 'be comfortable'
GRI iluaʀ- 'be right, honest, holy' [and iluaat- 'not be right', iluanaaʀ- 'be lucky', iluamik 'properly' and iluʀfak, NWG iluXXaq 'right side (of kayak)'; Tersis EG itiwaʀ- 'be correct, perfect', itiwati- 'be valuable']

PI əłuaqci- 'improve' [cf. ci- under li-[2]]
SPI iluaqsi- 'improve'
NAI iłuaqsi- 'get well, fix'
WCI Cop ihuaXXi- 'correct' [Lowe]
ECI isuaʀsi- 'have improved'
GRI iluaʀsi- 'have got better, put straight'

PE əłuʀaqə- or **əłuʀakə-** 'approve of' [cf. kə-[1]]
AAY —
CAY əłuakə- 'approve of'
NSY —
CSY —
Sir —
SPI —
NAI iłuaʀi- 'consider all right, be a good fit'
WCI Cop ihuaʀi-, Net, Car iłuaʀi- 'consider correct, suitable' [Pryde; Met. has Sig isuaʀiŋit- — for iłuaʀiŋit-? — 'not be pleased with']
ECI isuaʀi- 'be pleased with, find useful'
GRI iluaʀi- 'like, approve of'

PI əłuʀit- 'be bad' [cf. ŋit-]
SPI iluit- 'be beyond help, beyond one's control'
NAI iłuit- [or iluit-] 'not be right'
WCI Cop ihuit- 'be bad' [Ras.]
ECI isuit-
GRI — [compare iluaat- under əłuʀaʀ- above]

PI əłuʀʀi- 'put in order or be content' [cf. li-[1]?]
SPI —
NAI —
WCI Sig iluʀʀi- 'correct' [Lowe]
ECI isuʀʀi- 'feel at ease'
GRI iluXXit- 'recover, be content, put in order', iluXXišaaʀ- 'feel at ease, be content'

PY əma 'grandmother' [cf. ama(C)uʀ]
AAY əma, əmaaq 'grandmother'
CAY mauʀluq, maXłuɣaq
NSY əma 'grandmother' [əmaXpak 'great grandmother' Orr and L.-T.]
CSY —
Inu — [but note Net, Cop amaama 'mother']

PE əmə 'voice' [cf. napə and əməɣ-]
AAY əmtu-, AP mixtu- 'be loud' [the latter form influenced by əməɣ-?]
CAY [əmaitə- 'be silent', and mixtu- 'be loud' — influenced by əmə-?; opp. = mixkitə-]
NSY [əmŋitə-, əməłkiŋʀa- 'be silent' (ANLC); and L.-T. has əməmialuk 'unclear speech']
CSY ma 'voice' [base mə]
Sir əmə 'voice, noise' [from Em.'s files; Vakh. has əməməX from Rub.'s texts, also əmyəɣaʀ- 'speak' from Rub.'s texts — Em. has umyəʀaʀ- 'talk', and umiyəɣaʀəta 'talk, conversation, request', perhaps influenced by umyuɣžaq]
SPI Imaq əmait- 'be silent'
NAI ➟
WCI —
ECI —
GRI —

PE əməŋiʀ- 'become silent' [cf. ŋiʀ-]
AAY əmiiʀ- 'quiet down'
CAY əmaiʀ-
NSY —
CSY —
Sir —
SPI —
NAI imaŋiq- 'become silent'
WCI —
ECI —
GRI imaŋiʀ-

PE əməɣ- or **əmiɣ-** 'make a resonant or loud sound' [cf. əmə, also Aleut imat- 'shout, cry out', though there is a problem with the vowels]
AAY miɣ-, KP miɣyaʀ- 'make a racket' [also məxłuk 'buzzing, roaring', and PWS əmŋaXtə- 'echo, resound']
CAY mixpak 'sudden noise'
NSY imixtə- 'resonate' [ANLC]
CSY miik 'loud noise' [for ma 'voice' see əmə]
Sir əməɣcəkəɣləʀəX 'resonant' [Vakh. has əməɣca 'sound'; for əmə(məX) 'voice' see əmə]
SPI imik- 'resound'
NAI imik-, imik- 'resound, reverberate'

WCI imik- 'be resonant' [and imikpaluk- 'make a loud noise crashing down', and Car imiɣlutaq 'bull-roarer' — B.-S.; Ow. has imiɣluktaq]
ECI imia- 'resound'
GRI imiɣ- 'reverberate'

PE əməŋə(ʀ)- 'sing or hum'
AAY məŋə- 'hum a song'
CAY məŋə- 'sing first stanza of song with drumming prior to dance'
NSY —
CSY məŋ^{w}aak 'moan, groan', Chap məŋʀa(a)luk 'babble'
Sir əməŋəɬqutaʀ- 'babble' [Em. has məŋʀəluxtaX 'noise, sound of voices']
SPI Qaw imŋaaluk- 'hum'
NAI imŋaluk- 'hum, whine, mumble'
WCI Car EP imŋiq- 'sing', Cop imʀiuq-, Sig iminʀiuq- 'hum' [Met. has Cop imnaluk- 'sing softly to baby, murmur'; Pryde has Car, Net imŋiq- 'sing to accompoany song dance', but also Sp. Bay and Holman Island iŋiuq- 'sing a song' — in B. Lake 'sing a chorus or refrain']
ECI Lab imŋiq- 'sing' [Peck; Ras. has Igl ivnger- and Schn. has iŋŋiluttaarut 'song' for Tar; Saul has iŋŋiq- 'sing' for Tar]
GRI iŋŋiʀ-, SWG immiʀ- 'sing (esp. a traditional satyrical song)', NG iŋmiq-, EG iŋŋiʀ- 'sing to drum dance' [Egede has ivnger- for WG; there may be contam. with iŋəq-; note also iŋŋaaluɣ- 'clear one's throat']

PY-S məŋquq 'loud noise' [cf. əməŋə(ʀ)- above; there may be contam. with mapkuq- here]
AAY K məŋquq 'banging, clicking or whirring noise' [also verbal məŋquXtə-]
CAY məŋquXpak 'loud noise' [and cf. Nun məŋquX 'Japanese spherical glass fishnet float (that pops)'; NI məŋkuk 'labret' is probably not related]
NSY —
CSY məŋquq 'popping sound' [also 'goose bump, feather stem on birdskin' — a different base, going with NI məŋkuk above?]
Sir məŋqələXca 'loud noise' [and Vakh. has məŋqəɬaɣət(ə)- 'crackle, crack, rattle']

PE əməʀ(-) 'fresh water' [and as verb 'drink', trans. and intrans.; cf. Aleut maqða- 'suck breast or milk', with a p.b. qða-?]
AAY əməq* '(fresh) water' [verbally əməʀ- = 'drink']
CAY <ə>məq (and məʀʀa 'its water'), Nun əməX '(fresh) water' (and əmʀa 'its water') [<ə>məʀ-, Nun əməʀ- 'drink']
NSY əməq 'water' [əməʀ- 'drink']
CSY məq* '(fresh) water' [məʀ- 'drink']
Sir məX '(fresh) water' [Krup. has əməX; məʀ- 'drink' — Vakh.]
SPI imiq '(fresh) water' [verbal = 'drink']
NAI imɨq*
WCI imiq
ECI imiq
GRI imiq* '(fresh) water', EG also 'lake' [and imiʀ- 'drink']

PY əməqyaʀtuʀ- 'go to drink' [cf. yaʀ(tuʀ)-; see also anaqyaʀtuʀ- under anaʀ(-)]
AAY —
CAY məqsaXtuʀ- 'go to drink'
NSY əməqɣ̥aXtuʀ- [ANLC]
CSY məqsaXtuʀ-

PY-S əməqyuɣ- 'be thirsty' [cf. qyuɣ-; compare anaqyaʀtuʀ- under anaʀ(-), also the relat. between nəqə and nəʀə-]
AAY məqsuɣ- 'be thirsty'
CAY məqsuɣ- 'be thirsty'
NSY əməqɣ̥uɣ- 'be thirsty'
CSY məqsuɣ- 'be thirsty'
Sir məqɣuʀ- 'be thirsty', məqɣ̥uX 'thirst' [Em.]
Inu [imiʀuk- 'be thirsty' from əməʀ- plus yuɣ- is predictable everywhere]

PE əməʀtaʀ- 'fetch water' [cf. taʀ-]
AAY məXtaʀ- 'fetch water'
CAY məXtaʀ- 'fetch water' [compare məsaaɣ- 'fetch water from an accessible place (e.g. a well)' — see under taʀ-]
NSY əməXtaʀ- 'fetch water'
CSY məXtaʀ-
Sir məXtaʀ-
SPI imiqtaq-
NAI imɨqtaq- 'fetch or obtain water'
WCI imiqtaq-
ECI imiqta(q)- 'go to look for water'
GRI imiʀtaʀ- 'fetch water'

PI əmmiaq 'melted ice or snow (to drink)' [cf. li(C)aʀ]
SPI immiaq 'water from melted snow'
NAI immiaq 'beer'
WCI —
ECI immiaq 'water from melted snow'
GRI immiaq 'beer, melted ice or snow'

PE əmmit- '(provide with) water' [cf. lit-]
AAY —
CAY HBC, Nun miitə- 'provide with water'
NSY əmitə- 'provide with water'
CSY —
Sir —
SPI —
NAI immit- '(over)soak'
WCI Cop immit- 'put in water' [Pryde]
ECI immit- 'have filled with water'
GRI immit- 'give s.o. s.th. to drink' [for the homonym meaning 'have drifted out to sea' see immit- under ima(ʀ)]

PE əm(ə)ʀun and **əm(ə)ʀuciq** 'cup or dipper' [cf. un and uciʀ]
AAY C məʀa'un, məʀa'utaq 'water pail' [B.-S. also has C əmuun, as well as imiin 'dipper']
CAY məʀʀun, Nun əmʀun 'cup'

NSY [note əmʀusiʀ- 'give water to']
CSY məʀun, məʀuta 'dipper, cup'
Sir məʀəsəʀaX 'cup, jar, pot'
SPI iʀmun 'bottle, drinking glass'
NAI imʀun 'water pitcher, glass', imʀusiq 'horn dipper'
WCI imʀusiq 'cup'[Net, Car 'water dipper' in B.-S. and Ras.; Cop imʀun 'vessel to hold water' Jen.]
ECI SB iʀŋusiq, Aiv iʀmusiq 'glass, cup' [Ras. has the former as 'cup, water dipper' for Igl and Dor. has imʀusiq for Aiv; for Lab Peck has ermgusek]
GRI iʀmusiq, iʀŋusiq 'cup, mug, bottle', EG iŋŋut, iʀŋusiq 'cup'

PY məʀyaɣ- 'get mucus in eye' [cf. yaɣ-]
AAY məʀyaɣ-, məʀyaʀ- 'get mucus in eye'
CAY Y məʀyak 'mucus in eye'
NSY —
CSY —

PY miiciʀ- 'soak' [from əmmit- and c(c)iʀ-?]
AAY —
CAY miiciʀ- 'soak'
NSY —
CSY miisiʀ- 'soak'

PE əmət- 'ask to do s.th. for one'
AAY —
CAY əmutə-, NSU muutə- 'seek medical aid, take an item for repair'
NSY [note əmłuk 'obstinate, persistant' (ANLC)]
CSY muutə- 'ask someone to do s.th. for one'
Sir əmutaX 'material that one has asked to have work done on' [Orr; note also muXtuʀ- 'ask for s.th.']
SPI imit- 'give work to s.o.'
NAI imɨt-
WCI —
ECI —
GRI imit- 'give work to or order s.th. from someone'

PI əmətqutaq 'groin' [cf. EA umli-x, Att uvli-x 'groin']
SPI imitqutaq 'groin'
NAI ➟
WCI Car? imitqutaaq 'groin' [Schn. 'adg'; Ras. has imitqutakki- 'groin']
ECI imiqqutaaq 'groin'
GRI imiqqutak

PI əmətqutailaq '(arctic) tern' [cf. ŋit- for the apparent etymology here — literally 'one without a groin' as suggested by Ras. for the WCI term — compare NAI utcutcaakiq 'small bird with pinkish breast and forked tail that spreads out when it hovers, arctic tern', from utcuk 'female genitals']
SPI W imitqutailaq 'arctic tern' [Jen.]
NAI mitqutail[y]aq
WCI imitqutailaq
ECI imiqqutailaq
GRI imiqqutaalaq

PE əmmuɣ 'milk'
AAY muɣ- [Rezanov əmuɣ-] 'suck at breast', muk 'teat' [earlier 'milk']
CAY əmuk 'milk' [əmulək 'nipple' is probably a reanalysis of mulə(ɣ), q.v.; note also Nun, HBC muuɣək 'breast']
NSY umuɣ- 'suck breast' [umuɣniq 'sweet' (L.-T.)]
CSY muuɣatə- 'be sweet'
Sir [əmuɣnitə- 'be sweet' — Orr]
SPI immuk 'milk'
NAI immuk
WCI Car B. Lake immuk [Pryde]
ECI immuk
GRI immuk 'milk' [NWG also 'cheese', EG also 'sperm' (Robbe and Menn.)]

PE əna- 'play' [cf. ŋ(ŋ)uðaʀ- for the Yup forms; there may be two bases here]
AAY C, AP inaŋuaʀ- 'play (make believe)'
CAY naaŋuaʀ- 'play (make believe)', Eg inaŋuaʀ- 'play house'
NSY əna- 'play sports' [ANLC; L.-T. has ənałəq 'sports, play', also ənaʀun 'toy']
CSY naaŋ[w]aaʀaʀ- 'swing (at play)'
Sir —
SPI ina- 'play', inaun 'toy' [and Jen. has KI, W inat- 'order']
NAI ina- 'stop to play while migrating (whales)', inat- 'purposely distract', Mal 'care for, entertain', PH in[y]attuaq- 'play' [as nom. = 'toy']
WCI inaviqqi- 'waste time, be distracted', Cop inaviqqutaq 'obstacle' [Met.; Pryde has Cop inat- 'fool, deceive']
ECI inat- 'want to have as a companion or accomplice', Lab 'invite' [Peck has 'constrain, summon s.o. to s.th.' for Lab]
GRI inat- 'order, command' [compare the NAI equivalent above, but also maŋat- under maŋat-]

PE ənə 'place' [cf. Aleut naɣ-an 'in it' from *na-ɣa-ni, and probably also na(a)- 'west' (given that the Aleut house was entered from the east)]
AAY əna C 'house', K 'room, space' [base ənə]
CAY <ə>na, HBC, Nun əna 'house, place' [base ənə]
NSY ənə
CSY na 'home, place' [base nə]
Sir ənə 'place, dwelling'
SPI ini, Di ənə 'house'
NAI inɨ 'place, room' [and inɨt 'village']
WCI ini 'place, sledge track' [and note Car? iɣliniq 'beaten track' — Schn. 'adg']
ECI ini 'place, sledge track'
GRI ini 'place, nest, lair, sledge track' [and note iłłiniq* 'sledge track' (old ortho. iglineq) from *ən(ə)linəʀ with li-[1]]

PY ənələɣtə- 'put in place' [cf. ləɣ-?]
AAY KP ənləxtə-, PWS əŋləxtə- 'finish a job and put things away'
CAY —
NSY —
CSY nələxtə- 'put in place securely'

PI ənəllak- 'settle or place oneself' [cf. łłaɣ-]
SPI inilak- 'become full-grown, of age', Qaw also 'settle down, make a place for oneself, jell'
NAI inillak-, PH inillalak- 'find a place to stay, settle, become full (moon) or full-grown, situate'
WCI inillak- 'place oneself, settle for a while'
ECI inilla(k)- 'rest, lie down, place'
GRI —

PE ənəŋiR- 'take s.o.'s place' [cf. ŋiR-]
AAY —
CAY ənaiR- 'take s.o.'s place'
NSY ənŋiR- [ANLC]
CSY nəŋiR-
Sir —
SPI Qaw inaŋiq-
NAI ɨnaŋiq-
WCI inaŋiq-
ECI inaŋiq-
GRI inaŋiR-

PE ənli(C)aR 'womb' [cf. ənə and li(C)aR]
AAY —
CAY ənliaq, nəliaq 'uterus, womb'
NSY ənliaq 'uterus' [L.-T.]
CSY —
Sir —
SPI illi<ž>aq, illižak (du.)
NAI ɨlli<ž>aq
WCI illiaq
ECI illiaq [Peck has iɣliaq, as spelled also by Schn.]
GRI iłłiaq [old ortho. igliaq] 'womb' [Kroeber has idliviaq as 'stomach' as a NG shaman's word]

PE ənqa(R)- 'remember' [for the forms with a final uvular see R- under ŋ(ŋ)uR- and for those with a final kə-/ɣi- see kə-[1]]
AAY ənqaR- 'mention, bring to mind'
CAY nəqqaR- 'recall', ənqakə-, nəqqakə- 'remember, keep in mind with consideration'
NSY ənqaR- 'remember'
CSY nəqaR-
Sir — [but note ənqiR- 'establish'?]
SPI iqqa(q)- [W itqa(q)- acc. Jen.] 'remember' [Qaw also iqqai- 'keep in mind']
NAI ɨtqaq- 'remember', (trans.) ɨtqaɣɨ- 'remember'
WCI itqaq-, itqaɣi- 'remember'
ECI iqqa(q)-, iqqai- 'remember', iqqaɣi- 'be full of attention for, esteem' [and iqqatuq- 'judge s.o.', iqqanaqtuq 'favorite, one to whom one gives favors']
GRI iqqaa- [old ortho. erqai-] 'remember, mention', iqqaɣi- 'be anxious to get' [and iqqanaR- look threatening', iqqaRsaR- 'think about s.th.', iqqaRtuR- 'talk about, remind about']

PE ənqa(Ru)ma- 'keep in mind' [cf. (u)ma-]
AAY C ənqama- 'keep in mind'
CAY —
NSY —
CSY [nəqamikə- 'remember, not forget']
Sir —
SPI itqauma- 'keep in mind, remember'
NAI ɨtqauma-
WCI itqauma-
ECI iqqauma- 'bear in mind, remember a long time'
GRI iqqaama- '(can) remember, keep in mind' [and Ges. has EG iqqaamanaR- 'cause homesickness, longing']

PI ənqanaiq- 'make ready' [cf. naR- and ŋiR-]
SPI Qaw iqqanaiq- 'get or become ready' [iqqanait- 'be ready']
NAI ɨtqanaiq- 'become or make ready'
WCI itqanaiq- 'be ready, get ready' [Pryde]
ECI iqqanaiq- 'finish up (e.g. work)', NBI, SB iqqanaiyaq- 'work'
GRI iqqanaaR- 'have put by provisions in good time, put in a safe place' [old ortho. erqanaer-, as opposed to erqanâr- 'fear misfortune' going with iqqanaR- under ənqaR- above]

PE ənuR- 'fall short'
AAY nuRyuɣ- 'need', nuRnaR- 'be scarce, rare'
CAY ənuR- 'be insufficient, unable to reach', nuXtə- 'fall short, fail to reach'
NSY ənuR- 'not reach, be insufficient'
CSY nuuR- 'be in need, unable to reach'
Sir [Vakh. has əŋžuxt(ə)-, əŋcəXt(ə)- 'not reach' and Orr has əŋcəRutə- 'be insufficient']
SPI inuq- 'be insufficient, fall short, not reach'
NAI ɨnuq- 'fail to reach, be insufficient' [and ɨnuqtuq- 'run short of food, not quite reach one's destination']
WCI inuq- 'not reach (target)'
ECI inuq-
GRI inuR- 'fail to reach, cannot reach' [and inuRtuR- 'come too late to meet s.o.']

PE əŋə 'pubis'
AAY —
CAY —
NSY əŋə 'pubis, groin' [L.-T. has əŋək; and note əŋəłqaq 'protuberance, hillock']
CSY — [for inək 'groin, armpit' see inək]
Sir —
SPI iŋi 'pubis, mound of Venus'
NAI iŋɨ
WCI iŋik [Pryde]
ECI iŋi(q) [Dor.]
GRI iŋi(q) [Robbe and Menn. have iŋaq for EG]

PY-S əŋiɣ- 'press down on' [there may be a link to məŋik-, if not tənəɣ-]
AAY ŋiɣ-, niɣ-, ŋikə- 'put weight on, press, hold down'
CAY əniɣ-, niiɣ-
NSY —
CSY ŋiixtə-
Sir əŋiɣ- [Em.]

PY əŋki- 'prop'
AAY əŋki- 'prop', PWS 'lean on (with body at an angle)', əŋkiq 'prop'

CAY Nun ənki- 'prop'
NSY iŋki 'prop' [ANLC — Men. has əŋki]
CSY nəŋki-, nənki- 'prop' [also nominal]

PE əŋlaʀ- 'laugh'
AAY əŋlaʀ- 'laugh'
CAY ŋəllaʀ-, Nun, Eg əŋlaʀ-, HBC nəŋlaʀ-
NSY ənlaʀ-
CSY nəŋlaʀ-
Sir laʀ(ə)-
SPI iɣlaq-
NAI ɨɣlaq-
WCI iɣlaq-
ECI NBI iɣlaq- [B.-S. for Igl, Boas for Baf.]
GRI iłłaʀ- 'laugh'

PE əŋlu 'house'
AAY K əŋluq 'house'
CAY ŋəllu, nəllu, Y, HBC ənlu 'beaver house' [Nu ənluqfaɣaʀ 'little house']
NSY ənlu 'small semi-subterranean house'
CSY nəŋlu 'sod house'
Sir lu 'sod house' [also luvəx]
SPI iɣlu
NAI ɨɣlu 'house' [ɨɣlupiaq 'sod house']
WCI iɣlu 'snow house, igloo' [Lowe has 'house']
ECI illu, Lab iłłuk 'house' [illuviɣaq 'snow house']
GRI iłłu, EG ittiq 'house' [iłłuiɣaq 'snow house, hunting hut, bear's den']

PY əŋuɣ- 'eat meat from bone?'
AAY —
CAY —
NAY əŋukšak 'sour meat of whale or seal' [ANLC]
CSY ŋuuɣ- 'eat meat clinging to bone' [and ŋuuɣžaq 'whale flesh']

PE əpaɣ 'grain or fiber'
AAY paxaq 'grain' [paxtu- 'be rough-grained', paxkitə- 'be fine-grained']
CAY paɣaq 'grain in wood'
NSY —
CSY —
Sir —
SPI iva(a)
NAI ipak 'grain, fiber'
WCI ipak 'grain in wood'
ECI ipa(k)
GRI ipak 'grain, fiber, vein (in wood, bone, etc.)'

PE əpə- 'suffocate' [cf. perhaps Aleut Atkan m̥uqati-X, EA uqati-X 'gill cover'?]
AAY K, PWS əpə-, KP əppaXtə- 'suffocate'
CAY əpə- 'suffocate, drown'
NSY əpə- 'suffocate', gasp for breath'
CSY əpə- 'become stale, flat-tasting' [and pəkaʀ- 'gasp, suffocate']
Sir [pəkaʀmər- 'pant, gasp' — Vakh. has epəkəɣ-]
SPI ivi- 'suffocate, drown'
NAI ipɨ- 'suffocate, drown' [and ipɨt- 'suffocate']
WCI ipi-
ECI ipi- 'die of suffocation' [and ipit- 'suffocate']
GRI ipi- 'suffocate, drown'

PE əpyalŋu- 'feel suffocated' [cf. lŋu-]
AAY [əpsuɣ- 'feel stifled, suffocated']
CAY əpsalŋu- 'feel bad because of lack of fresh air'
NSY əpy̥alŋu- 'be suffocating, become stuffy (air)'
CSY —
Sir —
SPI ipyaŋu-, Qaw ipsanŋu- 'be short of breath, pant'
NAI ivyanŋu- 'be short of breath, feel faint'
WCI ivyanŋunaq- 'be stuffy, suffocating' [Pryde]
ECI iyyaŋu- 'suffocate' [also 'adg' in Schn.]
GRI issaŋu- [old ortho. ivsangu-] 'be short of breath, breathe painfully'

PE əpəɣ- or **əpəʀ(aʀ)-** 'release' [cf. Aleut im̥i- 'be torn off']
AAY pəxtə- 'let go of'
CAY pəxtə- 'drop, let go, give up, break up with'
NSY əpəxtə- 'release, suddenly let og' [ANLC]
CSY pəxtə- 'let go, release, divorce, get free, come loose'
Sir [note ipXəta 'harpoon' on p. 40 of Men.]
SPI iviʀaq- 'have s.th. slip from hand, let go'
NAI ipiʀaq- 'give up on, cast aside'
WCI ipiʀaq- 'let go'
ECI ipiʀaq- 'put aside' [and ipiqqaku 'abandoned object']
GRI ipiʀaʀ-, ipaʀaʀ-, NG ipaaq- 'let go, put aside' [for homonym 'hit with whip' see əpiqaʀ-]

PE əpəqaʀ 'lamp wick (of moss)' [there may be a relat. to əpəʀ]
AAY —
CAY — [note Nun pəquX 'piece of sod']
NSY əpəqaq 'oil lamp wick, moss'
CSY pəqaq 'moss used for oil-lamp wick'
Sir pəqəX 'wick'
SPI Qaw ipiʀaq 'wick' [Men. has ivuʀa- 'adjust wick' for Imaq]
NAI ipiʀaq 'wick' [Ras. has 'moss' for Nu]
WCI ipiʀaq 'wick' [Car 'moss for wick' — B.-S.]
ECI —
GRI ipiʀaq, EG, Up ipar̃aq 'wick, lamp moss' [also 'light bulb' in EG acc. Robbe and Menn.; for homonym meaning 'harpoon strap' see ipiʀaq under ipiq(-)]

PE əpəʀ 'dirt' [cf. əppaʀiʀ-]
AAY ➟
CAY ➟
NSY ➟
CSY pəXuq 'moist grime'
Sir pəʀnəX 'dirt' [and pəʀnəʀiʀ- 'clean']
SPI ivak- 'get dirty' [Jen. has 'get wet' for W]
NAI ipiq* 'dirt' [and ippak- 'get dirty', ipqu- 'be dirty']
WCI Car ipiq 'dirt' [Ras.], Cop ipqu- 'be dirty' [Jen.]
ECI ipiq 'dirt' [and ippa(C)- 'dirty (s.th.)'; for ippaq 'remains of food stuck to container' see əppaʀ-]
GRI ipiq* 'dirt' [and ippaɣ- 'dirty']

PE əpʀiʀ- and **əpʀit-** 'be clean' [cf. ŋiʀ- and ŋit- respectively]
AAY C pəXitə-, K pəʀitə- 'be clean'
CAY pəXiʀ-, Nun əpXiʀ- 'wipe', Y pəXXitə- 'be clean'
NSY əpXiXsaʀ- 'clean' [and əpXiʀ- 'clean' (ANLC)]
CSY pəXiʀ- 'wash hands'
Sir —
SPI ipqit- 'be clean'
NAI ipqit- 'be clean', ipqiq- 'clean, become clean'
WCI —
ECI [ipiiq- 'be clean']
GRI iqqit- 'be clean', iqqiaʀ- 'clean'

PE əpiqaʀ- 'hit with whip'
AAY piqəʀ- 'strike, club, swat'
CAY piqəʀ-
NSY —
CSY —
Sir —
SPI iviʀaq- 'hit with whip'
NAI ipiʀaq- 'hit with whip'
WCI Car EP ipiʀaqtuq- 'hit with whip' [Ow.]
ECI ipiʀaq- 'hit with whip'
GRI ipiʀaʀ-, ipaʀaʀ-, NG ipaaq- 'hit with whip' [the latter two forms influenced by ipaʀaʀ- under əpəɣ-?]

PE əpiq(a)ʀutaʀ 'whip or axe' [cf. un]
AAY piqXutaq, piqXuu'utaq 'whip, club, switch' [also piqəXtuutaq]
CAY piqXutaq, piqXun 'whip, switch used in steambath', Nun 'axe' [also piqəXtuutaq 'axe']
NSY —
CSY —
Sir —
SPI [iviʀa.tuun, Qaw ipiʀaqtuun 'whip']
NAI [note Nu ipiʀauttaq 'tap root of plant', but also 'axe']
WCI Net, B. Lake ipiʀautaq 'whip' [Dor.]
ECI ipiʀautaq 'whip'
GRI NG ipiʀaataq, Up ipaʀ̃aataq 'whip'

PY əpla- 'get lost'
AAY pəła- 'get lost, get tired of too much noise'
CAY pəła- 'fade out, to disappear, lose consciousness' [and pəłaa- 'lose one's way']
NSY —
CSY ifła- 'lose, get lost' [but also pəłaʀ(yuɣ)- 'feel lonely, bored']

PE əpləʀ- 'revulsed by s.th. or respect a taboo?' [there may be a link to əpəʀ]
AAY łəʀ(yuɣ)- 'feel squeamish about s.th. messy and wet'
CAY pəłəʀ(yuɣ)- 'feel squeamish about s.th. messy and wet' [pəłəʀnaʀ- 'be messy and wet']
NSY əpłəʀnaʀ- 'be damp, wet' [ANLC; Men. has əpłəʀutə- 'moisten, make or get wet, urinate']
CSY əfłəʀ(yuɣ)- 'feel discomfort (from wetness or stickiness on one's skin)'
Sir əfłəʀ(yuɣ)- 'feel discomfort' [Orr; in Em. 'itch, be uncomfortable because of tight clothing, etc.' — from CSY?]
SPI —
NAI —
WCI ivliʀi- 'be afraid of talking to a relative of one's wife, be afraid of dealing with s.o. or catching their illness' [and Ras. has Net ivliʀiik 'two that never speak to each other for religious reasons, being named after the same dead person']
ECI Lab ivliʀi- 'esteem' [Peck]
GRI iłłiʀi- 'value (one's possessions), honor, keep holy', iłłiʀnaʀ- 'be valuable', NG illiʀnaq- 'be filthy' [Fab. has WG ibler- 'be or keep clean'; note also EG ittiʀta- 'be clean, tidy', Up iłłiʀ̃iit(i)- 'value one's possessions, be stingy with']

PE əpnaʀ 'cliff'
AAY pəŋ̥aq 'cliff'
CAY pəŋ̥aq, əpŋ̥aq
NSY əpŋ̥aq
CSY pəŋ̥aq
Sir pənəX 'cliff' [Vakh. also has pənaX and pəŋ̥aX]
SPI ipnaq 'cliff'
NAI ɨmnaq, Mal ɨpnaq
WCI Sig imnaq
ECI innaq
GRI innaq

PE əpnaʀiʀ 'mountain sheep' [cf. (C)iʀ]
AAY C pəŋ̥aiq 'mountain sheep'
CAY UK, LI əpŋ̥aiq, Y pəŋ̥aiq 'Dall sheep'
NSY əpŋ̥iaq [ANLC]
CSY pəŋ̥iiq*
Sir pənəʀəX 'mountain sheep' [Vakh. pənəʀiX]
SPI Qaw ipnaiq
NAI ɨmnaiq, Nu ɨpnaiq '(mountain) sheep'
WCI Sig imnaiq 'Rocky Mountain goat' [Pet.]
ECI —
GRI —

PI əpnit- 'be stuck on or by a cliff' [cf. łit-]
SPI Qaw ipnit- 'be stuck on cliff, unable to climb any higher'
NAI ɨpnit-
WCI Net imnit- [Pryde]
ECI —
GRI innit- 'run up against slope and be stopped by it'

PE əppaʀiʀ- 'lick clean' [cf. əpəʀ- and ŋiʀ-; the immediate base to which the latter is attached is probably *əppaʀ as in Inu ippaq below — compare allaʀ(iʀ)-]
AAY əpaiʀ-, PWS əpiiʀ- 'clean (dirty utensil), lick (dish, finger)' [from *əppaʀ plus (ŋ)iʀ-]
CAY paiʀ- 'lick', Nun əpaaʀ- 'scrape food from a receptacle or utensil with finger then lick clean'
NSY əpaaʀ- 'lick' [ANLC; Men. has əpaXtuʀ- 'lick off']
CSY paaʀ- 'lick, clean with tongue, scrape and lick food from finger'
Sir —
SPI ippaq- 'lick clean, eat everything off plate' [Imaq

əp(p)aqtuq-]
NAI ippaq-
WCI ippaq- 'clean one's plate of food with finger or spoon'
ECI ippa(q)- 'remove remains of food by scraping or licking' [and nom. ippaq 'remains of food stuck to vessel']
GRI ippaʀ- 'lick clean (dish), gather all fragments of s.th.'

PE əpu 'handle' [cf. perhaps Aleut hutu-X 'handle']
AAY C puk 'straight handle'
CAY əpu
NSY əpu 'handle, knob' [Orr; L.-T. and Em. have upu, L.-T. has ipiaq also]
CSY puu 'shaft-type handle, stem of plant'
Sir —
SPI ivu 'handle' [and Imaq əvəqłuk 'handle (e.g. of cup)']
NAI ipu 'handle' [for Mal ipi in this meaning, see ipiq(-)]
WCI ipu 'handle of tool' [Ras. has Cop 'caribou lance', Net 'whip handle']
ECI ipu 'handle'
GRI ipu 'handle, shaft'

PY əpulquq 'stem of plant' [cf. quʀ]
AAY —
CAY əpułquq 'stem of plant'
NSY əpəłquq 'stem of plant' [Men. has əpułquq]
CSY — [for puu 'stem of plant' see under əpu above]

PI əpžaʀun 'dog muzzle' [cf. əpə-, ðaʀ- and un]
SPI —
NAI ivžaʀun, Nu ipžaʀun 'dog muzzle'
WCI ivyaʀun
ECI iyyaʀut 'dog muzzle, ring on pipe stem'
GRI iʀšaʀut, issaʀut [old ortho. ivsarut], EG ittaat 'dog muzzle' [the first WG form may be influenced by iʀšaq under iqšaq (iq(ə)ʀ), the second by issaŋu- under epyalŋu- (əpə-)]

PE əqðuɣ- 'carry on shoulder'
AAY quuɣ- 'carry on shoulder'
CAY əquɣ- 'carry on shoulder', Nun 'carry under arm' [and əquk, quuk 'thing carried on shoulder'; for Y əquk 'wood' see qəðuɣ]
NSY əquɣ- 'carry on shoulder' [ANLC, also for əquk 'load carried on shoulders']
CSY — [for quuk 'firewood', quuxtə- 'gather firewood' see qəðuɣ]
Sir —
SPI iqšuk- 'carry on shoulder'
NAI iqšuk-
WCI Sig iqsuk-, Cop iXXuk-
ECI Lab itsuk- 'carry on shoulder' [Ras. has Igl iʀsuk-]
GRI iʀšuɣ- 'carry on shoulder'

PE əqə-[1] 'shrink or contract' [cf. əqlu and əqəya- and Aleut qya- 'be tight']
AAY əqə- 'shrink'
CAY əqə- 'shrink, contract'
NSY →
CSY →
Sir →
SPI →
NAI iqɨ- 'contract, close (fist)'
WCI iqi- 'contract, shrink'
ECI iqi- 'bend (limbs), shrink'
GRI iqi- 'shrink, be eager' [and iqima- 'be crowded together']

PE əqət- 'squeeze' [cf. t-[1] and Aleut qyat- 'tighten']
AAY əqtə- 'squeeze, hug'
CAY qəttə-, Nun əqtə- 'squeeze, embrace' [and qəzzun 'drawstring, barrel hoop', qəppaɣ- 'hug or squeeze vigorously']
NSY əqətə- 'embrace, roll (flat), squeeze'
CSY qətə- 'embrace, squeeze'
Sir qət(ə)-
SPI iʀit- 'contract, hug'
NAI iqɨt- 'contract, embrace' [and iqɨt 'clenched fist', iqimmaaq-, PH iqimmat- 'embrace']
WCI iqit- 'squeeze, embrace'
ECI iqit- 'hug, squeeze'
GRI iqit- 'shrink, squeeze, embrace, shake hands'

PY qəłuʀtə- 'shrink'
AAY qəłuXtə-, qəłuxtə- 'pucker, purse, close with drawstring'
CAY Nun, HBC, NS qəłuʀ- 'shrink', qəłuXtə- 'crimp to decrease in size'
NSY qəłuxtə- 'shrink' [ANLC]
CSY qəłuXtə-

PY əqə-[2] 'be angry' [cf. perhaps Aleut aq- in Atkan aqla- 'be angry, hotheaded', aqmit- 'get angry', EA amqi-, Att avqi- 'be angry'; the relat. to qəvə(t)- is obscure — contam. with əqə-[1]?]
AAY [Tyzh. has kayšuɣ- 'get angry' for Kod]
CAY əqə-, NSK əqəvə-, Nun əqquXtə- 'be infuriated, suddenly become very angry' [əqn̥aXqə-, qənaXqə- 'be infuriating']
NSY [for qəvə- 'be angry, evil' see qəvə(t)-]
CSY —

PE əqlu 'rectum' [cf. əqə-[1] and lu(ʀ)]
AAY qəłuq 'colon' [C qəłuɣnəq, K qəłuʀnəq 'anus']
CAY qəłuq 'colon, rectum'
NSY əqłu
CSY qəłu
Sir qəła [Orr]
SPI iqłu
NAI iqłu
WCI Sig iqłu, Cop iXXu
ECI iʀsuq, Lab iłłuk [Saul for the first]
GRI iʀłuk, NG iʀluq, EG iʀsiq

PE əqmaɣ- 'fold up' [cf. əqə-[1], also əʀmalin]
AAY əqm̥əʀ- 'double over'
CAY —

NSY əqm̥aɣ- 'roll or fold up' [ANLC]
CSY —
Sir —
SPI iqmak- 'fold (legs and the like)'
NAI iʀmak- 'fold up', Nu iqmak- 'fold over'
WCI —
ECI —
GRI —

PE əq(ə)ya- 'be lazy'
AAY qəsa- 'be lazy'
CAY qəsa- 'feel lazy' [and qəsaitə- 'be hard-working']
NSY iqɣ̥ani- 'be lazy' [ANLC; L.-T. has iqɣ̥anitaq 'lazy person']
CSY iXsa- 'refuse to do s.th.', iXsanitaʀ- 'be lazy'
Sir iXsaŋit(ə)- 'be lazy' [Vakh. — for iXsanit(e)-?; note also əʀəməyuɣ- 'be lazy', not want to do s.th.']
SPI iʀiasuk- 'be lazy' [and Qaw iʀiani- 'be sleepy', iʀinaq- 'be a slowpoke']
NAI iqiasuk- 'be lazy' [and iqiyɨ- 'think s.o. lacks initiative', iqiŋnaq-, iqiŋnaq- 'lack initiative', iqiŋnait- 'work without having to be told']
WCI iqiasuk- 'be lazy' [iqqiit- 'be ready to do any work']
ECI iqiasuk- 'be lazy', iqiasutu- 'be very lazy (mainly of dogs)' [Saul for the first; and note Lab iqinait- 'be hardworking']
GRI iqiasuɣ- 'be lazy, not feel like s.th.' [and iqiɣ- 'be tired of being unemployed', iqinnaat- 'be hard-working, helpful', iqigi-, iqiššut(i)- 'apologize for one's passivity']

PI əqiiq- 'be awake' [cf. ŋiʀ-]
SPI iʀiiq- 'become wide awake'
NAI iqiiq-
WCI Sig iqiiq- 'be wide awake' [Jen.]
ECI —
GRI iqiiʀ- 'be awake'

PE əq(ə)yakə- 'not feel like doing or allowing' [cf. kə-[1]]
AAY —
CAY qəsakə- 'not permit'
NSY iqɣ̥akə- 'not permit' [Em.; but ANLC iqɣ̥aqə- 'banish, refuse']
CSY iXsake- 'refuse (s.o. or s.th.)'
Sir —
SPI iʀiayi- 'feel lazy about (doing s.th.)'
NAI iqiayi-
WCI iqiayi-
ECI —
GRI iqiayi- 'not feel like (doing s.th.)'

PE əʀði 'milt sac'
AAY əriq 'gonad' [and KP əriłək 'male']
CAY əʀiq 'milt sac'
NSY iʀik 'milt sac' [L.-T.]
CSY ʀii
Sir XiX, pl. Xiʀiy [Orr; from CSY?]
SPI iʀži
NAI iʀži 'milt sac' [and iʀžisik 'suspenders (du.)' — note the white decorative strips on the shoulders of parkas like milt sacs]
WCI —
ECI —
GRI —

PE əʀə-[1] 'run or fade (color)' [compare uʀə-]
AAY əʀə- 'run (of colors)'
CAY əʀə- 'run (of colors)' [and əʀvə-, HBC əʀmə- 'fade, run (colors)']
NSY əʀəvə- 'fade' [Em.; ANLC əʀ(ə)vu(u)tə- 'fade, lose color, get sober']
CSY ʀəvə- 'fade'
Sir əʀəvə(s)- 'fade, become pale or washed out' [Em.]
SPI Qaw iʀivit- 'erase' [for KI iʀivit- 'wash' see əʀ(ə)viɣ- below]
NAI ➡
WCI ➡
ECI ➡
GRI ➡

PE əʀmiɣ- 'wash face' [cf. miɣ-?]
AAY əʀmiɣ- 'wash face'
CAY əʀmiɣ-
NSY əʀmiɣ- 'wash face' [ANLC; L.-T. has əʀmi(i)n 'towel' əʀmiłəq 'washing']
CSY aʀmiɣ- 'wash face'
Sir əʀməɣ- 'wash, swill'
SPI iʀmik- 'wash face'
NAI —
WCI iʀmik- 'wash hands or face' [Pryde; Cop, Car iʀmiut 'soap']
ECI iʀmik- 'wash', Lab immik- 'wash face'
GRI iʀmiɣ- 'wash face', EG immiC- 'wash (s.o. or face)'

PE əʀʀuʀ- 'wash or rinse' [cf. EA Xula- 'wash', Xuusi-X 'sponge']
AAY AP Xuuʀ-, Xuuʀi-, Kod, KP uuʀi- 'wash hands, clothes'
CAY əʀuʀ- 'wash (not clothes)'
NSY əʀuʀ-. 'wash' [ANLC; Men. has əʀuXtuʀ-]
CSY —
Sir —
SPI iʀʀuq- 'rinse' [Imaq əʀuaq- 'rinse, wash', əʀu(u)tuq- 'wash']
NAI Mal iʀʀuq- 'wash, rinse'
WCI —
ECI iʀʀutuq- 'wash hands, rinse', Cape Dorset iʀʀuq- 'rinse' [Andersen et al. have Lab iggut- 'wash, clean oneself']
GRI iXXuʀ- 'wash (s.th.)', iXXuʀtuʀ- 'rinse', Up iqqiʀtiʀ- 'wash one's hands'

PE əʀ(ə)viɣ- 'wash clothes or skin'
AAY —
CAY əʀviɣ- 'wash clothes'
NSY əʀviɣ-
CSY aʀviɣ-
Sir əʀvəɣ-
SPI Qaw iʀvik- 'wash clothes', KI iʀivit- 'wash' [the

former at least may be from the Yup]
NAI [note ɪʀviaq 'tanned leather']
WCI — [note Sig aʀipa- 'soak' (Lowe) — contam. with aʀipa-?]
ECI — [note Lab aʀipa- 'be wet through (skin)' (Peck) —contam. with aʀipa-?; for iʀit- 'soak (skin)' see əʀi-]
GRI [note iʀuit-, iʀivit- 'be soaked, hairless (skin), bare (cliff)', Fab. also 'be clean', iʀfaq 'waterproof skin coat' — there is entanglement with əʀi- here]

PY-S əʀvuqaʀ- 'take a bath'
AAY —
CAY əʀvuqaʀ-, HBC əʀvuqə- 'take a bath'
NSY uʀvəXqə- 'wash (one's body)' [ANLC; Men. has uʀvəXqəvik 'bath']
CSY uʀvuXqə- 'bathe' [and uʀvuʀ- 'rinse, wash'; influenced by uʀə-?]
Sir aʀvuXqə(s)- 'take a bath' [and aʀvuXtuʀ- 'rinse' — Em.]

PY-S əʀə-[2] 'dawn' [cf. Aleut aʀa- 'appear, become open, be born, arrive, clear up (sky)']
AAY əXtə- 'dawn'
CAY əXtə- 'dawn'
NSY əXtəkatə- [ANLC əXtə-]
CSY aXtə-, əXtə- 'dawn, recur'
Sir əXsimaʀən 'at daybreak' [and Vakh. has əʀt(ə)- 'dawn' from Men.'s texts — this may be the same as əʀutə- below or as Em.'s əXtə- 'dawn']
Inu — [for GRI iʀšiʀ- 'become visible' see iðəʀ-]

PY əʀnəq 'day' [cf. nəʀ[1]]
AAY əʀnəq 'day'
CAY əʀnəq*
NSY əʀnəq
CSY aʀnəq*, əʀnəq*

PY əʀnəʀpak '(all) today' [cf. əʀnəq above and vaɣ]
AAY əʀnəXpak 'today'
CAY əʀnəXpak
NSY əʀnəXpak 'all day'
CSY — [compare aʀnəʀmi 'today', loc. of əʀnəq]

PY əʀutə- 'dawn on or recur' [cf. utə-]
AAY əʀutə- 'dawn on s.o. or s.th., be discovered by daylight, arrive (a special day)'
CAY əʀutə- 'recur, happen again'
NSY —
CSY əXtə- 'recur, repeat' [compare under əʀə- above]
Sir [for əʀtə- 'dawn' see under əʀə- above]

PE əʀəni(ʀ)- 'hurry to get s.th. done' [there is some entanglement between this base and əɣmiʀ- in Yup and esp. Sir]
AAY C ənʀian 'immediately'
CAY [note əɣnaaXtə- 'be in a hurry']
NSY —
CSY aʀnaɣan 'hurry up' [and əɣnaaŋitə- 'be habitually slow']
Sir [aʀnaɣən 'right away, definitely (must), on time' (Men. and Orr); Men. has əɣnaqiɣ- 'run quickly', iɣəʀunaʀən, iʀəʀunaʀən, əɣnaqəʀən 'quickly, right away' — the latter acc. Vakh. əɣnaɣən; Orr also has ənaŋətə- 'be slow'; Em. has əɣnaŋəlŋuX 'slow', also aʀnaxsaʀ- 'hurry along (trans.)'; some of these may be borrowed from the CSY]
SPI W iʀini- 'do quickly' [Jen., who also has iʀinŋinaq- 'will do or come soon'; Imaq iʀni(i)taʀa(q)- 'be lazy', iʀni(i)taq 'laziness']
NAI iʀniqšuq- 'hurry'
WCI iʀini- 'hurry to do s.th.' [and Ras. has Net iʀinisuminut 'through impatience']
ECI [Peck has Lab iʀini- 'think s.o. slow', also iʀŋi- 'have done with one's work'; Ras. has Igl iʀŋiqɫuni 'at once']
GRI iʀini- 'wait impatiently' [and iʀniʀ-, iʀŋiʀ- 'do right away', iʀniinnaq, SWG iʀŋiinnaq 'right away', NG iʀini(i)hukkut(i)- 'long for, be impatient for'; for iʀnuma- 'be worried' see inʀuma-]

PE əʀi- 'fall out (hair)' [there is contam. with əʀə-[1] in Inu]
AAY [note məʀi- 'fall out (of hair)' — by contam. with məqə-]
CAY əʀinʀaq* 'down feather, undercoat hair'
NSY ➟
CSY ➟
Sir ➟
SPI Qaw iʀi- 'fall out (hair)' [for iʀivit-'wash' see əʀ(ə)viɣ- under əʀə-[1]]
NAI iʀi- 'fall out (hair)'
WCI iʀi- 'lose hair' [and Car 'wear a hole in sole' — Ras.]
ECI iʀit- 'pluck loose hair' [also 'soak (of skin)', contam. with əʀ(ə)viɣ- under əʀə-[1], Lab iʀiviC- 'be bare, naked']
GRI iʀit- 'pluck hair or feathers' [for iʀuit-, iʀivit- 'be hairless (skin)' see əʀ(ə)viɣ- under əʀə-[1]]

PE əʀitaʀ- 'pluck (fowl)' [cf. t-[1] and ðaʀ-]
AAY [məʀitə- 'pluck (animal)' — by contam. with məqə-]
CAY əʀitaʀ-, nəʀitaʀ- 'pluck (fowl)'
NSY iʀitaʀ- [ANLC; Men. has iʀita-]
CSY Xiitaʀ- 'pluck'
Sir əʀətəʀ- 'pluck (bird or grass)'
SPI iʀitaq-
NAI iʀisaq-, iʀitcaq-
WCI iʀitaq- 'pluck (bird)'
ECI iʀitaq- [Saul]
GRI iʀisaʀ- 'pluck' [and iʀitaq 'skin from which hair or feathers has been removed', iʀisaaq 'watertight skin']

PI əʀiala- 'shout' [cf. əʀina(ʀ)? — but compare also uiʀuala-]
SPI —
NAI iʀiala- 'shout'
WCI Cop iʀiala- [Pryde; Pet. has iʀialuaq- 'shout' for Sig]

ECI —
GRI —

PE əʀina(ʀ) 'voice'
AAY əʀina(q) 'voice'
CAY əʀina(q)
NSY iʀina 'voice' [ANLC; Em. has iʀniaʀ- 'lose one's voice']
CSY —
Sir —
SPI iʀinaq 'voice' [Jen. has 'incantation' for W]
NAI iʀinʸa, iʀnʸa 'voice'
WCI Cop, Car, Net iʀinaliu(u)t 'magic word, charm' [Ras.], Sig iʀinaq 'incantation' [Pet.; Pryde has Cop iʀinaq 'tune, melody', as verb 'utter incantation or spell']
ECI Lab iʀina 'tune, sound' [Peck; Ras. also has iʀinaliuutit 'magic words' for Igl]
GRI iʀinaq 'voice, melody' [Fab has erina, Kl. also iʀinak]

PI əʀmalin or **əʀmalicaq** 'skin on floor of kayak?' [cf. əqmaɣ- and li- and un]
SPI —
NAI —
WCI Cop iʀmalin 'sealskin mat with upturned edges in kayak' [Pryde; Schn. has iʀmalik 'floor of boat or canoe (with bilgewater in it)' for 'adg', but this could be Aiv]
ECI —
GRI iʀmalisaq, NG iʀŋalit 'skin on floor of kayak'

PY əsuɣ- 'scrub'
AAY suuɣ- 'scrub (floors, walls)'
CAY suuɣi- 'scrub (floors, walls)' [suɣluku (rather than suuɣluku or suuɣiluku) reported but not verified for non-compressing speakers, and if this is so, base is əsuɣ-, but if not PY could be suuɣ- instead of əsuɣ-]
NSY —
CSY —

PE ət- 'be' [cf. əɬ(ə)ŋa, əɬuʀaʀ-, etc.; the t ~ l alternation as in Yup may be original PE or an innovation extended from ŋit ~ ŋil(a)- — əluciʀ below makes the former possibility seem more likely; compare also əlun and Aleut ma- under p.b. (u)ma-]
AAY əttə- 'be (exist or be situated)' [with tə ~ l alt. as in CAY]
CAY ətə- 'be' [with tə ~ l alternation as for neg. and adj. bases in tə — compare əluciʀ below]
NSY ətə- 'be, live'
CSY [fused in postbase mətə-, q.v. (with ŋuq = məlŋuq)]
Sir [note the p.b. in manaʀət(ə)- 'be here' and kəcəkəɬaʀət(ə)- 'live alone' — Vakh., who also has qukaʀit- 'be in the middle ' from qukaq, mənaʀət-, manaʀət- 'be here' from məna 'here' (note dem. root ma-) and nanəʀət- 'be where' from na-²]
SPI it- 'be (situated), exist', Imaq ət- 'be, live' [and əɬəq 'life, generation']
NAI it- 'be (situated)' [and note taimait-, tainnait- 'be thus' under taimait- (taðim(m)a)]
WCI Net, Sig it- 'be (situated)' [Ras.; Met. has ik- 'be here' and iktuaq- 'stay quietly']
ECI [fused in postbase miit 'be in, at' and in taimait-, etc., under taimait- (taðim(m)a); Peck also has i(C)- for Lab, and Ras. has Igl ikviat 'one with whom they are']
GRI it- 'be (situated or like s.th.)' [fused in p.b. miit- 'be in, on, at' under mətə-; and note imaat-, imaali-, imaasi-, EG imaasiʀ- 'become thus' from ima 'thus']

PE əluciʀ 'shape or nature' [cf. uciʀ and compare əlitquciq under əlit-; the l may be due to əlu(ʀ)-, but see above under ət- — note that žžusiq in the NAI form is the regular allomorph of uciʀ after t bases]
AAY luuciq 'nature' [also 'whole' with possessor endings — for which see əlu(ʀ)-]
CAY əluciq 'shape, form, nature'
NSY —
CSY —
Sir —
SPI [ižžuziq 'character, condition']
NAI [ižžusiq 'behavior, appearace', PH ilʀusiq 'habit'; Jen. has B ilisiq 'behavior, manner']
WCI [iyyusiq 'manner of being, habit']
ECI ilusiq 'habit' [and ilutsiq 'appearance']
GRI ilusiq 'shape, form'

PE ətə- 'be deep' [cf. ətəʀ and Aleut it- 'fall, drop down'?]
AAY K, KP əttu-, PWS ət<x>u- 'be deep' [the x in PWS could be due to ətɣat- below — but note also ət<x>u- under ətəvə-]
CAY əttu- 'be deep' [with tu-¹?]
NSY ətu- 'be deep' [ANLC; Men. has ətuqaq 'deep']
CSY [uusqaq 'deep or high place']
Sir — [note usquqnəX 'hill' — Vakh. has usquʀneʀaX; compare əXtəvalaX 'deep, high' under əkəʀ(tu)-]
SPI itisaq 'deep water', Imaq ətu- 'be expansive, deep'
NAI iti- 'be deep'
WCI iti-
ECI iti- 'be deep' [itsiniq 'submerged part of boat']
GRI iti- 'be deep' [and itisuuq, NG itituuq 'deep', itsiniq* 'part of floating object below surface']

PE ətɣalʀit- 'come into shallow water' [cf. ətkalʀuq below and ɬit-]
AAY —
CAY ətxaɬqitə- 'reach a shallow spot'
NSY [ətəkitə- 'get stuck in shallow water' — ANLC]
CSY —
Sir —
SPI ikka·lit- 'get stuck in shallow water'
NAI ikkalʀit-
WCI ikkalʀit- 'go aground'
ECI ikkaʀit- [Saul]
GRI ikkaʀɬit- 'run aground'

PE ətɣat- 'be shallow' [see CAY ɣatə, etc. under p.b. ŋit- and compare also ətəɣaq- and for a parallel converse derivative ipɣit- 'be blunt' under ipəɣ-

'be sharp'; some of the Yup forms have kit- rather than ŋit-]
AAY K, KP əkkitə-, PWS ətxatə- 'be shallow'
CAY ətxatə- 'be shallow', ətxalŋuq*, ətxałquq 'shallow place'
NSY [note ətəkitə- 'be shallow', ətəkitaʀaq 'shallow place' (with p.b. kit-), also ətxaXsi- 'flatten']
CSY — [for aXqəłi- 'lower, become shallow' see under əkəʀ(tu)-]
Sir — [for əXqətaʀałəʀəX 'shallow' see əkəʀ(tu)-]
SPI ikkat- 'be shallow' [and ikkatuužaq 'shallow water', Imaq ətəqituu- 'be shallow', ətkazi- 'flatten']
NAI ikkat- 'be shallow'
WCI itkat- 'be shallow' [Lowe; Met. has ikkat-]
ECI ikkat- 'be shallow'
GRI ikkat-

PI ətkalʀuq 'shallow place' [cf. ətɣat- above and quʀ]
SPI Qaw ikkalʀuq 'shallow place'
NAI ikkalʀuq
WCI ikkalʀuq 'shallow place' [Met.; Ras. has Net itkalʀuq 'rock under water']
ECI ikkaʀuq 'shoal, shallows'
GRI ikkaʀłuk 'skerry'

PE ətəɣ(taʀ)- and **əciɣ(taʀ)-** 'have diarrhea' [note that *tət at least goes to cət/cit in Yup (and compare tətaʀ- and also CAY qəcəɣ- under qətəɣ-); the Inu forms may have been influenced by ətəʀ; if the second form is original cf. perhaps Aleut cðaɣ- 'have diarrhea']
AAY —
CAY ciikaʀ- 'have diarrhea' [probably actually əcikaʀ-, which would be indistinguishable from ciikaʀ-]
NSY isixtə- [L.-T.; compare əciʀ for change of initial ə to i in NSY]
CSY siixtə- 'have diarrhea'
Sir [Orr has síxtuʀ- 'have diarrhea', probably borrowed from CSY]
SPI itiktaq- 'have diarrhea'
NAI ɨtiktaq-
WCI itiktaq-
ECI itittaq-
GRI —

PI ətəɣaq- 'hit without penetrating (weapon)'
SPI itiɣaq- 'hit without penetrating, misfire of gun'
NAI itiɣaq- 'fail to accomplish or penetrate (target)'
WCI Cop, Car itiɣaq- 'fail to do, cannot do' [Ras.]
ECI itiɣaq- 'hit a hard object, not be able to penetrate, meet with a refusal'
GRI itiyaʀ- 'not hit properly (wounded animal), meet with a refusal, not have any effect (instrument or person)'

PE ətəmaɣ 'palm of hand' [cf. ətə-]
AAY tumak 'palm of hand'
CAY tumak
NSY ətumak, ətumaq [listed both ways; L.-T. gives the first, ANLC also has itumak]
CSY tunak 'palm of hand' [also 'smooth trail']
Sir [note mətŋ̥əX 'palm of hand']
SPI itumak, Qaw utumak, Imaq ətəmaq 'palm of hand'
NAI utummak, ɨtummak, Nu tummak
WCI itimak
ECI itimak
GRI itumak, EG ilimaq

PE ətəʀ 'anus' [cf. ətə- and Aleut iti-X 'anus']
AAY ətaq 'anus', AP ətXua(ʀ)aq 'sea anemone'
CAY <ə>təq* 'anus, bottom, sea anemone', Nun ətəX* 'anus, bottom'
NSY ətəq 'anus'
CSY təq*
Sir təX
SPI itiq 'anus'
NAI itɨq* 'anus' [and itiʀžuk 'groove, notch']
WCI itiq 'anus'
ECI itiq 'anus' [Lab also 'dent, groove. notch' acc. Peck]
GRI itiq* 'anus' [and note immap iqqa 'the bottom of the sea']

PE ətəquʀ 'urine' [cf. quʀə-, also Aleut icXu- 'wipe one's anal area']
AAY ətquq 'urine' [C also 'honey bucket, chamber pot']
CAY təqquq, Nun ətquX 'urine' [and Nun ətxuiʀ- 'wipe one's anal area']
NSY ətəquq 'urine'
CSY təquq
Sir təqəX
SPI itiʀuq 'old urine used for cleaning, soaking skins'
NAI ɨtiʀuq 'sour urine, ammonia'
WCI itiʀuq 'urine'
ECI itiʀuq
GRI itiʀuq 'stale urine (for washing or soaking)'

PE ətəʀlaɣ 'depression'
AAY —
CAY təʀlak 'dry creek bed'
NSY ətəʀlaq 'ravine, hole, dip' [ətəʀlak on Men.'s comp. list and in L.-T., but with q acc. Em.]
CSY —
Sir —
SPI itiʀlak 'harbor'
NAI itiʀlak 'pouch on back of woman's parka'
WCI Cop itiXXaq 'hollow, dip' [Pryde]
ECI itiʀsaq 'depression, dimple', itiʀlak Lab 'flat valley' [Peck], Igl 'wide bay' [Ras.]
GRI itiʀłak 'depression (in mountains), kettle-shaped bay', NG itiʀlak, itiʀliumaniq 'bay'

PY ətəʀtuli(q) 'lynx' [cf. tu-[1]]
AAY C ətəXtuliq, AP ətəXtuli 'lynx'
CAY təXtuli
NSY —
CSY —

PI ətqaq 'bottom (of sea)' [cf. qaʀ]
SPI [note itqaq- 'go to west of King Island'?]
NAI [Jen. has itqaʀaun 'instrument for measuring

depth of snow']

WCI Sig itqa- 'bottom of lake or sea, out at sea' [Pet.; Pryde has Net, Cop iqqaq 'land, ground' as a shaman's word]

ECI iqqaq 'bottom of sea, river, lake', as posit. root, iqqa-(ŋani) 'at the bottom of (sea, container of clear liquid, etc.)', Lab also 'neighborhood, near' [Bourq.; Ras. has it as a shaman's word in Igl for 'earth, land']

GRI iqqa- 'near, in vicinity of' [posit. root as in iqqaani, but note also iqqaa 'his or her relative', iqqaʀłiq* 'relative'; for immap iqqa 'bottom of the sea' see under ətəʀ above]

PY təqsuqaq 'fin or tail feather'
AAY təqsuqaq 'plume, long feather, tail feather'
CAY təqsuqaq 'adipose fin of fish, tail of bird or plane'
NSY —
CSY —

PE ətəʀ- 'wake up'
AAY — [for əs<x>aʀ- 'wake up' see əsɣaʀaʀ- under əðə]
CAY ➞
NSY [taʀviʀ- 'become more alert, wake up from being sleepy' — ANLC; Men. has ətəkəsitaatuqaq 'attentive']
CSY təXtuʀ-, taXtuʀ- 'wake up' [and note təʀluxtə- 'roll one's eyes up', also təXutə- 'have sexual intercourse with'?]
Sir təXtuʀ-, təXtəʀ- 'wake up' [Vakh. also has trans. təxtuXt(ə)- and təXsaʀ-]
SPI ➞
NAI itɨq- 'wake up' [and itɨʀiaq- 'wake early']
WCI [Net itiʀuhuk 'one who wants to wake up' — Ras.]
ECI itiq- 'wake up'
GRI itiʀ- 'wake up' [and NG itiʀiaq- 'wake early']

PE ətəmli- 'sleepwalk' [cf. mli-]
AAY təmli- 'sleepwalk'
CAY təmli-
NSY ətəmliʀ- 'sleepwalk' [ANLC; L.-T. has ətəmlituqaq 'sleepwalker']
CSY təmli- 'sleepwalk, have a nightmare'
Sir təmli- [Orr]
SPI itivli(a)- 'walk or talk in one's sleep'
NAI itɨvli-
WCI itivli- 'sleepwalk' ['have nightmare' in EP acc. Ow.]
ECI itillima- 'sleepwalk'
GRI itiłłi(ɣ)-, NWG also itułłiɣ-, NG itulli-

PI ətquma- 'be awake' [cf. (u)ma-]
SPI —
NAI itquma- 'be awake'
WCI itquma-
ECI iqquma-
GRI iqquma-

PE ətəvə(t)- 'portage' [cf. ətəʀ or ətə- and vət- under vaʀ-?]
AAY C ət<x>u- 'portage, cross over'
CAY təvə-, Nun ətəvə- 'go over'
NSY ətəvə- 'portage, og up and over' [ANLC; and ətəftə- 'hang (trans.)', ətəvŋa- 'be hanging' (Orr); Men. has ətəvžaʀvik 'mountain pass']
CSY təvə- 'go over, overflow' [and Chap təvnəq* 'portage']
Sir təv(ə)- 'go over, overflow' [Orr; also təvyiXt(ə)- 'heave across, go across' — Vakh. from Rub.]
SPI itivit- 'cross over, pass top of hill and start down'
NAI itɨvɨt- 'portage' [also noun itivlɨq*]
WCI itivit- 'portage' [Pryde; and Net has noun itivliq acc. Ras.]
ECI itivit- 'portage' [and note itilliq 'distance between two sides of a peninsula' acc. Schn., but Lab 'isthmus' acc. Peck and Igl 'portage' in B.-S.; note also itivi(k) 's.th. on other side of land']
GRI ituit-, itivit- 'portage' [and as noun itinniq*, itunniq*, itiłłiq*, NG ituittiʀiaq 'portage', EG ilinniq 'valley']

PE ətəvyaʀaʀ 'portage' [cf. yaʀ]
AAY K təxcua(ʀ)aq, tuxcu(ʀ)aq 'portage'
CAY təvyaʀaq, Nun təvcaʀaX
NSY —
CSY Chap təvyaʀaq
Sir —
SPI Qaw itivyaaq
NAI itivyaaq
WCI Cop itivyaaq 'portage' [Met. has Sig itivvaq — Lowe ivyaʀia]
ECI —
GRI itussaaq 'portage' [old ortho. ituvsâq]

PI ətkəq 'red driftwood (hard)'
Yup — [CSY təxəq and CAY təxqaq 'hardwood' are from təɣəɣ-, q.v.]
SPI ikkiq 'hardwood from spruce'
NAI ikkɨq*, ikkikkii 'red spruce tree, hardwood'
WCI itkiq [Pryde has ikkiq for Cop]
ECI Lab ikki 'pinewood streaks' [Peck has ikkit 'reddish lines on some fir trees']
GRI ikkiq* 'hard red driftwood'

PE ətlu(ʀ)(-) 'hit with sling' [there may be a link to əlquʀ-]
AAY C łuqquq, K pəłqaq 'sling' [the second form by contam. with pətluɣ-[1]?]
CAY əłuqun, əłuquq, əłuqutaq 'sling, rock thrown with sling'
NSY łuuk 'sling' [L.-T.]
CSY łuu(q) [also du. łuuk] 'sling', łuu- 'use a sling'
Sir ələX, əłiX 'sling' [Vakh. from Rub.]
SPI iłłuk-, Qaw iłłuq- 'hit using a sling', iłłuk, Qaw iłłuq, FR iłłuuk 'sling'
NAI illu(u)t-, Nu itlu- 'hit with a sling', illuun, PH illuuk
WCI illuuq-, illusaq- 'hunt with a sling', illuutik 'sling'
ECI illuuq- 'hit with a slingshot' [as nom. = 'slingshot'],

Igl illuun 'sling' [B.-S.; Peck has illoreut for Lab]
GRI iłłu-, iłłusaʀ- 'hit with a sling' [old ortho. igdlu-], NG iɣluuk, iɣluuhat 'sling' [Holt. has both iɣluuk and illuuk; also WG iłłusaʀtaatit, EG ittiiyaʀtaat, Up iłłiiʀžiitit 'sling', iłłuʀ- 'practice using sling' — but Fab. has idlor- 'hit with a sling']

PI ətqik- or **itqik-** 'be at ease' [cf. ət- and nqiɣ-[1]]
SPI itqik- 'feel comfortable, at ease'
NAI —
WCI —
ECI iqqi(C)- 'be untied or loose (dog)'
GRI iqqiɣ- 'be comfortable, at peace'

PE əva- 'sit on eggs' [compare perhaps Aleut miɣa- 'incubate, sit on eggs' if m < *əv-]
AAY waa- 'sit on eggs (bird)'
CAY əva- 'sit on eggs, incubate'
NSY —
CSY —
Sir —
SPI iwa-, Qaw ua-, waa- 'sit on eggs, care for young or baby'
NAI iva- 'bear a litter, whelp, lay and sit on eggs, feed or care for young' [and ivaaq 'young of animal']
WCI iva- 'hatch' [Briggs has also 'cuddle' for Utk]
ECI iva- 'hatch'
GRI iva- 'hatch eggs (bird), lie up close to, lie with litter of puppies (bitch)', NG 'warm one's hands on another's body' [Holt.; ivaaq 'egg bird sits on', ivak 'spawn']

PE əvcuɣ- 'shake' [cf. əvə(ʀ)ləɣ- and perhaps əvəɣ-]
AAY K, PWS uxcuɣ-, KP ułcuɣ- 'shake'
CAY əfcuɣ- 'shake or brush off snow, dirt'
NSY ufsuɣ- 'remove snow, debris, etc. from clothing by beating or shaking' [ANLC; Men. has ufsuɣataaʀ- 'rock, sway', ufsutə- 'brush or knock off snow']
CSY ufsuɣ-, əfsuɣ- 'beat or shake off snow or dirt'
Sir əfsəɣut(ə)- 'shake off' [Vakh. has əfsuɣaʀ-, also ifsəɣut(ə)- from Rub.]
SPI ipsuk- 'brush (snow) off, shake out'
NAI ifsuk- 'vibrate, brush snow off' [and ifsulɨk- 'be wet from rain'; for ivuluk- 'flap' see əvə(ʀ)ləɣ-]
WCI ipsuk-, iffuk- 'shake (clothes, etc.)'
ECI itsu(k)- 'shake (to remove dust, etc.)'
GRI issuɣ- [old ortho. ivsug-] 'shake, tremble' [and issuliɣ- 'flap', issuɣiut(i)- 'shake or fling off']

PE əvəɣ 'grass' [cf. əvək-]
AAY wək 'grass'
CAY HBC əvək, Eg, NS <ə>vək 'grass' [and elsewhere as well vəxtaʀ- 'gather grass' and also vinəq 'grassy island']
NSY əvək 'grass'
CSY vək 'grass' [also vəɣaaq 'grass', vəxłuk, Chap vəɣət 'wash cloth'; vəxtaʀ- 'gather grass']
Sir əvəx 'grass'
SPI iwik, W wik 'blade of dead grass'
NAI ivɨk, iviɣaaq 'blade of grass'
WCI ivik
ECI ivik 'sedge, grease on fingers after having handled blubber or dog food'
GRI ivik, iviɣaq 'blade of grass', iffit, ivikkat (pl.) 'grass' [ivik also 'ship biscuit']

PE əvəɣtaʀ 'bee' [cf. taʀ]
AAY K məxta, məxtaq 'bumblebee' [perhaps by contam. with əmə(ɣ)-?]
CAY vəxtaq, məxtaq 'bumblebee'
NSY uməxtaq [L.-T.]
CSY vəxtaaq
Sir əvəxtəX [Orr]
SPI [iipsak, Qaw iipsaq 'bumblebee' is perhaps unrelat.]
NAI —
WCI Net iviktaq [Ras.]
ECI Baffin ivittaq [Boas]
GRI NG iviktaq 'bee'

PI əvək- 'wipe hands' [cf. əvəɣ and əvcuɣ- — perhaps there is contam. here]
Yup — [for CSY vəxłuk, Chap vəɣət 'washcloth' see əvəɣ]
SPI iwik-, W wik- 'wipe hands'
NAI ivɨk- 'wipe'
WCI Cop ivik-
ECI ivik- 'wipe grease from fingers'
GRI NG ivik- 'dry one's hands'

PI əvɣun 'cloth or towel' [cf. un]
SPI iɣvun 'towel'
NAI ivɣun
WCI ivɣun
ECI iɣɣut 'hand cloth'
GRI NG iɣɣut 'towel'

PE əvə(ʀ)ləɣ- 'flap about or vibrate?' [cf. ləɣ-, also əvcuɣ-]
AAY —
CAY HBC ləviaʀ- 'flap in the wind'
NSY —
CSY uvələxtaʀ-, əvələxtaʀ- 'bounce, vibrate'
Sir əɣələʀ- 'bounce, vibrate' [Orr; Em. has əvələɣ- 'shake' but uvələXtaʀ- 'shudder, shake (intr.)']
SPI iuluk- 'make a big noise'
NAI ivuluk- 'flap'
WCI —
ECI [note ivva(q)- 'skip (with rope)']
GRI [note iʀfala- 'flap', NG iʀvak- 'flap about']

PY əvəʀtə- 'get s.th. in eye'
AAY wəXtə- 'get s.th. in one's eye'
CAY (ə)vəXtə-, HBC əʀəftə-
NSY —
CSY —

PE əvtəʀ 'juice'
AAY —
CAY —
NSY [əftəqitə- 'render fat' — ANLC]
CSY əftəq* 'liquid component of sea mammal fat' [iimža 'oily broth from boiled meat' may be a loan from

Chukchi (m)iməl 'water']
Sir —
SPI —
NAI ifsa(q*), Nu ipsaq* 'juice of meat or fruit, saliva, sap' [and ifsak- 'become damp (e.g. ground)', ifsiq- 'provide with liquid', the latter with p.b. liʀ-, so the other forms may be back-formations; note also ifsulɨk- 'be wet from rain (ground, plants)' — contam. with əvcuɣ-?]
WCI Sig iptiʀit 'old pieces of blubber in which there is no oil left', Car iptiq 'juice, sap, oil from blubber' [Schn. 'adg']
ECI ittiq 'juice, sap, oil from blubber, water in soaked garment', Lab itti 'sap' [and ittaŋiq-, ittiŋiq- 'remove juice' and ittaqayaŋŋit- 'not let out any more oil (blubber)', itta(q)- 'be juicy, wet (ground)', ittaaq 'sperm']
GRI issiq* [old ortho. ivseq] 'juice' [perhaps a back formation from verbal expression with liʀ- — compare issiʀsuʀ- 'squeeze out juice, sweat' with p.b. liʀsuʀ- under liʀ- and compare NAI ifsiq- above]

PE əvyaŋ(ŋ)iʀ 'breast' [the relat. — if any — to əva- is obscure]
AAY Kod uxsaiq, muxsaiq, AP muɣyaiq 'female breast' [the last two forms by contamination with əm(m)uɣ-]
CAY əzvaiq, əzvaik, əzviaq, əvzaik 'female breast'
NSY əvyiaq [Taghyuq and L.-T.]
CSY —
Sir —
SPI iuaŋiq, Qaw iyaiŋiq, W iaŋiq
NAI iviaŋŋiq*
WCI Cop, Net, Car iviaŋiq
ECI iviaŋiq
GRI iviaŋiq(*)

PE əyyi(ʀ) 'yolk' [compare iyuʀ-, iyyuʀ- for the ts reflex of *yy in Inu, though the westerly Inu forms with ks are unexplained]
AAY AP əsiq 'yolk of egg' [Fisher]
CAY əzi(q), HBC əyi(q), Nun əssax 'yolk of egg'
NSY —
CSY —
Sir —
SPI iksiq 'yolk'
NAI [for Nu itciaq 'membrane inside eggshell or around internal organs' see əciʀ]
WCI Car ixxi 'yolk' [Schn., Dor; Lowe has iktiq for H. Island Cop]
ECI itsi, NBI iksi 'yolk'
GRI itsik, Up itsiq 'white of egg', NG itsiq 'yolk'

PI əžət- 'fall (into water)' [cf. əðəvkaʀ-]
Yup [for CSY əsiqXuutə-, isiqXuutə- 'fall into water with a splash' see ciqəʀ-]
SPI ižit-, Imaq əžət- 'fall (from a height)'
NAI ižɨt- 'fall accidentally'
WCI —
ECI —
GRI išit- 'fall into water', NG ihit- 'calve (glacier)' [and isiqqa-, EG ilaqqa- 'disintegrate and turn over (iceberg)' — the former perhaps a NWG form or influenced by ica-]

PI əžžuq- and **əžžuaq-** 'mimic'
SPI ižžuaq- 'mimic' [and Imaq əžužaq- 'be concerned about, assist, pay attention to'?]
NAI ižžuaq- 'mimic' [half-trans. ižžuaqɬiq-]
WCI iyyuaq-, Sig also iyyuq-, iyuq- 'imitate, mock' [Lowe has half-trans. Sig iyuqɬiq-, Cop iyyuaXXi- 'imitate s.o. mockingly'; Ras. has ijoor- 'imitate' for Net]
ECI iyyua(q)- 'copy, imitate' [and iyuq- 'laugh']
GRI iššuaʀ- 'imitate'

PI əž(ž)uʀə- 'express disapproval of' [cf. kə-[1]]
SPI —
NAI ižuʀɨ- 'express disapproval of, mock by imitating' [half-trans. ižuqɬiq-; ižurnaq- 'elicit unfavorable responses from others', ižuʀnaʀɨ- 'express disapproval of, be embarrassed by']
WCI [Ras. has iyuʀi- 'be amused at, deride' and iyuʀnaq- 'be amusing' for Car — Pryde has iyuʀi- 'laugh at' for Cop]
ECI iyuʀi- 'laugh at', iyyuʀi- 'be repelled by'
GRI išuʀi- 'criticize, rebuke, be offended by' [Kl. has half-trans. išuʀ-]

I

PE i(i)[1] 'ugh (exclamation of disgust)?' [cf. i(C)iʀ- and compare ikki]
AAY ii, ix 'how disgusting!'
CAY —
NSY —
CSY —
Sir —
SPI ii 'exclamation of fear'
NAI ii [with breathy voice] 'exclamation of fear' [and note i 'oops!', iaqi 'don't!']
WCI [Dor. has iiq 'no' for Net and Ras. iakak; Pryde has Net Sp. Bay iiqi 'no' and Cop iiq 'no, don't!' (to child)']
ECI —
GRI ii(q) 'how disgusting!, how could you?' [and note iii(q) 'help !', also EG i(i)qqi, iiq 'no']

PE i(i)[2] 'yes' [cf. a(a)ŋ — the nasalized forms in Inu here may be influenced by the latter]
AAY —
CAY ii-i 'yes'
NSY ii-i 'yes, that's how it is, aha'
CSY ii-i 'see, this is how it is'
Sir ii 'yes'
SPI ii-i
NAI ii [nasalized]
WCI ii
ECI NBI, SB ii
GRI NG, EG ii [nasalized] 'yes' [EG also iiyi (Robbe and Menn.), and iimilaa 'yes indeed' — compare aamilaa under a(a)ŋ]

PI ica- 'molt' [cf. perhaps Aleut isa- 'break, crack, chip']
Yup [note CAY Y isəŋquq 'young bird']
SPI Qaw isa- 'molt' [and isa 'molting bird']
NAI isa- 'molt' [and isa 'molting duck that cannot fly', isavik, itcavik 'July']
WCI Cop iha- 'molt' [Ras., who also has Net icavik 'July'; Met. has isat 'molting ducks']
ECI isaq 'molting bird that cannot fly' [and Lab isa- 'molt (bird)']
GRI isa- 'molt, fall apart (e.g. barrel)' [and isa, isaniq* 'molting bird that cannot fly'; Robbe and Menn. have EG isatsimaliq 'eider duck that has molted and cannot fly, gosling that is too young to fly' as well as isaC- 'cannot fly (bird)' — as if from iyaɣ-]

PE icavʀaʀ or **icavɣaʀ** 'baby walrus' [cf. ica- and some of the p.b. forms under vžəʀaʀ-?]
AAY—
CAY —
NSY isavʀaq 'baby walrus'
CSY isavʀaq, əsavʀaq 'person moving a boat on a sled across the ice' [also verbal]
Sir —
SPI izaɣvaq 'baby walrus'
NAI isavɣaq
WCI —
ECI —
GRI—

PY iciɣʷa 'that's what I thought' [cf. uci[2] and dem. root uv-; note esp. NAI usiuvva, to which this set corresponds — presumably it has been influenced by icivaʀ]
AAY Perry iciw̥ału, C iciw̥ami 'I thought it would be so'
CAY iciw̥a 'you know, remember . . .'
NSY —
CSY [note isiɣima 'I thought mistakenly that -']

PE icivaʀ 'recently' [cf. itcaq[1], which may have influenced the Inu forms below]
AAY K iciwaq 'recently', in Perry more distant past, C 'spring', PWS 'early summer' [note also iciwaXpak 'this spring/early summer', Kod 'some time ago', KP iciwaʀ- 'be spring, early summer']
CAY icivaq, iciwaq 'recently, a few days ago'
NSY isivaq 'not long ago' [ANLC; for inłəvaq 'yesterday' see ikpaq]
CSY —
Sir —
SPI —
NAI isvaq 'recently' [or 'in a few days in either direction from the present' acc. Murdoch; note also isivanniq 'seal carcass buried in sand to cure' — compare CSY iʀaluqaq under iʀaluq]
WCI —
ECI —
GRI issaq 'recently' [old ortho. ivsaq — Fabricius also gives ivsaʀšuaq 'long ago'; issaʀu 'in a few days'; and EG itsaŋutsiaai 'soon, in a moment' (Robbe and Menn.)]

PI icuma(-) 'think' [the link, if any, to cuməʀ(tə)- and cumiɣ- is obscure]
Sir — [for əsəmə- 'know how to do' see əlicima- under əlit-]
SPI izuma 'mind' [also Imaq has the initial i in izumaluaq- 'think' and izumaq 'mind, character, will']
NAI isuma- 'think' [and as nom. = 'mind'; also isumaaq- 'be worried, sad']
WCI isuma- 'think' [as nom. = 'thought'; Ras. has isumaq 'mind']
ECI isuma- [as nom. = 'thought' — also 'meaning' in Lab acc. Peck; isumaliuq- 'attribute unknown thoughts or intentions to', isumannik 'as you wish']
GRI isuma- 'think' [as nom. = 'mind, thought, meaning'; isumaliuʀ- 'think, ponder', isumannik 'as you like, on your own accord']

PI icumaaluɣə- 'worry about' [cf. aluk and kə-[1]]
SPI [izumaaluk- 'think']
NAI isumaaluɣɨ- 'worry about'
WCI Cop ihumaaluɣi- [Pryde]
ECI isumaaluɣi- 'think often about' [Saul has 'worry about' rather]
GRI isumaaluɣi- 'be worried about'

PI icumaɣə- 'think about' [cf. kə-[1]]
SPI izumai- 'think about'
NAI isumaɣɨ-
WCI isumaɣi-
ECI isumaɣi-
GRI isumaɣi-, EG isimaŋi- 'think about, worry, be concerned about' [for EG isimiiŋŋiC- 'not pay attention to' see cumiɣ-]

PI icumatu- 'be thoughtful' [cf. tu[1]]
SPI izumatu- 'be wise'
NAI isumatu-
WCI Cop ihumatu- 'be wise' [Pryde; Met. has Sig isumatuʀu- — for isumatuuʀu-? — 'have understanding']
ECI isumatu- 'be intelligent'
GRI isumatu- 'be thoughtful, have a deep meaning', NG ihumatuuq 's.o. who is cheeky or unsavory'

PE iðəʀ- 'hide' [cf. Atkan Aleut izana-, EA iðana- 'be almost invisible, undiscoverable', also Atkan iðaXta- + neg. 'know']
AAY iiʀ- 'hide'
CAY iiʀ-
NSY iiʀ-
CSY iiʀ-
Sir icəʀ- 'hide' [Vakh. has əcəʀ-, also əsX- from Men.'s texts and siʀ- from Rub.; note also əcXutaʀəɣəx 'ambush' and əcəpaniłəʀəX 'sly']
SPI ižiq-, Imaq əžəq- 'hide'
NAI ižiq-
WCI iyiq- 'hide' [and Ras. has Net isʀuti- 'hide from' — for ižʀut(i)-; Briggs has ilʀumiaq- 'hide s.th.' for Utk]

ECI iyiq- 'hide' [and Lab iXXuyi- 'hide oneself', iXXinaik- 'be dim'; Peck has erguti- 'hide FROM' and erger- 'become visible']
GRI išiR- 'hide' [and iRšut(i)- 'hide from', iRšiR- 'become visible' (i.e. 'no longer be hidden', with p.b. ŋiR-), iRšit-, EG iRtit- 'be clear, visible']

PE iðəRaR 'spirit being'
AAY ii<R>aq 'evil spirit, demon'
CAY iiRaq, iinRaq 'evil spirit, ghost' [the latter by contam. with ayanRu(CaR)?]
NSY iiRaq 'savage, wild man'
CSY — [for iRanaq 'disgusting thing' see iRa-]
Sir —
SPI ižiRaq 'hiding person — usually a stranger drifted ashore on ice floe', Qaw 'person believed to live as a hermit, having run away from the world' [compare GRI qivittuq under qəvə(t)-]
NAI PH ižiRaq 'prowler, hiding person' [for Nu iiRaaq 'wild baby (ferocious legendary being)' see i(C)iR-]
WCI Car iyiRaq 'mythical being with eyes and mouth set vertically in face, who lives under rocks' [Pryde]
ECI iyiRaq, iyuRaq, NBI iyuRuyuq 'ghost'
GRI išiRaq 'legendary creature living underground'

PY-S iɣa- 'be thankful or happy'
AAY —
CAY —
NSY —
CSY iɣamsiqa-, iyamsiqa- 'be thankful' [emot. root]
Sir iɣəyuy- 'be happy', iɣəyukə(s)- 'thank' [and iɣəyux 'happy', iɣəyułəX 'joy']

PY-S iɣaq 'mark' [an original geminate ɣ could explain the preservation of the ɣ in CAY, AAY]
AAY iɣaq, Perry ya(ɣ)aq, KP, PWS yaq 'letter, s.th. written' [in earlier K also 'tattoo'],
iɣaR-, yaaR- 'write' [note also yaXtuliq 'owl']
CAY iɣaq 'mark, letter', iɣaR- 'write', əyaq [as verb, əyaR-] 'tattoo' [and note yaaRuin 'story knife']
NSY —
CSY iɣaq, iyaq 'design, tattoo', iɣaR-, iyaR- 'write, make design, tattoo' [and pl. iɣat 'book' acc. Men.]
Sir əɣətəR- 'write', əɣətəX 'paper, book, tatoo' [Em. has əɣətXəməłəRəX 'pattern, picture']
Inu [SPI Qaw iyaq 'tattoo' and NAI Mal iya 'line, streak' (Jen.) are probably borrowed from Yup]

PY-S iɣataR- 'be hungry' [there could be a link to iŋaɣ-, by contam. with iɣə-]
AAY —
CAY —
NSY —
CSY iɣataR-, iyataR- 'be hungry'
Sir iɣətəR- 'be hungry' [Orr; may be borrowed from CSY]

PE iɣðuɣ 'testicle' [dual; there may be a relat. to iɣðuR-]
AAY iɣuk 'testicle'
CAY iɣuuk, Nun iŋcu
NSY ixuk
CSY iɣuk
Sir iɣcəx
SPI iɣžuk
NAI iɣžuk
WCI iɣyuk
ECI iyyuk
GRI iššuk

PE iɣðuR- 'congeal'
AAY C yuXtə-, K iɣuXtə- 'jell, congeal'
CAY (ə)yuR-, iɣuR- 'jell, congeal'
NSY iɣuXtə- 'congeal' [ANLC; Men. has iɣuRnəq 'congealed lump of fat in soup']
CSY iɣuXtə- 'congeal'
Sir iɣžuR- 'harden' [Vakh. from Rub.; Men. has iɣcəɣažakəliRəX 'transparent']
SPI iɣžuq- 'jell, congeal'
NAI iɣžuq- 'jell, congeal', PH iɣžuiqqaq 'lump'
WCI Baker Lake iɣyuq- 'thicken (of liquid)' [Schn.], Cop iɣyuXXiaq 'blubber left out to freeze' [Ras.]
ECI iyyu(q)- 'coagulate, get stiff' [Saul; Peck has iɣyuq- for Lab]
GRI iššuR- [old ortho. igssor-] 'stiffen, coagulate' [and iššuqqaq '(congealed) lump']

PE iɣə- 'swallow'
AAY iɣə- 'swallow'
CAY iɣə-
NSY iɣə-
CSY [for iɣataR-, iyataR- 'be hungry' see iɣataR-] ➟
Sir [for iɣətəR- 'be hungry' see iɣataR-] ➟
SPI ii- 'swallow, have caught many fish in trap'
NAI i<ɣ>i- 'swallow'
WCI ii-
ECI ii- 'swallow, take bait and be caught (bird)'
GRI ii- 'swallow' [and ixxit(i)- 'swallow with s.th. else']

PY-S iɣlak or **iɣlaq** 'esophagus'
AAY Kod, PWS iɣlaq 'esophagus'
CAY iɣlak, iɣlaq
NSY iɣlak 'seal esophagus' [L.-T.]
CSY iɣlak 'windpipe, throat, voice'
Sir iɣləx 'throat' [Orr; Vakh. has iRləx 'voice'; Em. has iɣləɣəRət(ə)- 'lose one's voice, lower sound of s.th.']
Inu [note Nu iɣlʸak 'cheek pocket of squirrel']

PE iɣɣaR(aR) 'throat' [cf. yaR]
AAY iɣɣa<R>aq 'outlet or neck of a lake'
CAY iɣɣaRaq 'throat, area of river at outlet of lake'
NSY iɣɣaRaq 'throat'
CSY —
Sir —
SPI iɣɣiaq
NAI iɣɣiaq 'throat, esophagus'
WCI iɣɣiaq 'throat'
ECI iɣɣiaq
GRI ixxiaq 'throat, gullet'

PE iɣəɣaʀ- or **iɣəɣaɣ-** 'lean (against)' [cf. iɣə-[2]; probably with haplology in Yup]
AAY ixaxtə- 'lean to side, recline'
CAY ixaɣ-, Nun iɣaɣ- lean against'
NSY ixaɣ- 'lean against' [Em.; also ixaŋɣalʀia 'steep' and trans. ixaxtə- 'tilt']
CSY ixaɣ- 'tilt', ixasiXtə- 'recline, leaning on elbow' [and ixaɣžakəxtə- 'be steep']
Sir iɣixt(ə)- 'lean against' [Vakh. also has ixaɣ- 'tilt'; iɣəʀəlŋuX 'straight', iɣəʀəʀ- 'straighten']
SPI Imaq iɣaŋa- [for iiɣaŋa-?] 'be sloping' [and Jen. has KI iiɣaq- 'walk stealthily']
NAI iiɣaq- 'lean, set on a slant'
WCI i(i)ɣaŋaq- 'lean against s.th.'
ECI iiɣaq- 'land (of boat)' [Dor. for Tar]
GRI iiɣaʀ- 'lean up against s.th.' [also 'calve' of glacier, iiɣaq 'wall' — originally 'wall covering (of skin)']

PY iɣtə- 'fall' [cf. iɣəɣaʀ- and perhaps ikciq-]
AAY iXtə- 'fall (down)' [and KP ixii-, PWS ixci- 'drop']
CAY ixtə- 'fall (from a height)'
NSY ixtə- 'fall (down or through)'
CSY —

PI iɣuživk 'temple (anat.)' [cf. ðvig]
SPI iiživk 'temple, temporal bone'
NAI iɣuživk
WCI iɣuyvik
ECI —
GRI —

PY-S iɣvaʀ- 'appear'
AAY iɣwaʀ- 'appear, emerge'
CAY iɣvaʀ-, ivɣaʀ- 'appear (from behind s.th.)'
NSY [iɣvaʀyaʀaq 'corner, turn' (Em.)]
CSY ivɣaʀ- 'go round corner into next room' [ivɣaʀa- 'be in a trance']
Sir iɣvəʀ- 'go around, appear' [Vakh.]

PY-S iɣžuʀ- 'defend verbally'
AAY K iɣuʀ-, Perry yu<ɣ>uʀ-, C yuuʀ- 'defend another person verbally'
CAY əyuʀ-, HBC, Nun, NS iɣuʀ- 'defend verbally'
NSY iɣuʀ- 'defend verbally' [Em.]
CSY iɣuʀ-
Sir iɣcəʀ- 'defend verbally' [Em.]

PE i(C)iʀ- 'cry hard?' [cf. i(i)[1]?]
AAY —
CAY —
NSY iXsuxtaʀ- 'sob'
CSY iiX^{W}aaŋə- 'fume with rage, have a tantrum, want to cry'
Sir —
SPI —
NAI iila- 'moan' [iiqtuaq- 'moan and groan continually'; note also Nu iiʀaaq 'wild baby (legendary being)']
WCI —
ECI —
GRI iiŋala- 'be a cry-baby, be always crying' [iiʀ- 'express disgust', iiʀi- 'be disgusted by']

PY iitaq 'cottongrass'
AAY AP iitaq 'tall cottongrass (esp. edible part of lower stem)'
CAY iitaq
NSY —
CSY —
Inu [Qaw iitaq 'cottongrass stem or root' is probably from the Yup]

PY iiyaq 'ventilator' [cf. əðiʀ and ŋiyaʀ-?]
AAY —
CAY —
NSY iiyaq 'vent, chimney' [L.-T.]
CSY iiyaq
Sir —
Inu [SPI KI iiyaq is probably a loan from Yup]

PE ikaɣ- 'be untidy or unruly'
AAY —
CAY NSU ikaŋa- 'be sloppy'
NSY —
CSY —
Sir —
SPI Qaw ikaŋa- 'be untidy'
NAI ikak- 'be dirty', ikaŋa- 'be untidy' [and ikakłiqi- 'play in the dirt']
WCI —
ECI —
GRI ikaɣ- 'gambol, play', ikkatiɣi- 'play around with (girl), tease', NWG ikaɣ- 'be many, a crowd' [note also italaɣ- 'be untidy', itaʀšuaq 'what an untidy person!']

PE ikamʀaʀ '(small) sled'
AAY C ikammaq 'sea otter', AP ikam<ʀ>ak (du.) 'sled'
CAY ikamʀaq '(dog) sled, car' [and ikamtaɣ, ikamtaʀ- 'go over surface (of snow, etc.)']
NSY —
CSY —
Sir —
SPI iɣaʀmaq 'small sled'
NAI PH ikamʀaq 'small sled for carrying seals'
WCI [Cop ikaaʀallak 'basket sled'; Pryde has Net Sp. Bay ikamŋaaq 'sled' as a shaman's word]
ECI —
GRI —

PE ikayuʀ- 'help'
AAY ikayuʀ- 'help'
CAY ikayuʀ- 'help' [ikayuutə- 'help out']
NSY ikayuʀ- 'help'
CSY ikayuʀ- 'agree with, help'
Sir —
SPI iɣayuq- 'help'
NAI ikayuq-
WCI ikayuq-
ECI ikayuq-
GRI ikiuʀ-, NG ikayuq-, EG iɣiiʀ- 'help' [and ikiuut(i)- 'give a hand']

PI ikciq- 'shake' [cf. iɣtə-?]
SPI Qaw iksiq- 'be an earthquake' [Jen. has 'tremble, shake' for KI]
NAI —
WCI Car? iksiq 'thunder, earthquake' [Schn. 'adg']
ECI —
GRI issaʀ- [old ortho. igsar-] 'swing back and forth'

PY ikə- 'remove (a piece)' [cf. ikuɣ-]
AAY —
CAY —
NSY ikə- 'remove a piece', ikuʀ- 'remove' [ANLC]
CSY iikə- 'remove, unfasten', ikuʀ- 'remove, cut off' [and ikutə- 'cut off a piece', iikaɣaʀ- 'suddenly come undone']
Inu — [but note EG iɣaat 'saw' acc. Ges.]

PE ikəɣ(ə)t- 'be few' [compare canəɣ(ə)t- 'be thin' for the negative p.b. probably contained here]
AAY KP əkxitə- 'be few', K ikəxtə-, PWS ikxətə- [cf. neg. p.b. ŋit-]
CAY ikxətə- 'be few' [with the same tə ~ l alternation as neg. p.b. ŋit-; and note ikxəli-, ikəɣli-, ikəxłi- 'become few']
NSY əxkitaʀaq 'a few' [ANLC]
CSY —
Sir —
SPI iɣik- 'be few'
NAI ikɨt-
WCI Cop ikit-
ECI ikit- 'be few' [and note Lab ikiɣli- 'get fewer' in Peck]
GRI ikiɣ- 'be few' [and ikiłłi-, ikili- 'get fewer']

PY ikiɣ- 'be bent or stooped'
AAY ikiɣ- 'be bent or stooped over (forward)' [postural root]
CAY ikiɣ-
NSY —
CSY —

PE iki(C)ituɣ 'plant species'
AAY —
CAY ikiituk 'wild celery'
NSY ikiituk [ANLC]
CSY —
SPI Qaw ikiituk, Unk ikiutuk 'wild celery'
NAI Mal ikuusuk
WCI [for Cop ixuun 'arctic heather' (acc. Lowe) see əɣzutət]
ECI —
GRI —

PE ikiʀ- 'open'
AAY ikiʀ- 'open' [postural root, i.e. also trans. ikiXtə-]
CAY ikiʀ-
NSY ikiʀ-
CSY ikiʀ-
Sir ikiɣžuʀ- 'open' [Vakh., who also has ikaXt(ə)- 'open (door), raise' from Rub.]
SPI Qaw FR ikikaq- 'open (door)' [and KI iɣiʀaaq 'tent floor'?]
NAI ikiʀaaq 'tent door made of two flaps' [verbal = 'open easily (tent door)']
WCI ikiqtit- 'open up (crevasse, etc.)' [and ikiʀiaqtuq 'door (that is) slightly open'; Ras. has Cop ikiqtuq- 'open slightly', Pet. has Sig ikiʀaq- 'uncover']
ECI — [for ikiqtu- 'be gaping wide (crevasse)' see əkəqtu- under əkəʀ]
GRI ikiʀsit- 'open ajar, spread out'

PE ikki 'ugh (exclamation of disgust)' [cf. i(i)^1]
AAY ikii 'ugh!' [reaction to s.th. sloppy or wet]
CAY ikii exclamation of discomfort because of wetness, dirtiness, etc. [also ikaai, ikkatak 'ugh' and ikkiq 's.th. ugly']
NSY —
CSY Chap iki 'you mustn't, don't!' [and SLI ikiqun 'but yet, wait until']
Sir iki 'but, you mustn't' [Vakh.]
SPI ikkii, iikii 'how dirty, foul smelling!'
NAI ikkii 'how dirty!' [and cf. Nu ikiaʀuk- 'feel cold', PH ikiaqtaq- 'shiver from cold']
WCI Cop ikki 'how cold, wet!' [Met.], Car ikkii 'it's cold!' [Ras.; Ow. has ikkiiq-, ikkiirnaq- 'be cold' for EP]
ECI ikii 'how cold!'
GRI ikkii 'how cold, wet!' [and ikkiiʀnaʀ- 'be cold or wet', NG ikkiʀihuk- 'feel cold']

PY iknaqə- 'be strong'
AAY —
CAY —
NSY ikn̥aqə- 'be strong'
CSY ikn̥aqə-

PI ikŋik 'point or tip'
SPI W iknik [for ikŋik?] 'point of s.th.' [Jen.; note also Qaw place name ikŋiituq near Rocky Point]
NAI in^{y}ŋik, iŋŋik, Nu ikŋiq 'sharp point' [as verb = 'sharpen pencil']
WCI iŋniɣik- 'be pointed' [and Sig igniʀa 'point' acc. Pet.; Ras. has Car iktaq 'nose of sledge runner']
ECI [Boas has ingi 'mountain tip' for Baffin and Peck has iksuk 'point of knife', iksuktaq- 'make point new again' for Lab]
GRI iŋŋik 'tip (of mountain or knife)' [and note Fab. ingirksoit 'mountains']

PI ikpaq 'yesterday or recently' [compare itcaq^1 and icivaʀ; most forms below contain p.b. kðaʀ]
Yup [NSY inłəvaq 'yesterday' — Enm. et al — from an earlier *iŋluvaq (see iŋlu?), possible source of this set; Men. has inłəvałak as an adjectival]
SPI ikpaq 'some time ago, a month or so ago' Qaw 'recently', ikpakšaq 'yesterday' [and ikpažaaq, Qaw ikpakšaaq, KI also itpažaaq 'recently', ikpažaʀuužaq 'in a few days'; note Imaq iɣluvaq 'evening', which probably goes with the NSY form above]
NAI ikpakšaq 'yesterday' [and ikpakšaaʀu(n) 'in a few days', ikpakšaaq 'a few days ago']
WCI ikpaksaq, ikpaxxaq 'yesterday' [and Sig ikpaksa(a)ʀu 'in a few days', ikpaksaani 'the other day, the day before yesterday']

ECI ippasaq, NBI ikpaksaq 'yesterday' [and ippasaani 'the day before yesterday']
GRI ippaššaq 'yesterday' [and ippaššaani 'the day before yesterday']

PE ikuɣ- 'hack at' [compare ipuɣ- and ikə-]
AAY ikuɣ- 'find, dig up'
CAY ikuɣ- 'lift, pry up' [and ikuʀ- 'remove, cut off']
NSY ikuŋ̥əq 'gouging, hollowing out' [and ikuxtutə- 'make a bar for games']
CSY — [for iikə- 'remove, unfasten' see ikə-]
Sir [note ikəɣ-, ikəxtəʀ- 'beat' — Vakh. from Men.'s texts]
SPI iɣuk- 'stretch with a skin scraper (hide)'
NAI ikuk- 'scrape (animal skin)'
WCI Sig ikuk- 'plane down' [Pet. has 'scrape', Ras. has 'chop off' for Net, and Schn. has 'adg' ikupik- 'cut a small piece off']
ECI ikupiɣaq- 'remove several pieces (of meat or tobacco)'
GRI ikuɣ-, NG ikuaq- 'cut, hack'

PE ikuɣutaʀ and **ikuɣun** 'instrument for hacking or scraping' [cf. un]
AAY ikusaq, ikuutaq 'laddle, dipper' [contamination from ipuɣ-]
CAY ikuutaq 'lever, crowbar'
NSY ikuxutə 'comb for dried grass, nail puller, crowbar' [ANLC; Em. has ikuɣun 'screwdriver, can opener']
CSY —
Sir — [for iɣlaʀ- 'sew' see il(l)aɣ-]
SPI iɣuun, iɣuutaq 'skin scraper'
NAI ikuun, Mal icuun 'skin scraper'
WCI ikuutaq 'drill' [meaning here and in ECI show possible contamination with niɣəðuʀ- and niɣəðuʀun; also B.- S. for Car; Ras. has 'adze']
ECI ikuutaq 'bow drill, bit' [and verbal = 'drill']
GRI NG ikuutaq 'axe' [WG ikuttaat 'axe']

PE ikuɣəɣ 'elbow' [cf. ikuɣ-; Inu strong i is regular after s, note]
AAY ikuwik 'elbow'
CAY ikuzək, ikuyək
NSY ikuyək
CSY ikuyək
Sir ikəyəx
SPI iɣusik, Di iɣusiq
NAI ikusik
WCI ikusik
ECI ikusik
GRI ikusik

PE ikviɣ- 'suffer' [cf. əlpəkə-, but the relat. — if any — is obscure]
AAY —
CAY —
NSY —
CSY ikfiqə- 'feel anguish, suffer'
Sir — [for kəpəqšuqə(s)- 'be tormented' and kəpəqšuqałəX 'torture' see kəpət-[2]]
SPI [ikpii-, Di əkpəə- 'have one's sleep disturbed by -', Imaq əkpəə- 'worry about' reflect contam. with əlpəkə-, q.v. for Qaw homonym 'feel sensation (e.g. pinprick)']
NAI ikpiɣi- 'feel a slight pain from', PH 'experience discomfort from'
WCI ikpiɣi-, ippiɣusuk 'suffer, feel pain from' [emot. root]
ECI ippiɣi-, ippiɣusuk- 'feel pain, suffer, notice s.th.' [the latter sense going with əlpəkə-; also ippinaq- 'be able to be felt (touch or pain)']
GRI ippiɣi- 'be troubled by' [intr. ippiŋiaɣ-, ippiɣusuɣ-; ippiɣuɣ- 'not be well', ippinnaʀ- 'be offensive' and probably also ippiʀnaq 'mosquito, gnat', ippiqi- 'be pestered by insects']

PE ila(-)[1] 'part' [and verbal 'add'; cf. Aleut ila 'part (of s.th.)']
AAY ila 'part (of), relative' [verbal = 'add']
CAY ila 'part (of), relative, associate' [verbal = 'add']
NSY ila 'friend' [ilii '(his) other'; verbal = 'add']
CSY ila 'part (of), relative, friend' [verbal = 'add']
Sir ila 'friend' [and as possessed root ilə(ŋa) '(the) other, second', and iləvałəX 'piece' [also ilikcəʀ- — for iləkcəʀ-? — 'add']
SPI ila 'relative, companion' [verbal = 'add']
NAI ilʸa 'part (of), relative, companion' [verbal = 'add, get a new participant'; note ilʸaži 'relative(s)']
WCI ila(k) 'part (of), relative, piece' [and Lowe has Sig ilaa- 'add']
ECI ila 'part (of), relative, piece ' [verbal = 'add piece to garment']
GRI ila 'part (of), relative, companion' [verbal = 'add, increase, exaggerate, get another helping'; and ilaqutaq 'family member', NG ilaluinnaq 'relative'; Tersis has EG ia as well as ilaq]

PE ila(C)aʀ 'patch or addition' [cf. Aleut ilaʀ-, ilaʀi-X 'patch'; compare ilaɣaʀ- below]
AAY ila<ɣ>aq 'addition'
CAY ilaaq 'patch' [and verbal ilaaʀ- 'patch']
NSY ilaaq 'patch' [ilaaʀ- 'sew on (patch)']
CSY ilaaq* 'patch' [and verbal ilaaʀ- ; note also iliʀaq 'patch on sole of boot']
Sir — [note iliʀaX 'patch on sole of boot' (Orr)]
SPI ilaaq 'patch' [also verbal]
NAI ilʸaaq 'patch' [verbal = 'put addition on']
WCI ilaaq 'patch'
ECI ilaaq-, ilaaqtu(q)- 'add pieces to a garment'
GRI ilaaq 'patch' [and ilaaʀ- 'patch', ilaaʀtuʀ- 'patch net or clothing, darn socks, increase in number']

PE ilaɣaʀ- 'join in' [cf. aʀ-?]
AAY ila<ɣ>aʀ- 'join (s.o.), join in'
CAY ilaɣaʀ-
NSY — [but note ilʀutkuaɣan 'song']
CSY [ilaɣaʀ- 'sing' — compare the Sir under ilatə below]
Sir —
SPI —
NAI —

WCI —
ECI —
GRI ilaaʀ- ‘imitate, keep (s.o.) company, do as (s.o. else)’

PE ilakə- ‘be part or one of’ [cf. kə-[1]]
AAY ilakə- ‘take along with one, include, be related to’
CAY ilakə- ‘be related to’
NSY ilakə- ‘have as friend’ [Enm. et al.]
CSY ilakə- ‘have as friend or relative’
Sir [Vakh. has iləq(ə)- — for iləkə-? — ‘be friends’ from Rub.’s texts]
SPI ilaɣi- ‘have as a friend, find a missing piece of s.th.’
NAI il^{y}aɣɨ- ‘include, have as a member’ [and cf. il^{y}au- ‘be a member, be included’, PH ‘give or receive shares of a whale’]
WCI ilaɣi- ‘be related to, add one more to’
ECI ilaɣi- ‘have as a relative or traveling companion’
GRI ilaɣi- ‘be a part or one of, be related to, accompany’ [and ilaa- ‘go along, be a passenger’]

PE ilali(C)uʀ- ‘make or be friends’ [cf. li(C)uʀ- and EA ilali- ‘make friends’]
AAY C ilaliuʀ-, PWS ilali- ‘fool around with one’s relatives, argue with relatives’ [and note Kod ilaliɣaaʀ- ‘gossip about relatives’]
CAY ilaliuʀ- ‘be sociable’ [and ilaliute- ‘mix, join’]
NSY ilaliitə- ‘befriend, intercede on s.o.’s behalf’
CSY ilaliiʀ- ‘make friends’
Sir —
SPI ilaliuti- ‘join’ [and ilali- ‘shake s.o.’s hand, Qaw ilaliq- ‘join, get imbued with’, ilałXuaq- ‘fool around, play the clown’]
NAI il^{y}aliuq- ‘make (s.o.) one’s relative’ [and il^{y}ali- ‘shake hands with, wave at’, il^{y}aliutɨ- ‘join (group), make a part of’]
WCI ilaliut(i)- ‘join’
ECI ilaliuq- ‘receive a guest, get a companion, found a family, acknowledge as a relative’
GRI ilaliut(i)- ‘join, add’ [compare ilaliʀ- ‘add to’]

PI ilamaaq- ‘treat as a relative?’ [cf. (u)maʀ(aʀ)- and compare pima(a)q-]
SPI ilamaaq- ‘call s.o. (as) one’s dear friend or relative’
NAI il^{y}amaaqtuq-
WCI —
ECI —
GRI ilamaaʀ- ‘give s.th. for the sake of one’s relationship with s.o.’ [also ‘increase (e.g. speed of boat with help of oars)’, a different derivative]

PE ilannaʀ ‘friend’ [cf. nnaq; the CAY could be a borrowing from Inu]
AAY —
CAY Y, HBC ilanaaʀaq ‘friend’
NSY —
CSY —
Sir —
SPI ilanaq ‘friend’
NAI il^{y}annaq ‘good friend’
WCI ilannaq ‘friend’
ECI ilannaaq
GRI ilannaʀi-, ilannaaʀi- ‘like, spend a lot of time with’ [ilanna(a)ʀiit ‘good friends’]

PE ilaŋa(t)ni ‘some time’ [loc. case 3rd person sing./pl. possessed]
AAY iliini, Perry iłiini ‘sometime(s)’
CAY (cam) iliini ‘sometime’ (cat) ilaitn̥i ‘once in a while’
NSY iliini ‘sometimes’
CSY ilaŋani ‘meanwhile’ [ilaŋakun ‘sometimes’]
Sir iləŋəni ‘sometime’ [and Vakh. has iləŋku ‘once, some time’]
SPI ilaatni ‘sometime(s)’
NAI il^{y}aanni, Mal il^{y}aatni ‘sometime(s)’
WCI ilaanni ‘some time(s)’, ilaannilu ‘goodbye’
ECI ilaani, ilaŋan(n)i ‘sometimes’
GRI ilaanni ‘sometime(s)’

PE ilaŋci- ‘treat as a relative’ [cf. nəɣ- and Inu si- under li-[2]]
AAY [note ilaŋə- ‘gain a relative, increase’, ilaŋcaʀ- ‘ask or want s.o. to go along with one’]
CAY ilaŋci- K, NI ‘pay attention to’, Y ‘ignore, leave alone’ [and ilaŋciaʀ(aʀ)- ‘tease in a friendly way’]
NSY ilaŋsi- ‘invite, propose’
CSY —
Sir —
SPI ilaksia- ‘bother physically by touching’
NAI il^{y}aksia- ‘bother’, Nu il^{y}aksiuq- ‘disturb, confuse’
WCI —
ECI —
GRI ilassi- [old ortho. ilagsi-] ‘receive in a friendly manner, greet, take to heart’ [and ilassiuʀ- ‘be polite, friendly’]

PE ilaŋiʀ- ‘remove or lose a part’ [cf. ŋiʀ-]
AAY ilaiʀ- ‘lose or remove part’
CAY ilaiʀ-
NSY ilaŋiʀ-
CSY —
Sir —
SPI ilaŋiq- ‘lose a loved one, take away a part or member’
NAI il^{y}aŋiq-
WCI ilaŋiq- ‘take away a part of’
ECI ilaŋiut(i)- ‘take a part of s.th., give a part to s.o.’, Iti ilaŋi(C)- ‘give a part of s.th. to’
GRI ilaŋiʀ- ‘get a part of ’

PE ilaŋŋaʀ- ‘remove or diminish’
AAY AAY ilaŋaXtə- ‘improve, get better’, AP ‘(let) die down (storm)’
CAY ilaŋaXtə- ‘subtract, remove’
NSY ilaŋaXtə- ‘die down, take a part of s.th.’
CSY —

Sir —
SPI ilaŋaq- 'break away (shore ice), take part of s.th.'
NAI ilʸaŋŋaq- 'reduce, be reduced'
WCI ilaŋŋaq- 'take a part of s.th.'
ECI ilaŋŋa(q)- 'remove, take a part of s.th.'
GRI ilaŋŋaʀ- 'take part of s.th., subtract, diminish' [and ilaŋŋaa- 'take s.th. another should have had', EG 'sleep']

PY-S ilatə- 'add [cf. t-[1]]
AAY ilatə- 'mix'
CAY —
NSY ilatə- 'add'
CSY ilatə- 'add, join in'
Sir ilat(ə)- 'join, add' [and note iłtəX 'song', iłtəʀəti- 'sing', also iłtəʀ- 'compete at singing or dancing' acc. Em.].

PI ilavinəq 'piece or part' [cf. vinəʀ]
SPI ilaviniq 'piece, part'
NAI ilʸavinʸɨq*
WCI —
ECI ilaviniq 'dead relative'
GRI ilaminiq* 'piece'

PI ila[2] 'just so (exclamation)' [there seems to be some entanglement with əł(ə)ŋa]
Yup — [for CSY łaŋaqa 'it looks, sounds as if' see əł(ə)ŋa]
Sir — [for iłəma 'indeed', iłəmaqun 'as if', iłəma tana 'perhaps' see əłmaʀ(ᴀʀ)]
SPI ilainaq 'in vain, for no reason', Imaq ila(a)qa 'thus, agreed, even, please', ilaqauva 'thus, however', ilaqami 'as if' [the last form seems to go rather with əł(ə)ŋa]
NAI ilʸainʸnʸaq 'to no avail' [for ɨlaa 'just like' see əł(ə)ŋa]
WCI Cop ila 'of course, yes indeed' [Jen.; for ilaannilu 'goodbye' see ilaŋa(t)ni under ila(-)[1]]
ECI ilaa 'I mean', ilaii 'it's true, isn't it?', ilaali 'you're right' [Dor., who also has Aiv iila; Bourq. has ila 'certainly, it's true' for Lab]
GRI ila 'indeed, that's true', ilaa 'isn't that so?' [and ilami 'yes indeed']

PE ilacciʀ- 'lack initiative?' [cf. ila(-)[1] and c(c)iʀ-?]
AAY [Perry ilatuʀyuɣ-, AP ilasuuɣ- 'feel self- pity']
CAY ilaciʀ- 'refrain from acting in the hope that others will act for one', Nun 'draw breath again after almost drowning', K 'act inappropriately when a close relative is dying'
NSY —
CSY —
Sir —
SPI ilasiq- 'leave food to ferment or fat to render, not clean oneself when dirty', Qaw 'remain passive, not defend oneself'
NAI ilʸatciq-, ilʸatciaq- 'not defend oneself, lack initiative, leave things alone'
WCI —
ECI —
GRI ilatsiʀ- 'be untidy or careless (about oneself or s.th. else), let decay' [and ilatsiinnaʀ- 'hesitate until one is set going']

PE il(l)aɣ- 'be entangled'
AAY ilaɣ- 'be tangled'
CAY ilaɣ-, ilaʀ-
NSY iɣlaɣ- 'be tangled' [ANLC; L.-T. has iɣlałəq 'tangled']
CSY iɣlaɣutə- 'tangle', Chap iɣlaɣ- 'tangle, mix up'
Sir iɣlaɣutə- [Orr; also cf. iɣlaʀ- 'sew' (Vakh. and Orr), both from CSY? — the latter may be by contam. with ila(C)ᴀʀ- under ila(-)[1] however]
SPI ilak- 'be tangled'
NAI ilʸlʸak- 'tangle, get entangled' [and Nu ilʸaksiuq- 'confuse']
WCI ilak- 'get tangled' [Pryde]
ECI Lab ilaqik- 'tangle'
GRI ilaɣ- 'be tangled, in a mess'

PE il(l)aɣiʀun and **il(l)aɣiʀusiʀ** 'comb' [cf. ŋiʀ- and un or uciq; the AAY and Inu forms are in the pl.]
AAY [ilaiXtuutət, PWS iliiXtuutət 'comb' — both forms may alternatively end in - at]
CAY Y ilaiʀin 'comb'
NSY [iɣliaʀinəq 'combing' (L.-T.)]
CSY iɣlaɣiisiq
Sir iɣləɣiʀəsiʀaX [Orr]
SPI illaiyutit, Qaw illaiɣutit 'comb'
NAI ilʸlʸaiɣutɨt
WCI illaiyutit
ECI illaiɣuti
GRI iłłaaɣutit [old ortho. igdlaigutit], iłłaayaatit, NG illaɣiutit

PY ilalʀu- 'torment' [cf. ila(-)[1] and ilaŋci- under it]
AAY KP ilalʀutə-, ilallutə-, PWS ilaləXtuuʀ-, Kod ilałəxtə- 'torment' [but elsewhere ilasaaʀ-, K ilanaXqə- 'torment, beat up']
CAY NSU ilalʀu- 'torment' [elsewhere ilałkə-, NSK ilasqitə-]
NSY —
CSY —

PY ilaq '(kind of) small fish' [cf. iłuuq?]
AAY Kod ilaʀnaq 'salmon or trout fry'
CAY NSU ilaʀaaʀaq 'small fish found in lakes' [and note NS ilaqcuugaq 'stickleback']
NSY —
CSY —

PI iləqə- 'shake head' [cf. iləquq and iləqšaq-?]
SPI —
NAI —
WCI Sig iliqitama(a)q- 'shake head (to say no)' [Lowe has iliqitamauq-]
ECI iliqiluk-, Iti iliqiluq- 'move head in all directions', iliqitamaak- 'let head loll around in all directions' [Boas has iliqimisaq- for Baf.]
GRI iliqila- 'shake head (in weakness)', iliqimisaaʀ- 'shake head to give sign'

PI iləqšaq- 'squirm or twist' [there may be a link to iləqə-]
SPI Qaw iliqšaq- 'move' [as nom. = 'split sinew for thread', but Imaq has iləqšaq, ələqšaq 'vein, tendon']
NAI ilʸiqšaq-, ilʸiʀšaq- 'squirm, quake, move around' [nom. = 'strip of split sinew to use as a thread'; note also Nu ilʸʀiq- 'become twisted']
WCI iliqsaq- 'struggle, squirm'
ECI Lab iliʀsat 'prepared reindeer sinew' [Peck]
GRI iliʀšaq 'sinew thread', pl. 'twine' [and iliʀši- 'make thread even by rolling between hands']

PY-S iləquq 'brain' [cf. iləqə- and quʀ?]
AAY iłquq 'brain'
CAY iłquq, HBC ilquq, NSU iłəquq 'brain' [similar distribution under aləqaʀ; also iłqiuɣnəq*, iłquinəq* 'empty skull']
NSY iləquq 'brain'
CSY iiłquq
Sir iłqəX 'brain' [and iłqupax 'skull' — Vakh. from Rub.'s texts]

PE iliɣ 'partner'
AAY ilik 'partner, assistant' [and ililiʀ- K 'be s.o.'s partner', C 'assist']
CAY iliq, Nun iliXaX 'partner'
NSY —
CSY —
Sir —
SPI — [for iliɣaaʀžuk 'boy' see əliɣaʀ(ᴀʀ)]
NAI —
WCI ilik 'friend who customarily provides assistance to one' [Pryde; Met. has iliɣiiktuk 'partners' — iliɣiik acc. Pryde]
ECI ilik 'partner, comrade' [and iliŋŋataq 'one who is alone, without a partner']
GRI ilik 'helper, friend, partner' [and iłłiʀ(suʀ)- 'support, take s.o.'s side']

PI illaatquciq 'porcupine' [cf. il(l)aɣ-?]
Yup [NS ilaanquciq 'porcupine' is probably a borrowing from SPI]
SPI illaatquziq 'porcupine'
NAI ilʸlʸaatqusiq ' porcupine' [but PH, Mal ilʸuqutaq]
WCI illa(a)tqusiq
ECI Lab illaaɣusik [Schn. has Tar illaaqutsiq for W. Bay, marked with a question mark]
GRI ilaqusiq 'hedgehog, porcupine'

PI illa(ɣa)užaq 'ice forming crystals in spring' [cf. perhaps il(l)aɣ- and ŋ(ŋ)uðaʀ]
SPI —
NAI ilʸlʸaɣaužaq 'dangerous spongy ice that has begun to melt through'
WCI illauyaq 'ice forming sharp crystals during spring break- up' [Pryde]
ECI illauyaq 'ice which forms sharp vertical crystals when it breaks up in spring, 'candle' ice' [also 'skin of basking seal']
GRI —

PE illuʀ(ᴀʀ) '(cross) cousin' [cf. iluŋaq]
AAY ilu(ʀ)aq, AP iluʀaq, AP iluq 'male cousin'
CAY iluʀ(aq*) 'male cross cousin of male'
NSY iluʀaq 'cross cousin, close friend, joking partner' [ANLC]
CSY iluʀaq* 'male cross cousin of male', iluq 'hey cousin!'
Sir ilux 'male cousin' [Vakh. has iluX 'brother, male cousin']
SPI illuq 'cross cousin'
NAI ilʸlʸuq 'cross cousin, joking partner'
WCI Sig illuq 'cousin — child of father's sister or mother's brother' [Ow. has illuq 'respected friend' for EP; Pryde has illuq 'cousin of same sex' for Net but 'cross-cousin of same sex' for Baker Lake — as at Igl]
ECI Igl illuq 'cousin', illuʀiit 'cross cousins' [B.- S.]
GRI iłłuq* 'cousin' [old ortho. igdloq due to iŋlu? — Top has idlo 'relative'; in NG 'cousin of same sex'; for NG iluliaq 'great grandchild' see iluliʀᴀʀ under ilu]

PY-S ilŋiʀ- 'have lost a tooth' [cf. ŋiʀ- ; for corresponding Inu forms see kəkŋiq under
kəkə-]
AAY ilŋiq 'gap, missing tooth'
CAY ilŋiʀ- 'lose a tooth'
NSY —
CSY iilŋiʀ- 'lose a front tooth' [also 'go out (flame in middle of oil lamp)' in Rub.; iilŋiq 'missing tooth']
Sir ilŋiʀ- 'be knocked out (tooth of comb, notch in blade)', also 'go out (flame in middle of oil lamp)' [Em.]

PE ilu 'inside' [cf. Aleut il-, western Aleut also ilu- 'inside']
AAY ilu- 'inside' [posit. root]
CAY ilu 'interior, inner feelings, intestinal tract' [ilutm̥un 'inward']
NSY ilu 'interior, inside'
CSY ilu 'interior, inner organs or feelings'
Sir ilmənu 'inward'
SPI ilu 'inside, entrails, rime frost'
NAI ilʸu 'inside, cavity, rime frost' [and as verb = 'be surrounded, surround']
WCI ilu- 'inside', iluk 'rime frost' [and as verb = 'surround'; Car? iluŋmut 'inward' — Schn. 'adg']
ECI ilu 'inside, rime frost' [verbal = 'surround'; Boas has Igl iluk; note also ilum(m)ut 'inward']
GRI ilu- 'inside', iluq 'rime frost (inside window or tent)' [the latter also 'lower belly' in NG; as verb = 'surround'; ilummut 'inward', and note EG iluʀut 'liver', ilivat 'nostrils' (Ges.) and ilaaʀnaq 'rime (frost)' — acc. Robbe and Menn. ilaaʀniq]

PE ilu- 'form rime frost (on inside surface)'
AAY ilu- 'become damp or frosted over (window)'
CAY ilu- 'become frosted'
NSY —
CSY —
Sir —
SPI ilu- 'form (frost)'
NAI ilʸu-
WCI ilu- [Lowe]

ECI ilu- 'be frosted (over)'
GRI ilu- 'make rime frost on inside of, freeze to bottom (river)'

PI iluit- 'be whole' [cf. ŋit-]
Sir — [for icəʀunaʀməłŋuX 'all, whole' see əlu(ʀ)-]
SPI —
NAI —
WCI iluit- Sig 'not be hollowed out', Cop 'be whole' [and Ras. has iliviliq 'mainland' for Net]
ECI iluit- 'be complete, full, not hollowed out' [and iluiliq 'mainland']
GRI iluit-, ilivit- 'be whole'

PE iluli(C)aʀ 'great grandchild?' [cf. li(C)aʀ]
AAY ilulia'un Kod 'grandchild', PWS 'great grandchild'
CAY Nun iluliaʀun 'great grandchild' [and ilupəʀaq, for which see ilupəʀ(aʀ) below]
NSY —
CSY —
Sir —
SPI iluliaq, iluliaʀun 'great grandchild' [but Ras. has 'great grandfather' for W]
NAI [note il^{y}ɨvlɨq 'grandchild', Nu il^{y}ullɨk 'great grandchild']
WCI Cop iluliaʀun 'great grandchild' [Pryde]; Ras. has iluliaʀut 'great grandfather' for Net]
ECI —
GRI NG iluliaq 'great grandchild'

PE ilul(l)iʀaʀ 's.th. inside?' [cf. ilulliʀ below and aʀ?]
AAY iluli<ʀ>aq 'lining,wallpaper'
CAY —
NSY —
CSY iluliʀaq 'drifting ice on inward side of pack ice'
Sir —
SPI iluliaq 'bay, inlet'
NAI il^{y}uliaq, Nu il^{y}ulliaq 'inlet, cove'
WCI —
ECI [iluliaʀusiq 'inner fillet of whale']
GRI iluliaq 'iceberg'

PI ilulli- 'hollow out or work on interior' [cf. ləɣ and li-[1] — i.e. 'make into a container'?]
SPI iluli- 'make a hollow in'
NAI [note il^{y}uʀži- 'become concave, make a hollow in', also il^{y}ulɨk 'container']
WCI [iluli-, iluliuq- 'hollow out', ilulik '(there is) s.th. inside', and with liʀ- ilulliq- 'put s.th. in']
ECI ilulli- 'sew waterproof inner stitch of boot' [and note ilulik 'container, content', iluli-, ilulli(C)- 'fill, load (gun)', iluliuq- 'hollow out']
GRI ilułłi- [old ortho. ilugdli-] 'make a hollow in, sew inner seam (of kayak seam)' [and EG iliʀsi- 'hollow out'; note also iluliq, NG ilulixxaq 'bullet, cartridge', NWG ilulissivik 'bullet pouch']

PE ilulliʀ and **iluqliʀ** 'inner thing or part' [cf. l(l)iʀ; the second form with qliʀ — compare civul(l)iʀ and civuqliʀ under civu-]
AAY iluqłiq 'inner part'
CAY iluqłiq*
NSY iluliq 'inner (e.g. clothing)'
CSY iluliq(*), ilulirnəq* 'inside part' [but ilukłiq* 'inner part']
Sir —
SPI ilulliq 'innermost one'
NAI il^{y}ulliq*
WCI ilulliq 'interior thing'
ECI ilulliq 'one furthest in'
GRI iluʀłiq*, NG iluɣliq 'innermost thing' [Fab. has illudlek; EG ilittiq, SWG ilułłiq* 'shirt', NWG iluʀłiit 'underwear']

PE ilulŋu- 'hurt inside' [cf. lŋu-]
AAY PWS ilulŋu- 'be prone to suffer from internal pain'
CAY ilulŋu- 'be upset and angry'
NSY —
CSY —
Sir —
SPI ilunŋu- 'have one's insides hurt'
NAI il^{y}unŋuɣi- 'be sorry for, be hurt inside', il^{y}unŋutcak- 'be emotionally moved'
WCI —
ECI —
GRI iluŋŋu- 'be moved or sad' [and iluŋu- 'be impressed by s.th.']

PE ilumiɣ or **ilum(m)iʀu** 'fetus' [cf. p.b. miɣ- or miʀu?]
AAY ilumiaq 'fetus, unborn child' [ilumiaʀ- 'carry child in womb']
CAY —
NSY ilumiaq [ANLC]
CSY ilumik 'fetus'
Sir —
SPI ilumiutaq 'fetus, s.th. inside of one'
NAI il^{y}umiutaq 'fetus' [and il^{y}ummiq* '(caribou) fetus, one thing inside another']
WCI ilumiut(i) [with possessor ending] 'unborn child within one' [Dor. has ilumik for Net]
ECI [Andrsen et al. have Lab ilumiutalik 'has s.th. inside it', ilumiutsi- 'have memorized s.th.']
GRI ilumiu 'fetus' [and ilumiɣ- 'conceive']

PE ilumun 'truly' [all. case form of nom. ilu in sense 'insides, feelings', distinct from ilutmun 'inward' with the the all. ending typical of posit. roots]
AAY —
CAY ilumun 'truly'
NSY ilumun
CSY —
Sir —
SPI ilumun
NAI il^{y}umun 'truly' [and Uum ilumuuq- 'be right, tell the truth']
WCI ilumut 'truly' [H. Island, Sig ilumuuq- 'be right, tell the truth']

ECI —
GRI ilumut 'truly' [ilumuuʀ- 'be right, tell the truth']

PI il(l)uŋa- 'be hollow' [cf. ilu and ŋa-[1]]
SPI iluŋa- 'have a depressed spot'
NAI ilʸuŋa- 'have a hollow part, depression or hole' [and compare ivlʸuŋa- 'be bowlegged' and ivlʸuq- 'bow one's legs' — contam. with amłuʀ-?]
WCI [Pryde has ivluŋa- 'be bowlegged', ivluk- 'bow one's legs' — contam. with amłuʀ-?]
ECI illuŋa- 'have bandy legs' [Iti allaŋa- — contam. with amłuʀ-?]
GRI iłłuŋa- 'have bandy legs' [old ortho. igdlunga- with spurious g]

PI iluŋiq- 'do thoroughly or with all one's might' [cf. ŋiʀ-]
Yup [note CAY iluŋə- 'have sudden enthusiasm']
SPI —
NAI Nu ilʸuŋiq- 'get between, best s.o. at target shooting (getting nearer bull's- eye)' [ilʸuŋiqšuq- 'desire deeply', Nu 'be in a hurry']
WCI Sig iluŋiqtuq- 'do with all one's might'
ECI iluŋiqtu(q)-, NBI iluŋiʀsuq-, iluŋiʀsaʀ-
GRI iluŋiʀ- 'freeze right to the bottom' [and iluŋiʀsuʀ- 'do with all one's might, be eager, take s.th. to heart', iluŋiʀsua- 'be worried' — EG also iliɣiviʀsiʀ-, Robbe and Menn. ilaɣiviʀsiʀ- 'do with all one's might']

PE ilupəʀ(aʀ) 'inner clothing'
AAY —
CAY ilupəq* 'underwear, undershirt' [and note ilupəʀaq 'great grandchild, great grandnephew or niece' — compare iluli(C)aʀ above]
NSY iləpXuaq 'lining of clothes, inner pants of reindeer skin' [ANLC; L.-T. has iləpXaq 'lining' and Men. iləpXuaʀək 'inner trousers of caribou hide']
CSY ilupəʀaq 'liner for clothes' [Chap also 'inner mittens']
Sir ilupəʀaʀiy 'inner mittens, lining of clothes' [Em.]
SPI ilupaaq 'lining, inner fur clothing'
NAI ilʸupaaq 'lining, inner fur clothing', ilʸupiʀuk 'pair of long- johns' [and PH ilupqaaq 'underwear']
WCI ilupa(a)t 'inner clothing' [and Pryde has Car ilupiʀuq 'caribou skin stocking with fur inside']
ECI ilupaaq 'underpants', Lab 'petticoat' [and ilupiʀuq 'inner woolen mittens', iluppiaq 'inner lining, one object inside another']
GRI ilupaaq NWG 'shirt', NG 'inner mitten' Holt., ilupaqut 'underclothing' [Holm has ilipaaq 'stocking' for EG]

PE ilutaʀ 'inner part of hollow?' [cf. taʀ]
AAY ilutak (du.), AP ilutaq 'hollow between tendons in nape of neck'
CAY Y ilutak 'valley, dip, bay'
NSY —
CSY —
Sir —
SPI —
NAI —
WCI —
ECI ilutaq 'inner part of thigh or trouser leg'
GRI ilutaq 'inner side'

PY ilutəqə- 'grieve' [cf. təʀ-]
AAY AP ilutəqə- 'grieve'
CAY ilutəqə- 'be emotionally pained, grieve'
NSY —
CSY iiłqə- 'be sad'

PY iluŋaq 'female cousin'[cf. illuʀ(aʀ)]
AAY AP iluŋaq 'female cousin'
CAY iluŋaq* 'female cross cousin (of woman)'
NSY —
CSY —

PY iłuɣ- 'be tilted'
AAY iłuɣ- 'be tilting' [postural root]
CAY iłuɣ- 'be tilting' [post. root; note also luqiʀ- in this meaning, contam. with əluʀ-]
NSY —
CSY —

PI iłuuq 'kind of freshwater fish' [perhaps a loan to or from Athabaskan found extensively in Inuit — cf. Kutchin łuk, Navajo łóó' 'fish' (general term) in both; there may be a relat. to əlquaʀnəq and/or ilaq, however]
Yup — [but note CSY luXtuʀaq 'small shiny fish, smelt']
SPI —
NAI iłuuqinʸɨq* 'blackfish (?)'
WCI Car iłuuʀaq 'freshwater trout' [B.- S.], Cop ihuuq 'big lake trout' [Lowe; Met has iluŋit, ituŋit 'any small fish, tadpoles' (?); Pryde has Net iłuuq 'lake trout', iłuuʀaq 'small lake trout']
ECI isuuq 'large lake trout', Igl iłuuʀaq 'freshwater trout' [Saul and B.-S. respectively; Peck has idlôk 'pond or river fish' for Lab]
GRI —

PE ima(ʀ) 'contents (esp. of sea)' [Aleut Atkan imða-, EA iðma-, Att ivya- 'fill', put contents in, fetus, pregnancy' may rather go with ita- 'contain' under itəʀ- acc. Berg.]
AAY imaq 'ocean, contents', K also 'pus, bullet'
CAY imaq 'ocean, contents, bullet, pus' [and NSU imaXpik, imaXpak 'ocean']
NSY imaq 'sea'
CSY imaq 'open sea, contents, pus'
Sir iməX 'sea, pus' [Vakh. also 'contents'; note also iməʀəlŋuX 'empty (of water)']
SPI imaq 'contents, sea' [usually possessed in first sense; note also imau- 'be wet' and Imaqłiq 'Big Diomede Island' with p.b. l(l)iʀ; KI also imaq- 'moisten (e.g. skin)']

NAI imaq 'sea, ocean, lake, water not for drinking', ima 'contents' [and imau- 'be wet', also imaq- 'moisten (skin for soaking)']
WCI imaq 'sea or river water (not for drinking)', ima 'contents' [and Ras. also has 'large lake' for Cop, Sig]
ECI imaq 'water, sea, contents' [and imaqpik 'deep water, ocean']
GRI imaq 'sea', ima(q) 'contents' [imaʀpik 'ocean']

PI imaaq- 'fall into water' [cf. q-]
SPI imaaq- 'get wet, soaked'
NAI imaaq- 'fall into water'
WCI imaaq- [Pryde]
ECI imaaq- 'go into water, drown'
GRI —

PE imanəɣ- 'leak or take in water' [cf. nəɣ- which can give Inu immak- by replacive suffixation]
AAY imaŋə- 'leak, become filled with fluid or pus'
CAY imaŋə- 'leak (e.g. boat)'
NSY imaŋə- [ANLC]
CSY imaŋə- 'leak, acquire pus, get soaked'
Sir —
SPI immak- 'take in water, develop pus'
NAI immak- 'accumulate liquid, take in water' [nom. = 'pus']
WCI immak- 'take in water'
ECI imma(k)- 'take in water, develop pus'
GRI immaɣ- 'take in water'

PI imaqtəq- 'wet or water' [cf. təʀ-]
SPI imaqtiq- 'wet, water'
NAI imaqtɨq-
WCI imaqtiq-
ECI —
GRI —

PY imaʀnin 'raincoat' [cf. naʀ[1] and perhaps li-[1] and un]
AAY C imaʀniutək 'gut rain gear' [Rez.]
CAY imaʀnin 'gut rain parka, kayak spray cover'
NSY [imaʀnaq 'rain']
CSY imaʀniitət 'gut raincoat used at sea'
[Inu SPI imaʀnitik 'raincoat' is presumably from Yup, but compare SPI ivʀaniq 'rain' under ivəʀ-]

PI imaʀuq- 'melt (to produce open water)' [cf. ŋ(ŋ)uʀ-]
SPI imaʀuq- 'be created (expanse of water, e.g. when river floods)'
NAI imaʀuq- 'melt into water (snow or ice), get water on self or s.o. else, open up (expanse of water)'
WCI — [for imaʀuq 'pus' see imaʀyaɣ below]
ECI imaʀuq- 'melt into water' [also 'hit on flotation line at water level when shooting']
GRI imaʀuʀ-, EG imaaʀ- 'break up (ice), become open water'

PE imaʀyaɣ 'bodily fluid or pus' [cf. yaɣ-?]
AAY —
CAY HBC imaʀyaq, imałəʀ(aq*), NI imaʀyuk 'phlegm, pus' [elsewhere imaqucuk, imaquq]
NSY imaʀyaq 'furuncle, boil' [L.-T.]
CSY —
Sir —
SPI —
NAI imaʀiak 'liquid, fluid in joint or other organ' [as verb = 'be wet (meat at bullet hole), be oozing (sore)']
WCI [note imaʀuq 'pus']
ECI imaʀiaq 'bodily fluid or pus' [Saul; note also in Schn. imaʀuvik 'watery fluid in eye or joint']
GRI imaʀiaq 'fluid in joint'

PE immiʀ- 'fill' [cf. liʀ-]
AAY imiʀ- 'fill (with liquid)'
CAY imiʀ- 'fill, put contents in'
NSY imiʀ- 'fill'
CSY imiʀ-
Sir [note iməsəʀ- 'fill with water' — Vakh. and Orr]
SPI immiq- 'fill'
NAI immiq-
WCI immiq-
ECI immiq- 'fill with water'
GRI immiʀ- 'fill, load'

PI immit- 'drift out to sea' [cf. łit-]
SPI immit- 'for ice to drift out to sea'
NAI immin^{y}n^{y}aužaq, PH immin^{y}aužaq, immin^{y}ɨq* 's.o. who has become antisocial after having been lost on tundra or ice', PH 's.o. who has landed after drifting away on ice floe, fugitive, prowler'
WCI —
ECI —
GRI immit- 'have drifted out to sea'

PE imanəʀ and **imanaʀ** '(kind of) mollusk' [cf. ima(ʀ) and nəʀ[1] or naʀ]
AAY imanaq 'food in the intestines or stomach'
CAY imanaq 'guts'
NSY imanəq 'kind of mollusk eaten by walrus' ['oyster' acc. L.-T.]
CSY imanaq 'clam, mollusk'
Sir —
SPI imaniq 'clam taken from walrus stomach'
NAI imanɨq*, imaanɨq* 'clam'
WCI —
ECI —
GRI imaniq* 'sandgaper, kind of mussel'

PE imðuʀ- 'be tearful'
AAY imuʀ(yuɣ)- 'be uncomfortable because of wet cold'
CAY imuʀ(yuɣ)- 'be uncomfortable because of wet cold', imuXpaɣ- 'start to cry', imuqitə- 'react vocally to a sudden chill (e.g. touching cold water)'
NSY imuʀ(yuɣ)- 'be uncomfortable because of damp clothes' [Enm. et al.; for imunəq 'wrinkle (in face)' and imuŋalʀia 'wrinkled' see imu-[2]]
CSY imuʀ(yuɣ)- 'be tearful, cry', imuXtəqə- 'sob (silently), fight back tears'

Sir imuXtəqə(s)- 'cry silently' [Em. — from the CSY?]
SPI —
NAI ivžuattuq- 'gasp, be unable to breathe (when swimming, walking in wind or from the cold)'
WCI —
ECI iyyuatuq- 'choke, sob after crying'
GRI iššuaʀ- 'be about to cry'

PE imə- and **iməɣ-** 'collapse' [cf. Atkan Aleut imla-X, Att ivla-X, uvla-X 'valley, gorge'; the Inu forms apparently by conflation with iməɣ-]
AAY imtə- 'conquer, overcome' [only in old sources for Kodiak]
CAY imə- 'collapse' [imtə- 'tear down'; for məʀiɣ- 'be caved in, folded over' see məʀiɣ-]
NSY —
CSY imə- 'develop a hollow or depression'
Sir imə-
SPI imik- 'collapse (house, ice)' [and Jen. has W imigsi-, imigigi- 'be full (moon)']
NAI imik- 'cave in, become twisted (dwelling)'
WCI imik- 'collapse (roof)'
ECI imik- 'collapse (dwelling), cave in, become dented' [and imiŋŋa(C)- 'be dented', imikkaatiq- 'smash in with repeated blows']
GRI imiɣ- 'dent', imiłłuɣ- 'be dented', NG imik- 'collapse'

PY-S iməɣ- 'roll or fold up' [cf. Aleut imɣuʀ- 'roll up', EA 'wrap' and imɣa- 'reel in (killed sea lion)' and compare imu-[1], also imu-[2]]
AAY iməɣ- 'roll up, wind' [cont. = im<ɣ>uʀ-, precipitously = 'im<ɣ>aʀ- ; im<ɣ>utə- 'roll up in']
CAY iməɣ- 'roll up, fold up' [and imɣutə- 'roll up in']
NSY iməɣ- 'roll up, fold, wrap' [ANLC]
CSY iməɣ- 'roll up, coil up' [and slang 'run'; iimɣutə- 'roll up in']
Sir iməɣ-, imɣut(ə)-, iməxtə- 'wrap around, roll up' [Vakh. and Orr]

PY iməɣłuɣ- 'wrinkle or be wrinkled' [cf. łuɣ(-)?]
AAY K iməluXtə-, KP iməɣluXqə- 'wrinkle, crinkle'
CAY iməxłuxtə- 'be or get wrinkled'
NSY — [for imuɣ- 'get wrinkled' see imu-[2]]
CSY —

PE imla(C)u(ɣ) or **imla(C)uʀ** 'fetus (of animal)'
AAY AP imlauq 'seal fetus'
CAY imlauk Y 'fish egg, roe', Nun 'dried herring egg', K 'slab of cottonwood bark (formerly used for roofing smokehouse)'
NSY imlaa 'white hide of of (unborn?) seal pup' ['seal cub' acc. L.-T.]
CSY imlaa 'unborn seal pup'
Sir imla, pl. imlay 'unborn seal pup' [Orr; note also mila 'unborn seal' on Men.'s comp. list]
SPI ivlauq 'animal fetus'
NAI ivlʸauq
WCI ivlauk [but Ras. has ivlauq]
ECI illauq
GRI iłłaaq 'fetus of marine animal or caribou, loose heart of wood, innermost shoot of angelica' [old ortho. igdlaoq probably by contam. with igdliaq 'uterus' — Fab. has iblau]

PE imma 'thus or there' [from obscured dem. root im-, Aleut um; cf. taðim(m)a]
AAY ima, AP imani, PWS also imamta, KP also imanaa 'I suppose, I guess'
CAY ima 'particle directing listener toward s.th. known to him and speaker' [and imumi 'at that time, long ago']
NSY ima 'there (in distance, invisible or in past)' [interjectional]
CSY ima(qun) 'too bad!', imamta 'even though I told him' [and note iimnaŋuq 'once upon a time']
Sir iməni 'somewhere there' [Vakh. also has ima 'long ago' and imina, imini 'very' from Rub.]
SPI imma Qaw 'quiet!', KI '(of) s.th. long past or lost', immakiaq 'I guess' [and Qaw imani 'remember when?']
NAI imma 'in the aforementioned past' [and imani 'in past, at last', immami 'maybe that's so', immakii 'maybe'; note also innasiq 'such a one' and inna, Mal itna 'thus', influenced by im(m)aatna below if not by ət-?]
WCI ima 'thus', Car? immaaluk 'long ago' [Schn. 'adg'; and note Net i'na 'thus' (Briggs); Dor. has B. Lake imaa 'yes']
ECI imak 'thus', immaqa(a) 'perhaps' [and Lab immali 'how beautiful', immasaq, immani 'recently' — Bourq.]
GRI ima 'thus' [and immaqa, NG ammaqa (influenced by amma) 'perhaps', imaluunniit (EG iminnaliinniit acc. Ges.) 'or', imani 'some time ago', NG 'long ago, some time ago', imuŋa 'for a long time'; 'for imaat- 'be thus' see ət-]

PI im(m)atna 'thus' [old aequalis form]
Sir — [but note imətən 'now, today', imətəžaX 'right away']
SPI imatna(a) 'thus'
NAI iminna 'thus' [influenced by inna under imma above?]
WCI imanna, Net ima'na 'thus', Cop 'no'
ECI Aiv imanna 'thus'
GRI imanna'thus' [Tersis has EG iminna, immaqa 'thus']

PE im(m)atuʀ 'hardly?' [cf. enclitic tuʀ]
AAY —
CAY —
NSY imatuq 'hardly'
CSY imatuq 'I don't think so'
Sir imatuX 'hardly, maybe'
SPI —
NAI —
WCI [note Car imatuaq 'who cares?' — Schn. for Esk. Point]
ECI —
GRI imatuq 'would that -'

PE imtuqaʀ and **imtuq(q)iʀ-** 'stammer' [the latter form with p.b. liʀ-?]
AAY K, PWS imtuqaq, C nimtuqaq, KP also limtuqaq 'stutter', AP, C 'the hiccups' [and verbal imtuqaʀ-, etc.]
CAY imtuqaʀ- 'stutter'
NSY imtuqaq 'stutterer, stuttering' [ANLC; Men. has imtuqa(a)lək 'stammering, stammerer']
CSY imtuqaq 'stutter' [and verbal imtuqiqə-]
Sir imtuqałəX 'stammering'
SPI —
NAI ipturiq- 'stammer'
WCI ipturiq- 'stammer, babble'
ECI Lab ittuɣik- 'stutter'
GRI ittuqiʀ-, uttuqiɣ- 'stutter' [Fab. has iptorer-]

PI imu-[1] 'roll up' [cf. EA imu- X 'circle, area around', imu- 'go around'; the relat. between this set and iməɣ- is not clear, but compare the relat. between məlu- and məlәɣ- and between nəŋə- and nəŋuɣ- under it]
SPI imu- 'roll, wind, crouch'
NAI imu- 'roll up, fold, wind, crouch, become stooped with age'
WCI imu- 'wind, fold'
ECI imu- 'wind, roll, fold, curl up on self'
GRI imu- 'wind, roll up, form pressure ridges' [for the latter compare PE iŋ(ə)yu- — contam.?]

PE imu-[2] 'get wrinkled' [compare imu-[1], also iməɣłuɣ- under iməɣ-]
AAY —
CAY —
NSY imuɣ- 'get wrinkled' [ANLC; and imunəq or imułəq 'wrinkle (in face)', imuŋalʀia 'wrinkled' acc. L.-T.]
CSY —
Sir —
SPI —
NAI —
WCI imuniq 'wrinkle'
ECI imulluk 'wrinkle, pleats around Inuit boot sole', Iti 'red of lower eye lid', Wakeham Bay 'eyelid', Iti imuʀluk 'wrinkle on face or body' [and Iti imuʀliu(q)- 'pleat']
GRI EG imuttut 'wrinkles' [Gessain; Robbe and Menn. have imaavaaq 'upper eyelid']

PY-S inək 'groin or armpit?' [the relat. — if any — to əŋə and unəʀ is obscure]
AAY —
CAY —
NSY inaɣžuʀaq 'groin' [inəʀžəʀaq 'armpit' on Men.'s comp. list]
CSY inək 'armpit, groin or similar bend in body or land', inəqəžəwaaq* 'armpit' [also inak (du.?) 'lap', iŋmiɣ- 'hold in lap', inəɣžəwaaq* 'middle of armpit or groin'; Rub. has inəʀžuwaq 'groin' for Chap]
Sir inəx 'pocket, small bag (e.g. attached to hunter's waist)', inaqužɣaX 'armpit', inəɣžəʀwaX 'groin' [Vakh. from Men.'s texts — Men. has inənəžɣ(w)aX 'groin', inəqəžawaq 'armpit', and Em. has inakužɣaX for the latter]

PI inəq- 'finish' [cf. PE inəʀ- and Aleut ina- 'finish']
Yup — [but Hinz has ineri- 'be mature' for CAY]
SPI iniq- 'finish', iniallak- 'be fully grown'
NAI inʸiq- 'finish'
WCI iniq- 'be finished (with)'
ECI iniq- 'be finished (with)'
GRI iniʀ- 'be finished (with), be fully grown, reach orgasm', iniʀit- 'be mature, complete'

PI innaq 'adult or mature animal' [cf. q under nəʀ[1]]
SPI innaq 'mature animal'
NAI [note inʸnʸaaluk 'son'; for inʸnʸarik- 'look nice', and PH inʸnʸaq* 'appearance, condition' see iŋŋaʀ-]
WCI innaq Sig 'adult', Net 'old man' [Ras.; Jen. has 'old loon' for Sig; Lowe has iniʀniq 'adult' rather for H. Island Cop]
ECI NBI innaq 'adult' [Ras.]
GRI innaq* 'fully grown seal' [for innaʀłuk 'the wrong (left) side of the kayak' and innaʀłuɣ- 'be in disorder, lie wrong' see iŋŋaʀ-]

PE inəqə- 'coo to a baby' [cf. Aleut iniXsi- 'feel well, be happy, rejoice']
AAY inqə- 'coo to, amuse (baby)'
CAY in(ə)qə- 'coo to a child (special words for that child)'
NSY inəqə- 'use a term of endearment or cooing words to a child' [ANLC; Men. 'cuddle']
CSY iinqə- 'coo to a child'
Sir inqət(ə)- 'amuse child with songs, cuddle', inəqsuqə(s)- 'caress, admire' [Em.]
SPI iniqui- 'find cute' [with p.b. kə-[1]]
NAI —
WCI [Net Sp. Bay, Car B. Lake iniquɣi- 'find pretty' — Pryde]
ECI iniqu(C)-, iniquɣi- 'find attractive' [and iniqu 'how beautiful!']
GRI iniqut-, iniquɣi-, EG iuʀuu- 'find pretty, sweet'

PY-S inəqun 'pet name' [cf. un]
AAY inqun 'pet name (for child)'
CAY inqutaq
NSY inəqun 'cooing words for a child', inəqutaq 'pet name for a child' [ANLC]
CSY iinqun 'customary made-up words used to a particular child'
Sir inqita 'song or game to amuse child' [Em.]

PE inəqyunaʀ- 'be cute' [cf. yu- and naʀ-]
AAY inəqsu(ɣ)naʀ- 'be cute' [and AP inəqsukə- 'be charmed by s.th. cute']
CAY inəqsunaXqə- 'be cute'
NSY ənəqɣunaʀ- 'be beautiful (woman)' [ANLC]
CSY inəqsunaʀ- 'be attractive (espc. of woman)' [and inəqsukə- 'find attractive']
Sir inəqsuʀnałəʀəX 'loving, tender' [Em.]
SPI iniqunaq- 'be cute'
NAI —
WCI Net iniqunaq- 'look pretty' [Ras.; Jen. has Cop inneqxiniq- 'find pleasant']

ECI iniqunaq-, Iti inaqunaq- 'be attractive'
GRI iniqunaʀ-, EG iuʀunaʀ- 'be pretty, cute'

PE inəʀ- 'stop s.o. from doing s.th.' [cf. inəq- and Aleut inaayu- 'persecute, not want people around one', also perhaps EA inʀasa- 'be angry at' and Atkan inʀaayna- 'be bad, ugly'; the Inu forms contain p.b. təʀ-]
AAY Perry inəXquʀ- 'admonish, warn'
CAY inəXquʀ- 'warn, tell not to'
NSY inəXtə- 'forbid, warn'
CSY inəXtə-
Sir —
SPI iniqtiq- 'warn against, tell not to do'
NAI inʸiqtɨq- 'rebuke, stop from doing'
WCI Sig iniqtiq- 'warn not to do s.th.'
ECI iniqti(q)- 'admonish'
GRI iniʀtiʀ- 'forbid'

PE ini- 'hang out to dry' [cf. Aleut (Atkan) ni-s, EA ni-n 'rack for drying fish', and inka- 'hang', Atkan inka-X, EA ini- X 'sky']
AAY ini- 'hang out to dry'
CAY ini- 'hang out to dry, hang in the air (mirage)'
NSY ini- 'hang out to dry'[ANLC]
CSY ini- 'hang out to dry'
Sir —
SPI ini- 'hang out to dry (fish or meat)'
NAI inʸi- 'hang out to dry'
WCI →
ECI ini- 'put out to dry'
GRI ini- 'hang up, lay out to dry'

PE inivkaʀ 'mirage' [cf. vkaʀ-]
AAY —
CAY inifkaq 'mirage'
NSY [note ni(i)ʀafkaq 'mirage' — perhaps influenced by nəʀžuy- or niʀaʀ-]
CSY —
Sir —
SPI inipkaq 'mirage'
NAI inʸipkaq, iŋipkaq
WCI —
ECI —
GRI —

PI inniq- and **inniaq-** 'stretch skin for drying' [cf. liʀ-?]
SPI inniaq- 'stretch animal hide for drying'
NAI inniaq-
WCI —
ECI inni(q)- 'stretch hide for drying' [and inniaq 'hide that is drying']
GRI inniʀ- 'stretch animal hide for drying'

PE innitaʀ 'drying rack' [cf. un]
AAY initaq 'drying rack', K 'clothesline' [PWS inin 'drying rack']
CAY initaq 'part of fish rack on which fish are directly hung'
NSY initaq 'drying rack in yaranga' [ANLC]
CSY —
Sir —
SPI innitaq 'drying rack'
NAI inʸnʸisaq
WCI innitaq
ECI innitait 'indoor drying rack'
GRI innisaq, EG, Up innitsat

PI innia(suk)- 'dazzle' [cf. qitŋiʀ-?]
SPI —
NAI —
WCI Sig inŋianaq- 'be dazzling' [Lowe; Pet. has ingniacuk- 'be dazzled' and Met. has iŋniasuk- 'be uneasy, embarrassed']
ECI —
GRI iŋŋiasuɣ- 'be dazzled'

PI inʀaq- 'leak or drip (oil)' [cf. PY əłŋaʀ-, perhaps both from the same PE source — *iŋəłʀaʀ-?]
SPI iʀnaq-, Qaw inʀaq- 'ooze, leak' [and iʀnausitaq 'burnt oil from stone lamp']
NAI inʸʀaq- 'leak'
WCI inʀausiniq 'dirty oil dripping from lamp'
ECI iʀŋa(q)- 'drip, leak'
GRI iʀnaʀ-, iʀŋaʀ-

PI inʀaun 'dirty oil from lamp' [cf. un]
Yup — [compare NSY, CSY əłŋaan 'greasy residue, dirty burnt oil from lamp' under əłŋaʀ-]
SPI iʀnaun 'dirty oil from lamp', Imaq əʀnun 'saucer' [for əʀnaun?]
NAI inʸʀaun 'pan under seal oil lamp'
WCI Cop inʀaun 'drip- bowl for lamp' [Pryde; Ras. has inɣaut]
ECI iʀŋaut 'dirty oil from lamp'
GRI iʀnaat, iʀŋaat 'dripping oil (from lamp)'

PI inʀuma- 'be anxious' [cf. inəʀ- and (u)ma-?]
SPI —
NAI —
WCI Cop inʀuma- 'be anxious' [Saul; Ras. has iŋŋuma- and Jen. has inʀuma- 'be idle'; Car inʀumana(ʀ)luni 'it is enough to drive one to despair' Ras.]
ECI [note iʀŋali- 'be exhausted or harassed']
GRI iʀnuma-, iʀŋuma- 'be worried, anxious' [and note NG iʀŋahuk- 'be tired']

PI inʀutaq 'grandchild' [there may be a link to inəq-, but cf. also inqun under inəqə-]
SPI —
NAI inʸʀutaq 'grandchild'
WCI Cop inʀutaq, Sig inʀutaaluk 'grandchild' [and Net inŋutaq — Ras.]
ECI iʀŋutaq 'grandchild'
GRI iʀnutaq, iʀŋutaq 'grandchild' [Sisimiut, Maniitsoq also 'nephew, niece']

PY iŋa(va)- or **iya(va)-** 'far away' [cf. dem. root iŋ- and iŋan; the relat. to uyavaʀ- and to uŋan and its related derivatives uŋavaq and uŋasik- is obscure]
AAY yaaqxʷani 'far away' [loc. case, also yaqsəɣ- 'be far' and yaatiini 'the day before yesterday']
CAY yaaqfani 'further away' [and yaaqsiɣ- 'be far', yaani from *iŋani 'over there', yaavət '(to) over there'

and yaaliagni 'the day before yesterday']
NSY iavani 'far away' [p. 316 in Men.; also iavək '(to) over there'; and both iani and yiani]
CSY Chap iivani 'far away' [iŋani 'over there' may be restructured from the pronominal form of iŋ- acc. Berg. — note also iŋavək '(to) over there'; for iŋan 'side area of house' see iŋan and for uyavaq 'distance' see uŋavaʀ-]
Sir — [for uyəvani 'far off' see uŋavaʀ-]
Inu [note Nu, Mal in[y]ani 'over there' corresponding to CSY iŋani above and place name Iŋaliq 'Little Diomede Island']

PE iŋaɣ- 'avoid (for cult reasons)' [cf. dem. root iŋ-?]
AAY yaɣ-, yaaɣ- 'fast' [iyaa'iXqə-, iyaiyaXqə- 'break one's fast']
CAY əyaɣ-, Nun, HBC yaaɣ- 'abstain from s.th. for cult reasons, fast'
NSY —
CSY yakuʀ(yuɣ)- 'be fearful', yakuXtə- 'be careful, quiet and cautious after a death or before a religious ceremony' [and yakuʀnaq 'dangerous thing or situation', Chap also yakuXsaʀaʀ- 'protect from danger'; for iɣataʀ- 'be hungry' see iɣataʀ-]
Sir əyəkuʀ(yuɣ)- 'be scared' [Em. — Vakh. has iyəquʀ(yuɣ)-], iyəkusqižaʀaʀən 'carefully', əyəkuʀnəX 'danger', əyəkuʀnəʀəlŋuX 'fearless' [Men.; Em. also has əyəkuXsaʀaʀ- 'protect from danger', əyəkuXsaʀałəX 'threat']
SPI —
NAI —
WCI —
ECI Lab iŋalak- 'pass by, not approach' [Peck]
GRI iŋalaɣ- 'avoid'

PI iŋaluk 'intestine (of animal)' [cf. iʀnəʀłuk]
SPI —
NAI iŋaluk, in[y]aluk 'sea mammal intestine, dried intestine of bearded seal', iŋaluaq, in[y]aluaq 'intestine' [the form with ŋ also Mal]
WCI inaluk 'intestine' [Jen. has Cop iŋaluk]
ECI inaluaq 'intestine' [and Peck has inaluk 'animal gut' for Lab, which Math. has as 'gutskin' for Igl — Saul has as 'intestine of big game' for Tar]
GRI inalu, inaluaq 'gut'

PY-S iŋan 'side wall of sleeping compartment' [cf. dem. root iŋ-, also uŋan and iŋa(va)- — contam.?]
AAY [yaatə- 'over from - ']
CAY [yaatə- 'over from - ']
NSY [note iŋaliq 'Little Diomede Island' — lit. 'off to the side' acc. Men.]
CSY iŋan, iŋata 'side area of traditional multifamily dwelling' [Chap 'side wall of winter sleeping compartment']
Sir iŋata 'side wall of winter sleeping compartment'
Inu [note place name Iŋaliq 'Little Diomede Island']

PI iŋat- 'overdo' [cf. dem. root iŋ-?]
SPI —
NAI iŋattaq- 'overdo, vigorously deflate or put s.o. down'
WCI Sig iŋattaq- 'get worse (ill person)', iŋattaumi- 'exaggerate, overdo'
ECI —
GRI iŋaɣ- 'go too far', iŋammik 'especially', iŋašaɣ- 'overdo it'

PY iŋciq 'engraving on wood'
AAY AP iŋciq 'decorative engraving on wood'
CAY Nun iŋciX
NSY —
CSY —

PI iŋəq- 'beg for s.th. or sing shamanistic song?'
SPI Qaw iŋiqšuq- 'beg, ask'
NAI iŋɨq- 'beg, ask, pray to' [and iŋiula- 'beg'; but note also iŋiuq- 'spy on']
WCI Cop iŋiq- 'sing shaman's songs' [Ras.], iŋiuq- 'sing' [Met.]
ECI iŋiuq- 'sing along with s.o. else' [for Lab imŋiʀ- see əmaŋə(ʀ)- under əmaɣ-]
GRI iŋiuʀ- 'sing or read aloud with, accompany' [for iŋŋiʀ-, immiʀ- 'sing a satirical song', NG iŋmiq-, EG iŋŋiʀ- 'sing to drum dance' see əmaŋə(ʀ)- under əmaɣ-]

PE iŋət- 'sit down' [cf. iŋləʀ and Aleut uŋut- 'sit down, be seated', uŋuci- 'be sitting']
AAY ➡
CAY [iŋcuʀ- 'lie in wait for, endeavor to capture']
NSY —
CSY ➡
Sir iŋsəX(ə)- 'lay, put down' [Vakh. from Rub.'s texts — whence he has also iŋət- 'return']
SPI ➡
NAI iŋɨt- 'sit down'
WCI iŋɨt-
ECI iŋit- 'kneel, sit in firing position', Lab 'sit down' [Saul has the latter meaning also for Tar]
GRI iŋit- 'sit down'

PI ikšək- 'squat' [or iŋšək-; cf. perhaps p.b. ðiɣ-, which would explain the GRI s, and compare makšək- under makət-]
SPI ikšik- 'protrude buttocks, sit on toilet'
NAI ikšik- 'bend over with buttocks raised'
WCI iksik- 'bend down turning one's back on s.o.'
ECI itsi(C)-
GRI issiɣ- [old ortho. igsig-] 'bend over, squat', issiʀ- [old ortho. igser-] 'be on point of sitting down, sit on haunches (animal)' [and issiʀfik, EG iʀsiʀpik 'piece of wood behind kayak manhole', issinniʀit 'stranded pieces of ice at low tide']

PI ikšəva- 'be sitting' [or iŋšəva- — cf. the preceding set (the p.b. could explain the problematical sibilant in NAI); perhaps (u)ma- is also involved]
SPI —
NAI iksiva- 'be sitting'
WCI Sig iksiva-, Cop ixxiva- 'be seated' [Met. has 'sit down']
ECI itsiva-, NBI, SB iksiva- 'be seated, sit down'
GRI issia-, NG ixxua- 'be sitting'

PI iktuRaq 'seat in skin boat'
SPI iktuRaq 'seat in skin boat'
NAI iksuRaq
WCI [Pryde has iktiRvik 'seat in skin boat' for Cop]
ECI ittuRaq 'bench in (whaling) boat'
GRI issuRaq 'thwart (in boat)'

PY iŋun 'seat in boat' [cf. un]
AAY PWS iŋun, Kod iŋuca<R>aq 'seat in baidarka'
CAY iŋun 'crosspiece on which one sits in boat'
NSY —
CSY iŋun, iŋuta 'boat seat'
Inu [note NAI iŋutaq '(pole for placing) owl trap']

PE iŋuqaR 'pad to sit on? [cf. iŋun above and qaR?]
AAY —
CAY iŋuqaq 'mat, pad'
NSY —
CSY —
Sir —
SPI —
NAI —
WCI Cop iŋuRiq 'underlayer skin for sled' [Ras.; Ow. has 'tarp' for EP]
ECI —
GRI iŋuRaq, iŋuRiq, inuRaq 'sled skin', EG iŋiiřiaq 'seat for use for hunting at seal's breathing hole' [and Robbe and Menn. have iŋiqqivik 'skin at bottom of kayak']

PI iŋilRa- 'move OR travel' [cf. əɣləR- and p.b. a-, though the relat. is obscure]
SPI —
NAI [note PH iŋiRaqtuq- 'be in pursuit of whale']
WCI Cop iŋilRa- 'move, travel', iŋilRaaq 'someone on a hunting trip' [Met. also has Cop iŋilRaniq 'current']
ECI iŋiRRa- 'move, travel'
GRI iŋiRła-, EG iiRta- 'move, travel'

PI iŋilRaan 'long ago' [cf. 3s rel. mood inflection variant ŋan?]
Yup — [for NSY inłəvaq 'yesterday' see ikpaq]
SPI iŋilRaan 'long ago'
NAI iŋil^{y}Raan 'long ago'
WCI iŋilRaat 'long ago' [and Ras. has iŋilRait 'ancestors']
ECI —
GRI —

PE iŋilqaR 'hook for retrieving seals?'
AAY —
CAY —
NSY iŋiłqataq 'sealing harpoon head' [Jen.]
CSY [note iiŋqaRyaR- 'catch by hooking' and aŋałqataq 'hook for catching seals or birds, sling' — by contamination with aŋaR-? — but compare also aŋilRaR- under aŋit-]
Sir —
SPI iiłXaq 'seal- retrieving hook'
NAI iŋił^{y}Xaq, iɣił^{y}Xaq, PH iŋilRaq
WCI —
ECI —
GRI —

PE iŋkiR 'gum'
AAY iŋki<R>at, əŋki<R>at 'gums'
CAY iŋkiq 'gum'
NSY —
CSY iiŋqaq*
Sir iŋqəX, pl. iŋqay [Orr]
SPI ikkiq
NAI Pt. Barrow itkiq 'gum', Nu ikkic 'gums'
WCI itki(q) 'gum' [Lowe]
ECI ikkiq
GRI ikkiq [old ortho. igkik or ivkik]

PE iŋləR 'sleeping platform' [cf. iŋət- 'sit']
AAY K əŋləq 'bed' [B.-S. has C ŋəluq]
CAY iŋləq* 'bed, sleeping platform'
NSY ➟
CSY iŋləq* 'living and sleeping area of traditional house'
Sir [Vakh. has iŋliX, iŋlaX 'sleeping platform', the latter from Rub.]
SPI iɣliq 'bench along wall, sleeping platform'
NAI iɣl^{y}ɨq*
WCI iɣliq 'sleeping platform' [Ow. has 'bed' for EP]
ECI illiq 'sleeping platform' [and illinaq 'ledge, raised part of ground']
GRI iłłiq* 'sleeping platform' [iłłiRnaq 'ledge']

PY iŋləRaq 'bed slat' [cf. aR]
AAY —
CAY iŋləRaq 'bed slat, bench'
NSY iŋləRat 'lattice work shelf' [L.-T.; Em. has inləRat 'bed slats']
CSY iŋləRaq 'bed slat'

PI iŋlin 'board for sleeping platform' [cf. li-[1] and un]
SPI iɣlin 'wooden floor'
NAI PH iɣlisiq, iɣlisit 'bench along wall of qažɣi sleeping platform, planks along back wall of sod house'
WCI iɣlin 'wooden rim at front of sleeping platform made of snow (to prevent snow breaking off)' [Pryde]
ECI illiti 'vertical part of wall of snow house, wood upright supporting tent wall' ['wood for consolidating sleeping platform' rather acc. Saul]
GRI iłłit [pl. iłłisit] 'sleeping platform or bed board'

PI iŋliq- 'move aside' [cf. iŋluaq-; from iŋlu plus liR-?]
SPI —
NAI iɣl^{y}iq- 'move and make room for, prevent from being hit by moving aside' [contrast with ɨɣliq- 'move' under əɣləR-]
WCI iɣliq- 'move aside to avoid being struck' [Pryde]
ECI [illi(q)- 'be born prematurely']
GRI iłłiR- [old ortho igdler-] 'push, move aside', NG iɣliq- 'replace' [for WG homonym meaning 'get into kayak'

see əklərviɣ under əkə-², and note iłłiʀaʀ- 'move back and forth, shake']

PE iŋlu 'other (of pair)' [cf. dem. root iŋ- and p.b. lu(ʀ), also perhaps Aleut iŋacaʀi- x 'pair, couple'; for the 'six' meaning note the Eskimo finger counting system, crossing to the other hand at six; the 'eight' sense is more obscure]
AAY iŋlu 'other of pair, mate, adversary' [and note iŋlulən 'eight']
CAY iŋlu 'other of pair, enemy, opponent' [and note BB, NR, LI iŋlulɣən 'eight']
NSY inlu 'the other side of' [Jen. and L.-T.]
CSY iŋlu 'one of a pair, half, partner, spouse' [Chap also 'other side of s.th., half of a carcass']
Sir iŋluŋani 'on the other side' [and iŋləx 'six', malʀuɣnəŋ iŋləkəlʀəX 'seven'; Em. has iŋluŋiy 'opponents in a competition']
SPI iɣlu 'other of pair, other side'
NAI iɣlʸu 'other of two'
WCI iɣlu 'one of a pair' [and Ras. has Cop iɣluani 'six']
ECI illu 'one of a pair' [and illuaq 'opponent']
GRI iłłu(k) [old ortho. igdlo] 'one of, other of two, other side, dance partner, end of twisted sinew' [also iłłuq 'slice of bread to eat with tea or coffee', NG iɣluani 'six']

PE iŋluɣtun 'on both sides' [aequalis case]
AAY iŋlucəstun 'on the other side'
CAY iŋluxtun 'with both sides or arms'
NSY —
CSY —
Sir —
SPI iɣlutun, Qaw iɣluktun 'with both hands'
NAI iɣlʸuktun
WCI iɣluktun 'with both hands or feet'
ECI illutut '(with) both at same time'
GRI iłłuttut 'on both sides, in both hands'

PE iŋluk(k)ita(C)aʀ- 'juggle'
AAY —
CAY iŋlukiitaq 'juggling'
NSY [note inlupəxtaaq (L.-T. ənlupəxtaq) 'juggling']
CSY —
Sir —
SPI iɣluɣitaaq- 'juggle, carry s.th. in each hand'
NAI iɣlʸukisaaq-, PH iɣlʸukusaaq- 'juggle' [nom. = 's.th. juggled']
WCI iɣlukitaaq- 'juggle' [Lowe; Met. also has iɣlukittaq 'ball (for juggling)']
ECI illukitaaq- 'juggle'
GRI iłłukisaaʀ- 'do s.th. on both sides to'

PI iŋluktu(u)q- 'do s.th. with both hands' [a verbalization of iŋluɣtun above]
SPI [Imaq iɣlutukaq- 'carry s.th. in both hands']
NAI iɣlʸuktuuq- 'do with both hands'
WCI iɣluktuq- 'do using both hands or feet'
ECI illutuq- 'use both hands'
GRI iłłuttuʀ- 'use both hands or sides'

PI iŋluaq- 'go or hit to one side?' [cf. iŋliq-; from iŋlu and vaʀ-?]
SPI —
NAI iɣlʸuaq- 'shoot wide of the mark, omit, miss'
WCI iɣluaq- 'shoot wide of the mark'
ECI —
GRI iłłuaʀ- 'move aside'

PI iŋniq- 'press down on' [cf. iŋət-?]
SPI iŋniq- 'hold down, press on, run over'
NAI —
WCI iŋniqi- 'get astride (e.g. horse)'
ECI Lab iŋniʀaq- 'sit upon' [Peck]
GRI NG iŋniq-, iŋniqqiut(i)- 'run over (sled over dog)'

PE iŋŋaʀ- 'lie down (to sleep)' [related to iŋət-? — compare iŋaluk for the change of *iŋ- to in-]
AAY inaʀ- 'lie down, go to bed' [Tyzh. has iŋagna-]
CAY inaʀ-
NSY inaʀ-
CSY iŋaʀ-
Sir iŋaʀ- 'lie down, go to bed' [also inaʀ- in Men. — Vakh. has iŋaʀ-, iŋaXtə- 'lie down']
SPI innaq- 'lie down'
NAI inʸnʸaq- 'lie down on side, go to bed' [and note PH inʸnʸaq* 'appearance, condition', inʸnʸaʀik- 'look nice' — there may be contam. with innaq under inəq-]
WCI innaq- 'lie down, go to bed'
ECI innaq- 'lie down on side', NBI 'lie under blankets' [Dor.]
GRI innaʀ- 'go to bed' [and note innaʀłuk 'the wrong (left) side of kayak', innaʀłuɣ- 'be in disorder, lie wrong']

PE iŋqiʀ 'louse nit' [cf. Aleut Atkan hiŋala-s, EA iŋala-n 'nits'?]
AAY iŋqiq 'louse nit'
CAY iŋqiq
NSY iŋqiq [L.-T.]
CSY iiŋqiq
Sir iŋqəX [Orr]
SPI iqqiq
NAI icqiq
WCI itqiq
ECI iqqiq
GRI iqqiq

PE iŋqiliʀ 'Indian' [cf. l(l)iʀ as also in unaliʀ]
AAY —
CAY iŋqiliq 'Indian'
NSY —
CSY —
Sir —
SPI iqqiliq, Qaw iqqiłiq
NAI icqilʸiq
WCI itqiliq 'Indian' [B. Lake 'Cree Indian' — Dor.]
ECI [Ras. has Igl itqiliq 'Chipewayan Indian']
GRI iqqiłłit 'a legendary underground people (half human, half dog)'

PE iŋʀiʀ 'mountain'
AAY iŋʀiq, iŋŋiq 'mountain'
CAY iŋʀiq
NSY iŋʀiq
CSY —
Sir iŋʀəX
SPI iʀʀiq
NAI iʀʀi, Mal inʸʀiq
WCI iʀʀi
ECI —
GRI [for iŋŋik 'tip (of mountain or knife)' see ikŋik]

PY iŋtə- 'molt'
AAY C iŋtə-, AP iŋtᴀʀ- 'molt' [and AP iŋtaq 'molting fowl']
CAY iŋtə- 'molt' [iŋtaq* 'fledgling']
NSY —
CSY iiŋtaq 'molted goose'

PE iŋuɣ 'human being' [for Inu forms inuk, etc., compare iŋŋᴀʀ- and iŋaluk, and for Yup yuk, etc., compare iŋa(va)- and iŋaɣ-; in possessed form (yua, inʸua, etc.) this base, the original Eskimo ethnonym, is everywhere attested also in the senses 'resident spirit', 'core of boil' and 'chick in egg'; cf. also perhaps Aleut iŋisxi- X 'owner', which may contain the p.b. mentioned under ləɣ, here in a post-consonantal form, and iŋ(i)yu-X 'flesh, living body' mentioned under PE iŋ(ə)yuləɣ, which may belong here]
AAY suk 'person, owner'
CAY yuk, pl. yuɣɣət, Nun, Chevak [but not HB] cu(u)k, pl. cuuɣət 'person, owner' [an initial ə occurs in some derived forms such as əyiʀ- 'be populated' (with liʀ-) — but this probably just reflects an intermediate stage from i to zero, as in (ə)yuʀ- 'jell' from iɣuʀ- (at *iɣðuʀ-)]
NSY yuk 'person, male person'
CSY yu(u)k, pl. yuɣət 'person, male person'
Sir yux 'person'
SPI inuk 'person, master, owner' [Di also 'man']
NAI inʸuk 'person, owner' [and inʸnʸuk- 'form a being (egg)', inʸnʸiqɨ- 'go visiting from house to house', also inʸnʸiq- 'become populated, acquire a companion' going with CAY əyiʀ- above]
WCI inuk 'person, owner'
ECI inuk 'person, owner' [as verb = 'form (chick in egg)' and innu(k)- 'get inhabitants, appropriate']
GRI inuk, EG ii(k) 'person, owner' [and innuɣ- 'meet people, murder s.o.', inniʀi- 'long for human beings', NG inuk- 'get a boil, form (chick in egg)']

PI inuaq- 'murder' [cf. ŋᴀʀ-?]
SPI inuaq- 'murder'
NAI inʸuaq-
WCI inuaq-
ECI inuaq-
GRI inuᴀʀ- 'murder' [inuʀiʀ- 'kill people']

PI inuilaq 'uninhabited place' [cf. ŋit-]
Yup — [but note CAY yuiɫquq 'wilderness', going with WCI inuilʀuq below]
SPI inuilaq 'deserted, uninhabited place'
NAI inʸuilʸa(a)q
WCI inuilaq 'uninhabited place' [Lowe; Met. has inuillaq, also inuilʀuq]
ECI inuilaq 'uninhabited place, person without help' [and note inuillitiq- 'go away from people because of bad humor']
GRI inuila(a)q, EG iivilaq 'deserted, uninhabited place' [and inuiɫɫi- 'seek solitude away from people']

PI inuɣaqutlək 'mythical dwarf' [cf. iŋuɣᴀʀ below, q(q)un and ləɣ]
Yup [AAY KP ina'uquɫuk, PWS inu'aquɫuk 'mythical dwarf' are probably Inu loans brought by Inupiaq migrants who are known to have come to the Alaska Peninsula, although the forms have not been recorded there — see also inuɣuaq in CAY under yuɣu(C)aq for a similar use of a derivative from an Inu form occurring in Yup]
SPI inuɣᴀʀuɫiq, Qaw inuɣᴀʀuɫik, FR inuɣaquɫik 'mythical dwarf'
NAI Nu inʸuaqutlik, Mal inʸuɣaquɫɫiɣaužaq 'country elf or midget' [Seiler; B has inʸuquɫɫiɣaužaq, inʸuquɫɫik 'ghost', PH 'dwarf' from inʸuqun 'spirit, prowler' — the same as inuqun below]
WCI inuɣaqulliq 'mythical dwarf' [Pryde has Cop inuᴀʀulliɣaq, Net inuᴀʀu'liɣaq]
ECI inuɣɣaɣulliɣaq, inuɣaɣulliq, Iti inuaɣulik, inuaɣulliq. Lab inuagullik 'mythical dwarf'
GRI inuᴀʀuɫɫiɣaq, NG inuɣᴀʀulliɣaq, EG iaayivatsiaq

PI inukšuk 'cairn' [cf. yuɣ (alternating with ðuɣ)]
SPI —
NAI inʸukšuk, inʸuksuk 'pile of rocks used in corralling caribou'
WCI inuksuk 'cairn of rocks'
ECI inutsuk
GRI inussuk 'cairn of rocks, beacon'

PI inuqun 'family member or servant?' [cf. q(q)un]
SPI —
NAI — [for inʸuqun 'spirit, prowler' see inuɣaqutlek above — contam.?]
WCI —
ECI inuquti 'follower, servant'
GRI inuqut 'member of one's family' [and compare inuɣluqut 'orphan taken into house and treated like a slave']

PI inuusuk- 'be young' [cf. ŋu- and yuɣ-?]
SPI —
NAI —
WCI Cop inuuhuktuq 'young man'
ECI inuusuttuq 'adolescent'
GRI inuusuɣ- 'be young', inuusuttuq, NG inuuhukaaq 'young person'

PE iŋŋimi(yuɣ)- 'be shy' [cf. iŋŋit- below?]
AAY —
CAY —

NSY —
CSY yimi(yuɣ)-, yumi(yuɣ)- 'be shy'
Sir —
SPI —
NAI —
WCI —
ECI —
GRI innimisuɣ- 'be shy, respectful, humble' [innimiɣi- 'respect, not want to disturb']

PE iŋŋit- 'come upon people' [cf. łit-]
AAY —
CAY yittə-, yiitə- 'come upon a stranger'
NSY —
CSY —
Sir —
SPI — [for yukpak- 'travel around' see nuɣət-]
NAI inʸnʸit- 'come upon s.o. unexpectedly, reach habitation' [note also inʸnʸiaqattaaq- 'visit people' with liyaʀ-, and inʸnʸiŋiat- 'be wary of people' (see under ŋiɣ-); for yuɣit- 'travel around' see nuɣət-]
WCI innit- 'come upon people, habitation' [Pryde]
ECI inni(t)- 'come upon while arriving from afar' [and note innia(C)- 'visit s.o. on the way']
GRI innit- 'come to a house, get refuge' [compare inniaʀ- 'visit settlements (priest)', probably with liyaʀ-, also inniŋiaɣ- 'shun society of men']

PE iŋuɣaʀ 'finger or toe' [cf. aʀ]
AAY K sua'aq 'finger'
CAY yuaʀaq, HBC yuɣaʀaq, cuɣaʀaq 'finger, toe'
NSY yuɣaq 'finger' [ANLC]
CSY —
Sir — [Miller has nuraka '(my) finger']
SPI inuɣaq
NAI inʸuɣaq
WCI inuɣaq 'finger, toe' [Lowe has 'finger' sense only for Cop, Met. has 'knuckle']
ECI inuɣaq 'knucklebone', Lab inuɣait 'checkers'
GRI inuaq, inuak 'finger or toe' [pl. inukkat — which in NWG means 'cards', earlier 'knucklebones (game)']

PE iŋuɣinnaʀ 'twenty' [cf. ŋinnaʀ; the reference is to the twenty digits of the hands and feet]
AAY suinaq 'twenty'
CAY yuinaq*
NSY yuinaq, yuɣinaq
CSY yuɣinaq*
Sir yuɣənaX
SPI inuinaq
NAI inʸuinʸnʸaq
WCI Sig inuinnaq
ECI —
GRI —

PE iŋuɣinnaʀunʀit- 'nineteen' [cf. iŋuɣinnaʀ above and ŋu-, utə- and nʀit- or ŋit- — compare quləŋŋuʀutəŋit- under qulə-]
AAY —
CAY yuinaunʀitaʀ(aq), yuinaunʀitaraan 'nineteen'
NSY yuinaʀutŋilŋuq [ANLC]
CSY —
Sir —
SPI inuinaʀutailaq
NAI inʸuinʸnʸaʀutailʸaq
WCI —
ECI —
GRI —

PE iŋuɣniʀ- 'be friendly' [cf. niʀ-]
AAY suɣniʀ- 'be friendly, good- tempered, jovial'
CAY yuɣniXqə- 'be friendly' [yuɣniitə- 'be unfriendly']
NSY —
CSY yuɣniitə- 'be ugly'
Sir —
SPI Qaw inuŋniq- 'be friendly, good'
NAI inʸuŋniq- 'be friendly'
WCI —
ECI —
GRI —

PE iŋuɣu- 'be alive' [cf. ŋu-]
AAY —
CAY yuu- 'be alive'
NSY [yuu- 'be a person' — ANLC]
CSY yuɣuma- 'be or stay alive'
Sir —
SPI inuu- 'be alive' [and inuułiq 'soul']
NAI inʸuu- 'be alive'
WCI inuu-
ECI inuu-
GRI inuu-

PE iŋuɣuciʀ 'life' [cf. iŋuɣu- above and uciʀ]
AAY —
CAY yuuciq 'life'
NSY yuusiq [ANLC]
CSY yuɣusiq 'body' [in SLI esp. a dead body]
Sir —
SPI inuusiq 'way of life', Qaw 'life force, soul'
NAI inʸuusiq 'way of life, habit, soul'
WCI inuusiq 'life, way of life'
ECI inuusiq 'life'
GRI inuusiq 'way of life, nature'

PE iŋuɣyaɣ- 'be many (people)' [cf. yaɣ-]
AAY suɣyaɣ- 'have many people, be populous'
CAY yuɣyaɣ-
NSY —
CSY yuɣyaɣ- 'increase (population), join in game (new players)'
Sir —
SPI inuɣiak- 'be numerous, have many people'
NAI inʸuɣiak-
WCI Sig inuɣiak- 'be many'
ECI inuɣiattut 'crowd, assembly' [and Ras. has Igl inuɣiaɣaaluit 'many people']
GRI inuiaɣ- 'be filled with human beings (house or boat)', inuiaat 'crowd, multitude' [and inuiaqatiɣiit 'nation, society']

PE iŋupiɣ or **iŋupiɣaʀ** 'Eskimo' [cf. piɣ(-)]
AAY suxpiaq 'Eskimo'
CAY yuppik, yupiaq
NSY yupik [ANLC]
CSY yupik
Sir [yupiɣaX 'human being' acc. Vakhtin]
SPI inupiaq 'Eskimo'
NAI inʸupiaq
WCI —
ECI —
GRI —

PY-S yuɣłiqə- 'be angry (man)' [cf. łuɣ and liqə-]
AAY suXłiqə- 'be grouchy, test' [note also suXluɣ- 'be angry, grouchy, testy']
CAY —
NSY yuxłiqə- 'be furious'
CSY —
Sir yuxłiqə(s)- 'be angry (man)'

PY-S yuɣtə- 'murder' [cf. t-[2]]
AAY —
CAY yuxtə- 'murder, commit manslaughter'
NSY yuxsinaqə- 'try to murder'
CSY yuxtaʀ- 'murder'
Sir yuxtəŋinəqət- 'try to murder'

PY yuɣtu- 'be tall or big' [cf. tu-[1]]
AAY —
CAY suxtu-, Nun, HBC, NI cuxtu- 'be tall'
NSY —
CSY yuutu- 'be big around the waist'

PY yuɣu(C)aq and **yuɣaq** 'doll' [cf. ŋ(ŋ)uðaʀ and aʀ]
AAY suŋaq, K suaʀuaq 'doll'
CAY yuɣaq, BB suɣaq, suɣuaq 'doll' [and note Y, K inuɣuaq 'small doll' — from the Inu form of the base]
NSY yuŋuaq 'statue' [ANLC]
CSY [note yuɣaaq SLI 'important person', Chap 'rock resembling a man']
Sir [note yuɣwa 'boss', from the CSY]

PY yu(u)nʀaq 'young person' [cf. ŋu- and n(ə)ʀaʀ(aʀ), also Aleut suɣanʀi-X 'young person' — a loan from AAY?]
AAY sunna<ʀ>aq 'young person'
CAY yunnəXaʀ(aq*) 'male teenager', Nun cunʀaX 'young man' [Hamm.], NSY yuunʀaq 'child'
NSY yunʀaq 'young person' [ANLC]
CSY —

PY yuŋcaʀ- 'treat (a patient)' [cf. iŋuɣu- above and ŋcaʀ-?]
AAY suŋcaʀ- 'treat (a patient)'
CAY yuŋcaʀ-, HBC cuŋcaʀ-
NSY —
CSY —

PE iŋut-[1] 'stir up'
AAY —
CAY Nun iŋulatə- 'stir' [influenced by aŋulat- under aŋala-; note also iŋulaq 'old time dance']
NSY —
CSY —
Sir —
SPI —
NAI iŋut-, iŋulit- 'stir'
WCI iŋut- 'move' [Pryde has Cop iŋulak- 'stir']
ECI iŋula-, NBI, SB iŋut- 'mix, beat' [Saul has iŋut- 'stir']
GRI —

PE iŋut-[2] 'scold or speak ill of' [cf. iŋuɣ if not iŋut-[1]]
AAY situug- 'bawl out, tell off'
CAY yitaaʀ- 'scold' [note also əliłxia- 'gossip about, slander, tattle on' — infl. by əlit-? — and yuliuʀ- 'slander', with a different suffix on base iŋuɣ]
NSY [note iliłxi- 'gossip about, slander, tattle on', going with the CAY and CSY of that meaning]
CSY yitə- 'advise, warn' [and note yiiłxi- 'gossip about, slander, tattle on'; for yumi-, yimi- 'be shy, cowering' see iŋŋimi(yuɣ)- under iŋuɣ]
Sir [note yumə- 'scold']
SPI W iŋut- 'speak ill of' [Jen.]
NAI —
WCI —
ECI —
GRI iŋut- 'talk ill of'

PE iŋutuʀ 'young whale'
AAY —
CAY —
NSY iŋutuq 'yearling whale'
CSY iŋutuq 'yearling bowhead whale' [and note yusłiʀaq 'young gray whale']
Sir iŋutəʀəX, iŋutəraX 'young animal' [Vakh. from Rub.'s and Men.'s texts respectively]
SPI iŋutuq 'young whale'
NAI iŋutuq
WCI —
ECI —
GRI —

PE iŋyaʀ- 'do ahead of another' [cf. dem. root iŋ-?]
AAY iŋyaʀ- 'beat in a race, get there ahead of s.o.'
CAY —
NSY —
CSY iŋyaʀaXtə- 'do ahead of another, surpass'
Sir iŋyaʀaʀ- 'go past, pass, appear before, do quicker than s.o. else' [Em.; note iŋəyaXta 'archer, marksman', also iŋəyax 'nose of kayak' — Vakh. from Rub.]
SPI iŋiaq- 'do ahead of another'
NAI iŋiaq- 'do before another, forestall' [and PH iŋiʀaqtuq- 'be in pursuit of a whale']
WCI Sig iŋiaq- 'do before another' [Jen.]
ECI iŋiaq- 'keep up with' [Bourq. has 'pass' for Lab]
GRI iŋiaʀ- 'do before another' [and iŋiałłuʀ-, EG iiyaʀalii- 'keep company, do as s.o. else']

PE iŋ(ə)yu- 'form pressure ridges (in ice)' [cf. iŋ(ə)yuləɣ and compare also iŋ(ə)yukaʀ]
AAY —
CAY əvu-, Nun uɣu- 'pile up (ice)' [əvunʀət 'piled up ice'; note also yuulʀaaq 'swell, thin sheet of ocean ice']
NSY uvu- 'pile up (ice)' [nom. = 'pressure ridge']
CSY vuu- 'pile up (ice)' [and vuunəq* 'pressure ridge'; compare əvluk, uvluk 'ocean wave' under iŋ(ə)yuləɣ]
Sir —
SPI iu-, Imaq əu- 'pile up (ice)' [and iuniq, Imaq əu 'pressure ridge']
NAI ivu- 'form pressure ridges' [ivunɨq* 'pressure ridge']
WCI ivu- 'form pressure ridges' [and ivunʀit 'piled up ice']
ECI ivu- 'form pressure ridges' [ivuniit, NBI ivvuit 'broken ice floes']
GRI iŋu-, NG ivu- 'form pressure ridges' [cf. also imu- 'form pressure ridges' under imu-[2]; iŋuniq* 'pressure ridge']

PE iŋ(ə)yukaʀ 'pintail duck' [compare iŋ(ə)yuləɣ]
AAY —
CAY HBC iyukaq, NSU yuukaq 'pintail duck'
NSY — [yuɣʷayu(k) 'loon' is from the Chukchi yokwayo, as is CSY yuɣayu]
CSY ŋiikaq 'pintail'
Sir —
SPI iuɣaq 'pintail' [Jen. also has for W]
NAI ivuɣaq 'pintail'
WCI Sig ivugaq [Jen.]
ECI ivuɣait 'small ducks'
GRI —

PE iŋ(ə)yuləɣ 'wave or swell' [cf. iŋ(ə)yu- and ləɣ- and compare iŋ(ə)yukaʀ, also perhaps Aleut iŋ(i)yu-X 'flesh, living body', iŋyuusa- 'wriggle', though these may go directly with PE iŋuɣ rather]
AAY [note KP yuʀluun 'undertow']
CAY yuulʀaaq 'wave, swell'
NSY iŋuluk [ANLC]
CSY əvluk, uvəluk 'ocean wave, swell'
Sir —
SPI Qaw iŋiulik 'wave' [and note KI iuluk 'booming']
NAI iŋiulik 'wave, swell' [note also yuayuk- 'point upward (of waves on ocean)']
WCI iŋiulik
ECI iŋiulik, Lab iŋiullik
GRI iŋiulik 'swell'

PE ipəɣ- 'be sharp'
AAY ipəɣ- 'be sharp', ipək K 'blade', C 'sharp edge, sharpness'
CAY ipəɣ- 'be sharp'
NSY ipəɣ- 'be sharp' [ANLC has əpəɣ-]
CSY ipəɣ-
Sir ipaqiɣlərək 'sharp' [and Vakh. has ipaqipiɣ- 'be very sharp' as well as ipəpiɣ-]
SPI ivik- 'be sharp' [and Imaq əvək 'blade']
NAI ipik- 'be sharp'
WCI ipik-
ECI ipik-
GRI ipiɣ-

PE ipɣit- 'be dull' [note the variant ɣatə of p.b. ŋit- occuring in the CAY, NSY, and AAY forms here and compare also ətɣat- under ətə-]
AAY ipxiatə- 'be dull'
CAY ipxiatə- 'be dull' [with the tə ~ l alternation]
NSY əpxialŋuq 'blunt'
CSY iipxitə- 'be dull'
Sir ipxilŋuX 'dull' [Em. has ipaŋilŋuX]
SPI ipkit- 'be dull'
NAI ipkit-
WCI Sig ipkit- 'be dull' [and Cop ipiit-, a regular derivation with ŋit-]
ECI ikkiit- 'be dull' [Saul also has ipiit-]
GRI ikkiit- 'be dull'

PE ipəɣcaʀ- 'sharpen' [cf. caʀ-[1]]
AAY ipəxcaʀ- 'sharpen'
CAY ipəxcaʀ-
NSY əpəxsaʀ-
CSY ipəxsaʀ-
Sir [Vakh. has ipaqiɣcəqə- 'sharpen']
SPI ipiksaq- 'sharpen'
NAI ipiksaq-
WCI ipiksaq-
ECI ipitsa(q)-
GRI ipissaʀ-

PE ipi(ɣ) 'limb of a quadruped?'
AAY ipi(k) 'arm', C 'arm tendon' [and ipixtu- 'have long arms', PWS 'be tall']
CAY ipik 'limb of quadruped or insect', Nun ipiX 'finger', Y ipiaq 'unit of twenty' [the latter also for Nun acc. Jen.; Nelson has ipik 'combined leg, foot and toes of an animal' and ipiak 'set of such combined units, twenty']
NSY ipiaq 'handle of bucket or pot' [L.-T.; perhaps with contam. from əpu; ANLC also has ipiitaq 'handle']
CSY ipixtu- 'come high up the leg (boots, socks)'
Sir —
SPI iviaq 'handle of bucket or pot' [note maʀluutiviaq 'forty', W ivia 'twenty' acc. Jen. and maʀlukiviaq 'forty']
NAI [malʀukipiaq 'forty', and similarly for other units of twenty]
WCI [Sig malʀukipiaq 'forty']
ECI —
GRI [note ippiʀtu- 'be wide (e.g. spit of land or stretch of ice)', also ipiniq* 'flesh near the bone'?]

PI ipiq(-) 'tie' [cf. Atkan Aleut iim̥isiX, EA im̥iisiX 'shoestring']
SPI [for Imaq əvəqłuk 'handle (e.g. of cup)' see əpu] ➡
NAI ipiq 'dog chain, rope, thin root' [as verb = 'tie with chain or rope'; note also ipiaq 'drawstring, mitten string' — also verbal for tying up with a drawstring— and Mal ipi 'handle' influenced by əpu?]
WCI ipiq- 'tie (up)', Net ipiq 'trace, line with which s.th. is tied up' [Ras.]

ECI ipiq- 'tie up (dog)', ipiq 'chain (for tying up dog, etc.)'
GRI [note ipi 'handle (on bucket, kettle or the like)', which may belong with əpu] ➟

PI ipiq(q)iq(-) 'splice' [cf. nqiɣ-[1]?]
SPI iviqiq- 'fit, join, splice'
NAI ipiqqiq 'joint'
WCI Sig ipiqqiq
ECI —
GRI ipiʀiɣ- 'overlap'

PI ipiʀaq 'harpoon strap' [cf. qaʀ]
SPI —
NAI —
WCI Net, Car ipiʀaq 'harpoon line' [Ras.]
ECI ipiʀaq 'harpoon line'
GRI ipiʀaq, ipaʀaq 'harpoon strap used in hunting seals on ice' [for homonym 'wick' see əpəqaʀ]

PI ipiutaq 'line or string' [cf. un]
Yup [NSU ipiutaq 'fishing line' is probably from Inu]
SPI iviutaq 'string for mitten or knife, fishing line' [Jen. has iviita 'thong fastening foreshaft of harpoon to handle' for W, = Imaq ivi(i)taq 'small fishing line']
NAI ipiutaq 'fishing line' [Mal also 'umbilical cord']
WCI ipiutaq 'rope or chain for attaching (e.g. dog)', Car? 'fishing line' [Schn. 'adg'; Pet. has 'isthmus' for Sig]
ECI ipiutaq 'rope tie, isthmus joining peninsula to mainland' [Ras. has 'dog trace' for Igl]
GRI ipiutaq 'isthmus', NG 'dog trace' [and note ipiutak 'optic nerve']

PE ipuɣ- 'lever up' [compare ikuɣ- in the 'levering' sense, also iput-]
AAY ipuɣ- 'pry up', PWS 'turn, steer (using rudder)'
CAY ipuɣ- 'ladle, move with bow high in air (boat)'
NSY ipuɣ- 'pry' [ANLC]
CSY ipuɣ- 'scoop, pry', ipuxtə- 'tilt head up, perk up'
Sir ipuɣ- 'scoop or pry up' [Em.]
SPI ivuk- 'tilt, pry'
NAI ipuk- 'lift with a lever, cock trigger'
WCI ipuk- 'lever'
ECI —
GRI ipiɣ- 'lever up' [and ipit- 'turn (vessel), move with a lever' — Fab. has 'turn using an oar']

PY ipuɣun and **ipuɣutaq** 'ladle or similar utensil' [cf. un]
AAY ipuun 'fish pew (for tossing fish)', Kod 'prying instrument' [Rez. has Kod ippun 'rudder']
CAY ipuun 'ladle', Nun ipuutaX 'dipper for water, saucepan'
NSY ipu(u)taq 'stick for controlling lamp' [and ANLC has ipuɣun 'long oar']
CSY ipuɣutaq 'fork'
Inu [Imaq ivu(u)taq 'lever, stick for controlling lamp', Qaw ipuutaq 'lever' are prob. from Yup]

PI ipummiq- 'close mouth' [there may be a relat. to ipuɣ-; compare uqummiq-]
SPI imumiq- 'hold one's lips sealed' [Jen. has ivumi(q)- for W]
NAI ipummiq-, upummiq- 'close mouth'
WCI ipummiq- 'have one's mouth closed' [Ras. has 'have no food' for Car]
ECI ipummi(q)-
GRI ipummiʀ- 'close one's mouth'

PI ipun 'oar' [cf. un — and compare ipuɣun above under ipuɣ-; the existence of a proto- form ipə- would explain the presence of this base and apparently related iput- below]
Yup [NSY ipun 'short oar' and iputə 'long (steering) oar' (ANLC — Men. has the reverse) probably represent the same loan from Inu; ANLC also has verbal iputə- 'steer with a steering oar']
SPI ivun 'oar'
NAI ipun
WCI iput
ECI iput
GRI iput

PI iput- 'row' [cf. ipun]
Yup [for NSY iputə- 'steer with oar' see under ipun above]
SPI ivut- 'row'
NAI iput-
WCI Sig iput- 'row' [also Car in B.S.]
ECI iput- 'row'
GRI ipuɣ- 'row with oar' [Fab. has iput-]

PE iqa(ʀ) 'dirt' [the Inu forms may be contracted derivations parallel to PY iqaŋiʀ- below — compare under əppaʀiʀ-]
AAY iqa(q) 'dirt', iqa(ʀ)- 'be dirty'
CAY iqa(q) 'diʀt', iqa- 'be dirty'
NSY iqa 'diʀt', iqaʀ- 'get dirty' [and ANLC iqa- 'be dirty']
CSY iqa 'dirt'
Sir —
SPI [iʀaqłiq- 'wash hands']
NAI [iqaʀi-, PH iqaqi- 'wash']
WCI Sig iqqa(q)- 'wash', iqaʀi- 'wash self' — Lowe; Met. has iq(q)aq- 'wash self', iq(q)aqtak 'clean clothes']
ECI —
GRI —

PY iqaŋiʀ- 'clean' [cf. ŋiʀ-]
AAY iqaiʀ-, PWS iqiiʀ- 'wash'
CAY iqaiʀ- 'wash, clean'
NSY iqaiʀ- 'clean'
CSY iqaŋiʀ- 'clean'

PE iqałuɣ 'fish (esp. salmon)'
AAY iqałuk 'fish (esp. salmon)'
CAY K iqałuk 'dog salmon' [note Nun nəqaluk 'dried fish', which is a blend with nəqə]
NSY iqałuk 'fish'
CSY iqałuk 'fish, salmon'

Sir iqəɬəx 'fish'
SPI iʀaluk
NAI iqaluk, Mal, Nu qaluk, PH aqaluk
WCI iqaluk 'fish — esp. salmon, char'
ECI iqaluk 'fish — esp. char', Iti 'salmon, char'
GRI iqaluk 'char, sea trout'

PE iqałuɣaʀ 'arctic cod' [cf. aʀ]
AAY AP iqałuaq 'boreal smelt'
CAY Y, Nun, HBC iqałuaq 'arctic cod', BB 'boreal smelt'
NSY iqałuaq 'herring'
CSY iqałuɣaq 'tomcod'
Sir —
SPI iʀałuaq
NAI iqaluɣaq, PH qaluaq 'tomcod, codfish'
WCI iqaluaq 'small fish, minnow' [Pryde]
ECI iqaluɣaq 'small fresh- water trout, spinner, (fish) bait'
GRI iqaluɣaq, iqaluaq, iqaluʀaq 'polar cod'

PE iqaluɣpiɣ 'arctic char' [cf. piɣ]
AAY AP iqałuxpik 'dolly varden, arctic char'
CAY iqałuxpik
NSY iqałupik [ANLC]
CSY iqałupik
Sir —
SPI iʀaluɣvik, Qaw iʀalukpik 'rainbow trout'
NAI iqalukpik
WCI iqalukpik'arctic char, salmon, trout'
ECI iqaluppik 'arctic char, trout'
GRI —

PI iqaq- 'be stiff' [cf. iqaʀtə, iqyuk and Aleut aqa- 'be stretched (fingers, by a weight)', also aqaXta- 'be straight, straighten (e.g. fish hook)', aqat- 'stretch (e.g. fish line)']
SPI iʀaq- 'be stiff'
NAI iqaq- 'be or become stiff' [and iqaʀɨ- 'have difficulty doing', iqaqłak 'sealskin boots']
WCI iqa(a)q- 'be stiff' [and Sig iqaqłak 'sealskin boots']
ECI iqaq- 'be stiff from cold', NBI, SB 'be numbed', iqaʀnaq- 'be cumbersome (garment)'
GRI iqaʀ- 'be stiff' [and iqaʀi- 'have difficulty doing']

PE iqaʀtə '(outer layer of) skin' [cf. iqaq-]
AAY —
CAY iqəXtaq 'sealskin boot with hair inward'
NSY —
CSY iqəXta 'hard wood used for seal hooks', Chap iqaXta 'skin, birch, color' [Men.; SLI iqəXtaq 'color']
Sir iqəXtəX 'skin' ['human skin, color' acc. Em.]
SPI —
NAI —
WCI —
ECI iqaqtik 'skin — esp. black seal skin' ['outer layer of skin' acc. Saul]
GRI iqaʀti 'outer layer of skin, grain side (of wood or skin), right side (of material)'

PI iqci- 'be afraid' [cf. iʀa- and iʀcuɣ-]
Yup [note Nun iXci 'legendary creature, half animal, half man']
SPI iqsi- 'be afraid'
NAI iqsi-
WCI iqsi-, iXXi- 'be afraid' [esp. of physical injury, acc. Briggs]
ECI iʀsi- 'be afraid'
GRI iʀsi-

PE iqə- 'width' [dimensional root; cf. iqə(ʀ), iqquʀ, and iqpaq-]
AAY AP, PWS iqtu- 'be wide' [and iqkitə-, AP iqəxkitə- 'be narrow']
CAY iqtu- 'be wide' [and iqkitə- 'be narrow']
NSY —
CSY iqətu- 'be wide' [and iqəkəstaaq* 'narrow thing']
Sir —
SPI [note ižaqtu- 'be wide', ižakituuraq 's.th. narrow' — contam. with əðəŋqi-?]
NAI —
WCI Sig iʀniq 'hand's width' [Pet.]
ECI Lab iʀniqtu- 'be too thick to span' [Peck]
GRI iʀniʀtu- 'have a broad handle (throwing board)' [and note also iʀnannaq, EG innaʀnaq 'winged harpoon']

PE iqə(ʀ) 'corner of mouth' [cf. iqšək, iqə- and Atkan Aleut iiqi-X '(inside) corner']
AAY iqəq 'corner of mouth or eye'
CAY iqəq*, Nun, HBC iqək 'corner of mouth'
NSY əqə 'cheek'
CSY iqa 'lower cheek, corner of mouth' [base əqə; and iqəŋə- 'smile']
Sir iqa, pl. iqiy 'lower cheek, corner of mouth' [Orr]
SPI iʀi 'corner of mouth'
NAI iqɨ(q)
WCI iqi 'corner of mouth'
ECI iqiq
GRI iqiq(*) 'corner of mouth', iqi(k) 'small bay (in fjord)' [and NG hikup iqiŋa 'place where ice edge meets land']

PI iqəžʀaq 'corner' [cf. iqšək]
SPI —
NAI iqižʀaq 'corner' [as verb = 'contract']
WCI Sig iqiyʀaq, Car EP iqilʀaq 'corner' [Ow. for the latter form — which Pryde also has for Cop]
ECI iqiʀʀaq 'internal angle'
GRI — [but note EG iʀiiqquq 'elbow']

PI iqšaq 'cheek'
Yup [note NSY əqšaXtə- 'slap on cheek' (L.-T.)]
SPI iqšaq 'cheek', Qaw 'infected parotid gland in neck under ear' [Imaq has in the first sense əʀəqšaq, əqšaq]
NAI iqšaq 'cheek' [and iqšaaq- 'slap (on cheek)']
WCI Sig iʀsak 'rear part of face behind cheek' [Met.; Pet. has iʀsaq 'band of white skin on woman's hood'; Ras. has Cop iXXaʀluaq 'with prominant cheeks']
ECI iʀsaq 'cheek', NBI, SB 'temple' [and note Iti

iʀsaŋa- 'have one's chin in one's hands or one's cheek against s.th.']
GRI iʀšaq 'cheek' [and iʀšaaʀ- 'slap (on cheek)']

PE iqəlquʀ 'little finger' [cf. iqə- and p.b. quʀ]
AAY iqəłquq, iqəłqiq 'little finger'
CAY iqəłquq
NSY iqəłquq [L.-T. has əqəłquq]
CSY iqəłquq 'little finger'
Sir iqəłqəX
SPI iʀitquq
NAI iqitquq, itiqquq
WCI iqitquq
ECI iqiqquq
GRI iqiqquq

PI iqəžɣaɣiaq '(kind of) gull'
SPI —
NAI iqižɣaɣiaq 'Sabine's gull'
WCI [Jen. has Sig ikigagyuaq 'Sabine's gull', and Ras. has Net eqixhagiaq]
ECI [Parry has erkeetyuggeearioo 'Sabine gull' for Igl]
GRI NG iqiɣaɣiaq 'rare species of tern' [Holt.]

PE iqlaɣ or **iqɣaɣ** 'hook (for fish)' [cf. iqə(ʀ)]
AAY iqsak 'fishhook'
CAY BB, NR, NI iqsak 'fishhook' [also verbal 'to fish with a hook']
NSY iqɣ̥ak 'bullhead fish' [L.-T.]
CSY iqsak
Sir iqɣ̥əx 'fish hook' [Orr]
SPI —
NAI iqłʸak 'hook and line, e.g. for snagging burbot through ice' [also as verb 'catch a burbot'; iqłaaq- 'get a hangnail, crack, split (wood)']
WCI Sig iqłak 'sealing hook'
ECI iqiak- 'hook (a fish)'
GRI [iʀłaq 'splinter']

PE iqlaɣ- 'bare one's teeth' [cf. iʀɣaɣ-, iqlaɣ and iʀcuɣ-]
AAY —
CAY —
NSY iqšaɣ- 'be crooked' [L.-T.; also iqšaɣutaq 'grimace']
CSY iqšaɣ- 'be crooked, uneven, distorted'
SPI —
NAI iqłʸak- 'wrinkle nose, bare teeth in anger', iqłʸaŋa- 'make funny face'
WCI —
ECI — [for Iti iʀsaŋa- 'rest chin on hands' see iqšaq under iqə(ʀ)]
GRI iʀłaɣ-, iʀsaɣ- 'show one's teeth' [note also iʀsaŋa- 'talk SWG (i-)dialect']

PE iqliʀ 'molar tooth' [cf. iqə(ʀ) and iqə-]
AAY [note PWS iqłitə- 'reach innermost recess of']
CAY iqłiXpak 'molar'
NSY —
CSY iqłiʀaɣiiłiqə- 'smile in an awkward way', Chap iqłiʀa(a)qə- 'smile sheepishly', iqłiXtə- 'smile'
Sir iqłiʀ- 'smile, grin (baring teeth)' [Vakh.; Men. has iqłəXtəX 'malicious smile']
SPI iqłavak 'molar'
NAI iqłʸit 'tangled hair, sinew, small pieces of lip at the roots of baleen' [note iqłʸiq- 'be frayed']
WCI iqłiqpak 'molar'
ECI iʀsipaq, Lab iqłiqpak [Peck] 'molar'
GRI iʀłippak, EG iʀsiʀpaq 'molar' [and Kl. has iʀłiq 'extreme end of s.th.', in Fab. 'small pieces of baleen innermost in whale's mouth']

PY-S iqlu- 'lie or deceive' [cf. iqə(ʀ) but also iqu-]
AAY iqłu- 'lie, deceive' [and iqłuɣaʀ- 'be a liar']
CAY iqłu 'wrong one', iqłu- 'lie, deceive, go astray' [Barnum has iqłuʀ- ; note also iqłutm̥un 'the wrong way']
NSY iqłuʀ- 'lie, deceive'
CSY iqłumʀu- 'doubt'
Sir [Vakh. has iqəłqaʀ(niɣ)- 'lie']
Inu — [for WCI iqu- 'lie' see iqu-]

PY-S iqluŋaʀ- 'be a liar' [cf. ŋaʀ-[2]]
AAY —
CAY iqłuŋaʀ- 'be a liar'
NSY iqłəŋaʀ- [ANLC]
CSY iqłəŋaʀ- 'be a liar', iqłəŋiqə- 'tell lies' [and Chap iqłəŋaq 'lie']
Sir iqłəŋəqə(s)- 'lie, pretend'

PY-S iqmiɣ- 'put or keep in one's mouth' [cf. iqə(ʀ) and p.b. miɣ- and compare also PI uqummiq-]
AAY iqm̥iɣ- 'put in corner of mouth' [and iqm̥ik 'snuff']
CAY iqm̥iɣ- 'hold or put in mouth' [and iqm̥ik 's.th. held in mouth, chewing tobacco']
NSY iqm̥iɣ-, iqm̥iaʀ- 'hold in mouth, chew tobacco' [ANLC]
CSY iiqm̥iɣ- 'put s.th. in mouth without eating it' [and iiqm̥ik 's.th. held in mouth, sugar cube'
Sir iqm̥əX 'sugar' [Em. has iqməɣ- 'put s.th. in cheek']

PI iqpaq- 'open or spread out' [cf. iqə-]
SPI [note iqpaq- 'move away from door' (?)]
NAI iqpaq-, iqpiq- 'open or be open (door, flap or lid)' [the second form influenced by makpiq-?]
WCI —
ECI iqpa(q)- 'open, spread (e.g. flower or seal being opened up)', iqpaaqi- 'spread out, pour out contents' [and iqpaŋa- 'have bandy legs'; note also Peck iqłiqtiq- 'make flame larger in lamp']
GRI [note iʀłiʀ- 'spread (fire, flame)']

PE iqquʀ or **iqquɣ** 'buttock or end of s.th.' [the forms ending in ɣ may be reformulated from the dual; cf. iqə- and Aleut iquX '(outside) corner']
AAY iquk 'end'
CAY iquk 'end, tip'
NSY iqu 'end' [and iqukłiq 'extreme']
CSY iquk 'end, tip' [and cf. iqšək of similar meaning under iqšək]
Sir [note iqcəx 'end, edge' under iqšək; perhaps also iquɣəX 'bone neck (?) of harpoon']

SPI iqquq 'buttock'
NAI iqquk, Nu itquk 'buttock' [the Nu form by contam. with ətəʀ?]
WCI iqquq 'buttock' [dual iqquk; Schn. has 'back of boat or vehicle' for 'adg']
ECI iqquq 'back end of long object (like pencil, cigarette or vehicle), upper back part of trousers', Lab 'buttock' [Bourq.]
GRI iqquq(*), iqquk 'backside', EG iqqiq 'tail of bird', NG iqquq 'share of whale at back of neck' [Holt.]

> **PI iq(q)uq-** 'wipe backside' [cf. uqəʀ-]
> SPI iʀuq- 'wipe backside'
> NAI iquq-
> WCI iqquq-
> ECI iquq- [Saul]
> GRI iquʀ-

PY-S iqšək 'point or edge' [cf. iqə(ʀ) (esp. iqəžʀaq under it) and EA iqða-X 'corner of bay']
AAY —
CAY —
NSY —
CSY iqšək 'point, tip'
Sir iqcəx 'border, end, edge' [and iqcəkcəX 'extreme']

PE iqu- 'tilt or be crooked' [there may be a relat. to iqə(ʀ) and iqlu-]
AAY iqu- 'fall over'
CAY iqu-
NSY iqu- 'fall over'
CSY iqu- 'fall over', iquniXt(ə)- 'tilt, slant'
Sir iqunəʀməlŋuX 'slanting' [Vakh. has iqə- 'fall']
SPI iʀu- 'become distorted on one side'
NAI iqu-
WCI iqu- 'lie, tell a lie'
ECI Lab iquŋa- 'be crooked' [and Peck has iqu- 'make wry faces'; Saul has iquŋa- 'grimace, be irregular in shape' for Tar]
GRI iqu-, EG iʀiC- 'become crooked', iquŋa- 'be crooked'

PY iqu(tə)- 'scrape (a skin)'
AAY —
CAY iqutə- 'scrape a skin to make it pliable'
NSY iquarun 'scraper' [ANLC]
CSY —

PY iqɣuk 'left (hand)' [cf. iqu- and/or iqaq-]
AAY iqsuk 'left (hand)'
CAY iqsuq, iqsuk
NSY —
CSY —

PY iq(ə)žə- 'chip' [cf. iqšək?]
AAY —
CAY —
NSY iqəšqaXłəq 'part, fragment'
CSY iqšəɣaXtə- 'chip'

PY iʀa- 'be horrified' [cf. Aleut iʀaXta- 'be afraid of', iʀayu- 'be respectful, behave well', iʀana- 'be terrible', EA iʀa- 'be afraid', also PI iqci-]
AAY iʀanaʀ- 'be wild', AP ' be fearsome', AP iʀa-, Perry yaʀa- 'be afraid'
CAY iʀa(yuɣ)- 'be amazed' [emot. root; also iiXa(yuɣ)- 'be amazed, horrified' and iiła(yuɣ)- 'be amazed']
NSY iXa- 'grow furious'
CSY iʀa(yuɣ)- 'feel aversion or disgust' [iʀanaq 'disgusting thing'; for iiX^{w}aaŋə- 'fume' see i(C)iʀ-]

> **PY iʀ(a)ʀi-** 'be astonished'
> AAY K iʀʀi- 'be or become astonished'
> CAY iXXi- 'be amazed, marvel, stare, watch'
> NSY —
> CSY —

PY iʀaluq 'moon' [cf. p.b. lu(ʀ); the relat. to nəʀžuɣ- (suggested by the Sir forms there) is obscure]
AAY iʀaluq, Perry ya'aluq 'month, moon'
CAY iʀaluq 'moon, month' [and iʀaliʀ- 'shine (moon)' with p.b. liʀ-?]
NSY iʀaluq 'moon'
CSY [note iʀaluqaq 'aged auklet (i.e. one kept for a month)'] ➡
Sir — [for nuʀəX 'moon' see nəʀžuɣ-]

> **PY iʀaləqətaaq** 'star' [cf. iʀaliʀ- under CAY above and p.b. k(k)ət(t)aʀ-]
> AAY —
> CAY —
> NSY iʀaləqitaaq 'star'
> CSY iʀaləqətaaq* 'star'
> Sir — [for nuʀasaX 'star' see nəʀžuɣ-]

PE iʀcaquʀ '(area around) heart' [cf. quʀ]
AAY —
CAY iXcaquq 'heart'
NSY iXsaquq
CSY iXsaquq
Sir —
SPI iqsaʀuq 'animal heart', Qaw 'sack surrounding heart'
NAI —
WCI —
ECI Lab itsaɣuk 'pit of stomach'
GRI iʀsaʀuq

PY iʀcuɣ- 'grimace (child)' [cf. iqə(ʀ) and iʀyaɣ-]
AAY iXcuxtə- 'grimace (as a child unwilling to do s.th. or about to cry)'
CAY iXcuɣ-, iXcuŋa-
NSY iXsuXtaʀaaʀ- 'grimace, be about to cry' [ANLC; Men. has iXsuɣ- 'sob']
CSY —

PY iʀiʀ- 'tilt' [cf. Atkan Aleut iiXi- 'limp'; the relat. — if any — to iɣəɣaʀ- and/or iqu- is obscure]
AAY iXiʀ- 'be tilted' [post. root]
CAY iʀiʀ- 'be tilting, slanted' [postural root; and note iʀia- 'waddle when walking']

NSY iXiXtə- 'tilt, move from one place to another' [ANLC]
CSY iʀiʀ- 'be tilting' [post. root; note also iʀəłəʀγiqə- 'limp']
Inu [note perhaps NAI iʀiiłuktaq- 'wriggle, wiggle']

PE iʀ(ə)ləγ- 'be stingy'
AAY PWS iʀləγ- 'be secretive, stingy'
CAY iʀəlγitə-, HBC, Nun iʀlaitə- 'be generous', NS iʀləγ- 'be stingy'
NSY iʀləγ- 'be stingy, greedy' [iʀləxtuqaq 'stingy']
CSY iʀləxtu- 'be stingy' [and iʀləγitə- 'be generous']
Sir —
SPI iʀlik- 'be stingy'
NAI Mal iʀlʸɨk-
WCI iʀlik-
ECI iʀli(k)- 'resist, not let s.o. take one's thing(s)'
GRI iʀłiγ- 'be stingy' [and iʀłittuuq, 'miser', iʀłinnaʀ-, iʀłiʀnaʀ- 'be precious'; note also EG iaʀsiluuq (Robbe and Menn. iiaʀsiluuq) 'miser', WG iasilaaʀ- 'be miserly, anxious about s.th.' — perhaps by contam. with source of iʀa-]

PE iʀləkə- 'be stingy with' [c f. kə-[1]]
AAY PWS iʀləkə- 'be secretive, stingy with'
CAY iʀləkə- 'be stingy with'
NSY —
CSY iʀləkə- 'be possessive about'
Sir —
SPI iʀlii- 'be stingy with s.th.', Qaw 'not want (s.o.) to leave'
NAI Mal iʀłʸɨγi- 'be stingy about'
WCI iʀliγi- 'be mean with, Car? 'be very fond of' [Schn. 'adg']
ECI iʀliγi- 'resist'
GRI iʀłiγi- 'be stingy with, value' [and note iʀiaγi- 'protect, preserve', NG iʀiaʀi- 'like', iʀiaʀnaq- 'be good, clean, beautiful', EG iaqqit(i)- 'be stingy toward', iaa- 'be protective toward' — Robbe and Menn. have iiaa- 'be jealous, miserly, desire']

PI iʀnaaq 'heartwood' [cf. iʀnəʀ and aʀ?]
Yup [cf. CSY iʀnəʀaq 'guts, intestines' under iʀnəʀłuk]
SPI Qaw iʀnaaq 'heartwood'
NAI iʀnʸaaq 'core of wood'
WCI [Cop iʀnaaq is 'son of husband's sibling, cousin' acc. Pryde — cf. iʀnəʀ]
ECI iʀnaaq 'wood that is soft and easy to cut, sapwood'
GRI —

PE iʀnəʀ 'son'
AAY ➞
CAY ➞
NSY iʀnəq 'son'
CSY iʀnəq*
Sir —
SPI —
NAI iʀnʸɨq*
WCI iʀniq
ECI iʀniq
GRI iʀniq* 'son' [and iʀniu- 'be born']

PI iʀnəkšaq 'stepson or adopted son' [cf. kðaʀ]
Yup — [note CSY iʀnəXqaq 'adopted son' with a different p.b.]
SPI —
NAI iʀnʸikšaq 'adopted son'
WCI iʀniksaq 'stepson' [Lowe]
ECI iʀnisaq 'son of spouse, stepson, adopted son'
GRI iʀniššaq 'stepson' [compare iʀniʀsiaq 'foster son']

PE iʀni- 'give birth' [cf. li-[1]]
AAY —
CAY iʀni- 'give birth'
NSY iʀni-
CSY iʀni-
Sir —
SPI iʀni-
NAI iʀnʸi-
WCI iʀni-
ECI iʀni- 'give birth to, beget'
GRI iʀni- 'give birth'

PE iʀni(C)aʀ 'offspring' [cf. li(C)aʀ]
AAY K iʀniaq 'cub, louse egg'
CAY iʀniaq 'offspring'
NSY iʀniaq [ANLC]
CSY —
Sir —
SPI iʀniaq 'child'
NAI iʀnʸiaq
WCI —
ECI iʀniaq 'begotten' [and iʀniayuk 'nephew-in-law']
GRI iʀniaq 'brood, spawn', EG 'louse egg' [possessed pl. = 'interest (on loan)'; iʀniaʀi- 'give birth to']

PI iʀnisuk- 'be in labor' [cf. iʀni- above and yuγ-]
SPI iʀnizuk- 'be in labor (woman)'
NAI PH, Nu iʀnʸisuk-
WCI iʀnisuk-
ECI iʀnisuk-
GRI iʀnisuγ-

PY iʀnəʀłuk 'guts' [cf. iŋaluk, though the relat. is phonologically problematical — contam. with iʀnəʀ?]
AAY —
CAY iʀnəXłuk 'seal gut'
NSY —
CSY iʀnəXłuk 'cleaned and dried walrus intestine' [and iʀnəʀaq 'guts, intestines']
Sir [note iʀnəʀəX 'guts, intestines' — Vakh. from Men.'s texts, also Orr]

PE iʀtuʀ- 'break or crack (skin)'
AAY —
CAY —
NSY iXtuʀ- 'break up' [ANLC; Men. has iXtuXtə- 'break']
CSY iXtuʀ- 'become soft through being flexed'
Sir iXtəqcəX 'crushed'
SPI iqtuq- 'break, shatter'
NAI iqsuq- 'break, crack, prepare skin that way, be

ready for tanning'
WCI iqtuq- 'scrape (skin)' [and iqtuqsit 'skin-scraper']
ECI iqtuʀsit 'skin-scraper'
GRI iʀsuʀ- 'scrape (land animal's skin, with a rough stone)' [and iʀsuʀsit 'stone to prepare skins with']

PY-S iʀyaɣ- 'grimace' [cf. iqə(ʀ), iqlak- and iʀcug-]
AAY PWS iʀyaxtə- 'grit one's teeth'
CAY Nun iʀyaxtə- 'have one's mouth open and stretched wide with teeth clenched' [and note Y iʀzəɣ- 'pout']
NSY —
CSY iʀyaxtə- 'frown', iʀyaXqə- 'grimace'
Sir iʀyaXqə(s)- 'frown, grimace (before crying)'

PY isaluq 'porcupine' [cf. Aleut isaluX 'flock of birds'?; the semantic relat. here may be based on the folk belief that porcupines shoot their quills, although Berg. discounts any relationship; note that PY words rarely have initial is- unless loans]
AAY AP isaluq 'porcupine' [Fisher]
CAY isaluq, isaluuq
NSY —
CSY —

PI isu(k) 'end' [from *iyu(ɣ)? — cf. iyuŋŋaʀ]
SPI izu 'end' [also Di]
NAI isu 'end' [and note place name Isuk 'Cape Halkett']
WCI isu 'end'
ECI isuk
GRI isu 'end', NG also 'right side of sleeping platform', EG isiq 'cape, hood, tip' [Robbe and Menn. for the latter; note also isuitsuq '(topping) sea' — i.e. 'breaker']

PI isuɣluk 'end of s.th.' [cf. łuɣ]
SPI izuɣluk 'rough end of wood, bone'
NAI isuɣluk 'end of bone containing marrow'
WCI isuɣluk
ECI isulluk 'butt of rifle'
GRI [note isułłuk 'short strap from front part of bladder dart to middle of shaft']

PI isukliq 'endmost' [cf. l(l)iʀ]
SPI izukłiq 'endmost'
NAI isukłiq* 'farthest extension'
WCI [Schn. has 'adg' — i.e. Car? — isulliq 'object nearest end']
ECI isutsiq 'endmost one'
GRI isułłiq*, isuʀłiq* 'endmost one', EG isitsiq 'big toe' [Robbe and Menn. — Robbe and Dorais have isitsi(k)]

PI isuʀaq 'trace (for dog)' [cf. qaʀ?]
SPI —
NAI isuʀaq 'harness rope'
WCI isuqqat 'harness traces for dogs' [and Sig isuʀaqtu- 'be long' [Pet.]
ECI isuʀaqtuyuq 'long dog trace'
GRI isuʀaʀtu- 'be long from one end to the other'

isuʀiq 'spotted seal' [loan from Aleut isuX, isuʀi-X 'spotted seal']
AAY K isu<ʀ>iq 'spotted seal'
CAY isuʀiq, Nun suuʀi
NSY —
CSY —

PE itaɣ- 'take care of (belongings)' [cf. EA ituʀ- as in ituʀisa- 'be merciful', ituXta- 'have mercy on'?]
AAY itaɣ(yuɣ)-, AP ita(yuɣ)- 'be careful (with belongings)' [emot. root]
CAY [note icaqə- 'hold in lap, baby sit', NSU icaXqə- 'fix, repair' — by contam. with caʀliɣaʀ?]
NSY itaɣ- 'be possessive, careful, greedy', itaɣyuɣ- 'be greedy, begrudge', itaxsi- 'be tidy (person)' [ANLC; Men. has itakə- 'be sorry for' and L.-T. has itaxtalʀia 'stingy (person)']
CSY itakə- 'take care of (belongings)', itaɣnaʀ- 'be satisfactory', itaɣnaʀyuɣ- 'be happy' [and itaxsinəq* 'thrifty person']
Sir [Em. has itaXsinəX (for itaxsinəX?) 'thrifty' — from CSY?]
SPI —
NAI —
WCI [Pet. has Sig itayeytuaq 'peaceful']
ECI itaɣi- 'treat gently, cautiously', itanna(q)- 'be fragile'
GRI [note perhaps ittanniq* (old ortho. igtangneq) 'shrewd, clever' and ittassaʀ- (old ortho. igtagsar-) 'be spoilt (child)']

PI itcaq[1] 'long ago' [cf. icivaʀ and ikpaq]
SPI issaq 'a long time ago'
NAI Nu itcaq
WCI itsaq
ECI Lab itsaq 'in ancient times' [Bourq. — Saul also for Tar]
GRI itsaq 'long ago, in the old days'

PI itcaʀnitaq 's.th. from long ago [cf. p.b. nitaq]
SPI issaʀnitaq 's.th. ancient'
NAI —
WCI Cop ittaʀnihaq 's.th. ancient' [Ras.], Car? itsa(ʀ)nitaq 'events that happened long ago' [Schn. 'adg'; note also Baker Lake itsaʀniaq 'great grandchild']
ECI Igl itsaʀnisaaluk 'very old' [Ras.]
GRI itsaʀnisaq 's.th. from long ago, old-fashioned'

PI itcaq[2] 'tent skin'
SPI —
NAI itca 'skin for tent, tent cover', itcat 'caribou skin tent made of many pieces of skin', itcalik 'frame for skin tent', Nu 'skin tent' [itcakšat 'six', literally 'material for a skin tent', refers apparently to the number of skins once considered normal for constructing a traditional tent]
WCI Cop ittat 'skin tent' [Jen.], Net itsaq 'skin tent' [B.-S.], Car itsaxxaq 'skin for tent from caribou that has just molted' [Ras.]
ECI itsaq 'roof of tent or house', NBI ittaq 'sealskin tent', Iti itsat 'tent and its inhabitants', Lab 'the skin of a tent, cabin roof on boat' [Bourq.]
GRI itsa, Up itsaq 'skin placed above roof of house to protect against rain', itsat 'inner layer of skin of

traditional tent', NG itsaq, ittaq 'skin tent' [in Holt. pl. itsat is 'double tent skin']

PE itðə 'cold' [cf. Atkan Aleut iciŋu- 'feel chilly']
AAY —
CAY —
NSY isikinaʀ- 'be cold to touch' [ANLC; Men. has isikiŋalʀia 'cold']
CSY isəkinaʀ- 'be cold to the touch'
Sir isikinəɬəʀəX 'cold'
SPI išši
NAI iẓẓi, Mal itẓi
WCI iyyi 'cold' [and Cop iyyilaqi- 'be cold' — Lowe; Schn. has iyyiŋa- for 'adg'; Dor. has itẓi 'cold' for Net and Briggs has iẓẓiliq- 'be cold' for Utk]
ECI iyyi 'cold'
GRI išši, EG ittiliq 'cold' [and iššiɣ-, EG ittiliʀ- 'be cold']

PE itəɣ 'toe-cap'
AAY itək 'toe-cap (of boot)'
CAY itək
NSY itək
CSY itək
Sir itəx 'toe-cap' [and itəɣ- 'kick' — Vakh. from Rub.]
SPI itik 'ankle skin of caribou'
NAI isik
WCI →
ECI →
GRI isi 'tip of boot'

PE itəɣaʀ 'foot' [cf. aʀ; the meaning 'eleven', for WCI and GRI, refers to the Esk counting system, shifting down to the digits of the first foot]
AAY C it<ɣ>aq, K itxaq 'foot'
CAY itɣaq, NSU itəɣaq
NSY itəɣaq
CSY itəɣaq
Sir itəɣəX 'foot' [also itəɣa; and note itxəm iŋləx 'fifteen']
SPI itiɣak 'foot'
NAI isiɣak
WCI Sig itiɣak, Cop itiɣaq, Net ihiɣak 'foot' [and Ras. has Cop ihikkani 'eleven' — Sig itiangnerat acc. Pet.]
ECI Igl isiɣak, Tar, Cape Dorset itiɣait, Iti itaɣait [pl. only], Lab itiɣak 'foot' [and itiɣammaaq 'shoe that is too big', Iti itaɣaq 'European shoe', note also Cape Dorset itikkanuuqtut 'eleven']
GRI isiɣak 'foot' [Kl. also has 'toe, part of foot with toes', pl. isikkat 'whole foot or both feet'; NWG isikkaniɬɬit, NG ihikkaniq 'eleven' as if from loc. case ihikkani, NG ihiɣammaak 'outer boots']

PE itəɣmiɣ- 'kick' [cf. miɣ-]
AAY —
CAY itəɣmiɣ- 'kick with top of boot, shoe'
NSY itəɣmiɣ- [L.-T. has this and ətəɣmiXqə-]
CSY itəɣmiɣ-
Sir [note itəɣ- 'kick' — Vakh. from Rub.; Men. has itəmɣətə- (for itəɣməɣ-?) 'stumble, limp'; Em. has itəɣməɬqutaq '(native) football']
SPI —
NAI isiŋmik- 'kick'
WCI Cop itiŋmik-
ECI itimmi(k)-
GRI isimmiɣ-

PE itəɣnaʀ 'jade' [cf. itəɣ and naʀ?]
AAY —
CAY NSU itəɣnaq* 'jade'
NSY itiɣnaq 'serpentine, nephrite' [Jen.]
CSY —
Sir —
SPI itiŋnaq 'jade' [Jen. 'serpentine, nephrite' for W]
NAI isiŋnaq 'jade'
WCI [Jen. has Sig isingnaq 'serpentine']
ECI —
GRI —

PY itəmə- 'break or come undone' [compare the p.b. in ciqumə(t)-; the relat. — if any — to əɣumə- is obscure]
AAY itəmə-, AP itumə-, PWS utəmə- 'come apart, get loose'
CAY itumə- 'break into pieces', NSU itumtə- 'undress', itumŋa- 'be naked'
NSY —
CSY itəmə-, iləmə- 'come undone', itəmtə- 'undo'
Sir —

PE itəʀ- 'enter' [cf. Aleut ita- 'contain, have in it', Atkan it- 'go in, have room', EA ica- 'fill' and compare under ima(ʀ)]
AAY itəʀ- 'enter, come in'
CAY itəʀ-
NSY itəʀ-
CSY itəʀ-
Sir itəʀ-
SPI itiq-, Di itəq-
NAI isiq-
WCI itiq-, Net ihiq-
ECI itiq-
GRI isiʀ-

PI itaa- 'enter (many)' [cf. a-]
SPI itaa- 'enter in large numbers, all at once'
NAI isaa-
WCI —
ECI itaa- 'come in one after the other'
GRI isaa- 'all come in'

PE itəʀaʀ- 'go farther in or up river' [cf. aʀ-]
AAY itXaʀ- AP 'go farther inside', Kod 'go toward north of island'
CAY itXaʀ- 'go upriver, go further in'
NSY —
CSY itəʀaʀ- 'go farther in'
Sir itXaʀ- 'go farther into bay, etc.'
SPI itaaq- 'enter river from sea'
NAI —
WCI itaaq- 'break in (as dog in snowhouse' [Pryde]
ECI itaaq- 'break into (house), invade (country)'
GRI —

PE itəʀcaʀnəʀ 'incoming current or wind' [cf. caʀ- and nəʀ[1]]
AAY AP itəXcanəq 'incoming tide'
CAY —
NSY —
CSY —
Sir —
SPI —
NAI isiqsaʀnaq 'river current flowing toward (in)land(?)'
WCI —
ECI —
GRI isiʀsaʀniq* 'wind up fjord'

PY itəʀnəq 'draft' [cf. nəʀ[1]]
AAY K, KP itəʀnəq 'draft entering building'
CAY itəʀnəq*
NSY itəʀnəq [ANLC]
CSY —

PE itʀutə- 'bring in' [cf. utə-]
AAY itXutə- 'bring in'
CAY itXutə-
NSY itXutə- [ANLC]
CSY itXutə- 'bring in', iitXutə- 'forcefully bring in'
Sir —
SPI itquti- 'bring in'
NAI [icqun 'admission charge']
WCI itqut(i)- 'have met s.o. inside'
ECI —
GRI iqqut(i)-, iXXut(i)- 'bring in'

PE ituɣ 'milk of animal'
AAY itumnaq, ituŋnaq 'sore that doesn't heal'
CAY ituk 'serum' [reported in old sources], NSU ituɣ- 'be sweet', NSU itulək 'jellyfish'
NSY ituk 'milk'
CSY ituk 'milk (not of humans)'
Sir itux [Orr]
SPI ituk 'baby walrus stomach full of milk'
NAI ituk 'congealed milk in caribou calf's stomach' [the t rather than s is unexplained — a borrowing from another dialect?]
WCI Cop ituk 'milk' [and Pet. has for Sig]
ECI NBI itu(k) 'caribou milk'
GRI —

PY itutə- 'dock (boat)'
AAY itutə-, PWS itu- 'dock (a boat)' [and C, Kod itu(q) 'one who accompanies by boat']
CAY itutə- 'put alongside (esp. a boat)'
NSY —
CSY —

PY ivalʀayak 'crab' [cf. ivaʀ-]
AAY AP, Kod iwalʀayak, PWS yualla<y>ak 'king crab', KP 'dungeness crab'
CAY Nun ivalʀiiyax, NSU yaləʀsaq 'king crab'
NSY —
CSY —

PE ivalu 'sinew'
AAY AP iwaluq, C yualuq 'sinew'
CAY yualuq, Nun, HBC ivalu(q)
NSY ivalu
CSY ivalu
Sir ivəla, pl. ivəluy [Orr]
SPI iwalu, Qaw ialu
NAI ivalu 'sinew' [as verb = 'thread (a needle)']
WCI ivalu 'sinew'
ECI ivalu 'sinew for sewing'
GRI uyalu, uyaluq, NG ivaluq 'sinew (for sewing with)' [as verb = 'thread (a needle)']

PE ivaʀ- 'look for'
AAY K iwa-, C yuaʀ- 'look for'
CAY yuaʀ-, HBC, Nun ivaʀ- 'look for, miss' [for yuaʀun, Nun ivaʀun 'song' see ivaʀun]
NSY ivaʀ- 'look for' [ANLC ivaaʀ- 'search']
CSY ivaʀ-
Sir —
SPI iwaq-, W iaq-, Qaw iaq-, yiaq- 'look for' [half-trans. iwaqłiq-, iaqłiq-]
NAI ivaq- 'look for' [half-trans. ivaqłiq-]
WCI Cop ivaq- 'look for' [Ras.; Schn. has Car? iva(a)q- 'look for a place or object known to be near' — 'adg'; Net half-trans. ivaqłiq- acc. Pryde]
ECI ivaa- 'look for actively, moving everything'
GRI uyaʀ-, NG ivaq- 'look for' [half-trans. uyaʀłiʀ-; uyaaʀi-, uyaasi- 'be out searching (for s.o.)']

PI ivaʀiatci- 'miss'
SPI —
NAI ivaʀiatci- 'miss s.o. who has left'
WCI —
ECI —
GRI uyaʀiatsi-, NG ivaʀiatsi- 'miss (s.th.)' [and ujaʀiaɣi- 'miss (s.o. or s.th. one has grown used to)']

PE ivayaʀ- ' steal or rob' [cf. yaʀ(tuʀ)?]
AAY —
CAY wayaʀ-, w̥ayaʀ-, Nun mayaʀ- 'rob' [the latter form may be influenced by mayitəqə-]
NSY wayaʀ- 'plunder, pillage' [ANLC]
CSY wayaʀ- 'despoil' [and wayaq 'slave'; note also mayaXtə- 'lose weight, become thin'?]
Sir [Orr has unayəʀ- 'take away' — a possible contam. with una-[1]]
SPI iwayaq- 'take without asking'
NAI ivayaq- 'get more than one should, take away a necessary part of s.th.', ivayaqtuq- 'rob, defraud'
WCI Sig ivayaq- 'steal'
ECI ivayaq- 'pick up s.th. somebody else has thrown away', Lab ivayak- 'steal, scrounge'
GRI uyaya(a)ʀ-, NG ivayaq- 'rob' [in WG also 'throw s.th. for scrambling']

PY ivaʀun 'song' [apparently from ivaʀ- with p.b. un, but cf. also ivəq-[2]]
AAY Kod iwaʀun 'song' [Rezanov]
CAY yuaʀun, HBC, Nun ivaʀun 'song, music'

NSY —
CSY Chap ivaʀutaq 'ceremonial song'

PI ivəq-[1] 'fit into or up against' [cf. ivəq-[2]?]
Sir — [for əvʀit- 'return' see uvəʀ-]
SPI — [for Imaq wiqma(q)- see uyiqə-]
NAI iviq- 'fit' [and iviqtit- 'make go back to same position as before', also iviʀak- 'please, be pleased'?]
WCI iviq- 'fit into s.th. else' [and iviqtit- 'put together, in place, return s.o. to good health']
ECI iviq- 'put or try on narrow garment (e.g. to see if it fits)'
GRI iviʀ- 'lie up against, penetrate' [Kl. also 'follow in all its angles and edges'; note also iviʀtit- 'attach, install'; for ippiʀ- 'penetʀate (floating ice)' see ivəʀ-]

PI ivəq-[2] 'sing (in song duel)' [cf. ivəq-[1] and ivaʀun?]
SPI uiq- 'sing a song about one's cross cousin'
NAI —
WCI iviq- 'sing lampoon' [Ras.], B. Lake 'compete in song duel' [Schn.]
ECI —
GRI iviʀ-, iffit- 'satirize in drum song' [and NG iviq 'competitor, opponent', iviʀiik 'regular opponents' — Holt.; compare iŋəq-]

PE ivəʀ- and **ipəʀ-** 'wade or step into water' [there may be a link to ivəq-[1]; there seems to be contam. with əpəʀ in Inu — note esp. the SPI there]
AAY PWS iwəʀ- 'wade'
CAY ivəʀ- 'step into water'
NSY ivəʀ- 'step in water' [Em.]
CSY ivəʀ- 'wade'
Sir iʀvə- 'wade' [Orr; Em. has iɣvəsinaʀ- 'wade, go into water']
SPI Qaw ipiq- 'enter water and begin to wade', KI iviʀaaq- 'wade' [and note ivʀa(a)niq, Qaw ivʀaniq, Di iaanəq 'rain' — compare under imaʀnin (ima(ʀ)) — contam.?]
NAI ipiʀaq- 'wade'
WCI ipiʀa(a)q- 'wade' [and note B. Lake ivʀaʀniq 'moderately soft snow' — Dor.]
ECI ipiʀaaq- 'wade'
GRI ipiʀaaʀ- 'wade' [and note ippiʀ-, ippikaʀ- 'penetrate (through ice floating on water)']

PY ivʀaʀ- 'wade around' [cf. aʀ-]
AAY PWS iwwaʀ-, KP yuɣɣaʀ- (old word) 'wade around'
CAY ivʀaʀ- 'wade'
NSY ivʀaʀ- 'wade, walk in water' [ANLC]
CSY ivʀaaʀ- 'wade around'

PY ivʀuciq 'waterproof boot' [cf. un]
AAY K iʀʀuciq 'skin knee- boot, shoe'
CAY ivʀuciq 'waterproof (skin) boot'
NSY ivʀusiik 'medium- sized boot of dehaired sealskin' [ANLC has ivʀusiq 'wading boot']
CSY [iivʀusiq 'any wading device']

PE ivitəʀaʀ 'red mineral'
AAY C wiitəq 'soft black rock used for paint'
CAY wiiitəʀaq 'red clay or ochre' [Jen. has Nun wiitix 'red paint, iron oxide']
NSY [witəXsi-, uitəXsi- 'prepare dye from alder bark — ANLC]
CSY [mitəʀa 'ochre' — Chap]
Sir —
SPI Qaw iitaaq 'ochre, red stone used as dye for wood or hide' [KI iʀitaq]
NAI ivisaaq
WCI Sig ivita(a)q 'red, vermillion, red iron' [Pet.; Jen. has 'red paint' and as verb 'be red'; Ras. has ivitaaq 'soft red stone used for coloring']
ECI Lab ivitaaq 'red earth or stone' [Bourq.]
GRI ivisaaq 'reddish brown earth or stone'

PI ivitaaʀuq 'arctic char (spawning)'
Yup [note CSY ivisa 'flounder, halibut'?]
SPI —
NAI —
WCI Cop ivitaaʀuq 'spawning char' [Lowe; Met. has ivitaʀuk 'red fish'; Ras. has Net ivitaaʀuq 'reddish trout']
ECI ivitaaʀuq 'red trout (in lakes)' [Dor.; Schn. has ivitaʀuq]
GRI ivisaaʀuq 'trout with reddish belly'

PE iyaɣ- 'extend arm' [cf. iyaquʀ, (i)yavə- and Aleut ya-X 'half fathom — from middle finger to chin']
AAY saxtə- 'stretch out arm'
CAY yaxtə-, HBC, Nun caxtə- 'stretch out arm'
NSY ➡
CSY yaaxtaʀ- 'pull hand over hand'
Sir yaxtaʀaʀ- 'fly' [Vakh. from Men.'s texts]
SPI izak- 'extend arm, reach and get'
NAI isaaq- 'raise one's arm'
WCI isak- 'extend arm (like priest at mass)', isaaq- 'raise arms above head' [Met.]
ECI isak- 'stretch arm', isaak- 'spread or stretch arms sideways' [also said of calving ice at high tide, of leaves and flowers that open, bloom']
GRI isaɣ- 'extend arm' [and Robbe and Menn. have EG isaaC- stretch out (limb)']

PI isaɣutə- 'reach for' [cf. utə-]
SPI izaɣu(ti)- 'start, begin', Qaw 'do in a hurry'
NAI isaɣuti- 'start, begin'
WCI Sig isaɣutiŋ(ŋ)it- 'not have done yet' [and note isaq(q)i- 'work at s.th.'; Ras. has isaɣuti- 'throw oneself on, attack']
ECI isaɣutaq- 'shine (sun)' [and isaɣutaq 'ray of sunlight'; Ras. has Igl isaʀayaq 'job']
GRI isaɣut(i)-, isaat(i)- 'reach for, take hold of, start working on' [and NG ihaʀaaluk- 'work, be busy']

PE iyaɣnəʀ 'span' [cf. nəʀ[1]]
AAY saɣnəq 'span, fathom'
CAY yaɣnəq*
NSY —
CSY yaaɣnəq* 'span from fingertips of one arm to bent elbow of other one, fathom'

Sir —
SPI —
NAI isaɣnɨq* 'fathom'
WCI isaŋniq
ECI —
GRI isanniq* 'span'

PE iyaqqi- 'flap wings' [cf. iyaquʀ below and li-[1]]
AAY saqi- 'flap wings'
CAY yaqiuʀ-
NSY yaqi- 'fly away' [ANLC]
CSY yaqii- 'move with wings'
Sir —
SPI izaqila- 'flap wings'
NAI isaqqilʸa- 'flap wings'
WCI —
ECI isaqqilaa- 'gesticulate'
GRI isaqqila-, EG isaqqala- 'flap wings' [Robbe and Menn. for the latter; for EG isaqqiiq 'butterfly' see caqələŋkitaʀ]

PE iyaquʀ 'wing' [cf. quʀ]
AAY saquq 'wing' [and saquləkʼbird']
CAY yaquq, HBC, Nun, Eg caquq 'wing' [and yaquləkʼbird', Nun 'angel']
NSY yaquq 'wing'
CSY yaquq 'wing' [and yaquləkʼangel']
Sir yaqəX 'wing, arm'
SPI izaʀuq 'wing'
NAI isaʀuq
WCI isaʀuq
ECI isaʀuq
GRI isaʀuq 'wing (bone)'

PI iyaŋa- 'be weak or tired' [cf. ŋa-[1]; the relat. — if any — to aʀ(ə)yu(ʀ)- or yaɣ(ə)- is obscure]
SPI [note iyaitqaa 'poor thing!']
NAI [Nu yaʀa- 'be lame, crippled']
WCI Sig iyaŋa- 'be weak' [and i(y)aŋi-, i(y)aŋatqi-, iaʀayi- 'tire', yaʀa- 'be tired, tire', yaʀaŋa- 'feel tired']
ECI [Ras. has Igl yaʀatiɣi- 'be tired of']
GRI iaŋa- 'be indeterminate, wishy-washy, tawny (dog)'

PE iyukuta(ʀ) 'moisture' [cf. Atkan Aleut yux 'moisture']
AAY sukuq, sukutaq 'dampness, moisture'
CAY yukutaq, HBC cukutaq [and yukutaXtə- 'be damp']
NSY —
CSY yukuta [and yukutatə- 'be damp']
Sir —
SPI izuɣutaq 'dew' [Jen.]
NAI —
WCI —
ECI —
GRI isuɣutaq, NG ihuutaq 'dew, moisture' [and suɣuta- 'be damp']

PE iyuŋŋaʀ 'jaeger' [cf. perhaps isu(k) — the bird has distinctive long mid- tail feathers]
AAY —
CAY yuŋaq, HBC cuŋaXłuɣaq* 'jaeger'
NSY — [but Ras. has tuŋ·aq 'arctic gull' — a misprint?]
CSY yuuŋaaʀaq* 'jaeger'
Sir —
SPI Qaw isuŋaq [and Jen. has izuŋaq for W]
NAI isuŋŋaq* 'long-tailed jaeger'
WCI isuŋŋaq 'kind of hawk' [Met., but Ras. has 'arctic gull' and B.-S. has 'jaeger' for Car]
ECI isuŋŋaq 'type of gull' [but in W. Bay 'bird with black head and long double tail' — prob. arctic tern]
GRI isuŋŋaq(*) 'arctic skua, jaeger'

PE iyuvʀiʀ- and **iyivʀiʀ-** 'examine' [cf. iyyuʀ-?]
AAY K suʀwiʀ-, C suʀʀiʀ- 'taste'
CAY yuvʀiʀ-, yuʀviʀ-, ivʀiʀ-, Nun cuvʀiʀ-, HBC, Eg cuʀviʀ- 'examine'
NSY yuvʀiʀ- 'check up, take a look, select' [ANLC has yuvʀiaʀ- 'examine, inspect']
CSY yuvʀiiʀ- 'examine'
Sir —
SPI iziʀlaq-, W izilʀaq- 'select, choose' [Imaq yuʀvi- 'check, select, look around', via Yup?]
NAI isivʀiq- 'judge, come out in open' [and note uyavɣaq- 'check on, take a look at']
WCI isivʀiuq- 'examine carefully'
ECI —
GRI —

PE iyyuʀ- 'poke head out for a look' [cf. iyuvʀiʀ- and yuʀžaʀ-]
AAY K su<ʀ>aʀ- 'poke head out of water, rise (sun)'
CAY yuʀaʀ-, Nun cuʀaʀ-, cuXtuʀ-, HBC cuʀaqəXtə- 'check outside'
NSY yuʀaʀ- 'poke head up to take a look' [Enm. et al.]
CSY ➟
Sir yuʀaʀ- 'look through something' [Orr — from CSY?; and note əcəqəX 'head', also icəqəX in Men.'s and Vakh.'s texts from *iyyuquʀ?; compare nacəʀaX 'young seal' under nayyiʀaʀ (nayyiʀ), also nay(ə)quʀ and uya(quʀ)]
SPI issuq- 'go out to check weather', Qaw 'go out and urinate, go out for a moment'
NAI itcuq- 'go out after waking'
WCI ➟
ECI itsu(q)- 'go out to take a look'
GRI itsuʀ- 'look outside for something', EG itsiiyaC- 'go out'

PI itcuaq- 'peek in or out'
SPI issuaq 'peek, look in or out'
NAI itcuaq- 'peek, look in'
WCI itsuaq- 'take a quick look outside'
ECI itsua(q)- 'peek in'
GRI itsuaʀ- 'peek in or out (through window, etc.)'

PY-S yuqaʀ- 'go outside' [cf. k(k)aʀ-]
AAY —
CAY yuqəXtə-, HBC, Nun cuqəXtə- 'relieve oneself in an appropriate place'
NSY yuqaXtə- 'go out of house briefly to look around' [ANLC]

CSY yuqəXtə- ‘go out for a moment (to check weather)’
Sir yuqaʀ- ‘go outside’ [Vakh. from Rub.’s texts]

PY-S ižuk ‘low tide’ [cf. niðuʀ-?]
AAY —
CAY —
NSY —
CSY iik^w ‘low tide’ [also verbal iiw-; for homonym ‘sip’ see niðuʀ-?]
Sir icəx ‘low tide’

K

PY kaa(kaa) ‘stop it (exclamation)’
AAY kaa ‘no, stop it!’
CAY kaak(a) ‘listen!’
NSY kakaa ‘stop it, you mustn’t’ [ANLC has kaakaa ‘don’t’]
CSY kaakaa ‘quit!’
Inu — [but note GRI kikkiik ‘expression of disgust’; for kakkaak ‘wow!’ see akka]

PE kacaɣ- or **katcaɣ-** ‘strike (with drumstick)’ [cf. kaðuɣ-]
AAY —
CAY —
NSY kasaxtə- ‘beat drum at start of dance’ [ANLC]
CSY —
Sir —
SPI kazak- ‘beat a drum’ [Jen. has kazaun ‘drumstick’]
NAI kasak- ‘make a noise by striking’, kasauti ‘drumstick’, Mal also katcaktuq- ‘knock on door’
WCI Net kahak- ‘hit’ [Ras.; Pet. has Sig kasaq- ‘fight’, for which Met. has ‘beat drum’, kasautik ‘drumstick’]
ECI —
GRI —

PE kaðəvə(t)- ‘revolve or spin’ [cf. kaspuɣtə-]
AAY —
CAY Nun kazvun ‘bow part of drill’
NSY kayəvə- ‘revolve, circle’ [ANLC has kayəvaʀ- ‘revolve, spin’, kayəftə- ‘revolve, rotate’]
CSY kazivə- ‘spin, whirl’ [compare the second vowel in uzivə- ‘revolve’]
Sir kacvə- ‘spin, whirl’ [and kažviminu ‘around’; Vakh. also has kacəfkitaʀ- ‘revolve’ from Rub.; Em. has kacəfkitaʀ- ‘go round in a circle’]
SPI kaivžaaq- ‘go in circle, spin’
NAI kaivɨt-, kiavɨt- ‘circle, spin’, kaivžaaq- ‘spin’ [and kaivžaaq ‘whirlpool’]
WCI kiavit-, kaivit- ‘go around’, Cop, Car kaivyaq- ‘turn, revolve’ [Ras. has Cop ka·vitit- ‘cut thong in spiral from skin’]
ECI kaivit-, kaivat- ‘turn, spin’ [and kaiyyaŋu- ‘be giddy’, kaivuti, kaivauti ‘Inuit drill’]
GRI kaaviɣ- [Fab. has ka(a)vit-], NG kaivit- ‘revolve, go around, go round s.th.’, EG kaaviC- ‘hover over’ [Holm; note also kaaššaaq (old ortho. kâvssâq), EG kaattiʀsiq (Robbe and Menn.) ‘whirlwind’; for kaaviq ‘top’ see kavžaq]

PI kaivca(a)q ‘top (game)’ [cf. caʀ-?]
SPI kaipsaq ‘top’
NAI kaifsaaq, kiafsaaq ‘top (game)’
WCI Cop kaiptaq, Car kaipqataq ‘top, seal-indicator’ [Pryde; Ras. has Net kaivsa(a)q ‘top’]
ECI kaittaq, NBI kaissaq ‘top’
GRI kaassaaq [old ortho. kâvsâq], NG kaussaq, EG, Up kaatsaq

PI kažəvallak- ‘go in a circle’ [cf. łłaɣ-]
SPI —
NAI kaivallak-, kiavallak- ‘go in a circle (once)’ [kaivaluk-, kiavaluk- ‘go around in circles, move in a circle’]
WCI Net kaival(l)ak- ‘go around’ [Ras.]
ECI kaivalla(k)- ‘turn around once’ [kaivalua- ‘turn around several times’, kaivaluaq ‘drill, wheel, roller’]
GRI kaayałłaɣ-, NG kaivallak- ‘go round (once)’ [kaayalui(t)- ‘surround’]

PE kaðuɣ- ‘strike (with instrument)’ [cf. katuk-, katyuɣ- and kacaɣ-; from *katðuɣ- (katə- plus ðuɣ) as suggested by Nu katžuutaq under kað(ð)uɣun below?]
AAY kauɣ- ‘strike with object’
CAY kauɣ-
NSY kaaw- ‘strike with hammer’
CSY kaaw- ‘strike with hammer’ [for kaxsaxtə- ‘whip’ see kakyaɣ-]
Sir —
SPI kauk- ‘strike with hammer, etc.’
NAI kauk- ‘hammer’, kažuk- ‘hit on head’, Nu kažži- ‘shape stone by pounding’ [and kažumit- ‘crush’; note also Nu has katžuaq- ‘break up frozen ground looking for roots’]
WCI kauk- ‘hammer’ [and Ras. has Cop kayuk- ‘beat with stone’ and kaɣyuk- (for kayyuk-?) ‘knock out’; Pryde has Cop kayuk- ‘strike with a stone, pound’ but kayyuk- ‘hit a heavy blow (esp. to release s.th. from the surroundings it is stuck to’]
ECI kauk- ‘hit with object’, kayyu(k)- ‘pound, hammer’ [and note kavvaq, NBI kaɣvaq ‘ice floe (fractured in spring, at sea in winter)’]
GRI kaat- [old ortho. kau(t)-] ‘hammer’ [and kaššuɣ- ‘knock loose’; note also kaššuit ‘bits of ice drifting in sea’ and apparently also NG kauktut ‘twenty’]

PE kað(ð)uɣun and **kaðuɣutaʀ** ‘hammer’ [cf. un]
AAY kau<ɣ>utaq K ‘club’, C ‘pounding instrument’
CAY NS kauɣun ‘hammer’
NSY —
CSY kaaɣusiq
Sir —
SPI kažžuun, kažžuutaq
NAI kautaq ‘hammer’, kažžuutaq, Nu katžuutaq ‘stone hammer’

WCI kautaq 'hammer'
ECI kautaq
GRI kaataq

PI kauɣaq- 'pound [cf. aʀ-]
SPI kauɣa(q)- 'knock at door'
NAI [note Nu, PH kauɣaq- 'flense with a large flensing knife' — also nom. for the knife]
WCI kauɣaq- 'beat blubber, etc.'
ECI kauɣaq- 'beat frozen blubber or peat for runners'
GRI kaavaʀ- 'beat frozen blubber'

PE ka(C)əɣ- 'be hungry'
AAY kaiɣ- 'be hungry'
CAY kaiɣ-
NSY kiaɣ-
CSY —
Sir —
SPI kaak- 'starve, go without food' [and kaaŋniuq- 'be hungry']
NAI kaak- 'be hungry'
WCI kaak-
ECI kaak- 'be hungry' [and kaattu(q)- 'devour food hungrily']
GRI kaaɣ- 'be hungry' [and kaattuʀ- 'eat for the first time in a long time']

PE kaɣa- 'come loose or strip'
AAY kii- 'come off as a layer, peel off, come loose', kiitə- 'peel, strip'
CAY kii- 'come off as a layer, peel off'
NSY —
CSY kaɣa- 'be unruly, disheveled' [for kiiXtə- 'split' see əkiðaʀ-]
Sir kaɣa- 'fall out (hair from skin taken from animal)' [Em.]
SPI —
NAI kaat- 'split or be split into two layers for boat cover (walrus hide)', PH 'slice blubber from whale skin, leaving muktuk'
WCI —
ECI —
GRI kaa- 'be loosened from s.th. (e.g. hair from skin, ice from beach)', kaaŋŋaʀ- 'become loose', EG kaattuʀ- 'be loose' [Robbe and Menn. for the latter]

PY kaɣataq 'piece of sod' [cf. ðaʀ, on base transitivized with t-[1] as AAY kiitə- under kaɣa- above]
AAY kiitaq AP piece of sod'
CAY kiitaq
NSY —
CSY —
Inu [note SPI kaataq 'whale skin with blubber, muktuk']

kaɣaluq 'stern of boat' [from Aleut kaɣalu-X 'stern, heel']
AAY Kod kaɣaluq 'stern of boat' [reported in early source (Milan)]
CAY kaɣaluq 'stern of kayak'
NSY —
CSY —

kaɣi- 'sweep' [loan from Aleut kaɣi- 'sweep (floor), dump (garbage)'; there may be a relat. to kaɣimə-]
AAY kaɣi- 'sweep'
CAY kaɣi-
NSY —
CSY —

PY- S kaɣimə- 'crumble' [compare ciqumə(t)-]
AAY —
CAY kaimə-, Nun kaamə- 'make or drop crumbs'
NSY kiamə- 'pound into large pieces, shed, molt' [ANLC]
CSY kaɣimə- 'crumble'
Sir kaɣvə- 'break to pieces' [Orr, who also has kavə- 'crumble'; also kaɣvəqə- 'scatter, smash to pieces' (Vakh. from Men.'s texts)]

PY kaɣtaʀ- 'be concealed'
AAY —
CAY —
NSY kaxtaʀ- 'be concealed' [ANLC]
CSY kaxtaʀ- 'be concealed, in seclusion'

PE kaɣu- 'reach into or under s.th.' [cf. EA kaxu- 'dig a pit (in the ground)']
AAY kau- 'reach under or inside'
CAY kau- 'reach into container or hollow place'
NSY kaa- [ANLC — also kaatuʀ- 'dig into with hands']
CSY kaɣu- 'reach into'
Sir kaɣə- [Orr]
SPI kau-
NAI kau-
WCI kau-
ECI kau- 'slip an empty object over an oblong one' [Saul; Schn. has 'reach into', also kautuq- 'thrust finger up anus']
GRI kaa- 'reach into or under' [kaatuʀ- 'feel in under, grope (a woman)']

PE kakaɣ- 'carry on head or shoulders' [cf. kakaŋcaʀ]
AAY —
CAY [note kakkacuk 'pompom on top of parka hood']
NSY kakəɣm̥iɣ- [Orr], kakəxm̥iɣ- [L.-T.] 'carry on shoulders' [and kakəxm̥ik 'load carried on nexk' (ANLC)]
CSY [note kakək 'uppermost part of trad. skin- covered house where roof poles meet']
Sir kakaməɣ- 'carry on back or shoulders' [Vakh. from Men. and Rub.'s texts]
SPI kaɣaaq- 'carry s.o. on one's shoulders'
NAI kakak- 'carry on head' [and kakaaq- 'carry s.o. on one's shoulders']
WCI kakak- 'carry on shoulders' [and Cop kakautaq 'head- strap for carrying pack' — Jen.]
ECI kakak- 'carry s.o. on one's shoulders' [Bourq. has 'carry on head' and Peck 'put tow rope on shoulders to pull' for Lab]
GRI kakaɣ- 'carry on head or (person) on shoulders, EG

kaɣaC- 'carry on back', NWG kakak 'head of needle or nail' [for homonym meaning 'go too far, be too bad' see akka]

PE kakaŋcaʀ 'crown of head' [cf. kakaɣ-]
AAY AP kakaŋsaq 'crown of head', C kakŋaq 'top, peak' [Fisher]
CAY kakxaq, NI, K kakaŋcaq, HBC kakəŋcaq 'crown of head'
NSY kaxkaq
CSY kaaxkaq
Sir kakiɣcəX 'crown of head' [for kakəɣsəX?; note kakəx 'uppermost part of skin- covered dwelling where roof poles meet' — Em.]
SPI —
NAI —
WCI Car B. Lake kakaxxaq 'head of nail' [Schn.]
ECI —
GRI SWG kakassaq 'head of needle or nail, bone peg at upper end of throwing board'

PY- S kakavə- 'shake or tremble'
AAY [note Perry kaxʷa-, Kodiak kaxʷaɣ- 'bustle with activity, rush, hurry']
CAY kakavə- 'clatter, shake (as from fright), tremble making noise'
NSY —
CSY kakavə- 'be terrified, panicky'
Sir kakav(ə)- 'be terrified', kakaftə- 'terrify', and kakavniʀ- 'be panic-stricken' [Em.], kakavniXtə- 'frighten' [Vakh. from Rub., who also has kakaft(ə)- 'beg for s.th.']
Inu — [but note NAI kakavyak- 'become dizzy from breathing fumes in unventilated place']

PE kaki- 'pierce or prick'
AAY kaki- 'pierce or hit in the right spot'
CAY kaki- 'take a stitch' [Jen. has 'spear' for Nun]
NSY kakitə- 'pin, begin sewing' [and ANLC kakiiquʀ- 'bind, interlace, intertwine']
CSY kaki- 'sew'
Sir kakit(ə)- 'fasten, pierce with needle, thrust'
SPI kaɣi- 'prick'
NAI kaki- 'prick' [Jen. also 'spear'; kakinʸɨq* 'tattoo']
WCI kaki- 'prick, tattoo' [also 'spear (fish)' acc. Jen.; and note Cop kakillaq- 'sew (shaman's word)' acc. Pryde]
ECI kaki- 'prick' [and kakiniq 'tattoo']
GRI kaki- 'sticks into it' [and kakiuʀniʀit 'tattoos', EG kaɣiniq 'tattoo']

PE kaki(C)aʀ 'fish spear' [for the forms ending in vak cf. p.b. vaɣ]
AAY AP kakiaXɬuut 'bone spear for fish' [Fisher; B.-S. has C kaki(i)vaq 'leister']
CAY kakiaq NSU 'large fork', Mountain Village 'fish spear' [the latter acc. Holtved]
NSY —
CSY kakiiq 'large fork, fish spear' [Orr; Rub. has kak(i)ʀət 'fork']
Sir kakiX 'large fork, fish spear' [Orr]
SPI kaɣiaq 'large fork', Qaw kakiak, kakiat 'fork' [and Ras. has W kakisat — for kakižat? — 'leister']
NAI kaki<ž>aq 'hook or prong at end of fish spear', kakiak PH 'roasting spit', Nu 'leister' [Jen. has kakivak 'fish spear']
WCI Sig kakiaq 'fork' [Ras. has Cop kakivfak, kakiva·k 'leister' and B.-S. has Car, Net kakivak 'trout spear']
ECI [kakivak 'fish spear' —for Igl Ras. has kakivSat 'meat fork']
GRI kakiak [pl. kakiššat], kakuyak, NG kakivvak 'leister'

PE kakiðviɣ 'needle case' [cf. ðviɣ]
AAY K, KP kakiwik, C kakiywik 'sewing kit' [and note K kakiswik 'foreshaft of harpoon, socket of arrow' in early sources]
CAY kakivik 'needle case, sewing kit', NSU kakizvik 'pin-cushion'
NSY kakivik [ANLC]
CSY —
Sir —
SPI kakkiwik 'pin-cushion'
NAI kakkivik
WCI kakkivik 'small bag for pins or needles' [Schn. has kakpik 'needle case' for 'adg', Pryde has Cop, Car kakpik 'pin-cushion']
ECI kakkivik 'pin-cushion' [Saul]
GRI kakkivik 'pin-cushion'

PE kakilla- 'have paresthesia' [cf. la(ʀ)-?]
AAY kakilacaɣ- 'have pins and needles feeling (paresthesia)'
CAY kakilacaɣ-
NSY kakilasaɣ- [ANLC]
CSY —
Sir —
SPI Qaw kakilauži-
NAI kakilʸlʸauži-
WCI Cop kakilahai-
ECI kakillaalitsi-, kakillaalatsi-
GRI kakiɬɬalaaʀ-

PI kakillaʀnaq 'thorn' [cf. la(ʀ)- and naʀ-?]
SPI —
NAI kakilʸlʸaʀnaq 'thorn'
WCI kakillaʀnaq
ECI kakillanaqutit 'plant with red thorns', kakillauti 'thorn'
GRI kakiɬɬaʀnaq 'thorn', kakiɬɬaʀnaqut, kakiɬɬaʀnat 'thorn bush'

PE kakkin 'pin' [cf. un]
AAY AP kakitaq 'skewer'
CAY kakin 'pin'
NSY kakin, kakitə 'brooch, pin'
CSY —
Sir —
SPI kakkin 'brooch, pin', kakkun 'safety pin'
NAI kakkinʸ 'pin'
WCI kakkin, kakkun

ECI [note kakiyyut 'safety pin']
GRI —

PI kakilacak 'stickleback' [cf. kaki-]
SPI Qaw kaki(i)lasak 'stickleback'
NAI kakilʸasak 'small fish'
WCI kakilasak [Pryde]
ECI kakilisaq 'stickleback'
GRI kakilisak

PY kakiŋəʀ- 'crunch or creak'
AAY K kakiŋəXtə- 'squeak, crunch, grate'
CAY kakiuŋqitə-, Y kakiŋəXtə- 'make a creaking or crunching sound when walking on snow/ice'
NSY —
CSY [note kaŋʀuk 'crunching sound, sound of fluid-filled lungs' and kaŋžaak 'crunchy, squeaky, grating sound']

PE kakkiɣ 'snot'
AAY kakəxłuk 'nasal mucus, snot'
CAY kakək, kakəxłuk 'snot'
NSY kakik 'snot' [and kakixłuXqə- 'blow nose']
CSY kakəxłuk 'snot'
Sir kakixłəqə(s)- 'blow nose'
SPI kakkik 'snot' [verbal = 'blow or wipe nose']
NAI kakkik [also verbal]
WCI kakkik [also verbal]
ECI kakkiq 'snot hanging from nose' [and kakki(k)- Tar 'wipe nose', Lab 'blow nose']
GRI kakkik 'snot', kakkiɣ- 'blow nose'

PY kakəɣtə- 'get or have a bloody nose'
AAY kakəxtə- 'have or get a bloody nose'
CAY kakəxtə-
NSY kakəxtə- [L.-T.]
CSY kakəxtə-

PI kakkivik '(groove above) upper lip' [cf. ðviɣ]
Yup — [but note CAY kakəxłiliyaʀaq 'groove above upper lip' and Nun kakəxłiyaʀvix 'September' from kakəxłiʀ- 'have a runny nose']
SPI Qaw kakkiwiaq 'groove above upper lip'
NAI kakkivik, kakkiviaq '(groove above) upper lip, space between nose and lip'
WCI kakkiviaq 'upper lip'
ECI kakkiviaq
GRI kakkiviaq

PY- S kakɣaɣ- 'whip'
AAY —
CAY —
NSY kakɣaɣun 'whip', kakɣaxtə- 'beat with whip' [but Jen. has qakkiaryun 'dog whip']
CSY kaxsaxtə- 'whip', Chap kaksaɣun 'whip', kaksaɣutə- 'beat with long object'
Sir kakɣaɣəta 'whip', kakɣaxt(ə)- 'beat with whip' [the latter Vakh. from Men.'s texts — Men. has kakɣaʀ]
Inu [note Imaq kaɣiaʀun 'whip' — Ras. has W kakiaʀun but Jen. has qaɣiaʀun 'dog whip' and qaɣiari-, KI qaɣiaqsuq- 'whip', perhaps all from the Yup]

kalaaliq 'Greenlander' [Norse loan- word in GRI — compare Icelandic skrælingi 'savage', apparently related to skrá 'dried skin (as worn, for example, by Eskimos)' — first attested in the 12th century, applied to Eskimos and/or North American Indians in Labrador; the present meaning of Danish skrælling (and dialectal Norwegian skræling), 'miserable wretch, weakling', is a later semantic extension]
SPI —
NAI —
WCI —
ECI Lab kaʀaaliq 'Greenlander' [Peck, spelled originally as karâlek; probably first introduced by Moravian missionaries from GRI — earliest attestation in Lab. 1765 (Drechert); see Kleinschmidt's correspondence with Bourquin pointing out that the spelling here suggests a spurious uvular 'ʀ']
GRI kalaaliq 'Greenlander' [in Fab. kalalek, karalek, reflecting an apical 'r' at the onset of the second syllable, as in Danish-Norwegian of the time]

kalaɣaq 'sculpin' [loan from Aleut kalaɣa-X 'yellow sculpin']
AAY kala<ɣ>aq 'sculpin'
CAY Nun kalaɣaX
NSY —
CSY —

PE kaləɣ-[1] and **kalət-** 'tow or drag' [the latter presumably with t-[1]; cf. kaləvə(t)- and Aleut kalat- 'drag along ground', kala- 'string (beads or fish on line)', EA 'lace up (boot), gather', Atkan kala-X 'string, row'; there is entanglement with kaləɣ-[2] if they are not directly related]
AAY —
CAY NS, Y kaluXaʀ- 'drag, pull behind one'
NSY kalə- 'tow' [and kaluʀaq 'tow line'; ANLC has kalaɣ-, kaluʀaʀ- 'tow'; L.-T. has kalałəq 'towing', probably from base kalatə-]
CSY kaalɣuʀ- 'haul dead whale to shore'
Sir —
SPI kalit-, Qaw kalik- 'drag, tow'
NAI kalit- 'drag, tow' [and kalɨ 's.th. dragged, towed', kaliɣaq- 'drag accidentally', probably also kalikłuk- 'wheeze, have a hard time breathing']
WCI kalit- 'tow' [and Schn. has B. Lake kalalutik as shaman's word for 'sledge']
ECI kalit-, kalik- 'tow, drag' [and Aiv kaliktaut 'sled brake of caribou horn']
GRI kaliɣ-, kalit-, NG kalik- 'tow, drag' [Fab. has only kalit-; note also kalisaɣ- 'breathe heavily']

PI kalɣun and **kalɣutaq** 'means for pulling' [cf. un]
SPI kalutaq 'tow rope'
NAI kaluutaq 'tow rope', Mal kalɣutaq 'rope used to tow another boat'
WCI Cop kalut, kalun 'tow rope behind kayak for towing dead caribou' [Pryde; Men. has kaliyyut 'tow rope' and Schn. has kaluktaq for 'adg']
ECI kaluti 'towing gear (hook with rope and handle

for dragging game behind kayak)'
GRI kalut [usually pl. kalutit] 'towing gear', kałłut, NG kaɣlut 'tow rope' [for homonym of the latter meaning 'bird net' see kaləɣ-[2]]

PE kaləɣ-[2] 'brush up against' [cf. kaləɣ-[1]?]
AAY PWS kałəktaɣ- 'graze' [and note kaliɣ- 'sweep', kalik 'broom']
CAY kaləɣ-, Nun katəɣ- 'brush against' [the latter also 'bump into' — contam. with katə-; also kalɣun 'weir' and Y, K kallutaq, HBC, NI kaluutaq 'stick used in hockey-like game'?]
NSY kalɣuuʀ- (for kalɣuaʀ-?), kalɣuaʀutə- 'brush against, carry along' [ANLC]
CSY —
Sir —
SPI —
NAI kalikłuk-, kaliukłuk-, kalixaaq-, kaliuxaaq- 'rub against and cause to fall'
WCI kalik- 'touch, rub against'
ECI [kalluʀaq- 'strike time and time again (waves against boat, wind against door)', kaluʀsu(q)- 'knock s.th. over inadvertently']
GRI kalit- 'strike against', kaluɣ- 'break s.th. in carelessness' [and NG kaɣlut(i)- 'knock against vertical edge (e.g. when one gets one's foot caught between sledge and ice)', perhaps also kaɣlut 'net for catching birds with']

PE kaləvə(t)- 'sink into mud (or water or snow)' [cf. kaləɣ- and perhaps vət- under vaʀ-]
AAY K kal<ɣ>u-, C kaluɣ- [AP also kaləfə-, kaləɣ-] 'set (sun)', kaluxtə- 'let down (into water)', Kod kaluxci- 'set a net'
CAY kalvə-, kalvaɣ- 'go down (into ground)', kaliftə- 'be stranded, inaccessible' [Jen. has 'carry a heavy load' for Nun]
NSY →
CSY kaləvə- 'sink into mud, snow or water, drown'
Sir —
SPI kalivit- 'get stuck'
NAI kalivit- 'get stuck or stranded' [kalivži- 'get s.th. stuck']
WCI kalivit- 'be stuck' ['not have anything' acc. Met.; Car? 'pull at traces or trap trying to get away (dog, fox in trap), get stuck (sledge dogs)' — Schn.; for Cop Pryde has 'get caught beneath sled runner (dog-trace)']
ECI —
GRI →

PE kaləvnəʀ 'chain (link)' [cf. nəʀ[1]]
AAY —
CAY kalivnəq, kalivnəʀət 'chain'
NSY kaləvnəʀət 'chain, shackles' [ANLC has kalivnəq, kaləvnəq 'chain']
CSY —
Sir —
SPI kalimniq 'chain'
NAI PH kalimniq*
WCI —
ECI —
GRI kalinniq*, kalunniq* 'link in chain' [pl. = 'chain']

kalikaq 'paper' [loan from Koryak kalikal 'book, letter, design' through EA kalika-X 'paper, mail, letter, (pl.) book']
AAY kalikaq 'paper, page, mail'
CAY kalikaq
NSY —
CSY —

PI kaliʀʀaq 'loud noise' [cf. katluɣ?]
SPI — [for kaluʀuaq 'loud noise' acc. Jen. see katluɣ]
NAI —
WCI —
ECI kaliʀʀaq 'sound of sled in snow' [and kaliʀʀi(t)- 'be heard approaching (sled)']
GRI kaliXXaq 'crash' [and kaliXXit- 'give a signal, scare away (animal)']

PY kalŋak or **kalŋaq** 'bag'
AAY kalŋaq, (archaic) Kod kalŋak, PWS qalŋak 'bag, knapsack'
CAY kalŋak 'bag made of reeds for carrying fish'
NSY kalŋaq 'bag (carried over shoulder)'
CSY kalŋak 'sealskin bag' [also 'shark']

kalukaq 'wooden bowl' [probably from EA kaluka-X 'dish, bowl, plate, trough', though the borrowing could have been the other way]
AAY kalukaq 'round spruce- root basket', Kod 'cask, barrel' [Rez.]
CAY Nun kalukaX 'wooden bowl' [and elsewhere kalukaq 'feast', if the same base; for kalukaq 'halo round sun or moon' see kaŋlu- — the relat. to this and to postural root kaluɣ- 'empty' is obscure]
NSY kalukaq 'dipper, scoop, circle' [L.-T.]
CSY —
Sir [note kalikəʀaX (for kaləkəʀaX?) 'bucket'; Vakh. has kaliquʀaX, but also kaluxtə- 'put, dump, throw away']

PY- S kałaɣ- 'rattle or drum' [cf. katluɣ]
AAY kałaxtə- 'make sharp noise' [and nom. kałak in C], kała<ɣ>aq 'supernatural power, evil spirit, sorcery' [and kała'alək 'shaman' — but compare Chukchi kelə 'spirit']
CAY kałaxtə- 'rattle' [and kałalək 'shaman' — compare qəlalək under qəla-[2], and the Chukchi under AAY above — source of contam.?]
NSY kałaxtə- 'beat drum (shaman)' [ANLC]
CSY kałaxtə- 'drum and sing' [kałaxtaak 'drum']
Sir kałaxtə- 'drum'
Inu — [but Ras. has Igl kalaaluk- 'crackle (?) on smooth ice (sledge)']

PE kama- 'be nervously attentive or intimidated?'
AAY [note K kakm̥ayuɣ- 'feel uneasy, intimidated around people']
CAY kama(yuɣ)- 'feel suspicious', Nun 'feel squeamish'

NSY —
CSY —
Sir [Vakh. has kaməɣəməkən 'in one's mind, to oneself']
SPI kamanaq- 'be great, skillful' [and kamait- 'be bothersome', kamaiqsiq- 'upset, cause disturbance']
NAI kamasuk- 'obey, be amazed' [and kamasaaq- 'boast', kamanaq- 'be bossy, strong']
WCI kamasuk- 'pay attention, be afraid' ['on the alert' acc. Pryde; and kamanaq- 'be menacing'; note also Car kammaluaq 'one easily excited' and Cop kaŋmaqtaaq (a name — for kammaqtaaq ?) 'one easily angered' acc. Ras.]
ECI kama- 'be busy with s.th., meddle with s.th.', Lab 'pay attention to, watch' [and kamasuɣi- 'look after']
GRI NG kamahuk- 'be agitated, busy', kamahuallak- 'be frightened' [and WG kamaɣ- 'be angry', kammaʀtuuq 'one easily angered', kamanaat- 'be irritating'; note also NG kamatsak- 'rush excitedly toward game', kamatsagiik 'two people who do not speak together out of respect (ritual avoidance)']

PE kamakə- 'pay attention to?' [cf. kə-[1]]
AAY [note K kakm̥akə- 'feel indimidated by, uneasy around']
CAY kamakə- 'suspect', Nun 'be squeamish about'
NSY —
CSY —
Sir —
SPI Qaw kamaɣi- 'praise, show respect toward'
NAI kamaɣi- 'obey'
WCI kamaɣi- 'pay attention to' [Pryde has it as Cop 'be wary of, on guard against', Net 'heed, respond to']
ECI kamaɣi- 'be busy with, meddle with'
GRI kamaɣi- 'put up with', NG 'pay attention to, consider important'

PE kaməɣ 'boot'
AAY kam<ɣ>uk 'shoe'
CAY kaməksak, Y, NS kamɣuk 'skin boot' [second form perhaps a reformulated dual — but compare piluɣ(uɣ)-; as verb kaməksaɣ-, kamɣuɣ- 'put on skin boot']
NSY kamək 'skin boot' [verbal kaməɣ- 'put on boots']
CSY kamək 'skin boot' [verbal kaməɣ-]
Sir kaməx 'skin boot' [verbal kaməɣ-]
SPI kamik 'skin boot' [also verbal]
NAI kamɨk 'skin boot' [as verb = 'put on boots', as in all Inu]
WCI kamik 'skin boot'
ECI kamik
GRI kamik 'skin boot' [older pl. kammit or kaŋŋit; kamiɣ- 'put on boots'; NG kamikpak 'outer skin boot with hair left on' = WG kamippak 'western style boot or shoe'; kamiʀuaq 'outer pull-over boot']

PI kamillaaq- 'go barefoot' [cf. kamillaʀ- below and aʀ-]
SPI kamilaaŋa- 'go barefoot'
NAI kamilʸlʸaaq- 'go barefoot or naked below waist'
WCI kamillaa(q)- 'go barefoot'
ECI kamillaa(q)- 'remain without shoes on'
GRI kamiłłaaʀ-, kamiłłaaŋa- 'go barefoot'

PE kamillaʀ- 'take off boots' [cf. ŋit-?]
AAY —
CAY kamilaʀ- 'remove shoes' [kamilaŋqa- 'be barefoot']
NSY —
CSY —
Sir —
SPI kamilaq- 'remove shoes'
NAI kamilʸlʸaq- 'take pants and/or boots off'
WCI Cop kamillaq- 'take boots off' [Jen. — also Ras. for Car]
ECI kamilla(q)- 'take boots off'
GRI kamiłłaʀ-

PE kamlu '(rounded) cap or mounting?' [there may be a loan from an unidentified source complicating the picture in Alaska]
AAY [note K kamlaq 'carrying case for ammunition']
CAY Y kavluun 'one hundred' [used originally for percussion caps which came in packages of a hundred — form from Inu?]
NSY kamlu 'cartridge case, tube'
CSY —
Sir —
SPI kavlu 'primer of bullet'
NAI Nu kavlu 'concave, rounded cover or percussion cap of gun?'
WCI [Cop kavlu 'mitt (shaman's word)' acc. Pryde]
ECI —
GRI kałłu [old ortho. kavdlo], EG kattuq [Ges.] 'bone mounting on end of paddle'

PE kanaɣ 'shin'
AAY kanaxtu- 'be tall', AP kanaɣaq 'shin'
CAY kanaɣaq 'leg, lower limb or part', kanaxtu- 'have long legs'
NSY kanaɣaq 'shin' [L.-T.]
CSY kanaɣaq 'shin'
Sir —
SPI kanaaq
NAI kanak 'inner leg (length from crotch to heel)', kanaɣaq, Nu kanaɣaaq 'shin bone, lower leg' [kanaktu- 'have long legs']
WCI kanaaq 'lower leg' [Lowe; Met. has kanaq 'leg bone', which Jen. has as 'shin bone', as does Ras. for Net]
ECI kanaaq 'shin, leg of boot'
GRI kanaaq 'shin'

PE kanaknaʀ 'west or west wind' [cf. dem. root kan- and p.b. knaʀ]
AAY [kanakəq C, AP 'west or southeast wind']
CAY kanakn̥aq, kanakn̥ak 'west wind'
NSY kanakn̥aq 'south-east name' [ANLC]
CSY —
Sir [note kanakšak 'south wind']
SPI kanakŋaq- 'blow south wind'

NAI kanaɣnaq 'northwest wind'
WCI kanaŋnaq 'north wind'
ECI [Bourq. has Lab kanaŋnaq 'sea (east) wind']
GRI kanannaq 'west wind', Up 'southwest wind', NG kanaŋniʀhuq 'there is a sea wind (into fjord)'

PE kanaʀ- 'fall over (headlong)' [cf. Aleut kanaʀ- 'fall headlong, bow']
AAY kanaʀ- 'be upside down', AP kanaqsaɣ- 'starve'
CAY kanaʀ- 'be bent forward' [also 'emerge from woods or water']
NSY kanaʀ- 'put inside' [ANLC]
CSY kanaʀ- 'step through soft ice (and drown), step into hole', kanaʀa- 'walk with difficulty through soft snow or dirt' [and kanaŋłuxtə- 'be bent over with sadness, pout unhappily', also kanaXtə- 'put into a container, store'?]
Sir kanaʀ- 'knock over, topple' [and kanaft(ə)- 'attack' — Vakh. from Rub.; he also has kanaXtə- 'put down, hang head']
SPI kanaq- 'die suddenly, fall over dead'
NAI —
WCI —
ECI —
GRI —

PY kanaʀaʀ- 'fall asleep' [cf. aʀ-]
AAY C kana<ʀ>aʀ- 'dream, daydream' [also nominal]
CAY kanaʀ(aʀ)- 'sleep, be falling asleep'
NSY —
CSY —

PE kanayu(ʀ) 'sculpin' [cf. PY kayu; Chukchi has kanayolgən 'sculpin', presumably borrowed from Eskimo]
AAY —
CAY [note NSU kanayuʀnaq 'burbot' — the base (without p.b. naʀ) may be borrowed from Inu, however]
NSY —
CSY —
Sir kanayu 'sculpin' [Krup.]
SPI kanayuq 'sculpin' [Jen. has W kaneyuaq]
NAI kanayuq 'sculpin'
WCI kanayuq
ECI kanayuq
GRI kanayuq [pl. kanassut], NWG kaniuq [pl. kanissut], EG kaniiřaq [Ges.]

PE kanəʀ 'frost' [cf. kanəvə-?]
AAY kanəq 'frost' [and kanəʀ- 'be frosty']
CAY kanəq* [verbal kanəʀ-; note also kanəfłuk 'light snow in rain', kanəfciʀ- 'have ice crystals in the air']
NSY kanəq '(hoar- *)frost'
CSY kanəq* 'frost' [verbal kanəʀ-]
Sir kanəX [Orr]
SPI kaniq 'frost' [also verbal]
NAI kaniq* [also verbal]
WCI [Car? kaniqsuit 'frost crystals on ice' — Schn. 'adg']
ECI kaniq 'frost crystal', Igl 'rime frost' [Ras.; and kaniq- 'be frosty', kaniʀyuit 'crystals of frost on ground', kaʀŋutit 'frost crystals on ice']
GRI kaniʀ- 'be dewy, covered with rime' [kaniʀniq* 'rime, dew', NG kaniq 'rime (frost)']

PY kanʀuyauciq 'lunar month (approx. = February)'
AAY kanʀuyauci(q), kanʀusauci(q) in old sources variously as 'September', 'October', or 'November'
CAY kanʀuyauciq 'February'
NSY kanʀuyaasiq 'February' [L.-T.; ANLC also 'November']
CSY —

PY kanəvə- 'sprinkle or scatter' [cf. kanʀaq- and kanəʀ — and compare kaɣimə-]
AAY —
CAY kanvə- 'sprinkle, scatter, pour out' [also kalmə- — influenced by kalvə- 'go down' under kaləvə(t)-?; kanəftə- 'scatter, sprinkle (tr.)']
NSY qanəftə- 'powder, grind up' [ANLC]
CSY —

PE kanivaʀun 'diaphragm' [cf. un]
AAY —
CAY —
NSY —
CSY kanivaan 'diaphragm'
Sir kanivʀətəX 'pleura' [Vakh. from Men.'s texts]
SPI —
NAI kanivaun 'diaphragm'
WCI kanivaun 'diaphragm' [Ras. has 'thin belly skin of seal' for Cop]
ECI kanivaut 'diaphragm'
GRI kanayaat, NG kanivaut

PE kannuyaʀ 'copper' [or perhaps kan(n)u(t)yaɣ as suggested by the GRI forms — cf. kanuɣ and tyaɣ, and Aleut kanu(u)ya-X 'copper', borrowed from Eskimo area where copper is found?]
AAY kanuyaq 'copper'
CAY kanuyaq
NSY kanuyaq
CSY kanuya [base kanuyə]
Sir kanuyə [Orr]
SPI kannuyaq 'sewing needle', Qaw 'copper',
NAI kannuyak, PH kannuyaq, Mal, Nu kanŋuyaq 'copper'
WCI kannuyaq, Baker Lake kanuhaq [Schn.]
ECI kannuyaq, Tar kaŋusaq
GRI kaŋŋussaq, kaŋŋussak, kannussak,
NG kannussaq

PI kanʀaq- 'scatter or drop (crumbs or hair)' [cf. kanəvə-; there may be a further relat. to kanəʀ]
SPI kaʀnaq- 'drop, scatter (seeds, crumbs)'
NAI kanʀaq- 'leak (non-liquid substance)' [and kanʀala(q) 'shedding animal', kanʀalluk, PH kanŋaluk 'crumb', also kanuqqait 'crumbs from table']
WCI Sig kanʀaq-, Cop kaŋalaq- [for kanŋalaq-?] 'fall

(like sand, seeds)' [and Sig kanʀaqqi-, Cop kaŋalaqqi- 'powder'; Dor. has kanʀalat 'herd of caribou' for B. Lake; Pryde has Cop kannŋala, kanʀala 'caribou that has not shed its winter coat yet', but also Cop, Net, Car kannŋalaq 'caribou which is shedding its winter coat']
ECI kaʀŋa(q)-, kaʀŋaluk- 'fall (dust, powder)' [and kaʀŋalak 'land animal losing its coat', kaʀŋaniit 'crumbs from table']
GRI kaʀnala- 'fall (e.g. hair of animal)' [and kaʀnalanikut 'crumbs, etc., that have fallen']

PE kanuɣ 'blood' [cf. Aleut kanuuX 'heart']
AAY [note K kanniXłuk 'heartburn']
CAY —
NSY —
CSY kanuk 'spot or streak of blood'
Sir —
SPI —
NAI PH kanuk- 'become angry', Nu kannuktit- 'become flushed with fever' [and note kanuŋŋiq* 'egg yolk']
WCI Cop, Net kanuk 'blood' [shaman's language — Ras.; Met. has kannuktit- 'make blush' and kannuumi- 'blush'; Ras. also has kanuaqtuq 'menstruating woman' in Net]
ECI Igl kanuk 'blood' [Ras.]
GRI EG kanik 'blood' [cited by Holt. from Thalbitzer; Kroeber has kanuk 'blood' as a shaman's word for NG]

PI kanuŋŋiq '(type of) driftwood?' [there may be a relat. to kanuɣ]
SPI —
NAI kanuŋŋiq* 'type of willow' [for homonym meaning 'egg yolk' see kanuɣ]
WCI —
ECI —
GRI kanunniq*, kanuŋŋiq* 'driftwood of a particularly sweet- smelling kind'

PE kaŋciʀ 'wall of house' [cf. kaŋlu-]
AAY —
CAY kaŋciq 'side wall of sod house'
NSY kansiq 'wall'
CSY —
Sir —
SPI kassiq 'house wall'
NAI katci 'interior house wall' [Nu kasiq, du. katcik]
WCI Cop kaxxi 'one of two small cairns set at either side of a hunter's hide' [Pryde]
ECI —
GRI —

PE kaŋəʀ 'top' [cf. Aleut kaŋ(a)- 'top' and kaŋayu-X 'upper part of body'; perhaps also EA kaxtu- 'be wide (clothing, opening)', comparable with CAY kaŋtu-]
AAY kaŋəq 'top'
CAY kaŋəq*
NSY —
CSY — [for kaŋəq* 'principle, cause' see kaŋiʀ]
Sir —
SPI kaq [3rd p. sing. possessed kaʀʀa] 'tip, peak' [Jen. has the latter as 'point, promontory' for W]
NAI [note Nu kaʀʀaq 'upriver end of island']
WCI kaŋiq 'head, promontory' [Ras; Pet. has kaʀʀa '(its) top' for Sig; Pryde has kaŋiʀun 'head (shaman's word)' for Cop; for Ras. kaaLhutaq 'top, peak' see kavžaq]
ECI Igl kaŋiq 'upper end, top' [Ras. and Boas; the former also has kangerSuaq as a shaman's word for 'head']
GRI kaŋiq* [in possessed form kaXXa, etc.] 'highest point, promontory, ear of corn, bunch of flowers on top of plant' [in the latter two senses only in inflected forms — note pl. kaXXit 'corn', also kaXXaqqut(i)- 'go round a promontory, go west of'; Kroeber has kaŋiq as a shaman's word for 'head' in NG; for kaaviq 'top' see kavžaq]

PY kaŋquq 'inflorescence on plant?' [cf. p.b. quʀ]
AAY Kod kaŋqutaq 'inflorescence, flowering top of grass'
CAY kaŋquq 'pussy-willow catkin'
NSY —
CSY [kaaŋquq 'core of tree, knot in wood, leader of village, headquarters']

PY kaŋtu- ' be wide ' [cf. tu-[1]]
AAY kaŋtu- 'have a big top or crown or crest, be wide or big'
CAY kaŋtu- 'be wide'
NSY —
CSY —

PE kaŋiʀ 'source or innermost part' [cf. Aleut kaŋaʀi- 'have meaning', kaŋta- 'mean' and EA kaŋi-n (pl.) 'interior, essence, meaning'; there seems to be some semantic overlap in Inu with kaŋəʀ]
AAY kaŋiq 'back of house, source', kaŋitm̥un 'upstream'
CAY kaŋiq 'source, meaning', kaŋiqutaq 'bay'
NSY kaŋiq 'bay' [also 'meaning, source, fjord' (ANLC)]
CSY kaŋiq 'indentation on shoreline' [also kaŋəq* 'principle, cause, bird down, underhair', by contam. with kaŋiʀ]
Sir [Em. has kaŋəX 'skin below hair, fur or feathers']
SPI kaŋiq 'origin, source, headwaters, towline of dogteam' [Jen. also 'part farthest inland' for W]
NAI kaŋiq 'root, source, headwater, place where peninsula joins mainland'
WCI kaŋi 'bottom of bay, direction toward land, source of river' [also 'rear part, back room' in Cop acc. Pryde]
ECI kaŋi 'solid firm part, direction toward land' [kaŋiqqut(i)- 'pass to inland side of'; Anderen et al. have Lab kangia 'west']
GRI kaŋi 'east, land side, place where smaller part of s.th. joins the larger part', EG 'upstream, inland' [kaŋiqqut(i)- 'go to the east of, pass inside of']

PE kaŋilliʀ and **kaŋiqliʀ** 'innermost one' [cf. l(l)iʀ and qliʀ]
AAY kaŋiqłiq 'back part, one toward back of bay or upstream'
CAY —

NSY —
CSY kaŋiqłiq* 'thing at end, wisdom tooth, molar'
Sir kaŋiqłiy 'molars' [Orr]
SPI kaŋiliq 'molar, innermost one'
NAI kaŋil^{y}l^{y}iq 'innermost one of group', kaŋil^{y}ipqaq, PH kaŋiliaq, kaŋilin^{y}aaq 'molar tooth'
WCI kaŋilliq Cop 'one nearer the land', Net 'easterly one' [Pryde]
ECI kaŋilliq 'thing farther inland than another' [Andersen et al. have Lab kaŋillik 's.th. farther inland, to the west']
GRI kaŋiłłiq* 'most easterly, innermost one' [and kaŋiliq 's.th. farther toward the east or toward land', kaŋiliniq* 'country to the east', NG 'wall behind lamp in trad. house']

PE kaŋiʀaʀ 'corner' [cf. aʀ]
AAY kaŋiʀaq 'bay', AP 'corner post'
CAY kaŋiʀaq 'corner'
NSY kaŋiʀaq 'corner' [ANLC]
CSY kaŋiʀaq 'corner, cove'
Sir kaŋiʀaX 'bay' [Orr; and Vakh. has 'angle' from Rub.'s texts]
SPI Qaw kaŋiʀaq 'corral', kaŋiʀaluk 'corner'
NAI kaŋiʀaq 'corral, blind for hunting caribou', kaŋiʀalluk 'corner'
WCI Cop, Net kaŋiʀalluk 'small storeroom built into wall of snowhouse' [Pryde]
ECI —
GRI —

PE kaŋiʀci- 'understand' [cf. ci- and EA kaŋcimat-, Atkan kaŋsimat- 'interpret']
AAY kaŋiXci- 'understand' [and K kaŋii(kə)-, Perry kaŋiił- (kə)- 'be curious about' — emot. root]
CAY kaŋiXci- 'understand'
NSY —
CSY —
Sir —
SPI kaŋiqsi-
NAI kaŋiqsi-
WCI kaŋiqsi- 'understand' [Jen. has Cop kaŋiq-]
ECI kaŋiisuk- 'suspect' [Lab 'become aware' acc. Peck], kaŋiitsa(C)- 'learn, find out'
GRI —

PE kaŋiʀłuɣ 'bay' [cf. łuɣ(-)]
AAY [C kaŋiquluk 'bay, cove']
CAY kaŋiXłuk 'bay'
NSY —
CSY —
Sir —
SPI —
NAI kaŋiqł^{y}uk
WCI kaŋiqłuk 'bay, fjord'
ECI kaŋiʀsuk 'bay'
GRI kaŋiʀłuk 'bay', EG kaŋiʀsik 'fjord'

PE kaŋivaʀ- 'go farther in' [cf. vaʀ-]
AAY C, AP kaŋiwaʀ- 'go toward back of house or bay'
CAY kaŋivaʀ- 'go toward source of river'
NSY —
CSY —
Sir —
SPI kaŋivaq- 'go inland on water, upriver, into a bay'
NAI —
WCI kaŋivaq- 'go farther in, right into house', Net also 'push back from blubber lamp (pot)' [Pryde]
ECI kaŋivaq- 'go farther inland or into house or bed, come down to horizon (sun), roll sleeves up a little'
GRI kaŋiaʀ-, NWG kaŋuyaʀ- 'move farther in (to land or on beach)'

PE kaŋivaʀtə(ʀ)- 'roll up sleeves' [cf. kaŋivaʀ- above and təʀ-]
AAY AP kaŋiwaXci- 'roll up one's sleeves'
CAY kaŋivaXtə-
NSY —
CSY —
Sir —
SPI kaŋiva(q)tiq-
NAI kaŋivaqtaaq-
WCI kaŋivaktiq- [for kaŋivaqtiq-?]
ECI kaŋivaqti(q)- 'roll up sleeves or trouser legs' [and see kaŋivaʀ- above]
GRI kaŋiaʀtiʀ-, NWG kaŋuyaʀtiʀ- 'tuck up (garment)'

PE kaŋŋit- 'reach source or end' [cf. łit-]
CAY K, BB kaŋitn̥əq* 'dog or chum salmon, old salmon after spawning'
NSY —
CSY —
Sir —
SPI kaŋŋit- 'reach end or highest point' [the latter sense from or influenced by kaŋəʀ?]
NAI kaŋŋit- 'pull or be pulled taut, reach destination or limit, arrive at root or source of'
WCI —
ECI —
GRI kaŋŋit- 'meet an obstacle, cannot make progress'

PY- S kaŋlu- 'surround' [cf. kaŋciʀ]
AAY Kod kaɣlu-, KP kal<ɣ>u- 'surround, encircle, corral, close in on'
CAY [note kalukaXtə- 'encompass, extend around', going with kalukaq 'halo around sun or moon' — influenced by kalukaq?]
NSY —
CSY kaŋlu-, kaŋłu- 'surround, crowd together' [and Chap kaŋłaaʀ- 'close in on game'; note also kaŋsuʀ- 'be too large to fit in an opening']
Sir kaŋlu- 'besiege' [and kaŋłuqəXtə- 'surround' — Vakh. from Rub.'s texts; note also kaŋsəʀ- 'get stuck (in opening)'; Em. has kaŋłu- 'surround']

PE kaŋuʀ ' snow goose'
AAY AP, KP kaŋuq, PWS kam̥uk 'brant goose'
CAY kaŋuq 'snow goose'
NSY kaŋgyuq [ANLC]
CSY kaaŋu
Sir —
SPI kaŋuq
NAI kaŋuq
WCI kaŋuq 'snow goose' [Pryde also has kaŋuuyaq 'cotton grass (used for lamp wicks)' — cf. ŋ(ŋ)uðaʀ]
ECI kaŋuq 'snow goose' [and kaŋuuyaq 'bog cotton (used for lamp wicks)']
GRI NG kaŋuq 'snow goose'

PE kapə- 'stab'
AAY kapə- 'stab, poke'
CAY kapə-
NSY kapə-
CSY kapə- 'stab, poke, pierce whale with harpoon'
Sir ➟
SPI kavi- 'stab, pierce'
NAI kapɨ-
WCI kapi-
ECI kapi-
GRI kapi-

PY kapəʀtə- 'pound blubber'
AAY —
CAY —
NSY kaapəXtə- 'pound blubber' [ANLC]
CSY kapəXtə- 'pound blubber to make it render'

PE kappun 'stabbing or pricking instrument' [cf. un; the forms like kapuut are presumably from kapuʀ- below]
AAY kaputaq C 'fish spear', Kod 'poker, instrument with pointed end' [= KP kapuu'utaq]
CAY kapun 'needle', Nun 'multipronged fish spear'
NSY kaputaq 'awl'
CSY —
Sir kaputaX 'awl'
SPI kappun 'needle, syringe' [kavutaq 'awl']
NAI kappun 'spear, dagger, needle', Nu kapuun 'long caribou spear' [and PH kaputtaun 'awl']
WCI kappun 'spear' [and Cop kapuʀaun 'fork'; Ras. has kapuut 'lance for caribou hunting' — also B.- S. for Net]
ECI kapuut 'spear'
GRI kapuut 'kayak knife, lancet, sting (of insect)'

PE kapputə- 'stick into' [cf. utə-]
AAY kaputə- 'stick into'
CAY kaputə-
NSY kaputə-
CSY kaaputə- 'poke, bump (fish), go into sea swell (boat)'
Sir —
SPI —
NAI kapputɨ- 'stick into'
WCI kapputi-
ECI kapput(i)-
GRI kapput(i)- 'stick into' [and kapušši- 'stick paddle under cross- strap on s.o.'s kayak to support them'

PE kapuʀ- 'stab repeatedly' [cf. (C)uʀ-]
AAY kapuʀ- 'stab or poke repeatedly'
CAY kapuʀ-
NSY kapuʀnalʀia 'prickly'
CSY kapuʀ- 'stab repeatedly, innoculate'
Sir kapuɣ- [for kapuʀ-?] 'pierce with awl'
SPI kavuq- 'spear repeatedly'
NAI Nu kapuq-
WCI kapuq-
ECI kapuq-
GRI kapuʀ- 'stab several times, vaccinate, feel a stitch (in one's side)'

PE kapəciʀ 'scale of fish' [cf. kapət-]
AAY —
CAY NSU kapəciq, kapciq 'scale of fish'
NSY kapəsi [ANLC]
CSY [kapəsəɣak (du.) 'woman's light overalls worn under parka']
Sir —
SPI —
NAI kavisiq 'scale of fish'
WCI kapisiq, kapisik
ECI kavisik, Iti kapisiq [Saul for the latter]
GRI EG kapisiq 'fish scale' [Tersis; WG kapisiq 'gutskin jacket' probably by contam. with kapitak at kapətaq under kapət-; for tattak 'fish scale' see under ta(a)vtaaq]

PI kapəciləк 'whitefish?' [cf. ləɣ]
SPI —
NAI —
WCI kapisilik 'kind of fish with scales' [Ras. has 'trout living both in lakes and salt water' for Net and Dor. has kavihilik 'whitefish']
ECI kavisilik 'kind of fish with scales', Lab 'salmon' [Dor. has 'whitefish' — also kapisilik for Iti; B.-S. has 'salmon' for Igl]
GRI kapisilik 'salmon'

PY kapəɣcuɣ- 'be anxious' [cf. kapət- and kappəya-, also cuɣ?]
AAY kəpəqsuuɣ-, qəpəqsu(u)ɣ- 'feel uneasy, restless'
CAY kapəxcuɣ(yuɣ)- 'dread, feel anxiety'
NSY —
CSY kaxpəsuɣ- 'feel claustrophobic, breathless'
Inu [note Qaw kapiksuk- 'panic, be terrified', from the Yup?; Jen. has kaviuraq- 'be anxious' for W]

PI kapəlʀak or **kapəlʀaq** 'polar night' [cf. kappəya- (esp. GRI kappi- there) and/or kapet-]
SPI —
NAI —
WCI Cop kapilʀaq 'dark period' [Ras., who also has Net kapisraq — for kapižʀaq?; Pryde has kapilʀaq also for Net]

ECI —
GRI kapiʀłak, NG kapiʀlaq 'polar night' [also NG kapiʀlak- 'stop coming up (sun in winter)' — Holt.]

PI kapəlʀuq or **kapəlʀuk** 'neck part of animal?' [cf. kapət-]
SPI kaviʀluk 'upper chest'
NAI —
WCI Cop kapilʀuq 'fatty meat from foreshoulders of caribou' [Pryde; and Schn. has Car Baker Lake kapilʀuq 'front part of caribou']
ECI —
GRI kapiʀłuk 'back bone of bird', NG kapiʀluk 'front part of salmon behind gills, part of backbone (e.g. seal's)'

PE kapət- and **kapəɣ-** 'fit tightly' [the first form may be from the latter plus t-[1], reanalysed as containing neg. p.b. ŋit- in Yup, parallel to ətɣat- under ətə- and ipɣit- under ipəɣ- ; cf. kapəciʀ, kapəɣcuɣ- and kappəya-; the Inu forms with kai-, kia- seem to be contaminated by kayəmə(t)- and/or kiapəʀuq under kiɣan]
AAY AP kapxitə-, Kod kapəxtə-, PWS kapkitə- 'be constricted, narrow' [the PWS form contains p.b. kit-]
CAY kapxitə- 'be narrow' [with the tə~l alternation reflecting ŋit-]
NSY —
CSY kaxpəsqʷaaq, kaxpəstaaq 'narrow opening' [with metathesis]
Sir [Vakh. has kaxpəsqi- 'be narrow' from Rub.'s texts]
SPI [kapputi- 'put outer garment over inner one']
NAI kapɨt- 'be tight-fitting' [and kapɨksi-, kaipiksisimaaq- 'cross one's arms', PH kapɨɣli- 'close (opening), come together (ice)', kaipik-, kiapik- 'fit together, pass over']
WCI kapit- 'be tight (garment)' [note also Cop kaipiktit- 'splice']
ECI kapit- 'pull outer garment over atigi' [and kaipiŋa- 'have hands pulled back in sleeves']
GRI kapit- 'pull outer garment over inner one' [and note NG kallutsi- 'pull outer boot over inner one']

> **PI kapətaq** 'waterproof outer garment' [cf. ðaʀ?]
> Yup [NSU kapittaq 'gut rain parka' is borrowed from Inu]
> SPI kavitak, Qaw kapitak 'gutskin rain parka'
> NAI PH kapitak 'outer fur parka'
> WCI Cop kapitaq 'outer (rain)coat' [Jen.]
> ECI kapitaq
> GRI kapitak 'waterproof jacket', NG kapatak 'outer fox skin coat' [Holt.], EG kapittaʀ̃aq 'outer clothing' [but compare also WG kapitaq 'inner garment (e.g. inner mittens or jacket)']

PE kappəya- 'feel anxious' [cf. kapəɣcuɣ-, kapəlʀaq and kapət- and perhaps ya-]
AAY —
CAY HBC kapia- 'be in great need, in desperate straits'
NSY —
CSY —
Sir — [but Vakh. has kapɣ̥əɣuʀ- 'make much noise' from Men.'s texts]
SPI —
NAI kappiasuk- 'feel oneself in imminent danger', kappiaɣɨ- 'feel worried about (e.g. someone leaving)' [emot. root]
WCI kappia(suk)- 'be anxious, anguished' [emot. root; Jen. has Cop kappiʀnaq- 'be annoying']
ECI kappia(suk)- 'be terrified' [and Boas has kapeʀnaʀ- 'be afraid' for Baffin]
GRI kappia(suɣ)- 'be worried (e.g. about sick person)', NG kappianaq- 'be frightful' [and note kappi- 'lack food, be in a sorry state']

> **PI kappiala-** 'cry out in fright' [cf. la(ʀ)-]
> SPI —
> NAI kappiala- 'feel oneself in great danger and cry out in fright'
> WCI —
> ECI —
> GRI kappiala- 'lament, wail'

PY kasiyuq '(bladder) feast' [cf. katə-?]
AAY C kasi<ɣ>uq, PWS kasiɣuun 'feast celebrating first catch of boy or young man, bladder feast' [and kasi<ɣ>uʀ- 'have a feast']
CAY kasiyuq 'an old time celebration'
NSY —
CSY —

PY-S kaspuɣtə- 'go (right) around' [cf. kaðəvə(t)- and kasuɣ-]
AAY Kod kaspətə-, C kaspəxtə- 'surround, go all the way around'
CAY —
NSY —
CSY kaspuxtə- 'pass through a specific time or place, go around'
Sir kasfut(ə)- 'go around' [Vakh. from Men's texts]

kassaq 'white person' [from Russian kazak 'cossack' via Aleut kasakaX 'Russian']
AAY kasaakaq 'Russian', PWS kas<ʀ>aq 'priest'
CAY kassaq 'white person'
NSY —
CSY —
Inu [SPI Qaw Unk kassaq 'white person' — from the CAY]

PY kasuɣ- 'go around' [cf. kaspuɣtə-]
AAY kasuɣ- 'surround', PWS 'meet again after splitting up' [the latter meaning influenced by kasuutə- 'meet each other' under katyuɣutə- (katyuɣ-); also apparently kasuutə- 'get married' belongs here, from the Russian Orthodox wedding ceremony where the couple go around the church together, though this may represent conflation — compare the meanings of katət- under katə-]
CAY kasuɣ- 'go around' [and kasutm̥un 'around'; and kasuutə- 'get married' — see note under AAY above]
NSY — [for kaasutə- 'bring' see katə-]
CSY —

Inu [SPI kassuuti- 'get married' is probably a loan from CAY]

PE kataɣ- 'fall or drop'
AAY kataɣ- 'dump or pour out, fall'
CAY kataɣ- 'fall out or off, drop'
NSY katə-, kataXtuʀ- 'pour out, drop, fall out' [ANLC has kataaʀ- 'spill out, pour out, empty']
CSY kataɣ- 'dump, empty'
Sir katəɣ- 'drop, pour out' [Vakh. — Men. has katəʀ-, Orr has kətəʀ-, also katət(ə)- 'pour, flood, spill']
SPI katak- 'dump, spill'
NAI katak- 'fall, drop'
WCI katak-
ECI katak- 'fall, drop, go downstairs'
GRI kataɣ- 'drop, fall, shed hair (animal), be loosened'

PI katak 'hole (down) to entrance passage in trad. house'
SPI —
NAI katak 'entrance hole from sod house into entrance passage'
WCI katak 'entrance previously in roof of house' ['entrance passage' in Ras.]
ECI katak 'house entrance'
GRI katak 'inner end of trad. Greenlandic house passage where one climbs into the interior'

PI katcuq- 'be settled' [there may be a relat. to katə-]
SPI kassuq- 'be finished, finish'
NAI katcuq- 'be pacified, settle'
WCI Sig katsuq- 'be satisfied, full' [old word acc. Met.]
ECI katsuŋa- 'be slow, without zeal' [katsuŋait- 'be zealous']
GRI katsuʀ- 'be calm, at peace' [katsuŋŋit- 'do in a hurry']

PE katə- 'meet' [cf. kaðuɣ-, katyuɣ- and katuk-, also katluɣ and Atkan Aleut kasaaɣ- 'tie (fish) together by the tails for drying']
AAY ➟
CAY [note katŋ̥əq* 'middle finger'; for Nun katəɣ- 'bump into, brush against' see kaləɣ-[2]] ➟
NSY kaatə- 'arrive, make a trip' [ANLC; Men. has kaasuʀ- 'arrive', kaasutə- 'bring', kaasuʀyuxsa- 'entice' — compare under katyuɣ-]
CSY kaatə- 'arrive' [and kaatutə- 'arrive with', kasivaɣ- 'encounter head- on or unexpectedly']
Sir katə- 'approach' [Men. has a macron over the first vowel; Vakh. has katəɣut(ə)- 'knock against each other' and kasivaXtə- 'approach (enemy)' from Rub.'s texts]
SPI kati- 'bump head'
NAI kati- 'bump head(s)' [and kałuk- 'bump heads (sheep)', PH katiʀžuʀniq* 'snowdrift']
WCI kati- 'bump head against s.th.' [and Sig kattuyyi- 'join up (against one person)']
ECI kati- 'join, come after' [Peck has 'bump head' for Lab; katut(i)- 'come together']
GRI kattut(i)-, NWG katut(i)- 'join, attack in a group' [and kanniq* 'joint']

PE katəma- 'be gathered' [cf. (u)ma-]
AAY —
CAY —
NSY katəma- 'gather' [and kasima- 'meet'; ANLC has katəmaʀ- 'gather, come together']
CSY [note kasima- 'have arrived']
Sir kasəmŋani [also kacəmɣani] 'approaching'
SPI katuma-, Imaq katəma- 'hold a meeting'
NAI kasima-, PH katima-
WCI katima- 'be gathered, piled up'
ECI katima- 'meet, remain continually with'
GRI katima- 'be gathered in a cluster'

PI katəqšat 'collection'
SPI katiqšat 'collection' [katiqsi- 'gather things']
NAI katiqšat 'pile, collection' [katiqši- 'gather together']
WCI [Ras. has katiXXi- 'cluster' for Cop — 'gather, bunch together' acc. Pryde]
ECI [note katiʀsu(q)- 'assemble']
GRI katiʀšat 'collection, gathering' [and note katiʀšuʀ- 'gather']

PE katət- 'join' [cf. t-[1]]
AAY —
CAY kacətə- 'arrive from wilderness', NSU 'gather'
NSY katətə- 'join, gather'
CSY —
Sir —
SPI katit- 'join, assemble, marry'
NAI katit- 'gather, get married'
WCI katit- 'gather'
ECI katit- 'join'
GRI katit- 'join, get married'

PE katŋuʀ- and **katuʀ-** 'assemble' [cf. ŋ(ŋ)uʀ-?]
AAY katuXtə- 'gather' [trans. or intrans.; also katu<ʀ>utə- 'meet with' and katunʀət 'flock']
CAY Y, Nun, NS katuʀ- 'be gathered' [post. root — katuŋqa- 'be gathered'; Hinz also has katŋat 'herd']
NSY [note kałəXtə- 'gather']
CSY kałŋuʀ- 'be gathered, assembled' [post. root — kałŋuʀŋa- 'be gathered'; note also SLI kałəXta 'a ball game'?]
Sir —
SPI —
NAI kanŋuq-, Nu katŋuq- 'assemble' [and kanŋut, Nu katŋut 'herd']
WCI —
ECI —
GRI —

PE katyaɣ 'place where two things come together'
AAY —
CAY kasiɣ- 'fork (river)'
NSY —
CSY [note kasivaɣ- under katə- above]
Sir kasix 'place where two poles meet' [Vakh. from Rub.'s texts]
SPI kassaaq 'fork in river'

NAI kayyaaq, Mal katyaaq
WCI [Pet. has katyaq — for kayyaaq? -, also kadjiarek 'confluence, fork of river' for Sig]
ECI —
GRI [kaayaaq 'groin']

PE katluɣ 'thunder' [cf. katə-, kaðuɣ-, kałaɣ-, and p.b. łuɣ(-), also (western) EA kału-, Atkan kalu- 'shoot with bow or gun']
AAY Kod, KP (archaic) kałuk 'thunder' [also kałiq, a nominalization with liʀ, which in Kod mean 'lightning'; kałuxtə- 'thunder (sound)' and kałkiq 'sparks']
CAY kałuk 'thunder and lightning, electricity'
NSY kałuk 'thunder, lightning'
CSY kałuk 'thunder, lightning'
Sir kałəx 'thunder, lightning, storm'
SPI kalliq- 'thunder', Qaw also nom. kalliq 'thunder', Imaq kaluk 'thunder, lightning' [the latter written with macron on first vowel, but Men. also has kałuk 'storm'; note also kalukaq 'jerry can, box drum'; Jen. also has kaluʀuaq 'noise, din']
NAI kalluk, Mal katluk, kalluk 'thunder' [also verbal; compare also Mal katliq- 'come together quickly'; note also kalukaq, kałukaq 'box drum', verbal 'beat a box drum' — compare kałaɣ-]
WCI kalluk 'thunder' [also verbal]
ECI kallu, Great Whale River kalli, Lab kalluk 'thunder' [as verb = 'strike (lightning)'- compare (with p.b. liʀ-) kalli(q)- 'sound (thunder)']
GRI kałłiq* [old ortho. kagdleq, but Fabr. kadlek] 'thunder' [back formation from verbal kałłiʀ-, as also EG kattiʀsiq; note also kałłiʀup inniʀa 'lightning, electricity']

PI katna(a)k 'bowsprit (of skin boat)' [cf. katə-]
Yup — [for CAY katn̥əq 'middle finger' see katə-]
SPI katnaak 'bowsprit'
NAI kannaak (du.) 'bowsprit, carved pieces of wood at either end of boat, projecting ends of umiaq's railing', Nu katnaak 'forked thing or place'
WCI —
ECI —
GRI kannak 'bowsprit, projecting end of skin boat railing, (usually pl.) male sexual organs'

PY katŋitə- 'insult with finger gesture' [cf. CAY katn̥əq 'middle finger' under katə- and lit-?]
AAY —
CAY katŋitə- 'insult with a finger gesture, hook finger under s.o.'s nose and push upward'
NSY katŋitaʀ- 'give the finger covered with spit (in derision)' [ANLC]
CSY —

PI katuk- 'beat drum' [cf. kacaɣ- and kaðuɣ-, and Aleut katuɣ- 'shake, flutter' but also EA kataɣ- 'beat']
Sir — [but Vakh. has qatuq(ə)- 'beat' from Rub.'s texts]
SPI —
NAI —
WCI katuk 'drumstick' [and verbal 'beat drum' — Ras.; also Schn. for 'adg']
ECI [katuk- 'tremble with old age'; and B.-S. has katuun 'drumstick' for Igl]
GRI katuɣ- 'beat drum' [and katu, katuut 'drumstick']

PE katyuɣ- 'knock into or meet' [cf. katə-, kacaɣ-, kaðuɣ- and Aleut kasu- 'find, hit upon']
AAY ➡
CAY — [for kasuɣ- 'surround' see kasuɣ-]
NSY kasuɣ- 'come over to, approach' [ANLC; Enm. et al. have kasuʀ- 'approach land (boat)' — but compare kaasuʀ- under katə-]
CSY kasuɣ- 'hit with a stick, hit shore (waves)' [for kasivaɣ- 'encounter head on' see katə-]
Sir kasuɣ- 'fling, lash' [Em. has kasuɣ- 'knock with head, splash against (wave)'; for kasix 'place where tent poles meet' see katyaɣ under kate-]
SPI kazuq- 'meet'
NAI kasuk- 'ram into each other (mountain sheep)' [and kasuq- 'meet', Nu kasuaq- 'go to meet']
WCI Sig kasuq- 'fight, meet' [Pet. has 'destroy'; Ras. has 'meet', Dor. 'land (boat)' for Net; Schn. has kasutuq-beat on door' for 'adg' and Ow. kahuk- 'knock head' for EP; Pryde has Net kasuq- 'meet, cross path of', Cop kahuk- 'bump one's head']
ECI kasuk 'flint for lighter', kasuq- 'join, grab' [B.-S. has kasuk 'fire- stone' and Ras. kasuaq- 'hammer' for Igl; note also kasu(a)- 'hold together']
GRI kasuɣ- 'strike, beat against'

PE katyuɣutə- 'come together' [cf. utə-]
AAY kasuutə- 'meet each other' [also 'get married' — for which see kasuɣ-, though kasuutə- with this meaning may also in fact be from this source]
CAY [for kasuutə- 'get married' see kasuɣ-]
NSY —
CSY —
Sir kasəɣut(ə)- 'hit with s.th., knock up against s.th.' [Em.]
SPI [for kassuuti- 'get married' see kasuɣ-]
NAI kasuuti- 'meet'
WCI —
ECI kasuut(i)- 'join'
GRI kasuut(i)- 'knock into, clink glasses (toast)'

PE ka(C)uɣ 'walrus skin (with blubber)' [cf. kaðuɣ-]
AAY [note Kodiak kauxkiqə- 'itch']
CAY Nun, NI, HBC kauxpak 'walrus'
NSY kaxu 'walrus skin with blubber'
CSY —
Sir —
SPI kauk
NAI kauk
WCI [Cop kau 'white of egg' acc. Pryde]
ECI kauk 'walrus skin' [also 'white of egg' — compare the NAI under natanquʀ]
GRI kaak 'walrus skin' [NG kauk also 'white of egg']

PY-S kavcak or **kavtak** 'make rattling or crunching sound' [cf. kaðuɣ- and kacak-]
AAY kauxtaq, AP also kauxtak 'hailstone'

CAY kafcak, kaftak, kaftuk 'hailstone', kafcaxtə- 'rattle, clatter'
NSY kafsaxtaʀ- 'tread heavily, tramp, rustle' [ANLC; Men. has kafsaXtałəq 'rustle']
CSY kafsak 'shuffling, crinkling or rustling sound', kaftəkšak 'hail' [Chap kapsak 'crunch, rustle' (verbal kapsaxtaʀ-); note also kavlək 'sharp clicking sound', Chap kavləŋunani 'soundlessly', kavləxtaʀ- 'bang, loud noise']
Sir kafsaxtaʀ- 'scrape, crunch, bang, rumble' [and kafcəɣca — for kafsəɣca? — 'scraping, crunching'; also kafsiX 'bell'?]
Inu — [but note NAI kapkaq- 'make noise with one's teeth']

PE kaviʀ- 'be red'
AAY kawiʀ- 'be red' [C kawiXqaq, K kawisqaq 's.th. red']
CAY kawiXtə- 'redden' [kawiXpak, kawiʀliq 'red thing']
NSY kaviʀ- 'be red' [ANLC; and Men. has kaviq 'red stone from which paint is made' and kaviʀžulŋuq 'reddish']
CSY kavitə- 'be red', kaviʀžuk, kavitažaak 'reddish thing'
Sir kavəʀəlŋuX 'red' [Vakh. from Rub; Men. has kavəɣəlŋuX, also kavisaɣənləŋuX 'reddish' and kavižuxtələX 'dawn'; Vakh. also has kavcuʀaX 'red' from Men.'s texts]
SPI kawiq- 'be red'
NAI kaviq-
WCI —
ECI —
GRI —

PE kav(v)i(C)aʀ '(red) fox'
AAY K kauɣya(ʀ)aq, C kauɣyaaq 'small red fox'
CAY kaviaq* 'red fox'
NSY [note kavilŋuq 'fox']
CSY kaviiq* 'fox'
Sir —
SPI —
NAI kavviaq 'red fox'
WCI —
ECI —
GRI —

PE kavlaɣ 'bearberry' [cf. kaviʀ-?]
AAY kauɣlaq 'bearberry'
CAY kavlak
NSY —
CSY kaavlak
Sir kavləx
SPI kavlak
NAI kavlaq
WCI kavlak
ECI kallak
GRI [note kałłannit- 'stink']

PI kavžaq and **kavžəq** 'crown of head' [cf. Aleut kamɣ-iX 'head' from *kavəɣ if not kaðəvə(t)- — two bases may be entangled here]
SPI kavžaq 'crown of head, peak of woman's parka'
NAI kavžaq 'crown of head'
WCI kavyiq 'crown of head' [Pryde has kavyaq 'crown of head' but kaavyaq 'peak of parka hood'; and Ras. has Cop kaavhera 'small tuft at back of man's hood' but also kaaLhutaq 'top (of tree), peak' — compare GRI kaaviq below]
ECI kayyiq 'crown of head' [SB, NBI also 'end of spiral of blocks in a snow house']
GRI kaššiq [old ortho. kavsseq] 'crown of head' [and kaaviq* 'top (of s.th.)' — 3s poss. kaaXXa or kaaʀfa, influenced by kaŋəʀ and/or kaðəvə(t)-?]

PY kaya(ɣ)- 'beg' [cf.kayəmə(t)- and kayu-]
AAY —
CAY kaiɣa- 'request, ask for s.th.'
NSY kaya- 'beg, appeal' [ANLC]
CSY [note kayaxtə- 'urge, send s.o.', kayaXqaʀ- 'cheer up, urge on']
Inu [for SPI kayuaq- 'ask for s.th.' see under kayu-]

PI kayaq- 'stay at home'
Yup [note AAY kayaɣnaʀ- 'be difficult', kayaɣyuɣ- 'balk at doing s.th.', which appears to be borrowed from Aleut kayaɣna- 'be heavy', however]
SPI kayaut(i)- 'stay at home when others go away' [Jen.]
NAI —
WCI —
ECI kayai- 'leave behind'
GRI kayaʀ- 'stay at home, not participate' [kayaat- 'always want to go along']

PE kayəmə(t)- 'push (forward)' [cf. perhaps Aleut kað- 'front, before, at tip of', if not PE kayu-]
AAY AP kayəmə-, kaimə- 'push, force in'
CAY kazmə-, HBC kaymə- 'poke, push'
NSY kayəmə- 'place on, help get up on'
CSY kayəmə- 'urge, encourage'
Sir [kaymər- 'order, send' (Vakh. from Men. and Rub.) and kayməqəX 'exile']
SPI kaimit- 'push into water (esp. boat)'
NAI kiamɨt-, kaimɨt- 'push before one, shove into water (boat)', kaimʀuaq- 'push sled, pole kayak against current' [for kaipik-, kiapik- 'fit together' see kapət-]
WCI kaimit- 'push into (e.g. one chimney tube into another)', kaimu(ʀ)aq- 'push sled' [Ras. has Car kaimig- 'push into water'; and Sig kaima- 'order', kaimaktuq- 'pursuade, order']
ECI kaimit- 'drive in, push in', Lab 'push out a boat' [Peck has kaiblar- 'exhort'; for kaipiŋa- 'have hands pulled back in sleeves' see kapət-]
GRI kaamit- 'push before one, shove into water (boat)', NG 'stuff, shove in (under)' [and note kaassuʀ- (old ortho. kâvsor-) 'push oneself forward in sitting position or in kayak over bad ice', NG kaussuaq- 'push sled']

PI kaivluaq- 'push continuously'
SPI [note kaivluaq- 'take boat out to sea in rough water']
NAI kaivlʸuaq- 'push from behind (trying to move sled, etc.)' [kaivlʸuk- 'push sled by stanchions']

WCI kailluaq- 'push s.th. ahead of one' [Pryde]
ECI kaillua(q)- 'push continually'
GRI EG kaattuaʀ- push' [Tersis, also for kaattuut (Robbe and Dorais kaattuulit) 'sled']

PE kayŋu- 'be ashamed'
AAY —
CAY kazu(yuɣ)-, HBC kayŋu(yuɣ)- 'be ashamed'
NSY kayŋu(yuɣ)-
CSY kayŋu(yuɣ)-
Sir kayŋə(yuɣ)-
SPI kanŋu(zuk)-
NAI kanŋu(suk)-
WCI kanŋu(huk)-
ECI kaŋŋu(suk)-
GRI kaŋŋu(suɣ)-

PY- S kayu 'sculpin' [may be cognate with PE kanayu(ʀ) despite the Sir form below — compare also PY qayu(q) with PI qanuq 'how' for parallel loss of n in Yup]
AAY kayuluk 'sculpin'
CAY kayu
NSY —
CSY kayu 'sculpin or any ocean fish other than salmon'
Sir kayəŋənʀaX 'small fish' [Orr; Miller has kaynirax 'sculpin']
Inu [Qaw kayuuqupak 'sculpin' is probably from the Yup]

PE kayu- 'be strong' [cf. kayəmə(t)-, kaya(ɣ)- and Aleut kayu-X 'strength, muscle', EA kayu- 'have hopeful expectation of s.o. coming' — there may be two bases entangled here]
AAY kayu- 'be strong'
CAY kayu- 'be strong' [esp. of wind in general CAY]
NSY ➟
CSY kayaatə- 'be weak' [and note kayaałqə- 'win']
Sir kayəX 'muscle', kayəŋəlŋuX 'rich (man)' [note also kayviʀ- 'get tired'; Em. also has kayaʀ- 'win, beat' — perhaps from the base of CSY kayaałqə- above; Men. has kayaXticaʀ- 'compete, quarrel, fight']
SPI kayuq 'upper arm' [and note kayuaq- 'ask for s.th., ask a favor']
NAI Nu kayuq 'outside of upper arm'
WCI ➟
ECI [kayusi- 'persevere (to the end)']
GRI [NG kayuhiqqa- 'keep running (under own steam — e.g. sledge)', kayuyuummi- 'persevere']

PE kay(y)u(C)aʀ 'biceps' [cf. aʀ?]
AAY K kasuaq 'biceps'
CAY —
NSY kayuaq 'muscle' [and note kayiiŋalʀia 'muscular']
CSY kayaaq 'biceps'
Sir kayaX [Orr]
SPI kayuaq 'biceps' [Jen.]
NAI —
WCI katsuaq 'biceps' [and Ras. has Net katjuaq 'sinew of seal's fore- flipper']
ECI katsuaq, kayyuaq 'biceps'
GRI katsuaq

PI kayumək- 'be strong or persevering'
SPI kayumik- 'be strong' [and note kayuuq(pak)- 'desire s.th. one can't have']
NAI kayumik- 'be fast, appetizing (food)' [and kayumŋiq- 'slow down, be eager to go but be held back, urge on, strain at harnass (dog)' — compare kayuŋŋiq- below]
WCI kayumik- 'be fast', Net kayumiktuq 'fresh breeze, gale' [Ras. has kayumik- 'blow' for Cop]
ECI Lab kayumik- 'cry a lot' [Schn.]
GRI kayumiɣ- 'be raring to go', EG kayimiɣ- 'persevere, be willing', kayiminnaʀ- 'be pleasant, amusing' [and Robbe and Menn. have EG ka(y)imii- 'like', Tersis kaimiC- 'persevere, have pleasure in doing']

PY-S kayun 'helper' [cf. un — perhaps influenced by ikayuʀ-]
AAY —
CAY —
NSY [kayun 'coeval, colleague']
CSY kayun 'helper' [kayusiʀ- 'help']
Sir kayuta 'help, helper' [Em.; Men. has kayusiʀ- 'help' — from CSY?]

PY kayuŋə- '(start to) blow (wind)' [cf. nəɣ-]
AAY kayuŋə- 'start to blow, blow hard (wind)'
CAY kayuŋə-
NSY —
CSY —

PI kayuŋŋiq- 'be eager to go' [cf. ŋiʀ-?]
SPI Qaw kayuŋiq- 'want or ask s.o. to go along with one'
NAI kayuŋŋiq- 'be eager to go'
WCI —
ECI kayuŋiq- 'pull on traces (dog), be raring to go s.where (person)'
GRI kayuŋiʀ- 'desire, long for s.th.' [kajuŋiʀi- 'desire']

PI kayuq- 'be reddish brown (animal)'
Yup — [but note CAY kayu 'coyote', which may be a loan from English]
SPI kayuqtuq 'red fox'
NAI kayuqtuq 'red fox' [Mal kayuun 'coyote' is surely a back-formation from the English which was rendered as kayuuti, perhaps influenced by kayuqtuq]
WCI Cop kayuqtuq 'red fox' [Ras. has kayuq 'red- brown (fox)' for Car]
ECI kayuq 'red, brown', kayuqtuq 'red fox' [Lab kajuk for both in Andersen et al.; and note kayuʀlaaq 'dog with reddish patches']
GRI kayuq 'brown dog or other animal', kayuʀ- 'be brown', NWG 'be yellow' [and SWG kayuʀuiq, NWG kayuaʀaq, Up kayavaʀ̃aq 'sandpiper, golden plover']

PE kəcit- 'count'
AAY —
CAY NS, Y, UK kəcətə- 'count'

NSY kisitə- [Em.]
CSY kəstə-
Sir kitə- [Em.]
SPI kizit-
NAI kisit-
WCI kisit-
ECI kisit-, Iti kitit-
GRI kisit-

PE kəði- 'alone or only' [quantifier/qualifier root, seeming to alternate morphologically with *kəðə-; compare the parallel phonological development of PE əðiʀ]
AAY C kii-, kiyi- [also kiɣi- in kiɣiin], K kii-, kəsi- 'only, alone'
CAY kii-, HBC kəyiʀ-, Y kəziʀ- 'only, alone' [and kəzianək, HBC kəyianəŋ 'always']
NSY kəyəmi 'alone' [ANLC; Men. has kəyəvək '(you) alone' on p. 317]
CSY kəzəXaʀ- 'only, alone'
Sir kəcəməlŋuX 'only (one)' [Vakh. has kəcəkəɬaʀmi 'alone', also kəcəmi, etc.]
SPI kizi- 'only'
NAI kisi- 'only' [both strong and weak i show up under inflection, e.g. kisiɣnʸik 'only they two' vs. kisɨpta 'we alone']
WCI kisi- 'only' [Ras. has Net, Sig kisianni '(it's) only (that)', Dor. has kisiani 'only']
ECI kisi- 'only' [and kisiani 'but, only'; for kiita 'a little, only' see ki(i)]
GRI kisi-, EG kiitsaaʀ- 'only' [and kisianni, kisiat 'but', kisiʀɬiuʀ- 'live alone', NG kihiani 'only, but']

> **PE kəðim(ʀ)aʀ** 'one who is alone'
> AAY [PWS kiimaaʀ- 'do s.th. by oneself']
> CAY [kiimiʀ- 'stand on its own (baby)']
> NSY kəyəmaq 'the only one'
> CSY kəzəmaq 'only child'
> Sir —
> SPI kiziʀmaaq 'person or animal alone'
> NAI PH kisimʀaaq 'person with no relatives', kisimʀiuq- 'be alone'
> WCI kisimʀiuq- 'be alone' [Pryde, who also has Cop kihimŋaaq 'rogue bull musk-ox']
> ECI [Aiv kisiʀmiutaq 'one who lives in solitude']
> GRI kisiʀmaaq 's.o. who is alone'

PE kəð(ə)kaviɣ 'falcon or hawk' [cf. kəði-?]
AAY —
CAY əskaviaq 'goshawk' [and Ras. has kitikagfiaq, also Nun skaf'viaq 'peregrine falcon']
NSY —
CSY —
Sir —
SPI kiɣžawik 'peregrine falcon' [Imaq kiakiaq 'hawk' acc. Men.]
NAI kižɣavik 'goshawk, falcon'
WCI kiɣɣavik, Cop kilɣavik 'falcon' [Ras. has Net kikSavik — for kiɣžavik?]
ECI kiɣɣavik 'hawk'
GRI kiššavik [old ortho. kigssavik] 'hawk'

PE kəɣaɣ- 'do fast' [cf. Atkan Aleut xaðaɣ- 'move or walk fast' with p.b. ðaɣ- under žaɣ- and loss of initial kə; with negation = 'move slowly']
AAY —
CAY kəxaɣ- 'be a fast eater'
NSY ɣaXtə- 'eat greedily' [ANLC; Men. has ɣaɣnəXsiq(aʀ)- 'eat ravenously']
CSY —
Sir —
SPI —
NAI —
WCI —
ECI —
GRI kiɣaat- [old ortho. kigait-] 'be slow' [with p.b. ŋit-; kiɣaaɬɬaɣ- 'slack (speed or eagerness)', EG kiaatsimik 'silently'; note also kiɣaaʀ- 'stop bleeding' with ŋiʀ- — influenced by kəɣək-?]

PE kəɣðaɣ- 'be rough' [cf. kəɣə- and žaɣ-?]
AAY xaɣ- 'be rough (surface)' [xak 'rough surface']
CAY kəxaɣ(cətə)- 'be rough (surface)'
NSY —
CSY xaak 'rasping, grating sound'
Sir —
SPI kiɣžak- 'be rough, coarse'
NAI kiɣžak-, Nu kiɣižak- 'be rough, coarse', Nu also 'be dull (blade)' [compare Nu kiɣlak- under kəɣlaɣ-]
WCI kiɣɣak- 'be rough'
ECI kiɣɣa(k)-
GRI —

PI kəɣaq- 'notch' [cf. kəɣə- and/or kəkə- — there is some entanglement between the two bases]
SPI kiaq- 'notch, etch' [Jen., who also has 'be worn by use (fur)']
NAI [note kiɣak- 'nibble']
WCI kiɣaq- 'cut with teeth'
ECI —
GRI kiɣaʀ- 'make a notch in, incise (edge)' [and note kixxaq* 'mountain pass, notch, scratch, furrow']

PE kəɣə- 'bite' [cf. kəɣlaɣ-, kəɣðaɣ- and Aleut kiɣ- 'bite']
AAY kəxə-, kəɣə- 'bite' [and note kiɣɣaɣ-, KP xiɣɣaɣ- 'be furious']
CAY kəxə- 'bite'
NSY kəxə-
CSY əxə- 'crimp boot soles with teeth', xiistə- 'clench teeth'
Sir [Em. has kəɣəžaʀ- 'crimp soles with teeth'; Orr has kižáx(tə)- 'crimp soles' and Men. has kižaX(tə)-]
SPI kii- 'bite' [and kiižaq- 'crimp soles']
NAI kii-, Mal kiɣi- 'bite, clench teeth' [and kiisi- 'take a bite']
WCI kii- 'bite' [Met. also has kiɣi-]
ECI kii- 'bite' [half-trans. kiisi-, kiinni(C)-]
GRI kii- 'bite, press together around s.th. (ice)', EG 'clench one's teeth' [and half-trans. kiisi-; note also kiɣuʀ- 'be worn off (surface)' and kixxit(i)- 'get jammed in s.th.']

PI kəɣɣəq 'bite or s.th. bitten' [cf. q under nəʀ[1]]
SPI —
NAI kiɣɣɨq* 's.th. bitten numerous times'
WCI [Pet. has kiɣ(ɣ)iq 'pimple' (?) for Sig]
ECI kiɣɣiq 'bite'
GRI kixxiq* 'bite'

PY kəɣ(ɣ)əvə- 'chafe'
AAY Perry xuɣ-, KP xuxtə- 'chafe, abrade'
CAY NSU kəxəvə- 'wear out'
NSY —
CSY —

PE kəɣi(C)aʀ 'beaver'
AAY —
CAY kəxiaʀnaq 'otter' [with p.b. naʀ]
NSY —
CSY —
Sir —
SPI —
NAI Nu kiɣiaq 'beaver'
WCI kiɣiaq
ECI kiɣiaq
GRI kixxiaq

PE kəɣmaʀ- 'bite repeatedly' [cf. maʀ-]
AAY kəxm̥a<ʀ>i- 'bite repeatedly'
CAY kəxm̥aʀ-
NSY kəxm̥aʀ-
CSY —
Sir —
SPI kiŋmaq-, Imaq kəɣma(q)-
NAI kiɣmaq-
WCI —
ECI [note kimmautiik 'pliers', kimmautiŋu- 'be tired of chewing or holding s.th. between one's teeth']
GRI kimmaʀ-, kimmaliɣ- 'chew to make soft' [the latter 'notch' in EG]

PE kəɣmi(C)- 'grip between teeth' [cf. miɣ-]
AAY C kəxm̥iɣ-, Kod kəɣmiɣ- 'grip between teeth' [kəxm̥iaq, kəɣmiaq 'thing thus gripped']
CAY kəxm̥iaq 'thing held between teeth' [Ras. has 'drill mouthpiece']
NSY [kəxəmsi- 'bite on to']
CSY əxm̥iiq* 'thing held between teeth'
Sir —
SPI kiŋmiaq 'drill mouthpiece'
NAI kiɣmi<ž>aq 'thing carried between teeth' [Jen. has 'mouthpiece of drill'; verbal = 'carry in teeth'; kiŋmiʀun 'sealskin edge between sole and fur part of boot']
WCI Net, Car kiŋmiaq 'mouthpiece of drill' [B.-S.; Ras. has verbal 'carry in mouth' for Cop]
ECI kimmi- 'clench teeth, be tightly shut (pliers)' [and kimmia(q)- 'hold between teeth' — nom. = 'thing thus held']
GRI kimmiaʀ- 'hold between teeth' [and kimmiaq 'thing thus held', kimmivik 'mouthpiece of pipe', kimmiqut 'strip (e.g. of dried skin) sewn into seam of boot']

PE kəɣun 'tooth' [cf. un]
AAY xun, xuutəq, PWS kəxun, kəxuta 'tooth'
CAY kəxun
NSY ɣutə
CSY xuta
Sir kəɣəta
SPI kiun, Qaw kiɣun
NAI kiɣun
WCI kiɣun
ECI kiɣuti
GRI kiɣut

PI kiimmi- 'clench teeth' [cf. umi-?]
SPI Qaw kiimi- 'clench teeth'
NAI kiimmi-
WCI —
ECI kimmi- 'clench teeth' [influen. by kəɣmi(C)-?]
GRI —

PI kəɣək- 'stop flowing (blood)' [cf. kəɣə-?]
SPI —
NAI —
WCI —
ECI Lab kiɣik- 'stop' [specifically of blood flowing in Peck and Bourq.]
GRI kiɣit- 'stop flowing (blood)' [as opposed to kixxit(i)- 'get (s.th.) jammed in s.th.'; Fab. has kigi(t)- or kigik- in the latter meaning, only kigi(t)- in the former; for kiɣaaʀ- 'stop flowing' see kəɣaɣ-]

PE kəɣinaʀ 'face or blade' [cf. kəɣə-]
AAY xiinaq 'face'
CAY kəxinaq 'face, blade of knife'
NSY ɣinaq 'face'
CSY xinaq 'face, blade of knife'
Sir kəx 'face' [Vakh. has kəkəX from Rub.]
SPI kiinaq 'face, blade or edge of knife'
NAI kiin^{y}aq, Mal kiɣin^{y}aq
WCI kiinaq
ECI kiinaq
GRI kiinaq, EG kiiaq 'face, blade of knife' [and kiinaʀpak, EG kiiappak, Up kiinappak 'mask' — EG also 'ghost']

PE kəɣinaquʀ 'mask' [cf. quʀ]
AAY AP xiinaquq 'mask' [Fisher]
CAY kəxinaquq 'mask' [kəxinaquʀ- 'put on a mask']
NSY ɣinaquq [ANLC]
CSY xinaq^{w}aaq* 'mask'
Sir —
SPI kiinauq, Qaw kiitnaʀuq
NAI kiin^{y}aʀuq 'mask' [and note kiin^{y}aaq 'male seal in mating season']
WCI —
ECI — [note kiinaaq, kiinaŋŋuaq 'mask']
GRI kiinaʀuq, kiinaaq 'black snout and eyes of saddleback seal'

PI kiinailitaq 'knife sheath' [cf. ŋilitaʀ, also kiɣlin, though the relat. is obscure]
SPI kiinailitaq 'knife sheath'

NAI PH kiinʸailʸisaq
WCI [note kiinait- 'be blunt']
ECI kiinailitaq 'sheath for covering instrument, veil for covering face'
GRI —

PI kiinnakcaq- 'sharpen' [cf. k- under nəɣ- and caʀ-]
SPI kiinaɣzaq- 'sharpen'
NAI PH kiinʸaksaun 'sharpening stone'
WCI kiinaksaq- 'sharpen'
ECI kiinna(k)-, kiinnasaq-
GRI kiinnaɣ-, NG kiinnaxxaq- 'whet, sharpen'

PI kiinaqci- 'see face to face' [cf. ci-]
SPI —
NAI Nu kiinʸaqsi- 'show one's face, see s.o.'s face'
WCI Cop kiinaXXi- 'see another's face' [Pryde]
ECI —
GRI kiinaʀsi- 'see s.o. face to face, show s.o. a friendly face (as greeting)'

PE kəɣiʀ- 'be in pain' [cf. kəɣə-]
AAY —
CAY kiXciuʀ-, NSU kəxiXciuʀ- 'be in pain, ill' [and kiXta 'pain']
NSY ɣiXtəŋə- 'be in pain from a wound, ache' [ANLC]
CSY xiiXsi- 'be in pain'
Sir —
SPI kiiqsiq- 'be in pain', kiiqsiuq- 'be in great pain' [kiiqti 'pain']
NAI kiiqsiuq- 'be in great pain'
WCI —
ECI —
GRI —

PI kəɣlu 'posts at bow or stern of skin boat' [cf. kəklu(ɣ), with which this set may share the same source]
SPI kiɣlu 'bow seat of umiaq'
NAI kiɣlu 'bow or stern seat of umiaq'
WCI —
ECI Baffin kiɣlu 'boat post' [Boas]
GRI umiap kiłłui 'bow and stern posts of skin boat' [for homonym (?) meaning 'fireplace' see kəklu(ɣ)]

PY kəɣlunəq 'wolf' [cf. kəɣə- and luʀ- plus nəʀ[1]?]
AAY PWS kəɣlunəq 'wolf' [elsewhere kaɣanaq, with taboo deformation?]
CAY kəɣlunəq* 'wolf'
NSY kəɣlunəq
CSY —

PE kəɣtuʀɣaʀ 'mosquito' [cf. kəɣə-, tuʀ-[2] and yaʀ]
AAY kəxtuʀyaq 'mosquito'
CAY əxtuʀyaq, Eg, Nun, NSU kəxtuʀyaq
NSY kəktuʀyaq 'mosquito' [L.-T. has kəktuʀiaq, poss. influenced by SPI]
CSY [note əxtuʀyaq 'unidentified creature like lemming with double claws or sea-squirt' (?)]
Sir —
SPI kiktuʀiaq, Imaq kəktuʀiaq 'mosquito'
NAI kiktuʀiaq
WCI kiktuʀiaq
ECI kittuʀiaq
GRI —

PI kəkcaq- 'think all the time about s.th.' [or kikcaq-?]
SPI —
NAI —
WCI kiksaq- 'think about s.th. all the time', Cop kixxaliʀi- 'desire' [Ras.], Sig kiksaɣi- 'think all the time about what to do, be worried about' [Met.]
ECI kitsa(q)- 'be worried', kitsa(ʀ)uti 'tribulation'
GRI kissaʀ- [old ortho. kigsar-] 'wish' [in Egede 'long for'; kissaatiɣi- 'wish for']

PI kəkcaun 'membrane around intestines' [or kikcaun?; cf. un]
SPI —
NAI —
WCI Cop kixxaut 'fat around internal organs or caribou' [Pryde]
ECI kitsauti 'membrane around intestines, peritonium'
GRI kissaatit [old ortho. kigsautit] 'reticulum (of animal)'

PI kəkə- 'break off (after notching)' [cf. kəklu(ɣ), kəklaɣ, and kəɣaq-]
SPI kiɣi- 'make a notch in'
NAI kiki- 'make a notch in, break off a piece (of wood)' [and kikkaq* 'notch, broken off piece'; for kikłuq- 'be notched, chipped' see kəklu(ɣ)]
WCI kiki- 'be split, cracked'
ECI ➟
GRI kiki- 'crack s.th. (e.g. a cup)'

PI kəkŋiq 'gap between teeth' [cf. ilŋiʀ-, with which there appears to be contam.]
SPI kiŋŋiq 'missing tooth'
NAI kiŋŋiq*, Nu kikŋiq* [also kɨɣnɨq*]
WCI Cop kiŋŋiq 'gap where tooth has been lost' [Pryde]
ECI kiŋŋiq 'gap between teeth, anything missing'
GRI kiŋŋiq* 'gap between teeth'

PI kəktuʀaq- 'break in two' [cf. ðuʀaʀ-?]
SPI kiktuaq-, W, Qaw kiktuʀaq-, Imaq kəktuaq- 'snap in two, break'
NAI kɨktuʀaq-
WCI kiktuʀaq- 'break (intr.)'
ECI kittuʀaq- 'break' [Bourq. has kiktuʀaq-]
GRI kittuʀaʀ- 'break, snap, pull apart'

PE kəklaɣ or **kəklaʀ** '(notch between teeth of) saw' [cf. kəkə- and ʀłaɣ; there may be some contam. with kəɣə- in Yup here]
AAY KP kəxłautə- 'notch (a log, where another is to join it)' [compare C kəxłacaɣ- 'nibble, take a few bites', going with kəɣə-]
CAY kəxłaq 'saw' [for HBC kəxsaq 'saw tooth' see kəkyaɣ]
NSY —

CSY —
Sir —
SPI —
NAI Nu kiɣlak 'flint blade' [as verb = 'be dull, rough (blade)' — compare under kəɣðaɣ-; Ras. has 'arrowhead of flint', Jen. has kiɣlaq 'skinning knife']
WCI Net kiɣlaaʀžuk 'little flint knife' [Ras.]
ECI killak, killaq 'interval between teeth of saw [Bourq. has kiklaq for Lab, but note also killait 'teeth of saw'; Ras. has killavait 'jagged (mountains)' for Igl]
GRI kiłłavaaq 'indentation, space between fingers, jagged crest' [kiłłavaaʀ- 'make indentations or notches in s.th.']

PE kəklu(ɣ) 'andiron (for cooking over)' [cf. kəkə- and perhaps lu(ʀ), also kəɣlu, which could represent the same base — note that PE kl becomes ɣl in NAI PH and also sporadically further east in some words; the base may originally have meant 'piece(s) of notched wood laid across each other (e.g. used as an andiron)']
AAY —
CAY —
NSY [note əkn̥aq 'stove', influenced by əkn̥əq 'fire' under əkə-[1]?]
CSY əxłuk 'stove' [also dual for one]
Sir kəkła 'stove' [Vakh. has 'fireplace']
SPI —
NAI [note kikłuq- 'be notched or chipped' from kəkə-]
WCI Car EP kikłut 'outdoor fireplace' [Ow.; Ras. has Car kiglut 'fireplace' but also kikłuvik 'cooking place' and Net kitlut 'oven'; Pryde has Cop killuk, kixxuk (the former also Net) 'one of a pair of firestones for supporting pot over camp fire']
ECI kitsuk 'support for teapot on Inuit lamp, stones to make open- aiʀ fiʀe', Lab kikłu 'fireplace, andiron' [Peck; note also kiɣluq- 'saw', nom. kiɣluuti — Dor.]
GRI kiłłu [old ortho. kigdlo], (pl.) kiłłut 'open air fireplace of stones, etc.' [Kl. has also 'two pieces of wood to lay flat stone on for drying tobacco for snuff'; NWG kiłłuut 'cooking range, hearth']

PE kəkyaɣ or **kəkyaʀ** 'nail' [cf. kəkə- and kəklaɣ; the Yup may be influenced by kəɣə-]
AAY —
CAY kəxsaʀaq 'mouthpiece of bow drill', HBC kəxsaq 'saw tooth'
NSY kəxɣ̥aq 'nail' [Jen. has kiikiak — from Inu?]
CSY kiksak 'ice creeper on sole of boot to prevent slipping'
Sir kikɣ̥iX (for kəkɣ̥əX?) 'stud on sole of boot to prevent slipping' [Vakh. from Rub.'s texts]
SPI kiɣiak 'nail'
NAI kiki<ž>ak 'nail' [also verbal]
WCI kikiak 'nail' [Lowe; Met. has kikiaq]
ECI kikiak 'nail'
GRI kikiak 'nail' [pl. kikiššat; verbal kikiaɣ-]

PE kəlaɣ- 'perfoʀate or get a hole' [cf. kəluɣ-]
AAY —
CAY —
NSY —
CSY kəlaɣ- 'come undone, unravel' [influenced by kəluaq- under kəluɣ-?]
Sir [kəlaxti- 'unpick, undo (s.th.)']
SPI kilak- 'pierce, make hole in'
NAI kiłak- 'pierce, get perforated' [and kiłaaq- 'be full of holes, perforate']
WCI kilak- 'pierce, get perforated'
ECI kilak- 'pierce, get perforated' [and kilaaq- 'make many holes in']
GRI kilaɣ- 'get a hole' [and kilak 'hole'; NG kilaaq- 'have a rash or sores on skin']

> **PI kəllaq** 'hole or tear' [cf. q under nəʀ[1]]
> SPI killaiq- 'sew'
> NAI kiłlaq* 'hole' [and kiłlaiyaq- 'sew, patch a hole']
> WCI killaq 'hole' [and killaiyaq- 'patch, repair']
> ECI killak 'hole, tear' [Bourq. has killaq for Lab; killai(q)- 'repair a garment']
> GRI kiłłaq* [old ortho. kigdlaq] 'hole' [and kiłłaaʀ- 'sew up a hole in s.th.']

PE kələ(t)- 'cut skin into strips (for rope)'
AAY —
CAY kəl(ə)və- 'cut skin into strips'
NSY kələvə- 'cut into strips' [L.-T.]
CSY kələvə- 'cut into strips (e.g. making thongs from hide)']
Sir [Vakh. has kəłit- 'twist' from Rub.'s texts]
SPI kilit- 'cut rope from hide'
NAI kiłit- 'cut into strips (hide, fish, etc.)' [and kiłtiq- 'slice', kiłtaq* 'strip of skin to be used for rope']
WCI [note Sig kilittaq 'section of beluga whale skin dried and pressed in a bag containing seal oil' (Pryde)]
ECI kilit- 'make a thong by cutting around edge of a tube of skin from a bearded seal'
GRI kilit- 'cut into strips (skin, baleen, bread, etc.), chap (teat)' [kilitiʀ-, kitsiʀ- 'cut into slices or strips' and kittaq* 'cut-off slice', in pl. 'small pieces of skin left from embroidering with skin strips']

PE kələɣ- 'inform' [cf. kələt-]
AAY kələɣ- 'inform, notify', AP also 'invite over'
CAY kələɣ- 'invite to one's house (to eat)' [and kəlɣuʀ- 'tell s.o. what s.o. else has said about him behind his back']
NSY —
CSY kələɣ- 'warn, inform, invite'
Sir kələʀyaʀ- [for kələɣyaʀ-?] 'invite, call together, inform' [and kəlɣitə- 'show'; Vakh. has kəlɣu(ʀ)- 'run', kəlɣ(ə)- 'go and call' and kəlɣət- 'show' from Rub.]
SPI kilik- 'summon, go to get'
NAI kiłik- 'inform, warn'
WCI Sig kilɣui- 'tell s.o. what s.o. else said about him, tell on s.o.' [kilɣuiyit 'informers, spies'; Car? kilikpaaq 'mark on meat, wood or iron recognizable to owner' — Schn. 'adg']
ECI —
GRI kiliɣ- 'inform' [and kilitsiššiaq 'spy, informer', kiłłuʀ- 'tell s.th. one shouldn't, betray']

PE kələt- 'be alert' [cf. kələɣ-]
AAY —
CAY kəłtə- 'be alert, wary'
NSY kələlŋa- 'observe, keep watch over'
CSY kələŋa- 'be wary, on guard'
Sir [note kənləʀəqə(s)- 'watch over', kənləʀanəX 'careful' — influenced by kənlə?]
SPI kilinŋa- 'be wary' [and Imaq kələnŋa- 'observe, keep an eye on s.th.']
NAI Mal kilinŋa- 'be wary'
WCI —
ECI —
GRI —

PE kəliɣ- 'scrape'
AAY kəliɣ- 'scrape' [and C kəlik 'edible strip of cambium layer of bark scraped from tree']
CAY kəliɣ- 'scrape' [especially to get edible strip of cambium layer of bark of tree]
NSY kəliɣ- 'scrape'
CSY kəliɣ-
Sir —
SPI kiliktuq- 'scrape, clean, rake'
NAI kil^{y}ik- 'scrape (skin)'
WCI [Cop kiliuq(tuq)- 'scrape off' — Pryde]
ECI kiliutaq 'scraping instrument for removing dirt from skins, etc.'
GRI kiliɣ- 'scrape' [and EG kiliilaq, Up kiliitaq 'mussel']

PE kəliɣaʀ- 'scrape repeatedly' [cf. aʀ-]
AAY —
CAY kəliɣaun 'skin scraper'
NSY —
CSY kəliɣaʀ- 'scrape with long, easy strokes'
Sir —
SPI —
NAI kil^{y}iɣaq- 'scrape fat off skin or baleen to desired size'
WCI kiliɣaq- 'scrape skin'
ECI kiliɣaq- 'clean by scraping, make oil by beating blubber', Lab 'scrape hair off skin'
GRI kiliɣaʀ- 'scrape frozen berries from heather in winter'

PE kəliɣvaɣ '(fossil) mammoth' [cf. vaɣ]
AAY —
CAY Y kəliɣvak '(fossil) mammoth' [Jen. also has this for Nun]
NSY [Ras. has kilivfak 'mammoth']
CSY —
Sir —
SPI kiliɣvak 'mammoth'
NAI kil^{y}iɣvak
WCI kiliɣvak
ECI —
GRI kiliffaq 'legendary animal (with six legs)'

PE kəlu 'area behind' [cf. Atkan Aleut klu- 'go in, get into (e.g. a bay)']
AAY kəlu- 'area behind, toward wall' [posit. root]
CAY kəlu- 'area behind (house), away from river' [posit. root]
NSY kəlu 'rear wall of house [and kəlua 'inland']
CSY kəlu 'area behind (house), back from shore'
Sir kəla 'sleeping platform' [Vakh. from Rub.'s texts; for kəła 'edge' see kənlə; Em. has kəlməzuʀ- 'go to neighbor in north, go in, up from sea to shore']
SPI Qaw kilusik- 'be far inland', Imaq kəlua 'inland', kəluk 'back wall'
NAI kɨlu 'part of house or tent opposite door'
WCI kilu- 'inland' [posit. root; also 'rear wall' acc. Ras.]
ECI kilu 'back of house'
GRI kilu, kilut 'foot end of bed or sleeping platform, back wall' [Tersis has EG kiliq 'interior of house, sleeping platform', and Robbe and Menn. have kiliʀ̌iit 'direction of interior, north' for EG]

PE kəluvaʀ- 'move back' [cf. vaʀ-]
AAY kəlu<w>aʀ- 'move back, out of way'
CAY kəluvaʀ- 'move back', NI kəluvaq 'east' [= Y kəlukŋ̥aq]
NSY kələva(a)q 'west (wind)'
CSY kələvaʀ- 'go back from house or behind building'
Sir kəlvaniʀ- 'move back from shore', kəlvaqun 'at the back' [Vakh. from Rub.]
SPI kiluva(q)tiq- 'move away from river, move north', Qaw kiluvaqtaaq- 'go farther upriver, into house', [and Imaq kələvaq 'west']
NAI kiluvaq- 'travel inland' [and Nu kɨluaɣnɨq 'east (wind)']
WCI kiluvaq- 'move toward back of house'
ECI kiluvaq- 'move toward back of snow house'
GRI kiluaʀ- 'move toward back of room'

PE kəluɣ 'seam or stitch' [cf. kəlaɣ-]
AAY kəluk 'seam'
CAY kəluk 'stitch'
NSY kəlu(k) 'seam' [ANLC]
CSY kəluk 'stitch'
Sir kələx 'stitch' [Orr and Em.]
SPI kiluk 'stitch, seam'
NAI kil^{y}uk
WCI kiluk
ECI kiluk
GRI kiluk

PI kəluaq- 'rip or become undone (seam)' [cf. aʀ-]
Yup [for CSY kəlaɣ- 'come undone, unravel' see kəlaɣ-]
SPI kiluaq- 'rip a seam'
NAI kɨluaq- 'become undone (seam)'
WCI kiluaq-
ECI kiluaq-
GRI kiluaʀ- 'rip up, become undone (seam)'

PE kəmaɣluɣ '(bitter) vegetable?' [cf. kəmnaq-]
AAY —
CAY —
NSY —
CSY kəmaɣluk 'sea vegetable' [so-called sea potato;

Chap. kəmaxłuk Orr]
Sir kəmaxłux [Orr]
SPI kimaɣluk 'bitter sourdock'
NAI PH kimaɣluk 'an edible green'
WCI —
ECI —
GRI —

PY- S kəmaɣnaq 'lung' [there may be a link to kəməɣ — cf. naʀ]
AAY K kəmaɣnaq, PWS kumaɣnaq 'lung'
CAY NSU kəməɣnəq* 'lung' [and note kəmaɣnaq 'sea urchin'?]
NSY kəmaɣnaq 'lung' [L.-T. has kəmaɣnaq and kəməɣnaq]
CSY kəmaɣnaq
Sir kəməɣnəX
Inu [Imaq kəmaɣnaq, kəmanŋaq 'lung(s)' is probably a loan from Yup]

PI kəmaktuun 'handle of woman's knife' [cf. kəmaliʀ and un]
SPI —
NAI kimaktuun 'handle of skin-scraper'
WCI Car? kimaktuun [Schn. 'adg']
ECI kimattuut(i) 'handle of ulu'
GRI kimattuut 'handle of ulu'

PE kəmaliʀ '(woman's) sewing knife' [cf. kəmaktuun]
AAY —
CAY —
NSY —
CSY —
Sir kəməsəX 'woman's knife' [Em. has kəməsiX; note also k'əmәny'әž'a 'handful']
SPI kimaliq 'small sewing ulu-type knife'
NAI kimaliq
WCI kimaliq
ECI Lab kimalik [Peck]
GRI —

PI kəmə- 'request'
SPI kimi- 'request, desire' [note personal name Di Kəmənaq]
NAI PH kimi- 'request personal or ancestor's song', kiminaq- 'request things habitually (esp. s.th. unavailable)' [and kimmun 'personal song played at messenger feast'; Spencer has kimik 'messenger feast partner']
WCI —
ECI —
GRI — [for kimiɣ- 'try and persuade' see kəməɣ]

PE kəməɣ 'flesh'
AAY kəmək 'flesh' [PWS also 'body']
CAY kəmək 'flesh'
NSY kəmək 'skin' [and kəməxtuqaq 'fat(ty)', 'stout' acc. L.-T., kəmi- 'be fat(ty)']
CSY kəmək 'flesh, skin'
Sir kəməx 'skin (human)' [Vakh. also 'body, flesh']
SPI —
NAI —
WCI Net kimikiliqtuq 'is not so strong' [Ras.]
ECI —
GRI kimik '(inner) force, power, influence' [and kimiɣ- 'influence, try to persuade, make impression on' (by contam. with kəmə-?); also kimikit- 'be weak, ineffective', kimittuuq 'strong, effective, one who wants his way, keeps on trying to persuade']

PE kəməɣit- 'be skinny' [cf. ŋit-]
AAY kəmmitə- 'be skinny'
CAY kəmɣitə-
NSY kəmɣilŋuq 'skinny' [person?]
CSY kəmɣitə- 'be skinny'
Sir kəmɣilŋuX 'thin' [person?]
SPI —
NAI —
WCI —
ECI —
GRI kimiit- 'be thin, weak (e.g. coffee), of no effect (medicine)'

PI kəmnaq- 'be bitter or strong-tasting' [cf. kəmaɣluɣ and kəmni-; there may be a link to kəməɣ]
Yup — [but note that Hinz has CAY kiminarkoq 'is effective (remedy)']
SPI kimnaq-, Imaq kəmnaq- 'be bitter'
NAI kimnaq- 'have a bitter or unpleasant taste'
WCI kimnaq- 'be strong (liquor, tobacco, etc.)'
ECI —
GRI —

PE kəmni- 'become dizzy from smoke' [cf. kəmnaq-]
AAY —
CAY kəmni- 'be light-headed, drugged'
NSY —
CSY —
Sir —
SPI kimni- 'feel ill or dizzy from smoking tobacco'
NAI kimni- 'become choked by tobacco while smoking'
WCI [Pet. has Sig kimi- 'swallow smoke' — for kimni-?]
ECI —
GRI —

kəna(a)yuq 'Tanaina (Athabaskan) Indian' [from Tanaina k'enaXt'ana, inc. -Xt'ana 'dweller in' which may have been replaced with an unidentifiable Eskimo suffix]
AAY K, KP kənaayuq, PWS kənaa<y>uq 'Tanaina'
CAY BB kənayuk, kənaayuq, NI kənaayuk 'Alutiiq (Pacific Eskimo), Tanaina Indian'
NSY —
CSY —

PE kənəʀ- 'be viscous'
AAY kənəʀ- 'be thick, viscous'
CAY kənəXtə- 'slow down progress, brake'
NSY kənəʀ- 'slow down, brake, be viscous' [ANLC; Men. has kənəXqə- 'thicken' and kənəxtə- 'brake' — ANLC has kənəXtə-]
CSY —

Sir —
SPI kiniq- 'be thick, viscous, not slide easily', Imaq 'brake'
NAI kiniq- 'be thick, viscous, not slide easily'
WCI kiniq- 'be thick, thicken' [Pryde — Sig 'be hard going through (viscous snow)' acc. Met]
ECI kiniq- Lab 'be viscous' [Peck], NBI, SB 'be without water' [Saul has kiniqtaq 's.th. viscous' for Tar]
GRI kiniʀ- 'be viscous, heavy (to transport or travel through)' [and EG kiʀnima- 'be heavy']

PE kənataɣ- 'apply brake'
AAY —
CAY Nun kənataɣun 'sled brake'
NSY —
CSY —
Sir —
SPI kinatak- 'apply sled brake'
NAI kinatak-, kiŋatak- 'resist, apply brakes'
WCI —
ECI Lab kinataɣut 'brake' [Peck]
GRI NG kinataqqut 'sled strap for braking on slope' [= WG kiniqut, kinaqut; Robbe and Menn. have kiaattiC- 'slow down' for EG]

PI kənəqtaq 's.th. viscous'
SPI —
NAI kiniqtat 'dried meat kept in seal oil'
WCI kiniqtaq 'viscous mixture of snow and water'
ECI kiniqtaq 's.th. of thick consistency'
GRI —

PE kəni- 'get soaked' [note the development of NAI *əni to inʸi, parallel to that of *əłi to ilʸi under PE əłi-; compare aʀipa- for the Inu forms]
AAY K kəni- 'get soaked'
CAY kəni- 'get soaked (to soften)'
NSY kinitə- 'soak' [ANLC; and L.-T. has kiniləq 'wet spot']
CSY ➟
Sir ➟
SPI ➟
NAI ➟
WCI kinipa- 'be wet, permeated with water'
ECI kinipa- 'be soaked through' [marked as 'rare' for Wakeham Bay by Schn.]
GRI kinipašuq 'soft (as opposed to frozen or dried) food'

PE kənit- 'soak' [cf. t-[1]]
AAY kənitə- 'soak'
CAY kənitə- 'soak in order to soften'
NSY —
CSY kənitə-
Sir kənitə- [also kənitivəx 'place in lake or river where walrus skins for covering skin boats are dipped for softening' — Em.]
SPI kinit- 'soak, immerse'
NAI kinʸit-
WCI kinit- 'soak' [Pryde also 'become wet, get soaked'; Ras. has kinik- 'soften (skin)' for Net]
ECI kinit- 'soak, dampen (skin, wood, etc.)'
GRI kinit- 'soak (in order to soften)'

PE kəniʀ 'front flap of parka'
AAY —
CAY kəniq 'front part of a parka cover gathered up and used as a means of carrying things'
NSY kənəq 'lap, front of shirt' [L.-T.; and kənəʀ- 'tie up hem of kamleika' (ANLC)]
CSY kəniq 'skirt of parka or dress'
Sir kənəX
SPI ➟
NAI ➟
WCI Car kiniq 'fore- flap of caribou skin coat' [Ras.; Pryde also for Cop]
ECI kiniq 'front flap of a woman's parka'
GRI NG kiniq 'front flap of parka'

PE kəniʀmiɣ- 'carry in front of parka' [cf. miɣ-]
AAY —
CAY kənimiɣ- 'put in the gathered front of one's parka cover' [and kənimikə- 'carry that way']
NSY kənəʀmiɣ- 'carry in lap of skirt' [ANLC]
CSY —
Sir kəniʀməɣ- 'carry inside front of parka' [Em.]
SPI kiniʀvik-, kiniʀmik- 'carry in the front of one's parka'
NAI kinʸiʀvik- 'carry something in the front of one's snowshirt or apron'
WCI —
ECI kiniʀmi(k)- 'carry in front of parka or apron'
GRI kiniʀfiɣ- 'carry s.th. before one (in an apron or folded arms)'

PE kənlə 'border or edge' [compare kənluʀ]
AAY kəŋla, Kod qəŋla, AP əŋla 'border, edge'
CAY (ə)ŋla, nəlla, HBC, Nun kəŋla 'border, edge' [also məŋla — for which see miŋlə; note also əŋəłqaq, HBC kəŋəłqaq 's.th. suitable, that fits']
NSY kənlə 'border, edge'
CSY kənla 'end, source, reason, limit, boundary' [and kənlə- 'get to the heart of a matter']
Sir kənlə(ŋa) 'limit, border' [but note also kəła (as in kəłəŋa) 'edge, divinity', kəliɣa 'universe, world', kəłəsiʀ- 'give a time limit' — perhaps with contam. from kətliʀ under kətə-]
SPI killi(q) 'border, edge, horizon' [Jen. also has killinaq 'wall of house to left of door' for KI]
NAI killi(q) [Jen. has kiɣlik] 'area next to wall or floor, goal, limit, reason, source of river, border, edge', Nu killik 'heel print where s.o. drives heel into earth or snow for support'
WCI kiɣli(k), kiɣliniq, killiniq 'limit'
ECI killi [Schn. has kiɣli] 'edge, limit', killiniq 'pack ice that stops at a distance' [and killaa(q)- 'cut along one side, get somewhere on time (e.g. to catch a boat)']
GRI kiłłik [old ortho. kigdlik] 'edge, limit' [and kiłłiɣ- 'have reached a limit, so far', NG killaaq- 'follow coast']

PE kənləkə- 'reach a limit' [cf. kə-[1]]
AAY kəŋəłkə-, AP qəŋəłkə-, KP əŋəłkə-, PWS ŋəłkə- 'have reached (a limit), from then on'
CAY —
NSY [kənləqłuku 'from that time or limit']
CSY Chap kənləkə- 'have as limit'
Sir [Vakh. has kəłəkə- 'limit, surround', and kəłəR- 'go to live with, live until' from Men. and Rub.'s texts]
SPI [Imaq kələluɣu 'from that time or point']
NAI Nu kɨlliɣɨ- 'reach a certain point, limit or goal'
WCI Cop kiɣliɣi- 'go no further than - (before turning back)' [Pryde]
ECI killiɣi- 'stop at (one's goal)'
GRI kiłłiɣi- 'reach a certain point and stop or return'

PI kənləŋiq- 'melt around edge (ice around object)' [cf. ŋiR-]
SPI —
NAI kɨlliŋiqsɨt- 'begin to thaw around the shore in spring (lake, river)'
WCI —
ECI —
GRI kiłłiŋiR- 'extend a boundary, have formed around an iceberg (open water)'

PE kənluR 'wrong (thing or direction)' [cf. kənlə?]
AAY K kəŋluq, Afognak kənluq, C ənluq 'wrong side or place' [kəŋlutmən, etc. 'in wrong direction']
CAY kənlu, Nun kəŋluX 'wrong one, sin' [kəŋlutmun 'contrary to the way it should be'; kənlu- 'do s.th. other than what one is meant to']
NSY —
CSY kənluq* 'opposite, contrary' [kənluRmun 'in opposite direction, acting to the contrary']
Sir —
SPI killuq 's.th. wrong, error' [killupmun 'in the wrong way']
NAI kɨlluq* 'wrong one' [kɨllunmun 'in the wrong direction or way', Nu kɨlluaq- 'err, betray']
WCI kiɣluq 'wrong, error' [kiɣluRmut 'in wrong way']
ECI killumut 'in other direction, to the contrary' [killu(q)- 'do or tell the opposite of what one should']
GRI kiłłuq* [old ortho. kigdloq] 'wrong, contrary', NG kiɣluq 'wrong, backward' [kiłłuRmut 'the wrong or opposite way', EG kittiRmiq, kittiRmik 'left side or hand'; for kiłłuR- 'tell s.th. one shouldn't, betray', see kələɣ-]

PI kənnaq 'fool'
SPI Qaw kinnaq 'fool'
NAI kinnaq 'fool, crazy person'
WCI —
ECI —
GRI —

PI kəŋək- 'be high'
Yup [note NSY kəəxta 'Cape Prince of Wales' — from the Di]
SPI kiŋik- 'be high' [and note Di kəəɣən, kəəkti 'Cape Prince of Wales']
NAI kiŋɨk- [note Mal. kɨŋik- where ŋ rather than n^{y} shows a preceding ɨ]
WCI kiŋik- 'be high' [and Ras. has kiŋŋaq 'mountain']
ECI kiŋik- [and Ras. has kiŋŋaq 'mountain' for Igl; note also place name Kiŋŋaq 'Cape Dorset']
GRI kiŋiɣ- 'be high' [and Ges. has EG kiiniq 'summit']

PI kəpa- 'joke' [cf. kəpəlŋu- under kəpət-[2]?]
SPI —
NAI kipaaq- 'joke', kipaɣɨ- 'tease, mock'
WCI Cop kipaqan 'joking partner', kipatti- 'banter with s.o.' [Pryde]
ECI —
ECI —

PE kəpə- 'cut or sever' [cf. Atkan Aleut kmatikða-, Att kavtiɣya- 'be brittle']
AAY kəpə- 'break, snap, cut crosswise'
CAY kəpə- 'cut off, sever'
NSY kəpə- 'cut (off)' [ANLC has 'sever, cut or snap in two'; kəpuR- 'cut in half']
CSY kəpə- 'cut off'
Sir kəpit(ə)- [for kəpət(ə)-?] 'cut off' [kəpqaR- 'chop off'; Vakh. has kəpəRət(ə)- 'cut off' and, from Men.'s texts, kəpəkaqut(ə)- 'be cut off']
SPI kivi- 'cut, sever'
NAI kipɨ-
WCI kipi-
ECI kipi- 'cut (across)'
GRI kipi- 'cut (off)'

PE kəpðaR- 'cut off (several or a lot)' [cf. ðaR-]
AAY [kəpparRnəq 'place where s.th. has been cut across', Kod 'block of wood']
CAY —
NSY kəpaR- 'cut up'
CSY Chap kəpaRaXtə- 'cut off'
Sir kəpšaR- 'cut'
SPI kipšaq- 'cut hair'
NAI kivžaq- 'cut hair'
WCI kivyaq- 'cut with scissors'
ECI kiyya(q)-
GRI kiššaR- 'cut (e.g. hair)'

PE kəpliR- 'cut (off)'
AAY PWS kəpłiaR- 'give or get a haircut'
CAY kəpłiaR- 'get or give a haircut'
NSY kəpłiaR- 'cut the bangs' [ANLC]
CSY kəpłiiR- 'cut hair, get a haircut'
Sir —
SPI —
NAI kivliq-, Mal kipliq- 'cut in two'
WCI —
ECI killi(C)- 'cut with a knife, file, or axe'
GRI —

PE kəpluR- 'cut or saw in pieces' [cf. luR-]
AAY —
CAY —
NSY kəpłəR- 'saw'
CSY —

Sir —
SPI kipłuq- 'cut in several pieces'
NAI kɨvluq-, Mal kɨpluq-
WCI kivluq- 'saw across'
ECI killu(q)- 'saw, cut'
GRI kiłłuʀ- 'cut off several pieces, slice, mow'

PE kəppaʀ 'piece cut off' [cf. q under nəʀ[1] and compare quppaʀ under qupə-]
AAY kəpa 'part broken off' [base kəpə-], AP kəppaq 'piece of fish cut up and aged, section, block of wood'
CAY [kəppalək 'greater scaup']
NSY —
CSY —
Sir —
SPI kippaq 'piece cut off', Qaw 'block of cut wood'
NAI kippaq* 'cut off part' [as opposed to kivžaq 's.th. that has been cut']
WCI kippaq 'block of cut wood'
ECI kippaq 'cut object'
GRI kippaq* 'cut off piece'

PI kəppaʀik- 'cut off straight' [i.e. kəppaʀ above and p.b. kiɣ-]
SPI —
NAI —
WCI kippaʀik- 'cut straight', Cop kikkaʀiktuq 'square' [Lowe — for kippaʀiktuq?]
ECI kippaʀittuq 's.th. with straight side, square'
GRI kippaʀiɣ- 'be cut of straight, at right angles'

PE kəpət-[1] 'dye or penetrate'
AAY —
CAY kəpətə- 'dye'
NSY —
CSY [note kəpsuʀ- 'have a full stomach'? — compare the SPI below]
Sir kəpcu!ʀaX 'de-haired and red-dyed seal skin' [Orr; note also kəpɣuʀ- 'be full (of food), eat one's full'?]
SPI kivit- 'dye, stain, be drunk' [and kipšuq- 'stain'; note also kivat-, Qaw kipat- 'be dirty, stained']
NAI kipɨt- 'dye, become brewed (tea), influence s.o. so their behavior resembles one's own' [and note PH kipak 'dirt, food on face']
WCI Cop kipit-, Sig kivyuq- 'dye'
ECI —
GRI —

PE kəpət-[2] and **kəpəqə-** 'long for' [cf. ʀqə- if not kə-[1] for the second form?]
AAY ➟
CAY kəpqə- 'be in need of s.th. and seek it'
NSY ➟
CSY —
Sir [note that Em. has kəpəqšuqə(s)- 'be tormented' and kəpəqšuqałəX 'torture']
SPI kiviʀi- 'long for'
NAI kipiʀɨ- 'be anxious to do, persist', kipiʀniuq- 'yearn, long for', kipiqšuq- 'keep on trying, urge on'
WCI ➟
ECI kipit- 'long for'
GRI kipit- 'die with longing for', kipiʀi- 'yearn for'

PE kəpəlŋu- 'be frustrated or annoyed?' [cf. lŋu-]
AAY kəpəlŋu(yuɣ)- 'be charmed by s.o. one finds cute' [emot. root]
CAY —
NSY kəpəlŋunalʀia 'mischievous, annoying' [and kəpəlŋunaXqə- 'make a noise, be a nuisance']
CSY —
Sir —
SPI kivinŋuzuk- 'be bothered by noise'
NAI kipinŋusuk- 'yearn to do but, being unable to, fret, speak one's mind without realizing it might hurt others' feelings'
WCI Net kipiŋŋu- 'be annoyed' [Ras.; Dor. has 'languish'; Pryde has kipiŋŋuq- 'starve to death']
ECI NBI, SB kipiŋŋu- 'languish' [Dor.; Ras. has Igl kipiŋŋu(v)ilitaq 'pastime' and adds 's.th. for keeping one from being bored']
GRI kipiŋŋu- 'be obtrusive, importune', NG kipiŋŋuɣi- 'hate', kipiŋŋuhuk- 'be angry, furious'

PE kəp(ə)kaʀ- 'break and gnaw a bone?' [cf. kəpə- and k(k)aʀ-]
AAY kəvkuaXtə- 'snap, break apart suddenly'
CAY kəfkaXtə-
NSY —
CSY kəpkaʀ- 'snap in two'
Sir kəpqaʀ- [for kəpkaʀ-?] 'chop off' [Vakh. has kəpəkaqut(ə)- 'be cut off' from Men.'s texts]
SPI kipkaq- 'gnaw on bone', Imaq kipkaq 'backbone'
NAI kipkaq- 'eat down to the bone' [and kipkaqsiʀiilʸat 'vertebrae above the lumbar']
WCI kipkaq- 'clean bone with a knife' [Ras. has 'gnaw meat off bone' for Net; nom. = 'bone good for gnawing']
ECI kikka(q)- 'gnaw remains of meat from a bone, be cleaned of meat (bone)' [nom. kikkaq = remains of meat on bone']
GRI kikkaʀ- 'gnaw meat off (bone)' [and kikkaq EG 'bone, tusk', NG 'meat nearest bone' — Holt.]

PY kəpnəʀaʀciq 'lunar month (approx. — March/April)' [cf. kəpə-]
AAY kəpna'aXciq Kod 'January or February'
CAY kəpn̥əXciq 'February or March'
NSY kəpn̥əʀaXsiq 'April' [ANLC; Menovshchikov. has kəpn̥əʀəxsiq]
CSY —

PE kətə- 'area in front or toward the water' [cf. Aleut kitxi- 'take out (food to camp), put out (away from village, e.g. on island)'?]
AAY kətə- 'toward the open or sea, away from wall' [posit. root]
CAY kətə- 'area toward river or sea, away from wall, down from in front' [posit. root]
NSY kətə- 'area in front or toward water' [ANLC]
CSY kətə- 'area in front, toward water' [posit. root], kətə- 'go out to sea'

Sir kətm̥ənu 'toward the sea', kətm̥ənužaX 'forward' [Vakh. from Men. and Rub.]
SPI kit(i)- 'south side of King Island' [posit. root], Imaq kəta 'south'
NAI —
WCI kit(i)- 'toward sea'
ECI kit(i)- 'toward sea' [and Andersen et al. have kitaanuu- 'travel out to sea, eastward' for Lab]
GRI kit(i)- 'toward sea, west (on east coast = east)' [posit. root, thus all. kitaani, EG kilaani; for EG kinniq 'ice edge' see kitnəʀ under kit-]

PE kətðiɣ- 'be far from shore or out in front' [cf. ðiɣ-]
AAY K kətəqsəɣ-, kətsiɣ-, C kətəqsəɣ-, kətseɣ- 'be far out in front, in the ocean' [the first K and C forms are newer more productive forms]
CAY kəsiɣ-, NS kətsiɣ- 'be far away from shore'
NSY —
CSY —
Sir —
SPI —
NAI —
WCI —
ECI —
GRI kitsiɣ- 'be far to the west, out to sea'

PE kətliʀ 'one far out in front or at sea' [cf. l(l)iʀ]
AAY kətłiq, kətəqłiq 'one out in front, toward open sea' [the latter a newer productive form]
CAY kəłiq*, kətłiq* 'one toward river, farthest from wall'
NSY —
CSY kəłii 'the sea, ocean (as seen from shore)'
Sir [for kəła 'edge' see kənlə]
SPI —
NAI —
WCI Cop ki(i)lliq, Net ki'liq 'one farthest from land' [Pryde]
ECI killiq 'one furthest out to sea'
GRI kiłłiq* 'most westerly, outermost one'

PE kətvaʀ- 'move forward or toward the water' [cf. vaʀ-]
AAY kətxʷaʀ- 'move out in front'
CAY kətfaʀ- 'go toward the water or edge'
NSY —
CSY kətfaʀ- 'go out to sea, bring out, recollect'
Sir kətfaniqəstaʀ- 'go out to sea' [kətfaXtə- 'remind, present' (Em.); Vakh. has kətfaniʀ- 'go out', kətfaniʀət(ə)- 'bring out, give']
SPI —
NAI —
WCI Cop kitpahik- 'be out at sea' [also kitpaq- 'bring or move farther forward or from land' — Pryde]
ECI kippa(q)- 'go or take out from shore, be out at sea, approach edge of sleeping platform in snow house'
GRI kippaʀ- 'move toward open sea, the west, or outermost islands (in spring to hunt)'

PE kətəɣ[1] 'pulverized rock' [cf. qətək, with which there may be a relat.]
AAY —
CAY —
NSY kətək 'crushed stone or sand used to dehair sealskin' [ANLC]
CSY —
Sir —
SPI —
NAI kitik 'white rock pulverized and used in tanning' [and kitci- 'pulverize']
WCI —
ECI —
GRI —

PE kətəɣ[2] 'strap for fastening s.th.'
AAY —
CAY kətɣaq, kətxaq 'thong tied around gutskin parka and kayak coaming'
NSY kətəkaq 'hoop of drum, string or strap for the hoop of the drum'
CSY —
Sir —
SPI kitiɣaɣžaq 'string which holds drumskin to frame' [and Jen. has kitiɣaq- 'tie waterproof coat to rim around kayak hole']
NAI Nu kitiɣaq 'string which holds drumskin to frame' [verbal = 'attach drumskin to frame with string']
WCI [Cop kitikkiut 'sinew braiding to bind drum head to frame' (Pryde)]
ECI —
GRI kitik 'strap (for fastening s.th. to s.th. else)', kitiɣaʀ- 'attach waterproof jacket round kayak ring, stretch drumskin'

PE kəvəɣ- 'lift' [cf. kəvɣaʀ- and Aleut kumsa- 'rise', kumsi- 'lift']
AAY kəwəɣ-, kʷəɣ- 'lift' [and kiwək 'load' — also verbal]
CAY kəvəɣ- 'lift', kəvək 'load'
NSY kəvəɣ- 'lift' [and kəvək 'load' (ANLC)]
CSY kəvəɣ- 'lift'
Sir kəvəɣ-
SPI kuik-
NAI kivɨk-
WCI kivik- 'lift' [also kivlik- 'raise']
ECI kivik- 'lift'
GRI kiviɣ-

PI kəvɣumiaq- 'carry in arms' [cf. miɣ-]
Yup [note CSY kəvɣaaʀ- 'hold after lifting (e.g. baby)']
SPI —
NAI —
WCI [for Sig Ras. has kixumiaʀ- 'carry in arms', and Pet. kiyigumear- 'carry a child' — both for kivɣumiaq-?]
ECI kiɣɣumiaq- 'hold in one's arms'
GRI kiššumiaʀ-, kixxumiaʀ- [old ortho. kivssumiar-, kivgumiar-] 'lift or carry in one's arms' [kiššumiaq, kixxumiaq 's.th. carried in arms']

PI **kəvvak-** ' lift gradually' [cf. nəɣ-?]
SPI kivvak- 'lift repeatedly'
NAI kivvak-
WCI Sig kivvak- 'lift up (e.g. sledge or heavy rock)' [Pryde]
ECI kivva(k)- 'raise from the ground'
GRI kiffattaʀ- 'raise little by little' [and note EG kivakisaq 'bearded seal that has hauled itself up on ice' — Tersis]

PE **kəvɣaʀ** 'messenger or helper' [cf. kəvəɣ- and Aleut kamɣa-X 'feast, religious service, prayer']
AAY Kod kəɣwaʀ- 'send as a messenger' [and kəɣwaq 'apostle (bibl.)']
CAY kəvɣaq 'helper, messenger, messenger feast', kəvɣiq 'messenger feast'
NSY kəvɣaq
CSY kəvɣaq 'messenger'
Sir kixpəX 'messenger' [Vakh., who also has kiɣpəqat(ə)- 'order, send' from Men.'s texts and kiɣpəʀaʀə- 'be a servant' from Rub.]
SPI kiɣvaq 'messenger'
NAI kivɣaq 'servant, messenger' [Nu kivɣaqtuq- 'serve and wait on'; also kivɣiq- 'hold messenger feast' acc. Pryde and Mal kivɣiq- 'hold messenger feast' — Seiler]
WCI kivɣaq 'servant'
ECI kiɣɣaq 'someone sent as a representative, spokesman, one who delivers a gift, apostle, missionary, servant'
GRI kiffaq, Up kikkaq, EG kippaq, NG kiɣvaq 'servant, hired worker, common sailor' [and kiffaʀtuʀ- 'serve as kiffaq', kiffaʀtuut 'errand']

PE **kəvɣaluɣ** 'muskrat' [cf. kuluk — i.e. 'little messenger moving to and fro between water and land'?]
AAY kufxaluk 'muskrat'
CAY Eg, NSU kəvɣaluk
NSY [kəvɣaluaq 'messenger' — L.-T.]
CSY —
Sir —
SPI kiɣvaluk, W kivɣaluk
NAI kivɣaluk 'muskrat, s.o. who runs errands' [and note kipaluk 'messanger boy, handy man' — influenced by kəpa-?]
WCI kivɣaluk 'muskrat'
ECI kiɣɣaluk 'muskrat' [but kipaluk 'servant, crew member', also 'salaried worker ' in Bourq.; Ras. has Igl kivɣaluaq 'man' as a shaman's word]
GRI [kiffaluɣaq, kiffalukak 'maid, helper']

PE **kəviʀ-** 'stuff'
AAY —
CAY kəviʀ- 'plug, stuff' [kəviq 'plug, stopper']
NSY kiviitaʀ- 'get in, fit, muffle up' [ANLC]
CSY kəviʀ- 'plug, stuff' [and Chap kəviq 'kind of reindeer meat sausage'; for kəpsuʀ- 'have a full stomach' see kəpət-[1]]
Sir kəvəX 'reindeer meat sausage'
SPI kiwiq-, W kuiq- 'stuff, put in container', kivviaq- 'feed s.o. who cannot eat by himself'
NAI kiviq-, kivviaq- 'stuff'
WCI kiviq-
ECI kivvia(q)- 'stuff' [Bourq. has kiviq- 'fill sack with blubber' for Lab]
GRI kiviʀ-, kiffiaʀ- 'stuff' [and NG kivi(ss)at 'dish prepared by fermenting auklets in blubber in a sealskin sack']

PI **kəvlək-** 'be effective' [or kəmlək-; cf. kəməɣ and/or kəmnaq-?]
SPI —
NAI —
WCI Cop kivlik- 'inflict a mortal blow to' [Pryde; Ras. has kiblerqati- 'have power' for Net; for kivlik- 'raise' see kəvəɣ-]
ECI killi(C)- 'manage to get what one wanted from s.o., affect, cast a spell on' [for homonym 'cut with a knife' see kəpə-; Bourq. has Lab kiblik- 'penetrate, affect']
GRI kiłłiɣ- [old ortho. kivdlig-] 'hit (with weapon), affect'

PI **kəžə(k)-** 'hesitate'
SPI —
NAI PH kiži- 'bow, lower head', kižuq- 'shun due to taboo'
WCI [Ras. has Net kisin·ar- — for kižiŋnaq-? — '(be such as to cause) fear']
ECI kiyiliq- 'hesitate to do s.th. (from timidity)' [Bourq. has Lab kiyik- 'be timid']
GRI kišiɣ- 'hold back, lack courage', kišiɣi- 'hold back from' [and kišiiʀ- 'take courage'; Robbe and Menn. have kilippii- 'respect' for EG]

PE **ki(i)** and **ki(i)ta** 'come on (exclamation)' [the ta is presumably the anaphoric or 'out-of-field' prefix in kiitaimma below, left as an enclitic after the rest of the form has dropped; Chukchi kita 'come on' is probably a loan from Esk]
AAY kita(kii) 'go ahead'
CAY kita(k) 'here, take it please', kiiki 'hurry!', kiitaɣʷani, kiituani 'finally, thereafter' [Lantis has Nun kiita in the latter sense — compare kiitaimma below]
NSY kii 'come on, then ' [but ANLC also kiiki 'don't (to children)' — cf. kaa(kaa)]
CSY kii 'gee, oh!'
Sir kita(qun) 'well then' [Vakh. has ki 'oh!' from Rub.]
SPI kii 'let's go!' [Imaq kiiki 'exclamation of surprise']
NAI kii 'see there, told you so!', kiita 'let's go', kiika(a) 'I want more!', kiiki(i) 'more, again, keep it up!'
WCI kiilu 'again, more!' [and Pet. has kii 'let's go!']
ECI kiita 'a little, only', Lab 'the only thing is -' [influenced by kəði-?]
GRI kii, kiiʀmi 'let's go, well now', kiiʀmiaasiit 'let me just take one as usual (of s.th. offered)', NG kiiha 'it sure is, believe me, great!', kiihalluaq 'even more' [for kikkiik 'expression of disgust' see kaa(kaa)]

PI **kiitaimma** 'finally' [cf. taðim(m)a]
SPI kiitaima 'finally'
NAI kiisaimma(a)
WCI Sig kiitaimma
ECI —
GRI kiisa(mi)

PE ki(na) 'who' [cf. Aleut kiin 'who', pl. Atkan kiinkus, EA kiinkun]
AAY kinaq [rel. kinam, pl. kinkut] 'who'
CAY kina [rel. kia, kiam or kitum, pl. kinkut]
NSY kina [pl. kinkut]
CSY kina [rel. kitum, pl. kinkut]
Sir kin [written with macron over the vowel; rel. kim, pl. kinəki]
SPI kina [rel. kia, pl. kitkut] 'who'
NAI kin^{y}a 'who' [rel. kia, pl. kitkut, Mal kisut]]
WCI kina [pl. Sig, Car kitut, Cop kitkut — compare kitu below for the former]
ECI kina [rel. kia or kinaup, pl. kikkut or kinakkut] 'who'
GRI kina [rel. kia, pl. kikkut]

PE kitu 'which or who' [cf. CSY natu 'which' under natə- (na-^{2})]
AAY kitu- 'who' [sg. non-abs. base]
CAY kitu- 'who' [sg. non-abs. base] as in kitumun 'to whom?'
NSY kitu- 'who' [sg. non-abs. base — from Jen. who has kituuwa 'who, which']
CSY kitu- 'who' [sg. non-abs. base]
Sir —
SPI kitu 'which'
NAI kisu 'which' [Ras. has 'who' for Nu; note also kisutliqa 'some people' and kisuiq- 'understand']
WCI Cop kitu 'which' [Pryde]
ECI kituuna 'who is that', SB, NBI kisuk 'what' [B.- S. has 'who' for Igl]
GRI NG kihu, EG kisi(k) 'what' [Fab. also has kisu 'what' for WG; note also kisuC- 'know thoroughly', kisunniʀ- 'know one's stuff' in Oqaatsit and NG kihuʀliq 'which']

PE kiðaɣ(-) 'heat or summer'
AAY kiak 'summer', kiaɣ- 'be summer'
CAY kiak 'summer', kiaɣ- 'become summer'
NSY kiak 'summer'
CSY kiik 'summer', kiiɣ- 'be summer'
Sir —
SPI ➡
NAI kižžak- 'be lukewarm (water)', kižžatciaq 'be sunny weather' [and Jen. has kiak 'heat, hot weather']
WCI kiyyak, Cop kiak 'hot weather' [as verb = 'be hot (weather or oven), dip in boiling water (skin)']
ECI kiak 'heat (of atmosphere, house)', kiak- 'be hot (of sun or oven), lose fur through overheating (skin)' [and Lab kiyyi(k)- 'be warm'; note also kiyyavalla(q)- 'be coming to boil (water)']
GRI kiak 'heat (in air)', kiaɣ- 'be hot, boil, treat skin with hot water', kišaq 'heat', kiššaɣ- 'get warm' [and NG kiaktaq 'skin with hair removed']

PE kiððiʀ- 'sweat' [cf. liʀ-]
AAY —
CAY kiiq 'heat in air', NS kiiʀyuɣ- 'feel hot and sweaty'
NSY kiiq, kiiʀyuk 'sweat' [and as verb kiiʀyuɣ-]
CSY kiiʀaXtaʀ- 'feel feverish'
Sir —
SPI kižžiq-, Qaw kižžiuq- 'sweat'
NAI PH kižžiq- 'have a fever'
WCI Cop kiyyiqi- 'run to cool off (caribou)' [Pryde; Schn. has kiyyiyaaq- 'sweat' for 'adg']
ECI kiyyiyaq- 'be too hot', Lab kiyyiyaaq- 'sweat'
GRI —

PE kiɣan (kiɣatə) 'upper part of body' [from dem. root kiɣ- and p.b. tə; cf. kiɣayəɣ and compare uɣan 'lower part of body' from uɣ-]
AAY xan 'upper part of torso'
CAY kəxan 'upper part of torso'
NSY ɣatə 'upper part of torso'
CSY xata 'upper part of torso'
Sir kiɣəta 'back' [Vakh. has 'shoulders']
SPI kian, Imaq kiatə 'upper part of body' [also W ki(ɣ)at(i)- 'north' in Jen.]
NAI kian 'upper part of body, blouse'
WCI kiataq 'upper part of body'
ECI kiati
GRI kiat, EG kialiq 'upper part of body' [but Tersis also has kiasiq 'blouse'; compare also EG kilani 'outside' based directly on dem. stem kiɣ- and perhaps influenced by kilaani 'out to sea' under kətə-; for EG kialaa 'north' see kivan — there seems to be contam. with the root of the present base here]

PI kiapəʀuq 'short inner jacket or vest' [compare ilupəʀ(aʀ) under ilu]
SPI Qaw kiapiʀuq 'blouse'
NAI kiapiʀuq 'short inner jacket, vest'
WCI kiapiʀuq [Pryde]
ECI —
GRI —

PE kiɣayəɣ 'shoulder blade' [cf. kiɣan and compare the ending of ikuyəɣ; note that strong i after s is regular in Inu]
AAY xaayək 'shoulder blade'
CAY kəxazək
NSY ɣayə(k)
CSY xayək
Sir —
SPI kiayik, Di kiaɣiq
NAI kiasik
WCI kiasik
ECI kiasik
GRI kiasik

PY kiɣlin 'cover for knife or spear' [cf. un; the relat. — if any — to kiinailitaq under kəyinaʀ is obscure]
AAY AP kiɣlin 'cover for spearhead' [Fisher]
CAY Nun kiɣlin 'knife sheath'
NSY —
CSY —
Inu [Nu kiɣlin^y 'sharpener for scraper made of horn' from kiɣli- 'sharpen' (Jen. also Sig kiɣlin 'flint-scraper') seems to go instead with kəklaɣ]

PI kikiik- 'put arms behind back' [or kəkiik-]
SPI [Jen. has W kiɣiq- 'turn wings back, put arms back']
NAI kikiik- 'bend back'

WCI [Schn. has 'adg' kikiiqsit 'sergeant of RCMP, one who puts you in prison']
ECI kikiik- 'put arms behind one's back'
GRI kikiiʀ- 'fly with wings back (bird of prey), put one's arms back'

PI kikkuləq 'seal hole in ice'
SPI kik(k)uliq 'seal hole in ice' [Jen.]
NAI —
WCI Net kikkuliq 'exposed seal hole in spring ice' [Pryde]
ECI kikkuliq, kiɣɣuliq
GRI kikkuliq* 'seal hole in ice' [an open one in the spring in NG]

PY kilɣaq 'wilderness'
AAY K kiłxaanun 'in vain'
CAY kilɣaq 'off the beaten track, anywhere at random'
NSY —
CSY kilɣaa 'tundra, uninhabited wilderness' [and Chap. kilɣmiqə- 'go wild']
Sir [kilɣamiqə(s)- 'go wild' — Em.; from the CSY?]

PE kiliʀ- 'cut or wound' [the Yup forms appear to be from əkiliʀ- under əki, but this probably conflation, as the NSY form there shows; cf. perhaps Aleut kli- 'dip hand (into water)', Atkan also 'pierce through']
AAY kiliʀ- 'cut (accidentally)'
CAY kiliʀ- 'cut, get cut, wound'
NSY kiliʀ- 'cut, wound' [ANLC]
CSY kiliʀ- 'cut, get cut' [also nominal kiliq]
Sir kəcəʀ- 'cut, get cut' [Orr]
SPI kiliq- 'cut, wound'
NAI kilʸiq- 'cut'
WCI kiliq-
ECI kiliq-
GRI kiliʀ- 'cut (self or s.o. else)' [kiliʀniq* 'wound']

PE killiʀ 'cut' [cf. q under nəʀ[1]]
AAY kiliq 'cut'
CAY —
NSY kili [ANLC]
CSY kiliq
Sir —
SPI killiq
NAI kilʸlʸiq* 'cut, sore'
WCI killiq 'cut, wound'
ECI killiq 'wound'
GRI NG killiq 'wound' [Holt.]

PE kinəʀ- 'drip dry' [cf. EA knaðɣu- 'dry, not dressed (hide)', knali- 'leak because of dried-up seams (kayak)' cf. possibly Al Att kinula-s 'grassless spots in between grass']
AAY kinəʀ- 'dry' [and note KP, AP kinəʀyuk 'dampness']
CAY kinəʀ- 'dry'
NSY —
CSY kinəʀ-
Sir —
SPI [Jen. has KI kiniq- 'fade, wither (leaf)']
NAI kinʸiq- 'filter' [nominal = 'discharge of water from skin (dog disease)']
WCI [Car. kinaq- 'sweat, let liquid flow in small quantities' — Schn.; Jen. has Sig, Cop kiniq- 'melt away'; Pryde has Net kiniut- 'sweat', also kinaaviin 'intestines' as a shaman's word]
ECI kiniʀitsi(C)- 'leave to drip' [kiniʀitsiaq 's.th. left to drip dry', kinnaq 'liquid run off by sweating', kinaa- 'trickle', also Lab kina- 'wet, dirty (with water, sweat, etc.) — Bourq.]
GRI kiniʀ- have run off (water)' [also EG kiaavik 'anus' — i.e. 'oozing place'? — compare kini-]

PY kinəʀtaq 'dried meat or fish' [cf. ðaʀ]
AAY kinəXtaq 's.th. dried or drying (meat or fish)'
CAY kinəXtaq 'dried meat'
NSY —
CSY kinəXtaq
Inu [Qaw kiniqtaaXaq 'string of dried tom cods' — from Yup?]

PE kini- '(hold child out to) urinate' [cf. kinəʀ-?]
AAY —
CAY Nun kənə- 'hold child (esp. male) out to urinate' [ANLC; perhaps infl. bu PE kəni-]
NSY —
CSY —
Sir —
SPI kini- 'hold child out to urinate'
NAI kinʸi- 'squat down on chamber pot (or help s.o. else do so)'
WCI Cop kini- 'tickle genitals of child to make it urinate' [Pryde]
ECI kini- 'hold child out to urinate'
GRI kini-

PE kiŋu- 'area behind or after' [cf. Aleut kiŋ- 'time after, younger sibling', kiŋuliʀ- 'generation']
AAY kiŋu- 'area behind, time after' [posit. root, also as noun 'rear (of boat)']
CAY kiŋu- 'area behind, time after' [as nom. = 'rear of boat'; and note kiŋuvəq* 'descendant']
NSY kiŋu- 'area behind, time after'
CSY kiŋu- 'area behind, time after' [and as noun = 'rear of boat'; kiŋutə- 'be late']
Sir kiŋə- 'area behind, time after' [and kiŋut(ə)- 'come too late']
SPI kiŋu- 'area behind, time after' [as noun = 'rear of boat'; as verb = 'have moved on, be gone (of game)']
NAI kiŋu- 'area behind, time after' [and as noun = 'rope used to wrap buoy in conjunction with whaling harpoon'; as verb = 'be late, over' — also 'move on (animal)' acc. Pryde]
WCI kiŋu 'area behind, time after' [for posit. root as in kiŋunʀa, etc. see kiŋunəʀ below]
ECI kiŋu 'area behind, time after, back of kayak' [for posit. root as in kiŋuʀŋa, etc. see kiŋunəʀ below]
GRI kiŋu 'hind part of kayak' [for posit. root as in kiŋuʀna, etc. see kiŋunəʀ below; note also kiŋu- 'have moved on (animals from place they lived)']

PE kiŋul(l)iʀ 'last or rearmost (one)' [cf. l(l)iʀ and kiŋuqliq below; there may be two derivations here, an earlier (kiŋuliʀ) and a later one (kiŋulliʀ) — compare civul(l)iʀ under civu-]
AAY —
CAY kiŋuliq* 'one toward the back'
NSY kiŋuliq 'last one' [ANLC; Men. has kiŋuliXpiɣaq 'last']
CSY kiŋuliq(*) 'descendant' [and kiŋuliXpiɣaq 'very last']
Sir kiŋəcəX 'last'
SPI kiŋuliq
NAI kiŋulliq* 'one previous'
WCI kiŋulliq 'last' [in plural = 'descendants']
ECI kiŋulliq 'last, one coming after' [and kiŋullipaaq 'last']
GRI kiŋułłiq* 'last', kiŋuliq 'next one, follower' [and kiŋułłiiq 'hind leg', kiŋułłiaʀšuit 'the younger generation', EG kiiliʀmi 'afterward, then' (Ges.)]

PE kiŋunəʀ 'behind or after (place or time)' [cf. nəʀ[1]]
AAY kiŋunəq 'place or person one has left behind'
CAY kiŋunəq* 'home, place of origin'
NSY kiŋunəq 'descendant' [L.-T.]
CSY kiŋunəq*
Sir —
SPI kiŋuniq 'home, ancestor'
NAI kiŋuniq*, kiŋuniiq* 'descendant'
WCI kiŋuniq 'space behind, time after' [posit. root with possessor endings]
ECI kiŋuniq 'space behind, time after' [posit. root — kiŋuʀŋa, etc.]
GRI kiŋuniq* 'consequence', NG also 'back of kayak' [Holt.; as posit. root = 'space behind, time after'; note also kiŋuniʀ- 'examine s.th. that has been done', EG kiŋuniC- 'rinse (sealskin)']

PI kiŋuppiaq- 'go backward' [cf. tmi(C)aʀtə-]
Yup [note CAY kiŋutm̥uXtə- 'back up']
SPI Qaw kiŋuupiaq- 'go backward'
NAI kiŋuppiaq- 'step backward' [and kiŋuppiaŋa- 'be born feet first (baby)']
WCI kiŋuppiaquq- 'go backward', Cop kiŋuppiq- 'go in backward', kiŋupik- 'run back, pour backward' [Pryde]
ECI kiŋuppia(q)- 'go out (tide), go backward'
GRI [kiŋupuʀsuʀ-, kiŋumuʀsuʀ- 'go backward, back out'; compare sanipiɣ- 'go sideways' under canivaʀ- (cani-)]

PY kiŋuqliq 'rearmost (one)' [cf. qliʀ and compare kiŋul(l)iʀ above]
AAY kiŋuqłiq 'rear part, one following, junior'
CAY kiŋuqłiq* 'one at rear, younger sibling'
NSY —
CSY —

PI kiŋuʀaq 'back part of s.th.' [cf. p.b. qaʀ]
SPI kiŋuʀaq 'hind portion, rear, ancestor' [and kiŋuʀaani 'before his/her/its time']
NAI kiŋuʀaq, kiŋuqqaq 'back of boot, calf of leg'
WCI Cop kiŋuʀaq 'back of leg' [Pryde]
ECI kiŋuʀaq 'back of leg between calf and thigh'
GRI kiŋuʀaq 'space behind'

PE kiŋuʀaʀ- 'be too late' [cf. ʀaq-?]
AAY —
CAY kiŋuʀaXtə- 'be late'
NSY —
CSY —
Sir —
SPI kiŋuʀaq- 'miss, having come too late'
NAI kiŋuʀaq-
WCI kiŋuʀai- 'be or come too late'
ECI kiŋuʀaq- 'miss (arriving late)'
GRI kiŋuʀaʀ- 'be too late for s.th. or s.o.' [and kiŋuʀaaʀ-, kiŋuaaʀ- 'come after, be s.o.'s successor', EG kiiʀ̃aʀ- 'regret']

PI kiŋuvaaq 'descendant' [cf. kiŋuvaʀ- below]
Yup [note CAY kiŋuvəq 'descendant']
SPI —
NAI Nu kiŋuvaaq 'descendant'
WCI —
ECI kiŋuvaaq
GRI kiŋuaaq

PE kiŋuvaʀ- 'move backward' [cf. vaʀ-]
AAY K kiŋu<w>aʀ- 'fall behind, go back to rear'
CAY kiŋuvaʀ- 'go to the rear, pass down from generation to generation'
NSY —
CSY kiŋuvaq^{w}aaqun 'later on'
Sir kiŋəvaqu
SPI kiŋuvaq- 'move toward the rear'
NAI kiŋuvaq- 'move toward the rear, miss, be late for'
WCI kiŋuvaq- 'move back, be slow (clock)'
ECI kiŋuvaq- 'carry to the back, arrive too late for s.o., act too late, delay' [and kiŋuvva(C)- 'come after, return (e.g. animals after disappearing)']
GRI kiŋuaʀ- 'move back, come later, be left behind' [and note kiŋuffaɣ- 'get another of the same kind, not be the only one of a kind']

PE kiŋuɣ 'worm?'
AAY kiŋuk, Perry kiŋuk 'insect, worm' [and note imaam kiŋua 'seafood']
CAY kiŋuk, kiŋuq 'worm'
NSY kiŋuk 'shrimp' [L.-T. — ANLC also 'water chestnut']
CSY kiŋuk 'worm, maggot'
Sir kiŋəx 'worm' [Vakh. has kiŋuX, kiŋəX]
SPI kiŋuk 'tiny brine shrimp found on ice'
NAI —
WCI Sig, Car kiŋuk 'shrimp' [Ras. — who has it as 'sand-skipper' for Cop]
ECI kiŋuk 'sand flea' [actually a shrimp acc. Saul]
GRI kiŋuk 'sand flea, shrimp'

PE kiŋyaʀ- 'look back' [there may be a link to kiŋu- and yaʀ(tuʀ)-]
AAY kiŋyaʀ- 'look back, turn and look'

CAY kiŋyaʀ- 'look back while moving'
NSY kinyaqu- 'look back'
CSY —
Sir —
SPI kiŋiaq- 'turn and look back'
NAI kiŋiaq- 'look back'
WCI kiŋiaq-
ECI —
GRI —

PE kiput- 'exchange or reverse'
AAY kiputə- Kod 'reverse, switch direction', AP 'buy', C 'return (home)' [KP rarely also 'reverse'; C kiputm̥ən 'back (home)']
CAY kiputə- 'buy', NSU 'exchange places'
NSY kiputə- 'exchange places' [ANLC]
CSY [kipuʀmun 'the other way'] ➟
Sir ➟
SPI kivut- 'to pass without knowing'
NAI kiput- 'cause to exchange places' [kipuyuŋa- 'not understand, be unable to distinguish things']
WCI kipuk- 'change places, sleep during day and be up during the night' [also kipuŋa- in the latter sense; Ras. has Sig kipuuri- 'take turns', and Pet. has kipuktuaq 'trader', kipusiq- 'replace'; Pryde has Cop, Net kipuuti- 'change (with each other)']
ECI kipuC- 'exchange, change places or marriage partners, shuffle cards' [and kipuŋa- 'put the other way round'; Bourq. has Lab kipuyuŋa- 'make lots of mistakes in reciting, stammer']
GRI [note kipu-, kiput- 'become warped', kipuŋa- 'be cut off crooked, not at right- angles', which may be by contam. with kəpə-]

PE kipułəɣ- 'exchange places or alternate' [cf. ləɣ-]
AAY kipułəxtə- 'take s.o.'s place'
CAY kipułəxtə- 'exchange places with' [and kipułxutə- 'miss, going in opposite direction, exchange unintentionally']
NSY —
CSY kipułəxtə- 'alternate, take turns, pass by (missing s.o.)'
Sir kipəłXit(ə)- 'alternate' [Em. has kipəłxət(ə)- 'go past or toward one another, carry past'; Vakh. has kipəłxinaqaʀələməŋ 'alternatingly']
SPI kivulik- 'miss, not see s.o.'
NAI —
WCI —
ECI —
GRI —

PE kit- 'sink' [cf. kitŋu- and Aleut kit- 'drain out, go down (tide)' and kiðuɣ- 'sink, become submerged']
AAY kittə- 'sink, set (of celestial body)'
CAY kittə- 'sink, fall into water, drown'
NSY kitə- 'sink, drown'
CSY —
Sir kit(ə)- 'drown' [but also kət(ə)- 'drop, fall' — influenced by kətə-?; Vakh. has kisi- 'sink']
SPI kit- 'sink, go out of memory'
NAI PH kit- 'settle (water)' [and kinʸɨtciq-, PH kitciaq- 'let settle (water)' — the former influenced by kinəʀ-]
WCI [Cop kitqaun 'sinker (stone)'; Jen. also has kitqaq- 'sink in water (stone)']
ECI [note kitsu(k)- 'dive when hit (seal)']
GRI kit- 'subside, precipitate (particles in water)' [and kitsima-, kitsuma- 'lie low in water (boat)', kitsuɣ- 'cannot float', kitsiʀ- 'let settle (water)', kitsit- 'have settled to bottom, have precipitated']

PE kicaʀ 'anchor' [cf. ðaʀ?]
AAY kicaq 'anchor'
CAY kicaq
NSY kisaq
CSY —
Sir kisəX [Vakh. also kisaX] 'stone', kisəʀəta 'anchor'
SPI kizaq 'anchor'
NAI kisaq
WCI kisaq
ECI kisaq
GRI kisaq

PE kitnəʀ 'sediment' [cf. nəʀ[1] — some Inu forms here seem to have contam. from kinəʀ-]
AAY [note kittanəq 's.th. sunk to bottom and stuck there']
CAY kiznəq*, HBC kiynəq* 's.th. settled at bottom of liquid'
NSY —
CSY —
Sir —
SPI kinniq 'sediment, dregs', Qaw kinnaqłuk 'dregs'
NAI [kinʸalluq, PH kinʸnʸaʀluk 'dregs']
WCI [Cop kinŋaaq 'dregs, liquid left at bottom of container' (Pryde)]
ECI — [for kinnaq 'liquid run off by sweating' see kinəʀ-]
GRI kinniq*, kinnikut, kiŋŋaniq* 'precipitate, dregs' [and note EG kinniq 'ice edge' — Robbe and Menn. have it as '(floating) pack ice']

PE kitmiɣ 'heel' [cf. p.b. miɣ- as also in itəɣmiɣ- 'kick' under itəɣ, and Aleut kita-X 'foot, hind flipper', Atkan and Att also 'root (of tooth)', as verb = 'kick'; there has been considerable entanglement with PE kitŋiɣ here]
AAY kitŋiq, kitŋik 'heel', PWS 'trigger of deadfall trap' [and KP kitŋiɣ- 'kick in one's grave (said to be heard just before one dies)']
CAY kitŋik 'heel' [and kitŋiɣ- 'kick with heel']
NSY kitŋik 'heel' [ANLC; Men. has kitŋiq]
CSY kətŋik 'heel' [and kətŋiɣ- 'kick forward with bottom of heel']
Sir kitŋəx 'heel' [Vakh.; Men. has kitŋ̥əX; kətqəX on his comp. list must be a misspelling]
SPI kikmik, Qaw kipmik 'heel'
NAI kimmik, Nu kipmik, Mal kikmik 'heel' [and kimmik- 'hit with heel']
WCI Sig kimmik, Cop kiŋmik 'heel' [kimmiaq- 'hit with heel']
ECI kimmik, NBI kiŋmik 'heel'
GRI kimmik 'heel' [old ortho. kingmik, though NG has kimmik]

PE kitmilquR 'heel-like appendage?' [cf. quR]
AAY —
CAY kitŋiłquq 'heel of sled runner'
NSY —
CSY —
Sir —
SPI —
NAI kimmitquq 'heel skin, top muscle of heel', PH kimmitquun 'heel tendon'
WCI Cop kiŋmitquq 'heel, bone heel' [Pryde]
ECI kimmiquaq 'heel of animal paw', kimmiqulluɣuti 'heel tendon'
GRI kimmiqquq 'prong or antler (projecting backward)'

PE kitŋiɣ 'lowbush cranberry' [cf. EA kiðŋa-X, Atkan kiŋða-X, Att kiɣya-X 'crowberry bush, berry patch, moss, soft grass', possibly with ðŋ from *tŋ acc. Berg.; compare, however, PE kitmiɣ, with which there has been contamination — *tŋ does not seem to have been a very stable PE cluster (compare atŋiR-)]
AAY —
CAY kitŋik 'lowbush cranberry'
NSY —
CSY kiitm̥ik 'lowbush cranberry'
Sir kitm̥əx 'lowbush cranberry'
SPI kikmik, Qaw kipmik
NAI kimmiŋn^{y}aq, Mal kikmik 'lowbush cranberry' [the former with p.b. naR]
WCI kimmiŋnaq 'cranberry'
ECI kimminaq
GRI kimmiRnaq

PE kitŋu- 'capsize' [cf. kit-]
AAY kitŋu- 'capsize'
CAY kitŋu-
NSY —
CSY —
Sir —
SPI kitŋu-, Qaw kipmu-
NAI kin^{y}ŋu-, Nu kikŋu- 'capsize (boat), turn over (sledge)'
WCI Sig [Met.], Car [Schn.] kiŋu-, Cop kinŋut(i)- [transitive], Net [Ras.] kiŋŋu- 'capsize' [Pryde has Cop kinŋu-, Net ki'ŋu-]
ECI Iti kiŋu- 'capsize'
GRI kiŋŋu-

PY kituR- 'pass'
AAY kituR- 'pass'
CAY kituR-
NSY kituR-
CSY kituR-

PE ki(C)u- 'answer' [cf. Aleut Atkan, EA Nikolski kiðu- 'help']
AAY kiu- 'answer'
CAY kiu-
NSY kiiw-
CSY kiimsiR- 'answer' [note ki(C)umɣa- below]
Sir —
SPI kiu-
NAI ki<γ>u- 'answer' [and kiɣɣun 'answer']
WCI kiu-, kiɣu- 'answer' [compare the ɣ in kiɣuRyak under ki(C)uRyaR; kiɣɣun 'answer']
ECI kiu- 'answer' [and Bourq. has Lab kiɣusi-]
GRI [kiuR- 'say yes to, admit to s.th.']

PE ki(C)umɣa- or **ki(C)umRa-** 'talk back all the time' [cf. a-?]
AAY kiumma- 'talk back' [i.e. kium<R>a- or kium<γ>a-, depending on dialect]
CAY kiumRa- 'talk back'
NSY —
CSY —
Sir —
SPI kiuRmaq- 'talk back, answer argumentatively'
NAI kiuma-, kiumŋa- 'keep talking back'
WCI —
ECI kiuma- 'answer at length'
GRI —

PE ki(C)uRyaR 'aurora borealis' [cf. yaR and perhaps ki(C)u-, referring to the alleged response of the aurora to calling?; compare EA yurya-n 'aurora', with loss of initial Cə, presumably an early borrowing from Eskimo]
AAY Kod, C kiuRyat, AP, KP qiuRyat 'aurora' [the q- initial forms here and in CAY are presumably influenced by PY qi(C)u(R)- 'be blue']
CAY qiuRyaq, qiuRyak, NS kiuRyaq, kiuRyak 'aurora' [Ras. has kigorv'jat for Nun]
NSY kiiR^{w}yak 'aurora'
CSY kiiR^{w}yaq
Sir kiiR^{w}yax [Orr; perhaps from the CSY]
SPI kiuRyaq, Qaw kiuRuya 'aurora'
NAI kiuRuya, Mal kiuRuyat, Nu, PH kiɣuRuya 'aurora' [also kiŋuyakkii]
WCI Cop kiɣuRyak, Sig kiuRyait [Lowe], Net kiuRuyaq [Pryde] 'aurora'
ECI —
GRI —

PE kivaknaR 'wind from a certain direction' [from dem. root kiv- and p.b. knaR; cf. kivan and see Fortescue 1988 for the different directional senses here]
AAY [note KP kiakəq, Kod kiuxkəq 'northeast' — Larionov for the latter]
CAY kiuxkənak '(north)east'
NSY —
CSY —
Sir —
SPI kiwaknaq 'west wind'
NAI kivaknaq Mal 'east wind', Nu 'wind blowing downstream', PH kivaŋnaq- 'blow (northeast wind)'
WCI Car B. Lake kivaŋnaq 'south wind' [Pryde]
ECI —
GRI [NWG kiɣaŋŋaq, Up kiaŋŋaq 'south wind' is from dem. root kiɣ-, but this has fallen together with kiv- in WG]

PE kivan (kivatə) 'area toward back or inside' [from dem. root kiv- and p.b. tə; cf. kivaknaʀ and see Fortescue 1988 for the various local senses here]
AAY —
CAY kian 'back of sleeping platform' [Barnum; and Lantis has 'back side of house' for Nun]
NSY —
CSY Chap kiwan 'rear of boat, house' [note that dem. kiw- refers to the west here]
Sir ➟
SPI kiwan 'west side of King Island'
NAI kivat(i) 'east side' [Wainwright 'north east'], kivan 'righthand wall when entering house', Wainwright 'place behind stove' [Jen.]
WCI kivat(i) Cop, Sig 'east', Car 'south'
ECI —
GRI kuyat(i) 'south' [= EG kialaa 'north' (in Robbe and Menn. also kialiʀ̃iit 'wind side, east'), which seems to have been influenced by derivatives of kiɣan, q.v. — Robbe and Dor. have kialiʀ̃aa 'wind side'; Tersis has EG kialiŋa 'windward side', also kujataa 'south part of Greenland' from the WG]

PE kival(l)iʀ 'one farthest to the back' [cf. l(l)iʀ; probably with an earlier and a later parallel derivation, the former (kivaliʀ) with the bare dem. root — compare civul(l)iʀ under civu-]
AAY [K, PWS kialiʀnəq 'area toward inside or northeast']
CAY —
NSY —
CSY —
Sir kivəciX 'behind' [Vakh. from Rub.'s texts]
SPI kiwaliq 'southwest'
NAI PH kivalliq 'front room of house'
WCI kivallit 'people in the south' [also for Cop acc. Ras., but Met. has 'people living at edge of sea']
ECI —
GRI kuyałłiq* 'southernmost one', kuyaliq 'southernmost area or part'

PE kivə- 'sink or settle' [cf. Aleut kim- 'sink, go down']
AAY AP kiwə- 'slip down (pants)'
CAY kivə- 'slip down (of one's pants), Nun 'sink part way (boat)', HBC also 'be depressed'
NSY kivə- 'ride low in water (heavily laden vessel)' [ANLC]
CSY kiivə- 'settle (child after crying, tub draining, sediment sinking, etc.)'
Sir —
SPI —
NAI kivi- 'sink' [also kiviqi- 'lower pants']
WCI kivi-
ECI kivi-
GRI kivi- 'sink' [and kiviŋa- 'slip down (pants), walk with pants around heels']

PY- S kiyaʀ- 'look around'
AAY kiaXtə- 'look around'
CAY kiaXtə-, HBC kiyaXtə- 'look around, scan'
NSY kiyaXtə- 'rest, take it easy' [ANLC; Men. has kiyaXsałəq 'leisure']
CSY kiyaXtə- 'be, reside, exist', kiyaʀutə- 'provide for, support' [and kiyaʀun 'pupil of eye']
Sir kiyaXt(ə)- 'search, hunt'

kuanniq 'angelica?' [presumed loan from Old Norse hvonn, pl. hvanniʀ 'angelica']
SPI —
NAI —
WCI —
ECI kuanniq 'type of edible seaweed' [in this sense in all of eastern Canada from Aivilik to Labrador, where Erdmann/Peck have it meaning 'sea grass eaten by Eskimos' — it is apparently reminiscent in form to angelica; only Bourquin has it as 'angelica', but this may be due to a confusion, since Kleinschmidt, with whom he was in communication, states that the word means 'edible seaweed' in Lab]
GRI kuanniq 'angelica' [Fab. has kuannek, kvannek; note that EG has a different name, quaʀ̃alik, for this plant, for which see quaʀaq]

PE kuccuʀ 'resin or gum' [cf. kutə]
AAY [KP kucəŋkaq, PWS qucəŋkaq 'spruce gum']
CAY Y, LI, NS kuccuq 'chewing gum'
NSY —
CSY —
Sir —
SPI kussuq 'resin, gum, chewing gum'
NAI kutcuq* 'resin, spruce gum'
WCI Sig kutsuq
ECI kutsuq 'resin, gum' [and Lab kutsuq- 'tar (a boat)' — Bourq.]
GRI kutsuk 'resin, gum'

PE kucukaʀ 'icicle' [cf. kutə and kuccuʀ]
AAY [note PWS kucuq 'nosepin (piece of bone worn through hole in septum)']
CAY kucukn̥aq 'icicle'
NSY kusuʀaq 'icicle'
CSY kusukaq 'glaciated spot where water has dripped and frozen on the ground'
Sir kusukaX, pl. kusukaʀiy [Orr]
SPI kuzuɣaq 'icicle'
NAI [kusuluɣaq, Nu kutuluɣaq 'icicle', kusiqaq 'place where melting snow drips']
WCI kusuɣaq 'icicle'
ECI kusuɣaq
GRI kusuɣaq

PE kuðə(ɣ)- 'feel protective or compassionate' [compare aluturʀ- for the semantics]
AAY —
CAY kuzɣu(yuɣ)- 'feel compassion for s.o.', kuzɣu(ʀ)-, HBC kuyɣuʀ- 'be protective (bird toward its young)' [and kuzɣua- 'help'; all with (C)uʀ-?]
NSY —
CSY —
Sir —

SPI —
NAI —
WCI —
ECI —
GRI kuši- 'feel pity toward' [Top], NG kuhihiq 's.o. one benefits from' [Fab. has kuši- 'become or make better (e.g. sick person)', also kužaɣ- 'become better (person or weather)' — compare modern kušaɣi- 'like, think beautiful', kušanaʀ- 'be beautiful']

PE kuðəɣ 'river' [there may be a relat. to kuvə-]
AAY kuik 'river'
CAY kuik
NSY kuik [also, L.-T. has kušiałəq 'swimming']
CSY kiik^{w}
Sir kucəx [Vakh. also kužax]
SPI ku<ž>uk, pl. kužɣit 'river' [and kuzžiq- 'flow, run (water)']
NAI ku<ž>uk, pl. kužɣit or kuuɣit 'river' [and kužži- 'make a stream (water)']
WCI Sig kuuk, Cop kuuɣaq 'river' [Cop kuuk = 'stream']
ECI kuuk 'river' [verbal = 'flow']
GRI kuuk 'river' [and kuuɣ- 'flow', EG kuu- 'sweat']

PY kuiɣət a(a)niit or **kuiɣət a(a)na(C)it** 'lunar month (approx. = Feb., Apr. or May)' [cf. a(a)na]
AAY Kod kuiɣət aaniit 'February — March'
CAY Nun kuiɣət aaniit 'February'
NSY kuiɣət a(a)ni(i)t 'May'
CSY [kiiɣəm aʀnaa 'May']

PI kužžinəq 'stream (bed)' [cf. li-^{1} and nəʀ^{1}]
SPI kužžiniq 'stream bed'
NAI kužžin^{y}ɨq* 'sea ice melted by a stream during break-up'
WCI Sig kuyyiniq 'stream'
ECI Lab kuyyinik 'dried up river bed' [Peck]
GRI kuššiniq* [old ortho. kugssineq] '(dry) river bed'

PE kuðuccɪʀ 'pelvis' [cf. Aleut kuðu-X 'leg, shank']
AAY ➟
CAY [note kucuquq 'pelvis' with quʀ] ➟
NSY kuusiq 'hip, back part of carcass' [ANLC; Jen. has qussiq; for quuyiq 'thighbone' see qu(C)əyiɣ]
CSY ➟
Sir kusəX 'pelvis' [Orr]
SPI kuusik, Imaq kuusiq 'pelvis' [for W kui 'thigh' in Jen. goes probably see qu(C)ək]
NAI kuutciq* 'bone containing hip socket' [and du. kuutciik 'pelvic bones (half of pelvic girdle)']
WCI Sig kuutsiq 'hipbone' [Met.; Lowe has kuutsik]
ECI kuutsiq 'hipbone'
GRI kuutsiq* 'socket of hip joint', NG kuutsiik 'pelvis'

PE kuðuccinəʀ 'pelvic bones or hips' [cf. li-^{1} and nəʀ^{1}?]
AAY AP kuucəṇaq, KP kuucəsṇiik 'pelvic bones'
CAY kuucṇaq 'hips'
NSY —
CSY kuusṇəq* 'pelvic bones (person or animal)' [usually dual about a person's]
Sir —
SPI kuusiniq 'pelvic area'
NAI kuutcin^{y}aaq 'pelvic bones', kuutcin^{y}ɨq* 'rump'
WCI —
ECI kuutsinaaq 'pelvis', kuutsiniq 'lumbar vertebra'
GRI kutsiniq* 'lumbar vertebra'

PY ku(C)imə- 'swim' [cf. kuvə- and kuðəɣ — this base may reflect puɣ(ə)mə(t)- under puɣə- with contam. from the latter]
AAY kuimaʀ- 'swim'
CAY kuimə- 'swim', kuimaʀ- 'be swimming'
NSY kuimə-, kuimaʀ-
CSY —

kuiŋiq 'pipe' [loan from Chukchi koyŋən 'pipe']
AAY —
CAY kuiŋiq, kuiniq 'tobacco pipe' [K 'cigarette or other smoking device'; kuiŋiʀ-, kuiniʀ- 'smoke']
NSY koyŋə [L.-T.]
CSY kuyŋa [base kuyŋə]
Sir kuyŋa, pl. kuyŋiy [Orr]
SPI kuiŋiq [W kuiniq acc. Jen.] 'pipe' [also verbal 'smoke']
NAI kuiŋiq 'pipe' [also verbal]
WCI kuiniq
ECI —
GRI —

PE kukðaɣ- 'be clumsy or unsure of oneself' [cf. kuk(k)u(ʀ)(-)]
AAY [note kuksuɣ- 'be off balance']
CAY Nun kuksaɣa- 'be bashful' [and note kuksuɣ-, kukiiŋaʀ- 'rock from side to side']
NSY —
CSY kukšak 'clumsy, unreliable person' [also kukšaɣnaʀ- 'be difficult' — Orr]
Sir [Em. has kukšaɣnaʀ- 'be difficult, harden oneself physically']
SPI —
NAI kukšasuk- 'be unsure, fail to do, do hesitatingly' [and Ras. has kugshavak 'woodpecker']
WCI Car kuxxa- 'be astonished, scared' [Schn. 'adg'; there appears to be contam. with qukəɣə-]
ECI kutsasuk- 'be frustrated, fearing to do s.th.' [Bourq. has 'be serious, worried about future' for Lab but Peck 'be anxious because of fear of doing s.th. wrong'; note also kutsanaq- 'cause anxiety', kutsagi- 'be irritably worried about', Iti kutsak- 'give a start']
GRI kuššasuɣ- [old ortho. kugsasug- in Ordb.] 'think s.th. too little', kuššaɣi- 'be charry with, not believe one can do it' [Fab. has kugšagi- 'be uncertain (about hitting s.th.)'; for kussaɣ-, kussiɣ- 'economize with s.th.' see kupci-, with which there could be contam. here]

PE kukəɣ 'pointed end of s.th.?' [cf. kukiɣ, at least for source of contam.]
AAY [Lis. has kukəɣluɣaq 'arrowhead']
CAY kukxaq 'large barbed harpoon used for seal hunting' [Barnum has 'ivory arrowhead']
NSY —
CSY —
Sir —
SPI —
NAI kukužvak 'arrowhead' [Nu kukiɣžalik 'flint arrowhead' — same as WCI kukummak acc. Pryde; Mal kukau 'arrow point' (Seiler), and PH kukuvlak 'spotted stone used for head of sealing club' — influenced by kukuɣ?]
WCI Net kukukpaaq 'peak of hood', Cop kukupquaq 'pointed end of walking stick' [Pryde, who also has Cop kukuk- 'bite (insect)' and kukummak 'blunt arrow to stun bird']
ECI kukuppaq 'peak of hood' [Lab also kukuk 'hood of garment' — Andersen et al.]
GRI —

PE kukəɣ- and **kukuɣ-** 'light a fire'
AAY kukək 'flint' [Rez.]
CAY kukəɣ- 'ignite readily, get singed'
NSY —
CSY kukəxtə- 'shine light (on s.th.)'
Sir —
SPI kuɣuk- 'make a fire'
NAI kukuk- 'light or build a fire', PH 'light a stove'
WCI kukuk-
ECI [Peck has Lab kuk(k)uk- 'discharge a cannon with a firebrand']
GRI kukuɣ- 'light (a fire, etc.)'

PE kukiɣ 'claw or nail'
AAY —
CAY K kukikcak 'glass- like stone' [for the p.b. see under kšak]
NSY kukikšak 'greenish stone used as chisel for ivory carving, stone or silicon knife' [ANLC]
CSY kukikšak 'grapnel hook'
Sir —
SPI kuɣik 'fingernail, toenail, claw, hoof'
NAI kukik 'hoof, fingernail' [also 'stone end of scraper' — contam. with kukəɣ?]
WCI kukik 'nail, claw, barb' [also 'head of caribou lance' and as verb 'steal' acc. Pryde for Cop; note also Car? kukiksaq 'flintstone, silex' — Schn. 'adg']
ECI kukik 'nail, claw'
GRI kukik

PY kukiyvak or **kukuyvak** 'glaucous gull' [cf. kukəɣ and vaɣ?]
AAY AP kukiswak 'glaucous gull'
CAY kukuzvak, Y kukizvak
NSY —
CSY —

PE kuk(k)u(ʀ)(-) 'act clumsily or like a baby' [cf. kukðaɣ-, also Aleut kuka-X 'grandmother'?]
AAY KP kukuq 'baby' [note kukuɣ- 'lie on one side']
CAY [note LI kuukuq 'younger brother', K kukkuq 'animal (child's word)']
NSY —
CSY [note kukumtuʀ- 'fear being left out, try to get to feed before the others'?]
Sir —
SPI —
NAI —
WCI [Cop H. Island kukuullit- 'giggle, say silly things (girls)' (Pryde); and note Sig kukapqu(ŋa)- 'act clumsily, not manage s.th., give up', and Car? kukuʀaq- 'belch' — Schn. 'adg'?]
ECI —
GRI kukku-, NG kukkuk- 'make a mistake', EG kuukuq 'baby, pet' [also kukkutuuq 'bungler, clumsy fellow']

PE kukuɣ '(s.th.) spotted'
AAY AP kukuk 'spot or strip of dark color'
CAY kukupak 'spot, freckle'
NSY kukupak 'Pribilof harbor seal' [Jen.], 'young seal' [L.-T.], 'spotted seal *(phoca largha)*' [ANLC; also kukumłəʀaq 'spotted thing (esp. seal)' (L.-T.)]
CSY kukupak 'ring seal'
Sir kukupax 'spotted seal'
SPI kuɣuʀik- 'be spotted, esp. of seal'
NAI — [for PH kukuvlak 'spotted stone used for head of sealing club' see kukəɣ]
WCI Sig kukuvainnat 'red spots on face' [and Car? kukuŋayuq 's.o. with a frost-bite spot' acc. Schn.; Pryde has Cop kukuvalak 'blotch' and kukuvalaattuq 'spotted, freckled']
ECI —
GRI —

PE kukuku(C)aʀ 'snipe' [probably onomatopoeic — but compare Aleut kukutuX 'young eider duck']
AAP AP, KP kukukuaq 'snipe'
CAY kukukuaq 'common snipe, dowitcher'
NSY —
CSY —
Sir — [for kuykunaX 'fledling' see kukumyaʀ-]
SPI —
NAI kuukukiaq 'common snipe'
WCI —
ECI —
GRI [note kuukuyuk 'young eider duck', also 'snail']

PY kukumyaʀ- 'whistle'
AAY kukumyaaʀ-, C sukumyaʀ-, sukumyaaʀ- 'whistle' [forms with s by contamination with culuɣ-?]
CAY kukumyaʀaʀ(aʀ)-, NS kukumsiʀ- 'whistle'
NSY —
CSY kukumyałqi-
Sir — [note kuykucəʀaʀ- 'whistle' (also nominal) and kuykunaX 'fledgling' — but cf. also kukuku(C)aʀ for the latter]
Inu [note EG kukkuyuuʀ- acc. Ras. and Cop kuummiuhaaq- acc. Lowe 'whistle' — Pryde has nom. kukummiuhaut]

PI kulavak 'caribou cow' [cf. vaɣ]
Yup — [but Holt. has Hooper Bay kula(a)vak 'caribou'; CAY kuluvak 'cow' is a Russian loan, probably blended with this base, thus explaining the final k]
SPI W kulavak 'caribou cow one year old' [Ras.]
NAI kulavak 'caribou cow', Nu 'ewe'
WCI kulavak 'caribou cow' [note B. Lake kula- 'be fat (winter caribou)' — Schn.]
ECI [Peck has kul(l)avak 'reindeer with white spot on side' for Lab]
GRI kulavak 'caribou cow'

PE kumaɣ 'louse' [cf. kuməɣ-?]
AAY ➟
CAY Eg, NSU kumak 'louse'
NSY kumak
CSY kumak
Sir kuməx
SPI Qaw kumak
NAI kumak
WCI kumak
ECI kumak
GRI kumak

PY kumakiʀ- 'delouse' [cf. kðaʀ and ŋiʀ-]
AAY AP kumakiʀ- 'delouse'
CAY kumakiʀ- 'look for lice'
NSY kumakiʀ- [L.-T.]
CSY kumakiʀ- 'delouse'

PI kumaʀuaq 'shamanic word for caribou' [cf. Inu ʀuaq 's.th. like' under ŋ(ŋ)uðaʀ; refers supposedly to the way caribou look to the shaman in flight above the land]
SPI —
NAI [Boas has qumaxoak as a shaman's word for 'caribou'; note Nu kumakšalliq 'reindeer, caribou covered with lice in spring', also kunaʀuu- 'be full of worms'; Pryde also gives kumaʀuq 'kind of freshwater worm or larva']
WCI Net kumaʀuaq 'caribou (shaman's word)' [Ras., who explains it as meaning literally 'big louse (of the land)', but the p.b. is not ðuɣaʀ (GRI šuaq); Pryde also has Car B. Lake kumaʀuq 'tiny fish or larva occurring in large numbers, food for fish']
ECI [kumaʀuaq 'tiny (land) insect' (in contrast to qumaʀuaq 'insect in river' under quma(ʀ)), in Igl shaman's language 'caribou' acc. Ras.]
GRI kumaʀuaq 'caribou (shaman's word)' [Fab.]

PE kuməɣ- 'scratch'
AAY [note kuməɣ- K, KP 'become angry', PWS 'scold, chide'?]
CAY kuməɣ- 'scratch (to relieve itch)'
NSY kuməɣ-
CSY kuməɣ-
Sir kuməɣ-
SPI —
NAI kumɨk- 'scratch' [and kumiɣaq- 'rake']
WCI kumik-
ECI kumik-
GRI kumiɣ- 'scratch' [and kumiɣaʀ- 'rake, scrub, scrape (soil)', NG kumik-, Up kumii- 'scrub']

PE kumɣun 'scratching implement' [cf. un]
AAY —
CAY —
NSY kumɣun 'back-scratcher'
CSY kuumɣun 'plant used for scouring cooking utensils'
Sir —
SPI Qaw kumiɣžaun 'ice scratcher for seals'
NAI kumŋun, Nu kumŋutɨt 'ice scratcher or the like'
WCI Cop, Car kumŋun 'back- scratcher' [Pryde]
ECI —
GRI kuŋŋut, kumiut 'scratching stick, louse rake' [and NG kumiutit 'scrubbing brush']

PE kumkaʀ 'food caught between teeth' [cf. Atkan Aleut kukmi-X 'chunk, lump', kukmila- 'be lumpy (flour or soup)'; Inu kupki(q) is probably a back-formation involving p.b. liʀ-]
AAY kumki- 'have food caught between one's teeth' [and kumkiaq, kumkiq 'food thus caught']
CAY kumkaʀ- 'have food stuck in teeth'
NSY kumkaq 'food particle between teeth' [L.-T.]
CSY kumkəɬəʀaq, kəmkəɬəʀaq
Sir kumkəɬəʀaX 'food particle between teeth' [Orr], kumkəʀži- 'clean teeth' [Em.]
SPI kukkiq 'food caught in teeth'
NAI kupki 'piece of s.th. stuck between teeth'
WCI [Pet. has Sig kupki 'remains of food between teeth']
ECI kukkiq 'piece of food caught between teeth' [verbal = 'get food between teeth'; Peck has Lab kupki- 'have s.th. between one's teeth']
GRI kukkaq 's.th. stuck between teeth' [and kukkaʀ- 'get s.th. caught between teeth']

PE kumka(C)ili- 'pick teeth' [cf. ŋit- and compare also ŋilitaʀ]
AAY [note kumkiutaq 'toothpick']
CAY kumkaili- 'pick teeth' [kumkailin, kumkailitaq, kumkailisuun 'toothpick']
NSY kumkiali- 'pick teeth' [Em.]
CSY kumkiili- 'pick teeth' [kumkiilin, kumkiilisiq 'toothpick']
Sir —
SPI kukkili- 'pick teeth' [kukkilin, kukkilitiq 'toothpick']
NAI kupkilʸi- 'pick teeth' [kupkilʸinʸ 'toothpick']
WCI kupkili-, kukkili- 'pick teeth' [Sig kupkilin 'toothpick' — Lowe]
ECI Iti kukkiliuti 'tooth pick' [but Aiv kukkiliti 'pin']
GRI kukkili- 'pick teeth' [kukkilit 'safety pin', kukkaayaat 'toothpick']

PY- S kumla- 'freeze'
AAY K kumla- 'freeze', C kumlatə- 'freeze (trans.), get frozen' [kumlanəq 'frozen food or part']
CAY kumla 'coldness, cold thing', kumlatə- 'be cold'

[kumlanəq* 'frozen fish']
NSY kumla- 'freeze' [ANLC; Men. has kumlatə- 'freeze', kumlałəq 'coldness', kumlaŋalʀia 'frozen']
CSY kumlatə- 'freeze', kumlama- 'be frozen' [kumlanəq* 'frozen part, permafrost']
Sir kumlə- 'freeze' [also kuməłtəX 'frozen meat']

PE kumlu 'thumb' [cf. lu(ʀ)]
AAY K kumluq 'thumb'
CAY kumluq
NSY kumlu
CSY kumlu
Sir kumla
SPI kuvlu
NAI kuvlu
WCI kuvlu
ECI kullu
GRI kułłuq

PI kunik- 'sniff or touch noses'
SPI kunik- 'kiss, sniff'
NAI kunik- 'kiss, sniff' [and kuniuʀaq- 'sniff repeatedly']
WCI kunik-
ECI kunik- 'kiss (with mouth or touching noses)' [and Saul has kuniuq- of a dog sniffing about]
GRI kuniɣ- 'kiss' [Kl. also 'sniff (face)', still the meaning of NG kunik-; kuniuʀaʀ- 'smell']

PE kunnaʀ 'kind of grass root'
AAY C kun<ʀ>aq 'underground leaf stem of fiddlehead fern'
CAY kunnaq* 'edible root of spreading-wood fern'
NSY —
CSY kunakaq 'type of marsh grass'
Sir —
SPI Qaw kunnaq 'fern'
NAI Mal kunnaq
WCI —
ECI —
GRI —

PI kupci- 'give little'
Yup — [but note CAY kupətə- 'provide for']
SPI [kupsik 'a little bit' and Qaw kupsik- 'get a little']
NAI kufsit- 'refuse to share, be overly economical'
WCI —
ECI kutsi(t)- 'give very little of s.th.', kutsiq 'one who gives little', kutsitaq 'one who gets little'
GRI kussiɣ-, kussaɣ- [old ortho. kugsig-, kugsag- — influenced by kukðaɣ-?] 'economize with s.th. there is little of, give small helpings'

PI kupkanaq- 'be sticky' [cf. kumkaʀ and naʀ-?]
SPI —
NAI kupkanaq- 'be sticky', PH kupkaq- 'not be fully baked (bread)' [and kupkaluk- 'have s.th. sticky on one', kupkaʀnaq- 'be flavorful, tender (meat)'
WCI —
ECI —
GRI kukkaʀnaaq 'dried seal blood, caramel'

PI kutak- 'speak in an indistinct way'
SPI —
NAI kutak- 'speak with a foreign accent'
WCI Car kutak- 'have a dialect accent' [Ras.; Schn. has kuttaq- 'stammer']
ECI kutak- 'make a mistake speaking', Lab 'stutter' [Peck has 'speak indistinctly' for Lab and kutaŋa- 'be deficient in one's work or actions']
GRI kutaɣ- 'lisp, speak indistinctly or like a child'

PE kutðuɣ- 'lower head' [cf. kutžaq- and perhaps EA kusu-lix 'be mad, angry, offended'; there is some entanglement with qussuɣ- under quvə- in GRI]
AAY K, KP kusu- 'be 'be lonesome, homesick, miss loved ones'
CAY —
NSY —
CSY —
Sir —
SPI —
NAI kužžuk- 'lower one's head (in shame, etc.)'
WCI —
ECI —
GRI kussuɣ- 'shorten, tuck, make self smaller, pull chin into hood' [old ortho. kugsug- with spurious g; note kussuɣaq 'short strap to sealing bladder' = EG kuttuaq; also kusuɣ- 'be pathetic to look at' (NWG or southern SWG form?), kuššuk (old ortho. kugssuk) 'witch', as verb kuššuɣ- 'bewitch' — Kl. has kugsug- 'shorten, bewitch', Rink kúsuineq 'witchcraft'; note also NG kuhuuɣi- 'be jealous of', kuhuuk- 'be jealous']

PE kutə 'drop' [cf. kucukaʀ and kuvə-]
AAY PWS kuta 'undripped drop' [base kutə-]
CAY kuta 'drop of liquid' [base kutə-]
NSY ➟
CSY —
Sir —
SPI kutau- 'drip continuously'
NAI [kutit- 'drip'] ➟
WCI kuti 'drop of liquid' [Sig 'lead (shot)'; Pet. has Sig kutit 'shower']
ECI kutuq 'drop' [verbal = 'drip']
GRI kuti 'drop' [kutiʀ- 'drip', kutsit, EG, Up kutsisaq 'skin stretched over ceiling to collect drips', NG kutuula- 'stream, pour']

PE kuciʀ- 'drip' [cf. liʀ-]
AAY kuciʀ- 'drip' [and kuciq 'drop']
CAY kuciʀ- 'drip' [and Barnum has kuciq 'drop']
NSY kusiʀ- 'drip' [and kusiłəq 'drop' — Jen. has kusiq]
CSY —
Sir —
SPI kuziq- 'drip'
NAI kusiq- 'drip' [and PH kutcitciq- 'place receptacle under to catch drips']
WCI kusiq- 'drip' [and as nom. 'drop']
ECI kusiq- 'drip ' [as nom. = 'drop']
GRI kusiʀ- 'drip' [kusiq 'drop']

PI kutžaq- 'lower head (below torso)' [cf. kutðuɣ-; there may be a relat. to kutə]
SPI kuššaq- 'turn upside down, invert' [and kuššaʀuaq- 'fall head first']
NAI kužžaq-, Mal kutžaq- 'put one's head lower than one's torso'
WCI kuyyaq- 'put head down, fall head first' [Pryde has Cop kuuyyaq- 'hang head-down']
ECI kuyya(q)- 'put oneself upside down' [Bourq. has 'fall head over heels' for Lab and Dor. 'fall in water, drown' for FB]
GRI kuššaʀ- [old ortho. kugssar-] 'be sunk in front, have head down lower than one's feet'

PI kutžaŋa- 'be steep' [cf. ŋa-[1]]
SPI kuššaŋa- 'be steep'
NAI kužžaŋa-
WCI —
ECI kuyyaŋa- 'hang upside- down' [Saul]
GRI kuššaŋa- 'be sloping, hold head downward' [and kuššaŋayaaq 'steep hill, slope']

PE ku(C)u(ɣ)- 'be pigeon-toed' [for the source of contam. for the q- initial forms cf. quðu-]
AAY Kodiak kuuŋa- 'be pigeon-toed'
CAY kuuxtə-
NSY —
CSY kuutu-, kuutuʀmətə-
Sir —
SPI quuŋa- 'keep legs together' kuuliŋa, Qaw also kuuŋa- 'be pigeon-toed'
NAI quuŋa- 'be pigeon-toed, knock-kneed'
WCI Sig quuŋa- 'be pigeon-toed' [Lowe; Met. has qutsuŋa- — compare ECI qutsuŋa- under quvə-; Pryde has Cop, Net kuutu- 'be pigeon-toed']
ECI kuuŋa- 'be pigeon-toed' [also said of sled whose runners are closer together in front], kuutu- 'walk pigeon-toed' [and kuqqut(i)- 'fire to the left of'; Pryde has quuŋa- 'be pigeon-toed' for Igl]
GRI kuuŋa- 'be bent inward, bend crookedly to the left, be pigeon-toed' [and kuuŋašuuʀ- 'go off crookedly to the left (harpoon)' (in Fab. = kóksuk-), kuusuɣ- 'be apt to go off crookedly to the left (harpoon, etc.)']

PE kuvðaʀ 'net' [cf. kuvə- and ðaʀ and Aleut kuðmaci-X 'seine net']
AAY kuɣyaq 'fish net' [and kuɣyasiq 'seine net']
CAY kuvya(q) 'fish net' [and kuvya- 'fish by drift-netting or purse-seining', kuvyatə- 'catch a fish with a net']
NSY kuvžaq 'net for sea mammals' [ANLC also 'cobweb']
CSY kuuvžaq 'seal net' [kuuvžaʀ- 'set a seal net']
Sir kuvžan 'seal net' [and Vakh. has kuvžaʀ- 'set a net']
SPI kuvžaq 'net' [verbal = 'fish using a net']
NAI kuvžaq 'net' [verbal = 'catch in a net']
WCI kuvyaq 'net' [verbal = 'visit one's nets, be caught in a net']
ECI —
GRI —

PE kuvə- 'pour or spill' [cf. kuvðaʀ and Aleut kum- 'pour out']
AAY kuɣə- 'pour out, spill' [and note kuxtə- 'drip (excess liquid)']
CAY kuvə-
NSY kuvə-
CSY kuuvə-
Sir kuvə-
SPI kui- 'spill'
NAI kuvi- 'spill, pour out'
WCI kuvi-
ECI kuvi- 'pour, flow'
GRI kui- 'pour' [also 'baptize']

PE kuyaɣ 'lumbar vertebra or keel of boat' [cf. Aleut kuyɣi-X 'loin vertebra, rump bone of bird', Atkan pl. kuyɣi-s 'sacrum, hips']
AAY ➟
CAY kuya(k) 'hip, keel of kayak'
NSY kuyaq 'keel'
CSY kuyak 'spine, keel of boat'
Sir kuyəx 'keel' [and kuyanaX 'vertebra']
SPI kuyak 'keel, lower back'
NAI kuyaic 'lumbar vertebrae, PH 'lower back'
WCI kuyak 'keel' [Ras. has Cop kuyaaq 'kayak keel' but Net kuyak 'keelson']
ECI kuyaq 'part of kayak frame to which bottom cross-members are attached'
GRI kuyak, pl. kutsat 'loin', kuyaaq 'keel'

PE kuyapəɣaʀ 'vertebra or spine'
AAY —
CAY kuyapəɣaq 'spine'
NSY kuyapəɣaq 'vertebra'
Sir —
SPI kuyapiaq
NAI kuyapiɣaq 'spine, vertebra', Mal kiyapiɣaq, kiyupiɣaq, kiipiɣaq 'spine'
WCI kuyapiɣaq 'vertebra'
ECI kuyapiɣaq
GRI kuyapiɣaq

PE kuyaɣ- 'have sexual intercourse' [cf. kuyaɣ]
AAY kuyaɣ- 'have sexual intercourse'
CAY Y kuyaɣ-, HBC kuyuɣ- 'have sexual intercourse' [the latter by contam., with uyuɣ-]
NSY —
CSY —
Sir —
SPI kuyak- 'have sexual intercourse'
NAI kuyak-
WCI kuyak-
ECI kuyak-
GRI kuyaɣ-

L

laɣiq 'Canada goose' [loan from Aleut lax, laɣi-X '(Alaskan) Canada goose'; note also Atkan laɣla-X '(Hutchins) Canada goose'; compare under nəʀlər]
AAY K laɣiq 'Canada goose'
CAY laɣiq 'goose', laɣiluxpiaq, laɣipiaq, laɣiXpak 'Canada goose'
NSY —
CSY —

ləvələvələʀaʀ 'sandpiper' [onomatopoeic — compare also some of the forms under nəʀlər and (ə)łəŋaðaʀ(-)]
AAY —
CAY NSU ləvləvləʀaq 'sandpiper' [from Inu?]
SPI Qaw livlivliXaq 'least sandpiper' [and livlivliXaqpak 'semipalmated sandpiper']
NAI nivilivilaaluk, livilivilaaluk, Mal livilivillakpak, livalivallakpak, Noatak River livalivak, alavluʀaužaq, navaluvaužaq, lavaluvaužaq, Nu livalivaq, Uum nivilivilaaq 'semipalmated sandpiper' [Pryde for all except the last two, from MacLean and Lowe respectively; he also has navaluʀaužaq, livilivillaužaq, Nu nivalivaužaq, N. River livalivaužaq 'least sandpiper']
WCI nivilivilaaq, Net livilivak 'semipalmated sandpiper' [Pryde, who also has Cop livalivak, nivalivak 'Baird's sandpiper']
ECI luviluvvilaaq 'sandpiper' [NBI also livilivilaaq, luviluvilaq acc. Pryde]
GRI —

(ə)łəŋaðaʀ(-) 'resonant or ringing sound?' [and (ə)łəʀaʀ and (ə)łəvəkluɣ — there may be several related onomatopoeic forms here]
AAY —
CAY [(ə)łəXaʀ(aq*), HBC əłaʀaq 'spinning toy that whirrs']
NSY łəŋa(a)Xtə- [ANLC łəŋaaʀ-] 'ring, sound', ła(a)Xaq 'sound, noise', łəŋa(a)lŋuq 'resonant' [and note łəvəkłuaq 'top, propeller' — ANLC, which also has səŋaaʀ- 'ring in ears (and nom. səŋaaq)]
CSY ləŋaaq 'sound of explosion, ringing noise', ləŋaaʀuutə- 'ring' [and note ləvəkłuk 'deep, hollow vibrating sound (like plane or thunder in distance)']
Sir ləŋacəʀca 'sound (musical)', ləŋacəłəʀəX 'resonant' [Em.; Men. has ləŋacəʀ- 'ring, rumble', ləŋacəXtaX 'little bell']
SPI Imaq łəŋa(a)k- 'sound, ring', łəŋa(a)ɣun 'bell' [and KI laʀlau- 'be a sudden sharp noise', laʀlaazit- 'bang, rattle, crackle']
NAI —
WCI —
ECI —
GRI —

M

PI maaq- 'yelp or howl in pain' [cf. maʀu-[2]]
SPI maaq- 'yelp with pain'
NAI maaq- 'yelp in pain', maʀaala-, Nu maala- 'howl in pain (dog)'
WCI maʀaaq- 'howl in pain'
ECI maaq- 'yelp in pain', maalaa-, maaʀala- 'yelp continuously'
GRI maaʀ-, maala- 'howl in pain'

PI macak or **maccak** 'moisture or slush' [cf. məcu(ɣ), məcuʀ and məcaɣ]
SPI massak 'slush' [and verbal 'be slushy and ready to slide']
NAI masak, matcak 'slush' [also misak, for which see məcaɣ; verbal = 'be slushy']
WCI masak 'slush' [but Pet. writes matsaq for Sig; Lowe has masak 'melting snow' but misak 'wet snow' — for which see məcaɣ]
ECI masak, matsaq 'wet snow' [masak- 'fall (soft snow)', NBI 'melt']
GRI masak 'moisture', masaɣ-' 'be wet on surface', EG masak, NG matsak 'wet snow' [and masaʀšuk 'marsh, tundra']

> **PI matcaktəq-** 'moisten' [cf. təʀ-]
> SPI —
> NAI matcaktɨq- [also misaktɨq-] 'moisten'
> WCI —
> ECI —
> GRI matsatsiʀ- 'moisten, water'

PE macaʀ 'sun' [cf. maqaq and matneq, though the relat. is not clear]
AAY C, Kod macaq 'sun'
CAY NSU macaq 'sun' [and verbal macaʀ- 'shine (sun)', elsewhere maciuʀ- 'warm oneself', Nun macaʀi- 'be hot (weather)']
NSY masaq 'sun' [and masaʀni- 'screw up eyes in (sun) light']
CSY Chap masaq '(sun's) heat', masaaʀi- 'warm up (weather in spring)', masiʀaʀ- 'warm up by stove']
Sir —
SPI mazaq 'sun' [Qaw masaq]
NAI masaʀni- 'sun oneself, be pleased, PH listen attentively', Nu masaXži- 'bask in the sun, listen with pleasure'
WCI —
ECI —
GRI —

PE maciɣ 'gill' [the Yup forms by assim. — compare patu and matu]
AAY pacik 'gill'
CAY pacik 'gill' [and paciɣuaq 'nostril']
NSY pasiɣuk 'nostrils'
CSY pasiŋuk 'area of face to side of nose'
Sir —
SPI Qaw masik 'gill'

NAI masik 'gill', Nu 'frame for laying paddle on deck of kayak in front of hole'
WCI masik 'gill' [and B.-S. has Car mahik 'crosspiece just forward of (kayak) man-hole']
ECI masiik [du.] 'gills, part of kayak deck that rises sharply just in front of the man-hole'
GRI masik 'gill, curved cross-beam or deck in front of man-hole of kayak' [EG masiq only in the second sense]

PI macuk 'edible root?'
Yup — [note AAY KP macuk (du.) 'female genitals', AAY maccutak 'codfish egg', and CAY Eg, Nun maccutaX 'dog salmon, chum (especially dried)']
SPI mazu 'root vegetable, potato'
NAI masu
WCI masu [Lowe, also Ras. for Net; Met. has massok]
ECI —
GRI [note NG massulala(a)q- 'become fibrous']

PE maðətən 'now' [aequalis case of dem. root mað-]
AAY maatən 'extremely, severely'
CAY maatən 'one observed that' [plus verb in part. or subord. mood]
NSY maatən 'now, today'
CSY maatən 'now, a little while ago'
Sir [Orr has iməcən 'now', but this may be from — or by contam. with — dem. root im- instead; Vakh. has imcəɣən from Men's texts]
SPI maatnami, Qaw maatnaɣu 'now'
NAI maanna 'now then', Mal maatna 'this time, now that the situation has been corrected' [in Nu 'now' acc. Berg.; Jen. has manago 'soon']
WCI Car? maanna(kut) 'now, immediately' [Schn. 'adg'; Pet. has manna 'now' for Sig, which Jen. also has for Cop, and Pryde has Net maa'na; note also Car ma'na 'thank you']
ECI maanna(kut), 'now', Iti 'soon', Lab maanna 'now'
GRI maanna, maannakkut 'now'

PI mait- 'be sensitive' [from *maŋit- with p.b. ŋit-? — cf. maŋtaɣ, maŋaɣ(-) and maŋuna(ɣ)]
SPI —
NAI —
WCI mait- 'be sensitive (to pain)' [and cf. maiaɣnait- (for maiyaɣnait-?) 'be strong']
ECI mait- 'be sensitive (to pain or touch)' [for maattu- 'be insensitive to pain' see maŋaɣ(-)]
GRI maat- [old ortho. mait-] 'be sensitive, sore (skin), spoiled or soft' [and Robbe and Menn. have EG maaŋa- 'be weak'; for maattu- 'be callous' see maŋaɣ(-)]

PI makcaq- 'sing a baby to sleep'
SPI —
NAI maksaq-, PH mapsaq- 'sing a baby to sleep'
WCI Sig maksaaq-, Cop maxxak- [Pryde]
ECI matsa(q)- 'sing a baby to sleep'
GRI massaʀ- [old ortho. mavsar-, but Fab. has maksar-]

PE makə- and **makuɣ-** come loose' [cf. maklaɣ and mak(k)utə-]
AAY — [for makəxtə- 'outdo, beat at a game' see mak(k)utə-]
CAY [note makuxtə- 'suffer hardship, work hard']
NSY makuɣ- 'shed hair, molt, come undone' [ANLC; Men. has makuxtə- 'undo or get loose, clear up (sky)']
CSY makuxtə- 'slip out of a loop that holds one, shed, molt' [and makšəɣ- 'peel']
Sir makuXqaʀži- 'unharness dogs' [for makuxqaʀži-?; Vakh. has makuxtə- 'sit down' from Rub.'s texts]
SPI maɣə- 'stand up, e.g. grain of wood, be whipped fluffy, e.g. tallow' [poss. contam. with makət-; Qaw makuktaq- 'overwork' goes with the CAY above]
NAI makɨ- 'come loose (of patch)' [also 'die', a usage due to white influence acc. MacLean; makłuaq- 'rip off']
WCI maki- 'come loose, come off (patch on sole)' [Pryde]
ECI maki- 'be unstitched (boot sole)'
GRI małłuʀ- 'tear up (grass, etc.)', maššaɣ- [old ortho. magssag-] 'loosen (skin with blubber attached)' [and mappilaɣ- 'be split or slashed']

PE makət- 'get up' [cf. makpiq- and Aleut haɣ- 'grow up (child)', also haxsa- 'open, become open (door)', Atkan also haxsi- 'open (door)'; there may be a link to makə-]
AAY maktə- 'get up'
CAY makətə- 'get up, set up'
NSY makətə-
CSY makətə-
Sir makət(ə)- 'sit up' [Vakh. from Rub.; Em. has 'get up']
SPI maɣit- 'get up, whip up food' [also 'open knife' acc. Jen.]
NAI makɨt- 'get up, set up'
WCI makit- 'get up' [and makitit- 'open knife' acc. Met.]
ECI makit- 'get up, set up, open (knife)' [and note makiaq- rise a little, splinter (wood)']
GRI makit- 'get up' [and makiaʀ- 'splinter, get splinter out']

> **PE makəta-** 'be upright' [cf. ta-]
> AAY —
> CAY makta- 'be up(right)'
> NSY —
> CSY —
> Sir —
> SPI maɣita- 'be up, no longer in bed'
> NAI makɨta- 'be standing'
> WCI Cop makita- 'stand upright' [Ras.]
> ECI makita- 'be up'
> GRI makita- 'be up, out of bed, be proud'
>
> **PI makətəq-** 'get up (gradually)' [cf. təʀ-]
> SPI —
> NAI makɨtɨq- 'get up (from bed), be up'
> WCI —
> ECI makitiq- 'get up, place face up in their right place (cards)' [also makitit-]

GRI makitiʀ- 'get up gradually (from bed or capsized kayak)'

PI makšək- 'get up partially or suddenly?' [compare ikšək- under iŋət-, though perhaps here with contam. from p.b. žaɣ-?]
Yup — [for CSY makšəɣ- 'peel' see makə-]
SPI makšik- 'get up suddenly with a start'
NAI makšik-
WCI —
ECI —
GRI maššit- 'sit up, get up partially from a sitting position'

PY-S makiʀ- 'remove edible parts?' [cf. mək(k)əɣ-; there may also be a link to makə-]
AAY — [for makəɣ- 'gnaw' see mək(k)ə-]
CAY makiʀa- 'gather greens or eggs to eat', makiuʀ- 'remove roots from plants'
NSY —
CSY makiʀ- 'gnaw on bone with meat attached to it'
Sir makiʀ- [Orr]

PE makitəʀ 'lumbar region' [there may be a relat. to makət-]
AAY PWS, AP makitək (du.) 'hip bones' [B.-S. has C makitXa 'his hip']
CAY —
NSY —
CSY —
Sir —
SPI —
NAI PH makisiq 'lower back'
WCI Cop makitiq 'anterior superior illiac crest, outer edge of hip bone' [Pryde; Pet. has Sig makitaq 'hip bone']
ECI makitiq 'hip bone' [Saul; Schn. has makiti, Lab, Aiv makitiq 'hip bone, iliac, lumbar region']
GRI makisiq, makit 'lower back', EG maɣisiq 'hip bone' [and Tersis has EG maɣittat '(game of) bones']

PI makkaq 'dome of head or snow house' [cf. makət-, and compare the semantics of kavžaq]
SPI —
NAI —
WCI Car? makkaq 'hood point, snow house dome, upper part of skull' [Schn. 'adg']
ECI Lab makkak 'upper part of skull, dome of snowhouse, tassle' [Andersen et al.; and note Iti makkaq 'raspberry']
GRI —

PE makkaʀ 'diaper' [cf. makə- and geminating -q under nəʀ[1]; however, this could be a loan from Chukchi maka (borrowed also into Even)]
AAY [note PWS makkaq 'pelvis bone of seal'? — but cf. PE makitəʀ]
CAY makaq 'diaper'
NSY makaq
CSY maka
Sir makaX 'flap of overalls' [Vakh. from Rub.]
SPI makkak 'diaper' [also verbal 'put on a diaper']
NAI makkaq 'diaper' [also verbal]
WCI makkaq 'diaper'
ECI [note Iti makkauyaq 'triangle']
GRI —

PE maklaɣ 'bearded seal' [there could be a relat. to makə-, the tough skin of this animal being removed and cut up to use as thongs]
AAY AP makłak 'spotted seal'
CAY makłak, makłaaq 'bearded seal'
NSY makłak
CSY makłak 'bearded seal' [and makławaaq* 'caterpillar' — cf. CAY uɣuɣuaq of the same meaning from *uɣðuɣ 'bearded seal']
Sir —
SPI [makłazuaq 'baby bearded seal']
NAI — [but note makłak- 'stand on end (animal hair, rising in anger),' going with makət-]
WCI Net makłaq 'bearded seal' [Ras., who also has maxak for Cop; Jen. has Coronation Gulf makcaluɣɣuaq, probably for maxxaluɣɣuaq, 'a large bearded seal in songs' — he lists it under maktak; Pryde has Cop maxxak 'bearded seal' in shaman's language]
ECI Igl makłak 'bearded seal' [shaman's word in Ras.]
GRI [NG maɣlaq 'shaman's word for bearded seal' in Kroeber, also perhaps SWG małłak (old ortho. magdlak) 'clever person', but compare małłaɣ- (old ortho. magdlag-) 'be split or torn' from makə-]

PI makpiq- 'open or fold back' [cf. makət-]
Yup — [but compare CAY maktaat 'book, magazine' from makət-]
SPI makpiq- 'fold back, open, turn over' [makpik- 'move s.th. stuck (e.g. in ground)']
NAI makpiq- 'open book, turn page' [makpiʀaat 'book']
WCI makpiq- 'open book, turn page, fold back (wound)' [makpiʀaat 'book'; cf. also Baker Lake makpiqtaut 'switch, lever of breachblock' in Schn.]
ECI mappi(q)- 'open, raise on one side (window, book, stone)' [mappitaq 'page of book', mappituʀaq- 'raise garment several times']
GRI mappiʀ- 'open (chest, door, book, etc.)' [mappiʀsakkat 'book', mappikaaʀ- 'be opened, lifted up (one after another)']

PY maksaq 'solar plexus?' [cf. makət-?]
AAY K maksaq 'solar plexus'
CAY maksak 'upper part of abdomen' [du.; note also maksaq 'spleen', by contam. with mamca(ʀ)]
NSY —
CSY Chap maksaq 'lower edge of rib arch'

PI mak(k)utə- 'overcome' [cf. makə- and utə-; there could be contam. with makət- here]
Yup [note AAY makəxtə- 'outdo, beat, get best of']
SPI —
NAI —
WCI Car? makkuti- 'take s.o.'s place' [Schn. 'adg'; Met. has makuti- 'get up with (s.th. in one's hands)' from makət-]
ECI makkut(i)- 'be stronger than (s.o. else), (for s.th. to)

be too small for (s.o.)'
GRI makut(i)- 'look down on, manage, overrule' [compare makkut(i)- 'get up again (e.g. from capsized kayak)' — a regular reflexive form from makət- and utə-]

PI malak or **malaq** 'front of throat' [cf. Aleut hala- 'turn head, look back, turn around', Atkan also 'look up']
SPI —
NAI PH malak 'chest'
WCI [Ras. has Net malatuaʀSuk 'one who throws his head back so that a hollow appears in the nape of the neck']
ECI malak 'upper part of breast of mammals' [and malaʀuti 'lower part of collar of dog harness']
GRI malaq 'front of throat', malaʀ- 'put head back, give in' [and malasiut 'towing hook to attach to neck of seal']

PI maląk 'wave' [cf. małəɣ- rather than maliɣ-]
SPI malik 'wave'
NAI malik 'wave' [verbal = 'have swells (sea)']
WCI malik
ECI malik 'wave' [verbal = 'be a storm']
GRI malik 'wave'

PI malliq- 'be rough (sea)' [cf. liʀ-]
SPI malliq- 'be rough (sea)'
NAI malliq- 'be rough (sea)' [nom. malliq* = 'tidal wave']
WCI malliq- 'be rough (sea)'
ECI malliq-
GRI małłiʀ-

PI maləʀi(q) 'loon?' [there may be a link to maląk and/or małəɣ-]
Yup [Barnum has CAY malləʀakiyaɣak 'little duck']
SPI —
NAI malʀi, Nu maliʀi 'arctic loon' [Jen. also has the second form for B]
WCI Cop maliʀiq 'loon' [Lowe has malʀiq; Ras. has maliʀaaluk for Sig]
ECI Igl maliʀaaluk 'long-tailed duck' [Ras.; for maliʀsuaq 'land game pursued for a long time' see maliqə- under maliɣ-]
GRI [EG maliiʀsaʀtaq 'eider duck'; and note WG note maliʀiq 'hunted sea mammal' — contam. with maliɣ-?]

PE maliɣ- 'follow or accompany' [cf. presumably unrelated maląk and małəɣ-, with which there is contam. in the Inu and Sir forms below]
AAY malixtə- 'go with, follow'
CAY maliɣ-, malikə- 'take, bring along', malik 'companion, thing taken along', malixtə- 'accompany, follow'
NSY malixtə- 'follow, accompany'
CSY malixtə-, malixtaʀ- 'follow, accompany' [and maliɣmun 'with the grain, following']
Sir maliɣ- 'follow, accompany' [Vakh. also has małiɣ- 'follow, accompany, approach'; note also maliʀmənu 'following, along' — for maliɣmənu?]
SPI malik- 'follow, accompany'
NAI malik- 'follow, accompany' [małak- 'follow everywhere' may be influenced by małəɣ-]
WCI malik- 'follow' [and Kroeber has maligna as the old name of the sun in Sig — cf. the myth of the moon following his sister the sun into the sky — compare under ciqinəʀ]
ECI malik- 'follow, accompany, try to catch s.o. when following' [and malinnaa(q)- 'follow everywhere']
GRI maliɣ- 'follow, imitate, conform to' [half-trans. malinniɣ-; note małłut(i)- 'take s.o. along after, follow along with s.th.', malinnaa- (old ortho. malingnau-) 'follow along behind'; cf. also the old name for the sun maliina in Fab. — from *maliŋnaq?]

PY maliɣcuaʀ- 'follow along after' [cf. yuɣ-?]
AAY [AP malixcuk 'one who always wants to go']
CAY malixcuaʀ- 'tag along after'
NSY —
CSY malixsaaʀ- 'follow without the permission of those being followed' [malixsaaXta 'follower']
Sir [note malixsaqaʀət(ə)- 'submit']

PI malikataq- 'pursue' [cf. k(k)attaʀ-]
Yup [for NSY maliɣataʀ- 'chase game' see maliʀqə- below]
SPI [and malikataq-, Imaq małqataq-, maləkataq- 'pursue' — the latter by contam. with małəɣ-?]
NAI malikataq- 'pursue'
WCI —
ECI [note Lab malikataak 'bitch in heat']
GRI —

PE maliqðuʀ- 'pursue persistently' [cf. qðuʀ-]
AAY maliXquʀ- 'chase continuously'
CAY malixquaʀ- 'chase persistently'
NSY maliXquʀ- 'go one after another' [Tein; ANLC 'chase']
CSY maliXquʀ- 'chase'
Sir —
SPI —
NAI maliqšuq- 'follow everywhere'
WCI maliqsuq- 'pursue' [for 'adg' Schn. has 'follow amphibious game into water']
ECI maliʀsu(q)- 'follow for a long time' [and maliʀsuaq 'land game pursued for a long time' — but Saul has both forms primarily of sea mammals]
GRI maliʀšuʀ- 'pursue'

PE maliʀqə- 'chase' [cf. p.b. ʀqə- and ðaʀ- in some of the forms]
AAY maliXqə- 'chase'
CAY maliXqaʀ-, malixqə-, malixkə- 'chase game'
NSY malixkə-, maliɣataʀ-
CSY maliXqaʀ- 'chase'
Sir maliXqaʀ(ži)- 'chase, hunt'
SPI Qaw maliqšaq- 'pursue'
NAI maliʀi- 'follow' [also malliq- 'follow, chase']
WCI [note Sig maliʀak- 'set out after' in Ras.]
ECI —
GRI — [for maliʀiq 'hunted sea mammal' see maləʀi(q)]

PE malʀuɣ 'two' [there may be a relat. to maliɣ-]
AAY malluk 'two'
CAY malʀuk
NSY malʀuk
CSY maalʀuk
Sir malʀux
SPI maʀluuk, Qaw malʀuk
NAI malʀuk
WCI malʀuk
ECI maʀʀuuk
GRI maʀłuk, EG maʀtit

PE malʀi 'twin' [a back-formation — cf. p.b. li-[1]]
AAY mal<ʀ>ik 'twins'
CAY malʀi 'twin' [malʀi- 'give birth to twins]
NSY malʀiik 'twins' [ANLC]
CSY malʀik 'twins' [and malʀi- 'give birth to twins']
Sir —
SPI malʀi 'twin'
NAI malʀi 'twin' [verbal = 'give birth to twins']
WCI malʀik, malʀiak 'twins'
ECI — [compare maʀʀuliak 'twins']
GRI — [compare maʀłuliaq, EG maʀtiʀ̃aliaq (Robbe and Menn.) 'twin' with li(C)aʀ]

PE malʀu(C)it 'two sets' [cf. it under ɣiik]
AAY malʀuin 'two sets'
CAY malʀuin
NSY —
CSY —
Sir —
SPI maʀluit 'two sets, pairs or groups'
NAI malʀuit
WCI —
ECI maʀʀuit
GRI maʀłuiit

PI maluɣə- 'notice that s.th. has changed for the worse' [cf. kə-[1]]
SPI maluknaq- 'be different, changed, not as good as before' [and maluknai- 'find s.th. that way'; Jen. has KI maliguga 'he notices it']
NAI maluŋnaq- 'be shameful, odd, seem wrong' [and maluŋnaʀi- 'consider it so']
WCI maluɣi- 'not like the way a thing is', Car? 'put a bad interpretation on s.th., cast doubt on' [Schn. 'adg'; maluŋnaq- 'be such as to cause that judgment', Car 'be liable to be mocked or criticized' acc. Schn. for 'adg' but 'be amusing' in Ras.]
ECI maluɣi- 'doubt s.th.'s value', Lab 'notice' [Bourq. for the latter; malunna(q)- 'cause suspicion, doubt', malunnia(q)- 'suspect, try to find out about s.o.' and maluɣusuɣuaq- 'be suspicious', Lab maluɣusuk- 'suspect, notice, feel one's drink']
GRI maluɣi- 'notice, discover, feel that' [and malunnaʀ- 'be striking, recognizable', maluɣusuɣ- 'be happy about receiving s.th. one lacked']

PI malukali- 'be crazy'
Yup [NSU malukkali- 'be rabid, insane' is probably borrowed from Inu]
SPI malukali- 'be crazy', malukaŋa- 'act crazy'
NAI malukali- 'be crazy' [and malukaɣɨ- 'consider inferior, be ashamed of', Nu malukaliq 'madman, rabid animal']
WCI Sig malukaliŋayuq 'idiot'
ECI —
GRI —

PY-S małəɣ- 'press up against' [cf. malək and Aleut hal-as in halim haðaa 'the windward side' and halmuðaʀ- 'go straight against the wind'; the relat. — if any — to maliɣ- is obscure]
AAY małəɣ- 'move up against (e.g. boat to dock)' [and AP małəɣnəq 'impassable place', małəɣnitə- 'be a very high tide']
CAY małəɣ- 'be close'
NSY małəɣ- 'draw near, get close to, become tight' [Em. has małəxtə-]
CSY małəɣ- 'be, get close'
Sir małəʀ- [for małəɣ-?] 'press against, pin down' [for małiɣ- 'approach, follow, accompany' see maliɣ- — Vakh. also has from Rub.'s texts małx- 'approach'; note also małəʀiʀətaX 'comb']
Inu — [for probable Inu cognates see malək, but note also Imaq malvək-, malvəža(a)q- 'press against']

PY-S mału(k) 'beached carcass' [cf. małəɣ- and malək]
AAY małuk 's.th. scavanged from beach'
CAY mału(k) 'beached carcass'
NSY mału
CSY mału
Sir masa 'edible thing washed up on beach' [Orr; and masəŋə- 'find thing washed up on beach']

PE mamaʀ(-) 'taste good or suck breast' [cf. ama(C)- — there may be only a single proto-form here]
AAY —
CAY —
NSY [L.-T. has mamaq 'baby, doll' (?)]
CSY mamaq 'breast, milk', mamaʀ- 'suck (breast)' [and note əmama 'child's word when it wants the breast']
Sir mamәʀ- 'suck breast, maməX 'milk', mamaʀənləŋuX 'sweet' [Vakh. has mamaX, maməX 'breast' from Men. and Rub., Orr has maməX, pl. mamay]
SPI Qaw mamaq- 'smell good' [for maamak- 'suckle' see ama-]
NAI mamaq- 'taste good' [mamaun 'udder']
WCI mamaq- 'taste good' [mamaun 'udder', in Cop also woman's breast]
ECI mamaq- 'taste good' [mamauti 'udder', mamaʀsaut 'perfume', mamaʀunaq 's.th. that looks delicious']
GRI mamaʀ- 'taste good' [and NG mamaXXaŋŋit- 'smell bad', mamaʀunaqtit- 'think delicious'; note also mamma 'food' (baby talk)]

PI mamait- 'taste bad' [cf. ŋit-]
SPI mamait- 'taste or smell bad'
NAI mamait-

WCI mamait- 'taste bad' [and Pryde mentions mamaitsuq 'sea' as a shaman's word in Net (as opposed to mamaqtuq 'lake)']
ECI mamait- 'taste bad' [and note Igl shaman's word mamaitsuq 'sea' in Ras.]
GRI mamaat- 'taste bad'

PI mamaʀə- 'like the taste of' [cf. kə-[1]]
SPI —
NAI mamaʀɨ- 'like (food)'
WCI mamaʀi- 'like the taste of'
ECI mamaʀi-
GRI mamaʀi- 'like (tasty food), take a liking to (s.o.)'

PE mamca(ʀ) 'spleen' [cf. mamə- and/or mamcaʀ-?]
AAY —
CAY LI mamcaq 'spleen' [elsewhere maksaq, for which see maksaq]
NSY mamsiq 'pancreas' (Men.), but mamsaq 'spleen' [L.-T.]
CSY maamsa
Sir mamsa [Orr]
SPI mapsa 'spleen, snow cornice' [the latter sense from the 'overhanging' position of the spleen?]
NAI mapsa 'spleen, snow cornice' [and mapsaq- 'fall down (snow cornice)']
WCI Cop maxxaq 'spleen' [Ras. — Pryde has mapsa]
ECI Aiv mapsa, Tar matsak 'spleen, earlobe'
GRI massak 'milt, spleen' [old ortho. mavsak]

PY mamcaʀ- 'flatten' [cf. mame]
AAY AP mamcaXtə- 'squeeze flat'
CAY mamcaʀ- 'flatten, be flattened' [postural root]
NSY mamsaXquʀ- 'flatten' [ANLC has mamsaŋʀa- 'be in a flattened state']
CSY —

PE mamə 'underside of skin' [cf. mamə- and/or mamcaʀ-?]
AAY ➞
CAY ➞
NSY mamə 'underside of skin' [Em.]
CSY —
Sir — [for mamiɣ- 'translate, turn over' see mumiɣ-]
SPI mami, Qaw mamiq 'underside of skin'
NAI mamɨq* 'underside of skin' [and note mamaaq 'gums of whale where baleen is attached']
WCI mami 'underside of skin' [and Car? mamaaq 'whale meat from between plates of baleen' — Schn. 'adg']
ECI mami 'underside of skin'
GRI mami 'blubber on fleshy side of skin', mamik 'fleshy side of skin, earth side of turf' [and mamaaʀ- 'molt (of seal), flake (whale skin), be hoarse in throat']

PE mamələɣ 'boot with hair or fur turned in' [cf. ləɣ]
AAY —
CAY Nun, Y mamlək 'skin boot with fur above knee and waterproof material below'
NSY —
CSY —
Sir —
SPI mamilaq 'waterproof sealskin boot, with hair turned in on lower part'
NAI mamɨlɨk 'caribou leg skin boot with fur inside', PH 'bearded sealskin boot with hair removed'
WCI —
ECI —
GRI —

PE mamtu- 'be thick or tough' [cf. tu-]
AAY mamtu- 'be able to withstand pain'
CAY mamtu- 'be thick'
NSY mamtu-
CSY —
Sir —
SPI maptu- 'be thick'
NAI maptu-
WCI maptu-
ECI mattu-
GRI mattu- 'be tough'

PE mamə- 'close over or heal' [cf. mamə and Aleut ham- 'heal, be healed']
AAY mamə- 'close over, heal'
CAY mamə- 'close in, close mouth, flatten, heal'
NSY mamə- 'heal, close over' [but note also papɣuɣnaʀ- 'can close' with p.b. yuknaʀ-]
CSY maamə- 'heal, close over'
Sir mamə- [Orr]
SPI ➞
NAI ➞
WCI [mamiŋa-, Cop mamiq- 'have mouth closed']
ECI mamilik- 'be bent double, folded out flat'
GRI mamia- 'be quick to heal', mamiliɣ- 'close, fold well'

PE mamət- 'close around or heal' [cf. t-[1]]
AAY —
CAY mamtə- 'close, flatten, heal'
NSY mamta(ʀ)- 'heal'
CSY mamtə- 'close in'
Sir —
SPI mamit- 'heal' [and Qaw mamitaq- 'bandage']
NAI mamɨt- 'heal' [mamɨtaq- 'bandage', Nu mamittaq- 'heal, close two halves of s.th. together']
WCI mamit- 'heal'
ECI mamit-
GRI mamit- 'heal' [note also maššut(i)- 'have closed in on (e.g. hole in ice on seal)', and SWG mamitaʀ- 'capsize, swing around and hang from s.th. (e.g. a branch)']

PI mapciq- 'convalesce or leave to heal' [cf. c(c)iʀ-]
SPI Qaw mapsiq- 'convalesce, rest'
NAI mafsiq- 'convalesce, rest' [mafsiʀiaq- 'leave to convalesce']
WCI —
ECI —
GRI massiʀ- 'wait until it is healed (sore)' [massiɣ-, massiʀiaʀ- 'heal quickly']

PI mavžak- 'scrape fat from skin' [cf. qapðaɣ- with which there is contam.]
SPI mavžak- 'flesh, remove blubber from (skin)'
NAI —
WCI Cop mavyak- 'scrape skin thin' [Ras., who spells it maujag-; B.-S. has mabiak- for Net; Pryde has mavyak- 'scrape oil and surface of hide from (e.g. seal) while still wet']
ECI mayya(C)- 'scrape (skin)' [B.-S. has mayyak- for Igl]
GRI —

PE mamtəʀaʀ 'cache or temporary dwelling' [with dissimilation in CSY; cf. mamə-]
AAY C mamtaaq 'smokehouse, barabara' [mamtəʀaa 'his smokehouse']
CAY Y, NS mamtəʀaq 'cache' [and place names mamtəʀiłəq 'Bethel' and mamtəʀat 'Goodnews Bay']
NSY mantəʀaq 'skin tent'
CSY maŋtəʀaq 'house'
Sir —
SPI maptiaq 'house, Qaw maptiʀaq 'cache', Di maptəaq 'Sib. Eskimo walrus skin house'
NAI [Nu maptiʀaq personal name]
WCI —
ECI —
GRI —

PE mam(ə)ya- 'be offended or annoyed' [there may be a link to mamə-; compare pumyuɣ- for the dissimiliation in AAY, though there could be contam. with papði- instead]
AAY papsaa(kə)- 'want to see, be suspicious of'
CAY — [for NSU papsi(kə)- 'find a nuisance' see papði-]
NSY [note pupɣaʀyuɣ- 'be ashamed']
CSY —
Sir —
SPI Qaw mamiat- 'have hurt feelings', W mamianaq- 'be nervous, afraid' [Jen.]
NAI mamiaɣɨ- 'feel hurt, distressed' [and mamiasaaq- 'tease, criticize', mamiat- 'have feelings hurt by scolding']
WCI mamianaq- 'be annoying', mamiasuk- 'be angry (at s.th.)' [emot. root; note also Car mamiavalaakkuni 'how annoying, what a pity' (Ras.) and mamiq- 'try to revenge self on weaker person' (Schn.) — but compare Cop mamiq- under mamə-]
ECI mamiasutsa(q)- 'try to annoy', mamiaɣi- 'detest'
GRI mamia(suɣ)- 'be offended' [emot. root; note also massua- (old ortho. mavssua-) 'scold because one is offended']

PE manaʀ 'lure (baited hook)'
AAY —
CAY manaq 'fishhook' [manaʀ- 'fish with hook or lure, esp. through ice']
NSY manaq 'lure' [ANLC has manaʀ- 'hook for fish' and Jen. has mannat 'fishing rod and line']
CSY Chap manaq 'lure, bait' [and as verb manaʀ-]
Sir manəX 'lure'
SPI manaq 'fishhook' [as verb = 'catch fish on hook']
NAI manaq 'seal retrieving hook' [verbal = 'catch with such a hook']
WCI manaq Sig 'grappling iron, baited hook left in water', Cop 'seal-retrieving apparatus', Net 'bait, gull hook' [Ras.]
ECI manaq 'baited fish line hanging from float' [as verb = 'be hooked on such a line (fish)']
GRI —

PE manəɣ- and **maŋə-** 'sob' [cf. nəɣ- (= Yup ŋə-)]
AAY maŋłəɣ- 'make involuntary gasping sounds after prolonged weeping'
CAY maŋəłpaɣ- 'sob loudly when through crying', maŋłəɣ- 'sob at intervals after crying'
NSY manyałaʀ-, manyaŋiXtaʀ- 'sob' [ANLC]
CSY maŋiʀ- 'stop crying' [and note maŋsiŋuʀ- 'soothe, calm' — influenced by maniɣuʀ- under maniɣ-?]
Sir [Em. also has maŋiʀ- 'stop crying' — from the CSY?]
SPI —
NAI manɨk- 'sob once' [manɨktuq-, maliktuq- 'be sobbing']
WCI Sig manik- 'burst into sobs' [Pet., who also has manilaqi- 'sob a lot']
ECI ➞
GRI maniɣ-, manittuʀ- 'sob, sniff when crying'

PE manəɣyuɣaʀ- 'sob (after crying)' [cf. uɣaq- and/or yu(C)aʀ-?]
AAY —
CAY maŋyuaʀiʀ-, HBC maŋyuaʀiʀ- 'sob from sadness'
NSY [maanaŋiXqə- 'sob after crying' — ANLC]
CSY maŋyaaŋiʀ- 'sob uncontrollably after crying'
Sir maŋyaŋiʀ- 'sob' [from CSY?]
SPI —
NAI —
WCI —
ECI maniyyuɣaq- 'sob after crying, have a heavy heart'
GRI —

PE manəʀ 'tussock (of moss)' [cf. Aleut hana- as in hanatu- 'be thick (log or rope)', Att as nom. 'big roundish mountain'? — note the parallel in EA tumtu- 'high roundish mountain', Atkan tumtatu- 'be thick']
AAY —
CAY NS manəq* 'tussock'
NSY —
CSY —
Sir —
SPI Qaw maniq 'tussock' [Jen. has 'tussock of moss']
NAI manɨq* 'tussock, moss for lamp wick'
WCI maniq
ECI maniq 'moss for lamp wick'
GRI maniq(*) 'moss for kindling a fire'

PE mani- 'display' [cf. maniɣuʀ-]
AAY mani- 'display, bring out'
CAY mani- 'display, put on stove'
NSY mani- 'display' [ANLC]
CSY mani- 'move close to'

Sir —
SPI mani- 'show, display, offer food, put on fire to cook'
NAI mani- 'show, present, display'
WCI mani- 'show, expose' [Pryde also 'stay put, stand fast, lie passively' for Cop; and maniɣuq- 'show to someone, present']
ECI mani- 'present, offer, introduce oneself'
GRI mani- 'offer to someone, reach out hand for s.th., expose to sun or air, hang out to dry'

PY mani(C)aʀ- 'roast over a fire' [cf. aʀ-]
AAY C maniaʀ- 'roast or fry over fire'
CAY maniaʀ- 'roast or fry over fire' [and maniaq 's.th. roasted, pancake']
NSY —
CSY —

PE maniɣ- 'be smooth or flat' [cf. perhaps Aleut hani-X 'lake' and/or hanika- 'float']
AAY K maniɣ- 'be flat' [Lis.]
CAY maniɣ- 'be smooth' [maniatə- 'be rough']
NSY maniq 'plain, valley, smooth spot', maniqsaq 'flat area', maniqsaʀ- 'flatten' [ANLC has manixtə- 'flatten']
CSY —
Sir —
SPI manik- 'be flat, smooth' [and Imaq manik 'valley']
NAI manik- 'be smooth'
WCI manik- 'be smooth (ice)'
ECI manik- 'be flat' [and Lab manitsak- 'smooth, iron']
GRI maniɣ- 'be smooth, level'

PI maniilaq 'rough ice' [cf. ŋit-]
SPI [maniilaq 'it is rough, uneven', from base maniit-]
NAI maniilʸaq 'surface that is not smooth'
WCI maniillat 'rough ice' [Ras. has maniilaq for Net]
ECI maniilaq 'surface of pack ice with icicles ' [Met.; Ras. has 'pack ice' for Igl and B.-S. 'rough ice']
GRI maniiłłat 'hummocky ice'

PI maniʀaq 'plain' [cf. qaʀ]
SPI —
NAI Nu maniʀaq 'tundra' [Jen. has maniqaq 'plain' for B]
WCI maniʀaq 'plain'
ECI maniʀaq
GRI maniʀak, EG maniʀ̃aq 'flat stretch (on ice, etc.)' [and note EG maniŋaq, manitsiq 'plain']

PE maniɣuʀ- 'soothe or cajole' [cf. mani- and (C)uʀ-, though there may be influence from maniɣ-]
AAY KP maniuʀ- 'soothe, try to comfort'
CAY —
NSY ➡
CSY maniɣuʀ- 'calm, soothe', maniɣuutə- 'worship, beg'
Sir maniɣuʀ- 'beg, plead' [Vakh. from Men. and Rub.]
SPI —
NAI —
WCI [Pryde has Cop maniɣuuti- 'give no opposition, back down'; for maniɣuq- 'show to s.o.' see mani-]
ECI Lab, Baffin (biblical) maniɣuq- 'console, pacify'
GRI maniɣuʀ- 'try to cajole, put in a good humor' [and cf. manuʀłuʀ-, manułłuʀ- 'be assuaged (pain)']

PE maniɣuʀutə- 'humble oneself before s.o.' [cf. utə-]
AAY —
CAY —
NSY maniɣutə- 'cajole, curry favor with' [ANLC has maniiʀutə- 'suck up to s.o.']
CSY maniɣuutə- 'worship, beg, present self as pitiful'
Sir —
SPI —
NAI —
WCI Car? maniɣut(i)- 'deceive with flattery, console' [Schn. 'adg']
ECI maniɣut(i)- 'humble oneself, confess'
GRI maniɣuut(i)- 'humble oneself before s.o.'

PE manniɣ 'egg' [there may be contam. from manŋəq- in NSY and SPI Di]
AAY K manik 'egg'
CAY NS manik 'egg', elsewhere maniɣnaq 'burbot (a fish with an egg-like belly)'
NSY manŋik 'egg' [ANLC; Men. has manŋiq]
CSY manik 'egg'
Sir manix
SPI mannik, Di manŋiq
NAI mannik
WCI mannik
ECI mannik
GRI mannik

PI manŋəq- 'be hard or lumpy' [cf. matŋa-?]
SPI —
NAI manŋɨqtuqqiq 'hard, lumpy rust' [and manŋait- 'be tough (meat)']
WCI Cop manŋiq- 'be hard, stiff' [Pryde]
ECI maŋŋiq 'rust' [and note maŋŋai(t)- 'be stubborn', Lab maŋait- 'be hard, not come off' — Peck]
GRI maŋŋiʀ- 'be hard, tough', maŋŋiʀtuʀniq* 'rust' [Kroeber has mangiq 'stone' as a shaman's word in NG]

PI manŋuk- 'thaw' [there may be a link to matnəq]
SPI manŋuk- 'thaw to point where it can be cut (frozen meat)'
NAI manŋuk- 'thaw to point where it can be cut (frozen meat)' [and Mal manŋuqsižžiutɨ- 'put out frozen food for thawing']
WCI Car B. Lake manŋuk- 'melt (snow)' [Dor. — Pryde has 'be thawed out (when brought inside)' for Cop]
ECI maŋŋu(C)- 'go down (level of melting snow)' [and Iti maŋŋuq 'melting snow']
GRI maŋŋuɣ-, maŋŋuʀ- 'get milder (weather)', maŋŋuk 'mild weather', EG maŋŋinniq 'summer'

PE manu 'front side of s.th. or area below chin' [or *manuR in some derivatives]
AAY PWS, AP manu 'lap' [and B.-S. has C manumi 'in the foremost hand (exclamation during stick game)' and manuani 'under it (a mountain)' — i.e. in front of it?]
CAY manu- 'front side of s.th.' [posit. root; note also manuqłiq* 'foremost one' and manusuuxtə- 'bow one's head']
NSY manu 'breast piece, bib of skin coat or parka' [and ANLC also 'front area of person'; manuxkaq 'front part of parka under chin']
CSY manu 'front side of s.th.'
Sir mana 'area in front of s.th., front part of clothing covering chin and neck' [Em.; note mancəRa 'north' — for manəcəRa with p.b. l(l)iR?; Vakh. has maŋcəX, maŋžaX 'north, right side' from Men.'s texts]
SPI manu 'area beneath chin, area of parka below neck'
NAI manu 'breast of shirt or parka' [and note manusuk- 'put one's chin inside one's parka and be idle']
WCI manu 'lower part of front of hood, lower part of fish head'
ECI manu 'lower part of fur of parka ruff under chin' [and Peck has mannorli- 'sink' for Lab]
GRI manu 'chin piece of Greenlandic jacket, place between neck and breast'

PE manuŋilitaR 'bib' [cf. ŋilitaR]
AAY —
CAY manuilitaq 'bib, apron'
NSY manuilitaq 'bib, breastplate, lamp support' [ANLC]
CSY manuŋiitaq 'bib'
Sir —
SPI manuilitaq
NAI manuilʸisaq 'bib' [also manuRun]
WCI manuilitaq 'bib'
ECI manuilitaq
GRI [note manuqut 'bib']

PE manuRaR 'threshold or front of house' [cf. aR]
AAY —
CAY —
NSY —
CSY manuRaq 'front of house'
Sir —
SPI —
NAI —
WCI Car manuaq 'threshold, edge of entrance hole from house passage' [Ras.]
ECI manuaq 'step down inside snow house entrance'
GRI NG manuaq 'threshold of house' [Holt.]

PI manuRmik- 'carry under chin' [cf. miɣ-]
SPI Qaw manuRmik- 'carry under one's chin'
NAI manuRmik-
WCI —
ECI —
GRI manuRmiɣ-

PE maŋaɣ(-) '(remove) outer layer of (whale) skin' [cf. maŋtaɣ and maŋuna(ɣ); there may be a further link to makə-]
AAY KP maŋak, AP maŋaq 'porpoise skin, callous' [in AP also 'sole of foot'; for maŋak 'porpoise' see maŋaq]
CAY maŋaɣ- K 'bevel edge of skin for sewing', Y 'cut with scissors' [and NS maŋak 'fortitude' — compare EG maatti- below]
NSY maanak 'bulge or swelling on heel, callous' [ANLC]
CSY maŋaxtə- 'remove outer layer of skin', maŋak 'outer layer of skin' [and maŋałquq 'callous']
Sir maŋəX 'outer layer of whale skin' [Em.]
SPI —
NAI —
WCI —
ECI maak- 'remove blubber from whale skin' [Lab also 'kiss, rub noses' — influenced by mait-?; maayyaq 'whale skin with blubber removed'; note also maattu- 'be insensitive to pain or touch'; Bourq. has maaktu- 'be strong, not tender' for Lab]
GRI maaššak [old ortho. maigssak influenced by mait-] 'skin of whale between blubber and rind' [and note maattu- 'be hard, callous, without feeling', EG maatti- 'be courageous, firm' (Robbe and Menn.), WG maakkit- 'be thin-skinned']

PY maŋaq 'porpoise?' [there appears to be a link to maŋtaɣ and maŋaɣ(-), but cf. Aleut maŋiða-X 'fin whale (?)', which with an initial m could not be directly cognate but could be a loan either from or to Esk — the relat. is obscure]
AAY K maŋaq 'porpoise' [B.-S. — Rez. has maŋak; note also C maŋaRniiq, PWS maŋaRnak 'minke whale', with naR?]
CAY maŋayaaq*, maŋaRniiq*, Nun maŋaqcuaR(aX*) 'porpoise'
NSY —
CSY —
Inu — [but note NAI maŋaq- 'be dark, black']

PE maŋiR- 'gnaw' [there may be a relat. to maŋtaɣ and maŋaɣ(-)]
AAY maŋiR- 'chew on (bone or gristle)'
CAY maŋiXə- 'chew on frozen food', HBC maŋiXaR-, maŋiryaɣ- 'chew, gnaw on s.th.'
NSY —
CSY maŋziXə- 'gnaw'
Sir maŋaXqə(s)-
SPI maŋiak-, W maŋiaq-
NAI maŋik- 'gnaw on', maŋiaq- 'tear at with teeth'
WCI maŋik- 'tear at food with teeth'
ECI maŋik-, maŋia(q)- 'gnaw at'
GRI maŋiaR- 'tear food with teeth'

PE maŋtaɣ 'whale skin (with blubber attached)' [cf. maŋiR-, maŋaɣ(-), mait- and maŋuna(ɣ)]
AAY PWS maŋtak 'porpoise skin, callous' [for KP maŋak, AP maŋaq in these meanings see maŋaɣ(-)]
CAY maŋtak, BB maŋəŋtak 'beluga skin with blubber'

NSY mantak 'whale skin with blubber' [L.-T. and Tein]
CSY maŋtak 'whale skin with blubber'
Sir maxtəɣəX 'whale skin with blubber' [Vakh.; also maŋtaX, which Vakh. indicates as from CSY; Em. has maXtəʀəX]
SPI maktak 'whale skin with blubber'
NAI maktak
WCI maktaq 'whale skin with blubber' [Pryde has maktak specifically of skin of bowhead whale for Sig]
ECI mattaq 'whale skin with blubber' [for Lab maŋait- 'be hard, not come off' see mannəq- and for maak- 'remove blubber' see maŋaɣ(-)]
GRI mattak, 'whale skin with blubber'

PI maŋtaaq 'edible skin of beluga (with blubber attached)' [cf. aʀ]
SPI —
NAI maktaaq 'edible skin and attached blubber of beluga'
WCI maktaaq [Pryde]
ECI mattaaq, NBI, SB maktaaq
GRI NG maktaaq 'whale skin with blubber'

PE maŋuna(ɣ) '(pad of) hard skin' [cf. mait-, maŋaɣ(-) and maŋtaɣ; the exact relat. between these is not clear, but probably all from an original *maŋə-]
AAY mauna(q), maunak 'sea lion flipper'
CAY —
NSY —
CSY maŋuna 'thick walrus skin with hair on'
Sir maŋəna, pl. maŋəniy 'walrus skin' [Vakh. and Orr]
SPI mauniq 'callous' [Jen. has 'palmar tips of fingers']
NAI maunna, maunni 'hard skin, callous' [the latter also verbal 'get calloused' with p.b. li-[1]; the double n of the first form affected by this too]
WCI maunaq 'finger tips, salient parts of interior of hand when one stretches it']
ECI maunaq 'hard skin on hands or paws'
GRI maanak 'pad, fingertip' [old ortho. mainak probably influenced by mait-], NG maunak 'pad under toes' [and maanni- 'become calloused', maanniniq 'hard skin, callous']

PE maŋut- or **maŋuk-** 'thrust or drive in' [some of the Inu forms may have been influenced by paɣuɣ-]
AAY —
CAY —
NSY maŋutə- 'thrust, shove, butt in'
CSY [maŋʀutə- 'tie a rope in a special knot'?]
Sir [maŋuʀ- 'seat, place, sit'?]
SPI maŋuk- 'drive s.th. in,' Qaw 'hide or put s.th. in or under s.th., thrust, pound in'
NAI maŋuk- 'drive in (peg, stick), be nailed, pegged'
WCI maŋuk- 'penetrate' [Met.; Ras. has Sig maŋut- 'plant, stick in']
ECI maŋuk- 'plant, stick in'
GRI maŋut- 'put, drive in to s.th.' [and maŋŋut(i)- 'thrust in (with several thrusts)'; for maxxut(i)- 'put in' see maʀu-[1]]

PI maŋŋuq 'foundation or root' [cf. q under nəʀ[1]]
SPI maŋŋuq 'foundation'
NAI maŋŋuq* 'root, foundation'
WCI maŋ(ŋ)uq 'root' [Met.]
ECI maŋŋuk 'part of s.th. stuck into ground, etc., trunk of tree above roots' [and note maŋŋiʀi- 'resew sole coming apart from shoe', maŋittuq 'skin on which food, etc., is placed, tablecloth', Iti 'table']
GRI maŋŋuq(*) 'root' [and maŋussiq (old ortho. manguvseq), NWG maŋussak 'underlayer made of skin']

PI mapkuq- 'pop or crackle'
Yup — [for AAY, CSY mənquq 'popping sound' and Nun mamqə- 'make a loud noise' see mənquq under əməɣ-]
SPI Qaw mapkuluk- 'pop, crackle'
NAI mapkuq- 'crackle, gather all one's strength for an effort' [nom. = 'bearded sealskin sewn together for blanket toss'; and note mapkuqtaun 'whip', mapqaq- 'explode, fire']
WCI Net mapkuq- 'hit with a slap', Cop makkuqtaq- 'make a noise or contact (e.g. striking bullet)' [Pryde; Met. has Sig mapqaq- 'fire (gun)', Cop makkaq 'shoot (object)'; Lowe has Cop makaq- 'shoot' and makkaXXuq- 'be good at shooting']
ECI makku(q)- 'make sound of hitting (bullet, etc.)', makkuluk- 'make sound falling on roof (rain)' [Peck has 'rattle' for Lab]
GRI makkuʀ- [old ortho. mavkor-], makkuluɣ- 'clatter, rattle', Up makkuʀnaʀ- 'hail' [as noun makkuʀnat, EG makkaʀtaʀniq (Robbe and Menn. makkaʀtaʀnaq, also corresponding verb) 'hail']

PI maqait- 'be absent' [cf. ŋit-; there may be a relat. to maqaq]
SPI —
NAI maqait- 'be absent' [Jen.]
WCI maqait- 'be absent', Car 'be away hunting' [Ras., Dor. has 'go on a hunting trip'; maqaiq- 'no longer be present']
ECI maqait- 'be absent, far away, go hunting' [latter meaning acc. Dor.]
GRI maqaaši- [old ortho. maqaissi-] 'miss s.o. or s.th.'

PY-S maqaq 'heat' [cf. macaʀ and matnəq]
AAY maqaq 'heat', maqaʀ- 'be warm' [and maqi- 'take a steambath', maqiq 'steambath' with p.b. li-[1]]
CAY maqaq 'warmth, heat', maqaʀ- 'be warm (clothes, bedding)' [and maqi 'steambath' — also verbal]
NSY maqaq 'warmth' [ANLC, also for maqaʀ- 'be warm (clothes)']
CSY maqaq 'warmth', maqaʀ- 'be warm'
Sir maqaX 'warmth', maqałəʀəX 'warm'
Inu [Qaw maʀi- 'take a bath' is probably from Yup]

PE maqə- 'ooze' [cf. maqu- and maʀʀaʀ]
AAY maqə- 'ooze, flow out'
CAY maqə-
NSY maqə- 'flow'

CSY maaqə- 'ooze, flow, drain out' [and maaqutə- 'be carried away by current']
Sir maqə- 'flow' [and maqn̥əX '(sea) current', maquɫəX 'current, flow'; Vakh. also has maqit(ə)- 'carry away (current)']
SPI maʀi- 'flow out, leak, sweat' [for Qaw homonym 'take a bath' see maqaq]
NAI maqɨ- 'flow out, leak, sweat'
WCI maqi- 'flow, suppurate'
ECI maqi-
GRI maqi- 'open (wound, abscess)' [and maʀši- 'get water in eyes']

PI maqənəq 'pus' [cf. nəʀ[1]]
SPI — [maʀiniq 'Saturday' is from CAY maqinəq 'Saturday' — see Qaw maʀi- under maqaq]
NAI —
WCI maʀniq, maqiniq 'pus'
ECI maʀniq, maqiniq
GRI maʀniq* 'pus'

PE maqət- 'drain liquid from' [cf. t-[1]]
AAY —
CAY maq(ə)tə- 'squeeze liquid out from'
NSY —
CSY maqətə- 'drain liquid from'
Sir —
SPI —
NAI —
WCI —
ECI —
GRI maqit- 'tap'

PE maqəɣ- 'carry on head (kayak)'
AAY maqəɣ- 'carry load on shoulders' [maqək 'shoulder load']
CAY —
NSY —
CSY —
Sir —
SPI —
NAI maqɨk- 'carry over portage' [Jen. has 'carry kayak on shoulders']
WCI maqik- 'carry kayak on shoulders' [Pryde]
ECI maqik- 'carry kayak on head'
GRI maqiɣ-

PE maqu- 'suppurate' [cf. maqə- and maʀʀaʀ and maʀuyuɣ-]
AAY maquxtə- 'drain (liquid from infected ear)' [and note məqu- 'be dirty, make a mess' — influenced by məqə-?]
CAY [note Y məquq 'human excrement' — influenced by məqə-?]➡
NSY maqusuɣniq 'unpleasant smell' [L.-T.]
CSY —
Sir —
SPI maʀusunit- 'smell moldy'
NAI maqu- 'become spoiled, deteriorate, defecate, urinate' [and maqut- 'destroy, have been destroyed', maqquq* 'body waste']
WCI —
ECI NBI maquk- 'rain' [for maquyuk- 'be revulsed, repelled by, disdain (biblical)', maquyunna(q)- 'be disgusting' see maʀuyuɣ-]
GRI —

PY maquluk 'drainage from infected ear' [cf. ɫuɣ(-)]
AAY maquluk 'drainage from infected ear'
CAY maquluk, maqulluk
NSY —
CSY —

PE maʀlaɣ- 'give gift after dance ceremony?'
AAY —
CAY Y maʀlaɣtuʀ- 'give or receive gifts according to reciprocal requests during the messenger feast'
NSY maʀlaɣ- 'exchange gifts during "berry" holiday' [ANLC; maʀlan 'gift exchange during "berry" holiday' (L.-T.)]
CSY maʀlak 'gift exchange ceremony after a particular dance traditionally held yearly'
Sir maʀlaX 'gift received after finishing dance at festival' [Em.]
SPI maʀlak- 'give present during dancing'
NAI maʀlak- 'give present during Inupiaq invitational dance' [also nom. for the present]
WCI Sig maʀlak-, maʀlaɣi- 'admire' [and maʀlaɣutsak- 'be amazed']
ECI —
GRI —

PE maʀʀaʀ 'mud' [from *maʀə-, ultimately the same as maqə-?; cf. maʀu-[1] and maqu- and compare maʀut- for the forms with initial mu- due to assimilation]
AAY maʀaq 'swampy area', KP maʀaɫaq, maʀaqcuk 'bog'
CAY maʀaq 'marshy, muddy low land' [and maʀayaq 'mud', NSU maqaɫaq 'sand']
NSY — [for uʀaq, uXaq 'clay' see uʀʀaʀ]
CSY Chap maʀaq 'marshy area'
Sir —
SPI maʀʀaq 'mud', maʀaɫɫak 'swampy ground', Qaw maʀa 'flat area, field' [Ras. has 'valley'], maʀluk 'mud', Di maXak 'sod insulation on building'
NAI maʀʀaq* 'gravel, sand', maʀia 'sand', maqaɫɫak, Nu maʀaɫɫak 'white powdery rock used for tanning' [and muʀalliq, PH muʀaliq 'slush']
WCI maʀʀaq 'mud' [Cop also maʀluk; Ras. has Net maʀukluk 'swamp' but maʀatla·ʀsuk 'little swamp'; Schn. has muʀuniq 'mixture of water and ice or water and clay' for Baker Lake]
ECI maʀʀaq 'clay' [and maʀlu 'dirt — esp. old oil and wicks in traditional lamp']
GRI maXXaq*, NG maʀʀak 'clay', maʀaɫɫuk, maʀuɫɫuk, maʀuyuk, maquɫɫuk 'marshy, swampy place' [also maxxuʀɫuk and maʀaniq* 'turbid seal oil', NG maʀulluk 'mud']

PY maʀtu- 'be thick or long?' [cf. tu-[1]; from a root *əmaʀ-?]
AAY maXtu- 'be thick' [opp. = maXkitə-]
CAY maXtu- 'be long (trail or distance overland)' [opp. = maXkitə-]

NSY —
CSY —
Inu [note KI maqtu- 'be wide (water)' — from CAY?]

PE maʀu-[1] 'sink into soft ground or snow' [cf. maʀut-, also maʀʀaʀ and muʀðuɣ-; the latter may have influenced the Yup, but compare maʀut- for the initial mu- here]
AAY muʀu- 'sink in mud, snow, etc.'
CAY muʀu-
NSY muʀułqa(ʀ)- 'get stuck or sink into deep snow'
CSY muʀu- 'sink into soft snow' [for muʀutə- 'hunt on ice' see maʀut-]
Sir məʀuqəmə- 'drown, sink in (person)', məʀuqə(s)- 'fall through' [Em.; note also muʀəX 'pressure ridge (in ice)?']
SPI mauɣaq- 'sink into soft ground, snow', maužaaq-, Qaw maʀuunaq- 'cross open water by jumping from floe to floe' [the latter form as nominal = 'ice floe']
NAI ma<ɣ>u- 'sink into soft ground or snow' [the ɣ is not historical, though note also maɣɣuti- 'sink with']
WCI Cop mau- 'put feet in snow or water' [Ras.; Schn. has muʀaq- 'be wet' for 'adg']
ECI mau- 'sink in' [and mauyaʀaq 'small ice floe that sinks when one steps on it']
GRI maa- 'sink into swampy ground or snow' [and maaɣaʀ-, maavaʀ- 'be soft to tread on', SWG maašaʀaq 'small ice floe'; note also maxxut(i)- 'put in (e.g. cork in bottle, hand in pocket)', by contam. with maŋut-?]

PE maʀuya(ʀ) 'soft snow' [cf. yaʀ?]
AAY [note KP ma<ʀ>uyaq 'wrinkle from exposure to water']
CAY —
NSY —
CSY muʀaya- 'walk through deep snow' [Chap also as nom. 'deep snow']
Sir —
SPI —
NAI mauyaq 'soft dirt or deep snow into which one may sink'
WCI mauyaq 'soft snow'
ECI mauyaq 'ground that gives in under one', Lab 'deep snow' [Baffin mauya acc. Boas]
GRI —

PE maʀu-[2] or **maɣu-** 'howl' [onomatopoeic or other distortions seem to have affected various forms here; cf. maaq-]
AAY —
CAY maʀuaʀa- 'howl'
NSY maXałəq 'howl of animal in pain', maXuaʀ- 'howl' [note also muʀža(ʀ)- 'bark']
CSY [note mulaaʀ- 'howl']
Sir [note mulaʀ- 'howl']
SPI maʀuaq-, Qaw mau- 'howl'
NAI maɣu- 'howl', PH maʀukpak- 'bay loudly' [and note maxuk-, maXuk- 'bark to get attention', Nu maXuq- 'give a short bark', maXak- 'whine (dog)']
WCI maɣu- 'howl' [Cop also muʀuq-], Car? miaɣaq- 'whine (dog)' [Schn. 'adg'; Ras. has miaɣɣuuʀ-, as in GRI — Pryde has miaɣɣuuq- 'howl' also for Cop]
ECI miaɣɣu(q)-, Lab muuxxuuk- 'howl' [Andersen et al. have miuggut- for Lab; also muʀaq- 'howl, cry (fox)']
GRI miaxxuuʀ- 'howl' [of wolves, also of dogs in SWG; and note muuXXuuʀ- 'bark (fox)']

PE maʀut- and **muʀut-** 'hunt on ice' [there may be a relat. to maʀu-[1]; the second, Yup form here may be by assimilation — compare similar forms with initial mu- under maʀu-[2] and maʀʀaʀ]
AAY —
CAY —
NSY muʀutə- 'hunt on sea ice' [ANLC; Men. has muʀusiłta 'hunter' and muʀufik 'hunting place']
CSY muʀutə- 'hunt on the ice'
Sir —
SPI maut- 'go out on ice to hunt' [and Imaq mausauq-, mauʀusauq- 'hunt (on the tundra)', also mauqšužə 'hunter', mauʀutəyauʀ- 'take hunting with one']
NAI maut-, mauq- 'go hunting out on ice'
WCI maut- 'go out on ice after seals' [and Net mauXXuq- 'go seal-hole hunting' — Ras.]
ECI mauliq- 'look for seal at breathing hole'
GRI maat- 'be out hunting at breathing hole in ice'

PE maʀuyuɣ- and **muʀuyuɣ-** 'feel disgusted' [cf. maqu- and yuɣ-; for the variants compare maʀut-, muʀut- above, also maqə- and maʀʀaʀ]
AAY —
CAY —
NSY muʀyu(ɣ)- 'be disgusted' [ANLC]
CSY —
Sir —
SPI muʀuyui- 'be repulsed'
NAI muayuk- 'feel repulsed, squeamish'
WCI muiyaŋu- 'feel sick'
ECI maquyuk- 'be revulsed, repelled by, disdain (biblical)', maquyunna(q)- 'be disgusting' [influenced by maqu-?]
GRI maayuɣ- [old ortho. mauyug-] 'be disgusted, be finicky about food', maayuɣi- 'feel loathing for', NG mauyuihuk- 'be disgusted'

PY-S maʀyaʀ- 'lead (esp. lead dog)'
AAY maʀyaXtə- 'lead (dog or person leading dog team)'
CAY maʀyaXtə-, maXtə-
NSY —
CSY maʀyaXquʀ-, məʀyaXquʀ- 'lead' [maʀyaXquXta 'leader, lead dog']
Sir maʀyaXqaXta 'leading dog or bird'
Inu — [but Ras. has W maʀiaʀit 'front crossbar of sledge']

PI matəqtə 'waistband'
SPI —
NAI matiqti 'waistband'
WCI —
ECI matiqti
GRI matiʀti
Yup [CAY Nun matəXta 'hip' is clearly related, but the original sense is unclear — contam. from PE makitəʀ?]

PY-S matnəq 'warmth' [cf. macaʀ and nəʀ[1]]
AAY Kod matn̥əq 'radiant heat'
CAY matn̥əq* 'warmth, heat' [and matn̥iʀ- 'produce a lot of heat', NS matŋiʀ- 'be burning']
NSY makn̥əq 'warmth' [L.-T.]
CSY maatn̥əq* 'heat, warmth' [and maatnəʀ- 'be hot']
Sir mantəʀyuɣ- 'feel sweaty' [Orr], mantəʀyupiɣ- 'be very warm' [Vakh.; and note mantəʀca 'sweat', also with metath.]
Inu [note Qaw matŋiʀ- 'burn, be on fire', from the NS above?]

PE matŋa- 'jolt or be jolted' [there may be a relat. to manŋəq-]
AAY matŋa- 'be speedy, fast (on feet or working)'
CAY matŋaxtə-, matŋała-, matŋitə- 'jolt (vehicle)'
NSY —
CSY —
Sir —
SPI —
NAI [manŋatcai- 'cause to tense up (muscles)', manŋaiqšuq- 'tense up in anticipation of being hit']
WCI [Car maŋat- 'run away (game, caribou)' — Schn.]
ECI maŋŋa(C)- 'move a little on being jolted', maŋŋaa- 'rock, budge several times (s.th. heavy like a rock)' [and maŋat- Iti 'move a little, budge (s.th. one is trying to loosen or remove)', Tar 'talk of s.o. behind their back']
GRI maŋat- 'order, enjoin to do s.th.', NG 'trick, tease'

PI matŋiaq 'wrist-guard for archer' [cf. matŋa-?]
Yup [note CAY NS maliŋuʀun 'wrist-guard for archer']
SPI [Jen. has man·iaq 'archer's wrist-guard' for KI and W]
NAI manŋiaq, Nu matŋiaq 'wrist-guard for archer'
WCI manŋiaq 'archer's wrist-guard' [Pryde]
ECI —
GRI —

PE mattaʀ- 'undress'
AAY mataʀ- 'become naked' [postural root as in all Yup]
CAY mataʀ- 'undress, unharness, be undressed, take off coat'
NSY mataʀ- 'undress' [and mataʀməlŋuq 'naked']
CSY mataʀ- 'take off clothes'
Sir mataʀ- 'take off clothes, molt (animal or bird)' [Vakh. has mataXt(ə)-]
SPI mattaq- 'remove parka or clothes'
NAI mattaq-
WCI mattaq- 'take off clothes, unharness dog'
ECI matta(q)- 'take off clothing, unharness dog' [Dor. has maktaq- for SB, NBI — influenced by maŋaɣ-?]
GRI mattaʀ- 'take clothing off, get out of harness (dog) or snare (ptarmigan)', EG mattaC- 'remove hair from sealskin' [also ma(a)ttamiiq 'water-tight skin with hair removed'?]

PE matu(-) 'cover' [the Yup forms with initial p may have been influenced by patuɣ if it is not simply a matter of assimilation]
AAY patu, matu 'cover' [also verbal]
CAY patu 'cover' [also verbal]
NSY matu [Jen.]
CSY —
Sir —
SPI matu 'lid, cover' [verbal = 'cover', as in all Inu]
NAI matu
WCI matu
ECI matu
GRI matu 'door, cover' [as verb = 'close, be closed']

> **PE matuŋiʀ-** 'uncover' [cf. ŋiʀ-]
> AAY patuiʀ-, matuiʀ- 'uncover'
> CAY patuiʀ-
> NSY —
> CSY —
> Sir —
> SPI matuiq-
> NAI —
> WCI matuiq-
> ECI matuiq-
> GRI matuiʀ- 'open, unlock'

PY mayitəqə- 'be eager for' [cf. kə-[1]]
AAY AP ma'itəqə- 'eagerly, anxiously await'
CAY mayitəqə- 'desire s.th. that one has been deprived of'
NSY —
CSY —

PE mayuʀ- 'climb' [cf. EA (h)ayuʀ- 'ascend, climb (a hill)']
AAY mayuʀ- 'climb'
CAY mayuʀ- 'climb, go hunting in mountains in spring or fall' [and mayuʀa- 'climb around']
NSY mayuʀ- 'climb'
CSY mayuʀ-
Sir mayəʀ- 'climb' [and mayuʀnəX 'breast, place where keel bends'?; and Em. has mayuXtə- 'pile up']
SPI mayuq- 'climb'
NAI mayuq- 'climb' [and mayuaq- Nu 'climb', Mal 'be climbing']
WCI mayuq- 'climb'
ECI mayuq- 'climb' [and mayuaq- 'be climbing']
GRI mayuʀ- 'rise (fish from deep or up river), build up toward bad weather' [mayuaʀ- 'climb, go up (person)']

> **PI mayuqqaq** 'slope or way up mountain' [cf. mayuʀaʀ(aʀ)- below and yaʀ?]
> Yup [note CAY mayuʀyaʀaq* 'ladder, stairs']
> SPI —
> NAI —
> WCI mayuqqaq 'place one ascends to cross mountain, etc.'
> ECI mayuqqaq 'slope (on road or mountain)', mayuqqaɣalak 'gently rising slope'
> GRI mayuqqaq 'slope one must go up, river one must sail up'

PE mayuʀaʀ(aʀ)- 'climb gradually' [cf. aʀ-]
AAY —
CAY mayuaʀ(aʀ)- 'climb gradually'
NSY —
CSY —
Sir —
SPI mayuaq- 'travel upward, uphill'
NAI —
WCI Car mayuʀaq- 'sail up river against tide' [Ras.]
ECI mayuʀaq- 'climb (steps or ladder)'
GRI mayuʀaʀ- 'go against current (boat)'

PE mayuʀaʀun 'ladder' [cf. mayuʀaʀ(aʀ)- above and un]
AAY C mayuʀuutaq, mayuʀuutat 'ladder'
CAY —
NSY —
CSY mayuʀaatak
Sir —
SPI mayuaXautit
NAI mayuʀautat
WCI mayuʀautit
ECI mayuʀauti
GRI —

PE məcaɣ 'swampy ground' [cf. məcaʀ- and məcu(ɣ); Aleut y̥a- 'rise (of tide), flood, high tide' may be related — Berg. suggests it is from *tya- and that the Esk base here could be from *mətyaɣ- — compare tucaʀ- and Aleut y̥u- under məcu(ɣ)]
AAY məcak, məcaxłuk, məcaɣuaq 'puddle'
CAY məcak, məcaxłuk 'puddle' [and məcqitə- 'step into a puddle'; Lantis has mesaq 'wet, soggy' for Nun]
NSY məsak 'puddle'
CSY məsak 'bog', məsaɣ- 'be swampy'
Sir məsax 'swamp', məsaxpałuX 'swampy'
SPI mizak 'liquid which soaks s.th.' [as verb = 'get soaked'; Jen. has W mizaq 'swamp']
NAI misak 'slush, swamp' [as verb = 'be slushy, wet (ground)'; mitcak- 'become damp or wet'; compare also masak under macak]
WCI Sig misak 'wet snow' [Lowe], misaktuq 'melting snow in spring' [B.-S. has misaluk 'swamp' for Net]
ECI —
GRI [note mitsaɣ-, mitsaʀ- 'have fermented (fish)']

PY məcaliqaq 'sleet'
AAY məcaliqaq 'sleet, wet snow' [also verbal]
CAY məcaliqaq
NSY —
CSY —

PE məcaʀ- 'make splashing or smacking sound' [cf. məcaɣ, məcu(ɣ) and macak — the exact relat. here is obscure]
AAY məcaXtə- 'make slapping or smacking sound'
CAY məcaXtə- 'make a splashing or smacking sound'
NSY məsaxtə- 'make slurping sound (water in shoes)' [infl. by məcaɣ?]
CSY məsaqə- 'smack lips' [and məsamsuɣ- 'nibble']
Sir məsaqaʀ- 'smack lips'
SPI Qaw misak- 'smack lips' [compare KI mizak- under məcaɣ]
NAI misaq- 'smack lips' [and misamatɨt- 'make slapping sound, slap hard']
WCI misaqpaluk-, Baker Lake misaluk- 'make splashing or smacking sound' [the latter Schn.; note also misamit- 'make noise while eating']
ECI misaq- 'smack lips' [Bourq. has 'eat noisily' for Lab]
GRI misaʀ- 'make splashing or smacking sound', NG mihaq- 'hit' [and note EG misaʀ̃aq 'bladder weed (kind of edible seaweed)', misaʀ̃aʀnat 'edible brown seaweed']

PE məcəɣ- 'jump' [cf. mətŋəʀ-]
AAY K məcəɣ- 'jump'
CAY NS məcəɣ-
NSY —
CSY —
Sir —
SPI mizik- 'jump over'
NAI misɨk- 'jump up, down, across' [and misiɣaq- 'hop']
WCI Cop mihik- 'jump across' [also Car. in Ras.]
ECI misik- 'jump up, down, across'
GRI [note EG miitsaaʀ- 'jump']

PE məciɣ- 'be clearly visible' [cf. Aleut six-ta- 'recognize'; kə-[1] is contained in many of these forms]
AAY [note AP mistu- 'be noisy' — influenced by əməɣ-?]
CAY məciɣ- 'be clearly visible, able to see well', məcikə- 'see clearly' [and note mistu- 'be clearly visible or audible'; opp. = miskite-]
NSY —
CSY —
Sir —
SPI miziɣi- 'observe'
NAI misiɣɨ- 'expect', misikši- 'watch over, tend reindeer'
WCI Sig misiɣi- 'watch over, protect, have noticed' [and Cop mihiɣi- 'discover, notice' in Ras.]
ECI misiɣi- 'discover, become aware of (usually of game animal getting wind)'
GRI misiɣi- 'feel, notice', NG mihii- 'get wind of (and be alarmed — animal)', EG misiisima- 'be careful' [and misiinaŋi 'not doing it voluntarily'; note also WG misiliɣ- 'examine, test']

PI məcikšuq- 'watch over or for' [cf. qðuʀ-]
SPI mizikšuq- 'watch from a look-out place'
NAI misikšuq- 'wait and watch for'
WCI misiksuq- 'watch over'
ECI —
GRI misiššuʀ-, EG miitsiʀ- 'examine, pay attention to, be careful'

PE məciʀaʀ- 'deny having done s.th.'
AAY məci<ʀ>aʀ- 'deny having done s.th.'
CAY məciʀ(aʀ)-
NSY məsiʀ- 'hide something out of greed' [L.-T.]
CSY məsiʀaʀ- 'deny having done something'

Sir məsiʀaʀ- [Orr]
SPI miziaq-
NAI —
WCI —
ECI misiaq-
GRI misiaʀ-

PE məcu(ɣ) or **məcuʀ** 'moisture or liquid' [cf. macak, məcaʀ- and məcaɣ, also perhaps Aleut ɣu- 'run (river), pour out (juice)', suggesting earlier *mətyu(ɣ) — compare ɣa- under məcaɣ; there could be two related sets here: verbal məcuɣ- and nominal məcuʀ]
AAY məcuq 'moisture', PWS 'juice' [and məcuu- 'be wet', məciʀ- 'get wet', Kod məcuxtə- 'make smacking noise in eating']
CAY məcuq 'sap, juice' [and məciʀ- 'soak', məci- 'get soaked', məcuʀ- 'get blood poisoning']
NSY məsu(k) 'sap, juice' [but Tein has məsuq; and məsuxtə- 'dip, moisten']
CSY məsuq 'liquid, juice'
Sir məsuX 'juice'
SPI mizu 'juice, sap', Qaw misuq- 'suck juice from plant'
NAI misuq 'juice, sap' [and misuk- 'dip, be dipped']
WCI misu 'juice, liquid squeezed out' [and misuk- 'dip in water'; Car? mihuk 'dew' — Schn. 'adg']
ECI misuk- 'dip'
GRI misuɣ- 'dip, dye'

PE məciʀaʀ 'oil dip' [cf. liʀ-?]
AAY —
CAY məciaq 'oil dip for food'
NSY məsiaq
CSY məsiiq*
Sir —
SPI miziʀaaq
NAI misiʀaaq
WCI Car mihiʀaq [Ras.]
ECI misiʀaq
GRI misiʀaq, misuʀaq

PY məcuŋə- 'get wet' [cf. nəɣ-]
AAY [PWS məcuŋyuilŋuq, AP məcuŋsuilŋuq 'bush cinquefoil']
CAY məcuŋə- 'be wet or soaked' [and note Nun məcuŋyuilŋuX 'type of plant']
NSY məsuŋə- 'get wet' [ANLC]
CSY məsuŋə- 'get wet, soaked'

PY məɣə- 'spend a long time (away)' [the relat. to the Chukchi given under Sir is unclear — perhaps there is contam. with it in CSY, though it may be a direct loan and thus not related to the AAY and CAY]
AAY PWS məɣə- 'take a long time, last a long time'
CAY məɣə- 'not want to go back to one's undesirable former living conditions'
NSY məɣə- 'take a long time' [ANLC]
CSY [muɣu- 'go far in the distance, move from place to place, be a caravan of travelers in the distance']
Sir [muɣul'iy 'caravan' (Vakh. from Men.'s texts) is from Chukchi muulə́n 'caravan' or Koryak məgulʀən — root muu-, -mgu- 'nomadic']

PE mək(k)əɣ- 'gnaw or bite off' [cf. makiʀ-, with which these may form a single set]
AAY AP məkəɣ-, KP makəɣ- 'gnaw'
CAY —
NSY məkəɣžaʀ- 'bite or tear into (meat)' [ANLC; L.-T. has məkəž(aqə)- 'bite, eat']
CSY məkəɣžaʀ- 'smooth off or make even with one's teeth'
Sir məkəɣžaʀ- 'eat biting food with front teeth or beak' [Em.]
SPI miɣik- 'take a bite out of, tear a piece out of with teeth'
NAI mikik- 'bite into and tear out a piece with teeth', mikkik- 'tear off pieces as one eats (meat)' [the second i of the first (uncommon) form probably weak]
WCI mik(k)ak- 'gnaw at (like puppy or fox)', Cop mik(k)ik- 'tear off meat with teeth' [Ras. has mikiC- 'bite', mikiɣiaq- 'snatch or bite at', mikiɣiaq 'deadfall trap']
ECI mikki(k)- 'bite off', mikiak- [Lab mikiaq- in Bourq.] 'bite pieces off with teeth', Iti? mikkali- 'gnaw at (of mouse, etc.)' [and mikiɣiaq '(fox) trap']
GRI mikiɣ- 'pull at with teeth to loosen', mikkaɣ- 'eat meat by tearing with teeth' [and NG mikixxuq- 'skin a fox']

PI məkəɣaq 'fermented meat' [cf. mək(k)əɣ-?]
SPI —
NAI mikiɣaq 'mixture of fermented whale meat, tongue and maktak' [verbal = 'be fermented (of such a mixture)']
WCI Cop mikiɣaq 'raw meat' [Ras. has mikiaq for Car]
ECI mikiɣaq 'raw meat'
GRI mikiaq, mikiɣaq 'fermented meat or fish', NG mikiaq 'raw meat' [mikiaʀ- 'have formented']

PI məkliaq 'umbilical cord' [cf. mək(k)əɣ- and li(C)aʀ?]
SPI —
NAI mikłiaq 'umbilical cord'
WCI mikłiaq [and Cop mixxiaq in Pryde]
ECI mitsiaq 'umbilical cord' [Bourq. has mikłiaq for Lab]
GRI miłłiaq 'umbilical cord' [also 'brother' as a shaman's word acc. Fab.]

PI məlak 'stain or spot'
Yup [note CSY məlaŋutə- 'see the outline of s.th. dimly']
SPI KI mila 'stain' [Jen.]
NAI [millit- 'become stained from being wet a long time']
WCI milait 'spots on skin of seals'
ECI milak 'round spot on skin' [Saul — Schn. has milaq]
GRI milak 'spot (of different coloration from surrounding area)'

PE mələɣ(-) 'plug or cover' [cf. məlu-; the relat. with məłaʀ- is obscure]
AAY—
CAY mələɣ- 'close', mələk 'door'
NSY —

CSY —
Sir — [for məłə- 'close'- see məlu-]
SPI — [for milaq 'plug' see məłaʀ-]
NAI miłɨk 'plug' [as verb = 'plug, close (window)']
WCI milik 'plug'
ECI milik 'cover, veil' [also verbal], Aiv 'bandage for eyes'
GRI milik 'plug, stopper, nail head', miliɣ- 'plug, close up'

PE məlŋuʀ 'water beetle' [cf. perhaps EA luuqaaya-X, Atkan n̥uuqaaya-X 'maggot, fly larva' — possibly from *lŋu- with loss of initial *mə- acc. Berg.]
AAY —
CAY məlŋuq 'water beetle'
NSY məlŋuq
CSY məlŋuq, məlŋu
Sir məlŋuX
SPI Qaw minŋuq
NAI minŋuq [min^{y}ŋuq is an innovation]
WCI Sig minŋuq
ECI miŋŋuq
GRI miŋŋuq

PE məlquʀ 'body hair (or fur) or feather' [cf. quʀ and Aleut imli-X 'hair of head']
AAY AP məłquq 'feather, human body hair, animal fur'
CAY məłquq
NSY məłquq 'fur, feather'
CSY məłquq 'feather, body hair, fur' [and note məlaŋaaq 'downy feather']
Sir məłqəX 'fur' [Vakh. also 'feather'; and note məlaŋaX 'down, cotton wool']
SPI mitquq 'feather, body hair, fur'
NAI miłquq
WCI mitquq
ECI miqquq
GRI miqquq 'feather, body hair, fur' [in EG miqqiq also 'eyebrow']

PY məlqupak 'shaggy dog' [cf. vaɣ]
AAY —
CAY məłqupayayaq 'shaggy dog'
NSY məłqupak [L.-T.]
CSY məłqupak

PY-S məlu- 'cover' [cf. mələɣ(-), and compare also iməɣ- and imu-]
AAY AP məlutə- 'cover eyes while playing hide-and-seek'
CAY məlu-
NSY —
CSY məłu- 'block, cover' [and məłutaq 'plug' — contam. with məłaʀ-?]
Sir məłə- 'close', məłutaX 'cover, opening (entrance)' [Vakh. from Rub.'s texts; contam. with məłaʀ-?]

PE məluɣ- 'suck (breast)' [cf. mulə(ɣ), with which there appears to be some contam.]
AAY məluɣ- 'suck', KP 'eat berries off bush' [and məlu<ɣ>aʀ- 'kiss']
CAY məluɣ- 'suck', məluk 'fish roe'
NSY məluɣ- 'suck' [ANLC; Em. has məluk 'baby's "pacifier" of walrus or reindeer fat'; məlu 'nipple' (ANLC)]
CSY məluɣ- 'suck'
Sir məłəɣ- 'suck or breathe in' [Vakh. from Rub.; Men. has məłəXtət- 'suck up, absorb']
SPI Imaq məlu 'nipple', Qaw 'breast, udder, milk'
NAI miłuk 'nipple, breast' [but in Mal 'milk' — also Jen. for 'Ingl.'; verbal = 'suck']
WCI miluk 'woman's breast' [verbal = 'suck'], Sig 'milk' [probably with influence from the English; Schn. has it for 'nipple' in 'adg' — also B.-S. for Car]
ECI miluk- 'suck' [and millua(q)- 'suckle']
GRI miluɣ-, miłłuɣ- 'suck' [and miłłuaʀ- 'suck in'; EG mittivaq, mittivaʀ̃aq 'breast']

PE məluɣyaʀ 'gnat (or other creature characterized by sucking)' [cf. yaʀ; there are some indep. parallel derivations here]
AAY K məluɣyaq 'big brown mussel', məluɣya(ʀ)aq 'bloodsucking insect, mosquito'
CAY məluɣyaʀ(aq*), NS məluxsaaʀaq 'small gnat', NS məluxsaq 'wasp' [and Nun məluɣyaX 'elephant' (!)]
NSY —
CSY [məluɣyaq 'jellyfish']
Sir —
SPI miluɣiaq 'gnat'
NAI miłuɣiaq 'solitary wasp', PH 'bee, sucker fish' [and note miłuɣiaq- 'go and suck']
WCI Cop miluɣiaq 'midge' [in Sig 'carp'; Schn. has 'midge, gnat, bee' for 'adg']
ECI miluɣiaq ' small wasp-like insect, carp, lampry', Lab 'black fly that sucks' [Bourq.]
GRI miluɣiaq 'bee'

PY məłaʀ- 'plug' [cf. mələɣ(-)]
AAY məłaʀ- 'plug'
CAY məłaʀ- 'plug' [nom. = məłaq]
NSY məłaʀ- 'plug' [and note məłəpxutə- 'knock or stick into ground']
CSY — [for məłutaq 'plug' see məlu-]
Sir — [for məłə- 'close' see məlu-]
Inu [note milaq- 'plug' (also nom.), Imaq məlaq 'plug for sealskin float' and məlupəuša(q)- 'knock into ground' — from the Yup?]

PE mənət- 'leave s.o. out during distribution'
AAY məŋtə- 'go straight to destination without stopping'
CAY məntə- 'leave none (for s.o.)'
NSY məntə- 'be left out when others eat, leave, etc.' [ANLC]
CSY —
Sir —
SPI minit- 'leave out, omit s.o. when distributing s.th.'
NAI minɨt-, nimɨt-
WCI minit-
ECI minit-
GRI minit- 'leave out when distributing s.th.' [also mittaʀi- (old ortho. migtari-), half-trans. minitsi-, missi-]

PI məŋik- 'get jammed' [or miŋik-?; compare PY əŋiɣ-?]
SPI miŋiaq- 'get squeezed, jammed, caught' [and note Qaw miŋialiʀžak 'shotgun']
NAI —
WCI —
ECI miŋik- 'pinch hand in door' [for Lab Bourq. has 'squeeze with one corner between s.th.'; note also Iti miŋiti, W. Bay piŋiti 'knuckles, articulations of hands or feet']
GRI miŋiɣ- 'get jammed (finger or toe, by a blow or pressure)'

PY-S məqə- 'shed hair'
AAY məqə- 'shed hair'
CAY məqə- 'shed hair' [for məquq 'excrement' see maqu-]
NSY məqə- 'shed (all one's) hair' [ANLC; Em. has məqəŋalʀia 'bald'; Tein has məqiłə 'worn or moldy spot on skin']
CSY məqə- 'shed hair'
Sir məqə(s)- 'shed hair' [Em.]
Inu [note Qaw məqqaq- 'shave bald']

PY-S məqəciʀ- 'loosen hairs from skin' [cf. c(c)iʀ-]
AAY —
CAY məqciʀ- 'soak so hair comes off (skin)'
NSY —
CSY məqəsiʀ- 'cause a skin to lose hair by letting it age'
Sir məqəsiʀ- 'remove hair from skin, leave skin for hairs to come loose' [Em.]

PY-S məʀiɣ- 'collapse?' [the relat. to imə- — if any — is obscure]
AAY Kod məʀiɣ- 'become steep, drop off into water' [postural root]
CAY məʀiɣ- 'be caved in, folded over, hemmed in'
NSY —
CSY —
Sir [Vakh. has məʀuqə- 'collapse, fall down' from Men.'s texts]

PE məʀnuʀ- 'be tired' [metathesis in Inu? — compare Sig qinʀiq- under qiʀnəʀ-; cf. məʀvi(k)-]
AAY K məʀnuʀ- 'be tired'
CAY məʀnuʀ-
NSY məʀnuʀ- 'be tired' [ANLC, but Men. has məɣnuʀ- — compare taɣnəʀaq under taʀ(ə)nəʀ]
CSY məʀnuʀ - 'be tired' [and Men. has Chap məʀnuq 'fatigue', məʀnali 'rest']
Sir —
SPI muʀnatuq-, Qaw minʀuq- 'be tired' [and Jen. has W munrautoq-, i.e. underlying munʀuqtuq-]
NAI mɨnʀuq-, mɨnʀuqtuq- 'be tired'
WCI [Met. has miŋiq- 'be tired' as an old word and Ow. has miŋuhuk- 'be tired' for EP, both from *minʀuq-?] ➡
ECI miʀŋutuq- 'be very tired'
GRI miʀŋuʀ- 'become faint, without strength' [and note Up miŋuʀtu- 'be in great trouble or agony'; for miʀfi- 'have lost one's strength because of heat' see məʀvi(k)-]

PE məʀnuʀiʀ- 'rest' [cf. ŋiʀ-]
AAY K məʀnuiXtuʀ- 'rest'
CAY məʀnuiʀ- 'recover from being tired'
NSY məɣnuiXsiʀ- 'rest'
CSY —
Sir —
SPI muʀnuiqsa(q)-, Qaw minʀuiqsiq- 'take a rest'
NAI PH mɨnʀuiqsiaq- 'rest'
WCI Car minʀuiXXiq- 'rest' [B.-S., who also gives Net miŋnueqseq- — Pryde has minʀuiqsiq- instead]
ECI miʀŋui(q)- 'be rested'
GRI miʀŋuiʀsiʀ- 'sit down for a rest'

PY məʀqə- 'rinse' [cf. əməʀ and ʀqə-?]
AAY məXqə-, muXqə- 'rinse (esp. dishes)'
CAY muXqə- 'rinse clothes'
NSY —
CSY məXqə- 'put water on'

PI məʀvi(k)- 'feel displeasure?' [cf. məʀnuʀ-?]
SPI —
NAI miʀviɣɨ- 'be stingy with', Nu 'dislike', miʀvisuk- 'be unwilling to pay the asking price', Nu 'dislike s.th.'
WCI miʀvik- 'dislike, feel displeasure', miʀviɣi- 'be envious of, not like s.o.'s way of acting (e.g. because he takes too much for himself)'
ECI —
GRI [miʀfi- 'have lost one's strength because of the heat' — contam. with məʀnuʀ-?]

PE mətaɣ- 'tease' [there may be a link to mətəŋłə(ʀ)-]
AAY mətqə-, Kod mətəqə- 'torture, be cruel toward, demean' [with ʀqə-?]
CAY Nun mətqə- 'suffer, be ill'
NSY —
CSY [note mətaʀ- 'smother'?]
Sir —
SPI mitaaq- 'joke' [and Jen. has nom. mitaq, also mitauti(gi)- 'fool' for W]
NAI mɨtaaq- 'joke' [Jen. also has nom. mitaq], mɨtautiɣɨ- 'mock'
WCI mitaaq- 'joke, play joke on s.o.', mita(a)qutiɣi- 'mock'
ECI mitak- 'joke, tease' [mitautiɣi- 'tease']
GRI mitaɣ- 'tease, make fun of' [half-translated mitałłiʀ-], mitaaʀ- 'pull faces, dress up for Twelfth Night (in grotesque disguise)'

PI mətək and **mətu** 'slush ice in fishing hole' [compare iməɣ- and imu- for the two forms]
SPI mitiŋiq- 'remove slush from fishing hole', mitiŋiun 'ice scoop'
NAI Nu mɨtik 'slush ice', mɨtu 'first chunks of ice clinging to nets in ocean in fall' [verbal = 'cling (new sea ice to nets)'; mɨtiŋiq-, PH pɨtiŋiq- 'remove slush from fishing hole', mɨtiŋiun, PH pitiŋiun '(baleen) ice scoop']
WCI mituit 'small pieces of ice forming a thin cover on water'
ECI mitu 'small piece of ice coming to surface in holes

cut through ice' [and mituiyaut 'ice scoop to remove them']
GRI — [for NWG mitiłłi- 'cannot close because of ice (door or window)' see mətəŋłə(ʀ)-]

PE mətəŋłə(ʀ)- 'spring up or flick' [cf. mətŋəʀ-; the CSY and Sir influenced by pətɣəʀ-?]
AAY — [for pət(ə)ŋə- 'come loose' see mətŋəʀ-]
CAY — [for pətəŋtə- 'set a trap', pətŋə-, NSU pətəŋə- 'spring off, snap out of position' see mətŋəʀ-]
NSY mətənłaqu(ʀ)- 'flick, give a fillip' [and mətənžan 'spring (metal)'; ANLC has mətəŋžaʀ- 'be elastic']
CSY pətəŋłaɣ(aʀ)- 'hit s.th. by flicking or snapping finger out from under ball of thumb'
Sir [Em. has pitəŋłəɣ- 'give a flick or fillip to s.o.']
SPI mitiɣliq- 'flick, give a fillup' [and mitiɣžalak- 'bounce forth, spring out']
NAI mɨtɨɣliɣaun 'bone catapult for springing pebbles', PH mɨtɨɣlak- 'flick, fillip, bounce away' [and mɨtɨɣžak- 'bounce off, fly off']
WCI Car? mitilliyaut [for mitiɣliyaut?] 'trigger' [Schn. 'adg', who also has mitiliʀaut 'flip, overthrow', mitilʀaqtuq 'spring'; Pryde has Net mitiɣlautik 'bow and arrow' as a shaman's word; Pet. has mitiɣliq- 'bounce' for Sig]
ECI —
GRI NG mitiɣli- 'give a flick', NWG mitiłłi- [old ortho. mitigdli-] 'be elastic (e.g. shark cartilage), not be able to close because of ice (door or window)' [contam. with mətək in the latter sense?]

PY mətəŋtaq 'fin (dorsal)' [cf. mətəŋłə(ʀ)-]
AAY — [for pətəŋtaq 'yarn, unraveled rope' see mətŋəʀ-]
CAY pətəŋtaq, pətŋałaq 'adipose fin of fish'
NSY [for mətənžan 'spring (metal)' see mətəŋłə(ʀ)-]
CSY mətəŋtaq 'dorsal fin'

PE mətəʀ 'eider duck' [cf. perhaps Aleut sa-X 'bird, duck' with loss of initial *mə -and for the s compare asa- under PE atəʀ]
AAY —
CAY mətXaq* 'eider'
NSY ➟
CSY mətXaq 'eider' [Chap. also 'bird-skin coat']
Sir [Em. has mətXaX 'coat made of bird skin']
SPI mitiq 'eider duck'
NAI mɨtɨq 'eider duck', Nu 'female eider'
WCI Cop mitiq 'duck', Sig 'female eider' [Met.], Car, Net 'eider' [Ras.]
ECI mitiq 'eider'
GRI mitiq*

PY-S mətəʀłuk 'raven' [cf. łuɣ]
AAY —
CAY —
NSY mətəXłuk 'raven'
CSY mətəXłuk
Sir mətəXłəX

PY mətəʀvik 'eagle' [cf. piɣ?]
AAY —
CAY mətəʀvik 'bald eagle
NSY mətəʀvik 'eagle' [L.-T.]
CSY —

PY-S mətəʀyaq 'eyebrow hair' [there may be a link to mətəʀ; cf. p.b. yaʀ]
AAY —
CAY —
NSY —
CSY mətəʀyaq 'eyebrow hair'
Sir mətəʀyaX 'eyebrow hair' [Orr — Men. has mətəʀyay 'eyebrows']
Inu [for EG miqqiq 'eyebrow' see məlquʀ]

PE mətləɣ 'knife for carving' [cf. mətŋəʀ-?]
AAY —
CAY məłxaʀ(aq*) 'small piece of metal, carving knife with curved blade'
NSY —
CSY —
Sir —
SPI miłłik and Qaw miłxaq 'curved carving knife' [the latter form could be a Yupik borrowing]
NAI millɨk, Nu mɨtlɨk 'long curved carving knife'
WCI —
ECI —
GRI —

PE mətŋəʀ- 'jump up' [cf. mətəŋłə(ʀ)- and pətɣəʀ-, also məcəɣ- and mətəŋtaq; there appears to be contam. from pətɣəʀ- in the p-initial Yup forms, but compare also patu under matu(-)]
AAY [note pət(ə)ŋə- 'come loose' and C pətəŋtaq 'yarn, unravelled rope']
CAY [pətŋə-, NSU pətəŋə- 'spring up, snap out of position', pətəŋtə- 'set a trap']
NSY [pətaŋə- 'spring up' — ANLC; Men. has pətaŋələq 'jump']
CSY mətŋəʀ- 'run away, steal away' [mətŋaamsiiɣ- 'hop around']
Sir [note məɣžaXqə(s)- 'run', məɣcaʀnəŋ 'at a run']
SPI [Jen. has W minyeq- 'leap straight in air'; note also mitik- 'unravel']
NAI mɨnŋɨq-, Nu mɨtŋɨq- 'jump up or over'
WCI miŋiqtaq- 'leap up', Net miŋŋiq- 'jump' [the latter Ras.; Met. also has miŋa- Sig 'be agile, able to jump high' — elsewhere 'have landed' from mit-; Pet. has Sig miŋrear- 'jump' and mingnerar- 'walk (bird)']
ECI miŋŋi(q)-, miŋiʀiaq- 'jump up (to catch s.th.)' [in Lab 'jump over']
GRI NG miŋŋiq- 'jump', Up miŋiʀ- 'jump up' [note also miŋŋa- 'have strength (rowing harder than others)']

PI mənŋəʀiaq 'kind of trout' [cf. yaʀ?]
SPI —
NAI —
WCI Cop, Net miŋŋiʀiaq 'kind of trout (that can jump)' [Ras., for minŋiʀiaq? — Pryde confirms minŋiʀiaq as a shaman's word for fish in Net;

Schn. has Baker Lake miŋʀiaq 'fish that goes for bait (?)']
ECI Igl miŋŋɪʀiaq 'jumping one (trout)' [Ras.; Bourq. has miŋɪʀiaq 'small fish' for Lab]
GRI [Eg. has miŋɪʀiaq 'capelin' as a shaman's word]

PE mi(C)ani(kə)- 'be careful' [cf. kə-[1]]
AAY —
CAY mianikə- 'be careful'
NSY miaɫkə- 'sense, feel, attend to' [ANLC; Men. has miaɫqaʀ- 'feel']
CSY —
Sir —
SPI —
NAI —
WCI —
ECI mianiʀi- 'direct, guide' [Peck has 'guard' for Lab]
GRI miani- 'take heed', mianiʀ(i)- 'be cautious (about)' [and mianiʀšuʀ- 'be careful', mianiʀnaʀ- 'get offended']

PE mikə- or mikət- 'be small'
AAY mik<ə>tə- 'be small' [and mikəlŋuq 'small one']
CAY mik<ə>tə-, HBC, NI, Nun mikə- 'be small' [with the tə ~ l alternation as for contrary/neg. p.b.s; also mikəlŋuq* 'child']
NSY mikaʀažaaʀaq 'small' [and mikisqiq 'child', mikaʀaq 'small one, small child']
CSY məkəstaaq 'small thing', məkəlʀiiq 'boy' [and məkəskəžaʀaX 'very small', also miksaɣaq 'smaller bull walrus', miɣliɣžuŋiq 'smaller walrus']
Sir mikəʀaɫəʀəX 'small' [and mikəsqižaʀaX 'small child' — the same as mikəskəžaʀaX 'little one'?; Vakh. has mikaʀaɫəʀəX 'small']
SPI mikšuaq 's.th. small' [mikšuq or mikšuužuq 'it is small'; for miɣiqɫiq 'child' see mikəqɫəqtuq]
NAI mikɨ- 'be small'
WCI miki- 'be small' [also Cop mikkaq 'small one' acc. Pryde]
ECI miki-, NBI, Aiv mikit- 'be small' [and note mikitsa(q)- 'find too small for s.o. (garment)']
GRI miki- 'be small' [and note mikiʀsaʀ-, NG mikixxaq- 'find s.th. or s.o. too small'; note also EG miikkaayu(mmi) 'a little']

PE mikəli- 'make or become smaller' [cf. li-[2]]
AAY mikɫi- 'make or become smaller'
CAY mikɫi-
NSY mikɫi- 'make or become smaller' [Em.]
CSY məkəɫi- 'make or become smaller'
Sir —
SPI mikɫi-
NAI mikɫi-
WCI mikɫi-
ECI mikili-
GRI miɫɫi-, EG mitsi-

PI mikəliʀaq 'ring (i.e. fourth) finger' cf. l(l)iʀ and aʀ?]
Yup [for HBC əkiliq, ikilipik 'ring finger' see akulipaq under aku(ʀ), though it could reflect (with contamination) the original PE form here]
SPI miɣiliaq, Qaw mikilʀaaq, mikiqɫiq 'ring finger' [Ras. has mikiliraq for W and Men. miɣliaq for Imaq]
NAI mikil^{y}ʀaq 'fourth, ring finger'
WCI mikiliʀaq [Jen. has mikilraq]
ECI mikiliʀaq 'fourth, ring finger'
GRI mikiliʀaq

PI mikəqləqtuq 'child' [cf. mikə-]
SPI miɣiqɫiq 'child'
NAI mɨqɫiqtuq
WCI — [for miʀayuq 'baby' see piiʀaq]
ECI Northern Lab miqɫiqtuk 'baby' [Peck]
GRI miʀɫiʀtuq, miʀɫaaq [esp. in bible translat.], EG miʀsiʀtiq 'child' [for miiʀaq 'child' see piaʀaq under pi(-)]

PI mikšə- 'direction (of s.th.)'
SPI —
NAI mikšaut- 'estimate', Mal mikšaaq- 'guess at'
WCI miksi- 'direction of, this side of' [posit. root; Dor. has mixxiqɫiq 'nearest' for Net]
ECI mitsi- 'direction of, in front of, this side of, on subject of' [also as possessed noun 'sense of s.th.', mitsilik 'true'; NBI miksiqɫiq 'the nearest']
GRI miššɨ- [old ortho. migsse] 'direction of, about' [posit. root, 3s possessed miššaa, older miššiŋa; miššiliuʀ- 'correspond to, approximate, resemble, guess, be on level with', miššiliuut(i)- 'compare'; EG mitsaani 'this side of -', but Robbe and Menn. have mitsaa '(its) normal place, surroundings']

PE miluʀ- 'hit with thrown object'
AAY K miluʀ- 'hit by throwing stones at'
CAY miluqu- 'throw s.th. (at — maliciously)' [and miɫqaʀ- 'throw (at)']
NSY miluʀ- 'throw (at)'
CSY miluʀ-
Sir miluʀ- 'throw' [Vakh.; Men. has miluʀaʀ- 'throw self', miluʀəqaqə(s)- 'throw out' and miluʀəsqaʀ- 'throw around']
SPI miluq- 'hit with thrown object'
NAI mil^{y}uq-
WCI miluq-
ECI miluq-
GRI miluʀ-

PI milluuq- 'throw things at s.th.' [cf. (C)uʀ-]
SPI milluuq- 'throw things at s.th.'
NAI mil^{y}l^{y}uuq-
WCI milluuq-
ECI millu(q)-
GRI miɫɫuuʀ-

PI miluʀiaq- 'throw object at' [cf. yaʀ(tuʀ)-]
SPI —
NAI mil^{y}uʀiaq- 'go and hit with thrown object'
WCI —
ECI miluʀiaq- 'throw s.th. at'
GRI miluʀiaʀ- 'throw stone at'

PE mimǝʀ 'haunch or hindquarter' [cf. mipquq]
AAY —
CAY mimǝq* 'thigh of bird or mammal'
NSY —
CSY —
Sir —
SPI mimiq 'haunch, hindquarter' [for mumiq 'drumstick (for drum), hindquarter' see mumǝʀ]
NAI mimɨq*, mumɨq* 'hindquarter, haunch, drumstick (bird's), upper part of thigh' [the second form influenced by mumǝʀ]
WCI mimiq 'hindquarters, buttocks'
ECI mimiq 'thigh, ham'
GRI EG mimiq 'hindquarter'

PE mimǝʀnaʀ 'stump of tree' [cf. naʀ]
AAY —
CAY mimǝʀnaq 'stump of old tree'
NSY —
CSY mimǝʀnaaq 'tree stump with roots' [Rub. has mǝmǝʀnaaq]
Sir —
SPI mumiʀnaq 'tree stump with roots that drifts ashore' [influenced by mumǝʀ]
NAI mumɨʀnaq 'tree root, stump' [infl. by mumǝʀ]
WCI —
ECI —
GRI —

PE minaʀ- 'set food aside for s.o.' [compare aminaʀ]
AAY minaʀ- 'give to, share with'
CAY minaq 'food set aside for s.o.', minaʀ- 'set aside food for' [ANLC 'food or other present set aside for a guest']
NSY minaq 'food set aside food for neighbors, present'
CSY minaq 'bait, food set aside for neighbors, present'
Sir minǝX [Orr]
SPI minaq- 'share what one has', Imaq minakšaq 'gift'
NAI min^{y}aq- 'set aside food for someone'
WCI minaq-
ECI minaq- [and nom. = 'food set aside for s.o.']
GRI minaʀ- 'take food home with one', EG miaʀ- 'give to (s.th. put aside for s.o.)' [minaaq 'food taken home']

PE minǝɣ[1] '(dried) oil of sea mammal?'
AAY minǝk 'mold' [perhaps influenced by minǝɣ[2]]
CAY minǝɣ- 'become moldy'
NSY —
CSY —
Sir —
SPI minik- 'ferment walrus hide, flipper in oil'
NAI —
WCI Car? minuk 'oil dried on a skin (shiny), frost shining on surface of s.th.' [Schn. 'adg'; Pryde has Cop minu 'kind of reddish purple seaweed, Irish moss']
ECI —
GRI minik 'coagulated seal oil for caulking, earwax' [miniɣ- 'caulk seams of boat with coagulated seal oil']

PE minǝɣ[2] 'drizzle'
AAY minixtǝ- 'drizzle'
CAY minuk, Nun minixłux 'drizzle' [and note minǝk 'wake of fish or boat'; miniʀ- 'drizzle']
NSY —
CSY —
Sir —
SPI Qaw miniqłiq 'misty rain'
NAI min^{y}ɨk 'mist, moisture, drizzle, splash made by fish or thrown object' [as verb = 'be misty, drizzle'; min^{y}ukula- 'drizzle, be light mist']
WCI miniq 'drizzle'
ECI mini
GRI mini 'drizzle' [verbal mini- 'drizzle', NWG 'squander']

PY-S miŋlǝ 'wall'
AAY —
CAY mǝŋla 'border, edge' [contam. with kǝnlǝ?; note also mǝŋǝlvaXtǝ- 'move out of the way' with vaʀ-]
NSY minłǝ 'wall, foot of mountain'
CSY miŋla 'wall' [and miŋłun 'wall, fence', miŋłuʀ- 'insulate with sods (house)']
Sir miŋla 'wall' [on Men.'s comp. list; also mǝŋłiɣmǝlŋuX 'well-made or decorated house' — Em.]

PY-S miŋłǝɣtǝ- 'put away' [cf. miŋlǝ]
AAY —
CAY — [for miŋǝlvaXtǝ- 'move out of way' see miŋlǝ]
NSY minłǝxtǝ- 'put away, store, pack' [ANLC]
CSY miŋłǝxtǝ- 'tidy up' [and note miŋłitǝ- 'put away', from miŋlǝ and łit-?]
Sir miŋłiqałǝX 'cleaning up'
[note SPI Imaq miŋłituʀnǝq 'cleaning up', from Yup]

PE miŋqǝ- 'sew'
AAY miŋqǝ- 'sew'
CAY miŋqe-
NSY miŋqǝ- 'sew' [but Jen. has minqǝ-, however L.-T. has miŋqǝ-]
CSY —
Sir →
SPI →
NAI miquq- 'sew' [Jen. has miqquq-]
WCI Sig miquq-, Cop miXXuq- 'sew' [Lowe; Met. has miqquq-, Jen. has Sig mitquq- and Ras. and B.-S. have Net meqSor-]
ECI miʀsu(q)- 'sew' [and miʀsaq 's.th. sewn, meat bag']
GRI miʀšuʀ- 'sew' [with qðuʀ-, as for the ECI and Cop]

PE miŋqun 'needle' [cf. un]
AAY miŋqun 'needle'
CAY miŋqun
NSY miŋqun 'needle' [ANLC — Jen. has minqun]
CSY —
Sir miŋqǝtaX 'needle for putting through gills'
SPI Qaw miqqun 'sewing needle'
NAI micqun 'needle' [also miqšuun]
WCI mitqun 'needle'
ECI miqquti
GRI miqqut, EG miʀsiit

PE miŋuɣ- 'smear'
AAY miŋuɣ- 'paint, rub, smear', AP miŋuk 'spot (e.g. of oil on clothing)' [and PWS miŋuutaq 'paint, liniment']

CAY miŋuɣ- 'smear, spread, paint', miŋuk 'paint, ointment, butter'
NSY miŋuɣ- 'rub, smear' [ANLC; L.-T. has miŋułəq 'rubbing']
CSY miŋuɣ- 'rub' [and miŋuXu- 'smear, get dirty']
Sir —
SPI miŋuk- 'rub s.th. on s.th'
NAI miŋuk- 'color, mark, smear' [and miŋuaqtuʀvik 'school']
WCI Cop, Baker Lake miŋuk-, Sig miŋuaq- 'paint', B. Lake 'mark, dirty oneself with fresh paint' [miŋut 'paint', B. Lake also 'sulphur of match' acc. Schn.; Ras. has Net miŋuk 'the wet (rain)' as a shaman's word, Jen. has miŋuyiq 'green, blue' and Pet. has Sig miŋutik 'nose tattoo'; Pryde also has miŋuaqtuqtitsiži 'teacher' for P. BayNet and miŋuaq- 'paint' for Repulse Bay]
ECI miŋuaq- 'paint'
GRI miŋuk 'dirt (wet or sticky), mud', miŋuɣ- 'be dirty' [and EG miŋuttuq 'blubber' acc. Holm]

PI miŋuləq- 'paint or smear' [cf. ləʀ-?]
SPI —
NAI miŋulɨq- 'paint'
WCI miŋuliq- 'paint' [and miŋuliq 'wet snow that sticks to clothing']
ECI miŋuliq- 'cover ground with fine snow' [and miŋuliq 'fine coat of powdered snow']
GRI [note miŋuliʀtiʀ- 'give chewed food to child to eat', also 'threaten with fist'(?)]

PI mipquq 'thigh of bird' [cf. mimәʀ and p.b. quʀ]
SPI W mipquq 'thigh of bird' [Jen., who also has mapqoq for KI]
NAI mipquq
WCI —
ECI —
GRI miqquq [old ortho. mevqoq]

PI mi(i)ʀayuq 'child or young animal' [cf. piaʀaq under pi(-); this base with initial m may be influenced by mikəqłəqtuq or be a baby talk variant of those with initial p]
SPI —
NAI miʀayaužaq 'young animal'
WCI Sig miʀayualuk, Car? miʀayuq 'newborn baby' [the latter Schn. 'adg'; Lowe has Cop miʀʀaq 'baby' — Pryde miʀʀaaq instead — and Dor. miʀaq, miʀaaluk for Net]
ECI Lab miʀayuq 'newborn child' [Peck; Schn. has this marked 'rare' for W. Bay]
GRI miiraq 'child' [WG only — see piaʀaq under pi(-) for NG piʀaaq; note also miiʀuyuk 'crybaby', miiʀuyuu- 'be indifferent, indisposed, spoiled (child)']

PE miʀyaʀ(-) 'vomit'
AAY miʀyaʀ- 'vomit'
CAY miʀyaʀ- [nom. miʀyaq]
NSY miʀyaʀ- 'feel like being sick, vomit'
CSY miʀyaʀ- 'vomit' [nom. miʀyaq]
Sir — [but Orr has milŋaX 'vomit', and Em. has milŋaʀ- 'vomit', and milŋayuɣ- 'feel like being sick', perhaps cognate]
SPI miʀiaq- 'vomit'
NAI miʀiaq-, muʀiaq- [and nom.]
WCI miʀiaq- 'vomit' [for muiyaŋu- 'feel like being sick' see maʀuyuɣ- — contam.?]
ECI miʀiaq- [and nom.]
GRI miʀiaʀ-, EG miiali- (Robbe and Menn. miialii-) 'vomit'

PE mit- 'land'
AAY mittə- 'land, alight'
CAY mittə-
NSY —
CSY —
Sir — [for mit(ə)- 'grow (plant), rise (sun)' see uvi(t)-]
SPI mit- 'land from flight'
NAI mit-
WCI mit- 'land' [Dor. has mik- for Car]
ECI mik- 'land'
GRI mit-

PI mitpəq- 'wait around to get s.th.' [or mətpəq-]
SPI mitpi(q)- 'observe closely, watch' [Jen.]
NAI —
WCI Cop mippiq- 'wait in passageway of snowhouse to be given allotted portion of seal catch' [Pryde]
ECI mippi(q)-, NBI also mippaq- 'wait (to receive s.th.)', mippii- 'wait around for'
GRI mippiʀ- 'wait to get s.th., beg' [mippaaʀ- 'beg (a crowd of people)']

PY muɣtu(yu)li(q) 'woodpecker' [cf. əməɣ- and tu-[1]]
AAY muxtuliq, muxtulia'aq '(hairy) woodpecker'
CAY puuxtuyuli 'woodpecker, flicker'
NSY —
CSY —

PE mulə(ɣ) 'nipple or tip' [cf. məluɣ- and EA, Att huli-X 'leaf', huluX Atkan 'noose (in trap), nipple, seed', in EA 'nipple' only]
AAY muulək 'nipple' (in old source only)
CAY [cf. əmulək under əmmuɣ 'nipple']
NSY —
CSY mula 'nipple'
Sir muła
SPI mulik
NAI mulu 'nipple, blade of paddle', muluk 'nipple of bottle'
WCI mulik 'woman's teat', muluk 'teat of bottle' [and Sig 'paddle blade' acc. Pet.; Pryde has mulik 'paddle blade' for B. Lake Car and muluk 'nipple' for Sig]
ECI mulik 'nipple' [and Peck has muli 'nipple, rudder, oar' for Lab; Math. for Igl and Boas for Baffin have 'paddle blade']
GRI muli(k) 'nipple, paddle blade, leaf of plant' [also muliq, a newer form in the first two senses; in NG mulik is also 'head of nail'; note also muliqut 'leaf' — compare under pəłu]

PY mulŋa- 'be careful or gentle' [there may be a link to munaʀ-]
AAY KP ulŋa(yuɣ)-, Kod uŋla(yuɣ)- 'be careful, gentle'
CAY mulŋakə- 'be careful or gentle (with)' [and mulŋaitə- 'be careless, reckless']
NSY —
CSY —

PE mulu- 'stay away a long time'
AAY mulu- 'be or take a long time doing s.th.'
CAY mulu-
NSY mulu-
CSY mulu-
Sir muli- [Vakh. — for mulə-?]
SPI mulu- 'stay away a long time, take long'
NAI mulu- 'stay away' [muluqtu- 'be in the habit of staying away long']
WCI [Lowe has Sig muluu(yuaq) 'stayed a short while', mulluqtu- 'is usually gone longer than intended']
ECI mulu- 'stay away a long time'
GRI mulu- 'stay away a long time' [mułłuʀtu- 'be in habit of staying away long'; EG muluuyaʀ- 'go visiting far away' — Ges.]

PE muməʀ(-) 'drumstick'
AAY —
CAY muməq* 'drumstick', muməʀ- 'beat a drum' [and Barnum has mumyuli 'expert dancer']
NSY muməq 'drumstick' [L.-T.]
CSY muməq*
Sir —
SPI mumiq 'drumstick, hindquarter' [the latter sense by contam. with miməʀ]
NAI Nu mumiq- 'dance in Canadian Inuit style' [for mumiq* 'drumstick of bird, haunch' see miməʀ but Jen. also has mumiq 'drumstick', so the modern meaning may be influenced by the secondary sense of English 'drumstick']
WCI mumiq- 'dance' [Ras. has for Cop 'sing and dance in festival house' and for Sig mumiq 'drum dancer', verbal 'do drum dance', but also muŋiq 'drum singer' (?), and Schn. for 'adg' has 'dance Inuit dance'; Lowe has Cop numiq- 'dance', as does Jen.]
ECI Igl mumiq- 'dance' [B.-S., also Boas for Baffin; Ras. has mumiʀniq 'combination of song, words and dance']
GRI mumiʀ- 'hum, sing without words', NG 'perform a drum dance'

PE mumiɣ- 'turn over'
AAY mumiɣ- 'turn over' [postural root as in other Yup]
CAY mumiɣ-
NSY mumiɣ- 'turn over, translate'
CSY mumiɣ-
Sir mamiɣ- [influenced by mamə]
SPI mumik- 'turn over, translate, stay awake at night and sleep during day'
NAI mumik-
WCI mumik- 'turn upside down', Cop numiktiʀi- 'translate' [Lowe; Sig mumiktitsiyi 'interpreter'; Pryde has Cop numik- 'shift to another direction (wind)']
ECI mumik- 'turn upside down'
GRI mumiɣ- 'turn over (e.g. page)', mumit- 'turn upside down, distort', mumik (old word) 'page of book' [but mumiŋa 'the reverse side' — influenced by mamə]

PE munaʀ- 'be careful'
AAY munaʀ- 'be skillful'
CAY munaʀ- 'be dexterous', munaqə- 'be skillful with', Y 'tend, watch over'
NSY —
CSY —
Sir —
SPI munaʀi- 'watch over, care for'
NAI munaʀi-, Nu nunaʀi- 'take care of, watch over' [and munaʀnaq- 'cause one to be cautious']
WCI munaʀi- 'take care of, watch over, be cautious'
ECI —
GRI —

PI muqpaq 'ball' [cf. muʀðuɣ-?]
SPI —
NAI muqpaaq 'ball made of whale flipper' [also as verb 'play ball'; compare muqpak- 'dive down' under muʀðuɣ-]
WCI muqpak 's.th. round, ball'
ECI —
GRI — [but compare muʀpaʀ- 'move down' under muʀðuɣ-]

PE muʀðuɣ- 'sink down (e.g. into soft snow or water)' [cf. Aleut huʀðu- 'be soft, downy', Atkan also huʀluɣ- 'be soft (wood)'; there may be a link to maʀu-[1], at least by contam.]
AAY [note C muu'uliʀ-, muu'iliʀ- 'let off bubbles, move so as to create a swell on the surface (submerged animal)', perhaps also mu<ʀ>i- 'be or do for a long time' unless this goes with məɣə-]
CAY muʀuxtə- 'sink down' [also 'gather cloth in sewing'], muʀua- 'sink in as one walks'
NSY muʀu- 'sink into snow as one walks' [ANLC; Em. has muʀułqə- sink in snow or mud' and L.-T. muʀuayaŋaq 'deep snow']
CSY muʀyuɣ- 'submerge (seal)' [for muʀu- 'sink into soft snow' see maʀu-[1]]
Sir —
SPI muʀžuk- 'disappear down a hole'
NAI muʀžuk- 'sink into snow, soft ground', PH 'enter sod house through tunnel' [and note muqpak- 'dive (of sea mammal arching high out of water)']
WCI muʀyuk- 'sink into snow' [note also Baker Lake muʀyuŋniq 'outlet of lake' acc. Schn.]
ECI Lab muyyu(k)- 'sink into snow or mud, enter cave or river' [Bourq. has muʀyuk-]
GRI muʀšuɣ- 'disappear down, slip into hole (seal)' [and note muʀfit- 'be stuck or wade in mud', muʀpaʀ-, EG nuppaʀ- 'move down (e.g. to bottom of boat)' — Ras. has EG nuʀpaʀ- 'go down (sun)' and Robbe and Menn. have muppaʀ-, nuppaʀ- 'sink down']

PY muʀnəqaq 'kind of skin boot' [cf. nəʀ[1] and qaʀ?]
AAY —
CAY [muʀuqaq, muʀun 'slipper, fur liner for skin boot']
NSY muʀnəqat 'footwear' [ANLC]
CSY muʀniqaq* 'high sealskin boot with hair in' [and note muʀnəq 'folded strip between sole and upper part of skin boot']

PI muʀiiq- 'sharpen' [cf. ŋiʀ-]
SPI —
NAI —
WCI [Ras. has Car muʀiilʀuʀyuaq 'big smooth one' and Ow. has muʀiittuq 'plain shore' for EP]
ECI Lab muʀiiq- 'grind, whet' [Peck; Schn. has muʀiq- 'be sharp, sharpen' for Tar; Saul also has muʀuit- 'be sharp']
GRI muʀiiʀ- 'grind', muʀiit- 'be blunt, rounded at end or edge' [muʀiiʀsivik, EG muŋuusivik, muʀ̃iiʀsit, NG muʀaiXXit 'whetstone']

N

PE na-[1] and **na(a)ɣɣa** 'no' [cf. Aleut naŋaa 'no', but also na(C)umi under na-[2]]
AAY K naa 'no!, don't (prohibition)'
CAY — [but note ina 'no' on Cook's word list; for naami(ki) 'I don't know' see na(C)umi under na-[2]]
NSY naami 'no'
CSY na(a), nakaa 'no' [the former often with final aspiration]
Sir náka 'no, I don't know'
SPI naaɣɣa 'no' [and na'aa 'expression of pain']
NAI naaɣɣa, naakka 'no' [for naumi 'no' see na(C)umi under na-[2]]
WCI Car naaɣɣa [Dor.], Sig naaɣɣai 'no' [Lowe — also Dor. and Ras. for Net; Pryde has naaɣɣa and Jen. naaka for Sig; note also Sig nana 'expression of pain' acc. Pet.]
ECI Igl naaɣɣa 'no' [B.-S. — alongside aaka, for which see aka(a); Peck has naukak alongside aukak 'no' for Lab, also naa-aak 'expression of pain' and naanaaq- 'say 'naa'; for Tar naakku 'expression of compassion' see naatki-]
GRI naaxxa, NG na'a 'no' [the latter older naaɣɣa; note also WG na'aa 'expression of pain' — also nanana in Kl.; for naami(k) 'no' see na(C)umi under na-[2]

PE na-[2] 'where' [i.e. locative nani, etc.; cf. nałə- and perhaps Aleut qana- under qaŋa]
AAY na- 'where' [abl. nakən 'from where']
CAY na- 'where' [all. natm̥un 'to where', abl. nakən 'from where']
NSY na- 'where' [and nakən 'from where']
CSY na- 'which' [and nakən 'from where', natm̥un 'to where']
Sir na- 'where' [and natm̥u, namu (Vakh. natm̥ənu) 'to where', nakənəŋ 'from where']
SPI na- 'where' [nakin 'from where']
NAI na- 'where' [nakin[y] 'from where', napmun 'to where']
WCI na- 'where' [nakit 'from where']
ECI na- 'where' [nakit 'from where', namut 'to where']
GRI NG nani 'where' [and nakit 'from where', namut 'to where']

PE naɣu and **na(C)uŋ** 'where (is it)' [apparently with the same 3s object ending as in the imperative and interrogative moods ɣu ~ uŋ]
AAY —
CAY nauw̯a, nauxa 'where', NSU nauŋ 'why have you come?'
NSY naa 'where'
CSY naaɣu 'where is it?' [pl. naaki, du. nakək 'where are they?']
Sir [Vakh. has naɣəla 'where is it or he?']
SPI nauŋ 'why have you come?'
NAI nauŋ 'where (exclamation)'
WCI nauk 'where' [and Pryde has nauk Cop 'I thought you said -', Car B. Lake 'no', the latter probably by contam. with na-[1]]
ECI nauk 'where (of s.th. nearby), what (did you say?)' [for Igl Schn. has 'no' — probably the same as Lab naukak under na-[1]]
GRI naak 'where', NG nauk 'how, why (exclamation)' [and NG nauŋayuq 'how annoying!']

PE nalliʀ 'which' [cf. p.b. l(l)iʀ]
AAY naliq 'which (of them)' [and note nalitutə-, nalituʀ- 'be undecided, hesitate']
CAY naliq 'which (of them)' [and note naliXuxtə- 'be undecided']
NSY naliq 'which (of them)'
CSY naliq
Sir nacəX 'which' [and naciqut(ə)- 'guess, foretell for s.o.'; Vakh. has nacəʀnam 'or']
SPI nalliq 'which'
NAI nalli(q)
WCI nalliat 'which of many', naliak 'which of two' [Lowe]
ECI nallia(q), Igl nali(aq) 'which' [Saul for the first form (Schn. has nalli-), Dor. for the latter]
GRI NG nalliq, EG nattiq 'which'

PY-S natə- 'which (part)' [cf. tə]
AAY natə- 'what part' [with possessor endings]
CAY natə-
NSY —
CSY natə- 'where (on possessor)' [and natətə- 'to which way, how, what kind', natu 'which one' — compare kitu under ki(na)]
Sir natəlŋuX 'which' [and natu 'where']

PY-S natən 'how' [aequalis case]
AAY —
CAY —
NSY natən 'how'
CSY [natən 'which way']
Sir natən 'how'

PE na(C)umi 'I don't know' [from same source as naɣu under na-² above plus enclitic mi?; compare na-¹ however — there is entanglement here]
AAY [note naama 'where is it?']
CAY naumi, naami(ki) 'I don't know'
NSY [for naami 'no' see na-¹]
CSY naami 'I don't know' [used by children on SLI acc. Orr]
Sir —
SPI naumi
NAI naumi 'no' [but PH, Nu, Mal naami 'where (is it)']
WCI Sig nauŋmi 'I don't know where' [for Cop nauna 'I don't know' see under nałunaʀ-]
ECI nau(mili) 'excuse me, move over, let me do it', naumik 'who' [Schn.; Bourq. has naumani 'yes, certainly' for Lab]
GRI naami(k) 'no, there is none' [Fab. distinguishes between naume 'where, I don't know where' and nâme in the latter meaning only ('in its most common pronunciation'); Hans Egede (1722) had nami 'I don't know what it is' but najmi 'no', the latter perhaps directly reflecting na-¹]

PI naalɣiuq- and **naalɣiuk-** 'suffer' [the relat. to naatki- and naŋłəɣ- is obscure]
SPI —
NAI naalɣiuq- 'lack s.th.', Mal naalɣiuk- 'be needy'
WCI —
ECI —
GRI naałłiuɣ-, NG naaɣliuq- 'suffer' [note also naałłii- 'torment, vex' and nałłi- 'be in labor']

PI naalu(n)ŋiaq 'infant'
SPI —
NAI naalunŋiaʀiik 'mother whale with baby' [and Nu naluŋiq 'wild baby (mythical rogue infant escaped from infanticide to plague travelers)']
WCI Cop, Net naaluŋiaq 'infant' [Ras.]
ECI —
GRI naaluŋiaq 'infant, youngest child', naaluŋiaʀšuk 'baby', NG nauliŋiaq 'infant, youngest sibling'

PI na(ž)aq 'belly or abdomen'
SPI nažžak 'abdomen, belly'
NAI na<ž>aq 'part of abdomen', nažžaak 'abdomen' [and PH naaq- 'have a full stomach']
WCI nayyak 'abdomen, belly' [Ras. has Cop naaq, pl. nagjat — for nayyat — 'stomach'; Pryde has Cop naaq as 'protruding stomach']
ECI naaq 'abdomen, belly'
GRI naaq, pl. naššat, older NG nassak 'abdomen, belly' [and naaʀtu- 'be pregnant', naaʀtu 'fetus']

PI nažžak- 'get a big belly' [cf. nəɣ-]
SPI nažžak- 'have a distended belly'
NAI nažžak- 'become pregnant, get a distended belly'
WCI Sig nayyak- 'have a big belly, be pregnant'
ECI —
GRI naššaɣ- 'get a pot belly'

PI naatki- 'pity' [cf. naŋłəɣ- and naalɣiuq-]
SPI —
NAI —
WCI Cop naatki- 'be sorry for' [Ras., who also has Net naagki-; Schn. has naapkiɣi-, naapkuɣi- for 'adg' in this sense; Pryde has Cop naapki- 'think one is stronger than, feel one could manage']
ECI naakki- 'be affectionate toward', naakkiɣi-, nakkuɣi- 'have pity on' [Bourq. has Lab naapkiɣi-, naapkiC-; note also naakkuuti 'pity' and naakku 'expression of compassion']
GRI naakki(ɣi)- [Fab. nâki-], half-trans. naakkiniɣ- 'feel pity for'

PI naatŋiq- 'hop on one foot' [cf. naɣət-]
SPI Qaw naatnižaq- 'hop on one foot'
NAI naanŋiq- 'hop on one foot (once), hop over'
WCI [Pet. has nánataʀ- 'hop on one foot' for Sig]
ECI naŋiyaq-, Lab naaŋŋi(C)- 'hop on one foot'
GRI naaŋŋi-

PE nacaʀ 'hood or hat'
AAY nacaq 'hairnet, cap'
CAY nacaq 'hat, hood' [and nacaʀ- 'put on hat or hood']
NSY nasaq 'hood' [acc L.-T.; also nasatə, nasan 'hat']
CSY nasaq 'hood' [and nasaʀ- 'put on hood']
Sir nasəX 'hood' [also verbal in Em.]
SPI nazaq 'hood' [and as verb = 'put hood up']
NAI nasaq 'hood' [as verb = 'put hood up']
WCI nasaq 'hood' [as verb = 'put hood on'; nasaʀaq 'hat' — Lowe]
ECI nasaq 'hat, hood' [as verb = 'put hat or hood on']
GRI nasaq 'hat, hood' [and nasaʀ- 'put hat or hood on']

PY nacałŋaq 'kind of gull?'
AAY nacałŋaayak 'duck of some sort'
CAY nacałŋaq, nacałŋaaʀ(aq*) 'Aleutian or Arctic tern, Sabine's gull'
NSY —
CSY nasałəŋuaq 'Sabine's gull'

PY naca(C)ułək 'kind of goose' [cf. ŋutə- and ləɣ?]
AAY AP nacaulək 'white-fronted goose'
CAY nacaułək 'emperor goose'
NSY —
CSY —
Inu [note NAI nasaullik 'a kind of ptarmigan', Cop nahaulik, Net nasaulliɣaq 'Lapland longspur' (Pryde) and ECI nasaulliɣaaq 'black-headed sparrow', parallel formations]

PE nacciɣ- 'cry because one wants to go along (child)'
AAY naciɣ- 'want to go along'
CAY naciɣ- 'cry or feel sad because of s.o. leaving'
NSY nasiɣ- 'cry after s.o. leaving (child)' [ANLC]
CSY nasiɣ- 'cry for s.o. leaving (child)'
Sir nasiɣ- [Orr and Em.]
SPI nassik- 'want to go along (though others oppose)'
NAI natcik- 'want to go along, cry wanting to go along (child)'

WCI Sig natsik-
ECI —
GRI —

PE nacit- 'survey one's surroundings from a height' [cf. łit-]?
AAY —
CAY nacətə-, Nun, HBC nastə- 'survey one's surroundings from a height'
NSY nasitə- 'climb to the top' [ANLC; Men. has nasi 'mountain above settlement']
CSY —
Sir —
SPI Qaw nasit- 'survey one's surroundings from a height'
NAI nasit-
WCI nasit-
ECI nasit-
GRI nasiɣ- [Fab. has nessípok, i.e. nasit-]

PE naðə- 'be completed'
AAY naa- K 'be completed', C 'burn'
CAY naa- 'become complete'
NSY ➟
CSY [note nasiqə- 'take home what one wants, take enough' and perhaps nažaŋitə- 'be loose'; for naasiiR- 'taste' see nay(ə)pət-] ➟
Sir — [note nažanRitə- 'be loose' (Orr)']
SPI ➟
NAI [naaRuq- 'be at zenith, be full (moon)']
WCI naa- 'be completed'
ECI naa- 'finish' [and (with non-historical ɣ) naɣɣati 'what one adds to an object to make it fit', Lab 'end' — Peck; naatsauŋittuq 'what is eternal']
GRI naa- 'finish, be finished' [and naxxat 'end', naari- 'finish, do from beginning to end', naaššaaŋŋit- (old ortho. nâgssáungit-) 'be endless']

PY naacuqə- 'measure out' [compare naðaqə- below]
AAY —
CAY HBC naacuqə- 'conserve, ration'
NSY —
CSY nasuqə- 'measure'

PI naammaɣə- 'fit or be satisfied with' [cf. naðama- below and kə-[1]]
SPI naamai- 'find sufficient'
NAI naamaɣi- 'fit'
WCI naamaɣi- 'be content with, be adequate for' [Pryde]
ECI naammaɣi- 'find sufficient or worthy, be satisfied with'
GRI naammaɣi- 'find sufficient, fit, be satisfied with'

PY naanəq 'complete set' [cf. nəR[1]]
AAY naanəq 'complete set (20–30 muskrat skins or set of eggs in a nest)'
CAY naanəq* 'complete bundle of skins sufficient for a parka (e.g., 45 squirrel skins)'
NSY —
CSY —
Inu [note NAI naaRniq* 'measurement of length of both arms outstretched']

PE naðama- 'be enough' [cf. (u)ma-]
AAY naama- 'be enough'
CAY naama-
NSY naama-
CSY naama-
Sir —
SPI naama- 'be enough, just right, fit'
NAI naama- 'be enough', naammak- 'be enough, of right size'
WCI naammak- Sig 'be enough', Cop 'be good' [Met.], Net 'be good' [Ras.; Briggs has 'be correct or convenient, feel comfortable or safe']
ECI naamma(k)- 'be enough' [naammasi- 'have become sufficient, have eaten enough']
GRI naammaɣ- 'be enough', NG naammak- 'be good' [Kl. also has 'be well done' for WG; naammassi- 'have become sufficient, have eaten enough', NG naammaxxi- 'be ready']

PE naðaqə- 'count out' [cf. qə-]
AAY naqə-, naaqi- 'read, count'
CAY naaqə-
NSY —
CSY nažaqə- 'figure out measurements'
Sir —
SPI Qaw naaqi- 'read' [prob. from CAY]
NAI —
WCI — [note Car naasaq- 'count' (Pryde)]
ECI —
GRI naaRi- 'finish, do from beginning to end'

PE naðat- 'complete' [cf. t-[1]]
AAY K naatə- 'complete'
CAY naatə-
NSY naatə- 'put together to make set or unit' [ANLC]
CSY naatə- 'complete, be complete, enough'
Sir nátə- 'complete, be complete, enough' [Orr; borrowed from CSY?]
SPI naat- 'finish, be enough, complete'
NAI naat- 'finish, be completed, finished'
WCI naat-
ECI —
GRI —

PE na(C)əvə(t)- 'pour from one container into another' [from *nayəvə(t)- or *nʸayəvə(t)-?]
AAY Kod nayyu- 'pour from one container to another' [continuative = nayyuXtuR-]
CAY naivə- 'pour from one container to another'
NSY niavə- 'pour from one container to another' [Em.]
CSY niivə- 'pour from one container to another, give birth' [and nivuR- 'pour into another container'; the preserved initial n suggests earlier *nayəvə- in both forms]
Sir yivə- 'pour from one container to another' [Orr]

SPI naavit- 'pour from one container to another'
NAI naavit- 'spill or pour non-liquid substance out', naaptiq- 'pour out, empty, dump'
WCI naavit- 'pour out, drop' [Ras., who also has Net naavik- 'fall out, be lost'; Met. has naaviq- 'be thrown out' as a rare word]
ECI naavit- 'pour out of container' [Ras. has 'throw away' for Igl; naaviraq- 'empty contents several times unintentionally']
GRI naaffiRaR- 'gradually fill a vessel from a smaller one, finish gradually, pay by installments'

PE naɣa(t)- 'hear'
AAY niitə- 'hear'
CAY niitə-
NSY niiquR- 'hear, understand'
CSY naɣatə- 'listen', naɣaquR- 'hear'
Sir —
SPI naalak- 'listen'
NAI naalak- 'listen' [naalaRni- 'listen to']
WCI naalak-
ECI naalak- 'listen to, hear, obey' [naalaɣaq 'master, the Lord']
GRI naalaɣ- 'listen, obey, be well-behaved' [naalaaR-, naalaRni- 'listen (carefully)', naalaɣaq 'master, officer, the Lord']

PY naɣacuɣni- 'listen' [cf. yuɣ- and ni-]
AAY niicuɣni- 'listen'
CAY niicuɣni-
NSY —
CSY naɣasuɣni- 'eavesdrop, watch for'
Inu — [but compare NAI naalaRni- 'listen' under naɣa(t)- above]

PY naɣaayuq 'small rocky island'
AAY naɣaayuk K 'small rock island, pinnacle rock', KP 'flat sandy island, sandbar'
CAY NSU naɣaayuq 'single rock standing alone in water, skerry'
NSY —
CSY —

PE naɣət- 'get caught or snagged' [cf. Aleut taɣaqu- 'be narrow, jammed']
AAY naxtə- 'get caught, stuck, stop'
CAY naxtə-, Eg laxtə- 'get snagged, caught'
NSY naxtə- 'get caught on s.th.', naxəsqiaR- 'stumble' [ANLC has naaxtə- 'stick, get stuck, catch on']
CSY naaxtə-, aaxtə- 'stumble'
Sir [note naŋcəR- 'slip' — Vakh. from Men.'s texts]
SPI Qaw naat- 'be snagged, caught on s.th.'
NAI naat- 'be snagged, caught on s.th.'
WCI naat- 'get caught' [and Ras. has Net naaktaq 'one remaining hanging']
ECI naat- 'get snagged, caught, trip' [naatit- 'snag, catch (intentionally)'; and note Iti naatsiviutaq 'hook']
GRI naaɣ- 'stumble against', naatit- 'hang up, catch on' [and naakkiut(i)- 'stumble and fall', naaqqavik, naatiffik, Up naatiqqavik, EG naalippik, NG naktittaRvik 'hook']

PE naɣci(t)- 'catch on bottom (hook)'
AAY —
CAY —
NSY naxsitaq 'hook (on clothes)' [and naxsitaR- 'fasten, buckle' (ANLC)]
CSY — [note nakšək, nəkšək 'hook' under nəɣciɣ — contam. seems to be involved]
Sir —
SPI naksi- 'catch on bottom (fish hook)' [Jen.; for naqsik- 'hook' see naRciɣ-]
NAI naksima- 'be hanging on hook' [and note naktit- 'get snagged, hang', naksatit- 'suddenly get snagged on s.th.]
WCI [note naktit- 'hook', but also Cop naxxit- 'uproot trap and escape (trapped animal)' acc. Pryde]
ECI Lab naksi- 'get stuck on bottom (hook)' [Bourq.]
GRI nassi- [old ortho. nagsi-] 'get hook stuck on bottom, get entangled with line to harpooned seal', nassiɣ- 'catch on bottom (line)'

PE naɣəkli(R)- '(cause to) trip'
AAY [note PWS nakkiłaɣ- 'trip (but not fall)']
CAY —
NSY —
CSY nakłiR- 'cause to trip'
Sir —
SPI —[for naŋikłiq- 'complain about, criticize' see naŋRu(R)-]
NAI naakłi(t)- 'cause to trip'
WCI naakłi-, Cop naaxxi(q)-
ECI Lab naałłi- 'trip' [Bourq. has naakłi-]
GRI naałłiR- 'cause to trip'

PE naɣtuqaR 'hook'
AAY —
CAY naxtuqaq 'belt buckle'
NSY naxtuqaq 'button'
CSY naxtuqaq
Sir —
SPI naktuaq 'button'
NAI nakturiq 'button, hook, peg for hanging clothes on'
WCI nakturaq 'hook' [Met.], Baker Lake 'button attaching trace to sled' [Schn.], Sig nakturiq 'latch' [Met.]
ECI natturaq 'belt button'
GRI natturaq, natsiraq 'whittled bone part of towing strap of kayak'

PI nakturalək 'eagle' [cf. naɣtuqaR above and ləɣ]
SPI —
NAI —
WCI Car, Net nakturalik 'eagle' [Ras.; also Sig acc. Pet.]
ECI natturalik 'eagle'
GRI natturalik, EG naRtařalik 'eagle'

PY naɣiquyaq 'kind of spear' [cf. nagət-]
AAY naɣiquyaq 'sea otter spear' [Fisher]
CAY naɣiquyaq 'spear used with throwing device'
NSY —
CSY —

PE naɣu- 'grow' [cf. Aleut taɣaða- 'be new, fresh, young (egg, grass, or (Atkan) fish)']
AAY nau- 'grow (of plant)' [and nauq, naucəstaaq 'plant']
CAY nau- 'grow' [and naucetaaq 'blossom, flower, plant']
NSY naa(w)- 'grow'
CSY naɣu-
Sir naɣu- [Orr]
SPI nau-
NAI na<ɣ>u- [and naɣɣuvik 'place where one grows up']
WCI nau- 'start growing up (seed), be conceived', naut- 'engender'
ECI Lab naulik- 'start to grow'
GRI naa- 'grow, spring out (plant), get green (ground)' [and naašuq 'flower, plant', naxxuik 'origin, place s.th. or s.o. comes from' (and in Fab. also a shaman's word for 'father'), EG nakkivik 'father']

PE naɣucciR- 'wait for s.th. to grow' [cf. c(c)iR-]
AAY —
CAY naucir- 'plant'
NSY naasiR- 'grow (plants)'
CSY —
Sir —
SPI [nausiziq- 'plant s.th.']
NAI PH nautciq- 'plant'
WCI [nautsiuq- 'examine']
ECI [nautsituq- 'try and find out what s.o.'s intentions are, see if dog wants to come in, etc., examine the sea or sky for the weather, investigate']
GRI naatsiR- 'wait for s.th. to grow' [naatsuRšuR-, SWG naatsiRšuR- 'wait to see how s.th. or s.o. will be (weather, invalid), calculate']

PE naɣucciRaR 'plant' [cf. naɣucciR- above]
AAY —
CAY Nun nauciaR(aq*) 'flower' [nauciq 'wild rhubarb']
NSY naasiRaq, naasiRamsiq 'flower'
CSY —
Sir —
SPI nausiaq 'plant, flower'
NAI nautci<ž>aq '(garden) flower'
WCI nautsiaq 'flower, plant' [and Pryde has Cop nauttiivik 'garden']
ECI —
GRI [naatsiiaq 'potato', naatsiivik 'garden']

PY naɣunRaq 'plant or sprout' [cf. n(ɔ)RaR(aR)]
AAY C naunnaq, K naunRaq 'sprout, new growth'
CAY naunRaq 'plant, vegetable, salmonberry'
NSY —
CSY —

PI naɣžuk 'antler' [cf. naɣət-]
SPI naɣžuk 'antler'
NAI naɣžuk 'antler' [verbal = 'fight, strike with antlers']
WCI naɣɣuk 'antler'
ECI naɣɣuk
GRI naššuk, EG nattiq 'antler, horn'

PE nakacuɣ 'bladder' [cf. naki- and Aleut EA, Att taka-X, Atkan (and western EA) takða-X 'codfish bladder']
AAY ➟
CAY nakacuk 'bladder'
NSY nakasuk
CSY nakasuk
Sir nakəsəx [Orr]
SPI naɣasuk
NAI nakasuk
WCI nakasuk
ECI nakasuk
GRI nakasuk

PE nakacuɣnaR 'calf (of leg)' [cf. naR]
AAY nakacuɣnaq 'calf of leg'
CAY nakacuɣnaq
NSY —
CSY —
Sir —
SPI naɣasuŋnaq
NAI nakasuɣnaq
WCI nakasuŋnaq
ECI nakasunnaq
GRI nakasunnaaq, NG nakahuŋnaq

PE nakaR 'stalk'
AAY —
CAY Y nakaaq 'wild rhubarb'
NSY nakaatə 'sourdock or pink plumes stalk' [ANLC, also for nakayiaXaq 'snowdrop'; L.-T. has nakayiaXat 'grass variety'; Jen. has nakanłat 'grass']
CSY —
Sir —
SPI naɣaaq 'flower of sourgrass'
NAI naka(a)q, nakaun, nakautaq 'stem of edible plant, stalk'
WCI nakaq 'stem'
ECI nakaq 'stem' [Peck has 'knot of roots' for Lab]
GRI —

PY nakaRyaq 'wind from a certain direction' [cf. nakkaR- and yaR — compare esp. GRI nakat- under the former, also CSY asivaq under acivaR- (aci[1]) for a parallel; Chukchi nik'eyen of the same meaning is probably a loan from the Esk.]
AAY [note K nakiXsaRiiq, nakiqsaRiiq 'southwest wind']
CAY —
NSY nakaRyaXtaq 'northeast wind' [and ANLC nakaRyaq 'northeast']
CSY SLI nakaRya 'east, northeast (wind)', Chap nakaRyaq 'northeast wind'
Sir [note nakiX 'northeast' — Vakh. from Men.'s texts]

PI nakataq 'object set up for aiming at?' [cf. nakəʀ- and nakciʀaq, but also napataʀ- under napa- and nakkaʀ- — there appears to be contamination]
SPI —
NAI nakataq 'sight on gun' [and Jen. has nakautaq 'stone set in a line to point to s.th. or as a barrier against caribou']
WCI nakataq 'sight on gun, mark left near cache for locating it' [Jen. has 'pointing barrier stone' for Cop]
ECI nakataq 'target set up for throwing stones at', Aiv 'sight of gun' [verbal = 'throw stones at nakataq'; for nakataq 's.th. cut over' see navəɣ-]
GRI nakataq 'object set up for throwing stones at', NG 'gun sight' [and nakataʀ- 'play at throwing stones at object'; NG nakatsiq- 'mark cache'; note also EG naɣalaȓaq 'ptarmigan'; for nakat- 'hang head, turn to the west (south wind)' see nakkaʀ-]

PI nakciʀaq 'target' [cf. nakataq, perhaps here with liʀ-]
Yup [note CSY nakəXsaʀ- 'target shoot' under nakəʀ-]
Sir [note nakəʀcaʀ- 'shoot at' under nakəʀ-]
SPI naksiaq, Qaw naksiʀaq 'target for shooting practice'
NAI naksiʀaq 'target for shooting practice' [verbal = 'fire at target'; note also naksiq 'goal (peg in ground) in game of qiputaq']
WCI [Ras. has nagyeʀit 'target' for Car]
ECI Lab naksiʀaq 'target for shooting practice' [Peck]
GRI nassiʀaq 'target' [nassiʀaʀ- 'shoot at target (with bow)']

PE nakəʀ- 'go straight (of harpoon or like)' [cf. nakciʀaq and EA Nikolski takinaaδa- 'shoot (seal) together with another' with p.b.s na- and aδa-?]
AAY nakəʀ- 'be lucky, bring luck'
CAY nakəʀ- 'be straight, shoot straight' [and note BB naki- 'be good at catching game']
NSY [note nakatə- 'give signal on sighting whale or accident at sea'?]
CSY nakəʀ- 'be an accurate shot', nakəXsaʀ- 'target shoot' [but also naaxsaʀ- 'shoot at target']
Sir nakəʀcaʀ- 'shoot at' [and nakəʀcaX 'target', nakəpixłəʀəX 'accurate']
SPI nakiq- 'go far'
NAI nakiq- 'go straight, shoot far'
WCI Sig nakiq- 'go straight, far' [and Car 'go quickly' acc. Schn. — Ras. has 'be quick (arrow), shoot over target'; Pryde has nakiq- 'be fast (arrow or bullet)' for Cop]
ECI nakiq- 'shoot far' [also nakili- 'carry farther, accelerate (motor)' and nakkiali- 'be strong (wind), be quick', Lab nakillaq- 'blow very hard (wind)' — the latter Peck, who also has naki- 'settle, become more constant (wind or person)'; Andersen et al. have Lab nakit- 'be fast and carry far (bullet)']
GRI nakiʀ- 'go straight, be accurate (gun or harpoon), be strong (current)', NG nakiq- 'hit beyond target' [note also nakiʀtit- 'increase in strength (wind or current)', nakkišaaʀ- 'blow a gale']

PE nakəʀit- 'go crooked' [cf. ŋit-]
AAY —
CAY nakXiatə- 'be crooked'
NSY —
CSY naakXitə- 'be a poor shot'
Sir —
SPI —
NAI —
WCI Sig nakiit- 'go crooked'
ECI nakiit- 'not carry far (gun or sling)'
GRI nakiit- 'not hit straight (gun or harpoon)' [and note NG nakiŋŋit- 'hit short of target']

PE naki- 'be unable to urinate?' [cf. nakacuɣ- and li-?]
AAY —
CAY [note nakaci- 'need to urinate'; for BB naki- 'be good at catching game' see nakəʀ-]
NSY —
CSY naki- 'have a bladder infection'
Sir —
SPI —
NAI naki- 'be unable to urinate because of urinary tract disorder'
WCI —
ECI —
GRI naki- 'be unable to urinate'

PE nakima- 'wander around in confusion' [cf. (u)ma- and perhaps nakəʀit- under nakəʀ-]
AAY —
CAY —
NSY nakima- 'get lost, wander around lost', nakimaka(a)ta(ʀ)- 'get lost, make a mistake, no longer be in control of oneself (from drink or a concussion)'
CSY nakimtaa- 'be lost and run around in a panic'
Sir nakimta- 'be at a loss as how to act, be lost, run round in different directions' [Em.]
SPI nagimaa- 'lose one's bearings' [and nagimaq- 'become unconscious, disoriented, lose one's memory, pass out, be insane']
NAI — [but note makimaq- 'not understand and perform accordingly']
WCI Cop nakima- 'have rabies' [Pryde; and note Cop nak(k)imayuq, nak(k)iŋayuq 'idiot' in Met.]
ECI Lab nakimaʀni- 'blow from all directions, be vacillating' [Bourq., who also has nakiliʀsi- 'be unstable, inconstant']
GRI nakima- 'hesitate' [nakimmaɣ-, nakimmaʀ- 'become vacillating']

PE nakkaʀ- 'plunge into water' [cf. Aleut taka- 'come off, get loose, go away', Att 'dive']
AAY —
CAY NSU nakaaʀ- 'dip one's head into water'
NSY —
CSY — [for nakaʀya(q) 'east wind' see nakaʀyaq]
Sir —
SPI Qaw nakkaq- 'dive, plunge'
NAI nakkaq- 'fall headlong, plunge'
WCI Sig nakkaq- 'plunge (seal)' [Ras. has Net 'fall through (ice?)' — Dor. 'drown'; Jen. has Cop nakak- 'bend' and Pet. has Sig nakkakak '(he) lowers his arms']
ECI nakka(q)- 'fall into water'

GRI nakkaʀ- 'fall down, fall through ice', EG nakkaʀ- 'drown', NG nakkaqtaaq- 'fish' [as noun = 'fish decoy'; note also nakat- 'hang head, hang straight down (fishing line), turn to the west (south wind)' — the latter meaning perhaps influenced by nakəʀ-]

PE naku(ʀ)- 'squint' [or *nʸaku(ʀ)-]
AAY naku-, Kod niki- 'be cross-eyed'
CAY naku- 'be cross-eyed' [and note nakukə- 'torment, fight'?]
NSY naku- 'cross one's eyes, squint'
CSY nakuʀ- 'cross one's eyes' [postural root]
Sir yakuʀ- [Orr]
SPI naɣu-
NAI naku- 'cross one's eyes' [and note nakut- 'entertain' — there may be contam. with naku(a)q(-) but compare nakkutiɣɨ- under nakkutə- below]
WCI naku- 'squint, be cross-eyed'
ECI naku- 'squint'
GRI naku- 'squint, get drunk' [and nakutit- 'fascinate, make commit a folly']

> **PI nakkutə-** 'stare at' [cf. utə-]
> SPI —
> NAI nakkutiɣɨ- 'have as source of enjoyment, tease'
> WCI nakuuti- 'squint at in order to see' [Pryde has Cop nakkut- 'stare' but nakut- 'squint, cross eyes' for Cop]
> ECI —
> GRI nakkut(i)- 'stare at', nakkutiɣi- 'have all one's attention directed at'

PI naku(a)q(-) 'be good or strong'
SPI naɣuu- 'be good'
NAI nakuu- 'be good' [and note naku<ž>aq 'caribou or moose fat, anything delicious', PH, Nu nakuqsi- 'improve, fix']
WCI nakuu- 'be good', nakuʀuq- 'become good', Net nakuq- 'be strong' [and Ras. has nakuʀut 'helping spirit' as a shaman's word; Pryde also has nakuq 'good' for Cop]
ECI nakuq- 'be worthy of praise, be a happy occasion, be glad', Lab 'be strong, good' [and nakuaq 'dog which fears nothing', nakuʀsi- 'be cured', nakuiɣi- 'find detestable, be displeased with']
GRI nakuu- 'be strong', nakuaq 'someone strong' [and nakuʀsaʀ- 'cure', nakuʀsaq 'doctor', nakuʀtit- 'recover', nakuit- 'be weak', nakuššaɣ- 'get stronger']

> **PI naku(a)ʀə-** 'like' [cf. kə-[1]]
> SPI naɣuaʀi- 'like'
> NAI nakuaʀi-
> WCI [note nakkuuɣi- 'like']
> ECI nakuʀi- 'thank, praise for' [and nakuʀmiik, Iti naku 'thank you']
> GRI nakkuʀi- 'like'

PE nala- 'be lying down'
AAY —
CAY nala- 'die (esp. plants), get numb'
NSY —
CSY —
Sir —
SPI —
NAI nala- 'be lying horizontally'
WCI nala-
ECI nala-
GRI nala- 'be lying down (plant, stone, person), be confined to bed'

> **PI nallaq-** 'lie down' [cf. ʀ- under ŋ(ŋ)uʀ-]
> SPI —
> NAI nallaq- 'lie down'
> WCI nallaq-
> ECI nalla(q)-
> GRI nałłaʀ- 'lie down, go to bed'

PE nalluɣ- or **naluɣ-** 'toss up'
AAY —
CAY naluɣ- 'throw into the air'
NSY —
CSY naluɣ- 'land from air' [and naluXqutaʀ- 'jump around', naluɣutə- 'jump across' — for homonym 'dive in' see naluɣ-]
Sir naləɣ- 'land from the air' [Vakh. from Men.'s texts]
SPI naluk- 'throw underhand, toss' [also nalluai-]
NAI naluk- 'throw underhand, toss up' [nallukataq- 'toss up and down', nalukataq- 'celebrate Nalukataq (whale festival with blanket tossing)'; Seiler also has nalluɣaq- toss into the air' for Mal]
WCI nalluk-, Net naluk- 'throw' [Ras. for the latter], nallukataq- 'toss in blanket' [Jen. has nalukataq- 'juggle with stones' for Coronation Gulf Cop]
ECI [Ras. has Igl naluksiɣi- 'throw']
GRI naluɣ- [also spelled nalut- in old ortho.] 'throw away from self', nałłuɣ- 'fish with line from shore' [possibly influenced by naluɣ-]

PE nalmiɣ 'crosswise slat in skin boat'
AAY —
CAY —
NSY —
CSY laalmik 'rib of boat, floorpiece across wooden boat'
Sir lalmix [Orr — from the CSY]
SPI nanmik 'crossbeam at bottom of boat' [Men. has nalmak for Imaq]
NAI Nu nanmik 'crosswise wooden slat in skin boat' [in the pl. 'cross-pieces that hold boat keel in place' in PH]
WCI —
ECI —
GRI nammik [old ortho. nangmik] 'crosswise slat in skin boat'

PY-S nalqu 'relative' [cf. nałə-]
AAY —
CAY — [for nałəqłiq 'relative' see nałə-]
NSY nałqu 'relative' [and nałqukułək 'family, tribe'; L.-T. has nałku]
CSY —
Sir nałqixtaX 'relative' [Vakh. from from Men.'s texts;

Men. has nałqixtəqałəX 'family, tribe', naʀəłxuta 'family (unit)' and nalɣuta 'relative on mother's side']
Inu [note Imaq nałqu 'relative', natku 'family, tribe' (Imaq also natkułəq), KI natkun 'close relative' — from the NSY?]

PE nalu(C)aʀ 'bleached sealskin' [there may be a relat. to naluɣ-]
AAY —
CAY NSU naluaq 'bleached sealskin'
NSY nałuaq
CSY —
Sir —
SPI naluaq 'white bleached sealskin' [and naluaʀmiu 'white man']
NAI nalu<ž>aq [and naluaʀmiu 'white man']
WCI naluaq 'dry skin' [Ow.; Schn. has it as 'sole of white (bleached) boot' for 'adg']
ECI nalluaq 'sole of white boot'
GRI —

PE naluɣ- 'wade or plunge into water?'
AAY naluɣ- 'wade'
CAY naluɣ- 'take a short cut by swimming (animal)'
NSY naluɣ- 'walk into water' [ANLC]
CSY naluɣutə- 'dive in' [for homonym (?) 'jump across' see nalluɣ-]
Sir —
SPI naluk- 'plunge into water'
NAI naluk- 'go into water up to chest, swim, wade'
WCI naluk- 'swim '
ECI naluk- 'be in water up to one's knees, swim' [Boas has also 'fall in water' for Baffin; naluʀaq- 'wade']
GRI naluɣ- 'swim (person, land animal)' [naluʀaaʀ- 'wade', EG naliŋaʀ- 'wade (caribou)']

PI nalluq 'ford or swimming place' [cf. q under nəʀ[1]]
SPI —
NAI —
WCI [Ras. has nabloq 'caribou crossing place' and Schn. nalluk 'place where caribou swim in number' for 'adg' — also nallaq for B. Lake in that meaning]
ECI nalluq 'place where caribou cross water' [Saul; Peck has nallok 'caribou track down to lake' for Lab]
GRI nałłuq* 'swimming place' [Kl. 'ford']

PE nałə- 's.th. corresponding in time or place or value' [pre-Eskimo *nat-lə? — cf. natə- under na-[2]; the Inu forms with geminate ll may be influenced by nałłiʀ- below]
AAY nałə- 'even with' [posit. root]
CAY nałə- 'that which corresponds in time or place'
NSY nałŋani 'opposite' [ANLC has nałə-]
CSY nała, nałə- 'that which corresponds in time or place' [and nałpiquʀ- 'compare' in Vakh. and Em.]
Sir nałə- 'around' [Vakh. from Men. and Rub.]
SPI nali- 'direction in line with something' [posit. root], naliq 'price' [and naliqšaq 'sight on gun']
NAI nali- 'place even, in line with s.th. [posit. root; as noun = 'price']
WCI nali- 'direction of s.th.' [posit. root]
ECI nali-, nalli- 'in front, facing', Lab nali 's.th. equal in value, direction, etc.' [posit. root; Saul distinguishes Tar nali- 's.th. facing, in front, or corresponding with respect to direction' and naliq 'an equal to another, worth, value', with nalliq only occurring in derivatives like nalliqaŋŋituq 'without equal']
GRI nali(k) (possessed naliŋa) 's.th. corresponding in time, place or value', nałłi(k) 's.th. equivalent or fitting' [usually with possessor endings; note also naliŋinnaq 'any (-body or -thing), common', EG 'Greenland seal']

PI naləmmak- 'be even or level'
SPI —
NAI nalimmak- 'be equal (to), be filled to the brim'
WCI —
ECI nalimma(k)- 'flatten, be flat or even'
GRI nalimmaɣ- 'flatten, be flattened or even' [nalima- 'be flat (terrain)']

PI naləʀaq 'place or thing level with s.th.' [cf. qaʀ]
SPI —
NAI [note naliʀak- 'make a choice, evaluate']
WCI [naliqqiyut(i)- 'have arrived facing or opposite']
ECI naliʀaŋiq- 'place oneself facing'
GRI naliʀaq 'landmark, mark of direction', Up naliʀ̃aq 'place one waits for seal to come' [and naliʀaʀ- 'happen the same time as', naliqqiʀ- 'be in line with, be just level with', EG 'hit (exactly)', NG naliqqiʀaq- 'screen']

PY-S nalkə- 'find' [cf. kə-[1], also nataqə-; perhaps the same as Inu nal(l)iɣi- under nalləɣiik below]
AAY nałkə- 'find'
CAY nałkə- 'find' [for nalaqə- 'find' see nataqə-]
NSY nałkə- 'find'
CSY naałkə-
Sir nałkə- [Vakh.]

PI nalləɣiik and **nalləʀiik** 'equals' [cf. ɣiik; there appears to be influence from nałłiʀ- below]
Yup [note CSY nałəqiiyaʀutə- 'even up, equalize']
SPI —
NAI nalliʀiik 'two equals in every respect' [compare naliɣi- 'be equal in ability to' with kə-[1]]
WCI nalliɣiik, nalliʀiik 'two equals' [and nal(l)iɣi- 'do as well as, go in direction of']
ECI nalliʀiik 'two equals in size or strength' [nalliɣi- 'have as equal']
GRI naliɣiit 'equals, coevals' [naliɣi- 'correspond with, be on a level with']

PE nalqiɣ- 'be or make straight' [cf. nqiɣ-[1]?]
AAY nałqiɣ- 'be straight' [nałqiatə- 'be crooked']
CAY nałqixtə- 'straighten, correct'
NSY nałqiʀ- 'be straight' [ANLC; Men. has nałqilʀia 'straight']

CSY nanqixtə- 'judge, test'; nałqiɣanitə- 'be careless, untidy' [for nałəqiiyaʀutə- 'even up, equalize' see under nalləɣiik above]
Sir — [for nałqixtəqałəX 'family' see nalqu]
SPI natqik- 'correct, fix, make s.o. notice one's presence'
NAI natqik- 'recover, correct' [and natqikšuq- 'correct s.o. when they have erred']
WCI —
ECI naqqi(k)- 'revive (animal thought dead)'
GRI naqqiɣ- 'correct, affirm, revive (animal thought dead)' [and naqqiššuʀ- 'confirm, try to convince, reprove']

PE nałaʀ- 'meet or hit the mark' [cf. q-?]
AAY nałłaXtə- 'hit just right'
CAY nałłaXtə- 'meet, hit the mark' [for nalaqə-, nataqə-, 'find' see nataqə-]
NSY —
CSY nałaʀ- 'run into, meet'
Sir —
SPI —
NAI —
WCI [nal(l)aaɣuq- 'head straight for']
ECI [nalaaɣuq- 'go straight, act rightly']
GRI nalaaʀ- 'head straight for, come across unexpectedly'

PE nałaʀutə- 'do s.th. right or at right time' [cf. nałaʀ- above and utə-]
AAY nałłautə- 'arrive at right time'
CAY —
NSY —
CSY —
Sir —
SPI nalaut(i)- 'get right answer, find, do just right'
NAI nalauti- 'go to, accompany, guess right'
WCI nalaut(i)- 'come at right time, guess'
ECI nalaut(i)- 'occur (predestined event)'
GRI nalaat(i)- 'meet, come across'

PE nałłiʀ- 'be or make equal' [cf. liʀ-]
AAY nałłiʀ- 'pay'
CAY —
NSY —
CSY —
Sir —
SPI —
NAI nalliq- Mal 'grow as big as', PH 'put a price on'
WCI nalliq- 'do as well as, give the equivalent'
ECI nalliut(i)- 'happen, take place, be time'
GRI nałłiʀ- 'reach, become equal to, come (time)' [and nałłiut(i)- 'occur, have a birthday', EG nattiit(i)- 'aim at, compare, go past']

PE nałʀu- 'be straight'
AAY —
CAY —
NSY nałXumailŋuq 'untidy'
CSY naałXutə- 'correct, repair, cure'
Sir nałXət(ə)- 'repair' [Vakh. has nałXətət- 'find, cure by sorcery']
SPI naʀlu- 'be straight'
NAI nalʀuq- 'straighten'
WCI nalʀu- 'be straight'
ECI Lab naXXu-
GRI naʀłu- 'be or go straight'

PE nałəkkaɣ 'crotch (of trousers)' [cf. nałə-]
AAY —
CAY nałkiik [du.] 'woman's panties, crotch'
NSY nałkiik 'rear part of pants' [L.-T.]
CSY naałkak 'seat of pants'
Sir — [for nacəʀcəX 'trousers' see nayyiʀ]
SPI nalikaak [du.] 'pair of trousers' [also Jen. for W; = Imaq naləqak — for naləkak?]
NAI nalikkaak 'crotch (of body or trousers)'
WCI Cop nalikkaak 'woman's trousers' [Ras. and Jen.; Met. has Sig nallikaq 'crotch (of trousers)']
ECI nalikkaaq 'crotch (body or trousers)'
GRI nalikkaaq 'crotch of trousers', NG nalikkaak 'crotch' [and note nalikkak, nalikkaɣut 'lamp stool']

PE nałmi(nəʀ) 'one's own' [cf. nałə- plus 4s inflection mi (and nəʀ[1]) — with influence from natə- under na-[2] in CAY and CSY?]
AAY C nałm̥ikun 'of own accord, in own time'
CAY [nakm̥iin 'one's own' (adverbial of emphasis)]
NSY —
CSY [nakm̥ikə- 'choose', nakm̥iiʀ- 'make a choice']
Sir —
SPI — [for natkun 'close relative' see nalqu]
NAI nanmin^{y}ɨq* 'peer, one with whom one can be free to express oneself, one's own property or relatives' [adverbial = 'definitely'], Mal natmiin^{y} 'close relative'
WCI naŋminiq 'one's own relatives, possessions' [Pryde has nanminiq 'own' for Cop]
ECI namminiq 'one's own possessions, blood relatives, oneself'
GRI namminiq* 'oneself, one's own'

PE nału- 'not know' [cf. natə- under na-[2]?]
AAY nału- 'not know' [nału(xku)- plus neg. inflections = 'know']
CAY nału- 'not know' [and as nom. with poss. endings = 'state of not knowing'; nałutə- 'not know what one is doing']
NSY nału- 'not know' [Em.]
CSY nału- 'be ignorant (due to immaturity)'
Sir nałəkə-, nałukə- 'not know' [Vakh.; Men. has nałəkaʀniqcəX 'drunk', and nałaqə(s)- 'lose, be lost' (from the CSY present tense nałaaquq, etc.? — but compare also under nałuyaɣutə- below); Em. has nałikə(s)- 'lose consciousness']
SPI nalu- 'not know'
NAI nalu-
WCI nalu-
ECI nalu-
GRI nalu- 'not know' [nom. = 'ignorance'; naluŋŋit- 'know']

PE nałunaʀ- 'be unknown or uncertain' [cf. naʀ-]
AAY nałunaʀ- 'be unrecognizable'
CAY —
NSY nałunalʀia '(s.th.) unknown'
CSY nałunaʀ- 'be difficult to know or perceive'
Sir — [but note nałənəX 'left side']
SPI nalunaq- 'be unknown or unclear'
NAI nalunaq- 'be indistinct, be doubtful'
WCI nalunaq- 'be inexplicable, unknown' [Pryde has naunaq- 'be uncertain, hard to say' for Cop — note also Cop nauna 'I don't know']
ECI nalunaqtuq 'what one cannot know', nalunaqi- 'act in a manner another cannot cope with'
GRI nalunaʀ- 'be unknown or uncertain'

PE nałunaʀilkutaʀ 'marker' [cf. nałunaʀ- above and ŋit- and compare ɣiitkutaq under ɣiit-]
AAY nałunaiłku(u)taq 'marker, sign' [and note nałunaitə- 'be recognizable']
CAY nałunaiłkutaq 'marker, insignia'
NSY —
CSY nałuniiłkutaq 'marker'
Sir —
SPI nalunailaq 'identifying mark'
NAI nalunail^{y}utaq 'marker, sign'
WCI Sig nalunaitkutaq, Cop naunaitkutaq 'marker, sign' [Lowe]
ECI nalunaikkutaq 'sign'
GRI nalunaaq(q)utaq 'marker, clock'

PE nałunaʀiʀ- 'show' [cf. nałunaʀ- above and ŋiʀ-]
AAY nałunaiʀ- 'explain, describe, interpret'
CAY nałunaiʀ- 'explain, instruct, show'
NSY —
CSY nałuniiʀ- 'mark so as to make easier to locate'
Sir [Vakh. has nałuniʀ- 'notice']
SPI nalunaiq- 'become clear'
NAI nalunaiq- 'become clear, signify, reveal'
WCI nalunaiq- 'explain, reveal' [Pryde has naunaiyaq- 'explain' for Cop; Schn. has nalunaiq- 'be no longer unaware of' for 'adg']
ECI nalunaiq- 'point out, show' [Saul; Schn. has nalunaiʀsa(q)- 'try to learn']
GRI nalunaaʀ- 'make known, explain'

PE nałunqutə- 'be in doubt about' [cf. utə-]
AAY —
CAY [note nałumquq 'dull-witted person']
NSY —
CSY —
Sir nałənqəsitən 'at random, in an unknown way'
SPI [nalutqii- 'doubt s.o.'s ability']
NAI —
WCI —
ECI naluqqut(i)- 'doubt that s.th. is good enough for s.th. or s.o.'
GRI naluqqut(i)- 'be uncertain about s.o., not rely on things going well for one'

PY nałuɣaɣutə- 'forget' [cf. ɣɣaɣ- and utə-]
AAY nałuɣa<ɣ>utə- 'forget'
CAY nałuɣaɣutə-
NSY nałuɣaɣutəfka(ʀ)- 'wean from, break from (habit)'
CSY nałuɣaɣutə- 'be unable to comprehend', Chap 'lose, lose one's way'

PE nanəʀ- 'weigh down' [there seems to be contam. with nəmniuq- in ECI and GRI]
AAY ➟
CAY nanəʀ- 'weigh down, press', NSU 'catch in a trap'
NSY nanəʀ- 'weigh down, press' [Em. — ANLC 'drop s.th. on']
CSY [note nanʀiiʀ- 'try, test, experience', Chap also 'get to know', nanqixtə- 'test, judge', going with the Sir below]
Sir [note nanitə- 'touch' — Vakh. has nanəkəʀ- from Rub.'s texts — also nanižaqaʀ- 'feel' if the link is not to nani-[1] instead]
SPI naniq- 'weigh down' [and Imaq nanəqsiiʀ- 'fall upon']
NAI nanɨq- 'weigh down, travel directly over, catch in a trap', Nu 'be caught in a trap' [and Nu nanʀutaq 'jaw of leg-hold trap']
WCI naniq- 'crush under a rock' [Ras. has 'press down' for Cop; Met. has Cop nanik- 'put flat, be flattened']
ECI naʀni(q)-, niiniq-, Lab niinik- 'press down on', naniq- 'extract oil from blubber' [Peck has 'grow less from pressure' for Lab, also nanok- 'press, print']
GRI naniʀ- 'press, weigh down', nanit-, NWG ninit- 'be pressed down by own weight, subside' [and naʀnut(i)-, naʀnualiut(i)- 'pin down, press down with one's weight', naʀniʀ-, naʀniɣ- 'paddle with all one's strength', naʀnuaʀi- 'wind tight (to compress)']

PE nanəʀɣaʀ 'trap (deadfall)' [cf. ɣaʀ]
AAY C nanaʀyaq 'trigger for deadfall'
CAY nanəʀyaq 'deadfall trap'
NSY nanəʀyaq [ANLC]
CSY —
Sir —
SPI naniʀiaq 'leghold trap' [as verb = 'trap an animal']
NAI naniʀi<ž>aq
WCI naniʀiaq '(leghold) trap' [Lowe]
ECI —
GRI —

PY-S nanəvɣaq 'old man' [there may be a link to nani-[2]; note also p.b. žaɣaq and compare the p.b. in icavʀaʀ]
AAY —
CAY —
NSY —
CSY nanəvɣaq 'old man' [nanəvɣaʀ- 'grow old']
Sir naniɣvəx 'old man', naniʀcəʀəX 'old woman' [Vakh. has naniʀcəX for the latter from Men.'s texts and Krup. naniʀcəɣaX; note also nancəXłətaX 'ancient'; Em. has naniɣvəX 'king (in cards)']

PI nani-[1] 'find' [from *nanə-? — in which case there could be a link to nažvaq- (compare nanvaʀ)]
Yup [for CSY nanʀiiʀ- 'try, test, experience' and nanqixtə- 'test, judge' see nanəʀ-]
Sir [for nanitə- 'touch' and nanižaqaʀ- 'feel' see nanəʀ-]
SPI —
NAI —
WCI Cop nani- 'find (s.th. one was looking for)' [also Schn. 'adg' and Pet. for Sig]
ECI nani- 'find (what one is looking for)' [half-trans. nanii-, nanisi-]
GRI nani- 'find (what one is looking for)' [half-trans. naniši-]

PY nani-[2] 'be unable to cope?'
AAY nanitu- 'not feel like doing s.th., be disinclined'
CAY nanikua- 'feel desperate, unable to cope' [and naniłiuʀ- 'be lonesome']
NSY —
CSY —

PE naniʀ 'lamp' [cf. Aleut tani- 'light up, give light to']
AAY K naniq 'lamp, light'
CAY Y, NS naniq lamp, HBC 'flashlight'
NSY naniq
CSY naniq 'oil lamp'
Sir nanəX 'lamp, light'
SPI naniq, Qaw also nanniq
NAI naniq
WCI Sig naniʀ- 'illuminate' [Ras., who also has naniyaq 'fire' and Cop nangeq 'lamp', Net nangneq 'fireplace'; Pet. has naniʀuaq 'candle']
ECI naniʀuaq, naniʀut 'kerosene lamp, lantern, makeshift lamp, torch' [Ras. has Igl nangeq 'lamp']
GRI naniʀuaq 'torch', naniʀuut 'candle' [naniʀuaʀ- 'illuminate with lamp for s.o.']

PY-S nanilʀaq 'lamp stand'
AAY [Milan has nanilak 'lamp stand' from Karluk]
CAY nanilʀaq 'lamp stand'
NSY —
CSY nanilʀaq
Sir nanilʀaX [Em.]

PE nanit- 'be short' [cf. nunanniʀ- for a similar case of loss of intervocalic n by dissimilation in Inu]
AAY nanitə- 'be short'
CAY nanitə- [with tə ~ l alternation]
NSY nanitə- 'be short'
CSY —
Sir —
SPI nait-
NAI nait-
WCI nait-
ECI nait-
GRI naat-

PE nanʀaʀ- 'praise or boast?' [from *nanəʀaʀ-? — there may be a link to nanəʀ-]
AAY nanʀaʀ- 'praise'
CAY nanʀaʀ- 'praise, honor'
NSY nanʀaʀ- 'praise, boast'
CSY — [for nanʀiiʀ- 'try, test' see nanəʀ-]
Sir — [for nanʀaʀ- 'watch' see naŋaʀ-[2]]
SPI —
NAI nanʀaq- 'praise'
WCI nanʀaut(i)- 'praise' [and nanʀaqtuq 'boaster'; Pryde has nanʀaq- Cop 'praise', Sig 'admire']
ECI [for naʀŋa(q)- 'criticize, speak ill of' see naŋʀu(ʀ)-]
GRI —

PI nanuk- 'rub s.th. on' [cf. naŋžuɣ-; from *nanəɣ-?]
SPI nanuk- 'rub s.th. on'
NAI nanuk-
WCI nanuk-
ECI nanuiɣut 'coat of ice that is painted onto the peat surface of the runners of a traditional sled'
GRI —

PE nanuʀ 'polar bear'
AAY —
CAY Y, HBC, NS nanuaq 'polar bear'
NSY nanuq
CSY nanuq* [or nanuq — there is some fluctuation here] 'polar bear'
Sir nanuʀaX 'polar bear'
SPI W, Qaw nanuq [and KI nanuayaaq 'polar bear cub']
NAI nanuq
WCI nanuq
ECI nanuq
GRI nanu(q) 'polar bear' [NG nannuk (du.) 'man's bearskin trousers']

PI nanuʀaq 'polar bear skin' [cf. aʀ]
Yup — [but CAY nanuaq above is probably the same]
Sir — [but nanuʀaX above is probably the same]
SPI nanuʀawiniq 'piece of polar bear skin'
NAI nanuʀaq
WCI nanuʀaq
ECI nanuʀaq 'polar bear skin (piece or whole)'
GRI NG nanuʀaq 'polar bear skin' [Holt.]

PI nanuʀluk- 'lie down on belly' [cf. nanəʀ- if not nanuʀ]
Yup — [but note CSY nanuʀuXtaaʀ- 'be crouching']
SPI —
NAI —
WCI —
ECI nanuʀlu(C)- 'lie down on belly like an animal does' [nanuʀluŋa- 'lie on belly (animal), remain on hands and knees']
GRI nanuʀłuaʀ- 'hold on to s.th., sit still and comfortably, lie on side, lie with front paws stretched out (dog)'

PE nanvaʀ 'lake' [from *nʸanvaʀ?; there appears to be dissimilation in CSY, Sir, and Inu, though there could be assimilation in CAY and AAY (also Sir) if from *naðvaʀ]
AAY nanwaq 'lake'
CAY nanvaq
NSY —

CSY naayvaq 'lake' [and note SLI naayvaʀ- 'freeze'?]
Sir yayvəX 'lake' [in Men.'s texts also nayvaX acc. Vakh.]
SPI navžaq 'lake'
NAI nažvaq
WCI Cop nalvaq, Sig nayvaq
ECI — [but Jen. has nachvak — for naɣvaq? — 'lake' in Lab]
GRI —

PE naŋaʀ-[1] 'skirt (and thus avoid)' [there seems to be some entanglement with naŋəʀ- — in the sense of s.th. standing in the way?]
AAY —
CAY —
NSY naŋa(ʀ)- 'go round extremity of s.th.' [for naŋnəq 'end' see naŋnəq under naŋə(t)-]
CSY [note naŋaXtə- 'form long snowdrift', Chap 'block way']
Sir —
SPI naŋaq-, naŋaa- 'skirt, thereby avoiding'
NAI naŋaq-, PH naŋaa-
WCI [Pryde has Cop naŋaq- 'cut across, not go round']
ECI Lab naŋaC- 'go past, not come toward s.o.' [Peck; Ras. has naŋaʀiaq 'short cut' for Igl]
GRI [note naŋaa- 'hesitate' (influenced by naŋyaʀ-?) and naŋaʀ- 'prevent from doing, forbid, contradict' (influenced by naŋəʀ-?)]

PE naŋaʀ-[2] 'open eyes (wide) or watch'
AAY —
CAY —
NSY —
CSY naŋʀayuɣ-, naŋʀaluɣ- 'feel excited, be interested', naŋlii- 'stare', naŋɬaXqə- 'open eyes wide' [perhaps with contam. from naŋəʀ-; also naŋaʀaɬəq*, naŋaʀnəq* 'way of life, behavior' — compare kiyaʀ- for a semantic parallel]
Sir naŋaʀ(cəʀ)- 'watch' [Vakh. from Men.'s texts; note also naŋət(ə)- 'see, watch', 'open eyes' (Orr), nəŋitaʀ- (Vakh. has nəŋətuʀ-, nəŋətituʀ-) 'go and look at', and nanʀaʀ- 'watch, observe', naʀət(ə)- 'live, be', naʀətəɬəx 'life']
SPI —
NAI —
WCI Car Baker Lake naŋaq- 'be amazed' [Schn.]
ECI —
GRI — [for naŋaa- 'be in doubt, hesitate' see naŋaʀ-[1]]

PE naŋcaʀ- 'take along'
AAY —
CAY naŋcaʀ- 'tow'
NSY nansaʀ- [ANLC]
CSY [note naŋsaɣaq 'exchange wife']
Sir —
SPI naksauti- 'carry along with one' [Jen.]
NAI —
WCI naksaq- 'take along'
ECI natsa(q)- 'carry, transport' [natsasaq 'object to be carried', natsaɣaq 'object usually carried']
GRI nassaʀ- [old ortho. nagsar-] 'have along, take with one' [nassataq, nassaɣaq 's.th. brought along', nassataʀi- 'bring, drag along with one']

PI nakcət- 'give to s.o. to take to another' [contracted from *naŋcaʀtət- with p.b. tət-?]
SPI —
NAI —
WCI Car Baker Lake naxxiutsi- 'give someone s.th. for another' [Schn.; with utə-]
ECI natsiut(i)- 'carry off unintentionally', FB 'send a gift to s.o.' [Dor.]
GRI nassit- [old ortho. nagsit-] 'send s.th. via (someone else), give s.th. to (s.o.) to take to another', nassiut(i)- 'send (to s.o.)'

PE naŋə- 'be used up' [cf. naŋɬəɣ- and naatki-, also perhaps naŋnəʀ-; compare the semantics of nuŋu-, with which there may be entanglement here]
AAY naŋə- 'finish off'
CAY naŋə- 'be used up, use up'
NSY naŋə- 'be used up' [note also naŋutə- 'eat everything up']
CSY naaŋə- 'be used up'
Sir naŋə- 'be finished' [for naŋɬəɣnaXqə(s)- 'torment' see naŋɬəɣ-]
SPI Imaq naŋu- 'be finished' [and Jen. has naksi- 'try for another (animal?)']
NAI [note naɣžutaq 'cause of suffering', naɣžuq-, PH naksi- 'finish off, slit animal's throat']
WCI ➟
ECI [note natti(t)- 'make fall ill again, finish off, kill']
GRI naŋima- 'become worse (sick person)' [and naŋitit- 'be unlucky', natsit- (old ortho. nagtit-) 'blow stronger (wind)']

PE naŋət- 'finish off or use up' [cf. t-[1]]
AAY —
CAY naŋtə- 'abuse, torment', Nun, NS 'be ill'
NSY naŋətə- 'finish'
CSY naaŋtə- 'use up' [and note naŋətəʀuʀ- 'give up hope']
Sir naŋət- 'finish' [and Em. has naŋətəʀuʀ- 'remain in one place, be held up, become rigid in fear, etc.']
SPI naŋit- 'be sick, suffer'
NAI naŋɨt- 'be sick', PH 'try to finish off (wounded animal)'
WCI naŋit- 'suffer' [Pryde also has naŋitit- 'mistreat']
ECI —
GRI naŋit- 'shoot again (at wounded animal) to finish it off' [half-trans. naŋii- or (older) naŋinniɣ-; for homonym 'continue' see naŋnəʀ-; note also naŋinniaʀ-, SWG naŋŋiaʀ-, nanniaʀ- 'try to finish off (a wounded animal)']

PY naŋnəq 'end or left over part' [cf. nəʀ[1]]
AAY C naŋnəq 'thumb, big toe, end part'
CAY naŋnəq* 'last one, end, vortex', Nun 'thumb'
NSY naŋnəq 'end of s.th.' [ANLC also 'last one']
CSY naaŋnəq* 'leftover'

PY naŋtəʀ- and **naŋtəqə-** 'suffer' [cf. təʀ-?]
AAY naŋtəqə- 'suffer'
CAY naŋtəqə- 'suffer pain', Y 'be sick'
NSY —
CSY [naŋətəʀuʀ- 'give up hope']

PE naŋəʀ- 'be standing'
AAY naŋaʀ- 'stand up' [postural root as in other Yup]
CAY naŋəʀ-
NSY —
CSY — [for naŋaXtə- 'form a long snowdrift' see naŋaʀ-[1] — there may be contam. here]
Sir —
SPI naŋiq- 'be standing'
NAI —
WCI naŋiq- 'be standing up'
ECI naŋiq-
GRI — [for naŋaʀ- 'prevent from doing, forbid, contradict' see naŋaʀ-[1]]

PE naŋiʀ 'diaper (skin put under baby)'
AAY naŋik 'menstrual pad'
CAY —
NSY —
CSY —
Sir —
SPI naŋiq- 'be standing'
NAI naŋiq 'waterproof cover placed under baby or invalid'
WCI —
ECI naŋiq 'skin put under baby in hood or bed'
GRI naŋiq 'diaper'

PE naŋłəɣ- 'feel sorry for s.o.' [cf. naŋət- under naŋə- and ləɣ-? — compare also naatki- and naalɣiuq-, with which there seems to be entanglement in Inu; there appears to be assimilation reflecting *ŋt + l in Alaskan Yupik and NSY]
AAY nakłəkə- 'love, cherish, have pity on' [nakłəŋ 'please, I beg you', nakłəɣnaa, AP akłinaa 'poor thingy']
CAY nakłəkə- 'feel compassion toward, be considerate of' [and nakłəɣnaXqə- 'cause to feel compassion', nakłəŋ, akłəŋ 'poor thing!']
NSY nakłəkə- 'pity' [ANLC also nakłəɣ- and nakłəɣnaʀ-; nakłəɣnaXqaʀ- 'torment']
CSY naŋłəɣ(yuɣ)- 'feel pity' [emot. root]
Sir naŋłəɣ-, naŋłəkə- 'pity' [Vakh. from Men.'s texts; Men. has naŋłəkət- 'pity', naŋłəɣnaXqə(s)- 'torment' in his dict.]
SPI naɣlii- 'pity' [Jen. also has 'love'; note also Qaw nakłiŋ 'poor thing!' — borrowed from Yup]
NAI naɣliɣi- 'pity', naɣliɣnaq- 'be pitiful' [and naɣliksaaq- 'suffer']
WCI naɣliɣi- 'pity, love'
ECI nalliɣi- [Baffin naɣliɣi-] 'love'
GRI nałłiɣi- 'feel pity for', NG naɣlii- 'love, feel pity for' [Tersis has nattii- 'be responsible for, look after affectionately, pity' for EG; Top has neglik- 'love' for WG; note also nałłiɣ- 'comfort (child)', nałłinnaʀ- 'be pitiful' and nałłi(nnaq) 'poor thing!']

PE naŋnəʀ- 'continue moving' [cf. naŋə-; probably with dissim. in Yup — compare CSY tuɣmaxtə- under tuŋvaʀ-]
AAY —
CAY —
NSY naɣnəʀ- 'continue moving (under own momentum or despite obstacles)' [ANLC]
CSY naɣnəʀ- 'go on without hesitating or despite obstacles' [and naŋənqaʀ- 'continue to one's destination']
Sir [naŋcəʀət(ə)- 'continue (on way)']
SPI —
NAI naŋniq- 'force, strain body by overworking, press on toward destination' [but PH 'beat badly' — contam. with naŋət- under naŋə-?]
WCI Cop naŋniuma- 'maintain a strong pull (sled dog)' [Pryde; Ras. has naŋit- 'continue' for Sig]
ECI —
GRI [note naŋit- (trans. and refl., half-trans. naŋitsi-) 'continue (having stopped for a while)', naŋiɣ- (intr.) 'have a relapse (s.o. ill), become as before again, revive (of s.o. thought dead)', SWG also nanniɣ- in the latter sense; Fab. has nangik- 'get worse, blow up (wind), finish off', of which the latter meaning goes with homonym 'finish off' under naŋət- (naŋə-) — there is some entanglement]

PE naŋquʀ 'arrowhead' [cf. perhaps naŋət- under naŋə- and quʀ — if the first Sir form below displays dissim.]
AAY —
CAY naŋquq 'end, arrowhead, spearhead'
NSY —
CSY naaŋquq 'piece of ivory' [Chap also 'walrus tusk']
Sir yaŋqułəɣaX 'arrow' [Vakh. from Men.'s texts — but compare also naŋłəX 'iron' (in Vakh. = 'tip of weapon'), naŋłəʀaX 'point, edge']
SPI naqquq 'arrowhead, tip of bullet'
NAI natquq
WCI natquq 'arrowhead'
ECI naqquq 'metal arrowhead, bullet of toy gun, bit of drill'
GRI naqquq 'arrowhead'

PY naŋʀu(ʀ)- 'criticize' [there may be a relat. to naŋə-]
AAY — [for alaŋ<ʀ>u- 'be critical' see alaŋʀu- under alaʀ-]
CAY naŋʀu(yuɣ)- 'be critical, find fault with people' [emot. root]
NSY naŋʀuʀ- 'curse' [and naŋʀu 'curse, damnation' (ANLC)]
CSY naŋʀu(ʀi)- 'disapprove, disagree', naŋʀukə- 'criticize' [and note Chap naŋʀitə- 'be right, correct']
Inu [but note KI naŋikłiq- 'complain about, criticize' and ECI naʀŋa(q)-, naʀŋaʀi- 'criticize']

PE naŋyaʀ- 'be afraid in a precarious place' [there may be a link to naŋaʀ-[1]]
AAY —
CAY naŋyaʀ- 'be afraid (of height)' [emotional root]

NSY nanyaxtalʀia 'careful', nanyakə- 'be careful with, act cautiously toward' [L.-T.]
CSY naŋyaʀ- 'wince, hesitate, be afraid'
Sir naŋyaʀ- 'wince, hesitate, be afraid' [Orr; also naŋyəqə(s)- 'be afraid of' Em.]
SPI naŋiaq- 'be afraid in a precarious place'
NAI naŋiaq- 'be afraid of falling (esp. from high place or into deep water)'
WCI naŋiaq- 'be afraid of danger' [Ras. has 'turn dizzy, anxious' for Cop]
ECI naŋiaq- 'be afraid of danger' [and naŋii 'I'm afraid (of falling)!']
GRI naŋiaʀ- 'be afraid or giddy in a precarious place, be dizzy in kayak' [naŋiaʀi- 'be afraid of']

PE naŋyaʀit- 'be brave' [cf. ŋit-]
AAY —
CAY —
NSY nanyailŋuq 'brave'
CSY naŋyiitə-, naŋyiiɣatə- 'be brave'
Sir —
SPI naŋiit-
NAI naŋiit-
WCI naŋiit-
ECI —
GRI naŋiit-

PY naŋžuɣ- 'chafe' [cf. nanuk- and ðuɣ?]
AAY naŋuɣ- 'chafe, abrade'
CAY naŋuxtə- 'chafe, abrade' [and naŋuɣun 'whetstone']
NSY —
CSY naŋžuɣ-
Sir [Orr has naŋžuɣ- 'chafe, abrade' — from CSY?]

PE napa- 'be standing (upright)' [or *nʸapa-]
AAY napaq 'tree' [note also napan 'heart']
CAY napa- 'stand upright' [as noun = 'tree, post']
NSY ➟
CSY ➟
Sir ➟
SPI Qaw napa- 'stand erect (of a dead tree)'
NAI napa- 'be standing upright (house, pole, etc.)'
WCI napa- 'be standing' [and Pryde has Cop nappan 'soul' as a shaman's word]
ECI napa- 'stand straight up'
GRI napa- 'be upright' [and note EG nappat 'neck']

PE napa(ʀ)aqtuʀ 'tree' [cf. aʀ- and ðuʀ?]
AAY —
CAY [for nəkəvʀaaXtuq, kəvʀaaXtuq 'spruce tree' see nəkəvʀaaʀtuq under nəkəvə(t)-]
NSY napaXtuq 'tree'
CSY —
Sir —
SPI navaaqtuq 'tree'
NAI napaaqtuq
WCI napaaqtuq
ECI napaaqtuq
GRI napaaʀtuq 'mountain ash'

PE napaðuʀ 'stanchion or upright' [cf. ðuʀ]
AAY —
CAY napayuq 'stanchion (of sled)'
NSY —
CSY —
Sir —
SPI [note navaaqtuq 'tree']
NAI napažuq 'sled stanchion, boat rib, frame support inside boat'
WCI —
ECI napayuq 's.th. upright'
GRI napašuq 'upright (along sides of umiaq)' in pl. 'props on which umiaq is laid' [and NG napahuqtaq 'dowel on harpoon for throwing board', EG napaliq 'kayak or umiaq stand' — Ges.]

PY-S napaquq 'pole' [cf. quʀ]
AAY —
CAY —
NSY —
CSY napaquq 'pole'
Sir yapaqaX

PE napaʀyaʀ 'pole' [cf. nappaʀ- below and p.b. yaʀ]
AAY napaʀyaq 'pole, post'
CAY NS napaʀyaq 'mast, pole'
NSY —
CSY napaʀyaq
Sir yapaʀyəʀaX
SPI navaʀiaq 'stilt support for house', Qaw napaʀiaq 'post, stanchion'
NAI napaʀiaq 'post'
WCI napaʀiaq 'post, stanchion (of sled)'
ECI napaʀiaq 'mast of boat' [Saul; Schn. has it for Aiv as 's.th. standing upright, stanchion']
GRI napaʀiaq 'stanchion (of sled), rib of umiaq'

PY napataʀ- 'target shoot' [cf. nappaʀtaʀ below and compare nakataq]
AAY napataʀ- 'target shoot' [napataq 'target']
CAY napataʀ- 'target shoot' [napataq 'dart']
NSY —
CSY [note napaqiliq 'game involving throwing rocks from a sitting position']

PE nappaqutaʀ and **nappaʀutaʀ** 's.th. raised up' [cf. un]
AAY napaqutaq 'cross on grave'
CAY napaʀutaq 'whale fin, mast, pole', napaqutaq 'mast'
NSY —
CSY napaqutaq, napaqətaq 'stake' [and napaataq 'pole and flag for signaling during hunt']
Sir —
SPI nappaʀutaq 'marker, signpost'
NAI nappaʀutaq 'piling, log driven into ground as support for structure'
WCI Cop nappaqqut 'headstone, marker of grave' [Pryde]
ECI napaʀutaq 'mast', Iti 'stem of plant resembling

a plantain'
GRI napaʀutaq, EG nappaat 'back fin of whale' [and nappaʀusiʀ- 'raise a mast on (a vessel)'; note also EG nappaalilik 'killer whale']

PE nappaʀ- 'raise or be raised' [cf. ʀ- under ŋ(ŋ)uʀ-]
AAY napaXtə- 'erect, stand' [postural root]
CAY napaXtə- 'erect, set upright' [napaŋqa- 'be upright']
NSY napaXtə- rise (nose of boat), stand (pole)'
CSY napaXtə- 'erect' [napaʀŋa- 'be erect']
Sir yapaʀ-, yapaXt(ə)- 'raise' [Vakh.]
SPI nappaq- 'stand or set straight'
NAI nappaq- 'erect, build'
WCI Cop nappaŋa- 'be up in the bow (boat)' [Pryde; Met. has note napaaq- 'raise']
ECI nappa(q)- 'raise up, stand upright, balance on hands, heave self out of water (seal)'
GRI nappaʀ- 'raise, be raised up'

PE nappaʀtaʀ 's.th. raised up (like a pole)' [cf. nappaʀ- above and ðaʀ]
AAY napaXta(q), napataq 'pole, post, target'
CAY napaXtaq 'post, pole, mast', Y, HBC also 'barrel'
NSY napaXtə 'mast', napaXtaq 's.th. established, walrus sleeping with head raised up' [ANLC also 'post'; Men. has napaqšaq 'post']
CSY —
Sir —
SPI navaqtaq, Imaq navaqtə 'mast'
NAI nappaqtaq 'circular tent with single pole'
WCI —
ECI —
GRI nappaʀtaq 'barrel, tub'

PI napatkaq- 'fall headfirst' [cf. napažaq- and k(k)aʀ-; there may be influence from nakkaʀ- here]
SPI —
NAI —
WCI Cop napatkaq- 'fall headfirst', Sig napatkaaq- 'do somersaults'
ECI napakka(q)- 'fall headfirst, head over heels', napakkataq- 'turn somersaults' [and napakkaŋa- 'lower head forward, do balancing act on hands']
GRI napakkaʀ- 'fall headfirst from s.th., swoop down on prey (bird)'

PI napažaq- 'do a somersault' [cf. napatkaq-, napə- and ðaʀ-?]
SPI Qaw napažaq- 'turn a somersault'
NAI napažaq- 'tumble over, turn a somersault' [napažaʀaaq- 'turn somersaults, do a handstand']
WCI napayaq- 'do a somersault' [napaayaʀaq- 'do somersaults']
ECI napayaʀaq- 'turn somersaults'
GRI napašaʀ- 'do a somersault' [napašaqattaaʀ- 'do several somersaults']

PE napə- 'break in two' [cf. naplu and navəɣ- — so perhaps *nʸapə-, given the Sir under the former]
AAY napŋ̥əq 'joint'
CAY Nun napŋ̥əX*
NSY —
CSY —
Sir —
SPI navi- 'break, cut in half'
NAI napi- 'break, cut in half'
WCI napi- 'break in two, have back broken', Car napqi- 'break, push out of joint' [Schn.]
ECI napi- 'break, be broken in two' [napit- 'open a shotgun', Lab napi(k)- 'be stiff']
GRI napi- 'break across or in two, be broken in two' [and note NG napakkaq- 'break (foreshaft from rest of harpoon)' acc. Holt. — influenced by napatkaq-?; also naffaʀ-, naššaʀ- (old ortho. nagvar-, nagssar-) 'get half of an animal']

PI napluq- 'break (in several places)' [cf. luʀ-]
SPI napłui- 'cut in half'
NAI —
WCI Cop H. Island navluq- 'cut into slices' [Pryde; Met. has navluaq 'piece of s.th. broken', and Schn. has Car? navluq- 'break a leg' for 'adg']
ECI nallu(q)- 'break in several places' [Saul; Schn. has nalluu(q)-]
GRI nałłuʀ-

PI nappaq 'half' [cf. q under nəʀ[1]]
SPI nappaq 'half'
NAI nappaq* 'half (s.th. cut or split), hump of hunchback'
WCI nappaq 'half' [and nappalik 's.o. with a broken back']
ECI nappaq 'half of s.th. broken in two, break, fracture'
GRI [note nappaq* 'illness' and nappaʀ- 'get ill', perhaps with PE ŋ(ŋ)uʀ- 'become']

PE napəʀ- and **napət-** 'snare' [the latter form with t-[1]?; from *nʸapəʀ-?]
AAY naptə- 'get caught (in mesh)'
CAY nap(ə)tə- 'be stuck, caught (in water or net)'
NSY napətaq 'thing caught in net' [L.-T.; note also napiʀ- 'harness, attach rope to in order to move', napitə- 'carry, go away with']
CSY naaptə- 'catch with trap or net' [and note napi- 'go hunting', Chap napŋ̥iiʀ- 'go trapping']
Sir yapəʀ- 'catch with a lasso' [Vakh., who also has yapəʀcaX (Men. yapəɣəcaX) 'lasso' and yapətəq(ə)- 'get a net' from Men.'s texts]
SPI navit- 'catch, trap'
NAI napit- 'trap, snare, be trapped'
WCI napit- 'be caught in trap or snare' [Net also 'catch in snare' — Ras., who also has Cop napiq- 'make a loop around']
ECI napiq- 'make a loop, catch with a lasso' [napiaʀuti 'lasso']
GRI napiʀ-, napiaʀ- 'snare (a bird)', napit- 'be caught in snare (bird)'

PE naplu 'knee joint' [or nʸaplu; cf. napə- and lu(ʀ)]
AAY —
CAY —
NSY [note pəɫəq 'joint']
CSY nafɫuq 'joint, hinge'[Chap. napɫuq acc. Orr]
Sir yapɫəX, yafləX 'joint' [second form acc. Orr]
SPI napɫuq 'knee joint'
NAI navlu, Mal naplu
WCI navluk 'knee joint' [Pryde has Net na'lu, Sig navluaq — also navlu 'shin-bone' for the latter]
ECI nalluk 'start of thigh above knee, knee articulation'
GRI naɫɫu, NG nalluq 'ham (of leg)'

PE napu 'crosspiece of sled'
AAY —
CAY NSU napu 'arch supporting bed of sled' [and Barnum has naput 'crosspieces of sled']
NSY naapu 'flesh between whale baleen' [ANLC; L.-T. has napu 'flesh between whale's whiskers']
CSY —
Sir —
SPI W navu 'crosspiece of sled' [Jen.]
NAI napu
WCI napu
ECI napu 'crossbar of sled' [and napuliuti 'rawhide thong binding crossbars of sled to runners']
GRI napu, NG napuq 'crosspiece of sled', NG also 'cross-rib of kayak' [and napuliutit 'rawhide thongs binding crossbars of sled to runners']

PE naqðaʀ 'valley' [cf. naqət-]
AAY —
CAY naqa 'valley'
NSY —
CSY —
Sir —
SPI naqšaq 'gentle slope atop King Island'
NAI naqšaq, Nu naXžaq 'pass, valley in mountains, ridge between watersheds'
WCI Cop naXXaq 'valley' [Lowe; Met. has naqsaq 'little valley or pass' for Sig; Pryde has Net naqšaq 'plain']
ECI naʀsaq 'mountain pass, valley without a river' [B.-S. has naqsaq 'plain' for Igl]
GRI naʀšaq 'plain, open field', EG naʀsaq 'mountain pass'

PE naqət- 'press down or tighten (load)' [or perhaps *nʸaqət-; cf. naqðaʀ and Atkan Aleut taqu- 'embrace']
AAY K naqtə- 'be tight, tighten, squeeze' [and AP naqiyutaq 'rope for tying']
CAY HBC naq(ə)tə- 'weave, braid' [and note naqiʀ- 'lash, bind', naquxtə- 'put on a belt']
NSY [note naqn̥iaʀun 'lock' (L.-T.)] ➡
CSY —
Sir [note yaqižaX 'haft, handle']
SPI naʀik- 'be low'
NAI naqɨt- 'be low, press down'
WCI naqit- 'be low, press' [and Car? naqitiq- 'squeeze, feel' — Schn. 'adg']
ECI naqit- 'be low, attach to a sled, pull s.th. attached' [and Baffin naqitiq- 'feel, squeeze' acc. Schn.]
GRI naqiɣ- 'be low', naqit- 'press down on' [and naqinniq* 'printed letter, seal (stamp), depression (low place)', naqitiʀi- 'print']

PI naqəkli- 'become lower' [cf. li-[2]]
SPI naʀiɣli- 'become lower'
NAI naqikɫi- 'set (sun), become lower, humble oneself'
WCI naqiɣli- 'lower, become lower'
ECI naqili- 'be stooped or low, lower', naqillitiq- 'lower, stoop'
GRI naqiɫɫi- 'become lower, lower', NG naqillihima- 'squat'

PE naqətaʀ- 'lash load to sled' [cf. ðaʀ-]
AAY —
CAY —
NSY naqətaXtə- 'tie up, secure, pack' [and ANLC naqəta 'package, bundle', but also nəqətə- 'secure a load']
CSY —
Sir —
SPI Qaw naʀitaq-, Imaq naʀataq- 'tie down a sled load' [and naʀiktaʀun 'rope to tie sled load']
NAI naqɨtak- 'be tied down, secured, a hindrance', naqɨtaqšuq- 'tie down'
WCI Car? naqitaq- 'tie load to sled' [Schn. 'adg'; Met. has Sig naqitaq(q)un 'rope for lashing load on sled' — Ras. has naqitaʀut for Net, Car and Cop]
ECI naqitaʀi-, Lab naqitaɣik- 'load things on sled' [and naqitaʀut 'rope for tying baggage down']
GRI naqitaʀi- 'lash, secure' [and NG naqataq 'rope for lashing to sled' — Holt.]

na(a)ʀa(a)yiq 'frog' [loan from Athabascan — cf. Kutchin nè:ʀai:, Tanana nɔʀυyə 'frog' and cognate Canadian Ath. forms meaning 'wolverine']
SPI — [Wales piliqpiliq 'frog' is probably onomatopoeic and borrowed to or from CAY where it appears as pələqpəlʀ(aq*)]
NAI naaʀaayiq 'frog', aaʀaayiq 'legendary little person with big head who travels by bouncing on hips'
WCI naaʀaayiq 'frog' [Lowe; Met. has naʀayiq]
ECI Lab naʀayi 'frog' [Peck]
GRI naʀasiq 'frog' [apparently taken by Kl. from the Lab form above to translate the word as used in the Bible; note also EG naaʀayiq 'specific creature of folklore, humanoid with fat belly acc. R. Petersen, though this could be from na(ž)aq]

PE naʀciɣ- 'wrinkle or push up one's nose' [cf. naʀə- and naʀʀu-]
AAY na<ʀ>isəxtə- 'offend by strong odor', na<ʀ>isəxn̥aʀ- 'be offensive'
CAY naʀitə-, NSU naXciɣ- 'show scorn by pushing up s.o.'s nose'
NSY [naʀžiɣtə- 'show scorn by pushing up another's nose — ANLC]
CSY [naʀžiɣtə- 'swipe one's wetted finger under another's nose as a gesture of scorn']

Sir —
SPI naqsik- 'hook, push s.o.'s nose up to show disdain' [the first sense by contam. with naɣci(t)- under naɣət-?; naqsiŋa- 'have a pug nose']
NAI naqsik- 'wrinkle one's nose', PH 'push one's nose up to show disdain' [nom. = 'pug-nose'; note also naqsiŋa- 'be pug-nosed']
WCI Sig naqsuŋa- 'be pug-nosed' [Ow. has naXXiktaq- 'make faces at s.o. (to show dislike)' for EP]
ECI naʀsi(C)- 'wrinkle up one's nose (as sign of displeasure)', naʀsu(C)- 'turn up one's nose', naʀsuŋa- 'be pug-nosed'
GRI naʀsiŋašuq 'pug-nosed'

PI naqciaq 'muffler'
SPI —
NAI naqsiaq 'face mask, muffler'
WCI Car naXXiaq 'piece of caribou skin under the chin of parka hood to gather rime from breath in cold weather' [Pryde; B.-S. has it as 'tippet of dearskin for children (?)']
ECI naʀsiaq 'scarf'
GRI —

PE naʀðuɣ- 'intercept or cross'
AAY [note Kod naɣuʀ- 'go to meet']
CAY naʀuɣ- 'meet', naʀuXtə- 'act against accepted standards of behavior'
NSY naʀuXtə- 'pass by' [ANLC]
CSY naʀuXtə- 'pass by'
Sir [note laʀluXtə- 'pass by, go past']
SPI naʀžuk- 'cut across s.o.'s path'
NAI —
WCI —
ECI [note Lab naʀsuktuq- 'outrun' — Peck]
GRI naʀšuɣ- 'cross, intercept, come up to s.o.'s side, forbid (s.o.) s.th. '

PE naʀə- 'smell' [cf. Aleut taʀa- 'try, test, taste, learn, understand']
AAY naʀə- 'detect smell' [and PWS naʀʀuʀ- 'keep smelling']
CAY naʀə-
NSY naʀə- 'smell, kiss, touch on nose with own nose' [ANLC; Men. has naʀuma- 'sniff, smell']
CSY naaʀ- 'smell, kiss'
Sir — [for naʀət(ə)- 'live' see naŋaʀ-[2]]
SPI nai- 'smell' [and naiyuq- 'smell s.th.']
NAI na<ʀ>i- [also na<ɣ>i-] 'smell, detect smell' [and naʀiuq- 'sniff']
WCI nai- 'smell'
ECI nai-, naima-
GRI naa- 'smell' [and naʀayuʀ-, NG naʀiuq- 'smell, sniff at', naXXat(i)- 'let (s.o.) smell s.th. evil-smelling', naama- 'have caught the scent of']

PE naʀ(ə)yaʀ 'bait' [cf. yaʀ]
AAY naʀyaaq 'bait'
CAY naʀyaʀ- 'be attracted by bait'
NSY —
CSY —
Sir —
SPI naʀiaq 'bait'
NAI naʀi<ž>aq 'bait' [and naʀiaq- 'detect smell']
WCI Sig naʀiaq 'bait' [and Cop naʀiaq- 'follow trail by smell']
ECI naʀiaq 'bait' [verbal = 'catch scent of s.th.']
GRI naʀayaq, pl. narassat, NG naʀiaq 'bait' [and naʀayaʀ-, NG naʀiaq- 'smell one's way to s.th.']

PY-S naʀiʀ- 'slacken' [or *n[y]aʀiʀ-]
AAY —
CAY —
NSY —
CSY naʀiʀ- 'slacken'
Sir yaʀiʀ- 'slacken' [Em.; Men. has yaʀiʀməlŋuX 'slack']

PI naʀlanŋu- 'be affected by a strong smell' [cf. naʀə- and lŋu-]
SPI —
NAI —
WCI naʀlaŋu-, Cop naʀlanŋunaq- 'have a headache from a strong smell' [Lowe for the latter form]
ECI —
GRI naʀłaŋŋunaʀ- 'smell bad'

PI naʀʀu- 'dislike or be disgusted by s.th.' [cf. naʀciɣ-]
SPI naʀʀu-, trans. naʀʀui- 'dislike, reject' [Men. has Imaq naʀu- 'curse']
NAI naʀʀu- 'dislike, refuse', naʀʀuɣɨ- 'reject'
WCI naʀʀu- 'be disgusted', naʀʀuɣi- 'not want, disdain'
ECI naʀʀuɣi- 'not want, be disgusted by' [Saul also has naʀʀu- 'be disgusted']
GRI naXXu-, (trans.) naXXuɣi- 'reject, despise' [and note naXXaɣ- 'get angry, offended', NG naʀʀutsi-, naʀʀuhuk- 'be offended, angry']

PE naʀułəɣ- 'harpoon' [cf. naʀułɣutə-]
AAY —
CAY ➡
NSY naʀułəɣ- 'harpoon'
CSY naʀułəɣ- 'harpoon' [and nom. naʀułxun]
Sir —
SPI naulik- 'harpoon' [and nom. nauliɣzaun]
NAI naulɨk- 'harpoon' [and naullaq 'object harpooned or speared', PH naulɣun 'sealing harpoon']
WCI naulik- 'harpoon' [Pryde has naulik Cop H. Island 'harpoon for throwing at seal', Sig 'kayak harpoon']
ECI naulik- 'harpoon' [and naulik 'harpoon' (Saul) — 'penis' in Lab acc. Bourq.]
GRI naaliɣ- 'harpoon'

PE naʀułəkaʀ 'harpoon or spear' [cf. kaʀ?]
AAY —
CAY naʀułkaq 'spear' [also verbal; Jen. has Nun nagułigaX — for naʀułiɣaX? — 'harpoon head with blade attached']
NSY —
CSY —
Sir —
SPI nauliaq, Qaw nauligaq 'harpoon' [and nauliaun 'toy harpoon']

NAI nauliɣaq 'small (i.e. non-whaling) harpoon for hunting seal' [PH 'for bearded seal and walrus'; as verb = 'use small harpoon, harpoon sea mammal']
WCI nauliɣaq 'harpoon' ['white whale lance' in Sig acc. Pryde; Ras. also has verbal 'throw harpoon' for Sig]
ECI —
GRI naaliɣaq, EG naalivaat 'toy harpoon', EG naalivaʀtaq 'arrow' [in Up naaliŋaq is the ordinary word for harpoon]

PI naulaq 'harpoon (head)'
SPI —
NAI naulaq 'harpoon, spear', Nu 'detachable spearhead' [Murdoch has 'toggle head of seal harpoon']
WCI naulaq 'blade of harpoon head (or whole harpoon)' [also 'two-pronged spear for catching Arctic char' in Cop and 'seal harpoon head of ivory for hunting at breathing hole' in Net acc. Pryde]
ECI naulaq 'point of sealing harpoon', Lab naulak 'harpoon' [also verbal]
GRI —

PI nautkiaq- 'throw harpoon' [cf. ɣiaq-]
SPI —
NAI [note nautkiaq- 'jump down']
WCI Car naukkiaq- 'throw harpoon' [Dor. for B. Lake; Pryde has nautkaq- 'throw harpoon at' for Cop]]
ECI naukkia(q)- 'throw harpoon' [and note naulaɣiaq- 'cast harpoon at', naukkataq- 'throw harpoons or darts or fire at']
GRI naakkiaʀ-, NG naukkiaq- 'throw harpoon' [and note naakkaluaʀ- 'wound a seal with harpoon', NG naukkiallaaluaq- 'miss with harpoon']

PE naʀułɣutə- 'plunge or dart?' [cf. naʀułəɣ- and utə-?; there may also be a link to naula(yu)q]
AAY —
CAY naʀułxutə-, LI naʀułkutə- 'die of a heart attack'
NSY [note perhaps naʀułəɣ- 'cover (ground) with snow (storm) or fog' — see homonym under naʀułəɣ-]
CSY naʀułxutə- 'dive into water, leap over s.th.'
Sir —
SPI —
NAI naulɣuti- 'suddenly get very ill, indulge in s.th.' [and note nauktaq- 'jump over' and compare nautkiaq- 'jump down' under nautkiaq- (naʀułəɣ-)]
WCI Utk naužɣuti- 'fall, have sudden collapse' [Briggs]
ECI —
GRI —

PE naʀuyaʀ 'seagull' [or *nʸaʀuyaʀ]
AAY naʀuyaq 'seagull'
CAY naʀuyaq
NSY naʀuyaq
CSY naʀuya
Sir yaʀəya
SPI nauyuak
NAI nauyaq
WCI nauyaq 'gull' [Cop 'glaucous gull' acc. Lowe]
ECI nauyaq 'gull'
GRI naaya

PE naʀuyavaɣ 'kind of gull' [cf. vaɣ]
AAY —
CAY naʀuzvak 'glaucous gull'
NSY —
CSY —
Sir —
SPI nauyuakpak
NAI nauyavak 'young glaucous gull'
WCI Sig nauyavatkusiq 'Ross's gull' [Lowe]
ECI —
GRI naayavaaʀšuk 'ivory gull'

PY na(a)šqaq or **na(a)škaq** 'head or scalp of animal?' [there could be a link to nay(ə)quʀ here]
AAY —
CAY —
NSY naškaq, naɣkaq 'head (of reindeer skin)' [also naskaq — ANLC]
CSY naašqaq 'scalp of animal including skin from face'

PE natanquʀ and **nataŋquʀ** 'cartilage' [cf. quʀ]
AAY tataŋquq 'cartilage in fish head' [and note also C tatałquq 'cheek']
CAY tataŋquq
NSY tataŋquq [L.-T.]
CSY taŋtaquq
Sir taŋtə́qəX [Orr]
SPI nataquq 'cartilage, soft fish bone' [Jen. also has 'white of egg']
NAI natatquq 'cartilage, egg white, soft bone'
WCI natatquq 'cartilage'
ECI nataqquq
GRI nataqquq

PI natanquaq 'cartilage (of nose)' [cf. aʀ]
SPI nataquaq 'cartilage'
NAI natatquaq 'cartilage, soft bones (of young animals or children)'
WCI natatquyyak 'nose wings'
ECI nataqquaq 'nose wing'
GRI nataqquaq 'nose cartilage'

PI natanquʀnaq 'hailstone' [cf. naʀ]
SPI nataqunak 'hailstone'
NAI natatquʀnaq
WCI natatquʀnaq 'hail'
ECI nataqqunaq 'hail, hailstone'
GRI nataqquʀnaq 'hail'

PY nataqə- 'find' [cf. nalkə- and nałaʀ- under nałə-, but also natə- under na-[2] — the relat. is obscure]
AAY Kod nataqə- 'find' [old sources — e.g. Tyzh.]
CAY nataqə-, nalaqə-, Nun alaqə- 'find' [the last two forms influenced by nalkə- or alakə- under alaŋkaʀ-?]
NSY —

CSY — [for nažaqə- 'figure out measurements' see naðaqə- under naða-]

PY natəcuɣ- 'be astonished?'
AAY [note natasuuɣ- 'deprive oneself, punish oneself']
CAY —
NSY natəsuɣnalʀia 'surprising'
CSY natəsuɣ- 'be astonished'

PE natəʀ 'floor'
AAY natəq 'floor (also of ocean)'
CAY natəq* 'floor'
NSY natəq 'entrance passage of old-style house, sole of shoe'
CSY natəq* 'floor, entry room of old-style house'
Sir natXa '(its) bottom (ocean)'; natəX 'entrance passage to traditional skin-covered house' [Em.]
SPI natiq 'floor, sole of shoe, ocean bottom'
NAI natɨq* 'floor, bottom', Nu 'plain (at bottom of mountain)', PH 'sole of sock or skin boot'
WCI natiq 'floor'
ECI natiq
GRI natiq* 'floor, bottom (of sea)'

PE naccin 'floorboard' [cf. li-[1] and un]
AAY nacitəq 'floorboard'
CAY nacin
NSY nasin 'floor'
CSY [Rub. has nati(i)n 'floor' for Chap]
Sir [natita 'floor']
SPI nassin 'floorboard'
NAI natcisit [pl.] 'wooden floor planks'
WCI —
ECI —
GRI natsit 'floorboard' [and note natsinnaq 'flat area', NG 'flat-topped iceberg']

PE natəquviɣ- 'drift (snow)'
AAY —
CAY natquik 'drifting snow or sand, etc.', natquixtə-, HBC natquvixtə- 'drift (snow)'
NSY —
CSY —
Sir —
SPI natiʀvik- 'blow at ground level (snow)'
NAI natiʀvik- 'blow or drift along the ground (snow, etc.)'
WCI natiʀuvik- 'drift (snow)' [Schn. has 'be a dust storm' for 'adg']
ECI natiʀuvik- 'come into house through window or entrance (powdery snow)' [Saul has 'blow along ground (drift snow)' instead; natiʀuvaaq 'drift snow']
GRI NG natiʀiviataaq-, natiʀivilaaluk- 'drift (a bit)' [compare WG natiʀnik 'drift snow', natiʀniɣ- 'drift' with p.b. nəɣ-]

PE natəʀaʀ 'bottom of s.th.' [cf. aʀ]
AAY nattaq 'sole of boot or shoe'
CAY natʀaq, NSU natəʀaq 'sole of skin boot'
NSY natəʀaq 'bottom of s.th.' [and nateXqaq 'material for sole' — ANLC has natXaq 'sole of boots']
CSY [note natəXqaq 'sole of skin boot']
Sir [note naciʀəX 'bottom of bedding' — Orr]
SPI nataaq 'bottom of container, sea or lake'
NAI nataaq 'bottom of container', PH 'soft skin sole'
WCI —
ECI nataaq 'bottom of container'
GRI nataaq 'bottom of container', SWG also 'solid cover of ice'

PE natəʀ(aʀ)naʀ 'flat fish' [cf. natəʀaʀ above and naʀ]
AAY —
CAY natəʀnaq 'flounder' [as if directly from natəʀ]
NSY natəʀaʀnaq 'flounder'
CSY —
Sir —
SPI nataaʀnaq
NAI nataaʀnaq
WCI nataaʀnaq
ECI nataaʀnaq 'flounder, flat-bottomed boat'
GRI nataaʀnaq 'halibut'

PE natəʀnaʀ 'plain or tundra' [cf. naʀ]
AAY —
CAY [for natəʀnaq 'flounder' see natəʀ(aʀ)naq above]
NSY natəʀnaq 'plain' [Ras.]
CSY —
Sir natəʀnəX 'valley' [Vakh. from Men.'s texts]
SPI natiʀnaq W 'plain' [Ras.], Qaw 'flat tundra'
NAI natiʀnaq 'flat valley, tundra'
WCI natiʀnaq 'plain'
ECI natiʀnaaq
GRI —

PE natmaɣ- 'carry on back' [cf. atə- for a possible source of contam. in Yup, also amaʀ-]
AAY atm̥aɣ- 'carry on back' [as nom. = 'backpack']
CAY atm̥aɣ-
NSY akm̥aɣ-
CSY akm̥aɣ-
Sir akm̥əɣ- 'carry on back' [and akm̥əx 'load, bundle on back' — Vakh.]
SPI maqmak-, Imaq makmak-, Qaw natmak- 'carry on back' [as nom. = 's.th. carried on back'; Jen. has W man'mak- 'carry on back' but natmaq 'pack']
NAI nanmak-, Mal, Nu natmak- 'carry on back' [also nominal]
WCI naŋmak- [Met.], nanmak- [Lowe], Net na'mak- [Pryde] 'carry on back' [and naŋmak 'load carried on back']
ECI namma(k)- 'carry on back' [and nammaq 'load carried on back', nammaɣaq 'rucksack']
GRI nammaɣ- [old ortho. naŋmaɣ-] 'carry on back' [and nammaaq 'load on back', nammaɣaq 'burden carried on back']

PI naucaaq 'ill omen' [or nausaaq]
Yup — [but note CSY naɣuyaq 'unnatural growth, tumor', from naɣu-?]
SPI —
NAI nausaaq 'omen, sign' [verbal = 'receive an omen']
WCI —
ECI —
GRI naasaaq [old ortho. nâsâq] 'ill omen' [naasaaʀ- 'have received an omen of death or misfortune', naasaaŋa- 'be afraid of imminent destruction']

PI naula(yu)q 'weasel' [there may be a link to naʀuɫɣutə-]
Yup [note CAY naʀuɫxiq, Nun naʀuɫkiaX 'ermine, weasel']
SPI Qaw naulayuq 'least weasel'
NAI naulayuq 'least weasel' [and PH naulayuužaq 'shrimp']
WCI ➞
ECI ➞
GRI ➞

PI naul(l)aʀnaq 'shrimp' [cf. naʀ]
SPI —
NAI naullaʀnaq 'small sea mollusk'
WCI Sig naulaʀnaq 'shrimp' [Pet.]
ECI naulaʀnaq
GRI naalaʀnaq

PI nauʀala- 'flare up' [cf. naɣu- and ala- under la(ʀ)-?]
SPI —
NAI nauʀala-, nauʀallak- 'flare up (fire)'
WCI nauʀalauqtuq 'cotton essence (?), s.th. that catches fire easily'
ECI —
GRI naaʀala- 'flare up'

PE navcu 'obscurity' [cf. navəɣ-?]
AAY —
CAY nafcuitə- 'be clear (weather)' [and Hinz has nafcuiʀ- 'make clear or visible']
NSY —
CSY [note naaftə- 'get stormy']
Sir —
SPI —
NAI —
WCI Sig navsuiq- 'try' [Met. has napsuiq-]
ECI —
GRI nassu [old ortho. navso] 'indistinctness', nassuit- 'be distinct' [and nassuu- 'be indistinct', nassuiaʀ- 'explain']

PE navəɣ- 'break' [cf. napə-]
AAY nawəɣ-, nauɣ-, nauxtə- 'break'
CAY navəɣ-, Eg lavəɣ- 'break' [and Nun naftə- 'collapse', NSU nafcaq 'snow hanging over a cliff ready to fall'; for (ə)lavə- 'crouch, bend over' see əlavə-]
NSY — [but note naavikələq 'thicket' (ANLC)]
CSY naavə-, naafqə- 'break'
Sir —
SPI nawik- 'break, fracture'
NAI navɨk- 'break'
WCI navik- 'break' [and Schn. has half-trans. navɣi- 'break a leg' for 'adg.' — Pryde has navɣi- 'be broken (leg, bone, etc.)' for Cop]
ECI [note nakaC- (from *naɣɣat-?) 'cut, separate', Lab 'break in two' — Ras. 'flense, cut across' for Igl; nakataq 's.th. cut across', naɣɣi- 'break a leg'] ➞
GRI naviɣ- 'soften by passing over a raised edge to make pliable (skin, thong)' [and EG nakkit 'piece of bone with holes for softening sealskin thongs']

PE navɣuʀ- 'break into pieces' [cf. (C)uʀ-]
AAY —
CAY navɣuʀ- 'break into pieces'
NSY —
CSY —
Sir —
SPI Qaw navɣuq-
NAI navɣuq-
WCI navɣuq- 'break into pieces' [and navɣut 'crack in ice']
ECI naɣɣu(q)- 'cut across a joint', naɣɣuaq limb, articulation'
GRI naxxuaq 'joint', NG naɣɣuq- 'break into pieces' [and naxxut 'lump of broken-off sea ice, biscuit', NG naɣɣut 'frozen-over crack in ice' — Holt.]

PY-S navəʀ(aʀ)- 'borrow or exchange' [or *n^{y}avəʀ(aʀ)-; there may be a relat. to niʀuvəʀ-]
AAY K naɣwaʀ-, naʀwaʀ-, KP naɣ^{w}ɣ^{w}aʀ- 'borrow'
CAY navəXtə- 'trade, sell', navʀaʀ- 'borrow'
NSY navʀaʀ- 'borrow', navəʀutə- 'exchange' [and note navəʀu- 'be reversed' and navəXtə- 'exchange, pay one's debt' (ANLC)]
CSY navʀutə- 'exchange', navʀaʀ- 'borrow'
Sir yavəʀətə- 'exchange' [Vakh. and Orr have also yavəʀutə- and yavəXtə-]

PY nav(ə)ʀitə- 'lend' [cf. lit-]
AAY K nauɣ'itə-, naʀwitə- 'lend'
CAY navʀitə-
NSY navʀitə- [ANLC]
CSY navʀiitə-

PI navia(ɣə)- 'consider dangerous' [cf. navəɣ-?]
Yup — [but note CSY naavyiʀ- 'become very tired']
SPI —
NAI naviaɣɨ- 'consider too dangerous', navianaq- 'be dangerous'
WCI —
ECI —
GRI naviaɣi-, naviasuɣ- 'consider dangerous, not dare to do (s.th.)', navianaʀ- 'be dangerous' [and note naviiʀ- 'be in danger', (trans.) 'scold']

PE nayaɣ 'man's younger sister'
AAY naya(ɣ)aq 'younger sister'
CAY nazzak, HBC nayyak 'unmarried girl, virgin', nayaɣaq 'younger sister'
NSY nayak, nayaɣaq 'sister'
CSY nayak 'older or younger sister of a male'

Sir —
SPI nayak '(younger) sister of male'
NAI nayak 'younger sister of male'
WCI nayak
ECI nayak 'sister of man' [Saul — Schn. glosses as 'word of elder brother to address younger sister']
GRI nayak 'younger sister of male' [4s possessed form naanni — old ortho. náine — compare qaanni under qayaʀ]

PE nayaŋaʀ- 'nod' [from a base *nayə- 'bend head' also in nay(ə)quʀ?].
AAY nayaŋaʀ- 'nod, bow, show respect'
CAY nayaŋaʀ- 'nod agreement', Y, NS 'dance Eskimo women's dance' [and nayaŋaq 'greeting']
NSY —
CSY —
Sir — [for ya(y)iŋucaʀ- 'spin' see uyivə-]
SPI nayaŋit-, Imaq nayaŋaq- 'be drowsy, nodding with sleep' [Jen. has W niaŋaq-, KI nayaŋaq- 'fall asleep while seated']
NAI nayaŋaq- 'nod with sleep' [and nayaksaq- 'move in time to music, be jolted', naiq- 'bend head to one side', nain^{y}n^{y}iq- 'bounce or roll torso in dancing']
WCI Car nayaɣaq- 'doze drowsily' [Ras.; Pet. has Sig nayanagyaq- 'rock' and note EP nayaŋaq 'dwarf seal' — Ow.]
ECI nayaŋaq- 'nod with sleep' [and naiq- 'hang head to side, let head drop involuntarily (e.g. when dying)']
GRI nayaŋaʀ- 'sit nodding with sleep'

PE nay(ə)pət- 'check or watch over' [with t-[1]?]
AAY naspətə- 'appraise'
CAY naspətə- 'try, taste'
NSY naɣ̥pətə- 'watch over, check on'
CSY naspətə-, naspəqə- 'estimate' [also nasiiʀ- 'taste' — there may be contam. with naacuqə- under naðə-]
Sir —
SPI naipit- 'try, taste (food)'
NAI naipit- 'watch'
WCI ➟
ECI naipit- 'catch (thief, game), find (lost object)' [and Bourq. has naipiqqunaq- 'be pitiful' for Lab]
GRI naapit- 'meet'

PE nay(ə)pəʀtuʀ- 'observe' [cf. tuʀ-[2]]
AAY —
CAY naspəXtuʀ- 'hesitate, consider alternatives' [and NS naspəʀyuɣ- 'watch covertly']
NSY —
CSY [note nałpəXtuʀ- 'feel one's way, try to guess one's location' — contam. with nałpiquʀ- 'compare' (cf. nałə-)?]
Sir —
SPI naipatuq- 'watch, observe'
NAI naipiqtuq- 'spy on, observe'
WCI Sig naipiqtuq- 'watch over'
ECI Lab naipiqtuq- 'pay attention to what one is told' [Peck]
GRI naapiʀtuʀ- 'pay attention to, do according to'

PE nay(ə)quʀ 'head' [cf. quʀ, also nayaŋaʀ- (esp. NAI naiq- under it); compare kayəmə(t)- for the diphthong in Inu]
AAY nasquq 'head'
CAY Y, HBC, NS nasquq
NSY naɣ̥quq 'head'
CSY naasquq 'head, skull' [and nasqunʀək (du.) 'walrus skull']
Sir nasqənəX 'skull of walrus' [Vakh. from Rub.'s texts — from CSY?; compare əcəqəX 'head' under iyyuʀ-; Vakh. also has əcəqupax, əyəqupax and (from Rub.) əsqənaX 'skull' — there may be entanglement between the two here]
SPI niaquq 'head, skull'
NAI niaquq
WCI niaquq
ECI niaquq 'head'
GRI niaquq

PE nay(ə)qulŋu- 'have a headache' [cf. lŋu-]
AAY nasqulŋu- 'have a headache'
CAY NS, HBC, Y nasqulŋu-
NSY naɣ̥qilŋu- 'have a headache' [ANLC; L.-T. has nasqilŋu-]
CSY —
Sir —
SPI niaquŋu-
NAI niaqunŋu-
WCI —
ECI niaqunŋu-
GRI niaquŋŋu- 'be giddy or dazed'

PE nay(ə)quʀun 'headdress' [cf. q(q)un]
AAY —
CSY nasquXun 'headdress'
NSY naɣ̥quʀun 'headdress, headband' [ANLC]
CSY Chap nasquʀun 'amulet previously worn on head, esp. by s.o. suffering from headaches'
Sir —
SPI niaquun 'crown'
NAI niaquʀun 'crown, headband'
WCI Net niaquun 'headband', Cop niaquut 'string around head for holding sun goggles in position' [Pryde]
ECI niaquuti 'crown'
GRI niaquʀut

PI niaquaq- 'hit on head' [cf. ŋaʀ-[1]]
SPI niaquaq- 'bump one's head'
NAI PH niaquaq- 'bang one's head (against)'
WCI —
ECI [niaqqua(q)- 'hit on the head' (Saul), and niaqqu(q)- 'bump or hurt head' (Schn.)]
GRI niaquaʀ- 'hit on the head'

PE nayuɣ- 'hollow out or skin an animal without splitting the skin' [or *n^{y}ayuɣ-]
AAY —
CAY nayuɣ- 'hollow out, skin a seal or other animal so the skin is not split lengthwise'
NSY nayuɣ- 'remove fur socks' [Tein — ANLC 'remove

fur like one removes a stocking (without splitting it)']
CSY nayuɣ- 'skin an animal without splitting the skin'
Sir yayəɣ- 'dig' [Orr and Vakh. from Men's texts — Men. has yayuXqə(s)- 'dig'; Berg. suggests a link to nivak- rather — there may be contam. at least; also yayunqaX 'hole for storing meat'; also yayuɣ- 'skin an animal without splitting the skin', from or infuenced by the CSY]
SPI —
NAI nayuk- 'remove skin of a seal through the mouth to make a poke'
WCI Sig nayuaq 'skin drawn off whole' [Ras.]
ECI nayuk- 'remove skin from seal without cutting it open' [and nayuaq 'skin flensed that way']
GRI nayuɣ- 'hollow out, remove sealskin whole, turn inside out (skin), pull stomach in' [and NG nayuaq 'cave hollowed out in snow']

PE nayuʀ- 'stay with or at'
AAY nayuʀ- 'stay with, look after'
CAY nayuʀ-
NSY nayuʀ- 'nurse, look after child' [and nayuqivik 'cradle'; also, acc. L.-T. nayułəq 'storing walrus skin for footwear' and nayuʀaq 'leather barrels for storage' though these may fit with nayuɣ- instead]
CSY nayuʀ- 'stay with, tend, watch, guard'
Sir nayuʀ- [Vakh.]
SPI nayuq- 'stay with, take care of'
NAI nayuq-
WCI nayuq- 'stay with'
ECI nayuq- 'sit with, keep company, look after house in someone's absence' [and note nayuɣaq 'residence' and nayuquti 'root of tree']
GRI nayuʀ- 'stay with, live with or at, be present' [for homonym 'suck through nose or mouth' see niðuʀ-; note also nayuɣaq 'residence' and nayuqqut 's.th. to hold on to, to support oneself by']

PI nayummi- 'hold on to s.th.' [cf. umi-?]
SPI —
NAI nayummi- 'lean on, hold on to keep steady' [and note nayummak- 'lean on']
WCI nayum(m)i- 'hold on to keep steady'
ECI nayummi 'hold on to prevent from moving' [and note nayummaʀut(i)- 'support oneself against']
GRI nayummi- 'hold on to, support, keep another's kayak steady' [and nayummaɣ- 'hold on (to support self)'

PE nayvaɣ- 'show' [there may be a relat. to na(C)əvə(t)-]
AAY —
CAY nazvaɣ- 'show, display' [and nazvaɣitə-, Y nazvitə-, nayvitə- 'show s.th. to']
NSY nayvaɣ- 'show' [ANLC]
CSY —
Sir —
SPI [naivažaaq- 'show, present']
NAI PH naivak- 'display for sale'
WCI —
ECI —
GRI —

PE nayyiʀ 'ringed seal' [compare nay(ə)quʀ and nayaŋaʀ- (the link being perhaps, as Berg. has suggested, the seal's head bobbing out of the water) — compare the geminate in the Inu reflexes of əyyi(ʀ)]
AAY —
CAY nayiq* 'ringed seal'
NSY ➟
CSY nazisuŋaq 'short-haired ringed seal'
Sir [note nacəʀcəX (pl. nacəʀžay acc. Orr) 'trousers'; Em. has nacəʀaʀəy 'light summer trousers of seal skin for men'] ➟
SPI Qaw nassiq 'ringed seal'
NAI natciq* 'seal' [Nu natciʀžuaq 'sealskin coat']
WCI natsiq 'seal'
ECI natsiq 'seal (esp. ringed seal)' [also 'sealskin parka']
GRI natsiq* 'ringed seal' [also 'sealskin coat'; natsiʀšuaq 'hooded seal']

PE nayyiʀaʀ 'young (ringed) seal' [cf. ʀaʀ]
AAY —
CAY —
NSY nayiʀaq 'young seal' [ANLC nayəʀaq]
CSY naziʀaq* 'long-haired ringed seal'
Sir naciʀaX 'young seal' [compare the reflex of *yy also in əcəqəX under iyyuʀ-]
SPI nassiaʀžuk 'young seal'
NAI natciaʀžuk 'small seal'
WCI Cop nattiaq 'young seal' [Lowe]
ECI natsiaq 'young seal'
GRI natsiaq 'young ringed seal', NG 'young seal'

PY nayiʀaʀciq 'month early in year' [cf. nayyiʀaʀ above and uciʀ?]
AAY —
CAY —
NSY nayəʀaXsiq 'March' [ANLC]
CSY naziʀaXsiq 'February'
Inu [SPI nassiaqsiq, Qaw natciaqciq 'February' is presumably from the Yup, whereas ECI Igl nattian 'April/May' — lit. 'young ring seals' — is an independent formation]

PY-S nažaʀcaq 'bottom part of fire-making apparatus?' [there may be a link to nauʀala-]
AAY —
CAY —
NSY —
CSY naaXsaq 'match' [but Em. has this in the same sense as the Sir cognate below]
Sir nacəXsəX 'bottom part (board of wood or bone) of apparatus for producing fire' [Men. has nacəXcəX 'match', presumably the same word]

PI nažvaq- 'find' [cf. nani-[1] though the relat. is obscure — dissim. of the second n as with nanvaʀ?]
SPI navžaaq- 'make a find' [as a noun = 'a find']
NAI navžaaq 'artifact, s.th. found while digging'
WCI Cop nalvaq-, Sig nayvaq- 'find by chance' [Met.; Pryde has nalvaaq- for Cop and Dor. has Net nažvaaq-]

ECI navvaa(q)-, Aiv naɣvaaq- 'find by chance' [Dor. for the latter — he also gives the Tar as 'find while searching or by chance']
GRI naššaaʀ- [old ortho. navssâr-] 'find, discover', naššaaq 'a find', EG nattaaři- 'find'

PE nəɣaʀ 'snare' [or *n^{y}əɣaʀ]
AAY nəɣaq 'snare'
CAY nəɣaq 'snare' [nəɣaʀ- 'catch or be caught in a snare'; note also nəɣaiʀ(aq*), nəɣaiq 'spider']
NSY nəɣaʀaq 'snare' [and compare nəɣiaq 'ant' (ANLC) with CAY nəɣaiʀ(aq) above]
CSY nəɣaq 'snare' [and nəɣaʀ- 'snare']
Sir yəɣəXpəx 'net'
SPI niaq, Qaw niɣaq 'snare' [verbal = 'be caught in a snare']
NAI niɣaq 'snare' [also verbal; niɣɣiq- 'set a snare for']
WCI niɣaq 'snare' [verbal = 'be snared']
ECI niɣaq 'snare' [verbal = 'be caught in a snare', niɣavit- 'wrap around (e.g. net around fish one catches)']
GRI niɣaq, NG nigaaq 'snare' [niɣaʀ- 'snare'; niɣavit- 'wrap around (e.g. strap around stone, thread around another thread)', nixxiʀ- 'set a snare for', nixxat 'spider's web']

PE nəɣciɣ 'gaff or hook' [or *n^{y}əɣciɣ; cf. nəɣar but also naɣci(t)- under naɣət- — the relat., if any, is obscure]
AAY —
CAY nəxcik, HBC, Nun ləxcix 'gaff'
NSY nəxsik 'gaff' ['fishhook' acc. L.-T.; ANLC nəxsiɣ- 'hook, catch or pull with a hook']
CSY nəkšək, nakšək 'fishhook' [second form contam. with naɣci(t)-?]
Sir yixsəX 'hook, gaff' [Em. also yixsiʀ- 'hook on to']
SPI niksik 'gaff' [also verbal]
NAI niksik 'fishhook, gaff' [also verbal]
WCI niksik 'fishhook' [also verbal]
ECI nitsik 'hook' [also verbal]
GRI nissik [old ortho. nigsik], EG nitsiq 'hook' [and nissit- 'hook, pull with hook']

PE nəɣəʀ 'wind (in Alaska from north)' [cf. Aleut ɣiðɣi-X 'breeze', ɣiðuɣ- 'blow' with a p.b. ðɣi-, ðuɣ-, and loss of initial nə-; see Fortescue 1988 for the specific directions involved]
AAY nəɣəq PWS 'west', KP 'north'
CAY nəɣəq* 'north'
NSY nəɣəq 'north'
CSY —
Sir —
SPI niiq 'north, north wind' [rel. niʀʀum], Qaw niiq, Di nəəq 'north'
NAI niɣɨq* 'north, northeast wind'
WCI niɣiq 'east wind' ['wind from east' in Cop and Pelly Bay and from southeast at B. Lake but from north in Utku acc. Pryde; Cop rel. case niʀʀum]
ECI niɣiq, niɣiiq, niɣɣiq 'sea wind' [east in Wakeham Bay; verbal niɣɣi(q)- 'blow (sea wind)']
GRI niɣiq* 'south wind' [and EG niqqayaaq '(north)east wind' — compare WG niXXaaq 'southerly breeze'; nixxiʀ- 'blow (south wind)']

PY nəɣiɣ- 'cut out or carve (decoration)?' [cf. nəɣžak and/or nəɣilaʀ?]
AAY —
CAY —
NSY nəɣižʀaʀ- 'carve bone' [and nəɣižʀaq 'instrument for carving bone']
CSY nəɣiɣ- 'cut out a piece of material or skin' [Rub. 'cut out from a whole'; also nəɣikšaʀ- 'cut out pattern' — Chap nəɣikšaqaq 'pattern' and nəɣikšaʀ^{w}aaq 'lace trimming']
Inu [Imaq nəɣžəɣa(a)qtə 'instrument for carving bone', nəɣžəɣaqtumažuaq 's.th. decorated by carving' — from NSY?]

PE nəɣilaʀ and **nəɣiliʀ** 'parka ruff or neck opening' [or *n^{y}əɣilaʀ, *n^{y}əɣiliʀ; cf. nəɣiɣ-? — two bases or derivatives may be entangled here, one involving (contam. with) nuɣə-]
AAY —
CAY nəɣiliq, Scammon Bay ləɣiliq 'parka ruff', Nun 'edge of hood where ruff is attached'
NSY nuilaq 'collar' [Em.], nuila(a)ʀun 'collar, fur fringe round hood' [influenced by nuɣə- if not from Inu]
CSY nəɣili 'neck opening, collar' [and nəɣilitaan 'trimming on neck of woman's hoodless garment']
Sir yəɣəcəx 'walrus gut rain coat (with crosstitching)', yəɣəcitaX 'collar' [Vakh. has yəɣəžułəɣaX 'raincoat' from Rub.; Em. has yəɣəca 'neck opening of parka, fur trimming at collar of parka' and yəɣətətaX 'collar of woman's overalls, fur ruff around hood of parka']
SPI nuilak 'parka ruff', Imaq nuilaq 'collar, head hole, fur fringe of parka hood', nuila(a)ʀun 'collar' [and note KI nuiyaaq 'head hole of garment']
NAI nuil^{y}ak 'neck opening of garment', nuik-, nuil^{y}atu- 'have a large neck opening'
WCI Sig, Cop nuilaq 'collar in dog harness' [and nuilaɣun 'dog collar' — Pryde has nuilaɣut 'string dog collar' for H. Island; B.-S. has Car nuilʀaaq 'neck opening in frock']
ECI nuilaq 'fur around hood of parka, also around sleeves and leggings'
GRI nuilaq, EG nuilaaq 'opening in garment for head', NG also 'neck opening in dog harness' [Holt.; note also nuilaʀmiut, Up nuilaqqitit 'bead collar']

PE nəɣituqaʀ- 'have the hiccoughs'
AAY C nimtuqaʀ-, limtuqaʀ-, K ni<ɣ>iɣ- 'have the hiccoughs' [and nom. nimtuqaq, etc.]
CAY nəɣituqaʀ- 'have the hiccoughs' [and nom. nəɣituqaq 'hiccough']
NSY nəɣituXqu- 'have the hiccoughs'
CSY —
Sir —
SPI niituaq-
NAI Uum niɣituʀaq-
WCI niituʀaq-
ECI niqituʀaq- 'have the hiccoughs' [contam. with nəqə?]
GRI niisuʀaʀ- 'have the hiccoughs' [NG niʀihuak- of this meaning probably by contam. with nəʀə-; note also niisuʀaq 'cavity of neck above breastbone']

PE nəɣuʀ- 'avoid or go around'
AAY C nəɣautə- 'make detour around'
CAY nəɣuʀ- 'go round obstacle in path'
NSY [nəɣaʀ- 'go round an obstacle' (ANLC)]
CSY nəɣuʀ- 'avoid, go around'
Sir —
SPI —
NAI niɣuq- 'leave (e.g. job) out of dissatisfaction' [and niɣuuti- 'remove self from another's presence']
WCI Sig niɣuq- 'flee, stay away from' [and niɣuuti- 'miss, go past each other' — Met.]
ECI niɣuq- 'make detour around'
GRI niɣuʀ- 'escape, try to get away from'

PE nəɣuʀluʀ 'loop' [cf. nəɣuʀ- and lu(ʀ), also nəɣaʀ; for the Siberian forms with ž compare the NSY form under taluʀtə- with sporadic ž for l]
AAY —
CAY Nun nəɣuʀluX 'loop on coat for use with a fastener'
NSY [nuɣžu 'loop, drawstring of hood' (ANLC); L.-T. has nəɣžik 'loop' but nuɣžu 'drawstring of hood']
CSY [nuɣžu, nužɣu 'noose, loop']
Sir [nuɣžu 'noose, loop' (Orr) — from CSY?]
SPI luʀluq 'loop on a rope'
NAI nuʀlu
WCI nuʀlu 'loop' [and Pryde has Car B. Lake nuʀluq 'loop on end of rope', Cop nuʀluk 'hand-loop']
ECI nuʀlu 'buckle made for string, mesh of net, eyelet of tent'
GRI nuʀłuq 'loop'

PE nəɣuyaʀ 'skin infection'
AAY KP nəɣuyak, Kod nəɣuyaq, AP nu'uya 'recurrent rash, pimples'
CAY [Y nəɣuyaq 'air bubble in ice']
NSY nəɣuyaq 'dandruff, scurf' [L.-T.; ANLC also has saɣuyak (also of a kind of lichen), which may indicate contam. from some other base]
CSY nəɣuya 'ringworm, skin infection' [but note also nəŋžak 'dermatitis']
Sir —
SPI —
NAI niɣuyaq 'ringworm, sunburn'
WCI —
ECI —
GRI —

PI nəɣvik 'membrane around intestines' [cf. nəŋə-?]
SPI —
NAI niɣvik 'membrane holding intestines in place, mesentery'
WCI Cop, Net niɣvik 'pouch opening to stomach of certain fishes, pyloric caeca' [Pryde]
ECI —
GRI niffik [old ortho. nivfik] 'internal (?) membrane of gut'

PI nəɣžak 'fringe on parka' [cf. nəɣiɣ- if not nəŋə-?]
SPI [Qaw niɣžapak 'seaweed']
NAI niɣžat 'fringe, hanging strip on dress parka'
WCI niɣyait
ECI —
GRI niššak [old ortho. nivssak with spurious v], niššaqattak, niššaqqataaq 'fringe'

PE nəka- 'feel inferior or unworthy'
AAY K nəka(yuɣ)- 'have hurt feelings'
CAY nəka(yuɣ)- 'find emotionally painful' [Hinz has 'feel insignificant']
NSY nəkaniiʀ^{w}- 'insult', nəkialŋuq 'one insensitive to insult' [L.-T.]
CSY —
Sir —
SPI niɣaɣi- 'give (s.th.) though one feels it is unworthy, inferior, give the best one has to (s.o.) even if the quality is doubtful', Qaw nikaɣi- 'doubt one's ability to do s.th.' [niɣasuk- 'doubt s.o.'s word']
NAI nika- 'be embarrassed, avoid eye contact with other, be silent through lack of confidence', nikasuk- 'not be confident', Nu 'quit', nikaɣɨ- 'feel (s.o./s.th.) is not good enough, incapable of s.th.'
WCI nikaɣi- 'not feel confident in, not consider good', [and nikalluq- 'calm down, quit, stop doing s.th. (e.g. running away when one feels safe)' — Ras. has 'be depressed' for this in Cop, Ow has nikahuk- 'be patient' for EP, and Dor. has nikalluŋa- 'show one's feelings' for B. Lake]
ECI nika- 'be bereaved (on death of s.o.)', nikaɣi- 'be sorry for' [Bourq. has 'spare (out of pity)' for Lab]
GRI nika- 'be sad, depressed, mourn over', nikaɣi- 'think (s.o.) insignificant, not much' [and nikałłuʀ- 'be depressed, calmed, quiet']

PI nəkait- 'be determined' [cf. ŋit-]
SPI niɣait- 'not be thankful when one should'
NAI nikait- 'be determined'
WCI nikait-
ECI —
GRI —

PE nəkəvə(t)- 'stand up' [or *n^{y}əkəvə(t)-]
AAY PWS nək<ɣ>u- 'stand up'
CAY Nun nək(ə)və- 'stand up' [and note HBC nəkəvyuk 'young man']
NSY nukuvə- 'stand up', nukuftə- 'build'
CSY nəkəvə- 'stand up', nəkəftə- 'build'
Sir yəfkə- 'stand up' [and yəfkəXti- 'build']
SPI nuɣuvit-, nuɣupit-, Qaw nikivit- 'stand up'
NAI nikuvɨt- 'sit on stool waiting for seal to emerge'
WCI Sig nikuvit- 'stand up'
ECI nikuvik-
GRI nikuit-

PE nəkəvʀa- and **nəkəvɣa-** 'be standing' [cf. a-]
AAY nəku<ɣ>a- 'be standing'
CAY nəkfa-
NSY nəkuvʀa- 'stand, be standing, be solid' [ANLC]
CSY nəkəvʀa- 'be standing'
Sir yəfkəʀə-
SPI —

NAI nikuvRautaq, PH nikivRautaq 'three-legged stool for waiting for seal at breathing hole'
WCI —
ECI nikuRRa- 'stand upright'
GRI nikuRfa-, EG niɣiqqa- 'be upright' [and SWG nikuRfaataq, NG nikuRvautaq 'footstool for seal hunting on ice']

PY nəkəvRAARtuq 'spruce tree' [cf. nəkəvRa- above]
AAY nəkuRaaxtuq 'spruce'
CAY nəkəvRaaXtuq, kəvRaaXtuq 'spruce'
NSY —
CSY —

PI nəkuvžaaq- 'stand on tiptoe'
SPI yuɣuvluɣitaaq-, Qaw nikivžaaq- 'stand on tiptoe' [and note KI yəfkəžaR- in Jen. 'jump up from kneeling position']
NAI —
WCI nikuvya(a)q- 'stand on tiptoe' [Schn. has nikuvraqtuq- for 'adg']
ECI nikuyyaa(q)- 'stand on tiptoe'
GRI SWG nikuššaaR-, NWG nikuXXaaRtuR-

PE nəkvaR- 'watch over seal hole' [cf. aR-]
AAY —
CAY Nun nəkfayaR- 'stand by river and work on net'
NSY nəkpaq 'seal hole in ice' [Tein]
CSY nəfkaR- 'watch for seal at breathing hole'
Sir —
SPI nikpaq- 'wait by breathing hole of seal'
NAI nikpaq- 'wait expectantly for seal, etc. to appear'
WCI nikpaq- 'await seal at hole' [Jen. also has mikpaq 'seal's breathing hole' for Cop]
ECI nikpaq-, nippa(q)- 'wait at seal's hole'
GRI nippaR-, NG nikpaq- 'watch over seal hole' [and NG nikpaaq 'seal caught at breathing hole']

PE nəlcaR- 'belch' [cf. nələt- under nələR and caR-; for the Inu forms compare under alpaɣ-]
AAY AP əɬaaR-, Kod əɬcaR-, C əɬaaqqaR- 'belch'
CAY əɬciaR-
NSY əɬsiaR- [ANLC]
CSY —
Sir —
SPI niksaak- 'belch'
NAI niksaak-
WCI niksaak- 'belch' [Lowe; Met. has niksaq-; Ras. has Car niksaaq- 'make a sound, sing, speak']
ECI nitsaa(C)- 'belch' [Bourq. has niksaaq- for Lab]
GRI nissaaɣ- 'belch'

PI nəkcaaktuq 'kind of ptarmigan' [cf. ðuR]
Yup — [note CAY əɬciayuli 'ptarmigan' from the same base]
SPI Qaw niksaaktuŋiq 'rock ptarmigan'
NAI niksaaktuŋiq 'all-white ptarmigan' [Jen. has niksaaktuq 'rock ptarmigan']
WCI Sig niksaaktualuk 'rock ptarmigan' [Lowe]
ECI nitsaatuq 'rock ptarmigan' [Saul; Lab nitsaaqtuq 'white ptarmigan' in Bourq.]
GRI —

PE nələR(-) 'fart' [cf. Aleut la- 'escape (air from inflated seal stomach)']
AAY ləq 'fart' [and verbal ləR-]
CAY <ə>ləq*, Nun, HBC nələq*, NS naləq* 'fart' [verbal <ə>ləR-, etc.]
NSY ələq 'fart, meteor' [ANLC, also for ələR- 'break wind'; note aɣyam anaa 'meteor' in CAY, lit. 'star's feces']
CSY ləq* 'fart' [and verbal ləR-]
Sir ələX [Orr]
SPI niliq 'fart' [also verbal]
NAI niɫiq* 'fart' [also verbal]
WCI niliq
ECI niliq [also verbal]
GRI niliq* 'fart' [and verbal niliR-]

PE nələt- 'let air out of s.th.' [cf. t-[1], also nəlcaR-]
AAY əɬtə- 'let air out' [for AP əɬcaaR-, Kod əɬcaR-, C əɬcaaqqaR- 'belch' see nəlcaR-]
CAY əɬtə-, HBC, Nun nəɬtə- 'let air out' [for əɬciaR- 'belch' see nəcaR-]
NSY —
CSY əɬtə- 'let air out'
Sir —
SPI nilit-
NAI niɫit- 'deflate, escape from bubble (air), ebb (tide)'
WCI [nilik- 'be deflated' — Pryde has 'digest, wait until food has been digested, settle down (stomach)' for Cop]
ECI —
GRI nilit- 'press the air out of bladder' [and note NG niɣluq- 'have air leak out (hunting bladder)']

PE nəlŋu(R)- 'be tough or flexible'
AAY əlŋuR- 'be tough but pliable' [and əlŋuq 'birch' — poss. contam. with ulɣilə]
CAY əlŋuR- 'be tough but pliable, be viscous' [and əlŋuq, nəlŋuq 'birch' — poss. contam. with ulɣilə]
NSY əlŋuR- 'be strong, tough' [Em.]
CSY —
Sir —
SPI ninŋuq- 'be hard to break'
NAI niɫnŋu-, PH niɫnŋuq- 'be hard to break or pull apart, be flexible' [and niɫnŋuq 'cottonwood']
WCI ninŋuq Cop 'type of tough flexible wood', Sig 'cottonwood' [Pryde; Met. has ni(n)ŋu- 'be hard to cut or tear' and niŋuk — for ninŋuq? — 's.th. hard to tear'; Ras. has niŋ·ut 'kind of wood with little grain' for Cop]
ECI niŋŋu- 'be thick (liquid), elastic' [Peck has 'be tough' for Lab]
GRI niŋŋu- 'be tough' [and EG niŋŋi- 'be bent'?]

PI nəmaaq- 'cry out in pain' [cf. nəpe]
SPI nimaaq- 'wail from pain'
NAI nima(a)q- [Jen.]

WCI —
ECI Lab nimaaC- 'cry in pain'
GRI nimaaʀ- 'groan'

PE nəməʀ(-) 'wrap around' [or *nʸəməʀ(-)?; cf. Aleut tmax 'long seaweed (nereocystis), formerly used for fishing line', tmaðɣi-X 'Atka mackerel' — conspicuous for the dark stripes around its body]
AAY nəməʀ- 'tie up'
CAY nəməq* 'binding, wrapping', nəməʀ- 'bind, wrap'
NSY nəməʀ- 'tie up, bind' [ANLC]
CSY nəməʀ- 'lash, tie' [Chap nəməʀvik 'groove in rim of drum for lashing to fit in']
Sir [Vakh. has yəmɣut(ə)- 'tie' from Rub., but also nəməsit(ə)- 'bind, bandage' from Men.'s texts; Em. has yəməʀvəx 'groove in rim of drum for lashing to fit in']
SPI nimiq- 'wrap, bandage'
NAI nimɨq* 'wrapping' [verbal = 'wrap, bind']
WCI nimiq 'binding, string' [verbal = 'bind']
ECI nimiq [also verbal]
GRI nimiq* 'wrapping, band', nimiʀ- 'wrap, wind around' [and niʀmut(i)-, niʀŋut(i)- 'lash to, wind around s.th.', also nimiʀuaʀtu-, ninniʀutitu-, nanniʀutitu-, NG nannikaaq- 'be striped' — contam. with nanəʀ-?; Robbe and Menn. have EG mimmiʀ- 'wrap or roll up']

PE nəməʀyaʀ 'eel-like creature' [cf. yaʀ]
AAY nəməʀyaq 'long seaweed, fishline'
CAY nəməʀyaq 'lamprey'
NSY nəməʀyak 'worm, snake'
CSY Chap nəməʀyaq 'sea snake'
Sir nəməʀyaX 'water worm, snake' [from the CSY?]
SPI nimiʀiaq 'eel'
NAI nimiʀiaq 'lamprey, water worm, snake'
WCI nimiʀiaq 'snake' [Jen. has 'worm found in pond' for Cop]
ECI nimiʀiaq 'centipede, snake'
GRI nimiʀiaq 'eel'

PI nəmniuq- 'be squeezed or tight-fitting' [cf. nəməʀ(-)]
SPI —
NAI —
WCI nimniuq- 'be too small or narrow (to hold — e.g. thread or nail)'
ECI ninniu(q)- 'be pressed, squeezed by others', ninniuʀi- 'press, squeeze continually' [and Saul has niŋŋiq 'snow piled up around snow house as wall or insulation' — ninniq or niŋŋisaq acc. Schn.]
GRI ninniuʀ- 'be squeezed (in crowd)', ninnit- [old ortho. nivnit-] 'be narrow or tight (clothing)' [ninniɣi- 'find too narrow, cannot get through (hole)']

PY-S nanəq 'bone' [cf. naʀə- and naʀ[1], but compare also PI caunəq]
AAY C nanəq, K nənəq 'bone'
CAY ənəq*, Nun, HBC nənəq*, NS, Eg nanəq* [and ənəXkuaq 'leftover bone']
NSY nənəq [L.-T. gives this form twice and nanəq once for 'bone']
CSY [note nəXquʀ- 'have bone or joint pain', nəXquʀžuk 'skeleton', and nəXqʷaaq* 'bone']
Sir ninəX 'bone', pl. ninʀiy [Orr; also ninəXquʀžux 'skeleton']

PY nənəqitə- 'choke on bone' [cf. łit- and compare caunnit- under caunəq]
AAY —
CAY nənʀitə-, ənʀitə-, nanʀitə- 'choke on a bone'
NSY nənəqitə- 'choke on bone' [ANLC]

PY-S nənəʀpaɣ(-) 'harpoon' [cf. p.b. vaɣ]
AAY —
CAY Y [for NS?] nanəXpak 'seal spear' [also verbal]
NSY —
CSY —
Sir ninəXpəɣ- 'harpoon'

PE nəŋ(ŋ)aʀ- 'be angry'
AAY nəŋaqaʀ- 'get angry, leave in a huff'
CAY nəŋaʀ- 'sulk angrily, be jealous on account of s.o. of opposite sex'
NSY nəŋaʀ- 'take offense' [ANLC; Em. has 'go off angrily']
CSY nəŋaʀ- 'go off angrily or sulking'
Sir —
SPI niŋaq- 'be angry'
NAI niŋaq- 'pout, sulk', PH 'beat one's wife'
WCI niŋaq- 'be angry', H. Island Cop 'fight' [the latter Lowe, also Dor. for Net; Ras. has niŋaqpak- 'be jealous (woman)' for Sig; Pryde also has Cop, Net niŋŋak- 'rage, get angry, go berserk']
ECI niŋŋa(C)- 'be or get angry', niŋŋaʀi- 'be angry with', Lab niŋak- 'be angry, bellow or break s.th. in rage', niŋaaC- 'beat up' [Saul has niŋŋa(q)- 'get angry' but niŋaq- 'be angry']
GRI niŋŋaɣ- 'be angry, be hysterical (child)', niŋaʀ-, NG niŋŋak- 'be jealous (woman)', EG niŋaC- 'be offended'

PE nəŋa(C)u(ɣ) 'son- or brother-in-law' [probably nəŋaʀuɣ — cf. Aleut ŋaru-X 'son-in-law', earlier also 'brother-in-law, wife's brother']
AAY nəŋau(k) 'son-in-law, brother-in-law (sister's husband)'
CAY nəŋauk
NSY nəŋaa 'son-in-law, brother-in-law' [ANLC; Tein's nəŋawitə- 'move to home of bride's parents' suggests underlying nəŋau-]
CSY nəŋaa 'son-in-law, brother-in-law' [aa from underlying au as shown by labialization in nəŋaawaq 'man working for future wife's parents']
Sir [Miller has nənəxna 'son-in-law, brother-in-law' (for nənəxka?)]
SPI niŋau(k) 'son-in-law, brother-in-law (sister's husband)'
NAI niŋau
WCI niŋauk
ECI niŋauk
GRI niŋaak, NG niŋauq 'son-in-law, brother-in-law'

[and in WG also of husbands of more remote female relatives]

PE nəŋðuʀ 'small spider' [cf. nəŋə- and ðuraʀ-, also aʀžuk for the p.b. in the Inu forms, yaʀ for that in Yup?]
AAY AP nəŋuʀyaq 'spider'
CAY Nun nəɣuʀyaX 'spider' [Ras. has niX'Xaq; for nəɣaiʀ(aq) see under nəɣaʀ]
NSY [nəŋžuʀ- 'collect eggs by rope on a cliff' (ANLC) — compare the SPI below]
CSY —
Sir —
SPI niɣžuaʀžuk 'spider' [note niɣžuq-, Imaq nəɣžuq-, 'let down by rope', Imaq nəɣžun 'rope for lowering self down cliff to bird nests']
NAI niɣžuaʀžuk 'small spider'
WCI Net niɣžuaʀžuk 'small spider' [B.-S. has Net niɣyuaʀzuk, Car niɣyuaʀyuk and Ras. has Cop nigyuq; Pryde has Cop, Car niɣyuq, Net niɣžuaʀžuk 'small web-making spider']
ECI Igl niɣyuq 'small spider' [Pryde], Tar niɣyuayuk, miɣyuayu(u)k 'small spider that hangs at end of thread and does not build web' [B.-S. has niɣyuk 'spider' for Igl]
GRI niššavaʀšuk [old ortho. nigssavarssuk], NG nixxaaXXuk, EG nittivaʀtik 'spider'

PE nəŋə- 'stretch or lower rope' [cf. EA ŋi(t)- in ŋiðusi-X 'rope with hook hanging under corner of anteroom', and ŋitaqa-X 'ear pendant'; there is probably a link to ni(i)łaʀ- too]
AAY nəŋə-, ləŋə- 'stretch'
CAY nəŋə- 'stretch, stand on tiptoe'
NSY ➟
CSY nəŋə- 'stretch, tighten (intr.)'
Sir nəŋtaʀəʀ- 'stretch (intr.)' [Vakh. has nəŋəmŋami 'stretching out' from Men.'s texts]
SPI ➟
NAI niŋi- 'descend gradually, as on a rope'
WCI ➟
ECI niŋi- 'descend on rope'
GRI ➟

PE nəŋət- 'lower or stretch on a rope' [cf. t-[1]]
AAY —
CAY nəŋtə- 'set a drift-net'
NSY —
CSY nəŋtə- 'stretch (trans.)'
Sir — [for nəŋət(ə)- 'see' see naŋaʀ-[2]]
SPI niŋit- 'lower by rope, set a net'
NAI niŋit- 'lower' [and Nu niŋitaq 'snare, trap']
WCI niŋit- 'be set (net)' [Pryde has 'lower on line' for Cop, and Ras. has 'lower' for Net]
ECI —
GRI niŋit- 'lower on rope'

PY-S nəŋuɣ- 'stretch out'
AAY neŋuxte- 'stretch out (trans.)'
CAY nəŋuxtə- 'spread, stretch out'
NSY nəŋuxtə- 'tighten' [and nəŋuŋɣalʀia 'hardy, strong']
CSY nəŋuɣ- 'reach across'
Sir nəŋuXpaqaʀ- 'tug at, pull out' [for nəŋuxpaqaʀ-?; Vakh. has nəŋuɣutə-, nəŋuɣət(ə)- 'raise']
Inu [note NG niŋuaq 'rope' as a shaman's word in Kroeber]

PY nəŋuləʀ- 'be stretchy?' [cf. nəŋuɣ- above and ləʀ-]
AAY sŋulʀaq, sŋullaq 'rubber band'
CAY nəŋulʀa- 'keep on stretching', nəŋulʀaq 'elastic'
NSY [nəŋulʀa 'motion of whole body in dance' (L.-T.)]
CSY ŋuləXtə- 'stretch boot soles with a stretching stick'

PE nəŋə(t)- and nəŋłi- 'be or get cold' [the latter form from nəŋət- plus li-[2]; CAY nəŋla and CSY nəŋlək may reflect nəŋə- without the t (t-[1]?); cf. Aleut ŋali- 'cool off', ŋat- 'get cool']
AAY ➟
CAY nəŋłi- 'have cooled down (food)', nəŋłiuʀ-, Nun nəŋtə- 'be cold (person)' [and nəŋla (base nəŋlə-) 'cold weather, cold']
NSY nənłi- 'be cold' [nənłi 'frost']
CSY nəŋli- 'be cool, chilled (liquid, etc.)' [and nəŋlək 'coldness']
Sir [Vakh. has nəŋcəpałəɣət(ə)- 'not have cooled down yet' from Rub.'s texts]
SPI niɣli- 'cool off'
NAI niɣli-
WCI ➟
ECI nilli- 'cool off' [and Iti nilluti- 'become colder']
GRI [nilłuʀ- 'have become cold']

PE nəŋłaʀ- 'cool down' [cf. ʀ- under ŋ(ŋ)uʀ-?]
AAY —
CAY nəŋła 'coolness, cool breeze', Nun nəŋłaʀ- 'have cooled down (e.g. food)'
NSY —
CSY naŋłaʀ- 'cool off (person)'
Sir —
SPI niɣlaq 'cool off'
NAI niɣlaq-
WCI niɣlaq- 'cool off' [as nom. = 'coolness']
ECI nilla(q)- 'become colder', nillasuk- 'have become colder (e.g. house)', NBI niɣlasuk- 'be cold'
GRI niłłaʀ- 'have cooled down (person)', NG niɣlaq- 'cool down (air in evening)'

PE nəŋłinaʀ- 'be cool' [cf. naʀ-]
AAY C nəŋłinaʀ- 'be cold'
CAY Nun nəŋłinaX 'spring of cool water'
NSY —
CSY —
Sir —
SPI niɣlina(q)- 'be cold'
NAI niɣlin^{y}aq-
WCI niɣlinaq- 'be cool'
ECI —
GRI —

PE nəŋłiʀ- 'be cold' [cf. liʀ-]
AAY nəŋliʀ- 'be cold' [and nəŋliq 'cold weather']
CAY nəŋłiʀ- 'be cold (weather)' [and Nun nəŋłəʀ- 'be cold (liquid)']
NSY nənłiʀ- 'be cold (air)' [ANLC]
CSY —
Sir —
SPI —
NAI —
WCI [Ras. has Net niɣliqtuq 'cold (water)']
ECI —
GRI niłłiq 'coldness', niłłiʀ- 'be cold (to touch)'

PE nəŋiʀ 'share of catch'
AAY nəŋiq 'share of catch' [also as verb nəŋiʀ- 'get share of catch']
CAY nəŋiq 'share of catch' [also as verb 'get share of catch']
NSY nəŋiq
CSY nəŋiq 'share of catch' [also as verb 'get share of catch']
Sir nəŋəX 'share of catch'
SPI niŋiq 'share of catch' [as verb = 'get share of catch']
NAI niŋiq
WCI niŋiq
ECI niŋiq
GRI niŋiq 'share of catch' [niŋiʀ- 'get share of catch']

PE nəŋyuʀ 'oldest woman in household'
AAY —
CAY NSU nəŋzuq 'grandmother'
NSY —
CSY nəŋyuq
Sir nəŋyəX 'grandmother' [and note nəŋəmastə- 'head woman in household' — Vakh. from Men.'s texts]
SPI W niŋiuq 'oldest woman in village' [Jen.]
NAI —
WCI Net niŋiuq 'grandmother' [Ras., also Pet. for Sig]
ECI niŋiuq 'old woman', Igl, Frob. Bay 'grandmother'
GRI niŋiuq 'oldest woman in household', SWG 'grandmother' [NG also 'bitch']

PE nəpə 'sound' [cf. nəmaaq-?]
AAY nəpa 'sound, noise'
CAY nəpa [base nəpə-] 'sound, noise' [note also nəpəŋyaʀ- 'come attracted by noise (animal or ghost)']
NSY ➟
CSY [for ma 'voice' see əmə; məŋyaʀ- 'attract unwanted spirits by excessive noise' is perhaps by contam. with əmə or əməɣ-] ➟
Sir [for əmə(məX) 'voice' see əmə] ➟
SPI nivi 'voice, sound'
NAI nipɨ
WCI nipi
ECI nipi 'voice, sound, melody'
GRI nipi 'voice, sound'

PI nəpaa(q)- 'make a noise or scream'
SPI nivaala- 'become noisy'
NAI nipaala- 'scream' [and nipat- 'make a sound']
WCI nipaaq- 'make a noise' [Schn. has nipaq- 'moan (sick person)' for 'adg']
ECI nipaa- 'moan, whimper'
GRI nipaaʀ- 'bawl', NG nipaa- 'shout, scream'

PE nəpəŋiʀ- 'fall silent' [cf. ŋiʀ-]
AAY nəpaiʀ- 'become silent'
CAY nəpaiʀ-
NSY nəpŋ̥iʀ-
CSY nəpiiʀ-
Sir nəpŋiʀ- 'become silent' [from Vakh.]
SPI nivaiq- 'become silent'
NAI nipaiq-
WCI nipaiqtit- 'silence' [Pryde]
ECI nipaŋiq- 'become silent'
GRI nipaŋiʀ-

PE nəpəŋit- 'be silent' [cf. ŋit-]
AAY nəpaitə- 'be noiseless'
CAY nəpaitə- 'be silent'
NSY nəpŋ̥itə- [ANLC]
CSY nəpiitə- [Rub.]
Sir [nəpŋ̥it- (for nəpŋit-?) 'be silent' — Vakh.]
SPI nivait-, Imaq nəvait- 'be silent'
NAI nipait-
WCI nipait-
ECI nipait-
GRI nipaat-, EG nipaala-

PE nəpliʀ- 'make a noise' [cf. liʀ-]
AAY nəpłiʀ- 'make a noise, say s.th. loudly'
CAY nəpłiʀ- 'be noisy'
NSY —
CSY —
Sir —
SPI nipłiq- 'utter a sound, yell'
NAI nɨvliq-, Nu nipliq- 'make a sound, speak' [nivlia- 'cry out feebly']
WCI nivliq-
ECI nilli(q)-
GRI niłłiʀ- 'make a sound, give a shout' [and niłłia- 'cry out']

PY nəpuɣ- 'speak or make noise'
AAY PWS nəpuxtə-, KP nupuxtə-, K niuxtə-, yuxtə- 'speak'
CAY Nun nəpuxtə- 'make noise' [and note niuxtə- 'rustle', niuk, HBC nivuk 'rustling sound']
NSY —
CSY nəpuk 'sound of many people talking at once'
Sir [nəpux 'sound of many people talking at once', probably borrowed from CSY — Orr]

PE nəpə- 'be extinguished or set (sun)' [or *nʸəpə-; the first vowel in the CAY form is unexplained, but the n would have dropped before an original i]
AAY —
CAY nipə- 'be extinguished', niptə- 'extinguish'
NSY —
CSY nəptə- 'dip into water' [and note nəpsaɣ- 'sponge up water' — contam. with nəpət-?]

Sir yupət- 'set (sun)' [and Vakh. has yupułəX 'west, sunset']
SPI Qaw nipi- 'set (of sun or moon)' [Jen. has nipšuq 'it sets' for W]
NAI nipɨ- 'set'
WCI nipi- 'set' [and Cop nipaq- 'stay away long, loiter on way', Car? nipama- 'be absent, hidden' — Schn. 'adg']
ECI nipi- 'set' [and nipaq- 'disappear from view'; Ras. has nipama- 'stay away a long time, hesitate' for Igl]
GRI —

PE nəpət- 'stick' [cf. nəpyuk, nəvə- (so perhaps from *nʸəpət-) and Atkan Aleut m̥at- in m̥ata- 'put in pocket under parka' with p.b. ta-, m̥aci- 'stick between s.th. (e.g. boat between rocks)', EA haci- 'get stuck' — compare uŋuci- 'be sitting' under iŋət- for the final vowel]
AAY nəptə- 'stick to, adhere'
CAY nəp(ə)tə-
NSY nəpətə-
CSY Chap nəpŋ̥əqaʀ- 'stick'
Sir — [for yəvət(ə)- 'stick' see nəvə-]
SPI nivit- 'stick'
NAI nipit-
WCI nipit-
ECI nipit-
GRI nipit- [also spelled nipig- in old ortho.], EG niput-

PI nəpətaq- 'stick together (of animals copulating)' [cf. ðaʀ-]
SPI nivitaq- 'copulate (animals)'
NAI nipɨtaq- 'copulate (animals), be stuck on it (female animal when mating)'
WCI —
ECI —
GRI nipitaʀ- 'be stuck together (dogs or foxes mating)', EG nipilaʀ- 'copulate'

PE nəpətya(ʀ)- 'be sticky' [cf. ya-?]
AAY nəpcanaʀ- 'be sticky', nəpcanaXtə- 'get stuck (in mud, etc.)'
CAY nəpsanaXqe- 'be sticky' [and Nun nəpcaX 'small type of sucker fish']
NSY nəpəsalŋuq 'sticky'
CSY nəpəsanaʀ- 'be drizzly, misty' [nəpəsənaq 'drizzle, mist']
Sir —
SPI nivisaq- 'be damp, sweaty'
NAI [nipitcaq 'octopus']
WCI [Car EP nipiha 'lumpfish' (Ow.), Sig nipisa 'loach-like fish' (Pryde)]
ECI [nipisaq 'sea fish with sucker — lamprey or sea-slug']
GRI [nipisa 'lumpfish']

PI nəpta- 'be clear (weather)' [there may be a link to nəpə-; cf. ta-]
SPI nəpta- 'be clear (weather)'
NAI nɨpta-
WCI nipta- 'be clear'
ECI nitta-
GRI nitta- 'have stopped (rain)'

PI nəptait- 'be overcast' [cf. ŋit-]
SPI niptait- 'be hazy'
NAI nɨptait-
WCI niptait-
ECI nittai(t)- 'be overcast, foggy', Lab nittaik 'fog'
GRI nittaat- 'be rainy or snowy' [and nittaalaq 'air thick with rain or snow', NWG nittaalaʀ- 'snow', EG nittaala- 'snow gently', NG nittaŋŋit- 'be obscured by snow or mist (way forward or air)' — Holt.]

PI nəptaq- 'become clear' [cf. ʀ- under ŋ(ŋ)uʀ-]
SPI niptaq- 'have cleared (of weather)'
NAI nɨptaq- 'become clear, come into view'
WCI niptaq- 'become clear' [Ras. has 'come into sight' for Cop and Net]
ECI nitta(q)- 'become clear' [Ras. has Igl nibtar- 'appear']
GRI nittaʀ- 'no longer rain or snow, exhibit, present'

PY-S nəpyuk 'rain' [or *nʸəpuk; cf. nəpət-?]
AAY —
CAY NI, NS ivzuk, HBC ivyuk 'rain'
NSY [note iamsuɣyak 'drizzle' — also verbal]
CSY nəpsuk 'rain, wet weather' [for nəpəsanaʀ- 'be drizzly' see nəpətya(ʀ)- under nəpət-]
Sir yəpy̥əX 'rain' [and yəpy̥uxłəX 'downpour']
Inu [note WCI nipaluk 'rain' (both noun and verb) though compare nəvəluɣ under nəvə- — and perhaps KI yiXXiq-, Di yaXXaq- 'drizzle'?; for SPI ivʀa(a)niq 'rain' see under ivəʀ- and for NAI ifsulɨk- 'be wet from rain' see əvcuɣ-]

PE nəqə 'food' [cf. nəʀə- and Aleut qa-X 'fish, meal', qa- 'eat']
AAY nəqa 'food'
CAY nəqa 'food, fish' [and nəqkaq 'food, a meal']
NSY nəqə 'food, meat'
CSY nəqa
Sir nəqa
SPI niʀi 'meat' [niʀikšaq 'food']
NAI niqɨ 'food, meat' [and niqqak- 'gain weight, catch game animal', PH 'get a share of polar bear meat s.o. else has killed']
WCI niqi 'food, meat'
ECI niqi, niqitsaq
GRI niqi 'meat' [and niqiššaq 'food', niqqaɣ- 'gain flesh (wound)'; NG niqi and EG niʀi(q) may also refer to human flesh]

PE nəqli(C)uʀ- 'prepare food' [cf. li(C)uʀ-]
AAY nəqłiuʀ- 'prepare food'
CAY nəqłiuʀ- 'serve food' [compare neqkiuʀ- 'prepare food' and nəqliuʀ- 'prepare fish']
NSY [note nəqłiʀ- 'poison']
CSY [note nəqłiʀ- 'poison', nəqłiXtuʀ- 'prepare food']

Sir —
SPI niqłiuq- 'cook, prepare food'
NAI niqłiuq- 'cook a meal' [niqikšiuq- 'prepare food']
WCI Sig niqłiuq- 'cook' [Cop niʀiXXiuq- 'cook a meal']
ECI niʀsiu(q)- 'cook'
GRI niʀłiuʀ- 'cook a meal' [and niqiliuʀ- 'cook meat', niʀłiʀ- 'provide food for, feed']

PY nəq(ə)niʀ- 'be tasty' [cf. n(n)iʀ-]
AAY —
CAY nəqn̥iXqə- 'be tasty'
NSY nəqn̥iʀ- 'be tasty, good to eat' [ANLC]
CSY nəqn̥iʀ-

PI nəqpik 'boneless meat' [cf. piɣ]
SPI —
NAI niqpik 'boneless meat (game or fish)'
WCI niqpik 'flesh' [Jen.; Ras. has 'fleshy meat of fish or loin of mammal']
ECI niqpik 'filet, fleshy loin part of seal'
GRI niʀpik, EG mappik 'fish meat', NG niqpik 'loin' [and note also NG niqpiaqtaq 'sealskin with hair removed to make waterproof boots' and EG mappimiiq 'meat without bone or fat']

PY nəqəcaq 'bait' [cf. nəqə]
AAY nəqcaq 'bait'
CAY nəqcaq
NSY nəqəsaq
CSY nəqəsXaq 'bait for trap'
Inu [SPI niʀisaq 'bait' probably from the Yup]

PE nəqu- 'width' [dimensional root]
AAY —
CAY nəqutu- 'be wide', nəqukit- 'be narrow'
NSY nuqutu- 'be wide' [ANLC; Men. has nuqukit- 'be narrow']
CSY nuqutu- 'be wide'
Sir —
SPI —
NAI niʀutu- 'be wide', niʀukit- 'be narrow'
WCI niʀutu- 'be wide'
ECI niʀutu- 'be spacious', niʀukit- 'be narrow' [niʀu 'space']
GRI niʀutu- 'be wide', niʀukit- 'be narrow'

PE nəʀcaʀ 'sea mammal?' [cf. nəʀə- and perhaps caʀ-]
AAY —
CAY —
NSY nəXsaq 'seal' [Tein has 'ringed seal']
CSY nəXsaq 'seal' [nəXsapik 'adult ringed seal']
Sir —
SPI niqsaq 'ringed seal'
NAI niqsaq 'sea mammal or animal living on sea ice', PH 'game animal' [as verb = 'catch game']
WCI Sig niqsaqsuqtuq 'good hunter'
ECI —
GRI —

PE nəʀə- 'eat' [trans. and intrans.; cf. nəqə]
AAY K nəʀə- 'eat'
CAY nəʀə-
NSY nəʀə-
CSY nəʀ(ə)-
Sir nəʀ(ə)- 'eat' [and nəʀyukcəX 'food, produce']
SPI niʀi- 'eat'
NAI niʀi-
WCI niʀi-
ECI niʀi-
GRI niʀi-

PE nəʀəðviɣ 'eating place' [cf. ðviɣ]
AAY nəʀwik 'restaurant'
CAY nərvik 'place to eat' NSU nəʀəzvik 'table'
NSY nəʀvik 'table, place of eating, dining room'
CSY nəʀvik 'place to eat'
Sir nəʀvəx 'place to eat' [Orr]
SPI niʀʀiwik 'table', Qaw 'restaurant' [and KI niXfik 'restaurant']
NAI niʀʀivik 'table'
WCI niʀʀivik
ECI niʀʀivik 'table, dining room' [and Spald. has niʀivvik 'restaurant, mythical woman at bottom of sea' for NBI]
GRI niXXivik 'eating time or place, table' [and NG niʀʀivik 'woman at bottom of sea (mythical figure releasing sea mammals from her cauldron)' — Holt.]

PY nəʀəsta 'louse' [cf. ðə]
AAY nəʀəsta, na'asta, nasta 'louse'
CAY neʀəsta
NSY —
CSY —

PE nəʀəvkaʀ- 'feed' [cf. vkaʀ-]
AAY K nəʀəxkʷaʀ- 'feed'
CAY nəʀəfkaʀ-
NSY —
CSY —
Sir —
SPI niʀipkaq- 'feed'
NAI niʀipkaq-
WCI niʀipkaq- [Lowe]
ECI niʀikka(q)-
GRI niʀikkaʀ-, niʀukkaʀ-

PY-S nəʀqə- 'feed (dogs)' [cf. ʀqə-]
AAY —
CAY nəXqə- 'feed (esp. dogs)'
NAY nəXqə- 'feed animals' [ANLC; Men. has nəXqusi-]
CSY nəXqə-
Sir nəXqə(s)- 'feed (animal)' [Em., who also has half-trans. nəXqasi-, nəXqusiʀ- 'prepare dog food', and nəXqatənəX 's.th. intended as food'; Men. has nəXqata 'food' and nəXqati- 'feed']

PI nəʀʀitu- 'eat a lot' [cf. tu-[1]]
SPI —
NAI niʀʀiqsu- 'eat too much'

WCI niʀʀitu- 'like to eat a lot'
ECI niʀʀituyuq 'one who eats a lot'
GRI niXXiʀsuuq

PY nəʀyaʀ- 'eat berries as one goes?' [cf. yaʀ(tuʀ)-]
AAY K nəʀya'aʀ- 'eat berries as one picks them' [but C predictable nəʀyaʀ- 'eat a meal, come to eat']
CAY nəʀyaʀ-, HBC nəʀliyaʀ- 'eat berries as one picks them'
NSY [note nəʀyaq 'small red edible flower' (ANLC)]
CSY [nəʀyaXtuʀ- is predictably 'go to eat']
Inu [forms like niʀiyaqtuq- predictably = 'go to eat' in all dialects]

PE nəʀiləɣ- 'choke on s.th.' [cf. nəʀə- and ləɣ-?; the strong i in Inu here is regular from *ə and compare CAY nəʀiləxtə- under nəʀyu(ɣ)- for the Yup]
AAY nəʀiləxtə- 'swallow the wrong way'
CAY nəʀiłkaʀ- 'choke on s.th. in windpipe'
NSY —
CSY —
Sir —
SPI —
NAI niʀil^{y}ɨk- 'choke on s.th.'
WCI —
ECI niʀilik- 'swallow s.th. the wrong way'
GRI niʀiliɣ-

PI nəʀiləktaq 'uvula' [cf. ðaʀ-?]
SPI —
NAI Nu niʀil^{y}ɨktaaq 'uvula'
WCI Cop niʀiliktaq 'nasal passage, uvula' [Pryde]
ECI Lab niʀiliktaq 'soft palate' [Bourq.]
GRI niʀilittaq, EG niilattaq 'uvula'

PE nəʀləʀ and **naqləʀ** 'goose' [cf. nəʀluq-?; there appears to be contam. with naqə and laɣiq in some of the forms, but onomatopoeia may also be involved]
AAY K naqłəq 'gray beach goose'
CAY naqłəq*, NS ləqłəq* 'white-fronted goose' [the latter form influenced by laɣiq?]
NSY łəqłəq 'swan, emperor goose'
CSY ləXłəq* 'emperor goose'
Sir ləXłəX 'gray goose'
SPI liʀliq 'goose' [Qaw 'Canada goose' but in Imaq 'white goose', contrasting with łəqłəq 'swan', presumably from NSY; Ras. has niʀliq 'brant goose' for W]
NAI nɨʀliq*, Mal liʀliq 'goose' [Ras. has lerlivik 'brant goose' for 'Norton', i.e. Mal]
WCI niʀliʀniq 'small wild duck — brant' [for Car Ras. has 'barnacle goose'], Cop niʀlivik 'white-fronted goose' [Lowe; Dor. has Car (Ahiarmiut) liʀliq 'goose', Ow. has niʀliq, liʀliq 'bean goose' for EP]
ECI niʀliq 'Canada goose'
GRI niʀłiq* 'goose'

PI nəʀluq- 'raise head' [cf. nəʀləʀ]
SPI niʀluq- 'break neck vertebra (of seal) and raise its head'
NAI nɨʀluq- 'throw head back, raise chin, sever head at first vertebra'
WCI Net niʀluqtit- 'break back near head (fish)'
ECI niʀlu(C)- 'raise head to listen, cut across promentary', niʀluŋayuq 'animal on the alert'
GRI niʀłuʀ-, niʀłiʀ- 'break back of s.th.' [and niʀłut (pl.) 'backbone of bird']

PE nəʀu(C)aʀ- 'choose'
AAY —
CAY —
NSY nəʀuaʀ- 'choose'
CSY —
Sir —
SPI Imaq nəʀuaq-
NAI —
WCI niʀuaq-
ECI niʀuaq-
GRI [note niʀuut(i)- 'give permission to take, offer assistance']

PI nəʀupkaq '(edible contents of) stomach of ruminant' [cf. nəʀuvəʀ-]
SPI Qaw niʀukaq 'first stomach of ruminant'
NAI niʀukkaq 'edible stomach contents (of caribou or deer)'
WCI niʀukkaq [Met. has nerrokark; Ras. has neruvkaq for Car and Net]
ECI niʀukkaq 'contents of first stomach of ruminant'
GRI niʀikkaq, niʀukkaq [old ortho. nerivkaq, etc.] 'stomach of ruminant or its edible contents'

PE nəʀuvəʀ- and **nəʀuvaʀ-** 'be soft and warm'
AAY Perry nu'uwaʀ- 'be soft and smooth'
CAY HBC nəʀuvəʀ- 'be soft and warm to the touch'
NSY nuʀuvatə- 'be soft, furry' [L.-T.]
CSY nəʀuvatə- 'be soft'
Sir luváʀətə- 'be soft' [Orr; Em. has luvaʀəlŋuX 'soft']
SPI niʀumaq- 'be smooth' [and note yavvau- 'be soft, pliable']
NAI niʀumɨk- 'be lukewarm', niʀummaak- 'be soft and warm'
WCI niʀumik- 'be lukewarm'
ECI niʀumik- 'be warm, maintain a mild heat (garment)'
GRI niʀumiɣ- 'yield when pressed, be tepid', niʀumaaʀ- 'be soft'

PE nəʀyu(ɣ)- 'eagerly expect' [the apparent relation in Yup with nəʀə- 'eat' and p.b. yuɣ- is probably coincidental]
AAY —
CAY nəʀyuniuʀ- 'eagerly expect s.th. good' [and note nəʀinitə- 'be anxious, impatient' and nəʀiləxtə- 'anticipate eagerly or anxiously', with which compare AAY nəʀiləxtə- 'swallow' under nəʀiləɣ- — contam.?]
NSY nəʀyu- 'hope, expect' [ANLC; Men. has nəʀyukələq 'hope' — compare nəʀyuɣnalʀia '(one that is) good to eat', nəʀyuɣnałəq 'good appetite' and nəʀyuxsaaʀ- 'want someone to eat s.th.' from nəʀə-]
CSY nəʀyu- 'hope, expect', nəʀyukə- 'have hope concerning'

Sir — [but note nəʀyuʀnaXaX — for nəʀyuɣnaX? — 'delicacy' from nəʀə-]
SPI niʀiuk- 'expect, hope' [trans. niʀiuɣi-]
NAI niʀiuk-, trans. niʀiuɣɨ- 'expect, hope' [as opposed to niʀisuk- 'want to eat']
WCI niʀiuk-, trans. niʀiuɣi- 'expect, hope'
ECI niʀiuk-, trans. niʀiuɣi-
GRI niʀiuɣ-, trans. niʀiuɣi-

PI nəʀiuqšuq- 'promise' [cf. qðuʀ-]
SPI niʀiuqšuq- 'promise'
NAI niʀiuqšuq-
WCI —
ECI —
GRI niʀiuʀšuʀ-

PY-S nəʀžuɣ- 'be bright' [or *n^{y}əʀžuɣ-; there may be a link to iʀaluq]
AAY —
CAY —
NSY — [for niʀafkaq 'mirage' see inivkaʀ under ini-]
CSY niʀuɣ- 'be light, daylight'
Sir yəʀcəɣəlŋuX 'bright', yəʀcəɣca 'light', yəʀcəɣuʀətəX 'ray of light' [but note also nuʀə- 'illuminate', nuʀəX 'moon' and nuʀasaX 'star'; Vakh. has niʀuʀ- 'be bright', niʀuX 'light', nuʀwaX, also (from Rub.'s texts) nuʀaX, nuʀəX 'moon' and (from Men.'s texts) nuʀəciX 'star']

PI nəʀžun 'land animal' [cf. nəʀə- and un, perhaps also yu-, ðu-]
SPI W niʀžun 'animal'
NAI niʀžun 'large animal'
WCI Sig niʀyun 'wild animal' [Lowe; Jen. has 'polar bear' in songs for Cop; Pryde has niʀyun 'migratory land animal' for Cop]
ECI NBI niʀyuti 'animal', Lab niyyut 'land animal' [Saul has both niʀyuti and niyyuti for Tar]
GRI niʀšut 'land animal'

PE nə(C)uʀ- 'be curved' [or ni(C)uʀ- to explain deletion of (C) in Inu; cf. niutaq]
AAY K nəmiXtə- 'curve, go all the way around'
CAY nəviXtə-, Nun nəmiXtə-, yuuXtə- 'curve (trail or river)'
NSY —
CSY [yuuŋiʀ- 'reduce in size by folding, rolling and/or tying' — Rub. has 'roll up, decrease, shrink' for Chap; for aɣuʀ- 'bend, turn' see PY-S aɣuʀ-]
Sir —
SPI —
NAI —
WCI Cop niuŋa-, niuqtit- 'be twisted' [Pryde]
ECI niuŋa- 'be crooked, bent' [and Iti niuŋaq 'curved American knife']
GRI niuʀ- 'curve, become crooked', niuŋa- 'be curved or crooked' [and nayuʀ- 'be curved', nayuŋašuq, NWG niuŋasuq 'rib', NG niuqtitaaq- 'be wavy']

PE nəvðuʀ or **əvðuʀ** 'sod or soil' [cf. nəvə-; umðu- is presumably the source of contamination in the Inu forms here]
AAY —
CAY nəvuq 'dirt, soil, mud' [note also nəvluk 'clinging debris, dirt' under nəvə-]
NSY nuvu(q) 'turf, sod'
CSY nəvuq 'sod, lump of soil'
Sir —
SPI Qaw ivžu, nivžu 'sod for housebuilding' [as in nivžulik ini 'sod house', also verbal nivžu- 'apply sod to walls of sod house'; Imaq uvžuq 'sod']
NAI ivžuq 'sod' [and ivžuqsi- 'cut sod in thick pieces for house walls']
WCI ivyu 'moss, piece of sod', Net ivžut 'earth' [Briggs; Ow. has ivyuq 'mud' for EP]
ECI iyyu(q)- 'apply liquid peat to sled runners'
GRI iššuq 'sod', NG 'moss' [for iššu-, EG nittu- 'be thick' see umðu-]

PE nəvə- 'cling to' [or *n^{y}əvə-; cf. nəpət-, nəvyuvaɣ and nəvɣur, also EA tmu- 'lean on, press', Atkan tmuusi-X 'cane'?]
AAY nuɣə- 'infect'
CAY nəvə-, HBC ləvə- 'have things clinging'
NSY ➟
CSY nəvə- 'stick, cling, adhere'
Sir yəvət(ə)- 'stick, adhere' [and yəvnəʀaqirləʀəX 'sticky'; Vakh. has yəvat(ə)-, yəvaʀ- 'stick' from Men. and Rub.; Em. has yəvnałəʀəX 'sticky']
SPI nui- 'flock to, be attracted to'
NAI nivi- 'be attracted to bait, flock around, cling, adhere' [nominal = 'place where animals or insects come'; niviɣaq- 'hover around, linger, scrutinize from all sides']
WCI Sig nivititsi- 'knead (dough)' [and Pryde has nivi 'non-biting midge-like insect occurring in swarms' for Cop]
ECI ➟
GRI nivi- 'seek out, keep close to (e.g. raven to carcass)' [nivitsiʀ- 'lure, wait for s.th. to come (whale, of krill)']

PE nəvəluɣ 'clinging dirt or snow' [cf. łuɣ(-)?]
AAY —
CAY nəvluk 'clinging debris, dirt'
NSY —
CSY —
Sir —
SPI —
NAI nivil^{y}uk- 'be sloppy, slushy, mixed rain and snow'
WCI niviluknaqtuq 'snow clinging to clothes' [and compare Cop nipaluk 'rain' under nəpyuk]
ECI —
GRI —

PI nəviŋa- 'be hanging' [cf. ŋa-^{1}]
SPI niuŋa- 'be hanging'
NAI niviŋa-
WCI niviŋa- 'be hanging' [also 'hang up' in Sig acc. Lowe]
ECI niviŋa- 'be hanging'
GRI niviŋa-

PI nəviŋŋaq- 'hang' [cf. nəviŋa- above and ʀ- under ŋ(ŋ)uʀ-]
SPI niuŋaq-, Qaw niiŋaq-, nuiŋaq- 'hang up'
NAI niviŋŋaq- 'hang, be hung up', PH 'be barely hanging'
WCI niviŋŋaq- 'hang up'
ECI niviŋŋa(q)-
GRI niviŋŋaʀ- 'hang up' [and note EG niiŋŋaʀ- 'hold on tight']

PI nəviuq- 'hang around near' [cf. (C)uʀ- unless this base is from *nəvyuʀ-]
SPI niu(u)q- 'stick to pan (burnt food), Qaw niwiuq-, nuwiuq- 'hang around, stick near (animal or child)'
NAI niviuq- 'hover, hang around'
WCI niviuq- 'hang around (animals or young men around girls)', Net niviuʀnaq- 'be charming' [Briggs, who also defines niviuq- as 'wish or arouse wish to kiss or touch affectionately' — Ow. has 'be worried' for EP]
ECI niviuq- 'remain close (by affection — as mother to child or bird close to nest)'
GRI niviuʀ- 'hover above, brood'

PY-S nəvtəɣtə- 'fasten or install' [or *nʸəvtəɣtə-; cf. t-[1]]
AAY —
CAY —
NSY nəftəxtə- 'put in, install, set up' [ANLC]
CSY nəftəxtə- 'fasten, hang up'
Sir yəftəʀ- 'put in' [Vakh. has yəftəɣ- 'tie']

PE nəvəʀ- 'lie down or fall on one's back' [or *nʸəvəʀ-; cf. Atkan Aleut tma- 'slip down (s.th. hanging on wall, fish out of hand)'?]
AAY C nuɣəʀ-, K nuʀ- 'lie on one's back' [postural root as in all Yup.]
CAY nəvəʀ-
NSY nəvaʀ-
CSY nəvəʀ-, navəʀ-
Sir yəvaʀmi 'reclining on back'
SPI ➞
NAI niviq- 'lie on one's back'
WCI niviq- 'fall backward'
ECI niviq-
GRI niviʀ-

PI nəvʀala- 'lie on one's back' [cf. la(ʀ)-?]
SPI niʀvalaq-, Qaw nivʀalaq- lie down on one's back' [and note Qaw nipqałak- 'fall on back']
NAI nivʀallaq- 'land on one's back' [with p.b. ʀ- under ŋ(ŋ)uʀ-]
WCI nivʀala- 'lie on one's back' [nivʀallaq- 'lie down on one's back']
ECI niʀʀala- 'sleep on back', niʀʀalaŋa- 'lie on one's back'
GRI niʀfala- 'lie on back' [niʀfałłaʀ- 'lie down on back']

PE nəvɣuʀ 'fish slime' [cf. nəvə-; the relat. to nuvaɣ is obscure — perhaps just contam.]
AAY — [for nuayaaq 'slime' see nuvaɣ]
CAY yuvɣəq, Nun cuvɣəX, HBC cuvayaaq 'fish slime' [for ŋəvva 'mucus' see nuvaɣ]
NSY —
CSY [for nuvaxłuk '(fish) slime' see nuvaɣ]
Sir —
SPI yuɣɣuq 'fish slime, fish scale' [Jen. has W nuɣu 'fish scale' and KI nuvvayaaq 'slime']
NAI nivɣuq, yuvɣuq 'fish slime'
WCI Cop nivɣuq [Pryde]
ECI niɣɣuq
GRI nixxuq [old ortho. nivɣu]

PE nəvi(C)aʀ 'girl' [cf. perhaps nəvə- and neviuq- under it if the first Sir below are from neighboring Sib. Yupik — compare the forms of nəvyuvaaʀžuk under nəvyuvak, so perhaps from *nəvyuɣaʀ; for the i in Yup compare CAY nəʀinitə- under nəʀyu(ɣ)-]
AAY —
CAY nəviaXcaq 'girl, young woman of marriageable age' [and note HBC nəvikci- 'act in a youthful manner' — from *nəvyuɣci-?]
NSY nəviaXsaq 'girl'
CSY —
Sir naXsəʀžaX, naXsəʀžaʀəX 'little girl' [Vakh. has the first as 'young woman' and naXsəʀžaʀaX 'young girl'; Men. also has naXsakiʀləʀəX 'pretty girl'; Krauss has from Pinaya naxsəɣžaX 'girl' — compare this with naxsəx (oblique naxsaɣ-) 'woman'; the relat. of the two bases to each other and — perhaps — to Chukchi ŋeɣəsqet 'woman' is obscure]
SPI niaqsiaq 'young unmarried woman', niaqsaaʀžuk 'girl'
NAI niviaqsiaq, niviaqsiaʀžuk 'girl' [the latter with aʀžuk]
WCI Sig niviaqsiʀaq [Pet. has niviyyaq], Car niviaXXiaq 'girl' [the latter Dor. — also Ras. for Cop; B.-S. has niviak and Dor. niviakkaq'young girl' for Baker Lake]
ECI niviaʀsiaq, NBI niviaʀsaaq 'girl'
GRI niviaʀsiaq, EG niiarsiaq, NWG niviaq [pl. nivissat] 'girl of marriagable age' [and niviaʀsiaʀaq 'little girl']

PE nəvku 'dried meat'
AAY —
CAY nəfkuq 'dried small fish, dried meat' [Jen. has mifku for Nun]
NSY nufku 'dried meat' [ANLC; L.-T. has nufkuʀaq]
CSY nəfku, nəfkuužaq 'meat hung outside to dry' [nəfkuʀ- 'hang meat to dry']
Sir —
SPI —
NAI mipku 'dried meat'
WCI mipku, Car nipku 'dried meat' [Ras. also has the latter for Net]
ECI nikku, Aiv nipku, mipku 'dried meat'
GRI nikku [old ortho. nivko], NG nikkuq

PI nəvyuvak 'fly' [cf. nəviuq- under nəvə- and p.b. vaɣ, and compare PY ciivak]
Yup [NSY ŋuyŋuaXaq, CSY ŋuuyŋaaʀaq* 'housefly' are apparently loans from Chukchi gəryoŋavət 'fly' — 'yellow meat fly' acc. de Reuse]
SPI niuuvak, Qaw nuyuuvak 'housefly' [and Imaq niiwaq — for niiuvaq? — 'fly, gadfly']
NAI nuviuvak 'housefly', PH niviuvak 'big housefly'
WCI nuviuvak, niviuvak 'housefly' [the former given as an alt. form for Cop by Lowe, who gives the latter as 'bluebottle' for Sig]
ECI nuviuvak, niviuvaq 'blowfly'
GRI niviuak, niviuɣak, NG niviuvak 'blowfly'

> **PI nəviuvaaʀžuk** 'small fly' [cf. aʀžuk and compare the Inu forms of ukyuʀaʀ under ukyuʀ]
> SPI nuyaʀžuk 'small fly'
> NAI niviaʀžuk 'small swamp fly'
> WCI —
> ECI niviaʀyuk 'kind of mosquito that doesn't bite, bug'
> GRI NG niviuvaaXXuk 'small fly'

PE niðuʀ- 'suck in or inhale' [cf. Aleut iðut- 'sniff, inhale', perhaps also iðʀut- 'swallow', EA iðʀuya- 'try to swallow']
AAY yuuXtə- 'suck in, inhale'
CAY yuuXm̥iuʀ- 'suck in mucus in nose', HBC yuuXtə- 'sip' [NSU niuXsiɣ- 'snuffle' may be from Inu]
NSY [iiʀʷmiiʀʷ- 'gasp for breath', iiʀʷyaɣ- 'have whooping cough', iiʀʷyak 'whooping cough' — ANLC]
CSY iiXʷtə- 'sip, go or wash out (tide)' [cf. ižuk, though there may be contam. here]
Sir ižuʀ- 'smell', ižuXtə- 'sniff' [also icəʀałəX 'inhalation'; Vakh. has əžuXtə-, ižuqaʀ- 'sniff, smell'; Em. has ižuɣ- 'sniff, kiss']
SPI niuq- 'suck, sip', niuʀmik- 'sniff'
NAI niuʀmik-, PH niuqsik- 'sniff'
WCI niuʀmik-
ECI niuq- 'inhale, swallow', Lab niutsi(k)- 'gulp'
GRI nayuʀ- 'suck through nose or mouth, drink a hot drink'

> **PE niðuʀqaʀ** 'hot drink' [cf. qqaʀ-?]
> AAY yuXqaq 'hot beverage' [single u probably from compression]
> CAY yuuXqaq
> NSY —
> CSY —
> Sir —
> SPI yuuqaq 'hot beverage' [also verbal; from Yup version of the base?]
> NAI niuqqaq 'refreshing drink, hot beverage' [Jen. has 'juice']
> WCI niuqqaq 'tea' [and niuqqaq- 'drink tea']
> ECI niuqqa(q)- 'drink in gulps'
> GRI [nayuuqqaʀ- 'gulp down, sniff up']

PE niɣəðuʀ- 'drill' [cf. Aleut iɣðaɣ- 'drill into' with p.b. ðaɣ- at žaɣ-?]
AAY ➞
CAY iɣuʀ- 'drill into'
NSY iɣuʀ- 'drill' [ANLC; Men. has iɣuXtuʀ- 'drill into']
CSY iɣažutaaʀ-, iyažutaaʀ- 'drill
Sir iɣžəpə-
SPI niuq-, Qaw niuqtuq-
NAI niuqtuq-
WCI niuqtuq-
ECI ➞
GRI niiuʀ-, NG niuq-

> **PE niɣəðuʀun** '(fire)drill' [cf. un]
> AAY Kod, PWS iɣuun 'drill'
> CAY iɣuun
> NSY iɣun
> CSY iɣažutaaq*, iyažutaaq*
> Sir —
> SPI niuun, W niuqtuun 'drill' [Jen.]
> NAI niɣɣuun 'fire drill' [Jen.]
> WCI niuqtuun 'drill' [B.-S., who also has Net niɣɣin 'drill bow']
> ECI Igl ni(i)uqtuun 'drill' [B.-S.; Math. has niiuqtuut 'drill bow' and niiun 'fire-drill bow'; Pryde has niɣɣin 'bow of bow-drill' for Igl]
> GRI NG niut 'fire drill' [Holt.; WG nixxit 'bow of drill']

PE niɣu- 'get or take out' [cf. Aleut iɣu- 'take, pull out', iɣa- 'get out (of boat, etc.), take off (bird)']
AAY yuu- 'get out, take out (of shallow container, boat, etc.)'
CAY yuu-
NSY iiw- [ANLC]
CSY iɣu- 'remove food from pot'
Sir iɣə- [Em.]
SPI niu- 'get out, take out (of boat, etc.)'
NAI niu- [niɣɣuinʸ 'get out of the boat!']
WCI niu-
ECI niu- 'get out, take out' [and note niuvviu(q)- 'be present at arrival or departure of a vehicle']
GRI niu- 'get out, take out, unload, ladle up (food)' [and note niuffiuʀ- 'go out to sled or boat to greet or see off'; for NG niuʀʀu- 'visit' see niuʀʀu-]

PI niiqquq- 'crunch (snow underfoot)'
SPI —
NAI —
ECI niiquq- 'crunch, creak', Lab also 'make cracking sound (gun, flag)' [and Peck has 'gnash teeth']
GRI niiqquʀ-, niiqquluɣ- 'creak, crunch (snow underfoot)'

niisa 'porpoise' [from Old Norse hnísa 'porpoise']
SPI —
NAI —
WCI —
ECI Tar, NB niisa, Lab niisaatsuk 'porpoise' [the former from Pryde, who also gives niisaʀnaq 'pilot whale' for Tar]
GRI niisa 'porpoise' [niisaʀnaq 'pilot whale']

PE nikət- 'shift position'
AAY nikiaʀii-, nikiqqəʀii- 'sprain ankle, dislocate' [compare nipała- and and niʀaʀ- for the retained n]
CAY —
NSY —
CSY — [for iikə- 'remove, unfasten' and iikaɣaʀ- 'suddenly come undone' see ikə-]
Sir ikəmtəʀ- 'twist, turn'
SPI niɣit- 'get out of adjustment, become askew, make uneven'
NAI nikit- 'have been made uneven'
WCI nikit- 'move a little' [but Schn. has 'move off far' for 'adg', also nikitaq- 'come forward, act one after another' for B. Lake — Met. has nikitaqtuq 's.th moving in the distance on the ice']
ECI Lab nikit- 'move, no longer be in line' [Bourq.; and note Lab nikisuittuk 'Pole Star']
GRI nikit- 'shift, change position, be dislodged' [nikitaat(i)- 'alternate']

PE nilaɣ 'freshwater ice'
AAY —
CAY —
NSY —
CSY ilaŋquq 'clear, fresh ice' [with p.b. quʀ]
Sir —
SPI nilak 'freshwater ice' [Imaq nilaq]
NAI nilʸak 'moist crushed ice, layer of granular snow under another (can be melted for potable water)'
WCI nilaq 'freshwater (river) ice', EP nilak 'chipped ice' [Ow.]
ECI nilak 'clear freshwater ice (potable)'
GRI nilak 'piece of freshwater ice' [nilaɣ- 'be glazed frost', EG, Up nilattaʀ- 'be covered with frozen earth (sled runners)', NG nilauhaq 'glass']

PY-S ni(i)łaʀ- 'stretch skin' [cf. nəŋə-; from *nəŋiłaʀ-?]
AAY niłaʀ- 'stretch (skin)' [niłaq 'skin stretcher']
CAY niłaʀ-, NSK ŋiłaʀ- 'stretch (skin)' [niłaq, niłaun 'skin stretcher']
NSY niʀ- 'stretch (skin)' [Em. — for niiʀ-?]
CSY niiłXək (du.) 'wooden stretching frame' [and niiXtuʀ- 'stretch a skin, lash skin to drying rack', niiʀiʀ- 'remove dried skin from rack (also flesh from skeleton)'; note also niita, niitət 'rack hanging from ceiling of house, lashing holding skin to boat frame', niiʀžaq 'cage, gate' and niiXtuutək 'drying rack for seal', Chap niiʀun 'cross-piece of frame of winter sleeping compartment']
Sir niłəX 'stretching frame', niʀətəy 'thongs for stretching walrus skin on boat' [Em. who also has niłəʀži- 'stretch skin on frame for drying', and niłqutəy 'strap for attaching skin to frame for drying']

PY-S nipała(ʀ)- 'be offended' [or nəpała-? — cf. the CAY form under nəpə-]
AAY —
CAY —
NSY nipała- 'be offended, emotionally hurt, despair'
CSY nipałaʀ-
Sir nipałaʀ-

PI niqtuq- 'praise' [cf. perhaps Aleut iʀamana- 'be good' with p.b. na- (PE naʀ-), Atkan also iʀamaXta- 'like' with p.b. Xta- 'have as']
SPI —
NAI —
WCI Net niqtuq- 'praise' [Ras.]
ECI niqtu(q)-
GRI niʀsuʀ- 'praise' [and note NG nissuk, nissuŋŋuayu 'well done, how clever', nissumaaq- 'boast']

PY niʀaʀ- 'cross' [or nəʀaʀ-?, but see also nipała- and the AAY at nikət- for the retained n]
AAY K niʀaq 'bridge'
CAY niʀaʀ- 'cross by a bridge, go by airplane'
NSY — [for niʀafkaq 'mirage' see inivkaʀ under ini-]
CSY —

PE niʀu 'leg'
AAY iʀu, iʀuq, yuuq 'leg'
CAY iʀu, iʀuq
NSY iʀu
CSY iʀu
Sir iʀa
SPI niu
NAI niu
WCI niu
ECI niu(k)
GRI niu [pl. nissut], EG, Up niiq 'leg' [compare perhaps pisuɣ- under piyuɣ- for the spurious *s the plural suggests]

PI niʀuliq 'first vertebra' [cf. l(l)iʀ]
SPI —
NAI —
WCI niuliq 'first vertebra'
ECI niuliq
GRI niuliq(*)

PE niʀulu 'root or foot of s.th.' [cf. lu(ʀ)]
AAY —
CAY iʀuluq NSU 'sourdock', elsewhere 'vein on tobacco leaf'
NSY irulu(q) 'metal holder for semi-lunar knife, leg of something' [L.-T.]
CSY —
Sir —
SPI niuli- 'get twisted root (tooth)'
NAI niulu 'root of tooth, leg of furniture'
WCI Baker Lake niuluk 'root' [Schn.]
ECI niuluk 'support for trad. lamp' [Peck has niulu 'leg of table, etc.' for Lab]
GRI niulu 'foot (of furniture), root (of plant)'

PE niʀuvəʀ- 'trade' [there may be a relat. to navəʀ(aʀ)-]
AAY K iɣu<ʀ>uʀ-, Perry yu<ʀ>uʀ- 'buy, trade'
CAY NSU iʀuvəʀ- 'buy'
NSY —
CSY —
Sir —
SPI niuviq- 'buy, trade'
NAI niuvɨq- 'buy, trade' [nom. = 'trading partner']

WCI niuviq- 'buy, trade' [nom. = 'trade partner' — Dor.]
ECI niuviq- 'buy, trade'
GRI niuiʀ- 'trade'

PI niuɣaq- 'rub skin in snow to dry'
SPI niuɣauti- 'rub skin in snow to dry'
NAI niuɣaq- 'clean skin by rubbing in snow'
WCI Net niuŋaut(i)- [for niuɣaut(i)-?] 'rub skin back and forth with feet to clean' [Ras.]
ECI niuɣaq- 'rub' [Peck has niogar- 'rub' and niC- 'be worn out by rubbing' for Lab]
GRI niuaʀ- 'clean skin by treading it in snow' [and niviuʀ- 'wear away by rubbing', nit- 'wear down by rubbing (skin cover of boat)' — Fab. also has the latter, intr., as 'be worn or rubbed down (skin)'; note also niuut(i)- 'gambol, roll around (dog), rub self against s.th.']

PI niulʀiq 'dragonfly' [cf. nəvyuvak, so perhaps from *nəvulʀiʀ, influenced by niʀu]
Yup [for AAY cilʀayuk, CAY ciilʀaaq* 'dragonfly' see ciilʀaq under ciɣi-, but they may belong here instead, with contam. from there and/or PY ciivak]
SPI —
NAI niulʀiq 'dragonfly'
WCI Sig niulʀiq
ECI —
GRI —

PI niuʀʀu- 'visit' [cf. niɣu-?]
SPI —
NAI —
WCI Car? niuʀʀu- 'visit a distant camp' [Schn. 'adg']
ECI niuʀʀu- 'visit a distant camp (and stay overnight)'
GRI NG niuʀʀu- 'visit' [also in Fab. for WG and in Holm for EG]

PI niutaq 'curved part of bow or stem of boat' [cf. nə(C)uʀ- and un]
SPI niutaq 'wooden piece on prow of kayak'
NAI niutaq 'curved part at bow and stern of skin boat frame'
WCI —
ECI niutaq 'lengthening of central stem in bow of kayak where it rises above water' [Peck has Lab niutak 'round hoop of whale bone covered with skin and fastened to strap to support seal bladder']
GRI niutak, niutaaq 'sternpost', NG niutak 'drag anchor'

PI nivak- 'dig' [cf. Aleut im- 'turn over']
Sir [for yayəɣ- 'dig' see nayuɣ-]
SPI niwak-, Qaw also nuak- 'dig, shovel' [Imaq nuɣayužaq- — for nuwayužaq-? — 'dig out']
NAI nivak- 'dig, shovel' [and nivaaq 's.th. dug out', nivviaq 'well']
WCI nivak- 'dig, shovel' [and niva(a)q 'hole dug in earth', also nivvak, nivaktak acc. Met.; Pet. has nivaʀiaq- 'throw out contents' for Sig]
ECI nivak- 'throw out contents of container' [and nivviaq 'hole for fresh water, well']
GRI nivaɣ- 'fling away, shovel (e.g. snow)'

PI nivaun 'shovel' [cf. un]
SPI niwaun, nuwaun, Imaq nuɣaun 'shovel'
NAI —
WCI —
ECI nivautaq
GRI nivaataq

PE nuccuɣ- 'pull or tug'
AAY nucuɣ- 'tug' [and note nucuq 'bow drill']
CAY nucuɣ- 'pull, pull out' [and nucuutaq 'bow drill']
NSY —
CSY nusuɣ- 'pull'
Sir nusəɣ-
SPI nuzuk- 'pull s.th. up from shore to houses — esp. sea mammal'
NAI nusuk-, nutcuk- 'pluck, snatch, pull out'
WCI nutsuk- 'pull on', Sig nusuk- 'run' [Lowe, like Pet. and Ras. for Net, has 'pull, scratch' for the latter and nusuqiq- 'run'; note also nusuksima- 'keep taut for a moment']
ECI nusuk- 'pull toward self, tear off', (of object pulled) 'reach puller', nutsu(k)- 'draw toward self (object on water), pluck (plant or s.th. on ground)'
GRI nusuɣ- 'pull toward self, pull out', nutsuɣ- 'pull toward self, pluck (heather for fuel)'

PI nucukaq- 'pull or jerk' [cf. k(k)aʀ-]
SPI —
NAI nusukaq- 'jerk and drag'
WCI Sig nusukaq- 'pull at harness to get going'
ECI —
GRI nusukaʀ-, nusukkaʀ- 'pull s.o. along against their will'

PI nuciləк- 'drop dead'
SPI —
NAI nusil^{y}ɨk- 'drop dead'
WCI Cop nuhilik- [Pryde]
ECI —
GRI —

PE nuðiʀ 'parent of child's spouse' [cf. nužə, nukaʀ, and nuʀaʀ(aʀ); for the l in Inu compare aðiʀ and ukaðiʀ]
AAY —
CAY —
NSY —
CSY nuziq 'parent of child's spouse'
Sir —
SPI —
NAI nulliq 'parent of child's spouse'
WCI nuliq [Pryde]
ECI —
GRI nuliq 'parent of child's spouse' [Fab. has nortlak, usually with poss. suffix as in nortla — this is the same as modern metathesized nuʀła 'father- or mother-in-law of one's son or daughter'; note also nuliʀiit- 'be related through one's children']

PE nuɣə- 'appear or rise (from water)' [cf. Aleut tuɣiða-X 'moon', probably with p.b. ða-, PE ðaʀ-]
AAY —
CAY nuɣə- 'get up on, climb out (from water)'
NSY nuɣə- 'rise (sun)'
CSY nuuɣ- 'surface, emerge' [nuuk 'surfaced seal']
Sir —
SPI nui- 'appear, rise'
NAI nu<ɣ>i- 'appear, rise, (trans.) see, look at', PH also 'take a look outside to see if s.o. is coming'
WCI nui- 'appear'
ECI nui-
GRI nui- 'appear, rise, (trans.) be able to see, appear before'

PY nuɣyaʀaq 'way up into s.th.' [cf. yaʀ]
AAY —
CAY nuɣyaʀaq 'neck opening of parka, ladder or path by which one gets up on s.th.'
NSY — [for nuilaq 'collar' see nəɣilaʀ]
CSY Chap nuɣyaʀaq 'entrance from passage up into interior of house'
Inu — [for nuilaq 'neck opening of parka' see nəɣilaʀ]

PI nuima- 'protrude' [cf. (u)ma-]
SPI nuipa-, Qaw nuimaaq- 'protrude, stand out'
NAI nuima-
WCI —
ECI —
GRI nuima-

PI nuita- 'be visible' [cf. ta-]
SPI nuita- 'be visible'
NAI nuisa-
WCI nuita-
ECI nuita- 'be visible' [but nuisayuq 'waxing crescent moon in first decade' — compare nuisaq- 'begin to show self from hiding place (e.g. seal appearing momentarily at sea)']
GRI nuisa- 'project behind or above s.th.'

PE nuɣət- 'move' [cf. nuɣə-?]
AAY nuxtaXtə- 'move (to new location or residence)'
CAY nuxtaXtə- 'move (from one place to another)'
NSY nuxtə-
CSY nuuxtə-
Sir [nuŋtaʀ- 'go or bring over', nuŋcaʀ- 'shift']
SPI nuut- 'move' [and note yukpak- 'travel around' — compare yuyik under nukəɣ for the y]
NAI nuut- 'move' [and note yuɣit- 'travel around', going with the SPI above]
WCI nuut- 'move'
ECI nuuk-
GRI nuuɣ- 'move' [and note nuxxiʀ- 'move (refl.)' parallel to ayyiʀ- under ayə-]

PI nuktəq- 'move to another dwelling' [cf. təʀ-]
SPI nuktiq- 'move to another dwelling'
NAI nuktɨq-
WCI nuktiq- 'move to another dwelling' [Pryde has 'move to another direction (wind)' for Net]
ECI nutti(q)- 'have moved to another dwelling (not far away)'
GRI nutsiʀ- [old ortho. nugter-] 'move to another house, translate'

PE nuɣiʀ 'three-pronged bird spear' [cf. Aleut pl. (Atkan) nuɣi-s, EA nuɣi-n 'three-pronged bird dart', borrowed from Eskimo]
AAY —
CAY nuik, nuiq 'dart for hunting birds'
NSY —
CSY Chap nuɣiq 'harpoon' [archaic acc. Rub.]
Sir —
SPI nuɣɣit 'bird dart, bird spear'
NAI nuiqsaq- 'throw bird dart' [and nuiyaaqpak 'spear for duck or fish, bird dart']
WCI Sig nuyaaqpak 'three-pronged spear' [Lowe; Ras. has nuiaqpak for Car; Pryde has Cop nuiyaaq 'blunt arrow used to stun or kill ptarmigan on ground', nuiyaaqpaak 'trident to spear fish with in shallow water in summer']
ECI nuit [pl.], Lab nuɣɣit [Bourq.] 'three-pronged spear'
GRI nuffit [pl., old ortho nugfit, 3s poss. nuii], Up nuit, EG nukkit 'three-pronged bird dart' [nuiʀ- 'hit with bird dart']

PI nuɣluk- 'jump up to reach or pierce suspended object?' [cf. nuɣə-?]
SPI —
NAI nuɣluk- 'play game of jumping up to reach suspended object' [Jen.]
WCI nuɣluk- 'catch, sieze', nuɣluɣaq- 'jump up' [Schn. has the former for 'adg' as 'pierce with pointer and win in game'; nuɣluktaun 'kind of pin game' — for 'adg' Schn. has nuɣluktaq 'bone suspended from tripod with hole to be pierced' (also verbal for to play that game) and nuɣluktauti 'pointer' for the game]
ECI nullu(k)- 'be thrust in (oblong wooden object in seal's breathing hole to make it go where it is awaited)' [Peck has 'play game aiming at holes in board or bone' for Lab]
GRI —

PE nukalpiɣaʀ 'young man' [cf. nukaʀ, and piɣ(-)]
AAY K nukałpiaq, C nupałkiaq 'man'
CAY nukałpiaq 'man in his prime'
NSY nukałpiaq
CSY nukałpiɣaq
Sir nukəłpəɣaX, nukałpəɣcəX 'young man' [Vakh. has nukəłpəʀcəʀaX 'boy' and, from Rub., nukəłpəʀaX 'youth']
SPI nuɣatpiaq 'young unmarried man', nuɣatpiaʀaaq 'boy'
NAI nukatpiaq 'young unmarried man', nukatpiaʀžuk 'young boy'
WCI nukatpiʀaq 'boy'
ECI nukappiaq 'boy'
GRI nukappiaq 'young unmarried man', nukappiaʀaq 'boy'

PE nukaR 'younger sibling (of same sex)' [cf. nukalpiɣaR, but also nuRaR and nužə and nutaRaq under nutaR-, and p.b. kaRaq]
AAY ➞
CAY nukaq, nukaR(aq*) 'beaver in second year', NSU 'younger sibling'
NSY [L.-T. lists nukaq without translation] ➞
CSY ➞
Sir nuka 'sister' [Vakh. has nukəx 'sister'; note also nu 'son' — Miller has nuka '(my) son' and nukəka '(my) sister']
SPI nuɣaq 'younger sibling' [Jen. has nugaga 'my sister's child' for KI]
NAI nuka(q) 'younger sibling'
WCI nukaq 'younger same-sex sibling'
ECI nukaq
GRI nuka(q) 'younger same-sex sibling' [and nukaɣ- 'be spoiled (child), be tired of one's work, be greedy for caresses']

PI nukaqliq 'youngest child' [cf. qliR]
SPI nuɣaqłiq 'youngest child'
NAI nukaqłiq*
WCI nukaqłiq
ECI nukaRsiq
GRI nukaRłiq*

PE nukaRaR 'second wife' [cf. aR]
AAY C nuka<R>aq 'second wife' [B.-S. has 'foster daughter']
CAY nukaRaq 'second wife'
NSY nukaRaq 'second wife' [Taghyuq]
CSY nukaRaq
Sir nukəRəX 'second wife' [Vakh. from Men.'s texts]
SPI —
NAI Nu nukaRaq 'second wife'
WCI [Sig nukaRaRiik 'two men who exchange wives' — Pryde]
ECI —
GRI —

PI nukaRiit 'siblings' [cf. ɣiik]
SPI nuɣaRiit 'siblings'
NAI nukaRiit
WCI nukaRiit
ECI nukaRiit [Saul]
GRI nukaRiit

PI nukatuɣaq 'young male animal'
SPI —
NAI [Nu nukataɣaq 'young bull caribou, young male animal']
WCI nukatukaq [for nukatuɣaq?] 'young bull caribou'
ECI nukatuɣaq 'caribou or bear yearling still with its dam' [also 'adg']
GRI nukatuɣaq 'bull caribou in its third year'

PI nukaunRuq 'junior co-in-law' [cf. nəR² and compare aŋayunRuq under aŋayuɣ]
SPI —
NAI nukaunRuq 'spouse's younger same sex sibling's spouse'
WCI nukaunRuq 'brother-in-law younger than one's wife'
ECI nukauRŋuq 'junior brother-in-law for a man or sister-in-law for a woman'
GRI nukaaRnuq 'wife's younger sister's husband, husband's younger brother's wife'

PI nukavluq 'walrus in its prime?'
SPI —
NAI Nu nukavluq 'large bull walrus'
WCI —
ECI nukalluq 'caribou or walrus in its prime'
GRI nukałłuq 'young walrus'

PE nukəɣ 'muscle or tendon'
AAY nukək 'tendon, root'
CAY Nun nuki- 'be physically strong' [and nukxiate- 'be weak'; Hinz has nukixsuɣ- 'be strong']
NSY —
CSY —
Sir —
SPI yuɣik 'strength, tendon' [compare under nuɣət- for the y; Jen. has W nuɣik]
NAI nukik 'strength, cartilage, tendon' [and nukinik- 'recover from illness']
WCI nukik 'strength, cartilage, tendon'
ECI nuki 'muscle, tendon, strength'
GRI nukik, EG nuɣiq 'muscle, tendon, strength' [nukiniɣ-, nukkaɣ- 'become strong', Up nukkatsaR- 'strengthen']

PI nukəŋiq- 'be weakened' [cf. ŋiR-]
SPI —
NAI [nukiɣiq- 'become unable to move']
WCI nukiiq- 'be weakened'-
ECI nukiŋiq- 'have had a tendon cut'
GRI nukiŋiR- 'make an effort, hurry', NG nukiŋiq- 'be tired'

PI nukəRuq 'nerve or sinew' [cf. quR]
SPI —
NAI nukiRuq 'nerve'
WCI nukiRuq 'filaments connecting two halves of wood one is chopping in half' [Pryde has Cop nukiRuq 'muscle fiber, gristle']
ECI nukiRuaq 'small tendons, fibers, small roots in peat used to shoe sled runners, rootlet'
GRI nukiRuaq [pl. nukiRukkat] 'root running out from tree', EG nuɣiřiq 'sinew thread, muscle, tendon'

PE nula- 'grow or increase'
AAY —
CAY —
NSY —
CSY nula- 'multiply, increase (in number or size)'
Sir —
SPI —
NAI —

WCI [note Cop nula 'frozen snow or slush', H. Island 'water frozen to s.th.' acc. Pryde]
ECI nula- 'grow up suddenly (in old stories)', Lab 'grow large (man or animal)' [Peck for the latter]
GRI —

PY nuləɣ- 'get cracked' [cf. nuŋŋaq; there appears to be a further relat. to nutəɣ-]
AAY nuləɣ- 'nick, get nicked'
CAY HBC, Nun, NS nuləɣ- 'crack, split'
NSY —
CSY —

PY nulɣaRiR- 'become expressionless' [cf. nuləɣ- and ŋiR-?]
AAY —
CAY nulɣaiR- 'become expressionless, unsmiling'
NSY —
CSY nulɣiiR-

PE nuliR(aR) 'wife' [though apparently based on a verbal base nul(l)iR- 'copulate (with female)' this may be a back-formation — the original sense of the verbal base may perhaps have been 'produce offspring', with p.b. liR- added to (the source of) Sir nu 'son' under nukaR — compare also nucəqəR- below; cf. nužə, nuðiR, nuRaR(aR) and nukaR]
AAY nuliX- 'wife' [from *nuliRaR; nuliR- 'copulate (with female)']
CAY nuliaq, nuliX- 'wife' [i.e. nuliXa or nuliaRa 'his wife', etc.; nuliXtə- 'copulate (animals)']
NSY nuliaq 'wife'
CSY nuliiq*, nuliX-
Sir nuciX 'wife' [Vakh. and Orr also nucəX; note nucəqəR- 'give birth' — also nuɣəR- from Rub.'s texts — and nuciRnəX 'daughter- or sister-in-law' (with liR- and nəR[1])?]
SPI nuliaq 'wife' [as verb = 'take a wife']
NAI nuliaq 'wife, female mate' [and as verb = 'take a wife or mate'; nulliq- 'pursue a bitch (dog)']
WCI nuliaq 'wife' [as verb = 'take a wife, cover (female animal)', Pryde also 'try to seduce a woman']
ECI nuliaq 'wife' [as verb = 'copulate with (female animal)']
GRI nuliaq 'wife' [and nuliaR- 'take a wife, copulate with female (animals)'; NG nuliaq- 'mate (animal)', EG nuliakkaaq 'woman, female']

PY nuli(R)aqəlRiik 'married couple' [compare nuliaRiik below, also kə-[1] and lRi(C)a(q) in dual]
AAY —
CAY nuliXqəłXiik 'married couple'
NSY nuliaqułəRiik
CSY nuliXqułXiik

PI nuliaRiik 'married couple' [compare ɣiik, and nuli(R)aqəlRiik above]
SPI nuliaRiik 'married couple, pair of mated animals'
NAI nuliaRiik 'married couple'
WCI nuliaRiik
ECI nuliaRiik
GRI nuliaRiit 'married couple, mated couple (animals)'

PI nuliasuk 'female lover' [cf. yuɣ — compare uɣiyuɣ under uɣi]
SPI —
NAI —
WCI nuliasuk 'female lover' [nuliasuɣiik 'lovers']
ECI nuliasuk 'concubine, partner in casual sex' [nuliasuɣiik 'two who commit adultery']
GRI nuliasuk 'female lover' [nuliasuɣiit 'lovers']

PI nulik- 'copulate' [a back-formation unless k- under nəɣ- is involved]
Yup — [compare AAY nuliR-, CAY nuliXtə- above]
SPI Qaw nulik- 'copulate'
NAI nulik- 'copulate (humans)', Nu 'mate (animals)'
WCI nulik- 'copulate'
ECI [Ras. has nuliC- 'go to bed with wife' for Igl]
GRI [EG nuliilaR- 'copulate (dogs)' — Robbe and Menn.]

PE nuliR(aR)iR- 'lose one's wife' [cf. ŋiR-]
AAY —
CAY nuliaRiR-, nuliXiR- 'lose one's wife'
NSY —
CSY nuliXiRaq 'widower'
Sir —
SPI nuliiɣliq-, Qaw nuliilɣaq- 'lose one's wife'
NAI nuliiq- 'lose one's wife', nuliiRn^{y}iq* 'widower' [Lowe has nuliaɣiiq- for Uum]
WCI Cop nuliilɣaq- 'lose one's wife' [Lowe; Met. has nuliilɣaqtuq 'widower']
ECI nuliiq- 'have lost one's wife', nuliiRniq 'widower'
GRI nuliiR- 'have lost one's wife', nuliiRniq* 'widower'

PY nuliR(aR)niaR- 'ask to marry' [cf. ni(C)aR-]
AAY nuliXn̥iaR- 'go ask parents for permission to marry'
CAY nuliXn̥iaR- 'ask to marry (man of woman)'
NSY —
CSY —

PY-S nuliR(aR)tuR- 'get married (man)' [compare the verbal uses of nuliaq- in Inu above and cf. tuR-[1]?]
AAY —
CAY nuliXtuR- 'get married (man)'
NSY nuliXtuR- [ANLC]
CSY nuliXtuR- 'get a wife'
Sir nucəRiXtəR- 'get married (man)' [Vakh. from Rub.'s texts — for nucəRəXtəR-?]

PI nuliu- 'be in heat (animal)' [cf. ŋu-?]
SPI —
NAI —
WCI —
ECI nuliu- 'be in heat (animal)'
GRI nuliušaRfik 'rutting', NG nuliu- 'be in heat (female animal)'

PI nullaq- 'come to a halt or camp (for the night)' [cf. nulqaʀ-]
SPI —
NAI nullaq- 'set up camp for the night' [and nullautaq 'evening meal']
WCI Sig nullaq- 'camp' [Pryde has Cop nullainnaq- 'go to bed without eating']
ECI nulla(q)- 'stop moving (e.g. sick person)' [and Peck has nullainaq- go to bed without supper', nullaʀumitaq- 'eat supper before going to bed' for Lab]
GRI [nułła- 'throw self down (on stomach)', nułłaŋa- 'lie around (on stomach)']

PE nulqaʀ- 'stop or be hindered' [cf. nullaq-]
AAY —
CAY [Nun nułtə- 'tarry, be gone a long time']
NSY —
CSY nułqaviiʀ- 'have a difficult time, be worried'
Sir —
SPI —
NAI nutqaq- 'stop, die', nutqai- 'cause to stop, go and stop on one' [and nutqallak- 'take a break']
WCI nutqaq- 'stop'
ECI nuqqa(q)-
GRI nuqqaa- [old ortho. norqai-] 'long, be drawn toward, can find no rest, beg for help' [there seems to be contam. with nuqaʀ-; note also NG nuqqaq- 'hit in the eye'?]

PE nuluʀ- 'lace snowshoes'
AAY —
CAY nuluq 'webbing on snowshoes or bottom of ice strainer', NS nuluʀ- 'fill in webbing of a snowshoe'
NSY —
CSY —
SPI nullut 'webbing as on snowshoe or ice-scoop' [Jen. has W nulik — also for B]
NAI nuluq 'fine webbing' [see nułu(ʀ) for homonym 'buttock'], nulluaq- 'break fine netting of snowshoes', Nu nuluun 'bone needle used to weave snowshoe webbing'
WCI Sig nuluq- 'lace snowshoes', nullut 'grill, lattice' [Pet.]
ECI nuluat 'net', nuluaq- 'catch, be caught in a net'
GRI nuluutit 'straps between stanchions of sled'

PE nuluʀ(aʀ)- 'beckon or lure'
AAY nuluʀ-, nulu(ʀ)aʀ- 'beckon'
CAY Y nuluʀ-, K nuluʀ(aʀ)-
NSY nuluʀ- 'beckon, lure' [ANLC nuluʀaʀ-]
CSY nuluʀ- 'fish through ice', nuluq 'ice-fishing gear, tea bag'
Sir —
SPI nulluaq-, Qaw nuluʀaq- 'gesture, wave to call attention'
NAI nuluʀaq-
WCI nuluʀaq-, Net nuluaqtuq- 'gesture, wave' [the second form Pryde, who also has Cop nulluaqtuq- 'wave s.th. to frighten an animal in a certain direction']
ECI nuluʀaq- 'gesture, wave to call attention'
GRI NG nuluʀaq-

PE nułu(ʀ) 'buttock
AAY nułuq 'buttock'
CAY nułuq
NSY nułuk 'buttocks'
CSY nułu 'buttock'
Sir nuła
SPI nuluq 'buttock'
NAI nuluq
WCI nuluq
ECI nuluq
GRI nuluq

PI nulluaq- 'hurt one's rump? [cf. ŋaʀ-]
Yup [note AAY nułuqqaʀ- 'sit down suddenly']
SPI —
NAI nulluaq- 'fall and hurt buttocks' [see nuluq- for homonym meaning 'break snowshoe webbing']
WCI [note Car B. Lake nulluaq- 'be sticking out, stand alone (mountain)' — Schn.]
ECI nullua(q)- 'hit on the rump'
GRI [note nułłuaʀ- 'lie on surface and sleep (seal)' — contam. with nullaq-?]

PE nuna 'land' [cf. Aleut tana-X 'land, island, space, place, earth, ground, settlement, country']
AAY nuna 'land, place, earth, village, country'
CAY nuna 'land, place, earth, village, country' [and luna reported in Curtis for Nun]
NSY nuna
CSY nuna [and suna 'soil, dirt']
Sir —
SPI nuna
NAI nuna 'land, earth, inland' [and nunaaqqiq 'village']
WCI nuna 'land' [and note Car EP nunataq 'higher ground']
ECI nuna 'land'
GRI nuna 'land, earth, dwelling place' [and note nunataq 'nunatak, mountain peak rising through inland ice', NG nuna- 'camp for the night', EG nunat 'land, country, earth' acc. Robbe and Menn.; note also EG nunat 'dandelions' (compare NG nunaʀluit 'vegetation'), and nunakkaaq 'stone' — nunaq acc. Holm]

PE nunałit- 'land' [cf. łit- and EA tanalit- 'run aground (ship)']
AAY —
CAY nunałitə-, nunitə- 'run aground'
NSY —
CSY —
Sir —
SPI —
NAI nunalit-, nunnit- 'reach land after being lost or drifting on ice'
WCI nunalit- 'land'
ECI nunalit- 'go inland' [Saul; Schn. has nunalitsa(k)- 'prowl around human dwellings (wolf, bear)']
GRI nunalit-, nunnit- 'land'

PY nunaŋitə- 'be restless' [cf. ŋit-]
AAY niniłkiʀ-, niŋiłkiʀ- 'play around, clown around'
CAY nunitə-, HBC ninitə- 'be restless' [and NSU nuniatə- 'be queasy']
NSY —
CSY nunaŋitə- 'not have enough room'

PI nunaʀžak or **nunaʀžaq** 'seal's den under surface of snow'
SPI —
NAI —
WCI Cop nunaʀyak, Net nunaɣžak 'den of seal beneath the snow beside breathing hole' [Pryde]
ECI nunaʀyaq 'ice shelf, lair where seal gives birth in extension of breathing hole'
GRI nunaʀsaq 'hollow in ice where seal lies'

PY nunatə- 'go to visit another settlement' [cf. t-[2], in the purely Yup sense of 'go to', and compare nunat-]
AAY nunatə- 'go to visit another town or village'
CAY nunatə-
NSY nunatə- 'visit from one village to another' [ANLC; Men. has nunataq 'person from another settlement']
CSY —

PI nunatqan 'fellow countryman' [cf. p.b. qan]
Yup [compare predictable nunalɣun with lɣun in this meaning in all Yup]
SPI —
NAI —
WCI Cop nuatqat, Sig nunaq(q)at 'fellow countryman' [the former also Net acc. Ras.]
ECI nunaqqati 'fellow countryman'
GRI nunaqqat

PE nunavaɣ or **nunavaʀ** 'walrus on ice' [cf. vaʀ-, contam. with vaɣ?]
AAY —
CAY —
NSY nunavaq 'walrus asleep on ice'
CSY nunavak 'walrus on ice'
Sir —
SPI nunavak
NAI nunavak
WCI —
ECI —
GRI —

PE nunivaɣ 'tundra (vegetation)' [seems to be a reformulation of nunapiɣ with p.b. piɣ — compare CAY nunapik and NAI nunavik below, otherwise cf. vaɣ]
AAY —
CAY [note place name Nunivaaq, also nunapik 'tundra'; for NSK nunataʀ- 'pluck greens' see unataʀ- under una-]
NSY nunivak 'rosewort' [L.-T. — ANLC 'roseroot, vegetation']
CSY nunivak 'tundra, roseroot plant' [and note nunavi- 'pluck greens']
Sir —
SPI nunivak- 'gather greens, pick berries' [Imaq as nom. 'leaf'; note Qaw nunavik 'large fertile area']
NAI [nunavik 'rolling tundra']
WCI [Ras. has Sig nunavaaq 'mainland' and Pryde has Car nunivaɣaq 'type of mouse' for B. Lake]
ECI nunivak- 'pick berries, collect clams' [and nunivaat 'berries or clams collected']
GRI nuniaɣ- 'pluck berries' [and nuniaat 'gathered berries (or basket to put them in)', NG nunivaaq 'leaf of willow shrub']

PE nunni- 'settle' [cf. p.b. li-[1]]
AAY —
CAY nuni- 'settle'
NSY —
CSY —
Sir —
SPI —
NAI nunni- 'acquire land'
WCI —
ECI —
GRI nunni- 'arrive in country or land, settle'

PY nunaki- 'enjoy oneself' [cf. nuna and nunanniʀ-]
AAY —
CAY Nun nunaki-, HBC nunakili- 'enjoy oneself'
NSY nunaki- 'enjoy oneself' [Em.]
CSY nunaki- 'enjoy oneself'
Sir [for nuŋəniqə(s)- 'enjoy oneself' see nunanniʀ-]
Inu [SPI nunaɣi- 'enjoy oneself', nunaɣinaq- 'be enjoyable' are probably from the Yup]

PE nunanniʀ- 'be enjoyable' [cf. nunaki-, nuna and n(n)iʀ-, with dissim. in Inu]
AAY nunaniʀ- 'be fun', nunaniqsaaɣ- 'have fun'
CAY nunaniq 'delight, happiness', nunaniXqə- 'be pleasant'
NSY nunaniʀ- 'be interesting', nunaniq 'fun' [ANLC; Men. has nunanilʀia 'interesting (thing)', nunaniXsaʀ- 'decorate']
CSY nunaniq 'enjoyable thing'
Sir [nuŋəniqə(s)- 'enjoy oneself' — Vakh. from Rub.'s texts]
SPI nunaɣi- 'enjoy oneself' [Jen. has nuanniq- 'be pleasant, enjoyable']
NAI —
WCI [Pet. has ananau- 'be beautiful' for Sig]
ECI [note Baf. aananau- 'be beautiful, cause to rejoice (biblical)', aanaugi- 'find beautiful', aanauniq 'beauty', and Lab aananak 'the beautiful' — Peck]
GRI nuanniʀ- 'be enjoyable' [and nuannaaʀ- 'be happy', nuannaʀi- 'like, be happy about' — with nnaq-; note also NG nannaat 'that's great!']

PI nunaŋiak 'alder' [cf. nuna]
SPI nunaŋiak 'alder'
NAI nunaŋiak 'red outer layer of willows used for drying hide, alder' [verbal = 'dye with willow dye']
WCI —

ECI —
GRI nunaŋiak 'alder, red fir bark (driftwood)' [and nunaŋiaɣ- 'dye (skin with red fir bark)'; the homonym meaning 'be dissatisfied with one's residence' contains ŋiaɣ under ŋiɣ- instead]

PI nunat- 'cache or accumulate' [cf. nuna and presumably t-[1], also Aleut tanat- 'bury, put in ground']
Yup — [for CAY nunatə- 'visit from village to village' see nunatə- under nuna]
SPI —
NAI nunat- 'cache (esp. caribou meat in a hole)'
WCI Sig nuat- 'accumulate, heap up' [with dissimilation; Pet. has nuamayut 'assembly']
ECI nuat- 'accumulate' [nuama- 'be assembled']
GRI —

PI nunataq 's.th. buried in ground' [cf. ðaʀ]
Yup [for NSY nunataq 's.o. from another settlement' see nunatə- under nuna]
SPI —
NAI nunataq 'meat cached in hole dug in ground and covered with sod'
WCI nunatat 'things cached in ground'
ECI —
GRI [for nunataq 'nunatak' see nuna]

PI nuniq or **nunəq** 'female jar seal'
SPI —
NAI —
WCI Sig nuniq 'mate of male stinking seal' [Pryde]
ECI Igl nuniq 'cow jar seal' [Pryde]
GRI —

PE nunu(ʀ)- 'squeeze or pinch together'
AAY —
CAY nunuʀ- 'pinch' [and note nuŋutə-, Nun nunutə- 'fasten (e.g. button), sew together', the former by contam. with nuŋiʀtə-?]
NSY nunutə- 'sew together, repair'
CSY nunuʀ- 'pinch' [and nunuXtuʀ- 'choke, strangle']
Sir —
SPI W nunu- 'restrain oneself' [Jen.]
NAI nunuq- 'pinch, tighten', nunu- 'restrain oneself from saying s.th. or expressing a desire' [trans. of the latter = nunut-; also nunui- 'choke, throttle']
WCI nunut- 'pinch together the two sides of an opening to close it'
ECI Lab nunu- 'hold to oneself' [Peck has 'restrain']
GRI nunu- 'restrain oneself, force oneself to do, refrain from', nunut-, nunuʀ- 'make narrower', NG nunuq- 'squeeze between thumb and finger'

PY nunuʀ- 'scold' [Al. tunu- 'sound, speak, say, scold, babble, roar, chirp, etc.', Bering Island 'swear, use dirty words' (Golovko), tunu-X 'word, meaning, language']
AAY nunuʀ- 'beat up, overpower'
CAY nunuʀ- 'scold', Nun also 'swear'
NSY —
CSY —
Inu [SPI nunuq- 'scold' is probably from the Yup]

PY-S nuŋiʀtə- 'fasten with drawstring'
AAY Kod nuŋiXtə-, C yuŋiXtə-, AP luŋiXtə- 'become pursed, closed with a drawstring'
CAY nuŋiXtə- 'fasten belt or drawstring' [nuŋiXta 'belt drawstring']
NSY nuŋiXtə- 'lace' [also nominal]
CSY nuŋiXtə- 'tie with drawstring' [nuŋiXta 'drawstring']
Sir nuŋiXta 'lace', nuŋiʀ- 'tie bootlaces' [Em.]

PI nuŋŋaq 'crack across s.th.?' [cf. nutəɣ- and/or nuləɣ-]
SPI —
NAI nuŋŋaq 'ridge along base of nose, crest, crown of bird'
WCI —
ECI —
GRI nuŋŋaʀut 'crack (across s.th.), vein in rock'

PI nuŋu- 'be used up'
Yup — [but note Nun nuŋu- 'be foggy'?]
Sir [note nuŋənamsi- 'doze off' — Vakh. from Men.'s texts]
SPI nuŋu- 'be used up'
NAI nuŋu- 'be used up, wear out, be new/old moon'
WCI nuŋu- 'be used up'
ECI nuŋu- 'be worn from use, wear out'
GRI nuŋu- 'be used up, disappear, be a new moon' [and note EG nuŋŋut(i) 'the last (of)' — Tersis]

PI nuŋut- 'use up' [cf. t-[1]]
SPI nuŋut- 'use up, finish'
NAI nuŋut- 'use up' [and PH nuŋŋit- 'finish']
WCI nuŋut- 'finish'
ECI nuŋut- 'finish, be finished' [and nuŋulla(q)- 'wear out by rubbing'
GRI nuŋut- 'finish, be finished' [nuŋułłaʀ- 'be worn down']

PE nuqaʀ- 'tighten' [cf. nuqət-]
AAY —
CAY —
NSY nuqaXtə '(bow)string'
CSY Chap nuqaXta 'spring'
Sir —
SPI nuʀaqti '(bow)string'
NAI nuqaq- 'be taut', nuqaqtɨ 'bowstring'
WCI nuqaqtaq 'violin string' [and note nuqqaqtaq- 'whip (esp. a man)' — contam. from nulqaʀ-?]
ECI nuqaq- 'tighten, contract muscles', nuqaqti 'spring'
GRI nuqaʀ- 'tighten, have an attack of cramp, be excited about s.th.', nuqaʀti '(bow)string', EG nuʀaʀ- 'tie, bind to s.th.', nuʀaalaq 'dog trace' [and nuqqaʀtaat 'whip' and nuqqiłłaɣ- 'be tightened, fastened', with contam. from nulqaʀ- and/or nuqət-]

PE nuqðaʀ 'throwing board (for harpoon)' [cf. nuqət-]
AAY nuqaq 'spear-throwing device' [B.-S. and older word lists]
CAY nuqaq
NSY —

CSY —
Sir —
SPI nuqšaq 'throwing board'
NAI Nu nuqšaq 'throwing board' [also Barrow acc. Jen. and Mal acc. Ras.]
WCI Sig nuqsaq 'throwing board' [also Car in B.-S]
ECI nutsaq, Igl nuʀsaq 'throwing board' [Saul and B.-S. respectively, the second also Peck for Lab]
GRI nuʀšaq 'throwing board'

PE nuqət- 'pull or hold back' [cf. nuqaʀ-]
AAY nuqtə- 'pull'
CAY nuq(ə)tə-
NSY —
CSY nuqətə- 'have fortitude, refrain from s.th. one feels like doing' [and nuqŋ̥əʀ- 'hold on (lest one fall)']
Sir [Em. has nuqət- 'hold back, delay']
SPI nuʀit- 'tug'
NAI nuqɨt- 'pull' [and nuqɨttaužžaq-, nuqiittaužžaq- 'pull at tug-of-war']
WCI nuqit- 'pull'
ECI nuqit- 'hold back with cable, etc.' [and nuqippuut(i)- 'play tug-of-war']
GRI nuqit- 'hold s.th. back, pull toward self, stand on stanchions of sled' [nuqqut(i)-, nuqquʀuut(i)- 'pull at tug-of-war']

PE nuʀaʀ(aʀ) 'nephew or niece of woman (through her sister)' [cf. nuʀʀaʀ, nužə and nukaʀ]
AAY —
CAY nuXXaq 'nephew or niece of a female through her sister' [from *nuʀaʀaq]
NSY —
CSY nuXaq 'woman's nephew or niece through sister'
Sir nuʀaX 'child' [Vakh. from Rub.'s texts; for nu 'son' see nukaʀ]
SPI [for nuɣaɣa 'my sister's child' acc. Jen. see nukaʀ]
NAI nuaʀaaluk 'nephew or niece of woman through her sister'
WCI nuaq, nuaʀaaluk 'sister's child (of woman)' [Pryde has nuaq for Car and Sig, nuʀʀaq for Net and Cop]
ECI nuaq 'sister's child (of woman)'
GRI nuaʀaluaq, EG nuʀ̃aalivaq

PE nuʀʀaʀ 'caribou calf' [cf. nuʀaʀ(aʀ)]
AAY nuʀaq, PWS nuwaq 'caribou calf'
CAY nuʀaq
NSY nuʀaq
CSY nuʀaq
Sir nuʀaX
SPI Qaw nuʀʀaq, KI nuʀʀayuaq
NAI nuʀʀaq*
WCI nuʀʀaq
ECI nuʀʀaq
GRI nuXXaq*

PE nutaʀ- 'renew' [there may be a link to nukaʀ, and cf. also p.b. taaq(-)]
AAY ➡
CAY ➡
NSY nutaXtə- 'renew'
CSY nutaXtə-
Sir nutaʀ- 'renew'
SPI ➡
NAI nutaq- 'renew, repair' [and note nutau- 'be young, new']
WCI ➡
ECI ➡
GRI nutaʀtiʀ- 'renew' [and nutaʀniq*, nutaʀmiq* 'new ice']

PY nuta(C)an 'just now' [cf. iŋilʀaan under iŋilʀa-]
AAY nutaan 'just now'
CAY nutaan 'exclamation expressing that s.th. good has just happened'
NSY nutaan 'just now'
CSY nutaan 'exclam. expressing that s.th. desired has just happened'

PI nutaʀaq 'child' [cf. nutaʀaʀ below, but with qaʀ?]
SPI nutaʀaq 'young person'
NAI nutaʀaq
WCI nutaʀaq 'infant' [Dor. has utaʀaq 'child' for Ahiarmiut Car]
ECI NBI, SB, Iti nutaʀaq, Lab nutagak 'infant'
GRI nutaʀaq 'young dog, young and inexperienced person'

PE nutaʀaʀ 'new thing'
AAY nuta<ʀ>aq 'new one'
CAY nutaʀaq 'new, fresh thing (e.g. fish)'
NSY nutaʀinʀaq 'new or young person or thing'
CSY nutaʀaq 'new thing'
Sir nutəʀ(ə)cəX 'new' [Vakh. has nutaʀžaX]
SPI nutaaq 's.th. new'
NAI nutaaq
WCI nutaaq 's.th. new' [and Pryde has nutaʀaq 'newly packled snow suitable for building snowhouse' for Net]
ECI nutaaq 'new thing, bit of news'
GRI nutaaq 'new (thing)'

PE nutəɣ- 'crack or explode' [cf. nuləɣ-]
AAY nutəɣ- 'shoot' [and nutək 'gun', nut<ɣ>aXtə- 'burst open']
CAY nutəɣ- 'shoot, explode, leap (spark from fire)' [and nutək 'gun']
NSY nutəɣ- 'jump'
CSY —
Sir —
SPI nutik- 'jump, leap'
NAI nutɨk-
WCI nutik- 'crack in heat'
ECI nutik- 'crack, break'
GRI nutiɣ- 'crack, burst' [and nuttaq(*) 'crack' — old ortho. nugtaq, with spurious g]

PI nuttak- 'crackle' [cf. nəɣ-]
SPI nuttak- 'keep jumping'
NAI nuttaɣaq-
WCI nuttak- 'crackle (ice cracking, wood in fire)'
ECI nuttalak- 'crack, snap' [and nutaraq- 'crackle

(fire), splutter (water in hot oil)', but SB nuktak-, NBI nuktaq- 'crack' acc. Dor.]
GRI nuttaɣ-, nuttaʀ- 'crack' [and note nutaʀaaluɣ- 'crackle, splutter, send off sparks']

PE nutəm 'always (from the beginning)'
AAY —
CAY nutəm 'from the beginning, originally'
NSY —
CSY nutəm 'like this from the beginning, always' [in Chap also 'it appeared (then)']
Sir [Vakh. has nutəm 'and so (then, there)' as in Chap]
SPI nutim 'originally, from the beginning'
NAI nutɨm
WCI Sig nutim 'really' [Ras. says that it intensifies or vivifies a statement]
ECI nuti 'see!' [Schn., who marks it as 'rare'; also Bourq. for Lab]
GRI —

PY nutŋaʀ- 'throb' [cf. nutəɣ- and ŋaʀ-^{2}?]
AAY nutŋaʀ- 'throb, pulse, beat (heart)'
CAY nutŋaʀ- 'throb' [nutŋaq 'pulse, heartbeat']
NSY —
CSY —

nuuniq 'porcupine' [an Athabaskan loan (note that it occurs in only two disconnected Eskimo areas, whereas it is in contiguous Ath. areas) — cf. Koyukon nu:nə, Inland Tanaina ni:ni:, Kuskokwim Ingalik neš:neš: 'porcupine']
AAY Kod nuuniq 'porcupine'
CAY NSK nuuniq
NSY —
CSY —

PE nuvaɣ 'saliva' [or *n^{y}uvaɣ; cf. nəvɣuʀ, though the relat. is obscure]
AAY C nuaxłuk, K nauxłuk 'saliva' [and nuayaaq 'slime']
CAY nuak, Nun, HBC nuvak 'saliva' [Jen. has 'cough' for Nun; compare ŋəvva (underling əŋva) 'mucus']
NSY nuvak 'saliva'
CSY nuvak 'saliva' [and nuvaxłuk '(fish) slime']
Sir yuvəx 'saliva' [and yuvaxłux '(fish) slime' — Orr]
SPI nuak, nuakłuk 'phlegm, mucus from cold' [Imaq nuɣaq 'saliva'; nuak- 'have a cold']
NAI nuvak- 'have a cold' [nom. = 'cold, mucus']
WCI nuvak 'saliva, saliva and sputum from a cold in the throat' [Sig also 'cold', nuvak- 'have a cold']
ECI nuvak 'saliva from a cold', nuvak- 'have a cold'
GRI nuak 'saliva', nuaɣ- 'have a cold' [and nuffaʀłiuʀ- 'suffer from a cold', nuałłuk 'influenza']

PY-S nuvakataq 'kind of kelp'
AAY —
CAY —
NSY nuvakataq 'blade kelp, sea tangle (laminaria)' [ANLC]
CSY nuvakatak 'type of kelp'
Sir [Vakh. has yuvəkətaX 'kind of grass?' from Men.'s texts]

PE nuvə- 'thread' [or *n^{y}uvə-]
AAY nuɣə- 'thread'
CAY nuvə-
NSY nuvə-
CSY nuuvə-
Sir yuvə- 'thread' [Vakh.; Men. has yuvit(ə)- 'thread, push through']
SPI nui- 'thread'
NAI nuvi-
WCI nuvi-
ECI nuvi-
GRI nui-, nuffit- 'pass thread through eye of needle', NG nui- 'harness dogs to sled' [NG also nuɣɣissaaq- 'unharness']

PI nuviqšaq- 'knit' [cf. ðaʀ-?]
Yup [note CSY nuvəšaʀ-, nəvəšaʀ- 'knit', a parallel derivation?]
SPI —
NAI nuviqšaq- 'thread one's way among'
WCI Cop nuviXXaq- 'knit'
ECI nuviʀsa(q)-
GRI nuiʀšaʀ- 'knit, sew basket, darn socks, pass in and out several times'

PI nuvvin 'line (for stringing fish)' [cf. un]
Yup [note CAY nuvun 'threading device', a parallel derivative]
SPI —
NAI nuvvin^y 'line used to string fish'
WCI —
ECI nuvviti 'long rope joining all dogs to sled, rawhide rope or stick on which fish are strung'
GRI nuffit 'line used to string fish or beads on', NG nuɣɣit 'foremost part of sled strap to which dog traces are attached'

PI nuviya 'cloud' [cf. nuvə-]
SPI W nuiya 'cloud' [Jen.]
NAI nuviya, nuvuya 'cloud'
WCI nuvuya 'cloud' [nuvuya- 'be cloudy']
ECI nuvuya(q) 'cloud' [Ras. also has nuviya; nuvuya- 'be cloudy']
GRI nuvuyaq, EG nuiaq, NG nuiɣaq 'cloud' [WG pl. nuiššat, the šš not historical; nuia- 'be cloudy']

PE nuvuɣ 'point or tip' [or *n^{y}uvuɣ]
AAY C nuɣu(k) 'tip'
CAY nuuk, Nun, HBC nuvuk 'point, tip' [and Ras. has Nun nuukataX 'naze']
NSY nuuk 'naze' [Ras.; note also the place name nuvuqaq 'Naukan' = Inu, CAY nuuʀaq]
CSY nuvuk 'point, tip'
Sir yuvəłqəX 'point, tip, top' [Vakh.]
SPI Qaw nuukataq 'point of land' [Jen. and Ras. both have nuuk for W]
NAI nuvuk 'point, tip'
WCI nuvuk
ECI nuvuk
GRI nuuk 'point (esp. of land)' [and as place name 'Godthaab']

PE nuyaʀ 'hair' [or perhaps *n^{y}uyaʀ]
AAY nuyaq 'hair'
CAY nuyaq
NSY nuyaq
CSY nuyaq
Sir nuyəX [Miller has yuyəX]
SPI nuyaq
NAI nuyaq [pl. nutsat]
WCI nuyaq
ECI nuyaq 'hair' [nuyappi(C)- 'have dissheveled hair']
GRI nuyaq, pl. nutsat 'hair' [and note nuyappiɣ- 'have dissheveled hair']

PE nuyuɣ- 'move away or be wary (wild animal)'
AAY [note nuuya- 'hide']
CAY nuyuXtaʀ- 'be wild'
NSY nuyuXtaʀ- 'be wary (animal)' [ANLC]
CSY nuyaaʀ-, nuyuXtuʀ- 'be timid, wary'
Sir —
SPI Qaw nuyuaq- 'be wary, timid', nuyuaqtu-, KI nuyatu- 'be wild' [and KI nuyaq- 'sense danger']
NAI nuyuaʀi- 'be wary of', nuyuaqtu- 'be timid, weary (animal)', PH nuyuɣaq- 'stalk'
WCI nuyuaqtuq 'wild animal that flees' [Lowe has Sig nuyuaqtuyuq, which for Met. is 'very wild']
ECI nuyuaq- 'be shy, wild'
GRI nuyuɣ- 'move to another place (animal)', nuyuaʀ- 'be shy (animal)'

PE nuyuɣit- 'be tame' [cf. ŋit-]
AAY —
CAY nuyuitə-, nuyuXitə- 'be tame' [the latter form from *nuyuɣaʀitə-?]
NSY —
CSY [nuyaaʀitə- 'not be timid']
Sir —
SPI Qaw nuyuit-, KI nuyaŋit- 'be fearless (animal)'
NAI nuyuit- 'be tame'
WCI nuyuit-
ECI nuyuit- 'be tame' [and nuyuisiq 'animal that often approaches hunter', nuyuisiʀviɣi- 'come close to (hunter, of animal)']
GRI nuyuit- 'be tame' [and nuyuisiʀ- 'approach (wild animal threatening to attack), threaten']

PI nuyuqqak- 'become wild or shy'
Yup — [but note CAY nuyuXqə- 'scare away (animals)']
SPI —
NAI nuyuqqak- 'be timid (animal)'
WCI —
ECI —
GRI nuyuqqaɣ- 'become timid, become wild (domestic animal)'

PY-S nužə 'elder sibling?' [cf. nuðiʀ, also Aleut luða-a '(his) older brother, (her) older sister', with dissimilation of n to l?]
AAY —
CAY —
NSY —
CSY nuyəkłiq* 'oldest (e.g. son)'
Sir nuca, nucəX 'older brother' [also nuskiX in Men.'s texts; nucəX is either younger or older brother in Rub.'s texts — Vakh.; for nu 'son' see nukaʀ]

P

PE pa(C)a- 'fight or struggle' [cf. patəɣ- and pasi-]
AAY paa- 'flap wings against surface of water (bird taking off)'
CAY —
NSY —
CSY [note pałuxtə- 'thrash around', and patimə- 'flap wings against water (bird)']
Sir [Orr has pałuxtə- 'thrash around', probably from CSY]
SPI —
NAI paa- 'have a convulsion, close in spasm (jaw, fist), block someone's way', PH 'fall forward, fall down flat on, pin down, pounce on' [the latter perhaps influenced by paŋałłaɣ-; note also paatcui- 'toss goodies for a scramble', pauq- 'flap wings while landing on water (bird)' and Mal pałuq- 'capsize']
WCI paa- 'fight'
ECI paa- 'beat, bite at wound in rage (bear)' [and paɣɣiniq 'wound, tear', paɣɣit- 'scrape skin, wound, become cold (house or garment)']
GRI paa- 'fight', NG 'attack' [the latter also Fab.; half-trans. paanniɣ-; note also paxxit(i)- (Ordbogi) 'fight (intr. plural)', paxxat(i)- 'fight over, scramble for s.th.' and paaʀtuʀ- 'flap wings flying over water' — compare pattattuʀ- under pattaɣ-]

PE pa(C)aməʀ- and **pa(C)ammaɣ-** 'crawl' [cf. paŋaləɣ- and paŋałłaɣ-]
AAY — [for paŋaləɣ- 'crawl' see paŋaləɣ- 'run on four legs']
CAY —
NSY paamaʀ- 'crawl, flicker (flame)' [ANLC; Orr also paamə- 'crawl']
CSY —
Sir —
SPI paamak-, Qaw paamʀuq-
NAI paamiq- 'keep close to ground', paammak-, paamʀuq- 'crawl'
WCI paamak- 'have face close to ground', paamʀuq-, H. Island Cop paamŋuq- 'crawl' [Lowe]
ECI paammak- 'lie prone', paaʀŋu(q)- 'crawl'
GRI paamaaʀ- 'be slow', paaʀᴍuʀ-, paaʀŋuʀ-, Up paaʀ̃uʀ-, EG paaʀɴuʀ- 'crawl' [NG pauʀŋuq-, corresponding to old ortho. WG paorngor-, as also in Fab. — the u perhaps reflects the *m; note also EG paaʀ̃alaaʀ- 'take one's time' and paaʀɴuaʀ- 'drift (snow)' — the latter from Holm]

PE paci- 'blame'
AAY paci- 'blame, accuse'
CAY paci(kə)- 'blame, accuse, suspect'

NSY pasi- 'suspect' [Em.]
CSY pasikə- 'blame, find fault with, accuse'
Sir — [for pasi- 'hit' see pasi-]
SPI pazi- 'blame, accuse'
NAI pasi- 'blame, accuse, suspect'
WCI patsi- 'blame, suspect'
ECI pasi- 'suspect, accuse' [Iti half-trans. pasinna(C)-]
GRI pasi- 'suspect' [half-trans. pasinniɣ-; pasiłłiʀ- 'accuse of s.th.']

PI patcin 'reason or excuse' [cf. un]
SPI passin 'reason, excuse'
NAI patcin[y], patcisɨ
WCI —
ECI patsiti 'excuse, alibi, s.o. accused or suspected of a misdeed'
GRI patsit 'reason, excuse'

PI pacik- 'get scorched'
SPI paziaq-, Qaw pasik- 'get scorched'
NAI pasik- 'get scorched', pasiaq- 'warm oneself (e.g. by fire)'
WCI Sig pasik- 'be hot (weather)' [and pasiaʀsiun 'hot-water bottle']
ECI —
GRI —

PE paðə 'opening or entrance' [there may be a relat. to paðəʀ- and more remotely to dem. roots paɣ-, pam-, etc.; cf. Aleut haðɣ-iX 'channel, narrow entrance to bay', haðɣa 'its channel']
AAY pai 'opening, mouth (of thing)'
CAY pai
NSY payə
CSY paya [pl. payət]
Sir paca [Vakh. from Men. and Rub.]
SPI paa 'entrance, opening, mouth'
NAI paa
WCI paa
ECI paa
GRI paaq 'opening, entrance, mouth, manhole of kayak', EG also 'clam' [and paasi- 'understand' — compare tukeci- under tukə-]

PE paðəʀ- 'meet' [cf. Aleut haða- 'direction toward']
AAY paiXtə- 'meet, encounter'
CAY paiXtə-
NSY payəʀ- 'meet'
CSY payəʀ- [and paaqutə- 'face (each other)'; note pasqamənu- 'go to meet' — Vakh. has pasqaʀ- 'go to meet' and, from Rub.'s texts, pažəl(səmə)-, pažvəXaʀutəqə- 'approach']
Sir pasqaʀət(ə)- 'meet' [from CSY?]
SPI paaq- 'meet' [and pažʀuti- 'meet up with']
NAI paaq- 'go to meet (s.o. as they arrive), travel into (wind, current)' [and pažʀuti- 'meet each other']
WCI paaq- 'meet' [and Cop palʀi- 'go to meet']
ECI paaq- 'meet' [and pa(a)ʀʀia(q)- 'go to meet'; Andersen et al. have patjaluuti- 'pass without seeing each other' for Lab]
GRI paaʀ- 'go to meet' [half.-trans. paaʀniɣ-; and note paššaʀłuɣ- 'miss, go past without seeing']

PI paaqlak- 'pass in the opposite direction' [cf. łłaɣ-?]
SPI paaqłak- 'disobey'
NAI paaqłak-
WCI —
ECI —
GRI paaʀłaɣ- 'pass in opposite direction, take s.o.'s place, fold hands', EG paaʀsaC- 'pass in opposite direction', NG paaʀlak-', cross s.o.'s path, meet on way'

PI paaqtuq- 'go (continually) toward s.th.' [cf. tuʀ-[2]?]
SPI paaqtuq- 'go to meet, go into wind'
NAI paaqtuq- 'come directly through door or flap (wind)', Nu 'travel into wind', PH 'go to meet'
WCI —
ECI paaqtu(q)- 'blow right through entrance of snow house (wind)'
GRI —

PE paðəʀcaʀ- 'go to meet' [cf. caʀ-]
AAY —
CAY paiXsaaɣ- 'go out to meet'
NSY —
CSY —
Sir —
SPI —
NAI paaqsaaq- 'encounter, experience'
WCI paaqsaq- 'pass (s.o.) coming in opposite direction', Cop 'challenge to fight' [and Schn. has paqsaq- 'go to meet, suspect, calumniate' for B. Lake]
ECI paaʀsaa(q)- 'go to meet' [and paʀsaʀiaqtu(q)- 'go to look for s.o. thought lost']
GRI [paʀsiaʀ-, paaʀsiaʀtuʀ-, NG paXXiaq-, EG paʀtiaʀ- 'go to meet' — all from *pa(a)ʀsaʀiaq(tuq)-]

PE paðviɣ 'wrist' [cf. paðəʀ- and ðviɣ?]
AAY K paswik 'ankle'
CAY Nun pasvix 'metacarpel in walrus flipper' [ANLC]
NSY pavžik 'joint of feet'
CSY [note paasłiq 'lower part of arm (esp. of garment)', paasłitaq 'wedge for splitting wood']
Sir —
SPI —
NAI paɣvik 'knee bone of seal' [for pažvik 'chopping block' see pasi-]
WCI —
ECI pavvik 'multiple boney articulation of many small bones such as the wrist, the feet, etc.'
GRI paffik, paššik, NG passik 'wrist'

PY pa(C)əvtə- 'prepare (for use)' [there may be a link to payuɣ-; compare na(C)əvə(t)- for the vowels]
AAY KP paixtə-, K paix[w]tə- 'get ready (to go)' [for PWS payuxtə- in this sense see payuɣ- — contam.?]
CAY paiftə-, Nun paftə- 'put where it can be used or seen' [for Nun payixtə- 'take supplies on ahead' see payug-]

NSY piaftə- 'prepare s.th. for, take food to s.o., put out for use'
CSY piiftə- 'set out for use'

PE paɣi- 'stay at home and look after house'
AAY pai- 'stay behind (and watch over baby)'
CAY pai-
NSY pia- 'stay behind (and watch over things)' [Em.]
CSY paɣi- 'stay behind (and watch over things)'
Sir paɣiti- 'nurse (child)'
SPI pai- 'stay at home'
NAI pa<ɣ>i-
WCI pai- 'stay at home' [and paiyiɣi- 'leave one's companion in the house']
ECI pai- 'stay at home, look after house' [and paiʀi- 'look after', paɣɣitatsaq 'food put aside for those who stay home', Lab paitsiC- 'look after', paiffik 'hospital']
GRI paa-, NG pai-, EG paaʀsi- 'be alone in house' [and paaʀi- (half-trans. paaʀši-), paaqqi- 'look after (e.g. child)', NG paɣɣit 'provisions for a waiting period (while hunter is away)']

PY-S paɣitə- 'inherit' [cf. t-[1]]
AAY paitaq 'inheritance'
CAY paitaq
NSY —
CSY paɣitə- 'inherit'
Sir paɣətaʀnəʀə- 'give as an inheritance' [Vakh. from Men.'s texts]

PE paɣnəʀ 'caribou bull'
AAY —
CAY [Turner's list for NS has pûngnûk 'bull caribou']
NSY paŋniq 'caribou bull' [ANLC]
CSY —
Sir [note paɣnəX 'maternal uncle']
SPI Qaw paŋniq 'old bull caribou'
NAI paɣniq* 'bull caribou'
WCI paŋniq 'male ruminant'
ECI panniq 'caribou bull'
GRI panniq*

PI paɣna(a)ʀyuk 'maternal uncle' [cf. yuɣ?]
Sir [note paɣnəX 'maternal uncle' under paɣnəʀ above]
SPI [Jen. has paɣnaʀyuk 'woman's father's brother' for W]
NAI [Jen. has paɣnaʀyuk 'woman's father's brother']
WCI Cop paɣnaaʀyuk 'uncle on father's side' [Lowe]
ECI —
GRI —

PE paɣu(la) 'soot'
AAY paula(q) 'ashes'
CAY paulaq 'spark from fire'
NSY —
CSY paɣula 'dust' [and Men. 1954 has paɣuq 'ripples on sea' for Chap]
Sir paɣula 'dust'
SPI paulaq, pau 'soot'
NAI paula 'soot'
WCI paula, pauq
ECI pauq 'soot' [paulaŋiq- 'remove soot from']
GRI paaq 'soot, (gun)powder' [and paxxiʀ- 'be sooted up', EG paaʀnaalak 's.th. dirty', NG paulaŋiit 'ramrod']

PE paɣuɣ- 'fasten down with pegs'
AAY pauk 'frame supporting roof of deadfall' [B.-S.]
CAY pauɣ- 'put a post in ground', pauk, pauɣun 'post, pole' [and note paukə- 'depend on']
NSY paawaʀ- 'stake out a sealskin on the snow to bleach it' [ANLC]
CSY paɣutə- 'pound a stake into the ground' [Orr]
Sir paɣutə- 'pound a stake into the ground' [Orr]
SPI pauɣaq 'peg, tent stake'
NAI pauk- 'stake to ground', also 'sting (insect)', pauɣaq 'big stake' [pauɣun, pauktuun 'tool for flattening arrows' — Jen.]
WCI pauk- 'fasten with peg, ram in stake', also 'sting (insect)' [pauɣaq 'peg for tent, etc.']
ECI pauɣuaq 'peg'
GRI paaɣ- 'fasten with a peg' [paaɣuaq 'guard holding sealing bladder in place on kayak', paaɣut, EG paaʀ̃it 'peg']

PI pauktuq- 'stake out skin to dry' [cf. tuʀ-[2]]
SPI pauktuun 'stake, peg for drying skin'
NAI pauktuq- 'be putting stakes in', Nu 'stake to ground (skin)'
WCI pauktuq- 'stake out to dry (skin)' [pauktutit 'stakes for stretching and drying skin']
ECI pauttu(q)- 'stake out with pegs' [and pauttuutit 'stakes for drying skin']
GRI paattuʀ- 'stake out to dry (skin)' [paattuut 'stake']

PE paɣunʀaʀ 'berry' [cf. p.b. n(ə)ʀaʀ(aʀ) and perhaps paɣuɣ-; note that all common names below probably signify *Empetrum nigrum*]
AAY —
CAY Eg, Nun, Y, NS paunʀaq* 'curlewberry'
NSY —
CSY paɣunʀaq 'curlewberry, berry'
Sir paɣnəʀəX 'berry' [Vakh. has paɣnəʀaX]
SPI paunʀaq 'crowberry'
NAI paunʀaq
WCI paunʀaq
ECI pauʀŋaq 'black camarine'
GRI paaʀŋaq, NWG paaʀnaq, SWG paaʀmaq 'berry', NG pauʀŋaq 'crowberry'

PI paunʀaqun 'juniper or crowberry bush? [cf. q(q)un]
SPI —
NAI paunʀaqutaq 'leaf of crowberry or blackberry'
WCI —
ECI pauʀŋaquti 'plant on which small black berries grow'
GRI paaʀŋaqutit, paaʀnaqutit, paaʀmaqutit

'crowberry, or ling berry' [and paaʀŋaquɫɫuk, etc., 'juniper bush']

PE pa(C)iʀ 'merganser' [cf. (C)iʀ?]
AAY paiq, paiXpak 'merganser, sawbill'
CAY payiq, payiXpak, Y paziq 'merganser'
NSY —
CSY [note payžuɣaq 'tufted puffin']
Sir [note paɣžuʀaX 'murre or merganser'? — Orr]
SPI pai 'merganser'
NAI paisuɣžuk
WCI pai
ECI Lab pai 'merganser' [Peck; Saul has paipasuk 'red-breated merganser' for Fort Chimo]
GRI paaq 'merganser'

PI pakak- 'knock into' [cf. pakiɣ-, with which there seems to be considerable entanglement, but also pa(C)a- and/or patəɣ-]
Yup [for CSY pakaɣ- 'pry with a lever' see pakiɣ-]
Sir [for pakaɣ(cəmə)- 'bend' see pakəɣ-]
SPI [Qaw pakak- 'rummage, search through things' — influenced by pakiɣ-?]
NAI [pakak- 'rummage through things, get into mischief', pakkaqtu- 'have habit of getting into everything' — influenced by pakiɣ-?]
WCI Sig pakaq- 'knock against and break' [Ras.; Pet. has 'go off (gun)', going with pakiɣ-?; and Met. has Sig paksak- 'touch things (child)'; Schn. has pakallak- 'touch and disturb everything (of child)' for 'adg']
ECI [note pakkii(C)- 'make someone drop s.th. by jostling him, pass and win'; Bourq. has paksaaq- 'fall' for Lab]
GRI pakaɣ-, pakamiɣ-, pakammiɣ- 'happen to jostle' [and note pakasaʀ- 'surprise, jostle', pakaksi- 'be disappointed', pakkiʀ- (old ortho. pagker-), NWG pakki- 'parry a thrust, jostle so as to make miss aim, tackle', EG pakki- 'slap ' — Robbe and Menn. have pakkiʀ- also as 'punch' for EG]

PE pakəɣ- 'bend or flex' [cf. pakiɣ-]
AAY —
CAY pakəxtə- 'start the upturn for the side of a basket'
NSY —
CSY pakəɣ- 'flex, bend (e.g. in old age)', pakəxtə- 'bend or flex at a joint, bend over forward' [and pakšəɣ- 'bend, curl, wrap, fold', pakšək 'curved carving knife']
Sir pakn̥əɣ- 'bend' [Vakh. from Men.'s texts but 'push away' in Rub.'s; Men. has pakaɣ(cəmə)- 'bend, bow down'; Vakh. also has pakaɣmətaləʀəX 'hunchbacked' from Rub. and pakaɣ-, pakaxtəXəʀ- 'pull legs up, curl up (body)' from Men.'s texts]
SPI paɣak- 'bend' [and pakši- 'hold on by fingers, pull trigger']
NAI —
WCI Baker Lake pakki 'finger twisted back' [Schn.]
ECI [note Lab pakik- 'perform sexual intercourse']
GRI [note pakkut 'prop for kayak support straps' and pakkut(i)- 'embrace']

PI pakəɣžumik- 'wrist wrestle' [cf. miɣ- and compare ažɣaɣmik- under aðɣa(ʀ)]
SPI —
NAI —
WCI Car BakerLake pakkiyɣumiut(i)- 'wrist wrestle' [Schn.; Pryde has Net pakilyu'miɣauti- 'pull arms' and pakiɣuŋmik- 'hook elbows in test of strength']
ECI pakayɣumiut(i)- 'compete at arm-pulling'
GRI pakaššit-, pakaššiumiɣ-, NG pakaxxaŋmik-

PE pakiɣ- 'dig finger(s) into or dig up?' [cf. pakəɣ-, pakaɣ-, and pəkutaq, with which there appears to be entanglement]
AAY [KP, Kod pakiɣ- 'go forward (boat), manage to reach (by pressing ahead)']
CAY pakiɣ- 'uncover by pulling back the top layer, go into ocean swimming'
NSY pakiɣ- 'pluck out, pick out, catch on' [ANLC; Men. has pakiɣžəʀuaʀ- 'dig', pakiɣvik 'support, hook, trigger'; for pəkuɣ- 'pry up' see pəkutaq]
CSY pakiɣ- 'hook one's hand onto and pull, grab much' [influenced by pakəɣ-?; note also pakaɣ- 'pry up with lever' — contam. with source of pakak-?; and pakaɣusiq 'lever']
Sir pakn̥iXqə(s)- 'dig out' [and Em. has pakəʀəsiʀaX 'lever']
SPI paɣik- 'scratch', Imaq also 'comb', pakši- 'hold on by fingers, pull trigger', Qaw pakik- 'pull the trigger'
NAI pakik- 'dig with hands or claws, pull the trigger' [in first sense also pakšaq-, PH paɣžaq-; Mal pakik-, pakak- 'search for' (the second form influenced by pakak-); note also pakkiq* 'hole, place dug out']
WCI pakik- 'scratch itself (of animal)' [and note pakkaq- 'make a hole through', pakkaq 'hole (right through)' — infl. by pakak-?]
ECI —
GRI ➟

PY paki(ɣ)uʀ- 'take a stroke' [cf. (C)uʀ-]
AAY pakiuʀ- 'row'
CAY pakiuʀ- 'take a stroke (swimming or paddling)'
NSY —
CSY —

PE pakinəɣ- 'hook or dig fingers into s.th.' [cf. nəɣ-?; compare SPI paɣik- and WCI pakik- under pakiɣ- above for the 'scratch' sense']
AAY pakinəɣ- 'scratch'
CAY —
NSY pakinəɣ- 'get scratched' [ANLC]
CSY pakinəɣ- 'scratch' [Men. has pakiŋuʀaq- for Chap]
Sir —
SPI —
NAI pakinʸik- 'pull toward self, pull oneself up, touch on shoulder'
WCI pakinik- 'pull the trigger, touch and pull' [Schn. has 'touch, catch, grasp' for 'adg', also pakinak- 'support with hand', and Ras. has pakinikturvik 'hand grip on kayak paddle' for Net]

ECI —
GRI NG pakinik- 'put forepaws on (edge of ice, of polar bear)' [and WG pakiniɣ-, pakaniɣ- 'lie with end across to weigh down (e.g. stone in wall)' — contam. with pakəɣ-?]

PE palaʀ- 'not give or get much'
AAY palaʀ- [plus negative] 'get plenty'
CAY palaʀ- 'not get or give enough' [and palaq 'it serves you right']
NSY palaXtə- 'wound, confuse, not pay in full, make mistake'
CSY palaʀ- 'not give or get enough', palaXtə- 'pacify' [and Chap palaXaq 'little']
Sir palaʀaXsəmələʀəX 'little' [Vakh.]
SPI palaq- 'not give enough'
NAI palaq- 'give or get less than one deserves, blame', Nu 'wrestle a bit, defeat effortlessly'
WCI Sig palaq- 'not give or get much', Car palaq- 'be good' [Ras], 'be calm, moderate' [Schn. 'adg'; and Net palait- 'be greedy' acc. Briggs]
ECI palaq- 'work badly' [and Spald. has NBI palaaqsi- 'become good (weather)']
GRI [NWG palak 'good', palaa-, panaa- 'be good' may also belong here, though it has been regarded as a borrowing from Norwegian-Danish bra, which means 'good' — perhaps a blend]

PI palaŋa- 'slacken or be loose' [cf. ŋa-[1]]
SPI —
NAI palaŋa- 'improve moderately (one's condition)'
WCI Sig palaŋa- 'be moderate, not very solid, not very strong (wind)', palaŋ(ŋ)aq- 'diminish'
ECI palaŋa- 'be loose, no longer held back' [Bourq. has pallak- 'make or become loose, not good', pallanga- 'not long-lasting, loose, open (door), apt to become ill', pallangaer- 'tighten, close' for Lab — compare Tar palaiq- 'lock' with the latter]
GRI palaŋŋaʀ- 'loosen (rheum)'

PE paliʀ- 'dry up or be tanned by the sun'
AAY paliXtə- 'sunburn'
CAY paliXtə- 'suntan'
NSY paliq 'sunburn, suntan' [and ANLC paliXtə- 'get sunburned']
CSY paliʀ- 'turn autumn colors, suntan'
Sir paliʀ- 'turn yellow'
SPI paliq- 'be dry' [and Jen. has W paliq- 'starve' — compare palu-]
NAI paliq- 'be dry'
WCI Cop paliq- 'dry up, waste away' [Jen.]
ECI paliq- 'go out for want of fuel (lamp or engine)', palli(q)- 'be dry' [and paliʀniq 'lamp that goes out for lack of fuel, suntanned person']
GRI paliʀ(sima)- 'be or make brown, sunburnt', paliʀsi- 'be sooted up, carbonized'

PI palliq 'dry willow twigs' [cf. q under nəʀ[1]]
Yup [note Nun pal(l)iaʀəX 'Alaskan cotton, cottongrass', with unexplained geminated l]
SPI palliq 'dry willow twigs'
NAI Nu palliq* 'dried plant, arctic cotton', Mal pallikšaq 'arctic cotton (used to start fires)' [Seiler for the latter]
WCI palliq 'dry willow' [Car paalliq 'dry willow used for fuel' acc. Pryde]
ECI palliq 'dried twigs, suntanned person']
GRI pałłiq* '(dwarf) willow' [in some areas 'alder' instead; pałłiit 'willow or alder scrub'; note also paliq, pałłit 'cover of capelin bag, wad (loaded in gun)']

PE palu- 'be lying on one's stomach' [cf. paŋałłaɣ- and pa(C)amaɣ- though the relat. — if any — is obscure]
AAY palu- 'be sad'
CAY palu- 'starve'
NSY palu- 'lie on stomach' [Orr]
CSY —
Sir —
SPI palu- 'become skinny'
NAI palu- 'be depressed, in bad condition', palut- 'turn upside down or over', Nu 'be covered in hard snow (trap)' [and pału- 'fall (dog's ears)']
WCI Cop palu- 'lie on face' [and Pet. has Sig paluŋaq- 'have hanging ears']
ECI palu- 'lower head' [Andersen et al. have also as 'collapse' in Lab]
GRI palu- 'lie on stomach', EG pali- 'lower head (seal)' [the latter Robbe and Menn.; and paluŋa- 'have hanging ears (dog)']

PE palluʀ- 'lie down on stomach' [cf. ʀ- under ŋ(ŋ)uʀ-]
AAY paluʀ- 'lie on belly' [and paluqsaɣ- 'trip and fall']
CAY paluʀ- 'lie face down' [post. root]
NSY paluXtə- 'lie face down'
CSY —
Sir —
SPI palluq- 'assume a prone position'
NAI palluq- 'assume a prone position' [and Nu paluq- 'have nothing more (e.g. to eat)']
WCI Cop pallukaq- 'fall on face' [Lowe; Met. has paalluq- 'be stretched out on stomach'; Dor. has palluq- 'fall flat on face' for Net]
ECI pallu(q)- 'lower self to ground', Iti 'fall down' [Peck has 'lie on belly' for Lab; palluŋa- 'be on all fours, on stomach']
GRI pałłuʀ- 'lie down on stomach' [pałłuŋa- 'be lying on stomach, lean forward toward s.th.; Up pałłittivi- 'creep after seal on ice']

PE paluʀtaʀ 'beaver' [cf. palluʀ- under palu-]
AAY Kod paluqtaq 'beaver'
CAY paluqtaq*
NSY paluqtaq 'otter?' [L.-T.]
CSY paluXtaq 'sea otter'
Sir paluXtəX
SPI paluqtaq 'beaver'
NAI pałuqtaq
WCI —
ECI —
GRI —

PY pama- 'flicker'
AAY —
CAY pama- 'be responsive, curve as it burns (candle wick)'
NSY pama- 'flicker (flame)'
CSY pama- 'flicker, be disheveled (hair)'
Inu [Imaq pamažaa(C)- 'flicker in wind (flame)' — from NSY?]

PI pamәq- 'raise (child)'
Yup [note CAY pamRiɣ- 'be adroit (growing child)', and AAY pamәRcәstә- 'stay up late']
SPI pamiq- 'raise, bring up'
NAI pamiq-, pamaRi- 'nurture', pamat- 'pamper, cater to'
WCI Cop pamiq- 'rear' [Ras.; Men. has pamiqtaituaq 'orphan under no one's protection' and pamatka 'the ones I raised']
ECI —
GRI NG pamiq-, pamiXXaq- 'grow up, rear'

PE pamyuR 'tail (of land animal)' [cf. papәɣ-]
AAY pamyuq 'tail', pamyuXsuun, 'anal fin', pamyuRualuk 'tailbone, coccyx'
CAY pamyuq 'tail' [and Y pamәsquq 'tailbone, coccyx', Y pamesqatak 'dried fish tail']
NSY pamyuq 'tail'
CSY [Rub. has pamyuk 'notch at base of harpoon'] ➡
Sir [note pamya 'harpoon notch (i.e. socket?)' — compare ECI, GRI pamiaq under pamyuRaR below] ➡
SPI pamiuq 'tail of a mammal'
NAI pamiuq 'tail of a land animal'
WCI pamiuq
ECI pamiuq
GRI pamiuq 'tail (on an animal with a round tail)'

PE pamyuRaR 'tailbone' [cf. aR; the Inu forms probably from *pamyuRal(l)uk — compare ukyuRaR under ukyuR]
AAY pamyuRualuk 'tailbone'
CAY HBC pamyuXauluq, LI pamyuqaq 'tailbone, coccyx' [for the first form see RuRluq]
NSY pamyuRaq 'tailbone' [ANLC]
CSY pamyuRaq 'tailbone (coccyx)'
Sir pamyuRaX 'back part of carcass of an animal'
SPI pamialuk 'tailbone, end of kayak'
NAI pamialluk, Mal pamiałłuk 'back flap of pants above belt, tailbone (coccyx)'
WCI pamialluk 'end of spine at buttocks'
ECI pamialluk 'tail of seal or walrus, coccyx (of human being)' [and note pamiaq 'tail of land animal, handle of saucepan, tail end of arrow or harpoon']
GRI pamiałłuk 'tail of seal or walrus, coccyx' [pamiaq 'terminal peg of harpoon']

PE pana 'lance'
AAY Kod panaq 'fish spear', KP panak 'spear'
CAY panaq 'large spear, lance' [and panaR- 'spear']
NSY pana 'spear'
CSY pana 'spear' [also verbal]
Sir pana 'spear' [Vakh. from Men.'s texts]
SPI pana 'long-handled spear' [Jen. = 'big two-edged knife']
NAI pana 'spear, double-edged blade, porcupine quill' [and as verb = 'spear']
WCI pana 'lance for killing enemies in war', Car 'point of caribou lance' [Ras.], 'snow knife' [B.-S. and Dor.]
ECI pana 'snow knife'
GRI pana 'large knife, sword' [pana-, panaR- 'hack with sword']

PE panәR- 'dry (out)'
AAY KP paanәɣ-, K pa(a)niR- 'roast over a fire, singe'
CAY —
NSY —
CSY panәR- 'starve to death, burn' [and panәłәq* 'ash, burned spot']
Sir pan(ә)R- 'be burnt', panәXtә- 'burn' [Vakh. from Rub., but from Men.'s texts he has the latter form as 'starve' as also Orr; Men. has panәXtәkcәX 'burnt'; Em. has panәłәX 'ash, burned spot']
SPI paniq- 'dry out'
NAI paniq- 'become dry, lose weight, become skinny, starve'
WCI paniq- 'be dry, be skinny, waste away'
ECI paniq- 'dry' [and paRŋi(C)- 'dry (by fire, sun, or wind)' — also perhaps paqqaa(q)- be hot']
GRI paniR- 'be dry, look like one doesn't have anything' [paqqiR- become dry, blanch (human in fear)', paqqit- 'be dry, destitute', paRni- 'be dried up in air (e.g. skin)']

PI pannaq 's.th. dried out or skinny' [cf. q under nәR[1]]
SPI pannaq- 'be getting dry', Qaw pannaRuq- 'dry out, get skinny'
NAI pannaq* 'skinny person or animal', pannaRik-, pannaqłuk- 'be very dry'
WCI Sig pannaq, pannaluk 'thin person'
ECI pannaq 'very dry wood', Lab 'dry tree with bark still on'
GRI pannaRiɣ- 'be very dry', pannaat-, EG pannaRaŋŋit-, Up panniqaŋŋit- 'not be completely dry'

PE paniɣ 'daughter'
AAY panik 'daughter'
CAY panik
NSY panik
CSY panik
Sir panәx, panix
SPI panik
NAI panik
WCI panik
ECI panik
GRI panik

PE paŋalәɣ- 'run on four legs' [cf. paŋałłaɣ- and lәɣ-]
AAY K paŋalәɣ- 'crawl'
CAY paŋalәɣ- 'run on four legs'
NSY paŋałәɣ- 'gallop' [Em.]

CSY paŋaləɣ- 'run on four legs'
Sir paŋələɣ-
SPI paŋałik-, Qaw paŋalik- 'gallop'
NAI paŋalik-
WCI paŋalik-
ECI paŋalik-
GRI paŋaliɣ-

PE paŋałłaɣ- 'fall forward' [cf. paŋaləɣ- and p.b. łłaɣ-]
AAY —
CAY paałaɣ- 'fall forward' [and paaʀvaɣ- 'fall forward hard']
NSY paałaɣ- 'fall forward' [ANLC; Em. has paałaa(ʀ)-]
CSY —
Sir —
SPI paalak-, Qaw paałak- 'fall forward', Qaw paalak- 'starve' [compare palu- for the latter]
NAI paałłak-, Mal paallak- 'fall forward' [and note paasaaq- 'fall forward (on s.th.)']
WCI paallak- 'fall forward' [also paasaq- 'stretch out on stomach']
ECI paalla(k)-
GRI paŋałłaɣ-, EG paŋakkaʀ- 'fall forward, stumble' [and paałłaɣ- 'glance off (harpoon, etc.), break off (foreshaft of harpoon)' — the latter meaning from Oqaatsit; NG paallak- 'fall forward']

PE paŋəʀ- 'paddle'
AAY AP paaŋəʀ- 'paddle'
CAY paaŋəʀ- 'paddle a kayak with a double-bladed paddle'
NSY —
CSY [note paŋəXtə- 'take a trip to Siberia from St. Lawrence Island' and compare paŋquqə- under paqət-]
Sir [note paŋəXtə- 'go from St. Lawrence Island to Siberia' — Orr]
SPI ➟
NAI paŋak- 'paddle swiftly' [for pauq- 'flap wings' see pa(C)a-]
WCI pauq- 'paddle' [influenced by pautik 'paddle' below?]
ECI pauq- 'paddle' [Lab also paaŋaq- 'paddle fast in a canoe' — Peck]
GRI paaʀ- [old ortho. paor-] 'paddle', paXXut(i)- 'compete at paddling', NG pauq- 'row, paddle' [influenced by paŋəʀun?; note also NG pauXXi- 'paddle quickly toward game']

PE paŋəʀun 'kayak paddle' [cf. un and Aleut Atkan, Att haasi-x (du.), EA Xaasi-X, earlier Xaasi-x 'double-bladed paddle' — from *haʀusi-x?]
AAY AP paaŋəXsuun 'paddle'
CAY paaŋʀun 'double-bladed kayak paddle'
NSY —
CSY Chap paŋʀun [Men.]
Sir —
SPI paaʀun, paaʀutik 'double-bladed paddle'
NAI paaʀutik
WCI pautik 'kayak paddle'
ECI pautiik 'kayak paddle' [also 'rudder, oar' in Lab acc. Peck]
GRI paatit (pl.) 'kayak paddle' [and NG paut 'oar', (du.) pautik 'paddle']

PI papaaq 'placenta (of animal)'
Yup — [note NSY papa 'raw core in boiled piece of meat' (Tein)]
SPI —
NAI papaaq 'animal placenta'
WCI papaat [Dor. has papaaq for B. Lake]
ECI papaaq 'placenta'
GRI —

PE papδi- 'be bothersome?' [there may be a link to papəɣ- — note the Sir below]
AAY papsi(ke)- 'find bothersome' [for papsaa(kə)- 'want to see, be suspicious of' see mam(ə)ya-]
CAY NSU papsi(kə)- 'find a nuisance' [emot. root]
NSY —
CSY papši- 'fidget' [and papšaŋitə- 'be active, vigorous']
Sir —
SPI Qaw papši- 'bother'
NAI papži- 'bother, annoy'
WCI —
ECI pavvi(C)- 'be impatient, bothered by s.o.', pavvinaq- 'be annoying'
GRI —

PE papəɣ 'tail' [cf. pamyuʀ]
AAY —
CAY papsałquq, papsałqitaq 'fish tail'
NSY papəkaq 'tail fin of fish' [L.-T.]
CSY papək 'tail of land mammal' [and papasquq 'fish tail', papəžəXti- 'wag tail']
Sir papəx 'tail' [and papələʀuʀ- 'quiver, swing', and papələʀ- 'move' — Orr]
SPI pavik 'bird tail'
NAI papik
WCI papik
ECI papik
GRI papik

PI papəqqila- 'wag tail' [cf. la(ʀ)-?]
SPI —
NAI papiqqilʸa- 'wriggle, jump around, wag tail'
WCI papiqqila- 'wriggle (fish in net)'
ECI —
GRI papiqila-, papikila- 'wag tail'

PI papəʀuq 'fish tail' [cf. quʀ]
SPI paviʀuq 'fish tail'
NAI papiʀuq
WCI papiʀuq
ECI papiʀuq 'fish tail' [also verbal of fish moving its tail]
GRI papiʀuq 'fish tail'

PE paqət- '(go and) find' [cf. paqna- and Aleut haqa- 'come', haqat- Atkan 'find, come across, learn, present oneself', EA, Att 'bring, give, bring about', and haqata- 'know']

AAY PWS paqtə- 'see if it is all right with someone'
CAY paq<ə>tə- 'check, investigate' [and note Y paquusiiɤ-, paŋquusiiɤ-, K paquusaaɤ- 'try to see (when not supposed to)']
NSY paqətə- 'encounter' [Em.]
CSY [note paŋquqə- 'go check on, pay a visit to' — contam. with paŋəʀ-?]
Sir [paŋquʀ- 'check on (something valuable)' — from the CSY? — Orr]
SPI paʀit- 'find'
NAI paqɨt-
WCI paqit-
ECI —
GRI —

PE paqna- 'prepare to leave [cf. paqət-]
AAY —
CAY paq̥na(yuɤ)- 'be curious about s.th.' [emot. root]
NSY paq̥nan 'supply'
CSY paq̥na(yuɤ)- 'be apprehensive', paq̥nan 'weapon, protection'
Sir paq̥na(yuɤ)- 'be apprehensive' [Orr]
SPI paqnak- 'get ready'
NAI paʀna-, Mal paqna- 'get ready to go', paʀnan, Nu paqnatit 'ammunition'
WCI paʀnak 'reserve, store of food', Net paʀnak- 'get ready to start' [Ras.]
ECI paʀna(k)- 'get ready to start' [and paʀnasima- 'be ready']
GRI ➟

> **PE paqnaŋiʀ-** 'secure' [cf. ŋiʀ-]
> AAY —
> CAY —
> NSY paq̥niaʀ- 'fasten, lock' [and paq̥naiʀun 'lock']
> CSY —
> Sir —
> SPI —
> NAI —
> WCI paʀnaiq- 'prepare to leave' [meaning due to paʀnak- above; Schn. has 'adg' (Car?) paʀnanaiqsivvik 'prison' and for Esk. Point pinaiq- 'lock, tie up']
> ECI paʀnai(q)-, paʀna(k)- 'get ready' [and paʀnanaiq- 'put in prison', paʀnanaiʀsivik 'prison']
> GRI paʀnaaʀ-, SWG payaʀnaaʀ- 'lash down, lock' [and paʀnaaʀut(i)- 'put in prison', paʀnaaʀuššivik 'prison']

PY-S paqʀitə- 'be missing' [cf. paqət- and ŋitə-?]
AAY —
CAY paqXitə- 'find something to be missing'
NSY —
CSY paaXqitə- 'be vacant, without people' [and paaXqilŋaatə- 'slip away, steal away']
Sir paqʀət(ə)- 'not have, be absent' [Vakh.; Men. has paqəʀitəX 'there is none, it is absent'

PE paqu(mi)- 'dread or be wary' [or paqqu(mi)-]
AAY —
CAY Nun paquminaXqə- 'be such as to make curious', paqumiyuɤ- 'be curious' [ANLC]
NSY —
CSY paqumiyuɤ- 'be wary of and hesitate to to act due to threatening weather'
Sir —
SPI paqqui- 'hesitate to do something dangerous,' paqquzuk- 'be cautious' [and Jen. has W paumi- 'dread, be superstitious about']
NAI paquʀɨ- 'shun (fearing contamination), regard with fear or caution'
WCI —
ECI Lab paqumi(suk)-, paqumiɤi- 'meditate (upon)' [Peck]
GRI paqumiɤi- 'be superstitious about, feel disgust for', paqumisuɤ-, EG qaqqimi(suC)- 'follow a taboo, be worried about s.th. for cult reasons' [and WG also paqinnaʀ- 'be taboo'; the EG could be by contam. with təqi- (cf. the SPI there) — Holm has EG paqumiɤi- 'be sad about']

PI paʀla- 'hurry eagerly toward' [there may be a link to paðəʀ-]
Sir [Em. has paʀləɤ- 'jump across something', paʀlaqənə 'at a jump', and paʀlaqə(s)- 'jump up and down']
SPI paʀliuq- 'welcome'
NAI paʀla- 'welcome, greet'
WCI paʀla- Net 'fight to be first', Car 'tremble with eagerness when hunting caribou' [Ras.]
ECI paʀla- 'throw things to them to eat, hurry to eat (to get most)' [Peck has for Lab 'pounce, fall on s.th.']
GRI —

PE paʀtə(ʀ) 'string or rope'
AAY —
CAY paXtak 'spruce root stretched above water's surface for a line of snares', paXtə- 'tighten drawstring or belt against cold or wind' [note also paqtil'ngut 'fish trap, single trap' in Barnum]
NSY —
CSY —
Sir paXtəX, pl. paXtay 'lace for boot' [Orr]
SPI ➟
NAI ➟
WCI paqti 'rope which connects sled to traces, sled draught line'
ECI —
GRI —

> **PE paʀtəʀžaʀ** 'drawstring'
> AAY —
> CAY paXtəʀaq 'drawstring', Nun, HBC taXpəʀaq 'drawstring' [may be influenced by taʀpaʀ-]
> NSY —
> CSY —
> Sir paXtəʀəX 'lace for boot' [Vakh.]
> SPI Qaw paqtiqšaq 'drawstring on mukluk top'
> NAI paqtiʀžaq 'kneestring of boot'
> WCI paqtiʀaq 'string at top of boot' [Pryde has paqtiʀiaq]
> ECI —
> GRI —

PY paʀuq 'bug'
AAY C paʀuq 'tiny bug'
CAY paʀuq
NSY paʀu 'very small insect found in wet places' [ANLC]
CSY —

PY-S pasi- 'smash or hit' [cf. patəɣ-?]
AAY pasi- 'smash' [pasinəq 'flat place']
CAY pasi-, masi- 'smash flat, be flattened'
NSY —
CSY — [but note Chap pasinəq* 'frame of house or window, hull of boat']
Sir pasi- 'hit'

PE patəɣ- 'slap' [cf. pattaɣ- and pasi-]
AAY PWS patəɣ- 'use paddle as brake'
CAY patəɣ- 'slap' [Hinz = 'lay a hand on']
NSY patəɣ- 'hit with palm of hand' [Em.]
CSY patəɣ- 'hit with palm of hand' [and note matəɣ- 'come up side by side with' — contam. with małəɣ-?]
Sir patəɣ- 'hit with palm of hand' [Em.]
SPI patik- 'lay an open hand on'
NAI patik- 'slap', PH 'lay hand on' [and note pažvik 'chopping block']
WCI patik- 'slap, beat, strike'
ECI patik- 'slap, lay a hand on, play cards, clap hands' [and patuk- 'touch self with hand']
GRI patiɣ- 'strike with the hand, lay a hand on, place paddle on another's kayak to support him', patit- 'strike with s.th. in hand' [and paššut(i)- 'treat (patient), beat, rape', pattuʀ- 'beat one's wife']

PI patəktət- 'slap together' [cf. tət-]
SPI patiktit- 'align so as to touch'
NAI patiktit-
WCI patiktit- 'put s.th. touching (e.g. wall), flatten with hand, clap hands with a child' [and note Net patitiktiq 'grounded ice floe' in Ras.]
ECI patitti(t)- 'make several things touch', Iti 'close (book), fold (skin)'
GRI patit(s)it- 'slap together (e.g. two pieces of bread)', NG patik(tit)- '(come to) land'

PE patɣutaʀ 'slapping instrument' [cf. un]
AAY C patxuta 'drumstick' [B.-S.; also patXutaq 'sled brake, paddle']
CAY —
NSY patkutaq 'whalebone fan with handle for slapping water during walrus hunt'
CSY pa(a)txutaq 'racket-like device used in a traditional game'
Sir —
SPI [patkutaq- 'play a game where ball is hit uphill']
NAI patkutaq 'fly swatter'
WCI [note Net patkutik 'child's mittens without fingers' — Ras.]
ECI —
GRI —

PE patəʀ 'marrow'
AAY patəq 'marrow'
CAY patəq* 'marrow' [patəʀ- 'eat bone marrow']
NSY patəq 'marrow' [patəʀ- 'swallow down, suck out bone marrow, kiss, permeate' (L.-T.)]
CSY patəq* 'marrow' [patəʀ- 'drain, evaporate']
Sir patəX 'marrow'
SPI patiq
NAI patiq* 'marrow' [verbal = 'eat bone marrow']
WCI patiq [and verbal = 'eat bone marrow'; patiʀiaq- 'have rheumatic aches']
ECI patiq 'marrow'
GRI patiq* 'marrow' [patiʀ- 'remove marrow from', NG patiʀiaXXi- 'ache (in bones)']

PE patət- 'be cold or frozen' [cf. patuɣ and patqaʀ-]
AAY pacəstə- 'be cold (body part), be chilled', pacesn̥aʀ- 'be cold (surroundings)' [pacesn̥aq 'cold draft']
CAY pacətə- 'be cool, chilled' [pacn̥aq 'chilly weather', and note patsaqaʀ- 'suffer a chill from going outside while sweaty']
NSY —
CSY [pasəʀaq 'frost on skin boat']
Sir —
SPI —
NAI patit- 'be frozen solid (shallow water)'
WCI Cop patit- [Pryde]
ECI —
GRI —

PI patlik- 'approach' [cf. patlitaʀ]
SPI pałłik- 'creep up on animal'
NAI pallik- 'be by the edge of s.th. or s.o.', Mal patliɣuti- 'approach, be near'
WCI Net Utku pa'liq- 'move closer' [Pryde]
ECI Lab palliɣuti- 'approach' [Peck]
GRI pałłiɣ-

PE patlitaʀ 'entrance passage' [cf. patlik-]
AAY —
CAY pałłitaq 'entrance passage (of trad. sod house)'
NSY pałitaq 'entrance in old-time semi-subterranean house'
CSY —
Sir —
SPI —
NAI pallisaq, pallitcat 'entrance mound or passageway to trad. sod house'
WCI —
ECI —
GRI —

PY patqaʀ- 'freeze over or form scab?' [cf. patuɣ and patət-, but compare also matu]
AAY AP patqaʀ- 'freeze or scab over'
CAY patqaʀ-
NSY —
CSY —

PE pattaɣ- 'slap or clap' [cf. patəɣ-]
AAY pataxtuʀ- 'hurry' [compare GRI pattattuʀ- below]
CAY pataɣ-, pataxtuʀ- 'hurry'
NSY —
CSY pataɣ- 'hit lightly', Chap pataɣaʀ- 'clap'
Sir pataɣaʀa(ci)- 'clap, slap'
SPI patak-, Qaw patakaq- 'hurry' [Jen. has W patak-]
NAI pattak- 'slap, spank' [and patala- 'get ready in a hurry, feel one's way in dark', PH 'clap hands', pattakula- 'applaud']
WCI pattak- 'applaud, clap, caress (an animal)' [Schn. has patta 'hand with outstretched fingers' for B. Lake]
ECI patta(k)- 'play ball', Lab 'slap' [pattak 'ball for playing with']
GRI pattaɣ- 'knock s.th. off s.o. with hand (e.g. snow of their clothing), pat, accompany (on musical instrument)' [pattaat(i)- 'play ball', pattaat 'ball, drum stick', pattattuʀ- 'flap wings']

PE patuɣ 'frost or ice forming a crust' [cf. patqaʀ- and patət-; for the 'brass' words compare ECI qakuʀnaq 'iron' under qakuʀnaʀ (qakuʀ-)]
AAY —
CAY patuxłuk 'ice fog, overcast weather' [note also patukpak 'brass' on old lists like Nelson's]
NSY —
CSY patuk 'crust of frost', patuɣ- 'become covered with ice'
Sir patux 'crust of frost' [Orr]
SPI patuk 'sleet' [note patukpak 'brass, copper']
NAI patuk 'frost of breath on ruff' [and verbal = 'be wet or frosty, form frost on ruff'; note also patukpak 'brass']
WCI patuk 'rime frost' [also verbal; Dor. has patuktuq 'thin snow on ground' for B. Lake]
ECI [Lab pat(t)utsauma- 'be frozen fast to s.th.' — Peck]
GRI — [but note patuɣut(i)- 'squeeze together around (e.g. ice around kayak, squid around its prey)' — contam. with patəɣ-?]

PY pauɣnaq 'brown bear' [cf. naʀ]
AAY PWS pauŋnaq, pauɣnaq 'bʀown bear' [in old sources]
CAY Nun pauɣnaX 'bear'
NSY —
CSY —

PE pa(C)umə(t)- 'itch'
AAY paumə- 'scratch an itch' [also C paumnaat 'nettle']
CAY Y NS paumə-, Nun paamə- 'scratch an itch'
NSY —
CSY —
Sir —
SPI paumit- 'itch'
NAI paumit-
WCI paumit-
ECI paumit- 'feel a slight tickle'
GRI paamiɣ- 'itch, scratch, be intrusive (person)' [and paamitsaɣ- 'get irritated']

PI pautnaq 'plant (edible)' [cf. naʀ and also paŋəʀun under paŋəʀ-?]
SPI —
NAI Nu pautnaq 'edible plant'
WCI —
ECI paunnaq 'mauve-colored subarctic wild flower of anenome family (used for Inuit tea)' [actually 'arctic fireweed' acc. Saul]
GRI NWG paannaq [old ortho. pângnaq], paannaat, NG paunnaak 'broad-leaved willow herb'

PY paviɣ- 'be lively
AAY pawiɣ- 'be deft, nimble, lively, fast'
CAY Y, Nun paviɣ- 'be lively, vigorous, fast'
NSY —
CSY —

PE pavlu 'drum handle' [cf. lu(ʀ)?]
AAY —
CAY NSU pakłuk, Nun papłu 'drum handle' [ANLC for the latter]
NSY —
CSY tafłu
Sir tafła [Orr]
SPI papłuq 'drum handle'
NAI pavlu
WCI —
ECI pallu 'vertical handle of cup or jug', palluaq 'handle of Inuit spade'
GRI —

PE pay(y)a(ɣ)- 'be unsteady or weak' [cf. Atkan Aleut hayamða- 'be unsteady']
AAY —
CAY Nun payaʀwaɣ- [or payaʀwaʀ-?] 'be faint from hunger'
NSY —
CSY —
Sir —
SPI Qaw payaŋa- 'be unsteady, loose-fitting'
NAI paya- 'be unable to manage, defeat or lift s.th.', payaŋa- 'be weak' [and payyaksaq- 'have difficulty overcoming, not be strong enough for s.th.']
WCI Sig paya- 'starve to death', payaŋa- 'be too weak to do s.th., be fragile, easy to make fall over' [and Car? payyaluk- 'change direction (wind)' — Schn. 'adg']
ECI —
GRI passaɣ- 'not be sure in kayak, tend to capsize' [and note pataya- 'be unsteady on feet or in kayak' — contam. with patəɣ- or piʀtuya- 'capsize easily' under pəʀə-]

PE payuɣ- 'bring food or supplies to' [cf. perhaps Aleut haya- 'request, ask for']
AAY payuxtə- 'take food to'
CAY payuxtə- 'take food to' [and Nun payixtə- 'take supplies on ahead — influenced by pa(C)əvtə-?]
NSY payuxtə- 'supply, present' [ANLC; L.-T. has payuxtaq 'boat arriving with delicacies']
CSY payuxtə- 'go check on'
Sir payuxtə- [Vakh.]
SPI payuk- 'bring food or supplies to'

NAI payuk-
WCI payuk- 'give food, clothing to those remaining'
ECI payuk- 'bring a gift to'
GRI payuɣ-

PE pəɣəɣaʀ- 'stay up all night' [cf. Atkan Aleut haɣlaɣ- 'have bad dreams'?]
AAY —
CAY pəxxaʀ- 'stay up late, all night' [and note pəɣla- 'walk or talk in sleep, have a nightmare' — for NSU pəlli- in the same meaning see pəllicci-]
NSY əpxaʀ- 'stay awake all night' [ANLC]
CSY pəxə-
Sir pəɣəɣ- [Vakh.]
SPI piaaq- 'stay up late'
NAI piɣaaq-
WCI piɣaaq-
ECI piɣaaq-
GRI piɣaaʀ- 'stay up late' [and pixxatiɣi- 'stay awake, keep vigil all night because of']

PE pəɣləʀ- 'bounce or jump up' [cf. pəkə- and Aleut hiɣit-, EA ixit- 'make a jump' with p.b. ləʀ-]
AAY —
CAY —
NSY pəɣləʀ- 'squat, sit down' [L.-T.; ANLC has pəʀləʀa- 'be squating']
CSY —
Sir pəɣlaʀ- 'squat'
SPI piɣliq- 'bounce, jump up'
NAI pɨɣlɨq- 'bounce, jump up' [and pɨɣla- 'be bouncy']
WCI piɣliq- 'bounce, jump up' [piɣlayuq 's.th. that bounces well']
ECI pilli(q)- 'bounce'
GRI piłłiʀ- 'hop, bounce'

PY-S pəɣnəm 'barely'
AAY —
CAY pəɣnəm 'after much effort, barely'
NSY pəɣnəm
CSY pəɣnəm
Sir pəɣnəm

PE pəkə- 'jump up (and move off)' [cf. pəkku(ɣ)- and pəɣləq-, and Aleut hiki- 'disappear']
AAY pəkaxtə- 'stir'
CAY pəkə- 'make a movement which attracts notice' [and note NSU pəkaʀa- 'stroll']
NSY — [for pəkuɣ- 'pry up' see pəkutaq]
CSY pəkuɣ- 'disperse quickly' [compare the sense 'become fully awake' under pəkku(ɣ)-]
Sir ➡
SPI ➡
NAI [piɣyuq- 'flee, migrate (birds)'; and note pikaala- 'writhe in pain', Nu pikak- 'break through thin ice to breathe (whale, seal)']
WCI piki- 'rise from nest and fly off' [and Pryde has piɣyuq- 'flee to avoid blood feud' for Cop]
ECI piki- 'rise from nest (bird), jump up' [and Lab pikallak- 'be rowdy'; Andersen et al. have Lab pikia- 'swim together in school (seals)']
GRI piki- 'get ready to leave' [and pikaala- 'go round the house busying oneself with all sorts of work'; Robbe and Menn. have piɣiq 'nest']

PE pəkət- 'move around' [cf. t-[1], which may be used reflexively, and Aleut hikit- 'lose, miss, cast'; there may be contam. from pakiɣ- and/or pəkutaq here]
AAY pək<ə>tə- 'work, be Monday', PWS 'walk'
CAY pək<ə>tə- 'move, walk', BB, LI, NR also 'work'
NSY [pəkətə- 'dig' (ANLC); for pəkutə- 'dig up' see under pəkutaq]
CSY [pəkətə- 'shovel, fire from work', pəkəqə- 'dig around in carelessly'; and pəkfiɣ- 'rummage, dig around in']
Sir [pəkətə- 'shovel, fire from work', and Vakh. has pəkfəʀ- 'dig up, expose, unfold' from Men. and Rub.; Em. has pəkət(ə)- 'dig up, work with shovel', pəkfəɣ- 'dig up' and pukfiʀ- 'dig in ground (animal)]
SPI piɣit- 'jump, move around'
NAI pikɨt- 'move constantly, cannot keep still'
WCI —
ECI —
GRI pikiɣ- 'become agitated, jump up' [old ortho. pikiɣ- but Fab. has piki(t)-]

PI pəkiaq- 'go out quickly' [cf. pəkyaɣ- below]
SPI piɣiaq- 'rush out, go out quickly'
NAI pikiaq- 'jump up suddenly and bolt, gush out (water)'
WCI pikiaq- 'leave the house in a rush' [and Schn. has 'break out of shell (chick)' for 'adg']
ECI pikiaq- 'pop up, stick up at surface' [Lab 'escape' in Bourq.]
GRI pikiaʀ- 'come up out of water (diving bird)', NG pikiaq- 'stick head out of breathing hole (seal)' [pikiala- 'gush forth (water)'; for EG pikkaatsaaʀ- 'hurry off' see pəkku(ɣ)-]

PE pəkyaɣ- or **pəkyəɣ-** 'fly off'
AAY —
CAY pəksałaɣ- 'fly off from eggs', HBC pəksaɣ- 'scatter'
NSY [pəkya̧ʀ- 'break up (river), have a heavy menstrual period' (ANLC)]
CSY Chap pəksaɣ- 'scatter'
Sir —
SPI piksik- 'fly off, bounce'
NAI piksak-, piksik- 'fly off, bounce off target, leave without preparation' [the form with i is unexplained, but note that strong i is regular after s]
WCI piksik- 'jump, bounce'
ECI pitsi(k)-
GRI pissiɣ-

PE pəkku(ɣ)- 'be alert or effective?' [cf. pəkə- and compare pillu(a)ʀik- under pi- for the contractions in some Inu forms]

AAY —
CAY —
NSY —
CSY pəkuɣ- 'become fully awake, alert'
Sir —
SPI —
NAI [note pikkaʀi- 'be very fond of' — from *pikkunaʀi-?]
WCI —
ECI pikkunaq- 'do things as they should be', pikkunaʀi- 'consider properly done' [and compare pikkaʀik- 'be capable' with p.b. kiɣ- and NBI pikkaniq- 'be clever'; also pikkaluk- 'be clumsy', pikutsuuq 'one who does bad work', pikatsiluk-, Iti pikutsu(k)- 'not do things right', with łuɣ(-)]
GRI pikkunaʀ- 'be effective, be strong (food)', pikkuɣi- 'think s.th. strong' [and pikkuʀiɣ- 'be capable' with p.b. kiɣ- (opp. = pikkuʀłuɣ- 'do clumsily'), and pikkusuɣ- 'do, eat eagerly', pikkutsaɣ- 'become enthusiastic', Fab. 'feel strengthened by s.th.'; Robbe and Menn. have pikkaaC- 'be fast' for EG — Ges. has pikkaʀ- 'be fast' and Robbe and Dor. pikkaaŋŋit- 'be slow', pikkaatsaaʀ- 'hurry (off)' as well as pikkaʀtiC- 'throw harpoon without hitting', with łuɣ(-)]

PE pəknəʀ 'kind of edible root'
AAY —
CAY Nun pəkn̥əq 'tall cottongrass'
NSY pəkn̥əq 'root of cottongrass plant' [ANLC]
CSY pəkn̥əq 'tuber of tall cottongrass'
Sir —
SPI pikniq 'tall cottongrass'
NAI piŋniq 'cache of food made by mice', Nu pikniq 'watergrass'
WCI —
ECI —
GRI —

PE pəku(ɣ) and **pəquʀ** 'upper back or nape of neck' [cf. pəqu- for the possible source of contam. in Yup — compare under pəkutaq; the Inu forms like pikusuk may have p.b. cuɣ — compare tunucuɣ under tunu]
AAY pəquq 'back of person or animal'
CAY pəquq 'scruff of the neck, upper back' [for Nun pəquX 'piece of sod' see pəqaq — contam.?; note also pəqumik 'back load'; for pəkutaʀuaq 'breastbone' see pəkutaq]
NSY —
CSY —
Sir [note pəkixtəX (for pəkəxtəX?) 'shoulder blade'; Vakh. has pəqəXtəX, piqəXtəX, pəqixta, pəqixtəX, pəkixtəX 'shoulder of whale, shovel' from Rub.'s texts — there is contam. here either from pəqu- or from pəkita 'shovel' under pəkutaq]
SPI —
NAI pikuk 'long vertebra under neck, wolf fur from below shoulders, area across shoulders', pikusuk 'big bone at shoulder, depression between shoulder blades, hump behind moose's head'
WCI pikuk 'bone between shoulder blades, hump of a hunchback'
ECI pikuq 'bump below nape of neck, nape of neck, hump on back' [and note pikkuluk 'hunchback']
GRI pikusuk, pukusuk, NG piku(huk) 'nape of neck'

PY-S pəkutaq 'shovel' [originally an animal shoulderblade used for this purpose? — cf. pəku(ɣ), also pəkə- (esp. pəkət- under it) and un; there may be contam. here from pakiɣ-]
AAY pəkutaq, pəkutaXsuun 'flat shovel' [the former from old sources; note also pəkutaʀuaq 'breastbone', with ŋ(ŋ)uðaʀ]
CAY LI, Nun, NS pəkutaq 'shovel'
NSY [pəkuɣ- 'pry up' (ANLC) — a back formation influenced by ipuɣ-?; Men. has pəkutə- 'dig up, dig over'; for pəkətə- 'dig' see pəkət-]
CSY pəkuutaq 'shovel' [also 'halibut, turbot']
Sir pəkita 'shovel' [for *pəkəta? — compare also under pəku(ɣ)]

PE pəkyu 'egg' [cf. pəkyaɣ- and pəkiaq- under pəkə-, also yuɣ-?]
AAY pəksu, pəksuq 'egg, to lay eggs'
CAY Y, UK, LI pəksuq 'egg', [elsewhere as well] pəksute- 'find eggs'
NSY —
CSY —
Sir —
SPI Qaw pikiuq 'wild egg', KI piɣiut- 'find eggs'
NAI pikiut- 'find a bird's nest with eggs or young'
WCI pikiut-
ECI pikiuk 'egg found' [verbal = 'find nest with eggs'; NBI, SB pikiusaq- 'gather eggs']
GRI EG piɣiik- 'find nest or eggs' [Tersis; Robbe and Dorais have EG pikkiC- 'gather eggs']

PE pəllicci- 'be unable to keep one's eyes open'
AAY pəlici(qə)- 'be sleepy after eating a lot, have eyes sticky with sleep'
CAY [note NSU pəlli- 'have a nightmare, walk in one's sleep']
NSY —
CSY —
Sir —
SPI —
NAI pillitci- 'be unable to keep one's eyes open'
WCI —
ECI pillisi-
GRI piłłitsi- [old ortho. pigdlitsi- with spurious g — Fab. has pillitsi-], NG pillutsi- 'be unable to keep one's eyes open'

PE pəlu(ʀ) 'dust or dirt'
AAY C pəlut 'ashes'
CAY pəluq 'ash of birch fungus or willow or cottonwood bark (mixed with chewing tobacco), volcanic ash'
NSY pəlužaq 'dust, dirt'
CSY pəluŋi 'cleanliness', pəluŋiʀ- 'clean up'
Sir pəluŋiXsaʀ- 'clean' [Em.]
SPI —
NAI —
WCI Car pilu 'clod of soil, remainder' [Schn., who also

has pillu]
ECI piluq 'caribou fur that has been shed' [and Ras. has pilu 'dust' for Igl]
GRI —

PE pəłu 'leaf'
AAY pəłuq 'leaf'
CAY pəłukutaq, pəłuqutaq 'leaf of coltsfoot plant', Nun 'leaf (any kind)'
NSY —
CSY [note pəłuməXtaq 'dish of frozen greens shredded by scraping', influenced by pəłuɣ-?]
Sir —
SPI [note Qaw miluɣataq 'coltsfoot' — influenced by məluɣ- or mulə(ɣ)]
NAI [note milukataq 'coltsfoot' — as the SPI]
WCI Car piluqut 'leaf' [Ras.]
ECI [for piluq 'caribou fur that is shed, has fallen off a pelt' see pəlu(ʀ); Peck has millukatak 'leaves of trees' for Lab]
GRI pilu 'leaf' [and piluqut 'bilberry shrub' — compare muliqut 'leaf' under mulə(ɣ)]

PY-S pəłuɣ- 'scrape skin'
AAY —
CAY Y pəłumʀun, K təłumʀun, BB əłumʀun 'skin scraper' [the latter forms apparently contam. with təluɣ-]
NSY pəłuxtə- 'shave s.o. completely bald' [ANLC, which also has ipłuk, upłuk 'skin scraper (without a handle)'; in Men. pəłuxtə- is 'cut hair' — compare the semantics of całiɣ-[1]]
CSY pəłuɣ- 'scrape dried fat off skin, process frozen greens' [contam. with pəłu in the latter sense?; pəłuɣək 'skin- scraping tool worked with both hands']
Sir pəłuXkət- 'scrape skin' [Vakh. from Rub.'s texts; pəłəɣutaX 'board for scraping skins on', pəłəx 'scraper without handle for scraping skins with' — Em.]

PE pəŋəɣ- 'be worried' [cf. EA ŋaaɣ- 'be afraid, apprehensive', ŋaaxta- 'be afraid of']
AAY pəŋəɣ(yuɣ)- 'be worried' [emot. root]
CAY pəŋəɣ(yuɣ)- 'be worried'
NSY pəŋəɣ- 'be worried' [Em]
CSY pəŋəɣ- 'worry about s.o. far away or whose return is expected', pəŋkə- 'worry about'
Sir pəŋəɣ- 'be worried about s.th.' [Vakh.; Men. has pəŋəʀ-]
SPI piŋiɣi- 'worry about s.o.'s safety' [intr. piŋikšaq-]
NAI piŋiɣɨ- 'worry about s.o.'s safety' [intr. piŋikšaq-]
WCI piŋiɣi- [Lowe]
ECI piŋiɣi- 'worry about s.o.'s safety' [intr. piŋiɣa(C)-]
GRI —

> **PY pəŋɣaʀtə-** 'worry' [cf. aʀ-]
> AAY pəŋŋaXtə- 'worry'
> CAY pəŋɣaXtə-
> NSY pəŋɣaXtə- 'worry'
> CSY —

PE pəŋiʀ '(kind of) wood'
AAY pəŋiq 'type of tree'
CAY — [for Y pəŋə- 'resume original shape after being bent (e.g. tree by wind)' see under pətɣəʀ-]
NSY —
CSY pəŋiq 'wood, pine wood'
Sir pəŋiX [Orr]
SPI Qaw piŋiq 'wood for harpoon handle,' KI piŋŋiq 'red cedar' [Jen. has 'birch wood' for W]
NAI —
WCI Cop piŋiq 'type of whitish wood' [Pryde; Car EP piŋilik 'hardwood for sled' (Ow.)]
ECI piŋiq 'birch tree'
GRI piŋiq 'red (drift) wood'

PE pəŋuʀ 'mound or hillock'
AAY pəŋuq 'hill'
CAY pəŋuq
NSY pəŋuq 'hill' [ANLC; Men. has pəŋuXqaq]
CSY pəŋuq 'rounded hill' [and pəŋuʀ- 'swell, rise in a lump']
Sir pəŋuɣnəX 'hillock', pəŋkułtaX 'hill'
SPI piŋu(q) 'dune, mound', Imaq pəŋuqšaq 'elevation, hill' [and piŋuaq- 'burst, rupture', piŋuaqłiq 'infected sore']
NAI piŋu 'mound, pimple' [verbal = 'develop pimple, swell (wave)'; piŋuktaaq, Mal piŋuqšaq 'small round hill isolated in flat area']
WCI piŋuq 'hill' [and Sig piŋuqsaaʀyuk 'hill formed by underground ice']
ECI piŋuq 'pimple' [also 'hill, mound' acc. Saul; verbal = 'have a pimple'; Boas has piŋu 'mountain' for Baf.]
GRI piŋu 'hillock, hummock'

> **PI pəŋuy(y)ak** or **pəŋuy(y)aq** 'swelling on skin' [cf. tyaɣ]
> SPI —
> NAI piŋuyaq 'ringworm, pimple', PH piŋuyyaq 'itchy type of pimple or sore'
> WCI Sig piŋuyaq 'wart' [Pet.]
> ECI —
> GRI piŋuyak 'blister'

PI pəqaluyak 'iceberg (old)' [cf. pəqliʀ-?]
SPI piʀaluyak 'freshwater Arctic ice'
NAI piqaluyak 'large chunk of freshwater ice'
WCI piqaluyaq 'old ice'
ECI piqaluyaq 'iceberg'
GRI NG piqaluyaq 'iceberg' [shaman's word in Kroeber]

PY pəqliʀ- 'harden with age or be wrinkled' [cf. pəqu-?]
AAY pəqlitə- 'be stiff, crunchy'
CAY pəqłiXtə- 'be wrinkled from soaking (skin)'
NSY— [for pəquʀ- 'wrinkle, bend' see pəqu-]
CSY pəqłiʀ-, pəqłiXtə- 'harden with age (esp. skins)'

PE pəqu- 'bend or be bent' [cf. pəʀə- and pəqliʀ-, though the relat. is obscure]
AAY —
CAY —
NSY pəqu- 'get turned inside, get folded or rolled up' [ANLC; Men. has pəquʀ- 'bend, wrinkle', pəqunəq 'bend, wrinkle']

CSY —
Sir —
SPI piʀuaq- 'for young ice to break and explode from pressure of heavier ice'
NAI piquaq- 'bend body when diving (seal)', piquniq* 'mound formed by pressure from below', Nu piqu- 'be pushed up and cracked by pressure from below (ice)'
WCI piquŋa- 'be weighed down, be bent over'
ECI piquniq 'ice dome or bulge on ice surface'
GRI piqu- 'bend up and then straighten out again' [and piqqut(i)- 'bend over', piqquk 'crayfish', NG piquk 'nose bone', also 'loin'; Tersis has piʀ̃iC- 'bend, be bent' for EG]

PE pəʀə- 'bend' [cf. pəqu- and pəʀləʀ-, also Aleut haXt- 'stand up, get up' and haʀit- 'lift up (one end), put upright, turn up (overturned kayak)'?]
AAY pəʀə- 'bend'
CAY pəʀə-
NSY [əpəʀ- 'bend]
CSY [note pəXtu(yuɣ)- 'be overwhelmed'; for pəʀləʀ- 'squat, bend over from cold' see pəʀləʀ-] →
Sir —
SPI →
NAI [piqsaq- 'bend the body while sounding (whale)']
WCI [Cop piqqiq 'bend in river' (Pryde)]
ECI →
GRI [note piqimi- 'pop up and go down again at once (seal)' (compare piqiŋa- under pəʀiŋa- below), piʀtuya- 'tend to capsize' (influenced by pay(y)a(ɣ)-?) and NWG piʀsala- 'fall headlong'] →

PE pəʀət- 'bend (trans.)' [cf. t-[1]]
AAY pəXtə- 'bend'
CAY pəXtə-, NSU pəʀətə-
NSY —
CSY pəXtə- 'fold, bend'
Sir —
SPI piʀit- 'bend' [and piqtaq 'bentwood bucket']
NAI piʀit- 'bend' [and piqtɨq- 'bend (wood)', piqta 'place where a line bends down, side of cliff, wall']
WCI piʀit- 'bend' [and note piqtaq 'wall, edge of well, outside of barrel']
ECI piʀit- 'bend'
GRI piqit- 'bend up, curve, bend' [influenced by pəqu-?; and piʀtaq 'dish made of curved baleen', piʀtiʀ- 'fold several times']

PI pəʀiŋa- 'be bent' [cf. ŋa-[1]]
SPI piʀiŋa- 'be bent'
NAI piʀiŋa-
WCI piʀiŋa- 'be bent (over or in two)' [for piquŋa- in this sense see pəqu-]
ECI piʀiŋa- 'be bent to the side (person)'
GRI piqiŋa- 'be bent (e.g. in old age)' [infl. by pəqu-]

PE pəʀnəʀ 'joint or bend' [cf. nəʀ[1]]
AAY pəʀnəq 'bent part of tree'
CAY —
NSY —
CSY pəʀnəq* 'joint, bend'
Sir —
SPI —
NAI [note place name Piʀniq* 'Birnirk', also Nu piʀliʀniq* 'inside of a joint', influenced by pəʀləʀ-]
WCI piʀniq 'curve of front of sled', Net Utku 'bend' [Pryde for the latter; Pet. has 'juncture of bay, joint' for Sig]
ECI piʀniq 'joint'
GRI piʀniq* 'joint, elbow' [piʀniʀ- 'fold together']

PY pəʀŋaliq 'rib' [cf. pəʀiŋa- above and l(l)iʀ]
AAY AP pəʀŋaliq 'rib'
CAY NSU pəŋʀaliq 'rib'
NSY —
CSY —

PE pəʀləʀ- 'be in dire need (starving or freezing)' [cf. pəʀə- and pəqu-]
AAY —
CAY pəXɫəqciiʀ(aʀ)-, pəʀləqciiʀ(aʀ)-, Nun pəʀləXcii- have stiff hands from cold'
NSY pəʀləʀ- 'squat down'
CSY pəʀləʀ- 'squat, bend over from the cold'
Sir pəʀlaʀ- 'squat down, bend over' [Em.]
SPI —
NAI piʀliq- 'become stiff with cold (hands)'
WCI Net, Car piʀliq- 'starve' [Pryde], Cop piʀla- 'starve to death'
ECI piʀli(q)- 'starve to death', piʀla- 'be in dire need (several)'
GRI piʀɫiʀ- 'starve to death' [and piʀɫasi-, piʀɫataaʀ- 'meet with an accident'; for piʀɫiʀuʀ-, piɫɫiʀuʀ- 'be mad' see pivli]

PE pəʀu(-) 'bury under stones (to cache)' [nominal for the stone(s) so used; cf. Aleut haʀu-X 'pack, burden', haʀu- 'pack on one's back']
AAY —
CAY Nun pəXu 'dried soil' [ANLC; for ciʀu- 'cover with snow, dirt, etc.' see ciʀu-]
NSY pəʀu- 'bury' [and pəʀut 'cache']
CSY pəʀu- 'bury, cover with earth or snow'
Sir pəʀə- 'cover' [pəʀutaX 'cover for boat or sled' (Orr)]
SPI piʀu-, Imaq pəʀu- 'bury, cache meat underground' [and pəʀuvik 'stones on meat cache']
NAI piʀu- 'put a cover over, cache' [piʀʀutaq 'rock weight to keep tent flap down']
WCI piʀu- 'cover meat cache with earth, stones, etc.'
ECI piʀuq 'stone weight for meat cache or to stop tent being blown away' [and piʀui- 'place such a stone']
GRI piʀu 'weight on s.th.' [and verbal = 'put a weight on s.th.'; piʀušaq 'meat covered with a stone' — Robbe and Menn. have EG piŋilaq for the latter; Up piʀ̃itsiaq 'wall']

PY pətaq 'pox or measles' [cf. pəttaq under pəte-]
AAY—
CAY —
NSY pətaʀaq 'chicken pox'
CSY pətaq 'measles or similar disease'

PE pətə- and **pətuʀ-** 'penetrate or pass through' [the latter with (C)uʀ-; cf. pətluɣ-²]
AAY pətuXtə- 'penetrate' [and note pəskuʀ- 'crack, chip'?]
CAY Nun pətuXtə- 'soak, penetrate'
NSY —
CSY [note pəskuɣ- 'slip off (rope), end (sadness)'?]
Sir [pəskəʀ- 'stick head out of water (animal)' — Vakh. has pəskəʀaXtə- 'emerge' (from Men.'s texts) and pəsqəʀ- 'stick head through'; Em. has pəskuɣ- 'release, become undone, be past' — all of these could be from CSY]
SPI W pitaq- 'enter' [Jen.]
NAI ➡
WCI Cop pitaq- 'break through (ice) to water' [Pryde; Jen. has Cop pitatkaq- 'enter']
ECI pitaaq- 'dent, break in, stave in', Lab 'drive an object through another' [and pitaaʀut(i)- 'appear through surface (e.g. pointed object penetrating through)']
GRI pitaʀ- 'pass, surpass', pitaʀut(i)- 'appear, come through (dampness)'

PI pəttaq 'hole' [cf. q under nəʀ¹]
Yup [for CSY pətaq 'measles' see pətaq]
SPI —
NAI pittaq* '(natural) hole in ice' [and pitak- 'have or make hole', Nu pitaq- 'get a hole in it (ice)']
WCI pittaq 'hole in ice' [as verb = 'make hole in ice'; Car 'surface of thin ice amidst thick ice' acc. Schn., who also has it as 'sound, narrows' for 'adg'; Pryde also has Cop pittaʀluk- 'cripple (an animal)']
ECI pittaq 'hole made by punching a pointed object through'
GRI —

PI pətuʀaq- 'come through or reach (from afar)' [cf. aʀ-?]
SPI pituʀaq- 'pass through'
NAI pituʀaq- 'arrive at body of water after long journey, come out to a lead in ice', Nu pituʀaaq- 'go down to shore from land'
WCI pituʀaq- 'go down to shore from land', Baker Lake 'reach a lake one doesn't know' [Schn.]
ECI pituʀaq- 'come from inland to shore' [and pituʀaaq 'one who goes down to shore']
GRI pituʀaʀ- 'come from afar (people), suddenly blow up (wind)', EG piliȓa(a)q, pilaȓaq 'violent foehn wind from inland ice' [verbal = piliȓaʀ-, pilaȓaʀ-]

PY-S pətɣəʀ- 'jump up' [cf. mətŋəʀ- and mətəŋtaq, perhaps influenced by pəkə-, but compare patu under matu for possible assimilation]
AAY pətxəʀ- 'fly, leap, bound through the air' [pətxəʀyaaq 'sand flea']
CAY pətxaʀ- 'spring up' [and note pətxeq* 'dandruff', Y pəŋə- 'resume original shape after being bent (e.g. tree by wind)' — influenced by apəŋə-?]
NSY pətxiʀ- 'rebound', pətxatə- 'be jumping, eager to jump or bounce' [ANLC; Men. has pətXələq 'rebounding']
CSY pətxəʀ-, pətxa(ʀ)- 'bounce off s.th.'
Sir pətxa- 'jump (up or across)' [Em.]
Inu [note Imaq pətaq '(a) jump']

PE pətluɣ-¹ 'dislocate a joint' [cf. pətɣəʀ- and pətŋu(ʀ)-]
AAY —
CAY [for pəɬuxtə- 'scrape a skin' see pəɬuɣ-]
NSY pəɬuɣ- 'dislocate a joint', pəɬuxtə- 'get out of joint' [for homonym 'cut one's hair' see pəɬuɣ-]
CSY [for pəɬuɣ- 'scrape dried fat off skin, process frozen greens by scraping' see peɬuɣ- and for pəɬuməXtaq 'dish of frozen greens shredded by scraping' see pəɬu]
Sir —
SPI piɬɬuk- 'get dislocated, out of joint', Qaw 'have an accident, come undone, come off'
NAI piɬlui- 'dislocate a joint' [for piɳŋui- of this meaning see pətŋu(ʀ)-]
WCI —
ECI pillu(k)- 'be bent over in pain', pillui- 'sprain a joint, be sprained'
GRI piɬɬuɣ- [old ortho. pigdlug-] 'fall from foundation, fail, get out of joint' [and piɬɬui- 'drop']

PE pətluɣ-² 'pass through or survive' [cf. pətə-]
AAY —
CAY pəɬuɣ- 'happen, pass'
NSY —
CSY —
Sir —
SPI Qaw piɬɬuk- 'be over with (esp. storm)'
NAI piɬluk-, Mal piɬluk- 'survive danger, illness or death'
WCI —
ECI —
GRI piɬɬuɣ- 'get through or past'

PI pətŋu(q)- 'get dislocated? [cf. pətluɣ-¹]
SPI pitŋuq- 'be dislocated,' pitŋui- 'become dislocated'
NAI piɳŋui- 'dislocate a joint (also of folding knife)' [and note pinʸŋuq- (for piɳŋuq-?) 'fold (knife)', Mal pitŋuqtaq 'folding knife']
WCI [Sig pinŋuqtaq 'pocket-knife' (Pryde)]
ECI —
GRI piŋ(ŋ)u-, piŋ(ŋ)uʀ-, piŋuɣ- 'rebound (harpoon)', piŋŋui- 'lose seal by having harpoon rebound'

PE pətuɣ 'lamp stand' [cf. pətuɣ-?]
AAY —
CAY —
NSY pətuk 'lamp stand'
CSY —
Sir —
SPI pitu 'stick supporting lamp' [Jen.]
NAI —
WCI [Ras. has Net pituɣSat 'two sticks under lamp']
ECI pituaq 'V-shaped sticks stuck in snow as lamp stand', pitsivik 'lamp stand'
GRI pitu 'lamp stand' [in NG pituk in this sense is specifically the two front legs of the three-legged lamp-stand, acc. to Holt.]

PE pətuɣ- 'fasten or secure'
AAY PWS pətuɣ- 'button, lace, zip' [and pətuk 'button, fastener, shoelace']
CAY pətuɣ- 'fasten, tether, tie to post' [as nom. pətuk = 'dog tether, chain, boat line']
NSY pətuɣ- 'tie up, tether' [and pətuk 'small hook' (ANLC) — compare under pətuɣ]
CSY pətuɣ- 'tie, tether, fasten'
Sir pətəxtəʀ- 'fasten' [Vakh. has pətuʀ-, pətəʀ-]
SPI pituk- 'chain or tie up'
NAI pituk- 'tie, chain to a stake or pole' [as nom. = 'chain']
WCI pituk- 'attach a dog to its chain', Car pitu(k) 'draught line on a sledge' [Ras.]
ECI pituk 'V-shaped part of rope that attaches dog harness to a sled' [as verb = 'attach to end of rope']
GRI pituɣ- 'attach, tether, harness, make fast' [and pitu(k), pituq, EG piliq, NG pituk 'front strap on sledge to which traces are joined']

PE pətuɣutaʀ 'tether' [cf. un]
AAY —
CAY [note Y pətuutaaʀutə- 'baste in sewing']
NSY —
CSY pətuɣutaq 'tether, tie rope or chain'
Sir pətəɣətaX 'chain'
SPI pituun 'chain', Qaw pituutaq 'dog's chain, boat rope'
NAI pɨtuutaq 'tether, tie rope'
WCI pituutait 'chain for dog, mitten cords'
ECI pituutaq, pituuti 'thong for attaching central trace to sled'
GRI pituutaq 'tether, tie rope'

PE pi(-) 'do s.th. (or thing)' [so-called empty root; cf. Aleut hi- 'say, call, ask for, tell']
AAY pi- 'do, say, act, go' [and possessed nom. = 'thing']
CAY pi- 'do, say, act, etc.' [and poss. nom. = 'thing']
NSY pi- 'say, ask for, turn to, happen, etc.'
CSY pi- 'do, say, act, go, etc. [poss. nom. = 'thing']
Sir pi- 'say, do' [nom. = 'something' acc. Vakh.]
SPI pi- 'do, say, get, etc.' [poss. nom. = 'thing', as in all Inu]
NAI pi-
WCI pi-
ECI pi- 'do, receive' [and piyyuti 'means, possibility, faculty']
GRI pi- 'do (to), say, get, go, happen, marry, concern, mean' [as poss. nom. = 'thing', piit, NG pit 'property', EG pit '(female) genitals'; note also pisataq 'part, property', piššut 'reason, cause', NG pissutit 'hunting equipment']

PI piaʀaq 'young (animal)' [cf. (V)ʀaq 'small' under ʀaʀ and compare piayaaq below and mi(i)ʀayuq]
SPI —
NAI [note piiʀaq 'gray-cheeked thrush']
WCI Net Utku piaʀaq 'young bird' [Pryde]
ECI piaʀaq 'small child, baby', Lab 'young animal' [Bourq.]
GRI piaʀaq 'young animal' [and NG piʀaaq 'child' — and compare WG piiʀaq 'girlfriend', a newer productive formation; EG piaʀ̃aq 'young caribou'; for WG miiʀaq 'child' see mi(i)ʀayuq]

PI piayaaq 'young animal' [cf. tyaɣ]
Yup [note CAY piyaɣaq* 'baby animal (esp. bird)' which may be the direct cognate]
SPI piayaaq 'young animal'
NAI piayaaq
WCI Cop piayaaq
ECI —
GRI —

PY piciatun 'any old way' [cf. uciʀ, here in the 3s possessed aequalis case form; compare also piciʀ]
AAY picaatun 'any old way'
CAY piciatun
NSY —
CSY —

PE piðqun 'request or order' [cf. ðqə- and un; note that most languages have predictable pisqə- (Yup), pitqu- (Inu) 'tell to do' from pi(-) plus ðqə-]
AAY —
CAY pisqun 'rule, law'
NSY —
CSY —
Sir —
SPI —
NAI pitqun 'request'
WCI —
ECI —
GRI piqqut 'reason' [compare more recent formation piqqušut 'order, permission']

PE piðviɣ 'place or time' [cf. ðviɣ; other languages/ dialects than those indicated below have this as a predictable combination in the sense 'time or place of doing s.th.']
AAY —
CAY pivik 'place, room, time, space'
NSY pivixkaq 'direction'
CSY pivik 'road' [also piviɣitə- 'be such that one feels disinclined to do anything, not be a good time to']
Sir pivəx 'road' [Orr; note also pivəɣitə- 'not have a road or place to go']
SPI puikšraq 'place for future use'
NAI pivik 'time or place', pivikšaq 'time or place for s.th.'
WCI —
ECI pivitsaq 'place where s.th. will be done'
GRI piffik 'counter, buffet', piffiššaq 'time'

PI piiyaq- 'remove (several things)' [cf. ŋiyaʀ-; all Alaskan and Canadian dialects also have predictable piiq- 'remove' from ŋiʀ-]
Yup [note predictable CAY piiʀ-, CSY piŋiʀ- 'remove' from ŋiʀ-]
SPI piiyaq- 'remove (several things)'
NAI piiyaq-

WCI piiyaun 'means for removing s.th.'
ECI piiyaq- 'remove, be removed, drip (water running along edge of snow house)'
GRI piiaʀ- 'remove, clean, take from' [piiʀ- 'remove, have gone away']

PE pikðaʀ 'lot (future possession)' [cf. kðaʀ]
AAY pikaXtə- 'get s.th. for (s.o.)', piksautə- 'get'
CAY pikaq 'future possession', pikaʀ- 'get s.th.'
NSY —
CSY —
Sir —
SPI pikšaq 'future possession'
NAI pikšaq 'future possession' [verbal = 'get s.th.'; pikšiaq 'share of s.th.']
WCI piksaʀsiuq- 'go look for s.th.' [piksaqsi- 'obtain s.th.', also Sig piksaŋayaʀa 'I'd like to have that', and Schn. has B. Lake pitsaq- (for piksaq-?) 'get what one needs']
ECI pitsaq 's.th. that can be used, thing destined for s.o.', pitsa(q)- 'bring together things one wants to own' [pitsasi- 'procure, get something', and pitsasiuq- 'look for s.th. another needs']
GRI piššaq 'lot, share' [piššiaq 'fiance, sweetheart', piššaʀsiaq 's.th. one has acquired', piššaʀsiuʀ- 'try to acquire s.th. (for self or another)']

PE pikə- 'own' [cf. kə-[1]]
AAY pikə- 'own'
CAY pikə-
NSY —
CSY pikə-
Sir [pikəŋə- 'obtain'; Vakh. has also pikŋ̥əʀəlŋuX 'having or doing nothing' from Rub.]
SPI pii- 'own'
NAI piɣɨ-
WCI piɣi-
ECI piɣi-
GRI piɣi-

PI pikšamaaq- 'desire or look forward to' [cf. pikðaʀ above and (u)maʀ(aʀ)-]
SPI pikšamaaq- 'want to get'
NAI pikšamaaq- 'desire, want to have'
WCI —
ECI —
GRI piššamaaʀ- 'look forward to s.th.' [piššamaat 's.th. saved for later, in reserve']

PI pilaaq- 'be late or long doing?' [cf. la(C)aʀ-?]
SPI —
NAI [note pilʸaaqtuaq- 'babysit', pilʸaaqtɨ 'babysitter']
WCI —
ECI pilaaq- 'will do later or tomorrow'
GRI pilaaʀ- 'be late, be a long time doing'

PE pili- 'make s.th.' [cf. li-; probably a productive combination in other languages/dialects than those indicated, with predictable meaning in other than GRI]
AAY pili- 'make s.th.'
CAY pili-
NSY —
CSY —
Sir —
SPI —
NAI pilʸi-
WCI pili-
ECI —
GRI pili- 'gather winter provisions' [piliat 'winter provisions']

PI pilliun 'gift?' [cf. liʀ- (esp. WG łłiʀ-) and un?]
SPI —
NAI Mal pilʸiun 'blessing'
WCI —
ECI piliutitsaq 'gift to give away free' [and note piliusaq 'charity gift (received)', piliuti- 'invite to take part in a game']
GRI piłłiut 'sacrifice' [and piłłiʀ- 'invite to feast', piłłii- 'make a sacrifice']

PI pillu(a)ʀik- 'be capable or clever' [cf. l(l)u(C)aʀ- and kiɣ-]
SPI —
NAI pilʸlʸuʀik- 'be cooperative, take the initiative'
WCI Car? pilluʀik- 'do well, succeed' [Schn. 'adg.']
ECI [pillaʀi(k)- 'do well, prosper' — compare piyyaʀik- under pižžaq(-)]
GRI piłłuʀiɣ-, piłłaqqiɣ-, NG pilluʀik- 'be clever or capable' [Holt.; compare pikkuʀiɣ- under pəkku(ɣ)-]

PE pi(t)lu(C)aʀ- or **pil(l)u(C)aʀ-** 'do or take (too) much' [cf. tluk- if not l(l)u(C)aʀ-]
AAY —
CAY piluaqaʀ- 'be fortunate, catch lots'
NSY piluaʀnəq 'cocky person', piluaXtaq 'insolence', piluałəq 'impertinent response' [L.-T.]
CSY —
Sir —
SPI piluaq- 'take too much'
NAI —
WCI —
ECI piluaq- 'do too much, be extravagant', piluaʀi- 'think another or oneself has taken or gotten too much'
GRI piluaʀi- [half-trans. piluaʀ-] 'reject, neglect'

PE piłuɣ- 'be bad or violent' [cf. łuɣ(-)]
AAY C piłuxqə- 'wreck, foul up, mess up'
CAY Nun piłuxtə- 'break'
NSY piłuɣ- 'fight', piłuk 'war'
CSY piłuɣaʀ- 'fight'
Sir —
SPI Qaw piłukataq- 'make excessive noise, do in a careless manner' [and Imaq piłuk 'war']
NAI pilʸuk- 'be bad' [and Mal piłʸłʸuktaq-, piłʸłʸukataq- 'do carelessly', = B pikałaktaq-]
WCI [Sig pilut 'sin']
ECI piluC- 'be poor', pilukaC- 'act badly, get angry'

GRI piluɣ- 'have bad equipment', [and note pilukat- 'play tricks', piʀłuɣ- 'meet with an accident, be plagued by bad weather', piʀłuk 'misfortune, bad weather', piʀłuut 'misfortune', piʀłukuq 'rubbish' NG piʀluk- 'break'; compare also pikataɣ- 'be careless' with the NAI above]

PE pinaʀ- 'be conducive?' [cf. naʀ-]
AAY KP pinaʀ- 'be good weather'
CAY —
NSY —
CSY pinaʀ- 'begin to melt (rivers and lakes in spring)'
Sir —
SPI —
NAI pinʸaq- 'be generous'
WCI pinaq- 'overflow (cup of tea)' [and note pinailaq 's.th. not allowed']
ECI Lab pinaq- 'be beautiful weather' [Peck; and note pinna(q)- 'be generous; pinnait- 'be miserly', contam. with pinnaʀ(naq)-?]
GRI pinaʀ- 'be easy to deal with' [and pinaat- 'refuse to do s.th.', pinaʀtuq 's.th. special']

PE pinəʀłuɣ- and **pinəʀłi-** 'act badly' [cf. nəʀłuɣ- and for the second form also li-[1]?]
AAY —
CAY pinəXłuxtə- 'have trouble'
NSY —
CSY pinəʀłuɣ-, pinəʀłiqə- 'be obstinate, stubborn or heedless'
Sir pinəXłiqə(s)- 'not obey' [Em.]
SPI —
NAI pinʸɨʀli- 'inadvertantly startle and cause to run away, be inadvertantly startled (game animal)'
WCI piniʀluk- 'act or do badly'
ECI piniʀlu(k)- 'damage', piniʀli(C)- 'do the wrong way, damage'
GRI piniʀłuɣ- 'act badly', piniʀłi- 'oppose, hinder (s.o.)'

PI piniaq- 'hunt or try to acquire' [cf. ni(C)aʀ-]
SPI piniaq- 'hunt'
NAI PH pinʸiaq- 'hunt' [pinʸiaqtɨ 'provider']
WCI —
ECI piniaq- 'try to do'
GRI piniaʀ- 'try to do or get, go hunting' [piniaʀtuq 'hunter', piniaʀti 'provider']

PE pinqiɣ- 'be careful or well?' [cf. nqiɣ-[1]]
AAY —
CAY pinqəx(tə)- 'be neat, precise'
NSY [note pinkəxtaq (for pinqəxtaq?) 'dilligent or wily person']
CSY [note pəXqinəʀ- 'be clever', pəXqiniqə- 'be sly, tricky']
Sir —
SPI pitqik- 'do well or again'
NAI [note picqik- 'cheat, be devious', picqiksiʀaq- 'do secretly, dishonestly']
WCI — [note pitqiɣiaq- 'get worse after abating (storm or fever)' — with nqiɣ-[2]?]
ECI —
GRI piqqiɣ- 'be well, healthy', EG 'be beautiful' [piqqissi- 'have got well', EG piqqitsi- 'have cleared up (weather)', and WG piqqissaaʀ- 'be careful, tidy', also perhaps piqqissimi(ɣi)- 'regret, repent']

PE piŋit- 'not have (anything) or be absent' [cf. ŋit-; the meaning 'not have' is predictable, but the meaning 'be absent' is not]
AAY piitə- 'not have any, be absent'
CAY Y piitə-
NSY piitə-
CSY piŋitə- 'not have any' [and note also piitə- 'eat the last meat clinging to a bone'?]
Sir —
SPI piit- 'not have any, be absent'
NAI piic- 'be absent, missing'
WCI piit- 'not have any (left)'
ECI [note Lab piittuk 'blunt (tool)' in Andersen et al.]
GRI piit- 'be poor'

PE piŋŋuðaʀ- 'play or pretend' [cf. ŋ(ŋ)uðaʀ(-)]
AAY piŋuaʀ- 'be fussy, particular'
CAY piŋuaʀ- 'pretend, play, act in a non-serious way'
NSY —
CSY piŋʷaaʀ-
Sir —
SPI piŋuaq- 'pretend to do s.th.'
NAI piŋŋuaq-
WCI piŋŋuaq- Sig 'pretend, make believe' [Lowe; Met. has 'play', as also B.-S. for Car]
ECI piŋŋua(q)- 'play' [as nom. = 'toy']
GRI piŋŋuaʀ- 'play' [and piŋŋuaq 'toy, trifle']

PI piqqun 'property' [cf. q(q)un]
SPI —
NAI — [compare piun 'possession' with un]
WCI Sig piq(q)utit 'belongings' [Schn. has piqquti for 'adg']
ECI piquti '(s.o.'s) property, collar, decoration on bottom of woman's parka' [Bourq. has piqquti for Lab]
GRI piqut '(s.o.'s) property, baggage', EG piʀilit 'material (for clothing)' [and note piquut '(permanent) stores', piqqumaat 'store, cache'; compare NG piʀluut 'belonging(s), property', EG piʀuyuulit 'belongings' (Robbe and Menn.); for piqqut 'reason' see piðqun above]

PI piʀuq- 'develop' [cf. ʀuq- under ŋ(ŋ)uʀ-]
SPI —
NAI piʀuq- 'be a success, amount to s.th., be haughty'
WCI piʀuq- 'become better'
ECI piʀuq- 'have grown or developed'
GRI piʀuʀ-, puyaʀuʀ- 'develop, grow' [and piXXuuʀ-, piʀuuʀ- 'be haughty', piʀuʀsaʀ- 'bring up, educate']

PY pisuʀ- 'hunt' [cf. ci(C)uʀ-]
AAY pisuʀ- 'hunt' [also trans.]
CAY pisuʀ-, NSU pisaaʀ- 'hunt' [the former also trans.; compare under ci(C)uʀ- for the latter]
NSY —
CSY —

PE pitaʀ 'animal caught' [pass. part. of pitə-[2] below — cf. also ðaʀ]
AAY pitaq 'game, thing caught' [pitaqə- 'catch']
CAY pitaq, pittaq 'thing caught, quarry, gift acquired at a feast' [and pitaqə- 'catch', with p.b. kə-[1]]
NSY —
CSY —
Sir —
SPI pitaʀi- 'catch (in hunting)'
NAI — [for pisaʀi- 'make an attempt at killing (animal)' see pityaqə-]
WCI pitaʀi- 'catch'
ECI [note pitaqaʀ- 'have, (impersonal) be', pitaʀi- 'own']
GRI [note pišaq 's.th. caught', pišaqaʀ-, pišaʀi- 'catch' — directly from pi- used transitively]

PI pitcu(q)- 'be a skilled hunter' [cf. pitə-[2] below and yu-]
SPI pissuq- 'be experienced at hunting'
NAI pitcuq-, pitcik- 'be a good hunter'
WCI —
ECI pitsuyuq 'good shot, good hunter'
GRI —

PY pitə-[1] 'come up' [cf. t-[1], here reflexive, and Aleut hit- 'go out, grow, become, make, etc.']
AAY —
CAY pittə- 'rise (sun)'
NSY —
CSY piitə- 'come into view or existence, sprout, rise (sun)' [and piitəsiʀaq 'flower' — compare PE naɣucciʀaʀ 'plant' under naɣu-]
Sir [for mit(ə)- 'rise, grow' see uvi(t)-; Vakh. has pitəsiʀaX 'flower', probably from CSY — compare mitita under uvi(t)-]

PY pitə-[2] 'take game' [cf. t-[2]]
AAY pitə- 'take game'
CAY pitə-, pittə- 'take game'
NSY —
CSY —
Inu [note Car pitaq- 'hunt seals in kayak' with related p.b. taʀ- — Pryde]

PY-S pivakə- 'value highly' [cf. vaɣ and kə-[1]]
AAY —
CAY pivakə- 'boast (of)'
NSY —
CSY pivakə- 'prize, value' [and pivaŋʀu- 'be thrifty or careful with']
Sir pivakə(s)- 'be thrifty or careful with, value' [Em.]

PE piciʀ '(song about) factual event?' [cf. pi- and uciʀ?]
AAY piciq 'proper way of doing things, religious law' [also picinək 'really']
CAY piciq 'fact, s.th. that really occurred' [and piciu- 'be true, correct'; for piciatun 'any old way' see piciatun under pi(-)]
NSY — [but note pisayŋa- 'sing a throat-song']
CSY —
Sir —
SPI Di piziq 'song or dance commemorating the deeds of an uncle or grandfather' [Jen.]
NAI —
WCI pisiq 'dance song'
ECI pisiq '(Eskimo) song with chorus'
GRI pisiq '(drum) song'

PE piðaɣ- or **piðaʀaɣ-** 'slide well' [cf. pi- and žak-?]
AAY piʀaʀ- 'be speedy, fast, capable of moving fast'
CAY piiʀaɣ-, HBC, NSU piiʀiɣ-, Nun nəpiʀaɣ- 'be slick, frictionless' [the last form influenced by nəpət-?]
NSY —
CSY piiʀaXtə- 'do or go quickly'
Sir pižaʀ- 'do or go quickly' [Orr]
SPI —
NAI piak- 'be slippery, slide easily, be thin (soup)' [and piaq- 'be waxed (thread)']
WCI piak- 'slide well'
ECI piak- 'slide well (sled runners), have a slightly salty taste (water)' [and piit- 'slide badly', piʀʀiyaq- 'use s.th. that slides well']
GRI puyaɣ-, piXXaɣ-, EG piaC-, NG piak- 'slide smoothly (boat or sled)' [note also piXXi- 'slip over edge, into sea']

PE piðaqə(naʀ)- and **piðaʀ(naʀ)-** 'be difficult' [cf. pi-, ðaʀ- (ðaqə-) and naʀ-?]
AAY ➡
CAY ➡
NSY —
CSY piyaqn̥aʀ- 'be difficult'
Sir piyaqn̥əʀ- 'be difficult' [Orr — from CSY]
SPI —
NAI —
WCI —
ECI piyaʀniit- 'be irritable, be difficult to do', Lab piyannit- 'be difficult' [and piyaʀiattu(q)- 'take a long time', piyaʀiatuɣi- 'find that (s.th.) takes too long, is too much work']
GRI pišaʀiu-, pišaʀi(a)tu- 'be complicated, require much effort' [and pišaʀiššiʀšuʀ- 'cause difficulty for']

> **PE piðaqəŋit-** 'be easy' [cf. ŋit-]
> AAY piaʀaitə- 'be easy'
> CAY piyaʀaitə-
> NSY [piyaqn̥aitə- 'be easy' — from *piðaqənaʀit-]
> CSY —
> Sir —
> SPI
> NAI —
> WCI —
> ECI [piyaʀnituq 'easy, docile', Lab piyanniŋit- 'be easy']
> GRI pišaʀiit- 'be easy or fast'

PY piɣinaq 'aged dried fish eggs'
AAY K piɣinaq, C piinaq 'aged fish eggs added to cooked salmon eggs (fish-egg cheese)'
CAY Y, NS piɣinaq 'aged dried fish eggs'
NSY —
CSY —

PE piɣinəʀ 'boot straw'
AAY —
CAY piinəq* 'insole'
NSY pi(i)nəq 'straw insole'
CSY piɣinəq*
Sir piɣənəX [Em.], píɣnəX [Orr] 'insole'
SPI piniq
NAI pinʸɨq* 'insole' [and pinʸnʸɨq- 'put insoles in boots']
WCI piniq 'felt slip-on shoe'
ECI piniq 'insole' [and piniʀait 'stockings']
GRI piniq*, pl. piʀnit, piʀŋit, EG piit 'straw for boot insoles' [piniʀ- 'put straw in boots']

PE pilaɣ- 'butcher' [cf. Atkan Aleut hilɣi- 'dig (e.g. for roots), dig out (fox — its den)']
AAY pilaɣ- 'butcher'
CAY pilaɣ- 'slit, cut into, butcher'
NSY pilaɣ- 'cut, perform surgery' [L.-T.]
CSY pilaɣ- 'slit up, butcher'
Sir —
SPI pilak-
NAI pilʸak-
WCI pilak-
ECI pilak-
GRI pilaɣ-

PE pilaɣtuʀ- 'cut up' [cf. tuʀ-[2]]
AAY —
CAY pilaxtuʀ- 'undergo or perform surgery'
NSY pilaxtuʀ- 'make a surgical incision' [ANLC]
CSY pilaxtuʀ- 'repeatedly cut, saw'
Sir —
SPI [pilaaqtuq- 'cut up (meat)', Qaw 'operate on']
NAI pilʸaktuq- 'perform surgery on'
WCI —
ECI pilattu(q)- 'cut up, operate on'
GRI pilattuʀ- 'cut or saw up, operate on' [pilattuut 'saw']

PI pilaun 'knife for butchering' [cf. un]
SPI pilaun 'large knife used for butchering'
NAI pilʸaun
WCI pilaun
ECI pilauti 'hunting knife, lancet'
GRI EG pilaalaq 'knife'

PI pil(l)aq- 'punish' [cf. pi(-) and p.b. łłaq-?]
SPI —
NAI —
WCI —
ECI pilaq- 'punish'
GRI piłłaʀ-

PI pilinʀu- 'be envious' [cf. pi(-)?]
SPI —
NAI pilʸinʸʀu- 'be unwilling to give up a possession, covet s.th. (esp. s.th. belonging to a dead relative)'
WCI pilinʀuɣi- 'be jealous of, want to keep for oneself'
ECI piliʀŋu- 'be jealous of s.o. who got s.th. while one got nothing oneself'
GRI piliʀnu- 'be envious, want everything s.o. else has'

PY piluɣ(uɣ)- 'put on clothes or footwear'
AAY —
CAY piluɣ-, piluɣuɣ- 'put on footwear', piluɣuk 'skin boot', NSU 'clothing' [for the latter compare kamɣuk under kaməɣ]
NSY —
CSY piluɣuɣ- 'put on clothes', piluɣuk 'clothing'

PI pima- 'provide for or look after others?' [cf. pi(-) and (u)ma- and compare also pima(a)q-]
SPI —
NAI —
WCI Sig pimayi 'attendant, overseer' [and Schn. has Baker Lake pimalliq- 'take care of' and pimayaq- 'give freely' for 'adg']
ECI pima- 'work on (s.th.) or for (s.o.)', pimayi 'servant' [but Igl 'hunter, provider' in Ras. — Hall has 'great man, chief' and Boas has pimain 'chief, experienced man'; Peck has pima- 'take care of, work for', intr. 'be made or procured' for Lab]
GRI [note pimmak 'experienced (person)', pimmaa- 'be experienced']

PI pima(a)q- 'claim (as)' [cf. pi(-) and (u)maʀ(aʀ)- and compare also pima-]
SPI —
NAI pimaaq- 'claim', pimaqtuq- 'claim as one's relative', Mal pimaktuq- 'be cordial toward' [and pimaʀi- 'have great affection for, regard as a relative']
WCI Baker Lake pimaq- 'want or desire a great deal' [Schn.]
ECI pimaq- 'own outright, not want others to have'
GRI — [but note p.b. maaʀ- under (u)maʀ(aʀ)- as in ilamaaʀ- 'give s.th. for sake of relationship']

PE pimci 'dried fish' [cf. pipək-?]
AAY PWS miŋciq 'dry fish'
CAY Nun piŋciX 'half-dried dolly varden' [with dissim.?]
NSY —
CSY —
Sir —
SPI pipsiʀaq 'dried fish'
NAI pipsi
WCI pipsi
ECI pitsik 'dʀied fish' [Peck has pipsi foʀ Lab]
GRI missi, nissi 'dried fish' [old oʀtho. mivse, nivse — Fab. has mipse, mivse, nipse]

PI pinnaʀ(naq)- 'be good or likable' [cf. nnaq and pinniʀ-]
SPI pinna(ʀ)naq- 'be beautiful'

NAI pinʸnʸaʀi- 'find good, pleasing, beautiful', pinʸnʸaʀnaq- 'be beautiful, pleasing'
WCI pinnaʀi- 'cherish, prefer', Sig pinnaknak- [for pinnaʀnaq-?] 'be likable'
ECI pinna(a)q 'friend, close companion', Baffin pinnaʀi- 'consider handsome (biblical)', Lab pinaʀnaq- 'be nice, pleasant' [Peck]
GRI pinnaʀi- 'to think or find beautiful'

PE pinniʀ- 'be good or beautiful' [cf. pi(-) and p.b. n(n)iʀ-; compare also pinnaʀ(naq)-]
AAY piniʀ- 'be good to do'
CAY piniʀ- 'be strong', Nun 'be good'
NSY piniʀ- 'be good' [L.-T.]
CSY piniʀ- 'be good, satisfying'
Sir [pinəqaX 'amulet' (Orr) is probably from Chukchi penaqalɣən 'tassle worn on clothing by shaman'] ➟
SPI ➟
NAI —
WCI Cop pinniq- 'be pretty' [Ras.]
ECI Lab piniq- 'be good' [Peck]
GRI pinniʀ- 'be beautiful'

PY piniqə- 'like or love' [cf. kə-1]
AAY —
CAY Nun piniqə- 'like, love'
NSY piniqə- 'love, become loved' [ANLC also 'gain respect, become a favorite']
CSY piniqə- 'like, love, approve'

PY pinitun 'well' [aequalis case]
AAY —
CAY —
NSY pinitun 'well' [ANLC]
CSY pinitun

PE pinniʀit- 'be ugly or bad' [cf. ŋit- — note the variant form in the Yup]
AAY —
CAY piniatə- 'be weak', Nun 'be bad'
NSY piniatə- 'be unwell, not good' [ANLC]
CSY —
Sir —
SPI Qaw pinniit- 'be ugly'
NAI —
WCI Cop pinniit- 'be ugly' [Lowe]
ECI Lab pin(n)iit- 'not be nice' [Peck]
GRI pinniit- 'be ugly'

PE pinquciʀ 'condition or manner' [cf. pi(-) and uciʀ and perhaps nqiɣ-[2]]
AAY —
CAY —
NSY —
CSY pinqusiq 'present state or condition'
Sir —
SPI piłquziq 'habit'
NAI pitqusiq, pilʸʀusiq 'habit' [pitqusiʀiit- 'have bad habits']
WCI pitqusiq 'habit' [and note Sig pitqutaq 'obstacle, cause of misfortune']
ECI piqqusiq 'tradition, culture, manner' [Saul; and note piqqusiʀaq- 'perform a certain dance (women)']
GRI [note piqqusiʀłuɣ- 'be hypocritical, false', piqqusiʀsuu- 'be cunning', piqqutsiʀ- 'dissimulate']

PE piŋayut 'three' [cf. dem. root piŋ- — the reference is to the middle finger in counting; the corresponding ordinal in Yup is regular — the base plus 3p possess. ending -at, piŋayuat, etc.]
AAY piŋa<y>un 'three'
CAY piŋayun
NSY piŋayut
CSY piŋayut
Sir piŋəyux
SPI piŋasut 'three' [and KI piŋayuak 'third, Wednesday', but Imaq piŋasuat 'third']
NAI piŋasut 'three' [and piŋayuat 'third']
WCI piŋasut 'three' [and Lowe has Holman Island piŋahuat 'third', Ow. piŋayuak 'Wednesday' for EP]
ECI piŋasut 'three' [and piŋayuat 'third']
GRI piŋasut 'three' [and piŋayuat 'third']

PE piŋu-[1] 'push (over)' [cf. Aleut hiŋu- 'push']
AAY
CAY —
NSY —
CSY —
Sir piŋə-, pəŋə- 'push' [Vakh.]
SPI Imaq piŋu- 'push, let fall'
NAI piŋu- 'go out' [for pinʸŋui- 'get a dislocated joint' see pətluɣ-[1]]
WCI piŋu- 'push', piŋuq- 'fall, push onto back'
ECI piŋu- 'push over (onto back)'
GRI piŋu(ɣ)- 'hit with fist' [also pikuɣ- (influenced by pəkə-?); for homonym meaning 'rebound (harpoon)' see pənŋu(ʀ)-; note also piŋuuʀ- 'berate, scold']

PE piŋu-[2] 'be useful or right' [cf. pi(-), postbase ŋu- 'be'?]
AAY piu- 'be the right one'
CAY piu- 'be the (right) one'
NSY —
CSY —
Sir —
SPI piu- 'be usable'
NAI piu- 'be it' [and piunʀiq- 'become useless, become angry, irrational', piuŋilʸaq 's.th. of no value', Mal piuŋŋilʸaq 'ghost']
WCI Cop piuŋŋilʀuq 's.th. that is (worth) nothing' [Ras.]
ECI piu- 'be good, holy' [piusaq- 'adorn, make pretty']
GRI piu- 'be usable' [and piuŋŋit- 'be useless', piuʀsaʀ- 'repair (house), adorn oneself', piukkut(i)- 'consider useful' — compare ayukkut(i)- 'feel humble' from ayuq- and pikkut(i)- 'feel embarrassed (from imposing on s.o. too much)' from pi(-)]

PI pipək- 'split lengthwise' [there may be a link to pimci]
SPI —
NAI —
WCI [Car pipinniq 'tidal crack in ice around shoreline' (Pryde)]

ECI pipiC- 'be divided lengthwise, open up along (e.g. join or line of holes)'
GRI NWG pipiɣ- 'have burst at the crotch' [and pipitiR- 'flense (seal) so the meat adheres to the skin']

PE piRðaR- 'braid or weave' [for the (metathesized?) Inu forms note that *ðR becomes lR regularly in PH and Cop at least; the X in Yup is from *RaR]
AAY ➡
CAY ➡
NSY piiXə- 'braid, weave'
CSY piiXə- 'braid'
Sir piRcəR- 'braid, weave'
SPI piRlaq-, Qaw pilRaq- 'braid'
NAI pilʸRaq- 'braid' [and pilʸRaiyuuRaq 'spider']
WCI pilRaq- 'braid' [and pilRaisuqtuq 'spider']
ECI piRRai- 'plait'
GRI piRłaR- 'twist', piRłaa- 'braid hair' [piRłaRniq* 'plait of hair']

PE piRðaRaR 'braid or woven thing'
AAY C piiXaq 'woven mat', AP 'insole'
CAY piiXaq 'two-ply cordage, string of interlaced fish'
NSY piiXaq 'braided hair'
CSY —
Sir [note piRžasaq 'braided hair']
SPI piRlaaq 's.th. braided (sinew, yarn, hair),' Qaw pilRaq 'braided hair, yarn',
NAI pilʸRa<R>aq 'braided sinew'
WCI pilRaqtat 'braids' [Ras. has pe(r)lrarnerut 'hair braid of caribou skin' for Car]
ECI piRRaaq 'plait of hair, whale ligament, thread' [and Parry has Igl piliRa 'line (platted) of sinew']
GRI piRłaaq 'twisted sinew thread' [and piRłaayaq 'braid']

PE piRlaɣ 'sled runner' [there may be a link to piðaɣ-]
AAY piRlak 'sled runner'
CAY piRlak
NSY —
CSY —
Sir —
SPI [note FR piRlaaŋa- 'be bowlegged']
NAI Nu piRlʸa<ž>aq 'long sled slat'
WCI pilRaak (dual) 'sled runners' [influenced by piRðaR-? — but compare Sig qinRiq- under qiRnəR-; Ras. has Car pelrat 'sledge shoes' — B.-S. has Car pilRaaq, Net pižRaaq 'sledge shoe']
ECI piRRaaq 'metal strip for sled runner'
GRI piRłaaq 'sled runner' [and piRłaaRi- 'run over']

PE piRtuR 'snowstorm'
AAY KP, AP piXtuq, K paiXtuq 'snowstorm' [the second form influenced by paiXtə- 'meet' under paðəR-?]
CAY piXtuk, piXta 'snowstorm'
NSY piXtuq 'snowstorm' [and ANLC has piXtə- 'be a snowstorm']
CSY piXtuq 'drifting snow'
Sir —
SPI Imaq piqtuq 'snowstorm'
NAI ➡
WCI piqtuq 'drift snow'
ECI piqtuq 'snow flurry' [Saul — Schn. has piiqtuq]
GRI piRsuq 'snowstorm' [and note also piRsuRi 'sea drift', as verb 'be whipped up by storm (water)']

PE piRciR- 'be a snowstorm' [cf. liR-]
AAY piXciq-, K paiXciq- 'be a snowstorm'
CAY piXciR- 'be a blizzard'
NSY piXsiR-
CSY —
Sir —
SPI piqsiq- 'be a snowstorm'
NAI piqsiq- 'be a wet snowstorm' [also nominal]
WCI piqsiq-, Net piqsilaqi- 'drift (snow)'
ECI piRsi(q)- [Tar also piiRsi(q)- acc. Schn.] 'snow'
GRI piRsiR- 'be a snowstorm'

PE piRtuRciRaR 'river otter'
AAY —
CAY Eg, NSU piXtuqciRaq 'river otter'
NSY piXtuXsiqaq 'river otter' [but ANLC has 'sable, marten']
CSY piXtuXsəRaq 'river otter or fur seal'
Sir piXtuXsəRaq 'river otter'
SPI piqtaziRaq, Qaw piqtuqsiRaq 'river otter'
NAI —
WCI Sig piqtuqsiRaq 'lynx'
ECI piqtusiRaq
GRI —

PI pitciulaaq 'black guillemot'
SPI —
NAI —
WCI Net, Car pitsiulaaq 'black guillemot' [B.-S.]
ECI pitsiulaaq
GRI —

PE pitəɣ- 'shoot with an arrow'
AAY pitəɣ- 'shoot with an arrow'
CAY pitəɣ-
NSY pitəɣ- [ANLC]
CSY pitəxtə-
Sir pitəɣ- [Orr]
SPI pitik- 'hit with a shot'
NAI pisik- 'hit with arrow or bullet'
WCI pitik- 'shoot at' [pitiksi 'bow']
ECI pitik- 'kill with an arrow'
GRI pisiɣ- 'shoot with a bow'

PE pitəɣcaR- 'shoot an arrow' [cf. caR-]
AAY pitəxcaR- 'shoot an arrow'
CAY [pitəxcaRaq 'lance', pitexcaun 'arrow']
NSY pitəxsaR- 'shoot an arrow' [ANLC]
CSY pitəxsaR- 'go shooting with bow and arrow'
Sir pitəxsiR- [for pitəxsəR-?] 'shoot, boom (of shot)'
SPI pitiksaq- 'shoot a bow and arrow or slingshot'
NAI pisiksaq- 'shoot an arrow, fire a gun'
WCI Sig pitiksaq- 'shoot with a gun'
ECI —
GRI pisissaaR- 'shoot with bow and arrow'

PI **pitəkcə** 'bow'
SPI —
NAI pisɨksɨ 'bow'
WCI pitiksi
ECI pitiksi
GRI pisissi(q) 'bow', EG pitsaq 'bow' [pisissani 'his (own) bow']

PE **pityaqə-** 'do deliberately' [cf. pi(-), tya- and ʀqə- or qə-?; there may be contam. with caʀ- in some forms here but see under that p.b. for its possible direct relat.]
AAY [note C pitaaʀ- 'do deliberately']
CAY pitsaqə- 'act intentionally (toward)' [trans. or intrans.]
NSY —
CSY —
Sir —
SPI pizaq- 'intend, do deliberately'
NAI pisaq-, pisaaʀɨ-, Mal pisaʀɨ- 'do s.th. (to s.o.) deliberately (trans. or intrans.)', Nu pityaq- 'rush to do s.th.' [and pisaʀɨ- 'try to kill (animal)', piyaaʀɨ- 'treat badly, roughly']
WCI pisaʀi- 'do deliberately' [Met. — Lowe has Sig pisaaʀima-; Schn. has piyaʀi- 'do on purpose' for 'adg', and Briggs has Utk piyaaʀi- 'say on purpose, joke']
ECI piyaaʀi- 'do s.th. on purpose (to s.o.), have killed (s.o. — of illness or persecutor), have killed a whale'
GRI piaaʀi- 'do s.th. on purpose' [and note pisaʀ- 'kill oneself']

PI **piuq-** 'move in on game' [cf. pi(-) and (C)uʀ-?]
Yup [note CAY piuʀ(aʀ)- 'keep acting or being as one is']
SPI KI, W piuq- 'paddle hard toward a seal, etc.' [Jen.]
NAI piuq- 'paddle toward'
WCI piuq- 'creep up on game (bent over but not crawling)'
ECI —
GRI piuʀ- 'paddle quickly toward sea mammal, swoop down on s.th. (bird of prey)'

PI **pivli(-)** 'be crazy or foolish?' [or pimli(-) — cf. perhaps pi(-) and mli-, in which case the original meaning could have been 'wander round at a loss']
SPI —
NAI —
WCI —
ECI Lab pivliŋait-, pivliŋaili- 'help oneself out of one's needy condition' [Peck, with ŋa-[1] or ŋa-[2] and ŋit- (and li-[2])?; Peacock, in his 1974 reworking of Erdman (Peck), gives the gloss as 'is making progress getting out of his poverty-stricken state' and Qumaq has for Tar 'is now OK, rich, can manage anything'; Spalding has NBI piłłaŋisaaqtuq 'mad dog', for or from *pilliŋasaaqtuq?]
GRI piłłi [Fab. peble, old ortho. pıvdle] 'mad or furious person', piłłiʀuʀ-, piʀłiʀuʀ- 'be mad' [the latter by contam. with pəʀləʀ-; Top also has piblilio- 'be murderous' and piblaror- 'be crazy'; Holt. has NG pilliʀuʀniq, pillaʀuʀniq as 'Arctic hysteria or drum-dance fit' — in modern NG it refers usually to rabies amongst dogs; note also piłłiŋayak 'one who acts foolishly', piłłiŋaaʀ- act crazy, treat s.o. harshly (so he starts to cry)']

PI **piyaʀəttuq-** 'wane and rise later and later (moon)' [cf. pi(-), ðaʀ- (ðaqə-) and tu-[1]]
SPI —
NAI piyaʀittuq- 'fall lower, wane and rise later than usual, come round more slowly (moon)'
WCI Sig piyaʀittuq- 'wane and rise later than usual (moon)'
ECI —
GRI —

PE **piyuɣ-** 'walk' [cf. pi(-) and yuɣ-?]
AAY ➟
CAY piyua-, Nun piuɣ-, HBC pəyuɣ-, pəyua- 'walk'
NSY pəyuɣ- 'walk' [ANLC, also for pəyua- 'take a long walk'; L.-T. has pəyuk 'pedestrian']
CSY piyuɣ- 'walk' [and piyaa- 'take a walk, hunt by walking on ice']
Sir piyəɣ-, piyuɣ- 'walk' [Vakh., who also has it as 'say' or 'do', the same as pi-; Men. has piyukšaʀaʀ- 'walk', piyuɣnəŋ 'on foot' and piyukasi- 'go hunting']
SPI Imaq pizukłiq- 'walking' [and pizuɣməŋ 'on foot', pizuaža(q)- 'hunt fur-bearing animal']
NAI pisuaq-, Nu pisuk-, Mal pišuk- 'walk'
WCI pisuk- 'walk' [and Sig pisuqi- 'go caribou hunting with bow and arrow' acc. Ras.]
ECI NBI, SB pisuk- 'walk' [and Tar pisuqitaq- 'walk up and down in a room']
GRI pisuɣ- 'walk'

PI **pisukkaaq** 'fox' [compare piyuɣte below]
SPI pizukaaʀžuk 'arctic fox'
NAI pisukkaaq 'fox', PH 'white fox, prey'
WCI Net pihukkaaq 'fox' [Ras.]
ECI [Spauld. has pisukkaq 'good walker' for NBI]
GRI —

PE **piyuɣtə** 'quadruped or walker' [cf. ðe]
AAY piuxta 'dog'
CAY —
NSY pəyuxtə 'foot hunter, pedestrian, tundra animal' [ANLC; L.-T. has pəyuałtə 'trapper, insect']
CSY —
Sir —
SPI pizuktə 'someone on foot, land animal'
NAI pisukti 'medium-sized fur-bearing animal — like fox'
WCI Sig pisukti 'colored fox' [and Ras. has Cop pihukti 'bear' as a shaman's word]
ECI pisukti 'land animal'
GRI —

PI **piyuɣaq-** 'stalk' [cf. piyuɣ-?; there may be contam. with piuq-]
SPI piyuaq- 'stalk an animal'
NAI piyuɣak- 'stalk an animal (crawling)', Nu piyuɣaq- 'pursue'

WCI [Cop piyuɣaq- 'attack' acc. Pryde; for piuq- 'creep up on game' see piuq-]
ECI piyuɣaʀi- 'long to go there (sea) to see if there is any game', Lab piyuɣaC- 'persecute, try to kill' [Bourq.]
GRI piuaʀłi-, piuaʀłiaʀi- 'creep up on' [and piuaat- (old ortho. piuait-) 'be gentle']

PI pižaʀiiq- 'have finished' [cf. piðaqə(naʀ)- and ŋiʀ-]
SPI —
NAI —
WCI Net pižaʀiiq- 'have finished' [Dor.]
ECI piyaʀiiq- 'have finished' [Dor. has piyaaʀi- 'finish' for NBI]
GRI piaʀiiʀ-, pišaʀiiʀ- 'have finished, prepared, arranged s.th., be ready'

PI pižək- 'get down (from sleeping platform)' [cf. pi(-) and perhaps p.b. ðiɣ-; compare makšək- under makət-]
SPI pižik- 'get down, take down' [note Imaq pəžək- 'take away, be blown away (by wind)']
NAI pižik- 'get down, jump down quickly', Nu 'go down to river'
WCI Car piyik- 'dress in the morning' [Schn.]
ECI piyik- 'reach solid ice from land (crossing ice floes)' [and piyitsima- 'be dressed']
GRI pisiɣ- 'get up and get dressed' [NG pihixxi- 'drop']

PI pižžaq(-) '(be) strong or dexterous?' [cf. pi(-) and ðaʀ-? — the GRI could be a back-formation from pižžaʀik- with p.b. kiɣ- as in most other dialects]
Yup — [note CSY piža(a)ʀaʀ- 'benefit, succeed, have advantage']
SPI pižža.luk- 'have a serious accident', pižža.luaŋa- 'be clumsy, do things wrong'
NAI pižžaʀik- 'be dexterous, graceful, do easily' [note geminating ʀik- under kiɣ- (involving a nominalization); also pižžaʀluk- 'do wrong unintentionally' with łuɣ(-)]
WCI piyyaʀik- 'be adroit' [Schn. has Car piyyu- 'be strong']
ECI piyyaʀik- 'can do well' [piyyait- 'cannot do (well)']
GRI piššaq 'someone strong, powerful', piššak 'strength, power' [and note NG pissaihua- 'be restless']

PI pualʀin 'shovel' [cf. un]
SPI Qaw pualʀin 'shovel'
NAI pualʀin[y]
WCI pualʀin
ECI puaʀʀit
GRI EG puaʀtit 'shovel' [and verbal puaʀti(kkaʀ)-]

PI pualu 'thick skin mitten' [cf. puɣə-, pu(ɣ)uq and Aleut EA huɣalu-X, huɣulu-X, old Atkan du. (h)uɣaluʀi-x 'sealskin mitten, glove', western EA also 'wrist-guard for bow']
SPI pualu 'elbow-length fur mitten'
NAI pualuk 'pair of trail mittens with fur outside'
WCI pualuk 'mittens' [Sig 'bear-skin mittens'; Pryde also has verbal pualu- 'put on mittens']
ECI pualu(k), Iti paaluk [Dor.] 'mitten'
GRI pualut [pl.], NG pualuk [du.] 'mittens for hunting on ice'

PE puci- 'lie face down' [cf. put-, also Aleut husuɣ- 'lie prostrate']
AAY —
CAY pucikaʀ- 'fall forward'
NSY —
CSY —
Sir —
SPI Qaw pusiiɣaq- 'roll, tumble forward'
NAI pusikaq- 'fall forward'
WCI pusi- 'be upside down' [and Ras. has Car puhik- 'capsize in kayak'; Pryde also has Cop puttikaq- 'fall on face (child)']
ECI pusiɣaq- 'bump head', Lab 'fall on face'
GRI pusi- 'be upside down (boat, etc.)', pusiɣaʀ- 'fall on face'

> **PI pucit-** 'turn upside down' [cf. t-[1]]
> SPI puzit- 'close (knife)' [Jen.]
> NAI pusit- 'turn upside down, with face down'
> WCI pusit- 'turn upside down'
> ECI pusit-
> GRI pusit-

PI pucitaq 'fringe around anorak hood?' [there may be a link to puci-]
SPI —
NAI —
WCI Cop puhitaq 'fringe around hood' [Ras.]
ECI —
GRI pusisaq 'cut-off end of boat skin used to cover tent pole and block opening', NG puhihaq 'fringe or anorak hood'

PE puɣə- 'surface or emerge' [cf. pu(ɣ)uq but also puvə- and perhaps Aleut huɣinɣi-X 'confined air (in stomach or bladder)']
AAY puɣə- 'surface, emerge from water'
CAY puɣə- 'come to surface, emerge halfway', puɣa 'surfaced seal'
NSY puɣə- 'come to surface'
CSY puuɣ- 'surface, come up for air (whale)' [and puɣnaan 'float, inflated poke']
Sir puɣ(ə)- 'appear (whale)'
SPI pui- 'emerge, surface'
NAI pu<ɣ>i-
WCI pui-
ECI pui- 'emerge, surface' [puiyi 'sea mammal' (in Tar one poking head out of water — any kind of seal); and puiɣaq- 'appear at surface (several whales)']
GRI pui- 'get out of water (sea mammal), rise to surface (fish)' [puiši, EG puiliq 'seal', NG puihi 'ringed seal', NG puiɣaq- 'come up to breathe (seal)'; also puisaʀtuʀtuq, Up puiqilaʀtiq 'seal in its breathing hole']

> **PY-S puɣlər-** 'float up' [cf. ləʀ-]
> AAY puɣləXtə- 'surface suddenly'
> CAY Nun puɣləXtə- 'float'

NSY puɣləʀ- 'surface (inanimate object or sea mammal)' [ANLC]
CSY puɣləʀ- 'surface, come out'
Sir puɣləʀ- 'float up'

PE puɣ(ə)mə(t)- 'swim' [compare ku(C)imə-]
AAY —
CAY —
NSY —
CSY puɣimə-, puɣimaʀ- 'swim'
Sir puɣmə-
SPI puivžaq-, Qaw, W puuvžaq-, FR puuɣžaq- 'swim'
NAI puumɨt-, puuvžaq-, puuvžaq- 'swim'
WCI puuvyaq- 'swim' [Pryde; Met. has puviaq-]
ECI —
GRI puumiɣ- 'dip head under water', EG 'swim' [and puumikaaʀ- 'pitch forward (vessel)']

PE puɣ(ə)nəʀ 'fat floating on surface' [cf. nəʀ[1]]
AAY puɣnəq 'membrane containing fish eggs which comes to the top of aged fish roe'
CAY puɣnəq* 's.th. floating on surface of liquid'
NSY puɣnəq 'dish of reindeer fat and minced meat'
CSY puɣnəq*
Sir —
SPI puiniq, Qaw also punniq 'fat risen to surface'
NAI puinʸɨq* 'fat rising to top of cooking broth' [and punnɨq* 'bread (esp. yeast bread)']
WCI puiniq 'fat floating on surface of cooking pot', Car punniʀnaq 'fat boiled from caribou bones' [Ras.]
ECI punniq 'fat risen to surface, shortening, kidney fat'
GRI punniq* [Fab. pungneq] 'butter', NG puiniq 'river water that has oozed up and refrozen on surface' [= WG putsinniq*, puffinniq*, the latter by contam. with puvə-]

PE puɣta- 'be afloat' [cf. ta-]
AAY puxta- 'be afloat', AP puxtatəq 'lung'
CAY puxta- 'be afloat', puxtaun 'buoy, float, lung'
NSY puxta- 'be afloat' [Em.; also puxtaq 'float' (L.-T.)]
CSY puxtaaʀʷaaʀ- 'stay surfaced (whale)'
Sir puxtaX 'float' [Em.]
SPI pukta- 'float'
NAI pukta-, Mal pupta- 'be afloat' [and puktaq- 'float to surface']
WCI pukta- 'float' [puktaʀutit 'bouy']
ECI putta- 'float'
GRI putta- 'float' [and puttałłaʀ- 'come up to surface', puttaʀsi- 'have a bad conscience']

PI puila- 'rise to surface' [cf. la(ʀ)-]
SPI —
NAI puilʸa- 'rise to surface (liquid)'
WCI Car puilayuq 'spring (in earth)' [Pryde]
ECI puila- 'well up through ice or ground, rise to surface of water, come out of tube (e.g. ointment)' [and Lab puilaa- 'come up to surface several times (fish)' — Bourq.]
GRI puila- 'well up'

PI puipkaq- 'appear over water (mirage)?' [cf. vkaʀ-]
SPI —
NAI —
WCI puipkaq- 'barely make it out of water', Car? 'loom large in distance from heat (mirage)' [Schn. 'adg']
ECI puikka(q)- 'begin to permeate ice softened by weather (sea water)', Iti 'loom large in distance from heat (mirage of hills)'
GRI puikkaʀ- 'be a mirage'

PI pukkit- 'be low (in water)' [cf. kit-; from *puɣnəkit-? — compare puqtu- below]
SPI pukkit- 'be low'
NAI pukkit- 'be low, ride low in water'
WCI Sig pukkit-
ECI pukkit- 'be low'
GRI pukkit- 'be low, ride low in water'

PI puktaaq 'iceberg' [cf. puɣta- above]
SPI puktaaq 'iceberg'
NAI puktaaq
WCI puktaaq 'ice-floe, piece of drift-ice' [Pryde]
ECI puttaaq 'autumn floating ice, broken shore ice in summer', Iti 'iceberg'
GRI puttaaq 'ice floe' [puttaaʀ- 'leap from ice floe to ice floe, dance']

PI puqtu- 'be high (in water)' [from *puɣnəʀtu- with nəʀ[1] and tu-[1]]
SPI puqtu- 'be high in water'
NAI puqtu-
WCI Sig puqtu- 'be high in water'
ECI puqtu- 'be placed high'
GRI puʀtu-, EG puʀtu-, pittu- 'be high'

PY-S puɣžaq 'beluga' [cf. puɣə- and ðaʀ-?]
AAY —
CAY —
NSY pu(u)ɣyaq 'beluga' [in Men. p. 24, not in vocab.]
CSY puuɣzaq 'beluga'
Sir puɣžaX

PE pukaɣ 'granular snow (crust)' [cf. puɣə-?]
AAY —
CAY Nun pukax 'granular snow (crust)' [ANLC]
NSY —
CSY [note pukanəq* 'foam, froth']
Sir [note pukanəX 'foam, froth' — Orr]
SPI Qaw pukak, KI puɣavžak 'grainy snow under top layer, preferred for drinking water' [Jen. has puɣaq for W]
NAI pukak 'granular snow crust, small pieces of ice under surface of snow', pukaɣžiŋa- 'be granular' [and Jen. has pukauyaq 'cube sugar'; also Nu pukaɣžalaaq 'small pieces of clear material in fish']

WCI pukaq 'granular snow' [and Pryde has Car, Sig pukayaaq 'firm snow']
ECI pukak 'crystalized snow'
GRI pukak 'snow crust' [pukaɣ- 'form a crust (snow)']

PI pukcinnaq- 'lie still (floating on surface)?' [cf. puɣə-]
Yup [note CAY puxci- 'skim oil from surface']
SPI puksinaq- 'kill with one shot'
NAI puksinʸnʸ- 'die suddenly or instantly'
WCI —
ECI —
GRI pussinnaʀ- [old ortho. pugsix̂nar-] 'lie still floating on surface (whale)' [Robbe and Menn. have putsinaʀ- 'come to breath at the surface briefly' for EG]

PE pukiʀ 'white belly fur'
AAY —
CAY pukiq 'trim at bottom of parka, white belly fur of animal'
NSY —
CSY —
Sir —
SPI W puɣiq 'white belly fur of caribou' [Jen.], KI puɣiviniq 'piece of reindeer belly fur'
NAI pukik
WCI Cop pukiq [also Ras. for Car]
ECI pukiq 'white belly fur of animal, similar white decoration on clothing'
GRI pukiq 'belly skin of land animal'

PE pukit- 'pick (up)' [cf. pukuɣ-]
AAY pukitə- 'squash, squeeze with fingernails'
CAY pukitə- 'pick and eat little things, pick lice and squash with teeth'
NSY pukitə- 'pick (and eat) lice' [ANLC]
CSY —
Sir —
SPI —
NAI pukit- 'pick up'
WCI Car? pukit- 'grab' [Schn. 'adg']
ECI —
GRI pukit- 'pick up, pick out, get (ptarmigan or seal one has seen)'

PI pukkuq 'mortice hole in side of sled or kayak frame' [cf. pukuɣ- and q under nəʀ[1]?]
SPI —
NAI pukkuq 'mortice hole', Nu 'hole in sled runner for upright pieces' [acc. Pryde the latter is 'mortice hole in side of sled frame to receive cross-strut']
WCI Cop pukkuq 'one of two holes in bow of sled's runners through which the sled-bridle is fastened' [Pryde, who also has this for Baker Lake as 'holes in gunwales of kayak to receive ends of transverse deck-struts']
ECI —
GRI —

PE pukuɣ- 'pick up (small things to eat)' [cf. pukit- — contam. with puvuɣ-?]
AAY pukuɣ- 'scrounge (e.g. from beach)'
CAY pukuɣ- 'pick meat off bones carefully'
NSY pukuk 'beak', pukuxtuʀ- 'pick at with beak' [L.-T.]
CSY —
Sir —
SPI Qaw pukuk- 'gather up (e.g. berries)'
NAI pukuk 'bend over and pick'
WCI Cop pukuk- 'pick up in beak' [Jen.; Schn. has pukuluk- 'peck about (bird)' for 'adg']
ECI pukuk- 'pick one by one'
GRI pukuɣ- 'pick and eat berries from bush' [and pukuluk- 'peck up seeds (bird)', EG puɣuŋaq 'crowberry']

PE pula- 'slip in under cover' [cf. Aleut hula- 'dawn, begin (month or day), be new (moon), happen in the morning', Atkan also 'bloom']
AAY pula- 'penetrate, go under cover, intoxicate'
CAY pula- 'go forward through thicket, clouds, etc.'
NSY [note L.-T. has pulaXtə- 'guess'] ➟
CSY pula- 'go into midst of things so as to be hidden from view'
Sir pulə- go into midst of things so as to be hidden from view' [Orr; Em. has puləqə- 'go into middle, go under ice (walrus or beluga)']
SPI pula- 'be eclipsed, break through, slip in'
NAI pula- 'be eclipsed (sun or moon)'
WCI pula-, pulak- 'go back under (e.g. water on surface back through ice), be eclipsed'
ECI pula- 'be eclipsed, go back under (e.g. in hole)' [pulama- 'be an eclipse, go in under, hide one's head under blanket']
GRI pula- 'go back in (e.g. hole)' [pulammaɣ- 'turn in to a fjord or harbor', NG pulama- 'be amongst scree (auk in nest)']

PE pula(C)aʀ- 'go visiting' [cf. aʀ-]
AAY pulaaʀ- 'go visiting'
CAY pulaaʀ(aʀ)- 'wander through woods', NSU pulaaʀ- 'go forward through thicket, etc.' [the latter also has a homonym meaning 'borrow', probably influenced by the English]
NSY pulaaʀ- 'visit locally' [ANLC]
CSY —
Sir —
SPI pulaaq- 'visit' [Jen. has 'visit neighbor to beg for food'; note also Qaw pulaktaq- 'go from house to house']
NAI pulaaq- 'go visiting'
WCI Cop pulaaq- 'visit'
ECI pulaaq-
GRI pulaaʀ-

PI pullan 'stone trap' [cf. un]
SPI —
NAI —
WCI Car pullati 'stone trap' [Schn.], Cop pullat 'stone trap for foxes (or wolves)' [Pryde]
ECI Aiv pullati 'stone trap'
GRI pułłat(it) '(fox or fish) trap'

PY pulǝŋtǝ- 'hit on the right spot or repeat?'
AAY pulǝŋtǝ- 'hit right on the right spot'
CAY pulǝŋtǝ- 'repeat one's action'
NSY —
CSY —

PE pumyuɣ- 'pinch thumb and forefinger together' [with dissimilation in most forms; the Inu via PI putyuk- from *pupyuk-]
AAY puksuɣ-, AP pupsuɣ- 'pinch'
CAY pupsuk 'pincer', pupsuɣ- 'pinch'
NSY pupɣuk 'pincer, thumb and forefinger' [and ANLC has pupɣuɣ- 'pinch']
CSY pumsuk 'thumb and forefinger', pumsuɣ- 'pinch'
Sir pumyuXqǝ(s)- 'pinch'
SPI putyuaq-, Qaw pussuk- 'pinch,' putyuuk 'pincer, thumb and forefinger'
NAI puyyuk-, Mal putyuk-, Nu pupsuk- 'pinch' [the latter form from Berg.; note also puyyuɣiaq 'crab']
WCI puyyuuk 'thumb and forefinger' [puyyuɣiaq 'crab']
ECI puyyuk 'thumb and forefinger'
GRI pussuɣ- 'pinch, wrinkle (because of becoming wet — skin)', EG puttuC- 'pinch' [pussuk 'thumb and forefinger pressed together']

PY pumsulǝk 'crab' [cf. lǝɣ]
AAY puksulǝʀyuwaq, AP pupsuɣayuk 'crab'
CAY pupsulǝk
NSY —
CSY —

PE pumyuɣðaʀ 'snowshoe' [cf. yaR]
AAY —
CAY [Nun pupsuxcǝtaaq 'snowshoe']
NSY pupɣuɣiaq 'snowshoe' [ANLC; L.-T. has pupɣuɣiaʀaq]
CSY —
Sir —
SPI putyuyaq
NAI Nu putyuɣiaq 'snowshoe with pointed tip'
WCI —
ECI —
GRI —

PY punǝʀtǝ- 'skim surface' [cf. puɣ(ǝ)nǝʀ under puɣǝ-?]
AAY punǝXtǝ- 'skim surface'
CAY punǝXtǝ- 'skim surface' [for puxci- 'skim oil from surface of liquid' see pukcinnaq-]
NSY punǝXtǝ- 'skim surface' [ANLC]
CSY —

PE pupiɣ '(raised?) sore or mange'
AAY pupik 'sore' [also verbal 'have sores']
CAY pupik 'sore' [and pupiɣnaq 'toadstool'; for pupiŋqua- 'have a frostbite spot' see pupiŋquʀ-]
NSY pupik 'sore'
CSY pupik
Sir pupilǝɣaX 'itch, mange'
SPI puvik 'sore on skin' [and verbal 'have sores']
NAI pupik 'itchy rash, scabies' [and verbal 'have itch']
WCI — [for Cop pupik 'species of lemming' see puvǝltu]
ECI —
GRI pupik 'mushroom, leprosy' [and pupiɣ- 'have leprosy', pupiłłaɣ- 'have sore in mouth']

PE pupiŋquʀ- and **puviŋquʀ-** 'get or feel frostbitten?' [there may be a relat. to pupiɣ, if only by contam. in Yup]
AAY —
CAY pupiŋqua- 'get frostbitten from touching s.th. cold, have a frostbite spot'
NSY [note pupiŋquXałǝq 'pock mark' (ANLC)]
CSY pupiŋquʀ- 'have a stinging sensation on one's skin from the cold'
Sir —
SPI —
NAI puvitquq- 'get frostbitten, be bleached white (caribou skin)'
WCI puvitquq- 'feel burning sensation from touching cold metal' [and Pryde has Cop puvitquq 'snow which is so cold that it causes going to be slow for sled']
ECI puviqqu(q)- 'feel burning sensation from touching s.th. very cold, receive an electric shock'
GRI puiqquʀ- 'be cool (air)'

PE puqiɣ- 'be intelligent'
AAY puqiɣ- 'be intelligent'
CAY puqiɣ-
NSY puqiɣ- 'be gifted, smart' [ANLC; L.-T. has puqilʀia 'intelligent']
CSY puqiɣ- 'be intelligent'
Sir puqiɣ- [Orr]
SPI puʀik-
NAI puqik-
WCI puqiq- 'be intelligent' [Lowe; Met. has puqit-]
ECI puqiC- 'be intelligent' [Peck has puqik- for Lab]
GRI puqiʀ- 'be quick to learn or understand'

PE puqiɣit- 'be stupid' [cf. ŋit-, esp. the variant form for Yup]
AAY puqiatǝ- 'be stupid'
CAY puqiatǝ- 'be stupid' [with the tǝ ~ l alt.]
NSY puqiatǝ- 'be stupid' [ANLC]
CSY —
Sir —
SPI puʀiit- 'be slow to learn'
NAI puqiit-
WCI puqiit- 'be stupid'
ECI puqiit-
GRI puqiit- 'be slow to learn or understand'

PE puqla 'heat or hot water' [cf. Aleut huʀ- in Atkan huʀðaɣ- 'boil', EA huʀðaŋu-X 'warm weather' and Atkan huʀnaaza- 'be warm (sun, boiled fish, person)', huʀnat- 'warm up']
AAY —
CAY puqła 'warmth, heat, hot water' [and Nun puqłanǝX* 'sun']
NSY puqłǝʀak 'thaw' [ANLC]
CSY puqła 'warmth, heat' [and puqłatǝ- 'be warm', puqłayuɣ- 'feel hot']

Sir puqłəʀaʀ- 'have fever' [Orr; note also perhaps pułəX 'summer' (Vakh. also pułaX, and pułəʀaX 'spring')]
SPI [note puqłaq 'plates of ice forming at freeze-up'? — also verbal]
NAI puqłaq- 'put in boiling water to remove feathers (bird)'
WCI puqłaqtaq 'boiling water' [and Sig puqłaq- 'boil a little'; note also Cop puʀʀiq- 'boil over' (Pryde)]
ECI —
GRI — [for NG puʀvila- 'bubble up (water boiling)' and puʀvitit- 'boil (food)' see under puvə-]

PY-S puʀətə- 'deceive'
AAY —
CAY —
NSY —
CSY puuXtə- 'deceive, pretend' [and note puuXə- 'be occupied or amused with s.th.', puuXun 'toy']
Sir puʀət(ə)- 'deceive, pretend' [and puʀuta 'game', puʀətəkə(s)- 'be amused with s.th.' — Em.]

PE put- 'stoop or bend forward' [cf. Aleut hut- 'tip over, capsize', perhaps also husa- (intr.), husat- (tr.) 'roll']
AAY C puttə- 'carve, fashion' [from bending over such work?]
CAY puttə- 'bend forward' [puza- 'be bent forward']
NSY —
CSY —
Sir putŋuʀ- 'bend forward' [Orr]
SPI put- 'bow, crouch, lower head'
NAI put- 'bow, kneel, crouch' [and punŋayuuq- 'walk bent over (e.g. hunter stalking game)']
WCI put- 'bend down, crouch'
ECI pu(C)- 'lower head so as not to be seen by game' [and puŋaq- 'nod head']
GRI puɣ- 'stoop' [and puŋŋaʀšuʀ- 'fish from the ice'; Fab. has put-]

> **PI punŋuuq** '(shaman's word for) dog' [lit. 'one going with bowed head']
> Sir [compare putŋuʀ- above]
> SPI —
> NAI [punŋuuq- 'walk with bowed head']
> WCI Car B. Lake puŋŋuuq 'shaman's word for dog' [Schn.; Ras. has Cop puŋŋuq, Net pu'ŋuq]
> ECI puŋŋuuq 'shaman's word for dog' [Schn. for W. Bay and Ras. has Igl]
> GRI [Kroeb. has NG punguaq and Egede WG pungok, pungvoak (for puŋŋu(u)q, puŋŋuaq) 'dog' as a shaman's word; note also puŋŋuyuuʀ- 'bend right over almost squatting']

PE putu(-)[1] 'hole (through s.th.)' [as verb 'make hole through'; cf. putžuq — there may be a further link to pətə-]
AAY — [but note putu- 'pout, look sad, stick out lower lip' — influenced by the English?]
CAY putu Nun 'leather piece on skin boot with hole for bootlace' [verbal = 'make a hole through']
NSY putu 'loop' ['hole, incision' acc. L.-T.]
CSY putu 'hole made at edge of skin for running rope for stretching and drying' [verbal = 'make such a hole']
Sir puta 'hole' [Orr]
SPI putu 'hole through s.th.' [verbal = 'pierce, have a hole' as in all Inu]
NAI putu 'hole'
WCI putu
ECI putu
GRI putu 'hole through s.th.' [verbal = 'perforate, look at stiffly so as to confuse, be perforated, be confused or drunk']

> **PI puttun** 'awl' [cf. un]
> SPI puttun 'awl'
> NAI puttun
> WCI [note putuʀun '(bow) drill']
> ECI [putuuʀʀiti, putuuʀsiti 'awl, bow drill, can opener, etc.']
> GRI puttut 'awl'

PY-S putu(-)[2] 'dance (a traditional dance)' [cf. putu(-)[1] — this 'dance' meaning may come from the practice of dancing with the upper part of the body protruding through a hole in the floor, partition, etc.; compare iyyuʀ- and yuʀžaʀ-]
AAY —
CAY Y putu 'women's welcome dance'
NSY putužaʀun 'woman's free-style dance' [L.-T.]
CSY putuuʀ- 'dance a whaling dance'
Sir putužaX 'Eskimo dance' [Orr]

PE putukuʀ 'big toe' [cf. putu(-)[1] and/or Aleut huta-X 'thumb']
AAY K putukuq 'big toe'
CAY putukuq
NSY putukuq
CSY putukuq
Sir putəkəX [Orr]
SPI putuɣuq
NAI putuɣuq
WCI putuɣuq
ECI putuɣuq
GRI putuɣuq

PI putžuq 'hole worn in s.th.' [cf. putu(-)[1]]
SPI [puššuq 'personal name']
NAI pužžuq* 'hole worn in boot sole', Nu putžuq- 'be worn out, have holes'
WCI —
ECI —
GRI puššuq(*) 'hole worn (e.g. in boot sole)' [puššuʀ- 'be worn through, wear a hole in']

PI pu(ɣ)uq 'bag or sealskin poke' [cf. puɣə-, also Aleut hux, huɣi-X 'bag, case', EA 'net, seine, sheath, vagina' and verbal 'fish, hunt (sea lion) with seine']
Yup [note CSY puɣnaan 'float, inflated poke' under puɣə-, which explains why the base here is puɣə- rather than expected puvə-]
SPI puuq 'poke, bag' [verbal = 'bandage, put in bag']
NAI pu<ɣ>uq [verbal = 'wrap']
WCI puuq 'bag' [verbal = 'wrap, put in bag']

ECI puuq 'bag' [verbal = 'wrap, put in bag']
GRI puuq [older pl. puxxut] 'bag, case' [puuʀ- 'wrap, pack']

PI puɣɣutaq and **puuɣutaq** 'bowl' [cf. un]
SPI puɣɣutaq 'dish, large bowl'
NAI puɣɣutaq 'pan, pot', PH puuɣutaq 'dish'
WCI puuɣutaq 'bowl' [Met.]
ECI puuɣutaq
GRI puuɣutaq 'bowl, dish, plate'

PI puukattaq 'sack (sealskin bag)' [cf. k(k)attaʀ-?]
SPI puuqataq 'container'
NAI puukataq 'sealskin bag, sack'
WCI puukattaq 'bag' [Lowe], Car? puuqattaq 'sack' [Schn. 'adg']
ECI puuqattaq 'bag'
GRI puuqattaq 'bag', NG puuqattak 'sledge bag' [and Robbe and Menn. have EG puuʀattaq 'small bag for putting berries in' — Robbe and Dor. puuʀattak]

PI puuʀuciq 'sack (for meat)' [cf. uciʀ]
SPI —
NAI [note Nu puuʀu 'wolf net']
WCI Sig puuʀusiq 'bag' [Schn. has 'tinder pouch' for B. Lake'; Pryde has Cop puuʀuhiq 'caribou-skin bag for holding dried meat']
ECI puuʀusiq 'meat sack'
GRI puuʀusiq 'sack for blubber, skin receptacle'

PI puvak 'lung' [cf. puvə- and Aleut humɣi-X, EA umxi-X 'lung', humɣix, umxix 'lungs']
SPI puwak 'lung'
NAI puvak
WCI puvak
ECI puvak
GRI puak 'lung'

PE puvała 'whaling festival'
AAY —
CAY Nun, Y, NS puała 'a certain type of dance'
NSY puała 'whaling festival'
CSY puvała 'a certain ceremony'
Sir puvəłaX 'holiday' [Vakh. also 'shamanistic seance']
SPI puala- ' dance (of a man)'
NAI PH puala-, Nu pualla- ' dance'
WCI —
ECI —
GRI —

PE puvə- 'swell' [cf. Aleut hum- 'inflate, swell', humta- 'be swollen', but possibly also w̥aX 'smoke' via *puvvaʀ acc. Berg.]
AAY puɣə- 'swell'
CAY puvə- 'swell'
NSY puvə-
CSY puuvə- [puufqə- 'become swollen in face']
Sir puvə- 'swell' [in Vakh. also 'become puffy, irritated (eyes)'; and note puvəX 'wind]
SPI puit- 'be swollen', puvžak- 'have a swelling' [also nominal], puvžuq- 'have puffy eyes'
NAI puvɨt- 'be swollen', puviq- 'inflate, be inflated', puptit- 'get puffy eyes', PH pupsaq- 'rise (dough)' [for puuvžaq-, 'swim' see puɣ(ə)mə(t)- under puɣə-]
WCI puvit- 'become swollen', puviq- 'inflate' [for puviaq- 'swim' see puɣ(ə)mə(t)- under puɣə-]
ECI puviq- 'be inflated, swell (from putrification)' [and puvittuq 'flesh that is swollen]
GRI pui(k) 'swelling, tumor', puiʀ- 'inflate, bulge, swell (sail)' [and puiɣ- 'have a swelling or tumor', puffaɣ- 'be cross, grumpy', also perhaps NG puʀvik 'seat of trousers', puʀvila- 'bubble up (water boiling)' and puʀvitit- 'boil (food)' (all from *puiʀvik(-)?)]

PI puvala- 'be fat' [cf. la(ʀ)-?]
SPI —
NAI puvala- 'be fat and round'
WCI puvala-
ECI —
GRI puala-

PI puvəʀaʀ 'ball or balloon-like thing'
AAY —
CAY —
NSY puvialuk puffball, grandfather's mushroom'
CSY —
Sir —
SPI —
NAI puviʀaq 'balloon, swim bladder'
WCI puviʀaq 'ball (for playing with)' [Schn. has puviɣaq 'small rubber balloon' for 'adg']
ECI puviʀaq 'small rubber balloon'
GRI [puiʀaašaq, puaašaq 'water-filled swelling' — the latter also 'bubble']

PE puvlaɣ or **puvlaʀ** 'bubble or air in s.th.' [back-formations from verbal forms? — but compare also puvlaʀ-]
AAY —
CAY —
NSY puvlaq 'gas'
CSY—
Sir —
SPI puvlak 'air in s.th., bubble' [Qaw also has puɣlak]
NAI puvlak 'bubble' [also puvžuk 'bubbles'; puvlak- 'rise, bubble up, spout (whale)', puvla(q) 'bubble from underwater']
WCI puvlak 'bubble' [as verb = 'swell']
ECI pullaq 'bubble, air pressure', Iti 'rotten meat' [pulla(k)- 'inflate']
GRI pułłaɣ- 'inflate, be inflated' [pułłaʀtaq 'bubble', pułłaq 'inflation, air inside bladder', EG puttaq 'bubble'; for NG puʀvila- 'bubble' see puvə- above]

PI puvliq- 'swell up' [cf. liq-?]
SPI puvliq- 'become swollen with air'
NAI puvliq-
WCI puvliq-
ECI pulli(q)-
GRI pułłiʀ- 'swell up (after a blow)'

puvəltu or **vuvəltu** 'lemming' [probably from Chukchi wewcelka-lɣən, ɣewcelk-lɣən (Bogo. vuvcelkalɣən) 'lemming', though it coulkd go the other way; the forms with initial p may be affected by PE puvlaʀ-]
AAY —
CAY puvəłtuk 'red-backed vole', Nun puɣułtu 'lemming'
NSY —
CSY puvəłtu, vuvəłtu creature not positively identified in SLI, listed there as 'frog, flounder, or rodent', Chap vuvəłtu 'lemming' [Rub.]
Sir puvəłəX 'lemming'
Inu [note Cop pupik 'species of lemming' acc. Pryde — contam. with pupiɣ?]

PY puvin 'ruff (of parka hood)' [cf. puvə- and un?]
AAY —
CAY — [but note puɣyaʀaq 'neck-opening of a pullover parka', from puɣə-]
NSY puvitə 'trim on hood of parka'
CSY puvin 'ruff'

PE puvlaʀ- 'be frightened away (animals scenting humans)' [cf. puvlaɣ under puvə-?]
AAY puɣlaʀ- 'run away (animal becoming aware of humans)'
CAY —
NSY —
CSY puuvlaʀ- 'scare away sea mammals (strange smells)'
Sir —
SPI puvlaq- 'be frightened away by smell (animals by people)'
NAI puvlaq-
WCI Sig puvlaq- [Pryde]
ECI pulla(C)- 'smell a hunter (seal)' [Saul; Schn. has pullauti 'stinking liquid from animal like ermine']
GRI —

PE puvuɣ- 'peck (bird)' [compare put- and pukuɣ-]
AAY pu'uɣ- 'peck up (bird)'
CAY puuɣ- 'bang head repeatedly on surface'
NSY ➡
CSY puvuɣ- 'peck (bird)'
Sir puvuXqə(s)-
SPI puuk- 'fall headlong'
NAI puuk- 'become bent with age', PH 'fall over from stroke, fainting' [and note also puufsaq- 'kill wounded animal']
WCI Sig pu(u)k- 'fall forward'
ECI puuk- 'let head fall forward when falling asleep, fold (knife)', Lab puuk- 'fall headlong to ground (shot animal)' [Bourq.]
GRI puut- 'be confused', puuŋa- 'be sleepy'

PE puvuk(k)aʀ- 'fall forward' [cf. k(k)aʀ- and compare CAY pucikaʀ- under puci-]
AAY puukaʀ- 'bump'
CAY puukaʀ- 'bump, sting (bee)'
NSY puukaʀ- 'bump' [ANLC]
CSY —
Sir —
SPI puukaq- 'fall forward'
NAI puukaq- 'stumble forward'
WCI —
ECI puukaq- 'pitch forward, nod head forward'
GRI —

PE puvyaʀ 'bird's crop' [cf. puvə- and yaʀ]
AAY —
CAY NSU puvzaq 'crop, craw of ptarmigan'
NSY puvyaq 'bladder' [ANLC also puyyaq]
CSY puuvyaq 'inflatable membrane in walrus mouth'
Sir puvyəx [for puvyəX?] 'crop'
SPI —
NAI puvi<ž>aq 'bird's crop, puffed out chest of walrus, inlet'
WCI puviaq 'bird's crop, (rubber) balloon'
ECI puviaq 'bird's crop, balloon, lamp mantle'
GRI puiaq 'bird's crop, lamp mantle' [and puiaašaq 'bottle']

PE puya 'rancid residue of oil' [cf. Aleut huða-X 'dried fish or meat', huða- 'dry (fish or meat)']
AAY AP puya- 'be permeated by stench (or stain)'
CAY puya-, puyaləXtə- 'be rancid (oil or grease)', NSU 'be dirty'
NSY puya 'fat condensed on side of barrel' [L.-T.; also verbal 'soot up, grease up' (ANLC)]
CSY puya 'rancid residue of oil from blubber'
Sir púya [Orr; Em. has puyapayɣŋuX 'smelling of rancid oil']
SPI puya 'dirt, grime' [and in Jen. 'blubber dried on surface']
NAI puya 'dirt, sticky oil, blubber used to waterproof skin boat'
WCI puyaq 'old oil or grease' [as verb = 'get dirty']
ECI puyaq 'residue of oil, rancid oil, earwax'
GRI puya(k), EG, Up, NG puyaq 'dried rancid blubber oil (with which umiaq is greased)' [puya- 'be rancid, have a layer of rancid blubber on it']

PE puyɣu(ʀ)- 'forget'
AAY —
CAY —
NSY —
CSY puyɣu- 'forget'
Sir puyəŋuʀ-
SPI puuyuʀ-
NAI puiɣuq-, piiɣuq-, PH puuɣuq- 'forget' [the second form influenced by piiq- 'remove, be removed' from pi(-) and ŋiʀ-?]
WCI puiɣuq- 'forget' [Pryde has piiyuʀ- for Sig]
ECI puiɣuq- 'have forgotten, forgive' [and note puijuittuq 'one who cannot forgive (insult)', puiɣutu- 'be forgetful']
GRI puiɣuʀ-, puiuʀ- [also more recent puuyuʀ-], EG, Up puiiʀ- 'forget' [and puiutu- 'be forgetful', puiɣunaat- 'be unforgetable']

PE puyuʀ 'smoke' [cf. Aleut huyuX 'smoke, steam']
AAY puyuq 'smoke'
CAY puyuq 'smoke' [and puyuXtə- 'smoke (fish)', NSU puyuŋuaq 'puffball (mushroom)']

NSY puyuq 'smoke, soot' [L.-T.]
CSY puyuq
Sir puyəX 'soot' [Vakh. has 'smoke ']
SPI puyuq 'steam', Qaw 'chimney smoke'
NAI puyuq 'smoke from chimney' [as verb = 'smoke, make smoke'; puyuuq- 'smoke (fire or chimney)']
WCI puyuq 'smoke' [also 'condensation in atmosphere from breath or whale spouting' acc. Pryde; verbal = 'give off smoke'; also puyuuʀvik 'smoke-hole, chimney']
ECI puyuq 'water vapor, tobacco smoke, puffball (mushroom)' [as verb = 'give off steam'; and Pryde has Igl puyuuʀvik 'chimney']
GRI puyuq 'smoke, steam, mist, fog' [puyuʀ-, puyuuʀ- 'give off smoke or steam', and in Kroeb. and Rink 'be infected by a dead person (a relative under taboo)', NG puyuq- 'smoke (pipe)']

PY puyuqə- 'be smoked or sooty' [cf. ʀqə-?]
AAY puyuqə- 'smoke (fish)'
CAY puyuqə- 'be smoked (food), be full of smoke (clothes)' [also trans. (impers. subj.); puyuqŋ̊əq* 'soot']
NSY puyuqə- 'be smoky or smoked' [ANLC]
CSY puyuqə-, puyuXqə- 'become sooty' [the former also trans. (impers. subject)']

PI puyuʀaq or **puyuʀak** 'frost smoke (snowy mist)'
SPI —
NAI puyuala-, putcuala- 'make steam or smoke'
WCI puyuaʀyuk 'kind of weather when powder snow in air is like smoke'
ECI puyuʀaq- 'be a light mist', Iti puyuʀaq, puyuqqiq 'light mist'
GRI puyuʀak 'frost smoke' [puyuʀaɣ- 'be mist from sea, frost smoke', puyuʀalak, puyualak 'dust', puyu(ʀ)ala- 'be dusty']

PY puyuʀnaq or **puyuʀniq** 'nagoonberry' [cf. naʀ]
AAY puyuʀniq, C also puyuʀnaq, K also puyuʀnik 'nagoonberry'
CAY Y puyuʀnaq, HBC puyuʀniq 'nagoonberry' [also K puyuʀaaʀ(aq*), NSU puyuʀuaʀaq]
NSY —
CSY —

Q

PI qaanaaq 'eroded cave' [cf. qaanəq and aʀ?]
SPI —
NAI qaanaaq 'eroded cave in ice or land'
WCI qa(a)nauŋaq 'cave toward foot of overhanging ice or cliff'
ECI [qaanauyaq 'cabin (in ship)']
GRI [note Qaanaaq 'Thule (place name)']

PI qaanəq 'empty space beneath s.th.' [cf. qaŋata- and nəʀ[1]?]
SPI —
NAI qaanɨq* 'space under sleeping platform, empty space under s.th.', Nu 'gentle slope at base of mountain levelling off to a plain'
WCI Cop qaaniq 'space under sleeping platform' [Pryde; for B. Lake qaanniq 'water heard trickling beneath snow or ice' see qaaptət-]
ECI —
GRI qaaniq* 'space under sleeping platform'

PI qaaptət- 'overflow (water over ice)' [cf. qaðə-, vət- under vaʀ- and tət-? — compare caavət- under caðə-]
SPI qaaptit- 'overflow onto ice (water)'
NAI qaaptɨt- 'spread over a surface (liquid), overflow from cracks in ice (water)'
WCI qaaptit- 'spread over surface (liquid)' [and note Baker Lake qaanniq 'water heard trickling beneath snow or ice' — Schn.]
ECI [note qaanniq 'water risen above lake or river ice or freed by floating away of pack ice', qaat- 'open up (stretch of water after the breaking away of the edge of pack ice)']
GRI qaatsinniq 'water that runs over the ice edge and freezes'

PI qaaqtuq- 'croak' [onomatopoeic, with p.b. (a)ʀ- plus tuʀ-[2]]
Yup [note AAY qaʀua'aq 'crow' and CAY Y qəXqaałəʀ(aq*) 'raven', also onomatopoeic]
SPI [note W qaqayuaʀuk (Jen.), Imaq qaqažuk 'raven']
NAI qaaqtuq- 'croak (raven)'
WCI —
ECI —
GRI qaaʀtuʀ- 'croak (raven)' [and EG qaaʀtuluk 'raven']

PE qa(C)aʀyaʀ 'fish eggs?' [cf. qaɣəʀ- and yaʀ?]
AAY qaʀyat 'fish eggs', qaʀyaq, qaʀyaʀuaq 'rash' [and note qaʀmit- 'be crunchy (fish eggs soaked in fresh water)']
CAY qaaʀyak 'pimple', Y, NS qaaʀzaq, Nun qiaʀyaX 'herring eggs' [so called because they crackle when eaten — note qiaʀyixtə-, qiaʀyəxtə-, LI qiaʀ- 'make a crackling noise']
NSY [qaɣžak 'fish eggs' (L.-T.)]
CSY —
Sir —
SPI —
NAI qaaʀiaq 'hernia'
WCI —
ECI qaaʀiaq 'fish eggs that have been laid'
GRI qaaʀiaq 'water bubble in ice'

PI qaatəq 'bone socket on end of harpoon shaft (for foreshaft)' [cf. qaðə-]
SPI qaatiq 'top of harpoon handle' [Jen. has 'bone socket of harpoon handle into which harpoon foreshaft fits']
NAI qaatɨq* 'piece of bone between harpoon shaft and point'
WCI Cop qaatiq 'bone socket of harpoon handle into which the foreshaft fits' [Jen.; Ras. has qatiq 'ring of horn on end of harpoon shaft' for Net]
ECI qaatiq 'piece of ivory of iɣimaq or sealing harpoon

or pivot of detachable barbed head'
GRI qaatiq* 'hoop, plate of bone or iron on a handle, knob'

PI qaayuq- 'shudder at cold or wet' [cf. qaʀaləʀ-]
SPI [qaalii- 'be squeamish about']
NAI PH qaayuʀɨ- 'be squeamish about' [and qaatcinɣa- 'feel uncomfortable from wet or dirty clothes']
WCI qaayuq- 'tremble with cold'
ECI qaayuq- 'feel very cold'
GRI qaayuʀ- 'be chilled, sensitive to cold', qaayuʀi- 'shudder at having to go out in (the cold)'

PE qacaɣ- 'feel one can handle more?'
AAY C, KP qacaɣyuɣ-, PWS qaca'uɣ- 'not be satisfied with what you get'
CAY [qaciɣnaXqə- 'be easy', qacixtə- 'be unoccupied']
NSY —
CSY [note qasikə- 'agree with, get along with']
Sir —
SPI —
NAI —
WCI Cop qahak- 'be easily moved or opened' [Pryde; Met. has Sig qasaɣi- 'can easily manage' with p.b. kə-[1]]
ECI Igl qasaɣi- 'consider inferior' [Ras.]
GRI qasaɣi- 'not get enough of' [Fab. has 'despise']

PE qac(c)aɣ- 'dance and shout?' [cf. qacaʀ- and western EA qacu-X 'bladder dance', verbal = 'dance, dragging feet on floor'; the relat. — if any — to qacu- is obscure]
AAY —
CAY qaccaɣ- 'make dancing motion with body in time with music'
NSY —
CSY —
Sir —
SPI —
NAI qasak-, qasala- 'burst out yelling and cheering', qatcak- 'make noise expressing pleasure when dancing (male)', qatcaq- 'shout with pleasure (e.g., whalers or dancers)'
WCI —
ECI —
GRI —

PI qacal(l)uq 'bark (of tree)' [there may be a relat. to CAY qacaxtə- under qacu-]
SPI qazałuq, Qaw qasaluq 'cottonwood bark'
NAI qasalluq 'cottonwood bark'
WCI Sig qasaluq 'bark of poplar' [Pet.; Cop qaihaluk 'bark of cottonwood' acc. Jen.]
ECI —
GRI qasaluq '(fir) bark'

PE qacaʀ- 'slap or clap' [cf. qac(c)aɣ-]
AAY qacaXtə- 'slap'
CAY qacaXtə-, qasaXtə- 'hit, slap, blow against (wind)'
NSY qasaXtə- 'clap'
CSY qasaXtə- 'slap with palm of hand'
Sir —
SPI qazaq-
NAI qasaq- 'crash against shore or ice (waves)'
WCI —
ECI —
GRI —

PE qacəli- 'sting or smart'
AAY qatłi- 'sting, smart (of body part)'
CAY NSU qacəłi-, qatłi- 'sting, whine'
NSY —
CSY qaasn̥i- 'suffer pain from burns, smart, burn with anger'
Sir —
SPI qazili- 'sting, smart'
NAI qasil^{y}i- 'beg, entreat, supplicate, smart'
WCI Sig qasilinaq- 'be bitter' [Pet.]
ECI qasili- 'have a prickling sensation in limbs'
GRI qasilit- 'be bitter, sharp tasting, sting (of wound)'

PI qaciŋŋuq- 'make a resonant noise' [cf. qatə]
Yup [cf. CAY qaci- 'have a deep voice' under qatə]
SPI —
NAI qasiŋŋuq- 'have a hollow, resonant sound'
WCI —
ECI —
GRI qasiŋuʀ- 'rattle, peal, ring'

PE qacu- 'become loose or slack' [for Aleut qacuX 'bladder dance' see qac(c)aɣ-]
AAY qacu- 'be wrinkled, shriveled up', qacu 'wrinkle'
CAY qacu- 'be loose, not taut, wrinkled, sag' [and K note qacaxtə- 'be loosely attached, come loose']
NSY qasu- 'weaken, slacken'
CSY —
Sir —
SPI qazu-, Qaw qasut-, 'become loose, slack'
NAI qasu- 'become slack, unwound'
WCI qasu- 'become loose, slack' [Ras. has 'fall (wind)' for Cop; qasut- 'loosen, slacken']
ECI qasu- 'unwind, slacken'
GRI qasu- 'be tired, exhausted', qasut- 'slacken', NG qahut- 'grow still (wind)' [and note qasuiʀ- 'have rested']

PI qatcuq- 'have slackened or become calm' [cf. ʀ- under ŋ(ŋ)uʀ-]
SPI —
NAI qasuq- 'stop, quit', qasuaq- 'become calm (wind)'
WCI [qasuŋa- 'drop (wind), be slack (rope)']
ECI Iti qatsu(C)- 'become calm (weather)' [and qasuŋa- 'have become calm']
GRI qatsuʀ- 'have become calm (wind, weather)' [qatsuŋa- 'be calm']

PE qaðə- 'top or surface of s.th.' [cf. perhaps p.b. tə for the second syllable, also Aleut qasa- 'surface after diving (sea mammal)' and/or Atkan qasmax 'fish scale', qacXi-X 'skin, peal, bark, earth cover (of house)']
AAY qai- 'on surface, top of ' [posit. root]
CAY qai-, Nun qaa-
NSY qayə-

CSY qayə-
Sir qacə- 'surface, top of' [posit. root; and qaca 'deck', qacəX 'grass insole']
SPI qaa- 'on surface, cover, top of' [posit. root]
NAI qaa- 'on surface, top of' [as posit. root; also 'cover, dorsal area of fish, right side of fabric']
WCI qaa- 'on surface, top of'
ECI qaa-
GRI qaa- 'on surface, top of' [as posit. root; also 'surface, deck']

PI qaaŋiq- 'pass' [cf. ŋiʀ-]
SPI qaaŋiq- 'pass by, be past, grow bigger than'
NAI qaaŋiq- 'pass, go over limit' [and qaaŋiuti- 'take past goal, be due (bill)']
WCI qaaŋiq- 'pass, overtake'
ECI qaaŋiq- 'pass, exaggerate'
GRI qaaŋiʀ- 'pass, surpass' [and qaaŋiut(i)- 'be past']

PI qaaq 'bed skin'
SPI qaaq, qaaʀažuk 'mattress'
NAI qaaq, qažžaaq 'skin mattress'
WCI qaaq 'bed skin'
ECI qaaq [Saul]
GRI qaaq

PE qaðəliʀ- 'cover' [cf. liʀ-]
AAY —
CAY [note qaliʀnəq* 'thing on top, roof']
NSY qayəliʀ- 'roof' [ANLC]
CSY qayəliʀ- 'cover'
Sir qaciʀ- 'heave up on (sled), cover' [Vakh. from Men.'s texts — he also has qaciɣ-]
SPI qalliq- 'cover'
NAI qalliq-
WCI qalliqtuq- 'heap up (on top)'
ECI qalli(C)- 'press down (once)' [and qalliniq 'upper part of body or boot']
GRI qałłiʀ- 'cover' [old ortho. qagdler-, but Fab. kadler-; qałłiniq* 'upper side of s.th.'; qałłiʀsaat 'overcoat']

PE qaðə(t)ʀutə- 'go over' [cf. tʀutə-]
AAY K qasʀutə-, C qayyutə- 'shoot over, overshoot'
CAY —
NSY qayətXutə- 'go over, overshoot'
CSY qayətXutə- 'exceed in value, do more than needed'
Sir — [but Vakh. has qasXižaXtə- 'overfill' from Men.'s texts]
SPI —
NAI qažʀut(i)- 'go over, pass over'
WCI Cop qalʀut(i)- 'shoot over, overshoot' [Pryde]
ECI qaʀʀut(i)- 'overshoot, pass over lightly (s.th. light that does not sink into snow)' [qaʀʀua- 'tread softly across snow without sinking in']
GRI qaʀšut(i)-, qaʀšua- 'flow over, inundate' [and note qaat(i)- 'graze, pass lightly over']

PE qaðliʀ or **qalliʀ** 'topmost or outermost thing' [cf. l(l)iʀ and qaliʀ below; the CAY and CSY could reflect a hypothetical *qatə- with tə as suggested above]
AAY —
CAY qałiq* 'one on top, outer layer' [note that the productive form of l(l)iʀ in CAY is qłiq under qliʀ]
NSY —
CSY Chap qaasłiq 'topmost' [Chap qaasłiXpaɣək 'overcoat']
Sir qałiX 'topmost' [Orr; Em. has qasłiXpəx 'overcoat' — from the CSY?]
SPI qalliq 'topmost one, scab'
NAI qalliq* 'outermost, topmost one', qalli 'scab' [Nu qalliq also 'cover of canvas' acc. Berg.]
WCI qalliq 'topmost one' [and qallili- 'form a scab']
ECI qalliq 'topmost one', qalli 'scab'
GRI qałłiq* 'outermost, topmost one, scab', EG qattiq 'surface' [EG also qattiʀit 'light outer garment, anorak', and qaʀtiʀsuit 'overcoat' (cf. qałłiʀsaat under qaðəliʀ- above)]

PE qaðqaʀ 'top of mountain' [cf. qaʀ; the verbal forms are with p.b. łit-]
AAY [note C qatqiyaʀ- 'go berry picking']
CAY qasqitə- 'scale, reach the top'
NSY qayqitə- [ANLC]
CSY qasqitə- 'reach the top'
Sir [Vakh. has qayɣəXtə- 'go up on s.th.' and qasXitəɣ- 'raise' from Men.'s texts]
SPI qatqit- 'reach the top'
NAI qatqit- 'be in one's prime, reach the top'
WCI Cop qatqaq 'mountain' [Ras. — also Net acc. Pryde, who further has Cop qatqiXXuq- 'stand on top of s.th. high'; Ow. has qatqa 'top of hill' for EP Car]
ECI qaqqaq 'mountain, hill'
GRI qaqqaq 'mountain', qaqqit- 'ascend a mountain, go into the mountains'

PE qaðvaʀ- 'rise or put on top' [cf. vaʀ- and compare qaɣvaʀ-, with which there seems to be contam.]
AAY C qaywaʀ- 'come out of water (animal)'
CAY qaivaʀ- 'rise to surface' [and HBC qayvaun 'spoon']
NSY qayvaʀ- 'take food from pot' [ANLC; also qayvaq 'spoon for turning over boiling meat, ladle']
CSY qavžaʀ- 'mingle (with crowd), lose an artifact one has dug up by mixing it with earth dug out' [also qavžaatat 'gulch, ravine' — but cf. also Aleut base qamða- 'deep']
Sir [note qavžátaX 'gulch, ravine' (Orr) — from CSY?]
SPI qavžaq- 'put s.th. above others, on top of pile', qavzazik- 'be on top of pile, lifted up'
NAI —
WCI [Pryde has Cop qalvaq- as equivalent of NAI qaɣvaq- 'rise or bring to surface' under qaɣvaʀ-]
ECI [for qavvi(ʀ)- 'raise onto s.th.' see qaɣvaʀ-]

GRI [note qaaʀpaʀ-, EG qaʀpaʀ- 'come higher up'; for qaffaʀ- 'lift, rise' see qaɣvaʀ-]

PE qaliqaʀ 'outer skin or cover' [cf. qaliʀ below and qaʀ]
AAY AP qaliqaq 'roof'
CAY qaliqaq
NSY —
CSY —
Sir —
SPI —
NAI —
WCI Cop qaliʀaq 'extra load lashed on top of main load' [Pryde; Met. has qaliʀaq- 'cover', qaliqqit- 'put on top']
ECI qaliʀaq 'overload, extra item carried' [as verb = 'carry things on one's back']
GRI qaliʀaq, EG qalaqqaq 'outer skin of tent, tarpaulin'

PE qaliʀ 'covering' [cf. qaðliʀ above — this seems to be an earlier derivation than the latter with the same p.b. l(l)iʀ, perhaps from a pre-PE root *qa-, which could further lie behind EA qalux 'coverlet, blanket' and EA qalɣ-a '(its) sod (on top of sod house)'; compare quliʀ under qulə-]
AAY qaliq 'outer covering', PWS 'overshoe', C 'blanket'
CAY qaliq 'top layer'
NSY qaliq 'outer layer, parka made of reindeer autumn skin' [ANLC]
CSY qaliq 'gut rain parka' [and qaližaaq* 'raincoat', qaliʀ- 'put on rain parka']
Sir [note qaližaX 'rain cape']
SPI qaliq 'low-lying cloud, like fog' [for the 'rust' sense of this form see qałəʀ; qalipaaq 'outer fur parka, with fur outside']
NAI qaliq 'roof covering' [for the homonym in sense 'rust' see qałəʀ; and note P. Hope qalipquaq 'shirt']
WCI Cop qaliq 'unshed winter hairs on caribou summer coat' [Pryde, who also has Sig qalipquaq 'shirt']
ECI —
GRI qaliq 'ribbon for hair topknot, table cloth', NG 'cloth parka' [Holt.; note also qalipak 'outer covering', qalipaɣ- 'paint', qalipaat 'paint', and qalipaaq SWG 'deerskin jacket', NWG 'white piece of embroidered linen above woman's short boots']

PI qal(l)iʀiik- 'lie on top of (one) another' [cf. qaðliʀ above and ɣiik-]
SPI qalliiik- 'lie on top of one another'
NAI qalliʀiik-, PH qaliʀiik-, Nu qalliʀik- 'lie on top of one another'
WCI [Cop qaliʀiiktittiaʀniq 'rafted ice (layers of sea ice ridden up on each other)' — Pryde]
ECI qaliʀiik- 'lie on top of one another'
GRI qaliʀiiɣ-

PE qaliʀuðaʀ 'outer covering?' [cf. qaliʀ above and ŋ(ŋ)uðaʀ]
AAY Kod qaliʀuak 'overshoes', PWS qaliʀuat 'quilt'
CAY qaliʀuaq 'overalls, slipper, sock'
NSY qaliʀuaʀək 'long sealskin gloves' [and ANLC has qaliʀužaq 'upper story of building, attic']
CSY —
Sir —
SPI —
NAI qaliʀuaq 'cover, tarpaulin, quilt'
WCI —
ECI —
GRI qaliʀuaq 'outer covering, cloak'

PY-S qaspəq 'parka cover' [or qaypəq; compare SPI qalipaaq and NAI qalipquaq under qaliʀ above, and ilupəʀ(aʀ) under ilu — also for the second CSY meaning]
AAY [note PWS qaspəq 'queen-like']
CAY qaspəq* 'cloth cover parka' [qaspəʀ- 'put on a parka cover']
NSY qaɣpəq 'thin cloth garment' [ANLC]
CSY qaspəraq 'outer layer or garment, great grandchild' [and note qaspiXtə- 'pile up, wear outer layer of clothes']
Sir [Em. has qaspiʀət- 'put s.th. on top, put on outer coat' — probably from CSY]

PI qatcik- 'be high up' [cf. p.b. ðiɣ-]
SPI Qaw qassik- 'stand out, protrude'
NAI qatcik-
WCI qatsik- 'be situated highest'
ECI qatsik- 'bulge out, be humped, stick up'
GRI qatsiɣ- 'be high up '

PE qaðəɣ- 'fish with seine net' [the Yup forms could be influenced by qalu(-)]
AAY —
CAY [qəłcaq, qəłcavak Y 'net into which fish are driven by people walking in and thrashing the water', K 'bird snare', NS 'seine']
NSY —
CSY aXqəła 'seine' [also verbal]
Sir qaciɣ- 'pull out, haul up' [Vakh. from Rub.'s texts, also 'moor, heave up (e.g. off sledge)' from his own texts; Men. has qaqəła 'seine net']
SPI qaak-, qaaktuq- 'seine', Qaw qažɣun 'seine'
NAI qaaktuq- 'seine', qaɣžun 'seine,' Qaw qažɣun
WCI qaaktuq- 'fish with a sweep net', qaaktat 'herrings'
ECI —
GRI NWG qaattaʀ-, SWG qaattuʀ- 'hunt with a net', qaššutit [old ortho. qagssutit] 'net, fishing net', Up qaattaq, EG qatsulimmilaq 'seal caught in net'

PE qaðɣi '(men's) communal house, kashim' [cf. qažɣitaq?]
AAY AP qasɣiq 'community house' [qasɣi-, Kod qazɣiʀ- 'have a potlatch']
CAY qazɣiq, qayɣiq 'men's communal house'
NSY qayɣi

CSY —
Sir —
SPI qaɣži, Qaw qažɣi
NAI qažɣi, PH qalɣi
WCI qayɣi(q) 'meeting house' [Jen. has Cop qalɣiq]
ECI qaɣɣiq 'assembly house' [marked as 'old word']
GRI qašši [old ortho. qaɣsse] 'Eskimo assembly house' [today used only of geographical formations = 'depression surrounded by peaks'; note also qaššimiuaaʀ- 'feast together']

PE qaðiɣɣaʀ 'spotted seal' [there may be a relat. to qatəʀ- — note esp. the GRI there]
AAY qaiɣɣaq 'seal'
CAY Nun qayiɣyaX, NSU qayiɣzaq 'spotted seal'
NSY qaziɣyaq 'spotted seal' [Tein]
CSY qaziɣyaq 'spotted seal'
Sir qaciɣyəX 'spotted seal' [listed in Menovschikov with initial k; Vakh. has qaciɣiyaX from Rub.'s texts]
SPI qaziɣiaq 'young spotted seal'
NAI qasiɣiaq 'spotted seal'
WCI Cop qahiɣiaq 'black seal' [Lowe adds: 'elsewhere harbor, spotted, freshwater seal'; Met. has qasiɣiaq 'seal as big as bearded seal but rare in central Arctic' and Ras. 'spotted seal' for Net]
ECI qasiɣiaq 'spotted seal' [Dor. — Saul has 'harbor seal']
GRI qasiɣiaq 'spotted seal'

PE qa(C)əʀu(ʀ) '(birch) bark' [there may be a relat. with qayəmɣu(ʀ)]
AAY Kod qasʀulək 'birch'
CAY qazʀuq [also kazʀuq] 'birch bark'
NSY ➟
CSY qaayʀu 'bark found on beach' [and note Chap qayəmɣu 'tree bark' — contam. with qayəmɣu(ʀ)?]
Sir qayʀu 'bark found on beach' [Orr]
SPI ➟
NAI qaiʀuq 'bark', Nun 'shelf in oven' [and Mal qaimʀuq 'birch bark', compare B qaimʀu 'first shore ice in fall' under qayəmɣu(ʀ), with which there appears to be contam.]
WCI qaiʀuq 'bark, envelope around tree trunk' [and qaiʀulik 'birch']
ECI —
GRI —

PE qa(C)əʀuləɣ 'ribbon seal' [cf. ləɣ]
AAY —
CAY qasʀuliq, qasʀulək, qasɣulək 'ribbon seal *(phoca fasciata)*'
NSY qayəʀulək [Enm. et al.], qayʀulək [L.-T. and Tein]
CSY —
Sir —
SPI qaiʀulik 'ribbon seal'
NAI qaiʀulik
WCI Car, Net qaiʀulik 'saddleback seal' [B.-S.; for qaiʀulik 'birch' see under qa(C)əʀu(ʀ) above]
ECI qaiʀulik 'Greenland seal, sea lion (?)' [actually 'saddleback or harp seal' acc. Saul]
GRI —

PY qaɣan 'lake at head of river [cf. dem. root qaɣ-]
AAY qaɣan 'lake at head of river'
CAY qaɣan
NSY —
CSY —

PE qaɣə(ʀ) 'wave (breaker)' [cf. qaɣəʀ-]
AAY [note K qaŋyuk 'wave, breaker', Kod qauɣyak 'wave, swell', perhaps influenced by qauɣyaq 'sand'] ➟
CAY qaiq 'wave'
NSY qia 'wave, storm', qaɣəq 'whitecap on sea' [L.-T.]
CSY qaɣi 'wave on shore, breaker', qaɣəq 'rough wave, swell'
Sir qaɣəy 'breakers' [Krup.; Vakh. has qaɣi 'breaker' from Men.'s texts]
SPI qai(q) 'wave on ocean'
NAI qaɣɣaq 'breaker', Nu qai 'ocean wave'
WCI qaɣɣat 'waves breaking on shore', Sig qaɣaaq 'whitecap'
ECI —
GRI —

PE qaɣəliʀ- 'have waves (sea) [cf. liʀ-]
AAY qailiq 'swell, wave'
CAY qailiʀ- 'be rough, have lots of waves (ocean)' [for qavlunaq 'wake made by fish or animal below surface' see qavlunaq]
NSY qialiʀ- 'be rough sea, a storm'
CSY —
Sir qaɣəɬəɣaX 'waves on sea'
SPI qailiq 'breaker, wave' [also verbal]
NAI qail^{y}l^{y}iq* 'wave on ocean' [also verbal; note also qail^{y}l^{y}iaržuit 'ripples in water' and Nu qaivl^{y}ɨk 'wave caused by passing boat' — also verbal]
WCI —
ECI —
GRI [note qaałłiʀ- 'cause ripples on surface (fish moving rapidly under water)'

PE qaɣəʀ- 'burst' [cf. qaɣə(ʀ) and Aleut qaɣa-, western EA qaxa- 'crack, make sharp noise, knock, echo']
AAY KP qaɣəʀ-, K qaɣaʀ- 'break (waves)' [also of infection breaking open]
CAY qaɣəʀ- 'explode, pop'
NSY qiaʀaXtə- 'explode' [ANLC]
CSY qaɣəʀ-
Sir qaɣəʀ- [Orr]
SPI qaaq- 'burst, explode' [and Qaw qaaqtaq 'breaker on shore']
NAI qaaq- 'burst, explode'
WCI qaaq-, qaɣaq- 'burst, break (waves)' [Sig qaɣaaq- in Ras.]
ECI qaaq- 'burst, explode' [and qaɣaq- 'be white with foam (sea)', Lab qagaat- 'breakers occurring due to heavy sea swells' [Andersen et al.]
GRI qaaʀ- 'burst, explode' [and qaaʀtit- 'have a wave break over one', qaaliʀ- 'be satisfied, full', qaʀtuʀaʀ-, qaʀaaʀ- 'burst', NG qaɣaaq- 'be white with breakers (sea)']

PI qaaqšuq- 'get a blister' [cf. qðuʀ-?]
SPI qaaqšuq- 'get a blister' [qaaqšaniq 'blister']
NAI qaaqšuq- 'get a blister'
WCI qaaqsuq- [Pryde]
ECI qaaʀsu(q)- 'get a blister' [Saul; Lab qaatsuk 'blister']
GRI [note qaaɣ- 'get a blister']

PE qaɣiŋŋiʀ '(kind of) duck or teal?' [cf. Aleut qaɣiða-X, western EA qaxiða-X 'horned puffin']
AAY qaiŋiaq, qaiŋi(ʀ)aq 'harlequin duck' [Kod qaɣiyaq 'horned puffin' is a loan from Aleut above]
CAY —
NSY —
CSY qaɣiŋiiq 'harlequin duck'
Sir —
SPI Qaw qaiŋiq 'green-winged teal'
NAI qaiŋŋiq*
WCI —
ECI —
GRI —

PY qaɣla(k) 'circular rim?'
AAY qaɣlawik 'ring outside manhole coaming of baidarka' [and qaɣla- 'carry (baidarka) by putting the hole over one's head'
CAY qaɣlak 'upper part of bucket (all except bottom)'
NSY —
CSY —

PE qaɣuʀ 'forehead'
AAY — [for qauq 'barnacle' see qa(C)uʀ-]
CAY Nun, NSU qauq, LK BB qauʀaq 'forehead'
NSY qaaqʷ
CSY qaɣuq
Sir qaɣəx
SPI qauq
NAI qauq
WCI qauq
ECI qauq
GRI qaaq, NG qauk

PI qauʀun 'headband' [cf. un]
SPI —
NAI qauʀutik 'bridle for sled reindeer', Nu qauʀun 'tattoo on forehead'
WCI Car qauʀut 'decorative brass plate on band worn across forehead by women' [Pryde]
ECI qauʀuti 'headband worn by Pallirmiut women'
GRI qaaʀut 'headband'

PE qaɣvaʀ- and **qakvaʀ-** 'rise or raise (to surface)' [cf. vaʀ- and qaðvaʀ- under qaðə- and compare also caɣvi(q)-; there appears to be contam. with qakə- in Yup at least — note CAY qakłitə- there; the eastern Inu forms could reflect qaðvaʀ- — see section B of Intro.]
AAY qakxʷaʀ- 'beat at a game', PWS 'come out of water onto land'
CAY qakfaʀ- 'emerge, remove from water, win' [as opposed to qaivaʀ- 'rise to surface' under qaðvaʀ-]
NSY qaɣvaXtə- 'rise up, raise, boast'
CSY —
Sir —
SPI qaɣvaq- 'rise, lift' [for qavžaq- 'put on top' see qaðvaʀ- under qaðə-]
NAI qaɣvaq- 'rise (sun), rise to surface'
WCI qaɣvaq- 'take out or be out of hole (stored meat)' [and qaɣviq- 'rise (sun), appear at surface' — infl. by caɣvi(q)-?]
ECI qavvaq- 'rise' [and note qavvi(q)- 'raise onto s.th., reach top of s.th. one is climbing']
GRI qaffaʀ- 'lift, heave up, rise, float' [old ortho. qagfar-, Fab. kabbar-, kagvar-; qaffaɣ- 'come up to surface (fish)', qaffiʀ- 'heave up, let rise, come into shallow water (fish)', NG qaɣvaxxama- 'have risen']

PI qaiq- 'be smooth'
SPI qaiqsaq- 'sand, smooth'
NAI qaiq- 'be smooth, flat, level'
WCI qaiq- 'be flat, smooth'
ECI qaiʀuq- 'plane, smooth', qaiʀayuk- 'scour', Lab 'be smooth, even, polished'
GRI qaaʀsaat 'water and blood rubbed on sledge runners and left to freeze'

PI qaiqtuq 'rock surface or cliff?' [cf. ðuʀ]
SPI [note qaiqtaq '(smooth expanse of) rock cliff']
NAI —
WCI Car B. Lake qaiqtuq 'rock' [Dor.; 'naked rock' in Cop acc. Pryde]
ECI qaiqtuq 'rock' [Saul]
GRI qaaʀsuq, NG qaiXXuq '(surface of) rock, cliff'

PE qa(C)iqu 'cave' [i.e. qayiqu? — cf. qaiq-]
AAY K qaiqunaq 'cave'
CAY —
NSY [qaɣɣiŋə 'cave' (L.-T.) is probably by contam. from qaðɣi[1]]
CSY —
Sir qayi 'cave' [Vakh. from Men.'s texts; Orr also has pl. qayiy]
SPI [Qaitquq 'cave on King Island (pl. name)']
NAI Nu qaiʀusuk, qaiʀułuk 'cave'
WCI Net qaiʀusuk [Pryde]
ECI qaiʀusuk 'cavern, cave', Lab 'cleft in rock' [Peck]
GRI qaaʀusuk 'cave'

PI qaiʀuaq- 'echo' [cf. qaʀya?]
SPI —
NAI qaiʀuaq- 'make a loud echoing sound' [qaiʀuatit- 'echo loudly']
WCI Cop qaiʀualiq- 'echo'
ECI —
GRI qaaʀuaʀpaluɣ- 'sound hollow'

PE qakə- 'climb up on s.th.' [there could be a link to qaðə-, but cf. also Aleut kaki- 'look up, raise bow (of boat)']
AAY —
CAY qakətə- 'resubmerge after coming to surface' [and qakłitə- 'scale a height']
NSY —

CSY qaakə- 'put up on elevated place'
Sir —
SPI qaɣi- 'climb out or up on'
NAI qakɨ- 'climb up on shore' [and qakšuq- 'bring boats up from whaling camp to village'; qakpik, qakitpik 'shelf']
WCI qaki- 'climb up on land' [and note Cop qakpik, Sig qaksaʀvik 'seal hole in spring ice']
ECI qaki-, qaqi- 'climb up on shore' [and Ras. has qaktuniq 'mountain' as a shaman's word for Igl]
GRI qaqi-, NG qaki- 'get up on something, e.g. land' [and qattuniq* 'hill' — old ortho. qagtuneq]

PI qakət- 'put or pull up' [cf. t-[1]]
SPI qaɣit- 'put above, on top'
NAI qakɨt- 'put up, pull up (on s.th.)'
WCI qakit- 'run up shore, pull ashore' [Pryde]
ECI —
GRI qaqit- 'pull up (from below)'

PI qakši- 'climb up on ice (sea mammal)' [cf. ði-?]
SPI Qaw qakšaq 'sea mammal out of water, on land or ice'
NAI qakši 'sea mammal on top of ice'
WCI Car qaxximayuq 'seal that has climbed up on ice' [Schn. 'adg'; note Sig qakisima- 'have crawled up on ice (seal)']
ECI —
GRI qašši- [old ortho. qagssi-] 'put s.th. on shore', qaššima- 'have crept up on ice or shore (sea mammal)'

PI qakšuɣaun 'carrying strap or belt' [cf. un]
Yup [note CAY qakəxtə- 'lift up parka, shirt, dress']
SPI qakšuaun 'belt for holding baby on back'
NAI qakšuɣautaq, qakšun 'one of two white bands along wolverine's back' [and note qakšukkak- 'pull clothing up and tie with belt']
WCI Sig qaksutaun 'door latch' [Pet.; Ras. has Car qaʀzuaut 'parka string' and Schn. has qaksuŋaut 'button on parka for attaching baby-carrying hood' for 'adg']
ECI qatsuŋauti 'belt for the parka' [Saul; Lab qaksuŋaut 'carrying strap (for baby-carrying hood) on parka' (Bourq.); Parry has Igl qakiumautik 'straps used by women for carrying children']
GRI qaššuaat 'waistband for an amaut' [old ortho. qagssuaut; and note, qaššuaʀ- 'tie up *amaut* for child to rest in']

PE qakə(ʀ)- 'be pale or bleached' [cf. qakuʀ-]
AAY —
CAY qaki-, HBC qakiXcətə- 'be pale, dry'
NSY ➟
CSY ➟
Sir ➟
SPI ➟
NAI ➟
WCI qakiq- 'be bleached in sun' [for homonym 'be moldy', which may have influenced this form, see qakəʀ-]
ECI qakiqtuq 's.th. bleached' [qakiʀniq 's.th. bleached in sun or air']
GRI —

PE qakcuʀ- 'be (bleached) white' [or qakəʀcuʀ-; compare quqcuq- under quʀə-?]
AAY —
CAY qəXcuXpak 'very white, bright thing'
NSY qəXsuʀ- 'be white' [ANLC; Jen. has qarsor- 'be white'; for qakšužak 'dawn' see qaʀu-]
CSY aXsuʀ- 'be pale, bleached' [for aqXuuxtə- 'be pale from illness' see qakuʀ-]
Sir qaXsəʀ- 'be white' [Vakh.; Em. has qaXsuʀžux 'whitish, grayish'; Men. has qaXsəɣ-, also qaXcəʀəłəX 'gray hair']
SPI qaqsuq- 'be white, esp. of bleached skin' [and qaqsatuq- 'have frostbite']
NAI qaqsuq- 'be bleached by weather'
WCI qaqsuqtaq 'sealskin bleached by sun or wind'
ECI —
GRI qaʀsuʀ- 'be bleached' [qarsurniq* 'skeleton', NG qaXXuqtitaq 's.th. bleached']

PE qakəʀ(luɣ) 'throat'
AAY ➟
CAY [Barn. has kákrlok 'throat'] ➟
NSY —
CSY ➟
Sir qaqəʀla 'throat' [Vakh. has qaqəʀləX from Men.'s texts; Orr has qaqəʀla]
SPI —
NAI qakiʀluk 'area under chin', qakɨq- 'hit on chin with fist'
WCI qakiqtaq- 'box', Sig qakiʀlut 'throat (under chin)' [Pet.]
ECI qakiʀluk 'area under face between neck and chin'
GRI qaqiʀłuk 'lower part of chin under neck' [and qaqiq 'opening in s.th., extension']

PE qakkit- 'have an irritated throat' [cf. łit-?]
AAY qakite- 'have mouth and throat irritated by rancid food'
CAY Y qakitə- 'have irritated throat'
NSY —
CSY qakitə- 'feel the undesirable effects of eating s.th. bitter'
Sir —
SPI qakkit- 'feel the effects of eating rancid oil'
NAI qakkit- 'get a thick feeling in mouth as from acrid food'
WCI —
ECI qakki(C)- 'feel stinging in eyes, nose or throat, be asphyxiated'
GRI —

PE qakəʀ- 'be rancid?' [the relat., if any, with qakəʀ(luɣ) is obscure]
AAY qakəʀ- 'be rancid'
CAY NSU qakiʀ- 'be rancid'
NSY qakəʀ- [ANLC], qakəXqə- [Men.] 'have a bitter

taste' [qakəlʀia 'bitter', qakəq 'bitter taste']
CSY qakəq 'bitter taste', qakəʀ- 'taste bitter' [for qakitə- 'feel the undesirable effect of eating s.th. bitter' see qakkit- under qakəʀ(luɣ)]
Sir —
SPI qaɣiq- 'become rancid (seal oil)' [qaɣiʀnit- 'taste or smell rancid']
NAI qakiʀnit- 'taste or smell rancid, irritate the throat', PH qakiq- 'get rancid (seal oil)' [for qakkit- 'get a thick feeling in mouth' see qakkit- under qakəʀ(luɣ)]
WCI qakiq- 'be moldy' [qakiʀnit- 'look moldy']
ECI [qakiq- 'have eroded (snow on ground or of snow house, owing to wind)'; Andersen et al. have qakkinagi- 'find too strong to eat because of aftertaste of eating shellfish, causing throat to have a tingling feeling' for Lab]
GRI qaqiʀnit- 'be rancid, irritate the throat'

PE qakəʀci- 'get irritant in eyes' [cf. ci-?]
AAY qakəXci- get soap or other irritant in eyes'
CAY qakəXci- 'have irritated eyes'
NSY —
CSY —
Sir —
SPI qaɣiqsi- 'have one's eyes sting'
NAI qakiqsi-, qaqiqsi-
WCI —
ECI qakiʀniq, qakiʀsinaqtuq 's.th. causing the eyes (or mouth or nose) to sting'
GRI qaqiʀsi- 'get water or smoke in eyes, smart (eyes)'

qakiiyaq 'salmon (silver)' [from Aleut qakiiða-X 'silver salmon']
AAY qakiiyaq 'silver salmon'
CAY qakiiyaq
NSY —
CSY —

PE qaku 'when (in future)' [with conditional mood marker ku-? — compare qaŋa]
AAY qaku 'when (in future)'
CAY qaku
NSY qaku 'when'
CSY qakun 'when (in future)'
Sir qaku 'when ' [in future? — note qakumənu 'in a while' on Men. p. 100]
SPI qaɣu(n), qaɣuʀun 'when (in future)'
NAI qakuɣu, Mal also qakuɣun
WCI Sig qaku(ɣu), Cop qakuɣu
ECI qaku 'when (at last, after lengthy waiting)', NBI qakuɣu(q) 'when (in future)' [Dor.]
GRI qaquɣu 'when (in future)' [and Robbe and Menn. have EG qaȓuliɣut, qaȓuluunniit 'at any time (in future)']

PI qakutiɣun 'rarely' [vialis case pl.]
SPI qaɣutiun 'rarely'
NAI qakkutiɣun
WCI qakutiɣut
ECI Lab qakutikkut 'from time to time' [Bourq.]
GRI qaqutiɣu(t), qaqutikkut 'now and then, seldom'

PE qakuʀ- 'be or turn white' [cf. qakə(ʀ)-]
AAY —
CAY ➟
NSY —
CSY aXquuxtə- 'be pale from illness'
Sir —
SPI ➟
NAI qakuq- 'be bleached by weather, turn white' [qakuak 'frost on ground']
WCI Cop qakuXXi- 'whiten', qakuqtaq 's.th. white' [Dor. has qaquqtuq 'white' for Net]
ECI qakuqtaq 's.th. white' [and Lab qaqutsi- 'whiten, pale']
GRI qaquʀ- 'be white' [(qilaluɣaq) qaquʀtaq, NG qakuqtaq 'white whale, beluga']

PE qakuʀnaʀ 'frost' [cf. naʀ]
AAY —
CAY qakuʀnaq 'frost on trees'
NSY —
CSY —
Sir —
SPI [qauʀnaq- 'have frost on ground', qaɣuʀniq 'ice fog']
NAI —
WCI qakuʀnaq 'autumn frost'
ECI qakuʀnaq 'white frost on ground' [also 'iron']
GRI qaquʀnaq, qaquʀnak, qaqunnak 'hoar frost'

PY-S qaləqə- 'tickle' [cf. qaʀaləʀ-]
AAY [for C Xalʀiucaaʀ- 'tickle' see qaʀaləʀ-]
CAY HBC qəlqəciʀ(ar)-, Nun qaləqm̥aciʀ(aʀ)- 'tickle'
NSY —
CSY qələqətaaʀ- 'tickle'
Sir qələqiyuɣ- [Orr]

PE qaləʀ- 'make characteristic cry (animal)' [cf. qała-[2] and Atkan Aleut qalXimiɣ- 'clear one's throat'; there may be a further relat. to qatə]
AAY qalliʀ-, AP qalriʀ- 'yell, ring, whistle, growl'
CAY qalʀiʀ- 'cry, make inarticulate vocal sound (animal)', qalʀiuʀ- 'twitter' [and note K, BB qalaXtə- 'talk, speak'; for K qałatə- 'talk, preach' see qała-[2]]
NSY qalʀiʀ- 'cry, whistle, shriek' [and ANLC has nominal qalʀiq 'cry']
CSY qalʀiʀ- 'cry, whine, twitter, make characteristic sound (animal)', qaləpaŋi- 'be outspoken' [for qałəɣ- 'speak, say' see qała-[2]]
Sir qaʀləʀ- 'make characteristic animal sound' [and qaʀləXtaʀ- 'howl (storm)'; Vakh. has qalʀiXtaʀ- 'call, cry' from Men.'s texts; Em. has qaʀləqaqu- 'cry out, sing rhythmic throat song', qalʀa- 'go into trance and shamanize, groan out during nightmare']
SPI qaʀluq- 'yell, call (animal)', W qalʀuq- 'make rumbling sound' [Jen.]
NAI qalʀuq- 'make characteristic sound (animal)'
WCI qalʀuq- 'bark (dog)' [Met.], Cop qalruqtuq- 'make

sound like bird' [Ras. has qalʀuut 'song']
ECI qaʀʀulaaq- 'yell, make inarticulate cries'
GRI qaʀłuʀ- 'twitter, squeak, squeal (also jocular of human speech)', qaʀłuusiq 'voice (of animal)', EG qaʀtiʀ- 'yelp (dog)' [but Robbe and Menn. have qattiʀ- 'howl (dog)' for EG and Tersis qalimaaʀ- 'growl'; note also qaʀłuʀtaat 'wind instrument', EG qaʀtiʀtaat 'larynx']

PI qaləŋu- 'growl'
SPI qaliŋužaaq- 'growl'
NAI qaliŋu-
WCI Sig qałiŋu- [Lowe]
ECI qaliŋulaaq-, qatiŋula(a)q- 'growl' [the latter influenced by qaciŋŋuq-? — but cf. also qatə]
GRI NG qaliŋuuq- 'growl, show teeth (dog)' [Holt.; for qaŋŋuʀ- 'boom' see qatŋuʀ-]

PE qalmaʀ- 'call to dogs' [cf. qaləʀ- and maʀ-?]
AAY —
CAY qalmaʀ- 'summon a dog vocally, try to attract a man by flirting (woman)'
NSY —
CSY qalmaʀ- 'summon a dog vocally'
Sir —
SPI —
NAI —
WCI qammaq- 'call, lure an animal' [Ras. — Pryde has qanmaq- for Cop]
ECI qammatuq-, NBI qaŋmaq- 'call (dogs)' [spelled qaŋmator- by Schn.; Peck has Lab kangmar-]
GRI qaʀmaʀ-, EG qammaa- 'call, lure (dog)' [but Robbe and Menn. have qammaʀ- for the latter; Fab. has kangmar-]

PY qalmi(t)yaq 'reef' [cf. qaluʀ?]
AAY qalmiyaq 'underwater reef where heavy swells break'
CAY —
NSY qalŋisaq 'reef'
CSY qalməsaq 'underwater reef'

qalqa 'axe' [a loan from Chukchi 'ałəgatte 'axe', from *'ałəgatga, derived from gatga 'Chukotkan adze' (note that initial glottal stop plus vowel is metathesized in the Chukchi orthography — see de Reuse: 419f.]
AAY —
CAY Y, NS, HBC, UK, NI qałqapak 'axe'
NSY qałqapak 'axe' [and aləɣatxa 'axe' — directly from the Chukchi]
CSY qałqalima 'axe' [contam. with ulima-]
Sir [aləɣatɣə 'axe' — directly from the Chukchi]
Inu [SPI qałXavak, Qaw qałXapak 'axe' — from the Yup?]

qalqaʀayaq 'magpie' [loan from EA qalqaʀaya-X 'raven, magpie', dimin. qalqaʀayaaða-X 'magpie'; compare also different base EA qalŋaaX, Atkan qaŋlaaX, Att qaɣlaaX 'raven' — both related to PE qaləʀ-?]
AAY K qałqayaq, qałqasaaq, C qałqana(a)q 'magpie' [and note Kod qalŋa'aq 'raven', a loan from Aleut]
CAY qałqəʀayak 'black-billed magpie'
NSY —
CSY —

PY qalʀu 'pike'
AAY K qalʀu 'pike (fish)'
CAY Eg, UK, UY qalʀu
NSY —
CSY —

PE qaltaʀ 'bucket' [cf. Aleut qal- 'bottom (of sea, bay, bucket, etc.)']
AAY C qałtaq 'container'
CAY qałtaq, Nun qałtauX 'bucket, pail'
NSY qałtaʀʷa(a)q 'bucket, pail' [and qałtat 'provisions'; ANLC has qałtaq 'provisions for journey, container for provisions']
CSY qałtaq 'bucket, pail'
Sir —
SPI qattauɣaq 'bucket, pail' [and qattausikaq 'barrel']
NAI qattaq 'water barrel with lid'
WCI qattaq 'bucket' [qattaʀyuk 'barrel']
ECI qattaq 'water bucket, pot, oven, cauldron'
GRI qattaq 'bucket (esp. for water)' [NWG qattaavaq 'leather water tub']

PY-S qaltə 'bark or scale' [cf. qaðə-?]
AAY qałta, qəłta 'bark, peeling'
CAY qəłta 'bark, peeling, scale'
NSY qałtə 'bark, scale, crust'
CSY qałta 'fish scale' [and qəšta 'matted hair']
Sir qałta 'scale, crust'

PE qalu(-) 'dip or scoop'
AAY qalu 'dipnet' [as verb = 'dip']
CAY qalu 'dipnet' [as verb = 'dip, bail boat'; qaluuʀin 'dipper']
NSY qalu 'dipnet' [and qalu- (Men. qaluʀ-) 'use dipnet (for fishing)']
CSY qalu 'dipnet' [verbal = 'dip, ladle, bail']
Sir qala 'dipnet' [and qalə(t)- 'scoop, dip' — Vakh. has qali- and Orr has qalə́kəʀaX 'bucket']
SPI qalu 'dipnet' [verbal = 'bail out, dish out']
NAI qalu 'dipnet' [verbal = 'use a dipnet, bail boat'; note also Nu qaluŋniq* 'small valley or cirque in mountains']
WCI qalu 'fish trap' [as verb 'dip, scoop out']
ECI qalu- 'dip, scoop out'
GRI qalu- 'scoop, bail out, receive hospitably' [qalut (pl.) 'net for catching birds', qałłut(i)- 'scoop up with', NG qallut(i)- 'get water in boots', qaluhiraut 'water dipper'; Ges. has EG qaliq 'capelin net']

PE qallun 'dipper' [cf. un]
AAY [B.-S. has qalun 'baidarka siphon']
CAY qalun 'dipper'
NSY qalun [ANLC]
CSY —
Sir —
SPI qallun 'dipper, cup'

NAI qallun 'dipper, cup, ladle'
WCI qal(l)un 'ladle, dipper'
ECI qallut 'dipper, gallon' [but qaluut 'mug, cup, scraper using liquid spread on skin'; Math. has qalut 'fish trap of baleen' for Igl]
GRI qałłut 'scoop, dip', Up qałłit, NG qallut 'mug, cup' [but qalut 'capelin dip']

PI qalunəq 'grease floating on stew' [cf. nər[1]]
SPI —
NAI —
WCI [note qaluniq 's.th. hollowed out']
ECI qaluniq 'melted grease floating on meat stew'
GRI qaluniq* 'fat, lard' [qalunni- 'skim off grease']

PI qaluqšaq 'valley or depression'
SPI qaluqšaq 'depression, hollow in ground,' Qaw 'canyon, deep valley'
NAI Nu qaluqšaq 'ditch, mountain cirque'
WCI —
ECI —
GRI qaluʀsaq 'depression, valley surrounded on three sides by cliffs' [Ordb. also qalumaniq*]

PE qalutaʀ(-) 'ladle or bail' [cf. qallun above]
AAY qalutaq 'dipper'
CAY Nun qalutaX 'wooden ladle'
NSY —
CSY —
Sir —
SPI —
NAI qalutaq- 'dip, bail out'
WCI [qalutaq 'dipper for bailing out']
ECI qalutaq- 'dip'
GRI qalutaat 'ladle, dipper', SWG 'spoon', NG qalutaq 'spoon'

PE qaluɣyaʀ 'whale lance' [cf. EA qalɣuya-X 'spear with stone point', probably a borrowing from Eskimo]
AAY [qaluɣyaq 'lance' appears on old word lists]
CAY qaluɣyaq 'harpoon head'
NSY qaluʀyaq [for qaluɣyaq?]
CSY qaluɣyaq 'whale lance'
Sir qaluɣyəx 'whale lance' [Em.; Orr has qalu!ɣyaX]
SPI qaluɣiaq 'harpoon head' ['whaling lance' in Jen. for W]
NAI qaluɣiaq 'whale lance'
WCI Sig qaluɣiaq 'whale lance' [Ras., who has it as 'copper snow knife' for Cop]
ECI Lab, Baffin qaluɣiaq 'hunting spear, lance'
GRI qaluɣiaq 'whale lance'

PE qaluʀ 'rock' [cf. qalmi(t)yaq; this may be a local loan into NSY rather than actual PE]
AAY —
CAY —
NSY qa(a)luq 'stone' [Jen.]
CSY —
Sir —
SPI qaluq 'round rock or pebble on shore'
NAI — [for Nu qaluqšaq 'ditch, valley' see qaluqšaq under qalu(-)]
WCI —
ECI —
GRI —

PE qała-[1] 'boil or churn' [cf. EA qału-n, Atk qalu-s 'hot springs', perhaps also old Atkan qałati-X 'well (of water)']
AAY qała- 'be boiling'
CAY qała(tə)- 'be boiling' [for K homonym meaning 'talk' see qała-[2]]
NSY qałat 'whirlpool' [Jen. also has as verb qałatə- 'boil']
CSY qała 'boiling, bubbling sound', qałatə- 'boil (food)' [and Chap qałəʀałəq* 'noise (of water)', qałəʀaxtaʀ- 'make noise (water)'; for qałəɣ- 'speak' see qała-[2]]
Sir qałažukaʀ- 'boil', qałažukaʀyutə- 'bubble' [Vakh. has qałažuʀ- 'boil']
SPI qalat- 'boil' [and qala 'wake of boat']
NAI qalat- 'boil', Nu 'churn (water)' [and qalak- 'burp' (Pryde also 'clear one's throat'), Nu qala, PH qalat 'wake of boat']
WCI qalat- 'boil' [and Cop qalak 'cough' (also verbal), Sig 'bubble rising to surface', qalaɣaq- 'gargle'; Pryde has qalaaq- 'sing, hiss (boiling water)' for Net]
ECI qalak- 'cook' [Lab also 'boil', nominal = 'wake of fish' — Bourq.; qala, P. Dorset qalaq 'disturbance in water from diving animal', qalaiq- 'be an eddy from diving animal', Igl qalaaq- 'be boiling']
GRI qalaɣ- 'boil', qalak 'bubble' [qalat- in the old (Kl.) ortho. is only used for the trans. but Fab. has for the intr. too; note also qalat- 'draw stomach in' — kallak- in Fab.]

PY qała-[2] 'talk' [cf. qaləʀ-, perhaps influenced by qała-[1]]
AAY qała-, qałaŋuaʀ- 'chat, talk away'
CAY K qałatə- 'talk, discuss, preach' [for qalaXtə- 'talk, speak' see qaləʀ-]
NSY qałapaŋəXsi- 'jabber, be talkative' [Em.]
CSY qałəɣ- 'speak, talk, say s.th. important' [compare qała 'sound of boiling water' under qała-[1]]
Sir [Em. has qałəɣ- 'speak' from CSY?; note also qažatəʀ- 'bawl out' — Orr]
Inu [cf. NAI qalak- under qała-[1]]

PE qałaciʀ 'navel' [there may be a link to qała-[1]]
AAY qałaciq 'navel'
CAY qałaciq
NSY qasałiq
CSY qałqasiq
Sir [note siłəX 'navel']
SPI qalasiq
NAI qalasiq
WCI qalasiq
ECI qalasiq
GRI qalasiq

PE qałəʀ 'mold or rust?' [there may be a link to qaðə-]
AAY K qałəq, C qałək 'mould'
CAY qałəq* 'rust'
NSY —

CSY —
Sir —
SPI qaliq
NAI qalɨq*, Mal qałɨq*
WCI [Pryde has Cop qattinnak- 'be rusty', qattiniq 'rust']
ECI —
GRI —

PY-S qałəvak 'coveralls' [cf. qaðliʀ under qaðə- and vaɣ, and compare SPI qalipaaq 'outer fur parka' under qaliʀ (qaðə-)]
AAY —
CAY qałuvak, du. qałuviik 'coveralls'
NSY qałəvak 'coveralls' [Men. has qałivik, also qałuk 'woman's thigh covering']
CSY qałəvak 'coveralls, woman's hoodless reindeer-skin suit' [and qałukaq 'fur from reindeer leg']
Sir qałəvɣiy [pl.] 'coveralls'

PE qama- 'be calm'
AAY —
CAY qama- 'be calm (water or wind)'
NSY —
CSY —
Sir —
SPI [note Qaw qamaayaaq 'whirlpool, snow whirling in wind']
NAI [note Nu qamatmuaq- 'travel with wind at one's back'] ➟
WCI Cop qama- 'hang suspended in water (dead seal or fish' [Pryde, who also has qamaq- 'be stopped dead in water (boat)']
ECI Igl qamaaʀvik 'place where one waits for seals' [Ras.]
GRI qama- 'wait for seal in one's kayak'

PE qamanəʀ 'calm stretch of river' [cf. nəʀ[1]]
AAY —
CAY qamanəq* 'place lacking current or wind'
NSY —
CSY —
Sir —
SPI —
NAI qamanɨq*, qamanaaq 'lee, shelter from weather or wind' [the latter means 'upstream current' in Nu]
WCI qamaniq 'place where current is neutralised (river)' [Pet. has 'bay of river' for Sig, Ras has 'broad (river)' and B.-S. has 'lake (in river)' for Car; qamanʀu- 'have no current']
ECI qamaniq 'widening of river' [Peck has 'pond, ditch, lake' for Lab]
GRI qamaniq 'widening in a river (below waterfall)'

PE qama(C)uɣ 'sled' [cf. qamuʀ-; perhaps from *qamiɣautəɣ — see qamiɣaʀ- under qamuʀ-, esp. the Qaw form qamiɣaun]
AAY KP qamuk (du.) 'sled'
CAY Nun, Y, NS qamauk
NSY qamaak[w]
CSY —
Sir —
SPI Imaq qamauk
NAI [note qamuɣaužat 'hand sled]
WCI qamauk 'toboggan'
ECI —
GRI —

PE qamə- 'go out (fire)'
AAY qamə- 'go out (fire, light), stop (machine) '
CAY qamə- 'die down, of fire, person depressed or drowning, or something that retreats from sight' [and qamłəq* 'ash from fire']
NSY qamə- 'be extinguished' [Jen.]
CSY qaamə- 'go out of fire, be extinguished, eclipsed' [and note qamaɣ- 'go through or consume all']
Sir [Vakh. has qaməxtə- 'go through, be or do all'] ➟
SPI qami- 'go out, die, of light or fire' [and Jen. has W qablit 'sediment on bottom of lamp']
NAI qamɨ- 'go out'
WCI qami-
ECI ➟
GRI qamiC- 'be extinguished' [qamig- in old orth. with spurious g — same as qamit- under qamət- below in Fab.; note also NG qattuaq- 'play the lamp-dousing game (men and women in dark)']

PE qamcuɣ- 'turn down light or become dim' [cf. mcuɣ-]
AAY —
CAY qamyuaʀ(ᴀʀ)- 'squint; close eyes part way'
NSY qamsuk 'gloomy weather', qaamsuxtə- 'wink, blink' [ANLC]
CSY qamsuuk 'gloomy weather with poor visibility', qamsuxtə- 'blink eyes', Chap qamsuuxtə- 'get worse (weather)' [and qamtə- 'close in (weather)']
Sir —
SPI —
NAI qafsuk-, Mal qapcuk- 'turn down (light), become dim or low (fire or light)'
WCI —
ECI —
GRI qassuɣ-, qassutsit- 'turn down (light)'

PE qamət- 'extinguish' [cf. t-[1]]
AAY qamtə- 'turn off (lamp), stop (machine)'
CAY qamtə- 'turn down (e.g. stove)'
NSY qamtə- 'put out fire'
CSY qamtə-
Sir qamət- 'put out (fire, lamp)' [Vakh.]
SPI qamit- 'put out fire, turn out light'
NAI qamɨt-
WCI qamit-
ECI qamit-
GRI qamit-

PI qaptəq- 'douse (a fire)' [cf. təʀ-]
SPI qaptiq- 'douse (a fire)'
NAI qaptɨq-
WCI qaptiq-
ECI —
GRI qatsiʀ-, qamitsiʀ-

PE qaməŋaʀ 'ankle bone'
AAY K qamaŋaq, C qapaŋaq 'ankle bone'
CAY qamaŋaq
NSY — [but note qamaaŋuaq 'pelvis']
CSY —
SPI —
NAI qamŋaq 'ankle'
WCI Net, Car qamŋaq 'ankle', Cop qamŋaaq 'ankle bone' [Pryde]
ECI —
GRI NG qaŋmak 'ankle or wrist bone'

PY qamqə- 'pull tight?' [there may be a link to qamuʀ-]
AAY K qamqə- 'tangle, get tangled'
CAY —
NSY —
CSY qaamqaXtə- 'pull on loop or noose to tighten'

PI qamʀui- and **qamŋui-** 'snore'
SPI qaŋŋui-, Qaw qamʀui- 'snore'
NAI qamŋui-
WCI Sig qamʀuq-, Cop qa(a)mŋuq- 'snore' [Pryde has qamŋuq-, qamŋui- for Cop]
ECI qaʀŋui-, Lab qaŋŋui- 'snore' [Peck has qamŋui-]
GRI qaŋŋui- [old ortho. qavngui-], EG qaʀŋumilaaʀ- 'snore' [Robbe and Menn. have qaŋŋumilaaʀ-]

PE qamuʀ- 'pull or tow' [cf. qama(C)uɣ and EA qamu- 'drag (stringed fish)']
AAY qamuʀ- 'drag, pull by rope'
CAY qamuʀ- 'pull, drag behind' [and qamuq 'sled or other pulled thing']
NSY qamuʀ- 'pull, drag' [and qamun 'rope for hauling game' — L.-T.]
CSY qamuʀ- 'pull, drag' [qamuq 'load pulled on sled']
Sir [note qamcəʀ- 'tow, carry on sled']
SPI Qaw qamuq- 'pull, tow'
NAI qamuk- 'pull, tow'
WCI qamuk- 'pull, tow' [Lowe — Met. has 'help dogs pull sled']
ECI [note qamuq 'dog that has been ill for some time'] ➟
GRI ➟

PE qamiɣaʀ- 'pull a small hunting sled' [cf. qamitə- below, perhaps extended by aʀ-, i.e. *ɣaʀ-]
AAY —
CAY qamiɣaʀ- 'go hunting with small sled and kayak during spring' [qamiɣaq 'small sled carried on kayak']
NSY qamiɣaʀ- 'hunt on the sea' [ANLC; Men. has qamiɣaʀnaqə- 'prepare to go hunting on sea']
CSY qamiɣaʀ- 'drag over ice or ground' [Chap 'move forward in sitting position']
Sir qamiɣəʀ- 'move forward in sitting position'
SPI qamiɣautit 'small sled for transporting kayak', Qaw qamiɣaq- 'pull such a sled by harness'
NAI —
WCI —
ECI —
GRI —

PY qamitə- 'give s.th. to take along on sled' [nominalized qamuq under qamuʀ- above plus lit-?]
AAY —
CAY qamitə- 'give s.th. to take along on a journey' [and Y qamizvak 'large freight sled']
NSY [qamilɣuʀ- 'drag (boat) overland, roam from place to place' (ANLC); L.-T. has qamilɣułəq 'dragging whales to shore at start of spring hunt']
CSY qamitə- 'give s.th. to take along' [and note qamilɣut 'family traveling by dog team', qamilɣuʀ- 'travel together by dog team', also qamiya 'sled']
Sir [note qamca 'sled' and qamcəʀ- 'tow, carry on sled' which may go with CSY qamiya above, but compare also qanžak]

PE qamuʀaʀ- '(help) pull sled' [cf. aʀ-]
AAY —
CAY Y qamuXaʀ- 'pull a sled' [and note HBC qamuʀaʀ-, qamuXi- 'write']
NSY qamuʀaʀ- 'pull sled by hand' [ANLC; Men. has qamuʀaq 'travois', qamuʀaXsiq 's.th. dragged, load']
CSY qamuʀaʀ- 'pull or drag by muscle power only' [qamuʀaq 'store-bought toboggan', Chap 'towed vessel']
Sir —
SPI qamuʀaq- 'help pull (dogsled)'
NAI Nu qamuʀaq-
WCI qamuʀaq- 'pull with a kind of harness (person pulling a load or boat or helping pull a sled)'
ECI qamuʀaq- 'help dogs pull sled'
GRI —

PI qamutək 'sled' [dual; cf. un]
SPI —
NAI qamutik 'low sled'
WCI Sig qamutik 'sled' [Dor. has qamutiik 'sled' for B. Lake]
ECI qamutiik du. 'sled'
GRI qamutit pl. 'sled', NG qamutik 'the two sled runners' [Holt.], EG qamulit 'little sled for supporting gun on when seal-hunting on ice' [and qamutiʀ- 'travel by sled'; for EG qamutsiq 'sled' see qimuciʀ]

PE qanaɣ 'tent pole or frame of shelter'
AAY qanak, qaŋ̥ak 'rafter, gate'
CAY qanak 'roof board'
NSY —
CSY —

Sir —
SPI qanak 'ceiling'
NAI qanak 'roof board, tent pole' [verbal = 'put roof boards on house']
WCI qanak 'tent pole'
ECI qanak
GRI qanak 'tent pole' [qanaɣ- 'fix tent poles in position', NG qanaɣuaq 'oblique tent pole']

PE qanəʀ(-) 'mouth' [verbal = 'speak'; cf. qaləʀ-]
AAY qanəq 'mouth' [qanəʀ- 'cuss']
CAY qanəq* 'mouth' [qanəʀ- 'speak']
NSY qanəq 'mouth, rumor, word' [qanəʀ- 'speak']
CSY qanəq* 'mouth' [qanəʀ- 'speak idly']
Sir qanəX 'mouth'
SPI qaniq 'mouth' [qaniq- 'speak']
NAI qaniq* 'mouth' [and qanaaq- 'quarrel']
WCI qaniq 'mouth' [verbal = 'insult, quarrel with'; Schn. has qanaaluk- 'argue, quarrel' for 'adg']
ECI qaniq 'mouth'
GRI qaniq*

PY-S qanəmcuk 'tale' [cf. mcuɣ-]
AAY —
CAY qanəmci- 'tell a tale'
NSY qanəmsuk 'incantation' [ANLC]
CSY qanəmsuɣ- 'incant'
Sir qanəmsuɣ- 'pray' [Orr; probably borrowed from CSY]

PY qanʀutə- 'talk' [cf. utə-]
AAY —
CAY qanʀutə- 'tell, talk to'
NSY qanʀutə- 'talk, chat'
CSY —

PE qanət- 'be near' [cf. qani-?]
AAY qantə- 'be near'
CAY qantə-
NSY qantə- 'encircle, surround' [Em.]
CSY →
Sir →
SPI qanit- 'be near (to)', qani- 'area near' [posit. root]
NAI qanit- 'be near', qani- 'area near' [posit. root; note the strong i as in PE qani- below — contam.?]
WCI qanit- 'be near' [qanilruq 'vicinity'; Pryde also has Sig qani(ŋa) as a posit. root 'vicinity of -']
ECI qanit- 'be near' [and qaniŋŋu(C)- 'sound near', qaniŋŋuu(C)- 'be closer than s.o. else or before']
GRI qaniɣ- 'be near (to)' [and qanimut 'close up', qanitaq 'relative', qaniŋŋuuʀ- 'stay nearby, appear close, loom up (distant land)']

PE qanli- 'approach' [cf. li-[2]]
AAY qanli- 'approach'
CAY qanli-
NSY qanli-
CSY —
Sir —
SPI qalli-
NAI qalli-
WCI Sig qaɣli-, Cop qaniɣli- 'approach' [the latter, more recent deriv. with Inu variant kli- of li-[2]]
ECI qalli-, qanilli- 'approach'
GRI qałłi- [old ortho. qagdli-], qaniłłi-, NG qaɣli-

PY-S qantaʀaq 'vicinity'[cf. (t)aʀaq]
AAY —
CAY —
NSY qantaʀaq 'vicinity' [qantaʀami 'near'; Jen. has qantaʀaʀ- 'be near']
CSY qantaʀaq 'area nearby', qantaʀałi- 'approach, be near'
Sir qantaʀani 'nearby', qantaʀantəX 'near' [and qantaʀanci- 'approach']
Inu [note ECI qanitani 'in the vicinity']

PE qani- 'see s.o. off' [the relat. — if any — to qanət- is obscure]
AAY K qani- 'get self ready (to go)'
CAY Nun qani- 'start on a journey'
NSY qaniłəq 'burial [and qanixtuʀ- 'admonish at parting, order'?]
CSY qani- 'see a person off by going with them a short way' [and qaniitə- 'take supplies ahead, caching them for coming journey']
Sir [note qanista 'provider', and qaniqažəɣaX 'small skin bag' — Orr]
SPI Qaw qaniži- 'take supplies part way along trail for future trip'
NAI qani-, Nu qaniuq- 'accompany part way to destination'
WCI qaniyi-, qaniuq- 'carry supplies forward for coming journey'
ECI qani- 'take supplies ahead, part way along trail', qaniyaq- 'see someone off', qaniuq- 'leave early on a short stage in order to make a longer one the next, do part of work before others, go ahead in short rushes'
GRI qani-, qaniuʀ- 'go part of way with person leaving'

PI qanilaaq- 'travel part of the way with s.o.' [cf. la(C)aʀ(-)]
SPI —
NAI qanil^{y}aaq- 'travel part of the way to one's destination, get gradually closer to it'
WCI —
ECI qanilaq- 'accompany (s.o.) part of the way on a journey'
GRI qanilaaʀ- 'be humble or docile'

PE qanit(t)aʀ 'porch of traditional house or midden'
AAY K qanitaq 'dump, midden'
CAY HBC, Nun qanitaq
NSY qanitaq 'dump' [L.-T.]
CSY —
Sir —
SPI qanitaq 'arctic entry, unheated storage porch'
NAI qanitcaq, qanitcat, Mal qanisaq 'storage shed, porch of house'
WCI Sig qanittat 'porch of house'
ECI —

GRI qanisaq 'sheltering wall (in front of entrance to house or tent)' [Holt. has qanitsat for NG]

PE qaniɣ 'falling snow' [cf. Aleut qanax, qanɣi-X 'winter', also deriv. qaniix 'snow', verbal qaniiɣ-]
AAY qaniq 'falling snow'
CAY qanuk 'snowflake' [and qanikcaq* 'snow on ground']
NSY qanik 'falling snow'
CSY qanik 'snowflake, falling snow' [qaniɣuXtə- 'fall (snow)']
Sir qanix 'falling snow'
SPI qanniq, Qaw qannik 'snowflake'
NAI qannik 'snowflake' [back formation from qannik- under qanniʀ- below?]
WCI Cop qanniq 'falling snow', Sig qanik 'falling snow' [and B. Lake qanniʀniq 'snow impeding sight' — Dor.]
ECI qannik 'snow which falls, snowflake', qanik, Lab qannik 'falling snow'
GRI qanik 'snowflake', qaniit 'snow in air'

PE qanniʀ- 'snow' [cf. liʀ-]
AAY qaniʀ- 'snow'
CAY qaniʀ-
NSY qaniXtə- [L.-T.]
CSY —
Sir —
SPI qanniq-, Qaw qanik-
NAI qannik-
WCI Cop qanniq-, Sig qanik-
ECI NBI, SB qanniq-, Lab qannik- 'snow' [and qanniq 'snowfall' — a back formation]
GRI SWG qanniʀ- 'be snowing'

PI qanima- 'have fever or gooseflesh'
SPI —
NAI —
WCI [Pryde has Cop qanima- 'be rehabilitating'; qanimayuq 's.th. brought to cache where one's things are stored' goes with qani-]
ECI qanima- 'be ill' [qanimmaq 'ill person'; note also qannima- 'be frozen from cold (face)']
GRI qanima- 'have gooseflesh (when ill or cold), have a fever, be susceptible to the cold' [and qanimaat- 'tolerate the cold'; Egede has kannima- (for qanima-) 'be an angakkoq' as a shaman's word]

PY qantaq 'container' [cf. qaltaʀ, though the relat. is obscure]
AAY qantaq 'container'
CAY qantaq 'plate, bowl, dish'
NSY qantaq 'sack, sheath, container, bandage', qantaʀ- 'bandage, wrap around' [and qantaružak 'barrel']
CSY qantaq 'container, wrapper, package', qantak 'womb, uterus'

PI qanuq 'how' [cf. qayu(q) and qaŋa]
SPI qanuq 'how' [and qanuqtun, Qaw qanutun 'how much', Fish River qanuʀmi 'I don't know']
NAI qanuq 'how' [and qanutun 'how much']
WCI qanuq 'how' [and Sig qanuʀmi 'I don't know']
ECI qanuq 'how'
GRI qanuq 'how' [and qanuʀmi 'yes indeed']

PI qanuqtuq 'let's hope' [cf. encl. tuʀ]
SPI —
NAI qanuqtuq 'I hope, I wonder why'
WCI qanuqtuq 'then how?'
ECI qanuqtuuq 'let's hope so'
GRI qanuʀtuq 'would that, if only'

PY qanžak 'small sled' [du.; possibly from *qamžak — cf. qamuʀ-]
AAY —
CAY —
NSY qanžak 'sled with walrus tusk runners' [qanžaxpik 'sled']
CSY qaanžak 'small sled used in pairs for hauling boats' [qaanŋ^{w}aaʀək 'toboggan of baleen']
Sir [for qamca 'sled' see qamitə- under qamuʀ-, though it may belong here]

PE qaŋa 'when (in past)' [cf. qaku, qanuq and Aleut qana- 'which, where', qanayaam 'when', qanaaŋ 'how many', the na- being perhaps the same as na-[2]; note the parallelism between the ŋa in this base — corresponding to the causative/consequential mood marker — and the ku in qaku corresponding to the condit. mood marker; for the meaning 'no', compare na-[1] versus na-[2]]
AAY →
CAY [note qaaŋ, qaŋŋa 'no'] →
NSY →
CSY →
Sir qaŋən 'when (in past?)' [and Em. has qaŋəsitaX 'long ago, earlier' Men. qaŋəsitanXaX 'just before']
SPI qaŋa 'when (in past)' [qaŋami 'in the past'; and note qaaŋ 'huh?' — but compare enclitic q(q)a(a) under the p.b.s]
NAI qaŋa 'when (in past)' [and note Mal qaŋŋaa 'no']
WCI qaŋa 'when (in past)' [also of future at B. Lake acc. Dor.; qaŋaʀnitaq 'thing from the past']
ECI qaŋa 'when', NBI 'when (in past)' [qaŋanitaq 's.th. from when?']
GRI qaŋa, EG also qař̃a 'when (in past), in the old days' [and qaŋanisaq 's.th. from the past, old-fashioned', EG qař̃anisaq 'old person, adult']

PY qaŋvaq 'when (in past)' [perhaps with p.b. vaʀ-]
AAY qaŋwaq 'when (in past)'
CAY qaŋvaq 'when (in past), for some time'
NSY qamvaq 'when (in past), earlier, long ago' [ANLC.; Men. has it as 'long ago']
CSY qavŋaq 'when (in past), some time ago'

PY qaŋanaq 'squirrel'
AAY qaŋanaq, qaŋa'ik 'squirrel'
CAY qaŋanaq*
NSY —
CSY —

PY qaŋanaʀuaq 'wormwood' [cf. ŋ(ŋ)uðaʀ]
AAY qaŋanaʀuaq, qaŋanaŋuaq 'yarrow'
CAY qaŋanaʀuaq 'artemesia, wormwood'
NSY —
CSY —

PI qaŋata- 'be elevated or have an empty space below' [cf. qaanəq and p.b. ta-, also qaŋłu(ʀ)]
SPI qaŋata- 'be elevated off the ground'
NAI qaŋata- 'be elevated off floor or ground' [and qaŋattaaq 'hollow area, ice or snow with one edge partly off the ground']
WCI qaŋat(t)a- 'be in the air'
ECI qaŋata- 'stay in the air'
GRI qaŋata- 'have a hollow space below' [and qaŋattaq 'cave', NG qaŋatavviɣi- 'pounce on']

PI qaŋattaq- 'rise above the ground' [cf. ʀ- under ŋ(ŋ)uʀ-]
SPI qaŋataq- 'rise from the ground'
NAI qaŋattaq-
WCI qaŋattaq- 'rise in the air, ascend, raise'
ECI qaŋatta(q)- 'rise in air' [and qaŋattauyaq- 'swing on a swing']
GRI qaŋattaʀ- 'rise from the ground'

PE qaŋiɣaʀ 'nephew or niece of man'
AAY qaŋa'aq 'daughter's daughter', qaŋiqłaa(ʀ)aq 'maiden, young woman, teenage girl'
CAY qaŋiaʀ(aq*) 'niece or nephew of a man through his brother'
NSY qaŋiaq
CSY qaŋiɣaq
Sir qaŋiɣəX
SPI qaŋiaq 'niece or nephew'
NAI —
WCI qaŋiaq 'niece or nephew through brother of man' [Jen. has qaŋiɣaq for Cop]
ECI qaŋiaq 'niece or nephew through brother of man'
GRI qaŋiaq

PE qaŋłu(ʀ) 'hollowed out place' [cf. qaŋata- and lu(ʀ)?]
AAY qaŋłuq 'hole in river bed, fishing hole'
CAY qaŋłuk, Y, HBC, NS qaŋłuq 'deep hole in river bed'
NSY —
CSY —
Sir —
SPI Qaw qaɣlu 'deep place in river' [and KI qaɣluaq 'dimple']
NAI qaɣlu
WCI qaɣlu
ECI qallu 'water-filled cavity in ice caused by heat (e.g. in the spring)'
GRI qałłu [old ortho. qagdlo] 'valley surrounded by mountains', NG qaɣluq 'hollow, dimple' [Fab. spells the WG form kaglo — S.-L. has qałłusuk 'depression, defile'; Kl. notes this base as especially found in place names — he equates it, erroneously, with qavlu 'eyebrow'; note also qałłuʀ- 'pull out from water (e.g. driftwood)'; Tersis has EG qattu- 'be dented', qattuniq 'dent']

PE qaŋquʀ- 'crunch with teeth'
AAY qaŋquʀ- 'chew cartilage', qaŋquq 'cartilage', qaŋkuʀ- 'nibble'
CAY qaŋquʀ- 'chew on, making a crunching noise' [and Y, NS qaqquq 'bread' — borrowed from Inupiaq]
NSY qaŋquq 'crab'
CSY [note kaŋʀuɣ- 'make a crunching noise']
Sir [note kaŋžuɣ- 'make a crunching noise' — Orr]
SPI qaqquq- 'crunch with teeth' [as noun = 'crab, bread']
NAI qaqquq- 'crunch with teeth' [qaqquaq 'nut']
WCI qaqqu(aq)- 'crunch with teeth' [qaqquq 'nut, crunchy dried seal intestines']
ECI qaqqu(q)- 'crunch with teeth' [Saul; Schn. has qaqquyaq- 'chew noisily', also qaqquq 'dried entrails']
GRI qaqquʀ- 'crunch with teeth, bite to death' [and qaqquaq 'boiled and dried seal meat (esp. liver and blood)', NWG qaqqut 'seaweed']

PI qapak- 'be emaciated and weak' [there may be a link to qapəq-]
Yup [note CAY qapacak 'bald head']
SPI —
NAI qapak 'physically weak person', qapaŋa- 'be physically weak'
WCI Cop qapak- 'be thin' [and qapak 'mild cloudy weather']
ECI —
GRI qapaɣ- 'be emaciated', qapak 'emaciated person or animal (owing to sickness)' [and qapasak 'weakling', qapasaɣ- 'steal s.th.', also qappat- 'bend one's back', qappaŋa- 'have a bent back' and qapaŋiinnaʀ- 'come to nothing'; Robbe and Menn. have EG qapaaŋa- 'be bent, tilted']

PE qapðaɣ- 'flesh or remove blubber from a skin' [cf. qapiʀ-, though the relat. is obscure]
AAY qapaxtə- 'take blubber off sealskin'
CAY Nun qapaxquʀ- 'remove seal blubber from skin' [ANLC]
NSY qapaxtə- 'take fat from s.th.'
CSY [note qapuk 'roll of fat on human body, rolling sea', which seems to show contam. with qapuɣ, also qapžaɣ- 'squirm, fidget, show signs of life'?]
Sir qapaxtə- 'remove fat from skin' [Orr and Vakh. from Rub.'s texts — compare the NSY]
SPI qapšak- 'flesh a skin'
NAI qažvak-, qavžak-, Nu qapžak- 'flense, remove blubber or oil from skin'
WCI qavyak- 'remove skin (from seal) or blubber from skin'
ECI qayyaa(C)- 'remove subcutaneous blubber from skin, skin animal leaving the blubber' [Lab qabsaq- acc. Peck, qabyaq- acc. Bourquin]
GRI qaššaɣ- [old ortho. qavssag-] 'remove blubber from skin (not scraping)'

PI qapəq- 'mock or (cause to) give up?' [cf. qapak-?]
SPI qaviq- 'lie', Imaq 'deceive', Qaw qapiq- 'be disappointed'
NAI qapɨq- 'give up, turn back' [and PH qapqutɨ- 'give up on, quit', B qappit- 'be unable to do any more (to s.o.), make give up, shove s.o.'s nose as a sign of disdain' — contam. with qappit-?]
WCI qap(p)ik-, qap(p)iqutiɣi-, qap(p)iqtu-, qap(p)iu- 'mock'
ECI —
GRI [note EG qapiŋayaaʀ- 'be bad, wicked' — Robbe and Menn.]

PY qapilaaq 'mussel' [cf. qappit-?]
AAY qapilaaq, qapiłaaq 'mussel, woman's genitals'
CAY qapila(a)q 'mussel'
NSY —
CSY —

PE qapiʀ- 'skin an animal without cutting?' [cf. qapðaɣ-, with which there appears to have been some contam.]
AAY K qapiʀ- 'remove fat and flesh from skin, remove skin from skin boat, qapiaʀ- 'scrape fat'
CAY qapiaʀ- 'skin a seal by pulling skin over body, not cutting skin'
NSY qapiłəq 'cutting the stomach of an animal (?)' [L.-T.; note also qapiqaq 'fresh walrus blubber']
CSY qapiʀ- 'skin an animal without cutting the skin'
Sir qapəʀ- 'cut up carcass'
SPI —
NAI [Nu qapiq- 'scoop fat from boiling meat']
WCI Cop, Net qapiq- 'scrape fat off hide of polar bear' [Pryde]
ECI —
GRI qapiʀ- 'scrape (pushing away from self), cut with scissors', qapiaʀ- 'scrape, plane, flesh a skin'

PE qappit- 'sink down' [cf. łit-, also perhaps qapuɣ]
AAY —
CAY qappitə- 'get mired down, stuck in mud'
NSY —
CSY —
Sir —
SPI qappit- 'put in water' [and note qavik- 'set (sun)']
NAI — [for qappit- 'be unable to do any more' see qapəq-]
WCI [note Cop qapuq- 'disappear below surface' (Ras.) and Sig qapqaluk 'submerged reef' (Pet.)]
ECI —
GRI qappi-, qapaŋit- 'disappear below water', qapit- 'disappear behind wave or horizon' [and qapi(t)-, qapitit- 'lose sight of s.th. below water or horizon'; EG qapittaʀ- 'swim and plunge down again rapidly (as porpoise)' — Robbe and Menn.]

PI qaptət- 'tighten'
Yup — [but Hinz has CAY qapniortek- 'have convulsions']
SPI qaptit- 'tighten'
NAI PH qaptɨt- 'tighten' [and Nu qapturaq 'band or loop around s.th.' — also verbal 'tie a band or loop around']
WCI Sig qaptit- 'tighten'
ECI [note qappa(C)- 'tighten strap over shoulder as tight as one can']
GRI —

PE qapuɣ 'foam'
AAY qapuk 'bubble, foam, pumice'
CAY qapuk, qapn̥əq* 'foam', qapuɣyaq 'pumice'
NSY qapuk 'foam'
CSY aXpuk 'foam' [also aXpumla 'deep powdery snow'; for qapuk 'roll of fat on human body, rolling sea' see qapðaɣ-]
Sir [Em. has aXpumłaʀaX 'powdery', from CSY]
SPI qavuk 'foam'
NAI qapuk
WCI qapuk
ECI qapu, Lab qapuk
GRI qapuk 'foam, froth, yeast, meerschaum'

PI qaqa- 'bob up and down (in pleasure)?' [cf. qaʀa-?]
SPI [for Imaq qaʀa- 'dance' see qaʀa-]
NAI [note qaqaq- 'bend backward', qaqaqtaq- 'move up and down']
WCI qaqa- Cop 'fondly dance or sing', Net 'display fondness or affection' [Ras.]
ECI qaqa- 'be joyful (child or dog)' [Peck has 'jump for joy' for Lab]
GRI qaqa- 'rock head in pleasure at lullaby (child)'

PE qaqðaʀ and **qaqða(C)uʀ** 'loon' [cf. Aleut qaqaX 'Arctic loon', borrowed from Yup?]
AAY K qaqaaqaaq 'red-throated loon'
CAY qaqaq, qaqataq, NSU qəXqauq
NSY —
CSY əXqaaq 'red-throated loon' [and note qaqsuŋiq 'red-throated kittiwake']
Sir [note qaqsuŋiX 'red-throated loon']
SPI qaqšauq 'red-throated loon'
NAI qaqšauq
WCI qaqsauq, qaXXauq
ECI qaʀsauq
GRI qaʀšaaq, EG qaqqaqqaaq, NG qaXXauq 'red-throated diver, loon' [Ras. has EG qaʀtiimayuʀtuq 'black-throated diver' (Arctic loon)]

PE qaqətaʀ or **qaqitaʀ** 'brain'
AAY —
CAY —
NSY qaqətaq 'small bone in fish head used as toy'
CSY —
Sir —
SPI qaʀitaq 'brain'
NAI qaqisaq, qaqasaq, qaʀasaq 'brain', Nu qaqisaq 'skull'
WCI qaʀitaq 'brain' [Lowe; Ras. has Cop also qaʀataq and Met. has qaʀiyaq (influenced by qaʀəyaq?) but also Sig qaʀitaʀnaq 'bowl']
ECI qaʀitaq 'brain'
GRI qaʀasaq, NG qaʀahaq, qaahaq

PY qaqitə- 'complete'
AAY qaqitə- 'complete, finish, become complete'
CAY qaqitə- 'complete, become complete' [and qaqima- 'be finished']
NSY —
CSY —

PE qaqluɣ 'lip'
AAY qəXłuk 'lip'
CAY qəXłuk 'lip, stones around fireplace'
NSY qəXłu 'lower lip, bow of sled'
CSY —
Sir —
SPI qaqłu 'lip', Qaw also 'gunwale of boat'
NAI qaqłuk (du.) 'lips' [and PH qaʀłunnak- 'get lip portion of whale as one's share of catch']
WCI Sig qaqłuk, Cop qaXXuk 'lower lip'
ECI qaʀsuk, Lab qaʀłuk [Bourq.], Igl qaqłuq, qaqłuk 'lower lip'
GRI qaʀłuq 'lip', NG qaʀluq 'lower lip'

> **PI qaqluaq** 'gunwale' [cf. aʀ]
> SPI —
> NAI —
> WCI Car qaʀluaq 'gunwale or crossbar of canoe', B. Lake 'lower part of caribou trap' [Schn.]
> ECI qaʀluaʀut 'gunwale of canoe, block on either side of snow house entrance'
> GRI [qaʀłuaq 'ring of capelin dipnet or net for catching birds']

PI qaqlutuuq '(kind of) duck' [cf. qaqluɣ and tu-[1]]
SPI qaqłutuuq 'shoveler duck'
NAI qaqłutuuq 'greater or lesser scaup, shoveler'
WCI Car qaʀłutuuq 'wild duck' [B.-S.; Ras. has qaaʀłutuuq]
ECI —
GRI qiiʀłutuuq [Fab. kaertlutôk] 'wild duck' [with onomatopoeic distortion?]

PE qaqu(ʀ) 'groove where throwing board fits against harpoon shaft?' [and verbally of sticking a finger or the like into a matching groove?; cf. Aleut qaʀu-, EA qaXu- 'butt of shaft, back part of shaft covered by spear-thrower']
AAY —
CAY Nun qaquaX 'crosspiece handle at upper end of single-bladed paddle' [ANLC; and note GCY aquq and in rhyming jingle qaquq 'middle finger'; Lantis has Nun kakoxtax 'crosspiece of paddle']
NSY —
CSY [note SLI qaquužaq 'cross' in bible translations]
Sir [note qəqusitaX 'middle finger' (Orr) — Men. has qəłqusitaX 'ring finger' — contam. with alqiliq?]
SPI qaʀu- 'dig through things'
NAI qaqu- 'stick one's finger or other object in' [and qaqutuq- 'search by reaching around in']
WCI Cop qaqu(ŋa) 'joint on arrow shaft' [Ras.; Pryde has Cop qaquq 'small boss of musk-ox horn on the top of a seal-indicator']
ECI qaqusaq- 'insert long object into orifice' [and qaquviʀaq 'cavity cut into vault of snow house by heat', also qaqiliq- 'try to force game or fish out from under s.th. with a stick', Iti 'unblock (e.g. drain)', perhaps via *qaq(q)iʀ- with liʀ-]
GRI qaqu 'gore, gusset (in garment)' [verbal = 'put a gore in, pierce from below (pain felt through whole body)'; note also qaquit, qaquisiq, EG qaʀivilisiq 'bone knob on hind part of bird- or bladder-dart with cavity for the knob of the throwing-board', and perhaps qaqiliʀ- 'rake up, scrape out']

> **PI qaquaq** 'hind part of spear or dart' [cf. ar]
> SPI W qaʀuaq 'back part of harpoon' [Jen.]
> NAI —
> WCI —
> ECI Lab qaquaq 'knob at end of bird arrow' [Peck]
> GRI qaquaq 'hind part of bird- or bladder-dart'

PE qaqutluɣ 'fulmar' [there may be a link to qaqa-, this bird bobbing up and down along the crests of waves]
AAY —
CAY —
NSY —
CSY aXqułuk 'fulmar'
Sir qaqə́łukáyəɣaX [Orr]
SPI Imaq qaʀułuk, Di qaʀułuaʀžuk
NAI —
WCI Net qaqulluk 'storm bird' [Ras., who spells it qaqukluk — Pryde has qaqu'luk 'fulmar']
ECI NBI Pond Inlet qaqulluk 'fulmar' [Pryde; Peck has Lab qaqul(l)uk, qaquʀluk 'storm petrel', which he spells kakkuluk, kakkorluk]
GRI qaqułłuk, EG qaʀattuk 'fulmar' [old ortho. qaqugdluk — but Fab. has kakordluk]

PY qaʀa 'decoration (on parka)' [cf. Aleut qaʀana-X 'paint (for trimming)', Atkan qaʀacuða-X 'design, decoration, trimming (of fur)', EA qaʀasi-X, qaXasi-X 'decoration for baskets and grass mats']
AAY [note qaʀataq 'underground leaf stem of fiddlehead fern']
CAY qaʀaliq 'spot, mark, decoration on parka'
NSY —
CSY qaʀa(ya), qaʀaaya 'dangling strip of fur died reddish on the back and used as parka decoration' [Rub. has 'amulet on parka']

PE qaʀa- 'dance or have fun' [cf. qaqa- and Aleut EA qaʀaðuʀ-, Atkan qaʀaðuuɣ- 'dance (men)', from qaʀa- 'be grateful, glad, thank'; there may be borrowing one way or the other here]
AAY KP Xattə-, PWS XaXtə- 'make merry, join in the fun', C Xai- 'be happy, merry'
CAY NSU qaʀa- 'have all that one wants'
NSY qaXa- 'dance non-Eskimo style dance' [L.-T.]
CSY qaʀa 'Eskimo dance done by dancers in sitting position' [also verbal in Chap at least]
Sir qaʀa- 'dance in squatting position'
SPI qaʀa- 'dance hard to a song one likes'
NAI qaʀa- 'live a carefree existence, take it easy', Nu 'make arm signals indicating that one has sighted

caribou' [qaʀanaq- 'be easy to do']
WCI qaʀauɣaq- 'take it easy at work'
ECI —
GRI—

PE qaʀaləʀ- 'get goose pimples or a tickling sensation' [cf. qaayuq- and qaləqə-]
AAY Xaaləʀ(yuɣ)- 'have a ticklish feeling' [and C Xalʀiucaaʀ- 'tickle']
CAY qəXaləʀyuɣ- 'get goose pimples, get chill down spine' [for HBC qəlqəciʀ(ᴀʀ)-, Nun qaləqm̥aciʀ(ᴀʀ)- 'tickle' see qaləqə-]
NSY —
CSY — [for qaləqətaaʀ- 'tickle' see qaləqə-]
Sir —
SPI [qaalii- 'be squeamish about']
NAI qaaliqta- 'feel repulsed by s.th. disgusting' [and qaaliŋa- 'hesitate to touch s.th. dirty']
WCI Car EP qaaliqta- 'have eery feeling' [Ow. — influenced by quiliqta-?' and note Sig qaaŋanaq- 'be dirty, repulsive']
ECI —
GRI qaaliʀta- 'be uncomfortable, damp' [and qaaliʀtanaʀ- 'be damp, slippery']

PE qaʀðuʀ 'arrow'
AAY K Xuuʀaq, C Xuq 'arrow, bullet'
CAY Eg, Nun, HBC, NS qəXuq
NSY Xu 'cartridge' [ANLC also ʀu]
CSY Xuuq* 'arrow, bullet'
Sir qaʀcəX 'arrow, bullet' [Vakh. also qaʀžuX; qaʀžuʀnəX 'bullet, lead']
SPI qaʀžuq 'arrow, bullet'
NAI qaʀžuq
WCI qaʀyuq, qaʀyuk
ECI qaʀyuk 'arrow', Aiv 'bullet'
GRI qaʀšuq 'arrow'

PI qaʀžuqcaq 'jigging hook'
SPI —
NAI qaʀžuqsaq 'skin-covered hook left in water' [also verbal; Nu 'long anchor fish hook']
WCI Cop qaʀyuXXaq 'special hook for jigging for salmon' [Ras. also for Net as 'fish hook']
ECI Lab qaʀyu(k)saq 'bait' [Bourq.; Peck has kakrusak 'fish hook with many barbs'; B.-S. has Igl qaqsorsaq, Math. qardjorsaq 'fish hook']
GRI qaʀsuʀsaq 'hook (esp. for fish)' [Fab. has karssursak; qaʀsuʀsaʀ- 'hook, put hook in']

PE qaʀə- 'come up (or away)' [originally of coming up into trad. house in Inu?; cf. qəʀaʀ- and qaʀu-]
AAY —
CAY —
NSY —
CSY qaʀləɣ- 'rise in the air' [and qaʀləɣutə- 'mill about in excitement (people)']
Sir qaXtəʀ- 'come' [Vakh. from Rub.'s texts — he has it as 'come apart or away, stay behind' from his own texts (compare under qəʀaʀ-); also qaʀləmi- 'hold up' from Rub.]
SPI qai-, Di qaə- 'come' [and qaʀʀiin, Qaw qaʀʀain 'come!', qaʀʀit(i)- 'transport, bring along']
NAI qa<ʀ>i- 'come' [and qaʀʀižži- 'bring s.th.'; note qaʀʀiinʸ, Mal qaʀʀainʸ 'come!']
WCI qai- 'come' [and qaʀʀit(i)- 'bring s.th. along']
ECI qai- 'come' [and Parry has qaʀʀii 'come here!']
GRI qaa- 'come, visit, be a guest' [older imperative = qaXXiit]

PI qaʀit- 'bring or hand over' [cf. t-[1]]
SPI qait- 'give'
NAI qait-
WCI Sig qait-
ECI qait- 'give, hand over'
GRI qaat- [old ortho. qait-] 'bring'

PI qaʀiaq 'storage alcove' [cf. qaʀə- and yaʀ?]
SPI —
NAI qaʀiaq 'storage hole in hallway of sodhouse'
WCI Net qaʀiaqłiq 'side room' [Ras.; Dor. has qaʀiaq 'room in a house' for Car]
ECI qaʀiaq 'second snow house opening onto the main snow house, bedroom of apartment' [and note Fort Chimo qaʀiuq- 'dig shelter or lair']
GRI qaʀayaq 'alcove, side compartment in Greenlandic house, bay encircled by rocks (in place names)', NG qaʀiaʀiik 'traditional double house with one entrance' [and note qaʀassi- 'hollow out'; Kroeb. has NG qaʀiuk 'liver' as a shaman's word]

PE qaʀ(u)łiɣ '(leg of) pants or fur breeches' [the NSY, CSY may be influenced by qulliʀ under qulə-]
AAY Xuulik 'fork of tree, etc.'
CAY qəXułiik 'pants', BB 'underpants' [du.; and note qəXulik 'Kotlik' — a place where the river forks']
NSY qułi(i)k 'pants'
CSY qułiɣək 'pants', qułiɣ- 'put on pants'
Sir —
SPI Qaw qaʀliaʀžuuk du. 'sealskin breeches' [Jen. has qaʀliik for W]
NAI qaʀliik 'fur pants, men's knee pants'
WCI qaʀliik
ECI qaʀliik 'long trousers'
GRI qaʀłiit 'trousers' [sing. qaʀłik; in NG qaʀliik is esp. 'women's short inner trousers']

PE qaʀmaʀ 'temporary dwelling with sod walls' [cf. qaʀə-?]
AAY qaʀmaq 'log shoring up fireplace'
CAY qaʀmaq 'piece of sod'
NSY —
CSY [note qaʀmaq 'mirage']
Sir [qaʀmaX 'mirage' — Orr]
SPI —
NAI qaʀmaqtuuq [name of one of the men's houses in Pt. Hope, lit. = 'one that has big qaʀmaqs']
WCI Car qaʀmaq 'shelter' [B.-S.; and Cop qaŋmaqtaq- 'put snow around a house']
ECI Lab qammak 'wall', NBI, SB qaʀmaq 'semi-subterranean house' [Dor., who also has the base for Tar as 'ruin of subterranean house, temporary

dwelling with snow walls and canvas roof']
GRI qaʀmaq, EG qammaq 'wall made of stone or sod', NG qaʀmaq 'temporary house with walrus skin covering over turf and stone walls' [Holt. for the latter; qaʀmaʀ- 'build in brick-work']

PE qaʀu- 'dawn' [cf. qaʀə- and qəʀiʀ-, also qa(C)u(ði)-]
AAY —
CAY [Holt. has qauwalaRts^{s}itoq 'it shines' for Mountain Village]
NSY [note qakšužak 'dawn' (marked 'affectionate' by Men.) — influenced by qakcuʀ- under qakə(ʀ)-?]
CSY —
Sir qaʀətiłəX 'dawn', qaʀətəqəstaʀ- 'dawn'
SPI qau- 'dawn'
NAI qa<ɣ>u- 'dawn, break (day)' [the ɣ, as in qaɣɣuvik 'dawn' is not historical; note also qaunɨq* 'shade of color']
WCI qau- 'be(come) day' [and EP qau- 'dawn']
ECI qau- 'become day', qauk 'dawn' [and qauppat 'tomorrow', qaummat 'the following day', qau tamaat 'every day', qaʀʀuyaq 'dying person who sees the light of day one more time']
GRI qaa- 'be(come) day', qaak 'daylight', qaXXut(i)- 'day breaks before one does s.th.'

> **PI qaulluq-** 'shine' [cf. luʀ-?]
> SPI —
> NAI qaulluq 'crystal'
> WCI [note Cop qaulluqtut 'small bone flap attached near shank of fish-hook to attract fish' and qaulluXXiq- 'stand out against dark background' — Pryde]
> ECI Aiv, NBI qaulluq- 'be white'
> GRI qaałłuʀ- 'shine', qaałłuʀiɣ- 'be shining white'

> **PI qauma-** 'be bright (daylight)' [cf. (u)ma-]
> SPI qauma- 'be (day)light' [and Imaq qaumaq 'light']
> NAI qaumanɨq* 'beam of light', qaummak- 'become daylight' [and qaummaq* 'daylight, light from source']
> WCI qauma- 'be daylight' [and Cop qaumaniq 'moon, moonlight, light' acc. Pryde]
> ECI qauma- 'be daylight, light (lamp), transparent', qaumma(q)- 'brighten'
> GRI qaama- 'be bright', qaammaʀ- 'become light' [the latter with ʀ- under ŋ(ŋ)uʀ-; and note EG qaamavaq 'sun' acc. Holm]

> **PI qaumman** 'light' [cf. qauma- above and un]
> SPI qauman 'light, lamp chimney'
> NAI qaumman 'light'
> WCI —
> ECI [Boas has qaumat 'moon', also qaumate 'sun' as shaman's words for Baf.]
> GRI qaammat 'moon, month'

PY qaʀutə- '(try to) induce?' [there may be a link to qa(C)u(ði)-]
AAY qautaaʀ-, qa'utaa'a-, qautaa<ʀ>a- 'pray'
CAY qaʀutə- 'persuade, convince, induce'
NSY —
CSY —

PY-S qaʀya 'deep voice' [the relat. (if any) to qatə and/or qaiʀuaq- is obscure]
AAY qəXsatu- 'have a deep voice' [qəXsi- 'lower one's voice', qəXsakitə- 'have a high voice']
CAY qəXsiɣ- 'have a deep voice' [also qaci-; see ðiɣ-]
NSY —
CSY qaʀi 'deep voice' [and qaʀya- 'brag, boast']
Sir qaʀya 'voice' [Em. has qaʀaX 'voice' and qaʀya- 'brag, boast'; also qaʀəpałuX 'bass voice']

PY qasaq 'raw meat'
AAY qasaq 'raw fish or meat' [qasaʀ- 'eat raw fish or meat']
CAY qasaq 'raw fish or meat' [and verbal qasaʀ-]
NSY —
CSY —
Inu [Qaw qasaq- 'eat raw meat' is probably from Yup]

PE qatə 'deep or loud voice' [cf. Aleut qasluɣ- 'quarrel', also qaciŋŋuq-, and perhaps qayaɣ- and qatəɣ; the relat. — if any — to qaʀya is obscure]
AAY ➟
CAY qastu- 'be loud' [with tu-?; for qaci- 'have a deep voice' see qaʀya]
NSY ➟
CSY —
Sir —
SPI qatitu- 'have deep voice' [and Qaw qatait- 'have a high voice']
NAI qatɨtu- 'have deep voice'
WCI qa(a)titu- 'have a deep voice' [and Baker Lake qataittuq 'high voice, soprano' — Schn.]
ECI qatitu- 'have deep voice' [note qatik 'voice' on Baffin acc. Schn.; also qatiŋulaq- 'growl']
GRI qati 'depth of voice', qatitu- 'have deep voice', qataat- 'have high voice' [and qatimaaɣ- 'growl, grumble']

> **PE qatðaʀ** 'bass or booming voice'
> AAY —
> CAY —
> NSY qašak 'bass' [but qay̱iaXłəq 'echo']
> CSY [note qayiiɣžuk 'echoing hollow sound']
> Sir —
> SPI Imaq qašaq 'bass' [for qaššaq?]
> NAI [note Nu qatžaq 'echo']
> WCI —
> ECI —
> GRI qaššaʀiɣ- 'have a good deep voice'

> **PE qatəkit-** 'have a soft or high voice' [cf. kit- and compare the forms with tu-[1] directly under qatə above]
> AAY qəskitə- 'be low (voice)' [compare also qəXsakitə- 'have a high voice' under qaʀya]
> CAY qaskitə- 'be soft or quiet'
> NSY —

CSY —
Sir —
SPI qatikiuužau- 'have a high voice'
NAI qatikit- 'have a high voice'
WCI Car? qatikit- [Schn. 'adg']
ECI qatikit-
GRI qatikit-

PE qatəɣ 'chest' [cf. qatə?]
AAY C qatək 'breast', C qat<ɣ>aq, K qataq 'chest (anat.)'
CAY qatək, qatɣaq
NSY qatək 'breast, chest'
CSY qatək 'bird's breast'
Sir qatə 'breast, chest' [Vakh. from Rub.]
SPI qatik 'breast of bird', qatiɣak 'chest'
NAI qatik 'breastbone of bird', qatiɣak, qatiɣaak, qatikkak 'front quarter of animal, breast of human'
WCI qatiɣak 'upper part of body'
ECI qatiɣaq 'upper part of body' [and qattaaq 'sternum or brisket, center bone of bird's chest', qatiɣaq- 'swim along with upper part of back and head showing (seal)']
GRI qatik 'breastbone (of a bird)', qatiɣak, EG qaliŋaq 'back' [and qatiɣaaʀ- 'swim with back visible above water (animal)']

PE qatəŋŋun 'half-sibling?' [there may be a link to qatəɣ — with p.b.s nəɣ- and un?]
AAY —
CAY qatŋun, qatŋuq 'half-sibling through traditional spouse-borrowing relationship'
NSY —
CSY —
Sir —
SPI qataŋun 'half-sibling from exchange wife'
NAI qataŋŋun, PH qataŋun 'step-sibling (through wife exchange)' [and qatak 'child by other than one's spouse']
WCI Cop qataŋŋun 'brother or sister' [Ras.; also Car qataŋ(ŋ)ut in B.-S.; Pryde has as 'parent's spouse-exchange partner's child' for all WCI]
ECI qataŋŋuti 'sibling of same mother or father, puppy of same litter' [and vocative qataaq, qataŋŋuuk 'my cousin!' acc. Schn.]
GRI qataŋŋut 'sibling'

PE qatəʀ- 'be white or pale' [cf. qatviaq]
AAY qatəʀ- 'be white'
CAY qatəʀ-
NSY qatəʀ- 'turn pale, bleach' [ANLC, also for qatəʀyiaXaq 'small white edible flower']
CSY qatəʀ- 'be white'
Sir [qatXaX 'dehaired and bleached sealskin' — Orr]
SPI qatiq- 'be white'
NAI qatiq-
WCI Sig qatiq- 'be white' [and Cop qatiŋa- 'be light-colored, faint', qatiŋayyit- 'be gray' acc. Pryde]
ECI qataak- 'be wan, pale, look sick' [and note Lab qayiq- 'be of a fine white color'? — Bourq.]
GRI EG qaliʀ- 'be colorless, vague, opaque' [Robbe and Menn., who also have qaliɣiliɣitsiq 'ring seal of two to three years'; compare WG qašaaʀ- 'be scoured white', qašiʀ- 'be gray, dusty, dust-colored', which may be influenced by qaðiɣyaʀ; EG qasiʀ- 'be gray, bleached' in Robbe and Dor. is from WG; Fab. also has qašiʀniq 'white dust, flour, chalk']

PE qatlin 'fat around internal organs?' [cf. qatəʀ- and and li-[1] un?]
AAY —
CAY qałin 'one of two fatty masses on sides of squirrel stomach'
NSY →
CSY —
Sir —
SPI Qaw qałłin
NAI Nu qatlin[y] 'fatty mass on side of squirrel stomach', B qallisik [du.] 'fat around bird's kidneys'
WCI Cop qa(a)llit 'stomach fat of bird or ground squirrel' [Pryde; Ras. has Cop qagLe·t 'fat around kidneys of animal', Sig 'suet']
ECI —
GRI [note qałłit, pl. qałłisit 'twisted sinew thread'?] →

PE qatliviɣ(aʀ) and **qatlipiɣ(aʀ)** 'pericardium (membrane surrounding heart)' [cf. piɣ]
AAY —
CAY —
NSY qałupik 'thin layer on ventricle of heart'
CSY —
Sir —
SPI —
NAI qalluviaq 'yellowish membrane surrounding heart'
WCI —
ECI qalluviaq 'membrane surrounding heart or other visceral membrane'
GRI qałłupiaq, qałłipiaq, EG qattipiaq, Up qatsipiaq 'pit of stomach', NG qallupiaq 'membrane between arteries and heart of animal'

PE qatŋuʀ- 'pry (heavy object) loose?' [cf. qa(C)uʀ-?]
AAY [note qatŋatə- 'fall hard, drop so that it lands hard', qatŋuXtə-, qatŋutə- 'injure self internally']
CAY [note qatŋitə- 'jolt']
NSY qatŋuʀ- 'start up, turn on or be turned on (e.g. radio), go away'
CSY —
Sir [note qatŋat(ə)- 'approach'?]
SPI qatŋuq- 'go away, remove, pry, lift up, take off (airplane)'
NAI qanŋuq-, Nu qatŋuq- 'move, budge a heavy object'
WCI qanŋuq- 'unstick, detach'
ECI —
GRI qaŋŋuʀ- 'boom, shoot (gun), be intoxicated' [Kl. has 'boom (e.g. stone or heavy object falling into water)' — contam. with qaciŋŋuq-?; EG qaŋŋiʀpalik 'noise' (also verbal)]

PY qatviaq 'kind of hide or skin' [there may be a relat. to qatəʀ-]
AAY qatxʷiaq 'soft (young) animal skin used for underwear, coat of caribou skin with fur on'
CAY qatfiaq 'moose hide tanned on both sides, tarpaulin'
NSY —
CSY —
Inu [note KI SPI qavžiaq 'patch, reinforcement']

PE qatviɣ or **qavciɣ** 'wolverine' [the Yup appears to have undergone metathesis via *qacviɣ- from qat(ə)viɣ — there may be a relat. to qatə, referring to the deep growling sound the animal makes]
AAY ➟
CAY NI, HBC, Y, NS qafcik 'wolverine'
NSY qafsik
CSY qafsik
Sir qafsəx
SPI qappik, Qaw qaffik
NAI qavvik, Mal, Nu qapvik
WCI Sig, Car qavvik, Cop qalvik, Net qa'vik [Pryde]
ECI qavvik, SB qaɣvik
GRI qappik 'mythical animal', NG qaɣvik 'wolverine'

> **PY qavcicuaq** 'marten' [cf. cuɣ]
> AAY qauxcicuaq 'marten'
> CAY qafcicuaq 'marten' [used even in areas where 'wolverine' is other than qafcik]
> NSY qafsisuaq 'marten' [ANLC]
> CSY —

PE qa(C)u(ði)- 'become conscious' [cf. qa(C)unaɣ- and perhaps also qaʀutə- and qaʀu-]
AAY —
CAY —
NSY qaaži- 'remember, come to senses, become aware, recognize' [and qaažima- 'be conscious, alert']
CSY [note qaažuʀyuɣ- 'feel that s.th. is wrong'?]
Sir —
SPI qauʀži- 'regain consciousness, become aware'
NAI qauži-, PH qauʀži- 'regain consciousness, come to one's senses' [and qaužima- 'be conscious, aware', qaužikłiq- 'understand']
WCI qauyi(ma)- 'know'
ECI qauyi- 'notice, become aware of', qauyima- 'know'
GRI qaatut-, qaaqqut(i)- 'come to one's senses' [and qaatusimašaqaŋŋit- 'be stupid']

PI qauciq- 'be wet'
SPI KI qausiq- 'be immersed in water' [Jen.]
NAI —
WCI [Pet. has kautcernak 'dew' for Sig]
ECI qausiq- 'be wet' [qausii- 'be wearing wet clothing'; Peck has kausek 'moisture' for Lab]
GRI qaasiʀ-, NG qauhiq- 'be wet through' [Fab. has kausek 'dampness'; note also qaasii- 'get wet feet' and NG qauhiʀnaq- 'be damp (weather)']

PE qa(C)unaɣ- 'be careful with s.th.' [cf. qa(C)u(ði)-?]
AAY —
CAY qaunqə- 'protect, care for'
NSY —
CSY —
Sir —
SPI qaunai- 'be aware of, attentive to', Qaw qaunak- 'be careful with', KI qaunaik- 'notice people'
NAI qaunaɣɨ- 'watch over, take care of', qaunaɣnaq- 'need attention' [and Mal qaunatqiit- 'be careless']
WCI Sig qaunaɣi- 'pay attention to'
ECI —
GRI —

PI qaunnaq 'solidified fat?'
SPI —
NAI qaunnaq 'solid animal fat (esp. back fat of caribou)'
WCI —
ECI qaunnaq 'Inuit chewing gum (dried oil with down or hair and boiled blood)'
GRI NG qaunnaq [Holt.]

PE qa(C)uʀ- 'pry loose' [the relat. — if any — to qatŋuʀ- is obscure]
AAY qauq 'barnacle'
CAY qauq, qaucuk 'sore on scalp', qauʀ- 'have sore on scalp'
NSY —
CSY qaa 'sore on head' [qaaXłaɣ- 'be covered with head sores']
Sir qaa 'sore on head' [Orr; borrowed from CSY?]
SPI qauq- 'pry loose, come unstuck'
NAI qauq-
WCI qauqtuq- 'unstick, detach'
ECI qauq- 'unstick'
GRI —

PE qavaʀ- 'sleep'
AAY K qawaʀ- 'sleep'
CAY qawaʀ-, HBC qavaʀ-
NSY qavaʀ- 'sleep' [and nom. qavaq 'sleep, sea animal sleeping on surface'; Jen. has qavaqsiq 'young walrus']
CSY qavaʀ- 'sleep'
Sir qavəʀ-
SPI qawaqtuq-, qawaqsiq- 'lie on back in water (seal)' [and qawaqsiaʀžuk 'yearling male walrus']
NAI qavaq- 'sleep on back in water (seal)'
WCI [Pryde has Cop qavaqtuq 'sleeping person' as a shaman's word; Ras. has Cop qavariaq 'dream' as a shaman's word; and note qavaqtu- 'be proud', Sig qavasuk- 'boast' in Met.]
ECI —
GRI —

> **PY qavaŋuq** 'dream'
> AAY qawaŋuq 'dream'
> CAY qawaŋuq, HBC qavaŋuq
> NSY qavaŋuq 'dream' [verbal qavaŋuʀ-]
> CSY qavaŋuq [verbal qavaŋuʀ-]

PY qavaŋuʀtuʀ- '(have a) dream' [cf. qavaŋuq above and tuʀ-[1]]
AAY qawaŋuʀtuʀ- 'dream'
CAY qawaŋuʀtuʀ-, HBC qavaŋuʀtuʀ-
NSY —
CSY —

PY qavaʀni- 'be sleepy' [cf. ni- and compare naɣacuɣni- under naɣa(t)-]
AAY qawaʀni- 'be sleepy'
CAY qawaʀni-, HBC qavaʀni-
NSY qavaʀninalʀia 'dozing'
CSY qavaʀni- 'be sleepy'

PY-S qavaʀvik 'bed or other sleeping place' [cf. ðviɣ]
AAY —
CAY qawaʀvik, HBC qavaʀvik 'sleeping bag, bedroom', Nun 'bed'
NSY qavaʀvik 'bed, time or place of sleeping'
CSY qavaʀvik 'bed, bedroom, place to sleep'
Sir qavəʀvəx 'bed'

PI qavaʀuciq 'outer skin of whale'
SPI [note qawausiq 'flake of dandruff' — contam. with qa(C)uʀ-?; for qawaqtiq- 'float on back (seal)' see qavaʀ-]
NAI PH qavausiq 'black outer skin of whale'
WCI —
ECI —
GRI qavaʀusiq

PE qavcit 'how many'
AAY qauxcin 'how many, so many'
CAY qafcin 'how many, several'
NSY qafsit 'how many'
CSY qafsina(t) 'how many' [and qafsiin 'which (in a series)']
Sir qafsi(ɣ-) 'how many, several' [the latter sense in Vakh.]
SPI qapsit 'how many'
NAI qafsit, Mal qapsit
WCI qapsit, Cop qaffit
ECI qatsit [Lab qapsit in Bourq.]
GRI qassit [old ortho. qavsit] 'how many', qassiit 'several'

PE qavəɣaɣ 'eider duck' [cf. EA qamɣaaŋ, Atkan qaɣmaŋ 'emperor goose']
AAY —
CAY qaɣʷəq*, qaɣʷiiq* 'spectacled eider'
NSY —
CSY qaɣʷaak 'bird' [Rub. has qawaaq '(any) small duck, bird other than the (very) smallest']
Sir qafqəX 'bird'
SPI Shishmaref qawiq 'eider'
NAI qauɣak 'duck', qavaasuk 'spectacled eider'
WCI qauɣaq 'eider'
ECI —
GRI —

PE qavəyaʀ 'sand'
AAY qauɣyaq 'sand'
CAY qaɣʷyaq
NSY qaɣʷyaq 'pebbles, sand'
CSY —
Sir qavi 'sand' [Vakh. has qaviX and Krup. has qavəy; and Em. has qavimcəʀaX 'fine sand']
SPI qayua(q) 'sand', Qaw qawia 'coarse sand, gravel'
NAI qavia 'fine sand'
WCI —
ECI —
GRI —

PY qaviʀ- 'curve'
AAY qawiXte-, qawite- 'go in a curve, make a u-turn'
CAY qaviXte- 'travel on a curved path'
NSY —
CSY qaviʀ- 'be slanted, diagonal' [postural root]

PE qavlu(ʀ) 'eyebrow' [cf. lu(ʀ) and Atkan Aleut du. qami-x (old Atkan sing. qam) 'eyebrows' = EA qamti-X, qamti-x, a derivative; compare also qavyuʀtə-]
AAY qauɣluq 'eyebrow'
CAY qavluq
NSY qavluq 'eyebrow' [ANLC has qavlu 'eyebrow, partition in oil lamp']
CSY —
Sir —
SPI qavlu 'eyebrow' [and qavlunaaq 'eyebrow ridge']
NAI qavlu 'eyebrow' [and qavluna(a)q 'eyebrow ridge']
WCI qavlu 'eyebrow' [and qavlunaq 'brow ridge'; note also Sig qavlalak- 'open and close eyes rapidly, blink'; Ow. has qavluXXuq- 'blink' for EP]
ECI qallu 'eyebrow' [and qalluqiaq- 'blink']
GRI qałłu 'eyebrow' [old ortho. qagdlo, qavdlo, Fab. kablo]

PI qavlunaaq 'white man' [the first contact with white men was at the end of the tenth century in Greenland, so this is not strictly PI; the traditional relation between this word and qavlu(ʀ) 'eyebrow', i.e. 'person with prominant/frowning brow(s)' may be tenable despite the verb form cited for earlier Greenlandic below, which could be the immediate source (i.e. 's.o. bleached or pale'?) — compare NAI naluaʀmiu under nalu(C)aʀ as R. Petersen has suggested — but it could in turn be related to qavlu(ʀ) (note the last meaning given for Kl.'s term below); for the p.b. see perhaps naaq- and compare under NAI below]
Yup [see qavlunaq for CAY qavlunaq 'wake of s.th. moving under the water'; the direct cognate of the present form (borrowed from Inu?) appears on an old word list for Y (Petroff 1881) — kablyuni 'white man' (glossed "heavy eyebrows")]
SPI —
NAI Nu qavluna 'white man' [and note p.b. naaq as in naŋinaaq 'ill person' and utuqqanaaq 'elder person'; for qavluna(a)q 'eyebrow ridge' see under qavlu(ʀ)]
WCI Cop qavlunaaq 'white man'
ECI qallunaaq 'white man, non-Inuit' [and note

qalluniaq- 'go to barter at trading post']
GRI qałłunaaq 'Dane, white man' [and qałłunniaʀ- 'travel to trading post'; note Kl. has qavlunâr- (Fab. kablunâr-) 'wither, deteriorate (of seaweed left too long in water or food that has got water into it), smart (of eyes, from getting old urine in them)']

PY qavlunaq 'wake of s.th. swimming under water' [apparently from qavlu(ʀ) and nar but see also qaɣə(ʀ) — there may be contam. here]
AAY qauɣlunəq, qayyuʀnəq 'ripple or wave from s.th. swimming just under water, wake of boat'
CAY qavlunaq 'wake made on surface by fish or animal swimming just below surface', HBC 'silver salmon'
NSY —
CSY —
Inu [note SPI qavlunaaq- 'swim just below water's surface' (from Yup?), but also Nu qaivl^{y}ɨk 'waves caused by passing boat' under qaɣəliʀ- (qaɣə(ʀ))]

PY qavyuʀtə- 'frown' [there may be a link to qavlu(ʀ)]
AAY PWS qauɣyuXtə- 'knit brows in anger'
CAY qavyuXtə- 'glower, frown'
NSY —
CSY —
Inu [note Sig qayyunaq- 'frown']

PY qayaɣ- 'shout' [there may be a link to qatə]
AAY qaya(ɣa)-, qaya'a- 'shout, yell'
CAY qayaɣa- 'shout repeatedly', qayaxpaɣ- 'shout loudly'
NSY — [note kaya(ʀ)- 'call, ask, challenge, cry out for help', and kayałəq 'request, call', going with or influenced by kayu-]
CSY —
Sir —

PI qayak(naq)- 'be fragile'
SPI —
NAI qayaɣnaq- 'be fragile'
WCI Cop qayaŋnaq- 'be fragile', qayaɣi- 'be careful with'
ECI —
GRI qayannaʀ- 'be fragile', qayaɣi- 'consider fragile, be careful with' [and qayaššuaʀ- 'be careful, gentle with s.th.]

PE qayaʀ 'kayak' [or *qan^{y}aʀ, as suggested by isolated GRI plural qaannat (old ortho. qáinat) and derivatives like qaanniuʀ- 'make a kayak' (also Canada)?; cf. Atkan Aleut (and western EA) iqya-X, EA iqa-X (Prib. Islands also niqa-X, a blend with niX 'baidar' if not reflecting *qan^{y}aʀ) 'kayak, baidarka' and compare the initial vowel in imli-X under məlqur; see kanayu(ʀ), kayu and qanu(q), qayuq for possible near-parallels if this base is from *qan(ə)yaʀ (to qaynaʀ by metath. — cf. qanət- and yaʀ) as Berg. has suggested, but compare also GRI qainni 'his (own) kayak' with (older) nainni 'his (own) little sister', from nayaɣ plus ni; alternatively, Jacobson 1984 suggests a link to qaðə- (plus yaʀ)]
AAY qayaq 'kayak' [originally 'baidarka', today any boat]
CAY qayaq 'kayak' [qayaʀ- 'use a kayak']
NSY qayaq 'kayak'
CSY qayaq
Sir qayaX
SPI qayaq 'kayak' [pl. qayyat; qayyi- 'build a kayak']
NAI qayaq 'kayak' [pl. qayyat; qayyi- 'build a kayak']
WCI qayaq 'kayak' [also of kayaker in his kayak acc. Pryde for Cop; Sig pl. qayyat or qainnat (Lowe) — Ras. has Net qainnanut 'to the kayaks' and Met. qainnaminut 'to his kayak' for Cop]
ECI qayaq 'kayak' [and qainniu(q)- 'make a kayak' with li(C)uʀ-]
GRI qayaq 'kayak, kayak with man in' [pl. qaannat (old ortho. qáinat), qaanni 'his (own) kayak', qaanniuʀ- (Fab. kaynior-) 'build a kayak', qaanni- 'leave one's kayak behind (on scaffold)']

PI qayaʀiaq 'canoe' [cf. yar or ɣiaq-?]
SPI —
NAI —
WCI qayaʀiaq 'canoe'
ECI qayaʀiaq
GRI qayaʀiaq 'canoe (from legends)'

PE qayaʀtuʀ- 'paddle in kayak' [cf. tuʀ-^{1}]
AAY —
CAY Nun qayaXtuʀ- 'hunt for seal (with or without kayak)'
NSY qayaXtuʀ- 'paddle in kayak'
CSY qayaXtuʀ-
Sir qayaXtuʀ-
SPI qayaqtuq-
NAI qayaqtuq-
WCI qayaqtuq- [Pryde]
ECI qayaqtu(q)-
GRI qayaʀtuʀ-

PI qayau- 'capsize in kayak' [cf. umiu-, on which this set might be based by analogy]
SPI qayau- W 'capsize in kayak' [but Qaw 'fall down']
NAI qayau- 'capsize in kayak'
WCI qayau- [Pryde]
ECI qayau- 'capsize and right kayak again with paddle' [not necessarily righting self again acc. Saul]
GRI qayaa- 'capsize and drown from kayak'

PE qayəmɣu(ʀ) 'shore ice' [cf. qa(C)əʀu(ʀ)]
AAY —
CAY qayəmɣu 'thick shorefast ice'
NSY qayəmɣu 'shore ice' [ANLC]
CSY Chap qayəmɣu 'shore ice' [for homonym meaning 'tree bark' see qa(C)əʀu(ʀ)]
Sir qayəmɣuX 'shore ice' [Vakh. from Rub.]
SPI qaimuq 'ice pan at freeze-up,' Imaq 'edge of ice'
NAI qaimŋuq, qaimʀu 'first shore ice in fall, white frozen edge of water' [for Mal qaimʀuq 'birch bark' see qa(C)əʀu(ʀ)]

WCI qaimɣuq [for qaimŋuq?] 'ice resembling ice crystals or snow which forms on sea or lake shore'
ECI qaiŋŋuq 'border of solid ice stuck to the shore', Lab qaimɣuq [Bourq.]
GRI qaaŋŋuq 'ice edge' [old ortho. qauŋŋuq with spurious u — Fab. has kaingok]

PY-S qayu(q) 'how' [cf. qanuq and qaŋa; compare Yup kayu 'sculpin' with Inu kanayuq for a possible parallel, but the common PE form could also have been *qan^y^ᴜʀ (compare qayaʀ)]
AAY qayu K 'how', KP 'really!'
CAY qayumi 'indeed, as expected', qayux^w^a 'this time, to my surprise', Y, NS 'how', HBC, Y, K qayutun 'how many or much'
NSY qay 'I wonder, is that so?', qaywa 'really, is that so?' [L.-T.]
CSY qayuq 'how' [and qayurmi 'how then?', qaywa 'wait', qaywaam 'surely', qayŋun 'probably' and qayuXłak 'because']
Sir [Vakh. has qayŋun 'really?' from Rub. and also qałuʀən 'because']

PY qa(y)itə- 'do how' [cf. ət-; the same as PI qanuq-ət-, GRI qanuʀit- 'be how'?]
AAY C qaiłun, qaiłuʀluni 'how' [4s subordinative mood; note also qaisuuɣ- 'be disappointed, let down, upset'?]
CAY qaił(un) 'how', NS qaitə- 'do how, have s.th. wrong with one'
NSY —
CSY —

PE qayuɣ- 'strike or hollow with adze'
AAY —
CAY —
NSY qayuɣ- 'hollow out, hew with an adze' [ANLC]
CSY qayuɣ- 'strike with an adze, create, shape'
Sir —
SPI qayuk- 'chop ivory or bone with adze'
NAI PH qayuk- 'shape s.th.'
WCI Cop qayuk- 'chop, hack with knife', Net qayuun 'adze' [Pryde]
ECI —
GRI —

PE qayuʀ 'meat broth' [for the 'tea' senses compare under caʀsa(q) for AAY saʀsaq 'tea' borrowed from Aleut caXsa-X 'fish broth']
AAY qayuq 'blood, broth, soup'
CAY qayuq
NSY qayuq 'tea, meat broth' [also qayuʀ- 'drink hot liquid' (ANLC)]
CSY qayuq 'broth, tea'
Sir qayəX
SPI qayuq 'blood soup, broth, Claytonia (plant)' [and qayusaaq 'flour boiled with water']
NAI qayuq 'tea, boiled blood, broth' [and note qayuqłaq, qayuqłak 'ripple on surface of snow'?]
WCI qayuq 'blood soup'
ECI qayuq 'soup, meat broth'
GRI qayuq 'soup' [and qayuušat 'flour', qayurłak 'froth on soup']

PE qayuʀutaʀ 'ladle' [cf. un]
AAY —
CAY Nun, NS qazuuciaq 'spoon' [Ras. has qautaX 'meat tray' for Nun]
NSY [qayuqaq 'wooden dish for meat'; Tein has qayutaq]
CSY qayuutaq 'wooden tray for meat'
Sir [note qayukəX 'tray for eating meat' — Em.]
SPI Qaw qayuutaq 'ladle, robin' [and qayuukaq 'wooden board for cutting meat']
NAI qayuuttaq 'ladle, dipper'
WCI qayu(u)taq 'cup which served for dipping broth'
ECI qayuutaq 'ladle'
GRI qayuutaq 'ladle' [NG qayuuttat 'antlers']

PI qažɣitaq 'pitfall trap' [cf. Aleut qaðɣi- 'penetrate', qaðɣit- 'put through, pierce'; there could be a relat. to qaðɣi]
SPI —
NAI qažɣisaq 'pitfall trap in snow (for caribou)' [also verbal for trapping with such a trap]
WCI qayɣitaq 'pitfall (old-style trap for caribou)' [Pryde has qalɣitaq for Cop and Car]
ECI qayɣitaq- 'fall into a hole'
GRI —

PE qəcaʀu(C)aʀ 'membrane around stomach of animal' [cf. ŋ(ŋ)uðaʀ?]
AAY qəcaq, qəcaʀuaq 'membrane with fat over stomach of goat'
CAY qəcaʀuaq 'tripe of caribou or moose'
NSY [note qəža 'tripe of reindeer or whale' (ANLC, Men. has it as 'whale fat') — contam. with qəža?]
CSY —
Sir —
SPI —
NAI qisaʀuaq 'first stomach of caribou, skin of first stomach'
WCI Cop qihaʀuaq 'membrane of caribou stomach' [Pryde; Schn. has Car? qisaʀuaq 'first stomach of ruminant' ('adg')]
ECI qisaʀuaq 'first stomach of ruminants (caribou), envelope containing the first stomach'
GRI qasaʀuaq 'stomach of ruminant'

PE qəciɣ 'skin (of animal)'
AAY qəcik 'scalp, bark, rind'
CAY qəcik 'skin, leather, rind'
NSY qəsi 'skin'
CSY —
Sir —
SPI qizik 'leather, skin'
NAI qisik 'skin with hair removed, leather'
WCI qisik 'leather' [Net 'sealskin' in Ras. — as also Schn. for 'adg']
ECI qisik 'skin' [NBI, SB 'sealskin' — also Lab acc. Bourq.]
GRI —

PI qəciqciun 'sharp twig or branch?' [or qiciqciun; there may be a link to qəc(c)uɣ-]
SPI —
NAI qisiqsiun 'tree branch, spruce needle'
WCI Sig qisiqsiutait, qisiqtuutit 'branches'
ECI [qisiqtuuti 'needles or spruce or fir']
GRI —

PE qəciʀ(-) 'spit'
AAY qəciq 'spit', qəciʀ- 'spit'
CAY qəciq, qəciʀ- 'spit'
NSY qəsiʀ- 'spit'
CSY qəsiʀ- 'spit' [and qəsiiʀaq 'mist, fog, drizzle']
Sir qəsiʀ- 'spit' [Vakh. and Orr have qəsəʀ-; note also qəcəʀətəɬəX 'tuberculosis']
SPI Di qisiq- 'spit' [Jen.]
NAI —
WCI Net qihiq- 'spit' [Ras.; also Pet. for Sig; Dor. has 'rain heavily' for B. Lake]
ECI qisiq 'spit' [also verbal; qisiʀi- 'be turning to drizzle (fog)']
GRI qisiq 'spit' [also verbal qisiʀ-]

PE qəc(c)uɣ- 'scratch or dig claws into' [cf. Atkan Aleut qiciʀ-, EA qicaʀ- 'be sharp' and EA qicaX, qicXi-X 'sharp (instrument)']
AAY qəcuɣ- 'grab with claws'
CAY qəcuɣ- 'pull out by roots' [qəcuɣmiɣ- 'grasp, scratch']
NSY qəsuɣ- 'pull out grass, take out weapon'
CSY qəsuɣ- 'pull out by roots' [for qəsuɣ(yuɣ)- 'be excited' see quvya(yuɣ)-]
Sir —
SPI qissuk- 'pull out by roots, Qaw 'scratch' [and Imaq qəzuk- 'pull out (grass)']
NAI qisuk-, qitcuk- 'scratch, grab with talons', PH 'grab roughly' [and qitcuq 'scratch mark']
WCI Cop qihuk- 'sieze (clasping to one's body)', qitsuk- 'scratch'
ECI qisuk- 'scratch, rake, brush', qitsu(k)- 'scratch, claw (several times)' [and qitsuq 'scratch']
GRI qisuɣ- 'dig one's nails into, be possessive about', qitsuɣ- 'scratch, dig nails into (several places)' [and intr. = 'hit water without causing a splash (harpoon or stone)'; note also qitsuk 'cat']

PY qəcuqitə- 'choke on liquid' [compare cittuqitə-]
AAY K qəcuɣitə- 'choke on food'
CAY qəcuqitə- 'drown, choke on liquid'
NSY qəsuqitə- 'choke on liquid' [L.-T.]
CSY qəsuqitə- 'choke on liquid'

PE qəðuɣ 'wood' [the Yup forms seem to be influenced by əqðuɣ-]
AAY [əquk 'wood' — in derivs. only]
CAY [NS, (mouth of) Y, Nun, Eg əquk 'wood', elsewhere only in derivatives; note also Y əqiʀ- 'stoke'; for əquk, quuk 'thing carried on shoulder' see əqðuɣ-]
NSY [əquk 'firewood, log' — by contam. with əquk 'load carried on shoulders' under əqðuɣ-; ΛNLC also has əkuq 'firewood, kindling', influenced by əkə-[1]?; Men. also əqiirivik 'furnace']
CSY [quuk 'firewood' could be via əqðuk; qiiʀ- 'stoke a fire']
Sir qəcəx, qəžux 'firewood' [Orr and Vakh.; Orr has pl. qəcəɣiy, Vakh. also has qəžŋuX 'tree', influenced by qəŋžuʀ-?]
SPI qižuk, Imaq qəžuk 'wood'
NAI qižuk
WCI qiyuk
ECI qiyuk
GRI qišuk, EG qilivatsiaq

PE qəðði(C)uʀ- 'chop wood' [cf. li(C)uʀ-]
AAY K [əqiuʀ- 'chop wood']
CAY [əqiuʀ- 'chop wood']
NSY —
CSY —
Sir —
SPI qižžiuq-
NAI qižžiuq-
WCI Sig qiyyiuq- [Lowe]
ECI qiyyiu(q)-
GRI —

PE qəðuɣtaʀ- 'gather wood' [cf. taʀ-]
AAY —
CAY [(ə)quxtaʀ- 'gather firewood', əquxtə- 'go for wood']
NSY —
CSY quuxtə- 'gather firewood'
Sir qəžuxtə-, qəžŋuX-'gather firewood' [second form influenced by qəžŋuʀ-?]
SPI qižuktaq- 'fetch wood'
NAI qižuktaq-
WCI qiyuktaq-
ECI qiyutta(q)- 'go to look for wood, carry wood'
GRI qišuttaʀ- 'gather wood'

PE qəla-[1] 'urge or be urged on'
AAY C, KP qəla- 'be in need', K 'wane (moon)', qəlatə- 'need'
CAY qəlapəxtə- 'hinder, be lethargic'
NSY —
CSY qəlaʀ- 'urge dogs on, shoo dogs away'
Sir qəlaʀ- [Orr]
SPI qilamik 'quickly'
NAI qilamik, Nu qilamiqaitciaq 'quickly, immediately'
WCI qilamik 'quickly'
ECI Aiv, Lab qilamik, Tar qilamiapik 'soon' [and note qilaiŋŋa(q)- 'die suddenly']
GRI qilamik 'soon' [and qilaɣ- 'be dying of thirst', qilaliʀ- 'be thirsty' (infl. bu qi(C)ət-?) and perhaps qilaŋŋaʀ- 'kill with one shot']

PE qəlanəʀ(aʀ)- 'want s.th. urgently'
AAY —
CAY qəlanəʀnaXqə- 'cause to waste time'
NSY —
CSY qəlanəʀ- 'long for'
Sir —
SPI [qilaniuq- 'be in a hurry']

NAI qiɫanaaq- 'want urgently'
WCI Cop qilanaaq- 'look forward to' [Ras.]
ECI qilanaaʀi- 'want urgently'
GRI qilanaaʀ- 'look forward', qilanaari- 'long for'

PE qəla-[2] 'invoke spirits (shaman)' [cf. Atkan Aleut qlat- 'tempt, offend, deceive (thus used by missionaries)']
AAY [note K qela- 'wane (of moon)']
CAY Y, Nun qəla 'spirit', qəla- 'practice shamanistic divination' [Lantis has nom. kal'a; Y qəlalək 'shaman' — compare kaɫalək under kaɫaɣ-]
NSY —
CSY [Bogoraz has kilrak 'shaman's helping spirit' as a shaman's word]
Sir qəla 'magic object that answers one's questions' [Vakh. from Rub., who also has kəla, as does Em. for 'master of sky' — compare Chukchi kelə 'spirit' under kaɫaɣ-]
SPI qila 'spirit of totem animal' [verbal = 'invoke spirit'], qilaŋniq 'shaman's trance'
NAI qila, qilʸa 'shaman's power or spirit' [verbal = 'invoke spirits'; qillan 'shaman's conjuring rod']
WCI Cop qila- 'perform sorcery' [and qila 'object used by sorcerer]
ECI Lab qila- 'practice sorcery by tying limb' [Peck]
GRI qila- 'conjure over, fish with rod' [trans. qilaɣ- in old ortho. for qilat-; qiɫɫat 'charm']

PI qəlaun 'drum' [cf. un; NAI qillan, GRI qiɫɫat above must be earlier parallel derivations]
SPI qilaun 'shaman's divining rod'
NAI qilʸaun 'drum'
WCI Cop qilaut 'Inuit drum' [also Car acc. B.-S. and Net acc. Ras., who also has Sig qilauvaqpaluk 'sound of drum']
ECI NBI, SB qilauti, Lab qilaut 'drum' [Bourq.]
GRI qilaat 'drum, violin', NWG also 'guitar'

PE qələɣ- and **qəluɣ-** 'get scorched or wrinkled' [cf. qəlu-, also EA qilɣu- 'scorch, roast, (intr.) shrivel, become crisp']
AAY qəɫtə- 'shrivel when burnt'
CAYqələŋtə- 'pleat, wrinkle'
NSY ➟
CSY —
Sir —
SPI qiluk- 'scorch'
NAI qiɫuk- 'warp, wrinkle from heat', PH 'get scorched'
WCI —
ECI qilukka(C)- 'twist'
GRI qiluɣ- 'scorch'

PY qələŋɫak 'scar' [cf. ʀɫaɣ?]
AAY qələŋɫak 'scar'
CAY qələŋɫak 'scar, wrinkle'
NSY qəɫəŋɫak 'scar' [Enm. et al.; ANLC also has ələŋžak 'scab']
CSY [note qəɫayək 'scar', qəɫayəɣ- 'undergo surgery']

PI qələʀuq 'scar' [cf. quʀ]
SPI qiliʀuq 'scar'
NAI qil(i)ʀuq
WCI Car? qiliʀuq [Schn. 'adg']
ECI qiliʀuq 'scar'
GRI qiliʀuq

PY-S qəlpaʀ- 'open'
AAY —
CAY HBC qəɫpəXtə- 'open a container' [Woodbury]
NSY qəɫpaʀ- 'open' [ANLC; L.-T. has qəɫpanəq 'crack, opening']
CSY qəɫpəXtə- 'open'
Sir qəɫpaʀ- 'open, be open' [Vakh.]
Inu [note WG qilu- 'open (bag)' — by contam. with PE qəlu-?]

PE qəlquðaʀ '(kind of) seaweed'
AAY əɫquaq 'fucus (seaweed with air hollows)' [note also C səqtuaq 'red seaweed']
CAY əɫquaq* 'herring eggs or roe', Nun əɫquaX 'seaweed', BB, NS qəɫquaq 'kelp' [the first meaning by contam. with the source of əlquaʀnəq]
NSY əɫquaq 'kind of seaweed' [ANLC 'sea cabbage']
CSY əɫqʷaaq 'kelp'
Sir qəɫqəcəX 'kind of seaweed'
SPI qitquaq 'seaweed'
NAI —
WCI Net qitquaq [Ras.]
ECI qiqquaq
GRI qiqquaq, pl. qiqquššat

PE qəlu- 'tighten or be cramped' [there may be a link to qələɣ-]
AAY qəlu- 'stoop, hunch, bend over', qəlui- 'get cramps'
CAY qəlu- 'pull up, tighten, be cramped (of muscle)' [for qəɫuq 'colon' see əqlu, for Nun, HBC, NS qəɫuʀ- 'shrink, crimp' see qəɫuʀtə- under əqə-[1]]
NSY —
CSY qəlu- 'have muscle cramp, be tied or fastened tightly, be taut' [for qeɫuXtə- 'shrink' see qəɫuʀtə- under əqə-[1]]
Sir [Vakh. has qəlutuqaX 'overall strap or lace']
SPI qilu- 'be cramped (of muscle), shrink, contract, pull up with hands'
NAI qilu- 'have a muscle cramp, attach tent ropes' [as noun = 'muscle cramp, tent rope'; qiluuq- 'stretch']
WCI qilu- 'have cramps, pull back on bow' [Cop also 'be open (bag), be drawn back (bowstring), spread apart' acc. Pryde]
ECI qilu- 'have a general nervous or muscular contraction', qilu 'fist, handle for carrying', Iti qiluk 'hammer and trigger of gun', Lab qilu 'trigger of gun' [Peck; Ras. has Igl qilu- 'pull up by hands']
GRI qilu- 'pull together, pull toward oneself, snare, draw bow' [for the sense 'open' see under qəɫpaʀ-; qiluuʀ- 'distend'; for qisua- 'have a spasm' see qi(C)ət-]

PI qəlummi(k)- 'clasp' [cf. miɣ-?]
SPI —
NAI Nu qilummi- 'hold on to (fishing line on which fish has bitten)'
WCI qilummi- 'hold open' [Pryde]
ECI qilummi- 'remain clasping on to s.th.'
GRI qilummi-, qilummiɣ- 'hold up while it is being filled (bag)'

PI qəluqqit- 'be taut'
SPI —
NAI qiłuqqit- 'stretch or be stretched to limit, pull a back muscle'
WCI Cop qiluqqit- 'be strained, overstretched' [Pryde]
ECI qiluqqi(t)- 'pull dog traces taut, shrink and stiffen (rope)', Iti 'stretch, tighten'
GRI NG qiluqqit- 'be taut'

PE qəl(l)uʀ(aʀ) 'string?'
AAY qəluq C 'rope', K 'bowstring'
CAY [note qəlun 'spring, bowstring, etc.']
NSY [qəluŋʀaləq 'jumprope (game)']
CSY —
Sir —
SPI qiluaq- 'catch bird in snare'
NAI [Nu qiluaq 'taut line attached to snare for catching squirrels' — also verbal for catching a squirrel that way]
WCI Car? qiluaqtuq- 'set snares' [Schn. 'adg']
ECI qilluaq 'belt, link, painter (for tying up up boat)'
GRI qiłłuaʀut 'string holding together fur jacket in crotch' [and qiluʀaʀtuʀ- 'catch small birds in snare', quluʀaʀtuut 'snare', qiłłuaq 'fork, crotch']

PY-S qəłi- 'get flattened or trampled down'
AAY —
CAY —
NSY —
CSY qəłi- 'get flattened down from pressure' [qəłistə- 'flatten']
Sir qəłitit(ə)- 'stamp down, trample' [Em.]

PE qəmaɣ- 'store away' [there is conflation between this set and qimaɣ- in Inu — see the 'leave behind' senses there]
AAY —
CAY qəmaɣ- 'put away for safekeeping' [also 'not want to leave (usually of a child)' perhaps a different base; qəmak 'thing put away as precious']
NSY —
CSY —
Sir —
SPI —
NAI qimatci- 'leave part of load behind when traveling'
WCI —
ECI —
GRI qimat- 'leave behind' [half-trans. qimatsi- 'leave s.th. for s.o.']

PI qəmatu(t) '(winter) cache or stores'
SPI —
NAI —
WCI Cop qimatu 'cache left to pick up later' [Pryde]
ECI qimatu 's.th. left in storage', qimatuli- 'make a storage cache'
GRI qimatut 'winter stores', qimatuli- 'lay in winter stores', EG qimululuik 'meat cache' [and note qimatuu- 'be left behind']

PI qəməlʀu- 'examine'
SPI —
NAI qimiłʀu- 'open and scrutinize, e.g. a box, book, bag'
WCI Cop qimilʀiuq- 'examine, sort the good things out'
ECI qimiʀʀu- 'glance at to see how s.th. is' [Saul has 'examine'; Schn. also has qimiʀʀua- consider, examine in detail']
GRI qimiʀłuuʀ- 'examine'

PE qəməʀyaʀ 'eyelash' [cf. qəməlʀu- and yaʀ?]
AAY qəməʀyaq 'eyelash'
CAY qəməʀyaq
NSY qəməʀyaq, [ANLC] qəməʀyak
CSY qəməʀyaq
Sir —
SPI qimiʀiaq
NAI qimiʀiaq
WCI qimiʀiaq [Pryde]
ECI qimiʀiaq
GRI qimiʀiaq

PE qəmiʀ[1] 'ridge' [cf. Aleut Att qimiyʀi-X, Atkan miðʀi-X 'breastbone', also EA qmi- 'ivory hook of spear-thrower']
AAY AP qəmiq 'long, low ridge'
CAY qəmiq 'hill, esp. part of ridge of hills' [for homonym meaning 'float line of net' see qəmiʀ[2]]
NSY —
CSY qəmiq 'hill, mound'
Sir qəmiX 'hill, ridge' [Vakh. from Men.'s texts]
SPI qimiq, Qaw qimmiq 'foothill, small hill, knoll', qimiʀaluk 'ridge'
NAI qimiʀaq 'hill'
WCI Cop qimiq 'ridge' [Pryde; Met. has Sig qimmialuit 'ridge' and qimiʀutit 'pole for hanging fish to dry on'; Schn. has qimmiʀut 'wooden pole supporting roof, keel of boat for 'adg' — Pryde qimiʀut Net 'side pole of tent', Cop 'beam of thong between uprights to support drying fish or meat'; Ras. has Sig qimiq 'ridge, mountain range']
ECI ➟
GRI NG qimiʀut 'tent ridge pole'

PI qəmiaʀžuk 'snowdrift' [cf. aʀžuk]
Sir [note qəməʀcəɣəta 'snowdrift']
SPI [note qimuɣžuk 'snowdrift, snow bank', Qaw qimuɣžuɣaq 'area of hard-packed snow']
NAI qimuaʀžuk 'high snowdrift, snowdrift in lee of building or blocking trail', Nu qimiaʀžuk 'low ridge'

WCI [Car EP qimuɣɣuit 'snowdrift' — Ow.; Pryde has Cop, Car qimuɣɣuk 'ridged snowdrift eroded by wind']
ECI [qimuyyuk 'snow drifts']
GRI NG qimiaXXuk 'snowdrift against side of iceberg or house'

PE qəmiʀłuɣ and **qəmiʀluʀ** 'spine' [cf. łuɣ(-) or lu(ʀ)?]
AAY K qəmiXłuk 'spine, backbone'
CAY qəmiXłuk
NSY —
CSY —
Sir —
SPI qimiʀluk
NAI qimiʀl^{y}uk
WCI Sig qimiʀluk 'human back' [Pet.; Pryde also 'backbone' in Cop]
ECI qimiʀluk 'dorsal spine, spinal column'
GRI qimiʀłuk, qimiʀłuq 'vertebra' [in pl. = 'back, spine']

PE qəmiʀ^{2} 'net line' [cf. qəmiʀ^{1} which may in fact be the same set]
AAY —
CAY qəmiq 'float line of net' [and qəmiʀ- 'string float line of net']
NSY —
CSY —
Sir —
SPI qimiq 'towline of dogsled, float line of net' [and Imaq qimiq- 'hang up net on string']
NAI qimiq 'net line'
WCI qimiaq 'net line', qimiq- 'raise net'
ECI qimiaq 'ropes attached to net'
GRI qimiaq 'string on which net or snares are hung'

PE qəmit- 'strangle'
AAY qəmitə- 'strangle'
CAY qəmitə-
NSY qimitə- [L.-T.]
CSY qəmitə- 'strangle, hang by the neck, get choked up'
Sir qəmət(ə)- 'strangle' [Vakh. has qəmit(ə)- 'overstrain, strangle (oneself)']
SPI qimit- 'strangle'
NAI qimɨt- 'choke by strangulation'
WCI qimit- 'hang oneself by the neck' [Cop also 'strangle' acc. Pryde]
ECI qimit- 'strangle, strangle oneself to death (e.g. by hanging), be numb (limb)'
GRI qimit- 'strangle'

PY-S qəmtaq 'roof?'
AAY qəmłite- 'become filled to the brim, become very high (tide)' [with łit-]
CAY —
NSY qəmtaq 'roof, ceiling'
CSY qəmtaq 'attic, upper level'
Sir qəmta 'ceiling, upper floor, attic'

PY qəna- 'be ill' [cf. qənəʀ-?; also — with loss of initial qə — Aleut naXta- 'have pain in', nat- 'hurt', nana- 'be painful']
AAY qəna- 'be sick, ill'
CAY BB, NR, LI qəna-
NSY —
CSY —

PE qənəʀ- 'be angry' [cf. qəna-?; the relat. — if any — with əqə-^{2} is obscure]
AAY qənəXtə- 'grunt, groan (from strain)'
CAY qənəXtə- 'be angry' [and qənŋə- 'get angry'; for əqə-, Nun əqquXtə- 'be infuriated' see əqə-^{2}]
NSY [for qinaʀyuɣ- 'be discontented with guests' see qiŋŋaʀ-]
CSY qənəXtə- 'feel slighted'
Sir qənəʀaʀ- 'be insulted'
SPI Qaw qiniqaʀiaʀait- 'be quick-tempered' [and Jen. has W qiŋnaʀuk- 'be angry']
NAI qɨniq- 'be angry', qɨnnak- 'be angry, fight'
WCI Cop qiniq- 'growl (dog)' [Jen.; Pryde has qinnak- 'become menacing, angry (dog)' for Cop]
ECI qinna(C)- 'show bad humor' [and Lab qinayuk- 'be fierce, furious with pain' (Bourq.) unless from qəna-]
GRI qiniʀ- 'groan, grumble' [qiniŋa- 'be ferocious (animal)']

PE qənəʀciʀ 'tonsil'
AAY K qənəXcəsn̥əq, C qənəXcəsn̥aq 'mph gland'
CAY qənəXcəXaq, qənəXciXaq, qənəXcinaq 'tonsil, swollen lymph node in neck'
NSY —
CSY [note qanlak 'tonsil']
Sir [note qanləx 'tonsil']
SPI —
NAI qiniqsiq 'tonsil'
WCI qiniqsik, qiniqsiniq
ECI qiniʀsiq
GRI qiniʀsiq 'gland, hard knot under skin'

PE qənŋu(ʀ) 'bridge of nose'
AAY PWS qənŋulək 'type of whale' [B.S. has it as 'humpback whale']
CAY Kwigillingok qənŋuq 'cartilage in fish head' [and qənŋiq 'bridge of nose']
NSY ➟
CSY qənŋu 'brow area'
Sir qənŋu
SPI qiŋŋuq 'root of nose'
NAI qinŋuq 'upper part of cheekbone under eye'
WCI qiŋuq 'part of caribou's head between nose and brain (when cooked)' [Pryde has Net qi'ŋuq 'spot between eyes, forehead of animal']
ECI qiŋŋuq 'lower middle of forehead'
GRI qiŋŋuq 'bridge of nose' [for homonym 'head of fjord, etc.' see qitəɣ, qitŋu(ʀ); note also qiŋŋuala- 'be cross, pout']

PE qənŋułiqə(t)- 'frown'
AAY —
CAY —

NSY qənŋułiqə- 'frown'
CSY qənŋułiqə-
Sir qənŋułiqə-
SPI —
NAI —
WCI [note Cop qiŋuRluk- 'frown']
ECI qinŋuliqit- 'frown' [Saul; Schn. has qiŋuliqit-]
GRI —

PE qənu 'slush ice'
AAY AP qənu 'water freezing on ice'
CAY qənu 'slush ice' [and qənu- 'freeze']
NSY qənu
CSY qənu
Sir qənu
SPI qinu
NAI qɨnu 'thin layer of new ice on water' [verbal = 'form a thin layer of new ice']
WCI qinu
ECI qinu 'thickening of sea ice close to shore before it freezes solid in autumn'
GRI qinuq 'slush snow'

PE qəŋaR 'nose'
AAY qəŋaq 'nose'
CAY qəŋaq [also dual for one nose]
NSY qəŋaq 'nose'
CSY qəŋaq
Sir qəŋəX
SPI qiŋaq, Di qəŋaq
NAI qiŋaq 'nose, house ventilator, blowhole of whale'
WCI qiŋaq
ECI qiŋaq 'nose, hole in roof for ventilation'
GRI qiŋaq 'nose, hole in roof for ventilation, protuberance at base of bird's bill' [S.-L. has 'nostril' with the plural as 'nose']

PE qəŋaləɣ 'king eider' [cf. ləɣ]
AAY qəŋałək 'king eider'
CAY qəŋałək
NSY qəŋałək
CSY qəŋalək
Sir —
SPI qiŋalik
NAI qiŋalik
WCI qiŋalik
ECI qiŋalik [Saul]
GRI qiŋalik

PE qəŋaRaR 'shin' [cf. aR]
AAY qəŋa(R)aq 'shinbone, tibia'
CAY qəŋaRaq
NSY —
CSY —
Sir [qəŋəRcəX 'shinbone' (Vakh. from Rub.'s texts)]
SPI W qiŋaaq 'fibula' [Jen.; note Qaw qiŋažaaq- 'hurt one's shin']
NAI qiŋaRaq 'shinbone, plateau', Nu 'ridge along front of nose' [and qiŋaaq 'bridge of nose']
WCI qiŋaaq, qiŋaRaq 'front of leg'
ECI qiŋaRRaq 'angular part of front of leg' [Saul — Schn. has qiŋaRaq]
GRI qiŋaaq 'front edge of shin' [and note qiŋaRtaq 'edge of shin, ridge of mountain or snow, roof ridge']

PY qəŋaRyak 'jellyfish' [cf. yag-?]
AAY qəŋaRyak 'jellyfish'
CAY BB qəŋaRyak 'striped jellyfish (eaten in fall)'
NSY —
CSY —

PY-S qəŋaRžuk 'snowdrift' [the Sir form suggests that p.b. ðuɣ is involved here, so 's.th. shaped like a nose', but compare qəmiaRžuk under qəmiR[1] — there may be contam. here]
AAY —
CAY K qəŋaRuk 'snowdrift'
NSY qəŋaRuq, [ANLC] qəŋaRuk 'snowdrift'
CSY qəŋaRuk
Sir qəŋəRcəx
Inu [Qaw qiŋaaRuq, Imaq qəŋaRuq 'snowdrift' — probably from Yup]

PE qəŋnəR 'cache' [cf. nəR[1] and perhaps qəŋžuR-]
AAY [note qəŋnəR-, qəŋłəR-, qəŋləR- 'be crowded, cramped']
CAY Nun qəŋnəX* 'water-filled storage hole in ground'
NSY —
CSY —
Sir —
SPI qiŋniq 'small underground cache' [and qiŋni- 'gather and store provisions' — Jen.]
NAI qiŋniq* 'small underground cache'
WCI qiŋniq 'fish cache' [and qiŋni- 'make a fish cache']
ECI qinniq 'cache, store of meat or fish walled in with stones'
GRI qinniq*, NG qiŋniq 'cold storage, winter cache' [and qinni-, NG qiŋni- 'gather winter stores', NG also 'bury']

PY-S qəŋžuR- and **qəŋžaR-** 'gather or assemble' [metathesized in CSY, perhaps due to influence from qəðuɣ; cf. qəŋnəR]
AAY — [for qəŋləR-, qəŋłəR-, qəŋnəR- 'be crowded together, cramped' see qəŋnəR]
CAY —
NSY —
CSY qəžŋuXtə- 'gather, assemble', qəžŋaR- 'together' [the latter in indep. rel. construction; also qəžŋuXuR- 'gather (things) by repeated action', Cap qəžŋaRnəqəxtaq 'dense (tree or shrub growth)', qəžŋuRnəq 'heap']
Sir qəžŋuX 'meeting' [Vakh., who marks this as being from Chap; for qəžŋuXtə- 'gather firewood' see qəðuɣtaR- under qəðuɣ]

PI qəpak- 'be angry' [cf. qəvə(t)- and vaɣ?]
SPI —
NAI —
WCI Car B. Lake qipak- 'make menacing gestures' [Schn., who also has qipasaq 'anger' for 'adg']
ECI qipak- 'send s.o. away, not wanting them around

(because they irritate or hold one too close)', qipaɣi- 'reject, send away', qipasuk- 'be fed up with s.o., be vengeful'
GRI NG qipak- 'be angry'

PE qəpə- 'tie' [there is conflation between this and qipə- in non-Imaq Inu]
AAY —
CAY Nun qəptə- 'roll up skirt of garment and tie at waist' [elsewhere qəpyun, qəpsun 'dancer's belt, sash']
NSY qəputaq 'strap given to shaman as partial compensation for treatment of patient' [ANLC]
CSY qəpə- 'tie' [and qəputə- 'tie up, lash', qəpn̥əq 'bundle' and qəputaq 'string, rope'; perhaps also qəpXaʀ- 'work']
Sir qəpəʀətaX 'rope', qəpəɬuɣət(ə)- 'join, attach', qəpəɬuxtə- 'gather' [and qəpuɬəX 'packing'; qəpənəX 'dog' (lit. 'one that is attached') probably belongs here also]
SPI qivižaq, Imaq qəvətaq 'bundle' [and Imaq qəvəžuziiža- 'give skin to shaman as compensation for treatment']
NAI qipitaq 'bundle'
WCI —
ECI qipisima- 'be rolled up (cloth or s.th. bound in string), roll up and tie with string' [for qipit- 'roll up' see under qipə-]
GRI — [for qipi- 'coil up, twist' see qipə-]

PY qəʀaʀ- and **qəʀataʀ-** 'rise up' [cf. qaʀə- and qəʀuʀ-]
AAY Xa-, XaXtə- 'get hollow, get blistered, come loose from surface', XaataXtə- 'lift up'
CAY qəXa- 'rise up, increase in volume', qəXataXtə- 'lift up by itself, be lifted by the wind'
NSY ʀataʀ-, Xataʀ- 'come off (from the surface), lift' [ANLC; Men. has Xata- 'go up, lift off, rise', Xatakumyu- 'raise', and Xata(ʀ)- 'cut up animal or lumps of frozen snow']
CSY Xataʀ- 'rise from surface (bird taking off, skin peeling off, etc.)' [and Xaa 'patch of epidermis come loose on an animal', XataXqə- 'peel off']
Sir [Vakh. has qaXtuXtə- 'rip off, separate' from Rub.'s texts]

PY qəʀaʀun 'sail' [cf. un]
AAY Xaa'un, Xaaʀun 'sail'
CAY qəʀaʀun, qəXəʀun
NSY —
CSY —

PY qəʀiʀ- 'be shiny' [cf. qaʀu-?]
AAY Xiʀ- 'be shiny, brightly gleaming'
CAY qəXiXcəte- 'be shiny', qəXiXcaʀ- 'polish, make shiny'
NSY —
CSY —

PE qəʀləʀ- 'push through or in under'
AAY qəXləXtə- 'jam in, get gammed in', [and qəXn̥aʀ-, qəXn̥iqe- 'feel cramped']
CAY qəXɬəʀ- 'be uncomfortably crowded (space)', qəXəɬqutə-, qəXəɬXutə- 'be uncomfortably crowded (people)', qəXtə- 'put into a confining space' [and Ras. has Nun qeRRsooraut 'wound plug']
NSY —
CSY — [for qaʀlu(-) 'harness' see əkəʀlu(-)]
Sir — [for qəʀlə- 'harness' see əkəʀlu(-)]
SPI qiʀlu- 'penetrate beneath' [Jen.]
NAI [PH qiʀluvaq- 'store away']
WCI Cop qiʀliq- 'lever up', qiʀluti- 'stick underneath' [Pryde]
ECI qiʀli(q)- 'try to squeeze into, put on (clothing, etc.)' [Lab 'push under or through s.th.' acc. Peck; qiʀliʀaq- 'try to touch another's sexual parts', qiʀlut(i)- 'put under s.th.']
GRI qiʀɬiʀ- 'push s.th. under or next to something, push one's way through', EG qiʀtiʀ- 'drive animal across ice', NG qiʀlit- 'hide away' [and qiʀɬut(i)- 'pass below, pass under the cross- strap of kayak', qiʀɬaaʀ- 'penetrate (rain or damp)', qiiʀɬiʀ- 'grab in the crotch']

PI qəʀləʀun 'marlin spike or similar tool' [cf. un]
SPI qiʀluun 'piece of ivory used to loosen a knot'
NAI qiʀlutaq 'marlin spike for adjusting back lashings of a bow' [Jen.]
WCI Cop qiʀlut 'marlin spike for bow' [Ras.]
ECI —
GRI —

PY qəʀtunəq 'gas in stomach' [cf. qəʀuʀ-, tu-[1] and nəʀ[1]]
AAY qəXtunəq 'gas in stomach'
CAY qəXtunəq*
NSY —
CSY aXpunəq*

PY qəʀu(C)aʀtə- 'get a splinter' [cf. qəʀaʀ- and qaʀə-?]
AAY əXuaXtə-, XuʀaaXtə- 'have a stick go through roof of mouth'
CAY qəXuaXtə- 'get a splinter'
NSY —
CSY —

PY qəʀuʀ- 'inflate' [cf. qaʀə- and qəʀaʀ-]
AAY Xuʀ- 'inflate'
CAY qəXuʀ- 'inflate' [for qəXuyaq 'goose pimple, air bubble under ice' see qiʀuya-]
NSY ʀuʀ-, Xuuʀ-, ʀuuʀ- 'inflate' [ANLC; Men. has Xuʀa(ʀ)-, XuʀaXtə-]
CSY Xuuʀ- 'inflate' [and XuuXpaxtaʀ- 'puff up, blister']

PE qətəɣ- and **qətɣəʀ-** 'jump (about)' [compare pətɣəʀ- for the second form]
AAY qətxəʀ- 'jump' [and qəcŋə-, qəcəŋŋə- 'run' — also kətxəʀ-]
CAY qəcəɣ- 'jump' [and qəcŋə-, qəcŋəXtə- 'bounce off, jump up']
NSY qətxaʀ- 'jump (up and down)' [ANLC; Men. has qətxəxtəʀ- 'attack']
CSY qətxəʀ- 'jump, endeavor to consummate marriage (man claiming bride at her parents' house)' [and note perhaps kətanqu- 'run fast']

Sir qətxəɣ- 'jump' [Vakh.; Em. has qətəʀ- 'throw self at, attack (animal or person), jump (in training)' and qətxaqə(s)- 'jump up and down in sport']
SPI ➟
NAI qɨtik- 'play games'
WCI qitik- Net 'amuse oneself with athletics' [Ras.], Car 'play cards' [Schn.]
ECI qitik- Aiv, NBI 'play (children)', Lab 'be joky, giddy' [Schn.]
GRI qitiɣ- 'dance' [and qittaʀ- 'be choppy (sea)']

PI qəžɣəq- 'jump up and down' [same source as second form qətɣəʀ- above?]
SPI qiɣžiq-, Qaw qižɣi-, 'do wolf dance'
NAI qižɣɨq-, qišɣɨq- 'do special kneeling dance', Mal qižɣiataq- 'jump for joy'
WCI Sig qiɣɣiq- 'jump' [and Pryde has Cop qilɣiq- 'jump over']
ECI qiɣɣɨ(q)- 'jump in place'
GRI qiššiʀ- [old ortho. qigsser-] 'leap into the air' [S.-L. has qiɣ- 'hop', but this may be spurious: Kl. suggests it is a 'deep root'; NG qixxik- 'jump', which appears as 'be born' as a shaman's word in Kroeb.; note EG qittaɣattaC- 'jump, take off (on skis or sled)' (Robbe and Menn.)]

PY qətək 'tuber of mare's-tail (black clump)' [compare kətəɣ, with which there may be contam.]
AAY qətək 'coal' [and note qəXqaq, XəXtaq 'plant that swans eat from bottom of lakes']
CAY qətək 'underground tuber of mare's-tail, piece of coal' [and note NSU qəXqaq 'Eskimo potato']
NSY —
CSY —

PE qətəʀ 'middle (of body)' [cf. Aleut quc(i)ɣ- 'space between, interval']
AAY qətəʀ- 'bend over backward' [postural root]
CAY qətəʀ- 'lie on back' [postural root], NSU qətəq* 'middle'
NSY qətəʀ- 'lean back' [ANLC]
CSY qətəq* 'spinal area, back, swim bladder of fish', qətəʀ- 'bend backward'
Sir [note perhaps qətəX 'morning, early']
SPI qitiq 'middle, lower back' [Imaq also verbal 'lean back']
NAI qɨtɨq* 'waist, middle'
WCI qitiq 'waist, middle, small of back' [and qitiʀaq- 'shoot in middle']
ECI qitiq 'middle, waist' [and qitiq- 'be noon', qitiʀaq- 'reach half way in a journey, handle by the middle']
GRI qitiq* 'middle, waist, half' [and qitiʀaʀ- 'be half way']

PI qətəqliq 'middle finger' [cf. qliʀ]
Yup [NSU qətəqłiq* 'middle finger' is probably a loan from Inu]
Sir [for qəɬqusitaX 'ring finger' see qaqu(ʀ)]
SPI qitiqłiq 'middle finger'
NAI qitiqłiq*
WCI qitiqłiq
ECI qitiʀsiq
GRI qitiʀłiq*

PI qətəqpaq- 'reach the middle' [cf. vaʀ-]
SPI qitiqpaq- 'reach the middle'
NAI qɨtiqpaq- 'be or put in the middle'
WCI —
ECI qitiqpa(q)- 'fill or empty so that s.th. is half full'
GRI qitiʀpaʀ- 'have reached half way across (stretch of water)'

PI qətəqquq- and **qətəqqaq-** 'be halfway'
SPI qitiquq- 'be noon, reach halfway point' [and Imaq qətqaun '(in) half']
NAI qitiqqaq- 'be halfway, be noon'
WCI qitiqqaq- 'cut across middle, be noon'
ECI qitiqqaq 'half' [and qitiqqut(i)- 'half fill']
GRI qitiqqut(i)- 'be halfway through', qitiqquut 'half'

PE qətəʀaʀ 'spinal cord' [cf. aʀ]
AAY qət<ʀ>aq PWS, AP 'fish kidney, dark meat under skin of fish', KP 'tail of whale'
CAY [note qətxaq (for qətXaq?) 'neural arch of spinal disk in fish backbone']
NSY —
CSY —
Sir —
SPI Imaq qitiʀaq 'spinal cord'
NAI qɨtɨʀaq
WCI qitiʀaq
ECI qitiʀaq
GRI qitiʀaq 'spinal cord, marrow'

PE qətunʀaʀ 'offspring' [cf. qətut- and n(ə)ʀaʀ(aʀ)?]
AAY —
CAY qətunʀaq* 'son', Nun 'offspring'
NSY —
CSY —
Sir —
SPI qituʀnaq 'son' [and Ras. has W qitunʀa(q) 'trace']
NAI qitunʀaq 'offspring' [also 'individual dog trace']
WCI Sig qitunʀaq 'young of animal (esp. bear), Cop qitunʀaq 'offspring (animal or human)' [Met. also has 'dog trace', as does Dor. for B. Lake; Pryde has Cop, Net qitunŋaq 'adult offspring']
ECI qituʀŋaq 'child'
GRI qituʀnaq

PI qətusuk- 'chuckle or feel like laughing' [cf. qətut- and yuɣ-?]
SPI —
NAI qɨtusuk- 'chuckle over s.th.' [qɨtusuŋnaq- 'be funny']
WCI qitusuk- 'feel like laughing' [qitusuŋnaq- 'be funny' — Lowe]
ECI —
GRI qitusuɣ- 'be loose-limbed (person), have slept too long, behave in an unseemly manner' [qitutsaɣ- 'crack up with laughter']

PE qətut- 'be soft and pliable'
AAY KP, AP qətutə- 'be soft, pudding-like'
CAY qətutə- 'be soft, pudding-like'
NSY —
CSY qətusqaaq, qətusqʷaaq 'soft thing', qətumla 'soft dirt, snow'
Sir qətutaʀałəʀəX 'soft, crumbly' [Em.]
SPI Qaw qitut- 'be soft, pliable', qituɣli- 'get soft'
NAI qitut- 'be soft, tender, pliable', qituɣli- 'become pliable'
WCI qitut- 'be supple, soft'
ECI qitut- 'be flexible, supple'
GRI qituɣ- 'be pliable, soft'

PE qəvcaɣ- 'splatter or splash'
AAY —
CAY qəfcaa- 'splatter repeatedly' [qəfcəXtə- 'splatter, scatter']
NSY —
CSY —
Sir —
SPI qipsak- 'bounce off, ricochet'
NAI qifsak-, Nu qipsak- 'fly off after impact (e.g. chip)' [PH qipsak 'wooden top']
WCI qipsaɣaq- 'splash, sprinkle with water'
ECI qitsa(C)- 'flick some drops of water at'
GRI qissaɣ- [old ortho. qivsag-] 'jerk (e.g. fishing rod)' [and qissattuʀ- 'jerk back and forth, wriggle', SWG qissattuʀfiɣi- 'splash (s.o.)', qissirłuk 'slushy, drizzly weather', NG qissiʀluk 'rain' — also verbal]

PE qəvə(t)- 'go away angrily' [cf. qəpak-; the relat., if any, to əqə-[2] is obscure]
AAY Kod quxtə- 'give up (on)'
CAY qəftə- 'neglect, forsake', NS 'be angry, frustrated' [for NSK əqəvə- 'be angry' see əqə-[2] — it could be a blend]
NSY qəvə- 'be angry' [ANLC also 'be evil']
CSY qəfłiqə- 'be angry (of men)'
Sir — [but note yuXłiqə- 'be angry (of men)' (Orr) — compare with yumə- 'scold' under iŋut-[2]]
SPI qiwit-, quit- 'go away angry, turn back on' [Jen. has 'be ashamed' for W]
NAI qivɨt- 'go off in a huff, act indignantly' [and qivži- 'cause to go away indignant']
WCI qivit- 'be fed up, turn one's back on s.o. and leave', also 'commit suicide' [Met. spells these differently, though the second is presumably a secondary sense of the first; note also qiviyyuti- 'be disgusted, disconcerted by']
ECI qivit- 'be disconcerted, angry, dispairing' [and note Aiv qipit- 'turn one's back', as if from PE qipə-; Ras. has qibsigi- 'make objections against' for Igl]
GRI qivit- 'go into mountains in disappointment or anger', qissima- [old ortho. qivsima-] 'have hidden in anger (of child)'

PE qəvləʀ- 'glitter' [cf. Aleut qum̥a- 'be white', Atkan qmaaluɣ- 'be dry and white at low tide (beach)']
AAY C qiuɣlər-, PWS, Kod quɣləʀ- 'glitter, shine' [and quɣləq 'fish scale']
CAY qəvləXtə-, Nun qəvli-, NSU qəvlia- 'shine, glitter, sparkle'
NSY qəvləʀ- [and nom. qəvləq 'luster, shine, sparkle' (ANLC)]
CSY qavləʀ- 'glitter', qəlməʀ- 'be shiny' [also uvləʀ- and əvləq 'gloss, sheen']
Sir —
SPI qivliq- 'be greasy, oily', qivlaik- 'be shiny'
NAI qɨvlaaq-, qɨvlɨqtaq- 'glitter'
WCI qivliq- 'glitter, shine'
ECI qilli(q)- 'glitter, shine' [Saul — Lab qivliq- 'glitter' in Bourq.; Schn. has qillitit- 'make shine with s.th.' and qilliili- 'lose brilliance']
GRI qiłłiʀ- 'be bright, shine, glitter', qiłłaaʀ- 'glitter' [and Kroeb. has NG qeblâ 'knife' as a shaman's word; note also qiłłi- 'get blotchy (face of pregnant woman)']

PI qəvlaʀik- 'be glittery' [cf. kig-]
SPI qivlaik- 'be shiny'
NAI —
WCI qivlaʀik- 'be very shiny' [and Schn. has qillarittuq 'fir tree' for 'adg']
ECI qillaʀik- 'be brilliant or sparkling'
GRI qiłłaʀiɣ- 'be shiny'

PI qəvləqiak 's.th. shiny'
SPI qivlaʀiaq 's.th. shiny'
NAI qivliqiak 'silk, shiny material'
WCI Cop qivliqiak 'mica' [Pryde]
ECI qillaqiaq 'mica, brilliant stone'
GRI qiłłakiak 'glitter'

qəža '(hacked up) whale blubber' [apparently a loan from Chukchi qəren 'remains of hacked up frozen blubber']
AAY —
CAY —
NSY qəža 'whale blubber'
CSY qəža 'aged whale skin' [SLI — Rub. has qəža(t) 'whale skin with blubber' for Chap.]

PI qianʀaqtuq '(blue or cross?) fox' [cf. qiʀnəʀ- and qiðəʀ — contam.?, but note the metathesis of *ʀn to nʀ in Sig under qiʀnəʀ-]
Yup [NSY qiaʀnaqtuq 'blue fox' is prob. a loan from SPI]
SPI Imaq qiaʀnatuq 'blue fox'
NAI qianʀaq 'cross fox'
WCI Cop qianʀaqtuq 'blue fox'
ECI qiaʀŋatuq 'silver fox'
GRI —

PE qi(C)aʀ 'lining of intestines?' [cf. qi(C)aʀ-?]
AAY PWS qiak 'thin layer of meat with fat on, meat between ribs and fat of seal'
CAY qiaq 'edible lining of seal intestine' [and note Nun qiɣaX 'seal flesh with blubber' (ANLC)]
NSY qiaq 'outer layer of intestine' [but ANLC 'walrus gut outer layer'; for qəža 'tripe' see qəcaʀu(C)aʀ]
CSY —
Sir —

SPI qiaq 'outer layer of bearded seal intestine'
NAI qia(q), pl. qižžat
WCI qiaq
ECI qiaq 'peritonium, membrane that covers intestines'
GRI qia(k), NG qiaq 'epidermis of stomach, gut or gullet when pulled off to use'

PY qi(C)aʀ- 'slip' [cf. qi(C)aʀ and EA qðina- 'be slippery', qðili- 'walk in a slippery place', qðit- 'slip or glance off']
AAY —
CAY —
NSY qiaʀni- 'skate (on ice)', qiaʀnaq 'treacherous ice' [L.-T.; ANLC also 'moss and lichen, slippery place' for the latter]
CSY qiiʀnaʀ- 'be slippery', qiiʀnitə- 'slip on the ice'
Inu [Imaq qiaʀnižaʀnəq 'skating (on ice)' is probably a loan from NSY]

PE qiðə- 'cry' [cf. Aleut qiða- 'cry'; the Sir form may be borrowed from the CSY replacing an earlier form *qicə-, accounting for the y]
AAY qi<y>a- 'cry'
CAY qia-, HBC, UY, UK, LI qəya-
NSY qiya-
CSY qiya-
Sir qiyə- 'cry' [Vakh. also has qəyə-]
SPI qia- 'cry'
NAI qi<ž>a- 'cry' [and qižžan 'lament, reason for crying']
WCI qia-
ECI qia- 'cry' [and note qiaʀsu(k)- 'whistle, moan (wind)']
GRI qia- 'cry' [and as nominal qia(k) 'crying'; qiaʀsuɣ- 'make a whining sound']

PE qiðəʀ 'gray hair' [cf. Atkan Aleut qiðaayu-s, EA qiðaaya-n, qiðaayu-n 'gray hair']
AAY qiiq 'gray hair'
CAY qiiq*
NSY qiiq
CSY qiiq^{w}*
Sir —
SPI qiʀžiq, Qaw qižʀiq
NAI qižʀiq 'gray hair'
WCI qiiq, Sig qiyʀiq 'gray hair' [Dor. has qižiq for Net]
ECI qiiq 'gray hair' [and qiiʀattuq 'silver fox' — compare qianʀaqtuq]
GRI qiiq 'gray hair'

PE qi(C)ət- and **qit-** 'be convulsed' [the second form contracted from *qiðət-? — but cf. Aleut qit- 'contract, be cramped (sinews or other parts of body)', eastern EA 'be twisted (rope)', western EA 'turn (e.g. walking)']
AAY qistə- 'have a convulsion'
CAY qistə-
NSY —
CSY —
Sir —
SPI qiit- 'have a convulsion'
NAI ➞
WCI Cop qiiqi- 'convulse, jerk, throw a fit', qiiXXuq- 'have a fit' [Pryde, who also has qiihuk- 'want to take revenge'; Met. has qiillaqtuq- 'work with all one's strength']
ECI qiit- 'have a great desire for', Lab 'be parched with thirst', qiitiq- 'be in death agony' [and qiitsiaq 's.th. longed for', qiimitiC- 'want'; Peck has ke'mituk- 'long for s.th.'; Andersen et al. have qii- 'die of thirst' for Lab]
GRI qiit- 'long for s.th.' [also spelled qiiɣ-; also qisua- 'get a spasm, shiver, give a start', qiitsat 'food longed for', and note qiila- 'be agile', qiima- 'be in high spirits']

PE qi(C)əliʀ- 'be worked up (with longing)?'
AAY —
CAY qiiləXtə- 'experience and show strong joyful feelings'
NSY [qiləʀyuxsaʀ- 'encourage to do s.th.']
CSY qiliʀ(yuɣ)- 'covet, desire' [emot. root]
Sir —
SPI —
NAI qiiliɣžuk- 'clench fists and teeth in frustration'
WCI qiilik- 'have a great desire for, make a grimace (with mouth and teeth when work goes badly)'
ECI —
GRI qiiliʀ- 'long for s.th.' [part. mood qiiliʀsuq, etc.]

PI qiiŋa- 'grimace (rolling eyes)' [cf. ŋa-[1]]
SPI —
NAI qiiŋa- 'roll eyes (person having a fit)'
WCI —
ECI qiiŋa- 'look to one side of person one is talking to (eyes)'
GRI qiiŋa- 'be oblique (Mongoloid eyes)'

PI qiiqšuq- 'have a seizure' [cf. qðuʀ-]
SPI Qaw qiiqšuq- 'have a convulsion'
NAI qiiqšuq- 'have an epileptic convulsion'
WCI qiiqsuq- 'have a seizure, fall into an epileptic convulsion'
ECI qiiʀsu(q)- 'have an epileptic seizure'
GRI qiiʀsuʀ- 'be in agony of death (esp. of animal)'

PE qiɣɣu 'talus of rocks'
AAY qiuq 'rock, cliff'
CAY qiuq* 'bluish-gray rock or mountain [influenced by qiyu(ɣ)(-) — compare qiɣuiq 'squirrel' under qiɣuiq]
NSY —
CSY —
Sir —
SPI qiɣɣut 'pile of rocks, talus'
NAI —
WCI Car qiɣɣuq 'talus' [Ras., who writes it qixoq; he also has Net qiXoq 'heap of stones']
ECI qiɣɣuit 'rocks of medium size', qiɣɣulait 'heap of stones' [Peck has kiggut 'heap of stones' for Lab]
GRI qiXXut, NG qiɣɣut 'heap of rocks at foot of mountain'

PI qiɣluk- 'regret a loss' [the relat. (if any) with qivʀu- is obscure]
SPI qiʀluk- 'regret a loss'
NAI qiɣlʸuk- 'regret a loss' [trans. qiɣluɣi-]
WCI qiɣluɣi- 'feel anguish over', Cop, Net qiɣluk- 'avenge' [Ras.]
ECI qiɣluk- 'take revenge'
GRI qiłłuɣ- 'be angry because of something lost' [old ortho. qigdlug-; Oqaatsit has qiłłuɣ-, qiłłuɣi- 'not want to lose (s.th. or s.o.)']

PY qiɣuiq 'squirrel' [cf. qiɣɣu and (C)iʀ?]
AAY —
CAY qiɣuiq 'tree squirrel'
NSY qiiwiik 'ground squirrel' [ANLC]
CSY —

PE qiɣuʀ- 'cut hair' [cf. Aleut qiɣaɣ- 'cut, mow', qiiɣa-X 'grass', Atkan also qiɣumluɣ-, qiɣamluɣ- 'clip, sheer, give a haircut to']
AAY qiuʀ- 'cut down brush'
CAY qiuʀ- 'shear, clip off growth, cut closely', Nun qiuqłax 'hair'
NSY — [for qiŋuq 'long hair of reindeer skin' see qivyu(ʀ)]
CSY qiɣuʀ- 'cut hair short, shear, mow'
Sir qiɣəʀ- 'trim' [Em. has 'remove hairs from skin']
SPI qiuq- 'thin, trim fur'
NAI qiuq-
WCI qiuq-
ECI qiuq 'cut hair' [and qiuralik 'powder snow'?]
GRI qiuʀ- 'cut, pare down'

PI qiɣuʀvik 'cutting board' [cf. ðviɣ]
Yup — [CSY qiɣuʀvik 'barber shop' is a recent independent parallel development]
SPI —
NAI qiɣuʀvik 'wooden board for scraping skin or cutting leather'
WCI Car? qiuʀvik 'wooden board for cutting tobacco' [Schn. 'adg']
ECI —
GRI qiuʀfik 'cutting board (for working skin)'

PI qiiqluq- and **qiilluq-** 'have something hanging from rectum?' [the relat. — if any — to qilu is obscure]
SPI Qaw qiiqłuʀniq 'internal organ of caribou or reindeer'
NAI qiiłłuaq 'piece of excrement hanging from rectum'
WCI Cop qilluaq 'turd hanging from rectum' [Pryde]
ECI qilluaqatsi(t)- 'have s.th. indigestible hanging from anus (dog)' [qilluaqatsiq 's.th. hanging from anus']
GRI qiiʀłuaqatsi- 'have s.th. hanging (e.g. sinews) out of rectum'

PE qikaʀ- 'stand (around)' [there may be a link to qikə-[1]]
AAY — [but note qikaXłuk 'sinew']
CAY qikaʀ- 'ponder, standing still and worrying about the future' [and perhaps qikiq 'tripod for holding pot over fire' — compare the NG below]
NSY —
CSY —
Sir —
SPI qiɣaq- 'stay home from work or hunting' [and Imaq qiɣaləq 'life'?]
NAI qikaq-, qikaaluk- 'stand around, loiter', PH 'stand up', Nu 'be standing'
WCI Sig qikaq- 'stop' [Pet.]
ECI qikaq- Tar 'do nothing, hang around at home', NBI, SB 'be stopped' [Dor.]
GRI qiqaʀ-, NG qikaq- 'stand upright' [NWG also 'be confirmed'; NG qikaut 'tripod, stand']

PE qikə-[1] 'be shy or respectful'
AAY qiki- 'be bashful' [and note PWS qikiXtə- 'cock head to side']
CAY qikcuɣ(yuɣ)- 'feel respect'
NSY —
CSY qiiksuɣ- 'feel uneasy due to being watched, feel bashful, self-conscious'
Sir —
SPI ➟
NAI qiki- 'feel insecure' [Seiler has 'be embarassed or intimidated by s.o.' for Mal; qikiɣi- 'respect, admire'; for qukiɣi- 'feel that s.o. is too clean and orderly so hesitate' see qukəɣə-]
WCI ➟
ECI ➟
GRI qissaaʀ- 'be shy, embarassed'

PE qikciɣ- 'look askance at s.o.'
AAY qixciɣ- 'look under one's eyebrows at (e.g. older person admonishing s.o.)'
CAY qixciɣ- 'look sideways without turning head or out of corner of one's eye' [Hinz has 'fear, be wary of'; qikciɣnaXqə- 'cause one to feel respectful']
NSY qixsiɣ- 'look sideways, out of corner of eye' [ANLC]
CSY qiŋsiɣ- 'look sideways at, glance at' [influenced by qiŋiʀ-?]
Sir —
SPI qiksik- 'fear' [Jen.]
NAI qiksiɣi- 'feel shy, diffident toward'
WCI qiksiŋaq- 'look at sideways, moving only the eyes, not the head' [Pryde has Cop qixxik-, (trans.) qixximik- 'glance out of corner of eye (at)']
ECI qitsimiɣaq- 'look sideways, moving the eyes'
GRI qissiɣi- 'be shy, afraid of, have caught a glimpse of' [old ortho. qigsigi-; qissimiɣ- 'glance at, look askance at'; and note EG qitsumaliq 'frowning']

PI qikə-[2] and **qikaaq-** 'crunch underfoot (snow)' [the second form with aʀ-; there seems to be contam. with qiʀə- in some forms here here]
SPI qiʀʀaq- 'make crunching noise walking on dry snow' [influenced by qiʀə-?]
NAI qikaallit- 'creak underfoot (packed snow)', qikiʀʀaq 'creaking of snow underfoot', qiʀiiluk-, Nu qikaaluk- 'make squeaking noise walking on ice' [the latter elsewhere = 'loiter, stand around' — see qikaʀ-; note also PH qiʀʀiʀʀaq- 'creak (footsteps in snow)' and Nu

qiqiʀʀit- 'startle with sound of one's feet in snow']
WCI qikaq 'sound of footsteps outside on gravel', Car B. Lake qikaluk- 'be sound of footsteps' [Schn. for the latter; Pryde has Cop qikaak-, Net qikiʀʀiq- and Sig, Cop qikiʀʀaq- 'make noises walkiong in snow']
ECI qikiʀʀaq 'crunching sound underfoot' [Schn. also has qiqiʀʀaq, and qiqiʀʀi(C)-, qiqiʀʀiyaq- 'crunch underfoot (snow)']
GRI qiʀaaʀ-, NG qikaaqpaluk- 'crunch underfoot (snow)'

PE qikəʀtaʀ 'island'
AAY qikəXtaq 'island'
CAY qikəXtaq 'island' [and cf. qikəXtə- 'go up and scan surrounding area']
NSY qikəXtaq 'island' [Jen.]
CSY qiiXqaq
Sir qiqəX
SPI qiɣiqtaq 'island'
NAI qikiqtaq
WCI qikiqtaq
ECI qikiqtaq
GRI qiqiʀtaq, NG qikiqtaq

PE qikmiʀ 'dog' [there could be a link to qikə-[1] — cf. p.b. miqə-]
AAY AP qikm̥iq 'dog'
CAY [Nun qikm̥iXtaləx — place name, lit. 'place with lots of dogs'] ➡
NSY qiqm̥iʀaq 'dog'
CSY qikm̥iq 'dog'
Sir — [for qəpənəX 'dog' see qəpə-]
SPI qipmiayak 'puppy', Di qipmiq 'dog'
NAI qimmiq, Mal qipmiq, Point Barrow qiŋmiq 'dog'
WCI qiŋmiq, qimmiq, Net, Car qi'miq 'dog' [Dor. has qiŋmiq for B. Lake and Net; Lowe has Cop qinmiq — also Pryde]
ECI qimmiq, qiŋmiq 'dog' [the latter in Bourq. Ras., Boas and B.-S.; note also Aiv qimmiʀi- 'feed dogs' and qimmiqqutiksaq 'dog food' — Schn.]
GRI qimmiq 'dog' [old ortho. has qingmeq; and note qimmiʀi- 'have as a house pet (e.g. fox or bird)', NG qimiʀi- 'feed dogs', qimiqqut 'dog food']

PY qikmiʀuaq 'upper arm' [cf. ŋ(ŋ)uðaʀ; compare qikmi(C)uðaʀ below, a parallel formation]
AAY —
CAY —
NSY qiqm̥iʀuaq 'upper arm'
CSY qikm̥iʀʷaaq* 'bone in upper arm, ulna'
Inu [Imaq qiqmiŋuaq 'upper arm' — from Yup?]

PE qikmi(C)uðaʀ 'willow catkin' [cf. ŋ(ŋ)uðaʀ]
AAY qikm̥iɣuaq 'pussy willow'
CAY qikm̥iʀuaq 'willow catkin'
NSY —
CSY —
Sir —
SPI [note Qaw qipmiayaŋuaq 'catkin']
NAI qimmiužaq 'willow catkin'
WCI —
ECI qimmiŋuaq
GRI —

PE qiku 'clay'
AAY qikuq 'clay, mud'
CAY qiku, qikuq 'clay, clay oil lamp'
NSY qiku
CSY qiku 'clay'
Sir —
SPI qiɣu, Qaw qikuyaq
NAI qiku
WCI qiku
ECI qiku 'cement'
GRI qiquq 'lime, whitewash', NG qikuq 'lead', EG qiʀik 'clay' [qiqik in Holm's list]

PE qilaɣ 'sky' [cf. apparently Aleut qila-X 'morning', qilam 'in the morning', qilaɣan 'tomorrow']
AAY qilak 'sky'
CAY qilak
NSY qilak 'sky, cloud'
CSY qilak 'sky' [qilaɣʷaaq 'cloud']
Sir qiləx 'sky'
SPI qilak 'sky, cloud, ceiling'
NAI qilʸak 'sky, roof, ceiling'
WCI qilak
ECI qilak 'sky, palate' [and note qilaŋŋua(q)- 'stand out in silhouette against the sky']
GRI qilak, EG qilaq 'sky' [qilaŋŋuuʀ- 'stand out in silhouette against the sky']

PE qilaɣaʀ 'roof of mouth or ceiling' [cf. aʀ]
AAY K qila(ɣ)aq 'roof of mouth'
CAY qilaɣaq
NSY qilaɣaq
CSY Chap qilaɣaq 'ceiling, palate'
Sir —
SPI qilaɣaq 'palate'
NAI qilʸaɣaq 'palate' [and qilʸaaq 'thin maktak from whale's mouth']
WCI qilaɣaq 'palate'
ECI —
GRI qilaaq 'palate, ceiling'

PE qilaɣłuɣ 'cloud' [cf. łuɣ(-)]
AAY K qilaxłuk 'cloud'
CAY Nun qilaxłux
NSY qilaxłuk
CSY Chap qilaxłuk
Sir qilaxłəx
SPI qilaɣluk
NAI qilaɣluk- 'be cloudy and windy'
WCI —
ECI —
GRI —

PE qilaɣmi(C)utaʀ '(kind of) lemming' [cf. miʀu, the creature is supposed to have fallen down out of the sky onto the snow acc. to folklore in various areas]
AAY —

CAY qilaɣmiutaq 'lemming'
NSY —
CSY —
Sir —
SPI qilaŋmiutaq 'white lemming'
NAI qilʸaŋmiutaq 'collared lemming'
WCI qilaŋmiutaq 'white lemming'
ECI —
GRI —

PE qilaɣ- 'knit or weave' [the relat. to qiłəʀ- is obscure]
AAY K qilaɣ-, C qilaʀ- 'knit, make net'
CAY qilaɣ-
NSY qilaɣ- 'knit' [ANLC; Men. has qilaʀ- 'knit, weave']
CSY qilaɣ- 'make a net'
Sir qiləɣ- [Orr]
SPI qilak- 'knit, weave net'
NAI qilʸak- 'knit'
WCI qilak-
ECI qilak-, Igl qilaksuq- 'tie'
GRI NWG qilattaa- [old ortho. qilagtai-] 'knit', NG qilaxxuq- 'tie', qilaxxama- 'be tied'

PI qilaluɣaq 'beluga'
SPI —
NAI qilʸaluɣaq, pl. qilʸalukkat 'beluga, white whale'
WCI qilaluɣaq, Net qinaluɣaq [Ras.]
ECI qilaluɣaq, Igl qinaluɣaq 'beluga' [the latter with dissimilation]
GRI qilaluaq, qilaluɣaq qaquʀtaq, EG qialivaʀnaq 'beluga, white whale' [pl. qilalukkat; qilalu(ɣ)aq qiʀniʀtaq, EG qialivaq 'narwhale']

PI qilamət- or **qilavət-** 'catch with a bola' [there may be a relat. to qilaɣ-]
SPI qilavitaun 'bola, jumprope', qilavitaaq- 'play jump-rope'
NAI qilʸamitaun 'bola', qilʸamit(aq)- 'kill with a bola', PH qilavitautit 'bola'
WCI qilamitautit 'whip with bones at end'
ECI qilaviq- 'cast something above or over (long object)'
GRI —

PE qilaŋŋaʀ 'puffin' [cf. perhaps EA qiðaŋa-X, Atkan qizaŋa-X 'ancient murrelet', but the correspondance is irregular]
AAY qilaŋaq 'horned puffin'
CAY qilaŋaq 'tufted puffin'
NSY —
CSY —
Sir —
SPI qilaŋaq
NAI qilʸaŋŋaq 'horned puffin'
WCI —
ECI NBI qilaŋŋaq 'puffin' [Pryde]
GRI qilaŋŋaq

PE qilʀi(q) 'rough-legged hawk'
AAY K qilʀiq 'rough-legged hawk'
CAY Nun qilʀi 'hawk' [ANLC]
NSY —
CSY —
Sir —
SPI Qaw qilʀiq 'rough-legged hawk'
NAI qilʸʀiq
WCI qilʀiq
ECI —
GRI —

PY-S qilu 'intestine' [the relat. (if any) to qiiqluq- is obscure]
AAY qiluq 'intestine'
CAY qiluq 'intestine' [for qəłuq 'colon' see eqlu]
NSY qilu 'intestine'
CSY qilu
Sir qila 'intestine' [and qilunaX 'dried piece of intestines, innards'; Vakh. has qiləʀyiX 'intestines with fat', also qiłəX, qiłəkałuX 'guts' from Rub. — influenced by əqlu?]
Inu [Qaw qilut 'intestine' is probably from Yup]

PE qiluɣ- 'bark' [cf. Aleut qiłuɣ- 'bark']
AAY qiluɣ- 'bark'
CAY qiluɣ-
NSY —
CSY qiluɣ-
Sir —
SPI qiluk-
NAI qilʸuk-
WCI qiluk-
ECI qiluk-
GRI qiluɣ-

PE qiłəʀ- 'tie' [cf. Aleut qisaXtaX 'tied', qisat- 'tie', EA qisa- 'be tied up (kayak)', but also qilʀ-, qilʀi-X 'umbilical cord', qilʀi- 'coil, bend']
AAY qiłəXtə- 'tie'
CAY qiłəXtə-
NSY qiłəXtə-
CSY qiłəXtə-
Sir qiłəXqaʀətə- 'tie', qiłəXtəłəX 'knot'
SPI qiliq- 'tie'
NAI qilʸɨq- 'tie' [and qilʸɨqšuq- 'tie knots in']
WCI qiliq- 'tie'
ECI [note qillaq 'place where sack is laced together, umbilical cord', qiliʀmik 'two kayaks lashed together to make a raft' — also verbal for traveling this way]
GRI qiliʀ- 'tie' [and qiłłaq* 'string around sealing dart, weft or threads of material', qiliʀmiɣ-, qilimmiɣ- 'lash two kayaks together to make a raft', qiliʀšuʀ- 'tie up (e.g. by hands or feet)']

PI qiləqtə 'woman's top-knot (hair)' [cf. ðaʀ or ðə?]
SPI — [but qiliqtat 'bundles tied together']
NAI — [but note qilʸɨqtat 'things lashed together, bundle of five ducks tied together', with ðaʀ]
WCI Car? qiliqtit 'tuft of hair' [Schn. 'adg'; compare qiliqtait 'things lashed together, bundles']
ECI qiliqtit 'traditional woman's chignon'
GRI qiliʀti(t) '(woman's) top-knot' [compare qiliʀtaq 'bundle']

PE qiłəRnəR 'knot' [cf. nəR[1]]
AAY qiłəRnəq 'knot'
CAY qiłəRnəq*
NSY qiłəRnəq
CSY qiłəRnəq*
Sir —
SPI qiliRniq 'knot'
NAI qil^{y}iRniq*
WCI qiliRniq
ECI qiliRniq
GRI qiliRniq*

PE qiłəRutaRiR- 'untie' [cf. utə, ðaR and ŋiR-]
AAY —
CAY qiłXutaiR- 'untie' [qiłXutaq 'rope or string for tying']
NSY [note qiłəRutaq 's.th. to tie with']
CSY —
Sir —
SPI qiliRutaiq- 'untie'
NAI qil^{y}iRutaiq- 'untie, become untied' [and note qil^{y}iRutik 'handcuffs', PH qil^{y}iRun 'string holding drum skin to frame' with un]
WCI qiliRutaiq- 'untie'
ECI [qilaɣuyyai(q)- 'untie']
GRI qiliRuššaaR-, EG qiliiRtaaR- 'loosen, open' [and note qiliRut 's.th. to tie with']

PE qimaɣ- 'run away' [there has been conflation with qəmaɣ- in Inu]
AAY qimaɣ- 'run away'
CAY qimaɣ-
NSY qimaɣ-
CSY qimaɣ-
Sir [Men. has kimawə- 'turn from, flee' — for qimaɣ-?]
SPI qimak- 'run away' [also qimaa-]
NAI qimak- 'flee, leave behind'
WCI qimak- 'leave behind', qimaa- 'flee'
ECI qimak- 'leave behind', qimaa- 'flee' [and qimatsi- 'run away from', qimattuq 'one who is abandoned']
GRI qimaɣ- 'leave (trans.)', qimaa- 'flee'

PI qimmuk- 'go beyond (so s.th. is no longer even)?' [or qəmmuk-]
SPI —
NAI qimmuktit- 'pucker, sew two pieces together so that one side is puckered up'
WCI —
ECI —
GRI qimmut- 'go beyond (e.g. one's goal), put oar alongside boat when one has finished rowing', qimmuut(i)- 'be past' [Kl. has 'put behind one what should be alongside, go further than one should have' for the former]

PE qimuɣ- 'pull (sled)'
AAY AP qimuɣ- 'pull heavy object, tow'
CAY qimuɣ- 'pull vigorously (of dogs) [qimulvak 'big dog']
NSY qimuɣ- 'train (dog or reindeer) to pull a sled'
CSY qimuɣ- 'train to pull sled' [qimuk 'game animal']
Sir [Vakh. has qəmpəłəRaR- 'leave by sled' from Rub.'s texts]
SPI [qimuk 'dragline']
NAI qimuk- 'tow, pull (esp. of dogs) [compare qamuk- 'pull, tow (of humans)' under qamuR-]
WCI qimuk- 'pull a sled'
ECI qimuk- 'tow'
GRI qimuɣ- 'pull (of animal), pull hunting float after it (harpooned seal)' [qimuttuq 'draught animal']

PE qimuɣciR(-) '(travel by) dog team' [cf. qimuɣtə below and liR-]
AAY —
CAY qimuxciR- 'run dogs'
NSY qimuxsiq 'dog team', qimuxsiXtə 'rider (on sled)'
CSY qimuxsiR- 'travel by dog team', qimuxsiq 'dog team'
Sir [Vakh. has qəmcəłəRaX 'dog team']
SPI —
NAI —
WCI Net qimuksiq- 'travel by dog sled' [Pryde, who also has Car qimuksiq 'traveler']
ECI qimutsi(q)- 'travel by dog sled', qimutsiq 'dog team, sled with man on'
GRI qimussiR- 'travel on a sled', qimussiq 'sled (with man on)', qimussit 'sled (with dogs and passengers)' [EG qamutsiq 'sled' is influenced by qamuR-]

PE qimuɣtə 'draught dog (or other animal)' [cf. ðə]
AAY —
CAY qimuxta 'dog' [base qimuxtə-]
NSY —
CSY —
Sir —
SPI qimukti, qimuɣin, Qaw qimuɣun 'dog'
NAI qimukti 'reindeer trained to pull sled'
WCI —
ECI —
GRI qimutsiɣi- 'have or use as draught animal'

PE qinəR- 'look around or through s.th.' [cf. old Atkan Aleut qinaamu- 'keep, observe']
AAY qinəXtə- 'look in through s.th.'
CAY qinəXtə- 'sight (e.g. with binoculars), look out through window, etc.' [and qinRun 'binoculars'; for qinikə-, qiŋiXtə- 'watch s.th. closely and critically' see qiŋiR-]
NSY [note qənəqsitaaq 'movie, cinema, TV' — from SPI?]
CSY qinəXtə- 'look through s.th., sight' [and qiinRutə- 'aim at']
Sir —
SPI qiniq- 'look at, watch' [and qiniraq- 'look through binoculars', qiniRaun, Qaw qinRutik 'binoculars'; qiniqsitaaq 'movie']
NAI qin^{y}iq- 'look at, watch' [and qin^{y}n^{y}aq* 'appearance', qin^{y}iRaun 'camera', Nu 'telescope', Nu, PH qin^{y}iRaq- 'look at with binoculars']
WCI qiniq- 'look around for' [qiniRaq- 'look through binoculars']

ECI qiniq- 'look around for, ask for s.th. (as loan or gift), check nets or traps' [and qiniʀuti, qiʀŋuti 'telescope']
GRI qiniʀ- 'look around for s.th., choose, elect', NG qiniq- 'look through binoculars' [and SWG qiʀnut(it), NWG qiŋŋut(it) 'binoculars, telescope', qinnaʀissaaʀ- 'look good'; Robbe and Menn. also have EG qiʀniʀ- 'choose']

PI qinaa- 'search for' [cf. a-]
SPI —
NAI qinʸaa- 'search for'
WCI qinaa- [Pryde]
ECI qinaa- 'look around for (s.o.)'
GRI qinaaʀi- 'look around for (s.o.)' [intr. qinaaši-]

PY qinki(q) 'kind of sedge'
AAY PWS qiŋkiaq 'three-cornered sedge used for weaving baskets'
CAY Y qinkiq 'female sedge'
NSY —
CSY —

PI qinluq 'carcass'
SPI qilli- 'find a carcass' [and as noun 'carcass' acc. Jen.]
NAI qilʸlʸi- 'find a carcass', Nu qilʸlʸuq* 'remains of dead animal'
WCI qilluq 'carcass'
ECI qilluk 'dead animal that is still flexible, not stiff'
GRI qilluq* [old ortho. qigdloq] 'carcass (of land animal)' [Fab. kigdlok; note also qiłłi-, qiłłuʀ-, qiłłuli- 'find a carcass']

PI qinŋucaaq 'knife for whittling'
SPI —
NAI [Murdoch has qin͡nusa 'antler chisel' and Jen. has qiŋusaq 'tool for cutting bone'; note also qin͡ŋusaaq- 'tie, fasten with twine'?]
WCI Car qiŋŋusaaq 'knife for cutting wood, etc.' [Ras., who also has Cop qinnuhaaq 'implement for cutting horn' — Pryde has qinŋuhaaq]
ECI Igl qiŋŋusaq 'whittling knife' [Math.]
GRI —

PI qinʀaq- 'utter an incantation' [cf. qinaʀ-?]
SPI —
NAI —
WCI qinʀaq- 'pray' [Ras. has qiŋŋaq- 'utter a magic prayer' for Car — Pryde has it as 'seek aid of helping spirit (shaman)']
ECI —
GRI qiʀnaʀ-, qiŋŋaʀ- 'call helping spirit, summon wind (shaman)', NG qiʀŋaq- 'summon good weather by incantation' [the second WG form perhaps by contam. with qiŋŋaʀ-]

PE qinu- 'whine or fuss'
AAY ➡
CAY qinu- 'be upset and fuss (often of child)'
NSY —
CSY qinu- 'be annoyed, disinclined to act'
Sir —
SPI qinu- 'grieve, mourn, die of grief', qinuuq- 'whine, beg, express a desire for'
NAI qinʸu- 'mourn, cry fitfully (of baby), search and cry after young (of animal)' [and note qinʸnʸuaq- 'beg, ask, appeal to someone's sympathy']
WCI qinu- 'ask', Net qinu- 'snarl of dog' [Ras.]
ECI qinu- 'ask, whimper, fuss (of child)', Lab 'beg, ask for, be impatient' [and qinnuaʀaq- 'yell for']
GRI qinu- 'pray, beg', qinuɣi- 'persecute, seek someone's life' [qinnuluuʀ- 'go begging'; note also qiʀnuala- 'shriek in fear']

PE qinuŋit- 'be quiet' [cf. ŋit-]
AAY qinuitə- 'be humble, meek, quiet'
CAY qinuitə- 'be quiet (child), calm (weather)'
NSY —
CSY —
Sir —
SPI qinuit- 'be humble, meek'
NAI qinʸuit-
WCI —
ECI qinuit- 'seldom cry (child), never complain or ask for help', Lab, Iti 'be patient'
GRI —

PE qinuʀaʀ- 'pester s.o.?' [cf. aʀ-]
AAY —
CAY qinuXqə- 'pester' [with ʀqə-?]
NSY —
CSY [note qinunaXqə- 'pester, tease, provoke']
Sir [note qinaʀ- 'bark (dog)'?]
SPI —
NAI —
WCI —
ECI qinuʀaq- 'whine (of dog)' [and note qinuaʀi- 'ask for a woman's hand in marriage']
GRI qinuaʀ- 'shriek, give an alarm, say no'

PE qiŋcuɣ(-) '(get) damaged fingernail'
AAY KP qiŋcuk 'bruised fingernail'
CAY —
NSY —
CSY qiŋsuɣaXtə- 'get a hangnail or broken fingernail'
Sir qiŋsuɣaXtə- [Orr]
SPI —
NAI —
WCI —
ECI —
GRI qissuk [old ortho. qigsuk], qitsuk 'dead flesh below nail' [there may be contam. with qəc(c)uɣ in the second form]

PY qiŋiʀ- 'watch closely' [the relat. — if any — to qinəʀ- and/or quŋyaʀ- is obscure]
AAY PWS qiŋiʀŋa- 'watch closely' [but not use much]
CAY qiŋiXtə-, qinikə- 'watch closely and critically' [the latter influenced by qinəʀ-?]
NSY qiŋixtaʀ- 'look askance at, out of corner of eye' [ANLC]
CSY — [for qiŋsiɣ- 'look at sideways' see qikciɣ- under qikə-^{1}]

PE qiŋŋaʀ- 'show displeasure' [there may be a second set in AAY and CAY here referring to pregnancy, although the semantic link based on a pregnant woman's shunning certain foods suggests one set as given here]
AAY qiŋaʀ- C 'whelp', K 'dislike'
CAY qiŋaq 'fetus', qiŋaʀ- 'be pregnant', Nun, HBC 'dislike certain foods'
NSY qiŋa- 'have an aversion for food' [ANLC; Em. has qiŋaɬəq 'aversion', Men. has qinaʀyuɣ- 'be dissatisfied with guests' — for qiŋaʀyuɣ-, or with contam. from qinu-?]
CSY qiŋaʀ- 'dislike certain foods'
Sir qiŋaʀ(naʀ)- 'be frightening' [Vakh. from Rub.]
SPI Imaq qiŋaʀyu(k)- 'not want to receive guests', qiŋanəq 'disgust' [and Jen. has qingnyarak- 'be angry' for W]
NAI qiŋałłuak- 'show displeasure by being sullen'
WCI Sig qiŋaq- 'have a fierce look'
ECI —
GRI qiŋŋaʀ- 'suffer because one has broken the cultic rules, be irritated', NWG qiŋŋaʀi- 'despise, be angry at'

PI qipaluaq 'inner corner of eye' [cf. qipə-]
SPI —
NAI qipaluaq 'inside corner of eye, steep undercut riverbank, curve'
WCI Sig qipaluaq 'corner of eye' [Pet.]
ECI qipaluaq 'corner of eye near nose' [Saul, also Peck for Lab and Boas for Baf.]
GRI qipaluaq, EG qipilivaaq 'inner corner of eye'

PI qipci- 'be prevented from sleeping' [cf. qipə-?]
SPI Qaw qipsi- 'be unable to go to sleep because of disturbances'
NAI qifsi-, Nu qipsi-
WCI —
ECI qitsi- 'be unable to sleep, snore', Aiv qipsi- 'be prevented from sleeping through anger'
GRI qissi- [old ortho. qivsi-] 'be unable to fall asleep'

PE qipə- 'twist' [cf. Aleut qim̥aɣ- 'be twisted', Atkan also qim̥u- 'twist, be twisted', EA qimðu- 'be twisted', perhaps also Atkan qiim̥i- 'whirl, go round'; there is conflation with PE qəpə- in Inu apart from Imaq]
AAY qipə- 'twist'
CAY qipə- 'twist' [and qipsaq, qipsak, Nun qifsaX 'screw']
NSY qipə- 'twist' [and qipɣaq 'screw' (Em.)]
CSY qiipə- 'twist' [and qipuʀ- 'wind (clock, etc.)']
Sir qipə- 'twist, knit' [Vakh. from Rub.; Men. has qipəʀ-, also qipəstəʀ- 'open'; Em. has qipəʀ- 'wind, unwind']
SPI qivi- 'twist' [and note qivaɣluk 'appendix'; Imaq qivət- 'twist, turn']
NAI qipi- 'twist, wind, writhe' [and qipit- 'wind around', Mal qipiʀuq- 'run around, not keep still (children)']
WCI qipi- 'twist' [and Cop qipiʀuaq- 'trot here and there trying to find place to cross water (caribou)' — Ras.]
ECILab qipi- 'turn, twist' [and qipiŋŋuq 'appendix'; for qipisima- 'roll up and tie' see qəpə-]
GRI qipi- 'twist, turn', NG 'coil up' [and qipilua- 'twist and turn, trying to get loose', qippaq* 'twist', qipiŋŋuq 'appendix']

PE qipðaʀ 'braided sinew' [cf. ðaʀ]
AAY —
CAY qippaq 'thick hand-twisted thread'
NSY qipaq 'thread'
CSY qiipaq 'thread' [note also qiipzaq 'fat on intestines of walrus']
Sir [note qipšay 'fat on intestines']
SPI qipšaq 'braided sinew'
NAI qivžaq, Nu qipžaq 'twine'
WCI qivyat 'caribou sinew thread, tresses in the Indian style'
ECI qiyyaq 'twist of thread or tobacco'
GRI qiššaq 'thread' [and qiššaʀ- 'twist, get tangled']

PE qipði- 'twist sinew for thread' [cf. li-[1]]
AAY —
CAY qipi- 'make thread'
NSY —
CSY Chap qipiłəq* 'making thread'
Sir —
SPI qipši- 'twist sinew for thread'
NAI qivži- 'make thread by twisting, cause to toss and turn in bed' [compare qipci-]
WCI Cop, Car qivyi- 'braid sinews' [Pryde]
ECI —
GRI qišši- 'spin'

PI qipək 'blanket'
SPI qivik 'blanket'
NAI —
WCI Cop qipik 'Eskimo caribou-skin bed, sleeping bag' [Jen.; note also Net qipiɣiaq 'deadfall trap' in Ras.]
ECI qipik 'blanket, wrap' [usually in plural]
GRI qipik 'blanket' [qipiɣ- 'cover with blanket']

PE qiputaʀ 'twisting instrument' [cf. un]
AAY —
CAY —
NSY —
CSY —
Sir qipətaX 'key'
SPI qivutaq 'hard stick used for reinforcing bow, game like horseshoes'
NAI qiputaq 'game like horseshoes played with hard stick'
WCI qiputaq 'sinew twister' (backing reinforcement to bow)' [Pryde]
ECI —
GRI —

PI qipuk- 'scratch'
SPI —
NAI qipuak-, Nu qipuk- 'scratch'
WCI qipuk-, qipuɣaq-
ECI qipuqqi(C)- 'scratch, mark with a scratch' [and

qipiʀuq- 'clean out interior of pipe with a knife', Lab 'carve' in Peck]
GRI [qipiʀuq, qipiqquq 'furrow, channel', qipiʀuʀ- 'hollow out, carve' — influenced by qipə-?; qipuʀaq 'furrow on whale's belly' (compare qipuqqaʀ)]

PE qipuqqaʀ 'humpback whale' [cf. qipuk-]
AAY —
CAY —
NSY qipuqaq 'humpback whale'
CSY Chap qipuqaq
Sir qipuqaX
SPI Imaq qivuqaq 'rorqual' [and K qivuqanilik]
NAI —
WCI —
ECI Baffin qipuqqaq 'fin whale' [Boas]
GRI qipuqqaq 'humpback whale' [EG qipuʀaq acc. Ges.; for qipuʀaq 'furrow on belly of whale' see under qipuk-]

PE qiʀə- or **qiqə-** 'freeze' [cf. qiʀu-; the second form could be by contam. with qikə-[2]]
AAY qəXcu- 'get frostbitten' [and qəXcunəq 'frostbite']
CAY qəXcua-, Nun qəXcuʀ- 'get frostbitten' [and qəXpəXtaq 'Eskimo ice cream', Nun qiqłi- 'harden (of prints in snow)' — ANLC]
NSY ➟
CSY [for qiiʀnaʀ- 'be slippery' see qi(C)aʀ-] ➟
Sir qiʀəʀ- 'shiver, freeze' [Vakh. has qəʀəʀ-]
SPI qiʀit-, Di qəʀət- 'freeze' [with vowel assimilation between the two vowels, as also in Imaq qəʀəłəq 'thin ice'; note also Qaw qiqłiwik 'freezer', qiqšaq 's.th. frozen']
NAI qiqɨ- 'be frozen', qiqit- 'freeze' [for qiʀiiluk- 'creak (footsteps in snow)', Nu qiqiʀʀit- 'startle with sound of one's feet in snow' see qikə-[2]]
WCI qiqi 'the cold', qiqit- 'freeze', Car? qiqi- 'be frozen' [Schn. 'adg'; Dor. has B. Lake qiqiuhivik 'freezer' — Pryde has Cop qiqittivik 'freezer, fridge']
ECI Aiv, NBI qiqi- 'be frozen' [and qiqumaaq 'snow whose surface is refrozen after a first thaw']
GRI qiʀi- 'be frozen stiff', qiʀit- 'freeze' [and EG qiiʀsimaʀtiq (Robbe and Menn. qiʀsimaaʀtiq), qiitsiaq 's.th. frozen']

PI qiʀa(ta)- 'be stiff' [cf. ta-]
Yup [for CAY qəXa- 'rise up', qəXataXtə- 'lift up' see qəʀaʀ-]
SPI — [for qiʀʀaq- 'make creaking noise walking on dry snow' see qikə-[2]]
NAI qiʀata- 'be stiff' [and qiʀʀaq- 'have stiff limbs']
WCI qiʀata- 'be stiff (e.g. frozen)' [qiʀʀaq- 'be stiff (limbs)']
ECI qiʀata-, Lab qiɣata- 'be stiff' [Saul for the first form; Schn. has qiʀattatiq- 'stiffen' and qiʀʀa(C)- 'have caused someone to stiffen (death or cold)']
GRI qiʀata-, EG qaala- 'be stiff'

PI qiʀətəq- or **qiqətəq-** 'get frostbitten' [cf. təʀ-]
SPI qiʀitiq- 'get frostbitten'
NAI qiqɨtiq-, PH qiʀittiq-
WCI —
ECI qiqitiq- 'have frozen feet, chillblains'
GRI —

PY qiʀətʀaʀ- or **qiqətʀaʀ-** 'form hard crust (snow)' [cf. qiʀətəq- above and aʀ-]
AAY XətXaʀ- 'get hard crust (snow)'
CAY qətXaʀ-, NSU qəXətXaʀ- 'form hard ice crust'
NSY kətxaXtə- 'crust over (snow)' [ANLC]
CSY aXqətXaq 'frozen crust on snow, frozen ground in spring'
Sir [Vakh. has qiʀituʀaʀ- 'freeze' from Men. and Rub.]

PE qiʀnəʀ- 'be black or dark (as blue fox)' [cf. PI qianʀaqtuq]
AAY —
CAY əʀnəXtuʀ(aq) LI, BB 'blue, gray fox' [and note Nun əqyəʀəX 'blue fox' — ANLC]
NSY — [for qiaʀnaqtuq 'blue fox' see qianʀaqtuq]
CSY [qənʀaXtu 'blue fox']
Sir [note qətXima 'blue fox'?]
SPI W qiʀniq- 'be dark colored, black' [Jen.]
NAI qiʀn^{y}ɨq- 'be black, dark', qiʀn^{y}ɨqtaq 'black, silver fox', Nu qiʀn^{y}ɨqtaaluk 'black wolf'
WCI Sig qinʀiq- 'be dark, black' [Lowe], Cop qiʀnaʀik- 'be black', qiʀniʀaqtuq 'blue fox' [Jen.], Car qiʀniqtaq 'black' [Dor.; for the Sig form compare WCI pilʀak under pirlaɣ, also under mənʀuʀ-]
ECl qiʀnitaq 's.th. black', qiʀnili- 'become dark'
GRI qiʀniʀ- 'be black' [also qinniʀ- in Sisimiut and Maniitsoq acc. R. Petersen; and note tiʀianniaq qiʀniʀtaq 'blue fox']

PI qiʀnəʀaq 'dark ripple on water'
SPI —
NAI Nu qiʀn^{y}iʀaq 'dark ripple on water'
WCI —
ECI qiʀniʀaq [Saul]
GRI qiʀniʀaaq 'ripple or breeze over water', EG qiʀnaak 'medium-sized wave' [but Holm has qiʀniʀtaq 'dark ripple on water'; qiʀniʀaaʀ- 'be dark (sea, owing to wind)', EG qiʀnaaliʀ- 'be rather stormy sea']

PE qiʀu- 'freeze to death' [cf. qiʀə-]
AAY ➟
CAY qəXu- 'freeze to death'
NSY ʀu- 'freeze (person)' [ANLC]
CSY Xuu- 'freeze (to death)'
Sir qiʀə- [Orr]
SPI qiu- 'freeze to death'
NAI qi<ɣ>u- 'freeze to death' [probably with spurious ɣ; also qiunŋu- 'shiver from illness', qiʀuviak 'refrozen slush']
WCI qiu- 'freeze to death'
ECI qiu-
GRI qiu- 'freeze to death' [and qiunŋuyuuʀ- 'be freezing cold', qiʀut- 'get frostbite, frost sores']

PY qiRutə- 'feel cold' [cf. utə-]
AAY —
CAY qəXutə- 'feel cold'
NSY Xutə- 'shiver from cold, freeze'
CSY Xuutə- 'feel cold'
Sir [note qiRə́x(tə)- 'feel cold' — Orr]

PE qiRuya- 'feel cold' [cf. ya-; Aleut qiŋana- 'be cold', EA qiŋa-X 'cold' is probably unrelated]
AAY Kod quyaXtə- 'be cold (person)' [and Xuuya 'goose-pimple (from cold)', perhaps influenced by qəRUR-]
CAY qəXuyanaXqə- 'be cold (weather)' [qəXuyaq, qəXuyak 'goose-pimple, air bubble under ice', perhaps influenced by qəRUR-; for qəXaləRyuɣ- 'get goose-pimples' see qaRaləR-]
NSY Xuyanaq 'chill'
CSY —
Sir —
SPI —
NAI qiiya- 'feel cold', qiiyanaq- 'be cold (weather)'
WCI —
ECI Igl qiiya- 'feel cold' [B.-S., who for Baffin has qia- 'be frozen stiff']
GRI qiia- 'freeze (of person)' [as possessed plural noun = 'gooseflesh'; qiianaR- 'be cold (weather)']

PY qisiq 'lip' [there may be a link to qitəvə(t)-]
AAY [note qisiXtə- 'be bent out of shape']
CAY Nun qisiX 'lip' [and note HBC qisəXtə- 'pout']
NSY —
CSY qəziq 'lip'

PY qitəR- 'beat'
AAY —
CAY —
NSY qitəR- 'beat'
CSY qitəR- 'beat one's wife'

PE qitəvə(t)- 'speak unintelligibly'
AAY PWS qituxtə- 'speak well, have a way with words'
CAY qitəftə- 'jabber, speak a foreign language, speak English'
NSY qitəftə- 'speak Chukchi' [ANLC; Men. has qitəvŋaq 'Chukchi']
CSY qitəvə- 'jabber, speak a foreign language'
Sir qitə́vzukaR- [Orr]
SPI qitimŋa- Di qitəmŋa- 'speak Chukchi'
NAI Mal qitivɨt- 'speak Indian'
WCI —
ECI —
GRI qituit-, qitivit- 'twitter (bird), speak unintelligibly, speak Danish'

PE qitŋiR- and **qitŋaR-** and **qitŋuR-** 'dazzle' [the second form may be from *qitŋiRaR- with aR- while GRI qiŋŋuR- has (C)uR- instead; but see also qunŋuq for possible source of contam.]
AAY qitŋiR- 'be blinded, dazzled'
CAY qitŋiR- 'dazzle' [and qitŋiqə- 'be dazzled']
NSY —
CSY qətŋiR- 'dazzle' [and qətŋŋiqə- 'be dazzled']
Sir —
SPI qikŋaq- 'be blinded by light'
NAI qiŋŋaq-, Nu qikŋaq- 'be blinded' and qikŋuq 'ray' [Nu qikŋuaqtuun 'telescope' — by contam. with qinəR- 'watch' and/or qutŋuq?]
WCI Cop qiŋnaq- 'be dazzled' [and Ow. has qiŋaq- for qi'ŋaq-? 'be bothered by bright light (eyes)']
ECI Lab qiŋŋak- 'squint from the sun'
GRI qiŋŋuR-, qinnuR- [old ortho. qingnor-] 'shine', qiŋŋuRniq 'beam', qiŋŋuaq, qinnuaq 'ray' [and NWG qiŋŋuR-, SWG qiŋŋuaR- 'look through binoculars' — compare the Nu form above, also NWG qiŋŋutit 'binoculars, telescope' under qinəR-; for iŋŋia(suɣ)- 'be dazzled' see iŋŋia(suk)-]

PE qitŋu(R) 'inner recess (of bay or river or cave)'
AAY [qitək 'head of bay or inlet, house or cave']
CAY —
NSY —
CSY —
Sir qitŋuX 'hall, storage room' [Vakh. from Men.'s texts]
SPI qikŋuq 'corner (inside or outside),' Qaw 'bend in river'
NAI qin^{y}ŋuq, Nu qitŋuq 'part of lake farthest inside', qin^{y}ŋuqłiq* 'hindmost'
WCI Car EP qiŋuq 'west side of lake' [Ow. — for qi'ŋuq?; Pryde has Net qi'ŋaRnaitkut, Cop qinŋaRnaipkut 'shade for lamp']
ECI qiŋŋu 'end of a fjord or creek, back of room or cave'
GRI qiŋŋuq 'head of fjord, inner recess of cave, bottom of gun' [for homonym 'root of nose' see qənŋu(R); also qiŋiR- 'go round bottom of fjord (to cross it)', qiŋŋuRłiq* 'innermost']

PI qivaaqi 'male sculpin' [cf. qivə(R)-?]
SPI —
NAI —
WCI —
ECI qivaaqi 'male sea scorpion, sculpin' [Saul; Schn. has qivaaRi]
GRI qivaaqi 'male sea scorpion (sculpin)', EG qivaaRiq 'sculpin'

PE qivə(R)- 'turn (back)' [cf. Atkan Aleut qimɣa- 'bent to the side (of fish hook, as it is meant to be)']
AAY qiuxtə- 'curl (hair)'
CAY qiivə- 'tremble, shake, curl (hair)' [the long vowel is unexplained]
NSY qi(i)və- 'turn around' [with macron on first vowel, but qivałəq 'turn' without]
CSY qiivə- 'turn body or head' [ANLC also 'make a U-turn'; qiiftə- 'turn']
Sir qivaR- 'turn'
SPI qiwiq- 'bend backward'
NAI qivi- 'lie on back', qiviq- 'lean backward'
WCI Cop qiviq- 'lean backward (esp. pregnant woman or s.o. having eaten a lot, to counterbalance weight of stomach)' — Pryde]

ECI qiviq- 'turn on pivot, outward or to rear' [and qiviʀsinaq- 'give up, stop']
GRI qiviʀ- 'lean backward, throw self on back (of stubborn child)'

> **PI qiviaq-** 'turn to look back' [cf. yaʀ(tuʀ)-?]
> SPI —
> NAI qiviaq- 'turn head and look'
> WCI qiviaq- 'turn head back'
> ECI qiviaq- 'turn to look'
> GRI qiviaʀ-

PY qiviʀ- 'add to (food)'
AAY qiwiʀ- 'add to (food)'
CAY qiviʀ-
NSY qiviʀ- 'fill, make full' [ANLC]
CSY —

PE qivʀu- 'grieve or be sorry' [there may be a link to qiɣluk-, but cf. also qivə(ʀ)- — contam.?]
AAY —
CAY qivʀu- 'be heartbroken, mourn'
NSY qivʀu- 'grieve, feel condolence' [ANLC]
CSY qivʀu- 'be sorry, grieve, regret'
Sir —
SPI —
NAI PH qivʀu-, Nu qivuʀu- 'mourn, grieve'
WCI —
ECI —
GRI —

PE qivyu(ʀ) 'down' [cf. qivə(ʀ)-, unless from earlier *qinavyuʀ, forms reflecting qivyu(ʀ) being by contam. with the former; there could be entanglement here with the source of quniɣuq, however, q.v.]
AAY [qinuk, qinuɣyuk, qinuɣyak 'underhair, down']
CAY qivyuq, NS qivzuq, Nun qinavyuX, LI qənavyuq 'underhair, down'
NSY — [but note qinuq 'long hair of reindeer skin']
CSY —
Sir —
SPI Qaw qiwiu 'down, underfeather, musk ox wool'
NAI qiviu 'down (of waterfowl), wool (of musk ox)'
WCI qiviu 'down' [for Car quniuq 'unhaired caribou neck skin' see quŋiaq (quŋəʀ)]
ECI qiviuq 'little short curled hair'
GRI qiviu 'down, woolly animal hair (below fur proper), down on a plant'

PE qiyu(ɣ)(-) '(become) blue (esp. berry)' [compare piyuɣ- for the s in Inu; the ɣ in CSY by assimilation to the final velar?]
AAY qiu- 'become ripe', qiuq 'color', C qiyuiʀ-, K qəsuiʀ- 'lose color, fade' [and qiulʀaaq 'fruit, vegetable', AP qiułʀiaq 'berry', C qiuʀcəstaak 'blue jeans']
CAY qiu-, HBC qəyu- 'become bluish, bruised', qiuq* 'blueberry, bluish reflection in sky from open water' [for homonym of the latter meaning 'bluish-gray rock' see qiyuʀ; and qiuʀliq, qiuɣliq, qəzuqliq, HBC qəyuʀliq 'blue color or thing', Nun qəXsuʀyax 'blue thing']
NSY qəyuʀ- 'be blue' [ANLC; Men. has qəyuk 'green', qəyuXqə- 'appear green (land) or blue (person)', qəyuʀalŋuq 'light blue', and qəyuaqəXtaq 'blue'; L.-T. has qəyulʀia 'blue' and ANLC also has qəstuʀałəʀia 'green (vegetation?)' and qəstuaqəXtaq 's.th. blue']
CSY qiɣuk 'reflection of open water shown by dark sky', Chap qiɣuʀaaq, qiɣuʀməlŋuq 'green' [and qiɣuʀžuk 'smoke, smog']
Sir —
SPI qizuk- 'be a dark cloud over open water'
NAI qisuk 'dark cloud over open water' [also verbal]
WCI qisuk
ECI qisuk 'vapor given off by sea during intense cold' [also verbal]
GRI qisuk 'darkness in sky which shows open water'

PE qu(C)aɣðuɣ 'ridge or edge' [cf. quɣðaʀ- and Aleut quɣðu-X 'edge, ridge']
AAY ➟
CAY quaɣuk 'ridge'
NSY quaɣžuk 'ridge, facet of three-edged needle' [ANLC]
CSY —
Sir —
SPI quaɣžuk 'groove, edge'
NAI quaɣžuk 'ridge'
WCI quaɣyuk 'edge'
ECI quayyuk 'facet', Lab 'point of land' [Bourq. has 'angle, corner' for Lab]
GRI quaššuk 'ridge'

> **PE qu(C)aɣðuləɣ** 'three-edged needle' [cf. ləɣ]
> AAY AP qua'ulək 'three-edged needle'
> CAY quaɣulək
> NSY quaɣžulək [ANLC]
> CSY —
> Sir —
> SPI KI quaɣžuilik 'three-edged needle', Imaq quaɣžulək 'beluga' [from fatty ridges on back; also quaɣžuilaq 'needle']
> NAI quaɣžulik 'three-edged needle'
> WCI quaɣyulik
> ECI quayyulik 'three-edged needle' [Bourq. has 'any object with corners, e.g. timber' for Lab]
> GRI quaššulik 'three-edged needle'

PI quaqcaaq- 'get a shock' [cf. quŋluɣ-]
Yup [for CAY HBC, Nun quxcuaqəʀ- 'be startled' see quŋluɣ-]
SPI quaqsaaq-, quaqsiaq- 'tingle, feel pins and needles', Qaw quaqsai- 'get a shock' [note also Qaw quksalaq- 'be startled']
NAI quaqsaaq- 'get an electric or emotional shock'
WCI quaqsa(a)q- 'get a shock in one's bones' [and quaqsa(a)ʀautit 'batteries']
ECI quaʀsaa(q)- 'be surprised, start, jump', Lab quatsaaC- 'be startled' [and note qutsalak- 'jump in surprise']
GRI quaʀsaaʀ- 'be frightened,' [Kl. has 'be startled from a sudden fright']

PE qu(C)aʀ 'frozen meat'
AAY —
CAY quaq 'frozen meat or fish to be eaten raw' [and note quaʀnaq 'larch, tamarack']
NSY quaq 'frozen meat or fish to be eaten raw' [Orr; ANLC also quaʀ- 'eat a kind of frozen fish']
CSY —
Sir —
SPI quaq 'raw frozen meat or fish', qužži- 'make frozen meat or fish'
NAI qu<ž>aq 'raw frozen meat or fish' [and verbal for eating it]
WCI quaq 'frozen meat or fish' [Lowe; and note Car quaʀnaq 'hard wood' acc. Ras.]
ECI quaq 'anything frozen stiff' [verbal = 'freeze (also weather)'; note quʀʀaq 'frostbite' and Lab quannatuk 'sub-zero weather']
GRI quaq 'raw frozen meat' [and note quaasi- (old ortho. quaisi-) 'store meat', also perhaps qui(k) 'shed for provisions', quiʀšuaq 'warehouse', Up quiʀsawaq 'blubber depot'; Tersis has quiq 'reserves of food, shed for storing food' for EG]

PI quaʀaq 'dwarf willow leaf?' [there may be a link to quɣəlŋiʀ]
SPI —
NAI quaʀaq, Nu quaʀuq 'sour dock, wild spinach, edible willow leaf'
WCI quaʀaq 'willow leaf'
ECI quaʀaq 'dwarf willow, osier'
GRI quaʀaq 'bunch of flowers or seeds' [Kl. has 'catkin'], EG quaʀ̃aq 'angelica root', quaʀ̃alik 'flowering angelica' [Ras. has quaatsut 'angelica' for EG]

PY qucaɣ- 'be messy or dissatisfied?'
AAY qucaɣ(yuɣ)- 'feel one hasn't received enough'
CAY qucaɣ- 'be messy' [qucak 'messy person']
NSY —
CSY —

PI qucuŋŋaq 'outer fur parka'
Yup — [but Ras. has qutjooyax 'caribou skin jacket' for CAY]
SPI quzuŋaq 'heavy reindeer parka,' Qaw qusuŋaq 'outer fur parka'
NAI qusuŋŋaq
WCI Sig qusuŋŋaq
ECI —
GRI —

PE quðu- 'close in' [cf. Aleut quðu-X EA 'valley, cleft', Atkan and old EA quðuɣ- 'narrow (e.g. door)']
AAY ➟
CAY quu- 'close in (e.g. hole in ice or eyelids swelling shut)' [and quutaaʀ- 'wink']
NSY [quɣnu- 'close in, lace up (clothes)' — ANLC]
CSY quusqə- 'pull head down and shoulders up' [and quunqaʀ-, qunqaɬəɣ- 'wink, blink', also perhaps qunaʀ-, qunəʀ- 'close eyes (post. root)']
Sir qusəɣəɣ- 'pull head down and shoulders up' [Orr; Vakh. and Orr have qunaʀ- 'close eyes' — from CSY?]
SPI quut-, Qaw quu- 'be closing in'
NAI quu- 'be closing in, turn feet inward', quut- 'become, make narrow' [and note quʀʀutɨ- 'close in and block path'; for quuŋa- 'be pigeon-toed' see ku(C)u(ɣ)-]
WCI quuyi- 'the throat contracts (in pain)', quuɣli- 'passage gets narrower', Net quuk- [for quut-?] 'close in' [Ras.; Met. also has quukilruq 'narrowest part of way or strait']
ECI quut- 'make narrower, have reduced opening, be angry', Lab 'get angry' [also quukit- 'have small opening', and note quki (for quuki?) 'narrowing of valley or river', quyuŋayuq 'something diminished in size such as a frosted-in hole in the ice, also said of a person who is angry'; NBI quukinniq 'strait' (Dor.)]
GRI quut-, quɣ- 'make narrower, shrink', EG quuʀ- 'converge, squeeze together' [Robbe and Menn. for the latter; and quuqqa(a)q 'larynx']

PE quðumiɣ- 'squeeze together' [cf. miɣ-]
AAY quumiɣ- 'grasp with sticks, tongs (e.g. hot rocks)'
CAY quumiɣ- 'squeeze legs together'
NSY —
CSY qumsəɣtə- 'close legs, scissors, door, wink'
Sir —
SPI quumik- 'squeeze legs together,' quumiŋa- 'be knock-kneed'
NAI quumik- 'squeeze legs together' [for qumik- 'put (e.g. arms) inside one's parka' see qumiɣ-]
WCI quumik- 'press between one's legs, press legs together' [Pryde — Schn. Car? 'take with pincers or the like' for 'adg']
ECI quummik- 'close legs, scissors, etc., dance opening and closing legs'
GRI quummiʀ- 'bring legs together'

PE quðuquʀ 'valley' [cf. quʀ]
AAY PWS ququuk 'ravine', KP ququuq 'steep incline' [and note AP quuqiya<ʀ>aq 'animal path']
CAY NS quuʀuq 'valley' [and note Eg quuqat 'narrows']
NSY —
CSY —
Sir —
SPI Qaw kuuʀuq 'stream running through a valley'
NAI kuuʀuq 'valley, furrow' [SPI and NAI probably by contamination with kuuk 'river']
WCI Net kuuʀuq 'valley' [B.-S.]
ECI kuuʀuq [Bourq. quuʀuq] 'valley, groove'
GRI quuʀuq, NWG, NG kuuʀuq 'valley, furrow' [and kuuqqiʀ- 'make a furrow or groove in']

PI quunʀuq 'narrow place' [cf. nəʀ[1] and quʀ?]
SPI —
NAI Nu quunʀut 'canyon'
WCI Cop quunʀuq 'narrow arm of sea leading into estuary or bay' [Pryde]
ECI quuʀŋuq 'narrows (between island and mainland, two lakes or two islands)'
GRI quuʀnuq 'narrow part of fjord (esp. as place name)'

PE qu(C)əyiɣ 'narrow bone in hind flipper of seal or walrus' [cf. Aleut quðɣuma-X 'shinbone', EA also 'instep', and quðɣ- 'top, backside']
AAY —
CAY —
NSY quuyiq 'thigh bone' [ANLC; Jen. has kuyiq 'thigh bone']
CSY —
Sir —
SPI quiivak 'set of bones in seal's hind flipper', Imaq quyəq 'thigh bone' [and Jen. has W quik 'thin bone in hind leg of seal' but also kui 'thigh']
NAI quɨk 'seal bone next to hind flipper'
WCI [Ras. has Cop quinia 'seal's hind limb']
ECI quik 'femur, thighbone — esp. of seal' [Ras. has quuvik 'thigh bone' for Igl]
GRI quuik 'narrow bone in hind flipper of seal', NG quɣiit 'femural pieces of walrus carcass' [Holt.]

PE quɣaʀta(ʀ) 'anal itch'
AAY quaXtaq 'pinworms, anal itch'
CAY quaXta 'anal itch' [verbal = 'have anal itch']
NSY quaXta 'pinworm' [ANLC]
CSY quɣaXtaq 'anal itch' [for homonym meaning 'type of small fish' see quɣðaʀutnaʀ under quɣðaʀ-]
Sir — [for qumaXtaX 'anal itch' see quma(ʀ)]
SPI quaqta 'anal itch' [also verbal]
NAI quaqta [also verbal]
WCI quaqta(q) 'anal itch'
ECI quaqtaq [also verbal]
GRI quaʀtaq 'anal itch' [and verbal quaʀta-]

PE quɣðaʀ- 'split with wedge' [cf. quɣðuɣ and qu(ɣ)aɣðuɣ and Aleut quxsu-X 'wedge', quxsu- 'chop'; there is varying suffixation to root *quɣ- here]
AAY C qu(u)ɣuutaq 'wedge'
CAY [quxcuun 'wedge, canine tooth' also əquxcuun, influenced by əquk, quuk 'wood'; HBC qucxutaq 'story knife' may belong here too]
NSY quɣaʀ- 'chisel, gouge, hollow out, hammer on a wedge' [ANLC; Men. has quɣan, quwataq 'chisel, sledgehammer']
CSY quɣaXsiiʀ- 'chop wood' [and quɣaʀ- 'hit hard, club']
Sir —
SPI quɣžaq- 'chisel, knock in' [and quɣžaun 'chisel']
NAI Nu quɣžaqtuq- 'drive in a wedge', quɣžautaq 'wooden wedge'
WCI Cop quɣyauttaq 'wedge' [Pryde]
ECI Iti quyyataq 'place for splitting wood', Lab quyyaatak 'wedge'
GRI quššaʀ- 'split with a wedge' [and quššaat 'wedge' (old ortho. quvssaut with non-historical v due to qupə- 'split'), quššaataq 'chisel']

PE quɣðaʀutnaʀ 'eel or wolf fish?' [cf. un and naʀ]
AAY KP quɣuutn̥aq 'eel'
CAY Nun, NI quɣautn̥aq 'wolf fish' [and note quaXuuk 'stickleback']
NSY —
CSY [note quɣaXtaq 'type of small fish']
Sir —
SPI —
NAI —
WCI Cop quɣyaunnaq, Net quɣžaunnaq 'polar eelpout' [Pryde; Ow. has Car EP quɣyauknaq 'eel']
ECI Iti quyyaunaq 'fish like an eel'
GRI quššaannaq 'butterfish, gunnel'

PE quɣðuɣ 'swan' [cf. quɣðaʀ- and Atkan Aleut qukinʀi-X, quqinʀi-X, EA qunki-X, qunqi-X 'swan', though the exact relat. is problematic]
AAY quɣyuk 'swan'
CAY quɣyuk
NSY quɣyuk [ANLC]
CSY quuk 'whistling swan'
Sir —
SPI quɣžuk 'swan' [but Men. has Imaq 'white goose']
NAI quɣžuk 'swan'
WCI quɣyuk
ECI quyyuk 'swan' [also 'white dog with black head']
GRI quššuk [old ortho. qugssuk] 'swan'

PY-S quɣələʀ- 'be sour' [quɣəlŋiʀ and EA quɣali- 'eat s.th. sour', quɣalina-, quɣul(i)na-, quɣilna-, Atkan quɣuulina- 'be or taste sour']
AAY K quuləxtə- 'be soured' [and C quunaʀliq 'sourdock', quunaʀ-, K quun̥aʀ- 'be sour']
CAY quuləXtə- 'be sour', quuləciraq, Y, HBC quuləq* 'sourdough, homebrew' [also Y quunaq 'sourdock']
NSY quulərnaʀ- 'be sour' [ANLC also has quilima- 'be aged ("soured")']
CSY [note quɣaak 'sour flavor'; also Chap. quɣalʀii 'sour' — evidently from a base quɣa(ɣ/ʀ)-]
Sir quɣəɬtaʀanɬəŋuX 'sour' [Em. has quwəɬtaləʀəX]

PE quɣəlŋiʀ 'sorrel or sourdock' [cf. quɣələʀ- and EA Aleut quuɣulnaaða-X 'sourgrass', Nikolski quuɣuulaaða-X 'wild rhubarb']
AAY —
CAY —
NSY qu(u)lŋiq 'sorrel'
CSY quɣəlŋiq 'sourdock'
Sir quɣəlŋiX 'sorrel'
SPI quŋuliq
NAI quŋulliq* 'mountain sorrel', Nu quŋuliq 'caribou intestine mixed with liver, etc.'
WCI quŋuliq 'sorrel' [Jen.]
ECI quŋuliq 'sorrel' [and Lab quŋuliuyaq 'cochlearia'; note also quŋuq 'white liquid from certain plants, sperm', though this is more likely to refer to dandelion than sorrel]
GRI quŋuliq*, Up quʀ̃uliq 'scurvy grass (cochlearia), cabbage' [Ras. has quulit 'sorrel' for EG]

PE quɣi- 'be fat' [cf. quɣinaɣ-?]
AAY K quili- 'be fat, of person'
CAY —
NSY —
CSY quɣinaq 'fat, blubber', Chap quɣili- 'become fat or strong'

Sir quɣinaX 'fat' [Vakh.; Men. has quvənaʀ- 'get fat']
SPI quiktit-, Qaw quini-, Imaq quyiqtiaq- 'be fat'
NAI quinʸi-, quivsit- 'be fat' [and quinnʸak- 'get fat']
WCI quini-
ECI quini- 'be fat' [and Ras. has quittit- 'become thick, broad, fat' for Igl]
GRI [quini- 'be fat (of terrestrial animals, esp. caribou)' is mentioned by Ras. for WG in his Igl word-list — a mistake?]

PE quɣinaɣ- 'be ticklish or squeamish' [cf. quiliqta-?]
AAY —
CAY Y, HBC, NS quinaɣ(yuɣ)- 'be disgusted by s.th.'
NSY quinaxsaʀ- 'tickle'
CSY quɣina(yuɣ)- 'be ticklish' [and note quɣinaɣ(yuɣ)- 'be terrified']
Sir —
SPI quinaktaaq- 'tickle'
NAI quinʸnʸak-, PH quinʸak- 'feel tickling sensation' [PH also 'be squeamish, scared of mice']
WCI quinak- 'tickle' [emot. root], quinaɣi- 'be disgusted by', Net 'feel touchy about, be afraid of (esp. insects)' [Ras.]
ECI quinak- 'be ticklish', quinaɣi- 'be disgusted by'
GRI quinaɣ-, EG quaaC- 'be ticklish, tickled', NG quinaŋnaq- 'feel nasty'

PI quɣluk- 'fold or pleat' [or quŋluk- — cf. quŋluɣ- and/or quŋcuʀ-]
SPI [Jen. has qulluk- 'fold over']
NAI quɣluk- 'fold, pleat'
WCI quɣluk- 'fold'
ECI qullu(k)- 'fold, tear in two'
GRI quɫɫuɣ- 'fold up, tuck, hemstitch'

> **PI quɣluɣiaq** 'caterpillar or similar creature' [cf. yaʀ]
> SPI Qaw quɣluʀiaq 'centipede'
> NAI Nu quɣluɣiaq 'small water worm (that moves by twisting itself)' [for Mal quɣluɣiaq '10-legged mythical polar bear' see qupquʀiaq]
> WCI Car? qulluɣiaq [for quɣluɣiaq?] 'worm, snake' [Schn. 'adg']
> ECI qulluɣiaq 'white, hairless caterpillar', Lab 'worm'
> GRI quɫɫuɣiaq 'caterpillar, leech'

PE quɣ(ə)nəʀ 'calm water or weather' [cf. nəʀ[1]]
AAY —
CAY quunəq* 'calm weather'
NSY quɣnəq 'calm'
CSY —
Sir —
SPI quuniq 'calm water'
NAI quuniq 'calm, glassy water'
WCI —
ECI —
GRI —

PE quɣtuqaʀ 'thigh'
AAY quxtuqaq 'ham of moose, etc.'
CAY quxtuqaq 'thighbone'
NSY quxtuqaq 'thigh'
CSY quxtuqaq
Sir quŋtəqəX 'thigh' [influenced by quŋcuʀ-?]
SPI quqtuaq 'thigh'
NAI quqtuʀaq, Mal quptuʀaq
WCI quqtuʀaq [Lowe; Met. has quktuʀaq]
ECI quqtuʀaq 'thigh'
GRI quttuʀaq [old ortho. qugtoraq], EG quʀtuʀ̃aq

PI quiliqta- 'tremble?' [there may be a link to quɣinaɣ- and or quɣi-]
SPI — [but note quivlaŋa- 'fidget']
NAI quilʸiqta- 'tremble with happiness'
WCI Cop quiliqta(huk)- 'think uncanny' [Ras.]
ECI quiliqta(suk)- 'be scared' [emot. root]
GRI quiliʀta- 'fear suffering damage'

PI qukaaq- 'be indistinct' [cf. qukaq?]
SPI —
NAI —
WCI Car? qukaaq- 'be pale, unclear' [Schn. 'adg']
ECI qukaaq- 'blend into distant surroundings, be indistinct'
GRI quqaaq 'reflection of land in water' [and note quqašši- 'sneak up on'?]

PY-S qukaq 'middle (of back)'
AAY qukaq 'middle, waist'
CAY qukaq
NSY qukaq 'middle, small of back, axis'
CSY qukaq 'middle, lower back'
Sir qukəX 'middle, small of back' [Vakh.; Men. has quxəX 'small of back' on his comp. list]

> **PY qukaqliq** 'middle one' [cf. qliʀ]
> AAY qukaqɫiq 'middle one'
> CAY qukaqɫiq*
> NSY qukaqɫiq
> CSY Chap qukaqɫiq*
> Sir [note qukəcəX 'middle one' — with l(l)iʀ instead]

PI qukəɣə- 'feel cowed before s.o. better than oneself?' [cf. kə-[1]; the relat. (if any) to qikə-[1] and/or quŋyaʀ- is obscure — contam.?]
SPI —
NAI qukiyi- 'feel s.o. is too clean and orderly so hesitate to do anything' [qukisuɣ- 'feel unworthy, not clean enough']
WCI [Ras. has Car quxxanaq- 'be silly', adding that it really means 'be ashamed of s.th.'; Ow. has quxxahuk- 'be nervous, hesitate', quxxallak- 'be suddenly aware' — but compare under kukðaɣ-]
ECI —
GRI [note quqiʀi- 'like (s.o.)', also perhaps qussala- (old ortho. qugsala-) 'be worried, timid', qussaɫɫaɣ- 'become timid', and qussi- 'find s.th. worse than expected, be disappointed in' direct from *qukə-; for qussuɣ- 'stoop, pull chin into hood' see quvə-]

PE qukiʀ- 'be deafened by a loud noise'
AAY qukiʀ- 'be bothered by noise'
CAY qukiʀ- 'hurt or be hurt in ears by loud noise'
NSY —
CSY —

Sir —
SPI quɣiq- 'be deafened, have ears hurt by noise'
NAI qukiq-
WCI qukiʀnaq- 'be dizzying, tiring (of noise)' [and Net qukiut 'gun' — Ras.]
ECI qukiq- 'fire on with a gun' [and qukiʀvaluk 'gun detonation, sound of gunshot', qukiʀnatuq 'something fired from a gun which makes one's ears buzz', qukiut 'gun']
GRI quqiʀ-, NG qukiq- 'become stunned, deafened (with noise)'

PY qukviʀ- 'part hair' [cf. qukaq]
AAY [qupw̥iɣ- 'part hair' — contam. with qupə- and viɣ)?]
CAY qukfiʀ- 'part hair'
NSY qukpiʀ- 'part hair' [ANLC]
CSY qukfiʀ- 'remove hair from ears'

PI qulaq- 'doubt'
SPI —
NAI qulaʀnaq- 'be incomprehensible'
WCI qulaʀi- 'suspect', qulaʀnaq- 'probably be so', Cop qulaq- 'doubt' [Ras.]
ECI qulaq- 'doubt'
GRI qulaʀ-, trans. qulaʀi- 'doubt' [qulaʀnaʀ- 'be doubtful']

PE qulə- 'area above' [positional root; cf. qutə and Aleut qul- plus ablative 'for the sake of, because of' but also ku- 'top surface', perhaps with assimilation due to such oblique forms as ku-ɣan 'on it'; for Aleut quðɣ- 'upside, backside' see qu(C)ək, but it could also be related to this set from a deep root *qu-]
AAY qulə- 'area above'
CAY qulə- 'area above' [qulətm̥un 'upward']
NSY qulə- 'area above' [also 'top rail on sled' (ANLC); qulmun 'upward']
CSY qula 'upper part, gunwale'
Sir qulə- 'area above' [Vakh.; also qulmənu 'upward']
SPI quli- 'area above' [qunmun 'upward']
NAI quli- 'area above' [and PH 'gunwale', Mal 'mukluk top trim'; qunmun 'upward']
WCI quli- 'area above' [qunmun 'upward']
ECI quli- 'area above' [and as verb 'put roof on, be overcast (sky)', qulisima- 'have put the last block on dome of snow house'; qummut 'upward']
GRI quli- 'area above' [and qulisima- 'be overcast (weather)'; qummut, NG quŋmut 'upward']

PI qulautə- 'pass over' [cf. utə-]
SPI qulaut(i)- 'pass over, overshoot'
NAI qulaut(ɨ)- 'pass overhead, shoot high, jump an obstacle'
WCI qulaut(i)- 'shoot high, pass over (bullet)'
ECI qulaut(i)- 'pass or fly over'
GRI qulaat(i)- 'go over, shoot over'

PE qulðiɣ- 'be high up' [cf. ðiɣ-]
AAY K qussiɣ-, C qussəɣ- 'be high up'
CAY quyiɣ-, Nun qusiɣ-
NSY —
CSY [note quyiɫək 'Chukchi' — i.e. one living inland — compare qutliq under qutə]
Sir —
SPI qussik- 'be high up'
NAI qutcik-
WCI Sig qutsik-
ECI Lab qutsik- 'be above'
GRI qutsiɣ- 'be high up'

PE qulə(t) 'ten' [same as qulə- above but usually in the plural, referring to the ten fingers extended upward in counting; the final n in AAY, CAY is found on all the basic numeral bases above two]
AAY qula, qulən 'ten'
CAY qula, qulən
NSY qulə, qulət
CSY qula, qulət
Sir —
SPI qulit
NAI qulɨt
WCI qulit
ECI qulit
GRI qulit 'ten' [and quliŋat 'tenth']

PE quləmciʀun 'cooking pot' [cf. un]
AAY —
CAY —
NSY qulumsiin 'pot'
CSY qulməsiin 'small cooking pot with handle, sea urchin'
Sir qulməsiʀətaX 'pot' [Orr and Em.]
SPI qulipsiun
NAI PH qulipsiun 'old style cooking pot used with lamp, wooden rack where ice and snow are placed to give water by dripping'
WCI Net qulipsiq- 'cook over blubber lamp' [Pryde]
ECI qulitsiut 'oil stove with a wick' [qulitsi(q)- 'cook (over lamp)', Lab qul(l)ipsiut 'vessel to put over lamp to cook in' Peck]
GRI qulissiut 'pot, kettle in which food is cooked over lamp', NG 'pan' [old ortho. qulivsiut; qulissiʀ- 'cook over lamp']

PE quləŋiʀ- 'be or pass over' [cf. ŋiʀ-]
AAY qulaiʀ- 'go by or over'
CAY qulaiʀ- 'pass over'
NSY —
CSY —
Sir quliŋəʀətə- 'fly over, hang over' [Em.]
SPI qulaŋiq- 'be above, overhead'
NAI qulaŋiq- 'hover over, become parallel or level with boat or person'
WCI Car B. Lake qulaŋiq- 'stand above it (kayakers heading off caribou downstream from them)', Net qulaŋiqsi- 'stand over an open breathing hole of seal in sea-ice' [Pryde]
ECI qulaŋiaq- 'overhang, jut out over', NBI qulaŋiqsi- 'hunt at seal breathing hole'
GRI qulaŋiʀ- 'hover over, take up position above'

PE quləŋŋuʀutəŋit- 'nine' [cf. ŋ(ŋ)uʀ-, utə- and ŋit-; there may be more than one independent derivation here, with ŋu- rather than ŋ(ŋ)uʀ-]
AAY qulŋuyan 'nine'
CAY qulŋunʀitaʀaan, qulŋunʀita'aʀ, BB, LI qulŋuyan, NSU qulŋuʀutailŋuut 'nine'
NSY qulŋuɣutŋilŋuq 'nine' [ANLC; Men. has qulŋuʀutŋilŋuq]
CSY —
Sir —
SPI quliŋuutailat
NAI quliŋŋuʀutailʸat
WCI Sig quliŋiluat [Lowe], Car quliŋiluaqtut [Dor.]
ECI [quliuŋŋiɣaqtut, Igl quliqaŋŋituinnaqtut 'nine' — Dor.]
GRI quliŋiluat, qulaaluat 'nine'

PE qulɪʀ 'upper part' [cf. l(l)ir and compare qullɪʀ below; this may be an earlier derivation, on an underlying *qu-?]
AAY —
CAY quliq 'upper side rail of sled', NSY qulik, HBC quliit 'back'
NSY qulik 'spine, back' [L.-T.]
CSY [quliʀnəq* 'upper part']
Sir quliXpiɣaX 'high place'
SPI quliq 'gunwale, upper sled rail'
NAI Nu quliit 'back (of man, animal or fish)' [Jen. has quliq 'back of man' for B]
WCI Cop quliik 'back (of person)' [Pryde, who also has quliiɣut 'dorsal fin of fish' and quliiɣutaq 'thin layer of fat on back of fish']
ECI quliiq 'back'
GRI SWG qulit '(embroidered) knee pieces of trad. women's trousers'

PI quliʀuaq 'shelf?' [cf. qulɪʀ above and ŋ(ŋ)u(C)aʀ]
SPI —
NAI PH quliʀuaq 'first level of ice cellar'
WCI Car EP quliʀuaq 'shelf' [Ow.]
ECI quliʀuaq
GRI quliʀuaq 'gunwale, railing (of boat)', EG quliivaq 'shelf'

PE qulit- 'wash hair' [cf. lit-?]
AAY qulitə- 'wash hair'
CAY qulitə-
NSY qulitə- [ANLC]
CSY qulitə-
Sir —
SPI qulit-
NAI —
WCI —
ECI —
GRI qulit-

PE qullɪʀ 'uppermost one' [cf. l(l)ɪʀ and compare qulɪʀ above — but for the Yup forms also qutliq under qutə]
AAY quɬɬiq* 'upper part'
CAY quɬiq* 'topmost one, attic' [compare qaɬiq under qaðlɪʀ and note that the productive form corresponding to l(l)ɪʀ in CAY is qɬiq rather]
NSY —
CSY — [for quɬiɣək 'pants' see qaʀ(u)ɬiɣ]
Sir —
SPI qulliq 'highest' [for quɬɬiq 'Siberia' see qutə]
NAI qulliq* 'uppermost, lamp' [the uppermost oil lamp in the trad. house, contrasting with alliq (see atlɪʀ under at(ə)-)]
WCI qulliq 'lamp'
ECI qulliq
GRI quɬɬiq* 'uppermost, lamp'

PY qulqin 'raised platform or shelf' [cf. qaʀ, li-[1]) and un?]
AAY —
CAY quɬqin 'shelf'
NSY —
CSY quuɬqin 'loft in a semi-subterranean house'

PE qulvaʀ- 'rise or raise' [cf. vaʀ-]
AAY qulwaʀ- 'rise'
CAY qulvaʀ- 'elevate' [and qulvani 'high up']
NSY —
CSY qulvaʀ- 'raise, go up', Chap qulvaq 'top'
Sir qulvanɪʀ- 'raise. rise, go up' [Vakh. and Em.]
SPI quvlaq- 'ascend, rise'
NAI qulvaq-, qužvaq- 'move up into room farther from door, roll sleeves up' [and qulvasik- 'be high up']
WCI [Pryde has qulvaq- (without translation) and Cop qulvahik- 'be placed far up']
ECI quvva(q)- 'raise' [quvvasik- 'be situated higher up']
GRI quɬɬaʀ- 'raise (e.g. on line), be hung up'

PY quliɣ- 'crack from drying'
AAY K quliɣ-, qulixtə-, C quləxte-, quləXqə- 'split, crack (esp. from drying)'
CAY quliɣ- 'crack from drying'
NSY —
CSY —

PI quliktaq 'outer caribou skin coat' [cf. quliɣ- and ðaʀ?]
SPI —
NAI quliksaak 'caribou skin pants with fur outside' [Tein has qultat 'woman's fur pants']
WCI Cop qulittaq 'outer caribou skin parka', Car B. Lake quliktaq 'parka with long fur' [Dor.; Pryde has qulitsaq 'man's winter parka' for Net]
ECI qulittaq 'caribou skin overcoat with fur outside'
GRI qulitsaq, NG qulittaq 'outer (caribou) skin parka'

PE quliʀaʀ- 'tell about'
AAY quliʀaʀ- 'tell about'
CAY quliʀaq 'story, legend' [quliʀaXta 'storyteller, Protestant minister']
NSY quliʀaʀ- 'tell a (true) story' [ANLC; Men. has quliʀamsuk 'story, account']
CSY —
Sir —

SPI quliaq- 'tell about'
NAI quliaq- 'tell about' [and quliaqtuaq 'story, life experience']
WCI quliaq 'story, esp. a true one' [also verbal]
ECI —
GRI —

PI qulliquliaq 'plover' [cf. qulliʀ under qulə-?]
SPI —
NAI —
WCI Sig qul(l)iliquliaʀluk 'semipalmated plover' [Jen.; Ras. has qutlequliaq for Net (Pryde has qu'liquliaq), also qublequliaq 'ringed plover' for Car; Pet. has Sig qobleqolearluk 'turnstone']
ECI qulliquliaq 'plover'
GRI —

PE qulucuɣ 'back (of bird)' [cf. qulə- and cuɣ and compare tunucuk under tunu]
AAY qulucuk 'occipital bump'
CAY [note quluxtə- 'be hunchbacked or stooped']
NSY —
CSY —
Sir —
SPI qulusuk 'back part of bird'
NAI qulusuk, qulutcuk
WCI —
ECI qulusuk
GRI qulusuk 'back of bird'

PY quluk 'aged fish'
AAY PWS quluŋuaq 'aged fish or fish eggs'
CAY Nun qulux 'aged fish made in fall for winter consumption', NS quluŋnaq 'aged blackfish'
NSY —
CSY —

PI quluk- 'rumble (stomach)'
SPI quluuk(taq)- 'rumble (stomach)'
NAI quluk-, quluula-
WCI Cop quluktaq- 'retch (dog)', quluxxitiɣi- 'rumble (belly)' [Pryde]
ECI quluaraq-, Lab quluaq- 'rumble (stomach)'
GRI qulua- 'rumble (stomach)' [and note qulussuɣ- 'gulp food down']

PI qulumiq- 'hold athletic or song festival?'
SPI —
NAI —
WCI Cop qulumiq- 'hold athletic or song festival' [Ras.]
ECI Igl qulumiqtut 'a game' [Ras.; Peck has kullumer- 'sing against each other' for Lab]
GRI —

PE qulvi 'tear(drop)' [cf. qunik, but also PY aluvik, with which there may be some entanglement]
AAY —
CAY—
NSY —
CSY — [for quni 'teardrop' see qunik]
Sir qulva 'tear' [Orr has qulvi]
SPI qulvi 'teardrop', qulvi- 'weep'
NAI qulvi 'teardrop', qulvi- 'weep'
WCI Cop qulvik, Sig qulvi 'teardrop' [and Pryde has Cop qulvi- 'weep']
ECI quvvik 'tear'
GRI qułłi(q) [old ortho. quvdle]

PE quma(ʀ) 'intestinal worm' [cf. qumaq-?]
AAY —
CAY qumaq 'tapeworm in fish or seal'
NSY qumaq 'tapeworm', qumaaq- 'wither, dry up'
CSY quma 'intestinal worm'
Sir qumaX, pl. qumaʀiy or qumay [Orr; also qumaXtaX 'anal itch']
SPI qumaq 'intestinal worm'
NAI PH qumak 'worm in bearded seal intestine'
WCI Cop qumaq 'tapeworm' [also verbal for having one — Pryde]
ECI qumaq 'intestinal worm' [qumaʀuaq 'water insect']
GRI qumaq 'tapeworm'

PI qumaq- 'be hunched over' [cf. quma(ʀ); there may be a link to quvə-]
SPI —
NAI qumaq- 'bend forward, crouch'
WCI qumaŋa- 'be hunchbacked'
ECI qumaq- 'pull one's head down between one's shoulders, bend down', qumaŋa- 'be hunched over'
GRI qumaʀ- 'become shorter when pushed together (e.g. a person with his head pulled down)'

PY qumci(ʀ)- 'feel ticklish'
AAY qumcaa(yuɣ)- 'feel ticklish'
CAY Nun qumciʀ(yuɣ)-
NSY qumsiaʀ- 'become numb'
CSY —

PE qumiɣ- 'put object or arms inside parka sleeves' [compare quðumiɣ- under quðu-]
AAY qumiɣ- 'put something inside clothing, be pregnant'
CAY qumik 'enclosed thing, thing inside, fetus', qumiɣ- 'put something inside clothing'
NSY qumiɣ- 'put thing or arms inside clothing' [ANLC]
CSY qumik 'thing carried inside parka' [and qumiɣ- 'put something inside parka']
Sir [quɣməx 'fetus' acc. Orr, 's.th. carried inside front of clothing' acc. Em., and Vakh. (from Rub.'s texts) and Em. have quɣməɣ- 'hold against chest inside clothing, put s.th. inside front of clothing' from Rub.'s texts]
SPI qumik- 'put arms or s.th. else inside one's parka', Qaw qumi 'human fetus'
NAI qumik- 'put arms inside parka' [and qumiik- 'keep arms inside parka']
WCI qumik- 'put arms inside one's parka'
ECI qumik- 'carry something under parka' [qumi 'something carried under parka']
GRI qumiɣ- 'put arms in sleeves' [and qumiiŋa- 'have pulled arms up inside sleeves']

PI qumiu- 'bring or keep back food for s.o.' [compare qumiɣ-?]
SPI —
NAI qumiu- 'bring food to (s.o.)'
WCI —
ECI qumiu- 'reserve (food) for (s.o.)' [Saul; Schn. has qumiliuq- (for qumiluiuq-) 'put a part aside for (s.o.)']
GRI EG qumii- 'keep s.th. back for (s.o.)'

PI quniɣuq '(bird or caribou) down' [compare qivyu(ʀ); both bases suggest the meaning 'curly']
SPI —
NAI —
WCI [Pryde has Sig quniɣuq 'caribou skin thong'; Schn. has Car? quniktut 'caribou down' ('adg') — he also has B. Lake quniktitaq 'caribou down, coat sewn behind the shoulder'; Ras. has Car quniuq 'unhaired caribou neck skin (and thongs made from this)' — this and the Sig form above probably by contam. with quŋiaq under quŋəʀ (compare Cop quniaq there)]
ECI quniɣuq (usually pl.) 'bird down', Lab quniɣuk 'feather, caribou down' [and compare qunik- 'curl up because of cold (dog)', also quniʀuuyaq 'bog cotton']
GRI —

PY qunik 'matter in eye' [cf. qulvi, though the relat. is obscure]
AAY qunik, qun̥ik 'matter in eye'
CAY Nun, Eg qunik
NSY —
CSY quni 'teardrop'
Inu [note NAI quniqłuk 'indistinct horizon' and WCI qunak 'sea slush' (Pryde has quna(q))]

PE qunu- 'be reluctant to part with s.th.'
AAY —
CAY qunu- 'be reluctant to part with one's possessions'
NSY [quŋusxu- 'be reluctant to part with one's possessions' — for qunusxu-? (ANLC)]
CSY —
Sir —
SPI qunu- 'feel the absence of, miss', qunuɣi- 'cherish'
NAI qunu- 'coo to a baby, sing a dirge, mourn a dead person'
WCI qunu- 'pout'
ECI qunu- 'refuse to do s.th., e.g. participate in sexual acts' [and qunuɣi- 'refuse in this way' — Andersen et al. have 'not feel like doing' for Lab]
GRI qunu- 'acknowledge oneself to be powerless, offer no resistance, be afraid' [qunuɣi- 'be afraid of', perhaps also quniit-, EG quniŋŋiC- 'be ugly, clumsy' — Robbe and Menn. have qunirʀ- 'be beautiful' and qunii- 'find beautiful' for EG]

PY quŋatə- 'pack away' [cf. quŋuʀ(-)]
AAY quŋatə 'dress (s.o.), pack away'
CAY quŋatə- 'pack away'
NSY —
CSY [note quŋa (base quŋə-) 'middle, center, main idea']
Sir [note quŋə- 'between' — Vakh. from Men.'s texts]

PE quŋcuʀ- 'bend (legs)' [cf. quɣluk- and perhaps quŋuʀ(-)]
AAY quŋcuʀ- 'sit on one's heels', quŋcuXtə- 'flex knees' [for quŋcuXtə-, quŋcuxtə- 'make a grimace of dislike' see quŋluɣ-]
CAY quŋcuʀ- 'have knees flexed and legs folded toward body' [quŋcuq 'back of knee', quŋtə- 'fold one's legs'; for quxcuaqəʀ- 'be startled' see quŋluɣ-]
NSY [note uqumsuɣ- 'sit cross-legged' (ANLC)]
CSY quŋsuʀ- 'rest after giving birth with one's legs flexed and upper body bent over them'
Sir [Em. has quŋsuʀ- 'be in a certain position after giving birth']
SPI —
NAI —
WCI Car Baker Lake quxxu(C)- 'be bent, arched in two' [Schn.]
ECI [note qutsu(C)-, qutsuŋa- 'be flattened or warped', Iti 'crinkle, plait, warp']
GRI — [for qussuɣ- 'stoop, make oneself small, put chin into hood' see quvə-]

PE quŋəʀ 'neck' [cf. Aleut quŋ, quŋi-X 'hump, humpback', EA also quŋtu-X 'humpbacked']
AAY —
CAY —
NSY —
CSY quŋuq 'scruff of neck, top of back' [and quŋuXtə- 'hang one's head']
Sir [quŋuX(tə)- 'hang one's head' — Orr]
SPI quŋusiq 'neck'
NAI quŋusiq, Mal quŋisiq 'neck'
WCI Sig quŋisiq, Cop quŋuhiq [but Pryde has qunuhiilitaq 'scarf' for Cop]
ECI quŋasiq, quŋisiq
GRI quŋasiq, Up Kullorsuaq quȓasiq

PI quŋiaq 'throat skin of animal' [cf. aʀ]
SPI —
NAI quŋiaq 'caribou neck skin'
WCI [note Net quŋiaʀuklik 'white dog with black neck' in Ras., who also has it for Igl — for Car quniuq 'unhaired caribou neck skin' see quniɣuq, but note that Pryde has Cop quniaq 'white-haired front part of caribou' (contam.)]
ECI [Lab quŋiaʀulik 'dog with white neck' — Peck]
GRI NG quŋiaq 'throat skin of bear (for trousers)' [Holt.]

PE quŋluɣ- 'wince or jump in surprise' [cf. quaqcaaq-]
AAY C quŋcuXtə-, K quŋcuxtə- 'make a grimace of dislike' [poss. contam. with quŋcuʀ-]
CAY HBC, Nun quxcuaqəʀ- 'be startled' [poss. contam. with quŋcuʀ-]
NSY qunluɣ- 'be startled'
CSY quŋluɣ- 'dive (seal, walrus)'
Sir —
SPI quɣluk- 'be startled'
NAI quɣluk- 'wince when startled or suddenly frightened'
WCI quɣluk- 'jump in surprise, quiver'

ECI qullu(k)- 'jump in surprise'
GRI EG quttuattaC-

PE quŋuʀ(-) 'bury or grave' [also 'corpse'; there may be a relat. with quŋcuʀ- if not quŋatə]
AAY quŋuq 'grave', quŋuʀ- 'bury'
CAY quŋuq 'grave, coffin', quŋitə-, Nun quŋi- 'bury'
NSY quŋuq 'corpse' [Jen. has 'grave']
CSY quŋuʀ- 'bury' [for quŋa 'middle, core, source' see quŋatə-]
Sir quŋəX 'grave' [Vakh. has quŋuX, also quŋuXtuʀvəx 'burial', quŋiʀət(ə)- 'put down' from Men.'s texts]
SPI quŋuq 'grave', Imaq 'corpse' [Men. also mentions quŋa 'the grave' as a place name in Imaq]
NAI Nu quŋuq 'corpse'
WCI —
ECI — [for quŋuq 'white liquid from certain plants, semen' see quŋuliq under quɣəlŋiʀ]
GRI —

PY quŋutuʀaq 'pet (animal in house)' [cf. quŋuʀ-]
AAY quŋutu<ʀ>aq 'pet (not dog) kept in house'
CAY quŋutuʀaq
NSY —
CSY —

PE quŋuyuɣ- 'smile'
AAY —
CAY quuyuʀni- 'smile'
NSY —
CSY —
Sir —
SPI quŋuyuŋaaq-
NAI quŋuyuk-
WCI quŋuyuk-
ECI quŋat- 'smile' [and quŋa- Iti 'smile about', Lab 'smile at or about' — Bourq.]
GRI quŋuyuɣ-, Up Kullorsuaq quʀ̃uyuɣ- 'smile'

PE quŋyaʀ- 'observe jealously?' [there may be a relat. to qukəɣə- here]
AAY quŋyaʀ-, quŋyuɣ- 'be jealous (man of woman or v.v.)'
CAY quŋyaʀ-
NSY qunyaʀ- 'be jealous' [Em.]
CSY quŋyaʀ- 'be jealous (man of woman or v.v.)'
Sir quŋyəʀ- 'be jealous' [Em.]
SPI —
NAI —
WCI quniaq- [for quŋiaq-?] 'look at (pictures, etc.)' [Pet. has 'observe' for Sig; Ras. has Cop, Net quŋ·iar- 'take pleasure in looking at' and Jen. has Cop quŋiaq- 'watch a distant object']
ECI Lab quŋiaq- 'look at' [Peck]
GRI quŋiaʀ- 'observe (at a distance)', EG quŋiaʀ- 'observe closely'

PE qupaɣ 'fancy trim'
AAY —
CAY —
NSY —
CSY qupak 'girl's hair beads'
Sir qupax [Orr]
SPI quvak 'fancy trim' [and as verb 'trim, decorate']
NAI qupak 'fancy trim' [also verbal]
WCI qupait 'fancy trim'
ECI —
GRI —

PE qupan(n)u(C)aʀ 'bunting (or other small bird)' [cf. qupaɣ and perhaps ŋ(ŋ)uðaʀ?]
AAY C qupanua'aq 'small bird, e.g. bunting', PWS qupankicuaq 'sparrow' [and AP qupalaq 'kind of bird']
CAY qupanuaʀ(aq*) 'gray jay'
NSY —
CSY [note qupšuʀaq 'black puffin']
Sir [note quvəxsipayux 'snow bunting' and qupšuʀəX 'black puffin', qupəqšaX 'eider']
SPI quvanuaq 'arctic goose', quvanuaužaq [Imaq also quvanŋuaq] 'snow bunting'
NAI [qupałuk 'Lapland longspur']
WCI Cop qupanuaq 'sparrow' [Car EP 'bird'; note Sig, Cop qupanuaqpak 'eagle'; Pryde has Cop qupannuaq 'small bird', qupannuaqpak 'golden eagle', and qupannuaqpaaʀyuk 'horned lark']
ECI qupanuaq 'snow bunting' [and Schn. has qupanuaqpaq 'big sparrow — northern horned skylark?'; B.-S. has qupanuvaʀyuk 'bunting' for Igl]
GRI qupannaaq, qupanavaʀšuk, SWG qupalu(ʀa)aʀšuk, NG qupanuk 'snow bunting'

PE qupə- 'split (lengthwise)'
AAY qupə- 'split, crack' [quppaq 'crack']
CAY qupə-
NSY qupə- 'cut in half'
CSY quupə- 'split in two lengthwise'
Sir qupə- 'cut in half' [Vakh. also has quvə- and quvɣəlmi 'in half'; Men. has qupət(ə)-, also qupəqaʀ- 'crack']
SPI quvi- 'crack'
NAI qupɨ- 'split lengthwise'
WCI qupi-
ECI qupi-
GRI qupi-

PI qupcik- 'split easily'
SPI qupsik- 'split easily'
NAI qufsik-
WCI qupsik-
ECI qutsi(k)-
GRI qussiɣ-

PE qupðaʀ 's.th. split in two' [cf. ðaʀ]
AAY PWS 'dried split fish'
CAY Nun quppayaɣaX 'fish cut in half to hang'
NSY —
CSY —
Sir —
SPI —
NAI —
WCI [note Cop quvyat 'matches, esp. a bunch stuck together as traded in northern Canada' — Pryde]

ECI —
GRI SWG quššaq 'animal cut in half'

PI qupluq- 'split into pieces' [cf. luʀ-]
SPI qupłuq- 'split into pieces'
NAI quvluq- 'split in many places lengthwise' [quvluula- 'crack repeatedly (ice)']
WCI quvluq- 'be split'
ECI qullu(q)-, qulluu(q)- 'split lengthwise (in several places)'
GRI qułłuʀ- 'split (several times)', qułłuuʀ- 'crack repeatedly' [and qułłui- 'split, cut into strips']

PE qupnəʀ 'crack or split' [cf. nəʀ[1]]
AAY C, AP qupn̥əq 'crack'
CAY qupn̥əq* 'crack, fissure'
NSY qupn̥əq 's.th. cut off'
CSY qupn̥əq* 'whitefish'
Sir qupn̥əX 'half, part cut off' [also 'whitefish' acc. Krup.]
SPI qupniq 'crack'
NAI qumnɨq* 'crack' [also quʀʀiq]
WCI qumniq 'deep and dangerous crack' [and Net qu'niq 'narrow crack in ice' — Pryde]
ECI qunniq 'crack in ice' [compare qupiniq 'split in wood']
GRI qunniq* 'cleft in rock', NG quŋniq 'crack in rock or ice'

PE quppaʀ 's.th. cracked in two' [cf. q under nəʀ[1] and compare qupnəʀ above]
AAY qupa 'half' [base qupə- — compare kupa under kuppaʀ (kupə-); note also PWS qupaʀn̥əq, C qupaqn̥əq 'crack, crevice' with further nəʀ[1]]
CAY qqupa 'half' [base qupə-, probably a back formation]
NSY [note qupaxłəq 'crack, fissure' with łəʀ[1]]
CSY —
Sir [Vakh. has qupəʀ(ə)nu 'in the middle']
SPI quppaq 'crack'
NAI quppaq*
WCI quppaq
ECI quppaq 'crack, half a year, last quarter of moon', Iti 'half (lengthwise)'
GRI quppaq* 'crack, half (lengthwise)' [and Ges. has EG quppaalaq 'valley']

PI quppiʀnəq 'parting' [cf. quppaʀ above and liʀ- and nəʀ[1]]
Yup — [but note PWS qupəʀnəq 'length of finger joint'?]
SPI quppaniq 'parting (in hair)'
NAI quppiʀnʸɨq* 'parting (in hair)'
WCI Cop quppiʀniq 'parting' [Pryde]
ECI quppiniq 'aisle between benches in snow house', Iti 'parting'
GRI quppiʀniq* 'page, parting' [and note quppiʀ- 'part hair, look up (in book)']

PE qupəlʀuʀ 'maggot or worm' [cf. qupə- and quʀ]
AAY qəpəlluq, AP qafłuq 'maggot, grub'
CAY qupluq, Nun quvluX
NSY qəpəlʀuk 'worm' [L.-T. has qəpəlʀuq]
CSY —
Sir —
SPI quvaʀluq, Qaw qupalʀuq
NAI qupɨlʀuq 'maggot, grub, worm' [qupilʀuq- 'be infested with worms']
WCI qupilʀuq 'worm'
ECI qupiʀuq 'insect'
GRI qupiʀłuq 'maggot' [qupiʀłuʀ- 'have maggots (in s.th.)']

PI qupquʀiaq 'legendary giant polar bear' [also the Inu forms may be ultimately from the Chukchi given under Yup below, with local distortions]
Yup [CSY and Sir quXsatku, NSY qoqsatku 'giant polar bear' is from Chukchi qocatko, whereas CAY equivalent quqquyaq is borrowed from the Inu]
SPI quqquyak 'legendary giant polar bear'
NAI qupquʀiaq, Mal quɣluɣiaq 'mythical ten-legged polar bear' [the latter influenced by quɣluɣiaq under quɣluk-]
WCI ququʀiaq 'sort of dragon in legends'
ECI —
GRI —

PY-S ququŋaq 'leaf'
AAY —
CAY —
NSY ququŋaq 'leaf, polar willow' [L.-T.]
CSY ququŋaq 'leaf, edible willow leaf'
Sir ququŋaX

PE ququʀ- 'call'
AAY —
CAY —
NSY —
CSY —
Sir ququʀ- 'call, beckon'
SPI quʀuaq- 'call to, hail from a distance'
NAI ququq- 'entreat, summon supernatural forces', PH 'call to', ququaq- 'call by name'
WCI ququaq- 'call loudly', Sig ququa- 'call by name from a distance' [and Pryde has Net, Cop ququuq- 'call for help']
ECI ququq- 'call, make an articulate cry, shout', ququaq- 'make the sound of a siren, shout'
GRI —

PE quʀa(yaqit)- 'slip'
AAY K AP quasqitə-, Kod wasqitə- 'slip, slide', quasqinaʀ- 'be slippery'
CAY quXasqitə-, HBC quʀasqitə-, UK, UY, LI wasqitə-, Nun, NI, Eg quasqitə-, quasqiaXtə- 'slip' [and quXasqinaXqə-, HBC quʀayaʀnaXqə- 'be slippery']
NSY waɣ̥qəXtə- 'slip' [ANLC — Men. has wiɣ̥qiaʀnalʀia 'slippery'; for qiaʀnaq 'treacherous ice' see qi(C)aʀ-]
CSY — [for qiiʀnitə- 'slip on ice', qiiʀnaʀ- 'be slippery' see qi(C)aʀ-]
Sir —
SPI quayaʀit- [Qaw also quwait-] 'slip, slide', quaya(ʀ)naq- 'be slippery'

NAI quayaqit- 'slip and slide'
WCI quayaqit- 'slip and fall'
ECI quayaqit- 'slip and fall repeatedly', NBI quat- 'slip' [and quitaaRnaq- 'be slippery']
GRI quaat-, quaaqqi(t)-, NG quayaqqit-, EG quaaqqitsi- 'slip' [Robbe and Menn. for the latter; also quayaat 'slimy moss or seaweed (to tread on)', EG quayasiiq 'green seaweed']

PI quacak 'slippery place'
SPI —
NAI quasa, quasižaq 'bare, smooth ice where you slide' [and quasižaaq- 'skate, slide along swiftly']
WCI Cop quahak 'new ice without snow' [Ras.; Car EP quahaq 'ice on lake'; Pryde has Cop quaha 'slippery ice' and quahiyaq- 'skate']
ECI quasaq 'slippery ice', quasaq- 'slip', Iti 'skate on ice'
GRI quasak, EG quasaq, NG quahaq 'slippery place' [Holt.], quasaɣ-, EG quasaR- 'be slippery', NG quihahaaq-, quahahaaq- 'slide, skate' [and quasasiuR- 'be out on slippery ice', quasi- 'drop s.th. slippery, slip and fall', NG quihi- 'let harpoon line run out', NG quihaqqit- 'slip and fall']

PE quRə- 'urinate'
AAY quXə- 'urinate'
CAY quXə- [and quXsuun 'penis']
NSY quXə-
CSY uXə- 'urinate'
Sir [Vakh. has quxtəqə- 'urinate' (for quXtəqə-?) from Rub.'s texts]
SPI qui- 'urinate'
NAI qu<R>i- 'urinate' [and note quRRivik 'penis']
WCI qui- 'urinate' [and note quiqivik 'penis']
ECI qui- 'urinate'
GRI qui- 'urinate' [and note EG quuqquuq 'penis']

PI quqcuq- or **quqcuk-** 'be yellowish' [cf. quRəR below and compare tuŋuyuq- under tuŋu- and CSY cuŋaɣyuk under cuŋaɣ- (cuŋa(R)) — this could contain p.b. yuɣ, in which case it should be quqsuk-, but compare qakcuR- under qakə(R)-]
SPI quqsuq- 'be yellow'
NAI quqsuq- 'be yellow, stained', PH 'be brown'
WCI Sig quqsuilRaq 'old bear skin, yellow with age', Car quqsuqtuq 'yellow' [Dor.; Pryde has Cop, Car, Net quqsuktuq 'yellow, yellowish green']
ECI quRsutaq, NBI, SB quRsuqtuq 'yellow' [Peck has qursuktaq 'yellow thing' and qursuk- 'be yellow' for Lab]
GRI quRsuk, EG quRsuq 'green', Up quRsuq 'yellow' [and NWG quRsuRpaluttuq 'green', NG quXXuqpaluktuq 'yellow']

PE quRəR 'urine'
AAY quXəq 'urine'
CAY [Lantis has Nun quX 'urine']
NSY —
CSY —
Sir —
SPI quq 'urine'
NAI quq
WCI quq [Ras. has quuq]
ECI quik 'urine' [influenced by quik under qu(C)əyiɣ?]
GRI quuq 'urine'

PY quR(əR)maR- 'urinate repeatedly' [compare (u)maR(əR)-]
AAY quXm̥aR- 'urinate repeatedly or at length'
CAY quXm̥aR-
NSY quXm̥aR- [ANLC]
CSY [uXm̥aataq 'urethra']
Inu [note NAI quRmaala- 'urinate in small amounts at frequent intervals']

PY-S quRun 'chamber pot' [cf. p.b. un]
AAY —
CAY quXun 'chamber pot'
NSY quXun
CSY Xuta, Xʷuta
Sir [quRəsaX 'chamber pot']

PI quRvik 'chamber pot' [cf. p.b. ðɣɨɣ]
SPI quRvik 'chamber pot'
NAI quRvik
WCI quRvik
ECI NBI, SB quRvik
GRI quRvik, EG quppik

PI quRžinəq 'urine stain' [cf. ði- and nəR[1]]
SPI [quRžiq 'stain as from hard water or urine' — also verbal]
NAI quRžinʸɨq* 'urine stain' [verbal = 'become stained with urine']
WCI —
ECI —
GRI quRšiniq*, quššiniq* 'yellow patch of urine on snow or ice'

PE quRli(C)aR 'slobber or sap?' [cf. quRə- and liaq under li(C)aR]
AAY —
CAY —
NSY —
CSY quRlaa 'commercial corn or similar syrup' [perhaps a loan from Inu]
Sir quRla, pl quRlay 'syrup' [Orr — from the CSY; note quXɬəx 'residue of oil from lamp, container for drips from oil lamp' — Em.]
SPI quRliaq 'slobber' [also as verb]
NAI quRliaq 'slobber, sap, resin' [also as verb]
WCI quRliaq 'soft tree sap'
ECI quRliaq 'sap' [as verb = 'slobber']
GRI NWG quRɬiaR- 'slobber'

PE quRluR- 'stream or flow' [cf. quRə- and luR-]
AAY quXɬuR- 'fall, cascade (water)'
CAY quXɬuR- 'cascade'
NSY —
CSY uqɬuXtə- 'drip'
Sir quRluR- 'drip' [Vakh. has quRluXt(ə)-]

SPI quʀluq- 'cascade'
NAI quʀluq- 'sound of falling water' [and quʀluula- 'drip extensively']
WCI quʀluq 'waterfall' [also verbal]
ECI quʀluq- 'drip, flow (e.g. waterfall)'
GRI quʀłuʀ- 'stream, flow', quʀłuq 'spout, uretha' [and EG quʀtuʀniq 'drop'; quʀłuula- 'drip a lot']

PE quʀluʀtaʀ and **quʀluʀtuʀ** 'waterfall' [cf. ðaʀ- and ðuʀ?]
AAY quXłuXta, quXłuXtəq 'waterfall'
CAY quXłuxtaq
NSY —
CSY —
Sir —
SPI quʀluqtaq
NAI quʀluqtaq
WCI Cop quʀluqtuq Pryde]
ECI quʀluqtuq 'waterfall'
GRI quʀłuʀtuq

PE qutə '(steep) shore' [there may be a relat. to qulə- (with p.b. tə on underlying *qu-?)]
AAY quta 'shore, beach, under water'
CAY quta 'solid ground, as at bottom of pit', Nun qutiXtuʀ- 'walk on shore (as when beachcoming) as a boat accompanies one out on the water' and qutqiʀ- 'sit close to edge (as on cliff or chair)' [ANLC]
NSY —
CSY quta 'land seen from sea, landmass, Siberia'
Sir quta '(dry) land'
SPI —
NAI qutait- 'be steep' [and qužvaq 'highlands']
WCI Car EP qutailʀuq 'cliff above water' [Ow.]
ECI quti 'flat terrain at the foot of steep rock, natural plain at the foot of a cliff', qutiʀʀuluk 'rough cliff'
GRI qutaarłuk 'steep cliff', NG qutaiʀluq 'cliff or promentary going straight into the sea with no beach'

PI qutəʀuq- 'follow boat along shore'
SPI —
NAI qutiʀuq- 'walk to same destination as others going by boat'
WCI [Cop qutiXXuq- 'follow edge of coast' (Pryde)]
ECI qutiʀuq- 'follow on shore at foot of cliff'
GRI qutiʀuʀ- 'follow boat along shore of land'

PI qutliq 'Siberia(n)' [cf. l(l)iʀ]
Yup — [NSU qułłiq* 'Chukchi peninsula' — from SPI?; for CSY quyiłək 'Chukchi' see qulðiɣ- under qulə-]
SPI qułłiq 'Siberia, Siberian Eskimo'
NAI Mal qutliq 'Siberia, Siberian Eskimo'
WCI —
ECI —
GRI —

PI qutŋuq 'gleam of light' [the relat. to qitŋiʀ- is obscure — assim. in variant form qitŋuʀ-?]
SPI qutŋuq 'brightness on horizon indicating presence of ice on ocean'
NAI qunŋuq
WCI —
ECI —
GRI quŋŋuq 'gleam of light' [quŋŋuʀ- 'peep out, begin to shine (sun)']

PY qutŋuʀ- 'hump shoulders or bend forward?' [cf. quðu-?; EA qutŋu-X 'whale shoulder' in Joch. is probably borrowed from the AAY]
AAY qutŋuq 'hump on back of salmon that has gone upstream' [and note qutəxtə-, qucəxtə- 'become crestfallen']
CAY [note Nun qutŋuX 'sealskin parka', also qutəxte- 'gloat, boast'; for quluxtə- 'be hunchbacked' see qulucuk]
NSY — [but note qutaxtə- 'wrap around, surround']
CSY qutŋuʀ- 'bend over forward with head down while sitting' [postural root; qutŋuʀžuk 'upper back of animal or person']

PE qutu(ɣ) 'collarbone' [cf. western EA qutuɣnu- 'bird's breast']
AAY KP, Kod qutuk 'collarbone'
CAY qutuk
NSY qutuq, [ANLC] qutuk
CSY qutuq
Sir qutəX [Orr]
SPI qutuk
NAI qutuk
WCI qutuk
ECI qutu
GRI qutuk

PI qutuɣžuk 'constellation of four stars seen in winter' [cf. yuɣ]
SPI —
NAI qutuɣžuk 'constellation of four stars seen in winter'
WCI [Jen. has constellation kuttoryk for Cop]
ECI qutuʀyuuk 'Castor and Pollux' [Saul; Peck has kuttorsuk 'the ɨ stars Castor, Pollux, Sectatrix and Capella for Lab — MacDonald has Menkalinan as the third star]
GRI — [but Crantze mentions a constellation killab (qilaap) kuttuk (sic)]

PY-S qutuɣ- 'snore' [cf. Aleut quŋtuɣ- 'snore', with secondary ŋ?]
AAY qutuɣ- 'snore'
CAY qutuɣ-
NSY qutuɣ- snore', qutuk 'Adam's apple' [L.-T.]
CSY qutuɣ- 'snore'
Sir qutəɣ- 'snore' [Vakh. from Rub.]

PE quvə- 'stoop (e.g. in humiliation)?' [cf. qumaq- and /or quðu-]
AAY —
CAY quvə- 'decrease in size, shrink'
NSY quvə- 'be angry' [Enm. et al.]
CSY quuvə- 'decrease in size, feel sad, insecure or

insignificant' [Chap also quuvyuɣ- 'feel sad or humble' with yuɣ-]
Sir quv(ə)- 'be sad, lose heart' [Em.]
SPI —
NAI qufsuk- 'kneel', Mal qupsuŋaužaq- 'be crouching'
WCI — [for Baker Lake quxxu(C)- 'be bent, arched in two' see quŋcuʀ-; qua- 'have sexual intercourse' marked as 'adg' by Schn. probably belongs here too — see under quya-]
ECI [Schn. has quva- 'have sexual intercourse', for which compare Lab pakik- under pakəɣ- and the probable relat. of Yup uyuɣ- to uyuŋə-; note also qusu- Wakeham Bay 'have head drawn down between shoulders, be in a bad mood', Iti 'be boastful', also qutta(q)- 'draw chin into parka, hunch because of cold', and perhaps Lab kotsoalak- 'be downcast' (Peck)]
GRI [note qussuɣ- (old ortho. qugsug- may be spurious) 'stoop, try to make oneself small, pull chin into hood, abate (wind)', qussuŋa- 'be bent over in cold or humiliation' — contam. with quŋcuʀ- and/or kutðuɣ-?]

PY quvəɣci(q) 'sourdock?'
AAY C qauxcaaɣuaq 'skunk cabbage'
CAY quaxciq 'sourdock'
NSY quvəXsitaq 'kind of plant' [ANLC]
CSY quvəxsi *'Polygonum tripterocarpum* (sour plant)'
Sir [note quvəxsələŋ '(I) going for plants' — Vakh. from Rub.]

PI quvəq- 'catch off guard'
SPI quiq- 'catch off guard, surprise'
NAI quvɨq-
WCI quvi(q)-
ECI —
GRI —

PE quvəʀtə 'cataract (in eye)'
AAY —
CAY quaXta, Nun quvəXta 'cataract in eye'
NSY quvəXtə [L.-T.]
CSY quvəXta
Sir quvəXta [Orr]
SPI quiqti 'cataract'
NAI quviqtɨ
WCI quviqti 'cataract' [and note quvirsaq 'white of eye']
ECI quviqti 'white spot on eye, cataract' [and quviqsaq 'white of eye']
GRI quiʀtiq 'cataract' [and note quiʀšaq 'white of eye']

PE quvya(yuɣ)- 'be happy' [cf. Atkan Aleut qumyuxta- 'love' (as nom. = qumyux, both biblical), Att quvyux 'sadness, grief', quvyuxta- 'mourn, miss' — compare the 'love' sense of naŋłəɣ-]
AAY K quswayuɣ- 'be happy'
CAY Y, Nun, NS quzva(yuɣ)-, HBC quyva(yuɣ)- 'be happy' [emot. root]
NSY —
CSY [note qəsuɣ(yuɣ)- 'be happy, excited' — influenced by qəc(c)uɣ-?]
Sir [Em. has qəsuɣyuɣ- 'be excited' — from CSY?]
SPI quya(suk)-, Qaw quwia(suk)-
NAI quvia(suk)- 'be happy' [quviit- 'be unhappy']
WCI quvia(suk)- 'be happy' [and Pryde has quviiq- 'be out of sorts, be indisposed' for Cop]
ECI quvia(suk)- 'be happy'
GRI quia(suɣ)- 'be amused' [emot. root; also quiaɣ- 'take pleasure in', quiiʀ- 'no longer be interested in amusements']

PE quya- 'be thankful'
AAY quya-, PWS qua- 'be thankful'
CAY quya- 'be thankful, glad'
NSY quya- 'be happy', quyaqə- 'thank' [and quya 'joy' (ANLC)]
CSY quya- 'be happy'
Sir —
SPI quya- 'be thankful'
NAI quya-
WCI quya- 'thank', Baker Lake 'have sexual intercourse' [the latter may be a mistake for quva- as in Tar for this meaning, for which see quvə- — Schn. also has qua- for 'adg'; Dor. has quyahuk- 'be in a good mood' for Net]
ECI quyalli-, quyaɣi- 'thank' [and quyamaC- 'be happy, thankful'; Dor. has Tar quya(C)-, NBI quyaaq- 'be happy'; note also qutsasiq- 'give s.th. in gratitude']
GRI quya- 'thank' [quyamasuɣ- 'be thankful', qutsasiʀ- 'dance around for joy (old woman)']

PE quyanaʀ 'thank you' [cf. naʀ-]
AAY quyanaa, PWS quanaa 'thank you'
CAY quyana
NSY quyanaq [ANLC]
CSY quyanatun 'happily'
Sir —
SPI Qaw quyaana 'thank you'
NAI quyanaq
WCI Sig quyanainni [Lowe], quyanaqtutin [Met.], Cop quana, Net quyanaq
ECI quyana(q) 'it doesn't matter, so much the better', NBI, SB quyannamik 'thank you'
GRI quyanaq 'thank you'

PE quyəʀ- 'cough' [cf. Aleut quyXi- 'cough']
AAY quiʀ- 'cough' [and nom. quyəq, qusəq, quiq 'cough']
CAY quyəʀ-, quzəʀ- 'cough' [nom. = quyəq*, quzəq*]
NSY quyəq 'tuberculosis' [L.-T. adds meaning 'cough'; ANLC has quyəXtuq 'cough']
CSY qiiʀʷ- 'cough' [nom. = qiiqʷ* 'cough']
Sir quyəʀ- [Orr]
SPI Qaw quXiq- 'cough'
NAI quiq-, quXiq-, quiqsuq-, quXik-
WCI quiqtuq-
ECI quiqtuq-
GRI quiʀ-, quiʀsuʀ- 'cough' [and NG quiXXuq- 'have a cold, cough', quiʀuk- 'have a cough']

quyŋiq or **qužŋiq** 'domesticated reindeer' [from Chukchi qožaŋə 'reindeer']
AAY —
CAY quzŋiq, quyŋiq 'reindeer' [K also 'sheep', from Bible translations]
NSY quyŋiq 'reindeer'
CSY quyŋiq 'reindeer' [also qužəŋa 'large old reindeer' (in stories)]
Sir qužŋiq
SPI qunŋiq
NAI qunŋiq
WCI qunŋiq
ECI —
GRI —

PY quyuuq 'kind of small fish'
AAY AP qusuuk 'candlefish'
CAY quzuuq 'smelt'
NSY —
CSY —

S

saŋlak 'box' [from Chukchi ceŋəl 'box']
AAY —
CAY —
NSY sanlak 'box, suitcase, coffin'
CSY salŋak
Sir saŋləX 'box, coffin' [Vakh.]

sava 'sheep' [a loan from Danish-Norwegian in early colonial times; Petitot, like the Lab missionaries, would have had access to the early Greenlandic Bible translations, so that the presence of this word in WCI and ECI may represent a missionary borrowing which has gained currency in the language, rather than a natural diffusion]
SPI —
NAI —
WCI Sig sauɣaq '(bighorn) sheep' [Pet. — probably for 'Dall sheep']
ECI sauɣaq 'sheep'
GRI sava 'sheep'

T

PI taanəq 'size' [cf. nəʀ[1] and Aleut Atkan, western EA taðɣa-X, eastern EA taɣða-X 'span, measure from outstretched thumb to finger tip', also taaðɣaaða-X 'index finger']
SPI —
NAI taaniqtu- 'be larger than others, appear large', taanikit- 'be smaller than others'
WCI Sig taaniqtu- 'contain by its presence' [i.e. 'be larger than s.th. else'? — Pet.]
ECI taaniqtu- 'stand out in distance', taanikit- 'hardly stand out, be hard to discern'
GRI taaniq* 'size, extent', taaniʀtu- 'have a large circumference, be stout, loom large', taanikit- 'be slender, look small'

taaŋaq 'liquor' [borrowing from Aleut, where it means '(drinking) water', cf. kasakam taaŋaa 'liquor, vodka' (lit. 'white man's water')]
AAY taaŋaq 'liquor, water' [attested in latter sense for K since 1791]
CAY taaŋaq 'liquor' [as a verb, taaŋaʀ- 'drink liquor'; also listed in early NS word lists as 'water']
NSY —
CSY —
Sir —
SPI taaŋŋaq
NAI taaŋŋaq 'liquor', Nu, Mal taaŋŋaq- 'get drunk'
WCI taanŋaq 'liquor' [Lowe; Met. has ta(a)ŋaq, also taŋaq-, taŋuyaq- 'drink liquor'; Pryde has taaŋŋaq for Cop and Sig]
ECI —
GRI —

taaqaq 'cod-like fish' [from Aleut taaqa-X 'silverhake or walleye pollock (resembles a cod)'; reconstruction of a protoform to account for the CSY would be problematical]
AAY AP taaqaq, C taaqatak 'tomcod'
CAY —
NSY —
CSY [taqiiq 'Pacific cod (caught in slush in early winter)' may be a cognate with the Aleut rather than a loan]
Sir [Orr has taqiX, probably borrowed from CSY]

PY taaʀ(aʀ)i- 'swat self in steambath'
AAY taaXi- 'swat self in steambath'
CAY taaXi-
NSY —
CSY —

PE taci(ɣ)- 'stretch' [cf. taciʀ; there may be a further relat. to tatyuʀ-]
AAY —
CAY —
NSY —
CSY tasik, tasiq 'short piece of rope used for carrying something', Chap also tasiɣ- 'attach strap to shoulder bag'
Sir tasəx 'strap over shoulder' [and Vakh. has tasicəʀaXtitu '(going) fishing' from Men.'s texts]
SPI tazi-, Qaw tasit- 'stretch, extend' [the former also intr.; tazik 'wooden rack on which skin boats are stored']
NAI tasi- 'stretch (intr.)' [trans. tasit-]
WCI tasik- 'stretch, be stretched' [and B. Lake tasit 'scaffolding for drying clothes or meat' — Schn.; EP tahiit, acc. Ow.]
ECI tasi- 'stretch, extend, be stretched or lengthened' [and tasiC- 'carry a kayak between several people']
GRI tasi- 'stretch, extend' [and tasit- 'extend by pulling (several times)', tasitsaat 'implement for softening skin']

PI tacižuk- 'stretch (be elastic)'
SPI [note taziuq- 'stretch']
NAI tasižuk- 'make bigger by stretching' [and tasižaʀa(a)q 'rubber band']
WCI [note tasiuʀaq 'rubber band']
ECI tasiyuaq 'body garment of stretchable material', tasiuayuuq 'rubber band, elastic'
GRI tasišua- 'stretch, be elastic' [NWG tasišuaaʀtuq 'rubber band']

PE taciʀ 'spit or sand bar' [also 'narrow inlet'; cf. taci-]
AAY —
CAY taciq 'sandspit and bay formed by it'
NSY —
CSY — [for tasiq, tasik 'rope for carrying' see taci-]
Sir —
SPI taziq 'point of land', Qaw tasiq 'bay, lagoon'
NAI tasiq 'lagoon, inlet'
WCI tasiq 'lake'
ECI tasiq, SB also sasiq 'lake' [and tasiuyaq 'almost closed bay, interior tidal lake']
GRI tasiq 'lake' [tasiužaq 'narrow bay or inlet from the sea']

PE taðəɣ- 'split into layers'
AAY —
CAY taiq 'inner layer of seal gut removed before processing'
NSY tiaɣ- 'remove a layer or outer garment' [ANLC also kiaɣ-, by contam. with əkiðaʀ-?]
CSY tiiɣ-
Sir [taɣžuʀ- 'separate double mittens or two layers of outer coat']
SPI taak- 'split into layers, come unraveled'
NAI taak-'split into layers, remove article of clothing attached to another piece of clothing' [and taaksi- 'remove an article of clothing attached to another']
WCI taak- 'unravel, come apart, take off outer parka or boots'
ECI taak- 'take off (top layer of clothing)', Lab 'make oneself easy or comfortable, take off boots' [and taɣut(i)- 'take off another's clothing, separate layers of clothing']
GRI taaɣ-, taat- 'turn inside out, pull out, be pulled out (inner garment from outer one)' [and taxxaatsut 'kamiks taken off and not turned inside out']

PI taaktəq- 'separate layers of clothing' [cf. təʀ-]
SPI taaktiq- 'remove a layer of clothing'
NAI taaktɨq- 'remove article of clothing attached to another piece of clothing'
WCI taaktiq- 'take off outer parka, unravel tresses
ECI taatsi(q)- 'remove outer garment (esp. boots)'
GRI taatsiʀ- 'take off waterproof clothing'

PE taðim(m)a 'there or thus' [dem. adv. imma preceded by anaphoric/out-of-field prefix ta(ð)-]
AAY taima 'then, apparently, what if, (it's) gone'
CAY tayima, Y taima 'elsewhere, gone'
NSY tayima 'somewhere near'
CSY Chap tazimavək 'to somewhere or other, at random'
Sir —
SPI taima 'long ago,' taimau- 'take a long time' [and Jen. has W taima 'it is ended']
NAI taimma 'there, then', taima 'that's it, stop!' [and note tainna, Mal taatna, Nu taitna, taimanna 'thus' (compare under imma), taimain[y]aq 'suddenly', taimmalikii 'so what?'; Jen. has taimani 'at that time']
WCI taima, taimani 'at that time' [and Ras. has taipsumani 'long ago' for Net]
ECI taima 'is it ready?, I've stopped, then, it's certain', taimaak 'thus' [Ras. has taamak for Igl and B.-S. has taissumani 'long ago', and Pryde has taimau- 'have had enough, quit' for Igl]
GRI taama 'thus, stop!', EG 'probably, no doubt' [Robbe and Menn. for the latter; also taamak 'thus, it's gone!', taamaałłaat 'only', taamani 'at that time', taamannak, EG taaminna 'thus, always']

PI taimait- 'be thus' [cf. ət-, here fused with preceding taðim(m)a]
Yup — [but compare CSY tawatətə- 'be that way' under taɣʷatən (taðva)]
SPI —
NAI taimait- 'be thus' [also tainnait- from tainna; taimailli, tainnailli 'leave it alone!']
WCI taimailiuq- 'act thus' [and Pryde has taimait- 'be like that', taimaili- 'say or do that (to)' for Cop]
ECI taimait- 'be or treat thus' [taimaili- 'do or say thus', taimailiuq- 'do or say thus (several things)']
GRI taamaat- 'be thus' [taamaali-, taamaasi- 'have become thus', taamaaliuʀ- 'do thus', taamaałłi 'stop, enough!', taamaattuq 'however, enough!']

PI taimuŋaaq- 'do s.th. blindly?' [cf. q-, here with the all. case of taðim-; compare CSY tazimavək under taðim(m)a above]
SPI —
NAI taimuŋaaq- 'recite from memory' [note taimuŋa 'for ever, to that time']
WCI [Cop taimuŋnaq- 'disappear without a trace' — Pryde]
ECI taimuŋaaqta(q)- 'grope around, talk without really knowing'
GRI [taamuŋa, taamuŋaannaq 'at random']

PE taðva 'there (you are)' [from deictic prefix ta(ð)- plus demonstrative root uv-, taking oblique case endings like other such roots used adverbially; cf. Aleut tacim '(not) yet', also tataam 'again' with is rel. case ending, and Att anaphoric dem. tama; note the semantic differences that have arisen between the metathesized and non-metathesized forms in Cop and GRI]
AAY tawa, tua 'there (you are), that's enough'
CAY tua-i, HBC, NS tawa-i 'well then, that's enough' [and tuaX 'like', taɣʷaam 'however']
NSY tawa 'there, ready'
CSY taawa 'there, enough' [talwa 'even yet, not yet, in addition' is from Chukchi təlv- 'quite' = Vakh.'s talɣʷa for Sir]

Sir tava 'there, enough' [also tavənaʀit- 'be there', also in Vakh. — from CSY?; Vakh. also has tacəkamənu 'to there']
SPI tavža, Qaw tažža 'that's it, enough'
NAI tavža, tažva, PH talva, Mal tažža 'that's it, enough' [and Mal taža 'that's right!']
WCI Sig tayva, Net tavža, Cop talva 'there (you are)' [and Cop tayya 'now' (Lowe); Schn. has taɣvatuuq 'if only I could' for B. Lake, and Briggs has Net tavža 'there (you are)', Utk tapža 'here, right now']
ECI tavva [older Baffin, Aiv taɣva], Tar, Lake Harbour, Cape Dorset taɣɣa 'here it is, then' [also (alongside tavva) in NBI, Aiv acc. Dor., who has taɣa for Iti — Saul has taɣataɣa 'now'; Lab taffa 'then, because'; note also NBI, C. Dorset, taɣvauvutit, Iti tavvavusi, taavavusi 'goodbye']
GRI tašša 'there (you are), that's enough', taava 'then', NG taaya, EG taava 'there, then, stop, enough' [and taššuuɣu 'in a while', NG tassaɣu 'now'; Robbe and Menn. also have tatta 'you know' and Robbe and Dor. tattaalaa 'luckily, that is why' for EG, and Tersis has taa 'then' as well as taava]

PE taðvaŋinnaʀ 'only or right away' [cf. ŋinnaʀ- and compare tažvakŋinnaq below]
AAY —
CAY —
NSY tawaŋinaq 'right away'
CSY Chap taawaŋinaq 'only'
Sir tavəŋinaX
SPI tavžainaq 'suddenly', Imaq 'only'
NAI —
WCI Sig tayvainnaq 'suddenly' [and Schn has Car? taɣvain(n)aq 'immediately' for 'adg']
ECI taɣɣainaq, Iti taɣainnaq, tavvainaq, Lab taffainak 'right away, suddenly' [the Iti forms from Saul]
GRI taššaannaq 'just now'

PY taɣʷakən 'from then on?' [abl. case]
AAY tawakən
CAY taw̥kən 'even though, however' [compare regular taukən 'from there']
NSY taaxkən 'then, from here'
CSY taaxkən 'from here, from then on, then'
Sir [Em. has tavəknəŋ 'from here, from then on, then', with abl. knəŋ]

PY taɣʷatən 'thus' [aeq. case]
AAY tawatən 'that way'
CAY tuatən, HBC, NS tawatən 'like that' [and note tuatna- 'act that way']
NSY tawatən 'like that' [tawatəlŋuXta(ʀ)- 'do thus']
CSY tawatən 'like that' [and tawatətə- 'be that way' with ət-]
Sir [tavətən 'like that' and tavətəlŋuX 'thus' — from CSY?]

PI tažvakŋainnaq 'suddenly' [cf. ŋinnaʀ and taðvaŋinnaʀ above; the present forms have the ablative of the demon. adverbial]
SPI Qaw tažžakŋainaq 'suddenly' [Imaq also tavžaniinaq acc. Men.]
NAI [note tavžaŋŋatciaq, tažvaŋŋatciaq 'suddenly']
WCI [Sig tayvaŋatsiaq- 'happen suddenly', Net tavžaŋŋatsiaq 'suddenly' (Pryde)]
ECI —
GRI taššaŋŋaannaq 'suddenly'

PE taɣci- 'win s.th.' [cf. taɣə-?]
AAY —
CAY taxci- 'win' [taxtaq 'winnings in a game']
NSY taxsi- 'win in a card game' [ANLC]
CSY —
Sir —
SPI taksi- 'win s.th.'
NAI PH taksi- 'bring home meat from site of kill'
WCI tak(si)- 'win, esp. at gambling or cards'
ECI —
GRI —

PE taɣə- 'go up (on shore)' [cf. Aleut taaɣa-X 'breaker, rip tide', also taɣətuɣ-, taɣi- and taɣ(ɣ)iq-; compare naɣət- for the vowel in Inu]
AAY taɣə- 'go up'
CAY taɣə- 'go up (from shore or up a slope), move back from center of attention'
NSY taɣə- 'go up' [L.-T.]
CSY taɣlaʀ- 'go up from shore' [and taɣyuqa- 'come slowly toward shore (boat)', taɣuʀa- 'come in over shallow part of beach (surf)', Chap taɣluɣutə- 'pull whale ashore']
Sir — [taɣluɣut(ə)- 'pull whale ashore' — Em., probably from CSY]
SPI taat- 'move up, climb ashore, go north, return from hunting', Qaw also 'bring up from shore'
NAI Nu takšuq- 'come up to land or village' [and note taksaʀnaq 'ocean current flowing toward shore']
WCI ➟
ECI taaC- 'carry into house or up from beach'
GRI taat- 'bring home or up from beach' [Fab.]

PE taɣciʀ- 'get to come (up)' [cf. c(c)iʀ-]
AAY —
CAY taxciʀ- 'beckon to come up'
NSY taxsi- (for taxsiʀ-?) 'call to come', taxsiʀaʀ- 'summon a dog by licking the tongue against the lower teeth' [ANLC; L.-T. has taxsiyaq 'calling a dog']
CSY taxsiʀ- 'beckon or call to come'
Sir —
SPI taksatuq- 'call upon for help, name s.o. for a dead person'
NAI taksiqsuq- 'call to make it come (animal)'
WCI —
ECI —
GRI NG taxxiq- 'make (another person) come toward one by sorcery'

PE taɣðaʀ(-) 'come up on shore (waves)' [cf. ðaʀ-]
AAY —
CAY taɣyaq 'surf, tide bringing things ashore'
NSY taɣžaa 'surf'

CSY —
Sir —
SPI Imaq taɣžaʀa(q)- 'come to shore (wave)'
NAI taɣžaq- 'go up river'
WCI Sig taɣɣaq- 'go upstream' [Lowe, who spells it taɣiaq-; EP taɣɣaaʀaqtuq 'surf' — Ow.; Pryde has taɣɣaaʀniq 'swell on sea' for Cop, and Briggs has takžau- 'travel away from water' for Utk]
ECI Aiv taɣɣaq- 'go inland'
GRI [tassaaʀ- (old ortho. tagsâr-) 'break against shore (waves)', NG taxxaaq 'surf' may be with p.b. caʀ- instead, like NAI taksarnaq under taɣə- above]

PE taɣətuɣ 'fog' [cf. taɣə-]
AAY taituk 'mountain fog'
CAY taituk 'fog'
NSY tiatuk
CSY taɣituk
Sir taɣətəx
SPI taktuk 'fog bank in distance' [and taksiq-, Di taitu(k)- 'be foggy', the latter presumably from Yup]
NAI taktuk 'fog'
WCI taktuk 'fog' [B.-S. has taxxiq for Car; Pryde also has Cop, Net, Car taksiq- 'be foggy']
ECI tattuq, tatsiq, F. Bay saksik 'fog' [and tatsi(q)- 'be foggy']
GRI —

PY taɣituɣi(C)aq 'murrelet' [cf. p.b. (C)iʀ and aʀ]
AAY C taituuyak, taituiyaq 'marbled murrelet'
CAY —
NSY —
CSY taɣituɣiiq 'murrelet'

PY-S taɣi- 'come (toward speaker)' [the relat. to taɣə- and ta(ɣ)i- and taɣɣiq- is obscure; cf. Aleut taya- 'alight']
AAY tai- 'come to speaker'
CAY tai-, Nun taa- 'come to speaker' [and taikaniʀ- 'bring closer, explain, clarify'; taitai 'come here!' (esp. to children)]
NSY tia- 'come toward speaker' [ANLC; Em. has tiatə- 'carry'; Men. has tiaɣ̥qə- 'call to come to one, call back', tiasiɣ̥qə- 'call (s.o.)']
CSY taɣi- 'come (to speaker)'
Sir [Vakh. has taɣi- 'come', which he marks as probably being from CSY]

PI taɣ(ɣ)iq- 'go from place to place' [cf. taɣə- and compare aɣɣiʀ- under aɣə- and anəɣiʀ- under anə-]
SPI —
NAI taɣiq- 'go (calling) from place to place', taɣɣiqsuaq- 'continually move from place to place'
WCI taɣiq- 'go from place to place, go visiting'
ECI —
GRI —

PE taɣi(C)uʀ- 'sneeze'
AAY —
CAY —
NSY taɣiiʀʷ- 'sneeze'
CSY —
Sir [taɣəsaqə(s)- 'sneeze']
SPI tayuuq- 'sneeze'
NAI taɣiuq- 'sneeze' [nom. = 'larva of throat botfly, worm in nasal cavity of caribou' — Pryde has taɣɣuq for Cop; taɣik-, taɣiuqtuq- 'sneeze repeatedly']
WCI taɣiuq- 'sneeze' [and taɣiuit (for taɣuiɣit?) 'nasal worms of caribou']
ECI taɣiuq- 'sneeze' [and taɣiuk 'worm in nose, turbinate bones of nose, olfactory nerve']
GRI taŋayuʀ-, EG taŋiirtuʀ-, NG taɣiuq- 'sneeze'

PI ta(ɣ)i- 'name ' [there may be a relat. with taɣi- and/or taɣə- (the latter becoming regularly taɣi- in Inu) — note especially the GRI 'messenger' senses below]
Yup — [for NSY taɣ̥qə- 'call', CAY taikaniʀ- 'bring closer, explain' see taɣi- and for CAY taxciʀ- 'call to come' see taɣciʀ- under taɣə-]
SPI tai- 'utter (name)'
NAI ta<ɣ>i- 'utter' [and tainʸɨq* 'name, title']
WCI tai- 'name' [and note Car? tailaq 'name, nominal' — Schn. 'adg'; Pryde also has tainiq 'word']
ECI tai- 'mention, name' [and tainiq 'fact of naming oneself']
GRI taa- 'name, mention, call, vote for, send with a message' [Robbe and Menn. also have it for EG in the sense 'get s.o. to do s.th. for one'; half-trans. taasi-; taašaq 'messenger', taałłaq 'poem', taaniq 'spelling, pronunciation' (S.-L. 'naming'), and taxxaʀłuɣ- 'mispronounce']

PI taɣɣin 'name' [cf. un]
SPI taɣɣin 'name'
NAI taɣɣinʸ
WCI [Cop taɣɣihiq 'name' — Pryde]
ECI —
GRI taxxit 'name (of s.th.), noun'

PI taiɣuq- 'name one after another' [cf. (C)uʀ-]
SPI —
NAI taiɣuq- 'call names out' [taiɣuaq- 'read']
WCI taiɣuaq- 'read, call by name'
ECI taiɣuq- 'tell about (in story)'
GRI taayuʀ- 'name one after another'

PY ta(C)ivkaʀ- 'approach (e.g. storm)?' [cf. taɣi- and vkaʀ-?]
AAY taixkʷautə- 'have labor pains'
CAY taifkaʀ- 'be stormy (weather), be closing in (stormy weather)'
NSY —
CSY —

PY takaʀ-[1] '(be placed) crosswise or at an angle?' [cf. takə-]
AAY takaq 'stick to hang kettle over fire on'
CAY takanəq* 'stick placed into ground at an angle to hold pot over fire'
NSY —
CSY takaʀ- 'be crosswise, be caught in the opening and not be able to pass'
Sir — [for takaXtə- 'be long' see takə-]

PY takaR-[2] 'be shy or inhibited' [cf. takaR-[1], but also PI təqi- — a blend or deformation]
AAY PWS takaXtə- 'stiffen up, become rigid'
CAY takaR(yuɣ)- 'be shy, intimidated or respectful'
NSY —
CSY takaR(yuɣ)- 'feel inhibited'

PE takə- 'be long'
AAY takə- 'be long'
CAY takə- 'be long' [taktaciq 'length']
NSY takə- 'be long, tall' [takətalŋa '(its) length']
CSY taakə- 'be long' [taxtala 'length'; note also takəstaaq, takəstaaXaq 'short thing' and takəstaaXaa- 'be short', with ŋit- before p.b. (t)aRaq]
Sir takəvalaX 'long' [takula 'length'; Vakh. has takaXtə- 'be long' from Men.'s texts, also takutəqəpəyəX 'long' from Rub.'s, and takətaRałəRəX 'short']
SPI taɣisaq, Qaw takšuaq 's.th. long'
NAI taki- 'be long' [and takkiiq 's.th. long']
WCI taki- 'be long' [and Pryde has Cop takkaq 'a long one']
ECI taki- 'be long'
GRI taki- 'be long' [and takisuuq 's.th. long']

PE takəli- 'become or make longer' [cf. li-[2]]
AAY takłi- 'get or make long'
CAY takłi-
NSY —
CSY takəłi- 'shorten'
Sir —
SPI takłi- 'become or make long'
NAI takłi- [also takisi-]
WCI takłi-
ECI takili-
GRI tałłi-, EG tatsi-

PY-S taklaR- 'stretch out'
AAY KP takłaXtə- 'straighten out'
CAY takłaR- 'lie down, be bedridden'
NSY —
CSY takłaR- 'stretch out' [post. root]
Sir takłaXqə- 'stretch out' [Vakh.]

PY takšu(k) 'kind of large whale' [cf. takə- and ðuɣ?]
AAY taksukx^wak, taksuxpak, taksukaq 'type of large whale'
CAY —
NSY takšutaq 'fin whale'
CSY takəškak 'blue or fin whale'
Sir [Orr has takəškax 'blue or fin whale', probably borrowed from CSY]

PE taku- 'see or check on' [cf. takviɣ-]
AAY taku- 'check out'
CAY taku- 'check net, trap or snare'
NSY taku- 'visit'
CSY taku- 'go somewhere for a specific purpose'
Sir takə- 'find' [Vakh. has it as 'come to', also takuti- 'find' from Men. and Rub.; takəkcəX 's.th. found']
SPI taɣu- 'check'
NAI taku- 'visit, check on' [half-trans. takusi-, takuži-; and note takkun 'pupil of eye']
WCI taku- 'see' [half-trans. Cop takuhi- — Pryde, who also has Net takuŋnik- 'see a vision'; takuman 'pupil']
ECI taku- 'see' [takuRŋiu(q)- 'be happy to see again, be proud of', takutsau- 'be visible']
GRI taku- 'see' [half-trans. takunniɣ- (esp. of seeing a vision, otherwise zero, as ECI), EG taɣisi-; takuRniuR- 'show joy at seeing again', takkut(i)- 'show up', takuššaa- 'be visible']

PE takku(R) 'presence' [cf. q under nəR[1]]
AAY taku(q)-'presence,place in view, before' [used only with oblique case possessed endings]
CAY taku- 'presence' [used only with locative possessed endings]
NSY —
CSY —
Sir —
SPI takku- [with poss. endings] 'presence'
NAI takku-
WCI —
ECI takku- 'presence, sight'
GRI takku- [with poss. endings]

PE takumcuɣ- 'feel pity' [cf. mcuɣ-?]
AAY C takumcu-, takumcuɣ- 'have pity, compassion'
CAY takumcu(yuɣ)-
NSY —
CSY Chap takumsunalRii 'tender' [and note SLI takumsuɣ- 'go somewhere for pleasure']
Sir —
SPI —
NAI —
WCI —
ECI takutsuɣusuk- 'feel pity for, love'
GRI takussuɣi- [old ortho. takuvsuɣi-] 'find ugly to look at', takussunaR- 'look pitiful'

PI takuminaq- 'be attractive' [cf. umi- and naR-?]
SPI —
NAI —
WCI takuminaq- 'be attractive'
ECI takuminaq- 'be beautiful to look at' [and cf. Iti takumiɣi- 'find beautiful']
GRI takuminaR- 'be handsome, impressive' [but compare takuyuminaR- 'be good to look at' with yuminaq-; takumiɣi- 'think handsome']

PI takunnaq- 'stare at'
SPI —
NAI takunnaq- 'stare at'
WCI takun(n)aq- 'stare at'
ECI takunna(q)-, SB, NBI takunnaaq- 'look at' [takunnati 'pupil of eye']
GRI [takunnat 'pupil of eye']

PI takunRaq- 'see for first time' [cf. n(ə)RaR(aR)(-)]
SPI —
NAI —

WCI Sig takunʀaq- 'see for first time'
ECI takuʀŋa(q)- 'be afraid of seeing s.o. for first time or after a long time' [trans. takuʀŋaʀi-]
GRI takuʀnaʀ- 'see s.th. for first time', takuʀnaʀi- 'see for first time, not recognize' [and takuʀnaʀtaq 'stranger', takuʀnaʀniaʀ- 'come as a stranger, come to see s.th. new'; Robbe and Menn. have EG taɣiʀnaʀ- 'intimidate']

PI takuʀannaaq- 'take pleasure in looking at' [cf. n(n)iʀ-]
SPI —
NAI —
WCI —
ECI takuʀannaa(q)- 'take pleasure in looking at'
GRI takuʀannaaʀ- 'take pleasure in looking at' [and takuʀanniʀ- 'be pretty, fascinating', takuʀannaʀi- 'find pretty or fascinating'; Robbe and Menn. have EG taɣiʀnuuʀnaʀaalit 'I am glad to see you again']

PE takuyaʀ- '(turn and) look at' [cf. yaʀ(tuʀ)-?]
AAY takuyaʀ- 'take a look at'
CAY takuyaʀ- 'look (at) sideways or over shoulder'
NSY takuyaʀ- 'look at by turning head' [ANLC]
CSY —
Sir —
SPI —
NAI —
WCI Sig takusaq- 'stare at'
ECI takusaq- 'turn or rise to see'
GRI takusaʀ- 'keep an eye on, go to see'

PE takviɣ- 'see well' [from *takuviɣ-? — cf. taku-, also the ECI form takuvik below if it is not a reformulation based on taku- directly]
AAY takxʷiɣ- 'have good eyesight'
CAY takfik 'pupil of eye', takfixtu- 'have good eyesight'
NSY —
CSY —
Sir —
SPI takpik- 'have good vision'
NAI takpik-
WCI takpik- 'have good vision' [and Pryde has Cop takkuvik 'center of eye, pupil']
ECI tappi(k)- 'have good vision' [and note takuvik 'pupil of eye']
GRI tappiɣ- 'see well' [and EG tappiilaa 'pupil']

PE takviŋit- 'see badly' [cf. ŋit-, also for the variant (y)atə- in the Yup forms]
AAY takxʷiatə- 'have bad eyesight'
CAY takfiatə- 'have bad eyesight'
NSY —
CSY —
Sir —
SPI takpiit- 'have poor vision'
NAI takpiit-
WCI takpiit- 'be blind'
ECI tappii(t)- 'have bad vision'
GRI tappiit- 'have bad vision, be blind' [and note EG tappiʀ̃iʀ- 'become blind' — Robbe and Menn.]

PE tala(t)- 'be asphyxiated or intoxicated'
AAY tala-, talatə- 'be drunk, act crazy'
CAY —
NSY —
CSY —
Sir —
SPI —
NAI —
WCI —
ECI talat- 'be asphyxiated (by gas vapors or when eating s.th. intoxicating)' [Andersen et al. have tala- 'become intoxicated' for Lab]
GRI [note NWG talakkat- 'be careless, untidy']

talaaʀə 'kind of trout' [an Athabaskan loan — cf. Upper Inlet Tanaina təla:ʀə 'rainbow trout']
AAY PWS talaa'ik 'cutthroat trout'
CAY talaaʀiq 'rainbow trout' [compare talayaq, nalayaq 'spawning salmon' also an Athabaskan loanword — cf. Ingalik nalay 'chum salmon']
NSY —
CSY [talaʀitaʀ- 'jump up from surface of water (fish)' may not be related]

PI taləɣvak 'killdeer (or similar kind of bird)' [or taliɣvik; cf. vaɣ]
SPI —
NAI taliɣvak 'northern killdeer'
WCI Cop taliɣvak 'ruddy turnstone' [Pryde]
ECI —
GRI taliffak [old ortho. talivfak] 'snipe'

PY-S talmaɣ- '(come to) land' [the relat. — if any — to tulaɣ- is obscure; the CSY and Sir perhaps with contam. from təmə?]
AAY —
CAY [Nun talmaɣ- 'spawn (fish)']
NSY talmaɣ- 'land (boat)' [ANLC]
CSY tamlaɣ-
Sir tamcəɣ- 'approach, land'

PE talu(-) 'screen or partition'
AAY talu- 'be overcast'
CAY talu 'partition between two family areas in house'
NSY talu- 'watch for game (sea mammals)' [ANLC]
CSY ➟
Sir —
SPI talu 'shooting screen,' Qaw 'tent flap'
NAI talu- 'cover', Nu 'close door', talu 'shooting screen, covering', Nu 'door (originally of caribou skin)', Nu taalu 'shelter'
WCI talu- 'cover', talu(k), Net taluaq [Dor.] 'hunting screen', Car 'stone hide for caribou hunters' [Ras.; Net taluk is 'stone or snow blind' acc. Dor.]
ECI NBI talu 'curtain', Tar taalu 'hunting screen', Aiv, NBI, SB taluaq 'screen for hunting seal on ice' [also 'curtain' in 'adg' acc. Schn.; B.- S. has talut 'caribou fence' for Igl, Dor. has taluk 'stone or snow blind' for

NBI, Aiv, and SB]
GRI talu- 'put up partition', NG 'cordon off', talu 'shooting screen, partition on sleeping platform' [EG talivat, NG taluq 'fence' and NG talut 'shooting screen of stone for hunting caribou' (Holt.)]

PY talinəq 'shade' [cf. li-[1] and nəR[1]?]
AAY talinəq 'shadow, shade, hunting blind'
CAY talinəq* 'shadow, shade'
NSY —
CSY —

PE talit- 'go out of sight (behind shelter)' [cf. łit-]
AAY talitə- 'go out of sight, behind shelter, become obscured (also of sun)' [and taliyutaq 'screen'; for taliXtə- 'go out of sight' see talURtə- below]
CAY talitə- 'shelter from elements'
NSY —
CSY talitə- 'go out of sight behind s.th.'
Sir —
SPI talit- 'disappear from view (also of sun)'
NAI talit-
WCI talit-
ECI —
GRI talit- 'dock, lean up against s.th.' [and note taałłit- 'shade, stand in s.o.'s light' — influenced by taRRit- under taRəR?]

PY talURtə- 'move out of sight'
AAY taliXtə-, taluXtə- 'go out of sight, block one's sight of' [the first form by contam. with talit- above?]
CAY taluXtə- 'go out of sight' [and note Nun taliRnəX 'back of head']
NSY tažuXtə- 'move out of view' [L.-T.]
CSY taluXtə- 'move out of view'

PI ta(a)lutaq 'screen or curtain' [the forms with long aa have been influenced by taRəR — see taaRutaq below it]
SPI talutaq, taalutaq 'curtain' [verbal = 'close curtain']
NAI taalutaq 's.th. blocking one's view'
WCI [note Cop talutaq 'headband']
ECI taalutaq 'blind, curtain, protection from sun'
GRI taalutaq 'shooting sail on kayak' [and note EG taliilaq 'wall hanging'; for taalutaaR- 'get out of s.o.'s light' see taaRutaq under taRəR]

PY taluR- or tału(R)- 'split sinew'
AAY PWS taluR- 'split sinew'
CAY K taluR-, Nun, NI talu-
NSY —
CSY tału-, tałaaR-
Sir [Orr has tałaR- 'split sinew', probably borrowed from CSY]

PE taluyaR 'fish trap' [cf. talu(-) and yaR; this may, however, be PY, borrowed into Qaw and Nu]
AAY taluyaq 'fish trap'
CAY taluyaq
NSY —
CSY —
Sir —
SPI Qaw taluyat
NAI Nu taluyaq
WCI —
ECI —
GRI —

PE tałiR 'arm' [pre-Eskimo *tatliR? — cf. tatə-, tatyuR-, tayaR and tallimat, also Aleut talRi-X 'branch, tentacle'; Aleut tałiX, EA tali-X 'knot in wood, barb of harpoon' is probably not related acc. Berg., but note also taliR- 'dance' (in old Atkan with masks, the men with drums and the women with dancing shawls), probably borrowed from Esk]
AAY tałiq 'arm'
CAY tałiq 'arm' [and Y taliR- 'engage in Inupiaq-style dancing' — from Inu]
NSY tałiq 'arm'
CSY tałiq
Sir [tałəR- 'lead by hand' — Em.]
SPI taliq 'arm' [and taliq- 'do bench dance (seated women)']
NAI taliq 'arm' [and taliq- 'dance in sitting position gesturing with arms and hands', talliaq- 'break arm']
WCI taliq 'arm' [and Pryde has Cop talliaq- 'break arm']
ECI taliq 'arm' [taliaq- 'hurt arm']
GRI taliq 'arm'

PE tałiquR 'foreflipper' [cf. quR]
AAY —
CAY tałiquq 'flipper of seal, foreleg of animal'
NSY tałiquq 'flipper' [ANLC also 'wrist bone']
CSY tałiquq 'back fin'
Sir —
SPI taliRuq 'foreflipper'
NAI taliRuq
WCI taliquq
ECI taliRuq
GRI taliRuq, EG taliivaq

PE tałiRaR 'bracelet' [cf. aR]
AAY —
CAY tałiRaq 'bracelet'
NSY tałiRaq [ANLC]
CSY —
Sir —
SPI —
NAI Nu taliRaq 'large bracelet worn by woman'
WCI —
ECI taliaq 'bracelet'
GRI —

PE tałiRpiɣ 'right arm or side' [cf. piɣ]
AAY tałiXpik 'right side, right arm'
CAY tałiXpik
NSY tałiXpik
CSY tałiXpik
Sir —

SPI taliqpik
NAI taliqpik
WCI taliqpik
ECI taliqpik
GRI taliʀpik

PE tałłimat 'five' [cf. tałiʀ, li-[1] and pl. marker t (to n in all number words above two in Alaskan Yup), also perhaps CSY (u)man under (u)maʀ(aʀ)-; compare ətəmaɣ and probably unrelated Aleut caaŋ 'five' from ca-X 'hand']
AAY tałiman 'five'
CAY tałiman
NSY tałimat
CSY tałimat
Sir tasiməŋiy 'five' [and note tasixta 'ten']
SPI tallimat 'five'
NAI tallimat
WCI tallimat
ECI tallimat
GRI tałłimat

PE tałuʀ- 'be intimidated by s.o.' [emot. root]
AAY tałuʀ(yuɣ)- 'want to be in with others'
CAY tałuʀ(yuɣ)- 'be respectful, shy, inhibited' [tałuqə- 'be inhibited, etc., by']
NSY tałuʀnaq 'importance', tałuʀnalʀia 'respected, honored, severe' and tałuʀyuk 'shyness' [L.-T.]
CSY tałuʀ(yuɣ)- 'feel timid, intimidated'
Sir tałuʀni- 'be honorable, distinguished' [Em. has tałuʀyuɣ- 'be shy' — from CSY?]
SPI taluʀi- 'be wary of, fear s.o.'
NAI taluʀi- 'feel submissive toward, find s.o. unapproachable'
WCI taluʀi- 'be intimidated by s.o.'
ECI —
GRI taluʀi- 'keep back from, dare not approach s.o.'

PE tamaʀ- 'all' [quantifier/qualifier root; cf. Aleut tamaðax 'every (one)']
AAY tamaʀ- 'all, both, whole'
CAY tamaʀ-, tamałkuʀ- 'all, both, whole' [tamat 'all kinds']
NSY tamaXaʀ- 'all, both, whole'
CSY tamaXaʀ-
Sir [note tatəkəłaX 'all, every' on Men. p. 58, for taməkəłaX?]
SPI tamaq- 'all, every' [Jen. has W tamat — for tamaat? — 'all kinds of things']
NAI tamaq- 'all, both, whole'
WCI tamaq- 'all, both, whole'
ECI tama(q)-
GRI tama(ʀ)-

PI tamala- 'be scattered' [cf. la(ʀ)-]
SPI tamalak- 'be scattered (e.g. sea ice)'
NAI tamala- 'be scattered, loosely woven', tamallaq- 'scatter'
WCI —
ECI —
GRI tamałłaʀ-, tamałłaɣ- 'scatter' [and tamalaat 'all sorts']

PY-S tamaŋani 'everywhere' [3s poss. locative case]
AAY tamiini 'everywhere'
CAY tamiini
NSY tama(a)ni
CSY tamaŋani
Sir taməŋəni
Inu [note GRI tamaɣinni 'everywhere', also tamani tamaani, the second element apparently based on dem. root mað-]

PI tamatkiq- 'do or take all'
Sir — [but note taməŋkəX 'skin, hide' — Vakh.]
SPI —
NAI tamatkiq- 'take all'
WCI tamatkiq- 'do or take all'
ECI tamakki(q)- 'do two together']
GRI tamakkiʀ- 'do entirely'

PY-S ta(a)mlək 'darkness' [cf. taʀəʀ(-) and ləɣ; the Sib. Yup forms may be by contam. with the source of NAI maŋaq- 'be black' mentioned under maŋaq unless there is a link to mamə; perhaps there is taboo deformation here — compare taʀaʀnəʀ (taʀəʀ(-))]
AAY K tamlək 'darkness'
CAY taamlək 'darkness', K 'dwelling place of spirits' [and taamləxcətə- 'become dark'; for mamlək 'skin boot' see mamələɣ under mamə]
NSY [note mamžuk 'darkness' — compare tažuq under taʀəʀ(-)]
CSY mamlək 'darkness' [and mamləɣ- 'be dark']
Sir mamləɣ- 'be black, dark' [and mamlakətkaX 'darkness']
Inu — [for NAI mamiłik 'caribou skin boots with fur inside' see mamələɣ under mamə]

PE tamlu 'chin' [cf. lu(ʀ) and Aleut camlu-X 'chin' — with $*t_2$]
AAY tamlu(q) 'chin'
CAY tamluq
NSY tamlu
CSY tamlu
Sir tamla
SPI tavlu
NAI tavlu
WCI tavlu
ECI tallu
GRI tałłu

PE tamluʀun 'chin tattoo' [cf. q(q)un?]
AAY K tamlu<ʀ>un 'tattoo' [on old lists]
CAY tamluʀun 'chin tattoo'
NSY tamluʀutət [ANLC has tamluʀun]
CSY tamluʀun
Sir —
SPI tavluun
NAI tavluʀun
WCI tavluʀutit [also tavluʀun acc. Pryde]
ECI talluʀuti
GRI tałłuʀut 'chin tattoo, chin strap'

PE tammaʀ- 'lose or be lost'
AAY tamaʀ- 'lose, be lost'
CAY tamaʀ-
NSY tamaʀ-
CSY —
Sir —
SPI tamma(q)-
NAI tammaq-
WCI tammaq- 'get lost' [Pryde, who also has tammai- 'mislay' — Jen. has the first as 'lose']
ECI tamma(q)- 'get lost, make a mistake', NBI, SB 'be wrong' [Tar specifically 'make moral error of judgement' acc. Schn.; tammai- 'lose by wandering off or putting on wrong path']
GRI tammaʀ- 'lose, be lost, lose way, make a mistake' [tammaa- 'have lost'; for tavaɣ- 'wander about (e.g. at night)' see taʀaʀ-]

PE tamuʀ- 'chew' [cf. Aleut taamu- 'lick']
AAY [tamuuq 'dried fish']
CAY tamu- 'chew once', tamua- 'chew (repet.)'
NSY tamuaʀ- 'chew' [ANLC has tamua- 'chew' but tamuaʀ- 'eat berries while picking']
CSY tamaa- 'chew'
Sir tamər- 'eat' [Vakh. also tamuʀ-; note also tamuqət- 'give food to' — Vakh. also taməʀət-]
SPI tamuq 's.th. chewed', tamuq- 'eat greens raw, chew food for another', tamua- 'chew'
NAI tamuq- 'chew' [tamuluk- 'snack, eat a little']
WCI tamuq-, Car, Cop, Net tamua- 'chew'
ECI tamua- 'chew'
GRI tamuʀ- 'chew' [and tamua- 'chew (cud)' — Ras. has 'eat' for EG; tamuluɣ- 'chew, make chewing motions']

PE tamuʀaʀ 'mouthful' [cf. aʀ]
AAY —
CAY —
NSY tamua 'mouthful'
CSY Chap tamaak 's.th. being chewed'
Sir —
SPI tamuaq 's.th. being chewed'
NAI tamuaq 'single bite of food'
WCI tamuaq 'mouthful'
ECI tamuaq 'mouthful' [and tamuattuaq 'chewing gum'; compare tamuʀaq 's.th. held in mouth']
GRI tamuaq, tamuaaq 'mouthful' [and tamuʀasaaq 'taste of freshly caught game', NG tamuattaq 'chewing gum']

PE tanəɣ- or **tanə(t)-** 'wash' [cf. Atkan Aleut canikða- (with a p.b. kða-) 'skin (seal or reindeer) by cutting along the belly (and take the blubber off)']
AAY [PWS tanutaq 'washcloth']
CAY Nun, NS tanə-, HBC tanəxtə-, NI tanukaʀ- 'scrub, wash one's hands' [contin. taniuq-]
NSY tanə- 'wash, scrub (floor)' [ANLC also has tani-]
CSY taanə- 'scrub' [and tanuXqə- 'scrub a floor']
Sir —
SPI tanit- 'wash, scrub'
NAI —
WCI Sig tanik- 'wash clean' [Pet.]
ECI [Peck has tan(n)ik-, tan(n)iq- 'make a bone clean, take off meat' for Lab]
GRI tanit- 'grease, salve, put ointment on' [taʀnut 'ointment', taʀnut(i)- 'smear (ointment, etc.) on (s.o.)'; for taɣiaʀ-, taŋiaʀ- 'rub' see aɣiɣ-]

PY-S tanəm 'again'
AAY tanəm '- on earth' [as in 'why on earth?'; also takəq]
CAY tanəm '- on earth'
NSY tanəm 'again'
CSY tanəm 'finally, once again'
Sir tanəm 'again' [Vakh.]
Inu [SPI tani 'again' — also enclitic — is probably from the Yup]

PE tanəʀ- 'forbid'
AAY —
CAY —
NSY —
CSY —
Sir tanəʀ- 'forbid'
SPI —
NAI —
WCI taniqtiq- 'tell not to do'
ECI taniʀsa(q)- 'warn, caution, forbid'
GRI taniʀ- 'forbid', taniʀtaʀ- 'warn, forbid' [and NG taqqit 'command'?]

PY-S tanɣuʀaq 'child' [there could be a relat. to tannŋət; cf. ʀuʀluq and ʀaʀaʀ for the p.b.'s here]
AAY tanɣuXaq, tannuXaq, tanyuXaq, K tanəqn̥ak 'boy, lad'
CAY tanɣuXaq*, tanɣauʀluq*, NI tanəkcitaɣaq*, HBC tanəksaxłuɣaq* 'boy', Nun tanɣuXaX* 'child'
NSY tanŋuʀaq 'jack in cards' [Em.]
CSY taʀnuXaq* 'child'
Sir taŋaX '(one's own) child, baby' [and taŋasaX 'doll'; Orr has tanaʀnəka 'my child']

tannŋət 'strangers' [a borrowing from Chukchi pl. tannŋət 'strangers, Koryaks, members of a different tribe, Europeans'; the natural Yup. back formation for a singular would be as in CSY and the natural Inu. back formation would be as in NAI (with ɨ as shown); the Chukchi singular is tannŋətan, and therefore cannot be the source of the Esk.); there could be a further relat. to tanɣuʀaq]
AAY —
CAY —
NSY —
CSY tanŋa 'raider'
Sir tanŋiy 'enemies' [Vakh.]
SPI —
NAI B tanɨk 'Caucasian, White' [note also Nu tanɨktaaluk 'dog with hanging ears' — 'white or spotted dog' acc. Berg.]
WCI Sig tanik 'white man'
ECI —
GRI —

PE tanqiʀ or **tanqiɣ** 'light or moon'
AAY tanqik 'moon, light', tanqiɣ- 'be bright'
CAY tanqiɣ- 'be bright', Nun tanqix 'moon'
NSY taŋqiq 'light (day or moon)' [and taŋqiʀ- 'illuminate'; ANLC has taŋqik and taŋqiɣ- 'be bright']
CSY tanqiq 'moon'
Sir —
SPI taqqiq
NAI tatqiq
WCI tatqiq
ECI taqqiq
GRI EG taqqiq 'light' [Tersis]

PI tanqik- 'adjust lamp wick' [cf. nəɣ-]
SPI —
NAI tatqik- 'adjust lamp wick'
WCI [Men. has tatkrersor- 'trim wick of lamp' — for tatqiksuq-? — also tatkrertor 'bright light (of lamp)']
ECI taqqisuq-, Iti taqqi(C)- 'adjust lamp wick'
GRI taqqiɣ-, taqqiššuʀ- 'make it (the lamp) burn brightly'

PE taŋəʀ 'solid part of blubber left after rendering oil'
AAY —
CAY taŋəq*, taŋviaq, taŋviaXłuk, NI taŋəfkayak 'fatty material left when seal oil is rendered'
NSY [note perhaps taŋəsalʀia 'prosperous']
CSY taŋəq* 'solid part of something' [for homonym meaning 'reason behind something' see taŋəʀ-]
Sir [taŋəXtəvalaX 'firm']
SPI taŋiq 'strip of blubber remaining after oil renders' [also 'greens and/or blubber eaten along with meat or fish' — and verbal for that activity]
NAI taŋɨq* 'strip of blubber remaining after oil renders' [for homonym meaning 'evidence' see taŋəʀ-]
WCI taŋiq 'strip of blubber remaining after oil renders'
ECI taŋiq 'solid part of blubber after oil has run out of it, anything that remains good in the midst of spoilage' [and taŋiinnaq 'that which has no oil, is solid or good']
GRI taŋiq* 'strength, nourishment, piece of blubber (from blubber sack)', taŋikut 'coffee grounds'

PE taŋəʀ- 'see' [there may be a relat. with taŋəʀ]
AAY taŋəX- [for some KP taŋəʀ-] 'see', taŋəX̥niqə- 'watch out for'
CAY taŋəX- [from *taŋəʀᴀʀ-?] 'see', taŋXu- 'be visible', taŋvaɣ-, Y, NS taŋkə- 'look at, watch' [and taŋ 'look!']
NSY taŋəʀ- 'try, test, taste' [ANLC]
CSY taŋəq* 'reason behind s.th.' [also 'ancestor' — by contam. with kaŋəʀ?]
Sir —
SPI Qaw taŋiq 'truth, evidence'
NAI taŋɨq* 'evidence, proof' [taŋŋiq- 'become reality', taŋiʀit- 'be false']
WCI —
ECI —
GRI —

PE taŋluʀ 'snowshoe' [cf. lu(ʀ)]
AAY taŋluq 'snowshoe'
CAY taŋluq
NSY —
CSY —
Sir —
SPI —
NAI taɣlu
WCI taɣlu
ECI tallu
GRI —

PI taŋmaq- 'camp'
SPI taŋmak- 'come ashore to camp,' Qaw 'make camp'
NAI tanmaq- [for taŋmaq-?] 'stop to camp' [Jen.]
WCI taŋmaʀ- 'camp' [Pryde has taŋmaaq- for Cop]
ECI tammaa(q)- 'camp overnight on a journey, move into a newly built snow house', Lab 'pitch tent' [Peck]
GRI tammaaʀ- 'camp, tent'

PI taŋmik- 'graze or ricochet off'
SPI —
NAI taŋmik- 'swerve, turn aside, ricochet, be deflected'
WCI taŋmiluqit- 'have been grazed by hunter (animal)' [and taŋmiɣaq 'piece of wood on which boat slides into water'?]
ECI tammik- 'ricochet, rebound'
GRI tammiɣ- 'rebound, jump (thing)'

PY-S taŋpeq or **tanpəq** 'skin covering material (for hide house)' [cf. the -pəq in qaspəq under qaðə- and ilupəʀ(ᴀʀ) under ilu, perhaps also taŋəʀ]
AAY —
CAY NSK taŋpəq 'old skin from kayak'
NSY tampəq, tanpəq 'covering material for yaranga of dehaired deerskin or walrus skin' [ANLC — Men. has tampək 'covering']
CSY tanpəq 'dried walrus hide, especially as used on a traditional house or skin boat'
Sir tanpəX 'walrus skin, covering' [Vakh.]

PI tapak- 'show off or be unruly?'
SPI —
NAI PH tapaɣɨ- 'enjoy the company of'
WCI [note Cop H. Island tapattak- 'want more, be unsatisfied' — Pryde]
ECI tapaC- 'show off, try catching others off guard, make fools of others', Lab 'disobey, be bad-tempered'
GRI tapaɣ- 'be dirty', SWG tapaʀ- 'dance'

PE tapəʀ(-) 'add to' [cf. tapʀᴀʀ[1] and tapʀᴀʀ[2] and EA tam- 'bind in sheafs, hoop (barrel), finish edge (of basket), wrap or wind up', tami-X 'hoop, bundle, sinew binding frame of drum', Atkan tam̥iiɣasi-x (du.) 'bootstrings, garters']
AAY C tapəq 's.th. put alongside', K tapiʀ- [with liʀ-] 'reinforce, add', tapəqə- 'hem, put together with s.th. else'
CAY tapəq* 's.th. given along with s.th. else', tapiʀ- 'give s.th. along with'
NSY [note tapiʀ- 'harness dogs' — ANLC]

CSY —
Sir —
SPI taviq 's.th. added'
NAI tapɨq* 's.th. added' [verbal = 'widen by adding a piece, lie alongside, parallel with'; tappiq- 'side with', Nu 'enlarge by adding, be a friend to']
WCI tap(p)iq- 'add, fold'
ECI tapiq 's.th. added to widen a garment, partner, ally' [verbal = 'add cloth to widen, add a second layer']
GRI tapiq* 'addition, supplement', tapiʀ- 'add to'

PE tapət-[1] 'fold over or do double' [cf. t-[1]]
AAY tap<ə>tə- 'double over, fold'
CAY tap<ə>tə-
NSY —
CSY —
Sir —
SPI tavit- 'fold over', Qaw tapit- 'line up, double up, shoot with a single bullet' [and tapšun, tapšutaq 'strip of skin added between body and sole of mukluk']
NAI tapɨt- 'be folded over, walk side by side, shoot with one arrow or bullet (animal)'
WCI Cop tapit- 'shoot two with same shot' [Pryde, who also has Cop, Car tapitqut 'unhaired sealskin stocking']
ECI tapitaak 'two killed by one shot or cast of net'
GRI tapit- 'get with one shot' [tassutaq 'extra piece patched on', tapitaliʀiiɣ- 'be double', NG tapitaliʀiik- also 'get with one shot', NG tassuttaʀiik- 'place together (e.g. skins upon each other)', EG tattulaq 'woman's parka with hood for child']

PI taputə- 'include' [cf. utə-]
SPI tavuti- 'include'
NAI taput(ɨ)- 'include, influence'
WCI Cop taputi- 'get s.th. else into the bargain' [Pryde; Met. has tap(p)ut(i)- 'side with, follow']
ECI taputtaa(C)- 'hit after having crossed s.th. else (projectile)'
GRI taput(i)- 'take together with s.th. else'

PE tapət-[2] 'permeate' [there may be a link to tapəʀ(-)]
AAY tap<ə>tə- 'permeate, soak through'
CAY —
NSY tapətə-, tapuXtutə- 'seep, soak through'
CSY taapə-, taaputə- 'seep through'
Sir — [but Vakh. has tapə- 'get stuck (somewhere)' from Rub. — for tatə-? (see tatə-)]
SPI ➡
NAI PH tapɨt- 'soak (of wet clothing against the skin)'
WCI ➡
ECI ➡
GRI tapit- 'soak, seep through' [and tapinnaʀ- 'be insufficient (thin clothing)']

PI taplək- 'penetrate or get soaked' [cf. ləɣ-?]
SPI tapłik- 'get soaked', Imaq tapłaq- 'soak, seep'
NAI tavlɨk- 'penetrate', PH 'get soaked'
WCI [Pryde cites Cop tavlik- as in NAI]
ECI talli(k)- 'penetrate (needle through skin), scrape a skin to soften it'
GRI tałłiɣ- [old ortho. tavdlig-] 'penetrate (needle through skin, light through opening), influence, put pressure on (s.o.)'

PE tapʀaʀ[1] 'skin rope or strap' [cf. tapəʀ(-), p.b. aʀ and Aleut taamXaaX 'cross strap on kayak deck']
AAY PWS tapXaq 'skin rope'
CAY tapXaq(*) 'skin or root rope'
NSY tapXaq 'strap, cord'
CSY tapXaq 'rope'
Sir tapəʀaX 'strap, cord'
SPI tapqaq 'heavy rawhide rope'
NAI Nu tapqaq 'place (cross-strap?) on kayak where ropes are attached in front and back'
WCI —
ECI taqqaq 'cross strap on deck of kayak'
GRI taqqaq*

PY tap(ə)ʀaʀnaq 'kind of grass on seashore' [cf. naʀ]
AAY K tapəʀnaq, AP tapəXn̥aq 'basket grass'
CAY tapəXn̥aq 'coarse seashore grass'
NSY —
CSY —
Inu [SPI tapqa(ʀ)naq 'beach grass' — from the Yup?]

PE tapʀaʀ[2] 'isthmus or sand bank' [cf. tapəʀ(-) and aʀ — a parallel derivation to tapʀaʀ[1]?]
AAY —
CAY tapXaq(*) 'spit, isthmus' [and Jen. and Lantis have tapXaX 'tundra' for Nun]
NSY tapXaq 'isthmus'
CSY tapXaq 'isthmus, long sandy beach'
Sir tapXaX 'spit, cape' [Vakh.]
SPI tapqaq 'tundra, coastal flat land, beach'
NAI tapqaq'small island, sand bar off shore'
WCI tapqaq 'mud or sand bank'
ECI —
GRI —

PI taqammuq- 'fall into water'
SPI taʀuumaaq-, ittaʀuumaaq-, FR caqamuuq-, caʀamuuq- 'fall noiselessly into water' [perhaps with contam. from ciqəʀ- in Qaw; the second (KI) form is by contam. with ətə- — compare NAI ɨtiqquužži- 'cause to sink immediately, without splashing']
NAI taXammuq-, taXammuk-, Nu taqammuq- 'sink or cause to sink without a big splash, fall into water with a plop'
WCI Cop taqammuq- 'plunge into water'
ECI —
GRI taqammuʀ- 'fall into water with a splash' [and taqammi- 'strike water with flat of oar']

PE taqaʀ and **taqəʀ** 'vein'
AAY taqəq 'vein'
CAY taqəq*
NSY taqik

CSY taqəq*
Sir —
SPI taʀak
NAI taqak
WCI taqaq 'vein' [Pryde has taqak for Cop and Sig]
ECI taqaq 'vein' [Pryde has taqak for NBI]
GRI taqaq

PE taqə- 'stop or give up'
AAY C taqə- 'finish'
CAY taqə- 'quit, finish' [and taqsuqə- 'be tired', taqə-, taqm̥ixtə- 'be fully grown']
NSY taqə- 'finish'
CSY taaqə- 'finish, quit' [and taqm̥anpak 'adult (strong but small)']
Sir táqə- 'finish' [Orr has taqəmə- 'have finished']
SPI —
NAI taqɨt- 'give up'
WCI Net taqa- 'be tired' [Ras.]
ECI taqa- 'be tired' [taqaya- 'tire easily']
GRI [note taqayak 'foolish person'?]

PY taqmak 'dress'
AAY taqm̥ak 'dress'
CAY taqm̥ak
NSY —
CSY —
Inu [Imaq taqmaq 'dress' presumably from the Yup]

PE taqu(C)aʀ 'provisions for a journey'
AAY taquaq 'provisions for a journey'
CAY taquaq
NSY taquaq
CSY —
Sir —
SPI taʀuaq
NAI taquaq 'provisions for a journey' [and taqužžit- 'supply with provisions']
WCI taquaq 'provisions for a journey'
ECI taquaq
GRI taquaq

PY taqukaq 'brown bear' [there may be a link to taqiɣ-]
AAY takuka'aq 'brown bear, grizzly'
CAY taqukaq 'brown bear, grizzly' [but Nun, NI, HBC 'seal']
NSY —
CSY —
Inu [SPI KI taɣuʀaq 'polar bear' probably from Yup]

PY-S taquq 'braid or side of face'
AAY ➟
CAY taquq 'braid'
NSY taqu [ANLC]
CSY taquq 'side of face', taquXtə- 'braid hair'
Sir taquXta 'braid' [Em. has taqəX 'side of face, side part of hood or ear-flap of hat']
Inu — [but note ECI taqulik 'white mark over eyes of some dogs', NG taquliktuuq 'black dog with white mark over eyes']

PY taqulquq 'cheek' [cf. quʀ]
AAY KP, AP taqułquq 'cheek'
CAY —
NSY taqułquq 'side of the face from temple to the chin' [ANLC]
CSY —

PY-S taʀaʀ- 'wander about' [there could be a link to taɣə-; compare aʀaʀ-]
AAY —
CAY taXaXtə-, taXitə-, taXiXtə- 'wander around' [also taXanqəx(tə)- 'be active' and taXXu 'go away! (to dogs, etc.)']
NSY —
CSY —
Sir taʀaʀ- 'wander about' [Vakh.]
Inu [note GRI tavaɣ-, SWG taʀfi- 'drift about aimlessly (esp. at night)', the former also 'have disappeared, not amount to much', perhaps by contam. with tammaʀ-]

PE taʀəʀ(-) '(be) dark' [cf. taʀ(ə)nəʀ, ta(a)mlək, taʀu and Atkan Aleut taXt- 'get dark', taʀula- 'be the eve of'; 'deep root' taʀ-?]
AAY ➟
CAY Nun taaləx 'darkness' [with ləɣ — Jen. has taaX and Lantis has taalaxpax 'very dark place'; for taamlək 'darkness or dark place' see ta(a)mlək]
NSY [note tažuq 'darkness', tažuʀ- 'get dark'] ➟
CSY ➟
Sir — [but note taʀa 'soot' written with macron over final vowel]
SPI taaq 'darkness' [verbal = 'be black, dark'; taʀʀumi 'in the dark' — based on rel. case taʀʀum?]
NAI taaq 'darkness' [as verb = 'be dark', Nu 'be black']
WCI taaq 'darkness' [as verb = 'be dark'; Schn. has taɣɣalaq, taɣɣaliq 'total darkness' for B. Lake]
ECI taaq 'darkness' [as verb = 'be dark, make a shadow, darken, hide'; and note taɣɣatuʀyuinaq- 'be very dark']
GRI taaq 'darkness' [rel. sing. taXXup; taaʀ- 'be dark', taxxaʀiɣ- 'be pitch dark', NG taXXiq- 'shade, get in s.o.'s light', and EG taaʀtaq 'helping spirit' with taʀ; for EG taaq 'human being' see taʀu]

PI taaqsi- 'get dark [cf. si- under li-[2]]
Yup [CAY taaqsipak 'black person' is probably borrowed from Inu]
SPI taaqsi- 'get dark'
NAI taaqsi-
WCI taaqsi-
ECI taarsi- 'be nightfall'
GRI taaʀsi- 'get dark'

PI taaqtət- 'faint' [cf. tət-]
SPI Qaw taaqtipkaq- 'faint'
NAI taaqtipkaq-
WCI [taaqsipkai- 'lose consciousness' — influenced by taaqsi- above?]
ECI taaqtit- 'put in shadow or dark, hide, see only blue — from dazzlement or fainting' [and taarsit- 'faint', influenced by taaqsi- above?]
GRI taaʀtit- 'faint'

PI taaʀutaq 'shade (s.th. blocking view)' [cf. un]
SPI —
NAI taaʀutaq 'lampshade', Nu 'curtain' [for taalutaq 's.th. blocking view' see ta(a)lutaq under talu(-), with which this set has become entangled]
WCI Cop taʀutaq 'curtain, screen' [Pryde]
ECI —
GRI taaʀutaaʀ- [old ortho. târutaer-], NG tautaiq- 'get out of (s.o.'s) light' [WG also taalutaaʀ- by contam. with ta(a)lutaq under talu(-)]

PI taqšaq 'dark place'
SPI —
NAI —
WCI —
ECI taʀsaq 'isolated mark on skin or fur, tattoo, decoration on clothing, sign indicating a route' [and Iti taʀsi(C)- 'be underlined', taʀsapalla(C)- 'appear to have a visible mark']
GRI taʀšaq, taʀšak 'dark spot', NG taXXaq 'shooting screen (for hunting)' [and taʀšaɣ- 'lie in half-darkness, have a dark shadow above it', taʀšiałłaɣ- 'appear and disappear again at once (so one sees only s.th. dark moving quickly or jumping up in distance)']

PE taʀəʀnəʀ 'darkness or dark thing' [cf. nəʀ[1] and compare taʀ(ə)nəʀ; there appears to be taboo deformation in Yup (but note NSY məɣnuʀ- under məʀnuʀ-); cf. also Aleut tanʀaaX 'bear' — from the Yup?]
AAY C tannəq 'darkness', tannəʀ- 'be dark' [and note C tannəʀliq 'black bear']
CAY tanɣəq* 'darkness', taŋəʀ- 'be dark' [and note tanɣəʀliq 'black bear']
NSY tanɣəq 'black thing, darkness' [and taɣnəʀaq 'shadow' (ANLC also 'spirit'), for which compare taʀ(ə)nəʀ, also tanɣəlʀia 'becoming black' — ANLC has tanɣəʀ- 'be black']
CSY taɣnəq* 'darkness, dark thing', taɣnəʀ- 'be black'
Sir —
SPI —
NAI taaʀniq* 'darkness'
WCI Cop taaʀniq 'dark part or place' [Pryde]
ECI taaʀniq 'darkness' [in possessed form 'part of s.th. in shadow']
GRI taaʀniq* 'darkness'

PI taʀʀaq 'shadow' [cf. q under nəʀ[1]]
SPI taʀʀaq 'shadow'
NAI taʀʀaq*
WCI taʀʀaq 'shadow' [Cop also 'apparition (of a spirit)']
ECI taʀʀaq 'shadow, image in mirror, shady or north side, shooting screen' [and taʀʀaliniq 'reflected image in water, shadow cast, north side'; Ras. has taʀʀiyuq 'shaman' (with li-[1]) in Igl shaman language — compare tuɣənʀi- under tuɣənʀaʀ]
GRI taXXaq(*) 'shadow, image' [and NG taʀʀaliniq 'shady side'; Kroeber has NG taʀʀaq 'north', also in shaman's language for WG, and Fab. has WG tar'ak 'shade, (part of) soul' — from Egede]

PI taʀʀaqtuq- 'be reflected' [cf. taʀʀaq above and tuʀ-[1]?]
SPI taʀʀa.tuq- 'be reflected' [and taʀʀa.tuun, Qaw taʀʀaqtuun 'mirror']
NAI taʀʀaqtuq- 'cast a shadow, see one's reflection' [and taʀʀaqtuun 'mirror']
WCI taʀʀaqtuun 'mirror' [Pryde]
ECI taʀʀa(q)tuq- 'look at self in mirror, hide behind hunting screen' [and taʀʀa(q)tuuti 'mirror']
GRI taXXaʀtuʀ- 'be reflected' [taXXaʀsuut, NG taʀʀaqtuut 'mirror']

PI taʀʀit- 'move into shade (and be lost from view)' [cf. taʀʀaq above and łit-]
SPI taʀʀit- 'move into shade, become shaded'
NAI taʀʀit- 'move into shade, be thin like paper, disappear from view, cast a shadow' [the latter may rather be a homonym with p.b. lit-]
WCI —
ECI taʀʀit- 'vanish (behind hill), hide'
GRI taXXit- 'disappear behind s.th., set (sun), lose from view'

taʀ(a)nəq 'plant (cow parsley?)' [from Atkan Aleut taaʀanɣi-s, earlier taaʀanʀi-s 'lateral stalks of cow parsnip']
AAY C taʀ(a)niiŋuasaɣat 'plant — *Ligusticum hultenii*'
CAY taʀnaq, HBC, Y taʀvaq 'cow parsley, wild celery'
NSY —
CSY —

PE taʀ(ə)nəʀ 'soul or shadow' [cf. taʀəʀ(-) and nəʀ[1] and compare taʀəʀnəʀ and taʀʀaq under taʀəʀ; this base may be directly from 'deep root' *taʀ-]
AAY C tannaq, Kod tanʀaq, taŋənʀaq, Afog. taanəq 'shadow'
CAY taʀnəq* 'soul', taʀənʀaq 'shadow, image'
NSY — [for taɣnəʀaq 'shadow' see taʀəʀnəʀ under taʀəʀ]
CSY taʀnəʀaq 'shadow, image, ghost'
Sir taʀəncaX 'shadow'
SPI —
NAI Nu taʀniq* 'soul, life force'
WCI taʀniq 'soul'
ECI taʀniq, taʀnik
GRI taʀniq*, taʀnik

PE taʀpaʀ- 'open out or flare'
AAY —
CAY — [for Nun, HBC taXpəʀaq 'drawstring of boot or outer clothing' see paʀtə]
NSY taXpaʀ- 'open out, flare out' [ANLC]
CSY taXpaʀ- 'open, enlarge'
Sir —
SPI taqpaq- 'be funnel-shaped' [as noun 'nostril' — Jen.]
NAI taqpaq- 'open wide', taqpak 'nostril', PH 'flare of nostril'
WCI taqpak 'nostril'

ECI taqpa(C)- 'be funnel-shaped' [compare talavaaq 'utensil which becomes narrow at one end like a funnel or skirt', talaviq- 'be enlarged (sleeve, nostrils)', which seem to go rather with GRI talaʀtiq below]
GRI taʀpaʀ- 'widen into a funnel shape', NG taqpak '(flare of) nostrils' [Holt.; WG talaʀtiq 'funnel' is an early Scandinavian loan-word — compare Danish tragt of that meaning]

PE taʀtu 'kidney' [cf. Aleut ðaXtu-X 'kidney', influenced by ðaX 'eye' acc. Berg. — compare CSY iiskak 'kidney' (and Sir iskəx, probably borrowed from it), from əðə]
AAY taXtu(q) 'kidney'
CAY taXtuq
NSY taXtu
CSY —
Sir —
SPI Qaw taqtu 'kidney'
NAI taqtu
WCI taqtu
ECI taqtuq
GRI taʀtu

PI taqtunaq 'area around kidneys' [cf. naʀ]
SPI Qaw taqtuniq 'area around kidneys'
NAI taqtunak 'side of body toward front, above hip'
WCI taqtunaq 'groin (?) or midriff'
ECI —
GRI taʀtunaq 'small of back, broadside of boat'

PE taʀu 'human being (shamanistic term)' [cf. taʀəʀ(-) and taʀ(ə)nəʀ; the gloss of the EG form below suggests that p.b. ʀuq- under ŋ(ŋ)uʀ- may be involved here]
AAY AP taʀu 'human being'
CAY Eg taʀu(q) 'human being' [known but little used elsewhere in CAY; note also taʀuyamaaʀun 'dance fan'?]
NSY —
CSY taʀu 'human being' [shaman's language according to Bogoraz]
Sir taʀu 'human being' [shaman's language — Orr]
SPI —
NAI taʀutu- 'be fat, wide' [compare CAY cuxtu-/suxtu- 'tall' from yuk/cuk/suk 'human being' under iŋuɣ]
WCI Cop tauq 'man (shaman's language)' [Ras.; Pryde has Net tau 'human being' as a shaman's word]
ECI Igl tau 'man (shaman's language)' [Ras., who adds tauyaq 'white man'; tau is also known by older Iti speakers acc. Dor.]
GRI EG taaq 'man' [corresponding to older WG taušaq in shaman's language according to Egede — Ras. has EG taaq 'person whose name has left him after death', Holm just 'human being']

PE taʀyaqvaɣ 'king salmon' [cf. vaɣ]
AAY —
CAY taʀyaqfak, NSU taXsaqpak 'king salmon'
NSY —
CSY —
Sir —
SPI taʀya.vak, Qaw taʀyaqpak
NAI Nu taʀyaqpak
WCI —
ECI —
GRI —

PE taʀ(ə)yuʀ 'salt' [cf. Atkan Aleut taʀayu-X 'salt']
AAY taʀyuq 'salt'
CAY taʀyuq
NSY taʀyuq
CSY taʀyuq
Sir taʀyəX
SPI taʀiuq 'salt, sea, sea water'
NAI taʀiuq 'salt, sea, sea water' [taʀiuq- 'salt, use salt', PH 'be blue']
WCI taʀiuq 'sea, salt'
ECI taʀiuq
GRI taʀayuq 'salt water', pl. taʀatsut, EG taʀ̃ayut, Up taʀ̃ayit, NG taʀiuq 'salt' [and taʀayuʀ-, etc. 'salt']

PE tatamə(t)- 'be startled or terrified' [there may be a relat. to tatə-]
AAY tatamə- 'become agitated or nervous'
CAY tatamə- 'be startled'
NSY tatamə- 'be alarmed'
CSY tatamə- 'be startled'
Sir —
SPI tatamit- 'become scared, terrified', tatamaa- 'not know where to run or escape to' [tatait- 'feel scared']
NAI tatamɨt- 'become frightened enough to quit', tatamaa- 'be terrified' [and tataiɣɨ- 'be fearful of']
WCI [tatainaq- 'be afraid'; and tataisuk-, Cop tatiɣivak- 'tremble with fear']
ECI tatamit- 'be astonished' [tataiɣi- 'be on the alert because of']
GRI tatamit- 'get violently frightened, die of fright' [and tataaɣi- 'be frightened by']

PE tatə 's.th. secure (that one can rely on)' [cf. tatə-?]
AAY ➡
CAY cacətu-, NS tacəstu-, HBC, Nun castu- 'be unswerving, stable, strong' [opposite = cacəskit-, tacəskit-]
NSY —
CSY ➡
Sir — [Em. has tatəvali- 'cross, supporting oneself on s.th.']
SPI tatitu- 'be sedentary, not budge' [and note tatiɣiaq 'ivory piece on harpoon shaft through which thong is slipped']
NAI tatitu- 'be sensible, level-headed' [and Nu tatmiɣiaq- 'use a stick to steady oneself in snow or ice']
WCI tatituʀusi- 'look after, stay close to'
ECI tati 'protector, s.o. in whom one has confidence', Lab 'faith, love' [and tatituyuq 'one with self confidence, who obeys slowly']
GRI tati 'that which one sets one's confidence in', tatiɣi- 'rely on', tatitu- 'be self-confident, stubborn', EG tali- 'shove with shoulder'

PE tatəkə 'support (e.g. for keeping boat off ground)' [cf. kə(-)[2]?]
AAY tatkiq 'support pole of kayak, forked gun support'
CAY tatkik 'two pairs of crossed poles used to support a kayak off the ground'
NSY —
CSY taatxət 'intersection of poles at top of trad. house'
Sir —
SPI —
NAI tatiɣɨ 'frame cache for keeping skin boat off ground'
WCI Cop tatiɣiq 'paddle-brace (upright prong lashed in front of kayak cockpit to brace paddle against when using a weapon)' [Pryde]
ECI tatiɣit 'scaffolding to put things out of reach'
GRI —

PE tatə- 'jam in' [cf. tatə and Aleut caci- 'cover, close', but also PE taci- and tatyuʀ-; with $*t_2$]
AAY —
CAY ➟
NSY —
CSY tatəXtə- 'brake'
Sir [note tatəXtə- 'forbid' — contam. with tanəʀ-?]
SPI tati- 'bump into'
NAI tatɨ- 'be too tight, lean against, jam, squeeze up' [and tažžaq-, Nu tatžaq- 'brush against (repeatedly)']
WCI tati- 'squeeze up to', tatit- 'squeeze up, jam together'
ECI tati- 'have pushed s.th. away with shoulder' [also tatiɣiaq- 'tap or nudge to get attention', tayya(q)- 'push continuously']
GRI tati- 'pinch, jam', EG tali-, NG tatit- 'push with shoulders'

PI tat(t)at- 'be packed full'
SPI —
NAI tattalaužaq- 'be a tight fit'
WCI Cop tatat- 'fill to brim, squeeze into, be full'
ECI NBI, SB tatat- 'be full'
GRI NG tatat- 'have a swelling or boil' [and tattak- 'swell up (boil)'; WG tataɣ- 'be tender (body part), wince in pain']

PI tattuqun 'wedge' [cf. tat(ə)tuʀ- above and p.b. un]
SPI tattuʀun 'wedge'
NAI tattuqun 'wedge for supporting'
WCI tattuqusiq- 'wedge s.th. in, make fit'
ECI tattuqusiq- 'wedge s.th. in (with s.th. else)', Iti tattuqut 's.th. to wedge s.th. else in with'
GRI tattuqut, tatuɣut 'wedge'

PE tat(ə)tuʀ- 'be stuck or too big to fit' [cf. tuʀ-[2]]
AAY —
CAY tastuʀ-, całtuʀ- 'be too big to fit'
NSY [taxtuʀ- 'not fit, not be room enough for s.th.' — ANLC]
CSY [əłtuʀ- 'be stuck']
Sir — [but Vakh. has əłtə(ʀ)- 'touch' (?) and əłtəqayuX 'shaman' from Rub.'s texts; for tapə- 'be stuck' see tapət-[2]]
SPI tattuq- 'be stuck, tight, narrow', tattui- 'be constipated', tattuaut(i)- 'be crowded in'
NAI tattuq- 'be stuck', PH tattui- 'be constipated' [and tatumiaq- 'be in contact with']
WCI tattuqit- 'get stuck, jammed' [Pryde]
ECI tattu(q)- 'be too tight, squeeze, be unable to fit', tattui- 'be constipated' [and tattuqit- 'have jammed s.th. in']
GRI tattuʀ- be too small or narrow for' [and tattuqit- 'completely fill'; Robbe and Menn. also have EG tattiiC-, tattiʀsiʀ- 'be jammed']

PY-S tatək 'bridge of nose ' [cf. tatə- or tatəkə under tatə?]
AAY tatək 'forehead'
CAY UK, UY, HBC tatək, LI [also HBC and NI?] tautək 'forehead' [the latter form could be by contam. with the source of ta(C)utu(k-)]
NSY tatək 'bridge of nose'
CSY tatək 'bridge of nose' [and note tatŋułuk 's.th. that impedes visibility']
Sir tatəx 'bridge of nose' [only on Men.'s comparative list]
Inu [Imaq tatəkpałuk 'big-nosed' is probably from NSY]

PE tatəlɣaʀ 'crane' [there may be a link to tatə or tatə-]
AAY tatəłxaq 'crane'
CAY NSU tacəłxaq 'crane' [and Lantis has tasiłkax for Nun; compare also quciłxaq, quciłŋaq 'sandhill crane' for the ending]
NSY tasiłŋaq 'crane' [Enm. et al. and L.-T.; Men. has tasilŋaq]
CSY satəlɣaq 'crane'
Sir —
SPI tatiɣžaq
NAI tatižɣaq
WCI Sig tatiyɣaq, Cop tatilɣaq
ECI tatiyɣaq 'sandhill crane' [also 'jibe or jeer to s.o. who acts self-confidently', directly related to tatə?]
GRI [Ras. has tatiɣɣaq 'bird somewhat larger than snipe with fine neck' for EG]

PE tatyuʀ- 'lead by the hand' [cf. tatə- and taci-]
AAY C, Kod tassuqə- 'hold by the hand, give a hand', tassuʀ- 'take by the hand' [and Kod tassuq 'person one is holding by hand']
CAY tassuqə- 'hold hands with' [compare kasiɣ- under katə-]
NSY [taxsuʀ- 'hold hands with' — ANLC]
CSY tasłuʀ- 'hold hands with'
Sir — [for tałəʀ- 'lead by hand' see tałiʀ]
SPI taziuq- 'lead by hand'
NAI tasiuq- 'lead by hand' [and note tasikuaq- 'lead with a leash']
WCI tasiuq- 'lead by hand' [tasikuaq- 'lead with a leash']
ECI tasiuq- 'take or lead by the arm or hand'

GRI tasiuʀ- 'hold by hand' [and note tasiaq 'handle of kayak paddle', tasikumiaʀ- 'lead dog by traces']

PI tauʀciq- 'exchange or trade' [from ta(C)uʀtə as in GRI below plus liʀ-; cf. EA taaɣuya- 'trade, exchange, buy' (with p.b. ya-); Atkan taya- 'buy', tayana-X 'trader' and tayaʀu-X 'man' are probably not related, acc. Berg.]
SPI tauqsiq- 'trade'
NAI tauqsiq- 'buy'
WCI Uum tauqsiq- 'buy'
ECI tauʀsi(q)- 'exchange'
GRI taaʀti 'replacement, exchange', taaʀsiʀ- 'exchange, pay back (loan), barter for something else'

PI tautu(k)- 'look'
SPI —
NAI tautuk- 'see', Mal also 'focus on' [tautturik- 'look healthy']
WCI Cop tautuk- 'have seen' [Met.], Net 'catch sight of' [Ras. — Pryde also 'be acquiainted with, know personally' for Cop; Car EP tautuquuq 'vision']
ECI tautuk- 'look', Lab 'be able to see' [tauttu 'appearance, color of face, comportment', Lab tauttuk 'color (of face)'; note also Lab tautuk 'me too!' in Bourq.]
GRI taatuɣ- 'receive a distinct impression from s.o.'s appearance' [taattu 'appearance' (old ortho. táuto), taatturiɣ- 'look healthy' — Holm has 'be red' for the latter in EG; note also taatuuna 'what a nasty person!']

PE tavci 'belt'
AAY K tauxci, tauxciq 'belt'
CAY NSU tafci 'belt' [as verb = 'put belt on']
NSY tafsi 'belt' [and as verb = 'put belt on' (ANLC)]
CSY tafsi 'belt' [as verb = 'put belt on']
Sir tafsa
SPI tapsi
NAI tafsi, Nu tapsi 'belt' [as verb = 'put belt on']
WCI Sig tapsi, Cop taffi 'belt'
ECI tatsiq
GRI tassiq, tassik 'waistband, ribbon', NG 'belt' [tassiɣ- 'put belt or band on']

PY ta(a)vtaaq 'clam' [possibly from PE *tav(ə)taɣ if the Inu is cognate (there may be infl. from kapəciʀ there) — but cf. tapət-[1] under tapəʀ(-)]
AAY tauxtaaq 'cockle'
CAY HBC taftaaq [with compressed first vowel], NI taaftaaq, Nun aatəftaaX 'clam'
NSY —
CSY —
Inu [note NAI taptayuʀaq 'rib cartilage, ensiform appendage between floating ribs', and GRI tattak (old ortho. tavtak) 'fish scale' (corresponding to which Robbe and Menn. have EG tattaq, also in sense 'flake of skin on scalp')]

PI tayaq 'bracelet' [cf. tayaʀnəʀ]
SPI tayaat 'bracelet'
NAI tayaq
WCI tayat 'kind of cuff'
ECI tayaq 'bracelet'
GRI tayak, tayaq

PE tayaʀnəʀ 'wrist (or bracelet)' [cf. tayaq and nəʀ[1], also perhaps tatyuʀ- and Aleut ca-X 'hand, seal's flipper', caaŋ 'five'— with *t_2?]
AAY tayanəq 'wrist'
CAY tayaʀnəq*
NSY tayaʀnəq [ANLC]
CSY taŋyəq* 'wrist' [and Chap. taŋyəʀun 'bracelet']
Sir taŋyəXqaʀ- 'roll sleeves up' [from CSY?; and, on Men.'s comp. list, naŋcəX 'wrist', presumably cognate; Vakh. has taŋyəʀay 'bracelets' and nancəqəX 'wrist' from Men.'s texts]
SPI tayaʀniq 'wrist'
NAI tayaʀniq*
WCI tayaʀniq
ECI tayaʀniq 'foreflipper of seal'
GRI tayaʀniq* 'wristbone of seal or whale', EG tiaʀniq* 'wrist' [also 'bone of front flipper' in Robbe and Menn.]

PY tayu(ɣ)- 'be in a rush' [the relat. — if any — to tu(C)avə(t)- is obscure]
AAY tayu- 'rush, go (too) fast with work'
CAY —
NSY — [for tayuxpaɣ- 'tremble, be alarmed' and tayuxtə- 'twitch, kick' see cayuɣ-]
CSY taayuɣ(yuɣ)- 'be hurried, pressed for time'

PE təðatəða(C)iʀ and təʀatəʀa(C)iʀ 'kind of (noisy) bird' [onomatopoeic reduplication — cf. perhaps təðə(ʀ)- and (C)iʀ, but also cəqtaaq, which could form one irregular set here]
AAY —
CAY —
NSY —
CSY təžatəžiiq* 'dunkin, red phalarope, rock sandpiper'
Sir —
SPI —
NAI taasiŋiq, taatciŋiq 'loon', taatciŋižaq 'stale-colored junco' [and Pryde has tiqitiʀaaq 'kittiwake' for Noatak River; Seiler has taatciŋiq 'loon' for Mal
WCI [Pryde has Car tiʀatiʀaaq 'kittiwake']
ECI tiʀatiʀak 'three-toes gull' [Schn.; Pryde has Tar, NBI taatiʀaaq but Pond Inlet tiʀatiʀaaq 'kittiwake' and Tar, NBI taatiʀaaʀnaq 'Sabine's gull']
GRI taatiʀaaq, EG taalaqqaaq 'kittiwake'

PE təðə(ʀ)- 'make creaking or crunching noise'
AAY —
CAY — [for cəqcəXtə- 'make lots of noise' see cəqtaaq]
NSY təžətaaʀ- 'creak, crunch, squeak' [and təXtəq 'cracking or crashing noise' — ANLC]
CSY Chap təšqitak 'creak, crack, bang'
Sir —
SPI tižiniq- 'creak (e.g. door)' [Jen.]
NAI tižiq- 'make rubbing sound, gnash teeth'
WCI tiyitquɣluyaq- 'gnash teeth'
ECI [note tijittuq 'sealskin so dry that it cannot even be

soaked for softening']
GRI titiqquʀ-, titiqquluɣ- 'creak, gnash teeth'

PY təɣalquq 'rock (in water)' [cf. təɣəɣ- and quʀ?]
AAY C təxalquq 'rock or reef in water'
CAY təxałquq, HBC təɣałquq 'rock'
NSY —
CSY —

PE təɣəɣ- 'be hard or stiff' [cf. təɣɣaɣ and EA txa- 'be tight (rope)']
AAY təxə- 'be stiff, tough' [and note KP təxxiXtə- 'get uneasy, nervous']
CAY təxə- 'be hard, tough' [and təxxi- 'get hard, harden', təxxia- 'become tense, hard in parts', təxqaq, Nun təxsax 'hard wood']
NSY ətəɣ- 'be hard' (ANLC)]
CSY təxəq* 'hard wood' [and təxm̥ak 's.th. stiff', təkšuqaq 'lump or hard spot in flesh']
Sir təɣaʀəvalaX 'hard, resilient, unbending' [Em.]
SPI Qaw tiik- 'be hard (e.g. wood)', tiɣɣak- 'be stiff'
NAI tiɣɣaq- 'be stiff'
WCI [Cop tixxak-, Net tikšak- 'be erect (penis)' — Pryde]
ECI titsa- 'stiffen (penis)'
GRI tiiɣ-, tiiŋa- 'feel randy' [and tiššaɣ- 'have an erection', tiššaʀ- (old ortho. tigssar-) 'have lascivious thoughts']

PY tə(k)kaʀ- 'have an erection' [cf. k(k)aʀ-]
AAY —
CAY təkkaʀ- 'have an erection'
NSY —
CSY təkaʀ-

PI tiipak- 'be promiscuous or randy' [cf. vaɣ]
SPI —
NAI tiipak 'flirt', tiipaŋa- 'be coquettish, promiscuous' [and note tiiqtala- 'move about excitedly']
WCI [Pryde has tiitaŋa- 'act in a silly manner' for Cop]
ECI —
GRI tiipakusuɣ-, tiipaqusuɣ-, tiiqila- 'be exuberantly happy', tipaɣ- 'be wanton, frisky' [the latter in this form in Kl. and Oqaatsit, but (probably spurious) tipa- in S.-L.; note also piitaat- 'be wanton, unchaste' and tipaatsuɣ- 'be happy, gay', apparently influenced by təpə; Tersis has tippaC- 'dance' for EG]

PE təɣɣaɣ 'rutting seal' [cf. təɣəɣ-]
AAY —
CAY Y, Nun təɣak 'rutting seal' [compare also təxanəq*, Y, Nun, HBC təxn̥əq* 'elder person']
NSY təɣak 'rutting seal' [ANLC]
CSY təɣak 'rutting seal'
Sir təɣax [Orr]
SPI tiɣɣak
NAI tiɣɣak
WCI tiɣɣak
ECI tiɣɣaq 'rutting seal' [Spald. has 'male jar seal' for NBI']
GRI tixxak, NG tiɣɣaŋnitsuq [Holt.] 'male seal (esp. old, stinking one)', EG tikka(q) 'man', NG tiɣɣak 'large male narwhale, walrus or other mammal']

PE təɣləɣ- 'steal' [cf. Aleut cxa- 'steal' with $*t_2$]
AAY təɣləɣ- 'steal'
CAY təɣləɣ-
NSY təɣləɣ-
CSY təɣləɣ-
Sir təɣləɣ- [Orr]
SPI tiɣlik- 'steal'
NAI tiɣlik-
WCI tiɣlik-
ECI tiɣli(k)-
GRI tiłłiɣ-

PY təɣləŋaʀ- 'steal habitually' [cf. ŋaʀ-]
AAY —
CAY təɣləŋaʀ- 'habitually steal'
NSY təɣləŋaʀ- 'be a thief' [ANLC]
CSY Chap təɣləŋalʀii 'thief' [Rub.]

PI təɣləq- 'throb' [or təŋləq-?]
SPI tiɣliq- 'beat, throb (of pulse, heart)'
NAI tiɣliq-
WCI tiɣliq-
ECI tilli(q)- 'beat, throb' [and tillitaaq 'pulse']
GRI tiłłiʀ- 'beat, throb' [and tiłłiq, NG tiɣliqtaaq, EG tittiʀniq 'pulse']

PE təɣu- 'take' [cf. Aleut su- 'take'?]
AAY tuu-, təɣu- 'take' [half-trans. tuutə-, təɣutə-]
CAY təɣu- 'take' [half-trans. təɣutə-]
NSY tuɣu- 'take'
CSY tuɣu- 'take' [half-trans. tuɣutə-]
Sir təɣə- 'take'
SPI tiu-
NAI tiɣu- 'take' [half-trans. tiɣusi-]
WCI tiɣu-
ECI tiɣu- 'take' [half-trans. tiɣusi-]
GRI tiɣu-, EG tii-, NG tiu- 'take' [half-trans. tiɣusi-]

PE təɣɣun 'hook (for lifting)' [cf. un]
AAY —
CAY təɣun 'recovery hook for seals'
NSY —
CSY tuɣun, tuɣutaq 'potholder'
Sir [note təɣutəX 'roseroot' — Orr]
SPI tiɣɣun 'potholder'
NAI tiɣɣun
WCI Cop tiɣɣun 'tongs, pincers' [Pryde]
ECI tiɣɣuti 'means for lifting s.th. without touching it directly'
GRI NG tiɣɣut 'boat hook' [and Holm has EG tiɣɣit 'mitten']

PE təɣuðaʀ 'adopted child' [cf. ðaʀ]
AAY PWS təɣuaq 'captive, hostage'
CAY təɣuaq 'adopted child, s.th. taken, crimp in boot sole'

NSY təɣuaq 'adopted child, crimp in boot sole' [ANLC]
CSY —
Sir —
SPI tiuaq, Qaw tiɣuaq 'adopted child'
NAI tiɣuaq 'adopted child' [as verb = 'adopt']
WCI tiɣuaq
ECI tiɣuaq
GRI [note tiɣuaʀ- 'take over, conquer']

PI təɣu(ʀ)liq 'handle'
Yup [note CAY təɣuɬitaq, AAY tuuɬitaq 'pot-holder']
SPI tiuʀliq 'handle'
NAI tiɣuʀliq 'doorknob, hole in bow of kayak used as handle' [compare tiɣuʀiq 'handle, doorknob']
WCI —
ECI tiɣuliq 'handle of basket'
GRI tiɣuliq 'handle of kayak paddle'

PE təɣum(m)i(C)aʀ 's.th. held in hands' [cf. təɣummi- below]
AAY təɣumiaq, tuumiaq 's.th. held in hands'
CAY təɣumiaq
NSY tuɣumiaq
CSY tuɣumiiq*
Sir təɣəməɣəʀaX 's.th. held in hands' [təɣəməqə(s)- 'hold in hands'; for təma 'handle' see təmə]
SPI tiimiaq 's.th. held in hands' [verbal = 'carry in hands']
NAI tiɣummiaq 's.th. held in hands' [verbal = 'carry in arms']
WCI tiɣumiaq 's.th. held in hands' [also verbal]
ECI tiɣumiaq 's.th. held in hands' [and tiɣumiaq- 'hold in hands, keep in adoption (child)']
GRI tiɣumiaq 's.th. held in hands', EG tiimmuik 'handle' [and tiɣumiaʀ- 'hold in hands, present at font (child to be baptized)', tiɣumiššiʀ- 'give s.th. to hold to '; Holm has EG tiɣimiaq 'child' and Holt. NG tiimiaq- 'hold']

PI təɣummi- 'hold on' [cf. umi-?]
SPI —
NAI tiɣummi- 'hold on'
WCI tiɣummi- 'hold' [Pryde]
ECI tiɣummi- 'hold tight'
GRI tiɣummi- 'grasp'

PI təɣu(ɣ)aʀun 'handle of dog whip' [cf. təɣu-, aʀ- and un?]
SPI —
NAI —
WCI Car tiiɣaʀut 'short whip for driving dogs out of house', Net tiiaqut 'dog whip' [Ras.; Schn. has tiɣaʀut, tiɣaut 'hard part of whip' for B. Lake]
ECI Lab tiiɣaʀut 'short dog whip' [Peck]
GRI tiiaʀ- 'give (dog) a stroke with whip', tiiaʀut, tiiaqut, 'whip handle', NG tiuɣaʀut 'thick part of whip nearest handle'

PI təkaaɣun 'knob on harpoon shaft to prevent hand slipping' [cf. təkəʀ and un?]
Yup — [but note CSY təkəʀmiɣun 'knob on harpoon shaft to which line is attached']
SPI —
NAI [note tikiʀun 'protection for index finger']
WCI —
ECI tikaaɣuti 'piece of ivory on harpoon to prevent hunter's hand from slipping'
GRI tikaaɣut 'handle of shaft of harpoon or lance'

PI təkaaɣutlək 'fin whale' [cf. ləɣ]
SPI —
NAI —
WCI —
ECI NBI, SB tikaaɣullik 'fin whale' [Pryde]
GRI tikaaɣuɬɬik 'lesser fin whale'

PE təkðə(ʀ) 'wax or scales in ears' [compare the odd variation under žiɣtə, which could be a source of contam. in the CSY here at least]
AAY təkiq 'earwax'
CAY təkiq 'earwax' [also titiq reported for 'ear pus' from Kwethluk]
NSY əžiq 'earwax' [L.-T.]
CSY žiiq* 'earwax'
Sir —
SPI tiššiq, Qaw tižži 'earwax, scales in ear'
NAI siʀži, PH tiʀži 'scales in ear' [verbal = 'remove earwax from ear']
WCI Cop tixxik, Sig tiksi, Car tikti [Dor.] 'earwax' [see citciq- for B. Lake tixxiq- 'penetrate']
ECI —
GRI siššik [old ortho. sigssik], pl. siššiŋit 'scale in ear, small hard bone in head of fish'

PE təkəðquʀ 'angle or corner' [cf. təkəʀ and quʀ but also təʀu; there may be contam. with iqə(ʀ)]
AAY —
CAY —
NSY təkəšquq 'angle'
CSY təkəšqaq 'point, outer corner'
Sir [note təkəsiX 'angle, spit']
SPI tiʀitquq 'outside corner, right angle', Imaq təʀəsquq 'corner, end'
NAI tiʀitquq, Mal iqižʀuq 'corner' [the latter form influenced by iqə(ʀ) — compare NAI iqižʀaq there]
WCI Cop tiʀitquq 'corner' [for Sig iqiyʀaq see iqə(ʀ); Dor. has tiʀiqquq for B. Lake]
ECI tiʀiqquq 'corner'
GRI tiqiqquq, tikiqquq, EG tiɣiqqiq 'corner' [note also tiqiqquʀiɣ-, EG tiɣiqqiŋiC-, tiʀiqqittaaC- 'be right-angled']

PE təkəʀ 'index finger' [cf. təkkuk- and Aleut tikla-X (EA and late Atkan) 'middle finger', earlier 'ring finger', tikla- EA 'flip, snap with fingers', Atkan and western EA 'pull fingers']
AAY təkəq 'index finger, thimble'
CAY təkəq*

NSY təkəq
CSY təkəq*
Sir təkəX 'index finger' [and Vakh. has təkayuɣaX 'thimble']
SPI tikiq 'index finger, thimble'
NAI tikɨq* 'index finger, thimble' [and tikkivik 'thimble holder']
WCI tikiq 'index finger, thimble'
ECI tikiq
GRI tikiq* 'index finger, thimble' [and NG tikivik 'thimble']

PE təkəʀaʀ 'point of land' [cf. aʀ]
AAY —
CAY —
NSY təkəʀaq 'promontory, point of land'
CSY təkəʀaq 'point of land'
Sir — [for təkəsəX 'spit, angle' see təkəðquʀ]
SPI —
NAI tikiʀaq 'point of land'
WCI tikiʀaq
ECI tikiʀaq
GRI —

PE təkit- 'arrive (at)' [trans. or intrans.; cf. EA tiɣ- 'land (in boat)'; western Aleut siɣ- 'go up from shore' probably goes rather with EA siɣ- 'go up in the bed', a different base, acc. Berg.]
AAY təkitə- 'arrive, reach'
CAY təkitə-
NSY təkitə-
CSY təki(i)tə- 'land (s.th. thrown), land on, hit, stop'
Sir təkət- 'knock against, appear, show up' [Vakh. from Rub.]
SPI tiɣit- 'arrive, reach (goal)'
NAI tikit- 'arrive (at)'
WCI tikit-
ECI tikit-
GRI tikit-

PI təkicaqtuq- 'be nearing one's destination' [cf. yaq(tuʀ)-]
SPI Qaw tikisaq- 'be in a hurry to arrive'
NAI tikisaq-
WCI Car EP tikihaqtuq- 'be just arriving' [Ow. — Cop 'come into view, approach' acc. Pryde]
ECI tikisaqtu(q)- 'be nearing one's destination'
GRI tikisaʀtuʀ- 'be completing the last leg of the homeward journey'

PE təkiðutə- 'bring' [cf. utə-; probably appears as a predictable combination in other languages/dialects than those indicated below]
AAY təki<y>utə- 'arrive with or at same time as, have come (appointed time)'
CAY təki(y)utə- 'bring, arrive with'
NSY təkiitə-
CSY —
Sir —
SPI tiɣižuti- 'bring, arrive with'
NAI tikiut(ɨ)-, tikižžutɨ-
WCI tikiyuti- 'bring, (intr.) arrive'
ECI tikiut(i)- 'have brought, have as reason for arriving' [Lab also 'arrive' acc. Bourquin]
GRI tikiut(i)- 'bring, (intr.) have arrived, take place'

PI təkiʀaaq- 'arrive from afar' [cf. ʀaq- and aʀ-?]
SPI tikiʀaaq 'traveler from afar'
NAI —
WCI —
ECI tikiʀaaq- 'arrive from afar' [as nominal = 'one who arrives from afar']
GRI tikiʀaaʀ- 'come on a visit' [tikiʀaaq 'visitor, guest (traveling from elsewhere)']

PY təkiyaq 'tern' [cf. təkicaqtuq- under təkit-]
AAY AP təkiyaq 'common (arctic?) tern'
CAY təqiyaaʀ(aq*), Y təqiʀayuli, NSU təqəłquayaq 'arctic or Aleutian tern'
NSY təkəyiaXaq [ANLC]
CSY təkəyiiʀaq 'arctic tern'

PI təkkuk- 'stick out' [cf. təkəʀ]
SPI ➞
NAI tikkuk- 'bristle, stand out stiffly'
WCI ➞
ECI tikku(q)- 'have been stiffened by freezing after being damp (clothing)'
GRI tikkuʀ- 'stand on end (hair, fur)' [and note note EG tikkit, tikkiliq 'thumb']

PI təkkuaq- 'point at' [cf. aʀ-]
SPI tikkuaq- 'point with index finger' [tikkuun 'pointer', Imaq tək(k)uun 'index finger, thimble']
NAI tikkuaq- 'point at' [tikkuun 'signpost']
WCI tikkuaq- 'point at'
ECI tikkua(q)-, tikkutuq-
GRI tikkuaʀ-

PI təkpik 'kayak rib'
SPI tikpik 'side rib of kayak'
NAI tikpi 'side of rib of kayak' [Ras.; but MacLean has tippiq* 'piece of bent wood across width of kayak, kayak frame rib']
WCI titpik, Net tikpik 'side rib of kayak' [Ras.]
ECI tippi
GRI tippik [old ortho. tigpik] 'kayak rib'

PI təktaaliq 'burbot'
SPI Qaw tittaaliq 'ling cod, burbot'
NAI tɨttaaliq, Mal also tɨktaaliq
WCI Net tiktaaliq 'ling cod, burbot' [Ras. — also Cop acc. Pryde; Schn. has it as 'kind of fish with flat head and thin tail' for B. Lake]
ECI —
GRI —

PE təlaɣ- 'wipe (dry)' [cf. təluɣ-; two separate bases may have become entangled here]
AAY —
CAY əłai- 'stroke gently'
NSY —

CSY ➟
Sir ➟
SPI tilaktuq- 'wipe dry'
NAI tilak- 'scrub large surface'
WCI tilak- 'sweep, wipe away water'
ECI ➟
GRI —

PI təlaʀ(ʀ)i- or **təlaqqi-** 'sweep'
SPI tilaʀi- 'sweep with broom'
NAI tɨlaʀʀi-, tɨlai-
WCI tilaqqi- 'sweep' [Pryde has Cop tilaʀi-, H. Island tilaʀʀi-, also tilaʀʀit 'broom', brush']
ECI tillaʀi- 'remove snow from clothing', Lab tillaiyai- 'stroke'
GRI —

PY-S təlvə- 'smooth over or stroke'
AAY —
CAY Nun təłfə- 'sweep off' [ANLC]
NSY —
CSY əfłuʀ-, ufłuʀ- 'run hands or fingers over' [with metath.]
Sir təlvə- 'smooth, stroke' [Vakh.]

PE təli- 'tell s.o. to do s.th.'
AAY C łiiməʀ- 'order to do s.th.'
CAY əłiməʀ- 'request or order to do a task'
NSY łəməXtə- [ANLC]
CSY lipəXsaʀ- 'send for s.th., send s.o. with or leave instructions' [and Chap əłilatə- 'force, order']
Sir —
SPI tili- 'tell to do s.th., send (s.o.) on an errand'
NAI tɨli-
WCI tili-
ECI tili-
GRI tili- 'tell s.o. to do s.th., send on an errand' [and note tiliuq 'best friend' in Oqaatsit, SWG tiliaq 'companion' in S.-L.; also NG tiliŋitsuq 'busybody, fidgety, funny person']

PE təlqiðaʀ 'eyeshade'
AAY —
CAY əłqiaq 'visor, eyeshade'
NSY əłqiaq 'visor, cap'
CSY əłqiiq* 'visor'
Sir əłqiyəɣaX [Orr]
SPI titqiaq
NAI titqiaq, tatqiaq [the latter perhaps by contam. with tanqiʀ]
WCI Sig titqiaq 'visor' [Pet.]
ECI tiqqiaq
GRI tiqqiaq

PE təłuɣ- 'clean off by beating' [cf. təlaɣ-]
AAY —
CAY Y əłuXtuʀ-, Nun əłuɣ- 'shake or brush snow or dirt off', HBC əłuXtə- 'groom oneself' [for K təłumʀun, BB əłumʀun 'skin scraper' see pəłuɣ-]
NSY —
CSY —
Sir —
SPI Qaw tiluktuq- 'clean snow, mud off shoes'
NAI tɨluk(tuq)- 'clean by beating (snow, dirt) off'
WCI tiluk- 'beat dust, snow from clothes with a stick' [tiluktuun 'stick for beating snow off clothes']
ECI tiluk- 'beat with stick (clothing, rug) [tiluktu(q)- 'beat several times with stick'; for tillu(k)- 'give blow with fist, strike' see təŋluk-]
GRI tiluɣ- 'knock on s.th. to make snow, feathers, etc. fall off' [tiluttuʀ-, siluttuʀ- 'beat (bedding, clothing), beat snow off' the second form by contam. with ciluk-?]

PE təmci- 'be funny' [cf. Aleut tumci- 'copulate with (woman)']
AAY təmci(kə)- 'be (find) funny' [emot. root]
CAY təmci(kə)-
NSY —
CSY təmsiyaaʀaʀ- 'smile faintly, wanting to laugh but suppressing it'
Sir —
SPI tipsii- 'find funny, laugh at'
NAI tivsi(ɣɨ)-, Nu tipsi(ɣɨ)-
WCI Car? tipsiɣi- 'tease, joke' [Schn. 'adg'; Pryde has Net tipsisuk- 'feel like laughing' — Briggs tipsi(naq)- 'provoke laughter']
ECI —
GRI tissiɣi- 'think funny, laughable', tissinaʀ-, EG titsiaʀ- 'be amusing', NG tissihuk- 'laugh' [Robbe and Menn. have citsitsaaC- as well as titsitsaaC- 'laugh' for EG]

PE təmə 'body or main part' [cf. Aleut cma-X 'tail of fish or whale', with *t_2?; there may be some contam. with təmi in Inu]
AAY təma 'torso' [the base is təmə]
CAY təma 'body, main part to which s.th. is attached' [the base is təmə]
NSY təma 'body'
CSY təma 'body, close relative' [the base is təmə]
Sir [note təma 'handle' — Vakh. has təməX from Men.'s texts; by contam. with təɣum(m)i(C)aʀ- under təɣu-?]
SPI timi 'body, body of boot'
NAI timɨ 'body, body of boot above sole' [and '(toward) inland' in Jen.]
WCI timi 'body, main part of s.th., inland from shore' [3s poss. timaa in the latter sense, otherwise timiŋa]
ECI timi 'body, boot leg, area higher up from shore, upstream' [and timaani 'higher up than (s.th.)'; Lab timiʀliq 's.th. situated further inland' — Bourq.]
GRI timi 'body, top of boot, inland' [note also timiʀłiq* 's.th. situated most inland']

PY təmkaq 'type of seal or sealskin' [cf. kðaʀ?]
AAY —
CAY —
NSY təmkaq 'sealskin'
CSY təmkaq 'old spotted or ringed seal'

PI təmvaq- 'move inward or inland' [cf. vaʀ-; the ɣ in NAI and Sig may be by dissimilation via *təŋvaʀ-]
SPI —

NAI tiɣvaq- 'come in all the way (to room)' [and tiɣvasik- 'be well inside']
WCI Sig tiɣvaq- 'go up on land from sea', Car? tivvaq- 'bring ashore, inland' [Schn. 'adg'; and Sig tipsik-, Cop, Car tivvahik- 'be high up on shore, inland']
ECI Lab tivvaq- 'bring ashore, inland' [Bourq.]
GRI tiffaʀ- [old ortho. tivfaʀ-] 'move inland', tiffasiɣ- 'be far inland'

PI təmi 'marrow' [cf. EA tumtu-X, Atkan cumtu-X 'marrow']
SPI —
NAI —
WCI Cop timi 'pith of an antler' [Pryde]
ECI —
GRI timi 'marrow' [Fab. has 3s poss. form timia as opposed to timaa 'its body' from təmə]

PY təm(m)iʀ- 'make a rumbling noise' [cf. liʀ-?]
AAY AP təmmiXtə- 'make a rumbling noise'
CAY təmmiXtə- 'make a rumbling noise' [nom. təmmiq]
NSY —
CSY [note Chap təməXn̥aʀ- 'cure by sorcery'?]
Sir [note təməqnaŋaʀ- 'cure by sorcery, shamanize' — Vakh. from Rub.'s texts; Em. has təməʀnaʀ-]

PE tənəɣ- 'press down on or against' [with dissimilation except in NSY and KI; cf. tənət- and tənu- and compare əŋiɣ-; Aleut tiɣ- 'press down, weigh upon' may not be related acc. Berg.]
AAY kənəxtə- 'press (down)'
CAY nəxtə-, HBC, Nun kənəxtə- 'press down on'
NSY tənəxtə- 'press' [Taghyuq and Em.]
CSY kənəxtə- 'press'
Sir kəniʀ- 'press down against' [Vakh. has kənixtə- 'clasp (a stick), stab, prick' for kənəɣ-?'; Em. has kənət-]
SPI KI tinik- 'press down on'
NAI —
WCI —
ECI —
GRI —

PE tənət- 'ebb' [cf. tənəɣ-?; with dissimilation in Yup — compare tənu- and tənniʀ-]
AAY kəntə- 'go down, ebb (water)'
CAY əntə-, HBC, Nun kəntə- 'ebb'
NSY —
CSY —
Sir —
SPI tinit- 'be low tide'
NAI Nu tinit- 'be almost empty of water, be at ebb, low (river)'
WCI tinit- 'go out (tide)'
ECI tinit- 'go out (tide)' [and tinuɣyaq 's.th. left high and dry by tide']
GRI tini 'ebb tide', tinit-, tiniɣ- 'be low tide' [and note tinut(i)-, tinuɣut(i)- 'be exposed at low tide']

PY tən(n)aq 'tide flat' [cf. q under nəʀ]
AAY K, KP kənnaq, PWS kən<ʀ>aq 'tide flat, beach exposed by ebb tide'
CAY ənnaq* 'sand bar exposed at low tide'
NSY —
CSY — [kənmaaŋqaq 'water behind shoreline caused by high waves' is from Chukchi kənmaŋqə]
Inu [compare ECI tininniq 'ground uncovered by outgoing tide', GRI tininniq* 'low tide']

PE tənniʀ- 'point or nudge to get attention' [cf. tənu-]
AAY kəniʀ- 'point'
CAY əniʀ-, niiʀ-, kəniʀ-
NSY təniʀ- [ANLC]
CSY kəniʀ-
Sir [for kənixtə- 'clasp, prick, stab' see tənəɣ-]
SPI tinnaktaaq- 'keep touching'
NAI tinniq- 'touch or nudge to get s.o.'s attention'
WCI —
ECI tinniʀaq- 'surprise, attract attention by nudging'
GRI tinniʀ- 'touch or nudge to get s.o.'s attention'

PY-S tənputə- 'knock against (shore)' [cf. tənu-, but also Chukchi tənpə- 'pierce', borrowed directly into CSY and Sir in this sense — contam.?]
AAY —
CAY —
NSY tənputa(ʀ)- 'knock up against s.th., come ashore to'
CSY Chap tənputə- 'knock against s.th.' [also 'stick into s.th.' from the Chukchi; and note tənpututə- 'pull boat somewhere, take people somewhere (in boat, out to ship)']
Sir [tənpututə(ə)- 'pull boat somewhere, take people out to ship', also 'stick in' from CSY/Chukchi?; Vakh. has tənpižaqaʀ- 'knock into' and Men. tənpitə- 'land from sea']

PE tənu- 'push or poke' [cf. tənniʀ-, tənəɣ-, tənputə-, and perhaps Aleut n̥u- 'reach']
AAY kənu- 'poke, push, nudge'
CAY ənuuʀ-, HBC, Nun kənuuʀ- 'nudge', NSU ənu- 'push, shove'
NSY tənu- 'push, shove'
CSY kənu- 'poke, push with pointed instrument' [and note kənuk 'edge, ridge']
Sir [for tənpižaqaʀ- 'knock into' see tənputə-]
SPI tinu- 'push, shove'
NAI tinu-
WCI Sig tinu- [Lowe]
ECI tinu- 'flatten, pushing down bumps' [and note tinuyuq 'half moon']
GRI tinu-, tinupa- 'swell (like a boil)'

PE təŋaɣ or **təŋə** 'pubic hair' [cf. Aleut cŋa-X 'fur, body hair' — with *t_2]
AAY AP təŋak 'pubic hair'
CAY təŋak 'pubic hair'
NSY təŋə 'pubic hair' [L.-T.]
CSY təŋa 'pubic hair' [base təŋə-]
Sir —

SPI tiŋak
NAI tiŋak
WCI tiŋak 'pubic hair' [Cop, Sig tiŋaq acc. Pryde]
ECI tiŋiit [Saul]
GRI tiŋi

PI təŋaužaq 'kind of moss or lichen' [cf. ŋ(ŋ)uðᴀʀ]
SPI —
NAI tiŋaužaq 'dried black moss used as tinder', tiŋaužat 'lichen'
WCI Car? tiŋauyaq 'curly black or white grass' [Schn. 'adg'; Pryde has Cop, Car tiŋauyaq, Net tiŋaužaq 'blackbeard lichen']
ECI tiŋauyaq 'thin green curly grass growing on sand in place exposed to wind', Iti 'caribou moss, lichen', Lab 'white moss' [Bourq. for the latter]
GRI tiŋaašat 'black lichen'

PE təŋayuɣ 'throat hair of caribou' [cf. yuɣ]
AAY PWS təŋa<y>uk 'down feather'
CAY təŋayuk 'throat hair of caribou'
NSY təŋayuk 'reindeer beard' [L.-T.]
CSY təŋayuk 'decoration of caribou throat hair (on drum, etc.)'
Sir —
SPI tiŋayuk 'throat hair of reindeer'
NAI tiŋayuq, Nu tiŋayuk 'long white throat hair (beard) of caribou or moose'
WCI Cop tiŋayuk 'long hair on dewlap of caribou' [Pryde]
ECI —
GRI tiŋayuk 'caribou beard'

PE təŋə- 'fly (up)'
AAY təŋə- 'fly, take off'
CAY təŋə-
NSY təŋə-
CSY təŋə-
Sir təŋə-
SPI tiŋi-
NAI tiŋɨ-
WCI tiŋi-, Cop tiŋixxa- 'take off' [Lowe]
ECI tiŋi- 'fly'
GRI tiŋi- 'take off' [and note tiŋŋaɣ- 'jump out of water (whale)']

PI təkšaluk- 'spurt out' [or təŋšaluk-; cf. təŋmikaq- below, also ðᴀʀ- and łuɣ?]
SPI —
NAI —
WCI Cop tixxaluaq- 'ejaculate' [Pryde]
ECI titsalukaa- 'squirt out in a continuous jet'
GRI tiššaluɣ- [old ortho. tigssalug-] 'spurt out', tiššalukaᴀʀ- 'squirt'

PI təkši- 'frighten into flight' [or təŋši-; cf. ði-]
SPI tikši- 'frighten into flight (bird)'
NAI tiɣži-
WCI —
ECI tiyyi-
GRI tišši-

PE təŋəlʀᴀʀ- 'sail'
AAY —
CAY təŋalʀᴀʀ- 'sail' [and nominal təŋalʀaq 'sail']
NSY —
CSY —
Sir —
SPI tiŋiʀlaq- 'sail (a boat)'
NAI tiŋɨlʀautaq 'sail'
WCI Sig tiŋilʀautaq 'sail' [Lowe has tiŋilʀaun]
ECI tiŋiʀʀautaq 'sail'
GRI tiŋiʀłaat

PE təŋət- 'blow away (wind)' [cf. t-[1]]
AAY təŋtə- 'blow away (wind)'
CAY təŋtə-
NSY [təŋłəqə- 'blow away (wind)']
CSY təŋtə- 'blow away (wind)'
Sir təŋtə- 'carry out to sea' [Vakh.]
SPI tiŋit- 'blow away (wind)'
NAI tiŋɨt- 'be blown away, be caused to drift away' [and tiksiq- 'drift in a boat', Nu, PH tɨktaq 's.o. carried out to sea on an icefloe, s.th. swept out to sea', tɨktau- 'be carried out to sea, etc.']
WCI tiktau- 'be carried off by wind' [and tiktat 'things carried off by the wind']
ECI tittau- 'be carried off by wind'
GRI tiŋit- 'blow away (wind), be blown by the wind' [and tissikᴀʀ- (old ortho. tigsikar-), tissukᴀʀ- 'drift with wind', tissiʀ-, tissiataᴀʀ- 'sail', NG tiktaq 's.th. blown by the wind']

PI təŋmi- 'be flying' [cf. miɣ-? — note the Aleut sense there]
SPI tiŋmila-, Qaw tiŋmilra- 'be flying'
NAI tiŋmi-
WCI tiŋmi-
ECI timmi-
GRI timmi-

PE təŋmi(C)ᴀʀ 'bird'
AAY təŋmiaq, təmŋiaq 'goose'
CAY təŋmiaq 'bird'
NSY təɣmiaq [L.-T.]
CSY —
Sir —
SPI tiŋmiaq 'bird', Qaw 'duck' [and Qaw tiŋmiaʀžuk 'small bird']
NAI tiŋmiaq 'medium-sized bird', tiŋmiaʀžuk 'small bird'
WCI tiŋmiaq Sig 'white-fronted goose', Car 'goose' [and Sig tiŋmiaʀyuk 'small bird'; Pryde has Cop, Net, Car tiŋmiaq, Sig tiŋmiluk 'bird']
ECI timmiaq 'bird' [and NBI, SB timmiakuluk 'fulmar']
GRI timmiaq 'bird, birdskin coat (in Up rather of reindeer skin)' [pl. timmiššat, but note also timmik 'gannet' with a velar cons.; in SWG timmiaq is 'chicken', and Ras. has it as 'gull' for EG; Up timmiakiluk 'fulmar']

PI təŋmikaq- 'spurt' [cf. təŋmi- above and k(k)aʀ-]
SPI —
NAI —
WCI tiŋmikaq- 'spurt'
ECI timmikaq-
GRI NG timmikayaaq- 'spurt' [and note WG timmiɣ- 'have diarrhea']

PI təŋmiʀala- 'flap about' [cf. təŋmi- above and la(ʀ)-]
SPI [note Qaw FR tiŋmiʀalasuun 'airplane']
NAI tiŋmiʀala- 'fly in all directions'
WCI —
ECI timmiʀalaaC- 'flap wings (bird on ground)'
GRI timmiʀala- 'flap about'

PE təŋqa(ʀ)- 'fly up' [cf. təŋə- and k(k)aʀ-]
AAY —
CAY —
NSY təŋqaXtə- 'fly up'
CSY təŋqałuk 'windy wet weather'
Sir —
SPI —
NAI tiqqala- 'be flying around in the air'
WCI —
ECI tiqqalaa- 'flap in wind' [tiqqalaaq 's.th. flapping in the wind', Lab 'wind direction indicator']
GRI tiqqaʀ- 'blow up into the air (wind)', tiqqala-, tiqqakatta(a)ʀ- 'fly around in the air' [Robbe and Menn. have EG tiqqattaC- 'be blown away']

PE təŋluɣ(-) '(strike with) fist'
AAY teŋluɣ- 'strike with fist' [təŋluk 'fist']
CAY təŋluɣ- 'strike with fist' [təŋluk 'fist']
NSY tənluɣ- 'strike with fist'
CSY təŋluɣ-
Sir —
SPI tiɣluk-
NAI tiɣluk-
WCI tiɣluk- 'strike with fist' [tiɣluk 'fist']
ECI tillu(k)- 'strike with fist'
GRI tiłłuɣ-

PY təŋʀu- 'be enthusiastic'
AAY təŋʀu-, təŋŋu- 'be confident, sure of oneself'
CAY təŋʀu- 'be enthusiastic, eager'
NSY —
CSY təŋʀu(yuɣ)- 'be enthusiastic' [təŋʀuniqə- 'have fun']

PE təŋuɣ 'liver'
AAY təŋuk 'liver'
CAY təŋuk
NSY təŋuk
CSY təŋuk
Sir təŋəx
SPI tiŋuk
NAI tiŋuk
WCI tiŋuk
ECI tiŋuk
GRI tiŋuk

PY təŋuqə- 'strain' [cf. ciŋuk-]
AAY təŋuqə- 'strain (at stool, etc.)'
CAY təŋuqə-, təŋuqaaʀ- 'show strain by physical expression, as when lifting or defecating' [and note təŋuxtaaʀun 'tug-of-war' and təŋuɣaXtə- 'be unable to breathe because of blow to the solar plexus']
NSY təŋuqə- 'exert oneself, strain' [ANLC]
CSY təŋuqə- 'strain as when defecating or giving birth' [and note təŋuɣ- 'box, fight with fists' — contam. with təŋluɣ-?]

PE təpə 'smell' [cf. Aleut tum̥i-X 'fart']
AAY təpa 'odor, smell' [base təpə-]
CAY təpa 'odor, smell, fish aged underground as preparation for eating' [base təpə-]
NSY təpə 'odor, smell'
CSY təpa 'odor, smell' [base təpə-]
Sir təpa [base təpə-]
SPI tivi, Imaq təvə 'odor, smell'
NAI tipɨ
WCI tipi
ECI tipi, tipa 'smell, taste'
GRI tipi, tipik, EG tipiq 'odor, smell' [3s poss. tikka; tipiɣ- 'smell bad']

PI təppak- 'stink' [cf. nəɣ-]
SPI —
NAI tippak- 'develop a strong smell' [and tipaaq- 'stink'; note also PH tipaaqpak 'block of tobacco']
WCI tipaaq- 'stink' [and Car? tipaaq 'tobacco' — Schn. 'adg']
ECI tipaaɣɣi(C)- 'stink'
GRI tippaɣ- 'have developed a smell, have begun to go off (food)' [and note tipaaʀnaq 'thyme']

PY təptukuyuq or **təptukuuyaq** 'fleabane or similar plant' [cf. tu-[1]]
AAY C təptukuuyaq, təptukuiyaq 'fleabane, aster, arctic daisy'
CAY Y təptukuyuq 'fleabane, valerian'
NSY —
CSY —
Inu [Qaw tipitukuuwik 'wild onion' is presumably a loan from Yup]

PE təpə- 'drift ashore'
AAY təpə- 'drift ashore'
CAY təpə-
NSY təpə-
CSY təpə-
Sir təpə- 'drift ashore' [Vakh. also has təptaʀ- from Rub.'s tetxs]
SPI tivi-, Qaw tipi- 'drift ashore'
NAI tipɨ-
WCI tipi- 'drift ashore' [and tivliq 's.th. drifted ashore']
ECI tipiyuq 'flotsam, s.th. washed up on shore' [and tilliq 's.th. situated farther up inland' — for Lab timiʀliq see təmə, with which there is contam. here]
GRI tipi- 'drift ashore' [and NG tippussat 'flotsam'; and also timiʀłiq under təmə]

PE təpðaR 'flotsam or jetsam' [cf. ðaR]
AAY təppaq 'drift log'
CAY təppaq 'driftwood, s.th. drifted ashore'
NSY təpaq 's.th. drifted ashore' [ANLC also 'sea potatoes']
CSY təpaq 'edible sea creature such as sea cucumber found on beach'
Sir təptaRəX 's.th. drifted ashore' [Vakh. from Rub.]
SPI tipšaq 'flotsam'
NAI tivžaq, Mal tipžaq 's.th. washed ashore, driftwood'
WCI tivyat 'driftwood' [Schn. has tipiyaq for 'adg'], tivyak- 'find s.th. washed ashore', Car? tivyaRluk 'wreckage washed up on shore' [Schn. 'adg']
ECI tiyyaq 'floating wreck', tiyyaluk Tar 'wreckage thrown up on shore', Lab 'driftwood'
GRI tiššaq, tišaRłuk 'wreckage washed up on shore'

PE təpli 'food around mouth' [cf. Aleut cimci-X 's.th. caught between teeth' — with *t_2]
AAY təpłi-, təpłiɣ- 'have food around mouth left from eating'
CAY təpłi- 'have particles of food or the like around mouth'
NSY təpłiq 'dirty mouth' [L.-T.; ANLC also təpłiR- 'have a dirty mouth']
CSY təfłi 'particles of food or the like around mouth'
Sir təfłi 'particles of food around mouth' [Orr; Em. has təfłici- 'smear food round mouth' and təfłiŋəR- 'wipe mouth' — from CSY?]
SPI tipłiluk
NAI tivli [and Mal tipliiyaun 'napkin']
WCI tivlit 'food around mouth' [Met.]
ECI tilliq [Lab tivli — Peck]
GRI tiłłi 'grease from food around mouth'

PI təpuk 'whitefish'
Yup — [but note NSU tupuk 'whitefish', probably borrowed from Inu]
SPI Qaw tipuk 'whitefish'
NAI tipuk
WCI —
ECI —
GRI —

PI təqətuRaq 'young animal?' [cf. təRiɣ (esp. təRiɣluɣ under it), but also the p.b. in nukatuɣaq under nukaR?]
SPI —
NAI tiqituRaq 'young caribou' [tiqittut 'herd of cows and calves']
WCI tiRi(t)tuaq, Car tiRituRaq 'young animal' [the latter in Ras. — Dor. has 'adult from 30 to 35' for B. Lake]
ECI tiqituRaq 'young seal'
GRI —

PI təqi- or təRi- 'refrain from doing for cult reasons' [or təqə-; cf. təRiɣ, also PY takaR-[2], though the relat. is obscure]
Yup [note CAY HBC taqiɣ- 'have sexual intercourse (of humans)' and taqik 'genitalia' — compare the GRI forms below]
SPI [Jen. has qiɣi- 'refrain from mentioning a dead person's name']
NAI —
WCI Net tiRiɣi- 'refrain from because of superstition', tiRiŋnaq- 'be unclean' [and Schn. has tiRinaqtuq 'one who can practice sorcery, what is forbidden by sorcerer', tiRiɣi- 'practice sorcery on' for 'adg'; for Cop tiRiɣi- 'move or speak quietly so as not to arouse' see təRiɣ]
ECI —
GRI tiqiɣi- 'dare not mention a dead person who has not yet had s.o. named after him' [and tiqiłłiR- 'fear things will again turn out badly'; note also taqiɣ-, taqima- 'be reserved, shy, not want to go along, shrink back (of game animal)' (the former also 'be huddled up (bird)' — Fab. also has 'have a bad conscience because of one's behavior'); also taqassiɣi- 'be disgusted by' — perhaps infl. by taqə-]

PE təRiɣ 'game animal' [as verb = 'be alert or furtive', perhaps the original meaning; cf. təRlək- and perhaps also təqətuRaq and təqi-, with which there is some entanglement]
AAY [təRikə- 'creep up on'] ➟
CAY [note təRikaXtə- 'stand alert, be proud in a silly way'] ➟
NSY təRik 'sea animal' [ANLC also 'wild animal'; təRižaɣaq 'young of sea animal']
CSY təRik 'game animal' [also təRiɣniiR- 'hunt game', təRixsiR- 'sing a song to attract game (shaman)', and note emot. root təRiɣ(yuɣ)- 'have fun, be interested']
Sir təRix 'sea animal' [note also təRincaRaXtə- 'interest', nominal təRinəŋułəX — Em. has təRiŋyuxtə-]
SPI Imaq təRik 'animal' [and note FR tiRiɣuk- 'do noiselessly']
NAI [tiRii- 'try not to make noise (e.g. when stalking animal)']
WCI [Pryde has Cop tiRii- 'move or creep toward an animal so as not to be heard by it, move quietly so as not to arouse sleeping person' (also tiRiɣi- in the latter sense); for tiRit(t)uaq 'young animal' see təqətuaq]
ECI Lab tiɣik- 'do quietly' [and Tar tiRiŋŋuaq 'small sparrow']
GRI [note tiRiɣ- 'be small and narrow', tiRiit- 'be soft spoken, slow and careful in speaking'] ➟

PY təRi(C)aR- or təRiiR- 'pursue by stealth (animal)'
AAY —
CAY [təRiiR- 'react to strange animal by becoming alert and barking (e.g. dog)']
NSY təRiaR- 'sneak up on' [ANLC]
CSY təRiiR- 'pursue (another animal, of dog)'
Inu [note Imaq tiRiaɣaq- 'stalk game', but also NAI tiRiiɣaq- 'stalk (animal)' going with tiRii- under təRiɣ above]

PE təRiɣaR 'weasel or other small mammal?' [cf. aR]
AAY —
CAY təRiaq 'weasel'
NSY —
CSY təRiɣaq 'game animal'

Sir təʀiɣəX 'white fox' [compare təʀikanni(C)aʀ below; Vakh. has təʀiɣaX 'animal' from Men.'s texts]
SPI tiʀiaq 'weasel'
NAI itiʀiaq 'weasel, ermine', Mal tiʀiaq 'ermine' [the former influenced by ətəʀ-?]
WCI tiʀiaq
ECI tiʀiaq 'weasel, ermine'
GRI tiʀiaq 'mouse, lemming, weasel'

PE təʀiɣluɣ 'young bearded seal' [cf. ʀuluk?]
AAY —
CAY —
NSY təʀiɣluk 'young bearded seal' [ANLC]
CSY təʀiɣluk
Sir təʀiɣlux [Orr]
SPI tiʀiɣluk
NAI —
WCI tiʀiɣluk 'young bearded seal' [Pryde for Cop and Net, Ras. for Car; Ras. also has Net terikluak 'young fox' — Pryde tiʀiɣluaq]
ECI tiʀillu 'young bearded seal'
GRI NWG tiqiłłuk 'young bearded seal' [influenced by təqətuʀaq?]

PY təʀiɣluɣciq 'lunar month in early part of year'
AAY —
CAY —
NSY təʀiɣlusiq [L.-T.], təʀiɣluxsiq [Men. article] 'April' [and ANLC təʀiɣluxsiaq 'February']
CSY təʀiɣluxsiq 'February-March' [but Sergeeva has təʀiɣlusiq]
Inu [Peck has terrigluliut 'April' for Labrador; another ECI source has tirikluliut for 'April-May']

PE təʀikanni(C)aʀ 'arctic fox?' [cf. ni(C)aʀ-, also perhaps təʀiɣaʀ (with p.b. nəɣ-) and/or AAY təʀikə- under təʀiɣ above]
AAY —
CAY təʀikaniaq 'wolverine'
NSY —
CSY —
Sir [note təʀikəX 'animal' — Vakh. from Men.'s texts; for təʀiɣəX 'white fox' see təʀiɣaʀ above]
SPI —
NAI tiʀiɣanniaq 'white (arctic) fox'
WCI tiʀiɣanniaq
ECI tiʀiɣanniaq
GRI tiʀianniaq, NG tiʀiɣanniaq 'fox' [old ortho. teriangniaq but Top has terrienniak]

PI təʀikšuq- 'stalk or creep up on game' [cf. ðuʀ-?]
Yup [cf. AAY təʀikə- 'creep up on' under təʀiɣ above, and note CSY təʀiXtuʀ- 'stalk, pursue' with tuʀ-[2], and təʀikusaq 'animal']
Sir [note təʀikusaX 'land animal', from CSY?]
SPI Qaw tiʀikšuq- 'creep up on (game)' [= KI tiʀiktuq-, going with the CSY above?]
NAI tiʀikšuq- 'creep up on animal in crouching position' [for tiʀii- 'try not to make noise while stalking' see təʀiɣ above]
WCI tiʀiksuq- 'move in on animal silently' [Schn. has tiʀiqsuq- for B. Lake; compare also Cop tiʀii- 'creep up on' under təʀiɣ above]
ECI [tiʀiʀsu(q)- 'come creeping, surreptitiously']
GRI [note taqiššuʀ- 'steal up on (of game)']

PI təʀikšaq 'belt' [there may be a link to təʀiɣ — cf. GRI tiʀiɣ- there]
SPI tiʀikšaq 'belt worn under clothing'
NAI tiʀikšaq 'belt for pants'
WCI tiʀiksaq
ECI [note tiʀitti 'belt for pants'; Ras. has Igl tirissiq 'waist belt']
GRI —

PI təʀlək- 'think oneself safe (and thus be easy prey)' [cf. təʀiɣ]
SPI —
NAI —
WCI [tiʀliaq- 'surprise, creep up on' and tiʀlima- 'keep under careful observation'; Ras. has tiʀlaaq- 'come on from behind' for Cop]
ECI tiʀli(C)- 'be an unsuspecting victim', Lab tiʀlik- 'feel secure', tiʀliaq- 'deceive' [Peck; and tiʀlituʀnia(q)- 'stalk game that is unaware of being stalked', Iti tiʀli 'game unaware of being hunted', tiʀliani- 'creep up on']
GRI tiʀłik 'seal which lies safely in water and is easy to approach', tiʀłiɣ-, tiʀłaʀuʀ- 'feel safe, be unawares, have calmed down' [Top has 'sit still, be sad'; Robbe and Menn. have EG tiʀtaaʀ- 'relax' and tiʀtaaŋa- 'be lazy', tirtiɣaaʀ- 'be distrustful'; note also tiʀłisaaʀ-, tiʀłiŋaniiʀ-, tiʀłassi- 'creep up on, take by surprise']

PY təʀu 's.th. at an angle to s.th. else?' [cf. təkəðquʀ?]
AAY təʀuq 'fork of tree or river'
CAY təʀu 'foot of bed area, bed partner sleeping in opposite or perpendicular direction' [and note NI təʀuluk 'friend', also nəʀuvailitaq, LI təʀuvailitaq, təʀupailitaq 'great-great-grandchild' (with vaʀ- and ŋilitaʀ, the first form influenced by nəʀuvəʀ-?)]
NSY —
CSY [təʀuq 'fleshy part of bird tail, notch in end of arrow']

PE tətəʀ- 'mark'
AAY cətəʀ- 'mark'
CAY cətəʀ-, HBC citəʀ- 'mark' [nominal cətəq, citəq]
NSY təžəʀ- 'mark' [ANLC also 'underline, draw a line, cross out'; nom. təžəq 'line']
CSY təžəʀ- 'mark' [nom. təžəq]
Sir təžəʀ- 'mark' [from CSY?]
SPI titiq-
NAI titiq- 'mark' [and titiq* 'mark, dot']
WCI titiq- 'mark'
ECI titiq- 'write, mark' [and tittaq 'mark']
GRI tittaq(*) 'line'

PI tətəʀaq- 'draw or write' [cf. aʀ-]
SPI —
NAI [titiʀaq 'calendar month, mark']
WCI titiʀaq- 'write' [and Cop titiqqat 'letters']
ECI NBI, Aiv titiʀaq- 'write' [and Aiv titiqqat 'letters']
GRI titaʀ- 'draw (line)', NG tittaq- 'write' [and NG tittakkat 'letter']

PI təva- 'do a frolicsome dance'
Yup — [but note NSY təvəkitaŋʀalʀia 'clumsy']
SPI —
NAI —
WCI Cop tiva- 'dance frolicsome drum-dance' [Ras.]
ECI Igl tiva- 'dance with masks' [Ras.]
GRI tiva- 'leap about, do drum-dance, flap wings' [for tipaɣ- 'be wanton, fawn upon' see təɣəɣ-]

PY təviʀ- 'set (sun)'
AAY —
CAY təviʀ- 'disappear, set (sun)'
NSY təviʀ- 'set or disappear behind s.th. (sun)'
CSY təviʀ- 'set (sun or moon)'
Sir —

PY təvu(q) 'solid (added) ingredient'
AAY —
CAY təvuq 'solid ingredient', NSU 'bread accompanying tea or coffee'
NSY təvu 'added ingredient' [ANLC]
CSY —

PE təvvuɣ- 'spit'
AAY —
CAY təfaaʀ- 'spit' [and note Nun təpłuaʀ- 'spit' — influenced by təpli?]
NSY —
CSY [note təfaay 'expression said at end of story, said to represent spitting']
Sir —
SPI tivvuaq- 'spit'
NAI tivvuk-, tivvuaq- 'spit out', Mal tuvvuq-, tuvvuaq- 'spit'
WCI tivvuaq- 'spit'
ECI tivvuaq-, tivvualuk- 'spit s.th. out'
GRI tiffuɣ-, tixxuɣ- [old ortho. tivgug-] 'splash, squirt', tiffuaʀ-, tixxuaʀ- 'spit out', EG tippuɣaʀ- 'spit, splutter'

PI təža- 'slice for drying (fish or meat)'
SPI tiža- 'slice meat thin for drying', Qaw 'make cross cuts in fish for drying'
NAI tiža- 'cut fish across width for drying, make incision (in human) for bloodletting'
WCI tiya- 'cut fish or meat for drying'
ECI tiyaa- 'cut in thin slices', tiyak- 'cut into slices' [tiyaaq 'slice']
GRI tiša- 'cut meat, fish for drying' [tišaaq 'split fish']

PI təžžuq- 'dry out' [there may be a link to təža-]
SPI tižžuq- 'run dry, boil dry, have water run out of s.th.'
NAI —
WCI —
ECI tiyyu(C)- 'boil off excess water'
GRI tiššuʀ- 'be dried out, boiled off (water)'

PI tuat- 'be thin'
SPI —
NAI —
WCI Cop tuat- 'thin'
ECI tuat- 'be narrow, oblong, thin'
GRI tuaɣ- 'be thin'

PE tu(C)avə(t)- 'rush about' [cf. tayu(ɣ)-, though the relat. if any — is obscure]
AAY —
CAY HBC, Nun tuaftə- 'be very busy' [and note tavə-, Nun taavə- 'hurry be in a rush' — contam. with tayu(ɣ)-?]
NSY —
CSY [for taayuɣ- 'hurry' see tayuɣ-]
Sir —
SPI [note Imaq tavak- 'hurry', which Jen. also has for KI]
NAI tuavɨt- 'cheer, whoop it up at celebration' [and tuakšuit- 'be very calm']
WCI tuavit- 'make lot of noise (household, child)' [and tuavait- 'be quiet' — Met.; Schn. has Car? tuaviuq- 'hurry' for 'adg']
ECI tuaviq- 'hurry' [and tuavi 'hurry!']
GRI tuaviuʀ- 'hurry' [and tuavi 'hurry!', tuavisaaʀ- 'hurry (someone) along']

PE tucaʀ- 'hear or understand' [from *tutyaʀ-? — cf. Aleut tut- 'hear, get to hear', tuta- 'hear, be hearing', Atkan tutni-, EA tun̥i- 'inform']
AAY —
CAY —
NSY susaʀ- 'learn, hear from, find out'
CSY tusaqə- 'hear and comprehend' [and tusaqn̥əXłuɣ- 'misunderstand, hear badly']
Sir [note tunəʀaʀ- 'listen, understand']
SPI suzaa- 'understand'
NAI tusaa- 'hear', PH susaa- 'hear news'
WCI tusaq-, tusaa- 'hear' [and Cop sometimes 'understand' acc. Met.]
ECI tusaq- 'hear (once)', tusaa- hear (continually), understand'
GRI tusaʀ- 'hear', tusaa- 'can hear, listen, have understood' [and tutsiut(i)- 'be rumored, be heard from, be spoken about']

PI tucaqliq- 'inform' [cf. liʀ-?]
SPI suzaqɬiq- 'tell news to s.o.'
NAI tusaqɬiʀaq- 'complain or make offensive remark about s.o. so that they can hear'
WCI —
ECI —
GRI tusaʀɬiʀ- 'inform, give hint to'

PI tucaqšau- 'be audible' [cf. kðaʀ and ŋu-]
SPI —
NAI [tusaqšaʀi- 'be able to hear' — with trans. p.b. kə-[1]]
WCI Cop tuhaXXau- 'be audible' [Pryde; Met. has tusaksau- 'must be heard, listened to' and Schn. has Car? tusaʀsau- 'be audible' for 'adg']
ECI tusaʀsau- 'be audible'
GRI tusaʀšaa- 'be clear to hear, sound loud and clear'

PI tucaʀna(a)q- 'listen to s.th. pleasing' [cf. nnaq]
SPI — [suzaanaq- 'be understandable' is with naʀ-]
NAI — [tusaʀnaq- 'can be heard' is with naʀ-]
WCI [Schn. has tusaʀnaqtut 'pleasant things to listen to', tusaʀnaʀuti 'gramophone' for 'adg' — Pryde has tuhaʀnaaʀun for Cop]
ECI Lab tusaʀnaaq- 'listen to a pleasant tale, like to hear', tusaʀnaaʀi- 'like to listen to' [Peck]
GRI tusaʀnaaʀ- 'listen' [tusaʀnaaʀut 'gramophone', tusaʀnaʀi- 'find pleasant to listen to']

PI tutcaq 's.th. heard (news)' [cf. q under nəʀ[1]]
SPI —
NAI tutcaq* 'oral account, news' [tutcaʀik- 'be cause for good news', tutcaʀluk- 'hear bad news']
WCI Sig tutsaʀik- 'hear well', tusaʀluk- 'hear bad news' [Lowe]
ECI tutsaluk- 'hear bad news'
GRI tutsa(ʀ)- [with possessor endings] '(s.o.'s) hearing' [tutsaʀiɣ- 'hear well, receive good news', tutsaʀłuɣ- 'not hear well, receive bad news' — compare CSY tusaqŋ̥əXłuɣ- under tucaʀ- above]

PE tucilaʀ- 'be deaf' [cf. tucaʀ- and ŋit-?]
AAY tutłaʀ- 'be deaf'
CAY [note tuuskayaʀ- 'be disorientated']
NSY —
CSY tuusłaʀ- 'be hard of hearing, deaf' [and tuusłitə- 'hear well']
Sir tusłaʀməlŋuX 'deaf'
SPI —
NAI tusilʸlʸaq- 'become deaf'
WCI —
ECI tusilaq- 'be hard of hearing or disobedient' [Saull — Schn. has tusilaaq-, also tusilait- 'be obedient']
GRI tusilaʀ- 'be deaf', tusiłłaʀ-, tusiłłaɣ- 'have become deaf'

PE tucu- 'admire or envy'
AAY cucukə- 'admire'
CAY cucu- 'want to emulate'
NSY —
CSY —
Sir —
SPI suzu- 'covet, envy'
NAI tusu-
WCI tusu-
ECI tusu- 'desire, envy'
GRI tusu- 'desire', EG 'envy' (trans. tusuu- acc. Robbe and Menn.), NG tuhu-, tuhuyi- 'admire, envy' [and note tutsuʀiɣi- 'trust, rely on']

PE tuðiɣ 'snipe or plover (or similar shore bird)' [compare aðiʀ for the forms with l here; cf. tuuyuk under tuɣəʀ- and tu(C)utləɣ, with which there seems to be entanglement]
AAY [Ras. has tuikaxnigil'guk 'heron']
CAY tuuziik, tuuyiik, HBC tuliik 'plover, sandpiper', Nun, HBC tuyək 'snipe' [and note tuiʀ(aq) 'tree sparrow', BB tulikaq 'dowitcher']
NSY tužik 'snipe' [and ANLC has tužiaXaq 'tundra snipe']
CSY tužiik 'snipe, golden plover'
Sir tužix, tulix 'snipe' [the former on Men.'s comp. list, the latter also Vakh. from Rub.]
SPI Qaw tullik 'golden plover', Imaq tužik 'snipe'
NAI tulliɣnaq 'ruddy turnstone', Nu, Mal tullik 'golden plover' [and tužžaatužaq 'godwit']
WCI Cop tulliɣaq 'golden plover' [Ras. has Net tutlik 'black-billed plover' and tuituaq 'little plover'; Car EP tullik 'golden plover' acc. Ow. and Net tu'lik 'black-billed plover' acc. Pryde, who also has tuutuuq 'pectoral sandpiper' for Cop]
ECI Lab tullik 'kind of snipe' [Peck — for tuullik 'loon' see tu(C)utləɣ; Schn, has tulliʀunniq 'marsh bird (woodcock or harlequin duck?)' and Peck has Lab tuɣliʀunik 'black duck' — by contam. with tuɣliʀunnaq?]
GRI —

PE tuɣəkaʀ '(toggle) harpoon head' [cf. tuɣət- and kaʀ; the apparent relat. to tuɣəkaʀ(aʀ) under tuɣəʀ(-) may be coincidental]
AAY ➡
CAY ➡
NSY [ətuxkaiXsi- 'remove harpoon head'
CSY tuuxkaq, tuuXqaq 'harpoon head' [Rub. only has the first for Chap — the second may be by contam. with tuɣəʀ-]
Sir ➡
SPI tuukaq 'harpoon toggle head'
NAI tuukkaq*
WCI Net tuukkaq 'detachable walrus-harpoon head' [Pryde; Ras. has Cop tuuk(k)aXXiaq 'harpoon line of plaited caribou sinew'; Met. has tuɣaqsiaq 'line connecting harpoon head with rest of harpoon']
ECI tuukkaq 'detachable harpoon head' [Saul and Dor. for Tar and NBI respectively — Schn. has tukkak 'barbed detachable head of walrus harpoon', NBI, Aiv tuukaq 'tip of walrus harpoon', and B.-S. has tukkaʀsiaq 'harpoon line']
GRI tuukkaq(*) 'harpoon head'

PY-S tukaʀtə 'harpoon rope' [cf. perhasp p.b. ðə-]
AAY [B.-S. has tuqxiik 'harpoon line']
CAY Nun tukaXta 'harpoon rope (linking parts of harpoon and float)' [ANLC]
NSY tukaXtək 'rope on harpoon' [du.; ANLC]
CSY tukaXta 'rope on whaling harpoon attaching harpoon to float'
Sir tukəxta 'harpoon line'
Inu [SPI tuɣaqtik 'harpoon rope' seems to be a loan from Yup]

PE tuɣənRaR 'shaman's helping spirit' [cf. tuɣət- and n(ə)RaR(aR)- lit. 'one that has been secured'?]
AAY K tunRaq 'evil spirit, devil'
CAY tuunRaq, Nun tuunR(aX*) 'helping spirit, devil' [Nun tuunRam ciutii 'toadstool' (lit. 'devil's ear'); note Al quɣam tutuca or quɣam tutusii 'toad stool, mushroom' lit. 'devil's or demon's ear']
NSY tuunRaq 'devil' [ANLC also has tuRnəRaq 'shaman's spirit']
CSY tuRnəRaq* [tuuRnəRam siɣutŋa 'toadstool' (literally, 'devil's ear') — the occurrence of this idiom here and in CAY Nun may be from diffusion]
Sir tuɣnəRaX 'evil spirit'
SPI tuuRnaq 'shaman's helping spirit, devil' [Qaw has tuunRaq]
NAI tuunRaq* 'shaman's helping spirit, devil' [as verb = 'frighten, pretending to be a devil']
WCI tu(u)nRaq 'shaman's helping spirit, devil' [Pryde also Cop tuunŋaq- 'summon familiar spirit']
ECI tuuRŋaq 'helping spirit, devil'
GRI tuuRnaq 'shaman's helping spirit' [tuuRnaR-, tuuRnat- 'terrify (helping spirit appearing before s.o.']

PE tuɣənRi- 'traffic with spirits' [cf. li-[1]]
AAY —
CAY tuunRi- 'use spirit power, traffic with spirits'
NSY tuunRi- 'traffic with spirits' [ANLC; Tein has tunRiałkutat 'amulets']
CSY —
Sir —
SPI —
NAI —
WCI Cop tuunŋi-, tuunRi- [Pryde]
ECI tuuRŋi-
GRI tuuRni-

PI tuunRaaRžuk 'scoter or similar bird' [cf. aRžuk]
SPI Qaw tuunRaaRžuk 'black scoter'
NAI tuunRaaRžuk 'surf scoter'
WCI Car tuunRaviaq 'common scooter' [Pryde, who also has Sig tuunRavik 'white-winged scooter']
ECI —
GRI [note tuuRnaviaRšuk 'harlequin duck' and compare tuuRnaaRšuk 'special helping spirit, devil', a parallel formation]

PE tuɣəR(-) 'poke or strike ice pick' [cf. Aleut tuɣa- 'hit', tuɣa-X 'fist']
AAY C PWS tuɣəR- 'poke, beat with stick'
CAY tuɣəq*, tuuq 'ice pick' [and verbal tuɣəR- 'strike with ice pick, etc.']
NSY tuɣəq 'ice pick', tuɣəR- 'use ice pick on' [ANLC]
CSY tuɣəq*, tuɣaq 'ice pick' [and verbal tuɣəR-, tuɣaR- 'use an ice pick']
Sir tuɣəX 'ice pick' [Orr]
SPI tuuq 'ice pick' [and verbal tuuq- 'poke with s.th. sharp, sting']
NAI tu<ɣ>uq 'ice pick' [also tuuRniq* 'dot', and PH tuɣɣuq- 'chop ice with ice pick']
WCI tuuq 'ice pick' [and verbal tuuq- 'use an ice pick']
ECI tuuq 'ice pick' [and verbal tuuq- 'hit with long pointed instrument', tuɣɣaku 'chip of ice removed by ice pick']
GRI tuuq 'ice pick' [and verbal tuuR- 'thrust at, cut hole in ice, recoil (gun)', EG also 'point at, touch with finger' acc. Robbe and Menn.; and tuXXut(i)- 'press in against', tuuRniq* 'dot, mark from blow'; for tuɣ- 'strike against' see tut-]

PE tuɣəkaR(aR) '(walrus) tusk' [cf. perhaps Aleut tumɣa-X 'ivory, walrus tusk' if from *tuɣma-; the apparent relat. to tuɣəkaR may be coincidental, though there appears to be some contam.]
AAY tuxka<R>aq 'ivory, walrus tusk'
CAY tuxkaR(aq*) [also kuxkaR(aq*)] 'walrus tusk'
NSY tuxkaq 'walrus tusk' [L.-T. tuxkaRqaq]
CSY [note tuɣun 'tusk'; for tuuxkaq, tuuXkaq 'ivory, harpoon head' see tuɣəkaR]
Sir tuxkaX 'walrus tusk' [Vakh. has tuXkaX]
SPI tuuɣaaq 'tusk, ivory'
NAI tuuɣa<ž>aq 'walrus tusk, ivory'
WCI tuuɣaaq 'tusk, ivory'
ECI tuuɣaaq 'tusk, ivory' [Saul — Schn. has tuɣaaq, also tuɣaɣaq]
GRI tuuɣaaq,tuuaaq 'tusk, ivory'

PE tuɣəkaRaləɣ 'narwhale' [cf. tuɣəkaR(aR) above and ləɣ]
AAY —
CAY —
NSY tuxkaRalək 'narwhale'
CSY [note puuɣzaq tuɣutələk 'narwhale' (lit. 'tusked beluga')]
Sir —
SPI Imaq tuwaalək
NAI [qil[y]aluɣaq tuuɣaalik 'narwhale' (lit. 'tusked beluga')]
WCI Net tuuɣaalik 'narwhale' [Pryde]
ECI NBI tuuɣaalik [Spald.]
GRI tuuɣaalik

PE tuɣɣaR- 'strike or hack repeatedly' [cf. aR-]
AAY KP tuɣaR- 'beat with stick (to soften and remove skin)'
CAY [tuɣauR- 'strike repeatedly with ice pick']
NSY — [for tuqaXtə- 'knock against' see tut-]
CSY [for tuɣaR- 'use ice pick' see tuɣəR- above]
Sir —
SPI tuɣɣaq- 'push, prod'
NAI tuɣɣaq- 'prod, push away', tuɣaq- 'poke with stick'
WCI tuɣaq- 'hit several times'
ECI tuɣaq- 'hit several times', NBI tuɣɣaq- 'box'
GRI tuxxaR- 'cut or hack at'

PI tuuyuk or **tuuyuq** 'woodpecker?' [cf. yuɣ?]
SPI Qaw tuuyuk 'woodpecker'
NAI tuuyuq
WCI Sig tuuyuq [Pet.]
ECI [tuɣɣayuuq 'woodpecker'; but Pryde has tuuyuk 'ringed plover' for both Igl and Tar]
GRI tuuyuk 'ring plover' [contam. with tuðiɣ?]

PE tuɣət- 'lash or secure'
AAY [note C tuɣlər- 'heal, knit together (bone), C tuɣləXtə- 'pound, mash']
CAY ➟
NSY [tuxtaq 'ball of pickled walrus meat' — ANLC]
CSY tuuxtə- 'bundle securely, tighten parka hood round face'
Sir —
SPI tuut- 'put rawhide line through boat skin to lash it to boat frame'
NAI tuut- 'lash skin cover to boat frame' [and tuɣžut- 'lash, secure with rope', tuužvik 'horizontal pieces of wood to which umiaq skins are lashed', PH tuulvik 'brace board running length of boat frame']
WCI —
ECI —
GRI tuut- 'lash skin cover to boat frame' [and tuuffik (old ortho. tûvfik) 'side rib in umiaq over which tightening line is stretched']

PE tuɣətðar ridgepole' [cf. ðar?]
AAY —
CAY Nun tuusaX 'horizontal log in men's community house'
CSY —
NSY —
Sir —
SPI tuušaq 'beam across corner of men's house'
NAI tuužžaq, Nu tuutžaq 'ridgepole, ceiling beam'
WCI —
ECI —
GRI tuuššaq 'main roof beam in Greenlandic house, top beam of tent frame'

PI tuɣlərunnaq 'rosewort' [cf. tuŋlə(r)]
SPI —
NAI —
WCI Net tukłirunnaq 'rosewort' [Ras.]
ECI Baf tullirunniq *'Sedum radiola'* [Boas; Peck has Lab tuɣlirunak 'plant, orpine'; compare the bird sense homonyms under tuðiɣ]
GRI tułłirunnaq [old ortho. tugdleruᶍnaq], EG turtiirnaq 'rosewort'

PY tuka(r)- 'get sick from eating certain foods'
AAY Kod tuukar- 'have heartburn'
CAY [note Nun tukaayuX 'wild parsley']
NSY —
CSY tukaatə- 'get sick from eating incompatible foods'

PI tukə- 'lengthwise axis'
SPI —
NAI —
WCI tukimun 'lengthwise' [and Schn. has 'adg.' tukimiaq- 'shoot straight', tukilaq- 'go straight']
ECI tuki- 'axis, length' [tukiŋa 'its sense'; and tukimuak- 'go straight', tukit- 'become lined up with s.th. along its length', tukiŋa- 'be parallel with the axis of s.th.']
GRI tukik 'longitudinal direction' [e.g. of long island or mountain range seen from one's own perspective — Kl. has tukiŋa- 'have end turned against s.th. (e.g. coastline); also tukit- 'be positioned lengthwise', tukitit- 'place lengthwise', NG 'squeeze through narrow place' — Holt.]

PI tukəci- 'understand' [cf. ci- and compare the similar image of finding one's way back into a fjord under kaŋirci- (kaŋir) — GRI has a parallel form paasi- 'understand', with the same p.b. added to stem paðə 'mouth (of fjord)']
SPI —
NAI —
WCI Car tukihi- 'understand' [Pryde]
ECI tukisi-, tutsi- 'understand' [and NBI, SB tukisitsiaq- 'read']
GRI —

PE tukər- 'kick or push with foot' [cf. tutə- and tukkar-, also perhaps Aleut tukluɣ- 'scratch, tear with claw']
AAY tukər- 'kick'
CAY tukər- 'push or brace with feet, hatch (of chick)'
NSY tukər- 'push or brace with feet, hatch (of chick)' [Em.; ANLC also 'stretch a skin by dampening it and sitting on edge and pushing']
CSY tukər- 'brace with feet'
Sir tukər- 'lean, support self'
SPI tuɣiq- 'kick, pushing out with foot, hatch (of chick)' [and note F. River tukiq 'foot of moose or caribou']
NAI tukɨq- 'hatch, push with legs, extend legs'
WCI tukiq- 'push with foot'
ECI tukiq- 'push, hit with flat part of foot, tread on, hatch (of chick breaking shell)'
GRI tukir- 'push foot against, kick, creep out of egg'

PE tukkar- 'trample or kick repeatedly' [cf. tukər- and p.b. ar-, also tuku(q)]
AAY tukar- 'kick'
CAY tukar- 'kick with both feet from lying position'
NSY tukar- [ANLC]
CSY tukar- 'stamp feet'
Sir tukar- 'dance' [and Em. has tukarət- 'stamp, dance']
SPI tukkatuq- 'push with feet repeatedly', Qaw tukkaq- 'trample'
NAI tukkaq- 'push with one's feet repeatedly'
WCI —
ECI tukka(q)- 'push with feet continually' [and Iti tukailaa- 'move legs like scissors, pedal']
GRI tukkar- 'trample, tread on (e.g. bellows or lathe, turning it)' [and tukaala- 'shudder in agony (shot animal)]

PE tukku(r) 'host' [cf. Aleut tuku-X 'chief, master, rich man, boss, wealth', tuku- 'be rich']
AAY tuki- 'live comfortably', PWS tukiXtə- 'relax'
CAY tukuq Y, HBC 'host', K 'wealthy person', tukuu- 'be wealthy'
NSY tukuq 'wealth, goods, owner, boss' [and tukur- 'be rich' (ANLC)]
CSY tukuq 'host', tukuqə- 'be a guest'
Sir tukuX 'boss, leader, rich man' [and tukururcəɣəcəX 'powerful'; Vakh. has tukuriyurnəX 'rich']
SPI tukku- 'stay as a guest', tukkuu- 'have a house guest'

NAI tukku(q*) 'host', tukku- 'stay as a guest' [tukkumavik 'hotel']
WCI tukku(ma)- 'stay at someone's house'
ECI Lab tukku- 'not sleep beside one's mother (child)'
GRI tukku- 'sleep at a neighbor's house, be generous', tukkuʀ- 'be generous' [and note tukuma- 'be restless, enthusiastic, quick at work']

PY tukniɣ- 'be strong' [there may be a relat. to tukku(ʀ)]
AAY tukn̥iɣ- 'be strong'
CAY tukn̥i-
NSY —
CSY [note tukšunpak 'athletic agile person'
Sir — [for tukuʀuʀcəɣəcəX 'powerful' see tukku(ʀ)]

PI tukšuk- 'crush' [cf. tukəʀ-?]
SPI —
NAI tukšuk- 'crush, be crushed, crumple'
WCI tuksuk- 'flatten, dent'
ECI tutsu(k)-
GRI [note tuššuŋa- 'be on point of crying, emotionally moved']

PY-S tuku(q) 'foot?' [cf. tukəʀ- and tukkaʀ-]
AAY —
CAY Nun, HBC tukułək 'foot' [and Nun tukułəxaX 'beach greens, sea chickweed', parallel to itɣaXalək 'beach greens' — lit. 'one with little feet']
NSY —
CSY tukuʀaq 'ankle'
Sir tukəłqəX 'ankle' [Men.'s comp. list]

PY tukuʀnaq 'kind of seaweed' [cf. naʀ]
AAY —
CAY Nun tukuʀnaX 'edible yellow seaweed (yellow, looks like bloated tree branch)'
NSY —
CSY tukuʀnak 'edible sea plant'
Sir [Orr has tukuʀnax 'edible sea plant', which is probably borrowed from CSY]

PY-S tukviʀ- 'buy' [cf. tukku(ʀ)-?]
AAY —
CAY —
NSY tukpiʀ- 'buy' [and tukpiyaXqaq 'goods', tukpiʀaq 's.th. bought']
CSY tukfiʀ- 'buy' [tukfiʀaq 'store-bought thing']
Sir tukfəʀ- 'buy'

PE tulaɣ- 'land (come ashore)' [cf. tuluʀ- and western Aleut cala- 'land, come ashore' — with *t_2; there may be a link to tut-]
AAY —
CAY tulaɣ- 'arrive (esp. at land from sea)'
NSY —
CSY [note təʀluɣ- 'land from sea (onto beach)'; for tamlaɣ- 'land' see talmaɣ-]
Sir — [for tənpit(ə)- 'land' see tənputə-]
SPI tulak- 'come ashore'
NAI tulak- 'come ashore' [and tullaqi- 'come ashore for', tulaɣiaq 'landing place'; for Mal tullak- 'land gently' see tut-]
WCI tulak- 'land'
ECI tulak-
GRI tulaɣ- 'land, come ashore' [tulaɣiaq 'landing place']

PE tulimaʀ 'rib' [cf. Aleut tuli-X 'rafter, gablepost']
AAY tulimaq 'rib'
CAY tulimaq, tulimaʀaq
NSY tulimaq [L.-T.]
CSY tulimaq 'rib' [also 'rainbow' in Chap; note also Chap tułuməq 'pole in interior structure of skin-covered house', although this form with the Sir may in fact constitute a separate set]
Sir tułəməX 'cross-pole of skin tent' [Orr]
SPI tulimaq 'rib', tulimaaq 'rib of boat frame'
NAI tulima<ž>aq 'rib' [and tulim(m)aq 'rainbow']
WCI tulimaaq
ECI tulimaaq 'human rib', tulimaq, tulimayaaq 'rib of large mammal'
GRI Maniitsoq tulimaaq, NG tulimaq 'rib'

PI tulləq- 'trample' [cf. tutə-]
SPI —
NAI —
WCI tulliq- 'trample (snow) to flatten (e.g. for sleeping place in snow house)'
ECI tulli(q)- 'trample (snow) to flatten' [tullaaq 'snow house made with trodden snow', tulliʀaq 'linoleum', tulliʀaɣut 'door mat']
GRI EG tuttiC- 'tread on', NG tulliq- 'trample skin to soften it', WG tułłaʀ- [old ortho. tugdlar-] 'tread on, trample (flat or to clean skin)' [and note tułłaaʀi- 'have trodden s.th. down', tułłiʀaq 'mat, s.th. to tread on']

PE tulukaʀ 'raven'
AAY [note C tulukkuuləʀ- 'talk in an intelligible tongue to spirit']
CAY tulukaʀuk, tulukaʀuq 'raven'
NSY —
CSY —
Sir —
SPI ➡
NAI tuluɣaq 'raven' [pl. tulukkat]
WCI tuluɣaq
ECI tuluɣaq
GRI tuluɣaq 'raven' [tulukkaaq 'young raven']

PI tuluɣaʀnaq 'swallow (bird)' [cf. naʀ]
SPI Qaw tuluɣaʀnaq 'swallow'
NAI tuluɣaʀnaq
WCI —
ECI tuluɣaʀnaq 'small sparrow, black marine insect appearing after storm'
GRI tulu(ɣ)aʀnaq 'swallow'

PE tuluʀ- 'butt or bump into' [cf. tulaɣ-]
AAY ➡
CAY tuluʀ- 'lean on, be supported on', tuluq 'ivory, tusk'

NSY [note tuluʀaq 'drowsiness' (L.-T.) and tuluʀaʀ- 'nod head in drowsiness, doze' (ANLC) — influenced by nuluʀ(aʀ)-?]
CSY [note tuluʀaʀ- 'nod when sitting and falling asleep' and tuluʀ- 'sharpen, hone']
Sir —
SPI tuluq- 'hit with tusks'
NAI tuluq- 'butt, hit with head or tusk, attack (bird), reach shore (boat)'
WCI tuluq- 'bump into s.th.' [tululauq- 'pass close to land (fish, foxes in spring)']
ECI tuluq- 'give a blow with tusk or teeth, knock against' [tulua- 'touch land with bow (boat)'
GRI tuluʀ- 'lean up against, butt, poke'

PE tuluʀyaʀ 'canine tooth' [cf. yaʀ]
AAY tuluʀyaq, tuluʀnəq 'tusk of animal, canine tooth'
CAY tuluʀyaaq 'canine tooth'
NSY [note tuluk — with macron on second syllable — 'sharp, barb on fishing hook, notch']
CSY tuluʀyak 'canine tooth'
Sir —
SPI tuluʀiaq
NAI tuluʀiaq
WCI tuluʀiaq
ECI tuluʀiaq
GRI tuluʀiaq 'canine tooth, fang'

PE tumaɣ- 'taste bitter'
AAY tumaɣ- 'be dry'
CAY Nun tumaɣ- 'taste bitter'
NSY —
CSY tumaɣ- 'taste bitter'
Sir —
SPI —
NAI tumanŋu- 'feel one's food has not gone down completely and needs washing down'
WCI [Net tumak- 'be silent and withdrawn in unhappiness' — Briggs]
ECI —
GRI tumaŋŋu- 'feel faint (from lack of water), languish', NG 'have unpleasant sensation in throat from having eaten s.th. inedible or unfamiliar' [Holt.]

PY tumaɣliq 'plant type'
AAY AP tumaɣliq 'plant with heart-shaped leaves close to ground'
CAY tumaɣliq 'low-bush cranberry'
NSY —
CSY —

PE tumaʀ- 'harden or heal (broken bone)?'
AAY tumaʀ- 'get thick, lumpy, bunch or match up'
CAY tumaXtə- 'assemble, fix'
NSY tumaʀ- 'assemble, construct, be constructed, appear' [the homonym meaning 'follow behind' is from tumə]
CSY —
Sir —
SPI tumaq- 'become formed, made'
NAI tumaq- 'heal (of broken bone), repair'
WCI tumaq- 'repair clothing, harness'
ECI tumaq- 'harden and swell (of limb, broken bone, joint)'
GRI tumaʀ- 'become lame, stiff (of limb), be an invalid'

PE tumə 'track or footprint' [cf. Aleut cimi-X, old Atkan cim, westerm EA and Atkan also cim̥i-X (usually pl.) 'track, footprint(s)', with *t_2]
AAY tuma(q) 'track, footprint'
CAY tuma 'footprint, track, trail' [base tumə-]
NSY tumə 'footprint, track'
CSY tuma 'footprint, track, way, road' [base tumə-; and tumtə- 'follow, track']
Sir tuma 'track'
SPI tumi 'track' [and tupli- 'make tracks']
NAI tumɨ 'track, trail, footprint' [and tuvli- 'make tracks']
WCI tumi 'track, trail'
ECI tumi 'footprint' [and tuyyi- 'leave tracks from walking in s.th. dirty', tumiuyaq 'oval']
GRI tumi, EG tumiq 'track, footprint' [tumaašaq 'oval']

PE tumðaʀ- 'follow tracks' [cf. ðaʀ-]
AAY tummaXtə- 'track, follow tracks'
CAY tummaXtə-
NSY tumaʀ-
CSY tumaʀ-
Sir tumcaʀ-
SPI tuvžaq-
NAI tuvžaq-
WCI Sig tuvyaʀaq-, Cop tuvyaXXi- 'track' [Cop also tuvyaq-, Net tuvžaq- acc. Pryde]
ECI tuyya(q)-, Aiv tuvyaqsi- 'track, follow tracks'
GRI tuššaʀ- [old ortho. tuvssaʀ-] 'track'

PE tuməci- 'find tracks' [cf. ci-]
AAY —
CAY tumci- 'find tracks'
NSY tuməsi- 'find tracks' [and tumətə- 'find tracks of (s.th.)']
CSY —
Sir —
SPI —
NAI tufsi-, Nu tupsi- 'find tracks'
WCI tumisi-, tupsi-
ECI tumisi- 'see footprints'
GRI tumisi- 'find tracks'

PY tumənaq 'wooden bowl' [cf. tumə and naʀ]
AAY —
CAY Y, NS tumnaq 'large oval wooden bowl'
NSY tumənaq 'deep wooden bowl' [L.-T.]
CSY —
Inu [Imaq tumənaq 'wooden bowl' in Men. is probably from NSY]

PE tunə- 'give'
AAY tunə- 'give (away, back)'
CAY tunə- 'exchange, give, trade, sell'
NSY tunə- 'give, sell, be sold' [ANLC 'give back, return']

CSY tuunə- 'give'
Sir tunə- 'give' [for tunəʀaʀ- 'listen' see tucaʀ-]
SPI tuni- 'sell' [half-trans. tuniži-]
NAI tuni- 'sell, be sold' [half-trans. tuniži-, tunisi-]
WCI tuni- 'give, sell' [half-trans. tunisi- (Pryde)]
ECI tuni- 'give' [half-trans. tunisi-, tuniyi-]
GRI tuni- 'give s.th. to, sell' [half-trans. tuniši-], tunniut(i)- 'give (an object) to someone' [the latter influenced perhaps by nassiut(i)- under nakcət- (nakcaʀ-)]

PI tuniuqqaq- 'distribute' [cf. (C)uʀ- and qqaʀ-]
SPI —
NAI tuniuqqaq- 'sell several'
WCI tuniuqqa(q)- 'distribute'
ECI tuniuqqa(q)- 'give or distribute several'
GRI tuniuqqaatiγi-, tuniuʀaatiγi- 'distribute' [tuniuʀaʀ- 'distribute s.th. among']

PI tunəγə- 'go directly to' [cf. kə-[1], also tunəʀ-?; there may be contam. with the latter and/or tuŋə- (see esp. NAI tuŋaaʀɨ-) in ECI and GRI]
SPI tuniγi- 'travel directly to'
NAI PH tuniγɨ- 'go directly to'
WCI —
ECI [note Lab tunaaʀi- 'have eyes fixed on', tunaaq 'thing one especially wants' — Peck]
GRI [note tunaaʀtaʀi- 'steer toward, get support from', tunaaʀi-, half-trans. tunaaʀɫiʀ- 'rely on, put trust in']

PI tunənŋuq- 'be tired of lying on a hard surface' [cf. tunəʀ- and lŋu-?]
SPI tuniŋuq- 'be tired of lying on a hard surface'
NAI tunɨnŋuq- 'be tired of lying on hard surface, walking on hard ground'
WCI tuniŋunaq- 'be boring, tired of lying on bed'
ECI tuniŋŋuC- 'have pain in back or rump from lying, sitting a long time', tuŋŋaŋuq- 'tire of being in same position'
GRI —

PI tunəq 'legendary pre-Eskimo (Dorset?)' [this appears to be the native Inuit word for the Dorset people who preceded them in Canada and Greenland; it may be related to tunəʀ- — the people in question were thought to be strong]
Yup [CAY Nun tuniqtax 'jade' is prob. from Inu.]
SPI —
NAI [tunɨqtaq (with taʀ) 'soapstone, stone lamp' — this Inuit cultural item has been attributed to the Dorset people]
WCI tu(n)nit [for tunʀit?] 'fabulous beings who lived in houses of earth and had only one eye in the middle of their heads' [Met. adds that these were specifically not Indians; acc. Pryde 'a race of Eskimo-speaking people driven out by ancestors of present people of the region' or (Bathurst Inlet) 'legendary race of tiny people']
ECI tuniq 'inhabitant of great strength of country before the Inuit, (in Ungava) stone age people living in houses of large stones' [and in Lab claimed in legend to be 'chased out (from Labrador) by the Inuit whence they fled to Greenland' — Bourq.; note also tuniqtasayaq 'stone object made by the tuniit']
GRI tuniq*, pl. tuʀnit 'legendary figure living in interior, Indian or Eskimo of another tribe' [in EG timiʀsiq 'inland dweller' is used rather]

PE tunəʀ- 'strength or solidness'
AAY —
CAY tunəXtu- 'have a strong impact (of gun) [also tunʀiʀ- 'feel embarrassed because one is imposing or unable to reciprocate']
NSY —
CSY — [for tunəq* 'mat' see tuŋəʀ]
Sir —
SPI tuniqsi- 'have one's mind made up' [also tuʀniq-, Qaw tunʀiq- 'feel bad, ashamed, remorseful, hesitate to ask for s.th.']
NAI tunɨqtu- 'be emotionally stable, enduring, solid', tuniqsima- 'be faithful, enduring, hard to persuade' [and cf. Nu tunɨq 'thick snowshoe webbing']
WCI tuniqsi- 'be decided', Car 'be strong', Car? tuniqtu- have strong recoil (of gun)', B. Lake 'be more robust than others (man)' [Schn.; Pryde has Cop tuniqtu- 'be steadfast, determined']
ECI tuniqsi- 'pledge, give one's word of honor'
GRI — [for tunaaʀi- 'rely on' see tunəγə-]

PI tuniʀžuk 'breastbone' [cf. Aleut cuniX 'backbone' — with $*t_2$ — and yuγ, ðuγ; there may be a link to tunu]
SPI tuniʀžuat 'breastbone'
NAI —
WCI Net tuniʀžuk 'breastbone (of seal)', also 'kayak deck strap' [Pryde, who also has Cop tuniʀluaq in the first sense]
ECI tuniʀyuk 'breastbone'
GRI tuniʀšuk, EG tuniʀtik 'breastbone' [Robbe and Menn. have tunaʀtik rather, also tuniʀtia 'longitudinal piece of wood in kayak']

PE tunnuʀ 'back fat of caribou' [cf. tunu]
AAY AP, PWS tunuq 'tallow, back fat'
CAY tunuq
NSY tunuq 'reindeer fat'
CSY tunuq 'reindeer fat' [and note tunuʀaq 'quartz or other white rock']
Sir tunuX 'reindeer fat' [and note tunuʀca 'white']
SPI tunnuq 'fat of large land animal'
NAI tunnuq* 'back fat of caribou or moose'
WCI tunnuk, tunnuq
ECI tunnuk 'fat, caribou suet'
GRI tunnuq 'caribou tallow'

PY tunŋaq 'puffin'
AAY Kod tunŋaq 'puffin, sea parrot'
CAY Nun tunŋaX
NSY tunŋaq 'red-nosed puffin' [tunŋinaq (for tunŋainaq?) 'white-breasted puffin']
CSY —

PE tuntu 'caribou' [cf. tunnuʀ and tu-[1]; the CSY and eastern Inu forms reflect the merger of *nt and *ŋt]
AAY tuntu 'caribou'
CAY tuntu

NSY tuntuq [ANLC tuntu 'moose, caribou']
CSY tuŋtu 'caribou'
Sir tumta
SPI tuttu
NAI tuttu
WCI tuktu 'caribou' [tuktuk- 'kill a caribou' — Pryde has tuktut- for Cop]
ECI tuttu 'caribou' [and NBI, SB tuktuk- 'kill a caribou']
GRI tuttu [tugtu in old ortho.], NG tuktu 'caribou' [tuttut- 'kill a caribou']

PE tunturʀðuɣ 'the Big Dipper (constellation)' [cf. yuɣ]
AAY [note tuntuŋuaq 'the Big Dipper']
CAY tunturʀyuk 'the Big Dipper (Great Bear)'
NSY —
CSY [note tuŋtut 'the Big Dipper']
Sir [note tumtiy 'the Big Dipper']
SPI tuttažuk, Qaw tutturʀžuk 'the Big Dipper'
NAI tutturʀžuk
WCI Net tutturʀžuit [Ras.; Pryde has Cop tukturʀyuk, Net tukturʀžuin]
ECI tuttuyuit 'the Great Bear (Big Dipper)'
GRI [note NG tuktuuhat 'the Big Dipper' — Holt. has tuktuXXuit]

PE tuntuvaɣ 'moose' [cf. vaɣ]
AAY AP tuntuwak 'moose'
CAY tuntuvak
NSY —
CSY tuŋtuvak
Sir tumtuvax [Orr]
SPI Qaw tuttuwak
NAI tuttuvak
WCI tuktuvak
ECI tuttuvak
GRI —

PE tunu 'back' [cf. tunnuʀ, tunucuɣ and Aleut cunu-X 'back of neck' — with $*t_2$]
AAY tunuq 'back' [also as posit. root tunu- 'back of']
CAY tunu 'back of ' [posit. root]
NSY tunu
CSY tunu 'back' [as posit. root = 'back of']
Sir ➟
SPI tunu 'back'
NAI tunu 'back' [and tunumun 'with the back facing forward']
WCI tunu 'back'
ECI tunu 'back, outer side of snow block facing snow house builder' [tunumut 'back, behind']
GRI tunu, EG, Up tunuq 'back' [the former also 'East Greenland' and as posit. root; tunumut 'backward, toward land']

PE tunucuɣ 'nape of neck' [cf. cuɣ]
AAY Kod, C tunucuk 'nape of neck, lower back of head'
CAY tunucuk
NSY tunusuk
CSY tunusuk
Sir tuŋsəx 'nape of neck' [Orr; with dissim.]
SPI tunusuk 'nape of neck'
NAI tunusuk
WCI tunusuk [but Lowe has Cop tunuhiniq]
ECI tunusuk 'nape of neck'
GRI tunusuk

PE tunut- 'turn one's back on' [cf. t-[1]]
AAY tunutə- 'turn one's back, put backward'
CAY tunutə- 'turn one's back on'
NSY —
CSY tunutə- 'turn one's back on, turn away'
Sir —
SPI tunut- 'turn one's back on, turn and face the other way'
NAI tunut-
WCI tunut-
ECI tunut-
GRI tunut- 'turn one's back, turn away from' [intr. also spelled tunuɣ-]

PE tunuvaʀ- 'go back [cf. vaʀ-]
AAY —
CAY tunuvaʀ- 'go back'
NSY —
CSY tunuvaʀ- 'go or take back'
Sir —
SPI —
NAI tunuvaq- 'back up, go to the rear'
WCI tunuvak- 'go back'
ECI tunuvaq- 'push back, reserve for later'
GRI tunuaʀ- 'move back, remain behind' [and Kroeb. has NG tunuaq- 'die' as a shaman's word]

PI tunucitaq 'third stomach of ruminant' [cf. tunu?]
SPI —
NAI tunusisaq 'hard covering of the small stomach of caribou'
WCI tunusitaq 'third stomach of ruminant, grinding stomach of caribou' [Pryde]
ECI —
GRI —

PE tuŋciʀ- 'beg'
AAY [tuŋitə- 'beg, pester']
CAY tuŋciXtuʀ- 'ask to come or bring s.th.'
NSY —
CSY tuŋsiʀ- 'ask for'
Sir —
SPI —
NAI tuksiq- 'beg of someone' [tuksiaq- 'beg in prayer']
WCI tuksiq- 'ask for, pray (in request)' [and Ras. has 'send for' in Net; tuksiut(i)- 'pray for'; Car EP tuxxiaq- 'pray' acc. Ow.]
ECI tutsia(q)- 'ask for, ask (s.o.)', tutsiʀaq- 'ask for s.th.' [tutsianiq 'prayer', tutsiut(i)- 'pray for, bless']
GRI tussiaʀ- 'pray, sing a hymn' [for NG homonym tussiaq- 'hunt reindeer' see tumðaʀ- under tumə; note also tussiut(i)- 'pray for']

PE tuŋə- 'direction (of)'
AAY tuŋə- 'in direction of, toward' [posit. root]
CAY tuŋə-
NSY tuŋə- 'direction of, neighboring area' [Em.]
CSY tuŋa 'immediate vicinity, close relative outside of immediate family'
Sir tuŋa 'direction, side (of)' [Vakh., who also has tuŋaŋiʀ- 'approach' from Rub.'s texts]
SPI tuŋi- 'area toward' [posit. root]
NAI tuŋaaʀɨ- travel toward', tuŋiʀuq- 'come close to'
WCI tuŋi- 'in direction of' [posit. root]
ECI tuŋi- 'at foot of, side of' [posit. root]
GRI tuŋi- 'in direction of' [posit. root; tuŋalit- 'approach']

PE tuŋ(ə)liʀ 'next one' [cf. l(l)iq]
AAY tuŋliq 'ring finger' [and tuŋliʀ- 'put under or next to']
CAY tuŋliq* 'second one'
NSY tuŋiliaq 'neighbor, relative', tuŋliXtaq 'neighboring' [ANLC has suŋliq 'second, next']
CSY tuuŋliq*, tuŋəqłiq* 'next one'
Sir tuŋcəX
SPI tuɣliq
NAI tuɣli, Mal tuɣliq*
WCI tuɣliq 'next one' [tuɣliʀiit 'one after the other']
ECI NBI, SB tuɣliq, Tar tuŋalliq, Iti tulliq 'next, nearest', Lab tullik 'second, neighbor' [tulliʀiik 'two, one after the other']
GRI tułłiq* 'next, nearest' [tułłiʀiiɣ- 'follow in a row'; Robbe and Menn. have EG tualiq 'next, nearest' but tuttiq 'next (in time)']

PE tuŋəʀ 'pad or mat' [cf. Aleut cuŋu-X 'bird's down', in pl. 'nest, diaper' — with *t_2]
AAY —
CAY Y tuŋəq* 'menstrual pad'
NSY —
CSY tunəq* 'mat, floor covering' [perhaps influenced by tutə-]
Sir tunəX 'mat, floor covering' [Orr]
SPI tuniq 'floorboard in men's house'
NAI tuŋiun 'sleeping skin'
WCI Net tuŋilik 'one with hay in his stockings' [Ras.]
ECI —
GRI tuŋiq(*) [possessed tuŋia, etc.] 'bedsheet', NG tuŋi(q) 'insole, boot straw'

PY-S tuŋi(q) 'shaft or quill?'
AAY PWS tuŋiq 'quill(s) on porcupine's tail'
CAY —
NSY —
CSY SLI tuŋik 'ivory shaft between head and main shaft of whaling harpoon'
Sir tuŋəX 'wooden rod in device for obtaining fire'

PE tuŋlə(ʀ) 'hair at temples?'
AAY —
CAY —
NSY —
CSY tuŋlət 'bunch of cut grass over skin door to keep frost out, short hair at hairline'
Sir —
SPI —
NAI tuɣlɨ 'braided hair'
WCI tuɣlilik 'woman with braided hair' [Schn. has tullaat 'braid of hair over ears or chignon' and tullaq- 'put up hair in a chignon' for 'adg'; Pryde has for B. Lake tuɣlik, du. tuɣliik 'side locks wrapped around sticks on either side of woman's head']
ECI tullik 'coiled hair (chignon) above the ears'
GRI tułłiq* 'temple'

PI tuŋləʀun 'ornament for hair' [cf. un]
SPI —
NAI tuɣliʀun 'hairclip, barrette'
WCI tuɣliʀutit 'hair ribbons' [Pryde has Cop tuɣliʀutik 'support on foredeck of kayak for caribou spears']
ECI tulliʀuti 'ribbon for bun in hair' [Lab tuɣliʀut 'beads or other ornaments in the hair' acc. Peck; Pryde has tuɣliʀutit 'pieces of shaped antler for holding cross-strap on sled in position']
GRI tułłiʀut 'ornament (e.g. beads) for temple, earring, false sun or moon (paraselene)', NG tuɣliʀut 'bead'

PE tuŋu- 'be dark blue (as ripe berry)?' [as a nom. 'berry juice' as in ECI and GRI?]
AAY AP tuŋu(tə)- 'become tanned (by sun)' [on early word lists 'black']
CAY tuŋu- 'be black'
NSY —
CSY — [for tuŋu- 'stare vacantly into space' see under cuŋu-]
Sir —
SPI tuŋuq- 'be bluish, dark', Qaw Fish River tuŋuq- 'be brown (tanned)'
NAI tuŋuq- 'be blue (also of bruise)', tuŋu- 'be blue in face'
WCI tuŋu- 'be blue, dark (of cloud)' [and tuŋuniq 'bruise'; Dor. has tuŋuqtuq 'blue' for B. Lake Car; Schn. has tuŋuq- 'become green' for 'adg']
ECI tuŋuq- 'become blue', tuŋuniq, 'black cloud, blue-black ice', Lab tuŋu 'berry juice' [Peck]
GRI tuŋu 'berry juice'

PI tuŋuyuq- and **tuŋuyuk-** 'be bluish or green' [cf. yuɣ?]
SPI —
NAI Uum tuŋuyuqtaq 'blue'
WCI tuŋuyuq- 'be blue, green', Car tuŋuyuqtuq 'blue, green' [Dor. for the latter]
ECI tuŋuyuqtaq 's.th. blue or green' [Schn — 'blue' only acc. Saul, who also has tuŋuyuʀsi- 'become blue'; Dor. has tuŋuyuqtuq 'blue, green' for NBI]
GRI tuŋuyuʀ- 'be blue, bluish green' [in older NG tuŋuyuq- was 'green' (blue green?)]

PE tuŋvaʀ- and **tuŋvaɣ-** 'store away or bury' [there may be a link to tutquq-]
AAY tuŋmaXtə- 'get closer to finishing'
CAY tuŋmaxtə- 'bury (the dead)', NSU tuŋvaxtə- 'put

away for later use'
NSY tumɣaxtə- 'hide from view, conceal, store away' [ANLC; Men. has tumvaXtə- 'bury, acquire']
CSY tuɣmaxtə- 'store away for later use, murder'
Sir tuɣmaxtə- 'store away for later use' [Orr — from CSY]
SPI —
NAI tuɣvaq- 'put away'
WCI —
ECI —
GRI — [for tułłuaʀ- (old ortho. and Fab tugluar-) 'fit, be suitable' see tut-]

PY-S tuŋyuq 'tide (high)' [cf. tuŋə-?]
AAY tuŋyuq, tuŋŋiq 'high tide'
CAY Nun tuŋyuX 'incoming tide'
NSY —
CSY tuŋyuq 'high tide'
Sir tuŋyəłəX 'high tide' [and tuŋyəʀət(ə)- 'inundate']

PE tupaɣ- 'be startled' [cf. tupəkə- and EA tumða- 'produce a crack, shoot, explode'?]
AAY tupaɣ- 'startle'
CAY tupaɣ- 'wake up'
NSY tupaɣ-
CSY tupaɣ-, tupaxpaɣ- 'be startled'
Sir tupaxpaxt(ə)- [Vakh.]
SPI tuvak- 'awake'
NAI tupak- 'be surprised, startled, become fully awake'
WCI tupak- 'awake'
ECI tupak-
GRI tupaɣ- 'start, have a sudden fright, be roused suddenly by noise' [and EG tupaya- 'be quick' (Robbe and Menn.)]

PI tupaaq- 'keep waking up' [cf. aʀ-]
SPI tuvaaq- 'awaken'
NAI tupaaq- 'keep waking s.o. up by making noise'
WCI tupaaq- 'have awakened (s.o.)'
ECI tupaaq-
GRI tupaaʀ- 'keep waking up or waking s.o. up, disturb s.o.'s sleep' [and tupaatuʀ-, NG tupaluatuq- 'wake up suddenly']

PI tupə(nəq) 'tattoo' [cf. perhaps EA cumi-n 'ornamental dots', with *t_2]
Yup [note AAY tup 'small round tattooed spots on the cheek' in Merck]
SPI tupniq 'tattoo', W tuvi- 'tattoo' [Jen.]
NAI tupɨ 'small tattoo' [and as verb]
WCI tupiniq 'tattoo' [Pryde has Cop tuni 'cheek tattoo']
ECI tunniq 'woman's facial tattoo' [Pryde has tuni 'cheek tattoo' for Igl]
GRI tunni 'tattoo on cheek or under eyes' [old ortho. = tuvne]

PE tupəkə- 'be surprised or excited at' [cf. tupəlak, tupaɣ- and kə-[1]]
AAY —
CAY NSU tupəkə- 'be excited to see', tupkə- HBC 'agree', Nun 'take care of' [NSU also tupəɣ- 'be excited to see s.o.']
NSY —
CSY —
Sir —
SPI —
NAI [tupɨnŋa- 'be apprehensive, jumpy']
WCI —
ECI —
GRI tupiɣi- 'be surprised at' [tupiɣusuɣ- 'be surprised', tupinnaʀ- 'be surprising']

PI tupəlak 'spirit being sent out to attack one's enemy' [cf. tupəkə-, tupaɣ- and łaɣ-]
SPI —
NAI tupɨlak 'shaman's familiar spirit' [Jen.]
WCI tupilak 'demon' [in stories, it was a stone or wood figure believed to be magical and used by shamans to harm their enemies; Pryde also has Cop tupilauyaq 'lawyer for prosecution']
ECI Igl tupilak 'evil spirit' [Ras.]
GRI tupilak, EG tupilaq, tupiliq 'being composed of various parts brought to life by magic to kill an enemy' [and NWG tupilaɣ- 'frighten animals away from', NG tupilaxxuq- 'be frightening, do evil' — Søby]

PE tupəʀ 'tent or other temporary dwelling'
AAY —
CAY —
NSY tupəq* 'hut of branches, temporary dwelling' [and tupəʀ- 'make such a hut']
CSY tupəq* 'makeshift or temporary dwelling'
Sir —
SPI tuviq 'tent' [as verb = 'raise tent', as in all Inu]
NAI tupɨq* 'tent', Mal 'house'
WCI tupiq 'tent' [also verbal 'pitch tent']
ECI tupiq
GRI tupiq*

PE tupət- 'choke on food'
AAY tuxtə- 'choke on food'
CAY tuftə- 'choke on food, become choked with s.th.'
NSY tuftə- [Enm. et al.]
CSY tuuftə- 'choke on s.th., swallow accidentally, have hiccups'
Sir tuftə- [Orr]
SPI tuit- 'choke'
NAI tupɨt- 'have food stuck in throat'
WCI tupit- 'have difficulty swallowing a large mouthful'
ECI tupit- 'choke in swallowing, be constricted in anguish (throat)'
GRI tupit- 'have s.th. caught in throat and be on the point of choking'

PY tupiʀ- 'lace'
AAY tupiʀ- 'fasten, lace, button'
CAY tupiɣ- 'weave', tupiXtaaʀute- 'baste'
NSY
CSY —

PI tupquža(a)q 'larynx' [cf. tupət- and quR and ŋ(ŋ)uðaR?]
SPI —
NAI tupqužaak 'hyoid bones in throat'
WCI tupquyaq 'Adam's apple'
ECI tuqquyaaq 'throat, larynx' [tuqquyaaRsi- 'grab by the throat']
GRI tuqqušaaq 'larynx' [tuqqušašši- 'grab by the throat']

PI tuputaq 'wound plug' [cf. un; there could be a further link to putu- by metathesis]
Yup [CAY NS tupun (on old lists) 'wound plug' probably from Inu]
SPI W tuputaq 'wound plug' [Ras. for tuvutaq?]
NAI —
WCI tuputaq Net, Cop 'wound plug' [Ras.; but Met. has 'needle for making holes' for Sig]
ECI Igl tuputaq 'wound plug' [B.-S.]
GRI WG, NG tuputaq, EG tipulaq 'wound plug' [Ordbogêraq for the WG]

PE tuqlu(ɣ) and **tuqluR** 'windpipe' [cf. Aleut cuqa- 'throat, shout', with *t_2' and p.b. lu(R)]
AAY tuqłuq 'larynx, windpipe' [note KP cuqaq, Kod suqaq 'stomach', apparently directly from the Aleut above]
CAY tuqłuq 'throat, windpipe' [and Y tuXquq, tuXtuqaq 'throat, windpipe', NSU tuqłuk 'tunnel entrance' — with which compare tuqšuk]
NSY ➡
CSY ➡
Sir —
SPI tuqłu 'windpipe'
NAI tuqłuk
WCI tuqłu(k)
ECI tuRsuk, Lab tułłuk
GRI tuRłuk

PI tuqluaq 'tube (like a windpipe)' [cf. aR]
SPI tuqłuaq 'windpipe, spout, barrel of gun'
NAI tuqłuaq 'telescope, (drinking) straw'
WCI tuqłuaq 'barrel of gun'
ECI tuRsuaq '(drinking) straw, tube, siren, megaphone'
GRI tuRłuaq 's.th. tube-like, ear-trumpet'

PE tuqluR(aR)- 'call'
AAY tuqłuR- 'call out to'
CAY tuqłuR- 'call out'
NSY tuqłuR- 'call out' [ANLC 'call by shouting'; tuqłuRaXtə 'one who calls people to s.th.']
CSY tuqłuR- 'call out' [tuqłuRaR- 'call loudly']
Sir —
SPI tuqłuaq- 'call out'
NAI tuqłuq- 'call (by name or kinship term)' [tuqłuRaq- 'call out repeatedly from inside']
WCI tuqłuaq- 'call' [Ras. has tuXXulaq- 'shout' for Cop]
ECI tuRsu(q)- 'call by relationship name' [and tuRsuRaq- 'address by relationship name']
GRI tuRłuR-, EG tuRsuaaR-, cuRsuaaR- 'shout (to)' [the latter by contam. with cuɣaɣ-?; and tuRłuRaR- 'call, address as (e.g. mother)']

PY tuqmik 'container of some sort' [cf. Aleut tumqi-X 'wooden pail' — a loan one way or the other]
AAY tuqm̥ik 'wooden bottle' [from old sources]
CAY K, NR tuqm̥ik 'bucket'
NSY —
CSY —

PE tuqu(-) 'die' [or nom. 'death']
AAY tuqu- 'die' [tuquq 'death']
CAY tuqu- 'die' [nom. = 'death']
NSY tuqu- 'die'
CSY tuqu-
Sir tuqə- 'die' [tuqa 'death']
SPI tuRu- 'die' [nom. = 'death']
NAI tuqu- 'die' [nom. in certain (possessed) expressions = 'death']
WCI tuqu- 'die' [nom. = 'death']
ECI tuqu- 'die'
GRI tuqu- 'die' [nom. = 'death']

PI tuqucaq- 'kill a wounded animal' [cf. caR-]
SPI tuRusaq- 'try to kill a wounded animal'
NAI tuqusaq-
WCI Cop tuquhaq- 'kill a wounded animal'
ECI tuqusaq- 'kill, execute'
GRI tuqusaR- 'finish off a wounded seal after harpooning it'

PE tuqunaR- 'be poisonous' [cf. naR-]
AAY tuqunaR- 'be poisonous'
CAY tuqunaXqə-
NSY —
CSY tuqunaR-
Sir —
SPI tuRunaq- 'be poisonous, poison'
NAI tuqunaq-
WCI tuqunaq- 'be deadly'
ECI tuqunna(q)- 'be poisonous, deadly'
GRI tuqunaR-

PI tuquRaq- 'kill many' [cf. Raq-]
SPI tuRuRaq- 'kill many'
NAI tuquRaq- 'die or kill in large numbers'
WCI —
ECI tuquRaq- 'kill several'
GRI tuquRaR- 'slaughter (many)'

PE tuqut- 'kill' [cf. t-[1]]
AAY tuqutə- 'kill'
CAY tuqutə-
NSY tuqutə-
CSY tuqutə-
Sir tuqət(ə)-
SPI tuRut-
NAI tuqut-
WCI tuqut-
ECI tuqut-
GRI tuqut-

PI tuqšuk 'entrance tunnel to semi-subterranean house' [cf. tuqlu(ɣ)]
Yup [note CAY tuqsuk 'widening at mouth of river', also NSU tuqłuk 'tunnel entrance to traditional semi-subterranean house' under tuqlu(ɣ)]
SPI tuqšuk 'entry passage of house'
NAI tuqšuk
WCI Cop tuXXuk 'porch'
ECI tuʀsuuk, Frob. Bay suʀsuuk [du. forms]
GRI tuʀšuuq, EG cuʀsuuk (Tersis cuʀsuuq) 'house entry'

PI tuʀaaq- 'aim at' [cf. tut- and/or tunəɣə-?]
SPI —
NAI —
WCI Cop, Net tuʀaa(q)- 'head straight for s.th.' [Pryde]
ECI tuʀaaq- 'aim at' [and note tuqqa(C)-, tuqqa- 'look to see if one can make out what s.th. is']
GRI tuʀaaʀ-, tuqqaʀ- 'aim at', EG tuʀ̃aaʀ- 'be straight' [the second WG form also 'choose among'; note also tuXXałłaɣ- 'have done s.th. well', and tuʀiʀ- 'be clear, well made, correct' — influenced by tutqik-?; Robbe and Menn. have EG tuʀ̃aaʀ- 'be orderly, neat, straight' and tuqqaaʀ- 'aim at, go straight for, find s.th. one is looking for']

PI tuʀaayu- 'be good at hitting (with weapon)' [cf. yu-]
SPI —
NAI —
WCI Car? tuʀaayu- 'be a good shot' [Schn. for 'adg']
ECI tuʀaayu- 'be a good shot'
GRI tuʀaayu- 'be a good shot, good at hitting (with weapon)'

PE tut- 'land or arrive' [cf. tulaɣ-; there may also be a relat. to tutə-; in the Yup languages tut- and tutə- (q.v.) have coalesced]
AAY tuttə- 'arrive (person), occur'
CAY tuttə- 'arrive (not people), occur' [and note tuzzun, tuzzutaq 'prop, wedge']
NSY tutə- 'arrive, occur' [and tuqaXtə- 'knock against']
CSY tuutə- 'land (plane), fall (rain), step'
Sir tutaX(tə)- 'land' [Orr]
SPI tut- 'land, arrive'
NAI tut- 'touch ground, land, lie down' [and Mal tullak- 'land gently', tutpaliq- 'make a sound and seem to have landed'; and note tuɣluaq- 'protect' — with l(l)u(C)aʀ-?]
WCI tut- 'touch bottom (e.g. fishing line)' [trans. = 'put on ground']
ECI tuC- 'touch ground, hit' [and tuttit- 'adjust a block of snow to make it fall easily into place', tuppalia- 'go down more and more, be about to hit']
GRI tuɣ- [Fab. tut-] 'fall onto, strike against, come to rest' [and tuppałłiʀ- 'be comforted, in good spirits', tułłuaʀ-, NG tulluaq- 'fit, match', tułłuut(i)- 'come to rest against s.th., feel satisfied, comforted']

PE tutŋa- 'rest on' [cf. ŋa-[1]]
AAY —
CAY tuza-, HBC tuyŋa- 'rest on, depend on, be attached' [and tuzavik 'foundation']
NSY tuyŋa- 'rest on' [ANLC]
CSY —
Sir —
SPI tunŋa- 'be connected to'
NAI tunŋa- 'be based on, rest on'
WCI tuŋ(ŋ)a- 'rest on' [and tuŋ(ŋ)avik 'foundation']
ECI tuŋŋa- 'be placed (on s.th.)' [and tuŋŋavik 'foundation' — compare tuqqavik 'place where one was born', Lab 'home']
GRI tuŋŋa- 'rest on, be based on s.th.' [and tuŋŋavik 'foundation', NG 'cutting board' (Holt.) — compare tuqqavik 'trestle, lamp stool', EG 'foundation' (Robbe and Menn. for the latter), with variant qqa- from *ɴʀa- under ŋa-[1]]

PI tužvik 'landing place or support' [cf. ðviɣ]
SPI Qaw tužvik 'foundation'
NAI tužvik 'bleached skin frame used to stiffen a woman's sunburnt parka ruff', tužviatciaq 'solid ground'
WCI tuyvik 'place where s.th. was hit by a bullet'
ECI tuvvik 'place one can land'
GRI [WG tuššik 'chock on which a boat is lowered into the water']

PE tutə- 'step on' [cf. tukəʀ- and tulləq-; there may be a relat. to tut-; in the Yup languages tutə- and tut- (q.v.) have coalesced]
AAY tuttə- 'step on' [and C tuxxʷik 'step (of stairs)']
CAY tuttə- 'step on'
NSY ➞
CSY tuutə- 'step on, clean a skin by rubbing it in snow' [tuuta 'frozen-over place, ice bridge between floes']
Sir tutaqə(s)- 'trample on' [Vakh. tutaʀ- 'step on' from Rub.'s texts]
SPI tuti- 'step on'
NAI tuti- 'tread, step on'
WCI tuti- [Pryde]
ECI tuti- 'step on'
GRI tuti- 'tread on', NG 'cover roof with snow (blocks)' [Holt. for the latter]

PE tutmaʀ- 'tread on (repeatedly)' [cf. maʀ-]
AAY tutm̥aʀ- 'step on'
CAY tutm̥aʀ- 'step repeatedly, walk on'
NSY tutm̥aʀ- 'trample on' [ANLC 'stamp feet']
CSY tutm̥aʀ- 'walk all over'
Sir [Vakh. has tutəmqicaʀ- 'walk over']
SPI tupmaq- 'step on, stand on'
NAI tunmaq-, tuŋmaq-, PH tummaq-, Nu tutmaq- 'tread repeatedly on'
WCI Sig tunmaq- 'step on' [Lowe]
ECI tumma(q)- 'make footmarks' [Saul]
GRI tummaʀ- [old ortho. tungmar-] 'stand, tread on' [tummaaʀi- 'tread repeatedly on', tummi- 'tread on (to)', NG tuŋmaŋŋit- 'limp', and note EG tummaliq, tummat 'foot']

PE tutməqaʀ 'stair or step' [cf. qaʀ?]
AAY —
CAY tutəmqaq 'stair, rung', Y 'bridge' [tutm̥aʀyaʀaq 'mat, walkway']
NSY tutm̥iqaq 'ladder'
CSY tutəmqaq 'porch, stepstool'
Sir tutəmqicaX 'ladder, staircase'
SPI tupmiaq, Qaw tutmiʀaq 'stair, step, rung of ladder'
NAI tunmiʀaq, tuŋmiʀaq 'rung, stepstool, step' [pl. tunmiqqat, etc. = 'stairs, steps in entry to sod house'; also tutipqiq, by contam. with tutyaʀ(aʀ) below]
WCI tunmiʀaq 'stepstool, step, rung' [and tunmiʀautit 'stairs' Lowe; Schn. has tummiʀaut 'ladder' for B. Lake]
ECI tummiʀaq 'doormat, steps up to house'
GRI tummiʀaq 'step, stirrup' [pl. tummiqqat 'stairs, ladder', NG tuŋmiqqat 'Orion's Belt' — Holt.; note EG tummaʀ̃aq 'box']

PE tutyaʀ(aʀ) 'step or s.th. else on which to stand' [cf. yaʀ]
AAY —
CAY tutsaʀaq, tussaʀaq 'step, rung, rug'
NSY [note tuusaq 'beam in yaranga' — ANLC]
CSY tuusaq 'step, stool'
Sir —
SPI —
NAI tutiʀɨq 'stoop, step outside house door'
WCI [Cop, Net tutiʀiaq 'bag of caribou skin to carry sealing implements to breathing hole and to use as rug to stand on while waiting there' — Pryde]
ECI [note tutiʀiaq 'inner boots of caribou skin with fur outside', Iti 'sealskin disguise worn by hunter at seal's breathing hole']
GRI tutiʀaq, tutiʀiaq 'woolly sole for hunting on ice'

PE tutəɣ(-) 'lie next to s.o.' [and as a noun 'bedmate']
AAY tutəɣ- 'share bed with', tutək 'bedmate' [and PWS tutaaq 'loved one, spouse'; note also tutək, tuta 'female genitals']
CAY tutəɣ- 'sleep next to', tutək 'bedmate' [and tutxaq, tutxaʀ(aq) 'grandchild']
NSY —
CSY tutəɣ- 'be side by side' [tutu 'vagina' may be contam. with the source of tutuk]
Sir tutəɣ- 'be side by side' [Orr]
SPI tutik, Imaq tutə 'grandchild' [and Qaw Unalaq. tuttaaq- 'make oneself comfortable in bed']
NAI tutik 'grandchild' [and tuttaaq- 'go to bed']
WCI Sig tutik- 'lie with', tuti(i)k 'endearing term for wife or mistress' [Ras.]
ECI tutik- 'sleep under same blanket'
GRI tutiɣ- 'lie down beside, copulate with' [tutsiut(i)- 'lie down next to']

PI tutqik- 'be even or well arranged' [cf. tut- and nqiɣ-[1]]
SPI tutqik- 'be content, peaceful'
NAI tutqik- 'be content, peaceful' [tutqiksi- 'become content, at ease', tutqaasuk- 'feel ill at ease']
WCI tutqik- 'be well arranged, arrange well' [and tutqaasuk- 'be ill at ease'; Pryde has Cop tutqik- 'be flat, smooth']
ECI tuqqi(k)- 'suit well, be the right size for, make smooth'
GRI tuqqiɣ- 'be even, smooth', NG tuqqixxuq 'cube' [Holt. for the latter; tuqqissi- 'calm down']

PI tutquq- 'store away' [cf. tut-?; the relat. to tut-, tutqik- and/or tuŋvaʀ- is obscure]
SPI —
NAI tutquq- 'put away for future use' [cf. Mal tułhuq- 'keep s.th. in a safe place']
WCI tutquq- 'store, put aside'
ECI tuqqu(q)- 'put in its box or enclosed place'
GRI tuqquʀ- 'hide, keep s.th.'

PI tutuk 'dirt'
Yup — [for CSY tutu 'vagina' see tutəɣ(-)]
Sir —
SPI tutuk 'flakes of dry skin' [Jen. has 'dirt, stain' for W]
NAI Mal tutuk 'dirt' [and PH tutuk 'name of man in story so called because he flicks dirt']
WCI tutuk 'dirt, matted hair'
ECI tutu 'tangled hair'
GRI tutuk 'dirt on floor brought in by feet, ingrained dirt in skin' [tutuɣ- 'be full of ingrained dirt']

PE tutyaɣat- 'limp' [cf. tutə-]
AAY C tusitə- 'walk gingerly'
CAY tussitə- 'be lame, limp'
NSY —
CSY [tusiiɣatə- 'be comical']
Sir [Vakh. has tusiɣat(ə)- 'be amusing']
SPI [Jen. has KI tusiaʀ- 'limp, be lame']
NAI tusiat- 'be lame, limp'
WCI tusiat-
ECI tusiat-
GRI tusiaɣ- [Fab. tusiaʀ-]

PE tu(C)utaʀ 'labret' [cf. tuɣət-?]
AAY —
CAY tuutaq 'labret' [tuutaʀuaq 'rose hip']
NSY tuutaq 'labret, bead hanging on chin' [ANLC; tuutaʀuaq 'mushroom']
CSY tuutaq 'labret' [Orr]
Sir —
SPI tuutaq 'labret'
NAI tuutaq
WCI tuutak 'labret' [and note Car.? tuttaq (for tuutaq?) 'jewel' Schn. 'adg.'; Pryde has Sig, Cop tuutaq 'one of a pair of labrets worn by men below the lower lip']
ECI —
GRI —

PI tu(C)utcinəq 'bald place' [cf. li-[1] and nəʀ[1]]
SPI —
NAI—
WCI Cop tuutsiniq 'bald place on head' [Jen.]

ECI tuusiniq 'bald spot on temple'
GRI tuutsiniq* 'bald place on woman's temples (from wearing hair up in a top-knot for so long)'

PE tu(C)utləɣ 'loon or northern diver' [cf. ləɣ; the relat. — if any — to tuðiɣ is obscure]
AAY C tuułək 'loon' [B.-S. has 'northern diver']
CAY tuułək, tunutəłək, tunułək, HBC tunuciłək 'loon' [all except the first by contam. with tunu?]
NSY —
CSY —
Sir —
SPI Qaw tuułik 'arctic loon'
NAI tuullik, Nu, Mal tuutlik 'yellow-billed loon'
WCI Sig tuullik 'yellow-billed loon' [Ras. has Net to.tlik 'great northern diver' — tuu'lik 'yellow-billed loon' acc. Pryde]
ECI tuulliq 'loon with a collar, the biggest loon (common loon)', Aiv tuulliɣyuaq 'black-throated diver, Arctic loon' [Peck has Lab. tuullik 'northern diver' — 'common loon' acc. Andersen et al.]
GRI tuułłik 'great northern diver (common loon)'

PE tuvapaɣ 'gravel' [cf. tuvaʀ]
AAY tuwapak 'gravel'
CAY Nun tuwapax 'piece of gravel'
NSY —
CSY taapak
Sir —
SPI tuyakpak
NAI tuapak
WCI tuapak
ECI tuapak
GRI tuapak

PE tuvaʀ '(lumpy) shore ice' [perhaps from *tuvvaʀ — cf. CAY tuvə- below and q under nəʀ[1]]
AAY [note KP tumlaɣ-, AP tuŋlaɣ- 'tense up, become firm in texture' and tumlak, tuŋlak 'muscle']
CAY Nun tuvaX '(stranded) ice-cake one or more years old' [Jen.; note also tuvə- 'cake up, become lumpy', tuvlak 'lump of caked matter, e.g. snow']
NSY tuvak 'shore ice, mooring place' [ANLC tuvaq 'fast shore ice']
CSY tuvaq 'large stretch of shore ice'
Sir tuvəX 'shore ice'
SPI tuaq
NAI tuvaq*, PH tuɣaq*
WCI tuvaq 'thick, old land-locked ice'
ECI tuvaq 'ice of frozen sea or lake' [and tuvaiʀvik 'break-up time', tuvatsaniaq- 'go hunting on sea ice that is forming']
GRI tuaq(*) 'lump of old ice frozen into new ice' [Ordbogêraq], EG '(sea) ice, landfast ice', tuaaq 'landfast ice' [1997 version of Oqaatsit]

PY tuvcuk 'Adam's apple' [cf. tupquža(a)q and tupət-, with which the CAY may be contaminated, in which case tavcak rather]
AAY —
CAY tufcuɣuaq 'Adam's apple'
NSY tafsuk
CSY —

PE tuvəʀaʀ 'hunter on sea ice' [cf. tuvaʀ?]
AAY [note PWS tuxqaqə- 'be generous']
CAY [note tufqa- 'be generous with food']
NSY —
CSY tuvʀaq SLI 'hunter on sea ice', Chap 'one on whom you can depend'
Sir tuvʀaX 'hunter on sea ice' [Orr]
SPI tuwaaq 'person' [pl. tuwiʀat]
NAI tuvaaq, pl. tuviʀʀat, PH tuɣaaq 'hunter' [and note tuvaaq- 'chase caribou (e.g. into corral) by shouting'; and tuviʀʀat, tuvaužat 'three stars in Orion's Belt]
WCI Cop tuvaaq 'hunter on ice', tuvaaq- 'hunt' [the former 'hunter on sea ice' for all WCI acc. Pryde; Ras. has Net tupiʀat — in texts also tuveʀat — 'breathing hole hunters'; Pryde also has tuviʀʀat 'three stars in Orion's Belt']
ECI Igl tuvaaq 'one who acquires things for others' [Ras.; Schn. has Tar tuva 'man' marked as uncertain]
GRI —

> **PI tuvaaqan** 'hunting companion' [cf. qan]
> SPI tuwaaqan 'traveling companion'
> NAI tuvaaqan 'companion'
> WCI tuvaaqataq 'companion on hunting trip' [and Sig tuvaaqat 'spouse' acc. Pryde — a possible meaning also for NAI
> ECI Igl tuvaaqat 'hunting companion' [Ras.]
> GRI —

PE tuyə 'shoulder' [cf. Aleut cuyu-X 'arm' — with $*t_2$]
AAY tuyək, AP tusək, tuik, tuwik 'shoulder'
CAY tuzək, tuyək
NSY tuyə
CSY tuya [base tuyə]
Sir —
SPI tuik
NAI tui
WCI Cop tui
ECI tui
GRI tui

PE tuyuʀ- 'send (s.th.)' [cf. tuyuʀmi-]
AAY tuyuʀ- 'send'
CAY tuyuʀ- 'send (for)'
NSY tuyuʀ- 'send (s.th. to someone)' [tuyu(u)saq 'package, parcel' (L.-T.)]
CSY tuyuʀ- 'send, go to join a boat crew' [tuyuusaq 'package that's been sent']
Sir tuyəʀ- 'send'
SPI tuyuq-
NAI tuyuq-
WCI tuyuq- 'send s.th. (esp. letter)', tuyuqsiyaq 's.th. received like gift or letter', Net tuyuqtuaq- 'give as present' [Ras.]
ECI tuyuq- 'send gift by messenger from afar'
GRI tuyuʀ- 'give food to'

PI tuyuRmi- 'be a guest' [cf. tuyuR-?]
SPI tuyuRmiaq 'house guest'
NAI tuyuRmi- 'be a guest', tuyuRmiaq 'guest'
WCI tuyuRmiaq 'visitor' [Pryde has Cop tuuRmiaq 'person from other part of the country, stranger']
ECI tuyuRmi- 'be bored, not pleased visiting strangers', tuyuRmiaq 'guest' [on Baffin the former is 'be a guest' rather; Lab tuyummiuvik 'hotel']
GRI tuyuRmi- 'be houseless, feel uneasy (in a situation)', tuyuRmiaq 'person taken into home'

PI tužRu- 'have thick hair'
SPI tuRžu- 'have thick hair or fur'
NAI tužRu-
WCI Sig tulRu- [Ras.]
ECI tuRRu- 'have long hair'
GRI tuRšu- 'be thick-haired'

U

PI uaq- 'mix together' [cf. uRaR-, with which there may be contam.]
SPI uaq- 'mix bread dough'
NAI —
WCI — [for uaq- 'wash' see uRaR-]
ECI uaRusiq- 'add a condiment to', Iti uasaq- 'put in disorder' [and uaRuti 'thing mixed with another']
GRI —

PI uaqtaq 'plug for sealing bladder?'
SPI —
NAI —
WCI —
ECI uaqtaq 'button, hole in skin pulled out and bound around to block hole' [and uaqsi- 'bind around a hole in skin (e.g. of kayak)']
GRI uaRtaq 'block (in tackle), wooden plug (in sealing bladder)', NG uaqtiq 'plug for sealing bladder' [Holt.]

PE uci[1] 'load' [cf. Aleut husi-X 'load' — the h is secondary]
AAY K uci 'load'
CAY uci
NSY usi [also verbal]
CSY usi
Sir usa, pl. usiy 'load' [and verbal usə- — Em. has usi-]
SPI uzi(aq) 'load' [and uzi- 'take (s.o.) in one's boat']
NAI Nu usiq 'load, s.th. carried on sled or boat'
WCI usi 'load' [also verbal]
ECI usi 'load' [verbal = 'be loaded, transport (a load)']
GRI usi, EG usiq 'load' [verbal = 'be loaded']

PE uci(C)aR- 'carry a load' [cf. aR-]
AAY —
CAY uciaR- 'be heavily loaded'
NSY —
CSY —
Sir —
SPI uziaq- 'carry a load' [as noun = 'load, cargo']
NAI usiaq- 'haul, transport' [as noun = 'load, cargo']
WCI usiaq- 'add to one's load'
ECI usiaq- 'carry s.o. on top of one's kayak'
GRI usiaR- 'carry on one's kayak (load)' [usiaq 'load (on kayak)']

PE uciŋiR- 'unload' [cf. ŋiR-, Inu also ŋiyaR-]
AAY —
CAY uciiR- 'unload'
NSY usiiR-
CSY usiŋiR-
Sir usəŋiXta 'freight handler, docker'
SPI uziŋiiq-, uziiq- 'unload'
NAI usiiyaq-
WCI usiiyaq-
ECI usiŋiyaq-
GRI usiŋiaR-

PI utciqtu- 'have a large load capacity' [cf. tu-[1] and nəRtu-]
SPI —
NAI utciqsu- 'have a large load capacity'
WCI —
ECI —
GRI utsiRsu-

PI uci[2] 'that's what I thought' [cf. iciɣ^{w}a]
SPI uziŋi 'I thought that -'
NAI usii(n^y) 'you remember, you know', usiuvva 'oh, I thought -'
WCI usiuma 'I think that -'
ECI usi 'oh yes, I remember', usiimmalu 'I thought that - (but was mistaken)'
GRI usi, usiinna, usiima 'that's right, now I remember!' [and usiuffa 'I thought that - (but was mistaken)', NG uhiuɣɣa(li) 'I thought otherwise, that's a lie'; Tersis has isiippa 'alas, I thought otherwise' for EG]

PI uciq- 'overflow'
SPI —
NAI usiRaq- 'spill over, overflow' [utciqšuula- 'boil over']
WCI usiRaq-
ECI usiRaq- 'fill to overflowing'
GRI usiR-, usiRaR- 'splash water on' [utsiRaR- 'splash repeatedly', utsiRšuR- 'overflow, boil over']

PE uciR- 'undress'
AAY —
CAY [note HBC isəR- 'take clothes off']
NSY —
CSY —
Sir usiR- 'take off clothes or boots' [Vakh. and Orr]
SPI —
NAI usiq-, usil^{y}l^{y}aq- 'take off pants'
WCI usiq- 'undress (incl. pants and underpants)'
ECI usiq- 'undress, lie under a blanket'
GRI usiR- 'pull off boots (in order to sit down on sleeping platform)', Up usiRsiR- 'take clothes off'

PE ucuɣ 'sexual organ'
AAY ucuk 'penis'
CAY ucuk 'penis', (du.) ucuuk 'vagina'
NSY usuk 'penis, vagina' [ANLC also usu, and usuuk 'vagina']
CSY usuk 'penis'
Sir usəɣ 'penis' [usuɣəX 'animal penis' — Vakh. and Orr]
SPI uzuk 'penis', ussuk 'vagina'
NAI usuk 'penis', (du.) utcuk 'vagina' [and usuužaq 'clitoris']
WCI usuk 'penis', utsuk 'vagina' [and uhuuyaq 'prow of kayak' — Pryde]
ECI usuk 'penis', utsuk 'vagina' [usuuyaq 'carrot, sausage']
GRI usuk 'penis', utsuk 'vagina' [usuušaq 'tip of kayak']

PY ucukcaq 'peg or nail'
AAY K ucukcaq 'nail'
CAY usukcaq, NSU ucukcaq 'nail'
NSY —
CSY —

PE ucuʀ- 'praise or envy'
AAY ucuʀyuɣ- 'be astonished'
CAY ucuqə- 'praise, revere, respect'
NSY [note usuqpalak 'gold, silver' — ANLC]
CSY usuqə- 'praise' [usuqəsaqə- 'do s.th. showy']
Sir usəqə- 'praise' [Orr; Em. has usəqəsaqə(s)- 'do s.th. showy or ostentatious']
SPI uzuʀi- 'respect, revere' [uzuʀnaq- 'be great, do great deed']
NAI —
WCI Car, Net uhuʀnaq- 'be enviable' [Ras.]
ECI [note Lab usunnaC- 'save s.o.']
GRI usuʀi- 'envy (s.o.), wish to be in their place' [usuʀnaʀ- 'be enviable']

PE uða(t)- and **uðamə(t)-** 'play around' [cf. EA uðat- 'quit, give up plans'; compare uima- and uyviŋit- under uyvi, with which there may be contamination in Inu]
AAY wamtə- 'trick, coax, cajole into doing s.th., play (with kids)'
CAY waamə- 'waste time'
NSY uamtə- 'deceive, joke' [L.-T.]
CSY waamə- 'rush around', waamtə-, Chap užəmtə- 'tease, joke' [Men. has waamtə- 'cheat', also wakəstəŋunani 'confused', wakənʀilŋuq 'calm, indifferent']
Sir užmət(ə)- 'deceive' [and Vakh. has užmaXsəʀ- 'play around with woman, flirt' from Rub.'s and Men.'s texts]
SPI uamit- 'delight, please' [Jen.]
NAI uamɨt- 'dance Inupiaq style (of man)', uayuk- 'make loud noises, play loudly'
WCI [for uiyi- 'trick, cheat' see uyviŋit- under uyvi; for Net uvimmak- 'talk in delirium' see uima-]
ECI [note uaʀit- 'be disorderly or agitated', Iti uasaq- 'put in disorder'; for uima- 'hurry' see uima- and for uvisaq- 'cheat, tease' see uyviŋit- under uyvi]
GRI uat-, Up uataʀsiʀ- 'deceive' [for uššat 'proverb, saying' see užžiq- under uðəɣ-]

PE uðəɣ- 'try'
AAY wiɣnəq Kod 'distance between outstretched thumb and index finger', PWS 'one foot'
CAY Y, Nun wiiɣ- 'try, sample, measure'
NSY wixtə- 'try', uža- 'measure' [ANLC has uiɣ-; uža(a)n 'instrument', užatəlan 'competition']
CSY ➟
Sir ucəxtə- 'taste' [Orr; and Men. has ucəcicaɣ- 'measure', ucəxcəcaʀita 'ruler, measure' — Em. has ucəxsətaʀita for the latter]
SPI uuk- 'try on', užžaaq- 'measure'
NAI uuk- 'sample, try'
WCI Cop uuk- 'try, have a go at' [Pryde; note also Baker Lake uuxxitaq- 'compete at shooting at target' — Schn.]
ECI uuk- 'try, tast'
GRI uuɣ-, Up u(u)tsiʀ- 'try, measure' [note also uuqattaaʀ- 'try', EG uuʀattaaʀaʀ- 'be able to right one's kayak', Up uutsivik 'target']

PE uðəɣtuʀ- 'measure or try out' [cf. tuʀ-[2]]
AAY —
CAY wiixtua- 'try, taste'
NSY — [but note uixtaʀ- 'try clothes on' — ANLC]
CSY —
Sir —
SPI uuktaaq-, Qaw uuktuaq- 'try, test, sample'
NAI uuktuun 'measuring device'
WCI uuktuq- 'measure', uuktuun 'measure, ruler' [EP uuktuʀaq- 'practice']
ECI uttu(q)- 'taste, try', uutturaq- 'measure, sound out'
GRI uuttuʀ- 'measure, weigh', uuttaa- [old ortho. ûgtai-] 'shoot at mark' [in EG the first also 'hold back from doing s.th.'; NG uuktuq- also 'get a taste of']

PY uspəʀ- 'measure or weigh' [or uypəʀ-; compare ilupəq under ilu for the p.b.]
AAY uspəq 'weight, measure', uspəʀ- 'weigh, measure'
CAY uspəʀ- 'weigh', uspəq* 'weight'
NSY uɣpətə- 'weigh' [ANLC]
CSY uspəqə-, uspətə- 'measure'

PI užžiq- 'show what to do (by signs)?' [cf. un and liʀ-]
SPI užžatuq- 'give directions'
NAI užžiqsuq- 'give directions' [and užžaaq- 'gesticulate']
WCI uyyiqtuq- 'watch over (so that s.th. is not done to excess)', Cop uyyiqi- 'wave, call by waving', Car? uyyiq- 'look after', uyyiluk- 'reveal one's destitution in the hope of receiving s.th.' [Schn. 'adg'; Briggs has užžiq- 'worry' for Utk]
ECI uyyituq- 'watch over (to protect)' [mainly biblical; Spald. has uyyiʀi- 'notice' for NBI]

GRI uššiʀ- 'try, tempt, point at', uššiʀsuʀ- 'wave at, gesticulate', uššiʀsuut(i)- 'measure', NWG ussiʀsaʀ- 'measure, weigh' [and uššiʀaʀ- 'give signal to', uššat 'fixed expression, proverb'; Terrsis has uttiqqa(C)- 'gesticulate while speaking' for EG]

PE **uðukaʀ** 'cod'
AAY —
CAY —
NSY uukaq 'tomcod' [Jen.]
CSY uukaq 'cod'
Sir ucəkəX, pl. ucəkay 'cod' [Orr]
SPI W uuɣaužaq [Ras.]
NAI uuɣaq
WCI uuɣaq
ECI uuɣaq
GRI uuɣaq, uuaq

PE **uɣaknaʀ** 'wind from a certain direction' [cf. dem. root uɣ- and p.b. knaʀ; for the different directions involved see Fortescue 1988]
AAY [note waakəq 'south wind']
CAY Nun waknəX 'west wind' [with compressed first syllable], LI waaqnaq '(south)west wind'
NSY uaknaq 'east'
CSY —
Sir —
SPI —
NAI Nu uaknaq 'west wind'
WCI Car uaŋnaq 'northwest wind' [and Pryde has Net ua'naq 'south wind']
ECI NBI Igl uaŋnaq '(north)west wind', SB 'north wind', Tar uannaq, uanniq 'northwest wind, wind from land' [the second form with p.b. liʀ-], Lab uaʀnaq 'west wind' [Peck — but Andersen et al. have uanniluak 'southerly wind']
GRI —

PE **uɣan (uɣatə)** 'area or part near exit' [cf. dem. root uɣ- and p.b. tə, also uɣaknaʀ; compare kiɣan and kivan and also EA uɣikiŋa (from *uɣi(m) kiŋa), Att uŋikiŋ 'time before daybreak', EA abl. uɣik(i)ŋaan 'in the night (about midnight?)' — since kiŋ means 'after' uɣ(i)- must mean some time before midnight acc. Berg.; compare GRI ualiq under uɣal(l)iʀ below]
AAY ➡
CAY waatə 'area near exit'; waan 'body from waist down, skirt, haunch' [note NI wazək 'arctic hare' — contam. with ukaðiʀ?]
NSY uatək 'buttocks' [ANLC sg. uatə; for uaknaq 'east' see uɣaknaʀ]
CSY uɣatə 'area near exit (of passage)', Chap uɣan 'place on either side of entrance (in house)' [note also that dem. uɣ- refers to the direction to the east on the Chukotkan mainland but to the (north) west on St. Lawrence Island]
Sir [note that dem. root uɣ- refers to the (north)east here acc. Menovščikov] ➡
SPI uatit, Qaw waatik, uatik 'hips, lower part of body, hind part of animal' [and W uatmun 'toward the south' in Jen.]
NAI uan, PH uatɨ 'lower part of body, hind part of animal' [and Jen. has 'right hand wall when moving toward exit of house'; note also uanmun 'toward west']
WCI uat(i)- 'direction to west'
ECI uati 'edge of snow house on either side of door'
GRI ➡

PE **uɣal(l)iʀ** 'thing or place most toward exit' [cf. l(l)iʀ; as with civul(l)iʀ there appear to be earlier (uɣaliʀ) and later (uɣalliʀ) parallel derivations here, the former directly on the dem. root]
AAY —
CAY [waaqłiq* 'part of house toward door' — with qliʀ]
NSY ualəq 'Uelen' [place name]
CSY —
Sir uɣəciʀnəX 'northeast' [see p.b. liʀnəq]
SPI —
NAI ualliq* 'west wall or room', PH 'front room of house (nearest door)' [and note uali- 'grow late, be in the west (sun)']
WCI Cop ualliq 'westernmost one' [Pryde, who also has Car B. Lake ualiq 'west wind'; Schn. has for Back River ualiliq- 'set (sun)'; Met. has uavaq-, uavali- 'be toward the west (sun)' with vaʀ-]
ECI SB ualliq 'foremost (entrance) vault of snow house' [Boas]
GRI [note ualiq 'afternoon' and uali- 'decline (of day)']

PY **u(ɣ)atsaq** or **u(ɣ)atyaq** '(wind from or to) a certain direction' [from *uɣatyaʀ — cf. yaʀ(tuʀ)- and compare uɣaknaʀ]
AAY waasaaq 'north (wind)'
CAY NSU waasiaq 'west (wind)'
NSY —
CSY —

PE **uɣðuɣ** 'bearded seal' [cf. uɣət-?]
AAY ➡
CAY ➡
NSY ➡
CSY ➡
Sir uɣcəx 'bearded seal' [Vakh. also uɣžux]
SPI uɣžuk
NAI uɣžuk
WCI uɣyuk, Utk ukžuk [Briggs for latter]
ECI uɣyuk 'bearded seal'
GRI uššuk [old ortho. ugssuk]

PE **uɣðuɣnaʀ** 'shrew (or similar rodent)' [cf. naʀ]
AAY Afognak uɣnaq 'mouse'
CAY uuɣnaʀ(aq*) 'vole', NS uɣuɣnaʀaq* 'shrew'
NSY —
CSY uɣuɣnaʀaq* 'shrew'
Sir uɣuʀnaX 'shew' [from CSY?]
SPI uɣžuŋnaq
NAI uɣžuŋnaq
WCI uɣyuŋnaq

ECI uɣɣunaq
GRI uššunnaq [old ortho. ugssungnaq]

PY **uɣuɣuaq** 'caterpillar' [cf. ŋ(ŋ)uðaʀ; note also Sir ulʀətaX 'caterpillar, worm' from uʀəɬəX 'sea lion' under ulʀuaq]
AAY —
CAY uɣuɣuaq 'caterpillar'
NSY uɣuɣuaʀnaq 'caterpillar' [ANLC; Men. has uɣuɣuaʀŋaq and L.-T. uɣuɣuaʀnak]
CSY [compare makɬaɣʷaaq 'caterpillar', from makɬ ak 'bearded seal']

PE **uɣət-** 'get up on s.th.' [cf. uɣðuɣ; there is contam./ conflation with uɣut- under uɣu- in Inu]
AAY uxtə- 'get up on top of s.th.'
CAY uxtə- 'get up on s.th.' [also uɣiiXtə- 'beach or be beached (boat)']
NSY uuxtə- 'get up on s.th.' [ANLC — Men. has uxtə-]
CSY uuxtə- 'get up on s.th.' [and uxɬəŋaʀ- 'come up in a group' — influenced by uɣlaʀ-?]
Sir uxtənəqə(s)- 'get up on s.th. [but Men. also has uxtə- 'get out of boat' and Vakh. has uXtə- 'get into kayak' and (from Rub.) uXqaʀaxtə- 'jump out (onto shore)']
SPI —
NAI —
WCI —
ECI uut- 'warm self (seal on ice)' [uuttuq 'seal out warming itself on ice' [and NBI, SB uɣliq 'walrus rookery']
GRI NWG, NG uuttuq 'seal (in NG also walrus) warming self on ice'

PY **uɣtaq** 'sea animal on ice floe' [compare ECI, GRI uuttuq above]
AAY —
CAY uxtaq 'seal on ice-floe'
NSY uxtaq 'walrus on ice floe' [ANLC]
CSY uuxta 'sea mammal resting on ice or land'
Inu [SPI, KI uktaq 'sea mammal out of water' probably from Yup]

PE **uɣɣuʀ-** 'regret' [cf. uɣumi-]
AAY uXcaʀ- 'long for s.th. which one might have got but which is now inaccessible'
CAY uuXcaʀa- 'regret a loss which might have been prevented'
NSY uuXsaʀ- 'regret' [ANLC]
CSY —
Sir —
SPI uɣɣuaq- 'regret'
NAI —
WCI uɣɣualak- 'call, warn with a gesture of finger' [and note uɣɣaʀnaq- 'causing suffering (e.g. heat, illness)']
ECI uɣɣua(q)- 'regret', Lab 'mourn, grieve' [Peck]
GRI uxxuʀ-, uxxuaʀ-, EG ukkuʀsaʀ- 'be angry' [and uxxuʀnaʀ-, uxxuaʀnaʀ- 'be annoying', uxxuʀi- 'be annoyed at']

PE **uɣi** 'husband' [cf. Aleut uɣi-X 'husband']
AAY wi(k) 'husband'
CAY wii
NSY ui
CSY uɣi
Sir uɣa 'husband' [and note uɣəcəx 'bridegroom']
SPI ui, Qaw Unk wii 'husband'
NAI ui
WCI ui
ECI ui
GRI ui 'husband' [old ortho. uvə]

PE **uɣilɣaʀ-** 'lose one's husband' [cf. ŋit-?]
AAY wil<ɣ>aq 'widow'
CAY wiilɣaq 'unmar ried woman'
NSY uilɣaq [ANLC]
CSY —
Sir —
SPI uiɣlaq- 'lose one's husband'
NAI uilʸɣaq- 'lose one's husband', uilʸɣaʀniq* 'widow'
WCI uilɣaʀniq 'widow' [and uilɣasuk 'young marriageable woman without (and not looking for) a husband']
ECI uiɣɣa(q)- 'have lost one's husband', uiɣɣanaq, Lab uiXXanik 'widow' [and Lab uiXXasuk 'unmarried young woman, teenage girl']
GRI uiɬɬaʀ- [old ortho. uigdlar-] 'lose one's husband', uiɬɬaʀniq* 'widow' [and uiɬɬaat 'woman's dead husband']

PE **uɣinəɣ-** 'marry (of woman)' [cf. p.b. nəɣ- (= Yup ŋə-)]
AAY —
CAY wiiŋə- 'marry (of a woman)'
NSY —
CSY —
Sir —
SPI uinik-
NAI uinʸɨk-
WCI uinik-
ECI uinik-
GRI uiniɣ-

PE **uɣiŋ(ŋ)uðaʀ** 'man a woman lives with who is not her real husband' [cf. ŋ(ŋ)uðaʀ]
AAY —
CAY wiiŋuaq, wiiŋusaq 'lover, imaginary husband'
NSY —
CSY uɣiŋwaaq* 'exchange husband'
Sir —
SPI uiŋuaq 'boyfriend'
NAI uiŋŋuaq 'man a woman lives with not her real husband' [and Nu uiɣužaq 'boyfriend']
WCI —
ECI —
GRI —

PE **uɣiyuɣ** 'woman's lover' [cf. yuɣ]
AAY —
CAY —
NSY —
CSY uɣiyuləɣk 'woman said to be married to a dead man's spirit' [with p.b. ləɣ]

Sir —
SPI —
NAI —
WCI uisuk 'woman's lover' [uisuɣiik 'lovers']
ECI uisuk 'fornicator, woman's lover' [uisuɣiik 'lovers', uisuk- 'have casual sex with a man (woman, outside of marriage)']
GRI uisuk 'adulterer, woman's lover'

PY uicuŋaq 'male cross-cousin of female' [cf. cuŋaq]
AAY wiicuŋaq 'teasing word for son-in-law or brother-in-law'
CAY wiicuŋaq 'male cross cousin of female'
NSY —
CSY —

uɣinaq 'sea lion' [from EA uɣina-X 'broad-shouldered sea lion bull', but the latter could be related to uɣət-]
AAY wiinaq 'sea lion'
CAY uɣinaq
NSY —
CSY —
Inu [Nu has uɣiŋn^{y}aq, uɣiʀn^{y}aq 'sea lion', but this is obviously not native to the area]

PE uɣiʀ(ᴀʀ)- 'fight (dogs)'
AAY wiXə-, wiXtə- 'fight (of dogs)' [and C wiʀləʀ- 'growl']
CAY wiiXə- 'fight (of dogs)'
NSY ➞
CSY uɣiXə- 'fight (dogs), maul'
Sir —
SPI uyaaq- 'fight (dogs)', Qaw uɣiaq- 'maul'
NAI uɣik-, uɣiaq- 'fight viciously' [and uɣiayuk 'ferocious animal']
WCI uɣiaq- 'fight (of dogs)'
ECI uɣiaq- 'kill with snap of its jaws (e.g. bear of dog)', Lab 'kill from intense emotion or insanity'
GRI uiᴀʀtuʀ- 'tear to pieces (one dog another)'

PE uɣiʀanni- 'growl'
AAY —
CAY uiXani- 'snarl and growl'
NSY uiXani- 'growl' [ANLC, also for uɣ̥Xani- 'snarl (dog)']
CSY uɣini-, Chap uɣiXŋ̥iʀ- 'roar, growl (e.g. polar bear)'
Sir —
SPI —
NAI Nu uɣianižaaq- 'snarl (of dog)'
WCI —
ECI —
GRI uiannišaaʀ- 'growl'

PE uɣlaʀ- 'be many' [cf. Aleut uɣlaɣ-a 'another (than it)']
AAY —
CAY [note uɣlaniiq 'ferocious mythical bear' — influenced by uɣiʀ(ᴀʀ)-?]
NSY uɣlaq 'large number', uɣlaʀi- 'increase, spread' [and ANLC has uɣlaʀ- 'be many']
CSY uɣlaʀ- 'be many', uɣlaq 'large number or amount', uɣlaʀi- 'increase in number' [and note uɣlavə- 'spread out, disperse', uɣlafqə- 'be confused, scatter']
Sir —
SPI —
NAI —
WCI uɣlaq- 'run in and out of the house all the time (e.g. children playing)' [and Schn. has 'visit' for 'adg']
ECI NBI, Aiv uɣlaq- 'visit'
GRI [note ussaɣ- (old ortho. ugsag-) 'crowd together, have caught many -'?]

PE uɣu- 'be heated up or cooked'
AAY uuma- 'be cooked' [uu- 'get a rash']
CAY uu- 'be cooked' [uuɣaq 's.th. cooked']
NSY ➞
CSY uɣu- 'get burnt, ripen, get irritated (skin)'
Sir uɣu- 'be baked' [and note uqłaʀ- 'burn']
SPI ➞
NAI ➞
WCI ➞
ECI [note uulittaa(q)- 'toast (bread, etc.)'] ➞
GRI uu- 'be burnt, burn oneself, be boiled' [and uuniq* 'burn (sore)', uuliniq* 's.th. burnt', EG uulaq, uutsit 'food being cooked']

PE uɣukə 'boiled food' [cf. kə-[2]]
AAY —
CAY [uŋəłkaaq 'fish steak']
NSY uxkə 'boiled food'
CSY uxka 'cooked food' [compare uɣutkaq 'cooked food' from uɣut- below and kaʀ]
Sir uxka 'boiled meat, bread' [Em. has uɣəkcəX 'cooked, boiled']
SPI —
NAI —
WCI —
ECI Lab uuɣi 'meat, fish put to boil' [Andersen et al.]
GRI uui(q) 'meat or fish that is boiling'

PE uɣukli- 'cut up meat for cooking' [cf. uɣukə above and li-[1]]
AAY [C uxki- 'cut up food']
CAY ukłi- 'cut up, dice (meat)' [ukłiʀ-, ukliʀ- 'provide solid ingredients for soup', ukłiaq 'cooked pieces of fish']
NSY —
CSY uxkəłi- 'cut up meat for cooking'
Sir —
SPI uukłi- 'cut up for cooking (meat)'
NAI uukłi- 'cut up meat' [and uukłiaq 'cut-up meat', uukłiqpik 'grate inside oven'; Pryde also has uukłiq- 'put meat in pot']
WCI [Pryde has Cop uuxxiq- 'put ingredients in pot']
ECI uutsi-, uutsi(C)- 'cut up for stew (meat)'
GRI uułłi- [old ortho. ûgdli-] 'cut up for stew (meat)' [uułłiaq 'cut-up meat', uułłiʀ- 'put cut-up meat in oven']

PE uɣuŋilaʀ 'raw food' [cf. ŋit-]
AAY —
CAY uuvlaaɣ-, uuŋłəkaʀ-, HBC uvluaqaʀ-, umł uaqaʀ-, umłəkaʀ- 'cook rare'
NSY —
CSY —
Sir —
SPI —
NAI uilʸaq 'raw food' [as verb = 'eat raw food']
WCI Sig uilaq 's.th. raw, uncooked' [Lowe, who also has uittuq for Cop; Met. has uilaq 'wad (for chewing)', also as a verb]
ECI [note uuyuuŋŋituq 'uncooked, raw meat or fish']
GRI uuilaq 'raw food', EG 'kidney'

PY uɣuqə- 'burn or get burnt' [cf. kə-[1] ?]
AAY —
CAY —
NSY uuqə- 'burn or get burnt (flesh)' [ANLC]
CSY uɣuqə- 'get burnt'

PY uɣuqnaʀ- 'be burning hot' [cf. uɣuqə- above and naʀ- and also uunaq- below]
AAY —
CAY uuqn̥aXqə-, HBC, Nun uqn̥axqə- 'be burning hot' [with short u due to compression; note HBC uqn̥aq 'berries and blood cooked up, cooked tubers']
NSY uuqn̥aʀ- 'be hot (object)' [ANLC; Men. has uuqn̥aq 'heat', uuqn̥aXtə- 'heat up']
CSY uɣuqn̥aʀ- 'be burning hot'

PE uɣut- 'burn or cook' [cf. t-[1]]
AAY uutə- 'burn oneself'
CAY uutə- 'bake, roast, burn'
NSY uutə- 'cook'
CSY uɣutə-
Sir —
SPI uut- 'be cooked, get burnt'
NAI uut- 'be cooked, get sunburnt' [uunniq* 'burn']
WCI uut- 'be cooked, cook' [and Lowe has uunnaaq- 'be hot' for H. Island Cop]
ECI uut- 'burn' [for the 'warm self (seal on ice)' sense see under uɣət-; uunniq 'burn', uunna(q)- 'be burning (to touch)']
GRI uut- 'boil, bake, roast, burn' [and NG uunnaq- 'be burning (to touch)' and uuttuq 'meat or fish being boiled', EG uutsit 'cooking pot']

PI uunaq- 'be hot or burning' [cf. naʀ-]
Sir [note uɣnəʀətəX 'cold' with ŋit-]
SPI uuna(q)- 'be hot' [and Jen. has uunaq 'heat' for W]
NAI uunaq- 'be hot' [and uunnaak- 'be warm']
WCI Sig uunaq 'heat', uunaq- 'be burning hot' [Dor. has 'be warm (weather)' for Net]
ECI uunaq- 'be boiling (liquid), burning hot (e.g. stove)', Iti uunaʀniq 'heat, temperature', Lab uunak- 'be hot' [as noun = 'heat']
GRI uunaʀ- 'be burning hot (to touch)', NG uunaq- 'be hot, warm' [and uunnaɣ- 'warm up', unnaa- 'heat up water', also EG uunnaqqit 'oil lamp'; for NG uunnaq- 'be burning (to touch)' see uɣut- above]

PI uunni- 'feel hot' [cf. ni-?]
SPI uuni- 'feel hot'
NAI [note uunniqɨ- 'suffer from heat']
WCI Cop uunniuq- 'be bothered by heat' [Pryde]
ECI uunni- 'feel hot, heavy after eating'
GRI [note uniʀiffik 'hell' (biblical)]

PI uuq- 'have a heat rash'
Yup [note CAY uuzuXtə-, uuyuXtə- 'have diaper rash']
SPI uuq- 'have heat or diaper rash'
NAI uuq-
WCI [note Cop uuq- 'hurt oneself (child)' acc. Pryde]
ECI [Andersen at al. have uuɣimajuk 'baby with diaper rash' for Lab]
GRI [uuaʀaʀ- 'be blotchy, have a rash']

PI uutəq- 'burn or get burnt' [cf. təʀ-]
SPI uutiq- 'get sunburnt, scorched by the sun'
NAI uutiq-
WCI uutiq- 'burn', uutiʀnaq- 'be burning'
ECI uuti(C)- 'cause to be burnt, burn (intentionally)', uutiʀna(q)- 'have a fever' [and Lab uutaak- 'scorch, burn self']
GRI uutiʀ- 'bake'

PI uužuq 'boiled meat' [cf. ðuʀ]
SPI uužaq 'boiled fish'
NAI uužuq 'boiled meat'
WCI Cop uuyuq 'boiled meat' [Pryde]
ECI uuyuq 'boiled meat or fish'
GRI uušuq

PE uɣumi- 'be infuriated' [cf. uɣɣuʀ- — there may be a further link to uɣu-]
AAY —
CAY uumi(yuɣ)- 'be infuriated (at)' [emot. root; uuminaqfaa 'darn it!']
NSY uumi(yuɣ)- 'hate, be infuriated (at)'
CSY uɣumi(yuɣ)- 'feel hatred or frustration' [and uɣuminaXalək 'how annoying!']
Sir —
SPI Qaw uumiɣi- 'hate'
NAI uumiɣi- 'hate', uuminʸaq- 'be annoying'
WCI uumiɣi- 'hate'
ECI uumiɣi- 'have a grudge against, be angry at' [emot. root]
GRI uumiɣi- 'be furious with', uuminaʀ- 'be annoying', uumiššuʀ- 'hate' [perhaps uminaaʀ- 'have a sudden pain' is also related]

PI uumila- 'grimace' [cf. la(ʀ)-?]
SPI —
NAI uumilʸa- 'make a face'

WCI u(u)milauq- 'make a grimace'
ECI uumila- have as cause of one's sad expression' [and uumilli(q)- 'show disgust at']
GRI uumila-, uumiłłiʀ- 'look or feel cross, be a nuisance (child)', NG uumilliq- 'make a grimace'

PY-S uɣžiɣ- 'go down' [cf. dem. root uɣ- and p.b. ðiɣ-?]
AAY —
CAY —
NSY [Men. has place name uɣyuqiq, lit. '(place with) landslide', cape between Nunama and Pinakulem]
CSY [note ukiɣ- 'go or come down', ukixtə- 'bring down', by contam. with dem. root uk-?]
Sir uɣcəɣ- 'go or come down' [Em. and Vakh. — Men. has uɣcəʀ-; uɣcəxtə-, Men. uɣcəXtə- 'bring down']

PI uima- 'rush about?' [or uvima-? — cf. uvi(t)-, but also uða(t)-, at least as a source of contam.]
SPI —
NAI uima- 'be quick'
WCI uima- 'hang around men (girls)', uimaŋŋit- 'be calm' [Pryde has Net 'be crazy' and Sig 'be infatuated with s.o. (girl)' for the former; Ras. has Net uvimmak- 'talk in delirium']
ECI uima- 'hurry', NBI 'be dissipated', Lab 'not know where one is upon awakening'
GRI —

PI uiqšaq- 'get a child outside wedlock?' [cf. uɣi]
SPI —
NAI —
WCI [Cop uiXXaq- 'be sexually attracted to a woman' — Pryde]
ECI uiʀsaq 'male demon who has sexual relations with women, incubus'
GRI uiʀšaʀ- 'have a child outside wedlock', uiʀšaɣaq, NG uiXXaq 'child born outside wedlock' [and Gessain et al. have EG uiʀsaq 'bisexual spirit of initiation'; uiʀšaʀniq* 'woman who has got an illegitimate child']

PI uiʀuala- 'cry out in pain' [there may be a relat. to uvit-]
SPI —
NAI uiʀuala- 'yell, holler in distress'
WCI —
ECI —
GRI uiʀuala- 'speak in a high, squeaky voice', NG 'howl (in pain)' [compare uiʀuluɣ- 'open eyes wide']

PI u(ɣ)iyaq 'young beluga '
SPI Di uiyaq, uiaq 'young of beluga' [Men. has uyiaq for Imaq]
NAI —
WCI —
ECI Lab uɣiak 'young whiting (i.e. white whale?), blackfish or porpoise' [Peck]
GRI uiaq, NG uɣiaq 'young white whale or narwhale'

PE ukaðiʀ 'hare' [compare the reflexes of *ði in tuðiɣ]
AAY uka'iq 'hare'
CAY — [for wazək 'arctic hare' see uɣan] ➟
NSY ukayiq 'arctic hare'
CSY ukaziq
Sir ukacəX
SPI uɣaliq 'hare'
NAI ukalliq, ukallisuɣžuk 'arctic hare' [the latter also in Mal]
WCI ukaliq 'arctic hare'
ECI ukaliq
GRI ukaliq

PE ukaðiʀuðaʀ 'cottongrass' [cf. ŋ(ŋ)uðaʀ(-)]
AAY —
CAY ukaziʀuaq, ukayiʀuaq 'cottongrass'
NSY —
CSY —
Sir —
SPI —
NAI —
WCI —
ECI —
GRI ukaliušaq

PY-S ukaliq 'neighbor' [cf. dem. root uk- and p.b. l(l)iʀ]
AAY —
CAY — [but note ukatə- 'this side', ukaqsiɣ- 'be near']
NSY ukaliq 'neighbor'
CSY ukaliq SLI 'one on this side, lowest on the social scale', Chap 'nearest (of group)'
Sir ukəcəX 'neighbor' [and ukəncəX 'near']

PE ukamaʀ- 'tow a boat'
AAY —
CAY ukamaʀ- 'tow a boat with rope while walking along shore'
NSY ukamaXtə 'one who tows a boat'
CSY ukamaʀ- 'tow a boat from shore'
Sir ukəməXta 'one who tows a barge'
SPI uɣamaq- 'tow boat while walking along shore'
NAI ukamaq-
WCI ukamaq-
ECI ukamaq- 'tow s.th. floating by a cable'
GRI ukamaʀ-, ukumaʀ- 'rock one's body or kayak back and forth' [influenced by uku-?]

PI uki-[1] 'want more of s.th.'
SPI —
NAI —
WCI —
ECI uki- 'get to like s.th.' [Andersen et al. have 'want more and more' for Lab; and ukiyi-, ukkiyi- 'stare fixedly at a point']
GRI uki- 'want more of the same' [and ukkit(i)- 'want more, stare at s.th.', ukkat(i)- 'be absorbed in, intent on', ukkiši- 'stare straight ahead']

PE uki-[2] 'get a hole' [cf. Atkan Aleut ukinaX 'knife']
AAY uki- 'get a hole, get pierced'
CAY uki-
NSY uki- [ANLC]
CSY uki-
Sir ➟

SPI uɣizi- 'get a hole in mukluk sole' [and note uʀiłXaaq, Imaq uɣiłqa(a)q, Qaw ukiłXaaq 'cloth, pullover parka']
NAI [note ukił^{y}Xaaq 'cloth'] →
WCI →
ECI →
GRI →

PE ukit- 'pierce' [cf. Aleut uxt- 'prick (boil with needle), bleed (with lancet)']
AAY ukitə- 'make a hole in'
CAY ukitə-
NSY ukitə- 'make a hole in' [and ukiquʀ- 'make holes in']
CSY ukitə- 'make a hole in'
Sir ukəqaʀ- 'make holes in' [and ukənʀəX 'window, smoke hole, chimney, ear hole']
SPI uɣit- 'open hole in ice'
NAI ukit- 'cut oblong hole in'
WCI ukit- 'have round hole cut in it' [Pryde; Met. has ukkiq- 'tear away a piece']
ECI ukit- 'tear (garment or skin while cleaning), gash' [and Peck has ukkiC- 'make eye in needle' for Lab]
GRI ukit- 'drill eye in (needle)' [and EG uɣiȓit 'marlinespike' (Ges.)]

PY ukiy(u)qaq 'capable person'
AAY ukisqaq 'capable young man'
CAY NS ukisqaq 'strong capable person' [and, also elsewhere, ukisqiʀ- 'help']
NSY ukiy̯uqaq 'capable person' [ANLC]
CSY —

PI ukpan 'hindquarter of animal' [cf. un and perhaps uku-]
SPI —
NAI ukpan 'hindquarter, hip'
WCI ukpatik 'rump of animal'
ECI uppat
GRI uppat 'thigh, ham, hindquarter' [old ortho. ugpat]

PI uku- 'bend or bow'
SPI —
NAI —
WCI uku- 'bow body and head while bending' [and Net, B. Lake, Uum ukkuttaq 'jacknife' — Dor.]
ECI uku- 'bend forward', ukuŋa- 'be bent forward' [and NBI ukkutaqtuq 'jacknife' — Dor.]
GRI uku- 'bend head, fold together', NG 'collapse, fall, starve to death' [the latter ukaliʀ- in WG; ukuŋa- 'lean, tilt, be folded (pocketknife)', ukut- 'fold', ukusaʀtuq 'pocketknife' and ukutsiq 'pit of stomach (where one bends forward)']

PE uku(C)aʀ 'daughter- or sister-in-law'
AAY [for ukuXaq 'daughter-in-law' see uku(C)aʀaq below]→
CAY Nun, NS ukuaq 'daughter-in-law, sister-in-law (brother's wife)'
NSY ukuaq
CSY ukaaq*
Sir →
SPI uɣuaq 'daughter-in-law, sister-in-law (brother's wife)'
NAI ukuaq
WCI ukuaq 'sister-in-law (brother's wife) of a woman (term used by members of husband's family for his wife)'
ECI ukuaq 'daughter-in-law, sister-in-law, son's wife, nephew's wife, girl's first cousin's wife'
GRI ukuaq 'daughter-in-law, sister-in-law' [also of wife of more remote male relatives; ukuššiut(i)- 'marry into a family'; and note (older) NG ukuuq 'mother' — also in EG acc. Holm]

PY-S uku(C)aʀaq 'bride' [cf. aʀ]
AAY KP ukuXaq 'daughter-in-law'
CAY ukuXaq 'daughter-in-law, sister-in-law'
NSY ukuXaq 'new bride who has recently moved in with her husband's family'
CSY ukuXaq
Sir [ukəsqəX 'new bride who has recently moved in with her husband's family']

PE ukvəʀ- 'believe'
AAY ukxəʀ- 'believe'
CAY ukfəX- 'believe', ukfəq 'religion, faith'
NSY ukpəʀ- 'believe'
CSY uxpəʀ-
Sir uxpəʀ- 'believe in something' [Vakh. who also has əxpəʀ- from Rub.'s texts, as also in Em.]
SPI ukpiq- 'believe'
NAI ukpiq-
WCI ukpiq-
ECI uppi(q)-
GRI uppiʀ-

PE ukvəqə- 'believe in' [cf. kə-[1]]
AAY uk<x>əqə- 'believe in'
CAY ukfəqə-, ukfəkə-
NSY ukpəqə-
CSY uxpəqə-
Sir uxpəqə(s)- 'believe in' [Em.]
SPI ukpii-
NAI ukpiʀi-
WCI ukpiʀi-
ECI uppiʀi-
GRI uppiʀi-

PE ukyuʀ 'winter or year'
AAY uksuq 'winter, year' [uksuʀ- 'be winter']
CAY uksuq 'winter, year' [and uksuʀ- 'become winter']
NSY uky̯uq 'winter, year'
CSY uksuq 'winter, year' [and uksuʀ- 'be winter']
Sir →
SPI uɣiuq 'winter, year'
NAI ukiuq [as verb = 'become winter']
WCI ukiuq 'winter, year'
ECI ukiuq 'winter, year' [as verb = 'be winter']
GRI ukiuq 'winter, year' [and ukiuʀ- 'have become winter']

PE ukyi- 'spend the winter' [cf. li-[1]]
AAY uksi- 'spend the winter'
CAY uksi-
NSY ukỵi-
CSY —
Sir —
SPI uɣii- 'spend the year or the winter'
NAI ukii-
WCI ukii- 'spend the winter'
ECI ukii-
GRI ukii-

PE ukyuʀaʀ 'autumn' [cf. aʀ?; compare pamyuʀaʀ under pamyuʀ for a parallel to the Inu forms]
AAY uksuaq 'autumn, fall' [uksuaʀ- 'be fall', uksuali- 'spend the fall']
CAY uksuaq 'autumn, fall' [uksuaʀ- 'become fall', uksii- 'spend the fall']
NSY ukỵuaq 'autumn, fall'
CSY uksaaq* 'autumn, fall' [uksaaʀ- 'be fall']
Sir ukỵəʀaX 'autumn, fall'
SPI uɣiaq
NAI ukiaq 'autumn, fall' [and Nu ukiaqsiq- 'be fall, spend the fall']
WCI ukiaq 'autumn'
ECI ukiaq 'autumn, fall' [as verb = 'be autumn']
GRI ukiaq, EG uɣiatsaq 'autumn, fall' [ukiaʀ-, EG uɣiatsaʀ- 'have become autumn']

PY ulaɣaq 'arctic fox'
AAY —
CAY uliiq 'arctic fox'
NSY ulaɣaq
CSY —
Sir [note əlwa, əlɣʷa 'arctic fox']

PY ulakitaaʀ- 'play tag' [cf. ulapə(t)-]
AAY AP alakkiiʀ-, Perry alakkiitaʀ- 'play tag' [also nom.; influenced by alaʀ- or alaŋe-?]
CAY NSU ulakitaaʀ- 'play tag' [and elsewhere alakiitaaq 'game of tag' — influenced by alaʀ- or alaŋə-?]
NSY —
CSY ulakitaaʀ- 'play tag' [also nom. ulakitaaq 'game of tag']
Inu [cf. GRI ulikattaʀ- 'do somersaults' under ulət-]

PI ulamiq- 'be round'
SPI ulamiq- 'become fat and round (e.g., seal)' [Jen.]
NAI ulamiq- 'braid seal intestines for boiling'
WCI ulamiqtuq 'round, circle' [Pet. has for Sig 'compact, thick' and Ras. has for Car 'round piece of caribou sinew ready for use']
ECI ulamiqtaq 'cylindrical object'
GRI ulamiʀ- 'be cylindrical, round'

PE ulapə(t)- 'play around?' [cf. uləq-, with which there appears at least to have been contam. in Inu, also ulpəɣ-[2]]
AAY —
CAY ulapəqə- 'waste time, play around', ulapsaxtə- 'make a mistake, forget'
NSY ulapəsaʀ- 'keep from speaking or singing' [L.-T.; ANLC has ulapəsaʀaʀ-]
CSY ulapə- 'exercise physically' [for uɣlafqə- 'be confused' see ul(l)aʀ-]
Sir ulaftə- 'throw around' [Vakh.]
SPI ulapit- 'distract, confuse, bother' [Jen. has 'be busy']
NAI ulapɨt- 'get confused, lose s.th.' [Jen. also has ulapki- 'play a certain game'; for alapɨt- 'become confused' see alapənʀaʀ-; note also ulavži- 'become or make confused']
WCI ulapit- 'lose, be lost', Sig ulapaaq- 'live it up, act wild', Net ulapqi- 'play', Cop ulapqiuyaq- 'play with toys', ulapqutiɣi- 'occupy oneself with'
ECI ulapit- 'distract (oneself or another)'
GRI ulapit- 'be busy' [and ulaššut(i)- (old ortho. ulavssut(i)-) 'be confused by' — compare under uləq-]

ulaʀiq 'apple berry' [loan from EA hulaX, pl. hulaʀin 'bearberry']
AAY AP ulaʀiq 'apple berry'
CAY LI ulaʀiq
NSY —
CSY —

PE ulə(-) 'high tide or flood' [cf. EA ulʀi- 'overflow', Atkan ulut- 'go down and remain a long time under water', also Atkan ulʀi- 'go inside (cave or bay)'?]
AAY ula 'flood', ulə- 'flood, overflow'
CAY ula 'high tide' [and uləvə- NSU 'bubble, babble (when speaking)', Nun, NS 'be messy, mess up']
NSY [uluvŋa-, uluftə- 'overflow' (ANLC]
CSY uləvə- 'flood, overflow'
Sir —
SPI ulit- 'be a flood', Qaw ulima- 'be high tide'
NAI ulɨ, ulɨnniq* 'high water, flood', ulɨt- 'rise (water), flood'
WCI uliq 'high tide', ulit- 'be high tide'
ECI ulik- 'have risen (tide)', ulikki(C)- 'overflow' [and uliɣaq- 'wash over (tide)', uliɣiaq- 'begin to rise', Iti ulik 'rising tide' — influenced by ulik 'cover'?]
GRI uli 'high tide', ulit- 'be high tide' [and ulinniʀšuaq 'flood, high tide', biblical ulišsuaq 'the Flood']

PE uləvkaʀ- 'fill or be full' [cf. vkaʀ-]
AAY —
CAY —
NSY ulufkaq 'high tide' [and ulufkaiɬəq 'low tide']
Sir —
SPI —
NAI ulipkaaq- 'fill completely'
WCI Cop ulipkaaq 'fill to overflowing', Car? ulipkaq- 'be overflowing, flood (river)' [Schn. 'adg']
ECI —
GRI ulikkaaʀ-, EG ulukkaaʀ- 'be full, fill'

PE uləvlaʀ- 'overflow' [cf. CSY uləvə- under ulə(-) above]
AAY —
CAY uləvlaʀ- 'leak', ulevlaq 'spring (water)'
NSY —

CSY —
Sir —
SPI ulivlaq- 'overflow'
NAI uliv la-
WCI —
ECI —
GRI —

PE ulutə- 'be flooded over' [cf. utə-]
AAY ulutə- 'flood'
CAY ulutə-
NSY —
CSY —
Sir —
SPI [uližuti- 'be blocked by flood']
NAI ulluti-, PH uluti- 'be blocked (by flood)'
WCI —
ECI ulut(i)- 'cover (tide)'
GRI ulut(i)-, uluɣut(i)- 'come up over (water)'

PE ulə(t)luyaʀ 'whirlwind' [cf. ulət-; there is contam. with uyivə- in western Inu, it seems]
AAY PWS ułuaq, KP upłuyaq, Perry upłuya 'whirlwind'
CAY Y ucłuʀyaq, K, BB ułłuyaq 'whirlwind'
NSY —
CSY —
Sir —
SPI [uyayula, Qaw uwiayulak 'whirlwind' — also verbal]
NAI [uyalunaq, PH uyalulaq 'whirlwind' — also verbal; note PH uyalu 'man dressed up as woman who dances with masks (during messanger feast)']
WCI uyaluyaq, Sig ulayuyaq [Pet.] 'whirlwind'
ECI ulayuyaq
GRI ulušsaaq (old ortho. uluvssâq) 'whirlwind' [compare NAI ulivžaɣaq 'ocean swell' under ulət-?]

PI uləq- 'mistake or confuse' [there may be a relat. to ulapə(t)-]
SPI uliq- 'speak a dialect or language not one's own, get to like something or someone new and come back for more'
NAI uliq- 'speak a dialect not one's own, see or hear from afar'
WCI Sig uliq- 'make a mistake' [and Cop uleʀuftaʀ- 'confuse with' in Ras. — with uliʀut(i)-?]
ECI Igl uliq- 'make a mistake' [Ras.], Lab ulinnaik- 'recognize from afar'
GRI uliʀut(i)-, ulaʀut(i)- 'be confused by (because there are so many)', NG uliq- 'make a mistake', uliʀut(i)- 'mistake for another'

PE ulət- 'turn inside out' [cf. Aleut ula- 'be turned inside out', ulat- 'turn inside out']
AAY ułtə- 'turn inside out'
CAY ułtə-
NSY ułtə- 'turn inside out' [ANLC; and note ulŋan 'inside out' (L.-T.)]
CSY uułtə- 'turn inside out, gossip about s.o., change character at maturity' [and ulmiɣ- 'be inside out']
Sir [ulcət- 'turn inside out' — Vakh. from Rub.'s texts]
SPI ulit- 'turn inside out'
NAI ulit- 'turn inside out' [and note ulitcuil^{y}aq 'waterproof boot with fur inside' — literally 'which is never turned inside out' — and ulivžaɣaq 'large ocean swell with overhang', which as verb = 'form breakers']
WCI ulit- 'turn inside out'
ECI ulit- 'be turned inside out, be rolled up'
GRI ulit- 'turn inside out, do a somersault' [and ulikattaʀ- 'do somersaults']

PY-S ulpəɣ-[1] 'roll up'
AAY —
CAY —
NSY ułpəXquʀ- 'roll up (sleeves)'
CSY ułpəɣ- 'fold back (e.g. pants leg)'
Sir ułpəɣ- 'turn inside out, roll up (intr.)' [Em.]

ulɣilə 'birch' [apparently from Chukchi vəlgil in which case this is the only Chukchi loan in GRI]
AAY — [for əlŋuq 'birch' see nəlŋu(ʀ)-]
CAY — [for əlŋuq, nəlŋuq 'birch' see nəlŋu(ʀ)-, possibly by contam. with this set]
NSY —
CSY —
Sir wəlɣila 'birch tree' [perhaps a recent loan; Vakh. has wiła from Rub.]
SPI —
NAI užɣiil^{y}iq 'birch tree'
WCI Sig uyɣiiliq, Cop ulɣiiliq 'birch tree' [Pryde for the latter]
ECI —
GRI [uliɣiiliq, uliɣiilik 'loose, brittle driftwood']

PE uliɣ(-) 'cover or blanket'
AAY ulik 'blanket'
CAY ulik 'blanket' [uliɣ- 'use a blanket']
NSY ulikutaq 'blanket' [ANLC has ulik, also uliɣ- 'cover with a blanket']
CSY ulik 'blanket' [and uliɣ- 'cover with a blanket']
Sir —
SPI ulik 'cover, taupaulin', Qaw 'blanket'
NAI ulik 'blanket' [verbal = 'cover with a blanket']
WCI ulik 'blanket' [as verb = 'cover']
ECI ulik 'dress, robe, cover' [also verbal]
GRI ulik 'cover, bedspread, shawl, tarpaulin' [and uliɣ- 'cover'; EG uliivik 'skin (of animal or human)' probably belongs here too, influenced by uvinəɣ?]

PI uliɣžuaq 'cover or cape' [cf. ðuɣaʀ]
Yup — [but note NSU uliɣaaq 'coat']
SPI —
NAI uliɣžuaq 'heavy blanket or cover'
WCI —
ECI uliyyuaq 'coat'
GRI uliɣuaq 'cape'

PE ulima- 'make or fashion'
AAY [note C ulimaʀuaq 'bow' — B.-S.]
CAY —

NSY —
CSY ulima- 'make'
Sir ucəma-
SPI ulima- 'use an adze'
NAI ulima-
WCI ulima-
ECI ulimak- 'give (s.th.) a blow with an axe'
GRI ulima-, EG uluma- 'cut with an axe'

PI ulimaun 'adze or axe' [cf. un]
Yup [for CSY qałqalima 'axe' see qalqa]
SPI ulimaun 'adze'
NAI ulimaun
WCI ulimaun [Pryde]
ECI ulimaut 'axe'
GRI ulimaat, ulumaat

PE uli(C)un 'sinew from back of animal' [cf. un]
AAY PWS ułiun 'sinew from backbone of caribou'
CAY uliun 'sinew before it is split to be used for sewing'
NSY uliin, uliitə 'back sinew' [ANLC; and note ułiun 'back part of skin house' acc. L.-T.]
CSY —
Sir —
SPI uliun 'sinew from back'
NAI uliun, uliusinʸɨq*
WCI uliut 'sinew from back' [and uli(y)usiniq 'filet of caribou']
ECI uliuti 'whole bundle of tendons from a caribou or whale filet', Lab 'sinew in reindeer's back'
GRI uliut 'loin, back part (of seal or whale, esp. beluga)' [EG uliilit 'back muscles' acc. Robbe and Menn.]

PY ulmiʀtə- 'flare out' [cf. perhaps ulət- (esp. CSY ulmiɣ- there) and p.b. tmi(C)aʀtə-]
AAY ulmiXtə- 'flare (e.g. copper tubing)'
CAY ulmiXtə- 'flare'
NSY —
CSY —

PE ulpəɣ-[2] or **ulpət-** 'tumble' [cf. Aleut kaŋaa (= 'his top') ula- 'do somersault' and ulapə(t)-; compare alpaɣ- for the Inu cons. cluster; there may be some contam. here with ułəʀ- and ulpəɣ-[1] under ulət-]
AAY K ułpətə-, ułpəxtə- 'flip over, do a somersault, tumble'
CAY ułpiaXtə- 'somersault' [and Nun ułpəɣ- 'boil'?]
NSY ułpiaXtaqu(ʀ)- 'trip over' [ANLC has ułpiaXtə-, ułpitə- 'go head over heals']
CSY ułpəxtə-, ułpiɣ- 'run with all one's might'
Sir ułpaXtə- 'tumble, roll' [and ułpaXsuɣnaʀməlŋuX 'wheel'; Vakh. has ułpaʀ-, ułpaXt(ə)- 'roll' from Rub.'s texts']
SPI Qaw ukpitaq- 'do a somersault, tumble'
NAI ukpɨtaq- 'tumble over, cross highest point of hill and start descent'
WCI ukpit- 'fall headlong'
ECI uppikaq-
GRI uppit- 'fall over', uppikaʀ- 'be knocked aside'

PE ulqiʀ 'wild potato'
AAY —
CAY Nun ułqiX, NS utqiq 'wild potato' [the latter from Inu]
NSY ułqiq 'wild potato'
CSY uułqiq
Sir ułqi
SPI utqiq
NAI PH utqiq
WCI —
ECI —
GRI —

PY ulʀuaq 'sea lion' [the exact relat. to Chukchi 'otleq, Koryak uluul, Alutor ulwul 'sea lion' is unclear, but is slightly more likely to be a loan from Esk than vice versa (apart from the Sir, which is clearly from Chukchi) given the irregular reflexes in the Chukchi-Koryak forms and the fact that an Esk ʀ may turn up as a glottal stop in Chukchi (metathesized with an initial vowel here) in loans, as in Chukchi reduplicated te'yute'y 'salt' from CSY taʀyuq]
AAY — [for wiinaq 'sea lion' see uɣinaq]
CAY —
NSY ulʀuaq 'sea lion' [L.-T.]
CSY ulʀaaq
Sir [uʀəłəX 'sea lion' — from the Chukchi above]

PY ulʀuk 'pants' [dual]
AAY K ulʀuk, Perry ułłuk, KP ulluk 'pants'
CAY BB ulʀuk
NSY —
CSY —

PY-S ulu(q) 'tongue' [cf. ulu(ʀ), but also perhaps Aleut ulu-X 'meat'; this base could contain p.b. lu(ʀ), in which case compare uqaq]
AAY uluq 'tongue' [KP also uluk]
CAY ulu 'tongue'
NSY ulu 'tongue' [ANLC also 'tip or blade of harpoon' — cf. ulu(ʀ)]
CSY ulu 'tongue, language'
Sir ula 'tongue, language' [on Men.'s comp. list; Miller and Orr have uła]

PE ulu(ʀ) and **uluʀaʀ** '(semi-lunar) knife, ulu' [cf. uluʀaʀ-, also ulu(q), the apparent source of this set, i.e. 'little tongue' or 's.th. resembling a tongue', may or may not be fortuitous (it could be the source of contam.); note also Chukchi ulun 'blade of harpoon or spear', presumably borrowed from Esk]
AAY uluaq, ulukaq 'woman's semi-lunar knife' [the former with p.b. aʀ]
CAY uluaq 'woman's semi-lunar knife'
NSY uluaq 'semi-lunar knife'
CSY ulaaq* 'woman's semi-lunar knife' [and ulaɣ- 'cut with such a knife' — a back-formation? (but cf. uluʀaʀ-)]
Sir [Em. has ułəžaX 'flint knife', but this = 'little tongue' in Men.]
SPI ulu 'woman's semi-lunar knife' [and note Imaq ulutaq 'harpoon tip']

NAI ulu 'woman's semi-lunar knife'
WCI ulu ' woman's semi-lunar knife' [Met. has ulun — for uluun?]
ECI ulu 'semi-lunar knife'
GRI ulu, 'woman's semi-lunar knife, blade of harpoon', EG uluq 'blade of harpoon' [uluʀnaq, ulunnaq 'blade of lance, etc.', NG ulunnaq 'blade of kayak paddle' — Holt.]

PE uluɣ- 'soften skin by rubbing' [cf. Aleut uliɣ- 'rub (a hide)']
AAY uluɣ- 'rub to soften, massage'
CAY uluɣ- 'flex, soften (a skin)'
NSY uluɣ-
CSY uluɣ-
Sir uləɣ-
SPI uluk- 'rub and twist (skin)' [uluktuq- 'rub clothes', uluɣmaq- 'crumple']
NAI uluk- 'rub and twist (skin or clothing)' [ulluk-, ulluuq- 'become crumpled, wrinkled']
WCI uluk- 'rub clothing or skin'
ECI uluk-
GRI uluɣ-, uluttuʀ- 'rub to soften (e.g. skin)'

PE uluʀ- 'turn edgewise or on side' [cf. uluʀya-]
AAY uluʀ- 'avert eyes'
CAY uluʀ- 'turn one's head and eyes away'
NSY uluʀ- [ANLC]
CSY ulaaʀ- 'put in a position so that a narrow object can enter a slot'
Sir —
SPI uluq- 'turn sideways to pass through a narrow passage'
NAI uluq- 'turn sideways to pass through a narrow passage, lie down on side, move aside'
WCI uluq- 'put on side (e.g. block of snow), stretch out on one's side'
ECI — [for Iti uluq- 'cut s.th. hard, hammering with a cold chisel' see uluʀaʀ-]
GRI uluŋa- 'lie crooked (e.g. boat on support)' [and note uluʀtit-, ulutsit- 'distort, twist']

PE uluʀaʀ- 'cut with a saw' [cf. ulu(ʀ)?]
AAY —
CAY NS uluaʀ- 'saw', uluaʀun 'saw'
NSY uluaXtə 'blade' [ANLC, which also has uluaXtaq 'plank']
CSY —
Sir —
SPI uluun 'saw'
NAI uluaqtuun, uluun
WCI uluaq- 'saw'
ECI [note Iti uluq- 'cut s.th. hard, hammering with a cold chisel', iluʀsit 'chisel, crowbar']
GRI —

PE uluʀya- 'flinch (in fear)' [cf. uluʀ-?]
AAY uluʀ(yuɣ)- 'dread, be apprehensive'
CAY uluʀya(yuɣ)- 'wince, afraid of being hit'
NSY uluʀyaʀaʀ- 'wince' [ANLC]
CSY —
Sir —
SPI uluʀiasuk- 'flinch', Qaw uluʀiaɣi- 'be wary of'
NAI uluʀiasuk- 'flinch', uluʀiaɣi- 'be apprehensive about', PH 'draw back from'
WCI uluʀiasuk- 'terrify' [and Net uluʀiahaaq- 'threaten' — Ras.]
ECI uluʀi 'watch out!', Lab uluʀiaq- 'turn aside, avoid' [Peck]
GRI uluʀiaʀ- 'rush back in fear', uluʀiaɣi- 'be terrified of' [and NG uluʀiahaaq- 'threaten']

PE uluʀyanaʀ- 'be dangerous or threatening' [cf. naʀ-]
AAY uluʀyanaʀ- 'cause dread'
CAY uluʀyanaXqə- 'be threatening, cause to wince or quiver with fear'
NSY uluʀyanaʀ- 'be threatening' [ANLC]
CSY —
Sir —
SPI uluʀianaq- 'be physically unsafe'
NAI —
WCI uluʀianaq- Sig 'be dangerous (e.g. sharp knife, bad dog)', Cop 'be painful'
ECI uluʀianaq- 'be such as to make you leap out of the way', Lab 'be dangerous' [Peck]
GRI uluʀianaʀ- 'be dangerous, make one jump back in fear'

PE uɫəʀ- and **uɫʀu-** 'fall' [cf. ulpəɣ-[2]]
AAY —
CAY [note Nun uɫixtə- 'turn over']
NSY —
CSY uɫəʀ- 'fall over'
Sir uɫəʀ- 'fall, overturn' [Vakh. also has uɫəʀlaʀ- 'go to bed' from Men.'s texts]
SPI uʀlu- 'fall, topple, or tip over'
NAI ulʀu-
WCI ulʀu- 'fall over'
ECI uʀʀu-
GRI uʀɫu- 'fall oveʀ' [and uʀɫuŋa- 'be on point of falling' — Oqaatsit has uʀɫiŋa- 'stand crooked']

PE uɫiʀ- 'crack (open)'
AAY [note AP uɫixtə- 'rummage, dig around']
CAY uɫiXtə- 'open or cut s.th. so as to expose the inside' [and Y uɫiʀnəq* 'cut'; also K uɫixtə- 'cut fish for drying' — for Nun uɫixtə- 'turn over' see uɫəʀ-]
NSY —
CSY —
Sir —
SPI uliq- 'break (of glass, crockery, wood utensil)'
NAI uliq- 'crack, chip (china, enamel)'
WCI uliq- 'tear, crack'
ECI uliq- 'make a crack in (porcelain, glass, stone)' [uliʀniq 'crack']
GRI —

PE uɫuɣay 'cheek' [cf. Aleut uluɣa-X 'cheek']
AAY Kod uɫuɣaq, PWS uɫuwak 'cheek'
CAY uɫuvak 'cheek'
NSY uɫəŋik [ANLC]

CSY ułuŋak
Sir ułuŋəx 'cheek' [and ułənžaXpałuʀaX 'chubby']
SPI Qaw uluak 'cheek'
NAI ulu<ž>ak 'cheek' [with non-historical ž]
WCI uluak
ECI uluaq
GRI uluak, pl. uluššat, EG uluaq 'cheek'

PI umak 'stitch in boots'
SPI —
NAI —
WCI Car umaɣaq 'blind stitch' [B.-S.]
ECI Lab umak 'stitch in boots' [Peck; and Boas has umaŋ 'stitch on top of boot sole' for Baffin; B.-S. has Igl umaaqtuq 'blind stitch']
GRI —

PE umðu- 'be thick' [cf. Atkan Aleut and western EA umðu- 'be swampy, soft to walk on (ground)', also Bering Island umðu-X 'snowdrift' given by Men.; there appears to be contam. with nəvðuʀ in Inu — note especially the EG form]
AAY —
CAY —
NSY —
CSY umu- 'be thick' [also 'sleep dreamily', and (with metathesis from *um(u)ɣatə-?) uɣməłi- 'get thinner', uɣmitaʀaq 'sea ice with thin spots', also Chap uɣməlʀu 'thick sea ice alternating with thin']
Sir umžəvalaX 'thick' [and note uɣmətaʀaX 'thin ice' — from CSY?]
SPI uvžu- 'be thick (e.g. ice)'
NAI PH uvžu-
WCI ivyu-
ECI iyyu-
GRI iššu- [old ortho. ivssu-], EG nittu- 'be thick' [contam. from nəvðuʀ in the latter? — Tersis has ittu-]

PE uməɣ- 'close off or cover' [cf. umək and EA umta- 'weigh on, squeeze', Atkan umusi-X 'implement for squeezing, head piece of drill' and/or Aleut umna- 'be watertight, leakproof']
AAY KP uməɣ- 'be cloudy, foggy', Kod 'have nose blocked, stuffed', umək 'fog, cloud' [and K umtə- 'be fogged up']
CAY umək 'door', uməɣ- 'close' [and Y umtə- 'be foggy', umta 'fog']
NSY umək 'cover', uməɣ- 'close' [Enm. et al.]
CSY uməɣ- 'close', umək 'door, cover' [and umɣək 'box']
Sir uməɣ-, umət- 'close' [Vakh., who also has uməkax 'snowstorm' from Rub.; Men. has umɣaX 'box' — 'woman's needlework container' acc. Em.]
SPI umik- 'close'
NAI umɨk- 'cover' [and umŋit- 'now be open']
WCI umik- 'close', umiqpik 'door, boat cover', Car? umiq 'skin tent [Schn. 'adg'; note also Sig upsaʀniq 'air entering through open door' — compare an(ə)caʀnəʀ under anə-]
ECI umik- 'fill with snow (cracks between snow house blocks)'
GRI umiɣ- 'pull entrance cover closed', NWG 'get thick with approaching rain or snow (air)', umik 'entrance cover of tent', NG 'door' [also ummisit-, umitsit- 'begin to thicken, become hazy', ussaʀniq* 'draught through entrance', and NG uŋŋiut(i)- 'open for someone']

PE umciɣ- 'be airtight or watertight'
AAY umciɣ- 'be airtight', PWS 'be stuffy (nose)' [KP umci- in the latter sense]
CAY umciɣ- 'be airtight' [and umci-, HBC umciɣi- 'be plugged (esp. nose)']
NSY [umsiɣ- 'close in (weather)' — ANLC]
CSY Chap umsiʀ- 'repair, patch (s.th. with many holes)'
Sir umsiqə(s)- 'plug up, close'
SPI upsik- 'be tightly woven'
NAI ufsik- 'be dense, closely grouped, tightly woven', PH upsitqik- 'be finely woven, not highly porous' [and ufsiɣɨ- 'fill up (cracks)']
WCI Car upsiXXuliq- 'tighten (snow hut)'
ECI utsiʀi- 'block holes between blocks in snow house' [and utsi(C)- 'become airtight (snow house, by filling fissures between blocks; utsitaq 'tightly woven windproof cloth']
GRI ussiɣ- 'be watertight' [old ortho. uvsig-; note also ussiʀi- 'caulk, tar']

PI umənŋatci- 'have a blocked-up nose'
Yup [for AAY, CAY umci- 'be plugged (esp. nose)' see under umciɣ- above]
SPI —
NAI umɨnɣatci- 'have a plugged-up nose'
WCI [note umiŋa- 'be nasal because the nose is blocked (voice)']
ECI umiŋŋasi- 'be blocked (nose)' [but umiŋa- 'be blocked (ears)']
GRI umiŋŋatsi- 'have a blocked-up nose, talk with a snuffle'

PI umək 'beard' [cf. uməɣ- if the trad. metaphorical link in the 'entrance cover of tent' sense holds, but compare also uŋak, which may be the same set]
SPI umik 'beard, whisker'
NAI umik 'beard' [ummak- 'grow a beard']
WCI umik 'beard' [Dor. has pl. umŋit 'beard' for B. Lake]
ECI umik 'beard' [umma(k)- 'grow a beard']
GRI umik 'whisker', uŋŋit, NG umiit 'beard' [and ummaɣ- 'grow a beard']

PI uməŋmak 'musk ox' [cf. p.b. vaɣ]
Yup [CAY Nun umiŋmaʀ is prob. from Inu]
SPI Qaw umiŋmak 'musk ox'
NAI umiŋmak, Mal also imummak
WCI Sig, Cop umiŋmak [Lowe]
ECI umimmak [Saul — Schn. has umimmaq]
GRI umimmak [old ortho. umingmak]

PI umŋiyaq- 'shave' [cf. ŋiyaʀ-]
Yup — [compare uŋaɣiʀ- under uŋak]
SPI uŋmiyaq- 'shave'

NAI umŋiyaq-
WCI Cop umŋiyaq-
ECI uŋŋiyaq-
GRI uŋŋiaʀ-, ummiaʀ-

PI umǝlʀuq 'snout' [cf. quʀ and presumably umǝk]
Yup [note CAY uŋalʀuk 'snout' from uŋak]
SPI umaʀlut 'snout (of walrus)'
NAI umilʀuq 'snout of animal, lower face of human', Nu imilʀuuk 'snout, nose'
WCI umilʀuk 'lips of human', Cop umilʀuq 'snout' [Ras.]
ECI umiʀʀuq 'beard and snout of animal'
GRI umiʀłuk 'lip (of seal or reindeer)'

PE umǝʀ- or **umiʀ-** 'look closely at'
AAY —
CAY —
NSY umiXtǝ- aim'
CSY —
Sir —
SPI umiq- 'take aim' [Imaq umiɣ-, umiɣužaʀ- acc. Men.]
NAI umiq- 'look closely at' [umiʀuq- 'look over, trying to make one's choice']
WCI —
ECI —
GRI umiʀ- 'look closely at' [also umiʀuʀ- and umiʀalaaʀ-; umiut(i)- 'aim at', NG umiʀuaq- 'look out of door or window' — Holt.]

PY umi- 'be absent or distant'
AAY umiqsiɣ- 'be very distant, barely audible' [umiqx^{w}anǝk 'heard from a distance']
CAY umi- 'be absent' [and umiqsiɣ- 'be almost inaudible because of the distance', umiqfanǝk 'heard from the distance']
NSY —
CSY —

PI umiaq 'large skin-covered boat' [cf. yaʀ; there may be a link to umǝɣ-; compare PY aŋyaq]
SPI umiaq 'large skin-covered boat'
NAI umiaq 'boat' [as verb = 'launch a boat', PH 'be out in a whaling boat'; also umiʀʀiq- 'prepare to go whaling', umii-, umiʀʀi- 'make a boat']
WCI umiaq 'boat (previously seal-skin)'
ECI umiaq '(seal-skin) boat' [and umiiyaq- 'wreck a boat']
GRI umiaq 'traditional 'women's boat' [pl. umiat = 'woman's boat plus crew'; umiatsiaq 'boat', umiiaʀ- 'be shipwrecked', umii- 'put boat on land for a fairly long time']

PI umialǝk 'captain of whaling boat' [cf. lǝɣ]
Yup [the Inu term has been borrowed as umialǝk CAY NSU 'wealthy person', NSY 'strong man, leader' and CSY umiilǝk 'leader, boss']
SPI umialik 'boat owner, rich man'
NAI umialik 'whaling captain, boss, rich person'
WCI Sig umialik 'rich person'
ECI umialittaaq 'captain of ship'
GRI EG umialik 'captain' [Robbe and Menn.]

PI umiaʀluk- 'raft across open water' [cf. łuɣ]
SPI umiaʀluk- 'cross open water on an icefloe' [nom. = 'raft']
NAI umiaʀluk- 'cross open water on an icefloe' [nom. = 'raft, icefloe used to cross open water']
WCI umiaʀluk 'raft'
ECI umiaʀluk- 'sail on a piece of ice as if on a boat' [nom. = 'raft']
GRI umiaʀłuɣ- 'drift or travel on an icefloe'

PI umiiqǝ- 'prepare one's boat' [cf. liqǝ-]
SPI umiiqi- 'prepare one's boat'
NAI umiiqɨ-
WCI —
ECI umiiʀi- 'beach or launch a boat'
GRI umiiʀi- 'work on a boat (landing or putting it into the water)'

PI umiu- 'capsize' [cf. umiaq and compare qayau- under qayaʀ — the exact relat. is unclear]
SPI umiu- 'capsize, turn over in sled'
NAI umiu- 'capsize'
WCI —
ECI umiu- 'capsize, be thrown overboard'
GRI umiu- 'be shipwrecked'

PE umkuʀaʀ 'cover over doorway' [cf. umǝɣ- and upkaq?]
AAY —
CAY —
NSY umku 'temporary door' [Em.; but Men.'s umkǝ 'stronghold' ('lobby of men's house' acc. L.-T.), also umku as 'temporary dwelling, stronghold', and umkutak 'snow shelter for fishing through ice' are probably from Chukchi umǝkǝt- 'gather', and/or with contam. from upkaq]
CSY umkuʀaq 'door'
Sir —
SPI W upkuaq, ukkuaq 'curtain over doorway' [Jen.]
NAI upkuaq, ukkuaq 'door'
WCI upkuaq 'door', Net ukkuaq 'snow door block' [Ras.; Pryde has Cop, Net, Car ukkuaq 'block of snow to close entrance of snowhouse, door, gate']
ECI ukkuaq 'door' [and Lab ukkuk 'division wall between rooms']
GRI ukkuaq 'skin hung as door before entrance, or by shaman to curtain self during seance'

PE umłuʀ 'day' [or umluʀ — cf. lu(ʀ)?]
AAY —
CAY —
NSY —
CSY —
Sir umłǝX 'day' [and umłuXtułǝmi 'for a long time'; Em. has umłǝqu 'in the daytime' and umłułqusiX 'all day']
SPI uvluq 'day' [as verb = 'become day']
NAI NS uvluq 'day' [uvlupak, S Mal, Nu uɣlupak, N Mal uvluvak 'today', uvluq- 'become day']

WCI uvluq 'day'
ECI ulluq 'day' [ullu(q)- 'have become day']
GRI uɫɫuq 'day' [uɫɫuʀ- 'have become day']

PI umlaaq 'morning' [from *umlu(ʀ)aq with aʀ?]
SPI uvlaaq 'morning' [and uvlaakun 'tomorrow']
NAI uvlaaq 'morning' [and uvlaaku(n) 'tomorrow']
WCI uvlaaq 'morning' [and Sig uvlaakun 'tomorrow']
ECI ullaaq 'morning' [and ullaakut 'in the morning', ullaaʀuq- 'get up early']
GRI uɫɫaaq 'morning' [uɫɫaakut 'in the morning', uɫɫaaʀuʀ- 'leave early in the morning']

PI umli- 'spend the day' [cf. li-[1]]
SPI uvli- 'spend the day'
NAI uvli- 'spend the day, take a day's rest'
WCI uvliu- 'spend the day'
ECI ulli-
GRI uɫɫi- 'spend the day'

PI umlumi 'today' [loc. case of umluq 'day']
SPI [uvluminin 'today']
NAI [uvlumin^{y}in^y 'every day']
WCI uvlumi 'today'
ECI ullumi
GRI uɫɫumi

PI umluʀiaq 'star' [cf. yaʀ?]
SPI uvluʀiaq 'star'
NAI uvluʀiaq
WCI uvluʀiaq
ECI ulluʀiaq
GRI uɫɫuʀiaq [old ortho. uvdloriaq]

PY-S umyuɣžaq 'mind or thought' [there could be a link to uməʀ-]
AAY umyaaXtəqə- 'think', umyaaq, umyuaq 'mind'
CAY umyu(ɣ)aq, NS umsu(ɣ)aq 'mind, thought, idea', umyuaXtəqə-, umyuɣaXtuʀ- 'think' [and umyu(ɣ)aqə- 'think about'; note also NS umə- 'panic' and NSU umsuaXulaaʀ- 'be in a panic']
NSY umyuɣaq 'mind, character, will', umyuɣaazaXtə- 'think'
CSY umyuɣaq 'mind, character'
Sir umiɣcəɫəx 'sensible' [Vakh. has umiɣcəŋə- 'get wise'; Em. has umiɣcəX 'thought, consciousness, character'; for umyəʀaʀ- 'talk' see əmə]

PY umyuɣaʀitə- 'be stupid' [cf. ŋit-]
AAY —
CAY umyuaʀitə-, umyuɣaitə- 'be stupid, lack mental ability'
NSY umyuɣailŋuq 's.o. who has gone crazy, become stupid'
CSY umyuɣiitə- 'be thoughtless, insensitive'

PY-S una-[1] 'handle' [cf. unaðmi-, unataq-, unakə-, unaŋə- and Aleut una- 'cook, boil, bake, prepare food', EA also 'heat (steambath)']
AAY una- 'handle'
CAY una- 'work on by hand tool' [and unayaqə- 'invite along', unan 'hand, seal flipper', unaŋiɣ- 'be dexterous (especially at picking berries)']
NSY —
CSY ➡
Sir — [for unayəʀ- 'take, steal from' see ivayaʀ-] ➡

PY-S unakə- 'catch or manage to handle' [cf. kə-[1] and compare unaŋə- below]
AAY unakə- 'be able to lift or handle, persuade to do s.th.' [and KP unaksa'utə- 'tempt, try to talk into']
CAY unakə- 'go get'
NSY —
CSY unakə- 'catch by hunting, hit with bullet, etc.'
Sir unəkə- 'catch'

PY-S unaŋə- 'obtain or catch' [cf. ŋə- under nəɣ-?]
AAY unaŋə- 'obtain'
CAY unaŋə-
NSY —
CSY unaŋə- 'catch sea mammal' [and unaŋniitXa 'hunter']
Sir unəŋniXta 'hunter' [Vakh. also has unəŋə- 'catch']

PI una-[2] 'frolic' [cf. unasuk; there may be a link to una-[1] — note the 'pet' sense below]
Yup [note NSU una- 'play (of pups)' — from the Inu?]
SPI una- 'play, frolic'
NAI una- 'be playful (dog)'
WCI una- 'pet', Net 'wag tail, bark at game (dog)'
ECI una- 'show delight at return of master (dog)'
GRI una- 'fawn on, caress, wag tail' [and unaqut 'sweetheart', unaɫɫiʀ- 'tease, provoke (polar bear, of a dog)']

PE unaðmi- 'challenge' [cf. unataq- and una-[1]]
AAY —
CAY Nun unazmiuʀ- 'challenge'
NSY —
CSY unaymiʀ- 'feel capable of acting'
Sir —
SPI —
NAI —
WCI Sig unanmiɣi- 'believe one can do easily', Cop unaŋmi- 'try to emulate in singing and dancing' [Jen.], Car unanmia(C)- 'think self better than another' [Schn., who also has it as 'hate with idea of defeating, killing' for 'adg']
ECI unammi- 'believe self capable of doing, worthy of receiving' [also unammia(C)-]
GRI unammi- [old ortho. unangmi-] 'compete with, challenge'

PE unaliʀ 'person from another tribe or from the coast?' [cf. dem. root un- and p.b. l(l)iʀ, parallel to kival(l)iʀ under kivan; perhaps originally from a CAY point of view]
AAY —
CAY unaliq 'Norton Sound Yupik'
NSY unaliʀmii 'Norton Sound Alaskan Eskimo' [ANLC]

CSY —
Sir —
SPI unaliq 'Norton Sound Yupik'
NAI —
WCI Car unaliq 'Cree Indian' ['Dene Indian' at B. Lake acc. Dor.]
ECI unaliq 'enemy, soldier, dangerous person'
GRI —

PI unaŋuq- 'become tired' [cf. una(C)ɪʀ- and ŋ(ŋ)uʀ-?]
SPI unaŋuq- 'be tired, weak'
NAI unaŋuq- 'become tired'
WCI unaɣuq-
ECI —
GRI —

PE unaʀcɪʀ 'driftwood (used for making things)' [cf. una-¹?]
AAY unaʀsaak, unaʀsaaq 'splinter' [and unaʀcaaq 'game played with sticks']
CAY unaXciaq, munaXciaq 'straight-grained piece of wood useful for making things' [the second form contaminated by munaʀ- 'be dexterous'?]
NSY unaXsiq 'wood, log, plank' [L.-T. has unaXsiaq]
CSY unaXsiq 'wood for making s.th.'
Sir —
SPI unaqsiq 'driftwood', Qaw 'tree'
NAI PH unaqsiq 'wood'
WCI —
ECI —
GRI unaʀsivik 'driftwood used for bird or bladder dart'

PY-S unaʀɪʀ- 'become limp or numb' [cf. unaŋuq- and p.b. ŋɪʀ-]
AAY unaiʀ-, unaitə-, PWS uniiʀ-, uniitə- 'be or get soft' [and unaiqsi- 'get limp']
CAY unaiʀ- 'lose coordination, become numb, be spastic'
NSY uniaʀ- 'relax muscles, be limp' [ANLC]
CSY uniiʀ- 'become limp, paralysed, lose muscle control'
Sir unaʀəryuɣ- 'be depressed' [Em.; also unaʀəlŋuX 'weak', unaʀəci- 'get weak, unaʀunaʀən 'weakly, gently, quietly'; Vakh. has unaʀət(ə)- 'be weak' from Rub.'s texts]

PI unasuk 'next youngest child' [cf. una-² and yuɣ-?]
SPI —
NAI unasuk- 'be cranky sensing mother is pregnant with a second child'
WCI Car? unasuk 'next younger brother or sister' [Schn. 'adg']
ECI [unasuɣiik 'two siblings, one older than the other' — old word at W. Bay acc. Schn.]
GRI unasuŋiaq 'next youngest child (who would still be suckling if there weren't a younger child)'

PI unataq- 'beat or struggle' [cf. una-¹ and unaðmi-?]
Yup — [for AAY, CAY, CSY unataʀ- 'pick greens or berries' see unataʀ-]
SPI —
NAI unataq- 'persist, refuse to give up on s.th.' [Jen. has 'wrestle'; unataun 'club']
WCI unataq- Sig 'beat', Car 'whip up sea (wind)', Net 'kill', Cop unatai- 'fight' [Ras.; EP unataq- 'fight' acc. Ow.]
ECI unataq- 'try to kill (another human), struggle against' [unatauti 'weapon']
GRI unataʀ- 'beat, NWG 'kill harpooned animal with lance'

PY unataʀ- 'pick greens or berries' [this could be from *nunataʀ- with base nuna and p.b. taʀ-, contaminated by una-¹, though the NSK below could rather be contaminated by nuna, and this base could be from una-¹ and an unidentified postbase — cf. t(t)aʀ-?]
AAY AP unataʀ- 'pluck berries'
CAY unataʀ-, NSK nunataʀ- 'pluck berries'
NSY unataʀ- 'pick berries or greens' [ANLC; Men. has unataq 'sweet edible root']
CSY unataʀ- 'pick greens' [and Men. has unataq 'leguminous plant' for Chap]
Sir [unataʀ- 'pick greens' is probably borrowed from CSY — Orr]
Inu — [but compare NAI nunataq- 'fetch sod']

PE unəɣ- 'remain' [cf. unit-]
AAY unəxtə- 'remain, stay behind'
CAY unəxtə-
NSY unəxtə- 'remain, leave behind'
CSY unəxtə- 'stay or keep behind'
Sir unəxtə- 'remain behind' [Vakh.; Men. has unətə-, for which see unit-]
SPI unik- 'stay behind'
NAI unik- 'be left behind'
WCI unik- 'stay or leave behind' [and Sig uniɣautit 'brake for sled']
ECI unik- 'stop, give up'
GRI uniɣ- 'stop, remain, be taken to hospital'

PE unəʀ 'armpit' [cf. Aleut unʀ-im sitx-a 'armpit' (with sitx- 'under') and Atkan quɣanam unʀ-a 'narrow space between rocks'; the relat. — if any — to inək is obscure]
AAY unəq 'armpit'
CAY unəq*
NSY unəʀžəʀaq 'underarm' [ANLC has unəʀžəɣaq 'underarm, armpit', unəʀmiɣ- 'put under one's arm'; note also perhaps uaniq 'underarm odor, stink' (ANLC)]
CSY unəq* 'armpit, underarm' [for inək 'armpit, groin' see inək, and note unəʀžuxtaq 'bag or purse with shoulder strap carried hanging down under one's arm'; and note uuyni 'underarm odor']
Sir [Em. has unəʀžuxtaX 'bag carried over shoulder on strap containing amulets'; for inaqužɣaX 'armpit' see inək]
SPI uniq 'armpit'
NAI uniq*
WCI uniq
ECI uniq
GRI uniq*, EG uʀnaq

PE unəRaR 'harpoon' [the relat. — if any — to uRnəɣ- and/or uRniR- is obscure]
AAY Kod unRaat 'whaling spears' [Lisianski has uunxat]
CAY NSU unRaq 'spear with line attached' [and Jen. has unaRaq 'sealing harpoon' for Nun]
NSY unRaq 'harpoon'
CSY uunRaq* 'harpoon' [and uunRaaXsi- 'aim harpoon']
Sir [note unRaR- 'approach']
SPI unaaq 'harpoon'
NAI unaaq 'seal or walrus spear, stick used to test ice or water' [pl. uniRRat = 'toggleheads']
WCI Cop, Car unaaq 'harpoon' [Dor. has 'small harpoon' for Car but Schn. has 'handle of harpoon' for 'adg'; note also Cop unRaR- 'make sign of cross' — compaare CSY qaquuzaq under qaqu(R)]
ECI unaaq 'seal harpoon', NBI, Aiv 'small harpoon'
GRI unaaq 'harpoon (shaft)' [pl. unaXXat; unaaRiaR- 'throw harpoon']

PI uni(C)aq- 'pull or drag [the ž in NAI forms may be non-historical]
SPI uniaq- 'pull, drag', uniaRaq- 'travel by dogsled' [and pl. uniat 'sled', Qaw unižaqtuun 'sled reindeer']
NAI uni<ž>aq- 'tow, drag, pull', uniaRaq- 'travel with dog team' [and uniat 'sled', du. uniak 'sled runners', PH unižžat 'reindeer sled', Nu uniqqat 'toboggan']
WCI uniaq- 'tow, pull' [and uniqqat 'sled', Sig uniaq 'basket sledge' — rare, acc. Met.]
ECI uniaq- 'pull, drag' [and uniRRaq 'tracks of sled in snow']
GRI uniaR- 'drag' [and uniXXaq* 'traces left of seal being dragged along', uniaaq 's.th. dragged along']

> **PI uniun** 'tow rope' [cf. un]
> SPI uniutaq 'tow rope'
> NAI Nu, PH uniutaq 'tow line, drag line'
> WCI —
> ECI uniutaq 'rope for dragging (e.g. toboggan)'
> GRI uniut 'rope for pulling, leash'

PE unit- 'leave behind' [cf. unəɣ- — the relationship between the two bases is not clear, but this set probably with t-[1], so from *unəɣt-?]
AAY unitə- 'leave or be left behind'
CAY unitə- 'leave behind' [and uni- 'dissolve, disappear'?]
NSY unitə- 'leave behind, forget'
CSY unitə-
Sir [unətə- 'remain behind'; Vakh. has unat- 'leave behind']
SPI unit- 'leave behind'
NAI unit-
WCI —
ECI —
GRI —

PE uni(C)uR- 'miss the mark' [cf. Aleut unuqu- 's.o. else, other, foreign', earlier Atkan abl. 'from somewhere else, differently, otherwise' and unuqumuðaRan 'in a different direction, aside']
AAY uniuXtə- 'miss'
CAY uniuXtə- 'overlook, miss the mark'
NSY uniiX^{w}tə-, uniXsiR- 'miss the mark' [ANLC; Men. has uniuR-]
CSY —
Sir —
SPI uniuq- 'miss target, overlook, fall short'
NAI uniuq-
WCI uniuq- 'miss'
ECI uniuq- 'miss, pass by'
GRI uniuR- 'miss'

PE univkaRaR 'story' [or uŋivkaRaR? — cf. unniR- and vkaR- and Atkan Aleut uniika-X, eastern EA uŋiika-X, Unalaska uŋiika-X, Nikolski uŋ̊iika-X, Att uɣyi(i)ka-X 'tale' (and verbal 'tell a (fictive) story') — from the Esk.?]
AAY unixkuaq 'story, legend, myth'
CAY NS unifkaRaq
NSY unikpaRaq 'story, myth' [and Taghyuq has unikpaaq 'piece of news', L.-T. has unikpaRaq and unikpak 'news']
CSY uŋipaRaq 'story, legend' [uŋipaRaR- 'tell a story', uŋipaq 'news', uŋipaR- 'spread news, inform']
Sir [Vakh has uŋəpəR- 'tell a story' from Men.'s texts; for unəRcaX 'story' see unniR-]
SPI unipkaaq 'story, legend' [also verbal]
NAI unipkaaq, ulipkaaq, Mal unipcaaq 'old story, legend' [as verb = 'tell (story)']
WCI unipkaaq 'legend'
ECI unikkaaq 'story, gossip' [as verb = 'relate']
GRI unikkaaq [old ortho. univkâq] 'story' [unikkaaR- 'narrate, tell about s.th.', NG unikkaaq- 'tell', unikkaaqtuaq- 'tell a story']

PI unni(in) 'whatever' [cf. unniR- — from the 2s imperative?]
SPI unniin 'even' [enclitic]
NAI unnii 'regardless, anyway, even' [encl.]
WCI Sig un(n)in 'too bad' [rare acc. Met., used in stories; and luunnii(t) 'or, even, -ever' — encl.]
ECI unniit, unnit 'even, it doesn't matter', Lab 'so so, it is unsatisfactory because -' [also encl.]
GRI unnia 'it is said', unni(i)t 'although' [old ortho. uvnît with spurious v], NG unniit 'it doesn't matter' [also encl. luunniit 'or, even, -ever']

PE unniR- 'say or tell' [cf. univkaRaR and unni(in)]
AAY —
CAY —
NSY —
CSY —
Sir uniX '(piece of) news', uniRcaX 'story' [verbal = 'tell tale'; also uniXɬəɣuR- 'tell s.th.'; Vakh. has unəRcəX 'story' and uniRət- 'tell, speak']
SPI —
NAI ➟
WCI unniq- 'tell, narrate' [and unniqsiuq- 'tell s.th. about oneself']
ECI unnisiuq- 'tell of one's gratitude', Lab 'go to tell

someone, look for shelter or a defender'
GRI unniʀ- 'say (of one)', NG unniut(i)- 'be known, told' [unniʀsiuʀ- 'tell of s.th. happy that has happened']

PI unniqtuq- 'promise' [cf. tuq-²]
SPI unnatuq- 'promise'
NAI unniqsuq-
WCI unniqtuq-
ECI unnituq- 'tell to take and use s.th.' [and unnituqtaq 'person to whom s.th. is promised or permitted']
GRI unniʀsuʀ- 'promise' [and unniʀsuut(i)- 'show way, instruct']

PI unniʀluk- 'complain' [cf. łuɣ(-)]
SPI [note unnaziuq- 'complain']
NAI unniʀlʸuk- 'complain'
WCI Cop unniʀluk- 'blab' [Pryde]
ECI unniluk- 'complain, accuse'
GRI unniʀłuɣ- 'complain about s.th.'

PE unnuɣ 'night' [cf. EA unuɣ-ulux, Atkan unuɣ-ulax 'long ago' (lit. 'not tonight'?)]
AAY unuk 'night', unuɣ- 'be(come) night'
CAY unuk 'night, last night', unuɣ- 'become night'
NSY unuk 'night', unuɣ- 'become night'
CSY unuk 'night, last night', unuɣ- 'become night'
Sir unux 'night' [also verbal unuɣ-]
SPI unnuk 'evening'
NAI unnuk 'evening' [verbal = 'become evening'; unnui- 'spend the night, work during the night']
WCI unnuk 'evening' [as verb = 'become night']
ECI unnuk 'evening' [as verb = 'become night']
GRI unnuk 'evening', unnuɣ- 'fall (of evening)' [unnui- 'spend the night out']

PE unnu(C)aʀ '(early) morning' [cf. aʀ]
AAY unuaq 'morning'
CAY unuaq 'this morning'
NSY unua(q) 'morning'
CSY unaaq* 'morning, this morning' [and unaami 'tomorrow']
Sir —
SPI unnuaq 'night'
NAI unnuaq 'night, last night, PH 'yesterday'
WCI unnuaq 'night'
ECI unnuaq
GRI unnuaq 'night, last night' [old pl. unuššat]

PE unnuʀaqu 'tomorrow' [or tomorrow night; cf. ku]
AAY unuaqu 'tomorrow' [compare unuaka'aʀmi 'early this morning']
CAY unuaqu 'tomorrow'[but unuaku 'tomorrow morning', unuakuaʀ 'early in the morning', unuakuayaaʀ 'very early in the morning']
NSY unuaqu 'tomorrow' [L.-T., Men. has unuaku 'at the onset of night', also unuakuya 'tomorrow', for which Miller has unuaku]
CSY unaaqu 'postponed until tomorrow'
Sir unəʀaqu 'tomorrow'
SPI —
NAI unnuaʀu 'night still to come, tomorrow night'
WCI —
ECI —
GRI unnuaʀu 'tonight (to come)'

PY-S unuɣcaʀun 'gnat, mosquito' [cf. p.b. un, perhaps unnuɣ]
AAY —
CAY —
NSY —
CSY unuŋsaan 'gnat, midge'
Sir unuxsaʀəta 'mosquito' [Orr]

PI unuq- 'be many'
SPI —
NAI —
WCI Car unuʀniq 'most manifold' [i.e. 'many' — from Ras.'s texts]
ECI unuq- 'be many', unuʀniq 'many, majority', Lab ununnik 'amount, sum'
GRI —

PE uŋa- 'cling to (child to adult)' [cf. EA uŋaalʀi-X 'young of sea lion or seal (up to 4 months)']
AAY [note uxa- 'be satisfied, agreeable']
CAY uŋa- 'show affectionate attachment by clinging (usu. child to adult)'
NSY uŋa- 'fawn up to someone' [L.-T.]
CSY —
Sir —
SPI uŋa- 'act cute, childish'
NAI uŋa- 'act as if one wants to be loved and cuddled (of child)' [uŋaaq 'person who acts childishly, lets others do his work' — also as a verb for to act that way]
WCI uŋa- 'cry after parents (of child)' [Pryde also 'yearn for, miss']
ECI uŋa- 'feel affection for s.o. absent', Lab 'be attached to' [Peck; uŋanaq- 'be lovable', Iti 'be missed (a generous person)']
GRI uŋa- 'cling to (child to mother)' [and uŋaaq 'infant', uŋanaʀ- 'be liked so much that people don't want to leave it (place or person)']

PY-S uŋak 'beard or mustache' [compare uməɣ for the Inu equivalent — since morpheme-internal *mŋ does not seem to occur in Yup this base could be from the same base (via *umŋak?)]
AAY uŋak 'mustache or beard hair'
CAY uŋak
NSY uŋak
CSY uŋak
Sir uŋax 'mustache or beard hair' [Orr — Men. has pl. uŋəɣəy Men.]

PY-S uŋaɣiʀ- 'shave' [cf. ŋiʀ-]
AAY uŋaiʀ- 'shave'
CAY uŋaiʀ-
NSY uŋiaʀ-
CSY uŋaɣiʀ-
Sir uŋəɣiʀ-

PY-S uŋaɣžaq 'reindeer moss'
AAY [note napat uŋałʀit 'tree lichen']
CAY uŋaɣaq, uŋaxaq, uŋaɣuaq 'black reindeer moss'
NSY uŋaɣaq '(reindeer) moss'
CSY uŋaɣaq 'lichen, reindeer moss'
Sir uŋəɣcəx 'moss'

PE uŋan (uŋatə) 'area beyond (partition)' [from demonstrative-like root uŋ-, related perhaps to iŋ-, and p.b. tə; compare uɣan, but also PY iŋa(va)- and iŋan]
AAY ➞
CAY ➞
NSY [uŋavžaq 'current from north through Bering Strait']
CSY uŋavik 'temporary box-like sleeping quarters of reindeer skin or cloth within the trad. house'
Sir uŋəvəx, uŋəvɣəX 'canopy' [Vakh.; Men. has uŋavikutax 'blanket'; Orr has uŋəvikutaX 'blanket'; Em. has uŋəvəx 'sleeping compartment in summer skin tent']
SPI uŋati 'south'
NAI uŋati 'space beyond' [posit. root], uŋan 'partition in house, space beside bedding'
WCI uŋati 'space beyond' [posit. root; uŋatak 'part farthest away']
ECI uŋat(i) 'partition wall, something distant' [as posit. root 'beyond']
GRI uŋat(i) 'side wall', [as posit. root] 'other side', NG 'left side of sleeping platform (wife's)' [EG uali(q) 'side wall of traditional house, beyond, on far side' — Tersis]

PE uŋalaʀ 'wind from a certain direction' [cf. uŋal(l)iq below, though the relat. is unclear, also probably Aleut ŋa-, ŋu-, na-, nu- 'south'; see Fortescue 1988 for the specific local directions involved]
AAY uŋalaq 'east wind'
CAY uŋalaq 'south wind'
NSY uŋalaq
CSY —
Sir —
SPI uŋalaq, uŋaliq 'south wind' [the second form due to uŋal(l)iq below]
NAI uŋala(a)q 'southwest wind' [and place name uŋalaqłiit 'Unalakleet']
WCI uŋalaq 'west wind'
ECI —
GRI —

PI uŋal(l)iaɣu 'day after tomorrow' [cf. uŋal(l)iq below and ku following 3s poss. inflection]
SPI uŋaliaku 'the day after tomorrow' [compare uŋaliakni 'the day before yesterday']
NAI uŋaliaɣu, Nu uŋalliaɣu 'the day after tomorrow' [and compare uŋal(l)iani 'the day before yesterday']
WCI Sig uŋaliaɣu 'day after tomorrow' [compare uŋaliani 'day before yesterday']
ECI uŋalliaɣu 'day after tomorrow' [and uŋalliani 'day before yesterday']
GRI —

PI uŋal(l)iq 's.th. outermost or on the far side' [cf. l(l)iʀ; there may be an earlier deriv. uŋaliʀ (directly on the dem. root) and a later one uŋalliʀ — compare civul(l)iʀ under civu-]
Yup [note CSY place name uŋaziq 'Chaplino', possibly reflecting the Sir form below]
Sir [uŋəłəX 'elder brother', but note also uŋəcəX 'Chaplino' — Vakh.]
SPI [for uŋaliq 'south wind' see above under uŋalaʀ]
NAI uŋalliq* 'outer door'
WCI uŋalliq 'one farthest away, last'
ECI uŋalliq 'one farthest away'
GRI uŋaliq(*) 'one nearest on the other side, one farthest away', uŋałłiq* 'one next to side wall, outermost' [and note uŋalisaq 'wall covering']

PI uŋalu 'enclosure' [cf. lu(ʀ)]
SPI —
NAI —
WCI [Net uŋaluužaq 'makeshift cooking vessel made of flat stone slabs' — Pryde]
ECI uŋaluk 'foundation of snow house, first circle of blocks'
GRI uŋaluq 'fence, enclosure, cover (of book)' [and uŋalu- 'fence in']

PI uŋasik- 'be far' [cf. ðiɣ-]
Yup — [but compare AAY yaqsəɣ-, CAY yaaqsiɣ- 'be far' under iŋa(va)-]
SPI uŋasik- 'be far'
NAI uŋasik-
WCI uŋasik-
ECI uŋasik-
GRI uŋasiɣ- 'be far' [and EG uasinni 'elsewhere' — Robbe and Menn. have uasiani]

PI uŋavaq 'area beyond or far away' [cf. p.b. vaʀ- and compare PY-S uyavaʀ-]
Yup — [for AAY, CAY yaaqfa(ni) '(in) area farther away' see iŋa(va)-]
SPI uŋavaq- 'tear off, free from s.th., remove, cut off' [and note Imaq uŋavžaq 'current through Bering Strait' — from the NSY under uŋan above?]
NAI uŋavaq- 'stray to one side'
WCI uŋavaq 'distance' [verbal = 'go afar, remove']
ECI uŋava 'distance' [and uŋavva(q)- 'go into the distance']
GRI uŋavaq 'area beyond' [and uŋavariaʀ- 'go farther off (seal when hunter tries to lure it nearer to ice edge)']

PI uŋayu(t)- 'cut out?' [cf. perhaps EA uŋa- 'break, be broken, be torn (off)']
SPI uŋayu- 'cut out, extract'
NAI uŋayut- 'cut out, extract' [also uŋuyut- 'perform blood-letting on s.o.']

WCI —
ECI —
GRI —

PE uŋəʀ- 'lace up' [cf. uŋuʀ-]
AAY —
CAY —
NSY —
CSY uŋłəɣ- 'gather or draw together with folds or pleats, wrinkle with age, withdraw from activity' (with ləɣ-?)
Sir uŋləɣ- 'wrinkle, fold, pleat' [Em. has uŋłəɣ-; uŋlaɣaXłəX 'wrinkle']
SPI uŋiʀutaq 'drawstring', uŋiʀvik 'felt band around mukluk top'
NAI uŋiq- 'tie with drawstring' [and uŋižaq-, PH uŋižžaq- 'pleat, pucker, ruffle']
WCI uŋiq- 'tie up, lace up'
ECI uŋiq- 'tie a boot string' [and uŋŋitaq 'belt for caribou skin trousers', uŋŋuaq 'button'; Saul also has uŋiaq- 'gather, pucker (fabric)']
GRI uŋiʀ- 'lash, tie up (boots, sleeves with strings)' [and uŋŋiaʀ- 'put folds or pleats in', uŋŋiaq 'fold, pleat', uŋŋiʀsaq 'waist strap, belt'; for uŋŋutit 'creases in front of sole of boot by which it is drawn in to the upper' see uŋuʀ-]

PI uŋəʀlaun 'lace' [cf. un]
SPI —
NAI —
WCI Net uŋuʀlaun 'tent-flap lacing' [Pryde, who also has Cop uŋiʀlak 'sealskin bag for storing fish', and as a verb 'fasten with a lace'; Met. has Cop uŋiʀlaq 'meat sack closed with lacing strap']
ECI uŋiʀlauti 'lace to tie up meat or European boots' [uŋiʀla(k)- 'lace up, repair with big stitches']
GRI uŋiʀłaat 'lacing strap for capelin bag' [uŋiʀłattuʀ- 'lace up crosswise']

PY uŋi- 'get soggy'
AAY PWS uŋi- 'get soggy'
CAY uŋi-
NSY —
CSY —

PE uŋilaɣ- 'itch'
AAY uŋilaɣ(yuɣ)- 'be hateful' [compare kuməɣ-]
CAY uŋilaɣ- 'itch' [and uŋilak 'louse, spruce cone']
NSY uŋilaɣ- 'scratch' [ANLC; L.-T. has uŋilak 'combing']
CSY uŋilaɣ- 'itch'
Sir uŋələɣ- [Orr]
SPI —
NAI uŋilʸak-, uŋŋi- 'get an itchy rash, pimples, or hives, ripple (of water)' [Nu has uŋi- 'get a rash']
WCI uŋilak- 'itch'
ECI uŋilak-
GRI uŋilaɣ-, EG ualaaʀ- 'itch' [Robbe and Menn. for the latter]

PE uŋlu 'nest' [the m/v in forms like umlu due to assimilation?; there may be a link to uŋəʀ- (with lu(ʀ))]
AAY uŋluq 'nest'
CAY uŋlu
NSY umlu 'nest, lair'
CSY uŋlun 'nest' [and note uŋləʀ- 'nestle down in a ball (dogs, etc.)']
Sir uŋluta 'nest'
SPI uɣlu(t), Imaq uɣlun
NAI uɣlu, Mal uvluun
WCI uvlu, uvluun
ECI ullu 'nest'
GRI ułut [old ortho. uvdlut] 'down, bird's nest'

PE uŋpəɣ 'owl'
AAY —
CAY Nun uŋpaaʀ(aX), NSU uŋpək 'short-eared owl'
NSY ukpək 'forest owl' [from, or influenced by, Inu?]
CSY —
Sir —
SPI ukpik 'snowy owl'
NAI ukpik
WCI ukpik
ECI uppik
GRI uppik [old ortho. ugpik]

PE uŋu- 'drive game into area to be killed' [cf. Att Aleut uŋuuluX 'escape tunnel from native turf hut' with p.b. aluX 'place for'?]
AAY uŋu- 'drive game into an area to be killed'
CAY uŋu-
NSY uŋu-
CSY Chap uŋyuxtə-
Sir —
SPI uŋut-
NAI uŋu-, uŋužaq- 'drive game into area to be killed' [and uŋut-, PH uŋullaq- 'chase away so it will not return']
WCI uŋu-, uŋut- 'drive game into area to be killed' [and note Cop uŋu- 'come to breathing hole (seal)' in Jen.; Cop uŋullaq- 'whip (dog)' — Lowe]
ECI uŋu- 'drive into area to be killed' [and Peck has uŋu- 'flee to its breathing hole (seal)' for Lab]
GRI uŋu- 'drive game into area to be killed, surround, besiege'

PI uŋuuq- 'drive in front of one (animals)' [cf. (C)uʀ-]
Yup — [but note CAY uŋuuʀvik 'February']
SPI uŋuuq- 'drive animals'
NAI uŋuuq- 'drive in front of one (of game animal, toward waiting hunter)'
WCI uŋuuq- [Pryde]
ECI uŋuuʀaq- 'chase several animals' [and Peck has ungor- 'drive in front of one' for Lab]
GRI uŋuuʀ- 'drive in front of one (animal)'

PE uŋuləɣ- 'shake or tremble' [cf. ləɣ-]
AAY uuləɣ- 'shake'
CAY uuləxtə- 'shiver, shake'
NSY uuləxtə- 'shake, tremble' [ANLC]
CSY uŋələxtə- 'shake, tremble'
Sir —

SPI uulik- 'tremble, shiver, shake'
NAI uulik-
WCI uulik- 'tremble with cold or fear'
ECI uulik-
GRI uuliɣ-

PE uŋuma- 'be alive' [cf. (u)ma- — with dissim. in Yup]
AAY uŋuva- 'be alive'
CAY uŋuva- 'be alive' [and nominal = 'life']
NSY uŋuva- 'be alive' [L.-T. has umuva-]
CSY uŋuva-
Sir uŋəvə-
SPI uuma- 'be alive' [and uumažuaq 'animal']
NAI uuma- 'be alive (animal)'
WCI uuma- 'be alive'
ECI uuma- 'be alive (animal)' [uumayuq 'animal']
GRI uuma- 'be alive' [uumašuq 'animal']

PY uŋu(C)iʀ- 'come back to life' [compare uŋummaʀ- below]
AAY uŋuiʀ- 'come back to life'
CAY uŋuiʀ-
NSY uŋiiʀ- 'come back to life, regain consciousness' [ANLC]
CSY — [for uŋuvaʀ- in this meaning see uŋummaʀ- below]

PE uŋuman 'heart' [cf. un]
AAY K uŋuwan, uŋuan 'heart'
CAY LI, NR, BB, Nun, UK, NSU uŋuvan
NSY —
CSY —
Sir uŋəvata
SPI uuman
NAI uumman
WCI uumman
ECI uummati
GRI uummat

PE uŋummaʀ- 'come alive (again)' [cf. ʀ- under ŋ(ŋ)uʀ-; the relat. with Yup *uŋu(C)iʀ- above is obscure]
AAY —
CAY —
NSY —
CSY uŋuvaʀ- 'come to life'
Sir —
SPI uumaq- 'come back to life'
NAI [uummak- 'come to life, be revived', with k- under nəɣ-, and uummai- 'get or cause to have an erection', with ðì-]
WCI [Pryde has uummai- 'get an erection', and Met. has uummaksaq- 'bring to life']
ECI uumma(q)- 'come back to life' [and uumaʀi- 'be active (at work)', uummaʀi- come back to life' — compare uummaʀik- 'be full of life, active']
GRI uummaʀ- 'come alive (again)' [and uumaʀi- 'be quick at woʀk' — compare uummaʀiɣ- 'be in full vigor']

PI uummaq 'fresh green plant or wood' [cf. q under nəʀ[1]]
SPI uumaq 'fresh green wood'
NAI uummaq* 'fresh green plant or wood'
WCI —
ECI uummaq 'green wood'
GRI uummaq*, uummak 'fresh green plant or wood'

PY uŋuŋsiq 'animal' [cf. uŋuma-]
AAY AP uŋuŋsiq 'animal'
CAY uŋuŋsiq 'land animal (esp. bear)'
NSY uŋuŋsiq 'animal' [ANLC]
CSY —

PE uŋuʀ- 'pull back?' [cf. uŋəʀ- with which the Inu. part of this set is apparently contaminated, also Aleut uŋuʀ- 'pull up (fish line or anchor)'?]
AAY —
CAY —
NSY uŋuʀ- 'pull up' [L.-T.; and ANLC has uŋuʀaʀ- 'do pull-ups']
CSY uŋuXtə- 'take back'
Sir —
SPI —
NAI uŋuʀ- 'gather, pucker (fabric)'
WCI —
ECI —
GRI uŋŋutit 'creases in front part of the sole of a Greenlandic boot'

PE upaɣ- 'rush toward' [cf. upət-?]
AAY —
CAY upaɣ- 'change residence, move to fish camp', NSU 'run toward s.o.'
NSY —
CSY upaɣ- 'go to a boat to help or see those arriving' [and upłəɣ- 'rush over to']
Sir [Vakh. has upɣaɣ- 'go to meet' from Rub. and upłəX 'avenger']
SPI uvak- 'go after an animal,' uvakaq- 'chase after'
NAI upak-, upaktuq- 'go directly to, rush, charge'
WCI upak- 'go to meet' [and Jen. has 'follow after, pursue'; Ras. has Car upak-, upat- 'hunt large herds of caribou in migrating time, often from kayak', Net upaktuq- 'extend hands to help']
ECI upak- 'go to join, rush toward', Lab 'go after, attack, tell off'
GRI upaɣ- 'reach for food, lie in wait for (whale)', upattuʀ- 'seek bait (of fish)' [and upaat(i)- 'take some food home for s.o.', upanniɣ- 'attack', upaʀuaʀ- 'point at', upanniut 'whaling boat', NG upaatuq- 'suddenly become very busy'; Tersis has upa- 'share food' and upaC- 'receive a share of food' for EG]

PI upaluq- 'be unprepared or in a rush' [cf. luʀ-?]
SPI uvaluq- 'be tired out'
NAI upaluq- 'act swiftly, rush to check, be unprepared, be out of s.th.' [upaluŋaiyaq- 'get necessary supplies ready for a trip', upalui- 'catch by surprise']

WCI upaluq- 'hurry to carry out an order' [and Jen. has 'surprise, do unexpectedly']
ECI upaluq- 'arrive too late, be ready too late', upalui- 'join unexpectedly, surprise' [upalaŋaiRsa(q)- 'prepare in time to avoid rush']
GRI upaluR- 'be unprepared', upalui- 'surprise' [upaluŋaaR- 'be ready']

PE upən(ə)RaR 'spring (or summer)' [cf. upət- and n(ə)RaR(aR)]
AAY ➞
CAY ➞
NSY upənRaq 'spring'
CSY upənRaq
Sir upənəRəX
SPI uvaRnaaq, Qaw upanRaq 'summer' [Men. has Imaq uvaRnaq 'spring', reversed with uvaRnažaq under upən(ə)Rakðar below?]
NAI upinRaaq 'summer' [upinRaaq-, PH upinRaq- 'become summer']
WCI upinRaq, Net upinŋaaq 'spring' [B.S. for the latter; Dor. has upinRaaq for B. Lake]
ECI upiRŋaaq 'summer', Iti 'spring' [Dor.], Lab upiŋŋaak, NBI, SB upiRŋaq 'spring' [andupiRŋa(q)- 'be summer']
GRI upiRnaaq, SWG also upiRŋaaq 'spring' [and upiRnaR- 'have become spring']

PE upən(ə)Rakðar '(early) spring' [cf. kðaR]
AAY AP uɣnəXkaq 'spring'
CAY upnəXkaq, NSU upənəXkaq 'spring' [upnəXkaR- 'become spring']
NSY —
CSY —
Sir —
SPI uvaRnaɣžaq, Qaw upanRaqšaq 'spring' [Men. has Imaq uvaRnažaq 'summer', reversed with uvaRnaq above?]
NAI upinRakšaq 'spring'
WCI upinRaksaq 'spring' [Lowe; Dorais has upinRaXXaq 'early spring' for B. Lake]
ECI upiRŋasaq 'spring', Lab upiŋŋasaak 'early spring' [Dor. has upiRŋasaaq for Tar]
GRI upiRnaššaq 'beginning of spring'

PE upənRi- 'spend the spring (or summer)' [cf. li-[1]]
AAY —
CAY — [but note upnəXkivik 'spring camp']
NSY upənRi- 'spend the spring' [ANLC]
CSY —
Sir —
SPI uvaRni- 'spend the summer'
NAI upinRi-, Nu upinRai- 'spend the summer'
WCI upinRi- [Pryde]
ECI upiRŋivik 'place summer is spent'
GRI upiRni- 'spend spring', upiRnivik, upiRnavik 'place spring is spent'

PE upət- 'get excited or rush about' [cf. upaɣ- and upən(ə)RaR(aR)]
AAY up<ə>tə- 'become alert, be startled'
CAY up<ə>tə- 'get ready to go' [and uputə- 'gossip maliciously about'?]
NSY upətə- 'rush to' [ANLC]
CSY uuptə- 'burst out crying' [and upuR- 'be startled']
Sir [note upcəR- 'be scared', upšuR- 'frighten' — Vakh. has upciR- 'be afraid', also upułəX 'fear' and upuXłuku 'suddenly' from Men.'s texts]
SPI uvit- 'obey a command, rush urgently to s.th.'
NAI upit- 'get excited, rush about' [and uputi- 'pay heed — e.g. to noise']
WCI upit- 'go and do s.th. quickly' [and Sig upiŋ(ŋ)aq- 'be surprised'; Ras. has Sig upit- 'mourn, regret' — in B. Lake and Net acc. Dor. 'be surprised']
ECI Aiv upit- 'be astonished, admire' [and Tar upiɣi- 'be grateful toward', upiŋŋa(q)- 'surprise', upinnait- 'not be surprising, act normally', upinnaqut(i)- 'be surprised at', Lab upiɣunnik 'reverence']
GRI upit- 'complain, cry' [and upput 'lament']

PY-S upuRa- 'bustle about' [cf. (C)uR- and a-?]
AAY —
CAY —
NSY upuRa- 'bustle about hurriedly'
CSY upuRa- 'be hospitable' [and upuRat- 'be hospitable to']
Sir upuRa- 'bustle about' [Em. has 'be hospitable'; Vakh. has upuRat- 'meet']

PI upkaq 'part of room nearest door?' [cf. uməɣ-, umkuRaR, and kaR?]
Yup — [CAY umkaRyaRaq 'damper' is probably separately from uməɣ-; for L.-T.'s umkə 'lobby of men's house' see umku]
Sir — [umkə 'forest' is probably a borrowing from Chukchi umkuum '(dense) forest']
SPI —
NAI —
WCI upkakłiq 'part of room nearest door', upkani 'toward the door' [Met.], Car upka 'fire(place)' [Ras., who also has Net ukkaq 'front wall']
ECI ukkaq 'front entry'
GRI ukkaq [old ortho. uvkaq] 'front wall of house, outer side of island, space in front of door or sleeping platform'

PI uqaq(-) 'tongue' [as verb = 'speak, say']
SPI uRaq 'tongue'
NAI uqaq 'tongue' [uqaq- 'speak, say']
WCI uqaq 'tongue' [as verb = 'speak, say']
ECI uqaq 'tongue' [as verb = 'speak, say']
GRI uqaq 'tongue' [and uqaR- 'speak, say', uqami- 'make remark' — with p.b. umi-?]

PI uqallak- 'say something' [cf. łłaɣ-]
SPI —
NAI uqallak- 'say s.th.'
WCI uqallak-
ECI uqalla(C)- 'say little, only part'
GRI —

PI uqaluk- 'speak' [cf. GRI luɣ- under ʀuluk if not tluk- — compare GRI uqami- under uqaq(-) above]
SPI —
NAI uqaluk 'word' [and uqaluɣaaq- 'tell a story']
WCI Car, Net uqaluk- 'speak' [Ras.; compare homonym meaning 'speak too much, slander, tell malicious tales' with łuɣ(-) — Schn. for 'adg']
ECI Igl uqaluk- 'speak' [B.-S.; compare Tar homonym meaning 'have an ulcer on one's tongue', with łuɣ(-); Andersen et al. have uqaluqit- 'talk to amuse people, saying foolish things' for Lab]
GRI uqaluɣ-, EG uʀalivaʀ- 'speak' [and uqalualaaq 'story, legend, myth', uqalualaaʀ-, uqaluasaaʀ-, Up uqaliŋasaaʀ- 'tell a story (for entertainment)']

PI uqaluktuaq- 'tell a story' [cf. ðuʀaʀ-?]
SPI —
NAI uqaluktuaq 'story of recent historical events', uqaluktuaqti 'story-teller' [and compare Mal uqaaqtuaq- 'tell a story']
WCI Car uqaluktuaq- 'tell (a story?)' [B.-S.]
ECI —
GRI uqaluttuaʀ- 'tell a story' [uqaluttuaq 'story']

PI uqauciq 'word or speech' [cf. uciʀ]
SPI —
NAI uqausiq 'manner of speech, language, dialect, advice'
WCI uqausiq 'manner of speech, language'
ECI uqausiq 'word, name (of s.th.)' [Spald. also 'dialect' for NBI]
GRI uqaasiq 'word', uqaatsit (pl.) 'language'

PI uqautə- 'speak to' [cf. utə-]
SPI —
NAI uqaut(i)- 'speak, talk to'
WCI uqaut(i)-
ECI uqaut(i)- 'speak, talk to' [intr. = 'talk a lot']
GRI uqaat(i)- 'tell what to do, exhort' [and note uqqat(i)- 'quarrel']

PI uqciq 'toggle (on dog trace)'
SPI W uqsiq 'toggle' [Jen.]
NAI uqsi(q) 'loop or bone ring on lasso, loop of snare'
WCI uqsi 'belt buckle'
ECI uʀsiq 'ring on dog trace'
GRI uʀsiq 'piece of bone or bone ring on dog trace, noose, bow, eye (of hook)'

PE uqðuʀ 'blubber or seal oil'
AAY uquq 'oil, seal oil, blubber' [uquʀ- 'be fat']
CAY uquq
NSY uquq
CSY uquq 'oil, blubber'
Sir uqcəX
SPI uqšuq
NAI uqšuq
WCI uqsuq
ECI uʀsuq
GRI uʀšuq

PE uqðilŋu- 'feel sick from eating too much fat' [cf. li-[1] and lŋu-?]
AAY —
CAY uqilŋu- 'feel sick from eating too much oily food'
NSY —
CSY —
Sir —
SPI uqšiŋu-
NAI uqšit- 'feel sick from eating too much fat' [also 'soak in oil']
WCI uqsiŋu-
ECI uqsiŋu- 'be disgusted by the oil one is eating', Iti also 'be sorrowing'
GRI uʀšiŋŋu- 'feel sick from eating too much oily food'

PE uqðuʀ- and **uqðuʀtəʀ-** 'apply oil to' [cf. təʀ- for the second form]
AAY —
CAY uquXtə- 'apply oil to'
NSY uquXtə-
CSY uquXtə-
Sir —
SPI uqšuq-
NAI uqšuqtiq- 'rub oil into'
WCI uqsuqtiq- 'grease'
ECI uʀsutiq-
GRI uʀšuʀ- 'cover with oil or grease'

PE uqðuʀaʀ 'oil on surface' [cf. aʀ]
AAY —
CAY uquaq 'oil slick from boat or dead animal, fish oil from surface of fish broth'
NSY —
CSY —
Sir —
SPI uqšuaq 'oil slick on water around dead animal' [and verbal]
NAI uqšualaqi- 'leave trace of oil after being shot (animal)' [and uqšuʀa(a)q 'strip of rendered blubber']
WCI uqsuʀaq 'oil of cut-up seal' [uqsuaq- 'be calm (sea)']
ECI uʀsualaqi- 'produce oil slick on surface (wounded animal)' [and note uʀsua(q)- 'cover with coat of oil or grease']
GRI uʀšuaʀnišaaq, uʀšualikaq 'slick patch of water due to seal oil or blubber' [and NG uXXuʀaq- 'get smooth (sea)']

PE uqðumyaɣ 'mineral excrescence?' [cf. myaɣ-?]
AAY uqumyak 'quartz'
CAY uqumyak 'quartz' [because of light color, resembling seal fat']
NSY [uqšupaaniq 'salt mineral excrescence on cliffs, used in food']
CSY uqumyak 'tree pitch'
Sir —
SPI —
NAI Nu uqšuužaq 'quartz'

WCI —
ECI —
GRI uRšuɣiak 'cryolite'

PE uqəR 'lee or shelter' [cf. old Atkan Aleut uqma- 'hide'; the Inu forms apparently with quR]
AAY uqəq 'lee side'
CAY uqəq* [and note uqXaq 'windbreak', uquXsuk 'parka hood', uqənqaR-]
NSY [ukəq/ukXa 'south' — but ANLC also has uqaXm̥un 'going with the wind']
CSY uqəq* [loc. uuqXani] 'lee side', uuXqa [loc. uuXqaŋani] 'south, lee side'
Sir uqəRaX 'southern'
SPI uqqu 'lee side' [uqquuk- 'be sheltered from wind']
NAI uqquq 'sheltered place'
WCI uqqu 'lee side'
ECI uqqu 'lee side'
GRI uqquq 'lee side' [and uqquusimaaR- 'shelter in lee']

PE uqəRutaR 'windbreak' [cf. un]
AAY uqXutaq 'windbreak'
CAY uqXun, uqXutaq, Nun uqXiilitaX
NSY uXqutaq 'snow shelter by fishing hole' [L.-T.]
CSY —
Sir —
SPI Qaw uRuutaq
NAI —
WCI uquutaq 'windbreak' [Lowe; Met. has uqqutaq]
ECI uquutaq 'windbreak'
GRI uquutaq 'windbreak' [also 'flounder', by contam. with uqaq]

PE uqqit- 'take shelter' [cf. p.b. łit-]
AAY —
CAY uqitə- 'take shelter'
NSY uqitə- [ANLC]
CSY uqiitə-
Sir —
SPI uqqit-
NAI uqqit- 'take shelter, be safe'
WCI uqqisaq- 'take shelter'
ECI uqquit- 'bring self into shelter' [contam. from uqquq under uqəR above?]
GRI uqqit- 'bring oneself into the lee of s.th.' [also uqqui-; S.-L. has uqquit-, NWG uqqit- 'seek shelter, bring into shelter']

PI uqquq- 'be warm' [a back-formation from forms like uqquq under uqeR above, further verbalized with ŋu- in Sig, ECI uqquu- here?]
Sir — [but note uqiRnəX 'sun']
SPI uRuq- 'be warm (house, clothing)'
NAI uquq- 'be warm (especially clothing)' [and Nu uqut 'warm winter clothes']
WCI Cop uqquq-, Sig uqquu- 'be warm (clothes, house)' [Lowe]
ECI uquq- 'wear warm clothing' [and uqutsaq 'material for making warm clothes', uqqu(q) 'warm winter clothes', (as exclam.) 'how hot it is!', uqquu- 'be hot', uquRuti 'cover in which one is wrapped on sled']
GRI uquR- 'be warm (bed, clothes, etc.)' [uquRut 'piece of warm clothing or bedclothes'; EG uqqisaq (Robbe and Menn. uqqisiq) 'fur fringe around hood opening', also uRuRtuq 'warm (of water)' (Robbe and Menn.)]

PE uqumiɣ- 'move with wind behind one' [cf. miɣ-]
AAY —
CAY Nun uqumixtə- 'have wind blowing from behind when traveling'
NSY —
CSY —
Sir —
SPI [uqqumuaq- 'travel with wind at one's back']
NAI uqunmuɣaaq-, Nu uqunmuuq-, uqumiɣaaq 'walk with wind at one's back' [cf. muaq- for the p.b. in the first two forms]
WCI Cop uqumuu-, Sig uqunmuk- 'move with wind behind one' [Lowe; Met. has uqumaq- — cf. muaq- ?]
ECI uqumik- 'move with wind behind one' [also uqqumuaq-, with p.b. muaq-]
GRI uqumiɣaaR-, uqummukaR- 'move with wind behind one' [the latter with mukaR-under muaq-; Robbe and Menn. have uRumiC- 'be in the direction of the wind' for EG]

PY uqəR- 'wipe one's backside' [cf. iqquR]
AAY PWS uqXi- 'wipe backside'
CAY uqəR-
NSY —
CSY —

PE uqiɣit- 'be light' [presumably from *uqiɣ as in CSY uqik below plus ŋit-; cf. uqimaŋit-]
AAY uqxətə-, AP uqiatə- 'be light'
CAY uqixətə-, uqxətə-, HBC uqaxətə- 'be light'
NSY uqiɣ-, uqiɣitaRaR- 'be light' [ANLC; Men. has uqiɣitaaRalRia, uqitaaRaq 'light, əbrisk']
CSY uqiɣitə- 'be light', uqixtu- 'be heavy' [and uqik 'weight', uqəŋəstaaq 'light thing']
Sir uqəŋətaRałəRəX 'light'
SPI uRiktuužaq 's.th. light', Qaw uRik- 'be light'
NAI uqit- 'be light'
WCI uqit-
ECI uqit-
GRI uqit- 'be light'

PE uqiɣitli- 'become lighter' [cf. li-[2]]
AAY —
CAY uqiɣli-, uqixəli- 'become light'
NSY —
CSY uqəŋəłi- 'become light' [and compare uqəŋəXtə- 'be lighter, feel better after an illness, improve (weather), tidy up']
Sir uqəŋəcižaR- 'become lighter' [Vakh. from Men.'s texts]
SPI uRiɣli-
NAI uqiɣlʸi-, uqikłʸi- 'become light, happy'

WCI uqiɣli- 'become light'
ECI uqili- 'become or make light'
GRI uqili-, uqiłłi- 'become or make lighter'

PE uqila- 'be fast' [cf. uqiɣit- and la(ʀ)-?]
AAY Kod uqila- 'be fast'
CAY uqila- 'be fast (on one's feet)'
NSY uqila- 'run fast' [ANLC; Men. has uqilalʀia 'running']
CSY —
Sir —
SPI ᴜʀila- 'be a fast runner'
NAI uqilʸa-
WCI Cop uqila- [Ras.]
ECI uqila-
GRI uqila-

PE uqimaŋiʀ- 'have a nightmare' [cf. uqimaŋit- and ŋiʀ-]
AAY uqamaiʀaq 'nightmare', uqamai(ʀ)a- 'have a nightmare'
CAY uqamaiʀi- 'be partially awake, unable to move due to sleep paralysis'
NSY uqimiaʀ- 'have a nightmare' [ANLC]
CSY —
Sir —
SPI ᴜʀumaŋia- 'have a nightmare'
NAI uqumaŋia-, qumaŋia- 'have a nightmare', uqumaŋiaq- 'be half asleep' [with assimilation before m]
WCI Sig uqumaŋiaq- 'have a nightmare' [Lowe]
ECI uqumaŋiq- 'be lethargic, paralized or half asleep (from catalepsy, fear, etc.), unable to be wakened, lose one's head'
GRI uqimaŋiʀ- 'become heavy, have a nightmare', EG ᴜʀumaŋiʀ- 'have a nightmare'

PE uqimaŋit- 'be heavy' [cf. uqiɣit- and uqimaŋiʀ-; ŋit- has probably been added to a nominal form reflected by CAY uqamaq below (itself from *uqiŋimaʀ?); for the second vowel in the Yup forms here compare the CAY forms under uqiɣit-; there is further assimilation of the i before m in NAI, WCI and ECI]
AAY [uqamatu- 'be heavy' in Bible; note also Kod uqamaʀ- 'carry a load']
CAY uqamaitə- 'be heavy' [and uqamaq 'manageable weight, pound']
NSY uqamiatə- 'be heavy'
CSY —
Sir —
SPI ᴜʀumait-
NAI uqumait-
WCI uqumait- 'be heavy' [and uqumailitiksaq 'ballast']
ECI uqumait- 'be heavy' [and uqumailutaq 'lead weight on nets', Iti 'weight for scales']
GRI uqimaat- 'be heavy' [uqimaalutaq 'weight (e.g. for scales)']

PE uqliʀ- 'take aim at' [cf. ᴜʀniʀ-]
AAY uqłi(ʀ)- 'get into position to spear or shoot'
CAY uqłiʀ- 'be set or ready to act, take aim'
NSY uXłitə' 'aim at, make as if to strike'
CSY uqłiʀ- 'watch for game or person' [and uqłiitə- 'aim at']
Sir uXsiʀ- 'aim'
SPI W uqłiq- 'aim with missile' [Jen.]
NAI —
WCI Cop ᴜʀliq- 'raise harpoon to strike' [Pryde]
ECI ᴜʀliq- 'be ready to strike (game)', Lab ᴜʀliqtuq- 'aim' [Peck]
GRI ᴜʀłiʀ- 'aim and be ready to shoot, be ready to strike (of clock)'

PY uqsuq 'aged fish head'
AAY PWS, AP uqsuq 'aged fish head'
CAY uqsuq HBC, NS 'aged fish head', LI, UK 'head'
NSY —
CSY —

PE uquɣ 'mold'
AAY uquɣnilŋuq 'skunk or stink currant'
CAY uquxłuk 'mold'
NSY uquɣaq
CSY uquk
Sir uqux [Orr]
SPI ᴜʀuk
NAI uquk 'mold' [verbal = 'become moldy']
WCI uquk
ECI uquk 'mold' [uquq- 'become moldy']
GRI uquk 'mold, maggot' [uquɣ- 'be full of mold or maggots']

PY uquiq 'sandpiper or similar bird' [cf. uqðuʀ and (C)iʀ]
AAY PWS uquiyaq 'northern phalarope' [and uquiXpak 'swan']
CAY uquiʀ(aq*) 'pectural sandpiper, pomarine jaeger'
NSY —
CSY —

PI uqummiq- 'put s.th. in one's mouth' [cf. iqmiɣ- — contam. with uqaq(-)?]
SPI ᴜʀumiq- 'put s.th. in the mouth'
NAI uqummiq-
WCI uqummiq-
ECI uqummi(q)-
GRI uqummiʀ- 'put s.th. in mouth' [and note EG ᴜʀuluC- 'chew']

PI uqummiaq 's.th. kept in the mouth' [compare təɣum(m)i(C)aʀ under təɣu-]
SPI ᴜʀumiaq 'tobacco being chewed, s.th. kept in mouth' [as verb = 'chew tobacco']
NAI uqummiaq 's.th. kept in mouth' [as verb = 'keep in mouth']
WCI uqummiaq- 'keep in mouth' [and Sig uqummiaqataaq 'candy']
ECI Iti uqummiaq 'candy' [as verb also elsewhere = 'keep in mouth']
GRI uqummiaq 's.th. kept in mouth' [uqummiaʀ- 'keep in mouth'; Holt. has NG uqumissat 'lumps of blubber in lamp']

PE uqviɣ 'tree or shrub' [cf. uqəR and piɣ?]
AAY C uqxʷik, Kod uqXʷik 'alder'
CAY uqfik, uqfiaq, uqfiɣaq 'willow'
NSY uqpiɣaq 'shrub' [ANLC has uqpik, uqpiɣaaq 'bushes']
CSY uqfik 'tree'
Sir uqfəx 'tree' [and Vakh. has uxpix 'branch' from Men.'s texts]
SPI uqpik 'willow'
NAI uqpik
WCI uqpik
ECI uqpik
GRI uRpik 'tree', uRpiɣaq 'shrub', EG uRpiŋaq 'northern willow'

PE uRaR- 'wash away' [cf. uRə- and uRRaR]
AAY —
CAY —
NSY uaXtə- 'be washed out to sea' [ANLC; Men. mentions uaXɬəq 's.th. carried out to sea' in connection with the Imaq form below]
CSY uuXə- 'drift away with current' [for homonym 'get gooey' see uRə-]
Sir uRəR- 'carry away with current' [Vakh. from Rub.'s texts]
SPI uaq- 'wash out to sea, fade of color, wash away'
NAI uaq- 'cleanse, rinse, wash away' [uaqniq* 's.th. carried out to sea']
WCI uaq- 'wash, rinse, bathe, wash away'
ECI NBI, SB uasaq- 'wash' [for Iti uasaq- 'put in disorder' see uða(t)-]
GRI —

uRaRuq 'flounder or similar fish' [from Aleut uRaaRu-X 'starry flounder']
AAY C uRRa<y>uk 'starry flounder'
CAY uRaRuq, uRaluq 'starry flounder' (local meanings include also 'whitefish', 'sea slug', and 'wild celery')
NSY —
CSY —

PE uRðuR 'moss' [cf. Aleut uRðu-X, hu(u)Rðu-X 'moss', the last form perhaps influenced by huRðu- under muRðuɣ-]
AAY uRuq, uRRuq 'moss'
CAY uRuq
NSY uRžuk [ANLC]
CSY uRu
Sir uRuməžux 'moss' [Vakh. from Men.'s texts]
SPI uRžuq 'moss'
NAI uRžu(q)
WCI Cop uRiuRaliq [for uRyuRaliq?]
ECI uRyuk
GRI —

PY-S uRə- 'dissolve' [cf. uRaR-, uRyuR- and Aleut uRla- Atkan 'thaw, melt', EA 'become humid, wet', uRli- 'soak, dampen', perhaps also uRu-X 'juice, sap']
AAY uRə- 'disintegrate, rot, fall apart, become threadbare'
CAY uRə- 'dissolve, melt, run (colors), have dirty face'
NSY ➞
CSY uuXə- 'get gooey, dirty' [influenced by homonym meaning 'drift away with current' under uRaR-?; uuXtuR- 'wash hands']
Sir [Vakh. has uXtə- 'wet, wash hair' (the latter only acc. Em.); Vakh. also has uXtuR- 'wash' from Rub.]

PY-S uRuɣ- 'melt'
AAY uRuxtə- 'thaw, melt' [B.-S. has 'sweat' for C]
CAY uRuɣ- 'thaw, melt'
NSY uRuɣ- 'thaw, melt'
CSY uRuɣ- 'thaw, melt'
Sir uRuɣ- 'melt, thaw'
Inu [note NAI Nu uukturRniq* 'white gum from spruce']

PY-S uRluvəq 'bow' [cf. Aleut uRalu-X 'spear, lance', uRalu- 'hit with spear']
AAY —
CAY uRluvəq*, NSU uRluRaq 'bow'
NSY —
CSY uRluvəq*
Sir uRluvəX

PE uRnəɣ- 'go toward or turn to' [the relat. — if any — to unəRaR is obscure]
AAY —
CAY uRənkə- 'have free time, be unoccupied' [compare GRI uRniɣi- below]
NSY —
CSY uRnək 'handiwork, sewing, that which one is working on'
Sir [for unaRaR- 'approach' see unərar]
SPI —
NAI uRnikšuq- 'hurry, do quickly'
WCI Net uRnik- 'go to s.o.' [Ras.]
ECI Aiv uRnik- 'go to s.o.', Tar unnik- 'reach goal first, beat at game'
GRI uRniɣ- 'go to, approach' [uRniɣi- 'want, have time to occupy oneself with', uRniɣaq, NG uRnitaq 'goal']

PY uRniR- 'take aim' [cf. uqliR-, also uRnəɣ-, though the relat. is not clear]
AAY uRniR- 'get into position to spear or shoot'
CAY uRniR- 'take aim, be ready to act (esp. shoot)'
NSY —
CSY —

PE uRRaR 'clay or mud' [cf. uRə- and uRaR- — from *uRəRaR?]
AAY uRaɣ- 'be messy, sloppy, slimy'
CAY uXXaq, uXasquq, Nun uRasquX 'clay (mixed with caribou hair to make pottery)'
NSY uRaq, uXaq 'clay'
CSY uRaša 'mud' [and uuXXa 'porcelain']
Sir —
SPI Qaw uXXaq 'lead' [note KI uaqɬak 'lead']
NAI uRRaq, uXaq 'lead, tip of bullet'
WCI —
ECI —
GRI —

PI uRulu- 'be angry or grumpy'
SPI —
NAI —
WCI uRulu- 'anger easily' [and uRut- 'be angry']
ECI uRulu- 'be in a bad mood'
GRI uRulu- 'be grumpy, complain' [and NG uRuluiXXaaq- 'comfort', uRulut- 'complain, need help' — Holt.]

PI uRuni(q) 'intestines of ptarmigan'
SPI —
NAI —
WCI Cop Net uRunit 'ptarmigan intestines'
ECI uRuniq 'first intestine of ptarmigan'
GRI uRunit, uRuRnit 'ptarmigan intestines'

PY-S uRvik 'skin scraper' [cf. uRə- and ðviɣ?]
AAY —
CAY [uRuɣun 'skin scraper' — influenced by uRuɣ- under uRə-?]
NSY uRvik 'bone instrument for scraping gut of sea mammals'
CSY uRvik 'old-style scraper for skins' [and Em. has verbal uRviɣ-]
Sir uRvəx 'instrument for cleaning out gut' [= 'scraper for sea mammal gut made from walrus tusk' acc. Em., who also has uRvəXtə- 'work with scraper']

PE uRyuR- and **uRyaR-** 'spit out?' [cf. uRə-; the second form from *uRyuRaR-?]
AAY —
CAY uRyuR- 'overflow, spill'
NSY —
CSY uRyuR- 'spit on, seep out of ice (water)'
Sir uRyəR- 'spit on, seep out of ice (water)' [Orr]
SPI uRiaq- 'spit s.th. out'
NAI uRiaq-
WCI uRiuq-
ECI uRiaq- 'spit out', uRiuq- 'spit out oil from blubber one is chewing (e.g. onto food one is preparing)'
GRI uRiaR- 'spit out', uRiuR- 'spit out oil from blubber one is chewing' [and EG uŋiaR- 'spit']

PY utakinəq or **utakinaq** 'volcano'
AAY utakinəq 'volcano'
CAY NR utakinaq
NSY —
CSY —

PE utaqə- 'wait' [with p.b. a- in the Yup forms and with nqiɣ-[2] in the Inu forms?]
AAY utaqa- 'wait for' [K also 'wait']
CAY utaqa- 'wait (for)'
NSY utaqa-
CSY utaqa- 'wait for'
Sir utəqə(s)- 'wait for', utəqši- 'wait' [the latter half-trans.; Vakh. has utaqə-, utəqa- 'wait for']
SPI utaqi-, Imaq utaqə- 'wait for'
NAI utaqqi- 'wait for' [and utaqqik- 'continue to wait']
WCI utaqqi- 'wait for'
ECI utaqqi-, utaqqik-
GRI utaqqi- 'wait (for)' [and utaqqit- 'postpone']

PI utə- 'fall out (hair)' [cf. utuqqa(R) and Aleut usa- 'come off, shed (hair)', usat- 'remove hair from skin']
SPI uti- 'separate after fermenting (outer layer of skin)', Qaw 'fall out (hair)'
NAI uti- 'fall out (hair), grow bald', utitaq 'hairless skin'
WCI uti- 'lose hair (furs)'
ECI uti- 'lose hair, decompose (skin)' [Saul — Schn. has uuti-; Peck has uti- 'be rotten so hairs fall off' for Lab]
GRI uti- 'loosen (hairs)', utit- 'remove hairs from skin' [for EG uliivik 'skin, hide' see uliɣ-]

PI utənəq 'hairless skin or bald spot' [cf. nəR[1]]
SPI utiniq 'bald spot on skin'
NAI utiniq* 'bald spot'
WCI Net unniq 'skin with hair removed' [Pryde]
ECI utuniq [Saul]
GRI unniq* 'skin with hair removed, bleached skin' [and note unnaat 'festive white boots']

PE utəR- 'return'
AAY ➟
CAY utəXtə- 'return'
NSY utəXtə-, utəRaXtə- 'return' [ANLC; utəRmun 'back']
CSY utəXtə- 'come back, return, change plans' [and utəRmun 'back']
Sir utəR- 'return' [and utəRmənu 'back']
SPI utiq- 'return' [and utiRmun, Imaq utəRmu 'back']
NAI utiq- 'return' [and uttaqi- 'return to']
WCI utiq- 'return'
ECI utiq- 'return' [utiRsi- 'go look for s.th. one has left behind']
GRI utiR- 'return, repeat' [and utiRsi(ɣi)- 'regret, not want to lose']

PY utəŋqa- or **utəŋRa-** 'be back home' [cf. ŋa-[1]]
AAY —
CAY utəŋqa- 'be back home'
NSY utəŋRa- 'stay home'
CSY —

PE utəqi(C)aR- 'back up or turn back' [cf. nqiɣ-[2]?]
AAY utqiaR- 'go back, back up'
CAY [note HBC utqitə- 'bounce back, turn around and come back']
NSY utəqiaR- 'move backward'
CSY utqiiR-
Sir —
SPI utiRiaq-
NAI [note place name utqiaRvik 'Barrow']
WCI —
ECI utiRiaq- 'go down, deflate (bread, etc.)' [also 'turn back' acc. Saul; and utiRiikkuti 'chock put under wheel to stop vehicle moving backward']
GRI utiRiaR- 'go backward, calm down (wind), give in, backwater (oars)' [and utiRiit- 'be stubborn']

PY utəRniR- 'return (from trip)' [cf. nəR and liR-?]
AAY —
CAY —
NSY utəRniR- 'return' [ANLC]
CSY utəRniR- 'return from a trip'

PI utəʀžak- or **utəʀžaq-** 'make a return trip' [cf. žak-?]
SPI utiʀžaq- 'take a nap'
NAI utiʀžak- 'bounce back, make a round trip to where one started (usually in same day)'
WCI Cop utiʀyak- 'og and return the same day' [Pryde; Met. has utiʀyaɣaq- 'be flexible (like willow branch), make return trip on same day']
ECI utiʀya(q)- 'make return trip on same day'
GRI utiʀšaʀ- 'come back on same day, take same way back'

PE utətmun or **utətmən** 'back' [allative case]
AAY —
CAY utətm̥un 'homeward, back'
NSY —
CSY [uulmən 'backward' may be influenced by ulət-]
Sir —
SPI utiʀmun 'back'
NAI utɨnmun 'back again'
WCI utimut 'back'
ECI utimut
GRI utimut

PY-S utəvak or **utəmak** 'lump of turf or snow' [cf. u(u)tu(ɣ) and vaɣ?]
AAY —
CAY utfak 'snow carved into a block'
NSY —
CSY utumək 'earth, soil'
Sir utəvax 'turf' [Vakh. from Rub.'s texts, utəvəx acc. Orr]

PE utɣuciɣ 'cooking pot' [cf. uɣu(t)-?]
AAY —
CAY Nun utxucix 'cooking pot'
NSY —
CSY —
Sir —
SPI —
NAI utkusik
WCI utkusit
ECI ukkusik
GRI ukkusiššaq 'soapstone'

PE utlaɣ- 'appʀoach (in oʀder to see)'
AAY ułaɣ- 'come to see, go to or near (s.o.)'
CAY ułaɣ- 'approach'
NSY ułaɣ- [ANLC]
CSY —
Sir —
SPI ułłak- 'approach, go to'
NAI ullak-, Mal utlak- 'approach, go to'
WCI Car úlak- 'run' [Pryde, who also has Net úlaktut 'three stars forming belt of Orion'; Ras. has uklag- and ublasi- 'run' for Net]
ECI ullak- 'run', Iti 'run toward', Lab 'chase' [and Lab ullaktut 'Orion's Belt (constellation)' — Peck]
GRI EG uttaɣ- 'run in order to catch' [Holm, who also has ullattut 'three stars in constellation Orion' for EG]

PI utlacaun 'tower trap (for foxes)' [cf. caʀ- and un]
SPI —
NAI [Ras. has uvlihautit 'tower trap']
WCI Car? ullahaut 'trap, snare' [Schn. 'adg']
ECI ullasauti 'pit fall trap' [Saul]
GRI NG ullahaut 'tower trap for foxes', WG ułłasaat, ułłisaat '(old word for) men's community house'

PE utŋuʀ 'wart'
AAY utŋuq, utŋuk 'wart'
CAY utŋuk
NSY ɣutŋ̊uk [L.-T.]
CSY ŋuutŋuk
Sir ŋútŋəx [Orr — from the CSY]
SPI utŋuq 'wart'
NAI unŋuq*, Mal utŋuq*
WCI unŋuq
ECI uŋŋuq
GRI uŋŋuq* 'wart' [also iŋŋuq*]

PE u(u)tu(ɣ) or **utəvəɣ** 'dandruff or sebacea?' [if related to PY-S utəvak the original meaning may have been 's.th. come loose or removed' — cf. utə-; the double vowel in AAY, Nun, and GRI is unexplained, however]
AAY uutu 'dandruff'
CAY Nun uutuXłux 'flake of dandruff'
NSY —
CSY —
Sir —
SPI —
NAI utuvik 'scalp, skin under hair' [uncommon word — the i may be weak]
WCI utuvik 'scalp, skin under hair' [Pryde, who also has Cop uuyyaq 'skin which has lost its hair'; Met. also has utuviktu- 'be thick (skin)' and Sig utuvɣit- 'be thin']
ECI utuvik 'skin under hair on head' ['dandruff' in Andersen et al. for Lab
GRI uutuk 'ancher (on child's scalp), sebacea'

PE utuqqaʀ 's.th. old' [cf. perhaps utə- and p.b. tuqaq[2]]
AAY usuqqaʀ- 'wear out, fall apart'
CAY utuqa- 'be aged (of sealskin)'
NSY utuqaq 'old '
CSY utuqa 'old thing'
Sir [note usaX 'old' on Men.'s comp. list, also usatayəɣaX]
SPI utuqaq 's.th. old', utuqanaaq 'old person'
NAI utuqqaq* 's.th. old', utuqqanaaq 'old person'
WCI utuqqaq 's.th. old'
ECI Igl utuqqaviksuaq [for utuqqaviɣyuaq?] 'very old man' [Ras.]
GRI utuqqaq* 'someone old' [and utuqqałłak 'old animal', utuqqatsi(ʀ)- 'apologize, make excuses']

PY uupa(q) 'sea peach'
AAY —
CAY —
NSY uupaq 'sea peach' [L.-T.]
CSY uupa 'sea peach (edible sea organism)'

PY uutuk 'sea urchin' [cf. Aleut utu-X 'sea anemone']
AAY uutuk 'sea urchin'
CAY uutuk
NSY —
CSY —

PE uvakut 'we' [the kut seems to be the same as the 1pl verbal subject marker of that shape, but there has been restructuring in Yup with this kut plus relative person endings as found in the subord. mood attached apparently to singular uvaŋa; du. forms in Inu regular uvaɣuk, etc.; cf. uvaŋa]
AAY [w̯aŋkuta, du. w̯aŋkunuk 'we']
CAY [w̯aŋkuta, HBC, NS waŋkuta, Nun kʷaŋkuta, du. kʷaŋkuk 'we']
NSY [waŋkuta, du. waŋkuɣnuŋ 'we']
CSY [w̯aŋkuta, du. w̯aŋkutuŋ 'we']
Sir məkəta 'we'
SPI uaɣut, Unk waaɣut
NAI uvaɣut
WCI uvaɣut
ECI uvaɣut
GRI uaɣut, EG uaŋit

PE uvaŋa 'I' [apparently from dem. root uv- and 1s subject ending -ŋa; cf. uvakut]
AAY w̯i(i) 'I'
CAY w̯ii, w̯iiŋa, HBC, NS wii, wiiŋa, Nun kʷii, kʷiiŋa
NSY wi
CSY w̯aŋa
Sir məŋa
SPI uaŋa, Unk waaŋa
NAI uvaŋa
WCI uvaŋa
ECI uvaŋa 'I' [also uvaqa 'me (rather), myself' (Dor. has uvaʀa for Tar]
GRI uaŋa, EG uaña 'I' [and uaalu 'me too!']

PE uvəʀ- or əvəʀ- 'lean or tilt' [cf. perhaps əvə(ʀ)ləɣ-]
AAY wəʀŋa- 'slope'
CAY uvəʀ-, NS əvəʀ- 'be slanted, tilting'
NSY uvəʀ- 'tumble down', [ANLC] 'get overturned, fall flat', uvəXtə- 'knock down, tilt'
CSY uvəʀ- 'keel over' [and note vəXtə- 'take back', vəʀutə- 'give back', and Chap vəʀutataX 'elastic', also uvəxtaʀ- 'be tossed up in blanket toss' (nom. uvəxtaq) — going rather with əvə(ʀ)ləɣ-?; for uvəluk, əvluk 'sea swell' see iŋ(ə)yuləɣ]
Sir uvəʀ- 'keel over' [Em., who also has əvʀətataX 's.th. elastic, returning to same position' and uvəxtaX 'summer game of blanket toss' (from CSY?); Men. has əvʀižaqaʀ- 'turn head over heels', and Vakh. has əvʀit- from Rub. and əvəXt(ə)- from Men.'s texts for 'return']
SPI uiq- 'lean, list, tilt'
NAI uvɨq-
WCI uviq- 'lean to side'
ECI uviq- 'lean to side, capsize'
GRI uiʀ- 'slope'

PE uvə(C)a- or əvə(C)a- 'rock or roll' [from əvəʀa-?; cf. p.b. a-]
AAY uɣaa- 'rock, sway'
CAY uvaa- 'rock from side to side (boat)' [also əvəqaa-]
NSY —
CSY uvaʀaa- 'roll around, rub around (dogs, children)'
Sir —
SPI uaa- 'rock, roll, pitch'
NAI uvaaŋa- 'be tilted' [and uvaak- 'tilt, list, urinate with leg up (dog)' — as nom. = 'dog urine']
WCI —
ECI uvaa- 'roll from side to side' [and cf. ivva(q)- 'skip (with rope)']
GRI uaa-, uʀfaa-, uXXaa- 'roll (boat)' [note also EG uaayiiʀniq 'mask dance' in Oqaatsit]

PE uvi(t)- 'open eyes' [cf. uima-, uviluʀ and Aleut umla- 'wake up' for the la- of the latter compare uʀla- under uʀə-; the final t is presumably t-[1]]
AAY wiitə- 'open eyes'
CAY wiitə- 'open eyes, bloom'
NSY —
CSY —
Sir mit(ə)- 'grow (plant), rise (sun), appear' [and mitita 'flower']
SPI uit- 'open eyes', Qaw uit-, Unk wiit- 'open eyes, open in the ice (lead)'
NAI uit- 'open eyes, break away from shore ice to form open lead (pack ice)' [and ui- 'overreact, be too eager', uisi- 'be overexcited', uɣɣisiɣi- 'overreact about trivial matter' (with non-historical ɣ), uiži- 'open eyes for first time (newborn animal)']
WCI uit- 'open eyes' [and uiŋa- 'not understand', uiyut 'two young people sexually excited', uɣɣitiɣi- 'be mistaken about s.th.'; for uiyi- 'trick' see uða(t)-]
ECI uit- 'open eyes' [note also uiɣaq 'one who acts precipitously, nervously', uvikkaq 'young one (man or animal)'; for Lab uima- 'not know where one is upon awakening' see uima-]
GRI uit- 'open eyes' [and uisi- 'open eyes (newborn animal)', uissuummi- 'be surprised', uitsat(i)- 'rush around in confusion', uisuʀiʀ- 'blink']

PI uinəq 'open lead (in ice)' [cf. nəʀ[1]]
SPI uiniq 'open lead'
NAI uinʸiq*
WCI uiniq
ECI uiniq
GRI —

PI uinʀaq- 'be sleepy' [cf. n(ə)ʀaʀ(ᴀʀ)]
SPI uiʀnaq- 'be sleepy'
NAI uinʸʀaq-
WCI uinʀaq-
ECI uiʀŋa(q)-
GRI uiʀnaʀ-, NG iʀŋahuk-, EG uaʀnaʀ-

PI uitaq 's.o. who has drifted away on an ice floe [cf. uinəq, also NAI uit- above, here used transitively before ðaʀ?]
SPI —
NAI uisaq 's.o. who drifts off on ice floe'
WCI —
ECI uitaq 's.o. carried off by the break between the shore ice and the pack ice'
GRI uisaa- 'be carried out to sea on ice floe'

PI uivvak or **uivvaq** 'fern' [cf. vaɣ?]
SPI —
NAI —
WCI Cop uivvaq 'fragrant shield fern, club moss' [Pryde]
ECI —
GRI uiffak 'fern'

PE uvita- 'have eyes open' [cf. ta-]
AAY wiita- 'have eyes open'
CAY wiita- 'remain, live (somewhere)' [cf. kiyaʀ- 'look around' for a semantic parallel; note also uitan, uitasuun 'eye' on old word lists such as Wrangell 1839]
NSY —
CSY —
Sir —
SPI uita- 'have eyes open'
NAI uisa- 'have eyes open', PH 'go without eating'
WCI uita- 'have eyes open' [and Ras. has Cop uvita- 'rush around, be fidgety']
ECI uita- 'have eyes open'
GRI uisa- 'be busy, confused, have eyes open — e.g. in fright', NG uiha- 'be lively, run around excitedly [and note EG uitsat 'eye']

PE uviluʀ 'clam or mussel' [cf. uvi(t)- and lu(ʀ) and Aleut wayɣi-X 'blue mussel, small knife']
AAY —
CAY wiiluq 'clam, clamshell'
NSY iviluk 'mussel' [ANLC]
CSY ivilu 'clamshell'
Sir ivilu [Orr — from CSY]
SPI —
NAI uvil^{y}uq, ivil^{y}uq 'clamshell, seashell'
WCI uviluq 'seashell'
ECI uviluq 'mussel'
GRI uiluq 'bivalve, blue mussel'

PE uvinəɣ '(human) flesh or skin'
AAY —
CAY —
NSY uvinək 'body'
CSY uvinək 'human skin, close relative', Chap 'body' [and note uvin 's.th. around, surrounding, kinfolk, surface']
Sir uvənəX 'body, trunk' [Vakh. has uvənɣax; and note uvəłqaʀməlŋəX 'round thing, area around']
SPI uinik, Unk wiinik, wiiniq 'human skin', Imaq uiniq 'body'
NAI uvin^{y}ik, uvin^{y}iq* 'skin of human' [uvin^{y}n^{y}ak- 'become fat, fleshy']
WCI uvinik 'skin'
ECI uvinik 'skin covered flesh, esp. of humans' [usually 'skin of human' acc. Saul]
GRI uinik 'flesh' [uinnaɣ- 'have put on flesh (emaciated person)'; for EG uliivik 'skin' see uliɣ-]

PE uvinŋi(C)aʀ- and **uyu(n)ŋi(C)uʀ-** 'whistle'
AAY —
CAY —
NSY uyuŋiaʀ- 'whistle'
CSY —
Sir —
SPI uyuŋiaʀaq- 'whistle'
NAI uvin^{y}ŋiaqtuq-, uvin^{y}ŋiuʀaq-, uvin^{y}ŋiuqšaq-, PH uvin^{y}ŋiaʀžuk-
WCI Sig uviŋniuq- [Lowe has uvinŋiusuq-]
ECI uviŋŋiaq- 'whistle'
GRI uiŋŋiaʀ-, NG uiŋŋiak-

PE uvva 'here (you are)' [from demonstrative root uv-; cf. Aleut wa, Att ma under dem. roots — the direct cognate]
AAY w̥ału 'maybe', C w̥a, K w̥aa-i 'here you are' [also has enclitic uses]
CAY w̥ałłu 'or', w̥axxuq 'exclamation of disappointment, dissatisfaction', w̥aqaa 'hello, what's up?', w̥atua 'just now' [also, as +w̥a or +xa, has enclitic uses, e.g. when answering questions in conseq. mood or in conjunction with p.b. łi-; note also nauw̥a 'where is it?' under naɣu (na-^{2})]
NSY waninəŋ 'earlier', wasaq 'but', wiasam 'probably'
CSY w̥anikun 'later on, in the evening', w̥aaw̥a 'at least, again and again' [also enclitic '(when) ever, maybe' and as particle w̥aa used to intensify questions]
Sir mawənłu 'maybe', macicu 'if, it turns out'
SPI uvvaa 'here it is', uvvaa-aa 'expression of understanding' [and uvvaɣiaq 'I wonder']
NAI uvva 'here it is' [also enclitic], uvvahii, uvvii 'look, here it is'
WCI uvva 'here you are', Car? 'see, look' [Schn. 'adg']
ECI uvvalu 'or (else), maybe, isn't that so?'
GRI uffa, uxxa 'even though, there it is', uffami 'if only', EG uppa 'maybe'

PI uv(v)atciaq 'just now' [cf. tciaq]
SPI —
NAI —
WCI Cop [and 'adg' in Schn.] uvatsiaq 'a little while ago', uvatsiaʀu 'in a little while' [Dor. has uviatsiaʀu 'formerly' for B. Lake and Lowe uvattiaɣu for H. Island]
ECI Igl [Catholic part of population only acc. Dor.] uvattiaʀualuk 'formerly', uattiaʀu 'later' [also Aiv], Lab uvatsiaʀuk 'presently' [but Andersen et al. have uvatsiagu 'a long time ago']
GRI uatsi 'wait a bit', uatsiaq 'this morning', NG utsiaq 'just now', utsiaʀu 'wait a bit, in a while', utsiatsiaŋŋaaq 'a while ago', utsiaʀutsiaŋŋaaɣu 'soon', EG u(u)tsaaŋi 'in a while' [but EG uutsiaq 'a while ago' — Ras. has uvatsiaq 'during the

morning'; WG aatsaat (Top aitseit) 'just now, for first time' and EG aatsaatsiaayi 'a little while ago' probably belong here also]

PY ɣʷatən 'thus' [aequalis case]
AAY w̥atən 'like this'
CAY w̥atən 'like this' [exclam.; w̥atna- 'act like this']
NSY watən 'like this'
CSY w̥atən 'like this' [w̥atətə- 'be like this']

PI uvvaq- 'take a bath' [cf. əʀvuqaʀ- under əʀə-[1] but also əvəɣ- — there may be contam. here]
SPI uvva(q)tuq- 'take a bath'
NAI uvvaq(tuq)-, ivvaq(tuq)-
WCI Net uvvaq- 'take a bath' [Pryde; Met. has ivvaqtuq- 'take a bath'; for uaq- 'wash' see uʀaʀ-]
ECI uvva(q)- 'wash (with soap)'
GRI uffaʀ- 'take bath, wash body', NG uɣɣaq- 'wash body (with wash cloth, traditionally of guillemot skins)' [see hunauɣɣa under cuna-uvva (cu(na)) for the ɣɣ from *vv]

PE uya(quʀ) 'neck' [cf. uyaɣ- and quʀ and Aleut uyu-X 'neck', uyaʀ- 'spout, muzzle, neck of bottle']
AAY uyaquq, yuaquq, yaaquq 'neck'
CAY uya 'non-anatomical neck', uyaquq 'neck' [for uyatu- 'be wide (river, lake, etc.)' see uyatu-]
NSY uyaquq 'neck'
CSY uyaquq 'neck'
Sir uyəqəX 'neck'
SPI ➟
NAI ➟
WCI ➟
ECI [uyak 'upper part of bust' (Saul), Lab also 'forequarter of seal' (Peck)]
GRI ➟

PY uyalək 'cormorant' [cf. ləɣ]
AAY uyalək 'cormorant, shag'
CAY uyalək 'pelagic cormorant'
NSY —
CSY —

PE uyamiɣ 's.th. worn around neck' [cf. miɣ-]
AAY uyamik, yuamik 's.th. worn round neck'
CAY uyamik 'thing worn around neck'
NSY uyamiaq 'shoulder load' [Em.; L.-T. uyamiłquaq 'necklace']
CSY uyamik 'shoulder load'
Sir uyəməx 'shoulder load' [Orr and Em. who also gives gloss 'tube for carrying needles and thread fixed to upper clothing']
SPI uyamiɣžuaq 'necklace' [and uyamiataq 'bag worn round neck for picking greens']
NAI uyamik 'needle case, tube', Nu uyamitquq 'hair hanging under chin of cow moose, earring'
WCI Sig uyamitqun 'necklace' [and Ras. has Net uyamia 'caribou's necklace']
ECI uyamik 'necklace'
GRI uyamik 'necklace' [and uyamiɣ- 'have arm in sling']

PY-S uya(C)aq 'rope or line' [cf. uyukkuʀ(aʀ) though the relat. is obscure]
AAY —
CAY uzaaq*, Y uzaaʀaq 'line attached to a spear'
NSY uya(a)q 'rope for pulling animals out of water'
CSY [uyiiq* 'thick rope made from skin of baby walrus' — from *uyuðiʀ?; uyiiʀaq 'rope made from skin of bearded seal']
Sir ucəX 'skin rope' [Orr has uciX 'skin rope' which may be borrowed from CSY if not from *uyyaq]

PE uyaɣ- and **uyanəɣ-** 'stretch neck to see better' [cf. uya(quʀ) and nəɣ- for the second form]
AAY uyaŋtə- 'emerge from some place'
CAY uyaŋtə- 'look over and down, peek in'
NSY —
CSY uyaŋtə- 'stretch neck to see better'
Sir —
SPI [uyaʀaq- (for uyaɣaq?) 'stretch to look over s.th.' — Jen.]
NAI Nu uyak- 'hover at surface of water (of seal with neck coming in and out of water)'
WCI uyak- 'stand straight in water (of sea mammal)', Cop 'look or lean over abyss' [Ras.], Car? uyaq- 'appear, show oneself, appear from behind s.th.' [Schn. 'adg.']
ECI uyak- 'be half visible on the ice (of seal that raises chest above ice)' [Peck has uyaviɣi- 'look half out of hole (of seal)' for Lab]
GRI uyaɣ- 'stretch oneself', uyakkaʀ-, uyaŋit- 'bend over s.th. to see what is below'

PI uyakciutət 'shoulder harness or suspenders' [cf. un]
SPI —
NAI —
WCI uyatsiutik 'trouser braces, suspenders' [du.; Ras. has Car pl. uyattiutit 'harness']
ECI uyatsiutit 'trouser braces'
GRI uyatsiutit

PE uyaʀaɣ 'rock'
AAY —
CAY —
NSY uyʀak, uyaʀak 'rock'
CSY uyʀak
Sir —
SPI uyaʀak
NAI uyaʀak
WCI uyaʀak
ECI uyaʀak
GRI uyaʀak, pl. uyaqqat

PY uyatu- 'be wide [cf. uyavaʀ- and tu-[1], but compare also uya(quʀ)?]
AAY uyatu- 'spread out (tree branches), be wide (river, road)' [opp. = uyakite-]
CAY uyatu- 'be wide (water) [opp. = uyakitə-]
NSY —
CSY uyatu- 'be distant (in time or space)' [influenced by uyavaʀ-?]

PY-S uyavaʀ- 'go far away' [cf. uyatu- and vaʀ-; the relat. to iŋa(va)- and uŋavaq under uŋan is obscure]
AAY —
CAY —
NSY uyavaʀ- 'go far away' [ANLC]
CSY uyavaʀ- 'go far' [uyavaq 'distance']
Sir uyəvaX 'distance' [and uyəvani 'far off', uyəvaniʀ- 'go off']

PY-S uyəɣ- 'distribute' [from *uðəɣ-?; cf. Aleut uðiɣ- 'divide, distribute']
AAY —
CAY — [for uyiqə- 'keep going back for more (food)' see uyiqə-]
NSY —
CSY uyəxtə- 'distribute things'
Sir uyəxtə- 'distribute things' [Em.; Men. has uyixtə-]

PE uyɣu- 'add on'
AAY K usɣutə-, C uyɣutə- 'connect, attach, fasten'
CAY uzɣu- 'add on, extend', uzɣutə-, HBC uyɣutə- 'be attached'
NSY uyɣu- 'extend, add to length' [ANLC; Men. has uyɣutə- 'connect']
CSY uyɣu- 'add on, extend'
Sir uyɣułəku 'one after the other' [3s obj. subordinative form]
SPI uuyu- 'extend'
NAI uiɣu, iiɣu 'extension', uiɣu-, iiɣu- 'add on' [uiɣuqłiq* 'farthest extension']
WCI uiɣu- 'add on'
ECI uiɣu 'extension', uiɣu- 'lengthen'
GRI uiɣu(q), uiu(q) 'extension', uiɣu-, uiu- 'add on' [uiɣuʀłiq* 'outermost in a row, farthest appendage']

PE uyiqə- 'keep going back for more?' [cf. Aleut uyuXta- EA 'ask for, beg', Atkan 'like (to eat)' with p.b. (X)ta-, also EA uyuXsini- 'make feel happy']
AAY —
CAY uyiqə- 'keep going back for more, get a lot of food at a party' [and HBC uyəXqə- 'approach to get food (e.g. bait from trap)']
NSY —
CSY — [for uyəxtə- 'distribute things' see uyəɣ-]
Sir —
SPI Unk wiiʀi- 'get into an agreeable habit' [KI uiʀviili- 'bother s.o.', Imaq wiqma(q)- 'get used to, adapt to']
NAI uiʀit- 'get in the habit of doing s.th. enjoyable or fulfilling', uiʀn^{y}aaq-, Nu uiqn^{y}aaq- 'do s.th. frequently one has learned to enjoy'
WCI uiʀi- 'get used to s.th.'
ECI uiʀi- 'begin to get used to', Lab 'have s.th. one likes or longs for' [Peck]
GRI uiʀi- 'acquire the habit of', uiqqiʀiyi- 'keep on returning to (place one had a good time or s.th. one is addicted to)'

PE uyivə- 'go around (in a circle)' [the Inu forms by back-formation from uyivvaʀ below?]
AAY wiɣ-, PWS wiɣə-, AP wiuɣ- 'go in a circle' [and wiiɣaaXtə- 'spin (once)', PWS wiɣŋuaʀ- 'make a round trip']
CAY uivə-, HBC uyivə- 'circle, revolve' [and uivətm̥un 'around']
NSY uyutm̥un 'around'
CSY uzivə- 'revolve, rotate, go around s.th.'
Sir [yayiŋucaʀ- 'spin', yayiŋucəX 'spinning top']
SPI uivaq- 'come into sight, visit' [and Imaq uyutmun 'around' — from NSY?]
NAI uivaq-, uivvaq- 'come around (a promontory)'
WCI uivaq- 'go around (e.g. house)'
ECI uivaq- 'go around s.th.'
GRI uiaʀ- 'pass around headland or the like' [Holt. has NG uivaq- 'travel south on a long hunting trip in the spring']

PE uyivðaʀ- 'revolve or spin' [cf. ðaʀ-]
AAY —
CAY wiivaaʀ-, wiifaaʀ- 'revolve repeatedly'
NSY —
CSY —
Sir —
SPI uivžaaq- 'go in a (full) circle', uivžalak- 'go in a circle'
NAI uivžaluktaq- 'tumble, do somersaults'
WCI Car uivyaaq- 'spin around until dizzy (game)' [Pryde]
ECI uiyya(C)- 'turn round and round', uiyyaŋu-, uiyyaŋuq- 'see everything spinning around (when dizzy)'
GRI uiššaaʀ- [old ortho. uivssâʀ-] 'get dizzy (and fall)', uiššaŋu- 'be dizzy', NG uissaaq- 'turn round and round' [Holt.]

PE uyivvaʀ 'turning point' [cf. q under nəʀ[1]]
AAY K wiiwaq, KP iiwaq 'vertebra'
CAY wiivaq
NSY uyvaq 'turning point on coast (name of Cape Dezhnev)', uyuva(k) 'cartilagineous part of vertebra' [L.-T.]
CSY uziva 'circular thing, vertebra'
Sir —
SPI [uivaq- 'come into view, rounding a point']
NAI uivaq-, uivvaq- 'go around' [and Uivvaq 'Cape Lisbourne', Uum uivvaŋani 'around it' [Lowe]
WCI —
ECI uivvaq 'cape, point of land, trip around peninsula'
GRI uiffaq* 'promontory one must sail around (esp. as place name)'

PY uytə- 'erode or chip'
AAY ustə- 'slide down (earth in a landslide)'
CAY ustə- 'erode, chip, cave in', HBC uytə- 'cause to cave in'
NSY —
CSY [for uusqaq 'deep or high place' see ətə-] ➟

PY usnəq 'sandy bank?' [cf. nəʀ[1]]
AAY usŋ̥əq 'sandbank, dune'
CAY usŋ̥əq* 'chipped spot, caved in river bank'
NSY —
CSY uusŋ̥əq* 'river or ocean bank, small hill'

PY uyuɣ- 'have sexual intercourse' [cf. uyuŋə-?]
AAY uyuɣ- 'have sexual intercourse' [old sources]
CAY uyuɣ- 'have sexual intercourse'
NSY uyuɣ- [ANLC]
CSY uyuɣ-

PE uyukkuR(aR) 'fishing line' [there may be a relat. to uya(C)aq; cf. EA usxa-X 'string, line' — from the Yup?]
AAY [note uskuRuutaq 'type of berries on a long vine']
CAY uskuq 'rope, cord, umbilical cord', uskuRaq 'tether, harness, string of toy' [and NS uskuXtuliaRaq 'bog cranberry']
NSY —
CSY uskaaq 'cord on seal-retrieving hook or sling', uskuRaq 'cord, fishing line'
Sir uskəɣəRəX, uskəɣəX 'rope' [Vakh. from Rub.]
SPI —
NAI —
WCI uyukkuaq 'fishing line' [Dor.; Met. has uyupkuaq]
ECI uyukkuaq 'fishing line'
GRI uyukkuaq [old ortho. uyúkuaq] 'bait (blubber on a line used to catch gulls)'

PI uyuməq- 'shimmer in heat'
Yup [Drebert has uyungeriak (for uyuŋiRyaq?) 'heat waves over land or water' for CAY, perhaps by contam. with uyuŋe-]
SPI Qaw uyumiq- 'be heat waves visibly distorting horizon' [Jen. has 'mist, fog' for KI]
NAI uyumiq 'heat waves, heat mirage, refractory layer of atmosphere through which shamans pass to get to the moon' [also as verb; for Nu uyupkaq- 'dance moving a fan-like object from side to side' see uyuŋə-]
WCI uyumiaRaq- 'shimmer (of sun), be hazy (of earth)' [Schn. has uyumiRaq- 'dance or move (sun)' for 'adg', also uyuRumiRaq- for B. Lake]
ECI u(u)yuRumiali- 'move (of surrounding atmosphere when sun or rocks release heat)' [and uuyummi(C)- 'move like gelatin' — Saul has single u's in these forms]
GRI uyumik 'frost smoke, steam from sea in mild weather', uyumiɣ- 'be frost smoke', uyuviɣ- 'be foggy, dim' [and note uuyuRnu- 'make rings (stone in water)', NWG uyuŋŋuaRtuR-, SWG uuyuŋuyuuRtuR- 'have gooseflesh, freeze suddenly']

PY-S uyuŋə- 'squat' [cf. uyuɣ- and/or uyuməq-?]
AAY PWS uyuŋə- 'squat, sag posturally'
CAY uyuŋə- 'squat'
NSY —
CSY uyəŋpała- 'bob up and down' [uyəŋqaR- 'bob slowly']
Sir uyəŋpała- 'jump up and down, swing on s.th.' [Em.]
Inu [note NAI uyuk- 'dance Inupiaq style (of woman)', Nu uyupqaq- 'dance holding a fan and moving one's arms from one side to the other']

PY uyuRaq 'younger sibling' [cf. uyuRu(ɣ) and RaR, also perhaps Aleut huyu- '(woman's) brother', with unexplained h]
AAY uyuRaq, uyuwaq 'younger brother'
CAY uyuRaq* 'younger sibling'
NSY uyuRaq
CSY uyuRaq*
Sir [for uŋyəX 'younger sibling' see uŋi-X under Proto-Aleut bases]

PE uyuRu(ɣ) 'nephew or niece of man' [cf. uyuRaq and compare uyaRaɣ for the loss of the second vowel in Yup]
AAY uyRu(q), uyRu(k) 'niece or nephew of a man', K uzRuq, C uyyuq 'man's sister's child'
CAY uzRuq, HBC uyRuq 'niece or nephew of a man through his sister'
NSY uyRu [Enm.] 'nephew'
CSY uyRu 'nephew of a man, niece of a man through his sister'
Sir uyRu [Orr — Em. has uyRa]
SPI uyuRu 'nephew, niece' [Imaq also uyRu]
NAI uyuRu
WCI uyuRu(k) 'nephew or niece of a man'
ECI uyuRu(k) 'nephew, niece, man's sister's child'
GRI uyuRuk 'nephew, niece through sister (of man)', EG uyuȒuq 'brother's child'

PY uyvala- 'practice sorcery' [cf. uyvi]
AAY —
CAY —
NSY uyvala- 'practice sorcery, shamanize'
CSY uyvala- 'practice sorcery' [for uyviinəq* 'sorcerer' see uyviŋit- under uyvi]

PE uyvi 'mental ability' [cf. uyvala-]
AAY uswi 'intelligence, wits' [and K uswitu-, C uyyutu- 'be wise' with tu-[1] and K uswiiR-, C iɣuiR- 'be crazy' with ŋiR-]
CAY uzvi, HBC uyvi 'intelligence, wits' [and uzvitu- 'be wise']
NSY —
CSY ➡
Sir [Vakh. has uyviliR- 'annoy, persecute']
SPI ➡
NAI ➡
WCI [note uiviɣi- 'find too little (the price s.o. is willing to offer)', uivinaq- 'be too expensive', uivitu- 'feel that everything is too expensive' (Schn. has 'be vicious' for 'adg' and Ras. has uivitužuq 'miser' for Net)]
ECI [uivi(i)RRi(C)- 'cheat, harm' — Saul has long ii]
GRI uiviR-, uiviRsuR- 'gambol, run about' [these go with AAY uswiiR- above — compare also uyviŋit- below]

PE uyviŋit- 'be foolish' [cf. ŋit-]
AAY K uswiiłXaaq, C uɣuiłXaaq 'child' [and compare uswiiR- under uyvi above]
CAY uzviitə- 'be crazy'
NSY uyviatə- 'be unsuspecting' [ANLC]
CSY uyviinəq* 'sorcerer'
Sir —
SPI uiviit- 'be bold, mischievous, unruly' [and Qaw uiviilaq 'child', Imaq uivi(i)naq 'discontent']
NAI uiviit- 'be willing to go to any lengths to get what one wants' [uiviil^{y}aq 'one who does not mind

selling things at low cost or buying expensive things']
WCI —
ECI uiviit- 'do what one shouldn't, play tricks, be vicious, steal, lie, be a lecher', Lab 'be saucy' [also uiyi- 'cheat' and uivi(i)sa(a)q- 'cheat, annoy, tease' (with long ii acc. Saul), Lab uivisaaC- 'rape, mistreat']
GRI uavit-, uavat- 'be restless, noisy, in a mess' [the latter form influenced by uða(t)-?]

Y

PY-S yaɣ(ə)- 'crouch down' [cf. iyaŋa- and əlavə-? — the connection — if any — is obscure]
AAY —
CAY —
NSY —
CSY yaaɣ- 'crouch' [and yaxtaʀaʀ- 'fly low'; Chap also yaawaaʀ- 'hide' in Rub.]
Sir yaxpaɣ- 'crouch down (to avoid being seen)' [yaxpəʀ- 'hide (intr.)' — Em.]

PY yavə- 'row' [cf. iyaɣ-]
AAY ➟
CAY cavə-, LI savə-, NSU yavə- 'row'
NSY —
CSY yaavə- 'row'

PY yavun 'oar' [cf. un]
AAY KP saun 'arm'
CAY cavun, LI savun, HBC yavun 'oar'
NSY —
CSY yaavuquun

yayiaq(a) 'hawk' [apparently from Chukchi y'ayaq 'seagull', but cf. also the CAY under PE kəð(ə)kaviɣ — contam.?]
AAY —
CAY —
NSY yaɣiaq, yaɣuuq 'hawk' [ANLC]
CSY yayiiqa 'rough-legged hawk'

PY-S yuʀžaʀ- 'dance Eskimo dance?' [cf. iyyuʀ-, for the possible connection with which compare the KI gloss below; the Inu forms given are presumably borrowed from Yup]
AAY AP yuʀaq, PWS iwaq 'native-style dance'
CAY yuʀaʀ- 'dance trad. Eskimo style (NSU esp. women)', yuʀaq 'Eskimo dance'
NSY —
CSY yuʀaʀ- 'pray' [Em. has this as 'pronounce a charm' for Chap; yuʀaʀvik 'church', yuʀaXta 'minister, priest']
Sir yuʀcəX 'spell, charm', yuʀcəʀ- 'pronounce a charm' [Em.]
Inu [note KI yuʀaqtuat 'dancers who danced while half way through entrance hole of men's communal house' and NAI yuʀaisuq- 'invite dancers from another village, go in and out of house']

Ž

žiɣtə and **yiɣtə** '(fox's) den' [cf. Aleut cixti-X 'fox's den', but also ixti-X 'pit, grave', Atkan also '(eye) socket'; as Berg. suggests the CSY form at least is probably from Chukchi rəɣ- 'dig' — note corresponding Koryak yəɣ- for the CAY forms — these forms date at least from (Russian) colonial times; compare citə]
AAY nixta, ŋixta, ixta, nəxta, ləxta 'den'
CAY ixta, Nun iɣixta, sixta 'den' [reported from Stebbins; for Nun s(ə)tii 'cave' see citə]
NSY — [ɣəxtə, ɣətxə 'lake' is from Chukchi]
CSY žiixta 'den'
Sir əcixta 'den' [Krup. has əžixta]

PROTO-ALEUT BASES WITH NO OBVIOUS (OR A DOUBTFUL) ESKIMO COGNATE

These comprise in principle all lexical stems (discounting toponyms and clearly secondary derivations) occurring in Bergsland 1994 in at least two out of the three main Aleut 'dialects' — Atkan, Att, and EA — that have no obvious Eskimo cognates mentioned in the CED. They are only exceptionally indicated in the Aleut index. The orthography is that used elsewhere in this dictionary. Note that some tentative cognates given in the body of the dictionary may in fact belong instead on this list — e.g. su- 'take' mentioned under təɣu-. They may in some cases reflect Proto-Eskimo-Aleut stems lost in Eskimo (note that Aleut has a higher base to productive postbase ratio than Eskimo languages), though they may in other cases come from an unrelated — e.g. substratum — source. Some of them — especially ones referring to flora and fauna — have been borrowed into Alutiiq and/or CAY as indicated ('cf. Esk' refers to head forms in the main body of the CED if such loans are attested in more than one Eskimo language). Others represent 'deep' roots, in which case more concrete derived forms are supplied. The forms given correspond to those found in conservative Atkan (where attested), unless otherwise indicated. Alternative original forms follow obliques. For more detailed information see Bergsland 1994 (the tentative cross-references to PE stems added to some items below are also chiefly from that source).

a- 'blaze' (as in a-ðiga- 'be bright' and a-ni- 'light, set fire to')
aaci-X 'calm interval between waves' (EA; Atkan has aaci-s 'leave interval (breakers), abate (wind)')
aaðu-x 'loins'
aaɣlu-X 'fulmar'
aali- 'land' (as in aaliiluX 'landing place')
aalʀa- 'be bare, uncovered'
aalu- 'smile, laugh'
aalu-X 'swell, big wave' (cf. perhaps PI aluktətnəq)
aamatikna-X/am̥aatikna-X 'chip, shaving'
aamɣi-X/aamax 'blood' (and aamɣi- 'bleed')
aanaqliita-X, EA aaŋłiqiita-X 'sea cucumber' (> AAY anaqiitak)
aaqana-X 'cuttlefish, octopus'
aaʀi-X[1] 'liver'
aaʀi-X[2] 'mallard duck'
aaʀuliix 'hawk, falcon' (> AAY aaXuliq, aaXulik)
aaʀumikaaðax/haʀmikaaðɣi-X 'blowfly' (EA uuʀumikiðax/uuʀamikaðax, Att huurnimikayaX)
aaXuyaakða-X, EA aaquyaakða-X 'wart'
aci- 'press, crush' (as in acilaXsita-, EA acilat-; cf. perhaps PE at(ə)-)
aciɣ- 'fall' (cf. perhaps PE at(ə)-)
aciɣa-/acixa- 'learn'
acika-a 'inside (of it - skin)' (cf. perhaps PE at(ə)-)
acu-'feel cold'
acuuʀi- 'answer'
acxu- 'share food with' (> AAY 'feed')
að- 'landward side' (cf. perhaps PI aci[2])
aðalu- 'tell a lie'
aðɣayu-X 'pink salmon'
aðɣilax 'earthquake'
aði-X 'squid'
aðiɣasi-X 'large intestine' (EA; Atkan iðiɣasi-X 'anus' — a blend — cf. PE ətəʀ?)
aɣa-/axa- 'hiccup' (EA and Att)
aɣaðaX 'arrow, spear' (also aɣalʀi-X 'spear, harpoon (head)'; cf. perhaps PI aat- or aa(k))
aɣal- 'space behind' (cf. perhaps PI aat-)
aɣamaxci-X 'minke whale'
aɣamɣi-X 'chiton (mollusc)'
aɣamt- 'blame, judge'
a(a)ɣayuuX 'cormorant' (cf. Esk aɣayuuq)
aɣða-X 'crossbeam of baidar' (and probably also aɣðaaʀi-X, EA aaðxaaX 'backbone')
aɣðaXxi-X/aɣðiXxi-X 'sperm whale'
aɣðiɣ- 'cut, slice'
aɣðu- 'shake head'
aɣla- 'haul, transport'
aɣli- 'take care of, be careful'
aɣluXt- 'move, change place'
aɣu- 'make'
aɣu-lakan 'fear' (neg.; EA aɣuuqisa-lakan rather)
aɣuX 'part of beach left dry at low tide'
akaluX 'way, path' (cf. perhaps PE aɣə-)
akaʀusi-X 'toggle-head (harpoon)' (EA and Att)
akayu-X 'strait, pass' (cf. perhaps PE aɣə-)
akiiʀ- 'take along' (as in akiiʀasa-; cf. perhaps PE akkiʀ-)
akina-X 'leeward' (cf. perhaps PE aki(-))
al- 'middle (of)'
alaŋaX 'cottonwood (driftwood)'
alax 'two' (EA aalax, Att ulax; cf. perhaps PE p.b. ŋu- for the initial element, also the dual number infl.)
alaʀu-X 'sea, ocean' (cf. perhaps PE ala-, referring to game, and p.b. ʀu-)
alɣa-X 'animal'
aliɣ- 'vomit'
aliiɣaX 'leg'
alitxu- 'wage war'
aliX 'old man'
alqu- 'what, do what'
alʀi- 'submit' (as in alʀina- 'be difficult, be mighty')
alʀu- 'be shy, feel awe'
alu- 'side' (as in alum aŋaa 'side of body' and EA alu-n 'ribs')
aluɣa-X 'root bulb of black lily'
alut- 'count, reckon'
aluX 'line, letter' (and aluʀ- 'write'; cf. perhaps PE alŋaʀ(-))
ałaya-X 'board' (cf. Esk ałayaq)
ama- 'braid'
amax 'night' (cf. perhaps PE avəɣ-)

amaXu- 'race'
amayakna- 'be unclean' (also mayakna-, and perhaps also EA aama-li- 'remove dirt')
amcu- 'praise' (EA; Att avcu- 'tell a story')
amɣaaða-X 'walrus'
amɣi- 'attractive' (as in amɣiXsi- 'be beautiful')
amɣiʀ- 'keep (night) watch' (cf. perhaps PE avəɣ-)
ami-X 'maternal uncle'
amku-X 'inner layer of skin' (EA and Att)
amʀi- 'fight, wrestle' (cf. perhaps PE amit-)
amta- 'repent, regret'
amta-X 'bird's breastbone'
amti-X 'cliff'
amu-[1] 'be ready to, (with intent.) near future, (in past) long ago' (cf. perhaps PE amiʀ)
amu-[2] 'flash (lightning)' (cf. perhaps PE a(C)umaʀ)
amxi-X 'fish meat'
amXa-X 'sleeve' (cf. Esk amʀaq)
am̥iʀ- 'vicinity (of)'
anat-/anati-X '(property) mark' (also EA anata- 'keep'; perhaps from ana-t- 'procure (-t) something (ana-)')
anɣa-X 'line, rope'
anɣaxtaX 'young girl' (EA only, but cf. AAY C aŋyaXtaq 'young girl' — a loan?)
anɣu- 'drive in, nail'
aniiɣ- 'chop' (> AAY)
anu(ŋis) 'tarsal bones (of wrists and ankles)'
anu-[1] 'flow, stream' (also amnar- from an(u)maʀ-)
anu-[2] 'throw at, hit' (also amniɣ- from an(u)miɣ-)
anuɣ- 'be wanted, intend, think' (as in anuxta- and also anɣ- 'mind, idea, guts')
anXaɣ- 'beat hard (heart)'
aŋ̥i-X 'edible root of lupine' (cf. perhaps PE at(ə)-)
aŋaða- 'wash, wipe'
aŋaðaʀi-X/aŋiðaX 'canine tooth' (cf. perhaps aŋa- under PE aŋuðaʀ-)
aŋali-X 'daylight'
aŋayaX 'quickly'
aŋaza- 'be useful, profitable'
aŋiix-six 'rub' (EA only, but cf. CSY aŋiXə- 'smear, rub in, spread, paint' — a loan?)
aŋiqi- 'left (side)' (as in aŋiqim aðan and aŋiqiiʀi-X; > AAY aŋiqiq)
aŋiʀ- 'condemn' (EA 'menace')
a(a)ŋ(a)lax 'gill(s)' (EA aalŋaaX)
aŋli- 'be hard, solid' (cf. perhaps PE aŋ(ə)li- 'grow big' under aŋ(ə)-)
aŋu-X 'lamp'
aŋux/haŋux 'ditch, (dig) pit'
aŋyu- 'be cautious, unsteady', EA 'having a difficult time' (cf. perhaps PE aŋuðaʀ-)
aŋu-X 'birthmark, mole'
aqi-, EA iqi- 'run away, come off' (cf. perhaps PE aqva-)
aʀaaʀu-X 'cove'
aʀaɣ- 'sweat' (EA and Att)
aʀða-X 'bladder or stomach filled with oil, etc.'
aʀi- 'leave' (as in aʀiisa- 'leave, let go' and aʀiti-X 'remainder' and EA aʀiXta- 'remain'; cf. perhaps PE aʀ(ə)yu-)
aʀla- 'flap, flutter'
aʀliɣa-X 'black-footed albatross' (cf. Esk aʀli(ɣ)aq)
aʀlu- 'bail, ladle'
aʀu- 'disappear from view' (as in aʀut-)
aʀɣaaŋi- 'noise, shouting' (as in aʀɣaaŋina- 'shout, cry')
asaɣa-X 'cousin'
asanaqa-X 'daughter-in-law, sister-in-law'
asu-X 'cooking pot' (> AAY asuq)
asu- 'sneeze'
asux 'pit, hole in ground' (and verbal asuɣ- 'dig a pit'; EA and Att)
asxinu-X 'daughter, girl'
asxu-X 'peg, nail'
asXuðɣi-X 'girl'
asXukiða-X 'field mouse' (EA also asŋukiða-X)
atxi- 'stop'
atxiða-X 'arctic cod' (cf. Esk atɣiyaq)
awa- 'work'
axciɣa- 'move fast'
axsa- 'get a hole, be perforated'
axsiX 'black hematite' (> AAY)
ayaɣa-X 'wife' (cf. perhaps EA ayalu(ʀ)-)
ayaŋci-X 'mast'
ayaŋi-X 'fog'
ayaʀi- 'be ashamed'
ayɣi-X 'hill'
ayʀaʀ- 'shake, tremble'
ayuka- 'plait (grass rope)' (EA and Att)
ayuXa-X 'lumpfish' (Att ayuuʀi-X; > AAY)
ayxa-/ayga- 'exceed'
ayXa- 'travel, go by sea'
caaŋiqlu-X 'elbow' (cf. perhaps PE tayaʀnəʀ)
caati-X, EA and Att taaci-X 'forearm' (cf. perhaps PE tayaʀnəʀ)
cacXu-X 'belt' (cf. perhaps PE tatə-)
caðu-X 'fat, oil'
caɣ- 'split' (cf. perhaps PE ciðəɣ-)
caɣa-X/caxa-X 'red cedar (driftwood)'
caɣi-X 'halibut' (cf. Esk caɣiq)
cakna-X 'rotten, sour'
cakuXsi-X 'tinder (dried grass soaked in oil)'
cala-X 'clam' (> AAY salaq)
calu-X 'corner of oblong opening'
camli-X 'rack for skin boat'
cam̥a-X 'dish'
canki-/canku- 'pound, hammer open'
caŋa- 'crawl into' (also 'go fast (in baidarka)' (cf. perhaps PE ciŋə(t))
caŋi-X 'bow (of boat)'
caʀu- 'be wounded, cut'
cat-[1] 'slide down' (cf. perhaps PE citu-)
cat-[2] 'be partially dried (fish)'
catu- 'chip, flake off' (perhaps related to cat-[1])
caxa-X 'hollow, pit'

caXsa-X 'fish soup' (cf. Esk carsa(q))
caya-X 'fish pot in trap, weir'
ciðaʀ- 'space beside, border'
ciðɣi- 'hang loose' (and ciðɣi-ŋis, EA ciðɣa-n 'entrails'; cf. perhaps PE ciðaɣ-)
ciðʀi- 'be green, blue'
ciɣ- 'adhere, stick to' (as in ciɣit- and cit; also 'marry' and in EA 'drift ashore')
ciɣða-X 'gut parka'
ciɣli- 'undress' (EA also cilɣi-; cf. cilɣa- below)
ciiða-X 'young offspring' (and ciiðʀu-X 'baby' in Atkan and Att)
ciiðu-X 'beaked (?) whale'
ciikða-X 'eyeball, pupil'
ciikna-X 'limpet' (cf. perhaps PE citə(t)-)
ciilu- 'return'
ciimɣi- be nasty, foul, wet' (as in ciimɣi- na-)
cik- 'be in motion, agitated ' (as in ciklaɣ-)
ciku-X 'piece of food in pot for cooking'
cila- 'become loose'
cilɣa-, Att ciɣla- 'be torn apart' (and cilɣi- 'tear off', Att ciɣli- 'divide up (food)')
cilu-X 'Alaska longspur'
cimiɣi-X, EA ciimikaayu-X 'sea snail'
cimiɣnu-X 'big toe'
cimika-X 'all, whole' (EA and Att)
cimXa- 'splash' (cf. perhaps PE ciqəʀ-)
ciŋa-/ciŋa- 'stretch (body)'
ciŋa-X 'cut in fish meat (for drying)'
ciŋla-X 'fever'
ciqi-X 'earth, mud' (cf. perhaps PE ciqəʀ)
ciʀiisiŋi-X, EA ciXisŋi-X 'pectoral sandpiper'
ciʀu- 'paddle fast, chase (in baidarka)'
cisa- 'scatter' (also cisi- 'scatter, distribute')
citXi-X 'gall, gallbladder'
ciXtuðŋi-X, EA ciXtuðɣi-X 'boil' (cf. perhaps PE ciqəʀ-)
ciya- 'stretch out'
claʀ- 'dive'
cmaɣ- 'chase in baidarka, round up'
cmi-X pulp of tooth or bone' (EA and Att)
cu- 'put on clothes' (EA also cuɣa-; cf. Sir suɣakə- 'dress')
cucaɣ- 'stand upright'
cucuða- 'ring sharply'
cuðʀi-X 'edge, ridge'
cuya- 'be all there, sufficient'
cuɣaʀu-, EA cuɣaaʀu- 'point'
cuɣi-lakan, EA cuuɣi-lakan 'be silent' (negative form; cf. perhaps cuux- 'sizzle' and PI ciiq-[2])
culikða-X, EA culika-X 'rock sandpiper'
culu- 'feel cold'
cumli- 'whet (knife)'
cumnux 'brownish, yellowish'
cum̥u- EA 'fall in water' (Att cumu- 'step into soft snow')
cunku- 'lace (baidarka skin)'
cuŋi-X dam, weir' (EA and Att; Atkan cuŋut- 'dam up'; cf. perhaps cut- below)
cuŋiix 'thin ice on lake or bay'
cuqi- 'get many (game, etc.)'
cuquða- 'small'
cut- 'be clogged, plugged up'
cutx-a '(its) tip, point' (and cuŋ̊i-, cuni- 'stab')
cuuciiX 'least auklet'
cuuðu-X 'line'
cuyɣi-X, EA cuyŋi-X 'bar-tailed godwit' (cf. perhaps PE tuðiɣ)
cxu-X 'sponge' (> AAY)
cXa- 'be full'
cXuuʀ-, EA cXuʀ- 'wash'
ðaayu-, EA yaaðu- 'be springy'
ðaliiX 'snare' (perhaps from ðaX 'eye' under PE əðə)
ðaʀ-[1] '(on) attached surface'
ðaʀ-[2] 'know, remember, understand' (as in ðaʀ-lakan 'not know', ðaqas 'senses, wits'; cf. perhaps ðaʀ-[1] in sense 'grasp')
ðaXt- 'stop, stand still' (cf. perhaps ðaʀ-[1])
ðaya-X 'late evening'
ðuxsxa-X/ɣusxa-X 'hipbone, pelvic bone' (the latter perhaps influenced by ɣut- 'pierce')
ðuXtaX 'fishhook (of compound bone)' (EA and Att; cf. perhaps CAY uqtaq 'hookless fish lure')
ɣi- 'envy'
ɣixsx-X (EA; Att ixsxi-X '(sea lion) rookery'
ɣuciɣ-/uciɣ- 'swim' (perhaps from ɣu- 'penetrate, pass through' under PE əɣu-)
haaða- get better, calm down (wind)'
haaɣa- 'be hungry'
haaku- 'be at a loss' (as in haakut- 'make a mistake, do by accident', haakula- 'be ignorant')
haanu-X 'sockeye salmon' (cf. perhaps PE dem. paɣ- in sense '(moving) upward', but note also Wakashan haniX^w 'humpback salmon')
haaŋi- 'be stupid' (EA, and haaŋina- 'be difficult' also Atkan)
haaŋu- 'toil, strive for', EA 'feel sorry for, attached to'
haaʀa- 'stop, remain' (as in haaʀani-, haaʀat-)
haci-x 'back' (cf. perhaps PE paðə-)
haciʀi-/hacaʀi- 'wait' (cf. perhaps PE paðə-)
haðʀa-/haðaʀ- 'touch' (cf. perhaps PE paðəʀ-)
haɣit-/haxit- 'catch' (and haxt- 'get caught')
haka-X 'feather'
halaɣna-X 'salmonberry' (cf. Esk alaɣnaq)
halɣi-X 'root'
halu- 'sew'
hanaX 'surf'
hani-X 'lake' (cf. perhaps PE maniɣ-)
hanika- 'float' (cf. perhaps PE maniɣ-)
haŋa- 'rise, ascend' (and haŋaða- 'top'; cf. perhaps PE paɣ-)
haʀ- 'crumb, dust' (as in haʀliɣna-s, EA haʀlikna-X, haXsxi-n)
haʀut- 'beat, win' (also EA haʀuXsi-, and maʀusi-X

'reward', from *m̥aʀusi-X?)
hasi- 'be crowded, many' (as in hasina- 'occur in great number')
hasxi- 'go against the wind' (cf. perhaps PE paðə-)
hat- 'outside, opening' (cf. perhaps PE paðə-)
hataʀ- 'slip, slide'
hatat- 'start again, repeat'
hati-X[1] 'lip' (cf. hat- above and perhaps PE paðə-)
hati-X[2] 'ten' (cf. perhaps PE dem.
paɣ-)
hawaɣ- 'tow, pull'
hayu-X 'partition of sleeping place'
hiðalu-X 'long flat cape' (cf. perhaps PE pi-tə-[1] under pi-)
hiðaŋi- 'turn up (lamp)'
hiðati-X 'spring, water coming from underground' (also EA hiðʀa- 'come up from ground (water)' - cf. perhaps PE pi-tə-[1] under pi-)
hiiðu-X 'draft, breeze' (hiidu-, EA iðɣu- 'be drafty')
hiix 'black oystercatcher'
hilma-X 'wave'
hini-X 'wick'
hinu-X 'piece of sod, turf'
hiqa- 'stutter' (as in hiqamaɣ-, EA hiqaðaɣ-)
hiʀ- 'sprain' (as in hiʀni-, also hiXt- 'collapse, break')
hisax 'almost' (cf. perhaps PE pi-)
hitmi- 'pluck (bird)' (cf. perhaps PE pi-tə[2])
hitxi-X 'tail' (cf. perhaps PE pi-tə- in sense 'stick out')
hitXa- 'break (of waves)' (cf. perhaps PE pi-tə-[1])
hiXsa-, EA haXsa- 'find out, understand, recognize' (cf. perhaps PE paqət-)
huðʀu- 'breath hard, start coughing', EA 'gobble'
hukðu-X 'lump, piece'
hul- 'get red-cheeked' (as in huli- and EA hulaŋsa-)
hulɣi-X 'trunk, body' (Att huɣli-X 'upper part of mukluk')
hulma- 'melt'
huluʀ- 'wink, blink'
huna-X 'wound'
huqlu- 'be fuzzy, downy (fur)' (EA uqlu-X 'parka made of skins')
huʀu-X 'foam (from mouth)'
husi-x 'lower jaw'
hutxita- 'be obedient, well-behaved'
huuða- 'shout'
huya- 'go in some direction'
huzu- 'every, all' (EA husu-)
icaɣ- 'drip' (cf. perhaps PE ətə-)
iðɣi- 'be pulled out' (and iðɣit- 'pull out')
iðiya- 'be sweet'
iɣ- 'return, go back'
iɣa- 'freeze, be frozen'
iɣa-X 'slate'
iɣaci-X 'sinew'
iɣali- 'faint from seeing blood or from fear' (also perhaps iɣalina-X 'stingy'; cf. perhaps PE niɣu-)
iɣalu-X 'bridge'
iɣðaʀit-, EA iðɣarit- 'run (away)' (cf. perhaps PE əɣət-)
iɣiðɣu-X, EA iɣaðɣu-X 'waterfall' (EA also iɣaðʀu-X; cf. perhaps PE niɣu-)
iɣluqa-X 'skin, hide' (> AAY iɣluqaq 'dehaired (seal) hide')
iɣluʀ- 'wade' (also 'stumble')
iɣna-X 'weight'
iɣu-X 'bridge of nose' (and perhaps iɣunaX 'dorsal fin of whale'; cf. perhaps PE niɣu-)
iɣut- 'lengthen' (cf. perhaps PE niɣu-)
iɣuX 'spit (of land)'
iimit- 'choose'
iitikaalu-X 'cow parsnip (stem)'
ilɣa- 'search, look for'
ilɣu-X 'grandchild'
ilɣut- 'get', EA 'retain, stop' (EA also ilɣu- 'stop')
iluyaax, EA iliyuʀa-X 'decoy seal' (EA also iliyuʀ- 'attract seal or bird')
ilu- 'go round, skirt' (EA and Att; cf. perhaps PE ilu-)
ima-X, EA im̥a-X 'weft, woof' (and imaɣlu- 'weave')
imɣaʀi-'sealskin basket' (EA only, but cf. CSY imkutaq 'large skin basket')
imlaɣasi-X 'back scratcher' (EA and Att, EA also imlaɣ- 'scratch')
inaqa- 'alone, own'
ini-, Att nini- 'go to bed' (cf. perhaps PE iŋŋaʀ-)
inqi- 'fall on backside, sit deep (in water)' (cf. perhaps PE ətə-)
inu- 'be afraid' (as in inuuna-)
inu-X 'piece of food' (cf. perhaps CSY inpitə- 'distribute shares of catch')
iŋ- 'move backward' (as in iŋsa-, iŋt-; cf. perhaps PE dem. iŋ-)
iŋa(t)- 'throw spear' (> AAY i(i)ŋa(a)quq 'spear with blade')
iŋaaŋi-, EA inaaŋi- 'feel bad, in pain'
iŋacaʀi-X/iŋaciʀi-X 'pair, married couple' (cf. perhaps PE iŋlu)
iŋalu- 'human body', EA 'way of behaving' (EA also iŋaXta- 'behave'; cf. perhaps PE iŋuɣ and/or iŋ(i)yuləɣ)
iŋana-X 'steep cliff' (cf. perhaps iŋa(t)- below)
iŋatu-X 'red-faced cormorant'
iŋi-X 'dipnet'
iŋla-X 'whiskers (of animal)'
iŋlu-s, iŋłu-X 'leader of plaited threads' (cf. perhaps PY əɣlu(q))
iqana-X 'old woman' (and iqat- 'start to get old')
iʀu- 'leave, go away'
isuX 'spotted seal' (cf. Esk isuʀiq)
isxa-X 'place, dwelling, nest'
isXa-X corner of mouth (Atkan also miXsa-X)
isXati-X 'grass basket' (> CAY isʀan, Nun qəsʀan if not a loan the other way)
itaaŋ 'first'
itma-x, EA itma-n 'Big Dipper' (compare itmali-X 'post for tying boats to')

itu-s 'fish spear with three teeth' (Atkan only, but cf. ECI Lab ittuma-lik 'spear for stabbing auks' in Peck)
itxa- 'apart, different'
itxu- 'comb' (cf. perhaps itxa- above)
ituʀ- 'be affectionate, merciful' (as in iturnaazaasa- 'be gentle, affectionate' and EA ituXta- 'pity, love')
itXa- 'upper part' (cf. perhaps PE ətə-)
itXayax 'caribou'
itXut-, EA utXut- 'go out of sight'
ixcx(i)- 'slender connection (of)' (e.g. wrist of hand)
ixsa- 'calm down, slacken'
ixsaX 'bail, handle'
ixtula- 'be blamed' (and ixtusa- 'blame')
iXci-X 'worm'
iXsaaʀ- 'be brutalizing' (and iXsaaʀasa- 'torture, punish')
iXtuɣ- 'eat raw food'
kaaŋu- 'be in good health'
kaasxi-X 'sewing stand' (> AAY kas'iq)
kaaxaðɣi-X, EA kaaŋaðɣi-X 'harlequin duck'
kaci-X 'breast, chest'
kacix 'strong wind'
kað- 'in front of' (cf. perhaps PE kayəmə(t)-)
kaðɣi-X, EA kaðxi-X 'stake, post' (cf. perhaps kað- above)
kaɣalu-X 'stern, heel' (cf. Esk kaɣaluq)
kaɣi- 'sweep (floor), dump (garbage)' (cf. Esk kaɣi-)
kakaaŋa-X/kakaaŋa-X 'disks for throwing at target in game' (> AAY kakaŋaq)
kalaɣa-X 'yellow sculpin' (cf. Esk kalaɣaq)
kami- 'swing, rock'
kamu-X 'roof, turf for roofing'
kam̥aɣ- 'shake, wave' (cf. perhaps PI katuk-)
kani- 'be pleased' (as in kanita-, and kani-lakan 'be displeased')
kan̥u-s, EA kanu-n 'nasal mucus, snivel'
kaŋci-X 'crop, gizzard'
kaŋiiti-X 'pillow' (cf. perhaps kaŋi- below)
kaŋaðɣi-X/kaŋaðɣi-X 'bladder wrack' (cf. perhaps PE kaŋəʀ)
kaŋi-/qaŋi- 'bend, curve' (cf. perhaps PE kaŋir)
kasami-X 'common eider' (cf. perhaps PE katə- with ref. to flocking)
katmi- 'stretch (e.g. skin to ground)'
katxi-X 'flea'
kayaɣ- 'be heavy' (as in kayaɣna-; > AAY kayaɣnaʀ- 'be difficult')
kayuuʀ- 'work hard' (as in kayuuʀna- 'be hard' - cf. perhaps PE kayuɣ-)
kayux/kayix 'also, still, further'
kayuxta-X 'sinker'
kða-X 'ice'
kðaŋ(iX) 'Dall porpoise'
kiciɣ- 'itch' (as in kiciɣna-)
kikaɣna- 'be dirty'
kilʀi- 'ribs'
kimla-X, EA kilma-X 'stomach' (> AAY kilma(q))
kim̥itu(kða)-, EA kimitu-/mitu- 'pinch'
kini- 'bend over or down' (cf. perhaps qin̥i- below and/or PI kini-)
kinka-X 'spider'
kinuɣa- 'cache' (> AAY kinuɣaq 'leftover food')
kiŋsiiti-X 'grass wall cover' (cf. perhaps kiŋti-X below)
kiŋti-X 'river bank', EA 'wall, shelf covered with grass'
kiŋu- 'be sad' (and kin̥uXta- 'regret', EA 'love')
kitu-X 'louse'
kniix/kðiix 'whispered auklet' (EA and Att)
ku- 'on top of, on' (and kulix 'upper central rib or deck of baidarka'; cf. perhaps PE qutə- and/or qulə-)
kuci-X 'boulder'
kucu-s 'lips, gills'
kuka-X 'grandmother' (cf. perhaps PE kuk(k)u(ʀ)(-))
kulamax 'right whale' (> AAY kulamak 'whale')
kulu-X 'deep place in water'
kum 'hypothetical particle' (perhaps rel. case of ku- above)
kuna-/kina- 'dry and skinny' (cf. perhaps PI kinəʀ-)
kuumXu-X 'wild rye'
kyar- 'send on an errand'
lalu-X 'yellow cedar wood'
latuX 'grandfather'
lax 'Canada goose' (cf. Esk laɣiq)
lina-X 'mat'
lu- 'believe' (cf. perhaps PE ilumun under ilu-)
lukaʀi-x 'loins' (EA only, but cf. AAY K luqaq 'pelvis bone of seal')
ła-X 'son, boy'
łaaquða-X, EA laaquða-X 'fur seal'
maamanuuʀiða-X 'monkshood, aconite'
maɣ- 'be soaked, wet'
maliɣ- 'predict, have presentiment' (cf. perhaps ma- 'do' under PE p.b. (u)ma-)
manʀu- 'be falsely modest'
maŋi- 'ask, request' (and maŋiiyu- 'be devout', EA 'be a believer'; cf. perhaps PE maniɣuʀ-)
mayqu- 'be vigorous, healthy' (cf. perhaps ma- 'do' under PE p.b. (u)ma-)
miða-X 'fat (on skin)'
mika- 'play'
miquða-x 'nostrils'
m̥aaðu-X 'breeze'
m̥iiɣa- 'whistle' (as in m̥iiɣaaða-, EA iɣalaʀ-, miɣalaʀ-)
nam- 'sew together' (as in namt- and EA naamu- 'top seam of baidarka')
nami-X 'vein' (EA also mani-X)
nayu-X 'float (for baidarka in stormy weather)'
ni-X 'paternal aunt'
niiʀ- 'deny, swear' (as in niiʀasa-)
niX, Atkan iX 'baidar (skin boat)' (also niʀila X, Atkan, Att iʀila-X; cf. nuXa- below but compare also PE qayaʀ)
niXsu-X, Atkan iXsu-X 'temporary shelter, lean-to' (cf. niX above, with -su 'resemble' acc. Bergsland)

nuX 'stone'
nuXa- 'row (in baidar)' (EA, but also in Atkan uXaasi-X, uXaaða-X, EA nuXaaða-X, nuXaaða-X 'oar'; cf. niX above)
ŋalaʀ- 'bitter'
qaaɣu- 'dirt, dust'
qaaʀ- 'internal membrane'
qaata- 'where' (also qaatuuʀi- 'side'; cf. perhaps PE qaŋa)
qaayu-X 'berry' (cf. perhaps PE nəqə)
qaciiyu-X, EA qaciiya-X 'Steller's eider, kind of duck' (cf. AAY AP qacaaq 'type of duck' — a loan?)
qacima-X 'thigh(bone)'
qacuki-X/qaciiku-X 'shark' (> AAY qaacaq 'shark, sandpaper')
qaðu-X 'scab, crust' (cf. perhaps PE qaðə-)
qaɣaðaX 'braid' (> AAY qaɣataq)
qaɣalʀi-X 'claw, fingernail'
qaɣama-X 'cartilage'
qaɣðu-X 'sealskin parka'
qaɣna-X 'bone, shell'
qaka- 'be dry'
qakiiða-X 'silver salmon' (cf. Esk qakiiyaq)
qala- 'many'
qalaaʀ- 'mock'
qaliiɣu- 'accomplish, finish' (EA qaliiɣuXta- 'zealous'; cf. perhaps qal- 'bottom' under PE qaltaʀ)
qalit- 'resent, take offense against'
qama-X, qam̥a-X 'step, pace'
qamax 'skate (ray)' (cf. perhaps PE nəqə)
qamða- 'be deep' (cf. CSY qavžaatat 'gulch, ravine' under PE qaðvaʀ-)
qamli-X 'knife' (EA and Att)
qamti-X 'shoulder blade'
qam̥aqu-X 'cockle clam'
qam̥ix 'door' (cf. perhaps PI qipək under qipə-)
qanasi-X 'slit in meat or hide used as handle for dragging it'
qanku-s 'three' (EA qanku-n; also qamciiŋ 'eight')
qaŋa- 'be cooked, boiled'
qaŋlaaX, qalŋaaX 'raven' (cf. perhaps Esk qalqaʀayaq)
qaŋli-X 'shoulder'
qaŋu- 'enter'
qaŋ̊u-X, EA qaŋu-X 'seaweed' (> AAY qaŋuq 'giant kelp')
qata-X 'lateral half (of fish)' (also qati-X 'crack')
qatxa-X 'penis'
qatxuuya-X 'shirt, jacket'
qawa-X 'sea lion'
qaxat- 'throw rocks from a slingshot' (cf. perhaps PE qaɣəʀ-)
qaxcaɣ- 'be dark'
qaxsa- 'slide, slip'
qaxsa-X 'eyelash' (also 'baleen')
qaxu- 'be grumpy, fierce'
qaXlu-/qaʀlu- 'arch of foot' (also Atkan qaXluX 'ankle')
qaya- 'be tall' (and qaya-X 'mountain'; cf. perhaps PE qaðə-)
qayu-X 'anchor'
qayuqi- 'be forced' (and qayuqita- 'force')
qazaXa- 'be good' (EA qasaʀata- 'be right', and Atkan, Att qazaʀat- 'arrange')
qiðŋi- 'spit'
qiðʀu- 'earwax' (EA only, but cf. AAY K qiiɣuiʀ-, qiiɣuaʀ- 'clean out ear')
qiðʀu-n 'back of hand'
qiðuɣ- 'scrape blubber off'
qiɣða-X 'hook' (and EA qix 'barb, spine', crook of arm')
qi(i)ɣla(a)ɣiða-, EA qiɣðaɣla- 'make cracking noise'
qiɣlu-X 'knot'
qiɣna-X 'fire'
qiɣnu-/qiɣna- 'cuddle, caress'
qiɣu- 'gather' (and EA qiɣu-X 'precious thing, property')
qiɣux 'loon'
qiici-/qici- 'go around'
qiimayaaɣ-, EA qiyamaɣ- 'scratch oneself'
qiiqi-X 'storm-petrel'
qiiʀusi-X/kiiʀusi-X 'mountain' (cf. perhaps PE qiɣɣu)
qiitikila-X 'whirlwind' (cf. perhaps PE qi(C)ət-)
qiiXciiða-X 'green-winged teal (?)'
qiklu- 'clip, shear'
qiliŋi- 'close eye(s)' (Atkan qiliŋit- 'wink')
qiliʀi- 'brain' (pl.)
qilitaqa-X 'pelagic cormorant'
qilu-[1] 'imitate'
qilu-[2] 'curve' (EA and Att, also qilulaqaya- 'crooked'; cf. perhaps PE qələɣ-)
qim(i)-/qim̥(i)- 'creak, grit teeth' (as in qiimiʀ-, EA qi(i)miiða-, qim̥iiða-, qimuuʀ-)
qimðixti-s 'fern' (Att qivlixti-n)
qimɣi(i)ta-X 'crab'
qimnu- 'look away from'
qini- 'obey', EA 'bow down' (and EA qin̥i- 'get crick in back'; cf. perhaps kini- above and/or PE qi(C)ət-)
qiŋa-X 'cold' (and qiŋana- 'be cold')
qiŋu- 'kiss'
qiqi-X 'fish slime, bodily fluid'
qiqu- 'force'
qiʀu- 'be hard to get' (as in qiʀuna-)
qisi-X 'palm'
qisxi- 'turn with one end of paddle' (cf. perhaps PE qi(C)ət-)
qitiqða-X 'arctic tern'
qitx- 'lower end (of stomach)'
qixya-X 'shelf, raised cupboard' (in EA 'house platforms' in pl.)
qizaŋa-X, EA qiðaŋa-X 'ancient murrelet'
quðiiʀu-X 'clay'
quɣa-X 'assistant spirit' (> Nun acc. Lantis)
quɣaaŋ 'black scoter' (cf. perhaps quɣa-X)
quɣana-X 'rock'
quɣaqaaða-X, EA quɣaaðɣi-X 'mold'
quɣu- 'young bird' (as in quɣuuli-X, EA quɣuuyu-X)

qula- 'choke (on food)'
qula-X 'collarbone'
quli(i)ɣa-X 'aunt (uncle's wife)'
qulut- 'close eyes'
qulXuða- 'be bald-headed'
qumna-X 'grave'
qunquX, EA ququX 'milt'
qunʀuʀ- 'be afraid' (Atkan qunʀuumaliXta- 'be amazed')
qusa- 'space above' (cf. perhaps PE qulə- and/or qutə)
qutaɣ- ' blow (wind)' (as in qutaxt- 'blow away or up from the ground')
quxu- '(knob of) ankle' (as in quxulukða-X, EA quxutu-X)
quyu- 'go to bed'
qyuna- 'be difficult' (and EA qyu- 'be handicapped')
saaɣa- 'be drowsy' (cf. perhaps saɣni- below)
saaku-X 'king eider'
saakuut- 'turn over, put on belly'
saam̥la-X 'egg'
saaquða-X 'cow parsnip'
saaquðax 'summer' (early Att 'fall')
saasqayu-n 'fly eggs' (EA only; cf. AAY sasaq 'maggot egg' — a loan?)
saati- 'in-law' (as in saatimɣi-X 'parent-in-law')
saðaɣ- 'be fat'
saɣi- 'face' (as in saɣimaX, EA also siɣimaX)
saɣni- 'be distant' (also saxta- 'be lazy' and EA saxtana- 'take a long time')
saku- 'fight'
saliɣu-X 'cap' (> AAY)
salu-X 'cover, s.th. to hide behind'
sam- 'count' (and perhaps saamaax 'flock, herd')
samatXi-X coagulated (blood)' (EA and Att)
sanXu-X/sanʀu-X 'stomach (of animal)'
saŋa- 'respect' (as in saŋaʀa- 'be honored' - cf. perhaps PE caɣŋi-)
sasa-X 'layer'
sasuli- 'be annoyed'
sasxa- 'be solid, intact'
saxit- 'move slantwise'
saʀa- 'sleep' (> AAY)
sða-X 'star'
siɣ- 'go up' (in EA 'in the bed', in Atkan and Att 'from shore')
siɣa-X[1] 'fathom' (and EA siɣa- 'stretch out arms')
siɣa-X[2] 'traveling supplies, gifts' (cf. perhaps siɣa-X[1])
siɣnu-X 'instep, upper (of boot)'
siɣu- 'wrinkle(s)' (also saɣi-s 'lines, creases'; cf. saɣi- above — contam.?)
siim̥lu-X 'pigeon guillemot' (cf. CSY sipəlaaq 'guillemot')
siisXi- 'have nosebleed'
siknu- 'decay (fish, still alive after spawning)'
sil- 'proximity, close to'
silaʀ- 'tie strings of boots or or sleeves'
simaya- 'try to save, rescue'
simsi- 'chest, breast
siniɣ- 'inside (of)'
sinu- 'for first time after' (as in sinu-ɣaan)
sinu-X 'driftwood, things thrown up on beach' (cf. perhaps PE tənət-)
siŋða-X 'hip(bone)' (EA and Att)
siŋlaŋi-X 'small breeze (ripples on the sea)' (Atkan only, but cf. AAY ciŋłəq 'ripple, wake in water')
siŋli- 'close eyes, blink'
sisa- 'lose one's way'
sisa-X 'one hundred'
sismi- 'help, save'
sisuɣ- 'cross an isthmus or narrow place' (and sita-X 'isthmus' - cf. perhaps PI citə)
sitx- 'place under, below' (and sitxi-s 'excrement')
sitXi- 'be squeezed, tight'
slu-X 'summer' (cf. perhaps PE ciluʀ-)
sluka-X 'seagull'
smiiX 'wandering tattler (bird)' (Att sviiɣi-X 'golden plover')
sŋa-[1] '(to) fast' (and sŋanaaða-X 'bewitched, holy')
sŋa-[2] 'raise hand threateningly'
sŋaax 'pumice'
sŋaluʀ- 'gather and chat (men)'
suɣa- 'run, hurry' (and suɣat- 'chase')
suɣla- 'make a mistake'
suka- 'be dreary weather' (as in sukana-)
sukða-, EA suɣða- 'be envious' (cf. perhaps PE təɣu-)
suŋ̥u- 'move fast'
susa- 'become tangled'
susi- 'hurry up'
sxiixtu- 'be thick'
sXiðux 'drizzle'
taaman 'only, only then, indeed'
taaŋa-X 'fresh water' (borrowed into Alaskan Eskimo as taaŋaq 'liquor')
taaqa-X 'silver hake' (cf. Esk taaqaq)
taaʀna-X 'skin of sole or palm'
taða-lik 'step, tread' (cf. perhaps NAI tažžaq- 'touch, hit')
taðu- 'surprise' (as in taðut-)
taɣu- 'tie' (and taɣi-X 'bundle of grass')
taka-X 'braid'
talaaɣi- 'be dazzled, blinded'
tali- 'console, stop from crying'
tała-X/tala-X 'slave'
tamɣaalu-X 'white-winged scoter'
tani-X 'forehead'
tanʀaaX 'bear' (cf. perhaps taʀəʀnəʀ under PE taʀəʀ(-))
taʀa 'well, come on, but'
taʀatax 'first'
taʀuʀ- 'swim' (EA and Att)
tat- 'break, burst, erupt'
taxt- 'gather, call together' (and taxsa- 'collect, gather'; cf. perhaps taɣu- above if not PE naŋcaʀ-)
taya- 'buy, trade'

tayaʀu-X 'man (human being or male)' (> AAY tayaʀuq 'Aleut', but in CAY 'mare's tail (plant)')
tini- 'pitch (tent)' (cf. perhaps CAY təxtaq 'upturned part of front of sled runner')
tiʀ- 'tear out, jerk out' (as in tiʀi-, EA tiʀyu-)
tiʀla-X/tiXla-X 'eagle' (cf. perhaps tiʀ-)
tŋu- 'firm, steadfast'
tuðʀaalux 'bruise (from blow)' (cf. AAY K tuaʀyaʀtə- 'bruise, get bruised' — a loan?)
tuðu- 'light colored', EA 'be brown or purple'
tuðumali- 'speak, tell' (cf. perhaps PE tucaʀ-)
tuɣaaði-X 'urine, bladder' (> AAY tuɣaaʀiq 'bladder')
tuɣi- 'be stretched out, sloping' (also tuɣi-X artery, spinal cord')
tuɣla- 'touch, feel'
tuku-X 'black bass' (> AAY)
tula-X 'upper arm'
tumʀa- 'shut the mouth' (EA and Att)
tumsa- 'put away, store'
tumta-X ' thickness (around)', EA 'hill'
tuŋaʀ- 'be strong' (cf. perhaps tŋu- above)
tuqi- 'bow, look down'
tuta-x 'ear pendants' (cf. perhaps PE tucar-)
tutuutu-X 'owl'
tuutXa-X 'dried stem of grass or sedge (in winter)'
tuuxlu- '(bird's) tail (feathers)' (as in tuuxluuqiða-; EA and Att tuuɣlu-)
tuXi-X 'dot, spot, target'
ucXu- 'dip (fish or meat in oil)'
uða-X 'bay'
uðaɣa- 'go out in open sea'
uðayaX 'keel'
uðiʀ- 'sting, burn'
uðʀaaða-X, EA uðʀa- X/uðXa-X 'loop, noose'
uɣinʀi-X 'shadow, shade' (cf. perhaps PE uɣan)
uɣu- 'flatter' (as in Atkan uɣunisaXta-, EA uɣuya-)
uɣunu- 'forget'
uɣuX 'joint (of body)'
ukaɣ- 'fall backward, lie on back' (cf. perhaps PE dem. uk-)
ukałax, EA ukalaX 'bark (of tree)'
ukaxsi-X 'back of head' (cf. perhaps PE dem. uk-)
uku- 'see, find, turn in a direction' (cf. perhaps PE dem. uk-)
ula-X 'house'
uli-/ula- 'bend' (cf. perhaps PE ulət-)
uliix 'boots' (> CSY uliiʀək 'hunting boots', Rus. dialect ulegi, if not borrowed the other way)
uluX 'hatch (of baidarka), frame'
um- 'smell, get scent of'
umcu- 'suck' (EA also 'kiss')
umliɣ- 'be injured' (as in umliɣna- 'be harmful')
umna-X 'string, rope' (> AAY; cf. perhaps PE umciɣ-)
umni-X 'nephew'
umʀi-X 'bate' (cf. perhaps um- above)
umʀuli-X 'blue whale'
umsu-X 'tongue' (also 'paddle as support, lap', and EA 'fluke (whale's tail)')
um̥a-X, EA lum̥a-X 'flank' (<*num̥a-X?)
unamaax 'gunwhales of baidarka' (cf. perhaps PE dem. un-)
unaʀða-s 'bottom stringers, longitudinal ribs (of baidarka)' (> AAY unaʀat; cf. perhaps PE dem. un-)
unʀi- 'have hope' (as in unʀiXta-, EA unʀita-)
uŋ 'penis' (EA also huŋ, Att nuŋi-X)
uŋi-X 'sister (of man)' (cf. Sir uŋyəX 'younger sibling')
uŋla-X, EA hulŋa-X 'herring'
uŋlu-X 'rocky pillar or islet' (cf. perhaps uŋ above)
uŋuʀ- 'pull up' (cf. perhaps PE uŋəʀ-)
uqlaʀ- 'wash, bathe'
uqlu- 'dislike, abuse'
uʀa- 'go out, abate'
uʀaaŋi-X 'shower, squall'
uʀaaʀu-X 'starry flounder' (cf. Esk uʀaʀuq)
uʀlaaʀu- 'signal, wave to'
usxi-X 'willow bush'
usxu- 'shake, shiver'
ut- 'go down toward shore'
utm- 'center, middle (of)'
utuða-s 'temples
utuʀ- /uutuʀ- 'foment, treat with hot rock compress' (EA also utuX 'stove, cooking in pit on hot rocks')
utxi-s 'ashes'
utXu- 'be turbid, murky'
uuðuɣaari-X 'boulder den (of foxes)' uuquciiŋ 'blue fox' (> AAY uuquciik)
uxcu-X 'tufted puffin' (cf. perhaps CSY uɣžaaq 'puffin')
uxi-[1] 'extinguish'
uxi-[2], EA uɣi- 'skin (small animal or bird)'
uya- 'fetch'
uymi- 'be merry, vigorous'
uyuuɣ- 'beg for food'
wa- 'have pity for' (as in waXta-, also Atkan wana-X 'precious thing')
w̥aaða- 'howl, bark'
ya-[1] 'yesterday' (as in ya-m aŋalii, also yaXsina-X)
ya-[2] 'cape, rocky point' (as in ya(a)X, also ya-s 'reef')
yaaɣi- 'swing, sway back and forth'
yaali- 'move slowly'
yaɣ- 'be charitable toward' (and yaxta- 'give')
yu- 'crease, pleat, crimp, gather (seam)' (cf. perhaps PE nə(C)uʀ-)
yuXli-'leaves of cow parsnip' (cf. perhaps CSY yuXqutaq 'blade of grass')
y̥aaɣa-X 'wood, tree, stick'
Xa-X 'front of belly part of fish'

POSTBASES and ENCLITICS

POSTBASES AND ENCLITICS

AAY forms are from Leer's ms. list for Kenai Peninsula, CAY forms are from Jacobson 1977, NSY from Menovshchikov 1975 and 1987, CSY from Badten 1987, WCI Copper and Inu forms are in general from Fortescue 1983 (supplemented by Kaplan's SPI ms. dictionaries for King Island and Qawiaraq, MacLean et al.'s ms. dictionary for NAI, Schneider 1968 for ECI, Pryde's ms. list for WCI, and Hansen's ms. list for Car) unless otherwise specified. Aleut forms (principally from Bergsland and Dirks 1981) are for Atka unless otherwise specified.

The symbol '#' preceding a postbase or enclitic indicates non-productivity and '(#)' indicates limited productivity; otherwise the postbase is productive. The symbol '+' preceding a postbase or enclitic indicates additive/non-truncating suffixation; otherwise the postbase deletes stem-final consonants. An underlined uvular stop becomes velar after a velar base and vice versa for an underlined velar stop. Inuit initial ɣ alternates with ʀ following a uvular and Yupik initial X with x following a velar unless otherwise indicated. For Yupik, 'v-dr' indicates 'velar-dropping' (i.e. that a voiced velar or uvular continuant (velar only in CSY) is dropped under suffixation when occurring between single vowels) and 'ə-dr' indicates 'ə-dropping' (base-final ə dropped under suffixation). Initial bracketed consonants appear only after vowel bases unless otherwise indicated; other bracketed elements are optional.

It appears that PE postbases were essentially additive except when they began with a cluster or geminate. Note that the optional 'replacive' behavior of certain postbases that begin with an l (or n) is probably also PE. In these cases the initial consonant may drop and cause deletion of the final V (plus C) of the base (and gemination of remaining single C's at the end of the base in Inu), or combine with a preceding t to produce c (or s).

Apparently many PE postbases have been replaced in Sir and — to a somewhat lesser extent — also in CSY and NSY by particles borrowed from Chukchi.

A

PE a- 'repeatedly' [from *ɣa-? — cf. for example aqumɣa- under aqumə-]
AAY #a- 'repeatedly and rapidly' [and +aa-, (after tə) +(X)qaa-, qaa- 'intermittently' — for the latter cf. qə-]
CAY +a-, #a- 'repeatedly' [additive only after C]
NSY [+ažə-, (after tə-) qažə- 'repeatedly']
CSY — [for +aataʀ- see ʀataʀ-]
Sir —
SPI (#)a- 'en masse, all together'
NAI ayaa-, #a-
WCI (#)a- 'several do, do several times'
ECI (#)a-
GRI (#)a-

PI ala- 'with ease or a lot' [cf. a- and tla- and/or la(ʀ)-]
SPI —
NAI ala- 'a lot, intensely' [and note allak- 'begin to — a lot' with k under nəɣ-]
WCI ala- 'with ease, quickly'
ECI Aiv ala-
GRI #ala- 'be liable to' [Ordbogêraq; for ałłaɣ- 'suddenly a bit' see łłaɣ-]

PI aluk(-) 'big?' [cf. aʀ and either łuɣ(-) or tluk-?; compare ðuɣ for the combination of 'big' and 'bad' senses here]
Yup [compare CSY luk 'old' under luɣpiɣaq]
SPI aluk- 'at length'
NAI aluk 'old' [ɣaaluk after VV]
WCI Sig (and less productively Cop) aluk 'big' [with nuances of pity and amusement acc. Met. — Lowe has it as 'old' and in Cop it may be 'all of a period'; note also Cop ʀaaluk (ɣaaluk after k bases) 'big', verbally 'very', which may also be attached to adverbials, and (#)(+pa)aluk- 'very', Sig paaluk 'big']
ECI (ʀa)aluk 'big, bad' [also verbal; paaluk 'very big', SB also 'very, much'; note also lutsaq 'old, worn out']
GRI aluɣ- 'rather, here and there', (+(ʀ)pa)aluit 'several, a group of' [for nialuɣ- 'try a bit, catch small game' see ni(C)aʀ-]

PY (ŋ)am emphatic [enclitic]
AAY +am emphatic particle or enclitic — 'but, yet, still' [and amci, PWS amci-am 'go ahead']
CAY +am emphasis or contrast [and ampi, amci 'go ahead']
NSY [note eɣužŋam 'while', from eɣužŋa 'but, as if' plus modal enclitic -am acc. Men. p. 327]
CSY +ŋam emphasis — 'well then, how is it that, you should'

PE aʀ 'thing resembling s.th.' [from *ɣaʀ or *ʀaʀ? (the latter could be generalized from uvular bases) — cf. for example civu(C)aʀ under civu- manuʀaq under manu and əð(ə)ɣa(ʀ) under əðə; compare also aʀ-, to which the WCI and GRI verbal forms below seem to point]
AAY #+aq 'thing that resembles -, small'
CAY #+aq [only after C bases] 'thing that resembles -'
NSY #+aq
CSY #+aq [as in itəɣaq under itəɣ and taʀnəraq under taʀ(ə)nəʀ, but for the ʀaq* in aʀnaʀaq* 'girl', etc., see ʀaʀ]
Sir #+əX 'thing that resembles -'
SPI #aq
NAI #aq 'thing that resembles -' [also #ɣaq after velar, #ʀaq after uvular bases and note matuʀaq 'trap door' from matu, isuʀaq under isu and sakiʀaq under caki]
WCI #aq 'thing that resembles -' [and verbally 'be -ish' on color bases]
ECI #aq 'thing that resembles -'
GRI #aq 'thing that resembles -' [also ɣaq as in iviɣaq 'blade of grass' from əvəɣ; note also verbal #aʀ- = 'be -ish' on color bases — compare CAY (ɣ)aʀ(aʀ)- 'barely, rather' under ʀaʀaʀ-]

PE aʀ- 'repeated or prolonged activity' [from *ɣaʀ-? — cf. ɣaa- and the ɣ-initial allomorphs in Inu under ðaʀ-, also for example NAI niviɣaq- under nəvə-]
AAY #+aʀ- 'continuative'
CAY #aʀ- 'repeatedly'
NSY [note +aaʀ- in situXaaʀ- 'roll down']
CSY +aXtaʀ-, (#)aXtuʀ- 'repeatedly' Sir +aqaʀ- 'constantly, frequently' [note also the qəʀ- in cəqəʀ- under ðaʀ-, ðaqə- for the last element]
SPI —
NAI #(V)q- 'repeated, prolonged action' [geminating *q- in some forms]
WCI #aq- 'repeated, prolonged action'
ECI #aq-
GRI #aʀ-

PY aʀaʀtə- 'suddenly' [perhaps from *ɣaʀaʀ(tə)-]
AAY +aXtə-, (after unaccented syllable) aaXtə- 'suddenly' [the former after tə bases; suppletive to qqəXtə- under k(k)aʀ-, as also aaXtaʀ- 'in repeated sudden bursts' is to qqəXaa- under k(k)aʀ-]
CAY (+)(ɣ)aʀ(aX)tə- 'suddenly, immediately, for a short while' [compare qəXtə- under k(k)aʀ-]
NSY +aXtə- 'suddenly' [ANLC; Men. has +aXquʀ- 'quickly']
CSY +aXtə- 'suddenly' [compare qaXtə- under k(k)aʀ-]

PI aʀžuk 'little' [cf. aʀ and yuɣ]
Yup [cf. perhaps CSY saʀya under cuaʀžuk (cu(na))]
SPI Imaq aʀžuk 'little'
NAI aʀžuk 'younger'
WCI aʀyuk, +(ʀ)yuk 'dear little' [Briggs had Utk aqžuk]
ECI a(a)ʀyuk
GRI (v)aʀšuk 'poor, useless', NG aXXuk 'little' [and aʀšuɣ- 'half-heartedly']

C

PE caʀ-[1] 'try to cause to' [cf. Aleut ya- (after C aya-, with epenthetic a) 'try to make, become or effect (change of state or position)' and yaar- in am̥ayaar- 'try to find out, ask about'; if from *tyaʀ- there may be a link to tya- which would explain the unusual Aleut correspondence here — compare under pityaqə- (esp. Nu pityaq-), and cf. also yaʀaʀ-]
AAY (#)+caʀ- 'cause to be -' [with adj. roots]
CAY +caʀ- 'cause, try to induce to', +caaʀ(aʀ)- 'endeavor to', qcaaʀ(aʀ)- 'do one's best to' [and note saaɣ- 'try to']
NSY +saʀ- 'cause to, endeavor to induce to', +sa(a)qə- 'try to (by repeated action)'
CSY +saʀ- 'cause to', +saʀaʀ- 'try to induce to'
Sir +səʀ-, +saʀ- 'tell, ask to'
SPI +saq- 'cause to, try to', +saʀataq- 'try to (in future)' [for Qaw +saq- 'begin to, hurry to' see saaq-]
NAI +saq- 'cause, try, begin to' [the latter meaning by contam. with saaq-?; also 'definitely should, so that one -'; and +saaʀɪ- 'deliberately', (+)saaq- 'be in process of -ing, be just ing']
WCI +ha(a)q- 'try to get to -' [Lowe has Sig +saq- also as 'I hope that -'; note also Sig +saaʀɪ- 'on purpose', +saʀuma- 'intend']
ECI +sa(a)q- 'try to get to' [also used as imperative softener; +saaq- may cause gemination and has half-trans. +saaʀɪ-, reflex. saaq apparently truncating, but this could go with saaq-]
GRI +saʀ-, +saaʀ- 'try to get to -' [also intr. 'try to']

PE caʀ-[2] 'go to get' [cf. caʀ-[1]?]
AAY —
CAY [note saaɣ- 'fetch from accessible place'; for homonym 'try to' see caʀ-[1]]
NSY +saʀ- 'try to get, fetch'
CSY +saXtuʀ- 'be hunting -'
Sir —
SPI —
NAI +saq- 'fetch'
WCI Sig +saq- 'fetch' [Lowe — only after V, otherwise taq- under taʀ-]
ECI +saq- 'fetch s.th. already prepared' [but Lab 'set out to fetch' acc. Bourq.]
GRI NG +haq- 'fetch' [only after V, otherwise taq- under taʀ-]

PI caʀait- 'be quick to -' [cf. caʀ-[1]?]
SPI —
NAI —
WCI Cop +haʀait- 'be quick to, soon'
ECI +saʀait- 'easily, tend to, soon'
GRI —

PE ci- 'acquire' [cf. ci(C)uʀ- and Aleut si- 'gather, pick up, kill for storage (game)']
AAY —
CAY +ci- 'buy'
NSY —
CSY +si- 'acquire lots of, work on or with' [and +siiʀ- 'gather, get lots of']
Sir — [for si- 'make' see li-[1]]
SPI Qaw +si- 'buy', (#)(u)siaq 's.th. acquired by being given or sent' — usually with bases formed from un; as verb = 'to acquire in that way', +siaq- 'get a new -' [and as a nominal = 'new']
NAI —
WCI +hi- 'get, buy, find' [for Cop +haaq 's.th. received' see under taaq(-)]
ECI +si- 'get, buy, find' [also +siaq 's.th. bought, found'; Spald. has +siaq- 'come across (animal)' for NBI]
GRI +si- 'get, buy, find' [and +siaq 's.th. acquired, bought, found']

PY ciqə- 'future' [cf. c(c)iʀ- and ʀqə-?]
AAY +ciqə-, (+ciiqə- after dropped tə) 'planned future'
CAY +ciqə-, (+ciiqə- after dropped tə) 'future', Nun +ciqiaʀ- 'be about to'
NSY [+ɬəqə-, (with base in u(C)) +ɬuqə- 'future' — compare ɬəqɣaʀ- under c(c)iʀyaʀ-]
CSY [+ɬəqə- 'future', influenced by ɬi-? — but compare ŋɬaʀ- under ŋcaʀ-; also Chap nəXɬəqə -'be a long time -ing']

Inu [note SPI łiuq- 'future' (apparently siuq after t-bases in Imaq) if this is not from ləʀ[1] plus li(ʀ)uʀ-]

PI ciqtuq- 'pretend to' [cf. ciru(C)aʀ-; from c(c)iʀ- and tuʀ-[2]?]
SPI —
NAI siqtuq- 'pretend to' [Jen.]
WCI hiqtuq-
ECI siqtu(q)-
GRI —

PE c(c)iʀ- 'wait for s.o. or s.th. to' [cf. ciqə- and Aleut cXi- (old Atkan cXusa- with usa-) 'cause, let, wait for - to, think that -']
AAY nəXciʀ-, ŋciaqə- 'wait for - to' [and (#)ŋciʀ-, (#)+ciʀ- 'let sit and -, wait for - to']
CAY +ciʀ- 'let, wait for - to', +ciaʀ(aʀ)- 'wait patiently for - to' [and +(s)ciuʀ-, Y +(s)ciʀ- 'get -ed', +(s)ciiɣatə- 'be unable to']
NSY nəXsiʀ- 'wait for - to' [additive when preceding tə dropped?; also nəXsižaqə-, +sižaqə-]
CSY +siʀ- 'wait for, cause to', nəXsiʀ- 'wait for - to'
Sir — [note siʀ- in saluxsiʀ- 'dry (tr.)' from saluɣ- 'dry (intr.)'; for negative səɣətə- see under ŋit-]
SPI +siq- 'wait for - to, (intr.) be in process of -ing'
NAI (#)+(t)siq- 'let happen', +(t)sii-, +(t)siaʀɨ -'wait for - to'
WCI ttiq-, (after C) +hiq-, ttiaʀi-, (after C) +hiaʀi- 'wait for - to' [followed by contemp./subord. = 'while -ing'; intr. ttiq-, (after C) +hiq- can also be 'get oneself -ed']
ECI +(t)sii-, +(t)siaʀi- 'wait for - to', (intr.) +(t)si(q)- 'wait for self to -, be in process of -ing, get oneself -ed'
GRI +(t)siʀ-, +(t)sii- 'wait for - to' [the first form transitive or reflexive, the second trans. or half-transitive; +(t)siiaq- 's.th. left to be -ed']

PY ciʀu(C)aʀ- 'pretend to' [cf. ciqtuq-; from c(c)iʀ- and ŋ(ŋ)uðaʀ-?]
AAY —
CAY —
NSY +siʀuaʀ- 'pretend to' [and nom. +siʀuaq 'wretched little']
CSY siʀ^{w}aaʀ- 'pretend to, not put much effort into -ing'

PE c(c)iʀyaʀ- 'be easy to' [cf. c(c)iʀ- and yaʀ-]
AAY —
CAY +(s)ciʀyaʀ- 'be easily -ed' [compare (s)ciʀ- under c(c)iʀ-]
NSY [note +łəqɣ̥aʀ- 'almost (in past)', +łəqɣ̥aqə- 'barely, just a little' — compare łəqə- 'future' under ciqə-]
CSY —
Sir —
SPI +siaq-, Qaw +siʀiaq- 'be easily -ed'
NAI +(t)siʀiaq-
WCI ttiʀiaq-, (after C) +hiʀiaq- 'be easy to' [and ttiʀiit-, (after C) +hiʀiit- 'be difficult to -']
ECI +(t)siʀiit- 'be difficult to' [and +(t)si(k)- 'be easy to'; and Spald. has ttiʀiaq- 'be easy to' for NBI]
GRI +siʀiaʀ- 'be easy to', +siʀiit- 'be difficult to'

PE ci(C)un 'instrument for -ing' [cf. ci(C)uʀ- and un]
AAY +suun 'instrument for -ing'
CAY suun, (after C) +cuun, NI, HBC, Nun +suun 'device for -ing'
NSY —
CSY —
Sir —
SPI suun 'device for 'ing'
NAI +siun 'means for -ing' [Jen.]
WCI —
ECI +siut 's.th. used in -ing, for or during -'
GRI +siut 'means for acquiring or going in -'

PE ci(C)uʀ- 'look for' [cf. ci- and (C)uʀ- and ci(C)un; Atkan and Att Aleut saaʀu- 'hunt, look for, try to' is probably not related acc. Berg., but note NSU saaʀ- below]
AAY +(X)suʀ-, suʀ- 'hunt, look for' [also +(X)sua-, sua-]
CAY +suʀ-, (after C) cuʀ- 'hunt, look for, check' [NI, HBC and Nun +suʀ on all bases; note also NSU saaʀ- 'hunt', from *ci(C)uʀaʀ-?]
NSY —
CSY +suʀ- 'test, check how — s.th. is' [for +siiʀ- 'gather, get lots of' see ci-]
Sir —
SPI (#)+siuq- 'hunt, be among'
NAI +siuq- 'hunt, look for'
WCI +hiuq- 'look for, hunt, travel around in or on' [and Car +mihiuq- 'be in or at']
ECI +siuq- 'look for, hunt'
GRI +siuʀ- 'look for, travel around in, celebrate'

PE cuɣ 'big or bad' [cf. mcuɣ(-)]
AAY — [for ŋcuk, AP kcuk 'little' see mcuɣ(-)]
CAY cuk 'unpleasing, ugly old'
NSY suk 'bad'
CSY —
Sir —
SPI (a)suk, Imaq zuk 'old'
NAI suɣžuk 'huge' [note ðuɣ for the second element]
WCI Net suɣžuk, Cop huɣyuɣaaluk 'huge'
ECI #suyyuk
GRI #suššuk 'huge', NG huk 'wretched, bad' [the latter in 1st person verbal use = 'while I was -ing (s.th. unwished for happened)']

PY culŋu- 'be indisposed with respect to s.th.' [cf. lŋu- and perhaps cuɣ]
AAY #culŋu- 'be sick, characterized by -ing'
CAY culŋu- 'be indisposed with respect to -'
NSY —
CSY —

PY cuŋaq 'little?' [cf. mcuɣ(-)?]
AAY #cuŋaq 'relat. in a joking relationship'
CAY cuŋaq 'cute, little'
NSY —
CSY —
Inu [note SPI W suŋaq- 'more, most' and GRI (#)suŋaʀ- 'almost, just before'?]

ð

PE **ðaʀ** 'passive participial' [probably alternating with taʀ after a C in PE as the Inu forms suggest (the post-vocalic alternant generalized in Yup?) — see nappaʀtaʀ under napa-; compare kaʀ, with which this p.b. is suppletive in WCI, ECI and GRI at least; the initial ɣ in Yup only appears after VV to break up potential 3-vowel clusters]
AAY (#)+(ɣ)aq, (after Cə) +aaq 'product of -ing, s.th. -ed' [also trans. indicative marker]
CAY +(ɣ)aq 'passive participial' [geminates (C)VCə bases; ɣaq after VV; also +(ɣ)a(ʀ)- as trans. indic. marker and in passive postbase +(ɣ)au- with ŋu-; compare also for example under təɣuðaʀ (təɣu-) and təpðaʀ (təpə-)]
NSY ɣaq 'passive participial' [but also +aq, which is used as trans. indic. marker +a(ʀ)-]
CSY #+aq 'pass. part.' [productive as trans. indic. marker +a(ʀ)-]
Sir [(ma)žə(ʀ)- 'trans. indic. marker in past']
SPI (#)+žaaq, (after C) +taaq, #aq 'pass. part.' [the first two forms esp. after postbase k in sense 'the one s.o. has caught', in passive +žaaɣu-]
NAI +žaq, (after C) +taq, #aq, #+aq 'pass. part.' [+žaq-, +taq- also trans. indic. marker; passive +žau- with ŋu-]
WCI +ɣaq, +taq 'pass. part.' [also trans. indic.; passive +ɣau-]
ECI +ɣaq, (after C, truncating after t) +taq 'pass. part.' [also trans. indic.; passive +ɣau-; Lab +ɣaa-, +taa-(ŋani, etc.) 'while -ing']
GRI (#)+šaq, (after C, but with much irregularity) #(+)taq, #aq 'pass. part.' [for ɣaq after ʀ bases see kaʀ; stative passive +šaa-, etc.]

PE **ðaʀ-** and **ðaqə-** 'habitually or repeatedly' [probably alternating with taʀ-, taqə- after C in PE — there may have been generalization of the post-vocalic alternant in Yup (and Al.); cf. qə- in the second form, also t(t)aʀ-, ta(C)aʀ- and Aleut ða-, Atkan usually za-, Att ya- 'repeatedly', Atkan zaʀ-ulax, EA ðaʀ-ulux '(he) never'; note the suppletive forms with initial ɣ in Inu — cf. ɣaa-; the initial ɣ in Yup occurs only to break up 3-vowel sequences]
AAY +(ɣ)aqə- 'one at a time, more and more (of them)' [+(ɣ)aqa- 'whenever' with conj. mood]
CAY +(ɣ)aqə- 'would' [narrative repetition, also 'whenever' with conj. mood endings; ɣaqə- after VV bases, causes gemination in (C)VCə bases]
NSY +(ɣ)aqə- 'present tense, regularly', (with conj. mood) 'when(ever)' [and +(ɣ)aqəɣqə- with sub. mood = 'in order that — continually'; ANLC also has +žaʀ- 'repeatedly']
CSY +(ɣ)aqə- 'at present, habitually', (with sub. mood) now and then' [and +žaʀ-, +žaaʀ- 'repeatedly but unnecessarily, unsuccessfully']
Sir +cəqəʀ- 'present tense' [with aʀ-?; with preceding causative t = sqəʀ-]
SPI +žaq-, (after k/q) ɣaq-, (after t) taq- 'habitually', +žaʀɨ- 'always, continuously' [allomorphs as for žaq-]
NAI +žaq-, +žaʀaq-, (after C) +taq-, +taraq-, (after k/q) ɣaq- 'repeatedly', +(ž)aq-, +(ž)aʀɨ-, (after t) +taq-, +taʀɨ-, (after k/q) ɣaq-, ɣaʀɨ- 'would each time' [with some irregularity, esp. with bases in ɨt]
WCI +taq-'repeatedly'
ECI [Dor. has SB ɣaq- 'often']
GRI +šaʀ-, (after C) +taʀ- 'repeatedly, habitually', +šaʀɨ-, (after C) +taʀɨ- 'habitually' [also ʀaʀɨ- after ʀ bases — with aʀ- rather; +(š)araa- before -šuq and -luni, etc.; SWG +(š)aʀɨ- 'whenever' (with caus. ŋat, etc. — compare ɣaa-); note also +šaannaʀ- 'often, all the time'; for +šariaqaʀ- 'must' see ɣiaqaq-]

PE **ðə** and **tə** 'agent (-er)' [the two forms probably alternating in PE (respectively after V and C); cf. Aleut Xta-X, (after C) ta-X 'one skilled at -ing', verbally 'be skilled at -ing', with generalization of the post-cons. alternant?]
AAY +(s)ta 'agent, -er'
CAY +(s)ta 'agent, -er'
NSY +(ł)tə 'agent, -er'
CSY +(s)ta
Sir +(s)ta [and (s)kaʀ(aq*) '(the only) one who —', which is prob. from kaʀaq]
SPI ži, (after C) +ti 'agent, -er'
NAI žɨ, (after C) +tɨ
WCI ɣi, (after C) +ti [but ɣɣi with t bases]
ECI ɣi, (after C) +ti 'agent, -er'
GRI ši, (after C) +ti

PE **ði-** 'half-transitivizer (detransitivizer)' [cf. perhaps ðaʀ and li-[1]; note the post-consonantal variant +i (from a suppletive *ɣi? — see under ɣiit-), which might be relatable to the final element in Aleut half-transitivizer qaʀi-, consisting of pass. participial qa- plus ʀi- 'have' (possibly generalized from after uvular bases, acc. Berg.) which itself has verbal use as a passive of resultant state; the present p.b. detransitivizes trans. bases but also has transitive uses in an 'undergo s.th. detrimental' sense (more productively in Yup, where it can take intr. endings too on intr. only or agentive bases), either the object or — with intransitive-only bases — the subject being the undergoer]
AAY +(ɣ)i- 'half-transitivizer' [ci with tə bases; the initial ɣ only occurs to break up 3-vowel sequences; for (ɣ)itə- 'do for' see utə-]
CAY +(ɣ)i- 'half-transitivizer' [ci with tə bases; causes gemination of (C)VCə bases]
NSY +(ɣ)i- 'half-transitivizer' [si- at least with tə bases, apparently also others]
CSY +i- 'half-trans.-er' [si- with tə bases]
Sir +(ž)i- 'half-trans.-er' [ti- with tə bases]
SPI +ži-, (after k/q, fricativized) +i-, (#)+si- [the latter esp. to t bases, but +ši- after ut(i)] 'half-transitivizer'
NAI +ži-, (after most k/q bases) (#)i-, (after most t bases) (#)+si- 'half-transitivizer' [+zi- with ut(ɨ) and +i- with bases in ɨk/q or VV k/q; this p.b. also has restricted trans. use in the sense 'cause' on intr.-only bases]
WCI (#)ɣi-, (after C) (#)i-, #+hi- 'half-trans.-er' [Pryde has also trans. forms 'to - to s.o.'s detriment']
ECI (#)ɣi-, (after C) (#)i, #+si- 'half-transitivizer' [and note saaʀi-, half-trans. of saaq- under caʀ-[1]; ɣiaq 's.th.

unintentionally -ed', yiaqaʀ-, trans. yiaʀi- 'have happen to one's detriment']
GRI #+ši-, #+i-, #+si- 'half-transitivizer' [the first form after V or ut(i), the second after most ʀ/ɣ bases (the final C being dropped except ʀ after *ə or VV), the last after most t bases, but with much irregularity]

PE ðiɣ- 'be far in a direction' [cf. the lexicalized forms under qulðiɣ- 'be high up' (qulə-) and Aleut ðiɣa-, Atkan also ziɣa-, EA also siɣa- 'have a good or proper' (to verbal bases 'well, be well -ed'), Atkan ziɣat- 'well', ziɣata- 'well, for a long time', EA siɣat(a)- 'for a long time']
AAY #qsəɣ- 'be large or small in a dimension -ward' [also qsiɣ- as in umiqsiɣ- under umi-]
CAY #qsiɣ- 'be far in a direction' [compare qłiq under l(l)iʀ-]
NSY —
CSY —
Sir —
SPI #sik-
NAI #sik- 'lie in a direction' [additive to bases in t(ɨ); Jen. also has vasik-]
WCI #hik- 'lie in a direction'
ECI #(+va)sik- 'be far in a direction' [+vasik- 'lie in such a direction' more common acc. Saul; note vaʀ- for the first element; also pasik- 'almost']
GRI #siɣ- 'be (rather) far in a direction', +(ʀ)pasiɣ- 'lie to the (direction)', also 'seem or act like a -' [compare valuk- and contrast NWG passiɣ- 'more or less, almost' from vaɣ + ðiɣ-, also aaŋŋasiɣ- 'can almost not be seen/heard any longer' from aaŋa- under aɣa-]

PE ðqə- 'ask or tell to' [cf. perhaps t-[1] and ʀqə-; the vowel in the Inuit forms may be due to following affixed material like GRI indic. -vaa or p.b. un, hence pitqun under piðqun(-) — compare also NSY ɣ̥qur- below]
AAY sqə- 'ask, want - to' [cəqə- with tə bases; inserts ə after ʀ/ɣ bases]
CAY sqə- 'ask - to' [optionally inserts ə after ʀ/ɣ bases; also squma- 'want - to' with (u)ma-]
NSY ɣ̥qə- 'ask, tell - to' [with preceding half-trans. si- = siɣ̥qə-; may cause semi-final ə to drop before ɣ or ʀ, then reinserted right before the p.b.; ɣ̥quʀ- 'force - to', ɣ̥qusaʀ- 'encourage - to']
CSY sqə- 'ask, want - to' [inserts ə after ʀ/ɣ bases]
Sir sqə- 'ask, tell to' [Vakh. - from CSY?]
SPI (t)qu- 'ask, tell - to' [tqu- after V or t; (t)qusaaq- 'encourage - to (often against wishes)', (t)quinaq 'urge - to']
NAI (t)qu- 'ask, tell - to' [tqu- after V or t; (t)quuq- 'urge - to']
WCI tqu-, (after k/q) qqu- 'ask, want - to' [and Sig (t)quuq- 'urge to']
ECI qu-, Lab qqu- 'ask, want - to'
GRI qqu- [for speakers in some areas qu-] 'ask, want, tell - to' [and reflexive qqušaaʀ- 'try to get people to - one']

PE ðuɣ 'big?' [cf. ðuɣar, also NAI suɣžuk, etc., under cuɣ, the ðuɣ- of PE kutðuɣ- and Aleut ðuɣ- 'intensely, suddenly' as in ɪʀðuɣ- 'decay' and qaʀaðuuɣ- 'dance']
AAY —
CAY (#)ʀuk, (with velar base) +uk 'big' [the first form generalized from after uvular bases; for #(+)yuk 'thing like a -' see yuɣ]
NSY [note (#)ɣžuk 'weak, barely visible' and pižuɣ 'completely']
CSY +žuxłak 'big', (+)žuk 'big old' [the latter also verbal; and note +žukutaq 'very big' and qšuk '(good or bad) old, troublesome']
Sir [+žukutaX 'very ' — to adj. verbal bases only?]
SPI ɣžužuk, ɣžažuk '(big) old', +(ʀ)žuužaq 'bad' [verbal = 'badly'; Imaq has žuk 'little, weak' — from NSY?]
NAI Mal +žuk 'big' [also lexicalized elsewhere]
WCI —
ECI —
GRI —

PE ðuɣaʀ(-) 'big or a lot' [cf. ðuɣ and aʀ?]
AAY —
CAY ʀuɣaq*, (after velar base) uɣaq* 'a multitude of -', (pl.) ʀuɣaat, uɣaat 'many' [the first forms generalized from after uvular bases, as ʀuk under ðuɣ]
NSY žuɣaq 'good' [ANLC 'strong'], žuɣaʀ 'well' [and žuɣapixtəʀ 'very well']
CSY [note perhaps šuuk, šaak 'shabby, old']
Sir —
SPI —
NAI +(ʀ)žuaq(*) 'big, old, not quite proper' [pl. +(ʀ)žuit, verbal = 'against all odds'; in comb. with u 'be' = +(ʀ)žuuʀ]
WCI +(ʀ)yuaq 'big' [and note Baker Lake 'tuaq 'big, prominent', with lexicalized glottal stop acc. Dor.]
ECI +(ʀ)yuaq, Lab +(t)suak [verbal = 'a lot'; in comb. with u = +(ʀ)yuu]
GRI +(ʀ)šuaq*, southern SWG +(ʀ)sivasik/-(ʀ)suasik, EG +(ʀ)tivaq/-(ʀ)tuaq 'big' [also 'bad'; pl. +(ʀ)šuit, rel. +(ʀ)šuup; verbal = 'strongly' (NG intensifier xxaʀ-, after uvular XXaʀ- probably belongs here too); in comb. with u- 'be' = +(ʀ)šuu-]

PE ðuʀ and **tuʀ** 'intrans. participial' [the alternation (after respectively V and C) was already in PE; there may be a relat. to qðuʀ- and ðuʀaʀ- (note esp. the participial forms like žuaq in Inu below, whose past tense indic. uses seem to represent a conflation of the participial form with PI tuqaq[2] in a similar function elsewhere); this morpheme has both verbal (mood-marking) and nominal uses in Inu]
AAY +(ɣ/t)uq 'intrans. indicative marker' [ɣuq after VV, +tuq after C]
CAY +(ɣ/t)uq 'intrans. indicative marker' [as AAY, and note yuq in napayuq under napa-]
NSY +(ɣ/t)uq 'intrans. indicative marker'
CSY +(ɣ/t)uq 'intrans. indicative marker'
Sir cəX, (after C) +təX 'intrans. participial and recent past indic. marker'
SPI žuq, (after C) +tuq 'intrans. indic. marker' [and žuaq, (after C) +tuaq 'intr. participial (one that is -ing) ']
NAI žuq, (after C) +tuq 'intrans. participle or indic. marker' [and žuaq, (after t) +tuaq 'one that is -ing, past indic. marker']

WCI yuq, (after C) +tuq 'intrans. part. or indic. marker' [and Sig yuaq, (after C) +tuaq 'intrans. participial and indic. marker' — Lowe has yuaq as past indic, but participial yuaq, yualuk as ' the — one' but yuq as 'a — one' with qualitative bases]
ECI yuq, (after C) +tuq 'intrans. part. and indic. marker'
GRI šuq, (after C) +tuq 'intrans. participial' [for suuq in lexicalized forms like aŋisuuq 'big' see suu-; note also šuuʀ-, (after C) +tuuʀ- 'happen to (despite expectation)', with ŋ(ŋ)uʀ-?]

PE ðuʀaʀ- and **tuʀaʀ-** 'continually' [the alternation could be PE, with various generalizations since; cf. tuʀ-[2] and aʀ-, qðuʀ- and perhaps ðuʀ, also əkðuʀ(aʀ)- under əkə-[2] and atšuq- under atə-; the forms below with initial ɣ in Yup appear after VV to break up 3-vowel sequences; for the q-initial forms in Yup compare qðuʀ-]
AAY KP +tuaʀ-, AP +(ɣ)uʀaʀ-, (after C) +tuʀaʀ-, (after tə, which drops) quaʀ-'still, continue -ing'
CAY +(ɣ)uʀ(aʀ)-, (after C) +tuʀ(aʀ)-, (after tə, which drops) quʀ(aʀ)- 'keep on -ing', NSU also 'leisurely' [causes gemination in (C)VCə base, as do related +(ɣ/t)uʀainaʀ- 'finally', +(ɣ/t)uʀalaʀ-, Y +(ɣ/t)uʀ(aʀ)laʀ-, HBC, NI +(ɣ/t)uʀatu- 'always']
NSY +uaʀ- 'continually' [for tuaʀ- 'at last' see tu(C)aʀ-]
CSY —
Sir —
SPI —
NAI (#)+tuaq- 'continually' [Nu also 'whenever']
WCI (#)+tuaq- 'continually'
ECI ttuaq- 'continually, a long time'
GRI yuaʀ-, (after C) +tuaʀ- 'continually' [also #uaʀ- after V; there may be suppletion with uɣaq- here]

PE ðviɣ or **viɣ** 'place or time of' [the first form, as still reflected in NSU and Inu variant vvik, is probably the original one — note that the p.b. nowhere alternates with *piɣ after a C in the manner of virtually all other additive p.b.s with initial v after V; perhaps the initial ð(ə) goes with PE tə, Aleut ð(a); note that viɣ can be attached to nom. bases in CAY and (in lexicalizations) in GRI at least]
AAY +wik 'place, time of' [ə-dr; preceding tə drops leaving voicelessness only — though it can go to s in Kod]
CAY +vik 'place, time of' [+wik in core GCY after V; ə-dr; tə into z or (after a fric.) dropped leaving voicelessness; optionally zvik also after V in NSU; on nominal bases takes the form +(ʀ)vik 'place for -']
NSY +vik 'place, time of'
CSY +vik 'place, time of' [ə-dr, and tə causes devoicing (to fik), dropping after a fricative]
Sir +vəx 'place, time of' (underlyingly vix)
SPI +vik
NAI +vik 'place, time of' [geminating after V; preceding t goes to ž]
WCI +vik [geminating after V; preceding t to l (Copper) or ž (Net)]
ECI +vik 'place, time of' [may cause gemination in V base; in NBI both forms like iɣavvik and iɣɣavik from iɣa- occur acc. Dor.]
GRI +(f)fik 'place, time of' [also #vik causing gemination in V bases; the modern productive form could be due to redistribution of the gemination from the base to the p.b. if it does not directly reflect ðviɣ]

PE ðvikə- 'have as place or time of doing' [also with human object; cf. ðviɣ and kə-[1]]
AAY +wikə- 'have as place or time of -ing or person toward whom one is -ing'
CAY +vikə-
NSY —
CSY +vikə-
Sir [note vəkə(s)- as in sivəkə(s)- 'put on, place somewhere, pay off loan' in Em. — from si- under əɬi-]
SPI —
NAI +viɣɨ-
WCI +viɣi-
ECI +viɣi-
GRI +(f)fiɣi-, #viɣi-

ɣ

PI ɣaa- and **ɣai-** 'whenever' [with special forms of the causative -ŋat, etc.; cf. aʀ-, also ðaʀ-, with which this set is suppletive in Inu — note especially NAI forms like ɣarɨ -and SWG (š)aʀi- there, suggesting the source of the present set as a blend between aʀ- and ðaqə- under ðaʀ-]
SPI —
NAI [for ɣaq-, ɣaʀɨ- 'would each time' see ðaʀ-]
WCI +ɣaa-, +ɣaʀaa- 'whenever', +ɣai- 'whenever (in future)' [the latter with condit. kpat-, etc.]
ECI NBI +ɣaʀaa-, (after k/q) ɣaa-, SB +ɣai-, liʀai- 'whenever'
GRI +ɣaa-

PI ɣallaq- 'for time being or in a while?' [cf. ɬɬaq- and compare Sig ɣa- under na- for the first element, also kayuɣ- and ɣaluaq-]
SPI +ɣalaq- 'right away, quickly'
NAI —
WCI Net (+)ɣallaq- 'for time being or some time' [Ras.]
ECI —
GRI +ɣaɬɬaʀ- 'for time being, a while', [+ɣallaq- also 'first' in NG]

PI ɣaluaq- 'but . . .' [cf. l(l)u(C)aʀ-?; for the first element compare ɣallaq-, Sig ɣa- under na- and ɣayaq- under ɣaʀ-]
SPI +ɣaluaq- 'indeed, but . . .'
NAI +ɣaluaq- 'however, but . . .' [note also +luq- 'even if'; kkaluaq 'former -']
WCI +ɣaluaq- 'however, but . . .' [and Cop ɣaluaq 'former' — Pryde]
ECI +ɣaluaq- 'however, but . . .'
GRI +ɣaluaʀ- 'however, but . . . , in vain, formerly' [and as a nominal +ɣaluaq, rel. +ɣaluup, pl. +ɣaluit; uɣaluaq 'former']

PI ɣanək- 'already have -ed' [cf. nəɣ- and the same ɣa- as in ɣallaq- and under na-?]
SPI —
NAI +anik-, (optionally after t) +kanik-, Mal +ŋanik- 'have already -ed'
WCI Cop, Car anik-, Sig mmanik-
ECI Aiv (ʀa)anik-
GRI —

PI ɣiaq- and **ʀiaq-** 'set about -ing?' [the latter generalized from after uvular bases; cf. yaʀ(tuʀ)-]
SPI —
NAI —
WCI ɣiaq-, (after q) ʀiaq- 'set about, be in process of -ing' [also as an intensifier, e.g. with the causative mood 'when — (vivid action)' and in Net in the comb. ʀiaŋŋuaq — the latter dialect also has ɣiaq(tit)- (+ neg. contemp.) 'before -ing'; Pryde also has nom. ɣiaq plus possessed loc. forms 'before -ing' and ɣiami/yaami 'infinitive' for Cop]
ECI ɣiaq- 'begin' [and in more limited use as an enclitic = 'a little (in a direction)']
GRI ʀiaʀ-, Kap Farvel ʀayaʀ-, Paamiut +kiaʀ- after cons. bases 'set about, dynamic action or state, intensifier' [with contemp. mood = 'after -ing'; in EG (ʀ)iaʀ- is much used in comb. with certain mood paradigms such as caus. ia(ami, etc.), cond. iaʀ(pat, etc.), optative iatsi- (corresponding to WG ʀiassa- 'let's -'), and contingent aaȓia(ami) 'every time -']

PI ɣiaqaq- 'must' [cf. yaʀ- and ŋqaʀ-]
SPI —
NAI —
WCI ɣiaqaq- 'must' [Net also yaaqaq- after V) and nom. ɣialik]
ECI ɣiaqaq-, (nom.) ɣialik, NBI, SB also (with V bases) +yaʀiaqaq- 'must', (with t bases) tariaqaq- [with ðaʀ- as in the GRI below; also nom. yaʀialik, etc.]
GRI +šariaqaʀ-, (after C) +tariaqaʀ- 'must' [with preceding ðaʀ-; also #ɣiaqaʀ-, NG (nom.) yaʀialik 'must']

PI ɣiik (du.) ŋ **ɣiit** (pl.) 'pair or group in converse or mutual relationship' [dual and plural respectively; cf. kə-[1] and Inu it (GRI iit) as in malʀuit under malʀuɣ, added to numeral bases to form group nominals equivalent to CAY, AAY in, ik 'group, pair of', the nasal of which is the same as in all numeral bases above two in these languages]
Yup [note CAY k̠əłXiik 'pair of, mutual -s' from kə-[1] and lʀi(C)a(q) and compare PY nuli(ʀ)aqəlʀiik 'married couple' under nuliʀ(aʀ) — also CSY nałəqiiyaʀutə- under nalləɣiik (nałə-)]
SPI ɣiik, ɣiit 'pair, mutual group of -' [verbal = 'be mutual -s, in converse relationship', as in all Inu]
NAI ɣiik, ɣiit 'pair, mutual group of -'
WCI ɣiik, ɣiit
ECI ɣiik, ɣiit
GRI ɣiit 'pair, mutual group of -' [and verbal ɣiiɣ- 'be in a mutual/converse relationship']

PI ɣiiq- 'already' [cf. ki- and ŋiʀ-?]
SPI —
NAI —
WCI ʀiiq-, (after V only) yaʀiiq-, Sig ɣiiq- 'already' [the latter with preceding ðaʀ-; Lowe has yaʀiiq- only on all bases in Cop]
ECI ɣiiq-, (after V only) yaʀiiq-, (after t only) tsaʀiiq- 'already' [the latter allomorph taʀiiq on Baffin, where also vaɣiiq- is found; note Lab ɣiiʀi- 'again so soon']
GRI ʀiiʀ-, SWG +saʀiiʀ-, EG laȓaaʀ- 'already' [and compare pišaʀiiʀ-, piaʀiiʀ- under pižaʀiiq-]

PI ɣiit- 'can not' [cf. ŋit- and perhaps ɣi- discussed under ði-, i.e. originally 'not have s.th. unwanted happen to one' as in Sig ɣiitkutaq- below?]
Yup [AAY +(ɣ)ii- 'manage to', with neg. 'be unable to', is probably an extension of the half-transitive p.b. (ɣ)i- (under PE ði-) acc. Leer, so it could be related]
SPI —
NAI [note ɣiitkutaq in akšaɣiitkutaq under akðaɣ-]
WCI ɣiit- 'cannot (any longer)' [also ɣiiq- with ŋiʀ-; note also Sig ɣiitkutaq 'means for preventing'; and Pryde has ɣiit-/yaʀiit- 'does not need to -' for Cop]
ECI [note akšaɣiitkutaq under akðaɣ-]
GRI [note akšaɣiitkutaq under akðaɣ-]

PI ɣuciq 'secondary' [cf. ŋu- and un?]
SPI —
NAI ɣusiq 'secondary' [Jen.]
WCI —
ECI SB, Lab ɣusiq 'secondary, other kind of -'
GRI #ʀusiq 'not a real -'

I

PY i 'deictic used with demonstratives' [enclitic; cf. Aleut y, ya and see further under Demonstratives]
AAY K i 'deictic used with demonstratives'
CAY i
NSY —
CSY —

PI iqtuq- 'do so many times' [cf. tuʀ-[2]; added to numeral bases]
SPI —
NAI (#)iqtuq- 'do - times'
WCI (#)iqtuq-
ECI NBI iʀsuq-
GRI —

PE (C)iʀ 'animal connected with s.th.'
AAY #iq 'animal connected with -' [see for example under əpnaʀiʀ (əpnaʀ)]
CAY #iq, iʀ(aq^w)
NSY —
CSY #iq [in pəŋiiq under əpnaʀiʀ (əpnaʀ) at least]
Sir #iX [see under əpnaʀiʀ (əpnaʀ)]

SPI #iq [see under əpnaʀiʀ (əpnaʀ) as for all Inu]
NAI #iq
WCI #iq
ECI —
GRI —

PY (ŋ)iʀaʀ- 'be cold in one's (body part)' [cf. ŋiʀ- and aʀ-]
AAY (#)(ŋ)iʀaʀ- 'be cold in one's -'
CAY (#)(ŋ)iʀ(aʀ)-
NSY —
CSY —
Inu [for ECI iq- 'be cold in one's -' see ŋiʀ-]

PI ituq- 'fetch'
SPI —
NAI Mal isuq- 'fetch'
WCI ituq-
ECI ituq-
GRI isuʀ-

K

PI kapcak(-) 'almost' [or k(k)amcak? — cf. kkanniʀ-, k(k)aʀ- and mcaɣ- or myaɣ-]
Yup [AAY kcak 'big', kcaɣ- 'very much', and CAY kaca(ɣ)aʀ-, kacɣaʀ- 'very' may be related]
SPI —
NAI kafsak- 'rather, almost, on point of' [also kafsaaq- in the latter meaning]
WCI Sig kapsak- 'rather, almost, a bit', Cop kaffaaluk 'big, very much' [and compare B. Lake kahik- 'almost, fairly', with ðiɣ-]
ECI kasa(a)k- 'almost' [also nominal; Pryde has kasak for Aiv; note also kak 'tiny, bad']
GRI NWG kassak [old ortho. kavsak] 'bad, poor' [may be endearing or ironic; kasik is the more common equivalent elsewhere in WG, and the EG equivalent (ɣ)ayi may belong here too, perhaps combined with the second syllable of payuk and k(k)uyuɣ]

PE kaʀ 'passive participial' [cf. Aleut passive participial qa-X (generalized from after uvular bases), (after ɣ) ka-X, (after C) xa-X (used with poss. person endings for anaphoric object past tense), also in half-transitive qaʀi- mentioned under ði- and perhaps qaða-, (after ɣ) kaða-, (after t) xaða- 'have already ed, stop' (but cf. under kšaq) and qali- 'begin' mentioned under liq-]
AAY [note laakaq under əlakaq (əlaɣ-)]
CAY [note əlakaq 'water hole' under əlaɣ-]
NSY [note əlakaq under əlaɣ-, and also aɣlukaq 'work' from aɣluɣ- 'work' in Men.]
CSY k̲aq 'pass. part.' [also trans. past tense marker; ə-dr — also with tə bases, with t optionally into s; for past (active) participial homonym see kšaq]
Sir —
SPI [note (#)kaaq 'one that has been -ed (by possessor)' — after V bases only?]
NAI kkaq 'that which one has -ed' [also trans. participial mood marker — the gemination may be due to inflected forms as under GRI below; also liɣaaq 'that one has provided with -' from liʀ-]
WCI #ɣaq 'passive participial' [after some k and q bases]
ECI #ɣaq 'durable result of action' [and alternative trans. indic. marker qa(ʀ) after uvular bases; Spald. has passive participial ɣaq usual after k and q bases for NBI]
GRI ɣaq 'pass. participial' [pl. and inflected kka(t); usual with ʀ bases, causing the ʀ to drop, suppletive to ðaʀ]

PE k(k)aʀ- and **q(q)aʀ-** 'briefly or suddenly' [the latter form from after uvular bases; cf. kkanniʀ-, kapcak and also puvukaʀ- under puvuɣ-]
AAY (#)q̣q̣aʀ- 'briefly, a little' [not geminated as an imperative modifier], q̣q̣əXtə- 'suddenly' [for suppletive +aXtə- after tə bases (and ones with an unaccented final syllable) see aʀaʀtə-; note also q̣q̣əXaa-, aaXtaʀ- 'in repeated sudden bursts' with similar suppletive form under aʀaʀtə-]
CAY q̣aʀ- 'briefly, just (before), please (with imper.)', q̣əXtə- 'suddenly, fast, at same time as' [not with ɣ or — usually — tə bases, for which compare (ɣ)aʀ(aX)tə- under aʀaʀtə-]
NSY q̣aʀ- 'please, let's - (with opt.), suddenly, just' [note also łqaʀ- and (ANLC) qaXtə- 'suddenly']
CSY q̣aʀ- 'please (with imper.)', Chap also 'briefly', q̣aXtə- 'suddenly' [not with bases in ɣ or prime V; also +aXtə-]
Sir [note anqaʀaʀ- 'run out' from anə-]
SPI Qaw kainaq- 'right away' [and KI kalaq- 'already']
NAI #kaq- 'barely', kaŋit 'delay -ing' [additive to t bases], kallaiq-, Mal kalanʀit- 'not at once' [and aqsi-, (after t) +kaqsi- 'begin, be about to'?; for (+)kanik- 'already' see ɣanək-]
WCI kaq- 'suddenly, for a moment' [Pryde has 'already for Cop and Net; also kaallak- 'straight out, at a blow' (with łłaɣ-), Car ka(C)- 'a moment' and kalaaq- 'will soon']
ECI ka(a)lla(k)- 'suddenly', kapit- 'soon, at once', kainna(q)- 'for a moment' [and Lab kkaa- 'too much, precipitously', Aiv ka(C)- 'a moment', ka(ŋ)niaq- 'will soon']
GRI #kaʀ- 'suddenly', (#)kaałłaɣ- 'very much, hard' [compare under ala- for the latter, also EG kkaayu 'very' (a nominaizer), probably combining ʀuyuk under ʀuluk; for #kaa- 'several do' see qqaʀ-]

PY kaʀaq 'small' [cf. PE nukaʀ]
AAY —
CAY kaʀ(aq*) 'small' [only with bases in tə, which drops; see also (s)kaʀ(aq) under ðə, note also ŋkaʀaq 'exact area in a direction, right -']
NSY kaʀaq 'small' [ANLC]
CSY kaʀaq 'small'
Inu [note Car niviakkaq under nivi(C)aʀ and EG nuliakkaaq under nuliʀ(aʀ)?]

PE k(k)attaʀ- and **q(q)attaʀ-** 'repeatedly or habitually?' [cf. k(k)ətaʀ-, qqaʀ- and t(t)aʀ-; since there are far more uvular than velar bases in Esk. the generalization of a post-uvular allomorph to other positions (as in the second form here) is more likely than that of a post-velar one]
AAY q̣ataʀ- 'be -ing (progressive)' [usually drops tə], q̣ataaʀaʀ- 'slowly'
CAY q̣ataʀ- 'be about to', q̣ataaʀ(aʀ)- 'gradually, slowly start -ing' [for Nun kutaʀ(aʀ)- 'plan to' see kutaʀ-]
NSY ḵataaʀ- 'begin to' [ANLC has qataqə- 'near future, be about to', qataʀ- 'be about to', and qataaʀ(aʀ)- 'slowly start -ing']
CSY ḵataʀ(aʀ)- 'finally — despite feeling it wouldn't happen'
Sir —
SPI [note siniɣuminaitqataq- 'never sleep']
NAI #kataq- 'repeatedly' [also #qattaaq- and Mal #qataq-; #qattaliq- 'begin to regularly']
WCI qattaq-, Sig kattaq- 'repeatedly'
ECI qatta(q)- 'repeatedly' [also (#)kataq- after k bases]
GRI qattaaʀ- 'repeatedly', NG qattaq- 'habitually', qattaaq- 'repeatedly' [WG also #kattaʀ-, #kataaʀ- after certain velar bases]

PE kayuɣ(-) 'tend to (often)' [cf. yuɣ- and Sig ɣa- under na-, also Aleut Vka- 'can' under ya-]
AAY —
CAY —
NSY —
CSY ḵayuk 'one that - readily', ḵayuɣu- 'be able to'
Sir ḵayux 'one able to -'
SPI —
NAI Nu ɣayuk- 'often' [Jen. also for B; MacLean has #ayuuq-, #(ɣ)ayuk- 'one that (always) -']
WCI Net ɣayuk- 'tend to, often' [also Esk. Point in first sense]
ECI ɣayuk- 'tend to, often', ɣayuit- 'rarely'
GRI +ɣayuɣ- 'often, habitually' [and +ɣayuuq- 'one who habitually, often -']

PE kðaʀ '(s.th. for the) future' [cf. yaʀka(C)u- and žukšau-; the forms like kšau- added directly to verbal bases in Inu could represent a conflation with participial kšaq]
AAY +(X)kaq 'future', +kau 'be supposed to, should' [with ŋu-; for +yaʀau 'must' see yaʀka(C)u-]
CAY +kaq 'future, raw material for' [for +(ɣ)aXkaq 's.th. which is to be -ed' see yaʀka(C)u-]
NSY +(x)ḵaq ' material for' [ANLC also 'future']
CSY +ḵaq 'raw material for', ḵaXqaq 'future' [the former also 'raw material for -ing' on verbal bases]
Sir [Vakh. has kaXqaX 'future' — presumably from the CSY]
SPI kšaq 'material for' [and verbal = 'acquire material for']
NAI kšaq 'future' [verbal = 'get material for'; and note such lexicalized forms as tusaqšaʀɨ- 'be able to hear 'under tucaqšau- (tucaʀ-)]
WCI xxaq 'future' [verbal = 'get material for'; and xxau 'near future' — with ŋu- - and lexicalized forms like Cop tuhaXXau- 'be audible']
ECI tsaq 'future' [verbal = 'get material for'; also tsayaq 'material for -', and note tusaʀsau-under tucaqšau- (tucaʀ-)]
GRI ššaq 'future' [and note such lexical items as tusaššaa-, tusaʀšaa- 'be audible' from tucaʀ-; NG xxau-, (after uvular) XXau- 'be apt to, can easily']

PE kðit- 'supply with' [cf. kðaʀ and lit-]
AAY +(X)kitə- 'give, loan to'
CAY +kitə- 'give, supply with'
NSY —
CSY —
Sir —
SPI kšit-
NAI kšit-
WCI xxit-
ECI —
GRI ššit-

PE kə-[1] 'have as' [also a transitivizer of emotional roots — 'feel - toward'; compare also əðəkə- under əðə; for Aleut ʀi- 'have' see under ði-]
AAY ḵə- 'have as' [also 'find (too) -' with adj. bases]
CAY ḵə- [in the 'find (too)' sense causes tə to become l and does not alternate with q after a uvular]
NSY ḵə- 'have as'
CSY ḵə-
Sir ḵə- [kəs- before present tense qəXtəʀa, etc. — cf. t-[1], apparently added here]
SPI ɣi- 'have as' [for kaaq 'one that has been -ed' see kaʀ]
NAI ɣɨ -'have as' [and note kaaq 'that which one usually has as one's -']
WCI ɣi- 'have as, consider' [and note Car? ksaq- 'consider or find too -' — Schn. 'adg'
ECI ɣi- 'have as, consider' [and note tsa(q)- 'consider or find too -', based on this]
GRI ɣi- 'have as, consider' [before contemp. mood ɣa-, with indic. vaa (3s-3s), etc., contracts to ɣaa, etc.; note also NG xxaq- 'consider or find too -']

PE kə(-)[2] '(present passive) participial' [cf. kəŋaq, kšaq and kaʀ and Aleut present/participial marker ku-X (vowel influenced by 'lost' ðuʀ?), anaphoric trans. (3s object) kuu, etc., neg. (la)kaX; in Inu ɣa- before V in 3rd person inflections, otherwise ɣə-; note also the lexicalized forms uɣukə (under uyu-) and atəkə]
AAY kə- 'trans. past tense marker' [and in AP also a nominalizer as in CAY]
CAY ḵə- 'that which one is -ing' [and trans. participial mood marker; ḵəŋə- 'detransitivizer' (with ŋə- under nəɣ-) — compare kəŋaq]
NSY —
CSY ḵə- 's.th. one is -ing' [and transitive (present) participial mood marker]
Sir ḵə(ŋə)- 'transitive participial (may be used for indic.)'
SPI ɣi- 'trans. indic. marker'
NAI ɣɨ -

WCI ɣi-
ECI —
GRI ɣi- 'trans. participial marker'

PY-S kəcitə- or **kəcitaʀ-** 'slowly'
AAY —
CAY —
NSY k̲əsitə- 'slowly, peacefully'
CSY k̲əstaʀ- 'slowly, ahead of time' [and note k̲usiiʀ- 'casually, slowly']
Sir k̲əstaʀ- 'slowly' [perhaps from the CSY]

PY kəɣtaq 'one with a good' [cf. kiɣ-]
AAY —
CAY k̲əxtaq 'one with a good -'
NSY k̲əxtaq 'one with a good -' [ANLC also 'good']
CSY k̲əxtaq

PY kəŋaq 'one that is -ed (by s.o.)' [cf. kə-[2], nəɣ-, and ðaʀ]
AAY kəŋa(ʀ)- 'one that is -ed (by possessor)' [forms the present transitive participial mood]
CAY k̲əŋaq 's.th. that is being -ed (by possessor)'
NSY k̲əŋaq 'one that has (been) -ed (past participial)' [and note k̲əŋa(a)ma- 'distant past', k̲əŋauʀ- 'for a long time']
CSY —

PE k(k)ətaʀ- 'repeatedly' [cf. k(k)attaʀ- and t(t)aʀ-, also perhaps qə-]
AAY —
CAY q̲ətaaʀ- 'repeatedly back and forth' [and nominal q̲ətaaq 'device acting thus']
NSY (#)qitaaq, (#)kitaaq 'back and forth -, on and off -, thing that -s' [ANLC]
CSY k̲ətaʀ- 'tend to (by disposition)'
Sir — [cf. kacəfkitaʀ- under kaðəvə(t)-]
SPI —
NAI —
WCI —
ECI kitaq-, kitaaq-, (#)qitaq- 'one time after another, frequently' [also #qqitaʀ-, #qqiyaʀ- after certain q bases and note kutaaq-, qitaaq- 'a long time']
GRI — [for kula(aʀ)- 'habitually, often' see la(ʀ)-]

PE ki- 'in the future (and then)'
AAY k̲i 'in the future' [optative only]
CAY k̲i
NSY —
CSY —
Sir —
SPI —
NAI +ɣisi- 'future' [Jen. has ɣi- 'also'; note also lɣit- 'again', which could reflect the conflation of the present p.b. and another of this shape meaning 'although told not to, be bold enough to']
WCI ɣi-, +ki- 'again, too, and then'
ECI ɣi-, (esp. after t) kki-, (after ŋŋit) +ni- 'again, also' [for the latter compare the special form of the causative -nami, etc., after neg. ŋŋit-; generally with indic. but can also form less immediate imperatives; in Lab ɣi-, ɣialla(k)- 'again' is usually of unexpected, unfortunate occurrences]
GRI +ɣi- 'and then, moreover, also' [also older +ni- after ŋŋit-; used for less immediate imperatives; metathesized +ɣuyuq, etc., with intr. indicative]

PE k(k)i(C)aʀ 'I wonder' [enclitic]
AAY K +kiq 'I wonder, hope' [directly added to preceding word]
CAY +kiq 'I wonder' [and note +kin 'I wish' — used with opt. mood]
NSY —
CSY —
Sir —
SPI +kiaq 'I wonder'
NAI +kiaq, (after q) kkiaq 'I wonder' [and +kii, kkii 'because, too']
WCI kiaq 'I wonder'
ECI kiaq
GRI EG ɣiaq, NG #kiaq 'I wonder' [also in SWG suuʀłikiaq 'of course, I wonder why']

PE kiɣ- 'have a good' [cf. kəɣtaq, nqiɣ-[1] and ŋiɣ-, perhaps also Aleut Vcx(i)- as in slaacx-iX 'storm' from sla- 'wind' and Atkan Vcxuza- 'very (much), strongly']
AAY k̲əxtə-, q̲əxtə- 'have a good -' [and, with łəʀ-, KP łq̲əxtə-, Kod łk̲əxci-, PWS, AP łq̲əxci- 'enjoy -ing']
CAY k̲əxci- 'have a good -', k̲əxtə- 'be or have a good -' [and k̲əxłiq 'one that is or has a good-', k̲əxtaaʀ(aq) 'new, good', #ck̲əxtə- 'be very -, have a good -']
NSY k̲əxsaaqə- 'fix up'
CSY k̲əxtə- 'be or have a good -'
Sir nəxsəkəxtaX 'pretty' [and note qərlərəX on adj. bases 'one with a (esp. good) one']
SPI ɣik- 'have a good -' [and ɣiit- 'have a bad -', ɣiksaq 'fix']
NAI ɣik- 'be or have a good -' [also #ʀik- causing gemination in e.g. qaummaʀik- 'be bright' under qa(C)u(ði)-; also #ɣik-, Mal ɣiksaaq 'good', ɣiit- 'have a bad-, ache in one's -', (#)ɣiksaq- 'make nice']
WCI ɣik- 'have a good, plenty of -' [and less productively 'be a good -'; ɣixxaaq- 'properly, well']
ECI ɣik- 'have a good, big -' [and ɣitsi- 'have a better -']
GRI ɣiɣ-, ɣissaaʀ- 'have a good', ɣik 'one with a good -' [also ɣissi- 'have got a better -; 'for #qqiɣ- and geminating #ʀiɣ- 'be good at -ing' see nqiɣ-[1]]

PE k(k)it- 'have little' [this p.b. may be related to ŋit-, sharing the same tə/l alternation with it in Yup (compare also ipɣit- under ipəɣ-); the non-weakened k in Inu may indicate an earlier *nə(ʀ)kit- parallel to PE nəʀtu-]
AAY +kitə- 'have small, few -'
CAY +kitə- 'have small, few -' [with the tə ~ l alternation; note +kəłi-, HBC +kiłi- 'have to a decreasing degree']
NSY +kitə- 'have to a small degree' [ANLC]
CSY [cf. aXqəstaaq under əkəʀ(tu)-]
Sir [cf. əXqətaʀaʀ- under əkəʀ(tu)-]
SPI Qaw kit- 'have small, few -'

NAI kit- 'have small, few — ' [and kikł^{y}i- 'have smaller, fewer -']
WCI qqukit- 'have small, few -'
ECI (+ta)kit- 'have small, few -' [and Spald. has NBI kłi- 'have fewer, less -']
GRI kit-, kiłłiuʀ- 'have small, few' [and kišaaʀ- 'have rather little -', kiłłi-, NG ɣli- 'have smaller, fewer -']

PE kkanniʀ- 'rather (more)' [cf. k(k)aʀ-?]
AAY qaqaniiʀ-, AP qaniʀ-, PWS qaniiʀ-, Kod qa(qa)nia<ʀ>aʀ- 'a bit'
CAY k̲aniʀ- 'more intensely', k̲aniiʀ- 'a little more', k̲aniʀ(aʀ)- 'more and more' [all additive with tə bases — dropping the ə]
NSY —
CSY k̲aniʀ- 'rather, fairly'
Sir —
SPI —
NAI —
WCI Net, Car kkanniq- 'more, again' [Pryde has Cop ɣanniq-, (after t-stems) +kanniq- (also corresponding nom. forms)]
ECI Iti, NBI kkan(n)iq-
GRI kanniʀ-, NG kkanniq- 'somewhat, more or less' [also nominal kanniq, NG kkanniq-, which may be added to nominal forms in the allative case]

PE knaʀ 'wind from (a direction)' [from PE ablative case kən — cf. Inu kŋa on demon. stems]
AAY [note #kəq as in kanakəq 'south wind' (under kanaknaʀ)]
CAY #kŋ̥ak, Y #kŋ̥əq*, LI #kŋ̥aq 'wind from the -'
NSY #kŋ̥aq
CSY [note Chap akikŋ̥aq 'southwest wind' from aki(-)
Sir — [but note #kšaX in kanakšaX 'south wind']
SPI #kŋaq 'wind from the -' [as in KI iŋakŋaq 'east wind'; Imaq #knaq]
NAI #ŋnaq, Mal #knaq 'wind from the -'
WCI #ŋnaq
ECI #nnaq, Baf. #ŋnaq 'wind from the -' [and ŋ(ŋ)aq as in pinnaŋaq 'south wind']
GRI #nnaq, NWG, EG #ŋŋaq 'wind from the - direction' [and note #+naaʀ- 'blow strongly' as in avannaaʀ- 'blow strongly from the north']

PY kšak 'little' [cf. Aleut kδa-X 'small'; there seems to be some entanglement with tyaɣ]
AAY — [for kcak 'big' see under kapcak]
CAY — [for HBC kcak 'thing like a -' see tyaɣ]
NSY kšak 'a little bit of -' [ANLC also 'thing like a -'], kšaɣ- 'a little'
CSY kšak 'little, thing like a -'

PY-S kšaq 'past participial' [cf. kə^2, also Aleut qaδa- under kaʀ, which may belong here rather despite the problem with the vowels; compare also about Inu kšaq on verbal bases under kδaʀ]
AAY — [but note kaatə- 'too soon'?]
CAY —
NSY —
CSY k̲aq 'one that has -ed' [also a past tense marker; morphophonemics as for k̲aq under kaʀ; k̲aa- 'have — ed' (with ŋu-)]
Sir k̲cəX 'one that has -ed' [pl. k̲cəʀiy; can take personal endings, as k̲cəŋ 'I having -ed']

PE ku 'following (period)' [perhaps the same as conditional mood marker ku (see also qaku as opposed to qaŋa), though the vialis case marker kun may also be involved, at least as a source of contamination — compare Inu uvlaakun, etc. 'tomorrow, in the morning' under umlaaq (umłuʀ)]
AAY #k̲u 'following, future' [to time period bases]
CAY #k̲u 'following, future' [but note unuaku 'tomorrow morning' as opposed to unuaqu 'tomorrow' under unnu(C)aqu (unnuk)]
NSY #k̲u 'following, future'
CSY #k̲un, Chap #ku
Sir [note unəʀaqu 'tomorrow' under unnu(C)aqu (unnuɣ)]
SPI kun 'following, future' [but run in uɣiuʀun 'next winter']
NAI ku(n) 'following, future' [but uvlaaʀu 'tomorrow morning' as opposed to uvlaaku 'tomorrow']
WCI ɣu 'following, future'
ECI ɣu
GRI ɣu

PE k(k)u(C)aʀ- 'go via' [from vialis case marker kun; cf. q-, also muaq-]
AAY [note nunakuaʀ- 'go by land' from nuna, also (#)+xuiʀ- as in CAY]
CAY +kuaʀ- 'go via -' [drops weak q; also +kuiʀ- 'follow, go along', (#)+xuiʀ- with demonstr. roots]
NSY —
CSY —
Sir —
SPI kuaq- 'go via -'
NAI kuaq-, (with dual, plural bases) +tiɣuaq-
WCI kkuaq-, kkuuq-
ECI [kkuuq-, (with possessed bases) aɣuuq- 'go via -']
GRI [kkuuʀ-, (with possessed bases) aɣuuʀ- 'go via -']

PE k(k)uc(c)iʀ 'of such a kind' [cf. uciʀ?]
AAY (#)kuciq 'of such and such a kind' [to demonstr. roots]
CAY (#)kuciq 'one of same kind as -' [to demonstr. roots]
NSY —
CSY — [for łqusiq 'all of (time period)' see lquciq]
Sir —
SPI —
NAI —
WCI [Cop hukutsiq 'what part (of it)' — Pryde]
ECI (#)k(k)u(t)siq 'such a part ' [to demonstr. roots: the form with an initial geminate is used when the base concerned has a geminate in the plural, e.g. tamakku, otherwise kutsiq, e.g. with u(ku) — the initial element thus seems to reflect the plural morpheme on demonstr. roots]

GRI [note ukutsiq plus poss. endings 'such and such a part of (s.o.)' (while pointing) — with dem. root uv-]

PI k(k)uluk 'poor (little)' [cf. ʀuluk, łuɣ(-) and k(k)uyuɣ]
SPI —
NAI kuluk 'dear little'
WCI Car kuluk 'small, bad, poor' [Hansen]
ECI kuluk 'dear little'
GRI kkuluk 'poor, small, dear' [the latter meanings esp. SWG; also kuluɣ- 'somewhat' or 'poor/dear one does' and southern SWG kuluuq 'very big']

PY-S kumtaq 'usual?'
AAY —
CAY —
NSY k̲umta(a)q 'usual, reliable, familiar' [to nom. bases; to verbal bases 'frequently -ed thing']
CSY SLI qumtaq 'frequently or usually -ed thing' [on verbal bases, so containing *nəʀ[1]? — Rub. has qawaŋkumtaq 'constant (successful) hunter of birds' for Chap, with ŋə (nəɣ-)]
Sir kumtaX 'real, constant'

PE k(k)uʀ and **k(k)u(C)aʀ** 'remains of'
AAY #+kuaq 'part, piece' [and #łəXkuaq 'small remaining piece of']
CAY +kuaq 'left-over' [and łquq 'old broken piece of', #qucuk 'little bit of']
NSY +(x)k̲uaq 'old, discarded' [and +k̲usuk 'old']
CSY (+)k̲ʷaaq* 'left-over' [for Chap k̲uvinʀaq 'former' see vinəʀ]
Sir [see kuvinʀaX 'remains of, former' under vinəʀ]
SPI kuq, łikuq 'discarded' [and verbal ku 'leave - for', +nikuq 'one's act of -ing']
NAI ku 'left-over' [and note lexical items with gemination like kippaku 'cut-off piece' from kəppaʀ (kəpə-)]
WCI kuq 'remains of'
ECI (+ni)ku 'remains of' [ku causes gemination; +niku also = 'unfortunate result of -ing' and with the allative case in NBI and SB = 'because of one's -ing']
GRI kuq 'remains of, previous', +nikuq 'remains of, one who has -ed' [and +nikuu 'perfect (experiential) tense']

PY kutaʀ- or **kutaɣ-** 'be about to' [cf. k(k)ətaʀ- and also perhaps qu-]
AAY kutaʀ- 'near future'
CAY Nun, HBC kutaɣ- 'vague future', Nun kutaʀ(aʀ)- 'plan to' [elsewhere note kuxtə- 'be about to, plan to']
NSY —
CSY — [for kusiiʀ- 'casually, slowly' see kəcitə-]

PE k(k)uyuɣ 'poor little?' [cf. k(k)uʀ and perhaps yuɣ, also Aleut kuca-X 'small', EA kusa-X, Atkan kuza-X 'dear', Atkan also kuta-X 'poor'; the original geminate is reflected in the preserved intial k in GRI, as in parallel k(k)uluk]
AAY —
CAY kuyuk 'poor, small bit of'
NSY —
CSY —
Sir —
SPI —
NAI —
WCI —
ECI —
GRI kuyuɣ-, kuyuuʀ- 'somewhat' [and nominative plural kuyuit 'dear little ones (ironic)']

PY kyaɣutə- 'acquire' [cf. kə-[1], yyaɣ- and utə-]
AAY #k̲sayutə- 'adopt (as relative)'
CAY k̲sayutə- 'acquire as one's own -'
NSY —
CSY k̲sayutə-

PY kya(C)itə- 'not yet' [cf. ŋit-, perhaps also yyaɣ-]
AAY k̲siitə- 'not yet' [and +miksiitə 'have never or not in a long time -ed']
CAY k̲saitə- 'not yet' [with tə alternating with l]
NSY kyiatə- 'before, while still not -ing' [with subord. mood]
CSY —

PY kyu(C)aʀ- or **kya(C)aʀ-** 'a little' [from *tyu(C)aʀ- or *tya(C)aʀ-?; cf. tyaɣ, myaɣ- and mcuɣ- though the relat. is obscure — but note especially HBC kcak under tyaɣ]
AAY [note AP k̲cuk 'cute little']
CAY ksuaʀ(aʀ)- or k̲suaʀ(aʀ)-, ksaaʀ(aʀ)- 'in a small way', cuaʀ(aq*), (after tə that drops) ksuaʀ(aq*), HBC (all positions) kcuaʀ(aq*) 'little'
NSY kyuaʀ- 'barely'
CSY —

L

PE la(ʀ)- 'repeatedly' [cf. Aleut la- 'one after another, gradually'; the relat. to ðaʀ- is obscure — perhaps the forms like laʀ- are influenced by the latter]
AAY +laʀ- 'continually', #+laʀaa- 'intermittently' [and +milannətə 'no longer continually'],
CAY laʀ-, Y +laʀ- 'habitually' [ə-dr]
NSY laʀ- 'permanently, regularly' [ANLC]
CSY +laataʀ- 'again (once more)' [with ʀataʀ-]
Sir +lataʀ- 'again' [also +łataʀ acc. Men.]
SPI laq-, (after C) +taq 'be used to -ing' [drops preceding t; for lainaq- 'gradually' see tainnaq-]
NAI la- 'over and over' [after Vq 'say' and in limited use elsewhere; for ala- 'a lot' see ala-]
WCI la- Sig, Car 'say' [for senses 'can' and 'on point of' see tla-]
ECI la- 'say (once or several times)' [for laqi- 'and so' see ʀqə-]
GRI [note #la- lexicalized in meanings like 'back and forth, in all directions' — as in isaqqila- under iyaqqi- (iyaɣ-); also kula-, kulaaʀ- 'often', for the first element of which see qu-]

PE la(C)aʀ(-) '(a) little' [cf. Aleut laayakuca-X 'tiny']
AAY [note laayak 'horrible' (also verbal)?]
CAY —
NSY —
CSY #laaq* 'insignificant'
Sir —
SPI —
NAI Nu laaq- 'a little' [and note B (#)laaq- 'become or make more' after si-/li- 'become' and lexicalized in various nominal forms; for laaq-, (after C) +taaq- 'go so far as to' see tələ-]
WCI (#)laaq- 'a little', Net 'a while' [and laaŋŋit- 'not at all']
ECI laaq 'tiny, young', C. Dorset 'small' [for the NBI, SB sense 'one that is most' see łəʀ[2]]
GRI laaʀ- 'a little'

PI lauq- 'for a while?' [cf. la(ʀ)- and (C)uʀ-]
SPI —
NAI —
WCI lauq- Cop 'for a while', Car 'past', Sig 'suddenly' [the latter acc. Lowe; Cop lauŋŋit- 'not yet, in a while']
ECI lauq- 'past (at which speaker was present)' [and lauyu- 'distant past' — compare Baffin yuu under suu-]
GRI [note #laaʀ- in tuʀłulaaʀ- 'shout' — old ortho. tordlulaor-]

PE ləɣ 'one provided with or having' [the frequent dropping of the ə under inflection could have resulted in the truncating behavior of this p.b.; cf. Aleut passive p.b. lɣa-, (after C) sxa, Attuan lu, from *ləɣ plus a/u- 'be', also perhaps in certain place names ending in lɣi-X, sxi-X]
AAY lək 'one (provided) with'
CAY lək 'one (provided) with' [also +talək 'place with']
NSY lək 'one (provided) with'
CSY lək
Sir ləx 'owner of, one with'
SPI lik '(provided) with'
NAI lik '(provided) with' [and liɣaaq 'the one with a-; for verbal liɣaaq 'bring along' see lizaaq-]
WCI lik 'one (provided) with' [may also be verbal 'have'; also liɣaq 'one with, owner of', +talik 'there is/are']
ECI lik 'one (provided) with' [may also be used verbally; note also liɣaq 'catch, win'; also +talik 'there is/are -']
GRI lik 'one (provided) with' [rel. łłup or łłip, pl. łłit, NG ɣlit; may be used verbally in NG with person endings — also +talik 'there is/are -'; compare #+ləɣ in forms like saarułłik under caðəŋilitaʀ (under caðə-)?;]

PE ləɣ- 'back and forth'
AAY #ləɣ- 'back and forth' [as in uuləɣ- at uŋuləɣ- 'quiver']
CAY #ləɣ- [as in paŋaləɣ- 'run on four legs']
NSY #ləɣ- [as in paŋałxa- 'gallop' under paŋləɣ-]
CSY #ləɣ- [as in paŋaləɣ-]
Sir #ləɣ- [as in paŋaləɣ-]
SPI #lik- [as in paŋaləɣ- in all Inu]
NAI #lik-
WCI #lik-
ECI #lik-
GRI #liɣ-

PE ləʀ- and təʀ- 'quickly' [the relat. — if any — with (the other) təʀ- is obscure]
AAY —
CAY ləʀ-, Y +ləʀ- 'suddenly and willfully' [also (after C only, more lexicalized) +təʀ-, apparently by contam. with təʀ-; ləʀyaɣ- 'abruptly, in a huff']
NSY +ləʀ- 'quickly' [ANLC has təʀ- 'suddenly, rapidly']
CSY —
Sir —
SPI —
NAI liq-, (after C) +tiq- 'suddenly, quickly' [and liqtuq-, +tiqtuq- 'quickly'; the t-initial forms perhaps suppletive from təʀ-]
WCI Net liqtuq- 'quickly' [Met. tiqtuq- for Sig — compare təʀ-]
ECI —
GRI liʀtuʀ- 'quickly, for a short while', NG liqtaaq- 'quickly, early'

PE lɣiʀ- 'take along with one' [cf. ləɣ and liʀ-?]
AAY —
CAY lɣiʀ- 'take along'
NSY —
CSY lɣiʀ- 'travel using -'
Sir —
SPI —
NAI —
WCI lɣiq-, (trans.) lɣiaʀi- 'take, have with one'
ECI ɣɣi(q)-, (trans.) ɣɣiaʀi- [the ɣɣ doesn't change to uvular after q]
GRI —

PY lɣu- 'have' [cf. ləɣ and ŋu-]
AAY lɣu-, lʀuu- 'have lots of -'
CAY lɣu- 'be one that has -' [for ŋqəX- 'have' see ŋqaʀ-]
NSY lɣu- 'have'
CSY lɣu-

PY-S lɣun 'fellow (one sharing s.th. with one)' [cf. ləɣ and un]
AAY lɣun 'fellow -'
CAY lɣun 'one having the same -' [to verbal bases łxun rather]
NSY lɣutə [ANLC also lɣun] 'companion at -ing' [and note nunalɣutə 'fellow countryman' — compare PI nunatqan under nuna]
CSY lɣun 'one with same -'
Sir łxuta 'fellow -'

PE li-[1] 'make' [also 'spend the - (period)'; cf. li(C)uʀ-, lit-, liqə-, liyaʀ- and Aleut Xsi-, (after C) si- 'make, deal with, gather, store (in EA fish), celebrate, (refl.) become, be out in (weather), do in (morning)' (the first form generalized from the second after uvular bases) and compare also li- 'be engaged in, remove (from), lose at' (for the homonym meaning 'go to' see liyaʀ-),

liɣa-X 'material for', limaʀ-, (after C) simaʀ- 'deal with, cut (e.g. fish), check (weather), forecast (sea), Atkan liɣða-, EA likða- 'clean (fish or skin), punish (child)' — ul;timately the same as li-[2]?]
AAY li- 'make' [optionally replacive; and liɣaaʀ- 'work on, fool around with']
CAY li- 'make' [optionally replacive — especially in sense 'spend the -', optionally ci- with t(ə) bases]
NSY li- 'make' [ANLC; and note replacive i- in anyi- 'make a boat' from anyaq at least]
CSY (#) li- 'make' [and replacive (#)ii- 'cut up, butcher, prepare (game animal)']
Sir si- 'make'
SPI li- 'make' [optionally replacive]
NAI li- 'make, work on, cook' [optionally replacive — especially in 'spend the -' sense — in which case preceding t(ɨ) goes to s, as elsewhere]
WCI li- 'make' [optionally replacive]
ECI li- 'make'[optionally replacive]
GRI #li- 'make' [replacive especially in the 'spend the -' sense]

PE li-[2] 'become (more)' [cf. PE əłi-; the Yup allomorph (ʀ)i- may be suppletive — cf. ʀ- under ŋ(ŋ)uʀ- and compare also liq- (the vowel could be influenced by that of li- here); note also Aleut ŋali- 'cool off' under nəŋli- and the i in related lexical pairs like intr. la- 'ooze out' and trans. li- 'let out (air)', kumsa- 'rise' and kumsi- 'lift' — compare the transitive use of Esk li- below; the Inu variant si probably from combination with t bases as reflected in the GRI alternate imaasi- of imaali- under ət-, dissimilating allomorph kłi- later ousting it in most combinations — compare uqiɣitli- under uqiɣit- and amitli- under amit-]
AAY #+li-, +(ɣ/ʀ)i- 'become' [with adj. bases; li- after ə or tə — which drops -, ɣi- or ʀi- with bases in a prime vowel or ɣ/ʀ; (ɣ/ʀ)iuʀ-, (after tə bases) liuʀ- 'cause to become more', combined with ŋ(ŋ)uʀ-? — compare CAY liʀi- below]
CAY #+li-, +(ʀ)i- [as for AAY but with ʀi- only after prime V or ʀ, ɣi- after ɣ; note liʀi- 'become or cause to make more and more' (after bases ending in ə), seemingly composed of both allomorphs — but note under liq- — and compare also təxxi- 'harden' under təɣəɣ-]
NSY #+li-, +(ʀ)i- 'become (more)' [ANLC; and note +li- in anli- 'grow bigger' under aŋli- (aŋə-)]
CSY #+li-, +(ʀ)i- 'become' [li- after ə, ʀi- after prime V or ʀ]
Sir [note uqəŋicižaʀ- 'become lighter' under uqiɣitli- (uqit-)]
SPI #li- 'become' [also #+si-]
NAI #li-, (esp. after t and ɣɨ-) ɣli-, kłi- 'become, make become' [causes semifinal ɨ to drop; also #+si-]
WCI #(ɣ)li- 'become' [also #+si-; note Sig +si- 'begin to']
ECI #li- 'become, make become' [also #+si-; note si- 'begin to']
GRI #(+)li- 'become, make become' [esp. after t or V; also #+si-]

PE li(C)aʀ 'made thing' [cf. li-[1] and ðaʀ-]
AAY liaq 'made thing'
CAY liaq
NSY —
CSY —
Sir —
SPI liaq
NAI liaq
WCI liaq
ECI liaq
GRI liaq [pl. liššat]

PY linʀaq 'trace of or s.th. from' [cf. li-[1] and n(ə)ʀaʀ(aʀ)]
AAY —
CAY linʀaq* 'product, evidence, trace of -' [also #nʀaq]
NSY linʀaq 'piece of' [ANLC; and note kuvinʀaq under vinəʀ]
CSY linʀaq* 'thing of or from -' [and note kuvinʀaq under vinəʀ]

PI liq- 'begin to' [from *lliq-?; cf. valliq- and perhaps Aleut qali-, (after ɣ) kali-, (after t) xali- 'begin, make -ed', the first element being pass. part qa- as under kaʀ; from li-[2] plus geminating ʀ under ŋ(ŋ)uʀ-?]
Yup [for CAY liʀi- 'become or cause to make more and more', which may be cognate, see li-[2]]
SPI liq- 'begin' [and laliq-, +taliq- 'start -ing (after not -ing)']
NAI (#)liq- 'become, start -ing' [more productive is +žaʀaliq-, (after k/q) žaliq- 'start -ing frequently']
WCI liq- 'begin, be in in process of -ing'
ECI liqc
GRI liʀ- 'begin, be about to, in process of -ing' [in comb. with geminating (u)t(i) 'do with' = #siʀ- (compare EG imaasiʀ- under ət-); note also yumałłiʀ- under yuɣuma-]

PI liqaa 'any' [cf. łi and q(q)a(a)?]
SPI +liqaa 'any, every -'
NAI +liqaa 'any, -ever, so! (surprise)'
WCI +liqaa '-ever'
ECI —
GRI —

PE liqə- 'be occupied with' [cf. li-[1], qə- or ʀqə- and Aleut liXta- 'be busy with, have had too much of, suffer in' from li-[1] plus Xta- under ta-]
AAY (#)liqə- 'have pain in' [may be replacive; also +(X)łiqə- 'have problem with' and łiqə- 'have remnants of -ing on one']
CAY liqə- 'be afflicted in one's -, have problem with -, catch a lot of -' [may be replacive; with łuk = +łiqə 'have - of poor quality']
NSY liqə- 'have pain in or trouble with -' [ANLC]
CSY liqə- 'deal with, work with, have pain or trouble with' [optionally replacive]
Sir —
SPI (#)łiqi- 'have pain in one's -' [optionally replacive]
NAI (#)liqɨ- 'work on, deal with, have pain in one's -' [optionally replacive]

WCI liqi- 'occupy oneself with, hunt', Net liʀi- 'be occupied with, have pain in one's -' [optionally replacive]
ECI liʀi- 'occupy oneself with, have pain in one's -' [optionally replacive; Bourquin has liqi- 'get many' for Lab and Apald has NBI liqi- 'hunt']
GRI liʀi- 'be occupied with, have pain in one's -' [optionally replacive]

PE l(l)iʀ 's.th. or s.o. in a particular direction or position' [the geminated form could represent *nəʀ[2] + liʀ — compare related qliʀ apparently containing qaʀ; the (earlier) Inu forms in liq like GRI kiŋuliq under kiŋu- and siuliq under civu- may correspond to CAY li(q) below; cf. Aleut l(i)ʀ on demonstrative roots as in ukalʀa 'the village in here', perhaps also kiŋuliXtiŋis 'his descendants' from kiŋu-, also old Atkan kiŋuliʀ-a 'his lineage', and compare aqul- under aqu]
AAY #liq 'thing or area in a direction' [as in atłiq under at(-) and note qaliq under qaliʀ (qaðə-); also #liq 'one that is -' as in CAY]
CAY #liq* 'area or thing in a direction' [as in atłiq* under at(ə)- and kəłiq* under kətə-; also #li(q) 'one that is -' on verbal bases (which may fuse with a preceding t or l to łiq), also in tuli(q) under tu-[1] and yuli(q) under yu-]
NSY #liq 'the -most one, one in a certain direction'
CSY #liq(*) 'thing (most) in a direction' [and note ayuqłiq under ayuqə-]
Sir #ciX 'one most in a direction' [and note asiX 'lower one' under aci-[1], which may contain this p.b. — see also under atliʀ (at(ə)-)]
SPI #liq 'one most in a direction'
NAI #lliq* 'one most in a direction' [drops a preceding final ɨ and fuses with a t or l as in qulliq 'topmost' under qulliʀ (qulə-)]
WCI #lliq, #+hiq 'one most in a direction' [and lliqpaaq 'most to the -']
ECI #l(l)iq, #+(t)siq 'one most in a direction'
GRI #+(ł)łiq* 'one most in a direction' [and #liq(*) 'one in a certain direction', #+(ł)łiʀsaq 'one most to the-']

PE liʀ- 'provide with' [also used reflexively in sense 'there are/have come (s.th.)'; cf. li-[1] Aleut lʀi-, (after C) sXi- 'provide with', in which the i is auxiliary — compare imuunalʀasa- 'surround with' with p.b. asa- (under utə-) on base imuunu-; note also Inu half-transitive #kłiq- under aɣə- and ivaʀ- — from kaʀ or kə-[2] plus liʀ-?]
AAY liʀ- 'set up, put in, add to' [optionally replacive]
CAY liʀ- 'provide with, be well provided with' [optionally replacive]
NSY liʀ- 'attach, provide with, be provided with'
CSY liʀ- 'provide with, put in'
Sir [note cəʀ- in akəcəʀ- under akiliʀ- (aki(-)) and səʀ- in iməsəʀ- 'fill with water' under immiʀ- (ima(ʀ)), qəmtasəʀ- 'put up a ceiling' from qəmtaq (= CSY qəmtiʀ-), vuvəsəʀ- 'lay down walrus skin floor' from vuvəX (= CSY vuvəliʀ-)]
SPI liq- 'provide with' [optionally replacive]
NAI liq- 'provide with' [optionally repl.; also liqsuq]
WCI liq- 'provide with' [optionally repl.]
ECI liq- 'provide with' [optionally repl.]
GRI liʀ- 'provide with', liʀsuʀ- 'provide with several, bit by bit' [optionally repl.; note also łłiʀ- (old ortho. gdler) 'serve (of food and drink)']

PY-S liʀnəq 'area in a direction' [cf. l(l)iʀ and nəʀ[1]]
AAY #liʀnəq 'area in a direction' [as in PWS kiŋuliʀnəq 'area behind']
CAY #liʀnəq* 'area to the -'
NSY —
CSY #liʀnəq*
Sir [note ciʀnəX in uɣəciʀnəX 'northeast' under uɣal(l)iʀ (uɣan)]

PE lit- 'provide with?' [cf. liʀ-, also kðit-]
AAY —
CAY #itə- 'provide with (wherewithall to)'
NSY —
CSY —
Sir —
SPI —
NAI #lit- 'provide with'
WCI lit- 'give to'
ECI lit- 'give, take to'
GRI —

PE li(C)uʀ- 'prepare' [cf. li-[1] and (C)uʀ-]
AAY liuʀ- 'prepare, cook, fix' [optionally replacive]
CAY liuʀ- 'be occupied with, work or play with', Nun also 'cook' [optionally repl., with ciuʀ- after t(ə) bases]
NSY li(i)ʀ- 'prepare' [and li(i)q 'preparation of -' acc. Men., but ANLC has liiʀ[w]- 'be occupied with -']
CSY liiʀ- 'fix, prepare, cook, make' [optionally repl.]
Sir —
SPI liuq- 'make, prepare (food)' [optionally repl., as in all forms of Inuit]
NAI liuq-
WCI liuq- 'make, prepare' [in Car 'make several' acc. Pryde]
ECI liuq- 'make, prepare'
GRI liuʀ-, EG liiʀ-/luuʀ-

PE li(C)utə- 'make into' [cf. li-[1] and utə-]
AAY —
CAY k̲łiutə 'have obtained or claimed as one's -' [with kə-[1]]
NSY —
CSY liitə- 'have obtained as one's -'
Sir —
SPI (#)liuti- 'enter into a mutual relationship of -s'
NAI (#)liutɨ -'make into or out of'
WCI liut(i)- 'make into, compete at'
ECI (+mi)liut(i)- 'put into', liut(i)- 'invite or advise to — with one'
GRI liut(i)- 'use as a -, be caught in (e.g. storm)'

PE liyaʀ- 'go to' [cf. yaʀ(tuʀ)-, also Aleut li- 'go to, visit'; there may be a link to li-[1] and to łit-]
AAY —
CAY (#) liyaʀ-, liaʀ- 'go to participate in (group activity)' optionally repl.]

NSY —
CSY —
Sir —
SPI (#)liaq- 'go to'
NAI (#)liaq- 'go to, go hunting -'
WCI liaq- 'go to, hunt' [optionally repl.; also nominal 'one going to']
ECI liaq- 'go to, hunt'
GRI liaʀ- 'go to' [optionally repl.; also nominal liaq- 'one going to ']

PI liža(a)q- 'have along with one' [cf. li-[1] and ðaʀ-?]
SPI ližaq- 'use' [optionally replacive]
NAI liža(a)q- 'take along' [optionally replacive; note also liɣaaq- 'bring along' — contam. with lɣiʀ-?]
WCI Car liɣaq- 'bring along' [Hansen; Briggs has Utk ližaq- 'wear, be covered with']
ECI liɣaq- 'have with one, use' [and (#)liɣaaq- 'show one's -'?]
GRI lišaʀ- 'have with one' [also 'resemble' — a different p.b.?; lišaaʀ- 'be wearing']

PI llaa- 'once in a while' [cf. łłaɣ- and a-]
SPI —
NAI llaa- 'one by one, once in a while'
WCI llaa- 'once in a while'
ECI llaa- 'several times'
GRI #łłaa- 'continually' [Ordbogêraq]

PI lliq- 'be pained by s.th.?' [cf. łuɣ(-) and liʀ-? — but compare liqə- too]
Yup — [but note CAY (#)łiqə- 'have pain in one's -' (from łuɣ(-) and liqə-)]
SPI —
NAI —
WCI +(l)liq- 'have pain in one's -' [also (#)+(l)liuq-]
ECI #lli(q)- 'have pain in one's -' [note also (#)lliu(q)- 'be annoyed by -']
GRI #+(ł)łiʀ- 'be harmed by -' [also trans. 'harm'; note also #+(ł)łiuʀ- 'be pained or worried because of s.th.']

PE lŋu- 'have pain in (body part)' [cf. culŋu-]
AAY #lŋu- 'hurt in one's -'
CAY lŋu- 'be indisposed with respect to -, be tired of -ing'
NSY lŋu- [ANLC]
CSY —
Sir —
SPI (#)nŋu- 'have a sore -' [and productively 'ask for -']
NAI nŋu- 'have a sore -, be tired of -ing'
WCI (#)nŋu- 'have pain in -, be tired of -ing' [also nŋuq- when attached to verbal bases]
ECI (#)ŋu-, Lab ŋŋu- 'have pain in one's -' [and ŋŋu(q)- be tired of ing']
GRI #ŋŋu- 'have pain in one's -', NG ŋŋu- 'be tired of -ing'

PY lqu(C)aq 'old'
AAY —
CAY [cf. aʀnałquaʀ(aq*) 'old woman' under aʀnalqu(C)aʀ (aʀnaʀ)]
NSY [cf. aʀnałquaʀaq under aʀnalqu(C)aʀ (aʀnaʀ)]
CSY #łqʷaaq, #sqʷaaq 'old' [the latter as in maŋtəʀasqʷaaq, maŋtəʀašqʷaaq 'old house'; note also squq 'small', squXXaq* 'tiny']
Inu [cf. GRI aʀnaqquaššaaq and the other Inu 'old woman' words under aʀnalqu(C)aʀ (aʀnaʀ)]

PY-S lquciq 'whole or big' [cf. k(k)uciʀ]
AAY —
CAY —
NSY łqusiq 'whole, big'
CSY łqusiq 'all, throughout the -'
Sir łqusiX 'big' [Men. gives as equiv. of the CSY above, but note also umłułqusiX 'all day' under umłuʀ]

PI lʀammiq- or **tqammiq-** 'recently' [cf. łʀa(C)aʀ- and lʀaɣaq-]
Sir [note +miX 'one that has just -ed']
SPI ʀlamiq-, (after k/q — Qaw also after V) qamiq-, (after t) tqamiq- 'already, recently have -ed'
NAI qqammiq-, (after t) tqammiq- 'recently have -ed'
WCI lʀammiq-, (after k/q) qqammiq-, (after t) tqammiq- 'recently have -ed' [also nominal 'one who has just -ed']
ECI qqamiq- 'recently' [also nominal 'one who has just -ed'; qqamiŋŋi(t)- 'a long time ago']
GRI qqammiʀ- 'recently' [qammiŋŋit- 'some time ago']

PI lʀataq- or **ʀataq-** 'finally' [the relat. to ʀataʀ- is obscure; cf. also lʀammiq- and lʀaɣaq-]
Yup [note CSY lʀaXtuʀ- 'already, unexpectedly']
SPI ʀlataq-, (after k/q) ɣataq- 'about to' [and note +saʀataq- under caʀ-]
NAI lʀataq-, (after k/q) ɣataq- 'finally, until'
WCI (l)ʀataq-, Net ʀataq- 'at last' [also an intensifier]
ECI ʀataq- 'you see, it's a fact that -', ʀataŋŋi(t)- 'not yet' [and ʀataaq- 'one who has just -ed']
GRI ʀataʀ- 'at last, suddenly'

PI lʀaɣaq- or **tqaɣaq-** 'almost or barely' [cf. łʀa(C)aʀ- and ɣaʀ-, also ʀaʀaʀ- and lʀataq-, though the relat. is obscure]
Yup [note CSY lʀa-, (after C) Xa plus intr. indic. endings 'future optative']
Sir [note pilʀaɣaʀ- 'miss target' — Orr]
SPI qaɣaq-, (after t) tqaɣaq- 'barely, almost, start but not finishing'
NAI qqaɣaq-, (after t) tqaɣaq- 'almost', qqaɣaa(-nak, etc.) 'don't!'
WCI lʀaɣaq-, (after k/q) qqaɣaq-, (after t) tqaɣaq- 'almost' [Pryde has Cop lʀiaq-]
ECI qqaɣaq- 'can', Iti, NBI 'almost'
GRI qqaɣaʀ-, qqaɣaa-, EG qqiaʀ- 'almost, be about to', qqaɣaqi-, EG qqiaʀi- 'would'

PY-S lʀi(C)a(q) 'participial' [may also be used as an indic. mood marker; there may be a link to łəʀ[1]; for Aleut la(a)ʀana-X 'one who recently -ed' see łʀa(C)aʀ-]
AAY C lʀaa, pl. lʀiit, K ł<X>ia '(the) one who is -ing'
CAY lʀia(ʀ), '(the) one who is -ing' [optionally łXia(ʀ) after voiceless C; the final ʀ appears in inflected forms]

NSY lʀia 'one that is -ing'
CSY lʀii '(the) one that -ed' [used as a past tense marker]
Sir łəʀəX [Vakh. ləʀəX] 'one that is -ing or has -ed'
Inu — [but note Car nalʀiaq- 'probably', also nominal, as in tikittuunalʀiaq 'he probably came']

PY-S lʀutaq 'container for' [cf. q(q)un]
AAY —
CAY —
NSY lʀutaq 'container for -'
CSY lʀutaq 'container for -' [and note lʀun 'lots of -']
Sir [note lʀutaX in ažulʀutaX 'container for blood used in religious rites', from aðuɣ — Em.]

PE lu(ʀ) 'place or thing (for performing action)' [cf. Aleut aɣalu-X 'tooth', kaɣalu-X 'heel' and camlu-X 'chin'; found everywhere in anatomical terms like tamlu, qavlu(ʀ)]
AAY #(+)lu(q)
CAY #(+)lu(q)
NSY #(+)lu(q)
CSY #(+)luq
Sir #(+)la [probably *lu in underlying form]
SPI #(+)lu
NAI #(+)lu
WCI #(+)lu
ECI #(+)lu
GRI #(+)lu

PE l(l)u(C)aʀ- and **l(l)u(C)ataʀ-** 'well' [compare base əłuʀaʀ- with ət-, so from *l(l)uʀaʀ-?; there may be some entanglement with tluk- in Inu, if it is not related]
AAY luaʀ- 'well, carefully'
CAY luaqaʀ- 'well, enjoyably, beneficially', NSU luataʀ- 'well' [and nominal luataq]
NSY [note luataqu 'as soon as -' — a fixed form without further inflection in Men.]
CSY laataqu- 'have -ed well' [for +laataʀ- 'again' see la(ʀ)-]
Sir [note əłuraʀən 'truly' under əłuʀaʀ-]
SPI luataq- 'well' [and nominal 'good'; also KI luq- 'fortunately']
NAI lluataq- 'well' [and nominal 'good']
WCI lluaq- 'very' [as nominal 'real'], Net lluatsiaq- 'well', Eskimo Point lluaʀik- 'real, really'
ECI lluaq- 'exactly, just like' [can follow nominal in aequalis case; Lab has lluak 'one good at -, big enough'; note also (#)lluatsia(q)- 'exactly, just, very well', and llurik- 'well', llaʀik- 'real(ly)', Lab lluɣik- 'much, a lot' (all from *lluaʀik-?), and F. Bay +luinnaq- 'continually']
GRI +(ł)łuaʀ- 'well' [in comb. with ut(i) = +(ł)łuut(i)-; NG +(l)luaq- 'really, completely', +(l)luaŋŋaaq- 'exactly, just'; note also +(ł)łuataar-, +(ł)łuartaar-, NG +(l)luassaaq- 'at ease', +(r)łuinnaʀ- 'completely' and łłariɣ 'well']

PY luɣpiɣaq 'good old' [cf. viɣ(-) and perhaps tluk- and/or aluk(-)]
AAY —
CAY #luxpiaq 'authentic, original' [and compare HBC, Nun, NS Xłuɣaq* 'good old' under ʀuʀluq]
NSY —
CSY luxpiɣaq 'fine old' [and note luk 'old']

PI luktaaq 'all' [to nominal bases; cf. tluk-]
SPI —
NAI —
WCI Car luktaaq 'all' [as verb = 'completely'; note Cop lukta(a)q- 'poor or foolish one does s.th.', also apparently 'a lot']
ECI NBI, SB luktaaq 'all'
GRI —

PE luʀ- 'repeatedly' [cf. Aleut kiɣluʀ- 'chew on, bite through' from kiɣ- under kəɣə-]
AAY #łuʀ- [note under quʀluʀ- at least]
CAY #luʀ- [note quXłuʀ- 'cascade' under quʀluʀ- at least — also ayalu(ʀ)-]
NSY —
CSY #luʀ- [note under quʀluʀ-]
Sir #luʀ- [note under quʀluʀ- at least]
SPI #łuq- 'repeated action' [cf. under quʀluʀ- at least, as for all Inu]
NAI #luq-
WCI #luq-
ECI #luq-
GRI #luʀ-

Ł

PY łaq 'thing to do with (past time)'
AAY łaq 'thing to do with -'
CAY łaq* 'thing to do with — (past time)'
NSY łaq 'thing of -' [ANLC]
CSY —

PE łəʀ[1] 'nominalizer (participial or action)' [cf. łəʀ[2] and compare nəʀ[1] and nəʀ[2]; there may also be a link to łʀa(C)aʀ-; see the note to ləɣ concerning the truncating morphophonemics]
AAY łəq 'former, one that has -ed or was -ed (by possessor)' [and łXu- 'perfect tense']
CAY łəq* 'former, one that (has) -ed, act or state of -ing' [and łXu- 'perfect tense', HBC, Nun trans. łqə-; note also łəXkaq 'future -ing' — e.g. as object clause of futurity, and łəʀ plus rel. endings (but loc. for intrans.) as 'contemporary' mood marker]
NSY łəq 'action of -ing' [ANLC also 'thing that results from -ing']
CSY łəq* 'one that (has) -ed, or has been -ed, act of -ing' [corresponding negative = łXitə-]
Sir łəX 'action of -ing'
SPI łiq
NAI Mal łiq* 'action, result of -ing'
WCI —
ECI —
GRI —

PE łəʀ² 'one that is more or most' [cf. under łəʀ¹]
AAY łəq [possessed łXa, etc.] 'one that is more — (than possessor)' [and trans. łqə 'have — be more than (subject)'; only on tə bases, otherwise nəq (nəʀ²) is used — the same is true of łəXpaaq 'one that is most -']
CAY łəq [possessed łXa, etc.] 'one that is more or most -' [after tə bases only, as also łXu- 'be more']
NSY —
CSY łəXpiɣaq 'most'
Sir —
SPI —
NAI łXaaq 'one that is more, most -' [also verbal 'more, most'; compare lʀaaq under łʀa(C)aʀ-; for laaq- 'become or make more' see la(C)aʀ-]
WCI [note Sig (#)lʀuq 'the most -' on adjectival verb bases — the relat. if any to quʀ is obscure; for Cop łXaaq- 'vivid action intensifier' see ʀłaɣ; Briggs reports exclamatory 1s and 3s indic. equivalent łXa — compare the CAY above]
ECI NBI, SB laaq 'one that is most -'
GRI EG lii-, (after C) sii- 'more' [from *łəʀu-, alongside +nii- from nəʀ², both with ŋu-; note also nuɣaʀsiq, nuɣaʀsiqpaaq 'younger, youngest (sibling)' from PE nukaʀ]

PE ł(ə)ɣu- 'be good at'
AAY —
CAY lɣu- 'always'; NS lɣu- 'can' [influenced by lɣu-?]
NSY łək 'one able to (handle) -' [ANLC 'one good at -ing']
CSY łxu- 'well', łək 'one who — well'
Sir łəx 'one good at handling -' [compare under ləɣ]
SPI lɣu- 'well, can', Qaw lɣuit- 'be unable to -, badly' [and Imaq lik 'one good at making -']
NAI lɣu- 'be capable of -ing excessively or a lot'
WCI lɣu- 'be good at -ing' [and lɣuhaut(i)- 'compete at -ing']
ECI —
GRI —

PE łi 'but' [enclitic]
AAY —
CAY +łi 'emphasis in exclamations' [esp. with +paa, vaa 'so, very much' when used with localis noun; added directly to first word of clause]
NSY [cf. amałi under amma]
CSY +łi 'let's say -, what/when/where - again' [added directly to preceding word]
Sir —
SPI +li 'I wonder' [expresses wonderment — e.g. about s.th. lost]
NAI +li 'what about (contrasting topic), well, you see, (with condit.) ever'
WCI +li 'but, what about'
ECI +li 'but'
GRI +li 'but' [and with time expressions 'ever since']

PY łi- 'perhaps' [for Aleut łi- 'still, just' see mli-]
AAY AP łi- 'must (inferential)'
CAY łi- 'maybe' [and łini- 'apparently']
NSY [for +łəqə- 'future' see ciqə-]
CSY [for +łəqə- 'future' see ciqə-]
Inu — [for SPI +łiuq- 'future' see under p.b. ciqə-]

PE łit- 'come upon or reach' [cf. lit- and liyaʀ-, though the relat. is obscure — compare əɣyalʀit- under ətə- and nunałit- under nuna, the latter also for Aleut lit- as in tanalit- 'run aground']
AAY #qłitə- 'come to' [note qłiq under qliʀ]
CAY #(ł/q)itə- 'encounter, experience -ing' [and #qłiaXtə 'reach, extend to' — note qłiq under qliʀ]
NSY —
CSY #itə- 'come upon'
Sir —
SPI —
NAI #it- 'come upon' [and 'reach' in a few derivations like isukłit- 'reach the end of' from isu(k)]
WCI #lit- 'reach'
ECI #lit- 'go to, come across'
GRI #lit- 'have reached'

PE łłaɣ- or **llaɣ-** 'abruptly' [cf. ʀłaɣ, łłaq-, llaa-. and vałłaɣ-[1,2], also Aleut laɣ- 'spotwise, sporadically'; there seems to be some entanglement with ala- in Inu]
AAY —
CAY łaɣ- 'suddenly and surprisingly' [also #(C)ałaɣ- in some lexicalized forms; note also laaɣ- 'quickly']
NSY —
CSY [for łaaɣ- 'in a crude way' see ʀłaɣ, though it could belong here]
Sir —
SPI —
NAI llak- 'finally, briefly, non-stop for a period' [and llaɣžuaq- 'suddenly'; for allak- 'begin to - a lot' see ala- and for łłak(taq)- 'angrily' and Mal łak- 'big, bad, roughly' see ʀłaɣ- (they could go here)]
WCI llak- 'for some time, at a blow', allak- 'suddenly a bit' [with a-? (but see ala-); also llakpiaq- 'really']
ECI llak- 'once lightly', ɣialla(k)- 'suddenly a bit' [and SB (ra)allak- 'easily, imperative softener']
GRI ałłaɣ- 'suddenly a bit' [and łłattaaʀ- 'from time to time', łłatsiaʀ- 'for a short while']

PI łłaq- or **llaq-** '(narrative) intensifier' [cf. łłaɣ-; perhaps from *łłayaʀ- — compare the Yup forms under vałłaɣ-[1]]
SPI [for ɣalaq- 'right away, quickly' see ɣallaq-]
NAI llaq- 'vivid action (intensifier)' [with rel. endings = 'while ing'; Webster and Zibell also have łłaqtaq- 'roughly', corresponding to MacLean's łłaktaq- 'angrily' under ʀłaɣ, but she also has #łłaqtiq- in siqqiłłaqtiq- 'sprinkle']
WCI Sig, Net, Car łłaq 'vivid action' [Lowe has łłaq- 'anyway, regretfully' for Sig with intr. inflections, corresponding to tqa(q)- with trans. inflections — contam. with łʀa(C)aʀ-?]
ECI tsa(q)-, NBI, Lab łłaq- 'vivid action' [Spald. has łłaq- expressing annoyance as opposed to llaq- 'heavily, clumsily' for NBI']
GRI łłaʀ- 'vivid action'

PE łʀa(C)aʀ- 'first' [or lʀa(C)aʀ-; cf. perhaps łəʀ[1] and ʀaʀaʀ-, also n(ə)ʀaʀ(aʀ), which may have a parallel origin (from nəʀ[1] plus ʀaʀaʀ-), also Aleut Atkan laʀana-X, EA laaʀana-X, (after C) saaʀana-X 'recent past, one who recently -ed'; the Inuit forms with initial q may be from after t bases (cf. the CAY); Yup appears to have lost the original post-vocalic allomorph; compare also lʀammiq- and lʀayaq-]
AAY Xaaʀ-, (after ɣ) xaaʀ- 'first'
CAY Xaaʀ-, (after ɣ) xaaʀ-, (optionally with tə bases) qaaʀ- 'first' [Xaaʀ- plus contemp. endings = 'after -ing'; also q̣aXaaʀ-, containing qaʀ-, which with rel. endings (q̣aXaami, etc.) = 'when first -'; also note pilʀautə- 'compete at race', from pi-]
NSY łXaaʀ- 'after -ing' [ANLC]
CSY [yuxaaʀ- 'first'; for lʀaXtuʀ- 'already, unexpectedly' see lʀataq- and for lʀa- 'future optative' see lʀayaq-]
Sir —
SPI ʀlaaq-, (after C) qaaq- 'first' [tqaaq- after t bases; also nominal ʀlaaq- 'the first', with assimilation of the ʀ to a preceding ɣ as in iqaluɣlaaq-; Qaw qaaq-, (after t) tqaaq- 'first']
NAI qqaaq-, (after t) tqaaq- 'first' [also nominal and as enclitic; Mal lʀaaq 'one who for first time -', lʀautžaq-, (after t) tqautžaq- 'be first to -'; note also sikulʀaužaq 'new ice' from ciku; qqaaqtit — plus contemp. endings = 'after -ing']
WCI lʀaaq-, (after k/q) qqaaq-, (after t) tqaaq- 'first' [and lʀaaq-, qqaaq- plus contemp. mood = 'after -ing'; for Cop intensifier łXaaq- see ʀłaɣ]
ECI qqaa(q)- 'first' [with the (positive) contemporative = 'after ing', with the neg. = 'before -ing'; and Spald. has qqautau- 'be first to -' for NBI]
GRI qqaaʀ- 'first', NG qqaaq- 'have recently -ed' [and WG qqaaq 'one that has just -ed'; EG also 'still, for time being'; note also qqaanniut(i)- 'compete at -ing' and EG qqaaʀtaʀ- 'take care not to -, there's danger that -']

PE łu 'and' [enclitic]
AAY +łu 'and, also' [added directly to preceding word, as in rest of Yupik]
CAY +łu
NSY +łu
CSY +łu 'and, also, or, even'
Sir +łu 'and' [Vakh.]
SPI +lu 'and'
NAI +lu
WCI +lu
ECI +lu
GRI +lu

PE łuɣ (-) '(have a) bad' [cf. aluk, k(k)uluk and Aleut luɣ- 'have a bad, have a pain in -']
AAY +(X)łuxtə- 'have a bad -', +(X)łuk, łuk 'one with a bad -'
CAY (#)łuk 'bad, one with a bad -', łuɣ- 'have a bad -', Xłuxtə- 'have a bad, be afflicted in one's -', Xłuk 'departed from its natural state' [and note Xłuɣ- 'be dirtied with -, somewhat', Xłuaʀ(aʀ) 'a little bit'-, vluxtə- 'sloppily', NSY +łuk 'big' [and note vluɣaq 'wretched (little)']
NSY Xłuk 'big, large' [ANLC]
CSY (+)łuk 'poor, diseased', łuɣ- 'poor one does' [and note łuxaq 'dear little meek'; for +luʀ- 'a little' see ʀuʀluq]
Sir — [but cf. pałuX under vałuɣ(-)]
SPI +luk(-) 'badly', (with nominal bases) 'have a bad -, not like', #łuk 'bad, different from normal' [and łuɣvak- 'roughly', Imaq łuzaq 'wretched']
NAI ʀluk- 'badly', +luk- have undesirable, unhealthy -', (#)qłuk, (#)(+)luk 'big, bad' [and +ʀluaq- 'dislike, reject', #(+)łuk 's.th. resembling or associated with']
WCI +luk, Sig łuk 'bad' [Pryde has the latter for Net too; also verbal 'have a bad -']
ECI luk, lualuk 'bad', (+)luk- 'have a bad -'
GRI +luɣ- 'have a bad or painful -' [also #(ʀ)łuk 'bad' and #luaʀ(i)- 'be discontented with'; for geminating #(ʀ)łuɣ- 'be bad at -ing' see nəʀłuɣ-]

M

PE (u)ma- 'perfective (state of having done s.th.)' [probably alternating with ima- after t bases (if not cima-) and uma- after other C in PE as still in Yup; cf. (u)maʀ(aʀ)-, maŋa(aq)- and perhaps Aleut ma- 'be or do there or thus' (on demonstr. roots), also as a base ma- 'do so' (i.e. on a zero base from *ə- or *əl- (same as PE ət-?) and possibly masu-, EA musu- 'probably, perhaps']
AAY (+u)ma- 'be in state of having -ed or been -ed' [uma- after C or ə that drops; not used with bases in tə (see ŋa-[1] instead); also (+u)maʀi- (+u)maa'i- 'become (more) -ed' — not after tə bases]
CAY (+u)ma- 'be in state of having -ed or having been -ed (for a long time)' [as for AAY except that cima- results with bases in tə (that drops); also (+u)maʀi- 'have already -, have finished -ing' (see ʀi- under li-[2])]
NSY (+u)ma- 'past' [ANLC has 'be in a state of having -ed or having been -ed']
CSY (+u)ma- 'be in state of having -ed or been V-ed, evidently have -ed' [as for AAY but with sima- after tə bases; note also (+u)maŋitə- 'past negative']
Sir (+ə)ma- 'past tense' [səma- after bases in t(ə), which drops, ma- after prime V; also (+ə)macaʀ- 'passive (state)']
SPI +sima- 'evidential' [and +tuuma- (also (#)uma) 'be in state of having -ed or been -ed, already, distant past']
NAI ma-, (after C, replacing t) +sima- '(perfective) state, it is known that -'
WCI +hima- 'perfective state' [can passivize trans. bases; also #(u)ma-]
ECI +sima- 'perfective state, apparently' [also #(u)ma-; drops preceding t in older forms but may assimilate in the modern language; may be used for perfect or past tense, esp. following lauq-, and can passivize a trans. base; NBI, SB uma- 'have already -ed'; note also mmai(t)- 'not yet']

GRI +sima- 'perfective state, perfect tense, (evidential) apparently', NG +hama- 'perfective state' [usually drops t, can passivize a trans. base; also (#)ma- 'be in state of -ing']

PI maŋa(aq)- 'whether' [cf. (u)ma-; the same ŋa- as in the causative (consequential) mood?]
Sir — [note +məŋa- 'while -ing' under (u)maʀ(aʀ)-]
SPI Qaw +maŋaaq-, FR +maɣaaq- 'check whether', (with rel. person endings) 'whether'
NAI +m(m)aɣaaq- 'enquire whether', Mal +(p)maŋa- (plus rel. endings) 'whether'
WCI Sig +(ŋ)maŋa-, Car +(m)maŋa- (plus rel. endings) 'whether'
ECI +(m)maŋa- (plus rel. endings) 'whether'
GRI —

PE maʀ- 'repeated action' [there may be a relat. to (u)ma- and (u)maʀ(aʀ)-]
AAY #(+)maʀ- 'continuative (physical action)' [after bases ending in ə]
CAY #(+)maʀ- 'repeated physical action'
NSY #(+)maʀ- 'for a while?' [ANLC; and note tutmaʀ- under tutə-]
CSY #(+)maʀ- 'repeated action' [in tutmaʀ- under tutə- at least; note also Chap ma- 'at intervals, now and then']
Sir [note tutəmqicaʀ- under tutmaʀ- (tutə-)]
SPI [note tupmaq- under tutmaʀ- (tutə-)]
NAI #+maq- 'repeatedly' [in tunmaq- under tutmaʀ- (tutə-) and kiɣmaq- under kəɣmaʀ- (kəɣə-) at least]
WCI [note under tutmaʀ- (tutə-) and note (#)ma- 'catch many, all the time']
ECI —
GRI #+maʀ- 'repeated action' [in at least tummaʀ- 'tread on' under tutmaʀ- (tutə-) and kimmaʀ- under kəɣmaʀ- (kəɣə-); note also (#)ma- (esp. following qaʀ- 'have') 'catch a lot of - all the time']

PE (u)maʀ(aʀ)- 'continually (while -ing)' [cf. (u)ma- and aʀ- and compare base pima(a)q-]
AAY —
CAY (+u)maaʀ(aʀ)- K 'slowly', HBC 'to the surprise of others' [same morphophonemics as (tu)ma-]
NSY (+u)maʀ- (with rel. endings) 'while -ing'
CSY [note (+)man 'time while -ing' with un]
Sir [note +məŋa- (plus rel. endings) 'while -ing']
SPI Qaw maaq-, (after C) +simaaq- 'keep on -ing'
NAI +simaaq- 'prolonged casual state', +(m)maq- (with rel. endings) 'while at same time -ing' [and aeq. case nom. +(m)matun 'look like -ing']
WCI mmaaq- 'more and more'
ECI maaq- 'a little', Lab mmaak- 'a lot' [and Lab kammaa(k)- 'be wearing - too big for one']
GRI (#)+simaaʀ- 'continuing leisurely state' [NG maaq- 'pretend to', timaaq- 'say or think that -', WG niʀumaaʀ- 'a little more' and #maaʀ- 'be wearing -', ššamaaʀ- 'intend', and compare also ilamaaʀ- under ila[1]]

PE mcaɣ- 'finally or more?' [cf. myaɣ- and mcuɣ(-)?]
AAY —
CAY —
NSY —
CSY Chap msaɣ- 'finally'
Sir msaɣ- 'finally'
SPI —
NAI fsaaq- 'again, more', Nu psaaq- 'again' [and nominal to nom. base 'another']
WCI Cop ffaaq-, Sig psaaq- 'again, more'
ECI tsaaq- 'a second time'
GRI (#)ssaaʀ- [old ortho. vsaar] 'to especially high degree'

PE mcuɣ(-) '(a) little' [cf. myaɣ-, mcaɣ-, cuŋaq and cuɣ — the relat. between them is obscure]
AAY ŋcuk 'little', mcuaq 'almost a -'
CAY mcuxtə-, mzuXtə-, myuXtə-, NS mcauɣaʀ- 'in a small way' [the latter form entangled with mcaɣ-?; note also mciuʀ(aʀ)- 'a little at a time']
NSY msuXiinaq 'only -' [and verbal msuXiinaʀ- 'do nothing but -'; note also perhaps vyuaʀ- 'more or less, partially' — contam. with vyaɣ- under myaɣ-?]
CSY msuɣ- 'casually' [and note msuxiitə- 'completely lack -', msiiʀ- 'ineffectively, with little effort', msiiq* 'a litle, s.th. like', vziiʀ- 'carelessly' — contam. with vžəʀaʀ-?]
Sir —
SPI —
NAI [note pifsukaq- 'barely escape danger, barely miss hitting', from pi(-)?]
WCI Cop ffuk 'tiny', kaffuk- 'a little while' [Pryde; the first form also verbal = 'few, a little']
ECI [note pasuk- 'almost' and takutsusuɣuk- under takumcuɣ- (taku-)]
GRI (#)passuɣ- 'with difficulty' [and NG huk 'poor, miserable, useless']

PY mətə- 'be in or at' [after pl. or possessed nətə-; a transparent contraction of locative mi/ni plus ət- 'be']
AAY —
CAY +mətə- 'be at, in, etc.' [drops preceding 'weak q' and takes the form +nətə- with plural and demonstr. bases — the same pattern as everywhere else; see ət- for the tə ~ l alternation here]
NSY +mətə- 'be in or at'
CSY +mətə-, (with pl.) +nitə-, (with demonstr. bases) ntə-
Sir [note nanəʀət- 'be where' under na-[2] and manaʀət- 'be here' under ət-, a parallel but not identical development?]
Inu [note miit-, (after pl. or possessed bases) niit- (all dialects except Di, which has mit-, nit-) 'be in, on, at', a parallel development that must have occurred independently in different places at different times — it is still found side by side with the non-fused construction in various dialects]

PE mi 'what about [enclitic]
AAY +mi 'I wonder, how about' [used for light emphasis]
CAY +mi 'how about, contrast' [optionally a preceding t may go to z]

NSY #mi '- or other' [with Q-words]
CSY +mi 'how about, contrast'
Sir +mi 'emphatic enclitic' [Vakh. from Men.'s and Rub.'s texts]
SPI (+)mi 'why (not)'
NAI Uum +mi 'what about'
WCI —
ECI —
GRI +mi 'but, indeed, what about (contrastive emphasis)'

PE mi- 'and then (again)' [cf. enclitic mi, PI umi- and Aleut ma- 'also, too', EA also 'finally', Atkan maaya- 'finally'; the initial stop in conservative Inuit may be the same (evidential?) element as in certain forms of the contemp. mood — see under və(kə)- and in Mal (p)maŋa- under maŋa(aq)-]
AAY [for +mi- with neg. see la(ʀ)-]
CAY +mi- 'also'
NSY —
CSY —
Sir —
SPI +(p)mi-, Qaw +'mi- 'even though' [takes reduced intr. indic. uq, etc.]
NAI +(m)mi-, Mal +(k)mi- or +(p)mi- 'also', (with +lu) 'just after -ing, while someone or s.th. else is about to -' [takes reduced intr. indic. endings uq, etc.; for #+(m)mi- 'be in state of, continue -ing' see umi-]
WCI +(m)mi- 'again, too, and then'
ECI +(m)mi- 'again, also', Lab 'again, for sure, nevertheless'
GRI +(m)mi- 'and then — vivid narrative action', NG also 'too'

PE miɣ- 'hold in one's (body part)' [cf. Aleut miɣ- 'repeatedly (back and forth)', miɣða- 'several times (e.g. scratch)']
AAY #+miaqə- 'hold in one's -' [to body part base]
CAY (#)+miɣ- 'put in one's -' [and +mik, +miaq 'thing held in one's -']
NSY [(#)+miaq 'contents of -' — ANLC has 'thing held with the - or by -ing' (also +mik)]
CSY (#)+miɣ-, +miiʀ- 'hold in one's -' [and +mik, +miiq 'thing held in one's -']
Sir [note kənəʀməɣ- under kənəʀmiɣ- (kənəʀ) and məqə- in təɣəməqə(s)- under təɣumi(C)aʀ- (təɣu-)]
SPI #+mik- 'point one's - (finger)'
NAI #+mik- 'use one's - (body part)', (trans.) 'hit with one's -' [also 'repeatedly, back and forth' with some bases; and #+miaq 'thing held in one's -', as in all other Inu]
WCI #+mik- 'hit, do with one's - to someone' [distinct from #+mik- 'do with (instrument)' from instr. case mik?]
ECI #+mik- 'do with one's (body part)' [frequentative +miɣaaq-; #+mik- also 'have in one's - (container)' on some bases — by contam. with miʀu?; compare mik- 'give, transfer one's -', a different p.b., from instr. case mik-?]
GRI #+miɣ- 'do with one's - (body part)' [also with some other nom. bases in sense 'do with' (as if) from instr. case mik- — compare the ECI above; frequentative miɣaʀ- or misaʀ-; for (V)mišaaʀ- 'back and forth' see umi-]

PI minŋaq- 'come from' [cf. q-, here with the abl. case ending for nouns followed by that for demon. bases]
SPI —
NAI +min^{y}ŋaq- 'come from'
WCI +minŋaaq-
ECI NBI, SB +miŋŋaaq- 'come from' [#aŋŋau- on demon. bases]
GRI +miŋŋaʀ- 'come from' [also #miiʀ- and, on demon. bases, #aŋŋaʀ-]

PE miqə- 'compel to' [cf. PI catqummiq- and perhaps Aleut mi- 'let, make'; there may also be a link to ʀqə-]
AAY —
CAY [note anucimiXqə- under anucimiʀ- (annut-)]
NSY [note anuciminɬaʀvik under anucimiʀ- (annut-)]
CSY +miqə- 'compel to, make -'
Sir [note aʀəlmiqə- 'shake, move' from aʀula-]
SPI —
NAI —
WCI Utk miqsuq- 'cause' [Briggs; Pryde has Cop qiamiXXuq- 'make cry' from qiða-]
ECI —
GRI —

PE miʀu 'inhabitant of' [cf. ilumiɣ, ilum(m)iʀ under ilu, also ŋu-?]
AAY +(ʀ)miu(q) 'inhabitant of -'
CAY +miu 'inhabitant of' [and (#)+miutaq* 'animal living in -']
NSY +mii 'inhabitant of -'
CSY +mii
Sir +məʀa
SPI +miu 'inhabitant of -' [verbal = 'be in or at -']
NAI +miu(q) 'inhabitant of -' [also verbal on a few bases 'be in'; #+miutaq 's.th. inherently belonging to -']
WCI +miutaq 'inhabitant of -'
ECI +miuq, NBI, SB +miutaq
GRI +(ʀ)miu(q) 'inhabitant of -' [and +(ʀ)miu- 'live in or at -']

PE mli- 'casually (on and on)?' [cf. Aleut ɬi-, (after C) smi- (with metathesis) 'still, just, nevertheless, go on -ing', as nom. = 'only, rather, even' (for the correspondence l ~ s after C compare lʀi-, sXi- under liʀ-)]
AAY [note təmli- 'sleepwalk' under ətəmli- (ətəʀ-)]
CAY mli- 'casually, aimlessly'
NSY —
CSY [note mləʀaʀ-, etc. 'a little' under vlaɣ-, and təmli- 'sleepwalk' under ətəmli- (ətəʀ-)]
Sir —
SPI [note itivli(a)- 'sleepwalk' under ətəmli-]
NAI #vli- [as in iɫivli- under ətəmli- (ətəʀ-)]
WCI [note itivli- under ətəmli- and for Car vlak 'a little' see vlaɣ-]
ECI [note itillima- under ətəmli-]

GRI #łłi- [as in itiłłi(ɣ)- under ətəmli- (ətəʀ-); note also pivli-]

PI mmaʀik- 'well' [cf. kiɣ-, also (u)maʀ(aʀ)-?]
SPI —
NAI mmaʀiksi- 'better' [and note mmaʀłuk- 'badly']
WCI mmaʀik- 'really' [Pryde]
ECI mmaʀik- 'really' [and nom. 'real']
GRI #mmaʀiɣ- 'well' [and note #mmaʀłuɣ- 'badly']

PI muaq- 'go to(ward)' [also muuq- and (by contraction) muq-; based on allative case mut, on pl. (or demonstr.) bases nuaq- from nut; cf. q- and tmi(C)aʀtə- and compare k(k)u(C)aʀ-, also Aleut muðaʀ(an), ŋuðaʀ(an) '(move) toward' on directional and demonstr. bases]
Sir — [note asiməžuʀ- 'go down' from aci[1] in Em.]
SPI +muq- 'go to' [drops 'weak q' and has the form +nuq, etc. after pl. bases, the same pattern as elsewhere in Inuit; Qaw has +muk-]
NAI [note +muk- 'go to' — with k under nəɣ-?]
WCI Cop (#)+muaq-, (#)+muuq- 'go to' [the second form productive in Car; Sig and Net have +muk-; in Cop (#)+muk- and (#)+muliaq- are also found, but most productive are +muŋŋaq- 'go to' and +muŋŋau- 'go toward', the latter also B. Lake — compare the allative inflection on demonstratives, also NAI ɨɣlɨq- alongside ɨɣlau- under əɣləʀ-]
ECI +muaq-, +muuq- 'go to' [only with directional bases in Tar, but generally productive on Baffin, which also has +muŋŋau- 'go toward']
GRI [note +mukaʀ- 'go to' (with p.b. k(k)aʀ-?), also #+muuʀ-, and NG muak- in timmuak- 'go toward land' and haŋmuak- 'go toward sea' at least]

PE myaɣ- 'somewhat?' [cf. mcuɣ(-), ŋsi-, mcaɣ-, vlaɣ-, tyaɣ and vžəʀaʀ- — there could be phonaesthetic variation here]
AAY (#)myaxtə- 'briefly' [of weather phenomena]
CAY myaɣ- 'not enough'
NSY [vyaɣ -'almost'; for vyuaʀ- 'partially' see kyu(C)aʀ-]
CSY —
Sir [for młəɣaX 'very big' see ʀłaɣ]
SPI [note Imaq vyaq- — for vyaɣ-? — 'almost']
NAI —
WCI vyak- 'rather, more or less'
ECI —
GRI [note pissaɣ- (old ortho. pivsag-) 'wound by shooting (animal)', with base pi(-)]

N

PE na- 'might or so as to' [cf. na(C)uʀ-; for Aleut naaʀ- 'hunt for, try to' see ni(C)aʀ-]
AAY +na- 'so as to' [and +natə plus pers. endings 'until']
CAY +na- 'in order to' [plus sub. mood; also 2s imperative marker following p.b. ki-; note also +natkaq 'future time of -ing']
NSY — [for +naniʀ- 'stop -ing' see nʀiʀ-]
CSY +na- 'in order to, (with imp.) 'in the future' [for +naaʀ- 'be going to' see na(C)uʀ- and for +nayu- 'lest, may — not' see under yukə-]
Sir —
SPI — [for +nayaq- 'could have' see yaʀ-]
NAI — [for +nayaq- 'would' see yaʀ- and compare also +nasuyɨ- under yukə-]
WCI Sig +na-, (after k/q) ɣa- 'might' [with neg. imperative or conditional in the preceding clause], Net +na- 'may well', Utk +naqsuq- 'probably, I think' (Briggs), Eskimo Point yyanalauq- 'would probably', Cop +naxxa- 'might' [Cam. Bay +nixxa- acc. Pryde; with indic. vuq, etc.; with 2nd person = 'be careful or -'; the form ɣa- is probably influenced by the alt. form ɣa- of neg. contemporative marker na- mentioned in note 31 to the Inflections; for Car +na-, ɣa- 'would' see under yaʀ-]
ECI — [for +nayaq- 'would' see yaʀ-]
GRI +na- '2s imperative' [less immediate than ɣit-, often follows p.b. ɣi- from PE ki-, but is also found in some old 1/2 p. transitive forms; for qina 'watch out that you don't -, there's danger that -' see yaqu(naɣ); note also +naviiʀ- 'can no longer' and +navianŋit- 'certainly won't'; NG +na(alaaq)- 'I wish, would that']

PI naaq- 'make (too much) so?'
SPI —
NAI (#)naaq- 'make be so' [esp. with qualitative bases]
WCI —
ECI (#)naaq-, naaʀi- 'make be (too) -' [also 'arrive just as s.o. -']
GRI (#)naaʀ- 'find too -, more - than expected' [intr. 'do more than expected']

PE naci(C)aʀ- and **naca(C)aʀ-** 'take a long time doing' [cf. na- and c(c)iʀ-?; the Inu may be influenced by caʀ-[1]]
AAY —
CAY +naciaʀ- 'be late, take a long time -ing'
NSY —
CSY +nasiiʀ- 'put off -ing, angrily'
Sir —
SPI —
NAI [note #+nasaaq- in kiunasaaŋit- 'not hesitate to answer']
WCI +nahaaq- 'take a long time -ing'
ECI +nasaaq- 'late'
GRI (#)+nasaaʀ- 'hesitate -ing, be slow to -' [old ortho. nasaer, as if with ŋiʀ-]

PI naqci- 'be a good time to do s.th.' [cf. naʀ- and si- under li-[2]]
Yup [note CAY +naʀi- 'be time to -', for the second element of which see li-[2], a different (suppletive) allomorph than here]
SPI +naqsi- 'be time to -'
NAI +naqsi-
WCI +naXXi-, +naqi- 'be good time to -' [the latter with

ʀqə-? — compare ECI naqi- under naʀ-]
ECI +naʀsi- 'be a good time to -'
GRI [+naʀsi- 'become -able']

PY-S naqə- 'intend or try to' [cf. na- and ʀqə-]
AAY ŋnaqə- 'try to' [with preceding nəɣ-? — compare ŋcaʀ-]
CAY ŋnaqə- 'try to'
NSY +naqə- 'intend, be going to' [and +naqɣaʀ- (plus part./indic. tuq, etc.) 'although wanting to']
CSY +naqə- 'be going to (near future), try to'
Sir +nəqə- 'near future, intend to' [also +inəqə- after ʀ bases at least in some of Men.'s examples — he also has +inəqɣəXtəʀ- in the 'intend' sense; for +inəqatə- (plus rel. endings) 'as soon as' see ŋinnaʀ(-), with which there is some confusion here]
Inu — [for ECI naqi- 'be such as to' see naʀ-]

PE naʀ 's.th. resembling' [cf. perhaps Aleut na-X as in aɣuʀna-X 'sea urchin' from aɣuX 'beach']
AAY #+naq 's.th. like' [in names of animals, fishes and plants' elsewhere]
CAY #+naq
NSY #+naq
CSY #+naq
Sir [cf. natəʀnəX under natəʀnaʀ (natəʀ)]
SPI #+naq 's.th. like'
NAI #+naq
WCI #+naq
ECI #+naq
GRI #+(ʀ)naq

PE naʀ- 'be such as to or -able' [cf. Aleut na- 'be such as to, be -able']
AAY +naʀ-, (less frequently) +naXqə- 'be liable to, be -able' [opposite = +naitə-; +naXtə- 'be good weather for -ing']
CAY +naXqə- 'tend to cause one to -, be able to be -ed' [+naqə- before ə-dr p.b.s beginning CV (with ʀqə-); also #+naʀ-, nominal #+naq; opposite =+naitə-]
NSY +naʀ- 'tend to cause one to -' [ANLC; Men. has +naq 'a good time for -ing', +niatə- 'cannot (be -ed)']
CSY +naʀ- 'cause -ing' [nominal +naq]
Sir [cf. naŋłəɣnaXqə(s)- under naŋłəɣ- and nałuniʀ- under nałunaʀiʀ- (nału-)]
SPI +naq- 'able to be -ed'
NAI +naq- 'be or cause to -, be -able' [also nominal]
WCI +naq- 'be such as to -' [neg. +nait]
ECI +naq-, +naqi- 'be such as to -, be -able' [opp. +nait-]
GRI +naʀ- 'be such as to -, be -able' [also 'one -s' (depersonalized subject); opp. = +naat-]

PI nasuk- and **nasuaq-** 'try to' [cf. na- and yuɣ- and yu(C)aʀ-]
SPI +nasuaq-, (after k/q) ɣasuaq- 'try' [and +nasuaŋit- 'not bother']
NAI +nasuaq- 'hurriedly' [for Mal +našuk- see yukə-, but note Nu +nasuit-, ɣasuit- 'not at all']
WCI +nahuaq-, (after k/q) ɣahuaq- 'intend, prepare, try to -'
ECI ɣasuk-, ɣasuaq- (after t or V bases) nnasuk-, nnasuaq-, Aiv nasuk-, SB ɣasuk-, ɣasuaq- 'try to' [Tar ɣasuk- or ɣasuaq- after any but t bases]
GRI +nasuaʀ-, +ɣasuaʀ- 'quickly' [and NG +nahaaʀnaq- (from nahuaʀnaq-) 'be easy to -']

PY na(C)uʀ- 'be liable to?' [cf. na- and (C)uʀ-]
AAY C +nuuʀʀukə-, K +nauʀyukə- 'think that - might or would' [with yukə-]
CAY +nauʀ- 'habitually' [with 1st p. indicative equivalent to optative: 'let's, let me']
NSY —
CSY [+naaʀ- 'be going to eventually' and +naanʀitə- 'will not']
Sir [note +nəʀ- 'future'; also +inəʀ- after ʀ bases at least in some of Men.'s examples, for which compare under ŋinnaʀ(-)]

PE nəɣ- and **ŋ(ə)-** 'get' [the latter must have developed from the former already in PE, the direct reflex of the former only remaining in certain Inu forms — compare the correspondence in for example GRI innaɣ- 'catch fire', CAY kənŋə- 'start burning' (from base ək(ə)nəʀ under əkə-[1]) and also PE manəɣ-, (Yup) maŋə-; note the inchoative use on verbal bases in both Yup and Inu; the suppletive allomorph q in (some) Inu after uvular bases may reflect CSY +aʀ below; cf. also nnak- and nnək-]
AAY #ŋə- 'get' [also ŋə- 'begin to']
CAY ŋə- 'get' [also 'begin to']
NSY ŋə- 'get' [ANLC also 'begin to -']
CSY ŋə- 'get' [and note (#)+aʀ- 'catch (animal)', unrelated unless from *ŋaʀ-]
Sir ŋə- 'get, buy, kill (game animal)'
SPI nik- 'get', (#)k- 'kill by hunting' [and note Imaq ŋaq- 'acquire', going with CSY aʀ- above?]
NAI nik- 'get', #k- 'catch (animal), get or become (more) -' [causes gemination in the base; in the second, verbal use note uummak- 'come alive' under uŋummaʀ- (uŋuma-)]
WCI nik- 'get, find', #k-, (after q) #q- 'catch (animal)' [and Pryde has geminating k- 'get, grow' for Cop]
ECI #nik- 'get (e.g. spouse)', #(k)- 'catch (animal)' [causes gemination]
GRI (#)niɣ- 'get, have come', #ɣ- (after uvular #ʀ-) 'catch (animal)' [the latter, which can also refer to getting one's share in a catch of the animal concerned, cause gemination (and a preceding *ə to a as in aʀfaɣ- under aʀvak- (aʀvəʀ); note also such lexicalized forms as innuɣ- 'come across a human being', nippaɣ- alongside nipiniɣ- 'make a noise' (from nəpə) and, on a verbal base, qiimmaɣ- 'become happy' from qiima- under qi(C)ət-]

PE nəʀ[1] 'nominalizer' [cf. Aleut na-X 'participial', also 'non-anaphoric past tense marker'; for old geminating variant q* in sense of 'result of -ing' in Inu (the gemination caused by the loss of nə) see for example quppaq under qupə- and kəppaʀ under kəpə- (with Yup reflexes)]

AAY nəq 'act of -ing', #+nəq 'thing resulting from -ing' [and nRani, etc. 'while -ing', nRu 'be -able']
CAY nəq* 'act(ivity) of -ing', (#)+nəq* 'thing resulting from -ing' [also 'area of']
NSY (+)nəq 'act or result of act' [also (lexicalized?) 'one who is -ing' and 'caught (animal),' the latter by comb. with t-[2], like ŋnəq with ŋə (nəɣ-)'.]
CSY nəq* 'act(ivity) or state of -ing', #+nəq* 'thing resulting from or associated with -ing'
Sir #+nəX 'result of V-ing'
SPI +niq 'act of -ing' [also geminating #q]
NAI +niq* 'result, activity, condition, manner of -ing' [and geminating #q* as in kippaq* 's.th. cut off' from kipə-]
WCI +niq 'state, result or action of -ing' [also geminating #q]
ECI +niq [and geminating #q]
GRI +niq* [and geminating #q*]

PE nəR[2] 'one that is more or most' [perhaps the same as nəR[1] but used in different constructions (e.g. with ablative of standard in the present sense); cf. Aleut na- 'more, most' and compare łəR[1] versus łəR[2]]
AAY nəq 'be more - than (possessor)' [trans. nqə- used after V, k or q — compare łəR[2]]
CAY (#)nəq* 'one more or most (of them)' [not with tə bases; nRu- 'be more' (with ŋu-)]
NSY nRu- 'more' [and nəXpiɣaq 'one with the most -' (ANLC)]
CSY (#)nəq* 'one more or most (of them)'
Sir —
SPI +nažaq, Qaw +niqšaq 'the most - (of them)', +nažaRi- 'be more than'
NAI +niqšaq, (with taR?) +niqtaq 'the one that - most, more' [also #+niq*]
WCI +niXXaq 'the one that - most, more' [also #+niq]
ECI +niRsaq, (trans.) +niRsaRi- 'most, more - of two' [also #+niq]
GRI +niRšaq 'the most - (of small number)' [also #+niq*; +niRu-, EG +nii- 'more']

PE nəRłuɣ- 'badly' [cf. nəR[1] and łuɣ(-)]
AAY —
CAY nəXłuxtə- 'have trouble -ing'
NSY —
CSY nəXłuk 's.th. hard to -'
Sir —
SPI +niRluk- 'almost'
NAI niRluk- 'badly, with terrible consequences' [and #niqłuk- in kiuniqłuk- 'answer angrily' at least]
WCI +niRluk- 'badly'
ECI +niRlu(k)-
GRI +niRłuɣ- 'badly' [may syncopate and cause gemination of preceding base, as in kiitsiRłuɣ- from kiisi- 'bite into s.th.']

PE nəRpa(C)aR 'the most [cf. nəR[2] and vaɣ]
AAY nəXpaaq 'one that is most -' [compare łəXpaaq under łəR[2]]
CAY —
NSY — [compare nəXpiɣaq under nəR[2]]
CSY — [compare łəXpiɣaq under łəR[2]]
Sir —
SPI —
NAI —
WCI —
ECI +niqpaaq 'most, more '
GRI +niRpaaq 'the most -'

PE nəRtu- 'do a lot' [from nəR[1] and tu-[1]; there is contam. with tu-[2] in some Inu forms]
AAY nəXtu- 'be good at -ing, do a lot'
CAY nəXtu- 'habitually a lot'
NSY nəXtuaRaata(a)qə- 'a lot'
CSY —
Sir —
SPI +niqtu- 'always feel like -ing' [also qtu- 'a lot, all the time', causing gemination]
NAI (#)qtu- 'excessively, hard, a lot (by nature or disposition)' [causes gemination and final i into a; not used with t bases]
WCI qtu- 'always, a lot, for a long time'
ECI —
GRI +niRtu- 'a lot' [also geminating #Rtu-]

PE ni- 'say that' [cf. Aleut causative ni- 'make, produce (a state), put in motion, start, become (gradually)' and nisa- 'wait for - to, induce to'; note also the reflexive sense of ni- in uunni- under uɣu-, naɣacuɣni- under naɣa(t)-, and CSY qaasn̥i- under qacəli-, and compare the 'consider' sense of another causative p.b., tət-]
AAY +ni- 'say that -'
CAY +ni-
NSY +ni- 'think that -'
CSY +ni- 'say that -'
Sir —
SPI +ni-
NAI +ni- 'say that -', +niRaq- 'accuse of or describe as having a certain attribute' [the latter with Raq-?]
WCI +niRaq- 'accuse of -ing', Sig +ni- 'say that -'
ECI +niRaq- 'say that -'
GRI +niRaR-

PE ni(C)aR- 'try to' [probably *niRaR-; cf. Aleut naaR- 'hunt, try to, come close to -ing']
AAY +nia<R>aR- 'nearly, be about to', #+niaR- 'go hunting for -'
CAY +niaR- 'uncertain future, so that -', +niaRaR- 'be going to soon'
NSY +niaR- 'future', (with nom. base) 'look for' [ANLC also 'hunt', 'later', 'endeavor to'; Men. also #+niaq 'means for hunting -', #+niałəq 'hunting -']
CSY +niiR- 'hunt for, ask for, work with' [also 'carry out habitual or protracted activity'; for naaR- 'about to' see na(C)uR-]
Sir +niR 'hunt for -' [and nominal +niX 'hunter of -'; for nəR- 'future' see na(C)uR-]
SPI +niaq- '(go to) get, hunt for -'
NAI +niaq- 'future' [also sometimes 'hunt -'; note also +nit-, +niala-, +niatak- 'try to']

WCI +niaq- 'future, try to' [also, more limited 'hunt -'; for Cop +niaq- 'would' see yaʀ-]
ECI +niaq- 'near future, try to', Lab +(n)niaʀ- 'hunt -' [also an imperative softener]
GRI +niaʀ- 'future, try to' [also an imperative softener and a habitual marker with certain verbs of perceiving; in comb. with #ɣ- 'catch' (nəɣ-) can mean 'hunt' — nom. +(n)niaq 'one who is hunting -'; note also piniXXaʀiɣ- 'be a capable hunter' from piniaʀ- 'hunt' and +nialuɣ- 'try a bit, catch small game' with luɣ- under ʀuluk]

PI n(n)iq- 'apparently' [cf. ni- and liq- as also in valliq-?]
SPI —
NAI +niq- 'I (have) found out that - (evidential perfect)'
WCI +niq- 'apparently' [in Cop usually nniq- in combination with participials — intr. +yuunniq-, trans. +yaʀinniq-]
ECI +(n)ni(q)- 'evidential, narrative past' [+nni(q)- after V or t]
GRI +niʀ- 'I wonder, maybe', EG 'apparently', NG qaniq- 'apparently (unwitnessed past)' [and NG +niq- also 'ask if (s.o.) -' (with trans. endings]

PE n(n)iʀ- 'be good to do' [cf. pinniʀ- and compare pinnaʀ(naq)-, also nunanniʀ- — this p.b. could be from nnaq plus liʀ-]
AAY +niʀ- 'be pleasant to -' [opp. = +niitə- 'not be pleasant to']
CAY +niXqə- 'be pleasant to' [opp. = +niitə-]
NSY (#)+niʀ- 'be good to-'
CSY +niq 's.th. that is good to -'
Sir —
SPI —
NAI —
WCI #niq- 'be good to -'
ECI #niq- 'be good to -' [opp. #niit- 'not be good to -']
GRI #niʀ- 'be good to -' [opp. #niit- 'be bad to'; note also takuʀanniʀ- 'be pretty' under takuʀannaaq- (taku-)]

PE nit- and **cuɣnit-** and **paɣnit-** 'smell or taste of' [the second form with cuɣ, and the third with vaɣ(-); cf. Aleut nu- 'smell of'; there may be a further link to ni-]
AAY +(X)cuɣnitə- 'smell like'
CAY Y +cuɣninaXqə-, K cuɣninaXqə-, Nun, NSU +cuɣnilaXqə-, HBC +(cuɣ)nitə- 'smell or taste of' [with the tə ~ l alt.]
NSY +paɣnitə-, vaɣnitə- 'smell of, seem like a -' [with vaɣ-; also +suɣnitə- 'resemble', as CSY; ANLC has +niʀ- 'taste or smell of', also nominal +niq and +nitə- 'have the characteristics of -']
CSY +ni- 'smell of', +nitə- 'taste of' [and +paɣnitə- in both senses; note also +suɣnitə- 'resemble, seem to']
Sir [+suɣəntə- 'resemble' — note the CSY equivalent; Vakh. has qiɬəpaɣni- 'smell of guts' from Rub.]
SPI +sunit-, Qaw +suŋnit-, Imaq +suɣni- 'smell, taste of'
NAI +suɣnit- 'smell, taste of' [also #+nit-; for +nit- 'try' see ni(C)aʀ-]
WCI +huŋnit- 'smell of' [and, as nominal, +huŋni]
ECI #+(sun)ni(k)-, NBI +suŋnik- 'smell of' [and, as nominal, +sunniq]
GRI +sunnit-, NG +nit- 'smell of' [nominal +sunni]

PI nitaq 's.th. from a time or place' [cf. tar; nit could be the abl. case marker]
SPI +nitaq 's.th. from — (time or place)'
NAI +nisaq
WCI (#)nitaq
ECI nitaq
GRI nisaq 's.th. from -' [also lisaq — cf. linʀaq]

PE nkuɣ (du.) and **nkut** (pl.) 'and partner or family' [there may be a relat. to demonstr. dual/plural markers kuɣ/kut]
AAY nkuk (du.), nkut (pl.) '- and partner, family, etc.'
CAY nkuk, nkut
NSY nkuk, nkut
CSY nkuk '- and partner' [used on both conjoined nominals]
Sir +nəkux '- and (partner)' [Vakh. from Men.'s and Rub.'s texts he treats it as enclitic on both conjoined nominals]
SPI tkuk, tkut '- and partner, family, etc.'
NAI tkuk, tkut
WCI tkuk, tkut
ECI kkut
GRI kkut

PI nnak- 'get' [cf. nəɣ- ; nəʀ[1] may also be involved here]
SPI —
NAI nnak- 'get by winning or earning'
WCI nnak- Sig 'get', Cop 'have or catch many, be covered with'
ECI nna(q)- 'receive (as gift)' [Pryde gives nnak-]
GRI nnaɣ- 'get (esp. in quantity or as a gift)', NG nnak- 'get a share (of catch)'

PI nnaq 'favorite or dear' [cf. n(n)iʀ- and compare ilannaʀ under ila[1], also pinnaʀ(naq)-]
SPI —
NAI [Jen. has nnaq 'dear']
WCI nnaq 'favorite' [and note Car 'naaq '(dear) little' (with lexicalized glottal stop in B. Lake at least, written tnaaq), also verbal]
ECI nnaq 'favorite' [and cf. tusaʀna(a)q- under tucaʀ-]
GRI nna(a)q 'favorite'

PI nnək- 'half-transitivizer' [cf. nəɣ-, added perhaps to nəʀ[1] here]
SPI #+nik- 'half-transitivizer'
NAI #+(n)nik-
WCI Cop #+nik- [Pryde]
ECI #nik-, #nni(k)-
GRI #nniɣ- 'half-transitivizer' [old ortho. ngnig- but Fab. nnig- as in asannig- 'love' from asa-]

PE nqiɣ-[1] and **nqiɣca(C)aʀ-** 'be good at or do well' [from nəʀ[1] plus kiɣ-; compare nqiɣ-[2] and ŋiɣ-]
AAY nqəxtə- 'be a good -er' [and 'dark -' (of color)]
CAY nqəxcaaʀ(aʀ)- 'thoroughly' [also #nqəxtə-]
NSY —
CSY nqəxtə- 'easily, readily' [and nqəxtaq 'one that readily -', +yunqəxtə- 'love to'], Chap nqəxsaʀ- 'thoroughly'

Sir ŋ̥əqəxsaʀ- 'entirely, exactly'
SPI [tqi(ɣ)i- 'find too -']
NAI [note tqik- as in pitqik- 'be devious' under pinqiɣ-(pi-)]
WCI tqik- 'have or be a good -'
ECI —
GRI qqissaaʀ-, NWG qqinnaaʀ- 'carefully, exactly', #qqiɣ 'completely, be good at -ing' [and ššaqqiɣ- 'be good as a -', łłaqqiɣ- 'be good at -ing', also geminating #ʀiɣ- in the latter sense]

PE nqiɣ-² 'again' [cf. nəʀ² and nqiɣ-¹]
AAY nqixtə- 'again'
CAY nqixtə- 'again' [and linqixtə- 'get another, change one's -']
NSY nqixtə- 'again' [ANLC; Men. has nqiXtə-, also nqiʀ-, nqiłtə-]
CSY nqixtə- 'again'
Sir —
SPI tqik- 'again, more' [and on nom. base 'change one's -']
NAI tqik- 'again' [and on nom. base 'change one's -']
WCI tqik- 'again' [and nominalizer tqiyaq 'most, more (than possessor)', Sig tqinniq 'most']
ECI liqqi(k)- 'again' [and qqiyaqaʀ-, trans. qqiyaʀi- 'more']
GRI qqiɣ- 'again, further' [and #qqik-, NG qqihaq 'more (than possessor)']

PE n(ə)ʀaʀ(aʀ)(-) '(one who has) recently or for first time' [cf. nəʀ¹ and ʀaʀaʀ-?]
AAY nəXaq 'one that recently -ed or has begun to -'
CAY nəXaq*, nəXaʀ(aq*), Nun nəʀaʀ(aX*) 'new, one that has recently -ed' [and verbal nəXaʀ, etc. 'have recently -ed']
NSY nXaq 'new, young, one that has recently (been) -ed' [ANLC also nʀaq]
CSY nXaq 'one who has recently -ed' [nnəXaq after tə, which drops; verbal nXaa 'have recently -ed'; note also kənXaq 'newly made or acquired', with kə-¹?]
Sir —
SPI (#)+(ʀ)naq- 'catch one's first -'
NAI Uum nʀaq- 'for first time' [and nʀalait 'have never -ed'; note also PH aʀvanʀaqtuaq 'captain who has caught his first whale']
WCI nʀaq- 'for first time' [also nominal; nʀayuit 'have never -ed']
ECI ʀŋa(q)- 'for first time'
GRI (#)ʀŋa(a)ʀ-

PE nʀiʀ- 'stop doing' [cf. nəʀ¹ and ŋiʀ-]
AAY nʀiʀ- 'stop -ing'
CAY nʀiʀ- 'no longer -', +nanʀiʀ- 'stop -ing (for good)' [the latter with na-]
NSY +naniʀ- 'stop -ing'
CSY +naniʀ- 'stop -ing' [and +(tə)snaniʀ- 'tell not to ']
Sir —
SPI —
NAI nʀiq- 'stop -ing'
WCI nʀiq-
ECI —
GRI —

PE nʀit- 'not' [i.e. nəʀ¹ plus ŋit-; Aleut past neg. Atkan naʀ-ulax, EA naʀ-ulux (with na- under nəʀ¹) is perhaps reshaped from this; for the change to ŋŋit- in Inu compare the regular change of *nʀ to nŋ in Net and see the remark under ŋa-¹]
AAY C nnətə-, K nnitə- 'not' [and +minnətə- 'no longer', nnəʀaaʀ- plus rel. endings 'although not']
CAY nʀitə-'not' [with the tə ~ l alt.]
NSY nʀitə-
CSY nʀitə-
Sir nəXtə- 'neg. imperative' [in forms nəXtuzaŋ, etc.], +yunəXtə- 'will not'
SPI ʀnit-, ŋit- 'not' [the first form (with metathesis of ʀ and n) occurs with interrog. mood or when followed by p.b. +mi or by participial endings +žuaq, etc. 'one that -', and with assimilation of initial ʀ to ɣ following k base; the second form occurs with special indic. endings ŋilaq, etc.]
NAI Mal nʀit-, Nu ŋŋit-, B ŋit- 'not' [the B form is additive with t bases, producing nŋit-]
WCI ŋŋit- 'not'
ECI ŋŋi(t)- 'not' [indic. ŋŋituq or ŋŋilaq]
GRI ŋŋit-'not' [indic. ŋŋilaq, etc.]

ŋ

PE ŋa-¹ 'be in state of doing s.th.' [perhaps from *nʀa-, as the NSY forms suggest — compare Inu ŋŋit- under nʀit-; CAY ŋqa-, GRI qqa- may represent suppletion but could simply reflect a t base allomorph; the relat. with ŋa-² is unclear; cf. also yuɣŋa-]
AAY +ŋa- 'be in a state of -ing' [used rather than (u)ma- after tə bases, as also +ŋaʀi-, +ŋaa'i- 'become (more) -ed' (compare (u)maʀi- under (u)ma-)]
CAY (#)+ŋa- 'be in state of -ing or having been -ed' [only with bases in tə that drops, becomes s or goes to i; (#)ŋqa- is used instead with (mainly) postural roots ending in C(tə); note also NS +ŋaiʀ- 'stop -ing']
NSY ŋa-, ŋʀa- 'passive (state)' [ANLC 'be in state of having -ed or having been -ed'; and note ŋʀayaɣ — for ŋʀayaʀ-? — 'be recently -ed' (compare lʀayaq-), also, with kδaʀ-, ŋʀayaxqaa- 'should']
CSY +ŋa- 'be in state of -ing or having been -ed'
Sir —
SPI ŋa- 'be in a state of -ing' [and ŋaiq- 'stop -ing']
NAI (+)ŋa- 'perfect tense and perfective aspect' [drops preceding k/q but fuses with t to nŋa-, as also the following; (+)ŋait- 'have not (been) -ed', (#)(+)ŋaɣli- 'less than before', (+)ŋaiq- 'stop ing'; note also ŋŋaq-, (after t) nŋaq- plus rel. endings 'when -' compare (m)maq- under (u)maʀ(aʀ)-]
WCI (#)ŋa- 'be in state of'
ECI (#)ŋa- 'be in a state of' [and (#)ŋŋa(q)- 'begin to be in a state of']

GRI #ŋa- 'be in state of' [and qqa- 'be in state', NG 'perfect tense']

PE ŋa-[2] 'look like' [the relat. — if any — to ŋa-[1] is obscure]
AAY +(ʀ)ŋa- 'look like' [opp. = +(ʀ)ŋaitə-, but note also Kod +niŋaitə-, PWS +niŋiitə- 'will not'; for K +a(a)yaɣ-, ŋaayaɣ- 'kind of' see tyaɣ]
CAY +ŋaʀi- 'begin to be like, seem to be becoming -' [for the second element of which see li-[2]; +ŋatə- 'seem to be -ing, perhaps' has the tə ~ l alt. so perhaps containing ət-; note also +ŋaitə- 'not in future' with ŋit-; also +ŋalŋuq 'one similar to', and to nom. bases +(ʀ)ŋatə 'seem like (a) -']
NSY —
CSY —
Sir —
SPI —
NAI (#)(+)ŋaaq 'one with appearance or behavior of -ing or having -ed' [same morphophonemics as under ŋa-[1]]
WCI [note Sig ŋa(laaq)- 'somewhat, a little']
ECI — [for (#)ŋayaak- 'almost, rather (of state)' and (#)ŋayaaq- 'be in state of repeatedly -ing' see tyaɣ]
GRI ŋa- 'resemble' [for ŋayaɣ- 'almost' see tyaɣ]

PI ŋaaq- 'more or greatly?' [cf. ŋa-[1] and aʀ-?; compare the relat. of (u)maʀ(aʀ)- to (u)ma-]
SPI ŋaaq- 'more, most'
NAI ŋaaq-, (with t bases) nŋaaq- 'tend to be rather -'
WCI ŋaaq- Net 'greatly', Baker Lake 'more, greatly'
ECI ŋaaq- 'more than another, preferably' [also enclitic], Lab Rigolet 'good' [to nominals]
GRI ŋaaʀ- 'greatly', ŋaaq 'large, considerable' [and note piŋaaʀ- 'be important']

PE ŋaʀ-[1] 'hit or injure on the (body part)'
AAY (#)(ŋ)aXtə-, (after ə, which drops) +aaXtə- 'hit on the -'
CAY (#)(ŋ)aʀ(aX)tə- 'hit on the -' [v-dr; also #caʀ(aX)tə]
NSY —
CSY —
Sir —
SPI (#)aq- 'injure, break'
NAI (#)aq- 'injure, damage'
WCI (#)aq- 'hit on the -' [Pryde 'break, hurt']
ECI (#)aq- 'hit on the -, break one's -' [also 'apply (oil and the like) to']
GRI —

PY ŋaʀ-[2] 'habitually' [there may be a link to ŋa-[1]]
AAY #ŋaʀ- 'be a chronic -er (vice)'
CAY #ŋaʀ- 'tend to (chronically)', #ŋaʀli(q) 'one who tends to -'
NSY #ŋaʀ- 'habitually' [ANLC]
CSY #ŋaʀ-

PY ŋcaʀ- 'try to cause to' [cf. nəɣ- and caʀ-]
AAY ŋcaʀ- 'cause to be -' [with adjectival (verbal) bases]
CAY ŋcaʀ- 'try to cause to'
NSY [nła(ʀ)- 'make' on nominal bases, ANLC also 'make one -' with verbal bases]
CSY [ŋłaʀ- 'try to induce to', with nominal bases 'make' — compare łəqə- under ciqə-]

PE ŋicaɣ- 'be in need of' [cf. ŋit- and yyaɣ-]
AAY (ŋ)icaɣ- 'want, need'
CAY (ŋ)icaɣ-
NSY +isaɣ- 'be without' [and nom. +isak 'one without -']
CSY (ŋ)isaɣ- 'be in need of, lack'
Sir —
SPI —
NAI —
WCI ihak- 'have very few'
ECI NBI isak- [Spald.]
GRI isaɣ-

PY ŋiɣ- 'easily'
AAY +ŋiɣ- 'easily, quickly' [and +ŋiatə- 'with difficulty' — with the (ɣ)atə- variant of ŋit-]
CAY +ŋiɣ- 'be able to easily, be adapt at -ing' [and +ŋiatə- 'be inept at -ing']
NSY —
CSY —
Inu [note perhaps GRI #ŋiaɣ- 'be fed up with -ing', EG ŋiit- 'be discontented with -' — compare WG inniŋiaɣ- 'shun society of men' and NAI in in^{y}n^{y}iŋiat- 'be wary of people' from iŋŋit- under iŋuɣ]

PE ŋilitaʀ 'protection from or against' [cf. ŋit-, perhaps li-[1] and un, and yailkun; compare Aleut liisi-x 'protection against', apparently with li-[1]]
AAY —
CAY #ilitaq 'protection for or against' [in lexicalized forms with irregular contractions]
NSY #(ŋ)ilitaq 'protector for' [ANLC; for yiałkutaq 'device to prevent -ing' see yailkun]
CSY (#)+(ŋ)iitaq 'protection for (esp. body part)'
Sir —
SPI —
NAI #il^{y}isaq
WCI Cop (#)ilitaq [Pryde]
ECI #ilitaq
GRI [cf. akuilisaq under aku(ʀ)]

PE ŋiłiqə- 'suffer from lack of' [cf. ŋit- and liqə-]
AAY (ŋ)iłiqə- 'be short of'
CAY (ŋ)iłiqə- 'suffer from lack of'
NSY —
CSY —
Sir —
SPI —
NAI —
WCI iliqi- 'lack, need'
ECI iliqi-
GRI ššaaliqi- 'lack' [with kðaʀ]

PE ŋinnaʀ(-) 'only' [cf. qa(C)inaʀ-; forms with initial s are probably from allomorphs following t bases]
AAY +ŋinaa- (plus rel. endings) 'as soon as' [and K sinaq 'big'; for +(X)łiinaq 'only' see ʀłaɣ]
CAY +ŋinaq* 'merely' [also verbal +ŋinaʀ-; +(ŋ)iinaʀ- 'more and more', K (v-dr) (ŋ)inanʀa(ni), Y +ŋinanʀa(ni) 'while -ing', HBC inaʀ- 'finally' (only after prime V(C))]
NSY +(ŋ)inaq 'only' [verbal inaʀ-, with poss. endings = 'as soon as'; also inaqə-, (with tə base) sinaqə- 'only']
CSY (+)(ŋ)inaq* 'only' [v-dr; verbal (ŋ)inaʀ-, with conj. endings = 'only when'; note also staXiinaq* 'only -s, each a -']
Sir (+)ənaX 'only' [also tavəɣinaX under taðvaŋinnaʀ (taðva); for +(i)nəʀ- 'future', +(i)nəqə- 'about to' see na(C)uʀ- and naqə- — perhaps these are influenced by +inəqə- (plus conj. mood marker ya-) 'when (in past)' and +inəqatə- (plus poss. endings) 'as soon as', which belong here rather]
SPI +sinaq- 'only (verbal)', +siinaq- '(gradually) more and more'
NAI inʸnʸaq- 'continuously', Mal (ŋ)inʸaq 'only' [nom.; also (dropping preceding t) +sinʸnʸaq- 'only (verbal)'; for łXinʸaq, Mal łXainʸaq 'only' see ʀłaɣ-]
WCI innaq 'only (nom.)', +sinnaq-, (after k/q) ɣinnaq- 'only, all the time' [and Net, Car +hinnaq- + contemp. mood = 'after -ing']
ECI innaq 'only (nom.)', (ŋ)inna(q)- 'all the time' [also innaqi-; Lab +sinna(q)- 'finally']
GRI innaq* 'only, mere', innaʀ- 'only' [preceding 'weak i' to a before the nom. form; also (#)ɣinnaʀ- after ʀ or VV(C) and #+sinnaʀ- after ʀ — both more productive in NG; note also productive +sinnaʀ-(łuni, etc.) 'after -ing' and (with ŋu- and yaʀ- respectively) +sinnaa-, NG hinnaʀialik, ɣinnaʀialik 'can']

PE ŋiʀ- 'remove or be deprived of' [from *ŋŋiʀ-? — cf. ŋit- and ʀ- under ŋ(ŋ)uʀ-, also ŋiyaʀ- and (ŋ)iʀaʀ-]
AAY (ŋ)iʀ- 'remove, be deprived of' [v-dr; also (ŋ)i<ʀ>aXte- '(suddenly) lose one's -']
CAY (ŋ)iʀ- 'remove, be deprived of' [v-dr; and (ŋ)iXtə- 'be injured in one's -'; (ŋ)iʀ(aʀ)- 'have cold -', (#)(ŋ)iʀaXtə- 'be injured in one's -'; cf. ŋiyaʀ-]
NSY (ŋ)iʀ- 'become without-' [ANLC 'remove, lose one's -, cease -ing']
CSY (ŋ)iʀ- 'lose, remove, be injured in one's -' [v-dr]
Sir [cf. ŋiʀ- as in usəŋiXta 'docker' under uciŋiʀ- (uci[1])]
SPI iq- 'lose, be deprived of' [and #ŋiq- 'take position to - of']
NAI iq- 'remove, no longer have' [base-final ɨ to a, semi-final ɨ drops and following k/q fricativized, otherwise truncating; also #ŋiq- 'take position to - of, lose a -']
WCI iq- 'remove' [and iXXi- 'be short of'; Pryde has Cop #ŋiq- 'take position to - of, lose one's -']
ECI iq- 'remove, steal, be cold in one's -' [and #ŋiq- 'put in position to one's -', iʀsi-, isiq- 'have lost', Lab iqi- 'have one's - exposed']
GRI iʀ- 'remove, be deprived of, sell' [and iʀsiʀ- 'have lost', #ŋiʀ- 'position oneself to the - of']

PE ŋiʀutə- 'have no more' [cf. ŋiʀ- and utə-]
AAY (#)(ŋ)iʀutə- 'stop -ing' [of weather phenomena]
CAY (ŋ)iʀutə- 'no longer have'
NSY —
CSY (ŋ)iʀutə- 'have lost one's -'
Sir [cf. iɣləɣəʀət(ə)- lose one's voice, lower the sound of s.th.' under iɣlak (iɣə-)]
SPI iʀuti- 'remove, have no more'
NAI iʀuti- 'have no more' [morphophonemics as for iq- under ŋiʀ-]
WCI iʀut(i)- 'remove, break, have no more'
ECI iʀut(i)- 'remove, have no more'
GRI iʀut(i)-

PE ŋit- 'lack' [alternating with ŋil(a)-; cf. ŋiʀ-, ŋilitaʀ, nʀit-, ta(C)it-, ŋiłiqə-, təta(C)ili- and Aleut negative ula- 'be without' (the result of coalescence with a base-final a as in taaŋula- 'be thirsty' from taaŋa- 'water'), uli- 'lose, remove' (cf. li- under li-[1]), also laɣ in neg. imperative laɣaða, Att laɣuða, enclitic Atkan ulax, EA ulux (with u- 'be') and laka-X, the neg. equivalent of ku-X under kə(-)[2]; Inu negative indic. ŋŋilaq, etc., under nʀit- and SPI (ɣ)ilaq below probably reflect an original participial form; for the Yup variant atə- compare under ipəɣ-, also ətɣat- under ətə-, where it appears to be reflected in Inu too (see also under ŋiɣ- above) — perhaps from *aitə- < *ə(C) + ŋit- (cf. nəpait- under nəpə) then generalized to various other quality bases]
AAY (ŋ)itə- 'lack, have no -' [with the tə/l alternation as in CAY; also contrary negative of 'adjectival' bases; note atə- in takxʷiatə- 'have bad eyesight' under takviɣ-]
CAY (ŋ)itə- 'lack' [v-dr; ŋil before certain V- or voiced C-initial p.b.'s and endings; also forms the contrary of adj. bases (the tə/l alternation has apparently spread to contrary-like bases and p.b.'s in tə such as mikətə- 'be small'); optionally goes to ŋu before nani, etc. in combs. with k̲saitə- under kya(C)itə- and ŋaitə- under ŋa-[2]; note also lexicalized forms #atə-, #ɣatə-, #ɣiatə- (corresponding to CSY (ŋ)iɣatə- below and taking the tə/l alternation like (ŋ)it-; compare also HBC k̥ŋaɣaitə- 'not at all' (Woodbury 1981) and (s)ciiɣatə- 'not be able to' under c(c)iʀ-]
NSY (ŋ)itə- 'lack' [also contrary of adj. bases; u before nani, etc.; note also #atə- 'lack the -ness' — ANLC]
CSY (#)(ŋ)itə- 'lack' [v-dr; contrary of some adj. bases and neg. of lɣu- 'have', (ŋ)u- 'be' and in Chap yuɣ- 'want'; (ŋ)u- before nani, etc., (ŋ)ilŋuq with ŋuq; also (ŋ)iɣatə- 'never'; for msuxiitə- 'completely lack' see mcuɣ-]
Sir (ŋ)ət(ə)- 'not' [and səɣət(ə)- after t, which drops — Vakh. has iɣat(ə)- in tuniɣat(ə)- 'not give', presumably from the same source as CSY (ŋ)iɣatə- above; note also for the 'lack' sense luŋət- 'not have a house' and aŋayuqaʀilŋuX 'he is without parents' and the u before the neg. subordinative in iməʀunaʀən 'empty' from imaʀ]
SPI (ɣ)it- 'have no' [indic. = (ɣ)ilaq, etc.; for ŋit- 'not' see nʀit-]
NAI it- 'lack, have no' [also contrary neg. of 'adjectival'

bases; causes semi-final ɨ to drop, fricativizing remaining k/q, otherwise truncating; #il^{y}a(a)q 'one without -'; for (+)ŋit-, Nu ŋŋit- 'not' see nʀit-; note also il^{y}l^{y}iuq- 'need, lack', which causes final ɨ to drop]
WCI it- 'lack' [and illiuq-'need']
ECI it- 'be without -'
GRI (#)it- 'be without' [also contrary neg. of some adj. bases; note also ilatsi- 'be short of -']

PE ŋiyaʀ- 'remove (several?) or be cold in' [cf. ŋiʀ-]
AAY (#)(ŋ)iyaʀ-, ayaʀ- 'be cold in one's -' [for (ŋ)iʀaʀ- in this meaning see
(ŋ)iʀaʀ-]
CAY —
NSY —
CSY —
Sir —
SPI #iyaq-, #yaq- 'remove, break or have cold in one's -'
NAI iyaq- 'remove' [morphophonemics as for iq- under ŋiʀ-]
WCI iyaq- 'remove, have lost or have cold in one's -, break, kill'
ECI iyaq- 'remove (several), break s.o.'s -, be cold in one's -, sell'
GRI iaʀ- 'remove (several), break'

PI ŋŋiq- 'crave or want'
SPI —
NAI —
WCI Cop ŋŋiq- 'like, be fond of' [Pryde]
ECI NBI ŋŋiq 'one obsessed by -'
GRI ŋŋiʀ- 'crave, be wild about'

PE ŋqaʀ- 'have' [there may be a link to nəɣ- and ŋqa- (under ŋa-[1]) plus ʀ- (under ŋ(ŋ)uʀ-) and/or qan]
AAY ŋqəX- 'have'
CAY ŋqəX- 'have' [also impersonal +taŋqəX- '(for there to) be -', replaced by +taʀ- before subord. mood; note also +taŋə- 'for there to be - now' with taʀ- and ŋə- at nəɣ-]
NSY ŋqaʀ- 'have' [ANLC ŋqaX-]
CSY —
Sir —
SPI qaq-
NAI qaq-
WCI qaq- 'have' [and B. Lake Car +taqaq- '(for there to) be -' — Hansen]
ECI qaq- 'have' [also taqaq-]
GRI qaʀ- 'have' [and niqaʀ- 'passive' with nəʀ[1]; NG also +taqaq- '(for there to) be -']

PY ŋʀa(a)ʀ- 'although' [note CAY ŋqa- and NSY ŋʀa- at ŋa-[1]]
AAY ŋʀaaʀ- (plus relative person endings) 'although' [concessive mood marker]
CAY ŋʀ(aʀ)-
NSY ŋʀa(aʀ)-
CSY ʀŋaa(ʀ)-
Inu [Imaq ŋŋaʀ(mi)- 'although' may be from the NSY]

PY ŋsi- 'casually' [or msi-?; the relat. — if any — to mli- and/or tyaɣ is obscure]
AAY —
CAY (#)ŋsi-, (#)ŋsaɣ- 'to no particular end' [the latter influenced by mcaɣ- if not containing tyaɣ?]
NSY [note msi- 'a little' — infl. by mli-?]
CSY (#)ŋsi- 'briefly, casually'

PE ŋtaɣ- 'very'
AAY —
CAY ŋtaɣ- 'very, much', ŋtak 's.th. that is very -'
NSY —
CSY —
Sir —
SPI —
NAI —
WCI Cop tak 'very' [after derivations of qual. stems like aŋŋatak 'a very big one' from aŋə- — Pryde]
ECI [note lukatak- 'bad(ly)' with łuɣ(-)]
GRI [kataɣ- 'be tired of -ing' (compare under qqaʀ- perhaps for the first element), and note qasutaɣ- 'be exhaused' from qacu-]

PE ŋu- 'be' [cf. Aleut a-, Att u- 'be', usually an independent base, but suffixal in e.g. ayaɣaʀa- 'be married, had as a wife' and tanaʀa- 'be inhabited', the resultant ʀa- (or a- after C), Att ʀu- (generalized from position following uvular bases) now being the productive passive corresponding to Xta- 'have as'; could have been enclitic in pre-PE — compare also Aleut a-na-X 'something' and ulax under ŋit-]
AAY (ŋ)u- 'be' [v-dr after prime VC, also ə-dr]
CAY (ŋ)u- 'be' [as AAY]
NSY (ŋ)u-
CSY (ŋ)u- [v-dr and ə-dr]
Sir (ŋ)ə-
SPI (ɣ)u- 'be', Qaw also 'have many -' [same morphophonemics as NAI]
NAI (ɣ)u-, Mal (ŋ)u- 'be, have many -' [causes semifinal ɨ to drop, fricativizing following k/q, whereas final ɨ goes to a and the ɣ or ŋ is inserted only after double V, as in WCI and ECI too]
WCI (ŋ)u- 'be'
ECI (ŋ)u-
GRI (ɣ)u- 'be' [yu after double V; ŋu- in NG]

PE ŋ(ŋ)uðaʀ(-) 'small or like s.th. else' [cf. ŋuðaʀaʀ-; perhaps related to ŋu-, which might explain the geminated form in Inu, parallel with ŋ(ŋ)uʀ- from ŋu-; cf. ŋuža(a)q- and apparently Aleut aaðaX, (after V) Vða-X 'minor, young (animal)', EA 'small, s.th. resembling -, play', verbally 'a little, barely, resemble', EA also 'for nothing, pretend to, talk like', EA Vsa-, Atkan Vza- 'leisurely, well']
AAY C (ŋ)uaq 'imitation, s.th. like -', (ŋ)uaʀ- 'pretend to, for fun, casually', ŋuasa<ɣ>aq 'small', K ŋuaq 'small' [also verbal (ŋ)uaʀ-, with imper. (ŋ)uaʀ- – 'let's see you -']
CAY +(ŋ)uaq, ŋuaq 'imitation, s.th. like -', (+)ŋuaʀ-, ŋuaʀ- 'pretend to, without serious purpose'

NSY ŋuaq, (after ɣ/ʀ) +uaq 's.th. like -, small, toy' [and note ŋuža(ʀ)- 'for first time' (?); ANLC has (ŋ)užaq 'thing like -', and (ʀ)uaʀ- 'thoroughly' going with CSY +(ŋ)ʷaaʀ- below]
CSY +(ŋ)ʷaaq* 'imitation, toy, pretend, thing like -' [in Chap apparently also 'good, nice, tidy' and verbal equivalent; ɣʷaaq, ʀʷaaq after k/q bases; also +(ŋ)ʷaaʀ- 'diligently, thoroughly, at proper time' (going with the preceding Chap meaning?), and sŋʷaaʀaq 'tiny']
Sir (+)caX 's.th. like -' [for əcəX?; note also +ca(ɣa)łəx 'game of -' and +caʀ- 'well']
SPI ŋuaq 'fake, toy -' [verbal = 'pretend to'; also ŋuuži- 'play at, not properly, act like a -']
NAI ŋŋuaq 'fake, toy -' [verbal = 'pretend to'; also užaq (esp. Mal?) 'small version of', (with posit. base) 'in immediate vicinity of', which drops semifinal ɨ, and #ʀuaq 's.th. like or on top of' in some lexicalized forms]
WCI ŋŋuaq 'little' [verbal = 'pretend to, play at'; also nnuaq, ŋuyaq 'little', uyaq 'toy, s.th. like a -'; uyaq- 'imitate']
ECI ŋŋuaq 'toy' [verbal = 'play at, pretend to'; uyaq 's.th. like', uyaq- 'imitate']
GRI ŋŋuaq 'little' [pl. ŋŋuit, rel. ŋŋuup and with u 'be' ŋŋuu-, and verbal ŋŋuaʀ- 'dear little one does', ŋŋuaq 'play at'; also #ɣuaq, #ʀuaq 's.th. on top of s.th. else', uša(a)q 's.th. like a -', and ŋušaq, southern SWG, EG ŋŋuuyuk/ŋŋiiyuk 'dear little']

PE ŋuðaʀaʀ- 'leisurely or not seriously' [cf. ŋ(ŋ)uðaʀ(-), also EA Vsa-, Atkan Vza- 'leisurely' there]
AAY —
CAY [+miuyaaʀ- 'speak language of inhabitants of -', NSU usaaʀ- 'speak (language)']
NSY ŋuʀa(ʀ)- [for ŋuaʀaʀ-?] 'dear little one does s.th.' [disdainful when used of adults]
CSY +iižaaʀ- 'pretend to, play at' [to verbal or nom. base]
Sir —
SPI uža(a)q- 'gently, slowly' [and (#)užaaq- 'speak (a language)']
NAI (+ŋ)uža(a)q- 'slowly, leisurely, softly' [+ŋuža(a)q- with t bases; the form with single a also of old, young or handicapped person doing s.th.; also (#)užaaq- 'speak (language)']
WCI uya(a)q- 'a bit, leisurely, not seriously' [and Cop (+yu)uyaaq- 'act like, pretend to be']
ECI [uya(a)q- 'look like, imitate']
GRI ušaaʀ- 'act like, keep on -ing', NG uhaaq- 'pretend to, seem to, probably' [and ušaʀ- 'more or less', ʀu(u)šaaʀ-, NG luuhaq- 'slowly, at one's ease']

PY-S ŋuq 'participial' [with negative/contrary and other 'adjectival' bases, also ət(ə)- whose final tə goes to l; there may be a link to ŋu-]
AAY (#)ŋuq 'intr. participial of neg./contrary 'adjectival' bases [causes preceding tə to change to l; may also function as an indic. mood marker]
CAY (#)ŋuq* 'intr. participial' [as in AAY]
NSY (#)ŋuq
CSY (#)ŋuq*
Sir (#)ŋuX

PE ŋ(ŋ)uʀ- 'become' [cf. ŋu-, to which an inchoative/dynamic element ʀ- (from *Vʀ-?) causing gemination has been added that can also be found lexicalized in e.g. nappaʀ- under napa- and aʀullaʀ- under aʀula- (see also aŋvaʀ- under aŋva- and uŋummaʀ- under uŋuma-); note Inu non-geminating ɣuq-, ʀuq- below (for which compare the morphophonemics of NAI ɣu- under ŋu-) and the alternation between geminated and non-geminated Inu reflexes of PE ŋ(ŋ)uðaʀ(-); perhaps the geminating ʀ is cognate with the Yup ʀi allomorph under li-[2] (and CAY liʀi- there); cf. Aleut aʀ-, Attuan uʀ- 'put, give' from a-, Attuan u- 'be']
AAY (ŋ)uXtə- 'become'
CAY (ŋ)uXtə-
NSY (ŋ)uXtə-
CSY (ŋ)uXtə-
Sir [note ʀuʀ- as in aqəmaʀuʀ- 'become better' from aqəmaʀ- 'be good']
SPI ʀuq- 'become' [Qaw ɣuq- after k base]
NAI (#)ŋŋuq- 'become', ʀuq-, (after k, Uum also V base) ɣuq- 'become, turn into'
WCI ŋŋuq- 'become' [also (#)ʀuq]
ECI ŋŋu(q)- 'become', ɣuq- 'become, turn into'
GRI ŋŋuʀ- 'become' [and #ʀuʀ 'develop into']

PE ŋutə- 'one's supply of' [usually possessed; cf. un; the ŋ could perhaps reflect nəɣ- 'get']
AAY K (ŋ)utaq, (ŋ)un 'supply of, container for' [v-dr]
CAY (ŋ)un 'supply of, owned -' [v-dr]
NSY —
CSY —
Sir —
SPI uti 'supply of, owned' [note also usi- 'get a supply of -']
NAI un, utɨ 'supply of'
WCI ut(i)- 'owned, belonging to -'
ECI ut(i)- 'sack, bag of -', Aiv 'one's caught or stored thing'
GRI ut(i)- 'owned, belonging to -'

PE ŋu(C)uʀ or **ɣu(C)uʀ** quotative [enclitic; this could be from ŋu- 'be' plus participial ðuʀ — compare Aleut aXtaku-X 'it seems that' from a- 'be']
AAY PWS +xuq quotative, 'he or one says'
CAY +xuq
NSY +xuq
CSY +ŋuq [final k/q to ɣ/ʀ, otherwise no change to preceding word]
Sir +ŋuX quotative [Vakh.]
SPI ɣuuq, (after n or t) +uuq [preceding t to ž]
NAI ɣɣuuq, +(ɣ)ɣuuq [t to ž and c to y before the additive variant]
WCI ɣuuq, (after t) +ŋuuq quotative
ECI (+)ɣuuq
GRI ɣuuq, (after t or p) ŋŋuuq

P

PI payaaq- 'more?' [cf. vaɣ(-) and tyaɣ]
SPI —
NAI payaaq- 'more, most', Mal 'whenever' [also to nominal bases = 'every, each']
WCI Sig payaaq- 'most'
ECI —
GRI payaaʀ- 'more or less'

PI payuk(-) 'poor?' [cf. vaɣ and yuɣ, also forms like ʀuyuk under ʀuluk]
Yup [NSU pacuɣ- 'poor dear one does' could be from the SPI if it does not contain cuɣ]
SPI [note pasuk 'big old, funny old' (also verbal), which may contain cuɣ, however, and rather be from Yup]
NAI payuk 'poor' [also verbal]
WCI —
ECI [for pasuk- 'almost' (which may also be nominal) see mcuɣ-]
GRI payuk 'bad' [and payuɣ 'just a little']

PE piɣ(-) 'real or really' [the Inu vik may be a postvocalic variant due to lenition if it does not reflect a PE variant directly; forms like piaq are presumably with additional aʀ, q.v.]
AAY +(X)piaq 'real', +piaʀ- 'really'
CAY pik, piaq, NSU piɣaq 'real, genuine' [and piaʀ- 'really', #+pik, #+piaq 'most important form of -' and qapixtə-, qapiaʀ(aʀ)- 'very']
NSY pik 'real, correct', pixtə- 'much, very' [and pixłəʀia 'one that is very -' (to adj. bases); +(łəX)piɣaq 'most -', ŋqapixtə-'diligently'; ANLC has +piɣaq 'one that is very much a -']
CSY pik 'real', piɣ- 'very', (#)piɣaq '(fore)most'
Sir pix 'real' [also verbal in Vakh.]
SPI +piaq 'real' [also #piaq; verbal = 'really'; Imaq pik 'real']
NAI piaq 'real' [verbal = 'really'; also #vik 'real' (more productive in Nu, also as verbal 'really'); +viaq- 'might', viɣzuaq- 'without permission, regardless', Mal viksuq- 'carefully, completely']
WCI +(q)piaq, piaq 'real' [verbal = 'really'], Net vik, viɣaaluk 'real', Sig vik 'big, real', vialuk(-) 'real, really', Cop vik(-) 'unusually large, really' [Pryde]
ECI vik 'big', SB, NBI verbal 'really, for good'
GRI vik, +(ʀ)piaq 'real' [also #+pik], viɣ-, vissuʀ-, +(ʀ)piaʀ- 'really'

PI ptauq 'also' [or mtauq; enclitic — see also under amma]
Yup [note AAY +(m)ta 'again']
SPI +tauq 'also' [drops preceding t or n]
NAI +(p)ta 'as expected', +(p)tauq (or +(p)tuuq) 'also'
WCI +(p)tauq 'also'
ECI ı (t)tauq
GRI +(t)taaq

Q

PI q- 'go (to)' [added to allative case of (adverbial) demonstr. bases; from *aʀ-? — there may be a link to vaʀ-; cf. minŋaq-, k(k)u(C)aʀ-, viʀtə-, tmi(C)aʀte- and muaq-]
SPI #q- 'move (to)' [added to allative case of demonstrative bases; also unaaq- 'go via' with vialis]
NAI #q- 'go (to)' [with the allative = uŋaq-; note also #uunnaq- 'go via' with the vialis case]
WCI #q- 'go (to)' [with all. = unŋaq-; for +muŋŋaq- on noun bases see muaq-]
ECI #q- 'go (to)' [with all. = #uŋŋa(q)-; also #uunaq-, NBI, SB #uunau- 'go via'; for NBI, SB +muŋŋau- 'go toward' on nom. bases see muaq-]
GRI #ʀ- 'go (to)' [with all. = #unnaʀ-, NWG #uŋŋaʀ-]

PE q(q)a(a) 'is that so' [enclitic, but can also be an indep. particle in Yup]
AAY +qaa 'is that so?' [in yes/no questions]
CAY +qaa [qqaa after V]
NSY qaay 'is that so' [ANLC]
CSY +qaa 'is that so, perhaps, I wonder, let's -'
Sir [Vakh. has emphatic enclitic qa as in tavaqa 'well then']
SPI 'aa 'what about -?' [added straight to preceding word]
NAI Mal (+)qaa 'perhaps, isn't that so?' [added directly to preceding word — borderline case of enclisis, may be an independent particle]
WCI qaa 'I wonder, suppose' [and Sig (with condit. mood) 'if only ']
ECI qa(a) 'isn't that so?', +luqaa 'once upon a time', NBI qai 'maybe'
GRI EG ʀaa 'I wonder' [and note WG indep. particle qaa 'all right, try it, hurry']

PY qa(C)inaʀ- 'just (all the time)' [cf. ŋinnaʀ(-) and k(k)aʀ-]
AAY qiinaʀ- 'just - away'
CAY qainaʀ- 'only' [also nom. qainaq*]
NSY —
CSY qiinaʀ- 'only' [and de Reuse has łqi(i)naʀ- 'for a long time' — compare CAY Xłainaq under ʀłaɣ?]
Sir [note łqinaʀ- 'continually, for a long time']
Inu [for NAI łXinʸaq, Mal łXainaq 'only' see ʀłaɣ]

PI qan (qatə) 'companion (at doing s.th.)' [or nqan?; usually possessed; cf. Aleut qasi- 'fellow -, (the) other'; there may be a link to ŋqaʀ- — note the relat. of of PY lɣun, lɣutə- 'companion at -ing, one with same - as self' to lɣu- 'have' and compare anomalous Inu nunatqan under nuna]
SPI qan, (after t) tqan 'companion at -ing' [also +žuuqan]
NAI qan, (after t) tqan 'companion at -ing, one who has same - as self'
WCI qat
ECI qati
GRI qat

PE qaʀ 'area or part (in a direction)' [cf. qliʀ; mainly on positional bases — e.g. caniqaʀ 'side' under cani-]
AAY #qaq 'area or part in a direction'
CAY #qaq
NSY #qaq
CSY #qaq
Sir #qəX
SPI #ʀaq
NAI #ʀaq
WCI #ʀaq
ECI #ʀaq
GRI #ʀaq

PE qðuʀ- 'repeated action' [cf. qə- and ðuʀaʀ-; compare also tuʀ-[2]]
AAY ꝗuʀ-, +(X)quʀ- 'one after another, over and over' [only after tə base, otherwise (after V) uʀ-, (after ɣ/ʀ) +tuʀ-; also +quʀ- 'permanently' to motion bases, dropping tə]
CAY (#)quʀ- 'use repeated action to accomplish act'
NSY +(X)quʀ-, +(X)quža(ʀ)- 'in several places or times'
CSY (#)quʀ- 'all things available, completely' [only to bases in tə, which drops]
Sir —
SPI —
NAI (#)+(q)šuq-, qšuq- 'use repeated action to accomplish act' [on nominal bases = 'fetch, provide, reach into to get']
WCI —
ECI #+suq- 'repeated action' [on nom. bases = +(ʀ)suq- 'rummage through, work at']
GRI #+(ʀ)šuʀ- 'repeated action' [on nom. bases = 'work with or on']

PY qə- 'repeatedly' [cf. qu-, qðuʀ-, ðaʀ- (second form ðaqə-) and perhaps also ʀaq- and ʀqə-; the restriction to tə bases may indicate an earlier ʀ-initial form of which this is the te base allomorph — compare under łʀa(C)aʀ-) and aʀaʀtə-]
AAY ꝗə- 'repeatedly keep on -ing' [only after bases in tə, which drops]
CAY Xqə- 'one after another' [only with tə bases, otherwise ꝗu-, as under qu-; compare Xqə- under ʀqə-]
NSY —
CSY Xqə- 'divide into - groups' [with numeral bases]
Inu — [but note GRI naaʀi- under naðaqə- (naða-)]

PE qliʀ 'thing or part most or far in a direction' [cf. l(l)iʀ, here apparently added to qaʀ]
AAY #ꝗ łiq 'the -most one, the -ward part' [to positional bases; also #ꝗłiXpaaq 'the -most one']
CAY #ꝗłiq* 'the -most one, the -ward part'
NSY #ꝗłiq [ANLC]
CSY #ꝗłiq* 'thing far to the -'
Sir —
SPI —
NAI #qłiq, #kłiq 'thing or person far in a direction' [as in siuqłiq 'sailor' under civuqliʀ (civu-)]
WCI [Pryde has Net 'liq '-most one', also Car qłiq 'preferably' on demon. bases]
ECI —
GRI #ʀłiq* 'one most or far in a direction' [as in silaʀłiq under cilal(l)iʀ (cila) and siuʀłiq under civuqliʀ (civu-)]

PE qqaʀ- and **qqaqə-** 'one after another (now and then)' [perhaps from *k(k)aʀaʀ- (cf. ʀaq-), *k(k)aʀaqə- (cf. qə-) generalized from position after uvular bases — note in particular GRI kaa- and NSY kaʀ- below, though these could go with k(k)aʀ- rather, which could in turn be related (compare llaa- from łłaɣ-); cf. also k(k)attaʀ-]
AAY (+)(X)qaqə- 'one at a time, more and more' [and (#)ꝗaqu- 'repeatedly unexpectedly, momentarily'; for (X)qaa- see under a-]
CAY ꝗaqə-, (after unstressed syllable) ꝗaaqə- 'now and then' [underlyingly ꝗaʀaqə-; also 'one after another' or with subord. mood 'while now and then -ing' (only with bases in fricative plus tə, which drops) and ꝗaqu-, ꝗaquʀ(aʀ)- 'now and then' — cf. ꝗu- 'one after another' under qu-]
NSY [k̲aʀ- 'from time to time', k̲aataʀ-, k̲aažaʀ- 'repeatedly']
CSY ꝗaʀaqə- 'now and then'
Sir qaʀ- 'repeatedly, often'
SPI qa-, (after t base) tqa- '(all) do as a group'
NAI —
WCI qqa(ʀaaq) 'one after another' [for Car uqqaq see under (C)uʀ-]
ECI qqa(i)- 'one after another' [see under (C)uʀ- for qa(uq)-, uqqa(q)- 'several do'; and note Lab kaa- 'do - at a time' (with num. bases)]
GRI #qqaʀ- 'one after another' [and note (#)kaa- 'several do' (with a-); for NG uqqaq- see (C)uʀ-]

PI qquuq- 'probably' [there may be a link to k(k)uʀ — see under vinəʀ — and ŋ(ŋ)uʀ-]
SPI —
NAI — [for (t)quuq- 'urge to' see ðqə-]
WCI qquuq- 'no doubt' [Car tquuq- only after t base; Eskimo Point +nayaqquuq- 'probably, apparently', also uqquu as enclitic acc. Schn.]
ECI qquu(q)-, NBI quuyi- 'it seems'
GRI qquuʀ- 'undoubtedly'

PY qu- and **ʀqu-** 'one after another' [perhaps from *k(k)u-; cf. qə- and kutaʀ-]
AAY ꝗu- 'one after another'
CAY ꝗu- 'do one after another' [not with Ctə bases — cf. qqaʀ- and qə-; note also (#)Xqu- 'do so many times' (to numeral base with instr./abl. case ending)]
NSY — [for (X)quʀ- 'several times' see qðuʀ-]
CSY — [but note perhaps Xqu- 'go and get' (xku- after velar bases)' — compare the relat. between ʀaq- and ʀaaq-]
Inu [note GRI kula- 'often' under la(ʀ)- and kkuutaaʀ- 'do so many times' with numeral bases under ta(C)aʀ-]

PE q(q)un and **q(q)utaʀ** 's.th. associated with s.th.' [cf. quʀ and un?]
AAY (#)ꝗutaq 'forms plant name from berry, fruit or root base'

CAY [note (#)k̲utaq 'thing to be used as - would be, small version of -' from kə-[1]]
NSY —
CSY #(+)q̣utaq 'devise associated with -' [to nom. or verbal bases]
Sir —
SPI —
NAI #qutaq, #qun 'thing associated with -'
WCI #qutaq, #qut
ECI #q(q)ut [also qut(i) 'thing owned, belonging to possessor']
GRI #q(q)ut, #qutaq 'thing associated with or positioned on -' [and (#)qut(i) 'thing owned by possessor']

PE quR 's.th. associated with or attached to s.th.' [cf. the qu occuring in a few Aleut words like qam̥aqu-X 'cardium mussel' — original meaning difficult to determine as probably already non-productive in PE]
AAY #quq, #łquq 's.th. attached to, associated with or characterized by -' [esp. in anatomical terms; the second form resulting from attachment to neg. itə (under ŋit-)]
CAY #quq [also #łquq, #nquq, #mquq]
NSY #quq
CSY #quq
Sir #qəX
SPI #+quq, #Ruq 's.th. associated with or attached to' [the first form after t, as in all Inuit]
NAI #+quq, #Ruq [as SPI; also #lRuq from attachment to t bases, esp. ones containing neg. p.b. it — compare amilRuq under amit-, but also naqilRuq 'lower part of mountain' from naqət- and saalRuq 'thinner area of s.th. (e.g. ice)' from saat-]
WCI #+quq, #Ruq [as NAI; for Sig lRuq 'most' see under łəR[2]]
ECI #+quq, #Ruq 's.th. associated with or attached to'
GRI #+quq, #Ruq [as ECI; also #Rłuq as in naqiRłuq 'hollow' from naqət-]

PY qyuɣ- 'need to' [cf. yuɣ-]
AAY #qsuɣ- 'need to' [as under əməqyuɣ- (əməR(-)) and anaqyuɣ- (anaR(-))]
CAY #qsuɣ-
NSY #qɣ̥uɣ-
CSY #qsuɣ-
Sir [cf. məqɣ̥uR- under əməqyuɣ- (əməR(-))]

R

PE (V)R- 'say' [from *aR-?]
AAY +(R)- 'say (word or phrase)' [may be added to inflected forms]
CAY +R-, (after C) +aR- 'say'
NSY —
CSY +R- 'say' [de Reuse]
Sir —
SPI (#)Vq- 'call (by kinship name)'
NAI (#)Vq- 'say, call (by kinship name)'
WCI Vq- 'say, call'
ECI Vq-
GRI (#)VR- 'say' [can be added to (certain) inflected phrases as well as abs. nominal forms]

PI Raaq- 'catch so many' [cf. Raq-]
SPI —
NAI —
WCI Raaq- 'catch so many (on numeral base)'
ECI Raaq- 'catch or cost so much/many (numeral base)'
GRI RaaR- 'catch so many (numeral base)'

PI Raq- 'one after another' [cf. aR-]
Yup [cf. cituRaR- under citu-, also AAY aa-, (R)qaa- 'intermittently' under a-]
SPI Raq- 'do en masse, all together'
NAI —
WCI Raq- 'one after another' [Pryde, who also has Raaq-, ɣaaq- 'keep on -ing, slowly, at leisure']
ECI —
GRI #RaR-, #ɣaR- 'one after another, repeated action' [and yuRaR- (alongside yuRtuR-), EG yaR̃aR- 'one after another']

PE RaR and **aRaR** 'young or small' [cf. aR, of which this could be a doubling; compare RaRaR-, also piaRaq under pi(-)]
AAY #RaaRaq 'little extension of' [and +aRaR-, (esp. after V) RaaRaR-, (after tə) +(X)qaaRaR-, q̣aaRaR- 'for a bit (longer)']
CAY aR(aq*) 'little piece of' [and aR(aR)- 'a little, leisurely', as with aR(aq*) used only after CVC bases where V is a prime vowel; for Xaq* 'just a little, a little bit of' see RaRaR-]
NSY Raq 'small, thing like a -', Xaq 'small' [ANLC; Men. has Xaq 'young (animal)' — from *RaRaq, a doubling?]
CSY Raq* 'young, little -' [compare aq under aR; for Xaq* 'little, a little bit of' see RaRaR-]
Sir RaX 'new, young' [and note almiɣcəRaX, almiɣcəRaRaX '(small) seal', derived from almiɣžaq]
SPI [cf. nuɣatpiaRaaq 'young boy' under nukalpiɣaR]
NAI #Raq 'new, young'
WCI Sig aRaq, aRaaluk 'little', Cop, Car aq 'young (of animal)' [Pryde for the latter]
ECI aRaq 'little'
GRI aRaq, VRaq 'little, young', NG (#)Raaq 'little' [also #Raq as in nukappiaRaq under nukalpiɣaR — and compare NG nanuRaaq 'polar bear cub' from nanuR and uxxuɣaaq 'young bearded seal' from uɣðuɣ]

PY RaRaR- 'barely (a little)' [from *ɣaRaR-? — cf. RaR, but also aR, łRa(C)aR-, RataR-, n(ə)RaR(aR), lRataR-, lRayaq- and vqaR-; the exact relat. is obscure]
AAY XaXpiaR- 'barely' [and Xaq 'a little bit of']
CAY XaR- 'barely, a little' [and Xaq* 'just a little (bit of)', also +(ɣ)aR(aR)-'barely, rather', (with bases expresing a garment) 'go only with - or by -ing', which causes gemination in VCə bases]
NSY —

CSY Xaq* 'a little (bit of)'
Inu [note ECI ɣɣaa(q)- 'barely', also GRI aʀ- 'be -ish' under aʀ]

PE ʀataʀ- 'persistently or intensely?' [or ɣataʀ-?; the relat. to lʀataq- is unclear; an lʀ-initial post-vocalic allomorph could have been lost in Yup and eastern Inu, but contam. from lʀataq- in western Inu is perhaps more likely; most of the Yup forms seem to be preceded by a- or aʀ-]
AAY —
CAY —
NSY +aata(ʀ)- 'repeatedly, back and forth' [for variant kaataʀ-/qaataʀ- see under qqaʀ-]
CSY +aataʀ- 'repeatedly', #++aʀaataʀ- 'keep -ing' [for +laataʀ- 'again' see la(ʀ)-]
Sir — [for +lataʀ- 'again' see la(ʀ)-]
SPI [note Imaq ɣlataq- (for ʀlataq-?) 'slowly']
NAI lʀataq-, ataq- 'for a long time' [an ɨ preceding the latter alternate becomes a]
WCI Sig ataaq(sinnaq)- 'hard, on and on' [and note ʀataʀ(nani, etc.) 'without -ing'; see lʀataq- for Net intensifier ʀataq-, which could belong here]
ECI [note ataaluk- 'very badly', (+yu)ʀataq 'one which is really'; compare also enclitic ataq of pleasant surprise]
GRI ataaʀ-, ʀataaʀ- 'in a big way (often exclamatory)', NG ʀataaq- 'carefully' [and (yu/+ʀšu)ataaʀ- 'powerfully, hard', ʀiataaʀ- 'suddenly' (with ɣiaq-)]

PE ʀłaɣ 'big [cf. łłaɣ- — perhaps from a post-uvular allomorph of that p.b.]
AAY [(X)łiinaq 'only']
CAY #Xłak 'major' [and Xłainaq* 'nothing but -']
NSY —
CSY Xłak 'big, lots of' [and verbal Xłaɣ- 'in a big way, a long time', Xłaɣu- 'very'; note also łaaɣ- 'crudely', łaak, łəɣaq* 'crude, bad']
Sir — [for łqinaʀ- continually' see under qa(C)inaʀ-, and note młəɣaX 'very big']
SPI łXak- 'abruptly, roughly, angrily' [and +niqłak- 'badly', qłainaq, qłainat 'much, many']
NAI Mal łak(-) 'big, bad, rough(ly)', łallaq-, llapiaq- 'very, a lot', B łak(taq)- 'angrily' [though some of these could go directly with łłaɣ-; note also łXinʸaq, Mal łXainaq 'only', and Nu łʀinʸaq- 'finally', going with CAY Xłainaq above — entanglement with qa(C)inaʀ-?]
WCI Cop łXa(a)q- 'intensifier' [variously spelled lʀa(a)ʀ-, hʀa(a)ʀ-, etc. in Met.; also in Net in Ras.'s texts — Pryde has Net łhanaluk- 'at last' and łhaaluk- (for łXaaluk-?) 'intensifier']
ECI ʀlak 'big', ʀlaat 'lots of little -s'
GRI [note kanayuʀłak 'armed bull-head (kind of sculpin)' from kanayuʀ]

PE ʀqə- 'deliberate action?' [the relat. to qə- and/or ðqə-, if any, is obscure; this p.b. seems to be ingredient also in naqə- and miqə-]
AAY —
CAY Xqə- 'deliberately cause to -' [may optionally retain the uvular fricative after a velar base; note homonym of repetition under qə-]
NSY —
CSY [note (#)Xqə- (to noun base) 'apply - to' (as in məXqə- at məʀqə-); for homonym meaning 'divide into groups of -' with numeral bases, see qə-]
Sir [cf. nəXqə(s)- 'feed' under nəʀqə- (nəʀə-)]
SPI —
NAI [note #qɨ -as in aullaqɨ- 'set out' and saɣluqɨ- 'lie to' from saɣlu- 'lie', which may cause gemination as in nimmaqɨ- 'wrap s.th. around' from nəmər]
WCI #qi- 'cause to undergo' [the basic meaning seems to be of deliberate action; also trans. qisaq- and qipkaq-; note the seemingly meaningless qi scattered throughout Ras.'s Sigliq texts; also (#)laqi- 'begin to (and continue — of weather phenomena)', Baker Lake luqi- 'here and there', and alternative indic. forms -qquq-, etc., after uvular bases in Cop at least]
ECI #qi- 'spontaneous or deliberate action' [also (#)aqi- 'suddenly', laqi- 'and so' (with la(ʀ)-), Lab liaqi- 'become', llaqi- 'become a bit -', and note alternative indic. forms like qquq- with uvular bases (also kkuq- after other C bases acc. Schn.)]
GRI qi- 'very, intensifier' [qa-, EG ʀa- before v-initial intr. indic. endings (and contemp. mood); in NG qi- is a perfective marker on 'main line' narrative indicative forms, qa- before opt., interr., contemp. and caus. moods]

PI ʀuaq- 'have much' [cf. perhaps Aleut ʀu- 'have much or many']
Yup [for CAY (#)ʀuk, (after velar) +uk 'big', pl. ʀuɣaat 'many' see ðuɣ]
SPI —
NAI —
WCI Sig ʀuaq- 'have' [less productive also in Cop]
ECI —
GRI #uaʀ- 'have (too) much'

PI ʀuluk 'poor little?' [cf. k(k)uluk and łuɣ, also ʀuʀluq though the relat. is obscure; there appears to be phonaesthetic variation here]
SPI —
NAI [note luk- in sualuk- 'scold lightly' under cuɣaɣ-]
WCI Car ʀuluk 'little'
ECI ɣuluk 'dear or poor little' [also verbal], NBI, SB ʀuluk 'bad', Aiv 'small, miserable' [also verbal, including as imper. strengthener; note also ʀuyuk 'a little', ʀuyuit 'group of -', with yuɣ?]
GRI ʀuluɣ-, ʀuluuʀ- 'hard, violently' [and note NG luk- 'a little', WG #luɣ- 'a little' as in ikiuluɣ- 'help a little', also ʀuyuk 'bad', NWG 'big', ʀuyuɣ-, ʀuyuuʀ- 'a little' with the second syllable as in k(k)u yuk and payuk(-)]

PI ʀuq- 'hit on the (body part)'
SPI —
NAI [note ižaʀuq- 'hit in the eye' under əžaʀuq- (at əðə)]
WCI #ʀuq- 'hit on the — (body part)'
ECI #ʀuq-
GRI #ʀuʀ-

PY ʀuʀluq 'poor dear' [the relat. to ʀuluk is obscure — the first element at least is probably shared; perhaps from *ʀuʀluɣaq — compare apaʀuʀluq under ap(p)a[1]]
AAY Xuuʀluq 'poor'
CAY ʀ(uʀ)luq*, uʀluq*, HBC ʀuluq* 'poor dear' [+uʀluq* after velar or after a prime V in position for rhythmic stress; also verbal ʀ(uʀ)luʀ, etc. 'the poor dear one does'; compare also HBC, Nun, NS Xłuɣaq* 'good old']
NSY [note luaq 'minor sort of -' (ANLC)]
CSY [cf. Chap apaʀuʀluq 'great grandfather' under apaʀuʀluq (ap(p)a[1]), also luʀ- 'a little']
Inu [note SPI (ʀ)luusaaq 'poor, unfortunate']

S

PI saaq- and **lisaaq-** 'have just done or quickly do s.th.' [cf. yaʀaʀ- — there may be a further link to caʀ-[1]; the second form with liq-]
SPI [note Qaw +saq- 'begin to, hurry to' — going with or contam. with caʀ-[1]?]
NAI [for #(+)saaq- 'be in process of, just -ing' see caʀ-[1]]
WCI Cop, Car, Net haaq- 'have just -ed', Cop lihaaq- 'for first time' [also 'adg' acc. Schn. as nom. 'one who has just -ed', Met. also has saq- 'quickly' for Sig = Cop hak- acc. Lowe; Pryde has haaq 'new, recent' for Cop, which may be by contam. with +haaq under taaq(-)]
ECI saaq- 'quickly, at once', Lab saak- 'first, for time being', saałła(k)- 'quickly, right away', NBI, SB (li)saaq- 'have just -ed, for first time'
GRI —

PI sunŋu- 'be about to' [cf. yuɣ-, also lŋu-?]
Yup — [for CAY culŋu- 'be sick, characterized by -ing' see lŋu-]
SPI —
NAI [Jen. has suŋŋu- (for sunŋu-?) 'be about to']
WCI +hunŋu- 'intended future' [Lowe]
ECI (#)suŋŋu- 'be on point of'
GRI #suŋŋu- 'be on point of'

PI suu- 'habitually' [from nominal use of yuɣ- plus ŋu-?]
SPI +suu-, (after k/q) ɣuu- 'habitually'
NAI +suu-, (after k/q) ɣuu-
WCI +suu-, (after k/q) ɣuu- 'habitually'
ECI [note suuq, (#)yuuq 'one which habitually -s', (esp. the second form) 'instrument for -ing', which may be used verbally in the 3rd person, otherwise verbal suuŋu- 'habitually' — Schn. also has +su-; note also Baffin distant past yuu- (compare lauyu- under lauq-); for NBI, SB vaŋuu- 'used to' see vaɣ-]
GRI [note #suuq on adj. bases like aŋisuuq 'big', takisuuq 'long', pualasuuq 'fat' — perhaps by contam.with tu-[1]]

T

PE t-[1] 'transitivizer' [cf. Aleut transitivizer t-]
AAY #+tə- 'transitivizer' [and on postural roots 'assume such a position', with intr. endings]
CAY #+tə- 'cause to' [also with intr. and trans. postural roots; note +taaʀ- 'try to make others feel that one is -']
NSY #+tə- 'act on so as to cause to -' [ANLC; Men. has +təfkaqə- 'indirect causation' — i.e. cause someone else to perform a transitive action]
CSY #+tə- 'cause to' [also with postural roots]
Sir #t- 'transitivizer' [with present tense = s(qəXtəX, etc.); apparently added to many bases and postbases ending in qə before present tense endings]
SPI #t -'transitivizer' [only to V bases, as elsewhere in Inu]
NAI #t-
WCI #t-
ECI #t-
GRI #t-

PE t-[2] 'get or catch or go to' [cf. Aleut t- 'fetch, get, pick', and note the combination with pass. participial qa- and ʀi- 'have' in txaʀi- 'have caught -' mentioned under kə-[1] — compare pitaʀ under pi-; there may be a relat. to taʀ-]
AAY +(X)tə-, tə- 'kill, buy (food), go to'
CAY +tə- 'catch (game), go to, obtain, spend (time)' [and pass. part. +taq 'caught -']
NSY (#)+tə- 'catch, obtain'
CSY +tə- 'catch (game), go to, obtain' [and pass. part. +taq 'caught -']
Sir +t(ə)- 'go to'
SPI [(#)+k- 'catch' used with all animals]
NAI (#)+t- 'catch' [indistinguishable from k- under nəɣ- following k bases since it drops after C before C-initial endings; the corresponding pass. part. is +taaq as in natciqsaaq 'caught seal']
WCI #t- 'catch' [certain game animals — not those with which k- is used]
ECI #t- 'catch'
GRI #t-

PE ta- 'be in state of' [cf. Aleut Xta- (generalized from uvular bases), (after C) ta- 'for a time, have -ed, apparently']
AAY #(t)a- 'be in a state of -ing' [as in wiita- 'have eyes open', and puxta- 'float' from uɣit- and puɣə- respectively]
CAY #(t)a- 'be in a state of -ing'
NSY —
CSY —
Sir —
SPI #ta-
NAI #sa-
WCI #ta-
ECI #+ta-, #sa- [the latter in e.g. nuisa- 'wax (moon)' from nui-]
GRI #sa- 'be in a state of -ing'

PI taaq(-) '(get a) new' [cf. nutaʀaʀ under PE nutaʀ-, which may at least have influenced this set (if it is not a back formation from it), but also p.b. žaʀaq, though the relat. is obscure — there may be a link to taʀaq parallel to that between the Yup and Inu senses of tuqaq[1] and tuqaq[2] respectively]
SPI [note łaaq 'new', (verbal) 'use or wear a new -' — compare the Nun form under žaʀaq]
NAI [Jen. has +taq- 'have a new -'; note also #+taaq 'caught thing' under t-[2]]
WCI Car +taaq Eskimo Point 'new', Baker Lake +taaq- 'get' [the latter Hansen — Pryde has 'buy'; and note Cop +haaq 's.th. received' acc. Pryde (compare NBI +taasaaq below) ; for Cop haaq 'new, recent' see saaq-]
ECI +taaq- 'get', +taaq, NBI, SB +taasaaq = 'newly received' [and Cape Dorset +taaq 'adopted']
GRI +taaʀ- 'get a new -', +taaq 'new'

PE ta(C)aʀ- 'repeatedly' [cf. ðaʀ- and t(t)aʀ-]
AAY +taaʀ- 'repeatedly attempt to -' [and — with ŋu- — (#)(ŋ)utaaʀ- 'do - at a time', with numeral bases and conj. mood]
CAY #taaʀ- 'repeated action' [with tə bases only; also (#)(+)taaʀ- 'do - at a time' with numeral bases, utaaʀ- with maʀluk 'two' and piŋayun 'three']
NSY —
CSY —
Sir —
SPI (#)+taaq- '(move) some way'
NAI #+taaq- 'assume position or continue action in space or time, (move) some way' [and presumably also nom. +taaq 'some way (in a direction)' on directional expressions; for laaq, (after C) +taaq- 'go so far as to' see tələ]
WCI Sig +(llak)taaq- 'repeated action' [and note Cop (#) laaq- 'do - at a time', influenced by la(ʀ)-? — but see also under tələ]
ECI —
GRI #+taaʀ- 'repeated action' [and (#)kkuutaaʀ- 'do - at a time' with numeral bases — for the first element compare qu-]

PY taciaʀ- 'test -ness of' [cf. təkə-, esp. the AAY and CAY form taciq containing uciʀ as here]
AAY C +tasaaʀ-, K +tasua<ʀ>aʀ- 'test s.th.'s -ness'
CAY +tasiiʀ-, +tasiaʀ-, +taciaʀ-
NSY —
CSY —

PI tainnaq- 'finally' [cf. ŋinnaʀ(-)]
SPI [note lainaq- 'gradually' — with lenition after V (apparently the only position it is found in) unless it goes rather with la(ʀ)-]
NAI +tainʸnʸaq-, (after t also) lainʸnʸaq- 'finally'
WCI +tainnaq- 'finally', Car 'have just -ed, for first time'
ECI Lab +tainna(k)- 'finally, be late -ing', SB, NBI +tainnaq- 'at last', Aiv 'have just -ed' [Schn. — but Dor. has 'really'; Tar litainna(q)- 'for first time']
GRI —

PE taʀ 's.th. pertaining to s.th.' [cf. Aleut Xta- 'have as -']
AAY #+taq 'of such a type'
CAY +taq 'thing pertaining to -'
NSY +taq
CSY +taq 'thing pertaining to -' [#kaXtaq, #kəXtaq on demonstr. bases]
Sir +taX, sitaX 'thing pertaining to-' [also kaXtaX, distribution not clear]
SPI +taq 'thing pertaining to -'
NAI +taq
WCI +taq
ECI +taq
GRI +taq

PE taʀ- 'fetch or gather' [cf. t-[2]; there is suppletion with caʀ-[2] in Inu]
AAY #+taʀ- 'fetch, gather'
CAY +taʀ-
NSY +taʀ- [ANLC]
CSY #+taʀ-
Sir [note #+taʀ- in məXtaʀ- 'fetch water' under əmərtaʀ- (əmər) at least]
SPI +taq- 'fetch' [and +taaq- 'habitually fetch']
NAI +taq-, +saq- 'fetch'
WCI +taq- 'fetch' [Sig has saq- after V, +taq- after C acc. Lowe — compare caʀ-[2]]
ECI +taq-, +saq-
GRI +taʀ-, NG +haq-, (after C) +taq-

PE t(t)aʀ- 'habitually?' [cf. ðaʀ- and ta(C)aʀ-]
AAY #+taʀ- 'do by nature or disposition' [opp. #+taitə-]
CAY (#)+taʀ- 'do by nature or disposition' [esp. with emotional roots]
NSY +taʀ- [ANLC]
CSY +taʀ- 'do by disposition or nature' [and 'repeatedly occur' on bases indicating sounds]
Sir —
SPI +taq- 'keep -ing'
NAI —
WCI +taq- 'repeated action'
ECI Lab +tak- 'repeated action' [(#)+taq- found less productively elsewhere]
GRI [note #ttaʀ-, neg. #ttaat-, as in naakkittaat- 'be merciless' (Fab. nâkiteit-) from naakki- 'pity' and kamaɣittaʀ- 'be patient' from kamaɣi-]

PY-S taʀaq 'one that is of such a quality' [on adj. bases of a negative /diminutive quality, usually in combination with kit- or ŋit- — compare under taaq(-)]
AAY —
CAY —
NSY (t)aʀaq 'one that is -' [as in amitaʀaq 'thing that is narrow' under amit-]
CSY staaq, staaXaq* 'one that is -' [as in aməstaaXaq under amit- and aməlkəstaaXaq under amələ 'narrow thing' and iqəkəstaa(Xa)q under iqə-]
Sir taʀałərəX 'one that is -' [with lʀi(C)a; as in amətaʀałərəX 'thin' under amit-]

PE taʀit- 'not be any -' [cf. taʀ and ŋit-]
AAY —
CAY +taitə- '(for there) not to be any -' [the opp. of +taŋqəX(tə)- under ŋqaʀ-]
NSY —
CSY —
Sir —
SPI +tait- 'not be/have any -'
NAI +tait- 'lack, have no -'
WCI Car +tait- 'not have any -'
ECI +tait-
GRI —

PY tatəkə- 'to same extent as -' [cf. təkə-, un and kə-[1]]
AAY +tatəkə- 'have one of the right -ness, fit' [and +tatə 'degree of (possessor's) -ness']
CAY +tatəkə- 'to the same extent' [and +tatə 'one that is - to the same extent as possessor']
NSY —
CSY —
Inu [note Cop +titkutaʀi- 'be the same -th as -' and +titkiik- 'make or be as - as', from tələ? — Pryde has tikkiik- 'be of equal - to' and tikkuhiq 'degree of' rather]

PI tciaq 'fairly big or good?' [cf. tyaɣ — esp. CAY ya(ɣ)aq and AAY caxaq there; the unusual inflected forms below reflect the connection]
SPI —
NAI tciaq 'new', Mal 'small' [on directionals = 'a bit (in direction)', verbal 'get a new', and in some nom. lexicalizations 'small, s.th. like a -'; in Mal and Nu the inflected form of tciaq is tcaa(mi, etc.), and note variant tcaužaq 'little']
WCI Cop (#)ttiaq 'good' [verbal ='a little, well, very (e.g. small)'], Sig, Car, Net tsiaq 'small, nice' [also verbal for subjective coloration of 'niceness', in the latter two dialects 'be a good, really' and in Sig 'only' on numerals; note also Car, Net tsau- 'be or have a good'; Pryde also has atciaq 'piece or bit of -' for Sig]
ECI tsiaq 'good, beautiful' [verbal = 'well, plenty'; (#)atsiaq 'young (of animal)', Aiv ttau 'have or be a good -'; note also exclamatory base (with pi-) pitsiaq 'how beautiful!']
GRI tsiaq 'fair sized', NG 'small' [inflected form tsiaa(mi, etc.), pl. tsiaat, NWG ttaa(mi, etc.), EG tsaa(mi, etc.); tsiaʀ- 'rather, a bit' — also #atsiaq, verbal #atsiaʀ-; note also tsiaʀšuaq 'good — of s.th. desired but not got' and exclam. base pitsak 'great!' from pi(-)]

PE tə 'area in such a direction' [usually possessed; forms positional bases from demonstr. roots; otherwise word-finally n; cf. the t in CAY allative case tm̥un 'toward' and perhaps Aleut ð(a) in positional bases like sað- 'outside' corresponding to Esk caðə-, so the ðə in the latter could perhaps also be related]
AAY #tə 'area in such a direction (from possessor)'
CAY #tə
NSY #tə
CSY #tə
Sir #tə
SPI #ti
NAI #tɨ
WCI #ti
ECI #ti
GRI #t(i) 'area in such a direction' [3rd person possessed taa, etc.]

PE təkə- and **ta-** 'to such an extent or degree' [from *tə?; cf. kə-[1] for the first form, also tələ, tatəkə-, taciaʀ- and Aleut Vt-, (after C) aat- (possessed 3s Vca, etc.) 'its -th' on adjectival bases, (derived from the former with (X)ta 'have as') Vta-, (after C) aata- 'have same -th as -, have such and such a length']
AAY +ta- 'so', +taciq 'quality, fact of, that or whether' [the latter with uciʀ]
CAY +ta- 'so, to such a degree', (#)+taciq 'degree, extent of -'
NSY —
CSY [+tutka- 'to such a degree' — with tu-[1] preceding *təkə-?]
Sir —
SPI +tiɣi- 'so, to such a degree'
NAI +tiɣi-'to such a degree' [drops preceding t and sometimes also a preceding ɨ]
WCI +tiɣi- 'so'
ECI +tiɣi- 'so'
GRI +tiɣi-

PE tələ and **talə** 'extent of' [cf. təkə-; with 'adjectival' verbal bases]
AAY —
CAY —
NSY +talə 'extent, degree of' [also +tutalə — with tu-[1]]
CSY (#)(+)tala 'extent, degree of'
Sir (ta)la
SPI +tikłaaq 'extent of' [influenced by teke-?; with allative case = 'until', verbal = 'measure how - s.th. is'; Imaq talə '-ness' — from the Yup]
NAI +tɨlaaq 'degree, quality of -' [also forms object clauses 'that -; verbal = 'measure degree or quality of'; note also laaq-, (after C) +taaq- (+ contemp. mood) 'go so far as to -' (compare ta(C)aʀ-?) and +suqtɨlaaq-, (after k/q yuqtɨlaaq- 'do one's best at, measure one's ability to' (with yu-)]
WCI +tilaaq 'extent of' [also forms object clauses and (restricted) verbal = 'measure extent of' — Lowe]
ECI —
GRI —

PE təʀ- 'repeatedly' [cf. ləʀ-, with which there appears to be contam.]
AAY +(X)təʀ- 'keep on repeatedly'
CAY [note #təqə- in anəXtəqə- 'breathe' under anəʀ- at least]
NSY —
CSY —
Sir —
SPI —
NAI [note anɨqtiʀi- 'breathe' under anəʀ-]
WCI +tiq-, +tiʀi- 'one after another, bit by bit' [also 'quickly' acc. Met. — compare ləʀ-]

ECI (#)+tiq-, +tiʀi- 'repeated, ongoing action' [the first form transitive, the second intransitive]
GRI +tiʀ-, +tiʀi- 'one by one, gradually' [on nominal bases = 'cover, smear with -']

PE tət- 'cause or let' [cf. t-[1] and vkaʀ-, with which this must have been in complementary distribution already in PE; in most languages/dialects can be used with the subord./contemp. mood (in Inu in the specific senses 'while -ing' or neg. 'before -ing') as a 'subject adjuster' if the subjects of the two clauses do not coincide]
AAY +cəstə- 'cause, let' [only with C bases]
CAY +cətə-, HBC +citə- 'cause, let' [only with C bases; with adj. bases used reflexively in sense 'have become -'; tə into l before rel. endings as in 3s consequential +cəlan in the latter reflexive sense only; also tə(tə) as a 'subject adjuster']
NSY +sitə- 'cause, let'
CSY +təstə-, (after V) stə-
Sir +tət(ə)- 'make, cause' [in present tense +tətəqəXtəʀa, etc.]
SPI +tit- 'cause, let' [only after C in Qaw; drops t]
NAI +tɨt- 'cause, let' [only after C, causes t to drop; reflexive with adj. bases = 'become']
WCI +tit- 'cause, let' [only after C]
ECI +tit- 'cause, let' [drops t]
GRI +tit- 'cause, let, consider' [in older language drops preceding t]

PE təta(C)aʀ- 'cause repeatedly' [cf. tət- and ta(C)aʀ-]
AAY +cəstaaʀ- 'try to cause to (repeatedly)'
CAY +cətaaʀ-, HBC +citaaʀ- 'try to cause to'
NSY —
CSY —
Sir —
SPI —
NAI [note +tɨtaq-, (after V) pkaqtɨtaq- 'force to', with ðaʀ-?]
WCI [note +titaq-, +titiq-, +titiʀaaq- 'cause repeatedly or several to', the second and third forms with təʀ-]
ECI [note +titiq- 'cause repeatedly or gradually, (reflexive) consider oneself -']
GRI +titaaʀ- 'cause repeatedly or several to -' [also +titiʀ]

PE təta(C)ili- 'prevent from doing' [cf. tət-, ðaʀ- and ŋit-, also ŋilitaʀ]
AAY —
CAY NSU +təstaili-, (after V) staili- 'prevent from -ing' [with trans. endings also (+tə)stailitə-]
NSY —
CSY —
Sir —
SPI +taili-
NAI +(t)sail^{y}i- 'try to prevent from -ing'
WCI +(t)taili(tqu)- 'prevent from -ing' [and +(t)tai- plus contemp. mood 'don't -']
ECI +(t)taili- 'refrain from, refuse to -' [Lab also 'prevent from -ing']
GRI tsaali(uʀ)-, (after C only) +taali(uʀ)- 'prevent from -ing' [NG also reflexively 'refuse to -']

PI tla- 'can or be apt to' [cf. ala- and la(ʀ)-, though the relat. is obscure — compare tya- in relat. to ya- for the t]
SPI —
NAI lla-, Mal, Nu, Uum tla- 'can, be good at, apt to', Nu also 'would, may', lait-, Mal tlait- 'cannot, never', Nu lait-, tlaiq- 'can or could not, be unable' [the Nu forms from Berg.]
WCI Cop lla- 'can', lait- 'cannot', Sig la- 'can', Car la- Baker Lake 'on point of -ing' [but at Eskimo Point = 'easily, tend to', going rather with ala-; laŋŋit- 'cannot, will not', Sig laŋa- 'be -able', Car laaq- 'future'; Pryde has laaq- 'easily' for Cop]
ECI [note laaq- 'further future, prepare to', laŋa- 'near future']
GRI [note pilaŋa- 'promise well (a future hunter)']

PI tluk- '(too) much' [cf. Atkan łuɣ- 'straight away', + neg. = 'not as much as expected', also l(l)u(C)aʀ- and/ or łuɣ(-), though the relat. is obscure]
SPI —
NAI Mal, Nu tluk- 'more, most'
WCI —
ECI luaq-, luaŋŋuaq- 'much, too', Lab luałła(k)- 'too' [and ŋŋiluaq- 'not enough', also Lab ɣumaluaq- at yuɣuma-]
GRI (#)luaʀ- '(a little) too', (#)ŋŋiluaʀ- 'hardly' [and (#)luuʀ- 'still, (quite) a lot']

PY tmi(C)aʀtə- and **tmuʀtə-** 'go toward' [from allative case tmən, tmun on demon. adverbials and posit. roots plus the source of q-?; cf. muaq- and viʀtə-, also vaʀ-]
AAY #tm̥iaXtə-'go toward' [on demon. adverbials and posit. bases]
CAY #tm̥muXtə-
NSY #tm̥uaʀ- [ANLC]
CSY #tm̥iiXtə- 'go toward' [as in sanitm̥iiXte- 'go to the side']
Inu [cf. the forms under kiŋuppiaq- (kiŋu-)]

PE tʀutə- 'pass to the (direction) of' [cf. utə-, also təʀ-?; compare cažʀutə- under caðə-]
AAY #txutə- 'come ahead of, pass to the - of' [as in CAY]
CAY #tXutə- 'miss by passing too much toward the -' [with dem. roots or positional bases]
NSY #tXutə- 'miss the mark by shooting to the - side of the object' [ANLC]
CSY #tXutə-
Sir —
SPI #tqut(i)- 'pass to the - of' [with positional bases]
NAI #tqut(ɨ)- 'pass to the - of' [also #ut(ɨ)- with bases in ɨ(C) acc. MacLean]
WCI #tqut(i)- 'pass to the - of' [Cop also lʀut(i)-, from *žʀutə- — compare under cažʀutə- (caðə-)]
ECI #qqu(t)- 'pass to the - of' [also 'hit on the - (body part)']
GRI #qqut(i)- 'pass to the - of' [and note ut(i)- in qulaat(i)- 'pass above', as in NAI qulaut(ɨ)-]

PE tu-[1] 'have much or a big' [note Aleut tu- 'have much, a big', also tu- with emotional roots such as iʀatu- 'be afraid']
AAY +tu- 'have much' [and to verbal bases also 'be of great -ness'; note also (#)+tuuʀ- 'put on lots of']
CAY +tu- 'have to a large extent' [+tuli 'one that has — to a large extent']
NSY +tu- 'have many'
CSY +tu- 'have a lot'
Sir [cf. amtuʀ- under aməcu- and luXtəvalaX under əluʀ-]
SPI (#)+tu- 'have a lot or a big'
NAI (#)+tu- 'have (a) big -' [Jen. also has qquqtu-; note also llatu- 'enjoy -ing' — with which compare Aleut Vtu- under tu-[2]]
WCI +tu-, qquqtu- 'have a big or much -' [the second form with qquʀ?; Sig +tuuq 'one with a big -']
ECI +tu-, +taqtu- 'have a big or much -' [and +tuuq 'one with lots of -', #ttu(q)- 'get more']
GRI +tu-, qquʀtu- 'have a big or much -' [and +tuuq 'one with a big or much -', #ttuʀ- 'become more, get more' (with ʀ- under ŋ(ŋ)uʀ-)]

PE tu-[2] 'habitually' [note tu-[1] and tuʀ-[2] and perhaps Aleut Vtu-, (after C) aatu- 'want to, tend to'; there is some entanglement in Inu with nəʀtu-, q.v.]
AAY —
CAY tu- 'continually' [and tuli 'one who habitually -', NSU +tuinaʀ- 'always']
NSY [note tu- in nəXsatu- 'often catch seal']
CSY (+)tu- 'habitually'
Sir —
SPI tu- 'a lot, all the time' [+tuinaq- 'still, keep on -ing']
NAI (#)tu- 'excessively, hard, a lot (by nature or disposition)' [for qtu- in this sense see nəʀtu-; +tuin^{y}n^{y}aq- 'continually']
WCI tu- 'always, a lot, for a long time', +tuinnaq- 'all the time' [the former also 'be by nature' acc. Pryde, and in Car the latter 'just, only -' on nom. bases]
ECI tuin(n)aq- 'just, only' [also nominal]
GRI +tuinnaʀ-, ttuinnaʀ- 'all the time' [more commonly yuaannaʀ-, (after C) +tuaannaʀ- from yuaʀ- under ðuʀaʀ-]

PI tuaq 'only' [cf. tu-[2]?]
SPI —
NAI +tualuk 'only' [nominal; and Nu (nom. to nom. base) 'whichever']
WCI tuaq, Net pituaq 'only'
ECI tuaq 'only' [and note verbal +tuaq- 'play at -ing' in Lab 'only' acc. Bourq.]
GRI tuaq 'only'

PE tu(C)aʀ- 'finally' [there may be a link to tuaq]
AAY —
CAY —
NSY tuaʀ- 'at last'
CSY —
Sir —
SPI +tuaq- 'finally, for first time'
NAI [note Nu, Uum verbal tuaq(ami) 'every time']
WCI [note tuaq- 'as soon as' [with causative mood]
ECI [note tuaq- 'as soon as' (with caus. mood), tualli(C)- 'once', and Lab tua(ɣuni, etc.) 'I hope that, as long as -']
GRI (łła)tuaʀ- 'for once, at last'

PY tuqaq[1] 'one having to a high degree' [cf. tu-[1] and/or tu-[2], also PI tuqaq[2] and compare for the ending NSY p.b. yuqaq under yu-]
AAY #+tuqaq 'one that has - to a high degree' [and note C (#)+qaq, K (#)sqaq 'one that is -' with adjectival bases]
CAY #+tuqaq 'one that has - to a high degree'
NSY +tuqaq
CSY +tuqaq 'one that has - to a high degree' [and to verbal bases, when it may be truncating, 'one who habitually -s']

PI tuqaq[2] 'old' [from *tuqqaʀ? — cf. PE utuqqa(ʀ) (from which this could be a back formation), but compare also PY tuqaq[1] and the Inu past tense indic. forms under p.b. ðuʀ]
SPI —
NAI [Jen. has tuqaq 'old']
WCI (#)tuqaq 'same old', +yutuqaq 'always, still' [the latter may be used verbally as a 3rd person indic.]
ECI tuqaq 'old' [and verbally 'for a long time before or since']
GRI tuqaq 'old', NG hutuqaq, (after C) +tutuqaq 'still, all the time' [in NG can be used verbally as an indic. marker for all persons (optionally following past tense qqa-) in the sense 'has for a long time already', as a nominal 'one who long ago -ed, who has for a long time been -ing']

PE tuʀ 'would that' [enclitic]
AAY +tuq 'would that, I wish' [added directly to preceding word]
CAY +tuq 'would that, I wish' [preceding stop optionally fricativized]
NSY +tuq [ANLC]
CSY +tuq [preceding t optionally into s]
Sir +tuX 'would that' [Vakh. from Men.'s and Rub.'s texts — he also has it as an emphatic and as 'I wonder' with question words]
SPI +tuq 'would that'
NAI +tuq
WCI Car +tuq [Hansen]
ECI +tuuq
GRI +tuq 'would that' [also 'I wonder' with question words]

PE tuʀ-[1] 'use or consume'
AAY +(X)tuʀ-, tuʀ- 'eat'
CAY +tuʀ- 'eat' [less commonly 'use, wear']
NSY +tuʀ- 'eat' [ANLC also 'use, wear']
CSY +tuʀ- 'eat'
Sir [+cəʀ- 'eat]
SPI +tuq- 'eat' [less commonly 'use', Qaw also 'wear']
NAI +tuq- 'use, eat, wear'

WCI +tuq- 'eat, use'
ECI +tuq- 'eat, use, put on'
GRI +tuʀ- 'eat, use'

PE tuʀ-[2] 'repeated action' [cf. qðuʀ-, ðuʀaʀ- and Aleut tuʀ- 'many or several do']
AAY [for +tuʀ- 'one after another' see qðuʀ- (it is suppletive and belongs here)]
CAY #+tuʀ- 'for some time, repeatedly'
NSY +tuʀ- 'keep on -ing' [ANLC]
CSY +tuʀ- 'keep on -ing, do by repeated actions'
Sir +tuʀuʀ- 'for a short while' [also in trans. imperatives 'please, let's'; for +tuʀ- 'go after' see yaʀ(tuʀ)-; note also +tuʀ- 'almost', dropping preceding tə]
SPI (#)+tuq- 'repeated or prolonged action'
NAI #+tuq- 'repeated or prolonged action' [and 'habitually call (kin name)'; note also +tuq- or +tuula- after k/q bases in the sense 'quickly' — compare also liqtuq- at ləʀ-]
WCI +tuq- 'repeated action' [in Car 'pretend to' — compare ciqtuq-]
ECI +tuq- 'repeated action' [and (#)+tuuma 'several days in a row']
GRI (#)+tuʀ- 'repeated action' [mainly in comb. with (V)ʀ- 'say']

PY tu(C)uma- 'do or use together with?' [cf. tuʀ-[1] and (u)ma-]
AAY +(X)tuuma- 'have on, be equipped with'
CAY +(X)tuuma- 'act together with one's -, with one's - on' [plus sub. mood or in quantifier/qualifier construction]
NSY +tuuma- 'together with one's -' [in indep. rel. construction]
CSY +tuuma(ʀ)-
Inu [note Imaq +tuuma- 'while doing s.th. with -', presumably from the NSY, also ECI +tuuma- 'use or eat often' and GRI +tuuma- 'use or eat often, like to use or eat']

PI tuuq- 'act or speak like' [verbalization of aequalis case — compare q- with other cases]
Yup [note CSY +ti- 'speak (a language)']
SPI —
NAI —
WCI +tuuq- 'speak (a language)'
ECI +tuuq- 'act or speak like'
GRI #+tuuʀ-

PI tya- 'intend or be about to' [cf. ya- but also caʀ-; perhaps the t is t-[1]]
SPI tyaŋa-, 'yaŋa- 'intend to'
NAI —
WCI yya- 'shall, should' [esp. in orders and suggestions — also 'I wonder if -' (with subord. mood) in Cop acc. Pryde; takes indic. vuq, etc., older negative yyailaq, etc.; Net 'ya- 'vague future', 'yait- 'cannot', Car yyaŋŋit- 'will not (at all)']
ECI yyaŋ(ŋ)it-, SB, NBI yyaaŋŋit- 'will (definitely) not', yyai(t)- 'can or will not'
GRI ssa- (from *yya-), southern SWG, NWG also ssu-, EG tsu-/tsi- 'future, should ' [also modal 'must'; ssaŋa(tit)- 'think - will', EG tsaŋanaʀ- 'probably'; for NG ya- 'future' see ya-]

PE tyaɣ 'little or thing resembling s.th.' [cf. myaɣ-, payaaq- and tciaq — compare especially the forms like atsiaq there — preceded perhaps by ŋa-[2] as in the corresponding AAY and Inu forms below (compare also piayaaq under pi(-)); cf. also perhaps Aleut EA cxisa-X (with neg. ciða-X), Atkan cxiza-X, Att cixt[r]a-X 'nice, pretty' — but compare under kiɣ-]
AAY Kod caxaq 'little' [and note saaɣ- K pitiable one does', C 'pleasurable action', and K +a(a)yak, ŋaayak 'kind of a -', also verbal +a(a)yaɣ-, etc.]
CAY (#)+yak, HBC kcak 'thing similar to -, little' [compare the latter form with kšak, where it may belong, and with kyu(C)aʀ; for ya(ɣ)aq 'small, baby' see žaɣaq]
NSY —
CSY [note saaɣ-, yaaɣ- 'in a strange way', siiq* 's.th. like a -, little']
Sir —
SPI atyaaq, #asaaq 'young (of animal)' [Di has aɣaaq in some combinations]
NAI #ayaaq 'young'
WCI [note ŋayak, a nominalizer as in mmariŋayak 'one who -s well']
ECI [note (#)ŋayaak- 'almost, rather (of state)' and (#)ŋayaaq- 'be in a state of repeatedly -ing'; see tciaq for atsiaq 'young (animal)']
GRI NG yaaq- 'be -ish' [on adjectival quality bases; note WG ŋayaɣ-, #ŋayaaʀ- 'almost' (also nom. ŋayak) — with ŋa-[1] or ŋa-[2]? — and compare also tusaXXayaɣ- 'have heard s.th. or other' from tucaʀ- and #ayaaq 'rather' as in siłłayaaq '(s.th.) rather broad' from ciləɣ-; for atsiaʀ- 'a bit' see tciaq]

PI tyaiq- 'no longer' [cf. tya- and ŋiʀ-]
SPI —
NAI —
WCI yyaiq- '(can) no longer'
ECI yyai(q)- 'can or will no longer'
GRI ssaaʀ-, NG ssiiq- 'stop -ing, no longer'

U

PE uciʀ 'manner or means of doing s.th.' [cf. un]
AAY (u)ciq 'fact of -, quality of -' [usually supplanted today by +taciq under təkə-; note also (u)ciXkaitə- 'have no need or opportunity to -']
CAY (u)ciq 'condition of possessor with respect to -' [v-dr, uciq after C or ə and preceding tə to y]
NSY (u)siq 'devise for -ing' [ANLC]
CSY (u)siq 'device for -ing' [v-dr; usiq after C or ə]
Sir (ə)siʀaX 'device for -ing'
SPI usiq, (after V or t) žusiq 'means for, way of -ing' [drops semi-final weak i; note also (ž)usiuq 'make s.th.

for use in -ing']
NAI usiq, (with t bases) žžusiq 'manner, fact of -ing'
WCI uhiq 'manner of -ing' [but in Net rather 'device for -ing']
ECI usiq 'manner, action of -ing' [and Frob. Bay at least 'fact of -ing'; Spald. has NBI jjusiq after V]
GRI usiq 'manner of -ing' [and -ššusiq 'quality of -, -ness' with adj. bases']

PI uɣaq- 'continually' [the relat. — if any — to yuɣaʀ- and aʀ- is obscure, but compare manəɣyuɣaʀ- under manəɣ-]
SPI —
NAI uɣaq- 'continually'
WCI Sig uɣaq- 'continually' [and note Car uɣaq 'long and straight'?]
ECI uɣaq- 'a long time, slowly'
GRI [for variant #uaʀ- of yuaʀ- 'continually' see ðuʀaʀ-, though it may belong here]

PI umi- and **žuumi-** 'a little (more)' [the second form with ðuɣ?; there may be a relat. to ummiʀ- and/or miɣ-]
SPI —
NAI (ʀ)žuumi- 'begin to a little' [and note #+(m)mi- 'be in a state of, continue -ing' and +(m)mižaq- 'once in a while']
WCI Cop yuumi- 'a bit more'
ECI (yu)umi- 'a little more' [and umiɣi-, umiyaaq- 'still more'; NBI has y(y)uumi- 'a little']
GRI Vmi- 'a little' [also Vmiaʀ-; and note mišaaʀ- 'a little' and Vmišaaʀ- 'back and forth']

PE ummiʀ- 'suddenly (feel)' [from *ɣummiʀ? — cf. umi- and liq-?; compare with the Yup forms below ECI yumalliq- 'want intensely to', and GRI yumałłiʀ- 'get an urge to' under yuɣuma-]
AAY +yuumiʀ- 'want to' [with yuɣ-]
CAY +yuumiʀ- 'yearn to' [with yuɣ-]
NSY —
CSY —
Sir —
SPI —
NAI [note Mal ummi- 'enter state of -ing', additive after VVq at least]
WCI —
ECI ummi(q)- 'suddenly (feel)'
GRI ummiʀ-, ummi- 'suddenly (feel)' [and note NG allayuaʀummiq- 'feel shy' fʀom allayuaq- under atlayuɣ-]

PE un (utə-) 'means for doing' [alternating with geminating n, after full V tə- in PE; cf. uciʀ and q(q)un and Aleut Vsi-X, (after C) usi-X, old Atkan un (possessed uc-a, etc.) 'means, instrument for -ing'; Berg. points out that certain Aleut derivatives with a short V like iɣasi-X 'wing' from iɣa- 'take off' reflect the same kind of contraction-with-gemination as in Inu with this p.b.; perhaps the forms like utaq below reflect the origin in verbal utə- 'do with or for' (<*untə-?) plus pass. part. ðaʀ (compare 3s. rel. inflection -(ŋ)an, 3pl. -(ŋ)ata)]
AAY (#)un, (u)taq 'instrument for, cause of -ing' [with possessed endings and locative 'as soon as', with allative 'until']
CAY (u)n, (u)taq 'device for -ing' [v-dr; un after C or ə, fully productive only in HBC]
NSY (u)n, (u)tə, (u)taq 'instrument for -ing' [v-dr and drops semi-final ə; un after C or ə; ANLC also has kutaq 's.th. that one has for a -', with kə-[1]]
CSY (u)n, (u)ta(q) 'device for -ing' [v-dr; forms object clause of indirect questions 'whether, what' with abs. person endings]
Sir +(ə)ta, +(ə)taX 'devise for -ing' [probably secondary, from the inflected form of the base utə-]
SPI (u)n 'instrument, reason for -ing' [geminating n after V, drops semifinal weak i, fricativizes remaining k/q]
NAI (u)n 'means, cause, reason for -ing' [geminating n after vowel base, with ɨ into u, +un after VVk/q, +žun with t base, un with Vk/q base, dropping semi-final ɨ, fricativizing final k/q; also (#)(u)taq, #qun, #qutaq, #ŋutaq in 'means, instrument' sense]
WCI ut, (after V/t) yyut, (after VVk/q or weak ik/q) ɣut 'means, reason for -ing'
ECI ut, (after VVC) ɣut 'means, reason for -ing' [also lut with negative base; ɣut generalized in 'reason for' sense — as in NBI, SB yyut, which also occurs after VVC in 'means for' sense]
GRI (šš)ut 'means, reason for -ing' [ššut generalized in 'reason for' sense, but also found on V/t bases in 'means for' sense; also #ʀut, #q(q)ut and geminating #t after V]

PE (C)uʀ- 'repeated or prolonged action' [probably from *ɣuʀ-, going with Aleut frequentative causative ðɣu- 'make (several) -', where the ð represents causative t-[1] — cf. also anəɣuʀ- under anə- and taiɣuq- under ta(ɣ)i-]
AAY #uʀ- 'continuative, repeated action' [compare uʀ under qðuʀ-]
CAY #uʀ- 'purposeful repeated action'
NSY #uʀ-
CSY #uʀ- 'completely'
Sir [compare #uʀ- under atuʀ- at least]
SPI (#)uq- 'several do, collectively'
NAI #uq- 'repeated or prolonged action' [deletes penultimate ɨ, in which case it does not truncate a preceding C]
WCI #uq- 'repeated or prolonged action' [and Car uqqaq- 'several do'; Cop also uʀaq- acc. Pryde]
ECI #(qa)uq-, #uqqa(q)- 'several do'
GRI #uʀ-, #ɣuʀ- 'repeated or prolonged action', NG uqqaq- 'one after another'

PE utə- 'do with or for' [alternating with tə- after full V; cf. un, tʀutə- and Aleut Vsa-, (after t, which goes t, and m) usa-, (after polysyllabic bases in ɣ or ʀ) asa- 'do with, for, etc.', and note contracted Atkan tayasa- 'sell' from taya- 'buy'; probably not fully productive anywhere]
AAY (u)tə-, (after tə, which is dropped) citə 'do with, for,

reciprocally' [v-dr; utə- after C or ə; citə- also in other positions in K; also +(ɣ)itə-, (after tə) citə- 'do for' and intr. ʀutə- 'become' with neg./contrary tə bases; (u)tə- also sometimes a half-transitivizer]
CAY (u)tə- 'do with, for, reciprocally' [v-dr; utə- after C or ə and tə dropped or into y or (with neg./contrary base) l; intr. also used as a half-transitivizer on certain bases; note also (u)citə- 'do for, in place of']
NSY (u)tə- 'do for' [morphophonemics presumably as under un, but note iliɣ̥utə- under əlit-]
CSY (u)tə- 'do with, for, reciprocally' [v-dr; note also uutə-, (after C) +tuutə- 'do together, as a group'; also used as a half-transitivizer on certain bases]
Sir +(ə)tə- 'do with' [present = +(ə)təqəXtəʀa, etc., half-trans. əti-]
SPI uti- 'do with, for' [geminating ti- after V, drops semi-final weak i, fricativizing k/q, zuti after t and also sometimes V]
NAI (u)tɨ- 'do with, for, reciprocally' [morphophonemics as under un, with geminating tɨ- after V, etc.; note also (#)kkiuti- in comb. with ɣɨ- 'have as, etc.']
WCI (yy)ut(i)- 'do with or for, reciprocally' [morphophonemics as under un]
ECI ut(i)-, (after VVC) ɣut(i)- 'do with or for, in a group, reciprocally' [also #ɣɣut(i)-, #qqut(i)-, #kkut(i)-]
GRI (#)(šš)ut(i)-, (after VVC) yut(i)- 'do with or for, in a group, reciprocally' [ššut(i)- esp. in sense 'do for' (productive in this use) but also in other senses after V or t base; also lexicalized #ʀut(i)-, geminating #t(i)- and #kkut(i)- 'consider -' from comb. with ɣi- 'have as, consider', and XXat(i) 'in a group, many']

PE utəkə- 'have as means or reason for doing' [cf. un and kə-[1]; morphophonemics everywhere as for the former]
AAY (u)təkə- 'concerning, on account of' [with trans. conjunctive endings = 'as soon as']
CAY (u)təkə- 'concerning, on account of'
NSY [cf. anlanitəkə- under aŋla-]
CSY (u)tkə- 'on account of'
Sir —
SPI utiɣi- 'have as means or reason for -ing'
NAI utiɣɨ- 'have as means or reason for -ing' [followed by lla(q) and rel. endings = 'as soon as, at same time as']
WCI (yy)utiɣi- 'have as means or reason for -ing'
ECI utiɣi-
GRI (šš)utiɣi- 'have as means or reason for -ing' [ššutiɣi- generalized in 'have as reason' sense; also itiɣi- following bases in i(ʀ); utiɣi- plus contemp. = 'at same time as']

V

PE vaɣ(-) 'big or much' [vaɣ(-) only after V — the form is paɣ(-) after C, an alternation probably already in PE; cf. Aleut Vɣamax, (after C) iiɣamax 'main, major, adult (bird)', EA also 'favorite', Vɣamaxsi- 'too' (for the first element of which see yaɣ-) and note max in alamax 'humpback whale' from ala- 'whale' and some place names; the fixed forms with initial post-vocallic p are by generalization of the postconsonantal alternant; cf. vakaʀ-, vałłaɣ-[1] and vałuɣ(-)]
AAY #+(X)pak 'big' [also 'this or last -' on season/time bases], +waɣ, (after C) +paɣ- 'and then' [takes interrog. endings; also +(X)paɣuaʀ- 'greatly']
CAY Xpak 'big' [also (#)vak, esp. with bases in tə, which goes to l, with some irregular contractions], +vaɣ- 'so well', Xpaɣ-, HBC ʀvaɣ-, Nun ʀvaʀ- 'hard, very' [also (#)paɣ-, #vaɣ-, with irregular attachment patterns; and note uninflected exclamation +vaa 'how -!']
NSY Xpak 'major, large', #vak 'big' [ANLC, which also has paɣ- 'in a big way'; Men. has +pak '(frightening) big' (also pažaq), +vaqə- 'a lot', paaqə- 'any old way, carelessly' (also paxtuʀ-), and +vazuxtə- 'continuously']
CSY (#)Xpak 'big', vaɣ- 'hard, intensely'
Sir +pax, vax 'big'
SPI +(q)pak 'big' [verbal = 'a lot'], apak 'big'
NAI +(q)pak 'big' [verbal = 'much, hard'; also #vak(-), which is apparently more productive in Mal, esp. verbally in the 'much, hard' sense; in lexicalised forms it may indicate repetition, and (#)pak with time period bases = 'present or past -']
WCI +(q)pak, Sig +vak [i.e. +pak after C] 'big', +vak- 'repeated, habitual action, (experiential) perfect tense' [Sig +vakkaluaq- 'used to', 'big, very much'; Harper has vaŋuu- (for vaŋu-?) 'used to' for Baffin; Pryde also has +vaaq- 'strongly, very much for Cop]
ECI +pak- 'greatly, imperative strengthener', +vak- (or vak-) 'habitually' [may be nominal 'big' in Cape Dorset — Dor. has vaq-; also uninflected paa 'how -!', Lab 'very much', probably convergent with the similar CAY form]
GRI +(ʀ)paat, +(ʀ)paššuit 'many -', NG (q)paxxuaq- 'strongly, a lot' [also palaaʀ- 'more or less, half-heartedly', palaaq 'bad' and vaaʀ- 'greatly']

PY vaɣələɣ- 'before -ing' [initial p after C; cf. vaɣəl(l)uɣ-]
AAY K +wailɣaʀ-, C +wiillaʀ- (plus relative person endings) 'before -ing'
CAY +vailəɣ- (plus rel. endings) 'before -ing'
NSY —
CSY +vaɣiləɣ- (plus rel. endings) 'before -ing'

PE vaɣəl(l)uɣ- 'finally?' [initial p after C; cf. vaɣələɣ- and perhaps vaɣ(-)]
AAY —
CAY +vaaluɣ-, +vailuɣ- 'for first time (in a long time)'
NSY —
CSY —

Sir —
SPI Qaw +paaluk- 'have just -ed or begun to -'
NAI +vaalluk- 'finally' ['for first time' in Web. and Zib.]
WCI —
ECI vaallu(k)- 'too early, at bad time'
GRI —

PY vakaʀ- 'so much' [cf. vaɣ(-) and k(k)aʀ-]
AAY +wakaʀ-, +(X)pakaʀ- 'too much'
CAY +vakaʀ- 'so long', Nun Xpakaʀ- 'so much, so long'
NSY —
CSY —

PI valliq- 'appear to have started -ing?' [initial p after C; cf. valuk-, so from vaʀ- and liq-?; compare also vałłaɣ-[2]]
SPI +valia- 'probably'
NAI +valliq- 'appear to, probably, somewhat, sound like -ing' [also 'probably a -' on nom. bases]
WCI Sig +valliq- 'have started -ing', Cop +vallia(liq)- 'more and more' [Pryde has +vaalliq- 'more than before' and Cop +valiq- 'start -ing']
ECI (+)valli(q)- '(begin to) a bit more'
GRI —

PI valuk- 'sound or seem like' [initial p after C; cf. vaʀ- and tluk- if not the NG luk- under ʀuluk — also vałłaɣ-[2] and valliq-; compare GRI +(ʀ)pasiɣ- 'seem or act like' (with vaʀ-) under ðiɣ-, however there may be contam. here, the ultimate relationship being obscure]
SPI —
NAI +valuk- 'apparently, appear to be -ing' [and Web. and Zib. have vaaluk- 'sound of -']
WCI +valuk- Cop 'be heard, look like', Sig, Net 'look like a -, probably' [Pryde has +(q)paluk- 'look like, seem or act like' for Cop]
ECI +valuk- 'sound, seem like' [and nominal 'sound of']
GRI +(ʀ)paluɣ- 'seem like', +(ʀ)paluk 'sound of', NG +(q)paluk- 'sound like, speak (a language)'

PE vałłaɣ-[1] 'very much' [the p-initial forms from the post-consonantal PE alternants; cf. vaɣ and łłaɣ-; forms like Inu vallaaq- have an additional aʀ-]
AAY —
CAY +vałaɣ- 'intensely'
NSY vałaaq 'especially, above all' [attached to nom. bases]
CSY —
Sir +valaʀ-, +palaʀ- 'very' [on adjectival bases]
SPI +pałak- 'a lot, too much'
NAI +vallaaq-, Uum also +vałłaaq 'too much'
WCI +vallaaq- 'too much'
ECI —
GRI pałłaɣ- 'quickly', +vałłaaʀ- 'too much'

PE vałłaɣ-[2] 'seem or sound like' [cf. valuk-]
AAY —
CAY #Xpałaʀ- 'make the sound of -'
NSY —
CSY —
Sir —
SPI —
NAI —
WCI +vallak- 'perhaps, it is said, can be heard', Net, Car +valaaq- 'sound like' [Pryde has +(q)pallak- 'sound like -' for Cop]
ECI +vallak- 'sound, seem like', +vallai 'apparently', Lab ppalaaq- 'sound like', ppalai- 'seem like' [also nominal +vallaaq 'sound of']
GRI +(ʀ)pałłaɣ- 'it is said that, act like', +(ʀ)palaaʀ- 'seem, sound like' [for palaaq 'bad' see vaɣ]

PE vałuɣ(-) '(one that is) especially (big)?' [cf. vaɣ and łuɣ(-) if not tluk-]
AAY +(X)pałuk 'one especially or mostly -' [to nom. bases; to verbal bases +wałuʀ 'mostly']
CAY (X)pałuk 'one mostly -' [and on verbal bases +vałuɣ-, +vałuʀ- 'mostly'; note also paaXłuk, HBC vaaXłuk 'big']
NSY +vałuk 'one with a big -'
CSY +vałuq 'one with a big —, mostly -'
Sir +pałuX 'one with a big, much -'
SPI —
NAI pałłuk, Nu pałuk 'bad' [and verbal 'badly'; also paluk 'what a big -' — exclamatory, verbal = 'a lot, too much']
WCI [note Sig paluk- 'be glad that -' in Lowe; for Sig paaluk 'big' see aluk(-); Pryde has valuk 'a piece of, any old -' for Cop]
ECI [note SB, NBI paluk- 'a little', as enclitic = 'I guess, sort of']
GRI [NG paluk, Up palik 'poor little, naughty little' and NG paluxxuaq 'bad']

PE vaʀ- 'go toward' [may have alternated with paʀ- after C though the only evidence in Yup is CAY Xpałaʀ under vałłaɣ-[2]; cf. q-, viʀtə- and Aleut Vʀa-, uuʀa- 'come to, arrive at' with dem./positional bases (via *uaʀa- before the merger of v and m in Aleut); compare also the Yup allative case marker vət on dem. roots — the latter may also be the source of certain Inu verb bases with a fossilized p.b. vət- (or mət-) corresponding to Yup və- (or mə-) as in aqumə-, aquvət- or ətəvə(t)-]
AAY #+waʀ- 'go to, move toward' [on positional roots; note also trans. +waXtə 'move toward']
CAY #+vaʀ- 'go toward' [and note qfa(aq) 'area far in a direction'; note also +viaʀ- 'act toward in such an area' on dem. roots]
NSY #(+)vaʀ- [ANLC]
CSY #(+)vaʀ- 'go toward'
Sir [cf. uyəvaX under uyavaʀ- and kiŋuvaqu undcer kiŋu-]
SPI #+vaq-
NAI #+vaq- 'go toward' [does not regularly alternate with p after C, but note atpaq- 'go downward' under at(ə)-, the form found also in Canada and (as appaʀ-) Greenland; note also the locative extension (#)qpa(ni) 'area in a direction']
WCI #+vaq- 'go toward'
ECI #+vaq- 'go toward' [and note (+va)sik- under ðiɣ-, with +pasik- after C]
GRI #vaʀ-, +(ʀ)paʀ- 'go toward' [also lexicalized #aʀ-; note +(ʀ)pasiɣ- under ðiɣ-]

PY-S və(kə)-'negative subordinative' [the kə is probably part of the original neg. subordinative marker *kəna-; the və may be related to CSY evidential ftə- mentioned in note 31 to the Inflections, the negative lying originally in the special k(ə)na- forms of the subord. mood itself, as in Inu today; note the evidence for PE *k(ə)na- in the initial stop of Mal 2s neg. contemporative (= subordinative) tnak after a V (but e.g. qnaq after q), in Barrow just +nak causing gemination in the base — SPI has both patterns; note also neg. contemp. pinnani, etc., from pi- in GRI]
AAY +(x)ku-, AP +(x)kʷə- '(with neg. endings) negative' [Tyzhnev has +pəku- after C for Kod; used in conjunction with special forms of subordinative nani, etc., otherwise only found with negative/converse adj. bases in itə — compare yaqu(naɣ)]
CAY +fkə-, (after C) +pəkə-, HBC, Nun, NI +pəɣə [used as in AAY]
NSY +xpə- [used as in AAY; for fqa(a)(-vək) 'don't -' see vqaʀ-]
CSY +xpə- [used as in AAY; for neg. imp. fqaa- see vqaʀ-]
Sir +pə(-naŋ, etc.) 'negative imperative' [and Vakh. has aŋəpalaXpənani 'small' from aŋəpalaʀ- 'be large']

PE vinəʀ 'remains of or former' [the Yup forms are preceded by k(k)uʀ; for the ECI tense sense compare GRI nikuu- under k(k)uʀ]
AAY —
CAY —
CSY Chap k̠uvinʀaq 'remains of, former'
NSY k̠uvinʀaq 'remains of, former' [ANLC has quvinʀaq 'piece of -']
Sir kuvinʀaX 'remains of, former'
SPI [note sawiviniq 'piece of metal' under caviɣ]
NAI vinʸɨq* 'remains of, piece of -'
WCI viniq 'former, remains of -' [Cop miniq 'former' acc. Pryde]
ECI viniq, Cumb. Peninsula miniq 'former, remains of' [and verbally +yuviniq, trans. +yaviniq, etc. 'past tense'; for other than 3rd person subject viniu- with u 'be']
GRI miniq* 'piece of', NG 'former, remains of' [and miniʀ- 'a little']

PY viʀtə- 'go toward' [with the source of PI q- following allative ending vət?; cf. vaʀ- and tmi(C)artə-, also CAY xuiʀ- under k(k)u(C)aʀ-]
AAY +wiXtə- 'go toward (on dem. roots)'
CAY +viXtə- 'go toward' [on dem. roots and posit. bases taking allative case vət]
NSY —
CSY —

PE vkaʀ- 'cause or let' [cf. tət-, with which this p.b. is in complementary distribution in many forms of Eskimo (and probably PE)]
AAY xkʷaʀ- 'cause, let' [only after V bases]
CAY fkaʀ- 'cause, let' [only after V and optionally tə bases]
NSY fkaʀ- 'cause, let, compel to -' [ANLC; Men. has fkaqə- 'cause, let' — only after vowel base]
CSY —
Sir —
SPI Qaw pkaq- 'cause, let' [only after V; in KI only in lexicalized forms like niʀipkaq-]
NAI pkaq- 'cause, let' [only after V]
WCI pkaq- [only after V]
ECI (#)kka(q)-, Aiv pkaq- 'cause, try to get to ' [not just after V bases; more protracted than tit- according to Schn.]
GRI [note #kkaʀ- as in pikkaʀ- 'kill by magic']

PE vlaɣ- or **vəlaɣ-** 'a little' [perhaps from *vəl(l)aɣ-/pəl(l)aɣ- based on *vəɣ-/pəɣ- as reflected in the ECI below; cf. myaɣ-, žaɣaq and vžəʀaʀ- — phonaesthetic variation and/or contam. seems to be involved here]
AAY —
CAY vlaaɣ- 'insufficiently' [and note vɣuaʀ- 'a little bit' — from *vəɣ + ŋ(ŋ)uðaʀ(-)?]
NSY —
CSY vlaaʀ-, mlaaʀ-, vləʀaʀ-, mləʀaʀ- 'a little' vlaaq*, mlaaq* 'little thing like a -, a little bit of -' [and note (#)pəžaq 'small', also the vɣaq in nanəvɣaq 'old man']
Sir —
SPI —
NAI —
WCI Car vlak-, vla'naaq- '(a) little'
ECI [note vik- 'almost', also apik 'dear little' and NBI #pillak- 'a little, briefly']
GRI [note #pilaɣ-, #piłłaɣ-, #piʀaaʀ- 'a little, -ish']

PE vqaʀ- 'barely?' [cf. perhaps *vəɣ- at vlaɣ- above plus ʀaʀaʀ-?]
AAY —
CAY —
NSY fqa(a)žaʀ- 'with difficulty, barely, rarely' [and fqa(ami) 'although not', fqa(a)(-vək, etc.) 'don't -', fqažaq- 'only']
CSY fqa(ʀ)- (+ consequential endings) 'without -ing' [and in the neg. imperative fqaa(-vək, etc.) 'don't -']
Sir —
SPI pqaužaq- 'barely manage to' [also nominal]
NAI pqaq- 'barely', pqaŋa- 'enjoy -ing after so long' [and pqauzaq-, Uum pqaq- plus caus./condit. mood 'as soon as']
WCI pqaq- 'barely, just a bit'
ECI qqau- 'recent past'
GRI qqaʀ- 'barely', NG qqaq- 'recently' [and note qqaŋŋit- 'a lot']

PY-S vžəʀaʀ- 'a little (more)' [cf. myaɣ- and vlaɣ-; there seems to be considerable entanglement of these sets, esp. in CSY — phonaesthetic variation?]
AAY —
CAY vziaʀ-, HBC vyiaʀ- '(even) more'
NSY vžiaʀ- 'again' [and note vžəɣ-, mžəɣ- 'barely', vžəɣaq 'little' (ANLC 'thing like a -'); for vyuaʀ- 'barely' see mcuɣ-]
CSY vžaaʀ-, vzaaʀ-, mžaaʀ-, mzaaʀ-, vžəʀaʀ-, vzəʀaʀ-, mžəʀaʀ-, mzəʀaʀ- 'a little' [and note vziʀ- 'almost'; for

msiiʀ- 'ineffectively' see mcuɣ-]
Sir vžəʀaX 'tiny', vžəʀ- 'barely, almost' [the latter Vakh. from Men.'s texts — Men. has vžiʀ- and cf. mcəʀaX in qavimcəʀaX under qavəyaʀ]
Inu [note Imaq vžiʀaq- 'repeatedly' — from the NSY? — and Car EP vʀaq-, vva(q)- 'a little, almost' acc. Schn.]

Y

PE ya- 'be liable or apt to' [cf. tya-, yaʀ- and Aleut Vka- (after C) iika-, earlier saka after t (that dropped) 'can, should', the ka of which may correspond to that of PE kayuɣ-; Yup and SPI forms have ŋ(ŋ)uʀ- fused on.]
AAY +yauXtə- 'begin to', +yanaʀ- 'seem to, look like —ing' [opp. = +yanaitə-]
CAY +yauXtə- 'learn to'
NSY yauxtə- [for yauXtə-?] 'have begun to'
CSY +yaaXtə- 'learn to'
Sir —
SPI +yauq- 'know how to'
NAI ya- 'easily', yasi- 'be about to, make easy to -'
WCI —
ECI —
GRI ya- 'be apt to, can easily', NG ya- 'vague future ' [and yaat- 'be not likely to', yaŋŋit- 'cannot (ever)', NG yaaq 'one who tends to -']

PE yaɣ- 'have many' [cf. Al yaɣ- in Atkan yaɣða-/yaɣza- + neg. 'rarely', also perhaps the first element in Aleut Vɣamax under vaɣ(-), and Vɣatumasu- 'probably']
AAY —
CAY Nun, HBC +yaɣ- 'be much, many', and elsewhere in yuɣyaɣ- 'to have many people' only [and perhaps siyaaɣ-, Y saaɣ- 'too' (with adj. bases) — preceded by ðiɣ-?]
NSY +yaɣ- 'have lots of -' [ANLC; Men. has +yak 'a lot of -']
CSY (#)+yaɣ- 'increase in number', +yaɣət 'lots of -'
Sir +yax- 'group of -'
SPI [note ayaat 'lots of']
NAI [note #ɣiak- in inʸuɣiak- 'be many' from inʸuk 'human being']
WCI ɣiak- 'have many' [generalized from combination with inuk as in NAI?; ɣiaktut 'crowd or group of -']
ECI (#)ɣiattut 'many, crowd of -'
GRI #iaɣ- 'be full of -', #(ɣ)iak 'collection of -'

PY yailkun and **yailkutaq** 'means for preventing' [cf. yaʀ-, ŋit- and perhaps kə[1] and un, and compare ŋilitaʀ]
AAY —
CAY +yaiłkutaq, +yaiłkun 'device to prevent -ing'
NSY +yiałkutaq [ANLC]
CSY —

PY-S ya(a)qə- 'hypothetical or irrealis condition [cf. yaʀ- and perhaps ʀqə-]
AAY +yaaqə- Kod 'almost', C 'because -' [with conj. mood]
CAY +yaaqə- 'in vain, but . . .'
NSY +yaqə- 'if (hypothet./irrealis)' [with condit. mood]
CSY — [compare contrafactual yaʀ- under yaʀ-]
Sir yəqə-, məyəqə- 'if (irrealis)' [with condit. mood]

PE yaqu(naɣ) negative imperative [cf. yaʀ- and Aleut neg. optative Vʀana-, (after ɣ or ʀ) iiʀana-, (after t, deleted) saaʀana-; naɣ is the special 2s negative contemp./subordinative mood marker, so the qu probably reflects the original neg. contemp./sub. marker *kəna as under və(kə)-]
AAY —
CAY +yaqu(nak) negative imperative [the same special neg. subord. endings are used with neg. imperative viiq-, (after C) +piiq- 'stop -ing', probably containing vaɣ(-)]
NSY —
CSY +yaqu(naŋ) neg. imperative, 'don't (ever)' [and compare fqaa- under vqaʀ-]
Sir —
SPI —
NAI —
WCI —
ECI —
GRI łłaʀiaa(nak) neg. imperative (strengthener) [in Ordbogêraq older łłariaʀu(nak) — note łłaq- for the first element; note also neg. imperative qi-nak, etc., and p.b. qina-, southern SWG also qinu- 'watch out (since s.th. untoward might or is about to happen)', which seem to represent reanalyses, the former as if with intensifier qi- under ʀqə-]

PE yaʀ 'place or thing where action takes place?' [the exact meaning is difficult to determine, perhaps already non-productive in PE; cf. yaʀka(C)u- and ɣiaqaq-, also yaʀ-?]
AAY #yaq [as under aŋyaq and taluyaʀ; for +yaʀau 'must' see yaʀka(C)u-]
CAY #yaq [as under aŋyaq and taluyaʀ; note also productive +yaʀaq 'way of or device for -ing'
NSY +yaʀaq 'way to -, instrument for -ing' [ANLC; and note yaq in anyaq at least]
CSY [note yaq in aŋyaq at least and note Chap nuɣyaʀaq 'entrance from passage into interior of house' in nuɣyaʀaq under nuɣə-]
Sir [note aŋyaq under aŋyaq at least, also itəʀyaʀaX 'entrance from passage into interior of house (from itəʀ-) in Em.]
SPI —
NAI (#)iaq 'area where action occurs'
WCI #ʀiaq 'place where action occurs', ɣiaq, (after V, with ðaʀ) yaʀiaq 'action of -ing' [also forms object clauses of asking, etc., as does Cop ɣiaxxaq, (after V) yaaxxaq, (after t) +taaxxaq with poss. endings]
ECI ɣiaq, NBI, SB also (after V/t) +yaʀiaq '(one's) action of -ing'
GRI (#)ʀiaq, (#)ɣiaq 'place or thing where one -'

PE yaʀ- 'would' [cf. ya-, yaʀ, ya(a)qe-, yaqu(naɣ) and perhaps yaʀ(tuʀ)-, also Aleut optative and intentional mood markers Vʀ-, (after C) iiʀ-, (after t, deleted) saʀ-, from earlier yaʀ-; note also Aleut aaʀa- 'miss, not get or find anything', (as aux.) Atkan, Att 'in vain', EA Vʀ(a)li-, (after C) iiʀ(a)li-, (after t) saʀ(a)li- 'in vain, for a long time, nevertheless']
AAY +nayaʀ- 'would, could (have)' [with na-]
CAY +yaʀ- 'would (contrafactual)' [and +yaXpiaʀ-, HBC +yaXpiɣaʀ-, NSU +yaʀ- 'almost']
NSY +nayaʀ- 'would', (u)mayaʀ- 'would have (but didn't)' [and qɣaʀ- plus part. tuq, etc. 'although -'; for łəqɣaʀ- 'almost' see c(c)iʀyaʀ-; ANLC has +yaʀ- 'in vain']
CSY +yaʀ- 'in vain, but...' [saʀ- after tə base; also +yaXpətə- 'evidently in vain', +nayaʀ-, Chap also mayaʀ- 'would (irrealis)', the former also 'could' in polite requests]
Sir [Vakh. has yaʀ- in qivaʀyaXtəX 'he was about to turn']
SPI +nayaq-, (after k/q) ɣayaq- 'could have (if one had wanted)', Qaw 'should' (have)'
NAI +nayaq-, +ɣayaq- 'would' [in Uum the second variant only after k/q; opp. +nayait-, etc.; Nu +nayautnaq- 'might, maybe'; Jen. has yaʀiaq- 'be about to']
WCI Net +nayaq-, Car +nayaq-, (after k/q at least) ɣayaq- 'would' [in the latter often 'reduced' to +na-, ɣa-, esp. by children, acc. Schn. — compare Sig +na-, ɣa- under na-; Pryde has Cop +niaq- 'would', also 'let's hope that -' (with neg. subord. mood), probably influenced by ni(C)aʀ-]
ECI ɣayaq-, nayaq-, (after V/t only) +(n)nayaq- 'would'
GRI —

PE yaʀ(tuʀ)- 'go (in order to)' [cf. tuʀ-[2] and ɣiaq- and perhaps also yaʀ-; the ɣ-initial Inu forms may be influenced by ki-]
AAY +yaʀ-, +ya(X)tuʀ- 'go in order to, go -ing'
CAY +yaXtuʀ- 'go in order to -', #+yaʀ- 'go -ing'
NSY +yaXtuʀ 'go in order to -' [and note +yalʀia- (plus pers. endings) 'when, after -ing'; ANLC has +yaʀ- 'go -ing, because of -ing']
CSY +yaʀ- 'go in order to -' [with nom. base = 'hunt'], +yaXtuʀ- 'be about to, go somewhere in order to -' [and note (#)+saXtuʀ- 'hunt' only after C bases]
Sir [note +tuʀ- 'go after']
SPI yaqtuq- (Qaw yaqtuaq-), (after t only) saqtuq-, (after k/q only) ɣiaq- 'go in order to -'
NAI yaqtuq-, yaqtuaq-, (after t) +saqtuq-, +saqtuaq-, (after k/q) ɣiaq- [and yyaq- causing gemination after (C)VCV bases, Mal tyaq-, as in niʀʀiyyaʀin[y], Mal niʀityaʀin[y] 'come and eat' and note Nu pityaq- 'hurry to do s.th.']
WCI yaqtuq-, (after k/q) ɣiaq(tuq)- 'go in order to -' [ɣiaq as nom. = 'someone going to -']
ECI yaqtu(q)-, (after k/q) ɣiaqtu(q)-, (after t) +saqtu(q)- 'go in order to -' [the second form may also be used after a V or t base]
GRI +ɣiaʀtuʀ-, (after V) yaʀtuʀ-, +ɣiaʀ- 'go in order to', (+ɣi)yaʀtuʀ-, (+ɣi)yaʀtuaaʀ- 'more and more' [forms like ɣiaʀ- after V presumably generalized from after velar bases]

PE yaʀaʀ- 'early' [cf. yaʀ(tuʀ)- and saaq-, also tya- and caʀ-[1], though the relat. is obscure]
AAY +yaaʀ- 'do early'
CAY +yaʀaʀ-
NSY +yaʀaʀ- ' (too) early'
CSY +yaʀaʀ- 'early' [saʀaʀ- with bases in tə and after voiceless C in general]
Sir —
SPI [note Qaw +naʀiaq- 'early' — compare nasuk-]
NAI [note +naʀiaq- 'early', also #ɣiaq — compare ɣiaq-]
WCI yaaq- Net 'soon, early, about to', Sig 'be -ing, for a long time' [the latter may reflect a link to ɣiaq-; Met. has yaʀaq- 'quickly' and #ɣiaq- 'early']
ECI —
GRI yaaʀ- 'early', NG yaaq- 'future, be about to'

PY yaʀka(C)u- 'must' [cf. yaʀ, kðaʀ- and ŋu-, also zukšau-]
AAY [note +yaʀau- 'must', yaʀaitə- 'not have to' and +yaʀauXtə- 'be time to -' — directly from yaʀaq as in CAY under yaʀ?]
CAY [note +(ɣ)aXkaq 'thing which will -, which is to be -ed', +(ɣ)aXkau- 'should, will eventually', with ðaʀ rather than yaʀ, as in žakšau- under žukšau- although it is used on both transitive and intransitive bases — contam.?]
NSY +yaXqaa(w)-, (after tə which drops) saXqaa(w)- 'should' [and +yaXqa(a)piyu- 'will definitely']
CSY +yaXqaq 's.th. that will -, s.th. that is to be -ed', +yaXqaa-, trans. +yaXqaqə- 'should'
Sir [for +yukcəʀə- 'have to' see žukšau-]
Inu [for Cop ɣiaxxaq-, yaaxxaq- in object clauses of asking see yaʀ-]

PE yu- or **ðu-** 'be good at -ing' [cf. yunaʀ-, yu(ŋ)it- and Aleut zu-, EA su- 'be good at -ing', also ðu- 'fast'; this p.b. has largely gone over to yu- in Esk, but note especially the second SPI form below — there may be contam. with qðuʀ- in suppletive (?) forms like suq-]
AAY yu- 'be good at -ing'
CAY yu- 'be good at -ing' [ə-dr; note also yuli(q) 'one good at -ing']
NSY yu- 'well' [ANLC; Men. has +yuqaq 'one good at -ing'; for žuɣaq 'good' see ðuɣaʀ]
CSY yu- 'be good at -ing' [also as nominal 'one good at -ing']
Sir —
SPI yu- '(habitually) well' [also žuq-, (after C) +suq- 'well' — usually in combination with k 'catch' in sense 'always get lots of (in hunting)']
NAI [+suq-, (after k/q) yuq- 'well' and compare aŋusu(q)- 'be a good hunter' under aŋu-; for yuk- 'tend to' see yuɣ-]
WCI Net, Car (Esk. Point) yu-, Sig yu-, (after C) +suq-, Cop (#)+huq- 'do well (esp. of catching animals)' [B. Lake Car yu- 'usually, can' acc. Hansen]
ECI #yu-, #su- 'be good at -ing' [and note aŋusuqtuq 'good hunter' under aŋusu(q)-
(aŋu-)]
GRI [note tuʀaayu- 'be good at hitting (with weapon)' under tuʀaaq- and aŋuʀsuɣ- under aŋusu(q)- (aŋu-)]

PE yu(C)aʀ- 'might or be liable to' [cf. yuɣ- and aʀ-? — but also nasuk-, nasuaq-]
AAY +yuaʀ- 'lest, might (of s.th. bad happening)' [and nnəcuaʀ- plus indic. PWS 'so that - not', but in KP and Kod apparently in positive sense 'in order to']
CAY +yuaʀ- (plus indic.) 'lest -'
NSY —
CSY —
Sir —
SPI —
NAI ŋisuaq- (plus condit.) 'unless, until'
WCI Car +huaq-, (after k/q) ɣuaq- 'want to'
ECI ɣuaq-, suaq- 'can easily, tend to', Aiv +suaq-, (after k/q) ɣuaq- 'want to' [and ɣuit- 'have difficulty -ing, tend not to']
GRI —

PE yuɣ or **ðuɣ** 'thing resembling s.th.' [presumably from *ðuɣ — compare yu-, ðu-; cf. aʀzuk, k(k)uyuɣ and Aleut ðux 'approximately' as in aliʀðux 'middle-aged man' from aliX 'old man'; see respectively tuntuʀðuɣ under tuntu and təŋayuɣ under təŋaɣ for PE post-consonantal and post-vocalic allomorph examples; largely limited in Inuit to names of constellations and string figures]
AAY #yuk 's.th. like a -' [in təŋayuɣ under təŋaɣ at least]
CAY #(+)yuk 'thing like a -'
NSY #yuaq, #suaq 'non-normal sort of -, special, small, thing like a -' [ANLC, but cf. also təŋayuk under təŋayuɣ (təŋaɣ)]
CSY #yuk [in təŋayuɣ under təŋaɣ at least; note also pəžuk 'thing like a -']
Sir —
SPI #yuk
NAI #yuk, #žuk 'thing like a -'
WCI [Pryde has Cop (#)huk 'substitute, makeshift -' and note Net #žuk under tuntuʀðuɣ (tuntu) at least]
ECI #yuk, #suk 'thing like a -' [the latter as in nuliasuk under nuliʀ(aʀ)]
GRI #yuk, #suk

PE yuɣ- 'want or tend to' [cf. kayuɣ(-), nasuk-, yuɣŋa-, yukə-, suu- and Aleut yu- with a few emotional bases such as irayu- 'be afraid, respectful' and qumyuɣ- 'love', also Atkan yuuɣ- 'try or want not to' with the neg. (as yuuɣlakaX, cont. yuuɣlakan; also 'a little') and perhaps EA yuɣaaða-, Atkan yuɣaaʀ- 'for a short while' (the first form with Vða- under ŋ(ŋ)uðaʀ-); this p.b. apparently also had a nominalizing/participial function (compare kayuɣ)]
AAY +yuɣ- 'tend to', (with nom. bases) +(ʀ)yuɣ- 'want -' [with emot. roots (#)+yuɣ- 'feel (for the moment)']
CAY +yuɣ- 'want to, tend to', (with emot. roots) 'feel' [+(ʀ)yuɣ- 'want -' with nominal bases; note also NS +yuɣaʀ- 'enjoy -ing']
NSY +yuɣ- 'want, promise to', (with emot. roots) 'feel'
CSY +yuɣ- 'want to', (with emot. roots) 'feel' [also less productively 'want' with nom. bases]
Sir +yuɣ- 'want to' [and cf. unaʀəʀyuɣ- under una(C)iʀ-; also apparently used in optative mood — note yukə-]
SPI +suk-, (after k/q) ɣuk- 'want to, future tense', (#)suk- (with emot. roots) 'be in state of -ing' [and +(s)ukpak-, Qaw +(s)uɣuu- 'like to' — with which compare suu-]
NAI +suk-, (after k/q) ɣuk- 'want to', (#)yuk- 'have a tendency to', (to emotional roots) (#)suk- 'be in state of -ing' [note also nom. qinʸiyuk 'one who peeks' from qinəʀ-]
WCI yuk- 'tend, want, like to, often, be quick to', ɣuk- 'want to' [to nom. bases = 'want -'; (#)(ɣu)huk- 'be inclined to' (esp. to emot. roots), Sig +suk-, Net +huk- (after k/q) ɣuk- 'want to'; note also +(s)ulait- 'would not']
ECI ɣusuk-, suk- 'want, need, be inclined to' [the first form a doubling; also to emot. roots and, as ɣuk- 'want', with nom. bases; for Baffin yuu- 'distant past' see suu-]
GRI ʀusuɣ-, (after ɣ or t) +ɣusuɣ-, EG ŋusuɣ- 'want to' [a doubling of the p.b. with the uvular or velar allomorph first; yuɣ- 'thirst or long for' on nominal bases and (#)suɣ- 'feel' on emot. roots]

PY yuɣŋa- 'be able or ready to' [cf. yuɣ- and ŋa-[1]]
AAY —
CAY K, BB +yuɣŋa- 'be able to' [compare Y yuuma- under yuɣuma-]
NSY +yuŋɣa- 'intend'
CSY —

PE yuɣuma- 'want to' [cf. yuɣ- and (u)ma-, also yumaaq-]
AAY +yuuma- 'could (in polite requests)' [+yuumu- before u]
CAY +yuuma- Y, NS, HBC 'be able to', K, BB 'be ready to' [for +yuumiʀ- 'yearn to -' see ummiʀ-]
NSY —
CSY +yuɣuma- 'be easy to -'
Sir +yuɣumə- 'please (let) -' [used in requests]
SPI yuma-, (after k/q) ɣuma-, (after t) suma(uq, etc.) 'so that, should, it is to be hoped that -'
NAI +yuma-, (after k/q) +kuma-, ɣuma- 'be eager, willing to, should, so that' [takes short form uq, etc. of indic.]
WCI +yuma- 'want to' [morphophonemics as for yuŋnaq- at yuknaʀ-; llaɣuma- 'feel like -ing', Sig +yuma(a)llak- 'get a desire to -', Net (nominal) 'one fond of -ing', Car kkuma- 'want as a -']
ECI ɣuma-, (optionally to V bases) yuma- 'want to' [with t optionally tsuma-; note also ɣumalli(q)- 'want intensely to' (with liq-?) and Lab ɣumaluaq- 'prefer to']
GRI +yuma- 'want to', EG (ŋ)ima-, NG +yama-, ɣama- [morphophonemics as for +yunnaʀ(si)- under yuknaʀ-; note also +yumałłiʀ- 'get an urge to']

PI yuiq- and **suiq-** 'can no longer' [cf. yu- and yuɣ-, apparently entangled here, and ŋiʀ- and compare yu(C)it-]
SPI —
NAI suiq-, (after k) ɣuiq-, (after q) ʀuiq- 'no longer want to'
WCI Cop huiq-, ɣuiq- 'no longer'
ECI suiq-, ɣuiq- '(can) no longer'
GRI #yuiʀ-, #suiʀ- 'no longer'

PE yu(C)it- 'never or cannot' [cf. yu- and/or yuɣ- and ŋit- — the two NSY forms suggest conflation elsewhere]
AAY +yuitə- 'seldom, not be good at -ing'
CAY yuitə- 'never' [ə-dr; with tə ~ l alt.]
NSY yiitə- '(habitually) not, never have -ed' [but yuitə- 'poorly' — ANLC]
CSY [yiitə- 'poorly']
Sir —
SPI +suit- 'habitually not' [indic. +suilaq, etc.; Qaw also yuit-]
NAI (+)suit-, (after k/q only) yuit- 'never, not be able to - well' [suit- is additive to t base but may be truncating to k/q ones; nominal #yuilʸaq, suilʸaq]
WCI yuit, (+)huit- 'cannot, never' [Sig suit- after V, yuit- after C]
ECI yuit-, suit- 'cannot any more, never'
GRI yuit- 'never, cannot' [also #suit- — in NG yuit- is 'never' and +huit- 'can never'; yuinaaʀ- 'not - despite expectations']

PY yukaʀ- 'be about to' [cf. yukə- and aʀ-?]
AAY —
CAY +yukaaʀ(aʀ)- 'be ready to, about to'
NSY —
CSY +yukaʀ- [de Reuse]

PE yukə- 'think that' [from yuɣ- and kə-[1]? — cf. yuknaʀ-; for the forms with initial na or ɣa see na-]
AAY +yukə- 'think that -' [for +nauʀyukə- see under na-]
CAY +yukə- 'think that one is -ing', +nayukə- 'think that — might'
NSY +nayukə- (plus subordinative mood) 'thinking that, so as to -' [some of Men.'s examples require the gloss 'lest', i.e. have a negative sense]
CSY [for +nayu- plus condit. 'lest -', used principally as a negative optative 'may - not' (probably a reanalysis of nayukə-), see na-]
Sir +yukə- (with 3rd person subj.) +yuŋə- 'let - (transitive optative)' [this may go directly with yuɣ-]
SPI —
NAI +nasuɣɨ-, (alternatively after C) +ɣasuɣɨ-, Mal +našuk- 'think that -' [note also +suɣa-, (after k/q) ɣuŋa(uq, etc.) 'don't you recall that -']
WCI +nahuɣi-, (after k/q) ɣahuɣi- 'think that' [and less commonly (#)+yuʀi-, (#)+huɣi-; Sig +suɣi-, (after k/q) ɣuɣi-]
ECI +yuʀi-, NBI, SB +nasuɣi-, (after k/q) ɣasuɣi- 'think that' [the latter also given for Lab by Bourq.]
GRI +(ɣa)suɣi-, +(ɣa)suʀi-, +nasuɣi-, +nasuʀi- 'think that -' [i.e. +suɣi- or +ɣasuɣi-, etc. following any base; the alternative forms with initial na are particularly common in NWG, NG and in EG, which has +nasii- = NG +nahii-, +nihii-]

PI yuknaiq- 'no longer (can)' [cf. yuknaʀ- and ŋiʀ-, also yuknaʀit-]
SPI —
NAI —
WCI +yuŋnaiq- 'can no longer'
ECI (yya)ɣunnai(q)-, yunnai(q)-, NBI, SB yun(n)iiq-, ɣun(n)iiq- 'no longer'
GRI +yunnaaʀ-, ɣunnaaʀ-, EG ŋinnaaʀ-, ŋunnaaʀ-, NG yuŋniiq-, ɣuŋniiq- 'no longer'

PE yuknaʀ- 'probably' [cf. yukə- and naʀ- (and esp. the Mal form below), also yuknaʀit- and yuknaiq-; the ɣ in the Yup forms like yuɣnaʀ may be due to yuɣ-, but note also the general entanglement with yunaʀ-, q.v.]
AAY +yuɣnaʀ- 'maybe' [Perry also +yunaʀ-, influenced by yunaʀ-?]
CAY +yuɣnaXqə- 'probably' [morphophonemics as for yuɣ-]
NSY —
CSY [for +yuɣnaʀ- 'be easy to -' see yunaʀ-]
Sir [Vakh. has uɫəʀyuɣnaʀunaʀən 'in order not to fall' from Men.'s texts]
SPI yuŋnaq-, (after k/q) ɣuŋnaq-, (after t) suŋnaq- 'may, must have -ed'
NAI +suɣnaq-, (after k/q) ɣuɣnaq-, Mal +suknaq-, ɣuknaq- 'probably'
WCI +yuŋnaq-, (after k/q) ɣuŋnaq-, (after t) +tuŋnaq- 'no doubt, probably, can' [also +yuŋnaXXi- or, acc. Lowe, +yunaXXi-; Sig +suŋnaq- also after V/t in Met.; note also +yunaq- 'really, sure' (influenced by yunaʀ-?) — with caus. mood = exclamatory 'how -!' — Pryde has 'presumably' rather]
ECI ɣunna(q)-, yunna(q)- 'can' [second form optional with V base only, tsunaq- optional with t base; note also ɣunatsa(q)- 'be likely to, probably' and, with a nuance of wishing acc. Schn., ɣunaitsa(q)-, influenced by yunaʀ-?; as a nominalizer ɣunaq- = 's.th. which seems to be -']
GRI +yunnaʀ(si)- 'probably, no doubt' [i.e. +kunnaʀ(si)- after ɣ/t, +ʀunnaʀ(si)- after ʀ; note also piunnaʀtut 'those that can' with pi(-) and +ɣunaʀ- 'it seems, looks like', influenced by yunaʀ-?]

PE yuknaʀit- 'probably not' [cf. yuknaʀ- and ŋit-, also yuknaiq-]
AAY [for K +yuɣnaitə- 'not readily' see yunaʀ-]
CAY +yuɣnaitə- 'definitely not'
NSY —
CSY [for +yuɣniitə- 'not be easy to -' see yunaʀ-]
Sir —
SPI —
NAI Mal +(š)uknait- 'probably not' [morphophonemics as for +(s)suɣnaq under yuknaʀ-]
WCI +yuŋnait- 'will certainly not'
ECI yyaɣunnai(t)-, Lab ɣunait- 'will definitely not' [and Harper also has yun(n)aŋŋit- 'cannot, never' for Baffin — entanglement with yunaʀ-?]
GRI +yunnaŋŋit-, +ɣunaŋŋit- 'probably not, I don't think that —'

PI yumaaq- 'vague future' [cf. yuɣuma- and aʀ-]
SPI —
NAI +yumaaq- 'intend to'
WCI +yumaaq- 'vague future'
ECI ɣumaaq-, (optionally to V bases) yumaaq-
GRI +yumaaʀ- 'vague future' [and Ges. has (ŋ)imaaʀ- 'future' for EG]

PI yuminaq- 'be good or easy to' [cf. yu-, umi- and naʀ- — influenced by yuɣ- and yuknaʀ- for the morphophonemics; compare yunaʀ- and also takuminaq- under taku-]
SPI +yuminaq- 'be able to' [morphophonemics as for +yuma- at yuɣuma-]
NAI +yuminʸaq- 'be possible, all right to -', Nu 'can, could, would' [contrary = +yuminʸait-]
WCI +yuminaq-, +yuminaXXi- 'can now, be easy to -' [and +yuminait- 'cannot, will not']
ECI +yuminaq- 'be desirable to' [morphophonemics as for +yuma-, ɣuma-, but with quyuminaq- for 3rd person subject; with nom. base kkuminaq 'be good as a - ']
GRI +yuminaʀ-, EG (ŋ)imiaʀ- 'be easy, good to -' [morphophonemics as under yuknaʀ-; contrary = +yuminaat-; with nom. base kkuminaʀ- 'be good as a -']

PE yunaʀ- 'be easy or possible to' [cf. yu- and naʀ-, also yuknaʀ-, with which there has been considerable entanglement]
AAY [note K +yuɣnaitə- 'not readily, not be conducive to', for Perry yunaʀ- 'maybe' see yuknaʀ-]
CAY yunaXqə-, yuɣnaXqə- 'be possible to, tend to induce one to -' [ə-dr; the second form influenced by yuknaʀ-; contrary = yunaitə- 'be impossible to, not tend to induce one to -'; note also yunaʀi- 'be the proper time to -']
NSY yunaʀ- 'be such as to cause one to -' [ANLC; contrary = yuniatə-; Men. has +yuɣnalʀia 'one capable of -ing' — by contam. with yuknaʀ-?]
CSY [note +yuɣnaʀ- 'be easy to -', +yuɣniitə- 'not be easy to, not want to -', influenced by yuɣuma- and/or yuknaʀ-]
Sir —
SPI —
NAI +suʀnaq-, (after k/q) yunaq- 'be easy to -'
WCI [for Cop yunaq- 'presumably' see yuknaʀ-]
ECI —
GRI [for +ɣunaʀ- 'it seems, looks like' see yuknaʀ-]

PY yu(u)q 'vocative'
AAY (#)+yuuʀaa 'sing. vocative of demon. pronouns' [removes -na from abs. bases]
CAY (#)+yuuq [as AAY]
NSY —
CSY (#)+yuq [as AAY; note also voc. y on vowel bases such as apaay grandfather!'; compare non-sing. equivalent ʀsi, as also in Inu]
Sir [Em. has uyuX 'hey you' from una — from CSY equivalent uyuq?]
Inu — [compare lengthened forms like uumaak, pl. ukuʀsii 'hey you!' based on the rel. case of demonstrative una, uku]

PE yyaɣ- 'reach state of'
AAY +yaɣutə- 'finally' [with utə-]
CAY +yaɣutə- 'reach state of -ing' [ə-dr; can be used directly with emot. roots]
NSY +yaɣutə- [ANLC]
CSY +yaɣutə- 'reach state of -ing' [ə-dr; can be added directly to emot. roots]
Sir —
SPI —
NAI (#)tcak- 'become' [with emot. roots]
WCI (#)tsak-
ECI (#)tsak-
GRI (#)tsaɣ-

Ž

PY-S žaɣ- 'quickly' [cf. Aleut ðaɣ- as in xaðaɣ- 'move fast' under kəɣaɣ-]
AAY —
CAY [note kəxaɣ- 'be a fast eater' under kəɣaɣ-]
NSY +aXquʀ- 'fast' [with qðuʀ-?]
CSY (#)žaxkiiʀ- 'quickly' [de Reuse also žakəxtə- and žakxuuʀ — all with kiɣ-?]
Sir žaxkiʀ- 'quickly' [perhaps from CSY]
Inu [compare perhaps under kəɣðaɣ- and piðaɣ-]

PY žaɣaq 'small' [compare some of the forms under vžəʀaʀ-, vlaɣ- and žaʀaq, also the p.b. in cuŋavžəɣaq (cuŋaʀ)]
AAY [cf. aʀya<ɣ>aq 'young woman' under aʀnaʀ]
CAY yaɣaq* 'baby, small, thing like a -' [this could go rather with tyaɣ however; also verbal: 'the dear little one does']
NSY žaɣaq 'baby, small' [Men. also has sužaɣaq]
CSY +žəɣaq 'bit of a -, thing like a -'

PY-S žaʀaq 'new' [cf. ʀaʀ and perhaps taaq(-) though the relat. to the latter is obscure — compare žaɣaq and ʀaʀ, also təžəʀ- under tətəʀ- for the ž?]
AAY —
CAY [Nun laaʀ(aʀ)- 'get a new -']
NAY žaaq 's.th. like a -, a not normal type of -, fancy'
CSY žaaq* [de Reuse also žəʀžaq] 'new-fangled', +žaʀaq 'brand new' [and note šaʀ- 'in a new or fancy way']
Sir žaʀaX 'good' [compare ʀaX 'new, young' under ʀaʀ]
Inu [note WG #ššaaq 'great, grand'?]

PI žukšau- and **žakšau-** 'must' [respectively on intr. and trans. bases; cf. ðuʀ and ðaʀ, kðaʀ and ŋu- and compare yaʀka(C)u-]
Yup [for CAY (ɣ)aXkau- 'should' see yaʀqa(C)u-]
Sir [note yukcəX 'one that has to -', +yukcəʀə- 'have to', which appear to have yuɣ- for the first element rather]
SPI [+tuakšaq 'one who should -' — with žuaq under ðuʀ]
NAI +žukšau-, (trans.) +žakšau- 'must'
WCI +yuxxau-, (trans.) +yaxxaʀi- 'must, should' [and +yaxxauŋŋit 'cannot be -ed']
ECI +yutsau-, (trans.) +yatsaʀi- 'must', NBI +yuksau- 'probably (will)'
GRI +šuššaa-, (trans.) +šaššaa- 'be supposed to'

INFLECTIONS

INFLECTIONS

There have been numerous local developments away from the system tentatively reconstructed here, details of which cannot all be entered into. In particular, there has been much restructuring of dual forms in the various contemporary languages — only the most important deviations are pointed out in the footnotes that follow. Sir, note, like SWG and EG, has completely lost the category of dual number. Possessor number is marked in the leftmost vertical column (non-possessed forms on the top line) and possessum number horizontally above.

1. Nominal

Absolutive and Relative Cases

	Absolutive			Relative		
	s.	p.	d.	s.	p.	d.
unposs.	Ø	t[1] *cf. Al. s*[1]	ɣ[1] *cf. Al. x*	m[1] *cf. Al. m*	t[1]	ɣ[1]
poss. 3s	ŋa *cf. Al. a*	ŋi	ɣ[2]	ŋan *cf. Al. ɣan*	ŋin *cf. Al. (ŋ)in*	kənʀ *cf. Al. kin*
3p	ŋat	ŋit *cf. Al.(ŋ)is*[4]	kət[2]	ŋata	ŋita	kətaʀ
3d	ŋaɣ	ŋiɣ[2]	kəɣ[2] *cf. Al. kix*	ŋanəɣ[3]	ŋiɣta[3]	kənka[3]
1s	ka *cf. Al.ŋ*	nka *cf. Al.niŋ*	ɣka *cf. Al.kiŋ*	ma[5]	ɣma	
1p	vut[6] *cf. Al. mas*	put	ɣput	mta	ɣəmta	
1d	vuɣ[6]	puɣ	ɣpuɣ	mtuɣ[7]	ɣəmtuɣ	
2s	n[8] *cf. Al.Vn*	tən *cf. Al. t(xin)*	ɣkən *cf. Al. kin*	vət, ɣpət[8] *cf. Al. mis*	ɣpət *cf. Al. kimis*	
2p	ði *cf. old EA ci*	ci	ɣci	vci *cf. old EA mci*	ɣpəci	
2d	ðəɣ[9] *cf. Al.ðix*	təɣ	ɣtəɣ	vtəɣ[9] *cf. Al.məðix*	ɣpətəɣ[2]	
4s	ni[9] *cf. Al.Vn*	ni *cf. Al. t(xin)*	ɣni *cf. Al. kin*	mi *cf. Al.Vm*	ɣni *cf. old Atk. kiim*	
4p	ðəŋ[9] *cf. EA ðin*	təŋ	ɣtəŋ	məŋ *cf. old EA maŋ*	ɣməŋ	
4d	ðəɣ[9] *cf. Al. ðix*	təɣ	ɣtəɣ	məɣ *cf. old Al. max*	ɣməɣ	

The 3s-sing., 3p-pl., 3d-du. and other person s./pl. relative case endings are also used in the 'quantifier/qualifier' construction, with a distinction between 3rd person forms in object function and 4th person ones in subject function (no distinction in other persons; see for example under tamaʀ-).

Oblique cases

	s.	p.	d.
Loc.	mi[10]	ni	ɣni
Abl./instr.	məɣ[11]	nəɣ	ɣnəɣ
All.	mun[12]	nun	ɣnun
Vial.	kun[13]	təkun	ɣkun
Aeq.	tun[14]	tətun	ɣtun

The following non-possessed endings may cause a base-final weak ə to drop, with compensatory gemination in Inu. Initial m reflects the singular relative marker. The forms with initial n (or k or t) are combined to produce possessed oblique with the corresponding abs. endings in the case of 3rd person (xkə for dual possessum in CAY), but with variants of the rel. endings for the other persons: 1s m, 1p mtə (Inu ptɨt), 1d mtəɣ[7]; 2s v (Inuit ɣ but not vialis p-kun), 2p vci (Inu vsit), 2d vtəɣ; 4s mi, 4p/d məɣ, all preceded by ɣ for dual possessum in Yup. The original proto-Eskimo-Aleut nominal oblique cases have been collapsed to two in Aleut (loc./all. and abl./vial.), restricted to positional nouns and demonstratives. The ablative/instrumental distinction on nominals may well have been an Inuit innovation, as Bergsland (1989: 26–27) suggests, though this is not completely certain.

Similar endings appear on demonstrative pronominals (see the section on Demonstratives for the abs. and rel. cases). Inu appears to have innovated by expanding upon the relative case forms plus a final vowel borrowed from the adverbial forms of the roots such as uvva from uv-. The partially distinct adverbial oblique cases are: loc. ni (cf. Al. n); abl. kən (Inu (a)kŋa, Sir knəŋ — compare Al. Att ka between rel. and person markers, EA ki plus rel. person on location words, and compare also Inu nakin, etc., under na-[2]); all. vət, (CSY and NSY vək, Sir mu and Inu uŋa, probably all reflecting the same source as Al. allative ŋus, EA ŋun on demonstrative adverbials); and vial. ɣun (Yup ɣun, xun, Inu (u)una; cf. note 13 for the Al. cognate). Inu, apart from Sig and Di/Imaq, also has an instrumental on demonstrative pronouns (u)miŋa (= Sig anŋa) distinct from the adverbial ablative mentioned above and Tar has aequalis tunaq (cf. naʀ) alongside tut. The full set of oblique pronominal cases in Inu are thus as in NAI loc. taaptumani, all. taaptumuŋa, abl. taaptumaŋa, vial. taaptumuuna, aeq. taaptumatun and instr. taaptumiŋa from taamna (uv-). The plural is declined similarly with n rather than m and the dual is built up on base form taapkuak, loc. taapkunaŋi, etc. In Yup the endings are as for nouns. In Sir the oblique form of dem. pronouns are the same for singular and plural, namely loc. kənəti, all. kənətu, etc. (compare note 10).

2. Verbal *(see next page)*

Indicative / Participal

subj.	intransitive		transitive										
	intrans. marker	subject marker	trans. marker	object marker									
				3s	3p	3d	1s	1p	1d	2s	2p	2d
3s 3p 3d	(ðu[15])	ʀ t ɣ	(ða[16])	ŋa ŋat ŋaɣ	ŋi ŋit ŋiɣ[17]	ɣ kət[17] kəɣ[17]	ŋaŋa[18] ŋatŋa ŋaɣŋa	ŋakut[19] ŋatkut ŋaɣkut	ŋakuɣ ŋatkuɣ ŋaɣkuɣ	ŋatən ŋatkən ŋaɣtən	ŋaci ŋatəci ŋaɣci	ŋatəɣ ŋatətəɣ ŋaɣtəɣ
1s 1p 1d	(ðu[15])	ŋa[18] kut[19] kuɣ[20]	(ða[16])	ka vut vuɣ[20]	nka put puɣ	ɣka ɣput ɣpuɣ				*same as relative mood endings*		
2s 2p 2d	(ðu[15])	tən ci ðəɣ	(ða[16])	n ði ðəɣ	tən ci təɣ	ɣkən ɣci ɣtəɣ	*same as relative mood endings*					

Subordinative (Contemporative)

subj.	intransitive		transitive										
	intrans. marker	subject marker	trans. marker	object marker									
				3s	3p	3d	1s	1p	1d	2s	2p	2d
4s 4p 4d	(lu[31])	ni təŋ təɣ	(lu)	ku[22]	ki[22]	kəɣ	ŋa	ta	tuɣ, nuɣ[32]	tən	ci	təɣ
1s 1p 1d	(lu[31])	ŋa ta tuɣ, nuɣ[32]	(lu)	*same as above*						*same as above*		
2s 2p 2d	(lu[31])	tən ci ðəɣ	(lu)	*same as above*			*same as above*					

Interrogative

<table>
<tr><td></td><td colspan="2">**intransitive**</td><td colspan="10">**transitive**</td></tr>
<tr><td rowspan="2">**subj.**</td><td rowspan="2">**intrans. marker**</td><td rowspan="2">**subject marker**</td><td rowspan="2">**trans. marker**</td><td colspan="9">**object marker**</td></tr>
<tr><td>**3s**</td><td>**3p**</td><td>**3d**</td><td>**1s**</td><td>**1p**</td><td>**1d**</td><td>**2s**</td><td>**2p**</td><td>**2d**</td></tr>
<tr><td>3s
3p
3d</td><td>(ða[21])</td><td>Ø
t
ɣ</td><td>(ða[21])</td><td>ɣu, ku[22]
təɣu[22]
nəɣu[17]</td><td>ki[22]
təki
nəki</td><td>kəɣ
təkəɣ
nəkəɣ</td><td colspan="3">*same as relative mood endings*</td><td colspan="3">*same as relative mood endings*</td></tr>
<tr><td>1s
1p
1d</td><td>(ði[21])</td><td>ŋa
ta[24]
tuɣ, nuɣ[24]</td><td>(ði[21])</td><td>ku[23]
təku
(təɣ)nəɣu[25]</td><td>ki[23]
təki
(təɣ)nəki</td><td>kəɣ[23]
təkəɣ
(təɣ)nəkəɣ</td><td colspan="3"></td><td colspan="3">*same as relative mood endings but without initial m*</td></tr>
<tr><td>2s
2p
2d</td><td>(ði[21])</td><td>n
ci
təɣ</td><td>(ði[21])</td><td>ɣu
ciɣu
təɣu</td><td>ki
ciki
təɣki</td><td>kəɣ
cikəɣ
təɣkəɣ</td><td colspan="3">*same as relative mood endings but without initial v*</td><td colspan="3"></td></tr>
</table>

See the relevant information in the notes for Al. cognates.

Optative / Imperative

<table>
<tr><td></td><td colspan="2">**intransitive**</td><td colspan="10">**intransitive**</td></tr>
<tr><td rowspan="2">**subj.**</td><td rowspan="2">**intrans. marker**</td><td rowspan="2">**subject marker**</td><td rowspan="2">**trans. marker**</td><td colspan="9">**object marker**</td></tr>
<tr><td>**3s**</td><td>**3p**</td><td>**3d**</td><td>**1s**</td><td>**1p**</td><td>**1d**</td><td>**2s**</td><td>**2p**</td><td>**2d**</td></tr>
<tr><td>3s
3p
3d</td><td>(li[26])</td><td>Ø
t
ɣ</td><td>(li)</td><td>ku[22]
təɣu
nəɣu</td><td>ki
təki
nəki</td><td>kəɣ
təkəɣ
nəkəɣ</td><td colspan="3">*same as relative mood endings*</td><td colspan="3">*same as relative mood endings*</td></tr>
<tr><td>1s
1p
1d</td><td>Ø</td><td>(la)ŋa
(l)ta[27]
(l)tuɣ[27]</td><td>(la)</td><td>ku[23]
təku[28]
(təɣ)nəɣu[28]</td><td>ki
təki
(təɣ)nəki</td><td>kəɣ
təkəɣ
(təɣ)nəkəɣ</td><td colspan="3"></td><td colspan="3">*same as relative mood endings*</td></tr>
<tr><td>2s
2p
2d</td><td>Ø</td><td>ɣin[29]
(ɣi[30])ci
(ɣi[30])təɣ</td><td>Ø</td><td>ɣu[29]
ciku
təɣu</td><td>ki
ciki
təɣki</td><td>kəɣ
cikəɣ
təɣkəɣ</td><td colspan="3">*same as interrogative mood endings*</td><td colspan="3"></td></tr>
</table>

Relative Moods[33]

	intrans.	transitive											
		object marker											
subj.	subject marker	3s	3p	3d	1s	1p	1d	2s	2p	2d	4s	4p	4d
3s	n[24]	ku[22]	ki	kəɣ	ŋa	kut[19]	kuɣ	tən	ci	təɣ	ni[42]	təŋ	təɣ
3p	ta	tkən[22]	tki	tkəɣ	tŋa	tkut	tkuɣ	tkən	təci	tətəɣ	tni	tətəŋ	tətəɣ
3d	nəɣ[35]	nɣu[17]	nki	nkəɣ	ɣŋa	ɣkut	ɣkuɣ	ɣtən	ɣci	ɣtəɣ	ɣni	ɣteŋ	ɣtəɣ
1s	ma	mku	mki	mkəɣ				mkən[39]	mci	mtəɣ	mni	mtəŋ	mtəɣ
1p	mta	mtəku	mtəki	mtəkəɣ				mtəkən	mtəci	mtətəɣ	mtəni	mtətəŋ	mtətəɣ
1d	mtuɣ[36]	m(təɣ)nəɣu[36]	m(təɣ)nəɣki	m(təɣ)nəɣkəɣ				m(t)əɣtən[40]	m(t)əɣci	m(t)əɣtəɣ	mtəɣni[43]	mtəɣtəŋ	mtəɣtəɣ
2s	vət[37]	vku	vki	vkəɣ	v(ə)ŋa[41]	vkut	vkuɣ				vni	vtəŋ	vtəɣ
2p	vci	vciku	vciki	vcikəɣ	vciŋa	vcikut	vcikuɣ				vcini	vciteŋ	vciteɣ
2d	vtəɣ	vtəɣu[36]	vtəɣki	vtəɣkəɣ	vtəɣəŋa	vtəɣkut	vtəɣkuɣ				vteɣni	vteɣteŋ	vteɣteɣ
4s	mi[38]	miɣu	miki	mikəɣ	miŋa	mikut	mikuɣ	mitən	mici	mitəɣ			
4p	məŋ	məɣtəku	məɣki	məɣkəɣ	məɣtəŋa	məɣtəkut	məɣtəkuɣ	məɣtəkən	məɣtəci	məɣtətəɣ			
4d	məɣ	məɣnəɣu[36]	məɣnəki	məɣnəkəɣ	məɣəŋa	məɣkut	məɣkuɣ	məɣtən	məɣci	məɣtəɣ			

3. Notes to Inflections

1) The non-possessed forms (plus 3s possessor du. k in CAY) cause base-final weak ʀ to drop (with compensatory gemination observable in Inuit). In Inu the dual may cause gemination (even with strong C bases, with iɨ to a) or lengthening of the base, according to base type, and rel. sing. um and plural it occur specifically after strong cons. bases — by assimilation from *əm, *ət; compare Sir pl. y, (after strong C base) iy. Aleut has pl. s (EA n), du. x also in the relative.

2) Most Yup has forms with double dual-marking of the du. possessum here, e.g. CAY abs. pl. possessor xkət and du. xkək (also corresponding rel. sing. possessor xkən, etc.), which presumably first developed in the du.-du. forms. Abs. 3d possessor-pl. possessum ŋiɣ, has apparently been replaced in CAY by kək (by analogy with the du. possessum form); on the other hand, CSY has ʀs possessor-du. possessum kək (again by analogy with the other dual possessum form?). In Inu the du. possessum forms have generally been replaced by (ŋ)ik (when not causing gemination in the base) — also in verbal object inflections, in line with the pl. possessum forms.

3) Note that the 3d possessor rel. forms have a dual marker (k/ɣ) following the rel. marker n (also in the pl. possessum form — by analogy?) — these have been largely restructured outside of CAY, e.g. NAI 3s (ŋ)akta, 3d (ŋ)iksa, 3p (ŋ)iksa, CSY (ŋ)ita, (ŋ)ita, xkənka, but cf. NG du. possessum kkit, Sig kita, for all 3rd person possessors (NAI s./du. (ŋ)iksa, but pl. (ŋ)isa). CAY has apparently replaced 3d ŋanəɣ (reflected in Inu rel. mood forms) with (ŋ)aɣnək and 3d pl. possessum ŋiɣta with kənka in line with the dual possessum (Bergsland 1989:15). In the quantifier/qualifier construction Inu has 3d (i)ɣnik.

4) Al. Atkan (ŋ)is, EA (ŋ)in also covers Esk ŋi and ŋat in function, as kix also covers ŋaɣ and 3s du. possessum ɣ).

5) Al. miŋ in loc. phrases. Perhaps from *m + ŋa, as Berg. suggests (1989:9); he also suggests that corresponding Esk. verbal 1s ending ŋa could be from hypothetical p1s pronominal *tə(kə) + ŋa. The PE 1s abs. form ka may be from comb. with cons. bases on the other hand (note that *ŋa would have conflicted with the corresponding 3s ending).

6) With initial p after C, as for all v-initial forms. To kput, kpuk after a V in Inu (as for du. possessum). The Al. is probably by generalization of the post-vocalic alternant reflected in PE. Note CSY has du. vuŋ, etc.

7) As reflected in CSY mtuŋ, ɣəmtuŋ (also mtəɣ(ni, etc.) with obl. case); most other languages reflect mnuɣ, ɣəmnuɣ (with assimilation?), thus CAY has məɣnuk or mnuk (the former also in the quantifier/qualifier construction) and məɣ(ni, etc.), NSY mnung and NAI mnuk. Note however that NSY has mtəɣ(ni, etc.) and NAI ptiɣ(ni, etc.), also reflecting the form with original t.

8) Following a strong cons. in Inu abs. in (compare plural it), with the same vowel apparently transferred to (metathesized) rel. vit/kpin, perhaps from earlier *mkən as Berg. has suggested. CAY has rel. vət (after C +pət), CSY xpək, NSY vək and NAI kpin^y on all bases. Compare note 18 for hypothetical pronominal *(tə)kən that could be involved here, also 2s intrans. imperative ɣin. Atkan Al. has 2s rel. mis, EA min on ordinary nominal bases, also 2s loc. for locational words. Al. has probably generalized the post-vocalic alternant (PE vət).

9) The ð-initial forms alternating with initial t after C in PE (in contrast to 2p ði, alternating with ci after C). Inu has ktik (and 2p ksi) after a V. Note CAY 2d-s./pl. mənuk in the quantifier/qualifier construction. See note 42 as regards 2s/d ni.

10) Note Al. qila-m 'in the morning', etc., but compare also postpositional -m naɣan 'in' from *-m. The m in ataqaðim 'once' may be a relic of the instrumental acc. Berg. Sir has (n)i (and similarly instr. (n)əŋ, all. (n)u, the n dropping after bases in ə in the abs.) for both sing. and pl. (Compare the Sir 3p possessor form iti (for sing. or pl. possessum), also 4p məxti (and the demonstrative inflections mentioned above), all apparently containing plural marker t).

11) CSY, NSY, Sir HBC and SPI have məŋ rather (and Sir (n)əŋ). Perhaps from rel. m + kən (the ablative of adverbial forms of the demon. roots), i.e. originally ablative in function. Inu abl. min, etc. is probably an innovation influenced by the locative acc. Berg. (and cf. the final n in the all. and vial. cases). Note that in SPI_{DI}, the ablative is not min as in other Inu; this function is served instead by the locative mi.

12) Note Al. muð in at-muð-ᴀʀan 'downward', etc. (also ŋuð-ᴀʀan as in waŋuðᴀʀan 'to here'), and AAY tmən, CAY tmun 'toward' on demon. adverbials and posit. roots (cf. under ilu-, also for Inu equivalents) — with p.b. tə? For the vowel in AAY compare that of all. vət and aeq. tən on demon. roots; mun could be from rel. marker m plus the same all. vət (compare Bergsland 1989:70, foot 68). Sir has (n)u.

13) Inu kkun (kun in some western dialects) is probably secondary (from combinations following a C or from the dual as in CAY xkun alongside ɣnəyun?) — compare 3s possessor forms aɣun, etc., and old Al. vialis — now ablative -ɣaan from *-ɣa-ɣun.

14) Yup tən on demon. adverbials — influenced by ablative kən (and also the vowel in vət)? Note however madeten in the base section, with reflexes of this form of the aequalis also in Inu, so it is also possible that tun on nouns came from tən, influenced by the vowel of the vialis and allative.

15) i.e. indicative/participial (WG only the latter) mood marker ðuʀ under the p.b.s, alternating with tur after a C. The same endings occur with Inu mood marker +vu(q) (initial p after a C) the ordinary indic. in GRI, elsewhere a 'narrative' one — and with Yup lʀi(C)a(q) under the p.b.s. Aleut has present tense 3s kuX, 3d kux, ʀp kus, EA kun (also for 1p), 1s kuqiŋ. 2s kuXtxin, 2p kuXtxicix, EA kuXtxici(n), 2d kuXtxiðix, the ku of which may go with Eskimo trans. participial p.b. kə², but with the vowel of (lost) ðuʀ (compare also neg. lakaX, etc.). Similar endings occur on participial morpheme na- (cf. nə¹ under the p.b.s) for the remote past tense.

16) i.e. passive postbase ðaʀ (taʀ after a C as in Inu but no longer in Yup). Inu has mood marker +va(q) rather for the 'narrative' indicative — compare intr. -vu(q) (though a paradigm based on ðaʀ is also found outside of GRI). A parallel paradigm (WG participial mood only) uses participial postbase kə² with these endings. See foot 2 for the Inu 3d object forms. Corresponding to the 3rd person object forms of Esk. Aleut has (for anaphoric reference only) 3s/p/d-ʀs kuu (from *ku-a), 3s/d/p-ʀp kuŋis, EA kuŋin, 3s/d/p-ʀd kukix, 1s-3s kuŋ, 1s-3p kuniŋ, 1s-3d kukiŋ, 1p-3s/p/d ŋin or mas, 2s-3s kuun, 2s-3p kutxin, 2s-3d kukin, 2d-3s/p/d kuðix, and 2p-3s/p/d kucix, EA kucin. Participial morpheme qa- is used with the same endings for the anaphoric remote past tense (cf. postbase kaʀ).

17) Most Yup has forms with double dual marking (compare note 2 for the parallel nominal inflections). Also the 3d-3s/p/d interr., imper. and rel. forms are preceded by an 'extra' dual marker as in CSY ɣnəɣu, etc. (but compare CAY 3d-3s rel. mood xku and Inu tku). CAY has apparently replaced indic. 3d-3p ŋiɣ with kək (as for the equivalent nom. ending).

18) The relative mood 1st/2nd person object forms for ʀrd person subject appear to have been transferred to the indicative along with the other subject forms with 1st/2nd person object and added to the 3s-3s and 3p-3s forms of the indicative. In Yupik the 3p subject forms for non-singular 1st/2nd person object are added to the 3p-3p form rather, an innovation that has spread back to the relative moods outside of CAY (see Bergsland 1989:25). 1s forms (subject and object) are ŋ without the final a in Sir (and Aleut — thus present tense qing from q + 1s pronominal ting); note also Inu 1s interr. vik (from vi + *ŋ?). The personal subject/object markers seem to reflect (enclitic) pronominals with stem *tə(kə)- or *tə(ɣə)-, corresponding to independent forms in Aleut, as in 2s/4s txin, 2p txici and 2d txiðix, so 1s *tə(kə)ŋ(a)? Compare uvaŋa (with different demon. root) under the bases.

19) Perhaps from pronominal stem *tə(kə) plus vut acc. Berg. (1989:10) — compare Al. timas (earlier also tximas) 'we', Sir ki. The corresponding object marker in the relative and indicative moods for 3s subject is tiɣut (du. tiɣuk) in Inu, which could reflect the hypothetical pronominal stem directly or, more likely, be transferred from the 3p subject forms.

20) CSY kuŋ, vuŋ, etc. (the final nasal occurs in all other intr. 1d forms there).

21) Inuit has mood markers +va, +vi instead (by analogy with indic. +vu(q), +va(q)?); 1s vik.

22) Inu 3s uŋ, 3p žžuŋ (also imperative and rel. moods — including 4th person subject forms in the latter such as miuŋ); ku preserved as such in CAY opt. and rel. moods (CSY ɣu). cf. Al. 3s ka, 3p kis, 3d kix. 3p object ki to ɣit in most Inu (as with this ending in other moods).

23) CSY has kun, ŋi, ɣŋək rather (optative kun, ŋi, ŋak). CAY does not use 1st person trans. object forms in the interr. Neither has 2nd person object forms except 1s-2s kən.

24) CSY has 1s (s)ta, 1d (s)tuŋ (but CAY and Inu nuk, NSY nuŋ for the latter, for which compare the corresponding nom. ending in note ŋ).

25) As in CSY (s)təɣnəɣu, etc., also for 2d subject (conflation?).

26) Sir has 1st and 3rd person optative marker la throughout (intr. only in Men. — see p.b.s yuɣ- and yukə- for the trans. equivalents).

27) Additive 1p ta, 1d luk in Inu, 1d łuŋ in NSY, luk in CAY and łtuŋ in CSY — compare note 24. GRI distinguishes 1p inclusive lata from exclusive ta.

28) 1p/d forms are the same as the indic. in most contemporary languages (with mood marker la), but CSY and WGI still reflects these old forms (with conflation between the 1d and 2d forms in the former as with the interr., however; see also note 17 regarding the dual forms).

29) The intr. ending is zero after full Vs in Yup, +a after ʀ or ɣ in CAY and Sir (but i in CSY when no velar-dropping — Yup generally has much irregularity in reflexes of this form); compare Al. 2s ða (also older ʀs object form txa, EA also 3p txin) with the CAY form — this may represent the earlier form of the imperative to which ɣin was later added (for the latter compare the Al. 2nd person pronominal forms under note 18). NAI has (+)in^{y}, which may cause gemination in the preceding syllable — but +tin after t bases, and 2s-3s uŋ.

30) The ɣi found in Inu is apparently transferred from 2s ɣin — it is optional in CAY (after ə or VV) and not found in CSY or NSY. In CSY the 2p imper. form is tək (like the 2d) rather than *ci.

31) cf. Al. conjunctive marker l(ix), (after C, absorbing t) s(ix). Sir has rel. endings like additive 4s ləmi, 1s ləma

instead. The negative counterpart of lu is (kə)na (found in Yup after və(kə)/pə(kə) and neg./contrary bases in tə), with special 2s form naɣ (CSY naŋ) and Inu ɣa-/ʀa- rather than na- in certain combinations/dialects. In Inu there is a distinction between a 'past' or 'realized' and a 'future' or 'unrealized' contemporative paradigm. Whereas the latter takes simple forms like additive luni (also ɣuni, ʀuni with k and q bases in NAI), the former takes forms like pluni/vluni after V bases (and ḷuni after C — alternatively xuni, Xuni with k and q bases in some NAI). The 'past' paradigm may well contain evidential p.b. vət-/pət- as still productive in CSY ftə-, after C ptə- (also doubled pətəftə-) 'evidently'. This would explain its absence in the 'future' paradigm. Compare also p.b. və(kə)-.

32) CSY tuŋ, NSY (lu)ŋ, CAY and most Inu nuk (but HBC and SPI nuŋ) — compare note 24.

33) i.e. those subordinate moods containing rel. case marker *m in their non-3rd person forms, specifically the 'causative (consequential)', with mood marker ya (CSY and Sir +ya), ŋa (rest of Yup) or ka (Inu, where it is generally +ɣa — but NAI also ka and Mal 'a after V — perhaps influenced by the conditional; WCI, ECI, and GRI na after neg. ŋŋit-). Note also the Inu variant ŋa- in combination with contingent p.b. ɣaa- (ɣaaŋat, etc.) and in maŋa(aq)-, q.v., and cf. Al. anterior marker Vŋ, (after C) iiŋ, (after t) saŋ, from *yaŋ (perhaps from *yaŋ(a) acc. Berg.). The other principal rel. mood marker is conditional ku (Sir has kəɣə, but just ɣə after yəqə under ya(a)qə-, which suggests a reanalysis, the mood marker itself being ɣə); correspondingly Aleut has Atkan (i)ɣu, with k weakened intervocalicaly to ɣ, EA (after k) ku, (after t) xu, (after q) qu.

34) Inu causative pman (via *pŋan ?), conditional kpan (the same initial clusters also for 3d and 3p). The evidential p.b. vət-/pət- mentioned in note 31 may be involved in the causative forms and the conditional ones may be influenced by the latter. Yup consequential -(ŋ)an, -yan, conditional -kan (the same vowel in all transitive forms too). Note that the -n (and pl. -ta) is from *-an (and *-ata), as in the nominal possessed relative paradigm.

35) But CSY has yək/kənka acc. Jacobson for SLI (Chap xta acc. Men.), NSY ɣnəŋ (compare note 3 for corresponding nominal forms).

36) CAY has 1d məɣnuk, 1d-3s məɣnəɣu, etc., CSY mtuŋ (but NSY mnuŋ), mtəɣnəɣu, etc., NAI mnuk, ptiɣu, etc. CSY has 2d-3s ftəɣnəɣu, perhaps influenced by the corresponding 3d form (also the 1d and 4d — the latter is məɣnəɣu); Inu has 2d-3s ptitku and 4d-3s mitku. The reconstruction of the original forms is problematic here, but again compare note 7.

37) Initial p following a C; CSY, NSY vək, Inu vit/vin (the latter NAI; compare note 8).

38) But 4s ni, 4p nəŋ, 4d nəɣ, CSY ni, yəŋ, yək) in the conditional except in NSY, NAI, Sig, and Cop at least.

39) In western Inu metathesized to kpin.

40) NSY mtəɣənkən, etc., Inu ptəɣin (but Sig ptitkin), etc. Replaced by the 1s subj. forms in CSY.

41) To kma in Inu (metathesis?).

42) Perhaps from pronominal *təkəni via *tni, acc, Berg. (1989:9). The corresponding nominal 4s ending ni may cause gemination in certain bases in Inu, note, the n being dropped (replacive pattern).

43) Inu ptəɣni (but readjusted 1d-4p ptəɣit, 1d-4d ptəɣik), etc. Replaced by 3rd person object forms in CSY. CAY məɣni, etc. (compare note 7).

DEMONSTRATIVES

DEMONSTRATIVES

Proto-Eskimo Demonstrative Roots

	Extended	Restricted	Obscured
1) Near speaker	mað-	uv-	im-
2) Away from speaker on level			
a) More accessible	av-	iŋ-	am-
b) Less accessible (across barrier)	aɣ-	ik-	akəm-
3) Inside /outside			
a) More accessible (inside, upriver)	qav-	kiv-	qam-
b) Less accessible (outside)	qaɣ-	kiɣ-	qakəm-
4) Down from speaker			
a) More accessible (down below, down-slope)	un-	kan-/kað-	cam-
b) Less accessible (toward exit, dowriver)	unəɣ-	uɣ-	cakəm-
5) Up from speaker			
a) More accessible (up-slope)	pav-	piŋ-	pam-
b) Less accessible (up above)	paɣ-	pik-	pakəm-

Also: uk- 'approaching speaker'

In the above, 'extended' means moving, long or spread out, 'restricted' means not moving (or moving around in a confined area) but visible, and 'obscured' means not visible.

Below, 'pronoun' refers to the set of forms for each demonstrative which includes absolutive and relative as well as the oblique cases, differentiates between singular, dual (except Sir and GRI) and plural and can function like (other) nouns except for being subject to the limitation of taking few or no postbases and no possessive endings, and are characterized by the ending -na for the absolutive singular, -ðu- (Yup -u-, Inu -tu/žu-) as a marker for the non-absolutive singular, and -ku- as a marker for the non-singular. Note that the interrogative pronoun PE ki(na) 'who' is inflected much like a demonstrative pronoun, and the interrogative adverb PE na-[2] 'where' is inflected much like a demonstrative adverb. They can be found in the section on bases.

'Adverbs' are the sets of forms for each demonstrative which include only oblique cases (and in most cases special forms of these), have no distinction of number, and are characterized by the marker -a(-). The 'predicative' (or interjectional) form of a demonstrative adverb is the form without an oblique case ending that is used with or without a noun to indicate that something is in the place denoted by the particular adverb, and that the person spoken to should turn his or her attention to that area. This is the form of the AL. cognates given. Note the extra -i in AAY and CAY behaves like a consonant-initial syllable as far as prosody is concerned. These forms correspond to interjectional ones with -y in Al. (e.g. way from wa-). The gemination in the Inu forms was doubtless also PE.

'Prefixed forms' are those with the prefix ta(ð)- and its variants used for anaphora or for shifting the frame of reference from speaker to person spoken to (compare Al. tataam 'again' under taðva). It may be noted here that for AAY and CAY (except for NSU) such forms exist only for the first row of demonstrative roots on the chart above. In NSU_{CAY}, NSY, CSY, Sir, and Inuit these forms exist for most or all demonstratives. Apparently modeled after these prefixed forms with ta(ð)- are a few special forms of demonstratives in NSKCAY (see under iŋ- and piŋ- — there may be more such forms than just these), and in NSY (see under aɣ- and uv-). In GRI aa- can be prefixed to all forms instead of ta(ð)- in a purely deictic sense (it appears elsewhere in Inu as a particle for drawing attention).

SPI forms are for Wales and WCI ones for Cop (Lowe 1985b); additional Aiv forms are from Denny 1980.

The additional 'oblique' forms in Aleut with final -u are, acc. Bergsland, the direct cognates of the Esk 'obscured' items ending in -əm. The corresponding forms in final -a result from generalized formulation of converse pairs to (for example) restricted ika versus obscured aku (from *akəm), namely iku versus aka, etc.

In NAI forms where ɣ precedes a nasal, the entire cluster is optionally nasalized in North Slope, and obligatorily nasalized in Malimiut. Thus aɣna is alternatively aŋna in NS and must be aŋna in Malimiut.

Gaps in paradigms, such as missing relative case pronouns where the absolutive form is given, probably represent forms that are merely not attested.

PE **aɣ-** 'across' (extended); cf. Al. aɣa 'over there (as on other side of river)'

Language	abs. sing. pronoun	rel. sing. pronoun	abs. / rel. plural pronoun	localis adverb	predicative	prefixed abs. sing. pronoun	prefixed adverb	prefixed predicative
AAY	aɣna	aɣɣum	axkut	aaɣani	aaɣa	——	——	——
CAY	aɣna	aɣɣum	axkut	aɣaani[1]	aɣaa-i	taaɣna[2]	taaɣani[3]	——
NSY	aaɣna[4]	——	aaxkut[5]	aɣani	——	taaɣani[6]	——	taaɣa
CSY	aaɣna	aɣum	aaxkut	aɣani	aɣa	taaɣna	taaɣani	taaɣa
Sir	aɣna	aɣcəma	axkəža	aɣəni	aɣa	——	——	——
SPI	aŋna	aktuma[7]	akkua	aani	aɣɣaa[8]	taaɣaŋna	taaɣani	taaɣa
NAI	aɣna	aktuma	akkua	aani	aɣɣa	taaɣaɣna	taaɣani	taaɣɣa
WCI	aŋna	axxuma[9]	akkuat	aɣani	aɣɣa	——	taaɣani	taaɣa
ECI	——	——	——	aani[10]	——	——	——	——
GRI	——	——	——	——	——	——	——	——

Notes to demonstratives
1 also iini in Nun, NSU
2 NSU only
3 NSU only
4 for aɣna?
5 for axkut?
6 also sXaɣna (probably for əsXaɣna) 'see, that one', from əsXa- 'see'
7 KI aɣžuma
8 with special meaning, 'in the east'
9 Sig aɣɣuma
10 Lab. only; with meaning 'in the south'

PE **akəm-** 'across' (obscured); cf. Al. aku 'obliquely over there', also aka 'straight out there'

Lan-guage	abs. sing. pronoun	rel. sing. pronoun	abs. / rel. plural pronoun	localis adverb	predicative	prefixed abs. sing. pronoun	prefixed adverb	prefixed predicative
AAY	akəmna	akmum	akəmkut	akm̥ani	akm̥a	——	——	——
CAY	akəmna	akmum	akəmkut	akm̥ani	akm̥a	taakəmna[11]	taakmani[12]	——
NSY	akəmna	——	akəmkut	akm̥ani	——	——	——	——
CSY	akəmna	akm̥um	akəmkut	akm̥ani	akm̥a	taakəmna	taakm̥ani	taakm̥a
Sir	akəmna	akm̥um	akəmkəža	akm̥əni	akm̥a	——	——	——
SPI	aɣimna	aɣiptuma[13]	aɣipkua	akmani	akma	taakimna	taakmani	taakma
NAI	akimna	akiptuma	akipkua	aŋmani[14]	aŋma[15]	taakimna	taaŋmani	taaŋma
WCI[16]	akimna	akivyuma	akipkuat	aŋmani	aŋma	——	taaŋmani	taaŋma
ECI	——	——	——	——	——	——	——	——
GRI	——	——	——	——	——	——	——	——

[11] NSU only
[12] NSU only
[13] KI aɣivžuma
[14] Mal akmani
[15] Mal akma
[16] Sig. only

PE am- 'over' (obscured) [see also amma in section on bases — also for Al. cognate]

Language	abs. sing. pronoun	rel. sing. pronoun	abs. / rel. plural pronoun	localis adverb	predicative	prefixed abs. sing. pronoun	prefixed adverb	prefixed predicative
AAY	amna	ammum	amkut	amani	ama-i[17]	——	——	——
CAY	amna	ammum	amkut	amani	ama-i	taamna[18]	taamani	——
NSY	amna	——	amkut	amani	——	tamna[19]	——	——
CSY	aamna	amum	aamkut	amani	ama	taamna	taamani	taama
Sir	amna	——	amkəža	——	——	——	——	——
SPI	amna	aptuma[20]	apkua	amani	amma	taamamna	taamani	taama
NAI	amna	aptuma	apkua	amani	amma	taamamna	taamani	taamma
WCI[21]	——	——	——	——	——	taamamna	taamani	taama
ECI	——	——	——	——	——	——	——	——
GRI	——	——	——	——	——	——	——	——

[17] K only; C has ama
[18] NSU only, and similarly for taamani
[19] for taamna
[20] K: avžuma
[21] Sig. only on this line

PE av- 'over' (extended); cf. Al. awa 'over there or going away' [and see avan in section on bases]

Language	abs. sing. pronoun	rel. sing. pronoun	abs. / rel. plural pronoun	localis adverb	predicative	prefixed abs. sing. pronoun	prefixed adverb	prefixed predicative
AAY	aɣ^{w}na	aɣ^{w}ɣ^{w}um	aw̥kut	awani	awa-i[22]	——	——	——
CAY[23]	aɣ^{w}na	aɣ^{w}ɣ^{w}um	aw̥kut	awani	awa-i	tauɣ̥na[24]	taawani	——
NSY	awna	——	aw̥kut	awani[25]	——	——	——	——
CSY	——	——	——	awani	——	——	taawani	taawa
Sir	——	——	——	——	——	——	——	——
SPI[26]	amna	avžuma	apkua	awani	avvaa[27]	taavamna	taavani	taava
NAI	amna	aptuma	apkua	avani	avva	taavamna	taavani	taavva
WCI	avamna	avaffuma	avapkuat	——	——	taavamna	taavani	taavva[28]
ECI	anna	atsuma	akkua	avani	avva[29]	taavanna	taavani	——
GRI	anna[30]	aššuma	akku(a)	avani	affa	taayanna	taavani	taava

[22] K only; C has awa
[23] also 'going away from speaker' or 'from whom speaker is going' [as with Al. cognate awa]
[24] NSU only, and for taawani
[25] and see under avan
[26] this row KI
[27] with special meaning 'east'
[28] Sig taava
[29] Aiv
[30] usual meaning = 'in north' (EG 'in south'); old ortho. avaa but NG aŋna 'that one over there', by conflation with aɣ-

PE cakəm- 'toward exit, downriver' (obscured); cf. Al. saka 'down there (as on bottom of sea)'

Lan-guage	**abs. sing. pronoun**	**rel. sing. pronoun**	**abs. / rel. plural pronoun**	**localis adverb**	**predicative**	**prefixed abs. sing. pronoun**	**prefixed adverb**	**prefixed predicative**
AAY	cakəmna	cakmum	cakəmkut	cakm̥ani	cakm̥a	——	——	——
CAY	cakəmna	cakmum	cakəmkut	cakm̥ani	cakm̥a	tascakəmna[31]	tascakmani	——
NSY	sakəmna[32]	——	sakəmkut	sakm̥ani	sakm̥a	——	——	——
CSY[33]	sakəmna	sakm̥um	sakəmkut	sakm̥ani	sakm̥a	təsakəmna[34]	təsakm̥ani[35]	təsakm̥a
Sir	——	——	——	——	——	——	——	——
SPI	saɣimna	saɣiptuma[36]	saɣipkua	sakmani	sakma	satakimna	satakmani	satakma
NAI[37]	sakimna	sakiptuma	sakipkua	saŋmani[38]	saŋma	tasakimna	tasaŋmani	tasaŋma
WCI[39]	sakimna	sakivyuma	sakipkuat	saŋmani	saŋma	——	tasaŋmani	tasaŋma
ECI	——	——	——	——	——	——	——	——
GRI	——	——	——	——	——	——	——	——

[31] NSU only, and similarly for tascakmani
[32] with special meaning 'on the north side, on left looking out to sea', and similarly for sakm̥a
[33] this row also meaning 'in west, in outer room, toward Savoonga' but 'in east' in Chap
[34] also əsakəmna, and similarly for təsakm̥ani and təsakm̥a
[35] with additional meaning 'west' in SLI, 'southwest' in Chap
[36] KI saɣivžuma
[37] with special meaning 'in porch' when speaker is in house
[38] sakmani Mal, and similarly for saŋma, and tasaŋmani
[39] from Sig.

PE **cam-** 'down below, down-slope' (obscured)[40]

Language	abs. sing. pronoun	rel. sing. pronoun	abs. / rel. plural pronoun	localis adverb	predicative	prefixed abs. sing. pronoun	prefixed adverb	prefixed predicative
AAY	camna	cammum	camkut	camani	cama-i[41]	——	——	——
CAY	camna	cammum	camkut	camani	cama-i[42]	tascamna[43]	tascamani	——
NSY	samna	——	samkut	samani	sama	tasamna	tasamani	tasama
CSY	saamna	samumi	saamkut	samani	sama	təsamna[44]	təsamani[45]	təsama
Sir	samna	——	samkəža	saməni	sama	——	——	——
SPI	samna	savžuma	sapkua	samani	samma	satamna	satamani	satama
NAI[46]	samna	saptuma	sapkua	samani	samma	tasamna	tasamani	tasamma
WCI[47]	hamna	haffuma	hapkuat	hamani	hamma	tahamna	tahamani	tahamma
ECI	sanna	satsuma	sakkua	samani	——	tasanna	——	——
GRI	sanna[48]	saššuma	sakku(a)	samani	samma	tasanna	tasamani	tasama

[40] occurs in Aleut place name samalʀa
[41] K only; C has cama; see cama-i under bases
[42] see cama-i under bases
[43] NSU only, and similarly for tascamani
[44] also əsamna
[45] also əsamami, and similarly for təsama
[46] with additional meaning 'near speaker', but obscured, as in a container
[47] '(this one) here' in Cop (but sam- 'down there' in Sig)
[48] old ortho. savna with spurious v; also 'in west' — EG 'in east'

PE ik- 'across' (restricted); cf. Al. ika 'right over there (in front)', also iku 'right there to the side'

Lan-guage	abs. sing. pronoun	rel. sing. pronoun	abs. / rel. plural pronoun	localis adverb	predicative	prefixed abs. sing. pronoun	prefixed adverb	prefixed predicative
AAY	ikn̥a	ikkum	ikəxkut	ikani	ika-i[49]	——	——	——
CAY	ikn̥a[50]	ikkum	ikəxkut	ikani	ika-i	taikn̥a	taikani[51]	——
NSY	ikna	——	ikəxkut	ikani	——	——	——	——
CSY	iikn̥a	ikum	ikəxkut	ikani	ika	tazikn̥a	tazikani[52]	tazika
Sir	——	——	——	——	——	——	——	——
SPI	ikna	iktuma[53]	ikkua	iɣani	ikkaa	taikna	taikani	taika
NAI	iɣnʸa[54]	iktuma	ikkua	ikani	ikka[55]	taiɣnʸa	taikani[56]	taikka
WCI	iŋna	ixxuma	ikkuat	ikani	ikka	——	taikani	taika
ECI	inna[57]	itsuma	ikkua	ikani	ikka[58]	tainna	taikani	taika
GRI	iŋŋa[59]	iššuma	ikku(a)	ikani	——	taaŋŋa	taakani	taakka

49 K only; C has ika
50 also ikəxn̥a in some areas
51 NSU only, and similarly for taikani
52 with additional meaning 'south' in SLI, 'west' in Chap
53 KI iɣžuma
54 Mal iknya
55 Mal icani, icca
56 Mal taicani
57 NBI iŋna
58 Aiv only (Denny)
59 also (older) 'in north'

PE im- 'here' (obscured) — also 'aforementioned'; cf. Al. uma 'heard, felt, smelled, but not seen' [see also imma and taðim(m)a in the base section]

Language	abs. sing. pronoun	rel. sing. pronoun	abs. / rel. plural pronoun	localis adverb	predicative	prefixed abs. sing. pronoun	prefixed adverb	prefixed predicative
AAY	imna	immum	imkut	imani[60]	——	——	——	——
CAY	imna	immum	imkut	imani[61]	ima[62]	taimna	taimani	tayima[63]
NSY	imna	——	imkut	imani	ima	——	——	tayima[64]
CSY	iimna	imum	iimkut	imani	ima	tazimna	tazimani	tazima
Sir	imna	——	imkəža	——	ima	——	——	——
SPI	imna	ivžuma	ipkua[65]	imani	imma	taimna	taimani	taima
NAI	imnʸa	iptuma	ipkua	imani	imma	taimnʸa	taimani[66]	taimma
WCI	imna	iffuma	ipkuat	imani	——	——	taimani	taima
ECI[67]	imna	ipsuma	ipkua	——	——	tainna	——	——[68]
GRI	inna[69]	——	ikku(a)[70]	——	——[71]	taana[72]	——	——

[60] with special limited use in meaning 'I suppose' only in certain areas
[61] NSU only
[62] as an enclitic throughout CAY
[63] or taima; with special meaning: 'not present' (the predicative form used as an adverb or interjection)
[64] with special meaning: 'not present' (interjection)
[65] Mal ipcua
[66] with special meaning: 'in the past, aforementioned, in the future, unrealized'
[67] except for tainna this line is Aiv; NBI inna, rel. issuma, pl ikkua (see also under imma)
[68] see under taðim(m)a
[69] old ortho ivna; enclitic only today
[70] old ortho ivkua; enclitic only today
[71] see under imma
[72] old ortho taivna

PE iŋ- 'over' (restricted); cf. Al. iŋa 'right there in front'

Lan-guage	abs. sing. pronoun	rel. sing. pronoun	abs. / rel. plural pronoun	localis adverb	predicative	prefixed abs. sing. pronoun	prefixed adverb	prefixed predicative
AAY	iŋna	iŋŋum	iŋkut	yaani	yaa-i[73]	——	——	——
CAY	iŋna	iŋŋum	iŋkut	yaani	yaa-i	taiŋna[74]	taziaŋi[75]	——
NSY	iɣna	——	inkut	iɣani	——	tayiɣna[76]	tayiani	——
CSY	iiɣna	iŋum	iiŋkut	iŋani[77]	iŋa	taziɣna	taziɣani	taziɣa
Sir	iɣna	iŋcəma	iŋkəža	iŋkənəti[78]	iŋ	——	——	——
SPI	iŋna	iɣžuma	ikkua	iani[79]	iŋŋaa[80]	taiŋna	taiŋani	taiŋa
NAI[81]	in^{y}n^{y}a	iɣžuma	ikkua	in^{y}ani	in^{y}n^{y}a	tain^{y}n^{y}a	tainyani	tain^{y}n^{y}a
WCI	——	——	——	——	——	——	——	——
ECI	——	——	——	——	——	——	——	——
GRI	——	——	——	——	——	——	——	——

[73] K only; C has yaa
[74] NSU only
[75] NSU only; alternate form: taiŋani (but also yayaani (emphatic form) in NSK)
[76] plural is tayinkut
[77] but vial. is iiŋxun and abl. is iiŋken
[78] loc. is iŋkənəti, all. is iŋkənətu, abl. is iŋkənəməŋ
[79] KI iŋani
[80] with special meaning 'east'
[81] this row Mal only

PE kan- or **kað-** 'down below, down-slope' (restricted); cf. Al. ukna 'down there (as on beach seen from house above)' [the Al. reshaped after una (un-) unless related — via metathesis? — to unəɣ- rather; the rel. sing. pronominal forms may reflect *kanðum]

Lan-guage	abs. sing. pronoun	rel. sing. pronoun	abs. / rel. plural pronoun	localis adverb	predicative	prefixed abs. sing. pronoun	prefixed adverb	prefixed predicative
AAY	kanna[82]	kattum[83]	kankut	kanani	kana-i[84]	——	——	——
CAY	kanna[85]	kattum	kankut	kanani	kana-i	taskanna[86]	taskanani	——
NSY	kaana	kaatum	kaankut	kanani	kana	——	taɣ̥kanani	taɣ̥kana
CSY	kana[87]	kanum	kaankut	kanani[88]	kana	təskana[89]	təskanani[90]	təskana
Sir	kana	——	kankəža	——	kana	——	——	——
SPI	kanna	kažžuma	katkua	kanani	kanna	taɣana	taɣanani	taɣana
NAI	kanna	kattuma	katkua	kanani	kanna	takanna	takanani	takanna
WCI	kanna	katuma	katkuat	kanani	kanna	——	takanani	takanna
ECI	kanna	katsuma / katuma	kakkua	kanani	kanna[91]	takanna	takanani	——
GRI	kanna[92]	katuma[93]	kakku(a)	kanani	kana	takanna	takanani	takanna[94]

[82] voc. K kacuuq, PWS kacuuʀaa, KP kanyuuʀaa
[83] K and PWS, but kannum in KP
[84] K only; C has kana
[85] voc. kacuuq
[86] NSU only, and similarly for taskanani
[87] voc. kaanyuq or kaasuq
[88] but vial. is kaanxun and ablative is kaankən or kanakən
[89] also əskana
[90] also əskanani. and similarly for the prefixed predicative
[91] Aiv. only
[92] also 'in west'
[93] EG kattima, NG kassuma
[94] in special sense 'please take some food, go ahead and eat'; also, takašša

PE kiɣ- 'out' (restricted); cf. Al. qiɣa 'there by door (obsolete) or in east', also qika 'out there (near entrance)' and qiku 'back there, in there (as on wall in room one is in)[95]

Language	abs. sing. pronoun	rel. sing. pronoun	abs. / rel. plural pronoun	localis adverb	predicative	prefixed abs. sing. pronoun	prefixed adverb	prefixed predicative
AAY	kəxn̥a	kəxxum	kəxkut	kəxani	kəxa-i[96]	——	——	——
CAY	kəxn̥a	kəxxum	kəxkut	kəxani	kəxa-i	taskəxn̥a[97]	taskəxani	——
NSY	kəxn̥a	——	kəxkut	kəxani	——	——	——	——
CSY	——	——	——	——	——	——	——	——
Sir	——	——	——	——	——	——	——	——
SPI	kiŋna	kiktuma[98]	kikkua	kiani	kiɣɣaa	tatkiŋna	tatkiani	tatkiɣa[99]
NAI	kiɣnʸa[100]	kiktuma	kikkua	kiani	kiɣɣa	tatkiɣnʸa[101]	tatkiani	tatkiɣɣa
WCI[102]	kiŋna	kiɣyuma	kikkuat	kiani	kiɣɣa	——	tatkiani	tatkiɣa
ECI	kinna	kitsuma	kikkua	kiani	——	takkina	takkiani	takkiɣa
GRI	kiŋŋa[103]	kiššuma	kikku(a)	kiɣani[104]	kixxa	takkiŋŋa	takkiɣani[105]	takkiɣa

95 brought into line with the other q-initial in/out forms; the latter pair modeled on qaka versus qaku under qakəm
96 K only; C has kəxa
97 NSU only, and similarly for taskəxani
98 also kikšuma, KI kigžuma
99 KI tatkia
100 or kiŋnʸa
101 or tatkiŋnʸa
102 Sig only
103 also 'in south' and both 'out there' and 'in there' (the latter still in NG today) — i.e. conflation with kiv-
104 EG kilaani (cf. under kiɣan)
105 with special meaning 'south'

PE **kiv-** 'in, upriver' (restricted) [and see kivan under section on bases]

Lan-guage	abs. sing. pronoun	rel. sing. pronoun	abs. / rel. plural pronoun	localis adverb	predicative	prefixed abs. sing. pronoun	prefixed adverb	prefixed predicative
AAY	kiɣʷna	kiɣʷɣʷum	kiw̥kut	kiani	kia-i[106]	——	——	——
CAY	kiuɣna[107]	kiuɣum[108]	kiuxku[109]	kiani[110]	kia-i	taskiuɣna[111]	taskiani	——
NSY	——	——	——	——	——	——	——	——
CSY	kiiwna[112]	kiwum[113]	kiiw̥kut	kiwani	kiwa	təskiwna[114]	təskiwani	təskiwa
Sir[115]	——	——	——	——	——	——	——	——
SPI	kimna	kivžuma	kipkua	kiwani	kivvaa[116]	tatkimna	tatkiwani	tatkiwa
NAI	kimnʸa	kiptuma	kipkua	kivani	kivva	tatkimnʸa	tatkivani	tatkivva
WCI[117]	kimna	kivyuma	kipkuat	kivani	kivva	——	tatkivani	tatkiva
ECI	——	——	——	——	——	——	——	——
GRI[118]	——	——	——	——	——	——	——	——

[106] K only; C has kia
[107] HBC kiɣʷna
[108] HBC kiɣʷɣʷum
[109] HBC kiw̥kut
[110] kaani in Kotlik is also 'left along coast facing ocean'
[111] NSU only, and similarly for taskiani
[112] in SLI also special meaning 'that toward northeast, toward Savoonga'
[113] also kiɣum
[114] also əskiwna, and similarly for təskiwani, and təskiwa; (t)əskiwna/(t)əskiwani has additional meaning 'northeast'
[115] cf. kivan for kiv- 'in the west, inside' acc. Em.
[116] with special meaning 'west'
[117] this row for Sig
[118] note vestigial form takkiva 'in from sea' given by Berg. and compare kuyati- 'south' under kivan

PE **mað-** 'near speaker' (extended); cf. Al. uða 'here (on floor or an island)' [the initial vowel influenced by uv-?; see also maðətən in bases section]

Language	abs. sing. pronoun	rel. sing. pronoun	abs. / rel. plural pronoun	localis adverb	predicative	prefixed abs. sing. pronoun	prefixed adverb	prefixed predicative
AAY	manna	mattum	makut	maani	maa-i[119]	tamana[120]	tamaani	— —
CAY	manna	mattum	makut	maani	maa-i[121]	tamaana[122]	tamaani[123]	tamaa-i
NSY	mana	matum	makut	maɣni[124]	maa	— —	tamaɣni	— —
CSY	mana	matum	maakut	maani	maa	tamana	tamaani[125]	tamaa
Sir	mana	macəma	makəža	maɣni	— —[126]	— —	— —	— —
SPI	manna	mažžuma	maɣua	maani	mažžaa[127]	tamana	tamaani	tamaža
NAI	manna	mattuma[128]	makua	maani	mažža	tamanna	tamaani	tamažža
WCI[129]	manna	matuma	makuat	maani	mayya	— —	tamaani	tamayya
ECI	manna	matsuma / matuma	makua	maani	mayya[130]	tamanna	tamaani	tamayya
GRI	manna	matuma[131]	makku(a)	maani	mašša[132]	tamanna	tamaani	tamašša[133]

119 K only; C has maa
120 prefixed forms are also used for listener- centered reference; similarly for tamaani
121 also in sense 'now' maa-iXpak 'now, in this season'
122 rel. is tamaatum, pl. is tamaakut; prefixed forms are also used for listener-centered reference
123 prefixed forms are also used for listener-centered reference
124 for maani?
125 prefixed forms are also used for listener-centered reference
126 mažuma 'to here'; Vakh. also has tamina 'this' and tamiža 'there'; similarly for prefixed adverb and prefixed predicate
127 with special meaning 'here it is!' used upon finding something
128 also: mažžuma, maššuma
129 this row for Sig
130 Aiv only
131 EG mattuma
132 in special sense 'although, to be sure, for'; mašakkut 'now'
133 also in special meaning 'come in!', EG tamatta 'now'

PE paɣ- 'up above' (extended); cf. Al. haɣa 'up along there (as on clothesline or along hill)'

Lan-guage	abs. sing. pronoun	rel. sing. pronoun	abs. / rel. plural pronoun	localis adverb	predicative	prefixed abs. sing. pronoun	prefixed adverb	prefixed predicative
AAY	paɣna	paɣɣum	paxkut	paaɣani	paaɣa	——	——	——
CAY	paɣna	paɣɣum	paxkut	paɣaani[134]	paɣaa-i	taspaɣna[135]	taspiini	——
NSY	paɣna	——	paxkut	paɣani	——	——	taɣpaɣaani	——
CSY	paaɣna	paɣum	paaxkut	paɣani	paɣa	təspaɣna[136]	təspaɣani	təspaɣa
Sir	paɣna	——	paxkəža	——	——	——	——	——
SPI	paŋna	paktuma[137]	pakkua	paani	paɣɣaa	tatpaŋna	tatpaani	tatpaɣa[138]
NAI	paɣna[139]	paktuma	pakkua	paani	paɣɣa	tatpaɣna[140]	tatpaani	tatpaɣɣa
WCI	paŋna	paxxuma	pakkuat	paani	paɣɣa	——	tatpaani	tatpaɣa[141]
ECI	panna	patsuma	pakkua	paani	paɣɣa[142]	tappana	——	tappaɣa
GRI	——	——	——	——	——	——	——	——

[134] but piini in Nun and NSU
[135] NSU only, and similarly for taspiini
[136] also əspaɣna, and similarly for təspaɣani and təspaɣa
[137] KI paɣžuma
[138] KI takpaa and tak- for tat- in preceding forms
[139] or paŋna
[140] or tatpaŋna
[141] Sig tatpaɣa
[142] Aiv (Denny)

PE pakəm- 'directly up above' (obscured); cf. Al. haku 'up there aslant (as from beach inland), also haka 'up there (as in the air)'

Language	abs. sing. pronoun	rel. sing. pronoun	abs. / rel. plural pronoun	localis adverb	predicative	prefixed abs. sing. pronoun	prefixed adverb	prefixed predicative
AAY	pakəmna	pakmum	pakəmkut	pakm̥ani	pakm̥a	——	——	——
CAY	pakəmna	pakmum	pakəmkut	pakm̥ani	pakm̥a	taspakəmna[143]	taspakm̥ani	——
NSY	pakəmna	——	pakəmkut	pakmani	——	——	——	——
CSY	pakəmna	pakm̥um	pakəmkut	pakm̥ani	pakm̥a	təspakəmna[144]	təspakm̥ani[145]	təspakm̥a
Sir	——	——	——	——	——	——	——	——
SPI	paɣumna[146]	paɣuvžuma	paɣupkua	pakmani	pakma	tatpaɣumna[147]	——[148]	tatpaŋma[149]
NAI	pakimna	pakiptuma	pakipkua	paŋmani[150]	paŋma[151]	tatpakimna	tatpaŋmani	tatpaŋma
WCI[152]	pakimna	pakivyuma	pakipkuat	paŋmani	paŋma	——	tatpaŋmani	tapaŋma
ECI	——	——	——	——	——	——	——	——
GRI	——	——	——	——	——	——	——	——

143 NSU only, and similarly for taspakm̥ani
144 also əspakəmna
145 also əspakm̥ani, and similarly for əspakm̥a
146 KI paɣimna; i for u after ɣ
147 KI takpaɣimna
148 KI takpakmani
149 KI takpa'ma
150 Mal pakmani
151 Mal pakma
152 this row for Sig

PE pam 'above, up slope (obscured); cf. Al. hama 'over there (invisible) or as mentioned before'

Lan-guage	abs. sing. pronoun	rel. sing. pronoun	abs. / rel. plural pronoun	localis adverb	predicative	prefixed abs. sing. pronoun	prefixed adverb	prefixed predicative
AAY	pamna	pammum	pamkut	pamani	pama-i[153]	——	——	——
CAY	pamna	pammum	pamkut	pamani	pama-i	taspamna[154]	taspamani	——
NSY	pamna	——	pamkut	pamani	pama	——	tay̯pāmani[155]	tay̯pama
CSY	paamna	pamum	paamkut	pamani	pama	təspamna[156]	təspamani[157]	təspama
Sir	pamna	——	pamkəža	——	——	——	pamaf	——
SPI	pamna	pavžuma	papkua	pamani	pamma	tatpamna[158]	tatpamani	tatpama
NAI	pamna	paptuma	papkua	pamani	pamma	tatpamna	tatpamani	tatpamma
WCI[159]	pamna	pavyuma	papkuat	pamani	pamma	——	tatpamani	tatpama
ECI	——	——	——	——	——	——	——	——
GRI	——	——	——	——	——	——	——	——

[153] K only; C has is pama
[154] NSU only, and similarly for taspamani
[155] for tay̯pamani?
[156] also əspamna
[157] also əspamani, and similarly for əspama
[158] KI tak- for tat-
[159] Sig only

PE pəv- 'up-slope' (extended); cf. Al hawa 'there (in relat. to movement or as generally known)'

Language	abs. sing. pronoun	rel. sing. pronoun	abs. / rel. plural pronoun	localis adverb	predicative	prefixed abs. sing. pronoun	prefixed adverb	prefixed predicative
AAY	payʷna	payʷyʷum	paw̥kut	pawani	pawa-i[160]	——	——	——
CAY	payʷna	payʷyʷum	paw̥kut	pawani	pawa-i	taspayʷna[161]	taspawani	——
NSY	——	——	——	——	——	——	——	——
CSY	——	——	——	——	——	——	——	——
Sir	——	——	——	——	——	——	——	——
SPI	pamna	pavžuma	papkua	pawani	pavvaa	tatpamna	tatpawani	tatpava[162]
NAI[163]	pamna	paptuma	papkua	pavani	pavva	tatpamna	tatpavani	tatpavva
WCI	——	——	——	——	——	——	——	——
ECI	——	——	——	——	——	——	——	——
GRI	panna[164]	paššuma	pakku(a)	pavani[165]	paffa	tappanna	tappavani	tappava

[160] K only; C has pawa
[161] NSU only, and similarly for taspawani
[162] KI takpawa and tak- for tat- in all forms
[163] Mal only
[164] old ortho. pavna; also 'in east'
[165] EG puani

PE pik- 'up-above' (restricted); cf. Al. hika 'up there (as under ceiling)', also hiku 'up there slantwise'

Language	abs. sing. pronoun	rel. sing. pronoun	abs. / rel. plural pronoun	localis adverb	predicative	prefixed abs. sing. pronoun	prefixed adverb	prefixed predicative
AAY	pikn̥a	pikkum	pikəxkut	pikani	pika-i[166]	——	——	——
CAY	pikn̥a[167]	pikkum	pikəxkut	pikani	pika-i	taspikn̥a[168]	taspikani	——
NSY	pikna	——	pikəxkut	pikani	——	tay̥piłkani[169]	——	——
CSY	piikn̥a	pikum	pikəxkut	pikani	pika	təspikn̥a[170]	təspikani[171]	təspika
Sir	pikna	——	pixkəža	pikəni	pika	——	——	——
SPI	pikna	piktuma[172]	pikkua	piɣani	pikkaa	tatpikna	tatpiɣani	tatpiɣa[173]
NAI	piɣn^{y}a[174]	piktuma	pikkua[175]	pikani	pikka[176]	tatpiɣn^{y}a[177]	tatpikani[178]	tatpikka
WCI	piŋna	pixxuma	pikkuat	pikani	pikka	——	tatpikani	tatpikka[179]
ECI	pinna	pitsuma	pikkua	pikani	pikka[180]	tappina	tappikani	takpika
GRI	piŋŋa[181]	piššuma	pikku(a)	pikani	——	tappiŋŋa	tappikani	tappika

166 K only; C has pika
167 also pikəxn̥a in some areas
168 NSU only, and similarly for taspikani
169 for tay̥pikani?
170 also əspikn̥a
171 also əspikani, and similarly for əspika
172 KI piɣžuma
173 KI tak- for tat- in all forms
174 or piŋn^{y}a (Mal pikn^{y}a)
175 Mal piccua
176 Mal picani, picca
177 or tatpiŋn^{y}a (Mal tatpikn^{y}a)
178 Mal tatpicani
179 Sig tatpika
180 Aiv (Denny), and similarly for takpika
181 also 'in east', NG 'in west'

PE **piŋ-** 'up-slope' (restricted); cf. Al. hiŋa 'right there (close to you, as you know)'

Lan-guage	abs. sing. pronoun	rel. sing. pronoun	abs. / rel. plural pronoun	localis adverb	predicative	prefixed abs. sing. pronoun	prefixed adverb	prefixed predicative
AAY	piŋna	piŋŋum	piŋkut	piani	pia-i[182]	——	——	——
CAY	piŋna	piŋŋum	piŋkut	piani	pia-i	taspiŋna[183]	taspiaŋi[184]	——
NSY	piɣna	——	piŋkut[185]	——	——	——	taɣ̥piani	——
CSY[186]	piiɣna	piŋum	piiŋkut	piŋani	piŋa	təspiɣna[187]	təspiɣani[188]	təspiɣa
Sir	——	——	——	——	——	——	——	——
SPI	piŋŋa[189]	piktuma	pikkua	piani	piŋŋaa	tatpiŋa	tatpiani	tatpiŋa
NAI[190]	pinʸnʸa	——	pitʸkua	piani	pinʸnʸa	tatpinʸnʸa	tatpiani	tatpinʸnʸa
WCI	——	——	——	——	——	——	——	——
ECI	——	——	——	——	——	——	——	——
GRI	——	——	——	——	——	——	——	——

182 K only; C has pia
183 NSU only
184 NSU only, but also pipiani (emphatic) in NSK
185 for pinkut?
186 this row Chap only
187 also əspiɣna
188 also əspiɣani, and similarly for təspiɣa
189 KI pinŋa, piɣžuma, pitkua, piɣani, piŋŋaa, takpiŋna, takpiɣani, takpiŋa
190 this row Mal only

PE qaɣ- 'outside' (extended); cf. Al. qaɣa 'there outside (obsolete), there in east'

Lan-guage	abs. sing. pronoun	rel. sing. pronoun	abs. / rel. plural pronoun	localis adverb	predicative	prefixed abs. sing. pronoun	prefixed adverb	prefixed predicative
AAY	qaɣna	qaɣɣum	qaxkut	qaaɣani	qaaɣa	——	——	——
CAY[191]	qaɣna	qaɣɣum	qaxkut	qaɣaani[192]	qaɣaa-i	tasqaɣna[193]	tasqiini	——
NSY	qaɣna	——	qaxkut	qaɣani	——	——	——	——
CSY	qaaɣna	qaɣum	qaaxkut	qaɣani	qaɣa	təsqaɣna[194]	təsqaɣani[195]	təsqaɣa
Sir	qaɣna	——	qaxkəža	——	qaɣa	——	——	——
SPI	qaŋna	qaktuma[196]	qakkua	qaani	qaɣɣaa	tatqaŋna	tatqaani	tatqaɣa[197]
NAI	qaɣna	qaktuma	qakkua	qaani	qaɣɣa	tatqaɣna	tatqaani	tatqaɣɣa
WCI	qaŋna	qaxxuma	qakkuat	qaani	qaɣɣa	——	tatqaani	tatqaɣa[198]
ECI	qaŋna[199]	——	——	——	——	——	——	——
GRI	——	——	——	——	——	——	——	——

[191] additional meaning 'north' as in qaxkumiu 'northerner'
[192] but qiini in Nun and NSU
[193] NSU only, and similarly for tasqiini
[194] also əsqaɣna
[195] also əsqaɣani, and similarly for təsqaɣa
[196] KI qaɣžuma
[197] KI tatqaa
[198] Sig tatqaɣa
[199] Aiv (Denny)

PE qəkm- 'outside' (obscured); cf. Al. qaku 'in there (other room or bottom of bay)', also qaka 'out there, in east'

Language	abs. sing. pronoun	rel. sing. pronoun	abs. / rel. plural pronoun	localis adverb	predicative	prefixed abs. sing. pronoun	prefixed adverb	prefixed predicative
AAY	qakəmna	qakmum	qakəmkut	qakm̥ani	qakm̥a	——	——	——
CAY	qakəmna	qakmum	qakəmkut	qakm̥ani	qakm̥a	tasqakəmna[200]	tasqakm̥ani	——
NSY	qakəmna	——	qakəmkut	qakm̥ani	——	——	——	——
CSY	qakəmna	qakm̥um	qakəmkut	qakm̥ani	qakm̥a	təsqakəmna[201]	təsqakm̥ani[202]	təsqakm̥a
Sir	qamkəna	——	qakəmkəza	——	——	——	——	——
SPI	qaɣimna	qaɣiptuma[203]	qaɣipkua	qakmani	qakma[204]	tatqaɣimna	tatqaŋmani	tatqaŋma
NAI[205]	qakimna	qakiptuma	qakipkua	qaŋmani	qaŋma	tatqakimna	tatqaŋmani	tatqaŋma
WCI	qakimna	qakiffuma	qakipkuat	qaŋmani	qaŋma[206]	——	tatqaŋmani	tatqaŋma
ECI	——	——	——	——	——	——	——	——
GRI	——	——	——	——	——	——	——	——

200 NSU only, and similarly for tasqakm̥ani
201 also əsqakəmna
202 also əsqakm̥ani, and similarly for təsqakm̥a
203 KI qaɣivžuma
204 with special meaning 'next door'
205 Mal forms without assim: qakma, etc.
206 with special meaning 'right now' in Sig

PE qam- 'in' (obscured); cf. EA kama 'someone or something absent or where?'

Lan-guage	abs. sing. pronoun	rel. sing. pronoun	abs. / rel. plural pronoun	localis adverb	predicative	prefixed abs. sing. pronoun	prefixed adverb	prefixed predicative
AAY	qamna	qammum	qamkut	qamani	qama-i[207]	——	——	——
CAY	qamna	qammum	qamkut	qamani	qama-i	tasqamna[208]	tasqamani[209]	——
NSY	qamna	——	qamkut	qamani	qama	——	——	ta*kama
CSY	qaamna	qamum	qaamkut	qamani	qama	təsqamna[210]	təsqamani[211]	təsqama
Sir	qamna	——	qamkəža	qaməni	qama	——	——	——
SPI	qamna	qavžuma	qapkua	qamani	qamma	tatqamna	tatqamani	tatqama
NAI	qamna	qaptuma	qapkua	qamani	qamma	tatqamna	tatqamani	tatqamma
WCI	qamna	qaffuma	qapkuat	qamani	qamma	——	tatqamani	tatqamma[212]
ECI	qanna	qatsuma	qakkua	qamani	——	taqqana	——	——
GRI[213]	qanna	qaššuma	qakku(a)	qamani	qamma	taqqanna	taqqamani	taqqama

207 K only: C has qama
208 NSU only
209 NSU only
210 also əsqamna
211 also əsqamani, and similarly for təsqama
212 Sig tatqama
213 'outside (from within)' or 'inside (from without)' — conflation with qaɣ-

PE ʠav- 'in' (extended); cf. Al. qawa- 'in east' (in place names only)

Language	**abs. sing. pronoun**	**rel. sing. pronoun**	**abs. / rel. plural pronoun**	**localis adverb**	**predicative**	**prefixed abs. sing. pronoun**	**prefixed adverb**	**prefixed predicative**
AAY	qaɣ^{w}na	qaɣ^{w}ɣ^{w}um	qaw̥kut	qawani	qawa-i[214]	——	——	——
CAY	qaɣ^{w}na	qaɣ^{w}ɣ^{w}um	qaw̥kut	qawani	qawa-i	tasqaɣ^{w}na[215]	tasqawani	——
NSY	qawna	——	qaw̥kut	qawani[216]	——	——	——	——
CSY[217]	qaawna	qawum	qaaw̥kut	qawani	qawa	təsqawna[218]	təsqawani[219]	təsqawa
Sir	——	——	——	——	——	——	——	——
SPI	qamna	qavžuma	qapkua	qawani	qavvaa[220]	tatqamna	tatqawani	tatqava[221]
NAI	qamna	qaptuma	qapkua	qavani	qavva	tatqamna	tatqavani	tatqavva
WCI[222]	qamna	qavyuma	qapkuat	qavani	qavva	——	tatqavani	tatqava
ECI	——	——	——	——[223]	——	——	——	——
GRI[224]	qanna	qaššuma	qakku(a)	qavani	qaffa	taqqanna	taqqavani	taqqava

[214] K only; C has qawa
[215] NSU only, and similarly for tasqawani
[216] with special meaning 'on right side looking out to sea'
[217] additional meanings 'northeast' or 'toward Savoonga' in SLI
[218] also əsqaɣ^{w}na
[219] also əsqawani; and similarly for təsqawa
[220] with special meanings 'upriver, west'
[221] KI tatqawa
[222] Sig. only
[223] but note qavaŋŋaniq- 'blow from south (wind)'
[224] also 'in south', EG 'in north'

PE **uɣ-** 'toward exit, down river' (restricted); only in place names in Al. [see also uɣan in section on bases]

Lan- guage	abs. sing. pronoun	rel. sing. pronoun	abs. / rel. plural pronoun	localis adverb	predicative	prefixed abs. sing. pronoun	prefixed adverb	prefixed predicative
AAY	uɣna	uɣɣum	uxkut	waani	waa-i[225]	——	——	——
CAY	uɣna	uɣɣum	uxkut	waani[226]	waa-i	tauɣna[227]	tauɣani	——
NSY	——	——	——	——	——	——	——	——
CSY	uuɣna	uɣum	uuxkut	uɣani[228]	uɣa	taawna	taawani[229]	taawa
Sir	uɣna	——	uxkəža	——	——	——	——	——
SPI	uŋna	uɣžuma	ukkua[230]	uɣani	uɣɣaa	tauŋna	tauɣani	tauɣa
NAI	——	——	——	——	——	——	——	tauɣɣa[231]
WCI	uŋna	uxxuma	ukkuat	uɣani	uɣɣa	——	tauɣani	tauɣɣa
ECI	uŋna[232]	——	——	——	——	——	——	——
GRI	——	——	——	——	——	——	——	——

225 K only; C has waa
226 in Kotlik CAY waani is also right along coast facing ocean
227 NSU only, and similarly for tauɣani
228 special meaning 'near here'
229 additional meaning'west, northwest' in SLI, 'east' in Chap
230 KI utkua
231 Mal
232 Aiv (Denny)

PE uk- 'approaching speaker'; cf. Al. uka 'in here (e.g. house)' [if not PE, then PY-S — in which case SPI must have borrowed from Yup]

Lan-guage	abs. sing. pronoun	rel. sing. pronoun	abs. / rel. plural pronoun	localis adverb	predicative	prefixed abs. sing. pronoun	prefixed adverb	prefixed predicative
AAY	uk̥na	ukkum	ukəxkut	ukani[233]	uka-i[234]	——	——	——
CAY	uk̥na	ukkum	ukəxkut	ukani[235]	uka-i	tauk̥na[236]	taukani	——
NSY	ukna	——	ukəxkut	ukani[237]	——	——	——	tauka
CSY	uuk̥na	ukum	ukəxkut	ukani[238]	uka	$taak^{w}na$	$taak^{w}ani$	$taak^{w}a$
Sir	ukna	——	ukəxkəža	ukani	uka	——	——	——
SPI	ukna	ukšuma	uɣiɣua	uɣani	ukkaa	taukna[239]	tauɣani	tauka
NAI	——	——	——	——	——	——	——	——
WCI	——	——	——	——	——	——	——	——
ECI	——	——	——	——	——	——	——	——
GRI	——	——	——	——	——	——	——	——

[233] special meaning 'near here'
[234] K only; C has uka
[235] special meaning 'near here'
[236] NSU only, and similarly for taukani
[237] also with special meaning: 'near here'
[238] special meaning 'near here'
[239] pl. is taukiɣua

PE un- 'down below, down-slope' (extended); cf. Al. una, 'down there (as along beach as seen from land)' [also Aleut ethnonym Unaŋas, literally 'those down along coast']

Lan-guage	**abs. sing. pronoun**	rel. sing. pronoun	abs. / rel. plural pronoun	localis adverb	predicative	prefixed abs. sing. pronoun	prefixed adverb	prefixed predicative
AAY	unna	unnum	unkut	unani	una-i[240]	——	——	——
CAY	unna	unnum	unkut	unani	una-i	taunna[241]	taunani	——
NSY	——	——	——	unani	——	——	——	——
CSY	——	——	——	——	——	——	——	——
Sir	——	——	——	——	——	——	——	——
SPI	unna	užžuma	utkua	unani	unna	tauna	taunani	tauna
NAI	unna	uttuma	utkua	unani	unna	taunna	taunani	taunna
WCI[242]	unna	uyyuma	utkuat	unani	unna	taunna	taunani	taunna
ECI	unna	utsuma	ukkua	unani	——	taunna	taunani	——
GRI	——	——	——	——	——	——	——	——

[240] K only; C has una
[241] NSU only, and similarly for taunani
[242] this row for Sig

PE unɣ- ‘toward exit, downriver’ (extended)[243] [possibly PY-S rather than PE, in which case SPI must have borrowed from Yup]

Lan-guage	abs. sing. pronoun	rel. sing. pronoun	abs. / rel. plural pronoun	localis adverb	predicative	prefixed abs. sing. pronoun	prefixed adverb	prefixed predicative
AAY	unəɣna	unɣum	unəxkut	unɣani	unɣa-i	——	——	——
CAY	unəɣna	unɣum	unəxkut	unɣani[244]	unɣa-i[245]	taunəɣna[246]	taunɣani	——
NSY	unəɣna	——	unəxkut	——[247]	——	——	——	
CSY	unəɣna	unɣum	unəxkut	unɣani[248]	unɣa	taanəɣna	taanɣani	taanɣa
Sir	unəɣna	——	unkəža	——	——	——	——	——
SPI[249]	uniŋna	uniɣžuma	unitkua	unŋani	——	tauniŋna	taunŋani	——
NAI	——	——	——	——	——	——	——	——
WCI	——	——	——	——	——	——	——	——
ECI	——	——	——	——	——	——	——	——
GRI	——	——	——	——	——	——	——	——

243 perhaps by metathesis from *ukn-? influenced by un- and uɣ-
244 or unɣaani
245 or unɣaa-i
246 NSU only, and similarly for taunɣani
247 at least abl. unəxkən
248 but vial. uunxun, abl. unəxkən
249 apparently not in KI

PE uv- 'near speaker' (restricted); cf. Al. wa 'here' [see also uvva, and taδva in section on bases]

Language	abs. sing. pronoun	rel. sing. pronoun	abs. / rel. plural pronoun	localis adverb	predicative	prefixed abs. sing. pronoun	prefixed adverb	prefixed predicative
AAY	una	uum	ukut	w̥ani	w̥aa-i[250]	taɣʷna[251]	tawani[252]	tawa-i[253]
CAY	una	uum	ukut	w̥ani[254]	w̥aniw̥a	tauna[255]	tuani[256]	tua-i[257]
NSY	una	——	ukut	wani	——	taana[258]	tawani[259]	tawa
CSY	una	uum	ukut	w̥ani[260]	——	taana[261]	tawani[262]	——
Sir	una	——	——	məni	——	tána[263]	tavəni	——
SPI	una	uuma	uɣua	uani	uvvaa	taamna	tažani[264]	——
NAI	una	uuma	ukua	uvani	uvva	taamna[265]	tavžani[266]	——[267]
WCI	una	uuma	ukuat	uvani	uvva	taamna[268]	talvani[269]	——[270]
ECI	una	uuma	ukua	uvani	uvva	taana[271]	taɣɣani[272]	——[273]
GRI	una	uuma	uku(a)	uani	——[274]	taanna[275]	taššani	——[276]

250 K only; C has w̥a
251 rel. is taɣwɣwum; form used for listener-centered reference rather than anaphora
252 prefixed form used for listener-centered reference rather than anaphora
253 K only; C has tawa
254 NS, HBC wani; Nun kwani
255 prefixed form used for listener-centered reference rather than anaphora
256 NS, HBC tawani; prefixed form used for listener-centered reference rather than anaphora
257 NS, HBC tawa-i
258 prefixed form used for listener-centered reference rather than anaphora
259 also sXuna (probably for əsXuna) 'see, that one', from əsXa- 'see'; prefixed form used for listener-centered reference rather than anaphora, and similarly for tawa
260 vial. is w̥aɣun
261 prefixed form used for listener-centered reference rather than anaphora
262 prefixed form used for listener-centered reference rather than anaphora
263 'this right here'; plural is tavəkəža (but Vakh. has rel. sing. tacəma)
264 KI tavžani
265 prefixed form used for listener-centered reference rather than anaphora; rel. sing. taavžuma, taafšuma, or taaptuma
266 prefixed form used for listener-centered reference rather than anaphora
267 see under taδva
268 rel. taaffuma (Sig taavyuma)
269 acc. Lowe
270 see under taδva
271 rel. taatsuma
272 NBI tavvani
273 see under taδva
274 see under uvva
275 rel. taššuma; NG taunna
276 see under taδva

INDICES

ALEUT INDEX

Alphabetic order as in Bergsland 1980, which differs somewhat from that in Bergsland 1994 (where short/long vowel differences and initial h are ignored for alphabeticization); 'd.r.' = under demonstrative roots. Postbases are gathered at the end, with V (variable vowel)-initial ones listed last.

Aleut forms are written in the Aleut standard orthography. Equivalences between this orthography and the orthography used in this dictionary are given below. Symbols of the standard orthography are given in italics. If no equivalence is given it means that the standard practical orthography uses the same letter as our orthography. *ch* = c, *d* = ð, *g* = ɣ, *ĝ* = ʀ, *hl* = ł, *hy* = ɣ̥, *hw* = w̥, *x̂* = X, *ng* = ŋ (with an apostrophe used to distinguish *ng* (i.e. n'g) from ŋ), *hm* = m̥, *hn* = n̥, and *hng* = ŋ̥.

ALEUT	PROTOFORM
a-	ŋu- (p.b.)
aalngaa aalhngaax̂	ałɣiʀ
aang	a(a)ŋ
aataax	a(a)ta(a)ʀ
adag-	aðɣiʀ-
ada-	ata[1]
adguĝ-	aðɣuʀ-
adi- (lip)	aðiʀ
adi- (shore), adanga-	aci[2]
adu-	ayu-
aduĝ-	aðuʀ-
ag-	aɣə-
aga	aɣ- (d.r.)
aga-, agat-	aat-
agalux̂	aɣluʀ
a(a)gayuux̂	aɣayuuq
agi-, agit-	aɣittaʀ-
agig-, agiĝ-, agix̂	aɣiɣ-
agiit-, agiida-	aɣi
agisa-	aɣiɣtə-
aglu-	a(C)aʀłuɣ
aĝ-, uĝ-	ŋ(ŋ)uʀ- (p.b.)
aĝa-	əʀə-[2]
aĝdiikax̂	aqəðɣiʀ
aĝligax̂	aʀli(ɣ)aq
ax̂a-	aʀula-
aka, aku	akəm- (d.r.)
aki-, akiit-	aki(-)
akliga-	akləɣaʀ (under akəʀ)
ala-	ala-
alaqaada-	alaʀ-
alitxu-, alitxux̂	alikə-
alux̂	alŋaʀ
ahlayax̂	ałayaq
ama	amma
amax, amgix̂	avəɣ-
amgu-	avɣuq- (under avəɣ-)
amĝu-	amik(k)uʀ
amilgi-, amlig-	avi(C)u-
amilĝi-, amlu-	amu-
a(a)miyuung, amiyux̂	a(a)miyu(u)
amna-, amnaĝu-	aməlʀa(ʀ)-
amni-, amidgi-	amit-
amu-, amu-	amiʀ
ahmat-, ahmayaaĝ-	apə(ʀ)-
ana- (mother)	ana(a)na
ana- (something)	p.b. ŋu-
anax, ahnax, anag-	anaɣu-
analux̂, anqa-	anə-
an'gaxtax̂	(see Proto-Aleut bases)
anĝ(i)-, anĝaĝi-	anəʀ-
aniida-, aniqdu-	anə-
anga-, angaaĝu-	aŋuðaʀ-
angaduuti-	aŋuyaɣ
angax, angag-	aŋayuɣ
angayuĝ-	aŋŋi-
angi-	aŋi-
angiix-six	(see Proto-Aleut bases)
anglaax̂	ałɣiʀ
anguna-	aŋə-
aqa-, aqax̂ta-	iqaʀ-
aqamda-	aqəvðiɣ
a(a)qayax, aaqiyaayax	aq(ə)yaʀ
aqi-, iqi-	aqva-
aqla-, aqmit-, amqi-	əqə-[2]
aqul(i)-	aqu
asa-	atəʀ
asx̂a-	atʀaʀ- (undeʀ at(ə)-)
asl-, aslixt-, aslita-	atla
at- (straight), atxaĝ-	atə(ði)-
at- (down), atmudaĝan	at(ə)-
ataqan, atuung	ataʀuciʀ
ataqi-, atiqi-	ata-
atxida-	atɣiyaq
atxu-, adqu-	aðɣa(ʀ)
atuug-	atunem
awa	av- (d.r.)
aya-, ayu-	ayalu(ʀ)-
ayaasaqa-	ayaɣ-
ayax̂u-, ayaaĝu-	ayaʀuʀ (under ayaɣ-)
ayaqudaax̂, ayaqux̂	ayaɣ-
aygag-	ayaɣ-
ayqix̂ta-	ayuq-
ayug-	ayu-
ahyu-	at(ə)-
cha-	tayaʀnəʀ
chaamĝu-	ciðamʀu (under ciðaɣ-)
chaang	tayaʀnəʀ
chaaya-	caɣuyaq[1]
chachi-	tatə-
chagi-	caɣiq
chaxudax̂	caɣuyaq[2]
chaĝa	ciʀʀa-
chaĝalix, chaĝaligi-	caʀliɣaʀ
chaĝna-, chaĝat-	caʀvaʀ
chax̂sax̂	caʀsa(q)
chala-	tulaɣ-

ALEUT	PROTOFORM
cham-	cavət-
chamlu-	tamlu
chahmit-, chimit-	capə-
chanikda-	tanəɣ-
changa-	ciŋə(t)-
chdag-	ətəɣ(taR)-
chxa-	təɣləɣ-
chidag-	ciðaɣ-
chidigi-, chiidgiida-	ciɣəðqUR
chidu-	citu-
chixti-, ixti-	žiɣtə
chiĝanax̂	ciqəR-
chiiki-, chiikit-	cikə(t)-
chikiida-	caki
chim, chimi-, chihmi-	tumə
chimchi-	təpli
chimiglu-, chihmiglu-	civvUR-
chinga-	ciŋik
chiqa-, chix̂i, chix̂t(a)-	ciqəR-
chisu-	ciłuvaɣ
chma- (tail)	təmə
chma- (thick), chmat-	civa-
chnga-	təŋə
chngayux̂ta-, chagyux̂ta-	caniŋURtaq (under cani-)
chug-	ciURaq
chugu-	ciURaq
chumi-	tupə(-)
chumtux̂, tumtux̂	təmi
chunix̂	tuniRžuk
chunu-	tunu
chungux̂	tuŋəR
chuq(i)-	cuqlaɣ
chuqa-	tuqlu(ɣ)
chuyu-	tuyə
da-	əðə
dax̂tu-	taRtu
di-	əðIR
dux̂tax̂	(see Proto-Aleut bases)
galĝ(i)-	əɣaləR
gidgi-, gidug-	nəɣəR
gu-, gut-	əɣut-
xadag-	kəɣaɣ-
x̂ula-, x̂uusi-	əRRUR- (under əRə-[1])
haasi-, x̂aasi-	paŋəRun (under paŋəR-)
hada-	paðəR-
hadg(i)-	paðə
hag-, haxsa-, haxsi-	makət-
haga	paɣ- (d.r.)
haglag-	pəɣəɣaR-
haĝit-	pəRə-
haĝu-, haĝu-	pəRu(-)
haka, haku	pakəm- (d.r.)
hal-, halmudaĝ-	małəɣ-
hala-	malak
halagnax̂	alaɣnaq
ham-	mamə-
hama	pam- (d.r.)
hamrax̂	amRaq
hanatu-	manəR
hani-	maniɣ-
haqa-, haqat(a)-	paqət-
haqisnga-, haqisxa-	aqəstə-
hawa	pav- (d.r.)
haya-	payuɣ-
hayamda-	pay(y)a(ɣ)-
hayuĝ-, ayuĝ-	mayUR-
hi-	pi(-)
hig-	əkə-[1]
higit-, ixit-	pəɣləq-
hixt-	əkət- (under əkə-[1])
hika, hiku	pik- (d.r.)
hiki-	pəkə-
hikit-	pəkət- (under pəkə-)
hinga	piŋ- (d.r.)
hingala-, ingala-	iŋqIR
hit-	pitə-[1] (under pi(-))
huda-	puya
hugalux̂, hugulux̂	pualu
hugin'gi-	puɣə-
hux, hugi-	pu(ɣ)uq
huĝdag-, huĝdangux̂, huĝnat-	puqla
huĝdu-, huĝlug-	MURðuɣ-
hula-	pula-
hulax̂	ulaRiq
huli-, hulux̂, huluĝ-	mulə(ɣ)
hum-, humta-	puvə-
humgi-, umxi-	puvak
husi-	uci[1]
husug-	puci-
hut-, husa-, husat-	put-
huta-	putukUR
hutu-	əpu
huyu-	uyURaq
huyux̂	puyUR
ichx̂u-	ətəqUR (under ətəR)
ichingu-	itðə
idut-, idĝut-	niðUR-
igdag-	niɣəðUR-
igigna-	əɣə-
igim, iim, igiim	əłmi-
iglax	əɣət-
igni-	əɣət-
igu-, iga-	niɣu-
iĝa-, iĝax̂ta-, iĝayu-	IRa-
iĝamana-, iĝamax̂ta-	niqtuq-
iix̂i-	IRIR-
iiqi-	iqə(R)
ika, iku	ik- (d.r.)
ikla-	əkə-[1]
il-, ilu-	ilu
ila-	ila(-)[1]
ilaĝ(i)-	ila(C)aR (under ila[1])
ilg-	ələɣ-
im-	nivaR-
imaĝi-	(see Proto-Aleut bases)
imat-	əməɣ-
imda-, idma-, ivya-	ima(R)
imguĝ-, imga-	iməɣ-
imis, imin	əlpət

ALEUT	PROTOFORM
qahlu-, qahlati-	qała-
qam, qami-, qamti-	qavlu(R)
qamgaang, qagmang	qavəɣaɣ
qamu-	qamuR-
qana-, qanayaam, qanaang	qaŋa
qanax, qan'gix̂, qaniix	qaniɣ
qaqax̂	qaqðaR
qasa-	qaðə-
qaslug-	qatə
qasma-, qachx̂i-	qaðə
qdina-, qdili-, qdit-	qi(C)aR-
qichiĝ-, qichaĝ-, qichax̂	qəc(c)uɣ-
qida-	qiða-
qidaayu-, qidaaya-	qiðəR
qidanga-, qizanga-	qilaŋŋaR
qidĝu-	(see Proto-Aleut bases)
qiga	kiɣ- (d.r.)
qigag-, qiiga-, qigumlug-	qiɣuR-
qiihmi-	qipə-
qika, qiku	kiɣ- (d.r.)
qila-, qilam	qilaɣ
qilgu-	qələɣ-
qilĝi-	qiłəR-
qihlug-	qiluɣ-
qimga-	qivə-
qimiyĝi-, qmi-	qəmiR[1]
qihmag-, qihmu-, qimdu-	qipə-
qinaamu-	qinəR-
qingana-, qinga-	qiRuya- (under qiRu-)
qisa(t)-, qisax̂ta-	qiłəR-
qit-	qi(C)ət-
qlat-	qəla-
quch(i)g-	qətəR
qudg-, qudguma-	qu(C)ək
qudu-, qudug-	quðu-
qugali-, qugalina-, qugulna-	quɣələR-
qugdu-	qu(C)aɣðuɣ
quxsu-	quɣðaR-
qukinĝi-, quqinĝi-	quɣðuɣ
qul-	qulə-
qumyuxta-, qumyux, quvyux	quvya(yuɣ)-
quhma-, qmaalug-	qəvləR-
qunki-	quɣðuɣ
qung, qungi-, qungtu-	quŋəR
qungat-	quŋuR-
qungtug-	qutuɣ-
qutugnu-	qutu(ɣ)
quyx̂i-	quyəR-
qya-	əqə-[1]
qyat-	əqət- (under əqə-[1])
sa- (bird)	mətəR
sa- (blade)	caðə-
saalikdaasi-	całiɣ-
saalu-	caluɣ-
saami-, saahmi-	caviɣ
saasqayu-n	(see Proto-Aleut bases)
sad-, sadaĝu-	caðə-
saka	cakəm- (d.r.)
sakaĝ-, sakag-	cikaq-
sakiix, sakiigi-	caki(C)aɣ

ALEUT	PROTOFORM
sahmi-, sahmiisa-	capək-
sana-	cani-
sangax̂ta-	caŋyaR-
sangux̂ta-, sangu-	caŋuR-
sat-	caðku
saygi-	cayuɣ-
siching, sichin	citamat
signa-	ciɣi-
sixsa-, sixsi-	ciɣi-
sixta-	məciɣ-
six̂i-, six̂t-	ciqumə(t)-
siisag-	citə(ɣ)-
sikli-	ciklaR
sihmi-, sihmit-	cipə(ɣ)-
singlangi-x̂	(see Proto-Aleut bases)
sit- (sweat)	citciq-
sit- (be torn), sitmi-	citə
sla-	cila
slag-	ciləɣ-
sna-, snanga-, snuuĝi-	cinə
sngag-	ciŋək-
su-	təɣu-
suga-	cuɣaɣ-
suganĝi-	yu(u)nRaq (under iŋuɣ)
sukax̂	cukak-
sukalu-	cuk(k)a-
suklu-	cukluk
sulux, sulgi-, sulug-	culuɣ
taadgaada-	taanəq
taaga-	taɣə-
taaguya-	ta(C)uRciq-
taaĝangi-, taaĝanĝi-	taR(a)nəq
taamx̂aax̂	tapRaR[1]
taamu-	tamuR-
taanga-	taaŋaq
taaqa-	taaqaq
taata-	ata(a)ta
tachim, tataam	taðva
tada-lix	(see Proto-Aleut bases)
tadga-, tagda-	taanəq
taga-	taɣi-
tagada-	naɣu-
tagaqu-	naɣət-
taĝa-	naRə-
taĝayu-	taR(ə)yuR
tax̂t-, taĝula-	taRəR(-)
taka-	nakkaR-
takda-, taka-	nakacuɣ
takinaada-	nakəR-
talĝi-, taliĝ-	tałiR
tam-, tami-, tamiigasi-	tapəR(-)
tamadax	tamaR-
tana-	nuna
tanalit-	nunałit- (under nuna)
tanat-	nunat-
tanĝaax	taRəRnəR (under taRəR(-))
tani-	naniR
taqu-	naqət-
txa-	təɣəɣ-

ALEUT	PROTOFORM
ma- (act thus)	(u)ma-
mi-	miqə-
mig-, migda-	miɣ-
mudaĝ(an), ngudaĝ(an)	muaq-
na- (be such as to)	naʀ-
na- (participial)	nəʀ[1]
na- (more, most)	nəʀ[2]
na- (s.th. like)	naʀ
naaĝ-	ni(C)aʀ-
naĝ-ulax, naĝ-ulux	nʀit-
ni-, nisa-	ni-
nu-	nit-
qa-, qada-	kaʀ
qali-	liq-
qasi-	qan
qu-	quʀ
si- (gather)	ci-
si- (make)	li-[1]
t- (transitivizer)	t-[1]
t- (fetch), txaĝi-	t-[2]
tu-	tu-[1]
tuĝ-	tuʀ-[2]
ula-, uli-	ŋit-
ulax, ulux	ŋit-
usa-, Vsa-	utə-
usi-, Vsi-, un	un
ya-	caʀ-[1]
yag-	yaɣ-
yu-, yuuglakax̂, yux	yuɣ-
zigat(a)-	ðiɣ-
zu-, su-, du-	yu-
Vchxuza-	kiɣ-
Vĝ(a)li-	yaʀ-
Vka-, iika-	ya-
Vra-, uura-	vaʀ-
Vsa-, Vza-	ŋ(ŋ)uðaʀ(-)

CENTRAL ALASKAN YUPIK INDEX

Mainland dialects only (i.e. not Nunivak). Postbases, at the end, are generally given in their form following full vowels (and enclitics are preceded by '=').

Equivalences between the Central Alaskan Yupik standard orthography and the orthography used in this dictionary are given below. Symbols of the standard orthography are given in italics. If no equivalence is given it means that the standard practical orthography uses the same letter as our orthography. *v* = v and w, *s* = z, *g* = ɣ, *r* = ʀ, *vv* = f, *ll* = l, *ss* = s, *gg* = x, *rr* = X, *ng* = ŋ (with an apostrophe used to distinguish ng (i.e. *n'g)* from ŋ), *ḿ* = m̥, *ń* = n̥, *ńg* = ŋ̊, *u͡g* = ɣ^{w}, *u͡r* = ʀ^{w}, *w* = x^{w}, *u͡rr* = X^{w}, and *e* = ə. Initial *ua* = wa, and initial *ui* = wi. Pre-prosodic gemination is shown with an apostrophe following the geminated consonant (which is written single). A voiceless fricative is written single (as if it were voiced) next to a stop, after another voiceless fricative (which is written double), at the beginning of a word (in the case of s) and at the end of a word (in the case of X). A voiceless nasal is written without the accent mark after a stop or voiceless fricative. Exceptions to the above conventions are dealt with by means of an appropriately placed apostrophe. As in the orthography of this dictionary, vowel length and gemination which result from prosody are not explicitly shown, but ə deleted for prosodic reasons is omitted.

CAY	PROTOFORM
aa	a(a)
aa-ang	a(a)ŋ
aaggsak, aaggsaq	aðɣaʀuðaʀ (under aðɣa(ʀ))
aakaq	a(a)kaʀ
aamar-, aamaq	ama(C)-
aana	a(a)na
aarraaliq	a(a)-a(a)ŋliʀ
aarraangiiq	a(a)-a(a)ŋliʀ
aassaqe-, aassaqeq	a(a)tsaqə-
aata	ata[1]
aataak	a(a)ta(a)ɣ
aatunaq	aatunaq
aavcaaq	aavcaaq
acaluq	acaluʀ
aci-	aci[1]
acilquq	aci[1]
acir-	acciʀ- (under atəʀ)
acirneq	aciʀnəʀ (under at(ə)-)
acitmun, acitmurte-	at(ə)-
aciute-	acciʀutə- (under atəʀ)
acivar-	acivaʀ- (under aci[1])
acliq	atliʀ (under at(ə)-)
acuniar-	acu-
acuraq	acuʀaʀ
aga-	aɣ(ɣ)a(ʀ)-
ag'anga-	aɣ(ɣ)aɣ-
agaq	aɣ(ɣ)a(ʀ)-
agarte-	aɣ(ɣ)a(ʀ)-
agayu-	aɣayu-
agayuuq	aɣayuuq
agciun	aɣciun
age-, agute-	aɣə-
aggigte-	as(q)iɣte-
aggsuun	aɣcuun
agiirte-	aɣə
agler-	aɣləʀ(-)
agluma-	alɣu-
agluquq	aɣluquʀ (under aɣluʀ)
aglur-	aɣluʀ
agluryaq	aɣluʀyaq (under aɣluʀ)
agtar-	aɣtaʀ- (under aɣə-)
agtur-	aɣtuʀ-
aguumaq	aɣu(C)ummaʀ-
agyaq	aɣyaq
agyaur-	aɣyuʀ-
agyumciar(ar)-, agyumir-	aɣyumiʀ-
ai	ay
aiggaq	aðɣa(ʀ)
aipaq	a(C)ippaʀ
airraq	ayaʀaʀaʀ
aisgaaq, aasgaaq	aðɣa(C)aʀ (under aðɣa(ʀ))
aitar-	aɣittaʀ-
aitaur-	aɣittaʀuʀ- (under aɣittaʀ-)
ak'a	akka
akaa	aka(a)
akag-	akðaɣ-
akeka	aka(a)
akeq	akəʀ
akeqe-	akəqə-
akerta	akiʀ (under aki (-))
aki	aki(-)
aki-	aki(-)
akigar-	akiɣaʀ- (under aki(-))
akiite-	akiŋit- (under aki(-))
akilir-	akiliʀ- (under aki(-))
akimiaq	akimiɣaʀ (under aki(-))
akin	akin (under aki(-))
akiqliq	akil(l)iʀ (under aki(-))
akir-	akkiʀ-
akitmiar-	akitmi(C)-
akitmite-	akitmi(C)-
akiur-	akiʀuʀ- (under aki(-))
akivigte-	akiviɣ-
aklegaq	akləɣaʀ (under akəʀ)
aklu(q)	aklu-
akmaliarall'err(aq)	akmaliaʀaq
akngirte-	atŋiʀ-
aknirte-	atŋiʀ-
aku(q)	aku(ʀ)
akula	akulə (under aku(ʀ))
akulipeq, akulipraq	akulipaq (under aku(ʀ))
akuliq	akul(l)iʀ (under aku(ʀ))
akuliraq	akuliʀaʀ(aku(ʀ))
akulqucuk, akultuqucuk	akulqucuk (under aku(ʀ))
akultu-	akultu- (under aku(ʀ))
akuqar-	akuʀ-[1]
akuraq	akuʀaʀ (under aku(ʀ))
akurte-	akuʀ-[2]
akurtur-	akuʀ-[1]
akusrarte-	akpət-

CAY	PROTOFORM
akutaq	akutaʀ (under aku(ʀ))
akute-	akut- (under aku(ʀ))
akwarpak	ak(k)uvaʀ
akwaugaq	ak(k)uvaʀ
ala-a	a(a)
alagnaq	alaɣnaq
ala-i	a(a)
alai(yug)-	aliɣa-
alair-	allaʀ(-)
alaite-	alaʀitə- (under allaʀ(ɪʀ)-)
alake- (attracted to)	ala-
alake- (notice)	alaŋkaʀ-
alakiitaq	ulak(k)itaʀ-
alangaar-	alaŋʀu-
alange-	ala-
alangru(q)	alaŋʀu-
alap'aa	alappaa
alapen'erte-, alapeng'erte-	alapənʀaʀ-
alarte-	alaʀ-
alarute-	allaʀ(ɪʀ)-
alemqar-	aləmqaʀ-
al'erpak	al(ə)ʀaʀ(ᴀʀ) (under aləʀ]
alerqur-	aləʀaqðᴜʀ-
alia(yug)-	aliɣa-
alike-	alikə-
alinge-	aliŋə-
alingite-	aliŋitə-
alingtar-	aliŋtaʀ- (under aliŋə-)
aliq	aðɪʀ
aliqiliqiaq	alqiliq
aliurtuq	ali(C)ᴜʀtᴜʀ
alivtur-	alivtᴜʀ-
alla	atla
allaneq	atlanəʀ (under atla)
allayug-	atlayuɣ- (under atla)
alleg-	ałəɣ-[1]
allgiar(aq)	ałɣɪʀ
alliqaq	atliqaʀ (under at(ə)-)
alliraq	atlɪʀᴀʀ (under at(ə)-)
allirta	ałɪʀtə
allngik	ałŋiɣ
allragni	alʀani (under aləʀ)
allraku	alʀani (under aləʀ)
allungak	ałuŋžak
allurte-	ałᴜʀ-
alme-	aləmqaʀ-
almigaq	almiɣžaq
alngaq	alŋaʀ(-)
alpa	alpa(ɣ)
alqaq	aləqa(ʀ)
alqar-	aləmqaʀ-
alqiliq	alqiliq
alqunaq	alqunaʀ-
alrapak	alʀapak (under aləʀ)
alu(q)	alu(ʀ)
alunge-	aluɣ-
alungun	alu(C)un (under aluɣ-)
aluqaq, aluqun, aluqan	aluqaq
alutur-, alutuke-	alutᴜʀ-
aluvik	aluvik
amaqsuq	amaʀtᴜʀ
amar-	amaʀ-
amarullek	amaʀutləq
amauq	ama(C)ᴜʀ
amelkite-	amələ
amelraq	amiləqaʀ (under amit-)
ameltu-	amələ
amiik	amik
amikuk	amik(k)ᴜʀ
amili-	amitli- (under amit-)
aminaq	aminaʀ-
aminraq	aminʀaq (under amɪʀ)
amiq	amɪʀ
amirluq	amɪʀluq
amitatuk	amitatuk (under amit-)
amite-	amit-
amlek	amələ
amlleq	aməl(ə)ʀa(ʀ)-
amllir-	amłᴜʀ-
amqar-	amqaʀ-
amraq	amʀaq
amu-	amu-
amun	ammun (under amu-)
amyak	amyak
anaana	ana(a)na
anag-	annaɣ-
anagte-	anaɣtə- (under an(n)aɣ-)
anagute-	annaɣutə- (under an(n)aɣ-)
anaiq	anaʀɪʀ(yᴀʀ) (under anaʀ(-))
anaq, anar-	anaʀ(-)
anaqsartur-	anaqyaʀtᴜʀ- (under anaʀ(-))
anaqsug-	anaqyuɣ- (under anaʀ(-))
anau-	anaɣu-
anaute-	annaɣutə-
anautaq	anaɣutaq (under anaɣu-)
ancarneq	an(ə)cᴀʀɴəʀ (under anə-)
ane-	anə-
anelgun	anəłɣun (under anə-)
anerneq	anəʀɴəʀ (under anəʀ-)
anerteqe-	anəʀtəqə- (under anəʀ-)
aneryaar-	anəʀya(C)ᴀʀ- (under anəʀ-)
angak	aŋaɣ
angala-	aŋala- (under aŋaʀ-)
angalaci-	aŋalat- (under aŋala-)
angalkuq	aŋalkᴜʀ
angaqe-	aŋaqə-
ang'aqe-	aŋa(ʀ)-
an'garaq	an(ə)ɣaʀ(ᴀʀ)
angayite-	aŋaʀ-
angayuk	aŋayuɣ
angayukliq	aŋayuklɪʀ (under aŋayuɣ)
angayuqaq	aŋayuq(q)ᴀʀ (under aŋayuɣ)
ange-	aŋə-
angenquq	aŋənquq (under aŋə-)
angeq	aŋeq
angernak	ayəŋə
angeryuk	ayəŋə
anger-	aŋəʀ-
angi-	aŋi-
angimurte-	aŋit-

CAY	PROTOFORM
asgir-	aðɣiR-
asgur-	aðɣuR-
asgurake-	aðɣuRa- (under aðɣuR-)
asigarnaq	asiɣaRnaq
asigtaq	aciɣtaq (under at(ə)-)
asiite-	asiR-
asmegte-	ayəməɣtə- (under ayəmə-)
aspiar-	asiR-
asqigte-	asiR-
asriq	aɣži(R)-
assigtaq	aciɣtaq (under at(ə)-)
assigte-	as(q)iɣtə-
assike-	asikə- (under asiR-)
assingaq	at(ə)-
assipaq, assipek	at(ə)-
assir-	asiR-
assirneq	aciRnəR (under at(ə)-)
as'un	atžuq- (under atə-)
asvaite-, asvair-	ayva-
asveq	ayvəR
ata (father)	ata[1]
ata (listen)	ata[2]
ata-	ata-
ataata	ata(a)ta
ataku	ataku (under ata[2])
ataneq	atanəR (under ata-)
ataucikun	ataRuccikun (under ataRuciR)
atauciq	ataRuciR
ate-	atə-
ategtu-	atətu- (under at(ə)-)
ateq	atəR
ater-	atəR- (under at(ə)-)
aterte-	atəRtə- (under at(ə)-)
atgiaq	atɣiyaq
atkuk	atəkə
atliq	atliR (under at(ə)-)
atmak	natmaɣ-
atneq	atnəq (under at(ə)-)
atrar-	atRaR- (under at(ə)-)
atrilnguq	atRilŋuq (under atəR)
atsaq	atyaR
atunem	atunəm
atungar	atuŋaR
atur-	atuR-
atuun	atu(R)un (under atuR-)
au-	avu-
au͡'ar-, au͡'arite-	av(v)aR(iR)-
au͡tar-	aɣʷaR-
augyaq	aðuɣyaR (under aðuɣ)
auk	aðuɣ
auluke-	a(C)ulukə-
aumaq	a(C)umaR
aunrar-	aðun(ə)RaR- (under aðuɣ)
aur-	avuR-
aurre-	aðuR-
avaliq	avaliR-
avaq	avðaR
avaqutaq	avaqutaq
avataq	avataR
avate- (choke)	ava-
avate- (area around)	avan
avaur-	ava(C)uR-
avayaq	avayaq
avcellngaq	avəlŋaR
aveg-, avek	avəɣ-
avelngaq	avəlŋaR
avgur-	avɣuR- (under avəɣ-)
aviraute-	avðiR- (under avðaR-)
avirlurte-	avi(R)luR-
avite-	aɣʷitə-
aviu-	aviRu-
avler-	avləR-
avnguq	av(ə)ŋuq
avte-	avət- (under avəɣ-)
avu-	avu-
avur-	avuR-
ayag-	ayaɣ-
ayagaq	ayaɣaR- (under ayaɣ-)
ayagta	ayaɣta (under ayaɣ-)
ayagtuutaq	ayaɣtuR- (under ayaɣ-)
ayakutar(aq)	ayakutaq (under ayaɣ-)
ayallaq	ałayaq
ayalur-, ayalua-	ayalu(R)-
ayani-	ayani(R)-
ayaper-	ayapəR- (under ayaɣ-)
ayari-	ayaRi-
ayarr'aq	ayaRaRaR
ayaruq	ayaRuR (under ayaɣ-)
ayaun	ayaɣun (under ayaɣ-)
ayeme-	ayəmə-
ayi-	ayi-
ayu-	ayu-
ayuqe-	ayuqə-
ayuqucirtur-	ayuquciRtuR- (under ayuqə-)
ayute-	ayut- (under ayu-)
ca-	cu(na)
caaganeq, saaganeq	ci(ð)aɣanəR
caarrluk	cuRuyuk
caavte-	cavət-
caayuryaq	caayuR(y)aq
cacetu-	tatə
cagiq	caɣiq
cagmar-	ciðaɣma(R)- (under ciðaɣ-)
cagner-	caɣnəR-
cagni-	caɣni-
cagte-	ciðaɣ-
caite-	cu(na)ŋit- (under cu(na))
caiggluk, caggluk	caðəɣ(iR)
cakiak	caki(C)aR
cakiq	caki
cakiraq	cakiRaR (under caki)
cakite-	caki(tə)-
cakivte-	cakəvət-
cakuug-	cakəvət-
calaraq	calaRaq
cali	cu(na)li (under cu(na))
cali-	cu(na)li- (under cu(na))
calla-	cała-

CAY	PROTOFORM
ek'ur(ar)-	ək(ə)ðuʀ(aʀ)- (under əkə-[2])
ekvik	əkviɣ
elag-	əlaɣ-
elagayuli	əlaɣayuli (under əlaɣ-)
elagyaq	əlaɣyaq (under əlaɣ-)
elakaq	əlakaq (under əlaɣ-)
elalirte-	əlaliʀ-
elaqliq	cilalliʀ (under cila)
elara-	əlaʀa-
elaturraq	cilatuqaq (under cila)
elave-, lave-	əlavə-
elciar-	nəlcaʀ-
elgar-	əlɣaʀ-
elicar-	əlicaʀ- (under əlit-)
elicima-	əlicima- (under əlit-)
eligarte-	əliɣaʀtə- (under əlit-)
elillgia-	iŋut-[2]
elima-	əlima-
elingra(yug)-	əliʀa-
elirqe-	əliʀqə- (under əɬi-)
elitaqe-	əlitaqə- (under əlit-)
elite-	əlit-
elitnaur-	əlitnauʀ- (under əlit-)
eliveq	əɬivəʀ (under əɬi-)
elivte-, livte-	əlivtə-
ella	cila
ellai-	təlaɣ-
ellairute-	cilaŋiʀutə- (under cila)
ellaite-	cilaŋit- (under cila)
ellakegci-	cilakiɣ- (under cila)
ellalluk	cilaɬuɣ (under cila)
elleg-	ciləɣ-[1]
ellerrar(aq), llerrar(aq)	(ə)ɬəŋaðaʀ(-)
elli- (sharpen)	cili-
elli- (put, place)	əɬi-
ellii	əɬ(ə)ŋa
ellimer-	təli-
ellin	cillin (under cili-)
ellir-	əɬiʀ- (under əɬi-)
elliraq	əɬiɣaʀ(aʀ)
elliveq	əɬivəq (under əɬi-)
ellivik	əɬ(ɬ)iviɣ (under əɬi-)
ellmaar	əɬmaʀ(aʀ)
ellmi-	əɬmi-
ellngar-	əɬŋaʀ-
elluar-	əɬuʀaʀ-
ellumrun	pəɬuɣ-
elluqun	ətlu(ʀ)-
ellur-	ciluʀ-
elnguq	nəlŋu(ʀ)-
elpeke-	əlpəkə-
elpet	əlpət
elqiaq	təlqiðaʀ
elquaq	qəlquðaʀ
elraur-	əɣləʀ-
elravig	əlʀaviɣ
elturar	əltu(ʀa)q
eluciq	əluciʀ (under ət-)
elumar-	elimmaʀ-
elurtu-	əluʀ-
emuk	əmmuɣ
emute-	əmət-
ena	ənə
enair-	ənəŋiʀ- (under ənə)
en'aq	tən(n)aq (under tənət-)
eneq	nənəq
engelqaq	kənlə
englar-	əŋlaʀ-
enig-	əŋiɣ-
enir-	tənniʀ-
enki-	əŋki-
enliaq	ənli(C)aʀ
enqake-	ənqa(ʀ)-
ente-	tənət-
enur-	ənuʀ-
enuur-	tənu-
epaar-	əppaʀ-
epe-	əpə-
epnaiq	əpnaʀiʀ (under əpnaʀ)
epnaq	əpnaʀ
eprir-	əpʀiʀ-
epsalngu-	əpyalŋu- (under əpə-)
epu	əpu
epulquq	əpulquq (under əpu)
eqe-	əqə-[1]
eqiur-	qəðði(C)uʀ- (under qəðuɣ)
eqnarqe-	əqə-[2]
equg-	əqðuɣ-
equk (wood)	qəðuɣ
equk (thing in mouth)	əqðuɣ-
ere-	əʀə-[1]
erevte-	əvəʀtə-
erina(q)	əʀina(q)
erinraq	əʀi-
eriq	əʀði
eritar-	əʀitaʀ- (under əʀi-)
ermig-	əʀmiɣ-
erneq	əʀnəq (under əʀə-[2])
ernertur(aq)	qiʀnəʀ-
erte-	əʀə-[2]
erur-	əʀʀuʀ- (under əʀə-[1])
erute-	əʀutə- (under əʀə-[2])
ervig-	əʀ(ə)viɣ- (under əʀə-[1])
ervuqar-, ervuqe-	əʀvuqaʀ- (under əʀə-[1])
esiq	əɣyiʀ
eskaviaq	kəð(ə)kaviɣ
essmiar-	ciŋuʀ-
essngur-	ciŋuʀ-
esvaiq	əvyaŋ(ŋ)iʀ
ete-	ət-
etgalqite-	ətɣalʀit- (under ətə-)
etgate-	ətɣat- (under ətə-)
et'u-	ətə-
eva-	əva-
evate-	ava-
evcug-	əvcuɣ-
everte-, verte-	əvəʀtə-
evsiaq	əvyaŋ(ŋ)iʀ
evu-, evunret	iŋ(ə)yu-
eyag-	iŋaɣ-
eyur- (jell)	iɣðuʀ-

CAY	PROTOFORM
eyur- (stick up for)	iγžuʀ-
gilerte-	əγləʀ-
icivaq	icivaʀ
iciwa	iciγ^{w}a
igaq	iγaq
ige-	iγə-[1]
iggag-	iγəγaʀ-
igta	žiγtə
igte-	iγtə-
igur- (jell)	iγðuʀ-
igur- (stick up for)	iγžuʀ-
igur- (drill into)	niγəðuʀ-
iguuk	iγðuγ
iguun	niγəðuʀun (under niγəðuʀ-)
igvar-	iγvaʀ-
igyaraq	iγyaʀ(aʀ)
ii	əðə
ii-	aγa-
iigmiur-	əðəγmiγ- (under əðə)
iinraq	iðəʀaʀ (under iðəʀ-)
iinru(q)	aγanʀu(C)(aʀ)
iir-	iðəʀ-
iiraq (spirit)	iðəʀaʀ (under iðəʀ-)
iiraq (scar, gland)	əðəʀa(ʀ)
iitaq	iitaq
iivkar-	əðəvkaʀ-
ikamraq	ikamʀaʀ
ikanga-	ikaγ-
ikayur-	ikayuʀ-
ikgete-	ikəγ(ə)t-
ikig-	ikiγ-
ikii	ikki
ikiituk	iki(C)ituγ
ikir-	ikiʀ-
ikug-	ikuγ-
ikusek	ikuyəγ
ikuutaq	ikuγutaʀ (under ikuγ-)
ila	ila(-)
ilaaq	ila(C)aʀ (under ila(-)[1])
ilacir-	ilacciʀ-
ilag-, ilar-	il(l)aγ-
ilair-	ilaŋiʀ- (under ila(-)[1])
ilairin	il(l)aγiʀun (under il(l)aγ-)
ilake-	ilakə- (under ila(-)[1])
ilaliur-, ilaliute-	ilali(C)uʀ- (under ila(-)[1])
ilalke-, ilasqite-	ilalʀu-
ilalru-	ilalʀu-
ilanaaraq	ilannaʀ (under ila(-)[1])
ilangarte-	ilaŋŋaʀ- (under ila(-)[1])
ilangci-	ilaŋci- (under ila(-)[1])
ilaraaraq	ilaq
ilgar-	aŋilʀaʀ- (under aŋit-)
iliq	iliγ
illug-	iłuγ-
ilngir-	ilŋiʀ-
ilquq	iləquq
ilu	ilu
ilu-	ilu- (under ilu)
ilulngu-	ilulŋu- (under ilu)
ilumun	ilumun (under ilu)
ilungaq	iluŋaq (under illuʀ(aʀ))
ilupeq, iluperaq	ilupəʀ(aʀ) (under ilu)
iluqliq	ilulliʀ (under ilu)
ilur(aq)	illuʀ(aʀ)
ilutak	ilutaq (under ilu)
iluteqe-	ilutəqə- (under ilu)
ima	imma
imanaq	imanəʀ
imange-	imanəγ- (under ima(ʀ))
imaq	ima(ʀ)
imaquq	imaʀyaγ (under ima(ʀ))
imaryuk, imaryaq	imaʀyaγ (under ima(ʀ))
ime-	imə-
imeg-	iməγ-
imegglugte-	iməγłuγ- (under iməγ-)
imir-	immiʀ- (under ima(ʀ))
imlauk	imla(C)u(γ)
imtuqar-	imtuqaʀ-
imumi	imma
imur(yug)-	imðuʀ-
imurpag-, imuqite-	imðuʀ-
inar-	iŋŋaʀ-
ineqsunarqe-	inəqyunaʀ- (under inəqə-)
inerqur-	inəʀ-
ingcur-	iŋət-
ingkiq	iŋkiʀ
ingleq	iŋləʀ
ingleraq	iŋləʀaq
inglu	iŋlu
inglugtun	iŋluγtun (under iŋlu)
inglukiitaq	iŋluk(k)ita(C)aʀ- (under iŋlu)
ingqi-	əðəŋqi-
ingqiliq	iŋqiliʀ (under iŋqiʀ)
ingqiq	iŋqiʀ
ingriq	iŋʀiʀ
ingte-	iŋtə-
ingulaq	iŋut-[1]
ingun	iŋun (under iŋət-)
inguqaq	iŋuqaʀ (under iŋət-)
ini-	ini-
initaq	innitaʀ (under ini-)
inqe-	inəqə-
inqutaq	inqun (under inəqə-)
inuguaq	yuγu(C)aq (under iŋuγ)
ipegcar-	ipəγcaʀ- (under ipəγ-)
ipgiate-	ipγit- (under ipəγ-)
ipik	ipi(γ)
ipug-	ipuγ-
ipuun	ipuγun (under ipuγ-)
iqalluaq	iqałuγaʀ (under iqałuk)
iqalluk	iqałuk
iqa(q)	iqa(ʀ)
iqelquq	iqəlquq
iqeq	iqə(ʀ)
iqertaq	iqaʀtə
iqlirpak	iqliʀ
iqmig-	iqmiγ-
iqsak	iqlaγ

CAY	PROTOFORM
iqtu-	iqə-
iqu-	iqu-
iquk	iqquR
iqute-	iqu(tə)-
ira(yug)-	iRa-
iraluq	iRaluq
ircaquq	iRcaquR
ircug-	iRcuɣ-
irelgite-	iR(ə)ləɣ-
irir-	iRiR-
irleg-	iR(ə)ləɣ-
irleke-	iRləkə- (under iR(ə)ləɣ-)
irliqe-	ciRłəR-
irnerrluk	iRnəRłuk
irni-	iRni- (under iRnəR)
irniaq	iRni- (under iRnəR)
irr'i-	iR(a)Ri- (under iRa-)
irseg-	iRyaɣ-[1]
iru	niRu
iruluq	niRulu (under niRu)
iruver-	niRuvəR-
iryagte-	əðiRyaɣ(-) (under əðiR)
iryuqe-	aRyuqə- (under aR(ə)yu-)
issaluq, issaluuq	isaluq
issengquq	ica-
isser-	uciR-
issuriq	isuRiq
itegmig-	itəɣmiɣ- (under itəɣ)
itegnaq	itəɣnaR
itek	itəɣ-
iter-	itəR-
iterneq	itəRnəq (under itəR-)
it'gaq	itəɣaR (under itəɣ)
itrar-	itəRaR- (under itəR)
itrute-	itRutə- (under itəR-)
ituk	ituɣ
itume-	itəmə-
itute-	itutə-
ivalu	ivalu
ivar-	ivaR-
iver-	ivəR-
ivgar-	ivɣaR-
ivrar-	ivəR-
ivrir-	iyuvRiR-
ivruciq	ivRuciq (under ipəR-)
ivsuk, ivyuk	nəpyuk
iyukaq	iŋ(ə)yukaR
kaak(a)	kaa(kaa)
kacete-	katə-
kagaluq	kaɣaluq
kagi-	kaɣi-
kaig-	ka(C)əɣ-
kaiga-	kaya(ɣ)-
kaime-	kaɣimə-
kakangcaq, kakengcaq	kakaŋcaR
kakave-	kakavə-
kakeggluk	kakkiɣ
kakek	kakkiɣ
kaki-	kaki-
kakiaq	kaki(C)aR (under kaki-)

CAY	PROTOFORM
kakegte-	kakeɣtə- (under kakkiɣ)
kakilacag-	kakilla- (under kaki-)
kakin	kakkin (under kaki-)
kakingerte-, kakiungqite-	kakiŋəR-
kakivik, kakisvik	kakiðviɣ (under kaki-)
kalagaq	kalaɣaq
kaleg-	kaləɣ-[2]
kalgun	kaləɣ-[2]
kalikaq	kalikaq
kalivneq	kaləvnəR (under kaləvə(t)-)
kallagte-	kałaɣ-
kalluk	katluɣ
kalngak	kalŋaɣ
kalug-	kalukaq
kalukaq (halo)	kaŋlu-
kalukaq (feast)	kalukaq
kalurrar-	kaləɣ-[1]
kal'utaq, kaluutaq	kaləɣ-[2]
kalvag-	kaləvə(t)-
kalve-	kaləvə(t)-
kama(yug)-	kama-
kamake-	kamakə- (under kama-)
kameksak	kaməɣ
kamguk	kaməɣ
kamilar-	kamillaR- (under kaməɣ)
kanagaq	kanaɣ
kanaknaq, kanaknak	kanaknaR
kanar-	kanaR-
kanayurnaq	kanayu(R)
kaneq	kanəR
kangciq	kaŋciR
kangeq	kaŋəR
kangiq	kaŋiR
kangiqutaq	kaŋiR
kangiraq	kaŋiRaR (under kaŋiR)
kangirci-	kaŋiRci- (under kaŋiR)
kangirrluk	kaŋiRłuɣ (under kaŋiR)
kangivar-	kaŋivaR- (under kaŋiR)
kangivarte-	kaŋivaRtə(R)- (under kaŋiR)
kangquq	kaŋquq (under kaŋəR)
kangtu-	kaŋtu- (under kaŋəR)
kanguq	kaŋuR
kanruyauciq	kanRuyauciq (under kanəq)
kanuyaq	kannuyaR
kapciq	kapəciR
kape-	kapə-
kapeciq	kapəciR
kapegcug(yug)-	kapeɣcuɣ-
kapgite-	kapət-
kapia-	kappəya-
kapun	kappun (under kapə-)
kapur-	kapuR- (under kapə-)
kapute-	kapputə- (under kapə-)
kasme-	kayəmə(t)-
kasngu(yug)-	kayŋu-
kassiyuq	kasiyuq
kassug-	katyuɣ-
kassute-	katyuɣutə- (under katyuɣ-)
kasvun	kaðəvə(t)-
katag-	kataɣ-
katete-	katət- (under katə-)

CAY	PROTOFORM
katngite-	katŋitə-
katur-	katyuR- (under katə-)
kau-	kaɣu-
kaug-	kaðuɣ-
kaugpak	ka(C)uɣ
kaugun	kað(ð)uɣun (under kaðuɣ-)
kavcak	kavcak
kaviaq	kav(v)i(C)aR (under kaviR-)
kavirte-	kaviR-
kavlak	kavlaɣ
kavluun	kamlu
kavtak	kavcak
kayu (sculpin)	kayu
kayu- (strong)	kayu-
kayunge-	kayuŋə- (under kayu-)
kecete-	kəcit-
keggag-	kəɣaɣ-
keggagcete-	kəɣðaɣ-
keggan	kiɣan
keggasek	kiɣayəɣ
kegge-	kəɣə-
keggeve-	kəɣə-
keggiarnaq	kəɣi(C)aR (under kəɣə-)
kegginaq	kəɣinaR
kegginaquq	kəɣinaquR (under kəɣinaR)
kegglaq	kəklaɣ
keggmar-	keɣmaR- (under kəɣinaR)
keggmiaq	kəɣmi(C)- (under kəɣinaR)
keggun	kəɣun (under kəɣə-)
kegluneq	kəɣlunəq
kegturyaq	kəɣtuRyaR
keleg-	kəɫəɣ-
kelig-	kəliɣ-
keligaq	kəliɣaR (under kəliɣ-)
keligvak	kəliɣvaɣ (under kəliɣ-)
kellarvik	əkləRviɣ (under əkə-[2])
kelliq	kətliR (under kətə-)
kelu-	kəlu
keluk	kəluɣ
keluknaq	kəluvaR- (under kəlu)
keluvar-, keluvaq	kəluvaR- (under kəlu)
kelve-	kəl(ə)və-
kemegnaq	kəmaɣnaq
kemek	kəməɣ
kemgite-	kəmɣit- (under kəməɣ)
kemni-	kəmni-
kenatagun	kənataɣ- (under kənəR-)
kenayuk, kenaayuk	kənaayuq
keneq	ək(ə)nəR (under əkə-[1])
kenerte-	kənəR-
kengelqaq	kənlə
kengla	kənlə
keni-	kəni-
kenimig-, kenimike-	kəniRmiɣ- (under kəniR)
keniq	kəniR
kenir- (point)	tənniR-
kenir- (cook)	(ə)kəniR- (under əkə-[1])
kenite-	kənit- (under kəni-)
kenlu	kənluR
kennge-	ək(ə)nəɣ- (under əkə-[1])
kente-	tənət-
kenuraq	əkənuRaq (under əkə-[1])
kenuur-	tənu-
kep'alek	kəppaR (under kəpə-)
kepe-	kəpə-
kepete-	kəpət-[1]
kepnerciq	kəpnəRaRciq
kepqe-	kəpət-[2]
kerar-	əkəRaR-
ker'aq	əkəRaR
kesir-	kəði-
kessig-, ketsig-	kətðiɣ- (under kətə-)
kete-	kətə-
ketgaq	kətəɣ[2]
ketvar-	kətvaR-
keveg-	kəvəɣ-
kevgaluk	kəvɣaluɣ (under kəvɣaR)
kevgaq	kəvɣaR
kevir-	kəviR-
kevkarte-	kəpəkaR- (under kəpə-)
keyir-	kəði-
kiak	kiðaɣ(-)
kian	kivan
kiarneq	kiaRnəq (under kiðaR)
kiarte-	kiyaR-
kicaq	kicaR
kii- (come off as a layer)	kaɣa-
kii- (alone, only)	kəði-
kiiki	ki(i)
kiitaq	kiitaq (under kaɣa-)
kilgaq	kilɣaq
kilir-	kiliR-
kina	ki(na)
kiner-	kinəR-
kingu-	kiŋu-
kinguk	kiŋuɣ
kinguneq	kiŋunəR (under kiŋu-)
kinguqliq	kiŋuqliq (under kiŋu-)
kingurarte-	kiŋuRaR- (under kiŋu-)
kingutmurte-	kiŋutmuR- (under kiŋu-)
kinguvar-	kiŋuvaR- (under kiŋu-)
kingyar-	kiŋyaR-
kipullegte-	kipuɫəɣ- (under kiput-)
kipute-	kiput-
kirciur-, keggirciur-	kəɣiR-
kirta	kəɣiR-
kita(k)	ki(i)
kit'e-	kit-
kitngik (lowbush cranberry)	kitmiɣ
kitngik (heel)	kitŋiɣ
kitngilquq	kitŋilquR (under kitŋiɣ)
kitngu-	kitŋu-
kitur-	kituR-
kituuga	kitu (under ki(na))
kiu-	ki(C)u-
kiugkenak	kivaknaR
kiumra-	ki(C)umɣa- (under ki(C)u-)
kiuryaq	ki(C)uRyaR
kive-	kivə-
kiyarte-	kiyaR-

CAY	PROTOFORM
kucir-	kuciʀ- (under kutə)
kucuknaq	kucukaʀ
kuc'uq	kuccuʀ
kucuquq	kuðucciʀ
kuiɣ´t aaniit	kuiɣət aaniit (under kuðəɣ)
kuik	kuðəɣ
kuime-	ku(C)imə-
kuingiq	kuiŋiq
kukegte-	kukəɣ-
kukikcak	kukiɣ
kukkuq	kuk(k)u(ʀ)(-)
kuksaga-	kukðaɣ-
kuksug-	kukðaɣ-
kukukuaq	kukuku(C)aʀ
kukumyarar(ar)-	kukumyaʀ-
kukupak	kukuɣ
kukusvak, kukisvak	kukiɣvak
kuma-	əkuma-
kumak	kumaɣ
kumakir-	kumakiʀ- (under kumaɣ)
kumarte-	əkuma- (under əkə-[1])
kumeg-	kuməɣ-
kumkaili-, kumkailin	kumka(C)iʀ- (under kumkaʀ)
kumkar-	kumkaʀ-
kumla-	kumla-
kumluq	kumlu
kunnaq	kunnaʀ
kuta	kutə
kuucnaq	kuðuccinəʀ (under kuðucciʀ)
kuugaq	kukəɣ
kuugte-	ku(C)u(ɣ)-
kuukuq	kuk(k)u(ʀ)(-)
kuve-	kuvə-
kuvyaq	kuvðaʀ
kuya(k)	kuyaɣ
kuyag-	kuyaɣ-
kuyapegaq	kuyapəɣaʀ (under kuyaɣ)
lagiq	laɣiq
laqar-	aləmqaʀ-
leg-	əɬəɣ-
leq	nəɬəʀ(-)
leqleq	neqleq
maaten	maðətən
macaq	macaʀ
makete-	makət-
makira-, makiur-	makiʀ-
maklak	maklaɣ
maksaq	maksaq
makta-	makəta- (under makət-)
makugte-	makə-
malig-, malike-	maliɣ-
maligcuar-	maliɣcuaʀ- (under maliɣ-)
maligqe-, malirqe-	maliʀqə- (under maliɣ-)
maligte-	maliɣ-
malirqar-	maliʀqə- (under maliɣ-)
malleg-	maɬəɣ-
mallu(k)	maɬu(k)
mamcaq	mamca(ʀ)
mamcar-	mamcaʀ- (under mamə-)
mame-	mamə-
mamlek	maməlәɣ
mamte-	mamət- (under mamə-)
mamteraq	mamtəʀaʀ
mamtu-	mamtu- (under mamə-)
malri	malʀi
malruk	malʀuɣ
manaq	manaʀ
maneq	manəʀ
mangag-	maŋaɣ(-)
mangarniiq, mangayaaq	maŋaq
mangelpag-	manəɣ-
mangengtak	maŋtaɣ
mangirre-	maŋiʀ-
mangtak	maŋtaɣ
mangyuarir-, mangyaur(ar)-	manəɣyu(C)aʀ- (under manəɣ-)
mani-	mani-
maniar-	maniaʀ- (under mani-)
manig-	maniɣ-
manik	manniɣ
manu-	manu
manuilitaq	manuŋilitaʀ (under manu)
mangarniiq	maŋaʀniiq
maqaq	maqaq
maqe-	maqə-
maqete-	maqət- (under maqə-)
maquluk, maqulluk	maquluk (under maqu-)
maraq	maʀʀaʀ
marrlugaq	əma
maruara-	maʀu-[2]
martu-, markite-	maʀtu-
maryarte-	maʀyaʀ-
masi-	pasi-
matar-	mattaʀ-
matneq	matnəq
matngagte-, matngite-	matŋa-
maurluq	əma
mayiteqe-	mayitəqə-
mayur-	mayuʀ-
mayura-	mayuʀa(ʀ)- (under mayuʀ-)
mayuryaraq	mayuqqaq (under mayuʀ-)
mecak	məcaɣ
mecaliqaq	məcaliqaq (under məcaɣ-)
mecarte-	məcaʀ-
meceg-	məcəɣ
meciaq	məciʀaʀ (under mecu(ɣ)-)
mecig-	məciɣ-
mecir(ar)-	məciʀaʀ-
mecuq	mecu(ɣ)-
mege-	məɣə-
megtaq	əvəɣtaʀ
melek	mələɣ(-)
mellar-, mellaq	məɬaʀ-
mellgar(aq)	mətləɣ
melnguq	məlŋuʀ
melquq	məlquʀ
melu-	məlu-
melug-	məluɣ-

CAY	PROTOFORM
melugyar(aq)	məluɣɣaR (under məluɣ-)
menge-	əmənə(R)- (under əməɣ-)
mengla	miŋlə
mengqurpak	məŋquq (under əməɣ-)
mente-	mənət-
meq	əməR(-)
meqcir-	məqəciR- (under məqe-)
meqe-	məqə-
meqsartur-	meqsaRtuR- (under əməR(-))
meqsug-	əmeqyuɣ- (under əməR(-))
merig-	məRiɣ-
mernuir-	məRnuRiR- (under məRnuR-)
mernur-	məRnuR-
mertar-	əməRtaR- (under əməR(-))
mer'un	əm(ə)Run (under əməR(-))
meryak	məRyaɣ (under əməR(-))
metervik	mətəRvik (under mətəR)
metqe-	mətaɣ-
metraq	mətəR
mianike-	mi(C)ani(kə)-
migpak	əməɣ-
migtu-	əmə
miicir-	əmmit-
miite-	əmmit-
mike-	mikə-
mikete-	mikə-
mikli-	mikəli- (under mikə-)
miluqu-	miluR-
mimeq	mimər
mimernaq	mimərnaq (under mimər)
minaq	minaR-
mineg-	minəɣ-[1]
minek	minəɣ-[2]
mingqe-	miŋqə-
mingqun	miŋqun (under miŋqə-)
mingug-	miŋuɣ-
minuk	minəɣ-[2]
miryaq, miryar-	miRyaR(-)
mistu-, miskite-	məciɣ-
mit'e-	mit-
mulngaite-, mulngake-	mulŋa-
mulu-	mulu-
mumeq	muməR(-)
mumig-	mumiɣ-
munar-	munaR-
munarciaq	unaRciR-
murqe-	muRqə-
muru-	maRu-[1]
murugte-	muRðuɣ-
muute-	əmət-
na(ni)	na-[2]
naa-	naða-
naacuqe-	naacuqə- (under naða-)
naama-	naðama- (under naða-)
naami	na(C)umi
naaneq	na(C)aneq (under naða-)
naanguar-	əna-
naaqe-	naðaqə- (under naða-)
naate-	naðat- (under naða-)
nacallngaq, nacallngaar(aq)	nacałŋaq (under nacaR)

CAY	PROTOFORM
nacaq	nacaR
nacaullek	naca(C)ułək (under nacaR)
nacete-	nacit-
nacig-	naciɣ-
nacin	naccin (under natəR)
nagaayuq	naɣaayuq
nagiquyaq	naɣiquyaq
nagte-	naɣət-
nagtuqaq	naɣtuqaR (under naɣət-)
naive-	na(C)əvə(t)-
nakaaq	nakaR
nakaar-	nakkaR-
nakacugnaq	nakacuɣnaR (under nakacuɣ)
nakacuk	nakacuɣ
naker-	nakəR-
nakleke-	naŋłəɣ-
nakmiin	nałmi(nəR)
nakriate-	nak(ə)Rit- (under nakəR-)
naku-	naku(R)-
nala-	nala-
nalaqe-	nataqə-
naleq	nałəR
nali(q)	nalliR (under na-[2])
nalirrugte-	nalliR (under na-[2])
nalke-	nalkə- (under nałə-)
nalkiik	nałəkkaɣ
nall'arte-	nałaR- (under nałə-)
nalle-	nałə-
nallu-	nału-
nallunailkutaq	nałunaRilkutaR (under nału-)
nallunair-	nałunaRiR- (under nału-)
nalluyagute-	nałuyaɣutə- (under nału-)
nalqigte-	nalqiɣ- (under nałə-)
naluaq	nalu(C)aR
nalug- (throw in air)	nalluɣ-
nalug- (swim of animal)	naluɣ-
naneq	nənəq
naner-	nanəR-
nanerpak	nanəRpaɣ(-) (under nənəq)
naneryaq	nanəRyaR (under nanəR-)
nangcar-	naŋcaR-
nange-	naŋə-
nanger-	naŋəR-
nangete-	naŋət- (under naŋə-)
nangquq	naŋquR
nangru(yug)-	naŋRu(R)-
nangteqe-	naŋtəR- (under naŋə-)
nangugte-	naŋžuɣ-
nangyar(yug)-	naŋyaR-
nanikua-	nani-[2]
nanilliur-	nani-[2]
nanilraq	nanilRaq (under naniR)
naniq	naniR
nanite-	nanit-
nanrar-	nanRaR-
nanuaq	nanuR
nanvaq	nanvaR
napa, napa-	napa-
napartaq	nappaRtaR (under napa-)

CAY	PROTOFORM
naparte-	nappaʀ- (under napa-)
naparutaq	nappaqutaʀ (under napa-)
napataq, napatar-	napataʀ- (under napa-)
napayuq	napaðuʀ (under napa-)
napete-	napəʀ-
napu	napu
naqa	naqðaʀ
naqir-	naqət-
narcig-	naʀciɣ-
nare-	naʀə-
narite-	naʀciɣ-
narug-	naʀðuɣ-
narulkaq	naʀuɬəkaʀ (under naʀuɬəɣ-)
narulleg-	naʀuɬəɣ-
narullgute-, narulkute-	naʀuɬɣutə-
naruyaq	naʀuyaʀ
naryar-	naʀ(ə)yaʀ (under naʀə-)
nas'ak	nayaɣ
naspertur-	nay(ə)pəʀtuʀ- (under nay(ə)pət-)
naspete-	nay(ə)pət-
nasqulŋu-	nay(ə)qulŋu- (under nay(ə)quʀ)
nasquq	nay(ə)quʀ
nataqe-	nataqə-
nate-	natə- (under na-[2])
nateq	natəʀ
naternaq	natəʀ(aʀ)naʀ (under natəʀ)
natquigte-, natquvigte-	natəquviɣ- (under natəʀ)
natquik	natəquviɣ- (under natəʀ)
natraq	natəʀaʀ (under natəʀ)
nau-	naɣu-
naucetaaq	naɣu-
naucir-	naɣucciʀ- (under naɣu-)
naumi	na(C)umi
naunraq	naɣunʀaq (under naɣu-)
nauwa	naɣu
navcuite-	navcu
naveg-	navəɣ-
navgi-	nav(ə)ɣi- (under navəɣ-)
navgur-	navɣuʀ- (under navəɣ-)
nayagaq	nayaɣ
nayangar-	nayaŋaʀ-
nayiq	nayyiʀ
nayug-	nayuɣ-
nayur-	nayuʀ-
negaiq, negair(aq)	nəɣaʀ
negaq	nəɣaʀ
negcik	nəɣciɣ
negeq	nəɣəʀ
negiliq	nəɣilaʀ
negituqar-	nəɣituqaʀ-
negte-	tənəɣ-
negur-	nəɣuʀ-
neguyaq	nəɣuyaʀ
neka(yug)-	nəka-
nek(e)ve-	nəkəvə(t)-
nekevraartuq, kevraartuq	nəkəvʀaaʀtuq (under nəkəvə(t)-)
nekva-	nəkəvʀa- (under nəkəvə(t)-)
nekvayar-	nəkvaʀ- (under nəkəvə(t)-)
nel'a	kənlə
neleq	nəɬəʀ-
neliaq	ənli(C)aʀ
nelnguq	nəlŋu(ʀ)-
nemeq	nəməʀ(-)
nemeryaq	nəməʀyaʀ (under nəməʀ(-))
neneq	nənəq
nengar-	nəŋ(ŋ)aʀ-
nengauk	nəŋa(C)uɣ
nenge-	nəŋə-
nengiq	nəŋiʀ
nengla	nəŋə(t)-
nenglar-	əŋlaʀ-
nenglla	nəŋə(t)-
nenglli-	nəŋə(t)-
nengllir-	nəŋɬəʀ- (under nəŋə(t)-]
nengsuq	nəŋyuʀ
nengugte-	nəŋuɣ- (under nəŋə-)
nengulraq, nengulra-	nəŋuləʀ- (under nəŋə-)
nepa	nəpə
nepaite-	nəp'ŋit- (under nəpə)
neplir-	nəpliʀ- (under nəpə)
nepsenarqe-	nəpətya(ʀ)- (under nəpət-)
nep(e)te-	nəpət-
neqa	nəqə
neq'ake-	ənqa(ʀ)-
neq'ar-	ənqa(ʀ)-
neqcaq	nəʀcaʀ
neqleq	nəʀləʀ
neqliur-	nəqli(C)uʀ- (under nəqə)
nequtu-	nəqu-
nere-	nəʀə-
neresta	nəʀəsta (under nəʀə-)
neresvik	nəʀəðviɣ (under nəʀə-)
nerevkar-	nəʀəvkaʀ- (under nəʀə-)
nerilkar-	nəʀiləɣ-
nerqe-	nəʀqə- (under nəʀə-)
neruvailitaq	təʀu
neruver-	nəʀuvəʀ-
neryar-, nerliyar-	nəʀyaʀ- (under nəʀə-)
neryuniur-	nəʀyu(ɣ)-
neve-	nəvə-
never-	nəvəʀ-
neviarcaq	nəvi(C)aʀ
nevirte-	nə(C)uʀ-
nevkuq	nəvku
nevluk	nəvəluɣ (nəvə-)
nevuq	nəvðuʀ
ngel'a	kənlə
ngel'ar-	əŋlaʀ-
ngel'u, nel'u	əŋlu
ngillar-	ni(i)ɬaʀ-
niicugni-	naɣacuɣni- (under naɣa(t)-)
niig-	əŋiɣ-
niite-	naɣa(t)-
nillaq, nillar-	ni(i)ɬaʀ-
ninite-	nunaŋitə- (under nuna)

CAY	PROTOFORM
nipe-	nəpə-
nirar-	niRAR-
niugte-	nəpuɣ- (under nəpə)
nivuk	nəpuɣ- (under nəpə)
nuak	nuvaɣ
nucug-	nuccuɣ-
nuge-	nuɣə-
nugtarte-	nuɣət-
nugyaraq	nuɣyaRaq (under nuɣə-)
nuik	nuɣiR
nuiq	nuɣiR
nukalpiaq	nukalpiɣAR
nukaq	nukaR
nukar(aq)	nukaRAR (under nukaR)
nuki-	nukəɣ
nuleg-	nuləɣ-
nulgair-	nulɣaRiR-
nuliaq	nuliR(AR)
nuliarir-, nulirrir-	nuliAR(AR)iR- (under nuliR(AR))
nulirqellriik	nuli(R)aqəlRiik (under nuliR(AR))
nulirrniar-	nuliR(AR)niAR- (under nuliR(AR))
nulirtur-	nuliR(AR)tuR- (under nuliR(AR))
nullu	nułu(R)
nulte-	nulqaR-
nulur(ar)-	nuluR(AR)-
nuna	nuna
nunallite-	nunalit- (under nuna)
nunaniq	nunanniR- (under nuna)
nunate-	nunatə- (under nuna)
nungirte-, nungirta	nuŋiRtə-
nungute-	nunu(R)-
nuni-	nunni- (under nuna)
nunite-, nuniate-	nunaŋitə- (under nuna)
nunur-	nunuR-
nuqaq	nuqðAR
nuq(e)te-	nuqət-
nuraq	nuRRAR
nurr’aq	nuRAR(AR)
nurte-	ənuR-
nutaan	nutaan (under nutaRAR-)
nutaraq	nutaRAR (under nutaR-)
nuteg-	nutəɣ-
nutem	nutəm
nutngar-	nutŋAR-
nuuk	nuvuɣ
nuuniq	nuuniq
nuvak	nuvaɣ
nuve-	nuvə-
nuvuk	nuvuɣ
nuyaq	nuyAR
nuyuite-	nuyuɣit- (under nuyuɣ-)
nuyurrite-	nuyuɣit- (under nuyuɣ-)
nuyurtar-	nuyuɣ-
paallag-	paŋałłaɣ-
paame-	pa(C)umə(t)-
paanger-	paŋəR-
paangrun	paŋəRun (under paŋəR-)
pacete-	patət-
paci(ke)-	paci-
pacik	maciɣ
pacnaq	pacətə-
pagaq	əpaɣ
pai	paðə-
pai-	paɣi-
pair-	əppaiR-
pairsaag-	paðəRcAR- (under paðəR-)
pairte-	paðəR-
paitaq	paɣitə- (under paɣi-)
paivte-	pa(C)əvtə-
pakegte-	pakəɣ-
pakig-	pakiɣ-
pakiur-	paki(ɣ)uR- (under pakiɣ-)
pakluk	pavlu
palar-	palaR-
palirte-	paliR-
pall’itaq	patlitaR
palu-	palu-
palur-	palluR-
palurtaq	paluRtaR
pama-	pama-
pamesquq	pamyuR
pamyuq	pamyuR
panaq	pana
pangaleg-	paŋaləɣ-
pangquussiig-	paqət-
panik	paniɣ
pap’a	ap(p)a^2
papsalquq	papəɣ
papsi-, papsike-	papði-
paq(e)te-	paqət-
paqna(yug)-	paqna-
paqrite-	paqRitə-
paquussiig-, paquussaag-	paqət-
partak	paRtə(R)
parteraq	paRtəRAR (under paRtə)
paruq	paRuq
pasi-	pasi-
patag-	pattaɣ-
pateg-	patəɣ-
pateq	patəR
patqar-	patqaR-
patsaqar-	pacətə-
patu	matu(-)
patuggluk	patuɣ
patuir-	matuŋiR-
paug-	paɣuɣ-
paulaq	paɣu(la)
paume-	pa(C)umə(t)-
paunraq	paɣunRAR
pavig-	paviɣ-
payiq	pa(C)iR
pay’u-	pay(y)a(ɣ)-
payugte-	payuɣ-
peggar-	pəɣəɣaR-
pegnem	pəɣnəm
pegte-	əpəɣ-
peke-, pekara-	pəkə-

CAY	PROTOFORM
pekete-	pəkət- (under pəkə-)
peksallag-	pəkyaɣ- (under pəkə-)
peksuq	pəkyu
pekutaq	pəkutaq
pel'i-	pəllicci-
pella-	əpla-
peller(yug)-	əpləʀ-
pellug-	pətluɣ-[2]
pellukutaq	pəɫu
pellumrun	pəɫuɣ-
peluq	pəlu(ʀ)
penaiq	əpnaʀiʀ (under əpnaʀ-)
penaq	əpnaʀ-
penge-	pətɣəʀ-
pengeg(yug)-	pəŋəɣ-
pengraliq	pəʀŋaliq (under pəʀə-)
penguq	pəŋuʀ
peqlirte-	pəqliʀ-
pequq	pəku(ɣ)
pere-	pəʀə-
perrir-	əpʀiʀ-
perr'ite-	əpʀiʀ-
perrleqciir(ar)-	pəʀɫəə
perte-	pəʀət- (under pəʀə-)
petengtaq	mətəŋtaq
petengte-	mətəŋɫə(ʀ)-
petgar-	pətɣəʀ-
petgeq	pətɣəʀ-
pet'ngallaq	mətəŋtaq
pet'nge-, petenge-	mətŋəʀ-
petug-	pətuɣ-
peyug-	piyuɣ-
pi-	pi(-)
piciatun	piciatun (under piciʀ)
piciq	piciʀ
piginaq	piɣinaq
piineq	piɣinəʀ
piir-	piiyaq- (under pi(-))
piirag-	piðaɣ-
piirraq	piʀðaʀ-
piite-	piŋit- (under pi(-))
pikaq	pikðaʀ (under pi(-))
pike-	pikə- (under pi(-))
pilag-	pilaɣ-
pilagtur-	pilaɣtuʀ- (under pilaɣ-)
piluaqar-	pi(t)lu(C)aʀ- (under pi(-))
pillugte-	piɫuɣ- (under pi(-))
piluguk	piluɣ(uɣ)-
pingayun	piŋayut
pingcir-	pimci
pinguar-	piŋŋuðaʀ- (under pi(-))
piniate-	pinniʀit- (under pinniʀ-)
piniqe-	piniqə- (under pinniʀ-)
pinir-	pinniʀ-
pinqegte-	pinqiɣ- (under pi(-))
piqer-	əpiqaʀ-
piqertuutaq	əpiqaʀutaʀ (under əpiqaʀ-)
piqrutaq, piqrun	əpiqaʀutaʀ (under əpiqaʀ-)
pircir-	piʀciʀ- (under piʀtuʀ)
pirlak	piʀlaɣ
pirta	piʀtuʀ
pirtuk	piʀtuʀ
pirtuqciraq	piʀtuʀciʀaʀ
pisqun	piðqun (under pi(-))
pissur-	pisuʀ- (under pi(-))
pitaq, pitaqe-	pitaʀ (under pi(-))
pit'e- (rise)	pitə-[1] (under pi(-))
pite-, pit'e- (catch game)	pitə-[2] (under pi(-))
piteg-	pitəɣ-
pitegcaraq, pitegcaun	pitəɣcaʀ- (under pitəɣ-)
piu-	piŋu-[2] (under pi(-))
piug-	piyuɣ-
pivake-	pivakə- (under pi(-))
pivik	piðviɣ (under pi(-))
piyaraite-	piðaqəŋit- (under piðaqə(naʀ)-)
piyua-	piyuɣ-
pualla	puvaɫa
pucikar-	puci-
pugci-	pukcinnaq-
puge-	puɣə-
pugneq	puɣ(ə)nəʀ (under puɣə-)
pugta-	puɣta- (under puɣə-)
pukiq	pukiʀ
pukite-	pukit-
pukug-	pukuɣ-
pula-	pula-
pulaar(ar)-	pula(C)aʀ- (under pula-)
pulengte-	puləŋtə-
punerte-	punəʀtə-
pupik	pupiɣ
pupingqua-	pupiŋquʀ-
pupsug-	pumyuɣ-
pupsulek	pumsulək (under pumyuɣ-)
puqiate-	puqiŋit- (under puqiɣ-)
puqig-	puqiɣ-
puqla-	puqla
put'e-	put-
putu- (make hole)	putu(-)[1]
putu (dance)	putu(-)[2]
putukuq	putukuʀ
puugtuyuli	muɣtu(yu)li(q)
puukar-	puvuk(k)aʀ- (under puvuɣ-)
puve-	puvə-
puveltuk	puvəltu
puvsaq	puvyaʀ
puya-	puya-
puyuq	puyuʀ
puyuqe-	puyuqə- (under puyuʀ)
puyuraar(aq)	puyuʀnaq (under puyuʀ)
puyurniq, puyurnaq	puyuʀnaq (under puyuʀ)
qaaryak	qa(C)aʀyaʀ
qac'ag-	qac(c)aɣ-
qacagte-	qacu-
qacarte-	qacaʀ-
qacelli-	qacəli-
qaci-	qatə
qacu-	qacu-
qagan	qaɣan

CAY	PROTOFORM
qayuwa	qayu(q)
qecaruaq	qəcaʀu(C)aʀ
qeceg-	qətəɣ-
qecik	qəciɣ
qeciq	qəciʀ(-)
qecnge-, qecngerte-	qətəɣ-
qecug-	qəc(c)uɣ-
qecuqite-	qəcuqitə-
qela	qəla-[2]
qelanernarqe-	qəlanəʀ(aʀ)- (under qəla-[1])
qelapegte-	qəla-[1]
qelcaq, qelcavak	qaðəɣ-
qelengllak	qəłəŋłak (under qəłəɣ-)
qelengte-	qələɣ-
qelluq	əqlu
qellur-	qəłuʀtə- (under əqə-[1])
qelqecir(ar)-	qaʀaləʀ-
qelquaq	qəlquðaʀ
qelta	qaltə
qelu-	qəlu-
qemag-, qemak	qəmaɣ-
qemeryaq	qəməʀyaʀ
qemiq (hill)	qəmiʀ[1]
qemiq (float line)	qəmiʀ[2]
qemirrluk	qəmiʀłuɣ (under qəmiʀ[1])
qemite-	qəmit-
qena-	qəna-
qenarqe-	əqə-[2]
qenercinrraq	qənəʀciʀ
qenerte-	qənəʀ-
qengallek	qəŋaləɣ (under qəŋaʀ)
qengaq	qəŋaʀ
qengaraq	qəŋaʀaʀ (under qəŋaʀ)
qengaruk	qəŋaʀžuk (under qəŋaʀ)
qengaryak	qəŋaʀyak (under qəŋaʀ)
qenguq	qəŋu(ʀ)
qenu	qənu
qep'ag-	əqət- (under əqə-[1])
qepyun, qep'sun	qəpə-
qerar-	əkəʀaʀ-
qer'aq	əkəʀaʀ
qerarun, qerrarun	qəʀaʀun (under qəʀaʀ-)
qercua-	qiʀə-
qercurpak	qakcuʀ- (under qakə(ʀ)-)
qerkite-	əkəʀ(tu)-
qerqaaller(aq)	qaaqtuq-
qerqaq	qətək
qerqauq	qaqðaʀ
qerra-, qerratarte-	qəʀaʀ-
qerraleryug-	qaʀaləʀ-
qerrircete-, qerrircar-	qəʀiʀ-
qerrler-	qəʀłəʀ-
qerrluk	qaqluɣ
qerrsig-	qaʀya
qerru-	qiʀu-
qerruarte-	qəʀu(C)aʀte-
qerrulliik	qaʀułiɣ
qerruq	qaʀðuʀ
qerrur-	qəʀuʀ-
qerruyanarqe-	qiʀuya- (under qiʀu-)
qerruyaq, qerruyak	qiʀuya- (under qiʀu-)
qertu-	əkəʀ(tu)-
qertuneq	qəʀtunəq
qessa-	əq(ə)ya-
qessake-	əq(ə)yakə- (under əq(ə)ya-)
qes'un	əqət- (under əqə-[1])
qet'e-	əqət- (under əqə-[1])
qetek	qətək
qeter-	qətəʀ
qetrar-, qerretrar-	qiʀətəʀ- (under qiʀə-)
qetunraq	qətunʀaʀ
qetute-	qətut-
qevler-	qəvləʀ-
qevte-	qəvə(t)-
qeya-	qiða-
qeyu-	qiyu(ɣ)(-)
qia-	qiða-
qiaq	qi(C)aʀ
qiaryar	qa(C)aʀyaʀ
qigcig-	qikciɣ- (under qikə-[1])
qiguiq	qiɣuiq
qiilerte-	qi(C)əliʀ- (under qi(C)ət-)
qiiq	qiðəʀ
qiive-	qivə(ʀ)-
qikar-	qikaʀ-
qikcug(yug)-	qikə-[1]
qikertaq	qikəʀtaʀ
qikiq	qikaʀ-
qikmiruaq	qikmi(C)uðaʀ (under qikmiʀ)
qiku	qiku
qilag-	qilaɣ-
qilagaq	qilaɣaʀ (under qilaɣ)
qilaggluk	qilaɣłuɣ (under qilaɣ)
qilagmiutaq	qilaɣmi(C)utaʀ (under qilaɣ)
qilak	qilaɣ
qilangaq	qilaŋŋaʀ
qillerneq	qiłəʀnəʀ (under qiłəʀ-)
qillerte-	qiłəʀ-
qillerutair-	qiłəʀutaʀiʀ- (under qiłəʀ-)
qilug-	qiluɣ-
qiluq	qilu
qimag-	qimaɣ-
qimug-	qimuɣ-
qimugte	qimuɣtə (under qimuɣ-)
qinerte-	qinəʀ-
qingaq	qiŋŋaʀ-
qingirte-	qiŋiʀ-
qinike-	qiŋiʀ-
qinkiq	qinki(q)
qinu-	qinu-
qinuite-	qinu(C)it- (under qinu-)
qinurqe-	qinuʀaʀ- (under qinu-)
qip'aq	qipðaʀ (under qipə-)
qipe-	qipə-
qisserte-	qisiq
qiste-	qi(C)ət-
qitevte-	qitəvə(t)-
qitngir-	qitŋiʀ-
qiu-, qiuq (blueberry)	qiyu(ɣ)(-)

CAY	PROTOFORM
qiuq (rock)	qiɣuR
qiur-	qiɣuR-
qiurliq, qiugliq	qiɣu(ɣ)(-)
qiuryaq	ki(C)uRyaR
qivir-	qiviR-
qivru-	qivRu-
qivyuq	qivyu(R)
quagciq	quvəɣci(q)
quaguk	qu(C)aɣðuɣ
quagulek	qu(C)aɣðuləɣ (under qu(C)aɣðuɣ)
quaq, quarnaq	qu(C)aR
quarruuk	quɣðaRutnaq (under quɣðaR-)
quarta (anal itch)	quɣaRta(R)
quarta (cataract in eye)	quvəRtə
qucak, qucag-	qucaɣ-
qugarruuk	quɣðaR-
qugautnaq	quɣðaRutnaR (under quɣðaR-)
qugcuaqer-	quŋluɣ-
qugtuqaq	quɣtuqaR
qugyuk	quɣðuɣ
quinag(yug)-	quɣinaɣ-
qukaq	qukaR
qukaqliq	qukaqliq (under qukaR-)
qukir-	qukiR-
qukvir-	qukviR-
qulair-	quləŋiR- (under qulə-)
qule-	qulə-
qulen	qulə(t) (under qulə-)
qulig-	quliɣ-
quliq	quliR (under qulə-)
quliraq	quliRaR-
qulliq	qulliR (under qulə-)
qulngunritaraan	quləŋŋuRutəŋit- (under qulə-)
qulugte-	qulucuk
qulungnaq	quluk
qulvar-	qulvaR- (under qulə-)
qumaq	quma(R)
qumik	qumiɣ-
qungate-	quŋatə-
qungcur-	quŋcuR-
qunguq	quŋuR(-)
qunguturaq	quŋutuRaq
qungyar-	quŋyaR-
qunik	quniɣ
qunu-	qunu-
qupa	quppaR (under qupə)
qupanuar(aq)	qupan(n)u(C)aR
qupe-	qupə-
qup'luq	qupəłRuR
qupneq	qupnəR (under qupə-)
qurrasqite-, qurrasqinarqe-	quRasqit-
qurre-	quRə-
qurrlugtaq	quRluRtaR (under quRluR-)
qurrlur-	quRluR-
qurrmar-	quR(əR)maR- (under quRə-)
qurrsuun	quRə-
qurrun	quRun (under quRə-)
quser-	quyəR-
qusngiq, quyngiq	quyŋiq
qusuuq	quyuuq
qusva(yug)-	quvya(yuɣ)-
quta	qutə
qutug-	qutuɣ-
qutuk	qutu(ɣ)
quya-	quya-
quyana	quyanaR (under quya-)
quu-	quðu-
quuk	əqðuɣ-
quuleq, quuleciraq	quɣəłəR-
quulerte-	quɣəłəR-
quumig-	quðumiɣ- (under quðu-)
quunaq	quɣəłəR-
quuneq	quɣ(ə)nəq
quuruq	quðuquR (under quðu-)
quutaar-	quðu-
quuyurni-	quŋuyuɣ-
quve-	quvə-
quverta	quvəRtə
quyig-	qulðiɣ- (under qulə-)
sarsa-, carca-	caRsa(q)
segg'ar-	əsɣaR(aR)- (under əðə)
suugi-	əsuɣ-
suyute-, cuyute-	cuð(ð)u-
taamlek	ta(a)mlek
taangaq	taaŋaq
taarri-	taa(Ra)Ri-
taavtaaq, tavtaaq	ta(a)vtaaq
taayug(yug)-	tayu(ɣ)-
tacellgaq	tatəłɣaR
tacestu-	tatə
taciq	taciR
tagci-, tagtaq	taɣci- (under taɣə-)
tage-	taɣə-
tai-	taɣi-
taima	taðim(m)a
taiq	taðəɣ-
taituk	taɣətuɣ
taivkar-	taivkaR-
takaneq	takaR-[1]
takar-	takaR-[2]
take-	takə-
taklar-	taklaR- (under takə-)
takli-	takəli- (under takə-)
taku	takku (under taku-)
taku-	taku-
takumcu(yug)-	takumcuɣ- (under taku-)
takuyar-	takuyaR- (under taku-)
takvik	takviɣ-
talaariq	talaaR´
talineq	talinəq (under talu)
talirneq	taliR- (under talu)
talite-	talit- (under talu)
tallegte-	całiɣ-[1]
talliman	tałłimat
talliq	tałiR
talliquq	tałiquR (under tałiR)
tallirpik	tałiRpiɣ (under tałiR)

CAY	PROTOFORM
tallur(yug)-	taɫuʀ-
talu	talu
talur-, talu-	taluʀ-
talurte-	taliʀ- (under talu)
taluyaq	taluyaʀ
tamalkur-	tamaʀ-
tamar- (all)	tamaʀ-
tamar- (lose, be lost)	tammaʀ-
tamiini	tamaŋani (under tamaʀ-)
tamlag-	talmaɣ-
tamlu	tamlu
tamlurun	tamluʀun (under tamlu)
tamu-	tamuʀ-
tane-	tanəɣ-
tanegte-	tanəɣ-
tanem	tanəm
tangeq	taŋəʀ
tan'geq, tan'ger-	taʀəʀnəʀ (under taʀəʀ(-))
tan'gerliq	taʀəʀnəʀ (under taʀəʀ(-))
tangerr-	taŋəʀ-
tangevkayak	taŋəʀ
tangluq	taŋluʀ
tan'gurraq	tanɣuʀaq
tangviarrluk	taŋəʀ
tanqig-	tanqiʀ
tanukar-	tanəɣ-
tapeq	tapəʀ(-)
taperrnaq	tap(ə)ʀaʀnaq (under tapʀaʀ[1])
tapete-	tapət-[1] (under tapəʀ(-))
tapraq (rope)	tapʀaʀ[1]
tapraq (spit of land)	tapʀaʀ[2]
taqe-	taqə-
taqeq	taqaʀ
taqmak	taqmak
taqte-, taqmigte-	taqə-
taquaq	taqu(C)aʀ
taqukaq	taqukaq
taquq	taquq
tarenraq	taʀ(ə)nəʀ
tarnaq	taʀənəq
tarneq	taʀ(ə)nəʀ
tarperaq	paʀtəʀaʀ (under paʀtə)
tarranqegte-	taʀaʀ-
tarrarte-, tarrite-	taʀaʀ-
tartuq	taʀtu
taru	taʀu
taryaqvak	taʀyaqvaɣ
taryuq	taʀ(ə)yuʀ
tass'uqe-	tatyuʀ-
tastur-	tat(ə)tuʀ- (under tatə-)
tatame-	tatamə(t)-
tatangquq	nataŋquʀ
tatek	tatək
tatkik	tatəkə (under tatə)
tau͡a	taðva
tau͡ken	tayʷak'n (under taðva)
tavci	tavci
tayarneq	tayaʀnəʀ
tayima, taima	taðim(m)a
tegak	təɣɣaɣ
teggalquq, tegalquq	təɣalquq
tegge-	təɣəɣ-
tegg'i-	təɣəɣ-
tegleg-	təɣɫəɣ-
tegu-	təɣu-
teguaq	təɣuðaʀ (under təɣu-)
tegumiaq	təɣum(m)i(C)aʀ (under təɣu-)
tegun	təɣɣun (under təɣu-)
tek'ar-	tə(k)kaʀ- (under təɣə-)
tekeq	təkəʀ
tekiq	təkðə(ʀ)
tekite-	təkit-
teki(y)ute-	təkiðutə- (under təkit-)
tellumrun	pəɫuɣ-
temci(ke)-	təmci-
teme-	təmə-
tem'iq, tem'irte-	təm(m)iʀ-
temli-	ətəmli-
tengak	təŋaɣ
tengayuk	təŋayuɣ (under təŋaɣ)
tenge-	təŋə-
tengelraq	təŋəɫʀaʀ (under təŋə-)
tengluk	təŋluɣ(-)
tengmiaq	təŋmi(C)aʀ (under təŋə-)
tengru-	təŋʀu-
tengte-	təŋət- (under təŋə-)
tenguk	təŋuɣ
tenguqe-	təŋuqə-
tepa	təpə
tep'aq	təpðaʀ (under təpə-)
tepe-	təpə-
tepli-	təpli
teptukuyuq	təptukuyaq (under təpə)
teq	ətəʀ
teqiyaar(aq), teqirayuli	təkiyaq
teqsuqaq	teqsuqaq (under ətəʀ)
teq'uq	ətəquʀ- (under ətəʀ)
teriaq	təʀiɣaʀ (under təʀiɣ)
teriir-	təʀi(C)aʀ- (under təʀiɣ)
terikaniaq	tərikanni(C)aʀ (under təʀiɣ)
terlak	ətəʀlaɣ (under ətəʀ)
tertuli	ətəʀtuli(q) (under ətəʀ)
teru, teruluk	təʀu
teruvailitaq	təʀu
teve-	ətəvə-
tevir-	təviʀ-
tevuq	təvu(q)
tevvaar-	təvvuɣ-
tevyaraq	ətəvyaʀaʀ (under ətəvə-)
tua-i, tuar	taðva
tuaten, tuatna-	tayʷatən (under taðva)
tuavte-	tu(C)avə(t)-
tugeq	tuɣəʀ(-)
tuger-	tuɣəʀ(-)
tugkar(aq)	tuɣəkaʀ(aʀ) (under tuɣəʀ(-))
tukaate-	tuka(ʀ)-
tukar-	tukkaʀ-

CAY	PROTOFORM
tuker-	tukəR-
tukni-	tukniɣ-
tukullek	tuku(q)
tukuq	tukku(R)
tulag-	tulaɣ-
tuliik	tuðiɣ
tulimaq	tulimaR
tulukaruk	tulikaR
tuluq	tuluR-
tulur-	tuluR-
tuluryaaq	tuluRyaR (under tuluR-)
tuma	tumə
tumag-	tumaɣ-
tumagliq	tumaɣ-
tumak	ətəmaɣ
tumarte-	tumaR-
tum'arte-	tumðaR- (under tumə)
tumci-	tuməci- (under tumə)
tumnaq	tumənaR
tune-	tunə-
tunertu-	tunəR-
tungcirtur-	tuŋciR-
tunge-	tuŋə-
tungeq	tuŋəR
tungliq	tuŋ(ə)liR (under tuŋə-)
tungmarte-	tuŋvaR-
tungu-	tuŋu-
tungyur	tuŋyuq
tuntu	tuntu
tunturyuk	tunturðuɣ (under tuntu)
tuntuvak	tuntuvaɣ (under tuntu)
tunu-	tunu
tunucuk	tunucuɣ (under tunu)
tunullek	tu(u)tləɣ
tunuq	tunnuR
tunute-	tunut- (under tunu)
tunuvar-	tunuvaR- (under tunu)
tupag-	tupaɣ-
tupig-	tupiR-
tupirtaarute-	tupiR-
tup(e)ke-	tupəkə-
tuqluq	tuqlu(ɣ)
tuqlur-	tuqluR- (under tuqlu(ɣ))
tuqmik	tuqmik
tuqu-	tuqu(-)
tuqunarqe-	tuqunaR- (under tuqu(-))
tuqute-	tuqut- (under tuqu(-))
turquq, turtuqaq	tuqlu(ɣ)
tusek	tuyə
tusnga-	tutŋa- (under tut-)
tuss'araq	tutyaR(aR) (under tut-)
tussite-	tutyaɣat-
tus'un	tut-
tut'e- (arrive)	tut-
tut'e- (step on)	tutə-
tuteg-	tutəɣ(-)
tutemqaq	tutməqaR (under tutə-)
tutmar-	tutmaR- (under tutə-)
tutsaraq	tutyaR(aR) (under tutə-)
tuullek	tu(u)tləɣ
tuunraq	tuɣənRaR
tuunri-	tuɣənRi- (under tuɣənRaR)
tuusiik	tuðiɣ
tuuskayar-	tucilaR-
tuutaq	tu(C)utaR
tuvqa-	tuveRaR
tuvte-	tupət-
tuyek (snipe)	tuðiɣ
tuyek (shoulder)	tuyə
tuyur-	tuyuR-
uakner	uɣaknaR
uame-	uða(t)-
uan	uɣan
uaqliq	uɣal(l)iR (under uɣan)
uaqnaq	uɣaknaR
uassiaq	u(ɣ)a(t)saq (under uɣan)
uci	uci
uciar-	uci(C)aR- (under uci)
uciir-	uciŋiR- (under uci)
ucluryaq	ulə(t)luyaR
ucuk	ucuɣ
ucuqe-	ucuR-
u͡asqite-	quRa(yaqit)-
u͡ayar-	ivayaR- (under ivaR-)
uginaq	uɣinaq
ugtaq	uɣtaq (under uɣət-)
ugte-	uɣət-
uguguaq	uɣuɣuaq (under uɣðuɣ)
ugugnaraq	uɣðuɣnaR (under uɣðuɣ)
uicungaq	uicuŋaq
ui	uɣi
uig-	uðəɣ-
uigtua-	uðəɣtuR- (under uðəɣ-)
uilgaq	uɣilɣaR- (under uɣi)
uiluq	uviluR
uinge-	uɣinəɣ- (under uɣi)
uinguaq, uingusaq	uɣiŋ(ŋ)uðaR (under uɣi)
uirrani-	uɣiRani- (under uɣiR(aR)-)
uirre-	uɣiR-
uita-	uvita- (under uvi(t)-)
uite-	uvi(t)-
uiteraq	ivitəRaR
uivaar-	uyivðaR- (under uyivə-)
uivaq	uyivvaR (under uyivə-)
uive-	uyivə-
ukamar-	ukamaR-
ukasiruaq	ukaðiRuðaR (under ukaðiR)
uki-	uki-[2]
ukisqaq	ukiy(ə)qaq
ukisqir-	ukiy(ə)qaq
ukite-	ukit- (under uki-[2])
ukli-, uklir-	uɣukli- (under uɣu-)
uksi-	ukyi-
uksuaq	ukyuRaR (under ukyuR)
uksuq	ukyuR
ukurraq	ukuRaR
ukveqe-	ukvəqə- (under ukvəR-)
ukver-	ukvəR-
ula	ulə(-)
ulakitaar-	ulakitaaR-
ulapeqe-	ulapə(t)-

CAY	PROTOFORM
ulariq	ulaRiq
uleve-	uləvə- (under ulə(-))
ulevlar-	uləvlaR- (under ulə(-))
uliiq	ulaɣaq
ulik	uliɣ(-)
uliun	uli(C)un
ullag-	utlaɣ-
ulligte-	ułiR-
ullirte-	ułiR-
ulluvak	ułuɣaɣ
ull'uyaq	ulə(t)luyaR
ulmirte-	ulmiRtə-
ulpiarte-	ulpəɣ-[2]
ulruk	ulRuk
ulte-	ulət-
ulu	ulu(q)
uluaq	ulu(R)
uluar-	uluRaR-
ulug-	uluɣ-
ulur-	uluR-
ulurya(yug)-	uluRya-
uluryanar-	uluRyanaR- (under uluRya-)
ulute-	ulutə- (under ulə(-))
umci-	umciɣ- (under uməɣ-)
umcig-	umciɣ- (under uməɣ-)
ume-	umyuɣaq
umeg-, umek	uməɣ-
umi-, umiqsig-	umi-
umiqvanek	umi-
umte-	uməɣ-
umyu(g)aq, umyu(g)aqe-	umyuɣžaq
umyu(g)artur-	umyuɣžaq
umyugaite-, umyuarite-	umyuɣaRitə- (under umyuɣžaq)
una-	una-[1]
unair-	unaRiR-
unake-	unakə- (under una-[1])
unaliq	unaliR
unange-	unaŋə- (under una-[1])
unarciar-	unaRciR-
unasmiur-	unaðmi-
unatar-	unataR-
unegte-	unəɣ-
uneq	unəR
unga-	uŋa-
ungag(u)aq, ungaggaq	uŋaɣžaq
ungair-	uŋaŋiR- (under uŋak)
ungak	uŋak
ungalaq	uŋalaR (under uŋan)
ungi-	uŋi-
unguir-	uŋummaR- (under uŋuma-)
ungungsiq	uŋuŋsiq
unguva-	uŋuma-
unguvan	uŋuman (under uŋuma-)
ungilag-	uŋilaɣ-
unglu	uŋlu
ungpaar(aq)	uŋpəɣ
ungpek	uŋpəɣ
ungu-	uŋu-
unguir-	uŋu(C)iR- (under uŋuma-)
unite-	unit-
uniurte-	uni(C)uR-
univkaraq	univkaRaR
unraq	unRaR
unuaq	unnu(C)aR (under unnuɣ)
unuaqu	unnuRaqu
unuk	unnuɣ
upag-	upaɣ-
upete-	upət-
up'nerkaq	upən(ə)RakðaR (under upən(ə)RaR)
uqamairi-	uqimaŋiR-
uqamaite-	uqimaŋit-
uqamaq	uqimaŋit-
uqeq	uqəR
uqer-	uqəR-
uqiggete-, uqgete-	uqiɣit-
uqigli-, uqiggeli-	uqiɣitli- (under uqiɣit-)
uqila-	uqila-
uqilngu-	uqðilŋu- (under uqðuR)
uqite-	uqqit-
uqlir-	uqliR-
uqrun	uqəRutaR (under uqəR)
uqsuq	uqsuq
uquaq	uqðuRaR (under uqðuR)
uquggluk	uquɣ
uquir(aq)	uquiq
uqumyak	uqðumyaɣ (under uqðuR)
uquq	uqðuR
uqurte-	uqðuR- (under uqðuR)
uqvik	uqviɣ
uraruq	uRaRuq
ure-	uRə-
urluveq	uRluvəq
urnir-	uRniR-
urr'aq	uRRaR
urrasquq	uRRaR
urug-	uRuɣ- (under uRə-)
uruq	uRðuR
uryur-	uRyuR-
usaaq	uya(C)aq
usgu	uyɣu-
uskuq	uyukkuR(aR)
uskurtuliaraq	uyukkaR(aR)
usper-	uspəR- (under uðəɣ-)
usruq	uyuRu(R)
ussneq	usnəq (under uytə-)
ussukcaq, ucukcaq	ucukcaq
uste-	uytə-
usvi, usvitu-	uyvi
usviite-	uyviŋitə- (under uyvi)
utakinaq	utakinaq
utaqa-	utaqə-
utengqa-	utəŋqa- (under utəR-)
uterte-	utəR-
utetmun	utətmun (under utəR-)
utnguk	utŋuR
utqiq	ulqiR
utuqa-	utuqqaR
utvak	utəvak
uu-	uɣu-

CAY	PROTOFORM
uugnar(aq)	uɣðuɣnaʀ (under uɣðuɣ)
uulegte-	uŋuləɣ-
uumi(yug)-	uɣumi-
uunglekar-	uɣuŋilaʀ- (under uɣu-)
uuqnarqe-	uɣuqnaʀ- (under uɣu-)
uurcara-	uɣɣuʀ-
uute-	uɣut- (under uɣu)-
uutuk	uutuk
uuvlaag-	uɣuŋilaʀ- (under uɣu-)
uvaa-	uvə(C)a- (under uvəʀ-)
uver-	əvəʀ-
uyalek	uyalək (under uya(quʀ))
uyamik	uyamiɣ (under uya(quʀ))
uyangte-	uyaɣ-
uyaquq	uya(quʀ)
uyatu-, uyakite-	uyatu-
uyiqe-	uyiqə-
uyive-	uyivə-
uyte-	uytə-
uyug-	uyuɣ-
uyunge-	uyuŋə-
uyuraq	uyuʀaʀ
vegtaq	əvəɣtaʀ (under əvəɣ)
vek	əvəɣ
wa-	uvva
waten, watna-	ɣʷatən (under uvva)
wayar-	ivayaʀ- (under ivaʀ-)
wii	uvaŋa
yaaliagni	iŋa(va)-
yaani	iŋa(va)-
yaaqvani	iŋa(va)-
yaate-	iŋan
yagneq	iyaɣnəʀ (under iyaɣ-)
yagte-	iyaɣ-
yaqiur-	iyaqqi- (under iyaɣ-)
yaqulek	iyaquʀ
yaquq	iyaquʀ
yave-	yavə-
yavun	yavun (under yavə-)
yiite-	iŋŋit- (under iŋuɣ)
yitaar-	iŋut-[2]
yit'e-	iŋŋit-
yuar-	ivaʀ-
yuaraq	iŋuɣaʀ (under iŋuɣ)
yugaq	yuɣu(C)aq (under iŋuɣ)
yugnirqe-	iŋuɣniʀ- (under iŋuɣ)
yugte-	yuɣtə- (under iŋuɣ)
yugyag-	iŋuɣyaɣ- (under iŋuɣ)
yukutaq	iyukuta(ʀ)
yuinaq	iŋuɣinnaʀ (under iŋuɣ)
yuinaunritaraan, yuinaunrita'ar	yuinaunʀitaʀ(aq) (under iŋuɣ)
yuk, cuk	iŋuɣ
yungaq	iyuŋŋaʀ
yungcar-	yuŋcaʀ- (under iŋuɣ)
yup'ik	iŋupiɣ (under iŋuɣ)
yuqerte-	yuqaʀ- (under iyyuʀ-)
yurar-	yuʀžaʀ-
yurvir-	iyuvʀiʀ-
yuu- (live)	iŋuɣu- (under iŋuɣ)
yuu- (get or put in)	niɣu-
yuuciq	iŋuciʀ (under iŋuɣ)
yuukaq	iŋ(ə)yukaʀ
yuunerrar(aq)	yu(u)nʀaq (under iŋuɣ)
yuurqaq	niðuʀqaʀ (under niðuʀ-)
yuurrmiur-	niðuʀ-
yuvgeq	nəvɣuʀ
yuvrir-	iyuvʀiʀ-

Postbases and enclitics

a-	a-
(t)a-	ta-
aatar-	ʀataʀ-
allag-	łłaɣ-
(g)aq	ðaʀ
(g)aqe-	ðaʀ-
ar-	aʀ-
ar(aq)	ʀaʀ
(g)arar-	ʀaʀaʀ-
(g)arkaq, (g)arkau-	yaʀka(C)u-
(g)ar(ar)te-	aʀaʀtə-
(ng)ar(ar)te-	ŋaʀ-[1]
atarar-	ʀataʀ-
=am	(ŋ)am
caar(ar)-	caʀ-[1]
car-	caʀ-[1]
cetaar-	təta(C)aʀ-
cete-	tət-
ci-	ci-
ciar(ar)-	c(c)iʀ-
(u)ciq	uciʀ
ci(i)qe-, -ciqiar-	ciqə-
cir-	c(c)iʀ-
(s)ciryar-	c(c)iʀyaʀ-
cuar(aq)	kyu(C)aʀ-
cugninarqe-	nit-
cuk	cuɣ
culngu-	culŋu-
cungaq	cuŋaq
cuun, -ssuun	ci(C)un
gguir-	k(k)u(C)aʀ-
=gguq	ŋu(C)uʀ
(g)i-	ði-
(r)i-	li-[2]
(ng)icag-	ŋicaɣ-
ilitaq	ŋilitaq
(ng)illiqe-	ŋiłiqə-
(ng)inaq	ŋinnaʀ(-)
(ng)ir-	ŋiʀ-
(ng)irute-	ŋiʀutə-
ite-	lit-
(l/q)ite-	lit-
(ng)ite-	ŋit-
=i	i
kaca(g)ar-, kacgar-	kapcak(-)
kaniir-	kkaniʀ-
kanir-	kkaniʀ-
kanir(ar)-	kkaniʀ-
kaq	kðaʀ
(s)kar(aq)	kaʀ

CAY	PROTOFORM
karaq	kaʀaq
kcuar(aq), -kcuar(ar)-	kyu(C)aʀ-
ke- (have as)	kə-[1]
ke- (one acted on)	kə(-)[2]
kegci-	kiɣ-
kegtaq	kəɣtaq
kegte-	kiɣ-
ki-	ki-
=kiq	k(k)i(C)aʀ
kite-	kðit-
kliute-	li(C)utə-
knak	knaʀ
knaq	knaʀ
kneq	knaʀ
ksagute-	kyaɣutə-
ksaite-	kya(C)itə-
ku	ku
kuaq	k(k)uʀ
kuar-	k(k)u(C)aʀ-
kuciq	k(k)uciʀ
kugte-	kutaʀ-
kuir-	k(k)u(C)aʀ-
kutag-, kutar(ar)-	kutaʀ-
kutaq	q(q)un
kuyuk	k(k)uyuɣ
laag-	ɬaɣ-
lar-	la(ʀ)-
leg-	ləɣ-
lek	ləɣ
ler-	təʀ-
lgir-	lɣiʀ-
lgu-	ɬ(ə)ɣu-
li- (make)	li-[1]
li- (become more)	li-[2]
liaq	li(C)aʀ
liar-	liyaʀ-
linraq	linʀaq
liqe-	liqə-
lir-	liʀ-
liri-	li-[2]
lirneq	liʀnəq
liur-	li(C)uʀ-
liyar-	liyaʀ-
llag-	ɬaɣ-
lleq (nominalizer)	ɬəʀ[1]
lleq (one that is more)	ɬəʀ[2]
=lli	ɬi
lli-	ɬi-
=llu	ɬu
llug-	ɬuɣ
llugte-	ɬuɣ
lluk	ɬuɣ
lngu-	lŋu-
lria(q)	lʀi(C)a(q)
lu(q)	lu(ʀ)
luaqar-	l(l)u(C)aʀ-
lugpiaq	luɣpiɣaq
(u)ma-	(u)ma-
(u)maar(ar)-	(u)maʀ(aʀ)-
mar-	maʀ-
mcugte-	mcuɣ(-)
mete-	mətə-
=mi	mi
mi-	mi-
mig-	miɣ-
miu	miʀu
mli-	mli-
myag-	myaɣ-
(u)n	un
na-	na-
naciar-	naci(C)aʀ-
nanrir-	nʀiʀ-
naq	naʀ
narqe-	naʀ-
naur-	na(C)uʀ-
nayuke-	yukə-
neq (nominalizer)	nəʀ[1]
neq (on that is more)	nəʀ[2]
nerraq	n(ə)ʀaʀ(aʀ)(-)
nerrar(aq)	n(ə)ʀaʀ(aʀ)(-)
nerrlugte-	nəʀɬuɣ-
nertu-	nəʀtu-
nga-	ŋa-[1]
ngaite-	ŋa-[2]
ngar-	ŋaʀ-[2]
ngari-	ŋa-[2]
ngarli(q)	ŋaʀ-[2]
ngate-	ŋa-[2]
nge-	nəɣ-
ngig-	ŋiɣ-
ngnaqe-	naqə-
ngqerte-	ŋqaʀ-
ngr(ar)-	ŋʀ(a)ʀ-
ngssak, ngssag-	mcaɣ-
ngssi-	ŋsi-
ngtag-, ngtak	ŋtaɣ-
nguaq	ŋ(ŋ)uðaʀ(-)
nguq	ŋuq
ni-	ni-
niar-	ni(C)aʀ-
niarar-	ni(C)aʀ-
nirqe-	n(n)iʀ-
nkuk, nkut	nkuɣ
nqegcaar(ar)-	nqiɣ-[1]
nqigte-	nqiɣ-[2]
nrir-	nʀiʀ-
nrite-	nʀit-
peke-	və(kə)-
piaq	piɣ(-)
pik	piɣ(-)
=qaa	q(q)a(a)
qainar-, qainaq	qa(C)inaʀ-
qaq	qaʀ-
qaqe-, qa'aqe-	qqaqə-
qar-	k(k)aʀ-
qatar-	k(k)attaʀ-
qetaar-	k(k)ətaʀ-
qliq	qliʀ
qsig-	ðiɣ-
qu-	qu-
quq	quʀ

CAY	PROTOFORM
qur-	qðuR-
r-	(V)R-
r(ur)luq	RuRluq
rpak	vaɣ(-)
rpallar-	vałłaɣ-[2]
rqe-	Rqə-
rraar-	łRa(C)aR-
rrar-	łRaR-
rrlak, rrlainaq	Rłaɣ
rrlug-	łuɣ
rrlugaq	luɣpiɣaq
rrluk	łuɣ
rugaq, rugaat	ðuɣaR(-)
sqe-	ðqə-
ssaag- (try to)	caR-[1]
ssaag- (fetch)	caR-[2]
ssiyaag-, ssaag- (too, too much)	yaɣ-
ssur-	ci(C)uR-
(te)staili-	təta(C)ili-
ta-	tə-
(s)ta	ðə
taar-	ta(C)aR-
taite-	taRit-
(u)taq	un
taq	taR
tar- (get)	taR-
tar- (by nature)	t(t)aR-
tate-, tateke-	tatəkə-
te- (cause one to)	t-[1]
te- (catch, go to)	t-[2]
te- (area of)	tə
(u)te-	utə-
(u)teke-	utəkə-
ter-	təR-
tmurte-	tmi(C)aR-
trute-	tRutə-
tu- (have lots)	tu-[1]
tu- (habitually)	tu-[2]
=tuq	tuR
tuqaq	tuqaq[1]
tur- (eat, use)	tuR-[1]
tur- (repeatedly)	tuR-[2]
tuuma-	tu(C)uma-
(ng)u-	ŋu-
(ng)uaq	ŋ(ŋ)uðaR(-)
(ng)un	ŋutə-
(g/t)uq	ðuR
ur-	(C)uR-
(g/t)ur(ar)-	ðuR(aR)-
urluq	RuRluq
(ng)urte-	ŋ(ŋ)uR-
vaalug-	vaɣil(l)uɣ-
vag-	vaɣ-
vaileg-	vaɣəłəɣ-
vailug-	vaɣəl(l)uɣ-
vakar-	vakaR-
vallag-	vałłaɣ-[1]
vallug-	vałuɣ(-)
var-	vaR-
vguar-	vlaɣ-
vik	ðviɣ
vike-	ðvikə-
virte-	viRtə-
vkar-	vkaR-
vke-	və(kə)-
vlaag-	vlaɣ-
vsiar-	vžəRaR-
yaaqe-	yaaqə-
yag-	yaɣ-
yagute-	yyaɣ-
yak	tyaɣ-
yaq	yaR
yaqu(nak)	yaqu(naɣ)
yar- (would)	yaR-
yar- (go to)	yaR(tuR)-
yaraq	yaR
yarar-	yaRaR-
yarpiar-	yaR-
yartur-	yaR(tuR)-
yaurte-	ya-
yu-	yu-
yuar-	yu(C)aR-
yug-	yuɣ-
yugaq	žuɣaq
yugar-	yuɣ-
yugnaite-	yuknaRit-
yugnarqe-	yuɣnaR-
yugnga-	yuɣŋa-
yuite-	yu(C)it-
yuk	yuɣ
yukaar(ar)-	yukaR-
yuke-	yukə-
yuuma-	yuɣuma-
yuuq	yu(u)q

CENTRAL SIBERIAN YUPIK INDEX

Postbases, at the end, are generally given in their form following full vowel (and enclitics are preceded by '=').

Equivalences between the Central Siberian Yupik standard orthography (that is, the Roman orthography of St. Lawrence Island, Alaska, and not the Cyrillic orthography of Chukotka, Russia) and the orthography used in this dictionary are given below. Symbols of the standard orthography are given in italics. If no equivalence is given it means that the standard practical orthography uses the same letter as our orthography. *e* = ə, *g* = ɣ, *gg* = x, *gh* = ʀ, *ghh* = X, *ghw* = ʀ^{w}, *ghhw* = X^{w}, *kw* = k^{w}, *ll* = ł, *ng* = ŋ, *ngng* = ŋ̊, *ngw* = ŋ^{w}, *ngngw* = ŋ̊^{w}, *qw* = q^{w}, *rr* = š, *w* = ɣ^{w}, and *wh* = x^{w}. Letters written doubled are "undoubled" (*gg* to g, *ll* to l, *ghh* to gh, *ngng* to ng, etc.) when adjacent to certain other letters (see Jacobson 2001 for details). As in the orthography of this dictionary, vowel length which results from prosody is not explicitly shown. This index was compiled by Bent Nielsen.

CSY	PROTOFORM
aagtagh-	aɣtaʀ- (under aɣə-)
aagte-	naɣət-
aaghte-, aaghhaghte-	aʀaʀ-
aahaangwliq	a(a)-a(a)ŋliʀ
aakaq	a(a)kaʀ
aakw	aðuɣ
aalghaq	aləʀ
aane-	anə-
aanelgun	anəlɣun (under anə-)
aange-, a(a)ngeneq	aŋə-
aanghuute-	anəq
aangqaq	aŋqaq
aanngerquq, angangarquq	an(ə)ŋanquq
aantat	antat (under anə-)
aante-	anət- (under anə-)
aanvik	annəviɣ, anəðviɣ (under anə-)
aapte-	apət(ə)-
aarragh-	atšaʀ- (under atə-)
aastu-	atətu- (under at(ə)-)
aatak, aataqun	ata[2]
aataw	ata[2]
aate-	atə-
aatneq	atnəq (under at(ə)-)
aavgugh-, aavneq	avəɣ-
aavnguq	avŋuq (under avəɣ-)
aawyaq	aðuɣɣaʀ (under aðuɣ)
afsengaq	avəlŋaʀ
agagh-	aɣ(ɣ)a(ʀ)
agalghu-	aɣa-
agepsuq, agepsugh-	apyuʀ
agha	aʀða
aghenqigneq	aʀənqiɣ-
aghhmagte-	aʀ(caʀ)maɣ- (under aʀcaʀ-)
aghi-	aʀi(t)-
aghilluk	aʀin
aghinaq	aʀinaʀ- (under aʀi(t)-)
aghinwaaq	aʀʀi(t)naʀ
aghinwaq	aɣanʀu(Caʀ)
aghipa, aghipate-	aʀipa-
aghiva-	aʀiva-
aghliigh(yug)-	aʀli(C)-
aghmig-	əʀmiɣ- (under əʀə-[1])
aghnaasiq	aʀnauciq (under aʀnaʀ)
aghnagan	əʀəni(ʀ)-, (əʀəni(q)?
aghnaghaq	aʀnaʀaq (under aʀnaʀ)
aghnaghuq	aʀnaʀuq (under aʀnaʀ)
aghnalgun	aʀnalɣun (under aʀnaʀ)
aghnalqwaaq	aʀnalqu(C)aʀ (under aʀnaʀ)
aghnaq	aʀnaʀ
aghnasalek	aʀnacalluʀ (under aʀnaʀ)
aghnasqwaaq	aʀnalqu(C)aʀ (under aʀnaʀ)
aghneghwaalek	aɣanʀu(Caʀ)
aghneq	əʀnəq (under əʀə-[2])
aghpuk	qapuɣ
aghpuneq	qəʀtunəq
aghqella	qaðəɣ-
aghqestaaq, aghqelli-	əkəʀ(tu)-
aghqetghaq	qiʀətʀaʀ- (under qiʀə-)
aghqitaghaq	əkəʀ(tu)-
aghquugte-	qakuʀ-
aghqulluk	qaqutluɣ
aghsaghmete-	aʀcaʀ-
aghsaghte-, aghsaan	aʀcaʀ-
aghsug-	aqaɣcuɣ- (under aqaɣ-)
aghsugh-	qakcuʀ- (under qakə(ʀ)-)
aghte-	əʀə-[2]
aghtugh-	aʀtuʀ-
aghu-	aʀu-
aghula-	aʀula-
aghulaqe-, aghulaghqugh-	aʀullaʀ- (under aʀula-)
aghulate-	aʀulat- (under aʀula-)
aghuliigh-	aʀula(ŋ)iʀ- (under aʀula-)
aghuqe-	aʀuqə-
aghvak	aʀvaɣ
aghveghagetaq	aʀuvəʀ(aʀ)
aghvepik	aʀvəpiɣ (under aʀvəʀ)
aghveq, aghvequte-	aʀvəʀ
aghvesak	aʀəvcaɣ (under aʀvəʀ)
aghvetuq	aʀvətu(C)aq (under aʀvəʀ)
aghvig-	əʀ(ə)viɣ- (under əʀə-[1])
aghvigh-	aʀviʀ-
aghvinlek	aʀvin(ə)ləɣ (under aʀviʀ-)
aghyugh-	aʀ(ə)yu-
aghyuqe-	aʀyuqə- (under aʀ(ə)yu-)
aghyuugh-	aʀyuʀ-
agi	aɣi
agitagh-, agitagha-	aɣittaʀ-
aglagh-	aŋilʀaʀ- (under aŋit-)
agleghu-, agleq	aɣləʀ(-)
aglekesegaq	ałɣiʀ
aglug-	aɣluɣ-
agluk	aɣluʀ
agtugh-	aɣtuʀ-

CSY	PROTOFORM
agugh-	aɣuR-
agzighte-	aɣži(R)-
akamka	akðaɣ-
akangquq	akəquR
akeqe-	akəqə-
akevegte-	akiviɣ-
aki-	aki-
aki	aki(-)
akigh-	akkiR-
akiingqwaghte-	akiRuR- (under aki-)
akileghtugh-	akiliR- (under aki-)
akilghuu(gh)-	akiRuR- (under aki-)
akimigaq	akimiɣaR (under aki-)
akin	akin (under aki-)
akingite-	akiŋit- (under aki-)
akiniigh-	akini(C)aR- (under aki-)
akisqaghte-	akiR- (under aki-)
akite-	aki-
akivigte-	akiviɣ-
aklegaq	akləɣaR (under akəR)
aklek	aklək (under akəR)
aklu-	aklu-
aklungi, aklunaq	aklu-
akmag-	natmaɣ-
akmaliighaq	akmaliaRaq
aksaqe-	a(a)tsaqə-
akugaaq	ak(k)uvaR
akughaq	akuRaR (under aku(R))
akughte-	akuR-[2]
akughtugh-	akuR-[1]
akule-	akulə- (under aku(R))
akuliq	akul(l)iR (under aku(R))
akulqusuk	akulqucuk (under aku(R))
akultu-	akultu- (under aku(R))
akuq	aku(R)
akuutaq	akutaR (under aku(R))
akuute-	akut- (under aku(R))
alangghu(yug)-	alaŋRu-
aleq	aləR
alghapak	alRapak (under aləR)
alguma-	alɣu-
ali-	ali
aliftugh-	alivtuR-
aliga-	aliɣa-
alignagh-, alignaq	aliɣnaɣh- (under alikə-)
aliigh-	allaR(iR)-
aliite-	alaRitə- (under allaR(iR)-)
alike-	alikə-
alinge-	aliŋə-
alingite-	aliŋit-
alingnaq	aliŋə-
alingtagh-	aliŋtaR (under aliŋə-)
aliq	aðiR
alla	atla
allakagh-	atlakkaR (under atla)
allayug-	atlayuɣ- (under atla)
alleg-	aɬəɣ-[2]
allighaq	atliRaR (under at(ə)-)
allighta	aɬiRtə
allngik	aɬŋiɣ
allngugh-	aŋɬuR-
allughqi-	aɬuR-
allungak	aɬuŋak
alpa	alpa(ɣ)
alpag-	alpaɣ-
alpagh-	alpaɣ-
alqegkaq	alqəɣkaq
alqimagh-	alqimaR-
alqutaq	alqutaq
alunge-	aluɣ-
alungutelleq	aluktətnəq
aluq	alu(R)
ama	amma
amaa	amaquR
amagh-	amaR-
amaghtu	amaRtuR
ameltu-	amələ
amestaaghhaq	amit-
amigh-	amiR
amighaq	amiRaR (under amiR)
amik	amik
amikluk	amitatuk (under amit-)
aminaqe-	aminaR
aminghaq	aminRaq (under amiR)
amiq	amiR
amitelqaq	amiləqaR (under amit-)
amla	amələ
amllugh-	amɬuR-
amqeghte-	aləmqaR-
amu-	amu-
amyak	amyak
anaana	ana(a)na
anaavak	ana(C)uvaɣ
anag-	annaɣ-
angayuqaq	aŋayuqaR (under aŋayuɣ)
angegh-	aŋəR- (under a(a)ŋ)
anghungite-	an(ə)RutaR
angi-, angiqe-	aŋi-
angigh-	anəɣiR- (under anə-)
angiite-	aŋit-
angite-	aŋi-
anglaaq	anlu(C)aR (under anlu)
anglanagh-	aŋla-
angli-	aŋ (ə)li- (under anə-)
anglisagh-	aŋlicaR- (under aŋə-)
anglu	anlu
angqigh-	atŋiR-
angtaaq	aŋtuR(aR) (under anə-)
angu-	aŋu-
angukaq	aŋukaq
angumaasqitaghte-	aŋuma- (under aŋu-)
anguugh-	aŋuðuR-
anguyu-	aŋuyu(R)- (under aŋu-)
angvalluqegtaq	aŋvaluR- (under aŋva-)
angvaneq	aŋvanəq (under aŋva-)
angwaagh-	aŋuðaR-
angwaaghun	aŋuðaRun (under aŋuðaR-)
angyaq, angyagh-	aŋyaq
angyii-	aɣyuR-
anighta	aniRta
anigu	aniɣu

CSY	PROTOFORM
ege-	əγə-
egge-	kəγə-
eggmiiq	kəγmi(C)- (under kəγə-)
eghneq	əʀnəq (under əʀə-[2])
eghqaaq	qaqðaʀ
eghqaataqe-	əγqaʀ- (under əγət-)
eghte- (repeat)	əʀutə- (under əʀə-[2])
eghte- (dawn)	əʀə-[2]
egkuq	əγkuq
eglluk	kəklu(γ)
egmigh-	əγmiʀ-
egnaangite-	əʀəni(ʀ)-
egtaq	əγtaʀ
egte-	əγət-
egtug(yug)-	əγtuγ-
egtughyaq	kəγtuʀyaʀ
ellmaaghaghhaq	əɬmaʀ(aʀ)
ellmi-	əɬmi-
ellnga	əɬ(ə)ŋa
ellngagh-	əɬŋaʀ-
elpek	əlpət
elpeke-	əlpəkə-
elqiiq	təlqi(C)aʀ
elquaq	qəlquðaʀ
elqughaghte-	əlquʀ-
elte-	nələt- (under nələʀ)
eltugh-	tat(ə)tuʀ- (under tatə-)
eltughaq	əltuʀ
epe-	əpə-
epeqaq	əpəqaʀ
esghagh-	əsγaʀ(aʀ)- (under əðə)
esghapag-	əs(γa)ʀapaγ- (under əðə)
esla	cila
eslalluk, eslallugugh-	cilaɬuγ (under cila)
eslate-	cilan (under cila)
eslege- (be stout, thick)	ciləγ-[1]
esleqe- (be full)	ciləγ-[2]
eslequq	cil(ə)quʀ
eslevak	ciɬuvaγ
eslugh-	ciluʀ-
esna(q), esne-	cinə
esneghaq	cinəʀaʀ (under cinə)
esnek	cinək
esnighte-	ciniʀ- (under cinə)
estaaghagh-	cituʀaʀ- (under citu-)
estamat	citamat
esteqe-, esteqaq	citə(γ)-
estu-	citu-
estugh-	cittuʀ-
estuk	cituk
evelegtagh-	əvə(ʀ)ləγ-
evleq	qəvləʀ-
evluk	iŋ (ə)yuləγ
gaaghaq	əγa(C)aʀ (under əγa-)
gaaghusiq	əγγan (under əγa-)
geve-	əγə-
ggaak	kəγðaγ-
ggata	kiγan
ggayek	kiγayəγ
ggiighsi-	kəγiʀ-
ggiiste-	kəγə-
gginaq	kəγinaʀ
gginaqwaaq	kəγinaquʀ (under kəγinaʀ)
gguta	kəγun (under kəγə-)
gheve-	əʀə-[1]
ghhatagh-	qəʀaʀ- and qəʀataʀ-
ghhiitagh-	əʀitaʀ- (under əʀi-)
ghhuu-, ghhuute-	qiʀu-
ghhuugh-	qəʀuʀ-
ghhuuq	qaʀðuʀ
ghhwuta, ghhuta	quʀə- (under quʀə-)
giimaq	əγimaʀ
guute-	əγut-
ifkagh-	əðəvkaʀ-
ifla-	əpla-
igamsiqa-	iγa-
igaq	iγaq
igarutaaq	niγəðuʀun (under niγəðuʀ-)
igarutaagh-	niγəðuʀ-
igatagh-	iγataʀ-
iggag-	iγəγaʀ-
iggasighte-	iγəγaʀ-
igha(yug)-	iʀa-
ighaleqetaaq	iʀaləqətaq (under iʀaluq)
ighaluqaq	iʀaluq
ighanaq	iʀa-
ighigh-	iʀiʀ-
ighlegtu-	iʀ(ə)ləγ-
ighleke-	iʀləkə- (under iʀ(ə)ləγ-)
ighneghaq	iʀnəʀɬuk
ighneghlluk	iʀnəʀɬuk
ighneq	iʀnəʀ
ighni-	iʀni- (under iʀnəʀ)
ighsa-	əq(ə)ya-
ighsake-	əq(ə)yakə- (under əq(ə)ya-)
ighsaquq	iʀcaquʀ
ightugh-	iʀtuʀ-
ighu	niʀu
ighyagte-	əðiʀyaγ (under əd̲iʀ)
iglagiisiq	il(l)aγiʀun
iglagute-	il(l)aγ-
iglak	iγlak (under iγə-)
igleghte-	əγləʀ- or əγiləʀ-
igu-	niγu-
igugh-	iγžuʀ-
igughte-	iγðuʀ-
iguk	iγðuγ
ii-i	i(i)[2]
iigh-	iðəʀ-
iigha	aðγa(ʀ), aðγaγ
iighaq (glove)	aðγa(C)aʀ (under aðγa(ʀ))
iighaq (swollen gland)	əðəʀa(ʀ)
iighhaq	ayaʀaʀaʀ
iighhwaange-	i(C)iʀ-
iighhwe-	niðuʀ-
iighwigh-, iighwite	əŋlu(ʀ)-
iike-, ikugh-	ikə-
iikw	ižuk
iilngiq	ilŋiʀ
iilqe-	ilutəqə- (under ilu)

CSY	PROTOFORM
kaavlak	kavlaɣ
kaaw-	kaðuɣ-
kafsak, kaftekrak	kavcak
kaga-	kaɣa-
kagime-	kaɣimə-
kagpesqwaaq, kagpestaaq	kapət-
kagpesug-	kapəɣcuɣ-
kagsagte-	kakyaɣ-
kagtagh-	kaɣtaʀ-
kagu-	kaɣu-
kakave-	kakavə-
kakeglluk	kakkiɣ
kakegte-	kakəɣtə- (under kakkiɣ)
kakek	kakaɣ-
kaki-	kaki-
kakiiq	kaki(C)aʀ (under kaki-)
kaleve-	kaləvə(t)-
kallagtaak, kallagte-	kałaɣ-
kalluk	katluɣ
kalngak	kalŋak
kalngugh-, kalngughnga-	katŋuʀ- (under katə-)
kamek	kaməɣ
kanagaq	kanaɣ
kanagh-, kanagha-	kanaʀ-
kaneq, kanegh-	kanəʀ
kangighaq	kaŋiʀaʀ (under kaŋiʀ)
kangiq	kaŋiʀ
kangiqliq	kaŋilliʀ (under kaŋiʀ)
kanglu-, kangllu-	kaŋlu-
kanivaan	kanivaʀun
kanuk	kanuɣ
kanuya	kannuyaʀ
kape-	kapə-
kapeghte-	kapəʀtə- (under kapə-)
kapugh-	kapuʀ- (under kapə-)
kasima-	katəma- (under katə-)
kaspugte-	kaspuɣtə-
katag-	kataɣ-
kavighruk, kavitaraak	kaviʀ-
kaviiq	kav(v)i(C)aʀ (under kaviʀ-)
kavite-	kaviʀ-
kayaaq	kay(y)u(C)aʀ (under kayu-)
kayagte-, kayaghqagh-	kaya(ɣ)-
kayeme-	kayəmə(t)-
kayngu(yug)-	kayŋu-
kayu	kayu
kayu-	kayu-
kayun	kayun (kayu-)
kazive-	kaðəvə(t)-
keka	aka(a)
kelag-	kəlaɣ-
keleg-, kelenga-	kələɣ-
kelenga-	kələt-
kelevagh-	kəluvaʀ- (under kəlu)
keleve-	kələ(t)-
kelig-	kəliɣ-
keligagh-	kəliɣaʀ- (under kəliɣ-)
kelli(yug)-	əkli-
kellii	kətliʀ (under kətə-)
kelu	kəlu
keluk	kəluɣ
kemagluk	kəmaɣluɣ
kemagnaq	kəmaɣnaq
kemek	kəməɣ
kemgite-	kəməɣit- (under kəməɣ)
kemkelleghaq	kumkaʀ
kenegte-	tənu-
keneq	əkənəqk(ə)nəʀ (under əkə-[1])
kenigh-	tənniʀ-
keniq	kəniʀ
kenite-	kənit- (under kəni-)
kenla, kenle-	kənlə
kenluq, kenlughmun	kənluʀ
kenu-	tənu-
kepe-	kəpə-
kepkagh-	kəp(ə)kaʀ-
kepliigh-	kəpliʀ- (under kəpə-)
kepsugh-	kəpət-[1]
keste-	kəcit-
kete-	kətə-
ketfagh-	kətvaʀ- (under kətə-)
ketngik	kitmiɣ
keveg-	kəvəɣ-
kevgaq	kəvɣaʀ
kevigh-	kəviʀ-
kezeghhagh-	kəði-
kezemaq	kəðim(ʀ)aʀ (under kəði-)
kii (gee, oh)	ki(i)
kii (cut, wound)	əki
kiighaghtagh-	kiððiʀ- (under kiðaɣ(-))
kiighte-	əkiðaʀ-
kiighwyaq	ki(C)uʀyaʀ
kiik	kiðaɣ(-)
kiikw	kuðəɣ
kiimsigh-	ki(C)u-
kiiq, kiighmik	əkiðaʀ (under əkiðaʀ-)
kiitmik	kitŋiɣ
kiive-	kivə-
kiksak	kəkyaɣ
kilgaa	kilɣaq
kiligh-	kiliʀ-
kiliq	killiʀ (under kiliʀ-)
kina	ki(na)
kinegh-	kinəʀ-
kineghtaq	kinəʀtaq (under kinəʀ-)
kingu-	kiŋu-
kinguk	kiŋuɣ
kinguliq, kingulighpigaq	kiŋul(l)iʀ (under kiŋu-)
kinguneq	kiŋunəʀ (under kiŋu-)
kinguvaqwaaqun	kiŋuvaʀ- (under kiŋu-)
kipullegte-	kipułəɣ- (under kiput-)
kitu-	kitu (under ki(na))
kitugh-	lituʀ-
kiyaghte-, kiyaghute-	kiyaʀ-
kukegte-	kukəɣ
kukikrak	kukiɣ
kukrak	kukðaɣ-

CSY	PROTOFORM
metagh-	mətaɣ-
meteghlluk	mətəʀłuk (under mətəʀ)
meteghyaq	mətəɣhyaq
metengtaq	mətəŋtaq
metghaq	mətəʀ
metngaamsiig-, metngegh-	mətŋəɣh-
mighyagh-	miʀyaʀ-
migligrungiq	mikə-
miik	əməɣ-
miksagaq	mikə-
milugh-	miluʀ-
minaq	minaʀ-
mingla	miŋlə
mingllegte-	məŋłəɣtə-
mingug-	miŋuɣ-
mughaya-	maʀuya(ʀ) (under maʀu-[1])
mughneq, mughniqaq	muʀnəqaq (under muʀðuɣ-)
mughu-	maʀu-[1]
mughute-	maʀut-
mughyug-	muʀðuɣ-
mugu-	məɣə-
mula	mulə(ɣ)
mulaagh-	maʀu-[2]
mulu-	mulu-
mumeq	muməʀ(-)
mumig-	mumiɣ-
muugate-	əmmuɣ
muute-	əmət-
na	ənə
na-, naken	na-[2]
na(a), nakaa	na-[1], na(a)ɣɣa
naa	a(a)na
naafqe-	navəɣ-
naafte-	navcu
naagh-	naʀə-
naaghsaq	nažaʀcaq
naagte-	naɣət-
naagu	naɣu (under na-[2])
naakaghqaq	a(a)nakaq (under a(a)na)
naakghite-	nakəʀit- (under nakəʀ-)
naaki	naɣu (under na-[2])
naalkak	nałəkkaɣ
naalke-	nalkə- (under nałə-)
naama-	naðama- (under naða-)
naami	na(C)umi (under na-[2])
naange-	naŋə-
naangneq	naŋnəq (under naŋə-)
naangquq	naŋquʀ
naangte-	naŋət- (under naŋə-)
naangwaaghagh-	əna-
naapte-	napəʀ-
naarqaq	na(a)šqaq
naasquq	nay(ə)quʀ
naate-	naðat- (under naða-)
naave-	navəɣ-
nafluq	naplu
nagaqugh-	naɣa(t)-
nagasugni-	naɣacuɣni- (under naɣa(t)-)
nagate-	naɣa(t)-
naghigh-	naʀiʀ-
naghrigte-	naʀciɣ-
naghulleg-, naghullgun	naʀułəɣ-
naghullgute-	naʀułɣutə-
naghuya	naʀuyaʀ
nagnegh-	naŋnəʀ-
nagtuqaq	naɣtuqaʀ (under naɣət-)
nagu-	naɣu-
nakasuk	nakacuɣ
nakegh-, nakeghsagh-	nakəʀ-
nakek	naɣu (under na-[2])
naki-	naki-
nakimtaa-	nakima-
nakligh-	naɣəkli(ʀ)- (under naɣət-)
nakmike-	nałmi(nəʀ)
nakrek	nəɣciɣ
nakugh-	naku(ʀ)-
naliq	nalliʀ (under na-[2])
nalla, nalle-	nałə-
nallagh-	nałaʀ- (under nałə-)
nalleqiiyaghute-	nalqiɣ- (under nałə-)
nallghughqe-, nallghute-	nałʀu- (under nałə-)
nallu-	nałłu-
nallunagh-	nałunaʀ- (under nału-)
nalluniigh-	nałunaʀiʀ- (under nału-)
nalluniilkutaq	nałunaʀilkutaʀ (under nału-)
nalluyagute-	nałuyaɣutə- (under nału-)
nalpəghtugh-	nay(ə)pəʀtuʀ- (under nay(ə)pət-)
nalpiqugh-	nałə-
nalqiganite-	nalqiɣ- (under nałə-)
nalug-	nalluɣ-
nalughqutah-	nalluɣ-
nalugute-	naluɣ-
nanevgaq, nanevgagh-	nanəvɣaq
nangaghte-	naŋaʀ-[1]
nangenqagh-	naŋnəʀ-
nangeteghugh-	naŋtəʀ- (under naŋə-)
nangghalug-, nangghayug-	naŋaʀ-[2]
nangghu(ghi)-, nangghuke-	naŋʀu(ʀ)-
nanghiigh-, nanqigte-	nanəʀ-
nangllagh	nəŋłinaʀ- (under nəŋə(t)-)
nanglleg(yug)-	naŋłəɣ-
nangrug-	naŋžuɣ-
nangsagaq	naŋcaʀ-
nangyagh-	naŋyaʀ-
nangyiite-, nangyiigate-	naŋyaʀit- (under naŋyaʀ-)
nanilghaq	nanilʀaq (under naniʀ)
naniq	naniʀ
nante-	nantə- (under na-[2])
nanuq	nanuʀ
napaghte-, napaghnga-	nappaʀ- (under napa-)
napaghyaq	napaʀyaʀ (under napa-)
napaqiliq	napataʀ- (under napa-)
napaqutaq, napaqetaq	nappaqutaʀ (under napa-)
naraqe-	naðaqə- (under naða-)
narughte-	naʀðuɣ-
nasagh-	nacaʀ
nasallenguaq	nacałŋaq (under nacaʀ)

CSY	PROTOFORM
nasaq	nacaR
nasig-	nacciɣ-
naspete-, naspeqe-	nay(ə)pət-
nasqughhun	nay(ə)quRun (under nay(ə)quR)
nasqunghek	nay(ə)quR
nasuqe-	naacuqə- (under naða-)
nate-, natu	natə- (under na-²)
nateghqaq	natəRAR (under natəR)
naten	natən (under na-²)
nateq	natəR
natesug-	natəcuɣ-
natete-	natə- (under na-²)
navegh-	nəvəR-
navghagh-	navəR(AR)-
navghiite-	nav(ə)Ritə- (under navəR(AR)-)
navghute-	navəR(AR)-
nayak	nayaɣ
nayug-	nayuɣ-
nayugh-	nayuR-
nazighaghsiq	nayiRARciq (under nayyiR)
nazighaq	nayyiRAR (under nayyiR)
nazisungaq	nayyiR
nefkagh-	nəkvaR- (under nəkəvə(t)-)
nefku, nefkugh-	nəvku
neftegte-	nəvtəɣtə- (under nəvə-)
negagh-	nəɣaR
negaq	nəɣaR
negh(e)-	nəRə-
neghqe-	nəRqə- (under nəRə-)
neghqugh-, neghqughruk	nənəq
neghsaq, neghsapik	nəRcaR
neghuvate-	nəRuvəR-
neghvik	nəRəðviɣ (under nəRə-)
neghyaghtugh-	nəRyaR- (under nəRə-)
neghyu-, neghyuke-	nəRyu(ɣ)-
negig-	nəɣiɣ-
negikragh-	nəɣiɣ-
negili, negilitaan	nəɣilaR
negugh-	nəɣuR-
neguya	nəɣuyaR
nekeve-, nekefte-	nəkəvə(t)-
nekevgha-	nəkəvRa- (under nəkəvə(t)-)
nekrek	nəɣciɣ
nelegte-	ənələɣtə- (under ənə)
nemegh-	nəməR(-)
nengaa	nəŋa(C)u(ɣ)
nengagh-	nəŋ(ŋ)aR-
nenge-	nəŋə-
nengigh- (take the place of)	ənəŋiR- (under ənə)
nengiq, nengigh- (get share)	nəŋiR
nengki-	əŋki-
nenglagh-	əŋlaR-
nengli-, nenglek	nəŋə(t)-
nenglu	əŋlu
nengrak	nəɣilaR
nengte-	nəŋət- (under nəŋə-)
nengug-	nəŋuɣ- (under nəŋə-)
nengyuq	nəŋyuR
nenki-	əŋki-
nepesanagh-	nəpətya(R)- (under nəpət-)
nepiigh-	nəpaŋiR- (under nəpə)
nepiite-	nəpənɣit-
nepsuk	nəpyuk
nepte-	nəpə-
nepuk	nəpuɣ-
neqa	nəqə
neqamike-	ənqa(RU)ma- (under ənqa(R)-)
neqagh-	ənqa(R)-
neqesghaq	nəqəcaq
neqligh-, neqlightugh-	nəqli(C)uR- (under nəqə)
neqnighqe-	nəq(ə)niR- (under nəqə)
neve-	nəvə-
nevegh-	nəvəR-
nevuq	nəvðuR
ngiigte-	əŋiɣ-
ngiikaq	iŋ (ə)yukaR
nguleghte-	nəŋuləR- (under nəŋə-)
nguug-, nguugrag	əŋuɣ-
nguutngguk	utŋuR
nighug-	nəRžuɣ-
niighigh-	ni(i) łaR-
niightugh-	ni(i) łaR-
niillghek	ni(i) łaR-
niive-	na(C)əvə(t)-
nipallagh-	nəpała(R)-
nivugh-	na(C)əvə(t)-
nughaq	nuRRAR
nughhaq	nuRAR(AR)
nugru, nurgu	nəɣuRluR
nukaghaq	nukaRAR (under nukaR)
nukalpigaq	nukalpiɣaR
nula-	nula-
nulgiigh-	nulɣARIR-
nulighhighaq	nuliR(AR)IR- (under nuliR(AR))
nulighqullghiik	nuli(R)aqəlRiik
nulightugh-	nuliR(AR)tuR- (under nuliR(AR))
nuliiq, nulighh-	nuliR(AR)
nullu	nułu
nulqaghiigh-	nulqaR-
nulugh-	nuluR(AR)-
nuna	nuna
nunaki-	nunaki-
nunangite-	nunaŋitə- (under nuna)
nunaniq	nunanniR-
nunavak	nunavaR (under nuna)
nungighte-, nungighta	nuŋiRtə-
nunivak	nunivaɣ (under nuna)
nunugh-, nunughtugh-	nunu(R)-
nuqete-	nuqət-
nuqutu-	nəqu
nusug-	nuccuɣ-
nutaan	nuta(C)an (under nutaR-)
nutaghaq	nutaRAR (under nutaR-)
nutaghte-	nutaR-
nutem	nutəm

CSY	PROTOFORM
putukuq	putukuʀ
putuugh-	putu(-)[2]
puu	əpu
puug-	puɣə-
puughte-, puughhe-	puʀətə-
puugzaq	puɣžaq
puuve-	puvə-
puuvlagh-	puvlaʀ-
puuvyaq	puvyaʀ
puvalla	puvała
puveltu	puvəltu
puvin	puvin
puvug-	puvuɣ-
puya	puya
puygu-	puyɣu(ʀ)-
puyuq	puyuʀ
puyuqe-, puyughqe-	puyuqə- (under puyuʀ)
qaa, qaaghllag-	qa(C)uʀ-
qaake-	qakə-
qaame-	qamə-
qaamqaghte-	qamqə-
qaanrak	qanžak
qaasni-	qacəli-
qaayghu	qa(C)əʀu(ʀ)
qafsik	qatviɣ
qafsina(t)	qavcit
qagegh-	qaɣəʀ-
qageq	qaɣə(ʀ)
qagha	qaʀa-
qagha(ya), qaghaaya	qaʀa
qaghleg-, qaghlegute-	qaʀə-
qaghlu, qaghlu-	əkəʀlu
qaghya-	qaʀya
qagi	qaɣə(ʀ)
qagingiiq	qaɣiŋŋiʀ
qaguq	qaɣuʀ
qakeq, qakegh-	qakəʀ-
qakite-	qakkit- (under qakəʀ(luɣ))
qakun	qaku
qalghigh-	qaləʀ-
qaliq	qaliʀ (under qaðə-)
qalla	qała-[1]
qalleg-	qała-[2]
qallevak	qałəvak
qalmagh-	qalmaʀ-
qalmesaq	qalmi(t)yaq
qalqalima	qalqa
qalqasiq	qałaciʀ
qalta	qaltə
qaltaq	qaltaʀ
qalu	qalu(-)
qalugyaq	qaluɣyaʀ
qamigagh-	qamiɣaʀ- (under qamuʀ-)
qamite-	qamitə- (under qamuʀ-)
qamsuuk	qamcuɣ- (under qamə-)
qamte-	qamət- (under qamə-)
qamugh-	qamuʀ-
qamughagh-	qamuʀaʀ- (under qamuʀ-)
qanegh-	qanəʀ- (under qanəʀ)
qanemsug-	qanəmcuk (under qanəʀ(-))
qanegh-	qanəʀ(-)
qaneq	qanəʀ(-)
qangigaq	qaŋiɣaʀ
qangquq	qaŋquʀ-
qani-	qani-
qanik, qanigughte-	qaniɣ
qantaghaq, qantaghalli-	qantaʀaq (under qanət-)
qantaq, qantak	qantaq
qapigh-	qapiʀ-
qaquuraq	qaqu(ʀ)
qasaghte-	qacaʀ-
qasike-	qacaɣ-
qaspeghaq	qaspəq (under qaðə-)
qasqite-	qaðqaʀ (under qaðə-)
qategh-	qatəʀ-
qatek	qatəɣ
qavagh-	qavaʀ-
qavaghni-	qavaʀni- (under qavaʀ-)
qavaghvik	qavaʀvik (under qavaʀ-)
qavanguq	qavaŋuq (under qavaʀ-)
qavigh-	qaviʀ-
qavlegh-	qəvləʀ-
qavngaq	qaŋvaq (under qaŋa)
qavraatat	qaðvaʀ- (under qaðə-)
qavragh-	qaðvaʀ- (under qaðə-)
qaywaak	qavəɣaɣ
qayaghtugh-	qayaʀtuʀ- (under qayaʀ)
qayaq	qayaʀ
qaye-	qaðə-
qayeligh-	qaðəliʀ- (under qaðə-)
qayetghute-	qaðə(t)ʀutə- (under qaðə-)
qayngun	qayu(q)
qayug-	qayuɣ-
qayuq (broth, tea)	qayuʀ
qayuq (how)	qayu(q)
qayuutaq	qayu(C)utaʀ (under qayuʀ)
qazigyaq	qaðiɣyaʀ
qefliqe-	qəvə(t)-
qeghaq, qeghagh-	əkəʀaʀ
qelagh-	qəla-[1]
qelanegh-	qəlanəʀ(aʀ)- (under qəla-[1])
qeleqetaagh-	qaləqə-
qelli-	qəlli-
qellu	əqlu
qellughte-	qəłuʀtə- (under əqə-[1])
qelmegh-	qəvləʀ-
qelpaghte-	qəlpaʀ-
qelu-	qəlu-
qemeghyaq	qəməʀyaʀ
qemiq	qəmiʀ[1]
qemite-	qəmit-
qemtaq	qəmtaq
qeneghte-	qənəʀ-
qengaghuq	qəŋaʀuk (under qəŋaʀ)
qengalek	qəŋaləɣ (under qəŋaʀ)
qengaq	qəŋaʀ
qenngu	qənŋu(ʀ)
qenngulliqe-	qənŋułiqə(t)- (under qənŋu(ʀ))
qenu	qənu
qepe-,qepneq,	qəpə-

CSY	PROTOFORM
sakegh-	caki(tə)-
sakete-	cakəvət-
saki	caki
sakiiq, sakiighaq	cakiRaR (under caki)
sakimak	caki(C)aɣ
sakniqe-	cakə(t)-
salin	cu(na)li (under cu(na))
sallagte-	całiɣ-[2]
sallaqi-	cała-
sallek	całək
salligte-, sallegte-	całiɣ-[1]
sallmak, sallmag-	całmak
salŋak	saŋlak
salug-	caluɣ-
sanagte-	cana-
sanaghte-	canaRtə-
sangan	caŋan (under cu(na))
sangigte-	caniR-
sangite-	cu(na)ŋit-
sangwaa	cu(na)
sangyagh-	caŋyaR-
sangyite-	caŋyaR-
saniani	cani-
saningughtaq	caniŋuRtaq (under cani-)
saniquun	canniqun (under cani-)
sanivagh-	canivaR- (under cani-)
sanqun	canqun
sapeghhnagh-, sapeghhnaq	capəRnaR-
saqeghqe-, saqeghte-	caqə-[2]
saqeme-	caRəvə-
saqfigh-	caqviR- (under caqviɣ)
saqighqe-	caqə-[2]
saqlak	caqlaɣ
saqugneq	caqu-[2]
saquk, saqumig-	caqu-[2]
saquste-	caqu-[1]
sata	catə
satelgaq	tatəlɣaR
savek, saveg-	cavəɣ
savighqe(t)-	caviRuR- (under caviɣ)
savik, savilquq	caviɣ
saya	caðə-
sayug-	cayuɣ-
sayugh-	cayuR-
sayugpagtagh-	cayuɣ-
segesquq	ciɣəðquR
segesqwaaq	ciɣəðqu(C)aR (under ciɣəðquR)
seghe-	ciðəɣ-
seghhe-	əðiR
seghleq, seghleghqe-	ciRləR-
sengelqagh	ciŋələ-
seve-	civə-
sighla-	ciRlaɣ
sighuneq	ciRunəq
sigiqe-	ciɣi-
sii	əciR
siifte-	civtə-
siigh-	əcuRit- (under əcuR-)
siigte-	ətəɣ(taR)-
siimghu	ciðamRu (under ciðaɣ-)
siinge-	ciŋə(t)-
siipneq, siipneqllukek	cip(ə)nəR (under cipə(t)-)
siipte-	cipə(t)-
sikete-	cikə(t)-
sikik	cikðiɣ
siklaq	ciklaR
sikna(yug)-	cikna-
siku	ciku
sikuq	cikuR
sikwaavreghaq	ciku(C)aR (under ciku)
sikaaq	cika(C)aq
simigh-	cimmiR-
singagh-	ciŋaR-
singik	ciŋiɣ
singik	ciŋik
singiq	ciŋiR
sipelaaq	(cf. siim̥lu-X undeR Proto-Aleut basəs)
sipegte-	cipə(ɣ)-
sipsaq	cipyaR
siqineq	ciqinəR
siqite-	ciq(q)it- (under ciqəR-)
siqlugaq	ciqluɣaR
siqni-	ciqni-
sivu	civu-
sivug-	civ(v)uɣ-
sivugh-	civvuR-
sivugnga-	civ(v)uɣ-
sivuliq	civul(l)iR (under civu-)
sivuneq	civunəR (under civu-)
sivuqaq	civuqaR (under civu-)
sivuqliq	civuqliR (under civu-)
sivuughagh-	civu(C)uRa-
sivuyagta	civuyaɣtə
sivuyak, sivuyagta	civuyak (under civu)
sivaaq	civu(C)aR (under civu-)
suflu(q), sufluk	cupluɣ
sugag-	cuɣaɣ-
sughug-	cuRðuɣ-
sugruk, sugrugeq	cuɣðuɣ
sukangite-	cuk(k)aŋit- (under cuk(k)a-)
sukate-	cuk(k)a-
sukite-, sukitun	cukkit- (under cuki(R))
suklugraq	cukluk
sullevneq	cułəvnəq
suluk	culuɣ
sumeq	cuməR(tə)-
suna, sunami	cu(na)
sungaghteqe-	cuŋaR-
sungagyaak, sungagyuk	cuŋaɣ- or cuŋaR- (under cuŋa(R))
sungaq	cuŋa(R)
sungite-	cuŋitə-
supug-, supuk	cupə-
supugh-	cupuR- (under cupə-)
suqaq	cuqqaR
suqlaq	cuqlaɣ
suqlugh-	cuqluR-
susuq	ciqəR-

CSY	PROTOFORM
suugh-	əcuʀ-
suughaq	cuʀaq
suughite-	əcuʀit- (under əcuʀ-)
suume-	cumiɣ-
suupe-	cupə-
taagken	taɣwakən (under taðva)
taake-	takə-
taane-	tanəɣ-
taapak	tuvapaɣ
taape-, taapute-	tapət-[2]
taaqe-	taqə-
taatget	tatəkə (under tatə)
taawa	taðva
taayug(yug)-	tayu(ɣ)-
taflu	pavlu
tafsi	tavci
taghneghaq	taʀ(a)nəq
taghnughhaq	tanɣuʀaq
taghpagh-	taʀpaʀ-
taghu	taʀu
taghyuq	taʀ(ə)yuʀ
tagi-	taɣi-
tagitugiiq	taɣituɣi(C)aq (under taɣətuɣ)
tagituk	taɣətuɣ
taglagh-	taɣə-
tagneq, tagnegh-	taʀəʀnəʀ (under taʀəʀ(-))
tagsigh-	taɣciʀ- (under taɣə-)
tagtala	takə-
takagh-	takaʀ-[1]
takagh(yug)-	takaʀ-[2]
takelli-	takəli-
takerkak	takšu(k)
taklagh-	taklaʀ-
taku-	taku-
talaghitagh-	talaaʀə
talite-	talit- (under talu(-))
tallaagh-	taluʀ-
tallighpik	tałiʀpiɣ (under tałiʀ)
tallimat	tałłimat
talliq	tałiʀ
talliquq	tałiquʀ
tallu-	taluʀ-
tallugh(yug)-	tałuʀ-
talughte-	taluʀtə-
tamaa-	tamuʀ-
tamaghhagh-	tamaʀ-
tamangani	tamaŋani (under tamaʀ-)
tamlag-	talmaɣ-
tamlu	tamlu
tamlughun	tamluʀun (under tamlu)
tanem	tanəm
tangeq (reason behind)	taŋəʀ-
tangeq (part of blubber)	taŋəʀ
tangtaquq	natanquʀ
tangyeq	tayaʀnəʀ
tannga	tanəɣ
tanpeq	taŋpəq
tanqiq	tanqiʀ
tapghaq	tapʀaʀ[2]
tapghaq	tapʀaʀ[1]
taqeq	taqaʀ
taqiiq	taaqaq
taquq, taqughte-	taquq
tasik, tasiq	taci-
taslugh-	tatyuʀ-
tatame-	tatamə(t)-
tateghte-	tatə-
tatek	tatək
tawaten, tawatete-	taɣʷatən (under taðva)
tefaay	təvvuɣ-
tefli	təpli
tegak	təɣɣaɣ
teggeq	təɣəɣ-
teghigaq	təʀiɣaʀ (under təʀiɣ)
teghiglugsiq	təʀiɣluɣciq (under təʀiɣ)
teghigluk	təʀiɣluɣ
teghigniigh-	təʀiɣ
teghiigh-	təʀi(C)aʀ- (under təʀiɣ)
teghik	təʀiɣ
teghikusaq	təʀikšuq- (under təʀiɣ)
teghlug-	tulaɣ-
teghtugh-, taghtugh-	ətəʀ-
tegleg-	təɣləɣ-
teglengalghii	təɣləŋaʀ- (under təɣləɣ-)
tekagh-	tə(ɣ)kaʀ- (under təɣəɣ-)
tekeghaq	təkəʀaʀ (under təkəʀ)
tekeq	təkəʀ
tekerquq	təkəðquʀ
tekeyiighaq	təkiyaq
teki(i)te-	təkit-
tema	təmə
temkaq	təmkaq
temli-	ətəmli- (under ətəʀ-)
temsiyaaghagh-	təmci-
tenga	təŋə
tengayuk	təŋayuɣ (under təŋə)
tenge-	təŋə-
tengghu(yug)-	təŋʀu-
tenglug-	təŋluɣ(-)
tengqall	uktəŋqa(ʀ)-
tengte-	təŋət-
tenguk	təŋuɣ
tenguqe-	təŋuqə-
tepa	təpə
tepaq	təpðaʀ (under təpə-)
tepe-	təpə-
teq	ətəʀ
tequq	ətəquʀ (under ətəʀ)
terateriiq	təðatəða(C)iʀ
teregh-	tətəʀ-
teve-	ətəvə(t)-
tevigh-	təviʀ-
tevyaghaq	ətəvyaʀaʀ (under ətəvə(t)-)
tiig-	taðəɣ-
tungeqliq	tuŋ (ə)liʀ (under tuŋə-)
tugegh-, tugagh-	tuɣəʀ-
tugeq	tuɣəʀ (under tuɣəʀ-)
tughneghaq	tuɣənʀaʀ
tugmagte-	tuŋvaʀ-
tugu-	təɣu-

CSY	PROTOFORM
unaghsiq	unaRciR
unake-	unakə- (under una-[1])
unange-	unaŋə- (under una-[1])
unatagh-	unataR-
unaymigh-	unaðmi-
unegte-	unəɣ-
uneq	unəR
ungagaq	uŋaɣžaq (under uŋak)
ungagigh-	uŋaɣiR- (under uŋak)
ungak	uŋak
ungavik	uŋan
ungelegte-	uŋuləɣ-
ungilag-	uŋilaɣ-
ungipaghaq, ungipaq	univkaRaR
unglegh-	uŋlu
unglleg-	uŋəR-
unglun	uŋlu
ungughte-	uŋuR-
unguva-	uŋuma-
unguvagh-	uŋummaR- (under uŋuma-)
uniigh-	una(C)iR-
unite-	unit-
unuk, unug-	unnuɣ
unungsaan	unuɣcaRun
upag-	upaɣ-
upenghaq	upən(ə)RaR
upugh-	upət-
upugha-, upughat-	upuRa- (under upət-)
uqengelli-	uqiɣitli- (under uqiɣit-)
uqengestaaq	uqiɣit-
uqeq	uqəR
uqigite-	uqiɣit-
uqfik	uqviɣ
uqigite-	uqiŋit-
uqigtu-	uqiŋit-
uqiite-	uqqit- (under uqəR)
uqik	uqiŋit-
uqligh-, uqliite-	uqliR-
uqlughte-	quRluR-
uqughte-	uqðuR- (under uqðuR)
uquk	uquɣ
uqumyak	uqumyaɣ (under uqðuR)
uquq	uqðuR
usi	uci[1]
usingigh-	uciŋiR- (under uci[1])
uskaaq	uyukkuR(aR)
uskughaq	uyukkuR(aR)
uspeqe-, uspete-	uspəR- (under uðəɣ-)
usuk	ucuɣ
usuqe-	ucukcaq
utaqa-	utaqə-
uteghnigh-	utəRniR- (under utəR-)
uteghte-	utəR-
utqiigh-	utəqi(C)aR- (under utəR-)
utumek	utəvak
utuqa	utuqqaR
uughhe-	URə-
uughhe-	URaR-
uughqa	uqəR
uugta	uɣtaq (under uɣət-)
uugte-	uɣət-
uukaq	uðukaR
uulmen	utətmun (under utəR-)
uulqiq	ulqiR
uulte-	ulət-
uunghaq	unəRaR
uupa	uupa(q)
uupte-	upət-
uusneq	uytə-
uusneq	usnəq (under uytə-)
uusqaq	ətə-
uuyni	unəR
uvaghaa-	uva(C)a- (under uvəR-)
uvegh-	uvəR-
uvelegtagh-	əvə(R)ləɣ-
uveluk	iŋ(ə)yuləɣ
uvinek	uvinəɣ
uyamik	uyamiɣ (under uya(quR))
uyangte-	uyaɣ-
uyaquq	uya(quR)
uyatu-	uyatu-
uyavaq, uyavagh-	uyavaR-
uyegte-	uyəɣ-
uyengpalla-, uyengqagh-	uyuŋə-
uyghak	uyaRaɣ
uyghu	uyuRu(ɣ)
uygu-	uyɣu-
uyiighaq, uyiiq	uya(C)aq
uyug-	uyuɣ-
uyughaq	uyuRaq
uyvala-	uyvala-
uyviineq	uyviŋit- (under uyvi)
uziva	uyivvaR (under uyivə-)
uzive-	uyivə-
vegaaq	əvəɣ
veghte-	uvəR-
vegtaaq	əvəɣtaR (under əvəɣ)
vek	əvəɣ
vuu-, vuuneq	iŋ(ə)yu-
vuveltu	puvəltu
wayagh-, wayaq	ivayaR- (indəR ivaR-)
yaag-	yaɣ(ə)-
yaagneq	iyaɣnəR (under iyaɣ-)
yaagtagh-	iyaɣ-
yaave-	yavə-
yaavuquun	yavun (under yavə-)
yakugh(yug)-	iŋaɣ-
yakughte-	iŋaɣ-
yaqellengataq	caqələkitaR
yaqii-	iyaqqi- (under iyaɣ-)
yaquq, yaqulek	iyaquR (under iyaɣ-)
yiillgi-	iŋut-[2]
yimi(yug)-	iŋŋimi(yuɣ)- (under iŋuɣ)
yite-	iŋut-[2]
yu(u)k	iŋuɣ
yuggtagh-	yuɣtə- (under iŋuɣ)
yughagh-, yughaghta	yuRaR-
yuginaq	iŋuɣinnaR (under iŋuɣ)
yugniite-	iŋuɣniR- (under iŋuɣ)
yugtagh-	yuɣtə- (under iŋuɣ)

CSY	PROTOFORM
yuguma-	iŋuɣu- (under iŋuɣ)
yugusiq	iŋuɣuciʀ (under iŋuɣ)
yugyag-	iŋuɣɣaɣ- (under iŋuɣ)
yukuta, yukutate-	iyukuta(ʀ)
yumi(yug)-	iŋŋimi(yuɣ)- (under iŋuɣ)
yupik	iŋupiɣ (under iŋuɣ)
yuqeghte-	yuqaʀ- (under iyyuʀ-)
yuungaaghaq	iyuŋŋaʀ
yuutu-	yuɣtu- (under iŋuɣ)
yuvghiigh-	iyuvʀiʀ-

Postbases and enclitics

aatagh-	ʀataʀ
aghtagh-	aʀ
aatagh-	ʀataʀ
aghtagh-	aʀ
aghte-	aʀaʀtə
aghtugh-	aʀ
aghaatagh- (keep -ing)	ʀataʀ
angyali	li^{1}
angyi	li^{1}
aq	ðaʀ
(g)aqe-	ðaʀ
fik	ðviɣ
fqa(gh)-	vqaʀ
gh-	(V)ʀ
ghaq	ʀaʀ
ghhaq	ʀaʀaʀ
ghllag	ʀłaɣ
ghllagu-	ʀłaɣ
ghllak	ʀłaɣ
ghngaa(gh)-	ŋʀa(a)ʀ
ghpak	vaɣ( )
ghqe- (apply - to)	ʀqə
ghqe (divide into - groups)	qə
ghqu-, gku-	qu
gpe-	və(kə)
i- (half-trans.)	ði
(gh)i- (become)	li^{2}
(ng)igh-	ŋiʀ
(ng)ighute-	ŋiʀutə
ii-	li^{1}
iiraagh-	ŋuðaʀaʀ
(ng)iitaq	ŋilitaʀ
(ng)inagh-	ŋinnaʀ( )
(ng)inaq	ŋinnaʀ( )
(ng)isag-	ŋicaɣ
(ng)ite-	ŋit
kaghaq	kaʀaq
kaghqaq	kðaʀ
kaghtaq	taʀ
kanigh-	kkanniʀ
kaq (raw material for)	kðaʀ
kaq (past part.)	kšaq
katagh(agh-)	k(k)attaʀ
kayuk, kayugu	kayuɣ( )
ke- (s.th. one is -ing)	kə( )^{2}
ke- (have as)	kə^{1}
keghtaq	taʀ
kegtaq	kəɣtaq
kegte-	kiɣ
keq	knaʀ
kestagh-	kəcitə
ketagh-	k(k)ətaʀ
krak	kšak
ksagute-	kyaɣutə
kun	ku
kusiigh-	kəcitə
kwaaq	k(k)uʀ
laaq	la(C)aʀ( )
laataq	la(ʀ)
laataqu-	l(l)u(C)aʀ
leg	ləɣ
lek	ləɣ
lghii-	lʀi(C)aq
lghutaq	lɣhutaq
lgigh-	lɣiʀ
lgu	lɣu
lgun	lɣun
lqusiq	lquciq
li- (make)	li^{1}
li- (become)	li^{2}
ligh-	liʀ
lighneq	liʀnəq
liiq	li(C)uʀ
liite	li(C)utə
linghaq	linʀaq
liq	l(l)iʀ
liqe-	liqə
llaag	ʀłaɣ
llaak	ʀłaɣ
llegagh-	ʀłaɣ
lleghpigaq	łəʀ^{2}
llek	ł(ə)ɣu
lleq	łəʀ^{1}
llgu-	ł(ə)ɣu
lli-	łi
llu-	łu
lluggaq	łuɣ( )
lluk	łuɣ( )
lqusiq	k(k)uciʀ
lugh-	luʀ
lugpigaq	luɣpiɣaq
luq	lu(ʀ)
(u)ma-	(u)ma
magh-	maʀ
man	(u)maʀ(aʀ)
me	mə(t)
mete-	mətə
mi-	mi
mig-	miɣ
mii-	miʀu
miiq	miɣ
miqe-	miqə
mleghagh-	vlaɣ
mlaagh-, mlaaq	vlaɣ
mraaq, mzaaq	vžəʀaʀ
mreghaq, mzeghaq	vžəʀaʀ

CSY	PROTOFORM
yagh- (go in order to)	yaʀ(tuʀ)-
yaghagh-	yaʀaʀ
yaghpete-	yaʀ
yaghqaq	yaʀka(C)u
yaghqaa-	yaʀka(C)u
yaghtugh-	yaʀ(tuʀ)-
yagute-	yyaɣ
yaqu(nang)	yaqu(naɣ)
yayiiqa	yayiaq(a)
yiite-	yu(C)it
yu-	yu
yug-	yuɣ
yugnagh-, yugniite-	yunaʀ
yuguma-	yuɣuma
yuk	yuɣ
yukagh-	yukaʀ
yuq	yu(u)q

EASTERN CANADIAN INDEX
(Tarramiut Dialect)

Eastern Canadian forms are given in the Inuit Cultural Institute Roman orthography, that is with *qq*, *rr*, and *jj* rather than *rq*, *qr*, and *tj* as in the later Avataq Cultural Institute proposal. Equivalences between this orthography and the orthography used in this dictionary are given below. Symbols of the practical orthography are given in italics. If no equivalence is given it means that the practical orthography uses the same symbol(s) as our orthography. *g* = ɣ, *r* = ʀ, *j* = y, and *ng* = ŋ. Bases ending in a consonant not now determinable (owing mainly to Schneider's Law) end in 'C' and final consonants dropped because of Schneider's law are put in brackets. Postbases, gathered at the end, are given in post-vocalic form (enclitics preceded by '=').

TARRAMIUT — ECI	PROTOFORM
a'aa	aka(a)
aa	a(a)ŋ
aa-	aɣa-
aajjuuk	aaɣžuuk
aala	a(a)
aamai-	aɣa-
aana	a(a)na
aangajaak-	aaŋa- (under aɣa-)
aannia(q)-	anniaq- (under atŋiʀ-)
aanni(q)-	atŋiʀ-
aaqqi(k)-, aaqqisur-	aʀənqiɣ-
aariak	aaʀiak
aarlu(q)-	aaʀluq-
aarluk	a(C)aʀłuɣ
aasiit	aaci(in)
aasivaq	aacivak
aat-	aat-
aatsuuk	acu
aattu(q)-	aak-
aggaa(q)-	aðɣa(ʀ)
aggajaak	aðɣa(C)aʀ (under aðɣa(ʀ))
aggak	aðɣa(ʀ)
aggamik	ažɣaɣmik- (under aðɣa(ʀ))
aggaujaq	aðɣaʀuðaʀ (under aɣða(ʀ))
aggauti	ažɣaun (under aðɣa(ʀ))
aggiq	ałɣiʀ
aggi(q)-	aɣɣiʀ- (under aɣə-)
aggiut(i)-	aɣiɣ-
aggu(q)-	avɣuʀ- (under avɣuʀ-)
agguq-, aggu	aðɣuʀ-
agiaq-	aɣiɣ-
agiuppiniq	aɣiuppak (under aɣiɣ-)
ai	ay
ai-	aɣə-
aikaluk	aɣi
ailaq-	aʀiłaʀ- (under aʀi-)
ailitaq	ailitaq
aipa-	aʀipa-
aippaq	a(C)ippaʀ
airaq	aiʀaq
aiq	aðiʀ
aiqqavaq	aitqan (under aðiʀ)
aitsi(q)-	aɣə-
aitta(q)-	aɣittaʀ-
aittau(q)-	aɣittaʀuʀ- (under aɣittaʀ-)
aittu(q)-	aittuq- (under aɣə-)
aiva-	aiva-
aiviq	aɣvəʀ
aiviqiak	aiviqižak
aivva(k)-	aivvak- (under aɣvəʀ)
ajaaq	ayaɣaʀ (under ayaɣ-)
ajagutaq	ayaɣun (under ayaɣ-)
ajak-	ayaɣ-
ajakuluk	ayak
ajapiq-	ayapəʀ- (under ayaɣ-)
ajaraaq	ayaʀaʀaʀ
ajauppiak	ayaʀuʀ (under ayaɣ-)
ajja(q)-	aɣžaq- (under aɣə-)
ajjitaaq	atə(ði)
ajju(q)-	atžuq- (under atə-)
aju-	ayu-
ajuaq	ayu(ž)aq
ajugaq	ayuq-
ajuji-	ayuži- (under ayu-)
ajuq-, ajuri-	ayuq-
ajuqiq-, ajuqiqtu(q)-	ayuquciʀtuʀ- (under ayuqə-)
ajurir-, ajurit-	ayuʀiʀ-
ajurnaq-	ayuʀnaq- (under ayuq-)
ajursa(q)-	ayuqšaq- (under ayuq-)
ajursit-	ayuqšit- (under ayuq-)
ajutit-	ayu-
ajuttaq, ajutta(q)-	ayuktaq-
ajuttauti	ayyutaʀ-

TARRAMIUT — ECI	PROTOFORM
angiq-	aŋəʀ- (under a(a)ŋ)
angirramut	aŋilʀaq- (under aŋit-)
angirra(q)-	aŋilʀaq- (under aŋit-)
angu-	aŋu-
anguaq-	aŋuðaʀ-
angula-	aŋula-
anguma-, angummati-	aŋuma- (under aŋu-)
angusalluk	aŋucalluʀ (under aŋun)
angusuqtuq, angusuyuq	aŋuyu(ʀ)- (under aŋu-)
anguti	aŋun
angutiviaq	aŋutəviaq (under aŋun)
anguuq-	aŋuðuʀ-
anguuti	aŋuðaʀun (under aŋuðaʀ-)
anguvigaq	aŋuviɣaq
ani-	anə-
ani(k)	anaya-
aniguq-, anigguq	aniɣuq- (under anə-)
aniiqtuq	anəɣiʀ- (under anə-)
aninga-	aniŋa- (under anə-)
aniqta	aniʀta
aniqtiri-	anəʀtəqə- (under anəʀ-)
anirniq	anəʀ-
anirsaatuq	anəʀya(C)aʀ- (under anəʀ-)
anit-	anət- (under anə-)
aniu	aniɣu
annaaqtu(q)-	aŋənaaq- (under aŋə-)
annak-	annaɣ-
anngaa-	aŋəʀ- (under a(a)ŋ)
anngaq	an(ə)ɣaʀ(aʀ)
anngi(C)-	ałŋiɣ
annikit-	annəq(tu)-
anniri-, annirusuk-	atŋiqə- (under atŋiʀ-)
annitu-	annəq(tu)-
annuraaq	atnuʀaaq (under atə-)
anu	anu
anuri	anuqə
anursili	anuqliʀ- (under anuqə)
apaak-	apəktət-
apaapa	ap(p)a^{2}
apiri-	apəʀə-
apirsu(q)-	apəqšuq- (under apəʀə-)
appa(q)-	atpaq- (under at(ə)-)
appai-	atpaq- (under at(ə)-)
appaq	alpa(ɣ)
apujjaq	apun (under apə-)
apujjasuq-	apun (under apə-)
apummaq	apummaʀ
apuq-	apuʀ-
aput	apun (under apə-)
aqajaq	aqayaɣ
aqajuani	aqaɣu
aqali	akka
aqaq-	aqaɣ-
aqi-	aqə-
aqiaq	aq(ə)yaʀ
aqiaruq	aq(ə)yaquʀ (under aq(ə)yaʀ)
aqiggiq	aqəðɣiʀ
aqilluqaaq	aqilluk (under aqit-)
aqit-, aqili-	aqit-
aqittuq	aqit-
aqpaa(q)-	aqva-
aqpasua-, aqpangiq-	aqva-
aqpik	aqəvðiɣ
aqqa(q)-	atʀaʀ- (under at(ə)-)
aqqala-	aləmqaʀ-
aqqunaq-	alqunaʀ-
aqqusaa(q)-	apqucaaq- (under apʀun)
aqqusiniq	apqucinəq (under apʀun)
aqquti	apʀun
aqtaq-	aʀcaʀ-
aqtuq	aʀtuʀ-
aqu	aqu
aqui-	aqu(C)i-
aqupi-	aqup(p)i- (under aqumə-)
aqut-	aqut- (under aqu)
aquuti	aqu(ʀ)un (under aqu)
aquvit-	aqumə-
ariu-, ariuk-	aʀ(ə)yu-
ariuniku	aʀ(ə)yu-
arli(k)-	aʀli(C)-
arnaluk	aʀnacalluʀ (under aʀnaʀ)
arnaq	aʀnaʀ
arnaviaq	aʀnaviaq (under aʀnaʀ)
arngilik-	an(ə)ʀilək- (under anəʀ-)
arnguaq	aɣanʀu(Caʀ)
arraani, arragu	alʀani (under aləʀ)
arri-	aʀʀi-
arsa(C)-	aqla-
arsaa(q)-	aʀʀaʀ-
arsairaut	aqla-
arsaniq	aqsaq
arsaquq	akðanquʀ
arsi-	aqci-
arsu(k)-	aqaɣcuɣ- (under aqaɣ-)
arviq	aʀvəʀ
arvitaqtuq	aʀviʀ-
asa(k)-	ažak-
asi, asiani	aci
asigiyaaq-	aciɣə- (aci-^{2})
asiruq-	aciʀuq- (under aci-^{2})
asiu-	aciu- (under aci-^{2})
asivaq	aacivak
asivaq	acivaq- (under aci-^{2})
asu-	acu-
asuila, asuguuq	acu
at(i)-	at(ə)-
ata-	ata-
ataaq-	ataaq- (under at(ə)-)
ataata	ata(a)ta
ataatatsiaq	ata(a)ta
atai	ata^{2}
ataniq	atanəʀ (under ata-)
atauq	ata-
atausiaq-	atauciʀaq- (under ataʀuciʀ)
atausiq	ataʀuciʀ
atauti	attan (under ata)
atautsikkut	ataʀuccikun (under ataʀuciʀ)
ati-	atə-
atii	ata^{2}

TARRAMIUT — ECI	PROTOFORM
atigi	atəkə-
atiq	atəʀ
atiq-	atəʀ- (under at(ə)-)
atsa, atsak	accaɣ
atsagiikkuti	akšaɣiitkutaq (under akðaɣ-)
atsa(k)-, atsakaa(q)-	akðaɣ-
atsalik-	akšalək- (under akðaɣ-)
atsalua-, atsaluaq	akðaɣ-
atsaq	aklaq
atsataq-	apcak-
atsi(q)-	acciʀ- (under atəʀ)
atsiuti-	acciʀutə- (under atəʀ)
atsu-	aklu-
atsunaaq	akluna(a)q
atsut	akcut
attagu	ataku (under ata[2])
attatuq-	attaq- (under ata-)
attu(q)-	aɣtuʀ-
attuq	atuʀ(aʀ) (under aŋə-)
atuaq-, atuarniq	atuaq- (under atuʀ-)
atungaq	atuŋaʀ
atunit	atunəm
atuq-	atuʀ-
au-	aʀu-
augiaq	aðuɣɣaʀ (under aðuɣ)
aujaq-	aužaq (under aʀu-)
auk	aðuɣ (under aʀu-)
auk-	auk- (under aʀu-)
auka	aka(a)
aukkaniq	aupkaʀnəq (under aʀu-)
aula-	aʀula-
aulaikkaq	aʀulaŋiʀ- (under aʀula-)
aulajaiq-	aulay(y)aŋiq- (under aʀula-)
aulajja(k)-	aulayyak- (under aʀula-)
aulasaq-	aulacaq- (under aʀula-)
aulat-	aʀulat- (under aʀula-)
aulikkaq	aulait- (under aʀula-)
aullaaq-	aullaaq- (under aʀula-)
aullaat	aullaaq- (under aʀula-)
aulla(q)-	aʀullaʀ- (under aʀula-)
auma-	aʀu-
auma, aumaq	a(C)umaʀ
aumajaaq-	a(C)umaʀ
aummisiq-	aummin
aunaaq-	aðun(ə)ʀaʀ- (under aðuɣ)
aunniq	aunnəq (under aʀu-)
aunnitu-	aunnəqtu-
aupaluutaq, aupalaqtuq	aukpaluk- (under aðuɣ)
aursaa(q)-	auqcaaq-
autsa(q)-	auk- (under aʀu-)
auviq	aʀuvəʀ(aʀ)
auvvik	aužvik
avaagi-	avaaɣə-
avaala-	avaala-
avaalaqiaq	avaalaqiaq
avaaq-	avaaq- (under ava-)
avagi-	avaaɣə-
avat(i-)	avan
avat-	ava-
avatangiq-	avatəŋiʀ- (under avan)
avataq	avataʀ
avik-	avəɣ-
aviliuq-	avi(ʀ)luʀ-
avinngaq	avəlŋaʀ
aviuji-, aviur-	aviʀu-
avuti-, avuyuq	avət- (under avəɣ-)
avvaq	avvaq (under avəɣ-)
avvia(q)-	avðiʀ- (under avðaʀ[2])
iga-, iga	əɣa-
igaarniq	əɣa(C)aʀ (under əɣa-)
igalaaq	əɣaləʀ
igavik	əɣɣaviɣ (under əɣa-)
iggaak	əð(ə)ɣaʀ (under əðə)
iggiaq	iɣɣaʀ(aʀ) (under iɣə-)
iggut	əvɣun (under əvək-)
igimaq	əɣimaʀ
igit-	əɣət-
igumii-	əɣumə(t)-
igunaruq-	əɣunaq
igutsaq	əɣutcaq
iguuti	əɣut-
ii-	əɣə-
iigaq	iɣəɣaʀ-
ijaruq-	əžəʀuq- (under əðə)
ijaruvak	əžaʀuaq (under əðə)
iji	əðə
ijiq-	əðəʀ-
ijimmik-	əðəɣmiɣ- (under əðə)
ijiraq	iðəʀaʀ (under iðəʀ-)
ijjangu-	əpyalŋu- (under əpə-)
ijjaq	əɣžaq
ijjarut	əpžaʀun
ijji	itðə
ijji(t)-	əžžit- (under əðə)
ijju(q)- (apply peat)	nəvðuʀ
ijju(q)- (coagulate)	iɣðuʀ-
ijjua(q)-	əžžuq-
ijjuatuq-	imðuʀ-
ijjuk	əɣðuɣ
ijjuri-	əžžuq-
ijukka(q)-	əðəvkaʀ- (under əðət-)
ijuq-	əžžuq-
ijuraq	iðəʀaʀ (under iðəʀ-)
ijuri-, ijjuri-	əž(ž)uʀə- (under əžžuq-)
ikaaq-	əkəʀaʀ-
ikajuq-	ikayuʀ-
iki, iki- (cut block of snow)	əki
iki- (embark, get in)	əkə-[2]
ikiaq	əkiðaʀ
ikii	ikki
ikiliq-	əkiliʀ- (under əki)
ikiq	əkəʀ
ikiqtu-	əkəqtu- (under əkəʀ)
ikirasaq	əkəʀacak (under əkəʀ)
ikirnguaq	əkənʀužaq
ikisaq-	əkə-[1]
ikit- (few)	ikəɣ(ə)t-
ikit- (ignite)	əkət- (under əkə-[1])
ikkaruq	ətkalʀuq (under ətə-)

TARRAMIUT — ECI	PROTOFORM
ikkarit-	ətɣalRit- (under ətə-)
ikkat-	ətɣat-
ikkiit-	ipɣit- (under ipəɣ-)
ikkiq	iŋkiR
ikuala-, ikuallarutiritsi-	əkuala- (under əkə-[1])
ikuma-	əkuma- (under əkə-[1])
ikupigaq-	ikuɣ-
ikuq-	əkuq-
ikurraq	əkəvRaq (under əkəRAR)
ikusik	ikuyəɣ
ikuutaq	ikuɣutaR (under ikuɣ-)
ila	ila(-)[1]
ilaa	ila[2]
ilaani	ilaŋa(t)ni (under ila(-)[1])
ilaaq, ilaaqtu(q)-	ila(C)AR (under ila(-)[1])
ilagi-	ilakə- (under ila(-)[1])
ilaii	ila[2]
ilaliuq-	ilali(C)uR- (under ila(-)[1])
ilangan(n)i	ilaŋa(t)ni (under ila(-)[1])
ilannaaq	ilannaR (under ila(-)[1])
ilannga(q)-	ilaŋŋaR- (under ila(-)[1])
ilanngiut(i)-	ilaŋiR- (under ila(-)[1])
ilaviniq	ilavinəq (under ila(-)[1])
ili-	əɬi-
iliarjuk	əɬiɣaR(AR)
ilik	iliɣ
ilima-, ilimasuk-	əlima-
ilinngataq	iliɣ
iliqiluk-	iləqə-
ilira-, ilirasuk-	əliRa-
ilirniku, iliq-	əliRqə-
ilisaq-	əlicaR- (under əlit-)
ilit-	əlit-
ilitari-	əlitaqə- (under əlit-)
ilisima-	əlicima- (under əlit-)
iliuq-	əɬi-
ilitti(q)-	əliktəq-
ilivvik	əɬ(ɬ)iviɣ (under əlu(R)-)
illaiguti	il(l)aɣiRun (under il(l)aɣ-)
illaujaq	illa(ɣa)užaq
illauq	imla(C)u(ɣ)
illi(q)-	iŋliq-
illiaq	ənlic(C)AR
illiq, illinaq	iŋləR
illiti	iŋlin (under iŋləR)
illu (house)	əŋlu
illu (one of a pair)	iŋlu
illuaq	iŋlu
illui-	əðəɬuɣ- (under əðə)
illukitaaq-	iŋluk(k)ita(C)AR-(iŋlu)
illunga-	il(l)uŋa (under ilu)
illutuq-	iŋluktu(u)q- (under iŋlu)
illutut	iŋlutun (under iŋlu)
illuuq	ətlu(R)-
ilu	ilu
ilu-	ilu- (under ilu)
iluit-	iluit- (under ilu)
iluliarusiq	ilul(l)iRAR (under ilu)
ilulli-	ilulli- (under ilu)
ilulliq	ilulliR (under ilu)
ilungiqtu(q)-	iluŋiq- (under ilu)
ilupaaq	ilupəR(AR) (under ilu)
ilupiraq	ilupəR(AR) (under ilu)
ilusiq	əluciR (under ət-)
ilutaq	ilutaR (under ilu)
iluti	əlun
iluunna-	əlu(R)-
iluviq	əɬivəR (under əlu(R)-)
imaaq-	imaaq- (under ima(R))
imak	imma
imaq, imaqpik	ima(R)
imariaq	imaRɣaɣ (under ima(R))
imaruq-	imaRuq- (under ima(R))
imia-	əməɣ-
imik-, imikkaatiq-	imə-
iminnga(C)-	imə-
imiq	əməR(-)
imiqqutaaq	əmətqutaq
imiqqutailaq	əmətqutailaq (under əmətqutaq)
imiqta(q)-	əməRtaR- (under əməR(-))
imiruk-	əməRuk- (under əməR(-))
imma(k)-	imanəɣ- (under ima(R))
immaq(a)	imma
immi-, imminiir-	əɬmi-
immi(q)- (fill with water)	immiR- (under ima(R))
immi(q)- (without stopping)	əɣmiR-
immiaq	əmmiaq (under əməR(-))
immit-	əmmit (under əməR(-))
immuk	əmmuɣ
imu-	imu-[1]
imulluk	imu-[2]
inaluaq	iŋaluk
inangiq-	ənəŋiR- (under ənə)
inat-	əna-
ingi(q)	əŋə
ingiaq-	iŋyaR-
ingirra-	iŋilRa-
ingit-	iŋət-
ingiulik	iŋ(ə)yuləɣ
ingiuq-	iŋəq-
ingula-	iŋut-[1]
iniq-	inəq-
ini-	ini-
ini	ənə
inilla(k)-	ənəllak- (under ənə)
iniqti(q)-	inəR-
iniqu(C)-, iniqugi-	inəqə-
iniqunaq-	inəqyunaR- (under inəqə-)
inna(k)-, innaq (flintstone)	əknənəɣ- (under əkə-[1])
innaq (cliff)	əpnaR
innaq-	iŋŋaR-
innganiq	əɬŋaR-
inngiluttaaruti	əməŋə(R)- (under əməɣ-)
inngiq	əməŋə(R)- (under əməɣ-)
innia(C)-	iŋŋit- (under iŋuɣ)
inni(q)-	inniq- (under ini)
inni(t)-	iŋŋit- (under iŋuɣ)
inniq	ək(ə)nəR (under əkə-[1])
innitait	innitaR (under ini-)
inuaq-	inuaq- (under iŋuɣ)

TARRAMIUT — ECI	PROTOFORM
itilliq	ətəvə(t)-
itimak	ətəmaɣ
itimmi(k)-	itəɣmiɣ- (under itəɣ)
itiq	ətəʀ
itiq- (wake up)	ətəʀ-
itiq- (enter)	itəʀ-
itirlak	ətəʀlaɣ (under ətəʀ)
itirsaq	ətəʀlaɣ (under ətəʀ)
itiruq	ətəquʀ (under ətəʀ)
itivit-	ətəvə(t)-
itsaq	itcaq
itsi	əyyi(ʀ)
itsi(C)-	ikšək- (under iŋət-)
itsigi-	əkli-
itsiva-	ikšəva- (under iŋət-)
itsivik	əkləʀviɣ (under əkə-[2])
itsu(k)-	əvcuɣ-
itsu(q)-	iyyuʀ-
itsua(q)-	itcuaq- (under iyyuʀ-)
itsuti	əɣžutət
itta(q)-	əvtəʀ
ittaaq	əvtəʀ
ittangiq-	əvtəʀ
ittaniku	əɣtaʀ (under əɣət-)
ittaqajanngit-	əvtəʀ
ittiq	əvtəʀ
ittuluk-	əɣtuɣ(-)
ittuq	əltuʀ
itturaq	iktuʀaq (under iŋət-)
iva-	əva-
ivaa-	ivaʀ-
ivajaq-	ivayaʀ- (under ivaʀ-)
ivalu	ivalu
iviangiq	əvyaŋ(ŋ)iʀ
ivik	əvəɣ
ivik-	əvək-
iviq-	ivəq-[1]
ivitaaruq	ivitaaʀuq (under ivitəʀaʀ)
ivu-	iŋ(ə)yu-
ivugait	iŋ(ə)yukaʀ
ivva(q)-	əvə(ʀ)ləɣ-
ivvit	əlpət
kaak-, kaattu(q)-	ka(C)əɣ-
kaillua(q)-	kaivluaq- (under kayəmə(t)-)
kaimit-	kayəmə(t)-
kaipinga-	kapət-
kaittaq	kaivca(a)q
kaivalla(k)-	kažəvallak- (under kaðəvə(t)-)
kaivalua-, kaivaluaq	kažəvallak- (under kaðəvə(t)-)
kaivit-, kaivat-	kaðəvə(t)-
kajai-	kayaq-
kajjiq	kavžaq
kajju(k)-	kauɣaq- (under kaðuɣ-)
kajjuaq	kay(y)u(C)aʀ (under kayu-)
kajungiq-	kayuŋŋiq- (under kayu-)
kajuq	kayuq-
kajusi-	kayu-
kakak-	kakaɣ-
kaki-	kaki-
kakijjut	kakkin (under kaki-)
kakilisaq	kakilacak
kakillaalitsi-	kakilla- (under kaki-)
kakillanaqutit	kakillaʀnaq (under kaki-)
kakivak	kaki(C)aʀ (under kaki-)
kakkiq	kakkiq
kakkivik, kakkiviaq	kakiðviɣ (under kaki-)
kalirraq	kaliʀʀaq
kalit-, kalik-	kaləɣ-[1]
kallak	kavlaɣ
kallu	katluɣ
kalluraq-	kaləɣ-[1]
kalursu(qC-	kaləɣ-[2]
kaluti	kalɣun (under kaləɣ-[1])
kama-	kama-
kamagi-	kamakə- (under kama-)
kamik	kaməɣ
kamilla(q)-	kamillaq- (under kaməɣ)
kamillaa(q)-	kamillaaq- (under kaməɣ)
kanaaq	kanaɣ
kanajuq	kanayu(ʀ)
kangi	kaŋiʀ
kangiisuk-	kaŋiʀci- (under kaŋiʀ)
kangilliq	kaŋilliʀ (under kaŋiʀ)
kangiqquti-	kaŋiʀ
kangirsuk	kaŋiʀłuɣ (under kaŋiʀ)
kangivaq-	kaŋivaʀ- (under kaŋiʀ)
kangivaqti(q)-	kaŋivaʀtə(ʀ)- (under kaŋiʀ)
kanguq	kaŋuʀ
kangusaq	kannuyaʀ
kaniq	kanəʀ
kanivaut	kanivaʀun
kanngu(suk)-	kayŋu-
kapi-	kapə-
kapit-	kapət-
kapitaq	kapətaq (under kapət-)
kappia(suk)-	kappəya-
kapput(i)-	kapputə- (under kapə-)
kapuq-	kapuʀ- (under kapə-)
kapuut	kappun (under kapə-)
karnga(q)-	kanʀaq-
kasuk	katyuɣ-
kasuq-	katyuɣ-
kasuut(i)-	katyuɣutə- (under katyuɣ-)
katak	katak (under kataɣ-)
katak-	kataɣ-
kati-	katə-
katima-	katəma- (under katə-)
katirsu(q)-	katəqšat (under katə-)
katit-	katət- (under katə-)
katsuaq	kay(y)u(C)aʀ (under kayu-)
katsunga-, katsungait-	katcuq-
katuk-	katuk-
kau-	kaɣu
kaugaq-	kauɣaq- (under kaðuɣ-)
kauk	ka(C)uɣ
kauk-	kaðuɣ-

TARRAMIUT — ECI	PROTOFORM
kautaq	kað(ð)uɣun (under kaðuɣ-)
kautuq-	kaɣu-
kavisik	kapəciʀ
kavisilik	kapəciłək (under kapəciʀ)
kia	ki(na)
kiak, kiak-	kiðaɣ(-)
kiasik	kiɣaɣəɣ
kiati	kiɣan
kiggaluk	kəvɣaluɣ (under kəvɣaʀ)
kiggaq	kəvɣaʀ
kiggavik	kəð(ə)kaviɣ
kiggiq	kəɣɣəq (under kəɣə-)
kiggumiaq	kəvɣumiaq- (under kəvəɣ-)
kigiaq	kəɣi(C)aʀ (under kəɣə-)
kiguk	kiɣuɣ
kiguti	kəɣun (under kəɣə-)
kii-	kəɣə-
kiinailitaq	kiinailitaq (under kəɣinaʀ)
kiinannguaq	kəɣinaquʀ (under kəɣinaʀ)
kiinaq	kəɣinaʀ
kiinna(k)-	kiinnakcaq- (under kəɣinaʀ)
kiita	ki(i)
kijiliq-	kəžə(k)-
kijja(q)-	kəpðaʀ- (under kəpə-)
kikiak	kəkyaɣ
kikiik-	kikiik-
kikka(q)-	kəp(ə)kaʀ-
kikkuliq	kikkuləq
kikkut	ki(na)
kilak-, kilaaq-	kəlaɣ-
kiligaq-	kəliɣaʀ- (under kəliɣ-)
kiliq-	kiliʀ-
kilit-	kələ(t)-
kiliutaq	kəliɣ-
killaa(q)-	kənlə
killak (teeth interval)	kəklaɣ
killak (hole or tear)	kəllaq (under kəlaɣ-)
killi	kənlə
killi(C)- (cut)	kəpliʀ- (under kəpə-)
killi(C)- (affect)	kəvləʀ-
killigi-	kənlekə- (under kənlə-)
killiq (wound)	killiʀ (under kiliʀ-)
killiq (farthest toward sea)	kətliʀ (under kətə-)
killu(q)-	kəpluʀ- (under kəpə-)
killumut	kənluʀ
kilu	kəlu
kiluaq-	kəluaq- (under kəluɣ)
kiluk	kəluɣ
kiluvaq-	kəluvaʀ- (under kəlu)
kimattuut(i)	kəmaktuun
kimmautiik	kəɣmaʀ-
kimmautingu-	kəɣmaʀ-
kimmi-	kəɣmi(C)- (under kəɣə-)
kimmia(q)-	kəɣmi(C)- (under kəɣə-)
kimmik	kitmiɣ
kimminaq	kitŋiɣ
kimmiquaq	kitmilquʀ (under kitmiɣ)
kina	ki(na)
kinaa-	kəni-
kingik-	kəŋək-
kingu-	kiŋu-
kingulliq, kingullipaaq	kiŋul(l)iʀ (under kiŋu-)
kinguniq	kiŋunəʀ (under kiŋu-)
kinguppia(q)-	kiŋutmuʀ- (under kiŋu-)
kinguraq	kiŋuʀaq (under kiŋu-)
kinguraq-	kiŋuʀaʀ- (under kiŋu-)
kinguvaaq	kiŋuvaaq (under kiŋu-)
kinguvaq-	kiŋuvaʀ- (under kiŋu-)
kini-	kini-
kinipa-	kəni-
kiniq	kəniʀ
kiniqtaq	kənəqtaq (under kənəʀ-)
kiniritsi(C)-, kiniritsiaq	kinəʀ-
kinirmi(k)-	kəniʀmiɣ- (under kəniʀ)
kinit-	kənit- (under kəni-)
kinnaq	kinəʀ-
kinngiq	kəkniq (under kəkə-)
kipaluk	kəvɣaluɣ (under kəvɣaʀ-)
kipi-	kəpə-
kipit-	kəpət-[2]
kippa(q)-	kətvaʀ- (under kətə-)
kippaq	kəppaʀ (under kəpə-)
kipparittuq	kəppaʀik (under kəpə-)
kipuC-	kiput-
kisaq	kicaʀ (under kit-)
kisi-, kisiani	kəði-
kisit-	kəcit-
kiti-	kətə-
kitsa(q)-, kitsa(r)uti	kəkcaq-
kitsauti	kəkcaun
kitsuk	kəklu(ɣ)
kitturaq-	kəktuʀaq- (under kəkə-)
kitturiaq	kəɣtuʀyaʀ
kituuna	kitu (under ki(na))
kiu-	ki(C)u-
kiuma-	ki(C)umɣa- (under ki(C)u-)
kivi-	kivə-
kivik-	kəvəɣ-
kivva(k)-	kəvvak- (under kəvəɣ-)
kivvia(q)-	kəviʀ-
kuanniq	kuanniq
kujak-	kuyaɣ-
kujapigaq	kuyapəɣaʀ (under kuyaɣ)
kujaq	kuyaɣ
kujja(q)-	kutžaq-
kujjanga-	kutžaŋa- (under kutžaq-)
kukik	kukiɣ
kukkiq	kumkaʀ
kukuppaq	kukəɣ
kullu	kumlu
kumak	kumaɣ
kumaruaq	kumaʀuaq (under kumaɣ)
kumik-	kuməɣ-
kunik-	kunik-
kuqqut(i)-	ku(C)u(ɣ)-
kusiq	kuciʀ- (under kutə)
kusugaq	kucukaʀ
kutak-	kutak-

TARRAMIUT — ECI	PROTOFORM
kutsasuk-	kukðaɣ-
kutsi(t)-, kutsiq	kupci-
kutsuq	kuccuR
kutuq	kutə
kuuk	kuðəɣ
kuunga-	ku(C)u(ɣ)-
kuuruq	quðuquR (under quðu-)
kuusug-	ku(C)u(ɣ)-
kuutsinaaq	kuðuccinəR (under kuðucciR)
kuutsiniq	kuðuccinəR (under kuðucciR)
kuutsiq	kuðucciR
kuutu-	ku(C)u(ɣ)-
kuvi-	kuvə-
luvviluvvilaaq	ləvələvələRaR
maajjaq	maŋaɣ(-)
maak-	maŋaɣ(-)
maalaa-	maRu-[2]
maannakut	maðətən
maaq-, maarala-	maaq-
maattu	maŋaɣ(-)
mait-	mait-
majja(C)-	mavžak- (under məmə-)
majuaq-	mayuRaR(aR)- (under mayuR-)
majuq-	mayuR-
majuqqaq	mayuqqaq (under mayuR-)
majuraq-	mayuRaR- (under mayuR-)
majurauti	mayuRaRun (under mayuR-)
maki-	makə-
makit-	makət-
makita-	makəta- (under makət-)
makitiq	makitəR
makitiq-	makətəq- (under makət-)
makku(q)-, makkuluk-	mapkuq-
makkut(i)-	mak(k)utə-
malak	malak
malik	malək
malik-	maliɣ-
malirsu(q)-, malirsuaq	maliqðuR- (under maliɣ-)
malliq-	malliq- (under malək)
malugi-	maluɣə-
mamait-	mamait- (under mamaR(-))
mamaq-	mamaR(-)
mamari-	mamaRə- (under mamaR(-))
mami	mamə
mamia-	mamə-
mamiasutsa(q)-	məm(ə)ya-
mamit-	mamət- (under mamə-)
manaq	manaR
mangat-	maŋat-
mangik-, mangia(q)-	maŋiR-
manguk-	maŋut-
mani-	mani-
maniilaq	maniilaq (under maniɣ-)
manijjugaq-	manəɣyuɣaR- (under manəɣ-)

TARRAMIUT — ECI	PROTOFORM
manik-	maniɣ-
maniq	manəR
maniraq	maniRaq (under maniɣ-)
manna	maðətən
mannga(C)-	matŋa-
manngait-	manŋəq-
manngiq	manŋəq-
manngu(C)-	manŋuk-
mannguk	maŋŋuq (under maŋut-)
mannik	manniɣ
manu	manu
manuaq	manuRaR (under manu)
manuilitaq	manuŋilitaR (under manu)
mappi(q)-	makpiq-
mappituraq-	makpiq-
maqait-	maqait-
maqi-	maqə-
maqik-	maqəɣ-
maqiniq	maqənəq (under maqə-)
maqujuk-	maRuyuɣ-
marraq, marlu	maRRaR
marruit	malRu(C)it (under malRuɣ)
marruuk	malRuɣ
masak	macak
masiik	maciɣ
matiqti	matəqtə
matsa(q)-	makcaq-
matsaq	macak
matta(q)-	mattaR-
mattaaq	maŋtaaq (under maŋtaɣ)
mattaq	maŋtaɣ
mattu-	mamtu- (under mamə)
matu	matu(-)
matuiq-	matuŋiR- (under matu(-))
mau-	maRu-[1]
maujaq	maRuya(R) (under maRu-[1])
mauliq-	maRut-
maunaq	maŋuna(ɣ)
mianiri-	mi(C)ani(kə)-
mik-	mit-
miki-	mikə-
mikiak-	məkəɣ-
mikigaq	məkəɣaq
mikili-	mikəli- (under mikə-)
mikiliraq	mikəliRaq (under mikə-)
mikki(k)-	mək(k)əɣ-
milaq	məlak
milik	mələɣ(-)
millu(q)-	milluuq- (under miluR-)
millua(q)-	məluɣ-
milugiaq	məluɣyaR (under məluɣ-)
miluk-	məluɣ-
miluq-	miluR-
miluriaq-	miluRiaq- (under miluR-)
mimiq	miməR
minaq-	minaR-
mingik-	məŋik-
mingiriaq	mənŋəRiaq (under mətŋəR-)
mingiriaq-	mətŋəR-
minguaq-	miŋuɣ-

TARRAMIUT — ECI	PROTOFORM
napariaq	napaʀyaʀ (under napa-)
naparutaq	nappaqutaʀ (under napa-)
napi-	napə-
napiaruti	napəʀ-
napiq-	napəʀ-
napit-	napə-
nappa(q)-	nappaʀ- (under napa-)
nappaq	nappaq (under napə-)
napu, napuliuti	napu
naqili-	naqəkli- (under naqət-)
naqit-	naqət-
naqitari-	naqət-
naqqi(k)-	nalqiɣ- (under nałə-)
naqquq	naŋquʀ
nariaq	naʀ(ə)yaʀ
narni(q)-	nanəʀ-
narru-, narrugi-	naʀʀu-
narsaq	naqðaʀ
narsi(C)-	naʀciɣ-
narsiaq	naqciaq (under naʀciɣ-)
narsu(C)-	naʀciɣ-
narsunga-	naʀciɣ-
nasaq	nacaʀ
nasit-	nacit-
nataaq	natəʀaʀ (under natəʀ)
nataarnaq	nataaʀnaq (under natəʀ)
nataqquaq	natanquaq (under natanquʀ)
nataqqunaq	natatquʀnaq (under natanquʀ)
nataqquq	natanquʀ
natiq	natəʀ
natiruvik-	natəquviɣ- (under natəʀ)
natsa(q)-, natsagaq	naŋcaʀ-
natsasaq	naŋcaʀ-
natsiaq	nayyiʀaʀ (under nayyiʀ)
natsiq	nayyiʀ
natsiut(i)-	nakcət- (under naŋaʀ-)
natti(t)-	naŋə(t)-
natturalik	nakturalək (under naɣət-)
natturaq	naɣtuqaʀ (under naɣət-)
naujaq	naʀuyaʀ
nauk	naɣu (under na-[2])
naukkia(q)-	nautkiaq- (under naʀułəɣ-)
naulagiaq-	nautkiaq- (under naʀułəɣ-)
naulaq	naulaq (under naʀułəɣ-)
naularnaq	naul(l)aʀnaq (under naula(yu)q)
naulik-	naʀułəɣ-
naumik	na(C)umi (under na-[2])
naumili	na(C)umi (under na-[2])
navvaa(q)-	nažaq-
niaqqua(q)-	niaquaq- (under nay(ə)quʀ)
niaquq	nay(ə)quʀ
nigaq, nigavit-	nəɣaʀ
niggiq	nəɣəʀ
nigguq	nivɣuʀ
nigiq, nigiiq	nəɣəʀ
niguq	nəɣuʀ-
niiniq-	nanəʀ-
niiquq-	niiqquq-
niisa, niisarnaq	niisa
nijjuti, nirjuti	nəʀžun
nika-, nikagi-	nəka-
nikku	nəvku
nikpaq-	nəkvaʀ- (under nəkəvə(t)-)
nikujjaa(q)-	nəkuvžaaq- (under nəkəvə(t)-)
nikurra-	nəkəvʀa- (under nəkə(t)-)
nikuvik-	nəkəvə(t)-
nilak	nilaɣ
niliq	nələʀ(-)
nilla(q)-, nillasuk-	nəɣlaq- (under nəŋə(t)-)
nilli-	nəŋə(t)-
nilli(q)-	nəpliʀ- (under nəpə)
nimiq	nəməʀ(-)
nimiriaq	məməʀyaʀ (under nəməʀ(-))
ningaq-	nəŋ(ŋ)aʀ-
ningauk	nəŋa(C)u(ɣ)
ningi-	nəŋə-
ningiq	nəŋiʀ
ningiuq	nəŋyuʀ
ninnga(C)-, ninngari-	nəŋ(ŋ)aʀ-
ninngiq	nəmniuq-
ninngu-	nəlŋu(ʀ)-
ninniu(q)-	nəmniuq-
nipaa-	nəpaa(q)- (under nəpə)
nipait	nəpaŋit- (under nəpə)
nipangiq-	nəpəŋiʀ- (under nəpə)
nipaq-	nəpə-
nipi	nəpə
nipi-	nəpə-
nipisaq	nəpətyaʀ- (under nəpət-)
nipit-	nəpət-
nippa(q)-	nəkvaʀ- (under nəkəvə(t)-)
niqi	nəqə
niqiliur-	nəqli(C)uʀ- (under nəqə)
niqitsaq	nəqə
niqituraq	nəɣituqaʀ-
niqpik	nəqpik (under nəqə)
niqtu(q)-	niqtuq-
niri-	nəʀə-
nirikka(q)-	nəʀəvkaʀ- (under nəʀə-)
nirilik-	nəʀiləɣ-
niriuk-, niriugi-	nəʀyu(ɣ)-
nirliq	nəʀləʀ
nirlu(C)-, nirlungajuq	nəʀluq-
nirrala-	nəvʀala- (under nəvəʀ-)
nirrituguq	nəʀʀitu- (under nəʀə-)
nirrivik	nəʀəðviɣ (under nəʀə-)
nirsiu(q)-	nəqli(C)uʀ- (under nəqə)
niru	nəqu-
niruaq-	niʀuaq-
nirukit-	nəqu-
nirukkaq	nəʀupkaq
nirumik-	nəʀuvəʀ-
nirutu-	nəqu-
nitsaa(C)-	nəlcaʀ-
nitsaatuq	nikcaaqtuq (under nəlcaʀ-)

TARRAMIUT — ECI	PROTOFORM
pallu	pavlu
pallu(q)-	palluʀ- (under palu-)
palluaq	pavlu
palu-	palu-
pamialluk	pamyuʀaʀ (under pamyuʀ)
pamiaq	pamyuʀaʀ (under pamyuʀ)
pamiuq	pamyuʀ
pana	pana
pangalik-	paŋaləɣ-
panik	paniɣ
paniq-	panəʀ-
pannaq	pannaq (under panəʀ-)
panniq	paɣnəʀ
papaaq	papaaq
papik	papəɣ
papiruq	papəʀuq (under papəɣ)
parla-	paʀla-
parnai(q)-	paqnaŋiʀ- (under paqna-)
parna(k)-	paqna-
parnanairsivik	paqnaŋiʀ- (under paqna-)
parnasima-	paqna-
parngi(C)-	panəʀ-
parria(q)-	paðəʀ-
parsariaqtu(q)-	paðəʀ-
pasi-	paci-
patik-	patəɣ-
patiq	patəʀ
patitti(t)-	patəktət- (under patəɣ-)
patsiti	patcin (under paci-)
patta(k)-	pattaɣ-
patuk-	patəɣ-
pauguaq	paɣuɣ-
pauk-	paɣuɣ-
pauktuq-	paɣuɣ-
paulangiq-	paɣu(la)-
paumit-	pa(C)umə(t)-
paunnaq	pautnaq
pauq	paɣu(la)-
pauq-	paŋəʀ-
paurngaq	paɣunʀaʀ
paurngaquti	paunʀaqun (under paɣunʀaʀ)
pautiik	paŋəʀun (under paŋəʀ-)
pauttu(q)-	pauktuq- (under paɣuɣ-)
pavvi(C)-	papði-
pavvik	paðɣiɣ
pi-	pi(-)
piak-	piðaɣ-
piaraq	piaʀaq (under pi(-))
pigaaq-	pəɣəɣaʀ-
pigi-	pikə- (under pi(-))
piijaq-	piiyaq- (under pi(-))
piiq-	piŋiʀ-
piirsi(q)-	piʀtuʀ
piit-	piðaɣ-
pijaari-	pityaqə-
pijariiq-	pižaʀiiq-
pijarniit-	piðaqə(naʀ)-
pijarnituq	piðaqəŋit- (under piðaqə(naʀ)-)
pijik-	pižək-
pijitsima-	pižək-
pijjait-	pižžaq(-)
pijjarik-	pižžaq(-)
pijjuti	under pi(-)
pijugari-	piyuɣaq-
pikatsiluk-	pəkku(ɣ)-
piki-	pəkə-
pikiaq-	pəkiaq- (under pəkə-)
pikiuk	pəkyu
pikkaluk	pəkku(ɣ)-
pikkarik-	pəkku(ɣ)-
pikkuluk-	pəku(ɣ)
pikkunaq-	pəkku(ɣ)-
pikuq	pəku(ɣ)
pikutsu(C)-	pəkku(ɣ)-
pikutsuuq-	pəkkuna(ɣ)-
pilaaq-	pilaaq- (under pi(-))
pilak-	pilaɣ-
pilaq-	pil(l)aq-
pilattu(q)-	pilaɣtuʀ- (under pilaɣ-)
pilauti	pilaun (under pilaɣ-)
pilirngu-	pilinʀu-
piliusaq	pilliun (under pi(-))
piliuti	pilliun (under pi(-))
piliutitsaq	pilliun (under pi(-))
pillarik-	pillu(a)ʀik- (under pi(-))
pilli(q)-	pəɣləq-
pillisi-	pəllitci-
pillu(k)-	pətluɣ-[1]
pillurik-	pillu(a)ʀik- (under pi(-))
pilu-, piluC-	piłuɣ- (under pi(-))
piluaq-	pi(t)lu(C)aʀ- (under pi(-))
piluari-	pi(t)lu(C)aʀ- (under pi(-))
pilukaC-	piłuɣ- (under pi(-))
piluq	pəlu(ʀ)
pima-, pimayi	pima-
pimaq-	pima(a)q-
pingaju, pingajuat	piŋayut
pingasut	piŋayut
pingigi-	pəŋəɣ-
pingu-	piŋu-[1]
pinguq	pəŋuʀ
piniaq-	piniaq- (under pi(-))
piniq	piɣinəʀ
pinirait	piɣinəʀ
pinirlu(k)-	pinəʀłuɣ- (under pi(-))
pinna(q)-	pinnaʀ- (under pi(-))
pinnaaq	pinnaʀ(naq)-
pinngua(q)-	piŋŋuðaʀ- (under pi(-))
pipiC-	pipək-
piqalujaq	pəqaluyak
piqqusiq, piqqusiraq-	pinquciʀ
piqtuq	piʀtuʀ
piqtusiraq	piʀtuʀciʀaʀ
piquniq	pəqu-
piquti	piqqun (under pi(-))
piringa-	piʀəŋa- (under pəʀə-)
pirit-	pəʀət- (under pəʀə-)
pirli(q)-	pəʀləʀ-
pirniq	pəʀnəʀ (under pəʀə-)

TARRAMIUT — ECI	PROTOFORM
pirraaq (braid)	piRðaRaR (under piRðaR-)
pirraaq (sled runner)	piRlaɣ
pirrai-	piRðaR-
pirrijaq-	piðaɣ-
pirsi(q)-	piRciR- (under piRtuR)
pirui-	pəRu(-)
piruq	pəRu(-)
piruq-	piRuq- (under pi(-))
pisiq	piciR
pisukti	piyuɣtə (under piyuɣ-)
pisuqitaq-	piyuɣ-
pitaaq	pətə-
pitaarut(i)-	pətə-
pitaqar-	pitaR (under pi(-))
pitik	pitəɣ-
pitiksi	pitəkcə (under pit´ɣ-)
pituk	pətuɣ-
pitsaq	pikðaR (under pi(-))
pitsa(q)-	pikðaR- (under pi(-))
pitsi(k)-	pəkyaɣ- (under pəkə-)
pitsik	pimci
pitsiulaaq	pitciulaaq
pitsivik	pətuɣ-
pitsuyuq	pitcu(q)- (under pi(-))
pittaq	pətuR-
pituaq	pətuɣ
pituraq-	pətuRaq- (under pətuR-
pituutaq	pətuɣutaR (under pətuɣ-)
pituuti	pətuɣutaR (under pətuɣ-)
piu-	piŋu-[2]
piusaq-	piŋu-[2]
pivitsaq	piðviɣ (under pi(-))
pu(C)-	put-
pualu(k)	pualu
puarrit	pualRin
pui-	puɣə-
puigaq-	puɣə-
puiguq-	puyɣu(R)-
puikka(q)-	puipkaq- (under puɣə-)
puila-	puila- (under puɣə-)
pujaq	puya
pujjuk	pumyuɣ-
pujuq	puyuR
pujuraq-	puyuRaq (under puyuR)
pukak	pukaɣ
pukiq	pukiR
pukkit-	pukkit- (under puɣə-)
pukuk-	pukuɣ-
pula-	pula-
pulaaq-	pula(C)aR- (under pula-)
pulama-	pula-
pulla(C)-	puvlaR-
pullaq	puvlaɣ (under puvə-)
pulli(q)-	puvliq- (under puvə-)
pungaq-	put-
punnguuq	punŋuuq (under put-)
punniq	puɣ(ə)nəR (under puɣ´-)
puqiC-	puqiɣ-
puqiit-	puqiɣit- (under puqiɣ-)
puqtu-	puqtu-
pusigaq-	puci-
pusit-	pucit- (under puci-)
putta-	puɣta- (under puɣə-)
puttaaq	puktaaq (under puɣə-)
putu	putu(-)[1]
putuguq	putukuR
putuurriti, putuursiti	puttun (under putu[1])
puugutaq	puɣɣutaq (under pu(ɣ)uq)
puuk-	puvuɣ-
puukaq-	puvuk(k)aR- (under puvuɣ-)
puuq	pu(ɣ)uq
puuqattaq	puukattaq (under pu(ɣ)uq)
puurusiq	puuRuciq (under pu(ɣ)uq)
puvak	puvak
puviaq	puvyaR
puviq-	puvə-
puviqqu(q)-	pupiŋquR-
puviraq	puviRaq (under puvə-)
puvittuq	puvə-
qaa-	qaðə-
qaajuq-	qaayuq-
qaanaujaq	qaanaaq
qaangiq-	qaaŋiq- (under qaðə-)
qaanniq	qaanəq
qaaq	qaaq ɣunder qaðə-)
qaaq-	qaɣəR-
qaariaq	qa(C)aRyaR
qaarsu(q)-	qaaqšuq- (under qaɣəR-)
qaat-	qaaptət-
qaatiq	qaatəq
qagaq-	qaɣəR-
qaggiq	qaðɣi
qai-	qaRə-
qainnguq	qayəmyu(R)
qainniu(q)-	qayaR
qaiqtuq	qaiqtuq (under qaiq-)
qairajuk-	qaiq-
qairulik	qaðəRuləɣ (under qaðəRu(R))
qairuq-	qaiq-
qairusuk	qa(C)iqu
qait-	qaRit- (under qaRə-)
qajaq	qayaR
qajaqtu(q)-	qayaRtuR- (under qayaR)
qajariaq	qayaRiaq (under qayaR)
qajau-	qayau- (under qayaR)
qajjaa(C)-	qapðaɣ-
qajuq	qayuR
qajuutaq	qayuRutaR (under qayuR)
qaki-	qakə-
qakiq-	qakə(R)-
qakiqtuq	qakə-[2]
qakirluk	qakəR(luɣ)
qakirniq (bleached)	qakə(R)-
qakirniq (stinging)	qakəRci- (under qakəR-)
qakirsinaqtuq	qakəRci- (under qakəR-)
qakki(C)-	qakkit- (under qakəR)
qaku	qaku
qakuqtaq	qakuR-

TARRAMIUT — ECI	PROTOFORM
qakurnaq	qakuʀnaʀ (under qakuʀ-)
qalak-	qała-[1]
qalasiq	qałaciʀ
qalingulaaq-	qaləŋu- (under qaləʀ-)
qaliraq	qaliqaʀ (under qaðə-)
qaliriik-	qal(l)iʀiik- (under qaðə-)
qalli-	qanli- (under qanət-)
qalli(C)-	qaðəliʀ- (under qaðə-)
qalliniq	qaðəliʀ- (under qaðə-)
qalliq	qaðliʀ (under qaðə-)
qallu (cavity in ice)	qaŋłu(ʀ)
qallu (eyebrow)	qavlu(ʀ)
qallunaaq	qavlunaaq
qalluniaq-	qavlunaaq
qalluqiaq-	qavlu(ʀ)
qallut	qallun (under qalu(-))
qalluviaq	qatliviɣ(aʀ) (under qatlin)
qalu-	qalu(-)
qaluniq	qalunəq (under qalu(-))
qalutaq-	qalutaʀ(-) (under qalu(-))
qaluut	qallun (under qalu(-))
qamaniq	qama-
qamit-	qamət- (under qamə-)
qammatuq-	qalmaʀ-
qamuq	qamuʀ-
qamuraq-	qamuʀaʀ (under qamuʀ-)
qamutiik	qamutək (under qamuʀ-)
qanak	qanaɣ
qanga	qaŋa
qangata-	qaŋata-
qangatta(q)-	qaŋattaq- (under qaŋata-)
qangattaujaq-	qaŋattaq- (under qaŋata-)
qangiaq	qaŋiɣaʀ
qani-	qani-
qanilaq-	qanilaaq- (under qani-)
qanilli-	qanli- (under qanət-)
qanima-	qanima-
qanimmaq	qanima-
qaninngu(C)-	qanət-
qaninnguu(C)-	qanət-
qaniq	qanəʀ(-)
qanit-	qanət-
qanitani	qanət-
qannik	qaniɣ
qannima-	qanima-
qanniq	qaniɣ
qanuq	qanuq
qanuqtuuq	qanuqtuq (under qanuq)
qappa(C)-	qaptət-
qapu	qapuɣ
qaqa-	qaqa-
qaqi-	qakə-
qaqiliq-	qaqu(ʀ)
qaqqaq	qaðqaʀ (under qaðə-)
qaqqitaq-	qažɣitaq
qaqqujaq-	qaŋquʀ-
qaqqu(q)	qaŋquʀ-
qaqusaq-	qaqu(ʀ)
qaquviraq	qaqu(ʀ)
qariaq	qaʀiyaq

TARRAMIUT — ECI	PROTOFORM
qaritaq	qaqətaʀ
qariuq-	qaʀiyaq
qarjuk	qaʀðuʀ
qarliik	qaʀ(u)łiɣ
qarluarut	qaqluaq (under qaqluɣ)
qarngui-	qamʀui-
qarrua-	qaðʀutə- (under qaðə-)
qarrujaq	qaʀu-
qarrulaaq	qaləʀ-
qarrut(i)-	qaðətʀutə- (under qaðə-)
qarsauq	qaqðaʀ
qarsuk	qaqluɣ
qasigiaq	qaðiɣyaʀ (under qaðə-)
qasili-	qacəli-
qasu-	qacu-
qataak-	qatəʀ-
qatannguti	qatəŋŋun
qatigaq	qatəɣ
qatigaq-	qatəɣ
qatikit-	qatəkit- (under qatə)
qatingulaq-	qasaq
qatitu-	qatə
qatsik-	qatcik- (under qaðə-)
qatsit	qavcit
qattaaq	qatəɣ
qattaq	qaltaʀ
qau-	qaʀu-
qau tamaat	qaʀu-
qauji-	qa(C)u(ði)-
qaujima-	qa(C)u(ði)-
qauk	qaʀu-
qauma-	qauma- (under qaʀu-)
qaumma(q)-	qauma- (under qaʀu-)
qaunnaq	qaunnaq
qauppat	qaʀu-
qauq	qaɣuʀ
qauq-	qa(C)uʀ-
qauruti	qauʀun (under qaɣuʀ)
qausii-	qauciʀ-
qausiq-	qauciʀ-
qavvaq-	qaɣvaʀ-
qavvi(q)-	qaɣvaʀ-
qavvik	qatviɣ
qia-	qiða-
qiaq	qi(C)aʀ
qiarngatuq	qianʀaqtuq
qiarsu(k)-	qiða-
qiggi(q)-	qəžɣəq- (under qətəɣ-)
qigguit	qiɣɣuʀ
qiggulait	qiɣɣuʀ
qiimitsi(C)-	qi(C)ət-
qiinga-	qiiŋa- (under qi(C)ət-)
qiiq	qiðəʀ
qiirattuq	qiðəʀ
qiirsu(q)-	qiiqšuq- (under qi(C)ət-)
qiit-	qi(C)ət-
qijjaq	qipðaʀ (under qipə-)
qijjiu(q)-	qəðði(C)uʀ- (under qəðuɣ)
qijuk	qəðuɣ
qijutta(q)-	qəðuɣtaʀ- (under qəðuɣ)
qikaq-	qikaʀ-

TARRAMIUT — ECI	PROTOFORM
qikiqtaq	qikəʀtaʀ
qikirraq	qikə-[2]
qiku	qiku
qilagujja(q)-	qiłəʀutaʀɪʀ- (under qiłəʀ-)
qilak	qilaɣ
qilak-	qilaɣ-
qilalugaq	qilaluɣaq
qilanaari-	qəlanəʀ(ᴀʀ)- (under qəla-[1])
qilaviq-	qilamət-
qiliqtit	qiləqtə (under qiłəʀ-)
qilirniq	qiłəʀɴəʀ (under qiłəʀ-)
qiliruq	qələʀuq (under qələɣ-)
qillaq	qiłəʀ-
qillaqiak	qəvlaqiak
qillarik-	qəvlaʀik- (under qəvləʀ-)
qilli(q)-	qəvləʀ-
qillitit-	qəvləʀ-
qilluaqatsi-	qiiɣluɣ-
qilluaqatsiq	qiiɣluɣ-
qilluk	qinluq
qilluk-	qiɣluk-
qilu-, qilu	qəlu-
qiluaqtuq	qəl(l)uʀ(ᴀʀ) (under qəlu-)
qiluk-	qiluɣ-
qilukka(C)-	qələɣ-
qilummi-	qəlummik- (under qəlu-)
qiluqqi(t)-	qiluqqit- (under qəlu-)
qimaa-	qimaɣ-
qimak-	qimaɣ-
qimat-	qimaɣ-
qimatsi-	qimaɣ-
qimatu, qimatuli-	qəmatu(t) (under qəmaɣ-)
qimiaq	qəmiʀ[2]
qimit-	qəmit-
qimiriaq	qəməʀʏaʀ
qimirluk	qəmiʀłuɣ (under qəmiʀ[1])
qimirru-	qəməlʀua-
qimirrua-	qəməlʀu-
qimminnguaq	qikmi(C)uðaʀ (under qikmiʀ)
qimmiq	qikmiʀ
qimuk-	qimuɣ-
qimutsi(q)-	qimuqcɪʀ(-) (under qimuɣ-)
qinaa-	qinəʀ-
qingalik	qəŋaləɣ (under qəŋaʀ)
qingaq	qəŋaʀ
qingarraq	qəŋaʀᴀʀ (under qəŋaʀ)
qiniq-	qinəʀ-
qinirsiq	qənəʀᴄɪʀ
qinisima-	qipə-
qinna(C)-	qənəʀ-
qinngu	qitŋu(ʀ)
qinnguliqit-	qənŋułiqə(t)- (under qənŋu(ʀ))
qinnguq	qənŋu(ʀ)
qinniq	qəŋnəʀ
qinu	qənu
qinu-	qinu-
qinuari-	qinuʀᴀʀ- (under qinu-)
qinuit-	qinu(C)it- (under qinu-)
qinuraq-	qinuʀᴀʀ- (under qinu-)
qipagi-	qəpak-
qipak-	qəpak-
qipaluaq	qipaluaq
qipasuk-	qəpak-
qipik	qipək (under qipə-)
qipiruq-	qipuk-
qipisima-	qəpə-
qipuqqi(C)-	qipuk-
qiqirri(C)-, qiqirrijaq-	qikə-[2]
qiqitiq-	qiʀətəq- (under qiʀə-)
qiqquaq	qəlquðaʀ
qiqumaaq	qiʀə-
qirata-, qirattatiq-	qiʀa(ta)- (under qiʀə-)
qirli(q)-	qəʀləʀ-
qirliraq	qəʀləʀ-
qirnguti	qinəʀ-
qirniraq	qiʀɴəʀaq (under qiʀɴəʀ-)
qirnitaq	qiʀɴəʀ-
qisik	qəciɣ
qisiq	qəcɪʀ(-)
qisiqtuuti	qəciqciun
qisuk	qiyu(ɣ)(-)
qisuk-	qəc(c)uɣ-
qitik-	qətəɣ-
qitiq, qitiq-	qətəʀ
qitiqpa(q)-	qətəqpaq- (under qətəʀ)
qitiqqaq	qətək
qitiqqauliq-	qitiq
qitiqqut(i)-	qətəqquq- (under qətəʀ)
qitiraq, qitiraq-	qətəʀᴀʀ (under qətəʀ)
qitirsiq	qətəqliq (under qətəʀ)
qitsa(C)-	qəvcaɣ-
qitsi-	qipci-
qitsimigaq-	qikciɣ- (under qikə-[1])
qitsu(k)-	qəc(c)uɣ-
qitsuq	qəc(c)uɣ-
qiturngaq	qətunʀᴀʀ
qitut-	qətut-
qiu-	qiʀu-
qiuq	qiɣuʀ-
qivaaqi	qivaaqi
qiviaq-	qiviaq- (under qivə(ʀ)-)
qiviq-	qivə(ʀ)-
qivit-	qəvə(t)-
qiviuq	qivyu(ʀ)
quajaqit-	quʀa(yaqit)-
quajjuk	qu(C)aɣðuɣ
quajjulik	qu(C)aɣðuləɣ (under qu(C)aɣðuɣ)
quaq	qu(C)ᴀʀ
quaqtaq	quɣᴀʀta(ʀ)
quaraq	quaʀaq
quarsaa(q)-	quaqcaaq-
quasaq, quasaq-	quacak (under quʀa(yaqit)-)
qugu-	quvə-
qui-	quʀə-
quik (urine)	quʀəʀ (under quʀə-)
quik (femur)	qu(C)əyiɣ

TARRAMIUT — ECI	PROTOFORM
sangu-, sangujaraq-	caɣu-
sani-	cani-
saniijaq, saniijauti	canŋiyaq- (under canəɣ)
sanik, saniit	canəɣ
sanilliq, sanilliriik	canil(l)IR (under cani-)
saniq-	canIR-
saniqqia(q)-	caniqqiaq- (under cani-)
saniraq	caniqAR
sanirva(q)-	canivAR- (under cani-)
sannaku	cannaq (under cana-)
sanngiit-, sanngit-	caɣŋi-
sanni(q)- (ache all over)	caɣnəR-
sanni(q)- (cross a line)	cannIR- (under cani-)
sanninga-	cannIR- (under cani-)
sanningajulik	cannIR- (under cani-)
sannirutaq	canniqun (under cani-)
sapangaq	capaŋaq
sapijji(C)-	capək-
sapiq-	capIR- (under capə-)
sapirria(C)-	capIR-
sapirsait-	capiqšaq- (under capə-)
saput(i)-	capə- (under capə-)
saqi-	caqə-
saqpik, saqpinga-	caqvIR- (under caqviɣ)
saqpiqut(i)-	caqvIR- (under caqviɣ)
saqqaq	catqaq
saqqijaaq-	catqaq
saqqit-	catqaq
saralikitaaq	caqələkətAR
saraliq-	cARaq-
sarat-	cARat-
sarliaq-	cARliɣAR
sarraa(q)-	cARaq-
sarrut-, sarruti-	cažRutə- (under caðə-)
sarvaq	cARVAR
satsagiaq	cakcakiq
satuq-	catuq-
sau-	cau-
saugaq	sava
saullu(C)-	caulluq-
saumik	cARumiɣ
sauniq	caunəq
saunnit-	caunnit- (under caunəq)
savik, savik- (plane)	caviɣ
savik- (mount head on harpoon)	cavəɣ
saviujaqtu(q)-, saviujarniku	caviužaq- (under caviɣ-)
savva(q)-, sarva(q)-	cažvaq- (under caðə-)
savvasik-	cažvasik- (under caðə-)
siak-	ciðaɣ-
siamma-, siammaga-	ciðaɣma(R)- (under ciðaɣ-)
sianiq	ci(ð)aɣanəR
siarri(C)-, siarrijauti	cialRi-
sigaq-, sigalak-	ciɣɣaq-
siggi(t)-	ciɣi-
sigguk	cuɣduɣ
siik-	ciðəɣ-
siimik-	ciimik-
siiq-	ciiq-[1]
siiqiagaq	ci(i)qiak
siiqqiniq	ciitqinəq
siiqquaq	ciɣəðqu(C)AR (under ciɣəðqUR)
siiqqumiaq-, siiqqumigaq-	cigəðqumiɣ- (under ciɣəðqUR)
siiqquq, siiqu(q)-	ciɣəðɣUR
siirnatuq	ciiRnaq- (under ciiq-[1])
sijjaq	ciŋdAR
sijjariaq	ciŋžARiaq (under ciŋðAR)
sikaga-	cikaq-
siki-, sikinga-	cikə(t)-
sikkaaqi-	cipə(ɣ)-
sikki(q)-	cipkiq- (under cipə(ɣ)-)
sikkitaq	citkik-
sikkutaq	cinkutaɣ
siku	ciku
sikuaq	ciku(C)AR (under ciku)
sikuiq-	cikuŋIR- (under ciku)
sikuliaq	cikuliaq (under ciku)
sikullaaq	cikulaaq- (under ciku)
sikunngit-	cikunRiq-
sila	cila
silaarniq	cilali- (under cila)
silait-	cilaŋit- (under cila)
silalliq	cilallIR (under cila)
silaluk	cilałuɣ (under cila)
silati-	cilan (under cila)
silatu-	cilatu- (under cila)
sili-	cili-
siliC-	ciləɣ-
silinniku	ciləɣ-
silliq	citə(ɣ)-
silliti	cillin (under cili-)
silu	cilu
siluk-	ciluk-
siluli-	ciluli- (under cilu)
simik-	cimək-
sinaaq	cinəRAR (under cinə)
sinarnaq	ciŋAR-
singai-	ciŋai-
singaq-	ciŋAR-
singaqti	ciŋaq-
singiq	ciŋIR
singirniq	ciŋIRnəq (under ciŋIR)
singit-	ciŋə(t)-
singu-, singutit-	ciŋuk-
singullu(k)-	ciŋullu(q)- (under ciŋuk-)
sini	cinə
sinik-	cinək-
siniqtuq	cinIR- (under cinə)
sinirsu(q)-	cinIR- (under cinə)
sinivvik	cinəɣvik (under cinək-)
sinna-	cikna-
sinnaliuq-	cinnaRliuq- (under cinək-)
sinnatuuma-	cinnaktuq- (under cinək-)
sinniku, sipinniku	cip(ə)nəR (under cipə(t)-)
sipi-	cipə(ɣ)-
sipit-	cipə(t)-
siqiaq, siiqiagaq	ci(i)qiak
siqiiq-	ci(i)qiak
siqiniq	ciqinəR

TARRAMIUT — ECI	PROTOFORM
siqinnaaniq	ciqinnak- (under ciqinəʀ)
siqinni(q)-	ciqinəʀ
siqiraq-	ciqəʀ-
siqpa(k)-	ciqpaɣ- (under ciqəʀ-)
siqpi	ciqviɣ
siqqataq-	ciqqaq- (under ciqəʀ-)
siqquq	cil(ə)quʀ
siqquq-, siqquqtit-	ciŋquʀ-
siqumi(C)-	ciqumə(t)-
siqutsiraq	ciqumə(t)-
siqutti(q)-	ciquptəq- (under ciqumə(t)-)
siraaq-	ciiq-[2]
siri-, siriilli-	ciʀi-
sirlaa(q)-	ciʀləʀ-
sirliqi-	ciʀləʀ-
sirluaq	ciqluɣaʀ
sirmiq	ciʀmiʀ
sirnaa(C)-, sirnigusuk-	ciqni-
sirngut(i)-	ciʀmiʀ
sitamat	citamat
siti	citə
siti-	citə(ɣ)-
sitsituq-, sitsijuit-	citciq-
sittuq-	cittuʀ-
sittuqiC-	cittuqit-
situ-	citu-
situraq-	cituʀaʀ- (under citu-)
siturauti	cituʀaʀ- (under citu-)
siuq-	ciʀuʀðuɣ
siuraq	ciuʀaq
siuti	ciɣun
siva	civa-
sivaniq	civanəq
sivi, sivitu-	civi
sivu	civu-
sivuaq	civu(C)aʀ (under civu-)
sivuliq-	civuləɣ- (under civu-)
sivuliqtaituq	civulliqtə (under civu-)
sivulliq	civul(l)iʀ (under civu-)
sivumik-	civumiɣ- (under civu-)
sivuniq	civunəʀ (under civu-)
sivunni(q)-	civunniʀ- (under civu-)
sivuraq, sivurarsiq	civuqaʀ (under civu-)
sivuura-	civu(C)uʀa-
sivuvaq-, sivuvaaq	civu-
sivviaq	cipɣaʀ
sivvu(q)-, sivvu	civvuʀ-
suaniq	cu(C)aniʀ
suak-	cuɣaɣ-
suanga-	cuaŋa- (under cuɣaɣ-)
sugaluk-	cuɣaɣ-
suinnaq	cuviɣnit-
sujuk-, sujunga-	cuʀuɣuk
sujuraq-	cuʀuɣuk
sukaq	cukaʀ
sukat-	cuk(k)a-
sukkait-	cuk(k)aŋit- (under cuk(ka)a)
sukkit-	cukki(ʀ)
sukuuq-	cukuiq-
suli	cu(na)li (under cu(na))
suliaq, suli-	cu(na)li- (under cu(na))
sulluk	cupluɣ
suluk, sulutsuk	culuɣ
suluppaugaq	culuɣpa(C)uɣ (under culuɣ)
suluraq	culuʀaq (under culuɣ)
sumigi-	cumiɣ-
suna, su-	cu(na)
sunauvva	cuna-uvva (under cu(na))
sungaq	cuŋa(ʀ)
sungiq-	cuŋiʀ-
sungiuti-	cuŋiq-
supi-	cupə-[1]
supiniq	cupə-[1]
supput(i)-	cupputə- (under cupə-[1])
suqqaatiq-	cuqqa(C)aʀ-
suqqaq	cuqqaʀ
suqulajuq	cuqula-
suqutigi-, suqutaunngit-	cuq(q)utə- (under cu(na))
surluk	cuʀlu
surra(q)-	cuʀʀait-
surrait-	cuʀʀait-
surruq	cuʀ(ʀ)uk(-)
sursaq	cuqlaɣ
surujuk	cuʀuɣuk
surusiq	cuʀuciq
suvak	ciłuvaɣ
suviq	cuvəq
taaC-	taɣə-
taak-, taguti-	taðəɣ-
taalu	talu
taalutaq	ta(a)lutaq (under talu(-))
taanikit-	taanəq
taaniqtu-	taanəq
taaq	taʀəʀ(-)
taaqtit-	taaqtət- (under taʀəʀ(-))
taarniq	taʀəʀnəʀ (under taʀəʀ(-))
taarsi-	taʀəʀ(-)
taarsit-	taaqtət- (under taʀəʀ(-))
taatiraq	təðatəða(C)iʀ
taatsi(q)-	taaktəq- (under taak-)
tagga	taðva
taggainaq	taðvaŋinnaʀ (under taðva)
taggaturjuinaq-	taʀəʀ(-)
tagiuk	taɣi(C)uʀ-
tagiuq-	taɣi(C)uʀ-
tai-	ta(ɣ)i-
taiguq-	taiɣuq- (under ta(ɣ)i-)
taima	taðim(m)a
taimaak	taðim(m)a
taimaili-, taimailiuq-	taimait- (under taðim(m)a)
taimait-	taimait- (under taðim(m)a)
taimungaaqta(q)-	taimuŋaaq- (under taðim(m)a)
tajaq	taɣaq
tajarniq	taɣaʀnəʀ
tajja(q)-	tatə-
taki-	takə-
takili-	takəli- (under takə-)

TARRAMIUT — ECI	PROTOFORM
takku-	taku-
taku-	taku-
takuminaq-	takuminaq- (under taku-)
takunna(q)-	takunnaq- (under taku-)
takurannaa(q)-	takuʀannaaq- (under taku-)
takurnga(q)-	takuʀannaaq- (under taku-)
takurngiu(q)-	taku-
takusaq-	taku-
takutsau-	taku-
talat-	tala(t)-
talavaaq	taʀpaʀ-
taliq	tałiʀ
taliqpik	tałiʀpiɣ (under tałiʀ)
taliruq	tałiquʀ (under tałiʀ)
talli(k)-	tapląk- (under tapət-[2])
tallimat	tałłimat
tallu	tamlu
tallu	taŋluʀ
talluruti	tamluʀun (under tamlu)
tama-	tamaʀ-
tamakki(q)-	tamatkiq- (under tamaʀ-)
tamaq-	tamaʀ-
tamma(q)-	tammaʀ-
tammaa(q)-	taŋmaq-
tammai-	tammaʀ-
tammik-	taŋmik-
tamua-	tamuʀ-
tamuaq	tamuʀaʀ (under tamuʀ-)
tamuraq	tamuʀ-
tangiinnaq	taŋəʀ
tangiq	taŋəʀ
tanirsa(q)-	tanəʀ-
tapaC-	tapak-
tapiq	tapəʀ(-)
tapitaak	tapət-[1] (under tapəʀ(-))
tappii(t)-	takviŋit- (under takviɣ-)
tappi(k)-	takviɣ-
taputtaa(C)-	tapəʀ(-)
taqa-	taqə-
taqaja-	taqə-
taqaq	taqaʀ
taqissu(q)-	tanqik- (under tanqiʀ)
taqpa(C)-	taʀpaʀ-
taqqaq	tapʀaʀ[1]
taqqiq	tanqiʀ
taqqisuq-	tanqiʀ
taqtuq	taʀtu
taquaq	taqu(C)aʀ
tariuq	taʀ(ə)yuʀ
tarnik, tarniq	taʀ(ə)nəʀ
tarraliniq	taʀʀaq (under taʀəʀ(-))
tarraq	taʀʀaq (under taʀəʀ(-))
tarrit-	taʀʀit- (under taʀəʀ(-))
tarsaq	taqšaq (under taʀəʀ(-))
tasi-	taci(ɣ)-
tasiC-	taci(ɣ)-
tasijuaq	tacižuk- (under taci(ɣ)-)
tasiq	taciʀ
tasiuq-	tatyuʀ-
tataigi-	tatamə(t)-
tatamit-	tatamə(t)-
tati	tatə
tati-	tatə-
tatiggaq	tatəlɣaʀ
tatigiaq-	tatə-
tatigit	tatəkə (under tatə)
tatsi(C)-	captək- (under cavət-)
tatsiq (fog)	taɣətuɣ
tatsiq (belt)	tavci
tattu(q)-	tat(ə)tuʀ- (under tatə-)
tattui-	tat(ə)tuʀ- (under tatə-)
tattuq	taɣətuɣ
tattuqusiq-	tattuqun (under tatə-)
taursi(q)-	tauʀciq-
tauttu	tautu(k)-
tautuk-	tautu(k)-
tavva	taðva
tiggaq	təɣɣaq
tigguti	təɣɣun (under təɣu-)
tigli(k)-	təɣləɣ-
tigu-	təɣu-
tiguaq	təɣuðaʀ (under təɣu-)
tiguliq	təɣu(ʀ)liq (under təɣu-)
tigumiaq	təɣum(m)i(C)aʀ (under təɣu-)
tigummi-	təɣummi- (under təɣu-)
tijaa-	təža-
tijaaq	təža-
tijak-	təža-
tijittuq	təðə(ʀ)-
tijjaq	təpðaʀ (under təpə-)
tijji-	təkši- (under təŋə-)
tijju(C)-	təžžuq-
tikaaguti	təkaaɣun
tikiq	təkəʀ
tikiqaqtu(q)-	təkit-
tikiraaq-	təkiʀaaq- (under təkit-)
tikiraq	tekəʀaʀ (under təkəʀ)
tikisaqtu(q)-	təkicaqtuq- (under təkit-)
tikit-	təkit-
tikiuti-, tikiuti	təkidutə- (under təkit-)
tikkua(q)-	təkkuaq- (under təkkuk-)
tikku(q)-	təkkuk-
tili-	təli-
tillari-	təlaʀ(ʀ)i- (under təlaɣ-)
tilli(q)-	təɣləq-
tilliq (s.th. inland)	təpə-
tilliq (food around mouth)	təpli
tillu(k)-	təŋluɣ(-)
tiluk-	təłuɣ-
tiluktu(q)-	təłuɣ-
timi	təmə
timmi-	təŋmi- (under təŋə-)
timmiaq	təŋmi(C)aʀ (under təŋə-)
timmikaq-	təŋmikaq- (under təŋə-)
timmiralaaC-	təŋmiʀala- (under təŋə-)
tingaujaq	təŋaužaq (under təŋə-)
tingi-	təŋə-
tingiit	təŋaɣ
tingirrautaq	təŋəlʀaʀ- (under təŋə-)
tinguk	təŋuɣ

TARRAMIUT — ECI	PROTOFORM
tinninniq	tən(n)aq (under tənət-)
tinit-	tənət-
tinniraq-	tənniR-
tinu-	tənu-
tinujuq	tənu-
tinujjaq	tənət-
tipa, tipi	təpə
tipaaqqi(C)-	təppak- (under təpə)
tipijuq	təpə-
tippi	təkpik
tiqituraq	təqətuRaq
tiqqalaa-	təŋqa(R)- (under təŋɣə-)
tiqqalaaq	təŋqa(R)- (under təŋə-)
tiqqiaq	təlqiðaR
tiratirak	təðatəða(C)iR
tiriaq	təRiɣluɣ (under təRiɣ)
tiriganniaq	təRikanni(C)aR (under təRiɣ)
tirinnguaq	təRiɣ
tiriqquq	təkəðquR
tirirsu(q)-	təRiɣtuR- (under təRiɣ)
tirli(C)-	təRlək-
tirliturnia(q)-	təRlək-
titir-	tətəR-
titsa-	təɣəɣ-
titsalukaa-	təkšaluk- (under təŋə-)
tittau-	təŋət- (under təŋə-)
tivvualuk-	təvvuɣ-
tivvuaq-	təvvuɣ-
tuC-	tut-
tuapak	tuvapaɣ
tuat-	tuat-
tuavi	tu(C)avə(t)-
tuaviq-	tu(C)avə(t)-
tugajaq	tuɣəkaR(aR) (under tuɣəR(-))
tugaq-	tuɣɣaR- (under tuɣəR(-))
tuggajuuq	tuuɣuk (under tuɣəR(-))
tuggaku	tuɣəR(-)
tui	tuɣə
tujja(q)-	tumðaR- (under tumə)
tujji-	tumə
tujuq-	tuɣuR-
tujurmi-	tuɣuRmi-
tuki-	tukə-
tukimuak-	tukə-
tukiq-	tukəR-
tukisi-	tukəci- (under tukə-)
tukit-	tukə-
tukka(q)-	tukkaR-
tulag-	tulak-
tulimaaq	tulimaR
tulimajaaq, tulimaq	tulimaR
tullaaq	tulləq-
tulli(q)-	tulləq-
tullik	tuŋlə(R)
tulliragut	tullaq-
tulliraq	tullaq-
tulliruti	tuŋləRun (under tuŋləR)
tulugaq	tulukaR
tulugarnaq	tuluɣaRnaq (under tulukaR)
tuluq-	tuluR-
tuluriaq-	tuluRɣaR (under tuluR-)
tumaq-	tumaR-
tumi	tumə
tumisi-	tuməci- (under tumə)
tumiuyaq	tumə
tummiraq	tutməqaR (under tutə-)
tungalliq	tuŋ(ə)liR (under tuŋə-)
tungi-	tuŋə-
tungujuqtaq, tungujursi-	tuŋuɣuq- (under tuŋu-)
tunguniq	tuŋu-
tuni-	tunə-
tuniq	tunəq
tuniqsi-	tunəR-
tunirjuk	tuniRžuk
tuniuqqa(q)-	tuniuqqaq- (under tunə-)
tunnga-	tutŋa- (under tut-)
tunnganguq-	tunənŋuq-
tunngavik	tutŋa- (under tut-)
tunniq	tupə(-)
tunnuk	tunnuR
tunu	tunu
tunummut	tunu
tunusuk	tunucuɣ (under tunu)
tunut-	tunut- (under tunu)
tunuvaq-	tunuvaR- (under tunu)
tupaaq-	tupaaq- (under tupaɣ-)
tupak-	tupaɣ-
tupiq	tupəR
tupit-	tupət-
tuppalia-	tut-
tuqqa(C)-, tuqqa-	tuRaaq-
tuqqi(k)-	tutqik-
tuqqujaaq	tupquža(a)q
tuqqujaarsi-	tupquža(a)q
tuqqu(q)-	tutquq-
tuqu-	tuqu(-)
tuqunna(q)-	tuqunaR- (under tuqu(-))
tuquraq-	tuquRaq- (under tuqu-)
tuqusaq-	tuqucaq- (under tuqu-)
tuqut-	tuqut- (under tuqu(-))
turaaju-	tuRaayu- (under tuRaaq-)
turaaq-	tuRaaq-
turru-	tužRu-
tursuaq	tuqluaq (under tuqlu(ɣ))
tursuk	tuqlu(ɣ)
tursu(q)-	tuqluR(aR)- (under tuqlu(ɣ))
tursuraq-	tuqluR(aR)- (under tuqlu(ɣ))
tursuuk	tuqšuk
tusaq-	tucaR-
tusarsau-	tucaqliq- (under tucaR-)
tusiat-	tutyiɣat-
tusilaq-	tucilaR-
tusu-	tucu-
tuti-	tutə-
tutik-	tutəɣ(-)
tutiriaq	tutyaR(aR) (under tutə-)

TARRAMIUT — ECI	PROTOFORM
tutsaluk-	tutcaq (under tucaR-)
tutsi-	tukəci- (under tukə-)
tutsia(q)-	tuŋciR-
tutsianiq	tuŋciR-
tutsiraq-	tuŋciR-
tutsiut(i)-	tuŋciR-
tutsu(k)-	tuksuk-
tuttit-	tut-
tuttu	tuntu
tuttujuit	tunturðuɣ (under tuntu)
tuttuvak	tuntuvaɣ (under tuntu)
tutu	tutuk
tuugaaq	tuɣəkaR(aR) (under tuɣəR(-))
tuukkaq	tuɣəkaR
tuulliq	tu(u)tləɣ
tuuq	tuɣəR(-)
tuuq-	tuɣəR(-)
tuurngaq	tuɣənRaR
tuurngi-	tuɣənRi- (under tuɣənRaR)
tuusiniq	tu(C)utcinəq
tuvaq	tuvaR
tuvvik	tužvik (under tut-)
uannaq	uɣaknaR
uanniq	uɣaknaR
uaqtaq	uaqtaq
uarit-	uða(t)-
uarusiq-	uaq-
uasaq-	uRaR-
uati	uɣan
ugiaq-	uɣiR-
uggua(q)-	uɣɣuR-
ui	uɣi
uigaq	uvi(t)-
uigga(q)-	uɣilɣaR- (under uɣi)
uigganaq	uɣilɣaR- (under uɣi)
uigu, uigu-	uɣɣu-
uijja(C)-	uɣivðaR- (under uɣivə-)
uijjangu, uijjanguq-	uɣivðaR- (under uɣivə-)
uima-	uima-
uinik-	uɣinəɣ- (under uɣi)
uiniq	uinəq (under uvi(t)-)
uiri-	uɣiqə-
uirnga(q)-	uinRaq- (under uvi(t)-)
uirsaq	uiqšaq-
uisugiik	uɣiɣuɣ (under uɣi)
uisuk, uisuk-	uɣiɣuɣ (under uɣi)
uit-	uvi(t)-
uita-	uvita- (under uvi(t)-)
uitaq	uitaq (under uvi(t)-)
uivaq-	uɣivə-
uiviit-, uiviiri(C)-	uɣviŋit- (under uɣvi)
uivisaq-	uɣvi
uivvaq	uɣivvaR (under uɣivə-)
ujak	uɣa(quR)
ujak-	uɣaɣ-
ujamik	uɣamiɣ (under uɣa(quR))
ujarak	uɣaRaɣ
ujatsiutit	uɣakciutət (under uɣaɣ-)
ujjituq-	užžiq- (under uðəɣ-)
ujju-	umðu-
ujjuk	uɣðuɣ
ujjunaq	uɣðuɣnaR (under uɣðuɣ)
ujukkuaq	uɣukkuR(aR)
ujuru(k)	uɣuRu(R)
ujurumiali-	uɣuməq-
ukaliq	ukaðiR
ukamaq-	ukamaR-
uki-	uki-[1]
ukiaq	ukɣuRaR (under ukɣuR)
ukii-	ukɣi- (under ukɣuR)
ukiji-	uki-[1]
ukit-	ukit- (under uki-[2])
ukiuq	ukɣuR
ukkaq	upkaq
ukkiji-	uki-[1]
ukkuaq	umkuRaR
ukkusik	utɣuciɣ
uku-	uku-
ukuaq	uku(C)aR
ukuna-	uku-
ulajujaq	ulə(t)luɣaR
ulamiqtaq	ulamiq-
ulapit-	ulapə(t)-
uligaq-	ulə(-)
uligiaq-	ulə(-)
ulijjuaq	uliɣžuaq (under uliɣ(-))
ulik	uliɣ(-)
ulik-	ulə(-)
ulikki(C)-	ulə(-)
ulimak-	ulima-
ulimaut	ulimaun (under ulima-)
uliq-	ułiR-
ulit-	ulət-
uliuti	uli(C)un
ullaakut	umlaaq (under umłuR)
ullaaq	umlaaq (under umłuR)
ullaaruq-	umlaaq (under umłuR)
ullak-	utlaɣ-
ullasauti	utlacaun (under utlaɣ-)
ulli-	umli- (under umłuR)
ullu	uŋlu
ullu(q)-	umłuR
ullumi	umlumi (under umłuR)
ulluq	umłuR
ulluriaq	umluRiaq (under umłuR)
ulu	ulu(R)
uluaq	ułuɣaɣ
uluk-	uluɣ-
ulurianaq-	uluRɣanaR- (under uluRɣa-)
ulut(i)-	ulutə- (under ulə(-))
umialittaaq	umialək (under umiaq)
umiaq	umiaq
umiarluk-	umiaRluk- (under umiaq)
umiiri-	umiiqə- (under umiaq)
umik	umək
umik-	uməɣ-
umimmaq	uməŋmak (under umək)
uminga-	umənŋatci- (under uməɣ-)
uminngasi-	umənŋatci- (under uməɣ-)

TARRAMIUT — ECI	PROTOFORM
uulittaa(q)-	uɣu(t)-
uuma-	uŋuma-
uumari-	uŋummaʀ- (under uŋuma-)
uumigi-	uɣumi-
uumila-	uumila- (under uɣumi-)
uumma(q)-	uŋummaʀ- (under uŋuma-)
uummari-	uŋummaʀ- (under uŋuma-)
uummati	uŋuman (under uŋuma-)
unna(q)-	uɣut- (under uɣu-)
uunaq-	uunaq- (under uɣu-)
uunni-	uunni- (under uɣu-)
uunniq	uɣut- (under uɣu-)
uut- (burn)	uɣut- (under uɣu-)
uut- (bask on ice)	uɣət-
uuti(C)-	uutəq- (under uɣu-)
uutirna(q)-	uutəq- (under uɣu-)
uutsi-, utsi(C)-	uɣukli- (under uɣu-)
uuttu(q)-	uðəɣ-
uuttuq	uɣət-
uutturaq-	uðəɣtuʀ- (under uðəɣ-)
uvaa-	uvə(C)a- (under uvəʀ-)
uvagut	uvakut
uvanga	uvaŋa
uvara	uvaŋa
uviluq	uviluʀ
uvinik	uvinəɣ
uvinngiaq-	uvi(n)ŋi(C)aʀ-
uviq-	uvəʀ-
uvvalu	uvva
uvva(q)-	uvvaq-

Postbases and enclitics

a-	a-
aguuq-	k(k)u(C)aʀ-
ala-	ala-
aluk	aluk(-)
apik-	vlaɣ-
aq	aʀ
aq- (repeated action)	aʀ-
aq- (hit on the)	ŋaʀ-[1]
aqi-	ʀqə-
araq	ʀaʀ
arjuk, aarjuk	aʀžuk
ataaluk-	ʀataʀ-
atsiaq	tciaq
gajaq-	yaʀ-
gajuit-	kayuɣ(-)
gajuk-	kayuɣ(-)
galuaq-	ɣaluaq-
gaq	kaʀ
gasuaq-	nasuk-
gasuk-	nasuk-
ggaa(q)-	ʀaʀaʀ-
ggiari-	lɣiʀ-
ggi(q)-	lɣiʀ-
gi- (have as)	kə-[1]
gi- (in the future)	ki-
gialik	yaʀ
gialla(k)-	łaɣ-
giaq	ɣiaq-
giaqaq	ɣiaqaq-
giaqtu(q)-	yaʀ(tuʀ)
giattut	yaɣ-
giik	ɣiik
giiq-	ɣiiq-
giit	ɣiit
gik-	kiɣ-
ginna(q)-	ŋinnaʀ(-)
gitsi-	kiɣ-
gu	ku
guaq-	yu(C)aʀ-
guk-	yuɣ-
guluk	ʀuluk
guma-	yuɣuma-
gumaaq-	yumaaq-
gunaq-	yuknaʀ-
gunatsa(q)-	yuknaʀ-
gunnai(q)-	yuknaiq-
gunna(q)-	yuknaʀ-
gusuk-	yuɣ-
=guuq	ŋu(C)uʀ
i	ði-
ijaq-	ŋiyaʀ-
iliqi-	ŋiłiqə-
ilitaq	ŋilitaʀ
innaq, innaqi-	ŋinnaʀ(-)
iq-	ŋiʀ-
irsi-	ŋiʀ-
irut(i)-	ŋiʀutə-
isiq-	ŋiʀ-
it-	ŋit-
ituq-	ituq-
jaq	ðaʀ
jaqtu(q)-	yaʀ(tuʀ)
jariaqaq-	ɣiaqaq-
jatsari-	žukšau-
jau-	ðaʀ
jiaq	ði-
ji	ðə
ji-	ði-
jjagunnai(t)-	yuknaʀit-
jjai(q)-	tyaiq-
jjangit-	tya-
ju-	yu-
juaq	duɣaʀ(-)
juiq-	yuiq-
juit-	yu(C)it-
juk	yuɣ
juma-	yuɣauma-
jumaaq-	yumaaq-
jumi-	umi-
juminaq-	yuminaq-
junnai(q)-	yuknaiq-
junna(q)-	yuknaʀ-
juq	ðuʀ
jurataq	ʀataʀ-
juri-	yukə-
jutsau-	žukšau-

TARRAMIUT — ECI	PROTOFORM
juuq	suu-
kaalla(k)-	k(k)aʀ-
kainna(q)	k(k)aʀ-
kalla(k)-	k(k)aʀ-
kapit-	k(k)aʀ-
kasaak	kapcak(-)
kasak	kapcak(-)
=kiaq	k(k)i(C)aʀ
kit-	k(k)it-
kitaaq-	k(k)ətaʀ-
kitaq-	k(k)ətaʀ-
kka(q)-	vkaʀ-
kki-	ki-
kkuminaq-	ɣuminaq-
kkut	nkuɣ
kkuuq-	k(k)u(C)aʀ-
ku	k(k)uʀ
kuluk	k(k)uluk
k(k)u(t)siq	k(k)ucciʀ
la-	la(ʀ)-
laaq	la(C)aʀ(-)
laaq-	tla-
langa-	tla-
laqi-	ʀqə-
lauju-	lauq-
lauq-	lauq-
=li	łi
li- (make)	li-[1]
li- (become)	li-[2]
liaq	li(C)aʀ
liaq-	liɣaʀ-
lijaaq-	liža(a)q-
lijaq-	liža(a)q-
lik	ləɣ
lik-	ləɣ-
liq	l(l)iʀ
liq- (begin)	liq-
liq- (provide with)	liq-
liqqi(k)-	nqiɣ-[2]
liri-	liqə-
lit- (give, take to)	lit-
lit- (go to, come across)	łit-
liuq-	li(C)uʀ-
liut-, -liuti-	li(C)utə-
llaa-	llaa-
llak-	łłaɣ-
llarik-	kiɣ-
lli(q)-	lliq-
lliu(q)-	lliq-
lluaq-, lluaq	l(l)u(C)aʀ-
llurik-	kiɣ-
=lu	łu
lu	lu(ʀ)
lualuk	łuɣ(-)
luannguaq-, luannguaq	tluk-
luaq, luaq-	tluk-
luk-, luk	łuɣ(-)
lukatak	ŋtaɣ-
luq-	luʀ-
ma-	(u)ma-
maaq-	(u)maʀ(aʀ)-
manga-	maŋa(aq)-
mi-	mi-
mik-	miɣ-
miliut(i)-	li(C)utə-
miuq	miʀu
mmanga-	maŋa(aq)-
mmarik-	mmaʀik-
mmi-	mi-
naaq-, naari-	naaq-
najaq-	ɣaʀ-
naq-, naqi-	naʀ-
narsi-	naqci-
nasaaq-	naci(C)aʀ-
nga-	ŋa-[1]
=ngaaq-	ŋaaq-
ngajaak, ngajaaq	tɣaɣ
ngiq-	ŋiʀ-
ngu- (have pain)	lŋu-
ngu- (be)	ŋu-
ni-	ki-
niaq-	ni(C)aʀ-
nik- (get)	nəɣ-
nik- (smell of)	nit-
niku	k(k)uʀ
niq (nominalizer)	nəʀ[1]
niq (more, most)	nəʀ[2]
niq-	n(n)iʀ-
niqpaaq	nəʀpa(C)aʀ
niraq-	ni-
nirlu(k)-	nəʀłuɣ-
nirsaq-, nirsari-	nəʀ[2]
nitaq	nitaq
nna(q)-	nnak-
nnajaq-	ɣaʀ-
nnaq (wind from the)	knaʀ
nnaq (favorite)	nnaq
nnasuaq-	nasuk-
nnasuk-	nasuk-
nnga(q)-	ŋa-[1]
nngiluaq	tluk-
nngi(t)-	nʀit-
nnguaq	ŋ(ŋ)uðaʀ(-)
nngu(q)- (have a pain)	lŋu-
nngu(q)- (become)	ŋ(ŋ)uʀ-
nni(C)-	nnək-
nni(q)-	n(n)iq-
paaluk	aluk(-)
pasuk-	mcuɣ(-)
(V)q- (say)	(V)ʀ-
q- (go to)	q-
=qa, =qaa	q(q)a(a)
qaq-	ŋqaʀ-
qati	qan
qatta(q)-	k(k)attaʀ-
qi-	ʀqə-
qitaq-, qqitar-	k(k)ətaʀ-
qqa-, qqai-	qqaʀ-
qqaa(q)-	łʀa(C)aʀ-
qqajaq-	lʀaɣaq-
qqaminngit	lʀammiq-

TARRAMIUT — ECI	PROTOFORM
qqamiq-	lʀammiq-
qqijaqar-, qqijari-	nqiɣ-^{2}
qqut	q(q)un
qqu(t)-	tʀutə-
qquu(q)-	qquuq-
qu-	ðqə-
quq	quʀ
qut(i)	q(q)un
raaluk	aluk(-)
raaq-	ʀaaq-
raq	qaʀ
rataaq-	lʀataq-
ratanngi(t)-	lʀataq-
rataq-, rataq-	lʀataq-
rjuaq	ðuɣaʀ(-)
rlaat	ʀłaɣ
rlak	ʀłaɣ
rnga(q)	n(ə)ʀaʀ(aʀ)(-)
rujuk	ʀuluk
ruq	quʀ
ruq-	ʀuq-
sa-	ta-
saaq- (try to), saari-	caʀ-^{1}
saaq- (quickly)	caaq-
saq- (try to get to)	caʀ-^{1}
saq- (fetch)	caʀ-^{2}
saqtu(r)-	yaʀ(tuʀ)-
sarait-	caʀait-
si- (buy)	ci-
si- (become)	li-^{2}
siari-	c(c)iʀ-
sii-	c(c)iʀ-
sik-	ðiɣ-
sima-	(u)uma-
siq- (wait for self to)	c(c)iʀ-
siq- (most in a direction)	l(l)iʀ
siqtu(q)-	ciqtuq-
siriit-	c(c)iʀyaʀ-
siuq-	ci(C)uʀ-
siut	ci(C)un
su-	yu-
suaq-	yu(C)aʀ-
suiq-	yuiq-
suit-	yu(C)it-
sujjuk	cuɣ
suk-	yuɣ-
sunngu-	sunŋu-
sunni(k)-, sunniq	nit-
suq-	qðuʀ-
(r)suq-	qðuʀ-
suuq	suu-
t- (transitivizer)	t-^{1}
t- (catch)	t-^{2}
ta-	-ta-
taaq-	taaq(-)
taili-	təta(C)ili-
tait-	taʀit-
takit-	k(k)it-
taq (passive participle)	ðaʀ
taq (thing pertaining to)	taʀ
taq-	taʀ-
taqtu-	tu-^{1}
=tauq	ptauq
ti (agent)	ðə
ti (area)	tə
tigi-	tə-
tiq-, tiri-	təʀ-
tit-	tət-
titiq-	təta(C)aʀ-
tsaaq-	mcaɣ-
tsak-	yyaɣ-
tsaq	kðaʀ
tsi-	c(c)iʀ-
tsiaq, tsiaq-	tciaq
tsiari-	c(c)iʀ-
tsii-	c(c)iʀ-
tsiq	l(l)iʀ
tsiriit-	c(c)iʀyaʀ-
tsuma-	yuɣuma-
tsunaq-	yuknaʀ-
ttaili-	təta(C)ili-
ttu(q)-	tu-^{1}
ttuaq-	ðuʀaʀ-
tu-	tu-^{1}
tualli(q)-	tu(C)aʀ-
tuaq	tuaq(-)
tuaq- (continually)	ðuʀaʀ-
tuaq- (as soon as)	tu(C)aʀ-
tuin(n)aq-	tu-^{2}
tuq	ðuʀ
tuq- (use, consume)	tuʀ-^{1}
tuq- (repeated action)	tuʀ-^{2}
tuqaq	tuqaq^{2}
tuuma- (several days)	tuʀ-^{2}
tuuma- (use or eat often)	tuʀ-^{1}
tuuq	tu-^{1}
tuuq-	tuuq-
=tuuq	tuʀ
u-	ŋu-
ujaq, ujaq-	ŋ(ŋ)uðaʀ(-)
uma-	(u)ma-
ut(i-)	ŋutə-
vasik-	ðiɣ-
vigi-	ðvikə-
vik (place)	ðviɣ
vik (almost)	vlaɣ-

GREENLANDIC INUIT INDEX
(West Greenlandic Dialect)

West Greenlandic forms are given in the new orthography. Postbases, gathered at the end, are alphabetized according to post-vocalic allomorphs, those with initial variable V given last. Enclitics are preceded by '='.

Equivalences between the Greenlandic standard orthography and the orthography used in this dictionary are given below. Symbols of the standard orthography are given in italics. If no equivalence is given it means that the standard practical orthography uses the same letter as our orthography. *o* = u, *e* = i, *g* = ɣ, *r* = ʀ, *j* = y, *ng* = ŋ, *nng* = ŋŋ, and *ss* = both ss and šš without differentiation. geminated fricatives are devoiced so *ll* = łł, *gg* = xx, and *rr* = XX.

WEST GREENLANDIC	PROTOFORM
aa	a(a)
aa- (have convulsions)	aɣa-
aa- (fetch)	aɣə-
aa- (be rotten)	aʀu-
aaffaffak	aužvik
aaffag-	aivvak- (under ayvəʀ)
aaffaq	auvaq-
aag- (skin)	aak-
aag- (bleed)	aðuɣ
aag- (melt)	auk- (under aʀu-)
aagiaq	aaɣiaq
aak	aðuɣ
aakkar-, aakkarneq	aupkaʀnəq (under aʀu-)
aala-	aʀula-
aalaakkaa-	aʀulaŋiʀ- (under aʀula-)
aalajanger-	aulay(y)aŋiq- (under aʀula-)
aalanngaat	aulait- (under aʀula-)
aalaq	aʀiłaʀ- (under aʀi-)
aalar-	aʀiłaʀ- (under aʀi-)
aalassag-	aulayyak- (under aʀula-)
aalat-	aʀulat- (under aʀula-)
aali	a(a)
aalisagaq	aulacaq- (under aʀula-)
aalisaq	ailitaq
aalisar-	aulacaq- (under aʀula-)
aallaa-	aʀullaʀ- (under aʀula-)
aallaar-	aullaaq- (under aʀula-)
aallar-	aʀullaʀ- (under aʀula-)
aallarner-	aullaʀniq- (under aʀula-)
aaller-	aʀiłaʀ- (under aʀi-)
aama(q)	a(C)umaʀ
aamma(lu)	amma
aammit	aummin
aanak, aanaq	a(a)na
aanaar-	aðun(ə)ʀaʀ- (under aðuɣ)
aanga-	aaŋa (under aɣa-)-
aannersaq	aunəq (under aʀu-)
aannertu-	aunnəqtu-
aanngaa-	aaŋa- (under aɣa-)
aap	a(a)ŋ
aapa-	aʀipa-
aappa(q)	a(C)ippaʀ
aappalug-, aappalaar-	aukpaluk- (under aðuɣ)
aaq (sleeve)	aðiʀ
aaq (lateral point)	aa(k)
aaqqat	aitqan
aaqqiak	aʀəŋqiɣ-
aaqqig-, aaqqissor-	aʀəŋqiɣ-
aar- (put arm in sleeve)	aðiʀ
aar- (stalk animal on ice)	aðuʀ-
aariak, ariak	aaʀiak
aarit	a(a)
aarleri-	a(C)aʀłuɣ
aarlor-	aɣaʀluʀ-
aarluk	a(C)aʀłuɣ
aarnuaq	aɣənʀu(Caʀ)
aarsaar-	auqcaaq-
aasaq	aužaq (under aʀu-)
aasiak, aasiaq	aacivak
aasiit, aasit	aaci(in)
aasik	aaci(in)
aassiit	aaɣžuuk
aassik	aužvik
aat	ay
aat-	aat-
aataaq	a(a)ta(a)q
aatak, aataq	ata[1]
aatsaar-	aɣittaʀuʀ- (under aɣittaʀ-)
aatsaat	uv(v)atciaq (under uvva)
aatsar-	aɣittaʀ-
aatsor-	aittuq- (under aɣə-)
aatsuineq	aittuq- (under aɣə-)
aattor-	aak-
aavar-	auvaq-
aaveq (roofing timber)	aʀuvəʀ(aʀ)
aaveq (walrus)	ayvəʀ
aaver-	auvəq
aaviak, aagiak	aðuɣɣaʀ (under aðuɣ)
affaq	avvaq (under avəɣ-)
aggaatsoq	aak-
agger-	aɣɣiʀ- (under aɣə-)
aggor-	avɣuʀ- (under avəɣ-)
agiaq	aɣiɣ-
agiar-	aɣiɣ-
agior-, agiuaar-	aɣɣuʀ-
agiut	aɣiɣ(aʀ)un (under aɣiɣ-)
ai	ay
aja(k)	ayak
ajaappiaq	ayaʀuʀ (under ayaɣ-)
ajaaq	ayaɣaʀ (under ayaɣ-)
ajag-	ayaɣ-
ajagaatit	ayaɣaq (under ayaɣ-)
ajagaq	ayaɣaq (under ayaɣ-)
ajagutaq, ajaagutaq	ayaɣun (under ayaɣ-)
ajalu-, ajalor-	ayalu(ʀ)-
ajaper-	ayapəʀ- (under ayaɣ-)
ajaraar-	aqayaɣ
ajassaat	ayaɣ-
ajattor	ayaɣtuʀ- (under ayaɣ-)
ajoqer-, ajoqersor-	ayuqucirtuʀ- (under ayuqə-)
ajoqi, ajoqiit	ayuqucirtuʀ- (under ayuqə-)
ajoqut	ayuq-

WEST GREENLANDIC	PROTOFORM
apusineq	apun (under apə-)
aput	apun (under apə-)
apuut(i)-	apuR-
aqagu, aqaguani	aqaɣu
aqagut-	aqaɣu
aqajak	aq(ə)yaR
aqajaroq	aq(ə)yaquR (under aq(ə)yaR)
aqar-	aqaɣ-
aqassug-	aqaɣcuɣ- (under aqaɣ-)
aqerloq	aqilRuR (under aqit-)
aqi-	aqə-
aqillug-	aqilluk (under aqit-)
aqisseq	aqəðɣiR
aqit-, aqili-	aqit-
aqqala-	aləmqaR-
aqqaluk, aqqaluaq	anqaluk
aqqaneq, aqqanillit	atRaR- (under at(ə)-)
aqqar- (eat greedily)	aləmqaR-
aqqar- (go down)	atRaR- (under at(ə)-)
aqqunar-	alqunaR-
aqqusaar-	apqucaaq- (under apRun)
aqqusineq	apqucinəq (under apRun)
aqqut	apRun
aqu	aqu
aquit-, aquimi-	aqumə-
aqupi-, aquppi-	aqup(p)i- (under aqumə-)
aqut-	aqut- (under aqu)
aquut	aqu(Ru)n (under aqu)
arajug-	aR(ə)yu-
arajutsi-	aR(ə)yu-
arfag-	ARVak- (under ARVəR)
arfak, arfaq	ARVaɣ
arfeq	ARVəR
arfivik	ARVəpiɣ (under ARVəR)
arfersanillit	ARVin(ə)ləɣ (under ARVaɣ)
arfinillit	ARVin(ə)ləɣ (under ARVaɣ)
arla(r)-	aləR
arlaagut	aləR
arlaanisaq	aləR
arlaaq	al(ə)RaR(aR) (under aləR)
arlaarsar-	aqla-
arlallit	aləR
arliar-, arliari-	aRli(C)-
arlig-	aRli(C)-
arnaaneq	ARNaRunəR (under ARNaR)
arnag-	ARNaR
arnaq	ARNaR
arnaqquassaaq	ARNalqu(C)aR (under ARNaR)
arnaviaq	ARNaviaq (under ARNaR)
arneri-	ARNiqə- (under ARNaR)
arngili(g)-	an(ə)Rilək- (under anəR-)
arpag-, arpat-	aqva-
arpingiag-	aqpik-
arrag-	ARRi-
arri-	ARRi-
arriit-	ARRi-
arror-	auk- (under ARu-)
arsaar-	aqcaaq- (under ARCaR-)
arsaarutit, arsaaqqat	aqcaaq- (under ARCaR-)
arsaq	aqšaq (under aqə-)
arsar-, arsarneq	aqšaq (under aqə-)
arsat	ARða
arsi-	aqci-
arsug-	aqakcuk- (under aqak-)
artor-, artornar-	ARtuR-
aruma-, arama-	ARu-
asa-, asaaRi-	ažak-
asaasakkaak	až(ž)aa
asag-	ažak-
asaloq, asallut	acaluR
asattuar-, asattuut(i)-	ažak-
aserneq	aciRnəR (under at(ə)-)
aseror-	aciRuq- (under aci[2])
asi	aci[2]
asiar-	acivaq- (under aci[2])
asiarpak	atyaR
asigi-, asissor-	aciɣə- (under aci[2])
asiila-	acinila- (under aci[2])
asinga-	aci[2]
asiu-	aciu- (under aci[2])
assaa	að(ð)a(a)
assaar-	avðaR[2]
assaasat	aɣðaRuðaR
assaat	ažɣaun (under aðɣa(R))
assaat(i)-	aðɣa(R)
assag- (dig)	aðɣa(R)
assag- (beat drum)	apcak-
assagiikkut	akšaɣiitkutaq (under akðaɣ-)
assak	aðɣa(R)
assakar-, assakaa-	akðaɣ-
assalig-	akšalək- (under akðaɣ-)
assallag-	akðaɣ-
assaq (load)	aɣžaq- (under aɣə-)
assaq (wart)	avðaR[1]
assaq (shield)	avðaR[2]
assaqqoq	akðanquR
assarneq	an(ə)caRnəR (under anə-)
assartor-	aɣžaq- (under aɣə-)
asseq	avðaR[2]
asser- (mix with blood)	aðuɣ
asser- (protect)	avðiR-
assi(k), assigi-	atə(ði)-
assiaq	avðiRaR- (under avðaR[2])
assiar-	avðiRaR- (under avðaR[2])
assili-	atžili- (under atə(ði)-)
assior-	ažžiuq- (under aðuɣ)
assiu-	avðiR- (under avðaR[2])
assoq	aðɣuR-
assor- (go against wind)	aðɣuR-
assor- (put on clothes)	atžuq- (under atə-)
assortor-	aðɣuR-
assuari-	aðɣuRa- (under aðɣuR-)
assut	akcut
asu	acu
asu-	acu-
asuki(aq)	acu
asuli	acu
at(i)-	at(ə)-
ata	ata[2]
ata-	ata-

WEST GREENLANDIC	PROTOFORM
erneq	iRnəR
erner-, ernger-	əRəni(R)-
ernersiaq	iRnəkšaq (under iRnəR)
ernertu-	iqə-
ernguseq	əm(ə)Run (under əRə-[1])
erni-	iRni- (under iRnəR)
erniaq	iRni(C)aR (under iRnəR)
erniinnaq	əRəni(R)-
ernissaq	iRnəkðaq (under iRnəR)
ernisug-	iRnisuk- (under iRnəR)
erniu-	iRnəR
ernuma-, ernguma-	inRuma-
ernutaq, erngutaq	inRutaq
error-, errortor-	əRRuR- (under əRə-[1])
ersaar-	iqšaq (under iqə(R))
ersag-, ersanga-	iqlaɣ-[1]
ersaq	iqšaq (under iqə(R))
ersaroq	iRcaquR
ersarut	əpžaRun
erser—	iðəR-
ersi-	iqci-
ersik	əðəRa(R)
ersit-	iðəR-
ersor-, ersorsit	iqtuq-
ersug-	əqðuɣ-
ersut(i)-	iðəR-
eruit-	əR(ə)viɣ- (under əRə-[1])
ianga-	iyaŋa-
iasilaar-	iR(ə)ləɣ-
iffit	əvəɣ
iffit-	ivəq-
iga-, iga	əɣa-
igaaq	əɣa(C)aR (under əɣa-)
igaleq	əɣaləR
iggaser-	əɣɣan (under əɣa-)
iggavik, igaffik	əɣɣaviɣ (under əɣa-)
iggiaq	iɣɣaR(aR)
igi-	əɣə-
igimaq, igimaaq	əɣimaR
iginneq	əɣ(ə)nəR (under əɣə-)
igit-	əɣət-
igunaq	əɣunaq
igut-	əɣut-
igutsak	əɣutcaq (under əɣut-)
iguut	əɣut-
ii(q)	i(i)[1]
ii-	iɣə-[1]
iigaq	iɣəɣaR-
iigar-	iɣəɣaR-
iingala-	i(C)iR-
ikaar-	əkəRaR-
ikaat	əkəRaR
ikag-	ikaɣ-
ikeq	əkəR
ikerasak	əkəRacak (under əkəR)
ikernuaq, ikernusser-	əkənRužaq
ikernuk	əkənRužaq
ikersit-	ikiR-
ikertu-	əkəqtu- (under əkəR)
iki	əki
iki- (be lit)	əkə-[1]
iki- (get in)	əkə-[2]
ikiaq	əkiðaR (under əkiðaR-)
ikiaqutit	əkiðaR (under əkiðaR-)
ikiar-	əkiðaR-
ikiarneq	kiaRnəq (under əkiðaR-)
ikiaroor-	əkiðaR (under əkiðaR-)
ikig-	ikəɣ(ə)t-
ikiler-	əkiliR- (under əki)
ikili-, ikilli-	əkəɣ(ə)t-
ikinngut	əkəŋŋun
ikior-	ikayuR-
ikit-	əkət- (under əkə-[1])
ikkarlit-	ətɣalRit- (under ətə-)
ikkarluk	ətkalRuq (under ətə-)
ikkat-	ətɣat- (under ətə-)
ikkatigi-	ikaɣ-
ikkeq (driftwood)	ətkəq
ikkeq (gum)	iŋkiR
ikkii, ikkeernar-	ikki
ikkiit-	ipɣit- (under ipəɣ-)
ikkut(i)-	əkə-[2]
ikor-	əkuq-
ikorfaq	əkəvRaq
ikuala-, ikuallag-	əkuala- (under əkə-[1])
ikug-	ikuɣ-
ikuma-	əkuma- (under əkə-[1])
ikusik	ikuyəɣ
ikuttaat	ikuɣutaR (under ikuɣ-)
ila (part)	ila(-)[1]
ila (indeed), ilaa	ila[2]
ila-	ila(-)[1]
ilaa-	ilakə- (under ila(-)[1])
ilaanni	ila(-)[1]
ilaaq, ilaar- (patch)	ila(C)aR (under ila(-)[1])
ilaaquseq	illaatquciq
ilaar- (imitate)	ilaɣaR- (under ila(-)[1])
ilaat	əlaun (under əlaɣ-)
ilag-	il(l)aɣ-
ilagi-	ilakə- (under ila(-)[1])
ilalaar-	ila(C)aR (under ila(-)[1])
ilaler-	ilali(C)uR- (under ila(-)[1])
ilaliut(i)-	ilali(C)uR- (under ila(-)[1]
ilamaar-	ilamaaq- (under ila(-)[1])
ilami	ila[2]
ilamineq	ilavinəq (under ila(-)[1])
ilanger-	ilaŋiR- (under ila(-)[1])
ilanna(a)ri-, ilanna(a)riit	ilannaR (under ila(-)[1])
ilanngar-, ilanngaa-	ilaŋŋaR- (under ila(-)[1])
ilaqutaq	ila(-)[1]
ilar-	əlaɣ-
ilassi-, ilassior-	ilaŋci- (under ila(-)[1])
ilatser-	ilacciR-
ilatsiinnar-	ilacciR-
ileqimisaar-, ileqila-	iləqə-
ileqqoq	əlitquciq (under əlit-)
ilerasug-, ileragi-	əliRa-
ilerniku(q)	əliRqə-
ilersaq	iləqšaq-
ilersi-	iləqšaq-
ili-	əɬi-

WEST GREENLANDIC	PROTOFORM
kikkar-	kəp(ə)kaʀ-
kikkiik	ki(i)
kikkuleq	kikkuləq
kilak, kilag-	kəlaɣ-
kiler-, kilerneq	kiliʀ-
kiliffak	kəliɣvaɣ (under kəliɣ-)
kilig- (inform)	kələɣ-
kilig- (scrape)	kəliɣ-
kiligar-	kəliɣaʀ- (under kəliɣ-)
kilit-	kələ(t)-
kilitser-, kitser-	kələ(t)-
kilitsissiaq	kələɣ-
killaq, killaar-	kəllaq (under kəlaɣ-)
killavaaq, killavaar-	kəklaɣ
killeq	kətliʀ (under kətə-)
killig- (reach limit)	kənlə
killig- (affect)	kəvlək-
killigi-	kənləkə- (under kənlə)
killik	kənlə
killinger-	kənləŋiq- (under kənlə)
killoq, killormut	kənluʀ
killor- (betray)	kənluʀ
killor- (slice)	kəpluʀ- (under kəpə-)
killu, killut	kəklu(ɣ)
killu(i)	kəɣlu
kilu, kilut	kəlu
kiluar- (move back)	kəluvaʀ- (under kəlu)
kiluar- (rip up seam)	kəluaq- (under kəluɣ)
kiluk	kəluɣ
kimattuut	kəmaḷiʀ
kimig-	kəməɣ
kimiit-	kəməɣit- (under kəməɣ)
kimik, kimittooq	kəmi-
kimmalig-	kəɣmaʀ- (under kəɣə-)
kimmar-	kəɣmaʀ- (under kəɣə-)
kimmeqqoq	kitmilquʀ (under kitmiɣ)
kimmequt	kəɣmi(C)- (under kəɣə-)
kimmernaq	kitŋiɣ
kimmiaq, kimmiar-	kəɣmi(C)- (under kəɣə-)
kimmik	kitmiɣ
kimmivik	kəɣmi(C)- (under kəɣə-)
kina	ki(na)
kinequt, kinaqut	kənataɣ- (under kənəʀ-)
kiner- (be viscous)	kənəʀ-
kiner- (have water run off)	kinəʀ-
kinerfig-	kəniʀmiɣ- (under kəniʀ)
kingig-	kəŋək-
kingoraq	kiŋuʀaq (under kiŋu-)
kingorar-	kiŋuʀaʀ- (under kiŋu-)
kingorna	kiŋunəʀ (under kiŋu)
kingu	kiŋu-
kingu-	kiŋu
kinguaaq	kiŋuvaaq (under kiŋu-)
kinguaar-	kiŋuʀaʀ- (under kiŋu-)
kinguar-	kiŋuvaʀ- (under kiŋu-)
kinguffag-	kiŋuvaʀ- (under kiŋu-)
kinguk	kiŋuɣ
kinguliarsuit	kiŋul(l)iʀ (under kiŋu-)
kingulleq, kinguleq	kiŋul(l)iʀ (under kiŋu-)
kinguneq, kingorna	kiŋunəʀ (under kiŋu-)
kinguner-	kiŋunəʀ (under kiŋu-)
kinguporsor-, kingumorsor-	kiŋutmuʀ- (under kiŋu-)
kini-	kini-
kinipasoq	kənipa- (under kəni-)
kinit-	kənit- (under kəni-)
kinneq, kinnikut	kitnəʀ (under kit-)
kinnganeq	kitnəʀ (under kit-)
kinngeq	kəkniq (under kəkə-)
kinngu-	kitŋu-
kior-	kiðu-
kiperi-	kəpəqə- (under kəpət-[2])
kipi-	kəpə-
kipinngu-	kəpəlŋu- (under kəpət-[2])
kipit-	kəpət-[2]
kippaq	kəppaʀ (under kəpə-)
kippar-	kətvaʀ- (under kətə-)
kipparig-	kəppaʀik- (under kəpə-)
kiput-, kipunga-	kiput-
kisaq	kicaʀ
kiseer-	kəžə(k)-
kiserlior-	kəði-
kisermaaq	kəðim(ʀ)aʀ (under kəði-)
kisi-	kəði-
kisianni, kisiat	kəði-
kisig-, kisigi-	kəžə(k)-
kisit-	kəcit-
kissaatigi-	kəkcaq-
kissaatit	kəkcaun
kissag-	kiðaɣ
kissaq	kiðaɣ
kissar- (cut)	kəpðaʀ- (under kəpə-)
kissar- (wish)	kikcaq-
kissavik	kəð(ə)kaviɣ
kissumiaq, kissumiar-	kəvɣumiaq- (under kəvəɣ-)
kit-	kit-
kit(i)-, kitaa	kətə-
kitik, kitigar-	kətəɣ[2]
kitser- (let settle), kitsit-	kit-
kitser- (slice)	kələ(t)-
kitsig-	kətðiɣ- (under kətə-)
kitsima-, kitsuma-	kit-
kittaq	kələ(t)-
kittorar-	kəktuʀaq- (under kəkə-)
kiver-	kəviʀ-
kivi-	kivə-
kivig-	kəvəɣ-
kivinga-	kivə-
kooroq, kooqqer-	quðuquʀ (under quðu-)
kuanneq	kuanniq
kui-	kuvə-
kujaaq	kuyaɣ
kujag-	kuyaɣ-
kujak	kuyaɣ
kujalleq, kujaleq	kival(l)iʀ (under kivan)
kujapigaq	kuyapəɣaʀ (under kuyaɣ)
kujat	kivan
kukik	kukiɣ
kukkaajaaq	kumka(C)ili- (under kumkaʀ)
kukkaq, kukkar-	kumkaʀ
kukkarnaaq	kupkanaq-
kukkili-	kumka(C)ili- (under

WEST GREENLANDIC	PROTOFORM
maqit-	maqət- (under maqə-)
maqulluk	maRRaR
maralluk, marulluk	maRRaR
maraneq	maRRaR
marluiit	malRu(C)it (under malRuɣ)
marluk	malRuɣ
marluliaq	malRi (under malRuɣ)
marneq	maqənəq (under maqə-)
marraq	maRRaR
marsi-	maqə-
marujuk	maRRaR
masak, masag-	macak
masarsuk	macak
masik	maciɣ
massag-	makə-
massak	mamca(R)
massar-	makcaq-
masser-	mapciq- (under mamə-)
massig-, masseriar-	mapciq- (under mamə-)
massit-	makšək- (under makət-)
massua-	mam(ə)ya-
materti	matəqtə
matsatser-	macak
mattak	maŋtaɣ
mattar-	mattaR-
mattu-	mamtu- (under mamə)
matu, matu-	matu(-)
matuer-	matuŋiR- (under matu(-))
meeraq	mi(i)Rayuq
meerujuk, meerujuu-	mi(i)Rayuq
meqqoq (body hair)	məlquR
meqqoq (thigh of bird)	mipquq
meqqut	minqun (under miŋqə-)
merfi-	məRvi(k)-
meriar-	miRyaR(-)
merlaaq	mikəqləqtuq (under mikə-)
merlertoq	mikəqləqtuq (under mikə-)
merngor-	məRnuR-
mernguerser-	məRnuRiR- (under məRnuR-)
merseri-	məqə-
mersor-	miŋqə-
miaggoor-	maRu-[2]
mianeri-, mianersor-	mi(C)ani(kə)-
miani-	mi(C)ani(kə)-
miki-	mikə-
mikiaq, mikigaq	məkəɣaq
mikig-	mək(k)əɣ-
mikileraq	mikəliRaq (under mikə-)
mikkag-	mək(k)əɣ-
milak	məlak
milik, milig-	mələɣ
milli-	mikəli- (under mikə-)
milliaq	məkliaq
milloor-	milluuq- (under miluR-)
millug-, milluar-	məluɣ-
milor-	miluR-
miloriar-	miluRiaq- (under miluR-)
milug-	məluɣ-
milugiaq	məluɣyaR (under məluɣ-)
minaaq	minaR-
minar-	minaR-
minger-	mətŋəR-
mingig-	məŋik-
minguk, mingug-	miŋuɣ-
mingulertor-	miŋuləq- (under miŋuɣ-)
mini, mini-	minəɣ[2]
minik, minig-	minəɣ[1]
minit-	mənət-
minnga-	mətŋəR-
minngoq	məlŋuR
mippaar-	mitpəq-
mipper-	mitpəq-
misar-	məcaR-
miseraq	məciRaR (under məcu(ɣ))
misiar-	məciRaR-
misigi-	məciɣ-
misilig-	məciɣ-
misissor-	məcikšuq- (under məciɣ-)
misoraq	məciRaR (under məcu(ɣ))
missi	pimci
missi- (leave out)	mənət-
missi- (direction of)	mikšə
missilior-, missiliuut(i)-	mikšə
misug-	məcu(ɣ)
mit-	mit-
mitaar-	mətak-
mitag-	mətak-
miteq	mətəR
mitilli-	mətəŋḷə(R)-
mitsag-, mitsar-	məcaɣ
mittari-	mənət-
moreer-, moreersivik	muRiq-
morfit-	muRðuɣ-
moriit-	muRiiq-
morpar-	muRðuɣ-
morsug-	muRðuɣ-
mulequt	mulə(ɣ)
muli(k), muleq	mulə(ɣ)
mullortu-	mulu-
mulu-	mulu-
mumer-	muməR(-)
mumig-, mumit-	mumiɣ
mumik, muminga	mumiɣ
na-aa	na-[1]
naa- (finish)	naða-
naa- (grow)	naɣu-
naa- (smell)	naRə-
naafferar-	na(C)əvə(t)-
naag-	naɣət-
naagga	na-[1]
naaja	naRuyaR
naak	naɣu (under na-[2])
naakkaluar-	nautkiaq- (under naRułəɣ-)
naakki(gi)-	naatki-
naakkiar-	nautkiaq- (under naRuḷəɣ-)
naakkiut(i)-	naɣət-
naalaar-	naɣa(t)-
naalag-	naɣa(t)-
naalagaq	naɣa(t)-
naalarnaq	naul(l)aRnaq (under naula(yu)q)
naalig-	naRułəɣ-

WEST GREENLANDIC	PROTOFORM
naaligaq	naʀuɫəkaʀ (under naʀuɫəɣ-)
naaller-	naɣəkli(ʀ)- (under naɣət-)
naallii-	naalɣiuq-
naalliug-	naalɣiuq-
naalungiaq	naalu(n)ŋiaq
naama-	naʀə-
naami(k)	na(C)umi (under na-^{2})
naammag-	naðama- (under naða-)
naammagi-	naammaɣə- (under naða-)
naammassi-	naðama- (under naða-)
naanngi-	naatŋiq-
naapertor-	naypəʀtuʀ- (under nay(ə)pət-)
naapit-	nay(ə)pət-
naaq	na(ž)aq
naaqqavik	naɣət-
naarala-	nauʀala-
naari-	naðaqə- (under naða-)
naartu, naartu-	na(ž)aq
naasaanga-	naucaaq
naasaaq, naasaar-	naucaaq
naasoq	naɣu-
naassaanngit-	naða-
naat-	nanit-
naatit-	naɣət-
naatser-	naɣucciʀ- (under naɣu-)
naatsiiaq	naɣucciʀaʀ (under naɣu-)
naatsiivik	naɣucciʀaʀ (under naɣu-)
naatsorsor-, naatsersor-	naɣucciʀ- (under naɣu-)
naffar-	napə-
naggat	naða-
nagguaq	navɣuʀ- (under navəɣ-)
nagguik	naɣu-
naggut	navɣuʀ- (under navəɣ-)
najak	nayaɣ
najangar-	nayaŋaʀ-
najoqqut	nayuʀ-
najor- (stay with)	nayuʀ-
najor- (suck in)	niðuʀ-
najor- (curve)	ni(C)uʀ-
najug-	nayuɣ-
najummag-	nayummi- (under nayuɣ-)
najummi-	nayummi- (under nayuɣ-)
najungasoq	ni(C)uʀ-
nakasuk	nakacuɣ
nakasunnaq	nakacuɣ
nakat-	nakkaʀ-
nakataq	nakataq
naker-, nakeri-	nakəʀ-
nakertit-	nakəʀ-
naki-	naki-
nakiit-	nak(ə)ʀit- (under nakəʀ-)
nakima-	naki-
nakimmag-, nakimmar-	naki-
nakkar-	nakkaʀ-
nakkisaar-	nakəʀ-
nakkori-	naku(a)ʀə- (under naku(a)q(-))
nakkut(i)-	nakkutə- (under naku(a)q(-))
nakkutigi-	nakkutə- (under naku(a)q(-))
nakorsaq, nakorsar-	naku(a)q(-)
naku-	naku(ʀ)-
nakuaq	naku(a)q(-)
nakuit-	naku(a)q(-)
nakussag-	naku(a)q(-)
nakutit-	naku(ʀ)-
nakuu-	naku(a)q(-)
nala-	nala-
nalaar-	naɫaʀ- (under naɫə-)
nalaat(i)-	naɫaʀutə- (under naɫə-)
naleqqer-	naɫəʀaq (under naɫə-)
naleraq, nalerar-	naɫəʀaq (under naɫə-)
nali(k)	naɫə-
naligi-	nalləɣiik (under naɫə-)
naligiit	nalləɣiik (under naɫə-)
nalikkaaq	naɫəkkaɣ
nalikkak, nalikkagut	naɫəkkaɣ
nalimmag-	naləmmak- (under naɫə-)
nalinginnaq	naɫə-
nallar-	nallaq- (under nala-)
naller-	naɫɫiʀ- (under naɫə-)
nalli(k)	naɫə-
nalli(nnaq)	naŋɫəɣ-
nalli-	naɫə-
nalligi-	naŋɫəɣ-
nalliut(i)-	naɫɫiʀ- (under naɫə-)
nalloq	nalluq (under naluɣ-)
nallor-	napluq- (under napə-)
nallu	naplu
nallug-	nalluɣ-
naloqqut(i)-	naɫunqutə- (under naɫu-)
naloraar-	naluɣ-
nalu-, nalunngit-	naɫu-
nalug- (swim)	naluɣ-
nalug- (throw away)	nalluɣ-
nalunaaq(q)utaq	naɫunaʀilkutaʀ (under naɫu-)
nalunaar-	naɫunaʀiʀ- (under naɫu-)
nalunar-	naɫunaʀ- (under naɫu-)
nammag-, nammagaq	natmaɣ-
nammik	nalmiɣ
nammineq	naɫmi(nəʀ)
naner-	nanəʀ-
naneruaq, naneruar-	naniʀ
naneruut	naniʀ
nangaa-	naŋaʀ-^{1}
nangar-	naŋaʀ-^{1}
nangeq	naŋiʀ
nangiar-, nangiari-	naŋyaʀ-
nangig-	naŋnəʀ-
nangiit-	naŋyaʀit- (under naŋyaʀ-)
nangima-	naŋə-
nanginniar-, nangingiar-	naŋə-
nangit- (finish off)	naŋət- (under naŋə-)
nangit- (continue)	naŋnəʀ-
nangitit-	naŋə-
nani-	nani-^{1}
nanit-, ninit-	nanəʀ-
nannerutitu-	nəmniuq-

WEST GREENLANDIC	PROTOFORM
nanniar-, nanngiar-	naŋət- (under naŋə-)
nannig-	naŋnəR-
nanoq	nanuR
nanorluar-	nanuRluk-
napa-	napa-
napaartoq	napa(R)aqtuR (under napa-)
napakkar-	napatkaq-
napariaq	napaRɣaR (under napa-)
naparutaq	nappaqutaR (under napa-)
napasar-, napasaqattaar-	napažaq-
napasoq	napaðuR (under napa-)
naper-, napiar-	napəR-
napi-	napə-
napit-	napəR-
nappaq	nappaq (under napə-)
nappar- (raise)	nappaR- (under napa-)
nappar- (get ill)	nappaq (under napə-)
nappartaq	nappaRtaR (under napa-)
napparuser-	nappaqutaR (under napa-)
napu	napu
napuliutit	napu
naqig-, naqit-	naqət-
naqilli-	naqəkli- (under naqət-)
naqinneq	naqət-
naqitari-	naqətaR- (under naqət-)
naqiteri-	naqət-
naqqig-	nalqiɣ- (under nałə-)
naqqissor-	nalqiɣ- (under nałə-)
naqqoq	naŋquR
narajaq, narajar-	naR(ə)ɣaR (under naRə-)
narajor-	naRə-
naraseq	na(a)Ra(a)yiq
narlanngu-	naRlanŋu-
narlu-	nałRu- (under nałə-)
narner-, narnig-	nanəR-
narnuari-	nanəR-
narnut(i)-, narnualiut(i)-	nanəR-
narrag-	naRRu-
narrat(i)-	naRə-
narru-, narrugi-	naRRu-
narsaq	naqðaR
nasaq, nasar-	nacaR
narsingasoq	naRciɣ-
narsug-	naRðuɣ-
nasig-	nacit-
nassaar-, nassaaq	nažvaq-
nassag-	nažžak- (under na(ž)aq)
nassar- (take with one)	naŋcaR-
nassar- (get half of animal)	navəɣ-
nassat	na(ž)aq
nassataq	naŋcaR-
nasseraq, nasserar-	nakciRaq
nassi-, nassig-	naɣci(t)- (under naɣət-)
nassit-, nassiut(i)-	naŋcit- (under naŋcaR-)
nassu, nassuit-	navcu
nassuier-	navcu
nassuk	naɣžuk
nataaq	natəRaR (under natəR)
nataarnaq	nataaRnaq (under natəR)
nataqqoq	natanquR
nataqqornaq	natatquRnaq (under natanquR)
nataqquaq	natanquaq (under natanquR)
nateq	natəR
naternik, naternig-	natəquviɣ- (under natəR)
natisit	natəR
natseq, natsersuaq	naɣyiR
natsiaq	naɣyiRaR (under naɣyiR)
natsinnaq	naccin (under natəR)
natsit	naccin (under natəR)
natsit-	naŋə(t)-
nattoralik	nakturalək (under naɣət-)
nattoraq	naɣtuqaR (under naɣət-)
naveer-	navia-
naviagi-, naviasug-	naviaɣə-
navianar-	naviaɣə-
navig-	navəɣ-
neeqqor-, neeqqulug-	niiqquq-
neqi	nəqə
neqilior-	nəqli(C)uR- (under nəqə)
neqqag-	nəqə
nerfala-, nerfallar-	nəvRala- (under nəvəR-)
neri-	nəRə-
nerikkaq, nerukkaq	nəRupkaq
nerikkar-	nəRəvkaR- (under nəRə-)
nerilig-	nəRiləɣ-
nerilittaq	nəRiləktaq (under nəRiləɣ-)
neriorsor-	nəRiuqšuq- (under nəRyu(ɣ)-)
neriug-, neriugi-	nəRyu(ɣ)-
nerleq	nəRləR
nerler- (feed)	nəqli(C)uR- (under nəqə)
nerlior-	nəqli(C)uR- (under nəqə)
nerlor-, nerler- (break back)	nəRluq-
nerlut	nəRluq-
nermut(i)-, nerngut(i)-	nəməR
nerpik	nəqpik (under nəqə)
nerraaq	nəɣəR
nerrersooq	nəRRitu- (under nəRə-)
nerrivik	nəRəðviɣ (under nəRə-)
nersor-	niqtuq-
nersut	nəRžun
nerukkar-	nəRəvkaR- (under nəRə-)
nerumaar-	nəRuvəR-
nerumig-	nəRuvəR-
nerutu-	nəqu-
neruut(i)-	nəRu(C)aR-
niaqoq	naɣ(ə)quR
niaquar-	niaquaq- (under naɣ(ə)quR)
niffik	nəɣvik
nigaq, nigar-	nəɣaR
nigavit-	nəɣaR
nigeq	nəɣəR
niggat	nəɣaR
nigger- (set snare)	nəɣaR
nigger- (blow from south)	nəɣəR
niggit	niɣəðuRun (under niɣəðuR-)

WEST GREENLANDIC	PROTOFORM
niggoq	niv(ə)ɣuR
nigor-	nəɣuR-
niior-	niɣəðuR-
niisa, niisarnaq	niisa
niisoraq	nəɣituqaR
niisorar-	nəɣituqaR-
nika-	nəka-
nikagi-	nəka-
nikallor-	nəka-
nikit-	nikət-
nikitaat(i)-	nikət-
nikku	nəvku
nikorfa-	nəkəvRa- (under nəkəvə(t)-)
nikorfaataq	nəkəvRa- (under nəkəvə(t)-)
nikorraartor-	nəkəvRa- (under nəkəvə(t)-)
nikuit-	nəkəvə(t)-
nikussaar-	nəkuvžaaq- (under nəkəvə(t)-)
nilag-	nilak
nilak	nilaɣ
nileq, niler-	nələR(-)
nilit-	nələt- (under nələR)
nillar-	nəŋlaR- (under nəŋə(t)-)
nilleq	nəŋə(t)-
niller- (be cold)	nəŋłəR- (under nəŋə(t)-)
niller- (shout), nillia-	nəpliR- (under nəpə)
nillor-	nəŋə(t)-
nimaar-	nəmaaq-
nimeq, nimer-	nəməR
nimeriaq	nəməRyaR (under nəməR)
nimeruartu-	nəmniuq-
ningaak	nəŋa(C)u(ɣ)
ningar-	nəŋ(ŋ)aR-
ningeq, ninger-	nəŋiR
ningioq	nəŋyuR
ningit-	nəŋət- (under nəŋə-)
ninnerutitu-	nəmniuq-
ninngag-	nəŋ(ŋ)aR-
ninngu-	nəlŋu(R)-
ninnior-	nəmniuq-
ninnit-, ninnigi-	nəmniuq-
nior-	nə(C)uR-
nipaar-	nəpaa(q)- (under nəpə)
nipaat-	nəpaŋit- (under nəpə)
nipanger-	nəpəŋiR- (under nəpə)
nipi	nəpə
nipisa	nəpətya(R)- (under nəpət-)
nipit-	nəpət-
nipitar-	nəpətaq- (under nəpət-)
nippar-	nəkvaR- (under nəkəvə(t)-)
nissaag-	nəlcaR-
nissak, nissaqattak	nəɣžak
nissavarsuk	nəŋðuR
nissi	pimci
nissik, nissit-	nəɣciɣ
nit-	niuɣaq-
nitta-	nəpta-
nittaalaq, nittaalar-	nəptait- (under nəpta-)
nittaat-	nəptait- (under nəpta-)
nittar-	nəptaq- (under nəpta-)
niu, nissut	niRu
niu-	niɣu-
niuar-	niuɣaq-
niuer-	niRuvəR-
niuffior-	niɣu-
niuleq	niuliq (under niRu)
niulu	niRulu (under niRu)
niunga-	nə(C)uR-
niutak, niutaaq	niutaq
niuut(i)-	niuɣaq-
nivaataq	nivaun (under nivaɣ-)
nivag-	nivak-
niver-	nəvəR-
nivi-	nəvə-
niviaq	nəvi(C)aR
niviarsiaq, niviarsiaraq	nəvi(C)aR
nivinga-	nəviŋa- (under nəvə-)
nivinngar-	nəviŋŋaq- (under nəvə-)
nivior- (wear away)	nəviuq- (under nəvə-)
nivior- (hover above)	niuɣaq-
nivitser-	nəvə-
niviuak, niviugak	nəvyuvak
noqar-	nuqaR-
noqarti	nuqaR-
noqit-	nuqət-
noqqaa-	nulqaR-
noqqillag-	nuqaR-
noqqut(i)-	nuqət-
norlaq	nəɣuRluR
norraq	nuRRaR(aR)
norsaq	nuqðaR
nuak, nuag-	nuvaɣ
nualluk	nuvaɣ
nuannaar-	nunanniR-
nuanner-	nunanniR-
nuaraluaq	nuRaR
nuer-	nuɣiR
nuersar-	nuviqšaq- (under nuvə-)
nuffarlior-	nuvaɣ
nuffit (bird dart)	nuɣiR
nuffit (line for stringing)	nuvvin (under nuvə-)
nuffit-	nuvə-
nugger-	nuɣət-
nui- (appear)	nuɣə-
nui- (thread)	nuvə-
nuia, nuia-	nuviya
nuilaq	nəɣilaR
nuilarmiut	nəɣiliR
nuima-	nuima- (under nuɣə-)
nuisa-	nuita- (under nuɣə-)
nujappig-	nuyaR
nujaq	nuyaR
nujoqqag-	nuyuqqak- (under nuyuɣ-)
nujuar-	nuyuɣ-
nujug-	nuyuɣ-
nujuiser-	nuyuŋit- (under nuyuɣ-)
nujuit-	nuyuŋit- (under nuyuɣ-)
nuka(q)	nukaR
nukaarnoq	nukaunRuq (under nukaR)
nukag-	nukaR

WEST GREENLANDIC	PROTOFORM
	paɣunʀaʀ)
paarngor-	pa(C)aməʀ-
paarsiar-, paarsiartor-	paðəʀaʀ- (under paðəʀ-)
paarsisoq	paɣi-
paartor-	pa(C)a-
paasi-	paðə
paatit	paŋəʀun (under paŋəʀ-)
paattor-, paattuut	pauktuq- (under paɣuɣ-)
paffik	paðviɣ
paggat(i)-	pa(C)a-
pagger-	paɣu(la)
paggig-	pa(C)a-
paggit(i)-	pa(C)a-
paggut(i)-	paŋəʀ-
pajarnaar-	paqnaŋiʀ- (under paqna-)
pajug-	paɣuɣ-
pakag-	pakak-
pakamig-, pakammig-	pakak-
pakassit-, pakassi(umi)g-	pakəɣžumik- (under pakəɣ-)
pakatsi-	pakak-
pakinig-, pakanig-	pakinəɣ- (under pakiɣ-)
pakker-	pakak-
pakki-	pakak-
pakkut	pakəɣ-
pakkut(i)-	pakəɣ-
palak	palaʀ-
palanngar-	palaŋa- (under palaʀ-)
paleq	palliq (under paliʀ-)
paler-, palersima-	paliʀ-
palersi-	paliʀ-
palleq	palliq (under paliʀ-)
pallig-	patlik-
pallit	palliq
pallor-	palluʀ- (under palu-)
pallunga-	palluʀ- (under palu-)
palu-	palu-
palunga-	palu-
pamialluk	pamyuʀaʀ (under pamyuʀ)
pamiaq	pamyuʀaʀ (under pamyuʀ)
pamioq	pamyuʀ
pana	pana
pana-, panar-	pana
panaa-	palaʀ-
paner-	panəʀ-
pangalig-	paŋaləɣ-
pangallag-	paŋaləɣ-
panik	paniɣ
pannaat-	pannaq (under panəʀ-)
pannarig-	pannaq (under panəʀ-)
panneq	paɣnəʀ
papeqila-, papikila-	papəqqila- (under papəɣ)
paperoq	papəʀuq (under papəɣ)
papik	papəɣ
paqinnar-	paqu-
paqqer-	panəʀ-
paqqit-	panəʀ-
paqumigi-, paqumisug-	paqu(mi)-
parnaar-	paqnaŋiʀ- (under paqna-)
parnaarut(i)-, parnaarussivik	paqnaŋiʀ- (under paqna-)
parni-	panəʀ-
pasi-	paci-
pasiller-	paci-
passag-	pay(y)a(ɣ)-
passarlug-	paðəʀ-
passik	paðviɣ
passut(i)-	patəɣ-
pataja-	pattaɣ-
pateq, pater-	patəʀ
patig-, patit-	patəɣ-
patitit-, patitsit-	patəktət- (under patəɣ-)
patsit	patcin (under paci-)
pattaat, pattaat(i)-	pattaɣ-
pattag-, pattattor-	pattaɣ-
pattor-	patəɣ-
patugut(i)-	patuɣ
peer-	piiyaq- (under pi(-))
peqimi-	pəʀə-
peqinga-	pəʀiŋa- (under pəʀə-)
peqit-	pəʀət- (under pəʀə-)
peqqig-, peqqissi-	pinqiɣ- (under pi(-))
peqqissimi(gi)-	pinqiɣ- (under pi(-))
peqquk	pəqu-
peqquserlug-	pinquciʀ
peqqusersuu-	pinquciʀ
peqqussut	piðqun (under pi(-))
peqqut	piðqun (under pi(-))
peqqut(i)-	pəqu-
peqqutser-	pinquciʀ
pequ-	pəqu-
pequt	piqqun (under pi(-))
pequut	piqqun (under pi(-))
perlaa-, perlaajaq	piʀðaʀ-
perlaaq (twisted thread)	piʀðaʀaʀ (under piʀðaʀ)
perlaaq (sled runner)	piʀlaɣ
perlar-, perlarneq	piʀðaʀ-
perlasi-, perlataar-	pəʀləʀ-
perler-	pəʀləʀ-
perleror-	pivli(-)
perlug-, perlukoq	piłuɣ- (under pi(-))
perluk, perluut	piłuɣ- (under pi(-))
perneq	pəʀnəʀ (under pəʀə-)
peroor-, perroor-	piʀuq- (under pi(-))
peror-, perorsar-	piʀuq- (under pi(-))
perrag-	piðaɣ-
persala-	pəʀə-
perser-	piʀciʀ- (under piʀtuʀ)
persoq	piʀtuʀ
persori	piʀtuʀ
pertaq	pəʀət- (under pəʀə-)
perter-	pəʀət- (under pəʀə-)
pertuja-	pəʀə-
peru, perusaq	pəʀu(-)
pi-	pi(-)
piaari-	pityaqə-
piaraq	piaʀaq (under pi(-))
piareer-	pižaʀiiq-
piffik, piffissaq	piðviɣ (under pi(-))
pigaar-	pəɣəɣaʀ-
piggaatigi-	pəɣəɣaʀ-

WEST GREENLANDIC	PROTOFORM
pigi-	pikə- (under pi(-))
piiar-	piiyaq- (under pi(-))
piit	pi(-)
piit-	piŋit- (under pi(-))
piitaat-	tiipak- (under təɣə(ɣ)-)
pikaala-	pəkə-
piki-	pəkə-
pikiar-	pəkiaq- (under pəkə-)
pikig-	pəkət- (under pəkə-)
pikki-	pəkku(ɣ)-
pikkorig-, pikkorlug-	pəkku(ɣ)-
pikkugi-, pikkusug-	pəkku(ɣ)-
pikkunar-, pikkugi-	pəkku(ɣ)-
pikkut(i)-	piŋu-[2]
pikusuk, pukusuk	pəku(ɣ)
pilaar-	pilaaq- (under pi(-))
pilag-	pilaɣ-
pilattor-, pilattuut	pilaɣtuʀ- (under pilaɣ-)
pilernu-	pilinʀu-
pili-, piliat	pili- (under pi(-))
pillaqqig-	pillu(a)ʀik- (under pi(-))
pillar-	pil(l)aq-
piller- (hop)	pəɣlə(ʀ)-
piller- (invite to feast)	pilliun (under pi(-))
pilleror-	pivli
pilli	pivli
pillii-, pilliut	pilliun (under pi(-))
pillingaar-	pivli(-)
pillitsi-	pəllitci-
pillorig-	pillu(a)ʀik- (under pi(-))
pillug- (get through)	pətluɣ-[2]
pillug- (get out of joint)	pətluɣ-[1]
pillui-	pətluɣ-[1]
piloqut	pəłu
pilu	pəłu
piluar-, piluari-	pi(t)lu(C)aʀ- (under pi(-))
pilug-, pilukat-	piłuɣ- (under pi(-))
pimmak, pimmaa-	pima-
pinaat-	pinaʀ- (under pi(-))
pinar-, pinasaar-	pinaʀ- (under pi(-))
pineq, pernit	piɣinəʀ
piner-	piɣinəʀ
pinerli-	pinəʀłuɣ- (under pi(-))
pinerlug-	pinəʀłuɣ- (under pi(-))
pingasut, pingajua	piŋayut
pingeq	pəŋiʀ
pingoor-	piŋu-[1]
pingu	pəŋuʀ
pingu(g)-	piŋu-[1]
pingujak	pəŋuy(y)ak (under pəŋuʀ)
piniar-, piniarti	piniaq- (under pi(-))
piniartuq	piniaqq- (under pi(-))
pinnari-	pinnaʀ(naq)-
pinner-	pinniʀ-
pinneri-	pinnaʀ-
pinngu-, pinngor-	piŋu-[1]
pinnguar-, pinnguaq	piŋŋuðaʀ- (under pi(-))
pinngui-	piŋu-
pinniit-	pinniʀit- (under pinniʀ-)
pior-	piuq-
piorsar-	piŋu-[2]
pipig-	pipək-
pipiter-	pipək-
pisaq, pisaqar-	pitaʀ (under pi(-))
pisar-	pityaqə-
pisareer-	pižaʀiiq-
pisari-	pitaʀ (under pi(-))
pisariit-	piðaqəŋit- (under piðaqə(naʀ)-)
pisarissersor-	piðaqə(naʀ)-
pisariu-, pisari(a)tu-	piðaqə(naʀ)-
pisataq	pi(-)
piseq	piciʀ
pisig- (shoot arrow)	pitəɣ-
pisig- (get up)	pižək-
pisissaar-	pətəɣcaʀ- (under pitəɣ-)
pisissi, pisisseq	pitəkcə (under pitəɣ-)
pissak	pižžaq-
pissamaar-	pikšamaaq- (under pi(-))
pissaq (share)	pikðaʀ (under pi(-))
pissaq (strong)	pižžaq-
pissarsiaq	pikðaʀ (under pi(-))
pissarsior-	pikðaʀ (under pi(-))
pissiaq	pikðaʀ (under pi(-))
pissig-	pəkyaɣ- (under pəkə-)
pissut	pi(-)
pisug-	piyuɣ-
pitar-	pətə-
pitarut(i)-	pətə-
pitorar-	pətuʀaq- (under pətə-)
pitu (sledge strap)	pətuɣ-
pitu (lamp stand)	pətuɣ
pitu(k), pitoq	pətuɣ-
pitug-	pətuɣ-
pituutaq	pətuɣutaʀ (under pətuɣ-)
piu-, piunngit-	piŋu-[2]
piuaat-	piyuɣaq-
piuarli-	piyuɣaq-
piukkut(i)-	piŋu-[2]
pooq, poor-	pu(ɣ)uq
pooqattaq	puukattaq (under pu(ɣ)uq)
pooruseq	puuʀuciq (under pu(ɣ)uq)
poqer-	puqiɣ-
poqiit-	puqiɣit- (under puqiɣ-)
portu-	puqtu- (under puɣə-)
puaasaq	puviʀaq
puak	puvak
puala-	puvala- (under puvə-)
pualut	pualu
pueqqor-	pupiŋquʀ-
puer-	puvə-
pueraasaq	puviʀaq (under puvə-)
puffag-	puvə-
puffinneq	puvə-
pug-	put-
pugguik	puɣə-
pui(k), puig-	puvə-
pui-	puɣə-
puiaq, puiaasaq	puyaʀ
puigor-, puior-	puyɣu(ʀ)-
puigunaat-	puyɣu(ʀ)-
puikkar-	puipkaq- (under puɣə-)
puila-	puila- (under puɣə-)

WEST GREENLANDIC	PROTOFORM
puisartartoq	puɣə-
puisi	puɣə-
puiutu-	puɣɣu(ʀ)-
puja-	puya
pujag-	piðaɣ-
pujak, puja	puya
pujaror-	piʀuq-
pujoor-	puyuʀ
pujoq, pujor-	puyuʀ
pujorak, pujorag-	puyuʀaq (under puyuʀ)
pujoralak, pujorala-	puyuʀaq (under puyuʀ)
pujualak, pujuala-	puyuʀaq (under puyuʀ)
pukak, pukag-	pukaɣ
pukeq	pukiʀ
pukit-	pukit-
pukkit-	pukkit- (under puɣə-)
pukug-	pukuɣ-
pula-	pula-
pulaar-	pula(C)aʀ- (under pula-)
pulama-, pulammag-	pula-
pullag-	puvlaɣ (under puvə-)
pullaq, pullartaq	puvlaɣ (under puvə-)
pullat, pullatit	pullan (under pula-)
puller-	puvliq- (under puvə-)
punneq	puɣ(ə)nəʀ (under puɣə-)
punngarsor-	put-
punngujoor-	punŋuaq (under put-)
pupik, pupig-	pupiɣ
pusi-	puci-
pusigar-	puci-
pusisaq	pucitaq (under puci-)
pusit-	pucit- (under puci-)
pussinnar-	pukcinnaq-
pussoq	putžuq
pussug-, pussuk	pumyuɣ-
putsinneq	puvə-
putta-, puttallar-	puɣta- (under puɣə-)
puttaaq, puttaar-	puktaaq- (under puɣə-)
puttarsi-	puɣta- (under puɣə-)
puttut	puttun (under putu[1])
putu, putu-	putu(-)[1]
putugoq	putukuʀ
puugutaq	puɣɣutaq (under pu(ɣ)uq)
puumig-	puɣ(ə)mə(t)- (under puɣə-)
puumikaar-	puɣ(ə)mə(t)- (under puɣə-)
puunga-	puvuɣ-
puut-	puvuɣ-
qaa	q(q)a(a) (enclitic)
qaa- (above)	qaðə-
qaa- (come)	qaʀə-
qaa- (become day)	qaʀu-
qaag-	qaaqšuq- (under qaɣəʀ-)
qaak	qaʀu
qaaler-	qaɣəʀ- (under qaɣəʀ-)
qaalerta(nar)-	qaʀaləʀ-
qaaller-	qaɣəliʀ- (under qaɣə(ʀ))
qaallor-, qaallorig-	qaulluq- (under qaʀu-)
qaama-	qauma- (under qaʀu-)
qaammar-	qauma- (under qaʀu-)
qaammat	qaumman (under qaʀu-)

WEST GREENLANDIC	PROTOFORM
qaaneq	qaanəq
qaanger-, qaangiut(i)-	qaaŋiq- (under qaðə-)
qaanngoq	qaɣəmɣu(ʀ)
qaaq (bed skin)	qaaq (under qaðə-)
qaaq (forehead)	qaɣuʀ
qaaqqut(i)-	qa(C)u(ði)-
qaar-, qaartit-	qaɣəʀ-
qaariaq	qa(C)aʀyaʀ
qaarsaat	qaiq-
qaarsoq	qaiqtuq (under qaiq-)
qaartor-	qaaqtuq-
qaaruarpalug-	qaiʀuaq-
qaarusuk	qa(C)iqu
qaarut	qauʀun (under qaɣuʀ)
qaaser-	qauciq-
qaat-	qaʀit- (under qaʀə-)
qaateq	qaatəq
qaatsinneq	qaaptət-
qaatsor-	qaʀu-
qaattar-, qaattor-	qaðəɣ-
qaatut-, qaatusimasaqqanngit-	qa(C)u(ði)-
qaffag-	qaɣvaʀ-
qaffar-	qaɣvaʀ-
qaffer-	qaɣvaʀ-
qajaa-	qayau- (under qayaʀ)
qajagi-, qajannar-	qayak-
qajaq	qayaʀ
qajariaq	qayaʀiaq (under qayaʀ)
qajartor-	qayaʀtuʀ- (under qayaʀ)
qajassuar-	qayak(naq)-
qajoq	qayuʀ
qajorlak	qayuʀ
qajuusat	qayuʀ
qajuutaq	qayuʀutaq (under qayuʀ)
qalag-	qała-[1]
qalak	qała-[1]
qalaseq	qałaciʀ
qalat-	qała-[1]
qaleq	qaliʀ (under qaðə-)
qaleraq	qaliqaʀ (under qaðə-)
qaleriig-	qal(l)iʀiik (under qaðə-)
qaleruaq	qaliʀuðaʀ (under qaðə-)
qalipaaq, qalipaat	qaliʀ (under qaðə-)
qalipak, qalipag-	qaliʀ (under qaðə-)
qalleq	qaðliʀ (under qaðə-)
qaller-	qaðəliʀ- (under qaðə-)
qalli-	qanli- (under qanət-)
qallineq	qaðəliʀ- (under qaðə-)
qallipiaq	qatluviɣ(aʀ) (under qatlin)
qallit, qallisit	qatliviaq (under qatlin)
qallu (eyebrow)	qavlu(ʀ)
qallu (surrounded valley)	qaɣḷu(ʀ)
qallunaaq	qavlunaaq
qallunniar-	qavlunaaq
qallupiaq	qatluviɣ(aʀ) (under qatlin)
qallut	qallun (under qalu-)
qallut(i)-	qalu-
qalorsaq	qaluqšaq (under qalu(-))
qalu-	qalu-
qalugiaq	qaluɣyaʀ

WEST GREENLANDIC	PROTOFORM
qaluma-, qalumaneq	qalu(-)
qaluneq	qalunəq (under qalu(-))
qalunni-	qalunəq (under qalu(-))
qalut	qallun (under qalu(-))
qalutaat	qalutaR(-) (under qalu(-))
qama-	qama-
qamaneq	qamanəq (under qama-)
qamig-, qamit-	qamət- (under qamə-)
qamitser-	qaptəq- (under qamə-)
qamuter-	qamutək (under qamuR-)
qamutit	qamutək (under qamuR-)
qanak, qanag-	qanaɣ
qaneq	qanəR(-)
qanga	qaŋa
qanganisaq	qaŋa
qangata-	qaŋata-
qangattaq	qaŋata-
qangattar-	qaŋattaq- (under qaŋata-)
qangiaq	qaŋiɣaR
qani-, qanior-	qani-
qanig-	qanət-
qanik, qaniit	qaniɣ
qanilaar-	qanilaaq- (under qani-)
qanima-	qanima-
qanimaat-	qanima-
qanimut	qanət-
qaninngoor-	qani-
qanior-	qani-
qanisaq	qanit(t)aR (under qani-)
qanitaq	qanət-
qanner-	qaniɣ
qanngor-	qatŋuR-
qanngui-	qamRui-
qanoq	qanuq
qanormi	qanuq
qanortoq	qanuqtuq (under qanuq)
qapag-, qapak	qapak-
qapangiinnar-	qapak-
qapangit-	qappit-
qapasag-, qapasak	qapak-
qaper-	qapiR-
qapi-, qapit-	qappit-
qapiar-	qapiR-
qappat-, qappanga-	qapak-
qappi-	qappit-
qappik	qatviɣ
qapuk	qapuɣ
qaqa-	qaqa-
qaqajuk	qaqaR
qaqeq	qakəR
qaqerluk	qakəR(luɣ)
qaqernit-	qakəR-
qaqersi-	qakəRci- (under qakəR-)
qaqi-, qaqit-	qakə-
qaqiler-	qaqu(R)
qaqor-	qakuR-
qaqoriar-	qaqu(R)
qaqornaq	qakuRnaR (under qakuR-)
qaqortaq	qakuR-
qaqqaq	qaðqaR (under qaðə-)
qaqqit-	qaðqaR (under qaðə-)
qaqqor-	qaŋquR-
qaqquaq	qaŋquR-
qaqu, qaqu-	qaqu(R)
qaquaq	qaquaq (under qaqu(R))
qaqugu	qaku
qaquit, qaquiseq	qaqu(R)
qaqulluk	qaqutluɣ
qaqunnak, qaqornak	qakuR-
qaqutigu(t)	qakutiɣun (under qaku)
qaraar-	qaɣəR-
qarajaq	qaRiaq
qarasaq	qaqətaR
qarassi-	qaRəyaq
qarliit	qaRuɫiɣ
qarloq	qaqluɣ
qarlor-	qaləR-
qarluaq	qaqluaq (under qaqluɣ)
qarluuseq	qaləR-
qarmaq	qaRmaR
qarmar- (build brickwork)	qaRmaR
qarmar- (call dog)	qalmaR-
qarrut(i)-	qaRu-
qarsaaq	qaqðaR
qarsoq	qaRðuR
qarsor-	qakcuR- (under qakə(R)-)
qarsorneq	qakcuR- (under qakə(R)-)
qarsorsaq	qaRžuqcaq (under qaRðuR)
qarsut(i)-, qarsua-	qaðətRutə- (under qaðə-)
qartorar-	qaɣəR- (under qaɣə(R))
qasaar-	qatəR-
qasagi-	qacaɣə-
qasaloq	qacalluq
qasaruaq	qəcaRu(C)aR
qaser-	qatəR-
qasigiaq	qaðiɣɣaR
qasilit-	qacəli-
qasinngor-	qaciŋŋuq-
qassag-	qapðaɣ-
qassarig-	qatðaR (under qatə)
qassi	qaðɣi
qassi-, qassima-	qakši- (under qakə-)
qassit, qassiit	qavcit
qassorar-	qakšuɣaun (under qakə-)
qassuar-, qassuaat	qakšuɣaun (under qakə-)
qassug-, qassutsit-	qamcuɣ- (under qamə-)
qassutit	qaðəɣ-
qasu-	qacu-
qasuer-	qacu-
qasut-	qacu-
qataat-	qatə
qatanngut	qatəŋŋun
qati, qatitu-	qatə
qatigak	qatə
qatik	qatəɣ
qatimaag-	qatə
qatser-	qaptəq- (under qamə-)
qatsig-	qatcik- (under qaðə-)
qatsor-, qatsunga-	qatcuq- (under qacu-)
qattaq	qaltaR
qattuneq	qakə-[1]
qavaruseq	qavaRuciq
qeeq	qiðəR

WEST GREENLANDIC	PROTOFORM
qipeqqoq	qipuk-
qiperoq, qiperor-	qipuk-
qipi-	qipə-
qipik, qipig-	qipək (under qipə-)
qipilua-	qipə-
qipinnguq	qipə-
qipoqqaq	qipuqqaʀ
qiporaq	qipuk-
qippaq	qipə-
qiseq, qiser-	qəciʀ(-)
qissaar-	qikə-[1]
qissag-, qissattor-	qəvcaɣ-
qissaq, qissar-	qipðaʀ (under qipə-)
qisser-	qəžɣəq- (under qətəɣ-)
qissi- (be unable to fall asleep)	qipci-
qissi- (spin)	qipði- (under qipə-)
qissigi-	qikciɣ- (under qikə-[1])
qissima-	qəvə(t)-
qissimig-	qikciɣ- (under qikə-[1])
qisua-	qi(C)ət-
qisug-	qəc(c)uɣ-
qisuk (wood)	qəðuɣ
qisuk (dark sky over water)	qiɣuɣ(-)
qisuttar-	qəðuɣtaʀ- (under qəðuɣ)
qiteq	qətəʀ
qiteqqut(i)-, qiteqquut	qətəqquq- (under qətəʀ)
qiteraq, qiterar-	qətəʀaʀ (under qətəʀ)
qiterar-	qətəʀ
qiterleq	qətəqliq (under qətəʀ)
qiterpar-	qətəqpaq- (under qətəʀ)
qitig-	qətəɣ-
qitivit-, qituit-	qitəvə(t)-
qitornaq	qətunʀaʀ
qitsug-	qəc(c)uɣ-
qitsuk, qissuk	qiŋcuɣ(-)
qittar-	qətəɣ-
qitusug-	qətusuk-
qitug-	qətut-
qitutsag-	qətusuk-
qiu-	qiʀu-
qivaaqi	qivaaqi
qiver-	qivə(ʀ)-
qiviar-	qiviaq- (under qivə(ʀ)-)
qivit-	qəvə(t)-
qiviu	qivyu(ʀ)
qooq	quʀəʀ (under quʀə-)
qooqqa(a)q	quðu-
qoornoq	quunʀuq (under quðu-)
qooroq	quðuquʀ (under quðu-)
qoqaaq	qukaaq-
qoqassi-	qukaaq-
qoqer-	qukiʀ-
qoqeri-	qukəɣə-
qorfik	quʀvik (under quʀə-)
qorliar-	quʀliaq
qorlor-, qorloq	quʀluʀ-
qorlortoq	quʀluʀtaʀ (under quʀluʀ-)
qorluula-	quʀluʀ-
qorsineq	quʀžinəq (under quʀə-)
qorsuk, qorsoq	quqcuq- (under quʀə-)
quaasi-	qu(C)aq
quaat-, quaaqqit-	quʀa(yaqit)-
quajaat	quʀa(yaqit)-
quaq	qu(C)aʀ
quaraq	quaʀaq
quarsaar-	quaqcaaq-
quarta-	quɣaʀta(ʀ)
quartaq	quɣaʀta(ʀ)
quasak, quasag-	quacaq (under quʀasqit-)
quasasior-	quacak (under quʀasqit-)
quasi-	quacak (under quʀasqit-)
quassuk	qu(C)aɣðuɣ
queer-	quvya(yuɣ)
quer-, quersor-	quɣəʀ-
quersaq	quvəʀtə
quersuaq	qu(C)aq
querteq	quvəʀtə
qug-	quðu-
qui(k)	qu(C)aʀ
qui-	quʀə-
quiag-	quvya(yuɣ)-
quiasug-, quiagi-	quvya(yuɣ)-
quilerta-	quiliqta-
quinag-	quɣinaɣ-
quja-	quya-
qujamasug-	quya-
qujanaq	quyanaʀ (under quya-)
qujarut(i)-	quya-
qulaaluat	quləŋŋuʀutəŋit- (under qulə-)
qulaat(i)-	qulautə- (under qulə-)
qulanger-	quləŋiʀ- (under qulə-)
qular(i)-, qularnar-	qulaq-
quli-	qulə-
qulingiluat	quləŋŋuʀutəŋit- (under qulə-)
qulisima-	qulə-
qulisser-, qulissiut	quləmci(C)un (under qulə-)
qulit (ten)	qulə(t) (under qulə-)
qulit (knee pieces)	quliʀ (under qulə-)
qulit-	qulit- (under qulə-)
qulitsaq	quliktaq
qullar-	qulvaʀ- (under qulə-)
qulleq (lamp)	qulliʀ (under qulə-)
qulleq (tear)	qulvi
qulloor-	qupluq- (under qupə-)
qullor-, qullui-	qupluq- (under qupə-)
qullug-	quɣluk-
qullugiaq	quɣluɣiaq (under quɣluk-[1])
qulua-	quluk-
qulussug-	quluk-
qulusuk	qulucuɣ
qulutsuk	qulucuk
qumaq	quma(ʀ)
qumar-	qumaq-
qumig-, qumiinga-	qumiɣ
qummar-	quʀə-
qungaseq	quŋəciq
qungiar-	quŋyaʀ-
qungujug-	quŋuyuɣ-

WEST GREENLANDIC	PROTOFORM
simer-	cimmiR-
simik, simig-	cimək-
simmer-	cimək-
sinaaq	cinəRaR (under cinə)
siner-	cinə
sineriak	ciniR- (under cinə)
sinersor-	cinəR- (under cinə)
singar-	ciŋaR-
singarnaq	ciŋaq-
singeq	ciŋiR
singerneq	ciŋiRnəq (under ciŋiR)
singig-	ciŋə(t)-
singullor-	ciŋulluq- (under ciŋuk-)
singunner-	ciŋuk-
sini	cinə
siniffik	cinəɣvik (under cinək-)
sinig-	cinək-
sinnarlior-	cinnaRliuq- (under cinək-)
sinnartoor-	cinək-
sinnattor-, sinnattugaq	cinnaktuq- (under cinək-)
sinneq	cip(ə)nəR (under cipə(t)-)
sinnequt	cip(ə)nəR (under cipə(t)-)
sinner-	cip(ə)nəR (under cipə(t)-)
sinnga-, sinngagi-	cikna-
sinnganeer-	cinək-
sinngoqut	cip(ə)nəR (under cipə(t)-)
sinngor-	ciŋuk-
sinnguseq	ciŋək-
sioora-, siooragi-	civu(C)uRa-
sioorasaar-	civu(C)aRa-
sioraq (sand)	ciuRaq
sioraq (front)	civuqaR (under civu-)
siorarleq	civuqaR (under civu-)
siorleq	civuqliR (under civu-)
siorna	civunəR (under civu-)
siorsug-, siorsuk	ciRuRðuɣ-
sipi-	cipə(ɣ)-
sippaq	cipə(ɣ)-
sipper-	cipə(ɣ)-
sippor-	cipə(ɣ)-
sipporut(i)-, sipput(i)-	cipə(ɣ)-
sisag-	citə(ɣ)-
sisak	citə(ɣ)-
sisamat	citamat
sisi	citə
sisorar-, sisoraatit	cituRaR- (under citu-)
sissag-	ciðəɣ-
sissaq (beach)	ciŋðaR
sissaq (split in garment)	cižžaq (under ciðəɣ-)
sissariarsuk	ciɣžaRiaq (under ciŋðaR)
sissik (squirrel), sissinnguaq	cikðiɣ
sissik (scale in ear)	təkðə(R)
sissuer-	cikcuiq-
sisu-	citu-
sisuat	citu-
sitser-	citciq-
sitsoqig-	cittuqit-
sitsor-	cittuR-
siu	civu-
siuaasaq	civu-
siuaq	civu(C)aR (under civu-)
siuaR-	civu-
siuleq	civul(l)iR (under civu-)
siulig-	civuləɣ-
siulittar-	civuləɣ- (under civu-)
siulleeq	civul(l)iR (under civu)
siulleq	civul(l)iR (under civu-)
siulliarsuit	civul(l)iRaR (under civu-)
siumig-	civumiɣ- (under civu-)
siuneq	civunəR (under civu-)
siuneri-, siunertari-	civunəR (under civu-)
siunersi-, siuneqar-	civunəqci- (under civu-)
siunner-, siunnerfik	civunniR- (under civu-)
siunnersor-	civunniR- (under civu-)
siut	ciɣun
siuteroq	ci(ɣ)utəquR (under ciɣun)
siuttoq	civu-
sivi, sivisu-	civi
sivikit-	civi
sivinga-	civəŋa-
sooq	cuuq (under cu(na))
soormi	cuuq (under cu(na))
soqqaar-	cuqqa(C)aR-
soqqaq	cuqqaR
soqula-	cuqula-
soqutaa-	cuq(q)utə- (under cu(na))
soqutigi-	cuq(q)utə- (under cu(na))
soraar-	cuRaiq-
soraluaq	cuRuciq
sorlak	cuqlaɣ
sorleq	cu(na)
sorluk	cuRlu
sorraat-	cuRRait-
sorruk, sorrug-	cuR(R)uk(-)
sorsug-	cuRðuɣ-
sorujuk	cuRuyuk
su-, suna	cu(na)
suaar-	cuɣaɣ-
suag-	cuɣaɣ-
suak	ciłuvaɣ
sualug-	cuɣaɣ-
suami	cu(na)
suanga-	cuaŋa- (under cuɣaɣ-)
suarsuit	cuaRžuk (under cu(na))
sueq, suer-	cuvəq
suilaaqi-, suilaaqqut	cu(na)ŋit- (under cu(na))
suinni, suinnit-	cuviɣnit-
sukag-, sukat-	cuk(k)a-
sukaq, sukar-	cukaR
sukka-, sukkasooq	cuk(k)a-
sukkaat-	cuk(k)aŋit- (under cuk(k)a-)
sukkit-	cukki(R)
sukorseq	cuRuciq
sukuiar-	cukuiq-
suli	cu(na)li (under cu(na))
suli-, suliffik	cu(na)li- (under cu(na))
suliaq	cu(na)li- (under cu(na))
sullineq	culuɣ
sulluaq	cupluɣ
sulluar-	cupluaq- (under cupə-)
sullugi-	cuɣluɣə-
suloraq	culuRaq (under culuɣ)

Postbases and enclitics

WEST GREENLANDIC	PROTOFORM
navianngit-	na-
neq	nəʀ[1]
ner- (be good to)	n(n)iʀ-
ner- (I wonder)	n(n)iq-
nerar-	ni-
nerlug-	nəʀłuɣ-
nerpaaq	nəʀpa(C)aʀ
nersaq	nəʀ[2]
nertu-	nəʀ[2]
neru-	nəʀ[2]
nerumaar-	(u)ma-
nga- (in state)	ŋa-[1]
nga- (resemble)	ŋa-[2]
ngaar-, ngaaq	ŋaaq-
ngajag-, ngajaar-	tyaɣ
nger-	ŋiʀ-
ngiag-	ŋiɣ-
ngusaq	ŋ(ŋ)uðaʀ(-)
nialug-	ni(C)aʀ-
niar-	ni(C)aʀ-
nig-	nəɣ-
nikoq, nikuu-	k(k)uʀ
nisaq	nitaq
nnag-	nnak-
nnaq	knaʀ
nna(a)q	nnaq
nnger-	ŋŋiq-
nngit-	nʀit-
=nngooq	ŋu(C)uʀ
nngor-	ŋ(ŋ)uʀ-
nngu-	lŋu-
nnguaq, nnguar-	ŋ(ŋ)uðaʀ(-)
nniaq	ni(C)aʀ-
nnig-	nnək-
or-	(C)uʀ-
(r)paaluit	aluk
(r)paat	vaɣ(-)
pajaar-	payaaq-
pajug-, pajuk	payuk(-)
palaaq, palaar-	vaɣ(-)
(r)palaar-	vałłaɣ-[2]
pallaar-	vałłaɣ-[1]
pallag-	vałłaɣ-[1]
(r)pallag-	vałłaɣ-[2]
(r)palug-, (r)paluk	valuk-
(r)par-	vaʀ-
(r)pasig-	ðiɣ-
passig-	ðiɣ-
passug-	mcuɣ(-)
(r)passuit	vaɣ
peraar-	vlaɣ-
(r)piaq, (r)piar-	piɣ(-)
pilag-, pillag-	vlaɣ-
q	nəʀ[1]
qar-	ŋqaʀ-
qat	qan
qattaar-	k(k)attaʀ-
qi-	ʀqə-
qina-	yaqu(naɣ)
qoq	quʀ
qqa-	ŋa-[2]
qqaar-	łʀa(C)aʀ-
qqajar-, qqajaa-	lʀayaq-
qqammer-, qqamminngit-	lʀammiq-
qqar- (barely)	vqaʀ-
qqar- (one after another)	qqaʀ-
qqig- (completely)	nqiɣ-[1]
qqig- (again)	nqiɣ-[2]
qqinnaar-	nqiɣ-[1]
qqissaar-	nqiɣ-[1]
qqoor-	qquuq-
qqu-, qqusaar-	ðqə-
qqut(i)-	tʀutə-
qut, qqut	un
q(q)ut, qutaq	q(q)un
r- (become)	ŋ(ŋ)uʀ-
r- (go to)	q-
r- (catch)	nəɣ-
raar-	ʀaaq-
raq	qaʀ
rar-	ʀaq-
ratar-	lʀataq-
reer-	ɣiiq-
riaannaa-	yaʀ
riaq, giaq	yaʀ
riar-	ɣiaq-
riataar-	ʀataʀ-
rig-	nqiɣ-[1]
rloq	quʀ
rnga(a)r-	n(ə)ʀaʀ(aʀ)(-)
roq	quʀ-
ror- (become)	ŋ(ŋ)uʀ-
ror- (hit on)	ʀuq-
rrat(i)-	utə-
ruaq	ŋ(ŋ)uðaʀ(-)
rujug-, rujoor-	ʀuluk
rujuk	ʀuluk
rulug-, ruloor-	ʀuluk
ru(u)saar-	ŋuðaʀaʀ-
ruseq	ɣuciq
rusug-, gusug-	yuɣ-
sa-	ta-
saannar-	ðaʀ-
saq	ðaʀ
sar-, saar- (try to cause)	caʀ-[1]
sar- (habitual)	ðaʀ-
sari-, tari-	ðaʀ-
sariaqar-, tariaqar-	ɣiaqaq-
sassaa-	žukšau-
ser-	liq-
(t)ser-, (t)sii-	c(c)iʀ-
seriar-, seriit-	c(c)iʀyaʀ-
si	ðə
si- (detransitivizer)	ði-
si- (get)	ci-
si- (become)	li-[2]
siaq	ci-
sig-	ðiɣ-
(t)siiaq	c(c)iʀ-
sima-	(u)ma-
simaar-	(u)maʀ(aʀ)-
sinnaa-	ŋinnaʀ(-)
sinnar-	ŋinnaʀ(-)

WEST GREENLANDIC	PROTOFORM
sior-	ci(C)uʀ-
siut	ci(C)un
sooq	suu-
soor-	ðuʀ
soq	ðuʀ
(r)sor-	qðuʀ-
sor-	tuʀ-[1]
sori-	yukə-
ssa-	tya-
ssaleqi-	ŋiliqə-
ssaaq (great)	žaʀaq
=ssaaq	ptauq
ssaar- (stop)	tyaiq-
ssaar- (greatly)	mcaɣ-
ssamaar-	kðaʀ
ssanga-	tya-
ssaq	kðaʀ
ssit-	kðit-
ssuseq	uciʀ
ssut	un
ssut(i)-	utə-
ssutigi-	utəkə-
(r)suaq, -(r)suar-	ðuɣaʀ(-)
sug-	yuɣ-
suangu-	yuɣ-
suer-	yuiq-
sugi-	yukə-
suit-	yu(C)it-
suk	yuɣ
sungar-	cuŋaʀ
sunnit-	nit-
sunngu-	sunŋu-
sussaa-	žukšau-
sussuk	cuɣ
t- (transitivizer)	t-[1]
t- (catch)	t-[2]
t, ti-	tə
taannar-	ðaʀ-
taaq	taaq(-)
=(t)taaq, -ssaaq	ptauq
taar- (get)	taaq(-)
taar- (repeatedly)	ta(C)aʀ-
taq (pertaining)	taʀ
taq (past part.)	ðaʀ-
tar- (fetch)	taʀ-
tar- (habitual)	ðaʀ-
ter-, teri-	təʀ-
ti	ðə
tigi-	tə-
tit-, -titer-	tət-
titaar-	təta(C)aʀ-
toor-	tuuq-
toq	ðuʀ
=toq	tuʀ
toqaq	tuqaq[2]
tor- (use)	tuʀ-[1]
tor- (repeatedly)	tuʀ-[2]
tsaali(or)-, taali(or)-	təta(C)ili-
tsag-	yyaɣ-
tsiaq, tsiar-	tciaq
ttar-	t(t)aʀ-
tu-	tu-[1]
tuaannar-	tu-[2]
tuaq	tuaq(-)
tuar- (for once)	tu(C)aʀ-
tuar- (continually)	ðuʀaʀ-
tuinnar-, ttuinnar-	tu-[2]
tuuma-	tuʀ-[1]
u-	ŋu-
uar- (continuously)	ðuʀaʀ-
uar- (have much)	ʀuaq-
ummer-, ummi-	ummiʀ-
unnar-, unngar-	q-
usa(a)q	ŋuðaʀ(-)
usar-, usaar-	ŋuðaʀaʀ-
useq	uciʀ
ut	un
ut(i)- (owned)	ŋutə-
ut(i)- (do with)	utə-
utigi-,	utəkə-
vaar-	vaɣ(-)
vallaar-	vałłaɣ-[1]
var-	vaʀ-
vig-	piɣ(-)
vik (real)	piɣ(-)
vik (place)	ðviɣ
vissor-	viɣ(-)
Vmi-	umi-
Vmisaar-	umi-
Vr-	(V)ʀ-
Vraq	ʀaʀ

NORTH ALASKAN INUIT INDEX
(Barrow Dialect)

Postbases, at the end, are generally given in their form following a full vowel (and enclitics are preceded by '=').

Equivalences between the Alaskan Inupiaq standard orthography and the orthography used in this dictionary are given below. Symbols of the standard orthography are given in italics. If no equivalence is given it means that the standard practical orthography uses the same symbol as our orthography. *g* = ɣ, *ġ* = ʀ, *h* = X, *ḷ* = l^y, *ł̣* = $ɬ^y$, *ñ* = n^y, *r* = ž, *sr* = š. Alphabetization is as follows: a, ch, g, ġ, h, i, k, l, ḷ, ł, ł̣, m, ñ, ŋ, p, q, r, s, sr, t, u, v, y.

NAI	PROTOFORM
aa (listen, oops)	a(a)
aa (yes)	a(a)ŋ
aa-	aɣa-
aagiaq	aaɣiaq
aagruuk	aaɣžuuk
aaġiak	aaʀiak
aaġlu	a(C)aʀɬuɣ
aaġluq-	aɣaʀluʀ-
aak-	aak-
aaka	a(a)kaʀ
aana	a(a)na
aanaakłiq	aanakliq
aanġu<r>aq	aɣanʀu(Caʀ)
aannagu	anaqa
aannugu	anaqa
aaŋ	a(a)ŋ
aaŋayaaq-	aaŋa- (under aɣa-)
aapa	ap(p)a[1]
aapi(y)aq	ap(p)a[1]
aaqagu(n)	aqaɣu
aaqan	aqaɣu
aaqhaaliq	a(a)-a(a)ŋliʀ
aaqhaalliq	a(a)-a(a)ŋliʀ
aaqqan	aitqan (under aðiʀ)
aaquaksraq	aʀnalqu(C)aʀ (under aʀnaʀ)
aaquaq-	aʀnalqu(C)aʀ (under aʀnaʀ)
aaquk	aʀnalqu(C)aʀ (under aʀnaʀ)
aasi(i)	aaci(in)
aasiiñ	aaci(in)
aasivak	aacivak
aat-	aat-
aatchaq-	aɣittaʀ-
aatchauq-	aɣittaʀuʀ- (under aɣittaʀ-)
aatqan	aitqan (under aðiʀ)
aatqik-	aʀənqiɣ-
agak-	aɣ(ɣ)aɣ-
aggaġiitkuq	aɣ(ɣ)a(ʀ)-
aggaq-	aɣ(ɣ)a(ʀ)-
aggiq-	aɣɣiʀ- (under aɣə-)
agiaq-	aɣiɣ-
agik-	aɣiɣ-
agiun	aɣiɣ(aʀ)un (under aɣiɣ-)
agiuppak	aɣiuppak (under aɣiɣ-)
aglaan	aɣlaan
aglak-	alŋaʀ(-)
aglaun	alŋaʀun (under alŋaʀ(-))
agli-	aŋ(ə)li- (under aŋə-)
agliġi-	aɣləʀ(-)
agliġuq	aɣluquʀ (under aɣluʀ)
aglu	aɣluʀ
agluq-	aŋɬuʀ-
agma-	aŋva-
agmaaq	akmaaq
agmaq-	aŋvaʀ- (under aŋva-)
agniq	aɣnəʀ (under aɣə-)
agraq	aɣ(ɣ)a(ʀ)-
agraq-	aɣžaq- (under aɣə-)
aguummak	aɣu(C)ummaʀ
aguummaq	aɣu(C)ummaʀ
aġġi-	aʀʀi-
aġġiññaq	aʀʀi(t)naʀ
aġġutaq	an(ə)ʀutaʀ
aġiñaq-	aʀinaʀ- (under aʀi(t)-)
aġit-	aʀi(t)-
aġiu-	aʀ(ə)yu-
aġligi-	aʀliɣə- (under aʀli(C)-)
aġlik-	aʀli(C)-
aġnaq	aʀnaʀ
aġnasalluq	aʀnacalluʀ (under aʀnaʀ)
aġnauniq	aʀnaʀunəʀ (under aʀnaʀ)
aġnaviaq	aʀnaviaq (under aʀnaʀ)
aġniqi-	aʀniqə- (under aʀnaʀ)
aġra	aʀða
aġvak	aʀvaɣ
aġvak-	aʀvak- (under aʀvəʀ)
aġviġluaq	aʀvəʀluaq (under aʀvəʀ)
aġviq	aʀvəʀ
ai	ay
ai-	aɣə-
aiġaaluk	aɣi
aiġaq	aiʀaq
aiḷaq-	aʀiɬaʀ- (under aʀi(t)-)
aiñiq	ainnəq
aippaq	a(C)ippaʀ
aitchuq-	aittuq- (under aɣə-)
aitqan	aitqan (under aðiʀ)
aiviq	ayvəʀ
aivvak-	aivvak- (under ayvəʀ)
aiy	ay
aki (opposite)	akəʀ
aki (cost)	aki(-)
akigaq-	akiyaʀ-, akiʀaʀ- (under aki(-))
akiġuq	akəquʀ
akiit-	akiŋit- (under aki(-))
akiḷiñaaq	akil(l)iʀ, akiqliʀ (under aki(-))
akiḷiq-	akiliʀ- (under aki(-))
akiḷḷiq	akil(l)iʀ, akiqliʀ (under aki(-))
akiḷuk	akisuk- (under aki(-))

NAI	PROTOFORM
akiḷuk(-)	akisuk- (under aki(-))
akima-	akima- (under aki(-))
akimiaq	akimiɣaR (under aki(-))
akiñ	akin (under aki(-))
akisi	akin (under aki(-))
akiuq-	akiRuR- (under aki(-))
akivik-	akiviɣ-
akkaaka	akkak
akkakaa	akka
akkiq-	akkiR-
akku	ak(k)uvaR
akkuaq-	akuR-[1]
akkumman	ak(k)uvaR
akkupak	ak(k)uvaR
akkusaaq	ak(k)uvaR
akłaq	aklaq
akłuna<r>aq	akluna(a)q
akpak-	alpaɣ-
akpit-	akpət-
aksik-	aɣtuR-
aksiŋa-	aɣtuR-
aksragiitkutaq	akšaɣiitkutaq (under akðaɣ-)
aksrak-	akðaɣ-
aksraligaq	akðaɣ-
aksralik-	akšalək- (under akðaɣ-)
akuliaq	akul(l)iRaR (under aku(R))
akullaq	akulə- (under aku(R))
akunna(a)q-	akunnak- (under aku(R))
akunniq	akunnəq (under aku(R))
akuq	aku(R)
akuqtuq-	akuR-[1]
akut-	akut- (under aku(R))
akutaq	akutaR (under aku(R))
akuttu-	akultu- (under aku(R))
alaaq	ala(a)q
alapigi-	alapənRaR-
alapit-	alapənRaR-
alappaa	alappaa
alappuu	alappaa
alaq-	alaR-
alatkaq-	alaŋkaR-
alavri-	alapənRaR-
algiq-	aðɣiR-
alġa(i)	aləR
alġaaġusiq	alRa(a)Ruciq (under aləR)
alġaani	alRaku, alRani (under aləR)
alġaaq	al(ə)RaR(aR) (under aləR)
alġaqsuq-	aləRaqðuR-
alianait-	aliɣanaRit- (under aliɣa-)
alianaq-	aliɣa-
aliit-	aliŋit-
alik-	ałəɣ-[1]
aliqa(q)	aləqa(R)
aliqsik	ałiRtə
aliuq-	ali(C)uRtuR-
alivsuk-	alivtuR-
alla	atla
allanaq-	atlanəR (under atla)
allaq	allaq
allayuaq-	atlayuɣ- (under atla)
alliaq	atliRaR (under at(ə)-)
alliġaq	atliqaR (under at(ə)-)
alliġauraq	atliqaR (under at(ə)-)
alliq	atliR (under at(ə)-)
allu	anlu
alluaq	anlu(C)aR (under anlu)
alu	alu(R)
aluk	aluɣ-
aluk-	aluɣ-
aluktinniq	aluktətnəq
alumiġait-	alumƏRaq-, alupəq (under aluɣ-)
alupaaġiik	alupak-, alupaq-
aluuttaq	alu(C)un (under aluɣ-)
aluuttaun	alu(C)un (under aluɣ-)
amaamak-	ama(C)-
amaaq (load on back)	amaR-
amaaq (roots)	amaaq
amaġuq	amaquR
amaq-	amaR-
amaqtuq	amaRtuR
amau	ama(C)uR
amaullik	amaRutləɣ
amaułłigaaluk	amautləɣaq (under amaRutləɣ)
amaułuk	ama(C)uR
amiami	a(a)mi(ila) (under a(a)ŋ)
amigaq-	aməɣaq-
amigḷi-	amitli- (under amit-)
amiġaq	amiRaR (under amiR)
amii	a(a)mi(ila) (under a(a)ŋ)
amikḷi-	amitli- (under amit-)
amiḷġaq	amiləqaR, amitə(l)qaR (under amit-)
amiḷġuq	amilRuq (under amit-)
amiq	amiR
amirġaq	amiləqaR, amitə(l)qaR (under amit-)
amirġaq-	aməl(ə)Ra(R)-
amirriaq	aminaR
amisut	aməcu-
amit-	amit-
ammun	ammun (under amu-)
amu-	amu-
amuaq-	amuRaR- (under amu-)
anaġlu	anaRluk (under anaR(-))
anak-	an(n)aɣ-
anaktaq-	an(n)aɣ-
anaq	anaR(-)
anaqami	anaqa
anau-	anaɣu-
anautaq	anaɣutaR (under anaɣu-)
anaya(suk)-	anaya-
ani-	anə-
ania-	anə-
aniguq-	aniɣuq- (under anə-)
aniguyyaq	aniɣutyaR (under aniɣu)
aniġniq	anəRnəR (under anəR-)
aniiq-	anəɣiR- (under anə-)

NAI	PROTOFORM
aniŋa	anəŋaʀ
aniŋa-	aniŋa- (under anə-)
aniŋak	anəŋaʀ
aniq-	anəʀ-
aniqan	anə-
aniqsa	aniʀta
aniqsaaq-	anəʀɣa(C)aʀ-
aniqtiġi-	anəʀtəqə- (under anəʀ-)
anisiq-	aniciq- (under anə-)
anit-	anət- (under anə-)
aniu	aniɣu
annak-	annaɣ-
annauti-	annaɣutə- (under annaɣ-)
anniaq-	atniaq- (under atŋiʀ-)
anniġi-	atŋiqə- (under atŋiʀ-)
anniq-	atŋiʀ-
annisi-	annitə- (under anə-)
annivik	anəðviɣ, annəviɣ (under anə-)
annuġaaq	atnuʀaaq (under atə-)
annut-	annuci-, annut-
annik	ałŋiɣ
annun	aɣŋun
anu	anu
anuaqsruit-	annuʀaqə-
anuaqun	annuʀaqə-
anuġi	anuqə
anuqłiq-	anuqliʀ- (under anuqə)
anusiñŋu(q)-	annucinŋu(q)- (under annut-, annuci-)
aŋ	a(a)ŋ
aŋ(i)naaq	aŋənaaq- (under aŋə-)
aŋaayyu-	aɣaɣu-
aŋak	aŋaɣ
aŋala-	aŋala-
aŋalat-	aŋalat- (under aŋala-)
aŋatkuaq-	aŋatkuaq- (under aŋalkuʀ)
aŋatkuq	aŋalkuʀ
aŋayu-	aŋa(ɣəɣ)-, aŋayu(ɣ)-
aŋayukłiq	aŋayukliʀ (under aŋayuɣ)
aŋayunġuq	aŋayunʀuq (under aŋayuɣ)
aŋayuqaak	aŋayuq(q)aʀ (under aŋayuɣ)
aŋayuqak	aŋayuq(q)aʀ (under aŋayuɣ)
aŋayuqaksraq	aŋayuq(q)aʀ (under aŋayuɣ)
aŋi- (be big)	aŋə-
aŋi- (revive)	aŋit-
aŋiḷġaq-	aŋilʀaʀ- (under aŋit-)
aŋiq-	aŋəʀ- (under a(a)ŋ)
aŋivit-	aŋi-
aŋivraq-	aŋi-
aŋmaġuq	aŋmaq
aŋmaluaq-	aŋvaluʀ- (under aŋva-)
aŋŋiq	aɣnəʀ (under aɣə-)
aŋŋaq-	aŋəʀ- (under a(a)ŋ)
aŋŋiqi-	aŋŋi-
aŋŋuu(ŋ)	aŋŋu
aŋu-	aŋu-
aŋuaq-	aŋuðaʀ-
aŋula-	aŋula-
aŋun	aŋun
aŋunnaq	aŋutnaq (under aŋun)
aŋunnuniq	aŋutŋunəʀ
aŋusalluq	aŋucalluʀ (under aŋun)
aŋusuq-	aŋuyu(ʀ)- (under aŋu-)
aŋutaat	aŋun
aŋuun	aŋuðaʀun (under aŋuðaʀ-)
aŋuuq-	aŋuðuʀ-
aŋuyak-	aŋuviɣaq
apaaluk	ap(p)a[1]
api-	apə-
apiġi-	apəʀə-
apiktit-	apəktət-
apiqsruq-	apəqšuq- (under apəʀə-)
apitchiq	apətciq (under apə-)
apqałak-	aləmqaʀ-
apqun	apʀun
apqusaaq-	apqucaaq- (under apʀun)
apqusi-	apqucinəq (under apʀun)
apta-	avta-
apummaaq	apummaʀ
apummak	apummaʀ
apun	apun (under apə-)
apuq-	apuʀ-
aqak-	aqaɣ-
aqargiq	aqəðɣiʀ
aqaya	aqayaɣ
aqi-	aqə-
aqiaġuq	aq(ə)yaquʀ (under aq(ə)yaʀ)
aqiaq	aq(ə)yaʀ
aqiḷġuq	aqilʀuʀ (under aqit-)
aqiḷḷuk	aqilluk (under aqit-)
aqit-	aqit-
aqiya	aqayaɣ
aqła	aqla-
aqpat-	aqva-
aqpigi-	aqpik-
aqpik	aqəvðiɣ
aqqaluk	anqaluk
aqsaaq-	aqcaaq- (under ᴀʀᴄᴀʀ-)
aqsak-	ᴀʀᴄᴀʀ-
aqsraaq	aqšaq (under aqə-)
aqtuq-	ᴀʀᴛᴜʀ-
aqu	aqu
aqui-	aqu(C)i
aquppi-	aqup(p)i- (under aqumə-, aquvət-)
aqut-	aqut- (under aqu)
aquun	aqu(ʀᴜ)n (under aqu)
aquvit-	aqumə-, aquvət-
araa	að(ð)a(a)
arak-	ažak-

NAI	PROTOFORM
ayalu-	ayalu(ʀ)-
ayapiq-	ayapəʀ- (under ayaɣ-)
ayappak-	ayapəʀ- (under ayaɣ-)
ayaqhaaq	ayaʀaʀaʀ
ayau-	aya(C)u-
ayauppiaq	ayaʀuʀ, aya(ʀu)viʀaʀ (under ayaɣ-)
ayu-	ayu-
ayuġak-	ayuʀiʀ-
ayuġit-	ayuʀiʀ-
ayuġnaq-	ayuʀnaq- (under ayuq-)
ayuktaq-	ayuktaq-
ayuq-	ayuq-
ayuqiqsuq-	ayuquciʀtuʀ- (under ayuqə-)
ayuqiqsuun	ayuquciʀtuʀ- (under ayuqə-)
i<g>i-	iɣə-
iga	əɣa-
iga-	əɣa-
igaaq	əɣa(C)aʀ (under əɣa-)
igalaaq	əɣaləʀ
igaliq	əɣaləʀ
igamaaqłuk	əɣama(C)aʀłuɣ (under əɣa-)
iggan	əɣama(C)aʀłuɣ (under əɣa-)
iggavik	əɣɣaviɣ, əɣaðviɣ (under əɣa-)
iggiaq	iɣɣaʀ(aʀ)
igił̣qhaq	iŋilqaʀ
igit- (render)	əɣə-
igit- (throw away)	əɣət-
iglaq-	əŋlaʀ-
iglau-	əɣləʀ-, əɣiləʀ-
igliġaq	əɣləʀaq
igliq-	əɣləʀ-, əɣiləʀ-
iglu	əŋlu
iglupiaq	əŋlu
igḷiq-	iŋliq-
igḷiq	iŋləʀ
igḷu	iŋlu
igḷuaq-	iŋluaq-
igḷukisaaq-	iŋluk(k)ita(C)aʀ- (under iŋlu)
igḷuktun	iŋluɣtun (under iŋlu)
igḷuktuuq-	iŋluktu(u)q- (under iŋlu)
igniq (rendered oil)	əɣ(ə)nəʀ (under əɣə-)
igniq (fire)	ək(ə)nəʀ (under əkə-[1])
igruk	iɣðuɣ
igruq-	iɣðuʀ-
iguk-	əɣut-
igumit-	əɣumə(t)-, əɣəmə(t)-
igunaq	əɣunaq
igurvik	iɣuʒvik
igutchaq	əɣutcaq, əɣutcak (under əɣut-)
iguvit-	əɣumə(t)-, əɣəmə(t)-
iġġi	iŋʀiʀ
iġi-	əʀi-
iġiala-	əʀiala-
iġiña	əʀina(ʀ)
iġisaq-	əʀitaʀ- (under əʀi-)
iġitchaq-	əʀitaʀ- (under əʀi-)
iġmak-	əqmaɣ-
iġniqsruq-	əʀəni(ʀ)-
iġña	əʀina(ʀ)
iġñaaq	iʀnaaq
iġñi-	iʀni- (under iʀnəʀ)
iġñiaq	iʀni(C)aʀ (under iʀnəʀ)
iġñiksraq	iʀnəkšaq (under iʀnəʀ)
iġñiq	iʀnəʀ
iġri	əʀði
iġrisik	əʀði
ii (exclamation of fear)	i(i)[1]
ii (yes)	i(i)[2]
iigaq-	iɣəɣaʀ-, iɣəɣaɣ-
iigu	uɣɣu-
iigu-	uɣɣu-
iila-	i(C)iʀ-
ikaaq-	əkəʀaʀ-
ikak- (cross water)	əkəʀaʀ-
ikak- (be dirty)	ikaɣ-
ikakłiqi-	ikaɣ-
ikayuq-	ikayuʀ-
iki	əki
iki- (burn)	əkə-[1]
iki- (get out of)	əkə-[2]
ikiaq	əkiðaʀ (under əkiðaʀ-)
ikiaq-	əkiðaʀ-
ikiġaaq	ikiʀ-
ikiġġat	əkəʀaʀ
ikinġu<r>aq	əkənʀuʒaq or ikənʀuʒaq
ikiq	əkəʀ
ikiqtu-	əkəqtu- (under əkəʀ)
ikit- (ignite)	əkət- (under əkə-[1])
ikit- (be few)	ikəɣ(ə)t-
ikivġaq	əkəvʀaq
ikkalġit-	ətɣalʀit- (under ətə-)
ikkalġuq	ətkalʀuq (under ətə-)
ikkat-	ətɣat- (under ətə-)
ikkii	ikki
ikkikkii	ətkəq
ikkiq	ətkəq
ikł̣igi-	əkli-
ikł̣igusuk-	əkli-
ikł̣iġvik	əkləʀviɣ (under əkə-[2])
ikpak	əkpak, ikpak
ikpaksraaġu(n)	ikpaq
ikpaksraaq	ikpaq
ikpaksraq	ikpaq
ikpiaġruk	əkvi(C)aʀ
ikpigi	əlpəkə-
ikpigi-	ikviɣ-
ikpik	əkviɣ
iksiva-	ikšəva- (under iŋət-)
iksuġaq	iktuʀaq (under iŋət-)
iksrik-	ikšək- (under iŋət-)
iksruq-	ək(ə)ðuʀ(aʀ)- (under əkə-[2])

NAI	PROTOFORM
iktaq	əɣtaʀ (under əɣət-)
ikuala-	əkuala- (under əkə-[1])
ikuk-	ikuɣ-
ikuma-	əkuma- (under əkə-[1])
ikusik	ikuyəɣ
ikuun	ikuɣutaʀ, ikuɣun (under ikuɣ-)
ikuvġaq	əkəvʀaq
ilaa	əɫ(ə)ŋa
ilaaq-	əlaɣ-
ilaun	əlaun (under əlaɣ-)
ilġaviich	əlʀaviɣ
ilik-	ələɣ-
ilimi-	əɫmi-
ilivich	əlpət, əɫvət
illi<r>aq	ənli(C)ᴀʀ
illu(u)t-	ətlu(ʀ)(-)
illuk-	əðəɫuɣ- (under əðə)
iluamik	əɫuʀᴀʀ-
iluaq-	əɫuʀᴀʀ-
iluit-]	əɫuʀit- (under əɫuʀᴀʀ-)
iluqa(q)-	əlu(ʀ)-
ilvich	əlpət, əɫvət
iḷa	ila(-)[1]
iḷaanni	ilaŋa(t)ni (under ila(-)[1])
iḷaaq	ila(C)ᴀʀ (under ila(-)[1])
iḷagi-	ilakə- (under ila(-)[1])
iḷaiññaq	ila[2]
iḷaksia-	ilaŋci- (under ila(-)[1])
iḷali-	ilali(C)uʀ- (under ila(-)[1])
iḷaliuq-	ilali(C)uʀ- (under ila(-)[1])
iḷannaq	ilamaaq- (under ila(-)[1])
iḷaŋiq-	ilaŋiʀ- (under ila(-)[1])
iḷaŋŋaq-	ilaŋŋᴀʀ- (under ila(-)[1])
iḷatchiaq-	ilacciʀ-
iḷatchiq-	ilacciʀ-
iḷaviñiq	ilavinəq (under ila(-)[1])
iḷi-	əɫi-
iḷiaġruk	əɫiɣᴀʀ(ᴀʀ)
iḷiappak	əɫiɣᴀʀ(ᴀʀ)
iḷiġa(suk)-	əliʀa-, əliŋʀa-
iḷiġniku	əliʀqə-
iḷiġniq	əliʀqə-
iḷiktiq-	əliktəq-
iḷima(suk)-	əlima-
iḷimagi-	əlima-
iḷimmaq-	əlimmᴀʀ-, əlummᴀʀ-
iḷiqsraq-	iləqšaq-
iḷisaġi-	əlitaqə- (under əlit-)
iḷisaq-	əlicᴀʀ- (under əlit-)
iḷisiiḷak	əliciit-
iḷisiiyaq-	əliciit-
iḷisima-	əlicima- (under əlit-)
iḷit-	əlit-
iḷitchuġi	əliccuqə-, əlityuqə- (under əlit-)
iḷitqun	əlitquciq (under əlit-)
iḷitqusiq	əlitquciq (under əlit-)
iḷḷaatqusiq	illaatquciq
iḷḷagauraq	illa(ɣa)užaq

NAI	PROTOFORM
iḷḷaigutit	il(l)aɣiʀun, il(l)aɣiʀusiʀ (under il(l)aɣ-)
iḷḷak-	il(l)aɣ-
iḷḷivik	əɫ(ɫ)iviɣ (under əɫi-)
iḷḷuq	illuʀ(ᴀʀ)
iḷu	ilu
iḷu-	ilu- (under ilu)
iḷuliaq	ilul(l)iʀᴀʀ (under ilu)
iḷulliq	ilulliʀ, iluqliʀ (under ilu)
iḷumiutaq	ilumiɣ, ilum(m)iʀu (under ilu)
iḷummiq	ilumiɣ, ilum(m)iʀu (under ilu)
iḷumun	ilumun (under ilu)
iḷunŋugi-	ilulŋu- (under ilu)
iḷuŋa-	il(l)uŋa- (under ilu)
iḷupaaq	ilupəʀ(ᴀʀ) (under ilu)
iḷupiġuk	ilupəʀ(ᴀʀ) (under ilu)
iḷuviq	əɫivəʀ (under əɫi-)
iłqhuaġniq	əlquaʀnəq
iłuaġi-	əɫuʀaqə-, əɫuʀakə- (under əɫuʀᴀʀ-)
iłuamik	əɫuʀᴀʀ-
iłuaq-	əɫuʀᴀʀ-
iłuaqsi-	əɫuaqci-
iłuit-	əɫuʀit- (under əɫuʀᴀʀ-)
iłuuqiñiq	iɫuuq
ima	ima(ʀ)
imaaniq	imanəʀ, imanᴀʀ
imaaq-	imaaq- (under ima(ʀ))
imaġiak	imᴀʀyaɣ (under ima(ʀ))
imaġuq-	imᴀʀuq- (under ima(ʀ))
imaniq	imanəʀ, imanᴀʀ
imaŋiq-	əməŋiʀ- (under əmə)
imaq	ima(ʀ)
imaqtiq-	imaqtəq- (under ima(ʀ))
imġun	əm(ə)ʀun, əm(ə)ʀuciq (under əməʀ(-))
imġusiq	əm(ə)ʀun, əm(ə)ʀuciq (under əməʀ(-))
imik- (make sound)	əməɣ-, əmiɣ-
imik- (cave in)	imə-, iməɣ-
iminná	im(m)atna (under imma)
imiq	əməʀ(-)
imiqtaq-	əməʀtᴀʀ- (under əməʀ(-))
imit-	əmət-
imma	imma
immak-	imanəɣ- (under ima(ʀ))
immiaq	əmmiaq (under əməʀ(-))
immiññauraq	immit- (under ima(ʀ))
immiq-	immiʀ- (under ima(ʀ))
immit-	əmmit- (under əməʀ(-))
immuk	əmmuɣ
imnaiq	əpnaʀiʀ (under əpnᴀʀ)
imnaq	əpnᴀʀ
imŋaluk-	əməŋə(ʀ)- (under əməɣ- or əmiɣ-)
imu-	imu-[1]
ina-	əna-
inaŋiq-	ənəŋiʀ- (under ənə)
inat-	əna-

NAI	PROTOFORM
ini	ənə
inillak-	ənəllak (under ənə)
init	ənə
inmi-	əłmi-
inniaq-	inniq-, inniaq- (under ini-)
inuq-	ənuʀ-
inuqtuq-	ənuʀ-
iñaluk	iŋaluk
iñġaq-	inʀaq-
iñġaun	inʀaun (under inʀaq-)
iñġutaq	inʀutaq
iñi-	ini-
iñipkaq	inivkaʀ (under ini-)
iñiq-	inəq-
iñiqtiq-	inəʀ-
iññaq-	iŋŋaʀ-
iññisaq	innitaʀ (under ini-)
iññit-	iŋŋit- (under iŋuɣ)
iñŋik	ikŋik
iñuaq-	inuaq- (under iŋuɣ)
iñugaq	iŋuɣaʀ (under iŋuɣ)
iñugiak-	iŋuɣyaɣ- (under iŋuɣ)
iñuiḷa(a)q	inuilaq (under iŋuɣ)
iñuiññaġutaiḷaq	iŋuɣinnaʀunʀit- (under iŋuɣ)
iñuiññaq	iŋuɣinnaʀ (under iŋuɣ)
iñuk	iŋuɣ
iñuksuk	inukšuk (under iŋuɣ)
iñuksruk	inukšuk (under iŋuɣ)
iñuŋniq-	iŋuɣniʀ- (under iŋuɣ)
iñupiaq	iŋupiɣ or iŋupiɣaʀ (under iŋuɣ)
iñuu-	iŋuɣu- (under iŋuɣ)
iñuusiq	iŋuɣuciʀ (under iŋuɣ)
iŋaluk	iŋaluk
iŋattaq-	iŋat-
iŋi	əŋə
iŋiaq-	iŋyaʀ-
iŋiḷġaan	iŋilʀaan (under iŋilʀa-)
iŋił̣qhaq	iŋilqaʀ
iŋipkaq	inivkaʀ (under ini-)
iŋiq-	iŋəq-
iŋit-	iŋət-
iŋiulik	iŋ(ə)yuləɣ
iŋmiq-	əɣmiʀ-
iŋŋik	ikŋik
iŋulit-	iŋut-[1]
iŋut-	iŋut-[1]
iŋutuq	iŋutuʀ
ipak	əpaɣ
ipi-	əpə-
ipiġaq	əpəqaʀ
ipiġaq- (cast aside)	əpəɣ-, əpəʀ(aʀ)-
ipiġaq- (whip)	əpiqaʀ-
ipiġaq- (wade)	ivəʀ-, ipəʀ-
ipik-	ipəɣ-
ipiksaq-	ipəɣcaʀ- (under ipəɣ-)
ipiq (dirt)	əpəʀ
ipiq (dog chain)	ipiq(-)
ipiqqiq	ipiq(q)iq(-) (under ipiq(-))
ipiutaq	ipiutaq (under ipiq(-))
ipkit-	ipɣit- (under ipəɣ-)
ipnit-	əpnit- (under əpnaʀ)
ippak-	əpəʀ
ippaq-	əppaʀiʀ-
ipqit-	əpʀiʀ-, əpʀit- (under əpəʀ)
iptuġiq-	imtuqaʀ, imtuq(q)iʀ-
ipu	əpu
ipuk-	ipuɣ-
ipummiq	ipummiq-
ipun	ipun
iput-	iput-
iqalugaq	iqałuɣaʀ (under iqałuɣ)
iqaluk	iqałuɣ
iqalukpik	iqaluɣpiɣ (under iqałuɣ)
iqaq-	iqaq-
iqi-	əqə-[1]
iqi(q)	iqə(ʀ)
iqiagi-	əq(ə)yakə- (under əq(ə)ya-)
iqiasuk-	əq(ə)ya-
iqiiq-	əqiiq- (under əq(ə)ya-)
iqirgagiaq	iqəžɣaɣiaq
iqirġaq	iqəžʀaq (under iqə(ʀ))
iqit-	əqət- (under əqə-[1])
iqitquq	iqəlquʀ
iqł̣u	əqlu
iqł̣ak	iqlaɣ, iqyaɣ
iqł̣ak-	iqlaɣ-
iqł̣it	iqliʀ
iqpaq-	iqpaq-
iqpiq-	iqpaq-
iqqaq-	əɣqaʀ- (under əɣət-)
iqquk	iqquʀ, iqquɣ
iqsi-	iqci-
iqsuq-	iʀtuʀ-
iqsraq	iqšaq (under iqə(ʀ))
iqsruk-	əqðuɣ-
iqu-	iqu-
iquq-	iq(q)uq- (under iqquʀ, iqquɣ)
iraġuaq-	əžaʀuq- (under əðə)
iraġuq-	əžaʀuq- (under əðə)
iraqsri-	əðəŋqi-
iraqumak	əžaʀuaq (under əðə)
iratqi-	əðəŋqi-
irgaak	əð(ə)ɣa(ʀ) (under əðə)
iri	əðə
iriŋmigaq-	əðəɣmiɣ- (under əðə)
iriq-	iðəʀ-
irit-	əžət-
irri	itðə
irrit-	əžžit- (under əðə)
irruaq-	əžžuq-, əžžuaq-
iruġi-	əž(ž)uʀə- (under əžžuq-, əžžuaq-)
irukkaqi	əðəvkaʀ-
irupkaq-	əðəvkaʀ-
isa-	ica-
isaa-	itaa- (under itəʀ-)
isaaq-	iɣaɣ-

NAI	PROTOFORM
isagniq	iyaɣnəʀ (under iyaɣ-)
isaguti-	isaɣutə- (under iyaɣ-)
isaġuq	iyaquʀ (under iyaɣ-)
isaqqiḷa-	iyaqqi- (under iyaɣ-)
isavgaq	icavʀaʀ, icavɣaʀ
isi	əciʀ
isigak	itəɣaʀ (under itəɣ)
isiġiak-	əðiʀyaɣ(-) (under əðiʀ)
isik	itəɣ
isik-	əciʀ
isiŋmik-	itəɣmiɣ- (under itəɣ)
isiŋnaq	itəɣnaʀ
isiq	əðiʀ
isiq-	itəʀ-
isiqsaġnaq	itəʀcaʀnəʀ (under itəʀ-)
isivġiq-	iyuvʀiʀ-, iyivʀiʀ-
isivit-	əcivət-
isivruk-	əcəmðuɣ-, əcumðuɣ-
isu	isu(k)
isugluk	isuɣluk (under isu(k))
isuġaq	isuʀaq (under isu(k))
isuit-	əcuʀit- (under əcuʀ-)
isukłiq	isukliq (under isu(k))
isuma-	icuma(-)
isumaalugi-	icumaaluɣə- (under icuma(-))
isumagi-	icumaɣə- (under icuma(-))
isumatu-	icumatu- (under icuma(-))
isuŋŋaq	iyuŋŋaʀ
isuq-	əcuʀ-
isvaq	icivaʀ
it-	ət-
itcha	itcaq^{2}
itchalik	itcaq^{2}
itchat	itcaq^{2}
itchuaq-	itcuaq- (under iyyuʀ-)
itchuq-	iyyuʀ-
iti-	ətə-
itigaq-	ətəɣaq-
itiġiaq	təʀiɣaʀ (under təʀiɣ)
itiġlak	ətəʀlaɣ (under ətəʀ)
itiġuq	ətəquʀ (under ətəʀ)
itiktaq-	ətəɣ(taʀ)-, əciɣ(taʀ)-
itiq	ətəʀ
itiq-	ətəʀ-
itiqquq	iqəlquʀ
itivit-	ətəvə(t)-
itivli-	ətəmli- (under ətəʀ-)
itivliq	ətəvə(t)-
itivyaaq	ətəvyaʀaʀ (under ətəvə(t)-)
itqagi-	ənqa(ʀ)-
itqanaiq-	ənqanaiq- (under ənqa(ʀ)-)
itqaq-	ənqa(ʀ)-
itqauma-	ənqa(ʀu)ma- (under ənqa(ʀ)-)
itqiḷiq	iŋqiliʀ (under iŋqiʀ)
itqiq	iŋqiʀ
itquma-	ətquma- (under ətəʀ-)
itquq-	əlquʀ-
ittuk-	əɣtuɣ(-)
ituk	ituɣ
itummak	ətəmaɣ
iva-	əva-
ivaaq	əva-
ivaġiatchi-	ivaʀiatci- (under ivaʀ-)
ivalu	ivalu
ivaq-	ivaʀ-
ivayaq-	ivayaʀ- (under ivaʀ-)
ivgun	əvɣun (under əvək-)
iviaŋŋiq	əvyaŋ(ŋ)iʀ
ivigaaq	əvəɣ
ivik	əvəɣ
ivik-	əvək-
iviḷuq	uviluʀ
iviq-	ivəq-^{1}
ivisaaq	ivitəʀaʀ
ivḷauq	imla(C)u(ɣ), imla(C)uʀ
ivraġun	əpžaʀun
ivruattuq-	imðuʀ-
ivruq	nəvðuʀ, əvðuʀ
ivruqsi-	nəvðuʀ, əvðuʀ
ivsa(q)	əvtəʀ
ivsuk-	əvcuɣ-
ivsulik-	əvcuɣ-
ivu-	iŋ(ə)yu-
ivugaq	iŋ(ə)yukaʀ
ivuluk-	əvə(ʀ)ləɣ-
ivvaq(tuq)-	uvvaq-
ivyanŋu-	əpyalŋu- (under əpə-)
kaak-	ka(C)əɣ-
kaat-	kaɣa-
kaimit-	kayəmə(t)-
kaivallak-	kažəvallak- (under kaðəvə(t)-)
kaivit-	kaðəvə(t)-
kaivḷuaq-	kaivluaq- (under kayəmə(t)-)
kaivsaaq	kaivca(a)q (under kaðəvə(t)-)
kakak-	kakaɣ-
kaki-	kaki-
kaki<r>aq	kaki(C)aʀ (under kaki-)
kakiḷasak	kakilacak
kakiḷḷaġnaq	kakillaʀnaq (under kaki-)
kakiḷḷauri-	kakilla- (under kaki-)
kalikhaaq-	kaləɣ-^{2}
kakkik	kakkiɣ
kakkin	kakkin (under kaki-)
kakkiviaq	kakkivik (under kakkiɣ)
kakkivik (needle case)	kakiðviɣ (under kaki-)
kakkivik (snot)	kakkivik (under kakkiɣ)
kalikłuk-	kaləɣ-^{2}
kalit-	kaləɣ-^{1}, kalət-
kaliukhaaq-	kaləɣ-^{2}
kalivit-	kaləvə(t)-
kalluk	katluɣ
kaluutaq	kalɣun, kalɣutaq (under kaləɣ-^{1}, kalət-)
kamagi-	kamakə- (under kama-)

NAI	PROTOFORM
kamanaq-	kama-
kamasaaq-	kama-
kamasuk-	kama-
kamik	kaməɣ
kamiḷḷaaq-	kamillaaq- (under kaməɣ)
kamiḷḷaq-	kamillaʀ- (under kaməɣ)
kanagaq	kanaɣ
kanagnaq	kanaknaʀ
kanak	kanaɣ
kanayuq	kanayu(ʀ)
kanġaq-	kanʀaq-
kaniq	kanəʀ
kanivaun	kanivaʀun
kannaak	katna(a)k
kannuyak	kannuyaʀ
kanŋu(suk)-	kayŋu-
kanŋuq-	katŋuʀ-, katuʀ- (under katə-)
kanuŋŋiq	kanuŋŋiq
kaŋiġalluk	kaŋiʀaʀ (under kaŋiʀ)
kaŋiġaq	kaŋiʀaʀ (under kaŋiʀ)
kaŋiḷipqaq	kaŋilliʀ, kaŋiqliʀ (under kaŋiʀ)
kaŋiḷḷiq	kaŋilliʀ, kaŋiqliʀ (under kaŋiʀ)
kaŋiq	kaŋiʀ
kaŋiqłuk	kaŋiʀłuɣ (under kaŋiʀ)
kaŋiqsi-	kaŋiʀci- (under kaŋiʀ)
kaŋivaqtaaq-	kaŋivaʀtə(ʀ)- (under kaŋiʀ)
kaŋŋit-	kaŋŋit- (under kaŋiʀ)
kaŋuq	kaŋuʀ
kapi-	kapə-
kapit-	kapət-, kapəɣ-
kappiagi-	kappəya-
kappiala-	kappiala- (under kappəya-)
kappiasuk-	kappəya-
kappun	kappun (under kapə-)
kapputi-	kapputə-
karruutaq	kað(ð)uɣun, kaðuɣutaʀ (under kaðuɣ-)
karuk-	kaðuɣ-
kasak-	kacaɣ-, katcaɣ-
kasauti	kacaɣ-, katcaɣ-
kasima-	katəma- (under katə-)
kasuk-	katyuɣ-
kasuuti-	katyuɣutə- (under katyuɣ-)
katak	katak (under kataɣ-)
katak-	kataɣ-
katchi	kaŋciʀ
katchuq-	katcuq-
kati-	katə-
katiqsrat	katəqšat (under katə-)
katit-	katət- (under katə-)
kau-	kayu-
kauk	ka(C)uɣ
kauk-	kaðuɣ-
kautaq	kað(ð)uɣun, kaðuɣutaʀ (under kaðuɣ-)
kaviq-	kaviʀ-
kavisiq	kapəciʀ
kavlaq	kavlaɣ
kavraq	kavžaq, kavžəq
kavviaq	kav(v)i(C)aʀ (under kaviʀ-)
kayumik-	kayumək- (under kayu-)
kayuŋŋiq-	kayuŋŋiq- (under kayu-)
kayuqtuq	kayuq-
kayyaaq	katyaɣ (under katə-)
ki<g>u-	ki(C)u-
kiamit-	kayəmə(t)-
kian	kiɣan (kiɣatə)
kiapiġuq	kiapəʀuq (under kiɣan (kiɣatə))
kiasik	kiɣayəɣ
kiavallak-	kažəvallak- (under kaðəvə(t)-)
kiavit-	kaðəvə(t)-
kiavsaaq	kaivca(a)q (under kaðəvə(t)-)
kiggiq	kəɣɣəq (under kəɣə-)
kiggun	ki(C)u-
kiglu	kəɣlu
kigmaq-	kəɣmaʀ- (under kəɣə-)
kigmi<r>aq	kəɣmi(C)- (under kəɣə-)
kigrak-	kəɣðaɣ-
kigun	kəɣun (under kəɣə-)
kii	ki(i), ki(i)ta
kii-	kəɣə-
kiiki	ki(i), ki(i)ta
kiimmi-	kiimmi- (under kəɣə-)
kiiñaġuq	kəɣinaquʀ (under kəɣinaʀ)
kiiñaq	kəɣinaʀ
kiiqsiuq-	kəɣiʀ-
kiisaimma(a)	kiitaimma (under ki(i), ki(i)ta)
kiki-	kəkə-
kiki<r>ak	kəkyaɣ, kəkyaʀ
kikiik-	kikiik-
kikłuq-	kəklu(ɣ)
kiktuġaq-	kəktuʀaq- (under kəkə-)
kiktuġiaq	kəɣtuʀyaʀ
kilak-	kəlaɣ-
kilik-	kələɣ-
kilit-	kələ(t)-
killaq	kəllaq (under kəlaɣ-)
killi(q)	kənlə
killiŋiqsit-	kənləŋiq- (under kənlə)
killuq	kənluʀ
kilu	kəlu
kiluaq-	kəluaq- (under kəluɣ)
kiluvaq-	kəluvaʀ- (under kəlu)
kiḷigaq-	kəliɣaʀ- (under kəliɣ-)
kiḷigvak	kəliɣvaɣ
kiḷik-	kəliɣ-
kiḷiq-	kiliʀ-
kiḷḷiq	killiʀ (under kiliʀ-)

NAI	PROTOFORM
kiḷuk	kəluɣ
kimaktuun	kəmaktuun
kimaliq	kəmaliR
kimmik	kitmiɣ
kimmiŋñaq	kitŋiɣ
kimmitquq	kitmilquR (under kitmiɣ)
kimnaq-	kəmnaq-
kimni-	kəmni-
kinatak-	kənataɣ-
kiniq-	kənəR-
kiniqtat	kənəqtaq
kiña	ki(na)
kiñalluq	kitnəR (under kit-)
kiñi-	kini-
kiñiġvik-	kəniRmiɣ- (under kəniR)
kiñiq-	kinəR-
kiñit-	kənit- (under kəni-)
kiññaq	kinnaq
kiñŋu-	kitŋu-
kiŋatak-	kənataɣ-
kiŋiaq-	kiŋyaR-
kiŋik-	kəŋək-
kiŋŋiq	kəkŋiq (under kəkə-)
kiŋu-	kiŋu-
kiŋuġaq-	kiŋuRaq (under kiŋu-)
kiŋulliq	kiŋul(l)iR (under kiŋu-)
kiŋuniiq	kiŋuppiaq- (under kiŋu-)
kiŋuniq	kiŋunəR (under kiŋu-)
kiŋuvaq-	kiŋuvaR- (under kiŋu-)
kipaaq-	kəpa-
kipi-	kəpə-
kipiġi-	kəpət-[2], kəpəqə-
kipiġniuq-	kəpət-[2], kəpəqə-
kipinŋusuk-	kəpəlŋu- (under kəpət-[2], kəpəqə-)
kipiqsruq-	kəpət-[2], kəpəqə-
kipit-	kəpət-[1]
kipkaq-	kəp(ə)kaR-
kippaq	kəppaR (under kəpə-)
kiput-	kiput-
kirgavik	kəð(ə)kaviɣ
kirrak-	kiðaɣ(-)
kisaq	kicaR (under kit-)
kisi-	kəði-
kisit-	kəcit-
kisu	kitu (under ki(na))
kitik	kətəɣ[1]
kittaq	kələ(t)-
kittiq-	kələ(t)-
kiuġuya	ki(C)uRyaR
kiuma-	ki(C)umɣa-, ki(C)umRa- (under ki(C)u-)
kiumŋa-	ki(C)umɣa-, ki(C)umRa- (under ki(C)u-)
kivaknaq	kivaknaR
kivan	kivan (kivatə)
kivat(i)	kivan (kivatə)
kivgaluk	kəvɣaluɣ (under kəvɣaR)
kivgaq	kəvɣaR
kivi-	kivə-
kivik-	kəvəɣ-
kiviq-	kəviR-
kivliq-	kəpliR- (under kəpə-)
kivluq-	kəpluR- (under kəpə-)
kivraq-	kəpðaR- (under kəpə-)
kivvak-	kəvvak- (under kəvəɣ-)
kivviaq-	kəviR-
ku<r>uk	kuðəɣ
kuiŋiq	kuiŋiq
kukik	kukiɣ
kuksrasuk-	kukðaɣ-
kukuk-	kukəɣ-, kukuɣ-
kukurvak	kukəɣ
kulavak	kulavak
kumak	kumaɣ
kumik-	kuməɣ-
kumŋun	kumɣun (under kuməɣ-)
kunik-	kunik-
kupkanaq-	kupkanaq-
kupki	kumkaR
kupkiḷi-	kumka(C)ili- (under kumkaR)
kurgich	kuðəɣ
kurraŋa-	kutžaŋa- (under kutžaq-)
kurraq-	kutžaq-
kurri-	kuðəɣ
kurriñiq	kužžinəq (under kuðəɣ)
kurruk-	kutðuɣ-
kusiq-	kuciR- (under kutə)
kusulugaq	kucukaR
kutak-	kutak-
kutchuq	kuccuR
kutit-	kutə
kuugich	kuðəɣ
kuuġuq	quðuquR (under quðu-)
kuukukiaq	kukuku(C)aR
kuutchiñaaq	kuðuccinəR (under kuðucciR)
kuutchiq	kuðucciR
kuvi-	kuvə-
kuvlu	kumlu
kuvraq	kuvðaR
kuvsit-	kupci-
kuyaich	kuyaɣ
kuyak-	kuyaɣ-
kuyapigaq	kuyapəɣaR (under kuyaɣ)
livilivilaaluk	ləvələvələRaR
ma<g>u-	maRu-[1]
maanna	maðətən
maaq-	maaq-
magu-	maRu-[2] or maɣu-
maġġaq	maRRaR
maġlak-	maRlaɣ-
maġluk	maRRaR
maki-	makə-, makuɣ-
makit-	makət-
makita-	makəta- (under makət-)
makkaq	makkaR
makpiq-	makpiq-
maksaq-	makcaq-

NAI	PROTOFORM
maksrik-	makšək- (under makət-)
maktaaq	maŋtaaq (under maŋtaɣ)
maktak	maŋtaɣ
malġi (loon)	maləʀi(q)
malġi (twin)	malʀi (under malʀuɣ)
malġuit	malʀu(C)it (under malʀuɣ)
malġuk	malʀuɣ
maliġi-	maliʀqə- (under maliɣ-)
malik	malək
malik-	maliɣ-
malikataq-	malikataq- (under maliɣ-)
maliktuq-	manəɣ-, maŋə-
maliqsruq-	maliqðuʀ- (under maliɣ-)
malliq-	malliq- (under malək)
malukali-	malukali- (under maluɣə-)
maluknai-	maluɣə-
maluŋnaq-	maluɣə-
mamaġi-	mamaʀə- (under mamaʀ(-))
mamait-	mamait- (under mamaʀ(-))
mamaq-	mamaʀ(-)
mamiagi-	mam(ə)ya-
mamiasaaq-	mam(ə)ya-
mamilik	mamələɣ (under mamə)
mamiq	mamə
mamit-	mamət- (under mamə-)
manaq	manaʀ
mani-	mani-
maniiḷaq	maniilaq (under maniɣ-)
manik- (sob)	manəɣ-, maŋə-
manik- (be smooth)	maniɣ-
maniktuq-	manəɣ-, maŋə-
maniq	manəʀ
mannik	manniɣ
manŋaiqsruq-	matŋa-
manŋait-	manŋəq-
manŋatchai-	matŋa-
manŋiaq	matŋiaq
manŋiqtuqqiq	manŋəq-
manŋuk-	manŋuk-
manu	manu
manuġmik-	manuʀmik- (under manu)
manuġun	manuŋilitaʀ (under manu)
manuiḷisaq	manuŋilitaʀ (under manu)
maŋiaq-	maŋiʀ-
maŋik-	maŋiʀ-
maŋŋuq	maŋŋuq (under maŋut-, maŋuk-)
maŋuk-	maŋut-, maŋuk-
mapkuq-	mapkuq-
mapsa	mamca(ʀ)
mapsaq-	mamca(ʀ)
maptu-	mamtu- (under mamə)
maqait-	maqait-
maqi-	maqə-
maqik-	maqəɣ-
maqu-	maqu-
maqut-	maqu-
masaġni-	macaʀ
masak	macak, maccak
masik	maciɣ
masu	macuk
matchak	macak, maccak
matchaktiq-	matcaktəq- (under macak, maccak)
matiqti	matəqtə
mattaq-	mattaʀ-
matu	matu(-)
maunna	maŋuna(ɣ)
maunni	maŋuna(ɣ)
mauq-	maʀut-, muʀut-
maut-	maʀut-, muʀut-
mauyaq	maʀuya(ʀ) (under maʀu-[1])
mavsiq-	mapciq- (under mamə-)
mayuġautat	mayuʀaʀun (under mayuʀ-)
mayuq-	mayuʀ-
miġayauraq	mi(i)ʀayuq
miġiaq-	miʀyaʀ(-)
miġvigi-	məʀvi(k)-
miki-	mikə-, mikət-
mikigaq	məkəɣaq
mikik-	mək(k)əɣ-
mikkik-	mək(k)əɣ-
mikłi-	mikəli- (under mikə-, mikət-)
mikłiaq	məkliaq
miksraut-	mikšə-
milik	mələɣ(-)
millik	mətləɣ
millit-	məlak
milugiaq	məluɣɣaʀ (under məluɣ-)
miluk	məluɣ-
miḷḷuuq-	milluuq- (under miluʀ-)
miḷuġiaq-	miluʀiaq- (under miluʀ-)
miḷuq-	miluʀ-
mimiq	miməʀ
minġuq-	məʀnuʀ-
minġuqtuq-	məʀnuʀ-
minit-	mənət-
minŋiq-	mətŋəʀ-
minŋuq	məlŋuʀ
miñaq-	minaʀ-
miñik	minəɣ[2]
miñŋuq	məlŋuʀ
miŋuaqtuġvik	miŋuɣ-
miŋuk-	miŋuɣ-
miŋuliq-	miŋuləq- (under miŋuɣ-)
mipku	nəvku
mipquq	mipquq
miqłiqtuq	mikəliʀaq (under mikə-, mikət-)
miquq-	miŋqə-
misak (slush)	macak, maccak
misak (swamp)	məcaɣ
misaktiq-	matcaktəq- (under macak, maccak)
misamatit-	məcaʀ-

NAI	PROTOFORM
misaq-	məcaR-
misigaq-	məcəɣ-
misigi-	məciɣ-
misiġaaq	məciRaR (under məcu(ɣ), məcuR)
misik-	məcəɣ-
misiksri-	məciɣ-
misiksruq-	məcikšuq- (under məciɣ-)
misuk-	məcu(ɣ), məcuR
misuq	məcu(ɣ), məcuR
mit-	mit-
mitaaq-	mətaɣ-
mitchak-	məcaɣ
mitigligaun	mətəŋłə(R)-
mitiq	mətəR
mitqun	miŋqun (under miŋqə-)
mitquq	məlquR
mitqutaiḷaq	əmətqutailaq (under əmətqutaq)
muayuk-	maRuyuɣ-, muRuyuɣ-
muġiaq-	miRyaR(-)
muġruk-	muRðuɣ-
mulu	mulə(ɣ)
mulu-	mulu-
mumik-	mumiɣ-
mumiq	miməR
munaġi-	munaR-
muqpaaq	muqpaq
na-	na-[2]
na<g>u-	naɣu-
na<ġ>i-	naRə-
na<r>aq	na(ž)aq
naagga	na-[1], na(a)ɣɣa
naaġaayiq	na(a)Ra(a)yiq
naakka	na-[1], na(a)ɣɣa
naakłi(t)-	naɣəkli(R)- (under naɣət-)
naalak-	naɣa(t)-
naalgiuq-	naalɣiuq-, naalɣiuk-
naalunŋiaġiik	naalu(n)ŋiaq
naama-	naðama-
naamagi-	naammaɣə- (under naða-ə
naammak-	naðama-
naanŋiq-	naatŋiq-
naaptiq-	na(C)əvə(t)-
naat- (snag)	naɣət-
naat- (finish)	naðat- (under naðama-)
naavit-	na(C)əvə(t)-
nagguvik	naɣu-
nagligi-	naŋłəɣ-
nagruk	naɣžuk
naġġu-	naRRu-
naġġugi-	naRRu-
naġi<r>aq	naR(ə)yaR (under naRə-)
naġiaq-	naR(ə)yaR (under naRə-)
naiññiq-	nayaŋaR-
naipiqtuq-	nay(ə)pəRtuR- (under nay(ə)pət-)
naipit-	nay(ə)pət-
naiq-	nayaŋaR-
nait-	nanit-
naka(a)q	nakaR
nakasugnaq	nakacuɣnaR (under nakacuɣ)
nakasuk	nakacuɣ
nakataq	nakataq
nakaun	nakaR
nakautaq	nakaR
naki-	naki-
nakiñ	na-[2]
nakiq-	nakəR-
nakkaq-	nakkaR-
nakkutigi-	nakkutə- (under naku(R)-)
naksiġaq	nakciRaq
naksima-	naɣci(t)- (under naɣət-)
naktuġiq	naɣtuqaR (under naɣət-)
naku-	naku(R)-
naku<r>aq	naku(a)q(-)
nakuaġi-	naku(a)Rə- (under naku(a)q(-))
nakuu-	naku(a)q(-)
nala-	nala-
nalauti-	nałaRutə- (under nałə-)
nalġuq-	nałRu- (under nałə-)
nali-	nałə-
nalikkaak	nałəkkaɣ
nalimmak-	naləmmak- (under nałə-)
nallaq-	nallaq- (under nala)
nalli(q)	nalliR (under na-[2])
nalliġiik	nalləɣiik, nalləRiik (under nałə-)
nalliq-	nałłiR- (under nałə-)
nalu-	nału-
nalu<r>aq	nalu(C)aR
naluk-	nalluɣ-, naluɣ-
nalunaiḷutaq	nałunaRilkutaR (under nału-)
nalunaiq-	nałunaRiR- (under nału-)
nalunaq-	nałunaR- (under nału-)
nanġaq-	nanRaR-
naniġi<r>aq	nanəRyaR (under nanəR-)
naniq	naniR
naniq-	nanəR-
nanmak-	natmaɣ-
nanmiñiq	nałmi(nəR)
nanuġaq	nanuRaq (under nanuR)
nanuk-	nanuk-
nanuq	nanuR
naŋaq-	naŋaR-[1]
naŋiaq-	naŋyaR-
naŋiit-	naŋyaRit- (under naŋyaR-)
naŋiq	naŋiR
naŋit-	naŋət- (under naŋə-)
naŋniq-	naŋnəR-
napa-	napa-
napaaqtuq	napa(R)aqtuR (under napa-)
napaġiaq	napaRyaR (under napa-)
naparaġaaq-	napažaq-
naparaq-	napažaq-

NAI	PROTOFORM
naparuq	napaðuʀ (under napa-)
napi-	napə-
napit-	napəʀ-, napət-
napmun	na-[2]
nappaġutaq	nappaqutaʀ, nappaʀutaʀ (under napa-)
nappaq-	nappaʀ- (under napa-)
nappaq	nappaq (under napə-)
nappaqtaq	nappaʀtaʀ (under napa-)
napu	napu
naqikłi-	naqəkli- (under naqət-)
naqit-	naqət-
naqitak-	naqətaʀ- (under naqət-)
naqsiaq	naqciaq (under naʀciɣ-)
naqsik-	naʀciɣ-
naqsraq	naqðaʀ
narraak	na(ž)aq
narrak-	nažžak- (under na(ž)aq)
narvaq	nanvaʀ
nasaq	nacaʀ
nasit-	nacit-
nataaġnaq	natəʀ(aʀ)naʀ (under natəʀ)
nataaq	natəʀaʀ (under natəʀ)
natatquaq	natanquaq (under natanquʀ, nataŋquʀ)
natatquġnaq	natanquʀnaq (under natanquʀ, nataŋquʀ)
natatquq	natanquʀ, nataŋquʀ
natchiaġruk	nayyiʀaʀ (under nayyiʀ)
natchik-	nacciɣ-
natchiq	nayyiʀ
natchisit	naccin (under natəʀ)
natiġnaq	natəʀnaʀ (under natəʀ)
natiġvik-	natəquviɣ- (under natəʀ)
natiq	natəʀ
natqik-	nalqiɣ- (under nałə-)
natqiksruq-	nalqiɣ- (under nałə-)
natquq	naŋquʀ
nauġala-	nauʀala-
nauġallak-	nauʀala-
naulaq	naulaq (under naʀułəɣ-)
naulayuq	naula(yu)q
naulguti-	naʀułɣutə-
nauligaq	naʀułəkaʀ (under naʀułəɣ-)
naulik-	naʀułəɣ-
naullaġnaq	naul(l)aʀnaq (under naula(yu)q)
naullaq	naʀułəɣ-
naumi	na(C)umi (under na-[2])
nauŋ	naɣu and na(C)uŋ (under na-[2])
nausaaq	naucaaq
nautchi<r>aq	naɣucciʀaʀ
nauyaq	naʀuyaʀ
nauyavak	naʀuyavaɣ (under naʀuyaʀ)
navguq-	navɣuʀ- (under navəɣ-)
naviagi-	navia(ɣə)-
navianaq-	navia(ɣə)-
navik-	navəɣ-
navlu	naplu
navraaq	nažvaq-
nayak	nayaɣ
nayaksaq-	nayaŋaʀ-
nayaŋaq-	nayaŋaʀ-
nayuk-	nayuɣ-
nayummi-	nayummi- (under nayuʀ-)
nayuq-	nayuʀ-
niaquġun	nay(ə)quʀun (under nay(ə)quʀ)
niaqunŋu-	nay(ə)qulŋu- (under nay(ə)quʀ)
niaquq	nay(ə)quʀ
nigaq	nəɣaʀ
niggiq-	nəɣaʀ
nigguun	niɣəðuʀun (under niɣəðuʀ-)
nigiq	nəɣəʀ
niglaq-	nəŋłaʀ- (under nəŋə(t)-, nəŋłi-)
nigli-	nəŋə(t)-, nəŋłi-
nigliñaq-	nəŋłinaʀ- (under nəŋə(t)-, nəŋłi-)
nigrat	nəɣžak
nigruaġruk	nəŋðuʀ
niguq-	nəɣuʀ-
niguuti-	nəɣuʀ-
niguyaq	nəɣuyaʀ
nigvik	nəɣvik
niġġivik	nəʀəðviɣ (under nəʀə-)
niġi-	nəʀə-
niġiḷik-	nəʀiləɣ-
niġipkaq-	nəʀəvkaʀ- (under nəʀə-)
niġiugi-	nəʀyu(ɣ)-
niġiuk-	nəʀyu(ɣ)-
niġiuqsruq-	nəʀiuqšuq- (under nəʀyu(ɣ)-)
niġliq	nəʀləʀ, nəqləʀ
niġluq-	nəʀluq-
niġrun	nəʀžun
niġukit-	nəqu-
niġukkaq	nəʀupkaq
niġumik-	nəʀuvəʀ-, nəʀuvaʀ-
niġummaak-	nəʀuvəʀ-, nəʀuvaʀ-
niġutu-	nəqu-
nika-	nəka-
nikait-	nəkait- (under nəka-)
nikasuk-	nəka-
nikit-	nikət-
nikpaq-	nəkvaʀ- (under nəkəvə(t)-)
niksaak-	nəlcaʀ-
niksaaktuŋiq	nəkcaaktuq
niksik	nəɣciɣ
nikuvġautaq	nəkəvʀa-, nəkəvɣa- (under nəkəvə(t)-)
nikuvit-	nəkəvə(t)-
niliq	nələʀ(-)
nilit-	nələt- (under nələʀ(-))
niḷak	nilaɣ
nima(a)q-	nəmaaq-

NAI	PROTOFORM
puvi<r>aq	puvyaʀ
puviġaq	puvəʀaʀ (under puvə-)
puvit-	puvə-
puvitquq-	pupiŋquʀ-, puviŋquʀ-
puvla(q)	puvlaɣ, puvlaʀ (under puvə-)
puvlak	puvlaɣ, puvlaʀ (under puvə-)
puvlak-	puvlaɣ, puvlaʀ (under puvə-)
puvlaq-	puvlaʀ-
puvliq-	puvliq- (under puvə-)
puvruk	puvlaɣ, puvlaʀ (under puvə-)
puya	puya
puyuala-	puyuʀaq, puyuʀak (under puyuʀ)
puyuq	puyuʀ
puyyuk-	pumyuɣ-
qa<g>u-	qaʀu-
qa<ġ>i-	qaʀə-
qaa-	qaðə-
qaaġiaq	qa(C)aʀyaʀ
qaaktuq-	qaðəɣ-
qaaliŋa-	qaʀaləʀ-
qaaliqta-	qaʀaləʀ-
qaanaaq	qaanaaq
qaaniq	qaanəq
qaaŋiq-	qaaŋiq- (under qaðə-)
qaaŋiuti-	qaaŋiq- (under qaðə-)
qaaptit-	qaaptət-
qaaq	qaaq (under qaðə-)
qaaq-	qaɣəʀ-
qaaqsruq-	qaaqšuq- (under qaɣəʀ-)
qaaqtuq-	qaaqtuq-
qaatiq	qaatəq
qaggaq	qaɣə(ʀ)
qaglu	qaŋłu(ʀ)
qagrun	qaðəɣ-
qagvaq-	qaɣvaʀ-, qakvaʀ-
qaġa-	qaʀa-
qaġasaq	qaqətaʀ, qaqitaʀ
qaġġiiñ	qaʀə-
qaġġirri-	qaʀə-
qaġiaq	qaʀiaq
qaġliik	qaʀ(u)łiɣ
qaġmaqtuuq	qaʀmaʀ
qaġruq	qaʀðuʀ
qaġruqsaq	qaʀžuqcaq (under qaʀðuʀ)
qaiġuaq-	qaiʀuaq-
qaiġulik	qa(C)əʀuləɣ (under qa(C)əʀu(ʀ))
qaiġuq	qa(C)əʀu(ʀ)
qail̡liq	qaɣəliʀ- (under qaɣə(ʀ))
qaimġu	qaɣəmɣu(ʀ)
qaimŋuq	qaɣəmɣu(ʀ)
qaiŋŋiq	qaɣiŋŋiʀ
qaiq-	qaiq-
qait-	qaʀit- (under qaʀə-)
qaki-	qakə-
qakiġluk	qakəʀ(luɣ)
qakiġnit-	qakəʀ-
qakiq-	qakəʀ(luɣ)
qakiqsi-	qakəʀci-
qakit-	qakət- (under qakə-)
qakitpik	qakə-
qakkit-	qakkit- (under qakəʀ(luɣ))
qakkutigun	qakutiɣun (under qaku)
qakpik	qakə-
qaksri	qakši- (under qakə-)
qaksrugautaq	qakšuɣaun (under qakə-)
qaksrun	qakšuɣaun (under qakə-)
qaksruq-	qakə-
qakuak	qakuʀ-
qakugu	qaku
qakuq-	qakuʀ-
qalasiq	qałaciʀ
qalat-	qała-[1]
qalġuq-	qaləʀ-
qaliġuaq	qaliʀuðaʀ (under qaðə-)
qaliŋu-	qaləŋu- (under qaləʀ-)
qaliq (roof covering)	qaliʀ (under qaðə-)
qaliq (mold)	qałəʀ
qalli	qaðliʀ, qalliʀ (under qaðə-)
qalli-	qanli- (under qanət-)
qalliq-	qaðəliʀ- (under qaðə-)
qalliq	qaðliʀ, qalliʀ (under qaðə-)
qallun	qallun (under qalu(-))
qalluviaq	qatliviɣ(aʀ), qatlipiɣ(aʀ) (under qatlin)
qalu	qalu(-)
qalugiaq	qaluɣyaʀ
qalutaq-	qalutaʀ(-) (under qalu(-))
qamanaaq	qamanəʀ (under qama-)
qamaniq	qamanəʀ (under qama-)
qami-	qamə-
qamit-	qamət- (under qamə-)
qamŋaq	qaməŋaʀ
qamŋui-	qamʀui-, qamŋui-
qamuk-	qamuʀ-
qamutik	qamutək (under qamuʀ-)
qanaaq-	qanəʀ(-)
qanak	qanaɣ
qani- (near)	qanət-
qani- (accompany)	qani-
qanil̡aaq-	qanilaaq- (under qani-)
qaniq	qanəʀ(-)
qanit-	qanət-
qanitchaq	qanit(t)aʀ (under qani-)
qanitchat	qanit(t)aʀ (under qani-)
qannik	qaniɣ
qannik-	qanniʀ- (under qaniɣ)
qanŋuq-	qatŋuʀ-
qanuq	qanuq
qanuqtuq	qanuqtuq (under qanuq)
qanutun	qanuq
qaŋa	qaŋa
qaŋata-	qaŋata-
qaŋattaaq	qaŋattaq- (under qaŋata-)

NAI	PROTOFORM
qapak	qapak-
qapaŋa-	qapak-
qapiq-	qapəq-
qaptiq-	qaptəq- (under qamə-)
qapuk	qapuɣ
qaqasaq	qaqətaʀ, qaqitaʀ
qaqiqsi-	qakəʀci-
qaqisaq	qaqətaʀ, qaqitaʀ
qaqłuk	qaqluɣ
qaqłutuuq	qaqlutuuq
qaqquq-	qaŋquʀ-
qaqsrauq	qaqðaʀ, qaqða(C)uʀ
qaqsuq-	qakcuʀ- (under qakə(ʀ)-)
qaqu-	qaqu(ʀ)
qaqutuq-	qaqu(ʀ)
qargi	qaðɣi
qargisaq	qažɣitaq
qarġut(i)-	qaðə(t)ʀutə- (under qaðə-)
qarraaq	qaaq (under qaðə-)
qarvak-	qapðaɣ-
qasak-	qac(c)aɣ-
qasala-	qac(c)aɣ-
qasalluq	qacal(l)uq
qasaq-	qacaʀ-
qasigiaq	qaðiɣyaʀ
qasiḷi-	qacəli-
qasiŋŋuq-	qaciŋŋuq-
qasu-	qacu-
qasuq-	qatcuq- (under qacu-)
qataŋŋun	qatəŋŋun
qatchak-	qac(c)aɣ-
qatchaq-	qac(c)aɣ-
qatchik-	qatcik- (under qaðə-)
qatigaak	qatəɣ
qatigak	qatəɣ
qatik	qatəɣ
qatikit-	qatəkit- (under qatə)
qatikkak	qatəɣ
qatiq-	qatəʀ-
qatitu-	qatə
qatqit-	qaðqaʀ (under qaðə-)
qattaq	qaltaʀ
qaugak	qavəɣaɣ
qauġutik	qauʀun (under qaɣuʀ)
qaulluq	qaulluq- (under qaʀu-)
qaumaniq	qauma- (under qaʀu-)
qaummak-	qauma- (under qaʀu-)
qaumman	qaumman (under qaʀu-)
qaummaq	qauma- (under qaʀu-)
qaunagi-	qa(C)unaɣ-
qaunagnaq-	qa(C)unaɣ-
qauniq	qaʀu-
qaunnaq	qaunnaq
qauq	qaɣuʀ
qauq-	qa(C)uʀ-
qauri-	qa(C)u(ði)-
qavaasuk	qavəɣaɣ
qavaq-	qavaʀ-
qavia	qavəɣaʀ
qavlu	qavlu(ʀ)
qavluna(a)q	qavlu(ʀ)
qavrak-	qapðaɣ-
qavsich	qavcit
qavsuk-	qamcuɣ- (under qamə-)
qavvik	qatviɣ, qavciɣ
qayagnaq-	qayak(naq)-
qayaq	qayaʀ
qayaqtuq-	qayaʀtuʀ- (under qayaʀ)
qayau-	qayau- (under qayaʀ)
qayuq	qayuʀ
qayuuttaq	qayuʀutaʀ (under qayuʀ)
qayyat	qayaʀ
qayyi-	qayaʀ
qi<g>u-	qiʀu-
qi<r>a-	qiða-
qia(q)	qi(C)aʀ
qianġaq	qianʀaqtuq
qigḷuk-	qiɣluk-
qiġata-	qiʀa(ta)- (under qiʀə-, qiqə-)
qiġġaq-	qiʀa(ta)- (under qiʀə-, qiqə-)
qiġiiluk- (be frozen)	qiʀə-, qiqə-
qiġiiluk- (creak)	qikə-[2], qikaaq-
qiġlutaq	qəʀlərun (under qəʀləʀ-)
qiġñiq-	qiʀnəʀ-
qiġñiqtaq	qiʀnəʀ-
qiġuviak	qiʀu-
qiiligruk-	qi(C)əliʀ- (under qi(C)ət-, qit-)
qiiłłuaq	qiiqluq-, qiilluq-
qiiŋa-	qiiŋa- (under qi(C)ət-, qit-)
qiiqsruq-	qiiqšuq- (under qi(C)ət-, qit-)
qiiya-	qiʀuya- (under qiʀu-)
qiiyanaq-	qiʀuya- (under qiʀu-)
qikaallit-	qikə-[2], qikaaq-
qikaaluk-	qikaʀ-
qikaq-	qikaʀ-
qiki-	qikə-[1]
qikiġġaq	qikə-[2], qikaaq-
qikiqtaq	qikəʀtaʀ
qiksigi-	qikciɣ- (under qikə-[1])
qiku	qiku
qil(i)ġuq	qələʀuq (under qələɣ-, qəluɣ-)
qila	qəla-[2]
qilagluk-	qilaɣłuɣ (under qilaɣ)
qilamik	qəla-[1]
qilanaaq-	qəlanəʀ(aʀ)-
qillan	qəla-[2]
qilu-	qəlu-
qiluk-	qələɣ-, qəluɣ-
qiluqqit-	qəluqqit- (under qəlu-)
qiluuq-	qəlu-
qiḷa	qəla-[2]
qiḷaaq	qilaɣaʀ (under qilaɣ)
qiḷagaq	qilaɣaʀ (under qilaɣ)
qiḷak	qilaɣ
qiḷak-	qilaɣ-
qiḷalugaq	qilaluɣaq

NAI	PROTOFORM
qiḷalugaq tuugaalik	tuɣəkaʀaləɣ (under tuɣəʀ(-))
qiḷalukkat	qilaluɣaq
qiḷamit(aq)-	qilamət-, qilavət-
qiḷamitaun	qilamət-, qilavət-
qiḷaŋmiutaq	qilaɣmi(C)utaʀ (under qilaɣ)
qiḷaŋŋaq	qilaŋŋaʀ
qiḷaun	qəlaun (under qəla-[2])
qilġiq	qilʀi(q)
qiḷiġniq	qiłəʀnəʀ (under qiłəʀ-)
qiḷiġutaiq-	qiłəʀutaʀiʀ- (under qiłəʀ-)
qiḷiġutik	qiłəʀutaʀiʀ- (under qiłəʀ-)
qiḷiq-	qiłəʀ-
qiḷiqsruq-	qiłəʀ-
qiḷḷi-	qinluq
qiḷuk-	qiluɣ-
qimak-	qimaɣ-
qimatchi-	qəmaɣ-
qimiġaq	qəmiʀ[1]
qimiġiaq	qəməʀyaʀ
qimiġḷuk	qəmiʀłuɣ, qəmiʀluʀ (under qəmiʀ[1])
qimilġu-	qəməlʀu-
qimiq	qəmiʀ[2]
qimit-	qəmit-
qimmiq	qikmiʀ
qimmiuraq	qikmi(C)uðaʀ (under qikmiʀ)
qimmuktit-	qimmuk-
qimuaġruk	qəmiaʀžuk (under qəmiʀ[1])
qimuk-	qimuɣ-
qimukti	qimuɣtə (under qimuɣ-)
qiniq-	qənəʀ-
qiniqsiq	qənəʀciʀ
qinnak-	qənəʀ-
qinŋuq	qənŋu(ʀ)
qinu	qənu
qiñaa-	qinaa- (under qinəʀ-)
qiñiġaun	qinəʀ-
qiñiq-	qinəʀ-
qiññaq	qinəʀ-
qiñŋuq	qitŋu(ʀ)
qiñu-	qinu-
qiñuit-	qinuŋit- (under qinu-)
qiŋaġaq	qəŋaʀaʀ (under qəŋaʀ)
qiŋalik	qəŋaləɣ (under qəŋaʀ)
qiŋałłuak-	qiŋŋaʀ-
qiŋaq	qəŋaʀ
qiŋniq	qəŋnəʀ
qiŋŋaq-	qitŋiʀ-, qitŋaʀ-, qitŋuʀ-
qipaluaq	qipaluaq
qipi-	qipə-
qipit-	qipə-
qipitaq	qəpə-
qipuak-	qipuk-
qiputaq	qiputaʀ (under qipə-)
qiqi-	qiʀə-, qiqə-
qiqitiq-	qiʀətəq-, qiqətəq- (under qiʀə-, qiqə-)
qirgiq-	qəžɣəq- (under qətəɣ-, qətɣəʀ-)
qirġi	qiðəʀ
qirġiq	qiðəʀ
qirran	qiða-
qirrat	qi(C)aʀ
qirriuq-	qəððì(C)uʀ- (under qəðuɣ)
qiruk	qəðuɣ
qiruktaq-	qəðuɣtaʀ- (under qəðuɣ)
qisaġuaq	qəcaʀu(C)aʀ
qisik	qəciɣ
qisiqsiun	qəciqciun
qisuk	qiyu(ɣ)(-)
qisuk-	qəc(c)uɣ-
qitchuk-	qəc(c)uɣ-
qitiġaq	qətəʀaʀ (under qətəʀ)
qitik-	qətəɣ-, qətɣəʀ-
qitiq	qətəʀ
qitiqł̣iq	qətəqliq (under qətəʀ)
qitiqpaq-	qətəqpaq- (under qətəʀ)
qitiqqaq-	qətəqquq-, qətəqqaq- (under qətəʀ)
qitugli-	qətut-
qituŋġaq	qətunʀaʀ
qitusuk-	qətusuk-
qitusuŋnaq-	qətusuk-
qitut-	qətut-
qiunŋu-	qiʀu-
qiuq-	qiɣuʀ-
qivi-	qivə(ʀ)-
qiviaq-	qiviaq- (under qivə(ʀ)-)
qiviq-	qivə(ʀ)-
qivit-	qəvə(t)-
qiviu	qivyu(ʀ)
qivlaaq-	qəvləʀ-
qivliqiak	qəvləqiak (under qəvləʀ-)
qivliqtaq-	qəvləʀ-
qivraq	qipðaʀ (under qipə-)
qivri- (go off)	qəvə(t)-
qivri- (make thread)	qipði- (under qipə-)
qivsak-	qəvcaɣ-
qivsi-	qipci-
qu<ġ>i-	quʀə-
qu<r>aq	qu(C)aʀ
quagruk	qu(C)aɣðuɣ
quagrulik	qu(C)aɣðuləɣ (under qu(C)aɣðuɣ)
quaġaq	quaʀaq
quaqsaaq-	quaqcaaq-
quaqta	quɣaʀta(ʀ)
quasa	quacak (under quʀa(yaqit)-)
quasiḷaq	quacak (under quʀa(yaqit)-)
quasiraaq-	quacak (under quʀa(yaqit)-)
quayaqit-	quʀa(yaqit)-
qugluk- (fold)	quɣluk-
qugluk- (wince)	quŋluɣ-
quġrik	quʀvik (under quʀə-)
qugruk	quɣðuɣ

NAI	PROTOFORM
sana-	cana(R)-
sanagi-	can(n)a(q)-
sanatu-	canatu- (under cana(R)-)
sani-	cani-
saniġaq	caniqaR (under cani-)
sanik	canəɣ
sanivaq-	canivaR- (under cani-)
sanmi-	canmi- (under caðə-)
sanmun	caðə-
sannan	cana(R)-
sannaq	cannaq (under cana(R)-)
sanniġutaq	canniqun, canniRun (under cani-)
sanniq-	canniR (under cani-)
sanniqi-	canəɣ
sanŋiyaq-	canŋiyaq-, canɣiyaq- (under canəɣ)
sanŋu-	canəɣ
saŋiak-	caŋiak-
saŋik-	caŋiɣ-
saŋimmiq-	caŋimmiR-
saŋniq-	caɣnəR-
saŋŋi-	caɣŋi-
saŋŋiqsruq-	caɣŋi-
saŋŋit-	caɣŋi-
sapaŋiak	capaŋaq
sapaŋirraq	capaŋaq
sapi-	capə-
sapiġnaq-	capəRnaR-
sapiq-	capiR- (under capə-)
sapiqsraq-	capiqšaq- (under capə-)
sappit-	capə-
saptaq-	captək- (under cavət-)
sapun	cap(p)un (under capə-)
saqit-	caqə-[1]
saqpik	caqviɣ
saqpik-	caqviR-, caqviɣ- (under caqviɣ)
saqsranikut	caqšanəkut
saqu-	caqu-[1]
saquŋa-	caqu-[1]
sarġut(i)-	cažRutə- (under caðə-)
sarvaq-	cažvaq- (under caðə-)
sarvasik-	cažvasik- (under caðə-)
satchik-	cažvasik- (under caðə-)
satku(q)	caðku
satqak	catqaq
satqummiaq-	catqummiq-
satqummiq-	catqummiq-
sau-	cau-
saulluq	caulluq-
saumik	caRumiɣ
sauniq	caunəq
saunnit-	caunnit- (under caunəq)
savak-	cavaɣ-
saviġuq-	caviRuR- (under caviɣ)
savik	caviɣ
savinnaq-	cavət-
savit-	cavət-
savitu-	cavət-

NAI	PROTOFORM
savri-	capə-
sayait-	caya(ɣ)
sayak	caya(ɣ)
sayuk-	cayuɣ-
sayuq-	cayuR-
si<ġ>i-	ciRi-
siaġaq-	civa-
siak-	ciðaɣ-
sialuk	cilałuɣ (under cila, ciła)
siamġu	ciðamRu (under ciðaɣ-)
siamit-	ciðamə(t)- (under ciðaɣ-)
siggaq-	ciɣɣaq-
siggit-	ciɣi-, ciɣɣi(t)-
sigguk	cuɣðuɣ, ciɣɣuɣ
sigña-	cikna-
sigraaq	ciŋða(C)aR
sigraq	ciŋðaR
siġġaqi-	ciRRa-
siġluaq	ciqluɣaR
siġḷiġnaq-	ciRləR-
siġḷiqi-	ciRləR-
siġñigi-	ciqni-
siġri	təkðə(R)
siġvaq	civuRaR, ciɣuRaR
sii	cii(q)
siiġñaq-	ciiRnaq- (under ciiq-[1])
siik-	ciðəɣ-
siiḷak-	ciiq-[2]
siimik-	ciimik-
siimmak-	ciRi-
siiq-	ciiq-[1]
siiqsinniq	ciiqtənnəq (under ciiq-[1])
siitqiñ(ñ)iq	ciitqinəq (under ciɣəðquR)
siitquaq	ciɣəðqu(C)aR (under ciɣəðquR)
siitquq	ciɣəðquR
siki-	cikə(t)-
sikkik-	citkik-
sikkutaq	cinkutaɣ
sikḷaq	ciklaR
siksraaq	cikðiɣ
siksrik	cikðiɣ
siksrikpak	cikðiɣ
siku	ciku
sikuaq	ciku(C)aR (under ciku)
sikuiġvik	cikuŋiR- (under ciku)
sikulaaq-	cikulaaq (under ciku)
sikuliaq	cikuliaq (under ciku)
sikuq	cikuR
silgatu-	cilatu- (under cila, ciła)
siḷa	cila, ciła
siḷagik-	cilakiɣ- (under cila, ciła)
siḷaiġuti-	cilaŋiRutə- (under cila, ciła)
siḷait-	cilaŋit- (under cila, ciła)
siḷali-	cilali- (under cila, ciła)
siḷalliq	cilalliR, cilaqliR (under cila, ciła)
siḷaluk	cilałuɣ (under cila, ciła)
siḷan	cilan (cilatə) (under cila, ciła)

NAI	PROTOFORM
siḷati	cilan (cilatə) (under cila, ciła)
siḷi-	cili-, ciłi-
siḷiak-	ciliRak-
siḷik-	ciləɣ-[1]
siḷivit-	ciləɣ-[2]
siḷḷiñ	cillin, ciłin (under cili-, ciłi-)
siḷu	cilu
siḷuk-	ciluk-
siḷuli-	ciluli- (under cilu)
siḷut-	ciluli- (under cilu)
simik-	cimək-
simmiq-	cimmiR-
siñaġaq	cinəRaR (under cinə)
siñi	cinə
siñigvik	cinəɣvik (under cinək-)
siñik-	cinək-
siñiqsraq-	ciniR- (under cinə)
siññaġliuq-	cinnaRliuq- (under cinək-)
siññaktuq-	cinnaktuq-, ciŋnaktuq- (under cinək-)
siŋai(yau)-	ciŋai-
siŋiġñiq	ciŋiRnəq (under ciŋiR)
siŋiq	ciŋiR
siŋit-	ciŋə(t)-
siŋuk-	ciŋuk-
siŋulluq-	ciŋulluq- (under ciŋuk-)
sipi-	cipə(ɣ)-
sipiksaa(ġa)q-	capək-, capkut-
sipiksaq-	capək-, capkut-
sipit-	cipə(t)-
sipkiq-	cipkiq- (under cipə(ɣ)-)
sippaq	cippaq (under cipə(t)-)
sippiq-	cipə(t)-
siqi-	ciqəR-, ciq(q)i-
siqiak	ci(i)qiak
siqił̣ł̣ak-	ciqəR-, ciq(q)i-
siqiñiq	ciqinəR
siqiññak-	ciqinnak- (under ciqinəR)
siqpik	ciqviɣ
siqqaq-	ciqqaq- (under ciqəR-, ciq(q)i-)
siqquq-	ciŋquR-
siqu-	cikunRiq-
siqumit-	ciqumə(t)-
siquptiq-	ciquptəq- (under ciqumə(t)-)
siquvsi-	ciqumə(t)-
sirraq (split section)	cižžaq (under ciðəɣ-)
sirraq (den)	citə
sisamat	citamat
sisi	citə
sisi-	citə(ɣ)-
sisu-	citu-
sisu<r>aq	citu(C)aR
sisugiaq-	cittuqit-
sisuġaaq-	citURaR- (under citu-)
sisuqhaaq-	citURaR- (under citu-)
sisuuk	citu-
sitchiq-	citciq-
sitchuq-	cittuR-
sitchuqit-	cittuqit-
sitkutaq	cinkutaɣ
sitquaq	cil(ə)quR, cił(ə)quR
sitqugmik-	ciɣəðqumiɣ- (under ciɣəðquR)
sitquq	cil(ə)quR, cił(ə)quR
siuġaq	ciuRaq
siuġruk-	ciRURðuɣ(-)
siun	ciɣun
siutiġu(q)	ciɣutəquR (under ciɣun)
sivanau-	civanəq
sivaniq-	civanəq
sivaniqtaq-	civanəq
siviiŋa-	civəŋa-
sivikit-	civi
siviksiq-	civi
sivisu-	civi
sivu-	civu-
sivuaq	civu(C)aR (under civu)
sivuġaq	civuqaR (under civu)
sivulik-	civuləɣ- (under civu)
sivulliq	civul(l)iR (under civu)
sivulliuqti	civulliqtə (under civu)
sivuniq	civunəR (under civu)
sivuniqsi-	civunəqci- (under civu)
sivunniq-	civunniR- (under civu)
sivuqłiq	civuqliR (under civu)
sivuuġa(gi)-	civu(C)uRa-
sivviaq	cipyaR
sivvuŋa-	civ(v)uɣ
sivvuq-	civvuR-
suaġruich	cuaRžuk (under cu(na))
suak-	cuɣaɣ-
suaŋa-	cuaŋa- (under cuɣaɣ-)
suġġait-	cuRRait-
suġliq	cuRləq
suġlu	cuRlu
suġluq	cuRlu
suġruk-	cuRðuɣ-
suiḷauri-	cu(na)ŋit- (under cu(na))
suiḷḷi-	cu(na)ŋit- (under cu(na))
suka-	cuk(k)a-
sukait-	cuk(k)aŋit- (under cuk(k)a-)
sukat-	cuk(k)a-
sukkit-	cukkit- (under cuki(R))
sukuiq-	cukuiq-
suli	cu(na)li (under cu(na))
suluk	culuɣ
sulukpaugaq	culuɣpa(C)uɣ (under culuɣ)
suna	cu(na)
sunauvva	cuna-uvva (under cu(na))
suŋaaq-	cuŋaɣ- or cuŋaR- (under cuŋa(R))
suŋaq	cuŋa(R)
suŋauraaqtaaq	cuŋaɣ- or cuŋaR- (under cuŋa(R))
suŋauraq	cuŋa(R)

NAI	PROTOFORM
supi-	cupə-[1]
supik-	cupiɣ-
supput(i)-	cupputə- (under cupə-[1])
suqqaq	cuqqaʀ
suqutau-	cuq(q)utə- (under cu(na))
suqutigi-	cuq(q)utə- (under cu(na))
surruiq-	cuð(ð)u-
suvak	ciɫuvaɣ
suviŋñiq	cuviŋnit-
suviŋñit-	cuviŋnit-
suvlu	cupluɣ, cupluʀ
suvluaq-	cupluaq- (under cupə-[1])
ta<g>i-	ta(ɣ)i-
taaġniq	taʀəʀnəʀ (under taʀəʀ(-))
taaġutaq	taaʀutaq (under taʀəʀ(-))
taak-	taðəɣ-
taaksi-	taðəɣ-
taaktiq-	taaktəq- (under taðəɣ-)
taalutaq	ta(a)lutaq (under talu(-))
taanikit-	taanəq
taaniqtu-	taanəq
taaŋŋaq	taaŋaʀ
taaq	taʀəʀ(-)
taaqsi-	taaqsi- (under taʀəʀ(-))
taaqtipkaq-	taaqtət- (under taʀəʀ(-))
taasiŋiq	təðatəða(C)iʀ, təʀatəʀa(C)iʀ
taatchiŋiq	təðatəða(C)iʀ, təʀatəʀa(C)iʀ
taatchiŋiraq	təðatəða(C)iʀ, təʀatəʀa(C)iʀ
taggiñ	taɣɣin (under ta(ɣ)i-)
taggiqsuaq-	taɣ(ɣ)iq-
tagiq-	taɣ(ɣ)iq-
tagiuq-	taɣi(C)uʀ-
taglu	taŋluʀ
tagraq-	taɣðaʀ(-) (under taɣə-)
taġġaq	taʀʀaq (under taʀəʀ(-))
taġġaqtuq-	taʀʀaqtuq- (under taʀəʀ(-))
taġġaqtuun	taʀʀaqtuq- (under taʀəʀ(-))
taġġit-	taʀʀit- (under taʀəʀ(-))
taġiuq	taʀ(ə)yuʀ
taġiuq-	taʀ(ə)yuʀ
taġutu-	taʀu
taiguaq-	taiɣuq- (under ta(ɣ)i-)
taiguq-	taiɣuq- (under ta(ɣ)i-)
taimailli	taimait- (under taðim(m)a)
taimait-	taimait- (under taðim(m)a)
taimma	taðim(m)a
taimuŋa	taimuŋaaq- (under taðim(m)a)
taimuŋaaq-	taimuŋaaq- (under taðim(m)a)
tainna	taðim(m)a
tainnailli	taimait- (under taðim(m)a)
tainnait-	taimait- (under taðim(m)a)
taiñiq	ta(ɣ)i-
taki-	takə-
takisi-	takəli- (under takə-)
takkiiq	takə-
takku-	takku(ʀ) (under taku-)
takkun	taku-
takɫi-	takəli- (under takə-)
takpiit-	takviŋit- (under takviɣ-)
takpik-	takviɣ-
taksiqsuq-	taɣciʀ- (under taɣə-)
taktuk	taɣətuɣ
taku-	taku-
takunnaq-	takunnaq- (under taku-)
takuri-	taku-
takusi-	taku-
taligvak	taləɣvak
taliġuq	taɫiquʀ (under taɫiʀ)
taliq	taɫiʀ
taliq-	taɫiʀ
taliqpik	taɫiʀpiɣ (under taɫiʀ)
talit-	talit- (under talu(-))
talliaq-	taɫiʀ
tallimat	taɫɫimat
talu-	talu(-)
taluġi-	taɫuʀ-
tamala-	tamala- (under tamaʀ-)
tamaq-	tamaʀ-
tamatkiq-	tamatkiq- (under tamaʀ-)
tammaq-	tammaʀ-
tamuaq	tamuʀaʀ (under tamuʀ-)
tamuluk-	tamuʀ-
tamuq-	tamuʀ-
tanmaq-	taŋmaq-
taŋiġit-	taŋəʀ-
taŋiq (blubber)	taŋəʀ
taŋiq (proof)	taŋəʀ-
taŋmik-	taŋmik-
taŋŋiq-	taŋəʀ-
tapiq	tapəʀ(-)
tapit-	tapət-[1] (under tapəʀ(-))
tapqaq	tapʀaʀ[2]
taput(i)-	taputə-
taqak	taqaʀ, taqəʀ
taqhammuk-	taqammuq-
taqhammuq-	taqammuq-
taqit-	taqə-
taqpak	taʀpaʀ-
taqpaq-	taʀpaʀ-
taqtu	taʀtu
taqtunak	taqtunaq (under taʀtu)
taquaq	taqu(C)aʀ
taqurrit-	taqu(C)aʀ
tarraq-	tatə-
tarva	taðva
tasi-	taci(ɣ)-
tasiq	taciʀ
tasiraġa(a)q	tacižuk- (under taci(ɣ)-)
tasiruk-	tacižuk- (under taci(ɣ)-)
tasiuq-	tatyuʀ-
tasuq-	catuq-
tataigi-	tatamə(t)-

NAI	PROTOFORM
tatamaa-	tatamə(t)-
tatamit-	tatamə(t)-
tati-	tatə-
tatigi	tatəkə (under tatə)
tatiḷgaq	tatəlɣaR
tatitu-	tatə
tatqiaq	təlqiðaR
tatqik-	tanqik- (under tanqiR, tanqiɣ)
tatqiq	tanqiR, tanqiɣ
tattalauraq-	tat(t)at- (under tatə-)
tattuq-	tat(ə)tuR-
tattuqun	tattuqun (under tatə-)
tauqsiq-	tauRciq-
tauttuġik-	tautu(k)-
tautuk-	tautu(k)-
tavlik-	tapłək- (under tapət-[2])
tavlu	tamlu
tavluġun	tamluRun (under tamlu)
tavra	taðva
tavsi	tavci
tayaġniq	tayaRnəR
tayaq	tayaq
tiggak	təɣɣaɣ
tiggaq-	təɣəɣ-
tiggun	təɣɣun (under təɣu-)
tiglik-	təɣləɣ-
tigliq-	təɣləq-
tigluk-	təŋluɣ(-)
tigri-	təkši- (under təŋə-)
tigu-	təɣu-
tiguaq	təɣuðaR (under təɣu-)
tiguġliq	təɣu(R)liq (under təɣu-)
tigummi-	təɣummi- (under təɣu-)
tigummiaq	təɣum(m)i(C)aR (under təɣu-)
tigvaq	təmvaq- (under təmə)
tigvasik-	təmvaq- (under təmə)
tiġiganniaq	təRikanni(C)aR (under təRiɣ)
tiġii-	təRiɣ
tiġiksraq	təRikšaq
tiġiksruq-	təRikšuq- (under təRiɣ)
tiġitquq	təkəðquR
tiipak	tiipak- (under təɣəɣ-)
tiipaŋa-	tiipak- (under təɣəɣ-)
tikiġaq	təkəRaR (under təkəR)
tikiq	təkəR
tikirruti-	təkiðutə- (under təkit-)
tikisaq-	təkicaqtuq- (under təkit-)
tikit-	təkit-
tikiut(i)-	təkiðutə- (under təkit-)
tikkivik	təkəR
tikkuaq-	təkkuaq- (under təkkuk-)
tikkuk-	təkkuk-
tikkuun	təkkuaq- (under təkkuk-)
tikpi	təkpik
tiksiq-	təŋət- (under təŋə-)
tilaġġi-	təlaR(R)i-, təlaqqi- (under təlaɣ-)
tilak-	təlaɣ-
tili-	təli-
tiluk(tuq)-	təłuɣ-
timi	təmə
tinniq-	tənniR-
tinu-	tənu-
tiŋak	təŋaɣ, təŋə
tiŋauraq	təŋaužaq (under təŋaɣ, təŋə)
tiŋaurat	təŋaužaq (under təŋaɣ, təŋə)
tiŋayuq	təŋayuɣ (under təŋaɣ, təŋə)
tiŋi-	təŋə-
tiŋilġautaq	təŋəlRaR- (under təŋə-)
tiŋit-	təŋət- (under təŋə-)
tiŋmi-	təŋmi- (under təŋə-)
tiŋmiaġruk	təŋmi(C)aR (under təŋə-)
tiŋmiaq	təŋmi(C)aR (under təŋə-)
tiŋmiġala-	təŋmiRala- (under təŋə-)
tiŋuk	təŋuɣ
tipaaq-	təppak- (under təpə)
tipi	təpə
tipi-	təpə-
tippak-	təppak- (under təpə)
tipuk	təpuk
tiqittut	təqətuRaq
tiqituġaq	təqətuRaq
tiqqala-	təŋqa(R)- (under təŋə-)
tira-	təža-
tiriq-	təðə(R)-
titiq-	tətəR-
titiq	tətəR-
titqiaq	təlqiðaR
tittaaliq	təktaaliq
tivli	təpli
tivraq	təpðaR (under təpə-)
tivsi(gi)-	təmci-
tivvuaq-	təvvuɣ-
tivvuk-	təvvuɣ-
tu<g>uq	tuɣəR(-)
tuaksruit-	tu(C)avə(t)-
tuapak	tuvapaɣ
tuavit-	tu(C)avə(t)-
tugaq-	tuɣɣaR- (under tuɣəR(-))
tuggaq-	tuɣɣaR- (under tuɣəR(-))
tugli (next one)	tuŋ(ə)liR (under tuŋə-)
tugli (hair at temples)	tuŋlə(R)
tugliġun	tuŋləRun (under tuŋlə(R))
tugrut-	tuɣət-
tugvaq-	tuŋvaR-, tuŋvaɣ-
tui	tuyə
tukiq-	tukəR-
tukkaq-	tukkaR-
tukku-	tukku(R)
tukku(q)	tukku(R)
tuksıaq-	tuŋciR-
tuksiq-	tuŋciR-
tuksruk-	tukšuk-
tulagiaq	tulaɣ-
tulak-	tulaɣ-

NAI	PROTOFORM
tulim(m)aq	tulimaR
tulima<r>aq	tulimaR
tullaqi-	tulaɣ-
tullignaq	tuðiɣ
tulugaġnaq	tuluɣaRnaq (under tulukaR)
tulugaq	tulukaR
tuluġiaq	tuluRyaR (under tuluR-)
tulukkat	tulukaR
tuluq-	tuluR-
tumanŋu-	tumaɣ-
tumaq-	tumaR-
tumi	tumə
tuni-	tunə-
tuninŋuq	tunənŋuq-
tuniqsima-	tunəR-
tuniqtaq	tunəq
tuniqtu-	tunəR-
tuniuqqaq-	tuniuqqaq- (under tunə-)
tunmaq-	tutmaR- (under tutə-)
tunmiġaq	tutməqaR (under tutə-)
tunnuq	tunnuR
tunŋa-	tutŋa- (under tut-)
tunu	tunu
tunumun	tunu
tunusisaq	tunucitaq
tunusuk	tunucuɣ (under tunu)
tunut-	tunut- (under tunu)
tunuvaq-	tunuvaR- (under tunu)
tuŋaaġi-	tuŋə-
tuŋiġuq-	tuŋə-
tuŋiun	tuŋəR
tuŋmaq-	tutmaR- (under tutə-)
tuŋmiġaq	tutməqaR (under tutə-)
tuŋu-	tuŋu-
tuŋuq-	tuŋu-
tupaaq-	tupaaq- (under tupaɣ-)
tupak-	tupaɣ-
tupi	tupə(nəq)
tupilak	tupəlak
tupinŋa-	tupəkə-
tupiq	tupəR
tupit-	tupət-
tupquraak	tupquža(a)q
tuqɫuaq	tuqluaq (under tuqlu(ɣ), tuqluR)
tuqɫuġaq-	tuqluR(aR)- (under tuqlu(ɣ), tuqluR)
tuqɫuk	tuqlu(ɣ), tuqluR
tuqɫuq-	tuqluR(aR)- (under tuqlu(ɣ), tuqluR)
tuqsruk	tuqšuk
tuqu-	tuqu(-)
tuquġaq-	tuquRaq- (under tuqu(-))
tuqunaq-	tuqunaR- (under tuqu(-))
tuqusaq-	tuqucaq- (under tuqu(-))
tuqut-	tuqut- (under tuqu(-))
turġu-	tužRu-
turviatchiaq	tužvik (under tut-)
turvik	tužvik (under tut-)
tusaa-	tucaR-
tusaġnaq-	tucaRna(a)q- (under tucaR-)
tusaqɫiġaq-	tucaqliq- (under tucaR-)
tusaqsraġi-	tucaqšau- (under tucaR-)
tusiat-	tutyaɣat-
tusiḷḷaq-	tucilaR-
tusu-	tucu-
tut-	tut-
tutchaġik-	tutcaq (under tucaR-)
tutchaq	tutcaq (under tucaR-)
tuti-	tutə-
tutiġiq	tutyaR(aR) (under tutə-)
tutik	tutəɣ(-)
tutqaasuk-	tutqik-
tutqik-	tutqik-
tutqiksi-	tutqik-
tutquq-	tutquq-
tuttaaq-	tutəɣ(-)
tuttu	tuntu
tuttuġruk	tuntuRðuɣ (under tuntu)
tuttuvak	tuntuvaɣ (under tuntu)
tuuga<r>aq	tuɣəkaR(aR) (under tuɣəR(-))
tuuġniq	tuɣəR(-)
tuukkaq	tuɣəkaR
tuullik	tu(C)utləɣ
tuunġaaġruk	tuunRaaRžuk (under tuɣənRaR)
tuunġaq	tuɣənRaR
tuurraq	tuɣətðaR (under tuɣət-)
tuurvik	tuɣət-
tuut-	tuɣət-
tuutaq	tu(C)utaR
tuuyuq	tuuyuk, tuuyuq (under tuɣəR(-))
tuvaaq	tuvəRaR
tuvaaqan	tuvaaqan (under tuvəRaR)
tuvaq	tuvaR
tuviġġat	tuvəRaR
tuvli-	tumə
tuvraq-	tumðaR- (under tumə)
tuvsi-	tuməci- (under tumə)
tuyuġmi-	tuyuRmi-
tuyuq-	tuyuR-
ualliq	uɣal(l)iR (under uɣan (uɣatə))
uamit-	uða(t)-, uðamə(t)-
uan	uɣan (uɣatə)
uaq-	URAR-
uaqniq	URAR-
uayuk-	uða(t)-, uðamə(t)-
uggisigi-	uvi(t)-
ugiaq-	uɣiR(aR)-
ugiayuk	uɣiR(aR)-
ugik-	uɣiR(aR)-
uglu	uŋlu
ugruk	uɣðuɣ
ugruŋnaq	uɣðuɣnaR (under uɣðuɣ)
uġġaq	URRAR
uġiaq-	URYUR-, URYAR-

NAI	PROTOFORM
uŋaliagu	uŋal(l)iaɣu (under uŋan (uŋatə))
uŋalliq	uŋal(l)iq (under uŋan (uŋatə))
uŋan	uŋan (uŋatə)
uŋasik-	uŋasik- (under uŋan (uŋatə))
uŋati	uŋan (uŋatə)
uŋavaq-	uŋavaq (under uŋan (uŋatə))
uŋayut-	uŋayu(t)-
uŋiḷak-	uŋilaɣ-
uŋiq-	uŋəʀ-
uŋiraq-	uŋəʀ-
uŋŋi-	uŋilaɣ-
uŋu-	uŋu-
uŋuġ-	uŋuʀ-
uŋuraq-	uŋu-
uŋut-	uŋu-
uŋuuq-	uŋuuq- (under uŋu-)
uŋuyut-	uŋayu(t)-
upak-	upaɣ-
upaktuq-	upaɣ-
upalui-	upaluq- (under upaɣ-)
upaluŋaiyaq-	upaluq- (under upaɣ-)
upaluq-	upaluq- (under upaɣ-)
upiŋġaaq	upən(ə)ʀᴀʀ
upiŋġaaq-	upən(ə)ʀᴀʀ
upiŋġaksraq	upən(ə)ʀakðᴀʀ (under upən(ə)ʀᴀʀ)
upiŋġi-	upənʀi- (under upən(ə)ʀᴀʀ)
upit-	upət-
upkuaq	umkuʀᴀʀ
upummiq-	ipummiq-
uputi-	upət-
uqallak-	uqallak- (under uqaq(-))
uqalugaaq-	uqaluk- (under uqaq(-))
uqaluk	uqaluk- (under uqaq(-))
uqaluktuaq	uqaluktuaq- (under uqaq(-))
uqaluktuaqti	uqaluktuaq- (under uqaq(-))
uqaq	uqaq(-)
uqaq-	uqaq(-)
uqausiq	uqauciq (under uqaq(-))
uqaut(i)-	uqautə- (under uqaq(-))
uqhaq	uʀʀᴀʀ
uqigḷi-	uqiɣitli- (under uqiɣit-)
uqikł̣i-	uqiɣitli- (under uqiɣit-)
uqiḷa-	uqila-
uqit-	uqiɣit-
uqpik	uqviɣ
uqqit-	uqqit- (under uqəʀ)
uqquq	uqəʀ
uqsi(q)	uqciq
uqsrit-	uqðilŋu- (under uqðuʀ)
uqsrualaqi-	uqðuʀᴀʀ (under uqðuʀ)
uqsruġa(a)q	uqðuʀᴀʀ (under uqðuʀ)
uqsruq	uqðuʀ
uqsruqtiq-	uqðuʀ-, uqðuʀtəʀ- (under uqðuʀ)
uquk	uquɣ
uqumait-	uqimaŋit-
uqumaŋia-	uqimaŋiʀ-
uqumaŋiaq-	uqimaŋiʀ-
uqummiaq	uqummiaq (under uqummiq-)
uqummiq-	uqummiq-
uqunmugaaq-	uqumiɣ- (under uqəʀ)
uquq-	uqquq- (under uqəʀ)
urgiiḷiq	ulɣilə
urraaq-	užžiq- (under uðəɣ-)
urriqsuq-	užžiq- (under uðəɣ-)
usiaq-	uci(C)aʀ- (under uci[1])
usiġaq-	uciq-
usii(ñ)	uci[2]
usiiyaq-	uciŋiʀ- (under uci[1])
usiḷḷaq-	uciʀ-
usiq-	uciʀ-
usiuvva	uci[2]
usuk	ucuɣ
usuuraq	ucuɣ
utaqqi-	utaqə-
utaqqik-	utaqə-
utchiqsu-	utciqtu- (under uci[1])
utchiqsruula-	uciq-
utchuk	ucuɣ
uti-	utə-
utiġrak-	utəʀžak-, utəʀžaq- (under utəʀ-)
utiniq	utənəq (under utə-)
utinmun	utətmun, utətmən (under utəʀ-)
utiq-	utəʀ-
utitaq	utə-
utkusik	utɣuciɣ
Utqiaġvik	utəqi(C)aʀ- (under utəʀ-)
uttaqi-	utəʀ-
utummak	ətəmaɣ
utuqqanaaq	utuqqaʀ
utuqqaq	utuqqaʀ
utuvik	u(u)tu(ɣ), utəvəɣ
uugaq	uðukaʀ
uuk-	uðəɣ-
uukł̣i-	uɣukli- (under uɣu-)
uukł̣iaq	uɣukli- (under uɣu-)
uukł̣iqpik	uɣukli- (under uɣu-)
uuktuun	uðəɣtuʀ- (under uðəɣ-)
uulik-	uŋuləɣ-
uuma-	uŋuma-
uumigi-	uɣumi-
uumiḷa-	uumila- (under uɣumi-)
uumiñaq-	uɣumi-
uummai-	uŋummaʀ- (under uŋuma-)
uummak-	uŋummaʀ- (under uŋuma-)
uumman	uŋuman (under uŋuma-)
uummaq	uummaq (under uŋuma-)
uunaq-	uunaq- (under uɣu-)

NAI	PROTOFORM
uunnaak-	uunaq- (under uɣu-)
uunniq	uɣut- (under uɣu-)
uunniqi-	uunni- (under uɣu-)
uuq-	uuq- (under uɣu-)
uuruq	uužuq (under uɣu-)
uut-	uɣut- (under uɣu-)
uutiq-	uutəq- (under uɣu-)
uvaak-	uvə(C)a-, əvə(C)a (under uvəʀ-, əvəʀ-)
uvaaŋa-	uvə(C)a-, əvə(C)a (under uvəʀ-, əvəʀ-)
uvagut	uvakut
uvaŋa	uvaŋa
uviḷuq	uviluʀ
uviñik	uvinəɣ
uviñiq	uvinəɣ
uviññak-	uvinəɣ
uviñŋiaqtuq-	uvinŋi(C)aʀ-, uɣu(n)ŋi(C)uʀ-
uviñŋiuġaq-	uvinŋi(C)aʀ-, uɣu(n)ŋi(C)uʀ-
uviñŋiuqsraq-	uvinŋi(C)aʀ-, uɣu(n)ŋi(C)uʀ-
uviq-	uvəʀ-, əvəʀ-
uvlaaku(n)	umlaaq (under umłuʀ)
uvlaaq	umlaaq (under umłuʀ)
uvli-	umli- (under umłuʀ)
uvluġiaq	umluʀiaq (under umłuʀ)
uvlumiñiñ	umlumi (under umłuʀ)
uvsik-	umciɣ- (under uməɣ-)
uvva	uvva
uvvahii	uvva
uvvaq(tuq)-	uvvaq-
uvvii	uvva
uyaġak	uyaʀaɣ
uyalunaq	ulə(t)luyaʀ
uyamik	uyamiɣ (under uya(quʀ))
uyuġu	uyuʀu(ɣ)
uyumiq	uyuməq-
yuvguq	nəvɣuʀ

Postbases and enclitics

NAI	PROTOFORM
a-	a-
(r)aġi-	ðaʀ-, ðaqə-
aġruk	aʀruk
ala-	ala-
aluk	aluk(-)
anik-	ɣanək-
aq (resembling)	aʀ
aq (passive part.)	ðaʀ
aq-	ŋaʀ-[1]
(r)aq-	ðaʀ-, ðaqə-
ayaa-	a-
ayaaq	tyaɣ
galuaq-	ɣaluaq-
gaq	aʀ
gaq-	ðaʀ-, ðaqə-
=gguuq, (g)guuq	ŋu(C)uʀ, ɣu(C)uʀ
gi- (have as)	kə-[1]
gi- (pres. passive part.)	kə(-)[2]
giik (du.), giit (pl.)	ɣiik, ɣiit
gik-, giksaq-	kiɣ-
gisi-	ki-
gusiq	ɣuciq
ġaq (thing resembling)	aʀ
ġaq (area or part)	qaʀ
ġaq (young, small)	ʀaʀ
ġluk-, luk-, qłuk, luk	łuɣ
iaq	ɣaʀ
iġuti-	ŋiʀutə-
iłisaq	ŋilitaʀ
iññaq-	ŋinnaʀ(-)
iq	C)iʀ
iq-	ŋiʀ-
iqtuq-	iqtuq-
it-	ŋit-
iyaq-	ŋiyaʀ-
kanik-	ɣanək-
kaq-, kaŋit, kallaiq-	k(k)aʀ-, q(q)aʀ-
kataq-	k(k)attaʀ-
kataq-	q(q)attaʀ-
kavsak-	kapcak(-)
=kiaq	k(k)i(C)aʀ
kit-	k(k)it-
kkaq	kaʀ
ksraq	kðaʀ
ksrit-	kðit-
ku(n)	ku
kuaq-	k(k)u(C)aʀ-
kuluk	k(k)uluk
la-	la(ʀ)-
łhaaq	łəʀ[2]
lit-	lit-
llak-	łłaɣ-, llaɣ-
llaq-	łłaq-
lgu-	ł(ə)ɣu-
lġataq-, ataq-	ʀataʀ-
lġataq-, gataq-	lʀataq-, ʀataq-
=li	łi
li- (make)	li-[1]
li-, gli-, kłi- (become)	li-[2]
liaq	li(C)aʀ
liaq-	liyaʀ-
lik	ləɣ
lik-	ləɣ-
liq- (begin to)	liq-
liq- (provide with)	liʀ-
liq-, tiq- (quickly)	ləʀ-
liqaa	liqaa
liqi-	liqə-
lira(a)q-	lira(a)q-
lit-	lit-
liuq-	li(C)uʀ-
liuti-	li(C)utə-
lla-	tla-
llaa-	llaa-
llaq-	llaq-
lliq	l(l)iʀ

NAI	PROTOFORM
lluataq-	l(l)u(C)aʀ-, l(l)u(C)ataʀ-
lu	lu(ʀ)
=lu	łu
luq-	luʀ-
m(m)agaaq-	maŋa(aq)-
ma-, sima-	(u)ma-
maq-	maʀ-
matuġaq	aʀ
(m)mi-	mi-
mik-, miaq	miɣ-
miñŋaq-	minŋaq-
miu(q)	miʀu
mmaġiksi-	mmaʀik-
(u)n	un (utə-)
naaq-	naaq-
naq	naʀ
naq-	naʀ-
naqsi-	naqci-
nasuaq-	nasuk, nasuaq-
nasugi-, gasugi-	yukə-
nayaq-, gayaq-	yaʀ-
nġiq-	nʀiʀ-
ni-, niġaq-	ni-
niaq-	ni(C)aʀ-
niġluk-	nəʀjuɣ-
nik-	nəɣ-, ŋ(ə)-
(n)nik-	nnək-
niq-	n(n)iq-
niq	nəʀ^{1}
niqsraq, niqtaq	nəʀ^{2}
nisaq	nitaq
nnak-	nnak-
nŋu-	lŋu-
ŋa-, ŋaiq-	ŋa-^{1}
ŋaaq	ŋa-^{2}
ŋaaq-	ŋaaq-
ŋisuaq-	yu(C)aʀ-
ŋnaq	knaʀ
ŋŋuaq	ŋ(ŋ)uðaʀ(-)
ŋŋuq-, ġuq-, guq-	ŋ(ŋ)uʀ-
pałłuk	vałuɣ(-)
(q)pak	vaɣ(-)
payaaq-	payaaq-
payuk	payuk(-)
piaq, vik	piɣ(-)
pkaq-	vkaʀ-
pqaq-	vqaʀ-
q-	q-
(V)q-	aʀ-
qan, tqan	qan (qatə)
qaq-	ŋqaʀ-
qłiq, kłiq	qliʀ
qqaaq-, tqaaq-	łʀa(C)aʀ-
qqammiq-, tqammiq-	lʀammiq-, tqammiq-
qqayaq-, tqayaq-, qqayaa	lʀayaq-, tqayaq-
qtu-	nəʀtu-
quq, ġuq	quʀ
qutaq, qun	q(q)un, q(q)utaʀ
(t)qu-	ðqə-
(t)quuq-	ðqə-
raġaq-	ðaʀ-, ðaqə-
raq (passive part.)	ðaʀ
raq- (repeatedly)	ðaʀ-, ðaqə-
ri-, i-, si-	ði- (detransitivizer)
(ġ)ruaq(*)	ðuɣaʀ(-)
ruksrau-, (trans.) raksrau-	žukšau-
ruq	ðuʀ, tuʀ
(ġ)ruumi-	umi-, ruumi-
sa-	ta-
saaġi-	caʀ-^{1}
saaq-	caʀ-^{1}
(t)saiłi-	təta(C)ili-
saq- (cause, try, begin)	caʀ-^{1}
saq- (fetch, go get)	caʀ-^{2}
(t)siaġi-	c(c)iʀ-
(t)siġiaq-	c(c)iʀyaʀ-
(t)sii-	c(c)iʀ-
sik-	ðiɣ-
simaaq-, (m)maq-	(u)maʀ(aʀ)-
(t)siq-	c(c)iʀ-
siqtuq-	ciqtuq-
siun	ci(C)un
siuq-	ci(C)uʀ-
(q)sruq-, qsruq-	qðuʀ-
sugnaq-, gugnaq-	yuknaʀ-
sugnit-	nit- (and cuɣnit-, paɣnit-)
sugruk	cuɣ
suġnaq-, yunaq-	yunaʀ-
suit-, yuit-	yu(C)it-
suk-, yuk-	yuɣ-
suu-, guu-	suu-
t- (transitivizer)	t-^{1}
t- (catch)	t-^{2}
taaq-	ta(C)aʀ-
taiññaq-, laiññaq-	tainnaq-
tait-	taʀit-
(p)ta, (p)tauq	ptauq
taq (past part.)	ðaʀ-
taq (pertaining)	taʀ
taq-	ðaʀ-, ðaqə-
taq-, saq-	taʀ-
taraq-	ðaʀ-, ðaqə-
tcak-	yyaɣ-
tciaq	tciaq
ti	tə
(u)ti-	utə-
tigi-	təkə-, ta-
tiguaq- (with dual, plural bases)	k(k)u(C)aʀ-
tilaaq	tələ, talə
tit-	tət-
tkuk, tkut	nkuɣ, nkut
tqik-	nqiɣ-^{2}
tqut(i)-	tʀutə-
tu- (much, big)	tu-^{1}
tu- (habitually)	tu-^{2}
tualuk	tuaq
tuaq-	ðuʀaʀ-, tuʀaʀ-
=tuq	tuʀ
tuq- (use, eat, wear)	tuʀ-^{1}

NAI	PROTOFORM
tuq- (repeated action)	tuʀ-[2]
(g)u-	ŋu-
ugaq-	uɣaq-
un, uti	ŋutə-
uq-	(C)uʀ-
(ŋ)ura(a)q-	ŋuðaʀaʀ-
usiq, rrusiq	uciʀ
utigi-	utəkə-
vaalluk-	vaɣəl(l)uɣ-
vallaaq-	vałłaɣ-[1]
valliq-	valliq-
valuk-	valuk-
vaq-	vaʀ
vigi-	ðvikə-
vik	ðviɣ, viɣ
viñiq*	vinəʀ
vli-	mli-
Vq-	(V)ʀ-
vsaaq-	mcaɣ-
ya-	ya-
yaqtuq-, yaqtuaq-, saqtuq-, saqtuaq-, giaq-	yaʀ(tuʀ)-
yuk, ruk	yuɣ lɨr ðuɣ
yuma-, kuma-, guma-	yuɣuma-
yumaaq-	yumaaq-
yumiñaq-	yuminaq-

PROTOFORM GLOSS INDEX

A

B

D

E

F

G

H

I

M

P

T

U

V

W

Y

REFERENCES

REFERENCES

Brackets denote description of unpublished material.

Amos, M.A., and H.T. Amos. 2003. *Cup'ig Eskimo Dictionary*. Fairbanks: Alaska Native Language Center.

Andersen, A., W. Kalleo, and B. Watts. 2007. *Labradormi ulinnaisigutet. An Inuktitut-English Dictionary of Northern Labrador Dialect*. Nain: Torngâsok Cultural Centre.

Badten, L., V.O. Kaneshiro, and M. Oovi. 1987. *A Dictionary of the St. Lawrence Island/Siberian Yupik Eskimo Language*. 2nd preliminary edition (with supplementary forms from revised 2008 edition). Edited by S.A. Jacobson. Fairbanks: Alaska Native Language Center.

Barnum, F. 1901. *Grammatical Fundamentals of the Innuit Language as Spoken by the Eskimos of the Western Coast of Alaska*. Boston: Ginn and Co. Republished 1970. Hildsheim: Georg Olms Verlag.

Bergsland, K. 1966. The Eskimo Shibboleth inuk/yuk. In *To Honour Roman Jakobson: Essays on the Occasion of his Seventieth Birthday* 1(Oct. 11): 203–221. The Hague: Mouton.

—. 1980. *Atkan Aleut-English Dictionary*. Anchorage: National Bilingual Materials Development Center.

—. 1986. Comparative Eskimo-Aleut Phonology and Lexicon. *Journal de la Société Finno-ougrienne* 80: 63–137. Helsinki.

—. 1989. Comparative Aspects of Aleut Syntax. *Journal de la Société Finno-ougrienne* 82: 7–80. Helsinki.

—. 1994. *Unangam Tunudgusii/Aleut Dictionary*. Fairbanks: Alaska Native Language Center.

Bergsland, K., and M. Dirks. 1981. *Atkan Aleut School Grammar*. Anchorage: National Bilingual Materials Development Center.

Berthelsen, C., I. Kleivan, F. Nielsen, R. Petersen, and J. Rischel. 1977. *Ordbogi*. Copenhagen: Ministeriet for Grønland. New expanded versions 1990, and 1997 under new title *Oqaatsit, grønlandsk-dansk ordbog*. Nuuk: Atuakkiorfik.

Birket-Smith, K. 1928. Five Hundred Eskimo Words: A Comparative Vocabulary for Greenland and Central Eskimo Dialects. *Report of the Fifth Thule Expedition 1921–1924*. Vol. 3(3). Copenhagen.

—. 1953. The Chugach Eskimo. *Nationalmuseets Skrifter, Etnografisk* Række 6. Copenhagen.

Boas, F. 1888. The Central Eskimos. In *6th Annual Report of the Bureau of Ethnology for the Years 1884–1885* pp. 399–669. Washington, D.C.: Smithsonian Institution.

Bogoraz, V.G. 1909. O tak nazyvayemom Yazyke Dukhov (Shamanskom) u Razlichnykh Vetvey Eskimosskogo Plemeni. *Izvestiya Akademii Nauk* Seriya 6 t. 13 no. 8–11: 489–495.

—. 1913. *The Eskimo of Siberia*. In Jessup North Pacific Expedition VII. Edited by F. Boas. Memoirs of the American Museum of Natural History. Washington: Smithsonian Institution.

—. 1937. *Luorovetlansko-russkiy Slovar'*. Moskva-Leningrad: Uchpedgiz.

Bourquin, T. 1891. *Grammatik der Eskimosprache, wie sie an der Labradorküste gesprochen wird*. London: Moravian Mission Agency.

Briggs, J. 1970. *Never in Anger*. Cambridge: Harvard University Press.

Briggs, J. N.d. Utkusiksalingmiut dictionary. Manuscript.

Cook, J., and J. King. 1784. *A Voyage to the Pacific Ocean Undertaken, by the Command of His Majesty, for Making Discoveries in the Northern Hemisphere. Performed under the Direction of Captains Cook, Clarke, and Gore, in His Majesty's Ships the Resolution and Discovery; in the Years 1776, 1777, 1778, 1779, and 1780*. 3 vols. London: G Nicol and T. Cadell.

Denny, J.P. 1980. *Semantics of the Inuktitut (Eskimo) Spatial Deictics*. Department of Psychology Research Bulletin 503, University of Western Ontario. London.

de Reuse, W. 1994. *Siberian Yupik Eskimo: The Language and Its Contacts with Chukchi*. Salt Lake City: University of Utah Press.

Dobrieva, E.A., E.V. Golovko, S.A. Jacobson, and M. Krauss. 2004. *Naukan Eskimo Dictionary*. Fairbanks: Alaska Native Language Center.

Dorais, L.-J. 1975a. *The Inuit Language in Cape Dorset, NWT*. Québec: Université Laval, Association Inuksiutiit Katimajiit.

—. 1975b. *Southeast Baffin Inuit Language*. Québec: Université Laval, Association Inuksiutiit Katimajiit.

—. 1976. *The Aivilik Inuit Language*. Québec: Université Laval, Association Inuksiutiit Katimajiit.

—. 1978. *The Inuit Language of Igloolik, NWT*. Québec: Université Laval, Association Inuksiutiit Katimajiit.

—. 1979. *The Inuit Language in Inujjuaq and Great Whale River*. Québec: Université Laval, Département d'anthropologie.

—. 1990a. *1000 Inuit Words*. Inuit Studies Occasional Papers 3. Université Laval, Association Inuksiutiit Katimajiit. Québec.

—. 1990b. *Inuit uqausiqatigiit, Inuit languages and dialects*. Iqaluit: Arctic College, Nunatta campus.

Dumond, D. 1987. A Reexamination of Eskimo-Aleut Prehistory. *American Anthropologist* 89(1): 32–55.

Egede, P. 1750. *Dictionarium Grönlandico-Danico-Latinum*. Havniae.

Emel'yanova, N. N.d. [Siberian Eskimo Languages.] Word-list from unpublished cardfile. University of St. Petersburg.

Fabricius, O. 1804. *Den grønlandske Ordbog forbedret og forøget*. Copenhagen: C.F. Schubart.

Fisher, W.J. 1882. Kodiak and Ugashik Vocabularies. Manuscript. Bureau of American Ethnology. Copy at Alaska Native Language Center, Fairbanks.

Fortescue, M. 1983. A Comparative Manual of Affixes for the Inuit Dialects of Greenland, Canada and Alaska. *Meddelelser om Grønland, Man and Society* 4, Copenhagen.

—. 1985. The Degree of Interrelatedness between Inuit Dialects as Reflected by Percentages of Shared Affixes. *International Journal of American Linguistics* 51(2): 188–221.

—. 1988. Eskimo Orientation Systems. *Meddelelser om Grønland, Man and Society* 11, Copenhagen.

—. 1991. *Inuktun: An Introduction to the Language of Qaanaaq, Thule*. Institute of Eskimology Skriftserie No. 15. University of Copenhagen.

—. 1985. [Upernavik dialect wordlist.] Typescript. Institute of Eskimology, Copenhagen.

Gessain, R., L.-J. Dorais, and C. Enel. 1982. *Vocabulaire du groenlandais de l'est*. Documents du Centre de Recherches Anthropologiques du Musée de l'Homme 5, Paris.

Hall, C.F. 1879. *Narrative of the Second Arctic Expedition Made by Charles F. Hall: His Voyage to Repulse Bay, Sledge Journeys to the Straits of Fury and Hecla and to King William's Land, and Residence Among the Eskimos During the Years 1864–69*. Edited by J. E. Nourse. Washington, D.C.: U.S. Government Printing Office.

Hammerich, L.L. 1950. [Lexicon for Nunivak.] Manuscript. Alaska Native Language Center, Fairbanks.

Hansen, K.F. 1968. Uqausilik: a dictionary of the Qairnirmiut dialect of Caribou Eskimo, introduction and suffix list. Manuscript. Institute of Eskimology, Copenhagen.

Harper, K. 1979. *Suffixes of the Eskimo Dialects of Cumberland Peninsula and North Baffin Island*. National Museum of Man. Mercury Series Paper 54. Ottawa.

Hinz, J. 1944. *Grammar and Vocabulary of the Eskimo Language, as Spoken by the Kuskokwim and Southwest Coast Eskimos of Alaska*. Bethlehem, Pa.: The Moravian Church Board of Foreign Missions.

Holm, G. 1888. Den østgrønlandske expedition udført i aarene 1883–85 (contains H. Rink: Den østgrønlandske dialekt, 207–235). *Meddelelser om Grønland* 10, Copenhagen.

Holtved, E. N.d. [Comparative Eskimo.] Cardfile. Institute of Eskimology, Copenhagen.

—. N.d. [Field notes for Mountain Village Yupik.] Institute of Eskimology, Copenhagen.

—. N.d. [Field notes for Nunivak.] Institute of Eskimology, Copenhagen.

Jacobson, S.A. 1984a. *Yup'ik Eskimo Dictionary*. Fairbanks: Alaska Native Language Center (and manuscript for forthcoming revised edition).

—. 1984b. Semantics and Morphology of Demonstratives in Central Yup'ik Eskimo. *Études/Inuit/Studies* 8 (Supplementary Issue): 185–192.

—. 1990a. *A Practical Grammar of the St. Lawrence Island/ Siberian Yupik Eskimo Language*. Fairbanks: Alaska Native Language Center.

—. 1990b. Comparison of Central Alaskan Yup'ik Eskimo and Central Siberian Yupik Eskimo. *International Journal of American Linguistics* 56(2): 264–286.

—. 1998. *Yup'ik Dialect Atlas and Study*. Fairbanks: Alaska Native Language Center.

Jacobson, S.A., and L.D. Kaplan. 1991. Lexicography of the Eskimo-Aleut Languages. In *Dictionaries: An International Encyclopedia of Lexicography*. Edited by F.J. Hausmann et al. Third Volume: 2631–2634. Berlin, New York: Walter de Gruyter.

Jeddore, R., ed. 1976. *Labrador Inuit Uqausingit*. St. John's, Newfoundland: Department of Education.

Jenness, D. 1928. Comparative Vocabulary of the Western Eskimo Dialects. *Report of the Canadian Arctic Expedition 1913–18* 15(A). Ottawa.

Kaplan, L.D. 1981a. *Phonological Issues in North Alaskan Inupiaq*. Alaska Native Language Center Research Papers No. 7. Fairbanks.

—. 1981b. On Yupik-Inupiaq Correspondences for ï: A Case of Inupiaq Innovation. *Études/Inuit/Studies* 5 (Supplementary Issue): 81–90.

—. 1982a. Nunamiut wordlist. Manuscript. Alaska Native Language Center, Fairbanks.

—. 1982b. Point Hope Inupiaq wordlist. Manuscript. Alaska Native Language Center, Fairbanks.

—. 1984. Little Diomede Inupiaq wordlist. Manuscript. Alaska Native Language Center, Fairbanks.

—. 1985. Seward Peninsula Inupiaq Consonant Gradation and Its Relationship to Prosody. In *Yupik Eskimo Prosodic Systems: Descriptive and Comparative Studies*. Edited by M. Krauss. Alaska Native Language Center Research Papers No. 7. Fairbanks.

—. 1988a. Dictionary of King Island Inupiaq. Manuscript. Alaska Native Language Center, Fairbanks.

—. 1988b. Dictionary of Qawiaraq Inupiaq. Manuscript. Alaska Native Language Center, Fairbanks.

Kleinschmidt, S. P. 1871. *Den grønlandske Ordbog omarbejdet*. Copenhagen: L. Klein.

Krauss, M.E. 1973. Eskimo-Aleut. In *Current Trends in Linguistics* 10 (part2): 796–902. Edited by Thomas Sebeok. The Hague, Paris: Mouton.

—. 1975. St. Lawrence Island Eskimo Phonology and Orthography. *Linguistics* 152: 39–72.

—, ed. 1985. *Yupik Eskimo Prosodic Systems: Descriptive and Comparative Studies*. Alaska Native Language Center Research Papers No. 7. Fairbanks.

Kroeber, A.L. 1900. The Eskimo of Smith Sound. *Bulletin of the American Museum of Natural History* 12(21): 265–327.

Krupnik, I. N.d. Unpublished field notes. Alaska Native Language Center, Fairbanks.

Lantis, M. 1946. The Social Culture of the Nunivak Eskimo. *Transactions of the American Philosophical Society* 35(3): 153–323. Philadelphia.

—. N.d. [Field notes for Nunivak.] Manuscript. Alaska Native Language Center, Fairbanks.

Leer, J. 1978a. *Conversational Alutiiq Dictionary, Kenai Peninsula Alutiiq*. Anchorage: National Bilingual Materials Development Center.

—. 1978b. *A Conversational Dictionary of Kodiak Alutiiq*. Fairbanks: Alaska Native Language Center.

—. 1985. Prosody in Alutiiq. In *Yupik Eskimo Prosodic*

Systems: Descriptive and Comparative Studies. Edited by M. Krauss. Alaska Native Language Center Research Paper No. 7. Fairbanks.

—. N.d. [Dictionary of Alutiiq Eskimo.] Manuscript. Alaska Native Language Center, Fairbanks.

Lisianski, Y.F. 1803. Kratkiy Slovar' Yazykov Severo-zapadnoy Chasti Ameriki s Rossiyskim Perevodom. In *Puteshestvie Vokrug Sveta v 1803, 4, 5 i 1806 godakh*. St. Petersburg.

Lowe, R. 1983. *Basic Kangiryuarmiut Eskimo Dictionary*. Inuvik: Committee for Original Peoples Entitlement.

—. 1984a. *Basic Uummarmiut Eskimo Dictionary*. Inuvik: Committee for Original Peoples Entitlement.

—. 1984b. *Basic Siglit Inuvialuit Eskimo Dictionary*. Inuvik: Committee for Original Peoples Entitlement. 2nd, expanded edition 2001, Quėbec, Ėditions Nota bene.

—. 1985a. *Basic Siglit Inuvialuit Eskimo Grammar*. Inuvik: Committee for Original Peoples Entitlement.

—. 1985b. *Basic Kangiryuarmiut Eskimo Grammar*. Inuvik: Committee for Original Peoples Entitlement.

MacDonald, John. 1998. *The Arctic Sky*. Royal Ontario Museum, Ontario and Nunavut Research Institute, Iqaluit.

MacLean, E. 1980. *Abridged Iñupiaq and English Dictionary*. Fairbanks and Barrow: Alaska Native Language Center and Iñupiat Language Commission.

MacLean, E. et al. 1987. Dictionary of North Slope Iñupiaq. Manuscript. Alaska Native Language Center, Fairbanks.

Marsh, G.H., and M. Swadesh. 1951. Kleinschmidt Centennial V: Eskimo-Aleut Correspondences. *International Journal of American Linguistics* 17(4): 209–216.

Mathiesen, T. 1928. Material Culture of the Iglulik Eskimo. *Report of the Fifth Thule Expedition, 1921–1924*. Vol. 6(1). Copenhagen.

Menovshchikov, G.A. 1954. *Eskimossko-russkiy Slovar'*. Leningrad: Uchpedgiz.

—. 1964. *Yazyk Sirenikskikh Eskimosov*. Moskva-Leningrad: Nauka.

—. 1975. *Yazyk Naukanskikh Eskimosov*. Leningrad: Nauka.

—. 1980. *Yazyk Eskimosov Beringova Proliva*. Leningrad: Nauka.

—. 1987. *Materialy i Issledovaniya po yazyku i fol'kloru Naukanskix Eskimosov*. Leningrad: Nauka.

Métayer, M. 1953. Dictionnaire Esquimau-Français. Typescript. Aklavik.

Miller, B.F. 1897. Ob Eskimosskikh Narechiyakh Anadyrskogo okruga (na osnovanii materialov sobrannykh N. L. Gondatti). *Zhivaya Starina* vyp. 2: 133–159. St. Petersburg.

Murdoch, J. 1892. Ethnological Results of the Point Barrow Expedition. In *9th Annual Report of the Bureau of American Ethnology for the Years 1887–1888* pp. 19–441. Washington D.C.

Orr, D. 1992. [Sirenikski field notes.] Manuscript. Alaska Native Language Center, Fairbanks.

Owingayak, D. 1986. *Arctic Survival Book*. Inuit Cultural Institute Cultural Series. Eskimo Point.

Parry, W.E. 1824. *Journal of a Second Voyage for the Discovery of a North-west Passage from the Atlantic to the Pacific: Performed in the Years 1821–22–23, in His Majesty's Ships Fury and Hecla*. London: John Murray.

Peck, E.J. 1925. *A Dictionary of the Eskimo Language* (based on F. Erdmann: Eskimoisches Wörterbuch, Budissin, 1864). Hamilton, Ont.: Mission Fund.

Petersen, J. 1967. *OrdbogêraK*. Copenhagen: Ministry for Greenland.

Petitot, E. 1876. *Vocabulaire Francais-Esquimau, dialecte des Tchiglit des Bouches du Mackenzie*. Paris: Pinart.

Pryde, D. N.d. Dictionary of Western Canadian Inuktitut. Manuscript plus card file. Copies (in part) at Alaska Native Language Center, Fairbanks and Institute of Eskimology, Copenhagen.

Qumaq, Taamusi. 1990. *Inuit Uqausillaringit*. Inuksiutikkunullu avatakkunullu nuititartitait. Quebec.

Rasmussen, K. 1930. Intellectual Culture of the Hudson Bay Eskimos. *Report of the Fifth Thule Expedition 1921–1924*. Vol. 7. Copenhagen.

—. 1931. The Netsilik Eskimos: Social Life and Spiritual Culture. *Report of the Fifth Thule Expedition 1921–1924*. Vol. 8. Copenhagen.

—. 1932. Intellectual Culture of the Copper Eskimos. *Report of the Fifth Thule Expedition 1921–1924*. Vol. 9. Copenhagen.

—. 1938. Knud Rasmussen's Posthumous Notes on the Life and Doings of the East Greenlanders in Olden Times. Edited by H. Ostermann. *Meddelelser om Grønland* 109(1). Copenhagen.

—. 1941. Alaskan Eskimo Words. *Report of the Fifth Thule Expedition 1921–1924*. Vol. 3(4). Copenhagen.

—. 1942. The Mackenzie Eskimos (after posthumous notes, edited by H. Ostermann). *Report of the Fifth Thule Expedition 1921–1924*. Vol. 10. Copenhagen.

Rezanov, N. P. 1805. Slovar' Unalashkinskago, Kad'yakskago, Kinayskago, Kolyuzhskago, Ugalyakhmutskago i Chugatskago Yazykov. Manuscript. Fond Adelunga, St. Petersburg.

Rink, H. 1868. Om grønlændernes gamle tro og hvad der af samme er bevaret under Kristendommen. In *Aarbøger for Nordisk Oldkyndighed og Historie,* 3e hefte. Gyldendalske forlag, Copenhagen.

—. 1885. The Eskimo Dialects as Serving to Determine the Relationship Between the Eskimo Tribes. *Journal of the Royal Anthropological Institute of Great Britain and Ireland* 15(2): 239–245. London.

—. 1887–1891. The Eskimo Tribes: Their Distribution and Characteristics, Especially in Regard to Language. 2 vols. *Meddelelser om Grønland* 11. Copenhagen.

Robbe, P., and L.-J. Dorais. 1986. *Tunumiit Oraasiat*. Centre d'Etudes Nordiques, Université Laval. Collection Nordica No 49. Québec.

Rubtsova, E.S. 1971. *Eskimossko-russkiy Slovar'*. Moskva: Izdatel'stvo Sovetskaya Entsiklopediya.

Saul, Mark. 1997. Comments and additions to ECI forms in first edition of CED. Personal communication to M. Krauss, ANLC archives, Fairbanks.

Schneider, L. 1966. *Dictionnaire alphabético-syllabique du langage esquimau de l'Ungava et contrées limitrophes*. Centre d'Etudes Nordiques, Université Laval. Travaux et Documents 3. Québec.

—. 1968. *Dictionnaire des infixes de l'Esquimau de l'Ungava*. Québec: Ministère des Richesses Naturelles.

—. N.d. *Grammaire Esquimaude du sous-dialecte de l'Ungava*. Québec: Ministère des Richesses Naturelles.

—. 1985. *Ulirnaisigutiit* (based on Schneider 1966). Edited by D. Collis. Québec: Université Laval Press.

Schultz-Lorentzen, C.W. 1974 (earlier editions 1926, 1964). Det grønlandske ordbog. Sydgrønlands bogtrykkeri.

Seiler, Wolf. 2005. *Iñupiaq Eskimo Dictionary*. NANA Regional Corporation, Kotzebue, Alaska.

Smith, L.R. 1978. *A Survey of the Derivational Postbases of Labrador Inuttut (Eskimo)*. National Museum of Man. Mercury Series Paper 45. Ottawa.

Søby, R. 1977–78. *The Kinship Terminology in Thule*. Folk 19–20: 49–84.

Spalding, A. 1979. *Learning to Speak Inuktitut*. Centre for Research and Teaching of Canadian Native Languages, University of Western Ontario. Native Language Research Series No. 1. (Vol. 2 published in 1993 by Wuerz, Winnipeg, under the title Inuktitut Grammar of North Baffin Dialects.)

Spencer, R.F. 1959. *The North Alaskan Eskimo*. Washington, D.C.: Smithsonian Institution.

Sun, S., et al. 1979. *Kobuk Inupiat Junior Dictionary*. Anchorage: National Bilingual Materials Development Center.

Swadesh, M. 1952. Unaaliq and Proto Eskimo, V: Comparative Vocabulary. *International Journal of American Linguistics* 18(4): 241-256.

Tein, T. 1992. *I Bylo Tak* . . . Magadan: Tsentr Narodnogo Tvorchestva u Dosuga.

Teplilek-Leonova, I.A. N.d. [Naukanski wordlist.] Photocopied manuscript. Alaska Native Language Center, Fairbanks.

Tersis, N. 2008. *Forme et sens des mots du Tunumiisut*. Louvain, Paris: Peeters Press.

Thalbitzer, W. 1904. A Phonetical Study of the Eskimo Language Based on Observations Made on a Journey in North Greenland 1900–1901. *Meddelelser om Grønland* 31. Copenhagen.

—. 1916. Et Manuskript af Rasmus Rask om Aleuternes Sprog, sammenlignet med Grønland. *Kongelige Danske Videnskabernes Selskabs Oversigt* 3: 211–249.

—. 1922. The Aleutian Language Compared with Greenlandic: A Manuscript by Rasmus Rask, Dating from 1820, Now in the Royal Library at Copenhagen. *International Journal of American Linguistics* 2(1–2): 40–57.

—. 1923. The Ammassalik Eskimo, part 2. *Meddelelser om Grønland* 40(2): 113–564. Copenhagen.

Top, A. 1727. Manuscript Greenlandic wordlist. In *Pioneers of Eskimo Grammar,* edited by K. Bergsland and J. Rischel, vol. 21. Copenhagen: Travaux du cercle linguistique de Copenhague. 1986.

Tyzhnov, I. 1848. *Kik'tam Shuida Ashmukat, Aleutsko-Kad'yakskiy Bukvar'*. St. Petersburg: Sunodal'snoy Tipografiya.

Uhlenbeck, C.C. 1905. Uralische Anklänge in den Eskimosprachen. *Zeitschrift der deutschen morgenländischen Gesellschaft* 59: 757–765. Leipzig, Germany.

Vakhtin, N.B. 2000. *Jazyk Sirenikskix Eskimosov* (The Old Sirenik Language). Muenchen: Lincom Europa.

Vakhtin, N.B., and N.M. Emel'yanova. 1988. *Praktikum po Leksike Eskimosskogo Yazyka*. Leningrad: Izdatel'stvo Prosveshchenie.

Veniaminov, I. 1846. Zamechaniya o Koloshenskom i Kad'yakskom Yazykakh. St. Petersburg: Nauk.

Vibæk, M. 2001. *Tusarn!* Nuuk: Atuakkiorfik.

Walunga, W. 1987. *St. Lawrence Island Curriculum Resource Manual*. Gambell, Alaska: Bering Strait School District.

Walunga, W., and A. Apassingok. 1988. St. Lawrence Island Yupik Terminology. Manuscript. Alaska Native Language Center, Fairbanks.

Webster, D.H., and W. Zibell. 1970. *Inupiat Eskimo Dictionary*. Fairbanks: Summer Institute of Linguistics.

Woodbury, A. 1981. Study of the Chevak Dialect of Central Yup'ik Eskimo. Ph.D. dissertation, University of California, Berkeley.

—. 1984. Eskimo and Aleut Languages. In *Handbook of North American Indians* Vol. 5: 49–63. Washington D.C.: Smithsonian Institution.